BALDWIN'S

OHIO REVISED CODE

ANNOTATED

Title 29

Crimes
Procedure
Chapters 2935 to 2949

Mat# 40401336

DEDICATION

To the Bench and Bar
whose members preserve and protect
the rule of law in American society

STATE OF OHIO
OFFICE OF THE SECRETARY OF STATE

Pursuant to the authority vested in me, I, J. Kenneth Blackwell, Secretary of State, do hereby state that I have provided copies of the enrolled acts of the Ohio General Assembly, as filed in my office, to this publisher for publication of the Ohio Revised Code.

Given under my hand and the seal of the office of the Secretary of State, in the city of Columbus, this 30th day of August, 2006.

J. Kenneth Blackwell
Secretary of State

PREFACE

Baldwin's™ Ohio Revised Code Annotated has been published and maintained since 1921. Through the years, Banks–Baldwin™ met the changing needs of Code users by continuously improving both editorial content and the level of service provided to subscribers. Now published by West in casebound format, *Baldwin's ORC* sets the standard for quality editorial information and user-friendliness. With every content feature known to have value in an annotated Code, and all information presented for maximum user convenience, it is the first state code designed for practice in the 21st century. (Please consult the User's Guide in Volume 1 for additional information.)

This volume contains statutes current through legislation approved by the Governor on or before October 1, 2006, and is kept up to date by means of annual cumulative pocket parts and issues of *Baldwin's Ohio Legislative Service Annotated* (OLS). This system assures the fastest possible availability of the laws, rules, and judicial constructions and the fastest access to the full text of decisions and opinions in *Ohio Official Reports* and in Westlaw electronic research.

Editorial features include:

LEGISLATIVE HISTORY

A complete legislative history, in reverse chronological order, follows each section of law.

UNCODIFIED LAW

Provisions of uncodified law affecting statutory interpretation are printed under related Revised Code sections. See the User's Guide in Volume 1 for a complete explanation of this feature.

HISTORICAL AND STATUTORY NOTES

Editorial notes are inserted where necessary to supplement and clarify legislative history or interpretation; they typically call attention to matters such as endorsements or opinions from the Legislative Service Commission, legislative discrepancies, and statutes repealed and reenacted under the same or different section numbers.

"Pre–1953 H 1 Amendments" are noted in reverse chronological order for each section that existed prior to creation of the Revised Code by 1953 House Bill 1.

Amendment notes summarizing the nature and extent of legislative changes to the Revised Code have been editorially prepared and printed under sections of special interest to the Bench and Bar.

UNIFORM LAWS

Uniform Laws and model acts, as promulgated by the National Conference of Commissioners on Uniform State Laws and adopted by the Ohio General Assembly, contain references to identical or similar provisions in West's *Uni-*

form Laws Annotated®. Uniform Laws Tables specify other jurisdictions that have adopted the same Uniform Laws enacted in Ohio.

COMPARATIVE LAWS

Comparative Laws cite selected references to other state statutes on the same or analogous topic.

COMMENTARY

Where appropriate, commentary from the Ohio Legislative Service Commission, the National Conference of Commissioners on Uniform State Laws, committees of the Ohio State Bar Association, and other professional groups is included to assist in statutory interpretation. In addition, selected Rules of Practice carry Staff Notes from the Supreme Court of Ohio.

CROSS REFERENCES

There is an obvious kinship among various laws included in volumes of *Baldwin's Ohio Revised Code Annotated.* Facilitating full use of these interrelationships, time-saving cross references are provided to related or qualifying constitutional, statutory, and court rule provisions.

OHIO ADMINISTRATIVE CODE REFERENCES

Relevant references are provided to *Baldwin's Ohio Administrative Code,* the complete compilation of state agency rules published by West.

UNITED STATES CODE ANNOTATED

Cross references to federal laws as published in West's *United States Code Annotated*® (U.S.C.A.®) are also provided where deemed relevant or useful.

LIBRARY REFERENCES

A special feature that will appeal to users consists of references to West's Key Numbers ⚿, Westlaw® Digest topic numbers, and sections of *Corpus Juris Secundum*® (C.J.S.®). These references open the door to constructions and interpretations of statutory law throughout the country.

RESEARCH REFERENCES

Research References include citations to *Ohio Jurisprudence* (OJur), *American Jurisprudence* (Am Jur), and *American Law Reports* (ALR®). In addition, this feature contains references to West's comprehensive line of practice manuals, handbooks, journals, and other secondary sources on specific subjects of law. References in this category cite pertinent parts of these publications where explanatory text, forms, or other practice and study aids can be found.

LAW REVIEW AND JOURNAL COMMENTARIES

Informative articles and discussions in law reviews and bar journals are highlighted for users by references under this heading.

PREFACE

NOTES OF DECISIONS

Judicial constructions of the Ohio Revised Code, as contained in the annotations, are prepared and reviewed by the Publisher's editorial staff. Our objectives are to provide thorough and authoritative access to caselaw and agency opinions and to assist users in understanding the application and purpose of the statutes as determined by the courts and the agencies.

Coverage of this material in *Baldwin's ORC Annotated* is the most comprehensive available, including: all reported Ohio court decisions; selected unreported Courts of Appeals decisions since 1981; selected decisions of the Court of Claims; federal cases construing or affecting Ohio law; opinions of the Attorney General; and selected decisions from a number of state agencies, among them the Board of Tax Appeals, Civil Rights Commission, Public Utilities Commission, Ohio Ethics Commission, Unemployment Compensation Review Commission, and Board of Commissioners on Grievances & Discipline.

Closing dates for the annotations in this volume are indicated in the following table:

Reported decisions complete through:

107 Ohio St.3d

165 Ohio App.3d

136 Ohio Misc.2d

31 O.B.R. 610

125 S.Ct.

441 F.3d

420 F.Supp.2d

337 B.R.

233 F.R.D.

158 Fed.Appx.

Reported appellate decisions complete through: 4-16-2006

Selected unreported appellate decisions complete through: 2-26-2006

Agency opinions and decisions complete through: 7-31-2006

Law reviews complete through: 4-30-2006

General complete to date: 4-16-2006

SERB 2006-002

2006 SERB 4-8

OAG 05-027

Bd of Commrs on Grievances & Discipline Op 2006-04 (4-7-06)

BTA 2005-R-591 (12–29–05)

COC U87–62178 (10–22–87)

CRC 9281 (6–23–05)

EBR [please see now ERAC for decisions of the former Environmental Board of Review]

ERAC 745596 (12–16–04)

Elections Op 06–02

Ethics Op 99–002

Joint Legis Ethics Comm 99–002

PBR 86–MIS–07–1032 (9–25–86)

PUCO 88–716 to 720 GA–AIR (10–17–89)

RBR [please see now RC for decisions of the former Reclamation Board of Review]

RC 01–11 (10–19–01)

UCBR B–02–0212–0000 (9–17–02)[please see now UCRC for decisions of the former Unemployment Compensation Board of Review]

UCRC B2004–02537 (10–20–04) (12-2-2004)

HWFB 94–M–0475 (10–25–98)

Annotations are grouped by subject matter under descriptive headings, or catchlines, which are numbered and indexed alphabetically. The same arrangement and topic numbers will be used in supplementary pocket parts and in the "Case Notes and Journal References" section of *Baldwin's Ohio Legislative Service Annotated*™ (OLS); thus, Baldwin's Code users will always be able to locate quickly annotations to recent decisions construing a particular point of law. Further research beyond the closing dates indicated above can easily be accomplished by consulting first the annual pocket part, then the cumulative Case Notes and Journal References Table in the current year OLS.

All citations of these constructions give the full name of each case, the standard reporter where the case can be found, and complete case history.

WESTLAW ELECTRONIC RESEARCH GUIDES

Westlaw electronic research guides have been inserted to facilitate efficient access to West's computer assisted legal research system for the latest laws and cases. See page XIII.

GENERAL INDEX, RULES INDEX AND STATUTE INDEXES

The General Index is the most comprehensive, precise, reliable, and usable index to Ohio law ever published. It contains multiple, detailed references to the Ohio and U.S. Constitutions, the Ohio Revised Code, and the Ohio rules of practice.

Each title of the Revised Code carries its own index, found in the volume that concludes that title. When two titles are published in the same volume, the index combines both titles. An index to all rules of practice is found in the last court rule volume.

ANCILLARY RESEARCH AIDS

Other research aids in this set include a User's Guide (in Volume 1); a list of abbreviations; tables of titles and tables of contents; and analyses of chapters and sections.

ACKNOWLEDGMENT

We express our gratitude and appreciation to members of the Bench and Bar, Ohio's law librarians and law schools, the members and staff of the Ohio Secretary of State's Office, the Legislative Service Commission, and others whose timely suggestions have contributed materially to the successful planning and development of *Baldwin's Ohio Revised Code Annotated*.

WEST

Cleveland, Ohio
October, 2006

RELATED PRODUCTS FROM WEST

Baldwin's Ohio Practice, Business Organizations
Jason C. Blackford

Baldwin's Ohio Practice, Civil Practice
James M. Klein, Stanton G. Darling II & Dennis G. Terez

Baldwin's Ohio Practice, Criminal Law 2d
Lewis R. Katz, Paul C. Giannelli,
Beverly J. Blair, Judith P. Lipton

Baldwin's Ohio Practice, Ohio Criminal Justice
Lewis R. Katz, Paul C. Giannelli & Case Western Reserve University

Baldwin's Ohio Practice, Ohio Statutory Charges
Dennis G. Terez

Baldwin's Ohio Practice, Domestic Relations Law 4th
Beatrice K. Sowald & Stanley Morganstern

Baldwin's Ohio Practice, Evidence 2d
Paul C. Giannelli & Barbara Rook Snyder

Baldwin's Ohio Practice, Rules of Evidence Handbook
Paul C. Giannelli & Barbara Rook Snyder

Baldwin's Ohio Practice, Merrick–Rippner Probate Law 6th
Angela G. Carlin

Baldwin's Ohio Practice, Local Government Law—Township
Rebecca C. Princehorn

Baldwin's Ohio Practice, Local Government—Municipal
John E. Gotherman, Harold W. Babbit, & James F. Lang

Baldwin's Ohio Practice, Local Government—County
William T. Conard II

Ohio Appellate Practice
Judge Mark P. Painter and Douglas R. Dennis

Ohio Arrest, Search and Seizure
Lewis R. Katz

Ohio Consumer Law
Legal Aid Society of Cleveland,
Harold L. Williams, Ed.

RELATED PRODUCTS

Ohio Domestic Violence Law

Judge Ronald B. Adrine & Alexandria M. Ruden

Ohio Driving Under the Influence Law

Judge Mark P. Painter

Ohio Employment Practices Law

Bradd N. Siegel & John M. Stephen

Ohio Felony Sentencing Law

Judge Burt W. Griffin & Lewis R. Katz

Ohio Juvenile Law

Paul C. Giannelli &
Patricia McCloud Yeomans

Ohio Landlord Tenant Law

Frederic White

Ohio Personal Injury Practice

Ohio Planning and Zoning Law

Stuart Meck & Kenneth Pearlman

Ohio School Law Handbook

Susan C. Hastings, Richard D. Manoloff,
Timothy J. Sheeran & Gregory W. Stype

Trial Handbook for Ohio Lawyers

Richard M. Markus

Baldwin's Ohio School Law Journal

Mary A. Lentz, Ed.

Code News

David S. Collins, Ed.

Domestic Relations Journal of Ohio

Stanley Morganstern, Ed.

Finley's Ohio Municipal Service

Price D. Finley, Ed.

Probate Law Journal of Ohio

Robert M. Brucken, Ed.

Workers' Compensation Journal of Ohio

Jerald D. Harris, Ed.

Baldwin's Ohio School Law

Susan C. Hastings, Richard D. Manoloff,
Timothy J. Sheeran & Gregory W. Stype

RELATED PRODUCTS

Baldwin's Ohio Tax Law and Rules

Ohio Building Code and Related Codes

Know Your Code: A Guide to the OBC

The PREVIEW Group, Inc.

Ohio Workers' Compensation Law Practice Guide

Jo Ann Wasil, Mark E. Mastrangelo & Robert E. DeRose

Ohio Forms Legal and Business

Ohio Forms and Transactions

Ohio Jurisprudence Pleading and Practice Forms (CD–ROM)

Ohio Criminal Defense Motions (CD–ROM)

Michael C. Hennenberg & Harry R. Reinhart

Baldwin's Ohio Revised Code Annotated

Baldwin's Ohio Legislative Service Annotated

Ohio Administrative Code

Ohio Administrative Law Handbook and Agency Directory

Frederick A. Vierow & Michael B. Lepp, Eds.

Ohio Monthly Record

West's Ohio Cases

Ohio State Reports, 3d

Ohio Appellate Reports, 3d

Ohio Miscellaneous Reports, 2d

West's Ohio Digest

Ohio Rules of Court, Federal

Ohio Rules of Court, State

Ohio Rules of Court, Local

Westlaw®

West CD–ROM Libraries™

WESTCheck® and WESTMATE®

For more information about any of these Ohio practice tools, please call your West representative or 1–800–328–9352.

RELATED PRODUCTS

NEED RESEARCH HELP?

You can get quality research results with free help—call the West Reference Attorneys when you have questions concerning Westlaw or West Publications at 1–800–733–2889.

INTERNET ACCESS

Contact the West Editorial Department directly with your questions and suggestions by e-mail at west.editor@thomson.com.

Visit West's home page at west.thomson.com.

WESTLAW ELECTRONIC RESEARCH GUIDE

Westlaw—Expanding the Reach of Your Library

Westlaw is West's online legal research service. With Westlaw, you experience the same quality and integrity that you have come to expect from West books, plus quick, easy access to West's vast collection of statutes, case law materials, public records, and other legal resources, in addition to current news articles and business information. For the most current and comprehensive legal research, combine the strengths of West books and Westlaw.

When you research with westlaw.com you get the convenience of the Internet combined with comprehensive and accurate Westlaw content, including exclusive editorial enhancements, plus features found only in westlaw.com such as ResultsPlus™ or StatutesPlus.™

Accessing Databases Using the Westlaw Directory

The Westlaw Directory lists all databases on Westlaw and contains links to detailed information relating to the content of each database. Click Directory on the westlaw.com toolbar. There are several ways to access a database even when you don't know the database identifier. Browse a directory view. Scan the directory. Type all or part of a database name in the Search these Databases box. The Find a Database Wizard can help you select relevant databases for your search. You can access up to ten databases at one time for user defined multibase searching.

Retrieving a Specific Document

To retrieve a specific document by citation or title on westlaw.com click **Find&Print** on the toolbar to display the Find a Document page. If you are unsure of the correct citation format, type the publication abbreviation, e.g., **xx st** (where xx is a state's two-letter postal abbreviation), in the Enter Citation box and click **Go** to display a fill-in-the blank template. To retrieve a specific case when you know one or more parties' names, click **Find a Case by Party Name**.

KeyCite®

KeyCite, the citation research service on Westlaw, makes it easy to trace the history of your case, statute, administrative decision or regulation to determine if there are recent updates, and to find other documents that cite your document. KeyCite will also find pending legislation relating to federal or state statutes. Access the powerful features of KeyCite from the westlaw.com toolbar, the **Links** tab, or KeyCite flags in a document display. KeyCite's red and yellow warning flags tell you at a glance whether your document has negative history. Depth-of-treatment stars help you focus on the most important citing references. KeyCite Alert allows you to monitor the status of your case, statute or rule, and automatically sends you updates at the frequency you specify.

ResultsPlus™

ResultsPlus is a Westlaw technology that automatically suggests additional information related to your search. The suggested materials are accessible by a set of links that appear to the right of your westlaw.com search results:

- Go directly to relevant ALR® articles and Am Jur® annotations.
- Find on-point resources by key number.
- See information from related treatises and law reviews.

StatutesPlus™

When you access a statutes database in westlaw.com you are brought to a powerful Search Center which collects, on one toolbar, the tools that are most useful for fast, efficient retrieval of statutes documents:

- Have a few key terms? Click **Index**.
- Know the common name? Click **Popular Name Table**.
- Familiar with the subject matter? Click **Table of Contents**.
- Have a citation or section number? Click **Find by Citation**.
- Or, simply search with Natural Language or **Terms and Connectors**.

When you access a statutes section, click on the **Links** tab for all relevant links for the current document that will also include a KeyCite section with a description of the KeyCite status flag. Depending on your document, links may also include administrative, bill text, and other sources that were previously only available by accessing and searching other databases.

Additional Information

Westlaw is available on the Web at www.westlaw.com.

For search assistance, call the West Reference Attorneys at 1–800–REF–ATTY (1–800–733–2889).

For technical assistance, call West Customer Technical Support at 1–800–WESTLAW (1–800–937–8529).

TABLE OF TITLES
BALDWIN'S
OHIO REVISED CODE ANNOTATED

---

*

ABBREVIATIONS

A .... Amended
A B A J .... American Bar Association Journal
Abs .... Ohio Law Abstract
Admin L Rev .... Administrative Law Review, American Bar Association
Akron L Rev .... Akron Law Review
AFSCME .... American Federation of State, County and Municipal Employees
Alb L J Sci & Tech .... Albany Law Journal of Science and Technology
ALR .... American Law Reports Annotated
ALR2d .... American Law Reports Annotated, Second Series
ALR3d .... American Law Reports Annotated, Third Series
ALR4th .... American Law Reports Annotated, Fourth Series
ALR5th .... American Law Reports Annotated, Fifth Series
ALR Fed .... American Law Reports Annotated, Federal
Am .... Amended, Amendment
Am Crim L Rev .... American Criminal Law Review
Am Dec .... American Decisions
Am Jur .... American Jurisprudence
Am Jur 2d .... American Jurisprudence, Second Series
Am L Rec .... American Law Record
Am L Reg .... American Law Register
Am Rep .... American Reports
App .... Appellate Court
App .... Ohio Appellate Reports
App(2d) .... Ohio Appellate Reports, Second Series
App(3d) .... Ohio Appellate Reports, Third Series
App R .... Rules of Appellate Procedure
Ariz L Rev .... Arizona Law Review
Art .... Article
Assn .... Association
A–TF .... Amended and Transferred From
A–TT .... Amended and Transferred To
Auth .... Authority
B .... Weekly Law Bulletin
Babbit's Ohio Mun Serv ...... Babbit's Ohio Municipal Service
Baldwin's Ohio Sch L J ...... Baldwin's Ohio School Law Journal
Baldwin's Ohio Sch Serv ..... Baldwin's Ohio School Service
Bd .... Board
Bldg .... Building
B.R. .... Bankruptcy Reporter
Brook L Rev .... Brooklyn L Rev
BTA .... Ohio Board of Tax Appeals
B U L Rev .... Boston University Law Review
Bull .... Weekly Law Bulletin
Bus Law .... Business Lawyer
Cap U L Rev .... Capital University Law Review
Case W Res L Rev .... Case Western Reserve University Law Review

ABBREVIATIONS

CC .... Ohio Circuit Court Reports
CCA .... United States Circuit Court of Appeals
CC(NS) .... Ohio Circuit Court Reports, New Series
CCR .... Rules of Court of Claims of Ohio
CD .... Ohio Circuit Decisions
CFR .... Code of Federal Regulations
CF Stds .... Court Facility Standards
Ch .... Chapter
Cin B Ass'n Rep .... Cincinnati Bar Association Report
Cir .... Circuit Court
Cities & Villages .... Cities and Villages, Ohio Municipal League
CIV DISC .... Civil Discovery
Civ R .... Rules of Civil Procedure
CJC .... Code of Judicial Conduct
C.J.S. .... Corpus Juris Secundum
Clev B J .... Cleveland Bar Journal
Clev L Rec .... Cleveland Law Record
Clev L Reg .... Cleveland Law Register
Clev L Rep .... Cleveland Law Reporter
Clev–Marshall L Rev .... Cleveland–Marshall Law Review
Clev St L Rev .... Cleveland State Law Review
CMR .... Court–Martial Reports
Colum Hum Rts L Rev .... Columbia Human Rights Law Review
Colum J Gender & L .... Columbia Journal of Gender and Law
Colum J L & Soc Probs .... Columbia Journal of Law and Social Problems
Columbus B Briefs .... Columbus Bar Briefs
Co .... Company
COC .... Ohio Court of Claims
Comm .... Commission
Commr .... Commissioner
Com.Pl. .... Common Pleas Court
Conf .... Conflicting
Const .... Constitution
Cornell L Rev .... Cornell Law Review
Corp .... Corporation
CP .... Common Pleas Court
CPR .... Code of Professional Responsibility
CRC .... Ohio Civil Rights Commission
Crim L J Ohio .... Criminal Law Journal of Ohio
Crim R .... Rules of Criminal Procedure
CSCR .... Cincinnati Superior Court Reports
CSS .... Court Security Standards
Ct .... Court
D .... Ohio Decisions
Dayton .... Dayton Reports
Dayton B Briefs .... Dayton Bar Briefs
dba .... doing business as
DC .... District Court
Dept .... Department

ABBREVIATIONS

Dick L Rev ....Dickinson Law Review
Dist ....District
Div ....Division
Dom Rel ....Domestic Relations Court
Domestic Rel L J Ohio ......Domestic Relations Journal of Ohio
DPID Reg....................Death Penalty Indigent Defense Regulations
DR ....Disciplinary Rules, Code of Professional Responsibility
D Repr ....Ohio Decisions, Reprint
Duq L Rev ....Duquesne Law Review
E...........................Enacted
EBR.........................Environmental Board of Review (pre 1997)
EBR.........................Environmental Review Appeals Commission (1997 and after)
EC ....Ethical Considerations, Code of Professional Responsibility
Ed ....Education
eff. ....Effective
Elections Op ....Ohio Elections Commission Opinions
Envtl L J Ohio..............Environmental Law Journal of Ohio
Envtl Monthly ....Environmental Monthly
ERAC ....Environmental Review Appeals Commission
Ethics Op ....Ohio Ethics Commission Opinions
Evid R......................Ohio Rules of Evidence
ex rel ....on the relation of
Fam L Quar..................Family Law Quarterly, American Bar Association
F ....Form
F. ....Federal Reporter
F.2d ....Federal Reporter, Second Series
F.3d ....Federal Reporter, Third Series
F. Cas ....Federal Cases
Fed.........................Federal
Fed Appx ....Federal Appendix
Finley's Ohio Mun Serv .....Finley's Ohio Municipal Service
Fla L Rev ....University of Florida Law Review
Forum.......................Forum, American Bar Association
F.R.D. ....Federal Rules Decisions
FR Serv ....Federal Rules Service
FR Serv(2d).................Federal Rules Service, Second Series
F.Supp ....Federal Supplement
F.Supp(2d)..................Federal Supplement, Second Series
GC ....General Code of Ohio
Geo L J ....Georgetown Law Journal
Gotherman's Ohio Mun Serv ..Gotherman's Ohio Municipal Service
Gov Bar R ....Supreme Court Rules for the Government of the Bar
Gov Jud R ....Supreme Court Rules for the Government of the Judiciary
H ....House Bill
Harv L Rev ....Harvard Law Review
HCR ....House Concurrent Resolution
Health L J Ohio ....Health Law Journal of Ohio
HJR ....House Joint Resolution

ABBREVIATIONS

HR .... House Resolution
HWFB .... Hazardous Waste Facility Board
Inc .... Incorporated
Ind L J .... Indiana Law Journal
Indus Rel Rep .... Industrial Relations Report
Iowa L Rev .... Iowa Law Review
IRC .... Internal Revenue Code
J Fam L .... Journal of Family Law (University of Louisville)
J L & Com .... Journal of Law and Commerce
J L & Educ .... Journal of Law and Education
J L & Health .... Journal of Law and Health
J Min L & Pol'y .... Journal of Mineral Law and Policy
J Nat Resources & Envtl L ... Journal of Natural Resources and Environmental Law
Joint Legis Ethics Comm .... Joint Legislative Ethics Commission
Jud Cond .... Code of Judicial Conduct
Juv .... Juvenile Court
Juv R .... Rules of Juvenile Procedure
Ky Bench & B .... Kentucky Bench and Bar
Ky L J .... Kentucky Law Journal
Lake Legal Views .... Lake Legal Views, Lake County Bar Association
Law & Fact .... Law & Fact, Cuyahoga County Bar Association
LBA Bull .... Louisville Bar Association News Bulletin
L.Ed. .... Lawyers' Edition, United States Supreme Court Reports
L.Ed.2d .... Lawyers' Edition, United States Supreme Court Reports, Second Series
Legal Reference Serv Q ..... Legal Reference Services Quarterly
Louisville Law .... Louisville Lawyer
LRA .... Lawyers Reports Annotated
LRA(NS) .... Lawyers Reports Annotated, New Series
Ltd .... Limited
May Ed R .... Mayor's Court Education and Procedure Rules
Md L Rev .... Maryland Law Review
Mental Disability L Rep .... Mental Disability Law Reporter
Mercer L Rev .... Mercer Law Review
Mfg .... Manufacturing
Misc .... Ohio Miscellaneous Reports
Misc(2d) .... Ohio Miscellaneous Reports, Second Series
M J .... Military Justice Reporter
Muni .... Municipal Court
Nat'l L J .... National Law Journal
N D L Rev .... North Dakota Law Review
N.D.Ohio .... Northern District Ohio
N.E. .... Northeastern Reporter
N.E.2d .... Northeastern Reporter, Second Series
NEA .... National Education Association
Neb L Rev .... Nebraska Law Review
N Ky L Rev .... Northern Kentucky Law Review
N Ky St L F .... Northern Kentucky State Law Forum
NP .... Ohio Nisi Prius Reports

ABBREVIATIONS

NP(NS) .... Ohio Nisi Prius Reports, New Series
Nw U L Rev .... Northwestern University Law Review
O .... Ohio Reports
OAC .... Baldwin's Ohio Administrative Code
OAG .... Opinions of the Ohio Attorney General
OAPSE .... Ohio Association of Public School Employees
OBR .... Ohio Bar Reports
OCA .... Ohio Courts of Appeals Reports
O Const .... Ohio Constitution
OCRC .... Ohio Civil Rights Commission
OEA .... Ohio Education Association
OFD .... Ohio Federal Decisions
OFT .... Ohio Federation of Teachers
Ohio .... Ohio Reports
Ohio App .... Ohio Appellate Reports
Ohio App.2d .... Ohio Appellate Reports, Second Series
Ohio App.3d .... Ohio Appellate Reports, Third Series
Ohio B Ass'n Serv Letter .... Ohio Bar Association Service Letter
Ohio C.C. .... Ohio Circuit Court Reports
Ohio C.C.N.S. .... Ohio Circuit Court Reports, New Series
Ohio C.D. .... Ohio Circuit Decisions
Ohio Civ Prac J .... Ohio Civil Practice Journal
Ohio Ct.Cl. .... Ohio Court of Claims
Ohio Com.Pl. .... Ohio Common Pleas Court
Ohio Dec. .... Ohio Decisions
Ohio Dec. Reprint .... Ohio Decisions, Reprint
Ohio F.Dec. .... Ohio Federal Decisions
Ohio L Rep .... Ohio Law Reporter
Ohio Law .... Ohio Lawyer
Ohio Law Abs. .... Ohio Law Abstract
Ohio Misc. .... Ohio Miscellaneous Reports
Ohio Misc.2d .... Ohio Miscellaneous Reports, Second Series
Ohio N.P. .... Ohio Nisi Prius Reports
Ohio N.P.N.S. .... Ohio Nisi Prius Reports, New Series
Ohio N U L Rev .... Ohio Northern University Law Review
Ohio Sch Boards Ass'n J .... Ohio School Boards Association Journal
Ohio St. .... Ohio State Reports
Ohio St.2d .... Ohio State Reports, Second Series
Ohio St.3d .... Ohio State Reports, Third Series
Ohio St B Ass'n Rep .... Ohio State Bar Association Report
Ohio St L J .... Ohio State Law Journal
Ohio Tax Rev .... Ohio Tax Review
Ohio Trial .... Ohio Trial, Ohio Academy of Trial Lawyers Education Foundation
OJur 3d .... Ohio Jurisprudence, Third Series
OLS .... Baldwin's Ohio Legislative Service Annotated
OMR .... Baldwin's Ohio Monthly Record
OO .... Ohio Opinions
OO(2d) .... Ohio Opinions, Second Series
OO(3d) .... Ohio Opinions, Third Series

ABBREVIATIONS

Or L Rev	Oregon Law Review
ORC	Baldwin's Ohio Revised Code
OS	Ohio State Reports
OS(2d)	Ohio State Reports, Second Series
OS(3d)	Ohio State Reports, Third Series
OSLJ	Ohio State Law Journal
OS Unrep	Ohio State Unreported
O.Supp.	Ohio Supplement
Otto	Otto's Supreme Court Reports
Pa B A Q	Pennsylvania Bar Association Quarterly
Pa Law	Pennsylvania Lawyer
Pa St B Ass'n Bull	Pennsylvania State Bar Association Bulletin
PBR	Personnel Board of Review
PConf	Possibly or Partially Conflicting
Pepp L Rev	Pepperdine Law Review
Prob	Probate Court
Prob & Trust J	Probate and Trust Journal
Prob L J Ohio	Probate Law Journal of Ohio
Civ Discovery Edition	PRO/GRAM Civil Discovery Edition
Civ Litig Edition	PRO/GRAM Civil Litigation Edition
PUCO	Public Utilities Commission of Ohio
R	Repealed
RBR	Reclamation Board of Review (pre 1997)
RBR	Reclamation Commission (1997 and after)
RC	Ohio Revised Code
R–E	Repealed and Reenacted
RRD	RC 119.032 rule review date(s)
Rep R	Supreme Court Rules for the Reporting of Opinions
RS	Revised Statutes of Ohio
S	Senate Bill
St Mary's L J	St. Mary's Law Journal
SCR	Senate Concurrent Resolution
S.Ct.	United States Supreme Court Reporter
SCt R	Rules of Practice of the Supreme Court of Ohio
S.D.Ohio	Southern District Ohio
SERB	State Employment Relations Board
Shingle	The Shingle, Philadelphia Bar Association
SJR	Senate Joint Resolution
SR	Senate Resolution
Stat	Statutes
State Employment Rel Board Q	State Employment Relations Board Quarterly
Sub	Substitute
Sup R	Rules of Superintendence for Courts of Ohio
TC	Tax Court (United States)
Temp L Q	Temple Law Quarterly
Temp L Rev	Temple Law Review
TF	Transferred From
Title Topics	Title Topics, Ohio Land Title Association
TJS	Trial Court Jury Use and Management Standards

ABBREVIATIONS

Tol B Ass'n News .... Toledo Bar Association Newsletter
Traf R .... Ohio Traffic Rules
Trial .... Trial, Association of Trial Lawyers of America
TT .... Transferred To
Twp .... Township
UCBR .... Unemployment Compensation Board of Review (pre 1997)
UCBR .... Unemployment Compensation Review Commission (1997 and after)
UCC .... Uniform Commercial Code
U Cin L Rev .... University of Cincinnati Law Review
U Colo L Rev .... University of Colorado Law Review
UCRC .... Unemployment Compensation Review Commission
U Dayton L Rev .... University of Dayton Law Review
U Pa L Rev .... University of Pennsylvania Law Review
U Pitt L Rev .... University of Pittsburgh Law Review
U Rich L Rev .... University of Richmond Law Review
U.S. .... United States Supreme Court Reports
USC .... United States Code
USCA .... United States Code Annotated
USLW .... United States Law Week
USP.Q. .... United States Patent Quarterly
USP.Q.2d .... United States Patent Quarterly, Second Series
U Tol L Rev .... University of Toledo Law Review
v .... versus
v .... volume, Ohio Laws
VCC R .... Rules of Court of Claims of Ohio, Victims of Crime Compensation Section
Vill L Rev .... Villanova Law Review
W .... Withdrawn
W .... Wright's Ohio Supreme Court Reports
Wall. .... Wallace's Supreme Court Reports
Wake Forest L Rev .... Wake Forest Law Review
Washburn L J .... Washburn Law Journal
WL .... Westlaw reference number
W.L.B. .... Weekly Law Bulletin
WLG .... Weekly Law Gazette
WLJ .... Western Law Journal
WLM .... Western Law Monthly
Workers' Compensation J Ohio .... Workers' Compensation Journal of Ohio
W Reserve U L Rev .... Western Reserve University Law Review
Wright .... Wright's Ohio Supreme Court Reports

*

TABLE OF CONTENTS

Title 29—Crimes—Procedure

(Chapters 2935 to 2949)

*

CITE THIS BOOK

OHIO REV. CODE ANN. §2935.01 (Baldwin 2006)

*

BALDWIN'S OHIO REVISED CODE ANNOTATED

Title XXIX

CRIMES—PROCEDURE

(Chapters 2935 to 2949)

Publisher's Note: Commentary is reprinted from the Ohio Legislative Service Commission's Summary of 1972 House Bill 511. Commentary should be read in light of the language of the statute as it was enacted by 1972 H 511.

Publisher's Note: 1995 S 2—the Omnibus Criminal Sentencing Act—became effective 7–1–96, and applies only to offenses committed on or after July 1, 1996. Prior law continues to apply to offenses committed prior to that date, and is provided as an appendix following the current Title XXIX.

CHAPTER 2935

ARREST, CITATION, AND DISPOSITION ALTERNATIVES

DEFINITIONS

2935.01 Definitions

As used in this chapter:

(A) "Magistrate" has the same meaning as in section 2931.01 of the Revised Code.

(B) "Peace officer" includes, except as provided in section 2935.081 of the Revised Code, a sheriff; deputy sheriff; marshal; deputy marshal; member of the organized police department of any municipal corporation, including a member of the organized police department of a municipal corporation in an adjoining state serving in Ohio under a contract pursuant to section 737.04 of the Revised Code; member of a police force employed by a metropolitan housing authority under division (D) of section 3735.31 of the Revised Code; member of a police force employed by a regional transit authority under division (Y) of section 306.05 of the Revised Code; state university law enforcement officer appointed under section 3345.04 of the Revised Code; enforcement agent of the department of public safety designated under section 5502.14 of the Revised Code; employee of the department of taxation to whom investigation powers have been delegated under section 5743.45 of the Revised Code; employee of the department of natural resources who is a natural resources law enforcement staff officer designated pursuant to section 1501.013 of the Revised Code, a forest officer designated pursuant to section 1503.29 of the Revised Code, a preserve officer designated pursuant to section 1517.10 of the Revised Code, a wildlife officer designated pursuant to section 1531.13 of the Revised Code, a park officer designated pursuant to section 1541.10 of the Revised Code, or a state watercraft officer designated pursuant to section 1547.521 of the Revised Code; individual designated to perform law enforcement duties under section 511.232, 1545.13, or 6101.75 of the Revised Code; veterans' home police officer appointed under section 5907.02 of the Revised Code; special police officer employed by a port authority under section 4582.04 or 4582.28 of the Revised Code; police constable of any township; police officer of a township or joint township police district; a special police officer employed by a municipal corporation at a municipal airport, or other municipal air navigation facility, that has scheduled operations, as defined in section 119.3 of Title 14 of the Code of Federal Regulations, 14 C.F.R. 119.3, as amended, and that is required to be under a security program and is governed by aviation security rules of the transportation security administration of the United States department of transportation as provided in Parts 1542. and 1544. of Title 49 of the Code of Federal Regulations, as amended; the house sergeant at arms if the house sergeant at arms has arrest authority pursuant to division (E)(1) of section 101.311 of the Revised Code; and an assistant house sergeant at arms; officer or employee of the bureau of criminal identification and investigation established pursuant to section 109.51 of the Revised Code who has been awarded a certificate by the executive director of the Ohio peace officer training commission attesting to the officer's or employee's satisfactory completion of an approved state, county, municipal, or department of natural resources peace officer basic training program and who is providing assistance upon request to a law enforcement officer or emergency assistance to a peace officer pursuant to section 109.54 or 109.541 of the Revised Code; and, for the purpose of arrests within those areas, for the purposes of Chapter 5503. of the Revised Code, and the filing of and service of process relating to those offenses witnessed or investigated by them, the superintendent and troopers of the state highway patrol.

(C) "Prosecutor" includes the county prosecuting attorney and any assistant prosecutor designated to assist the county prosecuting attorney, and, in the case of courts inferior to courts of common pleas, includes the village solicitor, city director of law, or similar chief legal officer of a municipal corporation, any such officer's assistants, or any attorney designated by the prosecuting attorney of the county to appear for the prosecution of a given case.

(D) "Offense," except where the context specifically indicates otherwise, includes felonies, misdemeanors, and violations of ordinances of municipal corporations and other public bodies authorized by law to adopt penal regulations.

(2002 H 675, eff. 3–14–03; 2002 H 545, eff. 3–19–03; 2002 H 427, eff. 8–29–02; 2002 S 200, eff. 9–6–02; 2000 S 317, eff. 3–22–01; 2000 S 137, eff. 5–17–00; 1999 H 163, eff. 6–30–99; 1998 S 187, eff. 3–18–99; 1996 H 72, eff. 3–18–97; 1995 S 162, eff. 10–29–95; 1995 S 2, eff. 7–1–96; 1991 S 144, eff. 8–8–91; 1991 H 77; 1988 H 708, § 1)

Historical and Statutory Notes

Ed. Note: A special endorsement by the Legislative Service Commission states, "Comparison of these amendments [2002 H 675, eff. 3–14–03 and 2002 H 545, eff. 3–19–03] in pursuance of section 1.52 of the Revised Code discloses that they are not irreconcilable so that they are required by that section to be harmonized to give effect to each amendment." In recognition of this rule of construction, changes made by 2002 H 675, eff. 3–14–03 and 2002 H 545, eff. 3–19–03, have been incorporated in the above amendment. See *Baldwin's Ohio Legislative Service Annotated*, 2002, pages 12/L–2109 and 12/L–2323, or the OH–LEGIS or OH–LEGIS–OLD database on Westlaw, for original versions of these Acts.

Ed. Note: Former 2935.01 repealed by 1988 H 708, § 2, eff. 4–19–88; 1988 H 708, § 18; 1987 H

231, § 1, 6, H 261, § 1, 3; 1986 H 428, § 15; 1984 H 129, § 1,3; 1982 H 738; 1978 H 588; 1977 H 219; 132 v H 1; 129 v 582; 128 v 97; 1953 H 1.

Amendment Note: 2002 H 675 made nonsubstantive changes to the section.

Amendment Note: 2002 H 545 inserted "a special police officer employed by a municipal corporation at a municipal airport, or other municipal air navigation facility, that has scheduled operations, as defined in section 119.3 of Title 14 of the Code of Federal Regulations, 14 C.F.R. 119.3, as amended, and that is required to be under a security program and is governed by aviation security rules of the transportation security administration of the United States department of transportation as provided in Parts 1542. and 1544. of Title 49 of the Code of Federal Regulations, as amended;" in division (B); and deleted "and" following "for the purpose of arrests within those areas," and "includes" following "those offenses witnessed or investigated by them," in division (B).

Amendment Note: 2002 H 427 inserted "officer or employee of the bureau of criminal identification and investigation established pursuant to section 109.51 of the Revised Code who has been awarded a certificate by the executive director of the Ohio peace officer training commission attesting to the officer's or employee's satisfactory completion of an approved state, county, municipal or department of natural resources peace officer basic training program and who is providing assistance upon request to a law enforcement officer or emergency assistance to a peace officer pursuant to section 109.54 or 109.541 of the Revised Code;" in division (B).

Amendment Note: 2002 S 200 inserted "employee of the department of taxation to whom investigation powers have been delegated under section 5743.45 of the Revised Code;" in division (B).

Amendment Note: 2000 S 317 deleted "and" following "police constable of any township" and inserted "the house sergeant at arms if the house sergeant at arms has arrest authority pursuant to division (E)(1) of section 101.311 of the Revised Code; and an assistant house sergeant at arms;" following "police officer of a township or joint township police district;" in division (B).

Amendment Note: 2000 S 137 inserted "special police officer employed by a port authority under section 4582.04 or 4582.28 of the Revised Code;" in division (B).

Amendment Note: 1999 H 163 substituted "enforcement agent" for "liquor control investigator or food stamp trafficking agent" and inserted "designated under section 5502.14 of the Revised Code" in division (B).

Amendment Note: 1998 S 187 rewrote division (B), which prior thereto read:

"(B) "Peace officer" includes, except as provided in section 2935.081 of the Revised Code, a sheriff, deputy sheriff, marshal, deputy marshal, member of the organized police department of any municipal corporation, including a member of the organized police department of a municipal corporation in an adjoining state serving in Ohio under a contract pursuant to section 737.04 of the Revised Code, member of a police force employed by a metropolitan housing authority under division (D) of section 3735.31 of the Revised Code, member of a police force employed by a regional transit authority under division (Y) of section 306.05 of the Revised Code, state university law enforcement officer appointed under section 3345.04 of the Revised Code, liquor control investigator or food stamp trafficking agent of the department of public safety, Ohio veterans' home policeman appointed under section 5907.02 of the Revised Code, police constable of any township, and police officer of a township or joint township police district, and, for the purpose of arrests within those areas, and for the purposes of Chapter 5503. of the Revised Code, and the filing of and service of process relating to those offenses witnessed or investigated by them, includes the superintendent and troopers of the state highway patrol."

Amendment Note: 1996 H 72 inserted ", except as provided in section 2935.081 of the Revised Code," in division (B); and deleted "to any of those persons" after "officer's assistants" in division (C).

Amendment Note: 1995 S 162 substituted "liquor control investigator or food stamp trafficking agent of the department of public safety" for "an" in division (B); substituted "any such officer's" for "his" in division (C); and made nonsubstantive changes.

Amendment Note: 1995 S 2 inserted "member of a police force employed by a regional transit authority under division (Y) of section 306.35 of the Revised Code," in division (B); and made other changes to reflect gender neutral language.

Cross References

Absent voter's ballots; peace officer, defined, 3509.02

Aggravated assault, peace officer as victim, 2903.12

Arrest of persons violating parole or pardon; peace officer, defined, 2941.46

Arrest of persons violating parole, pardon, or probation, 2967.15

Arrest of persons violating parole, pardon, or probation; peace officer, defined, 2301.31

Arrest of persons violating probation or community control sanctions; peace officer, defined, 2951.08

Arson; emergency personnel, defined, 2909.01

Campaign laws violations or noncompliance, expedited hearing; appropriate prosecutor, defined, 3517.155

Commercial driver's licenses; peace officer, defined, 4506.01

Complaint to keep the peace, 2933.02

Research References

Encyclopedias

OH Jur. 3d Businesses & Occupations § 220, Generally; Definitions.

OH Jur. 3d Cvl. Servants & Pub. Officers & Employ. § 176, Eligibility for Promotion.

OH Jur. 3d Cvl. Servants & Pub. Officers & Employ. § 490, Who is Prosecuting Attorney in Magistrates' Courts.

OH Jur. 3d Criminal Law § 994, Weight and Sufficiency, Generally.

OH Jur. 3d Criminal Law § 1643, Owner's Defenses.

OH Jur. 3d Criminal Law § 1919, Overview; What Constitutes Disability.

OH Jur. 3d Criminal Law § 2111, Generally; Peace Officers.

OH Jur. 3d Police, Sheriffs, & Related Officers § 6, Privileges and Exemptions; Disclosure of Home Address.

OH Jur. 3d Railroads § 421, Bylaws, Rules, and Regulations.

OH Jur. 3d Schools, Universities, & Colleges § 312, Free Tuition.

Treatises and Practice Aids

Katz, Giannelli, Blair and Lipton, Baldwin's Ohio Practice, Criminal Law, § 6:2, Arrest Defined.

Katz, Giannelli, Blair and Lipton, Baldwin's Ohio Practice, Criminal Law, § 7:6, Authority to Execute Arrest Warrants.

Katz, Giannelli, Blair and Lipton, Baldwin's Ohio Practice, Criminal Law, § 97:3, Assault.

Katz, Giannelli, Blair and Lipton, Baldwin's Ohio Practice, Criminal Law, § 97:4, Felonious Assault.

Katz, Giannelli, Blair and Lipton, Baldwin's Ohio Practice, Criminal Law, § 97:5, Aggravated Assault.

Katz, Giannelli, Blair and Lipton, Baldwin's Ohio Practice, Criminal Law, § 103:4, Aggravated Arson.

Katz, Giannelli, Blair and Lipton, Baldwin's Ohio Practice, Criminal Law, § 110:10, False Allegation of Police Officer Misconduct.

Katz, Giannelli, Blair and Lipton, Baldwin's Ohio Practice, Criminal Law, § 110:14, Disclosure of Confidential Information.

Katz, Giannelli, Blair and Lipton, Baldwin's Ohio Practice, Criminal Law, § 118:11.50, Shooting at a Police Officer.

Katz, Ohio Arrest, Search & Seizure § 3:2, Defining Arrest.

Adrine & Ruden, Ohio Domestic Violence Law § 3:3, Elements and Penalties—Felonious Assault Under RC 2903.11.

Adrine & Ruden, Ohio Domestic Violence Law § 3:4, Elements and Penalties—Aggravated Assault Under RC 2903.12.

Adrine & Ruden, Ohio Domestic Violence Law § 5:13, Case Preparation—Hearsay Exceptions—Generally.

Princehorn, Baldwin's Ohio Practice, Local Government Law—Township, § 11:15, Special Constables.

Law Review and Journal Commentaries

CRIMINAL PROCEDURE—Rejection of the Conduit Theory of Entrapment, Hampton v. United States, Note. 8 U Tol L Rev 473 (Winter 1977).

The Developing Role of the Magistrate in the Federal Courts, Jack B. Streepy. 29 Clev St L Rev 81 (1980).

The Gradation of Fourth Amendment Doctrine in the Context of Street Detentions: People v. DeBour, Comment. 38 Ohio St L J 409 (1977).

The Right to Resist an Unlawful Arrest: Judicial and Legislative Overreaction?, Comment. 10 Akron L Rev 171 (Summer 1976).

State v. Holbert: Limits on the Power of Township Police to Make Arrests on State Highways, Note. 2 Ohio N U L Rev 74 (1974).

Substantive Due Process and the Use of Deadly Force Against the Fleeing Felon: Wiley v. Memphis Police Dept & Mattis v. Schnarr, Note. 7 Cap U L Rev 497 (1978).

Notes of Decisions

Ed. Note: This section contains annotations from former RC 1731.03.

---

1. Peace officers generally

Enforcement agents with Department of Public Safety had statutory authority to stop defendant for suspected driving under influence of alcohol (DUI); agents' stop of defendant in parking lot of bar was result of their continuing investigation of alleged Title 43 liquor violations, and agents were vested with authority of peace officers to arrest and detain, until warrant could be obtained, any person found violating state law. State v. Robinson (Ohio App. 5 Dist., Stark, 03-29-2004) No. 2003CA00235, 2004-Ohio-1571, 2004 WL 621762, Unreported. Automobiles ⚿ 349(11)

Evidence of each necessary element of aggravated murder, aggravated robbery, and having a weapon under disability was sufficient to support defendant's convictions thereof, as well as related specifications; eyewitness testimony and forensic and documentary evidence, including DNA tests, autopsy results, and defendant's prior criminal record, indicated that victim, a deputy sheriff in performance of his duties, interrupted defendant's robbery of gas station, and that defendant repeatedly shot victim with victim's own gun, more than once in the head as victim lay prone, fled in his car, and went to residence of acquaintance, where he traded victim's gun for crack cocaine. State v. Gross (Ohio, 10-30-2002) 97 Ohio St.3d 121, 776 N.E.2d 1061, 2002-Ohio-5524, reconsideration denied 97 Ohio St.3d 1486, 780 N.E.2d 288, 2002-Ohio-6866, certiorari denied 123 S.Ct. 2079, 538 U.S. 1037, 155 L.Ed.2d 1068, rehearing denied 124 S.Ct. 20, 539 U.S. 976, 156 L.Ed.2d 685. Homicide ⚿ 1139; Robbery ⚿ 24.15(2); Weapons ⚿ 17(4)

Armed and uniformed institutional guards who were hired by city to transport prisoners were "peace officers" required by statute to be certified as such; duty of transporting prisoners involved preserving peace, protecting life and property and enforcing laws. Cleveland Police Patrolmen's Assn. v. Cleveland (Ohio App. 8 Dist., 03-17-1997) 118 Ohio App.3d 584, 693 N.E.2d 864, stay granted 78 Ohio St.3d 1470, 678 N.E.2d 579, motion to vacate denied 78 Ohio St.3d 1506, 679 N.E.2d 7, appeal not allowed 79 Ohio St.3d 1449, 680 N.E.2d 1022, reconsideration denied 79 Ohio St.3d 1492, 683 N.E.2d 793. Municipal Corporations ⚷ 184(2)

A privately employed security guard is not required to provide Miranda warnings upon detaining a shoplifting suspect because a private security guard is not a peace officer under RC 109.71(A)(1) or 2935.01(B). State v. Giallombardo (Portage 1986) 29 Ohio App.3d 279, 504 N.E.2d 1202, 29 O.B.R. 343.

One who is a reserve or special deputy sheriff qualifies as a peace officer as that term is utilized in RC 2929.04(A)(6), which section sets forth one of the criteria for imposing death or imprisonment for a capital offense. State v. Glenn (Ohio 1986) 28 Ohio St.3d 451, 504 N.E.2d 701, 28 O.B.R. 501, certiorari denied 107 S.Ct. 3219, 482 U.S. 931, 96 L.Ed.2d 705, rehearing denied 108 S.Ct. 18, 483 U.S. 1044, 97 L.Ed.2d 806, stay granted 33 Ohio St.3d 601, 514 N.E.2d 869, post-conviction relief denied, reconsideration denied, dismissed 57 Ohio St.3d 723, 568 N.E.2d 1226, certiorari denied 112 S.Ct. 110, 502 U.S. 833, 116 L.Ed.2d 79, habeas corpus granted 71 F.3d 1204, rehearing and suggestion for rehearing en banc denied, certiorari denied 117 S.Ct. 273, 136 L.Ed.2d 196.

A municipal police officer may make an arrest for a violation of a municipal ordinance, upon a properly issued warrant, anywhere within the jurisdictional limits of the issuing court. City of Fairborn v. Munkus (Ohio 1971) 28 Ohio St.2d 207, 277 N.E.2d 227, 57 O.O.2d 436. Arrest ⚷ 66(2)

Investigators for the state dental board are "peace officers," within the meaning of those words as used in RC 2935.01(B), and such investigators have the authority to file affidavits to cause prosecutions for violations of the laws regulating the practice of dentistry. State v. Colvin (Ohio 1969) 19 Ohio St.2d 86, 249 N.E.2d 784, 48 O.O.2d 94.

A police officer's testimony that he has been properly commissioned is sufficient evidence to prove the "peace officer specification," RC 2903.11(B); a certified copy of the officer's commission is not required. State v Watson, No. 56507 (8th Dist Ct App, Cuyahoga, 1–25–90).

A person appointed as a special constable pursuant to RC 1711.35 to assist in keeping the peace during a county agricultural society's annual fair is a "peace officer" as defined in RC 2935.01(B), but is not a "peace officer" as defined in RC 109.71(A). OAG 87–057.

Unless the superintendent of the state highway patrol approves the markings and design on motor vehicles and uniforms used by township police constables, such police constables will be incompetent to testify as a witness in any prosecution against a person charged with a violation of the motor vehicle or traffic laws of the state. 1963 OAG 259.

2. State highway patrol

Where a highway patrolman arrests a person found violating a law of this state, for which violation he is authorized to arrest, he must follow the procedure prescribed by RC 2935.03, RC 2935.05, RC 2935.08, and RC 2935.13. 1961 OAG 2214.

Where a person arrested by a highway patrolman under authority of RC 2935.03 posts bond in a municipal court for his appearance for trial at a later date, but does not appear on the date specified and the judge issues a warrant for his arrest and requests the highway patrolman to serve the warrant, the highway patrolman has a duty to serve the warrant as requested. 1961 OAG 2214.

State highway patrolmen are authorized to file and serve process relating to those offenses witnessed or investigated by them, such filing and service of process being the only ministerial duties which they are authorized to perform in county court procedures. 1959 OAG 1040.

RC 5503.02 does not require or authorize state highway patrolmen to deliver prisoners who have failed to post bond in a county court to the county jail or to deliver prisoners from the county jail to the county court for hearings of their cases. 1959 OAG 1040.

3. Prosecutor—in general

Courts of common pleas possess inherent power to appoint special prosecutors in criminal matters. State ex rel. Master v. Cleveland (Ohio, 03-04-1996) 75 Ohio St.3d 23, 661 N.E.2d 180, 1996-Ohio-228. District And Prosecuting Attorneys ⚷ 3(1)

Decision whether to prosecute is discretionary, and not generally subject to judicial review. State ex rel. Master v. Cleveland (Ohio, 03-04-1996) 75 Ohio St.3d 23, 661 N.E.2d 180, 1996-Ohio-228. District And Prosecuting Attorneys ⚷ 8

City prosecutor had no duty to initiate investigation into criminal wiretapping allegations that were already being investigated by other law enforcement personnel. State ex rel. Master v. Cleveland (Ohio, 03-04-1996) 75 Ohio St.3d 23, 661 N.E.2d 180, 1996-Ohio-228. District And Prosecuting Attorneys ⚷ 8

As an agent of the state, a prosecutor has a constitutional duty to assure a fair trial to the defendant; such constitutional duty includes the prosecutor's obligation to (1) reveal evidence favorable to the defendant, (2) correct testimony that he knows is untrue, and (3) refrain from the knowing use of perjured testimony. State v. Staten (Miami 1984) 14 Ohio App.3d 78, 470 N.E.2d 249, 14 O.B.R. 91.

Filing of affidavit by prosecuting attorney charging violation of RC 3773.24 was insufficient where there was no allegation that said affidavit was based upon the affidavit of a peace officer or private citizen filed with him before his own affidavit was filed. State v. Laughlin (Ohio Com.Pl. 1966) 10 Ohio Misc. 219, 225 N.E.2d 298, 39 O.O.2d 306. Sunday ⚷ 29(2)

4. —— Village or city solicitor, prosecutor

A village solicitor of a village with no police or municipal court, who has not contracted to be a "prosecutor," may be appointed to represent indigent defendants pursuant to RC Ch 120. OAG 76–069.

A city solicitor may not represent defendants in a criminal case wherein the state of Ohio is plaintiff. OAG 66–159.

It is the duty of a city solicitor to prepare affidavits and warrants of arrest for violations of the law which occur in the territorial area of the municipal court, to prosecute misdemeanor violations occurring in such area through to a final verdict except those violations which are specifically assigned to the prosecuting attorney by statute, and to represent the state on felony violations occurring in such area through the preliminary hearing stages. OAG 66–159.

5. Offense

The term "offense," as defined in RC 2935.01(D) and as used in RC 2953.32(C), is intended to include minor misdemeanors; therefore, a person convicted of permitting drug abuse does not qualify as a "first offender" under RC 2953.32 where he was previously convicted of the minor misdemeanor of disorderly conduct by intoxication. State v. Petrou (Summit 1984) 13 Ohio App.3d 456, 469 N.E.2d 974, 13 O.B.R. 546.

6. Actions of law enforcement officers

The fight against crime is not a game, and officers dealing with criminal suspects need not display the impeccable manners and sportsmanship characteristic of dealings between members of a horse riding club. U. S. v. Grimes (C.A.6 (Ohio) 1971) 438 F.2d 391, 13 A.L.R. Fed. 896, certiorari denied 91 S.Ct. 1684, 402 U.S. 989, 29 L.Ed.2d 155.

Police who hold the arm of an intoxicated and belligerent prisoner who is resisting arrest, without causing serious injury, and who use a "stungun" on his back, do not shock a federal court's conscience enough to result in a finding of excessive use of force in a suit under 42 USC 1983. Francis v. Pike County, Ohio (S.D.Ohio 1988) 708 F.Supp. 170, affirmed 875 F.2d 863.

Officers who arrest a belligerent drunk driver, use a "stungun" on him, and place him in a holding cell are not exposed to liability under 42 USC 1983 by the consequences of their failure to remove the man's belt where he did not "act disturbed"; thus, since no reasonable jury could find the officers acted with deliberation tantamount to an intent to punish the prisoner, summary judgment in their favor is in order. Francis v. Pike County, Ohio (S.D.Ohio 1988) 708 F.Supp. 170, affirmed 875 F.2d 863.

7. Bounty hunters

Pursuant to the bail contract, bail bondsmen have broad authority to use reasonable and necessary force against fugitives including a forced entry into the home of the fugitive; however, this broad authority does not extend to infringing upon third parties who are not parties to the bail contract. State v. Kole (Ohio App. 9 Dist., Lorain, 06-28-2000) No. 98CA007116, 2000 WL 840503, Unreported, appeal allowed 90 Ohio St.3d 1451, 737 N.E.2d 55, reversed 92 Ohio St.3d 303, 750 N.E.2d 148, 2001-Ohio-191.

Members of an association incorporated under GC 10200 (RC 1731.01) et seq. for the purpose of apprehending and convicting any person or persons accused of either felony or misdemeanor may make arrests anywhere within the state, subject to the limitations prescribed in GC 10203 (RC 1731.03) and GC 10204 (RC 1731.04). Fouts v. State (Ohio 1925) 113 Ohio St. 450, 149 N.E. 551, 3 Ohio Law Abs. 691, 23 Ohio Law Rep. 592.

A member of an association organized to apprehend felons and misdemeanants may not arrest without a warrant a person charged with a misdemeanor. 1931 OAG 3697.

2935.011 Officer or employee of bureau of criminal identification as peace officer

If an officer or employee of the bureau of criminal identification and investigation is included as a "peace officer" under division (B) of section 2935.01 of the Revised Code, both of the following apply:

(A) Division (D)(2) of section 109.541 applies to the officer or employee while so included.

(B) The officer or employee is not, as a result of the inclusion, a member of a police department for purposes of Chapter 742. of the Revised Code or a law enforcement officer or peace officer for purposes of any state or local retirement system.

(2002 H 427, eff. 8–29–02)

ARREST

2935.02 Accused may be arrested in any county

If an accused person flees from justice, or is not found in the county where a warrant for his arrest was issued, the officer holding the same may pursue and arrest him in any county in this state, and convey him before the magistrate or court of the county having cognizance of the case.

If such warrant directs the removal of the accused to the county in which the offense was committed, the officer holding the warrant shall deliver the accused to a court or magistrate of such county.

The necessary expense of such removal and reasonable compensation for his time and trouble, shall be paid to such officer out of the treasury of such county, upon the allowance and order of the county auditor.

(1953 H 1, eff. 10–1–53; GC 13432–10)

Historical and Statutory Notes

Pre–1953 H 1 Amendments: 113 v 141, Ch 11, § 10

Cross References

Extradition, Ch 2963
Warrant or summons, arrest, Crim R 4

Library References

Arrest ⚡66.
Westlaw Topic No. 35.
C.J.S. Arrest § 55.

Research References

Encyclopedias

OH Jur. 3d Counties, Townships, & Municipal Corp. § 260, Expenses Connected With Administration of Justice.

OH Jur. 3d Criminal Law § 2101, Territorial Extent of Power to Arrest With Warrant.

OH Jur. 3d Criminal Law § 2148, Arrest With Warrant; Detention, Custody, and Disposition of Arrested Person.

OH Jur. 3d Criminal Law § 3987, Liability of County.

Treatises and Practice Aids

Katz, Giannelli, Blair and Lipton, Baldwin's Ohio Practice, Criminal Law, § 7:7, Place of Execution.

Katz, Giannelli, Blair and Lipton, Baldwin's Ohio Practice, Criminal Law, § 35:7, Citizen's Complaint.

Law Review and Journal Commentaries

United States v *Alvarez–Machain*: The Supreme Court's Approval of the Abduction of Foreign Nationals, Comment. 25 U Tol L Rev 297 (1994).

Notes of Decisions

Territorial jurisdiction of municipal police 1

1. Territorial jurisdiction of municipal police

Police officers' arrest of motorist outside county where they were employed, in violation of statutes governing such extraterritorial arrests, did not rise to level of constitutional violation requiring suppression of evidence seized; officers arrested motorist in adjoining county where his vehicle came to rest after he had run stop sign located in county where officers were employed. Stow v. Riggenbach (Ohio App. 9 Dist., 10-26-1994) 97 Ohio App.3d 661, 647 N.E.2d 246. Criminal Law ⚡ 394.4(9)

A municipal police officer may make an arrest for a violation of a municipal ordinance, upon a properly issued warrant, anywhere within the jurisdictional limits of the issuing court. City of Fairborn v. Munkus (Ohio 1971) 28 Ohio St.2d 207, 277 N.E.2d 227, 57 O.O.2d 436. Arrest ⚡ 66(2)

A municipal police officer cannot execute a search warrant outside the boundaries of his municipality because such an act cannot be authorized by the legislative body of a municipality, within its power of local self-government, and has not been authorized by state statute. OAG 69–043.

2935.03 Arrest and detention until warrant can be obtained

(A)(1) A sheriff, deputy sheriff, marshal, deputy marshal, municipal police officer, township constable, police officer of a township or joint township police district, member of a police force employed by a metropolitan housing authority under division (D) of section 3735.31 of the Revised Code, member of a police force employed by a regional transit authority under division (Y) of section 306.35 of the Revised Code, state university law enforcement officer appointed under section 3345.04 of the Revised Code, veterans' home police officer appointed under section 5907.02 of the Revised Code, special police officer employed by a port authority under section 4582.04 or 4582.28 of the Revised Code, or a special police officer employed by a municipal corporation at a municipal airport, or other municipal air navigation facility, that has scheduled operations, as defined in section 119.3 of Title 14 of the Code of Federal Regulations, 14 C.F.R. 119.3, as amended, and that is required to be under a security program and is governed by aviation security rules of the transportation security administration of the United States department of transportation as provided in Parts 1542. and 1544. of Title 49 of the Code of Federal Regulations, as amended, shall arrest and detain, until a warrant can be obtained, a person found violating, within the limits of the political subdivision, metropolitan housing authority housing project, regional transit authority facilities or areas of a municipal corporation that have been agreed to by a regional transit authority and a municipal corporation located within its territorial jurisdiction, college, university, veterans' home operated under Chapter 5907. of the Revised Code, port authority, or municipal airport or other municipal air navigation facility, in which the peace officer is appointed, employed, or elected, a law of this state, an ordinance of a municipal corporation, or a resolution of a township.

(2) A peace officer of the department of natural resources or an individual designated to perform law enforcement duties under section 511.232, 1545.13, or 6101.75 of the Revised Code shall arrest and detain, until a warrant can be obtained, a person found violating, within the limits of the peace officer's or individual's territorial jurisdiction, a law of this state.

(3) The house sergeant at arms if the house sergeant at arms has arrest authority pursuant to division (E)(1) of section 101.311 of the Revised Code and an assistant house sergeant at arms shall arrest and detain, until a warrant can be obtained, a person found violating, within the limits of the sergeant at arms's or assistant sergeant at arms's territorial jurisdiction specified in division (D)(1)(a) of section 101.311 of the Revised Code or while providing security pursuant to division (D)(1)(f) of section 101.311 of the Revised Code, a law of this state, an ordinance of a municipal corporation, or a resolution of a township.

(B)(1) When there is reasonable ground to believe that an offense of violence, the offense of criminal child enticement as defined in section 2905.05 of the Revised Code, the offense of public indecency as defined in section 2907.09 of the Revised Code, the offense of domestic violence as defined in section 2919.25 of the Revised Code, the offense of violating a protection order as defined in section 2919.27 of the Revised Code, the offense of menacing by stalking as defined in section 2903.211 of the Revised Code, the offense of aggravated trespass as defined in section 2911.211 of the Revised Code, a theft offense as defined in section 2913.01 of the Revised Code, or a felony drug abuse offense as defined in section 2925.01 of the Revised Code, has been committed within the limits of the political subdivision, metropolitan housing authority housing project, regional transit authority facilities or those areas of a municipal corporation that have been agreed to by a regional transit authority and a municipal corporation located within its territorial jurisdiction, college, university, veterans' home operated under Chapter 5907. of the Revised Code, port authority, or municipal airport or other municipal air navigation facility, in which the peace officer is appointed, employed, or elected or within the limits of the territorial jurisdiction of the peace officer, a peace officer described in division (A) of this section may arrest and detain until a warrant can be obtained any person who the peace officer has reasonable cause to believe is guilty of the violation.

(2) For purposes of division (B)(1) of this section, the execution of any of the following constitutes reasonable ground to believe that the offense alleged in the statement was committed and reasonable cause to believe that the person alleged in the statement to have committed the offense is guilty of the violation:

(a) A written statement by a person alleging that an alleged offender has committed the offense of menacing by stalking or aggravated trespass;

(b) A written statement by the administrator of the interstate compact on mental health appointed under section 5119.51 of the Revised Code alleging that a person who had been hospitalized, institutionalized, or confined in any facility under an order made pursuant to or under authority of section 2945.37, 2945.371, 2945.38, 2945.39, 2945.40, 2945.401, or 2945.402 of the Revised Code has escaped from the facility, from confinement in a vehicle for transportation to or from the facility, or from supervision by an employee of the facility that is incidental to hospitalization, institutionalization, or confinement in the facility and that occurs outside of the facility, in violation of section 2921.34 of the Revised Code;

(c) A written statement by the administrator of any facility in which a person has been hospitalized, institutionalized, or confined under an order made pursuant to or under authority of section 2945.37, 2945.371, 2945.38, 2945.39, 2945.40, 2945.401, or 2945.402 of the Revised Code alleging that the person has escaped from the facility, from confinement in a vehicle for transportation to or from the facility, or from supervision by an employee of the facility that is incidental to hospitalization, institutionalization, or confinement in the facility and that occurs outside of the facility, in violation of section 2921.34 of the Revised Code.

(3)(a) For purposes of division (B)(1) of this section, a peace officer described in division (A) of this section has reasonable grounds to believe that the offense of domestic violence or the offense of violating a protection order has been committed and reasonable cause to believe that a particular person is guilty of committing the offense if any of the following occurs:

(i) A person executes a written statement alleging that the person in question has committed the offense of domestic violence or the offense of violating a protection order against the person who executes the statement or against a child of the person who executes the statement.

(ii) No written statement of the type described in division (B)(3)(a)(i) of this section is executed, but the peace officer, based upon the peace officer's own knowledge and observation of the facts and circumstances of the alleged incident of the offense of domestic violence or the alleged incident of the offense of violating a protection order or based upon any other information, including, but not limited to, any reasonably trustworthy information given to the peace officer by the alleged victim of the alleged incident of the offense or any witness of the alleged incident of the offense, concludes that there are reasonable grounds to believe that the offense of domestic violence or the offense of violating a protection order has been committed and reasonable cause to believe that the person in question is guilty of committing the offense.

(iii) No written statement of the type described in division (B)(3)(a)(i) of this section is executed, but the peace officer witnessed the person in question commit the offense of domestic violence or the offense of violating a protection order.

(b) If pursuant to division (B)(3)(a) of this section a peace officer has reasonable grounds to believe that the offense of domestic violence or the offense of violating a protection order has been committed and reasonable cause to believe that a particular person is guilty of committing the offense, it is the preferred course of action in this state that the officer arrest and detain that person pursuant to division (B)(1) of this section until a warrant can be obtained.

If pursuant to division (B)(3)(a) of this section a peace officer has reasonable grounds to believe that the offense of domestic violence or the offense of violating a protection order has been committed and reasonable cause to believe that family or household members have committed the offense against each other, it is the preferred course of action in this state that the officer, pursuant to division (B)(1) of this section, arrest and detain until a warrant can be obtained the family or household member who committed the offense and whom the officer has reasonable cause to believe is the primary physical aggressor. There is no preferred course of action in this state regarding any other family or household member who committed the offense and whom the officer does not have reasonable cause to believe is the primary physical aggressor, but, pursuant to division (B)(1) of this section, the peace officer may arrest and detain until a warrant can be obtained any other family or household member who committed the offense and whom the officer does not have reasonable cause to believe is the primary physical aggressor.

(c) If a peace officer described in division (A) of this section does not arrest and detain a person whom the officer has reasonable cause to believe committed the offense of domestic violence or the offense of violating a protection order when it is the preferred course of action in this state pursuant to division (B)(3)(b) of this section that the officer arrest that person, the officer shall articulate in the written report of the incident required by section 2935.032 of the Revised Code a clear statement of the officer's reasons for not arresting and detaining that person until a warrant can be obtained.

(d) In determining for purposes of division (B)(3)(b) of this section which family or household member is the primary physical aggressor in a situation in which family or household members have committed the offense of domestic violence or the offense of violating a protection order against each other, a peace officer described in division (A) of this section, in addition to any other relevant circumstances, should consider all of the following:

(i) Any history of domestic violence or of any other violent acts by either person involved in the alleged offense that the officer reasonably can ascertain;

(ii) If violence is alleged, whether the alleged violence was caused by a person acting in self-defense;

(iii) Each person's fear of physical harm, if any, resulting from the other person's threatened use of force against any person or resulting from the other person's use or history of the use of force against any person, and the reasonableness of that fear;

(iv) The comparative severity of any injuries suffered by the persons involved in the alleged offense.

(e)(i) A peace officer described in division (A) of this section shall not require, as a prerequisite to arresting or charging a person who has committed the offense of domestic violence or the offense of violating a protection order, that the victim of the offense specifically consent to the filing of charges against the person who has committed the offense or sign a complaint against the person who has committed the offense.

(ii) If a person is arrested for or charged with committing the offense of domestic violence or the offense of violating a protection order and if the victim of the offense does not cooperate with the involved law enforcement or prosecuting authorities in the prosecution of the offense or, subsequent to the arrest or the filing of the charges, informs the involved law enforcement or prosecuting authorities that the victim does not wish the prosecution of the offense to continue or wishes to drop charges against the alleged offender relative to the offense, the involved prosecuting authorities, in determining whether to continue with the prosecution of the offense or whether to dismiss charges against the alleged offender relative to the offense and notwithstanding the victim's failure to cooperate or the victim's wishes, shall consider all facts and circumstances that are relevant to the offense, including, but not limited to, the statements and observations of the peace officers who responded to the incident that resulted in the arrest or filing of the charges and of all witnesses to that incident.

(f) In determining pursuant to divisions (B)(3)(a) to (g) of this section whether to arrest a person pursuant to division (B)(1) of this section, a peace officer described in division (A) of this section shall not consider as a factor any possible shortage of cell space at the detention facility to which the person will be taken subsequent to the person's arrest or any possibility that the person's arrest might cause, contribute to, or exacerbate overcrowding at that detention facility or at any other detention facility.

(g) If a peace officer described in division (A) of this section intends pursuant to divisions (B)(3)(a) to (g) of this section to arrest a person pursuant to division (B)(1) of this section and if the officer is unable to do so because the person is not present, the officer promptly shall seek a warrant for the arrest of the person.

(h) If a peace officer described in division (A) of this section responds to a report of an alleged incident of the offense of domestic violence or an alleged incident of the offense of violating a protection order and if the circumstances of the incident involved the use or threatened use of a deadly weapon or any person involved in the incident brandished a deadly weapon during or in relation to the incident, the deadly weapon that was used, threatened to be used, or brandished constitutes contraband, and, to the extent possible, the officer shall seize the deadly weapon as contraband pursuant to section 2933.43 of the Revised Code. Upon the seizure of a deadly weapon pursuant to division (B)(3)(h) of this section, section 2933.43 of the Revised Code shall apply regarding the treatment and disposition of the deadly weapon. For purposes of that section, the "underlying criminal offense" that was the basis of the seizure of a deadly weapon under division (B)(3)(h) of this section and to which the deadly weapon had a relationship is any of the following that is applicable:

(i) The alleged incident of the offense of domestic violence or the alleged incident of the offense of violating a protection order to which the officer who seized the deadly weapon responded;

(ii) Any offense that arose out of the same facts and circumstances as the report of the alleged incident of the offense of domestic violence or the alleged incident of the offense of violating a protection order to which the officer who seized the deadly weapon responded.

(4) If, in the circumstances described in divisions (B)(3)(a) to (g) of this section, a peace officer described in division (A) of this section arrests and detains a person pursuant to division (B)(1) of this section, or if, pursuant to division (B)(3)(h) of this section, a peace officer described in division (A) of this section seizes a deadly weapon, the officer, to the extent described in and in accordance with section 9.86 or 2744.03 of the Revised Code, is immune in any civil action for damages for injury, death, or loss to person or property that arises from or is related to the arrest and detention or the seizure.

(C) When there is reasonable ground to believe that a violation of division (A)(1), (2), (3), (4), or (5) of section 4506.15 or a violation of section 4511.19 of the Revised Code has been committed by a person operating a motor vehicle subject to regulation by the public utilities commission of Ohio under Title XLIX of the Revised Code, a peace officer with authority to enforce that provision of law may stop or detain the person whom the officer has reasonable cause to believe was operating the motor vehicle in violation of the division or section and, after investigating the circumstances surrounding the operation of the vehicle, may arrest and detain the person.

(D) If a sheriff, deputy sheriff, marshal, deputy marshal, municipal police officer, member of a police force employed by a metropolitan housing authority under division (D) of section 3735.31 of the Revised Code, member of a police force employed by a regional transit authority under division (Y) of section 306.35 of the Revised Code, special police officer employed by a port authority under section 4582.04 or 4582.28 of the Revised Code, special police officer employed by a municipal corporation at a municipal airport or other municipal air navigation facility described in division (A) of this section, township constable, police officer of a township or joint township police district, state university law enforcement officer appointed under section 3345.04 of the Revised Code, peace officer of the department of natural resources, individual designated to perform law enforcement duties under section 511.232, 1545.13, or 6101.75 of the Revised Code, the house sergeant at arms if the house sergeant at arms has arrest authority pursuant to division (E)(1) of section 101.311 of the Revised Code, or an assistant house sergeant at arms is authorized by division (A) or (B) of this section to arrest and detain, within the limits of the political subdivision, metropolitan housing authority housing project, regional transit authority facilities or those areas of a municipal corporation that have been agreed to by a regional transit authority and a municipal corporation located within its territorial jurisdiction, port authority, municipal airport or other municipal air navigation facility, college, or university in which the officer is appointed, employed, or elected or within the limits of the territorial jurisdiction of the peace officer, a person until a warrant can be obtained, the peace officer, outside the limits of that territory, may pursue, arrest, and detain that person until a warrant can be obtained if all of the following apply:

(1) The pursuit takes place without unreasonable delay after the offense is committed;

(2) The pursuit is initiated within the limits of the political subdivision, metropolitan housing authority housing project, regional transit authority facilities or those areas of a municipal corporation that have been agreed to by a regional transit authority and a municipal corporation located within its territorial jurisdiction, port authority, municipal airport or other municipal air navigation facility, college, or university in which the peace officer is appointed, employed, or elected or within the limits of the territorial jurisdiction of the peace officer;

(3) The offense involved is a felony, a misdemeanor of the first degree or a substantially equivalent municipal ordinance, a misdemeanor of the second degree or a substantially equivalent municipal ordinance, or any offense for which points are chargeable pursuant to section 4510.036 of the Revised Code.

(E) In addition to the authority granted under division (A) or (B) of this section:

(1) A sheriff or deputy sheriff may arrest and detain, until a warrant can be obtained, any person found violating section 4503.11, 4503.21, or 4549.01, sections 4549.08 to 4549.12, section 4549.62, or Chapter 4511. or 4513. of the Revised Code on the portion of any street or highway that is located immediately adjacent to the boundaries of the county in which the sheriff or deputy sheriff is elected or appointed.

(2) A member of the police force of a township police district created under section 505.48 of the Revised Code, a member of the police force of a joint township police district created under section 505.481 of the Revised Code, or a township constable appointed in accordance

with section 509.01 of the Revised Code, who has received a certificate from the Ohio peace officer training commission under section 109.75 of the Revised Code, may arrest and detain, until a warrant can be obtained, any person found violating any section or chapter of the Revised Code listed in division (E)(1) of this section, other than sections 4513.33 and 4513.34 of the Revised Code, on the portion of any street or highway that is located immediately adjacent to the boundaries of the township police district or joint township police district, in the case of a member of a township police district or joint township police district police force, or the unincorporated territory of the township, in the case of a township constable. However, if the population of the township that created the township police district served by the member's police force, or the townships that created the joint township police district served by the member's police force, or the township that is served by the township constable, is sixty thousand or less, the member of the township police district or joint police district police force or the township constable may not make an arrest under division (E)(2) of this section on a state highway that is included as part of the interstate system.

(3) A police officer or village marshal appointed, elected, or employed by a municipal corporation may arrest and detain, until a warrant can be obtained, any person found violating any section or chapter of the Revised Code listed in division (E)(1) of this section on the portion of any street or highway that is located immediately adjacent to the boundaries of the municipal corporation in which the police officer or village marshal is appointed, elected, or employed.

(4) A peace officer of the department of natural resources or an individual designated to perform law enforcement duties under section 511.232, 1545.13, or 6101.75 of the Revised Code may arrest and detain, until a warrant can be obtained, any person found violating any section or chapter of the Revised Code listed in division (E)(1) of this section, other than sections 4513.33 and 4513.34 of the Revised Code, on the portion of any street or highway that is located immediately adjacent to the boundaries of the lands and waters that constitute the territorial jurisdiction of the peace officer.

(F)(1) A department of mental health special police officer or a department of mental retardation and developmental disabilities special police officer may arrest without a warrant and detain until a warrant can be obtained any person found committing on the premises of any institution under the jurisdiction of the particular department a misdemeanor under a law of the state.

A department of mental health special police officer or a department of mental retardation and developmental disabilities special police officer may arrest without a warrant and detain until a warrant can be obtained any person who has been hospitalized, institutionalized, or confined in an institution under the jurisdiction of the particular department pursuant to or under authority of section 2945.37, 2945.371, 2945.38, 2945.39, 2945.40, 2945.401, or 2945.402 of the Revised Code and who is found committing on the premises of any institution under the jurisdiction of the particular department a violation of section 2921.34 of the Revised Code that involves an escape from the premises of the institution.

(2)(a) If a department of mental health special police officer or a department of mental retardation and developmental disabilities special police officer finds any person who has been hospitalized, institutionalized, or confined in an institution under the jurisdiction of the particular department pursuant to or under authority of section 2945.37, 2945.371, 2945.38, 2945.39, 2945.40, 2945.401, or 2945.402 of the Revised Code committing a violation of section 2921.34 of the Revised Code that involves an escape from the premises of the institution, or if there is reasonable ground to believe that a violation of section 2921.34 of the Revised Code has been committed that involves an escape from the premises of an institution under the jurisdiction of the department of mental health or the department of mental retardation and developmental disabilities and if a department of mental health special police officer or a department of mental retardation and developmental disabilities special police officer has reasonable cause to believe that a particular person who has been hospitalized, institutionalized, or confined in the institution pursuant to or under authority of section 2945.37, 2945.371, 2945.38, 2945.39, 2945.40, 2945.401, or 2945.402 of the Revised Code is guilty of the violation, the special police officer, outside of the premises of the institution, may pursue, arrest, and detain that person for that violation of section 2921.34 of the Revised Code, until a warrant can be obtained, if both of the following apply:

(i) The pursuit takes place without unreasonable delay after the offense is committed;

(ii) The pursuit is initiated within the premises of the institution from which the violation of section 2921.34 of the Revised Code occurred.

(b) For purposes of division (F)(2)(a) of this section, the execution of a written statement by the administrator of the institution in which a person had been hospitalized, institutionalized, or confined pursuant to or under authority of section 2945.37, 2945.371, 2945.38, 2945.39, 2945.40, 2945.401, or 2945.402 of the Revised Code alleging that the person has escaped from the premises of the institution in violation of section 2921.34 of the Revised Code constitutes reasonable ground to believe that the violation was committed and reasonable cause to believe that the person alleged in the statement to have committed the offense is guilty of the violation.

(G) As used in this section:

(1) A "department of mental health special police officer" means a special police officer of the department of mental health designated under section 5119.14 of the Revised Code who is certified by the Ohio peace officer training commission under section 109.77 of the Revised Code as having successfully completed an approved peace officer basic training program.

(2) A "department of mental retardation and developmental disabilities special police officer" means a special police officer of the department of mental retardation and developmental disabilities designated under section 5123.13 of the Revised Code who is certified by the Ohio peace officer training council under section 109.77 of the Revised Code as having successfully completed an approved peace officer basic training program.

(3) "Deadly weapon" has the same meaning as in section 2923.11 of the Revised Code.

(4) "Family or household member" has the same meaning as in section 2919.25 of the Revised Code.

(5) "Street" or "highway" has the same meaning as in section 4511.01 of the Revised Code.

(6) "Interstate system" has the same meaning as in section 5516.01 of the Revised Code.

(7) "Peace officer of the department of natural resources" means an employee of the department of natural resources who is a natural resources law enforcement staff officer designated pursuant to section 1501.013 of the Revised Code, a forest officer designated pursuant to section 1503.29 of the Revised Code, a preserve officer designated pursuant to section 1517.10 of the Revised Code, a wildlife officer designated pursuant to section 1531.13 of the Revised Code, a park officer designated pursuant to section 1541.10 of the Revised Code, or a state watercraft officer designated pursuant to section 1547.521 of the Revised Code.

(2005 H 68, eff. 6–29–05; 2002 H 675, § 1.04, eff. 1–1–04; 2002 H 675, § 1.01, eff. 3–14–03; 2002 H 545, eff. 3–19–03; 2002 S 123, eff. 1–1–04; 2000 S 317, eff. 3–22–01; 2000 S 137, eff. 5–17–00; 1998 S 187, eff. 3–18–99; 1997 S 1, eff. 10–21–97; 1996 S 285, eff. 7–1–97; 1996 H 670, eff. 12–2–96; 1996 S 269, eff. 7–1–96; 1995 S 2, eff. 7–1–96; 1994 H 335, eff. 12–9–94; 1994 S 82, eff. 5–4–94; 1993 H 42, eff. 2–9–94; 1992 H 536; 1991 H 77; 1990 H 669, H 88; 1988 H 708, § 1)

Historical and Statutory Notes

Ed. Note: Former 2935.03 repealed by 1988 H 708, § 2, eff. 4–19–88; 1988 H 708, § 18; 1987 H 231, § 1, 6, H 261, § 1, 3; 1986 S 356, § 1, 3, H 284, § 1, 3; 1985 S 33, § 1, 3; 1984 H 129, § 1, 3, S 321; 1980 S 355; 1978 H 835, H 588; 1975 H 300; 1972 H 511; 132 v S 29; 1953 H 1; GC 13432–1.

Pre–1953 H 1 Amendments: 115 v 530; 113 v 140, Ch 11, § 1

Amendment Note: 2005 H 68 deleted "or" and inserted ", (4), or (5)" in division (C); and inserted "of the Revised Code" throughout division (G)(7).

Amendment Note: 2002 H 545 inserted ", or a special police officer employed by a municipal corporation at a municipal airport, or other municipal air navigation facility, that has scheduled operations, as defined in section 119.3 of Title 14 of the Code of Federal Regulations, 14 C.F.R. 119.3, as amended, and that is required to be under a security program and is governed by aviation security rules of the transportation security administration of the United States department of transportation as provided in Parts 1542. and 1544. of Title 49 of the Code of Federal Regulations, as amended," and ", or municipal airport or other municipal air navigation facility," in division (A)(1); substituted "arms's" for "arm's" in division (A)(3); inserted ", or municipal airport or other municipal air navigation facility," in division (B)(1); inserted "special police officer employed by a municipal corporation at a municipal airport or other municipal air navigation facility described in division (A) of this section," and "municipal airport or other municipal air navigation facility," in division (D); inserted "municipal airport or other municipal air navigation facility," in division (D)(2); and made other nonsubstantive changes.

Amendment Note: 2002 H 675 inserted "operated under Chapter 5907. of the Revised Code" in divisions (A)(1) and (B)(1); and made other nonsubstantive changes.

Amendment Note: 2002 S 123 substituted "(1), (2), or (3)" for "(B) or (C)" in division (C); substituted "section 4510.036" for "division (G) of section 4507.021" in division (D)(3); and made other nonsubstantive changes to the section.

Amendment Note: 2000 S 317 added new division (A)(3); and deleted "or" following "peace officer of the department of natural resources," and inserted ", the house sergeant at arms if the house sergeant at arms has arrest authority pursuant to division (E)(1) of section 101.311 of the Revised Code, or an assistant house sergeant at arms".

Amendment Note: 2000 S 137 inserted "special police officer employed by a port authority under section 4582.04 or 4582.28 of the Revised Code" in divisions (A)(1) and in the introductory paragraph in division (D); inserted "port authority" after "veteran's home" in divisions (A)(1) and (B)(1) and after "territorial jurisdiction" in the introductory paragraph in division (D) and in division (D)(2); and made nonsubstantive changes.

Amendment Note: 1998 S 187 designated division (A)(1); added division (A)(2); inserted "or within the limits of the territorial jurisdiction of the peace officer" and deleted "(1)" after "(A)" in division (B)(1); changed references to division (B)(1) to references to division (A) throughout divisions (B)(3) and (B)(4); inserted "township", ", peace officer of the department of natural resources, or individual designated to perform law enforcement duties under section 511.232, 1545.13, or 6101.75 of the Revised Code", and "or within the limits of the territorial jurisdiction of the peace officer" in the first paragraph in division (D); inserted "or within the limits of the territorial jurisdiction of the peace officer" in division (D)(2); added divisions (E)(4) and (G)(7); and made other nonsubstantive changes.

Amendment Note: 1997 S 1 deleted the phrase "or consent agreement" following "violating a protection order" throughout; and substituted "if violence is alleged, whether" for "whether" in division (B)(1)(d)(ii).

Amendment Note: 1996 S 285 inserted references to sections 2945.401 and 2945.402 throughout the section and made related nonsubstantive changes.

Amendment Note: 1996 H 670 substituted "commission" for "council" in divisions (E)(2) and (G)(1).

Amendment Note: 1996 S 269 deleted "member of a police force employed by a" following "metropolitan housing authority housing project," and substituted "facilities or areas of a municipal corporation that have been agreed to by a regional transit authority and a municipal corporation located within its territorial jurisdiction" for "under division (Y) of section 306.36 of the Revised Code" in division (B)(1); deleted "(A)(1) of this section intends to arrest a person pursuant to division (A)(2) of this section or a peace officer described in division" preceding "(B)(1) of this section intends" and "in either case" preceding "the officer" in division (B)(3)(g); made changes to reflect gender neutral language; and made other nonsubstantive changes.

Amendment Note: 1995 S 2 inserted "member of a police force employed by a regional transit authority under division (Y) of section 306.35 of the Revised Code," in divisions (A) and (B)(1) and the first paragraph in division (D); inserted "regional transit authority facilities or those areas of a municipal corporation that have been agreed to by a regional transit authority and a municipal corporation located within its territorial jurisdiction" in division (A), the first paragraph in division (D), and division (D)(2); substituted "peace officer described in division (A)(1) of this section" for "sheriff, deputy sheriff, marshal, deputy marshal, municipal police officer, township constable, police officer of a township or joint township police district, member of a police force employed by a metropolitan housing authority under division (D) of section 3735.31 of the Revised Code, state university law enforcement officer appointed under section 3345.04 of the Revised Code, or Ohio veterans' home policeman appointed under section 5907.02 of the Revised Code" in division (B)(1); substituted "that territory" for "the political subdivision, metropolitan housing authority housing project, college, or university in which he is appointed, employed, or elected" in the first paragraph in division (D); and made other changes to reflect gender neutral language.

Amendment Note: 1994 H 335 inserted "the offense of violating a protection order or consent agreement as defined in section 2919.27 of the Revised Code," in division (B)(1); deleted former division (B)(2)(a); redesignated former division (B)(2)(b) and the first paragraph of former division (B)(2)(c) as divisions (B)(2)(a) and (B)(2)(b), respectively; added division (B)(3); removed the designation of the first paragraph of division (G) as division (G)(1) and deleted "division (F) of" before "this section" therein; redesignated former divisions (G)(1)(a) and (G)(1)(b) as divisions (G)(1) and (G)(2); added divisions (G)(3) and (G)(4); redesignated former divisions (G)(2)(a) and (G)(2)(b) as divisions (G)(5) and (G)(6); and deleted "(2) As used in division (E) of this section:" before division (G)(5). Prior to amendment, division (B)(2)(a) read:

"(a) A written statement by a person alleging that an alleged offender has committed the offense of domestic violence against the person or against a child of the person;"

Amendment Note: 1994 S 82 substituted "a violation" for "division (A)" following "section 4506.15 or" and inserted "or section" in division (C).

Amendment Note: 1993 H 42 designated divisions (B)(1) and (B)(2)(a) and (b); added divisions (B)(2)(c), (F), and (G)(1); and redesignated former divisions (F)(1) and (2) as divisions (G)(2)(a) and (b), respectively.

Cross References

Appointment and use of state university law enforcement officers, 3345.04

Arrest and bail in civil actions, 2713.01 to 2713.29

Arrest of persons violating parole, arrest powers of law enforcement officers not limited, 2301.31

Arrest of persons violating parole or pardon; arrest powers of law enforcement officers not limited, 2941.46

Arrest of persons violating probation or community control sanctions, arrest powers of law enforcement officers not limited, 2951.08

Commercial driver's licenses, powers of peace officers; jurisdictional limits, defined, 4506.23

Convention facilities authorities, special policemen, 351.07

Disposition of fines and moneys, 4513.35

Duties and compensation of port authority employees, special policemen, 4582.04

Emergency assistance to peace officer by investigator for bureau of criminal identification and investigation, 109.541

Forest officer, authority, 1503.29

Freedom from unreasonable seizure; warrants, O Const Art I §14

General duties of police, 737.11

Highway patrol troopers rendering emergency assistance to peace officers, 5503.02

Metropolitan housing authorities, police powers, 3735.31

Motion for temporary protection order, domestic violence, 2919.26

Natural resources law enforcement staff officers, powers, 1501.013

Park officers, authority, 1541.10

Port authorities, special policemen, 4582.28

Power of arrest for violations on state highways, 4513.39

Preserve officers, authority, 1517.10

Privilege from arrest, 2331.11 to 2331.14

Public safety department enforcement agents, powers, 5502.14

Regional transit authority, powers and duties, 306.35

State highway patrol, special police officers, 5503.09

Warrant or summons, arrest, Crim R 4, 9

Watercraft division chief and state watercraft officers, authority, 1547.521

Wildlife division chief and game protectors, authority, 1531.13

Youth services department, arrest of child violating supervised release from, 5139.52

Library References

Arrest ⟹63.

Westlaw Topic No. 35.

C.J.S. Arrest §§ 9, 14 to 39, 42 to 44.

Research References

Encyclopedias

OH Jur. 3d Criminal Law § 116, Federal Constitutional Foundations.

OH Jur. 3d Criminal Law § 126, Exclusionary Rule as Remedy for Statutory Violation.

OH Jur. 3d Criminal Law § 277, Questioning Under Certain Circumstances.

OH Jur. 3d Criminal Law § 2105, Territorial Power to Arrest Without Warrant.

OH Jur. 3d Criminal Law § 2107, Violations Involving Alcohol.

OH Jur. 3d Criminal Law § 2108, Misdemeanors and Other Minor Offenses.

OH Jur. 3d Criminal Law § 2111, Generally; Peace Officers.

OH Jur. 3d Criminal Law § 2113, Special Police Officers Under Jurisdiction of Department of Mental Retardation and Developmental Disabilities.

OH Jur. 3d Criminal Law § 2126, Duty to Investigate.

OH Jur. 3d Criminal Law § 2130, Information Derived from a Trustworthy Source.

OH Jur. 3d Workers' Compensation § 126, in the Course Of, and Arising Out of Employment.

OH Jur. 3d Workers' Compensation § 139, "Special Hazard" Rule.

Forms

Ohio Jurisprudence Pleading and Practice Forms § 61:3, General Rule of Competency.

Treatises and Practice Aids

Markus, Trial Handbook for Ohio Lawyers, § 29:8, Search Incident to Valid Arrest.

Markus, Trial Handbook for Ohio Lawyers, § 4:61, Criminal Case—Defenses—Self-Defense and Justifiable Force.

Katz, Giannelli, Blair and Lipton, Baldwin's Ohio Practice, Criminal Law, § 6:6, Warrantless Misdemeanor Arrests—"In Presence" Rule.

Katz, Giannelli, Blair and Lipton, Baldwin's Ohio Practice, Criminal Law, § 6:7, "In Presence" Rule—Dui Cases.

Katz, Giannelli, Blair and Lipton, Baldwin's Ohio Practice, Criminal Law, § 6:9, Extraterritorial Misdemeanor Arrests.

Katz, Giannelli, Blair and Lipton, Baldwin's Ohio Practice, Criminal Law, § 7:6, Authority to Execute Arrest Warrants.

Katz, Giannelli, Blair and Lipton, Baldwin's Ohio Practice, Criminal Law, § 29:5, Exclusionary Rule—Statutes.

Katz, Giannelli, Blair and Lipton, Baldwin's Ohio Practice, Criminal Law, § 5:21, Statutory Designation of Probable Cause in Domestic Violence Cases.

Katz, Giannelli, Blair and Lipton, Baldwin's Ohio Practice, Criminal Law, § 89:2, Police Arrest.

Katz, Giannelli, Blair and Lipton, Baldwin's Ohio Practice, Criminal Law, § 109:15, Domestic Violence.

Sowald & Morganstern, Baldwin's Ohio Practice Domestic Relations Law § 5:3, Criminal Domestic Violence—Practice and Procedure.

Katz, Ohio Arrest, Search & Seizure § 4:3, Nature of the Offense—Misdemeanors.

Katz, Ohio Arrest, Search & Seizure § 4:4, Misdemeanors: Exceptions to the "In Presence" Requirement.

Katz, Ohio Arrest, Search & Seizure § 4:5, Extraterritorial Misdemeanor Arrests.

Katz, Ohio Arrest, Search & Seizure § 2:25, Statutory Designation of Probable Cause in Domestic Violence Cases.

Katz, Ohio Arrest, Search & Seizure § 27:3, Exclusion for Violation of State Law.

Katz, Ohio Arrest, Search & Seizure App. A, Appendix A. Arrest Provisions: Checklist.

Adrine & Ruden, Ohio Domestic Violence Law § 3:7, Elements and Penalties—Aggravated Trespass Under RC 2911.211.

Adrine & Ruden, Ohio Domestic Violence Law § 4:7, Enforcement of a Protection Order.

Adrine & Ruden, Ohio Domestic Violence Law § 5:2, Prosecutorial Discretion.

Adrine & Ruden, Ohio Domestic Violence Law § 5:3, Case Triage.

Adrine & Ruden, Ohio Domestic Violence Law § 7:4, Arrest Considerations—Determining the Primary Physical Aggressor.

Adrine & Ruden, Ohio Domestic Violence Law § 7:5, Pretrial Detention and Initial Appearance Issues.

Adrine & Ruden, Ohio Domestic Violence Law § 8:6, Parents and Children.

Adrine & Ruden, Ohio Domestic Violence Law § 11:3, Full Hearing—Participation of the Parties.

Adrine & Ruden, Ohio Domestic Violence Law § 12:3, Court Enforcement of Civil Protection Orders—Criminal Prosecution.

Adrine & Ruden, Ohio Domestic Violence Law § 13:2, Ohio Statutory Procedure.

Adrine & Ruden, Ohio Domestic Violence Law § 13:3, Arrest of the Perpetrator.

Adrine & Ruden, Ohio Domestic Violence Law § 13:4, Determination of Primary Physical Aggressor.

Adrine & Ruden, Ohio Domestic Violence Law § 13:5, False Arrest, Warrantless Arrests and Searches, and Weapons Confiscation.

Adrine & Ruden, Ohio Domestic Violence Law § 13:6, Law Enforcement Policies and Procedures.

Adrine & Ruden, Ohio Domestic Violence Law § 14:6, Ohio's Judicial Response to Domestic Violence.

Adrine & Ruden, Ohio Domestic Violence Law § 17:8, Firearm Offenses Under Vawa.

Adrine & Ruden, Ohio Domestic Violence Law § 5:11, Case Preparation—Physical Evidence.

Adrine & Ruden, Ohio Domestic Violence Law § 9:11, Parties Authorized to File for Civil Protection Orders.

Adrine & Ruden, Ohio Domestic Violence Law § 9:13, Jurisdiction and Venue—in Domestic Violence Cases.

Adrine & Ruden, Ohio Domestic Violence Law § 10:19, Ex Parte Protection Orders—Available Relief—Property Division.

Adrine & Ruden, Ohio Domestic Violence Law § 10:22, Ex Parte Protection Orders—Miscellaneous Issues.

Adrine & Ruden, Ohio Domestic Violence Law § 11:21, Remedies—Miscellaneous Issues.

Adrine & Ruden, Ohio Domestic Violence Law § 11:28, Mutual Protection Orders.

Adrine & Ruden, Ohio Domestic Violence Law § 13:12, Police Liability for Failing to Protect Victims of Domestic Violence—Legal Theories for Recovery—State Duty to Protect.

Adrine & Ruden, Ohio Domestic Violence Law § 13:14, Significant Cases Involving Police Officer Action or Inaction.

Adrine & Ruden, Ohio Domestic Violence Law § 13:15, Potential Police Liability in the Enforcement of Protection Orders.

Painter, Ohio Driving Under the Influence § 10:7, Jurisdiction to Stop, Detain, and Arrest—Existence of Jurisdiction.

Painter, Ohio Driving Under the Influence § 10:8, Jurisdiction to Stop, Detain, and Arrest—Extraterritorial Detention and Arrest.

Painter, Ohio Driving Under the Influence § 8:14, Burden of Proof—Warrant Requirement.

Painter, Ohio Driving Under the Influence § 8:29, Probable Cause for Arrest.

Painter, Ohio Driving Under the Influence § 8:33, Arrest—View Requirement.

Giannelli & Yeomans, Ohio Juvenile Law § 14:3, Custody, Arrests & Stops.

Gotherman, Babbit and Lang, Baldwin's Ohio Practice, Local Government Law—Municipal, § 26:4, Metropolitan Housing Authorities.

Gotherman, Babbit and Lang, Baldwin's Ohio Practice, Local Government Law—Municipal, § 8:23, Safety Forces.

Gotherman, Babbit and Lang, Baldwin's Ohio Practice, Local Government Law—Municipal, § 8:31, Arrest Powers.

Gotherman, Babbit and Lang, Baldwin's Ohio Practice, Local Government Law—Municipal, § 23:16, Extraterritorial Exercise of Municipal Power.

Gotherman, Babbit and Lang, Baldwin's Ohio Practice, Local Government Law—Municipal, § 28:41, Arrest of Violators.

Princehorn, Baldwin's Ohio Practice, Local Government Law—Township, § 5:1, Regional Councils.

Princehorn, Baldwin's Ohio Practice, Local Government Law—Township, § 11:9, Territorial Jurisdiction.

Princehorn, Baldwin's Ohio Practice, Local Government Law—Township, § 49:4, Enforcement.

Princehorn, Baldwin's Ohio Practice, Local Government Law—Township, § 52:1, Contract for Police Protection.

Princehorn, Baldwin's Ohio Practice, Local Government Law—Township, § 52:6, Authority to Arrest and Detain Until Warrant Can be Obtained.

Princehorn, Baldwin's Ohio Practice, Local Government Law—Township, § 52:7, Power to Make Arrests for Traffic Violations.

Princehorn, Baldwin's Ohio Practice, Local Government Law—Township, § 57:2, Authority to Make Arrests.

Princehorn, Baldwin's Ohio Practice, Local Government Law—Township, § 11:11, Duties of Constable—Criminal.

Princehorn, Baldwin's Ohio Practice, Local Government Law—Township, § 11:39, Police Officers—Territorial Jurisdiction.

Princehorn, Baldwin's Ohio Practice, Local Government Law—Township, § 11:40, Police Officers—Duties.

Princehorn, Baldwin's Ohio Practice, Local Government Law—Township, § 11:43, Police Officers—Authority to Arrest and Detain Until Warrant Can be Obtained.

Law Review and Journal Commentaries

Arrest and Detention Procedures, Arthur V. N. Brooks and David M. Liebenthal. 38 Clev B J 85 (March 1967).

Fundamentally Speaking: Application of Ohio's Domestic Violence Laws in Parental Discipline Cases—A Parental Perspective, Richard Garner. 30 U Tol L Rev 1 (Fall 1998).

International Law: The Supreme Court Rules On Government Authorized Abduction—United States v Alvarez-Machain, Note. 18 U Dayton L Rev 889 (Spring 1993).

Mandatory arrest: A step toward eradicating domestic violence, but is it enough?, Note. 1996 U Ill L Rev 533.

No-Drop Policies: Effective Legislation or Protectionist Attitude?, Note. 30 U Tol L Rev 621 (Summer 1999).

Spouse Battering and Ohio's Domestic Violence Legislation, Comment. 13 U Tol L Rev 347 (Winter 1982).

State v. Anderson: Misdemeanor Arrest Beyond Municipal Limits, Note. 4 Ohio N U L Rev 470 (1977).

Notes of Decisions

---

1. Constitutional issue—confessions and statements generally

Defendant was not subjected to custodial interrogation at time he made statements to police officer prior to his arrest for domestic violence, and thus no *Miranda* warnings were required, despite defendant's contention that, under preferred arrest policies in domestic violence cases, he was in custody the moment the officer entered his home; defendant voluntarily responded to officer and generally felt at ease with officer, and officer's questions were intended to investigate alleged incident, not to extract confession. Akron v. Sutton (Ohio Mun., 04-04-2000) 106 Ohio Misc.2d 46, 733 N.E.2d 690. Criminal Law ⚷ 412.2(2)

2. —— Warrantless arrest or pursuit to arrest, constitutional issues

Police officer lacked statutory authority to make warrantless arrest of defendant for disorderly conduct; officer did not have personal knowledge of events, which allegedly involved defendant repeatedly knocking on door of residence early in morning, officer's only information about events was based on hearsay statements of occupant of residence, and occupant's allegation did not involve violence, domestic violence, theft, illegal drugs, or any other enumerated exception in warrantless-arrest statute. State v. Benner (Ohio App. 3 Dist., Seneca, 10-11-2005) No. 13-05-14, 2005-Ohio-5374, 2005 WL 2495471, Unreported. Arrest ⚷ 63.4(13)

Police officer did not have probable cause to make warrantless arrest of defendant for disorderly conduct, even though occupant of residence told officer early in morning that man named "Jeremy" was banging on doors of residence, and defendant provided name of "Jeremy" when he was found near residence; officer did not have personal knowledge of events. State v. Benner (Ohio App. 3 Dist., Seneca, 10-11-2005) No. 13-05-14, 2005-Ohio-5374, 2005 WL 2495471, Unreported. Arrest ⚷ 63.4(13)

Counsel's failure to file motion to suppress based on warrantless arrest did not constitute deficient performance, as required to support claim of ineffective assistance of counsel, in trial for felonious assault; domestic violence complaint executed by defendant's girlfriend was sufficient to justify defendant's warrantless arrest and detention for that offense. State v. Christian (Ohio App. 7 Dist., Mahoning, 03-21-2005) No. 02 CA 170, 2005-Ohio-1440, 2005 WL 704866, Unreported. Criminal Law ⚷ 641.13(6)

Police officers' interview with assault victims in which victims gave description of attacker, followed by officers' immediate drive to location where victims believed defendant lived, amounted to "pursuit," within meaning of statute authorizing police officer to arrest an individual outside officer's territorial jurisdiction. State v. Williamson (Ohio App. 12 Dist., Butler, 05-03-2004) No. CA2003-02-047, 2004-Ohio-2209, 2004 WL 937326, Unreported. Arrest ⚷ 66(3)

Police officer had reasonable grounds to arrest defendant for domestic violence, and thus sheriff's mandatory arrest policy for potential domestic-violence situations, as applied to defendant, was not unconstitutional; officer determined defendant was primary aggressor based on victim's statements to him and injuries he saw on victim, and victim signed affidavit alleging defendant committed domestic violence against her. State v. Lampe (Ohio App. 1 Dist., Hamilton, 06-13-2003) No. C-020708, 2003-Ohio-3059, 2003 WL 21360725, Unreported. Arrest ⚷ 63.4(15)

Warrantless entry into suspect's home to arrest him for domestic violence did not violate the Fourth Amendment, where suspect's girlfriend consented to the entry by telling officers she would leave the back door unlocked, and officers' observation of girlfriend's injuries provided reasonable grounds to believe suspect had assaulted her. Alley v. Bettencourt (Ohio App. 4 Dist., 09-10-1999) 134 Ohio App.3d 303, 730 N.E.2d 1067. Arrest ⚷ 68(13)

Information derived from investigation by city police department prior to defendant's arrest provided the police with reasonable cause to believe defendant had committed an offense of violence within the city, as statutory basis for warrantless arrest. State v. Mesa (Ohio, 10-20-1999) 87 Ohio St.3d 105, 717 N.E.2d 329, 1999-Ohio-253. Arrest ⚷ 63.4(11)

Authority granted by statute to a police officer to effect a warrantless arrest outside territorial limits of his jurisdiction provided that pursuit is initiated within limits of political subdivision in which officer is appointed, employed, or elected does not confer authority upon a municipal officer to arrest without a warrant outside geographic boundaries of his municipality for traffic offenses observed by officer to have been committed outside municipal limits. State v. Coppock (Ohio App. 2 Dist., 05-05-1995) 103 Ohio App.3d 405, 659 N.E.2d 837. Arrest ⚷ 66(2)

To have executed a proper warrantless traffic arrest outside territorial limits of police officer's jurisdiction, police officer must have observed a misdemeanor violation which occurred within confines of his jurisdiction or on that portion of highway contiguous to city limits and initiated pursuit from within his jurisdiction or where adjoining jurisdictions are contiguous. State v. Coppock (Ohio App. 2 Dist., 05-05-1995) 103 Ohio App.3d 405, 659 N.E.2d 837. Arrest ⚷ 66(3)

Police officer failed to comply with statute in effecting a warrantless arrest for misdemeanor traffic offense outside of territorial limits of his jurisdiction given that officer did not possess probable cause of a traffic violation within his jurisdiction and he did not commence his pursuit until he was outside of his territorial jurisdictional boundaries; however, if stop did not violate constitutional law, the fact that it violated state law was not a bar to prosecution nor a defense to a valid conviction. State v. Coppock (Ohio App. 2 Dist., 05-05-1995) 103 Ohio App.3d 405, 659 N.E.2d 837. Automobiles ⚷ 349(12); Criminal Law ⚷ 99

Absent exigent circumstances, arrest of defendant for misdemeanor after warrantless entry of police into defendant's home was unlawful. State v. Lee (Ohio Mun. 1983) 8 Ohio Misc.2d 28, 457 N.E.2d 377, 8 O.B.R. 397. Arrest ⚷ 68(10)

RC 2935.03, as amended by 132 v S 29, eff. 12–13–67, which authorizes a police officer to arrest without a warrant any person he has reasonable cause to believe is guilty of certain enumerated violations, including assault and battery, a misdemeanor, is constitutional. City of Columbus v. Herrell (Franklin 1969) 18 Ohio App.2d 149, 247 N.E.2d 770, 47 O.O.2d 254. Arrest ⚿ 63.4(1)

Police officer is permitted to make arrest without warrant for misdemeanor committed in his presence. U.S. v. Smith (C.A.6 (Ohio), 01-25-1996) 73 F.3d 1414. Arrest ⚿ 63.3

Requirement that misdemeanor must have occurred in police officer's presence to justify warrantless arrest is not mandated by the Fourth Amendment; it is merely a rule of common law. U.S. v. Smith (C.A.6 (Ohio), 01-25-1996) 73 F.3d 1414. Arrest ⚿ 63.3

Under Ohio law, generally, misdemeanor must be committed in officer's presence for officer to make warrantless arrest for misdemeanor offense. U.S. v. Smith (C.A.6 (Ohio), 01-25-1996) 73 F.3d 1414. Arrest ⚿ 63.3

Offenses of possessing open container of alcoholic beverage in motor vehicle and consumption of alcohol in motor vehicle were committed in officers' presence, and thus they had authority to arrest defendant, even though defendant temporarily eluded officers after they saw him drinking beer in car and was not drinking beer when officers subsequently found him. U.S. v. Smith (C.A.6 (Ohio), 01-25-1996) 73 F.3d 1414. Automobiles ⚿ 349(6); Automobiles ⚿ 349(2.1)

The federal constitution does not guarantee that only people guilty of a crime will be pursued or arrested, and thus police do not "shock the conscience" of a federal judge by chasing an individual whose flight violates RC 2921.33 or 4511.02; consequently, state troopers' high-speed chase of a fleeing motorcyclist does not violate the cyclist's civil rights and a suit on his behalf under 42 USC 1983 will be dismissed. York v. Lamantia (N.D.Ohio 1987) 674 F.Supp. 17.

3. —— Probable cause, constitutional issues

City police officer had probable cause to arrest fellow officer for domestic violence in incident underlying arrested officer's action against city and city police officers for malicious prosecution, false arrest, and civil conspiracy, where alleged victim's sister called police after phone conversation with alleged victim abruptly ended when arrested officer told alleged victim to get off the phone and when the alleged victim told the officer to "get your hands off me", and alleged victim told arresting officer the arrested officer pushed her into a wall twice, scratched her neck, and put her in a choke hold. Wolford v. Sanchez (Ohio App. 9 Dist., Lorain, 12-30-2005) No. 05CA008674, 2005-Ohio-6992, 2005 WL 3556681, Unreported, appeal not allowed 109 Ohio St.3d 1481, 847 N.E.2d 1226, 2006-Ohio-2466. Arrest ⚿ 63.4(11); False Imprisonment ⚿ 13; Malicious Prosecution ⚿ 18(5)

Officer was authorized to execute traffic stop of defendant in jurisdiction adjacent to his territorial jurisdiction; officer observed defendant commit a speeding violation within his territorial jurisdiction to which points were chargeable, and officer effectuated investigatory traffic stop in the adjacent jurisdiction without unreasonable delay. City of Heath v. Johnson (Ohio App. 5 Dist., Licking, 02-03-2005) No. 04-CA-29, 2005-Ohio-485, 2005 WL 299710, Unreported. Automobiles ⚿ 349(12)

Police officer had reasonable suspicion to stop defendant's vehicle for speeding; officer activated police cruiser's radar unit and clocked defendant's vehicle's speed at 10 miles per hour over the 50 mile-per-hour posted speed limit. City of Heath v. Johnson (Ohio App. 5 Dist., Licking, 02-03-2005) No. 04-CA-29, 2005-Ohio-485, 2005 WL 299710, Unreported. Automobiles ⚿ 349(2.1)

Police investigating murders had probable cause to detain and arrest defendant based upon information supplied by friend of defendant; police learned from friend that defendant had borrowed his car under suspicious circumstances on night of murders, had not come back for a long time, had changed clothes, and had been in a fight; friend also disclosed that defendant had admitted to another friend that defendant and his brother had killed victims, and friend disclosed details about crime scene that only killer would have known. State v. Smith (Ohio, 10-15-1997) 80 Ohio St.3d 89, 684 N.E.2d 668, 1997-Ohio-355, reconsideration denied 80 Ohio St.3d 1471, 687 N.E.2d 299, certiorari denied 118 S.Ct. 1811, 523 U.S. 1125, 140 L.Ed.2d 949, dismissal of post-conviction relief affirmed 1998 WL 549964, dismissed, appeal not allowed 84 Ohio St.3d 1469, 704 N.E.2d 578, reconsideration denied 85 Ohio St.3d 1410, 706 N.E.2d 791, habeas corpus denied in part 2003 WL 24136073, habeas corpus denied 2005 WL 1969309. Arrest ⚿ 63.4(7.1)

Police officers who smelled burning marijuana when defendant opened door to his apartment did not have probable cause to arrest defendant for any criminal offense, so as to permit search incident to arrest; odor of burning marijuana provided probable cause only as to commission of minor-misdemeanor drug offense that would warrant only issuance of citation. State v. Robinson (Ohio App. 1 Dist., 06-07-1995) 103 Ohio App.3d 490, 659 N.E.2d 1292, dismissed, appeal not allowed 74 Ohio St.3d 1418, 655 N.E.2d 738, reconsideration denied 74 Ohio St.3d 1465, 656 N.E.2d 1300. Arrest ⚿ 63.4(5)

Issues of fact as to whether police officer employed as security guard at grocery store arrested and detained customer upon "probable cause" to believe that customer was guilty of shoplifting or upon "reasonable ground" to believe that theft offense was committed and "reasonable cause" to believe that customer was perpetrator, precluded summary judgment on customer's false arrest and false imprisonment claims against officer and store. Evans v. Smith (Ohio App. 1 Dist., 09-14-1994) 97 Ohio App.3d 59, 646 N.E.2d 217. Judgment ⚿ 181(33)

Where an arrest without a warrant violated probable cause requirements under US Const Am 4 and 14, evidence secured as an incident to such arrest should have been excluded from the trial. State v.

Timson (Ohio 1974) 38 Ohio St.2d 122, 311 N.E.2d 16, 67 O.O.2d 140. Criminal Law ⇐ 394.4(9)

Although the common law authorized a police officer to make an arrest without a warrant for a misdemeanor only in cases where the violation was committed in his presence and involved a breach of the peace, while permitting an arrest for a felony when the officer believed on reasonable grounds that the person arrested had committed such felony, there is no constitutional inhibition against modification of such common-law rules by legislation, so long as the "probable cause" requirements of O Const Art I §14 and US Const Am 4 are met. City of Columbus v. Herrell (Franklin 1969) 18 Ohio App.2d 149, 247 N.E.2d 770, 47 O.O.2d 254.

Respondents were properly convicted on charges of transporting illegal aliens where experienced border patrol agents took into account the totality of the circumstances before conducting an investigative stop of respondents' vehicle. U.S. v. Cortez (U.S.Ariz. 1981) 101 S.Ct. 690, 449 U.S. 411, 66 L.Ed.2d 621, on remand 653 F.2d 1253.

Where, on information furnished by an informer, an arrest is made without a warrant, it is incumbent upon the prosecution to show specifically what the informer actually said and why the officer thought the information was credible; good faith on the part of the officer is not sufficient to show probable cause. Beck v. State of Ohio (U.S.Ohio 1964) 85 S.Ct. 223, 379 U.S. 89, 3 Ohio Misc. 71, 13 L.Ed.2d 142, 31 O.O.2d 80.

Whether an arrest is constitutionally valid depends on whether, at the moment the arrest is made, the officer has probable cause to make it. U. S. v. Edwards (C.A.6 (Ohio) 1973) 474 F.2d 1206, certiorari granted 94 S.Ct. 160, 414 U.S. 818, 38 L.Ed.2d 50, reversed 94 S.Ct. 1234, 415 U.S. 800, 39 L.Ed.2d 771, vacated 497 F.2d 925.

There is probable cause to arrest a defendant where (1) the defendant and his companion are seen directly in front of the post office three minutes before a police officer receives a message that the silent alarm in the post office has been triggered, (2) the defendant and his companion are the only persons observed by the officer in that vicinity late on a Sunday night, and (3) the officer testifies that it appeared as though the two men had just turned out of the drive leading to the post office. U. S. v. Edwards (C.A.6 (Ohio) 1973) 474 F.2d 1206, certiorari granted 94 S.Ct. 160, 414 U.S. 818, 38 L.Ed.2d 50, reversed 94 S.Ct. 1234, 415 U.S. 800, 39 L.Ed.2d 771, vacated 497 F.2d 925. Arrest ⇐ 63.4(17)

Whether there was probable cause for arrest is decided by a standard based on the conduct of reasonable men, not legal technicians; there is probable cause for an arrest when the facts and circumstances known by an officer, based on reasonably trustworthy information, warrant a man of reasonable caution to believe an offense has been committed. O'Kelly v. Russell Tp. Bd. of Trustees (N.D.Ohio 1987) 675 F.Supp. 389.

A policeman who sees a car swerving, turns around to follow it, and finds a man who smells of liquor stumbling out of the driver's door has probable cause to arrest the man; the fact that the man's license is later restored upon proof his wife had been driving and had gone in the house before the police arrived has no bearing on the existence of probable cause. O'Kelly v. Russell Tp. Bd. of Trustees (N.D.Ohio 1987) 675 F.Supp. 389.

4. —— Force, constitutional issues

A police officer on duty who shoots and kills a civilian but not while attempting to effectuate an arrest is not entitled in a wrongful death action to an instruction that a police officer has no duty to retreat while acting in performance of his duties; the officer is entitled only to a standard self-defense instruction on the duty to retreat where he testifies that at the time of the shooting he was acting solely in defense of himself and not in pursuit of his official duties. Fields v. Dailey (Franklin 1990) 68 Ohio App.3d 33, 587 N.E.2d 400, motion to certify overruled 56 Ohio St.3d 703, 564 N.E.2d 707, rehearing denied 57 Ohio St.3d 706, 566 N.E.2d 171.

A Tennessee statute authorizing the use of deadly force to halt a fleeing felony suspect is unconstitutional insofar as it authorizes the unreasonable seizure of that suspect by the use of deadly force, in the absence of probable cause to believe he poses a physical danger to others or has committed a violent crime. (Ed. note: Tennessee law construed in light of federal constitution.) Tennessee v. Garner (U.S.Tenn. 1985) 105 S.Ct. 1694, 471 U.S. 1, 85 L.Ed.2d 1.

An individual has a right to not be shot by police unless he is perceived to pose a threat to the pursuing officers or to other people; where three officers shoot a paranoid schizophrenic, armed only with knives, twenty-two times in three volleys and where the record suggests that the third volley is ten or twelve minutes after the second and the wounded man had apparently dropped his weapons by this time, a genuine issue of fact exists whether the officers fired their second and third volleys at a man who posed no serious threat to them of physical harm. Russo v. City of Cincinnati (C.A.6 (Ohio) 1992) 953 F.2d 1036.

The fight against crime is not a game, and officers dealing with criminal suspects need not display the impeccable manners and sportsmanship characteristic of dealings between members of a horse riding club. U. S. v. Grimes (C.A.6 (Ohio) 1971) 438 F.2d 391, 13 A.L.R. Fed. 896, certiorari denied 91 S.Ct. 1684, 402 U.S. 989, 29 L.Ed.2d 155.

Assuming driver and passengers intended to state a racial profiling claim against police officers, officers' alleged use of foul language, in commanding passengers and driver to exit vehicle and get on ground, was not unusual under the circumstances, let alone racially motivated. Alexander v. Haymon (S.D.Ohio, 01-14-2003) 254 F.Supp.2d 820. Civil Rights ⇐ 1088(4)

Sheriff's deputy's alleged act of handcuffing nonthreatening arrestee too tightly after arrestee had informed deputy that he had preexisting nerve damage in his arm and shoulder, and refusing to loosen cuffs when requested, constituted violation of arrestee's constitutional right not to be subjected to unreasonable use of force, as required to support arrestee's 1983 action against deputy. Turek v. Saluga (C.A.6 (Ohio), 09-24-2002) No. 01-3986, No. 01-4018, 47 Fed.Appx. 746, 2002 WL 31119691, Unreported, certiorari denied 123 S.Ct. 2251, 539 U.S. 903, 156 L.Ed.2d 112. Arrest ⚷ 68(2)

"Clearly established" element was satisfied in arrestee's 1983 excessive-force action against sheriff's deputy alleging neurological injuries from too-tight handcuffs, precluding qualified immunity for deputy; deputy knew arrestee had preexisting arm and shoulder injury, yet declined to handcuff arrestee in front as permitted by sheriff's policy manual when health of suspect might be compromised, arrestee's crime was not severe, arrestee posed no threat to deputy, and arrestee made no attempt to resist arrest. Turek v. Saluga (C.A.6 (Ohio), 09-24-2002) No. 01-3986, No. 01-4018, 47 Fed. Appx. 746, 2002 WL 31119691, Unreported, certiorari denied 123 S.Ct. 2251, 539 U.S. 903, 156 L.Ed.2d 112. Civil Rights ⚷ 1376(6)

5. —— Search incident to arrest, constitutional issues

Unconstitutional excessive force alleged in §§ 1983 action occurred at time that cocaine possession suspect was arrested, and thus applicable Ohio statute of limitations began to accrue on day of arrest; although suspect purportedly did not realize permanent nature of his injuries until three months after arrest, actual harm resulted from alleged choking and hitting by officers during arrest. Hodge v. City of Elyria (C.A.6 (Ohio), 03-03-2005) No. 03-3296, 126 Fed.Appx. 222, 2005 WL 513486, Unreported. Limitation Of Actions ⚷ 58(1); Limitation Of Actions ⚷ 95(15)

Even if defendant was not on property of city housing authority at time of his arrest by housing authority police following suspected drug transaction, evidence found in inventory search of defendant's vehicle was not subject to suppression based on officers' alleged absence of jurisdiction; arrest would not have been violation of Fourth Amendment, but only of state law. State v. Fannin (Ohio App. 8 Dist., Cuyahoga, 11-21-2002) No. 79991, 2002-Ohio-6312, 2002 WL 31618484, Unreported, appeal not allowed 99 Ohio St.3d 1438, 789 N.E.2d 1118, 2003-Ohio-2902. Criminal Law ⚷ 394.4(12)

Police officers could conduct brief patdown search of driver before detaining him in back seat of patrol car after he failed to produce license following lawful stop for speeding; officers were statutorily authorized to arrest driver. State v. Mason (Ohio App. 7 Dist., 11-08-1996) 115 Ohio App.3d 187, 684 N.E.2d 1294. Automobiles ⚷ 349(2.1); Automobiles ⚷ 349.5(10)

A custodial search of the handbag of one lawfully arrested for a misdemeanor committed in the presence of a police officer is a reasonable search under US Const Am 4, and evidence so obtained is properly admissible in a criminal action. State v. Mathews (Ohio 1976) 46 Ohio St.2d 72, 346 N.E.2d 151, 75 O.O.2d 150.

Where police officers on cruiser patrol in April at 9:20 p.m. stop, for a traffic violation, a black Cadillac automobile occupied by three males, one whom, in the back seat, they had observed wearing a ski mask, and the automobile fits a police bulletin description of a car used in recent robberies, and at the time of one such robbery it was occupied by three males, and the police arrest the defendant and the driver of the car on outstanding traffic warrants, and the police observe inside the car a ski mask on the rear seat, another ski mask on the passenger side of the front seat and a portable police-band radio on the middle arm rest in the front seat, the totality of the circumstances is sufficient to make reasonable, incident to the arrests, a search of the car for weapons; and such search is not violative of US Const Am 4. State v. Reynolds (Ohio 1972) 32 Ohio St.2d 101, 290 N.E.2d 557, 61 O.O.2d 367.

Where a law enforcement officer lawfully arrests a motorist for a minor traffic offense, his contemporaneous search of the motorist and the vehicle for weapons, without a search warrant, is lawful, but the lawful scope thereof is limited to those areas reasonably necessary for the protection of the officer. State v. Coles (Ohio Com.Pl. 1969) 20 Ohio Misc. 12, 249 N.E.2d 553, 48 O.O.2d 309, 49 O.O.2d 21.

A police officer may not search, or seize articles found in, a motor vehicle following an arrest for "speeding," where the circumstances are such that there is no reasonable basis for believing that a search for weapons is necessary for such officer's protection or to prevent an escape, and such officer has no probable cause to believe that a crime had been or is being committed. State v. Call (Montgomery 1965) 8 Ohio App.2d 277, 220 N.E.2d 130, 37 O.O.2d 274.

The search of an individual's person on the honest belief of an arresting officer, based upon probable cause that a felony has been committed, does not constitute an unlawful search, and incriminating articles seized during the search may properly be received in evidence against the individual at his trial for having in his possession such articles. State v. Beck (Ohio 1963) 175 Ohio St. 73, 191 N.E.2d 825, 23 O.O.2d 377, certiorari granted 84 S.Ct. 664, 376 U.S. 905, 11 L.Ed.2d 604, reversed 85 S.Ct. 223, 379 U.S. 89, 3 Ohio Misc. 71, 13 L.Ed.2d 142, 31 O.O.2d 80. Arrest ⚷ 71.1(12); Criminal Law ⚷ 394.4(4)

Search incident to arrest exception to warrant requirement, motor vehicle searches, probable cause to arrest, issuance of citation. Knowles v. Iowa (U.S.Iowa, 12-08-1998) 119 S.Ct. 484, 525 U.S. 113, 142 L.Ed.2d 492.

6. —— Double jeopardy, constitutional issues

Assuming that an ordinance prohibiting the playing of excessively loud music is deemed unconstitutional subsequent to a defendant's arrest, any evidence obtained during a search incident to that arrest nevertheless need not be suppressed for lack of probable cause since music in the defendant's car so loud that police officers could "feel" it violates the anti-loud music ordinance so that a subsequent search is valid. State v. Harris (Ohio App. 8 Dist., Cuyahoga, 03-31-1994) No. 65520, 1994 WL 110938, Unreported.

If a defendant in a criminal case is charged, tried and discharged, he cannot be rearrested upon a complaint and warrant and retried for the same offense, because to do so would put him twice in jeopardy because jeopardy attaches the moment the jury is sworn; however, a person who was illegally arrested without a warrant and discharged before trial may subsequently be arrested with a warrant and tried for the same offense for which he was previously charged because he has not been placed in jeopardy, in violation of the constitutional prohibition against double jeopardy. State ex rel. Wilson v. Nash (Cuyahoga 1974) 41 Ohio App.2d 201, 324 N.E.2d 774, 70 O.O.2d 409.

7. Arrest or detention

Police officer had no authority to arrest defendant, as was required for entry and search of her home based on a valid arrest; there was no evidence defendant refused to sign citation for drug abuse of marijuana or that officer ever attempted to give defendant the citation before he entered her home. City of Akron v. Gardner (Ohio App. 9 Dist., Summit, 12-29-2004) No. CIV.A. 22062, 2004-Ohio-7165, 2004 WL 3017231, Unreported. Arrest ⚷ 68(9)

An officer's act of handcuffing a defendant for suspected drug activity constitutes an arrest rather than a mere detention; the officer manifests his intention to arrest the defendant and acts under the authority of a city police department when he seizes the defendant by handcuffing him. State v. Nelson (Cuyahoga 1991) 72 Ohio App.3d 506, 595 N.E.2d 475. Arrest ⚷ 68(3)

Defendant was "arrested" for violating city ordinance where police officer followed defendant to his home and then had defendant follow him back to police station at which time he was cited. Village of Brookville v. Louthan (Ohio Co. 1982) 3 Ohio Misc.2d 1, 441 N.E.2d 308, 3 O.B.R. 64. Arrest ⚷ 68(3)

The general assembly has not identified in RC 2935.03(B) the reasons a peace officer may consider for not arresting and detaining a person the officer has reasonable grounds to believe committed the offense of domestic violence. Rather, pursuant to RC 2935.032, the policy adopted by an agency, instrumentality, or subdivision to implement the domestic violence arrest provisions must set forth examples of reasons a peace officer may consider for not arresting and detaining a person in that situation. OAG 01–039.

8. Warrantless arrest

Warrantless arrest of defendant on misdemeanors at his apartment was not in-home arrest of type prohibited by Fourth Amendment, as there was no entry into defendant's apartment; deputy remained in hallway outside during his entire colloquy with defendant, and defendant did not attempt to close door or to retreat into his apartment, but voluntarily stepped into common hallway when asked to do so by deputy. State v. Norris (Ohio Mun., 06-17-1996) 81 Ohio Misc.2d 38, 674 N.E.2d 788. Arrest ⚷ 68(7)

The phrase "immediately adjacent," as used in statute permitting a police officer to effect a warrantless arrest outside territorial limits of his jurisdiction on the portion of any street or highway that is located immediately adjacent to the boundaries of municipal corporation in which police officer is appointed, elected, or employed, means that the jurisdictions must be contiguous. State v. Coppock (Ohio App. 2 Dist., 05-05-1995) 103 Ohio App.3d 405, 659 N.E.2d 837. Arrest ⚷ 66(2)

A resisting arrest conviction cannot stand where the warrantless arrest from which the charge stems is based on a misdemeanor not committed in a police officer's presence. State v. Miller (Highland 1990) 70 Ohio App.3d 727, 591 N.E.2d 1355.

An officer effecting a warrantless arrest for a misdemeanor must have reasonable grounds to believe that the person has committed a misdemeanor in his presence; further, probable cause must be based on personal knowledge, and hearsay statements from three witnesses are insufficient to permit such a warrantless arrest. State v. Reymann (Summit 1989) 55 Ohio App.3d 222, 563 N.E.2d 749, dismissed 42 Ohio St.3d 702, 536 N.E.2d 1171.

Information supplied by officers or agencies engaged in a common investigation with an arresting officer may be used to establish probable cause for a warrantless arrest. State v. Henderson (Ohio 1990) 51 Ohio St.3d 54, 554 N.E.2d 104, rehearing denied 52 Ohio St.3d 704, 556 N.E.2d 530. Arrest ⚷ 63.4(11)

Where a police officer at an accident scene reasonably concludes that a defendant was operating a motor vehicle while under the influence of alcohol shortly before the officer arrived on the scene, a warrantless arrest of the defendant is not precluded by RC 2935.03, because the defendant is "a person found violating a law of this state or an ordinance of a municipal corporation" within the meaning of RC 2935.03(A). City of Bucyrus v. Williams (Crawford 1988) 46 Ohio App.3d 43, 545 N.E.2d 1298. Automobiles ⚷ 349(6)

Even though it may be illegal under RC 2935.03 for an officer to arrest a suspect for a misdemeanor committed outside the officer's presence, a search based on such an arrest need not be suppressed if the arresting officer had a reasonable basis for the arrest in a radio report from another officer who did witness the misdemeanor. State v. Holmes (Hamilton 1985) 28 Ohio App.3d 12, 501 N.E.2d 629, 28 O.B.R. 21.

State patrolmen are governed by the same standards as are police officers in warrantless arrests for misdemeanors; the phrase "person... in the presence of" contained in RC 5503.01 is equivalent to the phrase "person found violating" contained in RC 2935.03. State v. Scherer (Ohio Mun. 1981) 69 Ohio Misc. 1, 430 N.E.2d 478, 23 O.O.3d 40.

A person suspected of the misdemeanor of drug abuse may not be arrested unless the violation is observed. State v. Pender (Ohio Mun. 1980) 66

Ohio Misc. 23, 419 N.E.2d 1141, 20 O.O.3d 148. Arrest ⚷ 63.1

Arrests for misdemeanors must be based upon a viewing by the arresting police officer or there must be present a probable cause exception of theft, violence or domestic violence. State v. Pender (Ohio Mun. 1980) 66 Ohio Misc. 23, 419 N.E.2d 1141, 20 O.O.3d 148.

An individual may be arrested for the minor misdemeanor of intoxication if the offender is unable to provide for his own safety. State v. Pender (Ohio Mun. 1980) 66 Ohio Misc. 23, 419 N.E.2d 1141, 20 O.O.3d 148.

Under RC 2935.03, as amended by 132 v S 29, eff. 12–13–67, the specified law enforcement officers may arrest without a warrant upon reasonable ground to believe that there has been a violation of certain misdemeanor sections, but may not so arrest as to any other misdemeanors. State v. Williams (Ohio Mun. 1969) 20 Ohio Misc. 51, 251 N.E.2d 714, 49 O.O.2d 97. Arrest ⚷ 63.4(5)

A police officer who does not see a misdemeanor committed and does not have warrants for the arrest of a defendant on his person, but does know about the existence of warrants for the arrest of a defendant for a misdemeanor, has the right to place said defendant under arrest. State v. Crockett (Ohio Mun. 1967) 10 Ohio Misc. 131, 226 N.E.2d 846, 39 O.O.2d 245.

The law of the case as enunciated by a common pleas court is as much a part of the law of this state to be observed and enforced as is a state statute, or city or village ordinance. State ex rel. Bruns Coal Co. v. United Mine Workers of America (Ohio Com.Pl. 1952) 110 N.E.2d 162, 63 Ohio Law Abs. 531, affirmed in part, reversed in part 96 Ohio App. 541, 123 N.E.2d 43, 55 O.O. 127, appeal dismissed 160 Ohio St. 320, 116 N.E.2d 203, 52 O.O. 208.

Where a breach of the peace is committed in the presence of a marshal of an incorporated village or city, he may, without warrant, arrest the persons who participate therein; if, however, the officer was absent when such offense was committed, and did not appear there until after the affray had ended, public order restored, and the guilty parties had departed from the vicinity, and all the information the officer had of the affray, and of the parties to it, was the statements of bystanders who witnessed it, he has no authority, in law, to pursue and arrest the persons charged with the offense, without first obtaining a warrant. State v. Lewis (Ohio 1893) 50 Ohio St. 179, 29 W.L.B. 180, 33 N.E. 405.

Under a proper construction of these sections, a marshal of a municipal corporation is authorized, without warrant, to arrest a person found on the public streets of the corporation carrying concealed weapons contrary to law, although he had no previous knowledge of the fact, if he acted bona fide, and upon such information as induces as honest belief that the person arrested is in the act of violating the law. Ballard v. State (Ohio 1885) 43 Ohio St. 340, 14 W.L.B. 22, 1 N.E. 76. Arrest ⚷ 63.4(5)

The ancient common-law rule empowering a peace officer to arrest without warrant any individual who commits a misdemeanor or felony in his presence still stands. Hoover v. Garfield Heights Mun. Court (C.A.6 (Ohio) 1986) 802 F.2d 168, certiorari denied 107 S.Ct. 1610, 480 U.S. 949, 94 L.Ed.2d 796.

Arrest of disorderly person and detention for police action not false imprisonment. Erie R. Co. v. Reigherd (C.C.A.6 (Ohio) 1909) 166 F. 247, 92 C.C.A. 590, 7 Ohio Law Rep. 485, 16 Am.Ann.Cas. 459.

Where police officers were informed that accused refused to leave premises, arrest of accused for criminal trespass was justified. U. S. v. Prescott (W.D.Pa. 1979) 480 F.Supp. 554.

Nonresident police officer is empowered to make a warrantless arrest for misdemeanors under RC 2935.03, notwithstanding a municipal residency requirement for police officers, where such residency ordinance is not self-executing, and the municipality has taken no steps to enforce the ordinance pursuant to RC 737.19(B). State v Artiaga, No. OT–86–41 (6th Dist Ct App, Ottawa, 3–27–87).

Where a defendant is standing at the threshold within the frame of an open door and while he is half in and half out of the building line of his residence, the defendant is considered to be in a public place and a warrantless arrest based on probable cause is valid. State v Seymour, No. CA 9060 (2d Dist Ct App, Montgomery, 8–29–85).

Pursuant to RC 2935.03(C), a township constable may, without a warrant and within the limits of the township, arrest a person for the commission of a misdemeanor only if the constable has viewed the commission of the offense. OAG 86–073.

A municipal police officer who is a member of a police task force that, by the terms of a contract under RC 737.04 includes several municipalities and provides for general police services, has the same authority to make warrantless arrests of misdemeanor offenders within the territory of the contracting municipalities that he has within the municipality that appointed him. OAG 86–065.

Pursuant to RC 2935.03, a municipal police officer may pursue, arrest, and detain until a warrant can be obtained, a misdemeanor offender outside the limits of the municipality that appointed the officer if the officer is authorized under RC 2935.03(A) or RC 2935.03(B) to arrest and detain the offender without a warrant within the jurisdiction that appointed the officer, if the pursuit is initiated within the officer's jurisdiction without unreasonable delay after the offense is committed, and if the offense is a first degree misdemeanor or a violation of a substantially equivalent municipal ordinance, a second degree misdemeanor or a violation of a substantially equivalent municipal ordinance, or any offense for which points are chargeable under RC 4507.021(G). OAG 86–065.

9. Summons in lieu of arrest

RC 2935.10 provides that when an affidavit is filed charging the commission of a misdemeanor or a violation of a municipal ordinance a warrant may issue, but is not required, so that the accused can be served by a summons in the same manner as in civil cases. State v. Hooper (Monroe 1966) 10 Ohio App.2d 229, 227 N.E.2d 414, 39 O.O.2d 435, certiorari denied 88 S.Ct. 292, 389 U.S. 928, 19 L.Ed.2d 281. Criminal Law ⚷ 216

10. Officer's presence—element of offense observed by officer

Defendant's warrantless misdemeanor arrest for trespass, which violated statute requiring that arresting officer observe the criminal conduct, did not invoke the exclusionary rule; defendant did not assert that his warrantless arrest was not based upon probable cause. State v. Mason (Ohio App. 2 Dist., Montgomery, 10-08-2004) No. 20243, 2004-Ohio-5777, 2004 WL 2436596, Unreported. Criminal Law ⚷ 394.4(3)

Defendant's warrantless misdemeanor arrest for trespass was prohibited, where arresting officer did not observe defendant's trespass violation. State v. Mason (Ohio App. 2 Dist., Montgomery, 10-08-2004) No. 20243, 2004-Ohio-5777, 2004 WL 2436596, Unreported. Arrest ⚷ 63.4(5)

To make a valid warrantless arrest for a misdemeanor committed in his presence, an officer need not have evidence sufficient to support a conviction, but need only be in a position to form a reasonable belief that a misdemeanor is being committed, based on evidence perceived through his own senses. City of Columbus v. Lenear (Franklin 1984) 16 Ohio App.3d 466, 476 N.E.2d 1085, 16 O.B.R. 548. Arrest ⚷ 63.1

The word "found" as used in RC 2935.03(A) means that an officer must actually witness the commission of an offense or be able to reach a reasonable conclusion that an offense has been committed from the surrounding circumstances, including defendant's admissions. State v. Stacy (Lorain 1983) 9 Ohio App.3d 55, 458 N.E.2d 403, 9 O.B.R. 74. Arrest ⚷ 63.4(4)

In a prosecution for drunken driving a plea in abatement would lie where the arresting officer failed to observe any unusual or abnormal traffic behavior upon the part of the accused. State v. Burns (Ohio Mun. 1966) 7 Ohio Misc. 275, 217 N.E.2d 57, 35 O.O.2d 173.

Pursuant to RC 2935.03(C), a township constable may, without a warrant and within the limits of the township, arrest a person for the commission of a misdemeanor only if the constable has viewed the commission of the offense. OAG 86–073.

11. —— Offense committed in, officer's presence

Police officers must generally witness an offense before they make a warrantless arrest for a misdemeanor. State v. Holt (Ohio Mun., 03-04-2002) 119 Ohio Misc.2d 1, 772 N.E.2d 203, 2002-Ohio-3345. Arrest ⚷ 63.4(5)

Warrantless arrest of defendant for misdemeanor assault was supported by probable cause, even though officers did not see defendant commit assault, where victim reported to officers that defendant pushed him, struggled with him, and put him in a headlock so that he could not breathe, officers observed that victim was visibly shaken and had abrasions and contusions on and about his face, and witness to confrontation substantially corroborated victim's version of the episode. Cleveland v. Murad (Cuyahoga 1992) 84 Ohio App.3d 317, 616 N.E.2d 1116, dismissed, jurisdictional motion overruled 66 Ohio St.3d 1437, 608 N.E.2d 1082. Arrest ⚷ 63.4(15)

Police detectives' witnessing live act of cunnilingus in theater was of such a nature and under such exigent circumstances as to justify prompt and immediate arrest, notwithstanding lack of prior judicial scrutiny. City of Cleveland v. Mart (Cuyahoga 1983) 10 Ohio App.3d 210, 461 N.E.2d 316, 10 O.B.R. 284. Arrest ⚷ 63.4(13)

Arrest within one and one-half hours of the commission of a misdemeanor offense is permissible under RC 2935.03(A), where an officer observed the commission of the offense by the suspect, and both the offense and the arrest occurred within the limits of the officer's jurisdiction. State v. Stacy (Lorain 1983) 9 Ohio App.3d 55, 458 N.E.2d 403, 9 O.B.R. 74.

When a driver of a vehicle receives a traffic citation for violating RC 4511.12 from a state highway patrolman who did not personally witness the commission of the traffic violation, the driver has not been "unlawfully arrested" for a misdemeanor offense not committed in the presence of the officer. State v. Darrah (Ohio 1980) 64 Ohio St.2d 22, 412 N.E.2d 1328, 18 O.O.3d 193.

Township constables in the exercise of their arrest powers do not fall within the exceptions to the view requirement of RC 2935.03. State v. Fields (Ohio Co. 1979) 62 Ohio Misc. 14, 405 N.E.2d 740, 16 O.O.3d 382.

The unlawful possession of an hallucinogen is a continuing offense, committed in the presence of an arresting officer who finds the contraband in the bedroom occupied and controlled by an accused, who appears during the search, and an arrest in such circumstances is lawful. State v. Wilson (Montgomery 1974) 41 Ohio App.2d 240, 325 N.E.2d 249, 70 O.O.2d 452. Arrest ⚷ 63.3

In a prosecution for publicly exhibiting an obscene motion picture film neither an arrest warrant nor a search warrant is required, since the offense is committed in the presence of the arresting officer and the film is not hidden. State v. Shackman (Ohio Mun. 1971) 29 Ohio Misc. 56, 278 N.E.2d 61, 58 O.O.2d 94.

A person found by a law enforcement officer violating a law of this state or an ordinance of a municipal corporation may be lawfully arrested by such officer without a warrant, regardless of what charge, if any, is thereafter made against him. State v. Hatfield (Greene 1965) 1 Ohio App.2d 346, 204 N.E.2d 574, 30 O.O.2d 350.

A police officer has no legal authority to pursue a person or enter upon his property without permission, where such officer does not see, or personally know of, any violation of law perpetrated by such person, and has no warrant for the arrest of such person, but is relying solely on hearsay evidence.

Huth v. Woodard (Summit 1958) 108 Ohio App. 135, 161 N.E.2d 230, 9 O.O.2d 173.

The arrest by an officer without a warrant of one found violating a statute or ordinance is authorized by this section, and detention for one hour without such warrant is not unreasonable. Conrad v. Lengel (Ohio 1924) 110 Ohio St. 532, 144 N.E. 278, 2 Ohio Law Abs. 406, 22 Ohio Law Rep. 176.

The ancient common-law rule empowering a peace officer to arrest without warrant any individual who commits a misdemeanor or felony in his presence still stands. Hoover v. Garfield Heights Mun. Court (C.A.6 (Ohio) 1986) 802 F.2d 168, certiorari denied 107 S.Ct. 1610, 480 U.S. 949, 94 L.Ed.2d 796.

Township constables are not named in RC 2935.03(B) and, therefore, do not fall within the exceptions to the view requirement set forth therein. OAG 86–073.

12. Traffic offenses

Even if officer's stop of defendant's vehicle for partial obstruction of his license plate was supported by a reasonable suspicion of articulable facts that defendant had committed a crime, the detention leading to the arrest was longer than necessary to effectuate the purpose of the stop; officer stopped defendant and asked him for his driver's license and registration, but officer did not wipe license plate to obtain the number and/or view registration information, and had officer examined license plate, he would have realized that it was fully legible, officer did not observe the marijuana cigarettes until inordinate amount of time had elapsed, and officer continued to question defendant after he had verified defendant's license and registration. State v. Molek (Ohio App. 11 Dist., Portage, 12-20-2002) No. 2001-P-0147, 2002-Ohio-7159, 2002 WL 31862665, Unreported, appeal not allowed 98 Ohio St.3d 1515, 786 N.E.2d 64, 2003-Ohio-1572. Automobiles ⚷ 349(17); Automobiles ⚷ 349(18)

Defendant's conduct within city limits of driving 20 miles per hour in 35 mile-per-hour zone for distance of .2 of mile and failing to stop immediately upon city police officer's activation of his vehicle's overhead lights and siren did not constitute offense of obstructing official business. State v. Ternes (Ohio Mun., 05-15-1998) 92 Ohio Misc.2d 76, 700 N.E.2d 435. Obstructing Justice ⚷ 7

Pursuant to RC 2935.03(C), a township constable has authority to arrest for misdemeanor traffic violations that are not listed in RC 4513.19(A). State v. Darga (Franklin 1985) 30 Ohio App.3d 54, 506 N.E.2d 266, 30 O.B.R. 109.

In a prosecution on a charge of speeding based on a reading taken by one police officer from a radar speed meter and radioed to another officer who thereupon arrested the offender, it is sufficient to show that the meter was properly set up and tested by a technician trained by experience to do so, and that at the time it was functioning properly; and it is not essential to the admissibility of such evidence to show, by independent expert testimony, the nature and function of or the scientific principles underlying such speed meter. City of East Cleveland v. Ferell (Ohio 1958) 168 Ohio St. 298, 154 N.E.2d 630, 7 O.O.2d 6. Criminal Law ⚷ 388.4(1)

A city has jurisdiction to stop, detain, cite or try defendant who ignores clearly posted "road closed" signs erected by the department of transportation and drives around construction barriers and enters a section of road that had been closed for a construction project; municipal corporations have authority under their police powers to adopt and enforce regulations that are not in conflict with general law as in a case where a municipal ordinance that prohibits driving upon a street posted as closed for repair is not in conflict with the general law in RC 4511.71. State v Spartz, No. CA99–11–026, 2000 WL 204280 (12th Dist Ct App, Madison, 2–22–00).

A municipal police officer who is a member of a police task force that, by the terms of a contract under RC 737.04 includes several municipalities and provides for general police services, has the same authority to make warrantless arrests of misdemeanor offenders within the territory of the contracting municipalities that he has within the municipality that appointed him. OAG 86–065.

Pursuant to RC 2935.03, a municipal police officer may pursue, arrest, and detain until a warrant can be obtained, a misdemeanor offender outside the limits of the municipality that appointed the officer if the officer is authorized under RC 2935.03(A) or RC 2935.03(B) to arrest and detain the offender without a warrant within the jurisdiction that appointed the officer, if the pursuit is initiated within the officer's jurisdiction without unreasonable delay after the offense is committed, and if the offense is a first degree misdemeanor or a violation of a substantially equivalent municipal ordinance, a second degree misdemeanor or a violation of a substantially equivalent municipal ordinance, or any offense for which points are chargeable under RC 4507.021(G). OAG 86–065.

13. Driving while intoxicated

A police officer has probable cause for a proper warrantless arrest for driving under the influence of alcohol where (1) a trail of antifreeze leads from the point of impact at a stone wall to the defendant's vehicle which is parked in her driveway, (2) the color of the vehicle corresponds with a witness' complaint, (3) the vehicle is severely damaged, consistent with an accident, (4) steam is escaping from the radiator and the airbag has been deployed, (5) the defendant's wallet and driver's license are found in the vehicle, and (6) the defendant has an odor of alcoholic beverage about her person and difficulty standing and speaking; the trial court properly overrules the motion to suppress and motion in limine. State v. Eves (Ohio App. 12 Dist., Warren, 11-06-1995) No. CA95-02-010, 1995 WL 645525, Unreported, motion to certify allowed 74 Ohio St.3d 1511, 659 N.E.2d 1288, affirmed 76 Ohio St.3d 597, 669 N.E.2d 1114, 1996-Ohio-78.

While police generally may not make a warrantless arrest for a misdemeanor such as driving under the influence of alcohol unless the offense is committed in the officer's presence, an exception is allowed if there has been an automobile "accident," which is a legal determination to be made by the trial court; a further exception is recognized if the officer has probable cause to believe the motorist was driving drunk or while on drugs. City of Middletown v. McGuire (Ohio App. 12 Dist., Butler, 10-09-1995) No. CA94-11-202, 1995 WL 591238, Unreported.

Police officers had probable cause to believe that defendant was operating a vehicle while under the influence of alcohol, justifying warrantless arrest of defendant even though officers had not witnessed the offense, where defendant admitted that he had been drinking prior, but not subsequent, to the accident, admitted that he was driving his vehicle at the time of the accident, officers observed physical manifestations consistent with intoxication, i.e., the defendant smelled of alcohol, had slurred speech, glassy, bloodshot eyes, and a slow gait. State v. Holt (Ohio Mun., 03-04-2002) 119 Ohio Misc.2d 1, 772 N.E.2d 203, 2002-Ohio-3345. Automobiles ⚷ 349(6)

Arresting defendant at his home for violating city ordinance proscribing driving under influence of alcohol (DUI) did not violate statute permitting warrantless arrests where person is "found violating" law or ordinance, since arresting officer could reasonably conclude that defendant was operating his vehicle under influence of alcohol just prior to his arrest, based on informant's tip that defendant was driving erratically and based on defendant's own admission. Beachwood v. Sims (Ohio App. 8 Dist., 10-03-1994) 98 Ohio App.3d 9, 647 N.E.2d 821, dismissed, appeal not allowed 71 Ohio St.3d 1465, 644 N.E.2d 1387. Automobiles ⚷ 349(6)

A stop for an alleged improper left turn is unlawful where university police erect an unauthorized "No Left Turn" sign and a subsequent "search" in taking a breath sample to test for alcohol violates US Const Am 4. State v. Grubb (Franklin 1993) 82 Ohio App.3d 187, 611 N.E.2d 516.

Warrantless arrest conducted inside motorist's home after deputy sheriff kicked in door was justified under "hot pursuit" exception to warrant requirement, where motorist exhibited slurred speech and strong smell of alcohol upon his person and had retreated into home contrary to deputy sheriff's express command while deputy was on police radio. State v. Rouse (Franklin 1988) 53 Ohio App.3d 48, 557 N.E.2d 1227, cause dismissed 40 Ohio St.3d 712, 534 N.E.2d 843, motion to certify overruled. Automobiles ⚷ 349(14.1)

Where a police officer at an accident scene reasonably concludes that a defendant was operating a motor vehicle while under the influence of alcohol shortly before the officer arrived on the scene, a warrantless arrest of the defendant is not precluded by RC 2935.03, because the defendant is "a person found violating a law of this state or an ordinance of a municipal corporation" within the meaning of RC 2935.03(A). City of Bucyrus v. Williams (Crawford 1988) 46 Ohio App.3d 43, 545 N.E.2d 1298. Automobiles ⚷ 349(6)

There is probable cause to arrest a driver for drunk driving on the basis of an odor of alcohol about the driver and an otherwise unexplained one-car accident. State v. Bernard (Wayne 1985) 20 Ohio App.3d 375, 486 N.E.2d 866, 20 O.B.R. 481.

A municipal police officer may make a warrantless arrest for a misdemeanor charge of drunk driving even though he did not observe the offense, when he finds the defendant's abandoned damaged car at an accident scene and soon thereafter finds the defendant intoxicated and injured, and the defendant admits he was involved in the accident but denies driving. City of Xenia v. Manker (Greene 1984) 18 Ohio App.3d 9, 480 N.E.2d 94, 18 O.B.R. 33.

The testimony of a police officer will not be suppressed, when in response to an accident call, he observes an automobile in the front yard of a private residence, with a person standing nearby who admits that he owns the automobile and had been driving it, whose speech is slurred and who otherwise appears to be intoxicated, and then arrests such person without a warrant for operating a vehicle while under the influence of alcohol. State v. Allen (Hamilton 1981) 2 Ohio App.3d 441, 442 N.E.2d 784, 2 O.B.R. 536. Criminal Law ⚷ 394.4(9)

Where a police officer appears at the scene of an accident and the operator of a vehicle involved voluntarily admits he was driving it and is visibly under the influence of alcohol, the officer is not required to obtain a warrant as a prerequisite to arresting such individual for driving while intoxicated. City of Oregon v. Szakovits (Ohio 1972) 32 Ohio St.2d 271, 291 N.E.2d 742, 61 O.O.2d 496.

A highway patrolman may legally arrest a person found in a state of intoxication in an automobile standing off the paved portion of a highway, and the fact that the charge subsequently made is driving while in a state of intoxication does not render the arrest illegal. State v. Hatfield (Greene 1965) 1 Ohio App.2d 346, 204 N.E.2d 574, 30 O.O.2d 350.

Where police officer arrived at scene of automobile accident and found one of the drivers of vehicles in a state of intoxication and party admitted that he was a driver of the automobile, the police officer was authorized to arrest the motorist, and the mere fact that affidavit was not filed against motorist until approximately four days later, did not make the arrest illegal. City of Columbus v. Glenn (Franklin 1950) 102 N.E.2d 279, 60 Ohio Law Abs. 449. Arrest ⚷ 63.4(15)

Police officer, who was outside his jurisdictional limits, had reasonable suspicion that defendant was driving under the influence of alcohol to conduct stop of defendant, and thus, evidence derived from stop was not subject suppression, even though stop outside jurisdiction may have violated statute; officer observed defendant's vehicle weaving, officer observed defendant's vehicle cross center line at least twenty times, and officer observed that defendant had slurred speech, glassy eyes, and balance problems. State v. Crump (Ohio App. 2 Dist., Montgomery, 06-28-2002) No. 19021, 2002-Ohio-3284, 2002 WL 1393655, Unreported. Automobiles ⚷ 349(6)

A police officer may lawfully arrest a person without a warrant for driving while intoxicated in violation of RC 4511.19 or similar municipal ordinances if he sees the offense being committed or the person admits to have been driving the car and it is obvious to the officer that the person is under the influence of alcohol, but if a police officer does not see a person driving the car and the person has not admitted to driving the car and it is not obvious to the officer that the person is under the influence of alcohol, it is necessary to file a complaint and obtain an arrest warrant before the person may be lawfully arrested. State ex rel. Wilson v. Nash (Cuyahoga 1974) 41 Ohio App.2d 201, 324 N.E.2d 774, 70 O.O.2d 409.

Even if a warrantless arrest is contrary to RC 2935.03, suppression of evidence is not required if there is probable cause for the arrest and there is no constitutional violation. Middleton v McGuire, No. CA94–11–202, 1995 WL 591238 (12th Dist Ct App, Butler, 10–9–95).

Where police officers discover a defendant's car crashed 75 feet from the defendant's house, they find the defendant intoxicated and he admits driving the car, the offense of driving while intoxicated has been committed in the presence of the officers under RC 2935.03 so that an arrest therefor is a legal arrest which the defendant may not resist under RC 2921.33. State v Parks, No. 1306 (4th Dist Ct App, Ross, 9–3–87).

14. Probable cause

Police officer could arrest defendant without warrant, even without written statements supporting accusations against defendant, where defendant's own statement to officer provided basis for charging defendant with felony. State v. Miller (Ohio App. 3 Dist., 10-26-1993) 91 Ohio App.3d 270, 632 N.E.2d 569, denial of habeas corpus affirmed 269 F.3d 609, rehearing and suggestion for rehearing en banc denied, certiorari denied 122 S.Ct. 1592, 535 U.S. 1011, 152 L.Ed.2d 509. Arrest ⚷ 63.4(15)

Information supplied by officers or agencies engaged in a common investigation with an arresting officer may be used to establish probable cause for a warrantless arrest. State v. Henderson (Ohio 1990) 51 Ohio St.3d 54, 554 N.E.2d 104, rehearing denied 52 Ohio St.3d 704, 556 N.E.2d 530. Arrest ⚷ 63.4(11)

Where probable cause exists to arrest a suspect, a police officer may arrest the suspect in reliance on a police radio report, even though the officer does not have personal knowledge of facts supporting the radio report. State v. Holden (Hamilton 1985) 23 Ohio App.3d 5, 490 N.E.2d 629, 23 O.B.R. 38.

When drug traffickers are arrested and interrogated immediately after a sale to undercover police officers, the arrestees' description of a confederate by appearance, location at a nearby restaurant, and type of car driven, provides probable cause, under the totality of the circumstances test, to arrest an individual meeting that description. State v. Farndon (Cuyahoga 1984) 22 Ohio App.3d 31, 488 N.E.2d 894, 22 O.B.R. 107.

In determining whether police had probable cause for a warrantless arrest, based in part on an informant's tip, the veracity or reliability of the informant and the basis of his knowledge are relevant considerations in the totality of circumstances analysis that has traditionally guided probable cause determinations. State v. Ingram (Butler 1984) 20 Ohio App.3d 55, 484 N.E.2d 227, 20 O.B.R. 58.

An arrest for disorderly conduct is lawful when, under circumstances, it is probable that a reasonable police officer would find arrestee's language and conduct annoying or alarming and would be provoked to want to respond violently. State v. Johnson (Clinton 1982) 6 Ohio App.3d 56, 453 N.E.2d 1101, 6 O.B.R. 268. Arrest ⚷ 63.4(15)

To have probable cause, the arresting officer must have sufficient information derived from a reasonably trustworthy source to warrant a prudent man in believing that a felony has been committed and that it has been committed by the accused. State v. Timson (Ohio 1974) 38 Ohio St.2d 122, 311 N.E.2d 16, 67 O.O.2d 140. Arrest ⚷ 63.4(2)

Where a felony is claimed to have been committed, proof of probable cause for arrest without a warrant rests on facts shown by substantial and credible evidence sufficient to warrant a man of reasonable caution in the belief that such an offense had been committed, and the mere opinion, conclusion, or belief, standing alone, of the arresting officer that such act had been committed is without probative value and insufficient to justify such arrest. State v. Thompson (Cuyahoga 1965) 1 Ohio App.2d 533, 206 N.E.2d 5, 30 O.O.2d 574. Arrest ⚷ 63.4(2)

Whether an arrest is constitutionally valid depends on whether, at the moment the arrest is made, the officer has probable cause to make it. U. S. v. Edwards (C.A.6 (Ohio) 1973) 474 F.2d 1206, certiorari granted 94 S.Ct. 160, 414 U.S. 818, 38 L.Ed.2d 50, reversed 94 S.Ct. 1234, 415 U.S. 800, 39 L.Ed.2d 771, vacated 497 F.2d 925.

There is probable cause to arrest a defendant where (1) the defendant and his companion are seen directly in front of the post office three minutes before a police officer receives a message that the silent alarm in the post office has been triggered, (2) the defendant and his companion are the only persons observed by the officer in that vicinity late on a Sunday night, and (3) the officer testifies that it appeared as though the two men had just turned out of the drive leading to the post office. U. S. v. Edwards (C.A.6 (Ohio) 1973) 474 F.2d 1206, certiorari granted 94 S.Ct. 160, 414 U.S. 818, 38 L.Ed.2d 50, reversed 94 S.Ct. 1234, 415 U.S. 800, 39 L.Ed.2d 771, vacated 497 F.2d 925. Arrest ⚷ 63.4(17)

Law enforcement officials can offer to pay an informer a fee contingent in amount upon the number of specified people convicted for crimes not yet committed; while it is true an informant may in such circumstances be prone to lie and manufacture crimes, this likelihood is no greater than that characterizing any of an informant's activities. U. S. v. Grimes (C.A.6 (Ohio) 1971) 438 F.2d 391, 13 A.L.R. Fed. 896, certiorari denied 91 S.Ct. 1684, 402 U.S. 989, 29 L.Ed.2d 155.

Police officer had probable cause to arrest defendant for failing to comply with lawful police order in violation of state law, where officer repeatedly ordered defendant to remain inside his vehicle during traffic stop and defendant exited his vehicle and began walking away from scene. U.S. v. Garner (N.D.Ohio, 07-19-2000) 108 F.Supp.2d 796. Automobiles ⚷ 349(8)

Police officer acted lawfully under search and seizure clause in ordering defendant to remain in his vehicle during traffic stop, as officer could reasonably conclude his safety was best protected by having passengers remain in stopped vehicle. U.S. v. Garner (N.D.Ohio, 07-19-2000) 108 F.Supp.2d 796. Automobiles ⚷ 349(14.1)

Alleged victim's allegations that his step-father threw him on the sofa, slapped him across the face, and punched him in the lower back and police observation of roundish red area in the lower region of the back provided probable cause to arrest step-father for domestic violence despite his version of events. Adams v. Township of Champion, OH (N.D.Ohio, 10-21-1999) 68 F.Supp.2d 906. Arrest ⚷ 63.4(9)

15. Extraterritorial arrest

Police officer was not statutorily prohibited from taking arrestee to hospital in another county to obtain blood draw following accident occurring within officer's territorial jurisdiction, especially where there was no pursuit involved and arrestee was already in custody at time he was transported. State v. Neely (Ohio App. 11 Dist., Lake, 12-29-2005) No. 2004-L-197, 2005-Ohio-7045, 2005 WL 3610426, Unreported. Automobiles ⚷ 349(12); Automobiles ⚷ 414

Police officer acted within his statutory authority in pursuing and stopping defendant's vehicle, even though officer did not immediately turn on overhead lights upon initiating pursuit, and officer was outside his territorial jurisdiction when he arrested defendant; pursuit was initiated within limits of officer's territorial jurisdiction for an offense for which points were chargeable, and the pursuit began immediately, without unreasonable delay, after the officer observed defendant's failure to signal and license plate violations. State v. Black (Ohio App. 6 Dist., Fulton, 01-16-2004) No. F-03-010, 2004-Ohio-218, 2004 WL 88857, Unreported. Automobiles ⚷ 349(12)

Evidence obtained as result of defendant's stop and arrest for driving under the influence (DUI) outside officer's jurisdiction, in violation of territorial limits imposed by statute upon police officer's extra-territorial arrest powers, was nevertheless admissible at trial; only impropriety with stop was its alleged extra-territorial nature, which was, at most, a statutory violation, rather than a constitutional violation. State v. Pierce (Ohio App. 2 Dist., Montgomery, 12-31-2003) No. 19926, 2003-Ohio-7244, 2004 WL 68754, Unreported. Criminal Law ⚷ 394.4(9)

If the totality of facts and circumstances demonstrate that police officer acting outside his statutory territorial jurisdiction had a reasonable, articulable suspicion of criminal conduct sufficient to warrant investigative stop and detention, and probable cause to arrest, then while that extraterritorial seizure may violate state law, it does not rise to the level of a constitutional violation requiring suppression of all evidence derived from the stop. State v. Underwood (Ohio App. 5 Dist., Tuscarawas, 01-09-2004) No. 2003-AP-030022, 2004-Ohio-125, 2004 WL 67250, Unreported. Criminal Law ⚷ 394.2(1)

Township police officer who, outside of township limits, but based on probable cause obtained within township limits, stopped motorist for traveling left of centerline and on suspicion that motorist was driving under the influence (DUI), did not act unreasonably per se under the Fourth Amendment, though officer was acting outside his statutory territorial jurisdiction, and thus, officer's statutory violation did not require suppression of evidence flowing from the stop, under the exclusionary rule. State v. Annis (Ohio App. 11 Dist., Portage, 10-25-2002) No. 2001-P-0151, 2002-Ohio-5866, 2002 WL 31411070, Unreported. Automobiles ⚷ 349(12); Criminal Law ⚷ 394.4(12)

Where a defendant drives his vehicle from a parking lot within the arresting officer's jurisdiction to a street outside of the officer's jurisdiction and parks the vehicle on the side of the road, when the officer, without observing any improper or erratic driving on the part of the defendant then pulls behind the vehicle, asks the defendant if everything is alright, smells alcohol on the defendant, submits the defendant to sobriety tests which the defendant fails, then places the defendant under arrest for DUI, it is reversible error for a municipal court to deny a motion to suppress and to take judicial notice that the portion of a street where the defendant was arrested is in fact in the arresting officer's jurisdiction, where the arresting officer testifies that he did not observe the defendant violate any ordinances within the officer's jurisdiction, and that he arrested the defendant outside of his jurisdiction; and RC 2935.03 does not apply as the arresting officer did not begin pursuing the defendant until the defendant was outside his jurisdiction. City of Lyndhurst v. Sadowski (Ohio App. 8 Dist., Cuyahoga, 09-02-1999) No. 74313, 1999 WL 684570, Unreported.

Sufficient justification for a traffic stop exists despite plaintiff's characterization of driving left of center as a "minor flaw in his driving" and where the officer initiates the pursuit within the officer's municipality, subsequent arrest in the neighboring city of Cleveland for driving while under the influence pursuant to RC 4511.19 is valid. City of Lakewood v. Sheehan (Ohio App. 8 Dist., Cuyahoga, 02-20-1997) No. 68728, 1997 WL 72144, Unreported.

Where a law enforcement officer, acting outside the officer's statutory territorial jurisdiction, stops and detains a motorist for an offense committed and observed outside the officer's jurisdiction, the seizure of the motorist by the officer is not unreasonable per se under the Fourth Amendment; thus, the officer's statutory violation does not require suppression of all evidence flowing from the stop, under the exclusionary rule. State v. Weideman (Ohio, 04-03-2002) 94 Ohio St.3d 501, 764 N.E.2d 997, 2002-Ohio-1484. Arrest ⚷ 66(2); Automobiles ⚷ 349(12); Criminal Law ⚷ 394.4(9)

Police officers' arrest of motorist outside county where they were employed, in violation of statutes governing such extraterritorial arrests, did not rise to level of constitutional violation requiring suppression of evidence seized; officers arrested motorist in adjoining county where his vehicle came to rest after he had run stop sign located in county where officers were employed. Stow v. Riggenbach (Ohio App. 9 Dist., 10-26-1994) 97 Ohio App.3d 661, 647 N.E.2d 246. Criminal Law ⚷ 394.4(9)

Police officer had specific statutory authority to make stop for running red light, and to make subsequent arrest for driving while intoxicated, even though officer both saw violation take place, and made arrest, in neighboring township, where officer detained suspect on portion of street immediately adjacent to boundaries of officer's township police district. State v Brown (Ohio Co. 1993) 64 Ohio Misc.2d 41, 639 N.E.2d 1268. Automobiles ⚷ 349(12)

Statute allowing an Ohio police officer to pursue and arrest a suspect in another political subdivision in Ohio does not preclude interstate arrests. State v. Thierbach (Ohio App. 1 Dist., 09-08-1993) 92 Ohio App.3d 365, 635 N.E.2d 1276, motion overruled 68 Ohio St.3d 1447, 626 N.E.2d 688. Arrest ⚷ 66(2)

Even if Ohio officer violated statute by making extraterritorial arrest in Kentucky, violation afforded no basis for suppression of evidence gathered during arrest, as exclusionary rule does not apply to an illegal arrest stemming from statutory rather than constitutional violation. State v. Thierbach (Ohio App. 1 Dist., 09-08-1993) 92 Ohio App.3d 365, 635 N.E.2d 1276, motion overruled 68 Ohio St.3d 1447, 626 N.E.2d 688. Criminal Law ⚷ 394.4(9)

Where a vehicle being pursued by a highway patrol officer stops across the state line and the officer's vehicle remains in Ohio, an invalid extraterritorial arrest does not occur when the officer asks the suspect to return to Ohio and enter the patrol car so long as the officer does not intend the request to return to Ohio to be an arrest. State v. Walden (Defiance 1988) 51 Ohio App.3d 209, 555 N.E.2d 686.

Where a police officer has a reasonable belief a driver is intoxicated and initiates a pursuit within the officer's township, a subsequent arrest outside of such township is consistent with RC 2935.03(D). State v. Beckwith (Lake 1987) 38 Ohio App.3d 30, 526 N.E.2d 105.

While municipal police officer has no authority to effect arrest beyond territorial jurisdiction of city involved, purchase of LSD by police informer, who was agent of municipality, while located outside territorial city limits, did not render indictment for that sale subject to dismissal or require evidence of that sale to be suppressed at trial; city was not precluded from protecting its citizens by initiating and conducting drug investigations in nearby areas, as drug traffic does not stop at city limits. State v. Dotson (Ohio App. 3 Dist. 1987) 35 Ohio App.3d 135, 520 N.E.2d 240. Criminal Law ⚷ 36.6; Criminal Law ⚷ 394.2(2)

Traffic laws may be enforced by a police officer of a foreign jurisdiction, providing such police officer is authorized by the local law enforcement agency to direct traffic within the jurisdiction of occurrence. State v. Gates (Ohio Mun. 1979) 60 Ohio Misc. 35, 395 N.E.2d 535, 14 O.O.3d 82.

The authority granted in RC 2935.03 to a police officer to "arrest and detain a person found violating a law of this state" does not confer authority upon a municipal police officer to arrest without a warrant outside the geographical boundaries of his municipality for traffic offenses observed by the officer to have been committed outside such municipal limits. City of Cincinnati v. Alexander (Ohio 1978) 54 Ohio St.2d 248, 375 N.E.2d 1241, 8 O.O.3d 224. Arrest ⚷ 66(2)

RC 2935.03 does not authorize a municipal police officer outside his jurisdiction to arrest one observed committing a misdemeanor. State v. Wallace (Franklin 1976) 50 Ohio App.2d 78, 361 N.E.2d 516, 4 O.O.3d 52.

Parma Municipal Court has jurisdiction to try a defendant charged with driving while intoxicated in the village of Brooklyn and arrested in such village by a Parma police officer where such defendant is physically before the court and its jurisdiction has been duly invoked by the filing of a valid affidavit charging the offense. State v. Zdovc (Cuyahoga 1958) 106 Ohio App. 481, 151 N.E.2d 672, 79 Ohio Law Abs. 102, 7 O.O.2d 217.

An officer's extra-territorial pursuit and detention of defendant for suspected DUI is proper under RC 2935.03(D) where (1) the pursuit is initiated in response to a citizen's cell phone call indicating defendant's erratic driving, (2) the pursuit begins without delay within the officer's jurisdiction and continues into a neighboring jurisdiction where the officer first observes defendant's vehicle, and (3) defendant is pursued on suspicion of DUI, a traffic offense for which points are chargeable under RC 4507.021(G). State v Hornsby, No. CA99–06–060, 2000 WL 197249 (12th Dist Ct App, Clermont, 2–22–00).

The term "pursuit" as contained in RC 2935.03(D)(1) and 2935.03(D)(2) means "following with intent to stop." Thus, where state university police officers observe an individual driving erratically within the university limits and follow this person and arrest him for drunk driving four blocks outside the university, the arrest is in compliance with RC 2935.03. State v Jackson, No. 90AP–457 (10th Dist Ct App, Franklin, 11–6–90).

The exclusionary rule is inapplicable where a police officer, outside of his jurisdiction, observes the commission of numerous misdemeanors by the driver of a motor vehicle who is obviously endangering the lives of others and, subsequently, makes an unauthorized extraterritorial arrest; the holding in Kettering v Hollen, 64 OS(2d) 232 (1980), is extended. State v Tennison, No. WD–88–41 (6th Dist Ct App, Wood, 4–14–89).

Where a police officer pulls over and stops an errant driver solely to protect other motorists, with no intention of arresting him, then calls the state highway patrol, which arrests him for driving under the influence and other offenses, no constitutional violation has occurred, and any arguable violation of RC 2935.03(D) does not require suppression of evidence obtained pursuant to the stop. State v Pruey, No. 11–246 (11th Dist Ct App, Lake, 2–6–87).

Where defendant was subject to an extraterritorial warrantless arrest for driving while intoxicated and where such arrest was made with probable cause (defendant was speeding), the results of an intoxilyzer test were properly admitted. Powell v Moss, No. 82–CA–11 (5th Dist Ct App, Delaware, 7–7–82).

A county sheriff has no authority outside of his jurisdiction except as expressly provided by statute. OAG 89–074.

Pursuant to RC 2935.03, a municipal police officer may pursue, arrest, and detain until a warrant can be obtained, a misdemeanor offender outside the limits of the municipality that appointed the officer if the officer is authorized under RC 2935.03(A) or RC 2935.03(B) to arrest and detain the offender without a warrant within the jurisdiction that appointed the officer, if the pursuit is initiated within the officer's jurisdiction without unreasonable delay after the offense is committed, and if the offense is a first degree misdemeanor or a violation of a substantially equivalent municipal ordinance, a second degree misdemeanor or a violation of a substantially equivalent municipal ordinance, or any offense for which points are chargeable under RC 4507.021(G). OAG 86–065.

16. Hot pursuit

An officer is justified in making a warrantless entry into the home of a DUI suspect on the basis of "hot pursuit" where the defendant is weaving in and out of traffic lanes and ignores the officer's emergency lights and audible siren, activates his left turn signal, and turns into his own private driveway where the officer follows, and the officer (1) forces the garage door open, (2) enters the garage, (3) pursues defendant inside his home, (4) grabs defendant by his arm and pulls him back into the garage where the officer notes an odor of alcohol on the defendant and that his eyes are red, and (5) effects an arrest for driving under the influence of alcohol. State v. Raszick (Ohio App. 5 Dist., Stark, 12-29-1994) No. 1994CA00114, 1994 WL 728339, Unreported, dismissed, appeal not allowed 72 Ohio St.3d 1518, 649 N.E.2d 278.

Where a police officer, having probable cause, arrested an accused at the scene of the stop for operating a motor vehicle while intoxicated, such police officer was authorized to pursue the fleeing accused into his home to complete the original arrest. State v. Jenkins (Ohio Co. 1983) 10 Ohio Misc.2d 7, 460 N.E.2d 1172, 10 O.B.R. 159. Automobiles ⚷ 349(9)

The exclusionary rule will not be applied to the testimony of an arresting police officer regarding the actions of a misdemeanant observed as a result of an extraterritorial warrantless arrest, even though the arrest is unauthorized under existing state law, if the arrest is based on probable cause that a crime was committed within the officer's jurisdiction, and if the officer was in hot pursuit of the misdemeanant. City of Kettering v. Hollen (Ohio 1980) 64 Ohio St.2d 232, 416 N.E.2d 598, 18 O.O.3d 435.

Where a police officer observed a defendant operating a motor vehicle in an unlawful manner and immediately pursued him to his home outside the municipality, and it appeared that he was intoxicated, the officer was justified in arresting him without a warrant. State v. Marshall (Ohio Mun. 1952) 105 N.E.2d 891, 61 Ohio Law Abs. 568.

The federal constitution does not guarantee that only people guilty of a crime will be pursued or arrested, and thus police do not "shock the conscience" of a federal judge by chasing an individual whose flight violates RC 2921.33 or 4511.02; consequently, state troopers' high-speed chase of a fleeing motorcyclist does not violate the cyclist's civil rights and a suit on his behalf under 42 USC 1983 will be dismissed. York v. Lamantia (N.D.Ohio 1987) 674 F.Supp. 17.

The exclusionary rule is inapplicable where a police officer, outside of his jurisdiction, observes the commission of numerous misdemeanors by the driver of a motor vehicle who is obviously endangering the lives of others and, subsequently, makes an unauthorized extraterritorial arrest; the holding in Kettering v Hollen, 64 OS(2d) 232 (1980), is extended. State v Tennison, No. WD–88–41 (6th Dist Ct App, Wood, 4–14–89).

Pursuant to RC 2935.03, a municipal police officer may pursue, arrest, and detain until a warrant can be obtained, a misdemeanor offender outside the limits of the municipality that appointed the officer if the officer is authorized under RC 2935.03(A) or RC 2935.03(B) to arrest and detain the offender without a warrant within the jurisdiction that appointed the officer, if the pursuit is initiated within the officer's jurisdiction without unreasonable delay after the offense is committed, and if the offense is a first degree misdemeanor or a violation of a substantially equivalent municipal ordinance, a second degree misdemeanor or a violation of a substantially equivalent municipal ordinance, or any offense for which points are chargeable under RC 4507.021(G). OAG 86–065.

17. Arresting officer—in general

County park ranger has authority to arrest individual under Ohio Revised Code, rather than only for violations of county metropark rules; "police powers" statutorily vested in rangers include enforcement of laws of state and regulations of board of park commissioners. State v. Nunnally (Lucas 1992) 83 Ohio App.3d 741, 615 N.E.2d 725. Arrest ⚩ 63.2

A municipal police officer may make an arrest for a violation of a municipal ordinance, upon a properly issued warrant, anywhere within the jurisdictional limits of the issuing court. City of Fairborn v. Munkus (Ohio 1971) 28 Ohio St.2d 207, 277 N.E.2d 227, 57 O.O.2d 436. Arrest ⚩ 66(2)

A police officer's power to arrest people does not enable him to "establish final government policy," nor is his decision to arrest someone per se a decision as to government policy; consequently, the municipality is not liable for an arrest in an action under 42 USC 1983. O'Kelly v. Russell Tp. Bd. of Trustees (N.D.Ohio 1987) 675 F.Supp. 389.

A county dog warden has the power to make an arrest without a warrant, subject to the provisions of RC 2935.03. OAG 74–084.

18. —— Conduct of officer, arresting officer

State university police officers' decision not to arrest and detain person for his verbal threats against student was reasonable, even though student was later shot and killed by a different person, where police were responding to an altercation at a crowded campus pub and had an obligation to protect all of pub's patrons by gaining control of unruly crowd. DeSanto v. Youngstown State Univ. (Ohio Ct.Cl., 07-31-2002) No. 99-08777, 2002-Ohio-4144, 2002 WL 31966960, Unreported. Colleges And Universities ⚩ 5

State university police did not owe special duty to student who was killed shortly after police broke up altercation at campus pub that was distinct and separate from the duty it owed to the general public, and thus, public duty rule applied to preclude liability, where student did not ask for help from officers or request protection from person who threatened him, and student was killed off campus nearly 30 minutes later. DeSanto v. Youngstown State Univ. (Ohio Ct.Cl., 07-31-2002) No. 99-08777, 2002-Ohio-4144, 2002 WL 31966960, Unreported. Colleges And Universities ⚩ 5

Student's parents failed to prove that state university police officers' decision not to arrest and detain person for his verbal threats against student was the proximate cause of student's death, where person that threatened student at campus pub was not the same person who later shot and killed student at an off campus residence. DeSanto v. Youngstown State Univ. (Ohio Ct.Cl., 07-31-2002) No. 99-08777, 2002-Ohio-4144, 2002 WL 31966960, Unreported. Colleges And Universities ⚩ 5

Officers who made warrantless entry into suspect's home to arrest him for domestic violence had qualified immunity from suspect's 1983 claim, where the entry did not violate the Fourth Amendment because the alleged assault victim consented to the entry and the victim's injuries provided reasonable grounds to believe the suspect had assaulted her. Alley v. Bettencourt (Ohio App. 4 Dist., 09-10-1999) 134 Ohio App.3d 303, 730 N.E.2d 1067. Civil Rights ⚩ 1376(6)

Regardless of whether police officer employed as security guard at grocery store was acting as store employee or police officer at time he arrested and detained customer, officer was acting under color of state law as required for 1983 action; authority to arrest and detain arose either under statute empowering municipal police officer to effectuate warrantless arrest or under statute authorizing mercantile establishment to detain and peace officer to arrest shoplifter. Evans v. Smith (Ohio App. 1 Dist., 09-14-1994) 97 Ohio App.3d 59, 646 N.E.2d 217. Civil Rights ⚩ 1326(8)

In a wrongful-death action against a police officer, a motion for summary judgment should be overruled where the pleadings considered together with the motion, accompanied by affidavits of the movant, show the existence of genuine issues of material fact for the jury of, inter alia, whether a felony had been committed, whether decedent was placed under arrest, whether the arresting officer saw or had reasonable ground to believe that a felony had been committed and whether the officer used excessive force. Oliver v. Kasza (Lucas 1962) 116 Ohio App. 398, 188 N.E.2d 437, 22 O.O.2d 230.

A city can be held liable under 42 USC 1983 for misconduct in the form of an arrest by a police officer who is not a policy-making employee only if the city is shown reckless or grossly negligent in its training or suspension of the officer. O'Kelly v. Russell Tp. Bd. of Trustees (N.D.Ohio 1987) 675 F.Supp. 389.

19. —— Line of duty, arresting officer

A county seat municipal police officer who is killed by a county jail inmate in the office of the sheriff, where such police officer had gone in response to a call to the municipal police department that a jail break was in progress, while such inmate and other inmates are attempting to escape therefrom, is killed in the performance of his duties as a police officer of such municipality. State v. Halleck (Pickaway 1970) 24 Ohio App.2d 74, 263 N.E.2d 917, 53 O.O.2d 195. Homicide ⚩ 554

Rights of police officer to disability benefits discussed in light of place of injury, existence of contributory negligence and whether injury occurs in discharge of official duty; definition of "official duty" also discussed. 1959 OAG 50.

20. —— Off-duty officer, arresting officer

Off-duty peace officer must arrest person whom officer observes committing crime within officer's territorial jurisdiction. State v. Butler (Ross 1991) 77 Ohio App.3d 143, 601 N.E.2d 510. Arrest ⚩ 68(1)

A duly appointed auxiliary police officer, upon whom the city has conferred full "police powers," is authorized to make warrantless misdemeanor arrests pursuant to RC 2935.03, regardless of "duty status." State v. Clark (Paulding 1983) 10 Ohio App.3d 308, 462 N.E.2d 436, 10 O.B.R. 513. Arrest ⚩ 63.2; Municipal Corporations ⚩ 188

An off-duty municipal police officer cannot arrest for a misdemeanor committed outside the territorial boundaries of his municipality without a warrant. State v. Vanbarg (Ohio Mun. 1975) 44 Ohio Misc. 11, 335 N.E.2d 765, 73 O.O.2d 74.

A deputy sheriff or township police officer, during the hours that he or she is not required to be on duty for work as a deputy sheriff or police officer, may use his or her county or township owned uniforms, equipment, and firearms, provided the county sheriff or township chief of police authorizes that use. OAG 91–063.

Pursuant to RC 2935.03, a municipal police officer may pursue, arrest, and detain until a warrant can be obtained, a misdemeanor offender outside the limits of the municipality that appointed the officer if the officer is authorized under RC 2935.03(A) or (B) to arrest and detain the offender without a warrant within the jurisdiction that appointed the officer, if the pursuit is initiated within the officer's jurisdiction without unreasonable delay after the offense is committed, and if the offense is a first degree misdemeanor or a violation of a substantially equivalent municipal ordinance, a second degree misdemeanor or a violation of a substantially equivalent municipal ordinance, or any offense for which points are chargeable under RC 4507.021(G). OAG 86–065.

An off-duty municipal police officer may arrest for a misdemeanor without a warrant only within the territorial jurisdiction in which he is appointed, which is the corporate limits of the municipality. OAG 74–094; overruled in part by OAG 86–065.

21. —— State highway patrol, arresting officer

Where a vehicle being pursued by a highway patrol officer stops across the state line and the officer's vehicle remains in Ohio, an invalid extraterritorial arrest does not occur when the officer asks the suspect to return to Ohio and enter the patrol car so long as the officer does not intend the request to return to Ohio to be an arrest. State v. Walden (Defiance 1988) 51 Ohio App.3d 209, 555 N.E.2d 686.

A state highway patrolman may, under appropriate circumstances, reasonably inquire of an automobile driver concerning his suspicious on-the-highway behavior in the absence of reasonable grounds to arrest. State v. Burns (Ohio Mun. 1966) 7 Ohio Misc. 275, 217 N.E.2d 57, 35 O.O.2d 173. Automobiles ⚷ 349(2.1)

Because troopers of the state highway patrol, forest officers under RC 1503.29, preserve officers under RC 1517.10, wildlife officers under RC 1531.13, park officers under RC 1541.10, and watercraft officers under RC 1547.521 are not peace officers described in RC 2935.03(B)(1), the troopers and officers are not subject to the domestic violence arrest provisions of RC 2935.03(B)(3), and the highway patrol and the department of natural resources are not required to adopt a domestic violence policy pursuant to RC 2935.032. OAG 96–014.

Where a person arrested by a highway patrolman under authority of RC 2935.03 posts bond in a municipal court for his appearance for trial at a later date, but does not appear on the date specified and the judge issues a warrant for his arrest and requests the highway patrolman to serve the warrant, the highway patrolman has a duty to serve the warrant as requested. 1961 OAG 2214.

22. —— Undercover agent, arresting officer

Individuals employed by a county as undercover narcotics agents for the purpose of investigating and gathering information pertaining to persons suspected of violating RC Ch 2925 and Ch 3719, are not authorized by RC 2935.03(A) to make warrantless arrests of persons found violating a law of this state. OAG 91–037.

23. —— Workers' compensation entitlement, arresting officer

Injuries sustained by off-duty university police officer when he attempted to prevent armed robbery of bank were sustained in the course of officer's employment, for purposes of workers' compensation, though officer was outside his geographical jurisdiction, he was transacting purely personal business at bank, he was not wearing police uniform or badge, he did not drive police vehicle, and he did not have gun, handcuffs, mace or baton with him; officer had duty to prevent an offense when it was within his ability to do so. Luketic v. Univ. Circle, Inc. (Ohio App. 8 Dist., 08-30-1999) 134 Ohio App.3d 217, 730 N.E.2d 1006, appeal not allowed 87 Ohio St.3d 1478, 721 N.E.2d 123. Workers' Compensation ⚷ 695

Injuries sustained by off-duty university police officer when he attempted to prevent armed robbery of bank arose out of his employment, for purposes of workers' compensation, though officer was outside his jurisdictional authority; officer's legal and moral duty to protect public and attempt to prevent a violent felony placed him in his "zone of employment," and such duty constituted a "special hazard" to employment as police officer, which was distinctive in nature and greater than the risk common to the public. Luketic v. Univ. Circle, Inc. (Ohio App. 8 Dist., 08-30-1999) 134 Ohio App.3d 217, 730 N.E.2d 1006, appeal not allowed 87 Ohio St.3d 1478, 721 N.E.2d 123. Workers' Compensation ⚷ 695

Off-duty police officer was acting in the course of his city employment while attempting to arrest shoplifting suspect and his injuries during arrest attempt arose out of that employment, and, thus, officer was entitled to workers' compensation benefits from city, despite fact that officer was not in uniform, was working as security specialist for retail grocery store when injured and had not received prior approval for work, where officer identified himself as police officer, displayed his badge and drew his revolver, was acting according to his mandatory duty to arrest and detain any person found in violation of state law, and his role as security specialist ended when he invoked his police authority. Cooper v. Dayton (Ohio App. 2 Dist., 06-06-1997) 120 Ohio App.3d 34, 696 N.E.2d 640, appeal not allowed 80 Ohio St.3d 1415, 684 N.E.2d 707. Workers' Compensation ⚷ 695

24. —— Private guard or investigator, arresting officer

RC 2935.03 does not bar a chartered municipality from granting authority to publicly commission private police officers to arrest for a misdemeanor without a warrant. City of Cleveland v. Kufrin (Ohio Mun. 1982) 3 Ohio Misc.2d 18, 446 N.E.2d 230, 3 O.B.R. 553.

A security employee employed by a department store, and acting solely on behalf of and for the benefit of such department store, has only such authority as is granted under RC 2935.041 and does not have authority to detain a person for interfering with the detention of a suspected shoplifter. State v. Griffin (Ohio Mun. 1977) 54 Ohio Misc. 52, 376 N.E.2d 1364, 6 O.O.3d 455, 8 O.O.3d 383. Arrest ⚷ 62

The taking of a person from a motor vehicle by a privately-employed industrial plant security guard for an alleged violation of RC 3719.41, and taking him to the plant guard station is not a lawful arrest, and the subsequent taking of such person into custody by the police does not constitute an arrest where such person was given to police custody without ever having been out of the custody of the plant security guard, and a search of said defendant's automobile was improper. State v. Lamb (Ohio Mun. 1973) 34 Ohio Misc. 104, 299 N.E.2d 317, 63 O.O.2d 410.

A private investigator may not arrest a person for the commission of a misdemeanor, except where the investigator is employed by a merchant and has probable cause to believe that the person arrested is guilty of shoplifting. OAG 74–041.

25. Effect of illegal arrest

City police officer who, outside of city limits, but based on probable cause, stopped motorist on suspicion that motorist was driving under the influence of alcohol (DUI), and detained motorist until state highway patrol officer arrived, did not act unreasonably per se under the Fourth Amendment, though officer was acting outside his statutory territorial jurisdiction, and thus, the officer's statutory violation did not require suppression of all evidence flowing from the stop, under the exclusionary rule. State v. Weideman (Ohio, 04-03-2002) 94 Ohio St.3d 501, 764 N.E.2d 997, 2002-Ohio-1484. Automobiles ⚷ 349(12); Criminal Law ⚷ 394.4(9)

Although defendant's warrantless arrest on misdemeanors, commission of which did not occur in arresting officer's presence, violated statute addressing unlawful restraint, evidence flowing from arrest in violation of that statute was not subject to suppression unless arrest also violated defendant's constitutional rights. State v. Norris (Ohio Mun., 06-17-1996) 81 Ohio Misc.2d 38, 674 N.E.2d 788. Criminal Law ⚷ 394.4(9)

An illegal arrest does not in itself invalidate an affidavit filed in a misdemeanor case, and is not a proper ground to sustain a motion to quash the affidavit, but it can affect evidence received as a result of such arrest, and when this happens, a motion to suppress the evidence or a plea in abatement will lie. State v. Hooper (Monroe 1966) 10 Ohio App.2d 229, 227 N.E.2d 414, 39 O.O.2d 435, certiorari denied 88 S.Ct. 292, 389 U.S. 928, 19 L.Ed.2d 281.

Contraband seized upon the search of an automobile incidental to an unlawful arrest is inadmissible as evidence and constitutes good cause for the granting of a motion to suppress such evidence filed and heard prior to a trial on the merits. State v. Thompson (Cuyahoga 1965) 1 Ohio App.2d 533, 206 N.E.2d 5, 30 O.O.2d 574. Criminal Law ⚷ 394.4(12); Criminal Law ⚷ 394.6(2)

Where a person who has title to an automobile, possession of which he has given to another, which other person also has been given possession of the certificate of title and keys, calls the police, after unsuccessfully seeking possession of the automobile, and a police officer, without a warrant, arrests such other person for refusal to comply with the police officer's order to transfer possession of the automobile, certificate of title and keys, such arrest is without legal foundation; and, in resisting such attempted arrest, such other person is not guilty of resisting and obstructing a police officer in the execution of his duties. City of Columbus v. Holmes (Franklin 1958) 107 Ohio App. 391, 152 N.E.2d 301, 78 Ohio Law Abs. 231, 8 O.O.2d 376, affirmed 169 Ohio St. 251, 159 N.E.2d 232, 8 O.O.2d 253.

26. Treatment of person being arrested

A law enforcement officer stands in a special relation to a prisoner in his custody and has a duty to reasonably care for and protect the prisoner from the time of arrest until release from custody; no obligation to act arises, however, until the officer knows or should know that the prisoner is ill, injured, endangered, or deranged. Clemets v. Heston (Williams 1985) 20 Ohio App.3d 132, 485 N.E.2d 287, 20 O.B.R. 166.

Ohio law imposes no duty on custodial officers to ensure that released prisoners are absolutely free from danger; thus, an officer who returns a motorist arrested for drunk driving to an auto which the officer knows contains a shotgun has no duty to prevent the motorist from turning the gun on himself unless that outcome is foreseeable because, e.g., the prisoner is despondent. Clemets v. Heston (Williams 1985) 20 Ohio App.3d 132, 485 N.E.2d 287, 20 O.B.R. 166.

A city cannot be held liable under 42 USC 1983 for jailers' deliberate indifference to the serious need for attention of a prisoner beaten by police after arrest who took his own life in a cell, absent evidence of a municipal policy, custom, or usage animating police behavior that resulted in the alleged constitutional violations, or a showing of more than mere municipal negligence in taking measures to prevent such incidents and train police properly. Molton v. City of Cleveland (C.A.6 (Ohio) 1988) 839 F.2d 240, certiorari denied 109 S.Ct. 1345, 489 U.S. 1068, 103 L.Ed.2d 814. Civil Rights ⚷ 1348

Evidence that a prisoner took his own life in a cell after being beaten by police and that the cries for help of a neighboring prisoner were ignored for ten minutes supports a finding in federal court that the city breached its duty under RC 341.01 to exercise reasonable care as to the health and safety of prisoners, and to guard against dangers known or that should have been known to jailers. Molton v. City of Cleveland (C.A.6 (Ohio) 1988) 839 F.2d 240, certiorari denied 109 S.Ct. 1345, 489 U.S. 1068, 103 L.Ed.2d 814.

Evidence that police knocked a drunken, handcuffed prisoner to the ground and then kicked and struck him as he lay helpless supports a jury's finding that the city employing these police is liable in an action under 42 USC 1983 for use of excessive force. Molton v. City of Cleveland (C.A.6 (Ohio) 1988) 839 F.2d 240, certiorari denied 109 S.Ct. 1345, 489 U.S. 1068, 103 L.Ed.2d 814.

Hospital expenses incurred by a probationer who has been arrested by a county sheriff and detained in the county jail must be borne by the county. Consequently, the adult parole authority is not responsible for the hospital expenses of a probationer under its supervision and control when such costs are incurred while the probationer is detained in a county jail after being arrested by a county sheriff pursuant to RC 2951.08. OAG 80–084.

The county is charged with the duty to house a prisoner charged with a misdemeanor under state law, both prior to and after conviction. OAG 79–008; overruled on other grounds by OAG 86–003.

The adult parole authority is responsible for hospital expenses of a probationer under its supervision and control when such costs are incurred when the probationer has been arrested and detained by a county sheriff pursuant to RC 2951.08. OAG 78–067; overruled by OAG 80–084.

A municipal prisoner is one who has been charged with or sentenced for violation of a municipal ordinance and responsibility for the sustenance and care of such a prisoner rests with the municipality; and a county prisoner is one charged with or sentenced by the county for violation of a state statute and responsibility for the sustenance and care of such a prisoner rests with the county. OAG 76–012.

Where a township police constable arrests a person for violation of a state statute, and said person is confined in a municipal jail pending trial, the township which said police constable serves is not liable for the costs of confinement. 1962 OAG 3405.

Where a highway patrolman arrests a person found violating a law of this state, for which violation he is authorized to arrest, he must follow the procedure prescribed by RC 2935.03, RC 2935.05, RC 2935.08 and RC 2935.13. 1961 OAG 2214.

27. Law enforcement agencies

The authority granted to townships and municipal corporations by RC 505.431 and 737.041, respectively, coupled with the sheriff's and his deputies' authority under RC 311.07 and 2935.03(A) to provide police protection throughout the territory of the county, empowers a county and various townships and municipal corporations located within that county to provide additional police protection to each other, if the participating townships and municipal corporations authorize, by appropriate resolutions, the provision of such additional police protection by their police departments. OAG 90–091.

Since a county sheriff and his deputies are authorized, pursuant to RC 311.07 and 2935.03(A), to provide police protection throughout the territory of the county in which they are appointed or elected, and the townships and municipal corporations located within that county are empowered under RC 505.431 and 737.041, respectively, to provide, by resolution, additional police protection to any county, township, or municipal corporation of this state, these same political subdivisions may form, pursuant to RC 167.01, a regional council of governments to provide additional police protection throughout the entire territory encompassed by the regional council, provided that each member township and municipal corporation adopts an appropriate resolution. OAG 90–091.

The term "law enforcement agency" as used in RC 4511.191(A) refers to a police department, division of state highway patrol, sheriff or board of township trustees. OAG 68–037.

28. Juvenile proceedings

The statutory law of arrest does not apply to special statutory proceedings in the juvenile court which are civil in nature and have for their purpose the securing for each child under the jurisdiction of the juvenile court such care, guidance and control... as will best serve the child's welfare. In re L— (Ohio Juv. 1963) 194 N.E.2d 797, 92 Ohio Law Abs. 475, 25 O.O.2d 369.

29. Domestic violence

Mother who was arrested and prosecuted for domestic violence, and who brought false arrest, abuse of process, and malicious prosecution claims against arresting police officers and city that employed officers, waived, for purposes of appellate review, her constitutional challenges to statute defining domestic violence and statute defining probable cause to arrest for domestic violence, and her argument that such statutes, as applied, were inconsistent with statute defining child endangerment, where mother did not raise such arguments in the trial court. White v. Roch (Ohio App. 9 Dist., Summit, 03-16-2005) No. 22239, 2005-Ohio-1127, 2005 WL 602684, Unreported, appeal not allowed 106 Ohio St.3d 1486, 832 N.E.2d 738, 2005-Ohio-3978. Appeal And Error ⚷ 170(2)

Statute articulating Ohio's preferred arrest policy in domestic violence cases does not entitle an investigating officer carte blanche freedom in questioning anyone involved in a domestic violence dispute without regard to applicable *Miranda* warnings. City of Cleveland v. Morales (Ohio App. 8 Dist., Cuyahoga, 10-24-2002) No. 81083, 2002-Ohio-5862, 2002 WL 31402003, Unreported. Criminal Law ⚷ 412.2(3)

Balancing of defendant's interests against governmental interests weighed in favor of denying defendant's application to seal the records from prosecution for domestic violence and assault, which had been dismissed on day of trial because of alleged victim's failure to appear for trial; if defendant were to be involved in an alleged domestic violence situation in the future, the records would be needed by law enforcement officials to fulfill statutory duty of determining who was primary aggressor for purposes of detention while awaiting arrest warrant, the records had not prevented defendant's present employment in insurance industry, and the effect the records would have on defendant's future employment possibilities was speculative. State v. Tyler (Ohio App. 10 Dist., Franklin, 08-20-2002) No. 01AP-1055, 2002-Ohio-4300, 2002 WL 1934995, Unreported, appeal not allowed 97 Ohio St.3d 1485, 780 N.E.2d 288, 2002-Ohio-6866. Records ⚷ 32

The provisions of RC 2935.03(B)(3)(b) establishing arrest as the preferred course of action in domestic violence situations are not applicable to juveniles. OAG 96–061.

A judge's consultation and participation may be sought in collaborative efforts regarding domestic violence, but written endorsement of the protocols that set forth the required behavior of peace officers, prosecutors, and judges, interferes with the independence of the judiciary, implies partiality of the judges, and appears to commit a judge with respect to cases and controversies that may come before the judge in a court of law. For these reasons, it is not prudent under Canons 1, 2(A), 3(A)(1), and 7(B)(2)(c), (d), (e) of the Ohio Code of Judicial Conduct for a judge to make a written endorsement of a protocol for responding to domestic violence. Bd of Commrs on Grievances & Discipline Op 96–005 (6–14–96).

30. Investigators of crime and duty as to exculpatory evidence

Under *Brady*, state failed its duty of disclosure by failing to weigh evidence so that exculpatory evidence could be provided to defense in aggravated murder case, where police removed exculpatory evidence from information given to prosecution, such that prosecutor was intentionally kept in dark regarding exculpatory evidence. Jamison v. Collins (C.A.6 (Ohio), 05-23-2002) 291 F.3d 380, amended on denial of rehearing. Criminal Law ⚷ 700(7)

31. Traffic offenses, passenger

Passenger did not violate Ohio statute making failure to comply with lawful order of a police officer a first degree misdemeanor and an offense for which a person could be arrested, as would justify search incident to his lawful arrest; although passenger exited vehicle and walked away from traffic stop after officer told him three times to remain in vehicle, he was not required to read inner workings of officer's mind to determine reason why officer relented after much badgering and gave him permission to exit vehicle, i.e., because officer did not want to risk confrontation alone with two suspects. U.S. v. Garner (C.A.6 (Ohio), 09-05-2002) No. 00-4395, No. 00-4409, 46 Fed.Appx. 278, 2002 WL 31007867, Unreported, certiorari denied 123 S.Ct. 1650, 538 U.S. 947, 155 L.Ed.2d 488. Obstructing Justice ⚷ 7

2935.031 Agencies employing persons with arrest authority to adopt motor vehicle pursuit policies

Any agency, instrumentality, or political subdivision of the state that employs a sheriff, deputy sheriff, constable, marshal, deputy marshal, police officer, member of a metropolitan housing authority police force, state university law enforcement officer, or veterans' home police officer with arrest authority under section 2935.03 of the Revised Code or that employs other persons with arrest authority under the Revised Code, shall adopt a policy for the pursuit in a motor vehicle of any person who violates a law of this state or an ordinance of a municipal corporation. The chief law enforcement officer or other chief official of the agency, instrumentality, or political subdivision shall formally advise each peace officer or other person with arrest authority it employs of the pursuit policy adopted by that agency, instrumentality, or political subdivision pursuant to this section.

(2002 H 675, eff. 3–14–03; 1989 S 49, eff. 11–3–89)

Historical and Statutory Notes

Amendment Note: 2002 H 675 made changes to reflect gender neutral language; and made other nonsubstantive changes.

Library References

Arrest ⚷66(3), 68(1).

Westlaw Topic No. 35.

C.J.S. Arrest §§ 51 to 53, 55.

Research References

Encyclopedias

OH Jur. 3d Police, Sheriffs, & Related Officers § 90, Liability of Corporation or Political Subdivision for Acts of Police.

Notes of Decisions

1. Negligent operation of emergency vehicle

Statute permitting adoption of a policy for the pursuit in a motor vehicle of any person violating state law or municipal ordinance could not be used as an independent basis of imposing liability on township for death of driver who was killed in an automobile accident that occurred during a high speed chase. Robertson v. Roberts (Ohio App. 11 Dist., Trumbull, 12-23-2004) No. 2003-T-0125, 2004-Ohio-7231, 2004 WL 3090216, Unreported, appeal not allowed 105 Ohio St.3d 1562, 828 N.E.2d 117, 2005-Ohio-2447. Automobiles ⚷ 175(2); Automobiles ⚷ 187(2)

Disregard of statute governing agencies employing persons with arrest authority to adopt motor vehicle pursuit policies, coupled with other proof, can constitute evidence of negligence on the part of a political subdivision that is subject to liability for the negligent operation of emergency or public safety vehicle. Wagner v. Heavlin (Ohio App. 7 Dist., 02-14-2000) 136 Ohio App.3d 719, 737 N.E.2d 989. Automobiles ⚷ 175(2); Automobiles ⚷ 187(1)

2. Officers' authority to initiate pursuit

Officers were authorized to initiate vehicular pursuit of defendant, where defendant fled in his vehicle after being pulled over for a traffic violation, and defendant, if allowed to flee, presented a danger to human life or could have caused serious injury in that he hastily abandoned his vehicle in a residential area and ran, and shortly thereafter, gunshots were fired at officers from the direction in which defendant had fled. State v. Hill (Ohio App. 8 Dist., Cuyahoga, 03-18-2004) No. 83078, 2004-Ohio-1248, 2004 WL 527958, Unreported, appeal not allowed 103 Ohio St.3d 1426, 814 N.E.2d 490, 2004-Ohio-4524, appeal after new sentencing hearing 2005-Ohio-1311, 2005 WL 678120, appeal allowed 106 Ohio St.3d 1504, 833 N.E.2d 1247, 2005-Ohio-4605, reversed in part 109 Ohio St.3d 313, 847 N.E.2d 1174, 2006-Ohio-2109. Automobiles ⚷ 349(2.1); Automobiles ⚷ 349(8)

2935.032 Domestic violence arrest policies

(A) Not later than ninety days after the effective date of this amendment, each agency, instrumentality, or political subdivision that is served by any peace officer described in division (B)(1) of section 2935.03 of the Revised Code shall adopt, in accordance with division (E) of this section, written policies, written procedures implementing the policies, and other written procedures for the peace officers who serve it to follow in implementing division (B)(3) of section 2935.03 of the Revised Code and for their appropriate response to each report of an alleged incident of the offense of domestic violence or an alleged incident of the offense of violating a protection order. The policies and procedures shall conform to and be consistent with the provisions of divisions (B)(1) and (B)(3) of section 2935.03 of the Revised Code and divisions (B) to (D) of this section. Each policy adopted under this division shall include, but not be limited to, all of the following:

(1) Provisions specifying that, if a peace officer who serves the agency, instrumentality, or political subdivision responds to an alleged incident of the offense of domestic violence, an alleged incident of the offense of violating a protection order, or an alleged incident of any other offense, both of the following apply:

(a) If the officer determines that there are reasonable grounds to believe that a person knowingly caused serious physical harm to another or to another's unborn or knowingly caused or attempted to cause physical harm to another or to another's unborn by means of a deadly weapon or dangerous ordnance, then, regardless of whether the victim of the offense was a family or household member of the offender, the officer shall treat the incident as felonious assault, shall consider the offender to have committed and the victim to have been the victim of felonious assault, shall consider the offense that was committed to have been felonious assault in determining the manner in which the offender should be treated, and shall comply with whichever of the following is applicable:

(i) Unless the officer has reasonable cause to believe that, during the incident, the offender who committed the felonious assault and one or more other persons committed offenses against each other, the officer shall arrest the offender who committed the felonious assault pursuant to section 2935.03 of the Revised Code and shall detain that offender pursuant to that section until a warrant can be obtained, and the arrest shall be for felonious assault.

(ii) If the officer has reasonable cause to believe that, during the incident, the offender who committed the felonious assault and one or more other persons committed offenses against each other, the officer shall determine in accordance with division (B)(3)(d) of section 2935.03 of the Revised Code which of those persons is the primary physical aggressor. If the offender who committed the felonious assault is the primary physical aggressor, the officer shall arrest that offender for felonious assault pursuant to section 2935.03 of the Revised Code and shall detain that offender pursuant to that section until a warrant can be obtained, and the officer is not required to arrest but may arrest pursuant to section 2935.03 of the Revised Code any other person who committed an offense but who is not the primary physical aggressor. If the offender who committed the felonious assault is not the primary physical aggressor, the officer is not required to arrest that offender or any other person who committed an offense during the incident but may arrest any of them pursuant to section 2935.03 of the Revised Code and detain them pursuant to that section until a warrant can be obtained.

(b) If the officer determines that there are reasonable grounds to believe that a person, while under the influence of sudden passion or in a sudden fit of rage, either of which is brought on by serious provocation occasioned by the victim that is reasonably sufficient to incite the person into using deadly force, knowingly caused serious physical harm to another or to another's unborn or knowingly caused or attempted to cause physical harm to another or to another's unborn by means of a deadly weapon or dangerous ordnance, then, regardless of whether the victim of the offense was a family or household member of the offender, the officer shall treat the incident as aggravated assault, shall consider the offender to have committed and the victim to have been the victim of aggravated assault, shall consider the offense that was committed to have been aggravated assault in determining the manner in which the offender should be treated, and shall comply with whichever of the following is applicable:

(i) Unless the officer has reasonable cause to believe that, during the incident, the offender who committed the aggravated assault and one or more other persons committed offenses against each other, the officer shall arrest the offender who committed the aggravated assault pursuant to section 2935.03 of the Revised Code and shall detain that offender pursuant to that section until a warrant can be obtained, and the arrest shall be for aggravated assault.

(ii) If the officer has reasonable cause to believe that, during the incident, the offender who committed the aggravated assault and one or more other persons committed offenses against each other, the officer shall determine in accordance with division (B)(3)(d) of section 2935.03 of the Revised Code which of those persons is the primary physical aggressor. If the offender who committed the aggravated assault is the primary physical aggressor, the officer shall arrest that offender for aggravated assault pursuant to section 2935.03 of the Revised Code and shall detain that offender pursuant to that section until a warrant can be obtained, and the officer is not required to arrest but may arrest pursuant to section 2935.03 of the Revised Code any other person who committed an offense but who is not the primary physical aggressor. If the offender who committed the aggravated assault is not the primary physical aggressor, the officer is not required to arrest that offender or any other person who committed an offense during the incident but may arrest any of them pursuant to section 2935.03 of the Revised Code and detain them pursuant to that section until a warrant can be obtained.

(2) Provisions requiring the peace officers who serve the agency, instrumentality, or political subdivision to do all of the following:

(a) Respond without undue delay to a report of an alleged incident of the offense of domestic violence or the offense of violating a protection order;

(b) If the alleged offender has been granted pretrial release from custody on a prior charge of the offense of domestic violence or the offense of violating a protection order and has violated one or more conditions of that pretrial release, document the facts and circumstances of the violation in the report to the law enforcement agency that the peace officer makes pursuant to division (D) of this section;

(c) Separate the victim of the offense of domestic violence or the offense of violating a protection order and the alleged offender, conduct separate interviews with the victim and the alleged offender in separate locations, and take a written statement from the victim that indicates the frequency and severity of any prior incidents of physical abuse of the victim by the alleged offender, the number of times the victim has called peace officers for assistance, and the disposition of those calls, if known;

(d) Comply with divisions (B)(1) and (B)(3) of section 2935.03 of the Revised Code and with divisions (B), (C), and (D) of this section.

(3) Sanctions to be imposed upon a peace officer who serves the agency, instrumentality, or political subdivision and who fails to comply with any provision in the policy or with division (B)(1) or (B)(3) of section 2935.03 of the Revised Code or division (B), (C), or (D) of this section.

(4) Examples of reasons that a peace officer may consider for not arresting and detaining until a warrant can be obtained a person who allegedly committed the offense of domestic violence or the offense of violating a protection order when it is the preferred course of action in this state that the officer arrest the alleged offender, as described in division (B)(3)(b) of section 2935.03 of the Revised Code.

(B)(1) Nothing in this section or in division (B)(1) or (B)(3) of section 2935.03 of the Revised Code precludes an agency, instrumentality, or political subdivision that is served by any peace officer described in division (B)(1) of section 2935.03 of the Revised Code from including in the policy it adopts under division (A) of this section either of the following types of provisions:

(a) A provision that requires the peace officers who serve it, if they have reasonable grounds to believe that the offense of domestic violence or the offense of violating a protection order has been committed within the limits of the jurisdiction of the agency, instrumentality, or political subdivision and reasonable cause to believe that a particular person committed the offense, to arrest the alleged offender;

(b) A provision that does not require the peace officers who serve it, if they have reasonable grounds to believe that the offense of domestic violence or the offense of violating a protection order has been committed within the limits of the jurisdiction of the agency, instrumentality, or political subdivision and reasonable cause to believe that a particular person committed the offense, to arrest the alleged offender, but that grants the officers less discretion in those circumstances in deciding whether to arrest the alleged offender than peace officers are granted by divisions (B)(1) and (B)(3) of section 2935.03 of the Revised Code.

(2) If an agency, instrumentality, or political subdivision that is served by any peace officer described in division (B)(1) of section 2935.03 of the Revised Code includes in the policy it adopts under division (A) of this section a provision of the type described in division (B)(1)(a) or (b) of this section, the peace officers who serve the agency, instrumentality, or political subdivision shall comply with the provision in making arrests authorized under division (B)(1) of section 2935.03 of the Revised Code.

(C) When a peace officer described in division (B)(1) of section 2935.03 of the Revised Code investigates a report of an alleged incident of the offense of domestic violence or an alleged incident of the offense of violating a protection order, the officer shall do all of the following:

(1) Complete a domestic violence report in accordance with division (D) of this section;

(2) Advise the victim of the availability of a temporary protection order pursuant to section 2919.26 of the Revised Code or a protection order or consent agreement pursuant to section 3113.31 of the Revised Code;

(3) Give the victim the officer's name, the officer's badge number if the officer has a badge and the badge has a number, the report number for the incident if a report number is available at the time of the officer's investigation, a telephone number that the victim can call for information about the case, the telephone number of a domestic violence shelter in the area, and information on any local victim advocate program.

(D) A peace officer who investigates a report of an alleged incident of the offense of domestic violence or an alleged incident of the offense of violating a protection order shall make a written report of the incident whether or not an arrest is made. The report shall document the officer's observations of the victim and the alleged offender, any visible injuries of the victim or alleged offender, any weapons at the scene, the actions of the alleged offender, any statements made by the victim or witnesses, and any other significant facts or circumstances. If the officer does not arrest and detain until a warrant can be obtained a person who allegedly committed the offense of domestic violence or the offense of violating a protection order when it is the preferred course of action in this state pursuant to division (B)(3)(b) of section 2935.03 of the Revised Code that the alleged offender be arrested, the officer must articulate in the report a clear statement of the officer's reasons for not arresting and detaining that alleged offender until a warrant can be obtained. The officer shall submit the written report to the law enforcement agency to which the officer has been appointed, employed, or elected.

(E) Each agency, instrumentality, or political subdivision that is required to adopt policies and procedures under division (A) of this section shall adopt those policies and procedures in conjunction and consultation with shelters in the community for victims of domestic violence and private organizations, law enforcement agencies, and other public agencies in the community that have expertise in the recognition and handling of domestic violence cases.

(F) To the extent described in and in accordance with section 9.86 or 2744.03 of the Revised Code, a peace officer who arrests an offender for the offense of violating a protection order with respect to a protection order or consent agreement of this state or another state that on its face is valid is immune from liability in a civil action for damages for injury, death, or loss to person or property that allegedly was caused by or related to the arrest.

(G) Each agency, instrumentality, or political subdivision described in division (A) of this section that arrests an offender for an alleged incident of the offense of domestic violence or an alleged incident of the offense of violating a protection order shall consider referring the case to federal authorities for prosecution under 18 U.S.C. 2261 if the incident constitutes a violation of federal law.

(H) As used in this section:

(1) "Another's unborn" has the same meaning as in section 2903.09 of the Revised Code.

(2) "Dangerous ordnance" and "deadly weapon" have the same meanings as in section 2923.11 of the Revised Code.

(3) "The offense of violating a protection order" includes the former offense of violating a protection order or consent agreement or anti-stalking protection order as set forth in section 2919.27 of the Revised Code as it existed prior to the effective date of this amendment.

(1997 S 1, eff. 10–21–97; 1994 H 335, eff. 12–9–94)

Historical and Statutory Notes

Amendment Note: 1997 S 1 deleted the phrase "or consent agreement" following "violating a protection order" throughout; inserted references to "another's unborn" in divisions (A)(1)(a) and (A)(1)(b); deleted "as defined in section 2923.11 of the Revised Code," in divisions (A)(1)(a) and (A)(1)(b); deleted "or the offense of domestic violence" in division (A)(2)(a); added division (F); and made changes to reflect gender neutral language and other nonsubstantive changes.

Library References

Arrest ⚷63, 70.

Westlaw Topic No. 35.

C.J.S. Arrest §§ 9, 14 to 39, 42 to 44, 58 to 61.

Research References

Encyclopedias

OH Jur. 3d Criminal Law § 2111, Generally; Peace Officers.

Treatises and Practice Aids

Adrine & Ruden, Ohio Domestic Violence Law § 4:7, Enforcement of a Protection Order.

Adrine & Ruden, Ohio Domestic Violence Law § 5:1, Prosecution's Challenge.

Adrine & Ruden, Ohio Domestic Violence Law § 7:5, Pretrial Detention and Initial Appearance Issues.

Adrine & Ruden, Ohio Domestic Violence Law § 7:9, Pretrial Motions.

Adrine & Ruden, Ohio Domestic Violence Law § 8:6, Parents and Children.

Adrine & Ruden, Ohio Domestic Violence Law § 13:2, Ohio Statutory Procedure.

Adrine & Ruden, Ohio Domestic Violence Law § 13:3, Arrest of the Perpetrator.

Adrine & Ruden, Ohio Domestic Violence Law § 13:4, Determination of Primary Physical Aggressor.

Adrine & Ruden, Ohio Domestic Violence Law § 13:5, False Arrest, Warrantless Arrests and Searches, and Weapons Confiscation.

Adrine & Ruden, Ohio Domestic Violence Law § 13:6, Law Enforcement Policies and Procedures.

Adrine & Ruden, Ohio Domestic Violence Law § 17:7, Other Remedies Under Vawa.

Adrine & Ruden, Ohio Domestic Violence Law § 9:13, Jurisdiction and Venue—in Domestic Violence Cases.

Adrine & Ruden, Ohio Domestic Violence Law § 11:14, Remedies—Orders to Vacate or Evict.

Adrine & Ruden, Ohio Domestic Violence Law § 11:19, Remedies—Orders to Refrain from Entering Separate Residence, School, or Place of Employment.

Adrine & Ruden, Ohio Domestic Violence Law § 11:21, Remedies—Miscellaneous Issues.

Adrine & Ruden, Ohio Domestic Violence Law § 13:12, Police Liability for Failing to Protect Victims of Domestic Violence—Legal Theories for Recovery—State Duty to Protect.

Adrine & Ruden, Ohio Domestic Violence Law § 13:14, Significant Cases Involving Police Officer Action or Inaction.

Adrine & Ruden, Ohio Domestic Violence Law § 13:15, Potential Police Liability in the Enforcement of Protection Orders.

Adrine & Ruden, Ohio Domestic Violence Law § 13:17, Enforcement of Out-Of-State Protection Orders.

Adrine & Ruden, Ohio Domestic Violence Law § 15:11, Legal Responsibilities of Law Enforcement and Medical Personnel.

Adrine & Ruden, Ohio Domestic Violence Law § 15:12, Evidentiary Considerations Involving Independent Documentation.

Law Review and Journal Commentaries

Mandatory arrest: A step toward eradicating domestic violence, but is it enough?, Note. 1996 U Ill L Rev 533.

No–Drop Policies: Effective Legislation or Protectionist Attitude?, Note. 30 U Tol L Rev 621 (Summer 1999).

Notes of Decisions

1. Peace officers covered

Because troopers of the state highway patrol, forest officers under RC 1503.29, preserve officers under RC 1517.10, wildlife officers under RC 1531.13, park officers under RC 1541.10, and watercraft officers under RC 1547.521 are not peace officers described in RC 2935.03(B)(1), the troopers and officers are not subject to the domestic violence arrest provisions of RC 2935.03(B)(3), and the highway patrol and the department of natural resources are not required to adopt a domestic violence policy pursuant to RC 2935.032. OAG 96–014.

2. "Felonious assault" construed

Even if officer obtained consent before entry into residence, consent was invalid where wife merely told officer that she wanted him to escort her solely to get keys to her car, no violence or threat of violence had occurred, and officer knew that, although wife had made a 911 telephone call, she had made a subsequent one to cancel that call; officer was thus not authorized to validate official investigation of domestic violence. State v. Samarghandi (Ohio Mun., 02-18-1997) 84 Ohio Misc.2d 6, 680 N.E.2d 738. Searches And Seizures ⚷ 184

Fact that officer is making a radio run for domestic "situation" does not show he is involved in domestic violence situation for purposes of statute mandating that officer investigate and arrest when circumstances show that felonious domestic violence has occurred. State v. Samarghandi (Ohio Mun., 02-18-1997) 84 Ohio Misc.2d 6, 680 N.E.2d 738. Arrest ⚷ 63.1

3. Withdrawing of report of incident

Where officer's entry into home was, at best, as a Good Samaritan to aid wife in obtaining keys to her car, any perceived consent or actual consent to the entry could be withdrawn at anytime. State v. Samarghandi (Ohio Mun., 02-18-1997) 84 Ohio Misc.2d 6, 680 N.E.2d 738. Searches And Seizures ⚷ 186

4. Nonarrest or detention

The general assembly has not identified in RC 2935.03(B) the reasons a peace officer may consider for not arresting and detaining a person the officer has reasonable grounds to believe committed the offense of domestic violence. Rather, pursuant to

RC 2935.032, the policy adopted by an agency, instrumentality, or subdivision to implement the domestic violence arrest provisions must set forth examples of reasons a peace officer may consider for not arresting and detaining a person in that situation. OAG 01–039.

2935.033 Peace officer may assist federal law enforcement with arrest authority under USA Patriot Act

(A) Any peace officer may render assistance to any federal law enforcement officer who has arrest authority under the "Uniting and Strengthening America by Providing Appropriate Tools Required to Intercept and Obstruct Terrorism (USA Patriot Act) Act of 2001," Pub. L. No. 107–056, 115 Stat. 272, as amended, if both of the following apply:

(1) There is a threat of imminent physical danger to the federal law enforcement officer, a threat of physical harm to another person, or any other serious emergency situation present.

(2) Either the federal law enforcement officer requests emergency assistance or it appears that the federal law enforcement officer is unable to request assistance, and the circumstances reasonably indicate that assistance is appropriate.

(B) "Federal law enforcement officer" has the same meaning as in section 9.88 of the Revised Code.

(2005 S 9, eff. 4–14–06)

Library References

Arrest ⚷63.

Westlaw Topic No. 35.

C.J.S. Arrest §§ 9, 14 to 39, 42 to 44.

2935.04 When any person may arrest

When a felony has been committed, or there is reasonable ground to believe that a felony has been committed, any person without a warrant may arrest another whom he has reasonable cause to believe is guilty of the offense, and detain him until a warrant can be obtained.

(1953 H 1, eff. 10–1–53; GC 13432–2)

Historical and Statutory Notes

Pre–1953 H 1 Amendments: 113 v 140, Ch 11, § 2

Cross References

Arrest of persons violating parole, arrest powers of law enforcement officers not limited, 2301.31

Arrest of persons violating parole or pardon; arrest powers of law enforcement officers not limited, 2941.46

Arrest of persons violating probation or community control sanctions, arrest powers of law enforcement officers not limited, 2951.08

Civil immunity of federal law enforcement officers, 9.88

Freedom from unreasonable seizure; warrants, O Const Art I §14

Youth services department, arrest of child violating supervised release from, 5139.52

Research References

Encyclopedias

OH Jur. 3d Criminal Law § 2106, Generally; Felonies.

OH Jur. 3d Criminal Law § 2114, Private Persons; Security Officers.

Treatises and Practice Aids

Markus, Trial Handbook for Ohio Lawyers, § 29:8, Search Incident to Valid Arrest.

Markus, Trial Handbook for Ohio Lawyers, § 4:61, Criminal Case—Defenses—Self-Defense and Justifiable Force.

Katz, Giannelli, Blair and Lipton, Baldwin's Ohio Practice, Criminal Law, § 6:4, Warrantless Felony Arrests in Public Places.

Katz, Giannelli, Blair and Lipton, Baldwin's Ohio Practice, Criminal Law, § 6:10, Arrests by Private Citizens.

Katz, Giannelli, Blair and Lipton, Baldwin's Ohio Practice, Criminal Law, § 89:3, Citizen Arrest.

Katz, Ohio Arrest, Search & Seizure § 4:2, Nature of the Offense—Felonies.

Katz, Ohio Arrest, Search & Seizure App. A, Appendix A. Arrest Provisions: Checklist.

Giannelli & Yeomans, Ohio Juvenile Law § 14:3, Custody, Arrests & Stops.

Princehorn, Baldwin's Ohio Practice, Local Government Law—Township, § 11:40, Police Officers—Duties.

Law Review and Journal Commentaries

Reality and Illusion: Defining Private Security Law in Ohio, Comment. 13 U Tol L Rev 377 (Winter 1982).

United States v *Alvarez-Machain*: The Supreme Court's Approval of the Abduction of Foreign Nationals, Comment. 25 U Tol L Rev 297 (1994).

Notes of Decisions

---

1. Constitutional issues—arrest in home

A warrantless arrest in a suspect's home may be valid if necessitated by exigent circumstances or performed in "good faith" compliance with standards of conduct which, at the time of the arrest, were permissible. State v. Williams (Ohio 1983) 6 Ohio St.3d 281, 452 N.E.2d 1323, 6 O.B.R. 345, certiorari denied 104 S.Ct. 554, 464 U.S. 1020, 78 L.Ed.2d 727. Arrest ⚷ 68(9)

Intrusion into home to effect warrantless arrest justified by exigent circumstances, such as (1) where persons within already know of officers' authority and purpose, or (2) where officers justified in belief that persons within are in imminent peril of bodily harm, or (3) persons within are made aware of someone outside, and engage in activity justifying officers in believing that escape or destruction of evidence is being attempted. Ker v. State of Cal. (U.S.Cal. 1963) 83 S.Ct. 1623, 374 U.S. 23, 10 L.Ed.2d 726, 24 O.O.2d 201.

Where a defendant is standing at the threshold within the frame of an open door and while he is half in and half out of the building line of his residence, the defendant is considered to be in a public place and a warrantless arrest based on probable cause is valid. State v Seymour, No. CA 9060 (2d Dist Ct App, Montgomery, 8–29–85).

2. —— Deadly force, use, constitutional issues

A Tennessee statute authorizing the use of deadly force to halt a fleeing felony suspect is unconstitutional insofar as it authorizes the unreasonable seizure of that suspect by the use of deadly force, in the absence of probable cause to believe he poses a physical danger to others or has committed a violent crime. (Ed. note: Tennessee law construed in light of federal constitution.) Tennessee v. Garner (U.S.Tenn. 1985) 105 S.Ct. 1694, 471 U.S. 1, 85 L.Ed.2d 1.

3. —— Search incident to arrest, constitutional issues

The taking of a person from a motor vehicle by a privately-employed industrial plant security guard for an alleged violation of RC 3719.41, and taking him to the plant guard station is not a lawful arrest, and the subsequent taking of such person into custody by the police does not constitute an arrest where such person was given to police custody without ever having been out of the custody of the plant security guard, and a search of said defendant's automobile was improper. State v. Lamb (Ohio Mun. 1973) 34 Ohio Misc. 104, 299 N.E.2d 317, 63 O.O.2d 410.

Contraband seized upon the search of an automobile incidental to an unlawful arrest is inadmissible as evidence and constitutes good cause for the granting of a motion to suppress such evidence filed and heard prior to a trial on the merits. State v. Thompson (Cuyahoga 1965) 1 Ohio App.2d 533, 206 N.E.2d 5, 30 O.O.2d 574. Criminal Law ⚷ 394.4(12); Criminal Law ⚷ 394.6(2)

The search of an individual's person on the honest belief of an arresting officer, based upon probable cause that a felony has been committed, does not constitute an unlawful search, and incriminating articles seized during the search may properly be received in evidence against the individual at his trial for having in his possession such articles. State v. Beck (Ohio 1963) 175 Ohio St. 73, 191 N.E.2d 825, 23 O.O.2d 377, certiorari granted 84 S.Ct. 664, 376 U.S. 905, 11 L.Ed.2d 604, reversed 85 S.Ct. 223, 379 U.S. 89, 3 Ohio Misc. 71, 13 L.Ed.2d 142, 31 O.O.2d 80. Arrest ⚷ 71.1(12); Criminal Law ⚷ 394.4(4)

Evidence obtained in a search incident to an invalid arrest by a security guard under RC 2935.04 is admissible because the exclusionary rule does not apply to actions by private citizens. State v Cullers, No. 8781 (2d Dist Ct App, Montgomery, 1–4–85).

4. —— Miranda warnings, constitutional issues

Private security officers or private detectives are not officers of the law in such capacity that they have to render a constitutional warning precedent to taking of a statement in nature of a confession.

State v. Peoples (Mahoning 1971) 28 Ohio App.2d 162, 275 N.E.2d 626, 57 O.O.2d 226. Criminal Law ⚷ 412.2(3)

5. Misdemeanor as basis for warrantless arrest

RC 2935.04 authorizes the warrantless arrest of a person for a misdemeanor when the arresting officer knows that the person has a previous conviction which will enhance the misdemeanor to a felony. State v. Wac (Ohio 1981) 68 Ohio St.2d 84, 428 N.E.2d 428, 22 O.O.3d 299. Arrest ⚷ 63.1

If a constable has knowledge of a previous conviction which will enhance an offense of domestic violence from a misdemeanor to a felony, and if the provisions of RC 2935.04 are satisfied, the constable may arrest the offender under RC 2935.04, even though the constable has not viewed the commission of the offense. OAG 86–073.

Pursuant to RC 2935.03, a municipal police officer may pursue, arrest, and detain until a warrant can be obtained, a misdemeanor offender outside the limits of the municipality that appointed the officer if the officer is authorized under RC 2935.03(A) or (B) to arrest and detain the offender without a warrant within the jurisdiction that appointed the officer, if the pursuit is initiated within the officer's jurisdiction without unreasonable delay after the offense is committed, and if the offense is a first degree misdemeanor or a violation of a substantially equivalent municipal ordinance, a second degree misdemeanor or a violation of a substantially equivalent municipal ordinance, or any offense for which points are chargeable under RC 4507.021(G). OAG 86–065.

6. "Reasonable" cause or probable cause—in general

Suspicion and good faith are not sufficient to justify an arrest and incidental search without a warrant. State v. Rogers (Ohio Com.Pl. 1963) 198 N.E.2d 796, 94 Ohio Law Abs. 110, 27 O.O.2d 105.

Probable cause for arrest exists when a police officer observes suspicious behavior of the driver of a car and is informed by a reliable source that the vehicle has been reported stolen even though such report is later proved erroneous. State v Kellough, No. 81–CA–14 (12th Dist Ct App, Fayette, 7–14–82).

7. —— Test, "Reasonable" cause or probable cause

The unlawful possession of an hallucinogen is a continuing offense, committed in the presence of an arresting officer who finds the contraband in the bedroom occupied and controlled by an accused, who appears during the search, and an arrest in such circumstances is lawful. State v. Wilson (Montgomery 1974) 41 Ohio App.2d 240, 325 N.E.2d 249, 70 O.O.2d 452. Arrest ⚷ 63.3

To have probable cause, the arresting officer must have sufficient information derived from a reasonably trustworthy source to warrant a prudent man in believing that a felony has been committed and that it has been committed by the accused. State v. Timson (Ohio 1974) 38 Ohio St.2d 122, 311 N.E.2d 16, 67 O.O.2d 140. Arrest ⚷ 63.4(2)

A person who sees another taking merchandise from a store counter and has reasonable grounds to believe that a felony is being committed may under RC 2935.04 make an arrest without a warrant. State v. Stone (Ohio Mun. 1968) 16 Ohio Misc. 160, 241 N.E.2d 302, 45 O.O.2d 123. Arrest ⚷ 64

To have probable cause to arrest without a warrant an officer must have sufficient information from a reasonably trustworthy source to warrant a prudent man in believing that a felony has been committed and that it has been committed by the accused. State v. Fultz (Ohio 1968) 13 Ohio St.2d 79, 234 N.E.2d 593, 42 O.O.2d 259, certiorari denied 89 S.Ct. 95, 393 U.S. 854, 21 L.Ed.2d 123. Arrest ⚷ 63.4(2)

Where a felony is claimed to have been committed, proof of probable cause for arrest without a warrant rests on facts shown by substantial and credible evidence sufficient to warrant a man of reasonable caution in the belief that such an offense has been committed, and the mere opinion, conclusion, or belief, standing alone, of the arresting officer that such act had been committed is without probative value and insufficient to justify such arrest. State v. Thompson (Cuyahoga 1965) 1 Ohio App.2d 533, 206 N.E.2d 5, 30 O.O.2d 574. Arrest ⚷ 63.4(2)

State law determines validity of arrest without warrant, and the knowledge of officers was sufficient to warrant arrest of defendant in the belief that he was guilty of a felony in the unlawful possession of narcotic drugs under RC 3719.02. U. S. v. Pierce (N.D.Ohio 1954) 124 F.Supp. 264, 70 Ohio Law Abs. 140, 56 O.O. 44, affirmed 224 F.2d 281.

RC 2935.04 authorizes any person, including a constable, to make a warrantless arrest when a felony has been committed or there is reasonable ground to believe that a felony has been committed and when the person making the arrest has reasonable cause to believe that the person arrested is guilty of the offense; the person making the arrest need not have viewed the commission of the offense. OAG 86–073.

8. —— Source of information, "Reasonable" cause or probable cause

In determining whether police had probable cause for a warrantless arrest, based in part on an informant's tip, the veracity or reliability of the informant and the basis of his knowledge are relevant considerations in the totality of circumstances analysis that has traditionally guided probable cause determinations. State v. Ingram (Butler 1984) 20 Ohio App.3d 55, 484 N.E.2d 227, 20 O.B.R. 58.

In assessing whether there is probable cause for an arrest, evidence within the knowledge of the arresting officer may be considered, even though the evidence, such as hearsay, is not legally competent evidence in a criminal trial. State v. Sampson (Belmont 1982) 4 Ohio App.3d 287, 448 N.E.2d 467, 4 O.B.R. 536. Arrest ⚷ 63.4(13)

Reasonable ground or probable cause for a warrantless arrest may be provided by the arresting officer's own observations, credible information from a reliable informant, or corroborated information from a less than reliable informant. State v. Sizer (Ohio Com.Pl. 1970) 25 Ohio Misc. 245, 265 N.E.2d 468, 54 O.O.2d 406. Arrest ⚿ 63.4(2)

Where a police officer has received information over the police radio and that information is such as to give the officer reasonable grounds to believe a felony has been committed, such officer has probable cause to make an arrest. State v. Fultz (Ohio 1968) 13 Ohio St.2d 79, 234 N.E.2d 593, 42 O.O.2d 259, certiorari denied 89 S.Ct. 95, 393 U.S. 854, 21 L.Ed.2d 123.

"Reasonable cause" for the arrest of a person by police officers without a warrant exists where such officers acted on information furnished by the police department of another city; and the defendant fails to show by evidence that the arresting officers had no reasonable cause to believe that a felony had been committed. State v. Ball (Franklin 1964) 1 Ohio App.2d 297, 204 N.E.2d 557, 30 O.O.2d 304, appeal dismissed 176 Ohio St. 481, 200 N.E.2d 325, 27 O.O.2d 443.

Where, on information furnished by an informer, an arrest is made without a warrant, it is incumbent upon the prosecution to show specifically what the informer actually said and why the officer thought the information was credible; good faith on the part of the officer is not sufficient to show probable cause. Beck v. State of Ohio (U.S.Ohio 1964) 85 S.Ct. 223, 379 U.S. 89, 3 Ohio Misc. 71, 13 L.Ed.2d 142, 31 O.O.2d 80.

Where police officers learned through listening to a conversation between defendant and an informer with the informer's consent at 11:00 p.m. that defendant would arrive at 5:37 a.m. with narcotics, arrest of the defendant without a warrant and search of his luggage was justified. U. S. v. Pierce (N.D.Ohio 1954) 124 F.Supp. 264, 70 Ohio Law Abs. 140, 56 O.O. 44, affirmed 224 F.2d 281.

9. Citizen's arrest generally

Evidence that defendant failed to act with requisite reasonable haste in attempting to notify police that he had effected citizen's arrest, and therefore was without privilege to restrain victim's liberty, was sufficient to support conviction of abduction; defendant and third party held victims in hallway outside third party's apartment for several minutes without calling police, defendant pursued one victim out of building after scuffle, told clerk at convenience store to which victim had fled to call police, and returned to third party's apartment, and neither defendant nor third party ever called police to report alleged attempted burglary. State v. Liddy (Ohio App. 11 Dist., Ashtabula, 03-04-2005) No. 2003-A-0048, 2005-Ohio-940, 2005 WL 516514, Unreported. Kidnapping ⚿ 36

Evidence that defendant lacked reasonable grounds to believe that victim was attempting to break into apartment of third party, and therefore was without privilege to restrain his liberty by effecting citizen's arrest, was sufficient to support conviction of abduction; victim testified that he had not tampered with third party's apartment door, arresting officer testified that there was no sign that door had been tampered with, and victim had told defendant his reason for being at third party's apartment. State v. Liddy (Ohio App. 11 Dist., Ashtabula, 03-04-2005) No. 2003-A-0048, 2005-Ohio-940, 2005 WL 516514, Unreported. Kidnapping ⚿ 36

A citizen's arrest must be based upon either the commission of a felony or reasonable cause to believe a felony has been committed; a misdemeanor cannot be the basis for a citizen's arrest, and an individual unlawfully grabbed or held in a misdemeanor arrest attempt has the right to use reasonable force to free himself. Jackson v. Gossard (Allen 1989) 48 Ohio App.3d 309, 549 N.E.2d 1234.

Where authorized to make an arrest pursuant to RC 2935.04, a private person, prior to attempting the arrest, must inform the person to be arrested of the intention to arrest, and of the cause of the arrest unless such cause is contemporaneous with the arrest. State v. Rogers (Ohio 1975) 43 Ohio St.2d 28, 330 N.E.2d 674, 72 O.O.2d 16, certiorari denied 96 S.Ct. 801, 423 U.S. 1061, 46 L.Ed.2d 653. Arrest ⚿ 68(1)

An off-duty municipal police officer may arrest and detain another person whom he has reasonable cause to believe is guilty of a felony until a warrant can be obtained, as may any other citizen, pursuant to RC 2935.04. OAG 74–094; overruled in part by OAG 86–065.

10. Treatment of arrested person

A citizen's arrest must be based upon either the commission of a felony or reasonable cause to believe a felony has been committed; a misdemeanor cannot be the basis for a citizen's arrest, and an individual unlawfully grabbed or held in a misdemeanor arrest attempt has the right to use reasonable force to free himself. Jackson v. Gossard (Allen 1989) 48 Ohio App.3d 309, 549 N.E.2d 1234.

In a wrongful-death action against a police officer, a motion for summary judgment should be overruled where the pleadings considered together with the motion, accompanied by affidavits of the movant, show the existence of genuine issues of material fact for the jury of, inter alia, whether a felony had been committed, whether decedent was placed under arrest, whether the arresting officer saw or had reasonable ground to believe that a felony had been committed and whether the officer used excessive force. Oliver v. Kasza (Lucas 1962) 116 Ohio App. 398, 188 N.E.2d 437, 22 O.O.2d 230.

The county is charged with the duty to house a prisoner charged with a misdemeanor under state law, both prior to and after conviction. OAG 79–008; overruled on other grounds by OAG 86–003.

A municipal prisoner is one who has been charged with or sentenced for violation of a municipal ordinance and responsibility for the sustenance and care of such a prisoner rests with the municipality; and a county prisoner is one charged with or sentenced by the county for violation of a state statute and responsibility for the sustenance and care of such a prisoner rests with the county. OAG 76–012.

11. Warrant issuance

The issuance of a warrant of arrest pursuant to RC 2935.04 by a clerk of courts, a nonjudicial officer, is not a violation of the US Constitution. State v. Fairbanks (Hamilton 1971) 33 Ohio App.2d 39, 292 N.E.2d 325, 62 O.O.2d 100, modified 32 Ohio St.2d 34, 289 N.E.2d 352, 61 O.O.2d 241. Criminal Law ⚷ 207(3)

12. Juvenile proceedings

Homeowner, who discovered that his home had recently been vandalized, did not conduct citizen's arrest of juvenile, where homeowner did not identify himself as off-duty police officer and did not tell juvenile he was under arrest, but simply detained and escorted juvenile to cruiser of police officer, whom homeowner had contacted regarding vandalism, which was parked in front of home and released juvenile to police officer. In re M.D. (Ohio App. 12 Dist., Madison, 11-08-2004) No. CA2003-12-038, 2004-Ohio-5904, 2004 WL 2505161, Unreported. Infants ⚷ 192

The statutory law of arrest does not apply to special statutory proceedings in the juvenile court which are civil in nature and have for their purpose the securing for each child under the jurisdiction of the juvenile court such care, guidance and control... as will best serve the child's welfare. In re L— (Ohio Juv. 1963) 194 N.E.2d 797, 92 Ohio Law Abs. 475, 25 O.O.2d 369.

2935.041 Detention of shoplifters; rights of museums and libraries; rights of motion picture facility owner or lessee

(A) A merchant, or an employee or agent of a merchant, who has probable cause to believe that items offered for sale by a mercantile establishment have been unlawfully taken by a person, may, for the purposes set forth in division (C) of this section, detain the person in a reasonable manner for a reasonable length of time within the mercantile establishment or its immediate vicinity.

(B) Any officer, employee, or agent of a library, museum, or archival institution may, for the purposes set forth in division (C) of this section or for the purpose of conducting a reasonable investigation of a belief that the person has acted in a manner described in divisions (B)(1) and (2) of this section, detain a person in a reasonable manner for a reasonable length of time within, or in the immediate vicinity of, the library, museum, or archival institution, if the officer, employee, or agent has probable cause to believe that the person has either:

(1) Without privilege to do so, knowingly moved, defaced, damaged, destroyed, or otherwise improperly tempered with property owned by or in the custody of the library, museum, or archival institution; or

(2) With purpose to deprive the library, museum, or archival institution of property owned by it or in its custody, knowingly obtained or exerted control over the property without the consent of the owner or person authorized to give consent, beyond the scope of the express or implied consent of the owner or person authorized to give consent, by deception, or by threat.

(C) An officer, agent, or employee of a library, museum, or archival institution pursuant to division (B) of this section or a merchant or employee or agent of a merchant pursuant to division (A) of this section may detain another person for any of the following purposes:

(1) To recover the property that is the subject of the unlawful taking, criminal mischief, or theft;

(2) To cause an arrest to be made by a peace officer;

(3) To obtain a warrant of arrest.

(D) The owner or lessee of a facility in which a motion picture is being shown, or the owner's or lessee's employee or agent, who has probable cause to believe that a person is or has been operating an audiovisual recording function of a device in violation of section 2913.07 of the Revised Code may, for the purpose of causing an arrest to be made by a peace officer or of obtaining an arrest warrant, detain the person in a reasonable manner for a reasonable length of time within the facility or its immediate vicinity.

(E) The officer, agent, or employee of the library, museum, or archival institution, the merchant or employee or agent of a merchant, or the owner, lessee, employee, or agent of the facility acting under division (A), (B), or (D) of this section shall not search the person detained, search or seize any property belonging to the person detained without the person's consent, or use undue restraint upon the person detained.

(F) Any peace officer may arrest without a warrant any person that the officer has probable cause to believe has committed any act described in division (B)(1) or (2) of this section, that the officer has probable cause to believe has committed an unlawful taking in a mercantile establishment, or that the officer has reasonable cause to believe has committed an act prohibited by section 2913.07 of the Revised Code. An arrest under this division shall be made within a reasonable time after the commission of the act or unlawful taking.

(G) As used in this section:

(1) "Archival institution" means any public or private building, structure, or shelter in which are stored historical documents, devices, records, manuscripts, or items of public interest, which historical materials are stored to preserve the materials or the information in the materials, to disseminate the information contained in the materials, or to make the materials available for public inspection or for inspection by certain persons who have a particular interest in, use for, or knowledge concerning the materials.

(2) "Museum" means any public or private nonprofit institution that is permanently organized for primarily educational or aesthetic purposes, owns or borrows objects or items of public interest, and cares for and exhibits to the public the objects or items.

(3) "Audiovisual recording function" and "facility" have the same meaning as in section 2913.07 of the Revised Code.

(2003 H 179, eff. 3–9–04; 1978 H 403, eff. 7–4–78; 1969 H 49; 131 v H 395; 127 v 765)

Historical and Statutory Notes

Amendment Note: 2003 H 179 added "of a merchant" to division (A) and (C); added new division (D); redesignated former divisions (D) through (F) as new divisions (E) through (G); added division (G)(3); made other nonsubstantive changes; and rewrote former division (D) and (E), which prior thereto read:

"(D) The officer, agent, or employee of the library, museum, or archival institution, or the merchant or his employee or agent acting under division (A) or (B) of this section shall not search the person, search or seize any property belonging to the person detained without the person's consent, or use undue restraint upon the person detained.

"(E) Any peace officer may arrest without a warrant any person that he has probable cause to believe has committed any act described in division (B)(1) or (2) of this section or that he has probable cause to believe has committed an unlawful taking in a mercantile establishment. An arrest under this division shall be made within a reasonable time after the commission of the act or unlawful taking."

Cross References

Freedom from unreasonable seizure; warrants, O Const Art I §14

Privilege, defined, 2901.01

Probable cause, 2933.22

Purposely, defined, 2901.22

Theft, 2913.02

Library References

Arrest ⚬64.

False Imprisonment ⚬10.

Westlaw Topic Nos. 168, 35.

C.J.S. Arrest §§ 11 to 13.

C.J.S. False Imprisonment §§ 18 to 19, 22, 36, 38, 46 to 47, 70.

Research References

Encyclopedias

OH Jur. 3d Criminal Law § 799, Unlawful Restraint.

OH Jur. 3d Criminal Law § 2109, Misdemeanors and Other Minor Offenses—Shoplifting.

OH Jur. 3d Criminal Law § 2110, Misdemeanors and Other Minor Offenses—Tampering and Like Interference With Property of Library, Museum, or Archival Institution.

OH Jur. 3d False Imprisonment & Malic. Prosecution § 13, by Private Individual; Merchants or Employees Thereof.

OH Jur. 3d False Imprisonment & Malic. Prosecution § 54, Reasonableness of Warrantless Arrest—Plaintiff Suspected of Retail Theft.

Treatises and Practice Aids

Katz, Giannelli, Blair and Lipton, Baldwin's Ohio Practice, Criminal Law, § 3:6, Private Security Guards.

Katz, Giannelli, Blair and Lipton, Baldwin's Ohio Practice, Criminal Law, § 6:6, Warrantless Misdemeanor Arrests—"In Presence" Rule.

Katz, Giannelli, Blair and Lipton, Baldwin's Ohio Practice, Criminal Law, § 6:10, Arrests by Private Citizens.

Katz, Ohio Arrest, Search & Seizure § 4:3, Nature of the Offense—Misdemeanors.

Katz, Ohio Arrest, Search & Seizure § 4:4, Misdemeanors: Exceptions to the "In Presence" Requirement.

Katz, Ohio Arrest, Search & Seizure § 25:12, Searches by Private Persons.

Katz, Ohio Arrest, Search & Seizure § 27:12, Searches by Private Persons.

Siegel & Stephen, Ohio Employment Practices Law § 5:19, False Imprisonment and False Arrest.

Gotherman, Babbit and Lang, Baldwin's Ohio Practice, Local Government Law—Municipal, § 8:31, Arrest Powers.

Gotherman, Babbit and Lang, Baldwin's Ohio Practice, Local Government Law—Municipal, § 28:41, Arrest of Violators.

Law Review and Journal Commentaries

Private Searches, Private Interrogations, Stanley B. Kent. 57 Clev B J 74 (January 1986).

Reality and Illusion: Defining Private Security Law in Ohio, Comment. 13 U Tol L Rev 377 (Winter 1982).

Notes of Decisions

1. Constitutional issues

Totality of circumstances surrounding defendant's confession to her employer in employer's office regarding suspected theft demonstrated that she gave her confession voluntarily; although defendant remaining in the office for three hours, she was informed within 15 minutes of entering office why she was there, no evidence was presented that defendant asked to leave or use phone and was denied, she was 22 years old at time of offense, and there was no evidence she was induced into confessing to the theft. State v. Coleman (Ohio App. 7 Dist., Mahoning, 05-28-2003) No. 02-CA-66, 2003-Ohio-2928, 2003 WL 21310569, Unreported. Criminal Law ⚷ 519(1)

Statute allowing mercantile establishment to detain shoplifter does not operate to confer upon merchant or its employee status of law enforcement officer for purposes of Fourth Amendment. Evans v. Smith (Ohio App. 1 Dist., 09-14-1994) 97 Ohio App.3d 59, 646 N.E.2d 217. Arrest ⚷ 64

Privately employed security guard was not "peace officer" as statutorily defined, and thus, was not required to give *Miranda* warnings prior to questioning defendant stopped for shoplifting. State v. Giallombardo (Portage 1986) 29 Ohio App.3d 279, 504 N.E.2d 1202, 29 O.B.R. 343. Criminal Law ⚷ 412.1(2)

A search made by a security employee employed by a department store, and acting solely on behalf of and for the benefit of such department store, does not constitute governmental action or participation, even though such employee is commissioned as a special deputy sheriff. State v. McDaniel (Franklin 1975) 44 Ohio App.2d 163, 337 N.E.2d 173, 73 O.O.2d 189. Criminal Law ⚷ 394.2(1)

Where, pursuant to RC 2935.041, an employee of a merchant has detained a person whom he has probable cause to believe has unlawfully taken items offered for sale by the mercantile establishment, an admission or confession made during such detention is not rendered inadmissible by the failure of such employee to fully explain to such detained person those constitutional rights set forth in Miranda v Arizona, 384 US 436, 86 SCt 1602, 16 LEd(2d) 694 (1966). State v. Bolan (Ohio 1971) 27 Ohio St.2d 15, 271 N.E.2d 839, 56 O.O.2d 8.

In a malicious prosecution case where a grocery store customer seeks damages under 42 USCA 1983 for malicious prosecution, the distinction between the defendant officer's status as a municipal police officer and his status as a grocery store security guard assume significance so that the 42 USCA 1983 claim may be presumed upon an arrest and detention undertaken by the officer in his capacity as a municipal police officer, but not upon a detention undertaken by the officer, pursuant to RC 2935.041, as a grocery store employee, and the store cannot be held liable for the conduct giving rise to the customer's 42 USCA 1983 claim. Evans v Smith, No. C–930443, 1994 WL 496745 (1st Dist Ct App, Hamilton, 9–14–94).

2. Authority to detain or arrest

Individual, who was arrested on charges related to cashing fraudulent payroll check, could not establish false arrest claim against store where check was cashed after charges were dropped, where store never restricted, arrested, or detained individual in any manner, but only contacted police when check was returned to store as being fraudulent. Barnes v. Meijer Dept. Store (Ohio App. 12 Dist., Butler, 04-05-2004) No. CA2003-09-246, 2004-Ohio-1716, 2004 WL 720906, Unreported, appeal not allowed 103 Ohio St.3d 1407, 812 N.E.2d 1289, 2004-Ohio-3980. False Imprisonment ⚷ 15(2)

Individual, who was arrested on charges related to cashing fraudulent payroll check, could not establish false imprisonment claim against store where check was cashed, where store never restricted, arrested, or detained individual in any manner, but only contacted police when check was returned to store as being fraudulent. Barnes v. Meijer Dept. Store (Ohio App. 12 Dist., Butler, 04-05-2004) No. CA2003-09-246, 2004-Ohio-1716, 2004 WL 720906, Unreported, appeal not allowed

103 Ohio St.3d 1407, 812 N.E.2d 1289, 2004-Ohio-3980. False Imprisonment ⚷ 15(2)

Store had probable cause to report fraudulent check to police for investigation, and thus, arrestee could not establish malicious prosecution claim against store after charges against her for cashing fraudulent check were dropped, where payroll check from bank made payable to person with arrestee's name and endorsed by person with arrestee's name was cashed at store and bank subsequently returned check to store and indicated that check was fraudulent. Barnes v. Meijer Dept. Store (Ohio App. 12 Dist., Butler, 04-05-2004) No. CA2003-09-246, 2004-Ohio-1716, 2004 WL 720906, Unreported, appeal not allowed 103 Ohio St.3d 1407, 812 N.E.2d 1289, 2004-Ohio-3980. Malicious Prosecution ⚷ 18(5)

Whether detention of customer who was suspected of shoplifting by employee in store's loss prevention department was unreasonable, and thus exceeded scope of statute granting merchants authority to detain a suspected thief for a reasonable period of time, was issue for jury in action in which customer asserted claims for false arrest and false imprisonment. Tucker v. Kroger Co. (Ohio App. 10 Dist., 09-09-1999) 133 Ohio App.3d 140, 726 N.E.2d 1111. False Imprisonment ⚷ 39

Genuine issues of material fact as to whether store had probable cause to detain customer for shoplifting and whether the ensuing detention of customer was conducted reasonably, so that the detention would be permitted under shopkeeper's privilege, precluded summary judgment on customer's false imprisonment claim against store. Hodges v. Meijer, Inc. (Ohio App. 12 Dist., 08-10-1998) 129 Ohio App.3d 318, 717 N.E.2d 806. Judgment ⚷ 181(33)

Regardless of whether police officer employed as security guard at grocery store was acting as store employee or police officer at time he arrested and detained customer, officer was acting under color of state law as required for 1983 action; authority to arrest and detain arose either under statute empowering municipal police officer to effectuate warrantless arrest or under statute authorizing mercantile establishment to detain and peace officer to arrest shoplifter. Evans v. Smith (Ohio App. 1 Dist., 09-14-1994) 97 Ohio App.3d 59, 646 N.E.2d 217. Civil Rights ⚷ 1326(8)

Customer who was arrested and detained by police officer employed as security guard at grocery store could assert claim based on officer's conduct either as claim for false arrest or for false imprisonment; while arrest and detention could be perceived as exercise of officer's legal authority, record also provided basis for perception that detention accompanying customer's arrest was purely matter between private persons for private end with no intention of securing administration of law. Evans v. Smith (Ohio App. 1 Dist., 09-14-1994) 97 Ohio App.3d 59, 646 N.E.2d 217. False Imprisonment ⚷ 16

If police officer employed as security guard at grocery store was acting as store employee when he arrested and detained customer, store could be held liable under doctrine of respondeat superior for even intentional or willful conduct of officer, if conduct was within scope of employment as security guard and was calculated to facilitate or promote business for which he was employed. Evans v. Smith (Ohio App. 1 Dist., 09-14-1994) 97 Ohio App.3d 59, 646 N.E.2d 217. Labor And Employment ⚷ 3055

Store owner violated "merchant's privilege" to detain person suspected of theft by handcuffing for seven hours employee suspected of taking state lottery proceeds without contacting police, thereby subjecting store owner to prosecution for unlawful restraint. E. Cleveland v. Odetellah (Ohio App. 8 Dist., 11-15-1993) 91 Ohio App.3d 787, 633 N.E.2d 1159, dismissed, jurisdictional motion overruled 69 Ohio St.3d 1414, 630 N.E.2d 376. False Imprisonment ⚷ 43

Township constables in the exercise of their arrest powers do not fall within the exceptions to the view requirement of RC 2935.03. State v. Fields (Ohio Co. 1979) 62 Ohio Misc. 14, 405 N.E.2d 740, 16 O.O.3d 382.

A security employee employed by a department store, and acting solely on behalf of and for the benefit of such department store, has only such authority as is granted under RC 2935.041 and does not have authority to detain a person for interfering with the detention of a suspected shoplifter. State v. Griffin (Ohio Mun. 1977) 54 Ohio Misc. 52, 376 N.E.2d 1364, 6 O.O.3d 455, 8 O.O.3d 383. Arrest ⚷ 62

The authority of "a merchant's employee" to detain one who he has probable cause to believe is unlawfully taking items offered for sale by "a mercantile establishment," as described by RC 2935.041, is not limited to such events when observed to occur in the store of the company by which he is employed. State v. Stone (Ohio Mun. 1968) 16 Ohio Misc. 160, 241 N.E.2d 302, 45 O.O.2d 123. Arrest ⚷ 64

Where an employee of a business requests police to apprehend a customer who is suspected of shoplifting and an unlawful detention results, the business is not protected from liability and summary judgment for the merchant is error where there is a genuine issue of fact whether the merchant's call to police was to request aid in the investigation of a potential shoplifting or whether the call was actually a request to apprehend the customer for which the store may be held liable for false imprisonment. Niessel v. Meijer, Inc. (Ohio App. 12 Dist., Warren, 12-17-2001) No. CA2001-04-027, 2001-Ohio-8645, 2001 WL 1598325, Unreported.

A private investigator may not arrest a person for the commission of a misdemeanor, except where the investigator is employed by a merchant and has probable cause to believe that the person arrested is guilty of shoplifting. OAG 74-041.

3. Probable cause

Issues of fact as to whether police officer employed as security guard at grocery store arrested and detained customer upon "probable cause" to believe that customer was guilty of shoplifting or upon "reasonable ground" to believe that theft offense was committed and "reasonable cause" to believe that customer was perpetrator, precluded summary judgment on customer's false arrest and false imprisonment claims against officer and store. Evans v. Smith (Ohio App. 1 Dist., 09-14-1994) 97 Ohio App.3d 59, 646 N.E.2d 217. Judgment ⚷ 181(33)

Issues of fact as to whether police officer employed as security guard at grocery store had probable cause to arrest and detain customer without warrant precluded summary judgment on customer's 1983 claim against officer. Evans v. Smith (Ohio App. 1 Dist., 09-14-1994) 97 Ohio App.3d 59, 646 N.E.2d 217. Judgment ⚷ 181(15.1)

State did not bear burden of proving that merchant lacked probable cause or acted in unreasonable manner with respect to asserted privilege to detain employee suspected of theft during prosecution for unlawful restraint; merchant had burden of proving privilege asserted as affirmative defense. E. Cleveland v. Odetellah (Ohio App. 8 Dist., 11-15-1993) 91 Ohio App.3d 787, 633 N.E.2d 1159, dismissed, jurisdictional motion overruled 69 Ohio St.3d 1414, 630 N.E.2d 376. False Imprisonment ⚷ 44

Probable cause to detain a suspected shoplifter is shown where (1) a shopper repeatedly triggers a theft detection device located at the store's exit, (2) the device has not been known to give false alarms, and (3) store merchandise for which the plaintiff had not paid is found at her feet. Ashcroft v. Mt. Sinai Medical Ctr. (Cuyahoga 1990) 68 Ohio App.3d 359, 588 N.E.2d 280.

A peace officer told by a merchant that a woman "forgot to pay for some merchandise" and "we think she shoplifted" has probable cause to arrest the woman and search her purse for items she was seen to put inside. State v. McAfee (Hamilton 1985) 26 Ohio App.3d 99, 498 N.E.2d 204, 26 O.B.R. 274.

In an action for malicious prosecution and false imprisonment against a merchant for an alleged theft from the merchant, a bind over order or a grand jury indictment will create a rebuttable presumption of probable cause to prosecute on the part of the merchant, unless the plaintiff can show the existence of perjury or other significant irregularities at those proceedings. Adamson v. May Co. (Cuyahoga 1982) 8 Ohio App.3d 266, 456 N.E.2d 1212, 8 O.B.R. 358. False Imprisonment ⚷ 13; Malicious Prosecution ⚷ 24(6); Malicious Prosecution ⚷ 24(7)

Where a merchant, or his employee, has probable or reasonable cause to believe that an apparent customer is in reality a thief planning to shoplift merchandise, the merchant, or his employee, may utilize a reasonable means of surveillance and observation of such person in order to detect and prevent thievery, including a reasonably limited invasion of the privacy of such person, but the wholesale observation of customers by invading their privacy is not justified, nor can such observation be predicated upon a mere suspicion or hunch. State v. McDaniel (Franklin 1975) 44 Ohio App.2d 163, 337 N.E.2d 173, 73 O.O.2d 189. Searches And Seizures ⚷ 39

Where a plaintiff shows that he has been subjected to false imprisonment by an employee of a mercantile establishment, and the establishment seeks to justify such conduct by reason of the terms of RC 2935.041, the burden of proof is upon it to show probable cause for believing that items offered for sale by the mercantile establishment have been unlawfully taken by the plaintiff. Isaiah v. Great Atlantic & Pacific Tea Co. (Summit 1959) 111 Ohio App. 537, 174 N.E.2d 128, 86 A.L.R.2d 430, 15 O.O.2d 291. False Imprisonment ⚷ 22

4. Detention

Sufficient evidence supported finding that store falsely imprisoned customer, because a reasonable person could have believed that confinement occurred, where a security guard who had just been called over the public address system ordered customer to come with him, walking behind her the entire way to the back office, and once in office guard accused her of shoplifting, being banned from another store for shoplifting, and made a phone call which appeared to have been placed to police. Kalbfell v. Marc Glassman, Inc. (Ohio App. 7 Dist., Columbiana, 06-26-2003) No. 02CO5, 2003-Ohio-3489, 2003 WL 21505264, Unreported. False Imprisonment ⚷ 5

Although shopkeeper's privilege gives a merchant authority under certain circumstances to temporarily detain a suspected shoplifter, that authority does not preempt all later claims for false imprisonment where there is evidence of unreasonable or improper continuation of the detention. Hodges v. Meijer, Inc. (Ohio App. 12 Dist., 08-10-1998) 129 Ohio App.3d 318, 717 N.E.2d 806. False Imprisonment ⚷ 11

Trial court's finding that employee suspected of taking money did not voluntarily cooperate with seven-hour detention by merchant was supported by evidence that employee called and informed friend that she was being detained by merchant who insisted that employee would not be released until money was returned. E. Cleveland v. Odetellah (Ohio App. 8 Dist., 11-15-1993) 91 Ohio App.3d 787, 633 N.E.2d 1159, dismissed, jurisdictional motion overruled 69 Ohio St.3d 1414, 630 N.E.2d 376. False Imprisonment ⚷ 44

The requirements of RC 2935.041 regarding detention in a reasonable manner for a reasonable time period were not met where (1) a defendant was held for five hours in a small office on his employer's premises without food, drink, contact with family or counsel, or use of the restroom; (2) at the time he signed a confession, the defendant had not eaten for almost twenty-four hours; (3) the defendant was only nineteen, with no previous criminal record; and (4) his interrogators led the defendant to believe that he would only be fired from his job if he confessed, but would be arrested and jailed if he did not confess. City of Cleveland

Heights v. Stross (Cuyahoga 1983) 10 Ohio App.3d 246, 461 N.E.2d 935, 10 O.B.R. 343.

Where there is nothing more before a court than that one claiming to have been unlawfully detained agreed voluntarily to act in conformity with the request of the defendant and there could be no reasonable apprehension of force, there is no imprisonment as a matter of law. Mullins v. Rinks, Inc. (Butler 1971) 27 Ohio App.2d 45, 272 N.E.2d 152, 56 O.O.2d 218. False Imprisonment ⚬⇒ 5

5. Escape from detention

An attempt by a defendant to leave a closed office in a grocery store while under detention of employees after having been apprehended for shoplifting constitutes the crime of escape since the storekeeper has authority to detain persons suspected of shoplifting. State v. Hughes (Ohio Com.Pl. 1992) 62 Ohio Misc.2d 361, 598 N.E.2d 916.

6. Injured officer's workers' compensation

Off-duty police officer was acting in the course of his city employment while attempting to arrest shoplifting suspect and his injuries during arrest attempt arose out of that employment, and, thus, officer was entitled to workers' compensation benefits from city, despite fact that officer was not in uniform, was working as security specialist for retail grocery store when injured and had not received prior approval for work, where officer identified himself as police officer, displayed his badge and drew his revolver, was acting according to his mandatory duty to arrest and detain any person found in violation of state law, and his role as security specialist ended when he invoked his police authority. Cooper v. Dayton (Ohio App. 2 Dist., 06-06-1997) 120 Ohio App.3d 34, 696 N.E.2d 640, appeal not allowed 80 Ohio St.3d 1415, 684 N.E.2d 707. Workers' Compensation ⚬⇒ 695

7. Use of force

Music store owner who accidentally shot juvenile, who attempted to rob the store, in the buttocks while detaining him so owner could call police did not violate a duty of care to juvenile, for purposes of juvenile's negligence action against owner; juvenile was a trespasser to whom owner owed only the duty to refrain from wanton or willful conduct, there was no evidence that owner shot juvenile intentionally, rather than accidentally, and owner was privileged to detain juvenile in a reasonable manner in order to cause an arrest to be made. Mitchell v. Pugh (Ohio App. 11 Dist., Trumbull, 09-02-2005) No. 2004-T-0109, 2005-Ohio-4652, 2005 WL 2133705, Unreported. Negligence ⚬⇒ 1045(3); Weapons ⚬⇒ 20

2935.05 Affidavit filed in case of arrest without warrant

When a person named in section 2935.03 of the Revised Code has arrested a person without a warrant, he shall, without unnecessary delay, take the person arrested before a court or magistrate having jurisdiction of the offense, and shall file or cause to be filed an affidavit describing the offense for which the person was arrested. Such affidavit shall be filed either with the court or magistrate, or with the prosecuting attorney or other attorney charged by law with prosecution of crimes before such court or magistrate and if filed with such attorney he shall forthwith file with such court or magistrate a complaint, based on such affidavit. (128 v 97, eff. 1–1–60; 1953 H 1; GC 13432–3)

Historical and Statutory Notes

Pre–1953 H 1 Amendments: 113 v 140, Ch 11, § 3

Cross References

Criminal complaint; contents, Crim R 3

Duties and powers of state highway patrol, 5503.02

Jurisdiction and venue, 2901.11, 2901.12

Library References

Arrest ⚬⇒70.

Westlaw Topic No. 35.

C.J.S. Arrest §§ 58 to 61.

Research References

Encyclopedias

OH Jur. 3d Criminal Law § 2149, Warrantless Arrest; Detention, Custody, and Disposition of Arrested Person.

Treatises and Practice Aids

Katz, Ohio Arrest, Search & Seizure App. A, Appendix A. Arrest Provisions: Checklist.

Notes of Decisions

1. Constitutional issues

If a defendant in a criminal case is charged, tried and discharged, he cannot be rearrested upon a complaint and warrant and retried for the same offense, because to do so would put him twice in jeopardy because jeopardy attaches the moment the jury is sworn; however, a person who was illegally arrested without a warrant and discharged before trial may subsequently be arrested with a warrant and tried for the same offense for which he was previously charged because he has not been placed in jeopardy, in violation of the constitutional prohibition against double jeopardy. State ex rel. Wilson v. Nash (Cuyahoga 1974) 41 Ohio App.2d 201, 324 N.E.2d 774, 70 O.O.2d 409.

A defendant's right of due process is violated, and reversible error committed, where the state refuses to afford the defendant the right to consult with his lawyer at the earliest possible time. State v. Domer (Stark 1964) 1 Ohio App.2d 155, 204 N.E.2d 69, 30 O.O.2d 193.

The mere detention of an accused for a period of time before he is taken before a magistrate and charged does not constitute an infringement of his constitutional rights so as to invalidate his subsequent conviction. Henderson v. Maxwell (Ohio 1964) 176 Ohio St. 187, 198 N.E.2d 456, 27 O.O.2d 59.

2. Warrantless arrest

Suspicion and good faith are not sufficient to justify an arrest and incidental search without a warrant. State v. Rogers (Ohio Com.Pl. 1963) 198 N.E.2d 796, 94 Ohio Law Abs. 110, 27 O.O.2d 105.

Where a police officer makes an arrest without a warrant at the request of another police agency, all reasonable doubts concerning the reasonableness of the information on which the arresting officer acts should be resolved in his favor, and if such action is upon reasonable information, the officer is not subject to liability for false arrest or imprisonment. Johnson v. Reddy (Ohio 1955) 163 Ohio St. 347, 126 N.E.2d 911, 56 O.O. 316. False Imprisonment 🔑 7(3)

Where a highway patrolman arrests a person found violating a law of this state, for which violation he is authorized to arrest, he must follow the procedure prescribed by RC 2935.03, 2935.05, 2935.08 and 2935.13. 1961 OAG 2214.

3. Affidavit; complaint

An affidavit or sworn complaint in a misdemeanor charge is not subject to amendment by the court. City of Hamilton v. Petty (Ohio App. 1 Dist. 1972) 33 Ohio App.2d 194, 293 N.E.2d 881, 62 O.O.2d 286. Indictment And Information 🔑 162

A clerk of a county court is authorized to take affidavits, and affidavits may be filed with such a clerk under RC 2935.05, 2935.06, and 2935.09. 1962 OAG 3141.

4. Detention of arrested person

A county sheriff has a duty to detain in the county jail an individual arrested without a warrant by a municipal police officer for any violation of the laws of this state. OAG 95–011.

A sheriff has a duty to detain in the county jail a prisoner charged with the commission of a misdemeanor under state law for the period between his arrest and his initial appearance before a court, magistrate, or clerk of courts as required by RC 2935.05 or 2935.13 or until he is otherwise released prior to such initial appearance. OAG 88–060, approved and followed by OAG 95–011.

Where a township police constable arrests a person for violation of a state statute, and said person is confined in a municipal jail pending trial, the township which said police constable serves is not liable for the costs of confinement. 1962 OAG 3405.

5. Without unnecessary delay

In an action for false arrest or imprisonment, where an arrest without a warrant was made at 3 p.m. and a complaint and warrant were issued at 9 a.m. the next day, the question of whether the defendant acted with "all practicable speed" in filing the complaint and warrant is a question of fact. Johnson v. Reddy (Ohio 1955) 163 Ohio St. 347, 126 N.E.2d 911, 56 O.O. 316. False Imprisonment 🔑 39

6. Failure to comply with procedure

The failure of the police to comply with RC 2935.05 does not invalidate a subsequent conviction on proper and sufficient evidence. State v. Sampson (Belmont 1982) 4 Ohio App.3d 287, 448 N.E.2d 467, 4 O.B.R. 536.

The action of a village marshal, designated chief of police, in releasing from custody for any purpose whatever, a person arrested for and who confessed to breaking and entering an inhabited dwelling, constitutes malfeasance and misconduct in office tantamount to gross neglect of duty and is sufficient cause for his removal from office. Vajner v. Village of Orange (Cuyahoga 1963) 119 Ohio App. 227, 191 N.E.2d 843, 92 Ohio Law Abs. 410, 27 O.O.2d 98.

Chief of police who arrested two individuals for breaking and entering and had obtained conclusive evidence against them and then released them to get certain stolen property so as to return it was guilty of conduct which justified his dismissal by village council. Vajner v. Village of Orange (Cuyahoga 1963) 119 Ohio App. 227, 191 N.E.2d 843, 92 Ohio Law Abs. 410, 27 O.O.2d 98.

Where defendant was lawfully arrested on charge of driving a motor vehicle while under influence of intoxicating liquor, but affidavit against defendant was not filed until four days after arrest, the defendant would not be entitled to a dismissal of affidavit upon the filing of a plea in abatement, since the court had jurisdiction over the defendant and if any of defendant's legal rights were violated by reason of delay of filing affidavit, he had other remedies to pursue but not a dismissal of the charge. City of Columbus v. Glenn (Franklin 1950) 102 N.E.2d 279, 60 Ohio Law Abs. 449. Criminal Law ⚷ 278(1).

Failure of the police to comply with RC 2935.05 does not invalidate a subsequent conviction. Cato v. Alvis (C.A.6 (Ohio) 1961) 288 F.2d 530, 16 O.O.2d 437.

7. Juvenile cases

The ten day period of limitations in Juv R 29(A) is procedural only and such rule confers no substantive right upon an accused to have his case dismissed if he is not tried within the designated time. In re Therklidsen (Franklin 1977) 54 Ohio App.2d 195, 376 N.E.2d 970, 8 O.O.3d 335.

The statutory law of arrest does not apply to special statutory proceedings in the juvenile court which are civil in nature and have for their purpose the securing for each child under the jurisdiction of the juvenile court such care, guidance and control... as will best serve the child's welfare. In re L— (Ohio Juv. 1963) 194 N.E.2d 797, 92 Ohio Law Abs. 475, 25 O.O.2d 369.

2935.06 Duty of private person making arrest

A private person who has made an arrest pursuant to section 2935.04 of the Revised Code or detention pursuant to section 2935.041 of the Revised Code shall forthwith take the person arrested before the most convenient judge or clerk of a court of record or before a magistrate, or deliver such person to an officer authorized to execute criminal warrants who shall, without unnecessary delay, take such person before the court or magistrate having jurisdiction of the offense. The officer may, but if he does not, the private person shall file or cause to be filed in such court or before such magistrate an affidavit stating the offense for which the person was arrested.

(128 v 97, eff. 1–1–60; 1953 H 1; GC 13432–4)

Historical and Statutory Notes

Pre–1953 H 1 Amendments: 113 v 140, Ch 11, § 4

Library References

Arrest ⚷64, 70.

Westlaw Topic No. 35.

C.J.S. Arrest §§ 11 to 13, 58 to 61.

Research References

Encyclopedias

OH Jur. 3d Criminal Law § 2148, Arrest With Warrant; Detention, Custody, and Disposition of Arrested Person.

Treatises and Practice Aids

Katz, Giannelli, Blair and Lipton, Baldwin's Ohio Practice, Criminal Law, § 6:8, Minor Misdemeanors.

Katz, Giannelli, Blair and Lipton, Baldwin's Ohio Practice, Criminal Law, § 6:10, Arrests by Private Citizens.

Katz, Ohio Arrest, Search & Seizure § 4:3, Nature of the Offense—Misdemeanors.

Katz, Ohio Arrest, Search & Seizure § 4:6, Minor Misdemeanors.

Notes of Decisions

Powers and duties of clerk 1

---

1. Powers and duties of clerk

A clerk of a county court is authorized to take affidavits, and affidavits may be filed with such a clerk under RC 2935.05, 2935.06, and 2935.09. 1962 OAG 3141.

A clerk of a county court may sign and issue a warrant for the arrest of a person charged with either a misdemeanor or a felony. 1962 OAG 2842.

A clerk of courts who also acts as clerk of a county court may sign and issue a warrant for the arrest of a person charged with either a misdemeanor or a felony. 1960 OAG 1297.

2935.07 Person arrested without warrant shall be informed of cause of arrest

When an arrest is made without a warrant by an officer, he shall inform the person arrested of such officer's authority to make the arrest and the cause of the arrest.

When an arrest is made by a private person, he shall, before making the arrest, inform the person to be arrested of the intention to arrest him and the cause of the arrest.

When a person is engaged in the commission of a criminal offense, it is not necessary to inform him of the cause of his arrest.

(1953 H 1, eff. 10–1–53; GC 13432–5)

Historical and Statutory Notes

Pre–1953 H 1 Amendments: 113 v 140, Ch 11, § 5

Library References

Arrest ⚷68(1).
Westlaw Topic No. 35.
C.J.S. Arrest §§ 51 to 53.

Research References

Encyclopedias

OH Jur. 3d Criminal Law § 2145, Generally; Notice of Intention; Use of Force.

Treatises and Practice Aids

Katz, Giannelli, Blair and Lipton, Baldwin's Ohio Practice, Criminal Law, § 6:4, Warrantless Felony Arrests in Public Places.

Katz, Giannelli, Blair and Lipton, Baldwin's Ohio Practice, Criminal Law, § 6:10, Arrests by Private Citizens.

Katz, Giannelli, Blair and Lipton, Baldwin's Ohio Practice, Criminal Law, § 89:3, Citizen Arrest.

Katz, Ohio Arrest, Search & Seizure § 4:2, Nature of the Offense—Felonies.

Law Review and Journal Commentaries

Reality and Illusion: Defining Private Security Law in Ohio, Comment. 13 U Tol L Rev 377 (Winter 1982).

Warrants for Arrest or Search: Impeaching the Allegations of a Facially Sufficient Affidavit, Lawrence Herman. 36 Ohio St L J 721 (1975).

Notes of Decisions

1. Constitutional issues

It is well settled that even if an arrest is illegal it does not amount to a denial of due process and does not, after conviction, furnish grounds for a release by habeas corpus. Brown v. Maxwell (Ohio 1962) 174 Ohio St. 29, 186 N.E.2d 612, 21 O.O.2d 285. Constitutional Law ⚷ 262; Habeas Corpus ⚷ 470

2. Duty to notify—in general

Defendant's arrest for domestic violence was lawful, even though police officer did not immediately announce defendant was under arrest, and thus defendant could be convicted for violation of municipal ordinance that prohibited resisting arrest; police officers were attempting to handcuff defendant when he refused to comply, struggle ensued which found both police officers on top of defendant and telling defendant to let go of handcuffs and quit resisting, and defendant was told during struggle that he was under arrest for domestic violence and resisting arrest. City of Warren v. Culver (Ohio App. 11 Dist., Trumbull, 01-16-2004) No. 2003-T-0023, 2004-Ohio-333, 2004 WL 144227, Unreported. Obstructing Justice ⚷ 8

Police did not violate statute requiring that officer making warrantless arrest inform person arrested of cause of arrest, where defendant was notified of offenses charged against him soon after he was taken into custody. State v. Davie (Ohio, 11-26-1997) 80 Ohio St.3d 311, 686 N.E.2d 245, 1997-Ohio-341, dismissal of post-conviction relief affirmed 1998 WL 684157, dismissed, appeal not allowed 84 Ohio St.3d 1483, 705 N.E.2d 364, reconsideration denied 85 Ohio St.3d 1411, 706 N.E.2d 791, denial of post-conviction relief affirmed 2001-Ohio-8813, 2001 WL 1647193, appeal not allowed 95 Ohio St.3d 1423, 766 N.E.2d 162, 2002-Ohio-1737, habeas corpus denied 291 F.Supp.2d 573, motion to amend denied, certificate of appealability granted in part, denied in part 324 F.Supp.2d 862. Arrest ⚷ 68(1)

Where authorized to make an arrest pursuant to RC 2935.04, a private person, prior to attempting the arrest, must inform the person to be arrested of the intention to arrest, and of the cause of the arrest unless such cause is contemporaneous with the arrest. State v. Rogers (Ohio 1975) 43 Ohio St.2d 28, 330 N.E.2d 674, 72 O.O.2d 16, certiorari denied 96 S.Ct. 801, 423 U.S. 1061, 46 L.Ed.2d 653. Arrest ⚷ 68(1)

3. —— **Failure to notify, duty to notify**

A police officer's initial lie to a defendant in his home that he is being arrested for burglary when in fact he is being arrested for rape and kidnapping does not invalidate the defendant's arrest where the police officers notify the defendant after he is put into the police cruiser that he is really being arrested on charges of rape and kidnapping; the arresting officer's testimony shows that the police felt that due to the emotional state of the defendant's family members who were present at the time of the arrest, they were in a volatile and potentially dangerous situation, thus justifying the initial lie, and the defendant is not prejudiced in any way by the officer's conduct since no evidence ultimately used at trial was obtained during the interval. State v. Gladding (Lake 1990) 66 Ohio App.3d 502, 585 N.E.2d 838, dismissed, jurisdictional motion overruled 52 Ohio St.3d 706, 557 N.E.2d 1212.

Where probable cause exists for an arrest by a police officer, the failure to notify the accused of the cause of his arrest does not render the arrest illegal if he is notified of the offense with which he is charged soon after he is taken into custody. State v. Fairbanks (Ohio 1972) 32 Ohio St.2d 34, 289 N.E.2d 352, 61 O.O.2d 241. Arrest ⚷ 68(1)

Where probable cause exists for an arrest by a police officer, failure to notify the accused of the cause of arrest does not render the arrest illegal if the defendant is notified of the offense with which he is charged soon after he is taken into custody. State v Zimmerman, Nos. 1308 and 1309 (2d Dist Ct App, Darke, 3–8–93).

2935.08 Issuance of warrant

Upon the filing of an affidavit or complaint as provided in sections 2935.05 or 2935.06 of the Revised Code such judge, clerk, or magistrate shall forthwith issue a warrant to the peace officer making the arrest, or if made by a private person, to the most convenient peace officer who shall receive custody of the person arrested. All further detention and further proceedings shall be pursuant to such affidavit or complaint and warrant.

(129 v 582, eff. 1–10–61; 128 v 97; 1953 H 1; GC 13432–6)

Historical and Statutory Notes

Ed. Note: 2935.08 contains provisions analogous to former 2935.10 and 2935.11, repealed by 128 v 97, eff. 1–1–60.

Pre–1953 H 1 Amendments: 113 v 140, Ch 11, § 6

Cross References

Warrant or summons, Crim R 4, 9

Library References

Criminal Law ⚷215.

Westlaw Topic No. 110.

C.J.S. Criminal Law §§ 334 to 335, 337 to 338.

Research References

Encyclopedias

OH Jur. 3d Criminal Law § 2149, Warrantless Arrest; Detention, Custody, and Disposition of Arrested Person.

Treatises and Practice Aids

Katz, Giannelli, Blair and Lipton, Baldwin's Ohio Practice, Criminal Law, § 6:5, Post-Arrest Warrants—Gerstein Hearings.

Katz, Giannelli, Blair and Lipton, Baldwin's Ohio Practice, Criminal Law, § 12:2, Validity of Arrest.

Katz, Giannelli, Blair and Lipton, Baldwin's Ohio Practice, Criminal Law, § 35:7, Citizen's Complaint.

Katz, Giannelli, Blair and Lipton, Baldwin's Ohio Practice, Criminal Law, § 133:26, Arrest Warrant on Complaint.

Katz, Giannelli, Blair and Lipton, Baldwin's Ohio Practice, Criminal Law, § 133:27, Arrest Warrant on Complaint (Additional Form).

Katz, Giannelli, Blair and Lipton, Baldwin's Ohio Practice, Criminal Law, § 133:28, Arrest Warrant on Complaint—Defendant's Name Unknown.

Katz, Giannelli, Blair and Lipton, Baldwin's Ohio Practice, Criminal Law, § 142:16, Warrant Upon Indictment or Information Issued by Court.

Katz, Ohio Arrest, Search & Seizure § 4:11, Post-Arrest Warrants.

Notes of Decisions

Ed. Note: *This section contains annotations from former RC 2935.10.*

1. Constitutional issues

If a defendant in a criminal case is charged, tried and discharged, he cannot be rearrested upon a complaint and warrant and retried for the same offense, because to do so would put him twice in jeopardy because jeopardy attaches the moment the jury is sworn; however, a person who was illegally arrested without a warrant and discharged before trial may subsequently be arrested with a warrant and tried for the same offense for which he was previously charged because he has not been placed in jeopardy, in violation of the constitutional prohibition against double jeopardy. State ex rel. Wilson v. Nash (Cuyahoga 1974) 41 Ohio App.2d 201, 324 N.E.2d 774, 70 O.O.2d 409.

A warrant of arrest issued under RC 2935.08 by the clerk of courts, a nonjudicial officer, does not violate a defendant's rights under US Const Am 4, which guarantees that a warrant will not issue except upon probable cause. State v. Fairbanks (Ohio 1972) 32 Ohio St.2d 34, 289 N.E.2d 352, 61 O.O.2d 241. Criminal Law ⚷ 207(3)

Absent some exception, a search or seizure cannot lawfully be made without the prior issuance of a warrant. U. S. v. Edwards (C.A.6 (Ohio) 1973) 474 F.2d 1206, certiorari granted 94 S.Ct. 160, 414 U.S. 818, 38 L.Ed.2d 50, reversed 94 S.Ct. 1234, 415 U.S. 800, 39 L.Ed.2d 771, vacated 497 F.2d 925. Searches And Seizures ⚷ 24

As record was clear that police had probable cause to arrest plaintiff for criminal trespass, which occurred when he misrepresented himself as a city official entitled to inspect the home he was visiting, he could not demonstrate that he had been deprived of his liberty without justification, as required for claim of false arrest. Riddle v. Egensperger (N.D.Ohio, 02-27-1998) 998 F.Supp. 812, affirmed 181 F.3d 103. False Imprisonment ⚷ 13

2. Issuance of warrant

As issued, an Ohio state patrol arrest record did not comply with RC 2935.08. State v. Wheeler (Ohio Mun. 1958) 157 N.E.2d 763, 80 Ohio Law Abs. 114.

A deputy clerk of the municipal court has authority to issue a warrant for the arrest of a person charged with a misdemeanor. State ex rel. Focke v. Price (Montgomery 1955) 137 N.E.2d 163, 73 Ohio Law Abs. 214, affirmed 165 Ohio St. 340, 135 N.E.2d 407, 59 O.O. 435, certiorari denied 77 S.Ct. 132, 352 U.S. 892, 1 L.Ed.2d 87.

Where a highway patrolman arrests a person found violating a law of this state, for which violation he is authorized to arrest, he must follow the procedure prescribed by RC 2935.03, RC 2935.05, RC 2935.08 and RC 2935.13. 1961 OAG 2214.

3. Summons in lieu of arrest

RC 2935.08 authorizes jurisdiction of an accused to be obtained in misdemeanor cases by service of a summons as well as by service of a warrant. City of Lyndhurst v. Beaumont (Ohio Com.Pl. 1959) 170 N.E.2d 291, 84 Ohio Law Abs. 103.

4. False arrest or imprisonment or malicious prosecution

Alleged assault victim had probable case to file charges against defendant, and thus, victim was not liable for malicious prosecution, although defendant was acquitted of criminal charges, where victim testified that defendant kicked and punched him. Pravitskyy v. Halczysak (Ohio App. 8 Dist., Cuyahoga, 12-24-2003) No. 82295, 2003-Ohio-7057, 2003 WL 23009105, Unreported, appeal not allowed 102 Ohio St.3d 1483, 810 N.E.2d 967, 2004-Ohio-3069. Malicious Prosecution ⚷ 18(5)

Arrest warrant was not void, as required to support claim for false arrest or false imprisonment; police sergeant was sufficiently informed to execute affidavit in support of arrest warrant, where sergeant read victim's 15—page statement before he swore out complaint, and complaint was prepared by prosecutor who had also read statement and discussed case with investigating officers. Durbin v. Ohio State Highway Patrol (Franklin 1992) 83 Ohio App.3d 693, 615 N.E.2d 694, motion overruled 66 Ohio St.3d 1446, 609 N.E.2d 173. False Imprisonment ⚷ 7(1)

To prevail on claim of malicious prosecution, plaintiff must prove the following: (1) malice in instituting or continuing the prosecution; (2) lack of probable cause; and (3) termination of prosecution in favor of the accused. Durbin v. Ohio State Highway Patrol (Franklin 1992) 83 Ohio App.3d 693, 615 N.E.2d 694, motion overruled 66 Ohio St.3d 1446, 609 N.E.2d 173. Malicious Prosecution ⚷ 0.5

Arrestee could not recover from police for malicious prosecution; arrest was supported by probable cause consisting of fact that truck driver and truck matched detailed descriptions given by victim and evidence that truck matching description given by victim was seen in area where victim was raped during relevant time period. Durbin v. Ohio State Highway Patrol (Franklin 1992) 83 Ohio App.3d 693, 615 N.E.2d 694, motion overruled 66 Ohio St.3d 1446, 609 N.E.2d 173. Malicious Prosecution ⚷ 18(1)

2935.081 Administering oaths; acknowledging complaints, summonses, affidavits, and returns of court orders

(A) As used in this section, "peace officer" has the same meaning as in section 2935.01 of the Revised Code, except that "peace officer" does not include, for any purpose, the superintendent or any trooper of the state highway patrol.

(B) A peace officer who has completed a course of in-service training that includes training in the administration of oaths and the acknowledgment of documents and that is approved by the chief legal officer of the political subdivision in which the peace officer is elected or of the political subdivision or other entity in which or by which the peace officer is appointed or employed may administer oaths and acknowledge criminal and juvenile court complaints, summonses, affidavits, and returns of court orders in matters related to the peace officer's official duties.

(C) Except as authorized by division (B) of this section, no peace officer who has completed a course of in-service training of a type described in division (B) of this section shall knowingly perform any act that is specifically required of a notary public unless the peace officer has complied with Chapter 147. of the Revised Code.

(1996 H 72, eff. 3–18–97)

Historical and Statutory Notes

Ed. Note: RC 2935.081 contains provisions analogous to former RC 109.745 and 5503.051, repealed by 1996 H 72, eff. 3–18–97.

Research References

Encyclopedias

OH Jur. 3d Criminal Law § 2111, Generally; Peace Officers.

2935.09 Accusation by affidavit to cause arrest or prosecution

(A) As used in this section, "reviewing official" means a judge of a court of record, the prosecuting attorney or attorney charged by law with the prosecution of offenses in a court or before a magistrate, or a magistrate.

(B) In all cases not provided by sections 2935.02 to 2935.08 of the Revised Code, in order to cause the arrest or prosecution of a person charged with committing an offense in this state, a peace officer or a private citizen having knowledge of the facts shall comply with this section.

(C) A peace officer who seeks to cause an arrest or prosecution under this section may file with a reviewing official or the clerk of a court of record an affidavit charging the offense committed.

(D) A private citizen having knowledge of the facts who seeks to cause an arrest or prosecution under this section may file an affidavit charging the offense committed with a reviewing official for the purpose of review to determine if a complaint should be filed by the prosecuting attorney or attorney charged by law with the prosecution of offenses in the court or before the magistrate. A private citizen may file an affidavit charging the offense committed with the clerk of a court of record before or after the normal business hours of the reviewing officials if the clerk's office is open at those times. A clerk who receives an affidavit before or after the normal business hours of the reviewing officials shall forward it to a reviewing official when the reviewing official's normal business hours resume.

(2006 H 214, eff. 6–30–06; 128 v 97, eff. 1–1–60)

Historical and Statutory Notes

Ed. Note: 2935.09 contains provisions analogous to former 2935.11, repealed by 128 v 97, eff. 1–1–60.

Ed. Note: Former 2935.09 repealed by 128 v 97, eff. 1–1–60; 1953 H 1; GC 13432–7.

Pre–1953 H 1 Amendments: 113 v 141, Ch 11, § 7

Amendment Note: 2006 H 214 rewrote this section, which prior thereto read:

"In all cases not provided by sections 2935.02 to 2935.08, inclusive, of the Revised Code, in order to cause the arrest or prosecution of a person charged with committing an offense in this state, a peace officer, or a private citizen having knowledge of the facts, shall file with the judge or clerk of a court of record, or with a magistrate, an affidavit charging the offense committed, or shall file such affidavit with the prosecuting attorney or attorney charged by law with the prosecution of offenses in court or before such magistrate, for the purpose of having a complaint filed by such prosecuting or other authorized attorney."

Cross References

Criminal complaint, Crim R 3

Freedom from unreasonable seizure; warrants, O Const Art I §14

Warrant or summons, arrest, Crim R 4

Library References

Criminal Law ⚷208, 215.

Westlaw Topic No. 110.

C.J.S. Criminal Law §§ 324 to 335, 337 to 338.

Research References

Encyclopedias

OH Jur. 3d Criminal Law § 2096, Requisites and Sufficiency of Form of Affidavit, Generally.

Treatises and Practice Aids

Katz, Giannelli, Blair and Lipton, Baldwin's Ohio Practice, Criminal Law, § 7:2, Complaint and Affidavit.

Katz, Giannelli, Blair and Lipton, Baldwin's Ohio Practice, Criminal Law, § 35:2, Essential Elements of Charge.

Katz, Giannelli, Blair and Lipton, Baldwin's Ohio Practice, Criminal Law, § 35:7, Citizen's Complaint.

Katz, Giannelli, Blair and Lipton, Baldwin's Ohio Practice, Criminal Law, § 132:1, Complaining Witness Affidavit.

Katz, Giannelli, Blair and Lipton, Baldwin's Ohio Practice, Criminal Law, § 132:3, Complaint by Prosecuting Attorney Upon Affidavit.

Katz, Giannelli, Blair and Lipton, Baldwin's Ohio Practice, Criminal Law, § 133:26, Arrest Warrant on Complaint.

Katz, Giannelli, Blair and Lipton, Baldwin's Ohio Practice, Criminal Law, § 133:27, Arrest Warrant on Complaint (Additional Form).

Katz, Giannelli, Blair and Lipton, Baldwin's Ohio Practice, Criminal Law, § 133:28, Arrest Warrant on Complaint—Defendant's Name Unknown.

Katz, Ohio Arrest, Search & Seizure § 5:2, Issuance of Arrest Warrants.

Painter, Ohio Driving Under the Influence § 2:1, Method of Charging.

Gotherman, Babbit and Lang, Baldwin's Ohio Practice, Local Government Law—Municipal, § 28:37, Enforcement Personnel and Equipment.

Notes of Decisions

Ed. Note: *This section contains annotations from former RC 2937.03.*

---

1. Commencement of prosecution

The filing of an affidavit in accordance with RC 2935.09 commences the prosecution of a misdemeanant under RC 1.18. State v. Hooper (Ohio 1971) 25 Ohio St.2d 59, 267 N.E.2d 285, 54 O.O.2d 194.

The arrest and prosecution of a person for violation of RC 3773.24 can be caused by two methods: (1) by filing an affidavit with a judge or clerk of a court of record or with a magistrate and (2) by filing an affidavit with the prosecuting attorney or attorney charged by law with the prosecution for the offense, who, in turn, shall file a complaint. State v. Maynard (Ohio 1964) 1 Ohio St.2d 57, 203 N.E.2d 332, 30 O.O.2d 32, certiorari denied 86 S.Ct. 105, 382 U.S. 871, 15 L.Ed.2d 110. Criminal Law ⚷ 209; Sunday ⚷ 29(2)

A charge of violating RC 3773.24 may be instituted either by the filing of an affidavit with a judge or clerk of court or by the filing of a complaint by the attorney prosecuting such matters on an affidavit filed with him. State v. Hamilton House Furniture, Inc. (Franklin 1963) 118 Ohio App. 63, 193 N.E.2d 299, 24 O.O.2d 389.

2. Affidavit; filing

Alleged victim of assault was entitled to probable cause hearing on his private criminal complaint against alleged perpetrator; statute governing procedure upon filing of affidavit or criminal complaint by private citizen did not give court discretion to reject complaint without hearing, as it governed procedure after court had made probable cause determination. State v. Moss (Ohio App. 5 Dist., Stark, 11-10-2003) No. 2003CA00218, 2003-Ohio-6053, 2003 WL 22672018, Unreported. Criminal Law ⚷ 212

Absence of filing a criminal complaint or charging affidavit against habeas corpus petitioner prior to driving under the influence (DUI) conviction was irrelevant, and thus did not void petitioner's conviction, where petitioner pled guilty to DUI charge that was brought by indictment. Peters v. Anderson (Ohio App. 9 Dist., Lorain, 12-11-2002)

No. 02CA008096, 2002-Ohio-6766, 2002 WL 31761490, Unreported. Habeas Corpus ⚷ 474

Statute providing procedure for offenses charged by affidavits submitted by private citizens does not place any duty upon city prosecutors to prosecute misdemeanors charged by affidavit. State ex rel. Evans v. Columbus Dept. of Law (Ohio, 09-23-1998) 83 Ohio St.3d 174, 699 N.E.2d 60, 1998-Ohio-128. Criminal Law ⚷ 210; District And Prosecuting Attorneys ⚷ 8

Private citizen seeking writ of mandamus to compel city prosecutor to prosecute misdemeanor charges contained in citizen's affidavit was not entitled to writ, where citizen failed to allege sufficient facts evidencing that city prosecutor abused his discretion in determining that charges lacked probable cause. State ex rel. Evans v. Columbus Dept. of Law (Ohio, 09-23-1998) 83 Ohio St.3d 174, 699 N.E.2d 60, 1998-Ohio-128. Mandamus ⚷ 154(2)

Statute providing that private citizen having knowledge of facts shall file with judge, clerk of court, or magistrate an affidavit charging offense committed in order to cause arrest or prosecution of person charged, must be read in pari materia with statute prescribing subsequent procedure to be followed. State ex rel. Evans v. Columbus Dept. of Law (Ohio, 09-23-1998) 83 Ohio St.3d 174, 699 N.E.2d 60, 1998-Ohio-128. Statutes ⚷ 223.2(8)

Statute allowing private citizen having knowledge of commission of criminal offense to file affidavit charging offense in order to cause arrest or prosecution of person charged must be read in pari materia with statute prescribing subsequent procedure to be followed. State ex rel. Strothers v. Turner (Ohio, 07-23-1997) 79 Ohio St.3d 272, 680 N.E.2d 1238. Statutes ⚷ 223.2(8)

The provision of RC 2935.09 requiring the filing of an affidavit "for the purpose of having a complaint filed" thereon, applies to a prosecution under RC 3773.24. State v. Bowman (Montgomery 1962) 116 Ohio App. 285, 187 N.E.2d 627, 22 O.O.2d 117.

This section and GC 13433–3 (RC 2937.04) are to be construed strictly; an affidavit is the act of an individual for the signing of which such individual is and holds himself or herself out to be responsible; no court or public officer has authority to force an individual to say something different from what that individual actually did say or express a willingness to say. Diebler v. State (Richland 1932) 43 Ohio App. 350, 183 N.E. 84, 13 Ohio Law Abs. 20, 37 Ohio Law Rep. 232.

A clerk of a county court is authorized to take affidavits, and affidavits may be filed with such a clerk under RC 2935.05, RC 2935.06, and RC 2935.09. 1962 OAG 3141.

3. Who may file affidavit

An off-duty patrolman, out of uniform and in his private vehicle, may effectuate a traffic arrest only as a private citizen under RC 2935.09. State v. Maxwell (Ohio Mun. 1978) 60 Ohio Misc. 1, 395 N.E.2d 531, 14 O.O.3d 44. Automobiles ⚷ 349(11)

Investigators for the state dental board are "peace officers," within the meaning of those words as used in RC 2935.01(B), and such investigators have the authority to file affidavits to cause prosecutions for violations of the laws regulating the practice of dentistry. State v. Colvin (Ohio 1969) 19 Ohio St.2d 86, 249 N.E.2d 784, 48 O.O.2d 94.

Filing of affidavit by prosecuting attorney charging violation of RC 3773.24 was insufficient where there was no allegation that said affidavit was based upon the affidavit of a peace officer or private citizen filed with him before his own affidavit was filed. State v. Laughlin (Ohio Com.Pl. 1966) 10 Ohio Misc. 219, 225 N.E.2d 298, 39 O.O.2d 306. Sunday ⚷ 29(2)

The Ohio civil rights commission may file an affidavit to cause the prosecution of a suspected violator of RC 4112.02(H), RC 4112.07 or RC 4112.11 at such time as the commission has a knowledge of the facts, but only the trial judge of a court of competent jurisdiction may impose the penalties as provided by RC 4112.99 after the trial and conviction of an accused violator. OAG 70–108.

Either a peace officer or a private citizen having knowledge of the facts may file an affidavit charging a person with committing an offense in this state. OAG 70–053.

RC 4513.39 does not prohibit a peace officer, who is excluded from making arrests under said section, from swearing out an affidavit for the issuance of an arrest warrant for the arrest of persons who have, in the presence of such peace officer, violated any of the sections enumerated therein. OAG 69–061.

RC 3721.99 imposes a duty upon the attorney general to see that a proper affidavit is filed in a court of competent jurisdiction in all cases where evidence is received by him indicating a violation of of RC 3721.02, RC 3721.05 or RC 3721.06. 1961 OAG 2279.

4. Knowledge of facts

An arrest warrant may be based on a complaint identifying the arrestee even though the complainant's identification of the arrestee is not based on first-hand knowledge, but on information from a friend of the complainant who witnessed the crime. State v. Moore (Summit 1985) 28 Ohio App.3d 10, 501 N.E.2d 1209, 28 O.B.R. 19.

A criminal complaint is sufficient where the complainant had no personal knowledge of the facts alleged and saw none of the acts committed; the relevant issue is the fact of the commission of the crime, rather than the complainant's personal knowledge of every element of the offense. City of Cleveland v. Weaver (Ohio Mun. 1983) 10 Ohio Misc.2d 15, 461 N.E.2d 32, 10 O.B.R. 227.

Personal knowledge of the commission of an offense is not a prerequisite to the filing of an affidavit therefor under RC 2935.09. State v. Biedenharn (Hamilton 1969) 19 Ohio App.2d 204, 250 N.E.2d 778, 48 O.O.2d 338.

A private citizen must possess "knowledge of the facts" before being authorized to file an affidavit under RC 2935.01, whereas no such restriction is placed upon a peace officer, and such knowledge must be based on more than hearsay. City of South Euclid v. Clapacs (Ohio Mun. 1966) 6 Ohio Misc. 101, 213 N.E.2d 828, 35 O.O.2d 203.

Prosecutorial immunity, application for arrest warrant, false statements of fact. Kalina v. Fletcher (U.S.Wash., 12-10-1997) 118 S.Ct. 502, 522 U.S. 118, 139 L.Ed.2d 471.

5. Issuance of complaint or warrant

Complaint charging defendant with one count of letting his dog run loose was not deficient, even though the evidence produced at trial showed that two of defendant's dogs were running loose; complaint stated that the dog at issue was not lawfully engaged in a hunting activity, that the dog was not confined on defendant's premises, and that the dog was not under reasonable control. State v. Byrd (Ohio App. 7 Dist., Belmont, 05-27-2005) No. 04 BE 40, 2005-Ohio-2720, 2005 WL 1301768, Unreported. Animals ⚷ 65

Defendant's indictment on charges different from those contained in the complaint originally filed against him did not render conviction invalid; indictment was a different charging instrument from a complaint, and indictment generally rendered any defects in the proceedings arising from the complaint moot. State v. Hess (Ohio App. 7 Dist., Jefferson, 12-02-2003) No. 02 JE 36, 2003-Ohio-6721, 2003 WL 22939443, Unreported, reconsideration denied 2004-Ohio-1197, 2004 WL 500825, appeal not allowed 102 Ohio St.3d 1422, 807 N.E.2d 367, 2004-Ohio-2003, appeal not allowed 102 Ohio St.3d 1533, 811 N.E.2d 1152, 2004-Ohio-3580, habeas corpus dismissed in part 2006 WL 1064056. Indictment And Information ⚷ 122(2)

The issuance of a warrant of arrest pursuant to RC 2935.04 by a clerk of courts, a nonjudicial officer, is not a violation of the US Constitution. State v. Fairbanks (Hamilton 1971) 33 Ohio App.2d 39, 292 N.E.2d 325, 62 O.O.2d 100, modified 32 Ohio St.2d 34, 289 N.E.2d 352, 61 O.O.2d 241. Criminal Law ⚷ 207(3)

Regardless of any recitation in an arrest warrant, the filing of an affidavit by either a police officer or a private citizen will support its issuance. State v. Sizer (Ohio Com.Pl. 1970) 25 Ohio Misc. 245, 265 N.E.2d 468, 54 O.O.2d 406. Criminal Law ⚷ 210

Where a misdemeanor prosecution is initiated upon a summons issued on an affidavit signed by a city prosecutor, but where no complaint is filed against the defendant, a court lacks jurisdiction to entertain the prosecution and the conviction will be reversed and the summons dismissed. Louisville v Girard, No. CA–6439 (5th Dist Ct App, Stark, 12–3–84).

A clerk of a county court may sign and issue a warrant for the arrest of a person charged with either a misdemeanor or a felony. 1962 OAG 2842.

6. Traffic violations

Uniform Traffic Ticket is necessary to commence moving traffic prosecution in court inferior to common pleas court, regardless of whether officer or private citizen is bringing complaint. Toledo v. Weber (Ohio Mun., 07-01-1997) 87 Ohio Misc.2d 26, 688 N.E.2d 1146. Automobiles ⚷ 351.1

Only law enforcement officer, not private citizen, can be issuing complainant on Uniform Traffic Ticket, which is necessary to commence moving traffic prosecution in court inferior to common pleas court; private citizen must seek his or her recourse through prosecuting attorney. Toledo v. Weber (Ohio Mun., 07-01-1997) 87 Ohio Misc.2d 26, 688 N.E.2d 1146. Automobiles ⚷ 351.1

RC 2935.09 is not preempted by the Traffic Rules; therefore, a prosecution for a traffic violation may be commenced by the filing of an affidavit and acknowledged complaint by a private citizen. State v. Bogadi (Licking 1982) 5 Ohio App.3d 124, 449 N.E.2d 785, 5 O.B.R. 282.

The issuance of a traffic violation citation to appear in court does not constitute an arrest. OAG 70–063.

A peace officer, excluded from making arrests under RC 4513.39, may issue traffic violation citations commanding persons to appear in court. OAG 70–063.

7. Service of summons

When a railroad company is claimed to have committed an offense in violation of RC 5589.21 and there is no regular freight or ticket agent in the county where the offense occurred, the proper method of service of summons upon the company is by service upon the statutory (designated) agent of the company, the secretary of state when standing as the agent of the company, or the appropriate persons listed in RC 2703.10. OAG 70–009.

2935.10 Procedure upon filing of affidavit or complaint; withdrawal of unexecuted warrants

(A) Upon the filing of an affidavit or complaint as provided by section 2935.09 of the Revised Code, if it charges the commission of a felony, such judge, clerk, or magistrate, unless he has reason to believe that it was not filed in good faith, or the claim is not meritorious, shall forthwith issue a warrant for the arrest of the person charged in the affidavit, and directed to a peace officer; otherwise he shall forthwith refer the matter to the prosecuting attorney or other attorney charged by law with prosecution for investigation prior to the issuance of warrant.

(B) If the offense charged is a misdemeanor or violation of a municipal ordinance, such judge, clerk, or magistrate may:

(1) Issue a warrant for the arrest of such person, directed to any officer named in section 2935.03 of the Revised Code but in cases of ordinance violation only to a police officer or marshal or deputy marshal of the municipal corporation;

(2) Issue summons, to be served by a peace officer, bailiff, or court constable, commanding the person against whom the affidavit or complaint was filed to appear forthwith, or at a fixed time in the future, before such court or magistrate. Such summons shall be served in the same manner as in civil cases.

(C) If the affidavit is filed by, or the complaint is filed pursuant to an affidavit executed by, a peace officer who has, at his discretion, at the time of commission of the alleged offense, notified the person to appear before the court or magistrate at a specific time set by such officer, no process need be issued unless the defendant fails to appear at the scheduled time.

(D) Any person charged with a misdemeanor or violation of a municipal ordinance may give bail as provided in sections 2937.22 to 2937.46 of the Revised Code, for his appearance, regardless of whether a warrant, summons, or notice to appear has been issued.

(E) Any warrant, summons, or any notice issued by the peace officer shall state the substance of the charge against the person arrested or directed to appear.

(F) When the offense charged is a misdemeanor, and the warrant or summons issued pursuant to this section is not served within two years of the date of issue, a judge or magistrate may order such warrant or summons withdrawn and the case closed, when it does not appear that the ends of justice require keeping the case open.

(1972 H 511, eff. 3–23–73; 129 v 582; 128 v 97)

Historical and Statutory Notes

Ed. Note: Former 2935.10 repealed by 128 v 97, eff. 1–1–60; 1953 H 1; GC 13432–8; see now 2935.08 for provisions analogous to former 2935.10.

Pre–1953 H 1 Amendments: 113 v 141, Ch 11, § 8

Legislative Service Commission

1973:

This section permits a misdemeanor warrant to be withdrawn from the files and the case closed, if the warrant is not served within two years from the date it is issued. Withdrawal of "stale" warrants is not mandatory, and a case may be kept open if the interests of justice require it.

Under former law, a warrant could not be withdrawn no matter how old, and once a warrant was issued a case theoretically remained open indefinitely.

Cross References

Citation optional for minor misdemeanor; form, Crim R 4.1

Complaint, Crim R 3

Freedom from unreasonable seizure; warrants, O Const Art I §14

Initial appearance, preliminary hearing, Crim R 5

Obstruction of public roads by railroad companies, 5589.21

Warrant or summons; summons in lieu of arrest allowed with misdemeanor, Crim R 4, 9

Library References

Criminal Law ⊂⊃208, 215.

Westlaw Topic No. 110.

C.J.S. Criminal Law §§ 324 to 335, 337 to 338.

Research References

Encyclopedias

OH Jur. 3d Criminal Law § 2096, Requisites and Sufficiency of Form of Affidavit, Generally.

OH Jur. 3d Highways, Streets, & Bridges § 620, Obstructions and Encroachments.

OH Jur. 3d Railroads § 248, Abandonment of Locomotive.

OH Jur. 3d Railroads § 249, Violation of Obstruction Provision.

Treatises and Practice Aids

Katz, Giannelli, Blair and Lipton, Baldwin's Ohio Practice, Criminal Law, § 7:3, Authority to Issue Arrest Warrants.

Katz, Giannelli, Blair and Lipton, Baldwin's Ohio Practice, Criminal Law, § 7:6, Authority to Execute Arrest Warrants.

Katz, Giannelli, Blair and Lipton, Baldwin's Ohio Practice, Criminal Law, § 7:8, Delay in Execution.

Katz, Giannelli, Blair and Lipton, Baldwin's Ohio Practice, Criminal Law, § 35:7, Citizen's Complaint.

Katz, Giannelli, Blair and Lipton, Baldwin's Ohio Practice, Criminal Law, § 7:14, Summons in Lieu of Arrest Warrants.

Katz, Giannelli, Blair and Lipton, Baldwin's Ohio Practice, Criminal Law, § 133:2, Direction to Issue Summons.

Katz, Giannelli, Blair and Lipton, Baldwin's Ohio Practice, Criminal Law, § 134:3, Return of Unexecuted Warrant.

Katz, Giannelli, Blair and Lipton, Baldwin's Ohio Practice, Criminal Law, § 134:5, Return on Warrant When Service is by Telegraph Order.

Katz, Giannelli, Blair and Lipton, Baldwin's Ohio Practice, Criminal Law, § 133:16, Summons Issued by Law Enforcement Officer in Lieu of Executing Warrant by Arrest in Misdemeanor Cases.

Katz, Giannelli, Blair and Lipton, Baldwin's Ohio Practice, Criminal Law, § 142:16, Warrant Upon Indictment or Information Issued by Court.

Katz, Ohio Arrest, Search & Seizure § 5:3, Who May Issue Arrest Warrants.

Katz, Ohio Arrest, Search & Seizure § 5:4, Summons in Lieu of Arrest.

Katz, Ohio Arrest, Search & Seizure App. A, Appendix A. Arrest Provisions: Checklist.

Notes of Decisions

Ed. Note: *This section contains annotations from former RC 2935.10 and 2935.19.*

---

1. Constitutional issues

The issuance of a warrant of arrest pursuant to RC 2935.04 by a clerk of courts, a nonjudicial officer, is not a violation of the US Constitution. State v. Fairbanks (Hamilton 1971) 33 Ohio App.2d 39, 292 N.E.2d 325, 62 O.O.2d 100, modified 32 Ohio St.2d 34, 289 N.E.2d 352, 61 O.O.2d 241. Criminal Law ⚩ 207(3)

An arrest warrant supported by an affidavit alleging only the statutory description of the offense charged, the issuing clerk making no determination of probable cause before issuing the warrant, is not issued "upon probable cause" as required by US Const Am 4. State v. Sizer (Ohio Com.Pl. 1970) 25 Ohio Misc. 245, 265 N.E.2d 468, 54 O.O.2d 406. Criminal Law ⚩ 211(3)

2. Who may file affidavit

Statute providing that private citizen having knowledge of facts shall file with judge, clerk of court, or magistrate an affidavit charging offense committed in order to cause arrest or prosecution of person charged, must be read in pari materia with statute prescribing subsequent procedure to be followed. State ex rel. Evans v. Columbus Dept. of Law (Ohio, 09-23-1998) 83 Ohio St.3d 174, 699 N.E.2d 60, 1998-Ohio-128. Statutes ⚩ 223.2(8)

Statute allowing private citizen having knowledge of commission of criminal offense to file affidavit charging offense in order to cause arrest or prosecution of person charged must be read in pari materia with statute prescribing subsequent procedure to be followed. State ex rel. Strothers v. Turner (Ohio, 07-23-1997) 79 Ohio St.3d 272, 680 N.E.2d 1238. Statutes ⚩ 223.2(8)

Either a peace officer or a private citizen having knowledge of the facts may file an affidavit charging a person with committing an offense in this state. OAG 70–053.

RC 4513.39 does not prohibit a peace officer, who is excluded from making arrests under said section, from swearing out an affidavit for the issuance of an arrest warrant for the arrest of persons who have, in the presence of such peace officer, violated any of the sections enumerated therein. OAG 69–061.

3. Sufficiency of affidavit or complaint

Alleged victim of assault was entitled to probable cause hearing on his private criminal complaint against alleged perpetrator; statute governing procedure upon filing of affidavit or criminal complaint by private citizen did not give court discretion to reject complaint without hearing, as it governed procedure after court had made probable cause determination. State v. Moss (Ohio App. 5 Dist., Stark, 11-10-2003) No. 2003CA00218, 2003-Ohio-6053, 2003 WL 22672018, Unreported. Criminal Law ⚩ 212

Statute providing procedure for offenses charged by affidavits submitted by private citizens does not place any duty upon city prosecutors to prosecute misdemeanors charged by affidavit. State ex rel. Evans v. Columbus Dept. of Law (Ohio, 09-23-1998) 83 Ohio St.3d 174, 699 N.E.2d 60, 1998-Ohio-128. Criminal Law ⚩ 210; District And Prosecuting Attorneys ⚩ 8

An illegal arrest does not in itself invalidate an affidavit filed in a misdemeanor case, and is not a proper ground to sustain a motion to quash the affidavit, but it can affect evidence received as a result of such arrest, and when this happens, a motion to suppress the evidence or a plea in abatement will lie. State v. Hooper (Monroe 1966) 10 Ohio App.2d 229, 227 N.E.2d 414, 39 O.O.2d 435, certiorari denied 88 S.Ct. 292, 389 U.S. 928, 19 L.Ed.2d 281.

The practice of signing the name of an arresting officer by another arresting officer to an affidavit charging an offense is to be condemned, but if affidavit is actually executed by the latter officer and is sufficient to apprise defendant of the offense with which he is charged, the false signature is surplusage and such irregularity is not prejudicial to defendant. City of Toledo v. Miscikowski (Lucas 1955) 99 Ohio App. 189, 132 N.E.2d 231, 58 O.O. 331.

An affidavit charging a person with contributing toward the delinquency of a minor child which neither charges that such child is a delinquent nor sets forth facts showing such child to be a delinquent and which does not set forth facts showing any conduct on the part of the accused which would tend to cause the delinquency of such child, does not charge an offense, and in a prosecution under such affidavit, it is error for the court to convict and sentence the accused, suspend execution of the sentence, and, thereafter, to revoke such suspension and order the sentence executed. State v. Holbrook (Logan 1954) 95 Ohio App. 526, 121 N.E.2d 81, 54 O.O. 135. Indictment And Information ⚿ 110(48)

There can be no valid conviction under an affidavit which does not charge an offense under the law, and such defect is not cured by a plea of guilty. State v. Holbrook (Logan 1954) 95 Ohio App. 526, 121 N.E.2d 81, 54 O.O. 135. Indictment And Information ⚿ 193

If the exact words of a city ordinance are used in charging an offense, it is not enough to attack the legal sufficiency of the affidavit; the ordinance must be attacked, for it is the ordinance that is at fault and not the affidavit. City of Cincinnati v. Schill (Ohio 1932) 125 Ohio St. 57, 180 N.E. 545, 11 Ohio Law Abs. 478, 36 Ohio Law Rep. 207.

4. Amendment of affidavit or complaint

An affidavit or sworn complaint in a misdemeanor charge is not subject to amendment by the court. City of Hamilton v. Petty (Ohio App. 1 Dist. 1972) 33 Ohio App.2d 194, 293 N.E.2d 881, 62 O.O.2d 286. Indictment And Information ⚿ 162

Specific authority is given for the amendment of an affidavit to the same extent and under the same limitations as applied in the case of indictments and information in the common pleas court. State v. Jackson (Franklin 1960) 190 N.E.2d 38, 90 Ohio Law Abs. 577.

5. Issuance of warrant or summons

A deputy clerk of the municipal court has authority to issue a warrant for the arrest of a person charged with a misdemeanor. State ex rel. Focke v. Price (Montgomery 1955) 137 N.E.2d 163, 73 Ohio Law Abs. 214, affirmed 165 Ohio St. 340, 135 N.E.2d 407, 59 O.O. 435, certiorari denied 77 S.Ct. 132, 352 U.S. 892, 1 L.Ed.2d 87.

A clerk of a county court may sign and issue a warrant for the arrest of a person charged with either a misdemeanor or a felony. 1962 OAG 2842.

A clerk of courts who also acts as clerk of a county court may sign and issue a warrant for the arrest of a person charged with either a misdemeanor or a felony. 1960 OAG 1297.

6. Arrest or service of process

A municipal police officer may make an arrest for a violation of a municipal ordinance, upon a properly issued warrant, anywhere within the jurisdictional limits of the issuing court. City of Fairborn v. Munkus (Ohio 1971) 28 Ohio St.2d 207, 277 N.E.2d 227, 57 O.O.2d 436. Arrest ⚿ 66(2)

RC 2935.10 provides that when an affidavit is filed charging the commission of a misdemeanor or a violation of a municipal ordinance a warrant may issue, but is not required, so that the accused can be served by a summons in the same manner as in civil cases. State v. Hooper (Monroe 1966) 10 Ohio App.2d 229, 227 N.E.2d 414, 39 O.O.2d 435, certiorari denied 88 S.Ct. 292, 389 U.S. 928, 19 L.Ed.2d 281. Criminal Law ⚿ 216

The citation issued under authority of RC 2935.10 is an invitation to appear, not an arrest, and its issuance is not tantamount to an arrest as used in RC 5577.14. State v. Frost (Ohio Co. 1961) 179 N.E.2d 564, 88 Ohio Law Abs. 321, 18 O.O.2d 119. Automobiles ⚿ 349(10)

When a railroad company is claimed to have committed an offense in violation of RC 5589.21 and there is no regular freight or ticket agent in the county where the offense occurred, the proper method of service of summons upon the company is by service upon the statutory (designated) agent of the company, the secretary of state when standing as the agent of the company, or the appropriate persons listed in RC 2703.10. OAG 70-009.

2935.11 Failure of person summoned to appear

If the person summoned to appear as provided in division (B) of section 2935.10 of the Revised Code fails to appear without just cause and personal service of the summons was had upon him, he may be found guilty of contempt of court, and may be fined not to exceed twenty dollars for such contempt. Upon failure to appear the court or magistrate may forthwith issue a warrant for his arrest.

(128 v 97, eff. 1-1-60)

Historical and Statutory Notes

Ed. Note: Former 2935.11 repealed by 128 v 97, eff. 1–1–60; 1953 H 1; GC 13432–9; see now 2935.08 and 2935.09 for provisions analogous to former 2935.11.

Pre–1953 H 1 Amendments: 113 v 141, Ch 11, § 9

Library References

Contempt ⚖17.

Westlaw Topic No. 93.

C.J.S. Contempt § 31.

Research References

Encyclopedias

OH Jur. 3d Contempt § 19, Disobedience of Subpoena or Process.

Treatises and Practice Aids

Katz, Giannelli, Blair and Lipton, Baldwin's Ohio Practice, Criminal Law, § 7:14, Summons in Lieu of Arrest Warrants.

Katz, Giannelli, Blair and Lipton, Baldwin's Ohio Practice, Criminal Law, § 133:5, Summons Upon Complaint, Indictment, or Information.

Katz, Giannelli, Blair and Lipton, Baldwin's Ohio Practice, Criminal Law, § 133:16, Summons Issued by Law Enforcement Officer in Lieu of Executing Warrant by Arrest in Misdemeanor Cases.

Katz, Giannelli, Blair and Lipton, Baldwin's Ohio Practice, Criminal Law, § 133:20, Summons in Lieu of Arrest Without Warrant (Additional Form).

Katz, Giannelli, Blair and Lipton, Baldwin's Ohio Practice, Criminal Law, § 133:29, Arrest Warrant of Arrest Upon Failure to Obey Summons.

Katz, Ohio Arrest, Search & Seizure § 5:4, Summons in Lieu of Arrest.

2935.12 Forcible entry in making arrest; execution of search warrant

(A) When making an arrest or executing an arrest warrant or summons in lieu of an arrest warrant, or when executing a search warrant, the peace officer, law enforcement officer, or other authorized individual making the arrest or executing the warrant or summons may break down an outer or inner door or window of a dwelling house or other building, if, after notice of his intention to make the arrest or to execute the warrant or summons, he is refused admittance, but the law enforcement officer or other authorized individual executing a search warrant shall not enter a house or building not described in the warrant.

(B) The precondition for nonconsensual, forcible entry established by division (A) of this section is subject to waiver, as it applies to the execution of a search warrant, in accordance with section 2933.231 of the Revised Code.

(1990 S 258, eff. 11–20–90; 128 v 97)

Historical and Statutory Notes

Ed. Note: 2935.12 contains provisions analogous to former 2935.15, repealed by 128 v 97, eff. 1–1–60.

Ed. Note: Former 2935.12 repealed by 128 v 97, eff. 1–1–60; 1953 H 1; GC 13432–11; see now 2935.13 for provisions analogous to former RC 2935.12.

Pre–1953 H 1 Amendments: 113 v 141, Ch 11, § 11

Cross References

Freedom from unreasonable seizure; warrants, O Const Art I §14

Library References

Arrest ⚖68.

Westlaw Topic No. 35.

C.J.S. Arrest §§ 2, 37, 46 to 49, 51 to 53, 56 to 57.

Baldwin's Ohio Legislative Service, 1990 Laws of Ohio, S 258—LSC Analysis, p 5–954

Research References

ALR Library

85 ALR 5th 1, What Constitutes Compliance With Knock-And-Announce Rule in Search of Private Premises--State Cases.

Encyclopedias

OH Jur. 3d Criminal Law § 128, Independent Source; Ultimate or Inevitable Discovery Exception.

OH Jur. 3d Criminal Law § 218, Service of Warrant; Knock and Announce Rule.

OH Jur. 3d Criminal Law § 219, Use of Force to Enter Building.

OH Jur. 3d Criminal Law § 223, Scope of Search—Warrant Containing Waiver of Statutory Precondition for Nonconsensual, Forcible Entry; Liability in Damages for Improper Execution of Warrant.

OH Jur. 3d Criminal Law § 2147, Nonconsensual Entry of Private Property; Exigent Circumstances.

Treatises and Practice Aids

Markus, Trial Handbook for Ohio Lawyers, § 29:30, Search and Seizure With Warrant—Knock and Announce Requirement.

Katz, Giannelli, Blair and Lipton, Baldwin's Ohio Practice, Criminal Law, § 10:4, Knock and Announce Rule.

Katz, Giannelli, Blair and Lipton, Baldwin's Ohio Practice, Criminal Law, § 29:5, Exclusionary Rule—Statutes.

Katz, Giannelli, Blair and Lipton, Baldwin's Ohio Practice, Criminal Law, § 7:10, Knock and Announce Rule.

Katz, Giannelli, Blair and Lipton, Baldwin's Ohio Practice, Criminal Law, § 134:2, Return of Executed Warrant.

Katz, Ohio Arrest, Search & Seizure § 6:2, Forced Entry.

Katz, Ohio Arrest, Search & Seizure § 7:9, Execution of Search Warrants—Reasonableness Standard.

Katz, Ohio Arrest, Search & Seizure § 7:11, Execution of Search Warrants—Knock and Notify Rule and the Use of Force.

Katz, Ohio Arrest, Search & Seizure App. A, Appendix A. Arrest Provisions: Checklist.

Katz, Ohio Arrest, Search & Seizure App. C, Appendix C. Search Warrant Provisions: Checklist.

Law Review and Journal Commentaries

Overgeneralization of the Hot Pursuit Doctrine Provides Another Blow to the Fourth Amendment in Middletown v Flinchum, Note. 37 Akron L Rev 509 (2004).

Notes of Decisions

---

1. Constitutional issues

Defense counsel's failure to file motion to suppress evidence on basis of alleged search violation was not ineffective assistance of counsel, in prosecution for possession of drugs and criminal tools; any motion to suppress on such basis would have been denied since defendant did not enjoy legitimate expectation of privacy in apartment where police observed defendant packaging illegal drugs. State v. Griffin (Ohio App. 8 Dist., Cuyahoga, 04-29-2004) No. 82979, 2004-Ohio-2155, 2004 WL 906086, Unreported. Criminal Law ⚷ 641.13(6)

Police officers' failure to knock and announce their presence before entering residence of suspect who had sold cocaine to informant did not violate suspect's Fourth Amendment rights against unreasonable searches and seizures, since suspect saw police ascending front steps of residence with a ram, suspect attempted to slam door shut and flee into residence, and any delay by officers would only have permitted suspect time to secure weapon to resist officers' entrance, to conceal or destroy evidence, or to flee from house. State v. Roberts (Ohio App. 9 Dist., Summit, 01-29-2003) No. 21169, 2003-Ohio-363, 2003 WL 187589, Unreported, appeal not allowed 99 Ohio St.3d 1435, 789 N.E.2d 1117, 2003-Ohio-2902. Controlled Substances ⚷ 130

Evidence did not establish exigent circumstances justifying forcible entry into dwelling house, to execute warrant to search for drugs, before occupants could respond to knock-and-announce; police officers were able to observe occupants through glass door and they therefore would have been able to observe any attempt at destroying evidence, and no rapid or threatening movements were made by occupants. State v. Hunter (Ohio App. 2 Dist., 08-08-2003) 153 Ohio App.3d 628, 795 N.E.2d 139, 2003-Ohio-4204. Controlled Substances ⚷ 153

Police officers did not wait long enough for a response, after the knock-and-announce, and thus, the forcible entry into defendant's home, to execute a search warrant, was an unreasonable search; presence of police was announced only two to five times before forcible entry, announcements occurred simultaneously with officers reaching glass door and one officer knocking quickly, and there was insufficient time for occupants to register anything other than shock, so that a refusal of entry could not be implied. State v. Hunter (Ohio App. 2 Dist., 08-08-2003) 153 Ohio App.3d 628, 795 N.E.2d 139, 2003-Ohio-4204. Searches And Seizures ⚷ 143.1

Law enforcement officers, who arrived at defendant's home to execute bench warrant, became engaged in a hot pursuit of defendant, who upon spotting officers entered home and locked door behind him despite continual admonishments from officers to stay where he was, and thus officers were justified in entering defendant's home via force in order to arrest him; defendant's action indicated attempt to evade arrest by hiding inside his residence with doors locked. State v. Stuber (Ohio App. 3 Dist., 11-21-2002) 150 Ohio App.3d 200, 779 N.E.2d 1090, 2002-Ohio-6309. Arrest ⚷ 68(12)

Where police officers knock and announce themselves but are denied admittance, police acting pursuant to a valid warrant are permitted to forcibly enter a suspect's house. State v. Stuber (Ohio App. 3 Dist., 11-21-2002) 150 Ohio App.3d 200, 779 N.E.2d 1090, 2002-Ohio-6309. Searches And Seizures ⚷ 143.1

If the provisions of knock and announce statute are not followed, law enforcement officer's search may be constitutionally unreasonable and the results of the search may be suppressed. State v. Stuber (Ohio App. 3 Dist., 11-21-2002) 150 Ohio App.3d 200, 779 N.E.2d 1090, 2002-Ohio-6309. Searches And Seizures ⚷ 54

Police officers' "no-knock" entry into defendant's apartment to execute search warrant for drugs was not justified by reasonable suspicion regarding officers' safety or preservation of evidence, and thus violated the Fourth Amendment, where there was no indication by pre-search surveillance or through the use of the police informant that the defendant would possibly be armed or that defendant was alerted to the presence of the police prior to the execution of the warrant. State v. King (Ohio App. 8 Dist., 12-13-1999) 136 Ohio App.3d 377, 736 N.E.2d 921, stay denied 87 Ohio St.3d 1483, 722 N.E.2d 89, dismissed, appeal not allowed 88 Ohio St.3d 1478, 727 N.E.2d 130. Controlled Substances ⚷ 153

Inevitable-discovery doctrine did not apply to drug evidence gathered directly as a result of a violation of Fourth Amendment and knock-and-announce statute, where State could not show that the evidence would have been gathered from an alternative legal method or procedure. State v. Taylor (Ohio App. 12 Dist., 10-25-1999) 135 Ohio App.3d 182, 733 N.E.2d 310, dismissed, appeal not allowed 88 Ohio St.3d 1424, 723 N.E.2d 1112, reconsideration denied 88 Ohio St.3d 1487, 727 N.E.2d 135. Criminal Law ⚷ 394.1(3)

Police officers, who were attempting to serve a warrant based on information that evidence of drug trafficking was inside defendants' residence, violated knock-and-announce statute and Fourth Amendment, where police knocked on door, and forcibly entered residence, after pausing approximately three to four seconds. State v. Taylor (Ohio App. 12 Dist., 10-25-1999) 135 Ohio App.3d 182, 733 N.E.2d 310, dismissed, appeal not allowed 88 Ohio St.3d 1424, 723 N.E.2d 1112, reconsideration denied 88 Ohio St.3d 1487, 727 N.E.2d 135. Controlled Substances ⚷ 153

Statute conditionally authorizing officer making arrest or executing warrant to break down outer or inner door or window of dwelling house or other building was inapplicable where officers knocked then walked into workshop through unlocked door that was ajar, as they did not have to break down door or break window to effectuate arrest. State v. Campana (Ohio App. 11 Dist., 07-01-1996) 112 Ohio App.3d 297, 678 N.E.2d 626. Arrest ⚷ 65; Arrest ⚷ 68(2)

Partially open door with occupant standing therein, without exigent circumstances, does not diminish or vitiate protection afforded by, and values inherent in, Fourth Amendment or statute conditionally authorizing officers making arrest or executing warrant or summons to break down outer or inner door or window of dwelling house or other building. State v. Campana (Ohio App. 11 Dist., 07-01-1996) 112 Ohio App.3d 297, 678 N.E.2d 626. Arrest ⚷ 68(11); Arrest ⚷ 68(12)

The execution of a valid search warrant was reasonable in a constitutional sense when the evidence showed a police officer entered the premises, without force or resistance, by walking through an open door, although no permission was requested or given. State v. Applebury (Hamilton 1987) 34 Ohio App.3d 376, 518 N.E.2d 977. Searches And Seizures ⚷ 143.1

Where police officers, in executing a search warrant pursuant to a gambling investigation, knocked on the door to the apartment and announced their authority and purpose, but forced entry without having been actually or constructively refused admittance as required by RC 2935.12, the trial court properly granted the defendants' motions to suppress for failure to comply with the requirements of US Const Am 4 and US Const Am 14, inasmuch as the state failed to show any exigent circumstances which would justify the otherwise unreasonable search and seizure. State v. DeFiore (Hamilton 1979) 64 Ohio App.2d 115, 411 N.E.2d 837, 18 O.O.3d 90.

Where police officers, in executing a warrant for the search of an occupied house for the purpose of seizing narcotics, announce their identity but not their intention to search, make an immediate entry without knocking, by opening an unlocked, front screen door, and confiscate materials inside, such conduct constitutes an unreasonable search and seizure in violation of US Const Am 4 and US Const Am 14, and evidence resulting from such acts should be suppressed at the trial of the occupants for narcotics violations prohibited by RC Ch 3719. State v. Furry (Wood 1971) 31 Ohio App.2d 107, 286 N.E.2d 301, 60 O.O.2d 196. Controlled Substances ⚷ 153

Where police officers who have a warrant for defendant's arrest wherein defendant is charged with murder in the first degree, enter defendant's house in execution thereof, and discover evidence of a second crime in plain sight therein, there has been no violation of defendant's rights under US Const Am 4, and such evidence of the second crime may not be suppressed. State v. Jemison (Ohio 1968) 14 Ohio St.2d 47, 236 N.E.2d 538, 43 O.O.2d

115, certiorari denied 89 S.Ct. 312, 393 U.S. 943, 21 L.Ed.2d 280.

A forcible entry by deputy sheriffs on direction of the county prosecutor into an office to serve capiases on employees who ignored grand jury subpoenas concerning an investigation of the employer, is an act sanctioned by official policy; the warrantless entry in violation of the employer's rights under US Const Am 4 is, therefore, grounds for a suit under 42 USC 1983 against the county. Pembaur v. City of Cincinnati (U.S.Ohio 1986) 106 S.Ct. 1292, 475 U.S. 469, 89 L.Ed.2d 452, on remand 792 F.2d 57.

If detective obtained second search warrant pursuant to addendum to search warrant affidavit, submitted to judge the day after issuance of first search warrant and including an additional address to be searched, without either taking an oath on the statements in the addendum or instead attaching the addendum to the first affidavit and first search warrant when he presented the addendum to the issuing judge, the error was more than a mere procedural error; it was a constitutional error which required suppression of evidence seized pursuant to the second search warrant. State v. Hardy (Ohio App. 2 Dist., Montgomery, 05-17-2002) No. 19029, 2002-Ohio-2371, 2002 WL 1000425, Unreported. Criminal Law ⚷ 394.4(6)

2. Search warrant; peace warrant

The unlawful possession of an hallucinogen is a continuing offense, committed in the presence of an arresting officer who finds the contraband in the bedroom occupied and controlled by an accused, who appears during the search, and an arrest in such circumstances is lawful. State v. Wilson (Montgomery 1974) 41 Ohio App.2d 240, 325 N.E.2d 249, 70 O.O.2d 452. Arrest ⚷ 63.3

A law officer in the process of making an arrest under a valid peace warrant, after compliance with RC 2935.12, may utilize the procedures of that section to force entrance. State v. Clark (Cuyahoga 1974) 40 Ohio App.2d 365, 319 N.E.2d 605, 69 O.O.2d 324. Arrest ⚷ 68(8)

A law officer making a valid arrest under a peace warrant may conduct a reasonable search incident to the arrest. State v. Clark (Cuyahoga 1974) 40 Ohio App.2d 365, 319 N.E.2d 605, 69 O.O.2d 324. Arrest ⚷ 71.1(1)

A search warrant on which the judge took the officer's affirmation but did not sign the command order to search is invalid. State v. Vuin (Ohio Com.Pl. 1962) 185 N.E.2d 506, 89 Ohio Law Abs. 193.

3. Knock and announce rule

Police officers failed to comply with knock and announce statute in executing search warrant of residence, thus requiring suppression of evidence seized during search of residence, in drug prosecution; police broke into residence without first having been refused admittance, in violation of statute, and none of the occupants of residence, including defendant, were sufficiently alerted to have refused admittance. State v. Oliver (Ohio App. 8 Dist., Cuyahoga, 08-25-2005) No. 85606, 2005-Ohio-4411, 2005 WL 2045792, Unreported. Criminal Law ⚷ 394.4(8)

No exigent circumstances existed to justify police officers' entry into residence to execute search warrant, which entry violated knock and announce statute; officers were able to observe occupants of house through picture window, and, as such, they would have been able to observe any attempt at destroying evidence, but no such attempt was observed, and officer testified that one of the men was lying on a couch, while the other was sitting on a chair with his back towards the window, and that neither man moved. State v. Oliver (Ohio App. 8 Dist., Cuyahoga, 08-25-2005) No. 85606, 2005-Ohio-4411, 2005 WL 2045792, Unreported. Searches And Seizures ⚷ 143.1

Police officers adhered to knock and announce rule before forcibly entering defendant's residence on suspicion of drug trafficking, where, although defendant's mother and sister inside the house did not hear knock before police entered, their failure to hear knock did not mean that police failed to knock, and officer testified that, while executing warrant, he knocked on screen door and yelled "Police, search warrant," and then, approximately 15 seconds after no response, he entered house by using a ram and apprehended defendant once inside. State v. Gates (Ohio App. 8 Dist., Cuyahoga, 03-17-2005) No. 84600, 2005-Ohio-1173, 2005 WL 616415, Unreported. Controlled Substances ⚷ 153

Law enforcement officers acted reasonably in obtaining and executing a search warrant that requested noncompliance with statutory knock and announce requirement, and thus warrant complied with requirements of Fourth Amendment; even though the State did not strictly comply with all technical requirements, supporting facts were known to the affiant officer. State v. Noethtich (Ohio App. 3 Dist., Seneca, 11-15-2004) No. 13-04-14, 2004-Ohio-6047, 2004 WL 2588427, Unreported. Searches And Seizures ⚷ 143.1

Trial court's refusal to reopen evidentiary hearing on defendants' motions to suppress evidence was abuse of discretion, where trial court granted motions to suppress based on finding that police had violated "knock-and-announce" rule, but defendants had failed to raise that issue in their motions to suppress. State v. Pilot (Ohio App. 12 Dist., Clermont, 07-12-2004) No. CA2003-03-023, No. CA2003-03-24, 2004-Ohio-3669, 2004 WL 1551517, Unreported. Criminal Law ⚷ 394.6(5)

Sufficient exigent circumstances existed to permit police officer, who was executing a search warrant for evidence of drug trafficking and drug possession, to dispense with requirements that officer knock and announce before entering residence, where woman inside residence yelled, when officers were about 15-20 feet away from residence, "the police are coming!," bullhorn announced police's presence, and officer was concerned suspected drugs would be flushed down a toilet or drain or the occupants would barricade the door and get weapons. State v. Blue (Ohio App. 2 Dist., Montgomery, 06-04-2004) No. 20136, 2004-Ohio-2953,

2004 WL 1254197, Unreported. Searches And Seizures ⚷ 143.1

State demonstrated existence of exigent circumstances that justified police officers' failure to knock and announce before entering defendant's home, or to obtain waiver of knock and announce requirements in prosecution for illegal cultivation of marijuana; police officers testified about their concerns regarding destruction of evidence and risk of injury to themselves and other officers. State v. Bickel (Ohio App. 5 Dist., Holmes, 12-17-2003) No. 03-CA-002, 2003-Ohio-6910, 2003 WL 22971449, Unreported. Controlled Substances ⚷ 153

Failure of police officers to knock and announce their presence before entering apartment to execute search warrant did not deprive defendant of notice of officers' presence, or opportunity to allow officers to enter apartment peaceably; man police saw standing in doorway of apartment went in and slammed door closed when police began approaching thereby demonstrating his intent not to allow officers into apartment, and exigent circumstances existed because, if officers had delayed, defendant would have had time to conceal or destroy evidence, secure weapon, or flee apartment. State v. Varner (Ohio App. 9 Dist., Summit, 02-19-2003) No. 21056, 2003-Ohio-719, 2003 WL 357526, Unreported, appeal not allowed 99 Ohio St.3d 1438, 789 N.E.2d 1118, 2003-Ohio-2902, appeal not allowed 101 Ohio St.3d 1424, 802 N.E.2d 155, 2004-Ohio-123. Searches And Seizures ⚷ 143.1

The knock and announce provisions are only applicable where a forcible, unauthorized entry is necessary which is not the case where police obtain a warrant for a residence where drug possession is involved and upon arriving at the home they notice one of the suspects in the side yard and ask to talk with her and her husband inside the house; although the officers do not disclose that they have a search warrant for the residence the suspect leads them into the house upon their request. State v. Lewis (Ohio App. 2 Dist., Montgomery, 11-19-1999) No. 17538, No. 17564, 1999 WL 1043901, Unreported.

Knock-and-announce statute did not apply to entry into home where defendant was located, as deputies entered the home through an open door and without the use of force. State v. Gibson (Ohio App. 4 Dist., 11-22-2005) 2005-Ohio-6380, 2005 WL 3220271. Searches And Seizures ⚷ 54

Statute allowing law enforcement officers, when executing search warrant for a house or other building, to break down an outer or inner door or window if they are refused admittance did not apply to case in which officers knocked and announced their presence and then entered home through unlocked door that had become ajar. State v. Dixon (Ohio App. 3 Dist., 03-28-2001) 141 Ohio App.3d 654, 752 N.E.2d 1005, 2001-Ohio-2120. Searches And Seizures ⚷ 143.1

Sufficient competent and credible evidence supported trial court's finding that the police did not "knock and announce" their presence prior to forcibly entering the defendant's home to execute search warrant, where three witnesses testified that they heard no knocking or announcements by police as they approached door of apartment. State v. King (Ohio App. 8 Dist., 12-13-1999) 136 Ohio App.3d 377, 736 N.E.2d 921, stay denied 87 Ohio St.3d 1483, 722 N.E.2d 89, dismissed, appeal not allowed 88 Ohio St.3d 1478, 727 N.E.2d 130. Searches And Seizures ⚷ 196

Statute providing that, when making an arrest, a police officer may break down a door if, after he notifies the parties inside of his intention to make the arrest, he is refused admittance, is limited to entries by violent, forcible action. Alley v. Bettencourt (Ohio App. 4 Dist., 09-10-1999) 134 Ohio App.3d 303, 730 N.E.2d 1067. Arrest ⚷ 68(8)

Police officers complied with requirements of "knock and announce" statute by pulling up to defendant's house in three vehicles, two of which were marked "Sheriff," wearing clothing marked "Deputy Sheriff," shouting "deputy sheriff, search warrant," pounding on casement of outer storm door, and applying battering ram to entrance door after hearing no response. State v. Amundson (Ohio App. 12 Dist., 01-22-1996) 108 Ohio App.3d 438, 670 N.E.2d 1083. Searches And Seizures ⚷ 143.1

Whether police officers executing nighttime search warrant of residence violated knock-and-announce rule, or whether exigent circumstances existed which excused the knock-and-announce requirement, were jury questions in civil rights suit by the residents seeking damages for alleged unconstitutional search. Knop v. Toledo (Ohio App. 6 Dist., 11-17-1995) 107 Ohio App.3d 449, 669 N.E.2d 27. Civil Rights ⚷ 1429

Police officers' failure to establish any particularized reason why, in course of executing search warrant for narcotics, they broke down door to arrestee's apartment without knocking and announcing themselves, other than general knowledge that evidence can be destroyed and weapons were often present in narcotics cases, and police officers' testimony which suggested that officers, as routine matter, failed to knock and announce at all or only identified themselves as police as they forced entry was evidence upon which reasonable minds might reach different conclusions as to whether there was particularized reason for police officers' failure to observe knock and announce rule and whether police, as matter of custom, violated knock and announce principle, such that directed verdict was improper on issue of whether search of arrestee's apartment was unconstitutional violation of her Fourth Amendment rights. Gaston v. Toledo (Ohio App. 6 Dist., 08-25-1995) 106 Ohio App.3d 66, 665 N.E.2d 264. Civil Rights ⚷ 1429

Unannounced, forced entries to execute search warrants are not always reasonable in narcotics cases on ground that narcotics violators are normally on alert to destroy any contraband at first notice of officer's presence. Gaston v. Toledo (Ohio App. 6 Dist., 08-25-1995) 106 Ohio App.3d 66, 665 N.E.2d 264. Controlled Substances ⚷ 153

Where officers hold reasonable belief that they are in danger of bodily harm or that suspects are trying to escape or destroy evidence, compliance with knock and announce principle is excused. Gaston v. Toledo (Ohio App. 6 Dist., 08-25-1995) 106 Ohio App.3d 66, 665 N.E.2d 264. Searches And Seizures ⚷ 143.1

Announcement of police officer's purpose is not required before forced entry if, before arriving to search, police have particular reasons to reasonably believe in particular case that evidence would be destroyed. Gaston v. Toledo (Ohio App. 6 Dist., 08-25-1995) 106 Ohio App.3d 66, 665 N.E.2d 264. Searches And Seizures ⚷ 143.1

Particularized reasons necessary to justify exception to knock and announce rule can involve evidence of any unusual activity, noise or conduct indicating destruction of evidence is being attempted, or evidence of additional knowledge by police officers that destruction of evidence will be attempted. Gaston v. Toledo (Ohio App. 6 Dist., 08-25-1995) 106 Ohio App.3d 66, 665 N.E.2d 264. Searches And Seizures ⚷ 143.1

Mere observation of police officers by occupant of premises to be searched is not sufficient to establish particularized need required to justify exception to knock and announce rule. Gaston v. Toledo (Ohio App. 6 Dist., 08-25-1995) 106 Ohio App.3d 66, 665 N.E.2d 264. Searches And Seizures ⚷ 143.1

Where police went to defendant's girlfriend's home to arrest him, having probable cause to believe he could be found there and knowing there was an outstanding felony warrant against him, and further having a reasonable belief that persons on the premises would be armed and dangerous, and when the police arrived they announced their presence but not their purpose, but were not refused admittance and did not use force to enter, the knock and notify requirements of RC 2935.12 were irrelevant, and a protective sweep of the premises that uncovered guns, drugs and a large amount of money was justified under the exigent circumstances exception to US Const Am 4. State v. Davis (Cuyahoga 1992) 80 Ohio App.3d 277, 609 N.E.2d 174, dismissed, jurisdictional motion overruled 65 Ohio St.3d 1462, 602 N.E.2d 1171.

In a prosecution for gambling, an illegal search and seizure is committed when (1) the police officer kicks the defendant's door in only three seconds after knocking and announcing his presence as an officer, (2) there was no evidence offered to show that an undercover policewoman inside was in danger, and (3) there was no proof that the evidence, such as telephones and betting slips, would be destroyed. State v. Valentine (Lawrence 1991) 74 Ohio App.3d 110, 598 N.E.2d 82, reconsideration denied.

Repeated responses of "just a minute" to an officer announcing his presence and intent to search pursuant to a warrant constitute a refusal of admittance and forcible entry to the premises is justified. State v. Morgan (Mercer 1988) 55 Ohio App.3d 182, 563 N.E.2d 307.

Failure to comply with the "knock and announce" statute prior to entry of premises can be asserted to suppress the product of the search only by those whose rights were violated by the search itself and not by those who are aggrieved solely by the introduction of damaging evidence. State v. Wac (Ohio 1981) 68 Ohio St.2d 84, 428 N.E.2d 428, 22 O.O.3d 299.

Where police officers are acting under a valid warrant based upon a proper affidavit to search a private residence, a demand for and a refusal of admittance are not prerequisites to a lawful search where there is no one at home to consent to or refuse admittance, and the officers make a proper announcement and give proper notice as soon as the occupants return. State v. Wilson (Montgomery 1974) 41 Ohio App.2d 240, 325 N.E.2d 249, 70 O.O.2d 452. Searches And Seizures ⚷ 143.1

Where officers executing a search warrant failed to make any announcement of an intention to search the premises, a search thereafter made by breaking in was illegal, and evidence obtained thereby must be suppressed. State v. Vuin (Ohio Com.Pl. 1962) 185 N.E.2d 506, 89 Ohio Law Abs. 193.

Statute setting forth "knock and announce" requirements that police officers must follow when executing a warrant at a dwelling house or building were inapplicable, where police were not executing a warrant at time of entry into residence. State v. Carr (Ohio App. 2 Dist., Montgomery, 08-16-2002) No. 19121, 2002-Ohio-4201, 2002 WL 1881158, Unreported. Searches And Seizures ⚷ 54

Police officers did not violate knock and announce rule, where officers knocked and announced their presence, played bullhorn to emphasize their presence was for purpose of executing search warrant, and rammed open defendant's back door approximately ten to 20 seconds later. State v. Edmonds (Ohio App. 2 Dist., Montgomery, 07-26-2002) No. 19129, 2002-Ohio-3807, 2002 WL 1728014, Unreported. Searches And Seizures ⚷ 143.1

4. Consent to entry; exigent circumstances

A warrantless search of a bathroom of a hotel suite is made in exigent circumstances where (1) an anonymous informant calls claiming the defendant and another named person are in a hotel suite trafficking in cocaine and heroin and gives police accurate and specific information, (2) a police check confirms that the two names given by the caller had drug records, (3) a third party answering the door at the defendant's hotel suite initially denies knowing him, and (4) upon entering the hotel suite detectives hear the bathroom door slam, observe $200 cash and a cellular phone in plain view on the bed, and hear the toilet flushing. State v. Lushch (Ohio App. 8 Dist., Cuyahoga, 12-01-1994) No. 66395, 1994 WL 677507, Unreported, dismissed, appeal not allowed 72 Ohio St.3d 1413, 647 N.E.2d 1388.

Exigent circumstances excuse police from strict compliance with RC 2935.12's requirement of a refusal of admittance where police wait ten to fifteen seconds after knocking and announcing their presence, and activity in the dwelling gives rise to suspicion that evidence of drug trafficking is being destroyed. State v Boyd, No. 13425, 1993 WL 169104 (2d Dist Ct App, Montgomery, 5–21–93).

Officers did not violate statute imposing a knock-and-announce requirement, and limiting breaking down of door, for entry into a home to make an arrest, where suspect's girlfriend told officers she left back door unlocked so they could arrest suspect for domestic violence. Alley v. Bettencourt (Ohio App. 4 Dist., 09-10-1999) 134 Ohio App.3d 303, 730 N.E.2d 1067. Arrest ⚷ 68(8)

Statute providing that, when executing search warrant, law enforcement officer may break down outer or inner door or window of dwelling, house or other building if, after notice of his intention to execute warrant, he is refused admittance applies only if officer breaks down a door to enter; statute involves violent, forcible entry. State v. Baker (Hamilton 1993) 87 Ohio App.3d 186, 621 N.E.2d 1347. Searches And Seizures ⚷ 143.1

RC 2935.12 does not authorize an officer to break into a home to make a warrantless arrest in the absence of exigent circumstance, but merely permits entry to be by force if the entry is otherwise legal. City of Middleburg Heights v. Theiss (Cuyahoga 1985) 28 Ohio App.3d 1, 501 N.E.2d 1226, 28 O.B.R. 9.

Officers executing a search warrant are excused from the requirement of RC 2935.12 that they be refused admittance before breaking into a dwelling if the evidence sought could be easily and quickly destroyed if they waited for admittance or a refusal. State v. Roper (Summit 1985) 27 Ohio App.3d 212, 500 N.E.2d 353, 27 O.B.R. 252.

The testimony relating to visual and audible sounds of such a search will be suppressed where a law enforcement officer without a legal arrest warrant or a proper search warrant and without probable cause to believe a felony is being or has been committed gains admission to a common passageway of a rooming house through the consent of a minor, the son of the landlord, and peers through a keyhole of a private room and while doing so makes such observations and eavesdrops on sounds emanating therefrom. State v. Person (Ohio Mun. 1973) 34 Ohio Misc. 97, 298 N.E.2d 922, 63 O.O.2d 406. Criminal Law ⚷ 394.4(3)

In the absence of consent or exigent circumstances, a police officer who is in possession of an arrest warrant must obtain a search warrant before he may enter a residence to arrest a nonresident. Steagald v. U.S. (U.S.Ga. 1981) 101 S.Ct. 1642, 451 U.S. 204, 68 L.Ed.2d 38, on remand 656 F.2d 109, on remand 664 F.2d 1242.

The "knock and announce" requirement is met when police give occupants of a small apartment reasonable opportunity to open the door and the occupants refusal to do so is a constructive refusal pursuant to RC 2935.12 where (1) the police know that an informant had just purchased cocaine from an occupant of the apartment within five to ten minutes of executing the search warrant, (2) it is 10:15 p.m. so it is likely the residents of the apartment are not in bed, (3) the residence is a small apartment so that the occupants could be expected to rather quickly open the door, (4) the police use a bullhorn and knock so it is likely the occupants know of the presence and purpose of the police, and (5) it is likely that drugs would be flushed down a toilet if police delay their entry. State v. Allen (Ohio App. 2 Dist., Montgomery, 01-18-2002) No. 18788, 2002-Ohio-263, 2002 WL 63105, Unreported.

5. Display of warrant

A search of premises pursuant to a lawfully issued warrant, when the officers learned after obtaining entry that the warrant had been left in their police car, and where otherwise reasonable, results in the lawful seizure of any contraband found in plain sight on the premises and a motion for its exclusion from evidence is properly overruled. State v. Johnson (Ohio Com.Pl. 1968) 16 Ohio Misc. 278, 240 N.E.2d 574, 45 O.O.2d 345.

6. Effective assistance of counsel

Defendant was not entitled to evidentiary hearing on postconviction motion based on alleged claims of ineffective assistance of counsel for failure to pursue motions to dismiss arising from police officers' failure to give notice of intent to execute search warrant prior to breaking down door and for counsel's failure to pursue motion to suppress before trial court when he entered plea agreement, where defendant failed to submit evidentiary documents, other than his own self-serving affidavit, to support his claim. State v. Williams (Ohio App. 9 Dist., Summit, 08-06-2003) No. 21395, 2003-Ohio-4154, 2003 WL 21804750, Unreported, appeal not allowed 100 Ohio St.3d 1509, 799 N.E.2d 187, 2003-Ohio-6161. Criminal Law ⚷ 1655(6)

2935.13 Proceedings upon arrest

Upon the arrest of any person pursuant to warrant, he shall forthwith be taken before the court or magistrate issuing the same, if such court be in session or such magistrate available, and proceedings had as provided in sections 2937.01 to 2937.46, inclusive, of the Revised Code. If such court be not in session and a misdemeanor or ordinance violation is charged, he shall be taken before the clerk or deputy clerk of the court and let to bail, as provided in sections 2937.22 to 2937.46, inclusive, of the Revised Code, if the magistrate be not available, or if the defendant is arrested in a county other than that of the issuing court or magistrate he shall forthwith be taken before the most convenient magistrate, clerk, or deputy clerk of a court of record, and there let to bail for his appearance before the issuing court or magistrate within a reasonable time to be set by such clerk.

(128 v 97, eff. 1–1–60)

Historical and Statutory Notes

Ed. Note: 2935.13 contains provisions analogous to former 2935.12, repealed by 128 v 97, eff. 1–1–60.

Ed. Note: Former 2935.13 repealed by 128 v 97, eff. 1–1–60; 1953 H 1; GC 13432–12.

Pre–1953 H 1 Amendments: 113 v 142, Ch 11, § 12

Cross References

Bail, Crim R 46

Elector arrested at poll for violating election law may still vote or register if entitled, 3501.33

Initial appearance, preliminary hearing, Crim R 5

Warrant or summons, arrest, Crim R 4

Library References

Arrest ⚷70.

Westlaw Topic No. 35.

C.J.S. Arrest §§ 58 to 61.

Research References

Encyclopedias

OH Jur. 3d Criminal Law § 2148, Arrest With Warrant; Detention, Custody, and Disposition of Arrested Person.

OH Jur. 3d Criminal Law § 2178, Clerks of Court.

Treatises and Practice Aids

Katz, Giannelli, Blair and Lipton, Baldwin's Ohio Practice, Criminal Law, § 7:11, Post-Arrest Custody of Arrestee.

Katz, Ohio Arrest, Search & Seizure § 6:5, Post-Arrest Procedures.

Katz, Ohio Arrest, Search & Seizure App. A, Appendix A. Arrest Provisions: Checklist.

Notes of Decisions

Bond 3
Detention or arrest 2
Procedure 1

---

1. Procedure

Where a highway patrolman arrests a person found violating a law of this state, for which violation he is authorized to arrest, he must follow the procedure prescribed by RC 2935.03, RC 2935.05, RC 2935.08, and RC 2935.13. 1961 OAG 2214.

2. Detention or arrest

A county sheriff has a duty to detain in the county jail an individual arrested without a warrant by a municipal police officer for any violation of the laws of this state. OAG 95–011.

A sheriff has a duty to detain in the county jail a prisoner charged with the commission of a misdemeanor under state law for the period between his arrest and his initial appearance before a court, magistrate, or clerk of courts as required by RC 2935.05 or 2935.13 or until he is otherwise released prior to such initial appearance. OAG 88–060, approved and followed by OAG 95–011.

3. Bond

A county sheriff may not accept cash appearance bonds in misdemeanor cases coming within the jurisdiction of the county court. 1960 OAG 1641.

2935.14 Rights of person arrested

If the person arrested is unable to offer sufficient bail or, if the offense charged be a felony, he shall, prior to being confined or removed from the county of arrest, as the case may be, be speedily permitted facilities to communicate with an attorney at law of his own choice, or to communicate with at least one relative or other person for the purpose of obtaining counsel (or in cases of misdemeanors or ordinance violation for the purpose of arranging bail). He shall not thereafter be confined or removed from the county or from the situs of initial detention until such attorney has had reasonable opportunity to confer with him privately, or other person to arrange bail, under such security measures as may be necessary under the circumstances.

Whoever, being a police officer in charge of a prisoner, or the custodian of any jail or place of confinement, violates this section shall be fined not less than one hundred nor more than five hundred dollars or imprisoned not more than thirty days, or both.

(128 v 97, eff. 1–1–60)

Historical and Statutory Notes

Ed. Note: 2935.14 contains provisions analogous to former 2935.16 and 2935.17, repealed by 128 v 97, eff. 1–1–60.

Ed. Note: Former 2935.14 repealed by 128 v 97, eff. 1–1–60; 1953 H 1; GC 13432–13.

Pre–1953 H 1 Amendments: 113 v 142, Ch 11, § 13

Cross References

Bail, Crim R 46

Right to counsel, O Const Art I §10

Right to counsel in juvenile court, 2151.352

Warrant or summons, arrest, Crim R 4

Library References

Arrest ⚡70.
Bail ⚡42.
Criminal Law ⚡221.
Westlaw Topic Nos. 110, 35, 49.

C.J.S. Arrest §§ 58 to 61.

C.J.S. Bail; Release and Detention Pending Proceedings §§ 6, 9 to 15, 17 to 18, 24 to 25, 31 to 32.

Research References

ALR Library

124 ALR 5th 1, Denial of Accused's Request for Initial Contact With Attorney in Cases Involving Offenses Other Than Drunk Driving--Cases Focusing on Presence of Inculpatory Statements.

109 ALR 5th 611, Denial of Accused's Request for Initial Contact With Attorney--Drunk Driving Cases.

Encyclopedias

OH Jur. 3d Criminal Law § 33, Effect of Violation of Statutory Right to Counsel.

OH Jur. 3d Criminal Law § 39, Upon Arrest or Confinement.

OH Jur. 3d Criminal Law § 55, Availability of Facilities.

OH Jur. 3d Criminal Law § 2150, Opportunity to Communicate With Attorney or Other Person.

OH Jur. 3d Family Law § 1575, Delivery of Child to Shelter or Detention Facility—Telephone and Visitation Rights.

Treatises and Practice Aids

Katz, Giannelli, Blair and Lipton, Baldwin's Ohio Practice, Criminal Law, § 24:14, Miranda Warnings--Telephone Calls.

Katz, Ohio Arrest, Search & Seizure § 21:2, Miranda Warnings.

Katz, Ohio Arrest, Search & Seizure App. A, Appendix A. Arrest Provisions: Checklist.

Painter, Ohio Driving Under the Influence § 10:8, Jurisdiction to Stop, Detain, and Arrest—Extraterritorial Detention and Arrest.

Gotherman, Babbit and Lang, Baldwin's Ohio Practice, Local Government Law—Municipal, § 28:17, Implied Consent, and Chemical Tests.

Law Review and Journal Commentaries

CONSTITUTIONAL LAW—Fifth Amendment—Suspect's Confusion About Miranda Rights—People v. Madison and State v. Jones, Note. 36 Ohio St L J 220 (1975).

State v. Magby: Application of the Miranda Doctrine to In–Custody Probationers, Note. 7 Cap U L Rev 103 (1977).

United States v McDowell: A Newer Standard For Waiver, Note. 19 U Tol L Rev 383 (Winter 1988).

Notes of Decisions

Ed. Note: *This section contains annotations from former RC 2935.16.*

---

1. Constitutional issues—Miranda warnings

Miranda warnings must be given prior to any custodial interrogation regardless of whether the individual is suspected of committing a felony or a misdemeanor. State v. Buchholz (Ohio 1984) 11 Ohio St.3d 24, 462 N.E.2d 1222, 11 O.B.R. 56. Criminal Law ⚿ 412.2(3)

Where a suspect, after being fully apprised of his constitutional rights under Miranda v Arizona, 384 US 436, 86 SCt 1602, 16 LEd(2d) 694 (1966), indicates an understanding of those rights, but subsequently acts in such a way as to reasonably alert the interrogating officer that the warnings given have been misapprehended, the officer must, before any further questioning, insure that the suspect fully understands his constitutional privilege against self-incrimination, as described in Miranda. State v. Jones (Ohio 1974) 37 Ohio St.2d 21, 306 N.E.2d 409, 66 O.O.2d 79. Criminal Law ⚿ 412.2(3)

A defendant detained before trial has an interest protected by the Due Process Clause in avoiding involuntary administration of antipsychotic drugs, and once the defendant moves to end treatment the state must establish both the need for and medical appropriateness of the drug; due process would be given if the state showed the treatment medically appropriate and with consideration given to less intrusive alternatives essential to the defendant's or other people's safety or showed that an adjudication of guilt or innocence could not be obtained by less intrusive means. Riggins v. Nevada (U.S.Nev. 1992) 112 S.Ct. 1810, 504 U.S. 127, 118 L.Ed.2d 479, on remand 109 Nev. 966, 860 P.2d 705.

2. —— Right to counsel, constitutional issues

Approval by the court of the permanent surrender of a child is purely an administrative matter, and not in the nature of an adversary proceeding; the court has no duty to advise the mother of her right to counsel or to appoint a lawyer for her in the event of indigency. In re K. (Ohio Juv. 1969) 31 Ohio Misc. 218, 282 N.E.2d 370, 60 O.O.2d 134, 60 O.O.2d 388.

An arrested person, regardless of the nature of the crime or offense for which he is being held, must be immediately offered an opportunity to communicate with an attorney or other person for the purpose of contacting an attorney, and such arrested person has the right to be immediately visited by the attorney of his choice. City of Dayton v. Nugent (Ohio Mun. 1970) 25 Ohio Misc. 31, 265 N.E.2d 826, 54 O.O.2d 31. Arrest ⚿ 70(1)

Where, during the investigation of a crime, a person not yet charged with the commission of such crime is informed prior to being interrogated by a deputy sheriff and an assistant prosecutor that he is not required to make any statement, and that any statement which he might make may be used against him, and where he has not requested that counsel be provided, such person has not been denied the assistance of counsel under US Const Am 6 and US Const Am 14. (See also Woodards v Maxwell, 303 FSupp 690, 24 Misc 157 (SD Ohio 1969).) State v. Woodards (Ohio 1966) 6 Ohio St.2d 14, 215 N.E.2d 568, 35 O.O.2d 8, certiorari denied 87 S.Ct. 289, 385 U.S. 930, 17 L.Ed.2d 212.

When a juvenile in custody asks to have his probation officer present, the question does not constitute a request for an attorney and subsequent statements by the juvenile are not taken in violation of the rule in Miranda v Arizona, 384 US 436, 86 SCt 1602, 16 LEd(2d) 694 (1966). (Ed. note: California law construed in light of federal constitution.) Fare v. Michael C. (U.S.Cal. 1979) 99 S.Ct. 2560, 442 U.S. 707, 61 L.Ed.2d 197, rehearing denied 100 S.Ct. 186, 444 U.S. 887, 62 L.Ed.2d 121.

Where a defendant is identified by the victim through a one-way mirror while the defendant is being fingerprinted and before any formal charges have been placed against him, the denial of the defendant's request for counsel is not unconstitutional. Hastings v. Cardwell (C.A.6 (Ohio) 1973) 480 F.2d 1202, certiorari denied 94 S.Ct. 1425, 415 U.S. 923, 39 L.Ed.2d 478.

Mandamus lies to compel police department, holding minor incommunicado under bond as material witness in felonious assault case, to permit attorney of minor to interview and counsel her. State ex rel. Chase v. City of Cleveland (Ohio 1936) 130 Ohio St. 587, 200 N.E. 840, 5 O.O. 222.

3. —— Bail, constitutional issues

State Constitution gives any defendant charged with a noncapital offense right to post bond and obtain his release from jail during the pendency of the criminal action. Gallagher v. Johnson (Ohio App. 11 Dist., 09-15-1998) 129 Ohio App.3d 775, 719 N.E.2d 60. Bail ⚿ 42

The denial of bail when the defendant has the ability to post bail and when the defendant is not physically, mentally, or emotionally in a condition to pose a danger to himself or the community is a denial of due process. State v. Meyers (Ohio Mun. 1978) 59 Ohio Misc. 124, 394 N.E.2d 1037, 13 O.O.3d 343. Constitutional Law ⚿ 262

4. Communication with relative or other person

RC 2935.14 and 2935.20 require effective communication with counsel which is to be determined on a case-by-case basis; unreasonable overt interference by a law enforcement officer in an accused's attempt to communicate with counsel constitutes a denial of effective communication with counsel. Varnacini v. Registrar, Ohio Bureau of Motor Vehicles (Franklin 1989) 59 Ohio App.3d 28, 570 N.E.2d 296.

Where law enforcement officers communicate with the brother of a person charged with the offense of operating a motor vehicle while under the influence of intoxicating liquor, there exists sufficient compliance with RC 2935.14. City of Toledo v. Dietz (Ohio 1965) 3 Ohio St.2d 30, 209 N.E.2d 127, 32 O.O.2d 16, certiorari denied 86 S.Ct. 432, 382 U.S. 956, 15 L.Ed.2d 360.

5. DWI; sobriety test

There can be no penalty attached to the refusal to take a test pursuant to RC 4511.191 where a police officer interferes with the alleged drunken driver's right to counsel afforded by RC 2935.14 and 2935.20. Varnacini v. Registrar, Ohio Bureau of Motor Vehicles (Franklin 1989) 59 Ohio App.3d 28, 570 N.E.2d 296.

A request to exercise the statutory right to counsel pursuant to RC 2935.14 and RC 2935.20 prior to taking a designated chemical sobriety test in and of itself does not constitute a refusal within the meaning of RC 4511.191. Snavely v. Dollison (Cuyahoga 1979) 61 Ohio App.2d 140, 400 N.E.2d 415, 15 O.O.3d 244.

A person "refuses" to take the test prescribed in RC 4511.191 where the attending law enforcement officers have complied with RC 2935.14 and RC 2935.20, and the accused continues to withhold his consent to submit to the test. McNulty v. Curry (Ohio 1975) 42 Ohio St.2d 341, 328 N.E.2d 798, 71 O.O.2d 317.

A good faith request of an arrested person to exercise his statutory right to call an attorney, before submitting to a chemical test required by RC 4511.191 does not constitute a refusal to take such test where the delay occasioned by the exercise of the statutory right will not unduly or unreasonably delay the administering of the test. Siegwald v. Curry (Franklin 1974) 40 Ohio App.2d 313, 319 N.E.2d 381, 69 O.O.2d 293. Automobiles ⚷ 144.1(1.20)

There is no denial of a constitutional right where a person under arrest for driving while intoxicated is denied the right to consult with counsel prior to determining whether to take a chemical test. Siegwald v. Curry (Franklin 1974) 40 Ohio App.2d 313, 319 N.E.2d 381, 69 O.O.2d 293.

A person under arrest for driving while intoxicated has a statutory right pursuant to RC 2935.14 and RC 2935.20 to communicate with an attorney, and where an exercise of such right is requested the police must forthwith permit the arrested person to use facilities to make such communication. Siegwald v. Curry (Franklin 1974) 40 Ohio App.2d 313, 319 N.E.2d 381, 69 O.O.2d 293. Automobiles ⚷ 349(14.1)

Whether a request to consult an attorney is made in good faith and whether the exercise of the right will unreasonably delay administering a chemical test are factual issues to be determined from the facts and circumstances involved. Siegwald v. Curry (Franklin 1974) 40 Ohio App.2d 313, 319 N.E.2d 381, 69 O.O.2d 293. Automobiles ⚷ 144.1(1.11)

A police department policy that no prisoner charged or under investigation for driving while intoxicated shall be permitted to place a call to an attorney or other person until after the expiration of a four-hour period from the time he is first booked, although required under RC 4511.19 to be offered an alcoholic content test within two hours from the alleged violation, is violative of RC 2935.14 and RC 2935.20, and deprives the prisoner of his statutory and constitutional rights to counsel. City of Dayton v. Nugent (Ohio Mun. 1970) 25 Ohio Misc. 31, 265 N.E.2d 826, 54 O.O.2d 31.

2935.15 Amount and disposition of bail

Amount of bail, and nature of security therefor in misdemeanor cases may be set by a schedule fixed by the court or magistrate, or it may be endorsed on the warrant by the magistrate or clerk of the issuing court. If the amount be not endorsed on the warrant, the schedule set by the court or magistrate before whom bail is taken shall prevail. All recognizances taken, or cash received shall be promptly transmitted to the court issuing the warrant, and further proceedings thereon shall be the same as if taken by the issuing court.

(128 v 97, eff. 1–1–60)

Historical and Statutory Notes

Ed. Note: Former 2935.15 repealed by 128 v 97, eff. 1–1–60; 1953 H 1; GC 13432–14; see now 2935.12 for provisions analogous to former 2935.15.

Pre–1953 H 1 Amendments: 113 v 142, Ch 11, § 14

Cross References

Bail, Crim R 46

Library References

Bail ⚷46, 50.
Westlaw Topic No. 49.

C.J.S. Bail; Release and Detention Pending Proceedings §§ 39 to 53, 66 to 70.

Research References

Treatises and Practice Aids

Katz, Giannelli, Blair and Lipton, Baldwin's Ohio Practice, Criminal Law, § 141:9, Motion for Show Cause Hearing.

WARRANT AND GENERAL PROVISIONS

2935.16 Prisoners held without process

When it comes to the attention of any judge or magistrate that a prisoner is being held in any jail or place of custody in his jurisdiction without commitment from a court or magistrate, he shall forthwith, by summary process, require the officer or person in charge of such jail or place of custody to disclose to such court or magistrate, in writing, whether or not he holds the person described or identified in the process and the court under whose process the prisoner is being held. If it appears from the disclosure that the prisoner is held solely under warrant of arrest from any court or magistrate, the judge or magistrate shall order the custodian to produce the prisoner forthwith before the court or magistrate issuing the warrant and if such be impossible for any reason, to produce him before the inquiring judge or magistrate. If it appears from the disclosure that the prisoner is held without process, such judge or magistrate shall require the custodian to produce the prisoner forthwith before him, there to be charged as provided in section 2935.06 of the Revised Code.

Whoever, being the person in temporary or permanent charge of any jail or place of confinement, violates this section shall be fined not less than one hundred nor more than five hundred dollars or imprisoned not more than ninety days, or both.

(128 v 97, eff. 1–1–60)

Historical and Statutory Notes

Ed. Note: Former 2935.16 repealed by 128 v 97, eff. 1–1–60; 1953 H 1; GC 13432–15; see now 2935.14 for provisions analogous to former 2935.16.

Pre–1953 H 1 Amendments: 113 v 142, Ch 11, § 15

Cross References

Accused unlawfully detained, 2937.34

Dereliction of duty, 2921.44

Habeas corpus, Ch 2725

Interfering with civil rights, 2921.45

Right to indictment, and to know nature of accusation, O Const Art I §10

Library References

Criminal Law ⚷216.

Westlaw Topic No. 110.

C.J.S. Criminal Law § 334.

Research References

Encyclopedias

OH Jur. 3d Criminal Law § 2050, Prisoners Held Without Commitment.

2935.17 Affidavit forms; authority of supreme court to prescribe

(A) An affidavit in either of the following forms is sufficient:

(1) "State of Ohio,

_________ County, ss:

Before me, A.B., personally came C.D., who being duly sworn according to law deposes and says that on or about the day of _________, _____, at the county of _________ one E.F. (here describe the offense as nearly according to the nature thereof as the case will admit, in ordinary concise language) C.D.

Swron to and subscribed before me this _____ day of ________, _____.

A.B., County Judge

Clerk of _________ Court"

(2) "State of Ohio,

_________ County, ss:

Before me, A.B., personally came C.D., who being duly sworn according to law says that on or about the day of _____, _____, one E.F. did: (here listing several common offenses, plainly but tersely described as: fail to stop at stop sign, pass at crest of grade, etc., with a ruled box before each, and then showing an X or distinctive mark in front of the offense claimed to be committed). C.D.

Sworn to before me and subscribed in my presence this ________ day of ________, _____

A.B., County Judge

Clerk of _________ Court"

(B) A complaint in the following form is sufficient:

"State of Ohio,

_________ County, ss:

The undersigned (assistant) prosecuting attorney of ________ County complains that on or about the ________ day of ________, _____, one E.F. did (here describing the offense committed as above) based on affidavit of ________ filed with me.

____

Prosecuting Attorney/City Director of Law"

Provided, that the supreme court of Ohio, may, by rule, provide for the uniform type and language to be used in any affidavit or complaint to be filed in any court inferior to the court of common pleas for violations of the motor vehicle and traffic acts and related ordinances and in any notice to violator to appear in such courts, and may require that such forms and no other, shall be received in such courts, and issued to violators.

(2000 H 495, eff. 5–9–00; 1977 H 219, eff. 11–1–77; 128 v 97)

Historical and Statutory Notes

Ed. Note: Former 2935.17 repealed by 128 v 97, eff. 1–1–60; 1953 H 1; GC 13432–16; see now 2935.14 and 2937.03 for provisions analogous to former 2935.17.

Pre–1953 H 1 Amendments: 113 v 143, Ch 11, § 16

Amendment Note: 2000 H 495 deleted references to nineteen hundred dates; and made other non-substantive changes.

Cross References

Freedom from unreasonable seizure; warrants, O Const Art I §14

Library References

Criminal Law ⟹211.

Westlaw Topic No. 110.

C.J.S. Criminal Law §§ 324, 327 to 332, 337.

Research References

Encyclopedias

OH Jur. 3d Criminal Law § 2339, Authorized Forms.

Treatises and Practice Aids

Katz, Giannelli, Blair and Lipton, Baldwin's Ohio Practice, Criminal Law, § 7:2, Complaint and Affidavit.

Katz, Giannelli, Blair and Lipton, Baldwin's Ohio Practice, Criminal Law, § 35:4, Oath Requirement.

Katz, Giannelli, Blair and Lipton, Baldwin's Ohio Practice, Criminal Law, § 35:8, Prosecutor's Complaint.

Katz, Ohio Arrest, Search & Seizure § 5:2, Issuance of Arrest Warrants.

Katz, Ohio Arrest, Search & Seizure App. A, Appendix A. Arrest Provisions: Checklist.

Gotherman, Babbit and Lang, Baldwin's Ohio Practice, Local Government Law—Municipal, § 28:40, Uniform Traffic Ticket.

Notes of Decisions

1. Commencement of prosecution

The arrest and prosecution of a person for violation of RC 3773.24 can be caused by two methods: (1) by filing an affidavit with a judge or clerk of a court of record or with a magistrate and (2) by filing an affidavit with the prosecuting attorney or attorney charged by law with the prosecution for the offense, who, in turn, shall file a complaint. State v. Maynard (Ohio 1964) 1 Ohio St.2d 57, 203 N.E.2d 332, 30 O.O.2d 32, certiorari denied 86 S.Ct. 105, 382 U.S. 871, 15 L.Ed.2d 110. Criminal Law ⚷ 209; Sunday ⚷ 29(2)

The provision of RC 2935.09 requiring the filing of an affidavit "for the purpose of having a complaint filed" thereon, applies to a prosecution under RC 3773.24. State v. Bowman (Montgomery 1962) 116 Ohio App. 285, 187 N.E.2d 627, 22 O.O.2d 117.

2. Sufficiency of affidavit

Where defendant and his counsel and the prosecution were unaware that the affidavit charging defendant with a traffic violation had not been verified until discovered by the judge at the end of the trial, a waiver may not be considered, and verification of the affidavit cannot be furnished at the end of the trial against objection of the defendant. Village of Pepper Pike v. LaMaida (Ohio Mun. 1970) 25 Ohio Misc. 252, 268 N.E.2d 296, 54 O.O.2d 410.

In order to sustain a conviction for reckless driving under RC 731.03 of the codified ordinances of the city of Dover, Ohio, the affidavit should allege facts and not conclusions, and the acts or omissions constituting the offense should be specifically charged so as to show how a person or persons or property was endangered. State v. Davis (Ohio Com.Pl. 1968) 16 Ohio Misc. 282, 241 N.E.2d 750, 45 O.O.2d 347. Automobiles ⚷ 351.1

An affidavit (traffic ticket) which does not charge that the speed at which a motor vehicle was allegedly operated is unreasonable (i.e., that the accused's speed was either greater or less than reasonable and proper) does not state an offense under a municipal ordinance which is identical to RC 4511.21. City of Willoughby v. Hugebeck (Lake 1964) 2 Ohio App.2d 36, 206 N.E.2d 234, 31 O.O.2d 75.

The failure to have an affidavit verified is jurisdictional and is not waived by a "not guilty" plea. City of South Euclid v. Samartini (Ohio Mun. 1965) 5 Ohio Misc. 38, 204 N.E.2d 425, 31 O.O.2d 87. Indictment And Information ⚷ 196(4)

3. Variance; amendment

An affidavit or sworn complaint in a misdemeanor charge is not subject to amendment by the court. City of Hamilton v. Petty (Ohio App. 1 Dist. 1972) 33 Ohio App.2d 194, 293 N.E.2d 881, 62 O.O.2d 286. Indictment And Information ⚷ 162

Amendments to affidavits filed in criminal actions are not permitted under authority of RC 2941.30. City of South Euclid v. Samartini (Ohio Mun. 1965) 5 Ohio Misc. 38, 204 N.E.2d 425, 31 O.O.2d 87.

The date the offense occurred is not such an immaterial part of the affidavit that it may be changed with impunity after the affidavit has been verified. City of South Euclid v. Samartini (Ohio Mun. 1965) 5 Ohio Misc. 38, 204 N.E.2d 425, 31 O.O.2d 87.

The fact that the charge in the indictment does not conform to that originally made in the affidavit does not affect the validity of the conviction. Stebelton v. Haskins (Ohio 1964) 177 Ohio St. 52, 201 N.E.2d 884, 29 O.O.2d 76.

4. Uniform traffic citation

Mayor, as conservator of peace, was "law enforcement officer" within limits of city and, as such, would have been empowered to sign Uniform Traffic Ticket charging defendant with traffic violation. Toledo v. Weber (Ohio Mun., 07-01-1997) 87 Ohio Misc.2d 26, 688 N.E.2d 1146. Automobiles ⚷ 351.1

Uniform Traffic Ticket is necessary to commence moving traffic prosecution in court inferior to common pleas court, regardless of whether officer or private citizen is bringing complaint. Toledo v. Weber (Ohio Mun., 07-01-1997) 87 Ohio Misc.2d 26, 688 N.E.2d 1146. Automobiles ⚷ 351.1

Only law enforcement officer, not private citizen, can be issuing complainant on Uniform Traffic Ticket, which is necessary to commence moving traffic prosecution in court inferior to common pleas court; private citizen must seek his or her recourse through prosecuting attorney. Toledo v. Weber (Ohio Mun., 07-01-1997) 87 Ohio Misc.2d 26, 688 N.E.2d 1146. Automobiles ⚷ 351.1

The Ohio Traffic Rules adopted pursuant to RC 2935.17 and RC 2937.46 are statutory in origin and therefore do not supersede statutes with which they conflict. City of Toledo v. Fogel (Lucas 1985) 20 Ohio App.3d 146, 485 N.E.2d 302, 20 O.B.R. 180. Courts ⚡ 85(1)

Variances between the Ohio uniform traffic ticket and a local traffic ticket prepared after the Ohio uniform traffic ticket was adopted are grounds for dismissal of the local-ticket complaint if the defendant is thereby prejudiced. City of Cleveland v. Winchell (Cuyahoga 1981) 3 Ohio App.3d 186, 444 N.E.2d 465, 3 O.B.R. 212.

The complaint (and summons) in traffic cases is the Ohio uniform traffic ticket set out in the appendix of the forms of Ohio uniform traffic rules and is binding on all courts inferior to the court of common pleas; see Traf R 1(A) and Traf R 3(A). City of Cleveland v. Austin (Cuyahoga 1978) 55 Ohio App.2d 215, 380 N.E.2d 1357, 9 O.O.3d 368.

2935.18 Contents of warrant, summons or notice

A warrant, summons, or notice of a peace officer shall either contain a copy of the affidavit or recite the substance of the accusation. A warrant shall be directed to a specific officer or to a department designated by its chief, and shall command such officer or member of department to take the accused and bring the accused forthwith before the magistrate or court issuing such warrant to be dealt with according to law. A summons shall be directed to the officer or department, and shall command the officer or department to notify the accused by serving a copy of such summons upon the accused. The following form of warrant is sufficient:

"The State of Ohio,

________ County, ss:

To the Sheriff (other Officer):

Greetings:

Whereas there has been filed with me an affidavit of which the following is a copy (here copy) or the substance, (here set forth the substance, omitting formal parts). These are therefore to command you to take the said E.F., if E.F. is found in your county, or if E.F. is not found in your county, that you pursue after E.F. in any other county in this state and take and safely keep the said E.F. so that you have E.F. forthwith before me or some other magistrate of said county to answer the said complaint and be further dealt with according to law.

Given under my hand this ____ day of ________, ____.

A.B., Judge of ________ Court

Clerk of ________ Court"

The following form of summons is sufficient:

"The State of Ohio, ________ County, ss:

To the Bailiff or ________ Constable:

Whereas there has been filed before me an Affidavit (Complaint) of which the following is a copy (here copy) or the substance (here set forth the substance, omitting formal parts). You are commanded to summon one said E.F. to appear before me on the ____ day of ________, ____, at ____ o'clock, ___. M., at ________ Building, ________, Ohio, to answer to said charge.

You will make due return of this summons forthwith upon service.

A.B., Judge of ________ Court

Clerk of ________ Court"

(2000 H 495, eff. 5–9–00; 128 v 97, eff. 1–1–60)

Historical and Statutory Notes

Ed. Note: 2935.18 contains provisions analogous to former 2935.20, repealed by 128 v 97, eff. 1–1–60.

Ed. Note: Former 2935.18 repealed by 128 v 97, eff. 1–1–60; 1953 H 1; GC 13432–17.

Pre–1953 H 1 Amendments: 113 v 143, Ch 11, § 17

Amendment Note: 2000 H 495 deleted references to nineteen hundred dates; made changes to reflect gender neutral language; and made other nonsubstantive changes.

Cross References

Freedom from unreasonable seizure; warrants, O Const Art I §14

Serving and filing papers, Crim R 49

Warrant and summons, form, Crim R 4, 9

Library References

Criminal Law ⚷218.

Westlaw Topic No. 110.

C.J.S. Criminal Law §§ 334, 338.

Research References

Encyclopedias

OH Jur. 3d Criminal Law § 2080, Form and Content of Summons; Multiple Summons.

Treatises and Practice Aids

Katz, Giannelli, Blair and Lipton, Baldwin's Ohio Practice, Criminal Law, § 7:4, Form of the Warrant and Summons.

Katz, Giannelli, Blair and Lipton, Baldwin's Ohio Practice, Criminal Law, § 133:5, Summons Upon Complaint, Indictment, or Information.

Katz, Giannelli, Blair and Lipton, Baldwin's Ohio Practice, Criminal Law, § 133:26, Arrest Warrant on Complaint.

Katz, Giannelli, Blair and Lipton, Baldwin's Ohio Practice, Criminal Law, § 133:27, Arrest Warrant on Complaint (Additional Form).

Katz, Giannelli, Blair and Lipton, Baldwin's Ohio Practice, Criminal Law, § 133:28, Arrest Warrant on Complaint—Defendant's Name Unknown.

Katz, Giannelli, Blair and Lipton, Baldwin's Ohio Practice, Criminal Law, § 142:16, Warrant Upon Indictment or Information Issued by Court.

Katz, Ohio Arrest, Search & Seizure App. A, Appendix A. Arrest Provisions: Checklist.

Princehorn, Baldwin's Ohio Practice, Local Government Law—Township, § 11:13, Service of Process.

Notes of Decisions

Directed to officer 1

1. Directed to officer

The fact that an arrest warrant is not directed to a specific officer or department as required by RC 2935.18 will not warrant a motion to quash where the accused is not prejudiced thereby. State v. Sizer (Ohio Com.Pl. 1970) 25 Ohio Misc. 245, 265 N.E.2d 468, 54 O.O.2d 406. Criminal Law ⚷ 218(2)

2935.19 Form of affidavit

An affidavit in the form following is sufficient:

"The State of Ohio,

________ County, ss:

Before me, A.B., personally came C.D., who being duly sworn according to law, deposes and says that on or about the ____ day of ________, ____ at the county of ________, one E.F. (here describe the offense committed as nearly according to the nature thereof as the case will admit, in ordinary and concise language.)

Sworn to and subscribed before me, this ____ day of ________, ____.

A.B., Judge"

(2000 H 495, eff. 5–9–00; 127 v 1039, eff. 1–1–58; 1953 H 1; GC 13432–18)

Historical and Statutory Notes

Pre–1953 H 1 Amendments: 113 v 143, Ch 11, § 18

Amendment Note: 2000 H 495 deleted references to nineteen hundred dates; and made other nonsubstantive changes.

Cross References

Freedom from unreasonable seizure; warrants, O Const Art I §14

Library References

Criminal Law ⇔208.

Westlaw Topic No. 110.

C.J.S. Criminal Law §§ 324 to 333, 337.

Research References

Encyclopedias

OH Jur. 3d Criminal Law § 2096, Requisites and Sufficiency of Form of Affidavit, Generally.

OH Jur. 3d Criminal Law § 2339, Authorized Forms.

Treatises and Practice Aids

Katz, Ohio Arrest, Search & Seizure App. A, Appendix A. Arrest Provisions: Checklist.

Notes of Decisions

Variance in charge 1

1. Variance in charge

The fact that the charge in the indictment does not conform to that originally made in the affidavit does not affect the validity of the conviction. Stebelton v. Haskins (Ohio 1964) 177 Ohio St. 52, 201 N.E.2d 884, 29 O.O.2d 76.

2935.20 Right of one in custody to be visited by attorney

After the arrest, detention, or any other taking into custody of a person, with or without a warrant, such person shall be permitted forthwith facilities to communicate with an attorney at law of his choice who is entitled to practice in the courts of this state, or to communicate with any other person of his choice for the purpose of obtaining counsel. Such communication may be made by a reasonable number of telephone calls or in any other reasonable manner. Such person shall have a right to be visited immediately by any attorney at law so obtained who is entitled to practice in the courts of this state, and to consult with him privately. No officer or any other agent of this state shall prevent, attempt to prevent, or advise such person against the communication, visit, or consultation provided for by this section.

Whoever violates this section shall be fined not less than twenty-five nor more than one hundred dollars or imprisoned not more than thirty days, or both.

(131 v H 471, eff. 11–1–65)

Historical and Statutory Notes

Ed. Note: Former 2935.20 repealed by 128 v 97, eff. 1–1–60; 127 v 1039; 1953 H 1; GC 13432–19; see now 2935.18 for provisions analogous to former 2935.20.

Pre–1953 H 1 Amendments: 113 v 143, Ch 11, § 19

Cross References

Dereliction of duty, 2921.44

Due process and equal protection, US Const Am 5, 14

Interference with civil rights, 2921.45

Right to counsel, US Const Am 6; O Const Art I §10

Right to counsel in commitment proceedings, 5122.15

Trial for crimes, witness, O Const Art I §10

Library References

Criminal Law ⇔641.3.

Westlaw Topic No. 110.

C.J.S. Criminal Law §§ 277, 282 to 289, 293.

Research References

ALR Library

124 ALR 5th 1, Denial of Accused's Request for Initial Contact With Attorney in Cases Involving Offenses Other Than Drunk Driving--Cases Focusing on Presence of Inculpatory Statements.

109 ALR 5th 611, Denial of Accused's Request for Initial Contact With Attorney--Drunk Driving Cases.

96 ALR 5th 327, Denial Of, or Interference With, Accused's Right to Have Attorney Initially Contact Accused.

Encyclopedias

OH Jur. 3d Criminal Law § 31, Nature of Proceedings to Which Right Applies; Seriousness of Offense.

OH Jur. 3d Criminal Law § 33, Effect of Violation of Statutory Right to Counsel.

OH Jur. 3d Criminal Law § 36, Generally; Critical Stages.

OH Jur. 3d Criminal Law § 55, Availability of Facilities.

OH Jur. 3d Criminal Law § 56, Interference With Conference.

OH Jur. 3d Criminal Law § 1557, Effect of Arrestee's Request to Consult Counsel.

OH Jur. 3d Criminal Law § 2150, Opportunity to Communicate With Attorney or Other Person.

Treatises and Practice Aids

Katz, Giannelli, Blair and Lipton, Baldwin's Ohio Practice, Criminal Law, § 27:4, Right to Counsel—Attachment.

Katz, Giannelli, Blair and Lipton, Baldwin's Ohio Practice, Criminal Law, § 29:5, Exclusionary Rule—Statutes.

Katz, Giannelli, Blair and Lipton, Baldwin's Ohio Practice, Criminal Law, § 75:5, Attachment of Right—"Critical" Stages.

Katz, Giannelli, Blair and Lipton, Baldwin's Ohio Practice, Criminal Law, § 151:1, Waiver of Right to Counsel.

Katz, Giannelli, Blair and Lipton, Baldwin's Ohio Practice, Criminal Law, § 151:3, Assignment of Counsel.

Katz, Giannelli, Blair and Lipton, Baldwin's Ohio Practice, Criminal Law, § 151:4, Entry as to Counsel Assigned.

Katz, Giannelli, Blair and Lipton, Baldwin's Ohio Practice, Criminal Law, § 24:14, Miranda Warnings--Telephone Calls.

Katz, Ohio Arrest, Search & Seizure § 21:2, Miranda Warnings.

Katz, Ohio Arrest, Search & Seizure § 24:2, Attachment of the Sixth Amendment Right to Counsel.

Katz, Ohio Arrest, Search & Seizure § 27:3, Exclusion for Violation of State Law.

Katz, Ohio Arrest, Search & Seizure App. A, Appendix A. Arrest Provisions: Checklist.

Katz, Ohio Arrest, Search & Seizure App. E, Appendix E. Provisions for Interrogation and Pretrial Identification of Suspect: Checklist.

Katz, Ohio Arrest, Search & Seizure § 17:12, Right to Counsel Prior to Taking Alcohol or Drug Tests.

Hennenberg & Reinhart, Ohio Criminal Defense Motions F 15.01, Motion for Access to Telephone-Miscellaneous Motions.

Painter, Ohio Driving Under the Influence § 10:8, Jurisdiction to Stop, Detain, and Arrest—Extraterritorial Detention and Arrest.

Painter, Ohio Driving Under the Influence § 6:17, Als Appeal Issues in Refusal Cases—Refusal of Test—Request for Counsel Prior to Testing.

Painter, Ohio Driving Under the Influence § 8:40, Right to Counsel.

Gotherman, Babbit and Lang, Baldwin's Ohio Practice, Local Government Law—Municipal, § 28:17, Implied Consent, and Chemical Tests.

Law Review and Journal Commentaries

Arrest and Detention Procedures, Arthur V. N. Brooks and David M. Liebenthal. 38 Clev B J 85 (March 1967).

Brewer v. Williams: Express Waiver Extended To Sixth Amendment Right to Counsel, Note. 4 Ohio N U L Rev 833 (1977).

The Effects of Tucker on the "Fruits" of Illegally Obtained Statements, Comment. 24 Clev St L Rev 689 (1975).

The Involuntary Confession and the Right to Due Process: Is a Criminal Defendant Better Protected in the Federal Courts Than In Ohio?, Barbara Child. 10 Akron L Rev 261 (Fall 1976).

Manipulated by *Miranda*: A Critical Analysis of Bright Lines and Voluntary Confessions Under *United States v. Dickerson*, Casenote. 68 U Cin L Rev 555 (Winter 2000).

The Right to Remain Silent: The Use of Pre–Arrest Silence in *United States v. Oplinger*, 150 F.3d 1061 (5th Cir. 1998), Casenote. 68 U Cin L Rev 505 (Winter 2000).

Representation Under the Ohio Public Defender Act, Note. 38 Ohio St L J 855 (1977).

State v. Sargent: Constricting the Right to Counsel, Note. 2 Ohio N U L Rev 811 (1975).

State v. Wellman: "Intelligent" and "Knowing" Waiver of Right to Counsel, Note. 2 Ohio N U L Rev 53 (1974).

United States v McDowell: A Newer Standard For Waiver, Note. 19 U Tol L Rev 383 (Winter 1988).

Notes of Decisions

Ed. Note: This section contains annotations from former RC 2935.16.

---

1. Constitutional issues generally

Even though defendant's statutory right to communicate with attorney was violated by police officer's unreasonable interference with her communication with her attorney after her arrest for operating motor vehicle while under influence of alcohol or drugs (OMVI), defendant's right to due process was not violated, and thus suppression of defendant's breath-alcohol test results was not necessary. State v. Layton (Ohio App. 10 Dist., 05-14-1996) 111 Ohio App.3d 76, 675 N.E.2d 862. Automobiles ⚷ 421; Constitutional Law ⚷ 268.1(3)

Officers' failure to provide driver with access to attorney when she expressed desire for attorney after refusing to sign waiver of rights form presented by officers during booking process violated driver's Fourteenth Amendment right to due process. Lakewood v. Waselenchuk (Ohio App. 8 Dist., 05-02-1994) 94 Ohio App.3d 684, 641 N.E.2d 767, dismissed, appeal not allowed 70 Ohio St.3d 1454, 639 N.E.2d 793. Constitutional Law ⚷ 266.1(2); Criminal Law ⚷ 641.3(4)

The denial of bail when the defendant has the ability to post bail and when the defendant is not physically, mentally, or emotionally in a condition to pose a danger to himself or the community is a denial of due process. State v. Meyers (Ohio Mun. 1978) 59 Ohio Misc. 124, 394 N.E.2d 1037, 13 O.O.3d 343. Constitutional Law ⚷ 262

2. Miranda warnings

Where a suspect, after being fully apprised of his constitutional rights under Miranda v Arizona, 384 US 436, 86 SCt 1602, 16 LEd(2d) 694 (1966), indicates an understanding of those rights, but subsequently acts in such a way as to reasonably alert the interrogating officer that the warnings given have been misapprehended, the officer must, before any further questioning, insure that the suspect fully understands his constitutional privilege against self-incrimination, as described in Miranda. State v. Jones (Ohio 1974) 37 Ohio St.2d 21, 306 N.E.2d 409, 66 O.O.2d 79. Criminal Law ⚷ 412.2(3)

The "right to counsel" does not mean a suspect can demand an attorney be produced "on call"; a suspect must simply be informed of his right to an attorney and to appointed counsel and be told that if the police cannot provide appointed counsel they will not question him until he waives the right. Duckworth v. Eagan (U.S.Ind. 1989) 109 S.Ct. 2875, 492 U.S. 195, 106 L.Ed.2d 166.

A written statement given to a suspect by police adequately apprises him of his rights when it states: "you have the right to remain silent. Anything you say can be used against you in court. You have a right to talk to a lawyer for advice before we ask you any questions, and to have him with you during questioning. You have the right to the advice and presence of a lawyer even if you cannot afford to hire one. We have no way of giving you a lawyer, but one will be appointed for you, if you wish, before you go to court. If you wish to answer questions now without a lawyer present, you have the right to stop answering questions at any time. You also have the right to stop answering at any time until you have talked to a lawyer"; this statement does not impermissibly link the right to counsel to some future time following police interrogation. Duckworth v. Eagan (U.S.Ind. 1989) 109 S.Ct. 2875, 492 U.S. 195, 106 L.Ed.2d 166.

3. Affording opportunity to contact attorney—constitutional right

Any violation of driver's statutory right to counsel occasioned by uncounselled administration of breath alcohol tests did not require exclusion of test results in subsequent prosecution, where no state constitutional protection was implicated by such action. State v. Perez (Ohio App. 1 Dist., Hamilton, 03-25-2005) No. C-040363, No. C-040364, No. C-040365, 2005-Ohio-1326, 2005 WL 678947, Unreported. Criminal Law ⚷ 394.1(3)

There is no constitutional right to counsel prior to taking breathalyzer test. Lexington v. Reddington (Richland 1993) 86 Ohio App.3d 643, 621 N.E.2d 758, motion overruled 66 Ohio St.3d 1510, 613 N.E.2d 1048. Criminal Law ⚷ 641.3(8.1)

RC 2935.14 and 2935.20 require effective communication with counsel which is to be determined on a case-by-case basis; unreasonable overt interference by a law enforcement officer in an accused's attempt to communicate with counsel constitutes a denial of effective communication with counsel. Varnacini v. Registrar, Ohio Bureau of Motor Vehicles (Franklin 1989) 59 Ohio App.3d 28, 570 N.E.2d 296.

There is no denial of a constitutional right where a person under arrest for driving while intoxicated is denied the right to consult with counsel prior to determining whether to take a chemical test. Siegwald v. Curry (Franklin 1974) 40 Ohio App.2d 313, 319 N.E.2d 381, 69 O.O.2d 293.

Where an accused is provided instructions as to his rights to remain silent (pursuant to Miranda v Arizona, 384 US 436, 86 SCt 1602, 16 LEd(2d) 694 (1966)), refuses to sign a waiver that he knowingly and intelligently relinquishes such rights, indicates that he will sign nothing before consulting an attorney, and is not denied the use of facilities for contacting counsel, his voluntary statements pertaining to the alleged crime are admissible in evidence and such allowance is not a violation of US Const Am 5 and US Const Am 14. State v. Jones

(Franklin 1973) 35 Ohio App.2d 92, 300 N.E.2d 230, 64 O.O.2d 208, reversed 37 Ohio St.2d 21, 306 N.E.2d 409, 66 O.O.2d 79, certiorari denied 95 S.Ct. 109, 419 U.S. 860, 42 L.Ed.2d 94. Constitutional Law ⚿ 266.1(1); Criminal Law ⚿ 412.2(5)

A police department policy that no prisoner charged or under investigation for driving while intoxicated shall be permitted to place a call to an attorney or other person until after the expiration of a four-hour period from the time he is first booked, although required under RC 4511.19 to be offered an alcoholic content test within two hours from the alleged violation, is violative of RC 2935.14 and RC 2935.20, and deprives the prisoner of his statutory and constitutional rights to counsel. City of Dayton v. Nugent (Ohio Mun. 1970) 25 Ohio Misc. 31, 265 N.E.2d 826, 54 O.O.2d 31.

An arrested person, regardless of the nature of the crime or offense for which he is being held, must be immediately offered an opportunity to communicate with an attorney or other person for the purpose of contacting an attorney, and such arrested person has the right to be immediately visited by the attorney of his choice. City of Dayton v. Nugent (Ohio Mun. 1970) 25 Ohio Misc. 31, 265 N.E.2d 826, 54 O.O.2d 31. Arrest ⚿ 70(1)

Where a defendant is identified by the victim through a one-way mirror while the defendant is being fingerprinted and before any formal charges have been placed against him, the denial of the defendant's request for counsel is not unconstitutional. Hastings v. Cardwell (C.A.6 (Ohio) 1973) 480 F.2d 1202, certiorari denied 94 S.Ct. 1425, 415 U.S. 923, 39 L.Ed.2d 478.

The refusal to allow consultation with counsel prior to the administration of a breath analysis test constitutes a denial of due process. State v Larson, No. 16–CA–88 (5th Dist Ct App, Fairfield, 12–8–88).

A refusal by the police to allow a person arrested for drunk driving to call her attorney where the call would not impede the police in obtaining either a timely blood-alcohol sample or a timely refusal to take the test violates the due process guarantee of the Fourteenth Amendment and necessitates exclusion of the blood-alcohol test results. State v Scarlett, No. CA 10378 (2d Dist Ct App, Montgomery, 9–3–87).

4. —— Statutory right, affording opportunity to contact attorney

Imposition of the exclusionary rule does not lie as remedy for police violation of an accused's statutory right to counsel in prosecutions for operating a motor vehicle under the influence (OVI). State v. Franz (Ohio App. 5 Dist., Knox, 04-13-2005) No. 04CA000013, 2005-Ohio-1755, 2005 WL 856929, Unreported, appeal not allowed 106 Ohio St.3d 1508, 833 N.E.2d 1250, 2005-Ohio-4605. Criminal Law ⚿ 394.1(1)

Exclusionary rule is not applicable as sanction for violation of statutory right of one in custody to be visited by attorney. State v. Lloyd (Ohio App. 7 Dist., 04-15-1998) 126 Ohio App.3d 95, 709 N.E.2d 913. Criminal Law ⚿ 394.1(1)

Audiotaping of telephone conversation between arrestee charged with driving under the influence of alcohol and her attorney violated arrestee's statutory right to effective communication with legal counsel; police could have ensured that arrestee did not consume some substance that would affect results of blood-alcohol test, without invading privacy of consultation with attorney, by videotaping without sound recording. Dobbins v. Ohio Bur. of Motor Vehicles (Ohio, 06-05-1996) 75 Ohio St.3d 533, 664 N.E.2d 908, 1996-Ohio-454. Automobiles ⚿ 421; Criminal Law ⚿ 641.3(7)

In absence of any constitutional violations, when police violate statutory right to counsel of arrestee charged with driving under the influence of alcohol, and arrestee refuses to submit to blood alcohol test until she effectively speaks with her attorney, arrestee remains subject to license suspension; by refusing to submit to test contingent on receiving advice of counsel, arrestee has, for purposes of implied consent statute, "refused" to take chemical-alcohol test. Dobbins v. Ohio Bur. of Motor Vehicles (Ohio, 06-05-1996) 75 Ohio St.3d 533, 664 N.E.2d 908, 1996-Ohio-454. Automobiles ⚿ 144.1(1.20)

Imposition of exclusionary rule does not lie as remedy for police violation of accused's statutory right to counsel in prosecution arising under statute prohibiting operation of vehicle if operator has concentration of ten hundredths of one gram or more by weight of alcohol per 210 liters of his breath, so as to preclude prosecution from presenting evidence of result of otherwise admissible breath alcohol content analysis of accused solely because of police failure to comply with statutory right to counsel. State v. Griffith (Ohio, 02-21-1996) 74 Ohio St.3d 554, 660 N.E.2d 710, 1996-Ohio-256. Criminal Law ⚿ 394.1(1)

Exclusionary rule is not applicable as sanction for violating arrestee's statutory right to communicate with attorney. Fairborn v. Mattachione (Ohio, 06-28-1995) 72 Ohio St.3d 345, 650 N.E.2d 426, 1995-Ohio-207, on remand 1997 WL 368366. Criminal Law ⚿ 394.1(1)

Defendant has statutory right to counsel upon arrest, detention or being taken into custody which goes beyond right to counsel guaranteed by State and Federal Constitutions and requires that suspect be given effective communication with attorney. State v. Mason (Ohio App. 1 Dist., 12-07-1994) 99 Ohio App.3d 165, 650 N.E.2d 144, dismissed, appeal not allowed 72 Ohio St.3d 1413, 647 N.E.2d 1388. Criminal Law ⚿ 641.3(4)

Suppression of breathalyzer results was appropriate remedy for police officers' violation of driver's statutory right to consult attorney and constitutional right to due process when they continued booking process for driving under influence of alcohol despite driver's expressed desire for attorney upon her refusal to sign waiver of rights form during booking process. Lakewood v. Waselenchuk (Ohio App. 8 Dist., 05-02-1994) 94 Ohio App.3d 684, 641 N.E.2d 767, dismissed, appeal not allowed 70 Ohio St.3d 1454, 639 N.E.2d 793. Automobiles ⚿ 411; Criminal Law ⚿ 394.1(2)

Officers violated driver's statutory right to consult attorney and to be permitted facilities to communicate with attorney when they continued booking process for driving under influence of alcohol after driver expressed desire for attorney by indicating, when presented second waiver of rights form, that she was "scared" and that she thought she should have an attorney; when confronted by prospective breathalyzer test and implied consent form one hour and fifteen minutes after her arrest she again expressed dismay at having to make such decision without advice of counsel. Lakewood v. Waselenchuk (Ohio App. 8 Dist., 05-02-1994) 94 Ohio App.3d 684, 641 N.E.2d 767, dismissed, appeal not allowed 70 Ohio St.3d 1454, 639 N.E.2d 793. Criminal Law ⚷ 641.3(8.1)

It was unnecessary to decide whether right to counsel superseded statutory requirement that breathalyzer test be given within two hours of arrest in case in which, had driver's request for counsel been heeded at outset of booking procedures when first expressed, there would have been ample time to allow attorney-client communication and still proceed with test within time limit. Lakewood v. Waselenchuk (Ohio App. 8 Dist., 05-02-1994) 94 Ohio App.3d 684, 641 N.E.2d 767, dismissed, appeal not allowed 70 Ohio St.3d 1454, 639 N.E.2d 793. Criminal Law ⚷ 641.3(8.1)

Officers who arrested defendant for driving while intoxicated did not provide defendant with reasonable opportunity to communicate with attorney of his choice or to communicate with any other person of his choice about obtaining counsel, where officers at 3 a.m. on New Year's Day gave defendant telephone and telephone book and told him he would have 20 minutes to use telephone to secure counsel; therefore, since officers failed to comply with statute permitting defendant to communicate with counsel, results of defendant's breath-alcohol test should have been suppressed. Lexington v. Reddington (Richland 1993) 86 Ohio App.3d 643, 621 N.E.2d 758, motion overruled 66 Ohio St.3d 1510, 613 N.E.2d 1048. Automobiles ⚷ 421

The refusal to permit a suspected drunk driver to make additional telephone calls to contact an attorney for advice about whether to comply with a request for a chemical test of his level of intoxication does not constitute compliance with RC 2935.20; thus, the suspect's failure to take the test does not constitute a refusal within the meaning of RC 4511.191 and the prisoner has not refused to take the test although the officer so marks the implied consent form with at least forty-two minutes of the two-hour test limitation period remaining. Stout v. McCullion (Franklin 1990) 70 Ohio App.3d 447, 591 N.E.2d 373.

RC 2935.14 and 2935.20 require effective communication with counsel which is to be determined on a case-by-case basis; unreasonable overt interference by a law enforcement officer in an accused's attempt to communicate with counsel constitutes a denial of effective communication with counsel. Varnacini v. Registrar, Ohio Bureau of Motor Vehicles (Franklin 1989) 59 Ohio App.3d 28, 570 N.E.2d 296.

There can be no penalty attached to the refusal to take a test pursuant to RC 4511.191 where a police officer interferes with the alleged drunken driver's right to counsel afforded by RC 2935.14 and 2935.20. Varnacini v. Registrar, Ohio Bureau of Motor Vehicles (Franklin 1989) 59 Ohio App.3d 28, 570 N.E.2d 296.

When a person arrested for drunk driving calls his attorney immediately upon being brought to a police station, then says he will not decide whether to submit to a chemical test until he has consulted with his attorney, and the attorney arrives within fifteen minutes but is denied access to his client, the person has not "refused" to submit to a chemical test within the meaning of RC 4511.191(D). Stone v. McCullion (Hamilton 1985) 27 Ohio App.3d 112, 500 N.E.2d 326, 27 O.B.R. 143.

Where a police officer extends ample courtesies to a plaintiff accused of driving while intoxicated in allowing him the use of a telephone to reach his attorney, the officer must inform the plaintiff at the time of the last request to take the test that no further use of the telephone will be allowed and that it is necessary for the plaintiff to make a decision, after failing to contact such attorney, as to whether he will refuse to take the test without the advice of his counsel. Lawton v. Bureau of Motor Vehicles (Franklin 1978) 57 Ohio App.2d 159, 386 N.E.2d 267, 11 O.O.3d 160. Automobiles ⚷ 421

Where a defendant who is charged with operating a vehicle while under the influence of alcohol is allowed to communicate with his attorney by telephone pursuant to RC 2935.20, and when his conduct is observed during that communication with his knowledge and without complaint of a request for privacy, testimony offered concerning such conduct does not deprive the defendant of the effective assistance of counsel. State v. Sargent (Ohio 1975) 41 Ohio St.2d 85, 322 N.E.2d 634, 70 O.O.2d 169.

A person under arrest for driving while intoxicated has a statutory right pursuant to RC 2935.14 and RC 2935.20 to communicate with an attorney, and where an exercise of such right is requested the police must forthwith permit the arrested person to use facilities to make such communication. Siegwald v. Curry (Franklin 1974) 40 Ohio App.2d 313, 319 N.E.2d 381, 69 O.O.2d 293. Automobiles ⚷ 349(14.1)

Mandamus lies to compel police department, holding minor incommunicado under bond as material witness in felonious assault case, to permit attorney of minor to interview and counsel her. State ex rel. Chase v. City of Cleveland (Ohio 1936) 130 Ohio St. 587, 200 N.E. 840, 5 O.O. 222.

Where an arresting officer provided defendant with telephone and Dayton phone directory upon his request to speak with an attorney, the officer complied with his duty to permit the defendant "facilities to communicate with an attorney at law of his choice who is entitled to practice in the courts of this state" per RC 2935.20, and trial court properly denied the defendant's motion to suppress breath test results. State v Hudd, No. 92–CA–37,

1993 WL 435562 (2d Dist Ct App, Greene, 10–25–93).

Following a criminal arrest where defendant is advised of his right to counsel, RC 2935.20 does not require that questioning officer force defendant to make a telephone call to an attorney. State v Williams, No. L–81–360 (6th Dist Ct App, Lucas, 5–28–82).

5. Waiver of right to counsel

Where defense had ample opportunity before trial to determine whether the police authorities adequately afforded the defendant his constitutional and statutory rights to counsel, and through the cross-examination of police officer became aware of the fact that defendant was not given the opportunity to make telephone calls on the day of his arrest, by failing to timely file his motion to suppress before trial, the defendant waived any error. State v. Moody (Ohio 1978) 55 Ohio St.2d 64, 377 N.E.2d 1008, 9 O.O.3d 71. Criminal Law ⚷ 698(1)

6. DWI and sobriety test

For purposes of implied consent statute, motorist refused to submit to chemical test when she asked to speak to her attorney before submitting to test, although motorist had statutory right to counsel; motorist remained subject to administrative license suspension (ALS) if police violated statutory right to counsel and motorist refused to submit to test until she effectively spoke with attorney. State v. Huffman (Ohio App. 6 Dist., Wood, 11-10-2005) No. WD-05-007, 2005-Ohio-6005, 2005 WL 3008902, Unreported, appeal not allowed 109 Ohio St.3d 1405, 845 N.E.2d 522, 2006-Ohio-1703. Automobiles ⚷ 144.1(1.20)

An arrestee remains subject to license suspension for refusal to submit to a breath test following arrest for driving under influence of alcohol where he declines to take the test pending advice from his attorney and after speaking with his attorney but within two hours of his arrest he agrees to take the test but police are unwilling to administer it to him. City of Shaker Heights v. Greenfelder (Ohio App. 8 Dist., Cuyahoga, 07-16-1998) No. 73046, 1998 WL 398217, Unreported, dismissed, appeal not allowed 84 Ohio St.3d 1433, 702 N.E.2d 1212.

A police officer is not required to have a defendant speak to his attorney again after he has voluntarily chosen not to follow the attorney's advice; additionally, the exclusionary rule is not a remedy for police violation of the statutory right to counsel pursuant to RC 2935.20 in a prosecution arising under RC 4511.19 such that the prosecution should be precluded from presenting evidence of the results of an otherwise admissible breath alcohol content analysis of the accused solely because of police failure to comply with RC 2935.20. State v. Luedy (Ohio App. 9 Dist., Summit, 03-20-1996) No. 17399, 1996 WL 122002, Unreported.

Under statute requiring that arrested defendant be given effective communication with attorney police must afford suspect believed to have driven with prohibited breath-alcohol content reasonable opportunity to speak to counsel, and must wait reasonable amount of time for suspect to attempt to contact counsel, provided that delay occasioned by exercise of right would not unduly or unreasonably delay administration of test. State v. Mason (Ohio App. 1 Dist., 12-07-1994) 99 Ohio App.3d 165, 650 N.E.2d 144, dismissed, appeal not allowed 72 Ohio St.3d 1413, 647 N.E.2d 1388. Automobiles ⚷ 421

Question whether police have waited for a reasonable time under the circumstances, to allow suspect believed to have driven automobile with impermissible breath-alcohol level to contact attorney before administering test, is matter to be determined on case-by-case basis. State v. Mason (Ohio App. 1 Dist., 12-07-1994) 99 Ohio App.3d 165, 650 N.E.2d 144, dismissed, appeal not allowed 72 Ohio St.3d 1413, 647 N.E.2d 1388. Automobiles ⚷ 421

Police violated statute requiring that suspects taken into custody be given opportunity to consult counsel, when officer conversing over telephone with father of suspect believed to have been operating vehicle with impermissible breath-alcohol level gave father 20 minutes to contact an attorney, changed his mind after father had hung up and compelled suspect to take test immediately, and father called back within 20–minute period; officer had violated promise and allowance of 20 minutes would not have impeded ability of police to administer breath test within two hours of violation, as required by statute. State v. Mason (Ohio App. 1 Dist., 12-07-1994) 99 Ohio App.3d 165, 650 N.E.2d 144, dismissed, appeal not allowed 72 Ohio St.3d 1413, 647 N.E.2d 1388. Automobiles ⚷ 421

When definite period of time was provided by police to father of arrestee suspected of driving automobile with impermissible breath-alcohol level, during which father could attempt to consult with attorney, and when there would have been time to proceed with test after waiting for allotted time, failure by police to abide by commitment to wait was police interference with suspect's ability to speak to attorney in violation of state statute, also violated defendant's due process rights, requiring that results of breath test be suppressed. State v. Mason (Ohio App. 1 Dist., 12-07-1994) 99 Ohio App.3d 165, 650 N.E.2d 144, dismissed, appeal not allowed 72 Ohio St.3d 1413, 647 N.E.2d 1388. Automobiles ⚷ 421; Constitutional Law ⚷ 287.3

Defendant has no Sixth Amendment constitutional right to counsel prior to taking breath alcohol test. State v. Mason (Ohio App. 1 Dist., 12-07-1994) 99 Ohio App.3d 165, 650 N.E.2d 144, dismissed, appeal not allowed 72 Ohio St.3d 1413, 647 N.E.2d 1388. Criminal Law ⚷ 641.3(8.1)

Defendant's refusal to take alcohol chemical test under implied consent statute was admissible evidence to prove defendant's physical impairment at time of his refusal, in prosecution for driving while under influence of alcohol, despite contention that defendant's refusal to answer any questions or take any chemical tests was conditioned only upon request to exercise statutory right to counsel; facts were conflicting as to whether defendant conditioned his taking test upon first talking to brother-in-law, who was attorney, and trial court could have reasonably concluded that defendant's refusal to take chemical test was outright refusal. State v. Bushey (Ohio App. 12 Dist., 11-28-1994) 98 Ohio App.3d 832, 649 N.E.2d 1243. Automobiles ⚷ 413

Good faith request to exercise one's statutory right to consult with counsel before submitting to chemical test required by implied consent statute does not constitute "refusal" to take such test, as long as delay which occurs as result of exercising the right will not unduly or unreasonably delay administration of test. State v. Bushey (Ohio App. 12 Dist., 11-28-1994) 98 Ohio App.3d 832, 649 N.E.2d 1243. Automobiles ⚷ 421

If request to consult with attorney is made as fraud or subterfuge to avoid taking blood-alcohol content test, or as attempt to delay matters beyond statutory two hours for taking test, there is "refusal" to take test within contemplation of implied consent statute. State v. Bushey (Ohio App. 12 Dist., 11-28-1994) 98 Ohio App.3d 832, 649 N.E.2d 1243. Automobiles ⚷ 421

Determination of whether one's refusal to submit to blood-alcohol content test is "refusal" within contemplation of implied consent statute or good faith request to exercise one's statutory right to consult with counsel is factual determination to be made by trial court based upon facts and circumstances of case. State v. Bushey (Ohio App. 12 Dist., 11-28-1994) 98 Ohio App.3d 832, 649 N.E.2d 1243. Automobiles ⚷ 426

If law enforcement officers fail to comply with statute permitting arrestee to communicate with counsel upon his arrest, detention or being taken into custody when they arrest person for driving while intoxicated, there can be no sanction for refusal to take breathalyzer test pursuant to implied consent statute and likewise, if accused elects under threat of implied consent to take breathalyzer, result should be excluded. Lexington v. Reddington (Richland 1993) 86 Ohio App.3d 643, 621 N.E.2d 758, motion overruled 66 Ohio St.3d 1510, 613 N.E.2d 1048. Automobiles ⚷ 421

Police officer's violation of a motorist's statutory right to an attorney, after her arrest for operating a motor vehicle while under the influence of alcohol but prior to her undergoing breath test, despite her repeated requests, did not warrant suppression of breath test; Ohio does not recognize applicability of an exclusionary rule for violation of such a state statutory right, and, although decision to take test is possibly most critical part of a "per se" OMVI case, expansion of law as to when Sixth Amendment right to counsel attaches, so as to include time before breath test, would be inappropriate. City of Columbus v. Reid (Franklin 1986) 32 Ohio App.3d 7, 513 N.E.2d 351. Automobiles ⚷ 421

A request to exercise the statutory right to counsel pursuant to RC 2935.14 and RC 2935.20 prior to taking a designated chemical sobriety test in and of itself does not constitute a refusal within the meaning of RC 4511.191. Snavely v. Dollison (Cuyahoga 1979) 61 Ohio App.2d 140, 400 N.E.2d 415, 15 O.O.3d 244.

A refusal to take a designated chemical sobriety test, conditioned by a suspected offender upon a timely and bona fide request to contact an attorney, does not constitute a rejection within the meaning of RC 4511.191. Raine v. Curry (Franklin 1975) 45 Ohio App.2d 155, 341 N.E.2d 606, 74 O.O.2d 171. Automobiles ⚷ 144.1(1.20)

A person "refuses" to take the test prescribed in RC 4511.191 where the attending law enforcement officers have complied with RC 2935.14 and RC 2935.20, and the accused continues to withhold his consent to submit to the test. McNulty v. Curry (Ohio 1975) 42 Ohio St.2d 341, 328 N.E.2d 798, 71 O.O.2d 317.

A good faith request of an arrested person to exercise his statutory right to call an attorney, before submitting to a chemical test required by RC 4511.191 does not constitute a refusal to take such test where the delay occasioned by the exercise of the statutory right will not unduly or unreasonably delay the administering of the test. Siegwald v. Curry (Franklin 1974) 40 Ohio App.2d 313, 319 N.E.2d 381, 69 O.O.2d 293. Automobiles ⚷ 144.1(1.20)

Whether a request to consult an attorney is made in good faith and whether the exercise of the right will unreasonably delay administering a chemical test are factual issues to be determined from the facts and circumstances involved. Siegwald v. Curry (Franklin 1974) 40 Ohio App.2d 313, 319 N.E.2d 381, 69 O.O.2d 293. Automobiles ⚷ 144.1(1.11)

Where a short and reasonable delay is occasioned in the taking of a test for intoxication on the ground that the person charged with operating a motor vehicle while under the influence of alcohol desires to call his or her attorney, such request followed by a denial by the arresting officer to let the accused use the telephone, does not constitute a refusal under RC 4511.191(F). Siegwald v. Curry (Ohio Mun. 1973) 39 Ohio Misc. 16, 314 N.E.2d 191, 68 O.O.2d 157, affirmed 40 Ohio App.2d 313, 319 N.E.2d 381, 69 O.O.2d 293. Automobiles ⚷ 144.1(1.20)

A violation of defendant's statutory right to confer with counsel after her arrest would not require the exclusion of evidence, in prosecution for driving under the influence of alcohol (DUI). State Of Ohio v. Shannon L. Grove (Ohio App. 5 Dist., Fairfield, 07-09-2002) No. 01 CA 41, 2002-Ohio-3677, 2002 WL 1528028, Unreported. Criminal Law ⚷ 641.12(4)

Even after an accused invokes his right to counsel, police are still permitted to ask whether he will submit to a test of blood alcohol content for purposes of a prosecution for driving while under the influence of alcohol (DUI). State v. Downing (Ohio App. 2 Dist., Greene, 03-22-2002) No. 2001-CA-78, 2002-Ohio-1302, 2002 WL 441353, Unreported. Automobiles ⚷ 418

In prosecution for driving while under the influence of alcohol (DUI), police officer complied with defendant's statutory right to consult with counsel upon arrest, where officer gave defendant a phone book and allowed him to consult with an attorney prior to administering test for blood alcohol content. State v. Downing (Ohio App. 2 Dist., Greene, 03-22-2002) No. 2001-CA-78, 2002-Ohio-1302, 2002 WL 441353, Unreported. Automobiles ⚷ 421

2935.21 Security for costs

When the offense charged is a misdemeanor, the magistrate or court, before issuing the warrant, may require the complainant, or if the magistrate considers the complainant irresponsible, may require that said complainant procure a person to be liable for the costs if the complaint is dismissed, and the complainant or other person shall acknowledge himself so liable, and such court or magistrate shall enter such acknowledgment on his docket. Such bond shall not be required of an officer authorized to make arrests when in the discharge of his official duty, or other person or officer authorized to assist the prosecuting attorney in the prosecution of offenders.

(1953 H 1, eff. 10–1–53; GC 13432–20)

Historical and Statutory Notes

Pre–1953 H 1 Amendments: 113 v 144, Ch 11, § 20

Library References

Costs ⚷301.1.

Westlaw Topic No. 102.

C.J.S. Criminal Law §§ 1742 to 1750.

Research References

Encyclopedias

OH Jur. 3d Criminal Law § 2099, Security for Costs.

OH Jur. 3d Criminal Law § 3985, Liability of Complainant or Informer for Costs; Security for Costs.

Notes of Decisions

Deposit for costs 1

1. Deposit for costs

A county court has no authority to provide, by rule of court, that a defendant in a misdemeanor case who requests a jury trial, must first deposit or secure the costs for subpoena and empaneling a jury. OAG 65–48.

2935.22 Issuing subpoenas for witnesses—Repealed

(128 v 97, eff. 1–1–60; 1953 H 1; GC 13432–21)

Historical and Statutory Notes

Pre–1953 H 1 Amendments: 113 v 144, Ch 11, § 21

2935.23 Felony investigation; examination of witnesses

After a felony has been committed, and before any arrest has been made, the prosecuting attorney of the county, or any judge or magistrate, may cause subpoenas to issue, returnable before any court or magistrate, for any person to give information concerning such felony. The subpoenas shall require the witness to appear forthwith. Before such witness is required to give any information, he must be informed of the purpose of the inquiry, and that he is required to tell the truth concerning the same. He shall then be sworn and be examined under oath by the prosecuting attorney, or the court or magistrate, subject to the constitutional rights of the witness. Such examination shall be taken in writing in any form, and shall be filed with the court or magistrate taking the testimony. Witness fees shall be paid to such persons as in other cases.

(1972 H 511, eff. 1–1–74; 1953 H 1; GC 13432–22)

Historical and Statutory Notes

Pre–1953 H 1 Amendments: 113 v 144, Ch 11, § 22

Library References

Criminal Law ⚷212.
Witnesses ⚷7.
Westlaw Topic Nos. 110, 410.
C.J.S. Criminal Law §§ 324, 327, 337.
C.J.S. Witnesses §§ 2, 20 to 31.

Research References

Encyclopedias

OH Jur. 3d Criminal Law § 667, Examination of Witnesses Concerning Felony.

Law Review and Journal Commentaries

Scientific Evidence in the Sam Sheppard Case. Paul C. Giannelli, 49 Clev St L Rev 487 (2001).

Notes of Decisions

Oral testimony under oath 1

1. Oral testimony under oath

In order for oral testimony regarding facts establishing probable cause to justify issuance of a warrant, such testimony must be under oath. Tabasko v. Barton (C.A.6 (Ohio) 1972) 472 F.2d 871, 65 O.O.2d 333, certiorari denied 93 S.Ct. 2288, 412 U.S. 908, 36 L.Ed.2d 974.

2935.24 Warrants transmitted by teletype or similar means

A judge of a court of record may, by an endorsement under his hand upon a warrant of arrest, authorize the service thereof by telegraph, teletype, wire photo, or other means whereby a written or facsimile copy may be transmitted, and thereafter a copy of such warrant may be sent by any such means to any law enforcement officer. Such copy is effectual in the hands of any law enforcement officer and he shall proceed in the same manner under it as though he held the orginal [*sic*] warrant issued by the court making the endorsement, except that a state university law enforcement officer shall not arrest for a minor misdemeanor on the basis of a written or facsimile copy of a warrant of arrest. Every officer causing copies of warrants to be sent pursuant to this section, shall certify as correct and file in the office from which such warrant was sent, a copy of such warrant and endorsement thereon, and shall return the original with a statement of his action thereunder.

(1978 H 588, eff. 6–19–78; 1972 H 511; 1953 H 1; GC 13432–23)

Historical and Statutory Notes

Pre–1953 H 1 Amendments: 113 v 144, Ch 11, § 23

Library References

Criminal Law ⚷215.
Westlaw Topic No. 110.
C.J.S. Criminal Law §§ 334 to 335, 337 to 338.

Research References

Encyclopedias

OH Jur. 3d Criminal Law § 2102, Arrest by Telegraph, Teletype, Fax, and Like Order.

Treatises and Practice Aids

Katz, Giannelli, Blair and Lipton, Baldwin's Ohio Practice, Criminal Law, § 7:7, Place of Execution.

Katz, Giannelli, Blair and Lipton, Baldwin's Ohio Practice, Criminal Law, § 134:4, Endorsement Authorizing Arrest by Telegraph Order.

Katz, Ohio Arrest, Search & Seizure § 6:1, Execution of Arrest Warrants: Introduction.

Notes of Decisions

1. Arrest in another state

Where police in one state arrest an individual at the teletyped request of foreign state authorities, no established federal right of the prisoner is violated and the arresting officers are immune from civil liability under 42 USC 1983 even where it is found the arrest lacked probable cause. Donta v. Hooper (C.A.6 (Ohio) 1985) 774 F.2d 716, certiorari denied 107 S.Ct. 3261, 483 U.S. 1019, 97 L.Ed.2d 760.

2935.25 Power of arrest

Sections 2935.02 to 2935.24, inclusive, of the Revised Code do not affect or modify the power of arrest vested by law in other persons or officers than those named in section 2935.03 of the Revised Code.

(1953 H 1, eff. 10–1–53; GC 13432–24)

Historical and Statutory Notes

Pre–1953 H 1 Amendments: 113 v 145, Ch 11, § 24

Library References

Arrest ⚷62, 63.2.
Westlaw Topic No. 35.
C.J.S. Arrest §§ 9 to 10, 15.

2935.26 When citation must be used rather than arrest; exceptions; procedures

(A) Notwithstanding any other provision of the Revised Code, when a law enforcement officer is otherwise authorized to arrest a person for the commission of a minor misdemeanor, the officer shall not arrest the person, but shall issue a citation, unless one of the following applies:

(1) The offender requires medical care or is unable to provide for his own safety.

(2) The offender cannot or will not offer satisfactory evidence of his identity.

(3) The offender refuses to sign the citation.

(4) The offender has previously been issued a citation for the commission of that misdemeanor and has failed to do one of the following:

(a) Appear at the time and place stated in the citation;

(b) Comply with division (C) of this section.

(B) The citation shall contain all of the following:

(1) The name and address of the offender;

(2) A description of the offense and the numerical designation of the applicable statute or ordinance;

(3) The name of the person issuing the citation;

(4) An order for the offender to appear at a stated time and place;

(5) A notice that the offender may comply with division (C) of this section in lieu of appearing at the stated time and place;

(6) A notice that the offender is required to do one of the following and that he may be arrested if he fails to do one of them:

(a) Appear at the time and place stated in the citation;

(b) Comply with division (C) of this section.

(C) In lieu of appearing at the time and place stated in the citation, the offender may, within seven days after the date of issuance of the citation, do either of the following:

(1) Appear in person at the office of the clerk of the court stated in the citation, sign a plea of guilty and a waiver of trial provision that is on the citation, and pay the total amount of the fine and costs;

(2) Sign the guilty plea and waiver of trial provision of the citation, and mail the citation and a check or money order for the total amount of the fine and costs to the office of the clerk of the court stated in the citation.

Remittance by mail of the fine and costs to the office of the clerk of the court stated in the citation constitutes a guilty plea and waiver of trial whether or not the quilty plea and waiver of trial provision of the citation are signed by the defendant.

(D) A law enforcement officer who issues a citation shall complete and sign the citation form, serve a copy of the completed form upon the offender and, without unnecessary delay, file the original citation with the court having jurisdiction over the offense.

(E) Each court shall establish a fine schedule that shall list the fine for each minor misdemeanor, and state the court costs. The fine schedule shall be prominently posted in the place where minor misdemeanor fines are paid.

(F) If an offender fails to appear and does not comply with division (C) of this section, the court may issue a supplemental citation, or a summons or warrant for the arrest of the offender pursuant to the Criminal Rules. Supplemental citations shall be in the form prescribed by division (B) of this section, but shall be issued and signed by the clerk of the court at which the citation directed the offender to appear and shall be served in the same manner as a summons.

(1978 S 351, eff. 10–25–78)

Historical and Statutory Notes

Ed. Note: Former 2935.26 repealed by 128 v 97, eff. 1–1–60; 1953 H 1; GC 13434–1.

Pre–1953 H 1 Amendments: 113 v 149, Ch 13, § 1

Cross References

Driver's license as bond in certain traffic violation arrests, 2937.221

Optional procedure in minor misdemeanor cases, Crim R 4.1

Library References

Automobiles ⚷351.

Criminal Law ⚷215.

Westlaw Topic Nos. 110, 48A.

C.J.S. Criminal Law §§ 334 to 335, 337 to 338.

C.J.S. Motor Vehicles §§ 1344 to 1345, 1365 to 1372, 1397 to 1401, 1442 to 1444, 1473 to 1475, 1486 to 1487, 1496, 1508 to 1509, 1518, 1526, 1532, 1543 to 1547, 1550.

Research References

Encyclopedias

OH Jur. 3d Criminal Law § 161, Validity of Arrest or Entry Upon Premises.

OH Jur. 3d Criminal Law § 1696, Bail.

OH Jur. 3d Criminal Law § 1701, Failure to Appear Pursuant to Ticket.

OH Jur. 3d Criminal Law § 2083, Generally; Issuance of Citation.

OH Jur. 3d Criminal Law § 2084, Contents.

OH Jur. 3d Criminal Law § 2085, Procedure in Lieu of Appearance.

OH Jur. 3d Criminal Law § 2086, Failure to Appear or Respond.

OH Jur. 3d Criminal Law § 2108, Misdemeanors and Other Minor Offenses.

OH Jur. 3d Criminal Law § 2219, Minor Misdemeanor.

OH Jur. 3d Criminal Law § 2221, Nonappearance of Defendant—Forfeiture of License.

OH Jur. 3d Family Law § 1570, Apprehension.

Treatises and Practice Aids

Markus, Trial Handbook for Ohio Lawyers, § 29:8, Search Incident to Valid Arrest.

Klein, Darling, & Terez, Baldwin's Ohio Practice Civil Practice § 1:100, Modern Courts Amendment of 1968 as Limiting Scope of Application of Civil Rules.

Katz, Giannelli, Blair and Lipton, Baldwin's Ohio Practice, Criminal Law, § 6:8, Minor Misdemeanors.

Katz, Giannelli, Blair and Lipton, Baldwin's Ohio Practice, Criminal Law, § 12:6, Search of Arrestee's Person.

Katz, Giannelli, Blair and Lipton, Baldwin's Ohio Practice, Criminal Law, § 12:7, Pretextual Arrests.

Katz, Giannelli, Blair and Lipton, Baldwin's Ohio Practice, Criminal Law, § 15:3, Request for License/Registration.

Katz, Giannelli, Blair and Lipton, Baldwin's Ohio Practice, Criminal Law, § 29:5, Exclusionary Rule—Statutes.

Katz, Giannelli, Blair and Lipton, Baldwin's Ohio Practice, Criminal Law, § 7:15, Summons Required—Minor Misdemeanor.

Katz, Giannelli, Blair and Lipton, Baldwin's Ohio Practice, Criminal Law, § 133:30, Minor Misdemeanor Citation.

Katz, Ohio Arrest, Search & Seizure § 4:6, Minor Misdemeanors.

Katz, Ohio Arrest, Search & Seizure § 10:5, Search of a Person Incident to Arrest—the Offense.

Katz, Ohio Arrest, Search & Seizure § 2:14, Factors to Consider—Criminal Behavior.

Katz, Ohio Arrest, Search & Seizure § 27:3, Exclusion for Violation of State Law.

Katz, Ohio Arrest, Search & Seizure App. A, Appendix A. Arrest Provisions: Checklist.

Hennenberg & Reinhart, Ohio Criminal Defense Motions F 10.06, Motion to Withdraw Guilty Plea-Post-Trial Motions-Alternative Petition for Post-Conviction Relief-Failure to Advise Noncitizen of Deportation.

Hennenberg & Reinhart, Ohio Criminal Defense Motions F 10.07, Motion to Withdraw Plea/Post-Conviction Petition-No Deportation Advice.

Painter, Ohio Driving Under the Influence § 8:14, Burden of Proof—Warrant Requirement.

Painter, Ohio Driving Under the Influence § 8:23, Basis for Motion to Suppress—Illegal Stop.

Giannelli & Yeomans, Ohio Juvenile Law § 14:3, Custody, Arrests & Stops.

Notes of Decisions

Arrest for minor misdemeanor 2
Constitutional issues 1
Content of citation 5
Procedural issues 6
Search incident to citation or arrest 3
Violations bureau 4

---

1. Constitutional issues

Defendant's arrest for minor misdemeanor possession of marijuana was unreasonable, given that incarceration was not possible for such offense; defendant gave his name, produced identification, and never indicated that he would be unwilling to sign a citation, and thus there existed no exception to statute generally requiring citations rather than arrests for minor misdemeanors. State v. Washington (Ohio App. 8 Dist., Cuyahoga, 02-09-2006) No. 86370, 2006-Ohio-568, 2006 WL 305454, Unreported. Arrest ⚷ 63.4(5)

Police officers were justified under Fourth Amendment in arresting defendant for failing to offer satisfactory evidence of his identity, where defendant ran from officers as they attempted to issue citation for jaywalking, defendant provided at least two different versions of his last name and conflicting dates of birth, and, moreover, making unsworn, false, oral statement to public official with purpose to mislead, hamper, or impede investigation was punishable conduct. State v. Dillon (Ohio App. 10 Dist., Franklin, 08-11-2005) No. 04AP-1211, 2005-Ohio-4124, 2005 WL 1910749, Unreported, appeal not allowed 108 Ohio St.3d 1414, 841 N.E.2d 319, 2006-Ohio-179. Arrest ⚷ 63.4(15)

Police officer reasonably concluded that defendant was unable to provide for his own safety and, thus, had probable cause to arrest defendant for minor misdemeanor public intoxication, where defendant had passed out behind wheel of vehicle, vehicle was parked in driveway of residence occupied by persons not known to defendant, officer observed that defendant smelled of alcohol, that his eyes were bloodshot, that his speech was slurred, that some of his answers were incoherent, and that he was stumbling around inside vehicle, and defendant told officer that he had been at nearby drinking establishment all night. State v. Harper (Ohio App. 2 Dist., Montgomery, 09-24-2004) No. 20279, 2004-Ohio-5286, 2004 WL 2245097, Unreported. Arrest ⚷ 63.4(5)

Passenger of vehicle stopped by state trooper for traffic violation failed to prove that troopers were without lawful privilege to detain him, and thus passenger could not maintain false imprisonment claim against state highway patrol; passenger was lawfully arrested for not wearing seatbelt and for refusing to offer satisfactory evidence of his identity while trooper was in process of issuing citation. Dale v. Ohio State Highway Patrol (Ohio Ct.Cl., 04-08-2004) No. 99-13703, 2004-Ohio-1925, 2004 WL 823367, Unreported, adopted 2004-Ohio-2754, 2004 WL 1191932, affirmed 2005-Ohio-3383, 2005 WL 1532421. False Imprisonment ⚷ 8

State trooper had probable cause to arrest passenger, who was riding in vehicle stopped by state trooper for traffic violation, and thus passenger could not maintain malicious prosecution claim against state highway patrol; trooper observed that passenger was not wearing seatbelt, and passenger did not offer satisfactory evidence of his identity while trooper was in process of issuing passenger citation. Dale v. Ohio State Highway Patrol (Ohio Ct.Cl., 04-08-2004) No. 99-13703, 2004-Ohio-1925, 2004 WL 823367, Unreported, adopted 2004-Ohio-2754, 2004 WL 1191932, affirmed 2005-Ohio-3383, 2005 WL 1532421. Malicious Prosecution ⚷ 18(2); Malicious Prosecution ⚷ 18(5)

Officer's search of defendant's person and seizure of drugs therefrom was lawful incident to defendant's arrest for disorderly conduct; officer was authorized to arrest, rather than cite, defendant for violation given officer's reasonable belief that defendant, intoxicated and having difficulty standing up while walking next to a roadway, posed a risk of physical harm to himself and others. State v. Storer (Ohio App. 3 Dist., Auglaize, 04-12-2004) No. 2-03-31, 2004-Ohio-1850, 2004 WL 765099, Unreported. Arrest ⚷ 71.1(3); Arrest ⚷ 71.1(6)

A warrantless pat-down search of a pedestrian who is issued a citation for walking on the side of the street while not facing traffic is not justified where the pedestrian is unable to produce identification upon request and the officer's decision to prolong the person's detention to verify his identity does not amount to a full custodial arrest; the search incident to a lawful arrest exception to the warrant requirement does not validate the officer's warrantless search which yields cocaine that must be suppressed. State v. Richardson (Ohio App. 10 Dist., Franklin, 12-07-1999) No. 98AP-1500, 1999 WL 1102690, Unreported, dismissed, appeal not allowed 88 Ohio St.3d 1479, 727 N.E.2d 131.

RC 2935.26 requires that a citation be issued and forbids arrest where none of the statutory exceptions apply; consequently, an arrest for jaywalking in violation of RC 2935.26 is an unreasonable seizure and crack cocaine discovered as a result of the arrest is subject to the exclusionary rule. State v. Jones (Ohio App. 2 Dist., Montgomery, 02-19-1999) No. 17382, 1999 WL 76817, Unreported, motion to certify allowed 86 Ohio St.3d 1404, 711 N.E.2d 232, appeal allowed 86 Ohio St.3d 1406, 711 N.E.2d 233, affirmed 88 Ohio St.3d 430, 727 N.E.2d 886, 2000-Ohio-374.

The arrest of a pedestrian for jaywalking is a lawful arrest where the offender (1) provides a name and date of birth, (2) has no corroborative documentation, (3) cannot recall a social security number, and indicates indigency; in addition, the trial court errs in suppressing evidence of four rocks of crack cocaine found in the offender's pockets where the court does not apply the objective "reasonable officer" standard in resolving the motion to suppress and rather grants the motion on subjective determinations that the officer "considered" defendant's conduct to demonstrate a violation of a jaywalking ordinance and "believed that the defendant was guilty of jaywalking." State v. Williams (Ohio App. 2 Dist., Montgomery, 11-21-1997) No. 16306, 1997 WL 822672, Unreported.

Defendant's full custodial arrest for minor misdemeanor offense of having an improper signal device on a bicycle was a violation of his state and federal constitutional rights to be free from unreasonable searches and seizures. State v. Anderson (Ohio App. 1 Dist., 07-25-2003) 153 Ohio App.3d 374, 794 N.E.2d 126, 2003-Ohio-3970. Automobiles ⚷ 349(15)

Police officers could conduct brief patdown search of driver before detaining him in back seat of patrol car after he failed to produce license following lawful stop for speeding; officers were statutorily authorized to arrest driver. State v. Mason (Ohio App. 7 Dist., 11-08-1996) 115 Ohio App.3d 187, 684 N.E.2d 1294. Automobiles ⚷ 349(2.1); Automobiles ⚷ 349.5(10)

Police officers who smelled burning marijuana when defendant opened door to his apartment did not have probable cause to arrest defendant for any criminal offense, so as to permit search incident to arrest; odor of burning marijuana provided probable cause only as to commission of minor-misdemeanor drug offense that would warrant only issuance of citation. State v. Robinson (Ohio App. 1 Dist., 06-07-1995) 103 Ohio App.3d 490, 659 N.E.2d 1292, dismissed, appeal not allowed 74 Ohio St.3d 1418, 655 N.E.2d 738, reconsideration denied 74 Ohio St.3d 1465, 656 N.E.2d 1300. Arrest ⚷ 63.4(5)

RC 2935.26, insofar as it creates a substantive right of freedom from arrest for one accused of the commission of a minor misdemeanor, and Crim R 4.1, which provides a procedure for disposition of minor misdemeanor cases where citations have been issued, are not unconstitutionally in conflict. The right of non-arrest for a minor misdemeanor is created, defined, and regulated by the statute. The statute does not pertain to the method of enforcing that right; Crim R 4.1 does. The rule reflects the statutory provision that while a citation may be issued, it need not be issued in circumstances where one of the statutory exceptions applies. State v. Slatter (Ohio 1981) 66 Ohio St.2d 452, 423 N.E.2d 100, 20 O.O.3d 383.

Defendant's arrest for minor misdemeanor of open container was a violation of defendant's state and federal constitutional rights to be free from unreasonable searches and seizures, and thus even if defendant failed to adequately raise such claim that evidence taken pursuant to his arrest was subject to suppression during motion to suppress or suppression hearing, admission of drug evidence obtained during search incident to arrest constituted plain error; officer testified at suppression hearing, upon questioning by defendant's counsel, that there were no outstanding warrants for defendant, officer testified he had no recollection of problems procuring satisfactory identification from defendant, and no indication in the record existed that defendant needed medical attention. State v. Dade (Ohio App. 10 Dist., Franklin, 09-30-2002) No. 02AP-73, 2002-Ohio-5251, 2002 WL 31175210, Unreported, appeal allowed 98 Ohio St.3d 1421, 782 N.E.2d 77, 2003-Ohio-259, affirmed 100 Ohio St.3d 30, 795 N.E.2d 668, 2003-Ohio-4755. Criminal Law ⚷ 1036.1(4)

2. Arrest for minor misdemeanor

Search for weapons or contraband was not justified based on police officers' act of lawfully stopping defendant, who was carrying open bottle of beer on public sidewalk, where violation of open-container statute was punishable as minor misdemeanor, statutory exceptions allowing for search did not apply, and officers did not have reasonable, articulable suspicion that criminal wrongdoing was afoot. State v. Riggins (Ohio App. 1 Dist., Hamilton, 08-13-2004) No. C-030626, 2004-Ohio-4247, 2004 WL 1800714, Unreported, stay denied 103 Ohio St.3d 1476, 816 N.E.2d 253, 2004-Ohio-5405, appeal not allowed 104 Ohio St.3d 1439, 819 N.E.2d 1123, 2004-Ohio-7033. Arrest ⚷ 63.5(9)

Intoxicated defendant who was alone, agitated, and unsteady on his feet was "unable to provide for his own safety" within exception to statute prohibiting police from arresting a person for a minor misdemeanor offense, and thus, defendant was not entitled to suppression of marijuana and marijuana pipe that were found during search incident to arrest. State v. Barnes (Ohio App. 4 Dist., Athens, 02-27-2003) No. 02CA28, 2003-Ohio-984, 2003 WL 754245, Unreported. Arrest ⚷ 71.1(7)

Defendant was arrested for persistent disorderly conduct, rather than disorderly conduct, and thus the statute prohibiting arrests for minor misdemeanor offenses did not render his arrest invalid; deputy who arrested defendant testified that defendant was arrested for persistent disorderly conduct, and two deputies described defendant as being disruptive and abusive in the visitor's room of the jail and on the street after he was ordered to leave. State v. Sutterfield (Ohio App. 4 Dist., Adams, 11-26-2002) No. 02CA735, 2002-Ohio-6611, 2002 WL 31712663, Unreported. Arrest ⚷ 63.4(5)

It was reasonable for police officers to believe that defendant posed danger to himself and others, thus justifying arrest for misdemeanor offense of public intoxication; defendant told officers he had been in a bar and drank five beers and was on the way to pick up his car, he failed horizontal gaze nystagmus test, he would have had to cross five lanes of heavy traffic in order to reach his car, and he was planning on driving in his vehicle in an obviously impaired state. State v. Greene (Ohio App. 2 Dist., Montgomery, 10-11-2002) No. C.A. 19193, 2002-Ohio-5530, 2002 WL 31316064, Unreported. Arrest ⚷ 63.4(15)

Where an arrest is made for persisting in disorderly conduct and there is sufficient evidence of resisting arrest, failure to instruct the jury on persisting in disorderly conduct as an arrestable offense is reversible error. State v. Kuehne (Ohio App. 1 Dist., Hamilton, 03-06-1996) No. C-940971, 1996 WL 97560, Unreported.

The state does not fail to establish the RC 2936.26(A)(2) exception to the prohibition against arrest for an open container misdemeanor simply because the defendant is not carrying any I.D. and her verbal representations as to her identity prove to be truthful and the officer is unable to verify with the computer in his cruiser the date of birth, name, and social security number of the defendant. State v. Satterwhite (Ohio App. 2 Dist., Montgomery, 01-25-1995) No. 14699, 1995 WL 29200, Unreported, dismissed, appeal not allowed 72 Ohio St.3d 1538, 650 N.E.2d 479.

Police had no justification for arresting defendant for minor misdemeanor traffic violation of having a cracked windshield, absent a showing that defendant required medical care or was unable to provide for his own safety, could not offer satisfactory evidence of his identity, refused to sign citation, had previously been issued a citation for commission of that misdemeanor and failed to appear at time and place stated in citation. State v. Dubose (Ohio App. 7 Dist., 12-06-2005) 164 Ohio App.3d 698, 843 N.E.2d 1222, 2005-Ohio-6602. Automobiles ⚷ 349(15)

Warrantless search of defendant's vehicle was not incident to her arrest for minor automobile-related misdemeanors, so as to violate statute prohibiting an arrest when a citation, instead, must be issued, but, rather, the search was made with probable cause established by use of a drug-sniffing dog while defendant was reasonably detained to run her name through L.E.A.D.S. (Law Enforcement Automated Data System) and to ascertain whether she had any outstanding arrest warrants. State v. Wilkenson (Ohio Com.Pl., 06-01-2001) 118 Ohio Misc.2d 10, 769 N.E.2d 430, 2001-Ohio-4354. Automobiles ⚷ 349.5(2); Automobiles ⚷ 349.5(7)

Vehicle passenger whose lack of seat belt use had been observed by police officer did not fail to offer satisfactory evidence of his identity, as would allow officer to make arrest for seat belt violation, rather than issuing citation; while passenger gave his name and date of birth, there was no indication that police officer made any attempt to verify or corroborate information, or that computer check was available. State v. Miller (Ohio App. 2 Dist., 09-30-1999) 134 Ohio App.3d 841, 732 N.E.2d 483. Automobiles ⚷ 349(15)

Police officers did not provide defendant with opportunity to offer satisfactory evidence of his identity before arresting him for minor misdemeanor of jaywalking, and therefore such arrest was unlawful and officers should have instead just issued defendant a citation, where officers never attempted to verify defendant's identity on an operational computer in police cruiser before arresting him, and officers made no attempt to question defendant's girlfriend privately to compare her identification with defendant's statements. State v. Satterwhite (Ohio App. 2 Dist., 09-05-1997) 123 Ohio App.3d 322, 704 N.E.2d 259. Arrest ⚷ 58

State has the burden of demonstrating the existence of the statutory exemption, under statute requiring officers to issue citations rather than arrest people for minor misdemeanors unless the offender cannot or will not offer satisfactory evidence of his identity. State v. Satterwhite (Ohio App. 2 Dist., 09-05-1997) 123 Ohio App.3d 322, 704 N.E.2d 259. Arrest ⚷ 58

Police officer may not arrest someone for misdemeanor if officer did not observe offense. State v. Lunsford (Ohio App. 12 Dist., 02-24-1997) 118 Ohio App.3d 380, 692 N.E.2d 1078. Arrest ⚷ 63.4(5)

Receipt of traffic citation is not functional equivalent of arrest. State v. Lunsford (Ohio App. 12 Dist., 02-24-1997) 118 Ohio App.3d 380, 692 N.E.2d 1078. Automobiles ⚷ 349(10)

Defendant's conduct, namely being found in front of his home holding paper bag with bottle inside it and then refusing to accompany officer to his patrol car to go through motions of full custodial arrest, did not rise to level of arrestable offense, and since there was no lawful basis on which to arrest defendant, he could not be convicted of resisting arrest; carrying open container of beer was punishable as minor misdemeanor, and statute created substantive right to be free from arrest for commission of minor misdemeanor. State v. Thompson (Ohio App. 1 Dist., 12-18-1996) 116 Ohio App.3d 740, 689 N.E.2d 86. Obstructing Justice ⚷ 3

Possession of open container of beer or intoxicating liquor while operating automobile is minor misdemeanor and not arrestable offense, and thus conviction of that offense does not subject automobile of defendant to seizure and sale. State v. Johns (Ohio App. 9 Dist., 09-15-1993) 90 Ohio App.3d 456, 629 N.E.2d 1069, dismissed, jurisdictional motion overruled 68 Ohio St.3d 1445, 626 N.E.2d 687. Automobiles ⚷ 349(2.1); Criminal Law ⚷ 27; Forfeitures ⚷ 4

A police officer properly makes a custodial arrest for a minor misdemeanor under RC 2935.26(A)(2) where the defendant gives the officer a driver's license belonging to another individual when asked to identify himself; additionally, such a response to the officer's request for identification is, standing alone, a violation of RC 4507.30(C) and a proper basis for the arrest. State v. Bronaugh (Hamilton 1984) 16 Ohio App.3d 237, 475 N.E.2d 171, 16 O.B.R. 260.

An individual may be arrested for the minor misdemeanor of intoxication if the offender is unable to provide for his own safety. State v. Pender (Ohio Mun. 1980) 66 Ohio Misc. 23, 419 N.E.2d 1141, 20 O.O.3d 148.

3. Search incident to citation or arrest

There was competent, credible evidence that defendant could not provide for his own safety, and as such, officer was authorized to arrest defendant pursuant to statute which permits officer to arrest an offender for a minor misdemeanor if he requires medical care or is unable to provide for his own safety; officer testified that defendant was unsteady on his feet and had a strong odor of alcohol on his breath, and since driver of vehicle had been arrested, defendant, who was passenger in vehicle, had no one to ensure his safety, and officer did not want to leave defendant alone on side of road in his intoxicated condition. State v. Scasny (Ohio App. 4 Dist., Ross, 09-14-2004) No. 04CA2768, 2004-Ohio-4918, 2004 WL 2072477, Unreported. Arrest ⚷ 63.4(5)

Arrest for minor misdemeanor of jaywalking violated state constitution and required suppression of crack cocaine seized in search incident to arrest. State v. Brown (Ohio, 08-06-2003) 99 Ohio St.3d 323, 792 N.E.2d 175, 2003-Ohio-3931. Arrest ⚷ 63.4(5)

Police officer did not have reasonable suspicion about defendant's identity, as was required to support arresting defendant on minor misdemeanor charge of possession of marijuana, where defendant furnished officer with his name, address, and Social Security number, officer verified defendant's name and Social Security number by computer, and, even though officer was unable to verify defendant's address, he did have additional information, including a proper date of birth and information about prior contacts with the police. State v. Ellison (Ohio App. 2 Dist., 06-14-2002) 148 Ohio App.3d 270, 772 N.E.2d 1222, 2002-Ohio-2919. Arrest ⚷ 63.4(15)

A police deputy does not have authority pursuant to an arrest or on the basis of probable cause to search a defendant's vehicle where the defendant is stopped by a deputy and issued a citation for an expired thirty-day tag in the rear window and excessive windshield tint (minor misdemeanors) and the defendant and his passenger are cooperative and do not make furtive gestures or attempt to escape, and the deputy testifies that he knew the defendant owned a gun and that he had received a tip from a confidential informant that the defendant was selling marijuana, but the facts do not reveal probable cause for the search, and since RC 2935.26(A) explicitly states that the officer shall not arrest the person but shall issue a citation unless certain conditions occur, none of which were present in this case, the arrest was unlawful and cannot be a proper predicate for the search. State v. Peay (Ohio Com.Pl. 1991) 62 Ohio Misc.2d 92, 592 N.E.2d 926.

The search of an automobile by police is not incident to a lawful arrest where (1) it is conducted after the stop of the vehicle for the absence of a light over the vehicle's rear license plate and the after arrest of the juvenile passenger for a curfew violation, (2) the police officers admit that they did not issue a citation or arrest the driver of the vehicle with respect to the absence of a license-plate light, and (3) the officers do not relate to the trial court any basis for a lawful arrest of the juvenile for a curfew violation since there is nothing in the record to indicate that the officers had probable cause to believe that the minor was not in the care and custody of the driver, an adult and operator of the motor vehicle, even if somehow they could have otherwise had probable cause to believe the minor was in violation of the curfew law while a passenger in an automobile driven by an adult; therefore, the requirements of a warrantless search and seizure are not met and the suppression of the evidence obtained as a result of the search is proper. Columbus v. Watson (Franklin 1989) 64 Ohio App.3d 6, 580 N.E.2d 494.

Defendant was arrested for a fourth degree misdemeanor, not for two minor misdemeanors, and thus custodial arrest did not violate statute governing arrests for minor misdemeanors, and subsequent search incident to that arrest, which produced stolen blank check that was basis of receiving stolen property charge, was reasonable and proper; police officers during traffic stop issued citations in lieu of arrest for minor misdemeanor traffic offenses of no taillights or brake lights and a license plates violation, and officers chose to arrest defendant instead for unauthorized use of a license plate after they discovered that validation sticker on defendant's plate belonged to another vehicle. State v. Hicks (Ohio App. 2 Dist., Greene, 06-14-2002) No. 01CA125, 2002-Ohio-2926, 2002 WL 1332480, Unreported. Automobiles ⚷ 349(15); Automobiles ⚷ 349.5(6)

A routine stationhouse inventory search of a defendant arrested pursuant to RC 2935.26(A)(1) for disorderly intoxication, a minor misdemeanor, is reasonable and justified based on the legitimate custodial purposes present in any arrest or detention and a defendant arrested pursuant to RC 2935.26(A)(1) has no greater expectation of privacy than a defendant arrested for any other offense. State v Raines, No. 1426 (4th Dist Ct App, Ross, 11–16–88).

4. Violations bureau

A traffic violations bureau is not required to allow an individual charged with an offense enumerated in Traf R 13(B) to pay a fine without a court appearance, notwithstanding RC 2935.26. OAG 79–059.

5. Content of citation

Parking tickets issued by city were fatally defective for lack of certain important information; tickets did not contain information concerning address or telephone number of issuing authority, they lacked information as to when to appear or, at the very least, where to appear to pay or contest the ticket, and contained no information regarding procedure to be utilized to contest ticket. Warren v. Granitto (Ohio App. 11 Dist., 03-28-1994) 93 Ohio App.3d 723, 639 N.E.2d 865. Automobiles ⚷ 351.1

6. Procedural issues

Genuine issues of material fact existed as to whether child, whose grandmother was at the scene, needed to be arrested for jaywalking for her own safety, whether officer acted with malicious purpose, in bad faith, or in a wanton or reckless manner in making the arrest, and whether probable cause existed for arrest, precluding summary judgment in favor of officer, on immunity grounds, as to state law claims, including false arrest; jaywalking is an offense except where crossroads are an unreasonable distance apart, and officer testified that there are no crosswalks nearby. Hicks v. Leffler (Ohio App. 10 Dist., 04-24-1997) 119 Ohio App.3d 424, 695 N.E.2d 777. Judgment ⚷ 185.3(1)

2935.27 Alternatives for security for appearance

(A)(1) If a law enforcement officer issues a citation to a person pursuant to section 2935.26 of the Revised Code and if the minor misdemeanor offense for which the citation is issued is an act prohibited by Chapter 4511., 4513., or 4549. of the Revised Code or an act prohibited by any municipal ordinance that is substantially similar to any section contained in Chapter 4511., 4513., or 4549. of the Revised Code, the officer shall inform the person, if the person has a current valid Ohio driver's or commercial driver's license, of the possible consequences of the person's actions as required under division (E) of this section, and also shall inform the person that the person is required either to appear at the time and place stated in the citation or to comply with division (C) of section 2935.26 of the Revised Code.

(2) If the person is an Ohio resident but does not have a current valid Ohio driver's or commercial driver's license or if the person is a resident of a state that is not a member of the nonresident violator compact of which this state is a member pursuant to section 4510.71 of the Revised Code, and if the court, by local rule, has prescribed a procedure for the setting of a reasonable security pursuant to division (F) of this section, security shall be set in accordance with that local rule and that division.

A court by local rule may prescribe a procedure for the setting of reasonable security as described in this division. As an alternative to this procedure, a court by local rule may prescribe a procedure for the setting of a reasonable security by the person without the person appearing before the court.

(B) A person who has security set under division (A)(2) of this section shall be given a receipt or other evidence of the deposit of the security by the court.

(C) Upon compliance with division (C) of section 2935.26 of the Revised Code by a person who was issued a citation, the clerk of the court shall notify the court. The court shall immediately return any sum of money, license, or other security deposited in relation to the citation to the person, or to any other person who deposited the security.

(D) If a person who has a current valid Ohio driver's or commercial driver's license and who was issued a citation fails to appear at the time and place specified on the citation, fails to comply with division (C) of section 2935.26 of the Revised Code, or fails to comply with or satisfy any judgment of the court within the time allowed by the court, the court shall declare the forfeiture of the person's license. Thirty days after the declaration of forfeiture, the court shall enter information relative to the forfeiture on a form approved and furnished by the registrar of motor vehicles, and forward the form to the registrar. The registrar shall suspend the person's driver's or commercial driver's license, send written notification of the suspension to the person at the person's last known address, and order the person to surrender the person's driver's or commercial driver's license to the registrar within forty-eight hours. No valid driver's or commercial driver's license shall be granted to the person until the court having jurisdiction of the offense that led to the forfeiture orders that the forfeiture be terminated. The court shall so order if the person, after having failed to appear in court at the required time and place to answer the charge or after having pleaded guilty to or been found guilty of the violation and having failed within the time allowed by the court to pay the fine imposed by the court, thereafter appears to answer the charge and pays any fine imposed by the court or pays the fine originally imposed by the court. The court shall inform the registrar of the termination of the forfeiture by entering information relative to the termination on a form approved and furnished by the registrar and sending the form to the registrar as provided in this division. The person shall pay to the bureau of motor vehicles a fifteen-dollar reinstatement fee to cover the costs of the bureau in administering this section. The registrar shall deposit the fees so paid into the state bureau of motor vehicles fund created by section 4501.25 of the Revised Code.

In addition, upon receipt of the copy of the declaration of forfeiture from the court, neither the registrar nor any deputy registrar shall accept any application for the registration or transfer of registration of any motor vehicle owned or leased by the person named in the declaration of forfeiture until the court having jurisdiction of the offense that led to the forfeiture orders that the forfeiture be terminated. However, for a motor vehicle leased by a person named in a declaration of forfeiture, the registrar shall not implement the preceding sentence until the registrar adopts procedures for that implementation under section 4503.39 of the Revised Code. Upon receipt by the registrar of an order terminating the forfeiture, the registrar shall take such measures as may be necessary to permit the person to register a motor vehicle owned or leased by the person or to transfer the registration of such a motor vehicle, if the person later makes application to take such action and the person otherwise is eligible to register the motor vehicle or to transfer the registration of it.

The registrar is not required to give effect to any declaration of forfeiture or order terminating a forfeiture unless the order is transmitted to the registrar by means of an electronic transfer system. The registrar shall not restore the person's driving or vehicle registration privileges until the person pays the reinstatement fee as provided in this division.

If the person who was issued the citation fails to appear at the time and place specified on the citation and fails to comply with division (C) of section 2935.26 of the Revised Code and the person has deposited a sum of money or other security in relation to the citation under division (A)(2) of this section, the deposit immediately shall be forfeited to the court.

This section does not preclude further action as authorized by division (F) of section 2935.26 of the Revised Code.

(E) A law enforcement officer who issues a person a minor misdemeanor citation for an act prohibited by Chapter 4511., 4513., or 4549. of the Revised Code or an act prohibited by a municipal ordinance that is substantially similar to any section contained in Chapter 4511., 4513., or 4549. of the Revised Code shall inform the person that if the person does not appear at the time and place stated on the citation or does not comply with division (C) of section 2935.26 of the Revised Code, the person's driver's or commercial driver's license will be suspended, the person will not be eligible for the reissuance of the license or the issuance of a new license or the issuance of a certificate of registration for a motor vehicle owned or leased by the person, until the person appears and complies with all orders of the court. The person also is subject to any applicable criminal penalties.

(F) A court setting security under division (A)(2) of this section shall do so in conformity with sections 2937.22 and 2937.23 of the Revised Code and the Rules of Criminal Procedure.

(2004, H 230, eff. 9–16–04; 2002 S 123, eff. 1–1–04; 1997 S 85, eff. 5–15–97; 1996 S 121, eff. 11–19–96; 1996 H 353, eff. 9–17–96; 1994 H 687, eff. 10–12–94; 1993 S 62, § 4, eff. 9–1–93; 1992 S 275; 1990 S 338; 1989 H 381; 1986 S 356; 1978 S 351)

Uncodified Law

1996 S 121, § 4, eff. 11–19–96, reads: The Registrar of Motor Vehicles shall not be required to give effect to the amendments contained in Section 1 of this act that prohibit the Registrar from issuing or transferring a certificate of registration for a motor vehicle when so prohibited by the amendments until six months after the effective date of this act.

Historical and Statutory Notes

Ed. Note: Former 2935.27 repealed by 128 v 97, eff. 1–1–60; 1953 H 1; GC 13434–2.

Ed. Note: The effective date of the amendment of this section by 1992 S 275 was changed from 7–1–93 to 9–1–93 by 1993 S 62, § 4, eff. 6–30–93.

Pre–1953 H 1 Amendments: 113 v 149, Ch 13, § 2

Amendment Note: 2004 H 230 substituted "forfeiture" for "suspension" throughout division (D); inserted "of forfeiture" following "declaration" and substituted "reinstatement" for "processing" preceding "fee to cover the costs" in the first paragraph of division (D); and inserted "The registrar shall not restore the person's driving or vehicle registration privileges until the person pays the reinstatement fee as provided in this division" in the third paragraph of division (D).

Amendment Note: 2002 S 123 substituted "has" for "appears before a court to have" before "security set" in division (B); and rewrote divisions (A)(2) and (D), which prior thereto read:

"(2) If the person is an Ohio resident who does not have a current valid Ohio driver's or commercial driver's license or if the person is a resident of a state that is not a member of the nonresident violator compact, of which this state is a member pursuant to section 4511.95 of the Revised Code, the officer shall bring the person before the court with which the citation is required to be filed for the setting of a reasonable security by the court pursuant to division (F) of this section.

"(D) If a person who has a current valid Ohio driver's or commercial driver's license and who was issued a citation fails to appear at the time and place specified on the citation, fails to comply with division (C) of section 2935.26 of the Revised Code, or fails to comply with or satisfy any judgment of the court within the time allowed by the court, the court shall declare the forfeiture of the person's license. Thirty days after the declaration of forfeiture, the court shall enter information relative to the forfeiture on a form approved and furnished by the registrar of motor vehicles, and forward the form to the registrar. The registrar shall suspend the person's driver's or commercial driver's license, send written notification of the suspension to the person at the person's last known address, and order the person to surrender the person's driver's or commercial driver's license to the registrar within forty-eight hours. No valid driver's or commercial driver's license shall be granted to the person until the court having jurisdiction of the offense that led to the suspension orders that the forfeiture be terminated. The court shall so order if the person, after having failed to appear in court at the required time and place to answer the charge or after having pleaded guilty to or been found guilty of the violation and having failed within the time allowed by the court to pay the fine imposed by the court, thereafter appears to answer the charge and pays any fine imposed by the court or pays the fine originally imposed by the court. The court shall inform the registrar of the termination of the forfeiture by entering information relative to the termination on a form approved and furnished by the registrar and sending the form to the registrar. The court also shall charge and collect from the person a fifteen-dollar processing fee to cover the costs of the bureau of motor vehicles in administering this section. The clerk of the court shall transmit monthly all such processing fees to the registrar for deposit into the state bureau of motor vehicles fund created by section 4501.25 of the Revised Code.

"In addition, upon receipt of the copy of the declaration of forfeiture from the court, neither the registrar nor any deputy registrar shall accept any application for the registration or transfer of registration of any motor vehicle owned or leased by the person named in the declaration of forfeiture until the court having jurisdiction of the offense that led to the forfeiture orders that the forfeiture be terminated. However, for a motor vehicle leased by a person named in a declaration of forfeiture, the registrar shall not implement the preceding sentence until the registrar adopts procedures for that implementation under section 4503.39 of the Revised Code. Upon receipt by the registrar of an order terminating the forfeiture, the registrar shall take such measures as may be necessary to permit the person to register a motor vehicle owned or leased by the person or to transfer the registration of such a motor vehicle, if the person later makes application to take such action and the person otherwise is eligible to register the motor vehicle or to transfer the registration of it.

"The registrar is not required to give effect to any declaration of forfeiture or order terminating a forfeiture unless the order is transmitted to the registrar by means of an electronic transfer system.

"If the person who was issued the citation fails to appear at the time and place specified on the citation and fails to comply with division (C) of section 2935.26 of the Revised Code and the person has deposited a sum of money or other security in relation to the citation under division (A)(2) of this section, the deposit immediately shall be forfeited to the court.

"This section does not preclude further action as authorized by division (F) of section 2935.26 of the Revised Code."

Amendment Note: 1997 S 85 added the second sentence in the second paragraph in division (D).

Amendment Note: 1996 S 121 substituted "If the person is an Ohio resident who does not have a current valid Ohio driver's or commercial driver's license or if the person is a resident of a state that is not a member of the nonresident violator compact, of which this state is a member pursuant to section 4511.95 of the Revised Code," for "If the person does not have a current valid Ohio driver's or commercial driver's license" in division (A)(2); rewrote the first paragraph of divisions (D) and division (E); added the second and third paragraphs of division (D); made changes to reflect gender neutral language; and made other nonsubstantive changes. Prior to being rewritten, the first paragraph of division (D) and division (E) read:

"(D) If a person who has a current valid Ohio driver's or commercial driver's license and who was issued a citation fails to appear at the time and place specified on the citation and fails to comply with division (C) of section 2935.26 of the Revised Code or fails to comply with or satisfy any judgment of the court within the time allowed by the court, the court shall declare the forfeiture of the person's license. Thirty days after the declaration of forfeiture, the court shall forward a copy of the declaration of forfeiture to the registrar of motor vehicles. The registrar shall cancel the person's driver's or commercial driver's license, send written notification of the cancellation to the person at his last known address, and order him to surrender his driver's or commercial driver's license to the registrar within forty-eight hours. No valid driver's or commercial driver's license shall be granted to the person for a period of one year after the cancellation, unless the court having jurisdiction of the offense that led to the cancellation orders that the forfeiture be terminated. The court shall so order the registrar if the person, after having failed to appear in court at the required time and place to answer the charge or after having pleaded guilty to or been found guilty of the violation and having failed within the time allowed by the court to pay the fine imposed by the court, thereafter appears to answer the charge and pays any fine imposed by the court or pays the fine originally imposed by the court."

"(E) A law enforcement officer who issues a person a minor misdemeanor citation for an act prohibited by Chapter 4511., 4513., or 4549. of the Revised Code or an act prohibited by a municipal ordinance that is substantially similar to any section contained in Chapter 4511., 4513., or 4549. of the Revised Code shall inform the person that if he does not appear at the time and place stated on the citation or does not comply with division (C) of section 2935.26 of the Revised Code, the person's driver's or commercial driver's license will be canceled, the person will not be eligible for the reissuance of the license or the issuance of a new license for one year after cancellation, and the person is subject to any applicable criminal penalties."

Amendment Note: 1996 H 353 substituted "enter information relative to the forfeiture on a form approved and furnished by the registrar of motor vehicles, and forward the form to the registrar" for "forward a copy of the declaration of forfeiture to the registrar of motor vehicles" and inserted the concluding sentence of the first paragraph in division (D); made changes to reflect gender neutral language; and made other nonsubstantive changes.

Amendment Note: 1994 H 687 substituted "send written notification of the cancellation to the person" for "notify the person of the cancellation by certified mail" and "forfeiture be terminated" for "registrar of motor vehicles to reissue the license to its original date of expiration without additional fee or to permit the person to apply for a new license" in division (D).

Cross References

Bail, Crim R 46

Motor vehicle registration application, prohibitions to acceptance, 4503.10

Motor vehicle registration renewal by mail, prohibitions, 4503.102

Motor vehicle, transfer of ownership and registration, 4503.12

Motor vehicles, transfer of ownership prohibited, 4503.12

Release of bail and sureties, use to satisfy fine or costs, when, 2937.40

Transfer of motor vehicle ownership and registration, prohibitions, 4503.12

Library References

Bail ⚷40.

Westlaw Topic No. 49.

C.J.S. Bail; Release and Detention Pending Proceedings § 8.

Research References

Encyclopedias

OH Jur. 3d Automobiles & Other Vehicles § 43, Transfer of Ownership and Registration—Effect of Merger or Consolidation of Corporations, or Incorporation of Proprietorship or Partnership.

OH Jur. 3d Criminal Law § 1696, Bail.

OH Jur. 3d Criminal Law § 2217, License as Bond; Generally.

OH Jur. 3d Criminal Law § 2219, Minor Misdemeanor.

OH Jur. 3d Criminal Law § 2221, Nonappearance of Defendant—Forfeiture of License.

2935.28 Property owners to be provided with names of persons charged with damaging their property

(A) As used in this section, "motor vehicle" has the same meaning as in section 4501.01 of the Revised Code.

(B) If damage is caused to real property by the operation of a motor vehicle in, or during the, violation of any section of the Revised Code or of any municipal ordinance, the law enforcement agency that investigates the case, upon request of the real property owner, shall provide the owner with the names of the persons who are charged with the commission of the offense. If a request for the names is made, the agency shall provide the names as soon as possible after the persons are charged with the offense.

(C) The personnel of law enforcement agencies who act pursuant to division (B) of this section in good faith are not liable in damages in a civil action allegedly arising from their actions taken pursuant to that division. Political subdivisions and the state are not liable in damages in a civil action allegedly arising from the actions of personnel of their law enforcement agencies if the personnel have immunity under this division.

(1984 H 666, eff. 3–14–85)

Historical and Statutory Notes

Ed. Note: Former 2935.28 repealed by 128 v 97, eff. 1–1–60; 1953 H 1; GC 13434–3.

Pre–1953 H 1 Amendments: 113 v 149, Ch 13, § 3

Library References

Criminal Law ⚷1220, 1222.1.
Westlaw Topic No. 110.
C.J.S. Criminal Law §§ 1724, 1729 to 1730, 1759, 1761 to 1786.

Research References

Encyclopedias

OH Jur. 3d Criminal Law § 1520, Duty to Keep and Convey Information Regarding Violations.

2935.29 Definition of fresh pursuit and state

As used in sections 2935.30 and 2935.31 of the Revised Code:

(A) "Fresh pursuit" includes fresh pursuit as defined by the common law, and also the pursuit of a person who has committed a felony or who is reasonably suspected of having committed a felony. It includes the pursuit of a person suspected of having committed a supposed felony, though no felony has actually been committed, if there is reasonable ground for believing that a felony has been committed. Fresh pursuit does not necessarily imply instant pursuit, but pursuit without unreasonable delay.

(B) "State" includes the District of Columbia.

(1953 H 1, eff. 10–1–53; GC 13434–7, 13434–8)

Historical and Statutory Notes

Pre–1953 H 1 Amendments: 117 v 671, § 4, 5

Comparative Laws

Ariz.—A.R.S. § 13-3831 to 13–3834.
Ark.—A.C.A. § 16-81-401 to 16–81–407.
Cal.—West's Ann.Cal.Pen.Code § 852 to 852.4.
Colo.—West's C.R.S.A. § 16–3–104.
Conn.—C.G.S.A. § 54-156.
D.C.—D.C. Official Code, 2001 Ed. § 23–901 to 23–903.
Del.—11 Del.C. § 1931 to 1935.
Fla.—West's F.S.A. § 941.31 to 941.37.
Idaho—I.C. § 19-701 to 19–707.
Ill.—S.H.A. 725 ILCS 5/107–4.
Ind.—West's A.I.C. 35–33–3–1 to 35–33–3–7.
Iowa—I.C.A. § 806.1 to 806.6.
Kan.—K.S.A. 22-2404.
La.—LSA-C.Cr.P. art. 231.
Mass.—M.G.L.A. 276, § 10A to 10D.
Md.—MD CRIM PROC, § 2–304 to 2–309.
Me.—15 M.R.S.A. § 151 to 155.
Mich.—M.C.L.A. § 780.101 to 780.108.
Minn.—M.S.A. § 626.65 to 626.72.

Mo.—V.A.M.S. § 544.155.
Mont.—MCA 46–6–411.
N.C.—G.S. § 15A-403.
N.D.—NDCC 29–06–05 to 29–06–07.
Neb.—R.R.S.1943, § 29–416 to 29–421.
Nev.—N.R.S. 171.154 to 171.164.
N.H.—RSA 614:1 to 614:6.
N.J.—N.J.S.A. § 2A:155-1 to 2A:155–7.
N.M.—NMSA 1978, 31–2–1 to 31–2–8.
N.Y.—McKinney's CPL 140.55.
Okl.—22 Okl.St.Ann. § 221 to 228.
Ore.—ORS 133.410 to 133.440.
Pa.—42 Pa.C.S.A. § 8921 to 8924.
R.I.—Gen.Laws 1956, § 12–8–1 to 12–8–6.
S.C.—Code 1976, § 25–3–180.
S.D.—SDCL 23A–3–10 to 23A–3–15.
Tenn.—T.C.A., §§ 40–7–201 to 40–7–205.
Tex.—Vernon's Ann.C.C.P. art. 14.051.
Utah—U.C.A.1953, 77–9–1 to 77–9–3.
Vt.—13 V.S.A. § 5041 to 5045.
Wash.—West's RCWA 10.89.010 to 10.89.080.
Wis.—W.S.A. 976.04.
W.Va.—Code, 62–11–1 to 62–11–7.
Wyo.—Wyo.Stat.Ann., § 7–3–301.

Cross References

Freedom from unreasonable seizure; warrants, O Const Art I §14

State university law enforcement officers, jurisdiction, 3345.04

Library References

Arrest ⚷66.

Westlaw Topic No. 35.

C.J.S. Arrest § 55.

Research References

Encyclopedias

OH Jur. 3d Criminal Law § 2263, Authority of Foreign Police, Generally.

Treatises and Practice Aids

Gotherman, Babbit and Lang, Baldwin's Ohio Practice, Local Government Law—Municipal, § 23:16, Extraterritorial Exercise of Municipal Power.

Notes of Decisions

Duty to pursue offender 1

1. Duty to pursue offender

An officer is justified in making a warrantless entry into the home of a DUI suspect on the basis of "hot pursuit" where the defendant is weaving in and out of traffic lanes and ignores the officer's emergency lights and audible siren, activates his left turn signal, and turns into his own private driveway where the officer follows, and the officer (1) forces the garage door open, (2) enters the garage, (3) pursues defendant inside his home, (4) grabs defendant by his arm and pulls him back into the garage where the officer notes an odor of alcohol on the defendant and that his eyes are red, and (5) effects an arrest for driving under the influence of alcohol. State v. Raszick (Ohio App. 5 Dist., Stark, 12-29-1994) No. 1994CA00114, 1994 WL 728339, Unreported, dismissed, appeal not allowed 72 Ohio St.3d 1518, 649 N.E.2d 278.

Where crimes (including misdemeanors) are committed in the presence of a law enforcement officer within his jurisdiction, he has the duty to pursue the offender beyond the geographical limits of his authority under the doctrine of "fresh" pursuit in order to apprehend and arrest the suspect. State v. Foster (Ohio Com.Pl. 1979) 60 Ohio Misc. 46, 396 N.E.2d 246, 14 O.O.3d 144. Arrest ⚷ 66(3)

2935.30 Authority of foreign police

Any member of an organized state, county, or municipal peace unit of another state of the United States who enters this state in fresh pursuit, and continues within this state in such fresh pursuit, of a person in order to arrest him on the ground that he is believed to have committed a felony in such other state has the same authority to arrest and hold such person in custody as has any member of any organized state, county, or municipal peace unit of this state to arrest and hold in custody a person on the ground that he is believed to have committed a felony in this state.

This section does not make unlawful any arrest in this state which would otherwise be lawful.

(1953 H 1, eff. 10–1–53; GC 13434–4, 13434–6)

Historical and Statutory Notes

Pre–1953 H 1 Amendments: 117 v 671, § 1, 3

Cross References

Freedom from unreasonable seizure; warrants, O Const Art I §14

Library References

Arrest ⚬62, 63.2.
Westlaw Topic No. 35.
C.J.S. Arrest §§ 9 to 10, 15.

Research References

Encyclopedias

OH Jur. 3d Criminal Law § 2263, Authority of Foreign Police, Generally.

2935.31 Hearing before magistrate in county of arrest

If an arrest is made in this state by an officer of another state under section 2935.30 of the Revised Code, he shall without unnecessary delay take the person arrested before a magistrate of the county in which the arrest was made, who shall conduct a hearing for the purpose of determining the lawfulness of the arrest. If the magistrate determines that the arrest was lawful be [1] shall commit the person arrested to await for a reasonable time the issuance of an extradition warrant by the governor of this state, or admit him to bail for such purposes. If the magistrate determines that the arrest was unlawful he shall discharge the person arrested. (1953 H 1, eff. 10–1–53; GC 13434–5)

[1] So in original; should this read "he"?

Historical and Statutory Notes

Pre–1953 H 1 Amendments: 117 v 671, § 2

Cross References

Freedom from unreasonable seizure; warrants, O Const Art I §14

Library References

Arrest ⚬70.
Westlaw Topic No. 35.
C.J.S. Arrest §§ 58 to 61.

Research References

Encyclopedias

OH Jur. 3d Criminal Law § 2263, Authority of Foreign Police, Generally.

OH Jur. 3d Criminal Law § 2264, Hearing Before Magistrate.

Treatises and Practice Aids

Gotherman, Babbit and Lang, Baldwin's Ohio Practice, Local Government Law—Municipal, § 23:16, Extraterritorial Exercise of Municipal Power.

2935.32 Broadcasting information of crime

The board of county commissioners or the prosecuting attorney of any county, with the consent of the court of common pleas, may contract with any company engaged in broadcasting by radio, for the purpose of immediate broadcasting of information concerning any violent felony, when the perpetrator thereof has escaped. The sheriff and heads of police departments, immediately upon the commission of any such felony and the escape of such perpetrator, shall furnish all information concerning said crime and the perpetrator thereof, to said company with which such contract may be made, for the purpose of broadcasting. The reasonable cost of such broadcasting shall be paid by the county, out of the county treasury, on the order of the board.

(1953 H 1, eff. 10–1–53; GC 13431–1)

Historical and Statutory Notes

Pre–1953 H 1 Amendments: 113 v 139, Ch 10, § 1

Library References

Criminal Law ⚷1222.1.
Westlaw Topic No. 110.
C.J.S. Criminal Law §§ 1724, 1729 to 1730.

Research References

Encyclopedias

OH Jur. 3d Criminal Law § 666, Broadcasting Information of Crime.

Treatises and Practice Aids

Adrine & Ruden, Ohio Domestic Violence Law § 5:1, Prosecution's Challenge.

2935.33 Commitment of alcoholics and intoxicated persons

(A) If a person charged with a misdemeanor is taken before a judge of a court of record and if it appears to the judge that the person is an alcoholic or is suffering from acute alcohol intoxication and that the person would benefit from services provided by an alcohol and drug addiction program certified under Chapter 3793. of the Revised Code, the judge may place the person temporarily in a program certified under that chapter in the area in which the court has jurisdiction for inpatient care and treatment for an indefinite period not exceeding five days. The commitment does not limit the right to release on bail. The judge may dismiss a charge of a violation of division (B) of section 2917.11 of the Revised Code or of a municipal ordinance substantially equivalent to that division if the defendant complies with all the conditions of treatment ordered by the court.

The court may order that any fines or court costs collected by the court from defendants who have received inpatient care from an alcohol and drug addiction program be paid, for the benefit of the program, to the board of alcohol, drug addiction, and mental health services of the alcohol, drug addiction, and mental health service district in which the program is located or to the director of alcohol and drug addiction services.

(B) If a person is being sentenced for a violation of division (B) of section 2917.11 or section 4511.19 of the Revised Code, a misdemeanor violation of section 2919.25 of the Revised Code, a misdemeanor violation of section 2919.27 of the Revised Code involving a protection order issued or consent agreement approved pursuant to section 2919.26 or 3113.31 of the Revised Code, or a violation of a municipal ordinance substantially equivalent to that division or any of those sections and if it appears to the judge at the time of sentencing that the person is an alcoholic or is suffering from acute alcohol intoxication and that, in lieu of imprisonment, the person would benefit from services provided by an alcohol and drug addiction program certified under Chapter 3793. of the Revised Code, the court may commit the person to close supervision in any facility in the area in which the court has jurisdiction that is, or is operated by, such a program. Such close supervision may include outpatient services and part-time release, except that a person convicted of a violation of division (A) of section 4511.19 of the Revised Code shall be confined to the facility for at least three days and except that a person convicted of a misdemeanor violation of section 2919.25 of the Revised Code, a misdemeanor violation of section 2919.27 of the Revised Code involving a protection order issued or consent agreement approved pursuant to section 2919.26 or 3113.31 of the Revised Code, or a violation of a substantially equivalent municipal ordinance shall be confined to the facility in accordance with the order of commitment. A commitment of a person to a facility for purposes of close supervision shall not exceed the maximum term for which the person could be imprisoned.

(C) A law enforcement officer who finds a person subject to prosecution for violation of division (B) of section 2917.11 of the Revised Code or a municipal ordinance substantially equivalent to that division and who has reasonable cause to believe that the person is an alcoholic or is suffering from acute alcohol intoxication and would benefit from immediate treatment immediately may place the person in an alcohol and drug addiction program certified under Chapter 3793. of the Revised Code in the area in which the person is found, for emergency treatment, in lieu of other arrest procedures, for a maximum period of forty-eight hours. During that time, if the person desires to leave such custody, the person shall be released forthwith.

(D) As used in this section:

(1) "Alcoholic" has the same meaning as in section 3793.01 of the Revised Code;

(2) "Acute alcohol intoxication" means a heavy consumption of alcohol over a relatively short period of time, resulting in dysfunction of the brain centers controlling behavior, speech, and memory and causing characteristic withdrawal symptoms.

(2002 H 490, eff. 1–1–04; 1995 S 2, eff. 7–1–96; 1994 S 82, eff. 5–4–94; 1989 H 317, eff. 10–10–89; 1985 H 475; 1984 H 37; 1976 H 907; 1975 H 1; 1972 H 240)

Historical and Statutory Notes

Amendment Note: 2002 H 490 deleted the second sentence of division (B); and made changes to reflect gender neutral language. Prior to deletion the second sentence read:

"A commitment to close supervision for a misdemeanor violation of section 2919.25 of the Revised Code, a misdemeanor violation of section 2919.27 of the Revised Code involving a protection order issued or consent agreement approved pursuant to section 2919.26 or 3113.31 of the Revised Code, or a violation of any substantially equivalent municipal ordinance shall be in accordance with division (B) of section 2929.51 of the Revised Code."

Amendment Note: 1995 S 2 substituted "a misdemeanor violation of section 2919.25 of the Revised Code, a misdemeanor violation of section 2919.27 of the Revised Code involving a protection order issued or consent agreement approved pursuant to section 2919.26 or 3113.31 of the Revised Code, or a violation of" for "2919.25, or 2919.27 of the Revised Code or" three times in division (B); substituted "(B)" for "(E)" before "of section 2929.51" in division (B); and made other nonsubstantive changes.

Amendment Note: 1994 S 82 inserted "division (A) of" before "section 4511.19" in division (B).

Cross References

Bail, physical condition of arrestee poses danger to himself or others, Crim R 46

Suspension of sentence; acute alcohol intoxication, defined, 2929.51

Library References

Chemical Dependents ⚩11, 13.

Westlaw Topic No. 76A.

C.J.S. Chemical Dependents §§ 12 to 16.

Research References

Encyclopedias

OH Jur. 3d Incompetent Persons § 149, Short-Term Commitment of Alcoholics and Intoxicated Persons.

Treatises and Practice Aids

Katz, Giannelli, Blair and Lipton, Baldwin's Ohio Practice, Criminal Law, § 108:6, Disorderly Conduct.

Painter, Ohio Driving Under the Influence § 12:8, Statutory Penalties—Low Tier—Incarceration of Second Offender.

Law Review and Journal Commentaries

Ohio's New Alcohol Impaired Driving Law—A Judicial Perspective, John F. Bender. 15 U Tol L Rev 117 (Fall 1983).

Notes of Decisions

1. Commitment for treatment in lieu of jail

Where a person is convicted of operating a motor vehicle while under the influence of alcohol pursuant to a city ordinance (essentially the same as RC 4511.19 and 4511.99, as amended by 1982 S 432, eff. 3–16–83), commitment to an alcoholic treatment and control center under RC 2935.33(B) is not a suspension of sentence under RC 4511.99(A)(5); rather, such a commitment is in lieu of imprisonment and thus its equivalent or substitute. City of Wadsworth v. Slanker (Medina 1983) 10 Ohio App.3d 300, 462 N.E.2d 191, 10 O.B.R. 475.

Mandamus will not lie to compel a judge to sentence a person convicted of driving while intoxicated to three days in jail rather than to a three-day term in a treatment center. State ex rel. Phillips v. Andrews (Ohio 1977) 50 Ohio St.2d 341, 364 N.E.2d 281, 4 O.O.3d 480.

2. Repeat DWI offender

RC 2935.33(B), which provides for commitment to a treatment center in lieu of imprisonment, does not apply to the ten-day and thirty-day terms of imprisonment required by RC 4511.99(A)(2) and 4511.99(A)(3) for subsequent offenses within five years. State v. Johnson (Ohio 1986) 23 Ohio St.3d 127, 491 N.E.2d 1138, 23 O.B.R. 283.

2935.36 Pre–trial diversion programs for adult offenders; limits; procedure

(A) The prosecuting attorney may establish pre-trial diversion programs for adults who are accused of committing criminal offenses and whom the prosecuting attorney believes probably will not offend again. The prosecuting attorney may require, as a condition of an accused's participation in the program, the accused to pay a reasonable fee for supervision services that include, but are not limited to, monitoring and drug testing. The programs shall be operated pursuant to written standards approved by journal entry by the presiding judge or, in courts with only one judge, the judge of the court of common pleas and shall not be applicable to any of the following:

(1) Repeat offenders or dangerous offenders;

(2) Persons accused of an offense of violence, of a violation of section 2903.06, 2907.04, 2907.05, 2907.21, 2907.22, 2907.31, 2907.32, 2907.34, 2911. 31, 2919.12, 2919.13, 2919.22, 2921.02, 2921.11, 2921.12, 2921.32, or 2923.20 of the Revised Code, or of a violation of section 2905.01, 2905.02, or 2919.23 of the Revised Code that, had it occurred prior to July 1, 1996, would have been a violation of section 2905.04 of the Revised Code as it existed prior to that date, with the exception that the prosecuting attorney may permit persons accused of any such offense to enter a pre-trial diversion program, if the prosecuting attorney finds any of the following:

(a) The accused did not cause, threaten, or intend serious physical harm to any person;

(b) The offense was the result of circumstances not likely to recur;

(c) The accused has no history of prior delinquency or criminal activity;

(d) The accused has led a law-abiding life for a substantial time before commission of the alleged offense;

(e) Substantial grounds tending to excuse or justify the alleged offense.

(3) Persons accused of a violation of Chapter 2925. or 3719. of the Revised Code;

(4) Drug dependent persons or persons in danger of becoming drug dependent persons, as defined in section 3719.011 of the Revised Code. However, this division does not affect the eligibility of such persons for intervention in lieu of conviction pursuant to section 2951.041 of the Revised Code.

(5) Persons accused of a violation of section 4511.19 of the Revised Code or a violation of any substantially similar municipal ordinance.

(B) An accused who enters a diversion program shall do all of the following:

(1) Waive, in writing and contingent upon the accused's successful completion of the program, the accused's right to a speedy trial, the preliminary hearing, the time period within which the grand jury may consider an indictment against the accused, and arraignment, unless the hearing, indictment, or arraignment has already occurred;

(2) Agree, in writing, to the tolling while in the program of all periods of limitation established by statutes or rules of court, that are applicable to the offense with which the accused is charged and to the conditions of the diversion program established by the prosecuting attorney;

(3) Agree, in writing, to pay any reasonable fee for supervision services established by the prosecuting attorney.

(C) The trial court, upon the application of the prosecuting attorney, shall order the release from confinement of any accused who has agreed to enter a pre-trial diversion program and shall discharge and release any existing bail and release any sureties on recognizances and shall release the accused on a recognizance bond conditioned upon the accused's compliance with the terms of the diversion program. The prosecuting attorney shall notify every victim of the crime and the arresting officers of the prosecuting attorney's intent to permit the accused to enter a pre-trial diversion program. The victim of the crime and the arresting officers shall have the opportunity to file written objections with the prosecuting attorney prior to the commencement of the pre-trial diversion program.

(D) If the accused satisfactorily completes the diversion program, the prosecuting attorney shall recommend to the trial court that the charges against the accused be dismissed, and the court, upon the recommendation of the prosecuting attorney, shall dismiss the charges. If the accused chooses not to enter the prosecuting attorney's diversion program, or if the accused violates the conditions of the agreement pursuant to which the accused has been released, the accused may be brought to trial upon the charges in the manner provided by law, and the waiver executed pursuant to division (B)(1) of this section shall be void on the date the accused is removed from the program for the violation.

(E) As used in this section:

(1) "Repeat offender" means a person who has a history of persistent criminal activity and whose character and condition reveal a substantial risk that the person will commit another offense. It is prima-facie evidence that a person is a repeat offender if any of the following applies:

(a) Having been convicted of one or more offenses of violence and having been imprisoned pursuant to sentence for any such offense, the person commits a subsequent offense of violence;

(b) Having been convicted of one or more sexually oriented offenses or child-victim oriented offenses, both as defined in section 2950.01 of the Revised Code, and having been imprisoned pursuant to sentence for one or more of those offenses, the person commits a subsequent sexually oriented offense or child-victim oriented offense;

(c) Having been convicted of one or more theft offenses as defined in section 2913.01 of the Revised Code and having been imprisoned pursuant to sentence for one or more of those theft offenses, the person commits a subsequent theft offense;

(d) Having been convicted of one or more felony drug abuse offenses as defined in section 2925.01 of the Revised Code and having been imprisoned pursuant to sentence for one or more of those felony drug abuse offenses, the person commits a subsequent felony drug abuse offense;

(e) Having been convicted of two or more felonies and having been imprisoned pursuant to sentence for one or more felonies, the person commits a subsequent offense;

(f) Having been convicted of three or more offenses of any type or degree other than traffic offenses, alcoholic intoxication offenses, or minor misdemeanors and having been imprisoned pursuant to sentence for any such offense, the person commits a subsequent offense.

(2) "Dangerous offender" means a person who has committed an offense, whose history, character, and condition reveal a substantial risk that the person will be a danger to others, and whose conduct has been characterized by a pattern of repetitive, compulsive, or aggressive behavior with heedless indifference to the consequences.

(2003 S 5, eff. 7–31–03; 2003 H 95, eff. 9–26–03; 1999 S 107, eff. 3–23–00; 1996 H 180, eff. 7–1–97; 1995 S 2, eff. 7–1–96; 1994 S 82, eff. 5–4–94; 1986 S 262, eff. 3–20–87; 1978 H 473)

Uncodified Law

1996 H 180, § 5, eff. 10–16–96, reads: Sections 109.57, 2935.36, 2950.02, 2950.04, 2950.05, 2950.06, 2950.07, 2950.08, 2950.10, 2950.11, 2950.12, 2950.13, 2950.99, 2953.35, and 2953.54 of the Revised Code, as amended or enacted in Sections 1 and 2 of this act, shall take effect on July 1, 1997. The repeal of existing sections 109.57, 2935.36, 2950.08, 2950.99, 2953.35, and 2953.54 and sections 2950.02, 2950.04, 2950.05, 2950.06, and 2950.07 of the Revised Code by Section 2 of this act shall take effect on July 1, 1997, and the provisions of those sections shall remain in effect and shall be applicable to habitual sex offenders, as defined in the version of section 2950.01 of the Revised Code that is repealed by Section 2 of this act, until that date. Notwithstanding the repeal of existing sections 2950.01 and 2950.03 of the Revised Code by Section 2 of this act, the definitions and the duty to provide notice to habitual sex offenders who are being released from correctional institutions that are contained in the versions of those sections that are so repealed shall remain applicable to habitual sex offenders, as defined in the version of section 2950.01 of the Revised Code that is so repealed, until July 1, 1997.

Historical and Statutory Notes

Ed. Note: A special endorsement by the Legislative Service Commission states, "Comparison of these amendments [2003 S 5, eff. 7–31–03 and 2003 H 95, eff. 9–26–03] in pursuance of section 1.52 of the Revised Code discloses that they are not irreconcilable so that they are required by that section to be harmonized to give effect to each amendment." In recognition of this rule of construction, changes made by 2003 S 5, eff. 7–31–03, and 2003 H 95, eff. 9–26–03, have been incorporated in the above amendment. See *Baldwin's Ohio Legislative Service Annotated*, 2003, pages 7/L–1922 and 6/L–605, or the OH–LEGIS or OH–LEGIS–OLD database on Westlaw, for original versions of these Acts.

Amendment Note: 2003 S 5 inserted "or child-victim oriented offenses, both" and "or child-victim oriented offense" in division (E)(1)(b) and made other nonsubstantive changes.

Amendment Note: 2003 H 95 inserted "The prosecuting attorney may require, as a condition of an accused's participation in the program, the accused to pay a reasonable fee for supervision services that include, but are not limited to, monitoring and drug testing." following the first sentence of Division (A); and added Division (B)(3).

Amendment Note: 1999 S 107 deleted "2903.07," after "2903.06," and substituted "July 1, 1996" for "the effective date of this amendment" in the introductory paragraph in division (A)(2); and substituted "intervention" for "treatment" in division (A)(4).

Amendment Note: 1996 H 180 substituted "sexually oriented" for "sex" throughout division (E)(1)(b); and made other nonsubstantive changes.

Amendment Note: 1995 S 2 deleted a reference to section 2929.01 from division (A)(1); deleted a reference to section 2905.04 from and inserted "or a violation of section 2905.01, 2905.02, or 2919.23 of the Revised Code that, had it occurred prior to the effective date of this amendment, would have been a violation of section 2905.04 of the Revised Code as it existed prior to that date" in division (A)(2); added division (E); and made changes to reflect gender neutral language and other nonsubstantive changes.

Amendment Note: 1994 S 82 deleted "division (A) of" before "section 4511.19" in division (A)(5).

Cross References

Minor, diversion program, 4301.69

Misdemeanor sentencing; repeat offender and dangerous offender, defined, 2929.22

Probation, supervision fees, 2951.021

Sealed criminal records, re-examination, 2953.32, 2953.53

Library References

Sentencing and Punishment ⇐2058 to 2079.

Westlaw Topic No. 350H.

C.J.S. Criminal Law §§ 425 to 444, 449.

Research References

Encyclopedias

OH Jur. 3d Criminal Law § 2304, Establishment of Pretrial Diversion Program.

OH Jur. 3d Criminal Law § 2305, Notice to Victims of Crime of Accused's Entry in Program.

OH Jur. 3d Criminal Law § 2306, Operation of Programs.

OH Jur. 3d Criminal Law § 2308, Repeat Offenders.

OH Jur. 3d Criminal Law § 2309, Persons Accused of Specific Offenses.

OH Jur. 3d Criminal Law § 2310, Persons Accused of Specific Offenses—Exceptions.

OH Jur. 3d Criminal Law § 2311, Drug-Dependent Persons.

OH Jur. 3d Criminal Law § 2312, Persons Driving While Under the Influence of Alcohol.

OH Jur. 3d Criminal Law § 2313, Waiver and Agreement by Person Entering Program.

OH Jur. 3d Criminal Law § 2314, Release of Person, Bail, and Sureties Upon Entering Program.

OH Jur. 3d Criminal Law § 2315, Dismissal of Charges; Effect of Successful Completion of Charges.

OH Jur. 3d Criminal Law § 2316, Dismissal of Charges; Effect of Successful Completion of Charges—Proceedings Upon Refusal of Accused to Participate in Program or Violation of Agreement.

OH Jur. 3d Criminal Law § 4009, Required Eligibility Findings.

Treatises and Practice Aids

Katz, Giannelli, Blair and Lipton, Baldwin's Ohio Practice, Criminal Law, § 35:10, Pretrial Diversion.

Katz, Giannelli, Blair and Lipton, Baldwin's Ohio Practice, Criminal Law, § 143:38, Motion for Pre-Trial Diversion.

Katz, Giannelli, Blair and Lipton, Baldwin's Ohio Practice, Criminal Law, § 143:39, Prosecutor's Consent to Place Defendant on Pre-Trial Diversion Program.

Hennenberg & Reinhart, Ohio Criminal Defense Motions F 5.11, Treatment in Lieu of Conviction-Pretrial Motions.

Hennenberg & Reinhart, Ohio Criminal Defense Motions F 5.111, Motion for Intervention in Lieu of Conviction.

Law Review and Journal Commentaries

Misdemeanor Diversion Gets Trial in Municipal Court, Douglas J. Powley. 39 Akron B Ass'n Examiner 8 (February 1998).

Notes of Decisions

1. Constitutional issues

Trial court violated constitutional concept of separation of powers by terminating, without prosecutor's consent, prosecution of defendant who had been discharged from pretrial diversion program for failure to satisfy restitution condition thereof, where defendant was before the court solely for sentencing on his previously entered guilty plea; while court could legitimately consider fact that defendant made complete restitution in determining his sentence, prosecutor did not recommend dismissal of charges, and state had legitimate expectation that trial court would sentence defendant pursuant to his guilty plea. State v. Curry (Ohio App. 9 Dist., 07-28-1999) 134 Ohio App.3d 113, 730 N.E.2d 435. Constitutional Law ⚷ 72

Absent one or more of the exceptions specified by statute, a full custodial arrest for a minor misdemeanor offense violates the Fourth Amendment and the state Constitution, and evidence obtained incident to such an arrest is subject to suppression in accordance with the exclusionary rule. State v. Jones (Ohio, 05-17-2000) 88 Ohio St.3d 430, 727 N.E.2d 886, 2000-Ohio-374. Arrest ⚷ 68(1); Criminal Law ⚷ 394.4(9)

Defendants convicted of theft for receiving food stamps and ADC benefits while having other income are not entitled to participate in a prosecutor's diversionary program under the Due Process Clause because they suffer no loss and have no interest in remaining free of prosecution that would allow protection. State v. Newberry (Ross 1991) 77 Ohio App.3d 818, 603 N.E.2d 1086, dismissed, jurisdictional motion overruled 63 Ohio St.3d 1428, 588 N.E.2d 128.

Defendant's waiver of speedy trial rights in connection with consent to participation in domestic violence diversion program was void as of date that he was removed from program by the court. State v. Mintz (Wood 1991) 74 Ohio App.3d 62, 598 N.E.2d 52, dismissed, jurisdictional motion overruled 62 Ohio St.3d 1431, 578 N.E.2d 823. Criminal Law ⚷ 577.10(9)

Once a defendant is admitted into a diversion program, participation in such a program is a statutory right and termination of such participation without a hearing, when requested in a timely fashion, is a violation of due process. State v Sneed, No. 8837 (2d Dist Ct App, Montgomery, 1-1-86).

2. Diversionary programs

A judge's belief following a diversionary program that the defendant is likely to engage in similar conduct again is not the same thing as the defendant failing to "satisfactorily complete… the diversion program"; consequently, if the diversion program is completed as designed, the charge must be dismissed. State v. Bennett (Ohio App. 2 Dist., Miami, 05-10-1995) No. 94 CA 52, 1995 WL 276763, Unreported.

Prosecuting attorney has statutory discretion regarding the determination of whether to prosecute an individual who might be eligible for pretrial diversionary programs. State v. Curry (Ohio App. 9 Dist., 07-28-1999) 134 Ohio App.3d 113, 730 N.E.2d 435.

Prosecution had discretion to determine whether defendant who violated restitution condition of his pretrial diversion program should be brought to trial on underlying charges. State v. Curry (Ohio App. 9 Dist., 07-28-1999) 134 Ohio App.3d 113, 730 N.E.2d 435.

Trial court's dismissal of domestic violence misdemeanor charge in return for defendant's completion of counseling program (AMEND) was dispositive of charge, where defendant entered long-established diversionary program based on agreement with prosecutor to recommend charges be dismissed, and state did not explicitly reserve right to further prosecute defendant for same offense. State v. Monk (Ohio Com.Pl., 01-05-1994) 64 Ohio Misc.2d 1, 639 N.E.2d 518. Sentencing And Punishment ⚷ 2096

Order denying admission to county's diversion program is not order made in "special proceeding," and thus, such an order was not final and appealable. State v. Newberry (Ross 1989) 65 Ohio App.3d 179, 583 N.E.2d 365. Criminal Law ⚷ 1023(3)

Even though RC 2935.36 grants discretion to a prosecuting attorney regarding a defendant's eligibility to participate in a pretrial intervention program, programs which existed before the enactment of RC 2935.36 are still valid, even if they vest discretion in the judiciary rather than the prosecution. City of Cleveland v. Mosquito (Cuyahoga 1983) 10 Ohio App.3d 239, 461 N.E.2d 924, 10 O.B.R. 334.

A county prosecuting attorney that has established a pre-trial diversion program pursuant to RC 2935.36 may not require participants in the program to pay a fee for supervision services. OAG 03-005.

3. Successful completion of program

Trial court has the authority to hold a hearing to determine whether the conditions of a pretrial diversion program have been satisfactorily met by an accused. State v. Curry (Ohio App. 9 Dist., 07-28-1999) 134 Ohio App.3d 113, 730 N.E.2d 435.

A successfully completed diversion contract under RC 2935.36 is the equivalent of served or probated time for the contractual offenses. State v. Urvan (Cuyahoga 1982) 4 Ohio App.3d 151, 446 N.E.2d 1161, 4 O.B.R. 244. Sentencing And Punishment ⚷ 2096

4. Juvenile offenses

The violation of RC 2903.07, vehicular homicide, when committed by a juvenile is an act of delinquency, not a juvenile traffic offense. In re Fox (Ohio Com.Pl. 1979) 60 Ohio Misc. 31, 395 N.E.2d 918, 14 O.O.3d 80.

5. Termination of participation

Hearing is not mandated every time an accused is terminated from a pretrial diversion program; in order to be entitled to a hearing, an accused who claims that he or she was wrongfully terminated from a diversion program must bring the issue to the attention of the court in a timely manner. State v. Curry (Ohio App. 9 Dist., 07-28-1999) 134 Ohio App.3d 113, 730 N.E.2d 435.

Defendant's failure of polygraph test violated diversion agreement's conditions that she provide truthful information at all times and submit to polygraph test if requested, justifying termination of her participation in pretrial diversion program, though agreement did not expressly state that passing test was required; implicit in requirement that defendant submit to polygraph examination was concomitant requirement that she pass examination. State v. Pickens (Ohio App. 2 Dist., 02-07-1996) 109 Ohio App.3d 147, 671 N.E.2d 1116. Sentencing And Punishment ⚷ 2087

Prosecutor need not present clear and convincing evidence establishing violation of diversion agreement before terminating individual's participation in pretrial diversion program. State v. Pickens (Ohio App. 2 Dist., 02-07-1996) 109 Ohio App.3d 147, 671 N.E.2d 1116. Sentencing And Punishment ⚷ 2092

Once prosecutor established reasons for terminating defendant's participation in pretrial diversion program, defendant had burden of establishing, by greater weight of evidence, that state violated diversion agreement and abused its discretion when it revoked defendant's participation. State v. Pickens (Ohio App. 2 Dist., 02-07-1996) 109 Ohio App.3d 147, 671 N.E.2d 1116. Sentencing And Punishment ⚷ 2092

CHAPTER 2937

PRELIMINARY EXAMINATION; BAIL

PRELIMINARY EXAMINATION

BAIL

UNIFORM PROCEDURES IN TRAFFIC CASES

PENALTY

PRELIMINARY EXAMINATION

2937.01 Definitions

The definition of "magistrate" set forth in section 2931.01 of the Revised Code, and the definitions of "peace officer," "prosecutor," and "offense" set forth in section 2935.01 of the Revised Code apply to Chapter 2937. of the Revised Code.

(128 v 97, eff. 1-1-60; 1953 H 1)

Cross References

Additional costs in criminal cases in all courts to fund reparations payments; bail, defined, 2743.70

County court, jurisdiction, 1907.02

Proceedings upon arrest, 2935.13

Research References

Encyclopedias

OH Jur. 3d Cvl. Servants & Pub. Officers & Employ. § 490, Who is Prosecuting Attorney in Magistrates' Courts.

Treatises and Practice Aids

Katz, Giannelli, Blair and Lipton, Baldwin's Ohio Practice, Criminal Law, § 38:2, Right to a Preliminary Hearing.

Adrine & Ruden, Ohio Domestic Violence Law § 7:7, Temporary Protection Orders and Initial Felony Appearances.

Law Review and Journal Commentaries

CRIMINAL PROCEDURE—Preliminary Hearing Required To Satisfy Due Process for Pretrial Incarceration—*Gerstein v. Pugh*, Note. 37 Ohio St L J 170 (1976).

The Developing Role of the Magistrate in the Federal Courts, Jack B. Streepy. 29 Clev St L Rev 81 (1980).

2937.02 Announcement of charge and rights of accused by court

When, after arrest, the accused is taken before a court or magistrate, or when the accused appears pursuant to terms of summons or notice, the affidavit or complaint being first filed, the court or magistrate shall, before proceeding further:

(A) Inform the accused of the nature of the charge against him and the identity of the complainant and permit the accused or his counsel to see and read the affidavit or complaint or a copy thereof;

(B) Inform the accused of his right to have counsel and the right to a continuance in the proceedings to secure counsel;

(C) Inform the accused of the effect of pleas of guilty, not guilty, and no contest, of his right to trial by jury, and the necessity of making written demand therefor;

(D) If the charge be a felony, inform the accused of the nature and extent of possible punishment on conviction and of the right to preliminary hearing. Such information may be given to each accused individually or, if at any time there exists any substantial number of defendants to be arraigned at the same session, the judge or magistrate may, by general announcement or by distribution of printed matter, advise all those accused concerning those rights general in their nature, and informing as to individual matters at arraignment.

(128 v 97, eff. 1-1-60)

Historical and Statutory Notes

Ed. Note: Former 2937.02 repealed by 128 v 97, eff. 1-1-60; 1953 H 1; GC 13433-1.

Pre-1953 H 1 Amendments: 115 v 530; 113 v 145, Ch 12, § 1

Cross References

Initial appearance, explanation of rights, Crim R 5

Rights of accused, O Const Art I §10

Library References

Criminal Law ⚩229.

Westlaw Topic No. 110.

C.J.S. Criminal Law §§ 282, 345.

Research References

Encyclopedias

OH Jur. 3d Criminal Law § 34, Informing Accused of Right to Attorney.

OH Jur. 3d Criminal Law § 41, Arraignment.

OH Jur. 3d Criminal Law § 59, Presumption of Competence; Burden of Proof.

OH Jur. 3d Criminal Law § 2606, to Secure Counsel and Prepare Case.

OH Jur. 3d Criminal Law § 3669, Prejudicial Error, Generally.

Treatises and Practice Aids

Katz, Giannelli, Blair and Lipton, Baldwin's Ohio Practice, Criminal Law, § 36:1, Introduction.

Katz, Giannelli, Blair and Lipton, Baldwin's Ohio Practice, Criminal Law, § 36:2, Procedure.

Katz, Giannelli, Blair and Lipton, Baldwin's Ohio Practice, Criminal Law, § 36:3, Pleas.

Katz, Giannelli, Blair and Lipton, Baldwin's Ohio Practice, Criminal Law, § 36:5, Rule 5(A) Violations.

Katz, Giannelli, Blair and Lipton, Baldwin's Ohio Practice, Criminal Law, § 38:1, Introduction.

Katz, Giannelli, Blair and Lipton, Baldwin's Ohio Practice, Criminal Law, § 43:2, Right to Counsel.

Katz, Giannelli, Blair and Lipton, Baldwin's Ohio Practice, Criminal Law, § 43:13, Understanding the Waiver of Rights.

Katz, Giannelli, Blair and Lipton, Baldwin's Ohio Practice, Criminal Law, § 75:14, Waiver of Right.

Law Review and Journal Commentaries

Manipulated by *Miranda*: A Critical Analysis of Bright Lines and Voluntary Confessions Under *United States v. Dickerson*, Casenote. 68 U Cin L Rev 555 (Winter 2000).

The Right to Remain Silent: The Use of Pre–Arrest Silence in *United States v. Oplinger*, 150 F.3d 1061 (5th Cir. 1998), Casenote. 68 U Cin L Rev 505 (Winter 2000).

Notes of Decisions

---

1. Illegal detention

A mere illegal detention prior to the preliminary hearing does not entitle an accused to release after conviction. Cook v. Maxwell (Ohio 1965) 2 Ohio St.2d 107, 206 N.E.2d 558, 31 O.O.2d 151. Habeas Corpus ⚩ 470

2. Right to counsel

Defendant, who understood charge of domestic violence and pled not guilty at arraignment, was not prejudiced by lack of counsel, and thus lack of counsel at arraignment did not require reversal of his conviction. Shaker Heights v. Hunte (Ohio App. 8 Dist., 07-30-2001) 145 Ohio App.3d 150, 762 N.E.2d 384. Criminal Law ⚩ 1166(3)

Counsel was not ineffective in allegedly failing to inform defendant that state's recommendation would be one of consecutive sentences where prosecutor recited entire plea agreement prior to defendant entering his plea, defendant's attorney asked if defendant wanted to enter the no-contest plea, and defendant responded, "Yes, sir," and court then accepted plea. State v. Moore (Ohio App. 7 Dist., 06-21-1996) 111 Ohio App.3d 833, 677 N.E.2d 408. Criminal Law ⚩ 641.13(5)

A preliminary hearing is a critical stage of the criminal process during which a defendant's fundamental right to counsel is protected by US Const Am 6 and 14. State v. Spates (Ohio 1992) 64 Ohio St.3d 269, 595 N.E.2d 351. Criminal Law ⚩ 641.3(4)

A defendant's plea of guilty entered into knowingly, intelligently, and voluntarily after a preliminary hearing waives defendant's right to challenge a claimed deprivation of the constitutional right to counsel at the preliminary hearing stage of a criminal proceeding. State v. Spates (Ohio 1992) 64 Ohio St.3d 269, 595 N.E.2d 351. Criminal Law ⚩ 273.4(1)

Right of counsel at a preliminary hearing of the character set forth in Coleman v Alabama, 399 US 1, 90 SCt 1999, 26 LEd(2d) 387 (1970), does not extend in Ohio to magistrate's arraignment of accused on felony charge, where accused has been informed of his rights by magistrate as prescribed by RC 2937.02, has pled not guilty and has affirmatively waived his right to preliminary hearing. State v. Simones (Marion 1971) 27 Ohio App.2d 9, 272 N.E.2d 146, 56 O.O.2d 198, affirmed 30 Ohio St.2d 100, 282 N.E.2d 573, 59 O.O.2d 113. Criminal Law ⚩ 264

Defendant in contempt proceeding accused of attempting to bribe and threatening a witness outside the courtroom was entitled to cross-examine witnesses against him, protection against self-incrimination, reasonable notice of the charge against him, to be advised of his right to counsel, but not to trial by jury unless the penalty imposed is imprisonment for more than a year. In re Neff (Stark 1969) 20 Ohio App.2d 213, 254 N.E.2d 25, 52 A.L.R.3d 970, 49 O.O.2d 312.

When a defendant is incarcerated and without counsel for three months after his arrest, his claim that he has been denied a fair trial may be raised before or at trial or on appeal, and where it is not, it is barred by the doctrine of res judicata, and defendant is not entitled to postconviction relief. State v. Johnson (Ohio 1968) 14 Ohio St.2d 67, 236 N.E.2d 552, 43 O.O.2d 126.

The mere fact that the testimony of alibi witnesses is weakened upon cross-examination so that such witnesses reveal a lack of distinct recollection of the accused's whereabouts at the time of the alleged crime is not a sufficient basis for arguing upon appeal that such lack of evidence-memory was attributable to delay in the appointment of counsel for the defendant so as to ground a claim of lack of counsel at a critical stage of prosecution. (See also State v Johnson, 14 OS(2d) 67, 236 NE(2d) 552 (1968).) State v. Childs (Ohio 1968) 14 Ohio St.2d 56, 236 N.E.2d 545, 43 O.O.2d 119, certiorari denied 89 S.Ct. 1596, 394 U.S. 1002, 22 L.Ed.2d 779.

There is no statutory or constitutional requirement in Ohio that a defendant charged with a misdemeanor in violation of a city ordinance which parallels a state statute be apprised of his right to counsel and, if indigent, to an assignment of counsel by the court at public expense. City of Toledo v. Frazier (Lucas 1967) 10 Ohio App.2d 51, 226 N.E.2d 777, 39 O.O.2d 123.

In a case tried after Escobedo but prior to Miranda, where there was no request for counsel and the accused was advised of his right to remain silent, a statement taken in the absence of counsel but otherwise voluntary in nature is admissible into evidence. State v. Carder (Ohio 1966) 9 Ohio St.2d 1, 222 N.E.2d 620, 38 O.O.2d 1. Criminal Law ⚷ 412.2(3); Criminal Law ⚷ 412.2(5)

Where a defendant was not represented by counsel, did not have his right to counsel explained to him and did not waive counsel, he is entitled to his release under Gideon v Wainwright, 372 US 335, 83 SCt 792, 9 LEd(2d) 799 (1963). Johnson v. Maxwell (Ohio 1964) 177 Ohio St. 72, 202 N.E.2d 417, 29 O.O.2d 193. Habeas Corpus ⚷ 484

A refusal to appoint counsel at a primary hearing is not a deprivation of constitutional rights. Smith v. Maxwell (Ohio 1964) 177 Ohio St. 79, 202 N.E.2d 415, 29 O.O.2d 197. Criminal Law ⚷ 232

If a violation of the US Const Am 6 right to counsel does not show prejudice or a major threat of prejudice, a remedy is not warranted. The criminal proceeding may go forward with recognition of the defendant's right to counsel. It is not appropriate to dismiss the indictment. U. S. v. Morrison (U.S.Pa. 1981) 101 S.Ct. 665, 449 U.S. 361, 66 L.Ed.2d 564, rehearing denied 101 S.Ct. 1420, 450 U.S. 960, 67 L.Ed.2d 385.

A criminal defendant who is also a lawyer and a judge has no right to defend himself and be defended by counsel at the same time; the court may insist he make a choice. U.S. v. Mosely (C.A.6 (Ohio) 1987) 810 F.2d 93, certiorari denied 108 S.Ct. 129, 484 U.S. 841, 98 L.Ed.2d 87.

The denial of counsel to a defendant at a preliminary hearing is not presumed to result in prejudice; it may be harmless error. Takacs v. Engle (C.A.6 (Ohio) 1985) 768 F.2d 122.

Where counsel is not appointed for a defendant in a prosecution for white slave traffic until the very day and hour of trial and such counsel testifies that his late appointment prevented him from adequately investigating and preparing the case, the defendant is denied the effective assistance of counsel guaranteed him by the Sixth Amendment. U. S. ex rel. Sanders v. State of Ohio (S.D.Ohio 1969) 322 F.Supp. 28. Criminal Law ⚷ 641.7(2)

3. Right to preliminary hearing

Once an indictment has been returned by the grand jury, a preliminary hearing before a magistrate is no longer necessary. (See also State v Wigglesworth, 28 OS(2d) 28, 274 NE(2d) 759 (1971).) State v. Wigglesworth (Ohio 1969) 18 Ohio St.2d 171, 248 N.E.2d 607, 47 O.O.2d 388, reversed 91 S.Ct. 2284, 403 U.S. 947, 29 L.Ed.2d 857, on remand 28 Ohio St.2d 28, 274 N.E.2d 759, 57 O.O.2d 102.

The only purpose of a preliminary hearing is to determine whether sufficient facts exist to warrant the court in binding the accused over to the grand jury and to set bail, and once an indictment has been returned by the grand jury a preliminary hearing before a magistrate is no longer necessary. State v. Minamyer (Ohio 1967) 12 Ohio St.2d 67, 232 N.E.2d 401, 41 O.O.2d 282. Criminal Law ⚷ 223

A defendant who has been arrested and charged with a felony does not have a constitutional right to demand that he be afforded a preliminary hearing before a magistrate; the grand jury, during the pendency of such action in the magistrate's court, may, on its own motion or by action of the prosecuting attorney, give consideration to the case and under proper circumstances and sufficient credible evidence, as provided by law, return an indictment against such defendant for whatever crime is justified by the evidence, and, upon the return of such indictment to the common pleas court, such court is vested with jurisdiction of the case, and the proceeding in the magistrate's court must be dismissed. State v. McClellan (Lucas 1966) 6 Ohio App.2d 155, 217 N.E.2d 230, 35 O.O.2d 315, certiorari denied 87 S.Ct. 1380, 386 U.S. 1022, 18 L.Ed.2d 462.

Denial of a preliminary hearing is not a ground for release on habeas corpus. Douglas v. Maxwell (Ohio 1963) 175 Ohio St. 317, 194 N.E.2d 576, 25 O.O.2d 185.

4. Right to jury trial

The provision of RC 1901.24 requiring that demand for a jury trial in the municipal court be made in writing "not less than three days prior to the date set for trial," means three days before the actual trial date, no matter how many continuances for whatever reasons may have been had. State v. Edwards (Washington 1965) 4 Ohio App.2d 261, 208 N.E.2d 758, 31 O.O.2d 390. Jury ⚡ 25(6)

A defendant in a prosecution for drunk driving is not denied the right to counsel at arraignment or to a jury trial where his arraignment judge sets a trial date without specifically informing the defendant that it is, in fact, a trial date and then fails to explain the mechanics of making a jury demand, since the arraignment itself is not a critical stage of the prosecution requiring counsel to be present; nineteen days allowed to the defendant to retain counsel was reasonable, and it was the defendant's delay in obtaining counsel and his attorney's failure to file a written jury demand which resulted in the defendant's loss of the right to a jury trial. Brady v. Blair (S.D.Ohio 1976) 427 F.Supp. 5.

Where at arraignment judge entered plea of not guilty for a defendant who requested counsel, and hearing on charge was set for nineteen days later, defendant had adequate opportunity to retain counsel and request jury trial. Brady v. Blair (S.D.Ohio 1976) 427 F.Supp. 5.

Conviction in Ohio on a charge of operating a motor vehicle under the influence of alcohol is a serious offense and one in which the accused has a federal constitutional right to trial by jury. Brady v. Blair (S.D.Ohio 1976) 427 F.Supp. 5.

5. Failure to inform accused person of rights—in general

Plea of no contest in misdemeanor case involving serious offenses punishable by confinement for more than six months could not be accepted where defendant was not advised as to effect of his plea or as to Fifth and Sixth Amendment rights being waived, the possible minimum and maximum penalties were not explained, and court did not address defendant personally to determine that his plea was intelligent and voluntary. State v. Moore (Ohio App. 7 Dist., 06-21-1996) 111 Ohio App.3d 833, 677 N.E.2d 408. Criminal Law ⚡ 275.4(1)

Failure of judge to comply with provisions of RC 2937.02 to RC 2937.07 invalidates a plea of guilty to a misdemeanor. City of Cleveland v. Whipkey (Cuyahoga 1972) 29 Ohio App.2d 79, 278 N.E.2d 374, 58 O.O.2d 86.

The failure of a municipal court to inform a defendant charged with a misdemeanor of his right to have counsel constitutes prejudicial error. City of Toledo v. Frazier (Lucas 1967) 10 Ohio App.2d 51, 226 N.E.2d 777, 39 O.O.2d 123.

Much more than an unsupported allegation by a petitioner should be necessary to lead this court to reasonably conclude that a trial judge in this state did not fulfill his statutory duty to inform an indigent accused of his right to have counsel without cost to him. Conlan v. Haskins (Ohio 1964) 177 Ohio St. 65, 202 N.E.2d 419, 29 O.O.2d 189, certiorari denied 85 S.Ct. 1773, 381 U.S. 940, 14 L.Ed.2d 703.

6. —— Silent record, failure to inform accused person of rights

The provisions of RC 2937.02 to RC 2937.07 (since superseded by Crim R 5 and Crim R 11) are mandatory upon the trial court, and it will not be presumed from a silent record that the trial court has complied with the statutory requirements; an appellant meets his burden of demonstrating such error by ordering a transcript of the proceedings which do not contain an explanation of his rights. State v. Boerst (Summit 1973) 45 Ohio App.2d 240, 343 N.E.2d 141, 74 O.O.2d 350.

To sustain the validity of a plea of no contest and the concomitant waiver of constitutional rights, the record must affirmatively demonstrate that the trial court discharged the mandatory duties imposed by RC 2937.02 of advising the accused of the effects of such plea. State v. Kristanoff (Hamilton 1972) 32 Ohio App.2d 218, 289 N.E.2d 402, 61 O.O.2d 222. Criminal Law ⚡ 1086.9

Where a defendant enters a pleas of guilty to a crime of sufficient seriousness to warrant a jury trial pursuant to RC 2945.17, compliance with the mandatory requirements of RC 2937.02 will not be presumed from a silent record. City of Fairborn v. Vannicola (Greene 1972) 31 Ohio App.2d 167, 287 N.E.2d 281, 60 O.O.2d 278. Criminal Law ⚡ 1144.4

Failure of the transcript of proceedings to show compliance with the mandatory statutory requirements as to the pretrial procedure of RC Ch 2937 invalidates the entire proceedings, and a judgment based on a guilty plea will be reversed by the reviewing court. City of Cleveland v. Whipkey (Cuyahoga 1972) 29 Ohio App.2d 79, 278 N.E.2d 374, 58 O.O.2d 86.

7. Defendant's statement at preliminary hearing

Even if an incriminating statement of a defendant read at his preliminary hearing was obtained by coercion as the defendant claims, that hearing is not a critical stage of the proceedings under Ohio law. Watmuff v. Perini (C.A.6 (Ohio) 1970) 29 Ohio Misc. 182, 427 F.2d 527, 55 O.O.2d 376, 58 O.O.2d 480.

2937.03 Arraignment; counsel; bail

After the announcement, as provided by section 2937.02 of the Revised Code, the accused shall be arraigned by the magistrate, clerk, or prosecutor of the court reading the affidavit or complaint, or reading its substance, omitting purely formal parts, to the accused unless the reading of the affidavit or complaint is waived. The judge or magistrate shall then inquire of the accused whether the accused understands the nature of the charge. If the accused does not indicate understanding, the judge or magistrate shall give explanation in terms of the statute or ordinance claimed violated. If the accused is not represented by counsel and expresses a desire to consult with an attorney at law, the judge or magistrate shall continue the case for a reasonable time to allow the accused to send for or consult with counsel and shall set bail for the later appearance if the offense is bailable. If the accused is not able to make bail, bail is denied, or the offense is not bailable, the court or magistrate shall require the officer having custody of the accused immediately to take a message to any attorney at law within the municipal corporation where the accused is detained, or immediately to make available to the accused use of a telephone for calling to arrange for legal counsel or bail.

(1999 S 8, eff. 7–29–99; 129 v 582, eff. 1–10–61; 128 v 97)

Historical and Statutory Notes

Ed. Note: 2937.03 contains provisions analogous to former 2935.17, repealed by 128 v 97, eff. 1–1–60.

Ed. Note: Former 2937.03 repealed by 128 v 97, eff. 1–1–60; 1953 H 1; GC 13433–2.

Pre–1953 H 1 Amendments: 113 v 145, Ch 12, § 2

Amendment Note: 1999 S 8 inserted "of the affidavit or complaint is" in the first sentence; inserted "judge or" in the third sentence; and made changes to reflect gender neutral language and other nonsubstantive changes.

Cross References

Arraignment, Crim R 10
Assignment of counsel, Crim R 44
Right to counsel, O Const Art I §10

Library References

Arrest ⚷70(2).
Bail ⚷41.
Criminal Law ⚷229.
Westlaw Topic Nos. 110, 35, 49.
C.J.S. Arrest §§ 58 to 61.
C.J.S. Bail; Release and Detention Pending Proceedings §§ 6, 9 to 38.
C.J.S. Criminal Law §§ 282, 345.

Research References

Encyclopedias

OH Jur. 3d Criminal Law § 34, Informing Accused of Right to Attorney.

OH Jur. 3d Criminal Law § 2606, to Secure Counsel and Prepare Case.

Treatises and Practice Aids

Katz, Giannelli, Blair and Lipton, Baldwin's Ohio Practice, Criminal Law, § 38:1, Introduction.

Katz, Giannelli, Blair and Lipton, Baldwin's Ohio Practice, Criminal Law, § 42:4, Arraignment Procedures.

Katz, Giannelli, Blair and Lipton, Baldwin's Ohio Practice, Criminal Law, § 138:1, Waiver of Reading of Indictment, Information, or Complaint at Arraignment.

Katz, Giannelli, Blair and Lipton, Baldwin's Ohio Practice, Criminal Law, § 139:36, Motion to Deny Bail.

Katz, Giannelli, Blair and Lipton, Baldwin's Ohio Practice, Criminal Law, § 139:37, Order to Deny Bail.

Law Review and Journal Commentaries

The Municipal Court Misdemeanor Arraignment Procedure of Hamilton County, Ohio: An Empirical Study, Note. 41 U Cin L Rev 623 (1972).

Notes of Decisions

Constitutional issues 1-4
- **In general 1**
- **Bail 2**
- **Right to counsel 3**
- **Right to jury trial 4**

Failure to follow procedure 6
Right to preliminary hearing 5

---

1. Constitutional issues—in general

Even if defendant was never formally arraigned, he waived right to arraignment by first entering pleas of not guilty, then not guilty by reason of insanity, and finally of no contest to rape of person under age 13. Palmer v. Wilson (Ohio App. 5 Dist., Richland, 05-12-2005) No. 2005-CA-2, 2005-Ohio-2346, 2005 WL 1125336, Unreported. Criminal Law ⚯ 262

Closed-circuit arraignment of capital murder defendant did not violate defendant's confrontational, due process or state statutory rights; arraignment procedure was open to public, created no additional publicity or attention and did not subject him to greater risk of prejudice than personal appearance would have done, trial court asked defendant if he was able to hear and see proceedings and he replied he could. State v. Phillips (Ohio, 11-22-1995) 74 Ohio St.3d 72, 656 N.E.2d 643, 1995-Ohio-171, reconsideration denied 74 Ohio St.3d 1485, 657 N.E.2d 1378, stay granted 74 Ohio St.3d 1503, 659 N.E.2d 795, rehearing granted, opinion recalled 75 Ohio St.3d 1504, 665 N.E.2d 219, certiorari denied 116 S.Ct. 1835, 517 U.S. 1213, 134 L.Ed.2d 938, denial of post-conviction relief affirmed in part, reversed in part 1999 WL 58961, dismissed, appeal not allowed 86 Ohio St.3d 1402, 711 N.E.2d 231, denial of post-conviction relief affirmed 2002-Ohio-823, 2002 WL 274637, appeal not allowed 95 Ohio St.3d 1488, 769 N.E.2d 403, 2002-Ohio-2625. Constitutional Law ⚯ 265.5; Criminal Law ⚯ 264; Criminal Law ⚯ 662.3

Arraignment is not a procedure required under the Due Process Clause of Fifth Amendment. State v. Phillips (Ohio, 11-22-1995) 74 Ohio St.3d 72, 656 N.E.2d 643, 1995-Ohio-171, reconsideration denied 74 Ohio St.3d 1485, 657 N.E.2d 1378, stay granted 74 Ohio St.3d 1503, 659 N.E.2d 795, rehearing granted, opinion recalled 75 Ohio St.3d 1504, 665 N.E.2d 219, certiorari denied 116 S.Ct. 1835, 517 U.S. 1213, 134 L.Ed.2d 938, denial of post-conviction relief affirmed in part, reversed in part 1999 WL 58961, dismissed, appeal not allowed 86 Ohio St.3d 1402, 711 N.E.2d 231, denial of post-conviction relief affirmed 2002-Ohio-823, 2002 WL 274637, appeal not allowed 95 Ohio St.3d 1488, 769 N.E.2d 403, 2002-Ohio-2625. Constitutional Law ⚯ 265.5

Failure to permit defendant to be present at arraignment does not implicate Sixth Amendment right of defendant to confront witnesses, as there are no witnesses involved at that stage. State v. Phillips (Ohio, 11-22-1995) 74 Ohio St.3d 72, 656 N.E.2d 643, 1995-Ohio-171, reconsideration denied 74 Ohio St.3d 1485, 657 N.E.2d 1378, stay granted 74 Ohio St.3d 1503, 659 N.E.2d 795, rehearing granted, opinion recalled 75 Ohio St.3d 1504, 665 N.E.2d 219, certiorari denied 116 S.Ct. 1835, 517 U.S. 1213, 134 L.Ed.2d 938, denial of post-conviction relief affirmed in part, reversed in part 1999 WL 58961, dismissed, appeal not allowed 86 Ohio St.3d 1402, 711 N.E.2d 231, denial of post-conviction relief affirmed 2002-Ohio-823, 2002 WL 274637, appeal not allowed 95 Ohio St.3d 1488, 769 N.E.2d 403, 2002-Ohio-2625. Criminal Law ⚯ 662.3

Failure of capital murder defendant to assert claim before Court of Appeals, that his arraignment over closed-circuit television violated his confrontation and due process rights because he was not physically present in courtroom, resulted in waiver of right to assert claim before Supreme Court absent showing of plain error. State v. Phillips (Ohio, 11-22-1995) 74 Ohio St.3d 72, 656 N.E.2d 643, 1995-Ohio-171, reconsideration denied 74 Ohio St.3d 1485, 657 N.E.2d 1378, stay granted 74 Ohio St.3d 1503, 659 N.E.2d 795, rehearing granted, opinion recalled 75 Ohio St.3d 1504, 665 N.E.2d 219, certiorari denied 116 S.Ct. 1835, 517 U.S. 1213, 134 L.Ed.2d 938, denial of post-conviction relief affirmed in part, reversed in part 1999 WL 58961, dismissed, appeal not allowed 86 Ohio St.3d 1402, 711 N.E.2d 231, denial of post-conviction relief affirmed 2002-Ohio-823, 2002 WL 274637, appeal not allowed 95 Ohio St.3d 1488, 769 N.E.2d 403, 2002-Ohio-2625. Criminal Law ⚯ 1031(4)

Arraignment of an accused via closed-circuit television is constitutionally adequate when procedure is functionally equivalent to live, in-person arraignment. State v. Phillips (Ohio, 11-22-1995) 74 Ohio St.3d 72, 656 N.E.2d 643, 1995-Ohio-171, reconsideration denied 74 Ohio St.3d 1485, 657 N.E.2d 1378, stay granted 74 Ohio St.3d 1503, 659 N.E.2d 795, rehearing granted, opinion recalled 75 Ohio St.3d 1504, 665 N.E.2d 219, certiorari denied 116 S.Ct. 1835, 517 U.S. 1213, 134 L.Ed.2d 938, denial of post-conviction relief affirmed in part, reversed in part 1999 WL 58961, dismissed, appeal not allowed 86 Ohio St.3d 1402, 711 N.E.2d 231, denial of post-conviction relief affirmed 2002-Ohio-823, 2002 WL 274637, appeal not allowed 95 Ohio St.3d 1488, 769 N.E.2d 403, 2002-Ohio-2625. Criminal Law ⚯ 264

The denial of bail after arrest is a nonjurisdictional irregularity which cannot be raised by habeas corpus after conviction. Dodds v. Haskins (Ohio 1965) 1 Ohio St.2d 82, 204 N.E.2d 229, 30 O.O.2d 190. Habeas Corpus ⚯ 469

2. —— Bail, constitutional issues

The right of counsel at a preliminary hearing of the character set forth in Coleman v Alabama, 399 US 1, 90 SCt 1999, 26 LEd(2d) 287 (1970) does not extend in Ohio to a magistrate's arraignment of an accused on a felony charge, where the accused has been informed of his rights by the magistrate as prescribed by RC 2937.02, has plead not guilty and has affirmatively waived his right to a preliminary hearing. State v. Simones (Marion 1971) 27 Ohio App.2d 9, 272 N.E.2d 146, 56 O.O.2d 198, affirmed 30 Ohio St.2d 100, 282 N.E.2d 573, 59 O.O.2d 113. Criminal Law ⚯ 264

The mere fact that the testimony of alibi witnesses is weakened upon cross-examination so that such witnesses reveal a lack of distinct recollection of the accused's whereabouts at the time of the alleged crime is not a sufficient basis for arguing upon appeal that such lack of evidence-memory was attributable to delay in the appointment of counsel for the defendant so as to ground a claim of lack of counsel at a critical stage of prosecution. (See also State v Johnson, 14 OS(2d) 67, 236 NE(2d) 552 (1968).) State v. Childs (Ohio 1968) 14 Ohio St.2d 56, 236 N.E.2d 545, 43 O.O.2d 119, certiorari denied 89 S.Ct. 1596, 394 U.S. 1002, 22 L.Ed.2d 779.

Cases tried before Miranda v Arizona, 384 US 436, 86 SCt 1602, 16 LEd(2d) 694 (1966), are controlled by the law of the case of Escobedo v Illinois, 378 US 478, 84 SCt 1758, 12 LEd(2d) 977 (1964), with regard to advising a defendant in a felony case of his constitutional right to counsel, which case requires that a request therefor must be made and refused before such failure constitutes a denial of due process. State v. White (Cuyahoga 1967) 9 Ohio App.2d 271, 224 N.E.2d 377, 38 O.O.2d 330, reversed 15 Ohio St.2d 146, 239 N.E.2d 65, 44 O.O.2d 132.

A defendant's right of due process is violated, and reversible error committed, where the state refuses to afford the defendant the right to consult with his lawyer at the earliest possible time. State v. Domer (Stark 1964) 1 Ohio App.2d 155, 204 N.E.2d 69, 30 O.O.2d 193.

If a violation of the US Const Am 6 right to counsel does not show prejudice or a major threat of prejudice, a remedy is not warranted. The criminal proceeding may go forward with recognition of the defendant's right to counsel. It is not appropriate to dismiss the indictment. U. S. v. Morrison (U.S.Pa. 1981) 101 S.Ct. 665, 449 U.S. 361, 66 L.Ed.2d 564, rehearing denied 101 S.Ct. 1420, 450 U.S. 960, 67 L.Ed.2d 385.

A criminal defendant who is also a lawyer and a judge has no right to defend himself and be defended by counsel at the same time; the court may insist he make a choice. U.S. v. Mosely (C.A.6 (Ohio) 1987) 810 F.2d 93, certiorari denied 108 S.Ct. 129, 484 U.S. 841, 98 L.Ed.2d 87.

Where counsel is not appointed for a defendant in a prosecution for white slave traffic until the very day and hour of trial and such counsel testifies that his late appointment prevented him from adequately investigating and preparing the case, the defendant is denied the effective assistance of counsel guaranteed him by the Sixth Amendment. U. S. ex rel. Sanders v. State of Ohio (S.D.Ohio 1969) 322 F.Supp. 28. Criminal Law ⚿ 641.7(2)

3. —— Right to counsel, constitutional issues

Trial court never obtained jurisdiction over attorney whom defendant had incorrectly named as representing him at time of defendant's arraignment, so that court could not appoint attorney to represent defendant, and could not hold attorney in contempt after he failed to appear for trial, where attorney never made a predicate appearance on behalf of defendant with regard to offense, and never consented to his appointment. State ex rel. Bradley v. Stralka (Ohio App. 8 Dist., 09-02-1999) 134 Ohio App.3d 256, 730 N.E.2d 1034. Contempt ⚿ 44; Trial ⚿ 21

In inferring waiver of right to counsel when defendant refuses to take effective action to obtain counsel and on day of trial requests continuance in order to delay trial, court must consider total circumstances of case, including background, experience and conduct of defendant. State v. Boone (Ohio App. 1 Dist., 12-29-1995) 108 Ohio App.3d 233, 670 N.E.2d 527. Criminal Law ⚿ 641.4(2)

Defendant charged with drug abuse, possession of drug paraphernalia and criminal trespass who failed to secure legal counsel despite being given ample time and opportunity to do so by trial court and who did not ask for continuance on day of trial in order to obtain counsel waived by inference his right to legal representation. State v. Boone (Ohio App. 1 Dist., 12-29-1995) 108 Ohio App.3d 233, 670 N.E.2d 527. Criminal Law ⚿ 641.4(4)

Court may, under proper conditions, be permitted to infer waiver of right to counsel when defendant refuses to take effective action to obtain counsel and on day of trial requests continuance in order to delay trial. State v. Boone (Ohio App. 1 Dist., 12-29-1995) 108 Ohio App.3d 233, 670 N.E.2d 527. Criminal Law ⚿ 641.4(2)

A defendant in a prosecution for drunk driving is not denied the right to counsel at arraignment or to a jury trial where his arraignment judge sets a trial date without specifically informing the defendant that it is, in fact, a trial date and then fails to explain the mechanics of making a jury demand, since the arraignment itself is not a critical stage of the prosecution requiring counsel to be present; nineteen days allowed to the defendant to retain counsel was reasonable, and it was the defendant's delay in obtaining counsel and his attorney's failure to file a written jury demand which resulted in the defendant's loss of the right to a jury trial. Brady v. Blair (S.D.Ohio 1976) 427 F.Supp. 5.

Where at arraignment judge entered plea of not guilty for a defendant who requested counsel, and hearing on charge was set for nineteen days later, defendant had adequate opportunity to retain counsel and request jury trial. Brady v. Blair (S.D.Ohio 1976) 427 F.Supp. 5.

Conviction in Ohio on a charge of operating a motor vehicle under the influence of alcohol is a serious offense and one in which the accused has a federal constitutional right to trial by jury. Brady v. Blair (S.D.Ohio 1976) 427 F.Supp. 5.

4. —— Right to jury trial, constitutional issues

Where a defendant receives a prior warning that he is under arrest and may be charged with the crime of murder and that the law gives him a right to make a statement which may be used against him at trial, such statement is admissible in a case tried after Escobedo v Illinois, 378 US 478, 84 SCt 1758, 12 LEd(2d) 977 (1964), but before Miranda v Arizona, 384 US 436, 86 SCt 1602, 16 LEd(2d) 694 (1966), where defendant voluntarily surrendered to police in order to make the statement, and the warning is followed by a request for a statement suggesting no obligation on the part of defendant to make the statement. State v. White (Ohio 1968) 15 Ohio St.2d 146, 239 N.E.2d 65, 44 O.O.2d 132. Criminal Law ⚿ 412.2(3)

5. Right to preliminary hearing

Once an indictment has been returned by the grand jury, a preliminary hearing before a magistrate is no longer necessary. (See also State v Wigglesworth, 28 OS(2d) 28, 274 NE(2d) 759 (1971).) State v. Wigglesworth (Ohio 1969) 18 Ohio St.2d 171, 248 N.E.2d 607, 47 O.O.2d 388, reversed

91 S.Ct. 2284, 403 U.S. 947, 29 L.Ed.2d 857, on remand 28 Ohio St.2d 28, 274 N.E.2d 759, 57 O.O.2d 102.

A defendant who has been arrested and charged with a felony does not have a constitutional right to demand that he be afforded a preliminary hearing before a magistrate; the grand jury, during the pendency of such action in the magistrate's court, may, on its own motion or by action of the prosecuting attorney, give consideration to the case and under proper circumstances and sufficient credible evidence, as provided by law, return an indictment against such defendant for whatever crime is justified by the evidence, and, upon the return of such indictment to the common pleas court, such court is vested with jurisdiction of the case, and the proceeding in the magistrate's court must be dismissed. State v. McClellan (Lucas 1966) 6 Ohio App.2d 155, 217 N.E.2d 230, 35 O.O.2d 315, certiorari denied 87 S.Ct. 1380, 386 U.S. 1022, 18 L.Ed.2d 462.

6. Failure to follow procedure

Defendant failed to demonstrate sufficient breakdown in attorney-client relationship to warrant removal and substitution of his court-appointed counsel; defendant's motion for continuance to obtain new counsel was made on first day of trial, and defendant had not expressed any dissatisfaction or concern with counsel up to that point. State v. Hill (Ohio App. 2 Dist., Montgomery, 04-23-2004) No. 20028, 2004-Ohio-2048, 2004 WL 870439, Unreported. Criminal Law ⚷ 641.10(2)

The provisions of RC 2937.02 to RC 2937.07 (since superseded by Crim R 5 and Crim R 11) are mandatory upon the trial court, and it will not be presumed from a silent record that the trial court has complied with the statutory requirements; an appellant meets his burden of demonstrating such error by ordering a transcript of the proceedings which do not contain an explanation of his rights. State v. Boerst (Summit 1973) 45 Ohio App.2d 240, 343 N.E.2d 141, 74 O.O.2d 350.

Failure of the judge to comply with the provisions of RC 2937.02 to RC 2937.07 invalidates a plea of guilty to a misdemeanor. City of Cleveland v. Whipkey (Cuyahoga 1972) 29 Ohio App.2d 79, 278 N.E.2d 374, 58 O.O.2d 86.

Failure of the transcript of proceedings to show compliance with the mandatory statutory requirements as to the pretrial procedure of RC Ch 2937 invalidates the entire proceedings, and a judgment based on a guilty plea will be reversed by the reviewing court. City of Cleveland v. Whipkey (Cuyahoga 1972) 29 Ohio App.2d 79, 278 N.E.2d 374, 58 O.O.2d 86.

2937.04 Motion for dismissal

If accused does not desire counsel or, having engaged counsel, appears at the end of granted continuance, he may then raise, by motion to dismiss the affidavit or complaint, any exception thereto which could be asserted against an indictment or information by motion to quash, plea in abatement, or demurrer. Such motion may be made orally and ruled upon by the court or magistrate at the time of presentation, with minute of motion and ruling made in the journal (if a court of record) or on the docket (if a court not of record) or such motion may be presented in writing and set down for argument at later time. Where the motion attacks a defect in the record by facts extrinsic thereto, proof may be offered by testimony or affidavit.

(128 v 97, eff. 1–1–60)

Historical and Statutory Notes

Ed. Note: Former 2937.04 repealed by 128 v 97, eff. 1–1–60; 1953 H 1; GC 13433–3.

Pre–1953 H 1 Amendments: 113 v 145, Ch 12, § 3

Cross References

Bail, Crim R 46
Motions, Crim R 47
Motions before trial, Crim R 12

Library References

Criminal Law ⚷219, 239.
Westlaw Topic No. 110.
C.J.S. Criminal Law §§ 334, 352.

Research References

Encyclopedias

OH Jur. 3d Criminal Law § 2409, Motion to Dismiss on Initial Appearance.

Treatises and Practice Aids

Katz, Giannelli, Blair and Lipton, Baldwin's Ohio Practice, Criminal Law, § 47:2, Motions.

Katz, Giannelli, Blair and Lipton, Baldwin's Ohio Practice, Criminal Law, § 47:7, Rulings on Motions.

Katz, Giannelli, Blair and Lipton, Baldwin's Ohio Practice, Criminal Law, § 43:13, Understanding the Waiver of Rights.

Katz, Giannelli, Blair and Lipton, Baldwin's Ohio Practice, Criminal Law, § 143:15, Entry on Motion to Dismiss Overruled and Plea of Not Guilty.

Notes of Decisions

1. Nature of motion to dismiss affidavit or complaint

A motion to dismiss an affidavit is the equivalent of a motion to quash, a plea in abatement, or a demurrer, and comes within the exception reserved by Euclid v Heaton, 15 OS(2d) 65, 238 NE(2d) 790 (1968). State v. Seta (Hamilton 1968) 16 Ohio App.2d 97, 242 N.E.2d 349, 45 O.O.2d 270.

2. Grounds for motion

There is no provision under Ohio's criminal procedure for a motion to dismiss criminal charges premised upon a lack of probable cause. State v. Hartley (Medina 1988) 51 Ohio App.3d 47, 554 N.E.2d 950, motion overruled 41 Ohio St.3d 705, 534 N.E.2d 1211.

The invalidity of a municipal ordinance is an objection which may be taken advantage of by a motion, pursuant to RC 2937.04, and such objection is waived by the entry of a plea made pursuant to RC 2937.06. Carsey v. City of Mansfield (Richland 1973) 37 Ohio App.2d 141, 310 N.E.2d 263, 66 O.O.2d 361.

3. Effect of failure to follow procedure

Failure of the judge to comply with the provisions of RC 2937.02 to RC 2937.07 invalidates a plea of guilty to a misdemeanor. City of Cleveland v. Whipkey (Cuyahoga 1972) 29 Ohio App.2d 79, 278 N.E.2d 374, 58 O.O.2d 86.

Failure of the transcript of proceedings to show compliance with the mandatory statutory requirements as to the pretrial procedure of RC Ch 2937 invalidates the entire proceedings, and a judgment based on a guilty plea will be reversed by the reviewing court. City of Cleveland v. Whipkey (Cuyahoga 1972) 29 Ohio App.2d 79, 278 N.E.2d 374, 58 O.O.2d 86.

4. Appeal by prosecution

Where a motion to dismiss an affidavit in a misdemeanor case, made pursuant to RC 2937.04, raises the issues that could be asserted against an indictment by a motion to quash, or a plea in abatement, or a demurrer, the prosecutor may institute proceedings to review a judgment sustaining such motion. City of Columbus v. Youngquist (Franklin 1972) 33 Ohio App.2d 317, 294 N.E.2d 910, 62 O.O.2d 456.

2937.05 Discharge on motion to dismiss; amendment of complaint

If the motion pursuant to section 2937.04 of the Revised Code be sustained, accused shall be discharged unless the court or magistrate finds that the defect can be corrected without changing the nature of the charge, in which case he may order the complaint amended or a proper affidavit filed forthwith and require the accused to plead thereto. The discharge of accused upon the sustaining of a motion to dismiss shall not be considered a bar to further prosecution either of felony or misdemeanor.

(128 v 97, eff. 1–1–60)

Historical and Statutory Notes

Ed. Note: Former 2937.05 repealed by 128 v 97, eff. 1–1–60; 1953 H 1; GC 13433–4.

Pre–1953 H 1 Amendments: 113 v 145, Ch 12, § 4

Cross References

Dismissal, Crim R 48
Motions before trial, Crim R 12
Right to indictment, O Const Art I §10

Library References

Criminal Law ⚷219, 220, 239.
Westlaw Topic No. 110.
C.J.S. Criminal Law §§ 334, 352.

Research References

Treatises and Practice Aids

Katz, Giannelli, Blair and Lipton, Baldwin's Ohio Practice, Criminal Law, § 143:15, Entry on Motion to Dismiss Overruled and Plea of Not Guilty.

Notes of Decisions

Dismissal not a bar; exceptions 2
Rebuttal evidence 1

1. Rebuttal evidence

Where a defendant alleges that prior convictions for theft used to enhance the charged offense of defrauding a livery were uncounselled, the court must allow the prosecution the opportunity to rebut the defendant's claims prior to dismissing the charge. State v. Daniels (Lorain 1988) 61 Ohio App.3d 17, 572 N.E.2d 129, motion overruled 46 Ohio St.3d 716, 546 N.E.2d 1334.

2. Dismissal not a bar; exceptions

In a criminal proceeding, a dismissal for want of prosecution is not a bar to reindictment unless one of the following occurs: the dismissal is constitutionally compelled; the dismissal is statutorily compelled and the statute requires a dismissal under that statute to be with prejudice; or the entry of dismissal specifically provides that the dismissal is with prejudice. State v. Stephens (Cuyahoga 1977) 52 Ohio App.2d 361, 370 N.E.2d 759, 6 O.O.3d 404. Double Jeopardy ⚷ 92

The discharge of a defendant provided for in RC 2937.21 is from custody and bail only, and is not a bar to a subsequent prosecution for the same offense. City of Columbus v. Nappi (Ohio 1966) 5 Ohio St.2d 99, 214 N.E.2d 83, 34 O.O.2d 222.

2937.06 Pleas

(A) After all motions are disposed of or if no motion is presented, the court or magistrate shall require the accused to plead to the charge.

(1) In cases of felony, only a plea of not guilty or a written plea of guilty shall be received and if the defendant declines to plead, a plea of not guilty shall be entered for the defendant and further proceedings had as set forth in sections 2937.09 to 2937.12 of the Revised Code.

(2) In cases of misdemeanor, the following pleas may be received:

(a) Guilty;

(b) Not guilty;

(c) No contest;

(d) Once in jeopardy, which includes the defenses of former conviction or former acquittal.

(B) Prior to accepting a plea of guilty or a plea of no contest under division (A) of this section, the court shall comply with sections 2943.031 and 2943.032 of the Revised Code.

(C) Entry of any plea pursuant to this section shall constitute a waiver of any objection that could be taken advantage of by motion pursuant to section 2937.04 of the Revised Code.

(1995 S 2, eff. 7–1–96; 1989 S 95, eff. 10–2–89; 128 v 97)

Uncodified Law

1989 S 95, § 3, eff. 10–2–89, reads: Section 2937.06 of the Revised Code as amended by this act and section 2943.031 of the Revised Code as enacted by this act shall apply to all felony and misdemeanor cases pending on the effective date of this act in which the court has not accepted a plea to the indictment, information, or complaint.

Historical and Statutory Notes

Ed. Note: Former 2937.06 repealed by 128 v 97, eff. 1–1–60; 1953 H 1; GC 13433–5.

Pre–1953 H 1 Amendments: 113 v 146, Ch 12, § 5

Amendment Note: 1995 S 2 added the reference to section 2943.032 in division (B); and made other changes to reflect gender neutral language.

Cross References

Pleas, Crim R 11

Trial for crimes, witness, O Const Art I §10

Library References

Criminal Law ⚖267 to 301.
Westlaw Topic No. 110.
C.J.S. Criminal Law §§ 365 to 418, 453.

Research References

Encyclopedias

OH Jur. 3d Criminal Law § 2409, Motion to Dismiss on Initial Appearance.

Treatises and Practice Aids

Katz, Giannelli, Blair and Lipton, Baldwin's Ohio Practice, Criminal Law, § 36:3, Pleas.

Katz, Giannelli, Blair and Lipton, Baldwin's Ohio Practice, Criminal Law, § 42:2, Types of Pleas.

Katz, Giannelli, Blair and Lipton, Baldwin's Ohio Practice, Criminal Law, § 144:1, Plea of Guilty.

Katz, Giannelli, Blair and Lipton, Baldwin's Ohio Practice, Criminal Law, § 144:2, No Contest Plea.

Katz, Giannelli, Blair and Lipton, Baldwin's Ohio Practice, Criminal Law, § 144:3, Entry of Not Guilty Plea.

Katz, Giannelli, Blair and Lipton, Baldwin's Ohio Practice, Criminal Law, § 43:19, Misdemeanor Cases.

Law Review and Journal Commentaries

Constitutional Law—Criminal Procedure—Defendant's Possible Objection to Attorney's Waiver of Cross Examination.—Brookhart v. Janis, Note. 36 U Cin L Rev 164 (Winter 1967).

Notes of Decisions

1. Constitutional issues

The action of the bureau of motor vehicles in suspending a driver's license for refusing, while such driver's faculties are allegedly impaired, to submit to a chemical test of the level of alcohol in body fluids, when, upon sober reflection he pleads "guilty" to the offense for which he was arrested, is in violation of his right to remedy by due course of law under O Const Art I, § 16. Appeal of Williamson (Ohio Com.Pl. 1969) 18 Ohio Misc. 67, 246 N.E.2d 618, 47 O.O.2d 125.

Municipal court proceedings at which guilty plea was received was a critical stage of the criminal process so that petitioner was entitled to counsel thereat. Sheely v. Whealon (C.A.6 (Ohio) 1975) 525 F.2d 713.

2. Entry of plea as waiver

The invalidity of a municipal ordinance is an objection which may be taken advantage of by a motion, pursuant to RC 2937.04, and such objection is waived by the entry of a plea made pursuant to RC 2937.06. Carsey v. City of Mansfield (Richland 1973) 37 Ohio App.2d 141, 310 N.E.2d 263, 66 O.O.2d 361.

3. Failure to follow procedure

Trial court failed to inform defendant of his right to compulsory process, and thus his guilty pleas to three separate charges of robbery required vacation. State v. Cummings (Ohio App. 8 Dist., Cuyahoga, 08-26-2004) No. 83759, 2004-Ohio-4470, 2004 WL 1902119, Unreported, appeal allowed 104 Ohio St.3d 1459, 821 N.E.2d 576, 2005-Ohio-204. Criminal Law ⚖ 273.1(4); Criminal Law ⚖ 1167(5)

Failure of the judge to comply with the provisions of RC 2937.02 to RC 2937.07 invalidates a plea of guilty to a misdemeanor. City of Cleveland v. Whipkey (Cuyahoga 1972) 29 Ohio App.2d 79, 278 N.E.2d 374, 58 O.O.2d 86.

Failure of the transcript of proceedings to show compliance with the mandatory statutory requirements as to the pretrial procedure of RC Ch 2937 invalidates the entire proceedings, and a judgment based on a guilty plea will be reversed by the reviewing court. City of Cleveland v. Whipkey (Cuyahoga 1972) 29 Ohio App.2d 79, 278 N.E.2d 374, 58 O.O.2d 86.

Breach of a plea agreement by a federal judge may be remedied by specific performance of the agreement or allowing withdrawal of the plea. U.S. v. Mandell (C.A.6 (Ohio) 1990) 905 F.2d 970. Criminal Law ⚖ 273.1(2); Criminal Law ⚖ 274(3.1)

4. Plea of no contest

Defendant's plea of no contest to charge of driving under the influence (DUI) was not knowing where judge failed to advise defendant of following rights: right to trial by jury, that burden was on prosecution to prove charge beyond reasonable doubt if he chose to go to trial, right to cross-examine his accusers, right not to testify, and right to compulsory process. State v. Filchock (Ohio App. 11 Dist., 12-02-1996) 116 Ohio App.3d 572, 688 N.E.2d 1063. Criminal Law ⚖ 275.4(1)

A finding of guilty by a judge pursuant to RC 2937.07, after the defendant has pleaded "no contest" under RC 2937.06(C), must be supported by sworn evidence which states facts substantiating the presence of each of the elements of the offense.

City of Lyndhurst v. McFarlane (Ohio Com.Pl. 1969) 21 Ohio Misc. 197, 256 N.E.2d 627, 50 O.O.2d 414.

A conviction, without trial, based merely on a no contest plea to an indictment which does not allege sufficient facts to constitute an offense is void. State v Hayes, No. 5–82–11 (3d Dist Ct App, Hancock, 1–14–83).

2937.07 Action on pleas of "guilty" and "no contest" in misdemeanor cases

If the offense is a misdemeanor and the accused pleads guilty to the offense, the court or magistrate shall receive and enter the plea unless the court or magistrate believes that it was made through fraud, collusion, or mistake. If the court or magistrate so believes, the court or magistrate shall enter a plea of not guilty and set the matter for trial pursuant to Chapter 2938. of the Revised Code. Upon receiving a plea of guilty, the court or magistrate shall call for an explanation of the circumstances of the offense from the affiant or complainant or the affiant's or complainant's representatives. After hearing the explanation of circumstances, together with any statement of the accused, the court or magistrate shall proceed to pronounce the sentence or shall continue the matter for the purpose of imposing the sentence.

A plea to a misdemeanor offense of "no contest" or words of similar import shall constitute a stipulation that the judge or magistrate may make a finding of guilty or not guilty from the explanation of the circumstances of the offense. If a finding of guilty is made, the judge or magistrate shall impose the sentence or continue the case for sentencing accordingly. A plea of "no contest" or words of similar import shall not be construed as an admission of any fact at issue in the criminal charge in any subsequent civil or criminal action or proceeding. (2002 H 490, eff. 1–1–04; 128 v 97, eff. 1–1–60)

Historical and Statutory Notes

Ed. Note: 2937.07 contains provisions analogous to former 2937.10, repealed by 128 v 97, eff. 1–1–60.

Ed. Note: Former 2937.07 repealed by 128 v 97, eff. 1–1–60; 1953 H 1; GC 13433–6.

Pre–1953 H 1 Amendments: 113 v 146, Ch 12, § 6

Amendment Note: 2002 H 490 rewrote this section which prior thereto read:

"If the offense be a misdemeanor and the accused pleads guilty thereto, the court or magistrate shall receive and enter such plea unless he believes it made through fraud, collusion; or mistake in which case he shall enter a plea of not guilty and set the matter for trial pursuant to Chapter 2938. of the Revised Code. Upon a plea of guilty being received the court or magistrate shall call for explanation of circumstances of the offense from the affiant or complainant or his representatives, and after hearing the same, together with any statement of accused, shall proceed to pronounce sentence or continue the matter for the purpose of imposing sentence or admitting the defendant to probation.

"If the plea be 'no contest' or words of similar import in pleading to a misdemeanor, it shall constitute a stipulation that the judge or magistrate may make finding of guilty or not guilty from the explanation of circumstances, and if guilt be found, impose or continue for sentence accordingly. Such plea shall not be construed to import an admission of any fact at issue in the criminal charge in any subsequent action or proceeding, whether civil or criminal."

Cross References

Pleas, Crim R 11

Library References

Criminal Law ⚷272, 275.
Westlaw Topic No. 110.
C.J.S. Criminal Law §§ 365 to 374, 384 to 407, 410 to 418.

Research References

Encyclopedias

OH Jur. 3d Criminal Law § 1410, Intent as Element of Offense.

OH Jur. 3d Criminal Law § 2461, Cases Involving Serious Offenses.

OH Jur. 3d Criminal Law § 2464, Particular Matters Waived by Plea of Guilty.

OH Jur. 3d Criminal Law § 2472, Misdemeanor Cases; Explanation of Circumstances.

Treatises and Practice Aids

Klein, Darling, & Terez, Baldwin's Ohio Practice Civil Practice § 1:100, Modern Courts Amendment of 1968 as Limiting Scope of Application of Civil Rules.

Katz, Giannelli, Blair and Lipton, Baldwin's Ohio Practice, Criminal Law, § 36:5, Rule 5(A) Violations.

Katz, Giannelli, Blair and Lipton, Baldwin's Ohio Practice, Criminal Law, § 43:7, Refusing to Accept Guilty Plea.

Katz, Giannelli, Blair and Lipton, Baldwin's Ohio Practice, Criminal Law, § 45:2, Guilty Pleas Distinguished.

Katz, Giannelli, Blair and Lipton, Baldwin's Ohio Practice, Criminal Law, § 43:19, Misdemeanor Cases.

Katz, Giannelli, Blair and Lipton, Baldwin's Ohio Practice, Criminal Law, § 80:21, Appeal After No-Contest Plea.

Gotherman, Babbit and Lang, Baldwin's Ohio Practice, Local Government Law—Municipal, § 28:43, Waiver of Appearance and Bail.

Law Review and Journal Commentaries

Constitutional Law—Criminal Procedure—Defendant's Possible Objection to Attorney's Waiver of Cross Examination, Brookhart v. Janis, Note. 36 U Cin L Rev 164 (Winter 1967).

The Municipal Court Misdemeanor Arraignment Procedure of Hamilton County, Ohio: An Empirical Study, Note. 41 U Cin L Rev 623 (1972).

Notes of Decisions

---

1. Plea of no contest—in general

Jeopardy attached, in case in which defendant entered plea of no contest to misdemeanor criminal trespass, at time defendant entered plea. State v. Courts (Ohio App. 2 Dist., Montgomery, 07-15-2005) No. 20689, 2005-Ohio-3694, 2005 WL 1705334, Unreported. Double Jeopardy ⚷ 57

Record supported finding that defendant, prior to entering plea of no contest to charge of playing loud music in a vehicle, waived his right to explanation of circumstances, where prosecutor stated that, as part of the plea agreement, defendant waived presentation of evidence and stipulated to a finding of guilt, and defendant's attorney agreed that the prosecutor's recitation of the plea agreement was correct. State v. Howell (Ohio App. 7 Dist., Mahoning, 06-06-2005) No. 04 MA 31, 2005-Ohio-2927, 2005 WL 1385713, Unreported. Criminal Law ⚷ 275.3

Retrial of defendant was not barred by double jeopardy after his conviction for reckless operation was reversed on appeal due to trial court's failure to pronounce circumstances of offense; holding of Court of Appeals did not require determination as to whether circumstances were sufficient to sustain conviction. State v. Spinazee (Ohio App. 6 Dist., Lucas, 04-15-2005) No. L-04-1274, 2005-Ohio-1780, 2005 WL 859434, Unreported. Double Jeopardy ⚷ 108

Trial court erred in finding defendant guilty on his no contest plea of misdemeanor offense of reckless operation, where state failed to set forth any statement of facts or explanation as to how defendant violated statute. State v. Spinazee (Ohio App. 6 Dist., Lucas, 04-15-2005) No. L-04-1274, 2005-Ohio-1780, 2005 WL 859434, Unreported. Criminal Law ⚷ 275.3

Trial court erred by finding defendant guilty without an explanation of the circumstances after a plea of no contest; there was no explanation by the trial court or the prosecution of the circumstances of the charged offenses of operating under the influence and driving under suspension, and although trial judge mentioned that he looked at the record and noted that defendant was driving at 1:47 a.m. at the time he was pulled over, this was insufficient to meet the requirements of statute providing that, in case of no contest plea, it shall constitute a stipulation that the judge or magistrate may make finding of guilty or not guilty from the explanation of circumstances. State v. Bennett (Ohio App. 9 Dist., Summit, 03-19-2003) No. 21202, 2003-Ohio-1289, 2003 WL 1240054, Unreported. Criminal Law ⚷ 275.3

Statute governing no-contest pleas in misdemeanor cases did not apply to no-contest plea in prosecution for criminal simulation; criminal simulation was a fourth-degree felony. State v. Primous (Ohio App. 2 Dist., 10-21-2005) 2005-Ohio-5586, 2005 WL 2697257. Criminal Law ⚷ 275.1

While court may consider argument from defendant that facts, as explained by state and admitted by no contest plea, do not constitute the offense charged, defendant, by pleading no contest, has waived right to present additional affirmative factual allegations to prove that she is not guilty. State v. Murphy (Ohio App. 9 Dist., 12-04-1996) 116 Ohio App.3d 41, 686 N.E.2d 553, dismissed, appeal not allowed 78 Ohio St.3d 1463, 678 N.E.2d 221. Criminal Law ⚷ 275.2

Defendant admitted truth of matters alleged in disorderly conduct complaint by pleading no contest, and other than presenting some evidence as to each element, prosecutor was relieved of burden of presenting evidence sufficient to prove these elements beyond a reasonable doubt. State v. Wood (Ohio App. 11 Dist., 07-15-1996) 112 Ohio App.3d 621, 679 N.E.2d 735. Criminal Law ⚷ 275.2

Court has no duty to take additional testimony regarding charge where defendant pleads no contest, prosecutor presents some evidence as to each element of charge, determination of guilt can be made from prosecutor's explanation of circumstances, and court determines that defendant made plea voluntarily, knowing the full effect thereof. State v. Wood (Ohio App. 11 Dist., 07-15-1996) 112 Ohio App.3d 621, 679 N.E.2d 735. Criminal Law ⚷ 275.3

No contest plea relieves prosecution of burden of presenting evidence sufficient to prove defendant guilty beyond reasonable doubt. Cincinnati v. Hawkins (Ohio Mun., 12-27-1993) 67 Ohio Misc.2d 4, 643 N.E.2d 1184. Criminal Law ⚷ 275.2

The finding of guilty of a lesser included offense constitutes a finding of not guilty of the greater offense, even though the trial court does not so state, and the defendant is placed in jeopardy when the court exercises its discretion and accepts the no-contest plea. State v. Rader (Hamilton 1988) 55 Ohio App.3d 102, 563 N.E.2d 304. Double Jeopardy ⚷ 57; Double Jeopardy ⚷ 165

Before relying on a no contest plea to convict a defendant for any misdemeanor, the court must comply with RC 2937.07. Pursuant to that statute, the court "shall call for explanation of circumstances of the offense from the affiant or the complainant or his representatives" together with "any statement of [the] accused." The court must then "make [a] finding of guilty or not guilty from the explanation of [the] circumstances." The record must show that the required explanation included a statement of facts which supports all the essential elements of the offense. The mere fact that the court's record includes documents which could show the defendant's guilt will not suffice. If the prosecution relies on such documents, the record must show that the court considered them. Village of Chagrin Falls v. Katelanos (Cuyahoga 1988) 54 Ohio App.3d 157, 561 N.E.2d 992.

A plea of no contest to a criminal charge allows the court to make a determination of guilty from the explanation of circumstances. City of Springdale v. Hubbard (Hamilton 1977) 52 Ohio App.2d 255, 369 N.E.2d 808, 6 O.O.3d 257.

RC 2937.07 includes substantive provisions of law and has not been superseded by Crim R 11. City of Springdale v. Hubbard (Hamilton 1977) 52 Ohio App.2d 255, 369 N.E.2d 808, 6 O.O.3d 257.

The state board of pharmacy cannot suspend the license of a registered pharmacist solely because on two occasions he entered pleas of nolo contendere in a US district court, for himself individually and as an officer and majority stockholder for a drug company (1) to charges that drugs were dispensed in such manner that they were misbranded, and (2) that a cough syrup containing narcotic was dispensed without proper record of the sale, and upon these pleas there were findings of guilty. Herman v. State Bd. of Pharmacy (Ohio Com.Pl. 1971) 27 Ohio Misc. 86, 272 N.E.2d 924, 56 O.O.2d 301.

Trial court did not make a perfunctory finding of guilt, but instead considered a sufficient set of circumstances to support defendant's conviction following his plea of no contest to the charge of underage consumption, even though there was no explicit statement of defendant's age prior to finding him guilty, where trial court was aware of defendant's age through its review of court file. State v. Nichols (Ohio App. 5 Dist., Coshocton, 07-31-2002) No. 01CA016, 2002-Ohio-4048, 2002 WL 1821811, Unreported. Criminal Law ⚷ 275.3

2. —— Explanation of circumstances, plea of no contest

Defendant was entitled to be found not guilty on his plea of no contest to misdemeanor criminal trespass, where plea court failed to explain circumstances of offense in support of each element thereof. State v. Courts (Ohio App. 2 Dist., Montgomery, 07-15-2005) No. 20689, 2005-Ohio-3694, 2005 WL 1705334, Unreported. Criminal Law ⚷ 275.3

Failure of defendant to object to lack of explanation of circumstances of each element of offense, prior to entry of conviction on defendant's plea of no contest to misdemeanor unauthorized use of property, did not result in waiver or trial court's error; deficient or absent explanation of circumstances was indication that evidence was legally insufficient to support conviction following no contest plea to misdemeanor, no contest plea in misdemeanor case preserved sufficiency of evidence argument for appeal and, even if error were waived, error would be subject to plain error analysis. State v. Osterfeld (Ohio App. 2 Dist., Montgomery, 06-24-2005) No. 20677, 2005-Ohio-3180, 2005 WL 1490452, Unreported. Criminal Law ⚷ 1031(4)

Defendant could not be convicted, on no contest plea, of first degree misdemeanor of unauthorized use of property, in absence of explanation as to circumstances of each element of offense, where deficiency or absence of explanation of circumstances meant evidence was legally insufficient to support conviction following no contest plea to misdemeanor. State v. Osterfeld (Ohio App. 2 Dist., Montgomery, 06-24-2005) No. 20677, 2005-Ohio-3180, 2005 WL 1490452, Unreported. Criminal Law ⚷ 275.3

Trial court's failure to provide "explanation of circumstances" before making a finding of guilty on a no-contest plea in misdemeanor prosecution was reversible error. State v. Harrier (Ohio App. 2 Dist., Montgomery, 06-24-2005) No. 20675, 2005-Ohio-3175, 2005 WL 1490132, Unreported. Criminal Law ⚷ 275.3; Criminal Law ⚷ 1167(5)

Trial court was not authorized to find defendant guilty upon no contest plea without fully explaining to defendant the circumstances surrounding the case. State v. Wellington (Ohio App. 7 Dist., Mahoning, 12-09-2004) No. 03 MA 199, 2004-Ohio-6807, 2004 WL 2913922, Unreported. Criminal Law ⚷ 275.3

Invited error doctrine precluded defendant from raising on appeal claim that trial court erred by finding him guilty of charges without providing explanation of circumstances at time defendant entered no contest plea, where trial counsel explicitly waived explanation of circumstances and trial court did not coerce counsel into waiving explanation of circumstances, but merely asked counsel whether there would be waiver. City of North Ridgeville v. Roth (Ohio App. 9 Dist., Lorain, 08-25-2004) No.

03CA008396, 2004-Ohio-4447, 2004 WL 1882644, Unreported. Criminal Law ⚷ 1137(2)

Trial court's finding of guilt following defendant's plea of no contest to charge of driving under the influence of alcohol (DUI) was improper, and thus conviction required reversal, where there was no explanation as to the circumstances giving rise to the finding of guilt, and trial court never informed defendant of the consequences of his plea. State v. Herbst (Ohio App. 6 Dist., Lucas, 06-18-2004) No. L-03-1238, 2004-Ohio-3157, 2004 WL 1368210, Unreported. Criminal Law ⚷ 275.3; Criminal Law ⚷ 1167(1)

Trial court erred by finding defendant guilty of menacing following no-contest plea, as the only explanation of circumstances arguably present in the record, defendant's own statement at the plea hearing, was insufficient to permit a finding of guilt; there was nothing in defendant's statement from which the trial court could have found that defendant's victim believed that defendant was going to cause physical harm to him, his property, or his family. State v. Stewart (Ohio App. 2 Dist., Montgomery, 06-10-2004) No. 19971, 2004-Ohio-3103, 2004 WL 1352628, Unreported. Criminal Law ⚷ 275.3

Assault defendant's statement that he did not have anything to say before court made a finding with regard to assault charge was not a waiver of requirement that court provide an explanation of circumstances before entering a conviction based on a no contest plea, and thus conviction was invalid, absent an explanation of circumstances that included a statement of the facts supporting all of the essential elements of the offense. State v. Smyers (Ohio App. 5 Dist., Muskingum, 02-19-2004) No. CT03-0039, 2004-Ohio-851, 2004 WL 351881, Unreported, on subsequent appeal 2005-Ohio-2912, 2005 WL 1384630. Criminal Law ⚷ 275.3

Trial court failed to fully explain circumstances surrounding charge of driving with a prohibited alcohol content following defendant's entry of no contest plea and prior to finding of guilt, and thus defendant's plea required vacation. State v. Hull (Ohio App. 7 Dist., Mahoning, 07-07-2003) No. 02 CA 47, 2003-Ohio-3715, 2003 WL 21640652, Unreported, opinion adhered to as modified on reconsideration 2003-Ohio-5306, 2003 WL 22284065. Criminal Law ⚷ 275.3

Trial court's failure to provide explanation of circumstances surrounding alleged offense prior to accepting defendants' pleas of no contest to child endangering constituted reversible error. State v. Myers (Ohio App. 3 Dist., Marion, 06-10-2003) No. 9-02-65, No. 9-02-66, 2003-Ohio-2936, 2003 WL 21321402, Unreported. Criminal Law ⚷ 275.3; Criminal Law ⚷ 1167(5)

Trial court erred in failing to elicit explanation of circumstances surrounding alleged offense prior to accepting defendant's plea of no contest to simple assault; defendant was never addressed concerning either the charge against him or the elements of that offense. State v. Malek (Ohio App. 7 Dist., Mahoning, 11-20-2002) No. 02CA97, 2002-Ohio-6431, 2002 WL 31654481, Unreported. Criminal Law ⚷ 275.3

To gain a conviction of a defendant who has entered a no contest plea, state must provide an explanation of circumstances to maintain the offense; explanation is sufficient if it supports all the essential elements of the offense. State v. Puterbaugh (Ohio App. 4 Dist., 03-28-2001) 142 Ohio App.3d 185, 755 N.E.2d 359, 2001-Ohio-2498. Criminal Law ⚷ 275.3

A defendant who pleads no contest should be found not guilty where the state's statement of facts does not establish all of the offense's elements. State v. Puterbaugh (Ohio App. 4 Dist., 03-28-2001) 142 Ohio App.3d 185, 755 N.E.2d 359, 2001-Ohio-2498. Criminal Law ⚷ 275.3

Trial court that accepted defendant's no contest plea to vehicular homicide and speeding was not required to read into record circumstances and reasons for finding defendant guilty, since state had set forth sufficient facts, incorporating complaint and testimony of police officer, to support each of the essential elements of crimes charged. State v. Murphy (Ohio App. 9 Dist., 12-04-1996) 116 Ohio App.3d 41, 686 N.E.2d 553, dismissed, appeal not allowed 78 Ohio St.3d 1463, 678 N.E.2d 221. Criminal Law ⚷ 275.3

In case of no contest plea to misdemeanor offense, court may make its finding from explanation of circumstances by state, and need not consider accused's statement; court is required to consider accused's statement only where guilty plea is entered. State v. Waddell (Ohio, 03-29-1995) 71 Ohio St.3d 630, 646 N.E.2d 821, 1995-Ohio-31. Criminal Law ⚷ 273(4.1); Criminal Law ⚷ 275.3

In order to obtain conviction of defendant who has pled no contest, state must offer explanation of circumstances to support charge; this explanation is sufficient if it supports all essential elements of offense. State v. Gilbo (Ohio App. 2 Dist., 08-03-1994) 96 Ohio App.3d 332, 645 N.E.2d 69. Criminal Law ⚷ 275.3

Defendant's no contest plea constitutes stipulation that court can make finding of guilty or not guilty from prosecution's explanation of circumstances. Cincinnati v. Hawkins (Ohio Mun., 12-27-1993) 67 Ohio Misc.2d 4, 643 N.E.2d 1184. Criminal Law ⚷ 275.2

Although in misdemeanor cases no contest plea constitutes stipulation that judge or magistrate may make finding of guilty or not guilty from explanation of circumstances, neither criminal rules nor statutes require similar explanation of circumstances to trial judge prior to finding of guilt in felony case. State v. Kutz (Lucas 1993) 87 Ohio App.3d 329, 622 N.E.2d 362, dismissed, jurisdictional motion overruled 67 Ohio St.3d 1463, 619 N.E.2d 698. Criminal Law ⚷ 273(4.1)

Trial court had no power or authority to find defendant, who pleaded no contest to sale of cocaine in an amount in excess of three times bulk amount and sale of cocaine in excess of bulk amount, guilty of lesser included offense of sale of cocaine in less than bulk amount, where trial court had no "evidence" before it to support conclusion that sales involved less than bulk amount, in that prosecutor recited facts sufficient to support charges of sale of cocaine in excess of bulk amount and in excess of three times bulk amount, and upon completion of prosecutor's statement, and without intervention by defense counsel and without questions from court, court found defendant guilty of lesser included offenses. State v. Rader (Hamilton 1988) 55 Ohio App.3d 102, 563 N.E.2d 304. Criminal Law ⚷ 275.3

The taking of sworn testimony upon the plea of "no contest" more than satisfies the requirements of RC 2937.07, in regard to an "explanation of circumstances," and the taking of such sworn testimony does not constitute error. State v. Ovens (Lucas 1974) 44 Ohio App.2d 428, 339 N.E.2d 853, 73 O.O.2d 540. Criminal Law ⚷ 275.3

For purposes of statute, which provides that plea of no contest to a misdemeanor charge shall constitute a stipulation that judge or magistrate may make findings of guilty or not guilty from the explanation of circumstances, the "explanation of circumstances" required to found a finding of guilty does not have to be by "sworn" testimony. City of Cincinnati v. Kinder (Hamilton 1974) 322 N.E.2d 906, 67 O.O.2d 44. Criminal Law ⚷ 275.3

RC 2937.07 does not require that sworn testimony be presented when a "no contest" plea is made and accepted and an explanation of the case is provided. City of Cincinnati v. Ohio Police Patrol (Hamilton 1971) 32 Ohio App.2d 268, 290 N.E.2d 193, 61 O.O.2d 309.

The plea of "no contest" as provided for in RC 2937.07 constitutes a stipulation that the judge may make a finding of guilty or not guilty from "the explanation of circumstances," and the statute does not indicate or require sworn testimony. State v. Herman (Lucas 1971) 31 Ohio App.2d 134, 286 N.E.2d 296, 60 O.O.2d 210. Criminal Law ⚷ 275.2

An oral reading in open court of the affiant officer's notes written on the back page of the affidavit setting forth the offense is a proper procedure, and meets the requirements of RC 2937.07 even though the officer is not present. State v. Herman (Lucas 1971) 31 Ohio App.2d 134, 286 N.E.2d 296, 60 O.O.2d 210.

"The explanation of circumstances" referred to in RC 2937.07 shall be made by the affiant or complainant or his representative. State v. Herman (Lucas 1971) 31 Ohio App.2d 134, 286 N.E.2d 296, 60 O.O.2d 210. Criminal Law ⚷ 275.3

Statements made by counsel for both parties at the time of trial and, as restated and amplified by both in their briefs, fall within the term "explanation of circumstances" as authorized by the statute in connection with pleas of no contest. Village of Fairlawn v. Fuller (Ohio Mun. 1966) 8 Ohio Misc. 266, 221 N.E.2d 851, 37 O.O.2d 312.

Before relying upon a no contest plea to convict a defendant for a misdemeanor offense, the trial court is required to receive an explanation of circumstances so that it may properly determine from an evaluation of the facts provided whether the defendant's conduct amounts to a violation of the offense as charged in the complaint. State v. Spence (Ohio App. 12 Dist., Clermont, 07-15-2002) No. CA2002-02-012, 2002-Ohio-3600, 2002 WL 1495341, Unreported. Criminal Law ⚷ 275.3

A prosecutor's explanation of circumstances does not support a conviction for possession of an open container in violation of RC 4301.62 where a deputy empties unopened bottles of beer and wine and retains a photograph of the "empties" after he approaches a parked car where defendant and his girlfriend are found kissing and partially clothed in the front seat and (1) in searching the car the deputy finds several bottles of unopened beer and wine in a duffle bag in the back seat, (2) after emptying the bottles cites defendant for under age possession of beer and intoxicating liquor, and (3) there is no indication that opened containers of beer or intoxicating liquor were discovered in defendant's possession. State v Hurchanik, No. CA97–05–050, 1998 WL 117166 (12th Dist Ct App, Warren, 3–16–98).

The requirement of an explanation of circumstances upon which to make a finding of guilt when a defendant enters a no contest plea is not met by a mere restatement of the elements of a statutory offense. State v McGlothin, No. CA–13460 (2d Dist Ct App, Montgomery, 2–10–93).

The "explanation of circumstances" requirement under RC 2937.07 does not preclude a trial court from going further and allowing formal introduction of testimony; such benefits the defendant rather than prejudicing him. State v Jordan, No. 13–85–40 (3d Dist Ct App, Seneca, 4–21–87).

3. —— Basis for finding of guilt, plea of no contest

Evidence at hearing on defendant's motion to suppress provided explanation of circumstances sufficient for trial court to find defendant guilty following his plea of no contest to misdemeanor driving under influence of alcohol (DUI). State v. Kiefer (Ohio App. 1 Dist., Hamilton, 09-24-2004) No. C-030205, 2004-Ohio-5054, 2004 WL 2244553, Unreported. Criminal Law ⚷ 275.3

Convictions on four counts of failing to register dogs were not against manifest weight of evidence; prosecutor stated in support of defendant's no contest plea that four unlicensed dogs were found in the basement of defendant's home. State v. Brown (Ohio App. 2 Dist., Montgomery, 06-10-2004) No. 19917, 2004-Ohio-3091, 2004 WL 1347609, Unreported. Animals ⚷ 2.5(3)

Suspension of a driver's license is error where a defendant pleads no contest to a speeding charge and there is no statement of facts in the record to support the relation of the speed violation to reckless operation. City of Garfield Heights v. Huber (Ohio App. 8 Dist., Cuyahoga, 09-22-1994) No. 65916, 1994 WL 521131, Unreported.

Defendant, by pleading no contest to charge of obstructing official business, waived right to present evidence of her innocence and the reasons for her actions. State v. Puterbaugh (Ohio App. 4 Dist., 03-28-2001) 142 Ohio App.3d 185, 755 N.E.2d 359, 2001-Ohio-2498. Criminal Law ⚿ 275.2

Essence of "no contest" plea is that the accused cannot be heard in defense; thus, any statement by him must be considered in mitigation of penalty. State v. Puterbaugh (Ohio App. 4 Dist., 03-28-2001) 142 Ohio App.3d 185, 755 N.E.2d 359, 2001-Ohio-2498. Criminal Law ⚿ 275.2

Prosecutor sufficiently established all elements of vehicular homicide and speeding, where prosecutor presented statement on record that defendant was traveling at approximately 52 m.p.h. on street with a 35 m.p.h. speed limit when she hit child with her automobile causing fatal injuries, eyewitnesses and police officer from accident reconstruction unit confirmed that defendant was traveling at rate of 52 m.p.h., and defendant entered plea of no contest thereby admitting state's claim of a speed of approximately 52 m.p.h. State v. Murphy (Ohio App. 9 Dist., 12-04-1996) 116 Ohio App.3d 41, 686 N.E.2d 553, dismissed, appeal not allowed 78 Ohio St.3d 1463, 678 N.E.2d 221. Automobiles ⚿ 355(5); Automobiles ⚿ 355(13)

By pleading no contest, defendant waives his or her right to present additional affirmative allegations to prove that he or she was not guilty. State v. Gilbo (Ohio App. 2 Dist., 08-03-1994) 96 Ohio App.3d 332, 645 N.E.2d 69. Criminal Law ⚿ 275.2

Conviction on plea of no contest is improper when statements of factual matter presented to court in support of complaint negate existence of essential element of offense charged. Cincinnati v. Hawkins (Ohio Mun., 12-27-1993) 67 Ohio Misc.2d 4, 643 N.E.2d 1184. Criminal Law ⚿ 275.3

The provision in RC 2937.07 requiring an explanation of circumstances following a plea of no contest has not been superseded by the enactment of Crim R 11 because the statutory provision confers a substantive right to a finding of not guilty upon a no contest plea where the statement of facts reveals a failure to establish all of the elements of the offense. City of Cuyahoga Falls v. Bowers (Ohio 1984) 9 Ohio St.3d 148, 459 N.E.2d 532, 9 O.B.R. 438. Criminal Law ⚿ 275.3

Trial court may, in its discretion, refuse to accept no contest plea; for example, in felony case, when it appears from facts recited by prosecutor that defendant did not commit offense charged in indictment, proper course is for trial court to refuse plea. State v. Thorpe (Cuyahoga 1983) 9 Ohio App.3d 1, 457 N.E.2d 912, 9 O.B.R. 1. Criminal Law ⚿ 275.3

A finding of guilty by a judge pursuant to RC 2937.07, after the defendant has pleaded "no contest" under RC 2937.06(C), must be supported by sworn evidence which states facts substantiating the presence of each of the elements of the offense. City of Lyndhurst v. McFarlane (Ohio Com.Pl. 1969) 21 Ohio Misc. 197, 256 N.E.2d 627, 50 O.O.2d 414.

Defendant who pleads no contest has a substantive right to be acquitted if the explanation of circumstances does not support all the elements of the offense. State v. Spence (Ohio App. 12 Dist., Clermont, 07-15-2002) No. CA2002-02-012, 2002-Ohio-3600, 2002 WL 1495341, Unreported. Criminal Law ⚿ 275.3

4. —— Admission of fact, plea as, plea of no contest

Defendant who pleads no contest has substantive right to be acquitted where state's statement of facts fails to establish all elements of offense; accordingly, court may consider argument of defendant that facts as admitted did not constitute offense charged. State v. Gilbo (Ohio App. 2 Dist., 08-03-1994) 96 Ohio App.3d 332, 645 N.E.2d 69. Criminal Law ⚿ 275.3

Plaintiff's prior conviction for disorderly conduct was admissible in his suit for declaratory judgment against insurer, notwithstanding that conviction was based on plea of no contest, which plea was itself not admissible in subsequent civil proceeding. Steinke v. Allstate Ins. Co. (Auglaize 1993) 86 Ohio App.3d 798, 621 N.E.2d 1275, motion overruled 67 Ohio St.3d 1423, 616 N.E.2d 506. Declaratory Judgment ⚿ 344

After defendant pleaded no contest to domestic violence, Municipal Court failed to provide an adequate explanation of the circumstances to support its finding of guilt, and thus Court of Appeals would vacate plea and remand the case for further proceedings; by pleading no contest, defendant admitted truth of facts alleged in affidavit-complaint, but only element that could be proven was that alleged victims were defendant's family members, and that statement was not made at plea hearing. State v. Maley (Ohio App. 7 Dist., Columbiana, 09-27-2002) No. 01 CO 38, 2002-Ohio-5220, 2002 WL 31168844, Unreported. Criminal Law ⚿ 273(4.1); Criminal Law ⚿ 1181.5(3.1)

Defendant's statement to the court, in which he admitted shoving and wrestling with victim, did not invalidate defendant's waiver of rights and plea of no contest to misdemeanor charge of domestic violence; although defendant claimed that statement clearly indicated that he asserted his innocence and claimed a defense, waiver and plea were knowing and voluntary, where defendant pleaded no contest after being advised a no contest plea was an admission of the facts set forth in the citation, defendant admitted he knowingly caused or attempt to cause physical harm to victim, and court was free to accept or reject defendant's versions of the facts portrayed in statement. State v. Roots (Ohio App. 5 Dist., Morrow, 05-31-2002) No. CA-938, 2002-Ohio-2853, 2002 WL 1162353, Unreported, appeal not allowed 96 Ohio St.3d 1524, 775 N.E.2d 864, 2002-Ohio-5099. Criminal Law ⚿ 275.3

5. Failure to follow procedures

Proper remedy for trial court's error in convicting defendant on no contest plea of misdemeanor unauthorized use of property, without giving explanation as to circumstances of each element of offense, was reversal of judgment and discharge of defendant from any criminal liability; defendant performed his end of plea bargain by tendering no contest plea, which was accepted, and double jeopardy principles barred retrial when conviction was reversed based on lack of explanation of circumstances following no contest plea. State v. Osterfeld (Ohio App. 2 Dist., Montgomery, 06-24-2005) No. 20677, 2005-Ohio-3180, 2005 WL 1490452, Unreported. Criminal Law ⟹ 1187

Trial court's failure, after ascertaining that defendant making initial appearance before it spoke little or no English but was fluent in Spanish, to assure that charges were explained to defendant in Spanish, or to inform defendant of his right to counsel, fact that he was not required to make any statement, and fact that he was required to request jury trial in petty offense case, was prejudicial error requiring vacation of defendant's guilty plea. State v. Fonseca (Ohio App. 11 Dist., 11-24-1997) 124 Ohio App.3d 231, 705 N.E.2d 1278. Criminal Law ⟹ 264; Criminal Law ⟹ 1166(3); Criminal Law ⟹ 1181.5(1)

Trial court's failure to inform pro se defendant of effect of his guilty plea and his right to attorney required rejection of guilty plea to misdemeanor petty theft. State v. Fonseca (Ohio App. 11 Dist., 11-24-1997) 124 Ohio App.3d 231, 705 N.E.2d 1278. Criminal Law ⟹ 273.1(4)

Defendant's plea of guilty to petty theft was not knowingly made, where defendant spoke little or no English, and where court accepted assurance of unknown courtroom bystander who claimed to be fluent in Spanish that defendant understood charges and wished to plead guilty; record of plea proceeding was silent as to exact content of defendant's responses to court's questions and did not demonstrate that defendant understood court's untranslated English description of charges against him. State v. Fonseca (Ohio App. 11 Dist., 11-24-1997) 124 Ohio App.3d 231, 705 N.E.2d 1278. Criminal Law ⟹ 273.1(1)

To sustain the validity of a plea of no contest and the concomitant waiver of constitutional rights, the record must affirmatively demonstrate that the trial court discharged the mandatory duties imposed by RC 2937.02 of advising the accused of the effects of such plea. State v. Kristanoff (Hamilton 1972) 32 Ohio App.2d 218, 289 N.E.2d 402, 61 O.O.2d 222. Criminal Law ⟹ 1086.9

Failure of the judge to comply with the provisions of RC 2937.02 to RC 2937.07 invalidates a plea of guilty to a misdemeanor. City of Cleveland v. Whipkey (Cuyahoga 1972) 29 Ohio App.2d 79, 278 N.E.2d 374, 58 O.O.2d 86.

Failure of the transcript of proceedings to show compliance with the mandatory statutory requirements as to the pretrial procedure of RC Ch 2937 invalidates the entire proceedings, and a judgment based on a guilty plea will be reversed by the reviewing court. City of Cleveland v. Whipkey (Cuyahoga 1972) 29 Ohio App.2d 79, 278 N.E.2d 374, 58 O.O.2d 86.

2937.08 Action on pleas of "not guilty" or "once in jeopardy" in misdemeanor cases

Upon a plea of not guilty or a plea of once in jeopardy, if the charge be a misdemeanor in a court of record, the court shall proceed to set the matter for trial at a future time, pursuant to Chapter 2938. of the Revised Code, and shall let accused to bail pending such trial. Or he may, but only if both prosecutor and accused expressly consent, set the matter for trial forthwith.

Upon the entry of such pleas to a charge of misdemeanor in a court not of record, the magistrate shall forthwith set the matter for future trial or, with the consent of both state and defendant may set trial forthwith, both pursuant to Chapter 2938. of the Revised Code, provided that if the nature of the offense is such that right to jury trial exists, such matter shall not be tried before him unless the accused, by writing subscribed by him, waives a jury and consents to be tried by the magistrate.

If the defendant in such event does not waive right to jury trial, then the magistrate shall require the accused to enter into recognizance to appear before a court of record in the county, set by such magistrate, and the magistrate shall thereupon certify all papers filed, together with transcript of proceedings and accrued costs to date, and such recognizance if given, to such designated court of record. Such transfer shall not require the filing of indictment or information and trial shall proceed in the transferee court pursuant to Chapter 2938. of the Revised Code.

(128 v 97, eff. 1–1–60)

Historical and Statutory Notes

Ed. Note: 2937.08 contains provisions analogous to former 2937.11, repealed by 128 v 97, eff. 1–1–60.

Ed. Note: Former 2937.08 repealed by 128 v 97, eff. 1–1–60; 1953 H 1; GC 13433–7.

Pre–1953 H 1 Amendments: 113 v 146, Ch 12, § 7

Cross References

Complaint, Crim R 3

Court not of record, mayor's court, Ch 1905

Mayor's court jurisdiction over violations of municipal ordinances comparable to driving under suspension, 1905.01

Pleas in certain misdemeanor cases, Crim R 11

Territorial jurisdiction, 2938.10

Library References

Criminal Law ⟹289, 299.

Westlaw Topic No. 110.

C.J.S. Criminal Law §§ 378, 381, 409.

Research References

Encyclopedias

OH Jur. 3d Criminal Law § 2025, Mayor's Courts—Specific Offenses.

OH Jur. 3d Criminal Law § 2184, Upon Initial Appearance.

OH Jur. 3d Criminal Law § 2443, in Misdemeanor Cases.

Treatises and Practice Aids

Katz, Giannelli, Blair and Lipton, Baldwin's Ohio Practice, Criminal Law, § 62:13, Ohio Mayors' Courts.

Notes of Decisions

Action on no contest plea 5
Certification to court of record 3
Constitutional issues 1
Court not of record 2
Setting trial date 4

---

1. Constitutional issues

Felonious assault and aggravated menacing convictions are not barred on double jeopardy grounds based on the defendant's previous no contest plea to a disorderly conduct charge arising from his arrest where the defendant's disorderly conduct is a distinct act committed at a separate time from the felonious assault and aggravated menacing offenses. State v. Stringfield (Medina 1992) 82 Ohio App.3d 705, 612 N.E.2d 1327, dismissed, jurisdictional motion overruled 66 Ohio St.3d 1436, 608 N.E.2d 1082, denial of post-conviction relief affirmed.

2. Court not of record

A mayor's court is not a court of record. City of Greenhills v. Miller (Hamilton 1969) 20 Ohio App.2d 313, 253 N.E.2d 311, 49 O.O.2d 401. Courts ⟹ 187

A mayor of a village presiding over a mayor's court may sentence a person to imprisonment for violation of a village ordinance if such person in writing waives a jury and consents to be tried by the mayor as magistrate. OAG 69–117.

3. Certification to court of record

Although mayor's courts and municipal courts have concurrent jurisdiction to hear cases arising from violations of municipal ordinances, a mayor's court lacks jurisdiction to conduct a jury trial; therefore, when a defendant pleads not guilty to a misdemeanor case commenced in a mayor's court and the defendant either requests a jury trial or fails to waive his right to a jury trial, the case must be transferred to the appropriate municipal court. City of Brunswick v. Giglio (Ohio Mun. 1988) 39 Ohio Misc.2d 5, 530 N.E.2d 37.

In prosecutions under RC 3773.22 a county court has original, but not exclusive, jurisdiction and where in such a case the defendant is entitled to a trial by jury, and does not waive such right, the case must be certified to a court of record. (Ed. note: County courts are now courts of record under RC 1907.012.) 1960 OAG 1548.

Where a solicitor or law director of a municipal corporation presents a case in a county court and such case is certified to a court of record pursuant to RC 2937.08, said solicitor or law director should present the case in the transferee court; and where the county prosecuting attorney presents such a case which is so certified, or where neither a solicitor, law director, or the prosecuting attorney presents a case in a county court, which case is so certified, the prosecuting attorney should present the case in the transferee court. (Ed. note: County courts are now courts of record under RC 1907.012.) 1960 OAG 1548.

Under RC 1907.012 a county court is not a court of record until January 1, 1963, and, in a criminal case in a county court where the defendant is entitled to a trial by jury, and does not waive such right, the judge is required to certify the cases to a court of record in the county. (Ed. note: County courts are now courts of record under RC 1907.012.) 1960 OAG 1548.

4. Setting trial date

The provision that a criminal matter be set for trial at a date subsequent to arraignment unless both prosecutor and accused expressly consent, is a mandatory requirement. State v. Willis (Monroe 1963) 200 N.E.2d 790, 94 Ohio Law Abs. 263, 30 O.O.2d 518. Criminal Law ⟹ 575

5. Action on no contest plea

A finding of guilty by a judge pursuant to RC 2937.07, after the defendant has pleaded "no contest" under RC 2937.06(C), must be supported by sworn evidence which states facts substantiating the presence of each of the elements of the offense. City of Lyndhurst v. McFarlane (Ohio Com.Pl. 1969) 21 Ohio Misc. 197, 256 N.E.2d 627, 50 O.O.2d 414.

2937.081 Duty of prosecutor to give victims of crime notice of certain facts concerning resulting prosecution; procedures; limits—Repealed

(1994 S 186, eff. 10–12–94; 1987 S 6, § 4, eff. 6–10–87; 1984 S 76, § 1, 2)

Historical and Statutory Notes

Ed. Note: The repeal of this section by 1984 S 76, § 2, eff. 7–1–87, was rescinded by 1987 S 6, § 4, eff. 6–10–87. See *Baldwin's Ohio Legislative Service*, 1984 Laws of Ohio, page 5–468, and 1987 Laws of Ohio, page 5–55.

2937.09 Procedure in felony cases

If the charge is a felony, the court or magistrate shall, before receiving a plea of guilty, advise the accused that such plea constitutes an admission which may be used against him at a later trial. If the defendant enters a written plea of guilty or, pleading not guilty, affirmatively waives the right to have the court or magistrate take evidence concerning the offense, the court or magistrate forthwith and without taking evidence may find that the crime has been committed and that there is probable and reasonable cause to hold the defendant for trial pursuant to indictment by the grand jury, and, if the offense is bailable, require the accused to enter into recognizance in such amount as it determines to appear before the court of common pleas pursuant to indictment, otherwise to be confined until the grand jury has considered and reported the matter.

(129 v 582, eff. 1–10–61; 128 v 97)

Historical and Statutory Notes

Ed. Note: 2937.09 contains provisions analogous to former 2937.11, repealed by 128 v 97, eff. 1–1–60.

Ed. Note: Former 2937.09 repealed by 128 v 97, eff. 1–1–60; 1953 H 1; GC 13433–8.

Pre–1953 H 1 Amendments: 113 v 146, Ch 12, § 8

Cross References

Classification of offenses, 2901.02

Initial appearance, preliminary hearing, Crim R 5

Penalties for felony, imposing sentence, factors to be considered, 2929.11 to 2929.14

Pleas, rights upon plea, Crim R 11

Library References

Criminal Law ⚷272, 289.

Westlaw Topic No. 110.

C.J.S. Criminal Law §§ 365 to 374, 381 to 391, 400 to 407, 410, 418.

Research References

Encyclopedias

OH Jur. 3d Criminal Law § 2184, Upon Initial Appearance.

Notes of Decisions

Constitutional issues 1

---

1. Constitutional issues

Right of counsel at a preliminary hearing of the character set forth in Coleman v Alabama, 399 US 1, 90 SCt 1999, 26 LEd(2d) 287 (1970), does not extend in Ohio to magistrate's arraignment of accused in felony charge, where accused has been informed of his rights by magistrate as prescribed by RC 2937.02, has pled not guilty and has affirmatively waived his right to preliminary hearing. State

v. Simones (Marion 1971) 27 Ohio App.2d 9, 272 N.E.2d 146, 56 O.O.2d 198, affirmed 30 Ohio St.2d 100, 282 N.E.2d 573, 59 O.O.2d 113. Criminal Law ⚷ 264

Municipal court proceedings at which guilty plea was received was a critical stage of the criminal process so that petitioner was entitled to counsel thereat. Sheely v. Whealon (C.A.6 (Ohio) 1975) 525 F.2d 713.

2937.10 Hearing set in felony cases

If the charge be a felony and there be no written plea of guilty or waiver of examination, or the court or magistrate refuses to receive such waiver, the court or magistrate, with the consent of the prosecutor and the accused, may set the matter for hearing forthwith, otherwise he shall set the matter for hearing at a fixed time in the future and shall notify both prosecutor and defendant promptly of such time of hearing.

(128 v 97, eff. 1–1–60)

Historical and Statutory Notes

Ed. Note: Former 2937.10 repealed by 128 v 97, eff. 1–1–60; 127 v 1039; 1953 H 1; GC 13433–9; see now 2937.07 for provisions analogous to former 2937.10.

Pre–1953 H 1 Amendments: 113 v 146, Ch 12, § 9

Library References

Criminal Law ⚷225, 266.

Westlaw Topic No. 110.

C.J.S. Criminal Law §§ 340, 342, 364.

Research References

Treatises and Practice Aids

Katz, Giannelli, Blair and Lipton, Baldwin's Ohio Practice, Criminal Law, § 38:3, Jurisdiction.

Notes of Decisions

Pretrial motions 2
Right to preliminary hearing 1

1. Right to preliminary hearing

The Summit county "career criminal program" bears a reasonable relationship to the legitimate interest of the state of Ohio in the speedy, but fair, prosecution of those who have demonstrated a propensity for crime, and does not, on its face, violate the Equal Protection Clause of US Const Am 14, O Const Art I, § 2 or O Const Art II, § 26. State v. Lamp (Summit 1977) 59 Ohio App.2d 125, 392 N.E.2d 1090, 13 O.O.3d 173.

There is no constitutional right to a preliminary hearing under RC 2937.10, once an indictment has been returned by a grand jury, and, absent a showing by a defendant of particularized need for the inspection of grand jury minutes, such later relief is not required. State v. Morris (Ohio 1975) 42 Ohio St.2d 307, 329 N.E.2d 85, 71 O.O.2d 294, certiorari denied 96 S.Ct. 774, 423 U.S. 1049, 46 L.Ed.2d 637.

Where an appellant requested and was denied an immediate preliminary hearing and then while awaiting such hearing was indicted by a grand jury, there is no clear legal requirement of a preliminary hearing. State ex rel. Haynes v. Powers (Ohio 1969) 20 Ohio St.2d 46, 254 N.E.2d 19, 49 O.O.2d 305.

A defendant who has been arrested and charged with a felony does not have a constitutional right to demand that he be afforded a preliminary hearing before a magistrate; the grand jury, during the pendency of such action in the magistrate's court, may, on its own motion or by action of the prosecuting attorney, give consideration to the case and under proper circumstances and sufficient credible evidence, as provided by law, return an indictment against such defendant for whatever crime is justified by the evidence, and, upon the return of such indictment to the common pleas court, such court is vested with jurisdiction of the case, and the proceeding in the magistrate's court must be dismissed. State v. McClellan (Lucas 1966) 6 Ohio App.2d 155, 217 N.E.2d 230, 35 O.O.2d 315, certiorari denied 87 S.Ct. 1380, 386 U.S. 1022, 18 L.Ed.2d 462.

2. Pretrial motions

A motion to suppress evidence allegedly obtained as the result of an illegal search does not lie at a preliminary hearing in a felony case, since Crim R 12(B)(3) and Crim R 12(C) require such motions to be filed "within thirty-five days after arraignment or seven days before trial, whichever is earlier." State

v. Mitchell (Ohio 1975) 42 Ohio St.2d 447, 329 N.E.2d 682, 71 O.O.2d 417.

2937.11 Presentation of state's case; videotaped or recorded testimony of child victims

(A)(1) As used in this section, "victim" includes any person who was a victim of a felony violation identified in division (B) of this section or a felony offense of violence or against whom was directed any conduct that constitutes, or that is an element of, a felony violation identified in division (B) of this section or a felony offense of violence.

(2) At the preliminary hearing set pursuant to section 2937.10 of the Revised Code and the Criminal Rules, the prosecutor may state, but is not required to state, orally the case for the state and shall then proceed to examine witnesses and introduce exhibits for the state. The accused and the magistrate have full right of cross examination, and the accused has the right of inspection of exhibits prior to their introduction. The hearing shall be conducted under the rules of evidence prevailing in criminal trials generally. On motion of either the state or the accused, witnesses shall be separated and not permitted in the hearing room except when called to testify.

(B) In a case involving an alleged felony violation of section 2905.05, 2907.02, 2907.03, 2907.04, 2907.05, 2907.21, 2907.24, 2907.31, 2907.32, 2907.321, 2907.322, 2907.323, or 2919.22 of the Revised Code or an alleged felony offense of violence and in which an alleged victim of the alleged violation or offense was less than thirteen years of age when the complaint or information was filed, whichever occurred earlier, upon motion of the prosecution, the testimony of the child victim at the preliminary hearing may be taken in a room other than the room in which the preliminary hearing is being conducted and be televised, by closed circuit equipment, into the room in which the preliminary hearing is being conducted, in accordance with division (C) of section 2945.481 of the Revised Code.

(C) In a case involving an alleged felony violation listed in division (B) of this section or an alleged felony offense of violence and in which an alleged victim of the alleged violation or offense was less than thirteen years of age when the complaint or information was filed, whichever occurred earlier, the court, on written motion of the prosecutor in the case filed at least three days prior to the hearing, shall order that all testimony of the child victim be recorded and preserved on videotape, in addition to being recorded for purposes of the transcript of the proceeding. If such an order is issued, it shall specifically identify the child victim concerning whose testimony it pertains, apply only during the testimony of the child victim it specifically identifies, and apply to all testimony of the child victim presented at the hearing, regardless of whether the child victim is called as a witness by the prosecution or by the defense.

(1997 S 53, eff. 10–14–97; 1996 H 445, eff. 9–3–96; 1986 H 108, eff. 10–14–86; 128 v 97)

Uncodified Law

1996 H 445, § 3, eff. 9–3–96, reads:

(A) When a complaint is filed alleging that a child is a delinquent child for committing felonious sexual penetration in violation of former section 2907.12 of the Revised Code and the arresting authority, a court, or a probation officer discovers that the child or a person whom the child caused to engage in sexual activity has a communicable disease, the arresting authority, court, or probation officer shall notify the victim of the delinquent act of the nature of the disease in accordance with division (C) of section 2151.14 of the Revised Code.

As used in division (A) of Section 3 of this act:

(1) "Child" has the same meaning as in section 2151.011 of the Revised Code.

(2) "Delinquent child" has the same meaning as in section 2151.02 of the Revised Code.

(3) "Sexual activity" has the same meaning as in section 2907.01 of the Revised Code.

(B) If a child is adjudicated a delinquent child for violating any provision of former section 2907.12 of the Revised Code other than division (A)(1)(b) of that section when the insertion involved was consensual and when the victim of the violation of division (A)(1)(b) of that section was older than the delinquent child, was the same age as the delinquent child, or was less that three years younger than the delinquent child, the juvenile court with jurisdiction over the child may commit the child to the legal custody of the department of youth services pursuant to division (A)(5)(a) of section 2151.355 of the Revised Code, as amended by this act, and all provisions of the Revised Code that apply to a disposition otherwise imposed pursuant to division (A)(5)(a) of section 2151.355 of the Revised Code, as amended by this act, apply to a disposition imposed in accordance with division (B) of Section 3 of this act.

As used in division (B) of Section 3 of this act:

(1) "Child" and "legal custody" have the same meanings as in section 2151.011 of the Revised Code.

(2) "Delinquent child" has the same meaning as in section 2151.02 of the Revised Code.

(C) Section 2151.3511 of the Revised Code, as amended by this act, applies to a proceeding in juvenile court involving a complaint in which a child is charged with committing an act that if committed by an adult would be felonious sexual penetration in violation of former section 2907.12 of the Revised Code and in which an alleged victim of the act was a child who was under eleven years of age when the complaint was filed.

As used in division (C) of Section 3 of this act, "child" has the same meaning as in section 2151.011 of the Revised Code.

(D) Division (E) of section 2743.62 of the Revised Code applies to a claim for an award of reparations arising out of the commission of felonious sexual penetration in violation of former section 2907.12 of the Revised Code.

(E) Section 2907.11 of the Revised Code, as amended by this act, applies to a prosecution for felonious sexual penetration committed in violation of former section 2907.12 of the Revised Code.

(F) Division (A) of section 2907.28 and sections 2907.29 and 2907.30 of the Revised Code, as amended by this act, apply to a victim of felonious sexual penetration committed in violation of former section 2907.12 of the Revised Code.

(G) Sections 2907.41 and 2945.49 of the Revised Code, as amended by this act, apply to a trial or other proceeding involving a charge of felonious sexual penetration in violation of former section 2907.12 of the Revised Code in which an alleged victim of the offense was a child who was under eleven years of age when the complaint, indictment, or information was filed relative to the trial or other proceeding.

(H) Divisions (B) and (C) of section 2937.11 of the Revised Code, as amended by this act, apply to a case involving an alleged commission of the offense of felonious sexual penetration in violation of former section 2907.12 of the Revised Code.

(I) Notwithstanding section 2967.13 of the Revised Code, as amended by this act, a prisoner serving a term of imprisonment for life for committing the offense of felonious sexual penetration in violation of former section 2907.12 of the Revised Code becomes eligible for parole after serving a term of ten full years' imprisonment.

(J) Notwithstanding section 2967.18 of the Revised Code, as amended by this act, no reduction of sentence pursuant to division (B)(1) of section 2967.18 of the Revised Code shall be given to a person who is serving a term of imprisonment for the commission of felonious sexual penetration in violation of former section 2907.12 of the Revised Code.

Historical and Statutory Notes

Ed. Note: Former 2937.11 repealed by 128 v 97, eff. 1–1–60; 127 v 1039; 1953 H 1; GC 13433–10; see now 2937.08 and 2937.09 for provisions analogous to former 2937.11.

Pre–1953 H 1 Amendments: 113 v 147, Ch 12, § 10

Amendment Note: 1997 S 53 added division (A)(1); designated division (A)(2); inserted references to Revised Code sections 2905.05, 2907.24 and 2945.481 in division (B); deleted references to Revised Code sections 2907.06 and 2907.14 in division (B); inserted "or an alleged felony offense of violence and" following "Revised Code" in division (B); substituted "less than thirteen" for "under eleven" in divisions (B) and (C); substituted "listed in division B of this section or an alleged felony offense of violence and" for "of section 2907.02, 2907.03, 2907.04, or 2907.05 of the Revised Code" in division (C); and made other nonsubstantive changes.

Amendment Note: 1996 H 445 removed references to section 2907.12 from divisions (B) and (C); and made other nonsubstantive changes.

Cross References

Bureau of criminal identification and investigation, recording and televising equipment for child sex offense victims, 109.54

Prosecutor's role at preliminary hearing, Crim R 5

Testimony of mentally retarded or developmentally disabled victim; videotaped testimony, 2945.491

Library References

Criminal Law ⚷234.

Westlaw Topic No. 110.

C.J.S. Criminal Law § 345.

Research References

Treatises and Practice Aids

Katz, Giannelli, Blair and Lipton, Baldwin's Ohio Practice, Criminal Law, § 38:9, Rules of Evidence.

Katz, Giannelli, Blair and Lipton, Baldwin's Ohio Practice, Criminal Law, § 38:10, Illegally Obtained Evidence.

1 Giannelli and Snyder, Baldwin's Ohio Practice, Evidence, Index, Index.

Notes of Decisions

1. Constitutional issues

A preliminary hearing cannot be closed to the public at the defendant's request and the request of a newspaper publisher for a transcript of the proceedings be denied unless specific facts are found and recorded demonstrating a closed hearing is "essential to preserve higher values and is narrowly tailored to serve that interest." Press–Enterprise Co. v. Superior Court of California for Riverside County (U.S.Cal. 1986) 106 S.Ct. 2735, 478 U.S. 1, 92 L.Ed.2d 1.

2. Denial of preliminary hearing

Denial of a preliminary hearing is not a ground for release on habeas corpus. Douglas v. Maxwell (Ohio 1963) 175 Ohio St. 317, 194 N.E.2d 576, 25 O.O.2d 185.

3. Preliminary hearing superseded by indictment

A defendant who has been arrested and charged with a felony does not have a constitutional right to demand that he be afforded a preliminary hearing before a magistrate; the grand jury, during the pendency of such action in the magistrate's court, may, on its own motion or by action of the prosecuting attorney, give consideration to the case and under proper circumstances and sufficient credible evidence, as provided by law, return an indictment against such defendant for whatever crime is justified by the evidence, and, upon the return of such indictment to the common pleas court, such court is vested with jurisdiction of the case, and the proceeding in the magistrate's court must be dismissed. State v. McClellan (Lucas 1966) 6 Ohio App.2d 155, 217 N.E.2d 230, 35 O.O.2d 315, certiorari denied 87 S.Ct. 1380, 386 U.S. 1022, 18 L.Ed.2d 462.

4. Pretrial motions

A motion to suppress evidence allegedly obtained as the result of an illegal search does not lie at a preliminary hearing in a felony case, since Crim R 12(B)(3) and Crim R 12(C) require such motions to be filed "within thirty-five days after arraignment or seven days before trial, whichever is earlier." State v. Mitchell (Ohio 1975) 42 Ohio St.2d 447, 329 N.E.2d 682, 71 O.O.2d 417.

2937.12 Motion for discharge; presentation on behalf of accused; finding of court

(A) At the conclusion of the presentation of the state's case accused may move for discharge for failure of proof or may offer evidence on his own behalf. Prior to the offering of evidence on behalf of the accused, unless accused is then represented by counsel, the court or magistrate shall advise accused:

(1) That any testimony of witnesses offered by him in the proceeding may, if unfavorable in any particular, be used against him at later trial;

(2) That accused himself may make a statement, not under oath, regarding the charge, for the purpose of explaining the facts in evidence;

(3) That he may refuse to make any statement and such refusal may not be used against him at trials;

(4) That any statement he makes may be used against him at trial.

(B) Upon conclusion of all the evidence and the statement, if any, of the accused, the court or magistrate shall either:

(1) Find that the crime alleged has been committed and that there is probable and reasonable cause to hold or recognize defendant to appear before the court of common pleas of the county or any other county in which venue appears, for trial pursuant to indictment by grand jury;

(2) Find that there is probable cause to hold or recognize defendant to appear before the court of common pleas for trial pursuant to indictment or information on such other charge, felony or misdemeanor, as the evidence indicates was committed by accused;

(3) Find that a misdemeanor was committed and there is probable cause to recognize accused to appear before himself or some other court inferior to the court of common pleas for trial upon such charge;

(4) Order the accused discharged from custody.

(128 v 97, eff. 1–1–60)

Historical and Statutory Notes

Ed. Note: 2937.12 contains provisions analogous to former 2937.14, repealed by 128 v 97, eff. 1–1–60.

Ed. Note: Former 2937.12 repealed by 128 v 97, eff. 1–1–60; 1953 H 1; GC 13433–11.

Pre–1953 H 1 Amendments: 113 v 147, Ch 12, § 11

Cross References

Procedure to move for discharge for failure of proof, Crim R 5

Library References

Criminal Law ⚷229, 239, 240.

Westlaw Topic No. 110.

C.J.S. Criminal Law §§ 282, 345, 352 to 353.

Research References

Encyclopedias

OH Jur. 3d Criminal Law § 2066, Presentation of State's Case—Defendant's Options After Presentation of State's Case.

Treatises and Practice Aids

Katz, Giannelli, Blair and Lipton, Baldwin's Ohio Practice, Criminal Law, § 38:8, Presentation of Case.

Katz, Giannelli, Blair and Lipton, Baldwin's Ohio Practice, Criminal Law, § 140:2, Motion for Discharge for Failure of Proof.

Katz, Giannelli, Blair and Lipton, Baldwin's Ohio Practice, Criminal Law, § 140:3, Finding of Probable Cause After Preliminary Hearing.

Katz, Giannelli, Blair and Lipton, Baldwin's Ohio Practice, Criminal Law, § 140:4, Finding After Preliminary Hearing that Probable Cause Establishes Commission of Misdemeanor.

Katz, Giannelli, Blair and Lipton, Baldwin's Ohio Practice, Criminal Law, § 140:5, Finding of Court After Preliminary Hearing Discharged Accused.

2937.13 Basis for finding; no appeal; further prosecution

In entering a finding, pursuant to section 2937.12 of the Revised Code, the court, while weighing credibility of witnesses, shall not be required to pass on the weight of the evidence and any finding requiring accused to stand trial on any charge shall be based solely on the presence of substantial credible evidence thereof. No appeal shall lie from such decision nor shall the discharge of defendant be a bar to further prosecution by indictment or otherwise.

(128 v 97, eff. 1–1–60)

Historical and Statutory Notes

Ed. Note: Former 2937.13 repealed by 128 v 97, eff. 1–1–60; 1953 H 1; GC 13433–12.

Pre–1953 H 1 Amendments: 113 v 147, Ch 12, § 12

Cross References

Determination as to probable cause at preliminary hearing, Crim R 5

Library References

Criminal Law ⚷238, 239, 1023(3).

Westlaw Topic No. 110.

C.J.S. Criminal Law §§ 345, 352, 1669, 1672, 1675.

Research References

Encyclopedias

OH Jur. 3d Criminal Law § 2068, Appealability of Decision on Preliminary Hearing.

OH Jur. 3d Criminal Law § 2069, Proceedings Subsequent to Preliminary Hearing Determination.

Treatises and Practice Aids

Katz, Giannelli, Blair and Lipton, Baldwin's Ohio Practice, Criminal Law, § 38:9, Rules of Evidence.

Katz, Giannelli, Blair and Lipton, Baldwin's Ohio Practice, Criminal Law, § 140:3, Finding of Probable Cause After Preliminary Hearing.

Katz, Giannelli, Blair and Lipton, Baldwin's Ohio Practice, Criminal Law, § 140:4, Finding After Preliminary Hearing that Probable Cause Establishes Commission of Misdemeanor.

Katz, Giannelli, Blair and Lipton, Baldwin's Ohio Practice, Criminal Law, § 140:5, Finding of Court After Preliminary Hearing Discharged Accused.

2937.14 Entry of reason for change in charge

In any case in which accused is held or recognized to appear for trial on any charge other than the one on which he was arraigned the court or magistrate shall enter the reason for such charge on the journal of the court (if a court of record) or on the docket (if a court not of record) and shall file with the papers in the case the text of the charge found by him to be sustained by the evidence.

(128 v 97, eff. 1–1–60)

Historical and Statutory Notes

Ed. Note: Former 2937.14 repealed by 128 v 97, eff. 1–1–60; 1953 H 1; GC 13433–13; see now 2937.12 for provisions analogous to former 2937.14.

Pre–1953 H 1 Amendments: 113 v 147, Ch 12, § 13

Cross References

Preliminary hearing procedure, Crim R 5

Library References

Criminal Law ⚷240.

Westlaw Topic No. 110.

C.J.S. Criminal Law § 353.

Notes of Decisions

Plea down to misdemeanor 1

1. Plea down to misdemeanor

Where a complaint charges a defendant with a felony, a plea of no contest to a lesser included misdemeanor may not be accepted in municipal court absent compliance with Crim R 5(B). State v. Minor (Lorain 1979) 64 Ohio App.2d 129, 411 N.E.2d 822, 18 O.O.3d 98.

2937.15 Transcript of proceedings

Upon the conclusion of the hearing and finding, the magistrate, or if a court of record, the clerk of such court, shall complete all notations of appearance, motions, pleas, and findings on the criminal docket of the court, and shall transmit a transcript of the appearance docket entries, together with a copy of the original complaint and affidavits, if any, filed with the complaint, the journal or docket entry of reason for changes in the charge, if any, together with the order setting bail and the bail deposit, if any, filed, and together with the videotaped testimony, if any, prepared in accordance with division (C) of section 2937.11 of the Revised Code, to the clerk of the court in which the accused is to appear. Such transcript shall contain an itemized account of the costs accrued.

(1986 H 108, eff. 10–14–86; 128 v 97)

Historical and Statutory Notes

Ed. Note: 2937.15 contains provisions analogous to former 2937.19, repealed by 128 v 97, eff. 1–1–60.

Ed. Note: Former 2937.15 repealed by 128 v 97, eff. 1–1–60; 1953 H 1; GC 13433–14.

Pre–1953 H 1 Amendments: 113 v 147, Ch 12, § 14

Cross References

Preliminary hearing procedure, Crim R 5

Library References

Criminal Law ⚷235, 244.
Westlaw Topic No. 110.
C.J.S. Criminal Law § 345.

Notes of Decisions

Furnishing transcript to indigent 1

1. Furnishing transcript to indigent

The state's burden of showing that a transcript of prior proceedings requested by an indigent defendant is not needed for an effective defense or appeal may be met by the state by a showing that the transcript is not valuable to the defendant in connection with the trial or appeal for which it is sought, or that there are alternative devices available to the defendant that would fulfill the same functions as a transcript. State v. Arrington (Ohio 1975) 42 Ohio St.2d 114, 326 N.E.2d 667, 71 O.O.2d 81. Costs ⚷ 302.1(1); Criminal Law ⚷ 1077.2(3)

2937.16 When witnesses shall be recognized to appear

When an accused enters into a recognizance or is committed in default thereof, the judge or magistrate shall require such witnesses against the prisoner as he finds necessary, to enter into a recognizance to appear and testify before the proper court at a proper time, and not depart from such court without leave. If the judge or magistrate finds it necessary he may require such witnesses to give sufficient surety to appear at such court.

(1953 H 1, eff. 10–1–53; GC 13433–15)

Historical and Statutory Notes

Pre–1953 H 1 Amendments: 113 v 147, Ch 12, § 15

Library References

Witnesses ⚷19.
Westlaw Topic No. 410.
C.J.S. Witnesses §§ 2, 67 to 68.

Research References

Treatises and Practice Aids

Katz, Giannelli, Blair and Lipton, Baldwin's Ohio Practice, Criminal Law, § 139:4, Recognizance of the Witnesses Without Security.

Katz, Giannelli, Blair and Lipton, Baldwin's Ohio Practice, Criminal Law, § 139:5, Entry for Recognizance of Witnesses.

Katz, Giannelli, Blair and Lipton, Baldwin's Ohio Practice, Criminal Law, § 139:7, Recognizance of Witness With Surety.

Katz, Giannelli, Blair and Lipton, Baldwin's Ohio Practice, Criminal Law, § 139:13, Commitment of Witness Who Refuses to Enter Into Recognizance.

Law Review and Journal Commentaries

State Control of the Operation of Professional Bail Bondsmen, John J. Murphy. 36 U Cin L Rev 375 (Summer 1967).

2937.17 Recognizance for minor

A person may be liable in a recognizance for a minor to appear as a witness, or the judge or magistrate may take the minor's recognizance, in a sufficient sum, which is valid notwithstanding the disability of minority.

(1953 H 1, eff. 10–1–53; GC 13433–16)

Historical and Statutory Notes

Pre–1953 H 1 Amendments: 113 v 148, Ch 12, § 16

Library References

Witnesses ⚷19.

Westlaw Topic No. 410.

C.J.S. Witnesses §§ 2, 67 to 68.

Research References

Encyclopedias

OH Jur. 3d Criminal Law § 2199, Recognizance of Minor.

2937.18 Detention of material witnesses

If a witness ordered to give recognizance fails to comply with such order, the judge or magistrate shall commit him to such custody or open or close detention as may be appropriate under the circumstances, until he complies with the order or is discharged. Commitment of the witness may be to the custody of any suitable person or public or private agency, or to an appropriate detention facility other than a jail, or to a jail, but the witness shall not be confined in association with prisoners charged with or convicted of crime. The witness, in lieu of the fee ordinarily allowed witnesses, shall be allowed twenty-five dollars for each day of custody or detention under such order, and shall be allowed mileage as provided for other witnesses, calculated on the distance from his home to the place of giving testimony and return. All proceedings in the case or cases in which the witness is held to appear shall be given priority over other cases and had with all due speed.

(1972 H 511, eff. 3–23–73; 1953 H 1; GC 13433–17)

Historical and Statutory Notes

Pre–1953 H 1 Amendments: 113 v 148, Ch 12, § 17

Legislative Service Commission

1973:

This section permits a court discretion in placing a material witness under various forms of open or close detention to insure his appearance when required. Also, the section raises the fee of material witnesses from $3 to $25 per day, and entitles them to mileage computed on the distance from their home to the place of giving testimony and return. Cases in which a material witness is held to appear must be given priority on the docket and heard with dispatch.

Existing law, not changed by the act, permits a court to require a witness to post bail for his appearance when there is good reason to suppose he will not appear to testify when required in a criminal case. Under former law, there was only one alternative if the witness was unable to post bail—commitment to jail. Also, former law only allowed material witnesses the same fee as other witnesses ($3 per day), and did not permit payment of mileage.

Cross References

Right to compulsory process to obtain witnesses, O Const Art I §10

Library References

Witnesses ⚷20.
Westlaw Topic No. 410.
C.J.S. Witnesses §§ 2, 69.

Research References

Encyclopedias

OH Jur. 3d Criminal Law § 2201, Witness' Refusal to Comply With Order of Recognizance.

Treatises and Practice Aids

Markus, Trial Handbook for Ohio Lawyers, § 11:5, Compensation.

Katz, Giannelli, Blair and Lipton, Baldwin's Ohio Practice, Criminal Law, § 61:10, Out-Of-State Witnesses.

Katz, Giannelli, Blair and Lipton, Baldwin's Ohio Practice, Criminal Law, § 139:13, Commitment of Witness Who Refuses to Enter Into Recognizance.

Giannelli and Snyder, Baldwin's Ohio Practice, Evidence, § 804.8, Unavailability: Unable to Procure Testimony.

Notes of Decisions

Constitutional issues 1

1. Constitutional issues

At a minimum, a warrant to detain a material witness must be supported by probable cause supported by oath or affirmation to believe that the witness is material and that the detention of the witness is necessary to procure her attendance at trial; therefore, the method by which a warrant to detain a material witness is issued does not satisfy the requirements of constitutional due process where a bare entry or order is presented for signing to a trial court judge, unattended by even so much as an affidavit alleging those facts from which the trial court could find, as it did, that the witness' detention would be necessary to procure her attendance as a witness at a criminal trial. State, ex rel. Dorsey, v. Haines (Montgomery 1991) 63 Ohio App.3d 580, 579 N.E.2d 541.

2937.19 Subpoena of witnesses or documents

The magistrate or judge or clerk of the court in which proceedings are being had may issue subpoenas or other process to bring witnesses or documents before the magistrate or court in hearings pending before him either under Chapter 2937. or 2938. of the Revised Code.

In complaints to keep the peace a subpoena must be served within the county, or, in cases of misdemeanors and ordinance offenses, it may be served at any place in this state within one hundred miles of the place where the court or magistrate is scheduled to sit; in felony cases it may be served at any place within this state. In cases where such process is to be served outside the county, it may be issued to be served either by the bailiff or constable of the court or by a sheriff or police officer either by the county in which the court or magistrate sits or in which process is to be served.

(129 v 582, eff. 1–10–61; 128 v 97)

Historical and Statutory Notes

Ed. Note: Former 2937.19 repealed by 128 v 97, eff. 1–1–60; 1953 H 1; GC 13433–18; see now 2937.15 for provisions analogous to former 2937.19.

Pre–1953 H 1 Amendments: 113 v 148, Ch 12, § 18

Cross References

Subpoenas, Crim R 17

Library References

Witnesses ⚷7 to 16.
Westlaw Topic No. 410.
C.J.S. Witnesses §§ 2, 20 to 52.

Research References

Encyclopedias

OH Jur. 3d Criminal Law § 2054, Subpoena of Documents; Protection Against Unreasonable Requests.

2937.20 Procedure in disqualification of inferior court judge—Repealed

(1996 S 263, eff. 11–20–96; 1995 H 151, eff. 12–4–95; 127 v 423, eff. 8–27–57; 1953 H 1; 13433–19)

Historical and Statutory Notes

Ed. Note: Former 2937.20 amended and recodified as 2701.031 by 1996 S 263, eff. 11–20–96.

Pre–1953 H 1 Amendments: 113 v 148, Ch 12, § 19

2937.21 Continuance

No continuance at any stage of the proceeding, including that for determination of a motion, shall extend for more than ten days unless both the state and the accused consent thereto. Any continuance or delay in ruling contrary to the provisions of this section shall, unless procured by defendant or his counsel, be grounds for discharge of the defendant forthwith.
(128 v 97, eff. 1–1–60)

Historical and Statutory Notes

Ed. Note: Former 2937.21 repealed by 128 v 97, eff. 1–1–60; 1953 H 1; GC 13435–1; see now 2937.22 for provisions analogous to former 2937.21.

Pre–1953 H 1 Amendments: 113 v 149, Ch 14, § 1

Cross References

Computation of days, 1.14

Procedure in preliminary hearing in felony cases, Crim R 5

Speedy trial, continuance, discharge for delay, 2945.71 to 2945.73

Library References

Criminal Law ⚷613.

Westlaw Topic No. 110.

Research References

Encyclopedias

OH Jur. 3d Criminal Law § 2052, Continuances.

OH Jur. 3d Criminal Law § 2851, Excessive Delay by Continuance or in Ruling on Motion.

OH Jur. 3d Family Law § 1743, Adults in Custody of Juvenile Court.

Treatises and Practice Aids

Katz, Giannelli, Blair and Lipton, Baldwin's Ohio Practice, Criminal Law, § 38:5, Time Limits.

Notes of Decisions

Ed. Note: *This section contains annotations from former RC 2937.11.*

In general 1
Application of section 2
Discharge of accused 3
Mandamus and prohibition 4

---

1. In general

Trial court did not abuse its discretion in denying defendant's motion for a continuance during bench trial on domestic violence charge; on day of trial, at the close of his presentation of evidence, defendant made oral motion for continuance of trial so that he could produce his parents to rebut officer's testimony, trial date was set nearly two months before trial and defendant had sufficient time prior to trial to subpoena his parents or request continuance, and defendant's unsubstantiated assertion that he failed to subpoena parents because he believed trial would not go forward did not excuse his error. Cleveland Hts. v. Watson (Ohio App. 8 Dist., Cuyahoga, 07-14-2005) No. 85344, 2005-Ohio-3595, 2005 WL 1654568, Unreported. Criminal Law ⚷ 254.1

Trial court abused its discretion in denying defendant's request for continuance on morning of trial on charge of resisting arrest; trial court failed to consider all relevant factors including that defense counsel was unprepared for trial, and clear and uncontroverted breakdown had occurred in attorney-client relationship between defendant and counsel. State v. Landingham (Ohio App. 6 Dist., Lucas, 03-18-2005) No. L-03-1339, 2005-Ohio-1216, 2005 WL 635033, Unreported. Criminal Law ⚷ 590(2)

Trial court did not abuse its discretion in denying motion for one-week continuance in misdemeanor prosecution to permit counsel to prepare for trial, despite brevity of continuance requested and fact that defendant requested no other continuances, where request was not made until date and time set for trial, and counsel's lack of time to prepare was attributable to inaction of defendant and defendant's family; defendant's family did not contact counsel to inform him that he was representing defendant until two days before trial, despite fact that defendant was released on bail over 100 days prior to trial. State v. Rosine (Ohio App. 7 Dist., Mahoning, 02-08-2005) No. 03 MA 00094, 2005-Ohio-568, 2005 WL 351329, Unreported. Criminal Law ⚷ 590(2)

Defendant's request for a continuance in order to obtain missing document was properly denied in theft and forgery prosecution, even though inconvenience caused by delay would have been minor, since information to be obtained from document was not relevant to the case and defendant contributed to the necessity for a delay by failing to secure a copy of the document before trial. State v. Crumedy (Ohio App. 8 Dist., Cuyahoga, 11-10-2004) No. 84083, 2004-Ohio-6006, 2004 WL 2578856, Unreported. Criminal Law ⚷ 595(.5)

Defendant was not entitled to continuance; the request for a continuance was not made until the parties had appeared for trial, and the timing of the request demonstrated a lack of respect for the judge, the prosecutor, and the State's witness, who was present and prepared to testify, and defense counsel failed to proffer any reasons for the requested continuance. State v. Suarez (Ohio App. 2 Dist., Montgomery, 08-27-2004) No. 20055, 2004-Ohio-4513, 2004 WL 1909135, Unreported. Criminal Law ⚷ 589(1); Criminal Law ⚷ 605

Evidence supported finding that defendant's motion for continuance to obtain new counsel was made in bad faith and for purposes of delay; motion was made on first day of trial, and defendant had not expressed any dissatisfaction or concern with his court-appointed counsel up to that point. State v. Hill (Ohio App. 2 Dist., Montgomery, 04-23-2004) No. 20028, 2004-Ohio-2048, 2004 WL 870439, Unreported. Criminal Law ⚷ 593; Criminal Law ⚷ 605

Trial court acted within its discretion in denying defendant's motion for continuance, despite defendant's claim that he needed more time to consult with counsel regarding plea bargain; many of the charges against defendant had been pending for a significant period of time, defendant received an additional day to confer with counsel regarding plea bargain, and defendant failed to identify any prejudice resulting from denial of motion for continuance. State v. Strange (Ohio App. 10 Dist., Franklin, 03-18-2004) No. 03AP-519, No. 03AP-522, No. 03AP-526, No. 03AP-520, No. 03AP-523, No. 03AP-521, No. 03AP-525, 2004-Ohio-1300, 2004 WL 541055, Unreported, appeal not allowed 103 Ohio St.3d 1405, 812 N.E.2d 1288, 2004-Ohio-3980 Criminal Law ⚷ 590(2)

Trial court acted within its discretion in denying assault defendant's motion for continuance, despite defendant's claims that State failed to provide name of potentially exculpatory eyewitness and that eyewitness was discovered only three days before trial; trial court ensured that defendant was able to both investigate additional issues involving the eyewitness and present the testimony of that witness to the jury. State v. Dave (Ohio App. 12 Dist., Warren, 03-08-2004) No. CA2003-04-041, 2004-Ohio-1032, 2004 WL 413582, Unreported. Criminal Law ⚷ 590(1); Criminal Law ⚷ 627.8(6)

Trial court abused its discretion in granting state's oral motion for continuance on day of trial for failure to control a motor vehicle resulting in a crash; state was required to set forth, in writing, its reasons for requested continuance. State v. Jacobucci (Ohio App. 8 Dist., Cuyahoga, 11-20-2003) No. 82813, 2003-Ohio-6177, 2003 WL 22724995, Unreported. Criminal Law ⚷ 603.2

Defendant was not entitled to a continuance based on his alleged need for additional time to prepare for additional charges against him, where motion was made the morning of trial, and defense counsel knew of additional charges a week before trial. State v. Goode (Ohio App. 2 Dist., Montgomery, 08-15-2003) No. 19273, 2003-Ohio-4323, 2003 WL 21949740, Unreported, motion for delayed appeal denied 101 Ohio St.3d 1485, 805 N.E.2d 537, 2004-Ohio-1293. Criminal Law ⚷ 590(2)

The addition of a plaintiff's witness five days prior to trial is valid reason to grant defendant's motion for a continuance where the witness is a drug task force member who allegedly made illegal marijuana purchases from defendant and whose identity was known to the plaintiff all along; denial of a continuance has a prejudicial effect on defendant and is an abuse of discretion. State v. Spack (Ohio App. 7 Dist., Columbiana, 05-17-1994) No. 93-C-48, 1994 WL 194150, Unreported.

In inferring waiver of right to counsel when defendant refuses to take effective action to obtain counsel and on day of trial requests continuance in order to delay trial, court must consider total circumstances of case, including background, experience and conduct of defendant. State v. Boone (Ohio App. 1 Dist., 12-29-1995) 108 Ohio App.3d 233, 670 N.E.2d 527. Criminal Law ⚷ 641.4(2)

Defendant charged with drug abuse, possession of drug paraphernalia and criminal trespass who failed to secure legal counsel despite being given ample time and opportunity to do so by trial court and who did not ask for continuance on day of trial in order to obtain counsel waived by inference his right to legal representation. State v. Boone (Ohio App. 1 Dist., 12-29-1995) 108 Ohio App.3d 233, 670 N.E.2d 527. Criminal Law ⚷ 641.4(4)

Court may, under proper conditions, be permitted to infer waiver of right to counsel when defendant refuses to take effective action to obtain counsel and on day of trial requests continuance in order to delay trial. State v. Boone (Ohio App. 1 Dist., 12-29-1995) 108 Ohio App.3d 233, 670 N.E.2d 527. Criminal Law ⚷ 641.4(2)

The denial of a continuance is neither unreasonable, arbitrary, nor unconscionable where (1) the defendant was present with appointed counsel on the date of trial, (2) the trial had been continued at defendant's request once before, (3) the state had been ready to proceed with its witnesses once before and this was the second time it was ready, (4) the request for a continuance did not reflect the specific time necessary for the delay, and (5) the need for the delay was attributable to the defendant (the defendant chose private counsel who was unavailable on the date of trial, knowing him to be unavailable). State v. Jones (Wayne 1987) 42 Ohio App.3d 14, 535 N.E.2d 1372. Criminal Law ⚷ 593; Criminal Law ⚷ 614(1)

Where RC 2938.03 specifically authorizes a continuance for good cause shown, and the continuance granted does not prevent the defendant from having a fair trial, the trial court may, in its discretion, grant a continuance on behalf of the prosecution. City of East Cleveland v. Gilbert (Ohio 1970) 24 Ohio St.2d 63, 263 N.E.2d 400, 53 O.O.2d 85. Criminal Law ⚷ 254.1

Where, on arraignment, under RC Ch 2937, the accused pleads not guilty to the commission of a misdemeanor, the court shall proceed to set the trial at a future time pursuant to RC Ch 2938. City of East Cleveland v. Gilbert (Ohio 1970) 24 Ohio St.2d 63, 263 N.E.2d 400, 53 O.O.2d 85.

Where an appellant requested and was denied an immediate preliminary hearing and then while awaiting such hearing was indicted by a grand jury, there is no clear legal requirement of a preliminary hearing. State ex rel. Haynes v. Powers (Ohio 1969) 20 Ohio St.2d 46, 254 N.E.2d 19, 49 O.O.2d 305.

Defendant was not entitled to continuance of trial date, where defendant's trial counsel was ready to proceed, notwithstanding that another of defendant's attorneys was not available for trial. City of Toledo v. Emery (Ohio App. 6 Dist., Lucas, 05-31-2002) No. L-01-1361, 2002-Ohio-2694, 2002 WL 1303147, Unreported, appeal not allowed 96 Ohio St.3d 1524, 775 N.E.2d 863, 2002-Ohio-5099. Criminal Law ⚷ 593

2. Application of section

The requirements of RC 2937.21 have no application in a court of common pleas. State v. Martin (Ohio 1978) 56 Ohio St.2d 289, 384 N.E.2d 239, 10 O.O.3d 415.

RC 2937.21 does not apply to proceedings in the common pleas court. State v. Fowler (Ohio 1963) 174 Ohio St. 362, 189 N.E.2d 133, 22 O.O.2d 416.

RC 2937.21 is not applicable after trial, judgment, and sentence. Maloney v. Court of Common Pleas of Allen County (Ohio 1962) 173 Ohio St. 226, 181 N.E.2d 270, 19 O.O.2d 45.

3. Discharge of accused

The discharge of a defendant provided for in RC 2937.21 is from custody and bail only, and is not a bar to a subsequent prosecution for the same offense. City of Columbus v. Nappi (Ohio 1966) 5 Ohio St.2d 99, 214 N.E.2d 83, 34 O.O.2d 222.

Continuing case indefinitely and releasing accused exhausted jurisdiction and constituted discharge. Jones v. Wells Co. (Ohio 1931) 123 Ohio St. 516, 176 N.E. 73, 10 Ohio Law Abs. 158.

Where a delay in trial results from the defendant's filing affidavits of bias and prejudice, he is not entitled to discharge under RC 2937.21. State ex rel. O'Leary v. Cuyahoga Falls Municipal Court (Ohio 1964) 176 Ohio St. 197, 198 N.E.2d 660, 27 O.O.2d 85.

In appropriate cases, where the commitment has been pursuant to order of a magistrate's court, the examining court shall apply RC 2937.21 limiting continuances without consent to ten days in determining whether the prisoner should be recommitted or should be released pending further proceedings. State ex rel. Justice v. Rone (Auglaize 1972) 33 Ohio App.2d 1, 291 N.E.2d 754, 62 O.O.2d 1.

4. Mandamus and prohibition

Writ of prohibition should not issue to prohibit a mayor's court from proceeding with a cause upon an allegation of a violation of RC 2937.21. State ex rel. Keyse v. Polonye (Ohio 1965) 4 Ohio St.2d 23, 211 N.E.2d 831, 33 O.O.2d 267.

When it appears that an examining court has conducted the proceedings prescribed by RC 2937.21 an action in mandamus does not constitute an appeal and will not reach any error, including an error of abuse of discretion, committed by the examining court in its conduct of such proceedings. State ex rel. Justice v. Rone (Auglaize 1972) 33 Ohio App.2d 1, 291 N.E.2d 754, 62 O.O.2d 1.

BAIL

2937.22 Forms of bail; receipts

Bail is security for the appearance of an accused to appear and answer to a specific criminal or quasi-criminal charge in any court or before any magistrate at a specific time or at any time to which a case may be continued, and not depart without leave. It may take any of the following forms:

(A) The deposit of cash by the accused or by some other person for him;

(B) The deposit by the accused or by some other person for him in form of bonds of the United States, this state, or any political subdivision thereof in a face amount equal to the sum set by the court or magistrate. In case of bonds not negotiable by delivery such bonds shall be properly endorsed for transfer.

(C) The written undertaking by one or more persons to forfeit the sum of money set by the court or magistrate, if the accused is in default for appearance, which shall be known as a recognizance.

All bail shall be received by the clerk of the court, deputy clerk of court, or by the magistrate, or by a special referee appointed by the supreme court pursuant to section 2937.46 of the Revised Code, and, except in cases of recognizances, receipt shall be given therefor by him.

(128 v 97, eff. 1-1-60)

Historical and Statutory Notes

Ed. Note: 2937.22 contains provisions analogous to former 2937.21, repealed by 128 v 97, eff. 1-1-60.

Ed. Note: Former 2937.22 repealed by 128 v 97, eff. 1-1-60; 1953 H 1; GC 13435-2; see now 2937.23 for provisions analogous to former 2937.22.

Pre-1953 H 1 Amendments: 113 v 149, Ch 14, § 2

Cross References

Additional costs in criminal cases in all courts to fund reparations payments; bail, defined, 2743.70

Bail, Crim R 46

Bail allowed pending hearing to revoke probation, Crim R 32.3

Bailable offenses; excessive bail prohibited, O Const Art I §9

Domestic violence, bail schedule, 2919.251

Procedure on affidavit or complaint, withdrawal of unexecuted warrants, 2935.10

Proceedings upon arrest, 2935.13

Library References

Bail ⚖39, 73.

Westlaw Topic No. 49.

C.J.S. Bail; Release and Detention Pending Proceedings §§ 2, 4 to 7, 31 to 32, 88 to 92.

Research References

Encyclopedias

OH Jur. 3d Criminal Law § 2164, Bail, In General.

OH Jur. 3d Criminal Law § 2165, Bail, in General—Recognizance.

OH Jur. 3d Criminal Law § 2182, Receipt of Bail and Recognizance; Who Authorized.

Treatises and Practice Aids

Katz, Giannelli, Blair and Lipton, Baldwin's Ohio Practice, Criminal Law, § 37:1, Introduction.

Katz, Giannelli, Blair and Lipton, Baldwin's Ohio Practice, Criminal Law, § 37:6, Types of Pretrial Release.

Law Review and Journal Commentaries

Revision of State Bail Laws, John J. Murphy. 32 Ohio St L J 451 (Summer 1971).

State Control of the Operation of Professional Bail Bondsmen, John J. Murphy. 36 U Cin L Rev 375 (Summer 1967).

The University and the Bail System: in Loco Altricis, Harry W. Pettigrew. 20 Clev St L Rev 502 (September 1971).

Notes of Decisions

Cash 5
Constitutional issues 1
Credit cards 2
Denial of bail in federal case 3
Security for payment of fine 4

---

1. Constitutional issues

Providing a name and social security number is satisfactory proof of possession of a driver's license where defendant who is stopped for driving through a traffic sign shows the officer a municipal court receipt pursuant to RC 2937.22 which displays his name and social security number; as a result the crack cocaine and PCP obtained after the arrest for not having a driver's license is the result of an unconstitutional search and seizure and should be suppressed. State v. Killingsworth (Ohio App. 8 Dist., Cuyahoga, 11-04-1999) No. 74999, 1999 WL 1000673, Unreported.

2. Credit cards

State highway patrol officer can accept credit cards on the highway from violators within the jurisdiction of those courts which have entered into an agreement with the credit card servicing agency for payment upon presentation of a completed sales draft with the only conditions being that the bail amount involved not exceed the dollar limitations contained in the agreement, the sales draft be legible and that the sales draft be drawn on an unexpired credit card, but may not accept credit cards within jurisdiction of courts which have not entered into such agreements. OAG 70–036.

3. Denial of bail in federal case

The government has the burden of proving that a defendant should be retained pending trial, and it carries that burden by proving a risk of flight by a preponderance of the evidence or by proving a risk of danger by clear and convincing evidence; for severe drug offenses, however, there is a rebuttable presumption under 18 USC 3142(e) that conditions cannot be set that will reasonably assure the defendant's appearance and the community's safety. U.S. v. Alexander (N.D.Ohio 1990) 742 F.Supp. 421.

4. Security for payment of fine

A bail bond undertaken by an insurance company, and conditioned solely on a defendant's court appearance, cannot be used to secure the payment of a fine. State v Austin, No. 95-CA-99, 1996 WL 391844 (2nd Dist Ct App, Greene, 5-5-96).

5. Cash

Evidence was insufficient to establish that defendant was released on his own recognizance, and thus he could not be convicted of failure to appear for trial; release on one's own recognizance required a written undertaking by a defendant that was unsecured by others on his behalf, and surety deposited $500 in cash to secure defendant's release and signed the recognizance along with defendant. State v. Fusik (Ohio App. 4 Dist., Athens, 03-08-2005) No. 04CA28, 2005-Ohio-1056, 2005 WL 567308, Unreported. Bail ⚷ 97(3)

The additional $13 in court costs imposed by 1981 H 694, § 169 and 167, eff. 11–15–81, must be collected in cash at the time bail is posted. OAG 82–050.

A county sheriff may not accept cash appearance bonds in misdemeanor cases coming within the jurisdiction of the county court. 1960 OAG 1641.

2937.221 Use of driver's or commercial driver's license as bond in certain traffic violation arrests

(A) A person arrested without warrant for any violation listed in division (B) of this section, and having a current valid Ohio driver's or commercial driver's license, if the person has been notified of the possible consequences of the person's actions as required by division (C) of this section, may post bond by depositing the license with the arresting officer if the officer and person so choose, or with the local court having jurisdiction if the court and person so choose. The license may be used as bond only during the period for which it is valid.

When an arresting officer accepts the driver's or commercial driver's license as bond, the officer shall note the date, time, and place of the court appearance on "the violator's notice to appear," and the notice shall serve as a valid Ohio driver's or commercial driver's license until the date and time appearing thereon. The arresting officer immediately shall forward the license to the appropriate court.

When a local court accepts the license as bond or continues the case to another date and time, it shall provide the person with a card in a form approved by the registrar of motor vehicles setting forth the license number, name, address, the date and time of the court appearance, and a statement that the license is being held as bond. The card shall serve as a valid license until the date and time contained in the card.

The court may accept other bond at any time and return the license to the person. The court shall return the license to the person when judgment is satisfied, including, but not limited to, compliance with any court orders, unless a suspension or cancellation is part of the penalty imposed.

Neither "the violator's notice to appear" nor a court- granted card shall continue driving privileges beyond the expiration date of the license.

If the person arrested fails to appear in court at the date and time set by the court or fails to satisfy the judgment of the court, including, but not limited to, compliance with all court orders within the time allowed by the court, the court may declare the forfeiture of the person's license. Thirty days after the declaration of the forfeiture, the court shall forward the person's license to the registrar. The court also shall enter information relative to the forfeiture on a form approved and furnished by the registrar and send the form to the registrar. The registrar shall suspend the person's license and send written notification of the suspension to the person at the person's last known address. No valid driver's or commercial driver's license shall be granted to the person until the court having jurisdiction orders that the forfeiture be terminated. The court shall inform the registrar of the termination of the forfeiture by entering information relative to the termination on a form approved and furnished by the registrar and sending the form to the registrar. Upon the termination, the person shall pay to the bureau of motor vehicles a reinstatement fee of fifteen dollars to cover the costs of the bureau in administering this section. The registrar shall deposit the fees so paid into the state bureau of motor vehicles fund created by section 4501.25 of the Revised Code.

In addition, upon receipt from the court of the copy of the declaration of forfeiture, neither the registrar nor any deputy registrar shall accept any application for the registration or transfer of registration of any motor vehicle owned by or leased in the name of the person named in the declaration of forfeiture until the court having jurisdiction over the offense that led to the suspension issues an order terminating the forfeiture. However, for a motor vehicle leased in the name of a person named in a declaration of forfeiture, the registrar shall not implement the preceding sentence until the registrar adopts procedures for that implementation under section 4503.39 of the Revised Code. Upon receipt by the registrar of such an order, the registrar also shall take the measures necessary to permit the person to register a motor vehicle the person owns or leases or to transfer the registration of a motor vehicle the person owns or leases if the person later makes a proper application and otherwise is eligible to be issued or to transfer a motor vehicle registration.

(B) Division (A) of this section applies to persons arrested for violation of:

(1) Any of the provisions of Chapter 4511. or 4513. of the Revised Code, except sections 4511.19, 4511.20, 4511.251, and 4513.36 of the Revised Code;

(2) Any municipal ordinance substantially similar to a section included in division (B)(1) of this section;

(3) Any bylaw, rule, or regulation of the Ohio turnpike commission substantially similar to a section included in division (B)(1) of this section.

Division (A) of this section does not apply to those persons issued a citation for the commission of a minor misdemeanor under section 2935.26 of the Revised Code.

(C) No license shall be accepted as bond by an arresting officer or by a court under this section until the officer or court has notified the person that, if the person deposits the license with the officer or court and either does not appear on the date and at the time set by the officer or the court, if the court sets a time, or does not satisfy any judgment rendered, including, but not limited to, compliance with all court orders, the license will be suspended, and the person will not be eligible for reissuance of the license or issuance of a new license, or the issuance of a certificate of registration for a motor vehicle owned or leased by the person until the person appears and complies with any order issued by the court. The person also is subject to any criminal penalties that may apply to the person.

(D) The registrar shall not restore the person's driving or vehicle registration privileges until the person pays the reinstatement fee as provided in this section.

(2004 H 230, eff. 9–16–04; 2002 S 123, eff. 1–1–04; 1997 S 85, eff. 5–15–97; 1996 S 121, eff. 11–19–96; 1996 H 353, eff. 9–17–96; 1994 H 687, eff. 10–12–94; 1989 S 49, eff. 11–3–89; 1989 H 381; 1986 S 356; 1978 S 351; 1975 H 1; 1973 H 234)

Uncodified Law

1996 S 121, § 4, eff. 11–19–96, reads: The Registrar of Motor Vehicles shall not be required to give effect to the amendments contained in Section 1 of this act that prohibit the Registrar from issuing or transferring a certificate of registration for a motor vehicle when so prohibited by the amendments until six months after the effective date of this act.

Historical and Statutory Notes

Amendment Note: 2004 H 230 added division (D) and rewrote the last two paragraphs of division (A), which prior to amendment read:

"If the person arrested fails to appear in court at the date and time set by the court or fails to satisfy the judgment of the court, including, but not limited to, compliance with all court orders within the time allowed by the court, the court may impose a class seven suspension of the person's license from the range specified in division (A)(7) of section 4510.02 of the Revised Code. Thirty days after the suspension, the court shall forward the person's license to the registrar. The court also shall enter information relative to the suspension on a form approved and furnished by the registrar and send the form to the registrar, and the registrar shall send written notification of the suspension to the person at the person's last known address. No valid driver's or commercial driver's license shall be granted to the person until the expiration of the period of the suspension or, prior to the expiration of that period, the court having jurisdiction orders that the suspension is terminated. If the court terminates the suspension, the court shall inform the registrar of the termination by entering information relative to the termination on a form approved and furnished by the registrar and sending the form to the registrar. Upon the expiration or termination of the suspension, the person shall pay to the bureau of motor vehicles a processing fee of fifteen dollars to cover the costs of the bureau in administering this section. The registrar shall deposit the fees so paid into the state bureau of motor vehicles fund created by section 4501.25 of the Revised Code.

"In addition, upon receipt from the court of the copy of the suspension, neither the registrar nor any deputy registrar shall accept any application for the registration or transfer of registration of any motor vehicle owned by or leased in the name of the person named in the suspension until the expiration of the period of the suspension or, prior to the expiration of that period, the court having jurisdiction over the offense that led to the suspension issues an order terminating the suspension. However, for a motor vehicle leased in the name of a person named in a suspension, the registrar shall not implement the preceding sentence until the registrar adopts procedures for that implementation under section 4503.39 of the Revised Code. Upon the expiration of the suspension or upon receipt by the registrar of an order terminating the suspension, the registrar also shall take the measures necessary to permit the person to register a motor vehicle the person owns or leases or to transfer the registration of a motor vehicle the person owns or leases if the person later makes a proper application and otherwise is eligible to be issued or to transfer a motor vehicle registration."

Amendment Note: 2002 S 123 rewrote division (A), which prior thereto read:

"(A) A person arrested without warrant for any violation listed in division (B) of this section, and having a current valid Ohio driver's or commercial driver's license, if the person has been notified of the possible consequences of the person's actions as required by division (C) of this section, may post bond by depositing the license with the arresting officer if the officer and person so choose, or with the local court having jurisdiction if the court and person so choose. The license may be used as bond only during the period for which it is valid.

"When an arresting officer accepts the driver's or commercial driver's license as bond, the officer shall note the date, time, and place of the court appearance on 'the violator's notice to appear' and the notice shall serve as a valid Ohio driver's or commercial driver's license until the date and time appearing thereon. The arresting officer immediately shall forward the license to the appropriate court.

"When a local court accepts the license as bond or continues the case to another date and time, it shall provide the person with a card in a form approved by the registrar of motor vehicles setting forth the license number, name, address, the date and time of the court appearance, and a statement that the license is being held as bond. The card shall serve as a valid license until the date and time contained in the card.

"The court may accept other bond at any time and return the license to the person. The court shall return the license to the person when judgment is satisfied, including, but not limited to, compliance with any court orders, unless a suspension or revocation is part of the penalty imposed.

"Neither 'the violator's notice to appear' nor a court granted card shall continue driving privileges beyond the expiration date of the license.

"If the person arrested fails to appear in court at the date and time set by the court or fails to satisfy the judgment of the court, including, but not limited to, compliance with all court orders within the time allowed by the court, the court may declare the forfeiture of the person's license. Thirty days after the declaration of forfeiture, the court shall forward the person's license to the registrar. The court also shall enter information relative to the forfeiture on a form approved and furnished by the registrar and send the form to the registrar, who shall suspend the license and send written notification of the suspension to the person at the person's last known address. No valid driver's or commercial driver's license shall be granted to the person until the court having jurisdiction orders that the forfeiture be terminated. The court shall inform the registrar of the termination of the forfeiture by entering information relative to the termination on a form approved and furnished by the registrar and sending the form to the registrar. The court also shall charge and collect from the person a processing fee of fifteen dollars to cover the costs of the bureau of motor vehicles in administering this section. The clerk of the court shall transmit monthly all such processing fees to the registrar for deposit into the state bureau of motor vehicles fund created by section 4501.25 of the Revised Code.

"In addition, upon receipt from the court of the copy of the declaration of forfeiture, neither the registrar nor any deputy registrar shall accept any application for the registration or transfer of registration of any motor vehicle owned by or leased in the name of the person named in the declaration of forfeiture until the court having jurisdiction over the offense that led to the suspension issues an order terminating the forfeiture. However, for a motor vehicle leased in the name of a person named in a declaration of forfeiture, the registrar shall not implement the preceding sentence until the registrar adopts procedures for that implementation under section 4503.39 of the Revised Code. Upon receipt by the registrar of such an order, the registrar also shall take such measures as may be necessary to permit the person to register a motor vehicle the person owns or leases or to transfer the registration of such a vehicle if the person later makes a proper application and otherwise is eligible to be issued or to transfer a motor vehicle registration."

Amendment Note: 1997 S 85 added the second sentence in the sixth paragraph in division (A).

Amendment Note: 1996 S 121 substituted "The registrar shall suspend the license and send written notification of the suspension to the person at the person's last known address. No valid driver's or commercial driver's license shall be granted to the person until the court having jurisdiction orders that the forfeiture be terminated. The court also shall charge and collect from the person a processing fee of fifteen dollars to cover the costs of the bureau of motor vehicles in administering this section. The clerk of the court shall transmit monthly all such processing fees to the registrar for deposit into the state bureau of motor vehicles fund created by section 4501.25 of the Revised Code." for "The registrar shall cancel the license and send written notification of the cancellation to the person at his last known address. No valid driver's or commercial driver's license shall be granted to the person for a period of one year after cancellation, unless the court having jurisdiction orders that the forfeiture be terminated." in division (A); added the last paragraph of division (A); substituted "the license will be suspended, and the person will not be eligible for reissuance of the license or issuance of a new license, or the issuance of a certificate of registration for a motor vehicle owned or leased by the person until the person appears and complies with any order issued by the court. The person also is subject to any criminal penalties that may apply to the person." for "the license will be canceled, the person will not be eligible for reissuance of the license or issuance of a new license for one year after cancellation, and the person is subject to any criminal penalties that may apply to the person." in division (C); made changes to reflect gender neutral language; and made other nonsubstantive changes.

Amendment Note: 1996 H 353 inserted "court also shall enter information relative to the forfeiture on a form approved and furnished by the registrar and send the form to the" and the concluding sentence in the final paragraph of division (A); made changes to reflect gender neutral language; and made other nonsubstantive changes.

Amendment Note: 1994 H 687 substituted "send written notification of the cancellation to the person" for "notify the person of the cancellation by certified mail" and "forfeiture be terminated" for "registrar of motor vehicles to reissue the license to its original date of expiration without additional fee or to permit the person to apply for a new license" in the final paragraph of division (A).

Cross References

Bail, Crim R 46

Motor vehicle registration application, prohibitions to acceptance, 4503.10

Motor vehicle registration renewal by mail, prohibitions, 4503.102

Motor vehicle, transfer of ownership and registration, 4503.12

Transfer of motor vehicle ownership and registration, prohibitions, 4503.12

Library References

Automobiles ⚷349(19).

Westlaw Topic No. 48A.

C.J.S. Motor Vehicles §§ 1321 to 1332, 1334 to 1335.

Research References

Encyclopedias

OH Jur. 3d Automobiles & Other Vehicles § 42, Transfer of Ownership and Registration—Death of Owner.

OH Jur. 3d Automobiles & Other Vehicles § 43, Transfer of Ownership and Registration—Effect of Merger or Consolidation of Corporations, or Incorporation of Proprietorship or Partnership.

OH Jur. 3d Criminal Law § 1696, Bail.

OH Jur. 3d Criminal Law § 2217, License as Bond; Generally.

OH Jur. 3d Criminal Law § 2218, Notice to Appear; Temporary License.

OH Jur. 3d Criminal Law § 2220, Nonappearance of Defendant.

OH Jur. 3d Criminal Law § 2231, Liability of Sureties; Generally.

Treatises and Practice Aids

Katz, Giannelli, Blair and Lipton, Baldwin's Ohio Practice, Criminal Law, § 37:6, Types of Pretrial Release.

Notes of Decisions

Additional court costs 1

1. Additional court costs

The additional $13 in court costs imposed by 1981 H 694, § 169 and 167, eff. 11–15–81, must be collected in cash at the time bail is posted. OAG 82–050.

2937.222 Hearing to deny bail; information to consider

(A) On the motion of the prosecuting attorney or on the judge's own motion, the judge shall hold a hearing to determine whether an accused person charged with aggravated murder when it is not a capital offense, murder, a felony of the first or second degree, a violation of section 2903.06 of the Revised Code, a violation of section 2903.211 of the Revised Code that is a felony, or a felony OVI offense shall be denied bail. The judge shall order that the accused be detained until the conclusion of the hearing. Except for good cause, a continuance on the motion of the state shall not exceed three court days. Except for good cause, a continuance on the motion of the accused shall not exceed five court days unless the motion of the accused waives in writing the five-day limit and states in writing a specific period for which the accused requests a continuance. A continuance granted upon a motion of the accused that waives in writing the five-day limit shall not exceed five court days after the period of continuance requested in the motion.

At the hearing, the accused has the right to be represented by counsel and, if the accused is indigent, to have counsel appointed. The judge shall afford the accused an opportunity to testify, to present witnesses and other information, and to cross-examine witnesses who appear at the hearing. The rules concerning admissibility of evidence in criminal trials do not apply to the presentation and consideration of information at the hearing. Regardless of whether the hearing is being held on the motion of the prosecuting attorney or on the court's own motion, the state has the burden of proving that the proof is evident or the presumption great that the accused committed the offense with which the accused is charged, of proving that the accused poses a substantial risk of serious physical harm to any person or to the community, and of proving that no release conditions will reasonably assure the safety of that person and the community.

The judge may reopen the hearing at any time before trial if the judge finds that information exists that was not known to the movant at the time of the hearing and that that information has a material bearing on whether bail should be denied. If a municipal court or county court enters an order denying bail, a judge of the court of common pleas having jurisdiction over the case may continue that order or may hold a hearing pursuant to this section to determine whether to continue that order.

(B) No accused person shall be denied bail pursuant to this section unless the judge finds by clear and convincing evidence that the proof is evident or the presumption great that the accused committed the offense described in division (A) of this section with which the accused is charged, finds by clear and convincing evidence that the accused poses a substantial risk of serious physical harm to any person or to the community, and finds by clear and convincing evidence that no release conditions will reasonably assure the safety of that person and the community.

(C) The judge, in determining whether the accused person described in division (A) of this section poses a substantial risk of serious physical harm to any person or to the community and whether there are conditions of release that will reasonably assure the safety of that person and the community, shall consider all available information regarding all of the following:

(1) The nature and circumstances of the offense charged, including whether the offense is an offense of violence or involves alcohol or a drug of abuse;

(2) The weight of the evidence against the accused;

(3) The history and characteristics of the accused, including, but not limited to, both of the following:

(a) The character, physical and mental condition, family ties, employment, financial resources, length of residence in the community, community ties, past conduct, history relating to drug or alcohol abuse, and criminal history of the accused;

(b) Whether, at the time of the current alleged offense or at the time of the arrest of the accused, the accused was on probation, parole, post-release control, or other release pending trial, sentencing, appeal, or completion of sentence for the commission of an offense under the laws of this state, another state, or the United States or under a municipal ordinance.

(4) The nature and seriousness of the danger to any person or the community that would be posed by the person's release.

(D)(1) An order of the court of common pleas denying bail pursuant to this section is a final appealable order. In an appeal pursuant to division (D) of this section, the court of appeals shall do all of the following:

(a) Give the appeal priority on its calendar;

(b) Liberally modify or dispense with formal requirements in the interest of a speedy and just resolution of the appeal;

(c) Decide the appeal expeditiously;

(d) Promptly enter its judgment affirming or reversing the order denying bail.

(2) The pendency of an appeal under this section does not deprive the court of common pleas of jurisdiction to conduct further proceedings in the case or to further consider the order denying bail in accordance with this section. If, during the pendency of an appeal under division (D) of this section, the court of common pleas sets aside or terminates the order denying bail, the court of appeals shall dismiss the appeal.

(E) As used in this section:

(1) "Court day" has the same meaning as in section 5122.01 of the Revised Code.

(2) "Felony OVI offense" means a third degree felony OVI offense and a fourth degree felony OVI offense.

(3) "Fourth degree felony OVI offense" and "third degree felony OVI offense" have the same meanings as in section 2929.01 of the Revised Code.

(2002 S 123, eff. 1–1–04; 1999 S 22, eff. 5–17–00; 1999 H 137, eff. 3–10–00; 1999 S 8, eff. 7–29–99)

Historical and Statutory Notes

Amendment Note: 2002 S 123 substituted "OVI" for "OMVI" throughout the section.

Amendment Note: 1999 S 22 deleted "fourth degree" before "felony OMVI offense" in the first paragraph in division (A); and rewrote division (E), which prior thereto read:

"(E) As used in this section:

"(1) 'Court day' has the same meaning as in section 5122.01 of the Revised Code.

"(2) 'Fourth degree felony OMVI offense' has the same meaning as in section 2929.01 of the Revised Code."

Amendment Note: 1999 H 137 inserted "a violation of section 2903.211 of the Revised Code that is a felony" in the first paragraph in division (A).

Library References

Bail ⚷49(5).

Westlaw Topic No. 49.

C.J.S. Bail; Release and Detention Pending Proceedings §§ 54 to 64.

Research References

Encyclopedias

OH Jur. 3d Criminal Law § 2167, Generally; Constitutional Guarantee.

Treatises and Practice Aids

Katz, Giannelli, Blair and Lipton, Baldwin's Ohio Practice, Criminal Law, § 37:3, Ohio Constitution.

Katz, Giannelli, Blair and Lipton, Baldwin's Ohio Practice, Criminal Law, § 37:4, Preventive Detention.

Katz, Giannelli, Blair and Lipton, Baldwin's Ohio Practice, Criminal Law, § 37:11, Excessive Bail Cases.

Katz, Giannelli, Blair and Lipton, Baldwin's Ohio Practice, Criminal Law, § 139:36, Motion to Deny Bail.

Katz, Giannelli, Blair and Lipton, Baldwin's Ohio Practice, Criminal Law, § 139:37, Order to Deny Bail.

Adrine & Ruden, Ohio Domestic Violence Law § 3:2, Effect of Certain Prior Convictions on New Charges of Domestic Violence.

Adrine & Ruden, Ohio Domestic Violence Law § 3:6, Elements and Penalties—Menacing by Stalking Under RC 2903.211.

Notes of Decisions

1. Evidence for denial

Statute providing procedure to be followed before a trial court could deny bail to a person charged with a noncapital felony offense did not authorize cash-only bail. Smith v. Leis (Ohio, 10-12-2005) 106 Ohio St.3d 309, 835 N.E.2d 5, 2005-Ohio-5125. Bail ⚷ 73

Defendant, who never requested an evidentiary hearing to determine whether the proof or presumption warranted a denial of bail in capital murder prosecution, waived appellate review of issue challenging lack of hearing. State v. Hughbanks (Ohio, 08-20-2003) 99 Ohio St.3d 365, 792 N.E.2d 1081, 2003-Ohio-4121, stay granted 100 Ohio St.3d 1479, 798 N.E.2d 615, 2003-Ohio-5993, denial of post-conviction relief affirmed 101 Ohio St.3d 52, 800 N.E.2d 1152, 2004-Ohio-6, denial of post-conviction relief affirmed in part, reversed in part 159 Ohio App.3d 257, 823 N.E.2d 544, 2004-Ohio-6429, appeal not allowed 105 Ohio St.3d 1500, 825 N.E.2d 623, 2005-Ohio-1666. Criminal Law ⚷ 1031(1)

Trial court's failure to hold bond hearing in capital murder case did not result in unfair denial of bond; subsequent conviction based largely on evidence available by date of arraignment showed that by that date the proof was evident and the presumption great, and defendant's indigency would have prevented his making any reasonable bond that would have been appropriate. State v. Nields (Ohio, 08-29-2001) 93 Ohio St.3d 6, 752 N.E.2d 859, 2001-Ohio-1291, reconsideration denied 93 Ohio St.3d 1452, 756 N.E.2d 116. Bail ⚷ 49(5)

2937.23 Amount of bail; domestic violence offenders; anti–stalking violations

(A)(1) In a case involving a felony or a violation of section 2903.11, 2903.12, or 2903.13 of the Revised Code when the victim of the offense is a peace officer, the judge or magistrate shall fix the amount of bail.

(2) In a case involving a misdemeanor or a violation of a municipal ordinance and not involving a felony or a violation of section 2903.11, 2903.12, or 2903.13 of the Revised Code when the victim of the offense is a peace officer, the judge, magistrate, or clerk of the court may fix the amount of bail and may do so in accordance with a schedule previously fixed by the judge or magistrate. If the judge, magistrate, or clerk of the court is not readily available, the sheriff, deputy sheriff, marshal, deputy marshal, police officer, or jailer having custody of the person charged may fix the amount of bail in accordance with a schedule previously fixed by the judge or magistrate and shall take the bail only in the county courthouse, the municipal or township building, or the county or municipal jail.

(3) In all cases, the bail shall be fixed with consideration of the seriousness of the offense charged, the previous criminal record of the defendant, and the probability of the defendant appearing at the trial of the case.

(B) In any case involving an alleged violation of section 2903.211 of the Revised Code or of a municipal ordinance that is substantially similar to that section, the court shall determine whether it will order an evaluation of the mental condition of the defendant pursuant to section 2919.271 of the Revised Code and, if it decides to so order, shall issue the order requiring the evaluation before it sets bail for the person charged with the violation. In any case involving an alleged violation of section 2919.27 of the Revised Code or of a municipal ordinance that is substantially similar to that section and in which the court finds that either of the following criteria applies, the court shall determine whether it will order an evaluation of the mental condition of the defendant pursuant to section 2919.271 of the Revised Code and, if it decides to so order, shall issue the order requiring that evaluation before it sets bail for the person charged with the violation:

(1) Regarding an alleged violation of a protection order issued or consent agreement approved pursuant to section 2919.26 or 3113.31 of the Revised Code, that the violation allegedly involves conduct by the defendant that caused physical harm to the person or property of a family or household member covered by the order or agreement or conduct by

that defendant that caused a family or household member to believe that the defendant would cause physical harm to that member or that member's property;

(2) Regarding an alleged violation of a protection order issued pursuant to section 2903.213 or 2903.214 of the Revised Code, or a protection order issued by a court of another state, as defined in section 2919.27 of the Revised Code, that the violation allegedly involves conduct by the defendant that caused physical harm to the person or property of the person covered by the order or conduct by that defendant that caused the person covered by the order to believe that the defendant would cause physical harm to that person or that person's property.

(C) As used in this section, "peace officer" has the same meaning as in section 2935.01 of the Revised Code.

(1999 H 202, eff. 2–9–00; 1999 S 142, eff. 2–3–00; 1998 H 302, eff. 7–29–98; 1997 S 1, eff. 10–21–97; 1995 S 2, eff. 7–1–96; 1992 H 536, eff. 11–5–92; 1985 H 475; 129 v 557; 128 v 97)

Historical and Statutory Notes

Ed. Note: A special endorsement by the Legislative Service Commission states, "Comparison of these amendments [1999 H 202, eff. 2–9–00 and 1999 S 142, eff. 2–3–00] in pursuance of section 1.52 of the Revised Code discloses that they are not irreconcilable so that they are required by that section to be harmonized to give effect to each amendment." In recognition of this rule of construction, changes made by 1999 H 202, eff. 2–9–00, and 1999 S 142, eff. 2–3–00, have been incorporated in the above amendment. See *Baldwin's Ohio Legislative Service Annotated*, 1999, pages 12/L–3344 and 10/L–2170, or the OH–LEGIS or OH–LEGIS–OLD database on Westlaw, for original versions of these Acts.

Ed. Note: 2937.23 contains provisions analogous to former 2937.22, repealed by 128 v 97, eff. 1–1–60.

Ed. Note: Former 2937.23 repealed by 128 v 97, eff. 1–1–60; 1953 H 1; GC 13435–3; see now 2937.281 for provisions analogous to former 2937.23.

Pre–1953 H 1 Amendments: 113 v 150, Ch 14, § 3

Amendment Note: 1999 H 202 added the first sentence in the introductory paragraph in division (B).

Amendment Note: 1999 S 142 designated divisions (A)(1), (A)(2), and (A)(3); inserted "or a violation of section 2903.11, 2903.12, or 2903.13 of the Revised Code when the victim of the offense is a peace officer" in divisions (A)(1) and (A)(2); deleted ", or, in a case when" after "fixed by the judge or magistrate" in division (A)(2); added new division (C); and made other nonsubstantive changes.

Amendment Note: 1998 H 302 deleted "temporary" before "protection order" and inserted "issued" and "approved pursuant to section 2919.26 or 3113.31 of the Revised Code" in division (B)(1); deleted "anti-stalking" before "protection order" and inserted "issued pursuant to section 2903.213 or 2903.214 of the Revised Code," in division (B)(2); and made other nonsubstantive changes.

Amendment Note: 1997 S 1 deleted "of the order or agreement" following "that the violation" in division (B)(1); inserted "or a protection order issued by a court of another state, as defined in section 2919.27 of the Revised Code," in division (B)(2); and deleted "of the order" before "allegedly involves" in division (B)(2).

Amendment Note: 1995 S 2 rewrote this section, which previously read:

"(A) In cases of felony, the amount of bail shall be fixed by the judge or magistrate. In cases of misdemeanor or violation of a municipal ordinance, it may be fixed by the judge, magistrate, or clerk of the court and may be in accordance with a schedule previously fixed by the judge or magistrate or, in cases when the judge, magistrate, or clerk of the court is not readily available, bail may be fixed by the sheriff, deputy sheriff, marshal, deputy marshal, police officer, or jailer having custody of the person charged, shall be in accordance with a schedule previously fixed by the judge or magistrate, and shall be taken only in the county courthouse, the municipal or township building, or the county or municipal jail. In all cases, it shall be fixed with consideration of the seriousness of the offense charged, the previous criminal record of the defendant, and the probability of his appearing at the trial of the case.

"(B) In any case involving an alleged violation of section 2919.27 of the Revised Code or of a municipal ordinance that is substantially similar to that section, if the court determines that the violation of the temporary protection order or consent agreement allegedly involves conduct by the defendant that caused physical harm to the person or property of a family or household member covered by the order or agreement or conduct by that defendant that caused a family or household member to believe that the defendant would cause physical harm to that member or his property, the court shall determine whether it will order an evaluation of the mental condition of the defendant pursuant to division (A) of section 2919.271 of the Revised Code and, if it decides to so order, issue the order requiring that evaluation before it sets bail for the person charged with the violation.

"(C) In any case involving an alleged violation of section 2903.214 of the Revised Code or of a municipal ordinance that is substantially similar to that section, if the court determines that the violation of the anti-stalking protection order allegedly involves conduct by the defendant that caused physical harm to the person or property of the person covered by the order or conduct by that defendant that caused the person covered by the order to believe that the defendant would cause physical harm to that person or his property, the court shall determine whether it will order an evaluation of the mental condition of the defendant pursuant to division (A) of section 2903.215 of the Revised Code and, if it decides to so order, issue the order requiring that evaluation before it sets bail for the person charged with the violation."

Cross References

Additional costs in criminal cases in all courts to fund reparations payments; bail, defined, 2743.70

Bail, Crim R 46

Bailable offenses; excessive bail, O Const Art I §9

Domestic violence, bail schedule, 2919.251

Library References

Bail ⚷50.

Westlaw Topic No. 49.

C.J.S. Bail; Release and Detention Pending Proceedings §§ 66 to 70.

Research References

Encyclopedias

OH Jur. 3d Criminal Law § 2208, What Constitutes Reasonable Amount; Considerations.

Treatises and Practice Aids

Katz, Giannelli, Blair and Lipton, Baldwin's Ohio Practice, Criminal Law, § 37:6, Types of Pretrial Release.

Katz, Giannelli, Blair and Lipton, Baldwin's Ohio Practice, Criminal Law, § 37:10, Relevant Factors in Release Decision.

Hennenberg & Reinhart, Ohio Criminal Defense Motions F 15.04, Motion for Admission to Bail-Miscellaneous Motions.

Hennenberg & Reinhart, Ohio Criminal Defense Motions F 15.05, Motion to Amend Bond Order-Miscellaneous Motions.

Notes of Decisions

Ed. Note: This section contains annotations from former RC 2505.30.

Bail fixed by clerk or officer 3
Constitutional issues 1
Fixing amount and terms of bail 4
Modification of bail 2

---

1. Constitutional issues

Judges were entitled to absolute immunity from action brought by individual, who was acquitted of felony sexual offenses, alleging that first judge acted outside his jurisdiction when he set bail on felony charges and that second judge violated individual's constitutional rights by setting excessive bail, where judges' action of setting bail in felony prosecution was judicial act, judges were acting within their jurisdiction when they set bail before individual was indicted, and second judge's action of allegedly setting excessive bail was at most act in excess of judge's jurisdiction, which was not same as judge acting without jurisdiction. Barstow v. Waller (Ohio App. 4 Dist., Hocking, 10-26-2004) No. 04CA5, 2004-Ohio-5746, 2004 WL 2427396, Unreported. Civil Rights ⚷ 1737; Judges ⚷ 36

2. Modification of bail

Proper procedure for seeking relief for excessive pretrial bail is through habeas corpus proceedings. State v. Patterson (Ohio App. 10 Dist., 04-04-1996) 110 Ohio App.3d 264, 673 N.E.2d 1001, dismissed, appeal not allowed 76 Ohio St.3d 1493, 670 N.E.2d 240. Habeas Corpus ⚷ 469

A court of appeals, in a hearing in an original action for a writ of habeas corpus challenging the bail set by the trial court, can modify the bail bond without specifically stating that the bail is excessive and that the trial court abused its discretion in setting the bail. In re DeFronzo (Ohio 1977) 49 Ohio St.2d 271, 361 N.E.2d 448, 3 O.O.3d 408. Habeas Corpus ⚷ 800

3. Bail fixed by clerk or officer

An allegation that the clerk of a municipal court improperly failed to fix bail for a defendant following an arrest fails to state a claim upon which relief can be granted, inasmuch as the charge refers to an act performed by the clerk within the scope of his official quasi-judicial duties and thus he is entitled to immunity. Denman v. Leedy (C.A.6 (Ohio) 1973) 479 F.2d 1097, 66 O.O.2d 368.

Pursuant to Crim R 46(D), where the clerk of a municipal or county court is unavailable and a person charged with a misdemeanor offense of which the municipal or county court has jurisdiction is brought to a facility of which the sheriff has charge, the sheriff may accept bail and release the accused in accordance with the provisions of the rule. OAG 81–091.

A special deputy sheriff who is employed on a salary basis for approximately two days per week may not act as a professional bondsman in criminal cases, because of a possible conflict between his public duties and his private pecuniary interests. OAG 68–112.

A police officer acting as special deputy clerk of county court under RC 1907.101 for the purpose of accepting bonds may not be paid $1 for each bond accepted, but must be compensated in semimonthly installments out of the county treasury. 1964 OAG 1516.

4. Fixing amount and terms of bail

Trial court did not abuse its discretion in increasing the bond amount from $120,000 to $500,000 for defendant charged with attempted murder, felonious assault, and having weapons under a disability; defendant was alleged to have shot victim five times in the chest and back, victim was sole witness to offense and could identify defendant as perpetrator, defendant had prior felony conviction and a history of failure to appear in court, and defendant was on bail on pending charges at time of offense. King v. Telb (Ohio App. 6 Dist., Lucas, 02-17-2005) No. L-05-1022, 2005-Ohio-800, 2005 WL 435170, Unreported. Bail ⚷ 53

Increasing defendant's bail, after his conviction for attempted felonious assault, was not an abuse of discretion; defendant's conviction was a change in circumstances since the pretrial determination of bail, and the conviction presented an inherently increased risk of flight. Miles v. Telb (Ohio App. 6 Dist., Lucas, 08-01-2003) No. L-03-1204, 2003-Ohio-4220, 2003 WL 21862853, Unreported. Bail ⚷ 53

Following conviction, any error concerning the issue of pretrial bail is moot. State v. Hughbanks (Ohio, 08-20-2003) 99 Ohio St.3d 365, 792 N.E.2d 1081, 2003-Ohio-4121, stay granted 100 Ohio St.3d 1479, 798 N.E.2d 615, 2003-Ohio-5993, denial of post-conviction relief affirmed 101 Ohio St.3d 52, 800 N.E.2d 1152, 2004-Ohio-6, denial of post-conviction relief affirmed in part, reversed in part 159 Ohio App.3d 257, 823 N.E.2d 544, 2004-Ohio-6429, appeal not allowed 105 Ohio St.3d 1500, 825 N.E.2d 623, 2005-Ohio-1666. Criminal Law ⚷ 1134(3)

In determining the amount of bail to be fixed, the standards set forth in RC 2937.23 and Crim R 46(F) must be applied. Petition of Gentry (Lucas 1982) 7 Ohio App.3d 143, 454 N.E.2d 987, 7 O.B.R. 187. Bail ⚷ 51

Where a defendant is charged with four felonies, is released on and complies with the conditions of a personal recognizance bond, and is subsequently indicted on six additional felony charges, it is an abuse of discretion to revoke the original bond and impose substantial bond requirements without ten per cent provisions on both indictments where the defendant has no prior criminal record and evidence that the defendant is a poor bail risk is lacking. Griswold v Telb, No. L–85–176 (6th Dist Ct App, Lucas, 5–15–85).

2937.24 Oath to surety; form of affidavit

When a recognizance is offered under section 2937.22 of the Revised Code, the surety on which recognizance qualifies as a real property owner, the judge or magistrate shall require such surety to pledge to this state real property owned by the surety and located in this state. Whenever such pledge of real property has been given by any such proposed surety, he shall execute the usual form of recognizance, and in addition thereto there shall be filed his affidavit of justification of suretyship, to be attached to said recognizance as a part thereof. The surety may be required in such affidavit to depose as to whether he is, at the time of executing the same, surety upon any other recognizance and as to whether there are any unsatisfied judgments or executions against him. He may also be required to state any other fact which the court thinks relevant and material to a correct determination of the surety's sufficiency to act as bail. Such surety shall state in such affidavit where notices under section 2937.38 of the Revised Code may be served on himself, and service of notice of summons at such place is sufficient service for all purposes.

Such affidavit shall be executed by the proposed surety under an oath and may be in the following form:

"State of Ohio, County of ________, ss:

________ residing at ________, who offers himself as surety for ________ being first duly sworn, says that he owns in his own legal right, real property subject to execution, located in the county of ________, State of Ohio, consisting of ________ and described as follows to wit: ________; that the title to the same is in his own name; that the value of the same is not less than _____ dollars, and is subject to no encumbrances whatever except ________; that he is not surety upon any unpaid or forfeited recognizance, and that he is not party to any unsatisfied judgment upon any recognizance; that he is worth not less than _____ dollars over and above all debts, liabilities, and lawful claims against him, and all liens, encumbrances, and lawful claims against his property."

(1953 H 1, eff. 10–1–53; GC 13435–4)

Historical and Statutory Notes

Pre-1953 H 1 Amendments: 113 v 150, Ch 14, § 4

Cross References

Bail, Crim R 46

Library References

Bail ⚬63.
Westlaw Topic No. 49.

C.J.S. Bail; Release and Detention Pending Proceedings §§ 107 to 117.

Research References

Encyclopedias

OH Jur. 3d Criminal Law § 2229, Justification of Sureties; Generally.

Treatises and Practice Aids

Katz, Giannelli, Blair and Lipton, Baldwin's Ohio Practice, Criminal Law, § 139:3, Recognizance of the Accused on Adjournment of Examination.

Katz, Giannelli, Blair and Lipton, Baldwin's Ohio Practice, Criminal Law, § 139:8, Affidavit to Qualify as Surety (Statutory Form).

Kuehnle and Levey, Ohio Real Estate Law and Practice § 10:29, Recognizance Bonds.

2937.25 Lien; form

Upon the execution of any recognizance in an amount in excess of two hundred dollars in the usual form, and an affidavit of justification under section 2937.24 of the Revised Code, there shall attach to the real property described in said affidavit of justification, a lien in favor of this state in the penal sum of the recognizance, which lien shall remain in full force and effect during such time as such recognizance remains effective, or until further order of the court. Upon the acceptance by the judge or magistrate of such recognizance, containing such affidavit of justification, the said recognizance shall be immediately filed with the clerk of said court, if there is a clerk, or with the magistrate. The clerk of the court or the magistrate shall forthwith, upon the filing with him of such recognizance, file with the county recorder of the county in which such real property is located, a notice or lien, in writing, in substance as follows:

"To whom it may concern:

Take notice that the hereinafter described real property, located in the county of ________, has been pledged for the sum of ________ dollars, to the state of Ohio, by ________ surety upon the recognizance of ________ in a certain cause pending in the ________ court of the county (or city) of ________, to wit: the state of Ohio, plaintiff, versus ________ defendant, known and identified in such court as cause No. ________

Description of real estate: ________ Clerk of the court for the county of ________ or ________ Magistrate.

Dated ________"

From the time of the filing and recording of such notice it is notice to everyone that the real property therein described has been pledged to this state as security for the performance of the conditions of a criminal recognizance in the penal sum set forth in said recognizance and notice. Such lien does not affect the validity of prior liens on said property.

(1953 H 1, eff. 10-1-53; GC 13435-5)

Historical and Statutory Notes

Pre-1953 H 1 Amendments: 113 v 151, Ch 14, § 5

Cross References

Bail, Crim R 46

Liens in favor of state, agency or political subdivision, limitation of actions, notice of continuation, 2305.26

Library References

Bail ⚩54.
Westlaw Topic No. 49.

C.J.S. Bail; Release and Detention Pending Proceedings §§ 3, 93 to 106.

Research References

Encyclopedias

OH Jur. 3d Criminal Law § 2232, Lien.

Treatises and Practice Aids

Katz, Giannelli, Blair and Lipton, Baldwin's Ohio Practice, Criminal Law, § 139:9, Lien on Property of Surety (Statutory Form).

Kuehnle and Levey, Ohio Real Estate Law and Practice § 10:29, Recognizance Bonds.

Kuehnle and Levey, Ohio Real Estate Law and Practice § 10:49, Six Years' Duration of Statutory Liens—Notice for Continuation.

Kuehnle and Levey, Ohio Real Estate Law and Practice § 43:11, Land Installment Contracts—Nature of Vendor's Title.

2937.26 Cancellation of lien; form

Whenever, by the order of a court, a recognizance under sections 2937.24 and 2937.25 of the Revised Code has been canceled, discharged, or set aside, or the cause in which such recognizance is taken has been dismissed or otherwise terminated the clerk of such court shall forthwith file with the county recorder of the county in which the real property is located, a notice of discharge in writing, in substance as follows:

"To whom it may concern:

Take notice that by the order of the court of ________ (naming court) ________ of the county (or city) of ________, the recognizance of ________ as principal, and _____ as surety, given in the cause of the State of Ohio, plaintiff, versus ________, defendant, known and identified as Cause No. _____ in said court, is canceled, discharged, and set aside, and the lien of the State of Ohio on the real property therein pledged as security, is hereby waived, discharged, and set aside.

________ Clerk of the court.

Dated _____"

(1953 H 1, eff. 10–1–53; GC 13435–6)

Historical and Statutory Notes

Pre–1953 H 1 Amendments: 113 v 151, Ch 14, § 6

Cross References

Bail, Crim R 46

Library References

Bail ⚩74.
Westlaw Topic No. 49.

C.J.S. Bail; Release and Detention Pending Proceedings §§ 118 to 135.

Research References

Encyclopedias

OH Jur. 3d Criminal Law § 2232, Lien.

Treatises and Practice Aids

Katz, Giannelli, Blair and Lipton, Baldwin's Ohio Practice, Criminal Law, § 139:10, Cancellation of Lien (Statutory Form).

Kuehnle and Levey, Ohio Real Estate Law and Practice § 10:29, Recognizance Bonds.

2937.27 Duties of county recorder

The county recorder of the county in which the property of a surety on a recognizance is located, shall keep and file all notices of lien and notices of discharge which are filed with him pursuant to section 2937.26 of the Revised Code, and shall keep in addition thereto, a book or record in which he shall index notice of liens and notice of discharges, as they are filed with him. When a lien has been released or discharged for a period of one year, the county recorder may destroy all notices of such lien.

(129 v 1033, eff. 10–26–61; 1953 H 1; GC 13435–7)

Historical and Statutory Notes

Pre–1953 H 1 Amendments: 113 v 152, Ch 14, § 7

Cross References

Appellate procedure, bond as lien, 2505.13

Bail, Crim R 46

Library References

Registers of Deeds ⚬⇒5.

Westlaw Topic No. 330.

C.J.S. Registers of Deeds §§ 10 to 13.

Research References

Encyclopedias

OH Jur. 3d Automobiles & Other Vehicles § 42, Transfer of Ownership and Registration—Death of Owner.

OH Jur. 3d Criminal Law § 2232, Lien.

Treatises and Practice Aids

Kuehnle and Levey, Ohio Real Estate Law and Practice § 10:29, Recognizance Bonds.

Kuehnle and Levey, Ohio Real Estate Law and Practice § 10:31, Supersedeas Bonds on Appeal.

Notes of Decisions

Recording 1

1. Recording

When the recorder elects to maintain two sets of records as set forth in RC 317.08(F), the recorder may, pursuant to RC 317.08, maintain a single volume for the indexing, keeping, and recording of, among other documents, notices of liens and notices of discharge of recognizances which he is required to maintain pursuant to RC 2937.27, or may maintain such notices in a book or record as otherwise required by RC 2937.27. OAG 84–044.

A county recorder may not charge a recording fee upon the filing of a release of a lien created pursuant to RC 5749.02 since the legislature failed to provide for such a fee, which failure does not relieve recorder of the duties imposed upon him by that section. OAG 72–104.

2937.28 Transmission of recognizance

All recognizances shall be returnable to and all deposits shall be held by or subject to the order of the court or magistrate before whom the accused is to appear initially, and upon the transfer of the case to any other court or magistrate shall be returnable to and transmitted to the transferee court or magistrate.

It is not necessary for the accused to give new recognizance for appearance in common pleas court for arraignment upon indictment or pending appeal after judgment and sentence, unless the magistrate or judge of the trial court or the court to which appeal is taken, shall, for good cause shown, increase or decrease the amount of the recognizance, but such recognizance shall continue and be in full force until trial and appeal therefrom is finally determined. When two or more charges are filed, or indictments returned, against the same person at or about the same time, the recognizance given may be made to include all offenses charged against the accused.

(128 v 97, eff. 1–1–60)

Historical and Statutory Notes

Ed. Note: Former 2937.28 repealed by 128 v 97, eff. 1–1–60; 1953 H 1; GC 13435–8.

Pre–1953 H 1 Amendments: 113 v 152, Ch 14, § 8

Cross References

Bail, Crim R 46

Library References

Bail ⟹54.
Westlaw Topic No. 49.

C.J.S. Bail; Release and Detention Pending Proceedings §§ 3, 93 to 106.

Research References

Encyclopedias

OH Jur. 3d Criminal Law § 2223, Duration of Bond or Recognizance.

OH Jur. 3d Criminal Law § 2224, Recordation, Filing, and Transmittal.

OH Jur. 3d Criminal Law § 2227, Coverage of Offenses.

Treatises and Practice Aids

Katz, Giannelli, Blair and Lipton, Baldwin's Ohio Practice, Criminal Law, § 139:6, Entry for Recognizance of Witnesses—Upon Application of Prosecuting Attorney.

Katz, Giannelli, Blair and Lipton, Baldwin's Ohio Practice, Criminal Law, § 56:19, Transfer of Defendant.

2937.281 Requirements of recognizance

In cases of felony, the recognizance shall be signed by the accused and one or more adult residents of the county in which the case is pending, who shall own, in the aggregate, real property double the amount set as bail, over and above all encumbrances and liable to execution in at least that amount; or it may be signed by the accused and a surety company authorized to do business in this state.

In cases of misdemeanor, the recognizance may be signed by the accused and one or more adult residents, qualified as set forth above or as to personal property ownership, by the accused and surety company, or, if authorized by judge or magistrate, by the accused alone. In cases of misdemeanors arising under Chapters 4501., 4503., 4505., 4507., 4509., 4511., 4513., 4517., and 4549. of the Revised Code, and related ordinance offenses (except those of driving under the influence of intoxicating liquor or controlled substances and leaving the scene of an accident) the court or magistrate shall accept guaranteed arrest bond with respect to which a surety company has become surety as provided in section 3929.141 of the Revised Code in lieu of cash bail in an amount not to exceed two hundred dollars.

(1975 H 300, eff. 7–1–76; 129 v 1401; 128 v 97)

Historical and Statutory Notes

Ed. Note: 2937.281 contains provisions analogous to former 2937.23 and 4549.17, repealed by 128 v 97, eff. 1–1–60.

Ed. Note: Former 2937.281 repealed by 128 v 97, eff. 1–1–60; 127 v 847; 126 v 625.

Cross References

Bail, Crim R 46
Bailable offenses, O Const Art I §9

Library References

Bail ⟹54.
Westlaw Topic No. 49.

C.J.S. Bail; Release and Detention Pending Proceedings §§ 3, 93 to 106.

Research References

Encyclopedias

OH Jur. 3d Criminal Law § 2225, Signature of Recognizances; Felony Cases.

OH Jur. 3d Criminal Law § 2226, Signature of Recognizances; Felony Cases—Misdemeanor Cases.

Treatises and Practice Aids

Katz, Giannelli, Blair and Lipton, Baldwin's Ohio Practice, Criminal Law, § 37:6, Types of Pretrial Release.

Katz, Giannelli, Blair and Lipton, Baldwin's Ohio Practice, Criminal Law, § 139:6, Entry for Recognizance of Witnesses—Upon Application of Prosecuting Attorney.

Notes of Decisions

Credit cards 1

1. Credit cards

State highway patrol officer can accept credit cards on the highway from violators within the jurisdictions of those courts which have entered into an agreement with the credit card servicing agency for payment upon presentation of a completed sales draft with the only conditions being that the bail amount involved not exceed the dollar limitations contained in the agreement, the sales draft be legible and that the sales draft be drawn on an unexpired credit card, but may not accept credit cards within jurisdictions of courts which have not entered into such agreements. OAG 70–036.

2937.29 Release of accused on his own recognizance

When from all the circumstances the court is of the opinion that the accused will appear as required, either before or after conviction, the accused may be released on his own recognizance. A failure to appear as required by such recognizance shall constitute an offense subject to the penalty provided in section 2937.99 of the Revised Code.

(131 v H 47, eff. 8–10–65)

Historical and Statutory Notes

Ed. Note: Former 2937.29 repealed by 128 v 97, eff. 1–1–60; 1953 H 1; GC 13435–9.

Pre–1953 H 1 Amendments: 113 v 152, Ch 14, § 9

Cross References

Penalty: 2937.99(A)

Bail, Crim R 46

Library References

Bail ⚷54.

Westlaw Topic No. 49.

C.J.S. Bail; Release and Detention Pending Proceedings §§ 3, 93 to 106.

Research References

Encyclopedias

OH Jur. 3d Criminal Law § 2166, Penalty Upon Failure to Appear.

Treatises and Practice Aids

Katz, Giannelli, Blair and Lipton, Baldwin's Ohio Practice, Criminal Law, § 37:6, Types of Pretrial Release.

Katz, Giannelli, Blair and Lipton, Baldwin's Ohio Practice, Criminal Law, § 45:5, Procedure for Accepting No Contest Plea.

Katz, Giannelli, Blair and Lipton, Baldwin's Ohio Practice, Criminal Law, § 139:11, Discharge of Accused on His/Her Own Recognizance.

Notes of Decisions

Ed. Note: This section contains annotations from former RC 2937.29.

"Appearance" defined 5
Bail in murder case 6
Bail pending appeal 2
Constitutional issues 1
Medical reason for release 7
Responsibility for person released 3
Violation of recognizance 4

1. Constitutional issues

Statute governing release of defendant on his or her own recognizance does not impinge upon any First Amendment guarantee, and thus is not subject to challenge under overbreadth doctrine. State v. Hiatt (Ohio App. 4 Dist., 03-26-1997) 120 Ohio App.3d 247, 697 N.E.2d 1025. Bail ⚷ 40; Constitutional Law ⚷ 82(6.1)

Provision of statute governing release of defendants on their own recognizance, under which failure to appear as required constituted offense subject to penalty provided in separate statute, was not void for vagueness; language of provision was clear and unambiguous and provided constitutionally adequate guidelines, and did not unreasonably infringe constitutionally protected freedoms. State v. Hiatt (Ohio App. 4 Dist., 03-26-1997) 120 Ohio App.3d 247, 697 N.E.2d 1025. Bail ⚷ 97(1); Constitutional Law ⚷ 258(3.1)

2. Bail pending appeal

The punishment of one convicted of murder in the second degree is not life imprisonment, and such imprisonment is only "until legally released," and upon appeal of such conviction any judge of the court of appeals may admit such defendant to bail. (See contra State v Sheppard, 97 App 489,

123 NE(2d) 544 (1955) and 97 App 493, 124 NE(2d) 730 (1955).) State v. Hawkins (Belmont 1954) 97 Ohio App. 477, 124 N.E.2d 453, 56 O.O. 127.

When a defendant has been found guilty of a crime for which the punishment provided by law is life imprisonment, neither the trial court nor the reviewing court can admit the defendant to bail pending appeal. State v. Sheppard (Cuyahoga 1955) 97 Ohio App. 489, 123 N.E.2d 544, 69 Ohio Law Abs. 286, 56 O.O. 425, motion denied 97 Ohio App. 493, 124 N.E.2d 730, 56 O.O. 451. Bail ⚷ 44(2)

If there be no suspension of sentence upon conviction for felony, the provisions of this section, continuing in force, pending proceedings in error, a recognizance previously furnished, are not operative. Ex parte Thorpe (Ohio 1936) 132 Ohio St. 119, 5 N.E.2d 333, 7 O.O. 224.

3. Responsibility for person released

The risk that defendant would fail to abide by the conditions of his recognizance bond and would leave the state of Ohio was foreseeable to the surety, and thus, defendant's incarceration in another state, which prevented defendant from appearing at preliminary hearing in Ohio, did not relieve surety from liability on the recognizance bond based on performance being rendered impossible by operation of law. State v. Sexton (Ohio App. 4 Dist., 03-23-1999) 132 Ohio App.3d 791, 726 N.E.2d 554, appeal not allowed 86 Ohio St.3d 1443, 713 N.E.2d 1052. Bail ⚷ 75.2(3)

Where accused's departure from charging state to nearby state was not illegal, as he was required by charging court to do so, his subsequent incarceration in nearby state did not proximately result from any negligence of the sureties in failing to prevent his leaving charging state. State v. Scherer (Ohio App. 2 Dist., 12-20-1995) 108 Ohio App.3d 586, 671 N.E.2d 545. Bail ⚷ 75.2(3)

As surety has not undertaken role of "defendant's guardian angel," the defendant's bad acts are not within the business risks the surety assumes when it writes a bail bond. State v. Scherer (Ohio App. 2 Dist., 12-20-1995) 108 Ohio App.3d 586, 671 N.E.2d 545. Bail ⚷ 75.2(3)

Ohio law imposes no duty on custodial officers to ensure that released prisoners are absolutely free from danger; thus, an officer who returns a motorist arrested for drunk driving to an auto which the officer knows contains a shotgun has no duty to prevent the motorist from turning the gun on himself unless that outcome is foreseeable because, e.g., the prisoner is despondent. Clemets v. Heston (Williams 1985) 20 Ohio App.3d 132, 485 N.E.2d 287, 20 O.B.R. 166.

4. Violation of recognizance

Sentence of 18 months incarceration, the maximum term authorized, for defendant who pled guilty to failure to appear, was not contrary to law; defendant had long history of alcohol related offenses, he had failed to respond favorably to prior sanctions, and his operator's license had been revoked or suspended 22 times. State v. Bowmer (Ohio App. 6 Dist., Ottawa, 03-21-2003) No. OT-02-018, 2003-Ohio-1397, 2003 WL 1447842, Unreported. Bail ⚷ 97(1)

Trial court's failure to make requisite findings in response to defendant's allegation that a domestic violence conviction and confinement in an out-of-state prison listed in his presentence investigation report were inaccurate was harmless error, even though the court imposed consecutive sentences for felonious assault and breach of recognizance convictions, where trial court relied on the quantum of prior criminal convictions, not the nature of, or the punishment imposed for, any single conviction. State v. Platz (Ohio App. 4 Dist., Washington, 09-27-2002) No. 01CA33, 2002-Ohio-6149, 2002 WL 31521569, Unreported. Criminal Law ⚷ 1177

Defendant's failure to turn himself in at sheriff's office at time designated by court after execution of his sentence was stayed and he was released on his own recognizance following conviction constituted offense of failure to appear; defendant had been granted time to put his affairs in order before beginning sentence, and his obligation to present himself at date and time specified was very clear. State v. Hiatt (Ohio App. 4 Dist., 03-26-1997) 120 Ohio App.3d 247, 697 N.E.2d 1025. Bail ⚷ 97(1)

Statute providing that defendant may be released on his own recognizance and that failure to appear as required by such recognizance shall constitute an offense states indictable offense, even though it does not follow usual format of other statutory sections that define and prohibit offenses; offense is readily ascertainable from statute and statute prohibits specific conduct. State v. Pounds (Montgomery 1993) 85 Ohio App.3d 207, 619 N.E.2d 487, dismissed, jurisdictional motion overruled 66 Ohio St.3d 1494, 613 N.E.2d 237. Bail ⚷ 97(1)

Service of process on counsel of a criminal defendant constitutes notice to the defendant; thus, where a criminal defendant released on personal recognizance pending sentencing removes himself from the state and leaves no forwarding address, the defendant is properly convicted for failure to appear at the sentencing hearing. State v. Balas (Wayne 1990) 68 Ohio App.3d 524, 589 N.E.2d 86.

That a criminal penalty is only imposed upon violation of a personal recognizance bond is not a violation of equal protection since there is a rational basis for differentiating between release under personal recognizance and other release undertakings. State v Pembaur, No. C-800856 (1st Dist Ct App, Hamilton, 2-10-82), reversed on other grounds by 9 OS(3d) 136, 9 OBR 385, 459 NE(2d) 217 (1984); cert denied 467 US 1219, 104 SCt 2668, 81 LEd(2d) 373 (1984).

Before a person may be convicted for failing to appear for trial, pursuant to RC 2937.29, there must be a showing that he knew or should have known the date upon which it was to be held. State v. Glover (Franklin 1976) 52 Ohio App.2d 35, 367 N.E.2d 1202, 6 O.O.3d 20. Obstructing Justice ⚷ 6

5. "Appearance" defined

Evidence was insufficient to establish that defendant was released on his own recognizance, and thus he could not be convicted of failure to appear for trial; release on one's own recognizance required a written undertaking by a defendant that was unsecured by others on his behalf, and surety deposited $500 in cash to secure defendant's release and signed the recognizance along with defendant. State v. Fusik (Ohio App. 4 Dist., Athens, 03-08-2005) No. 04CA28, 2005-Ohio-1056, 2005 WL 567308, Unreported. Bail ⚷ 97(3)

Statute providing that offense of failure to appear for sentencing, an unclassified felony, is subject to "not less than one nor more than five years" of imprisonment requires sentencing court to impose definite, not indefinite, term of imprisonment. State v. Quisenberry (Ohio 1994) 69 Ohio St.3d 556, 634 N.E.2d 1009. Bail ⚷ 97(4)

Only court appearances are "appearances" for purposes of statute defining offense of failure to appear as required by defendant's own recognizance; pertinent provisions of chapter in which statute is found discuss bail and alternative to bail solely in context of assuring defendant's appearance before court or magistrate and consequences of failure to appear before court or magistrate. State v. Pounds (Montgomery 1993) 85 Ohio App.3d 207, 619 N.E.2d 487, dismissed, jurisdictional motion overruled 66 Ohio St.3d 1494, 613 N.E.2d 237. Bail ⚷ 97(1)

Defendant's failure to keep scheduled appointment with pretrial services, which was condition of his own recognizance, was not indictable offense under statute defining offense of failure to appear as required by own recognizance; only court appearances are "appearances" for purposes of statute. State v. Pounds (Montgomery 1993) 85 Ohio App.3d 207, 619 N.E.2d 487, dismissed, jurisdictional motion overruled 66 Ohio St.3d 1494, 613 N.E.2d 237. Bail ⚷ 97(1)

6. Bail in murder case

Courts of common pleas have jurisdiction to hear and determine, before trial on the merits, the application of a person, indicted for murder in the first degree, to be admitted to bail. State ex rel. Reams v. Stuart (Ohio 1933) 127 Ohio St. 314, 188 N.E. 393, 39 Ohio Law Rep. 651.

7. Medical reason for release

Defendant who was being held in jail after he failed to post bail failed to demonstrate that his continued confinement would result in psychiatric problems sufficient to warrant his release on his own recognizance solely for medical reasons. Gallagher v. Johnson (Ohio App. 11 Dist., 09-15-1998) 129 Ohio App.3d 775, 719 N.E.2d 60. Bail ⚷ 40

2937.30 Recognizance when accused discharged

When a defendant is discharged by the trial court otherwise than on a verdict or finding of acquittal, or when the appellate court reverses a conviction and orders the discharge of the defendant and the state or municipality signifies its intention to appeal therefrom, or the record is certified to the supreme court, the defendant shall not be discharged if he is in jail, nor the surety discharged or deposit released if the defendant is on bail, but the trial court, or the court to which appeal is taken may make order for his release on his own recognizance or bail, or recommit him.

(128 v 97, eff. 1–1–60; 1953 H 1; GC 13435–10)

Historical and Statutory Notes

Pre–1953 H 1 Amendments: 113 v 153, Ch 14, § 10

Cross References

Bail, Crim R 46

Library References

Bail ⚷54, 74.
Westlaw Topic No. 49.
C.J.S. Bail; Release and Detention Pending Proceedings §§ 3, 93 to 106, 118 to 135.

Research References

Encyclopedias

OH Jur. 3d Criminal Law § 2197, Discharge of Defendant.

OH Jur. 3d Criminal Law § 2245, Discharge of Principal.

2937.31 Recognizance or deposit for appearance of accused

If an accused is held to answer and offers sufficient bail, a recognizance or deposit shall be taken for his appearance to answer the charge before such magistrate or before such court to which proceedings may be transferred pursuant to Chapter 2937. of the Revised Code, at a date certain, or from day to day, or in case of the common pleas court on the first day of the next term thereof, and not depart without leave.

(128 v 97, eff. 1–1–60; 1953 H 1; GC 13435–11)

Historical and Statutory Notes

Pre–1953 H 1 Amendments: 113 v 153, Ch 14, § 11

Cross References

Bail, Crim R 46

Library References

Bail ⚖54.
Westlaw Topic No. 49.
C.J.S. Bail; Release and Detention Pending Proceedings §§ 3, 93 to 106.

Research References

Treatises and Practice Aids

Katz, Giannelli, Blair and Lipton, Baldwin's Ohio Practice, Criminal Law, § 139:12, Entry as to Prisoner Admitted to Bail by Examining Court.

2937.32 Confinement for unbailable offenses, when bail is denied, and lack of sufficient bail

If an offense is not bailable, if the court denies bail to the accused, or if the accused does not offer sufficient bail, the court shall order the accused to be detained.

(1999 S 8, eff. 7–29–99)

Historical and Statutory Notes

Ed. Note: Former 2937.32 repealed by 1999 S 8, eff. 7–29–99; 128 v 97, eff. 1–1–60; 1953 H 1; GC 13435–12.

Pre–1953 H 1 Amendments: 113 v 153, Ch 14, § 12

Cross References

Bail, Crim R 46
Bailable offenses, O Const Art I §9

Library References

Criminal Law ⚖241.
Westlaw Topic No. 110.
C.J.S. Criminal Law § 354.

Research References

Encyclopedias

OH Jur. 3d Criminal Law § 2168, Duty to Inform of Right to Bail; Detention Where Bail Denied, Insufficient, for Nonbailable Offense.

Treatises and Practice Aids

Katz, Giannelli, Blair and Lipton, Baldwin's Ohio Practice, Criminal Law, § 139:36, Motion to Deny Bail.

Katz, Giannelli, Blair and Lipton, Baldwin's Ohio Practice, Criminal Law, § 139:37, Order to Deny Bail.

Notes of Decisions

Ed. Note: *This section contains annotations from former RC 2937.32.*

---

1. Detention

A county sheriff may not release from the county jail a person who has not served his entire term of imprisonment unless the early release has been ordered by a court or the Governor. OAG 05–026.

Pursuant to RC 2937.32, a county sheriff may not release from the county jail a person accused of committing a criminal offense when the person does not offer sufficient bail for his release. OAG 05–026.

A county sheriff may not refuse to admit and confine in the county jail, or confine in another jail or detention facility that the county sheriff is authorized to use, a person who has been sentenced by a court to a term of imprisonment in the county jail. OAG 05–026.

A person arrested by a township law enforcement officer, deputy sheriff, or state highway patrol trooper for violating a law of this state may be confined in either a county or city jail prior to arraignment, initial appearance, or trial. Except as provided in a court order issued pursuant to RC 2937.32, a person may not be confined in a city jail unless the city permits the confinement. OAG04–024.

A person arrested by a township law enforcement officer for violating a law of this state and confined in a city jail prior to arraignment, initial appearance, or trial is in the custody of the city officials operating the jail. OAG 04–024.

Absent a contract between a county and city providing otherwise, a city is responsible for paying the booking fee and other costs of confinement when a person arrested by a township law enforcement officer, deputy sheriff, or state highway patrol trooper for violating a law of this state is confined in the city's jail prior to arraignment, initial appearance, or trial. OAG 04–024.

Absent a contract between a county and city providing otherwise, a city is responsible for paying the booking fee and other costs of confinement when a person arrested by a township law enforcement officer, deputy sheriff, or state highway patrol trooper pursuant to a bench warrant issued by a municipal court is confined in the city's jail. OAG 04–024.

City officials operating a city jail are responsible for supervising and feeding a person arrested for violating a law of this state and placed in the city jail by the county sheriff for a brief time before and after the person's appearance in a municipal court on the violation. OAG 04–024.

A county sheriff has a duty to detain in the county jail an individual arrested without a warrant by a municipal police officer for any violation of the laws of this state. OAG 95–011.

A sheriff has a duty to detain in the county jail a prisoner committed to it for failure to post bond under RC 2937.32 during the period between his commitment and trial on a state misdemeanor charge. OAG 88–060, approved and followed by OAG 95–011.

2. Detention costs

The state highway patrol is not required to pay for the cost of the medical treatment provided to individuals arrested by its troopers and incarcerated, pursuant to RC 2937.32, in a regional jail facility established under RC 307.93. OAG 91–047.

Where a township police constable arrests a person for violation of a state statute, and said person is confined in a municipal jail pending trial, the township which said police constable serves is not liable for the cost of confinement. 1962 OAG 3405.

2937.33 Receipt of recognizance

When a transcript or recognizance is received by the clerk of the court of common pleas, or of any court of record to which proceedings are transferred, he shall enter the same upon the appearance docket of the court, with the date of the filing of such transcript or recognizance, the date and amount of the recognizance, the names of the sureties, and the costs. Such recognizance is then of record in such court, and is proceeded on by process issuing therefrom, in a like manner as if it had been entered into before such court. When a court having recognizance of an offense takes a recognizance, it is a sufficient record thereof to enter upon the journal of such court the title of the case, the crime charged, the names of the sureties, the amount of the recognizance, and the time therein required for the appearance of the accused. In making the complete record, when required to be made, recognizances whether returned to or taken in such court shall be recorded in full, if required by the prosecutor or the accused.

(128 v 97, eff. 1–1–60; 1953 H 1; GC 13435–13)

Historical and Statutory Notes

Pre–1953 H 1 Amendments: 113 v 153, Ch 14, § 13

Cross References

Bail, Crim R 46

Library References

Bail ⚬54.
Westlaw Topic No. 49.

C.J.S. Bail; Release and Detention Pending Proceedings §§ 3, 93 to 106.

Research References

Encyclopedias

OH Jur. 3d Courts & Judges § 207, Dockets.

OH Jur. 3d Criminal Law § 2224, Recordation, Filing, and Transmittal.

Treatises and Practice Aids

Katz, Giannelli, Blair and Lipton, Baldwin's Ohio Practice, Criminal Law, § 139:6, Entry for Recognizance of Witnesses—Upon Application of Prosecuting Attorney.

Katz, Giannelli, Blair and Lipton, Baldwin's Ohio Practice, Criminal Law, § 139:14, Entry of Record of Recognizance.

2937.34 Accused unlawfully detained; examining court to be held

When a person is committed to jail, charged with an offense for which he has not been indicted, and claims to be unlawfully detained, the sheriff on demand of the accused or his counsel shall forthwith notify the court of common pleas, and the prosecuting attorney, to attend an examining court, the time of which shall be fixed by the judge. The judge shall hear said cause or complaint, examine the witnesses, and make such order as the justice of the case requires, and for such purpose the court may admit to bail, release without bond, or recommit to jail in accordance with the commitment. In the absence of the judge of the court of common pleas, the probate judge shall hold such examining court.

(1953 H 1, eff. 10–1–53; GC 13435–14)

Historical and Statutory Notes

Pre–1953 H 1 Amendments: 114 v 479; 113 v 154, Ch 14, § 14

Cross References

Dereliction of duty, 2921.44

Habeas corpus, Ch 2725

Interfering with civil rights, 2921.45

Prisoners held without process, 2935.16

Library References

Bail ⚬49.
Westlaw Topic No. 49.

C.J.S. Bail; Release and Detention Pending Proceedings §§ 11, 18, 24, 54 to 64.

Research References

Encyclopedias

OH Jur. 3d Courts & Judges § 67, Miscellaneous Powers and Functions of Probate Judge.

OH Jur. 3d Criminal Law § 2051, Preliminary Examination of Person Alleged to be Unlawfully Detained.

OH Jur. 3d Criminal Law § 2175, Court of Common Pleas.

Forms

Ohio Jurisprudence Pleading and Practice Forms § 2:24, Powers and Duties Via Particular Courts—Probate Division.

Notes of Decisions

1. Duty of examining court

Inmate's failing to support his mandamus complaint with affidavit specifying the details of his claim, as was required by local court rule, warranted dismissal of complaint. Barber v. McFaul (Ohio App. 8 Dist., Cuyahoga, 12-19-2003) No. 83448, 2003-Ohio-6948, 2003 WL 22991164, Unreported. Mandamus ⚬ 155(1)

Inmate's failing to aver whether information was issued against him, thus precluding need for an indictment, or whether there was some other reason to hold him, such as a parole violation, and to specify dates at issue, so as to provide firm basis for determining merits of his claim, warranted dismissal of mandamus action which sought to compel sheriff to notify common pleas court to hold an examining court to determine whether inmate was unlawfully detained; without such information Court of Appeals was prevented from resolving its doubts as to whether mandamus should issue, and mandamus should not issue in doubtful cases. Barber v. McFaul (Ohio App. 8 Dist., Cuyahoga, 12-19-2003) No. 83448, 2003-Ohio-6948, 2003 WL 22991164, Unreported. Mandamus ⚷ 154(3)

The examining court no longer has power to discharge a prisoner from accountability on the charge for which he is held but may, as the justice of the case requires, order him released with or without bond, or order him recommitted to jail in accordance with the commitment for which he was imprisoned; it has no authority to examine into probable cause. State ex rel. Justice v. Rone (Auglaize 1972) 33 Ohio App.2d 1, 291 N.E.2d 754, 62 O.O.2d 1. Criminal Law ⚷ 239; Criminal Law ⚷ 241

Examining court proceedings pursuant to RC 2937.34 constitute a method for determining whether a prisoner who has not been indicted shall be released, with or without bail bond, pending further proceedings against him. State ex rel. Justice v. Rone (Auglaize 1972) 33 Ohio App.2d 1, 291 N.E.2d 754, 62 O.O.2d 1.

2. Preliminary examination

A preliminary examination is not required where there is an indictment on the charge for which defendant was arrested. State v. Wilkinson (Ohio 1969) 17 Ohio St.2d 9, 244 N.E.2d 480, 46 O.O.2d 114, certiorari denied 89 S.Ct. 2020, 395 U.S. 946, 23 L.Ed.2d 465.

2937.35 Forfeit of bail

Upon the failure of the accused or witness to appear in accordance with its terms the bail may in open court be adjudged forfeit, in whole or in part by the court or magistrate before whom he is to appear. But such court or magistrate may, in its discretion, continue the cause to a later date certain, giving notice of such date to him and the bail depositor or sureties, and adjudge the bail forfeit upon failure to appear at such later date.

(128 v 97, eff. 1–1–60)

Historical and Statutory Notes

Ed. Note: 2937.35 contains provisions analogous to former 2937.38, repealed by 128 v 97, eff. 1–1–60.

Ed. Note: Former 2937.35 repealed by 128 v 97, eff. 1–1–60; 1953 H 1; GC 13435–15.

Pre–1953 H 1 Amendments: 113 v 154, Ch 14, § 15

Cross References

Additional costs in criminal cases in all courts to fund reparations payments; bail, defined, 2743.70

Bail, Crim R 46

Library References

Bail ⚷75.

Westlaw Topic No. 49.

C.J.S. Bail; Release and Detention Pending Proceedings §§ 140 to 156, 158 to 159.

Research References

Treatises and Practice Aids

Katz, Giannelli, Blair and Lipton, Baldwin's Ohio Practice, Criminal Law, § 37:15, Sanctions and Forfeiture.

Katz, Giannelli, Blair and Lipton, Baldwin's Ohio Practice, Criminal Law, § 139:15, Forfeiture of Recognizance.

Katz, Giannelli, Blair and Lipton, Baldwin's Ohio Practice, Criminal Law, § 139:16, Entry for Recognizance Forfeited.

Katz, Giannelli, Blair and Lipton, Baldwin's Ohio Practice, Criminal Law, § 139:17, Notice to Defendant Upon Forfeiture of Bond.

Katz, Giannelli, Blair and Lipton, Baldwin's Ohio Practice, Criminal Law, § 139:18, Notice to Surety Upon Forfeiture.

Katz, Giannelli, Blair and Lipton, Baldwin's Ohio Practice, Criminal Law, § 139:19, Entry of Judgment Against Surety.

Hennenberg & Reinhart, Ohio Criminal Defense Motions F 4.04, Motion to Reinstate Appearance Bond-Administrative Motions.

Hennenberg & Reinhart, Ohio Criminal Defense Motions F 15.14, Motion for Remission of Forfeiture-Surety's Motion-Return of Bond Ordered Forfeited.

Notes of Decisions

Ed. Note: This section contains annotations from former RC 2937.28 and 2937.38.

---

1. Forfeiture proceedings; grounds

Trial court's order denying bail bond surety's motion for remittitur of bond forfeiture was necessarily arbitrary, having been entered without any consideration as to the ultimate appearance of defendant as grounds for recompensation, the State's inconvenience and delay, the expense involved, the willfulness of the violation, or any other mitigating circumstances; even though surety was primarily responsible for defendant's apprehension, the trial court denied request for remittitur, finding that surety "assumed the risk" due to the nature of its business. State v. Delgado (Ohio App. 2 Dist., Clark, 01-09-2004) No. 2003-CA-28, 2004-Ohio-69, 2004 WL 41404, Unreported. Bail ⚷ 79(1)

A person other than defendant, who allegedly actually posted the cash bail bond to secure defendant's appearance at trial, was not entitled to notice and a hearing prior to execution of bail bond forfeiture. City of Xenia v. Diaz (Ohio App. 2 Dist., Greene, 12-19-2003) No. 2003-CA-25, 2003-Ohio-6894, 2003 WL 22972039, Unreported. Bail ⚷ 77(1)

Notice and a hearing prior to execution of bail bond forfeiture were not required, where the bail was posted in cash, as a cash bond, to secure defendant's appearance at trial. City of Xenia v. Diaz (Ohio App. 2 Dist., Greene, 12-19-2003) No. 2003-CA-25, 2003-Ohio-6894, 2003 WL 22972039, Unreported. Bail ⚷ 77(1)

Trial court's forfeiture of defendant's bail bond for his failure to appear at trial in which he was accused of driving under suspension and failure to signal lane change was not final and appealable order, and thus, Court of Appeals lacked jurisdiction to review order on appeal. State v. Stuber (Ohio App. 3 Dist., Hancock, 06-10-2003) No. 5-02-49, 2003-Ohio-2938, 2003 WL 21316231, Unreported. Criminal Law ⚷ 1023(3)

Trial court erroneously ordered clerk of court to not accept bonds from either surety or its agent until surety paid its judgment on bail bond forfeiture, where court erred in forfeiting surety's bond without following requisite statutory procedures. State v. Green (Ohio App. 9 Dist., Wayne, 10-23-2002) No. 02CA0014, No. 02CA0019, 2002-Ohio-5769, 2002 WL 31386775, Unreported. Bail ⚷ 77(1)

Trial court erroneously failed to follow statutory procedure for bail bond forfeiture, where court only gave surety and agent five days notice to produce defendant in court and court did not provide any date in its letter for a show cause hearing for surety and agent. State v. Green (Ohio App. 9 Dist., Wayne, 10-23-2002) No. 02CA0014, No. 02CA0019, 2002-Ohio-5769, 2002 WL 31386775, Unreported. Bail ⚷ 77(1)

Trial court has statutory authority to order forfeiture of bail upon violation of a condition of bond even where no failure to appear has occurred. State v. McLaughlin (Ohio App. 10 Dist., 08-26-1997) 122 Ohio App.3d 418, 701 N.E.2d 1048. Bail ⚷ 75.1; Bail ⚷ 75.2(1)

Trial court acted within its statutory authority in ordering forfeiture of defendant's appearance bond based on his failure to comply with the bond condition that he have "no contact" with victim. State v. McLaughlin (Ohio App. 10 Dist., 08-26-1997) 122 Ohio App.3d 418, 701 N.E.2d 1048. Bail ⚷ 75.1

Summary judgment may not be taken in a civil action by a city for forfeiture of a bail bond, and the defendant surety must be given an opportunity to defend the action. City of Cleveland v. Loviness (Cuyahoga 1955) 125 N.E.2d 890, 71 Ohio Law Abs. 105.

Where a prisoner was released upon a deposit of a sum of money by his attorney, and does not appear upon the date set for trial, the court has authority to forfeit the bond although the attorney appears and a week later both the attorney and defendant appear. State v. Wilson (Ohio Mun. 1950) 115 N.E.2d 193, 65 Ohio Law Abs. 422.

The fact that a defendant is in jail on another charge when he is scheduled to appear is no defense to a forfeiture of bail under RC 2937.35. State v Laguta, No. CA 12921 (9th Dist Ct App, Summit, 6–10–87).

2. Disposition of proceeds

Where there is a bail forfeiture in a case involving an arrest by a state highway patrolman, the magistrate or clerk of the court adjudging forfeiture may satisfy the amount of the accrued costs in the case out of the amount of bail before paying the moneys arising from the forfeiture as directed in RC 5503.04. 1960 OAG 1466.

A bail forfeiture in a case arising under RC 1531.01 to RC 1531.26 and RC 1533.01 to RC 1533.69 unless otherwise directed by the director of natural resources should be paid to the director, except that the magistrate or clerk of the court adjudging forfeiture may satisfy the amount of the accrued costs in the case out of the amount of bail before paying the forfeiture to the director. 1960 OAG 1372.

3. Issuance of capias

Although Ohio law provides procedures for bringing a person before the court after a failure to appear when released on a form of bail other than a release on personal recognizance pursuant to RC 2937.29, there is no authority to arrest such person for a separate offense of failure to appear similar to that provided in RC 2937.43 or to impose penalties analogous to those set forth in RC 2937.99. When a person has been released on a form of bail other than a release on personal recognizance, the court is limited to the forfeiture of bail proceedings set forth in RC 2937.35 to RC 2937.39 as punishment for the failure to appear, but a writ of capias may be issued to secure that person's appearance. OAG 87–016.

Where a person arrested by a highway patrolman under authority of RC 2935.03 posts bond in a municipal court for his appearance for trial at a later date, but does not appear on the date specified and the judge issues a warrant for his arrest and requests the highway patrolman to serve the warrant, the highway patrolman has a duty to serve the warrant as requested. 1961 OAG 2214.

2937.36 Forfeiture proceedings

Upon declaration of forfeiture, the magistrate or clerk of the court adjudging forfeiture shall proceed as follows:

(A) As to each bail, he shall proceed forthwith to deal with the sum deposited as if the same were imposed as a fine for the offense charged and distribute and account for the same accordingly provided that prior to so doing, he may satisfy accrued costs in the case out of the fund.

(B) As to any securities deposited, he shall proceed to sell the same, either at public sale advertised in the same manner as sale on chattel execution, or through any state or national bank performing such service upon the over the counter securities market and shall apply proceeds of sale, less costs or brokerage thereof as in cases of forfeited cash bail. Prior to such sale, the clerk shall give notices by ordinary mail to the depositor, at his address listed of record, if any, of his intention so to do, and such sale shall not proceed if the depositor, within ten days of mailing of such notice appears, and redeems said securities by either producing the body of the defendant in open court or posting the amount set in the recognizance in cash, to be dealt with as forfeited cash bail.

(C) As to recognizances he shall notify accused and each surety by ordinary mail at the address shown by them in their affidavits of qualification or on the record of the case, of the default of the accused and the adjudication of forfeiture and require each of them to show cause on or before a date certain to be stated in the notice, and which shall be not less than twenty nor more than thirty days from date of mailing notice, why judgment should not be entered against each of them for the penalty stated in the recognizance. If good cause by production of the body of the accused or otherwise is not shown, the court or magistrate shall thereupon enter judgment against the sureties or either of them, so notified, in such amount, not exceeding the penalty of the bond, as has been set in the adjudication of forfeiture, and shall award execution therefor as in civil cases. The proceeds of sale shall be received by the clerk or magistrate and distributed as on forfeiture of cash bail.

(128 v 97, eff. 1–1–60)

Historical and Statutory Notes

Ed. Note: 2937.36 contains provisions analogous to former 2937.38, repealed by 128 v 97, eff. 1–1–60.

Ed. Note: Former 2937.36 repealed by 128 v 97, eff. 1–1–60; 1953 H 1; GC 13435–16; see now 2937.40 for provisions analogous to former 2937.36.

Pre–1953 H 1 Amendments: 113 v 154, Ch 14, § 16

Cross References

Additional costs in criminal cases in all courts to fund reparations payments; bail, defined, 2743.70

Bail, Crim R 46

Library References

Bail ⚷77.
Westlaw Topic No. 49.

C.J.S. Bail; Release and Detention Pending Proceedings §§ 156, 160 to 163.

Research References

Encyclopedias

OH Jur. 3d Criminal Law § 2235, Forfeiture Proceedings; Generally.

OH Jur. 3d Criminal Law § 2236, Securities.

OH Jur. 3d Criminal Law § 2237, Recognizances.

OH Jur. 3d Criminal Law § 2239, Notice of Forfeiture.

OH Jur. 3d Criminal Law § 2240, Disposition of Securities Deposited.

OH Jur. 3d Criminal Law § 2242, Requirement of Good Cause.

OH Jur. 3d Criminal Law § 2243, Production or Arrest of Principal.

Treatises and Practice Aids

Katz, Giannelli, Blair and Lipton, Baldwin's Ohio Practice, Criminal Law, § 37:18, Financial Responsibility of Sureties.

Katz, Giannelli, Blair and Lipton, Baldwin's Ohio Practice, Criminal Law, § 139:16, Entry for Recognizance Forfeited.

Katz, Giannelli, Blair and Lipton, Baldwin's Ohio Practice, Criminal Law, § 139:17, Notice to Defendant Upon Forfeiture of Bond.

Katz, Giannelli, Blair and Lipton, Baldwin's Ohio Practice, Criminal Law, § 139:18, Notice to Surety Upon Forfeiture.

Katz, Giannelli, Blair and Lipton, Baldwin's Ohio Practice, Criminal Law, § 139:19, Entry of Judgment Against Surety.

Katz, Giannelli, Blair and Lipton, Baldwin's Ohio Practice, Criminal Law, § 139:33, Motion to Exonerate Recognizance—Death of Defendant (Principal).

Katz, Giannelli, Blair and Lipton, Baldwin's Ohio Practice, Criminal Law, § 139:34, Motion to Exonerate Recognizance—Imprisonment of Defendant (Principal).

Katz, Giannelli, Blair and Lipton, Baldwin's Ohio Practice, Criminal Law, § 139:35, Motion to Extend Time to Surrender Defendant (Principal).

Notes of Decisions

Ed. Note: This section contains annotations from former RC 2937.38, 2937.41 and 2937.43.

1. Forfeiture proceedings; grounds

Presentence releasee's presence in court at show cause hearing, at time specified in notice of default and adjudication of forfeiture, constituted showing of good cause why judgment of partial forfeiture could not be entered against surety. State v. Sheldon (Ohio App. 6 Dist., Wood, 05-27-2005) No. WD-04-055, 2005-Ohio-2686, 2005 WL 1283681, Unreported. Bail ⚩ 75.2(1)

Trial court's order denying bail bond surety's motion for remittitur of bond forfeiture was necessarily arbitrary, having been entered without any consideration as to the ultimate appearance of defendant as grounds for recompensation, the State's inconvenience and delay, the expense involved, the willfulness of the violation, or any other mitigating circumstances; even though surety was primarily responsible for defendant's apprehension, the trial court denied request for remittitur, finding that surety "assumed the risk" due to the nature of its business. State v. Delgado (Ohio App. 2 Dist., Clark, 01-09-2004) No. 2003-CA-28, 2004-Ohio-69, 2004 WL 41404, Unreported. Bail ⚩ 79(1)

Notice and a hearing prior to execution of bail bond forfeiture were not required, where the bail was posted in cash, as a cash bond, to secure defendant's appearance at trial. City of Xenia v. Diaz (Ohio App. 2 Dist., Greene, 12-19-2003) No. 2003-CA-25, 2003-Ohio-6894, 2003 WL 22972039, Unreported. Bail ⚩ 77(1)

A person other than defendant, who allegedly actually posted the cash bail bond to secure defendant's appearance at trial, was not entitled to notice and a hearing prior to execution of bail bond forfeiture. City of Xenia v. Diaz (Ohio App. 2 Dist., Greene, 12-19-2003) No. 2003-CA-25, 2003-Ohio-6894, 2003 WL 22972039, Unreported. Bail ⚩ 77(1)

Trial court erred in refusing to vacate forfeiture of defendant's $4,000 cash appearance bond, where court failed to promptly enforce forfeiture statute by finalizing adjudication of forfeiture within 20 to 30 days, court had vacated a previous bond forfeiture upon receiving notice that defendant was incarcerated on federal charges, thereafter, without notice to defendant, court unilaterally forfeited bond without hearing even though court was apprised of defendant's incarceration, and all charges pending against defendant were dismissed in the interest of justice on grounds that charges had been pending for a great deal of time, yet trial court failed to notice any type of bond revocation hearing. City of Euclid v. Fullerton (Ohio App. 8 Dist., Cuyahoga, 10-24-2002) No. 81137, 2002-Ohio-5863, 2002 WL 31402005, Unreported. Bail ⚩ 79(1)

Trial court erroneously failed to follow statutory procedure for bail bond forfeiture, where court only gave surety and agent five days notice to produce defendant in court and court did not provide any date in its letter for a show cause hearing for surety and agent. State v. Green (Ohio App. 9 Dist., Wayne, 10-23-2002) No. 02CA0014, No. 02CA0019, 2002-Ohio-5769, 2002 WL 31386775, Unreported. Bail ⚩ 77(1)

Trial court erroneously ordered clerk of court to not accept bonds from either surety or its agent until surety paid its judgment on bail bond forfeiture, where court erred in forfeiting surety's bond without following requisite statutory procedures. State v. Green (Ohio App. 9 Dist., Wayne, 10-23-2002) No. 02CA0014, No. 02CA0019, 2002-Ohio-5769, 2002 WL 31386775, Unreported. Bail ⚷ 77(1)

Surety that agrees to pay a penalty if the accused fails to appear in court is on notice of fact that person in jeopardy of loss of liberty or property has some inducement to flee a jurisdiction that might impose those penalties for a crime of which the person stands accused, and inducement to flee is even greater when accused has been convicted and awaits imposition of a sentence. State v. Scherer (Ohio App. 2 Dist., 12-20-1995) 108 Ohio App.3d 586, 671 N.E.2d 545. Bail ⚷ 75.2(1)

The only method by which recovery can be obtained on a recognizance forfeited in a criminal action is that provided by RC 2937.36, which is a continuing process in the criminal action, and a judgment rendered by a court on a forfeited recognizance by civil action in a criminal proceeding is void for want of jurisdiction of the subject matter, so that neither the payment of such judgment nor the consent to its rendition by the defendant can vest such court with such jurisdiction. City of Cleveland v. Young (Cuyahoga 1963) 119 Ohio App. 19, 190 N.E.2d 42, 26 O.O.2d 102.

Where a prisoner was released upon a deposit of a sum of money by his attorney, and does not appear upon the date set for trial, the court has authority to forfeit the bond although the attorney appears and a week later both the attorney and defendant appear. State v. Wilson (Ohio Mun. 1950) 115 N.E.2d 193, 65 Ohio Law Abs. 422.

Although Ohio law provides procedures for bringing a person before the court after a failure to appear when released on a form of bail other than a release on personal recognizance pursuant to RC 2937.29, there is no authority to arrest such person for a separate offense of failure to appear similar to that provided in RC 2937.43 or to impose penalties analogous to those set forth in RC 2937.99. When a person has been released on a form of bail other than a release on personal recognizance, the court is limited to the forfeiture of bail proceedings set forth in RC 2937.35 to RC 2937.39 as punishment for the failure to appear, but a writ of capias may be issued to secure that person's appearance. OAG 87-016.

2. Defenses

In determining whether a surety has shown good cause for being excused from performing on its bond, the object of that bond must be kept in mind, which is accused's appearance in court, not his good behavior, and surety is obligated to pay the bond amount as a penalty for the defendant's nonappearance, not as a penalty for his bad acts; defendant's bad acts, though possibly foreseeable to the surety, do not themselves trigger the surety's duty to pay a penalty in the amount of its bond. State v. Scherer (Ohio App. 2 Dist., 12-20-1995) 108 Ohio App.3d 586, 671 N.E.2d 545. Bail ⚷ 75.1; Bail ⚷ 75.2(3)

Surety may be excused from its duty to pay the penalty for accused's nonappearance in court by demonstrating good cause why judgment should not be entered against the surety in the amount of its bond, and that showing may consist of producing the body of the accused, or otherwise. State v. Scherer (Ohio App. 2 Dist., 12-20-1995) 108 Ohio App.3d 586, 671 N.E.2d 545. Bail ⚷ 75.2(3)

While a defendant remains incarcerated in one state, a surety who is obligated on a bail bond that obtained the defendant's release in another state may be excused from paying the penalty the bond requires under impossibility of performance for defendant's nonappearance because the object of the surety's promise, the defendant's appearance, is forbidden by law; however, the surety must demonstrate that the condition that rendered defendant's appearance impossible was also unforeseeable prior to its occurrence. State v. Scherer (Ohio App. 2 Dist., 12-20-1995) 108 Ohio App.3d 586, 671 N.E.2d 545. Bail ⚷ 75.2(3)

In determining whether bond surety should be excused from producing accused's appearance at court based on accused's incarceration in another state, whether an event is foreseeable is a question of fact to be determined from all the relevant facts and circumstances. State v. Scherer (Ohio App. 2 Dist., 12-20-1995) 108 Ohio App.3d 586, 671 N.E.2d 545. Bail ⚷ 75.2(3)

When accused cannot appear before court because he is incarcerated in another jurisdiction, a surety who seeks to avoid the penalty for accused's nonappearance must demonstrate that the incarceration was not foreseeable to the surety or preventable by it. State v. Scherer (Ohio App. 2 Dist., 12-20-1995) 108 Ohio App.3d 586, 671 N.E.2d 545. Bail ⚷ 75.2(3)

Sureties demonstrated "good cause" for being excused from performing on their bond to ensure accused's presence where he was incarcerated in nearby state, where his inability to appear did not proximately result from any fault of sureties as his travel to nearby state was requirement of charging court, and where sureties diligently sought his return; fact that defendant's detention in nearby state resulted from his own misconduct was of no consequence to the obligations of sureties. State v. Scherer (Ohio App. 2 Dist., 12-20-1995) 108 Ohio App.3d 586, 671 N.E.2d 545. Bail ⚷ 75.2(3)

Accused's imprisonment in nearby state and that state's refusal to return him to charging state constituted "good cause" for the surety's failure to perform on its promise to produce defendant in charging court and prevented forfeiture of bond and entry of judgment against surety; surety's liability on bond should be suspended until defendant is released from imprisonment in nearby state. State v. Scherer (Ohio App. 2 Dist., 12-20-1995) 108 Ohio App.3d 586, 671 N.E.2d 545. Bail ⚷ 75.2(3)

Sureties were not exonerated from liability on bail bond by act-of-law defense, though sureties had located defendant after he fled from jurisdiction and procured his arrest and incarceration in foreign state, where sureties had not appeared at extradition hearing, foreign court had released defendant on extradition bond, and defendant had again fled. State v. Hughes (Ohio 1986) 27 Ohio St.3d 19, 501 N.E.2d 622, 27 O.B.R. 437. Bail ⚷ 74(1)

In forfeiture proceedings pursuant to RC 2937.36, a court errs in entering judgment against the surety where the surety has established good cause for its failure to produce the defendant by showing that such defendant is incarcerated in another county's jail. State v. Smith (Wayne 1984) 14 Ohio App.3d 14, 469 N.E.2d 945, 14 O.B.R. 17. Bail ⚷ 75.2(3)

In a bond forfeiture proceeding, the surety has an insufficient defense where the defendant voluntarily fled the country before his initial court appearance date, notwithstanding the fact that the defendant cannot be brought back into the country because of foreign policy decisions. State v. Ohayon (Cuyahoga 1983) 12 Ohio App.3d 162, 467 N.E.2d 908, 12 O.B.R. 486.

A three-month delay in notifying the surety of failure of its principal to appear in court is not good cause for not entering judgment against the surety and for giving an extension of time to produce the principal. State v. Ward (Ohio 1978) 53 Ohio St.2d 40, 372 N.E.2d 586, 7 O.O.3d 124.

Summary judgment may not be taken in a civil action by a city for forfeiture of a bail bond, and the defendant surety must be given an opportunity to defend the action. City of Cleveland v. Loviness (Cuyahoga 1955) 125 N.E.2d 890, 71 Ohio Law Abs. 105.

3. Disposition of proceeds

Court costs and additional fees may not be deducted from the gross amount of fines and moneys to be distributed under RC 5503.04, except that when there is a forfeiture of bail, a court adjudging forfeiture may, pursuant to RC 2937.36, deduct accrued costs from the amount of bail prior to distribution of the bail proceeds under RC 5503.04. OAG 87–023.

When a bail bond posted in a municipal court in connection with a charge of assault and battery under RC 2901.25 is ordered forfeited by the court, such bail bond is subject to RC 1901.31(F) and RC 2937.36, and required to be distributed to the county treasury after deduction of the municipal court costs. 1964 OAG 1410.

When a recognizance bond posted in a municipal court under RC 2947.16 is ordered forfeited by the court, such recognizance bond is subject to RC 1901.31(F) and RC 2937.36, and required to be distributed to the county treasurer after deduction of municipal court costs. 1964 OAG 1410.

In cases involving a violation of a state statute, other than traffic laws, and in the absence of any statutory provision for a specific distribution of the fine, bail or other money held by the clerk of municipal court, such fine or bail should be distributed in accordance with RC 2937.36 and RC 1901.31(F). 1964 OAG 1410.

When a bail bond is posted in connection with a charge of burglary under RC 2907.15 which does not prescribe a fine as a part of the sentence, and it is ordered forfeited by the municipal court, such bail bond is subject to RC 1901.31(F) and RC 2937.36. 1964 OAG 1410.

Money collected by a clerk of a municipal court from a bail bond forfeiture under RC 4511.01 to RC 4511.78, RC 4511.99, and RC 4513.01 to RC 4513.37, inclusive where the arrest was not made by a state highway patrolman, should be distributed as provided in RC 1901.31 and RC 4513.35, as if the amount of the forfeiture were imposed as a fine for the offense charged, except that the clerk may satisfy the amount of the accrued costs in the case out of the amount of the bail before making such distribution. 1962 OAG 3241.

4. Remission of forfeiture

On consolidated appeal from denial of bail bonding company's motions in separate proceedings for remission of forfeited bond, it was not necessary for company to include transcripts of bond forfeiture hearings, where issue in cases was not whether bond should have been forfeited, but whether any portion of forfeited bond should be remitted. State of Ohio v. Rich (Ohio App. 6 Dist., Lucas, 10-22-2004) No. L-04-1102, No. L-04-1103, 2004-Ohio-5678, 2004 WL 2390085, Unreported. Bail ⚷ 79(2)

Thirty-day time period in which bail bonding company had to file notice of appeal challenging denial of its motions in separate proceedings for remission of forfeited bond began to run when sentencing entries for defendants, for whom company posted bond, were journalized. State of Ohio v. Rich (Ohio App. 6 Dist., Lucas, 10-22-2004) No. L-04-1102, No. L-04-1103, 2004-Ohio-5678, 2004 WL 2390085, Unreported. Bail ⚷ 79(2)

On consolidated appeal, bail bonding company could challenge factual findings trial court made in denying company's first motions in separate proceedings for remission of forfeited bond, despite fact that company indicated in notices of appeal that orders it was appealing were trial court's judgment entries in separate proceedings denying company's second motions for remission, where judgment entries denying company's first motions for remission were attached to notices of appeal and trial court referenced and incorporated its earlier decisions when it issued judgment entries denying second motions. State of Ohio v. Rich (Ohio App. 6 Dist., Lucas, 10-22-2004) No. L-04-1102, No. L-04-1103, 2004-Ohio-5678, 2004 WL 2390085, Unreported. Bail ⚷ 79(2)

In a bail forfeiture proceeding, where the trial court fails to consider exonerating factors, such as the lack of willful violation and the ultimate appearance of the defendant before the court, the denial of remission of bail will be reversed. State v. Patton (Lucas 1989) 60 Ohio App.3d 99, 573 N.E.2d 1201.

Pursuant to RC 2937.36(C), production of the body of the defendant on the date or dates specified in the notice of default and adjudication of forfeiture constitutes a showing of good cause why judgment should not be entered against each surety of the defendant. State v. Holmes (Ohio 1991) 57 Ohio St.3d 11, 564 N.E.2d 1066. Bail ⟹ 75.2(1)

A judgment entry constitutes sufficient notice of continuation of a bail bond to a surety, and a subsequent forfeiture under RC 2937.36 is valid. State v. Stevens (Ohio 1987) 30 Ohio St.3d 25, 505 N.E.2d 972, 30 O.B.R. 30.

When a judgment has been entered on a forfeited recognizance and the sureties make payment in satisfaction of said judgment, and thereafter the court remits or reduces the judgment, in whole or in part, the surety who made the payment has a collectible claim against the county for the difference between the amount he paid and the amount of the judgment as modified by the court. 1959 OAG 43.

A court which renders judgment on a forfeited recognizance in a criminal case may remit the whole or part of such judgment at any time even though the recognizance has been returned to the county auditor. 1958 OAG 2684.

5. Voided bonds

A bondsman can properly rely on the representations of employees of the clerk's office that a bond is void due to a municipal court judge's action in telephoning the clerk's office to raise the bond from $50,000 to $250,000, despite the bondsman's knowledge of established clerk's office procedure. State v. Marte (Ohio App. 8 Dist., Cuyahoga, 05-23-1996) No. 69587, 1996 WL 273800, Unreported.

2937.37 Levy on property in judgment against surety

A magistrate or court of record inferior to the court of common pleas may proceed to judgment against a surety on a recognizance, and levy on his personal property, notwithstanding that the bond may exceed the monetary limitations on the jurisdiction of such court in civil cases, and jurisdiction over the person of surety shall attach from the mailing of the notice specified in section 2937.36 of the Revised Code, notwithstanding that such surety may not be within the territorial jurisdiction of the court; but levy on real property shall be made only through issuance, return, and levy made under certificate of judgment issued to the clerk of the court of common pleas pursuant to section 2329.02 of the Revised Code.

(128 v 97, eff. 1–1–60)

Historical and Statutory Notes

Ed. Note: 2937.37 contains provisions analogous to former 2937.38, repealed by 128 v 97, eff. 1–1–60.

Ed. Note: Former 2937.37 repealed by 128 v 97, eff. 1–1–60; 1953 H 1; GC 13435–17.

Pre–1953 H 1 Amendments: 113 v 155, Ch 14, § 17

Cross References

Bail, Crim R 46

Library References

Bail ⟹77, 93.
Westlaw Topic No. 49.
C.J.S. Bail; Release and Detention Pending Proceedings §§ 156, 160 to 163, 179, 187.

2937.38 Minority no defense in forfeiture proceedings

In any matter in which a minor is admitted to bail pursuant to Chapter 2937. of the Revised Code, the minority of the accused shall not be available as a defense to judgment against principal or surety, or against the sale of securities or transfer of cash bail, upon forfeiture.

(128 v 97, eff. 1–1–60)

Historical and Statutory Notes

Ed. Note: Former 2937.38 repealed by 128 v 97, eff. 1–1–60; 1953 H 1; GC 13435–18; see now 2937.35, 2937.36, and 2937.37 for provisions analogous to former 2937.38.

Pre–1953 H 1 Amendments: 113 v 155, Ch 14, § 18

Cross References

Bail, Crim R 46

Library References

Bail ⟹79(1).
Westlaw Topic No. 49.

C.J.S. Bail; Release and Detention Pending Proceedings §§ 167 to 170.

Notes of Decisions

Forfeiture proceedings 1

1. Forfeiture proceedings

The only method by which recovery can be obtained on a recognizance forfeited in a criminal action is that provided by RC 2937.36, which is a continuing process in the criminal action, and a judgment rendered by a court on a forfeited recognizance by civil action in a criminal proceeding is void for want of jurisdiction of the subject matter, so that neither the payment of such judgment nor the consent to its rendition by the defendant can vest such court with such jurisdiction. City of Cleveland v. Young (Cuyahoga 1963) 119 Ohio App. 19, 190 N.E.2d 42, 26 O.O.2d 102.

2937.39 Remission of penalty

After judgment has been rendered against surety or after securities sold or cash bail applied, the court or magistrate, on the appearance, surrender, or re-arrest of the accused on the charge, may remit all or such portion of the penalty as it deems just and in the case of previous application and transfer of cash or proceeds, the magistrate or clerk may deduct an amount equal to the amount so transferred from subsequent payments to the agencies receiving such proceeds of forfeiture until the amount is recouped for the benefit of the person or persons entitled thereto under order or remission.

(128 v 97, eff. 1–1–60)

Historical and Statutory Notes

Ed. Note: 2937.39 contains provisions analogous to former 2937.43, repealed by 128 v 97, eff. 1–1–60.

Ed. Note: Former 2937.39 repealed by 128 v 97, eff. 1–1–60; 1953 H 1; GC 13435–19.

Pre–1953 H 1 Amendments: 113 v 155, Ch 14, § 19

Cross References

Bail, Crim R 46

Library References

Bail ⟹78.
Westlaw Topic No. 49.

C.J.S. Bail; Release and Detention Pending Proceedings §§ 136, 167 to 175.

Research References

Encyclopedias

OH Jur. 3d Criminal Law § 2246, Remission of Forfeiture of Bail.

Treatises and Practice Aids

Katz, Giannelli, Blair and Lipton, Baldwin's Ohio Practice, Criminal Law, § 37:18, Financial Responsibility of Sureties.

Hennenberg & Reinhart, Ohio Criminal Defense Motions F 4.04, Motion to Reinstate Appearance Bond-Administrative Motions.

Hennenberg & Reinhart, Ohio Criminal Defense Motions F 15.14, Motion for Remission of Forfeiture-Surety's Motion-Return of Bond Ordered Forfeited.

Notes of Decisions

Ed. Note: *This section contains annotations from former RC 2937.38 and 2937.43.*

Constitutional issues 1
Judicial discretion 2
Remission; refund to surety 3

1. Constitutional issues

Trial court's failure to hold evidentiary hearing on surety's motion for remission of forfeited bond did not violate substantive due process, where surety did not request a hearing and did not present trial court with anything other than that criminal defendants had reappeared and that their cases had concluded. State v. Hardin (Ohio App. 6 Dist., Lucas, 12-31-2003) No. L-03-1131, No. L-03-1132, No. L-03-1133, 2003-Ohio-7263, 2003 WL

23167301, Unreported. Bail ⚖ 79(2); Constitutional Law ⚖ 262

Trial court's failure to hold evidentiary hearing on surety's motion for remission of forfeited bond did not violate procedural due process, where surety failed to produce the criminal defendants in court as it was obligated to do and thus lost its property interest in the bond. State v. Hardin (Ohio App. 6 Dist., Lucas, 12-31-2003) No. L-03-1131, No. L-03-1132, No. L-03-1133, 2003-Ohio-7263, 2003 WL 23167301, Unreported. Bail ⚖ 79(2); Constitutional Law ⚖ 262

Sureties waived claim, on appeal from trial court's decision to grant them only partial remission of forfeited bail bond, that court's failure to remit to them at least 90% of the forfeited bail bond violated their equal protection rights, where sureties failed to raise this claim in trial court. State v. Am. Bail Bond Agency (Ohio App. 10 Dist., 09-10-1998) 129 Ohio App.3d 708, 719 N.E.2d 13, dismissed, appeal not allowed 84 Ohio St.3d 1470, 704 N.E.2d 578. Criminal Law ⚖ 1031(1)

2. Judicial discretion

Trial court's refusal to remit forfeited bond, based solely on rejection of defendant's reason for failure to appear at initial hearing, that she had arranged with prosecutor to waive preliminary hearing, was abuse of discretion, where 25-day delay between initial hearing and subsequent hearing at which defendant voluntarily appeared did not prejudice State, charges were ultimately dismissed following grant of motion to suppress, and there was no showing that forfeiture of bond bore reasonable relation to costs and inconvenience incurred in gaining custody of defendant and preparing for trial. State v. Owens (Ohio App. 11 Dist., Ashtabula, 11-09-2004) No. 2003-A-0088, 2004-Ohio-5941, 2004 WL 2526412, Unreported. Bail ⚖ 79(1)

Purpose of bail is to secure the presence of the defendant and is not punitive so where (1) inconvenience and delay to the prosecution is minimal, (2) little expense is involved in securing her presence and (3) the failure to appear may not have been willful, forfeiture of the defendant's entire $10,000 bond is a clear abuse of discretion. State v. Christenson (Ohio App. 2 Dist., Greene, 04-16-1999) No. 98 CA 53, 1999 WL 218146, Unreported.

The provisions of RC Ch 2925 that relate to the disposition and use of forfeited bail do not preclude a court or magistrate from remitting all or a portion of forfeited bail pursuant to RC 2937.39. OAG 93–015.

3. Remission; refund to surety

Trial court that forfeited $20,000 bail bond when defendant charged with felonious assault fled after the first day of trial abused its discretion by remitting only $8,000 of the bond to surety after defendant was recaptured, even though surety conducted minimal investigation of defendant's flight risk before posting bond, and collected a premium for the possibility he might flee; surety located defendant after he fled and enabled police to recapture him, and State was not prejudiced by defendant's failure to appear for the remainder of trial. State v. Thornton (Ohio App. 2 Dist., Montgomery, 02-17-2006) No. 20963, 2006-Ohio-786, 2006 WL 401594, Unreported, appeal not allowed 110 Ohio St.3d 1411, 850 N.E.2d 72, 2006-Ohio-3306. Bail ⚖ 79(1)

Order denying defendant's request for remission of $50,000 bond that was ordered forfeited when defendant failed to appear at hearing for community control violation was not abuse of discretion, despite costs of extradition following her arrest in Florida of $6,331.58; defendant's subsequent appearance was involuntary, in that it was only due to her arrest and extradition back to Ohio, defendant willfully attempted to avoid prosecution for community control violation, defendant hid from authorities by fleeing from jurisdiction for 21 months, bail was not actually posted by third party, so there was no need for third party to expend resources to secure defendant's appearance, defendant waited until two years after forfeiture to seek remission, and defendant wasted time and resources of court and state. State v. Hodge (Ohio App. 12 Dist., Clermont, 11-07-2005) No. CA2004-10-079, 2005-Ohio-5904, 2005 WL 2936283, Unreported. Bail ⚖ 96

Trial court did not abuse its discretion in denying surety's motion for partial remittitur of bond forfeited upon defendant's failure to appear in court for preliminary hearing, despite defendant's ultimate recapture by authorities and appearance in court, where substantial evidence established efforts and expense incurred by local and federal agencies in attempting to capture defendant, and surety's investigator was paid less than $500 for his services in attempting to recapture defendant, surety never paid reward offered by it to tipster who assisted in defendant's capture, and surety was not involved in defendant's arrest, capture, or return. State v. Stoneman (Ohio App. 5 Dist., Guernsey, 06-09-2005) No. 04 CA 17, 2005-Ohio-2910, 2005 WL 1384662, Unreported. Bail ⚖ 79(2)

Denying bail bonding company's motion for remission of forfeited bond was abuse of discretion, where defendant for whom company posted bond had not previously failed to appear for trial and it was unclear whether defendant was aware of his arraignment date. State of Ohio v. Rich (Ohio App. 6 Dist., Lucas, 10-22-2004) No. L-04-1102, No. L-04-1103, 2004-Ohio-5678, 2004 WL 2390085, Unreported. Bail ⚖ 79(1)

Denying bail bonding company's motion for remission of forfeited bond was not abuse of discretion; although defendant for whom company posted bond was secured by company four months after defendant failed to appear for trial, defendant had previously failed to appear for trial and had been recaptured when company issued bond. State of Ohio v. Rich (Ohio App. 6 Dist., Lucas, 10-22-2004) No. L-04-1102, No. L-04-1103, 2004-Ohio-5678, 2004 WL 2390085, Unreported. Bail ⚖ 79(1)

Trial court's order denying bail bond surety's motion for remittitur of bond forfeiture was necessarily arbitrary, having been entered without any consideration as to the ultimate appearance of defendant as grounds for recompensation, the State's inconvenience and delay, the expense involved, the willfulness of the violation, or any other mitigating circumstances; even though surety was primarily responsible for defendant's apprehension, the trial court denied request for remittitur, finding that surety "assumed the risk" due to the nature of its business. State v. Delgado (Ohio App. 2 Dist., Clark, 01-09-2004) No. 2003-CA-28, 2004-Ohio-69, 2004 WL 41404, Unreported. Bail ⚷ 79(1)

Trial court acted within its discretion in failing to hold evidentiary hearing on surety's motion for remission of forfeited bond with respect to three different criminal defendants; surety simply made bare allegations of entitlement to relief and failed to request hearing, and defendants willfully failed to appear before trial court. State v. Hardin (Ohio App. 6 Dist., Lucas, 12-31-2003) No. L-03-1131, No. L-03-1132, No. L-03-1133, 2003-Ohio-7263, 2003 WL 23167301, Unreported. Bail ⚷ 79(2)

When considering request for post-appearance bond remission pursuant to statute on refund of bond to surety, trial court should balance reappearance of accused, and efforts expended by surety to effectuate reappearance, against inconvenience, expense and delay suffered by state and any other factors court finds relevant. State v. Jackson (Ohio App. 3 Dist., 05-02-2003) 153 Ohio App.3d 520, 795 N.E.2d 57, 2003-Ohio-2213. Bail ⚷ 79(1)

Trial court's denial of bail bond company's motion for post-appearance bond remission was arbitrary and abuse of discretion, where trial court did not set forth reasons for its denial of motion, and thus Court of Appeals could not ascertain trial court's reasons for denying motion or review propriety of trial court's considerations. State v. Jackson (Ohio App. 3 Dist., 05-02-2003) 153 Ohio App.3d 520, 795 N.E.2d 57, 2003-Ohio-2213. Bail ⚷ 79(2)

Trial court's remittance of only $18,750 on defendant's bail bond of $75,000 was proper, although bail bond company expended effort and funds to locate defendant, and defendant's failure to appear did not affect state's proof, where defendant's reappearance was involuntary, state was prejudiced by delay and inconvenience, defendant's failure to appear at suppression hearing was a willful attempt to avoid prosecution, and bail bond company was not instrumental in securing defendant's appearance. State v. Duran (Ohio App. 6 Dist., 05-25-2001) 143 Ohio App.3d 601, 758 N.E.2d 742. Bail ⚷ 76

Trial court acted within its discretion, following apprehension of the accused, in remitting to sureties only $150,000 of $500,000 forfeited bail bond, though accused was apprehended due in part to efforts of sureties; accused failed to appear for her preliminary hearing in willful attempt to avoid prosecution, such failure to appear wasted time and resources of court, and sureties neglected their duty to conduct reasonable investigation of accused's background and to take necessary steps to ensure her appearance. State v. Am. Bail Bond Agency (Ohio App. 10 Dist., 09-10-1998) 129 Ohio App.3d 708, 719 N.E.2d 13, dismissed, appeal not allowed 84 Ohio St.3d 1470, 704 N.E.2d 578. Bail ⚷ 80

Trial court properly found, in only partially remitting forfeited bail bond following apprehension of accused, that sureties failed to follow their own procedures for posting bail bonds and that they grossly neglected their duty to conduct reasonable investigation of accused's background and to take necessary and routine steps to ensure her appearance, despite sureties' contentions that traffic accident involving their agent excused agent's failure to follow proper procedure and that short duration of felony bonds posted in municipal court prevented them from conducting extensive investigation. State v. Am. Bail Bond Agency (Ohio App. 10 Dist., 09-10-1998) 129 Ohio App.3d 708, 719 N.E.2d 13, dismissed, appeal not allowed 84 Ohio St.3d 1470, 704 N.E.2d 578. Bail ⚷ 80

The practice of a municipal court clerk relative to execution on forfeited bail bonds, the policies governing that practice, and whether the practice was abruptly changed in particular case were questions of fact subject to reasonable dispute and, therefore, were not subject to being judicially noticed, on sureties' appeal from municipal court's decision granting only partial remission of bail bond forfeiture. State v. Am. Bail Bond Agency (Ohio App. 10 Dist., 09-10-1998) 129 Ohio App.3d 708, 719 N.E.2d 13, dismissed, appeal not allowed 84 Ohio St.3d 1470, 704 N.E.2d 578. Evidence ⚷ 42

In determining whether to remit previous revocation of bail, court should consider ultimate appearance of defendant as grounds for recompensation, inconvenience and delay to prosecution, expense involved, willfulness of violation as well as any other mitigating circumstances. State v. Patton (Lucas 1989) 60 Ohio App.3d 99, 573 N.E.2d 1201. Bail ⚷ 79(1); Bail ⚷ 80

When a judgment has been entered on a forfeited recognizance and the sureties make payment in satisfaction of said judgment, and thereafter the court remits or reduces the judgment, in whole or in part, the surety who made the payment has a collectible claim against the county for the difference between the amount he paid and the amount of the judgment as modified by the court. 1959 OAG 43.

A court which renders judgment on a forfeited recognizance in a criminal case may remit the whole or part of such judgment at any time even though the recognizance has been returned to the county auditor. 1958 OAG 2684.

2937.40 Release of bail and sureties; use to satisfy fine or costs only when deposited by accused

(A) Bail of any type that is deposited under sections 2937.22 to 2937.45 of the Revised Code or Criminal Rule 46 by a person other than the accused shall be discharged and released, and sureties on recognizances shall be released, in any of the following ways:

(1) When a surety on a recognizance or the depositor of cash or securities as bail for an accused desires to surrender the accused before the appearance date, the surety is discharged from further responsibility or the deposit is redeemed in either of the following ways:

(a) By delivery of the accused into open court;

(b) When, on the written request of the surety or depositor, the clerk of the court to which recognizance is returnable or in which deposit is made issues to the sheriff a warrant for the arrest of the accused and the sheriff indicates on the return that he holds the accused in his jail.

(2) By appearance of the accused in accordance with the terms of the recognizance or deposit and the entry of judgment by the court or magistrate;

(3) By payment into court, after default, of the sum fixed in the recognizance or the sum fixed in the order of forfeiture, if it is less.

(B) When cash or securities have been deposited as bail by a person other than the accused and the bail is discharged and released pursuant to division (A) of this section, or when property has been pledged by a surety on recognizance and the surety on recognizance has been released pursuant to division (A) of this section, the court shall not deduct any amount from the cash or securities or declare forfeited and levy or execute against pledged property. The court shall not apply any of the deposited cash or securities toward, or declare forfeited and levy or execute against property pledged for a recognizance for, the satisfaction of any penalty or fine, and court costs, assessed against the accused upon his conviction or guilty plea, except upon express approval of the person who deposited the cash or securities or the surety.

(C) Bail of any type that is deposited under sections 2937.22 to 2937.45 of the Revised Code or Criminal Rule 46 by an accused shall be discharged and released to the accused, and property pledged by an accused for a recognizance shall be discharged, upon the appearance of the accused in accordance with the terms of the recognizance or deposit and the entry of judgment by the court or magistrate, except that, if the defendant is not indigent, the court may apply deposited bail toward the satisfaction of a penalty or fine, and court costs, assessed against the accused upon his conviction or guilty plea, and may declare forfeited and levy or execute against pledged property for the satisfaction of a penalty or fine, and court costs, assessed against the accused upon his conviction or guilty plea.

(D) Notwithstanding any other provision of this section, an Ohio driver's or commercial driver's license that is deposited as bond may be forfeited and otherwise handled as provided in section 2937.221 of the Revised Code.

(1990 S 338, eff. 11–28–90; 1989 H 381; 1986 S 356; 1980 H 402; 128 v 97)

Historical and Statutory Notes

Ed. Note: 2937.40 contains provisions analogous to former 2937.36, repealed by 128 v 97, eff. 1–1–60.

Ed. Note: Former 2937.40 repealed by 128 v 97, eff. 1–1–60; 1953 H 1; GC 13435–20.

Pre–1953 H 1 Amendments: 113 v 155, Ch 14, § 20

Cross References

Additional costs in criminal cases in all courts to fund reparations payments; bail, defined, 2743.70

Bail, Crim R 46

Library References

Bail ⚯78.

Westlaw Topic No. 49.

C.J.S. Bail; Release and Detention Pending Proceedings §§ 136, 167 to 175.

Research References

ALR Library

42 ALR 5th 547, Propriety of Applying Cash Bail to Payment of Fine.

Encyclopedias

OH Jur. 3d Criminal Law § 2075, Who May be Arrested.

OH Jur. 3d Criminal Law § 2216, Return of Bail or Recognizance.

OH Jur. 3d Criminal Law § 2243, Production or Arrest of Principal.

OH Jur. 3d Judgments § 404, Effect of Vacation or Reversal of Judgment.

OH Jur. 3d Mandamus, Procedendo, & Prohibition § 89, Role of Writ, Generally.

OH Jur. 3d Mandamus, Procedendo, & Prohibition § 166, Remedy as Preventative Rather Than Corrective; Moot Questions.

OH Jur. 3d Mandamus, Procedendo, & Prohibition § 173, Threatened Exercise of Judicial or Quasi-Judicial Power.

Treatises and Practice Aids

Katz, Giannelli, Blair and Lipton, Baldwin's Ohio Practice, Criminal Law, § 139:20, Entry as to Recognized Defendant Delivered and Committed to Bail.

Katz, Giannelli, Blair and Lipton, Baldwin's Ohio Practice, Criminal Law, § 139:21, Entry as to Defendant Delivered and New Recognizance Taken.

Katz, Giannelli, Blair and Lipton, Baldwin's Ohio Practice, Criminal Law, § 139:22, Entry as to Defendant Delivered in Vacation and Committed.

Katz, Giannelli, Blair and Lipton, Baldwin's Ohio Practice, Criminal Law, § 139:23, Entry as to Defendant Delivered in Vacation and Recognized.

Carlin, Baldwin's Ohio Practice, Merrick-Rippner Probate Law § 108:38, Juvenile Court—Civil Support Proceedings—Remedies for Failure to Comply With Support Order.

Notes of Decisions

---

1. Use of deposit

The trial court lacked authority to order bail money deposited by bailor to be applied toward payment of defendant's fines; defendant never failed to appear before the court, and there was no evidence that bailor expressly approved using the cash deposited by bailor toward the satisfaction of defendant's fines. State v. Warden (Ohio App. 6 Dist., Wood, 12-23-2005) No. WD-05-003, 2005-Ohio-6847, 2005 WL 3507844, Unreported. Bail ⚷ 96

Plain language of statute precluded application of cash bond, provided by defendant's father, toward satisfaction of defendant's mandatory fines for drug trafficking convictions, regardless of whether defendant was found to be indigent. State v. Lefever (Ohio App. 2 Dist., 10-27-1993) 91 Ohio App.3d 301, 632 N.E.2d 589. Bail ⚷ 96

Request for writ of prohibition preventing juvenile court judges from applying appearance bond funds to child-support arrearages was moot, where court had changed policy to require release of funds to the person posting the bond if a defendant appeared in court. Denton v. Bedinghaus (Ohio App. 1 Dist., Hamilton, 06–28–2002) No. C–000819, 2002–Ohio–3273, 2002 WL 1393563, Unreported. Prohibition ⚷ 13

It does not follow that, because RC 2937.40(B) prohibits use of cash or security deposits to pay fines and costs except with consent, a court may then require "consent" before permitting such deposits; such a construction, moreover, violates O Const Art I §9. State ex rel. Baker v. Troutman (Ohio 1990) 50 Ohio St.3d 270, 553 N.E.2d 1053.

The court may not, under RC 2937.40(C), apply a bail deposit to a child support arrearage of the defendant. State v Nixon, No. 663 (4th Dist Ct App, Highland, 4–26–88).

Pursuant to RC 2937.40(B), the clerk of the court of common pleas may not apply money deposited as bail by a person other than the defendant toward the payment of court costs, unless the person who deposited the money expressly approves the money being applied toward the payment of court costs. OAG 05–014.

Pursuant to RC 2937.40–.41, the clerk of the court of common pleas may not apply money deposited as bail toward the payment of court costs when the defendant is acquitted of all criminal charges in the case. OAG 05–014.

Pursuant to RC 2937.40, the clerk of the court of common pleas may not apply money deposited as bail toward the payment of court costs before the entry of a judgment by the court or magistrate. OAG 05–014.

2. Defenses to forfeiture

Sureties were not exonerated from liability on bail bond by act-of-law defense, though sureties had located defendant after he fled from jurisdiction and procured his arrest and incarceration in foreign state, where sureties had not appeared at extradition hearing, foreign court had released defendant on extradition bond, and defendant had again fled. State v. Hughes (Ohio 1986) 27 Ohio St.3d 19, 501 N.E.2d 622, 27 O.B.R. 437. Bail ⚷ 74(1)

In a bond forfeiture proceeding, the surety has an insufficient defense where the defendant voluntarily fled the country before his initial court appearance date, notwithstanding the fact that the defendant cannot be brought back into the country because of foreign policy decisions. State v. Ohayon (Cuyahoga 1983) 12 Ohio App.3d 162, 467 N.E.2d 908, 12 O.B.R. 486.

A surety on a criminal recognizance is not discharged from his obligation until the accused is presented and surrendered in open court in such manner that he can be detained and the court accepts the delivery. State v. Wilson (Ohio Mun. 1950) 115 N.E.2d 193, 65 Ohio Law Abs. 422. Bail ⚷ 80

3. Conflict of laws

A local rule of court requiring the clerk of the court of common pleas to apply money deposited as bail toward the payment of court costs does not control when it conflicts with RC 2937.40 or RC 2937.41. OAG 05–014.

2937.41 Return of bail; notice of discharge of recognizance

On the discharge of bail, the magistrate or clerk of the court shall return, subject to division (B) or (C) of section 2937.40 of the Revised Code, deposited cash or securities to the depositor, but the magistrate or clerk of the court may require presentation of an issued original receipt as a condition to the return. In the case of discharged recognizances, subject to division (B) or (C) of section 2937.40 of the Revised Code, the magistrate or clerk of the court shall endorse the satisfaction on the recognizance and shall forthwith transmit to the county recorder the notice of discharge provided for in section 2937.26 of the Revised Code.

(1980 H 402, eff. 5–13–80; 128 v 97)

Historical and Statutory Notes

Ed. Note: Former 2937.41 repealed by 128 v 97, eff. 1–1–60; 1953 H 1; GC 13435–21.

Pre–1953 H 1 Amendments: 113 v 155, ch 14, § 21

Cross References

Bail, Crim R 46

Library References

Bail ⚷75, 96.
Westlaw Topic No. 49.
C.J.S. Bail; Release and Detention Pending Proceedings §§ 140 to 156, 158 to 159, 189 to 190.

Research References

Encyclopedias

OH Jur. 3d Criminal Law § 2216, Return of Bail or Recognizance.

Notes of Decisions

Conflict of laws 3
Forfeiture proceedings 1
Liability for improper refund 2

---

1. Forfeiture proceedings

The only method by which recovery can be obtained on a recognizance forfeited in a criminal action is that provided by RC 2937.36, which is a continuing process in the criminal action, and a judgment rendered by a court on a forfeited recognizance by civil action in a criminal proceeding is void for want of jurisdiction of the subject matter, so that neither the payment of such judgment nor the consent to its rendition by the defendant can vest such court with such jurisdiction. City of Cleveland v. Young (Cuyahoga 1963) 119 Ohio App. 19, 190 N.E.2d 42, 26 O.O.2d 102.

2. Liability for improper refund

RC 2937.41 requires a municipal court clerk to return bail to the depositor rather than the defendant, and RC 2707.04 imposes liability for failure to do so; establishment of a bail return policy in contravention of these statutes is not a discretionary function for which immunity would attach under RC 2744.03. Sielaff v Dawson, No. CA 14725 (9th Dist Ct App, Summit, 1–9–91).

3. Conflict of laws

A local rule of court requiring the clerk of the court of common pleas to apply money deposited as bail toward the payment of court costs does not control when it conflicts with RC 2937.40 or RC 2937.41. OAG 05–014.

2937.42 Defect in form of recognizance

Forfeiture of a recognizance shall not be barred or defeated or a judgment thereon reversed by the neglect or omission to note or record the default, or by a defect in the form of such recognizance, if it appears from the tenor thereof at what court the party or witness was bound to appear and that the court or officer before whom it was taken was authorized to require and take such recognizance.

(128 v 97, eff. 1–1–60; 1953 H 1; GC 13435–22)

Historical and Statutory Notes

Pre–1953 H 1 Amendments: 113 v 156, Ch 14, § 22

Cross References

Bail, Crim R 46

Library References

Bail ⚷54, 78.
Westlaw Topic No. 49.

C.J.S. Bail; Release and Detention Pending Proceedings §§ 3, 93 to 106, 136, 167 to 175.

Research References

Encyclopedias

OH Jur. 3d Criminal Law § 2247, Vacation of Forfeiture of Bail.

Notes of Decisions

Effect of defect 1

1. Effect of defect

No defect in the form of a recognizance bond given in criminal action shall bar or defeat an action for judgment on it. State v. Johnson (Darke 1949) 92 N.E.2d 24, 56 Ohio Law Abs. 305. Bail ⚷ 84

2937.43 Arrest for failure to appear; issuance of warrant

Should the accused fail to appear as required, after having been released pursuant to section 2937.29 of the Revised Code, the court having jurisdiction at the time of such failure may, in addition to any other action provided by law, issue a warrant for the arrest of such accused.

(131 v H 47, eff. 8–10–65)

Historical and Statutory Notes

Ed. Note: Former 2937.43 repealed by 128 v 97, eff. 1–1–60; 1953 H 1; GC 13435–23; see now 2937.39 for provisions analogous to former 2937.43.

Pre–1953 H 1 Amendments: 113 v 156, Ch 14, § 23

Cross References

Bail, Crim R 46

Library References

Bail ⚷97.
Criminal Law ⚷215.
Westlaw Topic Nos. 110, 49.

C.J.S. Bail; Release and Detention Pending Proceedings §§ 73 to 79.

C.J.S. Criminal Law §§ 334 to 335, 337 to 338.

Research References

Encyclopedias

OH Jur. 3d Criminal Law § 2166, Penalty Upon Failure to Appear.

Notes of Decisions

Challenge to charge of failure to appear 2
Issuance of writ of capias 1

1. Issuance of writ of capias

Although Ohio law provides procedures for bringing a person before the court after a failure to appear when released on a form of bail other than a release on personal recognizance pursuant to RC 2937.29, there is no authority to arrest such person for a separate offense of failure to appear similar to that provided in RC 2937.43 or to impose penalties analogous to those set forth in RC 2937.99. When a person has been released on a form of bail other than a release on personal recognizance, the court is limited to the forfeiture of bail proceedings set forth in RC 2937.35 to RC 2937.39 as punishment for the failure to appear, but a writ of capias may be issued to secure that person's appearance. OAG 87–016.

2. Challenge to charge of failure to appear

Where a defendant signs a recognizance bond and then fails to appear for his arraignment, resulting in a further indictment for failure to appear in violation of the recognizance bond, the defendant's motion to dismiss the second indictment on the ground that he was never bound by the recognizance bond goes beyond the face of the indictment and he can only enter a motion for acquittal after the state presents its case. State v. Varner (Summit 1991) 81 Ohio App.3d 85, 610 N.E.2d 476.

2937.44 Form of recognizance

Recognizances substantially in the forms following are sufficient:

RECOGNIZANCE OF THE ACCUSED

The State of Ohio, __________ County, ss:

Be it remembered, that on the _____ day of __________, in the year _____ E.F. and G.H. personally appeared before me, and jointly and severally acknowledged themselves to owe the state of Ohio, the sum of __________ dollars, to be levied on their goods, chattels, lands, and tenements, if default is made in the condition following, to wit:

The condition of this recognizance is such that if the above bound E.F. personally appears before the court of common pleas on the first day of the next term thereof, then and there to answer a charge of (here name the offense with which the accused is charged) and abide the judgment of the court and not depart without leave, then this recognizance shall be void; otherwise it shall be and remain in full force and virtue in law.

Taken and acknowledged before me, on the day and year above written.

A.B., Judge

RECOGNIZANCE OF WITNESS

The State of Ohio, __________ County, ss:

Be it remembered, that on the __________ day of __________, in the year _____ E.F. and G.H. personally appeared before me and jointly and severally acknowledged themselves to owe the state of Ohio, the sum of __________ dollars, to be levied on their goods, chattels, lands, and tenements, if default is made in the condition following, to wit:

The condition of this recognizance is such that if the above bound E.F. personally appears before the court of common pleas on the first day of the next term thereof then and there to give evidence on behalf of the state, touching such matters as shall then and there be required of him, and not depart the court without leave, then this recognizance shall be void, otherwise it shall remain in full force and virtue in law.

Taken and acknowledged before me, on the day and year above written.

A.B., Judge

TO KEEP THE PEACE

The State of Ohio, __________ County, ss:

Be it remembered, that on the __________ day of __________, in the year of _____ E.F., and G.H. personally appeared before me, and jointly and severally acknowledged themselves to owe the state of Ohio, the sum of __________ dollars, to be levied on their goods, chattels, lands, and tenements, if default is made in the condition following, to wit:

The condition of this recognizance is such that if the above bound E.F. personally appears before the court of common pleas, on the first day of the next term thereof, then and there to answer unto a complaint of C.D. that he has reason to fear, and does fear, that the said E.F. will (here state the charge in the complaint), and abide the order of the court thereon, and in the meantime to keep the peace and be of good behavior toward the citizens of the state generally, and especially toward the said C.D., then this recognizance shall be void; otherwise it shall be and remain in full force and virtue in law.

Taken and acknowledged before me, on the day and year above written.

A.B., Judge

(127 v 1039, eff. 1–1–58; 1953 H 1; GC 13435–24)

Historical and Statutory Notes

Pre–1953 H 1 Amendments: 113 v 156, Ch 14, § 24

Cross References

Bail, Crim R 46

Library References

Bail ⚷54.
Westlaw Topic No. 49.
C.J.S. Bail; Release and Detention Pending Proceedings §§ 3, 93 to 106.

Research References

Encyclopedias

OH Jur. 3d Criminal Law § 2227, Coverage of Offenses.

Treatises and Practice Aids

Katz, Giannelli, Blair and Lipton, Baldwin's Ohio Practice, Criminal Law, § 139:24, Recognizance of Accused (Statutory Form).

Katz, Giannelli, Blair and Lipton, Baldwin's Ohio Practice, Criminal Law, § 139:25, Recognizance of Witness (Statutory Form).

Katz, Giannelli, Blair and Lipton, Baldwin's Ohio Practice, Criminal Law, § 139:26, Recognizance of Keep the Peace (Statutory Form).

Notes of Decisions

Credit cards 1
Forfeiture proceedings 2

---

1. Credit cards

State highway patrol officers can accept credit cards on the highway from violators within the jurisdictions of those courts which have entered into an agreement with the credit card servicing agency for payment upon presentation of a completed sales draft with the only conditions being that the bail amount involved not exceed the dollar limitations contained in the agreement, the sales draft be legible and that the sales draft be drawn on an unexpired credit card, but may not accept credit cards within jurisdiction of courts which have not entered into such agreements. OAG 70–036.

2. Forfeiture proceedings

Summary judgment may not be taken in a civil action by a city for forfeiture of a bail bond, and the defendant surety must be given an opportunity to defend the action. City of Cleveland v. Loviness (Cuyahoga 1955) 125 N.E.2d 890, 71 Ohio Law Abs. 105.

RC 2937.43 gives the trial court which renders a judgment of forfeiture of a recognizance in a criminal case the authority to remit or reduce the amount of such judgment at any time, during or after term, and whether or not any part or all of such judgment has been satisfied by payment to the clerk of courts and by him paid to the county auditor and deposited in the general fund. 1959 OAG 43.

2937.45 Forms of commitments

Commitments substantially in the forms following are sufficient:

COMMITMENT AFTER
EXAMINATION

The State of Ohio, ________ County, ss:

To the Keeper of the Jail of the County aforesaid, greeting:

Whereas, E.F. has been arrested, on the oath of C.D., for (here describe the offense), and has been examined by me on such charge, and required to give bail in the sum of ________ dollars for his appearance before the court of common pleas with which requisition he has failed to comply. Therefore, in the name of the state of Ohio, I command you to receive the said E.F. into your custody, in the jail of the county aforesaid, there to remain until discharged by due course of law.

Given under my hand, this ____ day of ____

A.B., Judge

COMMITMENT PENDING

EXAMINATION

The State of Ohio, ________ County, ss:

To the Keeper of the Jail of the County aforesaid, greeting:

Whereas, E.F. has been arrested on the oath of C.D., for (here describe the offense) and has been brought before me for examination and the same has been necessarily postponed by reason of (here state the cause of delay). Therefore, I command you, in the name of the state of Ohio, to receive the said E.F. into your custody in the jail of the county aforesaid (or in such other place as the justice shall name) there to remain until discharged by due course of law.

Given under my hand, this _____ day of _____

A.B., Judge

(127 v 1039, eff. 1–1–58; 1953 H 1; GC 13435–25)

Historical and Statutory Notes

Pre–1953 H 1 Amendments: 113 v 157, Ch 14, § 25

Cross References

Bail, Crim R 46

Library References

Criminal Law ⟹241.
Westlaw Topic No. 110.
C.J.S. Criminal Law § 354.

Research References

Encyclopedias

OH Jur. 3d Family Law § 1743, Adults in Custody of Juvenile Court.

Treatises and Practice Aids

Katz, Giannelli, Blair and Lipton, Baldwin's Ohio Practice, Criminal Law, § 139:38, Commitment After Examination (Statutory Form).

Katz, Giannelli, Blair and Lipton, Baldwin's Ohio Practice, Criminal Law, § 139:39, Affidavit in Support of Motion for Reduction in Amount of Bail.

Law Review and Journal Commentaries

The University and the Bail System: in Loco Altricis, Harry W. Pettigrew. 20 Clev St L Rev 502 (September 1971).

UNIFORM PROCEDURES IN TRAFFIC CASES

2937.46 Supreme court authorized to set uniform procedures in traffic cases

(A) The supreme court of Ohio, in the interest of uniformity of procedure in the various courts and for the purpose of promoting prompt and efficient disposition of cases arising under the traffic laws of this state and related ordinances, may make uniform rules for practice and procedure in courts inferior to the court of common pleas not inconsistent with the provisions of Chapter 2937. of the Revised Code, including, but not limited to:

(1) Separation of arraignment and trial of traffic and other types of cases;

(2) Consolidation of cases for trial;

(3) Transfer of cases within the same county for the purpose of trial;

(4) Designation of special referees for hearings or for receiving pleas or bail at times when courts are not in session;

(5) Fixing of reasonable bonds, and disposition of cases in which bonds have been forfeited.

(B) Except as otherwise specified in division (N) of section 4511.19 of the Revised Code, all of the rules described in division (A) of this section, when promulgated by the supreme court, shall be fully binding on all courts inferior to the court of common pleas and on the court of common pleas in relation to felony violations of division (A) of section 4511.19 of the Revised Code and shall effect a cancellation of any local court rules inconsistent with the supreme court's rules.

(2006 S 8, eff. 8–17–06; 2002 S 123, eff. 1–1–04; 129 v 582, eff. 1–10–61; 128 v 97)

Historical and Statutory Notes

Amendment Note: 2006 S 8 substituted "(N)" for "(L)" in division (B).

Amendment Note: 2002 S 123 rewrote the section, which prior thereto read:

"The supreme court of Ohio may, in the interest of uniformity of procedure in the various courts, and for the purpose of promoting prompt and efficient disposition of cases arising under the traffic laws of this state and related ordinances, makes uniform rules for practice and procedure in courts inferior to the court of common pleas not inconsistent with the provisions of Chapter 2937. of the Revised Code, including, but not limited to:

"(A) Separation of arraignment and trial of traffic and other types of cases;

"(B) Consolidation of cases for trial;

"(C) Transfer of cases within the same county for the purpose of trial;

"(D) Designation of special referees for hearings or for receiving pleas or bail at times when courts are not in session;

"(E) Fixing of reasonable bonds, and disposition of cases in which bonds have been forfeited.

"All of said rules, when promulgated by the supreme court, shall be fully binding on all courts inferior to the court of common pleas and shall effect a cancellation of any local court rules inconsistent therewith."

Cross References

Rules of evidence and procedure, 2938.15

Traffic rules, scope and applicability, authority and construction, Traf R 1

Library References

Automobiles ⚷349 to 358.

Westlaw Topic No. 48A.

C.J.S. Motor Vehicles §§ 1320 to 1335, 1344 to 1351, 1363, 1365 to 1379, 1395 to 1414, 1422 to 1425, 1434, 1442 to 1450, 1473 to 1483, 1486 to 1487, 1496 to 1502, 1507 to 1509, 1518 to 1523, 1526, 1531 to 1538, 1543 to 1547, 1550.

Research References

Treatises and Practice Aids

Gotherman, Babbit and Lang, Baldwin's Ohio Practice, Local Government Law—Municipal, § 28:40, Uniform Traffic Ticket.

Notes of Decisions

1. Uniform traffic rules

The Ohio Traffic Rules adopted pursuant to RC 2935.17 and 2937.46 are statutory in origin and therefore do not supersede statutes with which they conflict. City of Toledo v. Fogel (Lucas 1985) 20 Ohio App.3d 146, 485 N.E.2d 302, 20 O.B.R. 180. Courts ⚷ 85(1)

Traffic Rules were adopted by authority granted by statute and do not have the same force or effect as rules adopted pursuant to Section 5, Article IV of the Ohio Constitution. Linden v. Bates Truck Lines, Inc. (Butler 1982) 4 Ohio App.3d 178, 446 N.E.2d 1139, 4 O.B.R. 280. Automobiles ⚷ 11

2. Uniform traffic ticket

Variances between the Ohio uniform traffic ticket and a local traffic ticket prepared after the Ohio uniform traffic ticket was adopted are grounds for dismissal of the local-ticket complaint if the defendant is thereby prejudiced. City of Cleveland v. Winchell (Cuyahoga 1981) 3 Ohio App.3d 186, 444 N.E.2d 465, 3 O.B.R. 212.

The complaint (and summons) in traffic cases is the Ohio uniform traffic ticket set out in the appendix of the forms of Ohio uniform traffic rules and is binding on all courts inferior to the court of common pleas, see Traf R 1(A) and Traf R 3(A). City of Cleveland v. Austin (Cuyahoga 1978) 55 Ohio App.2d 215, 380 N.E.2d 1357, 9 O.O.3d 368.

3. Amendment of ticket

Where defendant and his counsel and the prosecution were unaware that the affidavit charging defendant with a traffic violation had not been verified until discovered by the judge at the end of the trial, a waiver may not be considered, and verification of the affidavit cannot be furnished at the end of the trial against objection of the defendant. Village of Pepper Pike v. LaMaida (Ohio Mun. 1970) 25 Ohio Misc. 252, 268 N.E.2d 296, 54 O.O.2d 410.

4. Violations bureau

A city council cannot force a municipal judge to establish a Traffic Violations Bureau. OAG 70–119.

Under Rule .18 of the Ohio Rules of Practice and Procedure in Traffic Cases promulgated by the Ohio Supreme Court a municipal court shall be the exclusive designator of the moving traffic offenses which are waiverable and of the fines. OAG 70–119.

5. Bond

A county sheriff may not accept cash appearance bonds in misdemeanor cases coming within the jurisdiction of the county court. 1960 OAG 1641.

PENALTY

2937.99 Penalties

(A) No person shall fail to appear as required, after having been released pursuant to section 2937.29 of the Revised Code. Whoever violates this section is guilty of failure to appear and shall be punished as set forth in division (B) or (C) of this section.

(B) If the release was in connection with a felony charge or pending appeal after conviction of a felony, failure to appear is a felony of the fourth degree.

(C) If the release was in connection with a misdemeanor charge or for appearance as a witness, failure to appear is a misdemeanor of the first degree.

(D) This section does not apply to misdemeanors and related ordinance offenses arising under Chapters 4501., 4503., 4505., 4507., 4509., 4510., 4511., 4513., 4517., 4549., and 5577. of the Revised Code, except that this section does apply to violations of sections 4511.19, 4549.02, and 4549.021 of the Revised Code and ordinance offenses related to sections 4511.19, 4549.02, and 4549.021 of the Revised Code.

(2002 S 123, eff. 1–1–04; 1999 S 107, eff. 3–23–00; 1994 H 571, eff. 10–6–94; 131 v H 47, eff. 8–10–65)

Historical and Statutory Notes

Amendment Note: 2002 S 123 deleted "charge of the commission of" before, and inserted "charge" after, "felony" in division (B); deleted "charge of the commission of" before, and inserted "charge" after, "misdemeanor" in division (C); inserted "4510" in division (D).

Amendment Note: 1999 S 107 rewrote this section, which prior thereto read:

"Whoever fails to appear as required, after having been released pursuant to section 2937.29 of the Revised Code, shall be sentenced as follows:

"(A) If the release was in connection with a charge of the commission of a felony or pending appeal after conviction of a felony, he shall be fined not more than five thousand dollars or imprisoned in a state correctional institution for not less than one nor more than five years, or both.

"(B) If the release was in connection with a charge of the commission of a misdemeanor or for appearance as a witness, he shall be fined not more than one thousand dollars or imprisoned not more than one year, or both.

"This section does not apply to misdemeanors and related ordinance offenses arising under Chapters 4501., 4503., 4505., 4507., 4509., 4511., 4513., 4517., 4549., and 5577. of the Revised Code, except that this section does apply to violations of sections 4511.19, 4549.02, and 4549.021 of the Revised Code and ordinance offenses related to such sections."

Amendment Note: 1994 H 571 substituted "a state correctional institution" for "the penitentiary" in division (A).

Cross References

Bail, sanctions, Crim R 46

Library References

Bail ⚩97.
Westlaw Topic No. 49.

C.J.S. Bail; Release and Detention Pending Proceedings §§ 73 to 79.

Research References

Encyclopedias

OH Jur. 3d Criminal Law § 2166, Penalty Upon Failure to Appear.

Treatises and Practice Aids

Katz, Giannelli, Blair and Lipton, Baldwin's Ohio Practice, Criminal Law, § 37:6, Types of Pretrial Release.

Katz, Giannelli, Blair and Lipton, Baldwin's Ohio Practice, Criminal Law, § 37:15, Sanctions and Forfeiture.

Notes of Decisions

Failure to appear 1

1. Failure to appear

Trial court improperly sentenced defendant convicted of aggravated burglary and failure appear to maximum, consecutive sentences; court did not specifically address defendant in regard to his offenses, court failed to provide reasons in support of its sentence, generalized statements regarding elements of crime for which defendant was charged did not suffice in determining that defendant should serve maximum term authorized, and broad statements about offense itself being "worst crime" did not address issue of whether that particular offender committed worst form of that particular offense. State v. Vincenzo (Ohio App. 11 Dist., Ashtabula, 06-24-2005) No. 2003-A-0090, 2005-Ohio-3269, 2005 WL 1503717, Unreported. Sentencing And Punishment ⚷ 373

Evidence was insufficient to establish that defendant was released on his own recognizance, and thus he could not be convicted of failure to appear for trial; release on one's own recognizance required a written undertaking by a defendant that was unsecured by others on his behalf, and surety deposited $500 in cash to secure defendant's release and signed the recognizance along with defendant. State v. Fusik (Ohio App. 4 Dist., Athens, 03-08-2005) No. 04CA28, 2005-Ohio-1056, 2005 WL 567308, Unreported. Bail ⚷ 97(3)

Record supported imposition of consecutive sentences for convictions of corrupting another with drugs, and failure to appear at sentencing, where trial court specifically found that consecutive sentences were necessary to protect public from future crime by defendant, and that sentences were required to adequately punish defendant, and defendant failed to provide trial court with clear and convincing evidence that consecutive sentences were disproportionate to his conduct. State v. Lehman (Ohio App. 3 Dist., Auglaize, 08-02-2004) No. 2-04-07, 2004-Ohio-4008, 2004 WL 1717659, Unreported. Sentencing And Punishment ⚷ 373; Sentencing And Punishment ⚷ 587

Trial court made proper on record findings, and record supported findings, for imposition of maximum sentence for conviction for failure to appear at sentencing; determinations that minimum sentence would not adequately protect public, and that defendant posed greatest likelihood of recidivism, were supported by findings that defendant was under release from confinement prior to sentencing when he committed offense, he had extensive history of criminal convictions that reflected fact that defendant had not responded favorably to sanctions in past, and that defendant showed no genuine remorse for crimes. State v. Lehman (Ohio App. 3 Dist., Auglaize, 08-02-2004) No. 2-04-07, 2004-Ohio-4008, 2004 WL 1717659, Unreported. Sentencing And Punishment ⚷ 66; Sentencing And Punishment ⚷ 114; Sentencing And Punishment ⚷ 116; Sentencing And Punishment ⚷ 373

Statute providing that offense of failure to appear for sentencing, an unclassified felony, is subject to "not less than one nor more than five years" of imprisonment requires sentencing court to impose definite, not indefinite, term of imprisonment. State v. Quisenberry (Ohio 1994) 69 Ohio St.3d 556, 634 N.E.2d 1009. Bail ⚷ 97(4)

Although Ohio law provides procedures for bringing a person before the court after a failure to appear when released on a form of bail other than a release on personal recognizance pursuant to RC 2937.29, there is no authority to arrest such person for a separate offense of failure to appear similar to that provided in RC 2937.43 or to impose penalties analogous to those set forth in RC 2937.99. When a person has been released on a form of bail other than a release on personal recognizance, the court is limited to the forfeiture of bail proceedings set forth in RC 2937.35 to RC 2937.39 as punishment for the failure to appear, but a writ of capias may be issued to secure that person's appearance. OAG 87–016.

CHAPTER 2938

TRIAL—MAGISTRATE COURTS

PRELIMINARY PROVISIONS

2938.01 Definitions

The definition of "magistrate" set forth in section 2931.01 of the Revised Code, and the definition of "peace officer," "prosecutor," and "offense" set forth in section 2935.01 of the Revised Code applies to Chapter 2938 of the Revised Code.

(128 v 97, eff. 1–1–60)

Cross References

Action on guilty and no contest pleas in misdemeanor cases, 2937.07

Subpoena of witnesses or documents, 2937.19

Research References

Encyclopedias

OH Jur. 3d Criminal Law § 1973, Municipal, Mayor's, and County Courts.

Law Review and Journal Commentaries

The Developing Role of the Magistrate in the Federal Courts, Jack B. Streepy. 29 Clev St L Rev 81 (1980).

The Quiet Revolution in the Criminal Law—A Foreward, Honorable Jack G. Day. 23 Clev St L Rev 1 (Winter 1974).

The Role of the Electronic Media in the Criminal Justice System, Note. 47 U Cin L Rev 417 (1978).

Notes of Decisions

Mayor's jurisdiction 1

1. Mayor's jurisdiction

A mayor of a village has jurisdiction to hear and determine all prosecutions for violations of ordinances where the defendants are not entitled to a trial by jury; and to hear and determine prosecutions for violations of ordinances where the defendants are entitled to trial by jury if, before the commencement of the trial, a waiver in writing, subscribed by the accused, is filed in the case, following the procedure prescribed in RC Ch 2938, but where the accused does not waive such right, the mayor is required to certify the case to a court of record. 1960 OAG 1208.

2938.02 Applicability of provisions

The provisions of Chapter 2938. of the Revised Code shall apply to trial on the merits of any misdemeanor, ordinance offense, prosecution for the violation of any rule or regulation of any governmental body authorized to adopt penal regulations, or to complaints to keep the peace, which may be instituted in and retained for trial on the merits in any court or before any magistrate inferior to the court of common pleas; provided that in juvenile courts, where the conduct of any person under the age of eighteen years is made the subject of inquiry and for which special provision is made by Chapter 2151. or 2152. of the Revised Code, such matters shall be tried, adjusted, or disposed of pursuant to Chapter 2151. or 2152. of the Revised Code.

(2000 S 179, § 3, eff. 1–1–02; 128 v 97, eff. 1–1–60)

Historical and Statutory Notes

Amendment Note: 2000 S 179, § 3, eff. 1–1–02, inserted "or 2152." twice.

Notes of Decisions

Setting case for trial 1

1. Setting case for trial

Where, on arraignment, under RC Ch 2937, the accused pleads not guilty to the commission of a misdemeanor, the court shall proceed to set the trial at a future time pursuant to RC Ch 2938. City of East Cleveland v. Gilbert (Ohio 1970) 24 Ohio St.2d 63, 263 N.E.2d 400, 53 O.O.2d 85.

2938.03 Setting and continuing cases; assignment of additional judges

The magistrate, or judge or clerk of court of record, shall set all criminal cases for a trial at a date not later than thirty days after plea is received, or in those cases in which the charge has been reduced on preliminary hearing or has been certified by another magistrate, then at a date not later than thirty days from fixing of charge or receipt of transcript as the case may be. Continuances beyond such date shall be granted only upon notice to the opposing party and for good cause shown.

Criminal cases shall be given precedence over civil matters in all assignments for trial and if the volume of contested criminal matters in courts of more than one judge is such as to require it, the chief justice or presiding judge of such court shall assign additional judges from other divisions of the court to assist in the trial of such criminal matters; in the case of county courts, the presiding judge of the court of common pleas shall assign county judges from other areas of jurisdiction within the county to assist those county judges whose volume of criminal cases requires assistance.

(128 v 97, eff. 1–1–60)

Historical and Statutory Notes

Ed. Note: Guidelines for Assignment of Judges were announced by the Chief Justice of the Ohio Supreme Court on 5–24–88, and revised 2–25–94 and 3–25–94, but not adopted as rules pursuant to O Const Art IV §5. For the full text, see 37 OS(3d) xxxix, 61 OBar A–2 (6–13–88) and 69 OS(3d) XCIX, 67 OBar xiii (4–18–94).

Cross References

Computation of days, 1.14
Precedence of criminal cases, Crim R 50
Speedy trial, continuances, discharge for delay, 2945.71 to 2945.73
Time, Crim R 45

Library References

Criminal Law ⚷577.1.
Westlaw Topic No. 110.
C.J.S. Criminal Law §§ 578, 593.

Research References

Encyclopedias

OH Jur. 3d Criminal Law § 2575, Assignment of Additional Judges.

Law Review and Journal Commentaries

The Municipal Court Misdemeanor Arraignment Procedure of Hamilton County, Ohio: An Empirical Study, Note. 41 U Cin L Rev 623 (1972).

Notes of Decisions

1. Setting case for trial

Where, on arraignment, under RC Ch 2937, the accused pleads not guilty to the commission of a misdemeanor, the court shall proceed to set the trial at a future time pursuant to RC Ch 2938. City of East Cleveland v. Gilbert (Ohio 1970) 24 Ohio St.2d 63, 263 N.E.2d 400, 53 O.O.2d 85.

2. Continuances

Trial court denial of defendant's second request for a continuance was not an abuse of discretion, during prosecution for aggravated murder; when the trial court granted defendant's first request for a continuance it impressed upon the parties the date scheduled for trial, defendant filed her second request for continuance on the day trial was scheduled to begin based on counsel and witnesses being on vacation and the need for additional time to prepare expert witness, the trial court noted that the first continuance had been granted in part because expert was not available for trial and to provide additional time for expert to prepare for trial, and the court found that additional delay would substantially interrupt the court's docket and would inconvenience the 60 jurors waiting to be impaneled and the numerous witnesses subpoenaed for trial. State v. Prom (Ohio App. 12 Dist., Butler, 05-09-2005) No. CA2004-07-174, 2005-Ohio-2272, 2005 WL 1077238, Unreported. Criminal Law ⚷ 614(1)

Trial court acted within its discretion in denying defendant's request for continuance to secure the appearance of two witnesses, where there was no indication that any additional time would have produced the desired witnesses. State v. Braddy (Ohio App. 8 Dist., Cuyahoga, 06-17-2004) No. 83462, 2004-Ohio-3128, 2004 WL 1364730, Unreported, motion to reopen denied 2005-Ohio-282, 2005 WL 174771, motion for delayed appeal denied 106 Ohio St.3d 1458, 830 N.E.2d 1167, 2005-Ohio-3490. Criminal Law ⚷ 594(3)

Trial court acted within its discretion in denying defendant's motion for continuance, even though defense counsel stated that she had had minimal contact with defendant; motion was filed on the day of trial and after matter had been pending for over a month, the facts surrounding the offenses were not complicated, and there was no indication that discovery had not been completed. State v. Brown (Ohio App. 2 Dist., Montgomery, 06-10-2004) No. 19917, 2004-Ohio-3091, 2004 WL 1347609, Unreported. Criminal Law ⚷ 590(2)

Trial court's failure to grant defendant's motion for continuance in which defendant claimed that State had seized and not returned privileged attorney-client communications constituted reversible error; defendant's allegations, if true, severely inhibited his ability to prepare a defense and possibly gave the State access to privileged materials. State v. George (Ohio App. 1 Dist., Hamilton, 06-04-2004) No. C-030216, 2004-Ohio-2868, 2004 WL 1231572, Unreported, appeal not allowed 103 Ohio St.3d 1525, 817 N.E.2d 408, 2004-Ohio-5852. Criminal Law ⚷ 1166(7)

Defendant was not entitled to obtain new counsel, where request for substitution of counsel was merely an attempt to get a continuance which had already been denied by the court, and defendant failed to provide any reasons for wishing to substitute counsel. State v. Goode (Ohio App. 2 Dist., Montgomery, 08-15-2003) No. 19273, 2003-Ohio-4323, 2003 WL 21949740, Unreported, motion for delayed appeal denied 101 Ohio St.3d

1485, 805 N.E.2d 537, 2004-Ohio-1293. Criminal Law ⚷ 641.10(2)

Defendant was not entitled to a continuance based on his alleged need for additional time to prepare for additional charges against him, where motion was made the morning of trial, and defense counsel knew of additional charges a week before trial. State v. Goode (Ohio App. 2 Dist., Montgomery, 08-15-2003) No. 19273, 2003-Ohio-4323, 2003 WL 21949740, Unreported, motion for delayed appeal denied 101 Ohio St.3d 1485, 805 N.E.2d 537, 2004-Ohio-1293. Criminal Law ⚷ 590(2)

Trial court had authority to grant continuance of psychiatric hearing in one of the cases against criminal defendant, where defendant asserted insanity defense in that case, initial psychiatric report in another case against defendant stated that defendant was sane at time of offenses and competent to stand trial, and defendant had requested independent psychiatric examination in the other case. Jackson v. Court Of Common Pleas (Ohio App. 8 Dist., Cuyahoga, 10-31-2002) No. 81589, 2002-Ohio-5980, 2002 WL 31429867, Unreported, cause dismissed 98 Ohio St.3d 1433, 782 N.E.2d 590, 2003-Ohio-374. Criminal Law ⚷ 625.20

The addition of a plaintiff's witness five days prior to trial is valid reason to grant defendant's motion for a continuance where the witness is a drug task force member who allegedly made illegal marijuana purchases from defendant and whose identity was known to the plaintiff all along; denial of a continuance has a prejudicial effect on defendant and is an abuse of discretion. State v. Spack (Ohio App. 7 Dist., Columbiana, 05-17-1994) No. 93-C-48, 1994 WL 194150, Unreported.

The denial of a continuance is neither unreasonable, arbitrary, nor unconscionable where (1) the defendant was present with appointed counsel on the date of trial, (2) the trial had been continued at defendant's request once before, (3) the state had been ready to proceed with its witnesses once before and this was the second time it was ready, (4) the request for a continuance did not reflect the specific time necessary for the delay, and (5) the need for the delay was attributable to the defendant (the defendant chose private counsel who was unavailable on the date of trial, knowing him to be unavailable). State v. Jones (Wayne 1987) 42 Ohio App.3d 14, 535 N.E.2d 1372. Criminal Law ⚷ 593; Criminal Law ⚷ 614(1)

The ten-day period of limitations in Juv R 29(A) is procedural only and such rule confers no substantive right upon an accused to have his case dismissed if he is not tried within the designated time. In re Therklidsen (Franklin 1977) 54 Ohio App.2d 195, 376 N.E.2d 970, 8 O.O.3d 335.

Where RC 2938.03 specifically authorized a continuance for good cause shown, and the continuance granted does not prevent the defendant from having a fair trial, the trial court may, in its discretion, grant a continuance on behalf of the prosecution. City of East Cleveland v. Gilbert (Ohio 1970) 24 Ohio St.2d 63, 263 N.E.2d 400, 53 O.O.2d 85. Criminal Law ⚷ 254.1

JURIES

2938.04 Jury trial

In courts of record right to trial by jury as defined in section 2945.17 of the Revised Code shall be claimed by making demand in writing therefor and filing the same with the clerk of the court not less than three days prior to the date set for trial or on the day following receipt of notice whichever is the later. Failure to claim jury trial as provided in this section is a complete waiver of right thereto. In courts not of record jury trial may not be had, but failure to waive jury in writing where right to jury trial may be asserted shall require the magistrate to certify such case to a court of record as provided in section 2937.08 of the Revised Code.

(129 v 582, eff. 1–10–61; 128 v 97)

Cross References

Computation of days, 1.14

Court not of record, mayor's court, Ch 1905

Jury trial, written demand, waiver of right, Crim R 23

Mayor's court jurisdiction over violations of municipal ordinances comparable to driving under suspension, 1905.01

Right to jury trial, O Const Art I §10

Right to jury trial inviolate, O Const Art I §5

Time, Crim R 45

Library References

Jury ⚷25, 29.

Westlaw Topic No. 230.

C.J.S. Juries §§ 166 to 179, 182, 186, 193, 207 to 219, 222.

Research References

Encyclopedias

OH Jur. 3d Courts & Judges § 25, Mayor's Courts.

OH Jur. 3d Criminal Law § 2025, Mayor's Courts—Specific Offenses.

OH Jur. 3d Criminal Law § 2443, in Misdemeanor Cases.

Law Review and Journal Commentaries

The Applicability of the Sixth or Seventh Amendment Right to a Jury Trial in OSHA Penalty Proceedings, Comment. 45 U Cin L Rev 108 (1976).

CRIMINAL PROCEDURE—Voir Dire—The Right to Question Jurors on Racial Prejudice. Ham v. South Carolina and Ristaino v. Ross, Note. 37 Ohio St L J 412 (1976).

The Right of Self–Representation and the Power of Jury Nullification, Frank A. Kaufman. 28 Case W Res L Rev 269 (Winter 1978).

Right to Trial by Jury—Sixth Amendment—A Five–Member Jury Does Not Satisfy the Jury Trial Guarantee of the Sixth Amendment.—Ballew v. Georgia, Note. 47 U Cin L Rev 524 (1978).

The Role of the Jury in Choice of Law, Willis L.M. Reese, Hans Smit and George B. Reese. 25 Case W Res L Rev 82 (Fall 1974).

Selecting a Jury in Political Trial, John Van Dyke. 27 Case W Res L Rev 609 (Spring 1977).

Smaller Juries and Non–Unanimity: Analysis and Proposal Revision of the Ohio Jury System, Note. 43 U Cin L Rev 583 (1974).

Notes of Decisions

---

1. Constitutional issues

Defense counsel's failure to prevent defendant charged with receiving stolen property, aggravated robbery, and kidnapping from waiving his right to jury trial did not amount to ineffective assistance, despite fact that defendant had, during prior plea hearing, made what amounted to confession before the trial court, where counsel explained defendant's trial alternatives, and trial court the explained in detail procedures and differences between jury trial and bench trial and questioned defendant's decision to waive jury trial. State v. Addison (Ohio App. 10 Dist., Franklin, 09-28-2004) No. 03AP-1102, 2004-Ohio-5154, 2004 WL 2803976, Unreported. Criminal Law ⚷ 641.13(2.1)

O Const Art I, §10 grants defendants the right to summon to trial witnesses on their behalf and where the state seeks to limit the right, it is the state who must demonstrate that the defendant's acts have interfered with the orderly conduct of the criminal trial and that this interference has prejudiced the prosecution to the extent that exclusion of the witness is warranted. State v. Brown (Ohio App. 6 Dist., Wood, 09-01-1995) No. WD-94-106, 1995 WL 516489, Unreported.

There is no unqualified constitutional right to know the identity of jurors. State v. Hill (Ohio, 07-05-2001) 92 Ohio St.3d 191, 749 N.E.2d 274, 2001-Ohio-141, on remand 2002-Ohio-227, 2002 WL 109297. Criminal Law ⚷ 631(1)

A jury need not reflect an exact cross-section of the community, and the use of voter registration lists as the source of names of prospective jurors is not unlawful even though it results in the exclusion of nonvoters; unless prejudice to the defendant or the systematic and intentional exclusion of a group is shown, the judgment will not be reversed because of minor and technical defects in the jury-selection procedure. State v. Strodes (Ohio 1976) 48 Ohio St.2d 113, 357 N.E.2d 375, 2 O.O.3d 271, vacated 98 S.Ct. 3135, 438 U.S. 911, 57 L.Ed.2d 1154.

In order to have a trial by an impartial jury, the array of a veniremen need not reflect an exact cross-section of the community, but the defendant is entitled to a jury panel selected by the best method that thoughtful men who are cognizant of the practicalities of selection and the inherent problems involved have been able to develop; the use of voter registration lists as the source of names of prospective jurors is not unlawful even though it results in the exclusion of nonvoters. State v. Strodes (Ohio 1976) 48 Ohio St.2d 113, 357 N.E.2d 375, 2 O.O.3d 271, vacated 98 S.Ct. 3135, 438 U.S. 911, 57 L.Ed.2d 1154.

The guaranty of a jury trial in criminal cases contained in the state and federal constitutions is not an absolute and unrestricted right in Ohio with respect to misdemeanors; and a statute, ordinance or authorized rule of court may validly condition the right to a jury trial in such a case on a written demand therefor filed with the court a specified number of days before the date actually set for the trial for the offense charged. City of Mentor v. Giordano (Ohio 1967) 9 Ohio St.2d 140, 224 N.E.2d 343, 38 O.O.2d 366. Jury ⚷ 22(1); Jury ⚷ 25(3)

If a petitioner charged with driving while intoxicated has a federal constitutional right to a trial by jury, habeas corpus may issue where the waiver of jury trial was the result of a default by his attorney. Brady v. Blair (S.D.Ohio 1976) 427 F.Supp. 5.

Conviction in Ohio on a charge of operating a motor vehicle under the influence of alcohol is a serious offense and one in which the accused has a federal constitutional right to trial by jury. Brady v. Blair (S.D.Ohio 1976) 427 F.Supp. 5.

2. Jury demand; waiver of jury trial

Defendant validly waived his right to jury trial, even though waiver was not signed in open court and waiver may not have been filed until trial was over; trial court conducted lengthy colloquy with defendant regarding his waiver of jury trial at forefront of trial, and waiver was in writing, signed by defendant, filed and journalized in the case, and made a part of the record. State v. Kiriazis (Ohio App. 8 Dist., Cuyahoga, 02-05-2004) No. 82887, 2004-Ohio-502, 2004 WL 231478, Unreported, appeal not allowed 102 Ohio St.3d 1485, 810 N.E.2d 968, 2004-Ohio-3069. Jury ⚷ 29(6)

Trial court had jurisdiction to proceed with bench trial in felonious assault prosecution, even though defendant's signed jury waiver was not journalized until the day after the trial had concluded. State v. Rivers (Ohio App. 8 Dist., Cuyahoga, 07-10-2003) No. 81929, 2003-Ohio-3670, 2003 WL 21555127, Unreported, appeal not allowed 100 Ohio St.3d 1486, 798 N.E.2d 1094, 2003-Ohio-5992. Jury ⚷ 29(6)

A written waiver of a defendant's right to a jury trial which is signed by the defendant is not effective where the waiver is not time-stamped and filed with the clerk's office as part of the record. State v McDonald, No. CA-9033, 1993 WL 271169 (5th Dist Ct App, Stark, 7-6-93).

Defendant's waiver of his right to a jury trial was voluntary and intelligent; defendant signed a written jury waiver form, which was filed and journalized, when trial court accepted the written waiver, defendant affirmed that his decision was voluntary, he also affirmed that his counsel had reviewed the waiver form with him and that he had discussed his decision with them, and his decision to waive a jury trial followed from his decision to plead guilty. State v. Fitzpatrick (Ohio, 07-07-2004) 102 Ohio St.3d 321, 810 N.E.2d 927, 2004-Ohio-3167, reconsideration denied 103 Ohio St.3d 1429, 814 N.E.2d 491, 2004-Ohio-4524, denial of post-conviction relief affirmed 2004-Ohio-5615, 2004 WL 2367987, appeal not allowed 105 Ohio St.3d 1499, 825 N.E.2d 623, 2005-Ohio-1666, motion to reopen denied 105 Ohio St.3d 1436, 822 N.E.2d 808, 2005-Ohio-531, certiorari denied 125 S.Ct. 2930, 162 L.Ed.2d 869. Jury ⚷ 29(6)

Because State has burden to prove beyond a reasonable doubt existence of prior conviction which enhances degree of subsequent offense, criminal defendant is not entitled to bifurcated proceedings in trial on subsequent offense, nor is he entitled to waive jury trial on that element alone. State v. Nievas (Ohio App. 8 Dist., 06-02-1997) 121 Ohio App.3d 451, 700 N.E.2d 339, dismissed, appeal not allowed 79 Ohio St.3d 1505, 684 N.E.2d 89. Criminal Law ⚷ 618; Jury ⚷ 29(2)

Although mayor's courts and municipal courts have concurrent jurisdiction to hear cases arising from violations of municipal ordinances, a mayor's court lacks jurisdiction to conduct a jury trial; therefore, when a defendant pleads not guilty to a misdemeanor case commenced in a mayor's court and the defendant either requests a jury trial or fails to waive his right to a jury trial, the case must be transferred to the appropriate municipal court. City of Brunswick v. Giglio (Ohio Mun. 1988) 39 Ohio Misc.2d 5, 530 N.E.2d 37.

It is prejudicial error for court to refuse to allow defendant a jury trial because he failed to file demand for such three days prior to trial, where he filed demand on the day following his receipt of notice of trial date, pursuant to RC 2938.04. City of Cincinnati v. Hill (Hamilton 1971) 29 Ohio App.2d 270, 281 N.E.2d 15, 58 O.O.2d 463. Criminal Law ⚷ 1166.6; Jury ⚷ 25(6)

Petitioner intelligently consented to waiver of jury, in favor of three-judge panel, for capital murder trial; counsel did not promise, or state as matter of law, that petitioner would not be sentenced to death by panel, and despite petitioner's intellectual limitations, he understood risks involved. Sowell v. Bradshaw (C.A.6 (Ohio), 06-23-2004) 372 F.3d 821, rehearing en banc denied, certiorari denied 125 S.Ct. 1645, 544 U.S. 925, 161 L.Ed.2d 485. Jury ⚷ 29(6)

State courts were not required to look beyond trial court's colloquy with petitioner, and petitioner's written waiver, in determining that petitioner intelligently consented to waive jury for capital murder trial, since petitioner presented no evidence to rebut presumption that proceeding on record was valid. Sowell v. Bradshaw (C.A.6 (Ohio), 06-23-2004) 372 F.3d 821, rehearing en banc denied, certiorari denied 125 S.Ct. 1645, 544 U.S. 925, 161 L.Ed.2d 485. Jury ⚷ 29(6)

While defendant may be deemed sufficiently informed to make intelligent waiver of right to jury trial if he is aware that jury is composed of 12 members of community, he may participate in their selection, verdict must be unanimous, and that judge alone will decide guilt or innocence upon waiver of jury, such elements are not constitutionally required. Sowell v. Bradshaw (C.A.6 (Ohio), 06-23-2004) 372 F.3d 821, rehearing en banc denied, certiorari denied 125 S.Ct. 1645, 544 U.S. 925, 161 L.Ed.2d 485. Jury ⚷ 29(6)

State trial court's failure, during colloquy on petitioner's waiver of jury for capital murder trial, to question petitioner on his understanding of his right to participate in jury selection and requirement of unanimity of recommendation to impose death sentence, or whether anyone had induced him to waive jury, did not render waiver unknowing. Sowell v. Bradshaw (C.A.6 (Ohio), 06-23-2004) 372 F.3d 821, rehearing en banc denied, certiorari denied 125 S.Ct. 1645, 544 U.S. 925, 161 L.Ed.2d 485. Jury ⚷ 29(6)

Where the record on appeal does not reveal a waiver of a jury trial by the defendant, who was convicted of draft evasion after a trial without a jury, the judgment must be reversed and the case remanded for a new trial. U. S. v. Davidson (C.A.6 (Ohio) 1973) 477 F.2d 136.

A defendant in a prosecution for drunk driving is entitled to a jury trial, but where neither the defendant nor his attorney file a written demand for a jury trial and go to trial without objecting to the court sitting without a jury, the right is completely waived. Brady v. Blair (S.D.Ohio 1976) 427 F.Supp. 5.

Where at arraignment judge entered plea of not guilty for a defendant who requested counsel, and hearing on charge was set for nineteen days later, defendant had adequate opportunity to retain counsel and request jury trial. Brady v. Blair (S.D.Ohio 1976) 427 F.Supp. 5.

3. Jury trial in municipal court

The right of an accused to a trial by jury in a criminal case in the municipal court is governed by RC 1901.24 and not by RC 2938.04. State v. Magana (Franklin 1961) 115 Ohio App. 106, 184 N.E.2d 525, 20 O.O.2d 216.

That part of RC 1901.24 which provides that "in any criminal case in which the accused is entitled to a jury trial, a demand for a jury trial must be made by the accused before the court shall proceed to inquire into the merits of the cause, otherwise a jury shall be deemed to be waived," was repealed by implication by RC 2938.04. Ex parte Milton (Ohio Com.Pl. 1961) 178 N.E.2d 846, 87 Ohio Law Abs. 168.

4. Mayor's court

Although mayor's courts and municipal courts have concurrent jurisdiction to hear cases arising from violations of municipal ordinances, a mayor's court lacks jurisdiction to conduct a jury trial; therefore, when a defendant pleads not guilty to a misdemeanor case commenced in a mayor's court and the defendant either requests a jury trial or fails to waive his right to a jury trial, the case must be transferred to the appropriate municipal court. City of Brunswick v. Giglio (Ohio Mun. 1988) 39 Ohio Misc.2d 5, 530 N.E.2d 37.

A mayor of a village presiding over a mayor's court may sentence a person to imprisonment for violation of a village ordinance if such person in writing waives a jury and consents to be tried by the mayor as magistrate. OAG 69–117.

A mayor of a village has jurisdiction to hear and determine all prosecutions for violations of ordinances where the defendants are not entitled to a trial by jury; and to hear and determine prosecutions for violations of ordinances where the defendants are entitled to trial by jury if, before the commencement of the trial, a waiver in writing, subscribed by the accused, is filed in the case, following the procedure prescribed in RC Ch 2938, but where the accused does not waive such right, the mayor is required to certify the case to a court of record. 1960 OAG 1208.

2938.05 Withdrawal of claim of jury

Claim of jury, once made, may be withdrawn by written waiver of jury but in such case the court may, if a jury has been summoned, require accused to pay all costs of mileage and fees of members of the venire for one day's service, notwithstanding the outcome of the case. No withdrawal of claim for jury shall effect any re-transfer of a case, once it has been certified to a court of record.

(128 v 97, eff. 1–1–60)

Cross References

Waiver of jury, Crim R 23

Library References

Jury ⚷29.
Westlaw Topic No. 230.
C.J.S. Juries §§ 167, 182, 207 to 219, 222.

2938.06 Number of jurors; challenges

If the number of jurors to be sworn in a case is not stated in the claim, the number to be sworn shall be twelve, but the accused may stipulate for a jury of six, provided in such case the number of pre-emptory [1] challenges shall be limited to two on each side.

(128 v 97, eff. 1–1–60)

[1] So in original.

Cross References

Number of jurors, Crim R 23
Peremptory challenges, number, manner of exercise, Crim R 24

Library References

Jury ⚷32, 134.
Westlaw Topic No. 230.

C.J.S. Juries §§ 264 to 267, 344, 421, 423 to 434, 436 to 442.

Law Review and Journal Commentaries

A New Peremptory Inclusion to Increase Representativeness and Impartiality in Jury Selection, Note. 45 Case W Res L Rev 251 (Fall 1994).

The Prosecutor's Exercise of the Peremptory Challenge to Exclude Nonwhite Jurors: A Valued Common Law Privilege in Conflict with the Equal Protection Clause, Comment. 46 U Cin L Rev 554 (1977).

Notes of Decisions

Peremptory challenges 1

1. Peremptory challenges

Murder defendant failed to prove purposeful discrimination with regard to state's use of peremptory challenges on two black potential jurors, and thus, trial court properly denied defendant's *Batson* objections; state exercised its challenge with respect to jurors on ground that jurors had attitudes that state believed favored defense, at time of state's challenge to second juror, there were four black potential jurors seated, and next replacement juror to take second juror's seat was black. State v. Melvin (Ohio App. 8 Dist., Cuyahoga, 05-12-2005) No. 84471, 2005-Ohio-2329, 2005 WL 1119959, Unreported. Jury ⚷ 33(5.15)

Prosecutor provided sufficient race-neutral explanations for striking two African-American prospective jurors in prosecution for robbery, assault, and receiving stolen property; State removed first juror because he had previously been convicted of theft, a crime of dishonesty, and State removed second juror because of his hypertechnicality. State v. Thomas (Ohio App. 1 Dist., Hamilton, 12-31-2002) No. C-010724, 2002-Ohio-7333, 2002 WL 31894850, Unreported, appeal not allowed 98 Ohio St.3d 1515, 786 N.E.2d 64, 2003-Ohio-1572. Jury ⚷ 33(5.15)

Defendant was not required, in making a prima facie case of discrimination in his *Batson* challenge to state's exercise of peremptory strike against African–American member of jury panel, to give a discriminatory reason for the strike. State v. Kiner (Ohio App. 1 Dist., 10-18-2002) 149 Ohio App.3d 599, 778 N.E.2d 144, 2002-Ohio-5578, appeal not allowed 99 Ohio St.3d 1412, 788 N.E.2d 648, 2003-Ohio-2454. Jury ⚷ 33(5.15)

African–American defendant made prima facie case of discrimination in state's exercise of peremptory juror strike, thus shifting burden to state to give race-neutral reason, where removed juror was the only African–American on jury panel, and prosecutor spent very little time questioning that juror during voir dire and obtained only the information that she lived in forum county and worked in market research. State v. Kiner (Ohio App. 1 Dist., 10-18-2002) 149 Ohio App.3d 599, 778 N.E.2d 144, 2002-Ohio-5578, appeal not allowed 99 Ohio St.3d 1412, 788 N.E.2d 648, 2003-Ohio-2454. Jury ⚷ 33(5.15)

The trial court, by asking defense counsel to state its reasons for its peremptory challenge of African–American juror, accepted African–American patient's prima-facie argument of racial discrimination, and thus, under *Batson* test, defendant hospital was required to articulate a race-neutral explanation for the strike, in the medical malpractice action. Cunningham v. St. Alexis Hosp. Med. Ctr. (Ohio App. 8 Dist., 04-12-2001) 143 Ohio App.3d 353, 758 N.E.2d 188, appeal not allowed 93 Ohio St.3d 1416, 754 N.E.2d 262, appeal not allowed 93 Ohio St.3d 1452, 756 N.E.2d 115. Jury ⚷ 33(5.15)

Trial court's abbreviated consideration of African–American patient's challenge to hospital's use of peremptory strike against African–American juror in medical malpractice action was grossly insufficient to indicate that trial court understood and applied the precise *Batson* test to adequately preserve patient's right to a constitutionally permissible jury-selection process; trial court interrupted defense counsel before defense counsel had concluded his explanation of race-neutral reason for using the strike, and trial court immediately denied patient's objection to the peremptory strike. Cunningham v. St. Alexis Hosp. Med. Ctr. (Ohio App. 8 Dist., 04-12-2001) 143 Ohio App.3d 353, 758 N.E.2d 188, appeal not allowed 93 Ohio St.3d 1416, 754 N.E.2d 262, appeal not allowed 93 Ohio St.3d 1452, 756 N.E.2d 115. Jury ⚷ 33(5.15)

Hospital's explanation that peremptory strike was used against African–American prospective juror because juror had stated during voir dire that she did not believe there should be a cap on damages was not a race-neutral explanation for the strike, in medical malpractice action brought by African–American patient; juror correctly stated the law, and hospital did not attempt to strike white jurors who had given the same answer as the African–American juror. Cunningham v. St. Alexis Hosp. Med. Ctr. (Ohio App. 8 Dist., 04-12-2001) 143 Ohio App.3d 353, 758 N.E.2d 188, appeal not allowed 93 Ohio St.3d 1416, 754 N.E.2d 262, appeal not allowed 93 Ohio St.3d 1452, 756 N.E.2d 115. Jury ⚷ 33(5.15)

Trial court misapplied *Batson* by attempting to make certain the first 12 jurors were not all white. State v. Holloway (Ohio App. 10 Dist., 09-17-1998) 129 Ohio App.3d 790, 719 N.E.2d 70, dismissed, appeal not allowed 84 Ohio St.3d 1472, 704 N.E.2d 579. Jury ⚷ 33(5.15)

Batson does not create a right to a jury of any particular composition. State v. Holloway (Ohio

App. 10 Dist., 09-17-1998) 129 Ohio App.3d 790, 719 N.E.2d 70, dismissed, appeal not allowed 84 Ohio St.3d 1472, 704 N.E.2d 579. Jury ⚷ 33(5.15)

Batson prohibition against racial discrimination in jury selection applies to both criminal and civil actions; whenever party opposes peremptory challenge by claiming racial discrimination, duty of trial court is to decide whether granting strike will contaminate jury selection through unconstitutional means. Hicks v. Westinghouse Materials Co. (Ohio, 04-02-1997) 78 Ohio St.3d 95, 676 N.E.2d 872, 1997-Ohio-227, certiorari denied 118 S.Ct. 159, 522 U.S. 859, 139 L.Ed.2d 104. Jury ⚷ 33(5.15)

Jury selection, peremptory challenges, sex discrimination. J.E.B. v. Alabama ex rel. T.B. (U.S.Ala., 04-19-1994) 114 S.Ct. 1419, 511 U.S. 127, 128 L.Ed.2d 89, on remand 641 So.2d 821.

Prosecution provided a valid, race-neutral justification for use of a peremptory challenge to remove only prospective African–American juror from venire; prosecutor explained that prospective juror had indicated on written juror questionnaire that she or a member of her family had been the victim of a crime, that during voir dire, she stated that she was referring to her son, who had been convicted of a crime and imprisoned, and that juror's inability to differentiate between victim of a crime and perpetrator, coupled with her subsequent evasiveness about her son's record, were the reasons for the peremptory strike. State v. Dockery (Ohio App. 1 Dist., Hamilton, 05-10-2002) No. C-000316, 2002-Ohio-2309, 2002 WL 944917, Unreported. Jury ⚷ 33(5.15)

PRACTICE AND PROCEDURE

2938.07 Authority of magistrate or judge

The magistrate or judge of the trial court shall control all proceedings during a criminal trial and shall limit the introduction of evidence and argument of counsel to relevant and material matters with a view to expeditious and effective ascertainment of truth regarding the matters in issue.

(128 v 97, eff. 1–1–60)

Cross References

Judge to control proceedings during criminal trial, 2945.03

Library References

Criminal Law ⚷633(1), 661, 730.
Westlaw Topic No. 110.
C.J.S. Criminal Law §§ 564, 656, 751, 1134, 1140, 1145 to 1146, 1191, 1202.

Research References

Treatises and Practice Aids

Giannelli and Snyder, Baldwin's Ohio Practice, Evidence, R 401, Definition of "Relevant Evidence".

Giannelli and Snyder, Baldwin's Ohio Practice, Evidence, R 611, Mode and Order of Interrogation and Presentation.

Giannelli and Snyder, Baldwin's Ohio Practice, Evidence, § 102.3, History of Rule.

Giannelli and Snyder, Baldwin's Ohio Practice, Evidence, § 401.3, Consequential (Material) Facts Defined.

Giannelli and Snyder, Baldwin's Ohio Practice, Evidence, § 611.3, Court Control of Trial: in General.

2938.08 Presumption of innocence

A defendant in a criminal action is presumed to be innocent until he is proved guilty of the offense charged, and in case of a reasonable doubt whether his guilt is satisfactorily shown, he shall be acquitted. The presumption of innocence places upon the state (or the municipality) the burden of proving him guilty beyond a reasonable doubt.

In charging a jury the trial court shall state the meaning of the presumption of innocence and of reasonable doubt in each case.

(128 v 97, eff. 1–1–60)

Cross References

Jury instructions, Crim R 30

Presumption of innocence, burden and degree of proof; reasonable doubt, defined, 2901.05

Library References

Criminal Law ⚷308, 561, 778(3), 789(1).
Westlaw Topic No. 110.
C.J.S. Criminal Law §§ 696, 1108, 1325 to 1327, 1342.

Research References

Encyclopedias

OH Jur. 3d Criminal Law § 2776, Reading Statutory Definitions.

OH Jur. 3d Criminal Law § 2897, Innocence.

Treatises and Practice Aids

Katz, Giannelli, Blair and Lipton, Baldwin's Ohio Practice, Criminal Law, § 71:6, Burden of Proof Instructions.

Katz, Giannelli, Blair and Lipton, Baldwin's Ohio Practice, Criminal Law, § 150:2, Proposed Jury Instructions.

Notes of Decisions

1. Constitutional issues

An accused contemnor has the due process right to the proper burden of proof, which is "beyond a reasonable doubt" in criminal contempt cases. The proper burden of proof in contempt cases is "beyond a reasonable doubt" for criminal contempt and "clear and convincing evidence" for civil contempt. In re Contemnor Caron (Ohio Com.Pl., 04-27-2000) 110 Ohio Misc.2d 58, 744 N.E.2d 787. Constitutional Law ⚷ 273

There is no provision in the Ohio Constitution or in the Ohio Revised Code which entitles a defendant in a criminal case to have the jury instructed that his failure to testify must not be considered for any purpose, and so it is discretionary with the trial court whether to charge on the defendant's right to elect not to testify. (See Griffin v California, 380 US 609, 85 SCt 1229, 14 LEd(2d) 106, 5 Misc 127 (1965).) State v. Nelson (Ohio 1973) 36 Ohio St.2d 79, 303 N.E.2d 865, 65 O.O.2d 222. Criminal Law ⚷ 787(1)

The presence of armed state troopers garbed in full uniform in the first row of the spectator's gallery, to compensate for a lack of courtroom guards usually assigned to defendants denied bail, does not deprive the defendant of a fair trial and need not be justified by an "essential state interest." Holbrook v. Flynn (U.S.R.I. 1986) 106 S.Ct. 1340, 475 U.S. 560, 89 L.Ed.2d 525.

2. Burden of proof

In a habeas corpus proceeding challenging the legality of the arrest and extradition of the defendant, the defendant's guilt is not at issue; thus, the burden of rebutting the presumed validity of the extradition documents and arrest is on the defendant. State v. Adkins (Wayne 1992) 80 Ohio App.3d 817, 610 N.E.2d 1143.

Argument that residual doubt was not a mitigating factor because all guilt issues had already been decided was a correct statement of Ohio law. Bonnell v. Mitchel (N.D.Ohio, 02-04-2004) 301 F.Supp.2d 698. Sentencing And Punishment ⚷ 1780(2)

3. Degree of proof

Trial court erred in applying a "clear and convincing" standard of guilt rather than the standard of "beyond a reasonable doubt" in imposing fines for criminal contempt for violation of a back-to-work order. Board of Educ. of Hamilton City School Dist. v. Hamilton Classroom Teachers Ass'n (Butler 1982) 5 Ohio App.3d 51, 449 N.E.2d 26, 5 O.B.R. 146.

Any adjudication of delinquency must be supported by clear and convincing evidence. In re Agler (Ohio 1969) 19 Ohio St.2d 70, 249 N.E.2d 808, 48 O.O.2d 85. Infants ⚷ 176

4. Evidence

Test for sufficiency of evidence is whether after viewing evidence in light most favorable to prosecution, any rational trier of fact could have found essential elements of crime beyond reasonable doubt. Cleveland v. Pugh (Ohio App. 8 Dist., 04-22-1996) 110 Ohio App.3d 472, 674 N.E.2d 759. Criminal Law ⚷ 1144.13(3); Criminal Law ⚷ 1159.2(7)

Statutory corroboration requirement does not mandate proof of facts which are very substance of crime charged. State v. Economo (Ohio, 07-10-1996) 76 Ohio St.3d 56, 666 N.E.2d 225, 1996-Ohio-426. Criminal Law ⚷ 568

A trier of fact may find a person guilty beyond a reasonable doubt even though the evidence presents a reasonable explanation of his innocence, where the evidence presented, even if it is circumstantial evidence, is sufficient to meet that burden of proof. State v. DeLeon (Montgomery 1991) 76 Ohio App.3d 68, 600 N.E.2d 1137, dismissed, jurisdictional motion overruled 63 Ohio St.3d 1409, 585 N.E.2d 834, appeal dismissed 63 Ohio St.3d 1435, 588 N.E.2d 862.

Circumstantial evidence is insufficient, as a matter of law, to sustain a conviction only where the connection between the direct evidence and the inference is so attenuated that no reasonable person could find that guilt beyond a reasonable doubt has been proved. State v. Griffin (Hamilton 1979)

13 Ohio App.3d 376, 469 N.E.2d 1329, 13 O.B.R. 458.

In a township zoning ordinance offense case, RC Ch 2938 applies to all trial proceedings; thus, where a party is charged with commercial use of property in a rural residential area, his guilt must be established beyond a reasonable doubt under RC 2938.08, and when there is no evidence that an exchange of money for goods took place ("commercial use") or any indicia tending to establish commercial nature, e.g., advertising, receipts, etc., then a violation is not proved beyond a reasonable doubt. Springfield Twp Bd of Trustees v Barnaby, No. L–88–069 (6th Dist Ct App, Lucas, 11–18–88).

2938.09 Grounds of objection to be stated

In the trial of any criminal case, the grounds of an objection to any ruling or action of the judge or magistrate shall be stated if required by him.

(1986 H 412, eff. 3–17–87; 128 v 97)

Cross References

Exceptions unnecessary, Crim R 51

Library References

Criminal Law ⚷660.

Westlaw Topic No. 110.

C.J.S. Criminal Law §§ 1150, 1180.

Research References

Treatises and Practice Aids

Giannelli and Snyder, Baldwin's Ohio Practice, Evidence, R 103, Rulings on Evidence.

Giannelli and Snyder, Baldwin's Ohio Practice, Evidence, § 103.4, "Exceptions" to Evidence.

2938.10 Territorial jurisdiction

The state or municipality in all cases must prove the offense committed within the territorial jurisdiction of the court, and in ordinance cases within the municipality, except as to those offenses in which the court has county wide jurisdiction created by statute and as to those cases in which certification has been made pursuant to section 2937.08 of the Revised Code.

(128 v 97, eff. 1–1–60)

Cross References

Action on not guilty and once in jeopardy pleas in misdemeanor cases, 2937.08

Jurisdiction, 2901.11

Venue, 2901.12

Venue and change of venue, Crim R 18

Library References

Criminal Law ⚷91, 106.

Westlaw Topic No. 110.

C.J.S. Criminal Law §§ 157 to 166, 177 to 178.

Research References

Encyclopedias

OH Jur. 3d Criminal Law § 2017, Jurisdiction as a Magistrate—Territorial Jurisdiction.

Treatises and Practice Aids

Katz, Giannelli, Blair and Lipton, Baldwin's Ohio Practice, Criminal Law, § 56:1, Introduction.

Notes of Decisions

Certification to court of record 2
Commission of offense within jurisdiction 3
Judicial notice of territory 1

1. Judicial notice of territory

A court may take judicial notice whether the Ohio turnpike passes through the territorial jurisdiction of the court or whether a specific interchange of the Ohio turnpike is located within its territorial jurisdiction; if the Ohio turnpike does pass through its territorial jurisdiction, a court may take judicial notice whether a particular milepost is within its territorial jurisdiction. State v. Scott (Trumbull 1965) 3 Ohio App.2d 239, 210 N.E.2d 289, 32 O.O.2d 360.

2. Certification to court of record

Where a judge of a county court is required to certify a case to a court of record, he may certify the case to the court of common pleas or to any municipal court in the county regardless of its territorial jurisdiction. 1960 OAG 1548.

3. Commission of offense within jurisdiction

Where a defendant is charged with rape based on the sexual abuse of a minor, and child endangering based on a separate incident of physical abuse, the acts are committed with a separate animus and there is no course of criminal conduct between the two acts, and where the victim repeatedly testifies the acts of sexual abuse all took place in North Carolina and the one incident of physical abuse took place in Ohio, a trial court has no jurisdiction over the acts which occurred in North Carolina and the rape conviction must be vacated. State v Kress, No. CA-9220, 1993 WL 471463 (5th Dist Ct App, Stark, 11-8-93).

2938.11 Order of proceedings of trial

The trial of an issue shall proceed before the trial court or jury as follows:

(A) Counsel may state the case for the prosecution, including the evidence by which he expects to sustain it.

(B) Counsel for the defendant may state his defense, including the evidence which he expects to offer.

(C) The prosecution then shall produce all its evidence, and the defendant may follow with his evidence, but the court or magistrate, in the furtherance of justice and for good cause shown, may permit evidence to be offered by either side out of its order and may permit rebuttal evidence to be offered by the prosecution.

(D) When the evidence is concluded, unless the case is submitted without argument, counsel for the prosecution shall commence, defendant or his counsel follow, and counsel for the prosecution conclude his argument either to the court or jury. The judge or magistrate may impose a reasonable time limit on argument.

(E) The judge, after argument is concluded in a jury case, forthwith shall charge the jury on the law pertaining to the case and controlling their deliberations, which charge shall not be reduced to writing and taken into the jury room unless the trial judge in his discretion shall so order.

(F) Any verdict arrived at by the jury, or finding determined by the judge or magistrate in trial to the court, shall be announced and received only in open court as soon as it is determined. Any finding by the judge or magistrate shall be announced in open court not more than forty-eight hours after submission of the case to him.

(1986 H 412, eff. 3–17–87; 128 v 97)

Library References

Criminal Law ⚷645, 680, 769.
Westlaw Topic No. 110.

C.J.S. Criminal Law §§ 1215, 1240 to 1244, 1258, 1302 to 1304.

Research References

Encyclopedias

OH Jur. 3d Criminal Law § 8, Under the Fourteenth Amendment.

OH Jur. 3d Criminal Law § 2655, Trial in Magistrate Court.

Treatises and Practice Aids

Markus, Trial Handbook for Ohio Lawyers, § 4:37, Sentencing—Delay in Sentencing or Executing Sentence.

Katz, Giannelli, Blair and Lipton, Baldwin's Ohio Practice, Criminal Law, § 68:2, Rules of Evidence.

Katz, Giannelli, Blair and Lipton, Baldwin's Ohio Practice, Criminal Law, § 68:9, Closing Argument.

Giannelli and Snyder, Baldwin's Ohio Practice, Evidence, R 611, Mode and Order of Interrogation and Presentation.

Giannelli and Snyder, Baldwin's Ohio Practice, Evidence, § 611.4, Court Control of Trial: Order of Proceedings.

Law Review and Journal Commentaries

Winning Arguments—In real life, the best measure of successful advocacy is prevailing at trial, James W. McElhaney. 82 A B A J 80 (September 1996).

Notes of Decisions

1. Procedural statutes as guidelines

RC 2938.11(F) and similar sections which purport to control the inherent functions of a court are mere directory guidelines suggested by a separate branch of government as an ideal format for judicial proceedings; therefore, "violation" of such sections does not affect the court's determination as to whether the defendant's due process rights have been violated. State v. Hatcher (Ohio Co. 1982) 2 Ohio Misc.2d 8, 436 N.E.2d 557, 1 O.B.R. 330.

Police officer's failure to preserve note taken on piece of scrap paper while talking to informant did not violate statute requiring government to produce any statement made by any witness after that witness has testified; if officer did take note, it only involved name and location of suspects, and would not constitute "statement" under statute. U.S. v. Braggs (C.A.6 (Ohio), 05-11-1994) 23 F.3d 1047, rehearing and rehearing en banc denied, certiorari denied 115 S.Ct. 262, 513 U.S. 902, 130 L.Ed.2d 181, certiorari denied 115 S.Ct. 274, 513 U.S. 907, 130 L.Ed.2d 191, certiorari denied 115 S.Ct. 329, 513 U.S. 933, 130 L.Ed.2d 288, denial of post-conviction relief affirmed 142 F.3d 432, certiorari denied 119 S.Ct. 437, 525 U.S. 978, 142 L.Ed.2d 356, denial of habeas corpus affirmed 142 F.3d 432, certiorari denied 119 S.Ct. 234, 525 U.S. 902, 142 L.Ed.2d 192, denial of post-conviction relief affirmed 181 F.3d 102, denial of habeas corpus affirmed 191 F.3d 455, certiorari denied 120 S.Ct. 993, 528 U.S. 1142, 145 L.Ed.2d 941, denial of habeas corpus affirmed 42 Fed.Appx. 678, 2002 WL 927031, certiorari denied 123 S.Ct. 1316, 537 U.S. 1216, 154 L.Ed.2d 1068, dismissal of habeas corpus affirmed 47 Fed.Appx. 396, 2002 WL 31164474. Criminal Law ⚿ 627.7(3); Criminal Law ⚿ 700(9)

2. Jury instructions

Instructing jury that it must accept stipulated facts as true did not constitute plain error, where defendant could not have been prejudiced by instruction as defendant testified that he was present at crime scene and only question was whether defendant committed certain crimes at scene. State v. McSwain (Ohio App. 8 Dist., Cuyahoga, 06-24-2004) No. 83394, 2004-Ohio-3292, 2004 WL 1402700, Unreported, appeal not allowed 104 Ohio St.3d 1425, 819 N.E.2d 709, 2004-Ohio-6585, certiorari denied 125 S.Ct. 2269, 544 U.S. 1040, 161 L.Ed.2d 1072. Criminal Law ⚿ 1038.1(5)

Claim that trial court deprived defendant of right to jury trial by instructing jury that it must accept stipulated facts as true could only be reviewed for plain error, where defendant failed at trial to object to instruction on stipulations. State v. McSwain (Ohio App. 8 Dist., Cuyahoga, 06-24-2004) No. 83394, 2004-Ohio-3292, 2004 WL 1402700, Unreported, appeal not allowed 104 Ohio St.3d 1425, 819 N.E.2d 709, 2004-Ohio-6585, certiorari denied 125 S.Ct. 2269, 544 U.S. 1040, 161 L.Ed.2d 1072. Criminal Law ⚿ 1038.1(5)

Jury instructions should be formulated to fit the facts of the individual case, and form instructions should not be followed blindly, but rather they should be used by the court as a guide in preparing its instructions to the jury. City of Avon Lake v. Anderson (Lorain 1983) 10 Ohio App.3d 297, 462 N.E.2d 188, 10 O.B.R. 472.

3. Speedy decision

Because the time frame imposed by RC 2938.11 is directory rather than mandatory, a ruling within a reasonable time is allowed and what constitutes a reasonable delay depends greatly on the individual circumstances of each case, thus, trial court's nineteen month delay, because of the state of flux of the law relevant to determining the question of appellant's double jeopardy challenge, was not unreasonable. State v. Rice (Ohio App. 7 Dist., Mahoning, 09-27-1999) No. 97 CA 74, 1999 WL 783955, Unreported.

The right to a speedy trial is not denied where court delayed its decision approximately six months in contravention to the forty-eight hour requirement of RC 2938.11 because the statutory provision is directory in nature and not a mandatory rule and defendant did not demand a decision through objection or motion nor did he show evidence of prejudice as he had been free on his own recognizance and his sentence was entirely suspended. State v. Trott (Ohio App. 7 Dist., Mahoning, 03-22-1999) No. 94 CA 73, 1999 WL 167844, Unreported.

Trial court's delay in pronouncing a judgment and sentence on conviction until forty days after trial was not unreasonable delay and did not deny defendant due process of law. State v. Echols (Ohio App. 12 Dist., 03-19-2001) 141 Ohio App.3d 556, 752 N.E.2d 314. Constitutional Law ⚿ 270(1); Criminal Law ⚿ 977(3); Sentencing And Punishment ⚿ 384

While the forty-eight-hour period to return a verdict prescribed in the statute is not mandatory, a defendant is entitled to judgment within a reasonable time after his case has been submitted to the court for determination and disposition. State v. Echols (Ohio App. 12 Dist., 03-19-2001) 141 Ohio App.3d 556, 752 N.E.2d 314. Criminal Law ⚿ 255.4; Criminal Law ⚿ 258; Criminal Law ⚿ 977(3)

Twenty days was not unreasonable time period for visiting judge to announce court's decision on complex nine-count indictment which required evaluation of 20 witnesses and numerous exhibits presented by both sides, though visiting judge determined other criminal matters between time case was submitted to him and read portions of transcript outside defendant's presence. State v. Fiorenzo (Ohio App. 11 Dist., 01-02-1996) 108 Ohio App.3d 500, 671 N.E.2d 287, dismissed, appeal not allowed 76 Ohio St.3d 1405, 666 N.E.2d 566. Criminal Law ⚷ 258

While statutory 48–hour period in which judge shall announce any finding after submission of case to him is not mandatory, defendant is entitled to judgment within reasonable time after case has been submitted to court for disposition. State v. Fiorenzo (Ohio App. 11 Dist., 01-02-1996) 108 Ohio App.3d 500, 671 N.E.2d 287, dismissed, appeal not allowed 76 Ohio St.3d 1405, 666 N.E.2d 566. Criminal Law ⚷ 258

The time limits of RC 2938.11(F) for findings by a judge are not mandatory, but merely directory, and where numerous legal issues are presented on four charges, a three-month delay in decision is not a violation of due process. City of Xenia v. Manker (Greene 1984) 18 Ohio App.3d 9, 480 N.E.2d 94, 18 O.B.R. 33.

Where a judgment of guilty in a criminal action tried without a jury is not announced until seven months after the defense rested, an accused has been denied his right to a speedy disposition of his case, contrary to the intent of RC 2938.11(F) and due process of the law. Village of Sheffield v. Nieves (Lorain 1976) 52 Ohio App.2d 187, 368 N.E.2d 1262, 6 O.O.3d 173. Constitutional Law ⚷ 268(4); Sentencing And Punishment ⚷ 380

Where a case was submitted at eleven a.m. and the judgment is announced at two p.m. on the second day following, there was sufficient compliance with RC 2938.11(F). State ex rel. Turrin v. County Court (Ohio 1966) 5 Ohio St.2d 194, 214 N.E.2d 670, 34 O.O.2d 350.

4. Opening and closing statements

Prosecutor's comment in closing argument that asked the jury to use reason and common sense when seeking justice did not deny defendant a fair aggravated robbery trial; the prosecutor did not implicitly or explicitly state that justice in the matter would be a conviction as opposed to an acquittal, nor did the prosecutor appeal to public demand or community pressures to convict. State v. Brown (Ohio App. 5 Dist., Stark, 02-21-2006) No. 2005CA00094, 2006-Ohio-826, 2006 WL 438692, Unreported. Criminal Law ⚷ 713

Prosecutor's statement in closing argument that commented on the credibility of the victim did not constitute plain error or deny defendant a fair aggravated robbery trial; comment was made in rebuttal to defendant's closing argument, during which defense counsel repeatedly emphasized alleged discrepancies between the victim's testimony and that of other witnesses, and the trial court advised the jury that closing arguments were not evidence and should not be treated as evidence. State v. Brown (Ohio App. 5 Dist., Stark, 02-21-2006) No. 2005CA00094, 2006-Ohio-826, 2006 WL 438692, Unreported. Criminal Law ⚷ 726

Prosecutor's comment during closing argument in a prosecution for possession with intent to distribute pseudoephedrine, asserting that defendant testified he was selling to "buying groups," and that there was no evidence other than from defendant's lips that there were buying groups, was supported by the evidence at trial, and thus, was not improper; defendant was the only person at trial who used the words "buying groups" when testifying, and the records showed no evidence of buying groups. U.S. v. Merkosky (C.A.6 (Ohio), 06-14-2005) No. 02-4332, 135 Fed.Appx. 828, 2005 WL 1400201, Unreported. Criminal Law ⚷ 720(7.1)

Prosecutor's impermissible comments regarding credibility of State's witnesses and asking jury to compare their credibility with defendant during closing argument did not prejudice defendant, in trial for petty theft, where jury would likely have found defendant guilty absent comments. Alliance v. Yin (Ohio App. 5 Dist., Stark, 06-13-2005) No. 2004CA00239, 2005-Ohio-2989, 2005 WL 1399269, Unreported. Criminal Law ⚷ 720(5)

Prosecutor's comments during closing argument that the State's witnesses were truthful "and you weigh that and the way they presented themselves with the way defendant presented himself" constituted improper vouching for credibility of witnesses, in trial for petty theft. Alliance v. Yin (Ohio App. 5 Dist., Stark, 06-13-2005) No. 2004CA00239, 2005-Ohio-2989, 2005 WL 1399269, Unreported. Criminal Law ⚷ 720(5)

Prosecutor's statement during rebuttal closing argument in murder prosecution, mentioning that defendant did not call his original counsel to bolster his claim that police witness was lying, was permissible response to defense counsel's statement during closing argument that state's case rested solely on testimony of police witness, that policc witness was lying about defendant's statement to police, and that defendant's former counsel had been present at time of statement but was not called to testify, and did not amount to misconduct. State v. Lewis (Ohio App. 7 Dist., Mahoning, 05-24-2005) No. 03 MA 36, 2005-Ohio-2699, 2005 WL 1300761, Unreported, appeal not allowed 106 Ohio St.3d 1556, 836 N.E.2d 581, 2005-Ohio-5531. Criminal Law ⚷ 726

Prosecutor's statement during rebuttal closing argument in murder prosecution, to effect that there were "evidentiary reasons" why jury had not seen defendant's videotaped statement to police and that defense counsel was aware of what those reasons were, were permissible response to defense counsel's prior attempt to cause jury to question state's reasons for failing to show videotape, and did not improperly shift any burden to defense. State v. Lewis (Ohio App. 7 Dist., Mahoning, 05-24-2005) No. 03 MA 36, 2005-Ohio-2699, 2005 WL 1300761, Unreported, appeal not allowed 106 Ohio St.3d

1556, 836 N.E.2d 581, 2005-Ohio-5531. Criminal Law ⚷ 726

Prosecutor's statements during rebuttal closing argument in murder prosecution, to effect that defendant was "hid[ing] behind the Constitution" and "waiv[ing] [*sic*] the flag" were permissible response to defense counsel's sweeping pronouncements during his closing argument with respect to the Constitution in attempt to elucidate his point about vengeance and state-induced sympathy for victim, and did not improperly shift any burden to defense. State v. Lewis (Ohio App. 7 Dist., Mahoning, 05-24-2005) No. 03 MA 36, 2005-Ohio-2699, 2005 WL 1300761, Unreported, appeal not allowed 106 Ohio St.3d 1556, 836 N.E.2d 581, 2005-Ohio-5531. Criminal Law ⚷ 726

The prosecutor's trial comments did not deprive defendant of a fair trial or constitute prosecutorial misconduct, during prosecution for drug abuse, carrying a concealed weapon, and having a weapon while under a disability; defendant did not cite in the transcript where the prosecutor referred to him as a drug dealer, and the court sustained two of defendant's objections to comments made by the prosecutor. State v. Westbrook (Ohio App. 5 Dist., Richland, 05-23-2005) No. 04CA0072, 2005-Ohio-2673, 2005 WL 1274779, Unreported. Criminal Law ⚷ 723(1); Criminal Law ⚷ 730(14)

Prosecutor's comment during rebuttal closing argument that, under defense counsel's own argument to effect that inconsistencies between eyewitness' testimony indicated that they were liars, defense counsel's misspelling of word would make him a liar, did not constitute impermissible denigration of defense counsel, in trial for aggravated murder, murder, and aggravated robbery; rather, prosecutor's comment was in response to defense counsel's assertion that eyewitnesses were liars and to expose weakness in counsel's argument, and prosecutor quickly pointed out that defense counsel was not liar but had simply made mistake. State v. Huges (Ohio App. 1 Dist., Hamilton, 05-20-2005) No. C-030489, 2005-Ohio-2453, 2005 WL 1190715, Unreported. Criminal Law ⚷ 726

State did not commit prosecutorial misconduct in referencing, during closing argument, defendant's failure to explain his possession of inculpatory evidence, a ring worn by murder victim, since, when viewed in context, statement was not an attempt to focus jury's attention on defendant's decision not to testify, and statement was truthful, underscoring what evidence had shown and what reasonable inferences may have been drawn therefrom. State v. Butler (Ohio App. 10 Dist., Franklin, 02-15-2005) No. 03AP-800, 2005-Ohio-579, 2005 WL 351759, Unreported, appeal not allowed 106 Ohio St.3d 1416, 830 N.E.2d 348, 2005-Ohio-3154. Criminal Law ⚷ 721(3)

Prosecutor's over zealous comments during closing argument of gross sexual imposition trial, in which she misstated the evidence by representing to the jury that defendant explained "sexual intercourse" and "pregnancy" to victim by reference to worms, eggs, and animals, did not deny defendant a fair trial so as to rise to the level of plain error; there was evidence before the jury that defendant had discussed with victim sexual intercourse, and the specifics were not relevant. State v. Novak (Ohio App. 11 Dist., Lake, 02-11-2005) No. 2003-L-077, 2005-Ohio-563, 2005 WL 336337, Unreported. Criminal Law ⚷ 1037.1(2)

Prosecutor's references to the "institutionalized mentally retarded" during closing argument of gross sexual imposition trial were not improper; defendant's defense was premised on equating the ability to resist with the ability to consent, and the prosecutor took the implications of such an argument to their logical extreme—even the severely mentally retarded possess the ability to resist. State v. Novak (Ohio App. 11 Dist., Lake, 02-11-2005) No. 2003-L-077, 2005-Ohio-563, 2005 WL 336337, Unreported. Criminal Law ⚷ 713

Comments by prosecutor during closing argument of gross sexual imposition trial, in which she characterized defendant's defense as a "whitewash" that he was attempting to "sell" the jury, though overly zealous, did not impugn defendant's veracity or defense counsel's integrity, so as to deny defendant a fair trial. State v. Novak (Ohio App. 11 Dist., Lake, 02-11-2005) No. 2003-L-077, 2005-Ohio-563, 2005 WL 336337, Unreported. Criminal Law ⚷ 720(5); Criminal Law ⚷ 723(1)

Prosecutor's statement during closing argument of gross sexual imposition trial, that she did not believe "that the law is that you can take advantage of somebody that is mentally retarded," was not improper as a misstatement of the law; during closing argument, prosecutor reviewed all the elements of gross sexual imposition with the jury using the technical terms used in the statute. State v. Novak (Ohio App. 11 Dist., Lake, 02-11-2005) No. 2003-L-077, 2005-Ohio-563, 2005 WL 336337, Unreported. Criminal Law ⚷ 717

Prosecutor's comment in closing argument in defendant's trial for sexual battery in which prosecutor evoked reptile imagery was an attempt to explain to the jury that they should not be misled by the defense's argument that the case was not what it appeared to be, rather than an impermissible comment comparing the defendant to a reptile. State v. Anderson (Ohio App. 6 Dist., Wood, 02-11-2005) No. WD-04-035, 2005-Ohio-534, 2005 WL 327179, Unreported. Criminal Law ⚷ 723(1)

Prosecutor's comments in closing argument in defendant's trial for sexual battery that victim remembered the events of the evening was not a comment about the victim's credibility, but rather was a response to the inference that she had blacked out from excessive drinking and could not remember what had happened. State v. Anderson (Ohio App. 6 Dist., Wood, 02-11-2005) No. WD-04-035, 2005-Ohio-534, 2005 WL 327179, Unreported. Criminal Law ⚷ 720(5)

Prosecutor's comment in closing argument in defendant's trial for sexual battery that witnesses were honest in their answers did not amount to an improper comment on the veracity of the witnesses; comment was made in the context of questions several jurors had proposed to witnesses regarding why the witnesses had allowed themselves to be placed in a position where the crime could have been committed, and it was not a comment on the credibility of the women with regard to their testimony against defendant. State v. Anderson (Ohio App. 6 Dist., Wood, 02-11-2005) No. WD-04-035, 2005-Ohio-534, 2005 WL 327179, Unreported. Criminal Law ⚷ 720(5)

The prosecutor's closing argument statement that medical expert had testified that "one blow can kill you" was a reasonable inference from the evidence presented during felonious assault trial, and therefore did not constitute prosecutorial misconduct; medical expert hypothesized that an unlucky hit could shear nerve fibers at the base of the brain, resulting in death, and expert testified about a case where a university student was killed with one blow. State v. Root (Ohio App. 2 Dist., Montgomery, 01-31-2005) No. CIV.A. 20366, 2005-Ohio-448, 2005 WL 281172, Unreported. Criminal Law ⚷ 720(7.1)

Defendant waived any prejudice that may have resulted from the prosecutor's closing argument statements that defense counsel had the "same subpoena power" as the State to call witnesses and that defendant was the "only person in this courtroom who picks witnesses," where defendant objected to both statements, the trial court sustained defendant's objections, and defendant failed to request any curative jury instructions. State v. Root (Ohio App. 2 Dist., Montgomery, 01-31-2005) No. CIV.A. 20366, 2005-Ohio-448, 2005 WL 281172, Unreported. Criminal Law ⚷ 728(5)

Prosecutor's argument to jury in prosecution for gross sexual imposition, telling jury that they should find defendant guilty if they would not let him be alone with their child, daughter, or granddaughter, and suggesting to the jury that they should feel like they were the victim, constituted prosecutorial misconduct. State v. Breland (Ohio App. 11 Dist., Ashtabula, 12-23-2004) No. 2003-A-0066, 2004-Ohio-7238, 2004 WL 3090222, Unreported, appeal not allowed 105 Ohio St.3d 1546, 827 N.E.2d 328, 2005-Ohio-2188. Criminal Law ⚷ 723(1)

Prosecutor's argument to jury in prosecution for gross sexual imposition, stating her personal opinion that defendant lied on the witness stand, constituted prosecutorial misconduct. State v. Breland (Ohio App. 11 Dist., Ashtabula, 12-23-2004) No. 2003-A-0066, 2004-Ohio-7238, 2004 WL 3090222, Unreported, appeal not allowed 105 Ohio St.3d 1546, 827 N.E.2d 328, 2005-Ohio-2188. Criminal Law ⚷ 720(5)

Prosecutor's argument to jury in prosecution for gross sexual imposition, wrongly asserting that defendant's claim of accident was irrelevant, constituted prosecutorial misconduct. State v. Breland (Ohio App. 11 Dist., Ashtabula, 12-23-2004) No. 2003-A-0066, 2004-Ohio-7238, 2004 WL 3090222, Unreported, appeal not allowed 105 Ohio St.3d 1546, 827 N.E.2d 328, 2005-Ohio-2188. Criminal Law ⚷ 717

Murder defendant failed to establish ineffective assistance based on trial counsel's failure to give opening statement, where decision to waive opening statement is matter of trial strategy. State v. Fayne (Ohio App. 8 Dist., Cuyahoga, 09-02-2004) No. 83267, 2004-Ohio-4625, 2004 WL 1944793, Unreported, motion for delayed appeal denied 106 Ohio St.3d 1502, 833 N.E.2d 1246, 2005-Ohio-4605. Criminal Law ⚷ 641.13(2.1)

Absent proof of alleged conversation between defendant and detective, it was improper for the State to refer to an "oral statement" defendant gave to the police in its "statement of the case and facts;" there was no evidence of any such statement at trial, and during defendant's cross-examination, the State asked him whether he made certain statements to questions by a police detective, and defendant denied making specific statements, and the State did not offer any proof relating to a conversation, nor did it present the testimony of the detective who allegedly heard these statements. State v. Paulk (Ohio App. 8 Dist., Cuyahoga, 08-05-2004) No. 83968, 2004-Ohio-4082, 2004 WL 1752956, Unreported. Criminal Law ⚷ 719(1)

Prosecutor's closing argument comment that only jury could correct injustices done to victims, when viewed in context of entire argument, was not prejudicial to defendant, who was convicted of kidnapping, aggravated robbery, aggravated burglary, and felonious assault, where such appeal to jury's sympathies was modest and prosecutor asked jury to use reason and common sense. State v. McSwain (Ohio App. 8 Dist., Cuyahoga, 06-24-2004) No. 83394, 2004-Ohio-3292, 2004 WL 1402700, Unreported, appeal not allowed 104 Ohio St.3d 1425, 819 N.E.2d 709, 2004-Ohio-6585, certiorari denied 125 S.Ct. 2269, 544 U.S. 1040, 161 L.Ed.2d 1072. Criminal Law ⚷ 723(1)

Claim that prosecutor's closing argument comment that only jury could correct injustices done to victims was improper could only be reviewed for plain error, where defendant failed at trial to object to such comment. State v. McSwain (Ohio App. 8 Dist., Cuyahoga, 06-24-2004) No. 83394, 2004-Ohio-3292, 2004 WL 1402700, Unreported, appeal not allowed 104 Ohio St.3d 1425, 819 N.E.2d 709, 2004-Ohio-6585, certiorari denied 125 S.Ct. 2269, 544 U.S. 1040, 161 L.Ed.2d 1072. Criminal Law ⚷ 1037.1(2)

Assuming Fifth Amendment right not to put forth any evidence in corroboration of defendant's testimony exists, prosecutor's closing argument comment that defendant offered version of events that was completely unsupported by anything else did not violate such right, where prosecutor did not comment on defendant's failure to offer corroborating testimony, but simply indicated that defendant's testimony was not consistent with other testimony. State v. McSwain (Ohio App. 8 Dist., Cuyahoga, 06-24-2004) No. 83394, 2004-Ohio-3292, 2004 WL 1402700, Unreported, appeal not allowed 104 Ohio St.3d 1425, 819 N.E.2d 709, 2004-Ohio-6585, certiorari denied 125 S.Ct. 2269, 544 U.S. 1040, 161 L.Ed.2d 1072. Criminal Law ⚷ 721.5(2)

Once robbery defendant waived his right against self-incrimination by testifying, his credibility was at issue and could properly be challenged by charge of recent fabrication. State v. McSwain (Ohio App. 8 Dist., Cuyahoga, 06-24-2004) No. 83394, 2004-Ohio-3292, 2004 WL 1402700, Unreported, appeal not allowed 104 Ohio St.3d 1425, 819 N.E.2d 709, 2004-Ohio-6585, certiorari denied 125 S.Ct. 2269, 544 U.S. 1040, 161 L.Ed.2d 1072. Witnesses ⚷ 337(1)

Prosecutor's closing argument comment that state's evidence was unchallenged was not improper personal opinion, but was proper comment directed at strength of state's case. State v. Gray (Ohio App. 8 Dist., Cuyahoga, 03-25-2004) No. 83097, 2004-Ohio-1454, 2004 WL 584187, Unreported, motion to reopen denied 2004-Ohio-4481, 2004 WL 1902381, motion for delayed appeal denied 103 Ohio St.3d 1476, 816 N.E.2d 252, 2004-Ohio-5405. Criminal Law ⚷ 719(3); Criminal Law ⚷ 720(1)

Prosecutor's improper use of bad character of defendant's friend to attack defendant's character during closing arguments in cocaine trafficking trial by suggesting defendant distanced himself from friend because "you are with whom you associate," did not deny defendant a fair trial so as to require reversal, even though evidence in case was not overwhelming; it was not clear that but for comment defendant would not have been convicted, case revolved around credibility of the witnesses, and to reverse on instant issue would necessarily have required appellate court to rule on witness credibility and supersede role of trier of fact. State v. Moman (Ohio App. 7 Dist., Columbiana, 03-18-2004) No. 02CO52, 2004-Ohio-1387, 2004 WL 549807, Unreported. Criminal Law ⚷ 1171.6

Prosecutor improperly used the bad character of defendant's friend to attack defendant's character during closing arguments in cocaine trafficking trial by suggesting defendant distanced himself from friend because "you are with whom you associate," even though prosecutor stated comments rebutted defense counsel's closing argument, where defense counsel did not state that defendant had distance himself from friend. State v. Moman (Ohio App. 7 Dist., Columbiana, 03-18-2004) No. 02CO52, 2004-Ohio-1387, 2004 WL 549807, Unreported. Criminal Law ⚷ 1171.6

Prosecutor's statement in closing argument that testimony of defendant's sister seemed to blame the drug charges against defendant on her deceased boyfriend did not constitute misconduct, even though sister never directly stated that her boyfriend was responsible for the drug sales, where she did state that defendant was not present on the date of one charge, that her boyfriend was present, and that her boyfriend was the individual who answered the door and spoke with the informant. State v. Moman (Ohio App. 7 Dist., Columbiana, 03-18-2004) No. 02CO52, 2004-Ohio-1387, 2004 WL 549807, Unreported. Criminal Law ⚷ 720(7.1)

Trial court did not commit plain error in failing to declare a mistrial for prosecutor's closing comments, during which prosecutor stated in response to assault defendant's argument that nobody saw stabbing that "the law still believe[d] that people [could] tell the truth," despite claim comments were disparaging to victim and defense counsel; comments were permissible argument in response to defense counsel's assertion of lack of physical evidence and to challenge of victim's credibility. State v. Hammond (Ohio App. 2 Dist., Montgomery, 04-25-2003) No. CIV.A. 19278, 2003-Ohio-2078, 2003 WL 1950370, Unreported. Criminal Law ⚷ 1037.1(2)

Prosecutor's comments during closing argument of murder trial that defendant should not have escaped punishment for aggravated murder by alleging sudden passion or fit of rage and words alone were not enough to allow someone to escape their punishment for aggravated murder were not prejudicial, where defense counsel objected, trial court sustained objection, and trial court gave a curative instruction. State v. Brandy (Ohio App. 10 Dist., Franklin, 04-10-2003) No. 02AP-832, 2003-Ohio-1836, 2003 WL 1848761, Unreported, appeal not allowed 99 Ohio St.3d 1515, 792 N.E.2d 201, 2003-Ohio-3957. Criminal Law ⚷ 730(1)

Prosecutor's characterization of murder defendant as a "drug dealer extraordinaire" was not plain error, where characterization was based on evidence presented at trial during which defendant admitted to a life of drug dealing. State v. Brandy (Ohio App. 10 Dist., Franklin, 04-10-2003) No. 02AP-832, 2003-Ohio-1836, 2003 WL 1848761, Unreported, appeal not allowed 99 Ohio St.3d 1515, 792 N.E.2d 201, 2003-Ohio-3957. Criminal Law ⚷ 1037.1(2)

Prosecutor's comment during closing argument of murder trial comparing defendant's actions in shooting victim to that of a dog hunting someone or something down, while it may have been a bit harsh, was merely an attempt by the prosecutor to explain to the jury defendant's actions and fell into the latitude afforded counsel during closing argument. State v. Brandy (Ohio App. 10 Dist., Franklin, 04-10-2003) No. 02AP-832, 2003-Ohio-1836, 2003 WL 1848761, Unreported, appeal not allowed 99 Ohio St.3d 1515, 792 N.E.2d 201, 2003-Ohio-3957. Criminal Law ⚷ 713

Three comments made by prosecutor during closing arguments, when read in full context, were neither materially prejudicial nor did they deny defendant convicted of murder and possession of cocaine a fair trial, but were an attempt by prosecutor to convince jury that defendant's defense of voluntary manslaughter must be rejected; prosecutor asked jury what else could defendant have said but that his actions were merely voluntary manslaughter, and prosecutor stated that defendant's claim that victim and his wife who were attempting to buy drugs from defendant had time to hide drugs and money on their person or in body cavities was "ridiculous." State v. Brandy (Ohio App. 10 Dist., Franklin, 04-10-2003) No. 02AP-832, 2003-Ohio-1836, 2003 WL 1848761, Unreported, appeal not allowed 99 Ohio St.3d 1515, 792 N.E.2d 201, 2003-Ohio-3957. Criminal Law ⚷ 1171.1(3)

Defendant failed to object to prosecutor's remarks during closing argument of murder trial and thus waived all but plain error. State v. Brandy (Ohio App. 10 Dist., Franklin, 04-10-2003) No. 02AP-832, 2003-Ohio-1836, 2003 WL 1848761, Unreported, appeal not allowed 99 Ohio St.3d 1515, 792 N.E.2d 201, 2003-Ohio-3957. Criminal Law ⚷ 1037.1(1)

Prosecutor's comment during closing argument characterizing defendant's actions as "open[ing] fire in a crowded apartment complex where kids are out playing, where people are all around," was not irrelevant or an improper appeal to jurors' emotions in trial for attempted murder and felonious assault, although defendant was not charged with an offense involving children or any other victims; statement was proper comment on evidence that defendant fired numerous shots at intended victim who was standing within group of people and that 12-year-old boy had been playing nearby. State v. Baker (Ohio App. 2 Dist., 01-07-2005) 159 Ohio App.3d 462, 824 N.E.2d 162, 2005-Ohio-45, motion for delayed appeal denied 106 Ohio St.3d 1408, 830 N.E.2d 342, 2005-Ohio-3154, appeal not allowed 106 Ohio St.3d 1417, 830 N.E.2d 348, 2005-Ohio-3154. Criminal Law ⚷ 720(1)

Prosecutor's characterization of defendant as "liar" during closing argument was reasonable inference from evidence presented at trial for attempted murder and felonious assault; defendant's version of shooting incident differed significantly from that of all other witnesses, defendant gave statements to police that were inconsistent with his testimony at trial, and his trial testimony was inconsistent with physical evidence. State v. Baker (Ohio App. 2 Dist., 01-07-2005) 159 Ohio App.3d 462, 824 N.E.2d 162, 2005-Ohio-45, motion for delayed appeal denied 106 Ohio St.3d 1408, 830 N.E.2d 342, 2005-Ohio-3154, appeal not allowed 106 Ohio St.3d 1417, 830 N.E.2d 348, 2005-Ohio-3154. Criminal Law ⚷ 720(5)

Prosecutor during closing argument of rape trial did not interject her personal beliefs about the veracity of victim's testimony, but rather merely argued that the evidence supported the theory that victim did not lie or concoct her story of abuse by her father, the defendant, and thus prosecutor did not commit misconduct. State v. Geboy (Ohio App. 3 Dist., 08-30-2001) 145 Ohio App.3d 706, 764 N.E.2d 451, 2001-Ohio-2214, appeal not allowed 94 Ohio St.3d 1410, 759 N.E.2d 787, appeal after new trial 2003-Ohio-343, 2003 WL 178616, appeal not allowed 99 Ohio St.3d 1412, 788 N.E.2d 648, 2003-Ohio-2454. Criminal Law ⚷ 720(5)

Statement by prosecutor during closing argument in murder prosecution that, while it is fundamental that law be upheld and rights of defendant be recognized, "On the other side of the coin it's just as important to all of us" that victim "did have a right to live," and that "no one has a right to extinguish the lives of others," was proper; comment did not constitute victim impact evidence, but merely pointed out that persons have a right to live and that murder takes away that right. State v. Getsy (Ohio, 12-23-1998) 84 Ohio St.3d 180, 702 N.E.2d 866, 1998-Ohio-533, reconsideration denied 84 Ohio St.3d 1488, 705 N.E.2d 368, certiorari denied 119 S.Ct. 2407, 527 U.S. 1042, 144 L.Ed.2d 805, dismissal of post-conviction relief affirmed 1999 WL 1073682, dismissed, appeal not allowed 88 Ohio St.3d 1425, 723 N.E.2d 1113, habeas corpus granted 456 F.3d 575. Criminal Law ⚷ 723(1)

Defense counsel's failure to make any opening or closing statement in support of sparing defendant's life in capital murder prosecution did not result in ineffectiveness per se. State v. Keith (Ohio, 10-01-1997) 79 Ohio St.3d 514, 684 N.E.2d 47, 1997-Ohio-367, reconsideration denied 80 Ohio St.3d 1450, 686 N.E.2d 276, certiorari denied 118 S.Ct. 1393, 523 U.S. 1063, 140 L.Ed.2d 652. Criminal Law ⚷ 641.13(7)

Defense counsel's failure to make opening or closing statement at sentencing in capital murder prosecution complied with defendant's decision not to present mitigating evidence and comported with claims of innocence and, thus, did not amount to ineffective assistance of counsel; even if counsel's performance had been deficient, defendant did not prove reasonable probability that result would have been different had counsel made closing argument against the death sentence. State v. Keith (Ohio, 10-01-1997) 79 Ohio St.3d 514, 684 N.E.2d 47, 1997-Ohio-367, reconsideration denied 80 Ohio St.3d 1450, 686 N.E.2d 276, certiorari denied 118 S.Ct. 1393, 523 U.S. 1063, 140 L.Ed.2d 652. Criminal Law ⚷ 641.13(7)

Defense counsel's decision not to make opening statement, in capital case, was legitimate tactical decision and did not prejudice defendant. Byrd v. Collins (C.A.6 (Ohio), 04-06-2000) 209 F.3d 486, rehearing en banc denied 227 F.3d 756, certiorari denied 121 S.Ct. 786, 531 U.S. 1082, 148 L.Ed.2d 682, rehearing denied 121 S.Ct. 1176, 531 U.S. 1186, 148 L.Ed.2d 1034. Criminal Law ⚷ 641.13(2.1)

Any error arising from prosecutor's introduction, in capital murder case, of videotape of television interview with victim and his family did not rise to level of due process violation, given key witness' testimony that defendant confessed to murder while watching interview in jail; any prejudice resulting from showing of videotape stemmed not from tape itself, but from admissible testimony regarding confession and defendant's callous remarks about victim. Byrd v. Collins (C.A.6 (Ohio), 04-06-2000) 209 F.3d 486, rehearing en banc denied 227 F.3d 756, certiorari denied 121 S.Ct. 786, 531 U.S. 1082, 148 L.Ed.2d 682, rehearing denied 121 S.Ct. 1176, 531 U.S. 1186, 148 L.Ed.2d 1034. Constitutional Law ⚷ 266(1); Criminal Law ⚷ 438(8)

In determining whether prosecutorial misconduct rises to level of due process violation, federal habeas court must bear in mind that the touchstone of due process analysis is the fairness of the trial, not the culpability of the prosecutor. Byrd v. Collins (C.A.6 (Ohio), 04-06-2000) 209 F.3d 486, rehearing en banc denied 227 F.3d 756, certiorari denied 121 S.Ct. 786, 531 U.S. 1082, 148 L.Ed.2d 682, rehearing denied 121 S.Ct. 1176, 531 U.S. 1186, 148

L.Ed.2d 1034. Constitutional Law ⚷ 268(8); Habeas Corpus ⚷ 497

Prosecutor's statements speculating about whether defendant had previously seen store clerk killed during robbery and whereabouts of missing evidence did not rise to level of due process violation, even if they were impermissible comments on facts not in evidence, given that statements were qualified with language suggesting their speculative nature, and thus did not mislead jury, remarks were relatively isolated, other evidence of guilt was strong, and defense counsel did not object or seek curative instruction. Byrd v. Collins (C.A.6 (Ohio), 04-06-2000) 209 F.3d 486, rehearing en banc denied 227 F.3d 756, certiorari denied 121 S.Ct. 786, 531 U.S. 1082, 148 L.Ed.2d 682, rehearing denied 121 S.Ct. 1176, 531 U.S. 1186, 148 L.Ed.2d 1034. Constitutional Law ⚷ 268(8); Criminal Law ⚷ 719(1); Criminal Law ⚷ 728(2)

Prosecutor's suggestion that defense counsel was trying to hide something about source of blood found on sweater alleged to have been worn by accomplice was suggestion of reasonable inference to be drawn from defense counsel's presentation of evidence and argument, and did not rise to level of due process violation. Byrd v. Collins (C.A.6 (Ohio), 04-06-2000) 209 F.3d 486, rehearing en banc denied 227 F.3d 756, certiorari denied 121 S.Ct. 786, 531 U.S. 1082, 148 L.Ed.2d 682, rehearing denied 121 S.Ct. 1176, 531 U.S. 1186, 148 L.Ed.2d 1034. Constitutional Law ⚷ 268(8); Criminal Law ⚷ 720(9)

Prosecutor's conduct in vouching for credibility of witness did not rise to level of due process violation, and thus did not warrant federal habeas relief; remarks did not mislead jury, which was told by prosecutor that his remarks were not evidence, trial court instructed jury immediately after arguments that arguments were not evidence, witness' testimony was reread at jury's request following initial deliberation, jury returned guilty verdict soon after again hearing witness' testimony, which was not complicated, and trial court instructed jury as to factors to consider in evaluating weight of witnesses' testimony. Byrd v. Collins (C.A.6 (Ohio), 04-06-2000) 209 F.3d 486, rehearing en banc denied 227 F.3d 756, certiorari denied 121 S.Ct. 786, 531 U.S. 1082, 148 L.Ed.2d 682, rehearing denied 121 S.Ct. 1176, 531 U.S. 1186, 148 L.Ed.2d 1034. Constitutional Law ⚷ 268(8); Criminal Law ⚷ 730(8); Habeas Corpus ⚷ 497

Statements in which prosecutor speculated as to whether defendant had previously seen store clerk who was killed during robbery due to store's close proximity to defendant's childhood home, as to whether witness had faulty recall as to color of one perpetrator's pants, and as to location of missing evidence were arguably reasonable inferences from the evidence presented at trial that prosecutor was allowed to draw. Byrd v. Collins (C.A.6 (Ohio), 04-06-2000) 209 F.3d 486, rehearing en banc denied 227 F.3d 756, certiorari denied 121 S.Ct. 786, 531 U.S. 1082, 148 L.Ed.2d 682, rehearing denied 121 S.Ct. 1176, 531 U.S. 1186, 148 L.Ed.2d 1034. Criminal Law ⚷ 720(9)

Prosecutor's use of term "predator" to describe murder defendant did not deprive defendant of fair trial. Byrd v. Collins (C.A.6 (Ohio), 04-06-2000) 209 F.3d 486, rehearing en banc denied 227 F.3d 756, certiorari denied 121 S.Ct. 786, 531 U.S. 1082, 148 L.Ed.2d 682, rehearing denied 121 S.Ct. 1176, 531 U.S. 1186, 148 L.Ed.2d 1034. Criminal Law ⚷ 724(1)

Defendant must show that the statement in question was indisputably false, rather than merely misleading, to establish a claim of prosecutorial misconduct or denial of due process based on knowing use of false or perjured testimony. Byrd v. Collins (C.A.6 (Ohio), 04-06-2000) 209 F.3d 486, rehearing en banc denied 227 F.3d 756, certiorari denied 121 S.Ct. 786, 531 U.S. 1082, 148 L.Ed.2d 682, rehearing denied 121 S.Ct. 1176, 531 U.S. 1186, 148 L.Ed.2d 1034. Constitutional Law ⚷ 268(9); Criminal Law ⚷ 706(2)

Witness' testimony that he had no pending charges against him at time of defendant's trial was not indisputably false, as required to support claim of prosecutorial misconduct or denial of due process based on state's alleged knowing use of false or perjured testimony, given that witness was not facing any criminal charges when he testified and that the record suggested that he, and the prosecutor, interpreted question raising issue as not encompassing parole revocation proceedings which witness faced at completion of workhouse sentence he was then serving. Byrd v. Collins (C.A.6 (Ohio), 04-06-2000) 209 F.3d 486, rehearing en banc denied 227 F.3d 756, certiorari denied 121 S.Ct. 786, 531 U.S. 1082, 148 L.Ed.2d 682, rehearing denied 121 S.Ct. 1176, 531 U.S. 1186, 148 L.Ed.2d 1034. Constitutional Law ⚷ 268(9); Criminal Law ⚷ 706(2)

Given extensive impeachment information elicited during defendant's cross-examination, witness' allegedly false testimony that he had no pending charges against him at time of defendant's trial was not "material," as required to support claim of prosecutorial misconduct or denial of due process based on state's alleged knowing use of witness' false or perjured testimony, even though witness faced parole revocation proceedings following completion of workhouse sentence he was then serving. Byrd v. Collins (C.A.6 (Ohio), 04-06-2000) 209 F.3d 486, rehearing en banc denied 227 F.3d 756, certiorari denied 121 S.Ct. 786, 531 U.S. 1082, 148 L.Ed.2d 682, rehearing denied 121 S.Ct. 1176, 531 U.S. 1186, 148 L.Ed.2d 1034. Constitutional Law ⚷ 268(9); Criminal Law ⚷ 706(2)

Conviction obtained by the knowing use of perjured testimony is fundamentally unfair, and must be set aside if there is any reasonable likelihood that the false testimony could have affected the judgment of the jury. Byrd v. Collins (C.A.6 (Ohio), 04-06-2000) 209 F.3d 486, rehearing en banc denied 227 F.3d 756, certiorari denied 121 S.Ct. 786, 531 U.S. 1082, 148 L.Ed.2d 682, rehearing denied 121 S.Ct. 1176, 531 U.S. 1186, 148 L.Ed.2d 1034. Criminal Law ⚷ 706(2)

Prosecutor's misconduct during penalty phase of capital murder trial, in indicating without evidence that petitioner had engaged in knife fight, commenting on petitioner's subsequent conviction after being admonished by trial court not to do so and exhibiting irrelevant photograph depicting petitioner next to marijuana plant, deprived petitioner of fundamentally fair penalty phase proceeding and, thus, warranted federal habeas relief; although there was overwhelming evidence of petitioner's guilt, prosecutor's misconduct destroyed petitioner's attempt to present mitigating evidence. DePew v. Anderson (S.D.Ohio, 03-31-2000) 104 F.Supp.2d 879, affirmed in part, reversed in part 311 F.3d 742, rehearing and suggestion for rehearing en banc denied, certiorari denied 124 S.Ct. 270, 540 U.S. 888, 157 L.Ed.2d 160, certiorari denied 124 S.Ct. 83, 540 U.S. 938, 157 L.Ed.2d 250. Habeas Corpus ⚿ 497

Trial counsel's failure to give an opening statement in murder trial did not constitute ineffective assistance of counsel; rather, that decision fell within the wide range of discretion afforded to counsel, particularly in light of fact that to do so would have required that defendant's counsel concede to the jury that their client was a murderer. Zuern v. Tate (S.D.Ohio, 03-30-2000) 101 F.Supp.2d 948, affirmed in part, reversed in part 336 F.3d 478, certiorari denied 124 S.Ct. 1456, 540 U.S. 1198, 158 L.Ed.2d 113. Criminal Law ⚿ 641.13(2.1)

Prosecutor's closing argument, that defendant's testimony was not logical because the police officers would gain nothing from planting a gun on his person, and consequently, that defendant must not be telling the truth, was proper, in prosecution for being a felon in possession of a firearm; the argument went to the question of whether the jury could reasonably infer from the evidence that defendant's version of the story was true. U.S. v. Vaughn (C.A.6 (Ohio), 12-22-2000) No. 99-4093, 12 Fed.Appx. 188, 2000 WL 1888793, Unreported. Criminal Law ⚿ 720(7.1)

In determining whether the prosecutor's closing remarks constitute reversible error, the Court of Appeals asks three questions: (1) whether the prosecutor's remarks were improper; (2) if they were improper, whether they were flagrant; and (3) if the statements were not flagrant, whether the court should nevertheless reverse. U.S. v. Vaughn (C.A.6 (Ohio), 12-22-2000) No. 99-4093, 12 Fed. Appx. 188, 2000 WL 1888793, Unreported. Criminal Law ⚿ 1171.1(2.1)

2938.12 When accused may be tried in his absence

A person being tried for a misdemeanor, either to the court, or to a jury, upon request in writing, subscribed by him, may, with the consent of the judge or magistrate, be tried in his absence, but no right shall exist in the defendant to be so tried. If after trial commences a person being tried escapes or departs without leave, the trial shall proceed and verdict or finding be received and sentence passed as if he were personally present.

(128 v 97, eff. 1–1–60)

Cross References

Defendant allowed to appear and defend in person, O Const Art I §1

Presence of the defendant, Crim R 43

Right to be present at trial, US Const Am 6; O Const Art I §10

Library References

Criminal Law ⚿636.

Westlaw Topic No. 110.

C.J.S. Criminal Law §§ 1161 to 1166.

Research References

Treatises and Practice Aids

Katz, Giannelli, Blair and Lipton, Baldwin's Ohio Practice, Criminal Law, § 138:4, Written Request of Defendant to be Tried in His/Her Absence.

Katz, Giannelli, Blair and Lipton, Baldwin's Ohio Practice, Criminal Law, § 138:5, Entry Granting/Denying Defendant's Request to be Tried in His/Her Absence.

2938.13 Responsibility for prosecution

In any case prosecuted for violation of a municipal ordinance the village solicitor or city director of law, and for a statute, he or the prosecuting attorney, shall present the case for the municipal corporation and the state respectively, but either may delegate the responsibility to some other attorney in a proper case, or, if the defendant be unrepresented by counsel may with leave of court, withdraw from the case. But the magistrate or judge shall not permit prosecution of any criminal case by private attorney employed or retained by a complaining witness.

(1977 H 219, eff. 11–1–77; 128 v 97)

Cross References

Asbestos violations, city law director may prosecute, 3710.99

Classification as misdemeanor, 2901.02

Library References

Criminal Law ⚡638.
District and Prosecuting Attorneys ⚡8.
Westlaw Topic Nos. 110, 131.

C.J.S. District and Prosecuting Attorneys §§ 20 to 21, 29.

Research References

Encyclopedias

OH Jur. 3d Cvl. Servants & Pub. Officers & Employ. § 490, Who is Prosecuting Attorney in Magistrates' Courts.

Treatises and Practice Aids

Gotherman, Babbit and Lang, Baldwin's Ohio Practice, Local Government Law—Municipal, § 27:6, Responsibility for Prosecution.

Notes of Decisions

1. Prosecution of state violations

Reference to city in caption of criminal complaint charging defendant with sexual imposition did not nullify conviction; reference was mere surplusage in identifying city as prosecuting authority, and city prosecutor was authorized to prosecute cases for violations of statutes in name of municipality and state respectively. State v. Gordon (Ohio App. 7 Dist., Mahoning, 06-23-2004) No. 03 MA 81, 2004-Ohio-3365, 2004 WL 1439825, Unreported. Indictment And Information ⚡ 54; Indictment And Information ⚡ 119

Once a prosecutor has, in the exercise of his discretion, determined that he will or will not prosecute a particular case, he has no continuing "duty" either to prosecute or to revisit his determination; prosecutor may, in exercise of his discretion, revisit that determination at any time until the statute of limitations expires and reverse or modify his decision, but he has no duty to do so, either during his term in office in which the potentially criminal conduct occurred, or in any subsequent term in office. Pengov v. White (Ohio App. 9 Dist., 10-31-2001) 146 Ohio App.3d 402, 766 N.E.2d 228, 2001-Ohio-1668, appeal not allowed 94 Ohio St.3d 1452, 762 N.E.2d 370, reconsideration denied 94 Ohio St.3d 1509, 764 N.E.2d 1038, 2002-Ohio-5738. District And Prosecuting Attorneys ⚡ 8

Pursuant to RC 2938.13, a prosecuting attorney is required to prosecute a criminal case brought before the county court for a state law misdemeanor occurring within a village that does not employ an attorney as village solicitor, unless the court grants the prosecuting attorney leave to withdraw from the case or he delegates the prosecution to some other attorney. OAG 99–042.

Both a county prosecutor and a city law director are, pursuant to RC 2938.13, under an obligation to either present the case for the state in a criminal prosecution in county court involving the violation of a state statute or ensure that the prosecutorial responsibility is otherwise carried out. OAG 81–094.

RC 3721.99 imposes a duty upon the attorney general to see that a proper affidavit is filed in a court of competent jurisdiction in all cases where evidence is received by him indicating a violation of RC 3721.02, RC 3721.05 or RC 3721.06. 1961 OAG 2279.

2. Prosecution of municipal violations

It is the duty of the solicitor or village attorney to prosecute violators of the village ordinances when village police file the charge or affidavit. OAG 68–117.

It is the duty of the solicitor or village attorney to prosecute for the violation of a village ordinance if any other county or state official files charges or an affidavit for a violation of such ordinance. OAG 68–117.

Where a solicitor or law director of a municipal corporation presents a case in a county court and such case is certified to a court of record pursuant to RC 2937.08, said solicitor or law director should present the case in the transferee court; and where the county prosecuting attorney presents such a case which is so certified, or where neither a solicitor, law director, or the prosecuting attorney presents a case in a county court, which case is so certified, the prosecuting attorney should present the case in the transferee court. 1960 OAG 1548.

3. Private attorney

To permit a private attorney, as amicus curiae, to participate in the trial of a criminal case in the municipal court and cross-examine the defendant, when such attorney's appearance was neither by application nor by invitation of the court, nor for the purpose of giving information to the court on a matter of law about which the court was doubtful, nor to call the court's attention to a legal matter which escaped or might have escaped the court's consideration, is an usurpation of the function of the city prosecutor, is manifestly irregular and constitutes error prejudicial to the defendant. City of Columbus v. Tullos (Franklin 1964) 1 Ohio App.2d 107, 204 N.E.2d 67, 30 O.O.2d 121. Amicus Curiae ⚖ 1; Criminal Law ⚖ 1166.9

RC 2909.25 does not authorize prosecution of an offender thereunder in the name of the state of Ohio as for a misdemeanor, by a private attorney employed or retained by a complaining witness. State v. Hartzell (Ohio Mun. 1962) 185 N.E.2d 88, 89 Ohio Law Abs. 191. Criminal Law ⚖ 640

4. Setting case for trial

The provision that a criminal matter be set for trial at a date subsequent to arraignment unless both prosecutor and accused expressly consent, is a mandatory requirement. State v. Willis (Monroe 1963) 200 N.E.2d 790, 94 Ohio Law Abs. 263, 30 O.O.2d 518. Criminal Law ⚖ 575

2938.14 Venires for juries

Venires for juries in courts of record inferior to the court of common pleas shall be drawn and summoned in the manner provided in the various acts creating such courts. But no challenge to the array shall be sustained in any case for the reason that some of the venire are not residents of the territory of the court, if it appears that the venire was regularly drawn and certified by the jury commissioners of county or municipality as the case may be.

(129 v 582, eff. 1–10–61; 128 v 97)

Cross References

Jury list, selection and summoning of venires, Ch 2313

Library References

Jury ⚖66, 67.
Westlaw Topic No. 230.
C.J.S. Juries §§ 271, 312 to 322.

Research References

Encyclopedias

OH Jur. 3d Jury § 191, Grounds for Challenge—Challenge in Inferior Courts.

Treatises and Practice Aids

Markus, Trial Handbook for Ohio Lawyers, § 6:2, Selection, Drawing, and Summoning of Jurors.

Notes of Decisions

Ed. Note: This section contains annotations from former RC 2945.18 and 2945.19.

Challenge 2
Change of venue 3
Constitutional issues 1
Special venire 4
Voir dire in capital case 5

---

1. Constitutional issues

Defendant failed to establish claim that African–Americans were unfairly and systematically underrepresented in jury venires relative to their numbers in the community in violation of Sixth Amendment's fair-cross-section requirement; there was no evidence that juries in the county had traditionally been void of African–Americans, and there was no evidence of systematic exclusion of African–Americans. State v. Jackson (Ohio, 11-23-2005) 107 Ohio St.3d 53, 836 N.E.2d 1173, 2005-Ohio-5981, reconsideration denied 108 Ohio St.3d 1418, 841 N.E.2d 321, 2006-Ohio-179, certiorari denied 126 S.Ct. 2940, motion to reopen denied 110 Ohio St.3d 1435, 852 N.E.2d 185, 2006-Ohio-3862. Jury ⚖ 33(1.15)

It is violation of defendant's equal protection rights to exclude members of his race from jury venire because of their race, or under false assumption that members of defendant's race are unqualified to serve as jurors. State v. Bryant (Ohio App. 6 Dist., 06-09-1995) 104 Ohio App.3d 512, 662 N.E.2d 846. Constitutional Law ⚖ 221(1); Jury ⚖ 33(1.15)

It is irrelevant how many minority jurors remain on panel if even one is excluded on basis of race. State v. Bryant (Ohio App. 6 Dist., 06-09-1995) 104 Ohio App.3d 512, 662 N.E.2d 846. Jury ⚖ 33(5.15)

Choosing jurors from a pool of jurors consisting of persons whose last names begin with the letters A through H does not violate a defendant's right to a jury chosen from a fair cross-section of the community. State v. Buell (Butler 1985) 29 Ohio App.3d 215, 504 N.E.2d 1161, 29 O.B.R. 260.

A defendant must demonstrate the following three factors in order to sustain a challenge to a jury-selection procedure on the grounds that the procedure involves a violation of the fair cross-section of the community requirement: (1) the group allegedly excluded constitutes a distinctive group in the community, (2) the representation of this group in venires from which juries are selected is not fair and reasonable in relation to the number of such persons in the community, and (3) the underrepresentation is due to a systematic exclusion of the group in the jury selection process. State v. Buell (Butler 1985) 29 Ohio App.3d 215, 504 N.E.2d 1161, 29 O.B.R. 260. Jury ⚷ 33(5.10)

A defendant is not denied due process of law where the composition of special venire called for his trial was constituted in such manner that only qualified electors were eligible for jury duty (RC 2945.18, RC 2945.19, RC 2313.06 and RC 2313.08 are constitutional). State v. Johnson (Ohio 1972) 31 Ohio St.2d 106, 285 N.E.2d 751, 60 O.O.2d 85.

A defendant is not denied due process of law where the composition of special venire called for his trial was constituted in such manner that only qualified electors were eligible for jury duty (RC 2945.18, RC 2945.19, RC 2313.06 and RC 2313.08 are constitutional). State v. Johnson (Ohio 1972) 31 Ohio St.2d 106, 285 N.E.2d 751, 60 O.O.2d 85.

2. Challenge

Denial of motion to dismiss jury venire after two codefendants pled guilty during jury selection process was not abuse of discretion, where court instructed jury, following guilty pleas, that jurors were not to draw any inference from fact that there were two fewer defendants at counsel table and three fewer lawyers at table representing defendants. U.S. v. Walker (C.A.6 (Ohio) 1993) 1 F.3d 423, rehearing denied, appeal after new trial 37 F.3d 1500. Jury ⚷ 133

3. Change of venue

The question of defendant's request for a change of venue on the alleged grounds that because of widespread publicity a constitutional trial by an impartial jury cannot be had is best considered during the process of impaneling the jury; and where the great majority of the prospective jurors summoned state under oath that they will not be influenced by any outside consideration and that they honestly believe they can afford the defendant a fair trial and state that they will do so, the jurors selected are accepted by the defendant after full examination without objection, and a jury is impaneled without the defendant using all his peremptory challenges out of the first venire of seventy-five, of which sixty-four appeared for examination, the overruling of such request does not constitute an abuse of discretion. State v. Sheppard (Cuyahoga 1955) 100 Ohio App. 345, 128 N.E.2d 471, 60 O.O. 298, affirmed 165 Ohio St. 293, 135 N.E.2d 340, 59 O.O. 398, certiorari denied 77 S.Ct. 118, 352 U.S. 910, 1 L.Ed.2d 119, rehearing denied 77 S.Ct. 323, 352 U.S. 955, 1 L.Ed.2d 245.

4. Special venire

Venire and special venire for jury in capital cases are applicable to one charged with aggravated murder, irrespective of whether such offense is not punishable by death due to lack of specifications of aggravating circumstances. State ex rel. Corrigan v. McMonagle (Ohio 1984) 12 Ohio St.3d 15, 465 N.E.2d 382, 12 O.B.R. 13. Jury ⚷ 70(1)

One accused of first degree murder is not entitled to a special venire allowed under RC 2945.19. State v. Gaines (Hamilton 1974) 40 Ohio App.2d 224, 318 N.E.2d 857, 69 O.O.2d 210. Jury ⚷ 70(2)

Prosecutor was not entitled to a writ of mandamus compelling trial court to provide special venire, as statute which had provided that aggravated murder was a capital offense had been amended to provide that a capital offense include only those offenses for which the death penalty may be imposed, RC 2901.02(B), and as this amendment relieved State of burden of providing a special venire to defendant who faced no threat that the death penalty would be imposed for his alleged aggravated murder of victim. State ex rel. Corrigan v. McAllister (Ohio 1985) 18 Ohio St.3d 239, 480 N.E.2d 783, 18 O.B.R. 296.

The requirements for venire for jury provided by RC 2945.18 and 2945.19 apply to prosecutions for aggravated murder in violation of RC 2903.01, even though no death penalty is sought, and may be compelled by a writ of mandamus issued against the trial judge at the request of the prosecuting attorney. State ex rel. Corrigan v. McMonagle (Ohio 1984) 12 Ohio St.3d 15, 465 N.E.2d 382, 12 O.B.R. 13.

The provisions of RC 2945.18 and RC 2945.19 are mandatory, and a trial judge has no discretion to refuse a request for a special venire, either as to the initial venire or subsequent venires. State v Jenkins, No. 45231 (8th Dist Ct App, Cuyahoga, 2–24–84), affirmed by 15 OS(3d) 164, 15 OBR 311, 473 NE(2d) 264 (1984).

5. Voir dire in capital case

Where a venireman was present while the judge asked others of the venire proper questions to learn whether they could recommend the capital penalty under any circumstances, the judge does not err to the defendant's prejudice by asking the venireman a question with a lesser standard, to wit, if it would violate his principles to vote a capital sentence, and by then excusing him when he answers "yes." Darden v. Wainwright (U.S.Fla. 1986) 106 S.Ct. 2464, 477 U.S. 168, 91 L.Ed.2d 144, rehearing denied 107 S.Ct. 24, 478 U.S. 1036, 92 L.Ed.2d 774, on remand 803 F.2d 613.

2938.15 Rules of evidence and procedure

The rules of evidence and procedure, including those governing notices, proof of special matters, depositions, and joinder of defendants and offenses set forth in Chapter 2945. of the Revised Code, which are not, by their nature, inapplicable to the trial of misdemeanors, shall prevail in trials under Chapter 2938. of the Revised Code where no special provision is made in such chapter, or where no provision is made by rule of the supreme court adopted pursuant to section 2937.46 of the Revised Code.

(129 v 582, eff. 1-10-61; 128 v 97)

Library References

Criminal Law ⚷254, 633(1).
Westlaw Topic No. 110.

C.J.S. Criminal Law §§ 564, 1134, 1140, 1145 to 1146, 1191.

Research References

Treatises and Practice Aids

Giannelli and Snyder, Baldwin's Ohio Practice, Evidence, R 101, Scope of Rules: Applicability; Privileges; Exceptions.

Giannelli and Snyder, Baldwin's Ohio Practice, Evidence, § 101.1, Introduction.

Law Review and Journal Commentaries

The Expungement or Restriction of Arrest Records, Comment. 23 Clev St L Rev 123 (Winter 1974).

A Guide to the Proposed Ohio Rules of Evidence, Kurt A. Philipps, Jr. 5 Ohio N U L Rev 28 (1978).

Impeaching A Defendant's Testimony By Proof Of Post–Arrest Silence: Doyle v. Ohio, Note. 25 Clev St L Rev 261 (1976).

The Proposed Ohio Rules of Evidence: The Case Against, Richard S. Walinski and Howard Abramoff. 28 Case W Res L Rev 344 (Winter 1978).

State v. Humphries: Who Bears the Burden of Proof for the Defense of Insanity?, Note. 5 Ohio N U L Rev 144 (1978).

State v. Souel: Ohio Turns the Corner on Polygraph Evidence, Note. 8 Cap U L Rev 287 (1978).

Notes of Decisions

1. Jurisdiction of mayor

A mayor of a village has jurisdiction to hear and determine all prosecutions for violations of ordinances where the defendants are not entitled to a trial by jury; and to hear and determine prosecutions for violations of ordinances where the defendants are entitled to trial by jury if, before the commencement of the trial, a waiver in writing, subscribed by the accused, is filed in the case, following the procedure prescribed in RC Ch 2938, but where the accused does not waive such right, the mayor is required to certify the case to a court of record. 1960 OAG 1208.

2. Speedy trial

RC 2945.71 to 2945.73, as enacted by 1972 H 511, eff. 1-1-74, apply to criminal prosecutions pending on that date, the arrests for which were made prior to such date. City of Columbus v. Vest (Franklin 1974) 42 Ohio App.2d 83, 330 N.E.2d 726, 71 O.O.2d 520.

CHAPTER 2939

GRAND JURIES

GRAND JURORS

2939.01 Definition of magistrate

The definition of "magistrate" set forth in section 2931.01 of the Revised Code applies to Chapter 2939. of the Revised Code.

(1953 H 1, eff. 10–1–53)

Cross References

Attorney general, investigations of patient abuse or neglect, presentation of evidence to grand jury, 109.86

Grand jury, Crim R 6

Investigation of organized crime, referral to grand jury, 109.83

Investigations and prosecutions for excess medicaid payments, 109.85

Powers of attorney general regarding antitrust matters, 109.81

Powers of attorney general regarding antitrust matters, antitrust fund, 109.82

Powers of attorney general regarding workers' compensation, 109.84
Right to indictment, O Const Art I §10

Law Review and Journal Commentaries

The Exercise of Supervisory Powers to Dismiss a Grand Jury Indictment—A Basis for Curbing Prosecutorial Misconduct, Note. 45 Ohio St L J 1077 (1984).

The Federal Grand Jury: Practice & Procedure, Note. 13 U Tol L Rev 1 (Fall 1981).

The Grand Jury: A Critical Evaluation, Ovio C. Lewis. 13 Akron L Rev 33 (Summer 1979).

The Grand Jury in Ohio: An Empirical Study, Ann Feder Lee. 4 U Dayton L Rev 325 (Summer 1979).

Understanding Prosecutorial Discretion in The United States: The Limits of Comparative Criminal Procedure as an Instrument of Reform, William T. Pizzi. 54 Ohio St L J 1325 (1993).

2939.02 Selection of grand jury

Grand juries shall consist of fifteen persons who satisfy the qualifications of a juror specified in section 2313.42 of the Revised Code. Persons to serve as grand jurors in the court of common pleas of each county shall be selected from the persons whose names are contained in the annual jury list and from the ballots deposited in the jury wheel, or in the automation data processing storage drawer, or from the names contained in an automated data processing information storage device as prescribed by sections 2313.07, 2313.08, and 2313.35 of the Revised Code.

At the time of the selection of the persons who are to constitute the grand jury, the commissioners of jurors shall draw from the jury wheel, or draw by utilizing the automation data processing equipment and procedures described in section 2313.07 of the Revised Code, ballots containing the names of not less than twenty-five persons. The first fifteen persons whose names are drawn shall constitute the grand jury, if they can be located and served by the sheriff, and if they are not excused by the court or a judge of the court. If any of the first fifteen persons whose names are so drawn are not located or are unable to serve and are for that reason excused by the court or by a judge of the court, whose duty it is to supervise the impaneling of the grand jury, the judge shall then designate the person whose name next appears on the list of persons drawn, to serve in the place of the person not found or excused and shall so continue to substitute the names of the persons drawn in the order in which they were drawn, to fill all vacancies resulting from persons not being found or having been excused by the court or the judge of the court, until the necessary fifteen persons are selected to make up the grand jury. If all of the names appearing on the list of persons drawn are exhausted before the grand jury is complete, the judge shall order the commissioners of jurors to draw such additional names as the judge determines, and shall proceed to fill the vacancies from those names in the order in which they are drawn.

The judge of the court of common pleas may select any person who satisfies the qualifications of a juror and whose name is not included in the annual jury list or on a ballot deposited in the jury wheel or automation data processing storage drawer, or whose name is not contained in an automated data processing information storage device, to preside as foreman of the grand jury, in which event the grand jury shall consist of the foreman so selected and fourteen additional grand jurors selected from the jury wheel or by use of the automation data processing equipment and procedures in the manner provided in this section.

(1984 H 183, eff. 10–1–84; 1969 H 424; 131 v S 20; 130 v S 103; 1953 H 1; GC 11419–34)

Historical and Statutory Notes

Pre–1953 H 1 Amendments: 114 v 203

Cross References

Grand jury, Crim R 6
Investigation of organized crime, referral to grand jury, 109.83

Library References

Grand Jury ⚷2.5 to 8.
Westlaw Topic No. 193.
C.J.S. Grand Juries §§ 13, 15, 18, 20 to 21, 23 to 44, 49 to 50, 53, 80, 92.

Research References

Encyclopedias

OH Jur. 3d Jury § 61, Generally; Number of Grand Jurors.

OH Jur. 3d Jury § 70, Selection; General Procedure.

OH Jur. 3d Jury § 104, Requirement that Jurors be Electors.

OH Jur. 3d Jury § 118, Foreman of Grand Jury; Deputy Foreman.

OH Jur. 3d Jury § 167, Number of Jurors Required for Indictment.

Treatises and Practice Aids

Katz, Giannelli, Blair and Lipton, Baldwin's Ohio Practice, Criminal Law, § 39:5, Selection Procedure.

Katz, Giannelli, Blair and Lipton, Baldwin's Ohio Practice, Criminal Law, § 39:6, Composition.

Katz, Giannelli, Blair and Lipton, Baldwin's Ohio Practice, Criminal Law, § 39:7, Foreman and Deputy Foreman.

Katz, Giannelli, Blair and Lipton, Baldwin's Ohio Practice, Criminal Law, § 39:8, Alternate Grand Jurors.

Katz, Giannelli, Blair and Lipton, Baldwin's Ohio Practice, Criminal Law, § 141:1, Order to Summon Grand Jury.

Katz, Giannelli, Blair and Lipton, Baldwin's Ohio Practice, Criminal Law, § 141:2, Order to Summon Grand Jury (Additional Form).

Katz, Giannelli, Blair and Lipton, Baldwin's Ohio Practice, Criminal Law, § 141:3, Summons for Grand Juror.

Katz, Giannelli, Blair and Lipton, Baldwin's Ohio Practice, Criminal Law, § 143:1, Motion to Dismiss Indictment—Challenge to Panel [Or Individual Grand Juror].

Katz, Giannelli, Blair and Lipton, Baldwin's Ohio Practice, Criminal Law, § 148:4, Order to Draw Jurors.

Katz, Giannelli, Blair and Lipton, Baldwin's Ohio Practice, Criminal Law, § 39:20, Finding and Return of Indictment.

Hennenberg & Reinhart, Ohio Criminal Defense Motions F 5.35, Motion to Quash the Venire-Pretrial Motions-Improperly Selected Venire.

Law Review and Journal Commentaries

CRIMINAL LAW—Naming of an "Unindicted Co–Conspirator" As Beyond the Scope of a Grand Jury's Power, United States v. Briggs, Note. 7 U Tol L Rev 245 (Fall 1975).

The Fourth Amendment Function of the Grand Jury, Charles A. Thompson. 37 Ohio St L J 727 (1976).

State v. Caudill: Court Dialogue to Ensure Intelligent Waiver of Defendant's Rights, Note. 4 Ohio N U L Rev 841 (1977).

State v. Singer: The State Alone Guards The Speedy Trial Right, Note. 4 Ohio N U L Rev 692 (1977).

Notes of Decisions

---

1. Constitutional issues

Trial court's error in relying on its own personal knowledge of the procedure used by the county court in appointing the grand jury foreperson when it denied defendant's claim of racial discrimination in appointment of the foreperson was harmless; trial court's dismissal of the racial discrimination claims were properly based upon either that fact that the claims were barred by res judicata or that defendant's evidentiary materials were insufficient to raise a prima facie showing of discrimination. State v. Jackson (Ohio App. 11 Dist., Trumbull, 03-03-2006) No. 2004-T-0089, 2006-Ohio-1007, 2006 WL 532105, Unreported, opinion superseded on reconsideration 2006-Ohio-2651, 2006 WL 1459757, cause dismissed 110 Ohio St.3d 1407, 850 N.E.2d 69, 2006-Ohio-3306. Criminal Law ⚷ 1166(2)

Trial court improperly relied on its own personal knowledge of the procedure used by the county court in appointing the grand jury foreperson when it denied defendant's claim of racial discrimination in appointment of the foreperson; any proceeding before the grand jury was distinct from the petit trial, the trial judge was not permitted to take judicial notice of any action separate from the proceeding before him, and the trial judge's own knowledge of county grand jury proceedings in general did not encompass all possible information on that topic. State v. Jackson (Ohio App. 11 Dist., Trumbull, 03-03-2006) No. 2004-T-0089, 2006-Ohio-1007, 2006 WL 532105, Unreported, opinion superseded on reconsideration 2006-Ohio-2651, 2006 WL 1459757, cause dismissed 110 Ohio St.3d 1407, 850 N.E.2d 69, 2006-Ohio-3306. Grand Jury ⚷ 21

Defendant's assertion that the county court selected a grand jury foreperson in a racially discriminatory manner was barred by res judicata in post-conviction relief proceeding; evidence as to the manner by which the grand jury foreperson was chosen could have been sought prior to defendant's actual trial. State v. Jackson (Ohio App. 11 Dist., Trumbull, 03-03-2006) No. 2004-T-0089, 2006-Ohio-1007, 2006 WL 532105, Unreported, opinion superseded on reconsideration 2006-Ohio-2651, 2006 WL 1459757, cause dismissed 110 Ohio St.3d 1407, 850 N.E.2d 69, 2006-Ohio-3306. Criminal Law ⚿ 1433(2)

No evidence supported capital defendant's claim in postconviction relief proceedings that the county grand jury that indicted him contained an underrepresentation of African-Americans, where defendant presented no evidence of an intentional exclusion of African–Americans from the grand jury. State v. Jackson (Ohio App. 11 Dist., Trumbull, 03-03-2006) No. 2004-T-0089, 2006-Ohio-1007, 2006 WL 532105, Unreported, opinion superseded on reconsideration 2006-Ohio-2651, 2006 WL 1459757, cause dismissed 110 Ohio St.3d 1407, 850 N.E.2d 69, 2006-Ohio-3306. Criminal Law ⚿ 1477

Indictment for aggravated murder and aggravated burglary returned by grand jury consisting of eleven jurors rather than fifteen, and signed by deputy foreperson rather than by grand jury foreperson, was not fatally defective, and thus, counsel's failure to challenge indictment did not constitute ineffective assistance of counsel, insofar as rule governing grand jury proceedings required only nine jurors and allowed for deputy foreperson to act as foreperson in appointed foreperson's absence. State v. Hughbanks (Ohio App. 1 Dist., Hamilton, 01-17-2003) No. C-010372, 2003-Ohio-187, 2003 WL 131937, Unreported, appeal not allowed 100 Ohio St.3d 1484, 798 N.E.2d 1093, 2003-Ohio-5992. Criminal Law ⚿ 641.13(2.1); Indictment And Information ⚿ 10.1(2); Indictment And Information ⚿ 10.1(3)

Any showing that county used only voter registration lists to select grand jurors, and that percentages of African–American and other minorities registered to vote in county was less than the percentage of racial minorities composing the voting age population of county, would not provide a basis for relief to defendant convicted and sentenced to death for capital murder, where defendant failed to claim purposeful discrimination or substantial underrepresentation in selection of grand jurors. State v. Nields (Ohio, 08-29-2001) 93 Ohio St.3d 6, 752 N.E.2d 859, 2001-Ohio-1291, reconsideration denied 93 Ohio St.3d 1452, 756 N.E.2d 116. Criminal Law ⚿ 1166(2)

Equal protection forbids intentional discrimination against any distinct group in choosing grand juries; however, not every grand jury has to represent a fair cross-section so long as selection process is non-discriminatory. State v. Williams (Ohio, 06-11-1997) 79 Ohio St.3d 1, 679 N.E.2d 646, 1997-Ohio-407, certiorari denied 118 S.Ct. 703, 522 U.S. 1053, 139 L.Ed.2d 646, denial of post-conviction relief affirmed 1999 WL 1059715, dismissed, appeal not allowed 88 Ohio St.3d 1425, 723 N.E.2d 1113, certiorari denied 121 S.Ct. 109, 531 U.S. 843, 148 L.Ed.2d 66, denial of habeas corpus affirmed 380 F.3d 932, rehearing en banc denied, certiorari denied 125 S.Ct. 1939, 544 U.S. 1003, 161 L.Ed.2d 779. Constitutional Law ⚿ 250.2(1); Grand Jury ⚿ 2.5

In order to obtain standing to challenge a grand jury array under the Equal Protection Clause, a defendant must prove the procedure employed in the selection process resulted in a substantial underrepresentation of his or her race or of the identifiable group to which he or she belongs and the group is one that is a recognizable, distinct class, singled out for different treatment under the laws, as written or as applied. State v. Fulton (Ohio 1991) 57 Ohio St.3d 120, 566 N.E.2d 1195, certiorari denied 112 S.Ct. 98, 502 U.S. 828, 116 L.Ed.2d 69. Constitutional Law ⚿ 221(5); Grand Jury ⚿ 17

Grand juries, discriminatory exclusion of blacks, standing of white defendant. Campbell v. Louisiana (U.S.La., 04-21-1998) 118 S.Ct. 1419, 523 U.S. 392, 172 A.L.R. Fed. 597, 140 L.Ed.2d 551.

Where a convict does not receive a full and fair hearing in state court on his claim that the grand jury indicting him was selected in a discriminatory manner, the claim may be raised in a federal habeas corpus proceeding; the federal court may grant the writ and reverse the conviction where discrimination is found, notwithstanding that the trial jury was selected without discrimination and there is no doubt concerning the sufficiency of the evidence of the convict's guilt. Vasquez v. Hillery (U.S.Cal. 1986) 106 S.Ct. 617, 474 U.S. 254, 88 L.Ed.2d 598.

Exclusion from a grand jury of lawyers, doctors, clergymen, students, felons, and elderly individuals is not a violation of the equal protection rights of a defendant who is not a member of any of the excluded groups of people. Aldridge v. Marshall (C.A.6 (Ohio) 1985) 765 F.2d 63, certiorari denied 106 S.Ct. 810, 474 U.S. 1062, 88 L.Ed.2d 785.

Irregularities in the selection of a grand jury do not constitute a violation of any constitutional right where there is no allegation they were not qualified, nor that the defendant was prejudiced, nor that any challenge was made to the array. Charles v. Maxwell (C.A.6 (Ohio) 1965) 5 Ohio Misc. 185, 348 F.2d 890, 33 O.O.2d 305.

Habeas petitioner was procedurally barred from claiming that African–Americans were underrepresented in county's grand jury pool where he failed to raise claim on direct appeal to state appellate court; failure to raise on appeal claim that appeared on face of record constituted procedural default under Ohio's doctrine of res judicata. Smith v. Anderson (S.D.Ohio, 02-22-2000) 104 F.Supp.2d 773, affirmed 348 F.3d 177, rehearing and rehearing en banc denied, certiorari denied 125 S.Ct. 278, 543 U.S. 841, 160 L.Ed.2d 65, rehearing denied, rehearing denied 125 S.Ct. 646, 543 U.S. 1016, 160 L.Ed.2d 488. Habeas Corpus ⚿ 366

Alleged underrepresentation of African–Americans in county's grand jury pool did not render capital murder conviction constitutionally infirm, such as would warrant habeas relief, absent showing that selection procedure used by county was susceptible to abuse or was not racially neutral, or that degree of alleged underrepresentation occurred over significant period of time. Smith v. Anderson (S.D.Ohio, 02-22-2000) 104 F.Supp.2d 773, affirmed 348 F.3d 177, rehearing and rehearing en banc denied, certiorari denied 125 S.Ct. 278, 543 U.S. 841, 160 L.Ed.2d 65, rehearing denied, rehearing denied 125 S.Ct. 646, 543 U.S. 1016, 160 L.Ed.2d 488. Habeas Corpus ⚷ 473

2. Size of grand jury

The number of jurors on a grand jury does not affect a substantive right. Accordingly, Crim R 6(A) controls the issue of how many grand jurors are needed to issue an indictment. RC 2939.02 and 2939.20 are superseded insofar as they conflict with this rule. State v. Brown (Ohio 1988) 38 Ohio St.3d 305, 528 N.E.2d 523, rehearing denied 39 Ohio St.3d 710, 534 N.E.2d 93, certiorari denied 109 S.Ct. 1177, 489 U.S. 1040, 103 L.Ed.2d 239, rehearing denied 109 S.Ct. 1774, 490 U.S. 1032, 104 L.Ed.2d 208. Grand Jury ⚷ 3

An issue pertaining to the number of persons comprising a grand jury in Ohio concerns a matter of procedure, and an indictment rendered by a body made up of less than fifteen members does not deny an accused any substantive right. State v. Juergens (Hancock 1977) 55 Ohio App.2d 104, 379 N.E.2d 602, 9 O.O.3d 262. Indictment And Information ⚷ 10.1(2)

3. Vacancies in venire

Except as to the foreman, vacancies occurring in a grand jury venire prior to the impanelling and swearing of the grand jury must be filled by persons whose names are contained in the annual jury list and from the ballots deposited in the jury wheel. State ex rel. Burton v. Smith (Ohio 1963) 174 Ohio St. 429, 189 N.E.2d 876, 23 O.O.2d 78. Grand Jury ⚷ 9

After a grand jury has been sworn the common pleas judge, in case of sickness, death, discharge, or nonattendance of a grand juror, may, in the exercise of his discretion, cause another person to be sworn in his stead, but prior to the administration of the oath to members of the grand jury the court has no authority to substitute another person to serve upon the panel of jurors drawn for service pursuant to RC 2939.02, 2313.07, 2313.08, and 2313.35 without compliance with the provisions of such sections. State ex rel. Burton v. Smith (Scioto 1962) 118 Ohio App. 248, 194 N.E.2d 70, 25 O.O.2d 90, affirmed 174 Ohio St. 429, 189 N.E.2d 876, 23 O.O.2d 78.

2939.03 Grand jurors subject to same provisions and regulations as other jurors

A grand jury is drawn and notified by the same persons, from the same jury wheel, automation data processing storage drawer, or automated data processing information storage device, and in the same manner as other jurors are drawn and notified under sections 2939.02 to 2939.04 and 2313.01 to 2313.46 of the Revised Code. Grand jurors so drawn and notified are not entitled to an exemption for any reason but may be excused from service or have their service postponed for the same reasons and in the same manner as other jurors under those sections and not otherwise. Grand jurors are subject to the same fines and penalties for nonattendance and otherwise as are other jurors under those sections. The duties and the powers of courts of common pleas, clerks of courts of common pleas, and commissioners of jurors in regard to grand jurors in all respects are the same as in regard to other jurors.

(1998 S 69, eff. 4–16–98; 1969 H 424, eff. 11–25–69; 131 v S 20; 1953 H 1; GC 11419–35)

Historical and Statutory Notes

Pre–1953 H 1 Amendments: 114 v 203

Amendment Note: 1998 S 69 inserted "are not entitled to an exemption for any reason but" and "or have their service postponed"; and made other nonsubstantive changes.

Cross References

Grand jury, Crim R 6

Library References

Grand Jury ⚷5 to 9.
Westlaw Topic No. 193.
C.J.S. Grand Juries §§ 13, 15, 18, 20 to 21, 23 to 40, 42 to 50.

Research References

Encyclopedias

OH Jur. 3d Jury § 6, Applicability to Grand Juries of Statutes Relating to Petit Juries.

OH Jur. 3d Jury § 70, Selection; General Procedure.

OH Jur. 3d Jury § 72, Notification and Summoning.

Treatises and Practice Aids

Katz, Giannelli, Blair and Lipton, Baldwin's Ohio Practice, Criminal Law, § 39:5, Selection Procedure.

Katz, Giannelli, Blair and Lipton, Baldwin's Ohio Practice, Criminal Law, § 148:4, Order to Draw Jurors.

Katz, Giannelli, Blair and Lipton, Baldwin's Ohio Practice, Criminal Law, § 141:18, Entry for Formation of New Grand Jury.

Katz, Giannelli, Blair and Lipton, Baldwin's Ohio Practice, Criminal Law, § 141:19, Entry for Formation of Special Grand Jury.

Hennenberg & Reinhart, Ohio Criminal Defense Motions F 10.15, Motion for New Trial-Rule 33-Irregularity in Venue.

Hennenberg & Reinhart, Ohio Criminal Defense Motions F 10.16, Motion for a New Trial-Improper Selection of the Venire-Discriminatory Exclusion of Jurors from Jury Wheel.

Notes of Decisions

Ed. Note: This section contains annotations from former RC 2939.05.

Improper selection and exemptions from service 2
Supervision of grand jury 1
Vacancies in venire 3

1. Supervision of grand jury

Although prosecutor may bring charge before grand jury so long as prosecutor has probable cause to believe that individual has committed offense defined by statute, grand jury is not subordinate to prosecutor, but is arm of common pleas court. State v. Asher (Ohio App. 1 Dist., 07-17-1996) 112 Ohio App.3d 646, 679 N.E.2d 1147, appeal not allowed 77 Ohio St.3d 1492, 673 N.E.2d 148. Grand Jury ⚿ 1; Grand Jury ⚿ 27

Court of common pleas has jurisdiction to supervise certain enumerated aspects of grand jury, and prohibition does not lie to control court's reasonable exercise of such powers. State ex rel. Shoop v. Mitrovich (Ohio 1983) 4 Ohio St.3d 220, 448 N.E.2d 800, 4 O.B.R. 575. Grand Jury ⚿ 33; Prohibition ⚿ 5(3)

Subject to express statutory limitations, the county grand jury is under the control and direction of the court of common pleas, which has authority after the disposition of matters pending at the beginning of the term to recess the grand jury for such further business as may arise during the term. State v. Schwab (Ohio 1924) 109 Ohio St. 532, 143 N.E. 29, 2 Ohio Law Abs. 196, 21 Ohio Law Rep. 602.

2. Improper selection and exemptions from service

Fact that grand juror had once worked at bar that defendant and victim visited on night of murder and was familiar with defendant carrying a knife into the bar did not demonstrate how grand juror was biased or incapable of carrying out duties of a grand juror in a fair and impartial manner or how brief statements of grand juror influenced grand jury's decision to indict, especially in light of testimony that defendant had used a knife to coerce witness to perform oral sex and sexual intercourse with him. State v. Myers (Ohio, 12-13-2002) 97 Ohio St.3d 335, 780 N.E.2d 186, 2002-Ohio-6658, reconsideration denied 97 Ohio St.3d 1500, 780 N.E.2d 1023, 2002-Ohio-7367, certiorari denied 123 S.Ct. 2254, 539 U.S. 906, 156 L.Ed.2d 116, motion to reopen denied 100 Ohio St.3d 1505, 799 N.E.2d 184, 2003-Ohio-6161. Grand Jury ⚿ 15

Where the selection of members of a grand jury and exemptions therefrom are made without adherence to the provisions of RC 2313.12, any indictment rendered by such jury is void. State v. Davis (Morgan 1978) 60 Ohio App.2d 355, 397 N.E.2d 1215, 14 O.O.3d 315. Indictment And Information ⚿ 10.1(2)

3. Vacancies in venire

Except as to the foreman, vacancies occurring in a grand jury venire prior to the impanelling and swearing of the grand jury must be filled by persons whose names are contained in the annual jury list and from the ballots deposited in the jury wheel. State ex rel. Burton v. Smith (Ohio 1963) 174 Ohio St. 429, 189 N.E.2d 876, 23 O.O.2d 78. Grand Jury ⚿ 9

2939.031 Alternate juror for grand jury; selection of

When it appears to the judge impaneling a grand jury that the inquiry is likely to be protracted, or upon direction of the judge, an additional or alternate juror shall be selected in the same manner as the regular jurors in the inquiry are selected. The additional or alternate juror shall be sworn and seated near the jury, with equal opportunity for seeing and hearing the proceedings, shall attend the inquiry at all times and shall obey all orders and admonitions of the court or foreman. When the jurors are ordered kept together, the alternate juror shall be kept with them. The additional or alternate juror shall be liable as a regular juror for failure to attend the inquiry or to obey any order or admonition of the court or foreman. He shall receive the same compensation as other jurors, and except as provided in this section shall be discharged upon the final submission of the bill to the foreman.

If before the final submission of the bill to the jury, a juror dies or is discharged by the judge or foreman due to incapacity, absence, or disqualification of such juror, the additional or alternate juror, upon order of the judge or foreman, shall become one of the jury and serve in all respects as though selected as an original juror during the absence or incapacity of an original juror.

(125 v 345, eff. 10–14–53)

Cross References

Alternate grand jurors, Crim R 6

Library References

Grand Jury ⚷8 to 13, 20.
Westlaw Topic No. 193.
C.J.S. Grand Juries §§ 6, 11, 13, 15, 18, 37 to 40, 42 to 52, 57 to 58, 66 to 67, 92.

Research References

Encyclopedias

OH Jur. 3d Jury § 238, Recess or Discharge of Grand Jury.

OH Jur. 3d Jury § 240, Compensation of Grand Jurors.

Treatises and Practice Aids

Katz, Giannelli, Blair and Lipton, Baldwin's Ohio Practice, Criminal Law, § 39:8, Alternate Grand Jurors.

Katz, Giannelli, Blair and Lipton, Baldwin's Ohio Practice, Criminal Law, § 143:1, Motion to Dismiss Indictment—Challenge to Panel [Or Individual Grand Juror].

Notes of Decisions

Vacancies in venire 1

1. Vacancies in venire

Except as to the foreman, vacancies occurring in a grand jury venire prior to the impanelling and swearing of the grand jury must be filled by persons whose names are contained in the annual jury list and from the ballots deposited in the jury wheel. State ex rel. Burton v. Smith (Ohio 1963) 174 Ohio St. 429, 189 N.E.2d 876, 23 O.O.2d 78. Grand Jury ⚷ 9

2939.04 Grand jurors; compensation

The compensation of grand jurors shall be fixed by resolution of the board of county commissioners, not to exceed forty dollars for each day's attendance, payable out of the county treasury. Except in counties of less than one hundred thousand population according to the last federal census, in which counties the judge of the court of common pleas shall make rules in the judge's own county applicable to subsequent grand juror and petit juror service, a person who has served as a grand juror at a term of court is prohibited from serving again, either as a grand juror or petit juror, in that jury year in which the service is rendered or in the next jury year. The person is entitled to a certificate of excuse or postponement in the same manner as a petit juror. The court of common pleas may order the drawing of a special jury to sit at any time public business requires it.

(1998 S 69, eff. 4–16–98; 1974 S 465, eff. 3–4–75; 1953 H 1; GC 11419–36)

Historical and Statutory Notes

Pre–1953 H 1 Amendments: 116 v 371; 114 v 204

Amendment Note: 1998 S 69 deleted "and regulations" after "rules"; substituted "to subsequent grand juror and petit juror service" for "thereto", "excuse or postponement" for "exemption", and "the same" for "like"; and made changes to reflect gender neutral language and other nonsubstantive changes.

Cross References

Grand jury, Crim R 6

Library References

Grand Jury ⚷14.
Westlaw Topic No. 193.
C.J.S. Grand Juries § 12.

Research References

Encyclopedias

OH Jur. 3d Jury § 113, Particular Exemptions and Grounds for Excuse—Previous Service as Juror.

OH Jur. 3d Jury § 240, Compensation of Grand Jurors.

Treatises and Practice Aids

Markus, Trial Handbook for Ohio Lawyers, § 6:3, Exemptions from Jury Service.

Notes of Decisions

Court orders 3
Special grand jury 1
Term of service 2

---

1. Special grand jury

RC 2939.04 and 2939.17 were enacted to deal with separate and distinct problems, and they are not to be read together and so narrowly as to defeat their separate purposes, so that error cannot be predicated on the ground that an indictment was returned by a special grand jury while the regular grand jury was then sitting, where the second jury was properly empaneled in order that timely and adequate consideration might be given to all matters then on the docket. State v. Pustare (Cuyahoga 1973) 33 Ohio App.2d 305, 295 N.E.2d 210, 62 O.O.2d 450.

2. Term of service

The term of service of a grand jury is one term of court. State v. Mirman (Summit 1955) 99 Ohio App. 382, 133 N.E.2d 796, 59 O.O. 162.

3. Court orders

The official act of a single judge of a court of common pleas composed of two or more judges is the act of the court; concurrence of the other judge or judges in such act is not necessary to its validity. State v. Phipps (Scioto 1964) 3 Ohio App.2d 226, 210 N.E.2d 138, 32 O.O.2d 322, certiorari denied 86 S.Ct. 434, 382 U.S. 957, 15 L.Ed.2d 361. Courts ⚷ 101

2939.05 Clerk to make list of persons required to appear—Repealed

(129 v 1201, eff. 9–11–61; 1953 H 1; GC 13436–1)

Historical and Statutory Notes

Pre–1953 H 1 Amendments: 113 v 158, Ch 15, § 1

2939.06 Oath to grand jurors

(A) When a grand jury is impaneled, the court of common pleas shall appoint one of the members of the grand jury as foreperson, and shall administer, or cause to be administered, to the jurors an oath in the following words to which the jurors shall respond "I do solemnly swear" or "I do solemnly affirm":

"Do you solemnly swear or affirm that you will diligently inquire into and carefully deliberate all matters that shall come to your attention concerning this service; and do you solemnly swear or affirm that you will keep secret all proceedings of the grand jury unless you are required in a court of justice to make disclosure; and do you solemnly swear or affirm that you will indict no person through malice, hatred, or ill will; and do you solemnly swear or affirm that you will not leave unindicted any person through fear, favor, or affection, or for any reward or hope thereof; and do you solemnly swear or affirm that in all your deliberations you will present the truth, the whole truth, and nothing but the truth, according to the best of your skill and understanding, as you shall answer unto God or under the penalties of perjury?"

(B) If, on or after the effective date of this amendment, a court impaneling a grand jury uses the grand juror's oath that was in effect prior to the effective date of this amendment instead of the oath set forth in division (A) of this section, the court's use of the former oath does not invalidate or affect the validity of the impanelment of the grand jury, any proceeding, inquiry, or presentation of the grand jury, any indictment or other document found, returned, or issued by the grand jury, or any other action taken by the grand jury.

(2002 S 218, eff. 3–24–03; 1953 H 1, eff. 10–1–53; GC 13436–3)

Historical and Statutory Notes

Pre–1953 H 1 Amendments: 113 v 158, Ch 15, § 3

Amendment Note: 2002 S 218 rewrote this section, which prior thereto read:

"When a grand jury is impaneled the court of common pleas shall appoint one of the members thereof as foreman, and shall administer, or cause to be administered, to said jurors an oath in the following words:

"'You and each of you do solemnly swear that you will diligently inquire, and true presentment make of all such matters and things as shall be given you in charge of otherwise come to your knowledge, touching the present service; the counsel of the state, your own, and your fellows, you shall keep secret unless called on in a court of justice to make disclosures; and you shall present no person through malice, hatred, or ill will, nor shall you leave any person unpresented through fear, favor, or affection, or for any reward or hope thereof, but in all your presentments you shall present the truth, the whole truth, and nothing but the truth, according to the best of your skill and understanding."

Library References

Grand Jury ⚷22.

Westlaw Topic No. 193.

C.J.S. Grand Juries § 56.

Research References

Encyclopedias

OH Jur. 3d Jury § 118, Foreman of Grand Jury; Deputy Foreman.

OH Jur. 3d Jury § 119, Oath of Grand Jurors.

OH Jur. 3d Jury § 155, Persons Subject to Secrecy Requirements.

Treatises and Practice Aids

Katz, Giannelli, Blair and Lipton, Baldwin's Ohio Practice, Criminal Law, § 39:7, Foreman and Deputy Foreman.

Katz, Giannelli, Blair and Lipton, Baldwin's Ohio Practice, Criminal Law, § 141:4, Oath to Grand Jurors (Statutory Form).

Katz, Giannelli, Blair and Lipton, Baldwin's Ohio Practice, Criminal Law, § 39:15, Subpoena and Immunity Power.

Katz, Giannelli, Blair and Lipton, Baldwin's Ohio Practice, Criminal Law, § 39:22, Grand Jury Secrecy.

Notes of Decisions

---

1. Grand jury organization; oath

Former analogous section cited in discussing the organization of grand jury. State v. Rhoads (Ohio 1910) 81 Ohio St. 397, 91 N.E. 186, 7 Ohio Law Rep. 614, 18 Am.Ann.Cas. 415.

Former analogous section cited with reference to the oath to be administered to a foreman of a grand jury. State v. Rhoads (Ohio 1910) 81 Ohio St. 397, 91 N.E. 186, 7 Ohio Law Rep. 614, 18 Am.Ann.Cas. 415.

2. Testimony before grand jury

An attorney who participates in conducting an inquiry under Rule XVIII of the Rules of Practice of the Supreme Court, and who is subpoenaed to appear before a grand jury to testify as to matters disclosed in such inquiry, is required to testify in accordance with such subpoena. In re Klausmeyer (Ohio 1970) 24 Ohio St.2d 143, 265 N.E.2d 275, 53 O.O.2d 346.

An indictment and subsequent proceedings based thereon are not rendered invalid on the ground that illegal and incompetent testimony was heard by the grand jury which voted such indictment, inasmuch as the grand jury does not exercise a judicial function. Wickline v. Alvis (Franklin 1957) 103 Ohio App. 1, 144 N.E.2d 207, 3 O.O.2d 105. Indictment And Information ⚷ 10.2(2)

3. Secrecy of grand jury proceedings

As a municipal court judge has no authority to order disclosure of grand jury testimony, a writ of prohibition will issue where a municipal court judge orders a prosecuting attorney, not a party to the civil action, as part of discovery in a civil action to disclose transcripts of a grand jury which returned a no bill against the defendant in a pending wrongful death action; the writ shall issue to prevent needless litigation over a possible contempt citation when the prosecutor fails to disclose the requested information. State, ex rel. Ney, v. Allen (Hamilton 1990) 64 Ohio App.3d 574, 582 N.E.2d 46.

Grand jury evidence may be disclosed to a committee investigating alleged attorney misconduct. Petition of Grievance Committee of Toledo Bar Ass'n (Ohio 1989) 47 Ohio St.3d 611, 548 N.E.2d 916.

Whether a state court order forbidding interviews or statements for publication by witnesses, jurors, and individuals summoned but excused from serving as jurors in connection with the special grand jury convened by the governor to investigate the Kent State tragedy is an order that violates US Const Am 1 is not a matter for federal courts to consider where the allegedly aggrieved individuals never applied to the state court to have the order modified or dissolved. King v. Jones (C.A.6 (Ohio) 1971) 450 F.2d 478, vacated 92 S.Ct. 956, 405 U.S. 911, 30 L.Ed.2d 780.

Advice given by attorneys which caused their clients or the members of the grand jury to disregard or ignore their oath of secrecy before the grand jury was, per se, an unlawful interference with the proceedings of the court, and, however honestly given, was at least a technical contempt. Schmidt v. U.S. (C.C.A.6 (Ohio) 1940) 115 F.2d 394, 21 O.O. 78.

An injunction restraining all grand jury witnesses from speaking out with reference to the comments of a special grand jury held to fall as being overly broad. King v. Jones (N.D.Ohio 1970) 25 Ohio Misc. 255, 319 F.Supp. 653, 54 O.O.2d 411, vacated 450 F.2d 478, vacated 92 S.Ct. 956, 405 U.S. 911, 30 L.Ed.2d 780. Constitutional Law ⚿ 90.1(2); Grand Jury ⚿ 41.40

4. Supervision of grand jury

The court of common pleas has jurisdiction to supervise aspects of the grand jury as enumerated in RC 2939.01 et seq. and Crim R 6, and prohibition does not lie to control the court's discretion in the exercise of these powers. State ex rel. Shoop v. Mitrovich (Ohio 1983) 4 Ohio St.3d 220, 448 N.E.2d 800, 4 O.B.R. 575.

2939.07 Charge of the court

The grand jurors, after being sworn, shall be charged as to their duty by the judge of the court of common pleas, who shall call their attention particularly to the obligation of secrecy which their oaths impose, and explain to them the law applicable to such matters as may be brought before them.

(1953 H 1, eff. 10–1–53; GC 13436–4)

Historical and Statutory Notes

Pre–1953 H 1 Amendments: 113 v 159, Ch 15, § 4

Cross References

Grand jury, Crim R 6

Library References

Grand Jury ⚿23.
Westlaw Topic No. 193.
C.J.S. Grand Juries §§ 74 to 75.

Research References

Encyclopedias

OH Jur. 3d Jury § 120, Charge by the Court.

OH Jur. 3d Jury § 155, Persons Subject to Secrecy Requirements.

Treatises and Practice Aids

Katz, Giannelli, Blair and Lipton, Baldwin's Ohio Practice, Criminal Law, § 39:10, Judicial Control.

Katz, Giannelli, Blair and Lipton, Baldwin's Ohio Practice, Criminal Law, § 141:13, Motion for the Court to Exercise Supervisory Authority Over the Grand Jury.

Notes of Decisions

Secrecy of grand jury proceedings 2
Testimony before grand jury 1

1. Testimony before grand jury

In the interest of justice, if prosecuting party is aware of any substantial evidence negating guilt he should make it known to grand jury, at least where it might reasonably be expected to lead jury not to indict. Mayes v. Columbus (Ohio App. 10 Dist., 08-17-1995) 105 Ohio App.3d 728, 664 N.E.2d 1340, reconsideration denied 1995 WL 600645, appeal after new trial 124 Ohio App.3d 411, 706 N.E.2d 402, dismissed, appeal not allowed 81 Ohio St.3d 1496, 691 N.E.2d 1058. Grand Jury ⚿ 36.8

An attorney who participates in conducting an inquiry under Rule XVIII of the Rules of Practice of the Supreme Court, and who is subpoenaed to appear before a grand jury to testify as to matters disclosed in such inquiry, is required to testify in accordance with such subpoena. In re Klausmeyer (Ohio 1970) 24 Ohio St.2d 143, 265 N.E.2d 275, 53 O.O.2d 346.

2. Secrecy of grand jury proceedings

Absent some evidence of perjury or some other irregularity in grand jury proceedings involving employee's alleged participation in scheme to commit theft against employer, employee failed to demonstrate a particularized need that outweighed the need for maintaining the secrecy of grand jury proceedings, and thus, disclosure of grand jury testimony was not warranted in employee's action for malicious prosecution. Tourlakis v. Beverage Distributors, Inc. (Ohio App. 8 Dist., Cuyahoga, 12-26-2002) No. 81222, 2002-Ohio-7252, 2002 WL 31875970, Unreported. Grand Jury ⚩ 41.50(5)

A state statute forbidding a witness to ever disclose testimony given before a grand jury impermissibly infringes rights protected by US Const Am 1 to the extent it applies to witnesses' disclosure of their own testimony after the grand jury's term has ended. (Ed. note: Florida statute construed in light of federal constitution.) Butterworth v. Smith (U.S.Fla. 1990) 110 S.Ct. 1376, 494 U.S. 624, 108 L.Ed.2d 572.

Under Ohio law, the secrecy of a grand jury proceeding must be preserved unless the ends of justice require disclosure and there is a showing that a particularized need for disclosure exists which outweighs the need for secrecy. Craig v. Lima City Schools Bd of Educ. (N.D.Ohio, 08-31-2005) 384 F.Supp.2d 1136. Grand Jury ⚩ 41.50(5)

2939.08 Duty of grand jury

After the charge of the court of common pleas, the grand jury shall retire with the officer appointed to attend it, and proceed to inquire of and present all offenses committed within the county.

(1953 H 1, eff. 10–1–53; GC 13436–5)

Historical and Statutory Notes

Pre–1953 H 1 Amendments: 113 v 159, Ch 15, § 5

Library References

Grand Jury ⚩24.

Westlaw Topic No. 193.

C.J.S. Grand Juries §§ 2, 10 to 11, 76 to 84, 86.

Research References

Encyclopedias

OH Jur. 3d Jury § 129, Inquisitorial and Investigatory Functions.

Law Review and Journal Commentaries

Antitrust Grand Jury Procedure, Carl Steinhouse. 23 Clev St L Rev 447 (Fall 1974).

Notes of Decisions

Compelling testimony 3
Indictment pending preliminary hearing or other proceeding 2
Limitations on grand jury's authority 4
Presentment of offenses within county 1

1. Presentment of offenses within county

A grand jury may inquire of and present only such offenses as have been committed within county for which it was impaneled. State v. Nevius (Ohio 1947) 147 Ohio St. 263, 71 N.E.2d 258, 34 O.O. 210, certiorari denied 67 S.Ct. 1521, 331 U.S. 839, 91 L.Ed. 1851. Grand Jury ⚩ 26

2. Indictment pending preliminary hearing or other proceeding

Whether a preliminary examination has been held or not, even though the defendant be in custody and charged in a municipal court with an offense over which it has jurisdiction, is of no moment so far as the power of the grand jury to indict is concerned. State v. Sallee (Ohio Com.Pl. 1964) 1 Ohio Misc. 50, 202 N.E.2d 438, 30 O.O.2d 176. Double Jeopardy ⚩ 54; Indictment And Information ⚩ 9

A grand jury may return an indictment against a person even though such person has been charged with the same offenses in a municipal court and has pleaded not guilty and requested a jury trial. State v. Karr (Ohio Com.Pl. 1959) 161 N.E.2d 559, 81 Ohio Law Abs. 280, 10 O.O.2d 329.

A county grand jury may return an indictment against a person even though such person has been charged with the same offense in a municipal court and has requested a preliminary hearing, which has not been held at the time the indictment is returned. State v. Miller (Greene 1953) 96 Ohio App. 216, 121 N.E.2d 660, 54 O.O. 263, appeal dismissed 161 Ohio St. 467, 119 N.E.2d 618, 53 O.O. 359. Double Jeopardy ⚷ 187

3. Compelling testimony

The privilege to withhold from disclosure the identity of an informer may be invoked by a police officer in the course of a grand jury proceeding where the inquiry is not directed to the determination of the possible guilt of a specified person, but rather a general quest as to who might have committed a crime, and a police officer invoking the privilege in such circumstances may not be held in contempt. State v. Roe (Ohio 1971) 26 Ohio St.2d 243, 271 N.E.2d 296, 55 O.O.2d 480. Grand Jury ⚷ 36.1

4. Limitations on grand jury's authority

A grand jury is without authority to issue a report that advises, condemns, or commends, or makes recommendations concerning the policies and operation of public boards, public officers, or public authorities. Hammond v. Brown (N.D.Ohio 1971) 323 F.Supp. 326, 62 O.O.2d 65, affirmed 450 F.2d 480, 64 O.O.2d 255. Grand Jury ⚷ 42

2939.09 Clerk of grand jury

The grand jury may appoint one of its members to be its clerk to preserve the minutes of its proceedings and actions in all cases pending before it. Such minutes shall be delivered to the prosecuting attorney before the jury is discharged.

(1953 H 1, eff. 10–1–53; GC 13436–6)

Historical and Statutory Notes

Pre–1953 H 1 Amendments: 113 v 159, Ch 15, § 6

Cross References

Grand jury, Crim R 6

Library References

Grand Jury ⚷40.

Westlaw Topic No. 193.

C.J.S. Grand Juries § 110.

Research References

Encyclopedias

OH Jur. 3d Jury § 121, Clerk of Grand Jury.

Treatises and Practice Aids

Katz, Giannelli, Blair and Lipton, Baldwin's Ohio Practice, Criminal Law, § 39:22, Grand Jury Secrecy.

OFFICIALS

2939.10 Who shall have access to grand jury

The prosecuting attorney or assistant prosecuting attorney may at all times appear before the grand jury to give information relative to a matter cognizable by it, or advice upon a legal matter when required. The prosecuting attorney may interrogate witnesses before the grand jury when the grand jury or the prosecuting attorney finds it necessary, but no person other than the grand jurors shall be permitted to remain in the room with the jurors while the jurors are expressing their views or giving their votes on a matter before them. In all matters or cases which the attorney general is required to investigate or prosecute by the governor or general assembly, or which a special prosecutor is required by section 177.03 of the Revised Code to investigate and prosecute, the attorney general or the special prosecutor, respectively, shall have and exercise any or all rights, privileges, and powers of prosecuting attorneys, and any assistant or special counsel designated by the attorney general or special prosecutor for that purpose, has the same authority. Proceedings in relation to such matters or cases are under the exclusive supervision and control of the attorney general or the special prosecutor.

(1986 S 74, eff. 9–3–86; 1953 H 1; GC 13436–7)

Historical and Statutory Notes

Pre-1953 H 1 Amendments: 113 v 159, Ch 15, § 7

Cross References

Grand jury, Crim R 6

Powers and duties of first assistant attorney general, 109.04

Sunshine law, grand jury proceedings not governed by, 121.22

Library References

Grand Jury ⚖34, 36, 41.

Westlaw Topic No. 193.

C.J.S. Grand Juries §§ 74 to 75, 101 to 109, 111 to 172, 174 to 176.

Research References

Encyclopedias

OH Jur. 3d Jury § 138, Who May be Present at Session of Grand Jury.

OH Jur. 3d Jury § 155, Persons Subject to Secrecy Requirements.

OH Jur. 3d State of Ohio § 134, Assistants and Employees.

Treatises and Practice Aids

Katz, Giannelli, Blair and Lipton, Baldwin's Ohio Practice, Criminal Law, § 143:4, Motion to Dismiss Indictment—Unauthorized Person Present With Grand Jury.

Katz, Giannelli, Blair and Lipton, Baldwin's Ohio Practice, Criminal Law, § 39:10, Judicial Control.

Katz, Giannelli, Blair and Lipton, Baldwin's Ohio Practice, Criminal Law, § 39:11, Prosecutor's Role.

Katz, Giannelli, Blair and Lipton, Baldwin's Ohio Practice, Criminal Law, § 39:13, Presence in Jury Room.

Katz, Giannelli, Blair and Lipton, Baldwin's Ohio Practice, Criminal Law, § 143:13, Motion to Dismiss Indictment—Violation of Grand Jury Secrecy.

Notes of Decisions

---

1. Supervision of grand jury

Court of common pleas has authority to recess grand jury for further business arising during term. Subject to express statutory limitations the grand jury in each county is under the control and direction of the court of common pleas, and that court has authority after the disposition of matters pending at the beginning of the term to recess the grand jury for such further business as may arise during the term. State v. Schwab (Ohio 1924) 109 Ohio St. 532, 143 N.E. 29, 2 Ohio Law Abs. 196, 21 Ohio Law Rep. 602.

The court of common pleas has jurisdiction to supervise aspects of the grand jury as enumerated in RC 2939.01 et seq. and Crim R 6, and prohibition does not lie to control the court's discretion in the exercise of these powers. RC 2939.10 does not alter the basic relationship between the court of common pleas and the grand jury. State ex rel. Shoop v. Mitrovich (Ohio 1983) 4 Ohio St.3d 220, 448 N.E.2d 800, 4 O.B.R. 575.

2. Special prosecutor

Quo warranto seeking a declaration that a special prosecutor obtaining indictments against the relator is a usurper of the office is unavailable as quo warranto may not be used as a substitute for appeal of the denial of the relator's motion seeking dismissal of the indictments. State ex rel. Jackson v. Allen (Ohio 1992) 65 Ohio St.3d 37, 599 N.E.2d 696.

3. Formal requirements for indictment

Absent showing of prejudice, indictment was not required to be dismissed for irregularities in grand jury selection and replacements, namely, replacements by the "Grand Jury Bailiff" rather than the trial court and fact that initial "draw" was conducted by jury commissioners two hours before trial court order authorizing drawing and was conducted more than 28 days prior to beginning of court term or that trial court failed to affirmatively determine that person selected possessed the requisite statutory qualifications. State v. Ross (Franklin 1982) 6 Ohio App.3d 25, 452 N.E.2d 339, 6 O.B.R. 76. Indictment And Information ⚖ 10.1(2)

The signature of the foreman of a grand jury is an indispensable requisite to a valid indictment, and in the absence thereof all subsequent proceedings are void; and habeas corpus will lie. Kennedy v. Alvis (Ohio Com.Pl. 1957) 145 N.E.2d 361, 76 Ohio Law Abs. 132.

In view of Const. Art. I, § 10, and GC 13556 (repealed 1929. See § 13436–3), the grand jury in its inquest of crimes and offenses and in its findings and presentation of indictments to the court of common pleas, does not exercise a judicial function, but only acts as the formal and constitutional accuser of crime and those it believes to be probably guilty thereof. State ex rel. Doerfler v. Price (Ohio 1920) 101 Ohio St. 50, 128 N.E. 173, 17 Ohio Law Rep. 488. Grand Jury 🔑 1; Indictment And Information 🔑 10.3

4. Access to grand jury

Under RC 2939.10, only the prosecuting attorney, assistant prosecuting attorney, and, in certain cases, the attorney general or special prosecutor appointed by the attorney general have access to the grand jury; thus, a private citizen does not have a right to present evidence before a grand jury nor may a private citizen require a judge of a common pleas court or a county prosecuting attorney to permit him to do so. Walton v. Judge (Ohio 1992) 64 Ohio St.3d 564, 597 N.E.2d 162.

Defense counsel is entitled to inspect prior statements of the state's principal witness where she admits in open court that her testimony is inconsistent with some or all of her prior statements to the police, and that these statements are inconsistent with each other, subject to an in camera inspection by the court at which counsel for the state and counsel for the defendant are present and participating. State v. White (Ohio 1968) 15 Ohio St.2d 146, 239 N.E.2d 65, 44 O.O.2d 132. Criminal Law 🔑 627.7(3)

Where a person conducts a private interview with one who afterwards is called and examined as a witness before the grand jury, which finds an indictment against the defendant concerning some matters disclosed in the interview which was stenographically recorded, written out and subsequently delivered to the prosecuting attorney for his use, and at trial the person interviewed is called and testifies for the state in support of the indictment, it is error for the court upon request of the defendant to order the prosecuting attorney to deliver the transcript of the interview to the defendant or his counsel, or to order the prosecutor to allow either of them an inspection of the interview. State v. Rhoads (Ohio 1910) 81 Ohio St. 397, 91 N.E. 186, 7 Ohio Law Rep. 614, 18 Am.Ann.Cas. 415. Criminal Law 🔑 627(2)

Former GC 13560 (Repealed) cited as to privilege of the prosecuting attorney to interrogate witnesses before the grand jury. State v. Rhoads (Ohio 1910) 81 Ohio St. 397, 91 N.E. 186, 7 Ohio Law Rep. 614, 18 Am.Ann.Cas. 415.

Where a special grand jury returned indictments against twenty-five persons and also filed a special report containing conclusions of the grand jury and assessing blame, the district court may order that special report be physically expunged and destroyed. Hammond v. Brown (C.A.6 (Ohio) 1971) 450 F.2d 480, 64 O.O.2d 255. Grand Jury 🔑 42

In proceedings before a special grand jury, the attorney general and his special counsel have and exercise the rights, privileges and powers of prosecuting attorneys. Hammond v. Brown (N.D.Ohio 1971) 323 F.Supp. 326, 62 O.O.2d 65, affirmed 450 F.2d 480, 64 O.O.2d 255. Grand Jury 🔑 34

Accused has no right to appear before grand jury, either personally or by counsel; and although a district attorney may examine witnesses before grand jury, even he has no right to be present during their deliberations if any juror objects. U.S. v. Central Supply Ass'n (N.D.Ohio 1940) 34 F.Supp. 241. Grand Jury 🔑 34; Grand Jury 🔑 35

5. Access to record of testimony

Where there has been no demonstration of prejudice from the fact that a witness who is an assistant prosecuting attorney was present during the testimony of other witnesses in the grand jury proceeding, the trial court errs in quashing the indictment based only upon a perceived inference of impropriety. State v. Crist (Ohio App. 12 Dist., Butler, 10-20-1997) No. CA 96-08-159, 1997 WL 656307, Unreported, dismissed, jurisdictional motion overruled 81 Ohio St.3d 1443, 690 N.E.2d 15.

Where a witness for the state in a criminal proceeding turns hostile while testifying on direct examination so that he is placed under cross-examination, his previous testimony drawn from a secret grand jury hearing may be used to attack his statements without opening the entire record of such hearing to the defendant's scrutiny. State v. Mullins (Scioto 1971) 26 Ohio App.2d 13, 268 N.E.2d 603, 55 O.O.2d 30.

Defense counsel is entitled to inspect prior statements of the state's principal witness where she admits in open court that her testimony is inconsistent with some or all of her prior statements to the police, and that these statements are inconsistent with each other, subject to an in camera inspection by the court at which counsel for the state and counsel for the defendant are present and participating. State v. White (Ohio 1968) 15 Ohio St.2d 146, 239 N.E.2d 65, 44 O.O.2d 132. Criminal Law 🔑 627.7(3)

Where the state's principal witness admits in open court that her testimony is inconsistent with some or all of her prior statements to the police, and that these prior statements are inconsistent with each other, the trial court must grant defense counsel's request to inspect the statements. State v. White (Ohio 1968) 15 Ohio St.2d 146, 239 N.E.2d 65, 44 O.O.2d 132. Criminal Law 🔑 627.7(3)

As to the power of the court to require the prosecuting attorney to permit counsel for the accused to examine the record of testimony taken before the grand jury with reference to his alleged offense. State v. Rhoads (Ohio 1910) 81 Ohio St. 397, 91 N.E. 186, 7 Ohio Law Rep. 614, 18 Am. Ann.Cas. 415.

Where a person conducts a private interview with one who afterwards is called and examined as a witness before the grand jury, which finds an indictment against the defendant concerning some matters disclosed in the interview which was stenographically recorded, written out and subsequently delivered to the prosecuting attorney for his use, and at trial the person interviewed is called and testifies for the state in support of the indictment, it is error for the court upon request of the defendant to order the prosecuting attorney to deliver the transcript of the interview to the defendant or his counsel, or to order the prosecutor to allow either of them an inspection of the interview. State v. Rhoads (Ohio 1910) 81 Ohio St. 397, 91 N.E. 186, 7 Ohio Law Rep. 614, 18 Am.Ann.Cas. 415. Criminal Law ⚷ 627(2)

2939.11 Official reporters

The official shorthand reporter of the county, or any shorthand reporter designated by the court of common pleas, at the request of the prosecuting attorney, or any such reporter designated by the attorney general in investigations conducted by him, may take shorthand notes of testimony before the grand jury, and furnish a transcript to the prosecuting attorney or the attorney general, and to no other person. The shorthand reporter shall withdraw from the jury room before the jurors begin to express their views or take their vote on the matter before them. Such reporter shall take an oath to be administered by the judge after the grand jury is sworn, imposing an obligation of secrecy to not disclose any testimony taken or heard except to the grand jury, prosecuting attorney, or attorney general, unless called upon in court to make disclosures.

(1953 H 1, eff. 10–1–53; GC 13436–8)

Historical and Statutory Notes

Pre–1953 H 1 Amendments: 113 v 159, Ch 15, § 8

Cross References

Grand jury, Crim R 6

Transcript of grand jury proceedings, discovery of, Crim R 16

Library References

Grand Jury ⚷38.

Westlaw Topic No. 193.

C.J.S. Grand Juries §§ 94, 110.

Research References

Encyclopedias

OH Jur. 3d Jury § 139, Who May be Present at Session of Grand Jury—Shorthand Reporter, Stenographer, or Operator of Recording Device.

OH Jur. 3d Jury § 155, Persons Subject to Secrecy Requirements.

OH Jur. 3d State of Ohio § 134, Assistants and Employees.

Treatises and Practice Aids

Katz, Giannelli, Blair and Lipton, Baldwin's Ohio Practice, Criminal Law, § 39:13, Presence in Jury Room.

Katz, Giannelli, Blair and Lipton, Baldwin's Ohio Practice, Criminal Law, § 39:22, Grand Jury Secrecy.

Notes of Decisions

Access to record of testimony 2
Impeachment of witness at trial with grand jury testimony 3
Secrecy of grand jury proceedings 1
Unauthorized special report 4

---

1. Secrecy of grand jury proceedings

Trial court was not required to conduct in camera review of grand jury minutes to ensure that grand jury had indicted defendant on appropriate grounds; as court reporter was required to withdraw from grand jury room prior to grand jury discussion of and vote regarding matters before them, transcripts would not reflect desired information. State v. Brown (Ohio App. 10 Dist., 12-29-1994) 99 Ohio App.3d 604, 651 N.E.2d 470. Criminal Law ⚷ 627.9(5)

An injunction restraining all grand jury witnesses from speaking out with reference to the comments of a special grand jury held to fall as being overly broad. King v. Jones (N.D.Ohio 1970) 25 Ohio Misc. 255, 319 F.Supp. 653, 54 O.O.2d 411, vacated 450 F.2d 478, vacated 92 S.Ct. 956, 405 U.S. 911, 30 L.Ed.2d 780. Constitutional Law ⚷ 90.1(2); Grand Jury ⚷ 41.40

2. Access to record of testimony

Defendant failed to show "particularized need" necessary to warrant disclosure of grand jury transcript, in prosecution for involuntary manslaughter and other offenses; there was no discrepancy between indictment and amended bill of particulars, which added receiving stolen property as underlying felony on which manslaughter charge was based, and in camera review of grand jury transcript showed that there was ample evidence presented to establish probable cause that defendant had received stolen property. State v. Elam (Ohio Com. Pl., 09-08-2004) 129 Ohio Misc.2d 26, 821 N.E.2d 622, 2004-Ohio-7328. Criminal Law ⚷ 627.9(2.1); Criminal Law ⚷ 627.9(5)

Defendant in capital murder prosecution failed to show particularized need for transcript of grand jury testimony by accomplice in robbery during which charged killing of security guard occurred, where accomplice never testified at trial. State v. Treesh (Ohio, 01-03-2001) 90 Ohio St.3d 460, 739 N.E.2d 749, 2001-Ohio-4, stay granted 91 Ohio St.3d 1435, 742 N.E.2d 135, certiorari denied 121 S.Ct. 2247, 533 U.S. 904, 150 L.Ed.2d 234. Criminal Law ⚷ 627.9(2.1)

Determining whether there is particularized need for disclosure of grand jury transcripts to defendant is matter within trial court's discretion. State v. Benge (Ohio, 03-04-1996) 75 Ohio St.3d 136, 661 N.E.2d 1019, 1996-Ohio-227, reconsideration denied 75 Ohio St.3d 1453, 663 N.E.2d 333, stay granted 75 Ohio St.3d 1493, 664 N.E.2d 1290, stay revoked 83 Ohio St.3d 1407, 698 N.E.2d 433, certiorari denied 117 S.Ct. 224, 519 U.S. 888, 136 L.Ed.2d 156, dismissal of post-conviction relief affirmed 1998 WL 204941, dismissed, appeal not allowed 82 Ohio St.3d 1482, 696 N.E.2d 1088, subsequent habeas corpus proceeding 2000 WL 1456911, habeas corpus dismissed 312 F.Supp.2d 978. Criminal Law ⚷ 627.9(1)

Accused is not entitled to see grand jury transcripts unless ends of justice require it and he shows that particularized need for disclosure exists which outweighs need for secrecy. State v. Benge (Ohio, 03-04-1996) 75 Ohio St.3d 136, 661 N.E.2d 1019, 1996-Ohio-227, reconsideration denied 75 Ohio St.3d 1453, 663 N.E.2d 333, stay granted 75 Ohio St.3d 1493, 664 N.E.2d 1290, stay revoked 83 Ohio St.3d 1407, 698 N.E.2d 433, certiorari denied 117 S.Ct. 224, 519 U.S. 888, 136 L.Ed.2d 156, dismissal of post-conviction relief affirmed 1998 WL 204941, dismissed, appeal not allowed 82 Ohio St.3d 1482, 696 N.E.2d 1088, subsequent habeas corpus proceeding 2000 WL 1456911, habeas corpus dismissed 312 F.Supp.2d 978. Criminal Law ⚷ 627.9(2.1); Criminal Law ⚷ 627.9(5)

Fact that grand jury indicted capital murder defendant on elevated charges of aggravated murder with death specifications, aggravated robbery, and gross abuse of corpse, even though he was bound over on charges of murder and theft, was not in and of itself sufficient showing of particularized need for disclosure of grand jury transcripts. State v. Benge (Ohio, 03-04-1996) 75 Ohio St.3d 136, 661 N.E.2d 1019, 1996-Ohio-227, reconsideration denied 75 Ohio St.3d 1453, 663 N.E.2d 333, stay granted 75 Ohio St.3d 1493, 664 N.E.2d 1290, stay revoked 83 Ohio St.3d 1407, 698 N.E.2d 433, certiorari denied 117 S.Ct. 224, 519 U.S. 888, 136 L.Ed.2d 156, dismissal of post-conviction relief affirmed 1998 WL 204941, dismissed, appeal not allowed 82 Ohio St.3d 1482, 696 N.E.2d 1088, subsequent habeas corpus proceeding 2000 WL 1456911, habeas corpus dismissed 312 F.Supp.2d 978. Criminal Law ⚷ 627.9(2.1)

Defense counsel is entitled to inspect prior statements of the state's principal witness where she admits in open court that her testimony is inconsistent with some or all of her prior statements to the police, and that these statements are inconsistent with each other, subject to an in camera inspection by the court at which counsel for the state and counsel for the defendant are present and participating. State v. White (Ohio 1968) 15 Ohio St.2d 146, 239 N.E.2d 65, 44 O.O.2d 132. Criminal Law ⚷ 627.7(3)

The reference by a trial judge outside of open court to the stenographic record of the testimony of witnesses before the grand jury either to constitute a foundation upon which the court might examine the defendant on the hearing of the motion to change his plea or as a means of convincing the court of the guilt of the defendant, constitutes an abuse of discretion and error prejudicial to the defendant for which the order overruling the motion to change the plea and the judgment and sentence entered on the unchanged plea will be reversed and vacated. State v. Amison (Lucas 1965) 2 Ohio App.2d 390, 208 N.E.2d 769, 31 O.O.2d 594.

Where a person conducts a private interview with one who afterwards is called and examined as a witness before the grand jury, which finds an indictment against the defendant concerning some matters disclosed in the interview which was stenographically recorded, written out and subsequently delivered to the prosecuting attorney for his use, and at trial the person interviewed is called and testifies for the state in support of the indictment, it is error for the court upon request of the defendant to order the prosecuting attorney to deliver the transcript of the interview to the defendant or his counsel, or to order the prosecutor to allow either of them an inspection of the interview. State v. Rhoads (Ohio 1910) 81 Ohio St. 397, 91 N.E. 186, 7 Ohio Law Rep. 614, 18 Am.Ann.Cas. 415. Criminal Law ⚷ 627(2)

Accused not entitled to copy of his testimony given before a grand jury indicting him. (See also State v Haugh, 4 NP(NS) 79, 16 D 477 (1906).) State v. Rhoads (Ohio 1910) 81 Ohio St. 397, 91 N.E. 186, 7 Ohio Law Rep. 614, 18 Am.Ann.Cas. 415.

A petition to the court which supervised a grand jury is the proper means of obtaining release of grand jury materials. In re Petition for Disclosure of Evidence Presented to Franklin County Grand Juries in 1970 (Ohio 1980) 63 Ohio St.2d 212, 407 N.E.2d 513, 17 O.O.3d 131.

RC 2939.11 allows the court which supervises a grand jury to disclose evidence presented to the grand jury where justice requires, in civil as well as criminal actions. In re Petition for Disclosure of Evidence Presented to Franklin County Grand Juries in 1970 (Ohio 1980) 63 Ohio St.2d 212, 407 N.E.2d 513, 17 O.O.3d 131.

3. Impeachment of witness at trial with grand jury testimony

Where a witness for the state in a criminal proceeding turns hostile while testifying on direct examination so that he is placed under cross-examination, his previous testimony drawn from a secret grand jury hearing may be used to attack his statements without opening the entire record of such hearing to the defendant's scrutiny. State v. Mullins (Scioto 1971) 26 Ohio App.2d 13, 268 N.E.2d 603, 55 O.O.2d 30.

4. Unauthorized special report

Where a special grand jury returned indictments against twenty-five persons and also filed a special report containing conclusions of the grand jury and assessing blame, the district court may order that special report be physically expunged and destroyed. Hammond v. Brown (C.A.6 (Ohio) 1971) 450 F.2d 480, 64 O.O.2d 255. Grand Jury ⚷ 42

A report of an Ohio grand jury is issued without authority if it violates the grand jury's secrecy against disclosure of evidence by purporting to summarize the evidence received by it or to make findings based thereon. Hammond v. Brown (N.D.Ohio 1971) 323 F.Supp. 326, 62 O.O.2d 65, affirmed 450 F.2d 480, 64 O.O.2d 255. Grand Jury ⚷ 42

A report of an Ohio grand jury that exceeds the jury's authority or violates the secrecy against disclosure is subject to expungement at the direction of a federal court. Hammond v. Brown (N.D.Ohio 1971) 323 F.Supp. 326, 62 O.O.2d 65, affirmed 450 F.2d 480, 64 O.O.2d 255.

2939.12 Clerk to issue subpoenas for witnesses

When required by the grand jury, prosecuting attorney, or judge of the court of common pleas, the clerk of the court of common pleas shall issue subpoenas and other process to any county to bring witnesses to testify before such jury.

(1953 H 1, eff. 10–1–53; GC 13436–9)

Historical and Statutory Notes

Pre–1953 H 1 Amendments: 113 v 160, Ch 15, § 9

Cross References

Grand jury, Crim R 6

Right to compulsory process to obtain witnesses, O Const Art I §10

Subpoenas, Crim R 17

Library References

Grand Jury ⚷36.4.

Westlaw Topic No. 193.

C.J.S. Grand Juries §§ 111, 114 to 128, 130, 132 to 140, 147.

Research References

Encyclopedias

OH Jur. 3d Criminal Law § 3113, Compelling Attendance.

OH Jur. 3d Jury § 148, Compelling Attendance and Testimony of Witnesses.

Treatises and Practice Aids

Katz, Giannelli, Blair and Lipton, Baldwin's Ohio Practice, Criminal Law, § 141:6, Subpoena for Witness to Grand Jury.

Katz, Giannelli, Blair and Lipton, Baldwin's Ohio Practice, Criminal Law, § 141:7, Subpoena Duces Tecum.

Law Review and Journal Commentaries

Subpoena, Note. 19 Am Crim L Rev 193 (Fall 1981).

Subpoenas and privilege—How they can coexist, Peter N. Cultice. 9 Ohio Law 12 (September/October 1995).

Notes of Decisions

Subpoena as public record 1

1. **Subpoena as public record**

Grand jury subpoenas, while in the possession of the clerk of courts prior to issuance in accordance with RC 2939.12, are not public records subject to disclosure under RC 149.43. OAG 84–079.

WITNESSES

2939.121 Employee's attendance before grand jury under subpoena; employer may not penalize

No employer shall discharge or terminate from employment, threaten to discharge or terminate from employment, or otherwise punish or penalize any employee because of time lost from regular employment as a result of the employee's attendance at any proceeding before a grand jury pursuant to a subpoena. This section generally does not require and shall not be construed to require an employer to pay an employee for time lost resulting from attendance at any grand jury proceeding. However, if an employee is subpoenaed to appear at a grand jury proceeding and the proceeding pertains to an offense against the employer or an offense involving the employee during the course of his employment, the employer shall not decrease or withhold the employee's pay for any time lost as a result of compliance with the subpoena. Any employer who knowingly violates this section is in contempt of court.

(1984 S 172, eff. 9–26–84)

Cross References

Victims' rights pamphlet, publication and distribution, 109.42

Victims' rights, retaliation by employer prohibited, 2930.18

Library References

Labor and Employment ⚷782.
Westlaw Topic No. 231H.

Research References

Treatises and Practice Aids

Employment Coordinator Benefits § 14:37, Ohio.

Notes of Decisions

Punishment of employee who is charged or indicted, distinguished 1

1. **Punishment of employee who is charged or indicted, distinguished**

Even assuming Ohio law evidenced clear public policy against employers terminating employee based upon fact that employee had been charged but not convicted of crime, employer did not violate any public policy by terminating truck driver who was arrested for driving under the influence (DUI), even though he was later acquitted of charges, and thus truck driver failed to support claim of public policy wrongful discharge under Ohio law. Roberts v. Alan Ritchey, Inc. (S.D.Ohio, 04-17-1997) 962 F.Supp. 1028. Labor And Employment ⚷ 767

2939.13 Oath to witnesses

Before a witness is examined by the grand jury, an oath shall be administered to him by the foreman of the grand jury or by the judge of the court of common pleas or the clerk of the court of common pleas, truly to testify of such matters and things as may lawfully be inquired of before such jury. A certificate that the oath has been administered shall be indorsed on the subpoena of the witness or otherwise made by the foreman of the grand jury, judge, or clerk certifying the attendance of said witness to the clerk of the court.

(1953 H 1, eff. 10–1–53; GC 13436–10)

Historical and Statutory Notes

Pre–1953 H 1 Amendments: 115 v 417; 113 v 160, Ch 15, § 10

Library References

Grand Jury ⚷36.
Westlaw Topic No. 193.
C.J.S. Grand Juries §§ 101, 111 to 172, 174 to 175.

Research References

Encyclopedias

OH Jur. 3d Jury § 147, Oath to Witnesses.

Treatises and Practice Aids

Katz, Giannelli, Blair and Lipton, Baldwin's Ohio Practice, Criminal Law, § 39:7, Foreman and Deputy Foreman.

Katz, Giannelli, Blair and Lipton, Baldwin's Ohio Practice, Criminal Law, § 39:22, Grand Jury Secrecy.

Notes of Decisions

Perjury 1
Secrecy of grand jury proceedings 2
Self–incrimination 3

1. Perjury

The giving of false testimony to a grand jury may form the basis of a perjury prosecution although, despite the witness' perjury, the grand jury returns an indictment against the subject of its inquiry. State v. Childress (Clark 1990) 66 Ohio App.3d 491, 585 N.E.2d 567.

A motion to quash an indictment charging perjury before a grand jury, where the indictment does not show affirmatively that the witness was not advised of his constitutional right to testify as to his own conduct, nor that he did not waive his constitutional privilege, presents no question of the invasion of his constitutional right under Const. Art. I, § 10. State v. Cox (Ohio 1913) 87 Ohio St. 313, 101 N.E. 135, 10 Ohio Law Rep. 600. Indictment And Information ⚷ 138

Fact that defendant charged with perjuring herself to grand jury had difficulty understanding grand jury proceedings because her counsel was not present and because defendant had difficulty understanding English did not require suppression of her grand jury testimony. U.S. v. Latouf (C.A.6 (Ohio), 12-18-1997) 132 F.3d 320, certiorari denied 118 S.Ct. 1542, 523 U.S. 1086, 140 L.Ed.2d 691, certiorari denied 118 S.Ct. 1543, 523 U.S. 1086, 140 L.Ed.2d 691, certiorari denied 118 S.Ct. 1572, 523 U.S. 1101, 140 L.Ed.2d 805, certiorari denied 118 S.Ct. 2307, 524 U.S. 920, 141 L.Ed.2d 165, denial of post-conviction relief affirmed 22 Fed.Appx. 605, 2001 WL 1631832. Criminal Law ⚷ 539(2)

2. Secrecy of grand jury proceedings

If grand jury witness claims his privilege against self-incrimination in any language which may be reasonably understood as invoking or asserting it, the prosecutor and the grand jury must honor the witness' decision to exercise it until immunity is granted or a valid waiver is secured. State v. Cook (Wood 1983) 11 Ohio App.3d 237, 464 N.E.2d 577, 11 O.B.R. 362. Witnesses ⚷ 297(6)

An injunction restraining all grand jury witnesses from speaking out with reference to the comments of a special grand jury held to fall as being overly broad. King v. Jones (N.D.Ohio 1970) 25 Ohio Misc. 255, 319 F.Supp. 653, 54 O.O.2d 411, vacated 450 F.2d 478, vacated 92 S.Ct. 956, 405 U.S. 911, 30 L.Ed.2d 780. Constitutional Law ⚷ 90.1(2); Grand Jury ⚷ 41.40

3. Self–incrimination

A witness is a "putative defendant," and thus entitled to be warned of the right to be free from compelled self-incrimination before testifying before the grand jury, if, at the time that the witness appears before the grand jury, the witness is potentially the focus of the investigation and is subject to possible indictment. State v. Cook (Wood 1983) 11 Ohio App.3d 237, 464 N.E.2d 577, 11 O.B.R. 362. Witnesses ⚷ 302

2939.14 Proceedings when witness refuses to testify

If a witness before a grand jury refuses to answer an interrogatory, the court of common pleas shall be informed in writing, in which such interrogatory shall be stated, with the excuse for the refusal given by the witness. The court shall determine whether the witness is required to answer, and the grand jury shall be forthwith informed of such decision.

(1953 H 1, eff. 10–1–53; GC 13436–11)

Historical and Statutory Notes

Pre–1953 H 1 Amendments: 113 v 160, Ch 15, § 11

Cross References

Granting immunity to witness, 2945.44

Right against compulsory self-incrimination, US Const Am 5; O Const Art I §10

Library References

Grand Jury ⚷36.

Westlaw Topic No. 193.

C.J.S. Grand Juries §§ 101, 111 to 172, 174 to 175.

Research References

Encyclopedias

OH Jur. 3d Contempt § 50, Particular Officers and Bodies.

OH Jur. 3d Jury § 149, Compelling Attendance and Testimony of Witnesses—Refusal to Testify or Produce Documents; Liability for Contempt.

Forms

Ohio Jurisprudence Pleading and Practice Forms § 100:10, Courts—Particular Officers and Bodies.

Treatises and Practice Aids

Markus, Trial Handbook for Ohio Lawyers, § 5:4, Direct Criminal.

Katz, Giannelli, Blair and Lipton, Baldwin's Ohio Practice, Criminal Law, § 41:4, Self-Incrimination—Witnesses.

Katz, Giannelli, Blair and Lipton, Baldwin's Ohio Practice, Criminal Law, § 141:8, Notice to Court that Witness Refuses to Answer Question Before Grand Jury.

Katz, Giannelli, Blair and Lipton, Baldwin's Ohio Practice, Criminal Law, § 141:9, Motion for Show Cause Hearing.

Katz, Giannelli, Blair and Lipton, Baldwin's Ohio Practice, Criminal Law, § 39:10, Judicial Control.

Katz, Giannelli, Blair and Lipton, Baldwin's Ohio Practice, Criminal Law, § 141:16, Dismissal of Contempt Charge.

Notes of Decisions

1. Privilege against self-incrimination

Where a grand jury witness is a putative or prospective defendant, he must be warned of his privilege against self-incrimination before he testifies; testimony gained without this warning will be deemed compelled and may not be used against the witness in a subsequent prosecution. State v. Cook (Wood 1983) 11 Ohio App.3d 237, 464 N.E.2d 577, 11 O.B.R. 362. Witnesses ⚷ 302

While being questioned, if a grand jury witness indicates a desire to claim his privilege against self-incrimination in a way which may be reasonably understood to invoke it, this decision must be honored by the prosecutor and the grand jury until immunity is granted or a waiver is obtained. State v. Cook (Wood 1983) 11 Ohio App.3d 237, 464 N.E.2d 577, 11 O.B.R. 362. Witnesses ⚷ 297(6)

An accused may be compelled to provide voice exemplars for identification purposes. State v. Sutton (Wayne 1979) 64 Ohio App.2d 105, 411 N.E.2d 818, 18 O.O.3d 83.

2. Compelling testimony—absence of immunity

Any error was harmless in special prosecutor's failure to present written list of interrogatories before trial court prior to trial court finding newspaper reporter in civil contempt for refusing to testify under subpoena before grand jury respecting reporter's interview with individual under criminal investigation, where there was no indication that defendant claimed qualified privilege as to only some of information sought by special prosecutor, and none of information sought was privileged or obtained from source promised confidentiality. In re Grand Jury Witness Subpoena of Abraham (Ohio App. 11 Dist., 11-30-1993) 92 Ohio App.3d 186, 634 N.E.2d 667, motion overruled 68 Ohio St.3d 1431, 624 N.E.2d 1068. Contempt ⚷ 66(7)

Order of trial court requiring physician to answer questions before grand jury and deliver to grand jury all medical records bearing name of patient was overbroad; there was no evidence that all records in patient's file were fraudulent. State ex rel. Buchman v. Stokes (Hamilton 1987) 36 Ohio App.3d 109, 521 N.E.2d 515. Grand Jury ⚷ 36.4(2)

Where a witness before a grand jury, in the absence of complete immunity, refuses to answer a series of questions, some of which are incriminating and others not, a trial judge, under RC 2939.14, must separate the incriminating from the nonincriminating questions, and the witness may be found in contempt for a refusal to answer the nonincriminating questions. State v. Prato (Mahoning 1965) 2 Ohio App.2d 115, 206 N.E.2d 917, 31 O.O.2d 197. Grand Jury ⚷ 36.1

3. —— Immunity granted, compelling testimony

Trial court's observation that grand jury transcript demonstrated that immunity had been granted to witness was both inadequate and incorrect. State v. Asher (Ohio App. 1 Dist., 07-17-1996) 112 Ohio App.3d 646, 679 N.E.2d 1147, appeal not allowed 77 Ohio St.3d 1492, 673 N.E.2d 148. Witnesses ⚷ 304(1)

Where statutory immunity has been conferred upon a witness, and such immunity is full and complete by preventing prosecutions against the witness on account of any transaction, matter or thing testified to, such witness may be compelled to testify and held guilty of contempt in refusing to do so, without violating the constitutional privilege against self-incrimination, but "where no written complaint or affidavit, information or indictment has been lodged against anyone such immunity provisions do not apply, as the witness is not called to testify "upon complaint, information, affidavit or indictment," and in such a case a witness may refuse to answer questions that have a tendency to incriminate himself." In re Lazzaro (Ohio Com.Pl. 1953) 111 N.E.2d 611, 65 Ohio Law Abs. 210, 51 O.O. 285.

4. Preventing testimony as obstruction of justice

City prosecutor's alleged statement to police chief encouraging him to write letter to city police officers telling them not to cooperate with grand jury investigation of mayor's court was insufficient to support officer's claim that city officials conspired to obstruct justice, absent evidence that city officials acted in concert with one another in order to prevent officer from testifying. Bragg v. Madison (C.A.6 (Ohio), 08-31-2001) No. 00-3237, 20 Fed.Appx. 278, 2001 WL 1041764, Unreported. Conspiracy ⚷ 2

2939.15 Court may proceed against witness for contempt

If the court of common pleas determines that a witness before a grand jury is required to answer an interrogatory and such witness persists in his refusal, he shall be brought before the court, which shall proceed in a like manner as if such witness had been interrogated and refused to answer in open court.

(1953 H 1, eff. 10–1–53; GC 13436–12)

Historical and Statutory Notes

Pre–1953 H 1 Amendments: 113 v 160, Ch 15, § 12

Cross References

Contempt, Crim R 17

Library References

Grand Jury ⚷36.5.

Westlaw Topic No. 193.

C.J.S. Grand Juries §§ 111, 123, 155 to 163.

Research References

Encyclopedias

OH Jur. 3d Contempt § 50, Particular Officers and Bodies.

OH Jur. 3d Jury § 149, Compelling Attendance and Testimony of Witnesses—Refusal to Testify or Produce Documents; Liability for Contempt.

Forms

Ohio Jurisprudence Pleading and Practice Forms § 100:10, Courts—Particular Officers and Bodies.

Treatises and Practice Aids

Markus, Trial Handbook for Ohio Lawyers, § 5:4, Direct Criminal.

Katz, Giannelli, Blair and Lipton, Baldwin's Ohio Practice, Criminal Law, § 41:6, Self-Incrimination—Immunity.

Katz, Giannelli, Blair and Lipton, Baldwin's Ohio Practice, Criminal Law, § 141:9, Motion for Show Cause Hearing.

Katz, Giannelli, Blair and Lipton, Baldwin's Ohio Practice, Criminal Law, § 39:10, Judicial Control.

Katz, Giannelli, Blair and Lipton, Baldwin's Ohio Practice, Criminal Law, § 141:15, Court Proceeding Against Witness for Contempt.

Katz, Giannelli, Blair and Lipton, Baldwin's Ohio Practice, Criminal Law, § 141:16, Dismissal of Contempt Charge.

Notes of Decisions

Imprisonment for contempt 1

1. Imprisonment for contempt

A commitment to jail for contempt of a person who refuses to answer questions before a grand jury, "until such time as he shall purge himself of the contempt or be otherwise released as provided by law" terminates of itself upon the discharge of such grand jury; and such person is thereupon "otherwise released as provided by law." State v. Granchay (Mahoning 1964) 1 Ohio App.2d 307, 204 N.E.2d 562, 30 O.O.2d 310. Grand Jury ⚷ 36.1

GENERAL PROVISIONS

2939.16 Court may appoint grand juror in case of death

In case of sickness, death, discharge, or nonattendance of a grand juror after the grand jury is sworn, the court may cause another to be sworn in his stead. The court shall charge such juror as required by section 2939.07 of the Revised Code.

(1953 H 1, eff. 10–1–53; GC 13436–13)

Historical and Statutory Notes

Pre–1953 H 1 Amendments: 113 v 160, Ch 15, § 13

Library References

Grand Jury ⚷11, 12.

Westlaw Topic No. 193.

C.J.S. Grand Juries §§ 49 to 50, 57 to 58, 66 to 67.

Research References

Encyclopedias

OH Jur. 3d Jury § 73, Completing Panel With Talesmen.

Treatises and Practice Aids

Katz, Giannelli, Blair and Lipton, Baldwin's Ohio Practice, Criminal Law, § 39:8, Alternate Grand Jurors.

Katz, Giannelli, Blair and Lipton, Baldwin's Ohio Practice, Criminal Law, § 39:9, Excusing Grand Jurors.

Katz, Giannelli, Blair and Lipton, Baldwin's Ohio Practice, Criminal Law, § 143:1, Motion to Dismiss Indictment—Challenge to Panel [Or Individual Grand Juror].

Katz, Giannelli, Blair and Lipton, Baldwin's Ohio Practice, Criminal Law, § 141:17, Entry for Jury Sworn in Place of One Who is Sick.

Notes of Decisions

Selection of jurors 3
Talesmen not on jury wheel as juror 2
Vacancies in venire 1

1. Vacancies in venire

A trial court may swear another qualified person to replace an excused grand juror after the grand jury has been sworn. State v. Ross (Franklin 1982) 6 Ohio App.3d 25, 452 N.E.2d 339, 6 O.B.R. 76.

Except as to the foreman, vacancies occurring in a grand jury venire prior to the impanelling and swearing of the grand jury must be filled by persons whose names are contained in the annual jury list and from the ballots deposited in the jury wheel. State ex rel. Burton v. Smith (Ohio 1963) 174 Ohio St. 429, 189 N.E.2d 876, 23 O.O.2d 78. Grand Jury ⚷ 9

After a grand jury has been sworn the common pleas judge, in case of sickness, death, discharge, or nonattendance of a grand juror, may, in the exercise of his discretion, cause another person to be sworn in his stead, but prior to the administration of the oath to members of the grand jury the court has no authority to substitute another person to serve upon the panel of jurors drawn for service pursuant to RC 2939.02, 2313.07, 2313.08, and 2313.35 without compliance with the provisions of such sections. State ex rel. Burton v. Smith (Scioto 1962) 118 Ohio App. 248, 194 N.E.2d 70, 25 O.O.2d 90, affirmed 174 Ohio St. 429, 189 N.E.2d 876, 23 O.O.2d 78.

2. Talesmen not on jury wheel as juror

It is not essential that a person selected to act as a substitute grand juror be chosen from the jury wheel, and the court may select a qualified talesman to sit as a member of such jury. State v. Mirman (Summit 1955) 99 Ohio App. 382, 133 N.E.2d 796, 59 O.O. 162.

3. Selection of jurors

It is not necessary that the records of the court should show how or by whom the grand jurors were selected and drawn, since the legal presumption is that duty was regularly performed by the proper officers. State v. Thomas (Ohio 1900) 61 Ohio St. 444, 43 W.L.B. 133, 56 N.E. 276. Criminal Law ⚷ 1144.2; Grand Jury ⚷ 8

2939.17 New grand jury may be summoned

After the grand jury is discharged, the court of common pleas, when necessary, may order the drawing and impaneling of a new grand jury, which shall be summoned and returned as provided by section 2939.03 of the Revised Code and shall be sworn and proceed in the manner provided by sections 2939.06 to 2939.24, inclusive, of the Revised Code. Whenever the governor or general assembly directs the attorney general to conduct any investigation or prosecution, the court of common pleas or any judge thereof, on written request of the attorney general, shall order a special grand jury to be summoned, and such special grand jury may be called and discharge its duties either before, during, or after any session of the regular grand jury, and its proceedings shall be independent of the proceedings of the regular grand jury but of the same force and effect.

Whenever a witness is necessary to a full investigation by the attorney general under this section, or to secure or successfully maintain and conclude a prosecution arising out of any such investigation, the judge of the court of common pleas may grant to such witness immunity from any prosecution based on the testimony or other evidence given by the witness in the course of the investigation or prosecution, other than a prosecution for perjury in giving such testimony or evidence.

(1970 H 956, eff. 9–16–70; 129 v 1201; 1953 H 1; GC 13436–14)

Historical and Statutory Notes

Pre–1953 H 1 Amendments: 113 v 160, Ch 15, § 14

Cross References

Alternate grand jurors, Crim R 6

Attorney general, investigations of patient abuse or neglect, presentation of evidence to grand jury, 109.86

Investigation of organized crime, referral to grand jury, 109.83

Powers and duties of first assistant attorney general, 109.04

Powers of attorney general regarding workers' compensation, 109.84

Library References

Grand Jury ⚷20.

Westlaw Topic No. 193.

C.J.S. Grand Juries §§ 6, 11, 51 to 52, 57 to 58.

Research References

ALR Library

29 ALR 5th 1, Propriety, Under State Constitutional Provisions, of Granting Use or Transactional Immunity for Compelled Incriminating Testimony--Post-Kastigar Cases.

Encyclopedias

OH Jur. 3d Criminal Law § 3115, Granting of Immunity.

OH Jur. 3d Evidence & Witnesses § 685, Particular Statutes.

OH Jur. 3d Jury § 9, Extent of Power of Special Grand Jury.

OH Jur. 3d State of Ohio § 134, Assistants and Employees.

Treatises and Practice Aids

Katz, Giannelli, Blair and Lipton, Baldwin's Ohio Practice, Criminal Law, § 39:3, Summoning Grand Juries.

Katz, Giannelli, Blair and Lipton, Baldwin's Ohio Practice, Criminal Law, § 143:1, Motion to Dismiss Indictment—Challenge to Panel [Or Individual Grand Juror].

Katz, Giannelli, Blair and Lipton, Baldwin's Ohio Practice, Criminal Law, § 141:18, Entry for Formation of New Grand Jury.

Katz, Giannelli, Blair and Lipton, Baldwin's Ohio Practice, Criminal Law, § 141:19, Entry for Formation of Special Grand Jury.

Notes of Decisions

1. Multiple grand juries

That former GC 13560 (Repealed) permitted the contemporaneous sitting of two grand juries in the same county was no objection to its validity. State ex rel. Doerfler v. Price (Ohio 1920) 101 Ohio St. 50, 128 N.E. 173, 17 Ohio Law Rep. 488.

2. Special grand jury

RC 2939.04 and 2939.17 were enacted to deal with separate and distinct problems, and they are not to be read together and so narrowly as to defeat their separate purposes, so that error cannot be predicated on the ground that an indictment was returned by a special grand jury while the regular grand jury was then sitting, where the second jury was properly empaneled in order that timely and adequate consideration might be given to all matters then on the docket. State v. Pustare (Cuyahoga 1973) 33 Ohio App.2d 305, 295 N.E.2d 210, 62 O.O.2d 450.

Where a special grand jury returned indictments against twenty-five persons and also filed a special report containing conclusions of the grand jury and assessing blame, the district court may order that special report be physically expunged and destroyed. Hammond v. Brown (C.A.6 (Ohio) 1971) 450 F.2d 480, 64 O.O.2d 255. Grand Jury ⚷ 42

The scope of a governor's call cannot enlarge the powers of a special grand jury. Hammond v. Brown (N.D.Ohio 1971) 323 F.Supp. 326, 62 O.O.2d 65, affirmed 450 F.2d 480, 64 O.O.2d 255. Grand Jury ⚷ 25

3. Immunity of witness

State failed to produce any evidence that defendant waived use immunity given to her compelled testimony before the legislative committee and, thus, prosecutor's use of compelled testimony tainted subsequent indictment. State v. Conrad (Ohio 1990) 50 Ohio St.3d 1, 552 N.E.2d 214. Indictment And Information ⚷ 10.2(2)

The different treatment of witnesses afforded under RC 2939.17 and 2945.44, whereby one class of witnesses may be offered full transactional immunity upon being compelled to testify and another class may only be offered limited use and derivative use immunity, does not violate the Equal Protection Clause. In re Special Grand Jury Investigating Medicaid Fraud & Nursing Homes (Franklin 1987) 38 Ohio App.3d 161, 528 N.E.2d 598.

RC 2939.17 allows a court to compel the testimony of a witness who invokes her Fifth Amendment privilege against self-incrimination after granting that witness use and derivative use immunity from the use of the compelled testimony against her. In re Special Grand Jury Investigating Medicaid Fraud & Nursing Homes (Franklin 1987) 38 Ohio App.3d 161, 528 N.E.2d 598.

A person's testimony before a grand jury under a grant of immunity cannot constitutionally be used to impeach him when he is a defendant in a later criminal trial. (Ed. note: New Jersey law construed in light of federal constitution.) New Jersey v. Portash (U.S.N.J. 1979) 99 S.Ct. 1292, 440 U.S. 450, 59 L.Ed.2d 501. Witnesses ⚷ 379(9); Witnesses ⚷ 393(3)

Where it is alleged that the government used immunized testimony to secure a conviction, the government must show that its evidence against the witness is neither directly nor indirectly traceable to the immunized testimony. U.S. v. Streck (C.A.6 (Ohio) 1992) 958 F.2d 141. Criminal Law ⚷ 42.6

4. Women as grand jurors

Under former GC 13568 (Repealed) women could be summoned as grand jurors under that section. Browning v. State (Ohio 1929) 120 Ohio St. 62, 165 N.E. 566, 7 Ohio Law Abs. 140, 28 Ohio Law Rep. 474. Grand Jury ⚷ 5

5. Supervision of grand jury

The official act of a single judge of a court of common pleas composed of two or more judges is the act of the court; concurrence of the other judge or judges in such act is not necessary to its validity. State v. Phipps (Scioto 1964) 3 Ohio App.2d 226, 210 N.E.2d 138, 32 O.O.2d 322, certiorari denied 86 S.Ct. 434, 382 U.S. 957, 15 L.Ed.2d 361. Courts ⚷ 101

2939.18 Fact of indictment shall be kept secret

No grand juror, officer of the court, or other person shall disclose that an indictment has been found against a person not in custody or under bail, before such indictment is filed and the case docketed, except by the issue of process.

(1953 H 1, eff. 10–1–53; GC 13436–15)

Historical and Statutory Notes

Pre–1953 H 1 Amendments: 113 v 161, Ch 15, § 15

Cross References

Secrecy of grand jury proceedings, grand jury procedures, Crim R 6

Library References

Grand Jury ⚷41.
Westlaw Topic No. 193.
C.J.S. Grand Juries § 176.

Research References

Encyclopedias

OH Jur. 3d Jury § 155, Persons Subject to Secrecy Requirements.

Treatises and Practice Aids

Katz, Giannelli, Blair and Lipton, Baldwin's Ohio Practice, Criminal Law, § 39:21, Sealing Indictments.

Notes of Decisions

Premature publication 3
Secrecy of proceedings 1
Use of testimony for impeachment 2

1. Secrecy of proceedings

Absent some evidence of perjury or some other irregularity in grand jury proceedings involving employee's alleged participation in scheme to commit theft against employer, employee failed to demonstrate a particularized need that outweighed the need for maintaining the secrecy of grand jury proceedings, and thus, disclosure of grand jury testimony was not warranted in employee's action for malicious prosecution. Tourlakis v. Beverage Distributors, Inc. (Ohio App. 8 Dist., Cuyahoga, 12-26-2002) No. 81222, 2002-Ohio-7252, 2002 WL 31875970, Unreported. Grand Jury ⚷ 41.50(5)

Whether a state court order forbidding interviews or statements for publication by witnesses, jurors, and individuals summoned but excused from serving as jurors in connection with the special grand jury convened by the governor to investigate the Kent State tragedy is an order that violates US Const Am 1 is not a matter for federal courts to consider where the allegedly aggrieved individuals never applied to the state court to have the order modified or dissolved. King v. Jones (C.A.6 (Ohio) 1971) 450 F.2d 478, vacated 92 S.Ct. 956, 405 U.S. 911, 30 L.Ed.2d 780.

The secrecy of grand jury proceedings may not be imposed upon witnesses who appear before a grand jury; such witnesses may be interviewed after their appearance and repeat what they said before the grand jury or otherwise relate their knowledge on the subject of the inquiry. In re Grand Jury Summoned October 12, 1970 (N.D.Ohio 1970) 26 Ohio Misc. 135, 321 F.Supp. 238, 55 O.O.2d 226. Grand Jury ⚷ 41.20

The secrecy surrounding grand jury proceedings which is to be upheld is the final action or inaction of the grand jury and not the specific questions propounded to and specific answers given by a particular witness. In re Grand Jury Summoned October 12, 1970 (N.D.Ohio 1970) 26 Ohio Misc. 135, 321 F.Supp. 238, 55 O.O.2d 226. Grand Jury ⚷ 41.30

2. Use of testimony for impeachment

Where a witness for the state in a criminal proceeding turns hostile while testifying on direct examination so that he is placed under cross-examination, his previous testimony drawn from a secret grand jury hearing may be used to attack his statements without opening the entire record of such hearing to the defendant's scrutiny. State v. Mullins (Scioto 1971) 26 Ohio App.2d 13, 268 N.E.2d 603, 55 O.O.2d 30.

3. Premature publication

Premature publication by a newspaper that a grand jury had voted to return an indictment prior to the return, filing or docketing of such indictment does not constitute contempt. State v. E.W. Scripps Co. (Ohio Com.Pl. 1960) 172 N.E.2d 178, 85 Ohio Law Abs. 596, 14 O.O.2d 237.

2939.19 Testimony of grand jurors

No grand juror may state or testify in court in what manner any member of the grand jury voted or what opinion was expressed by any juror on any question before the grand jury.

(1953 H 1, eff. 10–1–53; GC 13436–16)

Historical and Statutory Notes

Pre–1953 H 1 Amendments: 113 v 161, Ch 15, § 16

Cross References

Grand jury, Crim R 6

Library References

Grand Jury ⚷41.
Witnesses ⚷72.
Westlaw Topic Nos. 193, 410.
C.J.S. Grand Juries § 176.
C.J.S. Witnesses §§ 194 to 196, 198, 200.

Research References

Encyclopedias

OH Jur. 3d Jury § 155, Persons Subject to Secrecy Requirements.

Treatises and Practice Aids

Katz, Giannelli, Blair and Lipton, Baldwin's Ohio Practice, Criminal Law, § 39:22, Grand Jury Secrecy.

Notes of Decisions

1. Secrecy of proceedings

No evidence will be received from the grand jurors, the witnesses or any other person in the grand jury room, as to what evidence was presented to that forum by the prosecuting attorney or any other person. State v Kearns, 70 Abs 80 (CP, Franklin 1955).

2. Access to testimony

Trial court did not abuse its discretion by denying defendant's request to review grand jury testimony, absent demonstration of particularized need to inspect testimony; defendant merely asserted on appeal that he needed to examine grand jury testimony for inconsistencies in testimony of state witness. State v. Mack (Ohio, 08-30-1995) 73 Ohio St.3d 502, 653 N.E.2d 329, 1995-Ohio-273, stay granted 74 Ohio St.3d 1437, 655 N.E.2d 1321, certiorari denied 116 S.Ct. 822, 516 U.S. 1096, 133 L.Ed.2d 766, stay granted 75 Ohio St.3d 1418, 661 N.E.2d 1119, denial of post-conviction relief affirmed 2000 WL 1594117, dismissed, appeal not allowed 91 Ohio St.3d 1459, 743 N.E.2d 400, certiorari denied 122 S.Ct. 145, 534 U.S. 863, 151 L.Ed.2d 96. Criminal Law ⚷ 627.9(4)

Transcripts of grand jury proceedings may not be released to dispel or confirm unpleasant rumors and allegations reported in or made by the media and various local personalities as to the vigor with which prosecution was attempted; grand jury proceedings are traditionally secret and will not be opened to public view to satisfy the media's curiosity, and the controversy surrounding the grand jury's failure to indict county building inspectors suspected of misconduct does not involve matters of unique, statewide historical interest warranting disclosure of the grand jury transcripts to the general public. In re Grand Jury Investigation (Ohio Com. Pl. 1991) 61 Ohio Misc.2d 583, 580 N.E.2d 868.

Grand jury evidence may be disclosed to a committee investigating alleged attorney misconduct. Petition of Grievance Committee of Toledo Bar Ass'n (Ohio 1989) 47 Ohio St.3d 611, 548 N.E.2d 916.

Admission of grand jury testimony for the purpose of refreshing hostile witness' recollection rather than for proving crime was proper. State v. Diehl (Ohio 1981) 67 Ohio St.2d 389, 423 N.E.2d 1112, 21 O.O.3d 244.

Grand jury proceedings are secret, and an accused is not entitled to inspect grand jury transcripts either before or during trial unless the ends of justice require it and there is a showing by the defense that a particularized need for disclosure exists which outweighs the need for secrecy. State v. Patterson (Ohio 1971) 28 Ohio St.2d 181, 277 N.E.2d 201, 57 O.O.2d 422, certiorari denied 93 S.Ct. 242, 409 U.S. 913, 34 L.Ed.2d 174. Criminal Law ⚷ 627.9(1)

One charged with crime is not entitled before or at the trial to the minutes of evidence taken before the grand jury on which the indictment was found, nor to an inspection of the transcript thereof. State v. Rhoads (Ohio 1910) 81 Ohio St. 397, 91 N.E. 186, 7 Ohio Law Rep. 614, 18 Am.Ann.Cas. 415. Criminal Law ⚷ 627.9(1)

2939.20 Indictment by twelve jurors

At least twelve of the grand jurors must concur in the finding of an indictment. When so found, the foreman shall indorse on such indictment the words "A true bill" and subscribe his name as foreman.

(1953 H 1, eff. 10–1–53; GC 13436–17)

Historical and Statutory Notes

Pre–1953 H 1 Amendments: 113 v 161, Ch 15, § 17

Cross References

Concurrence of jurors, O Const Art I §10
Finding and return of indictment, Crim R 6

Library References

Indictment and Information ⚷10.
Westlaw Topic No. 210.

Research References

Encyclopedias

OH Jur. 3d Criminal Law § 1969, Power of Ohio Supreme Court to Prescribe Rules.

OH Jur. 3d Criminal Law § 2334, Signatures.

OH Jur. 3d Criminal Law § 2335, Indorsements.

OH Jur. 3d Habeas Corpus & Post Convict. Remedies § 13, Insufficiency of Information, Indictment, Complaint, or Grand Jury Proceedings.

OH Jur. 3d Jury § 61, Generally; Number of Grand Jurors.

OH Jur. 3d Jury § 167, Number of Jurors Required for Indictment.

Treatises and Practice Aids

Klein, Darling, & Terez, Baldwin's Ohio Practice Civil Practice § 1:26, Civ. R. 1(C)(1): Upon Appeal to Review Any Judgment, Order, or Ruling--Appeals in Supreme Court--Role of Revised Code Provisions Purporting to Control Application of Civil Rules.

Klein, Darling, & Terez, Baldwin's Ohio Practice Civil Practice § 1:29, Civ. R. 1(C)(1): Upon Appeal to Review Any Judgment, Order, or Ruling--Appeals in Courts of Appeals--Role of Revised Code Provisions Purporting to Control Application of Civil...

Klein, Darling, & Terez, Baldwin's Ohio Practice Civil Practice § 1:32, Civ. R. 1(C)(1): Upon Appeal to Review Any Judgment, Order, or Ruling--Appeals to Common Pleas Courts from Decisions of Governmental Entities--Role of Revised Code Provisions Purporting to...

Katz, Giannelli, Blair and Lipton, Baldwin's Ohio Practice, Criminal Law, § 39:6, Composition.

Katz, Giannelli, Blair and Lipton, Baldwin's Ohio Practice, Criminal Law, § 39:8, Alternate Grand Jurors.

Katz, Giannelli, Blair and Lipton, Baldwin's Ohio Practice, Criminal Law, § 143:2, Motion to Dismiss Indictment—Requisite Number of Grand Jurors Did Not Concur.

Katz, Giannelli, Blair and Lipton, Baldwin's Ohio Practice, Criminal Law, § 143:3, Motion to Dismiss Indictment—Not Properly Indorsed.

Katz, Giannelli, Blair and Lipton, Baldwin's Ohio Practice, Criminal Law, § 39:20, Finding and Return of Indictment.

Hennenberg & Reinhart, Ohio Criminal Defense Motions F 5.35, Motion to Quash the Venire-Pretrial Motions-Improperly Selected Venire.

Notes of Decisions

---

1. Size of grand jury

Indictment for aggravated murder and aggravated burglary returned by grand jury consisting of eleven jurors rather than fifteen, and signed by deputy foreperson rather than by grand jury foreperson, was not fatally defective, and thus, counsel's failure to challenge indictment did not constitute ineffective assistance of counsel, insofar as rule governing grand jury proceedings required only nine jurors and allowed for deputy foreperson to act as foreperson in appointed foreperson's absence. State v. Hughbanks (Ohio App. 1 Dist., Hamilton, 01-17-2003) No. C-010372, 2003-Ohio-187, 2003 WL 131937, Unreported, appeal not allowed 100 Ohio St.3d 1484, 798 N.E.2d 1093, 2003-Ohio-5992. Criminal Law ⚷ 641.13(2.1); Indictment And Information ⚷ 10.1(2); Indictment And Information ⚷ 10.1(3)

The number of jurors on a grand jury does not affect a substantive right. Accordingly, Crim R 6(A) controls the issue of how many grand jurors are needed to issue an indictment. RC 2939.02 and 2939.20 are superseded insofar as they conflict with this rule. State v. Brown (Ohio 1988) 38 Ohio St.3d 305, 528 N.E.2d 523, rehearing denied 39 Ohio St.3d 710, 534 N.E.2d 93, certiorari denied 109 S.Ct. 1177, 489 U.S. 1040, 103 L.Ed.2d 239, rehearing denied 109 S.Ct. 1774, 490 U.S. 1032, 104 L.Ed.2d 208. Grand Jury ⚷ 3

The numbers of jurors on a grand jury does not affect any substantive right of an accused and insofar as a conflict exists between RC 2939.20 and Crim R 6(A) the statute is of no further force or effect. State v. Wilson (Hamilton 1978) 57 Ohio App.2d 11, 384 N.E.2d 1300, 11 O.O.3d 8.

An issue pertaining to the number of persons comprising a grand jury in Ohio concerns a matter of procedure, and an indictment rendered by a body made up of less than fifteen members does not deny an accused any substantive right. State v. Juergens (Hancock 1977) 55 Ohio App.2d 104, 379 N.E.2d 602, 9 O.O.3d 262. Indictment And Information ⚷ 10.1(2)

2. Endorsement and signature on true bill

See for case under former GC 13571 (Repealed) wherein the indictment was properly indorsed. (See also Ruch v State, 111 OS 580, 146 NE 67 (1924).) Dun v. State (Ohio App. 1 Dist. 1922) 17 Ohio App. 10.

Statute providing that grand jury foreman shall indorse on indictment the words "A true bill" and subscribe his name as foreman is not contravened when the words "A true bill" are not handwritten, but pre-printed on indictment forms. Key v. State (Ohio App. 10 Dist., Franklin, 09-03-2004) No. 04AP-113, 2004-Ohio-5341, 2004 WL 2898757, Unreported. Indictment And Information ⚷ 34(6)

Grand jury foreperson's failure to sign indictment does not deprive trial court of jurisdiction or otherwise entitle criminal defendant convicted and sentenced on indictment to writ of habeas corpus. VanBuskirk v. Wingard (Ohio, 01-07-1998) 80 Ohio St.3d 659, 687 N.E.2d 776, 1998-Ohio-173, reconsideration denied 81 Ohio St.3d 1448, 690 N.E.2d 18. Habeas Corpus ⚷ 474; Indictment And Information ⚷ 33(3)

The signature of the foreman of a grand jury is an indispensable requisite to a valid indictment, and in the absence thereof all subsequent proceedings are void; and habeas corpus will lie. Kennedy v. Alvis (Ohio Com.Pl. 1957) 145 N.E.2d 361, 76 Ohio Law Abs. 132.

It is sufficient compliance with former GC 13571 (RC 2939.20) that the indictment have the words "a true bill" printed on it and that the foreman subscribe his name to it as foreman. Ruch v. State (Ohio 1924) 111 Ohio St. 580, 146 N.E. 67, 22 Ohio Law Rep. 669.

Though the better practice, it is not necessary, as a matter of law, that the foreman of a grand jury, in indorsing an indictment "A true bill," should describe himself as foreman; for, being appointed by the court, it is presumed to know who the foreman is. Whiting v. State (Ohio 1891) 48 Ohio St. 220, 25 W.L.B. 264, 27 N.E. 96.

Under Ohio law, public policy precludes use of testimony before grand jury as basis for civil action for malicious prosecution. Ventura v. Cincinnati Enquirer (S.D.Ohio, 02-11-2003) 246 F.Supp.2d 876, affirmed 396 F.3d 784, rehearing denied. Malicious Prosecution ⚷ 58(3)

The failure of a foreman of a grand jury to attach his signature to the endorsement "a true bill" on an indictment is a fatal defect and cannot be corrected by allowing the foreman to sign the indictment at a later time. State v Wilson, No. CA87–03–027 (12th Dist Ct App, Clermont, 11–30–87).

2939.21 Grand jury to visit county jail

Once every three months, the grand jurors shall visit the county jail, examine its condition, and inquire into the discipline and treatment of the prisoners, their habits, diet, and accommodations. They shall report on these matters to the court of common pleas in writing. The clerk of the court of common pleas shall forward a copy of the report to the department of rehabilitation and correction.

(1982 S 23, eff. 7–6–82; 1976 H 390; 1953 H 1; GC 13436–20)

Historical and Statutory Notes

Pre–1953 H 1 Amendments: 113 v 161, Ch 15, § 20

Library References

Grand Jury ⚷24, 42.

Westlaw Topic No. 193.

C.J.S. Grand Juries §§ 2, 10 to 11, 76 to 86.

Research References

Encyclopedias

OH Jur. 3d Jury § 132, Inquisitorial and Investigatory Functions—Visitation and Reports Relating Thereto.

Treatises and Practice Aids

Katz, Giannelli, Blair and Lipton, Baldwin's Ohio Practice, Criminal Law, § 39:25, Jail Visitation.

Notes of Decisions

Report on jail conditions 1

1. Report on jail conditions

The only type of grand jury report on civil matters specifically sanctioned by statute is the periodic report of county jail conditions authorized by RC 2939.21, and absent specific statutory authority, grand jury reports on civil matters are invalid and should not be issued. Simington v. Shimp (Sandusky 1978) 60 Ohio App.2d 402, 398 N.E.2d 812, 14 O.O.3d 422.

2939.22 Proceedings when indictments are returned

Indictments found by a grand jury shall by presented by the foreman to the court of common pleas, and filed with the clerk of the court of common pleas, who shall indorse thereon the date of such filing and enter each case upon the appearance docket and the trial docket of the term when the persons indicted have been arrested. The court shall assign such indictments for trial under section 2945.02 of the Revised Code, and recognizances of defendants and witnesses shall be taken for their appearance in court. When a case is continued to the next term of court, such recognizance shall require the appearance of the defendants and witnesses at a time designated by the court. Secret indictments shall not be docketed by name until after the apprehension of the accused.

(1953 H 1, eff. 10–1–53; GC 13436–21)

Historical and Statutory Notes

Pre–1953 H 1 Amendments: 113 v 161, Ch 15, § 21

Cross References

Grand jury, Crim R 6
Indictment information, Crim R 7

Library References

Indictment and Information ⚿10.
Westlaw Topic No. 210.

Research References

Encyclopedias

OH Jur. 3d Criminal Law § 2185, After Return of Indictment or Information; Assignment for Trial.

Treatises and Practice Aids

Katz, Giannelli, Blair and Lipton, Baldwin's Ohio Practice, Criminal Law, § 143:2, Motion to Dismiss Indictment—Requisite Number of Grand Jurors Did Not Concur.

Katz, Giannelli, Blair and Lipton, Baldwin's Ohio Practice, Criminal Law, § 39:21, Sealing Indictments.

Katz, Giannelli, Blair and Lipton, Baldwin's Ohio Practice, Criminal Law, § 141:21, Entry on Report Made by Grand Jury.

Law Review and Journal Commentaries

"Straight Release": Justice Delayed, Justice Denied, Timothy J. McGinty. 48 Clev St L Rev 235 (2000).

Notes of Decisions

Arrest of indicted individual 2
Signature on true bill 1

1. Signature on true bill

The signature of the foreman of a grand jury is an indispensable requisite to a valid indictment, and in the absence thereof all subsequent proceedings are void; and habeas corpus will lie. Kennedy v. Alvis (Ohio Com.Pl. 1957) 145 N.E.2d 361, 76 Ohio Law Abs. 132.

2. Arrest of indicted individual

County housing officer lacked a reasonable, articulable suspicion that defendant was engaged in criminal activity to justify a *Terry* stop of defendant, even though officer testified that he had received a "special attention" alert regarding drug activity and loitering in area, was patrolling an area of high drug activity, had made previous arrests for drug activity in area, and witnessed defendant engage in a brief conversation and a hand-to-hand transaction with a black male which, to officer, was suspicious activity, where officer failed to mention hand-to-hand transaction in his initial police report, and activity occurred during middle of day in the parking lot of a public housing estate which men, women, and children called their home. City Of Cleveland v. Fields (Ohio App. 8 Dist., Cuyahoga, 04-17-2003) No. 82070, 2003-Ohio-1965, 2003 WL 1901337, Unreported. Arrest ⚷ 63.5(5)

2939.23 Report to court when indictment not found

If an indictment is not found by the grand jury, against an accused who has been held to answer, such fact shall be reported by the foreman to the court of common pleas.

(1953 H 1, eff. 10–1–53; GC 13436–22)

Historical and Statutory Notes

Pre–1953 H 1 Amendments: 113 v 162, Ch 15, § 22

Cross References

Appeals, other postconviction remedies; court, defined, 2953.51

Finding and return of indictment, Crim R 6

Library References

Grand Jury ⚷42.

Westlaw Topic No. 193.

C.J.S. Grand Juries §§ 85 to 86.

Research References

Encyclopedias

OH Jur. 3d Jury § 168, Procedure Where Indictment Not Found.

Treatises and Practice Aids

Katz, Giannelli, Blair and Lipton, Baldwin's Ohio Practice, Criminal Law, § 141:21, Entry on Report Made by Grand Jury.

Notes of Decisions

Authority of special grand jury 2
Unauthorized report of grand jury 1

1. Unauthorized report of grand jury

A grand jury is without authority to issue a report that advises, condemns, or commends, or makes recommendations concerning the policies and operation of public boards, public officers, or public authorities. Hammond v. Brown (N.D.Ohio 1971) 323 F.Supp. 326, 62 O.O.2d 65, affirmed 450 F.2d 480, 64 O.O.2d 255. Grand Jury ⚷ 42

A report of an Ohio grand jury is issued without authority if it violates the grand jury's secrecy against disclosure of evidence by purporting to summarize the evidence received by it or to make findings based thereon. Hammond v. Brown (N.D.Ohio 1971) 323 F.Supp. 326, 62 O.O.2d 65, affirmed 450 F.2d 480, 64 O.O.2d 255. Grand Jury ⚷ 42

A report of an Ohio grand jury that exceeds the jury's authority or violates the secrecy against disclosure is subject to expungement at the direction of a federal court. Hammond v. Brown (N.D.Ohio 1971) 323 F.Supp. 326, 62 O.O.2d 65, affirmed 450 F.2d 480, 64 O.O.2d 255.

2. Authority of special grand jury

The scope of a governor's call cannot enlarge the powers of a special grand jury. Hammond v. Brown (N.D.Ohio 1971) 323 F.Supp. 326, 62 O.O.2d 65, affirmed 450 F.2d 480, 64 O.O.2d 255. Grand Jury ⚷ 25

2939.24 Disposition of person in jail and not indicted

If a person held in jail charged with an indictable offense is not indicted at the term of court at which he is held to answer, he shall be discharged unless:

(A) He was committed on such charge after the discharge of the grand jury.

(B) The transcript has not been filed.

(C) There is not sufficient time at such term of court to investigate said cause.

(D) The grand jury, for good cause, continues the hearing of said charge until the next term of court.

(E) It appears to the court of common pleas that a witness for the state has been enticed or kept away, detained, or prevented from attending court by sickness or unavoidable accident.
(1953 H 1, eff. 10–1–53; GC 13436–23)

Historical and Statutory Notes

Pre–1953 H 1 Amendments: 113 v 162, Ch 15, § 23

Cross References

Dismissal, Crim R 48

Library References

Indictment and Information ⚷16.

Westlaw Topic No. 210.

Research References

Encyclopedias

OH Jur. 3d Criminal Law § 2852, Limit on Time in Jail Without Indictment; Release from Custody.

OH Jur. 3d Jury § 168, Procedure Where Indictment Not Found.

OH Jur. 3d Jury § 239, Term of Grand Jury Service.

Treatises and Practice Aids

Katz, Giannelli, Blair and Lipton, Baldwin's Ohio Practice, Criminal Law, § 141:22, Entry of Order Discharging Prisoner Not Indicted.

Katz, Giannelli, Blair and Lipton, Baldwin's Ohio Practice, Criminal Law, § 141:23, Journal Entry When Recognizance Filed and No Indictment Found—Order to Discharge Defendant.

Notes of Decisions

---

1. Discharge

As used in RC 2939.24 "discharge" pertains only to release from jail and not to an acquittance of the charge laid in the indictment. State v. Sallee (Ohio Com.Pl. 1964) 1 Ohio Misc. 50, 202 N.E.2d 438, 30 O.O.2d 176.

2. Asserting right to speedy trial

By not seeking his discharge under RC 2939.24 and by not otherwise in any way having made a demand for a speedy trial prior to the filing of a motion for discharge from custody, a defendant waived the issue of a speedy trial. State v. Sallee (Ohio Com.Pl. 1964) 1 Ohio Misc. 50, 202 N.E.2d 438, 30 O.O.2d 176.

A defendant waives his right to a release from custody under RC 2939.24 by not seeking the remedy until after the return of an indictment and service of process thereon. State v. Sallee (Ohio Com.Pl. 1964) 1 Ohio Misc. 50, 202 N.E.2d 438, 30 O.O.2d 176.

The time limitation set forth in RC 2939.24 for the return of an indictment does not constitute a statute of limitation on the right to prosecute. State v. Sallee (Ohio Com.Pl. 1964) 1 Ohio Misc. 50, 202 N.E.2d 438, 30 O.O.2d 176.

3. Civil commitment of insane prisoner

A person committed to the Lima state hospital under the purported authority of RC 2945.37 and 2945.38, but who has not been indicted, is illegally restrained of his liberty and must be released forthwith from that hospital, provided, however, that if his mental condition is such that he is not sane and his release would result in his being dangerous to himself or to society the execution of the order of release will be suspended for a reasonable period of time to permit the probate division of an appropriate common pleas court, having jurisdiction, to cause his commitment to a proper institution. Burton v. Reshetylo (Allen 1973) 35 Ohio App.2d 113, 300 N.E.2d 249, 64 O.O.2d 234, affirmed 38 Ohio St.2d 35, 309 N.E.2d 907, 67 O.O.2d 53.

OUT–OF–STATE WITNESS

Comparative Laws

Uniform Act to Secure the Attendance of Witnesses from Without a State in Criminal Proceedings

Table of Jurisdictions Wherein Act Has Been Adopted.

For text of Uniform Act, and variation notes and annotation materials for adopting jurisdictions, see Uniform Laws Annotated, Master Edition, Volume 11.

Jurisdiction	Statutory Citation
Alabama	Code 1975, § 12–21–280 to 12–21–285.
Alaska	AS 12.50.010 to 12.50.080.
Arizona	A.R.S. § 13–4091 to 13–4096.
Arkansas	A.C.A. § 16–43–402 to 16–43–409.
California	West's Ann.Cal.Penal Code, § 1334 to 1334.6.
Colorado	West's C.R.S.A. § 16–9–201 to 16–9–205.
Connecticut	C.G.S.A. § 54–82i.
Delaware	11 Del.C. § 3521 to 3526.
District of Columbia	D.C. Official Code, 2001 Ed. § 23–1501 to 23–1504.
Florida	West's F.S.A. § 942.01 to 942.06.
Georgia	O.C.G.A. § 24–10–90 to 24–10–97.
Hawaii	HRS § 836–1 to 836–6.
Idaho	I.C. § 19–3005.
Illinois	S.H.A. 725 ILCS 220/1 to 220/6.
Indiana	West's A.I.C. 35–37–5–1 to 35–37–5–9.
Iowa	I.C.A. § 819.1 to 819.5.
Kansas	K.S.A. 22–4201 to 22–4206.
Kentucky	KRS 421.230 to 421.270.
Louisiana	LSA–C.Cr.P. arts. 741 to 745.
Maine	15 M.R.S.A. § 1411 to 1415.
Maryland	Code, Courts and Judicial Proceedings, § 9–301 to 9–306.
Massachusetts	M.G.L.A. c. 233 § 13A to 13D.
Michigan	M.C.L.A. § 767.91 to 767.95.
Minnesota	M.S.A. § 634.06 to 634.09.
Mississippi	Code 1972, § 99–9–27 to 99–9–35.
Missouri	V.A.M.S. § 491.400 to 491.450.
Montana	MCA 46–15–112, 46–15–113, 46–15–120.
Nebraska	R.R.S.1943, § 29–1906 to 29–1911.
Nevada	N.R.S. 174.395 to 174.445.
New Hampshire	RSA 613:1 to 613:6.
New Jersey	N.J.S.A. 2A:81–18 to 2A:81–23.
New Mexico	NMSA 1978, § 31–8–1 to 31–8–6.
New York	McKinney's CPL § 640.10.
North Carolina	G.S. § 15A–811 to 15A–816.
Oklahoma	22 Okl.St.Ann. § 721 to 727.
Oregon	ORS 136.623 to 136.637.
Pennsylvania	42 Pa.C.S.A. § 5961 to 5965.
Rhode Island	Gen.Laws 1956, § 12–16–1 to 12–16–13.
South Carolina	Code 1976, § 19–9–10 to 19–9–130.
South Dakota	SDCL 23A–14–1 et seq.
Tennessee	T.C.A., §§ 40–17–201 to 40–17–212.
Texas	Vernon's Ann.Texas C.C.P. art. 24.28.
Utah	U.C.A.1953, 77–21–1 to 77–21–5.
Vermont	13 V.S.A. § 6641 to 6649.
Virgin Islands	5 V.I.C. § 3861 to 3865.
Virginia	Code 1950, § 19.2–272 to 19.2–282.
Washington	West's RCWA 10.55.010 to 10.55.130.
West Virginia	Code, 62–6A–1 to 62–6A–6.
Wisconsin	W.S.A. 976.02.
Wyoming	Wyo.Stat.Ann., § 7–11–404 to 7–11–406.

2939.25 Definition of witness, state, and summons

As used in sections 2939.25 to 2939.29, inclusive, of the Revised Code:

(A) "Witness" includes a person whose testimony is desired in any proceeding or investigation by a grand jury or in a criminal action, prosecution, or proceeding.

(B) "State" includes any territory of the United States and District of Columbia.

(C) "Summons" includes a subpoena, order, or other notice requiring the appearance of a witness.

(1953 H 1, eff. 10–1–53; GC 13436–24)

Historical and Statutory Notes

Pre–1953 H 1 Amendments: 117 v 668, § 1

Research References

Encyclopedias

OH Jur. 3d Criminal Law § 3046, Generally; Unavailability of Witness.

OH Jur. 3d Criminal Law § 3113, Compelling Attendance.

OH Jur. 3d Jury § 148, Compelling Attendance and Testimony of Witnesses.

Treatises and Practice Aids

Markus, Trial Handbook for Ohio Lawyers, § 11:3, Out-Of-State.

Katz, Giannelli, Blair and Lipton, Baldwin's Ohio Practice, Criminal Law, § 61:10, Out-Of-State Witnesses.

Giannelli and Snyder, Baldwin's Ohio Practice, Evidence, § 804.8, Unavailability: Unable to Procure Testimony.

Notes of Decisions

1. Refusal of witness to appear

Prosecutor made good-faith effort to secure presence of out-of-state witness at new trial ordered after remand, even though prosecutor failed to use Uniform Act to Secure the Attendance of Witnesses from Without the State, RC 2939.25 et seq., 2939.29, where out-of-state witness at first appeared very willing to cooperate and then refused to appear to testify four days after start of trial; witness' testimony from prior trial was thus admissible pursuant to exception to the confrontation requirement of the Sixth Amendment. State v. Young (Cuyahoga 1984) 20 Ohio App.3d 269, 485 N.E.2d 814, 20 O.B.R. 332. Criminal Law 🔑 662.60

2939.26 Foreign court may compel witnesses

If a judge of a court of record in any state which by its laws has made provision for commanding persons within that state to attend and testify in this state, certifies under the seal of such court that there is a criminal prosecution pending in such court, or that a grand jury investigation has commenced or is about to commence, that a person being within this state is a material witness in such prosecution or grand jury investigation, and that his presence will be required for a specified number of days, upon presentation of such certificate to any judge of a court of record in the county in this state in which such person is, such judge shall fix a time and place for a hearing and shall make an order directing the witness to appear at a time and place certain for the hearing.

If at a hearing such judge determines that the witness is material and necessary, that it will not cause undue hardship to the witness to be compelled to attend and testify in the prosecution or grand jury investigation in the other state, and that the laws of the state in which the prosecution is pending, or grand jury investigation has commenced or is about to commence, and of any other state through which the witness may be required to pass by ordinary course of travel, will give to him protection from arrest and the service of civil and criminal process, he shall issue a summons, with a copy of the certificate attached, directing the witness to attend and testify in the court where the prosecution is pending, or where a grand jury investigation has commenced or is about to commence, at a time and place specified in the summons. In any such hearing the certificate is prima-facie evidence of all the facts stated therein.

If said certificate recommends that the witness be taken into immediate custody and delivered to an officer of the requesting state to assure his attendance in the requesting state, such judge may, in lieu of notification of the hearing, direct that such witness be forthwith brought before him for said hearing. If the judge at the hearing is satisfied of the desirability of such custody and delivery, for which determination the certificate is prima-facie proof of such desirability, he may, in lieu of issuing subpoena or summons, order that said witness be forthwith taken into custody and delivered to an officer of the requesting state.

If the witness, who is summoned as provided in this section, after being paid or tendered by some properly authorized person the sum of ten cents a mile for each mile by the ordinary traveled route to and from the court where the prosecution is pending and five dollars for each day, that he is required to travel and attend as a witness, fails without good cause to attend and testify as directed in the summons, he shall be punished in the manner provided for the punishment of any witness who disobeys a summons issued from a court of record in this state.
(1953 H 1, eff. 10–1–53; GC 13436–25)

Historical and Statutory Notes

Pre–1953 H 1 Amendments: 117 v 668, § 2

Cross References

Right to compulsory process to obtain witnesses, O Const Art I §10

Library References

Grand Jury ⚩36.
Witnesses ⚩6.
Westlaw Topic Nos. 193, 410.
C.J.S. Grand Juries §§ 101, 111 to 172, 174 to 175.
C.J.S. Witnesses §§ 2, 14 to 19.

Research References

Encyclopedias

OH Jur. 3d Criminal Law § 476, Persons Other Than Codefendants or Coconspirators.

Treatises and Practice Aids

Markus, Trial Handbook for Ohio Lawyers, § 11:3, Out-Of-State.

Katz, Giannelli, Blair and Lipton, Baldwin's Ohio Practice, Criminal Law, § 149:18, Motion to Compel the Appearance of a Witness Residing Outside the State of Ohio.

Katz, Giannelli, Blair and Lipton, Baldwin's Ohio Practice, Criminal Law, § 149:19, Certification of the Materiality of the Testimony of a Witness Located Outside the State of Ohio.

Katz, Giannelli, Blair and Lipton, Baldwin's Ohio Practice, Criminal Law, § 149:20, Order to Issue a Summons to a Witness Upon Certification of Materiality from the Court of Another State.

Katz, Giannelli, Blair and Lipton, Baldwin's Ohio Practice, Criminal Law, § 149:21, Journal Entry and Order Requiring an Out of State Witness to Appear and Provide Testimony.

Giannelli and Snyder, Baldwin's Ohio Practice, Evidence, § 804.8, Unavailability: Unable to Procure Testimony.

Notes of Decisions

1. Right of confrontation and unavailable witness

An out-of-state witness who disobeys a subpoena to appear at trial is unavailable for purposes of creating an exception to the confrontation requirement, even though the state does not proceed under the Uniform Act to Secure the Attendance of Witnesses from Without the State, RC 2939.25 et seq., so long as the state has made good faith efforts before trial to secure the witness' attendance, and the witness does not indicate his unwillingness to attend until trial is in progress. State v. Young (Cuyahoga 1984) 20 Ohio App.3d 269, 485 N.E.2d 814, 20 O.B.R. 332.

2. Material witness

In order for a newsperson to be declared a material necessary witness under RC 2939.26 for the purpose of obtaining either confidential information or the name of a confidential source, the record must demonstrate that the evidence sought from the newsperson or the confidential source is relevant and material in regard to guilt or innocence. Matter of McAuley (Cuyahoga 1979) 63 Ohio App.2d 5, 408 N.E.2d 697, 17 O.O.3d 222. Witnesses ⚩ 6

RC 2939.26 applies to all witnesses who are considered material and necessary regardless of their status, including news reporters. Matter of McAuley (Cuyahoga 1979) 63 Ohio App.2d 5, 408 N.E.2d 697, 17 O.O.3d 222.

3. Compulsory process to secure defense witnesses

Accused not entitled to habeas corpus because counsel failed to secure attendance of alleged alibi witnesses. Lancaster v. Green (Ohio 1963) 175 Ohio St. 203, 192 N.E.2d 776, 24 O.O.2d 283.

Any state court finding that witness who was incarcerated out-of-state was unavailable to testify at trial, for purposes of petitioner's Sixth Amendment right of confrontation, was contrary to clearly established Supreme Court precedent, so as to support federal habeas relief, given that both state in which trial was being conducted and state in which witness was incarcerated had enacted Uniform Act to Secure the Attendance of Witnesses from Without a State in Criminal Proceedings, which provided means for obtaining witness' presence, and that prosecution had employed such procedures to obtain witness' presence for related trial of his brother. Brumley v. Wingard (C.A.6 (Ohio), 10-11-2001) 269 F.3d 629. Habeas Corpus ⚷ 481

4. Hearsay exception where witness unavailable

State made good faith effort to secure attendance of absent out-of-state witness, notwithstanding its failure to use Uniform Act to Secure the Attendance of Witnesses from Without the State, and thus witness was unavailable for purposes of hearsay exceptions, where subpoena was issued for witness at her residence, airline ticket was provided for witness's use in traveling to trial location, detective received assurances from witness's mother that witness desired to testify, and detective secured help of local detective in effort to locate witness. State v. Carpenter (Ohio App. 8 Dist., 07-23-1997) 122 Ohio App.3d 16, 701 N.E.2d 10, dismissed, appeal not allowed 80 Ohio St.3d 1446, 686 N.E.2d 274, certiorari denied 118 S.Ct. 1534, 523 U.S. 1082, 140 L.Ed.2d 683. Criminal Law ⚷ 419(5)

2939.27 Certificate to specify time witness will be required; mileage and fees

If a person in any state, which by its laws has made provision for commanding persons within its borders to attend and testify in criminal prosecutions or grand jury investigations commenced or about to commence, in this state, is a material witness in a prosecution pending in a court of record in this state, or in a grand jury investigation which has commenced or is about to commence, a judge of such court may issue a certificate under the seal of the court stating these facts and specifying the number of days the witness will be required. Said certificate may include a recommendation that the witness be taken into immediate custody and delivered to an officer of this state to assure his attendance in this state. This certificate shall be presented to a judge of a court of record in the county in which the witness is found.

If the witness is summoned to attend and testify in this state he shall be tendered the sum of ten cents a mile for each mile by the ordinary traveled route to and from the court where the prosecution is pending, and five dollars for each day that he is required to travel and attend as a witness. A witness who has appeared in accordance with the summons shall not be required to remain within this state a longer period of time than the period mentioned in the certificate, unless otherwise ordered by the court. If such witness, after coming into this state, fails without good cause to attend and testify as directed in the summons, he shall be punished in the manner provided for the punishment of any witness who disobeys a summons issued from a court of record in this state.

(1953 H 1, eff. 10–1–53; GC 13436–26)

Historical and Statutory Notes

Pre–1953 H 1 Amendments: 117 v 668, § 3

Cross References

Right to compulsory process to obtain witnesses, O Const Art I §10

Library References

Witnesses ⚷6, 23.

Westlaw Topic No. 410.

C.J.S. Federal Civil Procedure § 585.

C.J.S. Witnesses §§ 2, 14 to 19, 70 to 86.

Notes of Decisions

Cost of transporting prisoner-witness 1

1. Cost of transporting prisoner-witness

The reasonable costs of transporting an out-of-state prisoner into the state of Ohio as a necessary witness in a criminal prosecution for violation of state law is taxable as a criminal cost and payable by the auditor of state under the criminal cost subsidy program. OAG 74–101.

2939.28 Exemption from arrest

If a person comes into this state in obedience to a summons directing him to attend and testify in this state, while in this state pursuant to such summons he is not subject to arrest or the service of process, civil or criminal, in connection with matters which arose before his entrance into this state under the summons.

If a person passes through this state while going to another state in obedience to a summons to attend and testify in that state or while returning therefrom, while so passing through this state he is not subject to arrest or the service of process, civil or criminal, in connection with matters which arose before his entrance into this state under the summons.

(1953 H 1, eff. 10–1–53; GC 13436–27)

Historical and Statutory Notes

Pre–1953 H 1 Amendments: 117 v 668, § 4

Library References

Arrest ⚷9, 60.
Process ⚷120.
Westlaw Topic Nos. 313, 35.
C.J.S. Arrest §§ 4 to 5, 77 to 81.
C.J.S. Process § 27.

Research References

Treatises and Practice Aids

Markus, Trial Handbook for Ohio Lawyers, § 11:1, Compelling Attendance.

2939.29 Construction

Sections 2939.25 to 2939.28, inclusive, of the Revised Code shall be so interpreted and construed as to effectuate their general purpose, to make the law of this state uniform with the law of other states which enact similar uniform legislation.

(1953 H 1, eff. 10–1–53; GC 13436–28)

Historical and Statutory Notes

Pre–1953 H 1 Amendments: 117 v 668, § 5

Research References

Encyclopedias

OH Jur. 3d Criminal Law § 3046, Generally; Unavailability of Witness.

OH Jur. 3d Criminal Law § 3113, Compelling Attendance.

OH Jur. 3d Jury § 148, Compelling Attendance and Testimony of Witnesses.

Treatises and Practice Aids

Markus, Trial Handbook for Ohio Lawyers, § 11:3, Out-Of-State.

Katz, Giannelli, Blair and Lipton, Baldwin's Ohio Practice, Criminal Law, § 61:10, Out-Of-State Witnesses.

Giannelli and Snyder, Baldwin's Ohio Practice, Evidence, § 804.8, Unavailability: Unable to Procure Testimony.

CHAPTER 2941

INDICTMENT

MAGISTRATE DEFINED

2941.01 Definition of magistrate

The definition of "magistrate" set forth in section 2931.01 of the Revised Code applies to Chapter 2941. of the Revised Code.

(1953 H 1, eff. 10–1–53)

Cross References

Indictment, Crim R 6, 7

Right to indictment, O Const Art I §10

Law Review and Journal Commentaries

FEDERAL JURISDICTION AND PROCEDURE—Federal Court Intervention in State Criminal Proceedings When Charges Are Brought After Filing of the Federal Complaint, Hicks v. Miranda, Note. 37 Ohio St L J 205 (1976).

Name Calling: Defendant Nomenclature in Criminal Trials, Arthur N. Bishop. 4 Ohio N U L Rev 38 (1977).

Some Legislative History and Comments on Ohio's New Criminal Code, Harry J. Lehman and Alan E. Norris. 23 Clev St L Rev 8 (Winter 1974).

INDICTMENTS AND INFORMATIONS

2941.02 Informations

All sections of the Revised Code which apply to prosecutions upon indictments, the process thereon, and the issuing and service thereof, to commitments, bails, motions, pleadings, trials, appeals, and punishments, to the execution of any sentence, and all other proceedings in cases of indictments whether in the court of original or appellate jurisdiction, apply to informations, and all prosecutions and proceedings thereon.

(1953 H 1, eff. 10–1–53; GC 13437–1)

Historical and Statutory Notes

Pre–1953 H 1 Amendments: 113 v 162, Ch 16, § 1

Cross References

Indictment and information, Crim R 7

Library References

Indictment and Information ⚷35 to 54.
Westlaw Topic No. 210.
C.J.S. Forgery §§ 45, 74, 76.
C.J.S. Larceny § 70.

Research References

Encyclopedias

OH Jur. 3d Criminal Law § 2325, Furnishing Accused Copy of Accusation.

Treatises and Practice Aids

Katz, Giannelli, Blair and Lipton, Baldwin's Ohio Practice, Criminal Law, § 142:14, Skeleton Information.

Notes of Decisions

Assignment of counsel 2
Commitment of insane prisoner 1

1. Commitment of insane prisoner

A criminal division of a common pleas court lacks jurisdiction to commit a person to the Lima state hospital until restored to reason under RC 2945.37 and 2945.38 unless that person has first been indicted by a grand jury. Burton v. Reshetylo (Allen 1973) 35 Ohio App.2d 113, 300 N.E.2d 249, 64 O.O.2d 234, affirmed 38 Ohio St.2d 35, 309 N.E.2d 907, 67 O.O.2d 53.

2. Assignment of counsel

The common pleas court has the authority to assign counsel where the defendant is prosecuted by information. 1963 OAG 105.

2941.021 Prosecution by information

Any criminal offense which is not punishable by death or life imprisonment may be prosecuted by information filed in the common pleas court by the prosecuting attorney if the defendant, after he has been advised by the court of the nature of the charge against him and of his rights under the constitution, is represented by counsel or has affirmatively waived counsel by waiver in writing and in open court, waives in writing and in open court prosecution by indictment.

(128 v 53, eff. 11–9–59)

Cross References

Right to indictment, O Const Art I §10

Waiving indictment, Crim R 7

Library References

Indictment and Information ⚷4, 5.
Westlaw Topic No. 210.

Research References

Encyclopedias

OH Jur. 3d Criminal Law § 2321, Indictment; Constitutional and Statutory Provisions—Waiver of Indictment.

OH Jur. 3d Criminal Law § 2464, Particular Matters Waived by Plea of Guilty.

Treatises and Practice Aids

Katz, Giannelli, Blair and Lipton, Baldwin's Ohio Practice, Criminal Law, § 40:3, Waiver of Right to Indictment.

Katz, Giannelli, Blair and Lipton, Baldwin's Ohio Practice, Criminal Law, § 142:4, Waiver of Indictment.

Katz, Giannelli, Blair and Lipton, Baldwin's Ohio Practice, Criminal Law, § 142:14, Skeleton Information.

Law Review and Journal Commentaries

Understanding Prosecutorial Discretion in The United States: The Limits of Comparative Criminal Procedure as an Instrument of Reform, William T. Pizzi. 54 Ohio St L J 1325 (1993).

Notes of Decisions

---

1. Constitutional issues

Where, after a crime has been committed, the procedural methods of charging crimes is amended to include the use of an information, the use of such an information against an accused charging him with the crime is constitutional. Wells v. Maxwell (Ohio 1963) 174 Ohio St. 198, 188 N.E.2d 160, 22 O.O.2d 147.

RC 2941.021 is constitutional, inasmuch as the privilege guaranteed by O Const Art I §10 in regard to presentment or indictment may be waived. Ex parte Stephens (Ohio 1960) 171 Ohio St. 323, 170 N.E.2d 735, 14 O.O.2d 1.

The constitutional provision for indictment cannot be waived by one accused of crime, so that a statute authorizing an information in a criminal case when the Ohio Constitution requires an indictment by a grand jury is void. State v. Centers (Ohio Com.Pl. 1959) 162 N.E.2d 925, 82 Ohio Law Abs. 385, 10 O.O.2d 246.

The constitutional requirement of a grand jury indictment in federal cases has no application to the states; indeed, a state need not indict at all if sufficient notice of the charges be given in another manner. Koontz v. Glossa (C.A.6 (Ohio) 1984) 731 F.2d 365.

2. In general

The manner by which an accused is charged with a crime is procedural rather than jurisdictional, and after a conviction for crimes charged in an indictment, the judgment binds the defendant for the crime for which he was convicted. Orr v. Mack (Ohio, 10-28-1998) 83 Ohio St.3d 429, 700 N.E.2d 590, 1998-Ohio-32. Criminal Law ⚷ 977(1); Indictment And Information ⚷ 4

After judgment of conviction for crimes charged in indictment, judgment binds defendant for crime for which he or she was convicted. State ex rel. Beaucamp v. Lazaroff (Ohio, 01-15-1997) 77 Ohio St.3d 237, 673 N.E.2d 1273, 1997-Ohio-277. Criminal Law ⚷ 990.1

Following conviction and sentence, defendant's remedy to challenge validity or sufficiency of indictment is by direct appeal rather than habeas corpus. State ex rel. Beaucamp v. Lazaroff (Ohio, 01-15-1997) 77 Ohio St.3d 237, 673 N.E.2d 1273, 1997-Ohio-277. Habeas Corpus ⚷ 292

Habeas corpus is not available to attack validity or sufficiency of information, since judgment on information binds defendant as long as trial court has jurisdiction to try defendant for crime on which he or she is convicted and sentenced. State ex rel. Beaucamp v. Lazaroff (Ohio, 01-15-1997) 77 Ohio St.3d 237, 673 N.E.2d 1273, 1997-Ohio-277. Habeas Corpus ⚷ 474

Manner by which accused is charged with crime, whether by indictment returned by grand jury or by information filed by prosecuting attorney, is procedural rather than jurisdictional. State ex rel. Beaucamp v. Lazaroff (Ohio, 01-15-1997) 77 Ohio St.3d 237, 673 N.E.2d 1273, 1997-Ohio-277. Indictment And Information ⚷ 4

A criminal prosecution by an information is subject to all the procedural and other statutory requirements which apply to a prosecution by indictment. Wells v. Sacks (Franklin 1962) 115 Ohio App. 219, 184 N.E.2d 449, 20 O.O.2d 304. Criminal Law ⚷ 633(1)

RC 2941.021 is to be strictly construed. Wells v. Sacks (Franklin 1962) 115 Ohio App. 219, 184 N.E.2d 449, 20 O.O.2d 304.

A judgment of conviction based on a void "information" is void for lack of jurisdiction of the subject matter. Wells v. Sacks (Franklin 1962) 115 Ohio App. 219, 184 N.E.2d 449, 20 O.O.2d 304. Indictment And Information ⚷ 10.1(1)

The offense of breaking and entering an inhabited dwelling in the night season may not be prosecuted by information, since it is punishable by life imprisonment. 1962 OAG 3387.

3. Waiver of indictment—in general

Trial court had jurisdiction to accept defendant's guilty pleas, though complaint was never filed and his accused did not initiate prosecution; defendant signed waiver of indictment in compliance with statute governing prosecution by information, bill of information filed by state complied with statute governing sufficiency of indictments or informations, and statute did not require state to attach affidavit or complaint from alleged victim. State v. Azan (Ohio App. 12 Dist., Butler, 06-28-2004) No. CA2003-09-247, 2004-Ohio-3347, 2004 WL 1447683, Unreported. Criminal Law ⚷ 273(4.1)

Alleged rape victim's failure to file an affidavit or a complaint against defendant did not deprive trial court of jurisdiction to accept defendant's guilty plea, where defendant was not charged with any crimes punishable by death or life imprisonment, and defendant signed a waiver of indictment. State v. Dotson (Ohio App. 4 Dist., Washington, 05-24-2004) No. 03CA53, 2004-Ohio-2768, 2004 WL 1188988, Unreported. Criminal Law ⚷ 273(4.1)

Defendant's plea of guilty to the offenses of attempted assault of peace officer and failure to comply with order of peace officer waived any claimed right to an indictment. State v. Pitts (Ohio App. 6 Dist., 03-25-2005) 159 Ohio App.3d 852, 825 N.E.2d 695, 2005-Ohio-1389, appeal after new sentencing hearing 2006-Ohio-3182, 2006 WL 1719846. Criminal Law ⚷ 273.4(4); Indictment And Information ⚷ 5

An accused may waive his right to be tried only on an indictment, and instead prosecution may be had on information. Stacy v Van Curen, 432 F(2d) 970 (6th Cir Ohio 1970).

A defendant charged with assault to commit rape who pleads guilty to an amended charge of assault with intent to commit robbery waives prosecution by indictment. Stacy v Van Curen, 432 F(2d) 970 (6th Cir Ohio 1970).

4. —— Knowing, intelligent, voluntary waiver, waiver of indictment

Defendant's guilty plea to charge contained in information waived any claimed right to indictment, where defendant was represented by counsel when he pled guilty and did not claim that his guilty plea was involuntary. State ex rel. Beaucamp v. Lazaroff (Ohio, 01-15-1997) 77 Ohio St.3d 237, 673 N.E.2d 1273, 1997-Ohio-277. Criminal Law ⚷ 273.4(4)

Claim that defendant did not knowingly, intelligently, and voluntarily waive his right to be prosecuted by indictment could not be raised in habeas corpus proceeding. State ex rel. Beaucamp v. Lazaroff (Ohio, 01-15-1997) 77 Ohio St.3d 237, 673 N.E.2d 1273, 1997-Ohio-277. Habeas Corpus ⚷ 474

Where in postconviction proceedings, instituted by an indigent prisoner, the record reflects that, before entering a plea of guilty, defendant was apprised of his "constitutional rights" and stated that he did not wish to be represented by counsel, but the record does not affirmatively show that defendant was specifically told of his right to state-appointed counsel if indigent, nor does the record specify the "constitutional rights" about which defendant was informed, or contain sufficient evidence to justify the conclusion that defendant knowingly and intelligently waived his constitutional right to counsel, the trial court is required to appoint counsel and conduct a hearing so that there may be a judicial determination, while defendant is represented by counsel, upon the issue of whether he knowingly and intelligently waived his right to counsel when he entered his plea of guilty. State v. Welch (Ohio 1971) 28 Ohio St.2d 31, 274 N.E.2d 756, 57 O.O.2d 103. Criminal Law ⚷ 1655(6); Criminal Law ⚷ 1606

Where, on motion to dismiss an action in habeas corpus, the evidence of petitioner, who had been prosecuted on an "information" supports a finding that he did not understand the nature or contents of the "waiver" (of prosecution by indictment) signed by him and was not advised of the nature of the charge against him prior to the execution of such "waiver" or of his constitutional rights, the petitioner has made a prima facie case for release from custody, the burden is on respondent (custodian of petitioner) to go forward with the evidence and the motion to dismiss will be overruled. Wells v. Sacks (Franklin 1962) 115 Ohio App. 219, 184 N.E.2d 449, 20 O.O.2d 304.

A so-called "felony information" is void where the accused does not intelligently and understandably waive his right to indictment. Wells v. Sacks (Franklin 1962) 115 Ohio App. 219, 184 N.E.2d 449, 20 O.O.2d 304. Indictment And Information ⚷ 5

Whether prosecution is by information or by indictment and whether appointment of counsel is waived either in writing or orally the court should advise the defendant of his rights in sufficient detail and make sufficient inquiry of the defendant to insure that such waiver was accomplished intelligently and understandingly. 1963 OAG 448.

5. —— Right to counsel, waiver of indictment

Where a defendant is prosecuted by information rather than by indictment he must either have counsel, be provided counsel or affirmatively and intelligently and understandingly waive counsel and prosecution by indictment by waiver in open court, preferably in writing. 1963 OAG 448.

The common pleas court has the authority to assign counsel where the defendant is prosecuted by information. 1963 OAG 105.

6. —— Withdrawal, waiver of indictment

Where one accused of crime regularly waives indictment and consents to proceed by information, but before trial files an application to withdraw such waiver and to have an examination by the grand jury, the allowance of such application is not a matter of absolute right but lies within the discretion of the trial court. State v. Coble (Montgomery 1962) 118 Ohio App. 258, 194 N.E.2d 64, 25 O.O.2d 93.

2941.03 Sufficiency of indictments or informations

An indictment or information is sufficient if it can be understood therefrom:

(A) That it is entitled in a court having authority to receive it, though the name of the court is not stated;

(B) If it is an indictment, that it was found by a grand jury of the county in which the court was held, of [*sic*] if it is an information, that it was subscribed and presented to the court by the prosecuting attorney of the county in which the court was held;

(C) That the defendant is named, or, if his name cannot be discovered, that he is described by a fictitious name, with a statement that his true name is unknown to the jury or prosecuting attorney, but no name shall be stated in addition to one necessary to identify the accused;

(D) That an offense was committed at some place within the jurisdiction of the court, except where the act, though done without the local jurisdiction of the county, is triable therein;

(E) That the offense was committed at some time prior to the time of finding of the indictment or filing of the information.

(1953 H 1, eff. 10–1–53; GC 13437–2)

Historical and Statutory Notes

Pre–1953 H 1 Amendments: 113 v 162, Ch 16, § 2

Cross References

Pleadings and motions before trial, defenses and objections, Crim R 12

Library References

Indictment and Information ⊂=55 to 123.
Westlaw Topic No. 210.
C.J.S. Breach of the Peace § 7.
C.J.S. Drugs and Narcotics § 225.
C.J.S. Elections § 339.
C.J.S. Embezzlement § 27.
C.J.S. Escape and Related Offenses; Rescue § 34.
C.J.S. Forgery §§ 45, 53, 74, 76.
C.J.S. Fraud § 103.
C.J.S. Homicide §§ 140 to 141.
C.J.S. Landlord and Tenant § 1246.
C.J.S. Larceny § 70.
C.J.S. Mayhem § 8.
C.J.S. Monopolies § 246.
C.J.S. Parent and Child § 368.
C.J.S. Receiving or Transferring Stolen Goods and Related Offenses §§ 17 to 20.
C.J.S. Robbery §§ 35, 83.
C.J.S. Telecommunications § 131.
C.J.S. Threats and Unlawful Communications § 23.

Research References

Encyclopedias

OH Jur. 3d Criminal Law § 2364, Designation of Accused.

OH Jur. 3d Criminal Law § 2375, Date.

Treatises and Practice Aids

Katz, Giannelli, Blair and Lipton, Baldwin's Ohio Practice, Criminal Law, § 142:1, Skeleton Indictment—Single Count.

Katz, Giannelli, Blair and Lipton, Baldwin's Ohio Practice, Criminal Law, § 142:2, Skeleton Indictment—Multiple Counts.

Katz, Giannelli, Blair and Lipton, Baldwin's Ohio Practice, Criminal Law, § 142:14, Skeleton Information.

Hennenberg & Reinhart, Ohio Criminal Defense Motions F 11.08, Motion to Dismiss-Lack of Specificity.

Notes of Decisions

---

1. Sufficiency of indictment

Indictment of defendant for rape and gross sexual imposition was properly filed and alleged sufficient facts to apprise defendant of charges; indictment recited definition of rape and gross sexual imposition as defined in relevant statutes, and indictment was not rendered invalid for failure to state exact date that offenses were committed, as range of years in indictment supported fact that victim was under age of 13. State v. Bogan (Ohio App. 8 Dist., Cuyahoga, 06-30-2005) No. 84468, 2005-Ohio-3412, 2005 WL 1541014, Unreported. Indictment And Information ⚷ 87(7); Indictment And Information ⚷ 110(3); Indictment And Information ⚷ 110(6)

Trial court had jurisdiction to accept defendant's guilty pleas, though complaint was never filed and his accused did not initiate prosecution; defendant signed waiver of indictment in compliance with statute governing prosecution by information, bill of information filed by state complied with statute governing sufficiency of indictments or informations, and statute did not require state to attach affidavit or complaint from alleged victim. State v. Azan (Ohio App. 12 Dist., Butler, 06-28-2004) No. CA2003-09-247, 2004-Ohio-3347, 2004 WL 1447683, Unreported. Criminal Law ⚷ 273(4.1)

In prosecution for multiple sex offenses, trial court's instruction to jury that it was not necessary for State to prove that the offenses were committed on the exact day as charged in indictment did not improperly open the door to "guesswork of the jury"; specificity as to the date and time of offenses was not required. State v. Braddy (Ohio App. 8 Dist., Cuyahoga, 06-17-2004) No. 83462, 2004-Ohio-3128, 2004 WL 1364730, Unreported, motion to reopen denied 2005-Ohio-282, 2005 WL 174771, motion for delayed appeal denied 106 Ohio St.3d 1458, 830 N.E.2d 1167, 2005-Ohio-3490. Rape ⚷ 35(4); Rape ⚷ 59(4)

Specific language of indictment, designating rape as a felony in the first degree, and exchange with court regarding proposed plea bargain placed defendant on notice that he was facing a possible sentence of life imprisonment and, thus, defendant was not prejudicially misled by omission of statutory numerical designation in indictment. State v. Sterling (Ohio App. 11 Dist., Ashtabula, 02-06-2004) No. 2002-A-0026, 2004-Ohio-526, 2004 WL 231514, Unreported, appeal not allowed 102 Ohio St.3d 1483, 810 N.E.2d 967, 2004-Ohio-3069. Indictment And Information ⚷ 108

Evidence was sufficient to establish that charged offenses of rape, attempted rape, and gross sexual imposition occurred during the time frame listed in the indictment, and thus, defendant was not entitled to judgment of acquittal; victim, defendant's adopted daughter, testified that sexual contact with defendant occurred during the summer she entered her fourth-grade year, which was the same as the dates listed in the indictment. State v. Hurd (Ohio App. 11 Dist., Trumbull, 12-20-2002) No. 2001-T-0086, 2002-Ohio-7163, 2002 WL 31862690, Unreported, appeal not allowed 98 Ohio St.3d 1566, 787 N.E.2d 1231, 2003-Ohio-2242. Infants ⚷ 20; Rape ⚷ 57(1)

Amendment of indictment to expand by approximately sixteen months the time frame of alleged rapes of child under age thirteen did not violate state constitutional requirement to try defendant on the same essential facts on which the grand jury found probable cause; the grand jury had found probable cause of sexual conduct with child under thirteen years and could easily have found probable cause of rape at a later time, and time was not an element. State v. Shafer (Ohio App. 8 Dist., Cuyahoga, 12-05-2002) No. 79758, 2002-Ohio-6632, 2002 WL 31722127, Unreported, appeal not allowed 98 Ohio St.3d 1540, 786 N.E.2d 902, 2003-Ohio-1946, appeal after new sentencing hearing 2004-Ohio-2555, 2004 WL 1118805, appeal not allowed 103 Ohio St.3d 1480, 816 N.E.2d 255, 2004-Ohio-5405, certiorari denied 125 S.Ct. 1663, 544 U.S. 928, 161 L.Ed.2d 491, rehearing denied, rehearing denied 125 S.Ct. 2249, 544 U.S. 1045, 161 L.Ed.2d 1083. Indictment And Information ⚷ 159(3)

Indictment was not invalid or insufficient because it did not describe the specific dates on which the crimes allegedly occurred; specificity as to the date and time of the offense was not required in the indictment. State v. Thompson (Ohio App. 8 Dist., Cuyahoga, 10-31-2002) No. 79334, 2002-Ohio-5957, 2002 WL 31426356, Unreported, dismissal of post-conviction relief affirmed 2002-Ohio-6845, 2002 WL 31771437, appeal not allowed 100 Ohio St.3d 1506, 799 N.E.2d 186, 2003-Ohio-6161, appeal not allowed 98 Ohio St.3d 1512, 786 N.E.2d 62, 2003-Ohio-1572, reconsideration denied 99 Ohio St.3d 1414, 788 N.E.2d 649, 2003-Ohio-2454, motion to reopen denied 2003-Ohio-4336, 2003 WL 21954760, as amended nunc pro tunc, appeal not allowed 100 Ohio St.3d 1509, 799 N.E.2d 187, 2003-Ohio-6161. Indictment And Information ⚷ 87(2)

Prohibition is not available to challenge the validity or sufficiency of indictments because such challenge is nonjurisdictional and can be raised on direct appeal. State ex rel. Jackson v. Callahan (Ohio, 07-07-1999) 86 Ohio St.3d 73, 711 N.E.2d 686, 1999-Ohio-84. Prohibition ⚷ 3(4); Prohibition ⚷ 5(4)

Habeas corpus was not available to attack the validity or sufficiency of the charging instrument, as petitioner had an adequate legal remedy by direct appeal to challenge the validity or sufficiency of the complaint and indictment. Orr v. Mack (Ohio, 10-28-1998) 83 Ohio St.3d 429, 700 N.E.2d 590, 1998-Ohio-32. Habeas Corpus ⚷ 275.1

Attacks on validity and sufficiency of indictments should have been raised by direct appeal, rather than habeas corpus petition. VanBuskirk v. Wingard (Ohio, 01-07-1998) 80 Ohio St.3d 659, 687 N.E.2d 776, 1998-Ohio-173, reconsideration denied 81 Ohio St.3d 1448, 690 N.E.2d 18. Habeas Corpus ⚷ 292

Indictment is sufficient if it contains elements of offense charged, fairly informs defendant what charge he must be prepared to meet, and enables defendant to plead acquittal or conviction in bar of future prosecutions for same offense. State v. Feliciano (Ohio App. 9 Dist., 11-20-1996) 115 Ohio App.3d 646, 685 N.E.2d 1307, appeal not allowed

78 Ohio St.3d 1442, 676 N.E.2d 1187. Indictment And Information ⚷ 71.2(3); Indictment And Information ⚷ 71.2(4); Indictment And Information ⚷ 71.3

Inmate's claims challenging admissibility of evidence and validity or sufficiency of his indictment were not cognizable in habeas corpus; inmate had adequate remedy by direct appeal to raise them. Davie v. Edwards (Ohio, 10-29-1997) 80 Ohio St.3d 170, 685 N.E.2d 228, 1997-Ohio-127.

Habeas corpus is not available to challenge either validity or sufficiency of indictment. Smith v. Seidner (Ohio, 04-16-1997) 78 Ohio St.3d 172, 677 N.E.2d 336, 1997-Ohio-224. Habeas Corpus ⚷ 474

Challenges to validity or sufficiency of indictments are cognizable on direct appeal but not by habeas corpus. State ex rel. Josso v. Seidner (Ohio, 01-15-1997) 77 Ohio St.3d 250, 673 N.E.2d 1284, 1997-Ohio-275. Habeas Corpus ⚷ 474

Inmates' claims that their indictments contained no allegation that charged offenses were committed within territorial jurisdiction of their sentencing courts were attacks upon validity or sufficiency of their indictments that were cognizable on direct appeal, rather than via habeas corpus. State ex rel. Yauger v. Seidner (Ohio, 11-06-1996) 77 Ohio St.3d 69, 671 N.E.2d 29, 1996-Ohio-348. Habeas Corpus ⚷ 292; Habeas Corpus ⚷ 474

Petitioner's claim challenging validity or sufficiency of his indictment was nonjurisdictional in nature, and, thus, should have been raised on appeal of his criminal conviction rather than in habeas corpus. State ex rel. Richard v. Seidner (Ohio, 11-06-1996) 77 Ohio St.3d 68, 671 N.E.2d 28, 1996-Ohio-349. Habeas Corpus ⚷ 292

Habeas corpus is not available to challenge either validity or sufficiency of indictment; such claims can be raised on direct appeal. State ex rel. Wilcox v. Seidner (Ohio, 08-21-1996) 76 Ohio St.3d 412, 667 N.E.2d 1220, 1996-Ohio-390, reconsideration denied 77 Ohio St.3d 1417, 670 N.E.2d 1004. Habeas Corpus ⚷ 292; Habeas Corpus ⚷ 474

Habeas corpus was not available to challenge alleged insufficiency of indictment in allegedly failing to contain any allegation that charged offenses were committed at some place within territorial jurisdiction of sentencing courts. State ex rel. Wilcox v. Seidner (Ohio, 08-21-1996) 76 Ohio St.3d 412, 667 N.E.2d 1220, 1996-Ohio-390, reconsideration denied 77 Ohio St.3d 1417, 670 N.E.2d 1004. Habeas Corpus ⚷ 474

Habeas corpus is not available to challenge sufficiency of indictment. State ex rel. Simpson v. Lazaroff (Ohio, 06-05-1996) 75 Ohio St.3d 571, 664 N.E.2d 937, 1996-Ohio-201. Habeas Corpus ⚷ 474

Motion to dismiss indictment tests sufficiency of indictment, without regard to quantity or quality of evidence that may be produced by either state or defendant. State v. Silos (Ohio App. 9 Dist., 05-10-1995) 104 Ohio App.3d 23, 660 N.E.2d 1239. Indictment And Information ⚷ 144.1(1)

Failure of count of indictment charging defendant with aggravated burglary to specify what felony defendant intended when he broke into house where victim was staying was not plain error in prosecution for capital murder and aggravated burglary, where it was clear from specifications in other two counts that state intended to establish that defendant entered house with intent to commit aggravated burglary, and state did not present evidence of any felony other than aggravated murder. State v. Frazier (Ohio, 08-23-1995) 73 Ohio St.3d 323, 652 N.E.2d 1000, 1995-Ohio-235, stay granted 74 Ohio St.3d 1437, 655 N.E.2d 1321, certiorari denied 116 S.Ct. 820, 516 U.S. 1095, 133 L.Ed.2d 763, denial of post-conviction relief affirmed 1997 WL 764810, dismissed, appeal not allowed 81 Ohio St.3d 1496, 691 N.E.2d 1058, habeas corpus denied 188 F.Supp.2d 798, denial of habeas corpus reversed in part 343 F.3d 780, opinion supplemented on denial of rehearing 348 F.3d 174, rehearing and suggestion for rehearing en banc denied, certiorari denied 124 S.Ct. 2815, 541 U.S. 1095, 159 L.Ed.2d 261. Criminal Law ⚷ 1032(5)

Defendant was not prejudiced by state's failure to provide more specific date than 24—day time frame listed in indictment for allegation that defendant engaged in oral intercourse with minor victim, as defendant was acquitted of that offense, as to which minor's testimony was vague. State v. Daniel (Ohio App. 10 Dist., 08-30-1994) 97 Ohio App.3d 548, 647 N.E.2d 174, dismissed, appeal not allowed 71 Ohio St.3d 1455, 644 N.E.2d 1028. Criminal Law ⚷ 1167(1)

Indictment which contained no allegation of essential facts showing element of deception or any allegation that deception occurred was ineffective, and conviction of defendant on her plea of no contest to charge of theft by deception was void. State v. Luna (Ohio App. 6 Dist., 07-22-1994) 96 Ohio App.3d 207, 644 N.E.2d 1056. False Pretenses ⚷ 30

Defendant could be convicted of housing violation in connection with failure to secure change-of-use permits, although he alleged that complaint cited section of building code which merely referred to schedule of inspection fees, where text of complaint clearly indicated change-of-use violation of city building code. Cleveland v. Makris (Ohio App. 8 Dist., 08-11-1993) 90 Ohio App.3d 742, 630 N.E.2d 739, motion to certify overruled 68 Ohio St.3d 1461, 627 N.E.2d 1002. Zoning And Planning ⚷ 803

Ordinarily, precise times and dates are not essential elements of offenses, and thus, failure to provide dates and times in indictment will not alone provide basis for dismissal of charges. State v. Sellards (Ohio 1985) 17 Ohio St.3d 169, 478 N.E.2d 781, 17 O.B.R. 410. Indictment And Information ⚷ 144.1(1)

A complaint charging a violation of RC 3773.24 "on or about Sunday the 6th day of January, 1963," is not indefinite and vague; the use of the disjunctive "or" in such complaint in charging that the accused "did suffer or permit a building to be open for transaction of business on Sunday" does not render such charge indefinite and vague; the omission of the words "against the peace and dignity of the state of Ohio" does not render it defective; such complaint is not defective because it charges the accused with a violation of such statute as an individual and does not set out the capacity in which he is supposed to have acted; and such complaint is not defective because it does not negate the exceptions contained in such statute. State v. Whitt (Montgomery 1964) 3 Ohio App.2d 278, 210 N.E.2d 279, 32 O.O.2d 382.

An indictment which charges the commission of the offense of sodomy "in the year 1955 in the county of Miami on a Sunday night in January and on four successive Sundays... said acts having occurred in the car of" defendant "while parked in Fountain Park in Piqua... and on various roads in the area of Piqua" fully sets out the required material allegations and is sufficient to charge the offense of sodomy. State v. Carey (Miami 1958) 107 Ohio App. 149, 157 N.E.2d 381, 8 O.O.2d 49, appeal dismissed 168 Ohio St. 254, 153 N.E.2d 676, 6 O.O.2d 388. Sodomy ⚷ 5

Indictment charging defendant with attempting to evade or defeat income tax due and owing over a five-year period, through his failure to file a tax return during that time, was sufficient to charge defendant with tax evasion, even though indictment did not additionally indicate statute that makes an individual liable for an income tax, or statute that requires an individual to pay the income tax for which he is liable. U.S. v. Middleton (C.A.6 (Ohio), 04-18-2001) 246 F.3d 825, rehearing en banc denied. Indictment And Information ⚷ 108

Indictment that follows statutory language is generally sufficient to satisfy requirements of due process, but it need not quote statute verbatim. U.S. v. Clinkscale (N.D.Ohio, 02-22-2000) 86 F.Supp.2d 780. Indictment And Information ⚷ 110(3)

Indictment charging defendant with participation in drug conspiracy between certain dates, which tracked statutory language and alleged that he furthered conspiracy by engaging in both money laundering and structuring of currency transactions, was not unconstitutionally vague merely because it did not point to any act involving particular drugs. U.S. v. Clinkscale (N.D.Ohio, 02-22-2000) 86 F.Supp.2d 780. Indictment And Information ⚷ 110(3)

A conviction, without trial, based merely on a no contest plea to an indictment which does not allege sufficient facts to constitute an offense is void. State v Hayes, No. 5–82–11 (3d Dist Ct App, Hancock, 1–14–83).

2. Jurisdiction and venue

Trial court was vested with jurisdiction over prosecution of defendant for gross sexual imposition, where defendant had been charged with offenses via a valid indictment. State v. Bogan (Ohio App. 8 Dist., Cuyahoga, 06-30-2005) No. 84468, 2005-Ohio-3412, 2005 WL 1541014, Unreported. Criminal Law ⚷ 99

Since the original indictment did not show upon its face that the offense was committed at a place within the jurisdiction of the court, GC 13437–2 (RC 2941.03), counsel challenged the jurisdiction of the court to proceed. Breinig v. State (Ohio 1931) 124 Ohio St. 39, 176 N.E. 674, 10 Ohio Law Abs. 94, 34 Ohio Law Rep. 478.

3. Name of defendant

Bill of information was sufficient to properly charge defendant with multiple sex offenses, even though information did not include an affidavit or complaint prepared by alleged victim; bill of information indicated that it was entitled in a court having authority to receive it, that it was subscribed and presented to the court by the prosecuting attorney, that the offense was committed at some place within the jurisdiction of the court, and that the offense was committed prior to the time of the filing of the information, and the information included defendant's name. State v. Dotson (Ohio App. 4 Dist., Washington, 05-24-2004) No. 03CA53, 2004-Ohio-2768, 2004 WL 1188988, Unreported. Indictment And Information ⚷ 52(1)

Allegation that indictment mistakenly named "Mark Simpson," instead of true name of "Marcus Simpson," merely challenged sufficiency of indictment and not court's jurisdiction, and therefore habeas corpus was not available; inmate had adequate remedy by direct appeal. State ex rel. Simpson v. Lazaroff (Ohio, 06-05-1996) 75 Ohio St.3d 571, 664 N.E.2d 937, 1996-Ohio-201. Habeas Corpus ⚷ 292; Habeas Corpus ⚷ 474

Inclusion of alias in indictment and references to use of alias during trial were harmless errors. State v. Williams (Ohio, 08-16-1995) 73 Ohio St.3d 153, 652 N.E.2d 721, 1995-Ohio-275, reconsideration denied 74 Ohio St.3d 1409, 655 N.E.2d 188, stay granted 74 Ohio St.3d 1437, 655 N.E.2d 1321, stay terminated 75 Ohio St.3d 1439, 662 N.E.2d 1085, certiorari denied 116 S.Ct. 1047, 516 U.S. 1161, 134 L.Ed.2d 193, denial of post-conviction relief affirmed 1998 WL 330539, dismissed, appeal not allowed 83 Ohio St.3d 1449, 700 N.E.2d 332, reconsideration denied 84 Ohio St.3d 1413, 701 N.E.2d 1021. Criminal Law ⚷ 345; Criminal Law ⚷ 1167(1); Criminal Law ⚷ 1169.1(6); Indictment And Information ⚷ 81(5)

The name of the defendant on a criminal complaint cannot be changed by amendment to a corporation from an entity that is not a corporation; the plaintiff should instead dismiss the complaint and file another. City of Columbus v. Moretti's Poultry (Franklin 1988) 48 Ohio App.3d 79, 548 N.E.2d 285.

4. Bill of particulars

Although defendant claimed the bill of particulars led him to believe that the State alleged all three crimes occurred on the same night, he did not claim that his ability to defend himself was prejudiced by this fact, and thus, defendant did not show that the date of the offenses was material to his defense, such that the indictment was invalid because it did not describe the specific dates on which the crimes allegedly occurred. State v. Thompson (Ohio App. 8 Dist., Cuyahoga, 10-31-2002) No. 79334, 2002-Ohio-5957, 2002 WL 31426356, Unreported, dismissal of post-conviction relief affirmed 2002-Ohio-6845, 2002 WL 31771437, appeal not allowed 100 Ohio St.3d 1506, 799 N.E.2d 186, 2003-Ohio-6161, appeal not allowed 98 Ohio St.3d 1512, 786 N.E.2d 62, 2003-Ohio-1572, reconsideration denied 99 Ohio St.3d 1414, 788 N.E.2d 649, 2003-Ohio-2454, motion to reopen denied 2003-Ohio-4336, 2003 WL 21954760, as amended nunc pro tunc, appeal not allowed 100 Ohio St.3d 1509, 799 N.E.2d 187, 2003-Ohio-6161. Indictment And Information ⚿ 87(2)

Specific information regarding the date and time of a rape need not be included in the indictment but must be disclosed by the prosecution, if known; it is enough if the amended bill of particulars identifies the dates as falling within a specified twelve-month period. State v. Ambrosia (Lucas 1990) 67 Ohio App.3d 552, 587 N.E.2d 892, dismissed 58 Ohio St.3d 701, 569 N.E.2d 504. Indictment And Information ⚿ 87(1)

Although a bill of particulars is not amended to reflect a more specific identification of the date and time of one of three rape charges, there is no basis for granting a new trial where the defendant was notified of the specific information, and a continuance gave him ample time to prepare his defense in light of this information. State v. Ambrosia (Lucas 1990) 67 Ohio App.3d 552, 587 N.E.2d 892, dismissed 58 Ohio St.3d 701, 569 N.E.2d 504. Criminal Law ⚿ 1167(1)

Inexactitude in responding to defendant's request for a bill of particulars, even where State is simply unable to comply with times and dates more specific than those found in the indictment, may prove fatal to the prosecution; such would be the case if absence of specifics truly prejudices accused's ability to fairly defend himself. State v. Sellards (Ohio 1985) 17 Ohio St.3d 169, 478 N.E.2d 781, 17 O.B.R. 410. Indictment And Information ⚿ 121.4

5. Interlineation

Interlineation of the date of alleged occurence of an offense in an indictment does not render the indictment invalid as the interlineation does not alter the nature or identity of the offense charged. State v. Price (Crawford 1992) 80 Ohio App.3d 35, 608 N.E.2d 818.

6. Variance

An indictment charging a defendant conspired with other "persons" does not vary in any material respect from evidence at trial that he conspired with just one other person, where the prosecution disclosed the identity of that individual in response to a motion for a bill of particulars and never endeavored to identify other individuals as conspirators; consequently, there is no need to determine whether the difference affects substantial rights of the defendant and necessitates reversal. U.S. v. Bouquett (C.A.6 (Ohio) 1987) 820 F.2d 165.

2941.04 Two or more offenses in one indictment

An indictment or information may charge two or more different offenses connected together in their commission, or different statements of the same offense, or two or more different offenses of the same class of crimes or offenses, under separate counts, and if two or more indictments or informations are filed in such cases the court may order them to be consolidated.

The prosecution is not required to elect between the different offenses or counts set forth in the indictment or information, but the defendant may be convicted of any number of the offenses charged, and each offense upon which the defendant is convicted must be stated in the verdict. The court in the interest of justice and for good cause shown, may order different offenses or counts set forth in the indictment or information tried separately or divided into two or more groups and each of said groups tried separately. A verdict of acquittal of one or more counts is not an acquittal of any other count.

(1953 H 1, eff. 10–1–53; GC 13437–3)

Historical and Statutory Notes

Pre–1953 H 1 Amendments: 113 v 163, Ch 16, § 3

Cross References

Joinder of offenses and defendants, Crim R 8

Library References

Criminal Law ⚿619, 620.
Indictment and Information ⚿124 to 132.
Westlaw Topic Nos. 110, 210.
C.J.S. Criminal Law §§ 558 to 562.
C.J.S. Receiving or Transferring Stolen Goods and Related Offenses §§ 17 to 20.

Research References

Encyclopedias

OH Jur. 3d Criminal Law § 2393, Different Statements of the Same Offense.

OH Jur. 3d Criminal Law § 2402, Election Between Counts.

OH Jur. 3d Criminal Law § 2819, Multiple Counts.

Treatises and Practice Aids

Katz, Giannelli, Blair and Lipton, Baldwin's Ohio Practice, Criminal Law, § 57:3, Joinder of Offenses—Criminal Rule 8(a).

Katz, Giannelli, Blair and Lipton, Baldwin's Ohio Practice, Criminal Law, § 57:4, Consolidation of Indictments and Complaints—Criminal Rule 13.

Katz, Giannelli, Blair and Lipton, Baldwin's Ohio Practice, Criminal Law, § 57:5, Severance—Criminal Rule 14.

Katz, Giannelli, Blair and Lipton, Baldwin's Ohio Practice, Criminal Law, § 57:7, Severance—Cumulation of Evidence.

Katz, Giannelli, Blair and Lipton, Baldwin's Ohio Practice, Criminal Law, § 58:3, Multiple Indictments and Complaints—Criminal Rule 13.

Katz, Giannelli, Blair and Lipton, Baldwin's Ohio Practice, Criminal Law, § 142:2, Skeleton Indictment—Multiple Counts.

Law Review and Journal Commentaries

Multiple Prosecutions When Conduct Constitutes More Than One Offense, Comment. 2 Ohio N U L Rev 23 (1974).

Readjudicating Partial Verdicts: Wallace v. Havener, Comment. 39 Ohio St L J 380 (1978).

Notes of Decisions

---

1. Constitutional issues

It is a settled law of criminal procedure that a general jury verdict is valid so long as it is legally supportable on one of the submitted grounds, and neither the Due Process Clause of the Fifth Amendment nor the United States Supreme Court's precedents require, in a federal prosecution for a multiple-object conspiracy, that a general jury verdict be set aside if the evidence is inadequate to support a conviction as to one of the objects; although it would generally be preferable for the court to give an instruction removing from the jury's consideration an alternative basis of liability that does not have adequate evidentiary support, the refusal to do so does not provide an independent basis for reversing an otherwise valid conviction. Griffin v. U.S. (U.S.Ill. 1991) 112 S.Ct. 466, 502 U.S. 46, 116 L.Ed.2d 371, rehearing denied 112 S.Ct. 1253, 502 U.S. 1125, 117 L.Ed.2d 484.

2. Variance between affidavit and indictment

The fact that the charge in the indictment does not conform to that originally made in the affidavit does not affect the validity of the conviction. Stebelton v. Haskins (Ohio 1964) 177 Ohio St. 52, 201 N.E.2d 884, 29 O.O.2d 76.

3. Multiple counts

Indictment that charged defendant with complicity in aggravated murder of her husband in three counts, with each count alleging separate theory of complicity-solicitation, aiding and abetting, or conspiracy-was not duplicitous, and thus prosecution was not required to elect between complicity counts. State v. Hoop (Ohio App. 12 Dist., 08-02-1999) 134 Ohio App.3d 627, 731 N.E.2d 1177, dismissed, appeal not allowed 87 Ohio St.3d 1441, 719 N.E.2d 5, on subsequent appeal 2001 WL 877296, dismissed, appeal not allowed 93 Ohio St.3d 1484, 758 N.E.2d 185, denial of post-conviction relief affirmed 2005-Ohio-1407, 2005 WL 694545, appeal not allowed 106 Ohio St.3d 1506, 833 N.E.2d 1249, 2005-Ohio-4605. Indictment And Information ⚿ 125(29)

The several counts of an indictment containing more than one count are not interdependent and an inconsistency in a verdict does not arise out of inconsistent responses to different counts, but only arises out of inconsistent responses to the same count. State v. Lovejoy (Ohio, 09-24-1997) 79 Ohio St.3d 440, 683 N.E.2d 1112, 1997-Ohio-371, habeas corpus denied 2001 WL 506534, reversed 54 Fed.Appx. 617, 2002 WL 31890928, on remand 2003 WL 1338210. Criminal Law ⚿ 878(4)

Failure of count of indictment charging defendant with aggravated burglary to specify what felony defendant intended when he broke into house where victim was staying was not plain error in prosecution for capital murder and aggravated burglary, where it was clear from specifications in other two counts that state intended to establish that defendant entered house with intent to commit aggravated burglary, and state did not present evidence of any felony other than aggravated murder. State v. Frazier (Ohio, 08-23-1995) 73 Ohio St.3d 323, 652 N.E.2d 1000, 1995-Ohio-235, stay granted 74 Ohio St.3d 1437, 655 N.E.2d 1321, certiorari denied 116 S.Ct. 820, 516 U.S. 1095, 133 L.Ed.2d 763, denial of post-conviction relief affirmed 1997 WL 764810, dismissed, appeal not allowed 81 Ohio St.3d 1496, 691 N.E.2d 1058, habeas corpus denied 188 F.Supp.2d 798, denial of habeas corpus reversed in part 343 F.3d 780, opinion supplemented on denial of rehearing 348 F.3d 174, rehearing and suggestion for rehearing en banc denied, certiorari denied 124 S.Ct. 2815, 541 U.S. 1095, 159 L.Ed.2d 261. Criminal Law ⚷ 1032(5)

Commercial fisherman pled guilty to one of three charged counts of inaccurate reporting of fish catches and, thus, prosecution did not terminate in favor of fisherman for purposes of his subsequent malicious prosecution claim. Koch v. Ohio Dept. of Natural Resources (Ohio App. 10 Dist., 06-07-1994) 95 Ohio App.3d 193, 642 N.E.2d 27. Malicious Prosecution ⚷ 37

An indictment or information may charge two or more different offenses, connected together in their commission, or two or more different offenses of the same class of crimes under separate counts, and a prosecutor is not required to elect between the different offenses or counts. State v. Ryan (Hamilton 1984) 17 Ohio App.3d 150, 478 N.E.2d 257, 17 O.B.R. 250. Indictment And Information ⚷ 129(1); Indictment And Information ⚷ 130; Indictment And Information ⚷ 132(3)

Two or more different offenses may be charged in a single indictment if said offenses (1) are connected together in their commission; or (2) are set out in different statements of the same offense; or (3) are of the same class of crimes or offenses. State v. Atkinson (Ohio 1965) 4 Ohio St.2d 19, 211 N.E.2d 665, 33 O.O.2d 226. Indictment And Information ⚷ 127

4. Different offenses of same class

If court dismisses only one count of multiple counts indictment, remaining count or counts in indictment are unaffected and prosecutor may proceed on such counts. State v. Armstead (Allen 1993) 85 Ohio App.3d 247, 619 N.E.2d 513. Indictment And Information ⚷ 144.2

An indictment of three counts, each charging a single and separate offense of armed robbery, does not constitute duplicity. Parker v. Maxwell (Ohio 1963) 174 Ohio St. 471, 190 N.E.2d 271, 23 O.O.2d 116. Indictment And Information ⚷ 128

Where first count of indictment charged defendant with breaking and entering in night season of a building with intent to steal property of value, and second count of indictment charged defendant with taking property valued at $180, offenses charged were separate and distinct and defendant was properly sentenced under both counts. Wyatt v. Alvis (Franklin 1955) 136 N.E.2d 726, 73 Ohio Law Abs. 21. Sentencing And Punishment ⚷ 532

Where accused was indicted for two counts of armed robbery and one count of plain robbery, trial court was authorized in its discretion to permit the state to try accused on the counts of armed robbery after sustaining accused's motion to elect as to the count charging plain robbery, and was not required to require an election between the counts of armed robbery. State v. Barnett (Franklin 1942) 42 N.E.2d 919, 36 Ohio Law Abs. 104. Indictment And Information ⚷ 132(4)

5. Different statements of same offense

If defendant had been prosecuted under both subparts of criminal trespass statute, he could have been convicted of violating only one. State v. Imperatore (Ohio App. 9 Dist., 11-02-1994) 98 Ohio App.3d 384, 648 N.E.2d 842. Criminal Law ⚷ 29(5.5)

Each method listed in former RC 2901.01 (RC 2903.01) is a separate offense even though the murder victim is the same person, and the use of a combination of such means does not constitute the "same criminal act" as that term is used in RC 2941.32. State v. Trocodaro (Franklin 1973) 40 Ohio App.2d 50, 317 N.E.2d 418, 69 O.O.2d 28.

The killing of another purposely and in perpetrating or attempting to perpetrate a robbery, and the killing of the same person purposely and of deliberate and premeditated malice, are separate and distinct offenses of first degree murder and may properly be charged in separate counts of an indictment. State v. Ferguson (Ohio 1964) 175 Ohio St. 390, 195 N.E.2d 794, 25 O.O.2d 383, certiorari denied 84 S.Ct. 1938, 377 U.S. 1002, 12 L.Ed.2d 1051. Indictment And Information ⚷ 130

6. Offenses connected in commission

Probative value of extraneous offense or collateral crimes evidence of threatening e-mail defendant sent to victim one day after he was charged with assault for striking victim, along with pages from defendant's website linking e-mail to defendant, was not substantially outweighed by danger of unfair prejudice, at trial in which defendant stood accused of assault and, joined as offenses committed during single course of criminal conduct, intimidation and telecommunications harassment. State v. Taylor (Ohio App. 8 Dist., Cuyahoga, 12-18-2003) No. 82572, 2003-Ohio-6861, 2003 WL 22966270, Unreported. Criminal Law ⚷ 369.2(1)

Extraneous offense or collateral crimes evidence of threatening e-mail defendant sent to victim one day after he was charged with assault for striking victim, along with pages from defendant's website linking e-mail to defendant, was admissible as relevant to defendant's intent regarding intimidation and telecommunications harassment charges, all of which offenses were subject to joinder as committed throughout single course of criminal conduct; e-mail was not so remote in time as to be irrelevant to either intimidation count or telephone harassment count, and e-mail was relevant to defensive theory of innocent intent. State v. Taylor (Ohio App. 8 Dist., Cuyahoga, 12-18-2003) No. 82572, 2003-Ohio-6861, 2003 WL 22966270, Unreported. Criminal Law ⚷ 371(1)

Offenses with which defendant was charged, including felonious assault, intimidation, and telecommunications harassment, though allegedly perpetrated on different dates, were nevertheless part of a single course of criminal conduct, thus warranting joinder of offenses in same indictment; alleged assault on victim and her subsequent filing of charges was clearly relevant to defendant's intent to subsequently intimidate victim into dropping charges, and evidence of defendant's assault explained defendant's motive for repeatedly calling and threatening victim and her family to drop assault charges so he would not have to go back to prison. State v. Taylor (Ohio App. 8 Dist., Cuyahoga, 12-18-2003) No. 82572, 2003-Ohio-6861, 2003 WL 22966270, Unreported. Indictment And Information ⚷ 129(1)

An indictment containing three counts, viz., (1) conveying articles into a place of confinement to aid an escape; (2) illegal possession of an instrument for administering drugs; and (3) unlawful possession of a narcotic drug, does not violate RC 2941.04 and is not prejudicial to the appellant even though the first count is of a different class of crimes or offenses from the last two so long as there is ample proof in the record to connect the three counts in their commission. State v. Minnek-er (Ohio 1971) 27 Ohio St.2d 155, 271 N.E.2d 821, 56 O.O.2d 97.

Where an indictment contains three counts, as follows: (1) forging a check; (2) uttering a forged instrument; and (3) carrying a concealed weapon, to wit, a blackjack; the third of said counts is not connected together with the other two counts in its commission and is in a different class of crimes or offenses from the first two counts; and the indictment is therefore violative of RC 2941.04 and is subject to the remedy provided in RC 2941.28. State v. Atkinson (Ohio 1965) 4 Ohio St.2d 19, 211 N.E.2d 665, 33 O.O.2d 226.

Charges of burglary and larceny arising out of a single transaction may be united in one count. Carter v. Maxwell (Ohio 1964) 177 Ohio St. 35, 201 N.E.2d 705, 28 O.O.2d 455. Indictment And Information ⚷ 125(42)

Forgery and uttering a forged instrument are two separate and distinct crimes. Dean v. Green (Ohio 1964) 177 Ohio St. 22, 201 N.E.2d 598, 28 O.O.2d 421, certiorari denied 85 S.Ct. 1450, 381 U.S. 905, 14 L.Ed.2d 286.

An individual may at the same time and in the same transaction commit several separate and distinct crimes, and separate sentences may be imposed for each offense. Overmyer v. Sacks (Ohio 1962) 174 Ohio St. 129, 187 N.E.2d 50, 21 O.O.2d 389. Criminal Law ⚷ 29(1)

An accused may be indicted in separate counts for breaking and entering, driving a vehicle without the owner's consent, and for larceny. Matey v. Sacks (C.A.6 (Ohio) 1960) 284 F.2d 335, 15 O.O.2d 123.

Prosecution was not prohibited from charging defendant with both felonious assault and assault on a corrections officer, or from proceeding on both charges at trial, where such offenses where not allied offenses of similar import. State v. Karasek (Ohio App. 2 Dist., Montgomery, 05-24-2002) No. 17408, No. 17563, 2002-Ohio-2616, 2002 WL 1041939, Unreported, stay denied 96 Ohio St.3d 1455, 772 N.E.2d 125, 2002-Ohio-3819, appeal not allowed 96 Ohio St.3d 1516, 775 N.E.2d 857, 2002-Ohio-4950, reconsideration denied 97 Ohio St.3d 1461, 778 N.E.2d 1052, 2002-Ohio-6248, appeal not allowed 98 Ohio St.3d 1425, 782 N.E.2d 79, 2003-Ohio-259, reconsideration denied 98 Ohio St.3d 1492, 785 N.E.2d 474, 2003-Ohio-1189. Criminal Law ⚷ 29(9)

7. "Same evidence" rule

Where an offer of "any valuable thing" is made to influence the testimony of a person who has factual knowledge relevant to (but has not been subpoenaed or sworn in) grand jury proceedings pending against another, the ultimate and essential facts of, and the evidence used to prove, the offerer's violation of RC 2917.06 are identical to those which prove a violation of RC 2917.07 and there is but one offense, and the defendant-offerer may be sentenced only once; the failure of the defendant to challenge the sentencing under both statutes in the trial court does not waive the error of imposing two sentences under the two statutes. State v. Lieberman (Franklin 1961) 114 Ohio App. 339, 179 N.E.2d 108, 18 O.O.2d 25, rehearing denied 114 Ohio App. 339, 182 N.E.2d 569, appeal dismissed 172 Ohio St. 478, 178 N.E.2d 506, 17 O.O.2d 464, certiorari denied 83 S.Ct. 294, 371 U.S. 925, 9 L.Ed.2d 233, rehearing denied 83 S.Ct. 543, 371 U.S. 965, 9 L.Ed.2d 512.

A defendant may be indicted for and convicted of perjury and intimidation of the witness alleged to have committed perjury, but cannot be sentenced for both offenses. State v. Stiles (Cuyahoga 1962) 179 N.E.2d 76, 88 Ohio Law Abs. 412, 21 O.O.2d 240, appeal dismissed 174 Ohio St. 131, 186 N.E.2d 844, 21 O.O.2d 390. Indictment And Information ⚷ 130

RC 2941.04 does not permit an accused to be charged with and found guilty at one trial of two offenses where, if tried separately, conviction of one offense would be a bar to a conviction thereafter of the other. State v. Johnson (Cuyahoga 1960) 112 Ohio App. 124, 165 N.E.2d 814, 83 Ohio Law Abs. 437, 16 O.O.2d 51.

8. Joinder and severance

Defendant was not entitled to separate trials for charges of burglary and attempted burglary; defendant was acquitted on attempted burglary charge, evidence supporting burglary charge was overwhelming, evidence of attempted burglary did not add support to burglary charge and did not prejudice defendant, and there was nothing indicating that evidence from separate crimes could not be used in separate trials for each charge. State v. Bell (Ohio App. 1 Dist., Hamilton, 07-09-2004) No. C-030726, 2004-Ohio-3621, 2004 WL 1531904, Unreported, appeal not allowed 103 Ohio St.3d 1481, 816 N.E.2d 255, 2004-Ohio-5405. Criminal Law ⚷ 620(6)

Trial court did not err in refusing to order separate trials on each of three counts of gross sexual imposition; defendant failed to affirmatively demonstrate any prejudice in joinder of counts of indictment; moreover, jury was able to easily segregate evidence pertaining to each count in the indictment, and trial court instructed jury as to the importance of considering each count and evidence applicable to each count separately. State v. Strobel (Henry 1988) 51 Ohio App.3d 31, 554 N.E.2d 916. Criminal Law ⚷ 620(6)

Test for determining whether separate counts of indictment should be severed is not one of risk of prejudice, or even of fairness; instead, burden is on defendant to either affirmatively demonstrate before trial that his rights would be prejudiced by joinder or to show at the close of the state's case or at the conclusion of all the evidence that his rights actually have been prejudiced by joinder. State v. Williams (Ohio App. 10 Dist. 1981) 1 Ohio App.3d 156, 440 N.E.2d 65, 1 O.B.R. 467. Criminal Law ⚷ 620(3.1)

Abuse of discretion in denying an accused's request to be tried separately on each count of an indictment is not cognizable in habeas corpus. Braxton v. Maxwell (Ohio 1965) 1 Ohio St.2d 134, 205 N.E.2d 397, 30 O.O.2d 486.

Where indictment contained two counts, one charging accused with entering a bank and committing crime of robbery upon a person therein, and a second count charging that defendant entered bank with intent to steal money from bank, the two counts were properly joined in one indictment and a verdict of guilty could be returned on each count. Zenz v. Alvis (Franklin 1951) 118 N.E.2d 678, 66 Ohio Law Abs. 606. Indictment And Information ⚷ 129(1)

Where a defendant is indicted jointly with another defendant for burglary and for larceny and is indicted singly for receiving the same stolen property, knowing it to be stolen, as he is charged with stealing in the indictment for burglary and larceny, and the same evidence is necessary and used at the trial upon each indictment, it is not error for court to order such indictments consolidated and tried together. Beckman v. State (Ohio 1930) 122 Ohio St. 443, 5 N.E.2d 482, 8 Ohio Law Abs. 353, 32 Ohio Law Rep. 111.

Where an indictment charges three offenses and no objection is made thereto and no request is made for a severance, the sufficiency of the indictment cannot be reviewed in habeas corpus proceedings. Via v. Perini (C.A.6 (Ohio) 1969) 23 Ohio Misc. 358, 415 F.2d 1052, 50 O.O.2d 512, 52 O.O.2d 361.

Indictment for burglary and larceny against defendant and another *held* properly consolidated with indictment against defendant alone for receiving same stolen property, where same evidence supported each indictment. Beckman v. State (Ohio 1930) 172 N.E. 145.

9. Inconsistent verdicts

Individual counts in indictment are not interdependent and an inconsistency in a verdict does not arise out of inconsistent responses to different counts, but only arises out of inconsistent responses to same count. State v. Gleason (Ohio App. 9 Dist., 04-03-1996) 110 Ohio App.3d 240, 673 N.E.2d 985, appeal not allowed 77 Ohio St.3d 1416, 670 N.E.2d 1004. Criminal Law ⚷ 878(4)

A verdict of guilty of aggravated robbery, necessarily predicated on the defendant's possession or control of a deadly weapon, may stand even though it is inconsistent with the jury's not guilty verdict on a firearm specification. State v. Woodson (Franklin 1985) 24 Ohio App.3d 143, 493 N.E.2d 1018, 24 O.B.R. 231.

The offenses of kidnapping, gross sexual imposition, and rape each have a separate animus, so that verdicts of not guilty on two charges and guilty on the third charge are not inconsistent and invalid where there is testimony on temporary insanity. State v. Brown (Ohio 1984) 12 Ohio St.3d 147, 465 N.E.2d 889, 12 O.B.R. 186.

The general rule against attacks on inconsistent verdicts does not except cases in which a jury acquits of a predicate felony while convicting on a compound felony; thus, a conviction of a defendant for use of a telephone to facilitate both a conspiracy to possess cocaine and possession of cocaine need not be reversed merely because it cannot be reconciled with an acquittal of the defendant by the jury at the same trial on conspiracy and possession charges. U.S. v. Powell (U.S.Cal. 1984) 105 S.Ct. 471, 469 U.S. 57, 83 L.Ed.2d 461.

2941.05 Statement charging an offense

In an indictment or information charging an offense, each count shall contain, and is sufficient if it contains in substance, a statement that the accused has committed some public offense therein specified. Such statement may be made in ordinary and concise language without any technical averments or any allegations not essential to be proved. It may be in the words of the section of the Revised Code describing the offense or declaring the matter charged to be a public offense, or in any words sufficient to give the accused notice of the offense of which he is charged.

(126 v 392, eff. 3-17-55; 1953 H 1; GC 13437-4)

Historical and Statutory Notes

Pre-1953 H 1 Amendments: 113 v 163, Ch 16, § 4

Cross References

Indictment and information, Crim R 7

Library References

Indictment and Information ⚷55 to 123.

Westlaw Topic No. 210.

C.J.S. Breach of the Peace § 7.

C.J.S. Drugs and Narcotics § 225.

C.J.S. Elections § 339.

C.J.S. Embezzlement § 27.

C.J.S. Escape and Related Offenses; Rescue § 34.

C.J.S. Forgery §§ 45, 53, 74, 76.

C.J.S. Fraud § 103.

C.J.S. Homicide §§ 140 to 141.

C.J.S. Landlord and Tenant § 1246.

C.J.S. Larceny § 70.

C.J.S. Mayhem § 8.

C.J.S. Monopolies § 246.

C.J.S. Parent and Child § 368.

C.J.S. Receiving or Transferring Stolen Goods and Related Offenses §§ 17 to 20.

C.J.S. Robbery §§ 35, 83.

C.J.S. Telecommunications § 131.

C.J.S. Threats and Unlawful Communications § 23.

Research References

Encyclopedias

OH Jur. 3d Family Law § 1740, Commencement of Proceedings—Charges in an Affidavit.

Treatises and Practice Aids

Katz, Giannelli, Blair and Lipton, Baldwin's Ohio Practice, Criminal Law, § 40:5, Nature and Contents.

Katz, Giannelli, Blair and Lipton, Baldwin's Ohio Practice, Criminal Law, § 142:1, Skeleton Indictment—Single Count.

Katz, Giannelli, Blair and Lipton, Baldwin's Ohio Practice, Criminal Law, § 142:2, Skeleton Indictment—Multiple Counts.

Katz, Giannelli, Blair and Lipton, Baldwin's Ohio Practice, Criminal Law, § 142:14, Skeleton Information.

Notes of Decisions

---

1. Sufficiency of indictment

Trial court improperly dismissed count of indictment, charging defendant with making terroristic threats, based upon state's alleged failure to plead underlying specified offense; indictment averred material facts constituting essential elements of offense, affording defendant notice and an opportunity to defend, any alleged defect in indictment was remedied by defendant's requesting and state's rendering bill of particulars delineating nature of offense charged and conduct alleged to constitute offense, and bill of particulars clearly put defendant on notice actual felony offense of violence was felonious assault. State v. Roach (Ohio App. 5 Dist., 11-23-2005) 165 Ohio App.3d 167, 845 N.E.2d 537, 2005-Ohio-6301. Extortion And Threats ⚷ 30; Indictment And Information ⚷ 121.5

Indictment for conspiracy to commit aggravated robbery was fatally defective, in that it did not specifically identify substantial overt act committed by defendant in furtherance of offense. State v. Bunch (Ohio App. 7 Dist., Mahoning, 06-24-2005) No. 02 CA 196, 2005-Ohio-3309, 2005 WL 1523844, Unreported, appeal allowed 107 Ohio St.3d 1680, 839 N.E.2d 401, 2005-Ohio-6480. Conspiracy ⚷ 43(5)

Indictment which charged defendant with committing three counts of rape of a child under the age of 13 but failed to specify the exact date on which the rapes allegedly occurred did not deprive defendant of due process; defendant was charged with raping his step-daughter, defendant lived with victim for 16 months, indictment alleged that the rapes occurred in the family home on occasions when mother was running errands or was otherwise out of the house, defendant failed to file notice of an alibi defense, and the victim testified to generalized dates and times at trial. State v. Alicea (Ohio App. 7 Dist., Mahoning, 12-11-2002) No. 99 CA 36, 2002-Ohio-6907, 2002 WL 31813090, Unreported, appeal not allowed 98 Ohio St.3d 1515, 786 N.E.2d 64, 2003-Ohio-1572, habeas corpus denied 2005 WL 2280281. Indictment And Information ⚷ 87(7)

Trial court's consideration of defendant's motion to dismiss indictment for failure to make out offense charged therein should have been restricted to review of face of indictment, and should not have included review of facts included in bill of particulars. State v. Silos (Ohio App. 9 Dist., 05-10-1995) 104 Ohio App.3d 23, 660 N.E.2d 1239. Indictment And Information ⚷ 144.2

A complaint charging a violation of RC 3773.24 "on or about Sunday the 6th day of January, 1963," is not indefinite and vague; the use of the disjunctive "or" in such complaint in charging that the accused "did suffer or permit a building to be open for transaction of business on Sunday" does not render such charge indefinite and vague; the omission of the words "against the peace and dignity of the state of Ohio" does not render it defective; such complaint is not defective because it charges the accused with a violation of such statute as an individual and does not set out the capacity in which he is supposed to have acted; and such complaint is not defective because it does not negate the exceptions contained in such statute. State v. Whitt (Montgomery 1964) 3 Ohio App.2d 278, 210 N.E.2d 279, 32 O.O.2d 382.

Indictment for aggravated robbery and robbery was legally sufficient, though indictment misstated which convenience store employee the defendant had subjected to physical harm during the robbery; defendant was aware that he was charged with armed robbery, and prosecutor had offered at trial to amend the indictment if it perplexed defense counsel. State v. Fields (Ohio App. 1 Dist., Hamilton, 08-30-2002) No. C-010720, No. C-010688, 2002-Ohio-4451, 2002 WL 1988273, Unreported, motion for delayed appeal denied 97 Ohio St.3d 1495, 780 N.E.2d 600, 2002-Ohio-7200. Indictment And Information ⚷ 101; Robbery ⚷ 17(1)

2. Essential elements

Where the existence of a prior conviction enhances the penalty for a subsequent offense but does not elevate the degree thereof, the prior conviction is not an essential element and need not be alleged in the indictment or proven as a matter of fact. State v. Allen (Ohio 1987) 29 Ohio St.3d 53, 506 N.E.2d 199, 29 O.B.R. 436. Indictment And Information ⚷ 113; Indictment And Information ⚷ 166

To be sufficient, an affidavit must set forth the facts and not merely the conclusions of law constituting the crime, so that the accused may have notice of what he is to meet; of the act done which he must controvert; and so that the court, applying the law to the facts charged, may see that a crime has been committed. City of Lima v. Ward (Allen 1966) 8 Ohio App.2d 177, 220 N.E.2d 843, 37 O.O.2d 193, reversed 10 Ohio St.2d 137, 226 N.E.2d 737, 39 O.O.2d 123.

While the court recognizes and will apply the liberal provisions of criminal code, GC 13437–4 (RC 2941.05) et seq., it will uphold the constitutional right of an accused to be advised in the indictment of the nature and cause of the accusation he is expected to meet; and all necessary elements of the crime must be in the indictment. Harris v. State (Ohio 1932) 125 Ohio St. 257, 181 N.E. 104, 36 Ohio Law Rep. 328.

On motion to dismiss indictments charging operating a gambling house and illegal gambling, trial court properly refused to find that classification of poker as "game of chance" was unconstitutional; issue of whether poker was a game of chance or skill was not properly before trial court, as indictments did not specify type of gambling involved. City of Akron v. Buzek (Ohio App. 9 Dist., Summit, 04-24-2002) No. 20728, 2002-Ohio-1960, 2002 WL 712731, Unreported. Indictment And Information ⚷ 144.2

An indictment for violation of RC 4301.69 is not insufficient merely because it specifies the sale of "beer" rather than "intoxicating liquor" to a minor. State v Poe, No. CA 13693 (9th Dist Ct App, Summit, 3–8–89).

A conviction, without trial, based merely on a no contest plea to an indictment which does not allege sufficient facts to constitute an offense is void. State v Hayes, No. 5–82–11 (3d Dist Ct App, Hancock, 1–14–83).

3. Charge to be in words of statute—in general

That part of RC 2905.34 which provides that "No person shall knowingly... have in his possession or under his control... a drug, medicine, article, or thing intended for causing an abortion" is constitutionally valid and is separable from the remainder of such statute, and an indictment charging an offense in the language of the above quoted part is sufficient. State v. Guerrieri (Mahoning 1969) 20 Ohio App.2d 132, 252 N.E.2d 179, 49 O.O.2d 162. Statutes ⚷ 64(6)

An affidavit which charges the commission of an offense and is drawn in the words of a municipal ordinance is not void for indefiniteness, and the sufficiency of such affidavit should have been raised by motion to quash before issued joined. City of Lima v. Ward (Ohio 1967) 10 Ohio St.2d 137, 226 N.E.2d 737, 39 O.O.2d 123.

An indictment need not be in the exact language of the statute charging the offense, so long as all essential elements of the crime are contained in language equivalent to that used in the statute. State v. Childers (Ohio 1938) 133 Ohio St. 508, 14 N.E.2d 767, 11 O.O. 191. Indictment And Information ⚷ 110(2)

Indictment charging defendant with attempting to evade or defeat income tax due and owing over a five-year period, through his failure to file a tax return during that time, was sufficient to charge defendant with tax evasion, even though indictment did not additionally indicate statute that makes an individual liable for an income tax, or statute that requires an individual to pay the income tax for which he is liable. U.S. v. Middleton (C.A.6 (Ohio), 04-18-2001) 246 F.3d 825, rehearing en banc denied. Indictment And Information ⚷ 108

4. —— Mens rea, charge to be in words of statute

Indictment charging defendant with one count of child endangering, and one count involuntary manslaughter based upon underlying felony of child endangering, and was defective, where indictment failed to contain culpable mental state; recklessness was culpable mental state for crime of child endangering, and indictment did not include culpable mental state of reckless, and thus, since indictment did not include element of recklessness, indictment was insufficient and failed to charge offense. State v. Conley (Ohio App. 5 Dist., Perry, 06-14-2005)

No. 03-CA-18, 2005-Ohio-3257, 2005 WL 1503589, Unreported. Indictment And Information ⚷ 88; Infants ⚷ 13

It was not ineffective assistance for defendant's trial counsel to fail to object to child endangerment indictment against defendant, though indictment did not include requisite mens rea element of recklessness; outcome would not have been different had indictment included mens rea element. State v. Ivey (Ohio App. 8 Dist., 10-03-1994) 98 Ohio App.3d 249, 648 N.E.2d 519, dismissed, appeal not allowed 71 Ohio St.3d 1476, 645 N.E.2d 1257. Criminal Law ⚷ 641.13(2.1)

Where a city ordinance conflicts with a state statute in that the former does not specifically enunciate the requirement of mens rea prescribed in the latter, a conviction under ordinance will not be reversed upon the basis of such conflict where court charged jury that finding of mens rea was an essential prerequisite to a verdict of guilty. City of Cincinnati v. Hoffman (Ohio 1972) 31 Ohio St.2d 163, 285 N.E.2d 714, 60 O.O.2d 117, appeal dismissed, certiorari denied 93 S.Ct. 1370, 410 U.S. 920, 35 L.Ed.2d 583. Municipal Corporations ⚷ 642(1)

Where a criminal statute does not clearly make a certain specific intent an element of the offense, but judicial interpretation has made such intent a necessary element, an indictment charging the offense solely in the language of the statute is insufficient. State v. Ross (Ohio 1967) 12 Ohio St.2d 37, 231 N.E.2d 299, 41 O.O.2d 220. Indictment And Information ⚷ 110(4)

An indictment charging an offense under RC 2915.11 is legally sufficient if it contains a statement charging the offense in the words of such section, hence it is not essential that the indictment specifically alleges scienter (knowledge) or mens rea (guilty purpose). State v. Lisbon Sales Book Co. (Ohio 1964) 176 Ohio St. 482, 200 N.E.2d 590, 27 O.O.2d 443, appeal dismissed, certiorari denied 85 S.Ct. 703, 379 U.S. 673, 13 L.Ed.2d 609.

An allegation that an accused purposely killed is equivalent to an allegation that the accused intentionally killed. White v. Maxwell (Ohio 1963) 174 Ohio St. 186, 187 N.E.2d 878, 22 O.O.2d 140, certiorari denied 84 S.Ct. 151, 375 U.S. 880, 11 L.Ed.2d 112.

5. —— Omission of words and phrases, charge to be in words of statute

Indictment charging defendant with raping his son was not fatally deficient in failing to include statutory language, "whether or not the offender knows the age of such person"; omission of such language was not prejudicial to defendant in context of allegations against him. State v. Smelcer (Cuyahoga 1993) 89 Ohio App.3d 115, 623 N.E.2d 1219, dismissed, jurisdictional motion overruled 67 Ohio St.3d 1502, 622 N.E.2d 650, dismissal of post-conviction relief affirmed. Sodomy ⚷ 5

An indictment for the crime of attempt, RC 2923.02, is not insufficient in that it specifies the attempted crime only by its code section number and not its name. State v. Reyna (Lorain 1985) 24 Ohio App.3d 79, 493 N.E.2d 555, 24 O.B.R. 148.

An indictment under RC 4931.31 for threatening over a telephone to do bodily harm, is not fatally defective for failure to contain the exact words used constituting such "threat" within the scope of the statute; and it is sufficient if the language used in the indictment is, in substance, the language of the statute creating the offense. State v. Goode (Greene 1962) 118 Ohio App. 479, 195 N.E.2d 581, 25 O.O.2d 395, appeal dismissed 174 Ohio St. 232, 188 N.E.2d 421, 22 O.O.2d 224.

An indictment for armed robbery is not invalidated by the omission of the phrase "from the person of" therefrom. Salzer v. Maxwell (Ohio 1962) 173 Ohio St. 573, 184 N.E.2d 396, 20 O.O.2d 172.

Inclusion of the phrase "on the body of" is not essential in an indictment for assault with intent to rape. Boynton v. Sacks (Ohio 1962) 173 Ohio St. 526, 184 N.E.2d 377, 20 O.O.2d 146, certiorari denied 83 S.Ct. 299, 371 U.S. 928, 9 L.Ed.2d 235.

It is not necessary to allege in an indictment for armed robbery that the action was committed unlawfully. Boynton v. Sacks (Ohio 1962) 173 Ohio St. 526, 184 N.E.2d 377, 20 O.O.2d 146, certiorari denied 83 S.Ct. 299, 371 U.S. 928, 9 L.Ed.2d 235.

The omission of the words "against her will" in an indictment charging aggravated rape does not invalidate such indictment. Weaver v. Sacks (Ohio 1962) 173 Ohio St. 415, 183 N.E.2d 373, 20 O.O.2d 43, certiorari denied 83 S.Ct. 134, 371 U.S. 870, 9 L.Ed.2d 107.

An indictment charging unlawful possession of a narcotic drug without specifying the particular drug is valid. Williams v. Eckle (Ohio 1962) 173 Ohio St. 410, 183 N.E.2d 365, 20 O.O.2d 40, certiorari denied 83 S.Ct. 154, 371 U.S. 881, 9 L.Ed.2d 118. Controlled Substances ⚷ 65

6. —— Omission of section number, charge to be in words of statute

RC 2941.05 does not require that numerical designations of a section of the Revised Code immediately follow the charge in an indictment. State v. Hughley (Trumbull 1984) 20 Ohio App.3d 77, 484 N.E.2d 758, 20 O.B.R. 97.

The failure to include the section number of the statute alleged to have been violated does not invalidate an indictment. Foutty v. Maxwell (Ohio 1962) 174 Ohio St. 35, 186 N.E.2d 623, 21 O.O.2d 288.

There being a complete description of the crime in the indictment, the failure to designate the code section did not invalidate the indictment. Norton v. Green (Ohio 1962) 173 Ohio St. 531, 184 N.E.2d 401, 20 O.O.2d 148.

7. —— Overbroad charge, charge to be in words of statute

Where affidavit charged defendant with driving while under the influence of intoxicating liquor, narcotic drugs, or opiates in violation of RC 4511.19, defendant was entitled to a bill of particulars. State v. Fowler (Ohio 1963) 174 Ohio St. 362,

189 N.E.2d 133, 22 O.O.2d 416. Criminal Law ⚷ 1167(1)

A defendant's conviction for driving with a breath alcohol concentration over the legal limit in violation of RC 4511.19(A)(3) will be reversed where the Uniform Traffic Ticket issued to her by the arresting officer lists "B.A.C. Test" as the description of the offense charged but does not state any statute or ordinance upon which the offense is based; a statute or ordinance reference is a bare minimum requirement if the issuing officer uses an abbreviated or shorthand description of the offense. State v Quicci, No. 16642, 1994 WL 654865 (9th Dist Ct App, Summit, 11–23–94).

8. Notice of charge and its sufficiency

Indictment for aggravated robbery and robbery was legally sufficient, though indictment misstated which convenience store employee the defendant had subjected to physical harm during the robbery; defendant was aware that he was charged with armed robbery, and prosecutor had offered at trial to amend the indictment if it perplexed defense counsel. State v. Fields (Ohio App. 1 Dist., Hamilton, 08-30-2002) No. C-010720, No. C-010688, 2002-Ohio-4451, 2002 WL 1988273, Unreported, motion for delayed appeal denied 97 Ohio St.3d 1495, 780 N.E.2d 600, 2002-Ohio-7200. Indictment And Information ⚷ 101; Robbery ⚷ 17(1)

Indictment compels the government to aver all material facts constituting the essential elements of an offense, thus affording the accused adequate notice and an opportunity to defend. State v. Childs (Ohio, 03-15-2000) 88 Ohio St.3d 194, 724 N.E.2d 781, 2000-Ohio-298. Indictment And Information ⚷ 60; Indictment And Information ⚷ 71.2(3)

By identifying and defining the offenses of which the individual is accused, an indictment serves to protect the individual from future prosecutions for the same offense. State v. Childs (Ohio, 03-15-2000) 88 Ohio St.3d 194, 724 N.E.2d 781, 2000-Ohio-298. Indictment And Information ⚷ 71.2(4)

While ordinarily precise times and dates are not essential elements of offenses and temporal information is generally irrelevant in preparing a defense, the state must, in response to a bill of particulars or demand for discovery, supply specific dates and times with regard to an alleged offense where it possesses such information; adherence to this rule will insure that no constitutional right of an accused to due process or a fair trial will be transgressed. State v. Sellards (Ohio 1985) 17 Ohio St.3d 169, 478 N.E.2d 781, 17 O.B.R. 410.

The purpose of an indictment is to inform the accused of the crime with which he is charged; the indictment may be laid in any of the different forms set forth in RC 2941.05, and, inasmuch as the phraseology of the indictment is in the words of RC 2907.10 defendant was fully informed of the crime of which he was charged. State v. Flowers (Pickaway 1971) 29 Ohio App.2d 105, 278 N.E.2d 680, 58 O.O.2d 160.

In a criminal proceeding where defendant is indicted for for "willfully making an indecent exposure of his person in a public place," the words "indecent exposure" are not vague and indefinite, but have a well defined, well understood and generally accepted meaning sufficient to advise accused of the nature of his alleged act. State v. Borchard (Athens 1970) 24 Ohio App.2d 95, 264 N.E.2d 646, 53 O.O.2d 254.

An indictment is not made invalid for surplus allegations such as naming obsolete sections of the Ohio General Code, or for defects or imperfections in the sentence, or for other defects or imperfections when the words of the indictment are sufficient to give the accused notice of the offenses of which he is charged. State v. Turpin (Stark 1969) 19 Ohio App.2d 116, 250 N.E.2d 94, 48 O.O.2d 236.

An affidavit which charges, in the words of a municipal ordinance, the commission of the offense prohibited by such ordinance, is not sufficient when the words of the ordinance fail to set out the facts which constitute such offense so as to apprise the accused of the nature and cause of the accusation against him. City of Lima v. Ward (Allen 1966) 8 Ohio App.2d 177, 220 N.E.2d 843, 37 O.O.2d 193, reversed 10 Ohio St.2d 137, 226 N.E.2d 737, 39 O.O.2d 123. Municipal Corporations ⚷ 639(1)

A charge that one "unlawfully did disturb the peace and good order of the city of Akron by intoxication," in violation of a municipal penal ordinance providing that "no person shall disturb the peace and good order of the city by intoxication," is so specific as to give notice of the act made unlawful, and so exclusive as to prevent its application to any acts other than those made unlawful, and is therefore sufficient to sustain a conviction on constitutional grounds. City of Akron v. Sabol (Summit 1965) 2 Ohio App.2d 109, 206 N.E.2d 575, 31 O.O.2d 166. Municipal Corporations ⚷ 639(1)

9. Waiver of defects

An indictment which employs fully the words of the statute describing the offense will support the conviction of the accused where no bill of particulars is requested or where no objection to the sufficiency of the indictment is interposed before submission of the case to a jury. State v. Simmans (Ohio 1970) 21 Ohio St.2d 258, 257 N.E.2d 344, 50 O.O.2d 487. Indictment And Information ⚷ 110(3)

Where defendant moved to quash an affidavit charging reckless operation of a motor vehicle, which was overruled, and then proceeded to trial on the merits without requesting a bill of particulars, the objection to the sufficiency of the affidavit was waived. State v. Hutton (Ohio 1937) 132 Ohio St. 461, 9 N.E.2d 295, 8 O.O. 411.

10. Variance—between allegations and proof

Where it is claimed that prejudicial error intervened in trial of criminal case in that trial court charged on element not laid in indictment, and charge exacted of prosecution proof of additional facts not necessary to sustain charge as stated in valid indictment, such claim is not valid. State v. Stone (Ross 1971) 30 Ohio App.2d 49, 283 N.E.2d 188, 59 O.O.2d 115.

Where an indictment containing four counts of armed robbery alleges that the property taken from the person of the victim is owned by the one named therein, and the proof establishes that such property was the personal property of the several victims, the trial judge does not commit error when, on motion, he permits an amendment of such indictment to show the true owners of the thing of value stolen; armed robbery is an offense against the person, not against property. State v. Dye (Summit 1968) 14 Ohio App.2d 7, 235 N.E.2d 250, 43 O.O.2d 18. Indictment And Information ⚷ 159(2)

11. —— Between affidavit and indictment, variance

The fact that the charge in the indictment does not conform to that originally made in the affidavit does not affect the validity of the conviction. Stebelton v. Haskins (Ohio 1964) 177 Ohio St. 52, 201 N.E.2d 884, 29 O.O.2d 76.

12. Indictment pending preliminary hearing

Once an indictment has been returned by the grand jury, a preliminary hearing before a magistrate is no longer necessary. (See also State v Wigglesworth, 28 OS(2d) 28, 274 NE(2d) 759 (1971).) State v. Wigglesworth (Ohio 1969) 18 Ohio St.2d 171, 248 N.E.2d 607, 47 O.O.2d 388, reversed 91 S.Ct. 2284, 403 U.S. 947, 29 L.Ed.2d 857, on remand 28 Ohio St.2d 28, 274 N.E.2d 759, 57 O.O.2d 102.

2941.06 Form of indictment or information

An indictment may be substantially in the following form:

"The State of Ohio,)
ss.
________ County)
In the Year _____.

The jurors of the Grand Jury of the State of Ohio, within and for the body of the County aforesaid, on their oaths, in the name and by the authority of the State of Ohio, do find and present that A.B., on the _____ day of ________, _____, at the county of ________ aforesaid, did ________ (here insert the name of the offense if it has one, such as murder, arson, or the like, or if a misdemeanor having no general name, insert a brief description of it as given by law) contrary to the form of the statute in such case made and provided, and against the peace and dignity of the State of Ohio.

________ C.D. ________

(Indorsed) A true bill. Prosecuting Attorney
E.F., Foreperson of the Grand Jury."

(2000 H 495, eff. 5–9–00; 1976 H 390, eff. 8–6–76; 1953 H 1; GC 13437–5)

Historical and Statutory Notes

Pre–1953 H 1 Amendments: 113 v 163, Ch 16, § 5

Amendment Note: 2000 H 495 deleted references to nineteen hundred dates; made changes to reflect gender neutral language; and made other nonsubstantive changes.

Cross References

Indictment and information, Crim R 7
Indictment for violation of monopoly law; form, 1331.09
Style of process, prosecution, and indictment, O Const Art IV §20

Library References

Indictment and Information ⚷35 to 54, 55 to 123.
Westlaw Topic No. 210.
C.J.S. Breach of the Peace § 7.
C.J.S. Drugs and Narcotics § 225.
C.J.S. Elections § 339.
C.J.S. Embezzlement § 27.
C.J.S. Escape and Related Offenses; Rescue § 34.
C.J.S. Forgery §§ 45, 53, 74, 76.
C.J.S. Fraud § 103.
C.J.S. Homicide §§ 140 to 141.
C.J.S. Landlord and Tenant § 1246.
C.J.S. Larceny § 70.
C.J.S. Mayhem § 8.
C.J.S. Monopolies § 246.
C.J.S. Parent and Child § 368.
C.J.S. Receiving or Transferring Stolen Goods and Related Offenses §§ 17 to 20.
C.J.S. Robbery §§ 35, 83.

C.J.S. Telecommunications § 131.

C.J.S. Threats and Unlawful Communications § 23.

Research References

Encyclopedias

OH Jur. 3d Criminal Law § 2339, Authorized Forms.

OH Jur. 3d Criminal Law § 2374, Venue.

OH Jur. 3d Criminal Law § 2375, Date.

Treatises and Practice Aids

Katz, Giannelli, Blair and Lipton, Baldwin's Ohio Practice, Criminal Law, § 40:5, Nature and Contents.

Katz, Giannelli, Blair and Lipton, Baldwin's Ohio Practice, Criminal Law, § 142:1, Skeleton Indictment—Single Count.

Katz, Giannelli, Blair and Lipton, Baldwin's Ohio Practice, Criminal Law, § 142:2, Skeleton Indictment—Multiple Counts.

Katz, Giannelli, Blair and Lipton, Baldwin's Ohio Practice, Criminal Law, § 142:14, Skeleton Information.

Notes of Decisions

Form of indictment 1
Sufficiency of indictment 2

1. Form of indictment

The forms of indictment set forth in the statutes are not mandatory. Turpin v. Sacks (C.A.6 (Ohio) 1961) 291 F.2d 223, 17 O.O.2d 31, certiorari denied 82 S.Ct. 94, 368 U.S. 855, 7 L.Ed.2d 53.

2. Sufficiency of indictment

Indictment presented to grand jury adequately provided that crimes for which defendant was charged occurred within jurisdiction of court, by alleging that offenses were committed within certain county. State v. Carpenter (Ohio App. 7 Dist., 12-06-1996) 116 Ohio App.3d 292, 688 N.E.2d 14. Indictment And Information ⚿ 86(2)

An indictment for the crime of attempt, RC 2923.02, is not insufficient in that it specifies the attempted crime only by its code section number and not its name. State v. Reyna (Lorain 1985) 24 Ohio App.3d 79, 493 N.E.2d 555, 24 O.B.R. 148.

2941.07 Bill of particulars

Upon written request of the defendant made not later than five days prior to the date set for trial, or upon order of the court, the prosecuting attorney shall furnish a bill of particulars setting up specifically the nature of the offense charged and the conduct of the defendant which is alleged to constitute the offense.

(1972 H 511, eff. 1–1–74; 1953 H 1; GC 13437–6)

Historical and Statutory Notes

Pre–1953 H 1 Amendments: 113 v 164, Ch 16, § 6

Cross References

Bill of particulars, Crim R 7

Library References

Indictment and Information ⚿121.

Westlaw Topic No. 210.

C.J.S. Receiving or Transferring Stolen Goods and Related Offenses §§ 17 to 20.

C.J.S. Telecommunications § 131.

Research References

Encyclopedias

OH Jur. 3d Family Law § 1740, Commencement of Proceedings—Charges in an Affidavit.

Treatises and Practice Aids

Katz, Giannelli, Blair and Lipton, Baldwin's Ohio Practice, Criminal Law, § 40:9, Bill of Particulars.

Katz, Giannelli, Blair and Lipton, Baldwin's Ohio Practice, Criminal Law, § 142:9, Motion for Bill of Particulars.

Katz, Giannelli, Blair and Lipton, Baldwin's Ohio Practice, Criminal Law, § 142:10, Defendant's Motion for a Bill of Particulars or in the Alternative, for Inspection of Grand Jury Minutes or to Dismiss the Indictment on Constitutional Grounds.

Katz, Giannelli, Blair and Lipton, Baldwin's Ohio Practice, Criminal Law, § 142:11, Court Order for Bill of Particulars.

Katz, Giannelli, Blair and Lipton, Baldwin's Ohio Practice, Criminal Law, § 142:12, Bill of Particulars.

Hennenberg & Reinhart, Ohio Criminal Defense Motions F 2.22, Motion for Bill of Particulars-Conduct of Defendant-Discovery Demands and Motions.

Notes of Decisions

---

1. In general

Having withdrawn request for bill of particulars before state had opportunity to respond, defendant could not assert on appeal that he was prejudiced by state's failure to respond. State v. Feliciano (Ohio App. 9 Dist., 11-20-1996) 115 Ohio App.3d 646, 685 N.E.2d 1307, appeal not allowed 78 Ohio St.3d 1442, 676 N.E.2d 1187. Criminal Law ⚷ 1137(2)

Motion for bill of particulars and motion for change of venue both tolled time for speedy trial. State v. Grinnell (Ohio App. 10 Dist., 06-27-1996) 112 Ohio App.3d 124, 678 N.E.2d 231, appeal not allowed 77 Ohio St.3d 1474, 673 N.E.2d 138, appeal not allowed 77 Ohio St.3d 1475, 673 N.E.2d 138, denial of habeas corpus affirmed 215 F.3d 1326, certiorari denied 121 S.Ct. 232, 531 U.S. 898, 148 L.Ed.2d 166. Criminal Law ⚷ 577.10(8)

Bill of particulars cannot cure defects in indictment; rather, purpose of bill of particulars is merely to provide greater detail to accused of nature and cause of charge against him or her, not to provide missing pieces in indictment. State v. Lewis (Allen 1993) 85 Ohio App.3d 29, 619 N.E.2d 57, dismissed, jurisdictional motion overruled 66 Ohio St.3d 1494, 613 N.E.2d 236, rehearing denied 67 Ohio St.3d 1407, 615 N.E.2d 630, certiorari denied 114 S.Ct. 685, 510 U.S. 1041, 126 L.Ed.2d 652. Indictment And Information ⚷ 121.1(5)

Bill of particulars provision is a reasonable provision, procedural in substance, and denies no rights guaranteed to a person accused of crime. State v. Whitmore (Ohio 1933) 126 Ohio St. 381, 185 N.E. 547, 37 Ohio Law Rep. 560.

2. Sufficiency of charge

Bill of particulars provided by state in rape prosecution was sufficient to fulfill its intended purpose, as it set out date of alleged offenses, general nature of alleged conduct, and applicable statute. State v. Brown (Ohio App. 7 Dist., Mahoning, 06-07-2005) No. 03-MA-32, 2005-Ohio-2939, 2005 WL 1385715, Unreported, appeal not allowed 106 Ohio St.3d 1558, 836 N.E.2d 582, 2005-Ohio-5531. Indictment And Information ⚷ 121.4

Any error committed by trial court, during trial for personating an officer, in allegedly relying on bill of particulars to define legal term "personate" was harmless, where bill of particulars was consistent with statutory definition of crime of personating an officer. State v. Powell (Ohio App. 12 Dist., 07-19-1999) 134 Ohio App.3d 616, 731 N.E.2d 1170. Criminal Law ⚷ 1172.1(3)

Bill of particulars cannot save defective indictment. State v. Grinnell (Ohio App. 10 Dist., 06-27-1996) 112 Ohio App.3d 124, 678 N.E.2d 231, appeal not allowed 77 Ohio St.3d 1474, 673 N.E.2d 138, appeal not allowed 77 Ohio St.3d 1475, 673 N.E.2d 138, denial of habeas corpus affirmed 215 F.3d 1326, certiorari denied 121 S.Ct. 232, 531 U.S. 898, 148 L.Ed.2d 166. Indictment And Information ⚷ 121.1(5)

The serial numbers of stolen guns are not essential elements of the charge of receiving stolen firearms and a defendant's ability to defend himself is not compromised by the fact that the bill of particulars lists the wrong serial numbers. State v. Webb (Huron 1991) 72 Ohio App.3d 749, 596 N.E.2d 489.

An indictment need not be in the exact language of the statute defining the offense, so long as all the essential elements of the crime are contained in language equivalent to that used in the statute, and the accused is advised in the indictment of the nature and cause of the accusation he is expected to meet. State v. Oliver (Ohio 1972) 32 Ohio St.2d 109, 290 N.E.2d 828, 61 O.O.2d 371. Indictment And Information ⚷ 110(2)

Inclusion of the phrase "on the body of" is not essential in an indictment for assault with intent to rape. Boynton v. Sacks (Ohio 1962) 173 Ohio St. 526, 184 N.E.2d 377, 20 O.O.2d 146, certiorari denied 83 S.Ct. 299, 371 U.S. 928, 9 L.Ed.2d 235.

The omission of the words "against her will" in an indictment charging aggravated rape does not invalidate such indictment. Weaver v. Sacks (Ohio 1962) 173 Ohio St. 415, 183 N.E.2d 373, 20 O.O.2d 43, certiorari denied 83 S.Ct. 134, 371 U.S. 870, 9 L.Ed.2d 107.

The form authorized by RC 2941.07 for charging the crime of attempted burglary, permits the use of either the word, "steal," or the phrase, "commit a felony." In re Bolin (Franklin 1960) 113 Ohio App. 268, 177 N.E.2d 797, 88 Ohio Law Abs. 237, 17 O.O.2d 263. Indictment And Information ⚷ 19

An indictment for larceny is not defective because it fails to charge that the act was "unlawfully" done and that the accused did "feloniously take and carry away" the property, where the indictment conforms with RC 2941.07, and concludes with the phrase, "contrary to the form of the statute in such case made and provided, and against the peace and dignity of the state of Ohio." Hamilton v. Alvis (Franklin 1959) 109 Ohio App. 298, 160 N.E.2d 372, 81 Ohio Law Abs. 54, 11 O.O.2d 54.

In order to establish that a father's carnal knowledge of his ten-year-old daughter constitutes the crime of aggravated rape it is essential to prove that the carnal knowledge of the victim was "against her will," i.e., without her consent, even where the father was eighteen or over. State v. Daniels (Ohio 1959) 169 Ohio St. 87, 157 N.E.2d 736, 76 A.L.R.2d 468, 8 O.O.2d 56.

3. Right to bill of particulars—in general

State's delay in providing defendant with bill of particulars, while not to be condoned, did not prejudice defendant, in rape prosecution; county in which defendant was prosecuted had somewhat unique policy of "open discovery" in prosecutor's office, and, thus, all of state's evidence was available for defendant and his counsel to examine in preparation for trial, including police reports and witness statements, and thus defendant would have been able to determine what time of day alleged crimes occurred and what type of sexual conduct was alleged, as long as state had this information. State v. Brown (Ohio App. 7 Dist., Mahoning, 06-07-2005) No. 03-MA-32, 2005-Ohio-2939, 2005 WL 1385715, Unreported, appeal not allowed 106 Ohio St.3d 1558, 836 N.E.2d 582, 2005-Ohio-5531. Criminal Law ⚷ 1167(1); Indictment And Information ⚷ 121.4

The defendant in a prosecution for illegal sale of narcotics is entitled to a bill of particulars under RC 2941.07 stating to whom the sale allegedly was made. State v. Bennett (Ohio Com.Pl. 1969) 17 Ohio Misc. 196, 245 N.E.2d 386, 46 O.O.2d 281.

Where the accused, while represented by counsel, withdraws his plea of not guilty and enters a plea of guilty, the need for a bill of particulars no longer exists. Foutty v. Maxwell (Ohio 1962) 174 Ohio St. 35, 186 N.E.2d 623, 21 O.O.2d 288. Indictment And Information ⚷ 121.1(2)

4. —— Alternative charges, right to bill of particulars

Where an affidavit charges the defendant with violations in the alternative of a specified section of the Revised Code "et seq.," the defendant is entitled to either a bill of particulars which specifies the precise section or sections of the code under which defendant is being prosecuted and which sets up specifically the nature of the offense charged (and which clearly informs the defendant of the offense with which he is charged), or a substitute affidavit which specifies the precise section or sections of the code under which defendant is being prosecuted and which sets up specifically the nature of the offense charged (and which clearly informs the defendant of the offense with which he is charged) without allegations in the alternative. City of South Euclid v. Novak (Ohio Mun. 1965) 8 Ohio Misc. 235, 220 N.E.2d 736, 37 O.O.2d 292, 37 O.O.2d 312.

Where affidavit charged defendant with driving while under the influence of intoxicating liquor, narcotic drugs, or opiates in violation of RC 4511.19, defendant was entitled to a bill of particulars. State v. Fowler (Ohio 1963) 174 Ohio St. 362, 189 N.E.2d 133, 22 O.O.2d 416. Criminal Law ⚷ 1167(1)

5. —— Denial of request, right to bill of particulars

A person charged with a misdemeanor in a municipal court is not entitled to a bill of particulars, so that the placing of an attorney prosecuting a person for a misdemeanor in such court in the custody of a bailiff for contempt of court for refusal to comply with an order to furnish the accused with a bill of particulars is a denial of due process to such attorney and an illegal restraint of liberty, entitling such attorney to his release from custody. In re Schott (Hamilton 1968) 16 Ohio App.2d 72, 241 N.E.2d 773, 45 O.O.2d 168.

The failure or refusal to furnish a bill of particulars is not reviewable in a habeas corpus action. Foutty v. Maxwell (Ohio 1962) 174 Ohio St. 35, 186 N.E.2d 623, 21 O.O.2d 288.

Provision as to bill of particulars is a mandatory provision, and overruling of the defendant's timely motion to order prosecuting attorney to furnish bill of particulars is error. State v. Petro (Ohio 1947) 148 Ohio St. 473, 76 N.E.2d 355, 5 A.L.R.2d 425, 36 O.O. 152.

Whether failure of court to order prosecuting attorney to furnish bill of particulars setting up specifically nature of offense charged is prejudicial error requiring reversal by reviewing court, depends upon facts of the particular case. (See also State v DeRighter, 145 OS 552, 62 NE(2d) 332 (1945).) State v. Petro (Ohio 1947) 148 Ohio St. 473, 76 N.E.2d 355, 5 A.L.R.2d 425, 36 O.O. 152. Criminal Law ⚷ 1167(1); Indictment And Information ⚷ 121.1(2)

6. —— Indictment sufficiently specific, right to bill of particulars

Where a bill of particulars charges a defendant with a continuing course of conduct over an extended period of time, but the evidence at trial concerns three specific dates of misconduct, a defendant is prejudiced by being placed in a position where the defendant is not only unaware of the nature of the case against him, but is affirmatively misled by the bill of particulars provided by the state and a conviction will be reversed and remanded for a new trial. State v Luttrell, No. CA-9207, 1993 WL 370651 (5th Dist Ct App, Stark, 8-30-93).

Where an indictment informs the accused of the nature of the offense with which he is charged, he is not entitled to a bill of particulars. State v. Halleck (Pickaway 1970) 24 Ohio App.2d 74, 263 N.E.2d 917, 53 O.O.2d 195. Indictment And Information ⚷ 121.1(2)

Where the indictment fully advises defendant of the crime with which he is charged, he is not entitled to a bill of particulars. State v. Cron (Jackson 1967) 14 Ohio App.2d 76, 236 N.E.2d 671,

43 O.O.2d 201. Indictment And Information ⚷ 121.1(2)

If the indictment states specifically the nature of the offense charged, the court does not abuse its discretion in failing to order a bill of particulars. Boynton v. Sacks (Ohio 1962) 173 Ohio St. 526, 184 N.E.2d 377, 20 O.O.2d 146, certiorari denied 83 S.Ct. 299, 371 U.S. 928, 9 L.Ed.2d 235. Indictment And Information ⚷ 121.1(3)

When the specific nature of the offense charged is stated in the indictment the accused is entitled to no bill of particulars, and there is nothing in the statutes requiring that an indictment must contain an allegation as to any like act or similar offense the prosecutor expects to prove. State v. De Righter (Ohio 1945) 145 Ohio St. 552, 62 N.E.2d 332, 31 O.O. 194. Indictment And Information ⚷ 121.1(2)

Defendant indicted for sending money and equipment to Iran in violation of Executive Order was not entitled to bill of particulars, given government's furnishing or granting of access to all of its files and evidence in case, and given fact that indictment did not fail to apprise defendant of essential nature of charges against him. U.S. v. Anvari-Hamedani (N.D.Ohio, 02-04-2005) 354 F.Supp.2d 768. Indictment And Information ⚷ 121.2(1)

A bill of particulars to an affidavit charging an adult male with making indecent and improper proposals and suggestions to a sixteen-year-old child, which specified that the defendant made such proposals to a named child while alone with her in a driver training car on specified dates, is a sufficient statement to permit the denial of a motion for a bill of particulars to specify the language actually uttered. State v Poney, 19 Misc 51 (Juv, Cuyahoga 1966).

7. Information subject to disclosure

In a criminal prosecution the state must, in response to a request for a bill of particulars or demand for discovery, supply specific dates and times with regard to an alleged offense where it possesses such information. State v. Sellards (Ohio 1985) 17 Ohio St.3d 169, 478 N.E.2d 781, 17 O.B.R. 410. Criminal Law ⚷ 627.6(1); Indictment And Information ⚷ 121.1(4)

Purpose of bill of particulars is to set forth specifically nature of offense charged, not to require state to disclose its evidence, and a disclosure by prosecution in a bill of particulars of evidence relating to a specific offense charged does not bar state, at trial, from introducing supplemental evidence concerning such specified offense. State v. Chaffin (Ohio 1972) 30 Ohio St.2d 13, 282 N.E.2d 46, 59 O.O.2d 51.

RC 2921.14 requires the establishment of a conspiracy to defraud a subdivision of the state in some "manner"; and hence, in order to state specifically the nature of an offense under that statute in accordance with the requirements of the last sentence of RC 2941.07, an indictment or, if an indictment does not, and a bill of particulars is requested, the bill of particulars must specify some manner of defrauding that was a part of the conspiracy charged. State v. Lewis (Ohio 1970) 21 Ohio St.2d 203, 257 N.E.2d 59, 50 O.O.2d 441.

The prosecuting attorney, in filing a bill of particulars, is not required to set up the evidence by which he contemplates establishing the guilt of the accused. State v. McClellan (Lucas 1966) 6 Ohio App.2d 155, 217 N.E.2d 230, 35 O.O.2d 315, certiorari denied 87 S.Ct. 1380, 386 U.S. 1022, 18 L.Ed.2d 462.

Prosecuting attorney is not required to disclose state's evidence through a bill of particulars, but is required to state specifically the nature of the offense charged, including manner in which death was caused, where indictment charges murder in the first degree. (See also State v DeRighter, 145 OS 556, 62 NE(2d) 332 (1945).) State v. Petro (Ohio 1947) 148 Ohio St. 473, 76 N.E.2d 355, 5 A.L.R.2d 425, 36 O.O. 152. Indictment And Information ⚷ 121.4

8. Failure to request bill of particulars

An indictment which employs fully the words of the statute describing the offense will support the conviction of the accused where no bill of particulars is requested or where no objection to the sufficiency of the indictment is interposed before submission of the case to a jury. State v. Simmans (Ohio 1970) 21 Ohio St.2d 258, 257 N.E.2d 344, 50 O.O.2d 487. Indictment And Information ⚷ 110(3)

The failure to furnish a defendant in a criminal case with a bill of particulars, seasonably requested, is not reversible error, where no formal demand therefor was made on the prosecuting attorney and it was not otherwise brought to his attention, the defendant proceeded to trial without a request for a continuance, and no prejudice resulted or is claimed as the result of such delay. State v. Dinsio (Franklin 1964) 4 Ohio App.2d 309, 212 N.E.2d 606, 33 O.O.2d 353.

Habeas corpus will not lie on ground that no bill of particulars was supplied where no such bill was requested. Glowacki v. Sacks (Franklin 1960) 176 N.E.2d 844, 86 Ohio Law Abs. 249.

Where the accused in a criminal case fails to ask for a bill of particulars setting up specifically the nature of the offense charged, he will be deemed to have waived that right. Hamilton v. Alvis (Franklin 1959) 109 Ohio App. 298, 160 N.E.2d 372, 81 Ohio Law Abs. 54, 11 O.O.2d 54.

A failure by a defendant charged with larceny to ask for a bill of particulars constitutes a waiver of such right. Hamilton v. Alvis (Franklin 1959) 109 Ohio App. 298, 160 N.E.2d 372, 81 Ohio Law Abs. 54, 11 O.O.2d 54.

An objection that a "short form" affidavit, which uses the exact words of the statute describing an offense, fails to state an offense is without merit and will be overruled, where the defendant fails to request the prosecuting attorney to furnish or the court to order him to furnish a bill of particulars. State v. Parks (Franklin 1957) 105 Ohio App. 208, 152 N.E.2d 154, 6 O.O.2d 40.

Where defendant moved to quash an affidavit charging reckless operation of a motor vehicle, which was overruled, and then proceeded to trial on the merits without requesting a bill of particulars, the objection to the sufficiency of the affidavit was waived. State v. Hutton (Ohio 1937) 132 Ohio St. 461, 9 N.E.2d 295, 8 O.O. 411.

All objections to an indictment, because of vagueness, indefiniteness, uncertainty and insufficiency, are waived by failure to seasonably request a bill of particulars. State v. Whitmore (Ohio 1933) 126 Ohio St. 381, 185 N.E. 547, 37 Ohio Law Rep. 560. Indictment And Information ⚿ 196(5)

9. Specificity of bill of particulars

Lack of preciseness as to date in indictment and bill of particulars was not fatal to State's case against defendant charging him with corruption of a minor; precise time and dates were not essential elements of offense, and record did not indicate that failure to provide defendant with specific date was a material detriment to preparation of defendant's defense. State v. Gibson (Ohio App. 11 Dist., Trumbull, 10-24-2003) No. 2002-T-0055, 2003-Ohio-5695, 2003 WL 22427821, Unreported. Indictment And Information ⚿ 87(7)

Bill of particulars and indictment charging defendant with aggravated murder were sufficiently specific to advise defendant of charges and of nature of death specifications, where defendant was clearly fully aware of charges against him, of state's intent to try aggravated robbery and aggravated murder charges together, and indictment and bill of particulars specifically outlined capital specifications state intended to pursue. State v. Moulder (Ohio App. 8 Dist., Cuyahoga, 10-03-2002) No. 80266, 2002-Ohio-5327, 2002 WL 31195391, Unreported, appeal not allowed 98 Ohio St.3d 1512, 786 N.E.2d 62, 2003-Ohio-1572. Homicide ⚿ 831; Sentencing And Punishment ⚿ 1742

More detailed bill of particulars than that provided in capital murder prosecution was unnecessary, where defendant's original trial counsel filed motion for bill of particulars, defendant's second counsel obtained trial court order for state to supply bill, and state complied, and where counsel was conducting extensive discovery during process of obtaining bill of particulars. State v. Gross (Ohio, 10-30-2002) 97 Ohio St.3d 121, 776 N.E.2d 1061, 2002-Ohio-5524, reconsideration denied 97 Ohio St.3d 1486, 780 N.E.2d 288, 2002-Ohio-6866, certiorari denied 123 S.Ct. 2079, 538 U.S. 1037, 155 L.Ed.2d 1068, rehearing denied 124 S.Ct. 20, 539 U.S. 976, 156 L.Ed.2d 685. Indictment And Information ⚿ 121.4

Bill of particulars filed by the state for felonious assault charges adequately apprised defendant of conduct constituting the crime by describing all of the acts causing her children's serious physical harm, including repeated physical and sexual abuses, defendant's failure to protect each child from that abuse, and her numerous other acts and omissions, even though specific time periods for each act were not stated. State v. Cooper (Ohio App. 12 Dist., 07-24-2000) 139 Ohio App.3d 149, 743 N.E.2d 427, dismissed, appeal not allowed 90 Ohio St.3d 1468, 738 N.E.2d 381. Indictment And Information ⚿ 121.4

Purpose of bill of particulars is to elucidate or detail conduct of the accused which is alleged to constitute the charged offense. State v. Grinnell (Ohio App. 10 Dist., 06-27-1996) 112 Ohio App.3d 124, 678 N.E.2d 231, appeal not allowed 77 Ohio St.3d 1474, 673 N.E.2d 138, appeal not allowed 77 Ohio St.3d 1475, 673 N.E.2d 138, denial of habeas corpus affirmed 215 F.3d 1326, certiorari denied 121 S.Ct. 232, 531 U.S. 898, 148 L.Ed.2d 166. Indictment And Information ⚿ 121.1(1)

Bill of particulars is where prosecutor is to disclose manner or means by which death of homicide victim occurred. State v. Grinnell (Ohio App. 10 Dist., 06-27-1996) 112 Ohio App.3d 124, 678 N.E.2d 231, appeal not allowed 77 Ohio St.3d 1474, 673 N.E.2d 138, appeal not allowed 77 Ohio St.3d 1475, 673 N.E.2d 138, denial of habeas corpus affirmed 215 F.3d 1326, certiorari denied 121 S.Ct. 232, 531 U.S. 898, 148 L.Ed.2d 166. Indictment And Information ⚿ 121.2(5)

Purpose of bill of particulars is to provide defendant with greater detail of nature and causes of charges against him; accordingly, it cannot support or defeat motion to dismiss indictment, as it cannot create or cure defect in indictment. State v. Silos (Ohio App. 9 Dist., 05-10-1995) 104 Ohio App.3d 23, 660 N.E.2d 1239. Indictment And Information ⚿ 121.1(1); Indictment And Information ⚿ 144.2

Whether bill of particulars provides greater detail to charge contained in indictment is matter left to sound discretion of trial judge. State v. Lewis (Allen 1993) 85 Ohio App.3d 29, 619 N.E.2d 57, dismissed, jurisdictional motion overruled 66 Ohio St.3d 1494, 613 N.E.2d 236, rehearing denied 67 Ohio St.3d 1407, 615 N.E.2d 630, certiorari denied 114 S.Ct. 685, 510 U.S. 1041, 126 L.Ed.2d 652. Indictment And Information ⚿ 121.4

Second amended bill of particulars filed by prosecution provided defendant with sufficient specificity as to nature and cause of theft charges alleged in indictment, where bill of particulars clarified that defendant deprived victim of her money by deception, defined precise relation between defendant and victim and listed date and amount of each check written by victim to defendant. State v. Lewis (Allen 1993) 85 Ohio App.3d 29, 619 N.E.2d 57, dismissed, jurisdictional motion overruled 66 Ohio St.3d 1494, 613 N.E.2d 236, rehearing denied 67 Ohio St.3d 1407, 615 N.E.2d 630, certiorari denied 114 S.Ct. 685, 510 U.S. 1041, 126 L.Ed.2d 652. Indictment And Information ⚿ 121.4

2941.08 Certain defects do not render indictment invalid

An indictment or information is not made invalid, and the trial, judgment, or other proceedings stayed, arrested, or affected:

(A) By the omission of "with force and arms," or words of similar import, or "as appears by the record";

(B) For omitting to state the time at which the offense was committed, in a case in which time is not of the essence of the offense;

(C) For stating the time imperfectly;

(D) For stating imperfectly the means by which the offense was committed except insofar as means is an element of the offense;

(E) For want of a statement of the value or price of a matter or thing, or the amount of damages or injury, where the value or price or the amount of damages or injury is not of the essence of the offense, and in such case it is sufficient to aver that the value or price of the property is less than, equals, or exceeds the certain value or price which determines the offense or grade thereof;

(F) For the want of an allegation of the time or place of a material fact when the time and place have been once stated therein;

(G) Because dates and numbers are represented by figures;

(H) For an omission to allege that the grand jurors were impaneled, sworn, or charged;

(I) For surplusage or repugnant allegations when there is sufficient matter alleged to indicate the crime and person charged;

(J) For want of averment of matter not necessary to be proved;

(K) For other defects or imperfections which do not tend to prejudice the substantial rights of the defendant upon the merits.

(1953 H 1, eff. 10–1–53; GC 13437–7)

Historical and Statutory Notes

Pre–1953 H 1 Amendments: 113 v 165, Ch 16, § 7

Cross References

Harmless error and plain error, Crim R 52

Indictment and information, Crim R 7

Library References

Indictment and Information ⚷17 to 123.

Westlaw Topic No. 210.

C.J.S. Breach of the Peace § 7.

C.J.S. Drugs and Narcotics § 225.

C.J.S. Elections § 339.

C.J.S. Embezzlement § 27.

C.J.S. Escape and Related Offenses; Rescue § 34.

C.J.S. Forgery §§ 45, 53, 74, 76.

C.J.S. Fraud § 103.

C.J.S. Homicide §§ 140 to 141.

C.J.S. Landlord and Tenant § 1246.

C.J.S. Larceny § 70.

C.J.S. Mayhem § 8.

C.J.S. Monopolies § 246.

C.J.S. Parent and Child § 368.

C.J.S. Receiving or Transferring Stolen Goods and Related Offenses §§ 17 to 20.

C.J.S. Robbery §§ 35, 83.

C.J.S. Telecommunications § 131.

C.J.S. Threats and Unlawful Communications § 23.

Research References

Encyclopedias

OH Jur. 3d Criminal Law § 2356, Manner or Means of Committing Offense.

OH Jur. 3d Criminal Law § 2373, Value of Property.

OH Jur. 3d Criminal Law § 2374, Venue.

OH Jur. 3d Criminal Law § 2375, Date.

OH Jur. 3d Criminal Law § 2376, Time.

OH Jur. 3d Criminal Law § 2378, Repetition of Time and Place.

OH Jur. 3d Criminal Law § 2400, Repugnancy or Inconsistency.

OH Jur. 3d Criminal Law § 2403, Statutory Provisions.

OH Jur. 3d Criminal Law § 2405, Surplusage.

OH Jur. 3d Criminal Law § 2406, Matters Relating to Grand Jury.

Treatises and Practice Aids

Katz, Giannelli, Blair and Lipton, Baldwin's Ohio Practice, Criminal Law, § 40:5, Nature and Contents.

Katz, Giannelli, Blair and Lipton, Baldwin's Ohio Practice, Criminal Law, § 40:6, Surplusage.

Katz, Giannelli, Blair and Lipton, Baldwin's Ohio Practice, Criminal Law, § 40:7, Amendments to the Indictment.

Katz, Giannelli, Blair and Lipton, Baldwin's Ohio Practice, Criminal Law, § 142:1, Skeleton Indictment—Single Count.

Katz, Giannelli, Blair and Lipton, Baldwin's Ohio Practice, Criminal Law, § 142:2, Skeleton Indictment—Multiple Counts.

Katz, Giannelli, Blair and Lipton, Baldwin's Ohio Practice, Criminal Law, § 142:7, Motion to Strike Surplusage from Indictment.

Katz, Giannelli, Blair and Lipton, Baldwin's Ohio Practice, Criminal Law, § 142:8, Motion to Strike Aliases from Indictment.

Katz, Giannelli, Blair and Lipton, Baldwin's Ohio Practice, Criminal Law, § 40:10, Challenges to the Indictment.

Hennenberg & Reinhart, Ohio Criminal Defense Motions F 11.08, Motion to Dismiss-Lack of Specificity.

Notes of Decisions

---

1. In general

An indictment and proceedings based on it are not invalid on the ground that illegal and incompetent evidence was heard by the grand jury which voted the indictment. State v. Muenick (Summit 1985) 26 Ohio App.3d 3, 498 N.E.2d 171, 26 O.B.R. 171. Indictment And Information ⚷ 10.2(2)

RC 3719.44 does not require a finding of a specific intent to violate its prohibitions or knowledge that such statute was being violated before a violation is established; an indictment written in the words of the statute charges a crime. State v. Conley (Marion 1971) 32 Ohio App.2d 54, 288 N.E.2d 296, 61 O.O.2d 50.

A complaint charging a violation of RC 3773.24 "on or about Sunday the 6th day of January, 1963," is not indefinite and vague; the use of the disjunctive "or" in such complaint in charging that the accused "did suffer or permit a building to be open for transaction of business on Sunday" does not render such charge indefinite and vague; the omission of the words "against the peace and dignity of the state of Ohio" does not render it defective; such complaint is not defective because it charges the accused with a violation of such statute as an individual and does not set out the capacity in which he is supposed to have acted; and such complaint is not defective because it does not negate the exceptions contained in such statute. State v. Whitt (Montgomery 1964) 3 Ohio App.2d 278, 210 N.E.2d 279, 32 O.O.2d 382.

An indictment which charged that defendant "published and offered to sell" a medical diploma whereas the statute used the language "publish or sell" was not defective. State v. Broadwell (Cuyahoga 1956) 104 Ohio App. 37, 136 N.E.2d 72, 75 Ohio Law Abs. 47, 3 O.O.2d 217, certiorari denied 77 S.Ct. 668, 353 U.S. 911, 1 L.Ed.2d 665, rehearing denied 77 S.Ct. 1281, 353 U.S. 989, 1 L.Ed.2d 1147.

2. Essential elements

Trial court improperly dismissed count of indictment, charging defendant with making terroristic threats, based upon state's alleged failure to plead underlying specified offense; indictment averred material facts constituting essential elements of offense, affording defendant notice and an opportunity to defend, any alleged defect in indictment was remedied by defendant's requesting and state's rendering bill of particulars delineating nature of offense charged and conduct alleged to constitute offense, and bill of particulars clearly put defendant on notice actual felony offense of violence was felonious assault. State v. Roach (Ohio App. 5 Dist., Licking, 11-23-2005) No. 05-CA-57, 2005-Ohio-6301, 2005 WL 3150311, Unreported. Extortion And Threats ⚷ 30; Indictment And Information ⚷ 121.5

An indictment charging felonious assault is not fatally defective for its failure to include the names of the victims of the alleged crimes where it does include the elements of the crimes, the approximate date of the offenses, and the county in which they were committed; the victims' names are not an essential element of the crime of felonious assault. State v. Phillips (Montgomery 1991) 75 Ohio App.3d 785, 600 N.E.2d 825.

An indictment need not be in the exact language of the statute defining the offense, so long as all the essential elements of the crime are contained in language equivalent to that used in the statute, and the accused is advised in the indictment of the nature and cause of the accusation he is expected to meet. State v. Oliver (Ohio 1972) 32 Ohio St.2d 109, 290 N.E.2d 828, 61 O.O.2d 371. Indictment And Information ⚷ 110(2)

A waiver of the right to object to the insufficiency of an affidavit (or indictment) for its failure to allege a vital or material element identifying and characterizing the crime attempted to be charged cannot be based on passive conduct of the defendant or his counsel, but must be based only on affirmative action showing an active participation in the creation of the situation bringing about the conviction with the result that such conviction is induced or invited by the defendant's own conduct. State v. Culp (Marion 1971) 32 Ohio App.2d 39, 288 N.E.2d 308, 61 O.O.2d 42. Indictment And Information ⚷ 196(5)

Where it is claimed that prejudicial error intervened in trial of criminal case in that trial court charged on an element not laid in indictment, and charge exacted of prosecution proof of additional facts not necessary to sustain charge as stated in valid indictment, such claim is not valid. State v. Stone (Ross 1971) 30 Ohio App.2d 49, 283 N.E.2d 188, 59 O.O.2d 115.

The omission of the word "malicious" from an indictment charging entrance into a financial institution with intent to commit a felony, contrary to RC 2907.14, renders such indictment insufficient to charge an offense under such statute. State v. Mills (Hamilton 1967) 10 Ohio App.2d 152, 226 N.E.2d 572, 39 O.O.2d 272. Burglary ⚷ 18

An indictment in the language of the statute in using the word "bank," alleging defendants embezzled "bank" property, and concluding that the acts charged are contrary to the statute and against the peace and dignity of the state of Ohio, is not defective for failing to charge that bank was a state bank, rather than a national bank. Dorger v. State (Hamilton 1931) 40 Ohio App. 415, 179 N.E. 143, 11 Ohio Law Abs. 522, error dismissed 124 Ohio St. 659, 181 N.E. 881, certiorari denied 52 S.Ct. 265, 284 U.S. 689, 76 L.Ed. 581. Banks And Banking ⚷ 62; Embezzlement ⚷ 30; Indictment And Information ⚷ 110(13)

An allegation in an indictment descriptive of that which is essential to the charge therein made is a material allegation and cannot be rejected as surplusage. Goodlove v. State (Ohio 1910) 82 Ohio St. 365, 92 N.E. 491, 8 Ohio Law Rep. 119, 19 Am.Ann.Cas. 893. Indictment And Information ⚷ 120

An indictment under RS 7075 (See GC 13105), charging presentation to the county commissioners of a fraudulent claim and obtaining payment of the same, which in describing the claim avers it to have been "a certain false and fraudulent claim," but in no way avers wherein it was false and fraudulent, and states no facts, is bad on demurrer. Du Brul v. State (Ohio 1909) 80 Ohio St. 52, 87 N.E. 837, 6 Ohio Law Rep. 661. False Pretenses ⚷ 37

An indictment for violation of RC 4301.69 is not insufficient merely because it specifies the sale of "beer" rather than "intoxicating liquor" to a minor. State v Poe, No. CA 13693 (9th Dist Ct App, Summit, 3–8–89).

3. Fatal defects

Although defendant claimed the bill of particulars led him to believe that the State alleged all three crimes occurred on the same night, he did not claim that his ability to defend himself was prejudiced by this fact, and thus, defendant did not show that the date of the offenses was material to his defense, such that the indictment was invalid because it did not describe the specific dates on which the crimes allegedly occurred. State v. Thompson (Ohio App. 8 Dist., Cuyahoga, 10-31-2002) No. 79334, 2002-Ohio-5957, 2002 WL 31426356, Unreported, dismissal of post-conviction relief affirmed 2002-Ohio-6845, 2002 WL 31771437, appeal not allowed 100 Ohio St.3d 1506, 799 N.E.2d 186, 2003-Ohio-6161, appeal not allowed 98 Ohio St.3d 1512, 786 N.E.2d 62, 2003-Ohio-1572, reconsideration denied 99 Ohio St.3d 1414, 788 N.E.2d 649, 2003-Ohio-2454, motion to reopen denied 2003-Ohio-4336, 2003 WL 21954760, as amended nunc pro tunc, appeal not allowed 100 Ohio St.3d 1509, 799 N.E.2d 187, 2003-Ohio-6161. Indictment And Information ⚷ 87(2)

The failure to have an affidavit verified is jurisdictional and is not waived by a "not guilty" plea. City of South Euclid v. Samartini (Ohio Mun. 1965) 5 Ohio Misc. 38, 204 N.E.2d 425, 31 O.O.2d 87. Indictment And Information ⚷ 196(4)

The signature of the foreman of a grand jury is an indispensable requisite to a valid indictment, and in the absence thereof all subsequent proceedings are void; and habeas corpus will lie. Kennedy v. Alvis (Ohio Com.Pl. 1957) 145 N.E.2d 361, 76 Ohio Law Abs. 132.

4. Names

Defense counsel, who wanted to mention original two-count indictment in his opening statement because original indictment named wrong defendant and counsel intended to use this to present defense of mistaken identity, was properly precluded from mentioning original indictment in his opening statement; defense counsel admitted, after prosecutor's objection to reference to original indictment, that naming of wrong defendant had nothing to do with identity of defendant, but wrong name was only confusion during service of warrant and thus, original indictment had no relevancy to issues presented at trial. State v. Armstead (Allen 1993) 85 Ohio App.3d 247, 619 N.E.2d 513. Criminal Law ⚷ 704

It is not a ground for the granting of a habeas corpus petition that the indictment was amended during trial by changing the name of the person charged nor that upon it being found that he no longer needed mental care, he was transferred from a state hospital to the penitentiary. In re Stewart (Ohio 1952) 156 Ohio St. 521, 103 N.E.2d 551, 46 O.O. 436, certiorari denied 73 S.Ct. 61, 344 U.S. 845, 97 L.Ed. 657.

Affidavit charging defendant with having unlawful possession of intoxicating liquors in violation of GC 6212–15 (repealed 1933) need not specify or designate the particular kind of intoxicating liquor so unlawfully possessed, in view of sections 13583, 13588, 13589 (repealed 1929. See §§ 13437–13, 13437–19). State v. Marcinski (Ohio 1921) 103 Ohio St. 613, 134 N.E. 438, 19 Ohio Law Rep. 511. Criminal Law ⚷ 211(4); Intoxicating Liquors ⚷ 198

Where an indictment for manslaughter charges defendant with having unlawfully killed a person using that person's alias as well as his real name, and there is no evidence tending to prove the alias or that both names were that of the same person, such failure is not a fatal variance, being nonprejudicial to the merits of the case and the rights of defendant. State v. Schaeffer (Ohio 1917) 96 Ohio St. 215, 117 N.E. 220, 15 Ohio Law Rep. 122, Am.Ann.Cas. 1918E, 1137.

Describing a person in an indictment by a name that he has acquired by reputation is sufficient. Goodlove v. State (Ohio 1910) 82 Ohio St. 365, 92 N.E. 491, 8 Ohio Law Rep. 119, 19 Am.Ann.Cas. 893.

5. Time

State was properly allowed to amend indictment charging domestic violence in order to change date of offense for which defendant was charged, as amendment did not change name or identity of crime with which defendant was charged. State v. Dunderman (Ohio App. 3 Dist., Paulding, 06-30-2003) No. 11-03-01, 2003-Ohio-3411, 2003 WL 21487626, Unreported. Indictment And Information ⚷ 159(3)

State presented a justifiable reason for two-year delay in seeking indictment against defendant for corruption of a minor even if the delay prejudiced defendant; evidence indicated that after defendant gave his statement that he penetrated the victim's vagina, but it was consensual, the state continued its investigation of the incident to determine whether it had sufficient evidence to indict defendant for rape, and sought indictment for corruption of a minor after indictment it had secured for unlawful sexual conduct with a minor was dismissed due to technical errors. State v. Hahn (Ohio App. 4 Dist., Washington, 02-13-2003) No. 02CA22, 2003-Ohio-788, 2003 WL 369539, Unreported. Indictment And Information ⚷ 7

State's two-year delay in seeking indictment against defendant for corruption of a minor did not prejudice defendant, though a witness moved out of state in the intervening time, given that evidence did not indicate that the witness was unavailable to testify on defendant's behalf, and that defendant did not state how his inability to recall the events of night in question would prejudice his defense. State v. Hahn (Ohio App. 4 Dist., Washington, 02-13-2003) No. 02CA22, 2003-Ohio-788, 2003 WL 369539, Unreported. Indictment And Information ⚷ 7

Evidence was sufficient to establish that charged offenses of rape, attempted rape, and gross sexual imposition occurred during the time frame listed in the indictment, and thus, defendant was not entitled to judgment of acquittal; victim, defendant's adopted daughter, testified that sexual contact with defendant occurred during the summer she entered her fourth-grade year, which was the same as the dates listed in the indictment. State v. Hurd (Ohio App. 11 Dist., Trumbull, 12-20-2002) No. 2001-T-0086, 2002-Ohio-7163, 2002 WL 31862690, Unreported, appeal not allowed 98 Ohio St.3d 1566, 787 N.E.2d 1231, 2003-Ohio-2242. Infants ⚷ 20; Rape ⚷ 57(1)

Prosecution's failure to provide defense with more particular information about dates on which minor was alleged to have been sexually penetrated by defendant's boyfriend, despite having such information, did not prejudice defendant in prosecution for aiding and abetting felonious sexual penetration, despite defendant's argument that if she had known of more specific time period, she could have prepared alibi defense, where date was not element of offense, defendant did not file notice of alibi or indicate intention to use alibi, one year period was specific enough for defense, and defendant did not seek to cure defective bill of particulars in trial court. State v. Stepp (Ohio App. 4 Dist., 01-13-1997) 117 Ohio App.3d 561, 690 N.E.2d 1342. Criminal Law ⚷ 1167(1)

Ordinarily, state is not required to provide exact date and time of offense in bill of particulars because such information does not describe defendant's conduct; rather, it describes when conduct is alleged to have occurred, which is generally irrelevant to preparation of defense. State v. Stepp (Ohio App. 4 Dist., 01-13-1997) 117 Ohio App.3d 561, 690 N.E.2d 1342. Indictment And Information ⚷ 121.1(6.1)

Omission of time at which offense was allegedly committed will not render indictment invalid, in case in which time is not of the essence of offense charged. State v. Staples (Allen 1993) 88 Ohio App.3d 359, 623 N.E.2d 1313. Indictment And Information ⚷ 87(1)

A trial court's definition of "on or about" to mean "a reasonable time" does not prejudice a defendant who presents an alibi for the date on which the indictment alleges the offense occurred but the victim testifies that the offense occurred approximately two weeks before the date alleged in the indictment. State v. Price (Crawford 1992) 80 Ohio App.3d 35, 608 N.E.2d 818.

Specific information regarding the date and time of a rape need not be included in the indictment but must be disclosed by the prosecution, if known; it is enough if the amended bill of particulars identifies the dates as falling within a specified twelve-month period. State v. Ambrosia (Lucas 1990) 67 Ohio App.3d 552, 587 N.E.2d 892, dismissed 58 Ohio St.3d 701, 569 N.E.2d 504. Indictment And Information ⚷ 87(1)

Although a bill of particulars is not amended to reflect a more specific identification of the date and time of one of three rape charges, there is no basis for granting a new trial where the defendant was notified of the specific information, and a continuance gave him ample time to prepare his defense in light of this information. State v. Ambrosia (Lucas 1990) 67 Ohio App.3d 552, 587 N.E.2d 892, dismissed 58 Ohio St.3d 701, 569 N.E.2d 504. Criminal Law ⚷ 1167(1)

Where an indictment's failure to specify the exact date of an offense does not prejudice the defendant in his preparation of a defense or ability to protect himself from future prosecution for the same conduct, the indictment need not be dismissed. State v. Hill (Hamilton 1989) 59 Ohio App.3d 31, 570

N.E.2d 1138, dismissed 42 Ohio St.3d 707, 537 N.E.2d 226.

Inexactitude of dates and times in indictment, charging offenses of gross sexual imposition of person under 13 and rape, was not prejudicial, where defendant did not present alibi defense, conceded being alone with victims at various times throughout relevant time frame, and asserted as defense that alleged touchings never happened. State v. Barnecut (Fairfield 1988) 44 Ohio App.3d 149, 542 N.E.2d 353, dismissed 37 Ohio St.3d 716, 532 N.E.2d 765. Criminal Law ⚷ 1167(1)

Ordinarily, precise times and dates are not essential elements of offenses, and thus, failure to provide dates and times in indictment will not alone provide basis for dismissal of charges. State v. Sellards (Ohio 1985) 17 Ohio St.3d 169, 478 N.E.2d 781, 17 O.B.R. 410. Indictment And Information ⚷ 144.1(1)

Indictment which charged that defendant had engaged in sexual conduct with another person who was less than 13 years of age was not rendered invalid for failing to state time at which offense was committed, since exact date and time of the offense were not material elements of the crime nor essential to the validity of a conviction. State v. Madden (Warren 1984) 15 Ohio App.3d 130, 472 N.E.2d 1126, 15 O.B.R. 221. Indictment And Information ⚷ 87(1)

An averment of the precise date and time of an offense need not be included in an indictment or bill of particulars where the precise dates and times are not essential elements of the offense charged and the omission does not prejudice the accused's ability to defend himself; however, the state should supply the specific dates and times where it possesses such information. State v. Gingell (Hamilton 1982) 7 Ohio App.3d 364, 455 N.E.2d 1066, 7 O.B.R. 464. Constitutional Law ⚷ 265; Indictment And Information ⚷ 87(1)

The filing of an alibi does not alter the rule that in a criminal case the exact date and time of the offense are immaterial unless the nature of the offense is such that exactness of time is essential. State v. Dingus (Pike 1970) 26 Ohio App.2d 131, 269 N.E.2d 923, 55 O.O.2d 280, affirmed 26 Ohio St.2d 141, 269 N.E.2d 923, 55 O.O.2d 274.

The date the offense occurred is not such an immaterial part of the affidavit that it may be changed with impunity after the affidavit has been verified. City of South Euclid v. Samartini (Ohio Mun. 1965) 5 Ohio Misc. 38, 204 N.E.2d 425, 31 O.O.2d 87.

The rule is well established that the exact time and date of the commission of a crime, as may be alleged in an indictment, is not essential to the legal sufficiency of the charge therein alleged, unless it appears from the nature of the offense that exactness of time is material or essential. State v. Porcaro (Lucas 1956) 102 Ohio App. 128, 141 N.E.2d 482, 2 O.O.2d 122. Indictment And Information ⚷ 87(2)

A variance between an indictment showing murder on a certain day and on a bill of particulars showing deceased died over a month later is not reversible error where time was not of the essence of the offense, and no prejudice resulted to the defendant by reason of the variance. Massa v. State (Crawford 1930) 37 Ohio App. 532, 175 N.E. 219, 9 Ohio Law Abs. 408, 34 Ohio Law Rep. 49. Criminal Law ⚷ 1167(1); Indictment And Information ⚷ 176

In criminal trial it is not necessary for the state to prove that the offense was committed at the exact date and time charged; and in like manner evidence is admissible on behalf of the defendant, which tends to negative the commission of the offense by him, even though it departs somewhat from the date and time charged. (See also Massa v State, 37 App 532, 175 NE 219 (1930).) Tesca v. State (Ohio 1923) 108 Ohio St. 287, 140 N.E. 629, 1 Ohio Law Abs. 485, 1 Ohio Law Abs. 877, 21 Ohio Law Rep. 150, 21 Ohio Law Rep. 152.

6. Surplusage

An indictment is not made invalid for surplus allegations such as naming obsolete sections of the Ohio General Code, or for defects or imperfections in the sentence, or for other defects or imperfections when the words of the indictment are sufficient to give the accused notice of the offenses of which he is charged. State v. Turpin (Stark 1969) 19 Ohio App.2d 116, 250 N.E.2d 94, 48 O.O.2d 236.

Addition of the words "was prematurely delivered of such child" in an abortion indictment constitutes surplusage. State v. Roche (Franklin 1955) 135 N.E.2d 789, 72 Ohio Law Abs. 462, 72 Ohio Law Abs. 465.

In an indictment under this section which charges that defendant offered for sale and "actually sold" certain stock in violation of that section, the allegation as to the actual sale is surplusage and does not affect the validity of the indictment. Harrison v. State (Ohio 1925) 112 Ohio St. 429, 147 N.E. 650, 3 Ohio Law Abs. 267, 23 Ohio Law Rep. 210, affirmed 46 S.Ct. 350, 270 U.S. 632, 70 L.Ed. 771.

A valid charge of receiving and concealing stolen property is not affected by the further allegation of having concealed said property; the latter allegation is a mere legal conclusion and to be regarded as surplusage under the statute. State v. Schultz (Ohio 1917) 96 Ohio St. 114, 117 N.E. 30, 15 Ohio Law Rep. 83.

Mere matter of unnecessary particularity or immaterial description contained in an indictment is not sufficient upon which to base a charge of variance between pleading and proof. Such variance must be based upon some essential element of the offense or some essential part of such element. Tingue v. State (Ohio 1914) 90 Ohio St. 368, 108 N.E. 222, 12 Ohio Law Rep. 88, 12 Ohio Law Rep. 556, Am.Ann.Cas. 1916C, 1156. False Pretenses ⚷ 38

Charging that an officer did, on the first day of April, fail to pay into the treasury on the first Monday of April, the indictment being sufficient without the latter date, its presence does not invalidate indictment. State v. Van Gunten (Ohio 1911) 84 Ohio St. 172, 95 N.E. 664, 9 Ohio Law Rep. 62.

7. Technical defects

Under RC 2941.08(F) an indictment is not invalid for lack of an allegation as to the time or place of a material fact where that time or place has once been stated therein. State v. Williams (Franklin 1988) 53 Ohio App.3d 1, 557 N.E.2d 818. Indictment And Information ⚿ 86(2); Indictment And Information ⚿ 87(2)

A criminal indictment is not invalid because a properly appointed special prosecutor signs the indictment instead of the county prosecutor. State v. Bunyan (Auglaize 1988) 51 Ohio App.3d 190, 555 N.E.2d 980.

Indictment signed by assistant prosecuting attorney, rather than by county prosecutor, was not invalid where it could be said that assistant prosecutor's signature carried imprimatur of county prosecutor; mere absence of latter's signature on indictment did not violate defendant's constitutional rights or otherwise infringe upon substantial rights on the merits. State v. Sabbah (Sandusky 1982) 13 Ohio App.3d 124, 468 N.E.2d 718, 13 O.B.R. 155. Indictment And Information ⚿ 33(2)

Where the prosecuting attorney or his assistant fails to sign an indictment, but the prosecuting attorney's name is typed on the indictment, said indictment is not invalidated where defendant's substantial rights were not prejudiced and the indictment was sufficient to inform the defendant of the charges against him. State v. Ewing (Franklin 1983) 9 Ohio App.3d 285, 459 N.E.2d 1297, 9 O.B.R. 500. Indictment And Information ⚿ 33(1)

The failure to include the section number of the statute alleged to have been violated does not invalidate an indictment. Foutty v. Maxwell (Ohio 1962) 174 Ohio St. 35, 186 N.E.2d 623, 21 O.O.2d 288.

It is not a defect in an indictment that the words "A true bill" on the back of it are printed rather than written, or that the words "against the peace and dignity of the State of Ohio" are printed on a page of the indictment subsequent to that on which the body of the indictment is typewritten. Ruch v. State (Ohio 1924) 111 Ohio St. 580, 146 N.E. 67, 22 Ohio Law Rep. 669.

The constitution requires that all indictments shall conclude with the words "against the peace and dignity of the state of Ohio," but those words are not required to be at the conclusion of each count of an indictment. Olendorf v. State (Ohio 1901) 64 Ohio St. 118, 45 W.L.B. 203, 59 N.E. 892. Indictment And Information ⚿ 32(2)

An indictment for aggravated robbery lacking an allegation that the act was done knowingly does not give rise to any constitutional issue cognizable in a federal habeas corpus proceeding. Mira v. Marshall (C.A.6 (Ohio) 1986) 806 F.2d 636.

8. Amendment

The omission from an affidavit (or indictment) attempting to charge a violation of RC 3719.41 of the element of "intent to produce hallucinations or illusions" is a fundamental defect or omission resulting in an affidavit (or indictment) which fails to allege an offense and which is not subject to amendment. State v. Culp (Marion 1971) 32 Ohio App.2d 39, 288 N.E.2d 308, 61 O.O.2d 42.

Where the affidavit charging an offense was defective, and by agreement of counsel it was amended by completely rewriting and inserting by interlineation, but was not sworn to as amended, and defendant's counsel made no objection thereto, defendant by pleading not guilty and proceeding to trial waived objection to the want of verification. State v. Chrisman (Ohio 1966) 9 Ohio St.2d 27, 222 N.E.2d 649, 38 O.O.2d 16.

Amendment of an indictment to correct the date on which the crime is alleged to have occurred is not improper. McLean v. Maxwell (Ohio 1965) 2 Ohio St.2d 226, 208 N.E.2d 139, 31 O.O.2d 454.

Amendments to affidavits filed in criminal actions are not permitted under authority of RC 2941.30. City of South Euclid v. Samartini (Ohio Mun. 1965) 5 Ohio Misc. 38, 204 N.E.2d 425, 31 O.O.2d 87.

9. Variance between affidavit and indictment

Trial court had the requisite jurisdiction to try, convict, and sentence defendant for rape, even though no proper criminal complaint had ever been filed against him before he was indicted. Harris v. Bagley (Ohio, 10-23-2002) 97 Ohio St.3d 98, 776 N.E.2d 490, 2002-Ohio-5369. Criminal Law ⚿ 209

The fact that an indictment does not conform to a complaint made by the affidavit has no effect upon the validity of the indictment. Clinger v. Maxwell (Ohio 1964) 175 Ohio St. 540, 196 N.E.2d 771, 26 O.O.2d 219. Indictment And Information ⚿ 122(1)

10. Waiver of irregularities by guilty plea or otherwise

Defendant, by failing to object to alleged flaw in indictment until after prosecution finished presenting its case in chief, waived any argument concerning validity of indictment other than plain error. State v. Frazier (Ohio, 08-23-1995) 73 Ohio St.3d 323, 652 N.E.2d 1000, 1995-Ohio-235, stay granted 74 Ohio St.3d 1437, 655 N.E.2d 1321, certiorari denied 116 S.Ct. 820, 516 U.S. 1095, 133 L.Ed.2d 763, denial of post-conviction relief affirmed 1997 WL 764810, dismissed, appeal not allowed 81 Ohio St.3d 1496, 691 N.E.2d 1058, habeas corpus denied 188 F.Supp.2d 798, denial of habeas corpus reversed in part 343 F.3d 780, opinion supplemented on denial of rehearing 348 F.3d 174, rehearing and suggestion for rehearing en banc denied, certiorari denied 124 S.Ct. 2815, 541 U.S. 1095, 159 L.Ed.2d 261. Indictment And Information ⚿ 196(1)

Irregularities in a complaint against or in the arrest of an accused are not grounds for his release by habeas corpus after an indictment is returned against him and he has pleaded guilty to the charge. Mack v. Maxwell (Ohio 1963) 174 Ohio St. 275, 189 N.E.2d 156, 22 O.O.2d 335. Habeas Corpus ⚿ 276; Habeas Corpus ⚿ 474

2941.09 Identification of corporation

In any indictment or information it is sufficient for the purpose of identifying any group or association of persons, not incorporated, to state the proper name of such group or association, to state any name or designation by which the group or association has been or is known, to state the names of all persons in such group or association or of one or more of them, or to state the name of one or more persons in such group or association referring to the others as "another" or "others." It is sufficient for the purpose of identifying a corporation to state the corporate name of such corporation, or any name or designation by which such corporation has been or is known.

(1953 H 1, eff. 10–1–53; GC 13437–8)

Historical and Statutory Notes

Pre–1953 H 1 Amendments: 113 v 165, Ch 16, § 8

Cross References

Organizational criminal liability, 2901.23

Library References

Corporations ⚷533.
Indictment and Information ⚷81, 101.
Westlaw Topic Nos. 101, 210.

Research References

Encyclopedias

OH Jur. 3d Criminal Law § 2368, Identification of Corporation or an Unincorporated Group or Association.

Notes of Decisions

Amendment to substitute name 2
Name of corporation or other entity 1

1. Name of corporation or other entity

The purpose of this section is the identification of a corporation or any group or association of persons not incorporated and does not authorize a prosecution of any kind. State v. Fremont Lodge of Loyal Order of Moose (Ohio 1949) 151 Ohio St. 19, 84 N.E.2d 498, 38 O.O. 506.

2. Amendment to substitute name

The name of the defendant on a criminal complaint cannot be changed by amendment to a corporation from an entity that is not a corporation; the plaintiff should instead dismiss the complaint and file another. City of Columbus v. Moretti's Poultry (Franklin 1988) 48 Ohio App.3d 79, 548 N.E.2d 285.

2941.10 Indictment complete

No indictment or information for any offense created or defined by statute is objectionable for the reason that it fails to negative any exception, excuse, or proviso contained in the statute creating or defining the offense. The fact that the charge is made is an allegation that no legal excuse for the doing of the act exists in the particular case.

(1953 H 1, eff. 10–1–53; GC 13437–9)

Historical and Statutory Notes

Pre–1953 H 1 Amendments: 113 v 166, Ch 16, § 9

Library References

Indictment and Information ⚷111.
Westlaw Topic No. 210.
C.J.S. Homicide § 140.

Research References

Encyclopedias

OH Jur. 3d Criminal Law § 2355, Negating Exception, Excuse, or Proviso in Penal Law.

Treatises and Practice Aids

Katz, Giannelli, Blair and Lipton, Baldwin's Ohio Practice, Criminal Law, § 142:1, Skeleton Indictment—Single Count.

Katz, Giannelli, Blair and Lipton, Baldwin's Ohio Practice, Criminal Law, § 142:2, Skeleton Indictment—Multiple Counts.

Notes of Decisions

Sufficiency of indictment 1

---

1. Sufficiency of indictment

Lack of preciseness as to date in indictment and bill of particulars was not fatal to State's case against defendant charging him with corruption of a minor; precise time and dates were not essential elements of offense, and record did not indicate that failure to provide defendant with specific date was a material detriment to preparation of defendant's defense. State v. Gibson (Ohio App. 11 Dist., Trumbull, 10-24-2003) No. 2002-T-0055, 2003-Ohio-5695, 2003 WL 22427821, Unreported. Indictment And Information ⚷ 87(7)

Claim challenging validity or sufficiency of indictment was not cognizable in habeas corpus. State ex rel. Richard v. Seidner (Ohio, 04-02-1997) 78 Ohio St.3d 116, 676 N.E.2d 889, 1997-Ohio-230. Habeas Corpus ⚷ 474

An indictment charging unlawful possession of a narcotic drug without specifying the particular drug is valid. Williams v. Eckle (Ohio 1962) 173 Ohio St. 410, 183 N.E.2d 365, 20 O.O.2d 40, certiorari denied 83 S.Ct. 154, 371 U.S. 881, 9 L.Ed.2d 118. Controlled Substances ⚷ 65

PLEADING, AVERMENTS, AND ALLEGATIONS

2941.11 Pleading prior conviction

Whenever it is necessary to allege a prior conviction of the accused in an indictment or information, it is sufficient to allege that the accused was, at a certain stated time, in a certain stated court, convicted of a certain stated offense, giving the name of the offense, or stating the substantial elements thereof.

(1953 H 1, eff. 10–1–53; GC 13437–10)

Historical and Statutory Notes

Pre–1953 H 1 Amendments: 113 v 166, Ch 16, § 10

Library References

Indictment and Information ⚷113.

Sentencing and Punishment ⚷1363.

Westlaw Topic Nos. 210, 350H.

Research References

Encyclopedias

OH Jur. 3d Criminal Law § 2363, Prior Conviction.

Treatises and Practice Aids

Katz, Giannelli, Blair and Lipton, Baldwin's Ohio Practice, Criminal Law, § 40:5, Nature and Contents.

Adrine & Ruden, Ohio Domestic Violence Law § 2:7, Felony Violations.

Notes of Decisions

Proving prior conviction 3
Provisions mandatory 1
Uncounseled prior conviction 2

---

1. Provisions mandatory

To comply with the requirements of rule governing the language of an indictment, an indictment charging defendant with an elevated charge need only give fair and adequate notice that the state will seek to prove that the defendant has previously been convicted, and thus, where an indictment complies with that rule, the indictment does not need to allege that the accused was, at a certain stated time, in a certain stated court, convicted of a certain stated offense. State v. Midwest Pride IV, Inc. (Ohio App. 12 Dist., 12-28-1998) 131 Ohio App.3d 1, 721 N.E.2d 458, dismissed, appeal not allowed 85 Ohio St.3d 1486, 709 N.E.2d 1214, certiorari denied 120 S.Ct. 400, 528 U.S. 965, 145 L.Ed.2d 312. Indictment And Information ⚿ 113

Where indictment complies with criminal rule providing that indictments need not contain any technical averments or any allegations not essential to be proved, and gives defendant adequate notice that state will seek to prove that defendant previously had been convicted of theft offenses, indictment does not need to allege that defendant was, at a certain stated time, in a certain stated court, convicted of a certain stated offense. State v. Larsen (Lawrence 1993) 89 Ohio App.3d 371, 624 N.E.2d 766. Larceny ⚿ 28(4)

The provisions of RC 2941.11 are mandatory. State v. Winters (Ohio 1965) 2 Ohio St.2d 325, 209 N.E.2d 131, 31 O.O.2d 581.

2. Uncounseled prior conviction

Where a defendant alleges that prior convictions for theft used to enhance the charged offense of defrauding a livery were uncounselled, the court must allow the prosecution the opportunity to rebut the defendant's claims prior to dismissing the charge. State v. Daniels (Lorain 1988) 61 Ohio App.3d 17, 572 N.E.2d 129, motion overruled 46 Ohio St.3d 716, 546 N.E.2d 1334.

3. Proving prior conviction

It was not necessary for indictment charging defendant with enhanced felony operating a motor vehicle under the influence (OMVI) to allege that defendant was, on a specified date in a specified court, previously convicted of OMVI, where indictment gave defendant adequate notice that state was charging defendant with elevated felony OMVI offense and would seek to prove that he had prior convictions. State v. Jenkins (Ohio App. 4 Dist., Lawrence, 02-05-2003) No. 02CA5, 2003-Ohio-1058, 2003 WL 894807, Unreported. Indictment And Information ⚿ 113

Prior convictions referred to in indictment could be used to elevate the instant offenses into fourth degree felonies, even though the prior convictions were on appeal and had not yet been affirmed; certified copy of the entry of judgment in such prior conviction together with evidence sufficient to identify the defendant named in the entry as the offender in the case at bar, was all that was required. State v. Midwest Pride IV, Inc. (Ohio App. 12 Dist., 12-28-1998) 131 Ohio App.3d 1, 721 N.E.2d 458, dismissed, appeal not allowed 85 Ohio St.3d 1486, 709 N.E.2d 1214, certiorari denied 120 S.Ct. 400, 528 U.S. 965, 145 L.Ed.2d 312. Criminal Law ⚿ 28

Where the existence of a prior conviction enhances the penalty for a subsequent offense, but does not elevate the degree thereof, the prior conviction is not an essential element of subsequent offense, and need not be alleged in the indictment or proved as a matter of fact. State v. Allen (Ohio 1987) 29 Ohio St.3d 53, 506 N.E.2d 199, 29 O.B.R. 436. Indictment And Information ⚿ 113; Indictment And Information ⚿ 166

2941.12 Pleading a statute

In pleading a statute or right derived therefrom it is sufficient to refer to the statute by its title, or in any other manner which identifies the statute. The court must thereupon take judicial notice of such statute.

(1953 H 1, eff. 10–1–53; GC 13437–11)

Historical and Statutory Notes

Pre–1953 H 1 Amendments: 113 v 166, Ch 16, § 11

Library References

Indictment and Information ⚿107.

Westlaw Topic No. 210.

C.J.S. Breach of the Peace § 7.

C.J.S. Elections § 339.

C.J.S. Embezzlement § 27.

C.J.S. Escape and Related Offenses; Rescue § 34.

C.J.S. Forgery §§ 45, 74, 76.

C.J.S. Fraud § 103.

C.J.S. Homicide §§ 140 to 141.

C.J.S. Landlord and Tenant § 1246.

C.J.S. Larceny § 70.

C.J.S. Mayhem § 8.

C.J.S. Monopolies § 246.

C.J.S. Parent and Child § 368.

C.J.S. Receiving or Transferring Stolen Goods and Related Offenses §§ 17 to 20.

C.J.S. Robbery § 35.

C.J.S. Telecommunications § 131.

C.J.S. Threats and Unlawful Communications § 23.

Research References

Treatises and Practice Aids

Giannelli and Snyder, Baldwin's Ohio Practice, Evidence, R 201, Judicial Notice of Adjudicative Facts.

Giannelli and Snyder, Baldwin's Ohio Practice, Evidence, § 201.12, Judicial Notice of Law.

2941.13 Pleading a judgment

In pleading a judgment or other determination of, or a proceeding before, any court or officer, civil or military, it is not necessary to allege the fact conferring jurisdiction on such court or officer. It is sufficient to allege generally that such judgment or determination was given or made or such proceedings had.

(1953 H 1, eff. 10–1–53; GC 13437–12)

Historical and Statutory Notes

Pre–1953 H 1 Amendments: 113 v 166, Ch 16, § 12

Library References

Judgment ⟹948 to 950.
Westlaw Topic No. 228.
C.J.S. Judgments §§ 930 to 942.

Research References

Encyclopedias

OH Jur. 3d Criminal Law § 2380, Pleading Judgment or Proceedings.

2941.14 Allegations in homicide indictment

(A) In an indictment for aggravated murder, murder, or voluntary or involuntary manslaughter, the manner in which, or the means by which the death was caused need not be set forth.

(B) Imposition of the death penalty for aggravated murder is precluded unless the indictment or count in the indictment charging the offense specifies one or more of the aggravating circumstances listed in division (A) of section 2929.04 of the Revised Code. If more than one aggravating circumstance is specified to an indictment or count, each shall be in a separately numbered specification, and if an aggravating circumstance is specified to a count in an indictment containing more than one count, such specification shall be identified as to the count to which it applies.

(C) A specification to an indictment or count in an indictment charging aggravated murder shall be stated at the end of the body of the indictment or count, and may be in substantially the following form:

"SPECIFICATION (or, SPECIFICATION 1, SPECIFICATION TO THE FIRST COUNT, or SPECIFICATION 1 TO THE FIRST COUNT). The Grand Jurors further find and specify that (set forth the applicable aggravating circumstance listed in divisions (A)(1) to (10) of section 2929.04 of the Revised Code. The aggravating circumstance may be stated in the words of the subdivision in which it appears, or in words sufficient to give the accused notice of the same)."

(2002 S 184, eff. 5–15–02; 1997 S 32, eff. 8–6–97; 1981 S 1, eff. 10–19–81; 1973 H 716; 1972 H 511; 1953 H 1; GC 13437–13)

Historical and Statutory Notes

Pre–1953 H 1 Amendments: 113 v 166, Ch 16, § 13

Amendment Note: 2002 S 184 substituted "(10)" for "(9)" in division (C).

Amendment Note: 1997 S 32 substituted "divisions (A)(1) to (9)" for "divisions (A)(1) to (8)" in the final paragraph containing the form of the specification; and made other nonsubstantive changes.

Cross References

Criteria for imposing death or imprisonment for a capital offense, 2929.04

Homicide, 2903.01 to 2903.06

Indictment and information, Crim R 7

Library References

Homicide ⚷830 to 881.

Westlaw Topic No. 203.

Research References

Encyclopedias

OH Jur. 3d Criminal Law § 963, Murder and Aggravated Murder—Specification of Aggravating Circumstances.

OH Jur. 3d Criminal Law § 965, Manslaughter.

OH Jur. 3d Criminal Law § 1016, Determination by Trial Jury and Trial Judge or by Three-Judge Panel.

OH Jur. 3d Criminal Law § 1040, Aggravating Circumstances.

OH Jur. 3d Criminal Law § 2341, Advising Defendant of Charge and Facts—Indictments.

OH Jur. 3d Criminal Law § 2357, Manner or Means of Committing Offense—Aggravated Murder, Murder, Voluntary, or Involuntary Manslaughter.

OH Jur. 3d Criminal Law § 2381, Aggravated Murder; Death Penalty.

OH Jur. 3d Criminal Law § 2386, Objections To, and Amendment Of, Bill.

Treatises and Practice Aids

Katz, Giannelli, Blair and Lipton, Baldwin's Ohio Practice, Criminal Law, § 40:5, Nature and Contents.

Katz, Giannelli, Blair and Lipton, Baldwin's Ohio Practice, Criminal Law, § 124:16, Nonstatutory Aggravating Factors.

Hennenberg & Reinhart, Ohio Criminal Defense Motions F 13.39, Motion in Limine-Statutory Aggravating Circumstances-Death Penalty Motions.

Hennenberg & Reinhart, Ohio Criminal Defense Motions F 13.40, Motion to Prohibit Prosecutor from Arguing and the Court from Giving Instructions Regarding Non-Statutory and Statutory Mitigating Factors that Are Not Raised by the Defense-Death Penalty...

Hennenberg & Reinhart, Ohio Criminal Defense Motions F 13.41, Motion to Limit Prosecutor's Argument to the Aggravating Circumstances Proven at First Phase-Death Penalty Motions.

Notes of Decisions

1. In general

State's felony murder indictment did not need to specify the underlying felony; statute provided that, in an indictment for aggravated murder, murder, or voluntary or involuntary manslaughter, the manner in which, or the means by which, the death was caused need not be set forth, and defendant did not cite any authority that required the State to specify the underlying felony in his indictment of murder. State v. Jones (Ohio App. 8 Dist., Cuyahoga, 11-07-2002) No. 80737, 2002-Ohio-6045, 2002 WL 31478933, Unreported, motion for delayed appeal denied 98 Ohio St.3d 1509, 786 N.E.2d 60, 2003-Ohio-1572, appeal not allowed 98 Ohio St.3d 1513, 786 N.E.2d 63, 2003-Ohio-1572, motion to reopen denied 2003-Ohio-4397, 2003 WL 21981989, appeal not allowed 100 Ohio St.3d 1532, 800 N.E.2d 48, 2003-Ohio-6458, denial of post-conviction relief affirmed 2004-Ohio-3868, 2004 WL 1631122. Homicide ⚷ 850

Amended bill of particulars filed by state subsequent to defendant's indictment for involuntary manslaughter and other offenses, which set forth offense of receiving stolen property as predicate offense on which involuntary manslaughter charge had been based, did not change identity of crime that defendant had been charged with due to fact that indictment did not include receiving stolen property as predicate offense; pursuant to statute, indictment for involuntary manslaughter was not required to contain an allegation of the underlying felony, and thus there was no discrepancy between indictment and amended bill of particulars. State v. Elam (Ohio Com.Pl., 09-08-2004) 129 Ohio Misc.2d 26, 821 N.E.2d 622, 2004-Ohio-7328. Indictment And Information ⚷ 163

2. Multiple specifications in same count

Indictment for murder and involuntary manslaughter for causing a death during the commission of a felony did not need to specify the predicate felony offenses underlying the charges. State v. Talley (Ohio App. 8 Dist., Cuyahoga, 06-03-2004) No. 83237, 2004-Ohio-2846, 2004 WL 1234291, Unreported, appeal not allowed 103 Ohio St.3d 1494, 816 N.E.2d 1080, 2004-Ohio-5605, certiorari denied 125 S.Ct. 2548, 162 L.Ed.2d 280. Homicide ⚷ 850

Failure of indictment on rape count to allege that defendant compelled victim to "engage in sexual conduct" was not plain error with regard to aggravated murder charge and attached capital specification, where aggravated murder count specified that the victim was purposefully killed during the course of a rape, and specification charged defendant with committing the offense during the course of a rape. State v. Carter (Ohio, 09-13-2000) 89 Ohio St.3d 593, 734 N.E.2d 345, 2000-Ohio-172, stay granted 90 Ohio St.3d 1446, 737 N.E.2d 51. Criminal Law ⚷ 1032(5)

Indictment may charge aggravated murder based on legal theory involving aggravated burglary, or involving aggravated robbery, and prosecution may pursue either theory without engaging in impermissible multiplication of charges, as long as theories are not "stacked" to increase weight of aggravating circumstances for balancing with mitigating circumstances. State v. Haight (Ohio App. 10 Dist., 11-15-1994) 98 Ohio App.3d 639, 649 N.E.2d 294, leave to appeal denied 71 Ohio St.3d 1500, 646 N.E.2d 1125. Homicide ⚷ 850; Homicide ⚷ 876

The submission to a jury of one or more specifications of aggravation under one count in an indictment for aggravated murder, where each such specification presents a different premise of aggravating circumstances, does not necessarily constitute reversible error. State v. Hancock (Ohio 1976) 48 Ohio St.2d 147, 358 N.E.2d 273, 2 O.O.3d 333, vacated 98 S.Ct. 3147, 438 U.S. 911, 57 L.Ed.2d 1155. Criminal Law ⚷ 1172.1(3)

In an indictment for aggravated murder, a grand jury may state one or more specifications under one count when issuing the indictment. State v. Hancock (Ohio 1976) 48 Ohio St.2d 147, 358 N.E.2d 273, 2 O.O.3d 333, vacated 98 S.Ct. 3147, 438 U.S. 911, 57 L.Ed.2d 1155. Indictment And Information ⚷ 125(3)

Prior conviction under Florida's second-degree murder statute was insufficient to prove Ohio's specific intent capital specification, which required proof that, prior to offense at bar, defendant was convicted of offense involving purposeful killing of another. Johnson v. Coyle (C.A.6 (Ohio), 01-12-2000) 200 F.3d 987. Sentencing And Punishment ⚷ 1670

3. Short form of indictment for homicide

An indictment stating that on a specified date the accused caused the death of a named person as the proximate result of committing a felony in violation of RC 2903.04(A) complies with the requirements of Crim R 7(B) and RC 2945.75. State v. Mineer (Ohio Com.Pl. 1983) 8 Ohio Misc.2d 11, 456 N.E.2d 590, 8 O.B.R. 70. Indictment And Information ⚷ 71.4(5)

This section affords no excuse for failure to furnish defendant with a bill of particulars when seasonably requested and where, as in this case, the short form of indictment is used. State v. Petro (Ohio 1947) 148 Ohio St. 473, 76 N.E.2d 355, 5 A.L.R.2d 425, 36 O.O. 152.

The short form of indictment for manslaughter in the statute, does not violate the right to be advised of the nature of the accusation; and the unlawful act need not be averred. State v. Schaeffer (Ohio 1917) 96 Ohio St. 215, 117 N.E. 220, 15 Ohio Law Rep. 122, Am.Ann.Cas. 1918E, 1137.

4. Prior plea bargain's effect

State cannot indict defendant for murder after court has accepted negotiated guilty plea to lesser offense and victim later dies of injuries sustained in the crime, unless state expressly reserves the right to file additional charges on the record at the time of the defendant's plea. State v. Carpenter (Ohio 1993) 68 Ohio St.3d 59, 623 N.E.2d 66, rehearing denied 68 Ohio St.3d 1448, 626 N.E.2d 689, certiorari denied 114 S.Ct. 2741, 513 U.S. 1236, 129 L.Ed.2d 861. Double Jeopardy ⚷ 167

5. Aggravating circumstances

Trial court's error in giving instruction on aggravating circumstances at penalty phase of capital murder trial, describing defendant as causing victim's death with prior calculation and design "and" as principal offender in the aggravated murder, without requiring additional finding that the murder was committed while defendant was committing, attempting to commit, or fleeing immediately after committing or attempting to commit kidnapping, rape, aggravated arson, aggravated robbery, or aggravated burglary, and improperly using conjunctive "and" rather than disjunctive "or,", did not require reversal of death sentence; indictment accurately reflected statutory language for aggravating circumstance, instructions on alternative aggravating circumstances properly referred to kidnapping and aggravating robbery, jury unanimously found existence of alternative aggravating circumstances, there was dearth of mitigation evidence while overwhelming evidence established aggravating circumstances, and jury's conviction of defendant for aggravated murder, at guilt phase, constituted a specific finding of prior calculation and design. State v. Dixon (Ohio, 04-14-2004) 101 Ohio St.3d 328, 805 N.E.2d 1042, 2004-Ohio-1585, reconsideration denied 102 Ohio St.3d 1473, 809 N.E.2d 1159, 2004-Ohio-2830, certiorari denied 125 S.Ct. 875, 543 U.S. 1060, 160 L.Ed.2d 787. Sentencing And Punishment ⚷ 1789(9)

Although death penalty was never available as a sentencing option for 16-year-old defendant, due to his age, prosecution charging defendant with aggravated murder and aggravated robbery with specifications that would have made him eligible for the death penalty had he been an adult was required to be heard by a three-judge panel, as jurisdictional matter that could not be waived. State v. Koger (Ohio App. 6 Dist., 02-07-2003) 151 Ohio App.3d 534, 784 N.E.2d 780, 2003-Ohio-576, appeal allowed 99 Ohio St.3d 1451, 790 N.E.2d 1217, 2003-Ohio-3396, affirmed 102 Ohio St.3d 263, 809 N.E.2d 661, 2004-Ohio-2824. Criminal Law ⚷ 250; Sentencing And Punishment ⚷ 1643

RC 2941.14(B) limits the aggravating circumstances which may be considered in imposing the death penalty to those specifically enumerated in RC 2929.04(A). State v. Johnson (Ohio 1986) 24 Ohio St.3d 87, 494 N.E.2d 1061, 24 O.B.R. 282.

2941.141 Specification concerning possession of firearm essential to affect sentence

(A) Imposition of a one-year mandatory prison term upon an offender under division (D)(1)(a) of section 2929.14 of the Revised Code is precluded unless the indictment, count in the indictment, or information charging the offense specifies that the offender had a firearm on or about the offender's person or under the offender's control while committing the offense. The specification shall be stated at the end of the body of the indictment, count, or information, and shall be in substantially the following form:

"SPECIFICATION (or, SPECIFICATION TO THE FIRST COUNT). The Grand Jurors (or insert the person's or the prosecuting attorney's name when appropriate) further find and specify that (set forth that the offender had a firearm on or about the offender's person or under the offender's control while committing the offense.)"

(B) Imposition of a one-year mandatory prison term upon an offender under division (D)(1)(a) of section 2929.14 of the Revised Code is precluded if a court imposes a three-year or six-year mandatory prison term on the offender under that division relative to the same felony.

(C) The specification described in division (A) of this section may be used in a delinquent child proceeding in the manner and for the purpose described in section 2152.17 of the Revised Code.

(D) As used in this section, "firearm" has the same meaning as in section 2923.11 of the Revised Code.

(2000 S 179, § 3, eff. 1–1–02; 1999 S 107, eff. 3–23–00; 1995 S 2, eff. 7–1–96; 1990 H 669, eff. 1–10–91; 1990 S 258; 1982 H 269, § 4, S 199)

Uncodified Law

1982 S 199, § 6, eff. 1–5–83, reads: "Sections 2929.71 and 2941.141 of the Revised Code, as enacted by this act, and sections 2903.12, 2917.02, 2929.01, and 2929.41 of the Revised Code, as amended by this act, shall take effect on January 1, 1983, and shall apply only to offenses committed on or after January 1, 1983. Sections 2903.11, 2911.01, and 2911.11 of the Revised Code, as amended by this act, shall take effect on January 1, 1983; however, the amendments to those sections that change felonious assault to an aggravated felony of the second degree and aggravated robbery and aggravated burglary to aggravated felonies of the first degree shall not be applied to any acts occurring before July 1, 1983." Note that, pursuant to O Const Art II, § 1c, the effective date of 1982 S 199 was changed by 1982 H 269, § 4, eff. 1–5–83, from January 1, 1983 to January 5, 1983.

Historical and Statutory Notes

Amendment Note: 2000 S 179, § 3, eff. 1–1–02, added new division (C); and redesignated former division (C) as division (D).

Amendment Note: 1999 S 107 deleted "(i)" after "(D)(1)(a)" in divisions (A) and (B).

Amendment Note: 1995 S 2 rewrote this section, which previously read:

"(A) Imposition of a term of actual incarceration upon an offender under division (A) of section 2929.71 of the Revised Code for having a firearm on or about his person or under his control while committing a felony is precluded unless the indictment, count in the indictment, or information charging the offense specifies that the offender had a firearm on or about his person or under his control while committing the offense. A specification to an indictment, count in the indictment, or information charging the offender with having a firearm on or about his person or under his control while committing a felony shall be stated at the end of the body of the indictment, count, or information, and shall be in substantially the following form:

"'SPECIFICATION (or, SPECIFICATION TO THE FIRST COUNT), The Grand Jurors (or insert the person's or the prosecuting attorney's name when appropriate) further find and specify that (set forth that the offender had a firearm on or about his person or under his control while committing the offense).'

"(B) As used in this section, 'firearm' has the same meaning as in section 2923.11 of the Revised Code."

Cross References

Delinquent children, information provided to foster caregivers regarding, 2152.72

Library References

Indictment and Information ⚷113.
Westlaw Topic No. 210.
Baldwin's Ohio Legislative Service, 1995 S 2—LSC Analysis, p 8/L–2907
Baldwin's Ohio Legislative Service, 1990 Laws of Ohio, S 258—LSC Analysis, p 5–954

Research References

Encyclopedias

OH Jur. 3d Criminal Law § 1919, Overview; What Constitutes Disability.

OH Jur. 3d Criminal Law § 2369, Firearm Specification.

OH Jur. 3d Criminal Law § 3267, Specification as Prerequisite to Enhanced Penalty; State's Burden of Proof; Proof of Prior Conviction.

OH Jur. 3d Criminal Law § 3284, One-Year Term.

OH Jur. 3d Family Law § 1696, Commitment to Youth Commission.

OH Jur. 3d Family Law § 1698.5, Serious Youthful Offender.

Treatises and Practice Aids

Katz, Giannelli, Blair and Lipton, Baldwin's Ohio Practice, Criminal Law, § 40:5, Nature and Contents.

Katz, Giannelli, Blair and Lipton, Baldwin's Ohio Practice, Criminal Law, § 106:1, Introduction.

Katz, Giannelli, Blair and Lipton, Baldwin's Ohio Practice, Criminal Law, § 106:3, Firearm Possession in Liquor-Permit Premises.

Katz, Giannelli, Blair and Lipton, Baldwin's Ohio Practice, Criminal Law, § 106:4, Deadly Weapon or Ordnance on School Premises.

Katz, Giannelli, Blair and Lipton, Baldwin's Ohio Practice, Criminal Law, § 106:9, Discharging Firearm Into a School or Home.

Katz, Giannelli, Blair and Lipton, Baldwin's Ohio Practice, Criminal Law, § 117:2, Mandatory Prison Sentences.

Katz, Giannelli, Blair and Lipton, Baldwin's Ohio Practice, Criminal Law, § 118:7, Gun Enhancement.

Katz, Giannelli, Blair and Lipton, Baldwin's Ohio Practice, Criminal Law, § 153:9, Motion to Correct Improper Sentence—Firearm Specifications as Part of One Transaction.

Katz, Giannelli, Blair and Lipton, Baldwin's Ohio Practice, Criminal Law, § 118:11, Drive-By Shooting.

Carlin, Baldwin's Ohio Practice, Merrick-Rippner Probate Law § 107:84, Disposition of Delinquent Children—Prior to January 1, 2002.

Carlin, Baldwin's Ohio Practice, Merrick-Rippner Probate Law § 107:92, Enhanced Dispositions Due to Felony Specifications, Effective January 1, 2002.

Giannelli & Yeomans, Ohio Juvenile Law § 27:3, Department of Youth Services Commitment.

Law Review and Journal Commentaries

Constitutional Consequences of Ohio's New Sentencing Laws, Louis A. Jacobs. 15 U Tol L Rev 71 (Fall 1983).

Notes of Decisions

---

1. Constitutional issues

Defendant's guilty plea to robbery was not made voluntarily, where defendant expressed confusion regarding elements of robbery, court did not resolve defendant's confusion but rather simply asked if defendant was waiving his right to jury trial, defendant pleaded guilty to robbery, which was not a lesser included offense of charged crime of aggravated robbery, and defendant could not have been convicted of robbery under allegations in indictment. State v. Higgs (Ohio App. 11 Dist., 10-01-1997) 123 Ohio App.3d 400, 704 N.E.2d 308. Criminal Law ⚷ 273.1(4)

Double jeopardy precluded retrial of charge of having a weapon while under disability, where appellate court determined that trial court erred in reopening evidence sua sponte after closing arguments and taking judicial notice of prior proceedings in earlier case to supply crucial fact that state failed to prove in bench trial, and determined that, absent judicial notice of crucial fact, state's evidence was insufficient. State v. Lovejoy (Ohio, 09-24-1997) 79 Ohio St.3d 440, 683 N.E.2d 1112, 1997-Ohio-371, habeas corpus denied 2001 WL

506534, reversed 54 Fed.Appx. 617, 2002 WL 31890928, on remand 2003 WL 1338210. Double Jeopardy ⚷ 109

2. Penalty enhancement

Evidence in rape prosecution did not support imposition of one-year mandatory sentence for a firearm specification; although victim believed defendant had a gun in his coat pocket because he kept his hand in his pocket, there was no evidence that defendant threatened victim with a gun, or that victim felt an object or saw a shape which could be construed as a gun. State v. Evans (Ohio App. 8 Dist., Cuyahoga, 07-28-2005) No. 85396, 2005-Ohio-3847, 2005 WL 1792351, Unreported. Sentencing And Punishment ⚷ 323

Sentence of one year on the firearm specification plus three years on the firearm specification prior to and consecutively with twenty years to life on murder charge, and eleven months for having weapons while under a disability, with the counts to run concurrently to each other was proper; the sentences conformed with the sentencing guidelines. State v. Loyed (Ohio App. 8 Dist., Cuyahoga, 04-27-2005) No. 83075, 2005-Ohio-1965, 2005 WL 977833, Unreported. Sentencing And Punishment ⚷ 645

Trial court properly sentenced defendant for three-year and five-year firearms specifications attached to charged offenses of aggravated murder and attempted murder, even though defendant claimed both enhancements were based on same act; legislature required enhancements to be served consecutively to one another and to the prison terms for the base offense. State v. Gresham (Ohio App. 8 Dist., Cuyahoga, 02-20-2003) No. 81250, 2003-Ohio-744, 2003 WL 360922, Unreported. Sentencing And Punishment ⚷ 144

Imposition of two-level enhancement for possession of dangerous weapon in conjunction with defendant's conviction for conspiring to possess and distribute cocaine was not barred by defendant's conviction for being felon in possession of firearm. U.S. v. Bender (C.A.6 (Ohio), 12-11-2002) No. 02-3391, 52 Fed.Appx. 756, 2002 WL 31780940, Unreported.

Crime of aggravated assault to which defendant pleaded no contest contained proper gun specification, as required to impose three-year term of actual incarceration therefor. State v. Gaughan (Ohio App. 4 Dist., 04-27-1995) 103 Ohio App.3d 169, 658 N.E.2d 1113. Indictment And Information ⚷ 113

Statute regarding imposition of term of actual incarceration upon offender for having firearm on his person during commission of felony is penalty enhancement statute and provides for imposition of mandatory term of incarceration as penalty enhancement to actual sentence imposed for commission of crime as set forth in indictment. State v. Ervin (Ohio App. 8 Dist., 02-14-1994) 93 Ohio App.3d 178, 638 N.E.2d 104. Sentencing And Punishment ⚷ 77

Because possession of a firearm and conviction for a previous offense of violence are the essential allegations of the main indictment for having a weapon while under a disability, specification of those elements cannot be used to enhance the sentence. State v. Ellington (Cuyahoga 1989) 65 Ohio App.3d 473, 584 N.E.2d 784, dismissed 49 Ohio St.3d 716, 552 N.E.2d 945. Sentencing And Punishment ⚷ 139; Sentencing And Punishment ⚷ 141

An individual indicted for and convicted of aggravated robbery, RC 2911.01, and a firearm specification, RC 2941.141, is subject to a mandatory three-year term of actual incarceration under RC 2929.71, regardless of whether he was the principal offender or an unarmed accomplice. State v. Chapman (Ohio 1986) 21 Ohio St.3d 41, 487 N.E.2d 566, 21 O.B.R. 327. Robbery ⚷ 30

Where an indictment does not contain a firearm specification, it is plain error for a trial court to impose the three-year sentence provided by RC 2929.71. State v. Loines (Cuyahoga 1984) 20 Ohio App.3d 69, 484 N.E.2d 727, 20 O.B.R. 88.

Five firearms that were found during search of defendant's residence were admissible in his trial for assault and drug trafficking; although weapons were not the one that defendant discharged at a fleeing car on the night of his arrest, the firearms were relevant to enhancement to drug trafficking charge, and charge of tampering with evidence, and probative value of firearms outweighed any prejudicial effect. State v. McKinney (Ohio App. 11 Dist., Lake, 08-23-2002) No. 2000-L-210, 2002-Ohio-4360, 2002 WL 1961229, Unreported, appeal not allowed 98 Ohio St.3d 1411, 781 N.E.2d 1019, 2003-Ohio-60. Criminal Law ⚷ 404.65

3. Plea bargaining

Trial court was not required to advise defendant that state had to prove he possessed operable firearm in order to accept guilty plea to firearms specification, where defendant did not indicate confusion concerning elements of firearm specification. State v. Higgs (Ohio App. 11 Dist., 10-01-1997) 123 Ohio App.3d 400, 704 N.E.2d 308. Criminal Law ⚷ 273.1(4)

Defendant's guilty plea to robbery with a firearms specification was not given knowingly, where trial court erroneously stated maximum penalty when advising defendant of rights he was waiving. State v. Higgs (Ohio App. 11 Dist., 10-01-1997) 123 Ohio App.3d 400, 704 N.E.2d 308. Criminal Law ⚷ 273.1(4)

Defendant's guilty plea to firearms specification was not made knowingly, where trial court failed to make further inquiry regarding defendant's understanding of nature of the specification when defendant stated that he did not possess a firearm during the robbery. State v. Higgs (Ohio App. 11 Dist., 10-01-1997) 123 Ohio App.3d 400, 704 N.E.2d 308. Criminal Law ⚷ 273.1(4)

Where a defendant charged with felonious assault, which carries a firearm specification, agrees to plead guilty to the lesser offense of aggravated assault, with the understanding that he would be eligible for probation and that the firearm specification will be removed from the indictment, the court may not utilize a nunc pro tunc entry to alter the record and remove all references to firearms in the indictment after the defendant's conviction where nothing in the record indicates that the court intended to delete all references to firearms, even though the result is that the defendant is not eligible for probation although he thought he would be. State v. Hawk (Summit 1992) 81 Ohio App.3d 296, 610 N.E.2d 1082.

4. Probation

Defendant, who was convicted of aggravated robbery, was not eligible for probation, even though jury returned not guilty verdict on firearm specification; in returning guilty verdict on aggravated robbery count jury must have found that defendant had deadly weapon, a firearm, on or about his person or under his control during commission of crime, and not guilty verdict on firearm specification did nothing to change status of defendant's ineligibility for probation. State v. Ervin (Ohio App. 8 Dist., 02-14-1994) 93 Ohio App.3d 178, 638 N.E.2d 104. Sentencing And Punishment ⚷ 1861

That term of actual incarceration for gun specification has ended does not render inapplicable statutory prohibition against granting probation to persons who committed their offenses with firearms. State v. Brandon (Greene 1993) 86 Ohio App.3d 671, 621 N.E.2d 776. Sentencing And Punishment ⚷ 1840

A defendant convicted of an offense for which probation is not permitted, such as a crime containing a firearm specification under RC 2941.141, cannot be granted shock probation. State v. Young (Trumbull 1988) 47 Ohio App.3d 165, 547 N.E.2d 1022.

RC 2951.02 and 2941.141 do not conflict. State v. Fisher (Trumbull 1985) 26 Ohio App.3d 197, 499 N.E.2d 344, 26 O.B.R. 418.

5. Deadly weapon; firearm

Sufficient evidence demonstrated that gun that defendant allegedly possessed while committing underlying felony was operable or readily operable at time of offense, thus supporting imposition of firearm specifications; robbery victim testified that defendant pointed gun at victim, after striking victim in back of head with gun, defendant repeatedly threatened victim's life, detective testified that he retrieved loaded gun matching victim's description while executing search warrant at defendant's home, and defendant's written statement to police indicated that firearm was loaded at time of robbery. State v. Crawford (Ohio App. 8 Dist., Cuyahoga, 02-05-2004) No. 82833, 2004-Ohio-500, 2004 WL 229532, Unreported, motion for delayed appeal denied 103 Ohio St.3d 1461, 815 N.E.2d 677, 2004-Ohio-5056. Sentencing And Punishment ⚷ 323

For purpose of firearm enhancement specification, operability of weapon brandished by defendant or accomplice during robbery and burglary was established by codefendant's testimony that she saw what appeared to be a real handgun in a bag brought back from victim's residence, and victim's testimony that assailant pointed what had the appearance of a real gun at her and demanded her money. State v. Macias (Ohio App. 2 Dist., Darke, 03-28-2003) No. 1562, 2003-Ohio-1565, 2003 WL 1596472, Unreported. Sentencing And Punishment ⚷ 323

Defendant was "armed with a firearm," within meaning of statute rendering offender not eligible for probation if offense involved was committed while offender was armed with firearm, where prosecution proved beyond reasonable doubt that defendant had on or about his person or under his control firearm at time of offense pursuant to firearm specifications of indictment. State v. Brandon (Greene 1993) 86 Ohio App.3d 671, 621 N.E.2d 776. Sentencing And Punishment ⚷ 1840

A jury finding that an offense was committed while possessing a deadly weapon is insufficient to support a conviction for violating RC 2941.141, which requires possession of a firearm. State v. Thundercloud Way (Hamilton 1989) 49 Ohio App.3d 3, 550 N.E.2d 533, dismissed 45 Ohio St.3d 718, 545 N.E.2d 902.

A verdict of guilty of aggravated robbery, necessarily predicated on the defendant's possession or control of a deadly weapon, may stand even though it is inconsistent with the jury's not guilty verdict on a firearm specification. State v. Woodson (Franklin 1985) 24 Ohio App.3d 143, 493 N.E.2d 1018, 24 O.B.R. 231.

Imposition of departure sentence of 24 months' imprisonment for conviction of being felon in possession of firearm, for which recommended sentencing range under Sentencing Guidelines was 46 to 57 months, was reasonable based upon consideration of appropriate factors, including determination that defendant's criminal history category over-represented seriousness of his criminal history, that defendant's crime fell outside heartland of typical offenses, and that defendant had not been charged with any serious criminal conduct in more than decade. U.S. v. Williams (C.A.6 (Ohio), 12-14-2005) 432 F.3d 621. Sentencing And Punishment ⚷ 860; Weapons ⚷ 17(8)

Jury's verdict finding defendant guilty on gun specifications regarding kidnapping, aggravated burglary, and aggravated robbery was not against manifest weight of the evidence, although victim testified that she initially thought gun was a toy; evidence indicated that defendant had gun in his hand, that defendant hit victim with gun, and that victim suffered dark bruise on arm as result of being hit with gun. State v. MacDonald (Ohio App. 2 Dist., Montgomery, 09-20-2002) No. 19100, 2002-Ohio-4969, 2002 WL 31105391, Unreported. Sentencing And Punishment ⚷ 323; Kidnapping ⚷ 36; Robbery ⚷ 24.15(2)

A court is not empowered to impose a sentence of actual incarceration pursuant to RC 2929.71 where the indictment refers only to "a deadly or dangerous ordnance, to wit: a gun," but does not specify that the weapon was a firearm. State v Lumpkin, No. 47407 (8th Dist Ct App, Cuyahoga, 7–12–84).

6. Procedural issues

Defendant convicted of being felon in possession of firearm was not entitled to six-level downward departure on ground that weapon at issue was antique and was not used for any criminal purpose, where defendant's predicate offense was controlled substance offense. U.S. v. Fuson (C.A.6 (Ohio), 11-16-2004) No. 04-3050, 116 Fed.Appx. 588, 2004 WL 2590566, Unreported. Sentencing And Punishment ⚷ 855

Trial court's instruction to jury in felonious assault prosecution with firearm specification, in which jury was instructed that, for purposes of firearm specification, it could find that defendant could attempt to inflict physical harm upon his victims even where he did not intend to cause harm to victims, did not confuse jury with what they had to find regarding defendant's specific intent for assault offense; court limited the intent finding between assault offense and firearm specifications. State v. Finger (Ohio App. 8 Dist., Cuyahoga, 01-29-2003) No. 80691, 2003-Ohio-402, 2003 WL 194773, Unreported, motion to certify allowed 98 Ohio St.3d 1535, 786 N.E.2d 899, 2003-Ohio-1946, appeal allowed 99 Ohio St.3d 1470, 791 N.E.2d 985, 2003-Ohio-3801, reversed 104 Ohio St.3d 21, 817 N.E.2d 864, 2004-Ohio-6085, appeal decided 104 Ohio St.3d 157, 818 N.E.2d 1171, 2004-Ohio-6390. Weapons ⚷ 17(6)

Finding on specification that is inconsistent with guilty finding on principal charge will not undermine guilty finding on principal charge where sufficient evidence supports guilty finding on principal charge. State v. Boyd (Ohio App. 2 Dist., 03-22-1996) 110 Ohio App.3d 13, 673 N.E.2d 607. Criminal Law ⚷ 878(4)

Jury's failure to affirmatively find on firearm specification merely precludes imposition of mandatory actual term of incarceration. State v. Ervin (Ohio App. 8 Dist., 02-14-1994) 93 Ohio App.3d 178, 638 N.E.2d 104. Sentencing And Punishment ⚷ 77

In imposing three years' actual incarceration for using firearm in perpetration of offense, fact finder must separately address and respond to specification by way of substantive findings, apart from underlying criminal offense, in order to effect conviction; thus, trial judge must instruct jury as to elements of specification separately and apart from underlying offense and must provide jury form separately responsive to specification instructions. State v. Tyson (Hamilton 1984) 19 Ohio App.3d 90, 482 N.E.2d 1327, 19 O.B.R. 175. Criminal Law ⚷ 796; Sentencing And Punishment ⚷ 372

Assessment of valid indefinite sentence of incarceration under RC 2941.143 is necessary predicate to imposition of three years' actual incarceration for using firearm in perpetration of offense under RC 2929.71. State v. Tyson (Hamilton 1984) 19 Ohio App.3d 90, 482 N.E.2d 1327, 19 O.B.R. 175. Sentencing And Punishment ⚷ 77

The statutory procedure of RC 2929.12(D) and (E) for determining whether an individual is more or less likely to be a recidivist does not constitute a "separate proceeding" and does not deny the accused due process of law; in addition, a trial court does not err in considering that a firearm was used in the commission of the offenses despite the dismissal of the firearm specification against the defendant where use of a firearm by one of the perpetrators significantly increases the likelihood that the robbery victims could be subjected to serious injury or death and is relevant in determining the seriousness of the offense. State v Rose, No. CA96–11–106, 1997 WL 570695 (12th Dist Ct App, Clermont, 9–15–97).

Where trial court failed to reduce its ruling on defendant's Crim R 29(A) motion and RC 2929.71 requires a conviction of a RC 2941.141 firearm specification separate and apart from an underlying criminal offense, the trial court had to journalize its ruling on the firearm specification and its judgment is currently an interlocutory order; appeal dismissed. State v Johnson, No. 62540 (8th Dist Ct App, Cuyahoga, 5–20–93).

7. Weapon "on person" or "under control"

The fact that defendant did not have cocaine or weapons immediately on his person at time of police raid did not mean that he did not possess them or aid and abet in the possession of them. State v. Riley (Ohio App. 9 Dist., Summit, 09-15-2004) No. 21852, 2004-Ohio-4880, 2004 WL 2050521, Unreported. Controlled Substances ⚷ 28; Weapons ⚷ 4

Convictions for complicity to possess cocaine, with a gun specification, and complicity to illegal use or possession of drug paraphernalia was supported by testimony that drugs were found in bedroom occupied by defendants, that defendants carried handguns inside of socks, that two handguns and shotgun found on premises belonged to defendants, that one defendant had been selling drugs from house, and evidence that large amount of cash was found in defendant's pocket, shotgun was found between mattress and box springs of bed on which defendant was sitting when police arrived, and drugs were also found in same room. State v. Riley (Ohio App. 9 Dist., Summit, 09-15-2004) No. 21852, 2004-Ohio-4880, 2004 WL 2050521, Unreported. Controlled Substances ⚷ 80; Controlled Substances ⚷ 89; Sentencing And Punishment ⚷ 323

Evidence was sufficient to support conviction on one-year firearm specification applicable when defendant has firearm on or about his person or under his control while committing offense and three-year firearm specification applicable when offender has firearm on or about his person or under his control while committing offense and displaying firearm and conviction was not against manifest weight of evidence; store employee testified that defendant opened up defendant's coat and revealed gun tucked in defendant's pants, employee testified that defendant told employee to stand still, employee identified gun as revolver, and employee was familiar with guns from time spent in military and prior work in gun shop. State v. Marbury (Ohio App. 10 Dist., Franklin, 06-29-2004) No. 03AP-233,

2004-Ohio-3373, 2004 WL 1445224, Unreported, appeal not allowed 103 Ohio St.3d 1493, 816 N.E.2d 1080, 2004-Ohio-5605. Sentencing And Punishment ⚷ 323

Evidence supported finding that during the group assault of first victim and prior to the shooting of second victim, defendant had knowledge that at least one of his companions was armed with a gun, thus supporting gun specification convictions; during assault on first victim a gun fell to the floor and someone screamed, "Get your gun, get your gun," second victim's death resulted from gunshot wounds and occurred in propinquity to the crimes that were committed in first victim's apartment. State v. Brown (Ohio App. 10 Dist., Franklin, 06-10-2004) No. 03AP-130, 2004-Ohio-2990, 2004 WL 1277498, Unreported, appeal not allowed 103 Ohio St.3d 1481, 816 N.E.2d 255, 2004-Ohio-5405. Sentencing And Punishment ⚷ 323

Jury instruction that permitted conviction for carrying firearm during drug-trafficking offense based only on possession of the weapon was not plain error, though instruction was erroneous under *Bailey* and error was not waived; properly instructed jury would have concluded that defendant physically transported a firearm that was immediately available for use, as necessary for conviction, based on loaded gun found beneath car seat where defendant was sitting at time of arrest for cocaine possession, and thus defendant's substantial rights were not affected. U.S. v. Taylor (C.A.6 (Ohio), 12-10-1996) 102 F.3d 767, rehearing and suggestion for rehearing en banc denied, certiorari denied 118 S.Ct. 327, 522 U.S. 927, 139 L.Ed.2d 254. Criminal Law ⚷ 1038.1(4); Weapons ⚷ 17(6)

8. Firearm specification; lesser included offense

Evidence, including victim's testimony as corroborated by investigating officer, as to number, types, and operability of firearms stolen from victim's home, was sufficient to support conviction of burglary with firearm specification. State v. Elersic (Ohio App. 11 Dist., Lake, 09-30-2004) No. 2002-L-172, 2004-Ohio-5301, 2004 WL 2804809, Unreported, appeal not allowed 105 Ohio St.3d 1407, 821 N.E.2d 1027, 2005-Ohio-279. Burglary ⚷ 41(1)

Failing to give jury instruction on one-year firearm specification did not constitute plain error, where verdict forms required jury to make specific and separate factual findings as to one-year and three-year specifications and jury concluded that defendant engaged in behavior which satisfied both one-year and three-year specifications. State v. Marbury (Ohio App. 10 Dist., Franklin, 06-29-2004) No. 03AP-233, 2004-Ohio-3373, 2004 WL 1445224, Unreported, appeal not allowed 103 Ohio St.3d 1493, 816 N.E.2d 1080, 2004-Ohio-5605. Criminal Law ⚷ 1038.2

Giving jury instructions on element of aggravated robbery and three-year firearm specification related to use of weapon, which was not included in indictment, did not constitute plain error, where reasonable jury would not have found defendant not guilty of robbery and one-year firearm specification but guilty of aggravated robbery and three-year firearm specification, given store employee's testimony that defendant opened up defendant's coat, revealed gun tucked in defendant's pants, and told employee to stand still. State v. Marbury (Ohio App. 10 Dist., Franklin, 06-29-2004) No. 03AP-233, 2004-Ohio-3373, 2004 WL 1445224, Unreported, appeal not allowed 103 Ohio St.3d 1493, 816 N.E.2d 1080, 2004-Ohio-5605. Criminal Law ⚷ 1038.1(3.1); Criminal Law ⚷ 1038.1(4)

Evidence was sufficient to support finding that defendant was in possession of handgun while in possession of cocaine, as required to establish firearm specification in prosecution for possession of cocaine and conviction on firearm specification was not against manifest weight of evidence; sergeant testified that defendant admitted in interview following arrest that he was in possession of both crack cocaine and firearm on night in question and victim of abduction, of which defendant was also convicted, testified that defendant was in possession of handgun entire evening, including when he offered her crack cocaine. State v. Cerutti (Ohio App. 11 Dist., Lake, 06-22-2004) No. 2002-L-140, 2004-Ohio-3335, 2004 WL 1433656, Unreported. Sentencing And Punishment ⚷ 323

Evidence in prosecution for drug trafficking established defendant's constructive possession of weapon found in his residence, as required to support one-year firearm specification; firearm in question was located in defendant's bedroom and was operable and loaded, and defendant's occupancy of residence was established by testimony of detective who made controlled drug buys from defendant at residence and through utility checks. State v. White (Ohio App. 8 Dist., Cuyahoga, 01-22-2004) No. 82495, 2004-Ohio-228, 2004 WL 97595, Unreported. Sentencing And Punishment ⚷ 726(3)

Juvenile's waiver of preliminary bindover hearing was permissible, and thus, bindover judgment was sufficient to establish that transfer of jurisdiction from juvenile court to general division was done properly; juvenile's waiver of preliminary bindover hearing was essentially stipulation that there was probable cause to believe that he committed aggravated robbery, that he had used firearm in offense, and that he had firearm on or about his person, and juvenile's waiver of preliminary bindover hearing was not attempt to waive subject matter jurisdiction. State v. Pruitt (Ohio App. 11 Dist., Trumbull, 12-20-2002) No. 2001-T-0121, 2002-Ohio-7164, 2002 WL 32868031, Unreported. Infants ⚷ 68.7(3)

Trier of fact is to consider all the relevant facts and circumstances surrounding the crime, including any threats made by the suspect holding the firearm, when determining whether the suspect was in possession of a firearm, and thus is guilty of firearm specification in connection with underlying offenses. State v. Sanders (Ohio App. 1 Dist., 09-25-1998) 130 Ohio App.3d 92, 719 N.E.2d 619, dismissed, appeal not allowed 84 Ohio St.3d 1472, 704 N.E.2d 579. Weapons ⚷ 17(4)

Firearm specification must be charged in indictment and state that offender had firearm on or about his person or under his control while committing offense. State v. Nowlin (Ohio App. 4 Dist., 11-25-1996) 115 Ohio App.3d 778, 686 N.E.2d 334, dismissed, appeal not allowed 78 Ohio St.3d 1439, 676 N.E.2d 1186. Indictment And Information ⚖ 113

Trial court was bound by statute to impose determinate sentence for defendant who entered guilty plea to lesser included charge of aggravated assault where indictment never contained required specification providing notice that indefinite term would be sought; indictment originally charged felonious assault and was amended to state lesser included offense but was never amended to include notice specification required before indefinite term could be imposed for aggravated assault. State v. Hawes (Ohio App. 6 Dist., 08-30-1996) 113 Ohio App.3d 777, 682 N.E.2d 31. Assault And Battery ⚖ 100

Evidence was sufficient to sustain defendant's conviction for firearm specification while committing felony; record showed that officers found loaded, operable nine-millimeter handgun under mattress in defendant's bedroom, and that gun was about 10 to 12 feet from defendant at time of arrest, and officer testified that gun posed threat to officers since distance could be traveled in less than a second. State v. Brown (Ohio App. 3 Dist., 10-31-1995) 107 Ohio App.3d 194, 668 N.E.2d 514. Sentencing And Punishment ⚖ 323

Sentencing defendant for firearm specifications was improper where all firearm specifications had been dismissed at trial. State v. Williams (Ohio App. 8 Dist., 07-31-1995) 105 Ohio App.3d 471, 664 N.E.2d 576, cause dismissed 74 Ohio St.3d 1442, 656 N.E.2d 343, dismissed, appeal not allowed 74 Ohio St.3d 1444, 656 N.E.2d 345. Sentencing And Punishment ⚖ 372

Defendant's stipulation, for purposes of plea agreement, that aggravated assault was lesser included offense to original felonious assault, and defendant's express waiver of any right he may have had to grand jury and their consideration of the specification, amounted to waiver of claim that specification in original indictment did not allow imposition of three-year actual incarceration for gun specification, because aggravated assault was not a lesser included offense of felonious assault. State v. Gaughan (Ohio App. 4 Dist., 04-27-1995) 103 Ohio App.3d 169, 658 N.E.2d 1113. Criminal Law ⚖ 275.2

Where felonious assault counts for which defendant was indicted contained gun specifications, firearm specification applied to lesser aggravated assault charge to which defendant pled no contest. State v. Gaughan (Ohio App. 4 Dist., 04-27-1995) 103 Ohio App.3d 169, 658 N.E.2d 1113. Indictment And Information ⚖ 113

Where a defendant is convicted of a third- or fourth-degree felony that is a lesser included offense of a felony of greater degree, and where the felony of greater degree is charged in the indictment and is accompanied by a firearm specification, pursuant to RC 2941.141(A), the firearm specification applies to the lesser included offense. State v. Lytle (Ohio 1990) 49 Ohio St.3d 154, 551 N.E.2d 950, rehearing denied 50 Ohio St.3d 712, 553 N.E.2d 1368. Sentencing And Punishment ⚖ 77

Court did not impose a three-year or six-year mandatory prison term for underlying offense of receipt of stolen property, and thus, one-year prison sentence on firearm specification was not precluded. State v. Elersic (Ohio App. 11 Dist., Lake, 06-07-2002) No. 2000-L-145, 2002-Ohio-2945, 2002 WL 1270599, Unreported. Sentencing And Punishment ⚖ 77

2941.142 Specification concerning offense of violence while participating in criminal gang activity

(A) Imposition of a mandatory prison term of one, two, or three years pursuant to division (I) of section 2929.14 of the Revised Code upon an offender who committed a felony that is an offense of violence while participating in a criminal gang is precluded unless the indictment, count in the indictment, or information charging the felony specifies that the offender committed the felony that is an offense of violence while participating in a criminal gang. The specification shall be stated at the end of the body of the indictment, count, or information, and shall be in substantially the following form:

"SPECIFICATION (or, SPECIFICATION TO THE FIRST COUNT). The grand jurors (or insert the person's or the prosecuting attorney's name when appropriate) further find and specify that (set forth that the offender committed the felony that is an offense of violence while participating in a criminal gang.)"

(B) The specification described in division (A) of this section may be used in a delinquent child proceeding in the manner and for the purpose described in section 2152.17 of the Revised Code.

(C) As used in this section, "criminal gang" has the same meaning as in section 2923.41 of the Revised Code.

(2000 S 179, § 3, eff. 1–1–02; 1998 H 2, eff. 1–1–99)

Historical and Statutory Notes

Ed. Note: Former 2941.142 repealed by 1995 S 2, eff. 7–1–96; 1983 S 210, eff. 7–1–83.

Amendment Note: 2000 S 179, § 3, eff. 1–1–02, added new division (B); and redesignated former division (B) as division (C).

Cross References

Prison terms, gang related activity with specifications, 2929.14

Library References

Indictment and Information ⚷113.

Westlaw Topic No. 210.

Research References

Encyclopedias

OH Jur. 3d Criminal Law § 1918, Generally—Work-Related Need for Weapon.

OH Jur. 3d Criminal Law § 2370, Violence Specification; Sexual Motivation and Sexual Predator Specifications.

OH Jur. 3d Criminal Law § 3292, Participation in Criminal Gang Activity.

OH Jur. 3d Family Law § 1696, Commitment to Youth Commission.

Treatises and Practice Aids

Katz, Giannelli, Blair and Lipton, Baldwin's Ohio Practice, Criminal Law, § 40:5, Nature and Contents.

Katz, Giannelli, Blair and Lipton, Baldwin's Ohio Practice, Criminal Law, § 118:9, Criminal Gang Add-Ons.

Katz, Giannelli, Blair and Lipton, Baldwin's Ohio Practice, Criminal Law, § 62:10, Waiver of Jury Trial.

Carlin, Baldwin's Ohio Practice, Merrick-Rippner Probate Law § 107:92, Enhanced Dispositions Due to Felony Specifications, Effective January 1, 2002.

Giannelli & Yeomans, Ohio Juvenile Law § 27:3, Department of Youth Services Commitment.

Law Review and Journal Commentaries

A Brief History of Ohio Gang Trends—Changes in Legislation as a Result of Gangs and Successful Prevention Methods, Linda M. Schmidt. 10 Baldwin's Ohio Sch L J 69 (November/December 1998).

Preventing Violence in Ohio's Schools, Comment. 33 Akron L Rev 311 (2000).

Notes of Decisions

---

1. Specification as essential element

Trial court was warranted in permitting evidence of a prior conviction for burglary in prosecution for capital murder, where the prior conviction, representing a felony of violence, was a direct element of the principal offense charged of knowingly possessing a weapon while under disability. State v. Twyford (Ohio, 03-06-2002) 94 Ohio St.3d 340, 763 N.E.2d 122, 2002-Ohio-894, reconsideration denied 95 Ohio St.3d 1423, 766 N.E.2d 163, 2002-Ohio-1737, stay granted 95 Ohio St.3d 1429, 766 N.E.2d 996, 2002-Ohio-1924, certiorari denied 123 S.Ct. 302, 537 U.S. 917, 154 L.Ed.2d 203. Criminal Law ⚷ 369.2(3.1)

Where a prior conviction elevates the degree of a subsequent offense, it is an essential element of the subsequent offense and may not be bifurcated from the remainder of the elements of the subsequent offense under RC 2941.142 or 2941.143; thus, a defendant's prior conviction for domestic violence is an essential element of a later charged felony offense of domestic violence and accordingly, it cannot be bifurcated from the remainder of the elements of the latter offense. State v. Ireson (Ross 1991) 72 Ohio App.3d 235, 594 N.E.2d 165, dismissed, jurisdictional motion overruled 61 Ohio St.3d 1418, 574 N.E.2d 1089.

2. Improper inclusion of specification

A voluntary manslaughter prior conviction specification is improperly included in a murder indictment as the prior conviction is irrelevant to either the crime charged or the penalty for murder and the specification is not introduced to disprove a defense of mistake or accident nor is it relevant to intent. State v. Banks (Franklin 1992) 78 Ohio App.3d 206, 604 N.E.2d 219.

3. Separate determination of specification

In an appeal from a conviction of felonious assault with a gun specification, a defendant's claim of ineffective assistance of counsel and allegation that he was prejudiced by his counsel's failure to bifurcate the aggravated felony specification is not supported where the defendant chooses to testify;

the choice to forgo bifurcation is not unreasonable since evidence of the defendant's prior convictions would be admissible on the issue of his credibility. State v. Bell (Cuyahoga 1990) 70 Ohio App.3d 765, 592 N.E.2d 848.

Where a prior conviction specification contained in an indictment is not an element of the crime charged but rather goes solely to the matter of actual incarceration, and where the defendant requests that the trial judge, in a case tried to a jury, determine the existence of the specification at the sentencing hearing, it is prejudicially erroneous to permit evidence of the specification to go to the jury. State v. Swiger (Shelby 1987) 34 Ohio App.3d 371, 518 N.E.2d 972. Criminal Law ⚷ 1169.11

The language of RC 2941.142 is mandatory; thus, where prior crimes in violation of RC 2907.12 are disclosed to the jury in a rape trial, despite the felon's request that the specification be considered only during sentencing, the felon's subsequent conviction must be reversed. State v. Watters (Ohio App. 1 Dist. 1985) 27 Ohio App.3d 186, 500 N.E.2d 312, 27 O.B.R. 224.

A defense request that existence of earlier convictions be tried at a separate hearing by the jury cannot be granted, nor is it effective as a request that the judge determine the convictions apart from the jury under RC 2941.142. State v. Byrd (Cuyahoga 1985) 26 Ohio App.3d 91, 498 N.E.2d 217, 26 O.B.R. 266.

4. Penalty enhancement

Where an indictment under RC 2903.11(A)(2), constituting an aggravated felony of the second degree, fails to include a specification, the trial court abuses its discretion by sentencing the defendant to an indefinite term of imprisonment. State v Parker, No. 15–87–1 (3d Dist Ct App, Van Wert, 3–18–88).

Where an indictment labels the specification as a "violence" specification but substantially complies to the form required for a prior conviction specification, an enhanced sentence based on an aggravated felony specification is proper. State v Tate, Nos. 52730 to 52732 (8th Dist Ct App, Cuyahoga, 9–3–87).

Where an indictment fails to charge an aggravating specification, it is error for a court to impose an enhanced penalty based on the presence of an aggravating specification. State v Burke, No. C–840526 (1st Dist Ct App, Hamilton, 5–29–85).

2941.143 Specification concerning school safety zone

Imposition of a sentence by a court pursuant to division (J) of section 2929.14 of the Revised Code is precluded unless the indictment, count in the indictment, or information charging aggravated murder, murder, or a felony of the first, second, or third degree that is an offense of violence specifies that the offender committed the offense in a school safety zone or towards a person in a school safty[1] zone. The specification shall be stated at the end of the body of the indictment, count, or information and shall be in substantially the following form:

"SPECIFICATION (or, SPECIFICATION TO THE FIRST COUNT). The grand jurors (or insert the person's or the prosecuting attorney's name when appropriate) further find and specify that (set forth that the offender committed aggravated murder, murder, or the felony of the first, second, or third degree that is an offense of violence in a school safety zone or towards a person in a school safety zone)."

(1999 S 1, eff. 8–6–99)

[1] So in original; 1999 S 1.

Historical and Statutory Notes

Ed. Note: Former 2941.143 repealed by 1995 S 2, eff. 7–1–96; 1983 S 210, eff. 7–1–83.

Cross References

Prison terms, 2929.14

Research References

Encyclopedias

OH Jur. 3d Criminal Law § 2370, Violence Specification; Sexual Motivation and Sexual Predator Specifications.

OH Jur. 3d Criminal Law § 3293, Offense Within School Safety Zone.

Treatises and Practice Aids

Katz, Giannelli, Blair and Lipton, Baldwin's Ohio Practice, Criminal Law, § 40:5, Nature and Contents.

Katz, Giannelli, Blair and Lipton, Baldwin's Ohio Practice, Criminal Law, § 40:7, Amendments to the Indictment.

Katz, Giannelli, Blair and Lipton, Baldwin's Ohio Practice, Criminal Law, § 62:10, Waiver of Jury Trial.

Katz, Giannelli, Blair and Lipton, Baldwin's Ohio Practice, Criminal Law, § 80:23, Appellate Review of Sentencing.

Katz, Giannelli, Blair and Lipton, Baldwin's Ohio Practice, Criminal Law, § 118:10, School Safety Zone Add-on.

Adrine & Ruden, Ohio Domestic Violence Law § 2:7, Felony Violations.

Notes of Decisions

Ed. Note: *This section contains annotations from former RC 2941.143.*

1. Violence specification

Incest constitutes a crime of violence for purposes of the prior conviction specification of RC 2941.143. State v Jaynes, No. 2–92–3 (3d Dist Ct App, Auglaize, 1–29–93).

Escape is deemed by RC 2901.01(I)(1) to be an offense of violence for purposes of specifications pursuant to RC 2941.143. State v Van Houten, No. 88CA–000001 (5th Dist Ct App, Knox, 8–1–88).

2. Penalty enhancement

Indictment charging defendant with second-degree felony punishable by indefinite sentence put defendant on notice that prosecutor was seeking indefinite sentence and, thus, defendant could be sentenced to indefinite term upon pleading guilty to fourth-degree felony, even though indictment lacked specification charging elements ordinarily required for indefinite sentence for fourth-degree felony conviction, provided that facts would support finding that defendant satisfied one of prerequisites for indefinite sentence. State v. Carroll (Ohio App. 4 Dist., 06-06-1995) 104 Ohio App.3d 372, 662 N.E.2d 65. Sentencing And Punishment ⚷ 1367

Counsel was not ineffective for failing to object to enhanced sentence for breaking and entering, since sentence enhancement was result of defendant's plea agreement, by which he waived his right to have enhancement specification that he had previously been convicted of violent crime presented to grand jury for consideration, and plea bargain resulted in dismissal of other two counts of indictment. State v. Fryling (Logan 1992) 85 Ohio App.3d 557, 620 N.E.2d 862. Criminal Law ⚷ 641.13(7)

The imposition of an indefinite sentence is proper where a defendant dog owner is found guilty of violating RC 955.22(D) after his pit bull dog gets loose from a condominium patio and attacks and kills a two-year-old child. State v. Ferguson (Franklin 1991) 76 Ohio App.3d 747, 603 N.E.2d 345.

Where indictment charges accused with second-degree felony and indictment contains specification which would result in indefinite term, lesser included fourth-degree felony offense need not separately appear in indictment with its own specifications in order to impose indefinite term so long as original offense is accompanied by specification which places accused on notice that he faces possible indefinite term. State v. Valentine (Warren 1991) 77 Ohio App.3d 489, 602 N.E.2d 722. Indictment And Information ⚷ 188

A court of common pleas may impose the indefinite term of incarceration prescribed by RC 2929.11(B)(7) where an accused has been convicted of a fourth degree felony the commission of which caused physical harm to any person, provided the indictment which initiated the criminal proceeding contains the specification contained in RC 2941.143 and the accused was convicted thereon. State v. Witwer (Ohio 1992) 64 Ohio St.3d 421, 596 N.E.2d 451, rehearing denied 65 Ohio St.3d 1421, 598 N.E.2d 1172. Indictment And Information ⚷ 113

In a prosecution for possession of criminal tools, the sentencing court was permitted to find the existence of a violence specification for purposes of imposing a sentence of one and one half to five years where the defendant admits that he had a prior conviction for the offense of violence and the jury determines that the defendant is guilty of possession of criminal tools as charged. State v. Farris (Cuyahoga 1991) 71 Ohio App.3d 817, 595 N.E.2d 453.

Because an indictment containing no violence specification cannot give rise to an indefinite sentence, it is error to sentence a defendant convicted of the underlying definite term felony of having a weapon while under a disability to a mandatory three years' enhanced sentence. State v. Ellington (Cuyahoga 1989) 65 Ohio App.3d 473, 584 N.E.2d 784, dismissed 49 Ohio St.3d 716, 552 N.E.2d 945.

Where the indictment for aggravated vehicular homicide, RC 2903.06, contains a violence specification, RC 2941.143, an indeterminate sentence may be imposed upon conviction. State v. Runnels (Cuyahoga 1989) 56 Ohio App.3d 120, 565 N.E.2d 610, motion overruled 42 Ohio St.3d 711, 538 N.E.2d 123, rehearing denied 43 Ohio St.3d 713, 541 N.E.2d 78.

A violence specification pursuant to RC 2941.143 is not an element of the offense of aggravated vehicular homicide, but rather a factor permitting the imposition of an indefinite sentence, and a motion to strike the specification as surplusage will be denied. State v. Kavlich (Cuyahoga 1986) 33 Ohio App.3d 240, 515 N.E.2d 652.

As stated in RC 2941.143, a defendant may not be sentenced to an indefinite term pursuant to RC 2929.11(B)(6) or 2929.11(B)(7) unless his indictment includes the specification of physical harm set forth in RC 2941.143. State v. Howiler (Lake 1985) 26 Ohio App.3d 181, 499 N.E.2d 10, 26 O.B.R. 401.

A specification pursuant to RC 2941.143 is a prerequisite to the imposition of an indefinite sentence pursuant to RC 2929.11(B)(6) or 2929.11(B)(7). State v. Tyson (Hamilton 1984) 19 Ohio App.3d 90, 482 N.E.2d 1327, 19 O.B.R. 175.

In the absence of an admission, stipulation, or certified judgment of conviction, an enhanced penalty based on a prior conviction for an offense of violence may not be imposed. State v Thomas, No. S–91–32 (6th Dist Ct App, Sandusky, 9–30–92).

Where an indictment under RC 2907.05(A)(1), constituting a fourth degree felony, fails to include a specification, the trial court abuses its discretion by sentencing the defendant to an indefinite term of imprisonment. State v Parker, No. 15–87–1 (3d Dist Ct App, Van Wert, 3–18–88).

A defendant convicted of a fourth degree felony may be sentenced to an indefinite term of incarceration even if the indictment does not contain a physical harm specification where such indictment charged the defendant with a first or second degree felony. State v Gillenwater, No. 651 (4th Dist Ct App, Highland, 11–11–87).

A specification pursuant to RC 2941.143 is a prerequisite to the imposition of an indefinite sentence pursuant to RC 2929.11(B) absent a waiver of the right to a definite sentence. State v Dunn, No. 13093 (9th Dist Ct App, Summit, 10–7–87).

A trial court may impose an indefinite term of sentence on a defendant convicted of gross sexual imposition only if the indictment contains a specification that the defendant caused physical harm to his victim pursuant to RC 2929.143. State v Griswold, No. L–85–333 (6th Dist Ct App, Lucas, 3–20–87).

3. Amendment of indictment

Indictment could properly be amended to include specification that threat of physical harm had occurred during offense of attempted abduction when defendant knowingly and voluntarily assented to amendment pursuant to plea agreement with prosecution. State v. Childress (Ohio App. 3 Dist., 10-22-1993) 91 Ohio App.3d 258, 632 N.E.2d 562. Indictment And Information ⚷ 159(1)

Trial court properly amended indictment in open court to include specification that defendant had previously been convicted of crime of violence, without presenting it to grand jury, where amendment was made pursuant to plea agreement in which defendant pled guilty to fourth-degree felony charge and allowed amendment of indictment to provide prior crime specification, defendant attested in writing that he understood and agreed to plea, and defendant was advised that specification could result in enhanced sentence. State v. Fryling (Logan 1992) 85 Ohio App.3d 557, 620 N.E.2d 862. Indictment And Information ⚷ 159(1)

The state may not amend an indictment pursuant to Crim R 7(D) so as to include a specification contained in RC 2941.143 without first presenting the specification to the grand jury or following the other alternatives contained in RC 2941.143. State v. Dilley (Ohio 1989) 47 Ohio St.3d 20, 546 N.E.2d 937. Indictment And Information ⚷ 159(2)

State can add a specification to an indictment by stipulated amendment in accordance with plea negotiations in open court without first presenting the specification to the grand jury because under this procedure a defendant waives his right to have the specification presented to the grand jury and nothing in RC 2941.143 indicates that a defendant may not stipulate to the existence of a prior conviction of an offense of violence under Crim R 11(F). State v Wendt, No. 93–P–0042, 1993 WL 545125 (11th Dist Ct App, Portage, 12–3–93).

4. Separate determination of specification

A defendant is not entitled to have his offense of violence specification determined by a three-judge panel because his noncapital crimes are joined with a capital crime; RC 2941.143 offers defendant only two options: he may have the specifications determined by the jury or the trial judge and no statute allows him to try some issues to a jury and others to a panel. State v. Waddy (Ohio 1992) 63 Ohio St.3d 424, 588 N.E.2d 819, rehearing denied 63 Ohio St.3d 1470, 590 N.E.2d 1269, stay granted 64 Ohio St.3d 1424, 594 N.E.2d 625, certiorari denied 113 S.Ct. 338, 506 U.S. 921, 121 L.Ed.2d 255, rehearing granted, opinion recalled 71 Ohio St.3d 1418, 642 N.E.2d 384, dismissal of habeas corpus affirmed, dismissed, appeal not allowed 80 Ohio St.3d 1423, 685 N.E.2d 237, stay denied 80 Ohio St.3d 1479, 687 N.E.2d 474, certiorari denied 118 S.Ct. 1198, 140 L.Ed.2d 327.

RC 2941.143 grants an accused the option to have sentencing specifications litigated in a separate sentencing hearing before the trial judge, leaving only the underlying charge for the jury's consideration; thus, once the accused requests a bifurcated determination of the existence of sentencing specifications, it is error for the court to deny the request. State v. Riggins (Cuyahoga 1986) 35 Ohio App.3d 1, 519 N.E.2d 397.

5. Specification as essential element

Trial court did not commit plain error by instructing jury on firearm specifications, in prosecution for vandalism, even though defendant was not subject to indefinite term sentence for vandalism and, therefore, could not be sentenced on firearms specifications, where court did not impose any sentence for firearm specifications; defendant suffered no prejudice. State v. Wong (Ohio App. 4 Dist., 05-12-1994) 95 Ohio App.3d 39, 641 N.E.2d 1137, reconsideration denied 97 Ohio App.3d 244, 646 N.E.2d 538, dismissed, appeal not allowed 70 Ohio St.3d 1455, 639 N.E.2d 793. Criminal Law ⚷ 1038.1(3.1)

Statutory crime of breaking and entering was not "crime of violence," for purposes of using earlier conviction to elevate subsequent offense of robbery from misdemeanor to felony for use of concealed weapon and enhancing sentences for robbery and carrying concealed weapon; breaking and entering was not listed in statute listing crimes of violence and was not analogous to any listed offense. State v. Mosley (Hamilton 1993) 88 Ohio App.3d 461, 624 N.E.2d 297. Sentencing And Punishment ⚷ 1263

Where a prior conviction elevates the degree of a subsequent offense, it is an essential element of the subsequent offense and may not be bifurcated from the remainder of the elements of the subsequent offense under RC 2941.142 or 2941.143; thus, a defendant's prior conviction for domestic violence is an essential element of a later charged felony offense of domestic violence and accordingly, it cannot be bifurcated from the remainder of the elements of the latter offense. State v. Ireson (Ross 1991) 72 Ohio App.3d 235, 594 N.E.2d 165, dismissed, jurisdictional motion overruled 61 Ohio St.3d 1418, 574 N.E.2d 1089.

Where evidence of a prior conviction is already before a jury as an element of the crime of having weapons under a disability, it is not reversible error for a trial court to submit prior conviction specifications to a jury despite a defendant's request that the trial court determine the specifications, so long as the ultimate determination on the specifications is made by the trial court. State v. Thompson (Summit 1988) 46 Ohio App.3d 157, 546 N.E.2d 441, dismissed 38 Ohio St.3d 702, 532 N.E.2d 1317, denial of post-conviction relief affirmed.

A two-to-five year indefinite sentence imposed for a fourth-degree felony of aggravated assault is plain error where a second count of an indictment, which charges the defendant with felonious assault and under which the defendant is convicted of the lesser offense of aggravated assault, is not accompanied by a specification. State v Key, Nos. C–930205+, 1994 WL 25313 (1st Dist Ct App, Hamilton, 2–2–94).

6. Physical harm specification

Causation assumes some degree of intent by perpetrator of the act and, therefore, statute stating that imposition of indefinite term is precluded unless indictment specifies that, during commission of the offense, offender caused physical harm to any person does not impose strict liability. State v. Patton (Ohio App. 1 Dist., 10-11-1995) 106 Ohio App.3d 736, 667 N.E.2d 57, dismissed, appeal not allowed 75 Ohio St.3d 1405, 661 N.E.2d 755. Sentencing And Punishment ⚷ 68; Sentencing And Punishment ⚷ 85

Self-defense was a valid defense to the physical-harm specification in prosecution for having a weapon under disability, and thus, after jury returned its not guilty verdict on the murder charge on self-defense grounds, it was incumbent on trial court to enter a judgment of acquittal on the physical harm specification. State v. Patton (Ohio App. 1 Dist., 10-11-1995) 106 Ohio App.3d 736, 667 N.E.2d 57, dismissed, appeal not allowed 75 Ohio St.3d 1405, 661 N.E.2d 755. Sentencing And Punishment ⚷ 85; Sentencing And Punishment ⚷ 375

Trial court incorrectly rejected defendant's request for instruction on self-defense relative to the physical-harm specification. State v. Patton (Ohio App. 1 Dist., 10-11-1995) 106 Ohio App.3d 736, 667 N.E.2d 57, dismissed, appeal not allowed 75 Ohio St.3d 1405, 661 N.E.2d 755. Criminal Law ⚷ 796

Where there is insufficient evidence to support a physical harm specification and the indictment does not allege the defendant made an actual threat of physical harm with a deadly weapon, the imposition of an indefinite sentence with three years added for a firearm specification is contrary to law. State v Jimenez, No. 93CA005613, 1994 WL 45755 (9th Dist Ct App, Lorain, 2–9–94).

Where victim suffered two broken legs, broken wrist, and broken jaw after defendant dragged victim alongside his car, and grand jury indicted defendant for fourth degree felony of aggravated vehicular assault with specification of physical harm as provided in RC 2941.143, court did not err in denying defendant's motion to delete specification of physical harm and imposed an indefinite sentence on defendant after conviction. State v Hein, No. L–92–309, 1993 WL 313598 (6th Dist Ct App, Lucas, 8–6–93).

2941.144 Specification concerning possession of automatic firearm or firearm with silencer

(A) Imposition of a six-year mandatory prison term upon an offender under division (D)(1)(a) of section 2929.14 of the Revised Code is precluded unless the indictment, count in the indictment, or information charging the offense specifies that the offender had a firearm that is an automatic firearm or that was equipped with a firearm muffler or silencer on or about the offender's person or under the offender's control while committing the offense. The specification shall be stated at the end of the body of the indictment, count, or information and shall be stated in substantially the following form:

"SPECIFICATION (or, SPECIFICATION TO THE FIRST COUNT). The Grand Jurors (or insert the person's or the prosecuting attorney's name when appropriate) further find and specify that (set forth that the offender had a firearm that is an automatic firearm or that was equipped with a firearm muffler or silencer on or about the offender's person or under the offender's control while committing the offense)."

(B) Imposition of a six-year mandatory prison term upon an offender under division (D)(1)(a) of section 2929.14 of the Revised Code is precluded if a court imposes a three-year or one-year mandatory prison term on the offender under that division relative to the same felony.

(C) The specification described in division (A) of this section may be used in a delinquent child proceeding in the manner and for the purpose described in section 2152.17 of the Revised Code.

(D) As used in this section, "firearm" and "automatic firearm" have the same meanings as in section 2923.11 of the Revised Code.

(2000 S 179, § 3, eff. 1–1–02; 1999 S 107, eff. 3–23–00; 1995 S 2, eff. 7–1–96; 1990 S 258, eff. 11–20–90)

Historical and Statutory Notes

Amendment Note: 2000 S 179, § 3, eff. 1–1–02, added new division (C); and redesignated former division (C) as division (D).

Amendment Note: 1999 S 107 deleted "(i)" after "(D)(1)(a)" in divisions (A) and (B).

Amendment Note: 1995 S 2 rewrote this section, which previously read:

"(A) Imposition of a term of actual incarceration upon an offender under division (A) of section 2929.72 of the Revised Code for having a firearm that is an automatic firearm or that was equipped with a firearm muffler or silencer on or about his person or under his control while committing a felony is precluded unless the indictment, count in the indictment, or information charging the offense specifies that the offender did have such a firearm on or about his person or under his control while committing the offense. A specification to an indictment, count in an indictment, or information charging the offender with having a firearm that is an automatic firearm or that was equipped with a firearm muffler or silencer on or about his person or under his control while committing a felony shall be stated at the end of the body of the indictment, count, or information, and shall be stated in substantially the following form:

"'SPECIFICATION (or, SPECIFICATION TO THE FIRST COUNT). The Grand Jurors (or insert the person's or the prosecuting attorney's name when appropriate) further find and specify that (set forth that the offender had a firearm that is an automatic firearm or that was equipped with a firearm muffler or silencer on or about his person or under his control while committing the offense).'

"(B) As used in this section, 'firearm' and 'automatic firearm' have the same meanings as in section 2923.11 of the Revised Code."

Cross References

Delinquent children, information provided to foster caregivers regarding, 2152.72

Library References

Indictment and Information ⚷113.

Westlaw Topic No. 210.

Baldwin's Ohio Legislative Service, 1995 S 2—LSC Analysis, p 8/L–2907

Baldwin's Ohio Legislative Service, 1990 Laws of Ohio, S 258—LSC Analysis, p 5–954

Research References

Encyclopedias

OH Jur. 3d Criminal Law § 2369, Firearm Specification.

OH Jur. 3d Criminal Law § 3291, Automatic or Silencer-Equipped Firearm.

OH Jur. 3d Family Law § 1696, Commitment to Youth Commission.

OH Jur. 3d Family Law § 1698.5, Serious Youthful Offender.

Treatises and Practice Aids

Katz, Giannelli, Blair and Lipton, Baldwin's Ohio Practice, Criminal Law, § 40:5, Nature and Contents.

Katz, Giannelli, Blair and Lipton, Baldwin's Ohio Practice, Criminal Law, § 106:3, Firearm Possession in Liquor-Permit Premises.

Katz, Giannelli, Blair and Lipton, Baldwin's Ohio Practice, Criminal Law, § 106:4, Deadly Weapon or Ordnance on School Premises.

Katz, Giannelli, Blair and Lipton, Baldwin's Ohio Practice, Criminal Law, § 106:9, Discharging Firearm Into a School or Home.

Katz, Giannelli, Blair and Lipton, Baldwin's Ohio Practice, Criminal Law, § 117:2, Mandatory Prison Sentences.

Katz, Giannelli, Blair and Lipton, Baldwin's Ohio Practice, Criminal Law, § 118:7, Gun Enhancement.

Katz, Giannelli, Blair and Lipton, Baldwin's Ohio Practice, Criminal Law, § 106:11, Unlawful Possession of Dangerous Ordnance.

Carlin, Baldwin's Ohio Practice, Merrick-Rippner Probate Law § 107:84, Disposition of Delinquent Children—Prior to January 1, 2002.

Carlin, Baldwin's Ohio Practice, Merrick-Rippner Probate Law § 107:92, Enhanced Dispositions Due to Felony Specifications, Effective January 1, 2002.

Giannelli & Yeomans, Ohio Juvenile Law § 27:3, Department of Youth Services Commitment.

2941.145 Specification concerning use of firearm to facilitate offense

(A) Imposition of a three-year mandatory prison term upon an offender under division (D)(1)(a) of section 2929.14 of the Revised Code is precluded unless the indictment, count in the indictment, or information charging the offense specifies that the offender had a firearm on or about the offender's person or under the offender's control while committing the offense and displayed the firearm, brandished the firearm, indicated that the offender possessed the firearm, or used it to facilitate the offense. The specification shall be stated at the end of the body of the indictment, count, or information, and shall be stated in substantially the following form:

"SPECIFICATION (or, SPECIFICATION TO THE FIRST COUNT). The Grand Jurors (or insert the person's or the prosecuting attorney's name when appropriate) further find and specify that (set forth that the offender had a firearm on or about the offender's person or under the offender's control while committing the offense and displayed the firearm, brandished the firearm, indicated that the offender possessed the firearm, or used it to facilitate the offense)."

(B) Imposition of a three-year mandatory prison term upon an offender under division (D)(1)(a) of section 2929.14 of the Revised Code is precluded if a court imposes a one-year or six-year mandatory prison term on the offender under that division relative to the same felony.

(C) The specification described in division (A) of this section may be used in a delinquent child proceeding in the manner and for the purpose described in section 2152.17 of the Revised Code.

(D) As used in this section, "firearm" has the same meaning as in section 2923.11 of the Revised Code.

(2000 S 179, § 3, eff. 1–1–02; 1999 S 107, eff. 3–23–00; 1995 S 2, eff. 7–1–96)

Historical and Statutory Notes

Amendment Note: 2000 S 179, § 3, eff. 1–1–02, added new division (C); and redesignated former division (C) as division (D).

Amendment Note: 1999 S 107 deleted "(i)" after "(D)(1)(a)" in divisions (A) and (B); and substituted "count" for "county" in division (A).

Cross References

Delinquent children, information provided to foster caregivers regarding, 2152.72

Library References

Indictment and Information ⚷113.
Westlaw Topic No. 210.

Baldwin's Ohio Legislative Service, 1995 S 2—LSC Analysis, p 8/L–2907

Research References

Encyclopedias

OH Jur. 3d Criminal Law § 83, Other Actions or Omissions.

OH Jur. 3d Criminal Law § 868, Purpose or Intent.

OH Jur. 3d Criminal Law § 886, Purpose or Intent to Kill.

OH Jur. 3d Criminal Law § 896, Relationship to Other Offenses.

OH Jur. 3d Criminal Law § 994, Weight and Sufficiency, Generally.

OH Jur. 3d Criminal Law § 1919, Overview; What Constitutes Disability.

OH Jur. 3d Criminal Law § 2369, Firearm Specification.

OH Jur. 3d Criminal Law § 2584, Right to Hearing on Competency.

OH Jur. 3d Criminal Law § 2808, What Charge May be Given to Urge Agreement; Impossible Verdict Instruction.

OH Jur. 3d Criminal Law § 3283, Three-Year Term.

OH Jur. 3d Criminal Law § 3340, Determining Whether Offenses Are Allied and of Similar

Import—Where Separate Punishments Authorized by Statute.

OH Jur. 3d Criminal Law § 3572, Generally; Plain Error Doctrine.

OH Jur. 3d Family Law § 1696, Commitment to Youth Commission.

OH Jur. 3d Family Law § 1698.5, Serious Youthful Offender.

Treatises and Practice Aids

Katz, Giannelli, Blair and Lipton, Baldwin's Ohio Practice, Criminal Law, § 40:5, Nature and Contents.

Katz, Giannelli, Blair and Lipton, Baldwin's Ohio Practice, Criminal Law, § 106:3, Firearm Possession in Liquor-Permit Premises.

Katz, Giannelli, Blair and Lipton, Baldwin's Ohio Practice, Criminal Law, § 106:4, Deadly Weapon or Ordnance on School Premises.

Katz, Giannelli, Blair and Lipton, Baldwin's Ohio Practice, Criminal Law, § 106:9, Discharging Firearm Into a School or Home.

Katz, Giannelli, Blair and Lipton, Baldwin's Ohio Practice, Criminal Law, § 117:2, Mandatory Prison Sentences.

Katz, Giannelli, Blair and Lipton, Baldwin's Ohio Practice, Criminal Law, § 118:7, Gun Enhancement.

Katz, Giannelli, Blair and Lipton, Baldwin's Ohio Practice, Criminal Law, § 153:9, Motion to Correct Improper Sentence—Firearm Specifications as Part of One Transaction.

Carlin, Baldwin's Ohio Practice, Merrick-Rippner Probate Law § 107:84, Disposition of Delinquent Children—Prior to January 1, 2002.

Carlin, Baldwin's Ohio Practice, Merrick-Rippner Probate Law § 107:92, Enhanced Dispositions Due to Felony Specifications, Effective January 1, 2002.

Giannelli & Yeomans, Ohio Juvenile Law § 27:3, Department of Youth Services Commitment.

Notes of Decisions

---

1. Constitutional issues—disproportionate sentences

Imposition of consecutive sentences for aggravated robbery with a firearm, receiving stolen property, and failure to comply with the order or signal of a police officer was proper, where trial court found on the record that consecutive sentences were necessary to protect the public and to punish defendant and that they were not disproportionate to defendant's conduct, and it also considered but rejected mitigating factors. State v. Glenn (Ohio App. 11 Dist., Lake, 06-04-2004) No. 2003-L-022, 2004-Ohio-2917, 2004 WL 1238346, Unreported. Sentencing And Punishment ⚷ 587; Sentencing And Punishment ⚷ 600

2. —— Double jeopardy, constitutional issues

State court determination that imposition of multiple sentences following petitioner's convictions on multiple counts that each included two separate firearms specifications for using firearm to facilitate offense and for using firearm from motor vehicle did not violate Double Jeopardy Clause was not contrary to, and did not involve unreasonable application of, clearly established federal law in *Blockburger v. United States*, and thus did not warrant federal habeas relief, where relevant state statute required imposition of cumulative penalties for different specifications. Carter v. Carter (C.A.6 (Ohio), 02-14-2003) No. 01-3649, 59 Fed.Appx. 104, 2003 WL 356176, Unreported. Habeas Corpus ⚷ 466

3. —— Speedy trial, constitutional issues

State's decision to re-indict defendant four days before his trial and some 400 days after his arrest for felonious assault, in order to amend his firearm specifications, violated defendant's speedy trial rights; when the State re-indicted defendant with the new specifications, it added a new element for him to consider in his defense—that he discharged the firearm from a motor vehicle, and the new indictment increased the penalty defendant was subject to from three years to five years on each specification. State v. Carter (Ohio App. 7 Dist., Mahoning, 03-18-2005) No. 03-MA-245, 2005-Ohio-1347, 2005 WL 678569, Unreported. Criminal Law ⚷ 577.14

4. Stolen gun

Firearm that was object of defendant's theft from deputy sheriff also supported firearm specification for aggravated robbery charge arising from that theft, where defendant used firearm immediately after the theft to facilitate his flight by committing carjacking. State v. Campbell (Ohio, 12-20-2000) 90 Ohio St.3d 320, 738 N.E.2d 1178, 2000-Ohio-183, reconsideration denied 91 Ohio St.3d 1433, 741 N.E.2d 896, certiorari denied 121 S.Ct. 2606, 533 U.S. 956, 150 L.Ed.2d 762, dismissal of post-conviction relief affirmed 2003-Ohio-6305, 2003 WL 22783857, appeal not allowed 102 Ohio St.3d 1470, 809 N.E.2d 1158, 2004-Ohio-2830. Robbery ⚷ 24.15(2)

5. Evidence

Defendant's conviction for murder with a firearm specification was not against the manifest weight of the evidence; first witness testified that defendant was involved in altercation with victim, that defendant shot victim twice from close range, and that defendant then ran away, second witness testified that she saw defendant point gun at victim and fire shot, second witness identified defendant from photo array and in court as person who shot victim, and jury had opportunity to hear testimony and evaluate credibility of witnesses. State v. Bliss (Ohio App. 10 Dist., Franklin, 08-04-2005) No. 04AP-216, 2005-Ohio-3987, 2005 WL 1840128, Unreported, appeal not allowed 107 Ohio St.3d 1699, 840 N.E.2d 204, 2005-Ohio-6763. Homicide ⚷ 1181

Evidence was sufficient to support convictions for aggravated robbery with firearm specification, felonious assault with firearm specification, and having weapon under disability; victim was accosted, shot, and robbed of money, suffered life-threatening injuries, and positively identified defendant as one of his assailants, defendant was found sitting in rear passenger seat of vehicle carrying more than $900 and with handgun on floorboard, only shell casing found at scene of shooting came from handgun, handgun was operable, and defendant stipulated to having prior drug conviction. State v. Roberts (Ohio App. 1 Dist., Hamilton, 06-17-2005) No. C-040262, 2005-Ohio-3034, 2005 WL 1413357, Unreported, opinion vacated and superseded 2005-Ohio-4050, 2005 WL 1863401, appeal not allowed 106 Ohio St.3d 1559, 836 N.E.2d 583, 2005-Ohio-5531. Assault And Battery ⚷ 91.6(1); Robbery ⚷ 24.15(2); Weapons ⚷ 17(4)

Trial court's reasoning that defendant used firearm was sufficient to support finding that defendant committed worst form of voluntary manslaughter, as required for imposition of maximum sentence for offense, even though defendant was also convicted of firearm specification in connection with offense; conviction for firearm specification did not erase fact that gun was used during offense as response to argument between defendant and victim. State v. Crites (Ohio App. 7 Dist., Mahoning, 05-26-2005) No. 04 MA 146, 2004-Ohio-2704, 2005 WL 1300784, Unreported. Sentencing And Punishment ⚷ 144

Defendant's convictions for two counts of aggravated robbery with attendant firearm specifications were not against the manifest weight or the sufficiency of the evidence; bartender testified that as she was closing club, she was accosted by a man with a gun and a stick, the assailant took approximately $175 from bartender's purse and approximately $4,000 to $8,000 from the club, defendant could not be excluded as a possible source of DNA found on black stocking hat worn by the assailant, and upon his arrest, defendant informed police that the only person who could put him at the scene of the robbery was dead. State v. Bell (Ohio App. 5 Dist., Stark, 05-16-2005) No. 2004-CA-00087, 2005-Ohio-2418, 2005 WL 1163257, Unreported. Robbery ⚷ 24.15(2); Robbery ⚷ 24.40

Defendant's conviction for complicity to murder with a gun specification was not against the manifest weight or the sufficiency of the evidence; defendant suspected that victim had broken into his car, and, rather than involve the police, he went out searching for victim, defendant testified that he fired a loaded semi-automatic weapon at victim, but no bullets discharged, and further evidence indicated that defendant supplied accomplice with a second gun used to kill victim. State v. Alexander (Ohio App. 9 Dist., Summit, 05-18-2005) No. 22295, 2005-Ohio-2393, 2005 WL 1162984, Unreported. Homicide ⚷ 1207

Evidence that defendant knowingly caused serious physical harm to another, knowingly caused physical harm to another by means of deadly weapon, and displayed firearm and used in commission of his offenses, was sufficient to support convictions on two counts of felonious assault and findings of related firearms specifications; victim saw defendant remove short black gun from his pants and fire gun once, shooting victim in the thigh, victim was personally familiar with defendant, and victim told officer responding to report of shooting that defendant had shot him. State v. Holloway (Ohio App. 1 Dist., Hamilton, 04-29-2005) No. C-040113, 2005-Ohio-1998, 2005 WL 991830, Unreported. Assault And Battery ⚷ 91.7; Sentencing And Punishment ⚷ 323

Conviction for aggravated robbery with gun specification was not against manifest weight of evidence; defendant intended to rob victim at apartment and, during that attempt, aimed gun at victim's girlfriend, victim heard voice tell girlfriend to get down, heard girlfriend crying, jumped from apartment window and went for help, and saw flash of handgun toward apartment when he glanced back. State v. Dillard (Ohio App. 7 Dist., Jefferson, 03-28-2005) No. 03 JE 32, 2005-Ohio-1656, 2005 WL 775888, Unreported. Robbery ⚷ 24.15(2)

Sufficient evidence supported convictions for robbery and related firearm enhancement specifications; victim testified that he was familiar with firearms and was certain that gun under defendant's possession was a semiautomatic, defendant threatened victim by displaying black and chrome handle of semiautomatic gun located in his waistband in order to rob victim of his coat and hat, defendant's action of grabbing gun was a clear non-verbal threat that defendant was willing to use weapon to obtain what he wanted from victim, and it was only at this point that victim turned over clothing. State v. Rankin (Ohio App. 8 Dist., Cuyahoga, 03-31-2005) No. 84801, 2005-Ohio-1506, 2005 WL 730090, Unreported. Robbery ⚷ 24.10; Sentencing And Punishment ⚷ 323

Evidence was sufficient to support convictions for firearm specifications, despite defendant's claims that he did not personally possess the gun at issue and because the State failed to offer proof regarding the operability of the gun; robbery victim described the gun that was held on him as a .38 or .44 caliber revolver, and he further testified that the gun was pointed at him in a threatening manner during the robbery, that defendant told the man holding the gun to shoot the victim when he refused to take off his clothes, and that defendant then told the other man to give him the gun and that he would shoot the victim. State v. Hayes (Ohio App. 9 Dist., Summit, 03-30-2005) No. 22168, 2005-Ohio-1464, 2005 WL 711945, Unreported. Weapons ⚷ 17(4)

Evidence supported convictions for aggravated robbery and felonious assault with a firearm specification; although victim was physically larger than defendant and victim attempted to gain control of weapon, defendant entered victim's kitchen brandishing loaded rifle, victim testified that defendant pulled trigger and shot him, and defendant denied that his own hand was ever on trigger. State v. Edwards (Ohio App. 5 Dist., Stark, 02-14-2005) No. 2003CA00224, 2005-Ohio-576, 2005 WL 351756, Unreported. Assault And Battery ⚷ 91.6(1); Robbery ⚷ 24.15(2)

Evidence was sufficient to support finding that defendant had an operable firearm, thus supporting firearm specification in aggravated robbery prosecution; although victim never saw firearm and defendant never announced that he had a firearm, victim felt what he believed to be a firearm stuck into his side as defendant stood behind him and implicitly demanded submission to robbery, and loaded gun was found near vehicle identified as the same vehicle defendant had entered immediately after the robbery. State v. Watkins (Ohio App. 8 Dist., Cuyahoga, 12-16-2004) No. 84288, 2004-Ohio-6908, 2004 WL 2931008, Unreported. Robbery ⚷ 24.15(2)

Defendant's convictions for first-degree aggravated robbery with a firearm specification and second-degree robbery were not against the manifest weight of the evidence, even if teenage victim was only able to observe robber for less than a minute, robber had a sock pulled over much of his face, and defendant did not confess; victim was able to see bottom portion of robber's face, victim noticed details such as robber's long hair, leather coat, and black gun, victim readily identified defendant as robber after viewing photo array for no longer than 30 seconds, there was testimony that defendant "pitched" his black gun around time of robbery, defendant owned a black leather coat around time of robbery, and defendant had in his possession at time of robbery the approximate amount of cash taken in robbery. State v. Hayes (Ohio App. 6 Dist., Lucas, 12-03-2004) No. L-03-1221, No. L-03-1222, 2004-Ohio-6460, 2004 WL 2785290, Unreported, appeal not allowed 105 Ohio St.3d 1516, 826 N.E.2d 314, 2005-Ohio-1880. Robbery ⚷ 24.40

Conviction for aggravated murder with firearm specification was supported by sufficient evidence and was not against manifest weight of evidence, even though inconsistencies in testimonies of eyewitnesses raised questions as to credibility of some parts of testimonies; unarmed victim and defendant, who was armed with gun, were engaged in progressively escalating argument, eyewitnesses heard gunshot, one eyewitness looked to find defendant standing over victim holding gun, bullets and bullet fragments recovered from scene and from victim were consistent with being fired from gun that defendant was known to own, and eyewitnesses corroborated each other in significant aspects. State v. Towler (Ohio App. 10 Dist., Franklin, 12-02-2004) No. 04AP-141, 2004-Ohio-6445, 2004 WL 2757849, Unreported, appeal not allowed 105 Ohio St.3d 1499, 825 N.E.2d 623, 2005-Ohio-1666. Homicide ⚷ 1139

Defendant could be convicted of firearm specification with respect to offense of felonious assault, where felonious assault did not require use of firearm. State v. Elko (Ohio App. 8 Dist., Cuyahoga, 09-30-2004) No. 83641, 2004-Ohio-5209, 2004 WL 2340258, Unreported, appeal not allowed 105 Ohio St.3d 1441, 822 N.E.2d 811, 2005-Ohio-540. Sentencing And Punishment ⚷ 139

Defendant could not be convicted of firearm specification with respect to offense of improperly discharging firearm at or into habitation, where use of firearm was element of offense of improperly discharging firearm. State v. Elko (Ohio App. 8 Dist., Cuyahoga, 09-30-2004) No. 83641, 2004-Ohio-5209, 2004 WL 2340258, Unreported, appeal not allowed 105 Ohio St.3d 1441, 822 N.E.2d 811, 2005-Ohio-540. Sentencing And Punishment ⚷ 139

Convictions for murder with firearm specification, attempted murder with firearm specification, felonious assault with firearm specification, and kidnapping with firearm specification were not against manifest weight of evidence; although defendant claimed testimony of attempted murder victim and witness was not credible, credibility was issue for jury to resolve, and victim testified that defendant shot him and forced him out of vehicle with gun. State v. Fayne (Ohio App. 8 Dist., Cuyahoga, 09-02-2004) No. 83267, 2004-Ohio-4625, 2004 WL 1944793, Unreported, motion for delayed appeal denied 106 Ohio St.3d 1502, 833 N.E.2d 1246, 2005-Ohio-4605. Homicide ⚷ 1184; Kidnapping ⚷ 36; Weapons ⚷ 17(4)

Evidence was sufficient to support conviction for murder with firearm specification; police officer testified that defendant said he shot victim and that shooting involved gang dispute and detective testified that defendant admitted that he shot victim. State v. Fayne (Ohio App. 8 Dist., Cuyahoga, 09-02-2004) No. 83267, 2004-Ohio-4625, 2004 WL 1944793, Unreported, motion for delayed appeal denied 106 Ohio St.3d 1502, 833 N.E.2d 1246, 2005-Ohio-4605. Homicide ⚷ 1186

Evidence was sufficient to support conviction for felonious assault with firearm specification; victim testified that defendant and another gang member force victim out of vehicle and that defendant shot victim as victim fled. State v. Fayne (Ohio App. 8 Dist., Cuyahoga, 09-02-2004) No. 83267, 2004-Ohio-4625, 2004 WL 1944793, Unreported, motion for delayed appeal denied 106 Ohio St.3d 1502, 833 N.E.2d 1246, 2005-Ohio-4605. Assault And Battery ⚷ 91.6(3)

Evidence was sufficient to support conviction for attempted murder with firearm specification; victim testified that defendant and another gang member forced victim out of vehicle, that gang member hit victim, and that defendant shot victim as victim fled. State v. Fayne (Ohio App. 8 Dist., Cuyahoga, 09-02-2004) No. 83267, 2004-Ohio-4625, 2004 WL 1944793, Unreported, motion for delayed appeal denied 106 Ohio St.3d 1502, 833 N.E.2d 1246, 2005-Ohio-4605. Homicide ⚷ 1181

Evidence was sufficient to support conviction for kidnapping with firearm specification; victim testified that defendant and another gang member ran up to vehicle, that defendant put gun in victim's face and told victim to get out of vehicle or defendant would kill victim, and that victim got out of vehicle. State v. Fayne (Ohio App. 8 Dist., Cuyahoga, 09-02-2004) No. 83267, 2004-Ohio-4625, 2004 WL 1944793, Unreported, motion for delayed appeal denied 106 Ohio St.3d 1502, 833 N.E.2d 1246, 2005-Ohio-4605. Kidnapping ⚷ 36

Evidence was sufficient to show that defendant drove getaway car, and thus, convictions for aggravated robbery and kidnapping, both with firearm specifications, based on aiding and abetting, were not against manifest weight of evidence; eyewitness who saw perpetrator enter business and called police saw defendant waiting in vehicle nearby, police saw vehicle matching witness's description driving away from scene of crime, defendant was driving vehicle, perpetrator was passenger in car, and perpetrator testified to defendant's participation in offense. State v. Greene (Ohio App. 9 Dist., Summit, 07-28-2004) No. 21795, 2004-Ohio-3944, 2004 WL 1672270, Unreported. Criminal Law ⚷ 80; Robbery ⚷ 24.20

Evidence supported finding that during the group assault of first victim and prior to the shooting of second victim, defendant had knowledge that at least one of his companions was armed with a gun, thus supporting gun specification convictions; during assault on first victim a gun fell to the floor and someone screamed, "Get your gun, get your gun," second victim's death resulted from gunshot wounds and occurred in propinquity to the crimes that were committed in first victim's apartment. State v. Brown (Ohio App. 10 Dist., Franklin, 06-10-2004) No. 03AP-130, 2004-Ohio-2990, 2004 WL 1277498, Unreported, appeal not allowed 103 Ohio St.3d 1481, 816 N.E.2d 255, 2004-Ohio-5405. Sentencing And Punishment ⚷ 323

There was sufficient evidence to demonstrate that gun defendant allegedly possessed while committing aggravated robbery constituted a firearm, thus supporting three-year firearm specification; defendant was carrying in his waistband what appeared to victim to be real gun, defendant announced to victim that he intended to "empty full clips tonight," placed his hand on handle of gun, and told victim to pull phone cord out of wall and get money out of register. State v. Carothers (Ohio App. 8 Dist., Cuyahoga, 01-08-2004) No. 82860, 2004-Ohio-51, 2004 WL 35936, Unreported, appeal not allowed 102 Ohio St.3d 1460, 809 N.E.2d 33, 2004-Ohio-2569. Sentencing And Punishment ⚷ 323

Evidence was sufficient to support conviction of aggravated robbery with firearm specification; defendant admitted to having visible firearm on his person on night of robbery, witness testified defendant and his brother entered residence with guns, and there was testimony that defendant and his brother robbed victims of money and gold jewelry. State v. Pleasant (Ohio App. 5 Dist., Stark, 11-24-2003) No. 2003CA00087, 2003-Ohio-6365, 2003 WL 22828099, Unreported. Robbery ⚷ 24.15(2)

Conviction of aggravated robbery with firearm specification was not against manifest weight of evidence; jury did not lose its way in reaching conviction, and credibility of witness who testified defendant was armed with gun was issue for jury. State v. Pleasant (Ohio App. 5 Dist., Stark, 11-24-2003) No. 2003CA00087, 2003-Ohio-6365, 2003 WL 22828099, Unreported. Robbery ⚷ 24.15(2)

Sufficient evidence established that defendant possessed an operable firearm during commission of burglary, as required to support firearm specification of aggravated burglary charge; police deputy testified that when he arrived at scene, victim informed him that defendant pointed a gun at her face and stated that he was going to kill her, and that victim appeared very upset over the gun. State v. Thomas (Ohio App. 2 Dist., Montgomery, 10-24-2003) No. 19435, 2003-Ohio-5746, 2003 WL 22429536, Unreported, motion for delayed appeal denied 102 Ohio St.3d 1420, 807 N.E.2d 366, 2004-Ohio-2003. Weapons ⚷ 17(4)

Conviction for aggravated robbery with firearm specification was not against manifest weight of evidence, even though alleged victim and her boyfriend provided varying versions of events, where evidence indicating that alleged victim was robbed by a man she identified as defendant was uncontroverted. State v. Mitchell (Ohio App. 9 Dist., Summit, 10-22-2003) No. 21413, 2003-Ohio-5614, 2003 WL 22399720, Unreported. Robbery ⚷ 24.15(2)

Convictions for firearm specifications were not against manifest weight of evidence, despite claim of defendant, who was also convicted of attempted murder and armed robbery, that State failed to prove that recovered firearm was operable and that it was used in commission of offenses; alleged victim identified defendant and testified that defendant pointed a gun at him, ordered him to give defendant "everything," and shot him, and witness also identified defendant and testified that she saw him shoot alleged victim in the back, and thus facts and circumstances surrounding offenses, including defendant's implicit threats, were sufficient to show that defendant possessed an operable firearm while committing robbery. State v. Bush (Ohio App. 9 Dist., Summit, 08-06-2003) No. 21326, 2003-Ohio-4151, 2003 WL 21804683, Unreported. Sentencing And Punishment ⚷ 77

Evidence was sufficient to establish that defendant, in process of committing kidnapping, rape, aggravated robbery, felonious assault, and attempted murder, brandished a firearm that was operable, or could readily have been rendered operable, thus supporting his convictions for such offenses with firearm specification, where defendant threatened to kill victim, victim had ample opportunity to observe firearm, which was used to strike victim twice, and was described in victim's testimony as a shotgun with a wooden stock. State v. Axson (Ohio App. 8 Dist., Cuyahoga, 05-01-2003) No.

81231, 2003-Ohio-2182, 2003 WL 1994490, Unreported, appeal dismissed 99 Ohio St.3d 1517, 792 N.E.2d 730, 2003-Ohio-4009, appeal allowed 100 Ohio St.3d 1408, 796 N.E.2d 536, 2003-Ohio-4948, motion to dismiss appeal denied 100 Ohio St.3d 1425, 797 N.E.2d 92, 2003-Ohio-5232, reversed 104 Ohio St.3d 248, 819 N.E.2d 271, 2004-Ohio-6396, subsequent determination 2005-Ohio-4396, 2005 WL 2038692, appeal after new sentencing hearing 2005-Ohio-6342, 2005 WL 3219727, appeal allowed, reversed 109 Ohio St.3d 509, 849 N.E.2d 284, 2006-Ohio-2721, reconsideration denied 110 Ohio St.3d 1444, 852 N.E.2d 191, 2006-Ohio-3862. Sentencing And Punishment ⚿ 78

Evidence was sufficient to support defendant's aggravated robbery conviction with firearm specification, where victim identified defendant, from a photographic array two days after robbery and at trial, and two officers identified defendant from still photographs taken from videotaped surveillance of actual crime. State v. Harris (Ohio App. 5 Dist., Stark, 12-09-2002) No. 2002CA00121, 2002-Ohio-7053, 2002 WL 31839276, Unreported. Robbery ⚿ 24.40

Defendant knowingly, intelligently, and voluntarily entered guilty plea to complicity to commit murder and to a firearm specification; colloquy with defendant strictly complied with requirements regarding advisements of constitutional rights being waived, defendant responded "yes" when asked whether he understood he would be giving up nonconstitutional appeal rights, and trial court gave defendant opportunity to withdraw plea when defendant, on being asked whether there had been any promises or threats to secure his plea, vented frustration with a prosecutor in contemporaneous federal case. State v. Pough (Ohio App. 11 Dist., Trumbull, 12-13-2002) No. 2000-T-0151, 2002-Ohio-6927, 2002 WL 31813100, Unreported, appeal not allowed 98 Ohio St.3d 1538, 786 N.E.2d 901, 2003-Ohio-1946, dismissal of post-conviction relief affirmed 2004-Ohio-3933, 2004 WL 1663519. Criminal Law ⚿ 273.1(4)

Evidence that defendant pointed gun at police and discharged it during altercation was sufficient to show that he possessed firearm for purposes of facilitating felonious assault upon police officers, as required to enhance sentence based on firearm specification. State v. Hoffert (Ohio App. 1 Dist., Hamilton, 11-22-2002) No. C-020168, 2002-Ohio-6343, 2002 WL 31626896, Unreported, appeal not allowed 102 Ohio St.3d 1461, 809 N.E.2d 34, 2004-Ohio-2569, motion for delayed appeal denied 103 Ohio St.3d 1524, 817 N.E.2d 408, 2004-Ohio-5852. Sentencing And Punishment ⚿ 79

Defendant's conviction for aggravated robbery and accompanying firearm specification was not against the manifest weight of the evidence; inconsistencies in testimony of state's witnesses were minor and did not render testimony inherently unworthy of belief, defendant's version of events was far from plausible since in order to believe it, jury would have had to believe that victims invited defendant into their home, robbed him, and then called police to have them come and arrest him, and police found victim's wallet, money, and birth certificate in defendant's pocket, and defendant was unable to explain how wallet got in his pocket. State v. Berry (Ohio App. 12 Dist., 11-15-2004) 159 Ohio App.3d 476, 824 N.E.2d 543, 2004-Ohio-6027, appeal not allowed 106 Ohio St.3d 1488, 832 N.E.2d 739, 2005-Ohio-3978, reconsideration denied 106 Ohio St.3d 1537, 2005-Ohio-5146. Robbery ⚿ 24.15(2); Weapons ⚿ 17(4)

Failure of juvenile's counsel to move for competency evaluation in delinquency proceeding on charge of murder with a gun specification was not ineffective assistance, though psychological evaluation after delinquency adjudication showed juvenile had low IQ, where juvenile's testimony clearly demonstrated his understanding of the charge and of difference between purposefully shooting with intent to kill and acting without purpose, and he testified consistently that he did not intend to discharge gun toward victim. In re York (Ohio App. 8 Dist., 04-12-2001) 142 Ohio App.3d 524, 756 N.E.2d 191, as amended nunc pro tunc. Infants ⚿ 205

Evidence was insufficient, in delinquency proceeding on charge of murder with a gun specification based on fatal shooting of 10–year–old girl, to support finding of purposefulness on juvenile's part in victim's death; evidence indicated that defendant and victim were friends and were acting in friendly manner right up until moment that pistol discharged, that defendant earlier in the day had pulled trigger while pointing gun at cousin without consequence, and that juvenile was in process of lowering gun, albeit with finger on trigger, when it discharged. In re York (Ohio App. 8 Dist., 04-12-2001) 142 Ohio App.3d 524, 756 N.E.2d 191, as amended nunc pro tunc. Infants ⚿ 176

Court of Appeals was precluded, upon finding evidence insufficient in delinquency proceeding to support adjudication for murder with a gun specification, from remanding for entry of adjudication for negligent homicide, even if facts might be consistent with a finding of guilt on that offense, because it was not a lesser included offense of murder. In re York (Ohio App. 8 Dist., 04-12-2001) 142 Ohio App.3d 524, 756 N.E.2d 191, as amended nunc pro tunc. Infants ⚿ 254

Trial court's failure, in delinquency proceeding involving charge of murder with a gun specification, to order sua sponte that a competency hearing be conducted prior to trial, was not error; juvenile demonstrated at trial that he was able to assist effectively in his own defense and clearly understood nature and ramifications of charges against him. In re York (Ohio App. 8 Dist., 04-12-2001) 142 Ohio App.3d 524, 756 N.E.2d 191, as amended nunc pro tunc. Infants ⚿ 253

Conviction for aggravated murder with a firearm specification was not against the manifest weight of the evidence and thus was sufficient as a matter of law, in regard to a victim who was shot six times; state presented testimony that defendant, a police officer, had motive to kill victim, who was his ex-wife, due to financial and personal problems, two eyewitnesses testified that they saw defendant at the scene of the crime immediately before and after the murder, testimony established that defendant was proficient in shooting with both of his hands, and state's expert, a forensic odontologist, established that the bite mark left on victim was made by defendant. State v. Prade (Ohio App. 9 Dist., 08-23-2000) 139 Ohio App.3d 676, 745 N.E.2d 475, dismissed, appeal not allowed 90 Ohio St.3d 1490, 739 N.E.2d 816. Homicide ⚷ 1185; Homicide ⚷ 1184

Evidence supported conviction for illegal possession of a firearm in a liquor permit premises, conviction for having a weapon while under a disability, and attached firearm specification; defendant admitted having a firearm in his possession in a bar with a liquor permit, witness testified that she saw defendant with gun inside bar and that he shot a gun while outside, and defendant stipulated to earlier conviction for cocaine possession. State v. Johnson (Ohio App. 6 Dist., Lucas, 09-30-2002) No. L-01-1243, 2002-Ohio-5206, 2002 WL 31166939, Unreported. Sentencing And Punishment ⚷ 373; Weapons ⚷ 17(4)

Jury could infer from defendant's brief displays of gun underneath his tee shirt that gun was operable, thus supporting firearm specifications with respect to three counts of aggravated robbery. State v. Wilson (Ohio App. 12 Dist., Clermont, 09-09-2002) No. CA2001-09-072, 2002-Ohio-4709, 2002 WL 31008824, Unreported, appeal not allowed 98 Ohio St.3d 1422, 782 N.E.2d 77, 2003-Ohio-259. Robbery ⚷ 24.15(1)

Sufficient evidence existed that reasonable jury could have found essential elements of murder and felonious assault with gun specifications proven beyond a reasonable doubt, and thus defendant's motion to dismiss that was made at close of state's case was properly denied; evidence indicated that defendant removed pistol from right side of his pants during altercation at bar with assault victim, defendant pointed what appeared to be .380 pistol at assault victim, bullet entered and exited assault victim's upper thigh, murder victim was struck in head and killed by .380 caliber bullet, and only one gunshot was heard that night at bar. State v. Jackson (Ohio App. 12 Dist., Butler, 09-09-2002) No. CA2001-10-239, 2002-Ohio-4705, 2002 WL 31008812, Unreported, appeal not allowed 98 Ohio St.3d 1413, 781 N.E.2d 1020, 2003-Ohio-60. Assault And Battery ⚷ 91.6(3); Homicide ⚷ 1134

Defendant's conviction for felonious assault and involuntary manslaughter with gun specifications was not against manifest weight of the evidence; evidence indicated that defendant carried firearm into liquor establishment while under a disability, defendant pointed gun at assault victim during altercation, defendant admitted firing one gunshot to "scare those guys off of me," bullet entered and exited assault victim's upper thigh, and manslaughter victim was struck in head and killed by bullet. State v. Jackson (Ohio App. 12 Dist., Butler, 09-09-2002) No. CA2001-10-239, 2002-Ohio-4705, 2002 WL 31008812, Unreported, appeal not allowed 98 Ohio St.3d 1413, 781 N.E.2d 1020, 2003-Ohio-60. Assault And Battery ⚷ 91.6(3); Homicide ⚷ 1150

Five firearms that were found during search of defendant's residence were admissible in his trial for assault and drug trafficking; although weapons were not the one that defendant discharged at a fleeing car on the night of his arrest, the firearms were relevant to enhancement to drug trafficking charge, and charge of tampering with evidence, and probative value of firearms outweighed any prejudicial effect. State v. McKinney (Ohio App. 11 Dist., Lake, 08-23-2002) No. 2000-L-210, 2002-Ohio-4360, 2002 WL 1961229, Unreported, appeal not allowed 98 Ohio St.3d 1411, 781 N.E.2d 1019, 2003-Ohio-60. Criminal Law ⚷ 404.65

Verdict finding the defendant guilty of felonious assault with a firearm specification was not against the manifest weight of the evidence; defendant admitted firing the gun, and there was some competent credible evidence presented that defendant fired the gun at the car as it was leaving. State v. McKinney (Ohio App. 11 Dist., Lake, 08-23-2002) No. 2000-L-210, 2002-Ohio-4360, 2002 WL 1961229, Unreported, appeal not allowed 98 Ohio St.3d 1411, 781 N.E.2d 1019, 2003-Ohio-60. Assault And Battery ⚷ 91.6(3)

Firearm specification, in indictment charging aggravated assault, was sufficient, even though it deviated from statutorily mandated language required to be substantially followed by not including firearms within defendant's control when act was committed, as well as firearms on defendant's person. State v. Gamble (Ohio App. 2 Dist., Clark, 06-28-2002) No. 2001 CA 61, 2002-Ohio-3289, 2002 WL 1393718, Unreported. Indictment And Information ⚷ 113

6. Jury instructions

Trial court's failure to define "firearm" when instructing jury on firearm specification in connection with complicity to aggravated robbery was not plain error; sufficient evidence showed that defendant's accomplice used gun during robbery and that gun was operable and, thus, qualified as "firearm." State v. King (Ohio App. 5 Dist., Muskingum, 11-19-2004) No. CT2003-0057, 2004-Ohio-6277, 2004 WL 2676312, Unreported. Criminal Law ⚷ 1038.2

Failing to give jury instruction on one-year firearm specification did not constitute plain error, where verdict forms required jury to make specific and separate factual findings as to one-year and three-year specifications and jury concluded that defendant engaged in behavior which satisfied both one-year and three-year specifications. State v. Marbury (Ohio App. 10 Dist., Franklin, 06-29-2004) No. 03AP-233, 2004-Ohio-3373, 2004 WL 1445224, Unreported, appeal not allowed 103 Ohio St.3d 1493, 816 N.E.2d 1080, 2004-Ohio-5605. Criminal Law ⚷ 1038.2

Giving jury instructions on element of aggravated robbery and three-year firearm specification related to use of weapon, which was not included in indictment, did not constitute plain error, where reasonable jury would not have found defendant not guilty of robbery and one-year firearm specification but guilty of aggravated robbery and three-year firearm specification, given store employee's testimony that defendant opened up defendant's coat, revealed gun tucked in defendant's pants, and told employee to stand still. State v. Marbury (Ohio App. 10 Dist., Franklin, 06-29-2004) No. 03AP-233, 2004-Ohio-3373, 2004 WL 1445224, Unreported, appeal not allowed 103 Ohio St.3d 1493, 816 N.E.2d 1080, 2004-Ohio-5605. Criminal Law ⚩ 1038.1(3.1); Criminal Law ⚩ 1038.1(4)

Defendant failed to object to, and thus waived for appellate review, trial court's jury instruction defining "deadly weapon" as "any instrument, device or thing capable of inflicting death or designed or specifically adapted for use as a weapon, or possessed, carried or used as a weapon," which instruction was relevant to firearm specification attached to charges of kidnapping, rape, aggravated robbery, felonious assault, and attempted murder. State v. Axson (Ohio App. 8 Dist., Cuyahoga, 05-01-2003) No. 81231, 2003-Ohio-2182, 2003 WL 1994490, Unreported, appeal dismissed 99 Ohio St.3d 1517, 792 N.E.2d 730, 2003-Ohio-4009, appeal allowed 100 Ohio St.3d 1408, 796 N.E.2d 536, 2003-Ohio-4948, motion to dismiss appeal denied 100 Ohio St.3d 1425, 797 N.E.2d 92, 2003-Ohio-5232, reversed 104 Ohio St.3d 248, 819 N.E.2d 271, 2004-Ohio-6396, subsequent determination 2005-Ohio-4396, 2005 WL 2038692, appeal after new sentencing hearing 2005-Ohio-6342, 2005 WL 3219727, appeal allowed, reversed 109 Ohio St.3d 509, 849 N.E.2d 284, 2006-Ohio-2721, reconsideration denied 110 Ohio St.3d 1444, 852 N.E.2d 191, 2006-Ohio-3862. Criminal Law ⚩ 1038.1(4)

Trial court's instruction in aggravated robbery prosecution, when considered as a whole, substantially comported with instruction in *Howard*, which set forth charge given to jury that became deadlocked; language seized upon by defendant to demonstrate error appeared to be one of several mistakes that were made in transcribing court's statements, and slight difference in wording, which was use of "in" rather than "and," would not have caused jurors to disregard their oaths and decide case based upon views of other jurors rather than their own views. State v. Berry (Ohio App. 12 Dist., 11-15-2004) 159 Ohio App.3d 476, 824 N.E.2d 543, 2004-Ohio-6027, appeal not allowed 106 Ohio St.3d 1488, 832 N.E.2d 739, 2005-Ohio-3978, reconsideration denied 106 Ohio St.3d 1537, 2005-Ohio-5146. Criminal Law ⚩ 865(1.5)

Trial court's issuance of *Howard* charge, which was charge given to jury that became deadlocked, did not improperly coerce jury into convicting defendant of aggravated robbery; although defendant suggested that fact that jury deliberated for less than a half-hour after being given charge militated in favor finding that instruction was coercive, evidence of defendant's guilt was overwhelming, and his claim that he was the one who was actually robbed lacked credibility. State v. Berry (Ohio App. 12 Dist., 11-15-2004) 159 Ohio App.3d 476, 824 N.E.2d 543, 2004-Ohio-6027, appeal not allowed 106 Ohio St.3d 1488, 832 N.E.2d 739, 2005-Ohio-3978, reconsideration denied 106 Ohio St.3d 1537, 2005-Ohio-5146. Criminal Law ⚩ 865(1.5)

Trial court was not required in aggravated robbery prosecution to inquire of jury "whether further deliberations would result in a verdict" before giving them *Howard* charge, which was charge given to jury that became deadlocked. State v. Berry (Ohio App. 12 Dist., 11-15-2004) 159 Ohio App.3d 476, 824 N.E.2d 543, 2004-Ohio-6027, appeal not allowed 106 Ohio St.3d 1488, 832 N.E.2d 739, 2005-Ohio-3978, reconsideration denied 106 Ohio St.3d 1537, 2005-Ohio-5146. Criminal Law ⚩ 865(1.5)

Failure of trial court to give separate instruction that firearm specification had to be found beyond a reasonable doubt was not plain error; the instructions, viewed in their entirety, sufficiently apprised the jury of their obligation to find the firearm specification beyond a reasonable doubt, and the jury, by convicting defendant of two counts of felonious assault and one count of discharging a firearm into an occupied dwelling, obviously found the attendant firearm specification beyond a reasonable doubt. State v. Dubose (Ohio App. 7 Dist., Mahoning, 06-06-2002) No. 00-C.A.-60, 2002-Ohio-3020, 2002 WL 1376248, Unreported, appeal not allowed 96 Ohio St.3d 1525, 775 N.E.2d 864, 2002-Ohio-5099, motion to reopen denied 2002-Ohio-6613, 2002 WL 31718806, appeal not allowed 98 Ohio St.3d 1475, 784 N.E.2d 708, 2003-Ohio-904. Criminal Law ⚩ 822(1); Criminal Law ⚩ 1038.2

7. Prison term

Firearm specifications for displaying, brandishing, indicating possession of or using a firearm in the commission of an offense, and for discharging a firearm from a motor vehicle, did not merge prior to sentencing, where underlying felony of murder was one which included element of purposely causing the death of another. State v. Bates (Ohio App. 10 Dist., Franklin, 08-10-2004) No. 03AP-893, 2004-Ohio-4224, 2004 WL 1790068, Unreported. Sentencing And Punishment ⚩ 144

Trial court properly sentenced defendant for three-year and five-year firearms specifications attached to charged offenses of aggravated murder and attempted murder, even though defendant claimed both enhancements were based on same act; legislature required enhancements to be served consecutively to one another and to the prison terms for the base offense. State v. Gresham (Ohio App. 8 Dist., Cuyahoga, 02-20-2003) No. 81250, 2003-Ohio-744, 2003 WL 360922, Unreported. Sentencing And Punishment ⚩ 144

Defendant convicted of aggravated robbery used firearm in commission of such offense, within scope of such sentence enhancement, warranting three-year sentence. State v. Stadmire (Ohio Com.Pl., 03-26-2002) No. CR-410305, 2002 WL 32066755, Unreported, affirmed 2003-Ohio-873, 2003 WL 549912. Sentencing And Punishment ⚩ 80

Imposition of consecutive sentences for weapon under disability conviction and firearm specification violation was not contrary to law, even if trial court did not make required findings for imposing consecutive sentences, where consecutive sentences were mandated by law. State v. Patterson (Ohio App. 12 Dist., Butler, 11-04-2002) No. CA2001-09-222, 2002-Ohio-5996, 2002 WL 31443546, Unreported. Sentencing And Punishment ⚷ 372; Sentencing And Punishment ⚷ 578

Trial court's imposition of five-year prison term on defendant for aggravated robbery, rather than three-year minimum term, was not plain error; although defendant argued that under the Supreme Court's *Blakely v. Washington* decision, which decided defendant had right to have jury decide factual issues that would increase his sentence, court was obligated to sentence him to no more than statutory minimum sentence of three years, *Blakely* did not apply to state's indeterminate sentencing scheme, and to extent that *Blakely* did apply, court's imposition of sentence did not violate that decision, since five-year sentence was within range authorized by law. State v. Berry (Ohio App. 12 Dist., 11-15-2004) 159 Ohio App.3d 476, 824 N.E.2d 543, 2004-Ohio-6027, appeal not allowed 106 Ohio St.3d 1488, 832 N.E.2d 739, 2005-Ohio-3978, reconsideration denied 106 Ohio St.3d 1537, 2005-Ohio-5146. Criminal Law ⚷ 1042

8. Display of firearm

Evidence was sufficient to show that gun used by defendant's accomplice during robbery was operable, so as to support firearm specification in connection with complicity to aggravated robbery; store clerk testified that, after she fumbled with money, robber told her to hurry up and then jacked shotgun and dropped shell into chamber and that she was scared to death and feared for her safety as result, and robber's actions constituted implicit threat to discharge shotgun at time of robbery. State v. King (Ohio App. 5 Dist., Muskingum, 11-19-2004) No. CT2003-0057, 2004-Ohio-6277, 2004 WL 2676312, Unreported. Sentencing And Punishment ⚷ 323

Evidence was sufficient to show that defendant's accomplice used gun during robbery, so as to support firearm specification in connection with complicity to aggravated robbery; store clerk testified that she was familiar with guns and that robber pointed sawed-off shotgun at her and demanded money, and store videotape showed robber pointing gun at clerk. State v. King (Ohio App. 5 Dist., Muskingum, 11-19-2004) No. CT2003-0057, 2004-Ohio-6277, 2004 WL 2676312, Unreported. Sentencing And Punishment ⚷ 323

Evidence was sufficient to support conviction on one-year firearm specification applicable when defendant has firearm on or about his person or under his control while committing offense and three-year firearm specification applicable when offender has firearm on or about his person or under his control while committing offense and displaying firearm and conviction was not against manifest weight of evidence; store employee testified that defendant opened up defendant's coat and revealed gun tucked in defendant's pants, employee testified that defendant told employee to stand still, employee identified gun as revolver, and employee was familiar with guns from time spent in military and prior work in gun shop. State v. Marbury (Ohio App. 10 Dist., Franklin, 06-29-2004) No. 03AP-233, 2004-Ohio-3373, 2004 WL 1445224, Unreported, appeal not allowed 103 Ohio St.3d 1493, 816 N.E.2d 1080, 2004-Ohio-5605. Sentencing And Punishment ⚷ 323

Evidence was sufficient to support convictions for aggravated robbery and kidnapping with firearm specifications, despite defendant's claim that the State failed to prove that a "deadly weapon" or "firearm" was used; juvenile victim clearly testified to defendant's use of a firearm, stating that he felt the gun at his side and saw the black tip of the gun as defendant instructed him to go to back of building, and when victim's friends appeared, defendant displayed the gun and told them to leave. State v. Gooden (Ohio App. 8 Dist., Cuyahoga, 05-27-2004) No. 82621, 2004-Ohio-2699, 2004 WL 1172074, Unreported. Sentencing And Punishment ⚷ 323

Although not visible, defendant's threat of the use of a firearm was enough for a jury to find that defendant did, in fact, have an operable firearm, as would support gun specification attendant to aggravated robbery conviction. State v. Haskins (Ohio App. 6 Dist., Erie, 01-10-2003) No. E-01-016, 2003-Ohio-70, 2003 WL 99572, Unreported. Robbery ⚷ 24.15(2)

Evidence was sufficient to support conviction for gun specification attendant to aggravated robbery; during robbery of a gas station, defendant indicated that he would use the "pistol in my pocket" if the attendant did not give him the cash drawer money, and although no firearm was actually visible to the victim or found, the effect on the hearer was that defendant had a firearm and threatened to use it. State v. Haskins (Ohio App. 6 Dist., Erie, 01-10-2003) No. E-01-016, 2003-Ohio-70, 2003 WL 99572, Unreported. Robbery ⚷ 24.15(2)

Evidence was sufficient to support conviction for murder, with a firearm specification; witness testified that defendant shot victim with a firearm, and other witness testified that on day murder occurred, she saw defendant retrieve something from the trunk of his car and place it into his waistband. State v. Miller (Ohio App. 6 Dist., Lucas, 10-25-2002) No. L-00-1343, 2002-Ohio-5914, 2002 WL 31420125, Unreported, appeal not allowed 98 Ohio St.3d 1489, 785 N.E.2d 472, 2003-Ohio-1189, denial of post-conviction relief affirmed 2003-Ohio-4857, 2003 WL 22117594, appeal not allowed 101 Ohio St.3d 1422, 802 N.E.2d 153, 2004-Ohio-123. Homicide ⚷ 1134; Sentencing And Punishment ⚷ 323

Additional three years' incarceration for firearm specification was warranted where defendant briefly displayed, to carjacking victim, a gun from beneath his waistband and shirt. State v. Gest (Ohio App. 8 Dist., 12-29-1995) 108 Ohio App.3d 248, 670 N.E.2d 536. Sentencing And Punishment ⚷ 80

2941.146 Specification concerning discharge of firearm from motor vehicle

(A) Imposition of a mandatory five-year prison term upon an offender under division (D)(1)(c) of section 2929.14 of the Revised Code for committing a violation of section 2923.161 of the Revised Code or for committing a felony that includes, as an essential element, purposely or knowingly causing or attempting to cause the death of or physical harm to another and that was committed by discharging a firearm from a motor vehicle other than a manufactured home is precluded unless the indictment, count in the indictment, or information charging the offender specifies that the offender committed the offense by discharging a firearm from a motor vehicle other than a manufactured home. The specification shall be stated at the end of the body of the indictment, count, or information, and shall be stated in substantially the following form:

"SPECIFICATION (or, SPECIFICATION TO THE FIRST COUNT). The Grand Jurors (or insert the person's or prosecuting attorney's name when appropriate) further find and specify that (set forth that the offender committed the violation of section 2923.161 of the Revised Code or the felony that includes, as an essential element, purposely or knowingly causing or attempting to cause the death of or physical harm to another and that was committed by discharging a firearm from a motor vehicle other than a manufactured home)."

(B) The specification described in division (A) of this section may be used in a delinquent child proceeding in the manner and for the purpose described in section 2152.17 of the Revised Code.

(C) As used in this section:

(1) "Firearm" has the same meaning as in section 2923.11 of the Revised Code;

(2) "Motor vehicle" and "manufactured home" have the same meanings as in section 4501.01 of the Revised Code.

(2000 S 179, § 3, eff. 1–1–02; 1999 S 107, eff. 3–23–00; 1995 S 2, eff. 7–1–96)

Historical and Statutory Notes

Amendment Note: 2000 S 179, § 3, eff. 1–1–02, added new division (B); and redesignated former division (B) as division (C).

Amendment Note: 1999 S 107 substituted "(D)(1)(c)" for "(D)(1)(a)(ii)" in division (A).

Library References

Indictment and Information ⚷113.
Westlaw Topic No. 210.

Baldwin's Ohio Legislative Service, 1995 S 2—LSC Analysis, p 8/L–2907

Research References

Encyclopedias

OH Jur. 3d Criminal Law § 1942, Discharging Firearms at or Into Occupied Structure or School Safety Zone.

OH Jur. 3d Criminal Law § 2369, Firearm Specification.

OH Jur. 3d Criminal Law § 3290, Use of Firearm from Moving Vehicle.

OH Jur. 3d Family Law § 1696, Commitment to Youth Commission.

OH Jur. 3d Family Law § 1698.5, Serious Youthful Offender.

Treatises and Practice Aids

Katz, Giannelli, Blair and Lipton, Baldwin's Ohio Practice, Criminal Law, § 40:5, Nature and Contents.

Katz, Giannelli, Blair and Lipton, Baldwin's Ohio Practice, Criminal Law, § 106:1, Introduction.

Katz, Giannelli, Blair and Lipton, Baldwin's Ohio Practice, Criminal Law, § 106:9, Discharging Firearm Into a School or Home.

Katz, Giannelli, Blair and Lipton, Baldwin's Ohio Practice, Criminal Law, § 117:2, Mandatory Prison Sentences.

Katz, Giannelli, Blair and Lipton, Baldwin's Ohio Practice, Criminal Law, § 118:7, Gun Enhancement.

Katz, Giannelli, Blair and Lipton, Baldwin's Ohio Practice, Criminal Law, § 153:9, Motion to Correct Improper Sentence—Firearm Specifications as Part of One Transaction.

Katz, Giannelli, Blair and Lipton, Baldwin's Ohio Practice, Criminal Law, § 118:11, Drive-By Shooting.

Carlin, Baldwin's Ohio Practice, Merrick-Rippner Probate Law § 107:84, Disposition of Delinquent Children—Prior to January 1, 2002.

Carlin, Baldwin's Ohio Practice, Merrick-Rippner Probate Law § 107:92, Enhanced Dispositions

Due to Felony Specifications, Effective January 1, 2002.

Giannelli & Yeomans, Ohio Juvenile Law § 27:3, Department of Youth Services Commitment.

Notes of Decisions

1. Constitutional issues—Double jeopardy

State court determination that imposition of multiple sentences following petitioner's convictions on multiple counts that each included two separate firearms specifications for using firearm to facilitate offense and for using firearm from motor vehicle did not violate Double Jeopardy Clause was not contrary to, and did not involve unreasonable application of, clearly established federal law in *Blockburger v. United States*, and thus did not warrant federal habeas relief, where relevant state statute required imposition of cumulative penalties for different specifications. Carter v. Carter (C.A.6 (Ohio), 02-14-2003) No. 01-3649, 59 Fed.Appx. 104, 2003 WL 356176, Unreported. Habeas Corpus ⚷ 466

2. —— Speedy trial, constitutional issues

State's decision to re-indict defendant four days before his trial and some 400 days after his arrest for felonious assault, in order to amend his firearm specifications, violated defendant's speedy trial rights; when the State re-indicted defendant with the new specifications, it added a new element for him to consider in his defense—that he discharged the firearm from a motor vehicle, and the new indictment increased the penalty defendant was subject to from three years to five years on each specification. State v. Carter (Ohio App. 7 Dist., Mahoning, 03-18-2005) No. 03-MA-245, 2005-Ohio-1347, 2005 WL 678569, Unreported. Criminal Law ⚷ 577.14

3. Sentencing

Defendant, who was convicted of four counts of felonious assault, was properly given only one five year prison term pursuant to firearm specification addressing offender who discharges firearm from motor vehicle, where assaults stemmed from same act or transaction and involved four victim. State v. Dixson (Ohio App. 1 Dist., Hamilton, 05-21-2004) No. C-030227, 2004-Ohio-2575, 2004 WL 1124524, Unreported. Sentencing And Punishment ⚷ 80

4. Evidence

Evidence was sufficient to support convictions for two counts of felonious assault with gun specifications, and such convictions were not against the manifest weight of the evidence; victim testified that he was approached by defendant at gas station and that defendant began shooting at him when defendant pulled out of the gas station in his car, a bystander at the gas station was hit and seriously injured by the gunfire, and two witnesses identified defendant as the shooter at a photograph lineup. State v. Carter (Ohio App. 7 Dist., Mahoning, 03-18-2005) No. 03-MA-245, 2005-Ohio-1347, 2005 WL 678569, Unreported. Assault And Battery ⚷ 91.6(1)

2941.147 Sexual motivation specification

(A) Whenever a person is charged with an offense that is a violation of section 2903.01, 2903.02, 2903.11, or 2905.01 of the Revised Code, a violation of division (A) of section 2903.04 of the Revised Code, an attempt to violate or complicity in violating section 2903.01, 2903.02, 2903.11, or 2905.01 of the Revised Code when the attempt or complicity is a felony, or an attempt to violate or complicity in violating division (A) of section 2903.04 of the Revised Code when the attempt or complicity is a felony, the indictment, count in the indictment, information, or complaint charging the offense may include a specification that the person committed the offense with a sexual motivation. The specification shall be stated at the end of the body of the indictment, count, information, or complaint and shall be in substantially the following form:

"SPECIFICATION (OR, SPECIFICATION TO THE FIRST COUNT). The Grand Jurors (or insert the person's or the prosecuting attorney's name when appropriate) further find and specify that the offender committed the offense with a sexual motivation."

(B) As used in this section, "sexual motivation" has the same meaning as in section 2971.01 of the Revised Code.

(1996 H 180, eff. 1-1-97)

Uncodified Law

1996 H 180, § 4: See Uncodified Law under RC 2941.148.

Library References

Indictment and Information ⚷113.
Westlaw Topic No. 210.

Baldwin's Ohio Legislative Service, 1996 H 180—LSC Analysis, p 7/L–2553

Research References

Encyclopedias

OH Jur. 3d Criminal Law § 2370, Violence Specification; Sexual Motivation and Sexual Predator Specifications.

OH Jur. 3d Criminal Law § 3267, Specification as Prerequisite to Enhanced Penalty; State's Burden of Proof; Proof of Prior Conviction.

Treatises and Practice Aids

Katz, Giannelli, Blair and Lipton, Baldwin's Ohio Practice, Criminal Law, § 40:5, Nature and Contents.

Katz, Giannelli, Blair and Lipton, Baldwin's Ohio Practice, Criminal Law, § 121:2, Sentencing Violent Sexual Predators.

2941.148 Sexually violent predator specification

(A) The application of Chapter 2971. of the Revised Code to an offender is precluded unless the indictment, count in the indictment, or information charging the violent sex offense also includes a specification that the offender is a sexually violent predator, or the indictment, count in the indictment, or information charging the designated homicide, assault, or kidnapping offense also includes both a specification of the type described in section 2941.147 of the Revised Code and a specification that the offender is a sexually violent predator. The specification that the offender is a sexually violent predator shall be stated at the end of the body of the indictment, count, or information and shall be stated in substantially the following form:

"Specification (or, specification to the first count). The grand jury (or insert the person's or prosecuting attorney's name when appropriate) further find and specify that the offender is a sexually violent predator."

(B) In determining for purposes of this section whether a person is a sexually violent predator, all of the factors set forth in divisions (H)(1) to (6) of section 2971.01 of the Revised Code that apply regarding the person may be considered as evidence tending to indicate that it is likely that the person will engage in the future in one or more sexually violent offenses.

(C) As used in this section, "designated homicide, assault, or kidnapping offense," "violent sex offense," and "sexually violent predator" have the same meanings as in section 2971.01 of the Revised Code.

(2004 H 473, eff. 4–29–05; 1996 H 180, eff. 1–1–97)

Uncodified Law

1996 H 180, § 4, eff. 10–16–96, reads: Sections 2921.34, 2929.02, 2929.03, 2929.06, 2929.13, 2929.14, 2929.19, 2929.21, 2929.41, 2930.16, 2941.147, 2941.148, 2953.08, 2967.12, 2967.121, 2967.13, 2967.18, 2967.193, 2967.26, 2967.27, 2971.01, 2971.02, 2971.03, 2971.04, 2971.05, 2971.06, 2971.07, 5120.49, 5120.61, 5149.03, and 5149.10 of the Revised Code, as amended or enacted in Sections 1 and 2 of this act, shall apply only to persons who commit an offense governed by those amended and enacted sections on or after the effective date of this act.

Historical and Statutory Notes

Amendment Note: 2004 H 473 rewrote division (A); and changed "'sexually violent offense'" to "'violent sex offense'" in division (C). Prior to amendment, division (A) read:

"(A) The application of Chapter 2971. of the Revised Code to an offender is precluded unless the indictment, count in the indictment, or information charging the sexually violent offense or charging the designated homicide, assault, or kidnapping offense also includes a specification that the offender is a sexually violent predator. The specification shall be stated at the end of the body of the indictment, count, or information and shall be stated in substantially the following form:

"'SPECIFICATION (OR, SPECIFICATION TO THE FIRST COUNT). The grand jury (or insert the person's or prosecuting attorney's name when appropriate) further find and specify that the offender is a sexually violent predator.'"

Cross References

Sexually violent predator specification, defined, 2971.01

Library References

Indictment and Information ⚷113.
Westlaw Topic No. 210.
Baldwin's Ohio Legislative Service, 1996 H 180—LSC Analysis, p 7/L–2553

Research References

Encyclopedias

OH Jur. 3d Criminal Law § 3267, Specification as Prerequisite to Enhanced Penalty; State's Burden of Proof; Proof of Prior Conviction.

Treatises and Practice Aids

Katz, Giannelli, Blair and Lipton, Baldwin's Ohio Practice, Criminal Law, § 40:5, Nature and Contents.

Katz, Giannelli, Blair and Lipton, Baldwin's Ohio Practice, Criminal Law, § 117:2, Mandatory Prison Sentences.

Katz, Giannelli, Blair and Lipton, Baldwin's Ohio Practice, Criminal Law, § 121:2, Sentencing Violent Sexual Predators.

Katz, Giannelli, Blair and Lipton, Baldwin's Ohio Practice, Criminal Law, § 121:3, Sexual Offender Classifications.

Law Review and Journal Commentaries

Megan's Law affects public schools, Matthew DeTemple. (Ed. note: Notice of the release and whereabouts of sex-crime offenders is discussed.) 41 Ohio Sch Boards Ass'n J 2 (April 1997).

Notes of Decisions

1. Sentencing

Defendant did not subjectively understand that he could have received a mandatory prison time of two years for pleading guilty to 16 counts of gross sexual imposition, and that he could have been sentenced to life imprisonment for enhancement of such sentence based on sexually violent predator specification, and thus defendant's guilty pleas to gross sexual imposition charges were not knowingly, intelligently, and voluntarily given. State v. Sherrard (Ohio App. 9 Dist., Lorain, 01-29-2003) No. 02CA008065, 2003-Ohio-365, 2003 WL 187592, Unreported, appeal not allowed 99 Ohio St.3d 1435, 789 N.E.2d 1117, 2003-Ohio-2902. Criminal Law ⚷ 273.1(1)

2. Charged offense

Defendant's prior rape conviction was improperly used as basis for sexually violent predator specifications, in prosecution for rape, gross sexual imposition, and compelling prostitution, because it occurred some ten years prior to the enactment of statute which governs sexually violent predator specifications. State v. Robinson (Ohio App. 8 Dist., Cuyahoga, 09-29-2005) No. 85207, 2005-Ohio-5132, 2005 WL 2386608, Unreported. Sentencing And Punishment ⚷ 99

For purposes of sexually violent predator specification in prosecution for rape and kidnapping, charged offense of rape could not be used to establish that defendant had been "convicted" of a sexually violent offense, and thus evidence was insufficient to support sexually violent predator specification. State v. Smith (Ohio App. 5 Dist., Morrow, 06-19-2003) No. CA-957, 2003-Ohio-3416, 2003 WL 21489929, Unreported, appeal allowed 100 Ohio St.3d 1430, 797 N.E.2d 511, 2003-Ohio-5396. Mental Health ⚷ 454

3. Conviction on underlying offense

Defendant need not have a prior conviction for a sexually violent offense at the time of indictment in order for a sexually violent predator specification to attach; rather, a conviction on the underlying offense is enough. State v. Haven (Ohio App. 9 Dist., Wayne, 05-19-2004) No. 02CA0069, 2004-Ohio-2512, 2004 WL 1103957, Unreported. Mental Health ⚷ 469(2)

2941.149 Specification concerning repeat violent offenders

(A) The determination by a court that an offender is a repeat violent offender is precluded unless the indictment, count in the indictment, or information charging the offender specifies that the offender is a repeat violent offender. The specification shall be stated at the end of the body of the indictment, count, or information, and shall be stated in substantially the following form:

"SPECIFICATION (or, SPECIFICATION TO THE FIRST COUNT). The Grand Jurors (or insert the person's or prosecuting attorney's name when appropriate) further find and specify that (set forth that the offender is a repeat violent offender)."

(B) The court shall determine the issue of whether an offender is a repeat violent offender.

(C) At the arraignment of the defendant or as soon thereafter as is practicable, the prosecuting attorney may give notice to the defendant of the prosecuting attorney's intention to use a certified copy of the entry of judgment of a prior conviction as proof of that prior conviction. The defendant must then give notice to the prosecuting attorney of the defendant's intention to object to the use of the entry of judgment. If the defendant pursuant to Criminal Rule 12 does not give notice of that intention to the prosecuting attorney before trial, the defendant waives the objection to the use of an entry of judgment as proof of the defendant's prior conviction, as shown on the entry of judgment.

(D) As used in this section, "repeat violent offender" has the same meaning as in section 2929.01 of the Revised Code.

(2006 H 95, eff. 8–3–06; 1996 S 269, eff. 7–1–96)

Historical and Statutory Notes

Amendment Note: 2006 H 95 redesignated former division (C) as (D) and inserted new text in division (C).

Cross References

Delinquency adjudications deemed convictions, exceptions 2901.08

Prison terms imposed for felonies, 2929.14

Library References

Indictment and Information ⚷113.

Westlaw Topic No. 210.

Baldwin's Ohio Legislative Service, 1996 S 269—LSC Analysis, p 6/L–1143

Research References

Encyclopedias

OH Jur. 3d Criminal Law § 2363, Prior Conviction.

OH Jur. 3d Criminal Law § 2370, Violence Specification; Sexual Motivation and Sexual Predator Specifications.

OH Jur. 3d Criminal Law § 3267, Specification as Prerequisite to Enhanced Penalty; State's Burden of Proof; Proof of Prior Conviction.

Treatises and Practice Aids

Katz, Giannelli, Blair and Lipton, Baldwin's Ohio Practice, Criminal Law, § 40:5, Nature and Contents.

Katz, Giannelli, Blair and Lipton, Baldwin's Ohio Practice, Criminal Law, § 118:12, Repeat Violent Offenders.

Notes of Decisions

Constitutional issues 1

---

1. Constitutional issues

Defendant was constitutionally entitled to jury trial on facts relied upon by sentencing court in adjudicating him a repeat violent offender (RVO), and enhancing his sentence beyond statutory maximum for underlying offenses on basis of such finding, where such adjudication required additional findings with respect to defendant's prior felony convictions not apparent from face thereof, namely, whether prior convictions for conspiracy to aggravated robbery, conspiracy to aggravated burglary, and conspiracy to kidnapping resulted in death, serious harm, or physical harm to a person, and enhancement required additional findings as to seriousness and recidivism factors. State v. Payne (Ohio App. 11 Dist., Lake, 12-29-2005) No. 2004-L-118, 2005-Ohio-7043, 2005 WL 3610429, Unreported. Jury ⚷ 21.4

Application of statute governing repeat violent offender (RVO) specification, which required trial court to determine issue of whether defendant was RVO, would violate defendant's Sixth Amendment right to trial by jury; under facts of case, RVO specification would increase defendant's potential penalty. State v. Malcolm (Ohio App. 8 Dist., Cuyahoga, 08-11-2005) No. 85351, 2005-Ohio-4133, 2005 WL 1923593, Unreported, appeal allowed 108 Ohio St.3d 1412, 841 N.E.2d 317, 2006-Ohio-179. Jury ⚷ 34(7)

Defendant's counsel was deficient in allowing the jury to be made aware of defendant's prior robbery conviction, which was the basis of the specification alleging a prior violence conviction; counsel did not request that the judge decide the specification at the sentencing hearing as statutorily allowed and conviction could not have been used to impeach defendant at trial because he did not take the stand. State v. Black (Ohio App. 1 Dist., 12-12-1997) 124 Ohio App.3d 419, 706 N.E.2d 407, dismissed, appeal not allowed 81 Ohio St.3d 1496, 691 N.E.2d 1058. Criminal Law ⚷ 641.13(6)

2941.1410 Specification concerning major drug offender

(A) Except as provided in sections 2925.03 and 2925.11 of the Revised Code, the determination by a court that an offender is a major drug offender is precluded unless the indictment, count in the indictment, or information charging the offender specifies that the offender is a major drug offender. The specification shall be stated at the end of the body of the indictment, count, or information, and shall be stated in substantially the following form:

"SPECIFICATION (or, SPECIFICATION TO THE FIRST COUNT). The Grand Jurors (or insert the person's or prosecuting attorney's name when appropriate) further find and specify that (set forth that the offender is a major drug offender)."

(B) The court shall determine the issue of whether an offender is a major drug offender.

(C) As used in this section, "major drug offender" has the same meaning as in section 2929.01 of the Revised Code.

(1999 S 107, eff. 3–23–00; 1996 S 269, eff. 7–1–96)

Historical and Statutory Notes

Amendment Note: 1999 S 107 inserted "Except as provided in sections 2925.03 and 2925.11 of the Revised Code," at the beginning of division (A).

Cross References

Controlled substance violations, 3719.99
Corrupting another with drugs, 2925.02
Funding of drug or marihuana trafficking, 2925.05
Illegal dispensing of drug samples, 2925.36
Illegal manufacture of drugs or cultivation of marihuana, 2925.04
Pharmacists, drug violations, 4729.99
Prison terms imposed for felonies, 2929.14

Library References

Indictment and Information ⚷113.
Westlaw Topic No. 210.
Baldwin's Ohio Legislative Service, 1996 S 269—LSC Analysis, p 6/L–1143

Research References

Encyclopedias

OH Jur. 3d Criminal Law § 1774, Degrees of Offense; Penalties.

OH Jur. 3d Criminal Law § 1787, Illegal Dispensing of Drug Samples—Degrees of Offense; Penalties.

OH Jur. 3d Criminal Law § 2370, Violence Specification; Sexual Motivation and Sexual Predator Specifications.

OH Jur. 3d Criminal Law § 3221, Rules of Statutory Construction.

OH Jur. 3d Criminal Law § 3267, Specification as Prerequisite to Enhanced Penalty; State's Burden of Proof; Proof of Prior Conviction.

Treatises and Practice Aids

Katz, Giannelli, Blair and Lipton, Baldwin's Ohio Practice, Criminal Law, § 40:5, Nature and Contents.

Katz, Giannelli, Blair and Lipton, Baldwin's Ohio Practice, Criminal Law, § 107:5, Corrupting Another With Drugs—Penalties.

Katz, Giannelli, Blair and Lipton, Baldwin's Ohio Practice, Criminal Law, § 107:12, Funding Drug or Marihuana Trafficking.

Katz, Giannelli, Blair and Lipton, Baldwin's Ohio Practice, Criminal Law, § 107:23, Illegal Dispensing Drug Samples.

Katz, Giannelli, Blair and Lipton, Baldwin's Ohio Practice, Criminal Law, § 118:13, Major Offenders.

Notes of Decisions

1. Constitutional issues

Major drug offender specification in substitute indictment did not constitute new charge, for purpose of determining whether defendant's right to speedy trial on such specification was denied; although original indictment did not contain specification, original indictment included allegation that defendant possessed over 100 grams of crack cocaine, which would establish that defendant was major drug offender. State v. Barrett (Ohio App. 4 Dist., Scioto, 04-19-2004) No. 03CA2889, 2004-Ohio-2064, 2004 WL 878002, Unreported, on reconsideration in part 2004-Ohio-5088, 2004 WL 2260500, appeal not allowed 103 Ohio St.3d 1462, 815 N.E.2d 678, 2004-Ohio-5056. Criminal Law ⚷ 577.14

The major drug offender specification is not unconstitutional. State v. Edwards (Ohio App. 6 Dist., Lucas, 02-07-2003) No. L-00-1161, 2003-Ohio-571, 2003 WL 257383, Unreported, appeal not allowed 99 Ohio St.3d 1436, 789 N.E.2d 1117, 2003-Ohio-2902, certiorari denied 124 S.Ct. 809, 540 U.S. 1052, 157 L.Ed.2d 702. Sentencing And Punishment ⚷ 8

2. Law governing

Trial court properly sentenced defendant as a major drug offender following convictions for complicity in trafficking of drugs and complicity in the possession of drugs, where trial court submitted question of whether defendant was a major drug offender to jury when it asked the jury to determine whether the amount of drugs defendant was complicit in possessing and selling exceeded 1,000 grams, and jury answered such question in the affirmative. State v. McDermott (Ohio App. 6 Dist., Lucas, 04-29-2005) No. L-03-1110, 2005-Ohio-2095, 2005 WL 1007133, Unreported. Jury ⚷ 34(8)

Any error in trial court's imposition of additional five-year sentence upon major drug offender specification finding for which defendant was never indicted was harmless, as there was another basis for imposing enhanced sentence with which trial court fully complied, finding that defendant, convicted of trafficking in crack cocaine, engaging in pattern of corrupt activity, and possession of crack cocaine, demonstrated a great likelihood of recidivism, and that a ten-year prison term would have demeaned the seriousness of defendant's conduct. State v. Baker (Ohio App. 3 Dist., Hardin, 04-26-2004) No. 6-03-11, 2004-Ohio-2061, 2004 WL 877688, Unreported. Criminal Law ⚷ 1177

Sentence enhancement based on major drug offender specification did not violate *Apprendi v. New Jersey,* where specification was expressly dependent on a jury finding that the amount of drug possessed or sold by defendant was in excess of a certain amount. State v. Graves (Ohio App. 6 Dist., Lucas, 05-09-2003) No. L-02-1053, 2003-Ohio-2359, 2003 WL 21040652, Unreported, appeal not allowed 100 Ohio St.3d 1410, 796 N.E.2d 537, 2003-Ohio-4948. Jury ⚷ 34(8)

Amendment to indictment on morning of trial to indicate that amount of cocaine allegedly possessed exceeded 1000 grams of cocaine that was not crack cocaine, as opposed to 100 grams of cocaine that was not crack cocaine, was properly allowed; original indictment properly identified charged offense as a first-degree felony with a major drug offender specification, amendment merely corrected a clerical error, and defendant did not claim that he received inadequate notice of what state intended to prove or that he was otherwise prejudiced in preparing defense. State v. Jones (Ohio App. 3 Dist., Marion, 03-31-2003) No. 9-02-39, 2003-Ohio-1576, 2003 WL 1617979, Unreported, appeal not allowed 99 Ohio St.3d 1514, 792 N.E.2d 200, 2003-Ohio-3957. Indictment And Information ⚷ 159(2)

Statute providing that if an offender possesses an amount of drugs that equals or exceeds 100 times the amount necessary to commit a third-degree drug felony, the offender is statutorily specified to be a major drug offender for sentence enhancement purposes, as the later-enacted and more specific statute, was controlling over the statute leaving the determination of major drug offender status to the trial court instead of the jury. State v. Elkins (Ohio App. 10 Dist., 06-11-2002) 148 Ohio App.3d 370, 773 N.E.2d 593, 2002-Ohio-2914. Sentencing And Punishment ⚷ 11; Statutes ⚷ 223.4

2941.1411 Specification concerning use of body armor

(A) Imposition of a two-year mandatory prison term upon an offender under division (D)(1)(d) of section 2929.14 of the Revised Code is precluded unless the indictment, count in the indictment, or information charging the offense specifies that the offender wore or carried body armor while committing the offense and that the offense is an offense of violence that is a felony. The specification shall be stated at the end of the body of the indictment, count, or information and shall be stated in substantially the following form:

"SPECIFICATION (or, SPECIFICATION TO THE FIRST COUNT). The Grand Jurors (or insert the person's or the prosecuting attorney's name when appropriate) further find and specify that (set forth that the offender wore or carried body armor while committing the specified offense and that the specified offense is an offense of violence that is a felony)."

(B) As used in this section, "body armor" means any vest, helmet, shield, or similar item that is designed or specifically carried to diminish the impact of a bullet or projectile upon the offender's body.

(2000 S 222, eff. 3–22–01)

Library References

Indictment and Information ⚩113.

Westlaw Topic No. 210.

Research References

Encyclopedias

OH Jur. 3d Criminal Law § 2370.1, Body Armor Specification.

OH Jur. 3d Criminal Law § 3293.1, Offense While Carrying or Wearing Body Armor.

OH Jur. 3d Family Law § 1696, Commitment to Youth Commission.

Treatises and Practice Aids

Katz, Giannelli, Blair and Lipton, Baldwin's Ohio Practice, Criminal Law, § 40:5, Nature and Contents.

Katz, Giannelli, Blair and Lipton, Baldwin's Ohio Practice, Criminal Law, § 117:2, Mandatory Prison Sentences.

Katz, Giannelli, Blair and Lipton, Baldwin's Ohio Practice, Criminal Law, § 118:8, Body Armor.

Carlin, Baldwin's Ohio Practice, Merrick-Rippner Probate Law § 107:84, Disposition of Delinquent Children—Prior to January 1, 2002.

2941.1412 Discharging firearm at peace officer or corrections officer

(A) Imposition of a seven-year mandatory prison term upon an offender under division (D)(1)(f) of section 2929.14 of the Revised Code is precluded unless the indictment, count in the indictment, or information charging the offense specifies that the offender discharged a firearm at a peace officer or a corrections officer while committing the offense. The specification shall be stated at the end of the body of the indictment, count, or information and shall be in substantially the following form:

"SPECIFICATION (or, SPECIFICATION TO THE FIRST COUNT).

The Grand Jurors (or insert the person's or the prosecuting attorney's name when appropriate) further find and specify that (set forth that the offender discharged a firearm at a peace officer or a corrections officer while committing the offense)."

(B) As used in this section:

(1) "Firearm" has the same meaning as in section 2923.11 of the Revised Code.

(2) "Peace officer" has the same meaning as in section 2935.01 of the Revised Code.

(3) "Corrections officer" means a person employed by a detention facility as a corrections officer.

(4) "Detention facility" has the same meaning as in section 2921.01 of the Revised Code.

(2002 H 130, eff. 4–7–03)

Cross References

Disposition where child adjudicated delinquent, 2151.355

Felony specifications, 2152.17

Prison terms, 2929.14

Library References

Indictment and Information ⚩113.

Westlaw Topic No. 210.

Research References

Encyclopedias

OH Jur. 3d Criminal Law § 3267, Specification as Prerequisite to Enhanced Penalty; State's Burden of Proof; Proof of Prior Conviction.

OH Jur. 3d Family Law § 1740, Commencement of Proceedings—Charges in an Affidavit.

Treatises and Practice Aids

Katz, Giannelli, Blair and Lipton, Baldwin's Ohio Practice, Criminal Law, § 118:11.50, Shooting at a Police Officer.

Carlin, Baldwin's Ohio Practice, Merrick-Rippner Probate Law § 107:92, Enhanced Dispositions Due to Felony Specifications, Effective January 1, 2002.

Giannelli & Yeomans, Ohio Juvenile Law § 27:3, Department of Youth Services Commitment.

2941.1413 Specification concerning prior felony OVI offenses

(A) Imposition of a mandatory additional prison term of one, two, three, four, or five years upon an offender under division (G)(2) of section 2929.13 of the Revised Code is precluded unless the indictment, count in the indictment, or information charging a felony violation of division (A) of section 4511.19 of the Revised Code specifies that the offender, within twenty years of the offense, previously has been convicted of or pleaded guilty to five or more equivalent offenses. The specification shall be stated at the end of the body of the indictment, count, or information and shall be stated in substantially the following form:

"SPECIFICATION (or, SPECIFICATION TO THE FIRST COUNT). The Grand Jurors (or insert the person's or the prosecuting attorney's name when appropriate) further find and specify that (set forth that the offender, within twenty years of committing the offense, previously had been convicted of or pleaded guilty to five or more equivalent offenses)."

(B) As used in division (A) of this section, "equivalent offense" has the same meaning as in section 4511.181 of the Revised Code.

(2004 H 163, eff. 9–23–04)

Cross References

Driving while under the influence of alcohol or drugs; tests; presumptions; penalties; immunity for those withdrawing blood, 4511.19

Sentencing guidelines for various specific offenses and degrees of offenses, 2929.13

Library References

Indictment and Information ⚷113.

Westlaw Topic No. 210.

Research References

Encyclopedias

OH Jur. 3d Criminal Law § 897, Aggravated Vehicular Homicide, Generally.

OH Jur. 3d Criminal Law § 901, Vehicular Homicide, Generally; Death Caused by Negligence.

OH Jur. 3d Criminal Law § 934, Killing of Law Enforcement Officer.

OH Jur. 3d Criminal Law § 956, Aggravated Vehicular Homicide or Vehicular Homicide.

OH Jur. 3d Criminal Law § 963, Murder and Aggravated Murder—Specification of Aggravating Circumstances.

OH Jur. 3d Criminal Law § 3267, Specification as Prerequisite to Enhanced Penalty; State's Burden of Proof; Proof of Prior Conviction.

OH Jur. 3d Criminal Law § 3302, Omvi Offenses.

Treatises and Practice Aids

Katz, Giannelli, Blair and Lipton, Baldwin's Ohio Practice, Criminal Law, § 117:3, Mandatory Incarceration—Felony Omvi Offenses.

Carlin, Baldwin's Ohio Practice, Merrick-Rippner Probate Law § 107:92, Enhanced Dispositions Due to Felony Specifications, Effective January 1, 2002.

Painter, Ohio Driving Under the Influence § 1:1, Introduction—Historical Background.

Painter, Ohio Driving Under the Influence § 12:48, Recent Enactment—New Crimes.

Painter, Ohio Driving Under the Influence § 12:50, Penalty Charts.

Painter, Ohio Driving Under the Influence § 12:47.1, Recent Enactment—New Crimes.

2941.1414 Specifications concerning drug or alcohol related vehicular homicide of peace officer in construction zone

(A) Imposition of a five-year mandatory prison term upon an offender under division (D)(5) of section 2929.14 of the Revised Code is precluded unless the offender is convicted of or pleads guilty to violating division (A)(1) or (2) of section 2903.06 of the Revised Code and unless the indictment, count in the indictment, or information charging the offense specifies that the victim of the offense is a peace officer. The specification shall be stated at the end of the body of the indictment, count, or information and shall be stated in substantially the following form:

"SPECIFICATION (or, SPECIFICATION TO THE FIRST COUNT). The Grand Jurors (or insert the person's or the prosecuting attorney's name when appropriate) further find and specify that (set forth that the victim of the offense is a peace officer)."

(B) The specification described in division (A) of this section may be used in a delinquent child proceeding in the manner and for the purpose described in section 2152.17 of the Revised Code.

(C) As used in this section, "peace officer" has the same meaning as in section 2935.01 of the Revised Code.

(2004 H 52, eff. 6–1–04)

Cross References

Felony specifications, 2152.17
Prison terms, 2929.14

Library References

Indictment and Information ⚷113.
Westlaw Topic No. 210.

Research References

Encyclopedias

OH Jur. 3d Criminal Law § 899, Degrees of Aggravated Vehicular Homicide—Multiple Violations.

OH Jur. 3d Criminal Law § 901, Vehicular Homicide, Generally; Death Caused by Negligence.

OH Jur. 3d Criminal Law § 934, Killing of Law Enforcement Officer.

OH Jur. 3d Criminal Law § 956, Aggravated Vehicular Homicide or Vehicular Homicide.

OH Jur. 3d Criminal Law § 963, Murder and Aggravated Murder—Specification of Aggravating Circumstances.

OH Jur. 3d Criminal Law § 3267, Specification as Prerequisite to Enhanced Penalty; State's Burden of Proof; Proof of Prior Conviction.

OH Jur. 3d Criminal Law § 3321, Consideration of Other Criteria.

Treatises and Practice Aids

Carlin, Baldwin's Ohio Practice, Merrick-Rippner Probate Law § 107:92, Enhanced Dispositions Due to Felony Specifications, Effective January 1, 2002.

2941.1415 Specifications concerning drug or alcohol related vehicular homicide of peace officer in construction zone and prior convictions

(A) Imposition of a three-year mandatory prison term upon an offender under division (D)(6) of section 2929.14 of the Revised Code is precluded unless the offender is convicted of or pleads guilty to violating division (A)(1) or (2) of section 2903.06 of the Revised Code and unless the indictment, count in the indictment, or information charging the offense specifies that the offender previously has been convicted of or pleaded guilty to three or more violations of division (A) or (B) of section 4511.19 of the Revised Code or an equivalent offense, or three or more violations of any combination of those divisions and offenses. The specification shall be stated at the end of the body of the indictment, count, or information and shall be stated in substantially the following form:

"SPECIFICATION (or, SPECIFICATION TO THE FIRST COUNT). The Grand Jurors (or insert the person's or the prosecuting attorney's name when appropriate) further find and specify that (set forth that the offender previously has been convicted of or pleaded guilty to three or more violations of division (A) or (B) of section 4511.19 of the Revised Code or an equivalent offense, or three or more violations of any combination of those divisions and offenses)."

(B) The specification described in division (A) of this section may be used in a delinquent child proceeding in the manner and for the purpose described in section 2152.17 of the Revised Code.

(C) As used in this section, "equivalent offense" has the same meaning as in section 4511.181 of the Revised Code.

(2004 H 52, eff. 6–1–04)

Cross References

Felony specifications, 2152.17
Prison terms, 2929.14

Library References

Indictment and Information ⚷113.
Westlaw Topic No. 210.

2941.1416 Specification concerning prior misdemeanor OVI offenses

(A) Imposition of a mandatory, additional, definite jail term of up to six months upon an offender under division (E) of section 2929.24 of the Revised Code is precluded unless the information charging a violation of division (B) of section 4511.19 of the Revised Code specifies that the offender, within twenty years of the offense, previously has been convicted of or pleaded guilty to five or more equivalent offenses. The specification shall be stated at the end of the body of the information and shall be stated in substantially the following form:

"SPECIFICATION. (Insert the person's or the prosecuting attorney's name as appropriate) further finds and specifies that (set forth that the offender, within twenty years of committing the offense, previously had been convicted of or pleaded guilty to five or more equivalent offenses)."

(B) As used in division (A) of this section, "equivalent offense" has the same meaning as in section 4511.181 of the Revised Code.

(2004 H 163, eff. 9–23–04)

Cross References

Driving while under the influence of alcohol or drugs; tests; presumptions; penalties; immunity for those withdrawing blood, 4511.19

Misdemeanor jail terms, 2929.24

Library References

Indictment and Information ⚷113.

Westlaw Topic No. 210.

2941.15 Sufficiency of indictment for forgery

In an indictment or information for falsely making, altering, forging, printing, photographing, uttering, disposing of, or putting off an instrument, it is sufficient to set forth the purport and value thereof. Where the instrument is a promise to pay money conditionally, it is not necessary to allege that the condition has been performed.

(1953 H 1, eff. 10–1–53; GC 13437–14)

Historical and Statutory Notes

Pre–1953 H 1 Amendments: 113 v 166, Ch 16, § 14

Cross References

Forgery, 2913.31

Library References

Forgery ⚷25.

Westlaw Topic No. 181.

C.J.S. Forgery §§ 44 to 77.

Research References

Encyclopedias

OH Jur. 3d Criminal Law § 1376, Indictments.

2941.16 Sufficient description for forgery

In an indictment or information for engraving or making the whole or part of an instrument, matter, or thing, or for using or having the unlawful custody or possession of a plate or other material upon which the whole or part of an instrument, matter, or thing was engraved or made, or for having the unlawful custody or possession of a paper upon which the whole or part of an instrument, matter, or thing was made or printed, it is sufficient to describe such instrument, matter, or thing by any name or designation by which it is usually known.

(1953 H 1, eff. 10–1–53; GC 13437–15)

Historical and Statutory Notes

Pre–1953 H 1 Amendments: 113 v 166, Ch 16, § 15

Cross References

Counterfeiting, criminal simulation, 2913.32

Forgery, 2913.31

Library References

Forgery ⚷25.

Westlaw Topic No. 181.

C.J.S. Forgery §§ 44 to 77.

2941.17 Description by usual name or purport

In all cases when it is necessary to make an averment in an indictment or information as to a writing, instrument, tool, or thing, it is sufficient to describe it by any name or designation by which it is usually known, or by the purport thereof.

(1972 H 511, eff. 1–1–74; 1953 H 1; GC 13437–16)

Historical and Statutory Notes

Pre–1953 H 1 Amendments: 113 v 167, Ch 16, § 16

Library References

Indictment and Information ⚷103, 106.

Westlaw Topic No. 210.

Research References

Encyclopedias

OH Jur. 3d Criminal Law § 1376, Indictments.

OH Jur. 3d Criminal Law § 2371, Description of Writing, Instrument, Tool, or Thing.

Notes of Decisions

Description of promissory note 1

---

1. Description of promissory note

An indictment is sufficient which alleges the forgery of a "promissory note" with intent to defraud, and sets out in full a copy of the instrument, showing that it is an unconditional promise for the payment of a fixed sum of money on a day certain. Burke v. State (Ohio 1922) 104 Ohio St. 220, 135 N.E. 644, 19 Ohio Law Rep. 663, 19 Ohio Law Rep. 665.

2941.18 Allegations in perjury indictment

In an indictment or information for perjury or falsification, it is not necessary to set forth any part of a record or proceeding, or the commission or authority of the court or other authority before which perjury or falsification was committed.

(1972 H 511, eff. 1–1–74; 1953 H 1; GC 13437–17)

Historical and Statutory Notes

Pre–1953 H 1 Amendments: 113 v 167, Ch 16, § 17

Cross References

Perjury, 2921.11

Library References

Perjury ⚖18.
Westlaw Topic No. 297.
C.J.S. Perjury §§ 36, 57.

Research References

Encyclopedias

OH Jur. 3d Criminal Law § 1425, Indictment or Information.

Notes of Decisions

Averments in perjury indictment 1

1. Averments in perjury indictment

The requirements of state constitution and of former GC 13587 (Repealed) that a perjury indictment must contain an averment of the defendant's false testimony and an averment that such testimony was in respect to a matter material upon the trial were held to have been satisfied. McCaffrey v. State (Ohio 1922) 105 Ohio St. 508, 138 N.E. 61, 1 Ohio Law Abs. 229, 20 Ohio Law Rep. 166.

2941.19 Alleging intent to defraud

It is sufficient in an indictment or information where it is necessary to allege an intent to defraud, to allege that the accused did the act with intent to defraud, without alleging an intent to defraud a particular person or corporation. On the trial of such an indictment or information, an intent to defraud a particular person need not be proved. It is sufficient to prove that the accused did the act charged with intent to defraud.

(1953 H 1, eff. 10–1–53; GC 13437–18)

Historical and Statutory Notes

Pre–1953 H 1 Amendments: 113 v 167, Ch 16, § 18

Cross References

Criminal simulation, 2913.32
Defrauding a livery or hostelry, 2913.41
Forgery, 2913.31
Securing writings by deception, 2913.43
Tampering with records, 2913.42

Library References

Fraud ⚖69(2).
Westlaw Topic No. 184.
C.J.S. Fraud § 103.
Baldwin's Ohio Legislative Service, 1996 S 269—LSC Analysis, p 6/L–1143

Research References

Encyclopedias

OH Jur. 3d Criminal Law § 1370, Generally; Purpose and Intent.

OH Jur. 3d Criminal Law § 2359, Intent—Intent to Defraud.

2941.20 Allegations sufficient for unlawfully selling liquor

An indictment, information, or affidavit charging a violation of law relative to the sale, possession, transportation, buying, or giving intoxicating liquor to any person, need not allege the kind of liquor sold, nor the person by whom bought except that such charge must be sufficient to inform the accused of the particular offense with which he is charged.

(1953 H 1, eff. 10–1–53; GC 13437–19)

Historical and Statutory Notes

Pre–1953 H 1 Amendments: 113 v 167, Ch 16, § 19

Library References

Intoxicating Liquors ⚷199.

Westlaw Topic No. 223.

C.J.S. Intoxicating Liquors §§ 1 to 15, 17 to 43, 418 to 474.

Research References

Encyclopedias

OH Jur. 3d Criminal Law § 2367, Designation of Other Persons.

OH Jur. 3d Intoxicating Liquors § 271, Kind of Liquor.

OH Jur. 3d Intoxicating Liquors § 273, Name of Purchaser.

Notes of Decisions

Misnamed liquor 1

1. Misnamed liquor

An indictment for violation of RC 4301.69 is not insufficient merely because it specifies the sale of "beer" rather than "intoxicating liquor" to a minor. State v Poe, No. CA 13693 (9th Dist Ct App, Summit, 3–8–89).

2941.21 Averments as to joint ownership

In an indictment or information for an offense committed upon, or in relation to, property belonging to partners or joint owners, it is sufficient to allege the ownership of such property to be in such partnership by its firm name, or in one or more of such partners or owners without naming all of them.

(1953 H 1, eff. 10–1–53; GC 13437–20)

Historical and Statutory Notes

Pre–1953 H 1 Amendments: 113 v 167, Ch 16, § 20

Cross References

Theft, aggravated theft, 2913.02

Library References

Indictment and Information ⚷105.

Westlaw Topic No. 210.

Research References

Encyclopedias

OH Jur. 3d Criminal Law § 2372, Ownership of Property.

2941.22 Averments as to will or codicil

In an indictment or information for stealing a will, codicil, or other testamentary instrument, or for forgery thereof, or, for a fraudulent purpose, keeping, destroying, or secreting it, whether in relation to real or personal property, or during the life of a testator or after his death, it is not necessary to allege the ownership or value thereof.

(1953 H 1, eff. 10–1–53; GC 13437–21)

Historical and Statutory Notes

Pre–1953 H 1 Amendments: 113 v 167, Ch 16, § 21

Cross References

Effect of withholding a will, 2107.10

Securing writing by deception, 2913.43

Tampering with records, 2913.42

Who may enforce production of a will, 2107.09

Library References

Indictment and Information ⚷104, 105.

Westlaw Topic No. 210.

Research References

Encyclopedias

OH Jur. 3d Criminal Law § 1376, Indictments.

OH Jur. 3d Criminal Law § 2372, Ownership of Property.

OH Jur. 3d Criminal Law § 2373, Value of Property.

2941.23 Averments as to election

In an indictment or information for an offense committed in relation to an election, it is sufficient to allege that such election was authorized by law, without stating the names of the officers holding it or the person voted for or the offices to be filled at the election.

(1953 H 1, eff. 10–1–53; GC 13437–22)

Historical and Statutory Notes

Pre–1953 H 1 Amendments: 113 v 167, Ch 16, § 22

Library References

Elections ⚷328.

Westlaw Topic No. 144.

C.J.S. Elections § 339.

Research References

Encyclopedias

OH Jur. 3d Criminal Law § 2367, Designation of Other Persons.

OH Jur. 3d Elections § 282, Indictment.

2941.24 Counts for embezzlement and larceny—Repealed

(1973 H 716, eff. 1–1–74; 1953 H 1; GC 13437–23)

Historical and Statutory Notes

Pre–1953 H 1 Amendments: 113 v 168, Ch 16, § 23

2941.25 Multiple counts

(A) Where the same conduct by defendant can be construed to constitute two or more allied offenses of similar import, the indictment or information may contain counts for all such offenses, but the defendant may be convicted of only one.

(B) Where the defendant's conduct constitutes two or more offenses of dissimilar import, or where his conduct results in two or more offenses of the same or similar kind committed separately or with a separate animus as to each, the indictment or information may contain counts for all such offenses, and the defendant may be convicted of all of them.

(1972 H 511, eff. 1–1–74)

Uncodified Law

2005 S 20, § 3, eff. 7–13–05, reads:

The General Assembly hereby declares that it intends by the amendments made by Sections 1 and 2 of this act to prospectively overrule the decision of the Ohio Supreme Court in *State v. Yarbrough* (2004), 104 Ohio St. 3d 1.

Historical and Statutory Notes

Ed. Note: Former 2941.25 repealed by 1972 H 511, eff. 1–1–74; 1953 H 1; GC 13437–24.

Pre–1953 H 1 Amendments: 113 v 168, Ch 16, § 24

Legislative Service Commission

1973:

This section provides that when an accused's conduct can be construed to amount to two or more offenses of similar import, he may be charged with all such offenses but may be convicted of only one. If his conduct constitutes two or more dissimilar offenses, or two or more offenses of the same or similar kind but committed at different times or with a separate "ill will" as to each, then he may be charged with and convicted of all such offenses.

The basic thrust of the section is to prevent "shotgun" convictions. For example, a thief theoretically is guilty not only of theft but of receiving stolen goods, insofar as he receives, retains, or disposes of the property he steals. Under this section, he may be charged with both offenses but he may be convicted of only one, and the prosecution sooner or later must elect as to which offense it wishes to pursue. On the other hand, a thief who commits theft on three separate occasions or steals different property from three separate victims in the space, say, of 5 minutes, can be charged with and convicted of all three thefts. In the first instance the same offense is committed three different times, and in the second instance the same offense is committed against three different victims, i.e. with a different animus as to each offense. Similarly, an armed robber who holds up a bank and purposely kills two of the victims can be charged with and convicted of one count of aggravated robbery and of two counts of aggravated murder. Robbery and murder are dissimilar offenses, and each murder is necessarily committed with a separate animus, though committed at the same time.

Cross References

Joinder of offenses and defendants, Crim R 8

Library References

Criminal Law ⚷29.
Indictment and Information ⚷126.
Westlaw Topic Nos. 110, 210.
C.J.S. Criminal Law § 14.
C.J.S. Larceny §§ 50 to 51.

Research References

ALR Library

39 ALR 5th 283, Seizure or Detention for Purpose of Committing Rape, Robbery, or Other Offense as Constituting Separate Crime of Kidnapping.

42 ALR 5th 291, Validity, Construction, and Application of State Statutes or Ordinances Regulating Sexual Performance by Child.

29 ALR 5th 59, Participation in Larceny or Theft as Precluding Conviction for Receiving or Concealing the Stolen Property.

Encyclopedias

OH Jur. 3d Criminal Law § 81, Actions During Sentencing Phase.

OH Jur. 3d Criminal Law § 761, Effect of Acquittal.

OH Jur. 3d Criminal Law § 774, Identity of Offenses.

OH Jur. 3d Criminal Law § 776, Offenses Committed in Conspiracies.

OH Jur. 3d Criminal Law § 784, Illustrative Cases of Separate and Distinct Offenses.

OH Jur. 3d Criminal Law § 1179, as Lesser Included Offense of Rape; Merger With Rape Offense.

OH Jur. 3d Criminal Law § 1376, Indictments.

OH Jur. 3d Criminal Law § 2392, Connected Offenses.

OH Jur. 3d Criminal Law § 3236, Double Jeopardy, Generally.

OH Jur. 3d Criminal Law § 3338, Generally; Double Jeopardy.

OH Jur. 3d Criminal Law § 3339, Determining Whether Offenses Are Allied and of Similar Import.

OH Jur. 3d Criminal Law § 3340, Determining Whether Offenses Are Allied and of Similar Import—Where Separate Punishments Authorized by Statute.

OH Jur. 3d Criminal Law § 3342, Multiple Assault Offenses, or Assault and Another Offense.

OH Jur. 3d Criminal Law § 3343, Kidnapping and Rape.

OH Jur. 3d Criminal Law § 3349, Multiple Sex Offenses, or Sex Offense and Another Offense.

OH Jur. 3d Criminal Law § 3352, Multiple Drug Offenses, or Drug Offense and Another Offense.

OH Jur. 3d Criminal Law § 3355, Miscellaneous Other Combinations of Offenses.

OH Jur. 3d Criminal Law § 3566, Sentence.

OH Jur. 3d Criminal Law § 3817, for Resentence.

OH Jur. 3d Intoxicating Liquors § 262, Joinder of Defendants and Counts.

Treatises and Practice Aids

Markus, Trial Handbook for Ohio Lawyers, § 4:19, Joinder of Charges—Allied Offenses.

Katz, Giannelli, Blair and Lipton, Baldwin's Ohio Practice, Criminal Law, § 72:1, Introduction.

Katz, Giannelli, Blair and Lipton, Baldwin's Ohio Practice, Criminal Law, § 94:8, Scope—Multiple Crimes.

Katz, Giannelli, Blair and Lipton, Baldwin's Ohio Practice, Criminal Law, § 153:1, Motion to Merge Allied Offenses for Sentencing.

Katz, Giannelli, Blair and Lipton, Baldwin's Ohio Practice, Criminal Law, § 57:11, Allied Offenses of Similar Import.

Katz, Giannelli, Blair and Lipton, Baldwin's Ohio Practice, Criminal Law, § 73:10, Allied Offenses of Similar Import.

Carlin, Baldwin's Ohio Practice, Merrick-Rippner Probate Law § 106:4, Juvenile Court Jurisdiction—Delinquent Child—Non-Criminal Nature of Delinquency Proceedings.

Painter, Ohio Driving Under the Influence § 2:8, Election of Charges.

Painter, Ohio Driving Under the Influence § 1:18, Prohibited Alcohol Levels—in General—History.

Giannelli & Yeomans, Ohio Juvenile Law § 27:19, Plural Dispositions.

Law Review and Journal Commentaries

Multiple Convictions Statute in Ohio: Has It Achieved Its Intended Result?, Dale A. Nowak and Jeffery A. Key. 31 Clev St L Rev 295 (1982).

A Unified Theory of Multiple Punishment, George C. Thomas III. 47 U Pitt L Rev 1 (Fall 1985).

Notes of Decisions

1. Constitutional issues

Trial counsel's failure to raise in trial court claim that three kidnapping convictions merged with two rape convictions and one attempted rape conviction as they were allied offenses of similar import, which resulted in waiver of right to raise claim on appeal, did not constitute ineffective assistance, where record revealed that counsel was well-prepared and zealous advocate for defendant in face of overwhelming evidence of guilt and counsel could have decided as matter of trial strategy to be considerate of both jury's and court's patience. State v. Russell (Ohio App. 8 Dist., Cuyahoga, 09-23-2004) No. 83699, 2004-Ohio-5031, 2004 WL 2340125, Unreported, appeal not allowed 105 Ohio St.3d 1452, 823 N.E.2d 457, 2005-Ohio-763, motion to reopen denied 2005-Ohio-2998, 2005 WL 1406347, appeal not allowed 106 Ohio St.3d 1537, 835 N.E.2d 384, 2005-Ohio-5146. Criminal Law ⚿ 641.13(2.1)

Defendant failed to show that defense counsel's advising him to accept a plea bargain that stipulated to appropriateness of consecutive sentences, in exchange for dropping of pending charges, did not inure to his benefit and, thus, failed to establish that defense counsel was ineffective in failing to inform him that generally the court cannot sentence an individual to consecutive terms of imprisonment for allied offenses of similar import. State v. Yost (Ohio App. 4 Dist., Meigs, 08-31-2004) No. 03CA13, 2004-Ohio-4687, 2004 WL 1949367, Unreported. Criminal Law ⚿ 641.13(5)

Defendant's convictions for gross sexual imposition and rape were not based on the same conduct and did not constitute allied offenses in violation of double jeopardy; defendant had completed the act of cunnilingus when he turned victim over and placed his penis on her back. State v. Hawkins (Ohio App. 8 Dist., Cuyahoga, 02-26-2004) No. 82465, 2004-Ohio-855, 2004 WL 351871, Unreported, reversed 104 Ohio St.3d 582, 820 N.E.2d 931, 2004-Ohio-7124. Double Jeopardy ⚿ 148

Inmate failed to demonstrate that his television was lost as a proximate result of any negligent conduct attributable to correctional facility; evidence revealed that the sole cause of inmate's loss was the conduct of private repair shop in its refusal to return television. Spitler v. Southern Ohio Correctional Facility (Ohio Ct.Cl., 01-16-2004) No. 2003-06531-AD, 2004-Ohio-203, 2004 WL 95893, Unreported. States ⚿ 112.2(4)

Convictions for involuntary manslaughter and aggravated arson did not involve allied offenses of similar import, and thus trial court was permitted to impose consecutive sentences without offending principles of double jeopardy; statutory elements of the two offenses did not correspond to such a degree that the commission of one offense necessarily resulted in the commission of the other offense. State v. Cox (Ohio App. 4 Dist., Adams, 04-14-2003) No. 02CA751, 2003-Ohio-1935, 2003 WL 1889479, Unreported, appeal not allowed 99 Ohio St.3d 1543, 795 N.E.2d 682, 2003-Ohio-4671. Double Jeopardy ⚿ 29.1

Offenses of aggravated murder and child endangering did not correspond to such a degree that commission of one of the offenses would have resulted in commission of the other, and thus sentences for such offenses were not required to be merged; child endangering required that one in control or custody of a child under eighteen created a substantial risk to the child, while aggravated murder required that one purposefully caused the death of a child under thirteen. State v. Young (Ohio App. 8 Dist., Cuyahoga, 01-23-2003) No. 80059, 2003-Ohio-272, 2003 WL 152818, Unreported. Sentencing And Punishment ⚿ 530

Acts of gross sexual imposition by touching victim's breasts and putting fingers on her vagina were distinct and separate from each other and from the rapes, and, thus, defendant could be convicted of two counts of gross sexual imposition and rape without violating the Double Jeopardy Clause; there was no evidence that the defendant committed the acts while he was raping the victim. State v. Foust (Ohio, 12-29-2004) 105 Ohio St.3d 137, 823 N.E.2d 836, 2004-Ohio-7006, reconsideration denied 105 Ohio St.3d 1454, 823 N.E.2d 458, 2005-Ohio-763, motion to reopen denied 106 Ohio St.3d 1478, 832 N.E.2d 733, 2005-Ohio-3978. Double Jeopardy ⚿ 148

Touching victim's vagina with a knife and threatening to slice her open if she moved was conduct separate and distinct from rape before defendant tied victim to bathtub and threatened her, and, thus, defendant could be convicted of gross sexual imposition and rape without violating the Double Jeopardy Clause. State v. Foust (Ohio, 12-29-2004) 105 Ohio St.3d 137, 823 N.E.2d 836, 2004-Ohio-7006, reconsideration denied 105 Ohio St.3d 1454, 823 N.E.2d 458, 2005-Ohio-763, motion to reopen denied 106 Ohio St.3d 1478, 832 N.E.2d 733, 2005-Ohio-3978. Double Jeopardy ⚿ 148

By forcing victim into bathroom after raping her and then tying her hands and feet together and tying her to the leg of the bathtub with a belt before setting house on fire, defendant subjected victim to a substantial increase in the risk of harm and, therefore, could be convicted of kidnapping and rape without violating the Double Jeopardy Clause; the defendant committed kidnapping with animus separate from the rapes. State v. Foust (Ohio, 12-29-2004) 105 Ohio St.3d 137, 823 N.E.2d 836, 2004-Ohio-7006, reconsideration denied 105 Ohio St.3d 1454, 823 N.E.2d 458, 2005-Ohio-763, motion to reopen denied 106 Ohio St.3d 1478, 832 N.E.2d 733, 2005-Ohio-3978. Double Jeopardy ⚿ 149

Multiple punishments for robbery counts arising from a single incident but separately committed upon separate victims did not violate double jeopardy; General Assembly, in defining offense of robbery, intended to authorize cumulative punishments for each person robbed. State v. Madaris (Ohio App. 1 Dist., 02-13-2004) 156 Ohio App.3d 211, 805 N.E.2d 150, 2004-Ohio-653, appeal not allowed 102 Ohio St.3d 1473, 809 N.E.2d 1159, 2004-Ohio-2830. Double Jeopardy ⚿ 182

Separate convictions for engaging in corrupt activity, conspiracy to engage in corrupt activity, and multiple counts of tampering with evidence did not unconstitutionally subject defendant to cumulative punishment, based on claim that tampering with evidence provided predicate for corruption offenses; General Assembly provided for separate conviction for engaging in pattern of corrupt activity if jury found two or more predicate offenses.

State v. DeMastry (Ohio App. 5 Dist., 10-17-2003) 155 Ohio App.3d 110, 799 N.E.2d 229, 2003-Ohio-5588, appeal not allowed 101 Ohio St.3d 1488, 805 N.E.2d 539, 2004-Ohio-1293, appeal not allowed 103 Ohio St.3d 1495, 816 N.E.2d 1081, 2004-Ohio-5605, denial of post-conviction relief affirmed 2005-Ohio-4962, 2005 WL 2300288, appeal not allowed 108 Ohio St.3d 1440, 842 N.E.2d 64, 2006-Ohio-421. Sentencing And Punishment ⚿ 520(1)

Defendant's acquittal on one count of possession of crack cocaine did not raise double jeopardy bar to his subsequent prosecution for trafficking in crack cocaine, or to prosecution on other counts of possession of crack cocaine, where subsequent prosecutions did not involve allied offenses of similar import; trafficking and possession each required proof of additional fact, and elements of each did not correspond to such degree that commission of one would result in commission of the other. State v. Gonzales (Ohio App. 1 Dist., 09-20-2002) 151 Ohio App.3d 160, 783 N.E.2d 903, 2002-Ohio-4937, appeal not allowed 98 Ohio St.3d 1423, 782 N.E.2d 78, 2003-Ohio-259. Double Jeopardy ⚿ 146

Defendant's convictions and sentence did not violate double jeopardy or due process, where the trial court merged the three murder convictions into a single offense, the trial jury verdict referred to one death penalty, and the trial court imposed only a single death penalty. State v. Coley (Ohio, 10-03-2001) 93 Ohio St.3d 253, 754 N.E.2d 1129, 2001-Ohio-1340. Constitutional Law ⚿ 260; Double Jeopardy ⚿ 28; Double Jeopardy ⚿ 182

When determining whether two or more offenses are allied offenses of similar import, for double jeopardy purposes, the court should assess, by aligning the elements of each crime in the abstract, whether the statutory elements of the crimes correspond to such a degree that the commission of one crime will result in the commission of the other. State v. Cooper (Ohio App. 12 Dist., 07-24-2000) 139 Ohio App.3d 149, 743 N.E.2d 427, dismissed, appeal not allowed 90 Ohio St.3d 1468, 738 N.E.2d 381. Double Jeopardy ⚿ 136

Convicting defendant of felonious assault and rape did not subject her to double jeopardy, as each crime required the proof of acts not required in proving the other. State v. Cooper (Ohio App. 12 Dist., 07-24-2000) 139 Ohio App.3d 149, 743 N.E.2d 427, dismissed, appeal not allowed 90 Ohio St.3d 1468, 738 N.E.2d 381. Double Jeopardy ⚿ 148

Involuntary manslaughter and aggravated robbery are not allied offenses of "similar import," and thus, multiple count statute allows cumulative sentencing for the commission of those offenses, such that there is no double jeopardy violation; commission of one offense will not automatically result in commission of the other. State v. Rance (Ohio, 06-16-1999) 85 Ohio St.3d 632, 710 N.E.2d 699, 1999-Ohio-291. Double Jeopardy ⚿ 29.1

Double jeopardy did not require that defendant be subject to a single prison sentence, on ground that there was a single robbery and that two counts of aggravated robbery were allied offenses of similar import; because defendant inflicted injuries on each victim, offenses were separate. State v. Smith (Ohio, 10-15-1997) 80 Ohio St.3d 89, 684 N.E.2d 668, 1997-Ohio-355, reconsideration denied 80 Ohio St.3d 1471, 687 N.E.2d 299, certiorari denied 118 S.Ct. 1811, 523 U.S. 1125, 140 L.Ed.2d 949, dismissal of post-conviction relief affirmed 1998 WL 549964, dismissed, appeal not allowed 84 Ohio St.3d 1469, 704 N.E.2d 578, reconsideration denied 85 Ohio St.3d 1410, 706 N.E.2d 791, habeas corpus denied in part 2003 WL 24136073, habeas corpus denied 2005 WL 1969309. Double Jeopardy ⚿ 28

In issuing subsequent indictment, state is not subject to speedy-trial timetable of initial indictment, where additional criminal charges arise from facts different from original charges, or state did not know of these facts at time of initial indictment. State v. Baker (Ohio, 04-02-1997) 78 Ohio St.3d 108, 676 N.E.2d 883, 1997-Ohio-229, reconsideration denied 78 Ohio St.3d 1517, 679 N.E.2d 312. Criminal Law ⚿ 577.14

Indictment charging defendant, a pharmacist indicted for drug trafficking, with additional drug trafficking charges after audit of defendant's pharmacy disclosed additional offenses was not subject to speedy trial time limits of original indictment, since subsequent charges were based on new additional facts which state had no knowledge of at time of original indictment. State v. Baker (Ohio, 04-02-1997) 78 Ohio St.3d 108, 676 N.E.2d 883, 1997-Ohio-229, reconsideration denied 78 Ohio St.3d 1517, 679 N.E.2d 312. Criminal Law ⚿ 577.14

Additional crimes based on different facts should not be considered as arising from same sequence of events for purposes of speedy-trial computation for second indictment. State v. Baker (Ohio, 04-02-1997) 78 Ohio St.3d 108, 676 N.E.2d 883, 1997-Ohio-229, reconsideration denied 78 Ohio St.3d 1517, 679 N.E.2d 312. Criminal Law ⚿ 577.14

Allied offenses statute protects against multiple punishments for the same criminal conduct in violation of double jeopardy clauses of United States and Ohio Constitutions. State v. Moore (Ohio App. 1 Dist., 04-24-1996) 110 Ohio App.3d 649, 675 N.E.2d 13, dismissed, appeal not allowed 77 Ohio St.3d 1444, 671 N.E.2d 1283. Double Jeopardy ⚿ 5.1

Sentencing defendant on each of four charges for driving while under suspension, based on single act of driving while under different types of suspension, violated double jeopardy and was plain error; offenses were allied offenses of similar import. State v. Mergy (Ohio App. 1 Dist., 08-09-1995) 105 Ohio App.3d 646, 664 N.E.2d 1009, dismissed, appeal not allowed 74 Ohio St.3d 1475, 657 N.E.2d 783. Criminal Law ⚿ 1030(2); Double Jeopardy ⚿ 142

If offenses are allied offenses of similar import, court considering double jeopardy challenge must further determine whether offenses were committed separately or with separate animus as to each.

State v. Mergy (Ohio App. 1 Dist., 08-09-1995) 105 Ohio App.3d 646, 664 N.E.2d 1009, dismissed, appeal not allowed 74 Ohio St.3d 1475, 657 N.E.2d 783. Double Jeopardy ⚷ 132.1

Two statutory offenses are "allied offenses of similar import" for double jeopardy purposes if elements of respective offenses correspond to such degree that commission of one offense will result in commission of other offense. State v. Mergy (Ohio App. 1 Dist., 08-09-1995) 105 Ohio App.3d 646, 664 N.E.2d 1009, dismissed, appeal not allowed 74 Ohio St.3d 1475, 657 N.E.2d 783. Double Jeopardy ⚷ 135

Although first prong of allied offense test stresses commonality of elements and generally forbids cumulative punishments for both greater and lesser included offense, the two offenses need not be identical in constituent elements or in actual proof in order to be the same for double jeopardy purposes, and thus it is necessary to examine statutory elements of the two charged offenses in light of the facts and circumstances under which the two crimes were committed. State v. Lang (Ohio App. 1 Dist., 03-29-1995) 102 Ohio App.3d 243, 656 N.E.2d 1358. Criminal Law ⚷ 29(1); Double Jeopardy ⚷ 132.1

Illegal conveyance of prohibited items into detention facility and trafficking in drugs, knowingly selling controlled substance, as result of single incident in which defendant conveyed drugs into jail and then sold them to inmates were essentially same offense for double jeopardy purposes and trial court should have merged conviction for two offenses where sale was merely incidental to conveyance and defendant's commission of one crime resulted in his commission of other. State v. Oliver (Ohio App. 8 Dist., 03-06-1995) 101 Ohio App.3d 587, 656 N.E.2d 348, 72 A.L.R.5th 757, dismissed, appeal not allowed 73 Ohio St.3d 1409, 651 N.E.2d 1308. Criminal Law ⚷ 30; Double Jeopardy ⚷ 146

Contention by defendants that they received ineffective assistance of counsel due to counsel's failure to object to sentencing of defendants for both of allied offenses which did not involve separate animus or separate conduct, in violation of allied offenses statute, was rendered moot by determination on appeal that sentencing violated statute and remand for omission of impermissible sentence, even though failure to object fell below objective standard of reasonableness for counsel's performance required under *Strickland* test. State v. Fields (Ohio App. 1 Dist., 09-28-1994) 97 Ohio App.3d 337, 646 N.E.2d 866, motion for delayed appeal denied 84 Ohio St.3d 1427, 702 N.E.2d 903. Criminal Law ⚷ 1134(3)

Allied offenses statute mandates that court may not sentence defendant for two allied offenses; protection is rooted in concept that multiple punishments for single crimes violates double jeopardy clauses of State and Federal Constitutions. State v. Fields (Ohio App. 1 Dist., 09-28-1994) 97 Ohio App.3d 337, 646 N.E.2d 866, motion for delayed appeal denied 84 Ohio St.3d 1427, 702 N.E.2d 903. Sentencing And Punishment ⚷ 509

A criminal defendant is prejudiced by a nearly four-month delay in indicting him for robbery after his indictment in another county for receiving stolen property where the charges relate to the same act, motor vehicle theft. State v. DeLong (Franklin 1990) 70 Ohio App.3d 402, 591 N.E.2d 345.

Multiple prosecutions and sentences by dual sovereigns are not precluded by RC 2941.25. State v. Smith (Ohio Mun. 1991) 61 Ohio Misc.2d 165, 575 N.E.2d 1231.

To determine whether a subsequent prosecution is barred by the Double Jeopardy Clause of the Fifth Amendment, a court must first apply the Blockburger test; if application of the test reveals that the offenses have identical statutory elements or one that is a lesser included offense of the other, the subsequent prosecution is barred. State v. Tolbert (Ohio 1991) 60 Ohio St.3d 89, 573 N.E.2d 617, certiorari denied 112 S.Ct. 1215, 502 U.S. 1111, 117 L.Ed.2d 453. Double Jeopardy ⚷ 132.1; Double Jeopardy ⚷ 161

RC 2929.71, which requires actual incarceration for crimes committed with a firearm, does not create a separate offense, does not force a defendant to face multiple punishments for a single offense, does not violate the prohibitions against double jeopardy in the Ohio and United States Constitutions, and does not violate RC 2941.25. State v. Price (Cuyahoga 1985) 24 Ohio App.3d 186, 493 N.E.2d 1372, 24 O.B.R. 277. Sentencing And Punishment ⚷ 77; Double Jeopardy ⚷ 30

The protection against double jeopardy does not bar a prosecution for nonsupport based on facts stipulated to be identical, except for the date of the alleged offense, to facts in an earlier prosecution for nonsupport in which the defendant was acquitted. State v. Schaub (Cuyahoga 1984) 16 Ohio App.3d 317, 475 N.E.2d 1313, 16 O.B.R. 348.

Consecutive prison terms for felony murder (RC 2903.01(B)) and the underlying felony (RC 2941.25) do not constitute double jeopardy under the legislative intent standard of Albernaz v United States, 450 US 333, 101 SCt 1137, 67 LEd(2d) 275 (1981). State v. Royster (Franklin 1982) 3 Ohio App.3d 442, 446 N.E.2d 190, 3 O.B.R. 521.

The overruling of a motion to dismiss on the ground of double jeopardy is a final appealable order under RC 2953.02 and RC 2505.02. (See also State v Royster, 3 App(3d) 442, 3 OBR 521, 446 NE(2d) 190 (Franklin 1982).) State v. Thomas (Ohio 1980) 61 Ohio St.2d 254, 400 N.E.2d 897, 15 O.O.3d 262, certiorari denied 101 S.Ct. 143, 449 U.S. 852, 66 L.Ed.2d 64. Criminal Law ⚷ 1023(2)

Defendant's four convictions of receiving stolen property violate the United States and Ohio guaranty against double jeopardy which prohibits multiple punishment for the same offense and constitutes prejudicial error since the defendant's opportunity for pardon or parole are impaired by a multiplicity of sentences. State v. Sanders (Summit 1978) 59 Ohio App.2d 187, 392 N.E.2d 1297, 13 O.O.3d 209. Criminal Law ⚷ 1165(1); Double Jeopardy ⚷ 143

The Double Jeopardy Clause does not prohibit the state from continuing its prosecution of defendant on the charges of greater offenses after defendant has pleaded guilty to the lesser included offenses charged. Ohio v. Johnson (U.S.Ohio 1984) 104 S.Ct. 2536, 467 U.S. 493, 81 L.Ed.2d 425, rehearing denied 105 S.Ct. 20, 468 U.S. 1224, 82 L.Ed.2d 915, on remand.

The prohibition against double jeopardy applies not only to included or including offenses, but also to allied offenses of similar import committed with the same animus. State v James, No. WD–85–59 (6th Dist Ct App, Wood, 6–13–86).

2. Hearing; determination

Defendant was not entitled to hearing on issue of whether offenses of burglary and violation of a protection order were "allied offenses of similar import," such that he could not be convicted of both; trial court was first required to view elements of offenses in the abstract to determine whether elements of two offenses corresponded to such degree that commission of one offense would result in commission of the other and thus there was no need to hold hearing during initial step of inquiry. State v. Bates (Ohio App. 12 Dist., Fayette, 10-14-2002) No. CA2001-10-018, 2002-Ohio-5512, 2002 WL 31296867, Unreported. Criminal Law ⚷ 29(11)

If hearing is required on whether offenses to which defendant has pleaded guilty are alleged offenses of similar import and trial judge fails to conduct such a hearing, judgment of conviction must be reversed, and the matter remanded, but only for limited purpose of conducting proper hearing to determine whether defendant should be sentenced for one or all of the offenses. State v. Latson (Ohio App. 8 Dist., 10-12-1999) 133 Ohio App.3d 475, 728 N.E.2d 465, dismissed, appeal not allowed 88 Ohio St.3d 1412, 723 N.E.2d 118. Criminal Law ⚷ 1181.5(3.1)

In determining whether convictions are permissible on each count alleging same offense, court first compares elements of offense for which defendant is charged; if court finds that offenses are allied offenses with similar import, i.e., offenses that correspond to such degree that commission of one will result in commission of other, it must proceed to second step of analysis, which involves review of defendant's conduct to determine whether offenses were committed separately or with separate animus as to each. State v. Gregory (Ohio App. 12 Dist., 08-30-1993) 90 Ohio App.3d 124, 628 N.E.2d 86, motion overruled 68 Ohio St.3d 1421, 624 N.E.2d 195. Criminal Law ⚷ 29(1)

No hearing was required to determine if two counts of felonious assault were allied offenses of similar import committed separately or with separate animus; defendant did not plead guilty to multiple counts, but was found guilty of multiple counts following jury trial and, thus, trial court had heard all evidence necessary to make that determination. State v. Gregory (Ohio App. 12 Dist., 08-30-1993) 90 Ohio App.3d 124, 628 N.E.2d 86, motion overruled 68 Ohio St.3d 1421, 624 N.E.2d 195. Criminal Law ⚷ 29(9)

To determine if violations are allied offenses of similar import, elements of the two crimes are compared to determine if elements of crimes correspond to such a degree that commission of one crime will result in commission of the other and, if there is recognized similarity between elements of the crimes, then violations constitute allied offenses of similar import; analysis continues to second tier of test where defendant's conduct is reviewed and, if court finds either that crimes were committed separately or that there was separate animus for each crime, defendant may be convicted of both offenses. State v. Hankins (Ohio App. 3 Dist., 05-25-1993) 89 Ohio App.3d 567, 626 N.E.2d 965, dismissed, jurisdictional motion overruled 68 Ohio St.3d 1419, 624 N.E.2d 193. Criminal Law ⚷ 29(1)

When defendant pleads guilty to multiple offenses of similar import, and trial court accepts pleas, court has duty to conduct hearing and to make determination as to whether crimes were committed separately or with separate animus for each offense prior to entering judgment sentencing defendant for all offenses. State v. Mangrum (Clermont 1993) 86 Ohio App.3d 156, 620 N.E.2d 196, dismissed, jurisdictional motion overruled 66 Ohio St.3d 1499, 613 N.E.2d 645. Sentencing And Punishment ⚷ 509

The determination of an allied offense question under RC 2941.25 envisions the trial court hearing some evidence before deciding the issue in any given case. City of Cleveland v. Kufrin (Ohio Mun. 1982) 3 Ohio Misc.2d 18, 446 N.E.2d 230, 3 O.B.R. 553.

When a defendant enters a guilty plea to multiple offenses of similar import and the trial court accepts the plea, the trial court must conduct a hearing before entering a judgment of conviction and make a determination as to whether there were allied offenses of similar import committed with a single animus; whether there were offenses of dissimilar import; or whether there were similar offenses committed separately or with a separate animus as to each offense, and if the offenses are found to be allied offenses, a judgment of conviction may be entered for only one offense: but if the offenses are found not to be allied offenses, a judgment of conviction may be entered for each offense. State v. Kent (Cuyahoga 1980) 68 Ohio App.2d 151, 428 N.E.2d 453, 22 O.O.3d 223. Sentencing And Punishment ⚷ 513

Commission of importuning by soliciting would not necessarily result in the offense of sexual imposition, and commission of sexual imposition by engaging in sexual contact with a person 13 years of age or older but less than 16 years of age would not necessarily result in or involve soliciting by the perpetrator, and thus, defendant was not entitled to hearing to determine whether separate animus existed as to each of those offenses. State v. Butcher (Ohio App. 5 Dist., Stark, 07-15-2002) No. 2001CA00270, 2002-Ohio-3689, 2002 WL 1591742,

Unreported. Criminal Law ⚷ 296; Infants ⚷ 20; Rape ⚷ 1

A jury may determine that a pocketknife was possessed or carried as a weapon for the purpose of conviction under RC 2941.25(A) when other evidence supports such a finding. State v Massey, No. CA 1602 (2d Dist Ct App, Clark, 1–6–82).

3. Test for allied offenses of similar import

Domestic violence and unlawful restraint were not allied offenses of similar import within meaning of multiple-count statute, and thus defendant could be convicted of and sentenced for both offenses; each offense required proof of element that the other did not, in that unlawful restraint required that a person knowingly restrain another of his liberty, while domestic violence required that a person knowingly cause or attempt to cause physical harm to family or household member. State v. Brown (Ohio App. 4 Dist., Jackson, 05-03-2005) No. 04CA4, 2005-Ohio-2275, 2005 WL 1083257, Unreported. Criminal Law ⚷ 29(9)

Aggravated robbery and two counts of kidnapping were not allied offenses of similar import under multiple-count statute, and thus defendant could be convicted of and sentenced for all three offenses; defendant's acts with respect to each offense were separate and had different animi, in that defendant's acts in entering bank, brandishing knife, and ordering tellers to put money in bag that he had brought provided basis for aggravated robbery charge, defendant's acts in grabbing teller and threatening to kill her provided basis for one kidnapping charge, and defendant's acts of holding knife against other teller and threatening to kill her provided basis for second kidnapping charge. State v. Bright (Ohio App. 3 Dist., Marion, 05-09-2005) No. 9-04-61, 2005-Ohio-2247, 2005 WL 1077539, Unreported. Criminal Law ⚷ 29(13)

Offenses of trafficking in crack cocaine and possession of crack cocaine were not allied offenses of similar import such that it was impossible to commit one without committing the other, and thus defendant's conviction of both offenses did not violate double jeopardy; it was possible to obtain, possess, or use crack cocaine without preparing it for shipment or distributing it, and it was possible to distribute crack cocaine, or prepare it for distribution, without actually possessing it, such as by directing its transportation or serving as middle man in a drug sale. State v. McGhee (Ohio App. 4 Dist., Lawrence, 03-30-2005) No. 04CA15, 2005-Ohio-1585, 2005 WL 737581, Unreported. Double Jeopardy ⚷ 146

Aggravated robbery and having weapon while under disability are not of similar import, and thus, defendant could be convicted of both offenses; although defendant argued he could not have committed aggravated robbery without firearm, commission of having weapon under disability does not result in commission of aggravated robbery, and element of aggravated robbery is commission of or attempt to commit theft. State v. Nelson (Ohio App. 8 Dist., Cuyahoga, 06-03-2004) No. 83553, 2004-Ohio-2849, 2004 WL 1232155, Unreported, appeal not allowed 103 Ohio St.3d 1494, 816 N.E.2d 1080, 2004-Ohio-5605. Criminal Law ⚷ 29(15)

Drug trafficking and involuntary manslaughter are not allied offenses of similar import, and thus, defendant could be sentenced for both offenses; commission of one offense will not automatically result in commission of other. State v. Uselton (Ohio App. 5 Dist., Ashland, 05-12-2004) No. 03COA032, 2004-Ohio-2385, 2004 WL 1059505, Unreported, appeal not allowed 103 Ohio St.3d 1463, 815 N.E.2d 679, 2004-Ohio-5056. Sentencing And Punishment ⚷ 534

Imposition of multiple sentences for allied offenses of possession of criminal tools and possession of unauthorized device was plain error requiring remand for merger of offenses, even though sentences were imposed concurrently. State v. Sullivan (Ohio App. 8 Dist., Cuyahoga, 11-06-2003) No. 82816, 2003-Ohio-5930, 2003 WL 22510808, Unreported. Criminal Law ⚷ 1181.5(8)

Offenses of felonious assault and attempted murder committed by defendant who, in addition thereto, allegedly committed kidnapping, rape, and aggravated robbery were not allied offenses of similar import, and thus, defendant was properly sentenced separately for both offenses upon his conviction by jury trial; elements of each offense did not correspond to such a degree that the commission of one offense would result in commission of the other. State v. Axson (Ohio App. 8 Dist., Cuyahoga, 05-01-2003) No. 81231, 2003-Ohio-2182, 2003 WL 1994490, Unreported, appeal dismissed 99 Ohio St.3d 1517, 792 N.E.2d 730, 2003-Ohio-4009, appeal allowed 100 Ohio St.3d 1408, 796 N.E.2d 536, 2003-Ohio-4948, motion to dismiss appeal denied 100 Ohio St.3d 1425, 797 N.E.2d 92, 2003-Ohio-5232, reversed 104 Ohio St.3d 248, 819 N.E.2d 271, 2004-Ohio-6396, subsequent determination 2005-Ohio-4396, 2005 WL 2038692, appeal after new sentencing hearing 2005-Ohio-6342, 2005 WL 3219727, appeal allowed, reversed 109 Ohio St.3d 509, 849 N.E.2d 284, 2006-Ohio-2721, reconsideration denied 110 Ohio St.3d 1444, 852 N.E.2d 191, 2006-Ohio-3862. Sentencing And Punishment ⚷ 537

Defendant's child rape and gross sexual imposition offenses were not allied offenses of similar import, and thus, court was permitted to sentence defendant on each guilty finding, where defendant was convicted of multiple instances of rape and gross sexual imposition, involving different sexual activities on several separate occasions over a period of time. State v. Thomas (Ohio App. 12 Dist., Brown, 01-13-2003) No. CA2002-01-001, 2003-Ohio-74, 2003 WL 103411, Unreported. Criminal Law ⚷ 29(12)

Trial judge's failure to hold hearing and make determination on issue of whether rape and kidnapping charges were allied offenses of similar import prevented appellate review of consecutive sentences imposed against defendant and warranted remand for a hearing on the allied offense issue. State v. Banks (Ohio App. 8 Dist., Cuyahoga, 11-21-2002) No. 81191, 2002-Ohio-6331, 2002 WL 31618831,

Unreported, appeal after new sentencing hearing 2003-Ohio-6646, 2003 WL 22923434. Criminal Law ⚷ 1181.5(8)

Defendant preserved for appellate review his claim that three counts of illegal use of minor in nudity-oriented performance were allied offenses of similar import, which would preclude consecutive sentences; even though defendant did not raise that issue at sentencing hearing, he did file motion to correct his sentence day following sentencing hearing. State v. Douse (Ohio App. 8 Dist., 06-05-2000) 140 Ohio App.3d 42, 746 N.E.2d 649, dismissed, appeal not allowed 90 Ohio St.3d 1427, 736 N.E.2d 25, as amended nunc pro tunc. Criminal Law ⚷ 1044.2(1)

Defendant's two convictions for cruelty to animals under statutory provisions prohibiting recklessly torturing an animal and recklessly carrying or conveying an animal in a cruel or inhuman manner were not allied offenses of similar import, so as to preclude imposition of consecutive sentences under multiple-count statute; reckless transportation violation occurred when defendant dragged a dog behind his truck, while reckless torture violation occurred when he threw the injured dog into the bed of the truck. State v. Howell (Ohio App. 11 Dist., 05-30-2000) 137 Ohio App.3d 804, 739 N.E.2d 1219. Sentencing And Punishment ⚷ 605

Felonious assault and child endangering are not allied offenses of similar import, and thus convictions of both may stand, as child endangering requires proof of element distinct from elements of felonious assault. State v. Ross (Ohio App. 12 Dist., 10-25-1999) 135 Ohio App.3d 262, 733 N.E.2d 659, appeal not allowed 88 Ohio St.3d 1427, 723 N.E.2d 1115. Criminal Law ⚷ 29(9)

For purposes of analysis under the multiple count statute, the statutorily defined elements of offenses that are claimed to be of similar import are compared in the abstract; courts should assess, by aligning the elements of each crime in the abstract, whether the statutory elements of the crimes correspond to such a degree that the commission of one crime will result in the commission of the other, and if the elements do so correspond, the defendant may not be convicted of both unless the court finds that the defendant committed the crimes separately or with separate animus. State v. Rance (Ohio, 06-16-1999) 85 Ohio St.3d 632, 710 N.E.2d 699, 1999-Ohio-291. Criminal Law ⚷ 29(1)

Defendant's convictions for securities fraud, and making false representations in sale of securities, were for allied offenses of similar import, so that offenses merged, and defendant could be sentenced for only one offense; both offenses prohibit affirmative misrepresentation, so that commission of one crime will result in commission of the other, and defendant's conduct was not committed separately or with a separate animus, as he made affirmative misrepresentations and omissions during same conversations as to sale of securities. State v. Houston (Ohio App. 10 Dist., 08-12-1997) 122 Ohio App.3d 334, 701 N.E.2d 764. Criminal Law ⚷ 30; Sentencing And Punishment ⚷ 527

Only aggravating circumstances that are allied offenses of similar import, within meaning of rule providing that defendant can be convicted of only one such offense, are duplicative for purposes of principle that, where two or more aggravating circumstances arise from same act or indivisible course of conduct and are thus duplicative, the duplicative aggravating circumstances will be merged for purposes of sentencing. State v. Reynolds (Ohio, 01-14-1998) 80 Ohio St.3d 670, 687 N.E.2d 1358, 1998-Ohio-171, certiorari denied 118 S.Ct. 2328, 524 U.S. 930, 141 L.Ed.2d 702, denial of post-conviction relief affirmed 1999 WL 980568, dismissed, appeal not allowed 88 Ohio St.3d 1425, 723 N.E.2d 1113. Sentencing And Punishment ⚷ 146

Allied offenses of similar import do not merge until sentencing, since "conviction" consists of verdict and sentence. State v. McGuire (Ohio, 12-10-1997) 80 Ohio St.3d 390, 686 N.E.2d 1112, 1997-Ohio-335, reconsideration denied 81 Ohio St.3d 1433, 689 N.E.2d 52, dismissal of post-conviction relief affirmed 1998 WL 191415, dismissed, appeal not allowed 83 Ohio St.3d 1428, 699 N.E.2d 945, certiorari denied 119 S.Ct. 85, 525 U.S. 831, 142 L.Ed.2d 66, denial of post-conviction relief affirmed 2001 WL 409424, dismissed, appeal not allowed 93 Ohio St.3d 1411, 754 N.E.2d 259. Criminal Law ⚷ 30

In order to determine whether two or more crimes are allied offenses of similar import, so as to permit only one conviction based on same conduct, elements of the two crimes are first compared to see if commission of one crime results in commission of the other; if so, defendant's conduct is reviewed for determination of whether crimes were committed separately or separate animus existed for each crime. State v. Moore (Ohio App. 1 Dist., 04-24-1996) 110 Ohio App.3d 649, 675 N.E.2d 13, dismissed, appeal not allowed 77 Ohio St.3d 1444, 671 N.E.2d 1283. Criminal Law ⚷ 29(1)

Conviction for theft in office required proof that defendant was public official and that he used his office in aid of committing offense, but this evidence was not required for conviction for forgery, which also required proof that defendant forged writing, and therefore these crimes were not allied offenses of similar import, so that defendant could be convicted of both offenses. State v. Fiorenzo (Ohio App. 11 Dist., 01-02-1996) 108 Ohio App.3d 500, 671 N.E.2d 287, dismissed, appeal not allowed 76 Ohio St.3d 1405, 666 N.E.2d 566. Criminal Law ⚷ 29(10)

Trial court did not err in failing to merge the firearm specifications with the underlying weapons charges under statute providing that, where the same conduct by defendant can be construed to constitute two or more "allied offenses of similar import," indictment may contain counts for all such offenses, but defendant may be convicted of only one; firearm specification was not a separate offense and, thus, could not be "allied offense of similar import" for purposes of the statute. State v. Blankenship (Ohio App. 12 Dist., 04-17-1995) 102 Ohio App.3d 534, 657 N.E.2d 559, dismissed, appeal not allowed 73 Ohio St.3d 1426, 652 N.E.2d 799, denial of post-conviction relief affirmed 1995 WL 746232, dismissed, appeal not allowed 75 Ohio St.3d 1484, 664 N.E.2d 536, denial of post-conviction relief affirmed 74 Ohio St.3d 522, 660 N.E.2d 448, 1996-Ohio-58, denial of post-conviction relief affirmed 1997 WL 700073, dismissed, appeal not allowed 81 Ohio St.3d 1466, 690 N.E.2d 1287. Criminal Law ⚷ 29(15); Sentencing And Punishment ⚷ 139

In determining whether offenses are allied and of similar import, court must examine elements of the two offenses to determine if they correspond to such a degree that the commission of one will result in the commission of the other, and then inquire whether the two offenses were part of the same conduct and whether there was a separate animus for each crime. State v. Lang (Ohio App. 1 Dist., 03-29-1995) 102 Ohio App.3d 243, 656 N.E.2d 1358. Criminal Law ⚷ 29(1)

The "comparison of the elements" test for the purpose of determining allied offenses of similar import does not necessarily turn on whether each offense has technically a separate element. State v. Lang (Ohio App. 1 Dist., 03-29-1995) 102 Ohio App.3d 243, 656 N.E.2d 1358. Criminal Law ⚷ 29(1)

Conduct forming basis of defendant's conviction for robbery and grand theft was a single course of conduct with continuing animus, not offenses involving separate conduct, for purpose of determining whether they were allied offenses. State v. Lang (Ohio App. 1 Dist., 03-29-1995) 102 Ohio App.3d 243, 656 N.E.2d 1358. Criminal Law ⚷ 29(11)

Under doctrine of plain error as it applies to allied-offense issues, court must determine: (1) whether there was error; (2) whether it was plain error; and (3) whether the defendant was prejudiced. State v. Lang (Ohio App. 1 Dist., 03-29-1995) 102 Ohio App.3d 243, 656 N.E.2d 1358. Criminal Law ⚷ 1030(3)

In determining whether two criminal offenses are allied offenses, so that defendant may only be sentenced for both offenses if offenses were committed with separate animus or separate conduct, court is required to examine facts of alleged crimes in light of statutory elements to see if commission of one crime will result in commission of other. State v. Fields (Ohio App. 1 Dist., 09-28-1994) 97 Ohio App.3d 337, 646 N.E.2d 866, motion for delayed appeal denied 84 Ohio St.3d 1427, 702 N.E.2d 903. Sentencing And Punishment ⚷ 509

Under allied offenses statute, when two allied offenses are committed at separate times, at separate locations, or against different victims, offender may be sentenced for two crimes; however, when conduct is part of one continuous act, crimes are not separate. State v. Fields (Ohio App. 1 Dist., 09-28-1994) 97 Ohio App.3d 337, 646 N.E.2d 866, motion for delayed appeal denied 84 Ohio St.3d 1427, 702 N.E.2d 903. Sentencing And Punishment ⚷ 509

Defendant's robbery and kidnapping offenses were not allied offenses of similar import for purposes of sentencing; defendant completed robbery once he obtained combination to safe from victim, and then bound victim's wrists to facilitate his escape. State v. Perkins (Ohio App. 8 Dist., 03-16-1994) 93 Ohio App.3d 672, 639 N.E.2d 833, dismissed, appeal not allowed 70 Ohio St.3d 1425, 638 N.E.2d 87. Sentencing And Punishment ⚷ 537

Offenses charged in indictment constitute "allied offenses," such that bill of particulars must be provided in order to advise defendant of which acts are alleged to be violations of which offense, only if prosecutor has relied upon same conduct to support both offenses, if offenses and their elements correspond to such a degree that commission of one offense will result in commission of other, and if commission of both offenses was motivated by same purpose or animus. State v. Brown (Ohio App. 11 Dist., 07-12-1993) 90 Ohio App.3d 674, 630 N.E.2d 397. Indictment And Information ⚷ 121.1(1)

Under allied offense of similar import statute, trial court is authorized to convict and sentence defendant for two or more offenses that have as their origin same criminal conduct if offenses were not allied and of similar import, were committed separately, or were committed with separate animus as to each offense. State v. Tinch (Warren 1992) 84 Ohio App.3d 111, 616 N.E.2d 529, motion overruled 66 Ohio St.3d 1509, 613 N.E.2d 1047. Criminal Law ⚷ 29(1)

Under RC 2941.25, a two-tiered test must be undertaken to determine whether two or more crimes are allied offenses of similar import: in the first step the elements of the two crimes are compared and if the elements of the offenses correspond to such a degree that the commission of one crime will result in the commission of the other, the crimes are allied offenses of similar import and the court must then proceed to the second step; in the second step the defendant's conduct is reviewed to determine whether he can be convicted of both offenses, and if the court finds either that the offenses were committed separately or that there was a separate animus for each crime, the defendant may be convicted of both offenses. City of Newark v. Vazirani (Ohio 1990) 48 Ohio St.3d 81, 549 N.E.2d 520.

In order for there to be allied offenses of similar import, the court must determine that (1) the state relies upon the same conduct to support both offenses; (2) the offenses and their elements correspond to such a degree that commission of one of the offenses will result in the commission of the other; and (3) the the commission of both offenses was motivated by the same purpose. State v. Brown (Franklin 1982) 7 Ohio App.3d 113, 454 N.E.2d 596, 7 O.B.R. 145. Criminal Law ⚷ 29(1)

In determining whether actions of defendant in a criminal case constitute a single offense or multiple offenses, use of test consisting of whether each provision requires proof of fact which the other does not is appropriate only where defendant is charged with violating two statutes by commission of a single act. State v. Stratton (Erie 1982) 5 Ohio App.3d 228, 451 N.E.2d 520, 5 O.B.R. 513. Criminal Law ⚷ 29(1)

Before two separate offenses are considered allied offenses of similar import under RC 2941.25, a two-step inquiry must be undertaken and both steps must be satisfied in order for the offenses to be allied offenses. State v. Moralevitz (Cuyahoga 1980) 70 Ohio App.2d 20, 433 N.E.2d 1280, 24 O.O.3d 16.

Defendant's convictions for unlawful restraint and disorderly conduct were not allied offenses of similar import, and thus defendant could be convicted of both offenses; the offense of unlawful restraint required that a person knowingly restrain another of his liberty, and the offense of disorderly conduct required that a person recklessly cause inconvenience, annoyance, or alarm to another. State v. Beachy (Ohio App. 5 Dist., Stark, 09-03-2002) No. 2001CA00339, 2002-Ohio-4714, 2002 WL 31013425, Unreported. Criminal Law ⚷ 29(13)

Statute generally barring multiple convictions for allied offenses of similar import did not preclude defendant from being convicted of two counts of obstructing justice, where the false information that defendant had offered to police had obstructed the investigation of two different people. State v. Terry (Ohio App. 12 Dist., Fayette, 08-26-2002) No. CA2001-07-012, 2002-Ohio-4378, 2002 WL 1964694, Unreported. Criminal Law ⚷ 29(5.5)

Trial court could separately sentence defendant for rape and kidnapping, when defendant lured 14 year-old mentally handicapped girl to his basement with promise of candy, raped her and then detained her, while telling her mother he had not seen her; there was restraint over and above that required for actual rape, sufficient to sustain kidnapping as crime of dissimilar import from rape. State v. Brito (Ohio App. 8 Dist., Cuyahoga, 07-03-2002) No. 80529, 2002-Ohio-3421, 2002 WL 1454063, Unreported. Sentencing And Punishment ⚷ 531

Crime of kidnapping was more than incidental to rape offense, and thus trial court properly denied defendant's motion to merge convictions, where defendant's act of tying victim up and leading her throughout house had significance of its own; two crimes were committed with separate animus. State v. Hickman (Ohio App. 9 Dist., Summit, 07-03-2002) No. 20883, 2002-Ohio-3406, 2002 WL 1453759, Unreported, motion for delayed appeal denied 100 Ohio St.3d 1484, 798 N.E.2d 1092, 2003-Ohio-5992, appeal not allowed 102 Ohio St.3d 1412, 806 N.E.2d 563, 2004-Ohio-1763, appeal from denial of post-conviction relief dismissed 2005-Ohio-472, 2005 WL 293525. Criminal Law ⚷ 30

Convictions for theft under RC 2913.02 and receiving stolen property under RC 2913.51, both involving the same checkbook, ordinarily would constitute allied offenses of similar import and, therefore, the receiving stolen property charge would merge into the theft charge, however, where the convictions were the result of a plea agreement, jointly recommended by both the defendant and the prosecution, the defendant is barred from challenging his sentence. State v Coats, No. 98AP–927, 1999 WL 177575 (10th Dist Ct App, Franklin, 3–30–99).

4. Single conviction or sentence

Record supported trial court's determination that robbery and felonious assault were more serious based on victim's suffering serious physical, psychological, and/or economic harm, so as to support total sentence of eight years in prison for offenses, both of which included firearm specifications, where trial court stated that it had understanding that victim was beaten with a gun and that $300 was stolen from victim, that offenses were committed as part of organized criminal activity, and that because sentences for robbery and felonious assault would not be imposed consecutively, as they were committed with single animus, defendant committed two crimes for price of one. State v. Zenner (Ohio App. 11 Dist., Lake, 11-15-2005) No. 2004-L-008, 2005-Ohio-6070, 2005 WL 3047490, Unreported. Sentencing And Punishment ⚷ 645

Trial court committed plain error by entering convictions on two kidnapping counts arising from same incident, where there was only one "restraint" of victim's liberty, and thus, there was only one kidnapping. State v. Haines (Ohio App. 11 Dist., Lake, 04-08-2005) No. 2003-L-035, 2005-Ohio-1692, 2005 WL 820539, Unreported, motion to certify allowed 106 Ohio St.3d 1479, 832 N.E.2d 733, 2005-Ohio-3978, appeal allowed 106 Ohio St.3d 1483, 832 N.E.2d 736, 2005-Ohio-3978. Criminal Law ⚷ 1030(3)

Defendant's convictions of kidnapping and rape did not merge for sentencing purposes, despite fact that kidnapping and rape were offenses of similar import for merging purposes, where kidnapping and rape were committed separately and with separate, different animus; victims were abducted, confined and forced to ride in car with defendant and his two co-defendants for significant period of time before and after rapes, during which time victims were subjected to risk of harm from operation of automobile separate and distinct from rape injuries. State v. Flannery (Ohio App. 5 Dist., Richland, 04-01-2005) No. 03-CA-24, 2005-Ohio-1614, 2005 WL 750077, Unreported, appeal not allowed 106 Ohio St.3d 1486, 832 N.E.2d 738, 2005-Ohio-3978. Sentencing And Punishment ⚷ 501

Defendant's actions in shaking child and hitting child with blunt object was part of single course of conduct, and thus defendant's convictions for involuntary manslaughter and child endangerment were allied for sentencing purposes, where there was no evidence of separate motive of animus to shake child and then also hit his head against hard surface, and expert testified that victim's injuries were consistent with Shaken Baby Impact Syndrome, which begins with person shaking child and ends with person hitting hard surface with child. State v. Cooper (Ohio App. 3 Dist., Crawford, 08-11-2003) No. 3-02-02, 2003-Ohio-4236, 2003 WL 21904751, Unreported, appeal allowed 101 Ohio St.3d 1487,

805 N.E.2d 538, 2004-Ohio-1293, reversed 104 Ohio St.3d 293, 819 N.E.2d 657, 2004-Ohio-6553. Sentencing And Punishment ⚷ 530

Where the alleged criminal tool is a vehicle then the offenses of possessing criminal tools and permitting drug abuse are allied offenses of similar import pursuant to RC 2941.25, and the trial court commits error when it recognizes the merger of the two offenses by sentencing the defendant to concurrent sentences but fails to vacate one of the convictions and the sentencing order does not reflect the merger of the offenses or vacate one of the allied offense convictions. State v. Castellanos (Ohio App. 8 Dist., Cuyahoga, 09-14-1995) No. 67304, 1995 WL 546943, Unreported, dismissed, appeal not allowed 74 Ohio St.3d 1498, 659 N.E.2d 313.

Imposition of two separate concurrent sentences for aggravated robbery and grand theft during a carjacking incident are improper since the two charges are allied offenses of similar import under RC 2941.25 inasmuch as they stem from the same incident and share the same animus. State v. Clayton (Ohio App. 8 Dist., Cuyahoga, 01-27-1994) No. 64036, 1994 WL 24287, Unreported.

Defendant's contention that kidnapping and dissemination of matter harmful to juveniles were allied offenses and that he could therefore only be convicted and sentenced for one of those offenses was an argument more properly raised at sentencing, rather than at the appellate level as a question of the sufficiency of the evidence to support the convictions. State v. Colegrove (Ohio App. 8 Dist., 11-20-2000) 140 Ohio App.3d 306, 747 N.E.2d 303. Criminal Law ⚷ 1134(3)

Defendant's six convictions for cruelty to animals involved allied offenses of similar import and had to be merged into one conviction, and thus trial court should have sentenced defendant on only one of her offenses; elements of cruelty to animals charged in each complaint were identical, and defendant's offenses were part of same continuing pattern of neglect and did not rely on distinct abusive act for each dog. State v. Bybee (Ohio App. 1 Dist., 06-25-1999) 134 Ohio App.3d 395, 731 N.E.2d 232. Sentencing And Punishment ⚷ 516

It was prejudicial plain error to impose multiple sentences for robbery and grand theft even if sentences were made to run concurrently, where robbery and grand theft were allied offenses of similar import; prejudice arose from criminal record that revealed conviction for two felonies when in fact defendant had committed only one criminal act. State v. Lang (Ohio App. 1 Dist., 03-29-1995) 102 Ohio App.3d 243, 656 N.E.2d 1358. Criminal Law ⚷ 1030(3)

Where accused is sentenced for two crimes arising from what is indisputably a single theft, error is plain. State v. Lang (Ohio App. 1 Dist., 03-29-1995) 102 Ohio App.3d 243, 656 N.E.2d 1358. Criminal Law ⚷ 1042

Trial court committed plain and prejudicial error in improperly sentencing defendants for both of allied crimes which did not involve separate animus or separate conduct; despite complexity of analysis under allied offense statute, sentencing of defendants for aggravated robbery and robbery from one act of theft was violation of specific statutory prohibition, and had error not occurred defendants would only have been sentenced for one of crimes, even though sentence for robbery was to be served concurrently to sentence for aggravated robbery. State v. Fields (Ohio App. 1 Dist., 09-28-1994) 97 Ohio App.3d 337, 646 N.E.2d 866, motion for delayed appeal denied 84 Ohio St.3d 1427, 702 N.E.2d 903. Criminal Law ⚷ 1042

Finding a defendant guilty of multiple allied offenses does not violate RC 2941.25 where sentence is imposed for only one of the convictions. State v. Darga (Franklin 1985) 30 Ohio App.3d 54, 506 N.E.2d 266, 30 O.B.R. 109.

Where a defendant's singular criminal act is capable of being construed as "two or more offenses of similar import" within the meaning of RC 2941.25(A), he can only be convicted of one offense. State v. Sanders (Summit 1978) 59 Ohio App.2d 187, 392 N.E.2d 1297, 13 O.O.3d 209.

RC 2941.25(A) permits the submission to the jury of all counts of a multiple-count indictment, but prohibits conviction on more than one of those counts. State v. Osborne (Franklin 1976) 49 Ohio St.2d 135, 359 N.E.2d 78, 3 O.O.3d 79, vacated 98 S.Ct. 3136, 438 U.S. 911, 57 L.Ed.2d 1155.

In accordance with RC 2941.25(A), a defendant may be charged with violations of RC 4511.19(A)(1) and 4511.19(A)(3), found guilty of both, but may be sentenced only as to one. State v Turner, No. 89 CA 14 (4th Dist Ct App, Washington, 9–25–90).

5. Election by prosecution

Where defendant pleads no contest to and is found guilty of more than one allied offense of similar import, prosecution has power to specify allied offense upon which defendant will be sentenced, and trial court must respect prosecution's choice. State v. Redman (Warren 1992) 81 Ohio App.3d 821, 612 N.E.2d 416, motion to dismiss denied 65 Ohio St.3d 1442, 600 N.E.2d 684, dismissed, jurisdictional motion overruled 65 Ohio St.3d 1474, 604 N.E.2d 166. Sentencing And Punishment ⚷ 509; District And Prosecuting Attorneys ⚷ 8

Prosecution need not make its election, prior to trial, as to which of two allied offenses to pursue. State v. Redman (Warren 1992) 81 Ohio App.3d 821, 612 N.E.2d 416, motion to dismiss denied 65 Ohio St.3d 1442, 600 N.E.2d 684, dismissed, jurisdictional motion overruled 65 Ohio St.3d 1474, 604 N.E.2d 166. Indictment And Information ⚷ 132(7)

State's failure to include available allied offense charge in diversion contract constitutes contractual choice equivalent to election after conviction on two or more allied offenses, and contractual choice binds State unless and until diversion contract is breached by offender. State v. Urvan (Cuyahoga 1982) 4 Ohio App.3d 151, 446 N.E.2d 1161, 4 O.B.R. 244. Sentencing And Punishment ⚷ 2068

RC 2941.25 does not require the prosecution to elect which aggravated murder count will be submitted to the jury, but only prevents conviction under both counts. State v. Weind (Ohio 1977) 50 Ohio St.2d 224, 364 N.E.2d 224, 4 O.O.3d 413, vacated 98 S.Ct. 3137, 438 U.S. 911, 57 L.Ed.2d 1156.

Prosecution need not elect before trial a single count of allied multiple offenses upon which it will proceed, even though the defendant may be convicted of only one offense. State v Martin, No. 10629 (9th Dist Ct App, Summit, 10–13–82).

6. Separate animus, in general

Defendant was not entitled to merger of conviction for failing to obey a signal or order of a police officer with his conviction for receiving a stolen automobile, given that one may receive a stolen automobile without failing to obey a signal or order of a police officer. State v. Jordan (Ohio App. 10 Dist., Franklin, 12-16-2004) No. 04AP-42, 2004-Ohio-6836, 2004 WL 2913769, Unreported. Criminal Law ⚷ 30

Greater and lesser child endangering offenses are not allied offense of similar import, and thus, defendant may be convicted of both offenses, where greater offense, which may be committed by anyone, may be committed without committing lesser offense, which may only be committed by certain defined group of people. State v. Garcia (Ohio App. 10 Dist., Franklin, 03-23-2004) No. 03AP-384, 2004-Ohio-1409, 2004 WL 557343, Unreported, appeal not allowed 103 Ohio St.3d 1406, 812 N.E.2d 1288, 2004-Ohio-3980. Criminal Law ⚷ 29(1)

Two counts of burglary for which defendant was convicted should have been merged for sentencing purposes as arising from same conduct of similar import committed with single animus; evidence indicated that defendant entered one residence for purpose of committing criminal offense and, since he was apprehended within that residence before any further offense was committed, there was nothing from which it could be determined that crimes were committed with separate animus. State v. Allen (Ohio App. 8 Dist., Cuyahoga, 12-18-2003) No. 82618, 2003-Ohio-6908, 2003 WL 22972696, Unreported, appeal not allowed 102 Ohio St.3d 1458, 809 N.E.2d 32, 2004-Ohio-2569. Sentencing And Punishment ⚷ 519

Defendant's movements subjected victim to substantially increased risk of harm separate and apart from his sexual conduct and clearly demonstrated separate animus sufficient to sustain his convictions and sentences for both kidnapping and rape; defendant lured victim into house by deception, he then violently dragged her from first floor of house to his bedroom upstairs and closed door behind them, once in room, defendant placed both hands around victim's neck and began to choke her, thereafter, he proceeded to rape victim, following assault, defendant forbade victim to leave room, while threatening to kill her, later ordered victim to come downstairs, and again threatened to kill her if she told anyone, and it was not until defendant's sister arrived home that victim had opportunity to leave house. State v. Banks (Ohio App. 8 Dist., Cuyahoga, 12-11-2003) No. 82942, 2003-Ohio-6646, 2003 WL 22923434, Unreported. Criminal Law ⚷ 29(13); Sentencing And Punishment ⚷ 531

Defendant failed to produce clear and convincing evidence that trial court erred in imposing consecutive sentences for two counts of gross sexual imposition, where counts were based on separate and distinct acts, including touching victim's bare breast and then massaging her genitalia through her underwear, and each count had its own independent animus. State v. While (Ohio App. 11 Dist., Trumbull, 08-29-2003) No. 2001-T-0051, 2003-Ohio-4594, 2003 WL 22040803, Unreported, appeal not allowed 106 Ohio St.3d 1510, 833 N.E.2d 1250, 2005-Ohio-4605. Sentencing And Punishment ⚷ 561; Sentencing And Punishment ⚷ 591

Defendant's convictions for felonious assault and rape were not allied offenses of similar import, and thus, defendant could be convicted for both offenses; elements of those offenses did not overlap, as each required proof of facts not required in proving other. State v. Gallagher (Ohio App. 5 Dist., Morrow, 06-27-2003) No. CA941, 2003-Ohio-3581, 2003 WL 21530773, Unreported. Criminal Law ⚷ 29(12)

Defendant's felonious assault and attempted murder offenses, though committed against the same victim, were the result of separate acts, and thus, defendant was properly sentenced separately for both offenses upon his conviction by jury trial; felonious assault offense was complete when defendant struck victim in her head with a shotgun, whereas attempted murder offense was complete when defendant kidnapped victim by putting her into the trunk of her own vehicle and threatened to kill her with the shotgun. State v. Axson (Ohio App. 8 Dist., Cuyahoga, 05-01-2003) No. 81231, 2003-Ohio-2182, 2003 WL 1994490, Unreported, appeal dismissed 99 Ohio St.3d 1517, 792 N.E.2d 730, 2003-Ohio-4009, appeal allowed 100 Ohio St.3d 1408, 796 N.E.2d 536, 2003-Ohio-4948, motion to dismiss appeal denied 100 Ohio St.3d 1425, 797 N.E.2d 92, 2003-Ohio-5232, reversed 104 Ohio St.3d 248, 819 N.E.2d 271, 2004-Ohio-6396, subsequent determination 2005-Ohio-4396, 2005 WL 2038692, appeal after new sentencing hearing 2005-Ohio-6342, 2005 WL 3219727, appeal allowed, reversed 109 Ohio St.3d 509, 849 N.E.2d 284, 2006-Ohio-2721, reconsideration denied 110 Ohio St.3d 1444, 852 N.E.2d 191, 2006-Ohio-3862. Sentencing And Punishment ⚷ 529

Defendant's three convictions for robbery involved allied offenses of similar import and required merger for sentencing purposes; the offenses were not separated by time or conduct, and there was only a single animus underlying the three offenses. State v. Howard (Ohio App. 1 Dist., Hamilton, 03-21-2003) No. C-020389, 2003-Ohio-1365, 2003 WL 1389115, Unreported. Sentencing And Punishment ⚷ 501

A shoot-out with police in which one officer is murdered and a second feloniously injured are two different felonies committed simultaneously for which only one firearm specification is imposed.

State v. Vultee (Ohio App. 2 Dist., Montgomery, 06-03-1994) No. 13581, 1994 WL 237484, Unreported, appeal not allowed 71 Ohio St.3d 1413, 641 N.E.2d 1112.

Remand was required for resentencing hearing to determine whether defendant committed aggravated robbery, theft, and theft of drugs separately or with separate animus, for purpose of determining whether offenses should have merged. State v. Philpot (Ohio App. 12 Dist., 08-13-2001) 145 Ohio App.3d 231, 762 N.E.2d 443. Criminal Law ⚿ 1181.5(8)

Aggravated murder and kidnapping are not allied offenses of similar import, for double jeopardy purposes. State v. Coley (Ohio, 10-03-2001) 93 Ohio St.3d 253, 754 N.E.2d 1129, 2001-Ohio-1340. Double Jeopardy ⚿ 150(2)

If the elements of the crimes correspond, the defendant may not be convicted of both under merger statute, unless the court finds that the defendant committed the crimes separately or with separate animus. State v. Cooper (Ohio App. 12 Dist., 07-24-2000) 139 Ohio App.3d 149, 743 N.E.2d 427, dismissed, appeal not allowed 90 Ohio St.3d 1468, 738 N.E.2d 381. Criminal Law ⚿ 30

Offenses of obstructing justice by destroying or concealing physical evidence of a crime or act by another person with the purpose of hindering that person's apprehension and prosecution, and tampering with evidence, contain dissimilar elements, and thus, are not allied offenses of similar import, so that a defendant may be convicted of both offenses based on same course of conduct; while both crimes involve destruction or concealment of evidence, tampering with evidence also includes alteration, which obstructing justice does not, and intent required for each offense differs. State v. Baker (Ohio App. 12 Dist., 04-03-2000) 137 Ohio App.3d 628, 739 N.E.2d 819, dismissed, appeal not allowed 90 Ohio St.3d 1402, 734 N.E.2d 834, denial of post-conviction relief affirmed 2001 WL 1218888. Criminal Law ⚿ 29(5.5)

Offenses of aggravated robbery and involuntary manslaughter were committed separately and therefore did not merge for sentencing purposes; aggravated robbery was completed when defendant entered service station armed with a revolver in order to commit a theft, and involuntary manslaughter was committed when defendant aimed and fired loaded weapon at service station attendant's chest. State v. Mirmohamed (Ohio App. 10 Dist., 12-03-1998) 131 Ohio App.3d 579, 723 N.E.2d 152, dismissed, appeal not allowed 85 Ohio St.3d 1456, 708 N.E.2d 1010, dismissed, appeal not allowed 86 Ohio St.3d 1402, 711 N.E.2d 231. Sentencing And Punishment ⚿ 537

Crimes of robbery and aggravated robbery were allied offenses, and defendant could be sentenced for both crimes only if crimes were committed with separate animus or separate conduct, where defendants in committing theft against restaurant shoved metal box into ribs of employee of restaurant and closed her in cooler; commission of aggravated robbery, which included theft and infliction of serious physical harm, also resulted in commission of robbery, through theft and use of force against employee. State v. Fields (Ohio App. 1 Dist., 09-28-1994) 97 Ohio App.3d 337, 646 N.E.2d 866, motion for delayed appeal denied 84 Ohio St.3d 1427, 702 N.E.2d 903. Sentencing And Punishment ⚿ 537

Defendants were properly sentenced for both aggravated robbery of restaurant and robbery of employee of restaurant under allied offenses statute; two crimes had two complete and separate sets of elements, as robbery from employee required theft from and force against employee and aggravated robbery required theft from restaurant and serious physical harm against restaurant employee. State v. Fields (Ohio App. 1 Dist., 09-28-1994) 97 Ohio App.3d 337, 646 N.E.2d 866, motion for delayed appeal denied 84 Ohio St.3d 1427, 702 N.E.2d 903. Sentencing And Punishment ⚿ 537

Offenses of assault and hazing were not "allied offenses," such that bill of particulars was required to advise defendant of which acts were alleged to be violations of which offense; since hazing required no express animus, there was no way that defendant could have possessed same animus for both hazing and assault. State v. Brown (Ohio App. 11 Dist., 07-12-1993) 90 Ohio App.3d 674, 630 N.E.2d 397. Indictment And Information ⚿ 121.2(1)

Where defendant commits same offense against different victims during same course of conduct, separate animus exists for each offense, for purposes of determining whether multiple convictions are permissible. State v. Gregory (Ohio App. 12 Dist., 08-30-1993) 90 Ohio App.3d 124, 628 N.E.2d 86, motion overruled 68 Ohio St.3d 1421, 624 N.E.2d 195. Criminal Law ⚿ 29(1)

Because common-law doctrine of merger did not apply to multiple violations of same statute, statutory progeny of doctrine should not be interpreted to apply to multiple violations of same statute. State v. Larsen (Lawrence 1993) 89 Ohio App.3d 371, 624 N.E.2d 766. Criminal Law ⚿ 30

Dual prosecution may be pursued even if two crimes are allied offenses of similar import, so long as crimes were committed separately, or separate animus existed for each crime. State v. Frambach (Lorain 1992) 81 Ohio App.3d 834, 612 N.E.2d 424. Criminal Law ⚿ 29(1)

After dismissal with prejudice of a case including one of two related charges, trial of the second charge is permitted where each crime requires proof of an element not required for the others, without regard to whether an election among the charges would be required by RC 2941.25 if the offenses were jointly tried. State v. Fischer (Union 1984) 20 Ohio App.3d 50, 484 N.E.2d 221, 20 O.B.R. 53.

To support a conviction for each count in a multiple count indictment charging the commission of offenses of the same kind, committed at the same time, the state must prove that the defendant committed each offense with a separate animus. State v. Buck (Hamilton 1982) 3 Ohio App.3d 349,

445 N.E.2d 720, 3 O.B.R. 406. Criminal Law ⚷ 29(1)

Defendant did not commit rape and kidnapping separately or with separate animus, and therefore convictions of those offenses merged, where after victim let defendant into apartment where she was staying, defendant took victim by the hand from bathroom to living room, where he forced her to have sexual intercourse on the couch. State v. Williams (Ohio App. 10 Dist., Franklin, 09-03-2002) No. 02AP-35, 2002-Ohio-4503, 2002 WL 2005815, Unreported, appeal not allowed 98 Ohio St.3d 1412, 781 N.E.2d 1020, 2003-Ohio-60, denial of post-conviction relief affirmed 2006-Ohio-2197, 2006 WL 1174504. Criminal Law ⚷ 30

Defendant did not commit rape and kidnapping separately or with separate animus, and therefore convictions of those offenses merged, where victim was sleeping on a couch in apartment where she was staying when defendant forced himself on her and held her hands down as he had sexual intercourse with her. State v. Williams (Ohio App. 10 Dist., Franklin, 09-03-2002) No. 02AP-35, 2002-Ohio-4503, 2002 WL 2005815, Unreported, appeal not allowed 98 Ohio St.3d 1412, 781 N.E.2d 1020, 2003-Ohio-60, denial of post-conviction relief affirmed 2006-Ohio-2197, 2006 WL 1174504. Criminal Law ⚷ 30

Sufficient evidence of a separate animus supported independent convictions and sentences for kidnapping and rape in prosecution that also resulted in felony murder convictions for victim's death at defendant's apartment; testimony of neighbor who heard victim screaming and heard defendant threatening to tie her up, as well as timing of other events culminating in arrival of defendant's half-brother at scene, suggested fairly long period of restraint, and binding of victim's hands and feet not only facilitated rape, but substantially increased risk of asphyxiation separate and apart from rape. State v. Haynes (Ohio App. 10 Dist., Franklin, 08-27-2002) No. 01AP-430, 2002-Ohio-4389, 2002 WL 1969636, Unreported, dismissal of habeas corpus affirmed 2009 WL 675, appeal not allowed 97 Ohio St.3d 1484, 780 N.E.2d 287, 2002-Ohio-6866, appeal not allowed 98 Ohio St.3d 1463, 783 N.E.2d 521, 2003-Ohio-644, denial of post-conviction relief affirmed 2004-Ohio-591, 2004 WL 240011, appeal not allowed 102 Ohio St.3d 1473, 809 N.E.2d 1159, 2004-Ohio-2830, appeal not allowed 109 Ohio St.3d 1482, 847 N.E.2d 1226, 2006-Ohio-2466. Kidnapping ⚷ 36; Rape ⚷ 51(4)

7. Common elements, in general

Defendant was prejudiced by imposition of concurrent sentences for count of murder, and count of felony murder, where counts constituted alternative offenses for same behavior and should have merged. State v. Wymer (Ohio App. 6 Dist., Lucas, 04-15-2005) No. L-03-1125, 2005-Ohio-1775, 2005 WL 859445, Unreported, appeal allowed 106 Ohio St.3d 1505, 833 N.E.2d 1247, 2005-Ohio-4605, reversed 109 Ohio St.3d 313, 847 N.E.2d 1174, 2006-Ohio-2109. Criminal Law ⚷ 30; Criminal Law ⚷ 1177; Sentencing And Punishment ⚷ 529

Forgery and insurance fraud are allied offenses of similar import where a pharmacist submits to the insurance company for reimbursement a computer-generated record of costs for his wife's prescriptions and represents that it is an authentic record generated by the hospital computer and purports to be a record of drugs dispensed as prescribed by his physician, along with the amount paid for each drug, knowing the list to be false. State v. Shanely (Ohio App. 2 Dist., Miami, 02-09-1994) No. 92-CA-68, 1994 WL 37374, Unreported, dismissed, jurisdictional motion overruled 69 Ohio St.3d 1488, 635 N.E.2d 43.

For purposes of sentencing, assault on a police officer and failure to comply with the lawful order of a police officer would not be considered allied offenses of similar import, where elements of the two offenses did not correspond to such a degree that committing one offense necessarily resulted in commission of the other. State v. Evans (Ohio App. 7 Dist., 06-27-2003) 153 Ohio App.3d 226, 792 N.E.2d 757, 2003-Ohio-3475, cause dismissed 99 Ohio St.3d 1534, 795 N.E.2d 55, 2003-Ohio-4677, motion granted 100 Ohio St.3d 1429, 797 N.E.2d 510, 2003-Ohio-5396, appeal not allowed 100 Ohio St.3d 1530, 800 N.E.2d 47, 2003-Ohio-6458. Criminal Law ⚷ 29(9)

When deciding whether offenses are allied offenses of similar import, for purpose of determining whether defendant may be convicted of only one of the offenses, a court must compare the offenses in the abstract to see if their elements correspond to such a degree that committing one crime will result in committing the other. State v. Evans (Ohio App. 7 Dist., 06-27-2003) 153 Ohio App.3d 226, 792 N.E.2d 757, 2003-Ohio-3475, cause dismissed 99 Ohio St.3d 1534, 795 N.E.2d 55, 2003-Ohio-4677, motion granted 100 Ohio St.3d 1429, 797 N.E.2d 510, 2003-Ohio-5396, appeal not allowed 100 Ohio St.3d 1530, 800 N.E.2d 47, 2003-Ohio-6458. Criminal Law ⚷ 29(1)

Trial court was not required to merge defendant's abduction and robbery convictions pursuant to statute which prohibited multiple convictions based upon allied offenses of similar import, where victims of robberies were different from victims of abductions. State v. Garrison (Ohio App. 2 Dist., 09-19-1997) 123 Ohio App.3d 11, 702 N.E.2d 1222. Criminal Law ⚷ 30

Purpose of allied offenses statute is to codify judicial doctrine of "merger," which holds that a major crime often includes as inherent therein the component elements of other crimes and that these component elements, in legal effect, are merged in the major crime. State v. Moore (Ohio App. 1 Dist., 04-24-1996) 110 Ohio App.3d 649, 675 N.E.2d 13, dismissed, appeal not allowed 77 Ohio St.3d 1444, 671 N.E.2d 1283. Criminal Law ⚷ 29(1); Criminal Law ⚷ 30

Allied crimes of robbery and aggravated robbery arising out of theft of restaurant were committed with same animus and were part of same conduct, and defendants could not be sentenced for both crimes under allied offenses statute, where state proved only one theft to complete theft element of both crimes; animus for both was to deprive restaurant of money, robbery and aggravated robbery were part of one continuous act, and conduct was not separate as there was only one theft and crimes of aggravated robbery and robbery were committed at same time and location and against same victim. State v. Fields (Ohio App. 1 Dist., 09-28-1994) 97 Ohio App.3d 337, 646 N.E.2d 866, motion for delayed appeal denied 84 Ohio St.3d 1427, 702 N.E.2d 903. Sentencing And Punishment ⚿ 537

The prohibition against multiple convictions in RC 2941.25 applies where the two offenses have elements corresponding to such a degree that the commission of one will result in commission of the other; the elements should not be viewed abstractly but with reference to the facts of the case. City of Dayton v. McLaughlin (Montgomery 1988) 50 Ohio App.3d 69, 552 N.E.2d 965. Criminal Law ⚿ 29(1)

8. Complicity

Trial court's failure to merge convictions for complicity to aggravated robbery and complicity to theft, which were allied offenses of similar import, was not plain error; defendant was given concurrent sentences and, thus, suffered no prejudice. State v. King (Ohio App. 5 Dist., Muskingum, 11-19-2004) No. CT2003-0057, 2004-Ohio-6277, 2004 WL 2676312, Unreported. Criminal Law ⚿ 1030(3)

For purposes of sentencing, defendant failed to demonstrate that his convictions for complicity to commit aggravated murder and complicity to commit felonious assault constituted allied offenses of similar import; record revealed that defendant conspired to unlawfully terminate alleged victim's pregnancy, and thus the intent to harm separately extended to defendant's complicity in the contemporaneous assault on alleged victim's physical person. State v. Tarver (Ohio App. 5 Dist., Stark, 12-15-2003) No. 2002CA00394, 2003-Ohio-6840, 2003 WL 22958400, Unreported, appeal after new sentencing hearing 2004-Ohio-5508, 2004 WL 2315192, appeal not allowed 105 Ohio St.3d 1452, 823 N.E.2d 457, 2005-Ohio-763, denial of post-conviction relief affirmed 2005-Ohio-3119, 2005 WL 1463240, appeal not allowed 107 Ohio St.3d 1409, 836 N.E.2d 1229, 2005-Ohio-5859. Double Jeopardy ⚿ 150(1)

Defendant's convictions for complicity to commit sexual battery and endangering children were not allied offenses of similar import, and thus defendant was properly sentenced to concurrent terms for such offenses; each of the offenses requires different action or inaction on the part of the perpetrator of the crime. State v. Goff (Ohio App. 9 Dist., Summit, 03-12-2003) No. 21114, 2003-Ohio-1134, 2003 WL 1039443, Unreported, appeal not allowed 99 Ohio St.3d 1455, 790 N.E.2d 1219, 2003-Ohio-3396. Sentencing And Punishment ⚿ 522

State was not required to make pretrial election between counts charging defendant with conspiracy to commit aggravated murder and with complicity by conspiracy in completed crime of aggravated murder; offenses were allied offenses of similar import, such that defendant could be found guilty of both, but convicted of only one. State v. Hoop (Ohio App. 12 Dist., 08-02-1999) 134 Ohio App.3d 627, 731 N.E.2d 1177, dismissed, appeal not allowed 87 Ohio St.3d 1441, 719 N.E.2d 5, on subsequent appeal 2001 WL 877296, dismissed, appeal not allowed 93 Ohio St.3d 1484, 758 N.E.2d 185, denial of post-conviction relief affirmed 2005-Ohio-1407, 2005 WL 694545, appeal not allowed 106 Ohio St.3d 1506, 833 N.E.2d 1249, 2005-Ohio-4605. Criminal Law ⚿ 678(.5)

Convictions on counts charging conspiracy to commit aggravated trafficking under statutory subsections prohibiting shipment or distribution of controlled substances known to be intended for sale and prohibiting sale of a controlled substance in an amount equal to or exceeding three times the bulk amount did not have to be merged, despite claim that they related to a single conspiratorial agreement and were therefore multiplicitous; element of each underlying crime was unique, audio tapes revealed a series of agreements, not one agreement to commit a series of offenses, and evidence supported distinct conspiracies. State v. Childs (Ohio, 05-31-2000) 88 Ohio St.3d 558, 728 N.E.2d 379, 2000-Ohio-425, reconsideration denied 89 Ohio St.3d 1443, 731 N.E.2d 688. Criminal Law ⚿ 30

The elements of proof of the crimes of grand theft and complicity to commit arson do not correspond to such a degree that commission of the one offense will result in commission of the other; therefore, the two crimes are not allied offenses of similar import within the meaning of RC 2941.25. State v. Parks (Montgomery 1982) 7 Ohio App.3d 276, 455 N.E.2d 498, 7 O.B.R. 357.

Where a codefendant is charged with three counts of felonious assault as an aider and abettor, and the principal can be convicted of only one count under RC 2941.25, it is plain error to convict the codefendant of any count of felonious assault other than the one for which the principal can be convicted. State v. Cartellone (Cuyahoga 1981) 3 Ohio App.3d 145, 444 N.E.2d 68, 3 O.B.R. 163. Criminal Law ⚿ 80

A defendant may be properly convicted on three additional counts of rape where the jury is instructed on aiding and abetting and the evidence supports a finding that the defendant aided and abetted three other men in the act of rape. State v Pykare, Nos. 44652, 44756 and 44758 (8th Dist Ct App, Cuyahoga, 6–9–83).

9. Lesser included offenses

Defendant's separate sentences for robbery and unauthorized use of property did not violate double jeopardy; robbery and unauthorized use of property are offenses of dissimilar import since the commission of one did not automatically result in the commission of the other. State v. Colquitt (Ohio App. 2 Dist., Montgomery, 08-15-2003) No. 19707, 2003-Ohio-4318, 2003 WL 21949725, Unreported. Double Jeopardy ⚿ 145

An offense may be a lesser included offense of another if (i) the offense carries a lesser penalty than the other; (ii) the greater offense cannot, as statutorily defined, ever be committed without the lesser offense, as statutorily defined, also being committed; and (iii) some element of the greater offense is not required to prove the commission of the lesser offense. State v. Evans (Ohio App. 7 Dist., 06-27-2003) 153 Ohio App.3d 226, 792 N.E.2d 757, 2003-Ohio-3475, cause dismissed 99 Ohio St.3d 1534, 795 N.E.2d 55, 2003-Ohio-4677, motion granted 100 Ohio St.3d 1429, 797 N.E.2d 510, 2003-Ohio-5396, appeal not allowed 100 Ohio St.3d 1530, 800 N.E.2d 47, 2003-Ohio-6458. Indictment And Information ⚷ 191(.5)

If under any reasonable view of the evidence it is possible for the trier of fact to find the defendant not guilty of the greater offense and guilty of the lesser offense, the instruction on the lesser included offense must be given. State v. Wengatz (Portage 1984) 14 Ohio App.3d 316, 471 N.E.2d 185, 14 O.B.R. 381. Criminal Law ⚷ 795(2.5)

10. Specific offenses construed—animals and hunting

A defendant charged with twenty-eight counts of cruelty to animals arising out of his mistreatment of cattle resulting in malnutrition and dehydration is not entitled to have all the counts merged into one count since his conduct constitutes two or more offenses of dissimilar import. State v. Lapping (Trumbull 1991) 75 Ohio App.3d 354, 599 N.E.2d 416, dismissed, jurisdictional motion overruled 63 Ohio St.3d 1441, 589 N.E.2d 45.

An ordinance describing the offense of permitting a dog to bite another person and an ordinance as to keeping a vicious dog are allied offenses of similar import under RC 2921.45 where they have the same elements except for the additional element of biting or harming in the first ordinance. City of Dayton v. McLaughlin (Montgomery 1988) 50 Ohio App.3d 69, 552 N.E.2d 965.

Where a defendant is charged in separate complaints with taking several different species of fish contrary to law, and the taking was at the same time, at the same location, and in one net, the conduct of the accused constituted "two or more allied offenses of similar import," within the meaning of RC 2941.25(A), and he may be convicted on only one complaint. State v. Fisher (Lucas 1977) 52 Ohio App.2d 133, 368 N.E.2d 324, 6 O.O.3d 99.

Where a defendant is charged under valid laws in separate complaints with (1) the unlawful possession of fish and (2) their unlawful taking, and both events occurred at about the same time and location, the actions of the accused amounted to "conduct" which "constitutes two or more offenses of dissimilar import," within the meaning of RC 2941.25(B), and he may be convicted of both offenses. State v. Fisher (Lucas 1977) 52 Ohio App.2d 133, 368 N.E.2d 324, 6 O.O.3d 99. Criminal Law ⚷ 29(5.5)

As an adjudication of delinquency does not constitute a conviction for commission of a crime, RC 2941.25(A) does not apply to juvenile delinquency adjudications. In re Lugo, No. WD–90–38 (6th Dist Ct App, Wood, 6–14–91).

RC 2941.25 is not applicable to penalty enhancing factors involved in a single offense, as outlined in RC 2929.04. State v Jenkins, No. 45231 (8th Dist Ct App, Cuyahoga, 2–24–84), affirmed by 15 OS(3d) 164, 15 OBR 311, 473 NE(2d) 264 (1984).

11. —— Murder; homicide, specific offenses construed

Murder and aggravated arson were not allied offenses of similar import, and thus defendant could be convicted of both under multiple-count statute, even though defendant argued that she had to commit aggravated arson in order to commit murder; commission of one offense did not result in commission of other offense, in that defendant merely had to use fire to create physical harm to occupied structure to commit aggravated arson, while to commit murder, defendant's arson had to result in death of person. State v. Gipson (Ohio App. 3 Dist., Allen, 08-01-2005) No. 1-04-84, 2005-Ohio-3886, 2005 WL 1797964, Unreported, motion for delayed appeal granted 107 Ohio St.3d 1405, 836 N.E.2d 1226, 2005-Ohio-5859. Criminal Law ⚷ 29(14)

Defendant was prejudiced by imposition of concurrent sentences for count of murder, and count of felony murder, where counts constituted alternative offenses for same behavior and should have merged. State v. Wymer (Ohio App. 6 Dist., Lucas, 04-15-2005) No. L-03-1125, 2005-Ohio-1775, 2005 WL 859445, Unreported, appeal allowed 106 Ohio St.3d 1505, 833 N.E.2d 1247, 2005-Ohio-4605, reversed 109 Ohio St.3d 313, 847 N.E.2d 1174, 2006-Ohio-2109. Criminal Law ⚷ 30; Criminal Law ⚷ 1177; Sentencing And Punishment ⚷ 529

Convictions for murder with a gun specification and two counts of felonious assault each with a gun specification, which arose from defendant's act of firing handgun numerous times into a crowded hotel parking lot, did not merge for sentencing purposes; three individuals were shot during the incident. State v. Collins (Ohio App. 5 Dist., Richland, 04-05-2005) No. 2003-CA-0073, 2005-Ohio-1642, 2005 WL 774010, Unreported. Sentencing And Punishment ⚷ 529

Offense of child endangering and offense of felony murder were not allied offenses of similar import as would require merging of convictions for purposes of sentencing; commission of one offense would not automatically result in the commission of the other. State v. Hoover-Moore (Ohio App. 10 Dist., Franklin, 10-19-2004) No. 03AP-1186, 2004-Ohio-5541, 2004 WL 2341691, Unreported, appeal not allowed 105 Ohio St.3d 1453, 823 N.E.2d 457, 2005-Ohio-763. Criminal Law ⚷ 30

Felonious assault and attempted murder were not allied offenses of similar import, and thus, defendant could be sentenced on convictions for both offenses, where attempted murder is committed by purposely engaging in conduct that, if successful, would constitute or result in purposeful death of another and felonious assault is committed by knowingly causing or attempting to cause physical harm to another by means of deadly weapon or dangerous ordinance such that felonious assault may occur where elements of attempted murder would not be satisfied and attempted murder may be accomplished without use of deadly weapon or dangerous ordinance. State v. Bostick (Ohio App. 8 Dist., Cuyahoga, 04-01-2004) No. 82933, 2004-Ohio-1676, 2004 WL 637772, Unreported, motion to reopen denied 2005-Ohio-4003, 2005 WL 1846543, appeal not allowed 107 Ohio St.3d 1411, 836 N.E.2d 1230, 2005-Ohio-5859. Assault And Battery ⚷ 56; Homicide ⚷ 557; Sentencing And Punishment ⚷ 529

Multiple convictions for involuntary manslaughter as a result of committing or attempting to commit a felony, involuntary manslaughter as a result of committing or attempting to commit a misdemeanor, and voluntary manslaughter did not violate multiple-count statute, as offenses were not allied offenses of similar import within meaning of statute. State v. Mason (Ohio App. 6 Dist., Lucas, 11-07-2003) No. L-02-1211, No. L-02-1189, 2003-Ohio-5974, 2003 WL 22532865, Unreported, affirmed 105 Ohio St.3d 126, 823 N.E.2d 443, 2005-Ohio-791. Criminal Law ⚷ 29(14)

Absent separate animus for each count, offenses of involuntary manslaughter and two separate counts of child endangering were allied offenses of similar import, where general verdict did not indicate which form of child endangering was relied upon as predicate offense for involuntary manslaughter, and statutory elements of crimes corresponded to such a degree that cruelly abusing child resulting in death would necessarily result in abuse of a child. State v. Cooper (Ohio App. 3 Dist., Crawford, 08-11-2003) No. 3-02-02, 2003-Ohio-4236, 2003 WL 21904751, Unreported, appeal allowed 101 Ohio St.3d 1487, 805 N.E.2d 538, 2004-Ohio-1293, reversed 104 Ohio St.3d 293, 819 N.E.2d 657, 2004-Ohio-6553. Criminal Law ⚷ 29(14)

Aggravated murder with firearm specification and having weapon under disability were not allied offenses for sentencing purposes; firearm specification was a sentencing provision, not a separate offense. State v. Williams (Ohio App. 8 Dist., Cuyahoga, 07-24-2003) No. 81949, 2003-Ohio-3950, 2003 WL 21710766, Unreported, appeal not allowed 100 Ohio St.3d 1509, 799 N.E.2d 187, 2003-Ohio-6161. Sentencing And Punishment ⚷ 77

Statute allowing defendant to be convicted of only one offense when same conduct could be construed to constitute two or more allied offenses of similar import did not preclude defendant from being convicted for both involuntary manslaughter and domestic violence, since domestic violence charge arose from separate, earlier incident than later incident that resulted in victim's death. State v. Kitts (Ohio App. 11 Dist., Portage, 03-07-2003) No. 2001-P-0049, 2003-Ohio-1095, 2003 WL 943875, Unreported. Criminal Law ⚷ 29(14)

Offenses of attempted murder, felonious assault, and domestic violence were not allied offenses of similar import and, thus, court could impose separate sentences for each; statutory elements of offenses did not meet *Rance* requirements that, when viewed in the abstract and not upon particular facts, elements of crime corresponded to such degree that commission of one crime would result in commission of the other. State v. Williams (Ohio App. 5 Dist., Licking, 01-17-2003) No. 02-CA-82, 2003-Ohio-256, 2003 WL 149481, Unreported, appeal not allowed 99 Ohio St.3d 1411, 788 N.E.2d 647, 2003-Ohio-2454. Sentencing And Punishment ⚷ 529

Capital murder defendant's right to not be convicted of more than one offense based on same conduct was not violated, given that, trial court, in imposing sentence, merged separate murder counts relating to each victim. State v. Gapen (Ohio, 12-15-2004) 104 Ohio St.3d 358, 819 N.E.2d 1047, 2004-Ohio-6548, dismissal of post-conviction relief reversed 2005-Ohio-441, 2005 WL 281171, appeal not allowed 106 Ohio St.3d 1483, 832 N.E.2d 737, 2005-Ohio-3978, reconsideration denied 105 Ohio St.3d 1441, 822 N.E.2d 812, 2005-Ohio-531, certiorari denied 126 S.Ct. 97, 163 L.Ed.2d 112. Sentencing And Punishment ⚷ 501

State did not rely on same conduct to prove that defendant had committed offenses of involuntary manslaughter and child endangerment, and thus defendant could be convicted of both offenses and sentenced on each, under multiple-count statute; convictions did not originate from single act, but, rather, from defendant's separate acts of slamming victim against hard surface, which provided basis for underlying offense of child endangering in connection with involuntary manslaughter conviction, and shaking victim, which constituted separate count of child endangering. State v. Cooper (Ohio, 12-15-2004) 104 Ohio St.3d 293, 819 N.E.2d 657, 2004-Ohio-6553. Criminal Law ⚷ 29(14); Sentencing And Punishment ⚷ 530

Aggravated murder counts involving the same victim are to be merged for sentencing. State v. O'Neal (Ohio, 01-05-2000) 87 Ohio St.3d 402, 721 N.E.2d 73, 2000-Ohio-449, reconsideration denied 88 Ohio St.3d 1428, 723 N.E.2d 1115, denial of post-conviction relief affirmed 88 Ohio St.3d 179, 724 N.E.2d 423, 2000-Ohio-281, certiorari denied 121 S.Ct. 1997, 532 U.S. 1037, 149 L.Ed.2d 1001. Sentencing And Punishment ⚷ 529

Fact that jury considered two aggravated murder counts for a single victim did not unfairly affect penalty phase of capital murder trial. State v. O'Neal (Ohio, 01-05-2000) 87 Ohio St.3d 402, 721 N.E.2d 73, 2000-Ohio-449, reconsideration denied 88 Ohio St.3d 1428, 723 N.E.2d 1115, denial of post-conviction relief affirmed 88 Ohio St.3d 179, 724 N.E.2d 423, 2000-Ohio-281, certiorari denied 121 S.Ct. 1997, 532 U.S. 1037, 149 L.Ed.2d 1001. Sentencing And Punishment ⚷ 1788(10)

Aggravated murder and kidnapping are not allied offenses of similar import, so as to permit conviction of only one of them upon an indictment charging both, since kidnapping can take place without aggravated murder, and vice versa. State v. Keenan (Ohio, 02-25-1998) 81 Ohio St.3d 133, 689 N.E.2d 929, 1998-Ohio-459, reconsideration denied 81 Ohio St.3d 1503, 691 N.E.2d 1062, certiorari denied 119 S.Ct. 146, 525 U.S. 860, 142 L.Ed.2d

119, rehearing denied 119 S.Ct. 581, 525 U.S. 1035, 142 L.Ed.2d 484, denial of post-conviction relief affirmed 2001 WL 91129, dismissed, appeal not allowed 92 Ohio St.3d 1429, 749 N.E.2d 756, habeas corpus dismissed 262 F.Supp.2d 818, motion to amend denied 262 F.Supp.2d 826, vacated and remanded 400 F.3d 417. Criminal Law ⚷ 29(14)

Crimes of aggravated burglary and aggravated murder were not allied offenses of similar import, so as to require merger of aggravated burglary and aggravated murder specifications in capital murder case; elements of aggravated burglary and aggravated murder did not correspond to such degree that commission of one resulted in commission of the other. State v. Frazier (Ohio, 08-23-1995) 73 Ohio St.3d 323, 652 N.E.2d 1000, 1995-Ohio-235, stay granted 74 Ohio St.3d 1437, 655 N.E.2d 1321, certiorari denied 116 S.Ct. 820, 516 U.S. 1095, 133 L.Ed.2d 763, denial of post-conviction relief affirmed 1997 WL 764810, dismissed, appeal not allowed 81 Ohio St.3d 1496, 691 N.E.2d 1058, habeas corpus denied 188 F.Supp.2d 798, denial of habeas corpus reversed in part 343 F.3d 780, opinion supplemented on denial of rehearing 348 F.3d 174, rehearing and suggestion for rehearing en banc denied, certiorari denied 124 S.Ct. 2815, 541 U.S. 1095, 159 L.Ed.2d 261. Sentencing And Punishment ⚷ 1660

Indictment may charge aggravated murder based on legal theory involving aggravated burglary, or involving aggravated robbery, and prosecution may pursue either theory without engaging in impermissible multiplication of charges, as long as theories are not "stacked" to increase weight of aggravating circumstances for balancing with mitigating circumstances. State v. Haight (Ohio App. 10 Dist., 11-15-1994) 98 Ohio App.3d 639, 649 N.E.2d 294, leave to appeal denied 71 Ohio St.3d 1500, 646 N.E.2d 1125. Homicide ⚷ 850; Homicide ⚷ 876

Murders and kidnappings completed by restraint with duct tape were not allied offenses of similar import, and, thus, defendant could be convicted of kidnappings and aggravated murders; kidnappings were independent of the murders. State v. Luff (Lucas 1993) 85 Ohio App.3d 785, 621 N.E.2d 493, dismissed, jurisdictional motion overruled 67 Ohio St.3d 1464, 619 N.E.2d 698, certiorari denied 114 S.Ct. 1116, 510 U.S. 1136, 127 L.Ed.2d 426. Criminal Law ⚷ 29(14)

Multiple convictions for aggravated murder with death penalty specifications and underlying felony of aggravated arson do not violate multiple-count statute; aggravated murder and aggravated arson are not allied offenses of similar import within meaning of statute. State v. Grant (Ohio 1993) 67 Ohio St.3d 465, 620 N.E.2d 50, rehearing denied 68 Ohio St.3d 1412, 623 N.E.2d 568, certiorari denied 115 S.Ct. 116, 513 U.S. 836, 130 L.Ed.2d 62, rehearing denied 115 S.Ct. 617, 513 U.S. 1033, 130 L.Ed.2d 525. Criminal Law ⚷ 29(14)

Crimes of aggravated vehicular homicide and involuntary manslaughter were "allied offenses of similar import," such that accused could not lawfully be sentenced for both, in prosecution arising out of homicide occurring as result of accused's driving while intoxicated. State v. Redman (Warren 1992) 81 Ohio App.3d 821, 612 N.E.2d 416, motion to dismiss denied 65 Ohio St.3d 1442, 600 N.E.2d 684, dismissed, jurisdictional motion overruled 65 Ohio St.3d 1474, 604 N.E.2d 166. Sentencing And Punishment ⚷ 534

A defendant convicted on two counts of aggravated murder for a single killing should be given only a single life sentence. State v. Huertas (Ohio 1990) 51 Ohio St.3d 22, 553 N.E.2d 1058, certiorari granted 111 S.Ct. 39, 498 U.S. 807, 112 L.Ed.2d 16, certiorari dismissed 111 S.Ct. 805, 498 U.S. 336, 112 L.Ed.2d 837, rehearing denied 111 S.Ct. 1027, 498 U.S. 1115, 112 L.Ed.2d 1109, rehearing denied 57 Ohio St.3d 725, 568 N.E.2d 1230. Double Jeopardy ⚷ 150(1)

Where a defendant driving while under the influence of alcohol causes the death of another motorist and defendant is charged with both involuntary manslaughter and aggravated vehicular homicide, and where the facts of the case would support a charge of reckless operation, which requires a reckless mental state, involuntary manslaughter and aggravated vehicular homicide constitute allied offenses of similar import. State v. Torres (Lorain 1986) 31 Ohio App.3d 118, 508 N.E.2d 970, 31 O.B.R. 204.

Multiple convictions of vehicular homicide may be imposed where a single accident causes multiple deaths. State v. Stimson (Lorain 1985) 28 Ohio App.3d 69, 502 N.E.2d 231, 28 O.B.R. 110.

Multiple convictions of aggravated vehicular homicide may be imposed where a single accident causes multiple deaths, since the offenses are of dissimilar import within the meaning of RC 2941.25, and the legislature intended to authorize such cumulative punishment for violation of RC 2903.06. State v. Jones (Ohio 1985) 18 Ohio St.3d 116, 480 N.E.2d 408, 18 O.B.R. 148.

In weighing aggravating circumstances and mitigating factors, the specification under RC 2929.04(A)(3) should merge with the specification set forth under RC 2929.04(A)(7) under the principles espoused in considering the doctrine of merger under RC 2941.25. State v. Jenkins (Ohio 1984) 15 Ohio St.3d 164, 473 N.E.2d 264, 15 O.B.R. 311, certiorari denied 105 S.Ct. 3514, 472 U.S. 1032, 87 L.Ed.2d 643, rehearing denied 106 S.Ct. 19, 473 U.S. 927, 87 L.Ed.2d 697.

Aggravated vehicular homicide and involuntary manslaughter are allied offenses of similar import, since violation of aggravated vehicular homicide statute will of necessity result in violation of involuntary manslaughter statute; thus, indictment may contain count for each offense, and prosecution need not make its election prior to submission to the jury. State v. Davis (Clark 1983) 13 Ohio App.3d 265, 469 N.E.2d 83, 13 O.B.R. 329. Indictment And Information ⚷ 127; Indictment And Information ⚷ 132(3)

Aggravated murder is not an allied offense of similar import to aggravated robbery, for purposes of RC 2941.25(A), since clearly the crimes and their elements do not correspond to such a degree that commission of one offense constitutes commission of the other, nor is the commission of one merely incidental to the other. State v. Bickerstaff (Ohio 1984) 10 Ohio St.3d 62, 461 N.E.2d 892, 10 O.B.R. 352.

For purposes of RC 2941.25(A), aggravated murder, as defined in RC 2903.01, is not an allied offense of similar import to aggravated robbery, as defined in RC 2911.01. State v. Bickerstaff (Ohio 1984) 10 Ohio St.3d 62, 461 N.E.2d 892, 10 O.B.R. 352. Criminal Law ⚷ 29(14); Sentencing And Punishment ⚷ 537

Though the same conduct by defendant may be construed as both involuntary manslaughter and felonious assault, they are offenses of dissimilar import under RC 2941.25(B) in that each requires proof of an additional element not present within the other offense: proximate causation for involuntary manslaughter and purposefulness for felonious assault. State v. Williams (Lorain 1981) 2 Ohio App.3d 289, 441 N.E.2d 832, 2 O.B.R. 320.

Aggravated murder, as defined by RC 2903.01(B), is not an "allied offense of similar import" to aggravated burglary, as defined by RC 2911.11(A)(1), for purposes of application of RC 2941.25(A). State v. Moss (Ohio 1982) 69 Ohio St.2d 515, 433 N.E.2d 181, 23 O.O.3d 447, certiorari denied 103 S.Ct. 1183, 459 U.S. 1200, 75 L.Ed.2d 430. Criminal Law ⚷ 29(14)

Indictment could properly charge multiple counts of murder in connection with death of same victim, even though those charges may have merged at sentencing. State v. Blalock (Ohio App. 8 Dist., Cuyahoga, 09-05-2002) No. 80419, No. 80420, 2002-Ohio-4580, 2002 WL 2027520, Unreported, appeal not allowed 98 Ohio St.3d 1461, 783 N.E.2d 520, 2003-Ohio-644, denial of post-conviction relief affirmed 2003-Ohio-3026, 2003 WL 21360467, appeal not allowed 100 Ohio St.3d 1485, 798 N.E.2d 1093, 2003-Ohio-5992, appeal after new sentencing hearing 2003-Ohio-6627, 2003 WL 22922426, appeal not allowed 102 Ohio St.3d 1448, 808 N.E.2d 399, 2004-Ohio-2263. Indictment And Information ⚷ 125(29)

Trial court did not err in convicting and sentencing defendant for both aggravated arson and involuntary manslaughter, where since to consummate one offense, the other need not be committed, aggravated arson and involuntary manslaughter are not allied offenses of similar import within meaning of RC 2941.25. State v Bunnell, No. L–92–355, 1993 WL 323619 (6th Dist Ct App, Lucas, 8–27–93).

Reversible error for trial court to enter conviction for aggravated robbery where conviction was barred by RC 2941.25 because involuntary manslaughter and aggravated robbery are allied offenses of similar import because of nature of offenses and conduct involved as explained in jury instructions. State v Holland, No. 92AP–853, 1993 WL 238908 (10th Dist Ct App, Franklin, 6–24–93).

RC 2903.01(A) and 2903.01(B) are not allied offenses of similar import and sentencing on both crimes was proper under the facts of the case. State v Williams, No. 62040 (8th Dist Ct App, Cuyahoga, 4–22–93).

Aggravated murder, as defined in RC 2903.01(B), and aggravated arson, as defined in RC 2909.02(A), are not allied offenses of similar import within the contemplation RC 2941.25 because the crimes and their elements do not correspond to such a degree that commission of one offense constitutes the commission of the other, nor is the commission of one merely incidental to the other. State v Richey, No. 12–87–2 (3d Dist Ct App, Putnam, 12–28–89).

Convictions for aggravated murder, as defined in RC 2903.01(B), and child endangering, as defined in RC 2919.22(A) are not precluded under RC 2941.25. State v Richey, No. 12–87–2 (3d Dist Ct App, Putnam, 12–28–89).

Although attempted murder and attempted involuntary manslaughter are allied offenses of similar import, a guilty plea to an attempted involuntary manslaughter charge does not bar prosecution on the attempted murder charge; rather, where a defendant has already been sentenced on one count following a guilty plea, a prosecution on a charged offense of similar import should proceed, and upon a finding of guilt on the second count, one of the convictions must be vacated. State v Heisler, Nos. 1943 and 1951 (11th Dist Ct App, Portage, 4–21–89).

12. —— Resisting arrest, assaulting officer, disorderly conduct, specific offenses construed

Defendant's convictions for obstructing official business and failure to comply with an order or signal of a police officer were permitted under multiple count statute, and thus, convictions comported with the Double Jeopardy Clause; statutory elements of obstructing official business and of failure to comply with an order of a police officer did not correspond to degree that commission of one offense would result in commission of other offense, and thus, crimes of obstructing official business and failure to comply with an order of a police officer were not crimes of similar import. State v. Harris (Ohio App. 10 Dist., Franklin, 08-30-2005) No. 05AP-27, 2005-Ohio-4553, 2005 WL 2087926, Unreported. Criminal Law ⚷ 29(5.5); Double Jeopardy ⚷ 139.1

Offense of resisting arrest and offense of assault on peace officer were not allied offenses of similar import, and thus defendant could be convicted of both offenses; resisting arrest required proof of additional element of resistance of lawful arrest, and elements of offenses did not correspond to such degree that commission of one crime results in commission of other. State v. Loomis (Ohio App. 11 Dist., Ashtabula, 03-11-2005) No. 2002-A-0102, 2005-Ohio-1103, 2005 WL 583791, Unreported. Criminal Law ⚷ 29(9)

Disorderly conduct and criminal trespass are not allied offenses of similar import since each involves a unique element which is not the requisite for the other; trespass requires conduct on the "land or premises of another" and disorderly conduct requires "hindering or preventing the movement of persons" and the fact that the defendants' conduct in participating in an abortion protest at an abortion clinic violates both statutes does not result in the offenses being allied offenses. Akron v. Wendell (Summit 1990) 70 Ohio App.3d 35, 590 N.E.2d 380.

The offenses of obstructing official business and disorderly conduct do not constitute allied offenses of similar import since it is possible to commit one offense without committing the other; therefore, a motorist is properly convicted of both offenses where her convictions are based on separate conduct committed by her. Waynesville v. Combs (Warren 1990) 66 Ohio App.3d 292, 584 N.E.2d 9.

The offenses of resisting arrest and of assaulting a law officer in violation of municipal ordinances are not "allied offenses of similar import" in the purview of RC 2941.25. City of Cleveland v. Barnes (Cuyahoga 1984) 17 Ohio App.3d 30, 477 N.E.2d 1237, 17 O.B.R. 83.

13. —— Assault, specific offenses construed

Separate counts of felonious assault were not allied offenses of similar import, and thus defendant could be convicted of and sentenced for both offenses under multiple-count statute, even though assaults were against same victim; elements of offenses did not correspond to such degree that commission of one would result in commission of the other, in that first count required defendant to cause serious physical harm, while second count required defendant to cause or attempt to cause any degree of physical harm by means of deadly weapon. State v. Collins (Ohio App. 2 Dist., Montgomery, 07-29-2005) No. 20287, 2005-Ohio-3875, 2005 WL 1797510, Unreported, appeal allowed 107 Ohio St.3d 1680, 839 N.E.2d 402, 2005-Ohio-6480, reversed in part 109 Ohio St.3d 313, 847 N.E.2d 1174, 2006-Ohio-2109. Criminal Law ⚷ 29(9)

Defendant waived claim that his offenses were allied offenses of similar import, and thus, he should not have received consecutive sentences when he entered into plea agreement and stipulated that each assault was a separate and distinct event, and agreed to community control with possibility of consecutive sentences if he violated community control. State v. Yost (Ohio App. 4 Dist., Meigs, 08-31-2004) No. 03CA13, 2004-Ohio-4687, 2004 WL 1949367, Unreported. Sentencing And Punishment ⚷ 612

Felonious assault and child endangering are not allied offense of similar import, and thus, defendant may be convicted of both offense; although offenses both have causation and resultant serious physical harm in common, conviction for felonious assault requires proof that defendant acted knowingly, while child endangering conviction only requires proof that defendant acted recklessly. State v. Garcia (Ohio App. 10 Dist., Franklin, 03-23-2004) No. 03AP-384, 2004-Ohio-1409, 2004 WL 557343, Unreported, appeal not allowed 103 Ohio St.3d 1406, 812 N.E.2d 1288, 2004-Ohio-3980. Criminal Law ⚷ 29(9)

Even if felonious assault and kidnapping were of similar import, offenses were committed with a separate animus, such that defendant could be convicted of both offenses; defendant completed offense of felonious assault by slicing victim's hand with the knife and then continued to restrain victim by threatening him with the knife, committing kidnapping. State v. Cruz (Ohio App. 9 Dist., Medina, 09-10-2003) No. 03CA0031-M, 2003-Ohio-4782, 2003 WL 22093209, Unreported. Criminal Law ⚷ 29(13)

Defendant was subject to three separate convictions and sentences for felonious assault after defendant drove his brother's car into three victims who were walking in an alley, even if defendant meant to hurt only one of the victims, where defendant knew or should have known that he placed three separate people at serious risk of physical harm by his conduct. State v. Gibson (Ohio App. 6 Dist., Sandusky, 04-18-2003) No. S-02-016, 2003-Ohio-1996, 2003 WL 1904387, Unreported. Criminal Law ⚷ 29(9)

Two counts of felonious assault were not allied offenses of similar import, and therefore separate prison terms for those counts were appropriate, where defendant knew that both victims were in one victim's house when defendant fired shots into that home. State v. Ivey (Ohio App. 8 Dist., Cuyahoga, 04-10-2003) No. 80812, 2003-Ohio-1825, 2003 WL 1835513, Unreported, appeal not allowed 99 Ohio St.3d 1470, 791 N.E.2d 984, 2003-Ohio-3669. Sentencing And Punishment ⚷ 540

Offenses of felonious assault and child endangering are not allied offenses of similar import, such as would require merger of convictions. State v. Potter (Ohio App. 8 Dist., Cuyahoga, 03-20-2003) No. 81037, 2003-Ohio-1338, 2003 WL 1355230, Unreported, appeal not allowed 99 Ohio St.3d 1514, 792 N.E.2d 200, 2003-Ohio-3957, habeas corpus denied 2006 WL 988631. Criminal Law ⚷ 30

Defendant could commit felonious assault without committing kidnapping, and thus two offenses were not allied offenses, but rather were of dissimilar import, such that defendant could be convicted and sentenced for both. State v. Brown (Ohio App. 2 Dist., Montgomery, 11-22-2002) No. 19113, 2002-Ohio-6370, 2002 WL 31641092, Unreported, appeal not allowed 98 Ohio St.3d 1491, 785 N.E.2d 473, 2003-Ohio-1189, denial of post-conviction relief affirmed 2003-Ohio-5738, 2003 WL 22429289, appeal not allowed 101 Ohio St.3d 1469, 804 N.E.2d 42, 2004-Ohio-819. Criminal Law ⚷ 29(13); Sentencing And Punishment ⚷ 531

Aggravated arson and felonious assault were not two allied offenses of similar import as the commission of one offense could have occurred without commission of the other, and thus, trial court did not err by imposing consecutive sentences for the offenses; felonious assault did not have to be committed by fire or explosion, and involved activity directed to a specific individual or individuals, whereas, aggravated arson was necessarily committed with fire or an explosive and did not require that offender cause or attempt to cause harm to any person. State v. Kelly (Ohio App. 10 Dist., Franklin, 10-24-2002) No. 02AP-195, 2002-Ohio-5797, 2002 WL 31389009, Unreported, motion for delayed appeal denied 98 Ohio St.3d 1459, 783 N.E.2d 519, 2003-Ohio-644, reconsideration denied 98 Ohio St.3d 1516, 786 N.E.2d 65, 2003-Ohio-1572, appeal not allowed 100 Ohio St.3d 1433, 797 N.E.2d 512, 2003-Ohio-5396. Sentencing And Punishment ⚷ 557

Where convictions for child endangering and felonious assault are based on one occasion during which a defendant repeatedly struck a twenty-two month old child causing the child serious physical harm, the offenses constitute allied offenses of similar import and a sentence on both convictions constitutes error. State v Madison, No. 92AP-1461, 1993 WL 238941 (10th Dist Ct App, Franklin, 6-22-93).

Felonious assault offenses were committed separately and, thus, defendant could be convicted of multiple counts of felonious assault and sentenced to serve consecutive sentences on each count; defendant was aware of presence of two potential victims in car at which he fired multiple gunshots, and defendant attempted to cause physical harm to those two victims. State v. Gregory (Ohio App. 12 Dist., 08-30-1993) 90 Ohio App.3d 124, 628 N.E.2d 86, motion overruled 68 Ohio St.3d 1421, 624 N.E.2d 195. Criminal Law ⚷ 29(9); Sentencing And Punishment ⚷ 606

There is a separate and "dissimilar" import with respect to each person subject to the harm or risk of harm posed by one firing multiple shots from a passing car; a "drive-by shooter" who fires multiple shots which strike or come near five persons in a yard and in homes is properly convicted of five counts of felonious assault. State v. Phillips (Montgomery 1991) 75 Ohio App.3d 785, 600 N.E.2d 825.

Conviction for child endangering and felonious assault did not violate defendant's federal or state double jeopardy rights; felonious assault conviction required proof defendant acted knowingly, while conviction of child endangering could be obtained upon proof defendant acted recklessly, and child endangering required proof defendant acted in loco parentis, not required in felonious assault cases. State v. Barton (Hamilton 1991) 71 Ohio App.3d 455, 594 N.E.2d 702, dismissed, jurisdictional motion overruled 61 Ohio St.3d 1427, 575 N.E.2d 215, rehearing denied 62 Ohio St.3d 1419, 577 N.E.2d 664, certiorari denied 112 S.Ct. 1209, 502 U.S. 1109, 117 L.Ed.2d 448, denial of habeas corpus affirmed 91 F.3d 143, certiorari denied 117 S.Ct. 529, 136 L.Ed.2d 415. Double Jeopardy ⚷ 141

Even though both offenses are of similar import, a defendant may be convicted of two counts of felonious assault where the evidence shows that the offenses (1) were committed separately, (2) occurred at different times, and (3) occurred in different manners. State v. Campbell (Summit 1983) 13 Ohio App.3d 338, 469 N.E.2d 855, 13 O.B.R. 417.

Where a defendant fires three shots in continuous sequence at an intended victim and two other innocent bystanders are arguably within range, defendant may be charged with three counts of felonious assault, but convicted of only one under RC 2941.25, where (1) there was no animus against the innocent bystanders; (2) there was no evidence that the defendant knew of the presence of the innocent bystanders; and (3) the natural and probable consequences of defendant's act produced no consequence such as an injury to these bystanders. State v. Cartellone (Cuyahoga 1981) 3 Ohio App.3d 145, 444 N.E.2d 68, 3 O.B.R. 163. Criminal Law ⚷ 29(9)

RC 2941.25 does not preclude a defendant from being convicted and sentenced for rape and felonious assault, where the record establishes that the assaults upon the victim were far in excess of those required to force the victim to submit to the sexual acts. State v. Stewart (Licking 1980) 70 Ohio App.2d 147, 435 N.E.2d 426, 24 O.O.3d 198. Criminal Law ⚷ 29(12)

Defendant's convictions for felonious assault and for improperly discharging a firearm into an occupied structure, relating to a single incident in which he fired shots into a home, did not merge; the improper discharge offense did not require an occupant to actually be present at the time of the shooting, and thus, one who knowingly discharged a firearm at a home would commit the offense of felonious assault only if someone was at home when the discharge occurred. State v. Dubose (Ohio App. 7 Dist., Mahoning, 06-06-2002) No. 00-C.A.-60, 2002-Ohio-3020, 2002 WL 1376248, Unreported, appeal not allowed 96 Ohio St.3d 1525, 775 N.E.2d 864, 2002-Ohio-5099, motion to reopen denied 2002-Ohio-6613, 2002 WL 31718806, appeal not allowed 98 Ohio St.3d 1475, 784 N.E.2d 708, 2003-Ohio-904. Criminal Law ⚷ 30

Defendant's convictions for two counts of felonious assault, relating to a single incident in which he fired shots into a home, did not merge, where the offenses involved different victims and defendant had known that both victims were in the home. State v. Dubose (Ohio App. 7 Dist., Mahoning, 06-06-2002) No. 00-C.A.-60, 2002-Ohio-3020, 2002 WL 1376248, Unreported, appeal not allowed 96 Ohio St.3d 1525, 775 N.E.2d 864, 2002-Ohio-5099, motion to reopen denied 2002-Ohio-6613, 2002 WL 31718806, appeal not allowed 98 Ohio St.3d 1475, 784 N.E.2d 708, 2003-Ohio-904. Criminal Law ⚷ 30

To determine whether two crimes constitute allied offenses of similar import, it is not always necessary that both crimes are committed by the same conduct but, rather, is sufficient if both offenses can be committed by the same conduct; thus, where a mugging assault is committed to facilitate the theft of a victim's keys, there is little question that the two crimes were committed by the same conduct and occurred as a result of the same animus and as such constitute allied offenses of similar import. State v Mickens, No. 91AP–766 (10th Dist Ct App, Franklin, 2–13–92).

14. —— Kidnapping, specific offenses construed

Defendant's kidnapping and aggravated robbery convictions should have merged for sentencing purposes; although defendant admitted that the victims were restrained while the robbery was committed, there was no prolonged restraint or secretive confinement or substantial movement, and the restraint was merely incidental to the aggravated robbery. State v. Wheat (Ohio App. 10 Dist., Franklin, 12-29-2005) No. 05AP-30, 2005-Ohio-6958, 2005 WL 3551092, Unreported. Sentencing And Punishment ⚷ 537

Trial court did not commit plain error in convicting and sentencing defendant on kidnapping counts as well as on aggravated robbery counts, where restraint of victims subjected them to substantial increase in risk of harm and had significance independent of the robberies; victims, including nine-month-old baby, were restrained of their liberty by defendant and his accomplice as they were threatened with weapons, and were then duct-taped and left by defendant and his accomplice to free themselves. State v. Williams (Ohio App. 8 Dist., Cuyahoga, 07-21-2005) No. 85327, 2005-Ohio-3715, 2005 WL 1707016, Unreported, motion for delayed appeal denied 106 Ohio St.3d 1554, 836 N.E.2d 580, 2005-Ohio-5531, appeal allowed 108 Ohio St.3d 1470, 842 N.E.2d 1051, 2006-Ohio-665, reversed in part 109 Ohio St.3d 313, 847 N.E.2d 1174, 2006-Ohio-2109. Criminal Law ⚷ 1030(3); Criminal Law ⚷ 1042

Rape and kidnapping were not allied offenses of similar import, and thus, did not merge, for purposes of sentencing; victim was grabbed by defendant and others at her place of employment and taken substantial distance before she was raped. State v. Bunch (Ohio App. 7 Dist., Mahoning, 06-24-2005) No. 02 CA 196, 2005-Ohio-3309, 2005 WL 1523844, Unreported, appeal allowed 107 Ohio St.3d 1680, 839 N.E.2d 401, 2005-Ohio-6480. Sentencing And Punishment ⚷ 531

Defendant waived right to claim on appeal that his three kidnapping convictions merged with two rape convictions and one attempted rape conviction as they were allied offenses of similar import, where defendant failed to raise claim in trial court. State v. Russell (Ohio App. 8 Dist., Cuyahoga, 09-23-2004) No. 83699, 2004-Ohio-5031, 2004 WL 2340125, Unreported, appeal not allowed 105 Ohio St.3d 1452, 823 N.E.2d 457, 2005-Ohio-763, motion to reopen denied 2005-Ohio-2998, 2005 WL 1406347, appeal not allowed 106 Ohio St.3d 1537, 835 N.E.2d 384, 2005-Ohio-5146. Criminal Law ⚷ 1030(3)

Crime of aggravated robbery and crime of kidnapping required proof of element not included in other crime, and thus offenses were not allied offenses and did not merge in prosecution for aggravated robbery, kidnapping, and having weapon while under disability; aggravated robbery required proof that defendant brandished deadly weapon in order to facilitate theft offense, and kidnapping required proof that defendant restrained victim's liberty. State v. Dowdell (Ohio App. 8 Dist., Cuyahoga, 10-14-2004) No. 83829, 2004-Ohio-5487, 2004 WL 2306678, Unreported, appeal not allowed 105 Ohio St.3d 1441, 822 N.E.2d 812, 2005-Ohio-531. Criminal Law ⚷ 30

Kidnapping and felonious assault, committed by use of a vehicle, were not offenses of similar import, for purposes of determining whether sentences therefor were required to be merged pursuant to allied offenses statute; commission of kidnapping did not necessarily result in commission of felonious assault, and commission of felonious assault did not necessarily result in commission of kidnapping. State v. Totarella (Ohio App. 11 Dist., Lake, 03-12-2004) No. 2002-L-147, 2004-Ohio-1175, 2004 WL 473382, Unreported, appeal not allowed 102 Ohio St.3d 1484, 810 N.E.2d 967, 2004-Ohio-3069. Sentencing And Punishment ⚷ 534

Felonious assault and kidnapping were not allied offenses of similar import and, thus, defendant could be convicted of both offenses. State v. Cruz (Ohio App. 9 Dist., Medina, 09-10-2003) No. 03CA0031-M, 2003-Ohio-4782, 2003 WL 22093209, Unreported. Criminal Law ⚷ 29(13)

Aggravated burglary and kidnapping were not allied offenses of similar import, and thus defendant was properly convicted and sentenced for both such offenses; burglary offense required commission of felony in connection with a trespass, and such elements were not required to commit kidnapping. State v. Johnson (Ohio App. 8 Dist., Cuyahoga, 06-19-2003) No. 81692, No. 81693, 2003-Ohio-3241, 2003 WL 21419631, Unreported, appeal not allowed 100 Ohio St.3d 1433, 797 N.E.2d 513, 2003-Ohio-5396. Criminal Law ⚷ 29(13)

Rape and kidnapping were not allied offenses of similar import, and therefore, defendant's convictions for rape and kidnapping properly were not merged for sentencing purposes; defendant transported his victim from her bedroom to his apartment for singular purpose of raping her, and although duct—taping victim's mouth and pinning her on his sofa as defendant violated her would seem incidental to rape itself, carrying victim from her bedroom to defendant's living room was accomplished with separate animus and had its own independent significance—to avoid possible detection during the commission of the rape, and defendant prevented victim's rescue by placing duct tape on her mouth and moving her a substantial distance. State v. Rodrigues (Ohio App. 8 Dist., Cuyahoga, 03-20-2003) No. 80610, 2003-Ohio-1334, 2003 WL 1353256, Unreported, on subsequent appeal 2004-Ohio-6010, 2004 WL 2578892, appeal not allowed 105 Ohio St.3d 1465, 824 N.E.2d 93, 2005-Ohio-1024. Sentencing And Punishment ⚷ 501

Defendant was not entitled to merger of offenses of aggravated robbery and kidnapping, despite his assertion that conviction for both offenses subjected him to unconstitutional multiple punishments, where restraint and movement of the victim in this case was not merely incidental to the robbery but had a significance independent of the robbery, defendant and co-defendant forcibly restrained victim in her car for over four hours, drove to several locations while she was duct-taped, bound, and buried under blankets in back seat, extended detention satisfied requirements of prolonged restraint and substantial movement, confinement was secretive because she was buried under yoga mat and blankets in back seat, defendant also sexually assaulted victim after her movement was restrained . State v. Stadmire (Ohio App. 8 Dist., Cuyahoga, 02-27-2003) No. 81188, 2003-Ohio-873, 2003 WL 549912, Unreported. Criminal Law ⚷ 30

Defendant did not act with a separate animus when he restrained victim's liberty during course of the aggravated robbery of a restaurant, rather, any restraint or movement by defendant was merely incidental to underlying crime of aggravated robbery, and thus, kidnapping conviction concerning victim was impermissibly cumulative, where victim testified he first noticed defendant when he turned around after he finished ringing up a customer at the cash register, defendant, who had a weapon, stood to the left of him and made no other demands of him except to "get the money," after defendant instructed victim to hurry, defendant reached into the register, grabbed the remainder of the money and fled. State v. Savage (Ohio App. 10 Dist., Franklin, 12-12-2002) No. 02AP-202, 2002-Ohio-6837, 2002 WL 31771245, Unreported. Criminal Law ⚷ 29(13)

The trial court errs in sentencing a defendant for both kidnapping and rape where the restraint involves (1) the victim resting in a parked van, (2) the defendant and another male entering the van, (3) the van not moving, (4) after ten minutes both defendant and the other male leaving the victim in the van, and (5) both the restraint and rape of the victim occurring simultaneously so that there is no separate animus to sustain separate convictions. State v. McKinney (Ohio App. 8 Dist., Cuyahoga, 09-29-1994) No. 66319, 1994 WL 530864, Unreported, motion to reopen denied 2001 WL 1167157.

When a case involving a defendant convicted of and sentenced for the allied offenses of similar import of rape and kidnapping is remanded for retrial because it is found that no asportation exists, it is reversible error for the remand court to allow the kidnapping charge to stand and to retry only the rape charge when the defendant could not be convicted of kidnapping without first being found guilty of rape or a lesser included offense under the facts presented at trial. State v. Edmunds (Ohio App. 10 Dist., Franklin, 07-19-1994) No. 94APA01-54, 1994 WL 383781, Unreported.

Double jeopardy principles did not preclude punishing capital defendant for both felony-murder and underlying kidnapping in case in which state relied upon victim's murder to satisfy the "serious physical harm" element of kidnapping; felony–murder was not an allied offense of similar import to the underlying felony. State v. Campbell (Ohio, 12-20-2000) 90 Ohio St.3d 320, 738 N.E.2d 1178, 2000-Ohio-183, reconsideration denied 91 Ohio St.3d 1433, 741 N.E.2d 896, certiorari denied 121 S.Ct. 2606, 533 U.S. 956, 150 L.Ed.2d 762, dismissal of post-conviction relief affirmed 2003-Ohio-6305, 2003 WL 22783857, appeal not allowed 102 Ohio St.3d 1470, 809 N.E.2d 1158, 2004-Ohio-2830. Double Jeopardy ⚷ 150(2)

Defendant's stalking, which ended with him dragging the victim across a campus to a secluded stairwell, contained a separate animus from rape offenses, and thus, a kidnapping charge was not an allied offense to the rape charges, and did not have to be merged; defendant's restraint of the victim was so substantial both in terms of length and substance that it demonstrated a separate animus. State v. White (Ohio App. 8 Dist., 11-01-1999) 135 Ohio App.3d 481, 734 N.E.2d 848. Criminal Law ⚷ 30

Failure to conduct voir dire to determine whether kidnapping and aggravated robbery for which defendant received consecutive sentences were allied offenses of similar import was plain error; victim's testimony that defendant held gun to her head as she was entering her car, ordered her to move over to passenger side, and continued to hold gun to her head while demanding her money and car keys appeared to indicate that the restraint was not more than was necessary to complete the robbery. State v. Latson (Ohio App. 8 Dist., 10-12-1999) 133 Ohio App.3d 475, 728 N.E.2d 465, dismissed, appeal not allowed 88 Ohio St.3d 1412, 723 N.E.2d 118. Criminal Law ⚷ 1035(6)

Charges of kidnapping and aggravated robbery which arose from same incident had dissimilar elements, so that charges were not allied offenses of similar import, and defendant could be convicted of both offenses, where defendant asported victim in her vehicle before robbing her; while every robbery necessarily involves a kidnapping, in that restraint of victim is required, defendant's asportation of victim was more than merely incidental to robbery, and thus rendered offenses dissimilar. State v. Gore (Ohio App. 7 Dist., 02-17-1999) 131 Ohio App.3d 197, 722 N.E.2d 125. Criminal Law ⚷ 29(13)

When a kidnapping is committed during another crime, there exists no separate animus where the restraint or movement of the victim is merely incidental to the underlying crime, and the kidnapping specification thus merges with the other crime, but where the restraint is prolonged, the confinement is secretive, or the movement is substantial, there exists a separate animus as to each offense and merger does not occur. State v. Fears (Ohio, 09-08-1999) 86 Ohio St.3d 329, 715 N.E.2d 136, 1999-Ohio-111, reconsideration denied 87 Ohio St.3d 1421, 717 N.E.2d 1107, stay granted 87 Ohio St.3d 1423, 718 N.E.2d 441, denial of post-conviction relief affirmed 1999 WL 1032592, dismissed, appeal not allowed 88 Ohio St.3d 1444, 725 N.E.2d 284, certiorari denied 120 S.Ct. 1535, 529 U.S. 1039, 146 L.Ed.2d 349. Criminal Law ⚷ 30

Resentencing was not required after appellate court determined in capital murder case that the offenses of kidnapping and aggravated robbery were committed with no separate animus and therefore should have merged as aggravating circumstances at death sentencing, where the jury's consideration of duplicative aggravating circumstances did not affect the outcome of the penalty phase and the remaining aggravating circumstances outweighed the mitigating circumstances. State v. Fears (Ohio, 09-08-1999) 86 Ohio St.3d 329, 715 N.E.2d 136, 1999-Ohio-111, reconsideration denied 87 Ohio St.3d 1421, 717 N.E.2d 1107, stay granted 87 Ohio

St.3d 1423, 718 N.E.2d 441, denial of post-conviction relief affirmed 1999 WL 1032592, dismissed, appeal not allowed 88 Ohio St.3d 1444, 725 N.E.2d 284, certiorari denied 120 S.Ct. 1535, 529 U.S. 1039, 146 L.Ed.2d 349. Criminal Law ⚿ 1181.5(8)

Aggravated burglary and kidnapping were not "allied offenses of similar import," for purposes of rule providing that defendant could be convicted of only one such offense; even if restraint were element of burglary, defendant imposed further restraint on victim, beyond that involved in burglary, by tying her up. State v. Reynolds (Ohio, 01-14-1998) 80 Ohio St.3d 670, 687 N.E.2d 1358, 1998-Ohio-171, certiorari denied 118 S.Ct. 2328, 524 U.S. 930, 141 L.Ed.2d 702, denial of post-conviction relief affirmed 1999 WL 980568, dismissed, appeal not allowed 88 Ohio St.3d 1425, 723 N.E.2d 1113. Criminal Law ⚿ 29(13)

Kidnapping constituted separate offense from murder, attempted rape, and robbery charges, and defendant's kidnapping charge thus would not be merged into any of those other felonies, where defendant was in process of robbing victim when he noticed she was attempting to use the phone and struck her, then tied her hands behind her back, and killed her only after he had restrained her for a period of time. State v. Reynolds (Ohio, 01-14-1998) 80 Ohio St.3d 670, 687 N.E.2d 1358, 1998-Ohio-171, certiorari denied 118 S.Ct. 2328, 524 U.S. 930, 141 L.Ed.2d 702, denial of post-conviction relief affirmed 1999 WL 980568, dismissed, appeal not allowed 88 Ohio St.3d 1425, 723 N.E.2d 1113. Criminal Law ⚿ 30

Kidnapping and felonious assault were not allied offenses of similar import, so as to require felonious assault conviction to be set aside and merged with kidnapping conviction; defendant's participation in restraint of victim in defendant's apartment continued after felonious assault had been completed, so that restraint of victim was not merely incidental to crime of felonious assault. State v. Box (Ohio App. 8 Dist., 07-26-1993) 89 Ohio App.3d 614, 626 N.E.2d 996, motion overruled 68 Ohio St.3d 1406, 623 N.E.2d 564. Criminal Law ⚿ 30

Kidnapping and rape are not allied offenses of similar import, and a defendant may be convicted of both when he physically restrains the victim, removes her clothes, carries her to the kitchen and an upstairs bedroom where he rapes her, since the restraint did subject the victim to an increased risk of harm separate from that inherent in the underlying rape, thereby evidencing a separate animus for each offense. State v. Morgan (Franklin 1992) 80 Ohio App.3d 150, 608 N.E.2d 1114, denial of post-conviction relief affirmed, dismissed, appeal not allowed 75 Ohio St.3d 1449, 663 N.E.2d 330.

The crimes of aggravated robbery and kidnapping are not allied offenses of similar import since an accused cannot be convicted of kidnapping under RC 2905.01(A)(2) without having used force, threat, or deception, but he can be convicted of aggravated robbery under RC 2911.01(A)(1) without having used or threatened to use any force, as long as he merely possesses a deadly weapon or dangerous ordnance during the commission of a theft; moreover, the conduct which creates the culpability for kidnapping under RC 2905.01(A)(2) must be for the purpose of facilitating the commission of a felony, but the conduct proscribed in RC 2911.01(A)(1) includes the theft offenses listed in RC 2913.01, many of which are misdemeanors. State v. Parker (Marion 1991) 72 Ohio App.3d 456, 594 N.E.2d 1033, dismissed, jurisdictional motion overruled 61 Ohio St.3d 1418, 574 N.E.2d 1090. Criminal Law ⚿ 29(13)

Kidnapping by forcing victim into car, driving across town, and forcing victim into apartment had separate animus from rape in apartment; thus, defendant could be convicted of rape and kidnapping. State v. Ridgeway (Cuyahoga 1990) 66 Ohio App.3d 270, 583 N.E.2d 1123, dismissed, jurisdictional motion overruled 53 Ohio St.3d 703, 558 N.E.2d 57, reconsideration denied, dismissed, appeal not allowed 83 Ohio St.3d 1430, 699 N.E.2d 946. Criminal Law ⚿ 29(13)

Restraint or movement of a rape victim that is significantly independent of the rape, such as throwing the victim down a stairwell, striking her, and keeping her in the stairwell for a significant length of time after the sexual assault, demonstrates a separate animus or purpose for kidnapping and justifies a conviction for that crime as well as rape. State v. Mitchell (Cuyahoga 1989) 60 Ohio App.3d 106, 574 N.E.2d 573, cause dismissed 49 Ohio St.3d 709, 551 N.E.2d 1306.

Where a defendant renders a prison guard unconscious and ties the guard's legs together with rope, then afterwards strikes the guard's head with a piece of body-building equipment during the course of an escape plan, separate convictions for kidnapping and felonious assault will be upheld since the later blow to the guard's head cannot be said to be part of the kidnapping offense; thus, under these facts, kidnapping and felonious assault are not allied offenses of similar import. State v. Blankenship (Ohio 1988) 38 Ohio St.3d 116, 526 N.E.2d 816, rehearing denied 38 Ohio St.3d 721, 533 N.E.2d 1064.

Kidnapping and rape are not allied offenses of similar import within the meaning of RC 2941.25 when the restraint is for two-and-one-half hours, the victim is transported a substantial distance by automobile, and the confinement is secretive, because the farther the victim is transported and the longer the victim is restrained, the less likely it becomes that the victim will be returned safely and transporting the victim by automobile subjects the victim to a risk of injury from the operation of the motor vehicle, separate and distinct from the injuries exposed to from the rape. State v. Henry (Wood 1987) 37 Ohio App.3d 3, 523 N.E.2d 877.

Robbery and kidnapping are allied offenses of similar import where the charge of kidnapping is based on defendant's acts of placing a blanket over the victim's head and tying the victim's hands behind her back while committing a robbery, as the restraint used is merely incidental to the underlying offense of robbery. State v. Parker (Montgomery

1986) 31 Ohio App.3d 128, 508 N.E.2d 978, 31 O.B.R. 215.

A defendant may be sentenced for both aggravated robbery and kidnapping when he transported his victim ten miles and committed the two crimes separately or with a separate animus. State v. Muenick (Summit 1985) 26 Ohio App.3d 3, 498 N.E.2d 171, 26 O.B.R. 171.

Where a woman is induced by deception to leave a bar and is then forcibly removed to a secluded place and raped, the asportation by deception is a kidnapping sufficiently independent of the asportation incidental to the rape to support a separate conviction and sentence. State v. DePina (Medina 1984) 21 Ohio App.3d 91, 486 N.E.2d 1155, 21 O.B.R. 97.

Where a defendant and three other miscreants forcibly carry a girl from a sidewalk to behind a garage and rob and rape her until police arrive, the duration of the restraint and the short distance travelled do not sufficiently increase the risk of harm to show the separate animus necessary to impose a sentence for kidnapping, and a trial court errs in not merging the kidnapping conviction with the rape conviction. State v. Malone (Summit 1984) 15 Ohio App.3d 123, 472 N.E.2d 1122, 15 O.B.R. 214.

For purposes of applying RC 2941.25 and determining whether a kidnapping offense is merged with a subsequent rape offense, the question is whether the movement of the victim is substantial or the restraint of the victim's liberty is for a significant length of time, which serves to demonstrate a significant independence from the rape offense. State v. Moore (Franklin 1983) 13 Ohio App.3d 226, 468 N.E.2d 920, 13 O.B.R. 278. Criminal Law ⚷ 30

Convictions for rape and gross sexual imposition did not merge with kidnapping conviction, where defendant bound and gagged victim upon completion of sexual acts upon her, indicating that restraint was performed to facilitate his escape, not to facilitate sexual attack, and thus separate animus necessary to sustain convictions for kidnapping, rape, and gross sexual imposition was present. State v. Brown (Ohio 1984) 12 Ohio St.3d 147, 465 N.E.2d 889, 12 O.B.R. 186. Criminal Law ⚷ 30

Gross sexual imposition as defined by RC 2907.05(A)(3) and kidnapping as defined by RC 2905.01 are not allied offenses of similar import under RC 2941.25. State v. Moralevitz (Cuyahoga 1980) 70 Ohio App.2d 20, 433 N.E.2d 1280, 24 O.O.3d 16.

Where there was an act of asportation by deception which constituted kidnapping and which was significantly independent from the asportation incidental to the rape itself, conviction for kidnapping was not barred by RC 2941.25. State v. Ware (Ohio 1980) 63 Ohio St.2d 84, 406 N.E.2d 1112, 17 O.O.3d 51.

A rape conviction, pursuant to RC 2907.02(A)(1), and a kidnapping conviction, pursuant to RC 2905.01(A)(4), are allied offenses of similar import within the meaning of RC 2941.25(A), and cannot be punished multiply when they are neither committed separately nor with a separate animus as to each within the meaning of RC 2941.25(B). State v. Price (Ohio 1979) 60 Ohio St.2d 136, 398 N.E.2d 772, 14 O.O.3d 379, certiorari denied 100 S.Ct. 2169, 446 U.S. 943, 64 L.Ed.2d 798.

In establishing whether kidnapping and another offense of the same or similar kind are committed with a separate animus as to each pursuant to RC 2941.25(B), the Ohio Supreme Court adopts the following guidelines: (a) where the restraint or movement of the victim is merely incidental to a separate underlying crime, there exists no separate animus sufficient to sustain separate convictions; however, where the restraint is prolonged, the confinement is secretive, or the movement is substantial so as to demonstrate a significance independent of the other offense, there exists a separate animus as to each offense sufficient to support separate convictions; (b) where the asportation or restraint of the victim subjects the victim to a substantial increase in risk of harm separate and apart from that involved in the underlying crime, there exists a separate animus as to each offense sufficient to support separate convictions. State v. Logan (Ohio 1979) 60 Ohio St.2d 126, 397 N.E.2d 1345, 14 O.O.3d 373.

Kidnapping, as defined in RC 2905.01(A)(4), is an "offense of similar import" to rape, as defined by RC 2907.02(A)(1), for purposes of application of RC 2941.25(A). State v. Donald (Ohio 1979) 57 Ohio St.2d 73, 386 N.E.2d 1341, 11 O.O.3d 242.

Sufficient circumstantial evidence supported Ohio Supreme Court's finding that the State established that the restraint associated with the kidnapping specification and charge was distinguishable from the restraint associated with aggravated murder of victim; petitioner's tying of victim's leg to bed significantly increased her risk of harm of assault and rape but only marginally increased her risk of murder by strangulation and a slit throat. Hartman v. Bagley (N.D.Ohio, 08-31-2004) 333 F.Supp.2d 632. Sentencing And Punishment ⚷ 1660

Defendant was subject to separate sentences for both robbery and kidnapping; kidnapping required proof that defendant restrained victim for purpose of facilitating commission of a felony, but robbery required proof that force was applied merely to effect a theft offense, which is often a misdemeanor. State v. Dejanette (Ohio App. 1 Dist., Hamilton, 09-13-2002) No. C-010693, 2002-Ohio-4802, 2002 WL 31039669, Unreported, appeal not allowed 98 Ohio St.3d 1424, 782 N.E.2d 78, 2003-Ohio-259. Sentencing And Punishment ⚷ 537

Crimes of kidnapping and aggravated robbery to which defendant pled guilty were not allied offenses with a single animus, and were not required to be merged for sentencing purposes, where defendant restrained victim for prolonged period of time beyond commission of aggravated robbery; victim was attacked as she entered her apartment, at which point she ran to her bedroom and locked the door, defendant and co-defendant kicked in victim's door and hog-tied her with telephone cord, defendant began smashing victim's head with a padlock and demanding that she give him her credit cards and PIN numbers, and officers responded to emergency call heard assault upon approaching the home. State v. Moore (Ohio App. 8 Dist., Cuyahoga, 05-02-2002) No. 79353, 2002-Ohio-2133, 2002 WL 832488, Unreported, appeal after new sentencing hearing 2003-Ohio-3349, 2003 WL 21469163, appeal after new sentencing hearing 2004-Ohio-5383, 2004 WL 2252044, appeal allowed 105 Ohio St.3d 1451, 823 N.E.2d 456, 2005-Ohio-763, affirmed 109 Ohio St.3d 313, 847 N.E.2d 1174, 2006-Ohio-2109. Sentencing And Punishment ⚿ 537

Attempted felonious assault and kidnapping are allied offenses of similar import and should be merged under RC 2941.25 where a defendant attacks the victim and simultaneously restrains her by placing his hands around her throat and choking her. State v Williamson, No. CA93–04–034, 1994 WL 5322 (12th Dist Ct App, Clermont, 1–10–94).

If the court finds that under RC 2941.25 the commission of one offense will necessarily result in commission of the other offense, the offenses are allied offenses of similar import; the elements of abduction and felonious assault do not correspond to such a degree since abduction under RC 2905.02 has the element of restraint, while felonious assault under RC 2903.11 requires physical harm with a deadly weapon. State v Messineo, Nos. 1488 and 1493 (4th Dist Ct App, Athens, 1–7–93).

Kidnapping and escape from detention are not offenses of similar import; therefore, a conviction for both offenses is permitted. State v Burton, Nos. 1036 and 1037 (4th Dist Ct App, Ross, 7–26–84).

Where the evidence of restraint is only incidental to the crime of rape and the defendant is convicted on both kidnapping and rape, the kidnapping conviction must be vacated and judgment entered only on the allied offense of rape. State v Pykare, Nos. 44652, 44756 and 44758 (8th Dist Ct App, Cuyahoga, 6–9–83).

Trial court erred in convicting the defendant of the allied offenses of rape and kidnapping even though only one sentence was imposed. State v Fisher, No. 1–81–51 (3d Dist Ct App, Allen, 9–3–82).

Rape and kidnapping can be allied offenses only if a single animus exists; however, where a victim is transported miles from her original location, robbed, and then raped, a separate animus exists, as the asportation was not incidental to the rape but substantial and independent. State v Winters, No. 42799 (8th Dist Ct App, Cuyahoga, 7–22–82).

Kidnapping and rape are not allied offenses of similar import if they are committed separately or with separate animus. State v Bass, No. 81AP–999 (10th Dist Ct App, Franklin, 7–20–82).

15. —— Gambling and alcohol, specific offenses construed

Violations of statutes prohibiting operation of a motor vehicle while under the influence of alcohol, and operating a motor vehicle with a prohibited concentration of alcohol in one's breath are allied offenses of similar import, and thus, while a defendant may be charged and found guilty of both offenses, he can be convicted and sentenced for only one of them. State v. Lewis (Ohio App. 3 Dist., 03-04-1999) 131 Ohio App.3d 229, 722 N.E.2d 147, stay granted 85 Ohio St.3d 1451, 708 N.E.2d 724, dismissed, appeal not allowed 86 Ohio St.3d 1414, 711 N.E.2d 1010. Criminal Law ⚿ 29(7)

Where over one hour and a distance of two to three miles separate the acts of being in physical control of a motor vehicle while under the influence of alcohol and driving with a prohibited urine-alcohol content, the offenses are not allied offenses of similar import as the offenses were committed separately or with a separate animus. State v. Gabor (Wayne 1986) 33 Ohio App.3d 122, 514 N.E.2d 730.

Where a defendant driving while under the influence of alcohol causes the death of another motorist and defendant is charged with both involuntary manslaughter and aggravated vehicular homicide, and where the facts of the case would support a charge of reckless operation, which requires a reckless mental state, involuntary manslaughter and aggravated vehicular homicide constitute allied offenses of similar import. State v. Torres (Lorain 1986) 31 Ohio App.3d 118, 508 N.E.2d 970, 31 O.B.R. 204.

RC 4511.19(A)(1) and 4511.19(A)(3) create separate offenses, and, in accordance with RC 2941.25(A), a defendant may be charged with both, convicted of both, but may be sentenced as to only one. State v. Mendieta (Wood 1984) 20 Ohio App.3d 18, 484 N.E.2d 180, 20 O.B.R. 19. Criminal Law ⚿ 29(5.5); Sentencing And Punishment ⚿ 534

Driving under the influence of alcohol, RC 4511.19, and driving without reasonable control of a vehicle, RC 4511.202, are not allied offenses of similar import. State v. Butcher (Wood 1983) 12 Ohio App.3d 87, 466 N.E.2d 189, 12 O.B.R. 286. Criminal Law ⚿ 29(7)

RC 4511.19(A)(1) and RC 4511.19(A)(3) are allied offenses of similar import and conviction and sentencing for both operating a motor vehicle while under the influence of alcohol or drugs and operating a motor vehicle with a prohibited alcohol concentration is error. State v Schwartz, No. 01–CA–9, 2002 WL 193944 (5th Dist Ct App, Perry, 2–7–02).

The offenses of gambling under RC 2915.02(A)(2) and operating a gambling house under RC 2915.03 are allied offenses of similar import. State v FOE 2597 Delta Aerie, Inc, No. 92FU000002 (6th Dist Ct App, Fulton, 3–5–93).

RC 4511.19(A)(1) and 4511.19(A)(3) constitute allied offenses of similar import and multiple sentences upon conviction will be vacated. Cincinnati v Moore, No. C–880689+ (1st Dist Ct App, Hamilton, 11–15–89).

A defendant can be convicted under both a municipal drunk driving ordinance for conduct in one municipality and RC 4511.19 for the same conduct in an adjoining municipality without violating the double jeopardy provisions of RC 2941.25, as violation of the statute and ordinance represent two separate offenses. State v Babb, Nos. C–860005, C–860006, and C–860028 (1st Dist Ct App, Hamilton, 1–30–87).

16. —— Sex offenses, specific offenses construed

Rape and gross sexual imposition counts against defendant merged for purposes of sentencing; victim's testimony indicated that defendant was touching her at the same time he was orally assaulting her, and it appeared as though any touching was to assist in committing the rape. State v. Younger (Ohio App. 8 Dist., Cuyahoga, 01-26-2006) No. 86235, 2006-Ohio-296, 2006 WL 181914, Unreported, appeal allowed, reversed in part 110 Ohio St.3d 70, 850 N.E.2d 1168, 2006-Ohio-3663. Sentencing And Punishment ⚷ 501

Offense of possession of criminal tools and offenses of importuning were committed separately with a separate animus, and thus, offenses could not be merged as allied offenses; charges arose from internet conversations initiated by defendant with undercover FBI agent, whom defendant believed was a 13–year–old girl, and possession of computer as criminal tool was separate action, requiring separate animus from using computer to commit crime of importuning. State v. Feig (Ohio App. 8 Dist., Cuyahoga, 10-06-2005) No. 85734, 2005-Ohio-5341, 2005 WL 2467316, Unreported. Criminal Law ⚷ 29(12)

Each count of importuning constituted separate crime, exhibiting separate animus, and thus, five counts could not be merged as allied offenses into one count; although defendant asserted that internet conversations, initiated with undercover FBI agent, whom defendant believed was a 13–year–old girl, involved same victim and that conversations were actually one prolonged solicitation, rather than five distinct incidents of importuning, defendant contacted "child"/agent on separate occasions and used different approach each time he contacted her. State v. Feig (Ohio App. 8 Dist., Cuyahoga, 10-06-2005) No. 85734, 2005-Ohio-5341, 2005 WL 2467316, Unreported. Criminal Law ⚷ 29(12)

Complicity to rape and rape were not allied offenses of similar import, and thus, did not merge, for purposes of sentencing; complicity was committed separately or with separate animus, in that each act defendant committed to aid co-defendant in another act of rape, whether by holding her head while co-defendant orally raped her, pointing gun at her head while co-defendant raped her, or raping her vaginally while co-defendant orally raped her, furthered each successive act of rape against victim and further denigrated her integrity. State v. Bunch (Ohio App. 7 Dist., Mahoning, 06-24-2005) No. 02 CA 196, 2005-Ohio-3309, 2005 WL 1523844, Unreported, appeal allowed 107 Ohio St.3d 1680, 839 N.E.2d 401, 2005-Ohio-6480. Sentencing And Punishment ⚷ 522

Three counts of complicity to rape were not allied offenses of similar import, and thus, did not merge, for purposes of sentencing; defendant held victim's head and pointed gun at her while co-defendant orally raped her, he pointed gun at her while co-defendant vaginally raped her, and defendant vaginally raped victim to aid co-defendant in orally raping victim. State v. Bunch (Ohio App. 7 Dist., Mahoning, 06-24-2005) No. 02 CA 196, 2005-Ohio-3309, 2005 WL 1523844, Unreported, appeal allowed 107 Ohio St.3d 1680, 839 N.E.2d 401, 2005-Ohio-6480. Sentencing And Punishment ⚷ 522

Three counts of rape were not allied offenses of similar import, and therefore, did not merge, for purposes of sentencing, in view of victim's testimony that defendant raped her vaginally and orally, and witness' testimony that he saw defendant rape victim anally. State v. Bunch (Ohio App. 7 Dist., Mahoning, 06-24-2005) No. 02 CA 196, 2005-Ohio-3309, 2005 WL 1523844, Unreported, appeal allowed 107 Ohio St.3d 1680, 839 N.E.2d 401, 2005-Ohio-6480. Sentencing And Punishment ⚷ 522

Multiple counts of pandering sexually oriented matter involving a minor had separate animi, and thus defendant could be convicted on each count under multiple-count statute; children depicted in photographs with respect to each count appeared to be different individuals, and even assuming that some photographs were of identical children, photographs depicted children in separate positions and against different backgrounds. State v. Smith (Ohio App. 10 Dist., Franklin, 05-24-2005) No. 04AP-859, 2005-Ohio-2560, 2005 WL 1220742, Unreported, appeal not allowed 106 Ohio St.3d 1556, 836 N.E.2d 581, 2005-Ohio-5531. Criminal Law ⚷ 29(12)

Rape and kidnapping were committed with separate animus as to each offense, and thus convictions for those offenses were not required to be merged for sentencing purposes; restraint, confinement, and movement with respect to kidnapping were prolonged, secretive, and substantial, respectively, so as to demonstrate significance independent of rape. State v. Payton (Ohio App. 5 Dist., Stark, 02-22-2005) No. 2004-CA-00019, 2005-Ohio-737, 2005 WL 428034, Unreported, motion for delayed appeal denied 106 Ohio St.3d 1530, 835 N.E.2d 381, 2005-Ohio-5146. Sentencing And Punishment ⚷ 531

Eleven counts of pandering obscenity involving a minor were not allied offenses of similar import, for purposes of determining propriety of convictions on all 11 counts, where each count constituted separate act, and commission of one offense did not result in commission of any others; defendant had in his possession 11 different obscene photographs involving minor females, and possession of one such photograph did not establish his possession of other such photographs. State v. Cummings (Ohio App. 9 Dist., Medina, 12-08-2004) No. 04CA0009-M, 2004-Ohio-6535, 2004 WL 2806343, Unreported. Criminal Law ⚷ 29(12)

Defendant's convictions for rape and kidnapping did not merge, for sentencing purposes; defendant's acts of forcing the victim into the living room, then forcing her into the diningroom where he made her read his suicide note, followed by defendant forcing the victim back into the living room were not incidental to the rape that occurred later in the living room. State v. Marshall (Ohio App. 9 Dist., Summit, 09-29-2004) No. 21974, 2004-Ohio-5176, 2004 WL 2244104, Unreported, motion for delayed appeal denied 106 Ohio St.3d 1459, 830 N.E.2d 1167, 2005-Ohio-3490. Sentencing And Punishment ⚷ 531

Multiple offenses of possessing sexually oriented matter involving minor were not of similar import, and thus, neither statute nor double jeopardy clause precluded imposition of consecutive sentences, where defendant victimized several different minors by possessing graphic images of them involved in sexual abuse. State v. McCartney (Ohio App. 12 Dist., Clinton, 09-07-2004) No. CA2003-09-023, 2004-Ohio-4781, 2004 WL 2003606, Unreported, appeal not allowed 105 Ohio St.3d 1406, 821 N.E.2d 1027, 2005-Ohio-279. Double Jeopardy ⚷ 29.1; Sentencing And Punishment ⚷ 574

Gross sexual imposition and rape were not allied offenses of similar import, and thus defendant could be convicted of both charges; according to victim's testimony, the sexual contact necessary for the gross sexual imposition conviction was completed before the sexual conduct necessary for the rape convictions started, and sexual contact element of the gross sexual imposition offenses was not incidental to the sexual conduct element of the rapes because the rapes could have been committed without the preceding sexual contact. State v. Reid (Ohio App. 8 Dist., Cuyahoga, 04-22-2004) No. 83206, 2004-Ohio-2018, 2004 WL 859172, Unreported, appeal not allowed 103 Ohio St.3d 1428, 814 N.E.2d 491, 2004-Ohio-4524, reconsideration denied 103 Ohio St.3d 1496, 816 N.E.2d 1081, 2004-Ohio-5605, appeal after new sentencing hearing 2006-Ohio-3978, 2006 WL 2192039. Criminal Law ⚷ 29(12)

Evidence was sufficient to support finding that defendant raped victim while she was under 13 years of age, as required to support convictions for two counts of rape; victim testified that defendant raped her both before and after her thirteenth birthday. State v. Reid (Ohio App. 8 Dist., Cuyahoga, 04-22-2004) No. 83206, 2004-Ohio-2018, 2004 WL 859172, Unreported, appeal not allowed 103 Ohio St.3d 1428, 814 N.E.2d 491, 2004-Ohio-4524, reconsideration denied 103 Ohio St.3d 1496, 816 N.E.2d 1081, 2004-Ohio-5605, appeal after new sentencing hearing 2006-Ohio-3978, 2006 WL 2192039. Rape ⚷ 52(4)

Defendant's two sexual assault convictions, arising from defendant's conduct against his daughter on different occasions, were not for the same conduct, and thus two sexual battery counts would not merge. State v. Wilson (Ohio App. 5 Dist., Coshocton, 03-30-2004) No. 02CA030, 2004-Ohio-1692, 2004 WL 690176, Unreported, appeal not allowed 103 Ohio St.3d 1407, 812 N.E.2d 1289, 2004-Ohio-3980. Criminal Law ⚷ 30

Vaginal rape, anal rape, rape by fellatio, and rape by means of forcing victim to digitally penetrate her anus were not "allied offenses of similar import" within meaning of statute prohibiting conviction for more than one allied offense of similar import; each offense was distinct and separate sexual act. State v. Ludwick (Ohio App. 11 Dist., Ashtabula, 03-12-2004) No. 2002-A-0024, 2004-Ohio-1152, 2004 WL 454691, Unreported, appeal not allowed 102 Ohio St.3d 1484, 810 N.E.2d 968, 2004-Ohio-3069. Criminal Law ⚷ 29(12)

Defendant's conduct in putting his face and mouth on child victim's vagina, putting victim's hand on his penis and making her move it back and forth, and putting his hand on victim's vagina were three distinct, different sexual activities, each constituting a separate crime with a separate animus, and were not allied offenses of similar import, and thus defendant could be convicted and sentenced for all three offenses, even though offenses were committed in the course of the same encounter. State v. Grant (Ohio App. 2 Dist., Montgomery, 12-31-2003) No. 19824, 2003-Ohio-7240, 2003 WL 23167348, Unreported, appeal not allowed 102 Ohio St.3d 1459, 809 N.E.2d 33, 2004-Ohio-2569. Criminal Law ⚷ 29(12)

Each instance of rape defendant committed against victim was done with a separate animus and, as a result, permitted imposition of consecutive sentences; each of defendant's actions that victim testified to at trial formed a separate basis for the crime of rape when defendant used his hands, mouth, and penis in a systematic order to penetrate her vagina to see if she was sleeping with someone else, and when each of defendant's "tests" yielded no results, he raped her a different way. State v. Madsen (Ohio App. 8 Dist., Cuyahoga, 10-30-2003) No. 82399, 2003-Ohio-5822, 2003 WL 22457002, Unreported, appeal not allowed 101 Ohio St.3d 1489, 805 N.E.2d 540, 2004-Ohio-1293, motion to reopen denied 2004-Ohio-4895, 2004 WL 2065653, appeal not allowed 104 Ohio St.3d 1427, 819 N.E.2d 710, 2004-Ohio-6585, dismissal of post-conviction relief affirmed 2005-Ohio-3850, 2005 WL 1792337, appeal not allowed 107 Ohio St.3d 1425, 837 N.E.2d 1209, 2005-Ohio-6124. Sentencing And Punishment ⚷ 561; Sentencing And Punishment ⚷ 605

Assuming crimes of rape, unlawful sexual conduct with a minor and gross sexual imposition, when compared in the abstract, were allied of similar import under the *Rance* test, separate animus existed for each crime, which warranted sentencing defendant on each count; charges were based on events that occurred over period of time and involved different types of conduct. State v. Waters (Ohio App. 5 Dist., Ashland, 08-28-2003) No. 03-COA-002, 2003-Ohio-4624, 2003 WL 22039441, Unreported, appeal not allowed 100 Ohio St.3d 1545, 800 N.E.2d 751, 2003-Ohio-6879. Sentencing And Punishment ⚷ 522

Defendant committed three distinct sexual acts of dissimilar import when he inserted both his finger and the tip of his penis into victim's vagina and performed oral sex on her on several occasions, and thus, defendant's sentences for aggravated burglary, kidnapping, rape, and gross sexual imposition did not constitute multiple punishments for the same criminal conduct. State v. Reed (Ohio App. 10 Dist., Franklin, 05-13-2003) No. 02AP-694, 2003-Ohio-2412, 2003 WL 21060825, Unreported. Sentencing And Punishment ⚷ 531

Convictions for three counts of gross sexual imposition involving person less than 13 years of age did not constitute allied offenses of similar import, so as to require merger of offenses for purposes of sentencing, where offenses occurred on separate dates and therefore were committed separately and with separate animus. State v. Wayne (Ohio App. 7 Dist., Mahoning, 02-25-2003) No. 01-CA-94, 2003-Ohio-927, 2003 WL 684584, Unreported. Criminal Law ⚷ 29(12)

Six counts in indictment against defendant involving use of child pornography were not allied offenses; separate animus existed for each offense because offenses occurred at different times, images involved different children engaged in different acts, and defendant committed the same offense against different victims. State v. Yodice (Ohio App. 11 Dist., Lake, 12-31-2002) No. 2001-L-155, 2002-Ohio-7344, 2002 WL 31895121, Unreported. Criminal Law ⚷ 29(12)

Defendant did not suffer prejudice when he was given concurrent sentences for allegedly allied offenses of rape and kidnapping. State v. Worwell (Ohio App. 8 Dist., Cuyahoga, 12-05-2002) No. 80871, 2002-Ohio-6637, 2002 WL 31722382, Unreported, motion for delayed appeal denied 98 Ohio St.3d 1488, 785 N.E.2d 471, 2003-Ohio-1189, motion to reopen denied 2003-Ohio-4560, 2003 WL 22019526, appeal not allowed 100 Ohio St.3d 1532, 800 N.E.2d 48, 2003-Ohio-6458. Criminal Law ⚷ 1177

Multiple counts of rape are allied offenses of similar import when they involve penetration of the same orifice within a relatively short period of time and do not expose the victim to a different or significantly greater risk of harm. State v. Jones (Ohio App. 2 Dist., Montgomery, 08-04-1995) No. 14649, 1995 WL 461284, Unreported, appeal allowed 74 Ohio St.3d 1484, 657 N.E.2d 1377, affirmed in part, reversed in part 78 Ohio St.3d 12, 676 N.E.2d 80, 1997-Ohio-38.

Rape and kidnapping are allied offenses of similar import where the kidnapping is merely incidental to the commission of the rape and where there is not a substantial risk of harm other than that created by the rape. State v. Brooks (Ohio App. 10 Dist., Franklin, 03-31-1994) No. 93APA09-1281, 1994 WL 109711, Unreported, dismissed, appeal not allowed 70 Ohio St.3d 1426, 638 N.E.2d 88.

Where a defendant is charged with rape based on the sexual abuse of a minor, and child endangering based on a separate incident of physical abuse, the acts are committed with a separate animus and there is no course of criminal conduct between the two acts, and where the victim repeatedly testifies the acts of sexual abuse all took place in North Carolina and the one incident of physical abuse took place in Ohio, a trial court has no jurisdiction over the acts which occurred in North Carolina and the rape conviction must be vacated. State v Kress, No. CA-9220, 1993 WL 471463 (5th Dist Ct App, Stark, 11-8-93).

Rape by fellatio and vaginal rape are separate offenses, even when one is followed immediately by the other. State v. Adams (Ohio, 11-17-2004) 103 Ohio St.3d 508, 817 N.E.2d 29, 2004-Ohio-5845, reconsideration denied 104 Ohio St.3d 1442, 819 N.E.2d 1124, 2004-Ohio-7033, certiorari denied 125 S.Ct. 2271, 544 U.S. 1040, 161 L.Ed.2d 1072. Criminal Law ⚷ 29(12)

Defendant's two convictions for rape were not allied offenses of similar import, for the purpose of imposing multiple convictions and sentences for defendant's actions; each count of rape in the indictment referred to a separate incident or occurrence, defendant provided a written statement that indicated that he vaginally raped his daughter on two separate occasions, and defendant admitted to physician that he raped his daughter on two separate occasions. State v. Gopp (Ohio App. 9 Dist., 09-17-2003) 154 Ohio App.3d 385, 797 N.E.2d 531, 2003-Ohio-4908. Double Jeopardy ⚷ 148

Touching of victim's breast with one hand and kissing her breast with mouth were not "allied offenses of similar import" within meaning of statute prohibiting conviction for more than one allied offense of similar import, so as to require only one conviction, where both acts occurred separately but in close proximity of time during same extended assault of victim; each offense was of sufficiently separate character both in terms of animus of defendant and in terms of sense of violation experienced by victim. State v. Austin (Ohio App. 3 Dist., 08-02-2000) 138 Ohio App.3d 547, 741 N.E.2d 927, 2000-Ohio-1728, appeal not allowed 90 Ohio St.3d 1472, 738 N.E.2d 383. Criminal Law ⚷ 29(12)

Kidnapping and rape can be allied offenses of similar import and an offender may be punished for both offenses only if they are committed separately or with a separate animus as to each. State v. White (Ohio App. 8 Dist., 11-01-1999) 135 Ohio App.3d 481, 734 N.E.2d 848. Sentencing And Punishment ⚷ 531

Defendant's animus to rape victim was separate from his animus to commit burglary, robbery, kidnapping, and murder, and his attempted rape charge thus would not be merged into any of those other felonies. State v. Reynolds (Ohio, 01-14-1998) 80 Ohio St.3d 670, 687 N.E.2d 1358, 1998-Ohio-171, certiorari denied 118 S.Ct. 2328, 524 U.S. 930, 141 L.Ed.2d 702, denial of post-conviction relief affirmed 1999 WL 980568, dismissed, appeal not allowed 88 Ohio St.3d 1425, 723 N.E.2d 1113. Criminal Law ⚷ 30

Gross sexual imposition and rape are allied offenses of similar import within meaning of statute, so that single act by defendant may support conviction for only one of offenses. State v. Jones (Ohio

App. 2 Dist., 09-27-1996) 114 Ohio App.3d 306, 683 N.E.2d 87. Criminal Law ⚷ 29(12)

Vaginal penetration, loss of erection, withdrawal from vagina, and removal of tampon were "significant intervening acts" between two acts of oral rape, precluding merger of two oral rape convictions, even though all conduct occurred during short time period; first act of oral rape was separate from second act. State v. Jones (Ohio, 03-19-1997) 78 Ohio St.3d 12, 676 N.E.2d 80, 1997-Ohio-38. Criminal Law ⚷ 30

Loss of erection, withdrawal from vagina, removal of tampon, and oral rape were "significant intervening acts" supporting determination that act of vaginal rape was separate from subsequent act of attempted vaginal rape, precluding merger of convictions, even though all conduct was committed within short period of time. State v. Jones (Ohio, 03-19-1997) 78 Ohio St.3d 12, 676 N.E.2d 80, 1997-Ohio-38. Criminal Law ⚷ 30

Disseminating matter harmful to juveniles is not allied offense of similar import to either sexual battery or gross sexual imposition, and thus no hearing was necessary to determine whether they were committed separately prior to sentencing defendant for all offenses. State v. Mangrum (Clermont 1993) 86 Ohio App.3d 156, 620 N.E.2d 196, dismissed, jurisdictional motion overruled 66 Ohio St.3d 1499, 613 N.E.2d 645. Sentencing And Punishment ⚷ 530

Defendant's convictions on two counts of sexual battery were allied offenses of similar import because in each count elements of sexual battery were same, thereby imposing duty to hold hearing to determine whether each count of sexual battery was committed separately or with separate animus prior to sentencing defendant for both offenses. State v. Mangrum (Clermont 1993) 86 Ohio App.3d 156, 620 N.E.2d 196, dismissed, jurisdictional motion overruled 66 Ohio St.3d 1499, 613 N.E.2d 645. Sentencing And Punishment ⚷ 522

Crimes of sexual battery and gross sexual imposition are not allied offenses of similar import, so as to require hearing to determine whether crimes were committed separately or whether there was separate animus for each crime prior to sentencing defendant for convictions of both crimes. State v. Mangrum (Clermont 1993) 86 Ohio App.3d 156, 620 N.E.2d 196, dismissed, jurisdictional motion overruled 66 Ohio St.3d 1499, 613 N.E.2d 645. Sentencing And Punishment ⚷ 522

Vaginal intercourse, cunnilingus and digital penetration occurring during a single attack are separate crimes with separate anima, and thus do not constitute allied offenses of similar import. State v. Nicholas (Ohio 1993) 66 Ohio St.3d 431, 613 N.E.2d 225.

Attempted rape, under RC 2907.02(A)(2), and gross sexual imposition, under RC 2907.05(A)(1), are allied offenses of similar import where (1) the elements of the gross sexual imposition charge are included in those of the attempted rape charge, (2) the state relies on evidence of the same conduct to prove both offenses, and (3) both offenses were motivated by the same purpose, the latter two requirements being shown by the fact that the state's evidence relates to a single incident during which the defendant committed acts of gross sexual imposition while attempting to force the victim to have intercourse with him. State v. Brooks (Wood 1989) 65 Ohio App.3d 300, 583 N.E.2d 1035.

Verdicts finding defendant guilty of two counts of vaginal rape were not rendered unreliable by victim's testimony regarding three incidents of vaginal intercourse, in that two acts of vaginal intercourse that occurred in defendant's apartment constituted allied offenses of similar import, subject to only one conviction, and any confusion as to distinction between vaginal rape charges was dissipated by trial court's instruction that one count was alleged to have occurred in defendant's car and other count was alleged to have occurred in defendant's apartment. State v. Carmack (Hamilton 1989) 61 Ohio App.3d 351, 572 N.E.2d 794, dismissed 44 Ohio St.3d 703, 541 N.E.2d 622. Criminal Law ⚷ 878(1)

Because pandering sexually oriented matter involving minor and illegal use of minor in nudity-oriented material are not offenses of similar import, defendant was properly convicted of both offenses, even if those two offenses arose from same photographs that were taken at same location during same time period, and involved same parties. State v. Lorenz (Clermont 1988) 59 Ohio App.3d 17, 570 N.E.2d 285, dismissed 43 Ohio St.3d 710, 540 N.E.2d 725, denial of post-conviction relief affirmed, cause dismissed 66 Ohio St.3d 1409, 607 N.E.2d 9. Criminal Law ⚷ 29(12)

Defendant's entry into two separate bodily orifices of same victim constituted two separate acts of rape, permitting separate convictions, even though the sexual conduct occurred at one place and with no significant lapse of time between acts of rape. State v. Wilson (Cuyahoga 1982) 8 Ohio App.3d 216, 456 N.E.2d 1287, 8 O.B.R. 288. Criminal Law ⚷ 29(12)

A gross sexual imposition conviction, pursuant to RC 2907.05(A)(1), and an attempted rape conviction, pursuant to RC 2923.02(A), are allied offenses of similar import within the meaning of RC 2941.25(A), and cannot be punished multiply when they are neither committed separately nor with a separate animus as to each. State v. Earich (Columbiana 1982) 4 Ohio App.3d 183, 447 N.E.2d 121, 4 O.B.R. 285. Sentencing And Punishment ⚷ 522

Under RC 2941.25(B), entry into two bodily orifices constitutes two separate rape offenses of the same or similar kind for both of which a defendant may be convicted. State v. Barnes (Ohio 1981) 68 Ohio St.2d 13, 427 N.E.2d 517, 22 O.O.3d 126.

Rape and kidnapping arising out of the same incident constitute two offenses of dissimilar import, within the meaning of RC 2941.25(B). State v. Ware (Summit 1977) 53 Ohio App.2d 210, 372 N.E.2d 1367, 7 O.O.3d 280, affirmed 63 Ohio St.2d 84, 406 N.E.2d 1112, 17 O.O.3d 51.

Under RC 2941.25(B), entry into two bodily orifices are separate rape offenses of the same or similar kind. State v. Ware (Summit 1977) 53 Ohio App.2d 210, 372 N.E.2d 1367, 7 O.O.3d 280, affirmed 63 Ohio St.2d 84, 406 N.E.2d 1112, 17 O.O.3d 51.

Aggravated burglary and rape are not allied offenses of similar import within meaning of statute prohibiting conviction of more than one allied offense of similar import. State v. Grider (Ohio App. 8 Dist., Cuyahoga, 07-25-2002) No. 80617, 2002-Ohio-3792, 2002 WL 1728607, Unreported, appeal not allowed 97 Ohio St.3d 1471, 779 N.E.2d 237, 2002-Ohio-6347, appeal after new sentencing hearing 2003-Ohio-3378, 2003 WL 21473406, appeal not allowed 100 Ohio St.3d 1487, 798 N.E.2d 1094, 2003-Ohio-5992. Criminal Law ⚿ 29(12)

Defendant could be convicted and sentenced for abduction and attempted rape of the same victim, even if crimes were allied offenses of similar import; the abduction for several hours exceeded the scope of time necessary to commit attempted rape, and the defendant had a separate animus as to each offense. State v. McMillen (Ohio App. 4 Dist., Vinton, 06-13-2002) No. 01CA564, 2002-Ohio-2863, 2002 WL 1370655, Unreported. Criminal Law ⚿ 29(13)

Where a defendant commits multiple, independent acts of forcible sexual activity upon a victim, multiple convictions are permitted, but where the defendant's several acts constitute one uninterrupted assaultive episode without a separate animus as to each act, only one conviction is permitted. State v. Brindley (Ohio App. 10 Dist., Franklin, 05-21-2002) No. 01AP-926, 2002-Ohio-2425, 2002 WL 1013033, Unreported, appeal not allowed 96 Ohio St.3d 1515, 775 N.E.2d 857, 2002-Ohio-4950. Criminal Law ⚿ 29(12)

Defendant's conduct involved different acts, so that defendant's convictions for one count of gross sexual imposition, five counts of sexual battery, and six counts of rape were not "allied offenses of similar import" within meaning of statute prohibiting conviction of more than one allied offense of similar import; defendant engaged in vaginal intercourse, fellatio, cunnilingus, and anal intercourse with victim on separate occasions over period of years. State v. Carpenter (Ohio App. 6 Dist., Erie, 05-10-2002) No. E-00-033, 2002-Ohio-2266, 2002 WL 1003520, Unreported, appeal reopened 2002-Ohio-4824, 2002 WL 31053828, appeal not allowed 96 Ohio St.3d 1513, 775 N.E.2d 855, 2002-Ohio-4950, appeal reopened 2004-Ohio-1036, 2004 WL 413288, appeal after new sentencing hearing 2006-Ohio-3048, 2006 WL 1661781, cause dismissed 110 Ohio St.3d 1450, 852 N.E.2d 197, 2006-Ohio-4085. Criminal Law ⚿ 29(12)

Rape under RC 2907.02 and gross sexual imposition under RC 2907.05 constitute allied offenses of similar import when fondling of the victim is incidental to the act of fellatio and no separate animus for the conduct of fondling is established. State v. Abi–Sarkis (Cuyahoga 1988) 41 Ohio App.3d 333, 535 N.E.2d 745.

Abduction and gross sexual imposition are committed separately and separate convictions for the two offenses are appropriate under RC 2941.25 where a boy and girl in their early teens go for a ride with defendant who drives them to a secluded area and restrains the boy with force or the threat of force during the entire time that he rapes the girl to prevent the boy from soliciting help from others. State v Lusby, No. C–960472, 1997 WL 642988 (1st Dist Ct App, Hamilton, 10–17–97).

Elements of rape under RC 2907.02 and assault under RC 2903.13 do not correspond to such a degree so as to be allied offenses under RC 2941.25 when the force or threat of force necessary to commit rape does not require the infliction of physical harm; thus, where a victim is frightened of a defendant before she is raped, and the defendant's intimidation and threats are sufficient to compel her to submit to sexual acts, an assault on the victim prior to raping her is excessive and not necessary to force her to submit to rape. State v Jones, No. 54868 (8th Dist Ct App, Cuyahoga, 3–2–89).

Where offenses of rape, attempted rape, and gross sexual imposition, allied offenses of similar import, are committed without a separate animus, the defendant may not be subjected to multiple sentences pursuant to RC 2941.25. State v Pyotsia, No. 11–239 (11th Dist Ct App, Lake, 2–20–87).

A defendant who had vaginal intercourse with a seven-year-old, and on the same day had sexual contact with the same child by application of an electric vibrator to the child's genital area, was properly convicted of violating both RC 2907.02 and 2907.05, respectively, since the two acts were committed with a separate animus as to each, as required by RC 2941.25(B). State v Jackson, Nos. C–830331 and C–830343 (1st Dist Ct App, Hamilton, 4–11–84).

Where there is evidence from which the trier of fact could determine that there were three separate forcible, and therefore criminal, vaginal penetrations of the same victim, at least one of which culminated in ejaculation by the male, committed at the same location within a one-and-one-half to two hour period, the offenses were not "committed separately or with a separate animus as to each" within the meaning of RC 2941.25(B); the most important consideration in making such a determination is the "nature of the act and risk of harm to the victim." State v Elyel, No. C–830403 (1st Dist Ct App, Hamilton, 3–21–84).

Where defendant was convicted of rape of his daughter and of sexual battery by vaginal intercourse with the same victim, such defendant may be convicted on one charge only where both charges stem from one act of vaginal intercourse. State v Rodman, No. CA–595 (5th Dist Ct App, Morrow, 7–27–82).

17. —— Drug offenses, specific offenses construed

Trafficking in drugs and possession of cocaine were not allied offenses of similar import, and thus convictions for both did not violate double jeopardy and were allowed under multiple-count statute. State v. Greitzer (Ohio App. 11 Dist., Portage, 08-05-2005) No. 2003-P-0110, 2005-Ohio-4037, 2005 WL 1862121, Unreported, appeal allowed 107 Ohio St.3d 1696, 840 N.E.2d 202, 2005-Ohio-6763, reversed in part 109 Ohio St.3d 313, 847 N.E.2d 1174, 2006-Ohio-2109. Criminal Law ⚿ 29(8); Double Jeopardy ⚿ 146

Crimes of illegal processing of drug documents, deception to obtain dangerous drugs, and possession of drugs were not allied offenses of similar import, and thus offenses did not merge; each statutory violation could be committed without automatically violating one of other statutes. State v. Taylor (Ohio App. 8 Dist., Cuyahoga, 03-17-2005) No. 84532, 2005-Ohio-1169, 2005 WL 616083, Unreported. Criminal Law ⚿ 29(8); Criminal Law ⚿ 30

Drug trafficking and drug possession were not allied offenses of similar import, for purposes of allied offenses statute which protected against multiple punishments for the same criminal conduct. State v. Lyons (Ohio App. 8 Dist., Cuyahoga, 02-03-2005) No. 84377, 2005-Ohio-392, 2005 WL 273034, Unreported, stay denied 105 Ohio St.3d 1542, 827 N.E.2d 326, 2005-Ohio-2188, appeal not allowed 106 Ohio St.3d 1415, 830 N.E.2d 347, 2005-Ohio-3154. Criminal Law ⚿ 29(8)

Trafficking in cocaine and possession of cocaine are not allied offenses of similar import, and thus, offenses do not merge; statute proscribing possession does not include element of sale or offer to sell, while trafficking statute does not require actual possession or use of controlled substance. State v. Sanders (Ohio App. 11 Dist., Portage, 10-22-2004) No. 2003-P-0072, 2004-Ohio-5629, 2004 WL 2376014, Unreported, appeal not allowed 105 Ohio St.3d 1441, 822 N.E.2d 812, 2005-Ohio-531, appeal after new sentencing hearing 2006-Ohio-2147, 2006 WL 1133192. Criminal Law ⚿ 30

Offenses of drug trafficking and preparation of drugs for sale are not allied offenses of similar import; preparation of drugs for sale does not necessarily result in the sale of the drugs. State v. Thompson (Ohio App. 8 Dist., Cuyahoga, 06-10-2004) No. 83382, 2004-Ohio-2969, 2004 WL 1267124, Unreported. Criminal Law ⚿ 29(8)

Since the elements of the offenses did not correspond to such a degree that the commission of one crime would result in the commission of the other, trafficking in cocaine and possession of cocaine were not allied offenses, and thus, the trial court did not err in sentencing defendant for both; it was possible to obtain, possess, or use a controlled substance without preparing it for shipment, and it was also possible to sell or offer to sell cocaine without possessing it, e.g., when one serves as a middleman. State v. Alvarez (Ohio App. 12 Dist., Butler, 05-17-2004) No. CA2003-03-067, 2004-Ohio-2483, 2004 WL 1089110, Unreported. Sentencing And Punishment ⚿ 524

Defendant's drug trafficking and drug possession convictions were not allied offenses of similar import, and thus court could lawfully sentence defendant on both counts. State v. Moore (Ohio App. 6 Dist., Erie, 02-13-2004) No. E-03-006, 2004-Ohio-685, 2004 WL 291145, Unreported. Sentencing And Punishment ⚿ 524

Trafficking in cocaine and attempted possession of cocaine were not allied offenses of similar import, and thus defendant could be given multiple sentences for the two offenses, as it was possible to attempt to possess cocaine without preparing it for shipment, shipping, transporting or delivering or preparing it for distribution or distributing it. State v. Guzman (Ohio App. 10 Dist., Franklin, 09-11-2003) No. 02AP-1440, 2003-Ohio-4822, 2003 WL 22099257, Unreported, appeal not allowed 101 Ohio St.3d 1422, 802 N.E.2d 153, 2004-Ohio-123. Double Jeopardy ⚿ 146

Having a weapon while under disability and possession of cocaine are separate crimes and one can be committed without committing the other, and thus, defendant's convictions did not constitute a continuous, single course of conduct, which required concurrent sentencing, even though defendant was discovered committing the two offenses during the same traffic stop. State v. Campbell (Ohio App. 5 Dist., Stark, 08-25-2003) No. 2003CA00026, 2003-Ohio-4620, 2003 WL 22039321, Unreported. Criminal Law ⚿ 29(15)

Defendant's conduct for which he was tried and convicted of possession of cocaine and aggravated trafficking in cocaine in the vicinity of a school constituted two separate offenses of dissimilar import; it is possible to possess crack cocaine without offering it for sale, and it is possible to sell or offer to sell crack cocaine without possessing it, such as when one serves as a middleman. State v. Salaam (Ohio App. 1 Dist., Hamilton, 03-07-2003) No. C-020324, 2003-Ohio-1021, 2003 WL 832751, Unreported. Double Jeopardy ⚿ 146

Failure to merge, for sentencing purposes, two counts of possession of heroin arising from search of defendant's vehicle was not error; heroin found inside center console had been packaged for sale while heroin found inside trunk had yet to be prepared for sale, and therefore a separate animus could have existed with respect to each offense. State v. Fannin (Ohio App. 8 Dist., Cuyahoga, 11-21-2002) No. 79991, 2002-Ohio-6312, 2002 WL 31618484, Unreported, appeal not allowed 99 Ohio St.3d 1438, 789 N.E.2d 1118, 2003-Ohio-2902. Sentencing And Punishment ⚿ 501; Sentencing And Punishment ⚿ 524

Trafficking in drugs and conspiracy to commit trafficking are not allied offenses of similar import because conspiracy must be planned with another person while it is unnecessary for the underlying offense to be completed; on the other hand, trafficking requires only one individual and does not require any planning but does require the sale or offer to sell a controlled substance. State v. Ncehelser (Ohio App. 10 Dist., Franklin, 04-26-2001) No. 00AP-534, 2001 WL 422956, Unreported.

Offenses of theft by deception and aggravated trafficking, arising out of defendant's offer to sell cocaine and his theft of the payment, did not merge; defendant's offer to sell cocaine was a completed offense as soon as the words escaped his mouth, while theft by deception also required that defendant obtain and abscond with the money, with no intention of delivering the goods. State v. Byrd (Greene 1993) 86 Ohio App.3d 679, 621 N.E.2d 781, dismissed, jurisdictional motion overruled 66 Ohio St.3d 1507, 613 N.E.2d 1046. Criminal Law ⚿ 30

Giving cocaine away without accepting money constitutes a "sale" under RC 3719.01(EE), and if an amount of cocaine in excess of that given away is left over, the defendant may be convicted of both possessing and trafficking in cocaine, despite the fact that there is only one drug involved since there is a separate animus for each. State v. Adkins (Athens 1992) 80 Ohio App.3d 211, 608 N.E.2d 1152, dismissed, jurisdictional motion overruled 65 Ohio St.3d 1417, 598 N.E.2d 1169, certiorari denied 113 S.Ct. 1423, 507 U.S. 975, 122 L.Ed.2d 792.

Elements of trafficking in drugs and engaging in pattern of corrupt activity did not correspond to such degree that commission of one resulted in commission of the other, and thus sentencing upon both offenses was proper. State v. Thrower (Summit 1989) 62 Ohio App.3d 359, 575 N.E.2d 863, motion overruled 49 Ohio St.3d 717, 552 N.E.2d 951. Sentencing And Punishment ⚿ 524

Simultaneous possession of different controlled substances constitutes separate offenses under narcotics possession statute for double jeopardy purposes; overruling *State v. Stratton*, 5 Ohio App.3d 228, 451 N.E.2d 520. State v. Hedelsky (Erie 1985) 28 Ohio App.3d 78, 502 N.E.2d 241, 28 O.B.R. 120. Double Jeopardy ⚿ 146

Defendant's alleged simultaneous possession of marijuana, cocaine and methaqualone, in violation of statute providing that no person was to knowingly possess a controlled substance, constituted one offense permitting a single punishment. State v. Stratton (Erie 1982) 5 Ohio App.3d 228, 451 N.E.2d 520, 5 O.B.R. 513. Criminal Law ⚿ 29(8)

Double jeopardy clause did not prevent defendant from being prosecuted for felony of trafficking in drugs when facts indicated that after sale was made, defendant still possessed additional quantity of drugs in excess of amount of drugs sold, and that possession of that additional quantity of drugs, an act separate and distinct from the sale, was basis for previous misdemeanor conviction for possession of drugs. State v. Truitt (Hamilton 1981) 1 Ohio App.3d 65, 439 N.E.2d 452, 1 O.B.R. 344, certiorari denied 102 S.Ct. 588, 454 U.S. 1047, 70 L.Ed.2d 488. Double Jeopardy ⚿ 146

Defendant's offenses of drug trafficking, preparation of drugs for sale, possession of drugs, and possession of criminal tools were not allied offenses of similar import, and thus trial court had no duty to conduct hearing on issue, and trial court was not limited to imposition of only one sentence for one offense, but rather could sentence defendant for each offense. State v. Fort (Ohio App. 8 Dist., Cuyahoga, 09-26-2002) No. 80604, 2002-Ohio-5068, 2002 WL 31123871, Unreported, appeal not allowed 98 Ohio St.3d 1491, 785 N.E.2d 473, 2003-Ohio-1189. Double Jeopardy ⚿ 146

Convictions for trafficking in cocaine and possession of cocaine are not allied offenses of similar import and therefore do not merge, since trafficking imposes the additional element that possession of the controlled substance is incident to preparation for shipment, transportation, delivery or distribution of the drug through a sale. State v. Bridges (Ohio App. 8 Dist., Cuyahoga, 07-25-2002) No. 80171, 2002-Ohio-3771, 2002 WL 1728602, Unreported, appeal not allowed 97 Ohio St.3d 1484, 780 N.E.2d 287, 2002-Ohio-6866. Criminal Law ⚿ 30

The offenses of knowingly selling or offering to sell a controlled substance, as proscribed by RC 2925.03(A)(1), and knowingly selling or offering to sell a counterfeit controlled substance, in violation of RC 2925.37(B), are not allied offenses of similar import. State v. Mughni (Ohio 1987) 33 Ohio St.3d 65, 514 N.E.2d 870. Criminal Law ⚿ 29(8)

The offenses of drug trafficking, RC 2925.03(A)(2), and permitting drug abuse, RC 2925.13, are not allied offenses of similar import, as the latter includes the additional element of using a motor vehicle. State v Reese, No. 54105 (8th Dist Ct App, Cuyahoga, 8–18–88).

18. —— Robbery and burglary, specific offenses construed

Aggravated robbery and kidnapping were not allied offenses of similar import, and thus, did not merge, for purposes of sentencing; elements of offenses would not establish that commission of aggravated robbery would not necessarily result in kidnapping or vice versa. State v. Bunch (Ohio App. 7 Dist., Mahoning, 06-24-2005) No. 02 CA 196, 2005-Ohio-3309, 2005 WL 1523844, Unreported, appeal allowed 107 Ohio St.3d 1680, 839 N.E.2d 401, 2005-Ohio-6480. Sentencing And Punishment ⚿ 537

Aggravated robbery and receiving stolen property were allied offenses of similar import, and thus, trial court should not have imposed an additional sentence for receiving stolen property conviction; vehicle that defendant was accused of receiving under the receiving stolen property charge was the same vehicle that was stolen as part of the aggravated robbery charge. State v. Barnette (Ohio App. 7 Dist., Mahoning, 12-28-2004) No. 02 CA 65, 2004-Ohio-7211, 2004 WL 3090228, Unreported, opinion corrected on denial of reconsideration 2005-Ohio-477, 2005 WL 293804, appeal allowed 105 Ohio St.3d 1559, 828 N.E.2d 115, 2005-Ohio-2447, reversed in part 109 Ohio St.3d 313, 847 N.E.2d 1174, 2006-Ohio-2109. Sentencing And Punishment ⚿ 537

Attempted burglary and criminal damaging were not allied offenses of similar import, and thus defendant could be convicted and sentenced for both offenses; elements of offenses did not correspond to such degree that commission of one would result in commission of other, in that person could trespass on another's property, as required for attempted burglary, without damaging that property, as required for criminal damaging, just as person could damage another's property without trespassing. State v. Smith (Ohio App. 8 Dist., Cuyahoga, 11-18-2004) No. 84292, 2004-Ohio-6111, 2004 WL 2610526, Unreported, appeal allowed, reversed 105 Ohio St.3d 289, 825 N.E.2d 157, 2005-Ohio-1651. Criminal Law ⚿ 29(11)

Defendant's act of committing aggravated robbery of flower shop and aggravated robbery of employees at flower show were committed with a separate animus, and thus defendant was properly convicted and sentenced on each robbery; each offense was perpetrated against different victim and each victim was forced to relinquish their property to defendant. State v. Payne (Ohio App. 10 Dist., Franklin, 09-16-2003) No. 02AP-723, No. 02AP-725, 2003-Ohio-4891, 2003 WL 22128810, Unreported, appeal not allowed 101 Ohio St.3d 1421, 802 N.E.2d 153, 2004-Ohio-123, appeal not allowed 107 Ohio St.3d 1411, 836 N.E.2d 1230, 2005-Ohio-5859. Criminal Law ⚿ 29(11)

Defendant's act of committing aggravated robbery of credit union and aggravated robbery of individual at credit union were committed with a separate animus, and thus defendant was properly convicted and sentenced on for each robbery; each offense was perpetrated against different victim and each victim was forced to relinquish their property to defendant. State v. Payne (Ohio App. 10 Dist., Franklin, 09-16-2003) No. 02AP-723, No. 02AP-725, 2003-Ohio-4891, 2003 WL 22128810, Unreported, appeal not allowed 101 Ohio St.3d 1421, 802 N.E.2d 153, 2004-Ohio-123, appeal not allowed 107 Ohio St.3d 1411, 836 N.E.2d 1230, 2005-Ohio-5859. Criminal Law ⚿ 29(11)

Aggravated burglary and theft were not allied offenses of similar import, and thus defendant was properly convicted and sentenced for both such offenses; completion of theft was not a necessary element of burglary because purpose to commit any felony will suffice to supply requisite intent for burglary offense. State v. Johnson (Ohio App. 8 Dist., Cuyahoga, 06-19-2003) No. 81692, No. 81693, 2003-Ohio-3241, 2003 WL 21419631, Unreported, appeal not allowed 100 Ohio St.3d 1433, 797 N.E.2d 513, 2003-Ohio-5396. Criminal Law ⚿ 29(11)

Offenses committed by defendant, which were burglary and violation of protection order, were not "allied offenses of similar import," such that defendant could not be convicted of both; considered in the abstract, burglary would not automatically result from violation of a protection order or vice versa, given that burglary involved using force, stealth, or deception to trespass in habitation of any person when any person was present or likely to be present, but violation of a protection order required only that offender violated terms of order. State v. Bates (Ohio App. 12 Dist., Fayette, 10-14-2002) No. CA2001-10-018, 2002-Ohio-5512, 2002 WL 31296867, Unreported. Criminal Law ⚿ 29(11)

Prosecution for the offense of criminal damaging based on the same incident in which a defendant is convicted of burglary is barred by the double jeopardy clause. State v. Lugli (Ohio App. 6 Dist., Huron, 08-04-1995) No. H-94-043, 1995 WL 458671, Unreported, dismissed, appeal not allowed 74 Ohio St.3d 1475, 657 N.E.2d 783.

Aggravated burglary specification for death penalty did not merge with aggravated robbery specification; as soon as defendant entered the apartment by force armed with a deadly weapon with the intent to commit a theft, the aggravated burglary was completed. State v. Fears (Ohio, 09-08-1999) 86 Ohio St.3d 329, 715 N.E.2d 136, 1999-Ohio-111, reconsideration denied 87 Ohio St.3d 1421, 717 N.E.2d 1107, stay granted 87 Ohio St.3d 1423, 718 N.E.2d 441, denial of post-conviction relief affirmed 1999 WL 1032592, dismissed, appeal not allowed 88 Ohio St.3d 1444, 725 N.E.2d 284, certiorari denied 120 S.Ct. 1535, 529 U.S. 1039, 146 L.Ed.2d 349. Criminal Law ⚿ 30

Aggravated burglary and aggravated robbery were not "allied offenses of similar import," for purposes of rule providing that defendant could be convicted of only one such offense; defendant committed aggravated burglary by using deception to obtain entry into victim's home and used force to complete that entry in order to take her property, but committed aggravated robbery when he subjected victim to further injury in order to take her property. State v. Reynolds (Ohio, 01-14-1998) 80 Ohio St.3d 670, 687 N.E.2d 1358, 1998-Ohio-171, certiorari denied 118 S.Ct. 2328, 524 U.S. 930, 141 L.Ed.2d 702, denial of post-conviction relief affirmed 1999 WL 980568, dismissed, appeal not allowed 88 Ohio St.3d 1425, 723 N.E.2d 1113. Criminal Law ⚿ 29(11)

Aggravated robbery and aggravated murder are not "allied offenses of similar import," for purposes of rule providing that, where conduct of defendant can be construed as constituting two or more allied offenses of similar import, indictment may contain counts for all such offenses, but defendant may be convicted of only one. State v. Reynolds (Ohio, 01-14-1998) 80 Ohio St.3d 670, 687 N.E.2d 1358, 1998-Ohio-171, certiorari denied 118 S.Ct. 2328, 524 U.S. 930, 141 L.Ed.2d 702, denial of post-conviction relief affirmed 1999 WL 980568, dismissed, appeal not allowed 88 Ohio St.3d 1425, 723 N.E.2d 1113. Criminal Law ⚿ 29(14)

Aggravated burglary and aggravated murder are not "allied offenses of similar import," for purposes of rule providing that, where conduct of defendant can be construed as constituting two or more allied offenses of similar import, indictment may contain counts for all such offenses, but defendant may be convicted of only one. State v. Reynolds (Ohio, 01-14-1998) 80 Ohio St.3d 670, 687 N.E.2d 1358, 1998-Ohio-171, certiorari denied 118 S.Ct. 2328, 524 U.S. 930, 141 L.Ed.2d 702, denial of post-conviction relief affirmed 1999 WL 980568, dismissed, appeal not allowed 88 Ohio St.3d 1425, 723 N.E.2d 1113. Criminal Law ⚿ 29(14)

Aggravated robbery and felonious assault were not allied offenses of similar import, and thus defendant could be convicted of both charges. State v. Allen (Ohio App. 7 Dist., 11-20-1996) 115 Ohio App.3d 642, 685 N.E.2d 1304. Criminal Law ⚿ 29(11)

Aggravated robbery was not allied offense of similar import to aggravated murder, and thus merger of aggravated robbery conviction into aggravated murder conviction was not warranted. State v. Dennis (Ohio, 09-24-1997) 79 Ohio St.3d 421, 683 N.E.2d 1096, 1997-Ohio-372, denial of post-conviction relief affirmed 1997 WL 760680, dismissed, appeal not allowed 81 Ohio St.3d 1468, 690 N.E.2d 1287, certiorari denied 118 S.Ct. 1078, 522 U.S. 1128, 140 L.Ed.2d 136, habeas corpus dismissed 68 F.Supp.2d 863, affirmed 354 F.3d 511, certiorari denied 124 S.Ct. 2400, 541 U.S. 1068, 158 L.Ed.2d 971. Criminal Law ⚷ 30

Crimes of simple burglary and felonious assault were not allied offenses, and therefore defendant's convictions for both offenses were not prohibited under allied offenses statute. State v. Clark (Ohio App. 2 Dist., 10-27-1995) 107 Ohio App.3d 141, 667 N.E.2d 1262. Criminal Law ⚷ 29(11)

Offenses of burglary and receiving stolen property are not allied offenses of similar import, and thus conviction for both offenses arising out of same transaction is not prohibited by double jeopardy considerations; statutory elements of burglary and receiving stolen property do not correspond to such degree that commission of one crime will necessarily result in commission of the other. State v. Clelland (Hocking 1992) 83 Ohio App.3d 474, 615 N.E.2d 276, dismissed, jurisdictional motion overruled 66 Ohio St.3d 1437, 608 N.E.2d 1082. Double Jeopardy ⚷ 144

Allied offenses statute did not preclude defendant's burglary conviction, even though defendant had previously pled guilty to receiving stolen property charge regarding the same stolen items; statutory elements of burglary and receiving stolen property do not correspond with such degree as to constitute allied offenses of similar import. State v. Clelland (Hocking 1992) 83 Ohio App.3d 474, 615 N.E.2d 276, dismissed, jurisdictional motion overruled 66 Ohio St.3d 1437, 608 N.E.2d 1082. Criminal Law ⚷ 29(11)

Similar acts statute, which permits trial court to convict defendant of multiple offenses in single prosecution provided that offenses are not allied and of similar import, does not apply to felonious assault and aggravated robbery since assault requires actual use of deadly weapon or dangerous ordnance whereas aggravated robbery requires mere possession of deadly weapon or dangerous ordnance, and aggravated robbery is complete upon offender's purposeful attempt to inflict serious physical harm whereas felonious assault requires actual infliction of harm. State v. Ferguson (Butler 1991) 71 Ohio App.3d 342, 594 N.E.2d 23, dismissed, jurisdictional motion overruled 61 Ohio St.3d 1428, 575 N.E.2d 216. Criminal Law ⚷ 29(11)

Aggravated burglary, aggravated robbery and grand theft resulted from different conduct, and were not allied offenses of similar import, so that separate sentences could be imposed, where aggravated burglary occurred when defendant, in possession of deadly weapon, entered home for purpose of committing theft, aggravated robbery was committed when defendant took car keys and antique gun while in possession of deadly weapon, and grand theft was committed when defendant took victim's automobile. State v. Houseman (Allen 1990) 70 Ohio App.3d 499, 591 N.E.2d 405, dismissed 58 Ohio St.3d 717, 570 N.E.2d 1129, denial of post-conviction relief affirmed, dismissed, jurisdictional motion overruled 65 Ohio St.3d 1454, 602 N.E.2d 250. Criminal Law ⚷ 29(11); Sentencing And Punishment ⚷ 537

Aggravating specifications that defendant committed aggravated robbery of store employee and aggravated robbery of store were not required to be merged for purposes of sentencing of defendant for aggravated murder of employee, where defendant took cash from store's cash register, and took employee's watch, ring, and wallet. State v. Byrd (Ohio 1987) 32 Ohio St.3d 79, 512 N.E.2d 611, certiorari denied 108 S.Ct. 763, 484 U.S. 1037, 98 L.Ed.2d 780, rehearing denied 108 S.Ct. 1252, 485 U.S. 972, 99 L.Ed.2d 449, stay granted 39 Ohio St.3d 719, 534 N.E.2d 351, denial of post-conviction relief reversed, cause dismissed 60 Ohio St.3d 705, 573 N.E.2d 665. Sentencing And Punishment ⚷ 1660

Aggravated burglary and felonious assault are not allied offenses of similar import within the meaning of RC 2941.25. State v. Jackson (Cuyahoga 1985) 21 Ohio App.3d 157, 487 N.E.2d 585, 21 O.B.R. 168.

One who robs several patrons of a bar at the same time can be charged and convicted for separate offenses, as the offenses are of dissimilar import and are committed with a separate animus as to each victim. State v. Hughley (Trumbull 1984) 20 Ohio App.3d 77, 484 N.E.2d 758, 20 O.B.R. 97. Criminal Law ⚷ 29(11)

A defendant may be convicted of both breaking and entering and safecracking where the evidence shows that the defendant (1) broke into a bank, and (2) then tried to break into a safe inside the bank; the crime of breaking and entering was complete upon the defendant's breaking into the bank with intent to commit a theft offense, and the attempt to break into the safe was a separate offense. State v. Carroll (Clermont 1984) 14 Ohio App.3d 51, 469 N.E.2d 1348, 14 O.B.R. 56.

Under RC 2941.25(B), aggravated burglary and grand theft are offenses of "dissimilar import" where conviction of grand theft is predicated upon a prior theft conviction, involving independent conduct and a separate animus from the aggravated burglary conviction at issue. State v. Brown (Cuyahoga 1981) 3 Ohio App.3d 131, 443 N.E.2d 1382, 3 O.B.R. 148. Criminal Law ⚷ 29(11)

A defendant charged with aggravated burglary and aggravated robbery may be convicted of both offenses under the "separate acts" provision of RC 2941.25 since the offenses are not "allied offenses of similar import." State v. Moss (Ohio 1982) 69 Ohio St.2d 515, 433 N.E.2d 181, 23 O.O.3d 447, certiorari denied 103 S.Ct. 1183, 459 U.S. 1200, 75 L.Ed.2d 430.

The offense of aggravated robbery, committed in violation of RC 2911.01(A)(2), and the crime of aggravated burglary, a violation of RC 2911.11(A)(3), do not constitute "allied offenses of similar import" within the meaning of RC 2941.25(A). State v. Frazier (Ohio 1979) 58 Ohio St.2d 253, 389 N.E.2d 1118, 12 O.O.3d 263.

Felonious assault and aggravated robbery are not allied offenses of similar import under RC 2941.25(A). State v Sowell, No. 62601 (8th Dist Ct App, Cuyahoga, 5–27–93).

Aggravated robbery and felonious assault do not constitute allied offenses of similar import. State v Carter, No. 61502 (8th Dist Ct App, Cuyahoga, 1–14–93).

The offenses of theft of drugs, RC 2925.21(C), and aggravated robbery RC 2911.01(A)(1) are allied offenses of similar import, but conviction on both charges is permitted where the offenses were committed simultaneously at the same location but with separate objectives, theft to obtain cash and theft to obtain prescription drugs. State v Clements, No. C–880172 (1st Dist Ct App, Hamilton, 5–3–89).

Breaking and entering and possession of criminal tools are not allied offenses of similar import, and the relitigation of some factual issues in a prosecution for the latter after conviction for the former does not violate double jeopardy. State v Clemmons, No. 1409 (4th Dist Ct App, Ross, 3–29–88).

Defendant may be found guilty of both aggravated robbery and attempted murder since these offenses require two separate distinct animi; the evidence indicated that the robbery was complete at the time of the attempted murder. State v Thompson, No. 9–81–9 (3d Dist Ct App, Marion, 3–3–82).

19. —— Theft and other offenses, specific offenses construed

Defendant's convictions for money laundering and theft in office, as well as his convictions for theft in office and tempering with records, were not allied offenses of similar import; theft in office required a theft offense, by a public official, involving property owned by a government entity, neither money laundering or tampering with records had those same requirements, money laundering required either an intent to conceal the nature, location, source, or ownership of the proceeds from some unlawful activity, or a purpose to promote, manage, establish or carry on a corrupt activity, theft in office and tampering with records did not require those same purposes or intent, and tampering with records required falsification, destruction, removal, concealment, or alteration of some record, and theft in office and money laundering did not have that requirement. State v. Gray (Ohio App. 2 Dist., Greene, 01-06-2006) No. 04CA129, 2006-Ohio-40, 2006 WL 38282, Unreported, motion for delayed appeal granted 109 Ohio St.3d 1422, 846 N.E.2d 532, 2006-Ohio-1967. Criminal Law ⚿ 29(10)

Two counts of grand theft of firearms were not allied offenses of similar import for sentencing purposes merely because both subject firearms were stolen in course of single theft, where theft of each firearm was separate offense. State v. Helton (Ohio App. 3 Dist., Logan, 08-15-2005) No. 8-05-06, 2005-Ohio-4184, 2005 WL 1939437, Unreported, appeal not allowed 108 Ohio St.3d 1415, 841 N.E.2d 319, 2006-Ohio-179. Sentencing And Punishment ⚿ 532

Theft of money and receiving stolen property, i.e., checks, were committed separately and with separate animus, and thus, convictions did not merge at sentencing. State v. Austin (Ohio App. 8 Dist., Cuyahoga, 10-28-2004) No. 84142, 2004-Ohio-5736, 2004 WL 2425812, Unreported. Criminal Law ⚿ 30

Grand theft and unauthorized use of a motor vehicle were not allied offenses of similar import, and thus trial court was not required to merge defendant's convictions for both. State v. Whited (Ohio App. 2 Dist., Champaign, 10-24-2003) No. 02CA38, 2003-Ohio-5747, 2003 WL 22429696, Unreported. Criminal Law ⚿ 30

Although receiving stolen property is technically not a lesser included offense of theft, receiving stolen property and theft of the same property are allied offenses of similar import, for purposes of statute allowing a conviction for only one of the offenses, if the indictment or information contains counts for allied offenses of similar import. State v. Yarbrough (Ohio, 12-01-2004) 104 Ohio St.3d 1, 817 N.E.2d 845, 2004-Ohio-6087, reconsideration denied 104 Ohio St.3d 1437, 819 N.E.2d 1121, 2004-Ohio-7079. Receiving Stolen Goods ⚿ 6

Offenses of grand theft, motor vehicle and receiving stolen property should have been merged into sentence received for aggravated robbery where offenses were part and parcel of same conduct of carjacking of vehicle and there was no separate animus for each crime. State v. Gest (Ohio App. 8 Dist., 12-29-1995) 108 Ohio App.3d 248, 670 N.E.2d 536. Sentencing And Punishment ⚿ 537

Defendant's convictions of robbery and grand theft based on single bank robbery were allied offenses of similar import; although technically value of property stolen was an element of the crime for purpose of allocating to the state its burden of proof, property value did not alter fact that defendant committed only a single theft, theft was accompanied by threat of immediate force, thereby turning it into act of robbery, and thus commission of robbery automatically resulted in commission of theft. State v. Lang (Ohio App. 1 Dist., 03-29-1995) 102 Ohio App.3d 243, 656 N.E.2d 1358. Criminal Law ⚿ 29(11)

Defendant, by entering three guilty pleas, admitted that he committed three separate acts of theft, so that multiple sentences were permitted for each theft; as stated by defendant, thefts happened in three different places on two separate days. State v. Larsen (Lawrence 1993) 89 Ohio App.3d 371, 624 N.E.2d 766. Sentencing And Punishment ⚿ 532

A defendant may not be convicted for both theft and receiving stolen property where the second charge relates to the defendant's attempt to return for cash or other property at a Sears store in Lake County property she acquired at a Sears store in Cuyahoga County through the use of a stolen credit card. State v. Liston (Lake 1991) 70 Ohio App.3d 663, 591 N.E.2d 879.

A defendant may be convicted of theft in Cuyahoga County and attempted theft in Lake County, but not of receiving stolen property in Lake County, where the earlier theft charge relates to the defendant's obtaining property at a Sears store by using a stolen credit card and the charge of attempted theft relates to the defendant's attempt to return for cash or other property at a Sears store in Lake County property she had acquired at a Sears store in Cuyahoga County; where the defendant has been convicted of theft in Cuyahoga County, the charge of receiving stolen property in Lake County must be dismissed since theft and receiving stolen property charges are allied offenses of similar import and were not committed separately or with separate animus. State v. Liston (Lake 1991) 70 Ohio App.3d 663, 591 N.E.2d 879.

The two crimes of receiving stolen property and theft are allied offenses of similar import; where crimes are committed separately and have a separate animus a defendant can be convicted of both offenses. State v. Stone (Lorain 1990) 69 Ohio App.3d 383, 590 N.E.2d 1283. Larceny ⚷ 1; Receiving Stolen Goods ⚷ 1

Where the same criminal conduct results in convictions of bribery and theft in office, RC 2941.25 requires the trial court to merge the convictions for purposes of sentencing. State v. McCool (Cuyahoga 1988) 46 Ohio App.3d 1, 544 N.E.2d 933.

Aggravated robbery under RC 2911.01(A)(1) and theft of drugs using a firearm under RC 2925.21(C) are allied offenses of similar import. State v. Lundy (Hamilton 1987) 41 Ohio App.3d 163, 535 N.E.2d 664. Sentencing And Punishment ⚷ 537

Where a conviction for theft in office in violation of RC 2921.41 and a conviction for grand theft in violation of RC 2913.02 are committed with the same animus as part of a single plan to abscond with government funds, grand theft and theft in office constitute allied offenses of similar import under RC 2941.25. State v. McGhee (Cuyahoga 1987) 37 Ohio App.3d 54, 523 N.E.2d 864.

Although robbery and theft are allied offenses of similar import, a defendant may be convicted of both where he commits each crime separately or with a separate animus, by first robbing his victim of cash and car keys, and then stealing the car. State v. Reyna (Lorain 1985) 24 Ohio App.3d 79, 493 N.E.2d 555, 24 O.B.R. 148.

Separate counts of receiving stolen property are allied offenses of similar import where the defendant received, retained, or disposed of all the items involved in one transaction at one time; convictions of such counts should be merged for purposes of sentencing. State v. Wilson (Summit 1985) 21 Ohio App.3d 171, 486 N.E.2d 1242, 21 O.B.R. 182.

Theft and breaking and entering are dissimilar crimes for which a defendant may be separately punished. State v. Dunihue (Clinton 1984) 20 Ohio App.3d 210, 485 N.E.2d 764, 20 O.B.R. 256.

The offenses of breaking and entering, grand theft, and possessing criminal tools are not allied offenses of similar import inasmuch as these offenses have elements which do not correspond to such a degree that the commission of one offense will result in the commission of the other. State v. Talley (Ohio 1985) 18 Ohio St.3d 152, 480 N.E.2d 439, 18 O.B.R. 210.

Forgery as defined by RC 2913.01(G) and theft as defined by RC 2913.02 are not allied offenses of similar import. State v. Hunter (Cuyahoga 1983) 12 Ohio App.3d 75, 466 N.E.2d 183, 12 O.B.R. 273.

Where theft by deception offense was necessarily dependent upon evidence showing that a forgery offense was an integral part of the single transaction, the two offenses, when taken together under such circumstances, were allied offenses of similar import and defendants could be convicted of only one. State v. Wolfe (Montgomery 1983) 10 Ohio App.3d 324, 462 N.E.2d 455, 10 O.B.R. 530. Criminal Law ⚷ 29(10)

Defendant may not be sentenced for grand theft when defendant is also sentenced for aggravated robbery for the same theft. State v Bickerstaff, No. 1141 (9th Dist Ct App, Medina, 11-17-82), affirmed by 10 OS(3d) 62, 10 OBR 352, 461 NE(2d) 892 (1984).

Elements of aggravated burglary and theft do not correspond to such a degree as to constitute allied offenses of similar import and defendant may be convicted of both offenses. State v. Parson (Ohio 1983) 6 Ohio St.3d 442, 453 N.E.2d 689, 6 O.B.R. 485. Criminal Law ⚷ 29(11)

Theft is an allied offense of similar import to aggravated robbery, in that theft does not require the proof of any element not required to be proof of the offense of aggravated robbery, and defendant may not be convicted of both offenses for a single incident. State v. Parson (Ohio 1983) 6 Ohio St.3d 442, 453 N.E.2d 689, 6 O.B.R. 485. Criminal Law ⚷ 29(11)

Aggravated robbery is an "allied offense of similar import" to theft. State v. Johnson (Ohio 1983) 6 Ohio St.3d 420, 453 N.E.2d 595, 6 O.B.R. 466, certiorari granted 104 S.Ct. 994, 465 U.S. 1004, 79 L.Ed.2d 228, reversed 104 S.Ct. 2536, 467 U.S. 493, 81 L.Ed.2d 425, rehearing denied 105 S.Ct. 20, 468 U.S. 1224, 82 L.Ed.2d 915, on remand.

The elements of aggravated burglary and theft do not correspond to such a degree as to constitute allied offenses of similar import under RC 2941.25(A). State v. Mitchell (Ohio 1983) 6 Ohio St.3d 416, 453 N.E.2d 593, 6 O.B.R. 463. Criminal Law ⚷ 29(11)

Where it is charged in separate counts that the defendant, with purpose to commit theft, knowingly entered, forced an entrance into, tampered with, or inserted any part of an instrument into any coin machine, in violation of RC 2911.32, and that upon entry, theft of money or property contained therein was consummated by the defendant, in violation of RC 2913.02, the offenses together constitute "allied offenses of similar import" as to which the defendant may be indicted for both offenses but convicted of only one. State v. Baer (Ohio 1981) 67 Ohio St.2d 220, 423 N.E.2d 432, 21 O.O.3d 138. Criminal Law ⟹ 29(10)

A person may properly be tried and convicted for receiving stolen property after he admits the actual theft of that same property. City of Maumee v. Geiger (Ohio 1976) 45 Ohio St.2d 238, 344 N.E.2d 133, 74 O.O.2d 380.

While the Double Jeopardy Clause may protect a defendant against cumulative punishments for convictions on the same offense, it does not prohibit the state from prosecuting a defendant for such multiple offenses in a single prosecution; therefore, where a defendant pleads guilty to lesser charges while the more serious charges, to which he had pleaded not guilty, are dismissed, the double jeopardy clause does not prohibit the state from continuing its prosecution of the defendant on the more serious charges. Ohio v. Johnson (U.S.Ohio 1984) 104 S.Ct. 2536, 467 U.S. 493, 81 L.Ed.2d 425, rehearing denied 105 S.Ct. 20, 468 U.S. 1224, 82 L.Ed.2d 915, on remand.

Offenses of theft, safecracking, and breaking and entering were of dissimilar import and thus defendant could be convicted and sentenced for each of those offenses for a single course of conduct. State v. Evans (Ohio App. 1 Dist., Hamilton, 09-27-2002) No. C-020081, 2002-Ohio-5090, 2002 WL 31127509, Unreported. Criminal Law ⟹ 29(10)

Theft, safecracking, and breaking and entering were not allied offenses of similar import, and thus convictions for each could be had, even without finding of separate animus for each, given that, abstract comparison of elements indicated that theft required for conviction purpose to deprive owner of property, which was not required by safecracking or breaking and entering statutes, safecracking required showing of knowingly entering or forcing entry into safe, something not required in theft or breaking and entering statutes, and breaking and entering statute required showing of trespass, which was something not required in theft or safecracking statutes. State v. Tierney (Ohio App. 8 Dist., Cuyahoga, 05-23-2002) No. 78847, 2002-Ohio-2607, 2002 WL 1041727, Unreported, appeal not allowed 96 Ohio St.3d 1513, 775 N.E.2d 856, 2002-Ohio-4950, motion to reopen denied 2002-Ohio-6618, 2002 WL 31718863. Criminal Law ⟹ 29(11)

Defendant failed to establish that three counts of receiving stolen property for which he was convicted should have been merged into single count, under statute providing that, where same conduct by defendant can be construed to constitute two or more allied offenses of similar import, indictment may contain counts for all such offenses, but defendant may be convicted of only one, as record did not indicate that defendant received, retained, or disposed of property at same time and in same transaction, but record did reveal that defendant attempted to dispose of one stolen check in a separate transaction, while retaining other stolen checks in vehicle. State v. Early (Ohio App. 10 Dist., Franklin, 05-23-2002) No. 01AP-1106, 2002-Ohio-2590, 2002 WL 1290843, Unreported. Criminal Law ⟹ 30

Trial court did not err in sentencing defendant on counts of grand theft under RC 2913.02 and in trafficking food stamps under RC 2913.46(A) when the elements of the two crimes do not correspond to such a degree that commission of one crime will result in the commission of the other. State v Hill, No. 62791 (8th Dist Ct App, Cuyahoga, 6–17–93).

Where it appears from a presentence investigation report that a defendant's unlicensed sale of securities may have been the vehicle that he used to accomplish the offense of grand theft, and the relationship between the offenses cannot be conclusively determined from the undisputed facts recited in connection with the guilty plea proceedings, the trial court must hold a hearing to determine whether the offenses are allied offenses of similar import even though the defendant has not raised the issue before sentencing. State v Hartwell, No. 11422 (2d Dist Ct App, Montgomery, 12–13–89).

The offenses of theft of drugs, RC 2925.21(C), and aggravated robbery RC 2911.01(A)(1) are allied offenses of similar import, but conviction on both charges is permitted where the offenses were committed simultaneously at the same location but with separate objectives, theft to obtain cash and theft to obtain prescription drugs. State v Clements, No. C–880172 (1st Dist Ct App, Hamilton, 5–3–89).

While tampering with a coin machine under RC 2911.32 requires the purpose to commit theft or defraud, burglary under RC 2911.12 requires trespass as well as the purpose to commit theft or another felony, thus, these are not allied offenses of similar import and multiple sentences may be imposed. State v Brewer, No. E–86–25 (6th Dist Ct App, Erie, 3–13–87).

Where the offense of aggravated robbery of the victim included the taking of the victim's car keys, the later committed offense of grand theft of the victim's car remains a separate offense and therefore defendant may be convicted and sentenced on both offenses. State v Tyndall, No. C–810816 (1st Dist Ct App, Hamilton, 8–25–82).

20. —— Multiple theft, specific offenses construed

Three identical counts of theft charged in indictment were not "allied offenses of similar import," and thus, statute attempting to codify common-law doctrine of merger did not apply to permit sentencing of defendant on only one of three convictions. State v. Larsen (Lawrence 1993) 89 Ohio App.3d 371, 624 N.E.2d 766. Criminal Law ⟹ 30; Sentencing And Punishment ⟹ 532

Charges of racketeering and merged charges of theft and theft in office were not allied offenses of similar import permitting conviction on only one of those counts. State v. Burge (Franklin 1993) 88 Ohio App.3d 91, 623 N.E.2d 146. Criminal Law ⟹ 29(10)

Two thefts constitute a single act motivated by a single intent and should be merged under RC

2941.25(A) where the defendant in one act steals money from two purses which belong to different persons but are left in the same car. State v. Coffman (Franklin 1984) 16 Ohio App.3d 200, 475 N.E.2d 139, 16 O.B.R. 214.

Pursuant to RC 2941.25(A), an accused cannot be convicted of four separate crimes of receiving stolen property when there are only three theft offenses originally committed, and the state offers no evidence that the defendant either participated in the commission of the theft offenses or that defendant harbored a separate animus toward each individual owner. State v. Sanders (Summit 1978) 59 Ohio App.2d 187, 392 N.E.2d 1297, 13 O.O.3d 209. Criminal Law ⚷ 29(5.5)

The act of stealing a motor vehicle containing personal property constitutes one offense and a defendant may not be additionally convicted of stealing the personalty. State v. Fischer (Clermont 1977) 52 Ohio App.2d 53, 368 N.E.2d 332, 6 O.O.3d 40.

21. —— Forgery and uttering, specific offenses construed

Defendant's convictions for one count of possessing criminal tools, one count of tampering with evidence, and thirty counts of forgery were not allied offenses of similar import, for purposes of sentencing statute, and defendant was properly sentenced for all three offenses; when compared in the abstract, offenses did not correspond to the degree that the commission of one would result in the commission of the others, and multiple violations of the same statute are not allied offenses of similar import. State v. Brewster (Ohio App. 1 Dist., Hamilton, 06-11-2004) No. C-030024, No. C-030025, 2004-Ohio-2993, 2004 WL 1284008, Unreported, motion for delayed appeal denied 103 Ohio St.3d 1490, 816 N.E.2d 1078, 2004-Ohio-5605. Sentencing And Punishment ⚷ 536

Sentence of sixteen years' imprisonment was warranted for defendant convicted of one count of possessing criminal tools, one count of tampering with evidence, and thirty counts of forgery; sentence was within statutory limits, trial court made proper findings to justify sentences imposed and properly stated its reasons for those findings, evidence revealed that defendant and his brother conducted extensive check-forging operation, defendant had a lengthy criminal record for similar offenses, and sentence was less than half of maximum time that he could have received. State v. Brewster (Ohio App. 1 Dist., Hamilton, 06-11-2004) No. C-030024, No. C-030025, 2004-Ohio-2993, 2004 WL 1284008, Unreported, motion for delayed appeal denied 103 Ohio St.3d 1490, 816 N.E.2d 1078, 2004-Ohio-5605. Sentencing And Punishment ⚷ 645

Defendant's convictions of forgery of power of attorney and of uttering power of attorney were not allied defenses that would merge, though they related to same power of attorney, where offenses occurred at different times. State v. Beehive Ltd. Partnership (Ohio App. 8 Dist., 08-02-1993) 89 Ohio App.3d 718, 627 N.E.2d 592, motion overruled 68 Ohio St.3d 1429, 624 N.E.2d 1066. Criminal Law ⚷ 30

Under the definitions of forgery and uttering found in RC 2913.01, one who forges may not necessarily utter and one who utters a forged document need not have created the spurious writing; thus, a defendant may be convicted of both forgery and uttering in connection with the same transaction. State v. McGhee (Cuyahoga 1987) 37 Ohio App.3d 54, 523 N.E.2d 864. Forgery ⚷ 4; Forgery ⚷ 16

Forgery and uttering are not allied offenses where the defendant forges a check then later presents it to her bank for payment. State v. Hunter (Cuyahoga 1983) 12 Ohio App.3d 75, 466 N.E.2d 183, 12 O.B.R. 273.

Receiving stolen checks and forgery of checks are not allied offenses of similar import. State v Byrd, No. 87–CA–28 (2d Dist Ct App, Greene, 5–16–88).

22. —— Weapons violations and other offenses, specific offenses construed

Defendant's actions in committing aggravated murder, attempted aggravated murder, rape, and aggravated robbery constituted separate transactions rather than same act or transaction, thus subjecting defendant to consecutive sentences on firearm specifications applicable to each offense; acts involved two victims, shot in different places, defendant shot and killed murder victim, the mother of his child, because he believed that she had been with other men, and defendant raped both victims with expressed intent to give himself something to remember while in prison and robbed both victims to mislead police as to motive of their attacker. State v. Martin (Ohio App. 2 Dist., Montgomery, 09-02-2005) No. 20516, 2005-Ohio-4602, 2005 WL 2107858, Unreported, appeal allowed 107 Ohio St.3d 1681, 839 N.E.2d 402, 2005-Ohio-6480. Sentencing And Punishment ⚷ 599; Sentencing And Punishment ⚷ 605; Sentencing And Punishment ⚷ 611

Trial court improperly imposed three consecutive three-year terms of actual incarceration for firearm specifications on underlying counts of felonious assault and improperly discharging a firearm at or into a habitation; evidence established that defendant fired two shots in rapid succession at an inhabited dwelling in response to inhabitants' verbal attempts at thwarting an attempted burglary, and three felony convictions arose from a single transaction, and thus, defendant could be sentenced to only one three-year term of actual incarceration. State v. Gray (Ohio App. 10 Dist., Franklin, 09-01-2005) No. 04AP-938, 2005-Ohio-4563, 2005 WL 2100595, Unreported. Sentencing And Punishment ⚷ 604

Elements of municipal offense of possessing semiautomatic firearm and state offense of possessing firearm while under a disability do not correspond to such a degree that commission of one crime will result in commission of the other, and thus the two are not allied offenses of similar import for which only one conviction is allowed based on the same conduct; person convicted under ordinance who has no prior criminal record will not have violated weapons-under-disability statute, while person under a disability can violate statute by possessing a firearm which is not semiautomatic. State v. Moore (Ohio App. 1 Dist., 04-24-1996) 110 Ohio App.3d 649, 675 N.E.2d 13, dismissed, appeal not allowed 77 Ohio St.3d 1444, 671 N.E.2d 1283. Criminal Law ⚿ 29(15)

Firearm specification is not a separate offense and, thus, cannot be an "allied offense of similar import" for purposes of statute providing that, where the same conduct by defendant can be construed to constitute "allied offenses of similar import," indictment may contain counts for all such offenses, but defendant may be convicted of only one. State v. Blankenship (Ohio App. 12 Dist., 04-17-1995) 102 Ohio App.3d 534, 657 N.E.2d 559, dismissed, appeal not allowed 73 Ohio St.3d 1426, 652 N.E.2d 799, denial of post-conviction relief affirmed 1995 WL 746232, dismissed, appeal not allowed 75 Ohio St.3d 1484, 664 N.E.2d 536, denial of post-conviction relief affirmed 74 Ohio St.3d 522, 660 N.E.2d 448, 1996-Ohio-58, denial of post-conviction relief affirmed 1997 WL 700073, dismissed, appeal not allowed 81 Ohio St.3d 1466, 690 N.E.2d 1287. Sentencing And Punishment ⚿ 139

Unlawful transactions in weapons, in violation of RC 2923.20(A)(1) and possession of firearms with purpose to engage in unlawful transactions in weapons, in violation of RC 2923.20(A)(2) are allied offenses of similar import. State v. Wolfe (Lorain 1988) 51 Ohio App.3d 215, 555 N.E.2d 689. Criminal Law ⚿ 29(15)

The simultaneous possession of weapons by one under disability is but one offense; however, assuming arguendo that possession of each weapon constitutes a separate offense, the offenses are allied offenses of similar import pursuant to RC 2941.25(A). State v. Thompson (Summit 1988) 46 Ohio App.3d 157, 546 N.E.2d 441, dismissed 38 Ohio St.3d 702, 532 N.E.2d 1317, denial of post-conviction relief affirmed. Criminal Law ⚿ 29(15)

Having a weapon under disability in violation of RC 2923.13 and unlawful possession of a dangerous ordnance in violation of RC 2923.17 do not constitute allied offenses of similar import because the commission of one offense does not automatically result in the commission of the other offense. State v. Hines (Clark 1987) 39 Ohio App.3d 129, 529 N.E.2d 1286. Criminal Law ⚿ 29(15)

For committing robbery with a shotgun, a defendant may be sentenced for aggravated robbery, possession of criminal tools, and unlawful possession of dangerous ordnance. State v. Houston (Cuyahoga 1985) 26 Ohio App.3d 26, 498 N.E.2d 188, 26 O.B.R. 195.

The judgment of the court of appeals is reversed on authority of State v Preston, 23 OS(3d) 64, 23 OBR 197, 419 NE(2d) 685 (1986). State v. McKinley (Ohio 1986) 24 Ohio St.3d 208, 494 N.E.2d 1113, 24 O.B.R. 434.

Where an armed robber's pistol is struck from his hand by the victim after the robbery, recovered by the robber, and fired at the victim, the aggravated robbery and the felonious assault are not allied offenses of similar import. State v. Preston (Ohio 1986) 23 Ohio St.3d 64, 491 N.E.2d 685, 23 O.B.R. 197.

A robbery of several customers of a bar constitutes a single transaction within the meaning of RC 2929.71(B), and therefore only one three-year term of actual incarceration is permissible, even though there is a separate animus as to each victim, within the meaning of RC 2941.25(B). State v. Hughley (Trumbull 1984) 20 Ohio App.3d 77, 484 N.E.2d 758, 20 O.B.R. 97.

Because RC 2929.71 is a sentencing provision which creates no separate offense, a defendant may be convicted of both aggravated robbery and a firearm specification without violating the prohibition of RC 2941.25 against conviction of allied offenses of similar import. State v. Loines (Cuyahoga 1984) 20 Ohio App.3d 69, 484 N.E.2d 727, 20 O.B.R. 88.

Since a firearm specification pursuant to RC 2929.71 does not charge an offense separate from the related felony, the specification and felony are not allied offenses of similar import within the meaning of RC 2941.25. State v. Vasquez (Lucas 1984) 18 Ohio App.3d 92, 481 N.E.2d 640, 18 O.B.R. 455.

The offenses of carrying a concealed weapon, RC 2923.12, and having a weapon while under disability, RC 2923.13, are not allied offenses of similar import within the meaning of RC 2941.25(A). State v. Broadus (Franklin 1984) 14 Ohio App.3d 443, 472 N.E.2d 50, 14 O.B.R. 563. Criminal Law ⚿ 29(15)

Carrying a concealed knife, a misdemeanor in violation of RC 2923.12, and carrying a concealed loaded firearm, a felony in violation of RC 2923.12, are "offenses of dissimilar import" within the meaning of RC 2941.25(B). State v. Wilkin (Montgomery 1983) 11 Ohio App.3d 149, 463 N.E.2d 650, 11 O.B.R. 231.

The crimes of carrying a concealed weapon, RC 2923.12, and having weapons while under disability, RC 2923.13, are not allied offenses of similar import under RC 2941.25(A), and may be committed separately and with a separate animus under RC 2941.25(B). State v. Rice (Ohio 1982) 69 Ohio St.2d 422, 433 N.E.2d 175, 23 O.O.3d 374.

The offenses of carrying concealed weapons and possessing criminal tools do not constitute allied offenses of similar import pursuant to RC 2941.25(A) as a matter of law even in situations where dangerous ordnance is involved. State v. Moncrief (Cuyahoga 1980) 69 Ohio App.2d 51, 431 N.E.2d 336, 23 O.O.3d 61. Criminal Law ⚿ 29(15)

The offenses of possessing criminal tools and having weapons while under disability do not constitute allied offenses of similar import pursuant to RC 2941.25(A). State v. Moncrief (Cuyahoga 1980) 69 Ohio App.2d 51, 431 N.E.2d 336, 23 O.O.3d 61.

The offenses of carrying a concealed weapon and having a firearm while under disability are not allied offenses of similar import, and a defendant can be convicted of both offenses. State v Grooms, No. CA–1430 (4th Dist Ct App, Scioto, 12–7–83).

23. —— Arson, specific offenses construed

Defendant's conviction for aggravated arson for creating substantial risk of serious physical harm to a person, and conviction for aggravated arson for causing physical harm to an occupied structure were of dissimilar import, such that separate sentences were permissible; although the two counts involved the same fire set by defendant, each offense required proof of an element that the other did not. State v. Campbell (Ohio App. 1 Dist., Hamilton, 12-30-2003) No. C-020822, 2003-Ohio-7149, 2003 WL 23022038, Unreported, appeal not allowed 102 Ohio St.3d 1412, 806 N.E.2d 563, 2004-Ohio-1763. Sentencing And Punishment ⚷ 517

Aggravated arson and felonious assault were not two allied offenses of similar import as the commission of one offense could have occurred without commission of the other, and thus, trial court did not err by imposing consecutive sentences for the offenses; felonious assault did not have to be committed by fire or explosion, and involved activity directed to a specific individual or individuals, whereas, aggravated arson was necessarily committed with fire or an explosive and did not require that offender cause or attempt to cause harm to any person. State v. Kelly (Ohio App. 10 Dist., Franklin, 10-24-2002) No. 02AP-195, 2002-Ohio-5797, 2002 WL 31389009, Unreported, motion for delayed appeal denied 98 Ohio St.3d 1459, 783 N.E.2d 519, 2003-Ohio-644, reconsideration denied 98 Ohio St.3d 1516, 786 N.E.2d 65, 2003-Ohio-1572, appeal not allowed 100 Ohio St.3d 1433, 797 N.E.2d 512, 2003-Ohio-5396. Sentencing And Punishment ⚷ 557

Arson of another's property and arson with purpose to defraud are not "allied offenses of similar import" which prohibit conviction of the defendant under both offenses. State v. Saah (Cuyahoga 1990) 67 Ohio App.3d 86, 585 N.E.2d 999. Criminal Law ⚷ 29(5.5)

Causing physical harm to an occupied structure by means of fire and causing the deaths of victims located within the structure are offenses of dissimilar import; the two are not merged into one offense. State v. Willey (Guernsey 1981) 5 Ohio App.3d 86, 449 N.E.2d 471, 5 O.B.R. 200.

Three counts of aggravated arson with which defendant was charged were not "allied offenses of similar import," and therefore were not subject to merger, where indictment alleged conduct against two different victims and an occupied structure, and further indicated that only one victim had been bound prior to fire. State v. Garcia (Ohio App. 8 Dist., Cuyahoga, 08-15-2002) No. 79917, 2002-Ohio-4179, 2002 WL 1874535, Unreported, appeal not allowed 98 Ohio St.3d 1411, 781 N.E.2d 1019, 2003-Ohio-60. Criminal Law ⚷ 30

Felony murder and aggravated arson are not allied offenses of similar import where the case involves setting fire to the victim who is sitting in a car which is distinguished from setting fire to the car with the victim inside. State v. Brown (Ohio App. 2 Dist., Montgomery, 01-25-2002) No. 18643, 2002-Ohio-277, 2002 WL 91088, Unreported.

Multiple convictions and sentences for attempted arson will be upheld where the defendant made three separate offers to three different individuals to burn his house, even though all three attempts arose from the same animus. State v Giles, No. CA–1011 (5th Dist Ct App, Ashland, 2–24–93).

24. —— Multiple concealed weapons, specific offenses construed

Pursuant to RC 2909.01, another person does not have to be present in the house before it will be considered an occupied structure and so the offense of improper discharge can be committed without the element of a knowing attempt to cause harm to another person; thus the offenses of improperly discharging a firearm at or into a habitation and felonious assault are not allied offenses of similar import. State v. Mallet (Ohio App. 8 Dist., Cuyahoga, 08-17-2000) No. 76608, 2000 WL 1176880, Unreported, dismissed, appeal not allowed 90 Ohio St.3d 1490, 739 N.E.2d 815, appeal after new sentencing hearing 2001 WL 1456479.

When defendant conceals three weapons in one location at one time, his conduct is essentially one continuous, indivisible act, and a conviction of the defendant of three separate counts of carrying concealed weapons conflicts with RC 2941.25(A). State v. Woods (Cuyahoga 1982) 8 Ohio App.3d 56, 455 N.E.2d 1289, 8 O.B.R. 87.

Where the defendant placed a plastic bag containing two handguns in the glove compartment of a car, he can be convicted of only one count of carrying a concealed weapon since his motive must have been to conceal both weapons simultaneously. State v. Moore (Hamilton 1982) 7 Ohio App.3d 187, 454 N.E.2d 980, 7 O.B.R. 234.

25. —— Possession for sale and sale, specific offenses construed

Trafficking in cocaine and possessing cocaine are not allied offenses of similar import, and thus, defendant may be convicted of both offenses; possession offense requires proof that individual possessed or used cocaine, trafficking offense requires proof that individual sold or offered to sell cocaine, it is possible to possess cocaine without offering it for sale, and it is possible to sell or offer to sell cocaine without having it in one's possession. State v. Fair (Ohio App. 8 Dist., Cuyahoga, 06-10-2004) No. 82278, 2004-Ohio-2971, 2004 WL 1277153, Unreported, stay granted 103 Ohio St.3d 1425, 814 N.E.2d 489, 2004-Ohio-4524, appeal allowed 103 Ohio St.3d 1491, 816 N.E.2d 1079, 2004-Ohio-5605, affirmed 109 Ohio St.3d 54, 846 N.E.2d 1, 2006-Ohio-855, reconsideration denied 109 Ohio St.3d 1427, 846 N.E.2d 536, 2006-Ohio-1967. Criminal Law ⚷ 29(8)

Offering to sell a controlled substance under RC 2925.03(A)(1) and knowingly selling a counterfeit controlled substance under RC 2925.37(B) are not allied offenses of similar import, nor is RC 2925.37(B) a special provision that must prevail over the general provision of RC 2925.03(A)(1). State v Duette, No. 13502, 1993 WL 125449 (2d Dist Ct App, Montgomery, 4–20–93).

Where defendant was found to be in possession of plastic bag containing over thirty rocks of crack cocaine, trial court could convict defendant of both drug trafficking and possessing drug paraphernalia since plastic bag was deemed "a container or device for storing or concealing a controlled substance" under RC 2925.14(A)(10), and the two crimes are not allied offenses as a bulk amount of drugs need not be in a container pursuant to RC 2925.14(A)(10). State v Harris, Nos. 92CA005429+, 1993 WL 120346 (9th Dist Ct App, Lorain, 4–21–93).

Statutory elements of trafficking of marijuana and possession of marijuana did not correspond to extent required to prohibit multiple convictions on the charges. State v. McIntosh (Ohio App. 1 Dist., 08-31-2001) 145 Ohio App.3d 567, 763 N.E.2d 704, appeal not allowed 94 Ohio St.3d 1411, 759 N.E.2d 787, appeal not allowed 96 Ohio St.3d 1488, 774 N.E.2d 763, 2002-Ohio-4478, denial of post-conviction relief affirmed in part, reversed in part 2003-Ohio-3824, 2003 WL 21673323. Criminal Law ⚷ 29(1)

For purposes of sentencing, two separate counts charging defendant with possession of marijuana on different dates merged, so as to prohibit sentencing for but one count, where both counts involved same marijuana, elements for possession were identical and part of same continuing pattern of conduct by defendant, and facts did not demonstrate a separate animus. State v. McIntosh (Ohio App. 1 Dist., 08-31-2001) 145 Ohio App.3d 567, 763 N.E.2d 704, appeal not allowed 94 Ohio St.3d 1411, 759 N.E.2d 787, appeal not allowed 96 Ohio St.3d 1488, 774 N.E.2d 763, 2002-Ohio-4478, denial of post-conviction relief affirmed in part, reversed in part 2003-Ohio-3824, 2003 WL 21673323. Criminal Law ⚷ 30

Elements of possessing illegal drug and offering to sell illegal drug are sufficiently different so as not to constitute allied offenses of similar import. State v. Hankins (Ohio App. 3 Dist., 05-25-1993) 89 Ohio App.3d 567, 626 N.E.2d 965, dismissed, jurisdictional motion overruled 68 Ohio St.3d 1419, 624 N.E.2d 193. Criminal Law ⚷ 29(8)

Trial judge's comments from the bench at time of sentencing that possession of illegal drugs and selling illegal drugs were allied offenses of similar import were not assignable as error and were not reviewable by Court of Appeals, given that trial court's journal entry made no finding that offenses were allied and of similar import. State v. Hankins (Ohio App. 3 Dist., 05-25-1993) 89 Ohio App.3d 567, 626 N.E.2d 965, dismissed, jurisdictional motion overruled 68 Ohio St.3d 1419, 624 N.E.2d 193. Criminal Law ⚷ 1111(5)

Convictions for drug trafficking in the distribution of cocaine under RC 2925.03(A)(2) and possession of cocaine in an amount exceeding the bulk amount but less than three times that amount under RC 2925.03(A)(4) do not constitute allied offenses of similar import under RC 2941.25 since RC 2925.03(A)(2) imposes the additional element that possession of the controlled substance is incident to preparation for shipment, transportation, delivery, or distribution of the drug through a sale that is not present in RC 2925.03(A)(4). State v. Jordan (Cuyahoga 1992) 73 Ohio App.3d 524, 597 N.E.2d 1165, dismissed, jurisdictional motion overruled 64 Ohio St.3d 1413, 593 N.E.2d 4.

The charges of possession and transportation of a controlled substance stemming from a single transaction involving the same type and quantity of drugs constitute allied offenses of similar import for which only one sentence may be imposed. State v. Jennings (Hamilton 1987) 42 Ohio App.3d 179, 537 N.E.2d 685, dismissed, jurisdictional motion overruled 61 Ohio St.3d 1426, 575 N.E.2d 215. Criminal Law ⚷ 29(8)

Where a defendant is charged with the possession for sale of a narcotic drug in violation of RC 3719.20(A), and with the sale of a narcotic drug in violation of RC 3719.20(B), and the facts demonstrate that both charges are based upon a single sale and involve the same parties and the same type and quantity of drugs, and it is not proven that the defendant possessed a quantity of any type of narcotic drug in excess of the amount sold, the defendant may be indicted for both offenses but may be convicted of only one. State v. Roberts (Ohio 1980) 62 Ohio St.2d 170, 405 N.E.2d 247, 16 O.O.3d 201, certiorari denied 101 S.Ct. 227, 449 U.S. 879, 66 L.Ed.2d 102. Criminal Law ⚷ 29(8)

26. Miscellaneous offenses

Imposition of separate sentences upon convictions for attempted receiving stolen property and of possession of cocaine was warranted, as charges out of which convictions arose were not allied offenses of similar import. State v. Kelly (Ohio App. 2 Dist., Greene, 06-17-2005) No. 2004 CA 122, 2005-Ohio-3058, 2005 WL 1414446, Unreported. Sentencing And Punishment ⚷ 532

Offenses for which defendant was convicted, breaking and entering and receiving stolen property, were not allied offenses of similar import, and thus, defendant's prosecution for such offenses did not violate his right of protection against double jeopardy; evidence allowed conclusion that breaking and entering was accomplished at time of entry and that a new and different crime took place when theft within nursery was committed, and offenses had elements which did not correspond to such degree that commission of one would have resulted in commission of the other. State v. Judd (Ohio App. 5 Dist., Delaware, 05-17-2005) No. 04CAA07053, 2005-Ohio-2549, 2005 WL 1208841, Unreported. Double Jeopardy ⚷ 144

Defendant's three offenses of intimidation involving three different victims even though arising from one course of contract, were offenses of dissimilar import as a matter of law. State v. Wilhelm (Ohio App. 5 Dist., Knox, 10-15-2004) No. 03-CA-25, No. 03-CA-26, 2004-Ohio-5522, 2004 WL 2335192, Unreported. Criminal Law ⚷ 29(5.5)

Four counts of criminal nonsupport to which defendant pled guilty, which arose from his failure to pay child support for each of his four children, were not allied offenses of similar import; defendant's failure to pay child support separately affected each of the four children. State v. Ladson (Ohio App. 8 Dist., Cuyahoga, 06-10-2004) No. 83209, 2004-Ohio-2973, 2004 WL 1277176, Unreported. Criminal Law ⚷ 29(5.5)

Offenses of intimidation and retaliation were not allied offenses of similar import, and thus defendant could be convicted and sentenced for both offenses; intimidation required some threat or coercion intended to inhibit future activity, and retaliation required action taken in return for past activity. State v. Solomon (Ohio App. 3 Dist., Marion, 06-01-2004) No. 9-03-58, 2004-Ohio-2795, 2004 WL 1191966, Unreported, appeal not allowed 105 Ohio St.3d 1466, 824 N.E.2d 93, 2005-Ohio-1024. Criminal Law ⚷ 29(5.5)

Trial court was not required to merge convictions for engaging in pattern of corrupt activity and conspiracy to engage in pattern of corrupt activity for purposes of sentencing; General Assembly had specifically provided for separate punishments. State v. DeMastry (Ohio App. 5 Dist., 10-17-2003) 155 Ohio App.3d 110, 799 N.E.2d 229, 2003-Ohio-5588, appeal not allowed 101 Ohio St.3d 1488, 805 N.E.2d 539, 2004-Ohio-1293, appeal not allowed 103 Ohio St.3d 1495, 816 N.E.2d 1081, 2004-Ohio-5605, denial of post-conviction relief affirmed 2005-Ohio-4962, 2005 WL 2300288, appeal not allowed 108 Ohio St.3d 1440, 842 N.E.2d 64, 2006-Ohio-421. Criminal Law ⚷ 30

Course-of-conduct death penalty specification was not a separate criminal offense, and thus specification could not merge with substantive offense of attempted aggravated murder. State v. Dennis (Ohio, 09-24-1997) 79 Ohio St.3d 421, 683 N.E.2d 1096, 1997-Ohio-372, denial of post-conviction relief affirmed 1997 WL 760680, dismissed, appeal not allowed 81 Ohio St.3d 1468, 690 N.E.2d 1287, certiorari denied 118 S.Ct. 1078, 522 U.S. 1128, 140 L.Ed.2d 136, habeas corpus dismissed 68 F.Supp.2d 863, affirmed 354 F.3d 511, certiorari denied 124 S.Ct. 2400, 541 U.S. 1068, 158 L.Ed.2d 971. Criminal Law ⚷ 30

Police officer could not be convicted of both tampering with evidence and tampering with records, based on single filing of false duty report; commission of one offense automatically resulted in commission of other and crimes were committed with same animus. State v. McNeeley (Cuyahoga 1988) 48 Ohio App.3d 73, 548 N.E.2d 961, cause dismissed 38 Ohio St.3d 722, 533 N.E.2d 1059. Criminal Law ⚷ 29(5.5)

Child endangering and felonious assault did not constitute allied offenses of similar import within meaning of statute providing that where same conduct by defendant can be construed to constitute two or more allied offenses of similar import, indictment or information may contain counts for all such offenses, but defendant may be convicted of only one. State v. Anderson (Hamilton 1984) 16 Ohio App.3d 251, 475 N.E.2d 492, 16 O.B.R. 275. Criminal Law ⚷ 29(9)

Defendant's convictions for 12 counts of illegally storing hazardous wastes, based on one count for each of 12 days on which such waste was illegally stored, did not constitute conviction for allied offenses of similar import, since each day of such storage constitutes a separate violation. State v. Campbell (Medina 1983) 13 Ohio App.3d 348, 469 N.E.2d 882, 13 O.B.R. 428. Criminal Law ⚷ 29(5.5)

27. Delinquency proceedings

Statute providing that a defendant may be convicted of only one allied offense of similar import does not apply to delinquency proceedings. In re Bowers (Ohio App. 11 Dist., Ashtabula, 12-13-2002) No. 2002-A-0010, 2002-Ohio-6913, 2002 WL 31813014, Unreported. Infants ⚷ 153

28. Appeal

Appellate decision holding that defendant had waived challenge to allied offenses determination by failing to raise it at trial, was law of the case, and precluded trial court from considering defendant's claim on motion to withdraw guilty plea that absence of allied offenses determination rendered involuntary his guilty plea to offenses of aggravated robbery, kidnapping, theft of a motor vehicle, and failure to comply with the order of a police officer, and thus claim would have to be pursued by motion to reopen appeal. State v. Gaston (Ohio App. 8 Dist., Cuyahoga, 10-30-2003) No. 82628, 2003-Ohio-5825, 2003 WL 22456731, Unreported. Criminal Law ⚷ 1133

Court of Appeals, reviewing trial court's denial of defendant's motion to withdraw guilty plea, lacked jurisdiction to consider defendant's claim that trial court erred in imposing consecutive sentences, without first holding hearing to determine whether any of offenses were allied, in prosecution for aggravated robbery, kidnapping, theft of a motor vehicle, and failure to comply with the order of a police officer, where defendant had raised argument concerning allied offenses in his direct appeal, so relief would have to be sought in motion to reopen appeal; ruling in defendant's favor would be inconsistent with prior appellate decision. State v. Gaston (Ohio App. 8 Dist., Cuyahoga, 10-30-2003) No. 82628, 2003-Ohio-5825, 2003 WL 22456731, Unreported. Criminal Law ⚷ 1133

Where defendant failed to raise issue of whether his offenses were allied offenses of similar import at sentencing, appellate court was not prohibited from reviewing the issue at its own discretion to address plain error or defects affecting defendant's substantial rights so where the defendant's offenses included kidnapping and robbery, under circumstances of potentially similar import, the absence of a determination hearing was plain error and the matter was remanded for the limited purpose of conducting a proper hearing to determine the applicable sentencing provisions. State v. Latson (Ohio App. 8 Dist., 10-12-1999) 133 Ohio App.3d 475, 728 N.E.2d 465, dismissed, appeal not allowed 88 Ohio St.3d 1412, 723 N.E.2d 118.

Claim that trial court erred by entering judgment of conviction for violating two statutes which established allied offenses of similar import, which thus merged as matter of law, could constitute plain error, and thus would be considered on appeal even though it had not been raised in trial court, and would ordinarily be waived. State v. Houston (Ohio App. 10 Dist., 08-12-1997) 122 Ohio App.3d 334, 701 N.E.2d 764. Criminal Law ⚷ 1030(3)

Defendant who failed to object at trial to his conviction and sentence on basis that offenses were allied offenses of similar import resulted in waiver of allied offenses claim on appeal. State v. Perkins (Ohio App. 8 Dist., 03-16-1994) 93 Ohio App.3d 672, 639 N.E.2d 833, dismissed, appeal not allowed 70 Ohio St.3d 1425, 638 N.E.2d 87. Criminal Law ⚷ 1030(3)

Defendant's failure to raise, in her motion for bill of particulars, a claim that bill was required because offenses charged in indictment were "allied offenses of similar import" precluded Court of Appeals from addressing issue on appeal, absent plain error. State v. Brown (Ohio App. 11 Dist., 07-12-1993) 90 Ohio App.3d 674, 630 N.E.2d 397. Criminal Law ⚷ 1044.1(2)

If a defendant does not object at trial that his conviction and sentence on ten counts of engaging in a pattern of corrupt activity and theft in office violated RC 2941.25(A), which requires the merger of allied offenses of similar import, he waives the argument on appeal. State v. Burge (Franklin 1992) 82 Ohio App.3d 244, 611 N.E.2d 866, dismissed, jurisdictional motion overruled 65 Ohio St.3d 1495, 605 N.E.2d 949, reconsideration denied 88 Ohio App.3d 91, 623 N.E.2d 146, dismissed, jurisdictional motion overruled 67 Ohio St.3d 1479, 620 N.E.2d 852.

Defendant waived all but plain error in his appeal on issue of allied offenses of similar import by not raising it when he was convicted of possession of criminal tools and illegal processing of drug documents or in his first appeal of his sentence. State v. Denham (Ohio App. 2 Dist., Greene, 08-02-2002) No. 2001 CA 105, 2002-Ohio-3912, 2002 WL 1769798, Unreported. Criminal Law ⚷ 1030(2)

Defendant's concession, in first appeal from convictions and consecutive sentences for kidnapping and robbery, that those offenses were not allied offenses of similar import and thus did not merge for sentencing purposes, did not preclude him from arguing, on appeal from resentencing to the same consecutive sentences on remand, that the offenses were allied for sentencing purposes. State v. Brahler (Ohio App. 8 Dist., Cuyahoga, 05-09-2002) No. 79710, 2002-Ohio-2252, 2002 WL 973093, Unreported, motion for delayed appeal denied 99 Ohio St.3d 1466, 791 N.E.2d 982, 2003-Ohio-3669. Criminal Law ⚷ 1180

PROCEDURE

2941.26 Variance

When, on the trial of an indictment or information, there appears to be a variance between the statement in such indictment or information and the evidence offered in proof thereof, in the Christian name or surname, or other description of a person therein named or described, or in the name or description of a matter or thing therein named or described, such variance is not ground for an acquittal of the defendant unless the court before which the trial is had finds that such variance is material to the merits of the case or may be prejudicial to the defendant.

(1953 H 1, eff. 10–1–53; GC 13437–25)

Historical and Statutory Notes

Pre–1953 H 1 Amendments: 113 v 168, Ch 16, § 25

Library References

Indictment and Information ⚷164 to 184.
Westlaw Topic No. 210.

Research References

Encyclopedias

OH Jur. 3d Criminal Law § 2414, Variance.

OH Jur. 3d Criminal Law § 2415, Names.

OH Jur. 3d Criminal Law § 2418, Manner or Means of Committing Offense.

OH Jur. 3d Criminal Law § 2419, Description of Property; Place of Offense.

Treatises and Practice Aids

Katz, Giannelli, Blair and Lipton, Baldwin's Ohio Practice, Criminal Law, § 40:8, Variance Between Charge and Proof.

Notes of Decisions

Harmless variance 3
Material to merits 2

Variance between charge and proof 1

---

1. Variance between charge and proof

Where an indictment under RC 2921.14 for conspiracy to defraud specifies the manner of defrauding relied upon as the defrauding part of that conspiracy, the proof of a manner of defrauding that is not even suggested by any allegations of the indictment or by any bill of particulars thereunder will necessarily prejudice the accused. State v. Lewis (Ohio 1970) 21 Ohio St.2d 203, 257 N.E.2d 59, 50 O.O.2d 441. Conspiracy ⚷ 43(12)

Where an indictment for a conspiracy to defraud under RC 2921.14 specifies the manner or manners of defrauding relied upon as the defrauding part of that conspiracy, a conviction cannot be based upon evidence only establishing a manner of defrauding other than that so specified. State v. Lewis (Ohio 1970) 21 Ohio St.2d 203, 257 N.E.2d 59, 50 O.O.2d 441. Conspiracy ⚷ 43(12)

An indictment charging the obtaining of money by false representations is not proved by proof of the obtaining of a check for the specified amount. State v. Pittman (Ohio 1967) 9 Ohio St.2d 186, 224 N.E.2d 913, 38 O.O.2d 420.

That defendant, in inducing a hotel clerk to cash a check by falsely representing himself as a specific registered guest of the hotel, acknowledged that he had no account at the bank in question but asserted that he would redeem the obligation upon receipt of money the next morning did not constitute a defense to prosecution for forging a check. State v. Smith (Columbiana 1958) 159 N.E.2d 248, 80 Ohio Law Abs. 321.

Indictment for accepting money and proof of receiving check not fatal variance. Fleming v. State (Ohio 1930) 122 Ohio St. 156, 171 N.E. 27, certiorari denied 51 S.Ct. 39, 282 U.S. 800, 75 L.Ed. 719.

The evidence must show accused assaulted and killed one "Percy Stuckey alias Frank McCormick" if so charged in the indictment; and to sustain a verdict it must be shown that Frank McCormick, and Percy Stuckey were the same person and failure to so prove is not excused or rendered harmless by the curative provisions of statute. (But see State v Schaeffer, 96 OS 215, 117 NE 220 (1917).) Goodlove v. State (Ohio 1910) 82 Ohio St. 365, 92 N.E. 491, 8 Ohio Law Rep. 119, 19 Am.Ann.Cas. 893.

No variance exists where evidence shows accused personally conducted a bucket shop for which indictment charges him as permitting such place to be kept. State v. Murray (Ohio 1910) 82 Ohio St. 305, 92 N.E. 467, 8 Ohio Law Rep. 104.

Where in prosecution under RS 1892, § 6816 (See GC 12413, 12414), for carnally knowing and abusing female under 16 years with her consent, evidence established carnal knowledge and ages of parties, evidence tending to show want of consent of female does not constitute fatal variance. State v. Carl (Ohio 1905) 71 Ohio St. 259, 73 N.E. 463, 2 Ohio Law Rep. 372. Indictment And Information ⚷ 171; Rape ⚷ 35(4)

2. Material to merits

Where an indictment charged the defendant with operating a motor vehicle without the owner's consent and with stealing the vehicle, evidence that an officer saw the vehicle entering a parking lot from an alley is sufficient to establish operation on a public road and failure to prove value is immaterial, but failure to prove ownership requires a reversal of the conviction for operating the vehicle without the owner's consent (but not of the stealing conviction). State v. Givens (Franklin 1953) 133 N.E.2d 625, 72 Ohio Law Abs. 62, appeal dismissed 160 Ohio St. 172, 114 N.E.2d 729, 51 O.O. 385.

In a prosecution for selling intoxicating liquor wherein exactness of the time of the offense was not essential, it was the right of the state to prove the alleged acts on or about the time and the date formally charged, and defendant in the presentation of his defense had at least an equal right to depart from the exact time and date charged by the information or indictment or the testimony offered in support thereof. Tesca v. State (Ohio 1923) 108 Ohio St. 287, 140 N.E. 629, 1 Ohio Law Abs. 485, 1 Ohio Law Abs. 877, 21 Ohio Law Rep. 150, 21 Ohio Law Rep. 152. Indictment And Information ⚷ 176; Intoxicating Liquors ⚷ 223(4); Intoxicating Liquors ⚷ 223(5)

A variance material to the merits relates to matters that need to be pleaded and proved and not to unnecessary description; and if an indictment charges false pretenses in getting money to be invested in fictitious stock and the proof is that it was obtained as a loan, the variance is not material. Tingue v. State (Ohio 1914) 90 Ohio St. 368, 108 N.E. 222, 12 Ohio Law Rep. 88, 12 Ohio Law Rep. 556, Am.Ann.Cas. 1916C, 1156.

A decision of the trial judge on a question as to the materiality of a variance between an allegation of an indictment and the evidence offered in its support may be reversed if erroneous and prejudicial to the accused; and it may be the subject of an exception by the prosecuting attorney, with a view to obtaining a decision which shall determine the law for the government of similar cases. State v. Buechler (Ohio 1897) 57 Ohio St. 95, 38 W.L.B. 288, 48 N.E. 507. Criminal Law ⚷ 1024(10)

3. Harmless variance

An indictment charging larceny of nine "rungs" of a value of $360, in connection with and in the same count with a charge of burglary, is not fatal to burglary or larceny charge, where evidence shows that property stolen was not nine "rungs," but nine "rugs," of the value of $360. State v. Brozich (Ohio 1923) 108 Ohio St. 559, 141 N.E. 491, 1 Ohio Law Abs. 812, 2 Ohio Law Abs. 69, 21 Ohio Law Rep. 315, 21 Ohio Law Rep. 320.

A variance was not deemed fatal unless trial court made a finding that it was material to the merits or would be prejudicial. State v. Shoemaker (Ohio 1917) 96 Ohio St. 570, 117 N.E. 958, 15 Ohio Law Rep. 246, 15 Ohio Law Rep. 427.

The purpose of pleading an alias is to further advise the defendant of the identity of the person killed, to advise him that such person was known by different names, and to qualify that testimony of the different witnesses who may have known him under these different names; in no case is a mere alias a matter of such necessity and indispensable description that failure to prove the same should be considered by a court as prejudicial to the substantive merits of the case. State v. Schaeffer (Ohio 1917) 96 Ohio St. 215, 117 N.E. 220, 15 Ohio Law Rep. 122, Am.Ann.Cas. 1918E, 1137.

2941.27 Proof of dilatory plea

No plea in abatement, or other dilatory plea to the indictment or information, shall be received by any court unless the party offering such plan proves the truth thereof by affidavit, or by some other sworn evidence.

(1953 H 1, eff. 10–1–53; GC 13437–26)

Historical and Statutory Notes

Pre–1953 H 1 Amendments: 113 v 168, Ch 16, § 26

Cross References

Pleadings and motions before trial, defenses and objections, Crim R 12

Library References

Criminal Law ⚷277.

Westlaw Topic No. 110.

2941.28 Misjoinder of parties or offenses

No indictment or information shall be quashed, set aside, or dismissed for any of the following defects:

(A) That there is a misjoinder of the parties accused;

(B) That there is a misjoinder of the offenses charged in the indictment or information, or duplicity therein;

(C) That any uncertainty exists therein.

If the court is of the opinion that either defect referred to in division (A) or (B) of this section exists in any indictment or information, it may sever such indictment or information into separate indictments or informations or into separate counts.

If the court is of the opinion that the defect referred to in division (C) of this section exists in the indictment or information, it may order the indictment or information amended to cure such defect, provided no change is made in the name or identity of the crime charged.

(1953 H 1, eff. 10–1–53; GC 13437–27)

Historical and Statutory Notes

Pre–1953 H 1 Amendments: 113 v 168, Ch 16, § 27

Cross References

Joinder of offenses and defendants, Crim R 8

Relief from prejudicial joinder, Crim R 14

Library References

Criminal Law ⚷620, 622.

Indictment and Information ⚷124, 126.

Westlaw Topic Nos. 110, 210.

C.J.S. Criminal Law §§ 558 to 564.

Research References

Encyclopedias

OH Jur. 3d Criminal Law § 2404, Indefiniteness or Uncertainty.

OH Jur. 3d Criminal Law § 2422, Amendments to Cure Defects.

Treatises and Practice Aids

Katz, Giannelli, Blair and Lipton, Baldwin's Ohio Practice, Criminal Law, § 57:5, Severance—Criminal Rule 14.

Katz, Giannelli, Blair and Lipton, Baldwin's Ohio Practice, Criminal Law, § 57:10, Duplicity.

Katz, Giannelli, Blair and Lipton, Baldwin's Ohio Practice, Criminal Law, § 57:12, Multiplicity and Double Jeopardy.

Hennenberg & Reinhart, Ohio Criminal Defense Motions F 14.171, Objections to Magistrate's Report and Recommendation Dismissing Petition-Double Jeopardy.

Notes of Decisions

1. Misjoinder of offenses

Where an indictment contains three counts, as follows: (1) forging a check; (2) uttering a forged instrument; and (3) carrying a concealed weapon, to wit, a blackjack; the third of said counts is not connected together with the other two counts in its commission and is in a different class of crimes or offenses from the first two counts; and the indictment is therefore violative of RC 2941.04 and is subject to the remedy provided in RC 2941.28. State v. Atkinson (Ohio 1965) 4 Ohio St.2d 19, 211 N.E.2d 665, 33 O.O.2d 226.

2941.29 Time for objecting to defect in indictment

No indictment or information shall be quashed, set aside, or dismissed, or motion to quash be sustained, or any motion for delay of sentence for the purpose of review be granted, nor shall any conviction be set aside or reversed on account of any defect in form or substance of the indictment or information, unless the objection to such indictment or information, specifically stating the defect claimed, is made prior to the commencement of the trial, or at such time thereafter as the court permits.

(1953 H 1, eff. 10–1–53; GC 13437–28)

Historical and Statutory Notes

Pre–1953 H 1 Amendments: 113 v 169, Ch 16, § 28

Cross References

Effect of failure to raise defenses or objections, Crim R 12

Library References

Indictment and Information ⚷139, 144, 195.

Westlaw Topic No. 210.

Research References

Encyclopedias

OH Jur. 3d Criminal Law § 3573, Failure of Indictment, Generally.

Treatises and Practice Aids

Katz, Giannelli, Blair and Lipton, Baldwin's Ohio Practice, Criminal Law, § 42:7, Time Requirements.

Katz, Giannelli, Blair and Lipton, Baldwin's Ohio Practice, Criminal Law, § 47:4, Required Motions.

Katz, Giannelli, Blair and Lipton, Baldwin's Ohio Practice, Criminal Law, § 47:9, Waiver—Failure to Raise Issue.

Katz, Giannelli, Blair and Lipton, Baldwin's Ohio Practice, Criminal Law, § 56:17, Motion for Change of Venue.

Painter, Ohio Driving Under the Influence § 2:2, Sufficiency of Citation—Criminal Matters Generally.

Notes of Decisions

1. Jurisdictional defects

Appellate counsel's decision not to raise issue of lack of trial court's subject-matter jurisdiction due to typographical error as to amount of marijuana stated in indictment was reasonable appellate strategy and thus did not constitute ineffective assistance of counsel in prosecution for possession of drugs and possession of criminal tools, where trial counsel waived clerical error, and appellate counsel made much stronger argument that there was insufficient evidence to uphold conviction. State v. Smith (Ohio App. 8 Dist., Cuyahoga, 12-04-2002) No. 79301, 2002-Ohio-6620, 2002 WL 31718896, Unreported. Criminal Law ⚷ 641.13(7)

The failure to commence an action within one year after the violation of an ordinance or commission of an offense covered by RC 1905.33 deprives the court of jurisdiction to hear the prosecution, and if judgment is entered against the defendant it is void. City of Cleveland v. Hirsch (Cuyahoga 1971) 26 Ohio App.2d 6, 268 N.E.2d 600, 55 O.O.2d 26. Criminal Law ⚷ 145.5; Municipal Corporations ⚷ 636

RC 1905.33 may be asserted as a defense to a criminal prosecution for the first time after a trial and conviction of a defendant. City of Cleveland v. Hirsch (Cuyahoga 1971) 26 Ohio App.2d 6, 268 N.E.2d 600, 55 O.O.2d 26.

The failure to have an affidavit verified is jurisdictional and is not waived by a "not guilty" plea. City of South Euclid v. Samartini (Ohio Mun. 1965) 5 Ohio Misc. 38, 204 N.E.2d 425, 31 O.O.2d 87. Indictment And Information ⚷ 196(4)

An indictment charging that defendant, "in the night season, maliciously and forcibly broke and entered the… Farmer's Coop… with intent to steal… contrary to RC 2907.10" and which does not charge that a "building" was broken and entered, is insufficient to charge the crime of burglary, and the omission to state one of the material elements of such offense is fatal to the validity of such indictment. State v. Presler (Wyandot 1960) 112 Ohio App. 437, 176 N.E.2d 308, 16 O.O.2d 333.

The signature of the foreman of a grand jury is an indispensable requisite to a valid indictment, and in the absence thereof all subsequent proceedings are void; and habeas corpus will lie. Kennedy v. Alvis (Ohio Com.Pl. 1957) 145 N.E.2d 361, 76 Ohio Law Abs. 132.

Where in an indictment charging embezzlement there is an omission of any reference to defendant's official capacity, such deficiency cannot be supplied by amendment. State v. Kearns (Ohio Com.Pl. 1955) 127 N.E.2d 541, 70 Ohio Law Abs. 149.

This section and GC 13437–29 (RC 2941.30) apply to an indictment which as drawn is sufficient to charge an offense, but they do not contemplate the making of a good indictment out of one which states no offense. State v. Cimpritz (Ohio 1953) 158 Ohio St. 490, 110 N.E.2d 416, 49 O.O. 418. Indictment And Information ⚷ 159(2)

2. Timely objection

Defendant charged with possession of cocaine was not prejudiced by failure of indictment to allege that he knowingly possessed the cocaine, and thus defendant's failure to object to defective indictment waived issue for purposes of appeal; statute referenced in indictment clearly identified the charge against defendant. State v. Castile (Ohio App. 6 Dist., Erie, 01-07-2005) No. E-02-012, 2005-Ohio-41, 2005 WL 30509, Unreported, corrected. Criminal Law ⚷ 1032(5)

Burglary and sexual imposition defendant was not entitled to a hearing on his post-sentence motion to withdraw his no contest pleas in which he alleged that bill of information was void as being duplicitous, where defendant failed to raise objection before trial court. State v. Jain (Ohio App. 6 Dist., Wood, 02-27-2004) No. WD-03-037, 2004-Ohio-893, 2004 WL 368108, Unreported. Criminal Law ⚷ 275.5(4)

Error cannot be predicated, on appeal in a criminal proceeding, on the alleged ground that the panel of persons to serve as grand jurors was improperly drawn and not selected according to law and that the indictment was, therefore, invalid, where such issue was not, at any time, properly presented to the trial court, either by challenge to the array or a plea in abatement, and there is not a shred of evidence, or even argument, as to what such alleged impropriety in the selection of the grand jury was. State v. Lamonge (Trumbull 1962) 117 Ohio App. 143, 191 N.E.2d 207, 23 O.O.2d 314, appeal dismissed 174 Ohio St. 545, 190 N.E.2d 691, 23 O.O.2d 210, certiorari denied 84 S.Ct. 346, 375 U.S. 942, 11 L.Ed.2d 272.

Where a defendant is charged in an affidavit with a misdemeanor and pleads not guilty thereto, and goes to trial without questioning the validity of his arrest or the sufficiency of the affidavit, such defendant may not thereafter defend on the ground that he was unlawfully arrested or that the affidavit was falsely or improperly verified. City of Cleveland v. Ely (Ohio 1963) 174 Ohio St. 403, 189 N.E.2d 724, 23 O.O.2d 46. Criminal Law ⚷ 213

Objections to alleged defects either in form or substance of an indictment must be made prior to the commencement of the trial. Scott v. Sacks (Franklin 1960) 169 N.E.2d 312, 83 Ohio Law Abs. 417.

Any defect in an indictment should be raised at the time of trial under the indictment. Zenz v. Alvis (Franklin 1951) 118 N.E.2d 678, 66 Ohio Law Abs. 606. Indictment And Information ⚷ 133(1)

No objection within statute being filed, defects in indictment were immaterial on review, especially since record did not show affirmatively accused was prejudiced. Stover v. State (Putnam 1930) 37 Ohio App. 213, 174 N.E. 613, 9 Ohio Law Abs. 397, 33 Ohio Law Rep. 598. Criminal Law ⚡ 1032(1)

3. Collateral attack

Convicted party who failed to make direct attack on affidavit of charges, either in trial court or on appeal, cannot subsequently raise issue through a collateral attack on judgment. Plematis v. Berkemer (Franklin 1971) 30 Ohio App.2d 262, 285 N.E.2d 78, 59 O.O.2d 403. Judgment ⚡ 476

Where a defendant, while represented by counsel, pleads guilty to an offense and is sentenced, the judgment of conviction cannot be collaterally attacked on the ground that the indictment fails to state one or more essential elements of the offense. Midling v. Perrini (Ohio 1968) 14 Ohio St.2d 106, 236 N.E.2d 557, 43 O.O.2d 171. Judgment ⚡ 476

2941.30 Amending an indictment

The court may at any time before, during, or after a trial amend the indictment, information, or bill of particulars, in respect to any defect, imperfection, or omission in form or substance, or of any variance with the evidence, provided no change is made in the name or identity of the crime charged. If any amendment is made to the substance of the indictment or information or to cure a variance between the indictment or information and the proof, the accused is entitled to a discharge of the jury on his motion, if a jury has been impaneled, and to a reasonable continuance of the cause, unless it clearly appears from the whole proceedings that he has not been misled or prejudiced by the defect or variance in respect to which the amendment is made, or that his rights will be fully protected by proceeding with the trial, or by a postponement thereof to a later day with the same or another jury. In case a jury is discharged from further consideration of a case under this section, the accused was not in jeopardy. No action of the court in refusing a continuance or postponement under this section is reviewable except after motion to and refusal by the trial court to grant a new trial therefor, and no appeal based upon such action of the court shall be sustained, nor reversal had, unless from consideration of the whole proceedings, the reviewing court finds that the accused was prejudiced in his defense or that a failure of justice resulted.

(1953 H 1, eff. 10–1–53; GC 13437–29)

Historical and Statutory Notes

Pre–1953 H 1 Amendments: 113 v 169, Ch 16, § 29

Cross References

Indictment and information, Crim R 7

Library References

Indictment and Information ⚡155 to 163.

Westlaw Topic No. 210.

Research References

Encyclopedias

OH Jur. 3d Criminal Law § 764, for Mistake in Charging Proper Offense.

OH Jur. 3d Criminal Law § 2366, Designation of Victim.

OH Jur. 3d Criminal Law § 2386, Objections To, and Amendment Of, Bill.

OH Jur. 3d Criminal Law § 2422, Amendments to Cure Defects.

OH Jur. 3d Criminal Law § 2423, Amendment that Changes Substance of Offense.

OH Jur. 3d Criminal Law § 2604, Amendment to Indictment Upon Defendant's Request.

OH Jur. 3d Criminal Law § 3549, Motion for New Trial Unnecessary.

OH Jur. 3d Criminal Law § 3675, Continuance.

Treatises and Practice Aids

Katz, Giannelli, Blair and Lipton, Baldwin's Ohio Practice, Criminal Law, § 40:7, Amendments to the Indictment.

Katz, Giannelli, Blair and Lipton, Baldwin's Ohio Practice, Criminal Law, § 40:9, Bill of Particulars.

Katz, Giannelli, Blair and Lipton, Baldwin's Ohio Practice, Criminal Law, § 142:5, Motion to Amend the Indictment, Complaint or Information.

Painter, Ohio Driving Under the Influence § 2:2, Sufficiency of Citation—Criminal Matters Generally.

Notes of Decisions

1. Constitutional issues

Defendant was prejudiced by failure of trial court to grant defendant a continuance after State, just days prior to trial, amended indictment charging rape to include sexual battery, and thus, failure was abuse of discretion, where addition of sexual battery was a change in substance to indictment, in that in defense of rape charge defendant had to show that he did not force victim to engage in sexual conduct, whereas, to defend against sexual battery charge defendant had to show that victim was not substantially impaired when they engaged in sexual conduct, and although trial court offered to either continue trial for one day or, after conclusion of all other aspects of trial, have a one-week break thereafter defense could have presented any expert witnesses at that time, neither of those options would have given defendant sufficient opportunity to consult with an expert. State v. Hall (Ohio App. 11 Dist., Portage, 04-18-2003) No. 2002-P-0048, 2003-Ohio-1979, 2003 WL 1904070, Unreported. Criminal Law ⚿ 589(1)

A person charged with a misdemeanor in a municipal court is not entitled to a bill of particulars, so that the placing of an attorney prosecuting a person for a misdemeanor in such court in the custody of a bailiff for contempt of court for refusal to comply with an order to furnish the accused with a bill of particulars is a denial of due process to such attorney and an illegal restraint of liberty, entitling such attorney to his release from custody. In re Schott (Hamilton 1968) 16 Ohio App.2d 72, 241 N.E.2d 773, 45 O.O.2d 168.

Amendment of an affidavit, following the sustaining of a demurrer thereto, does not constitute double jeopardy. City of Columbus v. Burris (Franklin 1958) 151 N.E.2d 690, 78 Ohio Law Abs. 120.

GC 13437–29 (RC 2941.30) is not violative of any of provisions of constitution. It authorizes trial court to amend an indictment by inserting the venue or county where the alleged offense was committed, if no venue was stated; provided accused is not prejudiced thereby. Breinig v. State (Ohio 1931) 124 Ohio St. 39, 176 N.E. 674, 10 Ohio Law Abs. 94, 34 Ohio Law Rep. 478.

Where an indictment for the crime of arson under RC 2909.02(A)(2) is amended three days before trial, without a return to the grand jury, to charge conspiracy under RC 2909.02(A)(3), thereby rendering defendant's notice of alibi moot and requiring preparation of an entirely different defense, the defendant has insufficient notice of the crime charged and is denied the due process of law. Koontz v. Glossa (C.A.6 (Ohio) 1984) 731 F.2d 365.

Where accused was indicted for deliberate and premeditated murder, he was denied due process when he was required to defend against felony murder charge, even though the charge to the jury covered only premeditated murder. Watson v. Jago (C.A.6 (Ohio) 1977) 558 F.2d 330, 8 O.O.3d 307.

In a prosecution for the misdemeanor of failing to timely file federal income tax returns, where the government proceeds by indictment it is bound by the rules governing use of indictments, including amendment rules, and since an amendment to reflect dates to which the taxpayer had been given filing extensions is a material alteration, it can be undertaken only by grand jury action, and permitting an amendment by way of a bill of particulars is error. U. S. v. Pandilidis (C.A.6 (Ohio) 1975) 524 F.2d 644, certiorari denied 96 S.Ct. 1146, 424 U.S. 933, 47 L.Ed.2d 340. Indictment And Information ⚿ 159(3)

2. Variance between pleading and proof

Where an indictment for a conspiracy to defraud under RC 2921.14 specifies the manner or manners of defrauding relied upon as the defrauding part of that conspiracy, a conviction cannot be based upon evidence only establishing a manner of defrauding other than that so specified. State v. Lewis (Ohio 1970) 21 Ohio St.2d 203, 257 N.E.2d 59, 50 O.O.2d 441. Conspiracy ⚿ 43(12)

3. Allowable amendments

Defendant was not prejudiced by the State's amendment to the indictment prior to trial to accurately reflect the proper county for each offense, in prosecution involving numerous alleged sexual offenses occurring in three counties; the amendment did not affect a material element of the offenses, and the State's bill of particulars had already identified the city in which each offense occurred. State v. Ahmed (Ohio App. 8 Dist., Cuyahoga, 06-16-2005) No. 84220, 2005-Ohio-2999, 2005 WL 1406282, Unreported. Indictment And Information ⚿ 159(3)

An indictment may be amended at any time to name the victim or additional victims of a theft offense. State v. Wallace (Ohio App. 8 Dist., 04-14-2005) 160 Ohio App.3d 528, 828 N.E.2d 125, 2005-Ohio-1746, appeal not allowed 106 Ohio St.3d 1509, 833 N.E.2d 1250, 2005-Ohio-4605, reconsideration denied 107 Ohio St.3d 1411, 836 N.E.2d 1230, 2005-Ohio-5859. Indictment And Information ⚿ 159(4)

Trial court could allow amendment of indictment, alleging death penalty specification that murder had been committed to silence witnesses, so as to exclude from its coverage murder of any witness killed at same time witness observed offense, so as to conform to statutory description of specification; defendant was not prejudiced, as amendment narrowed rather than widened scope of specification. State v. Brooks (Ohio, 03-04-1996) 75 Ohio St.3d 148, 661 N.E.2d 1030, 1996-Ohio-134, reconsideration denied 75 Ohio St.3d 1452, 663 N.E.2d 333. Indictment And Information ⚷ 159(2)

The rights of a defendant, originally charged with aggravated murder, were not violated by filing of an amended bill of particulars nineteen days before trial adding a charge of complicity, since there was no change in the name or identity of the crime. State v. Ensman (Ashtabula 1991) 77 Ohio App.3d 701, 603 N.E.2d 303, dismissed, jurisdictional motion overruled 63 Ohio St.3d 1409, 585 N.E.2d 834.

A defendant charged with sexual abuse involving minors does not have his defense prejudiced nor is he denied due process of law by the trial court's granting of the state's motion to amend its indictment to expand the dates of the offenses where the defendant did not claim alibi as a defense and did not deny that the victims visited his residence. State v. Murrell (Butler 1991) 72 Ohio App.3d 668, 595 N.E.2d 982, dismissed, jurisdictional motion overruled 61 Ohio St.3d 1419, 574 N.E.2d 1090.

An amendment to an indictment which changes the name of the victim changes neither the name nor the identity of the crime charged. State v. Owens (Summit 1975) 51 Ohio App.2d 132, 366 N.E.2d 1367, 5 O.O.3d 290, denial of post-conviction relief affirmed, dismissed, jurisdictional motion overruled 66 Ohio St.3d 1443, 609 N.E.2d 170. Indictment And Information ⚷ 159(4)

Where an indictment containing four counts of armed robbery alleges that the property taken from the person of the victim is owned by the one named therein, and the proof establishes that such property was the personal property of the several victims, the trial judge does not commit error when, on motion, he permits an amendment of such indictment to show the true owners of the thing of value stolen; armed robbery is an offense against the person, not against property. State v. Dye (Summit 1968) 14 Ohio App.2d 7, 235 N.E.2d 250, 43 O.O.2d 18. Indictment And Information ⚷ 159(2)

An indictment which charges every essential element of a crime may be amended when no change is made in the name or identity of the crime charged. State v. Phipps (Scioto 1964) 3 Ohio App.2d 226, 210 N.E.2d 138, 32 O.O.2d 322, certiorari denied 86 S.Ct. 434, 382 U.S. 957, 15 L.Ed.2d 361.

Amendment of an indictment to correct the date on which the crime is alleged to have occurred is not improper. McLean v. Maxwell (Ohio 1965) 2 Ohio St.2d 226, 208 N.E.2d 139, 31 O.O.2d 454.

An amendment to an indictment for forgery or uttering, which merely changes the check numbers, amounts or the names of the payee as set forth in the indictment, is a matter of form, not of substance, and in no way affects the nature or identity of the offense as charged. Brookhart v. Haskins (Ohio 1965) 2 Ohio St.2d 36, 205 N.E.2d 911, 31 O.O.2d 20, certiorari granted 86 S.Ct. 104, 382 U.S. 810, 15 L.Ed.2d 59, reversed 86 S.Ct. 1245, 384 U.S. 1, 7 Ohio Misc. 77, 16 L.Ed.2d 314, 36 O.O.2d 141.

Amendment of indictment by interlineation to show name of person robbed was proper. State v. Murray (Trumbull 1962) 192 N.E.2d 517, 91 Ohio Law Abs. 513, 27 O.O.2d 192.

Amendment of an indictment for armed robbery to change the name of the person upon whom the crime was committed did not invalidate the indictment. Dye v. Sacks (Ohio 1962) 173 Ohio St. 422, 183 N.E.2d 380, 14 A.L.R.3d 1352, 20 O.O.2d 47.

An indictment which charges that an offense was committed subsequent to the date of its return may be amended by correcting thereon the date of the offense. McConnaughy v. Alvis (Franklin 1955) 100 Ohio App. 245, 136 N.E.2d 127, 60 O.O. 210.

In prosecution for driving while intoxicated, trial court was authorized to permit amendment of indictment by interlineation of word "motor" before word "truck" in each count in indictment. State v. Foster (Scioto 1936) 56 Ohio App. 267, 10 N.E.2d 786, 23 Ohio Law Abs. 278, 9 O.O. 363. Indictment And Information ⚷ 159(2)

Amendment to indictment charging "deputy clerk" of probate court with accepting bribe to award bribe giver contracts for purchase of clothing for patients, committed to insane asylum, which characterized accused as "employee," held not to change identity of crime, and amendment need not have been made on face of original indictment, but could be presented in another form of indictment. Roberts v. State (Franklin 1932) 45 Ohio App. 65, 186 N.E. 748, 13 Ohio Law Abs. 566, 38 Ohio Law Rep. 299, error dismissed 126 Ohio St. 429, 186 N.E. 93. Indictment And Information ⚷ 159(2)

Amendment of an indictment to correct a misdescription of the victim's name does not infringe upon defendant's constitutional rights. (See also Dye v Alvis, 170 OS 97, 162 NE(2d) 520 (1959).) Dye v. Sacks (C.A.6 (Ohio) 1960) 279 F.2d 834, 14 A.L.R.3d 1352, 86 Ohio Law Abs. 476, 13 O.O.2d 301.

Grant of state's motion to amend indictment on felonious assault charge so as to allege that defendant committed charged offense on or about the day after the date originally alleged in indictment was not error. State v. Curtis (Ohio App. 7 Dist., Jefferson, 06-07-2002) No. 01-JE-16, 2002-Ohio-3054, 2002 WL 1370901, Unreported, motion for delayed appeal denied 98 Ohio St.3d 1408, 781 N.E.2d 1017, 2003-Ohio-60, reconsideration denied 98 Ohio St.3d 1475, 784 N.E.2d 709, 2003-Ohio-904, certiorari denied 123 S.Ct. 2611, 539 U.S. 945, 156 L.Ed.2d 632, rehearing denied 124 S.Ct. 38, 539 U.S. 983, 156 L.Ed.2d 697. Indictment And Information ⚷ 159(3)

The trial court may properly grant the prosecutor's motion to amend an indictment from breaking and entering to that of aiding or abetting breaking and entering. State v Willison, No. 1157 (4th Dist Ct App, Athens, 12–9–83).

4. Unamendable defects

Where defendant and his counsel and the prosecution were unaware that the affidavit charging defendant with a traffic violation had not been verified until discovered by the judge at the end of the trial, a waiver may not be considered, and verification of the affidavit cannot be furnished at the end of the trial against objection of the defendant. Village of Pepper Pike v. LaMaida (Ohio Mun. 1970) 25 Ohio Misc. 252, 268 N.E.2d 296, 54 O.O.2d 410.

The provisions of RC 2941.30 do not apply when a vital element identifying or characterizing the offense is omitted from an indictment. State v. Ferguson (Miami 1967) 13 Ohio App.2d 151, 234 N.E.2d 598, 42 O.O.2d 268.

An affidavit, charging an accused with "indecent exposure" in violation of RC 2905.30, which does not contain an allegation or facts from which an inference can be made that the accused was eighteen or over, is not amendable. State v. Latham (Franklin 1964) 120 Ohio App. 176, 201 N.E.2d 603, 28 O.O.2d 430, appeal denied 177 Ohio St. 73, 202 N.E.2d 309, 29 O.O.2d 193.

An indictment which does not charge defendant with an intent which is one of the essential elements of a crime cannot be amended so as to include a charge of such intent. State v. Wozniak (Ohio 1961) 172 Ohio St. 517, 178 N.E.2d 800, 18 O.O.2d 58. Indictment And Information ⚷ 159(2)

An indictment charging that defendant, "in the night season, maliciously and forcibly broke and entered the... Farmer's Coop... with intent to steal... contrary to RC 2907.10" and which does not charge that a "building" was broken and entered, is insufficient to charge the crime of burglary, and the omission to state one of the material elements of such offense is fatal to the validity of such indictment. State v. Presler (Wyandot 1960) 112 Ohio App. 437, 176 N.E.2d 308, 16 O.O.2d 333.

Amendment of an indictment charging burglary in the night season to charge unlawful breaking and entering in the day season is improper. Hasselworth v. Alvis (Franklin 1956) 143 N.E.2d 862, 75 Ohio Law Abs. 238.

Where in an indictment charging embezzlement there is an omission of any reference to defendant's official capacity, such deficiency cannot be supplied by amendment. State v. Kearns (Ohio Com.Pl. 1955) 127 N.E.2d 541, 70 Ohio Law Abs. 149.

GC 13437–28 (RC 2941.29) and this section apply to an indictment which as drawn is sufficient to charge an offense, but they do not contemplate the making of a good indictment out of one which states no offense. State v. Cimpritz (Ohio 1953) 158 Ohio St. 490, 110 N.E.2d 416, 49 O.O. 418. Indictment And Information ⚷ 159(2)

An indictment charging a defendant with possession of a firearm on or about a certain date is constructively amended by a jury instruction that the defendant can be convicted of a felony if the jury found he had a prior felony conviction and possessed a firearm at any time from the time of the alleged purchase until the date of alleged possession, thereby warranting reversal of a conviction, because the jury may have convicted on the basis of a possession not intended by the grand jury as part of the charge or it may not have been unanimous in its determination of the date of the possession. U.S. v. Ford (C.A.6 (Ohio) 1989) 872 F.2d 1231, certiorari denied 110 S.Ct. 1946, 495 U.S. 918, 109 L.Ed.2d 309.

Amendment of indictment charging breaking and entering dwelling house in night time by inserting word "inhabited" before "dwelling" was improper. Horsley v. Alvis (C.A.6 (Ohio) 1960) 281 F.2d 440, 13 O.O.2d 320.

An indictment for assault with intent to commit rape cannot be amended to charge the crime of assault with intent to commit robbery. Stacy v Van Curen, 432 F(2d) 970 (6th Cir Ohio 1970).

5. Amendments to affidavits

RC 2941.35 and 2941.30 permit the amendment of affidavits upon which prosecutions for misdemeanors have been instituted by the court, at any time before, during or after a trial in respect to any defect, imperfection, or omission in form or substance, or of any variance with the evidence, provided no change is made in the name or identity of the crime charged. State v. Walker (Franklin 1969) 20 Ohio App.2d 179, 252 N.E.2d 646, 49 O.O.2d 245.

Amendments to affidavits filed in criminal actions are not permitted under authority of RC 2941.30. City of South Euclid v. Samartini (Ohio Mun. 1965) 5 Ohio Misc. 38, 204 N.E.2d 425, 31 O.O.2d 87.

Changing of affidavit alleging illegal possession of liquor to add allegation of holding for sale was more than mere amendment of the affidavit and required a reverification. State v. Jackson (Franklin 1960) 190 N.E.2d 38, 90 Ohio Law Abs. 577.

Specific authority is given for the amendment of an affidavit to the same extent and under the same limitations as applied in the case of indictments and informations in the common pleas court. State v. Jackson (Franklin 1960) 190 N.E.2d 38, 90 Ohio Law Abs. 577.

A "substitute" affidavit, filed in a criminal action in the municipal court, is not an amended affidavit but a new affidavit; and the defendant must be arraigned upon such new affidavit and be given an opportunity to enter a plea thereto; without such arraignment and opportunity to plead the court has no jurisdiction to proceed to trial. State v. Jennings (Wyandot 1959) 112 Ohio App. 455, 176 N.E.2d 304, 16 O.O.2d 346.

6. Waiver of defects

Defendant waived any error regarding the amended charge by not objecting at the time of the amendment. State v. Alvarez (Ohio App. 12 Dist., Butler, 05-17-2004) No. CA2003-03-067, 2004-Ohio-2483, 2004 WL 1089110, Unreported. Criminal Law ⚷ 1167(4)

Even assuming state had improperly amended indictment for gross sexual imposition, defendant waived any objection to amendment when it was result of plea negotiations pursuant to which defendant pled no contest to attempted abduction. State v. Mosley (Ohio App. 2 Dist., Montgomery, 05-09-2003) No. 19569, 2003-Ohio-2398, 2003 WL 21060820, Unreported. Criminal Law ⚷ 275.2

Where the affidavit charging an offense was defective, and by agreement of counsel it was amended by completely rewriting and inserting by interlineation, but was not sworn to as amended, and defendant's counsel made no objection thereto, defendant by pleading not guilty and proceeding to trial waived objection to the want of verification. State v. Chrisman (Ohio 1966) 9 Ohio St.2d 27, 222 N.E.2d 649, 38 O.O.2d 16.

A defendant charged with assault to commit rape who pleads guilty to an amended charge of assault with intent to commit robbery waives prosecution by indictment. Stacy v Van Curen, 432 F(2d) 970 (6th Cir Ohio 1970).

7. Form mislabeled as indictment

Defendant was not tried on amended indictment; form entitled "indictment" was actually a transcript of sentence or judgment of conviction. Lotz v. Sacks (C.A.6 (Ohio) 1961) 292 F.2d 657, 17 O.O.2d 206.

8. Appeal

Where petitioner alleged that he had been denied rights as a result of counsel's failure to appeal, he was entitled to an evidentiary hearing on the issue in a federal habeas corpus proceeding. Henderson v. Cardwell (C.A.6 (Ohio) 1970) 27 Ohio Misc. 4, 426 F.2d 150, 54 O.O.2d 248, 56 O.O.2d 230.

9. Amendment prior to judgment

Trial court's announcement that it was inclined to grant defendant's motion for acquittal in prosecution for patient abuse was not a final judgment, permitting state to subsequently amend indictment to charge attempted patient abuse, where trial court did not sign order granting motion. State v. Briscoe (Cuyahoga 1992) 84 Ohio App.3d 569, 617 N.E.2d 747, dismissed, jurisdictional motion overruled 66 Ohio St.3d 1485, 612 N.E.2d 1242. Criminal Law ⚷ 753.2(8); Indictment And Information ⚷ 159(2)

10. Crime charged and its name or identity

In prosecution for attempted abduction, prosecutor did not improperly amend indictment of gross sexual imposition, rather, state dismissed original indictment and proceeded by filing separate bill of information charging attempted abduction. State v. Mosley (Ohio App. 2 Dist., Montgomery, 05-09-2003) No. 19569, 2003-Ohio-2398, 2003 WL 21060820, Unreported. Indictment And Information ⚷ 159(2)

An amendment to an indictment which changes the name of the victim changes neither the name nor the identity of the crime charged. State v. Wallace (Ohio App. 8 Dist., 04-14-2005) 160 Ohio App.3d 528, 828 N.E.2d 125, 2005-Ohio-1746, appeal not allowed 106 Ohio St.3d 1509, 833 N.E.2d 1250, 2005-Ohio-4605, reconsideration denied 107 Ohio St.3d 1411, 836 N.E.2d 1230, 2005-Ohio-5859. Indictment And Information ⚷ 159(4)

Prisoner's claim that trial court improperly amended indictment on which he was convicted from murder to involuntary manslaughter was challenge to validity or sufficiency of indictment and was nonjurisdictional in nature, and should therefore have been raised on direct appeal from conviction rather than on petition for writ of habeas corpus. State ex rel. Raglin v. Brigano (Ohio, 07-29-1998) 82 Ohio St.3d 410, 696 N.E.2d 585, 1998-Ohio-222, reconsideration denied 83 Ohio St.3d 1436, 699 N.E.2d 950. Habeas Corpus ⚷ 292

Offense of attempted patient abuse was lesser included offense of patient abuse, permitting state to amend indictment charging patient abuse during trial to charge of attempted patient abuse. State v. Briscoe (Cuyahoga 1992) 84 Ohio App.3d 569, 617 N.E.2d 747, dismissed, jurisdictional motion overruled 66 Ohio St.3d 1485, 612 N.E.2d 1242. Indictment And Information ⚷ 189(1)

2941.31 Record of quashed indictment

In criminal prosecutions, when the indictment or information has been quashed or the prosecuting attorney has entered a nolle prosequi thereon, or the cause or indictment is disposed of otherwise than upon trial, a complete record shall not be made by the clerk of the court of common pleas unless ordered to do so by the court of common pleas.

(1953 H 1, eff. 10–1–53; GC 13437–30)

Historical and Statutory Notes

Pre–1953 H 1 Amendments: 115 v 530; 113 v 169, Ch 16, § 30

Cross References

Dismissal, Crim R 48

2941.32 Proceedings when two indictments pending

If two or more indictments or informations are pending against the same defendant for the same criminal act, the prosecuting attorney must elect upon which he will proceed, and upon trial being had upon one of them, the remaining indictments or information shall be quashed.

(1953 H 1, eff. 10–1–53; GC 13437–31)

Historical and Statutory Notes

Pre-1953 H 1 Amendments: 113 v 170, Ch 16, § 31

Cross References

Joinder of offenses and defendants, Crim R 8

Library References

Indictment and Information ⚬=132.

Westlaw Topic No. 210.

Research References

Encyclopedias

OH Jur. 3d Criminal Law § 2401, Election Between Indictments or Informations.

Treatises and Practice Aids

Katz, Giannelli, Blair and Lipton, Baldwin's Ohio Practice, Criminal Law, § 146:4, Motion for Election.

Katz, Giannelli, Blair and Lipton, Baldwin's Ohio Practice, Criminal Law, § 146:5, Order for Election Between Two Indictments.

Katz, Giannelli, Blair and Lipton, Baldwin's Ohio Practice, Criminal Law, § 146:6, Entry of Election Between Two Indictments.

Katz, Giannelli, Blair and Lipton, Baldwin's Ohio Practice, Criminal Law, § 146:7, Entry as Election Made at Time of Order.

Painter, Ohio Driving Under the Influence § 2:8, Election of Charges.

Notes of Decisions

Different criminal acts 2
Same criminal act 1

1. Same criminal act

Although indictment may contain a count for embezzlement and another count for obtaining the same money or property by false pretenses, the state must elect on which, and the same as if charged in separate indictments. Griffith v. State (Ohio 1915) 93 Ohio St. 294, 112 N.E. 1017.

2. Different criminal acts

Each method listed in former RC 2901.01 (RC 2903.01) is a separate offense even though the murder victim is the same person, and the use of a combination of such means does not constitute the "same criminal act" as that term is used in RC 2941.32. State v. Trocodaro (Franklin 1973) 40 Ohio App.2d 50, 317 N.E.2d 418, 69 O.O.2d 28.

RC 2941.32 does not apply where the accused is charged with offenses arising out of different criminal acts. Rodriguez v. Sacks (Ohio 1962) 173 Ohio St. 456, 184 N.E.2d 93, 20 O.O.2d 78.

2941.33 Nolle prosequi

The prosecuting attorney shall not enter a nolle prosequi in any cause without leave of the court, on good cause shown, in open court. A nolle prosequi entered contrary to this section is invalid.

(1953 H 1, eff. 10-1-53; GC 13437-32)

Historical and Statutory Notes

Pre-1953 H 1 Amendments: 113 v 170, Ch 16, § 32

Cross References

Dismissal, Crim R 48

Library References

Criminal Law ⚬=303.5.

Westlaw Topic No. 110.

C.J.S. Criminal Law §§ 419 to 424.

Research References

Encyclopedias

OH Jur. 3d Criminal Law § 2826, Dismissal by State.

OH Jur. 3d Criminal Law § 2827, Procedure to Secure Dismissal.

Treatises and Practice Aids

Markus, Trial Handbook for Ohio Lawyers, § 3:6, Nolle Prosequi, Criminal Case Dismissal.

Katz, Giannelli, Blair and Lipton, Baldwin's Ohio Practice, Criminal Law, § 44:2, Role in Criminal Justice System.

Katz, Giannelli, Blair and Lipton, Baldwin's Ohio Practice, Criminal Law, § 40:12, Dismissal of Indictment and Information.

Katz, Giannelli, Blair and Lipton, Baldwin's Ohio Practice, Criminal Law, § 142:13, Entry of Nolle Prosequi.

Adrine & Ruden, Ohio Domestic Violence Law § 5:2, Prosecutorial Discretion.

Notes of Decisions

1. Grounds for nolle prosequi

The mere recitation in the prosecution's motion to dismiss that there is "insufficient evidence" to prosecute a criminal complaint of domestic violence does not satisfy the "leave of court" and "good cause" provisions of Crim R 48(A) and RC 2941.33. Lakewood v. Pfeifer (Cuyahoga 1992) 83 Ohio App.3d 47, 613 N.E.2d 1079, motion to certify denied 66 Ohio St.3d 1444, 609 N.E.2d 171.

Separation of powers is not violated by requiring a prosecutor to give something more than a recitation that there is "insufficient evidence" to prosecute a domestic violence complaint in its motion for dismissal. Lakewood v. Pfeifer (Cuyahoga 1992) 83 Ohio App.3d 47, 613 N.E.2d 1079, motion to certify denied 66 Ohio St.3d 1444, 609 N.E.2d 171.

Insufficiency of proof has always been regarded as good cause for the nolle prosequi of an indictment. State v. Sutton (Wayne 1979) 64 Ohio App.2d 105, 411 N.E.2d 818, 18 O.O.3d 83. Criminal Law ⚷ 303.30(1)

Habeas petitioner procedurally defaulted claim that he was denied due process when state failed to show, and trial court failed to require, good cause for dismissal of original indictment against him; claim was raised for first time in first motion for state postconviction relief, failure to raise on appeal claim that appeared on face of the record was procedural default under Ohio's doctrine of res judicata, and petitioner did not allege cause or prejudice for failure to raise claim on direct appeal, nor did the record support such a finding. Sweet v. Carter (N.D.Ohio, 09-25-1998) 22 F.Supp.2d 707. Habeas Corpus ⚷ 366

Habeas petitioner alleged violation of state law for which federal habeas corpus relief was unavailable in claiming that he was denied due process when, in violation of Ohio statute, state failed to show, and trial court failed to require, good cause for dismissal of original indictment against him. Sweet v. Carter (N.D.Ohio, 09-25-1998) 22 F.Supp.2d 707. Habeas Corpus ⚷ 474

2. Consent to dismissal

Trial court abused its discretion, in prosecution on various charges related to aggravated vehicular homicide, in rejecting state's request for pretrial dismissal of charge of driving with a prohibited concentration of alcohol in bodily substances; good cause for dismissal was shown, in that sole evidence that blood draw occurred within two-hour time frame required by applicable statute was defendant's self-serving and implausible initial statement to police, and other evidence affirmatively established that blood draw occurred outside two-hour time frame. State v. Neely (Ohio App. 11 Dist., Lake, 12-29-2005) No. 2004-L-197, 2005-Ohio-7045, 2005 WL 3610426, Unreported. Automobiles ⚷ 422.1

Non-prosecution agreements made before criminal proceedings are initiated are not subject to court approval; in contrast, non-prosecution agreements which arise after there has been an indictment are subject to court approval. State v. Mucci (Ohio App. 7 Dist., 12-13-2002) 150 Ohio App.3d 493, 782 N.E.2d 133, 2002-Ohio-6896. Criminal Law ⚷ 42.5(1)

A prosecutor must have leave of court, granted after a showing of good cause, before an indictment can be dismissed. State v. Mucci (Ohio App. 7 Dist., 12-13-2002) 150 Ohio App.3d 493, 782 N.E.2d 133, 2002-Ohio-6896. Criminal Law ⚷ 303.15

Trial court acted within its discretion in refusing to grant joint motion to dismiss 16-count indictment charging defendant with obtaining and possessing prescription drugs illegally, even though state and defendant had agreed to dismissal of indictment if defendant cooperated with law enforcement and met other conditions; defendant was in nursing school, record established a pattern of drug-obtaining behavior that was more extensive than that reflected by indicted crimes, and there was no allegation of insufficient evidence. State v. Mucci (Ohio App. 7 Dist., 12-13-2002) 150 Ohio App.3d 493, 782 N.E.2d 133, 2002-Ohio-6896. Criminal Law ⚷ 303.30(4); Indictment And Information ⚷ 144.2

Trial court, at pretrial hearing, lacked discretion to dismiss case over prosecutor's objection solely on basis of "no prosecuting witness being present at this time"; record did not definitively indicate whether representative of police department was in courtroom or immediately available, trial court could have issued warrant for immediate appearance of arresting officer and/or victim, order of dismissal was not nolle prosequi in form or in substance, there were no findings of fact or reasons for dismissal having any reference to any alleged shortcoming or illegality of complaint, and any violation of requirement of local rule that prosecuting witness, arresting officer or law enforcement representative be present at pretrial hearing would not amount to "defect in the institution of the prosecution" under rule providing source of dismissal authority. State v. Spitzer (Franklin 1995) 107 Ohio App.3d 707, 669 N.E.2d 339. Criminal Law ⚷ 303.30(1)

A nolle prosequi cannot be entered without the affirmative consent of the prosecutor. City of Cleveland v. Mosquito (Cuyahoga 1983) 10 Ohio App.3d 239, 461 N.E.2d 924, 10 O.B.R. 334. Criminal Law ⚷ 303.15

A writ of mandamus may not issue directing a prosecuting attorney to dismiss indictments, since the consent of the court is necessary therefor. State ex rel. Lotz v. Hover (Ohio 1963) 174 Ohio St. 380, 189 N.E.2d 433, 22 O.O.2d 443.

3. No jeopardy

Double jeopardy did not preclude State from proceeding upon second indictment after first indictment was dismissed; State requested dismissal of first indictment prior to jury being sworn, to which defendant did not object and which court approved, and thus State had effectively dismissed first indictment prior to attachment of jeopardy. State v. Johnson (Lorain 1990) 68 Ohio App.3d 272, 588 N.E.2d 224, cause dismissed 55 Ohio St.3d 702, 562 N.E.2d 893, denial of habeas corpus affirmed 35 F.3d 566. Double Jeopardy ⚷ 89

Under Ohio law a nolle prosequi entered in accordance with RC 2941.33 completely terminates a prosecution, and if it is entered before a jury is sworn, the defendant has not been placed in jeopardy and another prosecution for the same offense is permissible. Sander v. State of Ohio (S.D.Ohio 1973) 365 F.Supp. 1251, 70 O.O.2d 418, affirmed 500 F.2d 1403, certiorari denied 95 S.Ct. 505, 419 U.S. 1026, 42 L.Ed.2d 301. Double Jeopardy ⚷ 59

4. Dismissal with prejudice

A dismissal for want of prosecution resulting from a plea bargain must be deemed to be with prejudice where it rests on a promise or agreement of the prosecutor and can be said to be part of the inducement or consideration for the plea bargain. State v. Malone (Ohio Mun. 1984) 14 Ohio Misc.2d 18, 471 N.E.2d 892, 14 O.B.R. 501. Criminal Law ⚷ 577.16(11)

Crim R 48(B) does not provide for the dismissal of an indictment with prejudice, and a court has inherent power to dismiss with prejudice only where it is apparent that the defendant has been denied either a constitutional or statutory right, the violation of which would, in itself, bar prosecution. If there has been no such denial, and if an application for a nolle prosequi meets the good cause and open court requirements of RC 2941.33 and Crim R 48(A), it should be granted. State v. Sutton (Wayne 1979) 64 Ohio App.2d 105, 411 N.E.2d 818, 18 O.O.3d 83.

2941.34 Lost or destroyed indictment

If an indictment or information is mutilated, obliterated, lost, mislaid, destroyed, or stolen, or for any other reason cannot be produced at the arraignment or trial of the defendant, the court may substitute a copy.

(127 v 847, eff. 9–16–57; 1953 H 1; GC 13437–33)

Historical and Statutory Notes

Pre–1953 H 1 Amendments: 113 v 170, Ch 16, § 33

Library References

Indictment and Information ⚷14.
Westlaw Topic No. 210.

Research References

Encyclopedias

OH Jur. 3d Criminal Law § 2326, Lost or Mutilated Pleading; Use of Copy.

MISDEMEANOR

2941.35 Prosecutions for misdemeanor

Prosecutions for misdemeanors may be instituted by a prosecuting attorney by affidavit or such other method as is provided by law in such courts as have original jurisdiction in misdemeanors. Laws as to form, sufficiency, amendments, objections, and exceptions to indictments and as to the service thereof apply to such affidavits and warrants issued thereon.

(1953 H 1, eff. 10–1–53; GC 13437–34)

Historical and Statutory Notes

Pre–1953 H 1 Amendments: 121 v 121; 113 v 170

Cross References

Indictment and information, Crim R 7

Library References

Criminal Law ⚩208.

Indictment and Information ⚩54.

Westlaw Topic Nos. 110, 210.

C.J.S. Criminal Law §§ 324 to 333, 337.

Research References

Encyclopedias

OH Jur. 3d Criminal Law § 2342, Advising Defendant of Charge and Facts—Affidavits and Complaints.

OH Jur. 3d Criminal Law § 2403, Statutory Provisions.

OH Jur. 3d Family Law § 1740, Commencement of Proceedings—Charges in an Affidavit.

Treatises and Practice Aids

Katz, Giannelli, Blair and Lipton, Baldwin's Ohio Practice, Criminal Law, § 40:2, Right to Indictment.

Katz, Giannelli, Blair and Lipton, Baldwin's Ohio Practice, Criminal Law, § 47:4, Required Motions.

Notes of Decisions

1. Affidavit—amendment

Where defendant and his counsel and the prosecution were unaware that the affidavit charging defendant with a traffic violation had not been verified until discovered by the judge at the end of the trial, a waiver may not be considered, and verification of the affidavit cannot be furnished at the end of the trial against objection of the defendant. Village of Pepper Pike v. LaMaida (Ohio Mun. 1970) 25 Ohio Misc. 252, 268 N.E.2d 296, 54 O.O.2d 410.

RC 2941.35 and 2941.30 permit the amendment of affidavits upon which prosecutions for misdemeanors have been instituted by the court, at any time before, during or after a trial in respect to any defect, imperfection, or omission in form or substance, or of any variance with the evidence, provided no change is made in the name or identity of the crime charged. State v. Walker (Franklin 1969) 20 Ohio App.2d 179, 252 N.E.2d 646, 49 O.O.2d 245.

Specific authority is given for the amendment of an affidavit to the same extent and under the same limitations as applied in the case of indictments and information in the common pleas court. State v. Jackson (Franklin 1960) 190 N.E.2d 38, 90 Ohio Law Abs. 577.

2. —— Contents, affidavit

RC 2941.05 applies equally to an affidavit charging crime. State v. Gundlach (Medina 1960) 112 Ohio App. 471, 174 N.E.2d 267, 15 O.O.2d 192.

3. —— Challenge, affidavit

Convicted party who failed to make direct attack on affidavit of charges, either in trial court or on appeal, cannot subsequently raise issue through a collateral attack on judgment. Plematis v. Berkemer (Franklin 1971) 30 Ohio App.2d 262, 285 N.E.2d 78, 59 O.O.2d 403. Judgment ⚩ 476

4. Alternate means to institute prosecution

The provisions of RC 103.35 directing that contempt proceedings shall be brought in accordance with RC 2705.03 to 2705.09 is not invalid, and it is immaterial if a charge of contempt takes the form of an indictment; contempt of the Ohio un-American activities commission is a misdemeanor, and, by RC 2941.35 misdemeanors may be prosecuted on information sworn to by the prosecuting attorney but such procedure is permissive, and the prosecution may be instituted by indictment. (See also State v Morgan, 164 OS 529, 133 NE(2d) 104 (1956); Morgan v Ohio, 354 US 929, 77 SCt 1403, 1 LEd(2d) 1535.) State v. Raley (Hamilton 1954) 100 Ohio App. 75, 136 N.E.2d 295, 60 O.O. 35, affirmed 164 Ohio St. 529, 133 N.E.2d 104, 58 O.O. 411, vacated 77 S.Ct. 1391, 354 U.S. 929, 1 L.Ed.2d 1532, vacated 77 S.Ct. 1403, 354 U.S. 929, 1 L.Ed.2d 1535, on remand 167 Ohio St. 295, 147 N.E.2d 847, 4 O.O.2d 342.

WARRANTS

2941.36 Warrant for arrest of accused

A warrant may be issued at any time by an order of a court, or on motion of a prosecuting attorney after the indictment, information, or affidavit is filed. When directed to the sheriff of the county where such indictment was found or information or affidavit filed, he may pursue and arrest the accused in any county and commit him to jail or present him in open court, if court is in session.

(1953 H 1, eff. 10–1–53; GC 13438–1)

Historical and Statutory Notes

Pre–1953 H 1 Amendments: 113 v 170, Ch 17, § 1

Cross References

Warrant or summons upon indictment or information, Crim R 9

Library References

Arrest ⚷65, 66.
Criminal Law ⚷215.
Westlaw Topic Nos. 110, 35.
C.J.S. Arrest §§ 6 to 8, 48, 55.
C.J.S. Criminal Law §§ 334 to 335, 337 to 338.

Research References

Treatises and Practice Aids

Katz, Giannelli, Blair and Lipton, Baldwin's Ohio Practice, Criminal Law, § 142:16, Warrant Upon Indictment or Information Issued by Court.

Notes of Decisions

Probable cause 1

---

1. Probable cause

County housing officer lacked a reasonable, articulable suspicion that defendant was engaged in criminal activity to justify a *Terry* stop of defendant, even though officer testified that he had received a "special attention" alert regarding drug activity and loitering in area, was patrolling an area of high drug activity, had made previous arrests for drug activity in area, and witnessed defendant engage in a brief conversation and a hand-to-hand transaction with a black male which, to officer, was suspicious activity, where officer failed to mention hand-to-hand transaction in his initial police report, and activity occurred during middle of day in the parking lot of a public housing estate which men, women, and children called their home. City Of Cleveland v. Fields (Ohio App. 8 Dist., Cuyahoga, 04-17-2003) No. 82070, 2003-Ohio-1965, 2003 WL 1901337, Unreported. Arrest ⚷ 63.5(5)

2941.37 Warrant when accused is nonresident

When an accused resides out of the county in which the indictment was found or information filed, a warrant may issue thereon, directed to the sheriff of the county where such accused resides or is found. Such sheriff shall arrest the accused and convey him to the county from which such warrant was issued, and there commit him to jail or present him in open court, if court is in session.

(1953 H 1, eff. 10–1–53; GC 13438–2)

Historical and Statutory Notes

Pre–1953 H 1 Amendments: 113 v 170, Ch 17, § 2

Cross References

Warrant or summons upon indictment or information, Crim R 9

Library References

Criminal Law ⚩215.
Westlaw Topic No. 110.
C.J.S. Criminal Law §§ 334 to 335, 337 to 338.

Research References

Encyclopedias

OH Jur. 3d Criminal Law § 2327, Issuance.

Treatises and Practice Aids

Katz, Giannelli, Blair and Lipton, Baldwin's Ohio Practice, Criminal Law, § 142:16, Warrant Upon Indictment or Information Issued by Court.

2941.38 Warrant when accused escapes

When an accused escapes and forfeits his recognizance after the jury is sworn, a warrant reciting the facts may issue at the request of the prosecuting attorney, to the sheriff of any county, who shall pursue, arrest, and commit the accused to the jail of the county from which such warrant issued, until he is discharged.

(1953 H 1, eff. 10–1–53; GC 13438–3)

Historical and Statutory Notes

Pre–1953 H 1 Amendments: 113 v 171, Ch 17, § 3

Library References

Criminal Law ⚩215.
Westlaw Topic No. 110.
C.J.S. Criminal Law §§ 334 to 335, 337 to 338.

CONVICTS

2941.39 Indictment of convicts

When a convict in a state correctional institution is indicted for a felony committed while confined in the correctional institution, the convict shall remain in the custody of the department of rehabilitation and correction, subject to sections 2941.40 to 2941.46 of the Revised Code.

(1997 S 111, eff. 3–17–98; 1994 H 571, eff. 10–6–94; 1953 H 1, eff. 10–1–53; GC 13438–4)

Historical and Statutory Notes

Pre–1953 H 1 Amendments: 113 v 171, Ch 17, § 4

Amendment Note: 1997 S 111 rewrote the section, which prior thereto read:

"When a convict in a state correctional institution is indicted for a felony committed while confined in the correctional institution, he shall remain in the custody of the warden or superintendent of the institution subject to the order of the court of common pleas of the county in which the institution is located."

Amendment Note: 1994 H 571 changed references to the penitentiary and reformatories to references to correctional institutions.

Library References

Criminal Law ⚩242.
Prisons ⚩13.5.
Westlaw Topic Nos. 110, 310.
C.J.S. Prisons and Rights of Prisoners §§ 130 to 143.

Research References

Encyclopedias

OH Jur. 3d Criminal Law § 4002, Generally; Custody of Indicted Convict.

Law Review and Journal Commentaries

The Core of Habeas Corpus: A New Definition, A New Test, Note. 3 Cap U L Rev 197 (1974).

Habeas Corpus—Prison Management–Custody and Control of Prisoners—Constitutional Law—Former Jeopardy (In Re Lamb), Note. 25 Case W Res L Rev 684 (Spring 1975).

Ohio Mail and Visitation Prison Regulations and the Evolving Recognition of Prisoners' Rights, Comment. 23 Clev St L Rev 109 (Winter 1974).

A Plan for Consistency and Fairness: Ohio's "Dead Time" Statute, Sheldon M. Slaybod, Julia K. Casey, Joan Torzewski. 9 U Tol L Rev 257 (Winter 1978).

Prison Discipline and the Eighth Amendment: A Psychological Perspective, Note. 43 U Cin L Rev 101 (1974).

Prisoners as Wards of the Court—A Nonconstitutional Path to Assure Correctional Reform by the Courts, Richard G. Singer. 41 U Cin L Rev 769 (1972).

Prisoners' Rights in the Hamilton County, Ohio Jail: The New Rules and Regulations, Comment. 45 U Cin L Rev 484 (1976).

Special Offender—Central Monitoring Case: Full Due Process Rights, Comment. 4 Ohio N U L Rev 658 (1977).

Surviving Justice: Prisoners' Rights to be Free from Physical Assault, Robert Plotkin. 23 Clev St L Rev 387 (Fall 1974).

Notes of Decisions

Speedy trial 1
Trial for misdemeanor 2

1. Speedy trial

Where an indictment is returned twenty-eight months after the affidavit against the accused was filed, the accused being imprisoned for another offense in the interim, there is a denial of a speedy trial. State v. Milner (Ohio Com.Pl. 1958) 149 N.E.2d 189, 78 Ohio Law Abs. 285, 6 O.O.2d 206.

2. Trial for misdemeanor

There is no statutory provision in the Revised Code for the removal of an inmate of a penitentiary or state reformatory to be tried on an indictment or information charging him with the commission of a misdemeanor. OAG 87–068.

2941.40 Convicts removed for sentence or trial

A convict in a state correctional institution, who escaped, forfeited his recognizance before receiving sentence for a felony, or against whom an indictment or information for felony is pending, may be removed to the county in which the conviction was had or the indictment or information was pending for sentence or trial, upon the warrant of the court of common pleas of the county.

(1994 H 571, eff. 10–6–94; 1969 H 508, eff. 10–24–69; 1953 H 1; GC 13438–5)

Historical and Statutory Notes

Pre–1953 H 1 Amendments: 113 v 171, Ch 17, § 5

Amendment Note: 1994 H 571 changed references to the penitentiary and reformatories to references to correctional institutions.

Library References

Criminal Law ⚷242.

Westlaw Topic No. 110.

Research References

Encyclopedias

OH Jur. 3d Criminal Law § 1436, Recapture of Escapee.

OH Jur. 3d Criminal Law § 4002, Generally; Custody of Indicted Convict.

OH Jur. 3d Criminal Law § 4003, Removal of Convict for Sentence or Trial.

OH Jur. 3d Criminal Law § 4004, Removal of Convict for Sentence or Trial—Warrant and Execution Thereof; Allowance of Fees.

Notes of Decisions

1. Trial for misdemeanor

There is no statutory provision in the Revised Code for the removal of an inmate of a penitentiary or state reformatory to be tried on an indictment or information charging him with the commission of a misdemeanor. OAG 87–068.

2. Transfer or removal of lifer

Release of a prisoner sentenced for life to another sovereign authority does not constitute a waiver of Ohio's right over his person. Bradley v. Cardwell (Ohio 1969) 20 Ohio St.2d 1, 251 N.E.2d 605, 49 O.O.2d 51. Criminal Law ⚷ 102

Even though sentenced to be imprisoned for life, a convict may be removed from a penal institution to attend a hearing on his petition for vacation of sentence under the so-called postconviction remedy procedures provided for in RC 2953.21 et seq.; the restriction in RC 2941.40 is not applicable to such proceedings. OAG 68–020.

3. Speedy trial

An accused is not denied his constitutional guaranty of a speedy trial where, following the filing of an affidavit charging him with a felony and his plea of not guilty, he is bound over to the common pleas court and then turned over to the authorities of another county for trial for felony, found guilty and sentenced to the penitentiary and, when released from confinement three years later he is delivered to the authorities of the first county to be tried for such previously charged felony on an information filed subsequent to his release from confinement and enters a plea of guilty thereto. State v. Henry (Gallia 1968) 13 Ohio App.2d 217, 235 N.E.2d 533, 42 O.O.2d 379.

Where an accused enters a plea of guilty without raising the question as to a denial of a speedy trial he waives his right thereto. Partsch v. Haskins (Ohio 1963) 175 Ohio St. 139, 191 N.E.2d 922, 23 O.O.2d 419.

4. Consecutive sentences

When a prisoner had been sentenced under a first conviction to two sentences for indeterminate terms of years and one sentence for life imprisonment, to be served concurrently, the date on which he would become eligible to be considered for parole is the same as the date of his eligibility to be considered for parole in relation to a sentence for life imprisonment, pursuant to a second conviction for the same criminal act after the first life sentence therefor had been set aside, which second life sentence was required by statute to be served consecutively with the two sentences for indeterminate years still being served at the time of the second conviction, and the eligibility of such prisoner to be considered for parole is not prejudiced by the trial court providing in its second judgment of conviction and sentence that the sentence for life imprisonment be served consecutively with the sentences which he was still serving arising from his first conviction, nor is the prisoner deprived of any constitutional rights when the trial court does not, in its second judgment of conviction and sentence, prescribe that the prisoner shall receive credit on his second life sentence for the time served on his first life sentence. State v. Packer (Marion 1969) 16 Ohio App.2d 171, 243 N.E.2d 115, 45 O.O.2d 492.

Where a prisoner at large on a revoked parole is convicted and sentenced for another offense, the unexpired term of his prior sentence will run consecutively with his subsequent sentence. King v. Maxwell (Ohio 1962) 173 Ohio St. 536, 184 N.E.2d 380, 20 O.O.2d 152, certiorari denied 83 S.Ct. 133, 371 U.S. 869, 9 L.Ed.2d 106.

Where a convict is tried for an offense in one of the circumstances stated in RC 2941.40 and is sentenced and returned to the penitentiary to serve consecutive sentences under RC 2941.43, such convict's eligibility for parole is determined by RC 2965.35. 1960 OAG 1451.

2941.401 Request by a prisoner for trial on pending charges

When a person has entered upon a term of imprisonment in a correctional institution of this state, and when during the continuance of the term of imprisonment there is pending in this state any untried indictment, information, or complaint against the prisoner, he shall be brought to trial within one hundred eighty days after he causes to be delivered to the prosecuting attorney and the appropriate court in which the matter is pending, written notice of the place of his imprisonment and a request for a final disposition to be made of the matter, except that for good cause shown in open court, with the prisoner or his counsel present, the court may grant any necessary or reasonable continuance. The request of the prisoner shall be accompanied by a certificate of the warden or superintendent having custody of the prisoner, stating the term of commitment under which the prisoner is being held, the time served and remaining to be served on the sentence, the amount of good time earned, the time of parole eligibility of the prisoner, and any decisions of the adult parole authority relating to the prisoner.

The written notice and request for final disposition shall be given or sent by the prisoner to the warden or superintendent having custody of him, who shall promptly forward it with the certificate to the appropriate prosecuting attorney and court by registered or certified mail, return receipt requested.

The warden or superintendent having custody of the prisoner shall promptly inform him in writing of the source and contents of any untried indictment, information, or complaint against him, concerning which the warden or superintendent has knowledge, and of his right to make a request for final disposition thereof.

Escape from custody by the prisoner, subsequent to his execution of the request for final disposition, voids the request.

If the action is not brought to trial within the time provided, subject to continuance allowed pursuant to this section, no court any longer has jurisdiction thereof, the indictment, information, or complaint is void, and the court shall enter an order dismissing the action with prejudice.

This section does not apply to any person adjudged to be mentally ill or who is under sentence of life imprisonment or death, or to any prisoner under sentence of death.

(1994 H 571, eff. 10–6–94; 1969 S 355, eff. 11–18–69)

Historical and Statutory Notes

Amendment Note: 1994 H 571 deleted "penal or" before "correctional" in the first paragraph.

Cross References

Interstate agreement on detainers, 2963.30 et seq.

Time within which hearing or trial must be held, 2945.71

Ohio Administrative Code References

Release to state or federal detainer, OAC 5120:1–1–33

Library References

Criminal Law ⚷577.10(1), 577.11(5).

Westlaw Topic No. 110.

C.J.S. Criminal Law §§ 583 to 588, 607.

Research References

Encyclopedias

OH Jur. 3d Criminal Law § 403, Applicability to Defendant Imprisoned for Another Offense; Imprisonment in Ohio.

OH Jur. 3d Criminal Law § 407, Effect of Failure to Demand Speedy Trial.

OH Jur. 3d Criminal Law § 409, Extension of Time for Hearing or Trial.

OH Jur. 3d Criminal Law § 411, Delay Attributable to Postponement of Trial.

OH Jur. 3d Criminal Law § 2834, Generally; Unavailability of Defendant.

OH Jur. 3d Criminal Law § 2855, Warden's Certificate; Delivery of Notice and Certificate.

OH Jur. 3d Criminal Law § 2856, Duty to Inform Prisoner.

OH Jur. 3d Habeas Corpus & Post Convict. Remedies § 18, Denial of Speedy Trial; Failure to Prosecute.

Treatises and Practice Aids

Markus, Trial Handbook for Ohio Lawyers, § 4:9, Speedy Trial—Statutory Time Limits—Accused Incarcerated or Arrested Outside Ohio.

Klein, Darling, & Terez, Baldwin's Ohio Practice Civil Practice § 6:4, Time--Computation--Day of Act, Event, or Default Not Included.

Katz, Giannelli, Blair and Lipton, Baldwin's Ohio Practice, Criminal Law, § 59:1, Introduction.

Katz, Giannelli, Blair and Lipton, Baldwin's Ohio Practice, Criminal Law, § 60:9, Extension—Unavailability of Accused.

Katz, Giannelli, Blair and Lipton, Baldwin's Ohio Practice, Criminal Law, § 59:11, Ohio Prisoners.

Katz, Giannelli, Blair and Lipton, Baldwin's Ohio Practice, Criminal Law, § 59:12, Interstate Compact on Detainers.

Notes of Decisions

---

1. Notice to prisoner of pending charge

Trial court's grant of defendant's motion to dismiss charges of failure to stop after an accident, driving under suspension, reckless operation, failure to control and driver's seatbelt requirement only a few days after motion was filed did not afford the prosecution its statutory opportunity to respond. City of Cleveland v. Austin (Ohio App. 8 Dist., Cuyahoga, 12-23-2004) No. 84451, 2004-Ohio-7022, 2004 WL 2979947, Unreported. Criminal Law ⚿ 303.20

Defendant, who was in county jail, did not properly follow procedures set forth in statute governing requests by prisoner for trial on pending charges, and as such, no speedy trial violation occurred in bringing defendant to trial; alleged notices and requests furnished by defendant at his speedy trial hearing showed that he had knowledge of charges pending against him, which his testimony confirmed, and because of this knowledge, once defendant was transferred to reception center from county jail, he was to send notices and requests to the proper court and prosecutor, but record did not show he did. State v. Siniard (Ohio App. 6 Dist., Huron, 03-05-2004) No. H-03-008, 2004-Ohio-1043, 2004 WL 413328, Unreported. Criminal Law ⚿ 577.10(10)

Defendant counsel's failure to file a motion to dismiss defendant's indictment for speedy trial violation constituted ineffective assistance, even though defendant was incarcerated at time she was indicted; State did not exercise due diligence in notifying defendant of indictment, and more than 180 days elapsed from date defendant was indicted until date defendant was arraigned. State v. Boone (Ohio App. 8 Dist., Cuyahoga, 03-03-2003) No. 81155, 2003-Ohio-996, 2003 WL 757603, Unreported. Criminal Law ⚿ 641.13(2.1)

When an untried indictment, information, or complaint is pending in Ohio against a prisoner and the pending charges are based on the alleged commission of additional crimes separate and apart from the crimes for which the prisoner is currently serving his sentence, the prosecution is required to notify the warden or superintendent having custody of the prisoner of the pending charge, and the warden or superintendent is, in turn, required to inform the prisoner in writing of the pending charge and his right to make a request for final disposition thereof. State v. Smith (Ohio App. 3 Dist., 09-29-2000) 140 Ohio App.3d 81, 746 N.E.2d 678, 2000-Ohio-1777. Criminal Law ⚿ 577.11(3)

Incarcerated defendant's duty under the speedy trial statute to request final disposition of an indictment is not triggered until and unless the defendant knows of the pending indictment. State v. Brown (Ohio App. 4 Dist., 11-23-1998) 131 Ohio App.3d 387, 722 N.E.2d 594. Criminal Law ⚿ 577.10(10)

Speedy trial statute places an affirmative duty upon the warden or superintendent having custody over a prisoner to promptly inform the prisoner of a pending charge. State v. Brown (Ohio App. 4 Dist., 11-23-1998) 131 Ohio App.3d 387, 722 N.E.2d 594. Criminal Law ⚿ 577.11(3)

State cannot avoid the requirements of the speedy trial statute by neglecting or refusing to send a copy of the indictment to the warden of the accused's institution of incarceration; although the statute does not explicitly require the state to give notice of an indictment to an accused who is incarcerated on a different charge, the statute would have no meaning if the state could circumvent its requirements by not sending notice of an indictment to the warden of the institution where the accused is imprisoned. State v. Brown (Ohio App. 4 Dist., 11-23-1998) 131 Ohio App.3d 387, 722 N.E.2d 594. Criminal Law ⚿ 577.11(3)

RC 2941.401 provides that the warden or superintendent having custody of a prisoner shall promptly inform him in writing of the source and contents of any untried indictment, information, or complaint against him, concerning which the warden or superintendent has knowledge, and of the prisoner's right to make a request for final disposition thereof; consequently, where a warden or superintendent fails to so inform the prisoner, the state cannot rely upon the prisoner's failure to make demand for speedy disposition of the pending indictment but must count the 180–day time period as commencing upon the first triggering of the state's duty to give notice of the right to make demand for speedy disposition. State v. Fitch (Coshocton 1987) 37 Ohio App.3d 159, 524 N.E.2d 912.

Delay in notifying a prisoner serving a sentence of new charges pending against him is excused, and does not deny the prisoner's right to a speedy trial, where the warden of the institution was without knowledge of the new charges, and police made diligent efforts to find and serve the prisoner with notice. State v. Martin (Franklin 1984) 16 Ohio App.3d 172, 475 N.E.2d 185, 16 O.B.R. 182.

The state need not notify a prisoner of new charges lodged against him on the same day the charges are filed, rather the state has a duty to notify the prisoner within a reasonable time and where the defendant is held in custody for only 196 days, the state's failure to inform a defendant of the formal filing of new charges within sixteen days so the defendant could demand a trial before he is released from prison will not be held unreasonable under RC 2941.401. State v Taylor, No. 92AP–1639, 1993 WL 268431 (10th Dist Ct App, Franklin, 6–29–93).

2. Request for final disposition

Statutory speedy trial period began to run when drug defendant, who was incarcerated, tendered to warden two copies of a notice of availability and a demand for final disposition of untried indictment, even though copy intended for clerk of court was improperly sent to county prosecutor's office due to an error by warden's office; record indicated that defendant fully complied with speedy trial statute for inmates, and the warden's error would not be imputed to inmate. State v. Gill (Ohio App. 8 Dist., Cuyahoga, 03-18-2004) No. 82742, 2004-Ohio-1245, 2004 WL 528449, Unreported. Criminal Law ⚿ 577.8(2)

Murder defendant was not deprived of his statutory right to speedy trial, where defendant was found guilty of another charge while awaiting trial on subject charge and defendant failed to petition state to bring him to trial as required to invoke statutory deadlines. State v. Chapman (Ohio App. 8 Dist., Cuyahoga, 08-07-2003) No. 73609, 2003-Ohio-4163, 2003 WL 21805616, Unreported. Criminal Law ⚿ 577.10(10); Criminal Law ⚿ 577.11(3)

Defendant scheduled for trial within 180 days of his request for disposition was not denied his statutory right to speedy trial. State v. Robison (Ohio App. 5 Dist., Licking, 12-19-2002) No. 02CA00015, 2002-Ohio-7216, 2002 WL 31875016, Unreported, motion for delayed appeal denied 98 Ohio St.3d 1473, 784 N.E.2d 707, 2003-Ohio-904, appeal not allowed 98 Ohio St.3d 1565, 787 N.E.2d 1230, 2003-Ohio-2242. Criminal Law ⚿ 577.10(10); Criminal Law ⚿ 577.15(1)

When reviewing a ruling on a speedy trial issue, Court of Appeals gives deference to trial judge's factual findings, but reviews the application of those facts to the law de novo. Cleveland v. Adkins (Ohio App. 8 Dist., 03-11-2004) 156 Ohio App.3d 482, 806 N.E.2d 1007, 2004-Ohio-1118. Criminal Law ⚿ 1139; Criminal Law ⚿ 1158(1)

Duty to bring an incarcerated defendant to trial within 180 days of the defendant's written notice of the place of his imprisonment and a request for a final disposition arises only after receipt of the statutory notice. State v. Hairston (Ohio, 03-17-2004) 101 Ohio St.3d 308, 804 N.E.2d 471, 2004-Ohio-969. Criminal Law ⚿ 577.11(3)

Prisoner who never caused the requisite notice of imprisonment and request for final disposition to be delivered to either the prosecuting attorney or the court never triggered the process to cause him to be brought to trial within 180 days of his notice and request. State v. Hairston (Ohio, 03-17-2004) 101 Ohio St.3d 308, 804 N.E.2d 471, 2004-Ohio-969. Criminal Law ⚿ 577.11(3)

Statute which applies when charges are pending against a prisoner does not require state to exercise reasonable diligence in locating an incarcerated defendant against whom charges are pending; rather, the statute requires the state to bring the defendant to trial within 180 days after he causes to be delivered to the prosecuting attorney and the appropriate court written notice of the place of his imprisonment and a request for a final disposition. State v. Hairston (Ohio, 03-17-2004) 101 Ohio St.3d 308, 804 N.E.2d 471, 2004-Ohio-969. Criminal Law ⚿ 577.11(3)

When a prisoner is notified of an untried indictment, information, or complaint in Ohio based on the alleged commission of additional crimes separate and apart from the crimes for which he is currently serving his sentence, he must cause to be delivered to the prosecuting attorney and the appropriate court in which the matter is pending written notice of the place of his imprisonment and a request for a final disposition to be made of the matter; if the action is not thereafter brought to trial within one hundred eighty days of the prisoner's written notice, no court has jurisdiction over the pending charges, and the charges must be dismissed. State v. Smith (Ohio App. 3 Dist., 09-29-2000) 140 Ohio App.3d 81, 746 N.E.2d 678, 2000-Ohio-1777. Criminal Law ⚿ 577.8(2); Criminal Law ⚿ 577.10(10); Criminal Law ⚿ 577.11(3); Criminal Law ⚿ 577.16(11)

The 180–day period under the speedy trial statute for bringing to trial a defendant who is already incarcerated begins to run after the defendant's notice of place of imprisonment and request for final disposition of the matter have been received by the prosecuting attorney and the appropriate court in which the charges are pending. State v. Smith (Ohio App. 3 Dist., 09-29-2000) 140 Ohio App.3d 81, 746 N.E.2d 678, 2000-Ohio-1777. Criminal Law ⚿ 577.8(2)

Indictment of defendant, who was incarcerated on separate conviction at time of indictment, should have been dismissed on speedy trial grounds, where state failed to notify warden of indictment, warden did not notify defendant of indictment or of right to make request for final disposition pursuant to speedy trial statute, and record did not reflect that trial court's order continuing case past speedy trial limit due to number of cases on its docket was entered in open court with either defendant or counsel present. State v. Miller (Ohio App. 11 Dist., 08-19-1996) 113 Ohio App.3d 606, 681 N.E.2d 970. Criminal Law ⚿ 577.11(3); Criminal Law ⚿ 577.16(2)

Period of 180 days in which defendant who is in prison on other charges must be tried on new charges does not begin to run until notice of request for disposition of the untried indictment has been filed with county prosecutor. State v. Grinnell (Ohio App. 10 Dist., 06-27-1996) 112 Ohio App.3d 124, 678 N.E.2d 231, appeal not allowed 77 Ohio St.3d 1474, 673 N.E.2d 138, appeal not allowed 77 Ohio St.3d 1475, 673 N.E.2d 138, denial of habeas corpus affirmed 215 F.3d 1326, certiorari denied 121 S.Ct. 232, 531 U.S. 898, 148 L.Ed.2d 166. Criminal Law ⚿ 577.8(2); Criminal Law ⚿ 577.11(3)

Although record reflected photocopy of letter sent by defendant to prosecutor stating that defendant was in county jail, defendant failed to comply with other requirements of statute allowing person serving term of incarceration to request adjudication on pending charges, in that letter was not filed with court and there was no certificate by warden or superintendent having custody of him, and absent compliance with statute, court was not obligated to bring defendant to trial within 180 days. State v. Brown (Cuyahoga 1992) 84 Ohio App.3d 414, 616 N.E.2d 1179, dismissed, jurisdictional motion overruled 66 Ohio St.3d 1467, 611 N.E.2d 325. Criminal Law ⚿ 577.10(10); Criminal Law ⚿ 577.11(1)

Letter requesting disposition of pending charges received by trial court from United States penitentiary comported with requirements of statute pertaining to interstate agreement on detainers, which essentially mirrored statute allowing person serving term of incarceration to request adjudication on pending charges, but which applied to prisoners held out of state, and, thus, defendant properly invoked his rights and was brought to trial within 180 days set forth in statute pertaining to interstate agreement on detainers. State v. Brown (Cuyahoga 1992) 84 Ohio App.3d 414, 616 N.E.2d 1179, dismissed, jurisdictional motion overruled 66 Ohio St.3d 1467, 611 N.E.2d 325. Extradition And Detainers ⚿ 59

Where a defendant avails himself of the speedy trial rights of RC 2941.401 by filing a motion for final disposition of any untried indictments in which he sets forth both the names used by him, the address and institutional location, and his penal system prison number, his failure to include the warden's certificate does not prevent the trial court from losing jurisdiction and the indictments against the defendant from becoming void after the expiration of the 180–day speedy trial period following the delivery of the motion to the court and the prosecuting attorney. State v. Drowell (Ohio Com. Pl. 1991) 61 Ohio Misc.2d 623, 581 N.E.2d 1183.

Before a defendant imprisoned on another charge can avail himself of RC 2941.401, he must first show that he delivered written notice to both the prosecuting attorney and the appropriate court, stating his place of imprisonment and requesting that there be a final disposition made of his case; thereafter, defendant must be brought to trial within 180 days. State v. Turner (Medina 1982) 4 Ohio App.3d 305, 448 N.E.2d 516, 4 O.B.R. 556. Criminal Law ⚿ 577.11(3)

Pursuant to RC 2941.401, when a prisoner in a state correctional institution provides appropriate officials written notice of his place of imprisonment and a request for final disposition of a pending misdemeanor charge that is set forth in a complaint filed with a municipal court, the prisoner may be removed from the institution and taken to the municipal court for final disposition of the matter. OAG 02-027.

When, pursuant to RC 2941.401, a prisoner in a state correctional institution provides appropriate officials written notice of his place of imprisonment and a request for final disposition of a pending misdemeanor charge that is set forth in a complaint, a municipal court in which the matter is pending may issue a warrant that requires a bailiff of the court, a municipal police officer, or a county sheriff to transport the prisoner to the court for final disposition of the matter. OAG 02-027.

3. Tolling speedy trial period

Speedy trial right of defendant who was a prisoner at the time of his indictment, but who was released from prison and held in county jail, was violated when he was not brought to trial within 90 days of his release from prison, where defendant was held in jail in lieu of bond solely on the pending charge, and there was no valid holder related to any other charge. State v. Beverly (Ohio App. 4 Dist., Ross, 09-13-2005) No. 04CA2809, 2005-Ohio-4954, 2005 WL 2293581, Unreported. Criminal Law ⚿ 577.11(1)

Defendant's failure to deliver to either prosecuting attorney or trial court the requisite notice of his imprisonment and request for final disposition tolled speedy trial period, on pending charges of escape. State v. Milner (Ohio App. 5 Dist., Morgan, 07-06-2005) No. 04 CA 5, 2005-Ohio-3467, 2005 WL 1580816, Unreported. Criminal Law ⚿ 577.11(5)

Statute which applies when charges are pending against a prisoner does not require state to exercise reasonable diligence in locating an incarcerated defendant against whom charges are pending; rather, the statute requires the state to bring the defendant to trial within 180 days after he causes to be delivered to the prosecuting attorney and the appropriate court written notice of the place of his imprisonment and a request for a final disposition. State v. Milner (Ohio App. 5 Dist., Morgan, 07-06-2005) No. 04 CA 5, 2005-Ohio-3467, 2005 WL 1580816, Unreported. Criminal Law ⚿ 577.11(5)

Statutory 180-day period for bringing defendant to trial under speedy trial statute was tolled while defendant was in prison on unrelated charges, where defendant never caused requisite notice of imprisonment and request for final disposition to be delivered to either prosecuting attorney or court. State v. Larkin (Ohio App. 5 Dist., Richland, 06-21-2005) No. 2004-CA-103, 2005-Ohio-3122, 2005 WL 1463255, Unreported. Criminal Law ⚿ 577.11(3)

Defendant's statutory right to a speedy trial was not violated, even though she was not brought to trial within 180 days after she caused delivery of written notice of the place of her imprisonment and a request for a final disposition; time was tolled while defendant was incarcerated as a result of other criminal charges, and the State exercised reasonable diligence in attempting to secure her attendance in the case. State v. Ray (Ohio App. 2 Dist., Greene, 05-27-2005) No. 2004-CA-64, 2005-Ohio-2771, 2005 WL 1322723, Unreported. Criminal Law ⚿ 577.11(3)

Defendant's speedy trial rights on pending charges were tolled while he was in prison on other charges, where he failed to file motion of availability. City of Cleveland v. Branham (Ohio App. 8 Dist., Cuyahoga, 03-24-2005) No. 84855, 2005-Ohio-1313, 2005 WL 678118, Unreported. Criminal Law ⚿ 577.10(10); Criminal Law ⚿ 577.11(3)

Delay caused by grant of defense counsel's motion for continuance was attributable to defendant for purposes of determining whether defendant was properly brought to trial within 180 days under statute governing prisoners' speedy trial rights. State v. Shepherd (Ohio App. 11 Dist., Ashtabula, 09-30-2004) No. 2003-A-0031, 2004-Ohio-5306, 2004 WL 2803407, Unreported. Criminal Law ⚷ 577.10(8)

Statutory 180-day period under speedy trial statute was tolled as result of conduct attributable to defendant, and thus defendant's right to speedy trial on charges of breaking and entering, and receiving stolen property, was not violated; defendant filed motion for evidentiary hearing which tolled statutory period for 22 days, defendant filed request for counsel, which resulted in tolling of period for 16 days until counsel was appointed, and defendant filed motion to dismiss which tolled period for 45 days until trial court ruled on motion and dismissed indictment. State v. Roberts (Ohio App. 6 Dist., Wood, 10-15-2004) No. WD-04-028, 2004-Ohio-5509, 2004 WL 2320338, Unreported. Criminal Law ⚷ 577.10(8)

Statutory 180-day period for bringing defendant to trial under speedy trial statute began to run not when defendant filed motion to dismiss on basis of violation of his right to speedy trial, but when trial court received defendant's completed "Certificate of Inmate Status" form. State v. Roberts (Ohio App. 6 Dist., Wood, 10-15-2004) No. WD-04-028, 2004-Ohio-5509, 2004 WL 2320338, Unreported. Criminal Law ⚷ 577.8(2)

Statute governing a request by a prisoner for trial on pending charges does not require state to exercise reasonable diligence in locating an incarcerated defendant against whom charges are pending. State v. Fairley (Ohio App. 3 Dist., Hancock, 05-24-2004) No. 5-03-41, 2004-Ohio-2616, 2004 WL 1146530, Unreported. Criminal Law ⚷ 577.11(1)

Defendant's speedy trial rights were not violated by four month delay between time when officer located crack pipe and the time when defendant was indicted for possession of cocaine; State was actively investigating the case by submitting crack pipe for scientific testing, and indictment was issued one month after officer became aware of results of scientific testing on pipe. State v. Fairley (Ohio App. 3 Dist., Hancock, 05-24-2004) No. 5-03-41, 2004-Ohio-2616, 2004 WL 1146530, Unreported. Indictment And Information ⚷ 7

Even assuming that request for trial was valid and proper, habeas action against judge to compel immediate release of drug defendant from custody, on grounds that his rights to a speedy trial had been violated, was premature; trial court had jurisdiction until 180 days from date of request and, then, defendant could enforce speedy trial rights through motion to dismiss and, if necessary, appeal. Henderson v. Lebarron (Ohio App. 8 Dist., Cuyahoga, 03-03-2004) No. 84030, 2004-Ohio-1002, 2004 WL 397155, Unreported. Habeas Corpus ⚷ 223

Jailed defendant's right to speedy trial on charges of domestic violence and assault was not violated, since his motions for bill of particulars, a discovery request, intent to use evidence, and dismissal tolled running of speedy trial period. City of Cleveland v. Sheldon (Ohio App. 8 Dist., Cuyahoga, 11-26-2003) No. 82319, 2003-Ohio-6331, 2003 WL 22804364, Unreported. Criminal Law ⚷ 577.10(8)

Speedy trial statute governing requests for trial by a prisoner, and not general speedy trial statute, controlled speedy trial period for defendant who was already incarcerated for a separate offense. State v. Pesci (Ohio App. 11 Dist., Lake, 12-20-2002) No. 2001-L-026, 2002-Ohio-7131, 2002 WL 31866167, Unreported, appeal not allowed 98 Ohio St.3d 1566, 787 N.E.2d 1231, 2003-Ohio-2242. Criminal Law ⚷ 577.5

In calculating speedy trial period for defendant who was already incarcerated for another offense, time was tolled for defendant's motions to dismiss and motion to suppress. State v. Pesci (Ohio App. 11 Dist., Lake, 12-20-2002) No. 2001-L-026, 2002-Ohio-7131, 2002 WL 31866167, Unreported, appeal not allowed 98 Ohio St.3d 1566, 787 N.E.2d 1231, 2003-Ohio-2242. Criminal Law ⚷ 577.10(8)

State's duty to inform defendant who was already incarcerated for a separate offense of his right to make a demand for a speedy disposition was triggered on date of arraignment, and thus, 180-day statutory time limit for bringing defendant to trial commenced on date of arraignment, where warden did not notify defendant of his right to demand a speedy disposition. State v. Pesci (Ohio App. 11 Dist., Lake, 12-20-2002) No. 2001-L-026, 2002-Ohio-7131, 2002 WL 31866167, Unreported, appeal not allowed 98 Ohio St.3d 1566, 787 N.E.2d 1231, 2003-Ohio-2242. Criminal Law ⚷ 577.8(2)

Statutory speedy trial time was tolled with respect to pending forgery charge against defendant until he was released from prison, as defendant failed to meet his initial duty to provide written notice requesting final disposition and to notify state of his whereabouts, under statute governing request by a prisoner for trial on pending charges. (Per Kline, J., with two judges concurring in judgment only.) State v. Roulette (Ohio App. 4 Dist., 10-04-2005) 2005-Ohio-5435, 2005 WL 2562639. Criminal Law ⚷ 577.8(2); Criminal Law ⚷ 577.11(1)

When a defendant who is imprisoned is aware of pending charges against him and fails to file a written notice requesting final disposition and notifying the state of his whereabouts, as permitted by statute governing request by a prisoner for trial on pending charges, the statutory speedy trial time period tolls until his release from prison; while statute governing extension of time for hearing or trial places a duty of reasonable diligence to secure a defendant's availability on the state, that duty is not triggered if the defendant is aware of the pending charges and fails to exercise his duty under statute governing request by a prisoner for trial on pending charges, and the state is not aware of his whereabouts. (Per Kline, J., with two judges concurring in judgment only.) State v. Roulette (Ohio App. 4 Dist., 10-04-2005) 2005-Ohio-5435, 2005 WL 2562639. Criminal Law ⚷ 577.8(2); Criminal Law ⚷ 577.11(1)

When reviewing a ruling on a speedy trial issue, Court of Appeals gives deference to trial judge's factual findings, but reviews the application of those facts to the law de novo. Cleveland v. Adkins (Ohio App. 8 Dist., 03-11-2004) 156 Ohio App.3d 482, 806 N.E.2d 1007, 2004-Ohio-1118. Criminal Law ⚷ 1139; Criminal Law ⚷ 1158(1)

Where prosecution of defendant who was already incarcerated on other charges was continued after first pretrial conference because parties needed more time to discuss case, 35 days between first and second pretrial conferences were tolled, for speedy trial purposes. State v. Smith (Ohio App. 3 Dist., 09-29-2000) 140 Ohio App.3d 81, 746 N.E.2d 678, 2000-Ohio-1777. Criminal Law ⚷ 577.10(4)

Where defendant fled jurisdiction in order to evade prosecution on instant charges, he could not claim that his right to a speedy trial was violated prior to his request, filed while he was incarcerated for other offenses, that those untried indictments pending against him be disposed of. State v. Smith (Ohio App. 3 Dist., 09-29-2000) 140 Ohio App.3d 81, 746 N.E.2d 678, 2000-Ohio-1777. Criminal Law ⚷ 577.11(2)

Delay of 19 months between indictment and commencement of trial was not unreasonable, for speedy trial purposes; because overriding factor preventing defendant's trial was his decision to flee jurisdiction, delay was solely within his control. State v. Smith (Ohio App. 3 Dist., 09-29-2000) 140 Ohio App.3d 81, 746 N.E.2d 678, 2000-Ohio-1777. Criminal Law ⚷ 577.11(2); Criminal Law ⚷ 577.15(4)

Statute setting 180–day period for bringing to trial defendant who was already incarcerated, rather than statute setting forth 270–day speedy trial period, governed prosecution of defendant who was incarcerated for other offenses after he failed to appear for arraignment on instant charges. State v. Smith (Ohio App. 3 Dist., 09-29-2000) 140 Ohio App.3d 81, 746 N.E.2d 678, 2000-Ohio-1777. Criminal Law ⚷ 577.5

In a prosecution for aggravated robbery with a firearms specification and breaking and entering, a defendant's speedy trial rights are not violated for failure to bring him to trial within 180 days of his demand for final disposition where (1) the defendant requested final disposition January 16, 1990; (2) the defendant's counsel agreed on March 26 to a continuance for purposes of preparing for trial; (3) the defendant, on September 10, 1990, moved to dismiss the indictment; and (4) the trial was held on October 22, 1990; the defendant's motion to dismiss tolled the 180–day period through the date of trial and the agreement of counsel to the continuance bound the defendant and waived his speedy trial right for a period of sixty-four days until he again requested final disposition, regardless of whether the defendant consented to the waiver. State v. Logan (Franklin 1991) 71 Ohio App.3d 292, 593 N.E.2d 395, dismissed, jurisdictional motion overruled 62 Ohio St.3d 1463, 580 N.E.2d 784, cause dismissed 75 Ohio St.3d 1427, 662 N.E.2d 376.

When a defendant is incarcerated on other charges, statute governing requests by a prisoner for trial on pending charges prevails over the general speedy trial statutes, governing the time within which the defendant must be brought to trial. State v. Cox (Ohio App. 4 Dist., Jackson, 05-14-2002) No. 01CA10, 2002-Ohio-2382, 2002 WL 1083897, Unreported. Criminal Law ⚷ 577.11(3)

Where a defendant already incarcerated on other charges is indicted, and he knows of the pending indictment but the warden of the facility in which he is incarcerated does not, a delay in notifying the court of the place of incarceration will be charged to the defendant and will thus toll the running of the speedy trial time period. State v Terrell, No. 90 CA 44 (7th Dist Ct App, Mahoning, 12–6–90).

Where an incarcerated defendant is indicted on unrelated charges, is aware of such indictment, and the state is unaware of his location, the state is under no duty to conduct a diligent search for him; where the defendant never notifies the state of his whereabouts the speedy trial time period in RC 2941.401 never commences to run. State v Himes, No. CA88–01–007 (12th Dist Ct App, Clermont, 12–12–88).

4. Discharge for delay

Statute which applies when charges are pending against a prisoner grants to an incarcerated defendant a chance to have all pending charges resolved in a timely manner, thereby preventing the state from delaying prosecution until after the defendant has been released from his prison term; it does not, however, allow a defendant to avoid prosecution simply because the state failed to locate him. State v. Hairston (Ohio, 03-17-2004) 101 Ohio St.3d 308, 804 N.E.2d 471, 2004-Ohio-969. Criminal Law ⚷ 577.11(3)

Once a defendant has demonstrated that the 180–day period under the speedy trial statute for bringing to trial a defendant who is already incarcerated has expired, he has established a prima facie case for dismissal; the burden then shifts to the state to demonstrate any tolling or extensions of time permissible under the law. State v. Smith (Ohio App. 3 Dist., 09-29-2000) 140 Ohio App.3d 81, 746 N.E.2d 678, 2000-Ohio-1777. Criminal Law ⚷ 577.16(8)

A defendant to a criminal charge is denied a speedy trial and entitled to discharge of the indictment when approximately seventeen months elapses from the date of indictment to date of service thereof, approximately two years and four months elapses between the date of indictment and the date of trial, during which period the only delay occasioned by the defendant has been created by his failure to enter his plea of not guilty by reason of insanity in writing resulting in a delay of some thirty days for pretrial observation, and during which period the defendant has on at least five separate occasions moved to dismiss the proceedings against him or quash the indictment because of the denial of a speedy trial. State v. Stapleton

(Allen 1974) 41 Ohio App.2d 219, 325 N.E.2d 243, 70 O.O.2d 440.

5. Mandamus to compel dismissal

Mandamus will not lie to compel dismissal of an indictment on the ground the case was not heard within 180 days after a demand for trial, since an adequate remedy at law is available. State ex rel. Bowling v. Court of Common Pleas of Hamilton County (Ohio 1970) 24 Ohio St.2d 158, 265 N.E.2d 296, 53 O.O.2d 355.

6. Interstate agreement on detainers, effect

Speedy trial time under the Intrastate Detainer Act did not begin to run until incarcerated defendant sent written request to prosecuting attorney and trial court requesting disposition of his untried indictment. State v. Mavroudis (Ohio App. 7 Dist., Columbiana, 06-16-2003) No. 02 CO 44, 2003-Ohio-3289, 2003 WL 21453468, Unreported. Extradition And Detainers ⚷ 59

Interstate Agreement on Detainers (IAD) does not create duty on part of state to promptly notify prisoners of detainers. State v. Wells (Ohio App. 10 Dist., 04-04-1996) 110 Ohio App.3d 275, 673 N.E.2d 1008, dismissed, appeal not allowed 77 Ohio St.3d 1413, 670 N.E.2d 1002. Extradition And Detainers ⚷ 57

2941.41 Warrant for removal

A warrant for removal specified in section 2941.40 of the Revised Code shall be in the usual form, except that it shall set forth that the accused is in a state correctional institution. The warrant shall be directed to the sheriff of the county in which the conviction was had or the indictment or information is pending. When a copy of the warrant is presented to the warden or the superintendent of a state correctional institution, he shall deliver the convict to the sheriff who shall convey him to the county and commit him to the county jail. For removing and returning the convict, the sheriff shall receive the fees allowed for conveying convicts to a state correctional institution.

(1994 H 571, eff. 10–6–94; 1981 H 145, eff. 5–28–81; 1953 H 1; GC 13438–6)

Historical and Statutory Notes

Pre–1953 H 1 Amendments: 113 v 171, Ch 17, § 6

Amendment Note: 1994 H 571 changed references to the penitentiary and reformatories to references to correctional institutions.

Library References

Criminal Law ⚷242.

Westlaw Topic No. 110.

Research References

Encyclopedias

OH Jur. 3d Criminal Law § 4004, Removal of Convict for Sentence or Trial—Warrant and Execution Thereof; Allowance of Fees.

2941.42 Convict to be confined

A convict removed as provided by section 2941.41 of the Revised Code shall be kept in jail subject to be taken into court for sentence or trial. If the case is continued or the execution of the sentence is suspended, the court may order him to be returned to the state correctional institution by the sheriff, who shall deliver him, with a certified copy of the order, to the warden, who shall again deliver the convict to the sheriff upon another certified order of the court.

(1994 H 571, eff. 10–6–94; 1953 H 1, eff. 10–1–53; GC 13438–7)

Historical and Statutory Notes

Pre–1953 H 1 Amendments: 113 v 171, Ch 17, § 7

Amendment Note: 1994 H 571 substituted “state correctional institution” for “penitentiary”.

Cross References

Classified civil service, report of violation of statutes or rules filed by employee, protection of reporting employee, 124.341

Library References

Criminal Law ⚷242.
Westlaw Topic No. 110.

Research References

Encyclopedias

OH Jur. 3d Criminal Law § 4005, Custody After Removal.

2941.43 Disposition of prisoner following trial for another offense

If the convict referred to in section 2941.40 of the Revised Code is acquitted, he shall forthwith returned [1] by the sheriff to the state correctional institution to serve out the remainder of his sentence. If he is sentenced to imprisonment in a state correctional institution, he shall be returned to the state correctional institution by the sheriff to serve his new term. If he is sentenced to death, the death sentence shall be executed as if he were not under sentence of imprisonment in a state correctional institution.

(1994 H 571, eff. 10–6–94; 1972 H 511, eff. 1–1–74; 131 v H 700; 1953 H 1; GC 13438–8)

[1] So in original; should this read "be returned"?

Historical and Statutory Notes

Pre–1953 H 1 Amendments: 113 v 172, Ch 17, § 8

Amendment Note: 1994 H 571 substituted "state correctional institution" for "penitentiary".

Cross References

Classified civil service, report of violation of statutes or rules filed by employee, protection of reporting employee, 124.341

Library References

Criminal Law ⚷241.
Westlaw Topic No. 110.
C.J.S. Criminal Law § 354.

Research References

Encyclopedias

OH Jur. 3d Criminal Law § 4006, Disposition After Trial.

Treatises and Practice Aids

Hastings, Manoloff, Sheeran, & Stype, Ohio School Law § 25:2, Statutory Standards for Student Conduct.

Notes of Decisions

1. Concurrent and consecutive sentences

Inasmuch as making sentences for different crimes run concurrently is in the nature of a reward to the convict, relieving him of paying a part of the penalty for his crimes, it follows that a positive act is required on the part of the sentencing court to cause sentences to run concurrently; and, in the absence of such action, if the entry is silent as to how sentences shall run, it is presumed such sentences will run consecutively. Stewart v. Maxwell (Ohio 1963) 174 Ohio St. 180, 187 N.E.2d 888, 22 O.O.2d 116.

Where a prisoner at large on a weekend parole is convicted and sentenced for another offense, the unexpired term of his prior sentence will run consecutively with his subsequent sentence. King v. Maxwell (Ohio 1962) 173 Ohio St. 536, 184 N.E.2d 380, 20 O.O.2d 152, certiorari denied 83 S.Ct. 133, 371 U.S. 869, 9 L.Ed.2d 106.

2. Parole eligibility

When a prisoner had been sentenced under a first conviction to two sentences for indeterminate terms of years and one sentence for life imprisonment, to be served concurrently, the date on which he would become eligible to be considered for parole is the same as the date of his eligibility to be considered for parole in relation to a sentence for life imprisonment, pursuant to a second conviction for the same criminal act after the first life sentence therefor had been set aside, which second life sentence was required by statute to be served consecutively with the two sentences for indeterminate years still being served at the time of the second conviction, and the eligibility of such prisoner to be considered for parole is not prejudiced by the trial court providing in its second judgment of conviction and sentence that the sentence for life imprisonment be served consecutively with the sentences which he was still serving arising from his first conviction, nor is the prisoner deprived of any constitutional rights when the trial court does not, in its second judgment of conviction and sentence, prescribe that the prisoner shall receive credit on his second life sentence for the time served on his first life sentence. State v. Packer (Marion 1969) 16 Ohio App.2d 171, 243 N.E.2d 115, 45 O.O.2d 492.

Where a convict is tried for an offense in one of the circumstances stated in RC 2941.40 and is sentenced and returned to the penitentiary to serve consecutive sentences under RC 2941.43, such convict's eligibility for parole is determined by RC 2965.35. 1960 OAG 1451.

3. Final release

The term "parole" is defined in RC 2965.01 to signify actual "release from confinement," and because the power of the pardon and parole commission to terminate a particular term of imprisonment by a "final release" is conditioned upon (1) such actual release on parole, and (2) the parolee's satisfactory conduct for at least one year in such parole status, the commission is without authority as to a convict sentenced under RC 2941.43 to give a "final release" as to his earlier term so as to permit him to begin serving in the term to which he was subsequently sentenced, the special situation described in RC 2941.43 being an exception to the general provisions of RC 5145.01. 1960 OAG 1333.

2941.44 Arrests and return of escaped convicts; expenses

Sheriffs, deputy sheriffs, marshals, deputy marshals, watchmen, police officers, and coroners may arrest a convict escaping from a state correctional institution and forthwith convey him to the institution and deliver him to the warden of the institution. They shall be allowed ten cents per mile going to and returning from the institution and additional compensation that the warden finds reasonable for the necessary expense incurred.

(1994 H 571, eff. 10–6–94; 128 v 542, eff. 7–17–59; 1953 H 1; GC 13438–9)

Historical and Statutory Notes

Pre–1953 H 1 Amendments: 113 v 172, Ch 17, § 19

Amendment Note: 1994 H 571 substituted "state correctional institution" for "penitentiary".

Cross References

Private investigators and security guards, 4749.01 to 4749.99

Library References

Arrest ⚖63, 70.

Westlaw Topic No. 35.

C.J.S. Arrest §§ 9, 14 to 39, 42 to 44, 58 to 61.

Research References

Encyclopedias

OH Jur. 3d Cvl. Servants & Pub. Officers & Employ. § 543, Duty to Act in Capacity of Sheriff or Constable.

OH Jur. 3d Criminal Law § 1436, Recapture of Escapee.

OH Jur. 3d Criminal Law § 2117, Convicts.

OH Jur. 3d Criminal Law § 4004, Removal of Convict for Sentence or Trial—Warrant and Execution Thereof; Allowance of Fees.

OH Jur. 3d Police, Sheriffs, & Related Officers § 47, Other Sheriff's Fees.

OH Jur. 3d Police, Sheriffs, & Related Officers § 49, Marshals' Fees and Expenses.

2941.45 Trial of persons serving sentence

Any person serving a sentence in jail or the workhouse, who is indicted or informed against for another offense, may be brought before the court of common pleas upon warrant for that purpose, for arraignment and trial. Such person shall remain in the custody of the jailer or keeper of the workhouse, but may be temporarily confined in the jail, if a prisoner in the workhouse.

If such prisoner is convicted and sentenced upon trial, he shall be returned to the jail or workhouse to serve out the former sentence before the subsequent sentence is executed. (1953 H 1, eff. 10–1–53; GC 13438–10)

Historical and Statutory Notes

Pre–1953 H 1 Amendments: 113 v 172, Ch 17, § 20

Library References

Criminal Law ⚷241.
Prisons ⚷13.5.
Westlaw Topic Nos. 110, 310.
C.J.S. Criminal Law § 354.
C.J.S. Prisons and Rights of Prisoners §§ 130 to 143.

Research References

Encyclopedias

OH Jur. 3d Criminal Law § 4007, Person Confined to Jail or Workhouse.

2941.46 Arrest of convict or prisoner violating pardon or parole

(A) If a convict has been conditionally pardoned or a prisoner has been paroled from any state correctional institution, any peace officer may arrest the convict or prisoner without a warrant if the peace officer has reasonable ground to believe that the convict or prisoner has violated or is violating any rule governing the conduct of paroled prisoners prescribed by the adult parole authority or any of the following that is a condition of his pardon or parole:

(1) A condition that prohibits his ownership, posession [*sic*], or use of a firearm, deadly weapon, ammunition, or dangerous ordnance;

(2) A condition that prohibits him from being within a specified structure or geographic area;

(3) A condition that confines him to a residence, facility, or other structure;

(4) A condition that prohibits him from contacting or communicating with any specified individual;

(5) A condition that prohibits him from associating with a specified individual.

(B) Upon making an arrest under this section, the arresting peace officer or his department or agency promptly shall notify the authority that the convict or prisoner has been arrested.

(C) Nothing in this section limits, or shall be construed to limit, the powers of arrest granted to certain law enforcement officers and citizens under sections 2935.03 and 2935.04 of the Revised Code.

(D) As used in this section:

(1) "State correctional institution," "pardon," "parole," "convict," and "prisoner" have the same meanings as in section 2967.01 of the Revised Code.

(2) "Peace officer" has the same meaning as in section 2935.01 of the Revised Code.

(3) "Firearm," "deadly weapon," and "dangerous ordnance" have the same meanings as in section 2923.11 of the Revised Code.

(1994 H 571, eff. 10–6–94; 1992 S 49, eff. 7–21–92; 130 v Pt 2, H 28; 1953 H 1; GC 13438–11)

Historical and Statutory Notes

Ed. Note: 2941.46 contains provisions analogous to former 2949.36, repealed by 1972 H 511, eff. 1–1–74.

Pre–1953 H 1 Amendments: 118 v 288, § 25; 113 v 172, Ch 17, § 11

Amendment Note: 1994 H 571 substituted "correctional" for "penal or reformatory" in the first paragraph of division (A) and in division (D)(1).

Cross References

Arrest of persons violating parole in custody of county probation department, 2301.31
Duties of adult parole authority, 5149.03
Pardon, parole and probation, Ch 2967
Private investigators and security guards, 4749.01 to 4749.99

Library References

Pardon and Parole ⚷80.
Westlaw Topic No. 284.
C.J.S. Pardon and Parole §§ 71 to 74.

Research References

Encyclopedias
OH Jur. 3d Criminal Law § 2117, Convicts.
OH Jur. 3d Criminal Law § 3888, Arrest; Detainer.
OH Jur. 3d Criminal Law § 4002, Generally; Custody of Indicted Convict.

Law Review and Journal Commentaries

Moody v. Daggett: Added Strength to Parole Violation Warrant, Note. 4 Ohio N U L Rev 683 (1977).

Notes of Decisions

Parole violation 1
Pursuit of parole violator 2
Warrantless arrest of parolee 3

---

1. Parole violation

Prisoner's parole was properly revoked on basis of assault committed while prisoner was on parole, although grand jury did not indict prisoner for assault; grand jury's failure to indict prisoner for assault did not remove all factual support for parole revocation based on that conduct. Duganitz v. Ohio Adult Parole Auth. (Ohio, 08-15-2001) 92 Ohio St.3d 556, 751 N.E.2d 1058, 2001-Ohio-1283. Pardon And Parole ⚷ 71

Whether a petitioner was rightfully or improperly convicted of a misdemeanor while he was on parole and for which he served a jail sentence is immaterial in a proceeding in which he seeks release through habeas corpus from the penitentiary and from the remainder of his sentence for the felony. Bussey v. Sacks (Ohio 1961) 172 Ohio St. 392, 176 N.E.2d 220, 16 O.O.2d 247.

2. Pursuit of parole violator

Where a parolee violates his parole there is no affirmative duty on the state to pursue him and return him to custody, and its failure to do so does not create any waiver of its right to exact penalty previously imposed when it once again takes him into custody. Whitaker v. Maxwell (Ohio 1966) 6 Ohio St.2d 202, 217 N.E.2d 223, 35 O.O.2d 313.

Where a paroled convict violates his parole, there is no affirmative duty upon the state to place detainers on him or pursue him so as to return him to custody, and the state by its inaction creates neither an estoppel nor a waiver of its right to exact the penalty imposed under the conviction when it once again takes him into custody. Cline v. Haskins (Ohio 1964) 175 Ohio St. 480, 196 N.E.2d 440, 26 O.O.2d 91. Pardon And Parole ⚷ 79

3. Warrantless arrest of parolee

In the absence of a written order of the chief probation officer, a deputy sheriff may not arrest a person as a probation violator; and a search of a motor vehicle and seizure of articles found therein incidental thereto is an invalid search and seizure. State v. Call (Montgomery 1965) 8 Ohio App.2d 277, 220 N.E.2d 130, 37 O.O.2d 274.

Where a parolee was arrested without a warrant in an automobile after midnight in the company of an ex-convict, a search of the automobile which found burglary tools was not unreasonable, and the arrest was valid. DiMarco v. Greene (C.A.6 (Ohio) 1967) 13 Ohio Misc. 63, 385 F.2d 556, 42 O.O.2d 121. Arrest ⚷ 71.1(7)

MISCELLANEOUS PROVISIONS

2941.47 Summons on indictments against corporations

When an indictment is returned or information filed against a corporation, a summons commanding the sheriff to notify the accused thereof, returnable on the seventh day after its date, shall issue on praecipe of the prosecuting attorney. Such summons with a copy of the indictment shall be served and returned in the manner provided for service of summons upon corporations in civil actions. If the service cannot be made in the county where the prosecution began, the sheriff may make service in any other county of the state, upon the president, secretary, superintendent, clerk, treasurer, cashier, managing agent, or other chief officer thereof, or by leaving a copy at a general or branch office or usual place of doing business of such corporation, with the person having charge thereof. Such corporation shall appear by one of its officers or by counsel on or before the return day of the summons served and answer to the indictment or information by motion, demurrer, or plea, and upon failure to make such appearance and answer, the clerk of the court of common pleas shall enter a plea of "not guilty." Upon such appearance being made or plea entered, the corporation is before the court until the case is finally disposed of. On said indictment or information no warrant of arrest may issue except for individuals who may be included in such indictment or information.

(1953 H 1, eff. 10–1–53; GC 13438–12)

Historical and Statutory Notes

Pre–1953 H 1 Amendments: 113 v 172, Ch 17, § 12

Cross References

Warrant or summons upon indictment or information, Crim R 9

Library References

Criminal Law ⚷627.

Westlaw Topic No. 110.

C.J.S. Criminal Law § 446.

Research References

Encyclopedias

OH Jur. 3d Criminal Law § 2329, Summons or Indictment Against Corporate Defendants.

OH Jur. 3d Criminal Law § 2431, Failure to Plead or Appear.

Notes of Decisions

Corporate officers' responsibilities 1

---

1. Corporate officers' responsibilities

Conviction of corporation's president for corporation's failure to file or pay municipal income tax violated president's right to due process, even though president appeared at trial and entered plea of no contest in city's proceeding against corporation, where president was not named in criminal complaint against corporation and was not served with summons in individual capacity. City of Cleveland v. Technisort, Inc. (Cuyahoga 1985) 20 Ohio App.3d 139, 485 N.E.2d 294, 20 O.B.R. 172. Constitutional Law ⚷ 263

2941.48 Recognizance of witnesses

In any case pending in the court of common pleas, the court, either before or after indictment, may require any witness designated by the prosecuting attorney to enter into a recognizance, with or without surety, in such sum as the court thinks proper for his appearance to testify in such cause. A witness failing or refusing to comply with such order shall be committed to the county jail until he gives his testimony in such case or is ordered discharged by the court. If a witness is committed to jail upon order of court for want of such recognizance, he shall be paid while so confined like fees as are allowed witnesses by section 2335.08 of the Revised Code. The trial of such case has precedence over other cases and the court shall designate any early day for such trial.

(1953 H 1, eff. 10–1–53; GC 13438–13)

Historical and Statutory Notes

Pre-1953 H 1 Amendments: 113 v 173, Ch 17, § 13

Library References

Witnesses ⚿19.
Westlaw Topic No. 410.
C.J.S. Witnesses §§ 2, 67 to 68.

Research References

Encyclopedias

OH Jur. 3d Criminal Law § 2201, Witness' Refusal to Comply With Order of Recognizance.

Notes of Decisions

Counsel's right to interview material witnesses 2
Warrant to detain material witness 1

1. Warrant to detain material witness

At a minimum, a warrant to detain a material witness must be supported by probable cause supported by oath or affirmation to believe that the witness is material and that the detention of the witness is necessary to procure her attendance at trial; therefore, the method by which a warrant to detain a material witness is issued does not satisfy the requirements of constitutional due process where a bare entry or order is presented for signing to a trial court judge, unattended by even so much as an affidavit alleging those facts from which the trial court could find, as it did, that the witness' detention would be necessary to procure her attendance as a witness at a criminal trial. State, ex rel. Dorsey, v. Haines (Montgomery 1991) 63 Ohio App.3d 580, 579 N.E.2d 541.

2. Counsel's right to interview material witnesses

Counsel for accused are entitled to interview accused's companions who are being held in jail as witnesses, in the presence of the sheriff, or of someone designated by the court. Atkins v. State (Ohio 1926) 115 Ohio St. 542, 155 N.E. 189, 4 Ohio Law Abs. 789, 5 Ohio Law Abs. 109, 25 Ohio Law Rep. 87, 25 Ohio Law Rep. 218, certiorari denied 47 S.Ct. 590, 274 U.S. 720, 274 U.S. 743, 71 L.Ed. 1324. Criminal Law ⚿ 666.5

A refusal to permit counsel for the accused to interview accused's companions who are then being held in jail as witnesses, when counsel does not request permission to interview witnesses in the presence of someone designated by court, is not prejudicial when the testimony which it is claimed would have been developed by interviewing the witnesses was within knowledge of the accused himself, and the additional testimony sought would have been cumulative to testimony adduced. Atkins v. State (Ohio 1926) 115 Ohio St. 542, 155 N.E. 189, 4 Ohio Law Abs. 789, 5 Ohio Law Abs. 109, 25 Ohio Law Rep. 87, 25 Ohio Law Rep. 218, certiorari denied 47 S.Ct. 590, 274 U.S. 720, 274 U.S. 743, 71 L.Ed. 1324.

2941.49 Indictment to be served on accused

Within three days after the filing of an indictment for felony and in every other case when requested, the clerk of the court of common pleas shall make and deliver to the sheriff, defendant, or the defendant's counsel, a copy of such indictment. The sheriff, on receiving such copy, shall serve it on the defendant. A defendant, without his assent, shall not be arraigned or called on to answer to an indictment until one day has elapsed after receiving or having an opportunity to receive in person or by counsel, a copy of such indictment.

(1953 H 1, eff. 10-1-53; GC 13439-1)

Historical and Statutory Notes

Pre-1953 H 1 Amendments: 113 v 173, Ch 18, § 1

Cross References

Arraignment, Crim R 10
Right to indictment, O Const Art I §10
Serving and filing papers, Crim R 49
Warrant or summons upon indictment or information, Crim R 9

Library References

Criminal Law ⚷627.
Westlaw Topic No. 110.
C.J.S. Criminal Law § 446.

Research References

Encyclopedias

OH Jur. 3d Criminal Law § 2322, Indictment; Constitutional and Statutory Provisions—Misdemeanors.

OH Jur. 3d Criminal Law § 2325, Furnishing Accused Copy of Accusation.

Treatises and Practice Aids

Katz, Giannelli, Blair and Lipton, Baldwin's Ohio Practice, Criminal Law, § 42:7, Time Requirements.

Katz, Giannelli, Blair and Lipton, Baldwin's Ohio Practice, Criminal Law, § 142:17, Prosecuting Attorney's Request for Issuance of Summons Upon Indictment or Information.

Notes of Decisions

1. Constitutional issues

A plea of former jeopardy cannot be based on a void judgment especially where the accused himself set in motion the proceedings which nullified the judgment. Foran v. Maxwell (Ohio 1962) 173 Ohio St. 561, 184 N.E.2d 398, 20 O.O.2d 166. Double Jeopardy ⚷ 60.1

2. Service of indictment

Alleged failure to properly serve indictment did not rise to level of plain error, where defendant received copy of indictment, court read charges to defendant, defendant stated he understood charges, and defendant proceeded to plead guilty. State v. Turner (Ohio App. 8 Dist., Cuyahoga, 09-18-2003) No. 81449, 2003-Ohio-4933, 2003 WL 22145816, Unreported. Criminal Law ⚷ 1035(2)

Defendant waived proper service of indictment, where defendant waived right to copy, notice, and reading of indictment at his arraignment and defendant pleaded guilty to charges. State v. Turner (Ohio App. 8 Dist., Cuyahoga, 09-18-2003) No. 81449, 2003-Ohio-4933, 2003 WL 22145816, Unreported. Criminal Law ⚷ 627(7)

An accused waives his right to service of an indictment by entering a plea of guilty. Click v. Eckle (Ohio 1962) 174 Ohio St. 88, 186 N.E.2d 731, 21 O.O.2d 343. Criminal Law ⚷ 627(7)

A criminal prosecution by an information is subject to all the procedural and other statutory requirements which apply to a prosecution by indictment. Wells v. Sacks (Franklin 1962) 115 Ohio App. 219, 184 N.E.2d 449, 20 O.O.2d 304. Criminal Law ⚷ 633(1)

A prosecutor has no authority to order the clerk of courts to delay the service of a criminal indictment and a dismissal of the indictment is an appropriate sanction under such circumstances. State v Colbert, No. 1950 (11th Dist Ct App, Portage, 4–28–89).

3. Immediate arraignment

The one-day delay between service of an indictment and arraignment mandated by RC 2941.49 is merely procedural; thus, the conflicting Crim R 10 permitting immediate arraignment controls and supersedes RC 2941.49. State v. Heyden (Summit 1992) 81 Ohio App.3d 272, 610 N.E.2d 1067.

There is no requirement under RC 2941.49 that the assent to being arraigned without the lapse of one day after service of the indictment must be in any particular form or be in writing. Click v. Eckle (Ohio 1962) 174 Ohio St. 88, 186 N.E.2d 731, 21 O.O.2d 343. Criminal Law ⚷ 264

2941.50 Assignment of counsel to represent indigents—Repealed

(1975 H 164, eff. 1–13–76; 132 v S 486; 131 v H 362; 130 v H 511; 1953 H 1; GC 13439–2)

Historical and Statutory Notes

Ed. Note: See now Ch 120 and Crim R 44 for provisions analogous to former 2941.50.

Pre–1953 H 1 Amendments: 113 v 173, Ch 18, § 2

2941.51 Person represented shall pay for part of costs if able

(A) Counsel appointed to a case or selected by an indigent person under division (E) of section 120.16 or division (E) of section 120.26 of the Revised Code, or otherwise appointed by the court, except for counsel appointed by the court to provide legal representation for a person charged with a violation of an ordinance of a municipal corporation, shall be paid for their services by the county the compensation and expenses that the trial court approves. Each request for payment shall be accompanied by a financial disclosure form and an affidavit of indigency that are completed by the indigent person on forms prescribed by the state public defender. Compensation and expenses shall not exceed the amounts fixed by the board of county commissioners pursuant to division (B) of this section.

(B) The board of county commissioners shall establish a schedule of fees by case or on an hourly basis to be paid by the county for legal services provided by appointed counsel. Prior to establishing such schedule, the board shall request the bar association or associations of the county to submit a proposed schedule. The schedule submitted shall be subject to the review, amendment, and approval of the board of county commissioners.

(C) In a case where counsel have been appointed to conduct an appeal under Chapter 120. of the Revised Code, such compensation shall be fixed by the court of appeals or the supreme court, as provided in divisions (A) and (B) of this section.

(D) The fees and expenses approved by the court under this section shall not be taxed as part of the costs and shall be paid by the county. However, if the person represented has, or reasonably may be expected to have, the means to meet some part of the cost of the services rendered to the person, the person shall pay the county an amount that the person reasonably can be expected to pay. Pursuant to section 120.04 of the Revised Code, the county shall pay to the state public defender a percentage of the payment received from the person in an amount proportionate to the percentage of the costs of the person's case that were paid to the county by the state public defender pursuant to this section. The money paid to the state public defender shall be credited to the client payment fund created pursuant to division (B)(5) of section 120.04 of the Revised Code.

(E) The county auditor shall draw a warrant on the county treasurer for the payment of such counsel in the amount fixed by the court, plus the expenses that the court fixes and certifies to the auditor. The county auditor shall report periodically, but not less than annually, to the board of county commissioners and to the Ohio public defender commission the amounts paid out pursuant to the approval of the court under this section, separately stating costs and expenses that are reimbursable under section 120.35 of the Revised Code. The board, after review and approval of the auditor's report, may then certify it to the state public defender for reimbursement. The request for reimbursement shall be accompanied by a financial disclosure form completed by each indigent person for whom counsel was provided on a form prescribed by the state public defender. The state public defender shall review the report and, in accordance with the standards, guidelines, and maximums established pursuant to divisions (B)(7) and (8) of section 120.04 of the Revised Code, pay fifty per cent of the total cost, other than costs and expenses that are reimbursable under section 120.35 of the Revised Code, if any, of paying appointed counsel in each county and pay fifty per cent of costs and expenses that are reimbursable under section 120.35 of the Revised Code, if any, to the board.

(F) If any county system for paying appointed counsel fails to maintain the standards for the conduct of the system established by the rules of the Ohio public defender commission pursuant to divisions (B) and (C) of section 120.03 of the Revised Code or the standards established by the state public defender pursuant to division (B)(7) of section 120.04 of the Revised Code, the commission shall notify the board of county commissioners of the county that the county system for paying appointed counsel has failed to comply with its rules. Unless the board corrects the conduct of its appointed counsel system to comply with the rules within ninety days after the date of the notice, the state public defender may deny all or part of the county's reimbursement from the state provided for in this section.

(1999 H 283, eff. 9–29–99; 1997 H 215, eff. 9–29–97; 1995 H 117, eff. 6–30–95; 1985 H 201, eff. 7–1–85; 1984 S 271; 1983 H 291; 1975 H 164; 132 v H 1; 131 v H 362; 128 v 54; 1953 H 1; GC 13439–3)

Uncodified Law

1997 H 215, § 191, eff. 6–30–97, reads: The client payment fund, which the public defender reimbursement fund was renamed in this act through the amendments to sections 120.04, 120.33, and 2941.51 of the Revised Code, is the continuation of the public defender reimbursement fund.

Historical and Statutory Notes

Pre–1953 H 1 Amendments: 122 v H 427; 117 v 279; 113 v 173

Amendment Note: 1999 H 283 inserted "a financial disclosure form and" and "that are" in division (A); inserted "of county commissioners" and added the fourth sentence in division (E); and substituted "120.04" for "102.04" in division (F).

Amendment Note: 1997 H 215 changed references to reimbursement to references to payment, inserted "Pursuant to section 120.04 of the Revised Code,", and substituted "client payment fund" for "public defender reimbursement fund", in division (D); and made changes to reflect gender neutral language and other nonsubstantive changes.

Amendment Note: 1995 H 117 inserted "or the standards established by the state public defender pursuant to division (B)(7) of section 102.04 of the Revised Code" and "county commissioners of" and substituted "the state public defender may deny all or part of the county's reimbursement from the state provided for in this section" for "the county's right to reimbursement from the state provided for in this section shall terminate at the end of the ninety day period" in division (F).

Comparative Laws

Ky.—Baldwin's KRS 453.190.

Cross References

Application fee, reports, 120.36

Competence to stand trial, appointment of counsel, 2945.37

Powers and duties of state public defender, funds, 120.04

Rights of person arrested, 2935.14

State public defender, collection of moneys due state for legal services, 120.04

State public defender, powers of representation, county representation fund, representation by private counsel, 120.06

State reimbursement in capital cases, 120.35

Testimony of prisoners in criminal proceedings, 2945.47

Verdict of not guilty by reason of insanity, representation by counsel, 2945.40

Ohio Administrative Code References

Denial of reimbursement to the counties in capital cases, OAC 120–1–13

Public defender commission, county reimbursement, denial, qualifications for assigned counsel and public defenders, OAC 120–1–10, 120–1–13

Library References

Costs ⊂=308.

Westlaw Topic No. 102.

Research References

Encyclopedias

OH Jur. 3d Cvl. Servants & Pub. Officers & Employ. § 504, Duties Regarding Reimbursement of Costs.

OH Jur. 3d Criminal Law § 103, Payment of Assigned Counsel.

OH Jur. 3d Criminal Law § 104, Payment of Assigned Counsel—Reimbursement by Accused.

OH Jur. 3d Criminal Law § 3324, Fines, Generally.

OH Jur. 3d Criminal Law § 3986, State Payment of Criminal Costs.

OH Jur. 3d Mandamus, Procedendo, & Prohibition § 16, Requirement that Act be One that the Law Specially Enjoins as a Duty.

Treatises and Practice Aids

Katz, Giannelli, Blair and Lipton, Baldwin's Ohio Practice, Criminal Law, § 119:6, Financial Sanctions.

Katz, Giannelli, Blair and Lipton, Baldwin's Ohio Practice, Criminal Law, § 151:2, Affidavit of Defendant's Inability to Obtain Counsel.

Katz, Giannelli, Blair and Lipton, Baldwin's Ohio Practice, Criminal Law, § 151:5, Entry Allowing Counsel Fee in Assigned Case.

Katz, Giannelli, Blair and Lipton, Baldwin's Ohio Practice, Criminal Law, § 151:6, Motion for Leave to Withdraw as Attorney on Grounds that Defendant is Not Indigent.

Law Review and Journal Commentaries

ATTORNEYS—Appointed Representation of Indigents—Right to Compensation—State v. Rush, Note. 28 Ohio St L J 156 (Winter 1967).

Notes of Decisions

---

1. Constitutional issues

Evidence supported finding that defendant was not financially eligible to reccive court-appointed counsel; defendant's financial disclosure affidavit of indigency indicated that he had assets totaling $106,000 and that he received $500.00 a month in income from rental property that he owned. State v. Barcharowski (Ohio App. 5 Dist., Stark, 08-11-2003) No. 2002CA00119, 2003-Ohio-4281, 2003 WL 21920952, Unreported. Criminal Law ⚷ 641.6(3)

Conviction will be vacated where defendant never understood that if he was indigent counsel would be appointed for him at the expense of the state. State v. Oney (Ohio 1967) 10 Ohio St.2d 186, 226 N.E.2d 114, 39 O.O.2d 195, 39 O.O.2d 267.

A convicted indigent defendant has a constitutional right to counsel on a direct appeal to the court of appeals from his judgment of conviction, and the fact that the Ohio statute failed to provide therefor at state expense prior to the effective date of RC 2941.50(B) cannot interfere with that right. State v. Catlino (Ohio 1967) 10 Ohio St.2d 183, 226 N.E.2d 109, 39 O.O.2d 194. Criminal Law ⚷ 1077.3

In the juvenile court in respect of proceedings to determine delinquency which may result in commitment to an institution in which the juvenile's freedom is curtailed, the child and his parent must be notified of the child's right to be represented by counsel retained by them, or if they are unable to afford counsel, that counsel will be appointed to represent the child. OAG 67–068.

2. Reimbursement for cost of assigned counsel

Evidence supported trial court's determination that defendant was able to pay for the cost of his appointed representation, thus supporting trial court's order that defendant pay costs; counsel indicated that defendant had been working up until the time of his arrest. State v. Nicholson (Ohio App. 6 Dist., Lucas, 11-24-2004) No. L-03-1256, 2004-Ohio-6314, 2004 WL 2690677, Unreported. Costs ⚷ 314

Record demonstrated that trial court properly considered whether defendant had or reasonably could be expected to have means to pay all or part of costs of legal services rendered to him before ordering him to pay costs; trial court asked defendant if defendant owned an interest in any real estate, defendant informed court that he owned a house which he intended to sell as soon as possible, and court noted that defendant had been gainfully employed his entire adult life. State v. Estes (Ohio App. 12 Dist., Preble, 10-06-2003) No. CA2002-05-008, 2003-Ohio-5283, 2003 WL 22283503, Unreported, denial of post-conviction relief affirmed 2005-Ohio-5478, 2005 WL 2626194, appeal not allowed 108 Ohio St.3d 1488, 843 N.E.2d 794, 2006-Ohio-962. Costs ⚷ 314

Sentencing order requiring defendant to pay fees of appointed counsel was plain error in absence of affirmative determination on record that defendant had, or reasonably could be expected to have, means to pay all or some part of costs; after accepting defendant's plea, trial court immediately proceeded to impose sentence, and trial court had no presentence investigation report (PSI) from which to glean information necessary to order payment of counsel costs. State v. Isbell (Ohio App. 12 Dist., Butler, 09-08-2003) No. CA2002-07-160, 2003-Ohio-4751, 2003 WL 22073131, Unreported, denial of post-conviction relief affirmed 2004-Ohio-2300, 2004 WL 1040699. Criminal Law ⚷ 1042

Sentencing court improperly required defendant to pay costs of court-appointed counsel and costs of confinement without making findings concerning his present and future ability to pay. State v. McGee (Ohio App. 7 Dist., Jefferson, 04-21-2003) No. 02-JE-39, 2003-Ohio-2239, 2003 WL 21000919, Unreported. Costs ⚷ 314

Trial court erred by ordering defendant who was convicted of unlawful sexual conduct with a minor and found to be a sexual predator to pay the cost of his court-appointed counsel without making an affirmative determination on the record of his ability to pay. State v. Black (Ohio App. 12 Dist., Butler, 04-28-2003) No. CA2002-04-082, 2003-Ohio-2115, 2003 WL 1956096, Unreported. Mental Health ⚷ 468

Trial court erred in ordering defendant convicted of aggravated robbery to pay the cost of his court-appointed counsel without first determining whether defendant had the ability to pay. State v. Robinson (Ohio App. 6 Dist., Lucas, 03-31-2003) No. L-02-1061, 2003-Ohio-1627, 2003 WL 1700570, Unreported. Costs ⚷ 314

Before trial court could order indigent defendant to pay court-ordered counsel fees as part of sentencing order following conviction for a fourth-degree felony, trial court was required to make affirmative determination on the record that defendant had, or reasonably may be expected to have, the means to pay all or some part of costs of legal services rendered on her behalf. State v. Bush (Ohio App. 12 Dist., Butler, 01-13-2003) No. CA2002-05-114, 2003-Ohio-81, 2003 WL 103596, Unreported. Costs ⚷ 314

Indigent criminal defendant was improperly required to pay fees of appointed counsel without requisite finding that he had, or reasonably could be expected to have, means to pay all or some part thereof. State v. Hite (Ohio App. 12 Dist., Butler,

12-23-2002) No. CA2002-03-050, 2002-Ohio-7141, 2002 WL 31862196, Unreported. Costs ⚷ 314

Trial court's failure to make an affirmative determination on the record that defendant had the means to pay all or some part of court appointed counsel fees constituted plain error. State v. Thomas (Ohio App. 12 Dist., Butler, 10-14-2002) No. CA2002-01-008, 2002-Ohio-5507, 2002 WL 31297654, Unreported. Criminal Law ⚷ 1042

Attorney fees and court costs could not be assessed against indigent defendant convicted of involuntary manslaughter in absence of court determination that defendant had, or reasonably may be expected to have, the means to pay all or some part of the cost of the legal services rendered to him. State v. Cooper (Ohio App. 12 Dist., 02-19-2002) 147 Ohio App.3d 116, 768 N.E.2d 1223, 2002-Ohio-617. Costs ⚷ 314

Trial court's assessment of attorney fees as a $1,000 fine against defendant charged with failure to comply with an order or signal of a police officer, was improper; defendant could not be assessed attorney fees as part of his sentence, the court's express announcement that it was assessing attorney fees as a fine demonstrated that the court failed to consider the proper statutory criteria in determining the appropriate sentence, the fine was not specially adapted to deter the offense or correct the defendant, recoupment of court-appointed attorney fees was a civil obligation. State v. Crenshaw (Ohio App. 8 Dist., 08-06-2001) 145 Ohio App.3d 86, 761 N.E.2d 1121. Costs ⚷ 308; Fines ⚷ 1.5

Awards of ordinary and extraordinary attorney fees for representing indigent defendant in capital murder case were not arbitrary, unreasonable, or capricious; $15,000 was awarded for case in which nolle prosequi was eventually filed, $20,000 was awarded for case through jury selection until change of venue was granted, $25,000 was awarded in case that went to trial, and extraordinary fees were $25,000. State v. Luff (Lucas 1993) 85 Ohio App.3d 785, 621 N.E.2d 493, dismissed, jurisdictional motion overruled 67 Ohio St.3d 1464, 619 N.E.2d 698, certiorari denied 114 S.Ct. 1116, 510 U.S. 1136, 127 L.Ed.2d 426. Attorney And Client ⚷ 132

Court need not list exact expenses denied to appointed counsel or counsel for indigent person. State v. Luff (Lucas 1993) 85 Ohio App.3d 785, 621 N.E.2d 493, dismissed, jurisdictional motion overruled 67 Ohio St.3d 1464, 619 N.E.2d 698, certiorari denied 114 S.Ct. 1116, 510 U.S. 1136, 127 L.Ed.2d 426. Attorney And Client ⚷ 132

Trial judge lacked judicial authority to require indigent criminal defendants to work to pay for appointed counsel. State ex rel. Carriger v. City of Galion (Ohio 1990) 53 Ohio St.3d 250, 560 N.E.2d 194. Costs ⚷ 318

Sentencing order requiring defendant to pay fees of court appointed counsel was plain error without an affirmative determination on the record that the defendant had or reasonably could be expected to have the means to pay all or some part of the costs. State v. Bogan (Ohio App. 12 Dist., Butler, 09-23-2002) No. CA2001-12-287, 2002-Ohio-4988, 2002 WL 31109443, Unreported. Criminal Law ⚷ 1042

Trial court's failure to affirmatively determine that defendant had or could be expected to have the means to pay all or some part of the costs of legal services rendered on his behalf was plain error, and required remand for determination regarding defendant's ability to pay fees. State v. Prom (Ohio App. 12 Dist., Butler, 08-26-2002) No. CA2002-01-007, 2002-Ohio-4376, 2002 WL 1965480, Unreported, appeal not allowed 98 Ohio St.3d 1411, 781 N.E.2d 1019, 2003-Ohio-60, on subsequent appeal 2003-Ohio-5103, 2003 WL 22227348, amended and superseded 2003-Ohio-6543, 2003 WL 22887906. Costs ⚷ 314; Criminal Law ⚷ 1181.5(3.1)

Trial court erred in ordering defendant to pay court-appointed counsel fees plus interest without first determining his ability to pay. State v. Byler (Ohio App. 5 Dist., Guernsey, 08-02-2002) No. 01CA30, 2002-Ohio-4055, 2002 WL 1821749, Unreported. Costs ⚷ 314

A rape victim for whom counsel is provided pursuant to RC 2907.02(F) must, under RC 2941.51(D), reimburse the county in such amount as is reasonable if such person has the means to meet some part of the cost of the services rendered. OAG 87–064.

A county is entitled to the reimbursement authorized by RC 2941.51 for costs incurred in providing appointed counsel for rape victims under RC 2907.02(F). OAG 87–064.

3. Compensation of counsel

Trial court was entitled to assess attorney fees on defendant in arson case after it found that defendant, due to his good health and ability to work, was able to meet his financial obligations. State v. Hawthorne (Ohio App. 6 Dist., Lucas, 03-31-2005) No. L-03-1120, No. L-03-1127, 2005-Ohio-1553, 2005 WL 736994, Unreported. Costs ⚷ 308

Sentencing court was not required to make separate finding with respect to indigent defendant's ability to pay costs of appointed counsel prior to ordering him to pay such costs, where record supported sentencing court's finding that defendant was expected to have future ability to pay costs. State v. Cole (Ohio App. 6 Dist., Lucas, 02-04-2005) No. L-03-1163, No. L-03-1162, 2005-Ohio-408, 2005 WL 280223, Unreported. Costs ⚷ 314

Trial court's sentencing order which included order requiring defendant to pay court-appointed attorney fees did not include requisite statutory finding as to whether defendant had means to pay fees, thus requiring remand for such finding; although error was independently identified by Court of Appeals after defendant's appellate counsel submitted *Anders* no-merit brief, which would have otherwise required Court to appoint new counsel to brief and argue issue, total absence in record of any finding constituted plain error, allowing Court to take immediate action. State v. Shannon (Ohio App. 12 Dist., Preble, 04-12-2004) No. CA2003-02-005,

2004-Ohio-1866, 2004 WL 766558, Unreported, dismissal of post-conviction relief affirmed 2006-Ohio-2720, 2006 WL 1493564. Criminal Law ⚷ 1181.5(8); Sentencing And Punishment ⚷ 2195

Trial court erred by ordering defendant, who pled guilty to sexual conduct with a minor and was classified as a sexual predator, to pay the cost of his court-appointed counsel without holding a hearing or making an affirmative determination on the record of his ability to pay. State v. Robinson (Ohio App. 12 Dist., Butler, 04-21-2003) No. CA2002-05-127, 2003-Ohio-2009, 2003 WL 1906476, Unreported. Costs ⚷ 314

Total absence in the record of any determination by the sentencing court that indigent defendant had, or reasonably could be expected to have, the means to pay all or some of the court-appointed counsel fees was plain error which the appellate court could take immediate action to remedy without appointment of new counsel to brief and argue the issue. State v. Isom (Ohio App. 12 Dist., Butler, 12-30-2002) No. CA2002-05-105, 2002-Ohio-7281, 2002 WL 31886667, Unreported. Criminal Law ⚷ 1042

Sentencing court could require indigent defendant to pay court-appointed counsel fees only after making an affirmative determination on the record that defendant had, or reasonably could be expected to have, the means to pay all or some of the costs of legal services rendered on his behalf. State v. Isom (Ohio App. 12 Dist., Butler, 12-30-2002) No. CA2002-05-105, 2002-Ohio-7281, 2002 WL 31886667, Unreported. Costs ⚷ 314

Trial court erred in ordering defendants to pay attorney fees for their court-appointed counsel, as court did not impose attorney fees as condition of probation, and did not make finding that defendants had ability to pay. State v. Watkins (Ohio App. 1 Dist., 07-20-1994) 96 Ohio App.3d 195, 644 N.E.2d 1049. Costs ⚷ 308

The amount of an award or allowance of attorney fees is a matter within the sound discretion of a trial court and, therefore, mandamus will not lie to compel a court to pay fees in the amount listed on an application for fees submitted by assigned counsel. State ex rel. Baerkircher v. Radcliffe (Ohio 1987) 31 Ohio St.3d 14, 508 N.E.2d 150, 31 O.B.R. 12.

The purpose of RC 2941.51 is to insure representation of an indigent defendant in a criminal case on the basis which would alleviate the burden on individual lawyers, but such statute does not purport to provide full compensation and it is not intended to permit the payment of fees in such cases that would regularly be charged nonindigent clients, and so where two attorneys are assigned to an appeal in a first degree murder case wherein they expended a total of 200 hours of time, the court will allow the maximum compensation for appeals in first degree murder cases, which is set at a total of $2,000. State v. Pruett (Ashtabula 1967) 10 Ohio App.2d 218, 227 N.E.2d 261, 39 O.O.2d 427. Attorney And Client ⚷ 132

A writ of mandamus will not issue to compel a judge to approve an attorney fee which is greater than the maximum amount set by the county commissioners pursuant to RC 2941.51(B). State ex rel. Marco v. Jaffe (Ohio 1986) 25 Ohio St.3d 236, 495 N.E.2d 958, 25 O.B.R. 295.

Counsel assigned to a case and removed by the court before completion of trial has a right to be paid for work performed, and the discretion of the trial judge under RC 2941.51(A) is limited to determining the amount of payment. State ex rel. Martin v. Corrigan (Ohio 1986) 25 Ohio St.3d 29, 494 N.E.2d 1128, 25 O.B.R. 24.

A local rule of court, requiring that applications for fees by counsel appointed to represent indigent criminal defendants be made within thirty days of sentencing, interferes with counsel's right to be paid pursuant to RC 2941.51, and is therefore invalid where the county's claim for reimbursement of fees from the state is not prejudiced. State ex rel. Wood v. Christiansen (Ohio 1984) 14 Ohio St.3d 27, 470 N.E.2d 895, 14 O.B.R. 329.

Counsel appointed as assigned counsel under RC 2941.50 to conduct appeals were entitled to a writ of mandamus ordering auditor to issue warrants in payment of their fees, ordering commissioners to create a fund if necessary for payment, and ordering the treasurer to pay such warrants. State ex rel. Giuliani v. Perk (Ohio 1968) 14 Ohio St.2d 235, 237 N.E.2d 397, 43 O.O.2d 366.

As used in RC 2941.51 "counsel" is used in the plural as well as the singular, and hence appointed defense counsel may receive a total fee of only $300. State ex rel. Thornburgh v. Davis (Ohio 1965) 2 Ohio St.2d 87, 205 N.E.2d 904, 31 O.O.2d 64.

Mandamus is not available to secure additional funding of appointed counsel in a postconviction relief action where the contract of appointment establishes a maximum amount of compensation that has been surpassed prior to the completion of the counsel's representation of the client in the action; RC 120.06(C) and 2941.51(A) provide an adequate mechanism to assure payment of appointed counsel fees. State, ex rel. Brown, v. Dana (Ohio App. 10 Dist. 1990) 66 Ohio App.3d 709, 586 N.E.2d 150.

In order for counsel to be paid by the county pursuant to RC 2941.51, a rape victim for whom representation is provided pursuant to RC 2907.02(F) must submit an affidavit of indigency on forms prescribed by the state public defender. A rape victim who is not indigent may complete such an affidavit by asserting that such person is not indigent but is otherwise unable to obtain the services of counsel. OAG 87–064.

A municipality has authority to provide by ordinance for compensation of counsel assigned to represent indigents accused before the municipal court of violations of municipal ordinances; except that if the jurisdiction of the municipal court extends beyond the territorial limits of the municipality, it has authority to compensate such counsel only in cases involving violations of municipal ordinances. OAG 73–113.

In the absence of specific legislation providing for payment of counsel appointed to defend indigents in misdemeanor cases involving a jail sentence, neither the county commissioners nor other state fiscal officers can appropriate funds for this purpose. OAG 72–095.

There is no provision under the statutes which permits the juvenile court to authorize compensation to attorneys appointed to represent indigents. OAG 67–068.

4. Legal aid; public defender

Attorneys seeking higher fees for public defender assignments stated proper claim in mandamus, where they alleged that county board of commissioners had a duty in establishing fees, and that there was no adequate remedy at law. State ex rel. Felson v. McHenry (Ohio App. 1 Dist., 09-28-2001) 146 Ohio App.3d 542, 767 N.E.2d 298, 2001-Ohio-4265, on subsequent appeal 2002-Ohio-4804, 2002 WL 31039688. Mandamus ⚷ 154(4)

A legal aid society and its legal aid defender department does not engage in the unlawful practice of law in referring indigents to lawyers working on a retainer or under a salary arrangement with such society, and such society does not engage in the unlawful practice of law because money paid by the county, pursuant to statute, for the defense of indigent persons to a "defender" attorney retained by such society on a retainer or salary basis is transferred by him into a trust fund from which his salary and office expenses are paid. Azzarello v. Legal Aid Soc. of Cleveland (Cuyahoga 1962) 117 Ohio App. 471, 185 N.E.2d 566, 90 A.L.R.2d 564, 90 Ohio Law Abs. 564, 24 O.O.2d 263.

Cleveland legal aid society's legal aid defender may receive compensation from state for services rendered as appointed counsel to indigent defendants. Azzarello v. Legal Aid Soc. of Cleveland (Cuyahoga 1962) 117 Ohio App. 471, 185 N.E.2d 566, 90 A.L.R.2d 564, 90 Ohio Law Abs. 564, 24 O.O.2d 263.

Attorney employed by Cleveland legal aid society is entitled to fee for defending indigent defendant. State ex rel. McCurdy v. Carney (Ohio 1961) 172 Ohio St. 175, 174 N.E.2d 253, 15 O.O.2d 326.

In order for counsel to be paid by the county pursuant to RC 2941.51, a rape victim for whom representation is provided pursuant to RC 2907.02(F) must submit an affidavit of indigency on forms prescribed by the state public defender. A rape victim who is not indigent may complete such an affidavit by asserting that such person is not indigent but is otherwise unable to obtain the services of counsel. OAG 87–064.

There is no statutory requirement that an affidavit of indigency must be submitted to the state public defender in order for a county to obtain reimbursement under RC 2941.51 for costs incurred in providing appointed counsel for a rape victim under RC 2907.02(F). OAG 87–064.

Imprisonment of indigents is a prerequisite to the payment of criminal costs by the Ohio public defender commission pursuant to RC 2949.12 et seq., and 1977 H 191, eff. 6–30–77. OAG 78–004.

5. Appeals

Arguable issue existed for appeal in trial court's imposition of costs of court-appointed counsel, and thus defendant's appeal was not wholly frivolous for purposes of defense counsel's request to withdraw pursuant to *Anders v. California,* where there was no indication in the record that defendant had the ability to pay the costs of court-appointed counsel. State v. Knight (Ohio App. 6 Dist., Sandusky, 08-19-2005) No. S-05-007, 2005-Ohio-4347, 2005 WL 2008144, Unreported. Criminal Law ⚷ 1077.3

Trial court's requirement that indigent defendant pay fees of his appointed counsel, in total absence in record of any determination that defendant had, or reasonably could be expected to have, means to pay all or some part thereof, amounted to plain error subject to immediate remedial action by reviewing court. State v. Hite (Ohio App. 12 Dist., Butler, 12-23-2002) No. CA2002-03-050, 2002-Ohio-7141, 2002 WL 31862196, Unreported. Criminal Law ⚷ 1042

Appointment of trial counsel as appellate counsel for an indigent who requests that trial counsel not be named appellate counsel, and who asserts ineffective assistance of trial counsel as error in his appeal constitutes a denial of the defendant's Sixth Amendment right to counsel, and is deemed to be prejudicial per se. State v. Fuller (Clark 1990) 64 Ohio App.3d 349, 581 N.E.2d 614.

There is no constitutional or statutory provision for the appointment or fixing of compensation of counsel for an indigent prisoner to prosecute an appeal from a judgment or order entered on a petition to vacate or set aside sentence filed under RC 2953.21. State v. Buffington (Van Wert 1966) 7 Ohio App.2d 211, 219 N.E.2d 614, 36 O.O.2d 344.

RC 2949.19 requires that the state of Ohio must bear the costs as provided in RC 2953.03 and counsel fees as provided in RC 2941.51 of an indigent defendant on appeal whether or not he has been committed prior to his appeal. OAG 68–098; overruled to the extent that it is inconsistent with OAG 80–099.

RC 2941.51(C) requires the state of Ohio to pay as costs, in addition to the counsel fees received for representation at the trial as provided in RC 2941.51(B), any counsel fees up to $300 resulting from an appeal as approved by the court of appeals. OAG 68–098; overruled to the extent that it is inconsistent with OAG 80–099.

6. Transcript

The state's burden of showing that a transcript of prior proceedings requested by an indigent defendant is not needed for an effective defense or appeal may be met by the state by a showing that the transcript is not valuable to the defendant in connection with the trial or appeal for which it is sought, or that there are alternative devices available to the defendant that would fulfill the same functions as a transcript. State v. Arrington (Ohio 1975) 42 Ohio St.2d 114, 326 N.E.2d 667, 71 O.O.2d 81. Costs ⚷ 302.1(1); Criminal Law ⚷ 1077.2(3)

The county is liable for the cost of providing an indigent defendant charged with a felony with a transcript of a probable cause hearing in the municipal court where the transcript is ordered by counsel assigned to the case under RC 120.16(E), 120.26(E), or otherwise, if the cost is approved by the court. The court may bill the county for such costs by certifying a statement of the charges from the court reporter and issuing a voucher to the county auditor. The county may then seek reimbursement from the state for fifty per cent of the cost of the transcripts. OAG 80–099.

7. Certification of costs

Trial court was not required to consider defendant's ability to pay before imposing fines, counsel costs, and fees, in prosecution for two counts of gross sexual imposition; the costs of prosecution were not considered punishment, the trial court stated that it considered defendant's ability to pay when it fined defendant $5,000.00 per offense, and the court stated that it considered defendant's presentence investigative report, which included financial data, when it determined that defendant had the means to pay all or part of the costs of legal services rendered to him. State v. Lane (Ohio App. 12 Dist., Butler, 03-17-2003) No. CA2002-03-069, 2003-Ohio-1246, 2003 WL 1193807, Unreported. Fines ⚷ 1.5

The court must enter a separate civil judgment for the fees or part thereof that the court finds the defendant has the ability to pay. State v. Crenshaw (Ohio App. 8 Dist., 08-06-2001) 145 Ohio App.3d 86, 761 N.E.2d 1121. Costs ⚷ 314

County commissioners may not refuse to pay fees awarded for representation of indigent defendants and certified to the auditor by the trial judge. State ex rel. Colgrove v. Supanick (Ohio 1975) 41 Ohio St.2d 141, 324 N.E.2d 183, 70 O.O.2d 261.

Where a judge refuses to order payment for a court-appointed attorney in the amount provided in a fee schedule established pursuant to RC 2941.51, a county treasurer has no authority to issue a warrant for that amount, and a writ of mandamus against the treasurer will be denied. State ex rel. Halloran v. Zapatony (Ohio 1984) 15 Ohio St.3d 73, 472 N.E.2d 357, 15 O.B.R. 166.

The auditor of state is required, upon certification to him of the statement of costs of a criminal conviction pursuant to RC 2949.19, to pay an amount equal to the moneys expended for fees and expenses of court-appointed counsel, approved and taxed as a part of the costs under RC 2941.51, provided there are sufficient funds in the state treasury appropriated for that purpose. State ex rel. Clifford v. Cloud (Ohio 1966) 7 Ohio St.2d 55, 218 N.E.2d 605, 36 O.O.2d 46.

8. Experts' compensation

Defendant must show more than mere possibility of assistance from expert in order to be entitled to public funds for retention of expert; defendant must show reasonable probability that expert would aid in his defense, that denial of expert assistance would result in unfair trial. State v. Peeples (Ohio App. 4 Dist., 03-23-1994) 94 Ohio App.3d 34, 640 N.E.2d 208, dismissed 70 Ohio St.3d 1445, 639 N.E.2d 113, affirmed 74 Ohio St.3d 153, 656 N.E.2d 1285, 1995-Ohio-30, denial of post-conviction relief affirmed 1997 WL 691474, dismissed, appeal not allowed 81 Ohio St.3d 1452, 690 N.E.2d 546, denial of post-conviction relief affirmed 1998 WL 975256, dismissed, appeal not allowed 85 Ohio St.3d 1464, 709 N.E.2d 170, certiorari denied 120 S.Ct. 133, 528 U.S. 852, 145 L.Ed.2d 112. Costs ⚷ 302.2(2)

Ex parte hearing was not required on defendant's motion for public funds to hire expert witness where ex parte protection was not necessary to protect counsel's defense strategy. State v. Peeples (Ohio App. 4 Dist., 03-23-1994) 94 Ohio App.3d 34, 640 N.E.2d 208, dismissed 70 Ohio St.3d 1445, 639 N.E.2d 113, affirmed 74 Ohio St.3d 153, 656 N.E.2d 1285, 1995-Ohio-30, denial of post-conviction relief affirmed 1997 WL 691474, dismissed, appeal not allowed 81 Ohio St.3d 1452, 690 N.E.2d 546, denial of post-conviction relief affirmed 1998 WL 975256, dismissed, appeal not allowed 85 Ohio St.3d 1464, 709 N.E.2d 170, certiorari denied 120 S.Ct. 133, 528 U.S. 852, 145 L.Ed.2d 112. Costs ⚷ 302.2(2)

Trial court properly limited funding for defense expert witnesses in prosecution for aggravated murder; defendant had benefit of one court-appointed psychiatrist and funds to pay for his services, and was provided with expert assistance sufficient to plead his case. State v. Peeples (Ohio App. 4 Dist., 03-23-1994) 94 Ohio App.3d 34, 640 N.E.2d 208, dismissed 70 Ohio St.3d 1445, 639 N.E.2d 113, affirmed 74 Ohio St.3d 153, 656 N.E.2d 1285, 1995-Ohio-30, denial of post-conviction relief affirmed 1997 WL 691474, dismissed, appeal not allowed 81 Ohio St.3d 1452, 690 N.E.2d 546, denial of post-conviction relief affirmed 1998 WL 975256, dismissed, appeal not allowed 85 Ohio St.3d 1464, 709 N.E.2d 170, certiorari denied 120 S.Ct. 133, 528 U.S. 852, 145 L.Ed.2d 112. Costs ⚷ 302.4

9. Hearing

Hearing was not necessary to determine defendant's ability to pay appointed counsel costs, where trial court considered defendant's pre-sentence investigation report (PSI), which contained information stating defendant was in excellent health and defendant expected to return to work when he was released; consideration of PSI demonstrated affirmative determination on record that court considered whether defendant had or reasonably could be expected to have means to pay costs of legal services rendered to him. State v. Bailey (Ohio App. 12 Dist., Butler, 10-06-2003) No. CA2002-03-057, 2003-Ohio-5280, 2003 WL 22283440, Unreported. Costs ⚷ 314

2941.52 Reasonable time to except—Repealed

(1975 H 164, eff. 1–13–76; 1953 H 1; GC 13439–4)

Historical and Statutory Notes

Pre–1953 H 1 Amendments: 113 v 174, Ch 18, § 4

2941.53 Exceptions to an indictment

An accused may except to an indictment by:

(A) A motion to quash;

(B) A plea in abatement;

(C) A demurrer.

(1953 H 1, eff. 10–1–53; GC 13439–5)

Historical and Statutory Notes

Pre–1953 H 1 Amendments: 113 v 174, Ch 18, § 5

Cross References

Motion in arrest of judgment, 2947.02

Library References

Indictment and Information ⚷133 to 154.
Westlaw Topic No. 210.

Research References

Encyclopedias

OH Jur. 3d Jury § 124, Effect of Rules of Criminal Procedure; Motion to Dismiss.

Notes of Decisions

Plea in abatement 1

1. Plea in abatement

Error cannot be predicated, on appeal in a criminal proceeding, on the alleged ground that the panel of persons to serve as grand jurors was improperly drawn and not selected according to law and that the indictment was, therefore, invalid, where such issue was not, at any time, properly presented to the trial court, either by challenge to the array or a plea in abatement, and there is not a shred of evidence, or even argument, as to what such alleged impropriety in the selection of the grand jury was. State v. Lamonge (Trumbull 1962) 117 Ohio App. 143, 191 N.E.2d 207, 23 O.O.2d 314, appeal dismissed 174 Ohio St. 545, 190 N.E.2d 691, 23 O.O.2d 210, certiorari denied 84 S.Ct. 346, 375 U.S. 942, 11 L.Ed.2d 272.

DEMURRERS AND MOTIONS

2941.54 Motion to quash

A motion to quash may be made when there is a defect apparent upon the face of the record, within the meaning of sections 2941.02 to 2941.35, inclusive, of the Revised Code, including defects in the form of indictment and in the manner in which an offense is charged.

(1953 H 1, eff. 10–1–53; GC 13439–6)

Historical and Statutory Notes

Pre–1953 H 1 Amendments: 113 v 174, Ch 18, § 6

Cross References

Motions, Crim R 47

Pleadings and motions before trial, defenses and objections, Crim R 12

Library References

Indictment and Information ⚷135 to 143.

Westlaw Topic No. 210.

Research References

Treatises and Practice Aids

Katz, Giannelli, Blair and Lipton, Baldwin's Ohio Practice, Criminal Law, § 47:2, Motions.

Notes of Decisions

Motion to quash affidavit 1
Motion to quash indictment 2

1. Motion to quash affidavit

An illegal arrest does not in itself invalidate an affidavit filed in a misdemeanor case, and is not a proper ground to sustain a motion to quash the affidavit, but it can affect evidence received as a result of such arrest, and when this happens, a motion to suppress the evidence or a plea in abatement will lie. State v. Hooper (Monroe 1966) 10 Ohio App.2d 229, 227 N.E.2d 414, 39 O.O.2d 435, certiorari denied 88 S.Ct. 292, 389 U.S. 928, 19 L.Ed.2d 281.

Question as to indefiniteness of affidavit can be raised only by motion to quash before issue joined. City of Cincinnati v. Schill (Ohio 1932) 125 Ohio St. 57, 180 N.E. 545, 11 Ohio Law Abs. 478, 36 Ohio Law Rep. 207. Criminal Law ⚷ 213; Indictment And Information ⚷ 139

2. Motion to quash indictment

Trial court erred as matter of law in dismissing without evidentiary hearing defendant's untimely motion to quash indictment on grounds that statutory requirements for certification and appointment of grand jury were not complied with, where Court of Common Pleas itself was implicated in failure to comply with statutory requirements in that one of its officers was among those required to certify venire and failed, along with those others, to do so. State v. Gunther (Ohio App. 11 Dist., 01-02-1998) 125 Ohio App.3d 226, 708 N.E.2d 242, dismissed, appeal not allowed 81 Ohio St.3d 1511, 692 N.E.2d 618. Indictment And Information ⚷ 141

An illegal arrest is not ground for motion to quash indictment under RC 2941.54. State v. Ramey (Ohio Com.Pl. 1971) 30 Ohio Misc. 89, 282 N.E.2d 65, 58 O.O.2d 442, 59 O.O.2d 405. Indictment And Information ⚷ 137(1)

The signature of the foreman of a grand jury is an indispensable requisite to a valid indictment, and in the absence thereof all subsequent proceedings are void; and habeas corpus will lie. Kennedy v. Alvis (Ohio Com.Pl. 1957) 145 N.E.2d 361, 76 Ohio Law Abs. 132.

2941.55 Plea in abatement

Plea in abatement may be made when there is a defect in the record shown by facts extrinsic thereto.

(1953 H 1, eff. 10–1–53; GC 13439–7)

Historical and Statutory Notes

Pre–1953 H 1 Amendments: 113 v 174, Ch 18, § 7

Cross References

Grand jury, Crim R 6

Pleadings and motions before trial, defenses and objections, Crim R 12

Library References

Criminal Law ⚷277.

Westlaw Topic No. 110.

Research References

Encyclopedias

OH Jur. 3d Jury § 124, Effect of Rules of Criminal Procedure; Motion to Dismiss.

Treatises and Practice Aids

Katz, Giannelli, Blair and Lipton, Baldwin's Ohio Practice, Criminal Law, § 39:5, Selection Procedure.

Katz, Giannelli, Blair and Lipton, Baldwin's Ohio Practice, Criminal Law, § 47:2, Motions.

Notes of Decisions

1. Challenge to grand jury array

Error cannot be predicated, on appeal in a criminal proceeding, on the alleged ground that the panel of persons to serve as grand jurors was improperly drawn and not selected according to law and that the indictment was, therefore, invalid, where such issue was not, at any time, properly presented to the trial court, either by challenge to the array or a plea in abatement, and there is not a shred of evidence, or even argument, as to what such alleged impropriety in the selection of the grand jury was. State v. Lamonge (Trumbull 1962) 117 Ohio App. 143, 191 N.E.2d 207, 23 O.O.2d 314, appeal dismissed 174 Ohio St. 545, 190 N.E.2d 691, 23 O.O.2d 210, certiorari denied 84 S.Ct. 346, 375 U.S. 942, 11 L.Ed.2d 272.

The question of the legality of the selecting and drawing of the grand jury may not be raised by plea in abatement to the indictment. State v. Deiter (Ohio 1909) 81 Ohio St. 504, 91 N.E. 1139, 7 Ohio Law Rep. 410, 7 Ohio Law Rep. 435.

2. Challenge to jurisdiction

In State v Klingenberger, 113 OS 418, 149 NE 395 (1925), it was held as follows: "A minor charged with felony waives his right to object to the jurisdiction of the court of common pleas on the ground of his minority, by not filing a plea in abatement to an indictment in the court of common pleas." Scopillitti v. State (Cuyahoga 1932) 41 Ohio App. 221, 180 N.E. 740, 11 Ohio Law Abs. 461, 36 Ohio Law Rep. 187.

2941.56 Misnomer

If the accused pleads in abatement that he is not indicted by his true name, he must plead his true name which shall be entered on the minutes of the court. After such entry, the trial and proceedings on the indictment shall be had against him by that name, referring also to the name by which he is indicted, as if he had been indicted by his true name.

(1953 H 1, eff. 10–1–53; GC 13439–8)

Historical and Statutory Notes

Pre–1953 H 1 Amendments: 113 v 174, Ch 18, § 8

Library References

Criminal Law ⟹280(4).

Westlaw Topic No. 110.

Research References

Encyclopedias

OH Jur. 3d Criminal Law § 2415, Names.

Treatises and Practice Aids

Katz, Giannelli, Blair and Lipton, Baldwin's Ohio Practice, Criminal Law, § 143:17, Motion to Correct Misnomer.

Katz, Giannelli, Blair and Lipton, Baldwin's Ohio Practice, Criminal Law, § 143:18, Entry on Motion to Correct Misnomer.

Notes of Decisions

1. **Alias**

It was not prejudicial error that defendants in a criminal proceeding were identified in the indictment by aliases where no evidence was offered of a claimed use of an alias. State v. Senzarino (Ohio Com.Pl. 1967) 10 Ohio Misc. 241, 224 N.E.2d 389, 39 O.O.2d 383.

2941.57 Demurrer

The accused may demur:

(A) When the facts stated in the indictment do not constitute an offense punishable by the laws of this state;

(B) When the intent is not alleged and proof thereof is necessary to make out the offense charged;

(C) When it appears on the face of the indictment that the offense charged is not within the jurisdiction of the court.

(1953 H 1, eff. 10–1–53; GC 13439–9)

Historical and Statutory Notes

Pre–1953 H 1 Amendments: 113 v 174, Ch 18, § 9

Cross References

Motions and pleadings, Crim R 47

Pleadings and motions before trial, defenses and objections, Crim R 12

Library References

Indictment and Information ⚷145 to 154.

Westlaw Topic No. 210.

Research References

Treatises and Practice Aids

Katz, Giannelli, Blair and Lipton, Baldwin's Ohio Practice, Criminal Law, § 47:2, Motions.

Katz, Giannelli, Blair and Lipton, Baldwin's Ohio Practice, Criminal Law, § 143:5, Motion to Dismiss—Lack of Jurisdiction.

Katz, Giannelli, Blair and Lipton, Baldwin's Ohio Practice, Criminal Law, § 143:8, Motion to Dismiss—Failure to State Sufficient Facts to Constitute an Offense.

Notes of Decisions

1. **Intent allegation**

Where a criminal statute does not clearly make a certain specific intent an element of the offense, but judicial interpretation has made such intent a necessary element, an indictment charging the offense solely in the language of the statute is insufficient. State v. Ross (Ohio 1967) 12 Ohio St.2d 37, 231 N.E.2d 299, 41 O.O.2d 220. Indictment And Information ⚷ 110(4)

Either "the intent to steal property" of some value or "intent to commit a felony" is an essential element of the crime specified in RC 2907.10, and an indictment which does not charge defendant with either such intent will not charge such defendant with the crime specified in that statute. State v. Wozniak (Ohio 1961) 172 Ohio St. 517, 178 N.E.2d 800, 18 O.O.2d 58. Burglary ⚷ 19

2. **Indefiniteness of allegations**

The first paragraph of the syllabus in State v Messenger, 63 OS 398, 59 NE 105 (1900): "Indefiniteness in the averments of an indictment should be taken advantage of by a motion to quash and not by demurrer," approved. City of Cincinnati v. Schill (Ohio 1932) 125 Ohio St. 57, 180 N.E. 545, 11 Ohio Law Abs. 478, 36 Ohio Law Rep. 207.

A judgment entered upon a plea of guilty to a criminal charge contained in an affidavit, information, or indictment is reviewable on error as to the question whether or not the act set forth in such written charge constitutes an offense against the statutes, in view of Bill of Rights, Art. I, § 10. State v. Marcinski (Ohio 1921) 103 Ohio St. 613, 134 N.E. 438, 19 Ohio Law Rep. 511. Criminal Law ⚷ 1134(8); Criminal Law ⚷ 1158(1)

3. Insufficient indictment against co-defendants

A single indictment which on appeal is found legally insufficient as to one defendant may not provide the basis for conviction of another defendant who is in the identical position and questions the sufficiency of that indictment on an appeal from his conviction thereunder. State v. Potts (Ohio 1968) 16 Ohio St.2d 111, 243 N.E.2d 91, 45 O.O.2d 460. Criminal Law ⚷ 1186.1

2941.58 Accused not discharged when indictment quashed

When a motion to quash or a plea in abatement is adjudged in favor of the accused, the trial court may order the case to be resubmitted to the grand jury, if then pending, or to the next succeeding grand jury. The accused then may be committed to jail or held to bail in such sum as the trial court requires for his appearance to answer at a time to be fixed by the court.

(1953 H 1, eff. 10–1–53; GC 13439–10)

Historical and Statutory Notes

Pre–1953 H 1 Amendments: 113 v 174, Ch 18, § 10

Cross References

Effect of determination of motion to dismiss, Crim R 12

Library References

Indictment and Information ⚷142.
Westlaw Topic No. 210.

Research References

Encyclopedias

OH Jur. 3d Criminal Law § 2187, After Grant of Motion to Quash; Plea in Abatement.

Treatises and Practice Aids

Katz, Giannelli, Blair and Lipton, Baldwin's Ohio Practice, Criminal Law, § 47:11, Effect of Motion to Dismiss.

Katz, Giannelli, Blair and Lipton, Baldwin's Ohio Practice, Criminal Law, § 143:15, Entry on Motion to Dismiss Overruled and Plea of Not Guilty.

Notes of Decisions

1. Not appealable order

An order quashing an indictment and holding the accused to bail for his appearance at the next term of court is not a final, appealable order. State v. Saygrover (Union 1964) 1 Ohio App.2d 360, 204 N.E.2d 549, 30 O.O.2d 358.

2. Multiple indictments

Where two of several indictments against a defendant are quashed, the cases should be held in abeyance until the other indictments are ruled upon before being resubmitted to the grand jury. State v. Kearns (Ohio Com.Pl. 1955) 127 N.E.2d 541, 70 Ohio Law Abs. 149.

2941.59 Waiver of defects

The accused waives all defects which may be excepted to by a motion to quash or a plea in abatement, by demurring to an indictment, or by pleading in bar or the general issue.

(1953 H 1, eff. 10–1–53; GC 13439–11)

Historical and Statutory Notes

Pre–1953 H 1 Amendments: 113 v 175, Ch 18, § 11

Cross References

Failure to raise defenses or objections, Crim R 12

Library References

Indictment and Information ⚷193 to 199.
Westlaw Topic No. 210.

Research References

Treatises and Practice Aids

Katz, Giannelli, Blair and Lipton, Baldwin's Ohio Practice, Criminal Law, § 47:9, Waiver—Failure to Raise Issue.

Hennenberg & Reinhart, Ohio Criminal Defense Motions F 15.12, Miscellaneous Motions-Petition for Writ of Habeas Corpus-Supplemental Memorandum-Single Judge Without Jurisdiction to Accept Plea in Capital Case.

Hennenberg & Reinhart, Ohio Criminal Defense Motions F 15.13, Supplemental Memorandum in Support of State Habeas Petition-Miscellaneous Motions.

Notes of Decisions

1. Waiver in general

Defendant, by failing to object to alleged flaw in indictment until after prosecution finished presenting its case in chief, waived any argument concerning validity of indictment other than plain error. State v. Frazier (Ohio, 08-23-1995) 73 Ohio St.3d 323, 652 N.E.2d 1000, 1995-Ohio-235, stay granted 74 Ohio St.3d 1437, 655 N.E.2d 1321, certiorari denied 116 S.Ct. 820, 516 U.S. 1095, 133 L.Ed.2d 763, denial of post-conviction relief affirmed 1997 WL 764810, dismissed, appeal not allowed 81 Ohio St.3d 1496, 691 N.E.2d 1058, habeas corpus denied 188 F.Supp.2d 798, denial of habeas corpus reversed in part 343 F.3d 780, opinion supplemented on denial of rehearing 348 F.3d 174, rehearing and suggestion for rehearing en banc denied, certiorari denied 124 S.Ct. 2815, 541 U.S. 1095, 159 L.Ed.2d 261. Indictment And Information ⚷ 196(1)

Where defendant and his counsel and the prosecution were unaware that the affidavit charging defendant with a traffic violation had not been verified until discovered by the judge at the end of the trial, a waiver may not be considered, and verification of the affidavit cannot be furnished at the end of the trial against objection of the defendant. Village of Pepper Pike v. LaMaida (Ohio Mun. 1970) 25 Ohio Misc. 252, 268 N.E.2d 296, 54 O.O.2d 410.

Error cannot be predicated, on appeal in a criminal proceeding, on the alleged ground that the panel of persons to serve as grand jurors was improperly drawn and not selected according to law and that the indictment was, therefore, invalid, where such issue was not, at any time, properly presented to the trial court, either by challenge to the array or a plea in abatement, and there is not a shred of evidence, or even argument, as to what such alleged impropriety in the selection of the grand jury was. State v. Lamonge (Trumbull 1962) 117 Ohio App. 143, 191 N.E.2d 207, 23 O.O.2d 314, appeal dismissed 174 Ohio St. 545, 190 N.E.2d 691, 23 O.O.2d 210, certiorari denied 84 S.Ct. 346, 375 U.S. 942, 11 L.Ed.2d 272.

2. Waiver by plea to general issue

A motion to quash an arrest warrant does not lie where, on arraignment, accused enters his appearance by waiving the reading of the indictment and entering a pleas of "not guilty." State v. Sizer (Ohio Com.Pl. 1970) 25 Ohio Misc. 245, 265 N.E.2d 468, 54 O.O.2d 406. Criminal Law ⚷ 219

Where a defendant is charged in an affidavit with a misdemeanor and pleads not guilty thereto, and goes to trial without questioning the validity of his arrest or the sufficiency of the affidavit, such defendant may not thereafter defend on the ground that he was unlawfully arrested or that the affidavit was falsely or improperly verified. City of Cleveland v. Ely (Ohio 1963) 174 Ohio St. 403, 189 N.E.2d 724, 23 O.O.2d 46. Criminal Law ⚷ 213

Entering a plea of not guilty waives all defects which may be excepted to by a motion to quash. State v. Foston (Miami 1954) 129 N.E.2d 307, 70 Ohio Law Abs. 540, appeal dismissed 162 Ohio St. 602, 124 N.E.2d 724, 55 O.O. 487, certiorari denied 76 S.Ct. 313, 350 U.S. 939, 100 L.Ed. 820.

Accused by his plea of "not guilty," waived his right to a motion to quash and it was lost to him unless he by leave of court withdrew such plea. City of Cincinnati v. Schill (Ohio 1932) 125 Ohio St. 57, 180 N.E. 545, 11 Ohio Law Abs. 478, 36 Ohio Law Rep. 207.

An earlier statute applied so that a minor accused of crime was held to waive a defect based on his minority where he pleaded not guilty without having filed in abatement. State v. Klingenberger (Ohio 1925) 113 Ohio St. 418, 149 N.E. 395, 3 Ohio Law Abs. 675, 23 Ohio Law Rep. 588.

3. Arraignment; appointment of counsel

Failure to appoint counsel to defend an indigent defendant prior to arraignment does not create grounds for release on habeas corpus. Dean v. Maxwell (Ohio 1963) 174 Ohio St. 193, 187 N.E.2d 884, 5 A.L.R.3d 1263, 22 O.O.2d 144.

Arraignment in Ohio is not always a "critical stage" of the trial process. Vitoratos v. Maxwell

(C.A.6 (Ohio) 1965) 7 Ohio Misc. 106, 351 F.2d 217, 34 O.O.2d 177, appeal dismissed, certiorari denied 86 S.Ct. 718, 383 U.S. 105, 15 L.Ed.2d 618. Criminal Law ⚷ 264

4. Challenge to defects

Where an affidavit alleged that the defendant was operating a gasoline truck under certain circumstances, whereas the defendant was actually operating a diesel truck, the affidavit is subject to a motion to quash but is not subject to demurrer. City of Cleveland v. Antonio (Cuyahoga 1955) 100 Ohio App. 334, 124 N.E.2d 846, 70 Ohio Law Abs. 518, 60 O.O. 289.

2941.60 Answer to plea in abatement

The prosecuting attorney may demur to a plea in abatement if it is not sufficient in substance, or he may reply, setting forth any facts which may show there is no defect in the record as charged in the plea.

(1953 H 1, eff. 10–1–53; GC 13439–12)

Historical and Statutory Notes

Pre–1953 H 1 Amendments: 113 v 175, Ch 18, § 12

Library References

Criminal Law ⚷281.
Westlaw Topic No. 110.

2941.61 After demurrer accused may plead

After a demurrer to an indictment is overruled, the accused may plead under section 2943.03 of the Revised Code.

(1953 H 1, eff. 10–1–53; GC 13439–13)

Historical and Statutory Notes

Pre–1953 H 1 Amendments: 113 v 175, Ch 18, § 13

Library References

Indictment and Information ⚷152.
Westlaw Topic No. 210.

Notes of Decisions

Arraignment 1

1. Arraignment

Failure to appoint counsel to defend an indigent defendant prior to arraignment does not create grounds for release on habeas corpus. Dean v. Maxwell (Ohio 1963) 174 Ohio St. 193, 187 N.E.2d 884, 5 A.L.R.3d 1263, 22 O.O.2d 144.

Even if an accused's pleas were withdrawn for the purpose of a demurrer, it was not an absolute withdrawal, and the court did not err in going to trial without a rearraignment. Douglas v. Maxwell (Ohio 1962) 174 Ohio St. 92, 186 N.E.2d 723, 21 O.O.2d 345, certiorari denied 83 S.Ct. 1885, 374 U.S. 836, 10 L.Ed.2d 1057. Criminal Law ⚷ 301

2941.62 Hearing on motions and demurrers

Motions to quash, pleas in abatement, and demurrers shall be heard immediately upon their filing, unless the trial court, for good cause shown, sets another time for such hearing.

(1953 H 1, eff. 10–1–53; GC 13439–14)

Historical and Statutory Notes

Pre–1953 H 1 Amendments: 113 v 175, Ch 18, § 14

Cross References

Pleadings and motions before trial, defenses and objections, Crim R 12

Library References

Criminal Law ⟹284.
Indictment and Information ⟹140, 150.
Westlaw Topic Nos. 110, 210.

Research References

Treatises and Practice Aids

Katz, Giannelli, Blair and Lipton, Baldwin's Ohio Practice, Criminal Law, § 47:7, Rulings on Motions.

2941.63 Counsel to assist prosecutor

The court of common pleas, or the court of appeals, whenever it is of the opinion that the public interest requires it, may appoint an attorney to assist the prosecuting attorney in the trial of a case pending in such court. The board of county commissioners shall pay said assistant to the prosecuting attorney such compensation for his services as the court approves.

(1953 H 1, eff. 10–1–53; GC 13439–15)

Historical and Statutory Notes

Pre–1953 H 1 Amendments: 113 v 175, Ch 18, § 15

Cross References

Change of venue; additional counsel for prosecuting attorney, Crim R 18
Employment of counsel, 305.14

Library References

District and Prosecuting Attorneys ⟹3, 4.
Westlaw Topic No. 131.
C.J.S. District and Prosecuting Attorneys §§ 36 to 64.

Research References

Encyclopedias

OH Jur. 3d Cvl. Servants & Pub. Officers & Employ. § 496, Appointment, by Court, of Counsel to Assist Prosecutor.

OH Jur. 3d Criminal Law § 2322, Indictment; Constitutional and Statutory Provisions—Misdemeanors.

Treatises and Practice Aids

Hennenberg & Reinhart, Ohio Criminal Defense Motions F 15.21, Objection to Order Removing Special Prosecutor from Case-Entry Void Ab Initio as Entered Without Jurisdiction-Miscellaneous.

Notes of Decisions

1. Assistant prosecutor

RC 309.10 and 2941.63 allow appointment of assistant prosecutors where the public interest requires, and appointment of an assistant prosecutor from one county in which part of a crime took place to serve without additional compensation as an assistant prosecutor in a different county where the alleged criminal is being tried is logical and reasonable; the fact that the victim's mother-in-law happens also to be employed by the first county's court system does not make the appointment erroneous. State v. Brewer (Ohio 1990) 48 Ohio St.3d 50, 549 N.E.2d 491, rehearing denied 49 Ohio St.3d 705, 551 N.E.2d 618, certiorari denied 111 S.Ct. 218, 498 U.S. 881, 112 L.Ed.2d 177, rehearing denied 111 S.Ct. 445, 498 U.S. 973, 112 L.Ed.2d 427, denial of post-conviction relief affirmed, dismissed, appeal not allowed 71 Ohio St.3d 1465, 644 N.E.2d 1387, certiorari denied 116 S.Ct. 101, 516

U.S. 830, 133 L.Ed.2d 55, dismissed, appeal not allowed 77 Ohio St.3d 1473, 673 N.E.2d 138.

An assistant prosecutor may be appointed by a single judge of a common pleas court having several judges. State ex rel. Williams v. Zaleski (Ohio 1984) 12 Ohio St.3d 109, 465 N.E.2d 861, 12 O.B.R. 153.

2. Special prosecutor

A criminal indictment is not invalid because a properly appointed special prosecutor signs the indictment instead of the county prosecutor. State v. Bunyan (Auglaize 1988) 51 Ohio App.3d 190, 555 N.E.2d 980.

CHAPTER 2943

ARRAIGNMENT; PLEAS

MAGISTRATE DEFINED

2943.01 Definition of magistrate

The definition of "magistrate" set forth in section 2931.01 of the Revised Code applies to Chapter 2943. of the Revised Code.

(1953 H 1, eff. 10–1–53)

ARRAIGNMENT

2943.02 Arraignment

An accused person shall be arraigned by the clerk of the court of common pleas, or his deputy, reading the indictment or information to the accused, unless the accused or his attorney waives the reading thereof. He shall then be asked to plead thereto. Arraignment shall be made immediately after the disposition of exceptions to the indictment, if any are filed, or, if no exceptions are filed, after reasonable opportunity has been given the accused to file such exceptions.

(1953 H 1, eff. 10–1–53; GC 13440–1)

Historical and Statutory Notes

Pre–1953 H 1 Amendments: 113 v 175, Ch 19, § 1

Cross References

Arraignment, Crim R 10

Library References

Arrest ⚩70(2).
Criminal Law ⚩261.
Westlaw Topic Nos. 110, 35.

C.J.S. Arrest §§ 58 to 61.
C.J.S. Criminal Law § 357.

Research References

Treatises and Practice Aids

Katz, Giannelli, Blair and Lipton, Baldwin's Ohio Practice, Criminal Law, § 42:4, Arraignment Procedures.

Katz, Giannelli, Blair and Lipton, Baldwin's Ohio Practice, Criminal Law, § 42:7, Time Requirements.

Law Review and Journal Commentaries

The Effect of the Double Jeopardy Clause on Juvenile Proceedings, James G. Carr. 6 U Tol L Rev 1 (Fall 1974).

The Rights of a Hearing–Impaired Litigant, Kenneth S. Resuick and Eleanor M. Stromberg. 8 Ohio Law 12 (March/April 1994).

Notes of Decisions

Withdrawal of plea 1

1. Withdrawal of plea

Motion to withdraw guilty pleas to rape, attempted rape, and gross sexual imposition was not appropriate remedy for claim that State, through parole board, breached plea agreement. State v. Bush (Ohio App. 11 Dist., Trumbull, 04-22-2005) No. 2004-T-0003, 2005-Ohio-1898, 2005 WL 940588, Unreported. Criminal Law ⚷ 274(3.1)

Inmate's mandamus petition seeking to compel judges to rule on his motion to withdraw guilty plea was moot, where motion to withdraw plea was denied. State ex rel. McGee v. Mahon (Ohio App. 8 Dist., Cuyahoga, 12-05-2002) No. 81753, 2002-Ohio-6647, 2002 WL 31723180, Unreported. Mandamus ⚷ 16(1)

Where an accused, after having pleaded not guilty upon arraignment, withdraws such plea and enters a plea of guilty, and subsequently withdraws such plea of guilty and re-enters a plea of not guilty, and such former plea of not guilty has been journalized, a court is without authority to vacate such plea of not guilty and re-establish such prior plea of guilty without the consent of such accused made in open court; and the sentencing of such accused on such prior plea of guilty is a denial of due process. State v. Evola (Cuyahoga 1955) 102 Ohio App. 419, 130 N.E.2d 166, 72 Ohio Law Abs. 607, 2 O.O.2d 425.

PLEAS

2943.03 Pleas to indictment

Pleas to an indictment or information are:

(A) Guilty;

(B) Not guilty;

(C) A former judgment of conviction or acquittal of the offense;

(D) Once in jeopardy;

(E) Not guilty by reason of insanity.

A defendant who does not plead guilty may enter one or more of the other pleas. A defendant who does not plead not guilty by reason of insanity is conclusively presumed to have been sane at the time of the commission of the offense charged. The court may, for good cause shown, allow a change of plea at any time before the commencement of the trial.
(1953 H 1, eff. 10–1–53; GC 13440–2)

Historical and Statutory Notes

Pre–1953 H 1 Amendments: 113 v 175, Ch 19, § 2

Cross References

Effect of plea, accused to be informed of, 2937.02

Effect of verdict of not guilty by reason of insanity, 2945.40

Inadmissibility of pleas, offers of pleas, and related statements, Evid R 410

Pleas, Crim R 11

Traffic rules, pleas, rights upon plea, Traf R 10

Withdrawal of guilty plea, Crim R 32.1

Library References

Criminal Law ⚷267 to 301.
Westlaw Topic No. 110.
C.J.S. Criminal Law §§ 365 to 418, 453.

Research References

Encyclopedias

OH Jur. 3d Criminal Law § 2445, Plea of Not Guilty by Reason of Insanity.

OH Jur. 3d Criminal Law § 2899, Sanity; Capacity.

Treatises and Practice Aids

Markus, Trial Handbook for Ohio Lawyers, § 4:58, Criminal Case—Defenses—Insanity—as Affirmative Defense.

Katz, Giannelli, Blair and Lipton, Baldwin's Ohio Practice, Criminal Law, § 42:2, Types of Pleas.

Katz, Giannelli, Blair and Lipton, Baldwin's Ohio Practice, Criminal Law, § 46:2, Criminal Rule 32.1.

Katz, Giannelli, Blair and Lipton, Baldwin's Ohio Practice, Criminal Law, § 47:2, Motions.

Katz, Giannelli, Blair and Lipton, Baldwin's Ohio Practice, Criminal Law, § 144:1, Plea of Guilty.

Katz, Giannelli, Blair and Lipton, Baldwin's Ohio Practice, Criminal Law, § 144:2, No Contest Plea.

Katz, Giannelli, Blair and Lipton, Baldwin's Ohio Practice, Criminal Law, § 144:3, Entry of Not Guilty Plea.

Hennenberg & Reinhart, Ohio Criminal Defense Motions F 5.09, Motion for Order Permitting Defendant to Enter a Written Plea of Not Guilty by Reason of Insanity-Pretrial Motions.

Law Review and Journal Commentaries

Affirmative Defenses, Defendant's Burden of Proof, Defense of Extreme Emotional Disturbance, Due Process, Lee Ann Johnson. 11 Akron L Rev 386 (Fall 1977).

Affirmative Defenses in Ohio After Mullaney v. Wilbur, Comment. 36 Ohio St L J 828 (1975).

CRIMINAL PROCEDURE—Multiple Representation and the Guilty Plea—United States v. Truglio, Note. 6 U Tol L Rev 559 (Winter 1975).

Epilepsy and the Alternatives for a Criminal Defense, Note. 27 Case W Res L Rev 771 (Spring 1977).

Failure to Plead Insanity as a Defense, Note. 6 U Cin L Rev 313 (1932).

Insanity as a Defense in Criminal Cases, Frank T. Cullitan. 18 Clev B J 75 (March 1947).

The Insanity Defense, Philip B. Lyons. 9 U Tol L Rev 31 (Fall 1977).

Patterson v. New York, Criminal Procedure—The Burden of Proof and Affirmative Defenses, Note. 9 U Tol L Rev 524 (Spring 1978).

The Role Of Plea Bargaining In The Criminal Justice System—What would happen if plea bargaining were to be abolished?, Dennis J. Langer. 40 Columbus B Briefs 11 (December 1990).

Notes of Decisions

Ed. Note: *This section contains annotations from former RC 2937.10.*

Constitutional issues 1
Guilty plea 3
Insanity 6
Pleas in bar 2
Withdrawal of guilty plea 4, 5
In general 4
After sentence 5

---

1. Constitutional issues

Sentencing hearing held after entry of guilty plea to burglary did not result in denial of defendant's due process rights, where court provided defense counsel and defendant opportunity to address court prior to sentencing, defendant did not object to proceeding with sentencing following acceptance of his guilty plea, and trial court adequately advised defendant he would be subject to post-release control. U.S.C.A. Const.Amend. 14. State v. Whitfield (Ohio App. 8 Dist., Cuyahoga, 03-27-2003) No. 81247, 2003-Ohio-1504, 2003 WL 1563801, Unreported. Constitutional Law ⚷ 270(1); Sentencing And Punishment ⚷ 354; Sentencing And Punishment ⚷ 359

The extraordinary original jurisdiction granted to an Ohio appellate court may be invoked to adjudicate the right of an accused to the benefit of the doctrine of collateral estoppel, made applicable to the state as being within the federal constitutional right against double jeopardy by Ashe v Swenson, 397 US 436, 90 SCt 1189, 25 LEd(2d) 469 (1970). Owens v. Campbell (Ohio 1971) 27 Ohio St.2d 264, 272 N.E.2d 116, 56 O.O.2d 158. Courts ⚷ 206(15.1)

Failure to appoint counsel to defend an indigent defendant prior to arraignment does not create grounds for release on habeas corpus. Dean v. Maxwell (Ohio 1963) 174 Ohio St. 193, 187 N.E.2d 884, 5 A.L.R.3d 1263, 22 O.O.2d 144.

Former jeopardy is a defense which must be pleaded in writing. State v. Downey (Cuyahoga 1960) 113 Ohio App. 250, 170 N.E.2d 75, 85 Ohio Law Abs. 253, 17 O.O.2d 227, appeal dismissed 171 Ohio St. 565, 173 N.E.2d 106, 15 O.O.2d 42.

The overruling of an oral motion for discharge of defendant in a criminal proceeding on the claim of "double jeopardy" is not a final appealable order. State v. Downey (Cuyahoga 1960) 113 Ohio App. 250, 170 N.E.2d 75, 85 Ohio Law Abs. 253, 17 O.O.2d 227, appeal dismissed 171 Ohio St. 565, 173 N.E.2d 106, 15 O.O.2d 42.

The guaranties contained in O Const Art I, § 10, and in US Const Am 5, that no person shall "be twice put in jeopardy," apply only to being placed in jeopardy more than once for the same offense—not the same transactions, acts, circumstances, or situation. State v. Orth (Allen 1957) 106 Ohio App. 35, 153 N.E.2d 394, 6 O.O.2d 300, appeal dismissed 167 Ohio St. 388, 148 N.E.2d 917, 5 O.O.2d 17. Double Jeopardy ⚷ 1

The constitutional right of a defendant to plead not guilty and to have a trial in which he can confront and cross-examine the witnesses against him cannot be waived by his counsel without defendant's consent. Brookhart v. Janis (U.S.Ohio 1966) 86 S.Ct. 1245, 384 U.S. 1, 7 Ohio Misc. 77, 16 L.Ed.2d 314, 36 O.O.2d 141. Attorney And Client ⚷ 77; Attorney And Client ⚷ 92

Arraignment in Ohio is not always a "critical stage" of the trial process. Vitoratos v. Maxwell (C.A.6 (Ohio) 1965) 7 Ohio Misc. 106, 351 F.2d 217, 34 O.O.2d 177, appeal dismissed, certiorari denied 86 S.Ct. 718, 383 U.S. 105, 15 L.Ed.2d 618. Criminal Law ⚷ 264

Failure of counsel to file a written plea of not guilty by reason of insanity in an action in which they relied on such defense made orally in the opening statement deprived accused of due process of law. Schaber v. Maxwell (C.A.6 (Ohio) 1965) 5 Ohio Misc. 81, 348 F.2d 664, 33 O.O.2d 377.

2. Pleas in bar

Where a defendant is acquitted of the charge of murder in the first degree while perpetrating a robbery, in which trial his only defense was that of alibi, the doctrine of res judicata does not apply to bar a subsequent prosecution for the crime of robbery, even though the robbery was a part of the same criminal act referred to in the indictment for murder. State v. Orth (Allen 1957) 106 Ohio App. 35, 153 N.E.2d 394, 6 O.O.2d 300, appeal dismissed 167 Ohio St. 388, 148 N.E.2d 917, 5 O.O.2d 17.

Where a defendant in a criminal action files a motion for leave to enter the defense of res judicata and submits to the court his defense of res judicata setting forth the facts he claims in support of his motion, the question presented is one of law for the court. State v. Orth (Allen 1957) 106 Ohio App. 35, 153 N.E.2d 394, 6 O.O.2d 300, appeal dismissed 167 Ohio St. 388, 148 N.E.2d 917, 5 O.O.2d 17.

A conviction in one county for a continuous transportation of intoxicating liquor through several counties may be pleaded in bar to a prosecution in another county. State v. Shimman (Ohio 1930) 122 Ohio St. 522, 172 N.E. 367, 73 A.L.R. 1502, 8 Ohio Law Abs. 386, 32 Ohio Law Rep. 208. Double Jeopardy ⚷ 183.1; Intoxicating Liquors ⚷ 176

3. Guilty plea

The law of the case doctrine prevented the Court of Appeals from vacating its prior decision, which vacated defendant's plea to murder, and reinstating defendant's prior plea agreement; the decision of the appellate court in a prior appeal will be followed in a later appeal in the same case in the same court, and defendant failed to demonstrate an extraordinary circumstance that would allow the Court of Appeals to question the finality of its former decision. State v. Prom (Ohio App. 12 Dist., Butler, 05-09-2005) No. CA2004-07-174, 2005-Ohio-2272, 2005 WL 1077238, Unreported, appeal not allowed 106 Ohio St.3d 1536, 835 N.E.2d 384, 2005-Ohio-5146, reconsideration denied 107 Ohio St.3d 1686, 839 N.E.2d 405, 2005-Ohio-6480. Criminal Law ⚷ 1180

Trial court was not required to enforce defendant's original plea agreement, which was vacated on appeal when her plea to the lesser charge of murder was set aside; the state was allowed to charge defendant with aggravated murder, which defendant was originally indicted for, after her plea was vacated on appeal, since the charge was within the limits of the original indictment. State v. Prom (Ohio App. 12 Dist., Butler, 05-09-2005) No. CA2004-07-174, 2005-Ohio-2272, 2005 WL 1077238, Unreported, appeal not allowed 106 Ohio St.3d 1536, 835 N.E.2d 384, 2005-Ohio-5146, reconsideration denied 107 Ohio St.3d 1686, 839 N.E.2d 405, 2005-Ohio-6480. Criminal Law ⚷ 273.1(2)

Trial court failed to substantially comply with rule requiring court, prior to taking defendant's guilty plea to gross sexual imposition, to determine that defendant fully understood maximum penalty involved, given that court failed to inform defendant that he was subject to five-year mandatory term of post-release control; although court reviewed plea agreement with defendant, plea agreement incorrectly stated that defendant was subject to post-release control of up to three years as to each offense. State v. Griffin (Ohio App. 8 Dist., Cuyahoga, 08-19-2004) No. 83724, 2004-Ohio-4344, 2004 WL 1846121, Unreported. Criminal Law ⚷ 273.1(4)

Filing of petition by Office of Victims' Services (OVS) for full parole board hearing after parole board granted murder defendant early release did not constitute breach of guilty plea agreement, where agreement provided that state would recommend early release and petition was not effort by prosecutor to circumvent agreement, but was filed on behalf of victim's relatives. State v. Hall (Ohio App. 2 Dist., Montgomery, 07-02-2004) No. 20025, 2004-Ohio-3561, 2004 WL 1490127, Unreported, appeal not allowed 103 Ohio St.3d 1527, 817 N.E.2d 410, 2004-Ohio-5852. Criminal Law ⚷ 273.1(2)

Letters by prosecutor and judge to parole board, which were sent after prosecutor and judge initially strongly opposed murder defendant's early release, were sufficient to constitute specific performance of guilty plea agreement in which prosecutor and judge agreed to recommend early release, where judge's letter strongly recommended early release and indicated that such recommendation was required by plea agreement, prosecutor's letter to parole board recommended early release, parole board granted rehearing and relied on such letters, nine out of ten board members did not receive initial negative recommendations, and board granted defendant early release. State v. Hall (Ohio App. 2 Dist., Montgomery, 07-02-2004) No. 20025, 2004-Ohio-3561, 2004 WL 1490127, Unreported, appeal not allowed 103 Ohio St.3d 1527, 817 N.E.2d 410, 2004-Ohio-5852. Criminal Law ⚷ 273.1(2)

Conduct of defense counsel did not prevent defendant from entering knowing and voluntary plea of guilty to total of six counts of burglary, in two separate cases, and did not amount to constitutionally ineffective assistance; defendant had been charged with seven counts of burglary, all second degree felonies, and one count of possessing criminal tools, a fifth degree felony, and faced maximum possible prison sentence of 57 years, negotiated guilty plea reduced her potential exposure to 48 years with generous recommendations from state, and defendant was ultimately sentenced to five years' imprisonment. State v. Ward (Ohio App. 6 Dist., Lucas, 12-12-2003) No. L-02-1281, No. L-02-1283, 2003-Ohio-6764, 2003 WL 22947441, Unreported. Criminal Law ⚷ 641.13(5)

Defense counsel did not render ineffective assistance of counsel by allowing a heavily medicated defendant to enter guilty pleas to attempted rape and gross sexual imposition, as guilty pleas were entered knowing and voluntarily, as demonstrated by defendant's assurance to trial court that the drugs did not alter his understanding of what was happening. State v. Richter (Ohio App. 11 Dist., Lake, 12-15-2003) No. 2002-L-080, 2003-Ohio-6734, 2003 WL 22941222, Unreported, motion for delayed appeal granted 102 Ohio St.3d 1420, 807 N.E.2d 366, 2004-Ohio-2003, appeal not allowed 103 Ohio St.3d 1425, 814 N.E.2d 489, 2004-Ohio-4524, denial of post-conviction relief affirmed 2004-Ohio-6682, 2004 WL 2860401, appeal not allowed 105 Ohio St.3d 1518, 826 N.E.2d 315, 2005-Ohio-1880, appeal not allowed 106 Ohio St.3d 1509, 833 N.E.2d 1250, 2005-Ohio-4605. Criminal Law ⚷ 641.13(5)

Defendant entered his guilty plea to one count of attempted rape and three counts of gross sexual imposition knowingly and voluntarily, even though he was medicated at time of plea hearing; trial court asked defendant if drugs caused him to be lethargic or unable to understand what was happening, to which defendant replied they did not, and provided trial court the correct date and time, before entering a verbal plea of guilty to each charge and signing the guilty plea form. State v. Richter (Ohio App. 11 Dist., Lake, 12-15-2003) No. 2002-L-080, 2003-Ohio-6734, 2003 WL 22941222, Unreported, motion for delayed appeal granted 102 Ohio St.3d 1420, 807 N.E.2d 366, 2004-Ohio-2003, appeal not allowed 103 Ohio St.3d 1425, 814 N.E.2d 489, 2004-Ohio-4524, denial of post-conviction relief affirmed 2004-Ohio-6682, 2004 WL 2860401, appeal not allowed 105 Ohio St.3d 1518, 826 N.E.2d 315, 2005-Ohio-1880, appeal not allowed 106 Ohio St.3d 1509, 833 N.E.2d 1250, 2005-Ohio-4605. Criminal Law ⚷ 273(2)

Defendant's plea of guilty to burglary was knowing and voluntary, even though trial court did not explain all elements of offense charged, where totality of circumstances indicated that defendant understood charges against him; court made extensive inquiry of defendant and his ability to understand and enter plea, court advised defendant of his constitutional rights, charges against him and consequences and penalties associated with plea, defendant indicated he understood his rights, charges against him and consequences of plea, and thus there was no indication that defendant did not understand nature of charge against him. State v. Whitfield (Ohio App. 8 Dist., Cuyahoga, 03-27-2003) No. 81247, 2003-Ohio-1504, 2003 WL 1563801, Unreported. Criminal Law ⚷ 273.1(4)

Record failed to show that defendant made knowing, intelligent, and voluntary plea of guilty to charged offense of attempted burglary, where trial court failed to specifically state at plea hearing that defendant could be subject to parole board supervision up to three years following completion of five-year sentence, defendant was not personally advised at plea hearing that parole board could impose up to nine months of prison for each violation of post-release control, and defendant was not notified at sentencing that parole board could impose a maximum of 50 percent of his original term for violations of post-release control. State v. Tucci (Ohio App. 7 Dist., Mahoning, 12-11-2002) No. 01 CA 234, 2002-Ohio-6903, 2002 WL 31812895, Unreported. Criminal Law ⚷ 273.1(4)

Record failed to show that defendant made knowing, intelligent, and voluntary plea of guilty to charged offense of attempted burglary, and thus plea required vacation, where trial court failed to inform defendant of his right against self-incrimination, his right to confront his accusers, and his right to compulsory process. State v. Tucci (Ohio App. 7 Dist., Mahoning, 12-11-2002) No. 01 CA 234, 2002-Ohio-6903, 2002 WL 31812895, Unreported. Criminal Law ⚷ 273.1(4)

Representations by detectives that defendant who pled no contest to attempted gross sexual imposition would more likely be dealt with leniently if he told the truth, were neither misleading nor unduly coercive, so as to render his no contest plea involuntary, where defendant received three years of community control with 30 days of intermittent incarceration in jail to be served during weekends, yet he could have been sentenced to incarceration for six months, up to 18 months, was originally charged with gross sexual imposition with a victim less than 13 years of age, and, had he not had the opportunity to plea to the lesser offense, could have been sentenced to a prison term of 1, 2, 3, 4 or 5 years. State v. Farley (Ohio App. 2 Dist., Miami, 11-15-2002) No. 2002-CA-2, 2002-Ohio-6192, 2002

WL 31528718, Unreported. Criminal Law ⚷ 275.4(1)

Defendant, who entered guilty plea to possession of crack cocaine and possession of heroin after original jury trial was declared mistrial, waived any error in trial court's denial of his motion for judgment of acquittal when he pled guilty. State v. Brooks (Ohio App. 2 Dist., Montgomery, 10-11-2002) No. C.A. 19152, 2002-Ohio-5527, 2002 WL 31316062, Unreported. Criminal Law ⚷ 273.4(1)

Defendant's guilty plea to three counts of aggravated murder with death specifications was knowing and intelligent, despite claim that trial court did not ensure that defendant understood the nature of the charges against him, specifically that the trial court should have explained to him the legal definitions of "purposely" and "prior calculation and design"; record of plea hearing contained express representations by defendant and his counsel that the nature of the charges had been explained to him and that he understood them. State v. Fitzpatrick (Ohio, 07-07-2004) 102 Ohio St.3d 321, 810 N.E.2d 927, 2004-Ohio-3167, reconsideration denied 103 Ohio St.3d 1429, 814 N.E.2d 491, 2004-Ohio-4524, denial of post-conviction relief affirmed 2004-Ohio-5615, 2004 WL 2367987, appeal not allowed 105 Ohio St.3d 1499, 825 N.E.2d 623, 2005-Ohio-1666, motion to reopen denied 105 Ohio St.3d 1436, 822 N.E.2d 808, 2005-Ohio-531, certiorari denied 125 S.Ct. 2930, 162 L.Ed.2d 869. Criminal Law ⚷ 273.1(4)

Defendant's guilty plea to three counts of aggravated murder with death specifications was voluntary, knowing, and intelligent, despite claim that plea colloquy was inadequate; trial court informed defendant that by pleading guilty, he would waive his privilege against self-incrimination and his rights to confront the State's witnesses before a jury, to subpoena witnesses for the guilt phase, to a jury trial, and to require the State to prove to a jury that he was guilty beyond a reasonable doubt. State v. Fitzpatrick (Ohio, 07-07-2004) 102 Ohio St.3d 321, 810 N.E.2d 927, 2004-Ohio-3167, reconsideration denied 103 Ohio St.3d 1429, 814 N.E.2d 491, 2004-Ohio-4524, denial of post-conviction relief affirmed 2004-Ohio-5615, 2004 WL 2367987, appeal not allowed 105 Ohio St.3d 1499, 825 N.E.2d 623, 2005-Ohio-1666, motion to reopen denied 105 Ohio St.3d 1436, 822 N.E.2d 808, 2005-Ohio-531, certiorari denied 125 S.Ct. 2930, 162 L.Ed.2d 869. Criminal Law ⚷ 273.1(4)

Defendant's guilty plea to charges of burglary and receiving stolen property was not voluntary; defendant was dissatisfied with his attorney's effort, defendant believed that a trial was not an alternative, and told the court no less than five times that he was only pleading guilty because he believed that to be his only alternative. State v. Gordon (Ohio App. 1 Dist., 06-07-2002) 149 Ohio App.3d 237, 776 N.E.2d 1135, 2002-Ohio-2761. Criminal Law ⚷ 273.1(3)

Defendant's failure to execute jury waiver before entering guilty pleas did not render pleas ineffective; entry of pleas constituted waiver of jury trial, and plea forms properly signed and filed by defendant and colloquy entered into by court demonstrated that defendant was aware that, by entering guilty pleas, he was waiving his right to jury trial. State v. West (Ohio App. 1 Dist., 06-11-1999) 134 Ohio App.3d 45, 730 N.E.2d 388, dismissed, appeal not allowed 87 Ohio St.3d 1418, 717 N.E.2d 1105. Criminal Law ⚷ 273(4.1)

Where an accused in effect pleads nolo contendere by requiring only that the state prove a prima facie case, which he will not contest, a conviction thereon is valid. Brookhart v. Haskins (Ohio 1965) 2 Ohio St.2d 36, 205 N.E.2d 911, 31 O.O.2d 20, certiorari granted 86 S.Ct. 104, 382 U.S. 810, 15 L.Ed.2d 59, reversed 86 S.Ct. 1245, 384 U.S. 1, 7 Ohio Misc. 77, 16 L.Ed.2d 314, 36 O.O.2d 141.

An oral plea of guilty is a waiver by a defendant charged with an offense of the necessity for a trial, and when the plea of guilty is journalized, it is of the same effect, within the meaning of the habitual criminal statute as a previous conviction which has been separately prosecuted and tried. State v. Sheridan (Summit 1959) 109 Ohio App. 482, 167 N.E.2d 530, 12 O.O.2d 21. Criminal Law ⚷ 273.4(1); Sentencing And Punishment ⚷ 1379(4)

Plea of guilty entered by counsel for defendant has same force and effect as a plea personally entered by defendant if latter was present in court and circumstances are such as to show clearly that he understood what was being done and acquiesced therein. Petition of Morelli (Franklin 1956) 148 N.E.2d 96, 76 Ohio Law Abs. 501. Criminal Law ⚷ 273(5)

A defendant who orally pleads guilty before one judge may subsequently be sentenced by another judge. State ex rel. Dake v. Alvis (Franklin 1957) 103 Ohio App. 38, 144 N.E.2d 223, 3 O.O.2d 124.

Breach of a plea agreement by a federal judge may be remedied by specific performance of the agreement or allowing withdrawal of the plea. U.S. v. Mandell (C.A.6 (Ohio) 1990) 905 F.2d 970. Criminal Law ⚷ 273.1(2); Criminal Law ⚷ 274(3.1)

4. Withdrawal of guilty plea—In general

Inmate's mandamus petition seeking to compel judges to rule on his motion to withdraw guilty plea was moot, where motion to withdraw plea was denied. State ex rel. McGee v. Mahon (Ohio App. 8 Dist., Cuyahoga, 12-05-2002) No. 81753, 2002-Ohio-6647, 2002 WL 31723180, Unreported. Mandamus ⚷ 16(1)

Defendant's pro se motion to withdraw his guilty plea was untimely, where factual issue relating to voluntariness of defendant's guilty plea to aggravated vehicular homicide had been previously decided by a trial judge more than two years prior to filing appeal of denial of identical motion; in both motions, defendant claimed he suffered from some medication-induced incoherence preventing him from being able to provide the judge with a knowing, voluntary and intelligent guilty plea, and that, had he known of the police reports, insurance adjuster reports or inmate's prospective testimony, he would not have pleaded guilty. State v. Sneed

(Ohio App. 8 Dist., Cuyahoga, 11-27-2002) No. 80902, 2002-Ohio-6502, 2002 WL 31667630, Unreported, appeal not allowed 99 Ohio St.3d 1409, 788 N.E.2d 646, 2003-Ohio-2454. Criminal Law ⚷ 274(9)

Defendant was not entitled to withdraw guilty plea to possession of heroin before sentencing, where defendant produced no evidence of a reasonable and legitimate basis for the withdrawal of the plea; trial judge's statement that interests of justice, in a broad sense, would not be served by granting defendant's motion to withdraw plea because defendant provided absolutely no reason why he wanted to withdraw his guilty plea was not consistent with defendant's claim that the judge wrongfully imposed upon him the burden of showing how the withdrawal of the plea would serve the ends of justice and not inconvenience the court. State v. Salti (Ohio App. 8 Dist., Cuyahoga, 11-27-2002) No. 80707, 2002-Ohio-6492, 2002 WL 31667612, Unreported. Criminal Law ⚷ 274(3.1)

Trial court did not abuse its discretion in denying defendant's presentence motion to withdraw guilty plea to aggravated robbery that was part of plea bargain; defendant's motion to withdraw his guilty plea merely stated that he was innocent but did not offer any evidentiary material to support such assertion, and prior to signing plea agreement, defendant had filed a notice of alibi, indicating that he was at his sister's home or in the surrounding neighborhood on the date and time that the aggravated robbery occurred, but, at the hearing on the motion to withdraw the guilty plea, defendant did not indicate that he had any possible defense to aggravated robbery charge. State v. McNeil (Ohio App. 1 Dist., 09-14-2001) 146 Ohio App.3d 173, 765 N.E.2d 884, motion for delayed appeal denied 102 Ohio St.3d 1457, 809 N.E.2d 31, 2004-Ohio-2569, appeal not allowed 104 Ohio St.3d 1408, 818 N.E.2d 710, 2004-Ohio-6364. Criminal Law ⚷ 274(8)

Prosecutor had no authority to fulfill plea agreement promise to allow defendant to withdraw his previously entered pleas of guilty, as decision to deny or grant a motion to withdraw a guilty plea was within sole discretion of the trial court. State v. Aponte (Ohio App. 10 Dist., 08-30-2001) 145 Ohio App.3d 607, 763 N.E.2d 1205, appeal not allowed 94 Ohio St.3d 1411, 759 N.E.2d 787. Criminal Law ⚷ 273.1(2); Criminal Law ⚷ 274(2)

Where an accused is allowed to withdraw a plea of guilty and enter a plea of not guilty prior to trial, it is error for the court to allow the written and signed original plea to be placed in evidence against the defendant and to permit it to be retained by the jury during its deliberations. State v. Gray (Hamilton 1979) 60 Ohio App.2d 418, 399 N.E.2d 131, 14 O.O.3d 432. Criminal Law ⚷ 858(3)

The reference by a trial judge outside of open court to the stenographic record of the testimony of witnesses before the grand jury either to constitute a foundation upon which the court might examine the defendant on the hearing of the motion to change his plea or as a means of convincing the court of the guilt of the defendant, constitutes an abuse of discretion and error prejudicial to the defendant for which the order overruling the motion to change the plea and the judgment and sentence entered on the unchanged plea will be reversed and vacated. State v. Amison (Lucas 1965) 2 Ohio App.2d 390, 208 N.E.2d 769, 31 O.O.2d 594.

The meaning of the term, "abuse of discretion," in relation to passing on a motion made under RC 2943.03 to allow a defendant in a criminal action to change his plea from guilty to not guilty connotes more than an error of law or of judgment; it implies an unreasonable, arbitrary or unconscionable attitude on the part of the court. State v. Amison (Lucas 1965) 2 Ohio App.2d 390, 208 N.E.2d 769, 31 O.O.2d 594. Criminal Law ⚷ 268

Trial court, by refusing to allow petitioner to withdraw guilty pleas, did not so deprive him of his rights as to give him a right to release by habeas corpus. Crider v. Maxwell (Ohio 1963) 174 Ohio St. 190, 187 N.E.2d 875, 22 O.O.2d 143, certiorari denied 83 S.Ct. 1919, 374 U.S. 852, 10 L.Ed.2d 1073.

5. —— After sentence, withdrawal of guilty plea

Motion to withdraw guilty plea, in which defendant claimed that his trial counsel was ineffective in wrongly informing him that he would receive one year prison sentence, was not ripe, where there was no information that defendant would not be released within one year of time he was sentenced. State v. McKinney (Ohio App. 9 Dist., Summit, 01-29-2003) No. 21123, 2003-Ohio-362, 2003 WL 187586, Unreported, appeal not allowed 99 Ohio St.3d 1413, 788 N.E.2d 648, 2003-Ohio-2454. Criminal Law ⚷ 274(9)

Claims that trial court failed to state plea agreement on the record and that negotiated plea agreement contained additional charges by prosecution did not entitle defendant to withdraw guilty plea, where state recited terms of plea agreement on record, and defendant answered affirmatively when asked by court if state's representations were accurate. State v. McKinney (Ohio App. 9 Dist., Summit, 01-29-2003) No. 21123, 2003-Ohio-362, 2003 WL 187586, Unreported, appeal not allowed 99 Ohio St.3d 1413, 788 N.E.2d 648, 2003-Ohio-2454. Criminal Law ⚷ 274(3.1)

Trial court's failure to specify at sentencing amount of restitution to be paid by defendant did not entitle defendant to withdraw his guilty plea based on claim that he did not know consequences of his plea, where, because court failed to specify amount, there was no valid order requiring defendant to pay restitution. State v. McKinney (Ohio App. 9 Dist., Summit, 01-29-2003) No. 21123, 2003-Ohio-362, 2003 WL 187586, Unreported, appeal not allowed 99 Ohio St.3d 1413, 788 N.E.2d 648, 2003-Ohio-2454. Criminal Law ⚷ 274(3.1)

Trial court's inquiry of defendant at plea colloquy was adequate to determine whether defendant sufficiently understood the proceedings and, thus, accept his plea of guilty to murder charge; in view of defendant's lack of education, trial court asked if anyone asked him to read anything or sign anything since time of his arrest, and whether he understood everything "we're doing here today," and also specifically inquired about whether defendant's medication interfered with his understanding. State v. Lawston (Ohio App. 8 Dist., Cuyahoga, 11-27-2002) No. 80828, 2002-Ohio-6498, 2002 WL 31667620, Unreported, appeal not allowed 98 Ohio St.3d 1514, 786 N.E.2d 63, 2003-Ohio-1572. Criminal Law ⚷ 273.1(4)

Defendant's affidavit was insufficient to require trial court to withdraw defendant's guilty plea to murder, though affidavit stated that victim had threatened defendant when victim asked for money and reached towards his back pocket just before defendant fired shotgun, and that defendant's lawyer would not defend him on the murder charge, given contradiction in defendant's oral statement to police that the victim was neither armed nor attempting to attack him, and absence of any statements during the plea proceeding or before sentencing about either victim's or lawyer's conduct. State v. Lawston (Ohio App. 8 Dist., Cuyahoga, 11-27-2002) No. 80828, 2002-Ohio-6498, 2002 WL 31667620, Unreported, appeal not allowed 98 Ohio St.3d 1514, 786 N.E.2d 63, 2003-Ohio-1572. Criminal Law ⚷ 274(3.1)

Prosecution's unfulfillable promise to allow defendant to withdraw his guilty plea upon compliance with certain conditions was likely to inculcate belief and reliance on part of defendant in assenting to the plea agreement, thus rendering defendant's plea involuntary in prosecution for felonious assault, having a weapon while under disability, and vandalism. State v. Aponte (Ohio App. 10 Dist., 08-30-2001) 145 Ohio App.3d 607, 763 N.E.2d 1205, appeal not allowed 94 Ohio St.3d 1411, 759 N.E.2d 787. Criminal Law ⚷ 273.1(2)

The administration of justice does not countenance the right of a person who formally declares his guilt to gamble with fate by pleading guilty in the expectation of receiving a suspended or a light sentence and then demanding as his right a withdrawal of his guilty plea when the sentence is greater than he expected. State v. Martin (Cuyahoga 1959) 158 N.E.2d 414, 81 Ohio Law Abs. 106. Criminal Law ⚷ 274(5)

A party will not be permitted to withdraw a plea of guilty after sentence is imposed unless he was falsely induced to enter such plea. Petition of Spensky (Franklin 1955) 133 N.E.2d 195, 71 Ohio Law Abs. 551.

6. Insanity

Defendant failed to demonstrate good cause to change plea to include not guilty by reason of insanity in prosecution for sexual battery; defendant knew at time of offense that having sex with his daughter was wrong. State v. Freeman (Ohio App. 7 Dist., 12-12-2003) 155 Ohio App.3d 492, 801 N.E.2d 906, 2003-Ohio-6730. Criminal Law ⚷ 286.5(1)

Defense counsel was not ineffective in failing to request psychiatric evaluation of defendant; record revealed that defendant's testimony was very clear with respect to dates, times, and events, there was no indication that defendant was unable to assist in his defense or that he was unable to understand nature of proceedings against him, and trial court conducted competency hearing in response to defendant's motion to discharge counsel. State v. Smith (Ohio App. 3 Dist., 11-20-1996) 115 Ohio App.3d 419, 685 N.E.2d 595.

Prosecutor was not entitled to argue that murder defendant would "walk out that door" if jury found him not guilty by reason of insanity; statement was incorrect statement of law and plainly sought to inflame passions of jury. State v. Awkal (Ohio, 08-14-1996) 76 Ohio St.3d 324, 667 N.E.2d 960, 1996-Ohio-395, certiorari denied 117 S.Ct. 776, 519 U.S. 1095, 136 L.Ed.2d 720, dismissal of post-conviction relief affirmed 1998 WL 827585, dismissed, appeal not allowed 85 Ohio St.3d 1442, 708 N.E.2d 209. Criminal Law ⚷ 717; Criminal Law ⚷ 723(1)

The legal presumption that a criminal is sane until the contrary is established by a preponderance of the evidence is not in conflict with RC 2945.04. State v. Johnson (Ohio 1972) 31 Ohio St.2d 106, 285 N.E.2d 751, 60 O.O.2d 85. Criminal Law ⚷ 311

Where, in a criminal prosecution, a defendant is charged with murder in the first degree, to which charge he enters a plea of not guilty and also an oral plea of not guilty by reason of insanity and he later enters a plea of guilty of murder in the second degree without first withdrawing his oral plea of not guilty by reason of insanity, such defendant thereby waives his oral plea of not guilty by reason of insanity. State v. Fore (Athens 1969) 18 Ohio App.2d 264, 248 N.E.2d 633, 47 O.O.2d 404. Criminal Law ⚷ 273.2(1)

In order to establish the defense of insanity where raised by plea in a criminal proceeding, the accused must establish by a preponderance of the evidence that disease or other defect of his mind had so impaired his reason that, at the time of the criminal act with which he is charged, either he did not know that such act was wrong or he did not have the ability to refrain from doing that act. (Superseded by statute as stated in State v Humphries, 51 OS(2d) 95, 364 NE(2d) 1354 (1977). (See also State v Staten, 25 OS(2d) 107, 267 NE(2d) 122 (1971); vacated by 408 US 938, 92 SCt 2869, 33 LEd(2d) 759 (1972).) State v. Staten (Ohio 1969) 18 Ohio St.2d 13, 247 N.E.2d 293, 47 O.O.2d 82. Criminal Law ⚷ 570(2)

A conviction upon a plea of guilty of violation of RC 2905.01 is not rendered invalid and subject to collateral attack by habeas corpus merely by reason of the fact that the subsequent examination required by RC 2947.25 resulted in a finding that the defendant was at that time, and for sometime prior thereto, mentally ill as defined by RC 5123.01. Krauter v. Maxwell (Ohio 1965) 3 Ohio St.2d 142, 209 N.E.2d 571, 32 O.O.2d 141.

A defendant who has pleaded not guilty may not after conviction and sentence attempt to raise a question of his sanity in a habeas corpus proceeding. Buck v. Maxwell (Ohio 1962) 173 Ohio St. 394, 182 N.E.2d 622, 19 O.O.2d 388.

Plea of not guilty by reason of insanity means not guilty by reason of insanity at time of crime's commission, if the only issue to be heard is the insanity at the time of trial, or if before or after trial it be suggested by accused's counsel, or if it otherwise comes to court's notice that the accused is not then sane, the court or jury must first determine that issue, and it must be tried before the accused is tried for the offense charged. State v. Smith (Ohio 1931) 123 Ohio St. 237, 174 N.E. 768, 9 Ohio Law Abs. 286, 34 Ohio Law Rep. 71.

By dictum Judge Allen expresses "grave doubt as to the constitutionality" of that part of former GC 13440–2 (RC 2943.03), which establishes a conclusive presumption of sanity from the failure of the attorney to file a written plea of not guilty by reason of insanity. Evans v. State (Ohio 1930) 123 Ohio St. 132, 174 N.E. 348, 9 Ohio Law Abs. 61, 33 Ohio Law Rep. 485.

A trial judge having recent psychological reports that a defendant is competent to stand trial has no duty to impose a defense of "not guilty by reason of insanity" on the defendant, particularly where the defendant rejected the advice of three attorneys to offer the defense, said he was able to counsel with his attorney, and understood both the charges and the possible penalties confronting him. Foster v. Marshall (S.D.Ohio 1987) 687 F.Supp. 1174.

2943.031 Court advising defendants on possibility of deportation, exclusion, or denial of naturalization prior to accepting pleas

(A) Except as provided in division (B) of this section, prior to accepting a plea of guilty or a plea of no contest to an indictment, information, or complaint charging a felony or a misdemeanor other than a minor misdemeanor if the defendant previously has not been convicted of or pleaded guilty to a minor misdemeanor, the court shall address the defendant personally, provide the following advisement to the defendant that shall be entered in the record of the court, and determine that the defendant understands the advisement:

"If you are not a citizen of the United States, you are hereby advised that conviction of the offense to which you are pleading guilty (or no contest, when applicable) may have the consequences of deportation, exclusion from admission to the United States, or denial of naturalization pursuant to the laws of the United States."

Upon request of the defendant, the court shall allow him additional time to consider the appropriateness of the plea in light of the advisement described in this division.

(B) The court is not required to give the advisement described in division (A) of this section if either of the following applies:

(1) The defendant enters a plea of guilty on a written form, the form includes a question asking whether the defendant is a citizen of the United States, and the defendant answers that question in the affirmative;

(2) The defendant states orally on the record that he is a citizen of the United States.

(C) Except as provided in division (B) of this section, the defendant shall not be required at the time of entering a plea to disclose to the court his legal status in the United States.

(D) Upon motion of the defendant, the court shall set aside the judgment and permit the defendant to withdraw a plea of guilty or no contest and enter a plea of not guilty or not guilty by reason of insanity, if, after the effective date of this section, the court fails to provide the defendant the advisement described in division (A) of this section, the advisement is required by that division, and the defendant shows that he is not a citizen of the United States and that the conviction of the offense to which he pleaded guilty or no contest may result in his being subject to deportation, exclusion from admission to the United States, or denial of naturalization pursuant to the laws of the United States.

(E) In the absence of a record that the court provided the advisement described in division (A) of this section and if the advisement is required by that division, the defendant shall be presumed not to have received the advisement.

(F) Nothing in this section shall be construed as preventing a court, in the sound exercise of its discretion pursuant to Criminal Rule 32.1, from setting aside the judgment of conviction and permitting a defendant to withdraw his plea.

(1989 S 95, eff. 10–2–89)

Uncodified Law

1989 S 95, § 3, eff. 10–2–89, reads: Section 2937.06 of the Revised Code as amended by this act and section 2943.031 of the Revised Code as enacted by this act shall apply to all felony and misdemeanor cases pending on the effective date of this act in which the court has not accepted a plea to the indictment, information, or complaint.

Cross References

Compliance prior to acceptance of plea, 2937.06

Library References

Criminal Law ⚷273(4.1), 273.1(4), 275.3.

Westlaw Topic No. 110.

C.J.S. Criminal Law §§ 384, 389, 398 to 407, 417.

Research References

Encyclopedias

OH Jur. 3d Criminal Law § 83, Other Actions or Omissions.

OH Jur. 3d Criminal Law § 2430, Due Process Requirements.

OH Jur. 3d Criminal Law § 2448, Degree of Compliance Required, Generally.

OH Jur. 3d Criminal Law § 2449, Use of a Signed Writing.

OH Jur. 3d Criminal Law § 2451, Requirement of Translation.

OH Jur. 3d Criminal Law § 2482, Hearing on a Post-Sentence Motion to Withdraw.

OH Jur. 3d Criminal Law § 2487, Plea by Noncitizen.

OH Jur. 3d Criminal Law § 3686, Pleas.

OH Jur. 3d False Imprisonment & Malic. Prosecution § 38, Res Judicata or Collateral Estoppel.

Treatises and Practice Aids

Markus, Trial Handbook for Ohio Lawyers, § 4:24, Plea of Guilty or No Contest—Requirements for Valid Plea.

Katz, Giannelli, Blair and Lipton, Baldwin's Ohio Practice, Criminal Law, § 46:2, Criminal Rule 32.1.

Katz, Giannelli, Blair and Lipton, Baldwin's Ohio Practice, Criminal Law, § 46:4, Postsentence Withdrawal.

Katz, Giannelli, Blair and Lipton, Baldwin's Ohio Practice, Criminal Law, § 144:1, Plea of Guilty.

Katz, Giannelli, Blair and Lipton, Baldwin's Ohio Practice, Criminal Law, § 144:2, No Contest Plea.

Katz, Giannelli, Blair and Lipton, Baldwin's Ohio Practice, Criminal Law, § 43:11, Understanding the Penalty.

Katz, Giannelli, Blair and Lipton, Baldwin's Ohio Practice, Criminal Law, § 43:12, Understanding Effect of Plea.

Hennenberg & Reinhart, Ohio Criminal Defense Motions F 10.06, Motion to Withdraw Guilty Plea-Post-Trial Motions-Alternative Petition for Post-Conviction Relief-Failure to Advise Noncitizen of Deportation.

Hennenberg & Reinhart, Ohio Criminal Defense Motions F 10.07, Motion to Withdraw Plea/Post-Conviction Petition-No Deportation Advice.

Adrine & Ruden, Ohio Domestic Violence Law § 7:11, Collateral Effects of a Guilty Plea or of Being Found Guilty—Immigration.

Notes of Decisions

1. Constitutional issues—In general

Defendant's plea of guilty to three counts of trafficking in drugs was not entered into knowingly, intelligently, and voluntarily, where defendant was noncitizen and plea court's advisement of immigration consequences did not satisfy statutory requirements. State v. Lucente (Ohio App. 7 Dist., Mahoning, 03-29-2005) No. 03 MA 216, 2005-Ohio-1657, 2005 WL 775886, Unreported. Criminal Law ⚷ 273.1(4)

Petitioner was entitled to evidentiary hearing on petition to withdraw guilty plea to robbery on basis that he pleaded guilty because his lawyer told him conviction after trial would lead to deportation, suggesting that guilty plea would ameliorate possibility of deportation, which was not true; petitioner alleged facts showing that his counsel was fully aware of petitioner's interest in deportation consequences, even after trial court informed him that deportation remained a possibility, petitioner could have relied on counsel's advice, and petitioner claimed that counsel effectively misinformed him regarding possible consequences, not that counsel merely misadvised him. State v. Creary (Ohio App. 8 Dist., Cuyahoga, 02-26-2004) No. 82767, 2004-Ohio-858, 2004 WL 351878, Unreported, stay granted 102 Ohio St.3d 1457, 809 N.E.2d 31, 2004-Ohio-2569, appeal not allowed 103 Ohio St.3d 1404, 812 N.E.2d 1287, 2004-Ohio-3980. Criminal Law ⚷ 274(1)

Statute requiring court to advise non-citizen defendant of deportation consequences of guilty plea, and providing right to withdraw plea if court failed to make the advisement and other statutory requirements were met, conferred substantive rights and, thus, was not superseded by conflicting provisions of rule of criminal procedure requiring showing of manifest injustice to withdraw guilty plea after sentencing. State v. Weber (Ohio App. 10 Dist., 12-31-1997) 125 Ohio App.3d 120, 707 N.E.2d 1178, dismissed, appeal not allowed 81 Ohio St.3d 1521, 692 N.E.2d 1023. Criminal Law ⚷ 273.1(4); Criminal Law ⚷ 274(3.1)

Although criminal aliens may be incarcerated pending removal, the time of incarceration is limited by constitutional considerations, and must bear a reasonable relation to removal. Ly v. Hansen (C.A.6 (Ohio), 11-26-2003) 351 F.3d 263, rehearing denied. Aliens ⚷ 53.9

Court of Appeals would treat postconviction relief movant's filing, styled as a "motion to vacate conviction," as a motion to withdraw his guilty plea to aggravated robbery and other offenses; while motion was not filed pursuant to a specific rule of criminal procedure, it was based on statute governing advisement of deportation consequences at guilty plea colloquy, it raised a constitutional issue, and movant substantively was seeking to withdraw his guilty plea. State v. Gomez (Ohio App. 9 Dist., Lorain, 10-02-2002) No. 02CA008036, 2002-Ohio-5255, 2002 WL 31175227, Unreported, appeal not allowed 98 Ohio St.3d 1565, 787 N.E.2d 1230, 2003-Ohio-2242. Criminal Law ⚷ 274(1); Criminal Law ⚷ 1576

2. —— Due process, constitutional issues

Incarceration of criminal alien for one and one-half years as part of a civil, nonpunitive removal proceeding when there was no chance of actual, final removal, was unreasonable, and therefore violated alien's substantive due process rights. Ly v. Hansen (C.A.6 (Ohio), 11-26-2003) 351 F.3d 263, rehearing denied. Aliens ⚷ 466; Constitutional Law ⚷ 274.3

Deportable aliens, even those who had already been ordered removed, possess a substantive Fifth Amendment liberty interest, and that interest is violated by indefinite detention. Ly v. Hansen (C.A.6 (Ohio), 11-26-2003) 351 F.3d 263, rehearing denied. Constitutional Law ⚷ 274.3

3. Effective date

Where defendant alien (1) was arrested and indicted on various counts for drug offenses, offenses of violence and related crimes, (2) was represented by competent counsel, and (3) entered guilty pleas to some of the drug counts after discussing the extensive aspects of a plea bargain with his counsel and the prosecutor and after a thorough explanation of his rights and consequences of his plea by the court pursuant to Crim R 11, his plea was voluntarily and intelligently made despite the fact that he was not advised that he would be subject to deportation, inasmuch as RC 2943.031, requiring that alien defendants be advised of the possibility of deportation, did not become effective until after defendant was indicted. State v. Odubanjo (Cuyahoga 1992) 80 Ohio App.3d 329, 609 N.E.2d 207, dismissed, jurisdictional motion overruled 65 Ohio St.3d 1430, 600 N.E.2d 675.

4. Withdrawal of plea—In general

Inmate could remedy trial court's failure to advise him on consequences of conviction for noncitizens, as required by statute, by filing a motion to withdraw his guilty plea, and thus existence of adequate remedy at law precluded mandamus relief. S/O ex rel. White v. Suster (Ohio App. 8 Dist., Cuyahoga, 09-12-2003) No. 83277, 2003-Ohio-4956, 2003 WL 22146532, Unreported, affirmed 101 Ohio St.3d 212, 803 N.E.2d 813, 2004-Ohio-719. Mandamus ⚷ 61

The trial court's decision on a noncitizen's motion to withdraw guilty or no-contest plea, based on allegedly inadequate advisement of immigration-related consequences of plea, is reviewed for abuse of discretion. (Per Alice Robie Resnick, J., with two Justices concurring, two Justices concurring in judgment only, and two Justices concurring in part and dissenting in part.) State v. Francis (Ohio, 12-22-2004) 104 Ohio St.3d 490, 820 N.E.2d 355, 2004-Ohio-6894. Criminal Law ⚷ 1149

Trial court's failure to advise defendant of possible consequences of pleading guilty, including exclusion from the United States and denial of naturalization under United States law, did not entitle defendant to withdraw his plea to trafficking in food stamps, where defendant did not provide court with any passport, affidavit, or other documentation on the record that he was not a United States citizen. State v. Almingdad (Ohio App. 8 Dist., 01-23-2003) 151 Ohio App.3d 453, 784 N.E.2d 718, 2003-Ohio-295. Criminal Law ⚷ 274(3.1)

Trial court's denial of non-citizen's motion to withdraw guilty plea was not abuse of discretion, even though criminal procedure rule governing withdrawal of pleas provided that statute was to be strictly construed against state and liberally construed in favor of the defendant, and, prior to accepting guilty plea, trial court failed to advise defendant regarding immigration and nationality consequences of his plea as required by immigration statute which allowed for withdrawal of pleas for such failures, and which lacked an explicit time limitation for such actions, where, without explanation for delay, defendant waited eleven and one-half years to move to withdraw his plea. State v. Tabbaa (Ohio App. 8 Dist., 01-21-2003) 151 Ohio App.3d 353, 784 N.E.2d 143, 2003-Ohio-299, motion to certify allowed 98 Ohio St.3d 1561, 787 N.E.2d 1227, 2003-Ohio-2242, appeal not allowed 98 Ohio St.3d 1567, 787 N.E.2d 1231, 2003-Ohio-2242, cause dismissed 100 Ohio St.3d 1417, 796 N.E.2d 939, 2003-Ohio-5098. Criminal Law ⚷ 274(9)

Trial court would be required to grant motion to withdraw no contest plea to domestic violence charge if following statutory requirements were met: (1) advisement that conviction could result in deportation was not given, (2) advisement was required to be given, (3) defendant was not a citizen of the United States, and (4) defendant could be deported, excluded, or denied naturalization as a result of his conviction. State v. Traish (Ohio App. 7 Dist., 03-29-1999) 133 Ohio App.3d 648, 729 N.E.2d 766. Criminal Law ⚷ 275.5(2)

Trial court had jurisdiction over, and was obligated to address, defendant's motion to withdraw no contest plea based on alleged lack of advisement about possible deportation consequences, even though appeal from conviction was pending when motion was brought. State v. Traish (Ohio App. 7 Dist., 03-29-1999) 133 Ohio App.3d 648, 729 N.E.2d 766. Criminal Law ⚷ 1083

Under statute requiring court to advise noncitizen defendant of deportation consequences of guilty plea, trial court was required to allow defendant to withdraw her guilty plea if she established that statutory advisement was required to be given, that court failed to give the advisement, that she was not citizen of United States and that plea resulted in adverse immigration consequence; defendant did not need to show that she would have not pled guilty if advisement had been given or that withdrawal of plea was necessary to correct manifest injustice. State v. Weber (Ohio App. 10 Dist., 12-31-1997) 125 Ohio App.3d 120, 707 N.E.2d 1178, dismissed, appeal not allowed 81 Ohio St.3d 1521, 692 N.E.2d 1023. Criminal Law ⚷ 274(3.1)

5. —— Actual prejudice, withdrawal of plea

Defendant, who filed postsentence motion to withdraw his guilty plea arguing that the trial court failed to advise him of the possibility of deportation, was required to make some showing of prejudicial effect caused by the trial court's failure to give the advisement before his motion would be granted. (Per Blackmon, P.J., with two judges concurring in judgment only). State v. Wahba (Ohio App. 8 Dist., Cuyahoga, 11-10-2004) No. 84012, 2004-Ohio-5978, 2004 WL 2538833, Unreported. Criminal Law ⚷ 274(3.1)

Failure to follow the explicit mandate of RC 2943.031(D) and permit the defendant to withdraw his plea is error where (1) the defendant is not a citizen of the United States, (2) the court fails to advise defendant of the possibility of deportation, and (3) the defendant demonstrates actual prejudice by his deportation order. State v. Felix (Ohio App. 8 Dist., Cuyahoga, 04-17-1997) No. 70898, 1997 WL 186838, Unreported.

A defendant who is not a citizen of the United States, and who did not receive the statutory warning from the trial court, before acceptance of guilty or no-contest plea, of possible immigration-related consequences of the plea is not required to demonstrate manifest injustice, to be entitled to withdraw the plea. (Per Alice Robie Resnick, J., with two Justices concurring, two Justices concurring in judgment only, and two Justices concurring in part and dissenting in part.) State v. Francis (Ohio, 12-22-2004) 104 Ohio St.3d 490, 820 N.E.2d 355, 2004-Ohio-6894. Criminal Law ⚷ 274(3.1); Criminal Law ⚷ 275.5(2)

Defense counsel's failure to file a motion to withdraw defendant's guilty plea prior to the trial court's imposition of sentence, after it became apparent that defendant would be deported as a result of his guilty plea, did not prejudice defendant, and thus could not amount to ineffective assistance; defendant failed to file a motion for post-conviction relief which sought the withdrawal of his guilty plea. State v. Abi-Aazar (Ohio App. 9 Dist., 09-25-2002) 149 Ohio App.3d 359, 777 N.E.2d 327, 2002-Ohio-5026. Criminal Law ⚷ 641.13(7)

6. —— Res judicata, withdrawal of plea

Post-sentencing motion to withdraw guilty plea based upon sentencing court's failure to comply with statute governing advisements to noncitizens of immigration consequences of guilty pleas was not barred on grounds of res judicata by movant's failure directly to appeal such defect in plea process. State v. Lucente (Ohio App. 7 Dist., Mahoning, 03-29-2005) No. 03 MA 216, 2005-Ohio-1657, 2005 WL 775886, Unreported. Criminal Law ⚷ 274(9)

Post-conviction movant's claim that motion court improperly denied his motion to withdraw guilty plea pursuant to statute was barred by res judicata, where movant failed to perfect appeal from his conviction and failed to appeal from denial of his first motion to withdraw guilty plea pursuant to rules of criminal procedure, and where issues raised in statutory motion to withdraw plea could have been fully litigated on direct appeal or raised in initial motion to withdraw plea. State v. Zhao (Ohio App. 9 Dist., Lorain, 06-23-2004) No. 03CA008386, 2004-Ohio-3245, 2004 WL 1397581, Unreported, appeal not allowed 103 Ohio St.3d 1495, 816 N.E.2d 1081, 2004-Ohio-5605. Criminal Law ⚷ 1433(2)

Doctrine of res judicata did not bar defendant on appeal from denial of his motion to withdraw plea from raising claim that trial court did not advise him of deportation consequences of his plea prior to accepting plea, as required by statute for noncitizens, where nothing in record at time of defendant's previous direct appeal evinced his non-citizen status. State v. Gegia (Ohio App. 11 Dist., Portage, 03-19-2004) No. 2003-P-0026, 2004-Ohio-1441, 2004 WL 574623, Unreported, appeal not allowed 103 Ohio St.3d 1525, 817 N.E.2d 408, 2004-Ohio-5852. Criminal Law ⚷ 1433(2)

Doctrines of law of the case and res judicata precluded review of post-conviction relief petitioner's motion to withdraw his guilty plea, where petitioner had raised issue of plea and sentence as being in violation of immigration advisement statute in several petitions for post-conviction relief, all of which had been denied. State v. White (Ohio App. 8 Dist., Cuyahoga, 03-11-2004) No. 83235, 2004-Ohio-1113, 2004 WL 440439, Unreported. Criminal Law ⚷ 1668(3)

Res judicata barred inmate from repeated attempts to raise his claim to withdraw guilty plea that trial court accepted without advising inmate of possible deportation. State ex rel. White v. Suster (Ohio, 03-03-2004) 101 Ohio St.3d 212, 803 N.E.2d 813, 2004-Ohio-719. Judgment ⚷ 751

Court of Appeals' decisions affirming denial of inmate's motions to withdraw guilty plea that trial accepted without advising inmate of possible deportation were res judicata barring inmate from resorting to mandamus. State ex rel. White v. Suster (Ohio, 03-03-2004) 101 Ohio St.3d 212, 803 N.E.2d 813, 2004-Ohio-719. Judgment ⚷ 559

7. —— Timeliness, withdrawal of plea

That nine years had elapsed since defendant's entry of guilty plea to trafficking in food stamps and possession of criminal tools did not render his motion to withdraw plea untimely, where defendant was not notified that he was to be deported until approximately 12 to 18 months prior to filing his motion to withdraw plea, defendant was not prejudiced by trial court's failure to properly advise him of deportation consequences until he received his deportation order, and defendant did not realize his waiver of his felony would not be granted until he appeared for his deportation hearing, before which time there was no reason for defendant to seek to withdraw his plea, as his work permit was being renewed annually, and the waiver of his felony was pending with the Immigration Department. State v. Sibai (Ohio App. 8 Dist., Cuyahoga, 06-02-2005) No. 84407, 2005-Ohio-2730, 2005 WL 1303215, Unreported. Criminal Law ⚷ 274(9)

Non-citizen defendant's motion to withdraw guilty plea based on trial court's failure to properly admonish him regarding the immigration consequences of such a plea was timely made, even though it occurred one year and eight months after the court accepted the plea, where at least one witness was still available to testify to the factual circumstances that resulted in defendant's indictment, and defendant filed his motion to withdraw two months after he received notice of hearing in removal proceedings. State v. Zuniga (Ohio App. 11 Dist., Lake, 04-29-2005) No. 2003-P-0082, No. 2004-P-0002, 2005-Ohio-2078, 2005 WL 1007173, Unreported, appeal not allowed 106 Ohio St.3d 1488, 832 N.E.2d 739, 2005-Ohio-3978. Criminal Law ⚷ 274(9)

Defendant's motion to withdraw guilty plea, based upon plea court's failure to comply with statutory requirements in advising him of potential immigration consequences of his plea, filed five months after imposition of sentence and four months after initiation of deportation proceedings, was not so untimely as to warrant denial of motion. State v. Lucente (Ohio App. 7 Dist., Mahoning, 03-29-2005) No. 03 MA 216, 2005-Ohio-1657, 2005 WL 775886, Unreported. Criminal Law ⚷ 274(9)

Drug defendant's motion to withdraw guilty plea was properly denied, even though trial court failed to inform defendant, a non-citizen, of the adverse effects that a conviction could have on his citizenship status; delay of seven and a half years between entry of plea and filing of motion to withdraw plea constituted an unreasonable delay, and defendant failed to present an order of deportation or any other indicia of actual prejudice. State v. Suleiman (Ohio App. 8 Dist., Cuyahoga, 08-26-2004) No. 83915, 2004-Ohio-4487, 2004 WL 1902526, Unreported, appeal not allowed 105 Ohio St.3d 1472, 824 N.E.2d 541, 2005-Ohio-1186. Criminal Law ⚷ 274(3.1); Criminal Law ⚷ 274(9)

Noncitizen defendant's motion to withdraw her guilty plea, alleging inadequate advisement regarding possible immigration-related consequences of the plea, was not untimely as a matter of law, where the motion was brought nine years after defendant had entered the plea. (Per Alice Robie Resnick, J., with two Justices concurring and two Justices concurring in judgment only.) State v. Francis (Ohio, 12-22-2004) 104 Ohio St.3d 490, 820 N.E.2d 355, 2004-Ohio-6894. Criminal Law ⚷ 274(9)

The timeliness of a motion to withdraw a guilty or no-contest plea because of allegedly inadequate advisement regarding possible immigration-related consequences of the plea is one of many factors the trial court should take into account when exercising its discretion in considering whether to grant the motion. (Per Alice Robie Resnick, J., with two Justices concurring and two Justices concurring in part and dissenting in part.) State v. Francis (Ohio, 12-22-2004) 104 Ohio St.3d 490, 820 N.E.2d 355, 2004-Ohio-6894. Criminal Law ⚷ 274(9)

8. —— Waiver, withdrawal of plea

Defendant waived claim that, prior to accepting plea to assault and conveying weapon into courthouse, trial court should have advised her of immigration and deportation consequences, where she failed to file motion to vacate plea at trial court level. State v. Akatova (Ohio App. 8 Dist., Cuyahoga, 01-23-2003) No. 80566, 2003-Ohio-279, 2003 WL 152931, Unreported. Criminal Law ⚷ 1044.1(2)

Defendant could not raise on appeal allegation that trial court failed to advise him of possible immigration consequences of guilty pleas, instead, defendant should have filed motion to withdraw guilty pleas and sought order setting aside pleas. State v. Rodriguez (Ohio App. 2 Dist., Clark, 09-11-2002) No. 01CA0062, 2002-Ohio-5489, 2002 WL 31266213, Unreported. Criminal Law ⚷ 274(3.1); Criminal Law ⚷ 1134(3)

Defendant waived his appellate argument that his guilty plea to possession of heroin and illegal use or possession of drug paraphernalia was unknowing and involuntary due to the trial court's erroneous advisement of the immigration consequences of his guilty plea, where defendant failed to file a motion to set aside the judgment and withdraw his guilty plea. State v. Abi-Aazar (Ohio App. 9 Dist., 09-25-2002) 149 Ohio App.3d 359, 777 N.E.2d 327, 2002-Ohio-5026. Criminal Law ⚷ 1044.1(2)

Defendant convicted on plea of guilty of aggravated vehicular assault and driving under the influence of alcohol waived appellate review of his contention that he never received statutorily required advisement with respect to deportation consequences of his conviction, where defendant failed to file motion with trial court to set aside judgment and withdraw his guilty plea. State v. Rodriguez (Ohio App. 12 Dist., Butler, 08-05-2002) No. CA2001-04-077, 2002-Ohio-3978, 2002 WL 1791115, Unreported. Criminal Law ⚷ 1044.1(1)

9. Court's duty to inform—In general

Alien defendant's guilty plea to gross sexual imposition was rendered unknowing, involuntary, and unintelligent when trial court ordered him to sign stipulation to permanent removal with Immigration and Naturalization Services, even though defendant agreed at plea hearing to condition of lifetime deportation, where, at time of plea, no mention was made of requirement that defendant sign stipulated removal. State v. Rattray (Ohio App. 8 Dist., Cuyahoga, 09-29-2005) No. 85708, 2005-Ohio-5152, 2005 WL 2388271, Unreported. Criminal Law ⚷ 273.1(4)

Claim of defendant, who was convicted pursuant to guilty plea of unlawful sexual contact, challenging trial court's alleged failure to advise him of possibility of deportation was not cognizable on direct appeal; exclusive remedy for alleged violation of statute governing deportation advisement was motion to withdraw plea, it was openly during sentencing discussed that defendant had Immigration Naturalization Service holder and that defendant would immediately be deported following any sentence court imposed, and defendant made no request before court to withdraw his guilty plea. State v. Bulgakov (Ohio App. 6 Dist., Wood, 04-08-2005) No. WD-03-096, 2005-Ohio-1675, 2005 WL 791403, Unreported. Criminal Law ⚷ 1012

Fact that state's plea agreement with noncitizen defendant was based in part upon dismissal of charges against defendant's brother did not negate responsibility of plea court to comply with statute governing advisements to noncitizens of immigration consequences of guilty pleas. State v. Lucente (Ohio App. 7 Dist., Mahoning, 03-29-2005) No. 03 MA 216, 2005-Ohio-1657, 2005 WL 775886, Unreported. Criminal Law ⚷ 273.1(4)

Plea court's statements to noncitizen defendant at sentencing, following defendant's plea of guilty to three counts of trafficking in drugs, were insufficient to constitute substantial compliance with statute governing advisements to noncitizens of immigration consequences of guilty pleas, where statute required that defendant be informed of immigration consequences prior to acceptance of his plea. State v. Lucente (Ohio App. 7 Dist., Mahoning, 03-29-2005) No. 03 MA 216, 2005-Ohio-1657, 2005 WL 775886, Unreported. Criminal Law ⚷ 273.1(4); Sentencing And Punishment ⚷ 422

Plea court was required to advise noncitizen defendant of immigration consequences of his guilty plea, where prior to accepting plea, court asked defendant if he was United States citizen and defendant responded that he was not, signed plea agreement filed with court indicated that defendant was not United States citizen, and guilty plea to crime with which defendant was charged, namely, trafficking in drugs, could result in defendant's deportation. State v. Lucente (Ohio App. 7 Dist., Mahoning, 03-29-2005) No. 03 MA 216, 2005-Ohio-1657, 2005 WL 775886, Unreported. Criminal Law ⚷ 273.1(4)

Only the court in whose jurisdiction petitioner is restrained has jurisdiction over petition for writ of habeas corpus. Waterhouse v. Warden of Belmont Correctional Inst. (Ohio App. 7 Dist., Belmont, 12-30-2004) No. 04 BE 44, 2004-Ohio-7207, 2004 WL 3090248, Unreported. Habeas Corpus ⚷ 632.1

Trial court's denial of defendant's first motion to withdraw his guilty plea, in which he alleged that trial court erred by failing to give him notice that his guilty plea could result in deportation, operated under res judicata to bar defendant's successive motion to vacate or set aside judgment and withdraw plea. State v. McDonald (Ohio App. 11 Dist., Lake, 11-26-2004) No. 2003-L-155, 2004-Ohio-6332, 2004 WL 2694945, Unreported, appeal not allowed 105 Ohio St.3d 1500, 825 N.E.2d 623, 2005-Ohio-1666. Criminal Law ⚷ 274(1)

Defendant's failure to raise claim that trial court erred by failing to give him notice that his guilty plea could result in deportation, on direct appeal, did not preclude him from raising claim in a motion to vacate or set aside judgment and withdraw plea. State v. McDonald (Ohio App. 11 Dist., Lake, 11-26-2004) No. 2003-L-155, 2004-Ohio-6332, 2004 WL 2694945, Unreported, appeal not allowed 105 Ohio St.3d 1500, 825 N.E.2d 623, 2005-Ohio-1666. Criminal Law ⚷ 274(3.1)

Defendant had no affirmative duty to inform trial court, at time of entry of guilty plea to forgery charges, that he was not a citizen of the United States, in order that he be given statutory advisement that conviction might lead to deportation or exclusion; duty was on the court to determine the defendant's citizenship status. State v. White (Ohio App. 11 Dist., 09-16-2005) 163 Ohio App.3d 377, 837 N.E.2d 1246, 2005-Ohio-4898. Criminal Law ⚷ 273.1(4)

Motion to set aside the judgment and withdraw guilty plea and appeal from denial of motion provide the exclusive remedies for an alleged violation of statutory requirement to advise alien of deportation consequence of guilty plea and conviction. State ex rel. White v. Suster (Ohio, 03-03-2004) 101 Ohio St.3d 212, 803 N.E.2d 813, 2004-Ohio-719. Criminal Law ⚷ 274(3.1)

Substantial compliance with the statutory requirement that the trial court personally advise a noncitizen defendant of immigration consequences of pleading guilty or no contest is the better rule to determine if the defendant knowingly entered his guilty plea, particularly in those cases where the defendant's claim comes after a lengthy lapse of time when witnesses or evidence are no longer available. State v. Yanez (Ohio App. 1 Dist., 12-20-2002) 150 Ohio App.3d 510, 782 N.E.2d 146, 2002-Ohio-7076. Criminal Law ⚷ 273.1(4)

That noncitizen defendant signed plea form, which recited statutory immigration consequences possible from guilty plea to aggravated vehicular assault, did not constitute substantial compliance with requirement that trial court personally advise defendant of immigration consequences prior to accepting plea; although defendant responded "yes" when asked if plea form had been read to him, there was no indication as to whether interpreter read warning in open court or if warning was read to him on same day he entered plea, and counsel remained silent during entire time. State v. Yanez (Ohio App. 1 Dist., 12-20-2002) 150 Ohio App.3d 510, 782 N.E.2d 146, 2002-Ohio-7076. Criminal Law ⚷ 273.1(4)

Since defendant failed to file a direct appeal of his conviction, the doctrine of res judicata barred his attempt to withdraw his guilty plea to correct manifest injustice, alleging that trial court erred when it denied his motion because he was not a United States citizen and the court did not advise him of the possibility of deportation when he pled guilty; those issues could have been fully litigated on direct appeal from that judgment. State v. White (Ohio App. 8 Dist., 04-02-2001) 142 Ohio App.3d 132, 754 N.E.2d 287, dismissed, appeal not allowed 92 Ohio St.3d 1443, 751 N.E.2d 482, motion to reopen denied 2001 WL 1249941, motion for delayed appeal denied 102 Ohio St.3d 1469, 809 N.E.2d 1157, 2004-Ohio-2830. Judgment ⚷ 751

Statutory provision requiring defendant to be advised of possible deportation consequences has no application when defendant pleads not guilty and is found guilty following jury trial. State v. Arnold (Ohio App. 2 Dist., Clark, 09-20-2002) No. 02CA0002, 2002-Ohio-4977, 2002 WL 31105404, Unreported. Criminal Law ⚷ 300

Defendant's motion to vacate his guilty plea was cognizable under statute requiring court to advise defendants on possibility of deportation, exclusion, or denial of naturalization prior to accepting pleas, where both parties argued case using elements of such statute. City of Lakewood v. Shurney (Ohio App. 8 Dist., Cuyahoga, 09-12-2002) No. 80885, 2002-Ohio-4789, 2002 WL 31031669, Unreported. Criminal Law ⚷ 274(1)

Under the doctrine of res judicata, the defendant's claim that his guilty plea was not knowing or voluntary, due to the trial court's alleged failure to inform the defendant that a plea would have deportation consequences, merged with the judgment of conviction, and the defendant's failure to directly appeal the judgment precluded his relitigation of the issue by way of a postconviction proceeding. State v. Idowu (Ohio App. 1 Dist., Hamilton, 06-28-2002) No. C-010646, 2002-Ohio-3302, 2002 WL 1393653, Unreported. Criminal Law ⚷ 1427; Judgment ⚷ 751

10. —— Deficient counsel, court's duty to inform

Counsel was not deficient, as element of ineffective assistance of counsel, in failing to address with defendant deportation consequences of conviction, in prosecution for unlawful sexual contact; duty to notify defendant regarding potential for deportation belonged to court, not counsel, and defendant knew that he was an illegal alien in country and, based on his own statements, acknowledged at arraignment that he was aware that he was facing potential deportation. State v. Bulgakov (Ohio App. 6 Dist., Wood, 04-08-2005) No. WD-03-096, 2005-Ohio-1675, 2005 WL 791403, Unreported. Criminal Law ⚷ 641.13(2.1)

11. —— Personally addressing defendant, court's duty to inform

Trial court, prior to accepting defendant's guilty plea to aggravated robbery and other offenses, advised defendant of deportation consequences of his plea; judge asked defendant if he was a United States citizen and defendant responded in the negative, and judge questioned if defendant understood that he could be deported and defendant answered in the affirmative, which established that defendant was aware of the fact that he could be deported at the time the plea hearing was conducted. State v. Gomez (Ohio App. 9 Dist., Lorain, 10-02-2002) No. 02CA008036, 2002-Ohio-5255, 2002 WL 31175227, Unreported, appeal not allowed 98 Ohio St.3d 1565, 787 N.E.2d 1230, 2003-Ohio-2242. Criminal Law ⚷ 273.1(4)

Trial judge, while addressing a group of people, "personally" advised defendant of possibility of deportation prior to entering his guilty plea, as required by statute, even though court did not advise defendant individually. City of Lakewood v. Shurney (Ohio App. 8 Dist., Cuyahoga, 09-12-2002) No. 80885, 2002-Ohio-4789, 2002 WL 31031669, Unreported. Criminal Law ⚷ 273.1(4)

Trial judge adequately determined that defendant understood its advisement of possibility of deportation prior to entering his guilty plea, even though defendant did not receive advisement individually, where judge engaged defendant in a colloquy that included an extensive discussion of the circumstances of the offense and showed defendant's understanding of the charge against him as well as his command of the English language. City of Lakewood v. Shurney (Ohio App. 8 Dist., Cuyahoga, 09-12-2002) No. 80885, 2002-Ohio-4789, 2002 WL 31031669, Unreported. Criminal Law ⚷ 273.1(4)

12. —— Review, court's duty to inform

Defendant waived all appellate review other than for plain error of his contention that trial court failed to advise him of immigration consequences of his guilty plea, by failing to raise such issue before trial court. State v. Encarnacion (Ohio App. 12 Dist., Butler, 12-27-2004) No. CA2003-09-225, 2004-Ohio-7043, 2004 WL 2980594, Unreported. Criminal Law ⚷ 1031(4)

Trial court's failure to substantially comply with provisions of immigration advisement statute, before accepting defendant's plea of guilty to gross sexual imposition, was harmless error in absence of showing of prejudice, even though defendant was not made aware that plea could result in him being denied reentry into United States, and he could be barred from becoming naturalized citizen; defendant did not assert that full advisement would have influenced his decision to plead guilty in return for entering of nolle prosequi on counts of kidnapping, rape, and attempted rape, plea arrangement benefited defendant, and there was no evidence defendant was facing exclusion from admission to country, or denial of naturalization, as result of guilty plea. State v. Batista (Ohio App. 10 Dist., Franklin, 09-23-2004) No. 03AP-1009, 2004-Ohio-5066, 2004 WL 2803421, Unreported. Criminal Law ⚷ 273.1(4); Criminal Law ⚷ 1167(5)

Case would be remanded to trial court to determine whether its advisement to defendant of possible immigration consequences of his guilty plea was in substantial compliance with statute requiring court to advise defendants on possibility of deportation, exclusion, or denial of naturalization prior to accepting pleas. State v. Badawi (Ohio App. 12 Dist., Clermont, 09-20-2004) No. CA2003-09-074, 2004-Ohio-4982, 2004 WL 2182659, Unreported. Criminal Law ⚷ 1181.5(3.1)

Defendant was not prejudiced by trial court's failure prior to accepting his guilty plea to advise him of deportation consequences of his plea, as required by statute for non-citizen defendants, where nothing in record showed that deportation proceedings had commenced against defendant, defendant did not claim that deportation was currently being sought against him, and defendant may have been subject to deportation on other grounds. State v. Gegia (Ohio App. 11 Dist., Portage, 03-19-2004) No. 2003-P-0026, 2004-Ohio-1441, 2004 WL 574623, Unreported, appeal not allowed 103 Ohio St.3d 1525, 817 N.E.2d 408, 2004-Ohio-5852. Criminal Law ⚷ 274(3.1)

Abduction defendant's claim that trial court failed to advise him of the potential consequences of his guilty plea to his status as an alien residing in, or seeking admission to, the United States was not cognizable on direct appeal; exclusive remedy for the alleged violation was a motion to withdraw plea. State v. Garmendia (Ohio App. 2 Dist., Montgomery, 07-11-2003) No. 2002-CA-18, 2003-Ohio-3769, 2003 WL 21658528, Unreported. Criminal Law ⚷ 274(3.1); Criminal Law ⚷ 1134(3)

Failure of a trial court to advise an alien resident that he could be deported as a result of entering a guilty plea in a criminal matter is not prejudicial error where the Department of Immigration and Naturalization Service (INS) has unrelated grounds for deportation pertaining to misrepresentations the resident made upon entering the United States. City of Broadview Heights v. Cvekic (Ohio App. 8 Dist., Cuyahoga, 11-21-2001) No. 77933, 2001 WL 1479231, Unreported.

Failure to give required advisement to defendant prior to entry of guilty plea to forgery charges, that conviction could subject him to deportation or exclusion, was prejudicial, as shown on motion to withdraw guilty plea, wherein defendant offered order of deportation that was based on his guilty pleas. State v. White (Ohio App. 11 Dist., 09-16-2005) 163 Ohio App.3d 377, 837 N.E.2d 1246, 2005-Ohio-4898. Criminal Law ⚷ 274(3.1)

Although the law mandated trial court to address the issue of citizenship and deportation prior to accepting defendant's guilty plea, court's error in failing to do so was harmless because, even though defendant stated that he was a Jamaican citizen, he failed to offer any documentation in support of that assertion and had not indicated the manner in which he had been prejudiced by the court's omission and he faced the possibility of deportation only as a result of his plea and that was insufficient to show prejudicial effect. State v. White (Ohio App. 8 Dist., 04-02-2001) 142 Ohio App.3d 132, 754 N.E.2d 287, dismissed, appeal not allowed 92 Ohio St.3d 1443, 751 N.E.2d 482, motion to reopen denied 2001 WL 1249941, motion for delayed appeal denied 102 Ohio St.3d 1469, 809 N.E.2d 1157, 2004-Ohio-2830. Criminal Law ⚷ 1167(5)

Defendant, an alien, suffered prejudice from judges' alleged failure at arraignment and sentencing on domestic violence charge to which defendant pleaded no contest to inform him of possible citizenship consequences of plea; defendant had no legal right to remain in country unless he changed his status from non-immigrant to immigrant, subsequent amendments to federal statute added domestic violence as a deportable offense for a legal immigrant, and the effect of that offense on one seeking immigrant status was clearly prejudicial. Euclid v. Muller (Ohio App. 8 Dist., 09-13-1999) 134 Ohio App.3d 737, 732 N.E.2d 410, appeal not allowed 87 Ohio St.3d 1494, 722 N.E.2d 527. Criminal Law ⚷ 275.3; Sentencing And Punishment ⚷ 354

13. —— Written advisement, court's duty to inform

Written advisement of potential immigration consequences of noncitizen defendant's guilty plea, without more, was insufficient to constitute substantial compliance with statute governing advisements to noncitizens of immigration consequences of guilty pleas, where statute required court to personally address defendant and inform him of such consequences. State v. Lucente (Ohio App. 7 Dist., Mahoning, 03-29-2005) No. 03 MA 216, 2005-Ohio-1657, 2005 WL 775886, Unreported. Criminal Law ⚷ 273.1(4)

14. —— Use of statutory language, court's duty to inform

Trial court's admonishment to non-citizen defendant that as a result of pleading guilty to a felony he could be deported failed to substantially comply with statute that required it to inform a non-citizen defendant of the possible consequences of a guilty plea; the court's general advisement failed to advise defendant that his conviction, standing alone, could result in immigration consequences, and thus, the court allowed for a broad interpretation of the advisement, which resulted in defendant's misguided belief that he would only be deported if he violated probation. State v. Zuniga (Ohio App. 11 Dist., Lake, 04-29-2005) No. 2003-P-0082, No. 2004-P-0002, 2005-Ohio-2078, 2005 WL 1007173, Unreported, appeal not allowed 106 Ohio St.3d 1488, 832 N.E.2d 739, 2005-Ohio-3978. Criminal Law ⚷ 273.1(4)

Plea court's advisement to noncitizen defendant of immigration consequences of his guilty plea to multiple counts of trafficking in drugs did not substantially comply with statutory requirements, where court stated only that prosecutor had advised that defendant's plea would not likely result in deportation, that court had allotted funds to defense counsel to obtain advice in that regard from attorney who was specialist in that field, and that if such attorney advised that deportation was possibility, court would permit defendant to withdraw plea and go to trial. State v. Lucente (Ohio App. 7 Dist., Mahoning, 03-29-2005) No. 03 MA 216, 2005-Ohio-1657, 2005 WL 775886, Unreported. Criminal Law ⚷ 273.1(4)

Trial court's advisement to noncitizen drug defendant with respect to immigration consequences of his guilty plea amounted to plain error, where advisement did not substantially comply with requirements of applicable statute, trial court's failure adequately to inform defendant was obvious defect in proceedings, and such failure affected defendant's substantial rights. State v. Encarnacion (Ohio App. 12 Dist., Butler, 12-27-2004) No. CA2003-09-225, 2004-Ohio-7043, 2004 WL 2980594, Unreported. Criminal Law ⚷ 1031(4)

When advising an accused of the possible immigration consequences of his guilty or no contest plea, trial court need only substantially comply with statute requiring court to advise defendants on possibility of deportation, exclusion, or denial of naturalization prior to accepting pleas. State v. Badawi (Ohio App. 12 Dist., Clermont, 09-20-2004) No. CA2003-09-074, 2004-Ohio-4982, 2004 WL 2182659, Unreported. Criminal Law ⚷ 273.1(4); Criminal Law ⚷ 275.3

Trial court's failure to provide a verbatim advisement to defendant that in pleading guilty to trafficking in food stamps, he was subject to exclusion from the United States and denial of naturalization under United States law, did not entitle defendant to withdraw his plea, where defendant failed to offer any proof that he was a non-citizen. State v. Almingdad (Ohio App. 8 Dist., Cuyahoga, 04-10-2003) No. 81201, 2003-Ohio-1829, 2003 WL 1849127, Unreported. Criminal Law ⚷ 274(3.1)

Trial court complied with statutory requirement to advise defendant of immigration consequences prior to accepting guilty plea to aggravated assault, where, during plea colloquy, trial court advised defendant that, by pleading guilty, he faced possibility of deportation, that he might be excluded from admission to the United States, or that he might be denied naturalization. State v. Marafa (Ohio App. 5 Dist., Stark, 01-21-2003) No. 2002CA00099, No. 2002CA00259, 2003-Ohio-257, 2003 WL 150093, Unreported. Criminal Law ⚷ 273.1(4)

If some warning of immigration-related consequences was given by the trial court when a noncitizen defendant's guilty or no-contest plea was accepted, but the warning was not a verbatim recital of the statutorily-required language, a trial court considering the defendant's motion to withdraw the plea must exercise its discretion in determining whether the trial court that accepted the plea substantially complied with the statute, i.e., whether under the totality of the circumstances the defendant subjectively understood the implications of her plea and the rights she was waiving. (Per Alice Robie Resnick, J., with two Justices concurring and two Justices concurring in part and dissenting in part.) State v. Francis (Ohio, 12-22-2004) 104 Ohio St.3d 490, 820 N.E.2d 355, 2004-Ohio-6894. Criminal Law ⚷ 274(3.1)

To ensure compliance with the statute requiring a trial court accepting a guilty or no-contest plea from a defendant who is not a citizen of the United States to warn the defendant of the possible immigration-related consequences of the plea, a trial court accepting a plea should never assume that any defendant is a United States citizen, but must give the warning verbatim to every criminal defendant, other than certain defendants pleading to a minor misdemeanor, unless the defendant affirmatively has indicated either in writing or orally on the record that he or she is a citizen of the United States. (Per Alice Robie Resnick, J., with two Justices concurring, two Justices concurring in judgment only, and two Justices concurring in part and dissenting in part.) State v. Francis (Ohio, 12-22-2004) 104 Ohio St.3d 490, 820 N.E.2d 355, 2004-Ohio-6894. Criminal Law ⚷ 273.1(4); Criminal Law ⚷ 275.3

A trial court accepting a guilty or no-contest plea from a defendant who is not a citizen of the United States must give verbatim the warning set forth by statute, which informs the defendant that conviction of the offense for which the plea is entered "may have the consequences of deportation, exclusion from admission to the United States, or denial of naturalization pursuant to the laws of the United States." (Per Alice Robie Resnick, J., with two Justices concurring, two Justices concurring in judgment only, and two Justices concurring in part and dissenting in part.) State v. Francis (Ohio, 12-22-2004) 104 Ohio St.3d 490, 820 N.E.2d 355, 2004-Ohio-6894. Criminal Law ⚷ 273.1(4); Criminal Law ⚷ 275.3

Trial court did not give defendant advisement called for in statute governing advisements to defendant concerning immigration consequences of pleading guilty, and thus defendant was entitled to withdraw guilty plea to charge of illegal use or possession of drug paraphernalia; although trial court told defendant that defendant was subject to deportation if defendant pled guilty; defendant was told that under certain conditions he could be deported if he pled guilty but then was told that conditions for deportation were not met. State v. Abi-Aazar (Ohio App. 9 Dist., 09-10-2003) 154 Ohio App.3d 278, 797 N.E.2d 98, 2003-Ohio-4780. Criminal Law ⚷ 274(3.1)

Although it may be a better practice for trial court to read verbatim statute governing advisements to defendant concerning immigration consequences of pleading guilty, literal compliance is not necessary. State v. Abi-Aazar (Ohio App. 9 Dist., 09-10-2003) 154 Ohio App.3d 278, 797 N.E.2d 98, 2003-Ohio-4780. Criminal Law ⚷ 273.1(4)

Postconviction relief movant was entitled to set aside guilty plea to felonious assault in order to correct manifest injustice that occurred when trial judge failed to provide proper statutory advisement on immigration effects of the plea; judge never mentioned the word "deportation," but merely referred to a "bad effect upon your ability to remain in the United States" and movant's not being able "to have any permanent residence here," judge never used the term "exclusion from admission" and he did not even elude to the concept of not being able to enter or re-enter the country, and he did not use the term "denial of naturalization," but he did explain "you probably will not be able to become a citizen." State v. Quran (Ohio App. 8 Dist., Cuyahoga, 09-19-2002) No. 80701, 2002-Ohio-4917, 2002 WL 31087704, Unreported. Criminal Law ⚷ 1482

Proof existed that defendant was present when trial judge gave to a group of individuals the statutorily mandated advisement of the possibility of deportation, exclusion, or denial of naturalization prior to accepting pleas, where judge took judicial notice of the municipal court's procedure, under which late-arriving defendants were checked in and forced to wait for a second arraignment session where the advisements are again stated. City of Lakewood v. Shurney (Ohio App. 8 Dist., Cuyahoga, 09-12-2002) No. 80885, 2002-Ohio-4789, 2002 WL 31031669, Unreported. Criminal Law ⚷ 273.1(4)

2943.032 Court to inform defendant prison term may be administratively extended for offenses committed during term before accepting plea

Prior to accepting a guilty plea or a plea of no contest to an indictment, information, or complaint that charges a felony, the court shall inform the defendant personally that, if the defendant pleads guilty or no contest to the felony so charged or any other felony and if the court imposes a prison term upon the defendant for the felony, all of the following apply:

(A) The parole board may extend the stated prison term if the defendant commits any criminal offense under the law of this state or the United States while serving the prison term.

(B) Any such extension will be done administratively as part of the defendant's sentence in accordance with section 2967.11 of the Revised Code and may be for thirty, sixty, or ninety days for each violation.

(C) All such extensions of the stated prison term for all violations during the course of the term may not exceed one-half of the term's duration.

(D) The sentence imposed for the felony automatically includes any such extension of the stated prison term by the parole board.

(E) If the offender violates the conditions of a post-release control sanction imposed by the parole board upon the completion of the stated prison term, the parole board may impose upon the offender a residential sanction that includes a new prison term up to nine months.

(1995 S 2, eff. 7-1-96)

Cross References

Compliance prior to acceptance of plea, 2937.06

Library References

Criminal Law ⚷273(4.1), 273.1(4), 275.3.
Westlaw Topic No. 110.
C.J.S. Criminal Law §§ 384, 389, 398 to 407, 417.

Baldwin's Ohio Legislative Service, 1995 S 2—LSC Analysis, p 8/L-2907

Research References

Encyclopedias

OH Jur. 3d Criminal Law § 2447, Felony Cases Generally.

OH Jur. 3d Criminal Law § 3636, Unnecessary or Immaterial Matter; Moot Questions.

Treatises and Practice Aids

Katz, Giannelli, Blair and Lipton, Baldwin's Ohio Practice, Criminal Law, § 120:5, Bad Time.

Katz, Giannelli, Blair and Lipton, Baldwin's Ohio Practice, Criminal Law, § 144:1, Plea of Guilty.

Katz, Giannelli, Blair and Lipton, Baldwin's Ohio Practice, Criminal Law, § 144:2, No Contest Plea.

Katz, Giannelli, Blair and Lipton, Baldwin's Ohio Practice, Criminal Law, § 43:11, Understanding the Penalty.

Notes of Decisions

1. Constitutional issues

Trial court's failure to advise defendant of correct maximum penalty for firearm specification and that he faced post-release control following sentence rendered his guilty plea invalid, thus necessitating remand for further proceedings. State v. Pendleton (Ohio App. 8 Dist., Cuyahoga, 06-23-2005) No. 84514, 2005-Ohio-3126, 2005 WL 1484020, Unreported. Criminal Law ⚷ 1181.5(3.1)

Issue of whether defendant's guilty plea for drug possession was not knowing and voluntary due to court's failure to notify him he was subject to "bad time" was rendered moot when Supreme Court found statute permitting Parole Board to extend sentences for bad behavior unconstitutional. State v. White (Ohio App. 8 Dist., 10-30-2003) 155 Ohio App.3d 215, 800 N.E.2d 84, 2003-Ohio-5816. Criminal Law ⚷ 1134(3)

2. Extension of sentence

Trial court failed to substantially comply with requirements of statute requiring court to inform defendant that prison term may be administratively extended for offenses committed during term before accepting plea, or rule governing pleas, and, thus, trial court erred in accepting defendant's guilty plea to burglary; trial court failed to inform defendant personally of three-year duration of his period of post-release control before accepting plea, or to include in its colloquy with defendant duration of any additional prison time for violations of post-release control conditions. State v. Gulley (Ohio App. 1 Dist., Hamilton, 09-02-2005) No. C-040675, 2005-Ohio-4592, 2005 WL 2106556, Unreported. Criminal Law ⚷ 273(4.1)

Trial court was not required to advise defendant, prior to accepting his plea of guilty to fifth-degree felony drug trafficking, with respect to potential administrative extensions of his sentence for committing criminal offense while serving his sentence, where "bad time" statute providing for such extensions was unconstitutional. State v. Reynolds (Ohio App. 8 Dist., Cuyahoga, 11-26-2003) No. 82914, 2003-Ohio-6338, 2003 WL 22805287, Unreported. Criminal Law ⚷ 273.1(4)

Record failed to show that defendant made knowing, intelligent, and voluntary plea of guilty to charged offense of attempted burglary, where trial court failed to specifically state at plea hearing that defendant could be subject to parole board supervision up to three years following completion of five-year sentence, defendant was not personally advised at plea hearing that parole board could impose up to nine months of prison for each violation of post-release control, and defendant was not notified at sentencing that parole board could impose a maximum of 50 percent of his original term for violations of post-release control. State v. Tucci (Ohio App. 7 Dist., Mahoning, 12-11-2002) No. 01 CA 234, 2002-Ohio-6903, 2002 WL 31812895, Unreported. Criminal Law ⚷ 273.1(4)

Trial court's failure to inform defendant prior to entry of guilty plea that only the commission of a crime in prison may authorize parole board to extend a prisoner's sentence and that statute establishes time limits for such extensions was not prejudicial, where defendant signed written plea agreement which outlined portions of statute which court failed to cover, and plea was entered as part of agreement under which defendant avoided gun specifications which carried actual incarceration terms of two to three years. State v. Gales (Ohio App. 7 Dist., 02-01-1999) 131 Ohio App.3d 56, 721 N.E.2d 497. Criminal Law ⚷ 1167(5)

Trial court's failure to advise defendant that post-release controls could have been part of his sentence in assault prosecution entitled defendant to have post-release control sanctions vacated, where post-release controls were imposed after defendant had served the term of imprisonment for assault. State v. Murphy (Ohio App. 8 Dist., Cuyahoga, 07-03-2002) No. 80460, 2002-Ohio-3452, 2002 WL 1453814, Unreported. Criminal Law ⚷ 1181.5(8)

3. Post release control

Trial court's failure to adequately inform defendant at plea hearing that he would be subject to mandatory five-year period of post-release control as part of his sentence for identity theft crimes rendered defendant's guilty plea invalid; although trial court informed defendant that he "might" be released on post-release control, by operation of law, defendant was subject to a mandatory five years of post-release control. State v. Crosswhite (Ohio App. 8 Dist., Cuyahoga, 03-09-2006) No. 86345, No. 86346, 2006-Ohio-1081, 2006 WL 562166, Unreported. Criminal Law ⚷ 273.1(4)

Trial court's failure to address post-release control issue as it pertained to offenses to which defendant was pleading guilty, attempted theft of a motor vehicle and felonious assault, rendered guilty plea invalid; post-release control constituted portion of maximum penalty involved, without which explanation defendant could not fully understand the consequences of his plea. State v. Douglas (Ohio App. 8 Dist., Cuyahoga, 02-09-2006) No. 85525, No. 85526, 2006-Ohio-536, 2006 WL 302134, Unreported. Criminal Law ⚷ 273.1(4)

Defendant's pleas of guilty to second-degree felonious assault, third-degree child endangering, and fifth-degree domestic violence were not knowing, where plea court failed to inform defendant prior to sentencing that he would be subject to three-year mandatory period of post-release supervision, and thus failed to inform defendant of his potential maximum sentence. State v. Kerin (Ohio App. 8 Dist., Cuyahoga, 08-11-2005) No. 85153, 2005-Ohio-4117, 2005 WL 1907324, Unreported. Criminal Law ⚷ 273.1(4)

Plea court's colloquy with defendant, prior to its acceptance of defendant's plea of guilty to felonious assault, was inadequate to explain that defendant would be subject to statutorily mandated three-year term of post-release control, where plea court merely stated that post-release control was mandatory. State v. Kerin (Ohio App. 8 Dist., Cuyahoga, 08-11-2005) No. 85153, 2005-Ohio-4117, 2005 WL 1907324, Unreported. Criminal Law ⚷ 273.1(4)

Trial court's failure to advise defendant at plea hearing of possibility of postrelease control or consequences of violating postrelease control rendered unknowing and involuntary his guilty plea to a third-degree felony. State v. Webster (Ohio App. 4 Dist., Hocking, 07-29-2005) No. 05CA9, 2005-Ohio-4036, 2005 WL 1847345, Unreported. Criminal Law ⚷ 273.1(4)

Trial court's failure to explain to defendant requirements of postrelease control was plain error, in sentencing for aggravated vehicular homicide after guilty plea; without adequate explanation, defendant was not informed of maximum penalty for offense and thus could not fully understand consequences of entering her plea. State v. Smith (Ohio App. 8 Dist., Cuyahoga, 07-28-2005) No. 85245, 2005-Ohio-3836, 2005 WL 1792456, Unreported. Criminal Law ⚷ 1031(4)

Defendant's plea of guilty to first-degree felony trafficking in drugs was not knowing, intelligent, and voluntary, where trial court failed adequately to inform him with respect to post-release control, in violation of requirements that he be informed of his potential maximum sentence and of consequences of his plea; court's only mention of post-release control occurred at very end of its imposition of sentence, at which time it merely informed defendant that upon his release he would be subject to five years' post-release control. State v. Oko (Ohio App. 8 Dist., Cuyahoga, 07-21-2005) No. 85049, 2005-Ohio-3705, 2005 WL 1707018, Unreported. Criminal Law ⚷ 273.1(4)

Sentencing court's explanation of post-release control sanctions was inadequate and did not substantially comply with court's responsibilities, where court failed to inform defendant, who was pleading guilty to two counts of aggravated arson, of consequences should he violate post-release control. State v. Owens (Ohio App. 8 Dist., Cuyahoga, 07-14-2005) No. 84987, 2005-Ohio-3570, 2005 WL 1648674, Unreported. Sentencing And Punishment ⚷ 354

Trial court did not adequately and accurately inform defendant of maximum penalties associated with his guilty pleas to first-degree felony trafficking in cocaine and fourth-degree felony trafficking in marijuana, and thus pleas were not knowingly, intelligently and voluntarily entered; trial court's description of maximum penalty for cocaine offense was unclear whether defendant would be subjected to discretionary or mandatory postrelease control, trial court failed to inform defendant of maximum penalty for marijuana offense, including possibility of postrelease control, and trial court failed to personally inform defendant of consequences of violating postrelease control. State v. Hill (Ohio App. 4 Dist., Lawrence, 06-30-2005) No. 04CA9, No. 04CA11, 2005-Ohio-3491, 2005 WL 1594834, Unreported. Criminal Law ⚷ 273.1(4)

Guilty plea to charge of trafficking in crack cocaine was not given with full knowledge of all potential penalties to which defendant was subject, where trial court informed defendant at plea hearing that he would be subject to post-release control, but trial court failed to inform defendant of consequences of violating post-release control. State v. Woods (Ohio App. 8 Dist., Cuyahoga, 04-07-2005) No. 84426, 2005-Ohio-1671, 2005 WL 798404, Unreported. Criminal Law ⚷ 273.1(4)

Requirement that sentencing court inform defendant who has pled guilty of possible nonprison sanctions for violation of terms of post-release control did not apply to defendant convicted after jury trial. State v. Panza (Ohio App. 8 Dist., Cuyahoga, 01-13-2005) No. 84177, 2005-Ohio-94, 2005 WL 77081, Unreported, appeal not allowed 106 Ohio St.3d 1413, 830 N.E.2d 346, 2005-Ohio-3154. Sentencing And Punishment ⚷ 354

Trial court in "sexual battery" proceeding was not required to inform inmate of post-release control; inmate was not subject to post-release control as a result of his conviction for sexual battery, and inmate was subject to post-release control when he was previously released from state prison since he had already served 30-month term imposed for his distinct conviction. Strzala v. Gansheimer (Ohio App. 11 Dist., Ashtabula, 12-03-2004) No. 2004-A-0049, 2004-Ohio-6472, 2004 WL 2785559, Unreported. Sentencing And Punishment ⚷ 354

Trial court's failure to inform defendant of post-release control sanctions at time of his guilty plea rendered his plea unknowing, unintelligent, and involuntary; defendant was not able to fully understand consequences of his plea, given that post-release control constituted portion of maximum penalty for offense. State v. Paris (Ohio App. 8 Dist., Cuyahoga, 11-10-2004) No. 83519, 2004-Ohio-5965, 2004 WL 2535759, Unreported, appeal not allowed 105 Ohio St.3d 1499, 825 N.E.2d 623, 2005-Ohio-1666. Criminal Law ⚷ 273.1(4)

Trial court's failure to inform defendant who pleaded guilty to fourth-degree felony driving under influence of alcohol (DUI) that she was subject to post-release control at discretion of parole board rendered her plea involuntary; defendant was not told necessary information regarding her maximum sentence in determining whether to enter plea. State v. Mercadante (Ohio App. 8 Dist., Cuyahoga, 07-08-2004) No. 81246, 2004-Ohio-3593, 2004 WL 1516841, Unreported. Criminal Law ⚷ 273.1(4)

Trial court's informing defendant that by pleading guilty to voluntary manslaughter he would be giving up his liberty, along with written guilty plea form notifying defendant that he could have up to five years of post-release control, was not sufficient to fulfill trial court's requirement to personally inform defendant of possibility of post-release control; defendant's alleged lack of prejudice by such error did not permit such error. State v. Johnson (Ohio App. 11 Dist., Lake, 01-16-2004) No. 2002-L-024, 2004-Ohio-331, 2004 WL 144202, Unreported. Sentencing And Punishment ⚷ 354

Trial court failed to substantially comply with rule requiring trial court, prior to taking defendant's guilty plea to aggravated robbery, rape, and kidnapping offenses, to determine that defendant had fully understood maximum penalty involved by failing to advise defendant that post-control release would be a part of his sentence; post-release control constituted a portion of maximum penalty involved in an offense for which a prison term would be imposed. State v. Perry (Ohio App. 8 Dist., Cuyahoga, 11-26-2003) No. 82085, 2003-Ohio-6344, 2003 WL 22805880, Unreported. Criminal Law ⚷ 273.1(4)

Even if trial court inadvertently misled defendant into believing he faced a longer possible prison sentence if he violated a condition of post-release control than was available under the law, defendant's guilty plea to fifth-degree felony receiving stolen property was knowingly and freely given; defendant could not seriously assert he entered guilty plea based on belief he faced possible additional nine-month sentence if he violated post-release control and that he would not have entered the plea if he had known that the possible sentence was only six months. State v. Carnicom (Ohio App. 2 Dist., Miami, 09-05-2003) No. 2003-CA-4, 2003-Ohio-4711, 2003 WL 22060583, Unreported. Criminal Law ⚷ 273.1(4)

Trial court's failure to inform defendant, prior to guilty plea to offense of driving under the influence of alcohol (DUI), that post-release controls could have been part of his sentence, entitled defendant to have conviction vacated. State v. Delventhal (Ohio App. 8 Dist., Cuyahoga, 03-27-2003) No. 81034, 2003-Ohio-1503, 2003 WL 1561948, Unreported. Criminal Law ⚷ 273.1(4); Criminal Law ⚷ 1167(5)

Statute mandated post-release control as part of sentence for felony sex offense, and thus trial court's failure to notify defendant convicted of rape that he would be subject to post-release control, or to include post-release control in its sentencing order, did not deprive Adult Parole Authority (APA) of jurisdiction to supervise defendant; remand for limited purpose of notifying defendant of post-release control and including this sanction in sentencing order was all that was required. State v. Johnson (Ohio App. 8 Dist., Cuyahoga, 09-05-2002) No. 80459, 2002-Ohio-4581, 2002 WL 2027521, Unreported, appeal allowed 98 Ohio St.3d 1460, 783 N.E.2d 519, 2003-Ohio-644, cause dismissed 98 Ohio St.3d 1544, 787 N.E.2d 7, 2003-Ohio-2002, reconsideration denied 99 Ohio St.3d 1416, 788 N.E.2d 1099, 2003-Ohio-2526. Sentencing And Punishment ⚷ 1913; Sentencing And Punishment ⚷ 354; Sentencing And Punishment ⚷ 373

2943.04 Form of plea

Pleas of guilty or not guilty may be oral. Pleas in all other cases shall be in writing, subscribed by the defendant or his counsel, and shall immediately be entered upon the minutes of the court.

(1953 H 1, eff. 10–1–53; GC 13440–3)

Historical and Statutory Notes

Pre–1953 H 1 Amendments: 113 v 176, Ch 19, § 3

Cross References

Pleas, Crim R 11

Library References

Criminal Law ⚷269, 273, 299.

Westlaw Topic No. 110.

C.J.S. Criminal Law §§ 375, 378, 384 to 389, 409.

Research References

Treatises and Practice Aids

Katz, Giannelli, Blair and Lipton, Baldwin's Ohio Practice, Criminal Law, § 42:2, Types of Pleas.

Katz, Giannelli, Blair and Lipton, Baldwin's Ohio Practice, Criminal Law, § 144:1, Plea of Guilty.

Katz, Giannelli, Blair and Lipton, Baldwin's Ohio Practice, Criminal Law, § 144:2, No Contest Plea.

Katz, Giannelli, Blair and Lipton, Baldwin's Ohio Practice, Criminal Law, § 144:3, Entry of Not Guilty Plea.

Katz, Giannelli, Blair and Lipton, Baldwin's Ohio Practice, Criminal Law, § 144:4, Plea of Not Guilty by Reason of Insanity at Arraignment.
Katz, Giannelli, Blair and Lipton, Baldwin's Ohio Practice, Criminal Law, § 144:5, Acceptance of Plea of Not Guilty by Reason of Insanity After Arraignment.

Notes of Decisions

---

1. Guilty pleas

Where the record affirmatively discloses that: (1) defendant's guilty plea was not the result of coercion, deception or intimidation; (2) counsel was present at the time of the plea; (3) counsel's advice was competent in light of the circumstances surrounding the indictment; (4) the plea was made with the understanding of the nature of the charges; and, (5) defendant was motivated either by a desire to seek a lesser penalty or a fear of the consequences of a jury trial, or both, the guilty plea has been voluntarily and intelligently made. State v. Piacella (Ohio 1971) 27 Ohio St.2d 92, 271 N.E.2d 852, 56 O.O.2d 52. Criminal Law ⚿ 273.1(1)

2. Oral pleas

Where, in a criminal prosecution, a defendant is charged with murder in the first degree, to which charge he enters a plea of not guilty and also an oral plea of not guilty by reason of insanity and he later enters a plea of guilty of murder in the second degree without first withdrawing his oral plea of not guilty by reason of insanity, such defendant thereby waives his oral plea of not guilty by reason of insanity. State v. Fore (Athens 1969) 18 Ohio App.2d 264, 248 N.E.2d 633, 47 O.O.2d 404. Criminal Law ⚿ 273.2(1)

There is no requirement that a plea of guilty to an indictment be in writing. Anderson v. Maxwell (Ohio 1963) 175 Ohio St. 210, 192 N.E.2d 779, 24 O.O.2d 286.

The overruling of an oral motion for discharge of defendant in a criminal proceeding on the claim of "double jeopardy" is not a final appealable order. State v. Downey (Cuyahoga 1960) 113 Ohio App. 250, 170 N.E.2d 75, 85 Ohio Law Abs. 253, 17 O.O.2d 227, appeal dismissed 171 Ohio St. 565, 173 N.E.2d 106, 15 O.O.2d 42.

An oral plea of guilty is a waiver by a defendant charged with an offense of the necessity for a trial, and when the plea of guilty is journalized, it is of the same effect, within the meaning of the habitual criminal statute as a previous conviction which has been separately prosecuted and tried. State v. Sheridan (Summit 1959) 109 Ohio App. 482, 167 N.E.2d 530, 12 O.O.2d 21. Criminal Law ⚿ 273.4(1); Sentencing And Punishment ⚿ 1379(4)

Under Crim R 11(A) a no contest plea may be made orally and need not be made in writing, notwithstanding RC 2943.04, since the rule controls over a conflicting statute. State v Sabo, No. 1273 (4th Dist Ct App, Athens, 9–5–86).

3. Written plea—In general

Former jeopardy is a defense which must be pleaded in writing. State v. Downey (Cuyahoga 1960) 113 Ohio App. 250, 170 N.E.2d 75, 85 Ohio Law Abs. 253, 17 O.O.2d 227, appeal dismissed 171 Ohio St. 565, 173 N.E.2d 106, 15 O.O.2d 42.

4. —— Failure to file, written plea

Failure of counsel to file a written plea of not guilty by reason of insanity in an action in which they relied on such defense made orally in the opening statement deprived accused of due process of law. Schaber v. Maxwell (C.A.6 (Ohio) 1965) 5 Ohio Misc. 81, 348 F.2d 664, 33 O.O.2d 377.

RIGHTS OF CRIME VICTIM

2943.041 Rights of crime victim in regard to prosecution of defendant—Repealed

(1994 S 186, eff. 10–12–94; 1994 H 571, eff. 10–6–94; 1987 S 6, § 1, eff. 6–10–87; 1987 S 6, § 3; 1984 S 172, § 1, 4)

DOUBLE JEOPARDY

Law Review and Journal Commentaries

Double Jeopardy Consequences of Mistrial Dismissal and Reversal of Conviction on Appeal, Sean T. Beeny. 16 Am Crim L Rev 235 (1979).

Government Appeals of Sentence: Double Talk with the Double Jeopardy Clause?, Comment. 9 Ohio N U L Rev 385 (1982).

2943.05 Form of plea of former conviction

If a defendant pleads that he has had former judgment of conviction or acquittal, or has been once in jeopardy, he must set forth in his plea the court, time, and place of such conviction, acquittal, or jeopardy. No claim of former judgment of conviction or acquittal, or jeopardy may be given in evidence under the plea of not guilty.

(1953 H 1, eff. 10–1–53; GC 13440–4)

Historical and Statutory Notes

Pre–1953 H 1 Amendments: 113 v 176, Ch 19, § 4

Cross References

Double jeopardy considerations, O Const Art I §10
Pleas, Crim R 11

Library References

Criminal Law ⚷292.
Westlaw Topic No. 110.
C.J.S. Criminal Law § 381.

Law Review and Journal Commentaries

The Effect of the Double Jeopardy Clause on Juvenile Proceedings, James G. Carr. 6 U Tol L Rev 1 (Fall 1974).

State v. Ikner: Examining the Merger Doctrine and Double Jeopardy in Terms of Auto Theft, Note. 4 Ohio N U L Rev 111 (1977).

Notes of Decisions

1. In general

Double jeopardy clause affords protection not only from multiple prosecutions, but also from imposition of multiple punishments in separate and successive proceedings; however, if pursued in a single proceeding, multiple punishment may constitutionally be imposed and the state may obtain the full range of both civil and criminal penalties. State v. Gustafson (Ohio, 07-30-1996) 76 Ohio St.3d 425, 668 N.E.2d 435, 1996-Ohio-425. Double Jeopardy ⚷ 5.1; Double Jeopardy ⚷ 28

Risk to which the double jeopardy clause refers is not present in proceedings that are not essentially criminal. State v. Gustafson (Ohio, 07-30-1996) 76 Ohio St.3d 425, 668 N.E.2d 435, 1996-Ohio-425. Double Jeopardy ⚷ 23

Separate prosecutions of a defendant for separate sales of narcotics to different persons on different dates in different counties do not constitute the placing of the defendant in double jeopardy on the basis of one course of criminal conduct. State v. Mutter (Cuyahoga 1983) 14 Ohio App.3d 356, 471 N.E.2d 782, 14 O.B.R. 459. Double Jeopardy ⚷ 146

In a bench trial, jeopardy does not attach until a witness is sworn in and gives testimony; therefore, before the first witness is sworn in, the trial court may correctly dismiss a defective complaint without prejudice and allow the trial to continue based on a substituted complaint. State v. Dallman (Wayne 1983) 11 Ohio App.3d 64, 463 N.E.2d 96, 11 O.B.R. 99.

Acquittal of a defendant in a municipal court trial on a charge of reckless driving is a bar to an indictment for vehicular homicide arising out of the same act. State v. Tolson (Ohio Com.Pl. 1973) 34 Ohio Misc. 55, 296 N.E.2d 705, 63 O.O.2d 217.

A conviction upon a charge of reckless driving is no bar to subsequent conviction on a charge of drunken driving arising out of the same accident. City of Akron v. Kline (Summit 1956) 170 N.E.2d 265, 84 Ohio Law Abs. 124, affirmed 165 Ohio St. 322, 135 N.E.2d 265, 59 O.O. 414.

The Double Jeopardy Clause precludes a second trial once the court has found the evidence legally insufficient to support the guilty verdict. Hudson v. Louisiana (U.S.La. 1981) 101 S.Ct. 970, 450 U.S. 40, 67 L.Ed.2d 30.

2. Separate crimes

Double jeopardy clause does not preclude criminal prosecution based on the fact that civil administrative proceedings based on the same conduct have previously been initiated. State v. Gustafson (Ohio, 07-30-1996) 76 Ohio St.3d 425, 668 N.E.2d 435, 1996-Ohio-425. Double Jeopardy ⚷ 24

Act of refusing chemical test for alcohol, standing alone, does not constitute a criminal "offense" of any kind for purposes of double jeopardy prohibition against multiple punishments for the same "offense." State v. Gustafson (Ohio, 07-30-1996) 76 Ohio St.3d 425, 668 N.E.2d 435, 1996-Ohio-425. Double Jeopardy ⚷ 21

The offenses of assault and resisting arrest each require proof of a fact which the other does not, and therefore a defendant is not placed in double jeopardy where (1) he is charged with both offenses, (2) he is acquitted of assault, (3) the jury cannot reach a verdict on the resisting arrest charge, and (4) a second trial on the resisting arrest charge is had. State v. Rhinehart (Summit 1983) 12 Ohio App.3d 156, 467 N.E.2d 902, 12 O.B.R. 480.

A conviction on one charge may not bar a subsequent conviction and sentence on the other charge arising out of the same act unless the evidence required to support the conviction on one would be sufficient to support the conviction on the other. City of Akron v. Kline (Ohio 1956) 165 Ohio St. 322, 135 N.E.2d 265, 59 O.O. 414. Double Jeopardy ⚷ 134

The same acts cannot be punished as two offenses by the municipal and state authorities; unless the case falls within the exceptions to the "same transaction" rule, the Double Jeopardy Clause bars a second trial. (See also Ashe v Swenson, 397 US 436, 90 SCt 1189, 25 LEd(2d) 469 (1970).) Waller v. Florida (U.S.Fla. 1970) 90 S.Ct. 1184, 397 U.S. 387, 25 L.Ed.2d 435, 52 O.O.2d 320, rehearing denied 90 S.Ct. 1684, 398 U.S. 914, 26 L.Ed.2d 79.

3. When jeopardy attaches

The rule that jeopardy attaches in a jury trial when the jury is sworn applies to state as well as federal courts. (Ed. note: Montana law construed in light of federal constitution.) Crist v. Bretz (U.S.Mont. 1978) 98 S.Ct. 2156, 437 U.S. 28, 57 L.Ed.2d 24, 10 O.O.3d 466. Double Jeopardy ⚷ 59

4. Collateral estoppel

The extraordinary original jurisdiction granted to an Ohio appellate court may be invoked to adjudicate the right of an accused to the benefit of the doctrine of collateral estoppel, made applicable to the state as being within the federal constitutional right against double jeopardy by Ashe v Swenson, 397 US 436, 90 SCt 1189, 25 LEd(2d) 469 (1970). Owens v. Campbell (Ohio 1971) 27 Ohio St.2d 264, 272 N.E.2d 116, 56 O.O.2d 158. Courts ⚷ 206(15.1)

Since the jury in defendant's first trial had acquitted him due to insufficient evidence, the state under the doctrine of collateral estoppel was constitutionally foreclosed from relitigating that issue in another trial arising out of the same robbery incident. Ashe v. Swenson (U.S.Mo. 1970) 90 S.Ct. 1189, 397 U.S. 436, 25 L.Ed.2d 469.

5. Dual sovereignty doctrine

Conviction of an individual by two states on the basis of the same act is not forbidden by US Const Am 5 as a second jeopardy "for the same offense," since the act is a distinct "offense" against each sovereign whose law it violates. Heath v. Alabama (U.S.Ala. 1985) 106 S.Ct. 433, 474 U.S. 82, 88 L.Ed.2d 387.

6. Rights of accused

Where a plea of guilty is entered by an accused, the failure to file a written waiver of jury does not deprive the accused of any of his constitutional rights or the court of jurisdiction. Click v. Eckle (Ohio 1962) 174 Ohio St. 88, 186 N.E.2d 731, 21 O.O.2d 343. Jury ⚷ 29(4); Jury ⚷ 31.3(1)

2943.06 Trial of issue on plea of former conviction

If a defendant pleads a judgment of conviction, acquittal, or former jeopardy, the prosecuting attorney may reply that there is no such conviction, acquittal, or jeopardy. The issue thus made shall be tried to a jury, and on such trial the defendant must produce the record of such conviction, acquittal, or jeopardy, and prove that he is the person charged in such record, and he may also introduce other evidence to establish the identity of such offense. If the prosecuting attorney demurs to said plea and said demurrer is overruled, the prosecuting attorney may then reply to said plea.

(1953 H 1, eff. 10–1–53; GC 13440–5)

Historical and Statutory Notes

Pre–1953 H 1 Amendments: 113 v 176, Ch 19, § 5

Cross References

Pleadings and motions before trial, defenses and objections, Crim R 12

Library References

Criminal Law ⚷296.

Westlaw Topic No. 110.

C.J.S. Criminal Law § 381.

Notes of Decisions

1. Constitutional issues

Administrative license suspension (ALS) ceases to be remedial and becomes punitive in nature to the extent that the suspension continues subsequent to adjudication and sentencing for driving under the influence (DUI) and thus, double jeopardy clauses of the Federal and State Constitutions preclude continued recognition of ALS following judicial imposition of criminal penalties for DUI. State v. Gustafson (Ohio, 07-30-1996) 76 Ohio St.3d 425, 668 N.E.2d 435, 1996-Ohio-425. Double Jeopardy ⚷ 24

There is no constitutional provision prohibiting a three man court in a case where the defendant is charged with murder in the first degree on a plea of guilty to the crime of homicide to determine the degree of guilt without the intervention of a jury. State v. Ferguson (Cuyahoga 1962) 119 Ohio App. 393, 184 N.E.2d 241, 89 Ohio Law Abs. 321, 28 O.O.2d 18, affirmed 175 Ohio St. 390, 195 N.E.2d 794, 25 O.O.2d 383, certiorari denied 84 S.Ct. 1938, 377 U.S. 1002, 12 L.Ed.2d 1051.

A state is not prohibited by the Double Jeopardy Clause from continuing a prosecution that was stopped by the trial court's acceptance, over objection of the state, of the defendant's plea of guilty to a lesser included or allied offense stemming from the same incident. Ohio v. Johnson (U.S.Ohio 1984) 104 S.Ct. 2536, 467 U.S. 493, 81 L.Ed.2d 425, rehearing denied 105 S.Ct. 20, 468 U.S. 1224, 82 L.Ed.2d 915, on remand.

Where a victim dies after a defendant has been convicted of felonious assault against him, a subsequent prosecution for murder is not barred by the Double Jeopardy Clause. State v Carpenter, No. 88AP–860 (10th Dist Ct App, Franklin, 3–14–89).

2. Jeopardy, defined

Where two persons were killed during the same controversy by different bullets discharged from a gun in the hands of the defendant, two indictments each charging the unlawful killing of one of such persons do not charge the "same offense" within Const. Art. I, § 10, providing that no person shall be twice put in jeopardy for the same "offense." State v. Billotto (Ohio 1922) 104 Ohio St. 13, 135 N.E. 285, 19 Ohio Law Rep. 548. Double Jeopardy ⚷ 182

Where accused conspired to steal certain automobiles and his confederate stole them at different times, each theft was a distinct and separate offense, and after an acquittal on a charge of one theft his trial for another did not place him twice in jeopardy. Patterson v. State (Ohio 1917) 96 Ohio St. 90, 117 N.E. 169, 15 Ohio Law Rep. 84, 15 Ohio Law Rep. 104. Double Jeopardy ⚷ 152; Larceny ⚷ 26

The capital sentencing procedure in Arizona, which provides a trial judge with exact guidelines for choosing between two sentencing options, constitutes a trial for double jeopardy purposes, and therefore the state may not sentence a defendant to death after the appellate court sets aside the life sentence initially imposed by a trial judge who misinterpreted the statute on capital punishment in the defendant's favor. (Ed. note: Arizona law construed in light of federal constitution.) Arizona v. Rumsey (U.S.Ariz. 1984) 104 S.Ct. 2305, 467 U.S. 203, 81 L.Ed.2d 164.

3. When jeopardy attaches

For double jeopardy purposes, jeopardy "attaches," so as to preclude subsequent criminal proceedings, at different points in time depending on nature of the proceeding in question. State v. Gustafson (Ohio, 07-30-1996) 76 Ohio St.3d 425, 668 N.E.2d 435, 1996-Ohio-425. Double Jeopardy ⚷ 51

Insofar as double jeopardy clause precludes successive criminal prosecutions, the proscription is against a second criminal trial after jeopardy has attached in a first criminal trial. State v. Gustafson (Ohio, 07-30-1996) 76 Ohio St.3d 425, 668 N.E.2d 435, 1996-Ohio-425. Double Jeopardy ⚷ 51

Where defendant has invoked the right to trial by jury, jeopardy does not attach so as to preclude subsequent criminal proceedings pursuant to double jeopardy clause until the jury is impaneled and sworn. State v. Gustafson (Ohio, 07-30-1996) 76 Ohio St.3d 425, 668 N.E.2d 435, 1996-Ohio-425. Double Jeopardy ⚷ 59

For double jeopardy purposes, jeopardy does not attach in criminal bench trial until the court begins to hear evidence and in other situations, jeopardy based on having undergone initial criminal trial attaches after acquittal or conviction. State v. Gustafson (Ohio, 07-30-1996) 76 Ohio St.3d 425, 668 N.E.2d 435, 1996-Ohio-425. Double Jeopardy ⚷ 59; Double Jeopardy ⚷ 60.1

In a non-jury case, a person has been placed in jeopardy when the accused is brought to trial and the court begins to hear evidence, even though the evidence does not bear directly on the guilt or innocence of the defendant. State v. Bryant (Ohio Mun. 1971) 31 Ohio Misc. 230, 277 N.E.2d 264, 57 O.O.2d 92, 60 O.O.2d 391.

4. Asserting double jeopardy

Trial court's prior ten-day sentence of incarceration of defendant for contempt based on failure to pay child support was civil in nature, and thus the one day he served of sentence did not bar on double jeopardy grounds state from subsequently bringing charges against defendant for criminal nonsupport of dependents, where civil order was suspended on condition that defendant pay portion of his monthly support and arrearage obligation, sentence was remedial in nature, and defendant could have avoided incarceration by complying with conditions of suspension. State v. Palmer (Ohio App. 2 Dist., Montgomery, 02-20-2004) No. 19921, 2004-Ohio-779, 2004 WL 316505, Unreported. Double Jeopardy ⚷ 34

Administrative license suspension (ALS) does not constitute a proceeding to which jeopardy attaches and thus, double jeopardy clauses of the Federal and State Constitution do not preclude criminal prosecution and trial of motorists for driving under the influence of alcohol (DUI) based upon, and subsequent to, the imposition of ALS; criminal prosecution after immediate ALS does not result in defendant being subjected to a second "trial" because he has not undergone a first "trial." State v. Gustafson (Ohio, 07-30-1996) 76 Ohio St.3d 425, 668 N.E.2d 435, 1996-Ohio-425. Double Jeopardy ⚷ 24

Administrative license suspension (ALS) and criminal driving under the influence (DUI) prosecution arising out of the same arrest constitute "separate" proceedings for double jeopardy purposes; suspension of driver's license becomes administrative fait accompli at time the license is physically seized by arresting officer, fact that General Assembly has provided opportunity for postsuspension administrative appeal of ALS in the court in which DUI charges are filed does not change this conclusion, and although administrative appeal of ALS may be presided over by the same judge as presides over the DUI case, that circumstance does not consolidate the ALS and DUI prosecution into the "same proceeding" for double jeopardy purposes. State v. Gustafson (Ohio, 07-30-1996) 76 Ohio St.3d 425, 668 N.E.2d 435, 1996-Ohio-425. Double Jeopardy ⚷ 24

Administrative license suspension (ALS), whether based on a test failure or test refusal, is a sanction based on the same offense or conduct as is subsequent prosecution on a charge of driving under the influence (DUI) for purposes of double jeopardy prohibition against multiple punishments for the same offense. State v. Gustafson (Ohio, 07-30-1996) 76 Ohio St.3d 425, 668 N.E.2d 435, 1996-Ohio-425. Double Jeopardy ⚷ 24

Administrative license suspensions (ALS) are, at least in their initial application, remedial in purpose and, thus, do not ab initio constitute "punishment" for double jeopardy purposes; however, while ALS in its initial application serves the goal of remediation, it may be applied so as to primarily serve goals of "punishment." State v. Gustafson (Ohio, 07-30-1996) 76 Ohio St.3d 425, 668 N.E.2d 435, 1996-Ohio-425. Double Jeopardy ⚷ 24

An indictment in the words of the prohibitory statute which alleges the obscenity of a film without naming it by its title and without setting forth the separate elements of obscenity does not prevent the defendant from successfully asserting a plea of double jeopardy and does not, by reason of such alleged deficiency, require the sustaining of a motion to quash. State v. Boyd (Allen 1972) 35 Ohio App.2d 147, 300 N.E.2d 752, 64 O.O.2d 260, certiorari denied 94 S.Ct. 3230, 418 U.S. 954, 41 L.Ed.2d 1175.

An order overruling an oral motion for release of a defendant on grounds of double jeopardy is not a final order. State v. Downey (Cuyahoga 1960) 113 Ohio App. 250, 170 N.E.2d 75, 85 Ohio Law Abs. 253, 17 O.O.2d 227, appeal dismissed 171 Ohio St. 565, 173 N.E.2d 106, 15 O.O.2d 42.

5. Hearing on plea

Where the state did not object to the trial court hearing on oral argument, without evidence being adduced, defendant's plea of once in jeopardy, the state cannot appeal an order finding the plea well taken and dismissing the indictment. State v. Boyle (Lucas 1972) 32 Ohio App.2d 255, 289 N.E.2d 913, 61 O.O.2d 285.

Where the prosecuting attorney files no demurrer or reply to a defendant's plea of former jeopardy pursuant to RC 2943.06, the issue of former jeopardy need not be tried by jury. State v. Bryant (Ohio Mun. 1971) 31 Ohio Misc. 230, 277 N.E.2d 264, 57 O.O.2d 92, 60 O.O.2d 391.

2943.07 What is not former acquittal

If a defendant was formerly acquitted on the ground of variance between the indictment or information and the proof, or if the indictment or information was dismissed, without a judgment of acquittal, upon an objection to its form or substance, or in order to hold the defendant for a higher offense, it is not an acquittal of the same offense.

(1953 H 1, eff. 10–1–53; GC 13440–6)

Historical and Statutory Notes

Pre–1953 H 1 Amendments: 113 v 176, Ch 19, § 6

Cross References

Double jeopardy, O Const Art I §10

Motion to discharge jury after amending of substance of indictment or where proof varies from charge; jeopardy does not attach, Crim R 7

Pleadings and motions before trial, defenses and objections, Crim R 12

Library References

Double Jeopardy ⚟103, 104.
Westlaw Topic No. 135H.
C.J.S. Criminal Law §§ 225, 230, 238.

Notes of Decisions

---

1. Constitutional issues

Former GC 13440–6 (RC 2943.07) and 13440–7 (RC 2943.08) are not violative of the Due Process Clause of US Const Am 14. Eastman v. State (Ohio 1936) 131 Ohio St. 1, 1 N.E.2d 140, 5 O.O. 248, appeal dismissed 57 S.Ct. 21, 299 U.S. 505, 81 L.Ed. 374.

2. Separate criminal acts

The fact that a defendant has been put in jeopardy upon a trial for one criminal act is no bar to a prosecution for a separate and distinct criminal act merely because they are closely connected in point of time, place and circumstance. (See also Halper v State, 36 App 331, 173 NE 253 (1930).) Dodge v. State (Ohio 1932) 124 Ohio St. 580, 180 N.E. 45, 81 A.L.R. 699, 11 Ohio Law Abs. 320, 36 Ohio Law Rep. 44.

Different offenses of the same character may be charged under one indictment, but they must be separately and distinctly numbered and stated; each offense cannot be added to the others and a sentence made upon the total. Halper v. State (Cuyahoga 1930) 36 Ohio App. 331, 173 N.E. 253, 8 Ohio Law Abs. 368, 32 Ohio Law Rep. 235. Indictment And Information ⚟ 130

3. Demurrer sustained

Trial court ruling discharging a defendant and sustaining demurrer to an indictment on the ground that a director of a bank is not an officer thereof within the purview of GC 710–174 (RC 1115.21), is not an acquittal on the merits under GC 13440–6 (RC 2943.07) and 13440–7 (RC 2943.08). Eastman v. State (Ohio 1936) 131 Ohio St. 1, 1 N.E.2d 140, 5 O.O. 248, appeal dismissed 57 S.Ct. 21, 299 U.S. 505, 81 L.Ed. 374.

4. Dismissal for delay

When a defendant deliberately chooses to seek termination of the proceedings against him by moving to dismiss the indictment because of prejudice due to delay, he suffers no injury under the Double Jeopardy Clause if the government is permitted to appeal from the trial court's ruling in favor of the defendant. U.S. v. Scott (U.S.Mich. 1978) 98 S.Ct. 2187, 437 U.S. 82, 57 L.Ed.2d 65, on remand 579 F.2d 1013, rehearing denied 99 S.Ct. 226, 439 U.S. 883, 58 L.Ed.2d 197. Criminal Law ⚟ 1024(2)

5. Mistrial

The Double Jeopardy Clause cannot be used to bar a retrial, where the defendant successfully moves for a mistrial on the basis of prosecutorial misconduct, unless the offending conduct was intended to provoke the mistrial motion. Oregon v. Kennedy (U.S.Or. 1982) 102 S.Ct. 2083, 456 U.S. 667, 72 L.Ed.2d 416, on remand 61 Or.App. 469, 657 P.2d 717.

6. Reversal on weight or sufficiency of evidence

The Double Jeopardy Clause does not bar a retrial of a defendant whose conviction is reversed on appeal due to weight of evidence as opposed to sufficiency of evidence. Tibbs v. Florida (U.S.Fla. 1982) 102 S.Ct. 2211, 457 U.S. 31, 72 L.Ed.2d 652.

2943.08 What is former acquittal

Whenever a defendant is acquitted on the merits, he is acquitted of the same offense, notwithstanding any defect in form or substance in the indictment or information on which the trial was had.

(1953 H 1, eff. 10–1–53; GC 13440–7)

Historical and Statutory Notes

Pre–1953 H 1 Amendments: 113 v 176, Ch 19, § 7

Cross References

Double jeopardy, O Const Art I §10

Library References

Double Jeopardy ⚟103, 104.
Westlaw Topic No. 135H.
C.J.S. Criminal Law §§ 225, 230, 238.

Research References

Encyclopedias

OH Jur. 3d Criminal Law § 750, Acquittal on Merits Under Defective Indictment or Information.

Notes of Decisions

1. Constitutional issues

GC 13440–6 (RC 2943.07) and this section, are not violative of the Due Process Clause of US Const Am 14. Eastman v. State (Ohio 1936) 131 Ohio St. 1, 1 N.E.2d 140, 5 O.O. 248, appeal dismissed 57 S.Ct. 21, 299 U.S. 505, 81 L.Ed. 374.

2. Separate criminal acts

An acquittal of a municipal zoning ordinance violation is not former jeopardy of a charge of a violation of a different zoning ordinance on a different day. Carsey v. City of Mansfield (Richland 1973) 37 Ohio App.2d 141, 310 N.E.2d 263, 66 O.O.2d 361. Double Jeopardy ⚷ 152

2943.09 Conviction or acquittal of a higher offense

When a defendant has been convicted or acquitted, or has been once in jeopardy upon an indictment or information, the conviction, acquittal, or jeopardy is a bar to another indictment or information for the offense charged in the former indictment or information, or for an attempt to commit the same offense, or for an offense necessarily included therein, of which he might have been convicted under the former indictment or information.

(1953 H 1, eff. 10–1–53; GC 13440–8)

Historical and Statutory Notes

Pre–1953 H 1 Amendments: 113 v 176, Ch 19, § 8

Cross References

Pleadings and motions before trial, defenses and objections, Crim R 12

Library References

Double Jeopardy ⚷164.
Westlaw Topic No. 135H.
C.J.S. Criminal Law § 251.

Research References

Encyclopedias

OH Jur. 3d Criminal Law § 787, Jeopardy on Greater Offense as Bar to Prosecution for Lesser.

Law Review and Journal Commentaries

Government Appeals of Sentence: Double Talk with the Double Jeopardy Clause?, Comment. 9 Ohio N U L Rev 385 (1982).

Notes of Decisions

1. Lesser included offenses

Trial court cannot find defendant not guilty of specific crime in one count and then attempt to convict defendant on same crime as lesser included offense of a separate offense. State v. Gary (Ohio App. 8 Dist., 12-20-1996) 117 Ohio App.3d 286, 690 N.E.2d 572. Criminal Law ⚩ 878(3)

Generally, trial court may enter judgment of conviction on offense which is lesser included offense, offense of inferior degree, or attempt to commit greater charged offense. State v. Peek (Ohio App. 1 Dist., 03-29-1996) 110 Ohio App.3d 165, 673 N.E.2d 938. Indictment And Information ⚩ 189(1); Indictment And Information ⚩ 191(.5)

Felonious assault of a peace officer is not a lesser included offense of attempted aggravated murder; thus, a conviction for felonious assault of a peace officer does not bar a subsequent retrial for attempted aggravated murder. State v. Hague (Summit 1989) 61 Ohio App.3d 756, 573 N.E.2d 1150, motion overruled 45 Ohio St.3d 704, 543 N.E.2d 810.

Where in a prosecution for first degree murder it was discovered after submission of some evidence but before submission of the matter to the jury that the indictment was so defective as to fail to charge first or second degree murder, but that it did charge manslaughter, the defendant has been placed in jeopardy and may not thereafter be tried for murder. State v. McGraw (Ohio Com.Pl. 1961) 177 N.E.2d 697, 86 Ohio Law Abs. 490, 19 O.O.2d 174.

2. Same transaction; same evidence

The rule as to former jeopardy under the US Const Am 5, is that, where the same act or transaction constitutes a violation of a distinct provision of an Ohio statute and a distinct provision of a city ordinance, the test to be applied to determine whether there are two offenses or only one is whether each provision requires proof of a fact which the other does not; a single act may be an offense against both the ordinance and the statute, and, if the statute requires proof of an additional fact which the ordinance does not, an acquittal or conviction under the ordinance does not exempt the defendant from prosecution and punishment under the statute. State v. Ikner (Ohio 1975) 44 Ohio St.2d 132, 339 N.E.2d 633, 73 O.O.2d 444. Double Jeopardy ⚩ 135

A defendant convicted of vehicular homicide may not thereafter be prosecuted for violating a municipal ordinance prohibiting drunken driving, but may be prosecuted for violating a municipal assured clear distance ordinance. State v. Best (Ohio 1975) 42 Ohio St.2d 530, 330 N.E.2d 421, 71 O.O.2d 517.

Both US Const Am 14 and O Const Art I §10, proscribe prosecution in Ohio after federal jeopardy for same act. State v. Fletcher (Cuyahoga 1970) 22 Ohio App.2d 83, 259 N.E.2d 146, 51 O.O.2d 183, reversed 26 Ohio St.2d 221, 271 N.E.2d 567, 55 O.O.2d 464, certiorari denied 92 S.Ct. 699, 404 U.S. 1024, 30 L.Ed.2d 675.

Where offenses charged are separate and distinct, either with respect to statutory definition or because, as charged, they grow out of different transactions and different evidence is needed to prove each, the constitutional inhibition against double jeopardy is not applicable; and, so long as the offenses charged are not factually inconsistent, an accused may be found guilty and sentenced as to each of the offenses charged. State v. Johnson (Cuyahoga 1960) 112 Ohio App. 124, 165 N.E.2d 814, 83 Ohio Law Abs. 437, 16 O.O.2d 51. Double Jeopardy ⚩ 132.1

RC 2941.04 cannot be construed to permit a defendant to be charged with and found guilty at one trial of two offenses when, if tried separately, conviction of one offense would be a bar to conviction thereafter of the other. State v. Johnson (Cuyahoga 1960) 112 Ohio App. 124, 165 N.E.2d 814, 83 Ohio Law Abs. 437, 16 O.O.2d 51.

3. Corrected complaint

The Double Jeopardy Clause does not bar the second trial of a criminal defendant under a new but corrected complaint for the same offense after the court dismisses the first complaint for failure to state an offense following the testimony of the first witness. City of Oakwood v. Ramnath (Montgomery 1987) 35 Ohio App.3d 156, 520 N.E.2d 261. Double Jeopardy ⚩ 91(1)

4. Dual sovereignty doctrine

The conviction or acquittal of a defendant in a federal court on charges of violation of federal law is not a bar to criminal prosecution in Ohio courts for violation of Ohio penal statutes, where both prosecutions relate to and arise from the same criminal acts. State v. Fletcher (Ohio 1971) 26 Ohio St.2d 221, 271 N.E.2d 567, 55 O.O.2d 464, certiorari denied 92 S.Ct. 699, 404 U.S. 1024, 30 L.Ed.2d 675. Double Jeopardy ⚩ 186

5. Attachment of jeopardy

Trial court's reversal of its decision acquitting defendant on all 4 firearm specifications was error even though there was evidence to show the use of a firearm in count 3 of the indictment, court's judgment of acquittal concludes a pending prosecution in which jeopardy attaches. State v Klopp, No. 63243, 1993 WL 290135 (8th Dist Ct App, Cuyahoga, 7–29–93).

2943.10 Proceedings after verdict on plea in bar

If the issue on the plea in bar under section 2943.06 of the Revised Code is found for the defendant he shall be discharged. If the issue is found against the defendant the case shall proceed and be disposed of upon his other pleas.

(1953 H 1, eff. 10–1–53; GC 13440–9)

Historical and Statutory Notes

Pre–1953 H 1 Amendments: 113 v 177, Ch 19, § 9

Library References

Criminal Law ⚷289.
Westlaw Topic No. 110.
C.J.S. Criminal Law § 381.

Research References

Encyclopedias

OH Jur. 3d Family Law § 1730, What is an Appealable Order.

Treatises and Practice Aids

Katz, Giannelli, Blair and Lipton, Baldwin's Ohio Practice, Criminal Law, § 143:9, Motion to Dismiss—Double Jeopardy.

CHAPTER 2945

TRIAL

PRELIMINARY PROVISIONS

TRIAL

Section

WITNESSES

2945.41 Rules applicable in criminal cases
2945.42 Competency of witnesses
2945.43 Defendant may testify
2945.44 Court of common pleas to grant transactional immunity; procedure; exceptions
2945.45 Subpoenas to issue to any county
2945.451 Employee's attendance at proceeding in criminal case under subpoena; employer may not penalize
2945.46 Attendance of witness enforced
2945.47 Testimony of prisoners in criminal proceedings
2945.48 Witness may be placed in jail
2945.481 Deposition of child sex offense victim; presence of defendant; additional depositions; videotaped deposition; admissibility of deposition; televised or recorded testimony
2945.482 Testimony of mentally retarded or developmentally disabled victim
2945.49 Testimony of deceased or absent witness; videotaped testimony of child victim
2945.491 Testimony of mentally retarded or developmentally disabled victim; videotaped testimony
2945.50 Deposition in criminal cases
2945.51 When deposition may be taken; expenses
2945.52 Counsel appointed shall represent the defendant
2945.53 Right of accused to examine witness
2945.54 Conduct of examination
2945.55 Testimony of previous identification
2945.56 Rebuttal of defendant's character evidence
2945.57 Number of witnesses to character

ALIBI

2945.58 Alibi

PROOF

2945.59 Proof of defendant's motive
2945.60 to 2945.63 Proof in cases of treason, unauthorized military expedition, perjury, and seduction—Repealed
2945.64 Prima–facie evidence of embezzlement

BILL OF EXCEPTIONS

2945.65 and 2945.66 Bill of exceptions; proceedings on filing—Repealed
2945.67 When prosecutor may appeal; when public defender to oppose
2945.68 Application by prosecutor, solicitor, or attorney general to file bill of exceptions—Repealed
2945.69 and 2945.70 Appointment of attorney by trial judge; decision of the court; appeal by the state—Repealed

SCHEDULE OF TRIAL AND HEARINGS

2945.71 Time within which hearing or trial must be held
2945.72 Extension of time for hearing or trial
2945.73 Discharge for delay in trial

DEGREE OF OFFENSE

2945.74 Defendant may be convicted of lesser offense
2945.75 Degree of offense; charge and verdict; prior convictions
2945.76 Circumstances for acquittal for carrying concealed weapon—Repealed

POST TRIAL PROCEDURE

2945.77 Polling jury
2945.78 Recording the verdict
2945.79 Causes for new trial
2945.80 Application for new trial
2945.81 Causes to be sustained by affidavits
2945.82 New trial
2945.83 When new trial shall not be granted
2945.831 Motion not necessary for appellate review
2945.832 Taking and recording exceptions—Repealed

Cross References

Rules of evidence and procedure, 2938.15

PRELIMINARY PROVISIONS

2945.01 Definition of magistrate

The definition of "magistrate" set forth in section 2931.01 of the Revised Code applies to Chapter 2945. of the Revised Code.

(1953 H 1, eff. 10–1–53)

Law Review and Journal Commentaries

The Rights of a Hearing–Impaired Litigant, Kenneth S. Resuick and Eleanor M. Stromberg. 8 Ohio Law 12 (March/April 1994).

2945.02 Setting and continuing cases

The court of common pleas shall set all criminal cases for trial for a day not later than thirty days after the date of entry of the plea of the defendant. No continuance of the trial shall be granted except upon affirmative proof in open court, upon reasonable notice, that the ends of justice require a continuance.

No continuance shall be granted for any other time than it is affirmatively proved the ends of justice require.

Whenever any continuance is granted, the court shall enter on the journal the reason for the same.

Criminal cases shall be given precedence over civil matters and proceedings. The failure of the court to set such criminal cases for trial, as required by this section, does not operate as an acquittal, but upon notice of such failure or upon motion of the prosecuting attorney or a defendant, such case shall forthwith be set for trial within a reasonable time, not exceeding thirty days thereafter.

(1953 H 1, eff. 10–1–53; GC 13442–1)

Historical and Statutory Notes

Pre–1953 H 1 Amendments: 113 v 178, Ch 21, § 1

Cross References

Criminal cases to have precedence over civil, Crim R 50

Magistrate courts, setting and continuing cases in, assignment of additional judges, 2938.03

Proceedings when indictments are returned, 2939.22

Speedy trial, continuances, discharge for delay, 2945.71 to 2945.73

Time, Crim R 45

Library References

Criminal Law ⚷577.5, 689, 632.

Westlaw Topic No. 110.

C.J.S. Criminal Law §§ 448 to 449, 455 to 458, 591 to 592, 599, 602, 1144, 1223.

Research References

Encyclopedias

OH Jur. 3d Criminal Law § 2574, Effect of Failure to Set Case for Trial.

Treatises and Practice Aids

Markus, Trial Handbook for Ohio Lawyers, § 4:7, Speedy Trial—Statutory Time Limits—Inapplicability.

Giannelli and Snyder, Baldwin's Ohio Practice, Evidence, R 611, Mode and Order of Interrogation and Presentation.

Giannelli and Snyder, Baldwin's Ohio Practice, Evidence, § 611.6, Continuances.

Law Review and Journal Commentaries

The Municipal Court Misdemeanor Arraignment Procedure of Hamilton County, Ohio: An Empirical Study, Note. 41 U Cin L Rev 623 (1972).

Notes of Decisions

---

1. In general

Granting of continuance is within discretion of trial court. State v. McMillen (Ohio App. 3 Dist., 06-26-1996) 113 Ohio App.3d 137, 680 N.E.2d 665. Criminal Law 🔑 586

Factors to be considered in determining whether to grant continuance requested by party include length of continuance requested, any prior continuance, inconvenience, reasons for delay, and whether defendant contributed to delay. Village of Glenwillow v. Tomsick (Ohio App. 8 Dist., 06-17-1996) 111 Ohio App.3d 718, 676 N.E.2d 1259. Criminal Law 🔑 578

Grant or denial of motion for continuance is matter within sound discretion of trial court. State v. Blankenship (Ohio App. 12 Dist., 04-17-1995) 102 Ohio App.3d 534, 657 N.E.2d 559, dismissed, appeal not allowed 73 Ohio St.3d 1426, 652 N.E.2d 799, denial of post-conviction relief affirmed 1995 WL 746232, dismissed, appeal not allowed 75 Ohio St.3d 1484, 664 N.E.2d 536, denial of post-conviction relief affirmed 74 Ohio St.3d 522, 660 N.E.2d 448, 1996-Ohio-58, denial of post-conviction relief affirmed 1997 WL 700073, dismissed, appeal not allowed 81 Ohio St.3d 1466, 690 N.E.2d 1287. Criminal Law 🔑 586

When reviewing trial court's decision regarding motion for continuance, reviewing court must weigh potential prejudice to defendant against trial court's right to control its own docket and public's interest in the prompt and efficient dispatch of justice. State v. Blankenship (Ohio App. 12 Dist., 04-17-1995) 102 Ohio App.3d 534, 657 N.E.2d 559, dismissed, appeal not allowed 73 Ohio St.3d 1426, 652 N.E.2d 799, denial of post-conviction relief affirmed 1995 WL 746232, dismissed, appeal not allowed 75 Ohio St.3d 1484, 664 N.E.2d 536, denial of post-conviction relief affirmed 74 Ohio St.3d 522, 660 N.E.2d 448, 1996-Ohio-58, denial of post-conviction relief affirmed 1997 WL 700073, dismissed, appeal not allowed 81 Ohio St.3d 1466, 690 N.E.2d 1287. Criminal Law 🔑 1134(3)

2. Continuance allowed

State was properly granted continuance in prosecution for felonious assault to secure complaining witness following witness's failure to return one afternoon, state proffered evidence that witness was material witness and had been willing to testify, and continuance was for limited duration. State v. Bean (Ohio App. 2 Dist., Montgomery, 06-06-2003) No. 19483, 2003-Ohio-2962, 2003 WL 21344620, Unreported. Criminal Law 🔑 594(3); Criminal Law 🔑 595(4)

Where defendant is charged with DUI and retains counsel, but this counsel fails to appear at the pretrial or trial, the trial court abuses its discretion in denying the defendant's motion for a continuance where (1) the defendant faces substantial jail time and loss of driving privileges, and (2) the trial court conducted a minimal inquiry into the circumstances of counsel's failure to appear. State v. Rosser (Ohio App. 9 Dist., Summit, 06-15-1994) No. 16455, 1994 WL 263207, Unreported.

Although clerk of court should not have advised defense counsel and prosecutor that trial continuance would be granted without prior judicial authorization to do so, no reversible error occurred thereby, as trial court independently considered and granted state's continuance request in a reasonable exercise of its discretion. Village of Glenwillow v. Tomsick (Ohio App. 8 Dist., 06-17-1996) 111 Ohio App.3d 718, 676 N.E.2d 1259. Criminal Law 🔑 578; Criminal Law 🔑 1166(7)

The allowance of a continuance is a matter that is entrusted to the sound discretion of the trial court, which should consider factors such as length of delay, inconvenience, the reason for the continuance and other relevant factors; therefore, where the defense asks for a continuance of under an hour to wait for a witness who was improperly subpoenaed and there is no inconvenience to anyone, the trial court abuses its discretion in denying a continuance and refusing to allow the testimony. State v. Holmes (Franklin 1987) 36 Ohio App.3d 44, 521 N.E.2d 479.

3. Continuance denied—In general

Defendant was not entitled to continuance based on amendment to indictment to correct the year the offenses at issue were allegedly committed; date of offenses was not an element of crimes, date originally shown in indictment was two months after defendant had been arrested and arraigned for the offenses, and police incident report in trial record indicated the correct date. State v. Mays (Ohio App. 11 Dist., Trumbull, 01-10-2003) No. 2001-T-0071, 2003-Ohio-63, 2003 WL 99535, Unreported, appeal not allowed 99 Ohio St.3d 1409, 788 N.E.2d 646, 2003-Ohio-2454. Criminal Law 🔑 589(1)

Trial court abused its discretion in failing to grant continuance in kidnapping prosecution when prosecutor failed to disclose address of complainant until day before trial, despite contention that there was no prejudice because complainant refused to discuss the case with counsel during attempting interview of morning of trial; noncompliance with discovery requirements was willful, lack of knowledge of address prevented defense counsel from speaking with complainant's neighbors or associates, and only evidence of attempted sexual activity as alleged in the indictment was the testimony of the complainant. State v. Parks (Montgomery 1990) 69 Ohio App.3d 150, 590 N.E.2d 300. Criminal Law ⚩ 589(1)

The denial of a continuance is neither unreasonable, arbitrary, nor unconscionable where (1) the defendant was present with appointed counsel on the date of trial, (2) the trial had been continued at defendant's request once before, (3) the state had been ready to proceed with its witnesses once before and this was the second time it was ready, (4) the request for a continuance did not reflect the specific time necessary for the delay, and (5) the need for the delay was attributable to the defendant (the defendant chose private counsel who was unavailable on the date of trial, knowing him to be unavailable). State v. Jones (Wayne 1987) 42 Ohio App.3d 14, 535 N.E.2d 1372. Criminal Law ⚩ 593; Criminal Law ⚩ 614(1)

4. —— Availability of counsel, continuance denied

Denial of defendant's request for a continuance due to illness of co-counsel was not an abuse of discretion in prosecution for rape and gross sexual imposition, where defense counsel did not indicate length of delay requested, defense counsel had previously requested and received two continuances, and rescheduling of trial would have been inconvenient, as case involved many witnesses. State v. Wagner (Ohio App. 5 Dist., Licking, 07-26-2004) No. 03 CA 82, 2004-Ohio-3941, 2004 WL 1672200, Unreported, appeal not allowed 104 Ohio St.3d 1426, 819 N.E.2d 709, 2004-Ohio-6585, appeal after new sentencing hearing 2005-Ohio-3821, 2005 WL 1785105, appeal allowed 107 Ohio St.3d 1681, 839 N.E.2d 402, 2005-Ohio-6480, reversed 109 Ohio St.3d 313, 847 N.E.2d 1174, 2006-Ohio-2109. Criminal Law ⚩ 589(2)

Defendant was not entitled to grant of motion for continuance, brought at the commencement of trial, based on claimed strained relationship with his attorney; trial date was set several months before trial was to commence, there had never been any indication of problems regarding defendant's relationship with attorney, no other attorney had been retained by defendant, and counsel indicated he was prepared to try the case. State v. Mays (Ohio App. 11 Dist., Trumbull, 01-10-2003) No. 2001-T-0071, 2003-Ohio-63, 2003 WL 99535, Unreported, appeal not allowed 99 Ohio St.3d 1409, 788 N.E.2d 646, 2003-Ohio-2454. Criminal Law ⚩ 593

Denial of defendant's motion for continuance of pretrial suppression hearing, when his retained counsel was unable to appear because of prior commitment, constituted abuse of discretion, where defendant had neither requested nor received any other continuances, was not seeking lengthy continuance, and sought continuance only for legitimate purpose of permitting him to exercise his constitutionally guaranteed right to counsel. Hudson v. South (Ohio App. 9 Dist., 12-14-1994) 99 Ohio App.3d 208, 650 N.E.2d 172. Criminal Law ⚩ 394.6(5)

Defendant waived right to counsel and, therefore, was not entitled to second continuance to obtain counsel after he had been granted continuance for purpose of seeking counsel; defendant was experienced with court system, knew nature of charges, knew scheduled trial date well in advance, had more than one month to obtain counsel after he was first summoned to court, and filed second motion for continuance on date of trial. State v. Crebs (Wayne 1987) 42 Ohio App.3d 50, 536 N.E.2d 52. Criminal Law ⚩ 593; Criminal Law ⚩ 614(1)

Where accused and his counsel jointly made motion requesting appointment of new counsel due to inability of counsel to properly represent defendant under circumstances, refusal of court to grant continuance for purpose of acquisition of new counsel constituted prejudicial error mandating reversal of subsequent conviction. State v. Bronaugh (Hamilton 1982) 3 Ohio App.3d 307, 445 N.E.2d 262, 3 O.B.R. 354. Criminal Law ⚩ 589(1); Criminal Law ⚩ 1166(7)

There was no abuse of discretion by trial judge in refusing a third continuance asked for by reason of illness of counsel. Stansbery v. State (Ohio 1932) 125 Ohio St. 150, 180 N.E. 711.

5. —— Availability of witnesses, continuance denied

Trial court acted within its discretion in denying defendant's request for second continuance during trial to procure witness; trial court had already granted continuance for defendant to produce witness, it was unclear how long that it would take to produce witness, given that witness had twice failed to appear, and defendant was not effectively deprived of any testimony, in that testimony on same matter to which witness would have testified was already elicited at trial from another witness. State v. Wright (Ohio App. 9 Dist., Summit, 05-04-2005) No. 22314, 2005-Ohio-2158, 2005 WL 1026498, Unreported. Criminal Law ⚩ 614(2)

Trial court acted within its discretion in denying defendant's requests for continuance to hire court-appointed psychologist and for court-appointed psychologist to assist him in sexual-predator hearing, even though defendant argued that he did not receive court-ordered examiner's report until shortly before hearing and that court-appointed psychologist was required to review that report; defendant made request days before hearing but could have sought to hire court-appointed psychologist after he was examined by court-appointed examiner more than one month before hearing, and defendant suffered little or no prejudice as result of trial court's denial of court-appointed psychologist. State v. Thomas (Ohio App. 2 Dist., Greene, 04-01-2005) No. 2004-CA-73, 2005-Ohio-1596, 2005 WL 742510, Unreported. Mental Health 🔑 469(4)

Defendant was not entitled to a continuance in order to locate a witness; at pretrial, defendant did not estimate how long it would take to locate witness, defendant was not sure of name of the witness he was looking for, defendant did not offer a reason why he was looking for this witness, defendant did not request a continuance at commencement of trial, and it was not until the State presented its evidence and defendant testified that defense counsel raised the issue of witness' testimony and his alleged appearance, but defense counsel did not renew his motion for continuance when trial court gave him an opportunity to do so. State v. Moore (Ohio App. 11 Dist., Trumbull, 07-02-2004) No. 2003-T-0028, 2004-Ohio-3542, 2004 WL 1485829, Unreported. Criminal Law 🔑 587; Criminal Law 🔑 594(1)

Trial court acted within its discretion in refusing to grant defendant's request for a further continuance, despite defendant's claim that such continuance was necessary to secure testimony of eyewitnesses; defendant's request for continuance occurred during trial, trial court provided a two-hour continuance, and defendant failed to indicate how eyewitnesses would have testified. State v. Rose (Ohio App. 8 Dist., Cuyahoga, 04-29-2004) No. 82635, 2004-Ohio-2151, 2004 WL 906022, Unreported, appeal not allowed 103 Ohio St.3d 1464, 815 N.E.2d 679, 2004-Ohio-5056. Criminal Law 🔑 649(2)

The addition of a plaintiff's witness five days prior to trial is valid reason to grant defendant's motion for a continuance where the witness is a drug task force member who allegedly made illegal marijuana purchases from defendant and whose identity was known to the plaintiff all along; denial of a continuance has a prejudicial effect on defendant and is an abuse of discretion. State v. Spack (Ohio App. 7 Dist., Columbiana, 05-17-1994) No. 93-C-48, 1994 WL 194150, Unreported.

Trial court acted within its discretion in refusing to grant continuance when murder defendant's arson expert died two days before defense began presentation of its case; delay in middle of trial would have placed jurors out of court's control for great deal of time, and defense called another expert who had inspected home with expert who died. State v. Franklin (Ohio, 10-16-2002) 97 Ohio St.3d 1, 776 N.E.2d 26, 2002-Ohio-5304, denial of post-conviction relief affirmed 2002-Ohio-2370, 2002 WL 1000415, appeal not allowed 98 Ohio St.3d 1422, 782 N.E.2d 77, 2003-Ohio-259, reconsideration denied 101 Ohio St.3d 1462, 804 N.E.2d 37, 2004-Ohio-823, appeal not allowed 108 Ohio St.3d 1475, 842 N.E.2d 1054, 2006-Ohio-665, reconsideration denied 97 Ohio St.3d 1486, 780 N.E.2d 288, 2002-Ohio-6866, stay granted 97 Ohio St.3d 1491, 780 N.E.2d 597, 2002-Ohio-7045, certiorari denied 123 S.Ct. 2249, 539 U.S. 905, 156 L.Ed.2d 115, denial of post-conviction relief affirmed 2005-Ohio-1361, 2005 WL 678925, appeal not allowed 106 Ohio St.3d 1464, 830 N.E.2d 1170, 2005-Ohio-3490, certiorari denied 126 S.Ct. 1352, 164 L.Ed.2d 64. Criminal Law 🔑 594(1)

Trial court acted within its discretion in refusing to grant continuance when murder defendant's arson expert died two days before defense began presentation of its case; delay in middle of trial would have placed jurors out of court's control for great deal of time, and defense called another expert who had inspected home with expert who died. State v. Franklin (Ohio, 10-16-2002) 97 Ohio St.3d 1, 776 N.E.2d 26, 2002-Ohio-5304, denial of post-conviction relief affirmed 2002-Ohio-2370, 2002 WL 1000415, appeal not allowed 98 Ohio St.3d 1422, 782 N.E.2d 77, 2003-Ohio-259, reconsideration denied 101 Ohio St.3d 1462, 804 N.E.2d 37, 2004-Ohio-823, appeal not allowed 108 Ohio St.3d 1475, 842 N.E.2d 1054, 2006-Ohio-665, reconsideration denied 97 Ohio St.3d 1486, 780 N.E.2d 288, 2002-Ohio-6866, stay granted 97 Ohio St.3d 1491, 780 N.E.2d 597, 2002-Ohio-7045, certiorari denied 123 S.Ct. 2249, 539 U.S. 905, 156 L.Ed.2d 115, denial of post-conviction relief affirmed 2005-Ohio-1361, 2005 WL 678925, appeal not allowed 106 Ohio St.3d 1464, 830 N.E.2d 1170, 2005-Ohio-3490, certiorari denied 126 S.Ct. 1352, 164 L.Ed.2d 64. Criminal Law 🔑 594(1)

Trial court did not abuse its discretion in denying request for continuance by defendant in kidnapping prosecution after defendant had scheduled expert medical witness on following Monday, but trial court had scheduled trial to continue until finished on Saturday, as trial court informed both counsel and jury that trial would occur all day on Friday and continue on Saturday if necessary. State v. Marine (Ohio App. 3 Dist., 02-14-2001) 141 Ohio App.3d 127, 750 N.E.2d 194, 2001-Ohio-2147, dismissed, appeal not allowed 92 Ohio St.3d 1414, 748 N.E.2d 547, denial of habeas corpus affirmed 86 Fed.Appx. 955, 2004 WL 237430. Criminal Law 🔑 594(1)

Even if trial court abused its discretion in denying kidnapping defendant's request for continuance so that he could present medical expert testimony, error did not prejudice defendant, as physician's proposed testimony regarding defendant's diminished capacity at time of offense was not admissible. State v. Marine (Ohio App. 3 Dist., 02-14-2001) 141 Ohio App.3d 127, 750 N.E.2d 194, 2001-Ohio-2147, dismissed, appeal not allowed 92 Ohio St.3d 1414, 748 N.E.2d 547, denial of habeas corpus affirmed 86 Fed.Appx. 955, 2004 WL 237430. Criminal Law 🔑 1166(7)

Trial court abused its discretion by denying defendant's motion for continuance, thereby denying defendant due process of law, where, after state unexpectedly rested its case on first day of trial scheduled for two and one-half days, defendant moved for continuance until following morning, at which time his witnesses would be available, defense counsel admitted that he misjudged length of state's case when notifying defense witnesses as to when they could expect to testify, and continuance would have delayed proceedings approximately 90 minutes. State v. Rash (Ohio App. 2 Dist., 05-24-1996) 111 Ohio App.3d 351, 676 N.E.2d 167. Constitutional Law ⚩ 268(3); Criminal Law ⚩ 649(2)

Trial court did not abuse its discretion by denying defendant's second motion for continuance to locate additional alibi witnesses; second motion for continuance was made one week prior to the scheduled trial date, trial court had previously granted defendant a 48—day continuance in order to locate alibi witnesses, and nothing suggested that further delay in proceedings would have allowed defendant to locate additional alibi witnesses. State v. Blankenship (Ohio App. 12 Dist., 04-17-1995) 102 Ohio App.3d 534, 657 N.E.2d 559, dismissed, appeal not allowed 73 Ohio St.3d 1426, 652 N.E.2d 799, denial of post-conviction relief affirmed 1995 WL 746232, dismissed, appeal not allowed 75 Ohio St.3d 1484, 664 N.E.2d 536, denial of post-conviction relief affirmed 74 Ohio St.3d 522, 660 N.E.2d 448, 1996-Ohio-58, denial of post-conviction relief affirmed 1997 WL 700073, dismissed, appeal not allowed 81 Ohio St.3d 1466, 690 N.E.2d 1287. Criminal Law ⚩ 605; Criminal Law ⚩ 614(3)

Defendant was not entitled to continuance based on discovery of the identities of two confidential informants, and receipt of transcripts, for the first time five days before scheduled trial date; defendant was not prejudiced insofar as trial counsel was not hampered in developing unsavory aspects of informants' backgrounds and character for consideration by jury, and prosecutor stated that he had informed defense counsel "very early on" that he would provide names of confidential informants but that in the event he did so there would be no plea negotiation and that, since their names had been revealed to defense counsel, informants or their families had received threatening telephone calls from defendant and his associates. State v. Taylor (Clark 1992) 76 Ohio App.3d 835, 603 N.E.2d 401. Criminal Law ⚩ 589(1); Criminal Law ⚩ 590(1)

The denial of a defendant's request for a third continuance for the purpose of securing the defendant's wife's attendance and testimony at trial or to declare a mistrial is not erroneous where a third continuance would not have secured the wife's attendance and the defendant was not prejudiced by his wife's failure to testify on his behalf. State v. Day (Ross 1991) 72 Ohio App.3d 82, 593 N.E.2d 456, motion overruled 60 Ohio St.3d 704, 573 N.E.2d 121. Criminal Law ⚩ 594(3); Criminal Law ⚩ 614(1); Criminal Law ⚩ 867

6. —— Change of strategy, continuance denied

Trial court acted within its discretion in denying rape defendant's request for continuance on first day of trial, where need for continuance apparently arose as a result of a change in defense strategy. State v. Kirkwood (Ohio App. 6 Dist., Lucas, 12-05-2003) No. L-00-1380, 2003-Ohio-6757, 2003 WL 22946477, Unreported, appeal not allowed 102 Ohio St.3d 1422, 807 N.E.2d 367, 2004-Ohio-2003. Criminal Law ⚩ 589(1)

Denying defense counsel's request for a continuance for more time to prepare defense in capital murder prosecution was not an abuse of discretion; lead counsel was appointed nearly two months before trial to replace previous lead counsel, who had withdrawn, co-counsel had been on the case fifteen months before trial, providing continuity, and previous lead counsel agreed to assist defendant's lawyers during portions of the trial. State v. Sanders (Ohio, 07-18-2001) 92 Ohio St.3d 245, 750 N.E.2d 90, 2001-Ohio-189, reconsideration denied 93 Ohio St.3d 1434, 755 N.E.2d 356, stay granted 93 Ohio St.3d 1437, 755 N.E.2d 900, stay revoked 98 Ohio St.3d 1453, 783 N.E.2d 514, 2003-Ohio-651, certiorari denied 122 S.Ct. 1795, 535 U.S. 1036, 152 L.Ed.2d 653, stay granted 98 Ohio St.3d 1506, 786 N.E.2d 57, 2003-Ohio-1573. Criminal Law ⚩ 593

7. —— Failure to present facts, continuance denied

Failing to grant continuance to allow sex offender to obtain records in support of his argument that he should not be classified as sexual predator was not abuse of discretion; although offender argued that clinical assessment presented in trial court contained error and that second assessment had been performed which was not included in materials submitted to court, offender failed to present any evidence to support this allegation, and offender had more than ample time to present all evidence in his defense. State v. Budreaux (Ohio App. 8 Dist., Cuyahoga, 05-20-2004) No. 83219, 2004-Ohio-2544, 2004 WL 1119590, Unreported, appeal not allowed 103 Ohio St.3d 1492, 816 N.E.2d 1079, 2004-Ohio-5605. Mental Health ⚩ 469(4)

Defendant was not entitled to continuance; defendant's proffered reasons for the requested continuance were weak, case had been pending for over three months, and the untimeliness of the request showed a lack of respect for the time of the others involved in the proceedings. City of Dayton v. Gregory (Ohio App. 2 Dist., Montgomery, 05-14-2004) No. 19912, 2004-Ohio-2421, 2004 WL 1077196, Unreported. Criminal Law ⚩ 605

In light of facts that defense counsel presented no facts to court to indicate identity of witnesses, materiality of their testimony, or reasonable likelihood that they could be found and that he gave no specific facts to support his contention that he needed more time to adequately prepare a proper defense, trial court did not abuse its discretion in denying defense motion for a continuance, which resulted in trial commencing within 11 days of defendant's arraignment for robbery. State v. Sowders (Ohio 1983) 4 Ohio St.3d 143, 447 N.E.2d 118, 4 O.B.R. 386. Criminal Law ⚩ 590(2)

8. —— Notice, continuance denied

Trial court acted within its discretion in denying defendant's request for continuance in proceedings to terminate his community control, despite defense counsel's claim that he did not have adequate notice of community control violation hearing; trial court noted that it had previously discussed with counsel both the date and purpose of the hearing.

State v. Stapleton (Ohio App. 4 Dist., Lawrence, 04-01-2004) No. 03CA28, 2004-Ohio-1859, 2004 WL 766416, Unreported. Sentencing And Punishment ⚷ 2025

9. —— Timeliness of motion, continuance denied

Trial court did not abuse its discretion in denying defendant's motion for continuance of trial, which had been set for three months, made one week before trial, in drug prosecution. State v. Miller (Ohio App. 2 Dist., Montgomery, 08-12-2005) No. 20513, 2005-Ohio-4203, 2005 WL 1939771, Unreported, appeal not allowed 107 Ohio St.3d 1700, 840 N.E.2d 204, 2005-Ohio-6763. Criminal Law ⚷ 605

Defendant was not entitled to continuance so that her "victim's advocate" could attend proceedings, in prosecution for disorderly conduct; defendant failed to file written motion for continuance despite her receipt of document form court informing her that she had to file such motion before scheduled trial date, but instead waited until day of trial to make her request, defendant did not explain why advocate was necessary to her defense, and there was no indication that advocate was licensed attorney who could represent defendant, or that advocate had witnessed events in question and had evidence to offer court. State v. Vance (Ohio App. 4 Dist., Athens, 09-24-2004) No. 03CA27, 2004-Ohio-5370, 2004 WL 2260498, Unreported. Criminal Law ⚷ 589(1)

Trial court acted within its discretion in denying rape defendant's request for continuance made on day of sexual predator classification hearing for stated purpose of obtaining independent psychological evaluation, where defendant chose, as a matter of strategy, to wait and evaluate doctor's report rather than to seek an independent evaluation at the earliest opportunity, and delayed release of doctor's report was direct result of defendant's refusal to participate in scheduled psychological evaluation. State v. Kirkwood (Ohio App. 6 Dist., Lucas, 12-05-2003) No. L-00-1380, 2003-Ohio-6757, 2003 WL 22946477, Unreported, appeal not allowed 102 Ohio St.3d 1422, 807 N.E.2d 367, 2004-Ohio-2003. Mental Health ⚷ 461

Trial court denial of defendant's motion for a continuance of capital murder trial, which was made on the day before voir dire began, was not an abuse of discretion; defendant gave counsel a list of approximately 60 witnesses the day before voir dire began, the list did not contain addresses or telephone numbers for the witnesses, the witness list contained a number of people who lived in Pakistan, and defendant did not offer a summary of what the testimony of the witnesses would have been. State v. Ahmed (Ohio, 08-25-2004) 103 Ohio St.3d 27, 813 N.E.2d 637, 2004-Ohio-4190, reconsideration denied 103 Ohio St.3d 1496, 816 N.E.2d 1081, 2004-Ohio-5605, certiorari denied 125 S.Ct. 1703, 544 U.S. 952, 161 L.Ed.2d 531, rehearing denied, rehearing denied 125 S.Ct. 2901, 162 L.Ed.2d 312. Criminal Law ⚷ 590(1)

Defendant was not wrongly denied a continuance on his claim that he needed more time to investigate and prepare for his murder trial, where he did not request one until eight days before trial, was represented by counsel for at least eight months before trial, received state funds for several investigators and experts, got additional help from the public defender's office, filed more than 50 pretrial motions, conducted several pretrial hearings, and called 31 trial witnesses. State v. Mason (Ohio, 06-17-1998) 82 Ohio St.3d 144, 694 N.E.2d 932, 1998-Ohio-370, reconsideration denied 82 Ohio St.3d 1483, 696 N.E.2d 1089, certiorari denied 119 S.Ct. 624, 525 U.S. 1057, 142 L.Ed.2d 562, habeas corpus denied 95 F.Supp.2d 744, affirmed in part, remanded in part 320 F.3d 604, on remand 293 F.Supp.2d 819, on remand 396 F.Supp.2d 837. Criminal Law ⚷ 590(1); Criminal Law ⚷ 605

Trial court was not required to grant defendant's motion for continuance, which was made on morning of trial; continuance had been granted on earlier request, and motion was made because defense witness was out of state, but sheriff received subpoena for service on witness only five days before start of trial. State v. McMillen (Ohio App. 3 Dist., 06-26-1996) 113 Ohio App.3d 137, 680 N.E.2d 665. Criminal Law ⚷ 605; Criminal Law ⚷ 614(3)

10. Unjournalized continuance

Only a court is vested with authority to grant trial continuance by proper journal entry. Village of Glenwillow v. Tomsick (Ohio App. 8 Dist., 06-17-1996) 111 Ohio App.3d 718, 676 N.E.2d 1259. Criminal Law ⚷ 578

Unjournalized continuances do not extend the time for speedy trial. State v. Benson (Cuyahoga 1985) 29 Ohio App.3d 321, 505 N.E.2d 987, 29 O.B.R. 448.

The granting of a sua sponte continuance may not be implied from the fact that the trial court originally set an accused's trial for a date beyond that permitted by RC 2945.71, and where the court's journal does not reflect that a continuance has been granted on or before the last day for trial permitted by RC 2945.71, the state may not rely upon RC 2945.72(H) to justify a delay in bringing the accused to trial. Village of Oakwood v. Ferrante (Cuyahoga 1975) 44 Ohio App.2d 318, 338 N.E.2d 767, 73 O.O.2d 374.

11. Speedy trial

For purposes of defendant's motion to dismiss assault indictments due to violation of right to speedy trial, Court of Appeals would not attempt to determine whether the journal entries accurately reflected which party requested the continuances of trial, where review of record indicated that various continuances were made at the request of defense counsel as reflected in the journal entries, and the docket and journal entries did not indicate any obvious error. State v. Barnett (Ohio App. 8 Dist., Cuyahoga, 11-27-2002) No. 81101, 2002-Ohio-6506, 2002 WL 31667667, Unreported, appeal not allowed 98 Ohio St.3d 1514, 786 N.E.2d 64, 2003-Ohio-1572, motion to reopen denied 2003-Ohio-3938, 2003 WL 21710610. Criminal Law ⚷ 1118

Defendant's right to speedy trial was not violated, where defendant was not held in jail in lieu of bail, and was brought to trial within 247 days, well within time limit of 270 days, considering defendant and his counsel's numerous requests for continuances, which were granted by the trial court, and period that jury was unavailable due to holidays. State v. Barnett (Ohio App. 8 Dist., Cuyahoga, 11-27-2002) No. 81101, 2002-Ohio-6506, 2002 WL 31667667, Unreported, appeal not allowed 98 Ohio St.3d 1514, 786 N.E.2d 64, 2003-Ohio-1572, motion to reopen denied 2003-Ohio-3938, 2003 WL 21710610. Criminal Law ⚷ 577.10(8); Criminal Law ⚷ 577.15(1)

Defendant's speedy trial right was not violated, although defendant objected to one continuance, where defendant waived right to speedy trial shortly after arrest, defendant never objected to other continuances and in some instances instigated them, and defendant at no time demanded trial or revoked or attempted to revoke waiver. Village of Glenwillow v. Tomsick (Ohio App. 8 Dist., 06-17-1996) 111 Ohio App.3d 718, 676 N.E.2d 1259. Criminal Law ⚷ 577.10(8); Criminal Law ⚷ 577.10(9); Criminal Law ⚷ 577.10(10)

The ten-day period of limitations in Juv R 29(A) is procedural only and such rule confers no substantive right upon an accused to have his case dismissed if he is not tried within the designated time. In re Therklidsen (Franklin 1977) 54 Ohio App.2d 195, 376 N.E.2d 970, 8 O.O.3d 335.

A defendant who was imprisoned in another state while awaiting trial in Ohio may not have the Ohio indictment dismissed for denial of a speedy trial, although he sent a request therefor to the Ohio court and prosecutor while serving his sentence outside the state, but there is no evidence he requested the governor of Ohio to institute extradition proceedings. State v. Moore (Ohio Com.Pl. 1968) 14 Ohio Misc. 139, 237 N.E.2d 628, 43 O.O.2d 349, appeal dismissed, certiorari denied 89 S.Ct. 460, 393 U.S. 221, 21 L.Ed.2d 393.

A trial commenced within approximately six weeks after a demand is made upon the court for a speedy trial is a compliance with the constitutional mandate. State v. Doyle (Hamilton 1967) 11 Ohio App.2d 97, 228 N.E.2d 863, 40 O.O.2d 251. Criminal Law ⚷ 577.15(1)

12. Review

Reviewing court will not reverse denial of motion for continuance unless defendant can show that trial court abused its discretion, meaning that court committed more than error of law or judgment and that attitude of court was, in fact, unreasonable, arbitrary, or unconscionable. State v. Rash (Ohio App. 2 Dist., 05-24-1996) 111 Ohio App.3d 351, 676 N.E.2d 167. Criminal Law ⚷ 1151

Appellate court must not disturb trial court's decision denying motion for continuance absent abuse of discretion. State v. Blankenship (Ohio App. 12 Dist., 04-17-1995) 102 Ohio App.3d 534, 657 N.E.2d 559, dismissed, appeal not allowed 73 Ohio St.3d 1426, 652 N.E.2d 799, denial of post-conviction relief affirmed 1995 WL 746232, dismissed, appeal not allowed 75 Ohio St.3d 1484, 664 N.E.2d 536, denial of post-conviction relief affirmed 74 Ohio St.3d 522, 660 N.E.2d 448, 1996-Ohio-58, denial of post-conviction relief affirmed 1997 WL 700073, dismissed, appeal not allowed 81 Ohio St.3d 1466, 690 N.E.2d 1287. Criminal Law ⚷ 1151

Denial of attorneys' timely motion for continuance was not error, even though, had attorneys proceeded to trial, they would have violated disciplinary rule which provides that lawyer shall not handle legal matter without adequate preparation; trial court found that attorneys were not adequately prepared due solely to their own neglect which is also violation of disciplinary rule. State v. Christon (Montgomery 1990) 68 Ohio App.3d 471, 589 N.E.2d 53. Criminal Law ⚷ 590(2)

Failure to grant attorney's timely motion for continuance was not abuse of discretion, where continuance would have presented great inconvenience to trial court, witnesses, and potential jurors, trial court specifically found that justification for continuance was result of attorneys' dilatory handling of case, and, even though cocounsel was ill, lead counsel was present, with no health problems to hinder his presentation of case, despite fact that attorneys had not received previous requested continuance, and, at time in question, only asked for two-week postponement. State v. Christon (Montgomery 1990) 68 Ohio App.3d 471, 589 N.E.2d 53. Criminal Law ⚷ 586

Trial court did not abuse its discretion in failing to continue criminal action for appearance of expert witness who did not arrive until after 1:40 p.m. where trial was scheduled to begin at 9:00 a.m. and only one prosecution witness was scheduled to testify. State v. Swisshelm (Wayne 1987) 40 Ohio App.3d 196, 532 N.E.2d 152. Criminal Law ⚷ 594(1)

It is an abuse of discretion to refuse a continuance for the defendant to subpoena witnesses in a probation revocation proceeding where counsel is appointed and given names of the witnesses only four days before the hearing, one of those days being the Fourth of July. State v Harris, No. C–840581 (1st Dist Ct App, Hamilton, 5–22–85).

2945.03 Control of trial

The judge of the trial court shall control all proceedings during a criminal trial, and shall limit the introduction of evidence and the argument of counsel to relevant and material matters with a view to expeditious and effective ascertainment of the truth regarding the matters in issue.

(1953 H 1, eff. 10–1–53; GC 13442–2)

Historical and Statutory Notes

Pre–1953 H 1 Amendments: 113 v 179, Ch 21, § 2

Cross References

Authority of magistrate in trial court, 2938.07

Evidence, relevancy of, Evid R 401 to 411

Library References

Criminal Law ⚷633(1), 661, 699.

Westlaw Topic No. 110.

C.J.S. Criminal Law §§ 564, 656, 751, 1134, 1140, 1145 to 1146, 1191, 1202, 1237.

Research References

Encyclopedias

OH Jur. 3d Criminal Law § 3716, Cross-Examination.

Treatises and Practice Aids

Markus, Trial Handbook for Ohio Lawyers, § 4:1, Criminal Procedure; in General.

Katz, Giannelli, Blair and Lipton, Baldwin's Ohio Practice, Criminal Law, § 64:2, Voir Dire.

Katz, Giannelli, Blair and Lipton, Baldwin's Ohio Practice, Criminal Law, § 68:4, Jail Garb and Security Measures.

Giannelli and Snyder, Baldwin's Ohio Practice, Evidence, R 401, Definition of "Relevant Evidence".

Giannelli and Snyder, Baldwin's Ohio Practice, Evidence, § 611.3, Court Control of Trial: in General.

1 Giannelli and Snyder, Baldwin's Ohio Practice, Evidence, Index, Index.

Hennenberg & Reinhart, Ohio Criminal Defense Motions F 8.03, Motion for Alternating Voir Dire-Jury-Related Motions.

Law Review and Journal Commentaries

The Meaning of the Term "Trial" Within the Ohio Rules of Civil Procedure, Note. 25 Clev St L Rev 515 (1976).

The Polygraph and Evidence Rule Making—A Proposal for Restraint in Ohio, Comment. 3 N Ky L Rev 214 (1976).

Notes of Decisions

---

1. Relevant and material evidence

Trial court acted within its discretion in limiting voir dire to 30 minutes per side in prosecution for felonious assault; trial court's restriction was not unreasonable or arbitrary. State v. Harris (Ohio App. 5 Dist., Stark, 03-29-2004) No. 2003CA00287, 2004-Ohio-1557, 2004 WL 614834, Unreported. Jury ⚷ 131(4)

Trial court was warranted in excluding a mask as a proffered demonstrative exhibit in prosecution for aggravated murder and aggravated robbery, though defendant claimed the mask would show that the victim could not have seen as much of the shooter's features as he claimed, given that the exhibit was wider and had a different mouth than mask used in the robbery, and thus, it was doubtful whether exhibit could give jury an accurate idea of how much victim could see. State v. Herring (Ohio, 02-27-2002) 94 Ohio St.3d 246, 762 N.E.2d 940, 2002-Ohio-796, reconsideration denied 95 Ohio St.3d 1423, 766 N.E.2d 163, 2002-Ohio-1737, stay granted 95 Ohio St.3d 1429, 766 N.E.2d 996, 2002-Ohio-1924, certiorari denied 123 S.Ct. 301, 537 U.S. 917, 154 L.Ed.2d 202, denial of post-conviction relief reversed 2004-Ohio-5357, 2004 WL 2334325, appeal not allowed 105 Ohio St.3d 1407, 821 N.E.2d 1027, 2005-Ohio-279. Criminal Law ⚷ 404.80

Trial court's limiting defense counsel's cross-examination of jailhouse informant during suppression hearing did not constitute abuse of discretion in capital murder prosecution. State v. Nields (Ohio, 08-29-2001) 93 Ohio St.3d 6, 752 N.E.2d 859, 2001-Ohio-1291, reconsideration denied 93 Ohio St.3d 1452, 756 N.E.2d 116. Criminal Law ⚷ 414

Decision not to admit into evidence composite sketch of murder suspect during defense counsel's cross-examination of witnesses in capital murder prosecution was not an abuse of discretion; trial court admitted the composite sketch into evidence at the close of the State's case-in-chief, and the jury considered it in deliberations. State v. Chinn (Ohio, 06-02-1999) 85 Ohio St.3d 548, 709 N.E.2d 1166, 1999-Ohio-288, reconsideration denied 86 Ohio St.3d 1444, 713 N.E.2d 1053, stay granted 86 Ohio St.3d 1446, 714 N.E.2d 398, certiorari denied 120 S.Ct. 944, 528 U.S. 1120, 145 L.Ed.2d 820, denial of post-conviction relief affirmed 2001-Ohio-1550, 2001 WL 788402, dismissed, appeal not allowed 93 Ohio St.3d 1473, 757 N.E.2d 772. Criminal Law ⚷ 680(1)

While statute grants prosecution and defense opportunity to conduct a reasonable examination of prospective jurors, trial court reserves right and responsibility to control proceedings, and must limit trial to relevant and material matters with a view toward expeditious and effective ascertainment of truth. State v. Getsy (Ohio, 12-23-1998) 84 Ohio St.3d 180, 702 N.E.2d 866, 1998-Ohio-533, reconsideration denied 84 Ohio St.3d 1488, 705 N.E.2d 368, certiorari denied 119 S.Ct. 2407, 527 U.S. 1042, 144 L.Ed.2d 805, dismissal of post-conviction relief affirmed 1999 WL 1073682, dismissed, appeal not allowed 88 Ohio St.3d 1425, 723 N.E.2d 1113, habeas corpus granted 456 F.3d 575. Jury ⚷ 131(1)

Trial court did not improperly limit voir dire of prospective jurors during capital murder prosecution; while court attempted to keep voir dire moving, counsel were rarely limited in questioning jurors, and court did not unreasonably or arbitrarily restrict examination of individual jurors. State v. Getsy (Ohio, 12-23-1998) 84 Ohio St.3d 180, 702 N.E.2d 866, 1998-Ohio-533, reconsideration denied 84 Ohio St.3d 1488, 705 N.E.2d 368, certiorari denied 119 S.Ct. 2407, 527 U.S. 1042, 144 L.Ed.2d 805, dismissal of post-conviction relief affirmed 1999 WL 1073682, dismissed, appeal not allowed 88 Ohio St.3d 1425, 723 N.E.2d 1113, habeas corpus granted 456 F.3d 575. Jury ⚷ 131(4)

The results of a polygraph test do not constitute relevant and material evidence within the meaning of RC 2945.03 and are not admissible in evidence even if the person tested has previously stipulated that such may be introduced against him at trial. State v. Hill (Montgomery 1963) 40 Ohio App.2d 16, 317 N.E.2d 233, 69 O.O.2d 9.

2. Fair trial—In general

Time limit on voir dire imposed by trial judge, allotting each side one-half hour to question each prospective juror, did not deprive defendant of the requisite latitude in voir dire questioning so as to amount to an abuse of discretion; defense counsel did not object to the time allotment or request more time to question a juror during voir dire, and trial court's statement to defense counsel that he had fourteen minutes left in questioning that juror was in response to defense counsel's inquiry as to the time. State v. Cornwell (Ohio, 09-22-1999) 86 Ohio St.3d 560, 715 N.E.2d 1144, 1999-Ohio-125, stay granted 87 Ohio St.3d 1414, 717 N.E.2d 714, stay revoked 98 Ohio St.3d 1475, 784 N.E.2d 709, 2003-Ohio-980, certiorari denied 120 S.Ct. 1200, 528 U.S. 1172, 145 L.Ed.2d 1103, denial of post-conviction relief affirmed 2002-Ohio-5177, 2002 WL 31160861, appeal not allowed 98 Ohio St.3d 1413, 781 N.E.2d 1020, 2003-Ohio-60. Jury ⚷ 131(4)

3. —— Restraint of defendant, fair trial

Imposing in-court restraint, in form of stun belt, on defendant during trial was not abuse of discretion where district court noted that defendant was fugitive from justice, having escaped from prison, that defendant was in desperate position in light of having already been sentenced to significant prison term, that defendant had no physical limitation which would prohibit his escape, that there was no less prejudicial alternative to use of stun belt, and that courtroom's facilities were not equipped to eliminate risk of escape. U.S. v. Waagner (C.A.6 (Ohio), 07-14-2004) No. 02-3953, 104 Fed.Appx. 521, 2004 WL 1595193, Unreported. Criminal Law ⚷ 637

Even if some potential jurors saw capital murder defendant handcuffed on the first day of voir dire, danger of prejudice to defendant was slight, since juror's view of defendant in custody was brief, inadvertent, and outside the courtroom. State v. Jalowiec (Ohio, 04-04-2001) 91 Ohio St.3d 220, 744 N.E.2d 163, 2001-Ohio-26, reconsideration denied 91 Ohio St.3d 1530, 747 N.E.2d 254, stay granted 92 Ohio St.3d 1401, 748 N.E.2d 76, certiorari denied 122 S.Ct. 374, 534 U.S. 964, 151 L.Ed.2d 284, stay revoked 100 Ohio St.3d 1441, 797 N.E.2d 1289, 2003-Ohio-5820. Criminal Law ⚷ 637

Capital murder defendant waived Supreme Court's review of claim that he was prejudiced when prospective jurors viewed him in shackles during voir dire, where issue was not properly raised before the Court of Appeals. State v. Jalowiec (Ohio, 04-04-2001) 91 Ohio St.3d 220, 744 N.E.2d 163, 2001-Ohio-26, reconsideration denied 91 Ohio St.3d 1530, 747 N.E.2d 254, stay granted 92 Ohio St.3d 1401, 748 N.E.2d 76, certiorari denied 122 S.Ct. 374, 534 U.S. 964, 151 L.Ed.2d 284, stay revoked 100 Ohio St.3d 1441, 797 N.E.2d 1289, 2003-Ohio-5820. Criminal Law ⚷ 1179

Capital murder defendant failed to demonstrate prejudicial error from prospective jurors' viewing him in shackles during voir dire; trial court suggested that defense counsel use voir dire to discover any possible prejudice, but defense counsel failed to do so. State v. Jalowiec (Ohio, 04-04-2001) 91 Ohio St.3d 220, 744 N.E.2d 163, 2001-Ohio-26, reconsideration denied 91 Ohio St.3d 1530, 747 N.E.2d 254, stay granted 92 Ohio St.3d 1401, 748 N.E.2d 76, certiorari denied 122 S.Ct. 374, 534 U.S. 964, 151 L.Ed.2d 284, stay revoked 100 Ohio St.3d 1441, 797 N.E.2d 1289, 2003-Ohio-5820. Criminal Law ⚷ 1166.8

Trial court's direction to jury to remain seated while deputies removed defendant from courtroom was not plain error; request did not rise to level of constant reminder of prison garb or shackles and was fairly related to trial court's authority to control proceedings. State v. Davie (Ohio, 11-26-1997) 80 Ohio St.3d 311, 686 N.E.2d 245, 1997-Ohio-341, dismissal of post-conviction relief affirmed 1998 WL 684157, dismissed, appeal not allowed 84 Ohio St.3d 1483, 705 N.E.2d 364, reconsideration denied 85 Ohio St.3d 1411, 706 N.E.2d 791, denial of post-conviction relief affirmed 2001-Ohio-8813, 2001 WL 1647193, appeal not allowed 95 Ohio St.3d 1423, 766 N.E.2d 162, 2002-Ohio-1737, habeas corpus denied 291 F.Supp.2d 573, motion to amend denied, certificate of appealability granted in part, denied in part 324 F.Supp.2d 862. Criminal Law ⚷ 1035(10)

Defendant suffered no prejudice from jury briefly viewing him in restraints, and therefore trial court properly did not give curative instruction and properly permitted defendant to examine only the two jurors who defendant's counsel requested be detained, where defendant did not ask that entire jury panel be examined, defendant did not request any kind of curative instruction, and jurors which were examined indicated that their brief glimpse of defendant did not affect their decision. State v. Powers (Ohio App. 9 Dist., 10-04-1995) 106 Ohio App.3d 696, 667 N.E.2d 32. Criminal Law ⚩ 637; Criminal Law ⚩ 868

The presence of armed state troopers garbed in full uniform in the first row of the spectator's gallery, to compensate for a lack of courtroom guards usually assigned to defendants denied bail, does not deprive the defendant of a fair trial and need not be justified by an "essential state interest." Holbrook v. Flynn (U.S.R.I. 1986) 106 S.Ct. 1340, 475 U.S. 560, 89 L.Ed.2d 525.

A state court judge abuses his discretion by deferring to the wishes of the sheriff that a criminal defendant charged with the first degree murder of an eighty-three-year-old woman be shackled during trial, where the defendant had engaged in no violence while in custody, and where the state judge's belief that certain items found in the defendant's cell suggested an intention to escape was rejected by a federal court, which ruled that the defendant's purpose in having a pencil, pieces of metal, a tee shirt, and a blank key was to construct "handicrafts" for his wife. Woodards v. Cardwell (C.A.6 (Ohio) 1970) 430 F.2d 978, 55 O.O.2d 405, certiorari denied 91 S.Ct. 874, 401 U.S. 911, 27 L.Ed.2d 809.

Defendant's due process rights were not violated by the jury having viewed him while he was shackled; given that jury knew that defendant had been incarcerated when prison guard was killed and, since he did not deny having killed guard, defendant did not suffer actual prejudice as a result of the jury observing him in shackles. Zuern v. Tate (S.D.Ohio, 03-30-2000) 101 F.Supp.2d 948, affirmed in part, reversed in part 336 F.3d 478, certiorari denied 124 S.Ct. 1456, 540 U.S. 1198, 158 L.Ed.2d 113. Constitutional Law ⚩ 268(2.1); Criminal Law ⚩ 637

4. —— Amicus curiae, fair trial

To permit a private attorney, as amicus curiae, to participate in the trial of a criminal case in the municipal court and cross-examine the defendant, when such attorney's appearance was neither by application nor by invitation of the court, nor for the purpose of giving information to the court on a matter of law about which the court was doubtful, nor to call the court's attention to a legal matter which escaped or might have escaped the court's consideration, is an usurpation of the function of the city prosecutor, is manifestly irregular and constitutes error prejudicial to the defendant. City of Columbus v. Tullos (Franklin 1964) 1 Ohio App.2d 107, 204 N.E.2d 67, 30 O.O.2d 121. Amicus Curiae ⚩ 1; Criminal Law ⚩ 1166.9

5. —— Judge's comments, fair trial

Trial judge's comments, that witness had long-standing reputation in community and that community in general hoped witness would soon be reinstated to practice of psychology, made in presence of jury, were prejudicial to defendant's right to fair trial in prosecution for aggravated murder; judge's comments, made during direct examination of witness, bolstered credibility of witness since she could not remember events to which she was testifying, and defendant's counsel was impaired by comments since counsel had task of cross-examining witness that judge had essentially endorsed as being credible witness and well regarded in community. State v. McCarley (Ohio App. 9 Dist., Summit, 03-15-2006) No. 22562, 2006-Ohio-1176, 2006 WL 625968, Unreported, appeal not allowed 110 Ohio St.3d 1441, 852 N.E.2d 189, 2006-Ohio-3862. Criminal Law ⚩ 656(5)

Trial court's restrictions on and interruptions of voir dire did not impair capital murder defendant's ability to use peremptory challenges effectively to remove prospective jurors or otherwise impair his defense, where trial court was not unduly restrictive, but rather balanced its obligation to control inquiry with according counsel latitude in questioning prospective jurors, and where court's only restrictions on particular areas of inquiry were well within its discretion. State v. Gross (Ohio, 10-30-2002) 97 Ohio St.3d 121, 776 N.E.2d 1061, 2002-Ohio-5524, reconsideration denied 97 Ohio St.3d 1486, 780 N.E.2d 288, 2002-Ohio-6866, certiorari denied 123 S.Ct. 2079, 538 U.S. 1037, 155 L.Ed.2d 1068, rehearing denied 124 S.Ct. 20, 539 U.S. 976, 156 L.Ed.2d 685. Jury ⚩ 131(4)

Statements by trial court which allegedly reflected impermissible bias and prejudice, but to which no objection had been made, including comments that court wished defense counsel would "move it along," that court had thought counsel would consult with his clients before trial, that counsel was "wasting time," and that counsel was not required to give a "long dissertation," but merely to object, did not rise to level of plain error. State v. Johnson (Ohio App. 1 Dist., 06-25-1999) 134 Ohio App.3d 586, 731 N.E.2d 1149. Criminal Law ⚩ 1035(8.1)

A judge's extensive involvement in a trial where he questions witnesses, interjects his own disdainful commentary during this questioning, and raises and sustains his own objections, is prejudicial to the jury and denies a defendant a fair trial. Mentor-on-the-Lake v. Giffin (Ohio App. 11 Dist., 07-25-1995) 105 Ohio App.3d 441, 664 N.E.2d 557.

6. —— Media coverage, fair trial

A state court rule which allows radio, television and still photographic coverage of a criminal trial for public broadcasting, despite defense objections, is not a prima facie violation of the US Constitution. To establish a due process violation, the defendant must show that media coverage of the trial compromised the ability of the jury to adjudicate fairly. (Ed. note: Case arose from Florida law. Facts and opinion in 376 So(2d) 1157.) Chandler v. Florida (U.S. 1980) 101 S.Ct. 348, 449 U.S. 947, 66 L.Ed.2d 211.

2945.04 Protective orders available if it is found likely that intimidation of crime victim or witness or domestic violence will occur; procedures; contempt of court

(A) If a motion is filed with a court before which a criminal case is pending alleging that a person has committed or is reasonably likely to commit any act prohibited by section 2921.04 of the Revised Code in relation to the case, if the court holds a hearing on the motion, and if the court determines that the allegations made in the motion are true, the court may issue an order doing any or any combination of the following, subject to division (C) of this section:

(1) Directing the defendant in the case not to violate or to cease a violation of section 2921.04 of the Revised Code;

(2) Directing a person other than a defendant who is before the court, including, but not limited to, a subpoenaed witness or other person entering the courtroom of the court, not to violate or to cease a violation of section 2921.04 of the Revised Code;

(3) Directing the defendant or a person described in division (A)(2) of this section to maintain a prescribed geographic distance from any specified person who is before the court, including, but not limited to, the victim of the offense that is the basis of the case or a subpoenaed witness in the case;

(4) Directing the defendant or a person described in division (A)(2) of this section not to communicate with any specified person who is before the court, including, but not limited to, the victim of the offense or a subpoenaed witness in the case;

(5) Directing a specified law enforcement agency that serves a political subdivision within the territorial jurisdiction of the court to provide protection for any specified person who is before the court, including, but not limited to, the victim of the offense or a subpoenaed witness in the case;

(6) Any other reasonable order that would assist in preventing or causing the cessation of a violation of section 2921.04 of the Revised Code.

(B) If a motion is filed with a court in which a criminal complaint has been filed alleging that the offender or another person acting in concert with the offender has committed or is reasonably likely to commit any act that would constitute an offense against the person or property of the complainant, his ward, or his child, if the court holds a hearing on the motion, and if the court determines that the allegations made in the motion are true, the court may issue an order doing one or more of the following, subject to division (C) of this section:

(1) Directing the defendant in the case not to commit an act or to cease committing an act that constitutes an offense against the person or property of the complainant, his ward, or child;

(2) Directing a person other than the defendant who is before the court, including, but not limited to, a subpoenaed witness or other person entering the courtroom, not to commit an act or to cease committing an act that constitutes an offense against the person or property of the complainant, his ward, or child;

(3) Directing the defendant or a person described in division (B)(2) of this section to maintain a prescribed geographic distance from any specified person who is before the court, including, but not limited to, the complainant or the victim of the offense, or a subpoenaed witness in the case;

(4) Directing the defendant or a person described in division (B)(2) of this section not to communicate with any specified person who is before the court, including, but not limited to, the complainant, the victim of the offense, or a subpoenaed witness in the case;

(5) Directing a specified law enforcement agency that serves a political subdivision within the territorial jurisdiction of the court to provide protection for any specified person who is before the court, including, but not limited to, the complainant, the victim of the offense, or a subpoenaed witness in the case;

(6) When the complainant and the defendant cohabit with one another but the complainant is not a family or household member, as defined in section 2919.25 of the Revised Code, granting possession of the residence or household to the complainant to the exclusion of the defendant by evicting the defendant when the residence or household is owned or leased solely by the complainant or by ordering the defendant to vacate the premises when the residence or household is jointly owned or leased by the complainant and the defendant;

(7) Any other reasonable order that would assist in preventing or causing the cessation of an act that constitutes an offense against the person or property of the complainant, his ward, or child.

(C) No order issued under authority of division (A) or (B) of this section shall prohibit or be construed as prohibiting any attorney for the defendant in the case or for a person described in division (A)(2) or (B)(2) of this section from conducting any investigation of the pending criminal case, from preparing or conducting any defense of the pending criminal case, or from attempting to zealously represent his client in the pending criminal case within the bounds of the law. However, this division does not exempt any person from the prohibitions contained in section 2921.04 or any section of the Revised Code that constitutes an offense against the person or property of the complainant, his ward, or his child, or provide a defense to a charge of any violation of that section or of an offense of that nature.

(D)(1) A person who violates an order issued pursuant to division (A) of this section is subject to the following sanctions:

(a) Criminal prosecution for a violation of section 2921.04 of the Revised Code, if the violation of the court order constitutes a violation of that section;

(b) Punishment for contempt of court.

(2) A person who violates an order issued pursuant to division (B) of this section is subject to the following sanctions:

(a) Criminal prosecution for a violation of a section of the Revised Code that constitutes an offense against the person or property of the complainant, his ward, or child;

(b) Punishment for contempt of court.

(E)(1) The punishment of a person for contempt of court for violation of an order issued pursuant to division (A) of this section does not bar criminal prosecution of the person for a violation of section 2921.04 of the Revised Code.

(2) The punishment of a person for contempt of court for a violation of an order issued pursuant to division (B) of this section does not bar criminal prosecution of the person for an offense against the person or property of the complainant, his ward, or child.

(3) A person punished for contempt of court under this section is entitled to credit for the punishment imposed upon conviction of a violation of the offense arising out of the same activity, and a person convicted of such a violation shall not subsequently be punished for contempt of court arising out of the same activity.

(1994 H 335, eff. 12–9–94; 1984 S 172, eff. 9–26–84)

Historical and Statutory Notes

Ed. Note: Former 2945.04 repealed by 1973 H 716, eff. 1–1–74; 1953 H 1; GC 13442–3; see now 2901.05 for provisions analogous to former 2945.04.

Pre–1953 H 1 Amendments: 113 v 179, Ch 21, § 3

Amendment Note: 1994 H 335 substituted "(C)" for "(B)" in the first paragraph of division (A); added division (B); and rewrote and redesignated former divisions (B) through (D) as divisions (C) through (E). Prior to amendment, divisions (B) through (D) read:

"(B) No order issued under authority of division (A) of this section shall prohibit or be construed as prohibiting any attorney for the defendant in the case or for a person described in division (A)(2) of this section from conducting any investigation of the pending criminal case, from preparing or conducting any defense of the pending criminal case, or from attempting to zealously represent his client in the pending criminal case within the bounds of the law. However, this division does not exempt any person from the prohibitions contained in section 2921.04 of the Revised Code or provide a defense to a charge of any violation of that section.

"(C) A person who violates an order issued pursuant to division (A) of this section is subject to the following sanctions:

"(1) Criminal prosecution for a violation of section 2921.04 of the Revised Code, if the violation of the court order constitutes a violation of that section;

"(2) Punishment for contempt of court;

"(D) The punishment of a person for contempt of court for violation of an order issued pursuant to division (A) of this section does not bar criminal prosecution of the person for a violation of section 2921.04 of the Revised Code. However, a person punished for contempt of court is entitled to credit for the punishment imposed upon conviction of a violation of that section, and a person convicted of a violation of that section shall not subsequently be punished for contempt of court arising out of the same activity."

Cross References

Menacing by stalking, bail, 2903.212

Victims' rights pamphlet, publication and distribution, 109.42

Library References

Breach of the Peace ⚷15.

Westlaw Topic No. 62.

C.J.S. Breach of the Peace §§ 14 to 19, 21 to 25.

C.J.S. Domestic Abuse and Violence §§ 2 to 23.

Research References

Encyclopedias

OH Jur. 3d Criminal Law § 1055, Bail.

OH Jur. 3d Criminal Law § 3500, Types of Protective Orders.

OH Jur. 3d Criminal Law § 3501, Types of Protective Orders—Penalties; Contempt of Court.

Treatises and Practice Aids

Markus, Trial Handbook for Ohio Lawyers, § 21:5, Innocence.

Markus, Trial Handbook for Ohio Lawyers, § 36:5, Criminal Case.

Markus, Trial Handbook for Ohio Lawyers, § 9:13, Criminal Case—Party Having Burden of Proof—Identity of Accused.

Adrine & Ruden, Ohio Domestic Violence Law § 4:8, Other Protection Orders Available in Criminal Cases.

Adrine & Ruden, Ohio Domestic Violence Law § 16:4, Confidentiality and Liability Concerns.

Law Review and Journal Commentaries

Empowering the Battered Woman: The Use of Criminal Contempt Sanctions to Enforce Civil Protection Orders, David M. Zlotnick. 56 Ohio St L J 1153 (1995).

TRIAL BY COURT

2945.05 Defendant may waive jury trial

In all criminal cases pending in courts of record in this state, the defendant may waive a trial by jury and be tried by the court without a jury. Such waiver by a defendant, shall be in writing, signed by the defendant, and filed in said cause and made a part of the record thereof. It shall be entitled in the court and cause, and in substance as follows: "I ________, defendant in the above cause, hereby voluntarily waive and relinquish my right to a trial by jury, and elect to be tried by a Judge of the Court in which the said cause may be pending. I fully understand that under the laws of this state, I have a constitutional right to a trial by jury."

Such waiver of trial by jury must be made in open court after the defendant has been arraigned and has had opportunity to consult with counsel. Such waiver may be withdrawn by the defendant at any time before the commencement of the trial.

(1953 H 1, eff. 10–1–53; GC 13442–4)

Historical and Statutory Notes

Pre–1953 H 1 Amendments: 113 v 179, Ch 21, § 4

Cross References

Trial by jury, O Const Art I §5

Waiver of jury, Crim R 23

Library References

Jury ⚬29.

Westlaw Topic No. 230.

C.J.S. Juries §§ 167, 182, 207 to 219, 222.

Research References

Encyclopedias

OH Jur. 3d Criminal Law § 82, Actions of Counsel on Appeal.

OH Jur. 3d Criminal Law § 83, Other Actions or Omissions.

OH Jur. 3d Criminal Law § 85, Ineffective Assistance of Appellate Counsel.

OH Jur. 3d Criminal Law § 98, Duty to Appoint.

OH Jur. 3d Criminal Law § 431, Ohio Constitutional and Statutory Bases.

OH Jur. 3d Criminal Law § 433, Necessity of Demand.

OH Jur. 3d Criminal Law § 438, Effect of Plea of Guilty.

OH Jur. 3d Criminal Law § 439, Withdrawal of Waiver.

OH Jur. 3d Criminal Law § 2612, Jurisdiction of Judge When Jury Trial is Waived.

OH Jur. 3d Criminal Law § 2614, Withdrawal of Waiver.

OH Jur. 3d Family Law § 1744, Trial by Jury.

OH Jur. 3d Habeas Corpus & Post Convict. Remedies § 23, Denial of Jury Trial; Strict Compliance With Waiver Statute.

OH Jur. 3d Mandamus, Procedendo, & Prohibition § 37, Failure to Appeal; Unsuccessful Appeal.

OH Jur. 3d Mandamus, Procedendo, & Prohibition § 102, Vacation or Modification of Judgment or Order.

Treatises and Practice Aids

Markus, Trial Handbook for Ohio Lawyers, § 4:32, Trial by Jury.

Katz, Giannelli, Blair and Lipton, Baldwin's Ohio Practice, Criminal Law, § 36:2, Procedure.

Katz, Giannelli, Blair and Lipton, Baldwin's Ohio Practice, Criminal Law, § 62:4, Petty Offense Exception—Demand Requirement.

Katz, Giannelli, Blair and Lipton, Baldwin's Ohio Practice, Criminal Law, § 43:18, Capital Cases.

Katz, Giannelli, Blair and Lipton, Baldwin's Ohio Practice, Criminal Law, § 62:10, Waiver of Jury Trial.

Katz, Giannelli, Blair and Lipton, Baldwin's Ohio Practice, Criminal Law, § 62:12, Waiver—Guilty Pleas.

Katz, Giannelli, Blair and Lipton, Baldwin's Ohio Practice, Criminal Law, § 75:15, Self-Representation.

Katz, Giannelli, Blair and Lipton, Baldwin's Ohio Practice, Criminal Law, § 148:22, Waiver of Jury Trial in Serious Offense Cases.

Katz, Giannelli, Blair and Lipton, Baldwin's Ohio Practice, Criminal Law, § 115:2.50, Right to Jury in Sentencing.

Law Review and Journal Commentaries

Convicting the Innocent Beyond a Reasonable Doubt: Some Lessons About Jury Instruction from the Sheppard Case, Lawrence M. Solan, 49 Clev St L Rev 465 (2001).

Law, Justice and Jury Waiver in the Ohio Supreme Court, Comment. 46 Case W Res L Rev 1113 (Summer 1996).

State v. Jones: When a "Waiver" Might Not be a Waiver, Note. 2 Ohio N U L Rev 65 (1974).

Notes of Decisions

1. Constitutional issues—In general

Trial court lacked jurisdiction to try defendant without a jury, where record failed to include a written waiver that defendant signed, relinquishing his right to a jury trial. State v. Baghdady (Ohio App. 10 Dist., Franklin, 09-27-2005) No. 05AP-142, 2005-Ohio-5092, 2005 WL 2364974, Unreported. Jury ⚬ 29(6)

There was no evidence that defendant's waiver of jury trial in prosecution for attempted gross sexual imposition was not intelligently or freely made; transcript indicated that trial court questioned defendant, asking him if he realized what Constitutional rights he was giving up, whether any one threatened defendant, whether defendant spoke with counsel, and defendant was found competent prior to start of trial. State v. Brooks (Ohio App. 8 Dist., Cuyahoga, 12-24-2003) No. 82336, 2003-Ohio-7060, 2003 WL 23009426, Unreported. Jury ⚷ 29(6)

A trial court entry correcting the court's record in a rape and sexual battery trial to reflect that the defendant waived in writing his right to a jury trial but the form was lost, made on the day that the state files its merit brief on appeal is inadequate to demonstrate that the defendant intelligently, knowingly, and voluntarily in writing waived his right to a jury trial where (1) contrary to statements in the entry, the certified record on appeal reflects that no form was signed in open court and (2) the purported correcting entry is not part of the record on appeal and has not been certified to the appellate court; furthermore, even if the entry had been certified and transmitted to the appellate court as a supplemental record, pursuant to App R 9(E), it would be insufficient on its face to establish the existence of a written waiver since to be proper, it would be necessary that a motion be filed and a hearing be held in open court so that the court can make a factual determination. State v. Harris (Franklin 1991) 73 Ohio App.3d 57, 596 N.E.2d 563, dismissed, jurisdictional motion overruled 62 Ohio St.3d 1405, 577 N.E.2d 358.

Division (E) of RC 2151.35 which authorizes the juvenile court to commit a male child over sixteen years of age, who has committed an act which if committed by an adult would be a felony, to the Ohio state reformatory (the same institution to which adults convicted of a felony are committed), without providing to such juvenile equal rights of due process of law, is an unconstitutional denial of rights secured by US Const Am 14. State v. Fisher (Tuscarawas 1969) 17 Ohio App.2d 183, 245 N.E.2d 358, 46 O.O.2d 247. Constitutional Law ⚷ 255(4); Infants ⚷ 132; Statutes ⚷ 64(6)

The constitutional right to a jury of one on trial for a felony may be waived on condition only that such waiver be in writing, signed by the defendant, filed in the cause, and made a part of the record, and such waiver must be made in open court, after the defendant has been arraigned and has had an opportunity to consult with counsel. State v. Fife (Ohio App. 9 Dist. 1954) 100 Ohio App. 550, 137 N.E.2d 429, 60 O.O. 419.

Former GC 13442–4 (RC 2945.05) and 13442–5 (RC 2945.06) are each constitutional and in the instant case were constitutionally applied. State v. Frohner (Ohio 1948) 150 Ohio St. 53, 80 N.E.2d 868, 37 O.O. 406.

Every person accused of crime has right to trial by jury but such right may be waived by defendant. State v. Frohner (Ohio 1948) 150 Ohio St. 53, 80 N.E.2d 868, 37 O.O. 406. Jury ⚷ 21.1; Jury ⚷ 29(2)

Former GC 13442–4 (RC 2945.05) and 13442–5 (RC 2945.06) giving accused the right to waive a jury and be tried by the court, do not violate the Ohio Constitution. State v. Smith (Ohio 1931) 123 Ohio St. 237, 174 N.E. 768, 9 Ohio Law Abs. 286, 34 Ohio Law Rep. 71. Jury ⚷ 29(1)

A record that does not contain a written waiver of defendant's right to a jury trial raises the issue of a trial court's jurisdiction to conduct a bench trial and renders a judgment of conviction on two counts of felonious assault with a gun specification void ab initio; failure to comply with RC 2945.05 in this case denies the defendant of his constitutional right to trial by jury and is prejudicial error requiring reversal and remand for a new trial. State v Peters, No. CA94–07–062, 1995 WL 103327 (12th Dist Ct App, Clermont, 3–13–95).

2. —— Effective assistance of counsel, constitutional issues

Defendant failed to raise a genuine issue as to whether he was deprived of effective assistance of counsel on appeal, as a result of appellate counsel's failing to challenge alleged jurisdictional defect resulting from a violation of jury waiver statute and failing to raise numerous other assignments of error on direct appeal; thus, defendant was not entitled to have his appeal reopened. State v. Frazier (Ohio, 08-21-2002) 96 Ohio St.3d 189, 772 N.E.2d 1182, 2002-Ohio-4011. Criminal Law ⚷ 641.13(7); Criminal Law ⚷ 1133

3. Procedure for written waiver—In general

Defendant's waiver of his right to jury trial on charge of felonious assault was knowing, intelligent, and voluntary, where written jury waiver was signed by defendant on date of trial, witnessed by trial court, and filed with court, court read waiver into record at commencement of trial, and defendant's trial counsel acknowledged that defendant wished to waive his right to jury trial. State v. Myers (Ohio App. 9 Dist., Lorain, 07-20-2005) No. 04CA008605, 2005-Ohio-3632, 2005 WL 1684778, Unreported. Jury ⚷ 29(6)

Jury waiver form signed prior to hearing was valid, where trial court addressed defendant at hearing with respect to signed waiver, defendant indicated that he understood waiver but had read it only briefly before signing it, court read the waiver in its entirety and then inquired as to whether defendant understood or had any questions, explained rights defendant was waiving, and asked whether defendant was induced to sign the waiver, and defendant acknowledged that he understood, that he was not pressured into signing waiver, and that he still chose to waive jury. State v. Cunningham (Ohio App. 8 Dist., Cuyahoga, 06-16-2005) No. 84960, 2005-Ohio-3007, 2005 WL 1406290, Unreported. Jury ⚷ 29(6)

Writs of mandamus or prohibition were not proper remedy for claimed violation of statutory requirements for waiver of jury trial, where direct appeal was sole and proper remedy for trial court's alleged failure to have relator execute jury waiver as to sexually violent predator specification, and sexual motivation specification, in prosecution for rape and felonious assault. State ex rel. Waver v. Gallagher (Ohio App. 8 Dist., Cuyahoga, 08-18-2004) No. 84662, 2004-Ohio-4355, 2004 WL 1853164, Unreported, affirmed 105 Ohio St.3d 134,

823 N.E.2d 449, 2005-Ohio-780. Mandamus ⚷ 4(4); Prohibition ⚷ 3(4)

Once presented with defendant's signed jury waiver form, the trial court only needed to satisfy itself that defendant executed the form knowing what the form entailed, and thus, no further "colloquy" was necessary as it would have merely restated that which defendant acknowledged in writing. State v. Campbell (Ohio App. 8 Dist., Cuyahoga, 08-05-2004) No. 83489, 2004-Ohio-4090, 2004 WL 1752978, Unreported. Jury ⚷ 29(6)

Defendant's written waiver of his right to jury trial fully complied with statute requiring waiver to be made in open court after defendant had been arraigned and had opportunity to consult with counsel, where defendant signed waiver prior to trial, specifically acknowledged to trial court that his signature appeared on waiver, and agreed that his decision to waive jury trial was his own decision based on advice of counsel. State v. Hogue (Ohio App. 8 Dist., Cuyahoga, 07-22-2004) No. 83483, 2004-Ohio-3871, 2004 WL 1631133, Unreported. Jury ⚷ 29(6)

Trial court fully complied with statute requiring defendant's written waiver of his right to jury trial to be filed and made part of record, where trial court filed waiver with clerk of court. State v. Hogue (Ohio App. 8 Dist., Cuyahoga, 07-22-2004) No. 83483, 2004-Ohio-3871, 2004 WL 1631133, Unreported. Jury ⚷ 29(6)

Written waiver of jury trial stating "I hereby waive my right to a jury trial ... and agree to a continuance of the jury trial of the same," which appeared at bottom of document titled "Waiver of Speedy Trial," did not substantially comply with language required by statute governing waiver of jury trial, and thus, trial court was without jurisdiction to try defendant without a jury. State v. Harrison (Ohio App. 7 Dist., Mahoning, 06-02-2004) No. 02-CA-157, 2004-Ohio-2933, 2004 WL 1240379, Unreported. Jury ⚷ 29(2)

Evidence supported finding that Somalian-speaking defendant knowingly, intelligently, and voluntarily waived his right to trial by jury; record demonstrated that defendant understood English well, defendant's waiver of his right to jury trial was made in open court after defendant had been arraigned and had consulted with counsel, waiver was written and signed by defendant in open court, and defense counsel specifically stated that, following his consultations with defendant, he was satisfied that, if defendant did waive his right to a jury trial, that his waiver was done knowingly, intelligently, and voluntarily. State v. Nasser (Ohio App. 10 Dist., Franklin, 11-06-2003) No. 02AP-1112, 2003-Ohio-5947, 2003 WL 22511552, Unreported, appeal not allowed 101 Ohio St.3d 1490, 805 N.E.2d 540, 2004-Ohio-1293. Jury ⚷ 29(6)

Trial court properly exercised its discretion in determining that Somalian-speaking defendant did not require assistance of interpreter at trial; videotape of police interrogation established that defendant was able to understand what detective was asking him, neither counsel nor trial court had any difficulty in understanding defendant's testimony at trial, and court reporter did not have any difficulty transcribing defendant's interrogation, defendant's 911 call, and defendant's testimony in front of court. State v. Nasser (Ohio App. 10 Dist., Franklin, 11-06-2003) No. 02AP-1112, 2003-Ohio-5947, 2003 WL 22511552, Unreported, appeal not allowed 101 Ohio St.3d 1490, 805 N.E.2d 540, 2004-Ohio-1293. Criminal Law ⚷ 642

Extraordinary relief in habeas corpus would not lie to correct trial court's failure to make written waiver of defendant's right to jury trial part of record, where record showed trial court's reference to defendant's waiver of right to jury trial; failure to comply with requirement that written waiver be made part of record was subject to remedy only on direct appeal from conviction. Rideau v. Russell (Ohio App. 12 Dist., Warren, 12-02-2002) No. CA2002-01-003, 2002-Ohio-6523, 2002 WL 31682353, Unreported, appeal not allowed 98 Ohio St.3d 1514, 786 N.E.2d 63, 2003-Ohio-1572. Criminal Law ⚷ 1088.8; Habeas Corpus ⚷ 501

In the case of a serious offense, waiver of right to jury trial must be in writing signed by defendant. State v. Riley (Ohio App. 2 Dist., 11-23-1994) 98 Ohio App.3d 801, 649 N.E.2d 914. Jury ⚷ 29(6)

In prosecution of defendant for aggravated trafficking with prior drug offense, trial court erred by removing from jury's consideration the element of the prior conviction for felony drug abuse offense without written waiver signed by defendant. State v. Riley (Ohio App. 2 Dist., 11-23-1994) 98 Ohio App.3d 801, 649 N.E.2d 914. Jury ⚷ 29(6)

Written waiver of jury trial stating "being fully aware that I have a constitutional and statutory right to trial by jury... I do hereby voluntarily waive and relinquish my right to be tried by jury, and I choose instead to be tried by a judge of this court," substantially complied with language required by statute governing waiver of jury trial. State v. Walker (Ohio App. 3 Dist., 09-15-1993) 90 Ohio App.3d 352, 629 N.E.2d 471. Jury ⚷ 29(6)

Statutory phrase "such waiver of trial by jury must be made in open court after the defendant has been arraigned and has had opportunity to consult with counsel" means that there must be further evidence on the record, in addition to signed writing, that defendant has voluntarily made informed waiver of his constitutional right to trial by jury. State v. Walker (Ohio App. 3 Dist., 09-15-1993) 90 Ohio App.3d 352, 629 N.E.2d 471. Jury ⚷ 29(6)

An ex-parte sua sponte statement by a trial court indicating that a signed written waiver of a defendant's right to a trial by jury has been lost is insufficient to establish a valid waiver of a defendant's right to a trial by jury. State v. Harris (Franklin 1991) 73 Ohio App.3d 57, 596 N.E.2d 563, dismissed, jurisdictional motion overruled 62 Ohio St.3d 1405, 577 N.E.2d 358.

The provision of RC 2945.05, that in a criminal case a waiver by the defendant of a trial by jury shall be in writing and signed by him, is mandatory. Winters v. Alvis (Franklin 1958) 106 Ohio App.

423, 152 N.E.2d 339, 78 Ohio Law Abs. 289, 7 O.O.2d 171.

A waiver of a timely jury demand must be in writing under RC 2945.05 and defendant's silent acquiescence to the earlier scheduled nonjury trial does not constitute a waiver. Warren v Wortman, No. 92–T–4735, 1993 WL 256753 (11th Dist Ct App, Trumbull, 6–30–93).

Although Crim R 23(A) purports to permit an oral waiver of jury trial made in open court, RC 2945.05 requires a written waiver; as a statute supersedes an analogous conflicting rule, RC 2945.05 requiring a written waiver supersedes Crim R 23(A). State v Hurt, No. 58882 (8th Dist Ct App, Cuyahoga, 9–12–91).

4. —— Duty of court, procedure for written waiver

Trial court's colloquy with defendant was sufficient to satisfy jury-waiver statute requiring colloquy such that trial court can make reasonable determination that defendant was advised and aware of implications of voluntarily relinquishing a constitutional right, where defense counsel presented trial court with three signed jury waivers, trial court asked defendant whether he had signed jury waivers, defendant acknowledged his signature, trial court asked defendant whether he understood that he was entitled to jury trial and that he was waiving that right by signing jury waivers, and defendant responded affirmatively. State v. Pace (Ohio App. 8 Dist., Cuyahoga, 07-14-2005) No. 84996, 2005-Ohio-3586, 2005 WL 1653588, Unreported. Jury ⚿ 29(6)

Because defendant filed proper jury demand, and there was no written, signed, and filed jury waiver, Municipal Court lacked jurisdiction to conduct bench trial and enter judgment of conviction on charges of assault, dereliction of duty, and aggravated menacing. Cleveland v. Fischbach (Ohio App. 8 Dist., Cuyahoga, 06-23-2005) No. 84944, 2005-Ohio-3164, 2005 WL 1490118, Unreported. Jury ⚿ 25(3); Jury ⚿ 29(1)

Requirement that defendant's waiver of jury trial be executed in open court was satisfied when trial court engaged in a colloquy with defendant extensive enough for trial judge to make a reasonable determination that defendant had been advised and was aware of implications of voluntarily relinquishing a constitutional right to a trial by jury and court reaffirmed waiver in open court. State v. Wilkens (Ohio App. 8 Dist., Cuyahoga, 10-21-2004) No. 84136, 2004-Ohio-5609, 2004 WL 2367339, Unreported. Jury ⚿ 29(6)

Trial court fulfilled statutory requirements related to waiver of jury trial right; jury waiver was filed before state rested its case and well before jury verdict, trial court asked defendant whether he understood what he was doing and whether he wanted to waive jury trial, defendant responded affirmatively, and court informed defendant of potential punishment. State v. Lowe (Ohio App. 8 Dist., Cuyahoga, 09-02-2004) No. 82997, 2004-Ohio-4622, 2004 WL 1944785, Unreported, appeal not allowed 104 Ohio St.3d 1461, 821 N.E.2d 578, 2005-Ohio-204, motion to reopen denied 2005-Ohio-5986, 2005 WL 3007146. Jury ⚿ 29(6)

Defendant's jury waiver was not rendered invalid by the fact that trial judge did not journalize her acceptance of the waiver until after trial, where record showed that waiver was validly considered and accepted before trial. State v. Corbin (Ohio App. 8 Dist., Cuyahoga, 06-03-2004) No. 82266, 2004-Ohio-2847, 2004 WL 1221670, Unreported, motion for delayed appeal denied 103 Ohio St.3d 1460, 815 N.E.2d 676, 2004-Ohio-5056, motion to reopen denied 2005-Ohio-4119, 2005 WL 1907342. Jury ⚿ 29(6)

Defendant's jury waiver was not rendered invalid by the fact that he did not sign the waiver in open court, where defendant acknowledged his signature and his waiver in open court, and trial judge engaged defendant in a discussion of his right to a jury trial. State v. Corbin (Ohio App. 8 Dist., Cuyahoga, 06-03-2004) No. 82266, 2004-Ohio-2847, 2004 WL 1221670, Unreported, motion for delayed appeal denied 103 Ohio St.3d 1460, 815 N.E.2d 676, 2004-Ohio-5056, motion to reopen denied 2005-Ohio-4119, 2005 WL 1907342. Jury ⚿ 29(6)

Record demonstrated that defendant's waiver of jury trial was knowing, voluntary, and intelligent, even though waiver was not signed in open court and was not journalized until after trial record demonstrated that waiver was signed by defendant and her counsel prior to trial, was file stamped, and was made part of record and that defendant indicated in open court that she understood the consequences of signing waiver and that she desired to have her case tried to the bench. State v. Shelton (Ohio App. 8 Dist., Cuyahoga, 03-11-2004) No. 83242, 2004-Ohio-1131, 2004 WL 449337, Unreported, appeal not allowed 102 Ohio St.3d 1484, 810 N.E.2d 968, 2004-Ohio-3069. Jury ⚿ 29(6)

Assuming petitioner's allegations that trial court's failing to obtain written waiver of his right to jury trial, prior to accepting his guilty plea, violated statute governing written jury waivers, petitioner had an adequate legal remedy through a direct appeal from the conviction and, thus, could not maintain viable habeas corpus action based on alleged violation. Hitchcock v. Wilson (Ohio App. 11 Dist., Trumbull, 03-05-2004) No. 2003-T-0131, 2004-Ohio-1073, 2004 WL 432323, Unreported. Habeas Corpus ⚿ 291

Defendant's jury trial waiver colloquy was made in open court, for purposes of determining whether waiver in prosecution for aggravated robbery was valid; court asked defendant if it was his signature on waiver, proceeded to question defendant regarding the waiver, and determined that waiver was knowing, intelligent, and voluntary. State v. Carothers (Ohio App. 8 Dist., Cuyahoga, 01-08-2004) No. 82860, 2004-Ohio-51, 2004 WL 35936, Unreported, appeal not allowed 102 Ohio St.3d 1460, 809 N.E.2d 33, 2004-Ohio-2569. Jury ⚿ 29(6)

Trial court's failure to strictly comply with mandates of code governing waiver of jury trials by failing to afford pro se defendant opportunity to consult with attorney prior to his waiver of jury trial amounted to prejudicial error. State v. Reese (Ohio App. 11 Dist., Trumbull, 12-31-2003) No. 2002-T-0068, 2004-Ohio-341, 2003 WL 23097097, Unreported, stay granted 101 Ohio St.3d 1457, 803 N.E.2d 830, 2004-Ohio-642, appeal allowed 102 Ohio St.3d 1457, 809 N.E.2d 32, 2004-Ohio-2569, reversed 106 Ohio St.3d 65, 831 N.E.2d 983, 2005-Ohio-3806. Criminal Law ⚷ 1166(1)

Trial court's failure to strictly comply with mandates of code governing waiver of jury trials by failing to afford pro se defendant opportunity to consult with attorney prior to his waiver of jury trial resulted in an improper waiver. State v. Reese (Ohio App. 11 Dist., Trumbull, 12-31-2003) No. 2002-T-0068, 2004-Ohio-341, 2003 WL 23097097, Unreported, stay granted 101 Ohio St.3d 1457, 803 N.E.2d 830, 2004-Ohio-642, appeal allowed 102 Ohio St.3d 1457, 809 N.E.2d 32, 2004-Ohio-2569, reversed 106 Ohio St.3d 65, 831 N.E.2d 983, 2005-Ohio-3806. Jury ⚷ 29(6)

Trial court failed to strictly comply with mandates of code governing waiver of jury trials by failing to afford pro se defendant opportunity to consult with attorney prior to his waiver of jury trial. State v. Reese (Ohio App. 11 Dist., Trumbull, 12-31-2003) No. 2002-T-0068, 2004-Ohio-341, 2003 WL 23097097, Unreported, stay granted 101 Ohio St.3d 1457, 803 N.E.2d 830, 2004-Ohio-642, appeal allowed 102 Ohio St.3d 1457, 809 N.E.2d 32, 2004-Ohio-2569, reversed 106 Ohio St.3d 65, 831 N.E.2d 983, 2005-Ohio-3806. Jury ⚷ 29(6)

Defendant's waiver of right to trial by jury on charges of driving while under the influence of alcohol or drugs (OMVI) and driving under suspension was valid as entered knowingly, intelligently, and voluntarily; colloquy between trial court, defense counsel, and defendant demonstrated defendant's awareness of right, and defendant signed waiver form that included language substantively similar to that which is suggested by jury trial waiver statute. State v. Townsend (Ohio App. 3 Dist., Marion, 12-22-2003) No. 9-03-40, 2003-Ohio-6992, 2003 WL 22994985, Unreported. Jury ⚷ 29(6)

Court of Appeals would presume that trial court transcript correctly reflected that defendant had executed jury waiver form in open court. State v. Bonner (Ohio App. 8 Dist., Cuyahoga, 12-04-2003) No. 82475, 2003-Ohio-6493, 2003 WL 22862794, Unreported. Criminal Law ⚷ 1144.9

Fact that trial court's journal entry setting forth jury waiver was not filed until after trial had ended did not divest trial court of jurisdiction to conduct bench trial, in prosecution for burglary of an occupied structure; strict compliance with statutory requirement was met upon filing waiver, and there was no rule pertaining to when filing must occur. State v. Thomas (Ohio App. 8 Dist., Cuyahoga, 11-20-2003) No. 82130, 2003-Ohio-6157, 2003 WL 22724619, Unreported, appeal not allowed 102 Ohio St.3d 1422, 807 N.E.2d 367, 2004-Ohio-2003, habeas corpus dismissed 2006 WL 1526061. Jury ⚷ 29(6)

Fact that trial court did not acknowledge defendant's signature on jury waiver in open court did not divest trial court of jurisdiction to conduct bench trial, in prosecution for burglary of an occupied structure; trial judge carefully examined defendant, explained his rights, and determined that his action in seeking waiver was knowingly, intelligently, and voluntarily made, and waiver was contained in and made part of record. State v. Thomas (Ohio App. 8 Dist., Cuyahoga, 11-20-2003) No. 82130, 2003-Ohio-6157, 2003 WL 22724619, Unreported, appeal not allowed 102 Ohio St.3d 1422, 807 N.E.2d 367, 2004-Ohio-2003, habeas corpus dismissed 2006 WL 1526061. Jury ⚷ 29(6)

Fact that defendant did not sign jury waiver in open court, but, rather, during recess from trial, did not divest trial court of jurisdiction to conduct bench trial, in prosecution for burglary of an occupied structure; statutory requirement that waiver be in open court was satisfied by colloquy between trial court and defendant, during which trial court asked defendant whether he understood that he had constitutional right to trial by jury, and, after defendant responded affirmatively, concluded that defendant had knowingly and intelligently waived his right to jury trial. State v. Thomas (Ohio App. 8 Dist., Cuyahoga, 11-20-2003) No. 82130, 2003-Ohio-6157, 2003 WL 22724619, Unreported, appeal not allowed 102 Ohio St.3d 1422, 807 N.E.2d 367, 2004-Ohio-2003, habeas corpus dismissed 2006 WL 1526061. Jury ⚷ 29(6)

Colloquy between trial court and defendant was sufficient to satisfy statutory requirement that waiver of right to jury trial be made in open court; record reflected that trial judge asked defense counsel to show defendant the signed jury waiver and then asked appellant whether that was his signature on the form, after defendant acknowledged his signature, the trial judge asked him whether he understood that he was entitled to a trial by jury and that by signing the form he was waiving that right, and upon defendant's affirmative response, the trial judge concluded that appellant had knowingly and intelligently waived his right to a jury trial. State v. Franklin (Ohio App. 8 Dist., Cuyahoga, 05-22-2003) No. 81426, 2003-Ohio-2649, 2003 WL 21193014, Unreported, appeal not allowed 100 Ohio St.3d 1424, 797 N.E.2d 92, 2003-Ohio-5232. Jury ⚷ 29(6)

Defendant's waiver of his right to a jury trial was voluntary and knowing; review of record indicated that trial court made required inquiry into determining whether defendant was aware of consequences associated with waiving his right to jury trial. State v. Merriweather (Ohio App. 8 Dist., Cuyahoga, 03-21-2003) No. 58089, 2003-Ohio-1498, 2003 WL 1561525, Unreported, appeal not allowed 99 Ohio St.3d 1457, 790 N.E.2d 1220, 2003-Ohio-3514. Jury ⚷ 29(6)

Trial court fulfilled all the statutory requirements for defendant's waiving trial by jury, and thus, court had jurisdiction to try the defendant without a jury; defendant signed his jury waiver before the beginning of his trial, defendant's counsel stated in open court that defendant was willing to waive trial by jury, defendant acknowledged the waiver and stated in open court that he was willing to waive trial by jury, and trial court filed the signed jury waiver eight days later and included it as part of the record. State v. Huber (Ohio App. 8 Dist., Cuyahoga, 10-24-2002) No. 80616, 2002-Ohio-5839, 2002 WL 31401616, Unreported, appeal not allowed 98 Ohio St.3d 1490, 785 N.E.2d 473, 2003-Ohio-1189, motion to reopen denied 2003-Ohio-3210, 2003 WL 21419177, motion to reopen denied 2004-Ohio-3951, 2004 WL 1681261, appeal after new sentencing hearing 2005-Ohio-2625, 2005 WL 1245629. Jury ⚷ 29(6)

A court speaks through its journal and thus a jury waiver where no journal entry is made and there is no time stamp or filing receipt of the clerk's office thereon is not "filed in the criminal action" and the conviction must be reversed. State v. Coleman (Ohio App. 8 Dist., Cuyahoga, 05-09-1996) No. 69202, 1996 WL 239878, Unreported, dismissed, appeal not allowed 77 Ohio St.3d 1446, 671 N.E.2d 1284.

In the absence of strict compliance with statute governing waiver of jury trial, a trial court lacks jurisdiction to try the defendant without a jury. State v. Thomas (Ohio, 12-11-2002) 97 Ohio St.3d 309, 779 N.E.2d 1017, 2002-Ohio-6624, reconsideration denied 97 Ohio St.3d 1498, 780 N.E.2d 1022, 2002-Ohio-7248, stay granted 98 Ohio St.3d 1403, 781 N.E.2d 221, 2003-Ohio-40, certiorari denied 123 S.Ct. 2295, 539 U.S. 916, 156 L.Ed.2d 133. Jury ⚷ 29(6)

Once the demand for a jury trial has been filed in a petty offense case, the trial judge may not try the defendant without a jury unless the defendant makes a knowing, voluntary, and intelligent waiver of his right to a jury trial, and that waiver is made a part of the record. State v. Pflanz (Ohio App. 1 Dist., 10-22-1999) 135 Ohio App.3d 338, 733 N.E.2d 1212. Jury ⚷ 29(6)

Any failure to comply with statute establishing requirements for waiver of defendant's right to jury trial may be remedied only in a direct appeal from a criminal conviction, and not by extraordinary writ. State ex rel. Billings v. Friedland (Ohio, 03-22-2000) 88 Ohio St.3d 237, 724 N.E.2d 1151, 2000-Ohio-317. Criminal Law ⚷ 1007

Trial court's failure to obtain a waiver of counsel, or an express waiver of jury trial from defendant charged with "serious offense" of operating motor vehicle while intoxicated (OMVI) with two prior offenses within six years, divested the trial court of jurisdiction to conduct the bench trial. State v. Garris (Ohio App. 3 Dist., 06-03-1998) 128 Ohio App.3d 126, 713 N.E.2d 1135. Criminal Law ⚷ 641.12(4); Jury ⚷ 29(1)

Statutory requirements for waiving jury trial in "criminal cases" do not apply to requests made by a defendant, under former prior conviction specification statutes, to have trial judge, in case tried by jury, determine specifications to support term of actual incarceration or specifications to support indefinite term. State v. Nagel (Ohio, 01-06-1999) 84 Ohio St.3d 280, 703 N.E.2d 773, 1999-Ohio-507. Sentencing And Punishment ⚷ 1355

Jurisdiction to try defendant was lacking, as waiver of jury trial was not filed in action, as evidenced by time stamp from clerk's office, or by admission into record during course of trial making paper exhibit to transcript, even though waiver appeared in record of case. State v. Ward (Ohio App. 8 Dist., 10-28-1996) 114 Ohio App.3d 722, 683 N.E.2d 1182, appeal not allowed 78 Ohio St.3d 1414, 675 N.E.2d 1251. Jury ⚷ 29(6)

Defendant was denied constitutional right to trial by jury and trial court did not have jurisdiction to conduct trial without jury even though defense counsel had moved the court to waive jury, which trial court agreed to, where written jury waiver was never signed or filed in the record. State v. Edwards (Ohio App. 8 Dist., 12-18-1995) 107 Ohio App.3d 783, 669 N.E.2d 521. Jury ⚷ 29(6)

Trial court is without jurisdiction to try defendant where record does not show strict compliance with jury waiver statute. State v. Edwards (Ohio App. 8 Dist., 12-18-1995) 107 Ohio App.3d 783, 669 N.E.2d 521. Jury ⚷ 29(6)

Criminal rules and revised code provision concerning jury waiver are satisfied by written waiver, signed by the defendant and filed with the court, and made in open court. State v. Edwards (Ohio App. 8 Dist., 12-18-1995) 107 Ohio App.3d 783, 669 N.E.2d 521. Jury ⚷ 29(6)

Statutory requirement that trial court file jury waiver with clerk and make it part of record in case was complied with when defendant's original waiver was made part of record and trial judge filed journal entry of waiver in clerk's office. State v. Billings (Ohio App. 8 Dist., 04-06-1995) 103 Ohio App.3d 343, 659 N.E.2d 799, belated appeal granted 73 Ohio St.3d 1412, 651 N.E.2d 1310, dismissed, jurisdictional motion overruled 74 Ohio St.3d 1455, 656 N.E.2d 950, subsequent mandamus proceeding 1999 WL 754508, affirmed 88 Ohio St.3d 237, 724 N.E.2d 1151, 2000-Ohio-317. Jury ⚷ 29(6)

In prosecution of defendant for aggravated trafficking with prior drug offense, it was harmless error for trial court to remove from jury's consideration the element of the prior conviction for felony drug abuse offense without waiver signed by defendant because any jury would necessarily have found for the state on that issue given defendant's stipulation to existence of the prior felony drug abuse offense conviction. State v. Riley (Ohio App. 2 Dist., 11-23-1994) 98 Ohio App.3d 801, 649 N.E.2d 914. Criminal Law ⚷ 1177.5(1)

Defendant voluntarily made knowing and intelligent waiver of jury trial, where language of written waiver of jury trial substantially complied with that required by statute and transcript revealed that defendant reaffirmed his waiver orally, in open court, following admonition and explanation by trial judge immediately preceding trial. State v. Walker (Ohio App. 3 Dist., 09-15-1993) 90 Ohio App.3d 352, 629 N.E.2d 471. Jury ⚷ 29(6)

Valid waiver of right to jury trial is accomplished by completion of two-step process: (1) defendant must sign written statement affirming that he is knowingly and voluntarily waiving his constitutional right to trial by jury, uninfluenced by promises or threats of any kind, and (2) there must occur, in open court, colloquy between trial judge and defendant himself extensive enough for judge to make reasonable determination that defendant has been advised and is aware of implications of voluntarily relinquishing constitutional right. State v. Walker (Ohio App. 3 Dist., 09-15-1993) 90 Ohio App.3d 352, 629 N.E.2d 471. Jury ⚷ 29(6)

For purposes of statute governing waiver of jury trial, written waiver need not be actually signed in open court as long as signed writing has been made part of record and waiver is reaffirmed in open court. State v. Walker (Ohio App. 3 Dist., 09-15-1993) 90 Ohio App.3d 352, 629 N.E.2d 471. Jury ⚷ 29(6)

In a prosecution on charges of rape and sexual battery, a trial court is without jurisdiction to try and convict the defendant without a jury where the court fails to obtain a written waiver of the defendant's right to a jury trial. State v. Harris (Franklin 1991) 73 Ohio App.3d 57, 596 N.E.2d 563, dismissed, jurisdictional motion overruled 62 Ohio St.3d 1405, 577 N.E.2d 358. Jury ⚷ 29(6)

There is no requirement for a trial court to interrogate a defendant in order to determine whether he or she is fully apprised of the right to a jury trial. State v. Jells (Ohio 1990) 53 Ohio St.3d 22, 559 N.E.2d 464, rehearing denied 54 Ohio St.3d 710, 561 N.E.2d 945, certiorari denied 111 S.Ct. 1020, 498 U.S. 1111, 112 L.Ed.2d 1101, dismissal of post-conviction relief affirmed, dismissed, appeal not allowed 83 Ohio St.3d 1431, 699 N.E.2d 946. Jury ⚷ 29(6)

Neither RC 2945.05 nor Crim R 23(A) requires that a court personally address an accused regarding his waiver of a jury trial, or that any underlying agreement regarding such a waiver be made a part of the record. State v. Griffin (Hamilton 1979) 13 Ohio App.3d 376, 469 N.E.2d 1329, 13 O.B.R. 458.

RC 2945.05 and Crim R 23(A) are satisfied by a written waiver signed by the defendant himself and filed with the court; these provisions do not require that the court personally inform the defendant of his right to a jury trial or make direct inquiry of the defendant as to the voluntariness of his waiver. State v. Morris (Cuyahoga 1982) 8 Ohio App.3d 12, 455 N.E.2d 1352, 8 O.B.R. 13.

Where defendant waived right to jury trial in municipal court of Toledo which is a court of record, granting state's request and trying defendant with jury *held* error (GC 1579–276, 1579–300, 13442–4). State v. Winters (Lucas 1931) 41 Ohio App. 146, 180 N.E. 559, 12 Ohio Law Abs. 164. Jury ⚷ 29(2)

5. —— Execution of waiver form, procedure for written waiver

Defendant's waiver of jury trial was valid, even though defendant did not sign waiver form in open court; statute did not require contemporaneous execution of jury waiver form in open court, transcript showed that defendant signed waiver form prior to trial, that he specifically acknowledged to court that his signature appeared on waiver, that he understood his right to jury trial, and that he agreed that decision to waive jury trial was his own decision, and written waiver, together with trial court's written acceptance of waiver, were filed on date trial began. State v. Shue (Ohio App. 8 Dist., Cuyahoga, 09-23-2004) No. 84007, 2004-Ohio-5021, 2004 WL 2340073, Unreported, appeal not allowed 105 Ohio St.3d 1452, 823 N.E.2d 457, 2005-Ohio-763. Jury ⚷ 29(6)

Defendant was not required to execute written waiver of right to jury trial in open court, and waiver executed in writing prior to entering courtroom and acknowledged by him in open court as knowing, intelligent and voluntary, was satisfactory. State v. Johnson (Ohio App. 8 Dist., Cuyahoga, 08-12-2004) No. 83117, 2004-Ohio-4229, 2004 WL 1795318, Unreported, appeal not allowed 104 Ohio St.3d 1461, 821 N.E.2d 577, 2005-Ohio-204. Jury ⚷ 29(6)

Defendant's written jury waiver, reaffirmed in open court and made part of the record, satisfied statutory requirements for waiver of jury trial, even though waiver was not actually signed in open court and was not filed until after trial had ended. State v. Dixon (Ohio App. 8 Dist., Cuyahoga, 05-13-2004) No. 82951, 2004-Ohio-2406, 2004 WL 1067527, Unreported, appeal not allowed 103 Ohio St.3d 1479, 816 N.E.2d 255, 2004-Ohio-5405. Jury ⚷ 29(6)

Trial court's failure to execute defendant's waiver of trial by jury in open court, or to file a contemporaneous journal entry that noted defendant's waiver, did not render waiver of jury trial invalid; statute only required that a signed waiver form be filed. State v. Phillips (Ohio App. 8 Dist., Cuyahoga, 02-05-2004) No. 82886, 2004-Ohio-484, 2004 WL 226120, Unreported, appeal not allowed 103 Ohio St.3d 1404, 812 N.E.2d 1287, 2004-Ohio-3980. Jury ⚷ 29(6)

6. —— Journalized forms, procedure for written waiver

Jury waiver form filed by trial court with clerk of courts on date of its signature was valid, irrespective of date on which filing was journalized. State v. Cunningham (Ohio App. 8 Dist., Cuyahoga, 06-16-2005) No. 84960, 2005-Ohio-3007, 2005 WL 1406290, Unreported. Jury ⚷ 29(6)

Defendant's waiver of jury trial was properly journalized, for purposes of determining whether waiver in prosecution for aggravated robbery was valid; record reflected that waiver form was signed by defendant and filed on day before trial, and that waiver was filed, time-stamped, and placed in the record. State v. Carothers (Ohio App. 8 Dist., Cuyahoga, 01-08-2004) No. 82860, 2004-Ohio-51, 2004 WL 35936, Unreported, appeal not allowed 102 Ohio St.3d 1460, 809 N.E.2d 33, 2004-Ohio-2569. Jury ⚷ 29(6)

Jury waiver was filed, time-stamped, and contained in record, and thus trial court had jurisdiction to conduct bench trial, even though waiver was not filed and placed in record before trial commenced. State v. Franklin (Ohio App. 8 Dist.,

Cuyahoga, 05-22-2003) No. 81426, 2003-Ohio-2649, 2003 WL 21193014, Unreported, appeal not allowed 100 Ohio St.3d 1424, 797 N.E.2d 92, 2003-Ohio-5232. Jury ⚷ 29(6)

Written jury waiver satisfied statutory requirements, and thus trial court had jurisdiction to conduct bench trial, even if waiver was not filed until after trial; waiver was in writing, signed by defendant, filed in the case, and made part of the record. State v. McKinney (Ohio App. 8 Dist., Cuyahoga, 12-26-2002) No. 80991, 2002-Ohio-7249, 2002 WL 31875967, Unreported. Jury ⚷ 29(6)

A written waiver of a defendant's right to a jury trial which is signed by the defendant is not effective where the waiver is not time-stamped and filed with the clerk's office as part of the record. State v McDonald, No. CA-9033, 1993 WL 271169 (5th Dist Ct App, Stark, 7-6-93).

Statutory requirement that a jury waiver form be "filed in said cause and made a part of the record thereof" means that the form must be time-stamped and included in the record. State v. Thomas (Ohio, 12-11-2002) 97 Ohio St.3d 309, 779 N.E.2d 1017, 2002-Ohio-6624, reconsideration denied 97 Ohio St.3d 1498, 780 N.E.2d 1022, 2002-Ohio-7248, stay granted 98 Ohio St.3d 1403, 781 N.E.2d 221, 2003-Ohio-40, certiorari denied 123 S.Ct. 2295, 539 U.S. 916, 156 L.Ed.2d 133. Jury ⚷ 29(6)

A second jury waiver form signed by defendant, which was date-stamped but not journalized, did not invalidate jury waiver, where jury waiver form containing identical language that defendant had signed 18 days earlier was date-stamped and properly journalized, thus meeting strict statutory requirements. State v. Thomas (Ohio, 12-11-2002) 97 Ohio St.3d 309, 779 N.E.2d 1017, 2002-Ohio-6624, reconsideration denied 97 Ohio St.3d 1498, 780 N.E.2d 1022, 2002-Ohio-7248, stay granted 98 Ohio St.3d 1403, 781 N.E.2d 221, 2003-Ohio-40, certiorari denied 123 S.Ct. 2295, 539 U.S. 916, 156 L.Ed.2d 133. Jury ⚷ 29(6)

7. —— Jurisdiction, procedure for written waiver

Lack of written jury waiver could not have deprived trial court of jurisdiction over defendant who entered guilty plea to one count of involuntary manslaughter and one count of endangering children and, thus, alleged violation of statute governing written jury waiver could not form basis for habeas corpus relief. Hitchcock v. Wilson (Ohio App. 11 Dist., Trumbull, 03-05-2004) No. 2003-T-0131, 2004-Ohio-1073, 2004 WL 432323, Unreported. Habeas Corpus ⚷ 496

Three-judge panel lacked subject matter jurisdiction to accept defendant's guilty pleas to two counts of aggravated murder with mass murder and felony murder specifications, as both counts still contained death penalty specifications, and defendant had not signed waiver of his right to jury trial. State v. Carley (Ohio App. 8 Dist., 09-25-2000) 139 Ohio App.3d 841, 745 N.E.2d 1122, appeal after new trial 2004-Ohio-1901, 2004 WL 794533, appeal not allowed 103 Ohio St.3d 1427, 814 N.E.2d 490, 2004-Ohio-4524, motion to reopen denied 2004-Ohio-5479, 2004 WL 2335805, appeal not allowed 104 Ohio St.3d 1463, 821 N.E.2d 578, 2005-Ohio-204. Criminal Law ⚷ 273(4.1); Jury ⚷ 29(4)

Absent strict compliance with statute requiring written waiver of right to jury trial, trial court lacks jurisdiction to try defendant without jury. State v. Haught (Ohio, 10-16-1996) 670 N.E.2d 232, 1996-Ohio-353. Jury ⚷ 29(6)

Three-judge panel had no jurisdiction to conduct aggravated murder trial due to court's failure to strictly comply with statute mandating that waiver of jury must be in writing, signed by defendant, filed in criminal action and made part of record; defendant's written waiver of right to trial by jury was never filed with trial court and never made part of record in case. State v. Pless (Ohio, 01-17-1996) 74 Ohio St.3d 333, 658 N.E.2d 766, 1996-Ohio-102, reconsideration denied 75 Ohio St.3d 1413, 661 N.E.2d 760, appeal after new trial 1998 WL 269093, dismissed, appeal not allowed 83 Ohio St.3d 1447, 700 N.E.2d 331. Jury ⚷ 29(6)

In absence of strict compliance with statute mandating that waiver of jury trial must be in writing, signed by defendant, filed in criminal action, and made part of the record thereof, trial court lacks jurisdiction to try defendant without jury. State v. Pless (Ohio, 01-17-1996) 74 Ohio St.3d 333, 658 N.E.2d 766, 1996-Ohio-102, reconsideration denied 75 Ohio St.3d 1413, 661 N.E.2d 760, appeal after new trial 1998 WL 269093, dismissed, appeal not allowed 83 Ohio St.3d 1447, 700 N.E.2d 331. Jury ⚷ 29(6)

Court of common pleas' lack of jurisdiction to try and convict defendant without jury, due to lack of evidence that written waiver was ever filed and made part of record, presented extraordinary circumstance warranting writ of habeas corpus. State ex rel. Jackson v. Dallman (Ohio, 09-14-1994) 70 Ohio St.3d 261, 638 N.E.2d 563, 1994-Ohio-235. Habeas Corpus ⚷ 496

8. —— Rejection by court, procedure for written waiver

Claimed violation of statute setting forth jury-trial waiver requirements is not the proper subject for habeas corpus relief and may be remedied only in a direct appeal from a criminal conviction. Bradford v. Moore (Ohio, 09-20-2000) 90 Ohio St.3d 75, 734 N.E.2d 828, 2000-Ohio-25. Habeas Corpus ⚷ 291

Claimed violation of statutory jury-trial waiver requirement was not proper subject for habeas corpus relief, and was subject to remedy only in direct appeal from criminal conviction. State ex rel. Earl v. Mitchell (Ohio, 12-01-1999) 87 Ohio St.3d 259, 719 N.E.2d 545, 1999-Ohio-54. Habeas Corpus ⚷ 496

Inmate who petitioned for writ of mandamus to compel trial judge to vacate inmate's conviction and sentence due to trial judge's alleged failure to comply with statutory jury-trial waiver requirements was not entitled to relief, as inmate essentially sought release from prison. State ex rel. Larkins v. Aurelius (Ohio, 12-09-1998) 84 Ohio St.3d 112, 702

N.E.2d 79, 1998-Ohio-661, certiorari denied 119 S.Ct. 1470, 526 U.S. 1072, 143 L.Ed.2d 554. Mandamus ⚩ 61

Failure to comply with statutory requirements for waiving jury trial may be remedied only in direct appeal from criminal conviction and is not proper subject of habeas corpus relief. Jackson v. Rose (Ohio, 06-18-1997) 79 Ohio St.3d 51, 679 N.E.2d 684, 1997-Ohio-179. Criminal Law ⚩ 1007; Habeas Corpus ⚩ 496

Trial court cannot reject defendant's waiver of right to jury trial. State v. Van Sickle (Ohio App. 10 Dist., 09-14-1993) 90 Ohio App.3d 301, 629 N.E.2d 39, dismissed, jurisdictional motion overruled 68 Ohio St.3d 1445, 626 N.E.2d 687. Jury ⚩ 29(2)

Denial of defendant's motion to sever for trial charge of aggravated murder and charge of abuse of corpse deprived defendant of her statutory right to waive jury trial on abuse of corpse charge since defendant desired jury trial on aggravated murder charge and to present defense on that charge. State v. Van Sickle (Ohio App. 10 Dist., 09-14-1993) 90 Ohio App.3d 301, 629 N.E.2d 39, dismissed, jurisdictional motion overruled 68 Ohio St.3d 1445, 626 N.E.2d 687. Criminal Law ⚩ 620(6); Jury ⚩ 29(2)

Trial court's denial of defendant's motion to sever for trial charge of aggravated murder and charge of abuse of corpse could not be deemed harmless error inasmuch as videotape of victim's body, which was admissible only as to abuse of corpse charge, was highly prejudicial with respect to murder charge, and denial of motion deprived defendant of her right to waive jury trial on abuse of corpse charge. State v. Van Sickle (Ohio App. 10 Dist., 09-14-1993) 90 Ohio App.3d 301, 629 N.E.2d 39, dismissed, jurisdictional motion overruled 68 Ohio St.3d 1445, 626 N.E.2d 687. Criminal Law ⚩ 1166(6)

Trial court has no power to reject defendant's waiver of right of trial by jury under this section, unless suggestion of his present insanity is made by counsel for accused or it otherwise comes to notice of court that accused is not then sane. State v. Frohner (Ohio 1948) 150 Ohio St. 53, 80 N.E.2d 868, 37 O.O. 406. Jury ⚩ 29(1)

The statutes giving accused the right to waive a jury and be tried by the court, are mandatory; and court has no power to reject accused's waiver, unless suggestion of his present insanity is made by counsel for accused or it otherwise comes to the notice of the court that accused is not then sane. State v. Smith (Ohio 1931) 123 Ohio St. 237, 174 N.E. 768, 9 Ohio Law Abs. 286, 34 Ohio Law Rep. 71.

9. —— Time requirements, procedure for written waiver

That signed jury waiver form was not processed for a couple days until after commencement of bench trial did not render it defective as to divest trial court of jurisdiction, in burglary prosecution; waiver was in writing, signed, filed, and made part of the record. State v. Stewart (Ohio App. 8 Dist., Cuyahoga, 03-09-2006) No. 86397, 2006-Ohio-1071, 2006 WL 562204, Unreported. Jury ⚩ 29(6)

Defendant's waiver of right to jury trial with respect to charge for having weapon under disability was not valid, where trial court did not file timely written waiver of jury trial, and there was no oral waiver on record or entry on docket indicating written waiver of jury trial prior to proceeding to trial on other charges. State v. Kennedy (Ohio App. 8 Dist., Cuyahoga, 12-02-2004) No. 83445, 2004-Ohio-6414, 2004 WL 2756211, Unreported, motion for delayed appeal granted 105 Ohio St.3d 1497, 825 N.E.2d 621, 2005-Ohio-1666, appeal not allowed 106 Ohio St.3d 1483, 832 N.E.2d 737, 2005-Ohio-3978. Jury ⚩ 29(6)

Jury waiver was obtained in accordance with statutory requirements where jury waiver form signed by defendant was filed on first day of trial, waiver occurred before trial, and waiver form was filed, time-stamped and placed in record. State v. Wilkens (Ohio App. 8 Dist., Cuyahoga, 10-21-2004) No. 84136, 2004-Ohio-5609, 2004 WL 2367339, Unreported. Jury ⚩ 29(6)

Defendant validly waived his right to jury trial, even though waiver was not signed in open court and waiver may not have been filed until trial was over; trial court conducted lengthy colloquy with defendant regarding his waiver of jury trial at forefront of trial, and waiver was in writing, signed by defendant, filed and journalized in the case, and made a part of the record. State v. Kiriazis (Ohio App. 8 Dist., Cuyahoga, 02-05-2004) No. 82887, 2004-Ohio-502, 2004 WL 231478, Unreported, appeal not allowed 102 Ohio St.3d 1485, 810 N.E.2d 968, 2004-Ohio-3069. Jury ⚩ 29(6)

Defendant lacked arguable claim that signed affidavit for waiver of jury trial on charges of aggravated murder, aggravated robbery, and aggravated burglary was not filed as required by statute, and thus appellate counsel was not ineffective for failing to raise issue, even though affidavit appeared to lack contemporaneous file stamp, where defendant attached photocopy of certified copy of signed jury waiver as exhibit to brief, nothing on face of copy indicated that signed waiver was not filed in trial court, and waiver showed certification of clerk of court of common pleas, which certified that copy was truly taken and copied from court file. State v. Otte (Ohio, 01-30-2002) 94 Ohio St.3d 167, 761 N.E.2d 34, 2002-Ohio-343. Criminal Law ⚩ 641.13(2.1)

Where a written jury waiver is not obtained prior to commencement of trial under RC 2945.05, the trial record is silent as to circumstances surrounding the mid-trial written jury waiver, and the record contains no clear reference to a jury waiver in open court, the waiver is invalid. State v. Johnson (Franklin 1992) 81 Ohio App.3d 482, 611 N.E.2d 414, dismissed, jurisdictional motion overruled 65 Ohio St.3d 1454, 602 N.E.2d 251.

A trial by jury in a criminal case may be waived at any time before it becomes known that the jury is deadlocked in reaching a verdict. City of Columbus v. Voyles (Franklin 1972) 32 Ohio App.2d 309, 291 N.E.2d 536, 61 O.O.2d 435. Jury ⚷ 29(6)

Where the jury in a criminal case is unable to reach a verdict after hearing all of the evidence, and counsel for the defendant thereafter attempts to orally waive the trial by jury and submit the cause to the court, it is not error for the court to declare a mistrial and to refuse to determine the question of guilt or innocence of the defendant. City of Columbus v. Voyles (Franklin 1972) 32 Ohio App.2d 309, 291 N.E.2d 536, 61 O.O.2d 435.

Appellate counsel did not render "deficient" performance by failing to anticipate decision on waivers of jury trial which would not be made for another ten years. Beckovich v. Coyle (N.D.Ohio, 10-15-1998) 22 F.Supp.2d 722. Criminal Law ⚷ 641.13(7)

An entry for a continuance, requested by a defendant in order to subpoena a witness, which notes that a jury is waived, does not strictly comply with the requirements for a written waiver of the right to a jury trial in RC 2945.05; thus, such a waiver is invalid and a conviction must be reversed and remanded. State v Brooks, No. 91AP–1498 (10th Dist Ct App, Franklin, 7–2–92).

10. —— Withdrawal by defendant, procedure for written waiver

An oral motion to withdraw a waiver of a jury trial made after witnesses have been sworn in is untimely and a trial court does not err in proceeding with a bench trial. Marysville v. Foreman (Union 1992) 78 Ohio App.3d 118, 603 N.E.2d 1155.

A waiver of trial by jury may be withdrawn by a defendant at any time before commencement of trial, under RC 2945.05, and it is error for the court to refuse to honor a written demand for jury trial duly filed under Crim R 23(A). State v. Grimsley (Hamilton 1982) 3 Ohio App.3d 265, 444 N.E.2d 1071, 27 A.L.R.4th 1060, 3 O.B.R. 308.

Defendant who has waived his right to trial by jury and has elected to be tried by a three-judge court, may withdraw such waiver at any time before commencement of trial but not after hearing. State v. Frohner (Ohio 1948) 150 Ohio St. 53, 80 N.E.2d 868, 37 O.O. 406. Jury ⚷ 29(7)

11. Guilty plea as waiver

The provisions of RC 2945.05 requiring the filing of a written waiver of a trial by jury are not applicable where a plea of guilty is entered by an accused. Martin v. Maxwell (Ohio 1963) 175 Ohio St. 147, 191 N.E.2d 838, 23 O.O.2d 423.

The entry of a plea of guilty by an accused constitutes a waiver of a jury trial. McAuley v. Maxwell (Ohio 1963) 174 Ohio St. 567, 190 N.E.2d 922, 23 O.O.2d 243.

In 1930 no written waiver of trial by jury was required where a defendant pleaded guilty to homicide generally before a one judge court. State ex rel. Evans v. Eckle (Ohio 1955) 163 Ohio St. 122, 126 N.E.2d 48, 56 O.O. 177.

A guilty plea is a waiver of a trial by jury. Matey v. Sacks (C.A.6 (Ohio) 1960) 284 F.2d 335, 15 O.O.2d 123.

Where defendant pleads guilty to first degree murder, neither failure of the court to appoint counsel nor failure to obtain a written waiver of the right to jury trial from such defendant is grounds for issuance of a writ of habeas corpus. Sims v. Alvis (C.A.6 (Ohio) 1958) 253 F.2d 114, 16 O.O.2d 185, certiorari denied 79 S.Ct. 67, 358 U.S. 844, 3 L.Ed.2d 78.

12. Capital cases

Post-conviction relief petitioner failed to prove that jury trial waiver was invalid because he underwent sodium pentothal interview on same day waiver was filed in capital murder prosecution, where it was not certain that waiver was executed on that day, defense counsel testified that he would not have allowed waiver proceeding to continue had he thought petitioner was incapable of understanding what was going on, and there was no evidence that sodium pentothal actually affected petitioner's judgment. State v. Moreland (Ohio App. 2 Dist., Montgomery, 10-08-2004) No. 20331, 2004-Ohio-5778, 2004 WL 2436589, Unreported, appeal not allowed 105 Ohio St.3d 1452, 823 N.E.2d 457, 2005-Ohio-763. Jury ⚷ 29(6)

Facts that jury trial waiver did not show date of signature or witness signatures, that there was no transcript of waiver proceeding, that newspaper article reported that waiver occurred on date petitioner was subjected to sodium pentothal interview, and that defense counsel lacked capital defense experience under 1981 revision of death penalty statutes were at most matters affecting weight of evidence in post-conviction proceeding in which petitioner claimed that jury waiver was invalid. State v. Moreland (Ohio App. 2 Dist., Montgomery, 10-08-2004) No. 20331, 2004-Ohio-5778, 2004 WL 2436589, Unreported, appeal not allowed 105 Ohio St.3d 1452, 823 N.E.2d 457, 2005-Ohio-763. Jury ⚷ 29(6)

Even if post-conviction relief petitioner was unaware of two-tiered sentencing process before he waived jury trial in capital murder prosecution, petitioner failed to prove that, if had he known of two-tiered sentencing process, he would not have waived jury trial, where defense counsel testified that, given gruesome evidence of five murders of which petitioner was accused, he believed best strategy for avoiding death penalty was trial before acceptable, presumably dispassionate, panel of judges, rather than jury trial, and that petitioner bought into this strategy. State v. Moreland (Ohio App. 2 Dist., Montgomery, 10-08-2004) No. 20331, 2004-Ohio-5778, 2004 WL 2436589, Unreported, appeal not allowed 105 Ohio St.3d 1452, 823 N.E.2d 457, 2005-Ohio-763. Jury ⚷ 29(6)

Post-conviction relief petitioner failed to prove that he was unaware of two-tiered sentencing process before he waived jury trial in capital murder prosecution, and thus, that jury trial waiver was invalid, where petitioner mischaracterized defense counsel's testimony in post-conviction proceeding regarding waiver of jury trial as irrelevant "habit and routine" evidence, counsel did not testify that he did not recall advising petitioner about two-tiered sentencing process, and instead, counsel testified that he could not recall precisely what he said to petitioner but that he was familiar with two-tiered sentencing procedure and that he believed he would have explained entire procedure to petitioner. State v. Moreland (Ohio App. 2 Dist., Montgomery, 10-08-2004) No. 20331, 2004-Ohio-5778, 2004 WL 2436589, Unreported, appeal not allowed 105 Ohio St.3d 1452, 823 N.E.2d 457, 2005-Ohio-763. Jury ⚷ 29(6)

Statutory requirements related to waiver of jury trial were met in capital murder prosecution, where jury waiver was signed by defendant, waiver language was identical to statutory language except that phrase "panel of three judges" was substituted in place of word "judge," and defense counsel indicated that waiver was executed in open court before judge. State v. Moreland (Ohio App. 2 Dist., Montgomery, 10-08-2004) No. 20331, 2004-Ohio-5778, 2004 WL 2436589, Unreported, appeal not allowed 105 Ohio St.3d 1452, 823 N.E.2d 457, 2005-Ohio-763. Jury ⚷ 29(6)

Murder defendant's waiver of jury trial was voluntary, even though defendant had told judge that he was waiving jury because his "counsel feels it's best," where defendant answered yes when asked if waiver was of his own volition, and even if, as defendant claimed, he did not know what "volition" meant because his IQ was only 74, context made inquiry comprehensible, coming as it did after question in which he was asked if waiver was of his own free will. State v. Bays (Ohio, 10-13-1999) 87 Ohio St.3d 15, 716 N.E.2d 1126, 1999-Ohio-216, reconsideration denied 87 Ohio St.3d 1454, 719 N.E.2d 969, certiorari denied 120 S.Ct. 1727, 529 U.S. 1090, 146 L.Ed.2d 647, denial of post-conviction relief reversed 159 Ohio App.3d 469, 824 N.E.2d 167, 2005-Ohio-47. Jury ⚷ 29(6)

Capital murder defendant's waiver of right to jury trial was knowing and intelligent, even though defendant argued that his waiver was because he believed particular jury would be unfair and did not understand that he was actually waiving right to a fair jury, and court did not explain that a single juror can block a death recommendation, or that a death sentence recommended by jury could not be reimposed if reversed on appeal. State v. Bays (Ohio, 10-13-1999) 87 Ohio St.3d 15, 716 N.E.2d 1126, 1999-Ohio-216, reconsideration denied 87 Ohio St.3d 1454, 719 N.E.2d 969, certiorari denied 120 S.Ct. 1727, 529 U.S. 1090, 146 L.Ed.2d 647, denial of post-conviction relief reversed 159 Ohio App.3d 469, 824 N.E.2d 167, 2005-Ohio-47. Jury ⚷ 29(6)

Record did not support capital murder defendant's claim that his jury waiver was not knowing, intelligent and voluntary due to fact that he was accidentally shocked with stun belt on morning of trial and was on medication as a result; record did not indicate voltage level of stun belt, court took recess after stun belt incident for remainder of morning, defendant's three attorneys, one of whom was a physician, never indicated that defendant would not be able to waive his right to jury, and defense counsel never asked court to revisit jury waiver issue. State v. Filiaggi (Ohio, 07-29-1999) 86 Ohio St.3d 230, 714 N.E.2d 867, 1999-Ohio-99, certiorari denied 120 S.Ct. 821, 528 U.S. 1090, 145 L.Ed.2d 691, denial of post-conviction relief affirmed 445 F.3d 851. Jury ⚷ 29(6)

Trial court's inquiry into capital murder defendant's understanding of nature and consequences of his waiver of right to jury trial was adequate, despite contention that court's knowledge of defendant's numerous intellectual deficiencies imposed absolute duty to conduct more thorough inquiry than that provided for by statute; trial court's inquiry met and exceeded requirements of waiver statute, jury waiver form itself apprised defendant of nature and consequences of decision to waive jury trial, and trial court specifically found that waiver was voluntarily made with full knowledge of consequences thereof. State v. Spivey (Ohio, 04-22-1998) 81 Ohio St.3d 405, 692 N.E.2d 151, 1998-Ohio-437, stay granted 82 Ohio St.3d 1435, 694 N.E.2d 1372, certiorari denied 119 S.Ct. 226, 525 U.S. 898, 142 L.Ed.2d 186. Jury ⚷ 29(6)

Defendant's waiver of jury trial in capital murder case was valid, despite defendant's contention that trial court failed to consider his limited intellectual ability; defendant had submitted written jury waiver and opted for trial before three-judge panel, trial court had questioned defendant about his jury waiver, record did not support defendant's contention that he was so mentally challenged as to be incapable of giving valid waiver, and trial court complied with all requirements of jury waiver. State v. Eley (Ohio, 12-18-1996) 77 Ohio St.3d 174, 672 N.E.2d 640, 1996-Ohio-323, reconsideration denied 77 Ohio St.3d 1549, 674 N.E.2d 1187, certiorari denied 117 S.Ct. 2522, 521 U.S. 1124, 138 L.Ed.2d 1023, dismissal of post-conviction relief affirmed 2001-Ohio-3447, 2001 WL 1497095, appeal not allowed 94 Ohio St.3d 1506, 764 N.E.2d 1036, 2002-Ohio-5738. Jury ⚷ 29(6)

Failure to comply with waiver of jury trial statute may be remedied only by direct appeal from criminal conviction. State v. Pless (Ohio, 01-17-1996) 74 Ohio St.3d 333, 658 N.E.2d 766, 1996-Ohio-102, reconsideration denied 75 Ohio St.3d 1413, 661 N.E.2d 760, appeal after new trial 1998 WL 269093, dismissed, appeal not allowed 83 Ohio St.3d 1447, 700 N.E.2d 331. Criminal Law ⚷ 1007

Where an accused, charged with a capital offense, knowingly, intelligently, and voluntarily waives his right to a trial by jury pursuant to RC 2945.05 and Crim R 23(A), and is subsequently tried before a three-judge panel, the panel may render a verdict upon a majority vote of its members pursuant to RC 2945.06. State v. Ruppert (Ohio 1978) 54 Ohio St.2d 263, 375 N.E.2d 1250, 8 O.O.3d 232, certiorari denied 99 S.Ct. 352, 439 U.S. 954, 58 L.Ed.2d 345.

A three-judge trial court has jurisdiction, upon a plea of guilty by an accused charged with unlawfully and purposely killing another while in the perpetration of a robbery, to determine the degree of the offense and to sentence the accused, even though no written waiver of trial by jury is filed. State ex rel. Scott v. Alvis (Ohio 1951) 156 Ohio St. 387, 102 N.E.2d 845, 46 O.O. 230. Jury ⚷ 29(4)

Where defendant pleads guilty to murder in first degree, waives right to trial by jury and elects to be tried by court and a court composed of three judges has examined the witnesses, determined degree of crime and pronounced sentence accordingly, such defendant has no right thereafter to trial by jury. State v. Frohner (Ohio 1948) 150 Ohio St. 53, 80 N.E.2d 868, 37 O.O. 406. Jury ⚷ 29(7)

Where minor, under eighteen years of age accused of first degree murder, who has been bound over to common pleas court, appears, with counsel he chose, before judge in open court and waives right to jury trial, and who later appears, with counsel, before a three-judge court and makes application to withdraw his former plea of not guilty and to plead guilty, no error can be predicated on the refusal of trial by jury after such court has determined degree of crime and pronounced sentence, if the judges are satisfied defendant had an intelligent understanding of such plea and of waiver of jury trial. State v. Frohner (Ohio 1948) 150 Ohio St. 53, 80 N.E.2d 868, 37 O.O. 406.

13. Petty offense cases

It was plain error to try defendant without a jury for misdemeanor assault, where defendant had filed jury demand, and written jury waiver was never filed with clerk of courts and made part of the record. State v. Pflanz (Ohio App. 1 Dist., 10-22-1999) 135 Ohio App.3d 338, 733 N.E.2d 1212. Criminal Law ⚷ 1035(1)

In accordance with RC 2945.05, a written waiver is required to waive a defendant's right to a jury trial in petty offense cases. An oral waiver by the defendant's attorney made during a discussion with the trial judge is ineffective. State v. Smith (Clark 1987) 38 Ohio App.3d 149, 528 N.E.2d 591.

A written demand for a trial by jury which is timely filed by a defendant charged with a petty offense may only be waived in writing by the defendant himself pursuant to RC 2945.05; thus, a defendant's silent acquiescence to a nonjury trial and written or oral waiver by defense counsel or the court do not constitute a valid waiver. State v. Cheadle (Union 1986) 30 Ohio App.3d 253, 507 N.E.2d 426, 30 O.B.R. 412.

Where a defendant in a petty offense case has a right to trial by jury and pleads not guilty and demands a jury trial in the manner provided by Crim R 23(A), it must appear of record that such defendant waived this right in writing in the manner provided by RC 2945.05, in order for the trial court to have jurisdiction to try the defendant without a jury. State v. Tate (Ohio 1979) 59 Ohio St.2d 50, 391 N.E.2d 738, 13 O.O.3d 36, certiorari denied 100 S.Ct. 456, 444 U.S. 967, 62 L.Ed.2d 379. Jury ⚷ 29(6)

RC 2945.05 does not supersede the provision of RC 1901.24 that "any cause in a municipal court, either civil or criminal, shall be tried to the court unless a jury trial is demanded in writing." City of Sidney v. Thompson (Shelby 1962) 118 Ohio App. 512, 196 N.E.2d 112, 26 O.O.2d 18.

RC 2945.05 is applicable to municipal courts. City of Lima v. Rambo (Allen 1960) 113 Ohio App. 158, 177 N.E.2d 554, 17 O.O.2d 133.

Where a defendant in a criminal case in the municipal court has a right to trial by jury and pleads not guilty and demands a jury trial, such court has no jurisdiction to proceed to trial without a jury unless such defendant waives such right to a trial by jury in the manner provided by RC 2945.05. City of Lima v. Rambo (Allen 1960) 113 Ohio App. 158, 177 N.E.2d 554, 17 O.O.2d 133.

14. Bench trial

Jury waiver was filed, time-stamped, and contained in record, and thus trial court had jurisdiction to conduct bench trial, even though waiver was not filed and placed in record before trial commenced. State v. Franklin (Ohio App. 8 Dist., Cuyahoga, 05-22-2003) No. 81426, 2003-Ohio-2649, 2003 WL 21193014, Unreported, appeal not allowed 100 Ohio St.3d 1424, 797 N.E.2d 92, 2003-Ohio-5232. Jury ⚷ 29(6)

Trial court strictly complied with mandates of code governing waiver of a jury trial, and thus, was not divested of jurisdiction to proceed with bench trial on charges of carrying a concealed weapon, even though signed waiver form was not filed in trial court and made part of the record until after trial had concluded, where defendant voluntarily signed waiver form, and transcript of bench trial demonstrated the trial court accepted the waiver and stated that it would be made part of the record and filed on same date. State v. Sekera (Ohio App. 8 Dist., Cuyahoga, 10-31-2002) No. 80690, 2002-Ohio-5972, 2002 WL 31429785, Unreported. Jury ⚷ 29(6)

Failure of trial court to formally file executed written waiver of petitioner's right to jury trial was not jurisdictional defect and did not affect trial court's authority to proceed with bench trial; defendant in fact executed written waiver of right to be tried by jury and elected to be tried by court. State ex rel. Larkins v. Baker (Ohio, 09-06-1995) 73 Ohio St.3d 658, 653 N.E.2d 701, 1995-Ohio-144. Jury ⚷ 29(6)

RC 2945.06 limits a court's jurisdiction to hear, try and determine cases without a jury to those in which the right to trial by jury has been waived in harmony with RC 2945.05. State v. McCoy (Hamilton 1969) 26 Ohio App.2d 62, 269 N.E.2d 51, 55 O.O.2d 86.

Where the record on appeal does not reveal a waiver of a jury trial by the defendant, who was convicted of draft evasion after a trial without a jury, the judgment must be reversed and the case remanded for a new trial. U. S. v. Davidson (C.A.6 (Ohio) 1973) 477 F.2d 136.

2945.06 Jurisdiction of judge when jury trial is waived; three–judge court

In any case in which a defendant waives his right to trial by jury and elects to be tried by the court under section 2945.05 of the Revised Code, any judge of the court in which the cause is pending shall proceed to hear, try, and determine the cause in accordance with the rules and in like manner as if the cause were being tried before a jury. If the accused is charged with an offense punishable with death, he shall be tried by a court to be composed of three judges, consisting of the judge presiding at the time in the trial of criminal cases and two other judges to be designated by the presiding judge or chief justice of that court, and in case there is neither a presiding judge nor a chief justice, by the chief justice of the supreme court. The judges or a majority of them may decide all questions of fact and law arising upon the trial; however the accused shall not be found guilty or not guilty of any offense unless the judges unanimously find the accused guilty or not guilty. If the accused pleads guilty of aggravated murder, a court composed of three judges shall examine the witnesses, determine whether the accused is guilty of aggravated murder or any other offense, and pronounce sentence accordingly. The court shall follow the procedures contained in sections 2929.03 and 2929.04 of the Revised Code in all cases in which the accused is charged with an offense punishable by death. If in the composition of the court it is necessary that a judge from another county be assigned by the chief justice, the judge from another county shall be compensated for his services as provided by section 141.07 of the Revised Code.

(1981 S 1, eff. 10–19–81; 1953 H 1; GC 13442–5)

Historical and Statutory Notes

Pre–1953 H 1 Amendments: 115 v 531; 113 v 179, Ch 21, § 5

Cross References

Pleas, rights upon plea, Crim R 11

Procedures in capital cases, 2929.022

Trial by the court, Crim R 23

Library References

Criminal Law ⚩247 to 259.

Jury ⚩29(7).

Westlaw Topic Nos. 110, 230.

C.J.S. Juries §§ 182, 207, 209, 219.

C.J.S. Summary Proceedings § 8.

Research References

Encyclopedias

OH Jur. 3d Courts & Judges § 52, Powers and Duties of Chief Justice; Acting Chief Justice—Assignment of Retired Judges.

OH Jur. 3d Courts & Judges § 104, Courts of Common Pleas and Divisions.

OH Jur. 3d Criminal Law § 969, Prosecution for Aggravated Murder.

OH Jur. 3d Criminal Law § 971, in Capital Cases.

OH Jur. 3d Criminal Law § 1014, Upon Plea of Guilty or No Contest.

OH Jur. 3d Criminal Law § 1016, Determination by Trial Jury and Trial Judge or by Three-Judge Panel.

OH Jur. 3d Criminal Law § 2464, Particular Matters Waived by Plea of Guilty.

OH Jur. 3d Criminal Law § 2612, Jurisdiction of Judge When Jury Trial is Waived.

OH Jur. 3d Criminal Law § 3560, Disqualification or Substitution of Judge.

OH Jur. 3d Criminal Law § 3561, Statements or Actions of Trial Judge.

OH Jur. 3d Mandamus, Procedendo, & Prohibition § 179, Effect of Jurisdiction in Inferior Tribunal, Generally.

Treatises and Practice Aids

Markus, Trial Handbook for Ohio Lawyers, § 4:32, Trial by Jury.

Katz, Giannelli, Blair and Lipton, Baldwin's Ohio Practice, Criminal Law, § 62:9, Unanimous Verdicts.

Katz, Giannelli, Blair and Lipton, Baldwin's Ohio Practice, Criminal Law, § 125:2, Indictment.

Katz, Giannelli, Blair and Lipton, Baldwin's Ohio Practice, Criminal Law, § 125:5, Jury and Bench Trials.

Katz, Giannelli, Blair and Lipton, Baldwin's Ohio Practice, Criminal Law, § 43:18, Capital Cases.

Katz, Giannelli, Blair and Lipton, Baldwin's Ohio Practice, Criminal Law, § 62:10, Waiver of Jury Trial.

Hennenberg & Reinhart, Ohio Criminal Defense Motions F 15.11, Miscellaneous Motions-Petition for Writ of Habeas Corpus-Supplemental Memorandum-Single Judge Without Subject Matter Jurisdiction to Accept Plea in Capital Case.

Law Review and Journal Commentaries

To Waive a Jury?, S. Adele Shank. 1 Crim L J Ohio 1 (July/August 1989).

Notes of Decisions

1. Constitutional issues

Defendant's decision not to present mitigating evidence in penalty phase of capital murder prosecution did not deprive state of its interest in seeing that sentence was imposed in conformity with reliability requirements of Eighth Amendment prohibition on cruel and unusual punishment, where state was required to present evidence of aggravating circumstances, trial court was required to determine if all elements of aggravated murder and death penalty specifications were proved beyond reasonable doubt before entering guilty verdict, court was required to afford defendant the opportunity to present mitigating evidence before court could impose death sentence, which it did, and to weigh aggravating circumstances against mitigating factors, if any, and Supreme Court was required to review evidence to determine if sentence was appropriate, proportionate, and not imposed in arbitrary or unreliable manner. State v. Ashworth (Ohio, 03-24-1999) 85 Ohio St.3d 56, 706 N.E.2d 1231, 1999-Ohio-204, reconsideration denied 85 Ohio St.3d 1468, 709 N.E.2d 173, certiorari denied 120 S.Ct. 252, 528 U.S. 908, 145 L.Ed.2d 212, denial of post-conviction relief affirmed 1999 WL 1071742, dismissed, appeal not allowed 88 Ohio St.3d 1434, 724 N.E.2d 810. Sentencing And Punishment ⚷ 1782

Alleged violation of statute setting forth procedures in case tried by court is not proper subject for habeas corpus relief and may be remedied only in direct appeal from criminal conviction. State ex rel. Collins v. Leonard (Ohio, 12-31-1997) 80 Ohio St.3d 477, 687 N.E.2d 443, 1997-Ohio-282. Habeas Corpus ⚷ 481

RC 2945.06 and RC 2945.74 are in pari materia, so that to the extent that an open-court confession, i.e., a plea to homicide generally, supersedes an in-custody confession, the alleged failure to comply with Miranda criteria is waived and is not prejudicial. State v. Place (Lucas 1971) 25 Ohio App.2d 158, 267 N.E.2d 832, 54 O.O.2d 337.

There is no constitutional provision prohibiting a three-judge court, where the defendant is charged with murder in the first degree, on a plea of guilty, to determine the degree of guilt without the intervention of a jury. State v. Ferguson (Cuyahoga 1962) 119 Ohio App. 393, 184 N.E.2d 241, 89 Ohio Law Abs. 321, 28 O.O.2d 18, affirmed 175 Ohio St. 390, 195 N.E.2d 794, 25 O.O.2d 383, certiorari denied 84 S.Ct. 1938, 377 U.S. 1002, 12 L.Ed.2d 1051. Jury ⚷ 29(4)

Former GC 13442–4 (RC 2945.05) and 13442–5 (RC 2945.06) are each constitutional and in the instant case were constitutionally applied. State v. Frohner (Ohio 1948) 150 Ohio St. 53, 80 N.E.2d 868, 37 O.O. 406.

Under normal circumstances, a plea of guilty precludes the defendant from attacking the sufficiency of the evidence under Ohio law. Carpenter v. Mohr (C.A.6 (Ohio), 12-18-1998) 163 F.3d 938, rehearing and suggestion for rehearing en banc denied, certiorari granted 120 S.Ct. 444, 528 U.S. 985, 145 L.Ed.2d 362, reversed 120 S.Ct. 1587, 529 U.S. 446, 146 L.Ed.2d 518, on remand 229 F.3d 1150. Criminal Law ⚷ 1026.10(4)

Under Ohio law, challenges to the sufficiency of the evidence by a party who pleads guilty to aggravated murder charges are expressly permitted. Carpenter v. Mohr (C.A.6 (Ohio), 12-18-1998) 163 F.3d 938, rehearing and suggestion for rehearing en banc denied, certiorari granted 120 S.Ct. 444, 528 U.S. 985, 145 L.Ed.2d 362, reversed 120 S.Ct. 1587, 529 U.S. 446, 146 L.Ed.2d 518, on remand 229 F.3d 1150. Criminal Law ⚷ 1026.10(4)

2. —— Habeas corpus relief, constitutional issues

Habeas petitioner convicted of capital murder did not state claim of violation of due process and equal protection rights when he alleged that trial court violated state statute governing selection of judges to form three judge panel, to decide guilt of capital murder defendant following waiver of jury trial, by selecting other judges himself rather than arranging for selection by presiding judge of his court or chief justice of supreme court. Cooey v.

Anderson (N.D.Ohio, 09-04-1997) 988 F.Supp. 1066. Habeas Corpus ⚷ 670(1)

3. —— Ineffective assistance of counsel, constitutional issues

Defendant's self-serving affidavit, claiming ineffective assistance of counsel, was insufficient to rebut evidence that defendant voluntarily and intelligently waived his right to jury or to three-judge panel in capital murder prosecution, where trial judge directly addressed defendant and determined that he waived those rights. State v. Swiger (Ohio App. 9 Dist., 01-28-1998) 125 Ohio App.3d 456, 708 N.E.2d 1033, dismissed, appeal not allowed 82 Ohio St.3d 1411, 694 N.E.2d 75. Jury ⚷ 29(6)

Appellate counsel's failure to challenge, on direct appeal, sufficiency of evidence supporting conditional guilty plea to aggravated murder, while pursuing significantly weaker claim, was constitutionally deficient; reasonably knowledgeable defense attorney would have known that challenge could and should have been raised under Ohio law, given that defendant consistently proclaimed his innocence and only entered plea to avoid death penalty, and that only information presented at culpability hearing was prosecution's recitation of case, which was not evidence. Carpenter v. Mohr (C.A.6 (Ohio), 12-18-1998) 163 F.3d 938, rehearing and suggestion for rehearing en banc denied, certiorari granted 120 S.Ct. 444, 528 U.S. 985, 145 L.Ed.2d 362, reversed 120 S.Ct. 1587, 529 U.S. 446, 146 L.Ed.2d 518, on remand 229 F.3d 1150. Criminal Law ⚷ 641.13(7)

4. —— Prosecutorial error, constitutional issues

Prosecutor's alleged misstatements concerning amount and quality of mitigating evidence presented in capital murder prosecution did not prejudicially affect substantial rights of defendant, as three-judge panel which heard case was presumed to have considered only relevant, competent and admissible evidence in its deliberations, and any prejudicial impact was minimized by Supreme Court's independent review. State v. Eley (Ohio, 12-18-1996) 77 Ohio St.3d 174, 672 N.E.2d 640, 1996-Ohio-323, reconsideration denied 77 Ohio St.3d 1549, 674 N.E.2d 1187, certiorari denied 117 S.Ct. 2522, 521 U.S. 1124, 138 L.Ed.2d 1023, dismissal of post-conviction relief affirmed 2001-Ohio-3447, 2001 WL 1497095, appeal not allowed 94 Ohio St.3d 1506, 764 N.E.2d 1036, 2002-Ohio-5738. Criminal Law ⚷ 260.11(2); Criminal Law ⚷ 260.11(6)

Any error committed by prosecutor, during penalty phase of capital murder prosecution tried to court, in allegedly urging three-judge panel to impose death penalty based on something other than individualized determination of appropriateness of sentence was harmless error, as three-judge panel was presumed to know law and to consider only relevant, competent and admissible evidence in its deliberations. State v. Eley (Ohio, 12-18-1996) 77 Ohio St.3d 174, 672 N.E.2d 640, 1996-Ohio-323, reconsideration denied 77 Ohio St.3d 1549, 674 N.E.2d 1187, certiorari denied 117 S.Ct. 2522, 521 U.S. 1124, 138 L.Ed.2d 1023, dismissal of post-conviction relief affirmed 2001-Ohio-3447, 2001 WL 1497095, appeal not allowed 94 Ohio St.3d 1506, 764 N.E.2d 1036, 2002-Ohio-5738. Criminal Law ⚷ 260.11(6)

5. Waiver—In general

An alleged violation of statute governing jurisdiction of judge when jury trial is waived is not cognizable in an extraordinary writ action and may be remedied only in a direct appeal from a criminal conviction. Kirklin v. Enlow (Ohio, 08-16-2000) 89 Ohio St.3d 455, 732 N.E.2d 982, 2000-Ohio-217. Courts ⚷ 207.1

Statute governing waiver of jury trials does not require an examination of witnesses, determination of guilt, and pronouncement of sentence by a three-judge court if the accused is not charged with an offense punishable by death. State ex rel. Henry v. McMonagle (Ohio, 01-19-2000) 87 Ohio St.3d 543, 721 N.E.2d 1051, 2000-Ohio-477. Criminal Law ⚷ 247

State waived objection to petitioner's presentation of theory not raised in state postconviction proceedings to support claim that his waiver of jury, in favor of three-judge panel, for capital murder trial was ineffective, by telling district court that it did not object to new testimony of neuropsychologist supporting claim. Sowell v. Bradshaw (C.A.6 (Ohio), 06-23-2004) 372 F.3d 821, rehearing en banc denied, certiorari denied 125 S.Ct. 1645, 544 U.S. 925, 161 L.Ed.2d 485. Habeas Corpus ⚷ 816

6. —— Habeas corpus relief, waiver

Direct appeal, and not habeas corpus relief, was sole remedy for defendant's claim that trial court lacked jurisdiction to accept guilty pleas and to sentence him for capital murder and aggravated arson, based on violation of rule requiring three-judge panel to preside over capital cases in which defendant has waived jury trial. State ex rel. Rash v. Jackson (Ohio, 05-12-2004) 102 Ohio St.3d 145, 807 N.E.2d 344, 2004-Ohio-2053. Habeas Corpus ⚷ 275.1

7. —— Jurisdiction, waiver

Trial court possessed jurisdiction to determine assault defendant's guilt in bench trial, even if defendant did not execute jury waiver form "in open court," where record demonstrated that defendant's waiver was made after defendant had been made aware of the implications of relinquishing his constitutional rights. State v. Bonner (Ohio App. 8 Dist., Cuyahoga, 12-04-2003) No. 82475, 2003-Ohio-6493, 2003 WL 22862794, Unreported. Jury ⚷ 29(6)

Holding that three-judge-panel requirement of statute governing waiver of jury trials was jurisdictional matter that could not be waived had to be interpreted to mean that a defendant need not raise error relative to compliance with statute at the trial level before raising it upon direct appeal, not that in motion for withdrawal of guilty plea, reversal was automatic upon showing of violation, in order to adhere to precedent holding that such jurisdiction did not mean subject matter jurisdiction and could not be attacked except upon direct appeal. State v.

Woods (Ohio App. 8 Dist., Cuyahoga, 05-15-2003) No. 82120, 2003-Ohio-2475, 2003 WL 21101507, Unreported, appeal allowed 100 Ohio St.3d 1422, 797 N.E.2d 91, 2003-Ohio-5232, affirmed 102 Ohio St.3d 89, 806 N.E.2d 1001, 2004-Ohio-1997. Criminal Law ⚷ 1035(1)

Three-judge panel lacked subject matter jurisdiction to accept defendant's guilty pleas to two counts of aggravated murder with mass murder and felony murder specifications, as both counts still contained death penalty specifications, and defendant had not signed waiver of his right to jury trial. State v. Carley (Ohio App. 8 Dist., 09-25-2000) 139 Ohio App.3d 841, 745 N.E.2d 1122, appeal after new trial 2004-Ohio-1901, 2004 WL 794533, appeal not allowed 103 Ohio St.3d 1427, 814 N.E.2d 490, 2004-Ohio-4524, motion to reopen denied 2004-Ohio-5479, 2004 WL 2335805, appeal not allowed 104 Ohio St.3d 1463, 821 N.E.2d 578, 2005-Ohio-204. Criminal Law ⚷ 273(4.1); Jury ⚷ 29(4)

Failure of trial court to formally file executed written waiver of petitioner's right to jury trial was not jurisdictional defect and did not affect trial court's authority to proceed with bench trial; defendant in fact executed written waiver of right to be tried by jury and elected to be tried by court. State ex rel. Larkins v. Baker (Ohio, 09-06-1995) 73 Ohio St.3d 658, 653 N.E.2d 701, 1995-Ohio-144. Jury ⚷ 29(6)

RC 2945.06 limits a court's jurisdiction to hear, try and determine cases without a jury to those in which the right to trial by jury has been waived in harmony with RC 2945.05. State v. McCoy (Hamilton 1969) 26 Ohio App.2d 62, 269 N.E.2d 51, 55 O.O.2d 86.

8. —— Withdrawal, waiver

Defendant who has waived right to trial by jury and elected to be tried by a three-judge court, may withdraw such waiver at any time before commencement of trial but not after hearing. State v. Frohner (Ohio 1948) 150 Ohio St. 53, 80 N.E.2d 868, 37 O.O. 406. Jury ⚷ 29(7)

9. Three-judge panel—In general

Court of Appeals would decline to extend rule of *State v. Parker*, providing that in capital case where defendant has waived right to jury trial three-judge panel is required even when death penalty is no longer available sentencing option, to case in which aggravated murder defendant did not waive right to jury trial and defendant entered into agreed stipulation providing that judge would decide sentence if jury convicted him. State v. Roper (Ohio App. 9 Dist., Summit, 12-31-2002) No. 20836, 2002-Ohio-7321, 2002 WL 31890116, Unreported, appeal not allowed 98 Ohio St.3d 1567, 787 N.E.2d 1231, 2003-Ohio-2242. Sentencing And Punishment ⚷ 335

There is no requirement, under statute governing the establishment of three-judge panel in prosecution for an offense punishable with death, that judge who signs order designating three-judge panel be a general division judge of court of common pleas. State v. Thomas (Ohio, 12-11-2002) 97 Ohio St.3d 309, 779 N.E.2d 1017, 2002-Ohio-6624, reconsideration denied 97 Ohio St.3d 1498, 780 N.E.2d 1022, 2002-Ohio-7248, stay granted 98 Ohio St.3d 1403, 781 N.E.2d 221, 2003-Ohio-40, certiorari denied 123 S.Ct. 2295, 539 U.S. 916, 156 L.Ed.2d 133. Criminal Law ⚷ 247

When a defendant pleads guilty to aggravated murder in a capital case, a three-judge panel is required. State v. Parker (Ohio, 06-26-2002) 95 Ohio St.3d 524, 769 N.E.2d 846, 2002-Ohio-2833, reconsideration denied 96 Ohio St.3d 1489, 774 N.E.2d 764, 2002-Ohio-4478. Criminal Law ⚷ 273(4.1)

Statement of facts by prosecutor does not satisfy evidentiary requirements of rule governing pleas or of statute governing cases in which defendant elects to be tried by three-judge panel in lieu of jury. State v. Green (Ohio, 02-18-1998) 81 Ohio St.3d 100, 689 N.E.2d 556, 1998-Ohio-454. Criminal Law ⚷ 254.2; Criminal Law ⚷ 273(4.1)

Trial transcript did not support defendant's contention that three-judge panel, in aggravated murder prosecution, had erroneously stated that it would consider lesser included offenses of murder and involuntary manslaughter only if any necessary elements of aggravated murder were not proven; viewed in context, panel merely asked prosecutor whether he thought lesser included offenses should be considered by panel, without expressing its own opinion or position. State v. Eley (Ohio, 12-18-1996) 77 Ohio St.3d 174, 672 N.E.2d 640, 1996-Ohio-323, reconsideration denied 77 Ohio St.3d 1549, 674 N.E.2d 1187, certiorari denied 117 S.Ct. 2522, 521 U.S. 1124, 138 L.Ed.2d 1023, dismissal of post-conviction relief affirmed 2001-Ohio-3447, 2001 WL 1497095, appeal not allowed 94 Ohio St.3d 1506, 764 N.E.2d 1036, 2002-Ohio-5738. Criminal Law ⚷ 260.7

RC 2929.03 and RC 2929.04 require an allegation and proof of an aggravating specification for imposition of a capital sentence; absent such an allegation, a defendant waiving jury trial is not entitled to the three-judge panel available under RC 2945.06. Ullman v. Seiter (Ohio 1985) 18 Ohio St.3d 59, 479 N.E.2d 875, 18 O.B.R. 92.

Where an accused, charged with a capital offense, knowingly, intelligently, and voluntarily waives his right to a trial by jury pursuant to RC 2945.05 and Crim R 23(A), and is subsequently tried before a three-judge panel, the panel may render a verdict upon a majority vote of its members pursuant to RC 2945.06 (Unanimous verdict required by amendment of RC 2945.06 by 1981 S 1, eff. 10–19–81.). State v. Ruppert (Ohio 1978) 54 Ohio St.2d 263, 375 N.E.2d 1250, 8 O.O.3d 232, certiorari denied 99 S.Ct. 352, 439 U.S. 954, 58 L.Ed.2d 345.

Where two valid sentences are imposed by a three-judge panel on separate counts for the first degree murder of one person, one of death and one of life imprisonment, that sentence which calls for the highest and most severe punishment, death, is the one that is actually imposed, the life sentence in practical effect being mere surplusage. State v.

Ferguson (Ohio 1964) 175 Ohio St. 390, 195 N.E.2d 794, 25 O.O.2d 383, certiorari denied 84 S.Ct. 1938, 377 U.S. 1002, 12 L.Ed.2d 1051.

10. —— Culpability hearing, three-judge panel

Three-judge panel fully complied with statutory requirements when conducting hearing to determine guilt and to pronounce sentence following defendant's guilty plea to two counts of aggravated murder, where panel heard testimony and accepted exhibits regarding offenses to which defendant had pled. State v. Hughes (Ohio App. 8 Dist., Cuyahoga, 01-16-2003) No. 81019, 2003-Ohio-166, 2003 WL 125252, Unreported, appeal not allowed 99 Ohio St.3d 1436, 789 N.E.2d 1117, 2003-Ohio-2902. Criminal Law ⚷ 273(4.1)

When defendant pleads guilty to aggravated murder in capital case, three-judge panel is required to examine witnesses and to hear any other evidence properly presented by prosecution in order to make determination as to guilt of defendant under rule governing pleas. State v. Green (Ohio, 02-18-1998) 81 Ohio St.3d 100, 689 N.E.2d 556, 1998-Ohio-454. Criminal Law ⚷ 273(4.1)

The state must prove material elements of crime of murder in first degree, including premeditation and deliberation, beyond a reasonable doubt, in order to resolve degree issue in hearing under RC 2945.06. State v. Taylor (Cuyahoga 1972) 30 Ohio App.2d 252, 285 N.E.2d 89, 59 O.O.2d 398. Criminal Law ⚷ 980(2)

Rule that defendant may not attack sufficiency of evidence on appeal after plea of guilty, is not applicable to appeal from decision after culpability hearing under RC 2945.06. State v. Taylor (Cuyahoga 1972) 30 Ohio App.2d 252, 285 N.E.2d 89, 59 O.O.2d 398. Criminal Law ⚷ 1134(8)

The aim of culpability hearing under RC 2945.06 is to safeguard defendant's rights by determining whether facts justify a finding of guilty to the offense of first degree murder, to a lesser included offense, or conceivably, a finding of not guilty, regardless of any apparent understanding defendant may have as to meaning of charge or nature of consequences, and tends to insure that defendant will not be found guilty of offense of more gravity than evidence will support and to protect him against his possible technical incompetence. State v. Taylor (Cuyahoga 1972) 30 Ohio App.2d 252, 285 N.E.2d 89, 59 O.O.2d 398.

Attempt to prove lack of premeditation and deliberation at degree of culpability hearing, after a plea of guilty to murder in first degree under RC 2945.06, is not so inconsistent with plea as to evidence lack of understanding of its nature and consequences. State v. Taylor (Cuyahoga 1972) 30 Ohio App.2d 252, 285 N.E.2d 89, 59 O.O.2d 398.

Plea in hearing under RC 2945.06 is not to be regarded as evidence of guilt absolute to crime charged because this would render procedures under statute pointless. State v. Taylor (Cuyahoga 1972) 30 Ohio App.2d 252, 285 N.E.2d 89, 59 O.O.2d 398. Criminal Law ⚷ 980(2)

A three-judge trial court has jurisdiction, upon a plea of guilty by an accused charged with unlawfully and purposely killing another while in the perpetration of a robbery, to determine the degree of the offense and to sentence the accused, even though no written waiver of trial by jury is filed. State ex rel. Scott v. Alvis (Ohio 1951) 156 Ohio St. 387, 102 N.E.2d 845, 46 O.O. 230. Jury ⚷ 29(4)

Determination of degree of crime by a three-judge court is reviewable; failure of such court to extend mercy to defendant determined guilty of murder in first degree is not reviewable; extension of mercy to such defendant rests within discretion of such court. State v. Frohner (Ohio 1948) 150 Ohio St. 53, 80 N.E.2d 868, 37 O.O. 406.

Upon plea of guilty of murder in first degree, a three-judge court shall, without intervention of jury, determine upon evidence the degree of crime, and, if found to be murder in first degree, has power to withhold or extend mercy. State v. Frohner (Ohio 1948) 150 Ohio St. 53, 80 N.E.2d 868, 37 O.O. 406. Sentencing And Punishment ⚷ 1774; Sentencing And Punishment ⚷ 1783

11. —— Duty of court, three-judge panel

Courts must strictly comply with the requirements that a defendant charged with an offense punishable with death who has waived a jury trial be tried by a court composed of three judges and, if such a defendant pleads guilty of aggravated murder, a court composed of three judges must examine the witnesses, determine whether the accused is guilty of aggravated murder or any other offense, and pronounce sentence accordingly. Pratts v. Hurley (Ohio, 05-05-2004) 102 Ohio St.3d 81, 806 N.E.2d 992, 2004-Ohio-1980. Sentencing And Punishment ⚷ 1774

In capital murder case in which defendant waived jury, three-judge panel was to determine all charges against defendant, including those for non-capital offenses, and defendant could not waive three-judge panel as to non-capital charges; thus, where presiding judge alone had determined all non-capital charges against defendant, remand was necessary to permit three-judge panel to decide those charges. State v. Filiaggi (Ohio, 07-29-1999) 86 Ohio St.3d 230, 714 N.E.2d 867, 1999-Ohio-99, certiorari denied 120 S.Ct. 821, 528 U.S. 1090, 145 L.Ed.2d 691, denial of post-conviction relief affirmed 445 F.3d 851. Criminal Law ⚷ 249; Criminal Law ⚷ 260.12

State's failure to examine witnesses or put on any evidence before three-judge panel so that panel could make determination as to defendant's guilt did not invalidate defendant's conviction, pursuant to guilty plea, for aggravated murder, where defense counsel stipulated that guilty plea was supported by facts. State v. Bolin (Ohio App. 8 Dist., 05-26-1998) 128 Ohio App.3d 58, 713 N.E.2d 1092. Criminal Law ⚷ 273(4.1)

Defendant did not receive valid conviction for aggravated murder after he elected to be tried by three-judge panel in lieu of jury and pleaded guilty, and his death sentence was therefore void, where panel did not take evidence, deliberate or make determination about appropriateness of charge, find that aggravated murder had been proven beyond reasonable doubt, or journalize finding of guilt. State v. Green (Ohio, 02-18-1998) 81 Ohio St.3d 100, 689 N.E.2d 556, 1998-Ohio-454. Sentencing And Punishment ⚷ 1736

A three judge panel considering a capital murder case on remand for resentencing does not err in separating during sentencing deliberations so as to allow individual consideration of the case over the weekend since the rules pertaining to jury sequestration need not apply to a three-judge panel which is presumed to consider only relevant, competent and admissible evidence in its deliberations. State v. Davis (Ohio 1992) 63 Ohio St.3d 44, 584 N.E.2d 1192, rehearing denied 63 Ohio St.3d 1433, 588 N.E.2d 132, stay granted 63 Ohio St.3d 1444, 589 N.E.2d 388, certiorari denied 113 S.Ct. 172, 506 U.S. 858, 121 L.Ed.2d 119, rehearing denied 66 Ohio St.3d 1489, 612 N.E.2d 1245, dismissal of post-conviction relief affirmed, dismissed, appeal not allowed 77 Ohio St.3d 1520, 674 N.E.2d 372.

12. —— Jurisdiction, three-judge panel

Failure to convene three judge panel to accept guilty plea to aggravated murder with death penalty specification was error only in exercise of jurisdiction, but did not deprive trial court of subject matter jurisdiction. Pratts v. Hurley (Ohio App. 4 Dist., Ross, 02-12-2003) No. 02CA2674, 2003-Ohio-864, 2003 WL 546423, Unreported, motion to certify allowed 99 Ohio St.3d 1406, 788 N.E.2d 644, 2003-Ohio-2454, appeal allowed 99 Ohio St.3d 1408, 788 N.E.2d 646, 2003-Ohio-2454, affirmed 102 Ohio St.3d 81, 806 N.E.2d 992, 2004-Ohio-1980. Criminal Law ⚷ 102; Criminal Law ⚷ 273(4.1)

Statute governing waiver of jury trials did not require determination of guilt or pronouncement of sentence by a three-judge panel if a defendant was not charged with an offense punishable by death, and thus, trial court did not lack subject matter or personal jurisdiction over defendant, nor was court required to convene three-judge panel to try defendant's prosecution for aggravated murder, aggravated arson, attempted murder, aggravated burglary, felonious assault, and attempted felonious assault, where defendant waived jury trial and State did not seek death penalty against defendant. State v. McDerment (Ohio App. 9 Dist., Lorain, 01-29-2003) No. 02CA008117, 2003-Ohio-361, 2003 WL 187582, Unreported, appeal not allowed 99 Ohio St.3d 1435, 789 N.E.2d 1116, 2003-Ohio-2902. Criminal Law ⚷ 247; Criminal Law ⚷ 250

Although the statute governing the jurisdiction of a judge when a jury trial is waived mandates the use of a three-judge panel when a defendant is charged with a death penalty offense and waives the right to a jury, the failure to convene such a panel does not divest a court of subject-matter jurisdiction so that a judgment rendered by a single judge is void ab initio; instead, it constitutes an error in the court's exercise of jurisdiction over a particular case, for which there is an adequate remedy at law by way of direct appeal. Pratts v. Hurley (Ohio, 05-05-2004) 102 Ohio St.3d 81, 806 N.E.2d 992, 2004-Ohio-1980. Criminal Law ⚷ 102; Sentencing And Punishment ⚷ 1774

Failure to convene three judge panel to accept guilty plea to aggravated murder with death penalty specification was error only in exercise of jurisdiction, but did not constitute a lack of subject-matter jurisdiction rendering the court's judgment void ab initio and subject to collateral attack in habeas corpus; statute governing the jurisdiction of a judge when a jury trial was waived established procedural requirements that a court was required to follow in order to properly exercise its subject-matter jurisdiction, and failure to follow requirements could result in reversible error; abrogating *State v. Brock*, 110 Ohio App.3d 656, 675 N.E.2d 18, and *State v. Noggle*, 1999 WL 446440. Pratts v. Hurley (Ohio, 05-05-2004) 102 Ohio St.3d 81, 806 N.E.2d 992, 2004-Ohio-1980. Criminal Law ⚷ 102; Criminal Law ⚷ 1166(1)

Statutory three-judge-panel requirement for capital cases in which defendant has waived his right to a jury is a jurisdictional matter that cannot be waived. State v. Parker (Ohio, 06-26-2002) 95 Ohio St.3d 524, 769 N.E.2d 846, 2002-Ohio-2833, reconsideration denied 96 Ohio St.3d 1489, 774 N.E.2d 764, 2002-Ohio-4478. Criminal Law ⚷ 254.1

For purposes of complaint for writ of prohibition to vacate conviction and sentence, single trial judge did not patently and unambiguously lack jurisdiction to accept defendant's guilty plea and to pronounce sentence on aggravated murder charge; examination of witnesses, determination of guilt, and pronouncement of sentence by three-judge panel was not required because indictment had been amended by time of plea to delete any death-penalty specification. State ex rel. Henry v. McMonagle (Ohio, 01-19-2000) 87 Ohio St.3d 543, 721 N.E.2d 1051, 2000-Ohio-477. Prohibition ⚷ 10(3)

Statutory requirement that a three-judge panel preside over capital cases is a procedural protection, such that trial court's failure to comply with requirement does not deprive court of subject matter jurisdiction. State v. Swiger (Ohio App. 9 Dist., 01-28-1998) 125 Ohio App.3d 456, 708 N.E.2d 1033, dismissed, appeal not allowed 82 Ohio St.3d 1411, 694 N.E.2d 75. Sentencing And Punishment ⚷ 1774

13. —— Rights of defendant, three-judge panel

Capital defendant, by failing to object at trial, waived claim that judge who signed order establishing three-judge panel lacked authority to establish that panel because he was not a general division common pleas judge. State v. Thomas (Ohio, 12-11-2002) 97 Ohio St.3d 309, 779 N.E.2d 1017, 2002-Ohio-6624, reconsideration denied 97 Ohio St.3d 1498, 780 N.E.2d 1022, 2002-Ohio-7248, stay granted 98 Ohio St.3d 1403, 781 N.E.2d 221, 2003-Ohio-40, certiorari denied 123 S.Ct. 2295, 539 U.S. 916, 156 L.Ed.2d 133. Criminal Law ⚷ 1035(8.1)

Defendant charged with a crime punishable by death who had waived his right to trial by jury had to have his case heard and decided by a three-judge panel, even though the state agreed that it would not seek the death penalty, as the state did not delete the death penalty specification, such that defendant was still charged with offense punishable with death, and therefore, a single trial judge lacked authority to accept defendant's plea; abrogating *State v Griffin,* 73 Ohio App.3d 546, 597 N.E.2d 1178. State v. Parker (Ohio, 06-26-2002) 95 Ohio St.3d 524, 769 N.E.2d 846, 2002-Ohio-2833, reconsideration denied 96 Ohio St.3d 1489, 774 N.E.2d 764, 2002-Ohio-4478. Criminal Law ⚷ 273(4.1)

Defendant who sought writ of prohibition to vacate conviction and sentence entered upon his guilty plea to aggravated murder had adequate legal remedy by way of appeal to raise claim that a single judge lacked authority to accept plea and impose sentence for that offense. State ex rel. Henry v. McMonagle (Ohio, 01-19-2000) 87 Ohio St.3d 543, 721 N.E.2d 1051, 2000-Ohio-477. Prohibition ⚷ 3(4)

Capital murder defendant's claim that probate judge could not serve on three-judge panel which presided over his trial was waived by his failure to object to probate judge's assignment during trial. State v. Bays (Ohio, 10-13-1999) 87 Ohio St.3d 15, 716 N.E.2d 1126, 1999-Ohio-216, reconsideration denied 87 Ohio St.3d 1454, 719 N.E.2d 969, certiorari denied 120 S.Ct. 1727, 529 U.S. 1090, 146 L.Ed.2d 647, denial of post-conviction relief reversed 159 Ohio App.3d 469, 824 N.E.2d 167, 2005-Ohio-47. Criminal Law ⚷ 1035(1)

Defendant, in capital murder prosecution tried to court, waived any objection to separation of three-judge panel prior to deliberations during both guilt and penalty phases, where defense counsel expressly declined to object to separation of judges during either phase of trial. State v. Eley (Ohio, 12-18-1996) 77 Ohio St.3d 174, 672 N.E.2d 640, 1996-Ohio-323, reconsideration denied 77 Ohio St.3d 1549, 674 N.E.2d 1187, certiorari denied 117 S.Ct. 2522, 521 U.S. 1124, 138 L.Ed.2d 1023, dismissal of post-conviction relief affirmed 2001-Ohio-3447, 2001 WL 1497095, appeal not allowed 94 Ohio St.3d 1506, 764 N.E.2d 1036, 2002-Ohio-5738. Criminal Law ⚷ 254.1; Sentencing And Punishment ⚷ 1774

Defendant, in capital murder prosecution tried to court, did not have right to voir dire members of three-judge panel and, therefore, did not have right to be present during selection of the panel. State v. Eley (Ohio, 12-18-1996) 77 Ohio St.3d 174, 672 N.E.2d 640, 1996-Ohio-323, reconsideration denied 77 Ohio St.3d 1549, 674 N.E.2d 1187, certiorari denied 117 S.Ct. 2522, 521 U.S. 1124, 138 L.Ed.2d 1023, dismissal of post-conviction relief affirmed 2001-Ohio-3447, 2001 WL 1497095, appeal not allowed 94 Ohio St.3d 1506, 764 N.E.2d 1036, 2002-Ohio-5738. Criminal Law ⚷ 254.1

Fact that petitioner was tried before single judge rather than three-judge panel did not entitle him to release from prison pursuant to writ of habeas corpus, even though he was charged with offenses punishable by death; petitioner was also charged and convicted of charge not punishable by death, i.e., kidnapping, for which one judge could try, convict, and sentence petitioner. Swiger v. Seidner (Ohio, 03-01-1996) 74 Ohio St.3d 685, 660 N.E.2d 1214, 1996-Ohio-237. Habeas Corpus ⚷ 227

An accused, charged with a capital offense, has not knowingly, intelligently, and voluntarily waived his right to a trial by jury where, prior to waiving this right, he is misinformed that the three-judge panel may render a verdict pursuant to RC 2945.06 only by unanimous vote (Unanimous verdict required by amendment of RC 2945.06 by 1981 S 1, eff. 10–19–81.). State v. Ruppert (Ohio 1978) 54 Ohio St.2d 263, 375 N.E.2d 1250, 8 O.O.3d 232, certiorari denied 99 S.Ct. 352, 439 U.S. 954, 58 L.Ed.2d 345.

14. —— Visiting judges, three-judge panel

Request by three-judge panel in capital murder case that a visiting judge not assigned to the case rule on admissibility at penalty of victim-impact statements was not authorized under statute governing the designation of three-judge panel in prosecution for an offense punishable by death. State v. Thomas (Ohio, 12-11-2002) 97 Ohio St.3d 309, 779 N.E.2d 1017, 2002-Ohio-6624, reconsideration denied 97 Ohio St.3d 1498, 780 N.E.2d 1022, 2002-Ohio-7248, stay granted 98 Ohio St.3d 1403, 781 N.E.2d 221, 2003-Ohio-40, certiorari denied 123 S.Ct. 2295, 539 U.S. 916, 156 L.Ed.2d 133. Sentencing And Punishment ⚷ 1781

Improper request by three-judge panel in capital murder case that a visiting judge not assigned to the case rule on admissibility at penalty phase of victim-impact statements did not go to the jurisdiction of the court or render the judgment void. State v. Thomas (Ohio, 12-11-2002) 97 Ohio St.3d 309, 779 N.E.2d 1017, 2002-Ohio-6624, reconsideration denied 97 Ohio St.3d 1498, 780 N.E.2d 1022, 2002-Ohio-7248, stay granted 98 Ohio St.3d 1403, 781 N.E.2d 221, 2003-Ohio-40, certiorari denied 123 S.Ct. 2295, 539 U.S. 916, 156 L.Ed.2d 133. Sentencing And Punishment ⚷ 1781

Retired judge was eligible to seat as panel member in capital murder trial. State v. Fox (Ohio, 05-04-1994) 69 Ohio St.3d 183, 631 N.E.2d 124, reconsideration denied 69 Ohio St.3d 1483, 634 N.E.2d 1029, stay granted 70 Ohio St.3d 1402, 636 N.E.2d 327, stay terminated 71 Ohio St.3d 1433, 643 N.E.2d 139, certiorari denied 115 S.Ct. 671, 513 U.S. 1060, 130 L.Ed.2d 604, stay granted 71 Ohio St.3d 1461, 644 N.E.2d 1384, dismissal of post-conviction relief affirmed 1997 WL 256659, dismissed, appeal not allowed 79 Ohio St.3d 1506, 684 N.E.2d 89, reconsideration denied 80 Ohio St.3d 1438, 685 N.E.2d 547. Judges ⚷ 4

Where a case has been tried before a three-judge panel and after an appeal the case is remanded to the trial court for a hearing on a motion to inspect, a judge appointed as a member of the three-judge panel to replace a judge of the original panel, who had resigned his office, may participate in such further proceedings in the case. State v. White (Ohio 1971) 27 Ohio St.2d 73, 271 N.E.2d 804, 56 O.O.2d 42, vacated in part 92 S.Ct. 2874, 408 U.S. 939, 33 L.Ed.2d 761. Judges ⚷ 32

15. Guilty plea

Trial court was not required to convene three-judge panel when it accepted defendant's guilty pleas to murder, kidnapping, aggravated burglary, and two counts of felonious assault; statute requiring convening of three-judge panel if defendant has been charged with crime punishable by death or has pleaded guilty to aggravated murder did not apply in defendant's case, as defendant was no longer charged with offense punishable by death at time he entered his guilty pleas. State v. West (Ohio App. 9 Dist., Lorain, 03-09-2005) No. 04CA008554, 2005-Ohio-990, 2005 WL 544820, Unreported, appeal not allowed 106 Ohio St.3d 1484, 832 N.E.2d 737, 2005-Ohio-3978. Criminal Law ⚷ 273(4.1)

Vacation of defendant's guilty plea to one count of aggravated murder with a capital, felony-murder specification, was not made necessary by manifest injustice in results of plea, notwithstanding fact that guilty plea was not made before statutorily-required three-judge panel; defendant potentially faced death penalty, but in exchange for plea, he avoided death penalty and possible prison terms associated with five other felony charges and mandatory gun specification prison sentence. State v. Woods (Ohio App. 8 Dist., Cuyahoga, 05-15-2003) No. 82120, 2003-Ohio-2475, 2003 WL 21101507, Unreported, appeal allowed 100 Ohio St.3d 1422, 797 N.E.2d 91, 2003-Ohio-5232, affirmed 102 Ohio St.3d 89, 806 N.E.2d 1001, 2004-Ohio-1997. Criminal Law ⚷ 274(3.1)

Although trial court received defendant's guilty plea to aggravated murder before dismissing death specifications, court considered the plea to be tendered only, and it was only subsequent to court's proper dismissal of death specifications, that court "accepted" defendant's plea and entered its finding of guilt as to the remaining counts and specifications, and consequently, when court entered its finding of guilt, defendant was no longer charged with an offense punishable by death, and therefore, statute providing that, if accused is charged with offense punishable with death, he shall be tried by a court to be composed of three judges was not applicable, and thus, single judge possessed jurisdiction to take the plea. State v. Jones (Ohio App. 6 Dist., Williams, 03-07-2003) No. WM-02-012, 2003-Ohio-1037, 2003 WL 859506, Unreported. Criminal Law ⚷ 273(4.1)

When a defendant pleads guilty to aggravated murder in a capital case, a three-judge panel is required to examine witnesses and to hear any other evidence properly presented by the prosecution in order to make a determination as to the guilt of the defendant, and following the presentation of evidence, the panel must unanimously determine whether the defendant is guilty beyond a reasonable doubt of aggravated murder or of a lesser offense; this finding of guilt must be properly journalized to constitute a valid conviction. Kelley v. Wilson (Ohio, 09-29-2004) 103 Ohio St.3d 201, 814 N.E.2d 1222, 2004-Ohio-4883. Criminal Law ⚷ 273(4.1)

Defendant's habeas corpus claim that trial court's acceptance by single judge of guilty pleas to capital murder and aggravated arson violated rule requiring three-judge panel to preside over capital cases when defendant waives jury trial was barred by doctrine of res judicata, where claim was raised and rejected on direct appeal. State ex rel. Rash v. Jackson (Ohio, 05-12-2004) 102 Ohio St.3d 145, 807 N.E.2d 344, 2004-Ohio-2053. Habeas Corpus ⚷ 276

Petitioner had remedy at law, in form of direct appeal, following common pleas court's failure to convene three-judge panel to accept guilty plea to aggravated murder with death penalty specification, and petitioner was thus not entitled to habeas corpus relief. Pratts v. Hurley (Ohio, 05-05-2004) 102 Ohio St.3d 81, 806 N.E.2d 992, 2004-Ohio-1980. Habeas Corpus ⚷ 292

Fed Crim R 11 requiring, upon plea of guilty, detailed inquiry as to defendant's understanding of his rights and full recital of consequences before accepting such plea, was not applicable to a state court hearing in 1964 under RC 2945.06, but effect of that statute, where applicable, was to extend to defendant much of the protection contemplated by Fed Crim R 11. State v. Taylor (Cuyahoga 1972) 30 Ohio App.2d 252, 285 N.E.2d 89, 59 O.O.2d 398. Criminal Law ⚷ 980(2)

After a plea to homicide generally is accepted, the determination of the degree of the crime requires competent, material and relevant evidence. State v. Place (Lucas 1971) 25 Ohio App.2d 158, 267 N.E.2d 832, 54 O.O.2d 337. Criminal Law ⚷ 980(2)

Under an indictment for larceny of property having a value of $80, a plea of "guilty as charged" includes the allegation of value contained in the indictment, and a judgment of conviction of "grand larceny" which does not include a determination by the court of the value of the property stolen, is not prejudicial to the defendant. State v. McCreary (Hamilton 1964) 120 Ohio App. 346, 200 N.E.2d 787, 29 O.O.2d 175.

In 1930 no written waiver of trial by jury was required where a defendant pleaded guilty to homicide generally before a one-judge court. State ex rel. Evans v. Eckle (Ohio 1955) 163 Ohio St. 122, 126 N.E.2d 48, 56 O.O. 177.

Where defendant pleads guilty to first degree murder, neither failure of the court to appoint counsel nor failure to obtain a written waiver of the right to jury trial from such defendant is grounds for issuance of a writ of habeas corpus. Sims v. Alvis (C.A.6 (Ohio) 1958) 253 F.2d 114, 16 O.O.2d 185, certiorari denied 79 S.Ct. 67, 358 U.S. 844, 3 L.Ed.2d 78.

Federal Constitution does not require that witness testimony be taken concomitantly with acceptance of guilty plea, as is required under Ohio statute. Shakoor v. Collins (N.D.Ohio, 09-23-1999) 63 F.Supp.2d 858. Criminal Law ⚷ 273(4.1)

Alleged failure of trial court to take witness testimony in connection with defendant's entry of guilty plea to charge of aggravated murder, as required under Ohio statute, did not create error in trial process so egregious that it denied fundamental fairness, as would provide basis for habeas corpus relief. Shakoor v. Collins (N.D.Ohio, 09-23-1999) 63 F.Supp.2d 858. Habeas Corpus ⚷ 475.1

16. Single-judge court

Alleged violation of statute governing waiver of jury trials, arising from acceptance of a guilty plea in a capital case by a single judge rather than a three-judge panel, was not a proper subject for habeas corpus relief and could be remedied only in a direct appeal from a criminal conviction. State ex rel. Frazier v. Brigano (Ohio, 05-12-2004) 102 Ohio St.3d 148, 807 N.E.2d 346, 2004-Ohio-2139, certiorari denied 125 S.Ct. 340, 160 L.Ed.2d 238. Habeas Corpus ⚷ 475.1

Although death penalty was never available as a sentencing option for 16-year-old defendant, due to his age, prosecution charging defendant with aggravated murder and aggravated robbery with specifications that would have made him eligible for the death penalty had he been an adult was required to be heard by a three-judge panel, as jurisdictional matter that could not be waived. State v. Koger (Ohio App. 6 Dist., 02-07-2003) 151 Ohio App.3d 534, 784 N.E.2d 780, 2003-Ohio-576, appeal allowed 99 Ohio St.3d 1451, 790 N.E.2d 1217, 2003-Ohio-3396, affirmed 102 Ohio St.3d 263, 809 N.E.2d 661, 2004-Ohio-2824. Criminal Law ⚷ 250; Sentencing And Punishment ⚷ 1643

Any challenge to propriety of defendant's waiver of three-judge panel in prosecution for aggravated murder with capital specifications could have been raised on direct appeal, and thus res judicata barred defendant's postconviction claim that trial court acted beyond its statutory authority by trying defendant before a single judge rather than a three-judge panel. State v. Swiger (Ohio App. 9 Dist., 01-28-1998) 125 Ohio App.3d 456, 708 N.E.2d 1033, dismissed, appeal not allowed 82 Ohio St.3d 1411, 694 N.E.2d 75. Criminal Law ⚷ 1429(2)

Death penalty statute and rule require that when plea of no contest is accepted to both charge and one or more specifications, panel of three judges shall make determination as to guilt of accused and, if guilty, whether offense was aggravated murder or lesser offense and impose sentence accordingly, and there is no provision for single trial judge to make that determination. State v. Brock (Ohio App. 3 Dist., 04-26-1996) 110 Ohio App.3d 656, 675 N.E.2d 18, dismissed, appeal not allowed 77 Ohio St.3d 1444, 671 N.E.2d 1283. Sentencing And Punishment ⚷ 1774

Defendant against whom judgment of conviction which was entered in death penalty case after trial court had improperly allowed single-judge court to make determination as to guilt following no contest plea, which rendered judgment void ab initio, was not in jeopardy on offense, and cause was remanded to proceed as if no plea had been entered. State v. Brock (Ohio App. 3 Dist., 04-26-1996) 110 Ohio App.3d 656, 675 N.E.2d 18, dismissed, appeal not allowed 77 Ohio St.3d 1444, 671 N.E.2d 1283. Double Jeopardy ⚷ 52

Single-judge court in capital murder case lacked jurisdiction to make determination as to guilt of accused after defendant entered no contest plea, and thus, judgment of conviction and subsequent jury proceedings regarding mitigation of death penalty phase were rendered void; court's actions, which it admitted imposed "some quirks" into procedure, were in violation of legislatively defined procedures for imposition of death penalty. State v. Brock (Ohio App. 3 Dist., 04-26-1996) 110 Ohio App.3d 656, 675 N.E.2d 18, dismissed, appeal not allowed 77 Ohio St.3d 1444, 671 N.E.2d 1283. Sentencing And Punishment ⚷ 1736

TRIAL PROCEDURE

2945.07 Recording presence of crime victim or member of family at trial; notices to be given—Repealed

(1994 S 186, eff. 10–12–94; 1994 H 571, eff. 10–6–94; 1987 S 6, § 1, eff. 6–10–87; 1987 S 6, § 3; 1984 S 172, § 1, 4)

Historical and Statutory Notes

Ed. Note: Former 2945.07 repealed by 1972 H 511, eff. 1–1–74; 1953 H 1; GC 13442–5a.

Pre–1953 H 1 Amendments: 120 v 707

2945.08 Prosecution in wrong county; proceeding

If it appears, on the trial of a criminal cause, that the offense was committed within the exclusive jurisdiction of another county of this state, the court must direct the defendant to be committed to await a warrant from the proper county for his arrest, but if the offense is a bailable offense the court may admit the defendant to bail with sufficient sureties conditioned, that he will, within such time as the court appoints, render himself amenable to a warrant for his arrest from the proper county, and if not sooner arrested thereon, will appear in court at the time fixed to surrender himself upon the warrant.

The clerk of the court of common pleas shall forthwith notify the prosecuting attorney of the county in which such offense was committed, in order that proper proceedings may be had in the case. A defendant in such case shall not be committed nor held under bond for a period of more than ten days.

(1953 H 1, eff. 10–1–53; GC 13442–6)

Historical and Statutory Notes

Pre–1953 H 1 Amendments: 113 v 180, Ch 21, § 6

Cross References

Jurisdiction, 2901.11

Right to trial in county where offense allegedly occurred, O Const Art I §10

Venue, 2901.12

Venue and change of venue, Crim R 18

Library References

Criminal Law ⚷115 to 144.

Westlaw Topic No. 110.

C.J.S. Corporations § 252.

C.J.S. Criminal Law §§ 187 to 191.

Research References

Encyclopedias

OH Jur. 3d Criminal Law § 2177, Where Another County Has Exclusive Jurisdiction.

OH Jur. 3d Criminal Law § 2572, Prosecution in Wrong County.

Notes of Decisions

Transfer of juvenile for trial as adult 1

1. Transfer of juvenile for trial as adult

Where a juvenile court in the jurisdiction in which an offender resides waives jurisdiction so that the offender will be tried by a common pleas court, such defendant is entitled to a trial in the county where the offense occurred. In re Davis (Ohio Juv. 1961) 179 N.E.2d 198, 87 Ohio Law Abs. 222, 22 O.O.2d 108.

2945.09 Grounds of objection to be stated

In the trial of any criminal case, the grounds of an objection to any ruling or action of the court shall be stated if required by the court.

(1986 H 412, eff. 3–17–87; 1953 H 1; GC 13442–7)

Historical and Statutory Notes

Pre–1953 H 1 Amendments: 113 v 180, Ch 21, § 7

Cross References

Exceptions unnecessary, Crim R 51

Magistrate courts, objections to rulings, 2938.09

Library References

Criminal Law ⚷660, 695.

Westlaw Topic No. 110.

C.J.S. Criminal Law §§ 1150, 1180, 1224.

Research References

Treatises and Practice Aids

Giannelli and Snyder, Baldwin's Ohio Practice, Evidence, R 103, Rulings on Evidence.

Giannelli and Snyder, Baldwin's Ohio Practice, Evidence, § 103.4, "Exceptions" to Evidence.

Notes of Decisions

Exception unnecessary 1

1. Exception unnecessary

When an objection to the introduction of testimony is made and overruled, even though no express exception is taken, it is available to the objecting party. Tatu v. State (Cuyahoga 1932) 43 Ohio App. 68, 182 N.E. 681, 12 Ohio Law Abs. 228, 36 Ohio Law Rep. 531.

2945.10 Order of proceedings of trial

The trial of an issue upon an indictment or information shall proceed before the trial court or jury as follows:

(A) Counsel for the state must first state the case for the prosecution, and may briefly state the evidence by which he expects to sustain it.

(B) The defendant or his counsel must then state his defense, and may briefly state the evidence which he expects to offer in support of it.

(C) The state must first produce its evidence and the defendant shall then produce his evidence.

(D) The state will then be confined to rebutting evidence, but the court, for good reason, in furtherance of justice, may permit evidence to be offered by either side out of its order.

(E) When the evidence is concluded, either party may request instructions to the jury on the points of law, which instructions shall be reduced to writing if either party requests it.

(F) When the evidence is concluded, unless the case is submitted without argument, the counsel for the state shall commence, the defendant or his counsel follow, and the counsel for the state conclude the argument to the jury.

(G) The court, after the argument is concluded and before proceeding with other business, shall forthwith charge the jury. Such charge shall be reduced to writing by the court if either party requests it before the argument to the jury is commenced. Such charge, or other charge or instruction provided for in this section, when so written and given, shall not be orally qualified, modified, or explained to the jury by the court. Written charges and instructions shall be taken by the jury in their retirement and returned with their verdict into court and remain on file with the papers of the case.

The court may deviate from the order of proceedings listed in this section.

(1953 H 1, eff. 10–1–53; GC 13442–8)

Historical and Statutory Notes

Pre–1953 H 1 Amendments: 113 v 180, Ch 21, § 8

Cross References

Jury instructions, Crim R 30

Trial, procedure, in civil case, 2315.01

Library References

Criminal Law ⚷645, 680, 769.

Westlaw Topic No. 110.

C.J.S. Criminal Law §§ 1215, 1240 to 1244, 1258, 1302 to 1304.

Research References

Encyclopedias

OH Jur. 3d Criminal Law § 2735, Written and Oral Instructions.

OH Jur. 3d Criminal Law § 2802, Generally; Transcripts; Written Charges and Instructions.

OH Jur. 3d Criminal Law § 3596, What Constitutes Record.

Treatises and Practice Aids

Markus, Trial Handbook for Ohio Lawyers, § 7:1, by Plaintiff.

Markus, Trial Handbook for Ohio Lawyers, § 7:2, by Defendant.

Markus, Trial Handbook for Ohio Lawyers, § 36:1, Requirements.

Markus, Trial Handbook for Ohio Lawyers, § 37:1, During Deliberations.

Markus, Trial Handbook for Ohio Lawyers, § 37:6, Items Taken to Jury Room.

Markus, Trial Handbook for Ohio Lawyers, § 4:46, Order of Proceedings of Trial.

Katz, Giannelli, Blair and Lipton, Baldwin's Ohio Practice, Criminal Law, § 68:2, Rules of Evidence.

Katz, Giannelli, Blair and Lipton, Baldwin's Ohio Practice, Criminal Law, § 68:9, Closing Argument.

Giannelli and Snyder, Baldwin's Ohio Practice, Evidence, R 611, Mode and Order of Interrogation and Presentation.

Giannelli and Snyder, Baldwin's Ohio Practice, Evidence, § 611.4, Court Control of Trial: Order of Proceedings.

1 Giannelli and Snyder, Baldwin's Ohio Practice, Evidence, Index, Index.

Hennenberg & Reinhart, Ohio Criminal Defense Motions F 8.03, Motion for Alternating Voir Dire-Jury-Related Motions.

Hennenberg & Reinhart, Ohio Criminal Defense Motions F 13.32, Motion to Allow the Defense to Argue Last and for Not Less Than Four (4) Hours-Death Penalty Motions.

Law Review and Journal Commentaries

Is Aggression Good Advocacy?, Bruce A. Allman. (Ed. note: A return to civility, courtesy, and cooperation by members of the Bar is urged.) 45 Dayton B Briefs 3 (November 1995).

Winning Arguments—In real life, the best measure of successful advocacy is prevailing at trial, James W. McElhaney. 82 A B A J 80 (September 1996).

Notes of Decisions

---

1. In general

Prosecution is entitled to certain degree of latitude in summation. State v. Eley (Ohio, 12-18-1996) 77 Ohio St.3d 174, 672 N.E.2d 640, 1996-Ohio-323, reconsideration denied 77 Ohio St.3d 1549, 674 N.E.2d 1187, certiorari denied 117 S.Ct. 2522, 521 U.S. 1124, 138 L.Ed.2d 1023, dismissal of post-conviction relief affirmed 2001-Ohio-3447, 2001 WL 1497095, appeal not allowed 94 Ohio St.3d 1506, 764 N.E.2d 1036, 2002-Ohio-5738. Criminal Law ⚷ 709

When a suppression motion is heard, it is not improper for the movant to present evidence first, since the movant has the initial burden of establishing whether a warrant authorized the search or seizure. State v. Malott (Highland 1992) 79 Ohio App.3d 393, 607 N.E.2d 508. Criminal Law ⚷ 394.5(4)

In the trial of a criminal case, it is not an abuse of discretion to deny defendant the right of surrebuttal. State v. Blanton (Lawrence 1960) 111 Ohio App. 111, 170 N.E.2d 754, 14 O.O.2d 13.

A defendant who announces he wishes to take the witness stand for the first time during the court's charge to the jury, and who has previously engaged in similar conduct during two plea proceedings, is not denied a fair trial where the trial court refuses to reopen the case for such testimony. State v Griggs, Nos. 52815 and 52923 (8th Dist Ct App, Cuyahoga, 10–8–87).

Where a trial judge rules that a criminal defendant is guilty before allowing defense counsel to present a closing argument and subsequently offers to withdraw the finding of guilty until the closing argument is made, defense counsel's failure to proceed with the closing argument does not constitute a waiver of the defendant's right to a closing argument. State v Patton, No. WD–83–51 (6th Dist Ct App, Wood, 12–30–83).

2. Discretion of court

Even if mortician's testimony that no monies had yet been received for funeral expenses for defendant's children, whom defendant allegedly killed, was not in rebuttal to defense testimony that defendant partially assigned life insurance proceeds to pay those expenses, trial court had discretion to deviate from order of proceedings. State v. Grant (Ohio 1993) 67 Ohio St.3d 465, 620 N.E.2d 50, rehearing denied 68 Ohio St.3d 1412, 623 N.E.2d 568, certiorari denied 115 S.Ct. 116, 513 U.S. 836, 130 L.Ed.2d 62, rehearing denied 115 S.Ct. 617, 513 U.S. 1033, 130 L.Ed.2d 525. Criminal Law ⚷ 680(1)

It is within the court's discretion to vary the order of trial proceedings set forth in RC 2945.10; thus, the trial court's denial of defense counsel's request for rebuttal of arguments made by the prosecution for the first time in the final portion of the prosecution's closing argument is not prejudicial error absent a showing of abuse of discretion. State v. Mahoney (Hamilton 1986) 34 Ohio App.3d 114, 517 N.E.2d 957.

Any decision to vary the order of proceedings in RC 2945.10 is within the sound discretion of the trial court, and any claim that the trial court erred in following the statutorily mandated order of proceedings must sustain a heavy burden to demonstrate the unfairness and prejudice of following that order. State v. Jenkins (Ohio 1984) 15 Ohio St.3d 164, 473 N.E.2d 264, 15 O.B.R. 311, certiorari denied 105 S.Ct. 3514, 472 U.S. 1032, 87 L.Ed.2d 643, rehearing denied 106 S.Ct. 19, 473 U.S. 927, 87 L.Ed.2d 697. Criminal Law ⚷ 633(1)

Any decision to vary the order of proceedings at trial in RC 2945.10 is within the sound discretion of the trial court, and any claim that the trial court erred in following the statutorily mandated order of proceedings must sustain a heavy burden to demonstrate the unfairness and prejudice of following that order. State v. Bayless (Ohio 1976) 48 Ohio St.2d 73, 357 N.E.2d 1035, 2 O.O.3d 249, vacated 98 S.Ct. 3135, 438 U.S. 911, 57 L.Ed.2d 1155. Criminal Law ⚷ 633(1)

3. Statements of case

Defendant was not denied effective assistance by counsel's opening statement allegedly admitting defendant's participation in burglary; record was unclear as to whether counsel was making such admission, jury was informed that opening statements were not evidence, and result of trial would not have changed had statement not been made, given overwhelming weight of evidence against defendant. State v. Robinson (Ohio App. 3 Dist., 01-19-1996) 108 Ohio App.3d 428, 670 N.E.2d 1077. Criminal Law ⚷ 641.13(2.1)

Trial court did not abuse its discretion in refusing to allow defense counsel to defer making opening statement until after state rested its case. State v. Gumm (Ohio, 08-30-1995) 73 Ohio St.3d 413, 653 N.E.2d 253, 1995-Ohio-24, reconsideration denied 74 Ohio St.3d 1423, 655 N.E.2d 742, certiorari denied 116 S.Ct. 1275, 516 U.S. 1177, 134 L.Ed.2d 221, rehearing denied 116 S.Ct. 1707, 517 U.S. 1204, 134 L.Ed.2d 806, denial of post-conviction relief affirmed 1997 WL 752608, dismissed, appeal not allowed 81 Ohio St.3d 1495, 691 N.E.2d 1057, certiorari denied 119 S.Ct. 195, 525 U.S. 884, 142 L.Ed.2d 159, denial of post-conviction relief affirmed 103 Ohio St.3d 162, 814 N.E.2d 861, 2004-Ohio-4755, reconsideration denied 104 Ohio St.3d 1411, 818 N.E.2d 712, 2004-Ohio-6364. Criminal Law ⚷ 645

Opening statements are not "evidence." State v. Smith (Greene 1992) 84 Ohio App.3d 647, 617 N.E.2d 1160, motion to certify denied 66 Ohio St.3d 1488, 612 N.E.2d 1244. Criminal Law ⚷ 702.1

The doctrine of invited error does not apply to remarks made in an opening statement; the purpose of an opening statement is to advise the jury what counsel expects the evidence to show, not to invite a line of questioning which invades the province of the jury. State v. McWhite (Lucas 1991) 73 Ohio App.3d 323, 597 N.E.2d 168, dismissed, jurisdictional motion overruled 62 Ohio St.3d 1463, 580 N.E.2d 784, dismissed in part 62 Ohio St.3d 1468, 580 N.E.2d 1098.

There is no change in a charge that a defendant sold LSD where the prosecution fully sets forth all the elements of the offense and then, by way of stating the evidence expected to sustain the charge, notes that the defendant called the tablets "chocolate mesc" but that these tablets were later tested and found to be LSD, as this is an evidentiary matter pertinent not to the material sold but to the defendant's knowledge or intent. State v. Dotson (Ohio App. 3 Dist. 1987) 35 Ohio App.3d 135, 520 N.E.2d 240.

A motion for judgment of acquittal may be made at the close of the state's opening statement in a criminal case, but should be granted only when the statement does not indicate that the accused was charged with the identical offense for which he was on trial, or contains admissions of fact showing that the accused had not committed or was not guilty of the offense charged in the complaint. State v. Scott (Fayette 1983) 8 Ohio App.3d 1, 455 N.E.2d 1363, 43 A.L.R.4th 979, 8 O.B.R. 1. Criminal Law ⚷ 703

An opening statement by the state in a criminal case as provided in RC 2945.10(A) is discretionary and not mandatory, and may be waived, and hence it is error for the trial court to discharge a defendant in a criminal case because the state did not make an opening statement. State v. Shaker (Cuyahoga 1980) 68 Ohio App.2d 135, 427 N.E.2d 537, 22 O.O.3d 165.

In a prosecution for practicing medicine without a license as required by GC 1269 et seq., the objection that the opening statement of defendant's counsel was unreasonably limited by trial judge when counsel undertook to show a conspiracy of persons in the county to prosecute defendant and deprive him of the rights of practicing medicine as a chiropractic and that the court unreasonably limited defendant by refusing his evidence tending to show such conspiracy, was without merit. Nesmith v. State (Ohio 1920) 101 Ohio St. 158, 128 N.E. 57, 18 Ohio Law Rep. 15, error dismissed 42 S.Ct. 186, 257 U.S. 622, 66 L.Ed. 402. Criminal Law ⚷ 704; Health ⚷ 186(4); Health ⚷ 187

Trial counsel's failure to give an opening statement in murder trial did not constitute ineffective assistance of counsel; rather, that decision fell within the wide range of discretion afforded to counsel, particularly in light of fact that to do so would have required that defendant's counsel concede to the jury that their client was a murderer. Zuern v. Tate (S.D.Ohio, 03-30-2000) 101 F.Supp.2d 948, affirmed in part, reversed in part 336 F.3d 478, certiorari denied 124 S.Ct. 1456, 540 U.S. 1198, 158 L.Ed.2d 113. Criminal Law ⚷ 641.13(2.1)

4. Introduction of evidence

Trial court acted within its discretion, at close of state's rebuttal case in capital murder prosecution, in refusing to admit reports of defense mental health experts; appropriate time for defense counsel to have requested admission of the reports was during defense's case. State v. Filiaggi (Ohio, 07-29-1999) 86 Ohio St.3d 230, 714 N.E.2d 867, 1999-Ohio-99, certiorari denied 120 S.Ct. 821, 528 U.S. 1090, 145 L.Ed.2d 691, denial of post-conviction relief affirmed 445 F.3d 851. Criminal Law ⚿ 680(1)

Trial court could allow mortician to testify in rebuttal that no monies had yet been received for funeral expenses for defendant's children, whom defendant allegedly killed; there had been earlier testimony that defendant partially assigned proceeds of life insurance policies she took out on children to pay funeral expenses. State v. Grant (Ohio 1993) 67 Ohio St.3d 465, 620 N.E.2d 50, rehearing denied 68 Ohio St.3d 1412, 623 N.E.2d 568, certiorari denied 115 S.Ct. 116, 513 U.S. 836, 130 L.Ed.2d 62, rehearing denied 115 S.Ct. 617, 513 U.S. 1033, 130 L.Ed.2d 525. Criminal Law ⚿ 683(1)

In prosecution for loitering with purpose to solicit sexual activity, trial court did not abuse its discretion by allowing city to reopen their case-in-chief at close of all evidence and commencement of closing arguments to allow police officer to make identification of defendant. City of Columbus v. Grant (Franklin 1981) 1 Ohio App.3d 96, 439 N.E.2d 907, 1 O.B.R. 399. Criminal Law ⚿ 687(1)

In trial of persons jointly indicted for robbery, where identity of the defendants is an issue, it is not error to receive testimony of other unconnected crimes, where sole purpose of such testimony is to establish identity and where the testimony is relevant to that issue and jury's consideration is limited thereto. Whiteman v. State (Ohio 1928) 119 Ohio St. 285, 164 N.E. 51, 63 A.L.R. 595, 6 Ohio Law Abs. 695, 27 Ohio Law Rep. 642.

The admission out of its order of evidence in a criminal case rests in the sound discretion of the court, and, unless some abuse appears when taken in connection with all the evidence in the case, such as to show that a party was prevented from having a fair trial, a verdict will not be disturbed upon such ground. Holt v. State (Ohio 1923) 107 Ohio St. 307, 140 N.E. 349, 1 Ohio Law Abs. 309, 21 Ohio Law Rep. 8. Criminal Law ⚿ 680(1)

5. Argument—In general

Prosecutor's statements during rebuttal closing argument in murder prosecution, to effect that defendant was "hid[ing] behind the Constitution" and "waiv[ing] [*sic*] the flag" were permissible response to defense counsel's sweeping pronouncements during his closing argument with respect to the Constitution in attempt to elucidate his point about vengeance and state-induced sympathy for victim, and did not improperly shift any burden to defense. State v. Lewis (Ohio App. 7 Dist., Mahoning, 05-24-2005) No. 03 MA 36, 2005-Ohio-2699, 2005 WL 1300761, Unreported, appeal not allowed 106 Ohio St.3d 1556, 836 N.E.2d 581, 2005-Ohio-5531. Criminal Law ⚿ 726

Prosecutor's statement during rebuttal closing argument in murder prosecution, to effect that there were "evidentiary reasons" why jury had not seen defendant's videotaped statement to police and that defense counsel was aware of what those reasons were, were permissible response to defense counsel's prior attempt to cause jury to question state's reasons for failing to show videotape, and did not improperly shift any burden to defense. State v. Lewis (Ohio App. 7 Dist., Mahoning, 05-24-2005) No. 03 MA 36, 2005-Ohio-2699, 2005 WL 1300761, Unreported, appeal not allowed 106 Ohio St.3d 1556, 836 N.E.2d 581, 2005-Ohio-5531. Criminal Law ⚿ 726

Prosecutor's statement during rebuttal closing argument in murder prosecution, mentioning that defendant did not call his original counsel to bolster his claim that police witness was lying, was permissible response to defense counsel's statement during closing argument that state's case rested solely on testimony of police witness, that police witness was lying about defendant's statement to police, and that defendant's former counsel had been present at time of statement but was not called to testify, and did not amount to misconduct. State v. Lewis (Ohio App. 7 Dist., Mahoning, 05-24-2005) No. 03 MA 36, 2005-Ohio-2699, 2005 WL 1300761, Unreported, appeal not allowed 106 Ohio St.3d 1556, 836 N.E.2d 581, 2005-Ohio-5531. Criminal Law ⚿ 726

Prosecutor's references to the "institutionalized mentally retarded" during closing argument of gross sexual imposition trial were not improper; defendant's defense was premised on equating the ability to resist with the ability to consent, and the prosecutor took the implications of such an argument to their logical extreme—even the severely mentally retarded possess the ability to resist. State v. Novak (Ohio App. 11 Dist., Lake, 02-11-2005) No. 2003-L-077, 2005-Ohio-563, 2005 WL 336337, Unreported. Criminal Law ⚿ 713

Prosecutor's comment in closing argument in defendant's trial for sexual battery in which prosecutor evoked reptile imagery was an attempt to explain to the jury that they should not be misled by the defense's argument that the case was not what it appeared to be, rather than an impermissible comment comparing the defendant to a reptile. State v. Anderson (Ohio App. 6 Dist., Wood, 02-11-2005) No. WD-04-035, 2005-Ohio-534, 2005 WL 327179, Unreported. Criminal Law ⚿ 723(1)

Prosecutor's comments in closing argument in defendant's trial for sexual battery that victim remembered the events of the evening was not a comment about the victim's credibility, but rather was a response to the inference that she had blacked out from excessive drinking and could not remember what had happened. State v. Anderson (Ohio App. 6 Dist., Wood, 02-11-2005) No. WD-04-035, 2005-Ohio-534, 2005 WL 327179, Unreported. Criminal Law ⚿ 720(5)

Defendant waived any prejudice that may have resulted from the prosecutor's closing argument statements that defense counsel had the "same subpoena power" as the State to call witnesses and that defendant was the "only person in this courtroom who picks witnesses," where defendant objected to both statements, the trial court sustained defendant's objections, and defendant failed to request any curative jury instructions. State v. Root (Ohio App. 2 Dist., Montgomery, 01-31-2005) No. CIV.A. 20366, 2005-Ohio-448, 2005 WL 281172, Unreported. Criminal Law ⚷ 728(5)

Absent proof of alleged conversation between defendant and detective, it was improper for the State to refer to an "oral statement" defendant gave to the police in its "statement of the case and facts;" there was no evidence of any such statement at trial, and during defendant's cross-examination, the State asked him whether he made certain statements to questions by a police detective, and defendant denied making specific statements, and the State did not offer any proof relating to a conversation, nor did it present the testimony of the detective who allegedly heard these statements. State v. Paulk (Ohio App. 8 Dist., Cuyahoga, 08-05-2004) No. 83968, 2004-Ohio-4082, 2004 WL 1752956, Unreported. Criminal Law ⚷ 719(1)

Assuming Fifth Amendment right not to put forth any evidence in corroboration of defendant's testimony exists, prosecutor's closing argument comment that defendant offered version of events that was completely unsupported by anything else did not violate such right, where prosecutor did not comment on defendant's failure to offer corroborating testimony, but simply indicated that defendant's testimony was not consistent with other testimony. State v. McSwain (Ohio App. 8 Dist., Cuyahoga, 06-24-2004) No. 83394, 2004-Ohio-3292, 2004 WL 1402700, Unreported, appeal not allowed 104 Ohio St.3d 1425, 819 N.E.2d 709, 2004-Ohio-6585, certiorari denied 125 S.Ct. 2269, 544 U.S. 1040, 161 L.Ed.2d 1072. Criminal Law ⚷ 721.5(2)

Once robbery defendant waived his right against self-incrimination by testifying, his credibility was at issue and could properly be challenged by charge of recent fabrication. State v. McSwain (Ohio App. 8 Dist., Cuyahoga, 06-24-2004) No. 83394, 2004-Ohio-3292, 2004 WL 1402700, Unreported, appeal not allowed 104 Ohio St.3d 1425, 819 N.E.2d 709, 2004-Ohio-6585, certiorari denied 125 S.Ct. 2269, 544 U.S. 1040, 161 L.Ed.2d 1072. Witnesses ⚷ 337(1)

Trial court did not improperly limit defendant's closing argument in prosecution for felonious assault by prohibiting defendant from arguing that he did not commit alleged offense; counsel's statements were properly limited to the evidence presented at trial. State v. Harris (Ohio App. 5 Dist., Stark, 03-29-2004) No. 2003CA00287, 2004-Ohio-1557, 2004 WL 614834, Unreported. Criminal Law ⚷ 711

Prosecutor improperly used the bad character of defendant's friend to attack defendant's character during closing arguments in cocaine trafficking trial by suggesting defendant distanced himself from friend because "you are with whom you associate," even though prosecutor stated comments rebutted defense counsel's closing argument, where defense counsel did not state that defendant had distance himself from friend. State v. Moman (Ohio App. 7 Dist., Columbiana, 03-18-2004) No. 02CO52, 2004-Ohio-1387, 2004 WL 549807, Unreported. Criminal Law ⚷ 1171.6

Defendant failed to object to prosecutor's remarks during closing argument of murder trial and thus waived all but plain error. State v. Brandy (Ohio App. 10 Dist., Franklin, 04-10-2003) No. 02AP-832, 2003-Ohio-1836, 2003 WL 1848761, Unreported, appeal not allowed 99 Ohio St.3d 1515, 792 N.E.2d 201, 2003-Ohio-3957. Criminal Law ⚷ 1037.1(1)

Prosecutor's comment during closing argument of murder trial comparing defendant's actions in shooting victim to that of a dog hunting someone or something down, while it may have been a bit harsh, was merely an attempt by the prosecutor to explain to the jury defendant's actions and fell into the latitude afforded counsel during closing argument. State v. Brandy (Ohio App. 10 Dist., Franklin, 04-10-2003) No. 02AP-832, 2003-Ohio-1836, 2003 WL 1848761, Unreported, appeal not allowed 99 Ohio St.3d 1515, 792 N.E.2d 201, 2003-Ohio-3957. Criminal Law ⚷ 713

Prosecutor's comments during closing argument of murder trial that defendant should not have escaped punishment for aggravated murder by alleging sudden passion or fit of rage and words alone were not enough to allow someone to escape their punishment for aggravated murder were not prejudicial, where defense counsel objected, trial court sustained objection, and trial court gave a curative instruction. State v. Brandy (Ohio App. 10 Dist., Franklin, 04-10-2003) No. 02AP-832, 2003-Ohio-1836, 2003 WL 1848761, Unreported, appeal not allowed 99 Ohio St.3d 1515, 792 N.E.2d 201, 2003-Ohio-3957. Criminal Law ⚷ 730(1)

Prosecutor's closing argument remark in prosecution for sex offenses allegedly committed by defendant against his minor daughters, that "we know where he penetrated [one daughter] because of that anal tear," was proper argument based on the evidence, even though the tear and examining physician's testimony did not compel such a conclusion. State v. Fitch (Ohio App. 2 Dist., Clark, 01-17-2003) No. 2002-CA-5, 2003-Ohio-203, 2003 WL 139761, Unreported, appeal not allowed 99 Ohio St.3d 1411, 788 N.E.2d 647, 2003-Ohio-2454. Criminal Law ⚷ 720(7.1)

Prosecutor's request that jury not "let down" the victims, during closing argument in prosecution for sex offenses allegedly committed by defendant against his minor daughters, was inappropriate. State v. Fitch (Ohio App. 2 Dist., Clark, 01-17-2003) No. 2002-CA-5, 2003-Ohio-203, 2003 WL 139761, Unreported, appeal not allowed 99 Ohio St.3d 1411, 788 N.E.2d 647, 2003-Ohio-2454. Criminal Law ⚷ 723(1)

Prosecutor improperly expressed his personal belief or opinion as to credibility of a witness or as to guilt of the accused, during closing argument in prosecution for aggravated robbery, where prosecutor stated, "I think the credibility of the State's witnesses, frankly, is unmatched by the credibility of the defense witnesses," and stated, "this defendant is as guilty as I think everybody in this jury knows he is." State v. Fields (Ohio App. 1 Dist., Hamilton, 08-30-2002) No. C-010720, No. C-010688, 2002-Ohio-4451, 2002 WL 1988273, Unreported, motion for delayed appeal denied 97 Ohio St.3d 1495, 780 N.E.2d 600, 2002-Ohio-7200. Criminal Law ⚿ 720(5); Criminal Law ⚿ 720.5

Prosecutor's characterization of defendant as "liar" during closing argument was reasonable inference from evidence presented at trial for attempted murder and felonious assault; defendant's version of shooting incident differed significantly from that of all other witnesses, defendant gave statements to police that were inconsistent with his testimony at trial, and his trial testimony was inconsistent with physical evidence. State v. Baker (Ohio App. 2 Dist., 01-07-2005) 159 Ohio App.3d 462, 824 N.E.2d 162, 2005-Ohio-45, motion for delayed appeal denied 106 Ohio St.3d 1408, 830 N.E.2d 342, 2005-Ohio-3154, appeal not allowed 106 Ohio St.3d 1417, 830 N.E.2d 348, 2005-Ohio-3154. Criminal Law ⚿ 720(5)

Prosecutor's comment during closing argument characterizing defendant's actions as "open[ing] fire in a crowded apartment complex where kids are out playing, where people are all around," was not irrelevant or an improper appeal to jurors' emotions in trial for attempted murder and felonious assault, although defendant was not charged with an offense involving children or any other victims; statement was proper comment on evidence that defendant fired numerous shots at intended victim who was standing within group of people and that 12-year-old boy had been playing nearby. State v. Baker (Ohio App. 2 Dist., 01-07-2005) 159 Ohio App.3d 462, 824 N.E.2d 162, 2005-Ohio-45, motion for delayed appeal denied 106 Ohio St.3d 1408, 830 N.E.2d 342, 2005-Ohio-3154, appeal not allowed 106 Ohio St.3d 1417, 830 N.E.2d 348, 2005-Ohio-3154. Criminal Law ⚿ 720(1)

Prosecutor can respond in argument to issues raised by an accused. State v. Cassano (Ohio, 08-07-2002) 96 Ohio St.3d 94, 772 N.E.2d 81, 2002-Ohio-3751, reconsideration denied 96 Ohio St.3d 1517, 775 N.E.2d 858, 2002-Ohio-4950, certiorari denied 123 S.Ct. 1359, 537 U.S. 1235, 155 L.Ed.2d 201. Criminal Law ⚿ 726

Prosecutor's statements during penalty phase closing argument in capital murder prosecution, to effect that future events might require abandoning single-cell policy of super-maximum security facility in which defendant was presently housed, or might require transfer of some of its inmates to other prisons, was proper rebuttal of defense argument that defendant would be restricted to single cell if given life sentence, defense assertions that defendant no longer represented danger since he would be under close scrutiny at his present facility, and defendant's optimistic speculation that his current conditions of confinement would continue indefinitely. State v. Cassano (Ohio, 08-07-2002) 96 Ohio St.3d 94, 772 N.E.2d 81, 2002-Ohio-3751, reconsideration denied 96 Ohio St.3d 1517, 775 N.E.2d 858, 2002-Ohio-4950, certiorari denied 123 S.Ct. 1359, 537 U.S. 1235, 155 L.Ed.2d 201. Sentencing And Punishment ⚿ 1780(2)

Both parties are permitted wide latitude during closing argument. State v. Eley (Ohio, 12-18-1996) 77 Ohio St.3d 174, 672 N.E.2d 640, 1996-Ohio-323, reconsideration denied 77 Ohio St.3d 1549, 674 N.E.2d 1187, certiorari denied 117 S.Ct. 2522, 521 U.S. 1124, 138 L.Ed.2d 1023, dismissal of post-conviction relief affirmed 2001-Ohio-3447, 2001 WL 1497095, appeal not allowed 94 Ohio St.3d 1506, 764 N.E.2d 1036, 2002-Ohio-5738. Criminal Law ⚿ 708.1

Prosecution was entitled to attack existence of murder defendant's alleged hallucinations when rebutting evidence of his insanity defense, where defendant placed his psychological status and competency at issue by presenting insanity defense and supporting that defense with evidence of hallucinations. State v. Awkal (Ohio, 08-14-1996) 76 Ohio St.3d 324, 667 N.E.2d 960, 1996-Ohio-395, certiorari denied 117 S.Ct. 776, 519 U.S. 1095, 136 L.Ed.2d 720, dismissal of post-conviction relief affirmed 1998 WL 827585, dismissed, appeal not allowed 85 Ohio St.3d 1442, 708 N.E.2d 209. Homicide ⚿ 1041

Robbery defendant had relinquished right to insist upon closing argument, by absenting herself from court after close of prosecution's case. State v. Harrison (Hamilton 1993) 88 Ohio App.3d 287, 623 N.E.2d 726. Criminal Law ⚿ 645

Permitting prosecution to argue last in capital sentencing proceedings did not violate defendant's constitutional rights. State v. Grant (Ohio 1993) 67 Ohio St.3d 465, 620 N.E.2d 50, rehearing denied 68 Ohio St.3d 1412, 623 N.E.2d 568, certiorari denied 115 S.Ct. 116, 513 U.S. 836, 130 L.Ed.2d 62, rehearing denied 115 S.Ct. 617, 513 U.S. 1033, 130 L.Ed.2d 525. Criminal Law ⚿ 645

Because the prosecution in a capital case has the burden of proof, pursuant to RC 2929.03(D)(1), that aggravating circumstances outweigh mitigating factors, the prosecution is properly permitted to open and close arguments in the penalty phase of the trial, pursuant to RC 2945.10(F). State v. Jenkins (Ohio 1984) 15 Ohio St.3d 164, 473 N.E.2d 264, 15 O.B.R. 311, certiorari denied 105 S.Ct. 3514, 472 U.S. 1032, 87 L.Ed.2d 643, rehearing denied 106 S.Ct. 19, 473 U.S. 927, 87 L.Ed.2d 697.

It is not error for trial court to refuse request of accused to address court or jury, where such is made after final submission of the case, unless it is shown that an unfair trial resulted from such refusal. Rehfeld v. State (Ohio 1921) 102 Ohio St. 431, 131 N.E. 712, 19 Ohio Law Rep. 67, 19 Ohio Law Rep. 68. Criminal Law ⚿ 699; Trial ⚿ 108

Defense counsel's decision not to make opening statement, in capital case, was legitimate tactical decision and did not prejudice defendant. Byrd v. Collins (C.A.6 (Ohio), 04-06-2000) 209 F.3d 486, rehearing en banc denied 227 F.3d 756, certiorari denied 121 S.Ct. 786, 531 U.S. 1082, 148 L.Ed.2d 682, rehearing denied 121 S.Ct. 1176, 531 U.S. 1186, 148 L.Ed.2d 1034. Criminal Law ⚿ 641.13(2.1)

Statements in which prosecutor speculated as to whether defendant had previously seen store clerk who was killed during robbery due to store's close proximity to defendant's childhood home, as to whether witness had faulty recall as to color of one perpetrator's pants, and as to location of missing evidence were arguably reasonable inferences from the evidence presented at trial that prosecutor was allowed to draw. Byrd v. Collins (C.A.6 (Ohio), 04-06-2000) 209 F.3d 486, rehearing en banc denied 227 F.3d 756, certiorari denied 121 S.Ct. 786, 531 U.S. 1082, 148 L.Ed.2d 682, rehearing denied 121 S.Ct. 1176, 531 U.S. 1186, 148 L.Ed.2d 1034. Criminal Law ⚷ 720(9)

Conviction obtained by the knowing use of perjured testimony is fundamentally unfair, and must be set aside if there is any reasonable likelihood that the false testimony could have affected the judgment of the jury. Byrd v. Collins (C.A.6 (Ohio), 04-06-2000) 209 F.3d 486, rehearing en banc denied 227 F.3d 756, certiorari denied 121 S.Ct. 786, 531 U.S. 1082, 148 L.Ed.2d 682, rehearing denied 121 S.Ct. 1176, 531 U.S. 1186, 148 L.Ed.2d 1034. Criminal Law ⚷ 706(2)

Counsel retort "No, sir," to a statement of opposing counsel is not an objection on which error can be assigned. Foster v United States, 16 OFD 444 (6th Cir Ohio 1910).

Prosecutor's statement on rebuttal during penalty phase of capital murder trial that jurors should remember defendant's lack of emotion when his mother testified did not deprive defendant of due process, despite defendant's contention that jury was left with incorrect impression that his lack of emotion was aggravating circumstance, where defendant had asserted that his good character was mitigating circumstance, prosecutor's statement was intended as comment on defendant's character, and court instructed jury that prosecutor's statements were not evidence. Lawson v. Warden, Mansfield Correctional Institution (S.D.Ohio, 03-29-2002) 197 F.Supp.2d 1072. Constitutional Law ⚷ 268(8); Sentencing And Punishment ⚷ 1780(2)

The fact that a defendant in an aggravated murder trial has the burden of going forward with evidence of mitigating factors does not change the prescribed order of final arguments found in RC 2945.10. State v Jenkins, No. 45231 (8th Dist Ct App, Cuyahoga, 2–24–84), affirmed by 15 OS(3d) 164, 15 OBR 311, 473 NE(2d) 264 (1984).

6. —— Fair trial, argument

Prosecutor's comment in closing argument that asked the jury to use reason and common sense when seeking justice did not deny defendant a fair aggravated robbery trial; the prosecutor did not implicitly or explicitly state that justice in the matter would be a conviction as opposed to an acquittal, nor did the prosecutor appeal to public demand or community pressures to convict. State v. Brown (Ohio App. 5 Dist., Stark, 02-21-2006) No. 2005CA00094, 2006-Ohio-826, 2006 WL 438692, Unreported. Criminal Law ⚷ 713

Prosecutor's statement in closing argument that commented on the credibility of the victim did not constitute plain error or deny defendant a fair aggravated robbery trial; comment was made in rebuttal to defendant's closing argument, during which defense counsel repeatedly emphasized alleged discrepancies between the victim's testimony and that of other witnesses, and the trial court advised the jury that closing arguments were not evidence and should not be treated as evidence. State v. Brown (Ohio App. 5 Dist., Stark, 02-21-2006) No. 2005CA00094, 2006-Ohio-826, 2006 WL 438692, Unreported. Criminal Law ⚷ 726

Prosecutor's comment during closing argument in a prosecution for possession with intent to distribute pseudoephedrine, asserting that defendant testified he was selling to "buying groups," and that there was no evidence other than from defendant's lips that there were buying groups, was supported by the evidence at trial, and thus, was not improper; defendant was the only person at trial who used the words "buying groups" when testifying, and the records showed no evidence of buying groups. U.S. v. Merkosky (C.A.6 (Ohio), 06-14-2005) No. 02-4332, 135 Fed.Appx. 828, 2005 WL 1400201, Unreported. Criminal Law ⚷ 720(7.1)

The prosecutor's trial comments did not deprive defendant of a fair trial or constitute prosecutorial misconduct, during prosecution for drug abuse, carrying a concealed weapon, and having a weapon while under a disability; defendant did not cite in the transcript where the prosecutor referred to him as a drug dealer, and the court sustained two of defendant's objections to comments made by the prosecutor. State v. Westbrook (Ohio App. 5 Dist., Richland, 05-23-2005) No. 04CA0072, 2005-Ohio-2673, 2005 WL 1274779, Unreported. Criminal Law ⚷ 723(1); Criminal Law ⚷ 730(14)

Prosecutor's over zealous comments during closing argument of gross sexual imposition trial, in which she misstated the evidence by representing to the jury that defendant explained "sexual intercourse" and "pregnancy" to victim by reference to worms, eggs, and animals, did not deny defendant a fair trial so as to rise to the level of plain error; there was evidence before the jury that defendant had discussed with victim sexual intercourse, and the specifics were not relevant. State v. Novak (Ohio App. 11 Dist., Lake, 02-11-2005) No. 2003-L-077, 2005-Ohio-563, 2005 WL 336337, Unreported. Criminal Law ⚷ 1037.1(2)

Comments by prosecutor during closing argument of gross sexual imposition trial, in which she characterized defendant's defense as a "whitewash" that he was attempting to "sell" the jury, though overly zealous, did not impugn defendant's veracity or defense counsel's integrity, so as to deny defendant a fair trial. State v. Novak (Ohio App. 11 Dist., Lake, 02-11-2005) No. 2003-L-077, 2005-Ohio-563, 2005 WL 336337, Unreported. Criminal Law ⚷ 720(5); Criminal Law ⚷ 723(1)

Prosecutor's closing argument comment that only jury could correct injustices done to victims, when viewed in context of entire argument, was not prejudicial to defendant, who was convicted of kidnapping, aggravated robbery, aggravated burglary, and felonious assault, where such appeal to jury's sympathies was modest and prosecutor asked jury to use reason and common sense. State v. McSwain (Ohio App. 8 Dist., Cuyahoga, 06-24-2004) No. 83394, 2004-Ohio-3292, 2004 WL 1402700, Unreported, appeal not allowed 104 Ohio St.3d 1425, 819 N.E.2d 709, 2004-Ohio-6585, certiorari denied 125 S.Ct. 2269, 544 U.S. 1040, 161 L.Ed.2d 1072. Criminal Law ⚷ 723(1)

Claim that prosecutor's closing argument comment that only jury could correct injustices done to victims was improper could only be reviewed for plain error, where defendant failed at trial to object to such comment. State v. McSwain (Ohio App. 8 Dist., Cuyahoga, 06-24-2004) No. 83394, 2004-Ohio-3292, 2004 WL 1402700, Unreported, appeal not allowed 104 Ohio St.3d 1425, 819 N.E.2d 709, 2004-Ohio-6585, certiorari denied 125 S.Ct. 2269, 544 U.S. 1040, 161 L.Ed.2d 1072. Criminal Law ⚷ 1037.1(2)

Prosecutor's improper use of bad character of defendant's friend to attack defendant's character during closing arguments in cocaine trafficking trial by suggesting defendant distanced himself from friend because "you are with whom you associate," did not deny defendant a fair trial so as to require reversal, even though evidence in case was not overwhelming; it was not clear that but for comment defendant would not have been convicted, case revolved around credibility of the witnesses, and to reverse on instant issue would necessarily have required appellate court to rule on witness credibility and supersede role of trier of fact. State v. Moman (Ohio App. 7 Dist., Columbiana, 03-18-2004) No. 02CO52, 2004-Ohio-1387, 2004 WL 549807, Unreported. Criminal Law ⚷ 1171.6

Trial court did not commit plain error in failing to declare a mistrial for prosecutor's closing comments, during which prosecutor stated in response to assault defendant's argument that nobody saw stabbing that "the law still believe[d] that people [could] tell the truth," despite claim comments were disparaging to victim and defense counsel; comments were permissible argument in response to defense counsel's assertion of lack of physical evidence and to challenge of victim's credibility. State v. Hammond (Ohio App. 2 Dist., Montgomery, 04-25-2003) No. CIV.A. 19278, 2003-Ohio-2078, 2003 WL 1950370, Unreported. Criminal Law ⚷ 1037.1(2)

Three comments made by prosecutor during closing arguments, when read in full context, were neither materially prejudicial nor did they deny defendant convicted of murder and possession of cocaine a fair trial, but were an attempt by prosecutor to convince jury that defendant's defense of voluntary manslaughter must be rejected; prosecutor asked jury what else could defendant have said but that his actions were merely voluntary manslaughter, and prosecutor stated that defendant's claim that victim and his wife who were attempting to buy drugs from defendant had time to hide drugs and money on their person or in body cavities was "ridiculous." State v. Brandy (Ohio App. 10 Dist., Franklin, 04-10-2003) No. 02AP-832, 2003-Ohio-1836, 2003 WL 1848761, Unreported, appeal not allowed 99 Ohio St.3d 1515, 792 N.E.2d 201, 2003-Ohio-3957. Criminal Law ⚷ 1171.1(3)

Prosecutor's characterization of murder defendant as a "drug dealer extraordinaire" was not plain error, where characterization was based on evidence presented at trial during which defendant admitted to a life of drug dealing. State v. Brandy (Ohio App. 10 Dist., Franklin, 04-10-2003) No. 02AP-832, 2003-Ohio-1836, 2003 WL 1848761, Unreported, appeal not allowed 99 Ohio St.3d 1515, 792 N.E.2d 201, 2003-Ohio-3957. Criminal Law ⚷ 1037.1(2)

Prosecutor's inaccurate statements during closing arguments that defendant's housemate had testified that defendant fanned stolen money out in front of him were not plain error, where housemate's actual testimony, if believed by jury, was equally incriminating, if not more so; housemate stated he recognized defendant's voice as robber outside, he recounted defendant's apparent admission, and testimony of other witnesses provided plausible link from victim's stolen money to defendant's rent money. State v. Carsten (Ohio App. 10 Dist., Franklin, 12-10-2002) No. 02AP-166, 2002-Ohio-6748, 2002 WL 31752187, Unreported. Criminal Law ⚷ 1037.1(2)

Murder defendant was not deprived of fair trial by prosecutor's comment in closing argument that defendant would not hesitate to come into courtroom and "lie to your faces," or by prosecutor's comment in rebuttal argument that defendant's wife still had one year to file medical malpractice claim against victim's physician, and thus defense counsel was not ineffective for failing to object to those statements. State v. Smith (Ohio App. 3 Dist., 11-20-1996) 115 Ohio App.3d 419, 685 N.E.2d 595.

A prosecutor's claim to "represent civilization" and his calling of jurors the "conscience of the community" do not prejudice the defendant. State v. Tyler (Ohio 1990) 50 Ohio St.3d 24, 553 N.E.2d 576, rehearing denied 51 Ohio St.3d 704, 555 N.E.2d 322, certiorari denied 111 S.Ct. 371, 498 U.S. 951, 112 L.Ed.2d 334, reconsideration denied 75 Ohio St.3d 1474, 663 N.E.2d 1302, stay granted 76 Ohio St.3d 1463, 669 N.E.2d 249.

Any error arising from prosecutor's introduction, in capital murder case, of videotape of television interview with victim and his family did not rise to level of due process violation, given key witness' testimony that defendant confessed to murder while watching interview in jail; any prejudice resulting from showing of videotape stemmed not from tape itself, but from admissible testimony regarding confession and defendant's callous remarks about victim. Byrd v. Collins (C.A.6 (Ohio), 04-06-2000) 209 F.3d 486, rehearing en banc denied 227 F.3d 756, certiorari denied 121 S.Ct. 786, 531 U.S. 1082, 148 L.Ed.2d 682, rehearing denied 121 S.Ct. 1176, 531 U.S. 1186, 148 L.Ed.2d 1034. Constitutional Law ⚷ 266(1); Criminal Law ⚷ 438(8)

Prosecutor's statements speculating about whether defendant had previously seen store clerk killed during robbery and whereabouts of missing evidence did not rise to level of due process violation, even if they were impermissible comments on facts not in evidence, given that statements were qualified with language suggesting their speculative nature, and thus did not mislead jury, remarks were relatively isolated, other evidence of guilt was strong, and defense counsel did not object or seek curative instruction. Byrd v. Collins (C.A.6 (Ohio), 04-06-2000) 209 F.3d 486, rehearing en banc denied 227 F.3d 756, certiorari denied 121 S.Ct. 786, 531 U.S. 1082, 148 L.Ed.2d 682, rehearing denied 121 S.Ct. 1176, 531 U.S. 1186, 148 L.Ed.2d 1034. Constitutional Law ⚷ 268(8); Criminal Law ⚷ 719(1); Criminal Law ⚷ 728(2)

Prosecutor's suggestion that defense counsel was trying to hide something about source of blood found on sweater alleged to have been worn by accomplice was suggestion of reasonable inference to be drawn from defense counsel's presentation of evidence and argument, and did not rise to level of due process violation. Byrd v. Collins (C.A.6 (Ohio), 04-06-2000) 209 F.3d 486, rehearing en banc denied 227 F.3d 756, certiorari denied 121 S.Ct. 786, 531 U.S. 1082, 148 L.Ed.2d 682, rehearing denied 121 S.Ct. 1176, 531 U.S. 1186, 148 L.Ed.2d 1034. Constitutional Law ⚷ 268(8); Criminal Law ⚷ 720(9)

Prosecutor's conduct in vouching for credibility of witness did not rise to level of due process violation, and thus did not warrant federal habeas relief; remarks did not mislead jury, which was told by prosecutor that his remarks were not evidence, trial court instructed jury immediately after arguments that arguments were not evidence, witness' testimony was reread at jury's request following initial deliberation, jury returned guilty verdict soon after again hearing witness' testimony, which was not complicated, and trial court instructed jury as to factors to consider in evaluating weight of witnesses' testimony. Byrd v. Collins (C.A.6 (Ohio), 04-06-2000) 209 F.3d 486, rehearing en banc denied 227 F.3d 756, certiorari denied 121 S.Ct. 786, 531 U.S. 1082, 148 L.Ed.2d 682, rehearing denied 121 S.Ct. 1176, 531 U.S. 1186, 148 L.Ed.2d 1034. Constitutional Law ⚷ 268(8); Criminal Law ⚷ 730(8); Habeas Corpus ⚷ 497

Prosecutor's use of term "predator" to describe murder defendant did not deprive defendant of fair trial. Byrd v. Collins (C.A.6 (Ohio), 04-06-2000) 209 F.3d 486, rehearing en banc denied 227 F.3d 756, certiorari denied 121 S.Ct. 786, 531 U.S. 1082, 148 L.Ed.2d 682, rehearing denied 121 S.Ct. 1176, 531 U.S. 1186, 148 L.Ed.2d 1034. Criminal Law ⚷ 724(1)

7. —— Prosecutorial misconduct, argument

Prosecutor's comment during rebuttal closing argument that, under defense counsel's own argument to effect that inconsistencies between eyewitness' testimony indicated that they were liars, defense counsel's misspelling of word would make him a liar, did not constitute impermissible denigration of defense counsel, in trial for aggravated murder, murder, and aggravated robbery; rather, prosecutor's comment was in response to defense counsel's assertion that eyewitnesses were liars and to expose weakness in counsel's argument, and prosecutor quickly pointed out that defense counsel was not liar but had simply made mistake. State v. Huges (Ohio App. 1 Dist., Hamilton, 05-20-2005) No. C-030489, 2005-Ohio-2453, 2005 WL 1190715, Unreported. Criminal Law ⚷ 726

State did not commit prosecutorial misconduct in referencing, during closing argument, defendant's failure to explain his possession of inculpatory evidence, a ring worn by murder victim, since, when viewed in context, statement was not an attempt to focus jury's attention on defendant's decision not to testify, and statement was truthful, underscoring what evidence had shown and what reasonable inferences may have been drawn therefrom. State v. Butler (Ohio App. 10 Dist., Franklin, 02-15-2005) No. 03AP-800, 2005-Ohio-579, 2005 WL 351759, Unreported, appeal not allowed 106 Ohio St.3d 1416, 830 N.E.2d 348, 2005-Ohio-3154. Criminal Law ⚷ 721(3)

Prosecutor's comment in closing argument in defendant's trial for sexual battery that witnesses were honest in their answers did not amount to an improper comment on the veracity of the witnesses; comment was made in the context of questions several jurors had proposed to witnesses regarding why the witnesses had allowed themselves to be placed in a position where the crime could have been committed, and it was not a comment on the credibility of the women with regard to their testimony against defendant. State v. Anderson (Ohio App. 6 Dist., Wood, 02-11-2005) No. WD-04-035, 2005-Ohio-534, 2005 WL 327179, Unreported. Criminal Law ⚷ 720(5)

The prosecutor's closing argument statement that medical expert had testified that "one blow can kill you" was a reasonable inference from the evidence presented during felonious assault trial, and therefore did not constitute prosecutorial misconduct; medical expert hypothesized that an unlucky hit could shear nerve fibers at the base of the brain, resulting in death, and expert testified about a case where a university student was killed with one blow. State v. Root (Ohio App. 2 Dist., Montgomery, 01-31-2005) No. CIV.A. 20366, 2005-Ohio-448, 2005 WL 281172, Unreported. Criminal Law ⚷ 720(7.1)

Prosecutor's argument to jury in prosecution for gross sexual imposition, telling jury that they should find defendant guilty if they would not let him be alone with their child, daughter, or granddaughter, and suggesting to the jury that they should feel like they were the victim, constituted prosecutorial misconduct. State v. Breland (Ohio App. 11 Dist., Ashtabula, 12-23-2004) No. 2003-A-0066, 2004-Ohio-7238, 2004 WL 3090222, Unreported, appeal not allowed 105 Ohio St.3d 1546, 827 N.E.2d 328, 2005-Ohio-2188. Criminal Law ⚷ 723(1)

Prosecutor's argument to jury in prosecution for gross sexual imposition, stating her personal opinion that defendant lied on the witness stand, constituted prosecutorial misconduct. State v. Breland (Ohio App. 11 Dist., Ashtabula, 12-23-2004) No. 2003-A-0066, 2004-Ohio-7238, 2004 WL 3090222,

Unreported, appeal not allowed 105 Ohio St.3d 1546, 827 N.E.2d 328, 2005-Ohio-2188. Criminal Law ⚷ 720(5)

Prosecutor's argument to jury in prosecution for gross sexual imposition, wrongly asserting that defendant's claim of accident was irrelevant, constituted prosecutorial misconduct. State v. Breland (Ohio App. 11 Dist., Ashtabula, 12-23-2004) No. 2003-A-0066, 2004-Ohio-7238, 2004 WL 3090222, Unreported, appeal not allowed 105 Ohio St.3d 1546, 827 N.E.2d 328, 2005-Ohio-2188. Criminal Law ⚷ 717

Prosecutor's closing argument comment that state's evidence was unchallenged was not improper personal opinion, but was proper comment directed at strength of state's case. State v. Gray (Ohio App. 8 Dist., Cuyahoga, 03-25-2004) No. 83097, 2004-Ohio-1454, 2004 WL 584187, Unreported, motion to reopen denied 2004-Ohio-4481, 2004 WL 1902381, motion for delayed appeal denied 103 Ohio St.3d 1476, 816 N.E.2d 252, 2004-Ohio-5405. Criminal Law ⚷ 719(3); Criminal Law ⚷ 720(1)

Prosecutor's statement in closing argument that testimony of defendant's sister seemed to blame the drug charges against defendant on her deceased boyfriend did not constitute misconduct, even though sister never directly stated that her boyfriend was responsible for the drug sales, where she did state that defendant was not present on the date of one charge, that her boyfriend was present, and that her boyfriend was the individual who answered the door and spoke with the informant. State v. Moman (Ohio App. 7 Dist., Columbiana, 03-18-2004) No. 02CO52, 2004-Ohio-1387, 2004 WL 549807, Unreported. Criminal Law ⚷ 720(7.1)

Prosecutor's misconduct during closing argument, in expressing his personal belief or opinion as to credibility of a witness or as to guilt of the accused, did not require reversal of aggravated robbery conviction, where evidence of defendant's guilt was overwhelming. State v. Fields (Ohio App. 1 Dist., Hamilton, 08-30-2002) No. C-010720, No. C-010688, 2002-Ohio-4451, 2002 WL 1988273, Unreported, motion for delayed appeal denied 97 Ohio St.3d 1495, 780 N.E.2d 600, 2002-Ohio-7200. Criminal Law ⚷ 1171.1(3); Criminal Law ⚷ 1171.3

Prosecutor during closing argument of rape trial did not interject her personal beliefs about the veracity of victim's testimony, but rather merely argued that the evidence supported the theory that victim did not lie or concoct her story of abuse by her father, the defendant, and thus prosecutor did not commit misconduct. State v. Geboy (Ohio App. 3 Dist., 08-30-2001) 145 Ohio App.3d 706, 764 N.E.2d 451, 2001-Ohio-2214, appeal not allowed 94 Ohio St.3d 1410, 759 N.E.2d 787, appeal after new trial 2003-Ohio-343, 2003 WL 178616, appeal not allowed 99 Ohio St.3d 1412, 788 N.E.2d 648, 2003-Ohio-2454. Criminal Law ⚷ 720(5)

The prosecutor's primary interest in a criminal prosecution is that justice shall be done; thus, while he may strike hard blows, he is not at liberty to strike foul ones. Lorraine v. Coyle (C.A.6 (Ohio), 05-23-2002) 291 F.3d 416, opinion corrected on denial of rehearing 307 F.3d 459, certiorari denied 123 S.Ct. 1621, 538 U.S. 947, 155 L.Ed.2d 489, rehearing denied 123 S.Ct. 2243, 538 U.S. 1069, 155 L.Ed.2d 1128. Criminal Law ⚷ 700(1)

A prosecutor may not make statements designed to arouse the passions or prejudice of the jury. Lorraine v. Coyle (C.A.6 (Ohio), 05-23-2002) 291 F.3d 416, opinion corrected on denial of rehearing 307 F.3d 459, certiorari denied 123 S.Ct. 1621, 538 U.S. 947, 155 L.Ed.2d 489, rehearing denied 123 S.Ct. 2243, 538 U.S. 1069, 155 L.Ed.2d 1128. Criminal Law ⚷ 723(1)

In determining whether prosecutorial misconduct rises to level of due process violation, federal habeas court must bear in mind that the touchstone of due process analysis is the fairness of the trial, not the culpability of the prosecutor. Byrd v. Collins (C.A.6 (Ohio), 04-06-2000) 209 F.3d 486, rehearing en banc denied 227 F.3d 756, certiorari denied 121 S.Ct. 786, 531 U.S. 1082, 148 L.Ed.2d 682, rehearing denied 121 S.Ct. 1176, 531 U.S. 1186, 148 L.Ed.2d 1034. Constitutional Law ⚷ 268(8); Habeas Corpus ⚷ 497

Defendant must show that the statement in question was indisputably false, rather than merely misleading, to establish a claim of prosecutorial misconduct or denial of due process based on knowing use of false or perjured testimony. Byrd v. Collins (C.A.6 (Ohio), 04-06-2000) 209 F.3d 486, rehearing en banc denied 227 F.3d 756, certiorari denied 121 S.Ct. 786, 531 U.S. 1082, 148 L.Ed.2d 682, rehearing denied 121 S.Ct. 1176, 531 U.S. 1186, 148 L.Ed.2d 1034. Constitutional Law ⚷ 268(9); Criminal Law ⚷ 706(2)

Witness' testimony that he had no pending charges against him at time of defendant's trial was not indisputably false, as required to support claim of prosecutorial misconduct or denial of due process based on state's alleged knowing use of false or perjured testimony, given that witness was not facing any criminal charges when he testified and that the record suggested that he, and the prosecutor, interpreted question raising issue as not encompassing parole revocation proceedings which witness faced at completion of workhouse sentence he was then serving. Byrd v. Collins (C.A.6 (Ohio), 04-06-2000) 209 F.3d 486, rehearing en banc denied 227 F.3d 756, certiorari denied 121 S.Ct. 786, 531 U.S. 1082, 148 L.Ed.2d 682, rehearing denied 121 S.Ct. 1176, 531 U.S. 1186, 148 L.Ed.2d 1034. Constitutional Law ⚷ 268(9); Criminal Law ⚷ 706(2)

Given extensive impeachment information elicited during defendant's cross-examination, witness' allegedly false testimony that he had no pending charges against him at time of defendant's trial was not "material," as required to support claim of prosecutorial misconduct or denial of due process based on state's alleged knowing use of witness' false or perjured testimony, even though witness faced parole revocation proceedings following completion of workhouse sentence he was then serving. Byrd v. Collins (C.A.6 (Ohio), 04-06-2000) 209 F.3d 486, rehearing en banc denied 227 F.3d 756, certiorari denied 121 S.Ct. 786, 531 U.S. 1082, 148 L.Ed.2d 682, rehearing denied 121 S.Ct. 1176, 531 U.S. 1186, 148 L.Ed.2d 1034. Constitutional Law ⚿ 268(9); Criminal Law ⚿ 706(2)

Prosecutor's misconduct during penalty phase of capital murder trial, in indicating without evidence that petitioner had engaged in knife fight, commenting on petitioner's subsequent conviction after being admonished by trial court not to do so and exhibiting irrelevant photograph depicting petitioner next to marijuana plant, deprived petitioner of fundamentally fair penalty phase proceeding and, thus, warranted federal habeas relief; although there was overwhelming evidence of petitioner's guilt, prosecutor's misconduct destroyed petitioner's attempt to present mitigating evidence. DePew v. Anderson (S.D.Ohio, 03-31-2000) 104 F.Supp.2d 879, affirmed in part, reversed in part 311 F.3d 742, rehearing and suggestion for rehearing en banc denied, certiorari denied 124 S.Ct. 270, 540 U.S. 888, 157 L.Ed.2d 160, certiorari denied 124 S.Ct. 83, 540 U.S. 938, 157 L.Ed.2d 250. Habeas Corpus ⚿ 497

8. Instructions—In general

Where, in the trial of a criminal case, the substance of instructions to the jury requested by the defendant is completely embraced in the court's general charge, the defendant is denied no constitutional or statutory right in the court's refusal to give such requested instructions. State v. Lakes (Adams 1964) 120 Ohio App. 213, 201 N.E.2d 809, 29 O.O.2d 12, appeal dismissed 176 Ohio St. 459, 200 N.E.2d 310, 27 O.O.2d 430. Criminal Law ⚿ 829(1)

9. —— Before argument, instructions

Prosecutor's impermissible comments regarding credibility of State's witnesses and asking jury to compare their credibility with defendant during closing argument did not prejudice defendant, in trial for petty theft, where jury would likely have found defendant guilty absent comments. Alliance v. Yin (Ohio App. 5 Dist., Stark, 06-13-2005) No. 2004CA00239, 2005-Ohio-2989, 2005 WL 1399269, Unreported. Criminal Law ⚿ 720(5)

Prosecutor's comments during closing argument that the State's witnesses were truthful "and you weigh that and the way they presented themselves with the way defendant presented himself" constituted improper vouching for credibility of witnesses, in trial for petty theft. Alliance v. Yin (Ohio App. 5 Dist., Stark, 06-13-2005) No. 2004CA00239, 2005-Ohio-2989, 2005 WL 1399269, Unreported. Criminal Law ⚿ 720(5)

Defendant was not prejudiced, in prosecution for aggravated burglary and felonious assault, by trial court's failure to include in written jury instructions the contents of writing on chalkboard clarifying the instructions on felonious assault, where defendant did not appeal felonious assault conviction and merely stated in appeal brief that omission of contents of chalkboard denied due process and right to appeal and required new trial. State v. Morton (Ohio App. 8 Dist., 03-29-2002) 147 Ohio App.3d 43, 768 N.E.2d 730, 2002-Ohio-813, appeal not allowed 96 Ohio St.3d 1469, 772 N.E.2d 1204, 2002-Ohio-3910, appeal after new sentencing hearing 2003-Ohio-4063, 2003 WL 21757725, appeal not allowed 100 Ohio St.3d 1531, 800 N.E.2d 48, 2003-Ohio-6458. Criminal Law ⚿ 1130(2)

A trial court does not err in refusing to give a defendant's special instruction on accomplice credibility to the jury when the substance of the requested instruction is already included in the court's general charge. State v. Sneed (Ohio 1992) 63 Ohio St.3d 3, 584 N.E.2d 1160, rehearing denied 63 Ohio St.3d 1433, 588 N.E.2d 132, stay granted 63 Ohio St.3d 1444, 589 N.E.2d 388, rehearing granted, opinion recalled 66 Ohio St.3d 1449, 609 N.E.2d 1270, certiorari denied 113 S.Ct. 1577, 507 U.S. 983, 123 L.Ed.2d 145, stay granted 66 Ohio St.3d 1504, 613 N.E.2d 1043.

Where a special instruction in writing before argument is given by the trial court, it is error for the court to identify to the jury the party who requested that instruction. State v. Stanton (Ohio 1968) 15 Ohio St.2d 215, 239 N.E.2d 92, 44 O.O.2d 191.

There is no requirement that, before final argument in a case, the trial judge reduce his general charge to the jury to writing, or that a party be furnished a written copy of such charge. State v. Gerhardt (Gallia 1961) 115 Ohio App. 83, 184 N.E.2d 516, 20 O.O.2d 204.

It is not mandatory upon a trial court to give any instructions to the jury in a criminal case before argument, but if requested special instructions reduced to writing are correct, pertinent and timely presented, they must be included, at least in substance, in the general charge. State v. Barron (Ohio 1960) 170 Ohio St. 267, 164 N.E.2d 409, 10 O.O.2d 299, certiorari denied 80 S.Ct. 1247, 363 U.S. 814, 4 L.Ed.2d 1153. Criminal Law ⚿ 801

Court is not required to give special instructions to jury before argument in criminal case. State v. Petro (Ohio 1947) 148 Ohio St. 473, 76 N.E.2d 355, 5 A.L.R.2d 425, 36 O.O. 152. Criminal Law ⚿ 801

Under the statute, it is not mandatory upon the court to give any instructions to the jury in a criminal case before argument, but a request made by defendant's attorney for a proper instruction before argument may not be ignored in the general charge, even though the request has not been repeated. Grossweiler v. State (Ohio 1925) 113 Ohio St. 46, 148 N.E. 89, 3 Ohio Law Abs. 361, 23 Ohio Law Rep. 301.

In a criminal case, the statute authorizes, though does not require, a charge before argument if requested by either party. Wertenberger v. State (Ohio 1919) 99 Ohio St. 353, 124 N.E. 243, 17 Ohio Law Rep. 43, 17 Ohio Law Rep. 66.

A federal court will not overturn a state criminal conviction on grounds the judge charged jurors about circumstantial evidence at the start of trial instead of at the close, where the convict cannot establish that this act violated some right guaranteed him by the Fourteenth Amendment. Mira v. Marshall (C.A.6 (Ohio) 1986) 806 F.2d 636.

RC 2945.10 allows for deviation from the usual practice of giving jury instructions after closing arguments as required under Crim R 30(A); consequently, in a case involving various theories of culpability for aggravated robbery and felonious assault, jury instructions given prior to closing arguments do not constitute plain error since written and oral instructions given after the closing arguments counteract the effects of "primacy" and "recency" on the jury. State v Watts, No. CA 10274 (2d Dist Ct App, Montgomery, 6–10–87).

10. —— After argument, instructions

Defendant's substantial rights were not violated when the trial court provided the jury with written instructions on self defense and later provided additional oral instructions on self defense during jury deliberations, in prosecution for felonious assault; the trial court was not prohibited from answering the jury's question during deliberations. State v. Hibbard (Ohio App. 12 Dist., Butler, 09-29-2003) No. CA2002-05-129, 2003-Ohio-5104, 2003 WL 22227350, Unreported, appeal after new sentencing hearing 2004-Ohio-7138, 2004 WL 3015385. Assault And Battery ⚷ 96(3); Criminal Law ⚷ 863(2)

Considering the charge to the jury as a whole, the court did not find that use of the language "It has been frequently said that justice is blind; justice is deaf and dumb as well," was prejudicial to the defendants. Galob v. State (Cuyahoga 1928) 6 Ohio Law Abs. 673, 27 Ohio Law Rep. 329. Criminal Law ⚷ 1172.1(2)

Defendant's due process right to appellate review was violated by trial court's failure to preserve for record any written instructions, which foreclosed comparison of any written instructions with allegedly insufficient verbal charge at beginning of trial. State v. Smith (Hamilton 1993) 87 Ohio App.3d 480, 622 N.E.2d 677, dismissed, jurisdictional motion overruled 67 Ohio St.3d 1479, 620 N.E.2d 851. Constitutional Law ⚷ 271; Criminal Law ⚷ 804(7)

A trial court's jury instructions in a capital murder prosecution that closing arguments are simply the attorneys' opinions about what they think the evidence has already shown and their opinions as to how the jury should apply the law to the evidence obviates any prejudice which may have occurred as a result of a prosecutor's closing statements. State v. Parrish (Franklin 1991) 71 Ohio App.3d 659, 595 N.E.2d 354, dismissed, jurisdictional motion overruled 60 Ohio St.3d 718, 574 N.E.2d 1079.

A defendant in an aggravated murder and aggravated robbery prosecution is not prejudiced by a trial court's refusal to repeat preliminary instructions as to circumstantial evidence where the court allows the defense counsel to remind the jury during closing arguments of those instructions. State v. Parrish (Franklin 1991) 71 Ohio App.3d 659, 595 N.E.2d 354, dismissed, jurisdictional motion overruled 60 Ohio St.3d 718, 574 N.E.2d 1079. Criminal Law ⚷ 1174(1)

Where written instructions are submitted to the jury pursuant to RC 2945.10(G), a conviction will be reversed if those written instructions are not returned along with the verdict and are not preserved on file as part of the record. Columbus v. Marcum (Franklin 1989) 65 Ohio App.3d 530, 584 N.E.2d 1233.

A trial court's submission of written instructions to a jury pursuant to a party's request which is made after closing arguments instead of prior to closing arguments is not reversible error. State v. Sneed (Ohio 1992) 63 Ohio St.3d 3, 584 N.E.2d 1160, rehearing denied 63 Ohio St.3d 1433, 588 N.E.2d 132, stay granted 63 Ohio St.3d 1444, 589 N.E.2d 388, rehearing granted, opinion recalled 66 Ohio St.3d 1449, 609 N.E.2d 1270, certiorari denied 113 S.Ct. 1577, 507 U.S. 983, 123 L.Ed.2d 145, stay granted 66 Ohio St.3d 1504, 613 N.E.2d 1043.

A trial court is under no obligation to instruct a jury in the penalty phase of a capital case that that state's pretrial negotiated plea offer constitutes a mitigating factor to be weighed against the aggravating circumstance. State v. Sneed (Ohio 1992) 63 Ohio St.3d 3, 584 N.E.2d 1160, rehearing denied 63 Ohio St.3d 1433, 588 N.E.2d 132, stay granted 63 Ohio St.3d 1444, 589 N.E.2d 388, rehearing granted, opinion recalled 66 Ohio St.3d 1449, 609 N.E.2d 1270, certiorari denied 113 S.Ct. 1577, 507 U.S. 983, 123 L.Ed.2d 145, stay granted 66 Ohio St.3d 1504, 613 N.E.2d 1043. Sentencing And Punishment ⚷ 1780(3)

In an aggravated murder case, a trial court's jury instruction that the jury should not be influenced in their deliberations by any consideration of sympathy or prejudice does not qualify as plain error where the outcome of the trial is not affected and the defendant does not object at the trial or raise the issue before the appellate court, thereby making waiver applicable. State v. Combs (Ohio 1991) 62 Ohio St.3d 278, 581 N.E.2d 1071, rehearing denied 62 Ohio St.3d 1503, 583 N.E.2d 974, certiorari denied 112 S.Ct. 2950, 504 U.S. 977, 119 L.Ed.2d 573, stay granted 65 Ohio St.3d 1446, 600 N.E.2d 1077, stay granted 66 Ohio St.3d 1470, 611 N.E.2d 328, stay granted 66 Ohio St.3d 1475, 611 N.E.2d 837, denial of post-conviction relief affirmed 100 Ohio App.3d 90, 652 N.E.2d 205, dismissed, appeal not allowed 71 Ohio St.3d 1472, 645 N.E.2d 735, reconsideration denied 71 Ohio St.3d 1494, 646 N.E.2d 469.

Where a jury, after substantial deliberation, sends a message to the trial judge stating that: (1) it is evenly deadlocked; (2) it has insufficient evidence to render a verdict; and (3) any verdict that it renders will be unfair; the trial judge must declare a mistrial sua sponte and dismiss the jurors; in less egregious cases, the trial judge should give a neutral supplementary instruction emphasizing the duty of the jury to make every reasonable effort to agree without compromising any individual's honest conviction; however, a statement by the trial judge that "this jury can reach a verdict if any jury can" is prejudicially coercive on the decision of the jury. State v. Sabbah (Sandusky 1982) 13 Ohio App.3d 124, 468 N.E.2d 718, 13 O.B.R. 155.

There is no provision in the Ohio Constitution or in the Ohio Revised Code which entitles a defendant in a criminal case to have the jury instructed that his failure to testify must not be considered for any purpose, and so it is discretionary with the trial court whether to charge on the defendant's right to elect not to testify. State v. Nelson (Ohio 1973) 36 Ohio St.2d 79, 303 N.E.2d 865, 65 O.O.2d 222. Criminal Law ⚷ 787(1)

Mere partial non-direction, if such be the case, as to a particular matter or issue, does not of itself constitute reversible error, in the absence of a request for more specific and comprehensive instructions upon the particular point or issue involved. State v. Perry (Athens 1972) 29 Ohio App.2d 33, 278 N.E.2d 50, 58 O.O.2d 25. Criminal Law ⚷ 1038.3

In a criminal case, if requested special instructions to the jury are correct, pertinent and timely presented, they must be included, at least in substance, in the general charge. City of Cincinnati v. Epperson (Ohio 1969) 20 Ohio St.2d 59, 253 N.E.2d 785, 49 O.O.2d 342. Criminal Law ⚷ 825(1)

A delay of twenty-five minutes between the conclusion of final argument to the jury and the charge of the court does not constitute error under RC 2945.10. State v. Eaton (Ohio 1969) 19 Ohio St.2d 145, 249 N.E.2d 897, 48 O.O.2d 188, vacated in part 92 S.Ct. 2857, 408 U.S. 935, 33 L.Ed.2d 750. Criminal Law ⚷ 801

RC 2945.10(G) is the only inhibition provided by statute that prohibits the court from performing any extraneous judicial function when a criminal trial is in progress. State v. Reardon (Ohio Com.Pl. 1964) 201 N.E.2d 818, 95 Ohio Law Abs. 56, 28 O.O.2d 394.

A court is correct in rejecting special charges offered dealing with entrapment when there is no evidence to warrant it, since a charge on a hypothetical case is calculated to mislead the jury. State v. Good (Franklin 1959) 110 Ohio App. 397, 169 N.E.2d 468, 13 O.O.2d 171, on reargument 110 Ohio App. 415, 165 N.E.2d 28, 83 Ohio Law Abs. 65, 11 O.O.2d 459.

In the prosecution of an accused for possessing for sale and selling narcotics, the defense of entrapment is inconsistent with the accused's claim that he neither had nor sold narcotics; and, where the accused's defense is that he is innocent of committing the acts charged, the trial court is bound to charge the jury only on the accused's theory of the case and not on any defense of entrapment. (See also State v Good, 110 App 397, 165 NE(2d) 28 (1959).) State v. Good (Franklin 1960) 110 Ohio App. 415, 165 N.E.2d 28, 83 Ohio Law Abs. 65, 11 O.O.2d 459.

Entrapment is an affirmative defense and where it is raised by the evidence, it is the duty of the court to instruct the jury on the subject. (See also State v Good, 110 App 397, 165 NE(2d) 28 (1959).) State v. Good (Franklin 1960) 110 Ohio App. 415, 165 N.E.2d 28, 83 Ohio Law Abs. 65, 11 O.O.2d 459.

RC 2945.10 is fully complied with if the final arguments of counsel in the case are concluded at the end of a court day, and the court instructs the jury as to its conduct during the adjournment, at which point court is adjourned, and, upon the court convening the next morning, it begins the reading of its charge as the first order of business, which written instruction does not include the instructions given the night before governing conduct of the jury during the adjournment. State v. Sheppard (Cuyahoga 1955) 100 Ohio App. 345, 128 N.E.2d 471, 60 O.O. 298, affirmed 165 Ohio St. 293, 135 N.E.2d 340, 59 O.O. 398, certiorari denied 77 S.Ct. 118, 352 U.S. 910, 1 L.Ed.2d 119, rehearing denied 77 S.Ct. 323, 352 U.S. 955, 1 L.Ed.2d 245.

In a criminal trial, it is duty of trial judge to tell jury all the essentials which constitute the crime charged, and which jury must find are sustained by the evidence beyond a reasonable doubt before jury can return a verdict of guilty. Miller v. State (Ohio 1932) 125 Ohio St. 415, 181 N.E. 890, 36 Ohio Law Rep. 372.

Postponement of charge after argument until time to which court was adjourned on following day held not error. Kahoun v. State (Ohio App. 1929) 33 Ohio App. 1, 168 N.E. 550, 29 Ohio Law Rep. 633. Criminal Law ⚷ 801; Trial ⚷ 220

A comment in a charge, admonishing the jury that "the shot that shoots down an officer reverberates with the echoes of anarchy and the flame that comes from the firing of that pistol gives suggestions of chaos," coming from the bench at the close of the trial, is prejudicial and especially so where purpose, wilfulness and intentional killing were in issue. Freeman v. State (Ohio 1928) 119 Ohio St. 250, 163 N.E. 202, 6 Ohio Law Abs. 387, 26 Ohio Law Rep. 562.

An instruction on the subject of alibi: "It is obviously essential to the satisfactory proof of an alibi that it should cover the whole of the time of the crime in question or so much of it as to render it impossible that the prisoner could have committed the act" is not reversible error, since it only defines the range of time and place covered by the alibi and has no relation to the quantum, degree or burden of proof. Sabo v. State (Ohio 1928) 119 Ohio St. 231, 163 N.E. 28, 6 Ohio Law Abs. 386, 26 Ohio Law Rep. 560.

In a criminal case where court omits to charge upon a feature of the law claimed to be applicable to the evidence, defendant, in order to predicate reversible error upon the court's omission, should call court's attention to that point and make specific request for such instruction. Rucker v. State (Ohio 1928) 119 Ohio St. 189, 162 N.E. 802, 6 Ohio Law Abs. 370, 26 Ohio Law Rep. 461.

RC 2945.10 allows for deviation from the usual practice of giving jury instructions after closing arguments as required under Crim R 30(A); consequently, in a case involving various theories of culpability for aggravated robbery and felonious assault, jury instructions given prior to closing arguments do not constitute plain error since written and oral instructions given after the closing arguments counteract the effects of "primacy" and "recency" on the jury. State v Watts, No. CA 10274 (2d Dist Ct App, Montgomery, 6–10–87).

Where identification of the defendant charged with possession of forged prescriptions is the crucial issue, and such identification is uncorroborated by evidence other than eyewitness testimony, the trial court commits reversible error in refusing to instruct the jury regarding the law concerning eyewitness testimony where both eyewitnesses had problems identifying the defendant from a police photo array. State v Turney, No. 82AP–580 (10th Dist Ct App, Franklin, 3–10–83).

11. —— Written or oral, instructions

Trial court's failure to include written jury instructions with the record on appeal as required by law, foreclosing any comparison of written instructions with erroneous and confusing oral instructions relating to assault charges, was not harmless error; error made it unknown whether the jury made its finding by applying the correct law or even that it had the correct law before it in the jury room. State v. Huckabee (Ohio App. 8 Dist., Cuyahoga, 10-21-2004) No. 83458, 2004-Ohio-5593, 2004 WL 2361817, Unreported. Criminal Law ⚷ 804(1); Criminal Law ⚷ 1173.1

Claim that trial court erred by failing to include written jury instructions in record, as required by rule, did not constitute plain error in felonious assault prosecution, where trial court fully and completely instructed jury prior to deliberations, parties had opportunity to review proposed written instructions, and neither party alleged variation between oral instructions and proposed written instructions. State v. Smith (Ohio App. 8 Dist., Cuyahoga, 07-01-2004) No. 82710, 2004-Ohio-3479, 2004 WL 1472081, Unreported, appeal not allowed 104 Ohio St.3d 1409, 818 N.E.2d 711, 2004-Ohio-6364. Criminal Law ⚷ 1038.1(6)

Failure of trial court to maintain written jury instructions with the papers of the case did not result in miscarriage of justice and was not plain error. City of Columbus v. Mullins (Ohio App. 10 Dist., Franklin, 03-09-2004) No. 03AP-623, 2004-Ohio-1059, 2004 WL 422717, Unreported. Criminal Law ⚷ 1038.1(6)

Failure of trial court to maintain written jury instructions with the papers of the case was not "structural error" and, thus, was not subject to automatic reversal. City of Columbus v. Mullins (Ohio App. 10 Dist., Franklin, 03-09-2004) No. 03AP-623, 2004-Ohio-1059, 2004 WL 422717, Unreported. Criminal Law ⚷ 1172.1(5)

The trial court's failure to include in the record the court's written jury instructions did not constitute reversible error; defendant failed to establish that he was prejudiced by the court's failure to preserve the instructions in the record. State v. Thompson (Ohio App. 8 Dist., Cuyahoga, 07-24-2003) No. 81322, 2003-Ohio-3939, 2003 WL 21710623, Unreported, appeal not allowed 100 Ohio St.3d 1487, 798 N.E.2d 1094, 2003-Ohio-5992. Criminal Law ⚷ 1109(3)

Trial court's failure to include written jury instructions in record did not warrant new trial, in prosecution for, among other things, rape, although defendant argued that said failure amounted to denial of due process by impairing his right to effective first appeal as of right, where defendant failed to demonstrate that said failure resulted in prejudice to him. State v. Gooden (Ohio App. 8 Dist., Cuyahoga, 06-05-2003) No. 81320, 2003-Ohio-2864, 2003 WL 21290932, Unreported, appeal not allowed 100 Ohio St.3d 1432, 797 N.E.2d 512, 2003-Ohio-5396. Criminal Law ⚷ 1109(3)

The failure of the trial court to maintain written jury instructions with the papers of the case was not a "structural error" and, thus, was not subject to automatic reversal; it was a statutory, rather than constitutional, defect, and the defendant did not allege that the written instructions deviated in any manner from the transcribed oral instructions in the record. State v. Perry (Ohio, 02-11-2004) 101 Ohio St.3d 118, 802 N.E.2d 643, 2004-Ohio-297, on remand 2004-Ohio-5152, 2004 WL 2804683. Criminal Law ⚷ 1109(1)

A trial court is required to maintain the written jury instructions with the papers of the case. State v. Perry (Ohio, 02-11-2004) 101 Ohio St.3d 118, 802 N.E.2d 643, 2004-Ohio-297, on remand 2004-Ohio-5152, 2004 WL 2804683. Criminal Law ⚷ 804(1)

A trial court is not required to reduce its instructions to writing, but even if it does, it is not prohibited from answering a jury's questions of law during deliberation. State v. Kersey (Ohio App. 1 Dist., 12-19-1997) 124 Ohio App.3d 513, 706 N.E.2d 818. Criminal Law ⚷ 804(7); Criminal Law ⚷ 864

Defendant waived any claimed error in trial court's refusal, during prosecution for having weapon while under a disability, to respond to jury's request for clarification of court's oral instructions on definition of "possession," where defense consented to note that trial court sent to jury and that stated that court could not answer jury's question. State v. Kersey (Ohio App. 1 Dist., 12-19-1997) 124 Ohio App.3d 513, 706 N.E.2d 818. Criminal Law ⚷ 1137(8)

Trial court's failure to make written jury instructions that were provided to jury a permanent part of record for use on appeal amounted to prejudicial error, in prosecution for rape, kidnapping, and gross sexual imposition. State v. Perry (Ohio App. 10 Dist., Franklin, 09-05-2002) No. 01AP-996, 2002-Ohio-4545, 2002 WL 2024677, Unreported, appeal allowed 98 Ohio St.3d 1421, 782 N.E.2d 76, 2003-Ohio-259, stay granted 98 Ohio St.3d 1487, 785 N.E.2d 470, 2003-Ohio-1189, reversed 101 Ohio St.3d 118, 802 N.E.2d 643, 2004-Ohio-297, on remand 2004-Ohio-5152, 2004 WL 2804683. Criminal Law ⚷ 1086.11; Criminal Law ⚷ 1109(3)

The trial judge did not commit plain error when he failed to give instructions orally to the jury at the conclusion of the arguments when the jury had written instructions which were the same as the preliminary instructions given by the judge and no objection was raised; furthermore, because the written instructions were in the record in compliance with RC 2945.10(G), this case is distinguishable from the holding in *State v Smith*, No. C–920350 (1st Dist Ct App, Hamilton, 4–7–93). State v Everson, No. C–920577 (1st Dist Ct App, Hamilton, 5–19–93).

12. Questions from jurors to witnesses—In general

Jurors in theft trial were allowed to question witnesses; jurors submitted questions to judge to ask witnesses following examination by counsel, judge and counsel discussed the questions at sidebar to determine whether they were legally acceptable, and if they were acceptable the judge read the questions to jury. State v. Smith (Ohio App. 8 Dist., 08-08-2002) 148 Ohio App.3d 665, 775 N.E.2d 554, 2002-Ohio-4091, motion to certify allowed 97 Ohio St.3d 1480, 780 N.E.2d 285, 2002-Ohio-6866, appeal allowed 97 Ohio St.3d 1481, 780 N.E.2d 286, 2002-Ohio-6866, affirmed 99 Ohio St.3d 143, 789 N.E.2d 236, 2003-Ohio-2772. Witnesses ⚿ 246(1)

13. —— Discretion of court, questions from jurors to witnesses

Trial court act of allowing jurors to submit questions to witnesses was not an abuse of discretion; trial court required the questions to be in writing, attorneys were provided an opportunity to object to juror questions, and jurors were instructed not to feel badly if their question was not presented to a witness. State v. Jones (Ohio App. 10 Dist., Franklin, 11-10-2003) No. 02AP-1390, 2003-Ohio-5994, 2003 WL 22533685, Unreported, appeal not allowed 102 Ohio St.3d 1409, 806 N.E.2d 561, 2004-Ohio-1763. Witnesses ⚿ 246(1)

The decision to allow jurors to question witnesses is a matter within the discretion of the trial court and should not be disturbed on appeal absent an abuse of that discretion. State v. Fisher (Ohio, 06-11-2003) 99 Ohio St.3d 127, 789 N.E.2d 222, 2003-Ohio-2761, denial of post-conviction relief affirmed 2005-Ohio-4065, 2005 WL 1869692, appeal not allowed 107 Ohio St.3d 1684, 839 N.E.2d 404, 2005-Ohio-6480, stay allowed 2006 WL 871194. Criminal Law ⚿ 1153(4); Witnesses ⚿ 246(1)

Practice of allowing jurors to question witnesses is matter committed to discretion of trial court; to minimize danger of prejudice, however, trial courts that permit juror questioning should: (1) require jurors to submit their questions to court in writing; (2) ensure that jurors do not display or discuss a question with other jurors until court reads question to witness; (3) provide counsel an opportunity to object to each question at sidebar or outside presence of jury; (4) instruct jurors that they should not draw adverse inferences from court's refusal to allow certain questions; and (5) allow counsel to ask follow-up questions of witnesses. State v. Fisher (Ohio, 06-11-2003) 99 Ohio St.3d 127, 789 N.E.2d 222, 2003-Ohio-2761, denial of post-conviction relief affirmed 2005-Ohio-4065, 2005 WL 1869692, appeal not allowed 107 Ohio St.3d 1684, 839 N.E.2d 404, 2005-Ohio-6480, stay allowed 2006 WL 871194. Witnesses ⚿ 246(1)

The right of a juror to question a witness during trial is within the sound discretion of the trial court. State v. Smith (Ohio App. 8 Dist., 08-08-2002) 148 Ohio App.3d 665, 775 N.E.2d 554, 2002-Ohio-4091, motion to certify allowed 97 Ohio St.3d 1480, 780 N.E.2d 285, 2002-Ohio-6866, appeal allowed 97 Ohio St.3d 1481, 780 N.E.2d 286, 2002-Ohio-6866, affirmed 99 Ohio St.3d 143, 789 N.E.2d 236, 2003-Ohio-2772. Witnesses ⚿ 246(1)

14. —— Ineffective assistance of counsel, questions from jurors to witnesses

Appellate counsel's failure to raise issue of whether trial court erred by allowing jurors to question witnesses did not constitute ineffective assistance of counsel in prosecution for possession of drugs and possession of criminal tools, where right of juror to ask questions of witness during trial had long been held to be within trial court's discretion, and appellate case holding that allowing such questions was not within trial court's discretion was not in existence at time that counsel filed appellate brief. State v. Smith (Ohio App. 8 Dist., Cuyahoga, 12-04-2002) No. 79301, 2002-Ohio-6620, 2002 WL 31718896, Unreported. Criminal Law ⚿ 641.13(7)

15. —— Objections, questions from jurors to witnesses

A trial judge should rule on any objections to juror questions when counsel objects at sidebar, including any objection that a question from a juror touches on a matter that counsel purposefully avoided as a matter of litigation strategy, and that, if asked, will cause particular prejudice to the party. State v. Fisher (Ohio, 06-11-2003) 99 Ohio St.3d 127, 789 N.E.2d 222, 2003-Ohio-2761, denial of post-conviction relief affirmed 2005-Ohio-4065, 2005 WL 1869692, appeal not allowed 107 Ohio St.3d 1684, 839 N.E.2d 404, 2005-Ohio 6480, stay allowed 2006 WL 871194. Witnesses ⚿ 246(1)

2945.11 Charge to the jury as to law and fact

In charging the jury, the court must state to it all matters of law necessary for the information of the jury in giving its verdict. The court must also inform the jury that the jury is the exclusive judge of all questions of fact. The court must state to the jury that in determining the question of guilt, it must not consider the punishment but that punishment rests with the judge except in cases of murder in the first degree or burglary of an inhabited dwelling.

(1953 H 1, eff. 10–1–53; GC 13442–9)

Historical and Statutory Notes

Pre–1953 H 1 Amendments: 113 v 181, Ch 21, § 9

Cross References

Jury instructions, Crim R 30

Presumption of innocence; reasonable doubt, defined, 2901.05

Library References

Criminal Law ⚷768, 769, 790.

Westlaw Topic No. 110.

C.J.S. Criminal Law §§ 1302 to 1304, 1308, 1346, 1350, 1499, 1540.

Research References

Encyclopedias

OH Jur. 3d Criminal Law § 2740, Refusal to Give Requested Instruction—Instructions Substantially Covered in General Instructions.

OH Jur. 3d Criminal Law § 2749, Alibi.

Treatises and Practice Aids

Markus, Trial Handbook for Ohio Lawyers, § 36:5, Criminal Case.

Katz, Giannelli, Blair and Lipton, Baldwin's Ohio Practice, Criminal Law, § 71:1, Introduction.

Katz, Giannelli, Blair and Lipton, Baldwin's Ohio Practice, Criminal Law, § 71:8, Fact-Finder and Credibility Instructions.

Katz, Giannelli, Blair and Lipton, Baldwin's Ohio Practice, Criminal Law, § 150:2, Proposed Jury Instructions.

Giannelli and Snyder, Baldwin's Ohio Practice, Evidence, § 607.7, Credibility of Witnesses.

Law Review and Journal Commentaries

Criminal Law—Actions and Defenses—Prisons and Prisoners—An Escape Defendant Presenting Some Evidence Showing that He Reasonably Believed Escape Was Necessary to Avoid Greater Injury Than Any Which Might Reasonably Result from the Escape and that He Did Not Occasion the Situation Is Entitled to a Jury Instruction on the Necessity Defense.—People v. Unger, Note. 46 U Cin L Rev 1079 (1978).

Criminal Law—Reading the Indictment—Jury Instructions, Alan Belkin and Lawrence Friedlander. 46 Clev B J 106 (March 1975).

State v. Abrams: Harmless Error in the Absence of the Accused—Additional Instructions, Note. 2 Ohio N U L Rev 596 (1975).

Notes of Decisions

1. Constitutional issues

Failure of appellate counsel to assign as error trial court's failure to instruct jury concerning defendant's history of marijuana use, as mitigating factor in capital sentencing, was not ineffective assistance of counsel; reasonable appellate counsel could have decided that history of marijuana use was of such little mitigation value that any error in failing to so instruct jury was harmless. State v. McGuire (Ohio, 12-10-1997) 80 Ohio St.3d 390, 686 N.E.2d 1112, 1997-Ohio-335, reconsideration denied 81 Ohio St.3d 1433, 689 N.E.2d 52, dismissal of post-conviction relief affirmed 1998 WL 191415, dismissed, appeal not allowed 83 Ohio St.3d 1428, 699 N.E.2d 945, certiorari denied 119 S.Ct. 85, 525 U.S. 831, 142 L.Ed.2d 66, denial of post-conviction relief affirmed 2001 WL 409424, dismissed, appeal not allowed 93 Ohio St.3d 1411, 754 N.E.2d 259. Criminal Law ⚷ 641.13(7)

A cautionary instruction to the jury that it is not to draw any adverse inference from defendant's refusal to testify on his behalf does not violate defendant's Fifth Amendment right against self-incrimination. Lakeside v. Oregon (U.S.Or. 1978) 98 S.Ct. 1091, 435 U.S. 333, 55 L.Ed.2d 319. Criminal Law ⚷ 787(1)

2. Instructions—In general

Upon determining that self-defense instruction was warranted on charge of felonious assault, trial court committed plain error in instructing jury that self-defense was not available as a defense to inferior degree offense of aggravated assault and the lesser included offense of assault; all offenses were based on the same facts, and jury apparently believed defendant's self-defense claim when it failed to find him guilty of felonious assault. State v.

Smith (Ohio App. 12 Dist., Butler, 12-30-2002) No. CA2002-01-019, 2002-Ohio-7280, 2002 WL 31883354, Unreported. Criminal Law ⚷ 1038.1(4)

Trial court, in its attempt to prevent jury from considering unrecognized defense of diminished capacity, negated through its instructions on aggravated robbery jurors' duty of finding culpable mental state of "knowingly," thereby essentially eliminating to defendant's prejudice necessary mens rea element required in conviction for crime charged, and thus committed reversible error; trial court stated, "You are hereby instructed that the defendant has not raised the defense of not guilty by reason of insanity, and as the State of Ohio does not recognize the partial defense of diminished capacity, you are to disregard any evidence of defendant's mental state." State v. Kincaid (Ohio App. 9 Dist., Wayne, 11-13-2002) No. 01CA007947, 2002-Ohio-6116, 2002 WL 31513544, Unreported. Criminal Law ⚷ 1172.1(3)

Trial court's jury instructions on aggravated robbery were misleading and prejudicial, and thus constituted reversible error; trial court's definition of "criminal attempt" was inappropriate for effectively transforming aggravated robbery from general intent to specific intent crime, that is, term criminal attempt required that a party act "purposely," whereas aggravated robbery did not require that defendant acted as such but rather "knowingly." State v. Kincaid (Ohio App. 9 Dist., Wayne, 11-13-2002) No. 01CA007947, 2002-Ohio-6116, 2002 WL 31513544, Unreported. Criminal Law ⚷ 1172.1(3)

Suggestion to jury that a defendant, if convicted of a certain offense, may be pardoned or paroled, is improper. State v. Santiago (Ohio App. 9 Dist., Lorain, 03-13-2002) No. 01CA007798, 2002-Ohio-1114, 2002 WL 388901, Unreported, appeal not allowed 96 Ohio St.3d 1466, 772 N.E.2d 1202, 2002-Ohio-3910. Criminal Law ⚷ 723(1)

Error by trial court in failing to give requested alibi instruction was not prejudicial in aggravated robbery prosecution. State v. Frost (Ohio App. 2 Dist., 10-14-2005) 164 Ohio App.3d 61, 841 N.E.2d 336, 2005-Ohio-5510. Criminal Law ⚷ 1173.2(3)

Jury instruction in capital murder prosecution with respect to inference from manner in which defendant made use of deadly weapon did not create impermissible mandatory presumption, where court's use of "may" adequately communicated that jury was free to accept or reject permissive inference; language "purpose to cause the death may be inferred from the use of the weapon" did not communicate conclusive presumption relieving state of its burden of persuasion on criminal intent. State v. Gross (Ohio, 10-30-2002) 97 Ohio St.3d 121, 776 N.E.2d 1061, 2002-Ohio-5524, reconsideration denied 97 Ohio St.3d 1486, 780 N.E.2d 288, 2002-Ohio-6866, certiorari denied 123 S.Ct. 2079, 538 U.S. 1037, 155 L.Ed.2d 1068, rehearing denied 124 S.Ct. 20, 539 U.S. 976, 156 L.Ed.2d 685. Homicide ⚷ 1388

Possibility of jury confusion with respect to instruction on complicity did not reach the level of plain error in prosecution for murder of corrections officer during prison riot; trial judge made several strong statements that defendant could be convicted of aggravated murder only if the state proved that he harbored the specific purpose to kill corrections officer and explained how the jury could determine whether purpose existed, thus underlining that purpose was necessary to a conviction. State v. Sanders (Ohio, 07-18-2001) 92 Ohio St.3d 245, 750 N.E.2d 90, 2001-Ohio-189, reconsideration denied 93 Ohio St.3d 1434, 755 N.E.2d 356, stay granted 93 Ohio St.3d 1437, 755 N.E.2d 900, stay revoked 98 Ohio St.3d 1453, 783 N.E.2d 514, 2003-Ohio-651, certiorari denied 122 S.Ct. 1795, 535 U.S. 1036, 152 L.Ed.2d 653, stay granted 98 Ohio St.3d 1506, 786 N.E.2d 57, 2003-Ohio-1573. Criminal Law ⚷ 1038.1(4)

Defendant waived claim that trial court erred in failing to specifically instruct that a solitary juror could block a recommendation of death by failing to object to penalty-phase instruction at trial. State v. Sanders (Ohio, 07-18-2001) 92 Ohio St.3d 245, 750 N.E.2d 90, 2001-Ohio-189, reconsideration denied 93 Ohio St.3d 1434, 755 N.E.2d 356, stay granted 93 Ohio St.3d 1437, 755 N.E.2d 900, stay revoked 98 Ohio St.3d 1453, 783 N.E.2d 514, 2003-Ohio-651, certiorari denied 122 S.Ct. 1795, 535 U.S. 1036, 152 L.Ed.2d 653, stay granted 98 Ohio St.3d 1506, 786 N.E.2d 57, 2003-Ohio-1573. Sentencing And Punishment ⚷ 1789(3)

Substance of jury instructions is of decisive importance, not necessarily exact words or form. State v. Roquemore (Franklin 1993) 85 Ohio App.3d 448, 620 N.E.2d 110. Criminal Law ⚷ 805(1)

Generally, if a juror dissents from verdict during polling, district court should either declare a mistrial or return jury to deliberate further; however, where a poll answer is ambiguous or appears coerced, district court may question a juror to ascertain whether verdict is unanimous. Bhat v. University of Cincinnati (C.A.6 (Ohio), 10-03-2001) No. 00-3529, 23 Fed.Appx. 280, 2001 WL 1216975, Unreported. Federal Civil Procedure ⚷ 2191

Trial court's action in informing jury of parties' stipulation of fact as to amount of crack cocaine involved in each transaction with which defendant was charged did not improperly remove matter of fact, credibility determination, or determination of weight of evidence from jury's consideration. State v. Sloan (Ohio App. 8 Dist., Cuyahoga, 05-30-2002) No. 79832, 2002-Ohio-2669, 2002 WL 1265578, Unreported. Criminal Law ⚷ 763(1)

3. —— When required, instructions

Where a defendant files a timely notice of alibi, presents evidence to support the contention, and relies on alibi as his sole defense, the trial court has a statutory duty to charge the jury on alibi; however, the trial court is not required to give such instruction in the exact form requested by the defendant and may, instead, frame the instructions in the court's own words. State v. Frost (Ohio App. 2 Dist., 10-14-2005) 164 Ohio App.3d 61, 841 N.E.2d

336, 2005-Ohio-5510. Criminal Law ⚯ 775(1); Criminal Law ⚯ 834(3)

A court must charge the jury with all the law required to return a verdict. State v. Mitchell (Cuyahoga 1989) 60 Ohio App.3d 106, 574 N.E.2d 573, cause dismissed 49 Ohio St.3d 709, 551 N.E.2d 1306.

Where the accused has seasonably filed a notice of alibi, presented testimony at trial in its support, and relies on alibi as his sole defense, the trial court's failure to instruct on the defense of alibi does not comply with its duty to instruct on "all matters of law necessary for the information of the jury in giving its verdict" as provided by RC 2945.11, and this omission may be noticed as plain error affecting the substantial rights of the accused, notwithstanding defense counsel's failure to request an instruction on alibi as provided by Crim R 30. State v. Bridgeman (Cuyahoga 1977) 51 Ohio App.2d 105, 366 N.E.2d 1378, 5 O.O.3d 275. Criminal Law ⚯ 775(2)

In a criminal case, it is not mandatory upon a trial court to give requested instructions to the jury verbatim, but if the requested instructions contain a correct, pertinent statement of the law and are appropriate to the facts they must be included, at least in substance, in the court's charge to the jury. State v. Nelson (Ohio 1973) 36 Ohio St.2d 79, 303 N.E.2d 865, 65 O.O.2d 222. Criminal Law ⚯ 834(2)

Where the evidence in a criminal case would support a finding by the jury of guilt of a lesser offense included in the offense for which defendant was indicted and tried, the refusal of the trial court to charge upon that lesser included offense is error prejudicial to the rights of defendant. State v. Loudermill (Ohio 1965) 2 Ohio St.2d 79, 206 N.E.2d 198, 31 O.O.2d 60.

Where one is being tried on an indictment charging malicious cutting with intent to kill, wound or maim, and the evidence discloses that the one assaulted was the aggressor; that a number of the aggressor's companions joined in making an attack upon the accused, including an attack with a chair; and that the aggressor reached for his pocket, giving the impression that he intended to use a knife, such facts are relevant for consideration by the jury in determining whether accused would be justified in using his pocketknife in self-defense, and it is prejudicial error for the court to refuse to give a requested charge on self-defense although the accused failed to testify and assert self-defense. State v. McDade (Lucas 1959) 113 Ohio App. 397, 178 N.E.2d 824, 17 O.O.2d 469.

4. —— When not required, instructions

Defendant was not entitled to a jury instruction on criminal trespass, as a lesser-included offense of aggravated burglary; victim testified that defendant and co-defendants possessed guns, that they physically attacked second victim, and that defendant threatened to kill the victims. State v. Garrett (Ohio App. 12 Dist., Butler, 09-22-2003) No. CA2002-05-111, 2003-Ohio-5000, 2003 WL 22170186, Unreported, appeal not allowed 101 Ohio St.3d 1423, 802 N.E.2d 154, 2004-Ohio-123. Criminal Law ⚯ 795(2.35)

Failure of trial counsel to request jury instructions based upon defendant's theory of the case in prosecution for cocaine possession and to request jury instructions in regard to the confidential informant's (CI) testimony was not deficient, as element of claim of ineffective assistance; record reflected that counsel made sound arguments to the court and jury, challenged testimony of witnesses by vigorous cross-examination, made timely objections, and was able to elicit conflicting testimony from the state's witnesses. State v. Edwards (Ohio App. 6 Dist., Lucas, 02-07-2003) No. L-00-1161, 2003-Ohio-571, 2003 WL 257383, Unreported, appeal not allowed 99 Ohio St.3d 1436, 789 N.E.2d 1117, 2003-Ohio-2902, certiorari denied 124 S.Ct. 809, 540 U.S. 1052, 157 L.Ed.2d 702. Criminal Law ⚯ 641.13(2.1)

Failure of trial counsel to request jury instructions based upon defendant's theory of the case in prosecution for cocaine possession and to request jury instructions in regard to the confidential informant's (CI) testimony did not prejudice defendant, as element of claim of ineffective assistance, absent showing of reasonable probability that, but for counsel's unprofessional errors, the result of the proceeding would have been different. State v. Edwards (Ohio App. 6 Dist., Lucas, 02-07-2003) No. L-00-1161, 2003-Ohio-571, 2003 WL 257383, Unreported, appeal not allowed 99 Ohio St.3d 1436, 789 N.E.2d 1117, 2003-Ohio-2902, certiorari denied 124 S.Ct. 809, 540 U.S. 1052, 157 L.Ed.2d 702. Criminal Law ⚯ 641.13(2.1)

Trial court's failure to give jury instructions based upon defendant's theory of the case in prosecution for cocaine possession and to give instructions in regard to the confidential informant's (CI) testimony was not plain error; trial court gave instructions on credibility of witnesses, and the application of tests of truthfulness and belief or disbelief of witnesses, as well as instructions on the elements of the crimes charged and, thus, accurately stated the law relevant to the case. State v. Edwards (Ohio App. 6 Dist., Lucas, 02-07-2003) No. L-00-1161, 2003-Ohio-571, 2003 WL 257383, Unreported, appeal not allowed 99 Ohio St.3d 1436, 789 N.E.2d 1117, 2003-Ohio-2902, certiorari denied 124 S.Ct. 809, 540 U.S. 1052, 157 L.Ed.2d 702. Criminal Law ⚯ 641.13(2.1)

Erroneous giving of instruction on duty to retreat in connection with capital murder defendant's claim of self-defense did not prejudice defendant and was harmless, where no reasonable jury could have believed that defendant acted in self-defense; defendant's own testimony established that he had been the aggressor in fatal encounter, had no basis for bona fide belief that he was in imminent danger of death or great bodily harm, and repeatedly stabbed victim after victim had ceased to pose any conceivable threat. State v. Cassano (Ohio, 08-07-2002) 96 Ohio St.3d 94, 772 N.E.2d 81, 2002-Ohio-3751, reconsideration denied 96 Ohio St.3d 1517, 775 N.E.2d 858, 2002-Ohio-4950, certiorari denied 123 S.Ct. 1359, 537 U.S. 1235, 155 L.Ed.2d 201. Criminal Law ⚷ 1172.1(4)

Instruction that would have relieved defendant in murder prosecution of criminal responsibility for death of cellmate after stabbing incident, if there was gross or willful maltreatment by medical personnel who attended to cellmate that was shown to be an independent intervening cause of death, was not warranted; pattern instructions adequately instructed on intervening cause and independent intervening cause of death, there was no evidence that cellmate was victim of gross or willful maltreatment, and defense expert agreed with coroner that attack by defendant was cause of death. State v. Hanna (Ohio, 05-22-2002) 95 Ohio St.3d 285, 767 N.E.2d 678, 2002-Ohio-2221, reconsideration denied 96 Ohio St.3d 1441, 770 N.E.2d 1050, 2002-Ohio-3344, certiorari denied 123 S.Ct. 554, 537 U.S. 1036, 154 L.Ed.2d 455. Criminal Law ⚷ 829(3)

Giving of jury instruction that defined causation in terms of foreseeability was not prejudicial error in aggravated murder prosecution arising from incident in which defendant thrust shank into sleeping cellmate's eye, where trial court provided jury with extensive instructions on the state's burden of proof and the requirement to prove purpose to kill both before and after giving foreseeability instruction. State v. Hanna (Ohio, 05-22-2002) 95 Ohio St.3d 285, 767 N.E.2d 678, 2002-Ohio-2221, reconsideration denied 96 Ohio St.3d 1441, 770 N.E.2d 1050, 2002-Ohio-3344, certiorari denied 123 S.Ct. 554, 537 U.S. 1036, 154 L.Ed.2d 455. Criminal Law ⚷ 1172.1(3)

Jury instruction on defense of voluntary intoxication was not warranted in capital murder prosecution, though police officers who encountered defendant in bar after murder would not allow him to drive home because he appeared intoxicated, where defendant just hours prior to murder told a bar patron he would "like to kill" the woman he lived with and did not appear intoxicated, other patrons who encountered him on night of murder did not think he had been drinking, and defendant clearly recalled murder when he recounted it to fellow inmate two days later. State v. Nields (Ohio, 08-29-2001) 93 Ohio St.3d 6, 752 N.E.2d 859, 2001-Ohio-1291, reconsideration denied 93 Ohio St.3d 1452, 756 N.E.2d 116. Homicide ⚷ 1506

Jury instruction on the law of accomplice liability was not unwarranted, even absent any evidence that someone other than defendant was the principal offender regarding aggravated murder charge; trial court did not specifically instruct the jury on accomplice liability in connection with the murder charge, and evidence tended to show that defendant was an aider and abetter in the aggravated robbery of the victim. State v. Chinn (Ohio, 06-02-1999) 85 Ohio St.3d 548, 709 N.E.2d 1166, 1999-Ohio-288, reconsideration denied 86 Ohio St.3d 1444, 713 N.E.2d 1053, stay granted 86 Ohio St.3d 1446, 714 N.E.2d 398, certiorari denied 120 S.Ct. 944, 528 U.S. 1120, 145 L.Ed.2d 820, denial of post-conviction relief affirmed 2001-Ohio-1550, 2001 WL 788402, dismissed, appeal not allowed 93 Ohio St.3d 1473, 757 N.E.2d 772. Criminal Law ⚷ 792(2)

Omission of standard jury instruction stating that circumstantial evidence "must be strong enough to support finding of proof beyond reasonable doubt" was not plain error; trial court instructed jury that circumstances must be "so convincing as to exclude reasonable doubt of defendant's guilt." State v. Grant (Ohio 1993) 67 Ohio St.3d 465, 620 N.E.2d 50, rehearing denied 68 Ohio St.3d 1412, 623 N.E.2d 568, certiorari denied 115 S.Ct. 116, 513 U.S. 836, 130 L.Ed.2d 62, rehearing denied 115 S.Ct. 617, 513 U.S. 1033, 130 L.Ed.2d 525. Criminal Law ⚷ 829(15)

Any claimed error with respect to a trial court's rejection of defendants' proposed jury instructions is waived by the defendants' subsequent waiver of their right to a jury trial. State v. Prince (Athens 1991) 71 Ohio App.3d 694, 595 N.E.2d 376. Criminal Law ⚷ 260.4

A defendant in an aggravated murder and aggravated robbery prosecution is not prejudiced by a trial court's refusal to repeat preliminary instructions as to circumstantial evidence where the court allows the defense counsel to remind the jury during closing arguments of those instructions. State v. Parrish (Franklin 1991) 71 Ohio App.3d 659, 595 N.E.2d 354, dismissed, jurisdictional motion overruled 60 Ohio St.3d 718, 574 N.E.2d 1079. Criminal Law ⚷ 1174(1)

A trial court does not err in refusing to give a defendant's special instruction on accomplice credibility to the jury when the substance of the requested instruction is already included in the court's general charge. State v. Sneed (Ohio 1992) 63 Ohio St.3d 3, 584 N.E.2d 1160, rehearing denied 63 Ohio St.3d 1433, 588 N.E.2d 132, stay granted 63 Ohio St.3d 1444, 589 N.E.2d 388, rehearing granted, opinion recalled 66 Ohio St.3d 1449, 609 N.E.2d 1270, certiorari denied 113 S.Ct. 1577, 507 U.S. 983, 123 L.Ed.2d 145, stay granted 66 Ohio St.3d 1504, 613 N.E.2d 1043.

A trial court is under no obligation to instruct a jury in the penalty phase of a capital case that that state's pretrial negotiated plea offer constitutes a mitigating factor to be weighed against the aggravating circumstance. State v. Sneed (Ohio 1992) 63 Ohio St.3d 3, 584 N.E.2d 1160, rehearing denied 63 Ohio St.3d 1433, 588 N.E.2d 132, stay granted 63 Ohio St.3d 1444, 589 N.E.2d 388, rehearing granted, opinion recalled 66 Ohio St.3d 1449, 609 N.E.2d 1270, certiorari denied 113 S.Ct. 1577, 507 U.S. 983, 123 L.Ed.2d 145, stay granted 66 Ohio St.3d 1504, 613 N.E.2d 1043. Sentencing And Punishment ⚷ 1780(3)

In a domestic violence action where the defendant is alleging the affirmative defense of self-defense, the trial court properly rejects a proposed jury instruction that the defendant had no duty to retreat from a place where he had a right to be, namely, the driveway since the duty to retreat extends to the driveway of one's home and is distinct from that presented when a person is attacked in his home. Cleveland v. Hill (Cuyahoga 1989) 63 Ohio App.3d 194, 578 N.E.2d 509.

A trial court's refusal to give a requested jury instruction is not error where the court provides a correct statutory definition to the jury in lieu of the expanded definition requested; the general rule is that amplification of statutory definitions is inadvisable, is likely to introduce error, and is to be done, if at all, only with extreme care not to prejudice either party to a criminal case. State v. Mahoney (Hamilton 1986) 34 Ohio App.3d 114, 517 N.E.2d 957.

A trial court is not required in all criminal cases to give a jury instruction on eyewitness identification where the identification of the defendant is the crucial issue in the case and is uncorroborated by other evidence. A trial court does not abuse its discretion in deciding that the factual issues do not require, and will not be assisted by, the requested instructions, and that the issue of determining identity beyond a reasonable doubt is adequately covered by other instructions. State v. Guster (Ohio 1981) 66 Ohio St.2d 266, 421 N.E.2d 157, 20 O.O.3d 249.

A defendant charged with first degree murder who pleads "not guilty" and "not guilty by reason of insanity" is not entitled to have the trial court instruct prospective jurors on voir dire, or the jury in the trial of the case, on the effect of a finding of not guilty by reason of insanity. State v. Siddle (Ohio 1971) 28 Ohio St.2d 135, 276 N.E.2d 641, 57 O.O.2d 367, certiorari denied 93 S.Ct. 148, 409 U.S. 860, 34 L.Ed.2d 107.

Where a defendant is being tried for crimes committed on four different dates, and does not assert an error in any of the dates, the trial court does not commit plain error by failing to instruct the jury regarding the date on which each offense was committed. State v Collier, No. 82AP–685 (10th Dist Ct App, Franklin, 1–17–84).

5. —— Tailored to case, instructions

Jury instruction on both subsections of statute defining the offense of unauthorized use of a motor vehicle, as a lesser included offense of the charged offense of grand theft of a motor vehicle, was proper, where defendant testified that he did not intend to steal the car, and thus the issue of whether defendant intended to permanently deprive the owner of property rather than merely use the property was before the jury. State v. Vrazalica (Ohio App. 8 Dist., Cuyahoga, 03-17-2005) No. 84412, 2005-Ohio-1164, 2005 WL 616082, Unreported. Criminal Law ⚷ 795(2.55)

Omission of a specific history, character, and background instruction was not plain error in prosecution for murder of corrections officer during prison riot; jury was instructed to consider "any other factors that are relevant to the issue of whether or not defendant should be sentenced to death," and it was likely that the jury considered defendant's history, character, and background under catchall category, especially since defense counsel argued that defendant's childhood "cried out for mercy." State v. Sanders (Ohio, 07-18-2001) 92 Ohio St.3d 245, 750 N.E.2d 90, 2001-Ohio-189, reconsideration denied 93 Ohio St.3d 1434, 755 N.E.2d 356, stay granted 93 Ohio St.3d 1437, 755 N.E.2d 900, stay revoked 98 Ohio St.3d 1453, 783 N.E.2d 514, 2003-Ohio-651, certiorari denied 122 S.Ct. 1795, 535 U.S. 1036, 152 L.Ed.2d 653, stay granted 98 Ohio St.3d 1506, 786 N.E.2d 57, 2003-Ohio-1573. Sentencing And Punishment ⚷ 1789(3)

Defense counsel's failure to request instruction that jury was not to deem police officer, by virtue of that status, to be more credible than any other witness and that officer's credibility and weight to be given his testimony are to be judged upon the same standard, did not amount to plain error, particularly as trial court gave standard charge that jury was sole judge of facts, credibility of witnesses, and weight of evidence. State v. Clark (Ohio App. 8 Dist., 02-27-1995) 101 Ohio App.3d 389, 655 N.E.2d 795, dismissed, appeal not allowed 72 Ohio St.3d 1548, 650 N.E.2d 1367. Criminal Law ⚷ 1038.2

Jury charge must state all matters of law necessary for the information of the jury in rendering its verdict and charge should be tailored to facts of case. State v. Shue (Ohio App. 9 Dist., 09-21-1994) 97 Ohio App.3d 459, 646 N.E.2d 1156, dismissed, appeal not allowed 71 Ohio St.3d 1476, 645 N.E.2d 1257. Criminal Law ⚷ 769; Criminal Law ⚷ 814(1)

It is duty of trial judge in jury trial to state all matters of law necessary for information of jury in giving its verdict. State v. Baker (Ohio App. 8 Dist., 12-20-1993) 92 Ohio App.3d 516, 636 N.E.2d 363. Criminal Law ⚷ 769

Jury instructions should be formulated to fit the facts of the individual case, and form instructions should not be followed blindly, but rather they should be used by the court as a guide in preparing its instructions to the jury. City of Avon Lake v. Anderson (Lorain 1983) 10 Ohio App.3d 297, 462 N.E.2d 188, 10 O.B.R. 472.

6. —— Charge relating to punishment, instructions

Penalty phase instruction in capital murder prosecution, stating that "whenever all 12 of you agree upon your verdict, you will complete the verdict form, sign it in ink, and summons the bailiff," was not misleading, despite defendant's contention that it failed to convey that single juror could vote so as to require life sentence, where instruction was intended merely to inform jurors that all of them had to sign verdict form, and where court gave defendant's requested instruction explicitly recognizing that single juror could preclude imposition of death penalty. State v. Cassano (Ohio, 08-07-2002) 96 Ohio St.3d 94, 772 N.E.2d 81, 2002-Ohio-3751, reconsideration denied 96 Ohio St.3d 1517, 775 N.E.2d 858, 2002-Ohio-4950, certiorari denied 123 S.Ct. 1359, 537 U.S. 1235, 155 L.Ed.2d 201. Sentencing And Punishment ⚷ 1780(3)

Penalty phase instruction in capital murder prosecution, stating that sentencing jury's weighing of evidence was "unlikely" to be disturbed and that it "should expect its sentence verdict to be carried out" was accurate reflection of state law and did not diminish jury's overall sense of responsibility for its verdict; in fact, court's strongly worded admonition as to importance of jury's verdict reinforced jury's sense of importance of its responsibility. State v. Cassano (Ohio, 08-07-2002) 96 Ohio St.3d 94, 772 N.E.2d 81, 2002-Ohio-3751, reconsideration denied 96 Ohio St.3d 1517, 775 N.E.2d 858, 2002-Ohio-4950, certiorari denied 123 S.Ct. 1359, 537 U.S. 1235, 155 L.Ed.2d 201. Sentencing And Punishment ⚷ 1780(3)

A judge does not violate a convicted murderer's constitutional rights by instructing the jury to avoid consideration of sympathy. State v. Jackson (Ohio 1991) 57 Ohio St.3d 29, 565 N.E.2d 549, rehearing denied 57 Ohio St.3d 725, 568 N.E.2d 1230, certiorari denied 112 S.Ct. 117, 502 U.S. 835, 116 L.Ed.2d 86, reconsideration denied 75 Ohio St.3d 1474, 663 N.E.2d 1302.

In a first degree murder case the court may, although it is better practice not to, explain the possibilities of pardon, commutation or parole in connection with a sentence of life imprisonment. State v. Meyer (Ohio 1955) 163 Ohio St. 279, 126 N.E.2d 585, 56 O.O. 256.

Explanation of the possibility of parole in the event of conviction of second degree murder was not prejudicial where the defendant was convicted of first degree murder without a recommendation of mercy. State v. Meyer (Ohio 1955) 163 Ohio St. 279, 126 N.E.2d 585, 56 O.O. 256.

Requirement that court state to jury that it must not consider the punishment, but that such rests with the judge, is not mandatory. State v. Moon (Ohio 1931) 124 Ohio St. 465, 179 N.E. 350, 11 Ohio Law Abs. 96, 35 Ohio Law Rep. 488.

The omission of an instruction, that jury must not consider the punishment, may be prejudicial to rights of the state, but is not to the detriment of defendant charged with an offense to which such provision applies, and he is not prejudiced thereby or prevented from having a fair trial. State v. Moon (Ohio 1931) 124 Ohio St. 465, 179 N.E. 350, 11 Ohio Law Abs. 96, 35 Ohio Law Rep. 488.

In view of express terms of GC 13442–9, providing that the court must state to the jury that in determining question of guilt, it must not consider the punishment, but that punishment rests with the judge, as may be provided by law, except in cases of murder in the first degree or burglary of an inhabited dwelling, failure to charge jury that it must not consider the punishment, but that the punishment rests with the judge, was not error in a prosecution for murder in the first degree, committed during attempted robbery of a filling station attendant. Dull v. State (Seneca 1930) 36 Ohio App. 195, 173 N.E. 26, 8 Ohio Law Abs. 398, 32 Ohio Law Rep. 358. Criminal Law ⚷ 796

7. —— Comment by judge on evidence, instructions

A trial judge commits plain error by telling a jury that the facts are not in controversy where the defendant asserts the defenses of alibi and mistaken identity. State v. Gover (Hamilton 1989) 61 Ohio App.3d 330, 572 N.E.2d 781, dismissed 43 Ohio St.3d 710, 540 N.E.2d 725.

Where, in the trial of an accused under RC 2905.06 (carnal knowledge of insane woman), the trial judge informs the jury of his ruling as to the competency of the woman-victim to testify, and intimates to the jury his opinion as to her sanity, insanity being an essential element of the crime charged, the court commits error prejudicial to the defendant which cannot be cured by later admonishing the jury to disregard such statements. State v. Nutter (Ohio 1970) 22 Ohio St.2d 116, 258 N.E.2d 440, 51 O.O.2d 178.

Where trial court, in prosecution for rape and gross sexual imposition, instructs the jury that the evidence is not in dispute that the victim was not the spouse of the defendant, it has failed to inform the jury that the jury is the exclusive judge of all questions of fact pursuant to RC 2945.11 and has committed error prejudicial to the defendant. State v Rudd, No. CA86–05–036 (12th Dist Ct App, Clermont, 3–2–87).

8. Partial or irrelevant instructions

An instruction which fails to inform the jury that the law requires a driver to be affected "to an appreciable degree" in the operation of his automobile before he may be found guilty of driving while under the influence of alcohol is erroneous as a matter of law and constitutes plain error. State v. Biggert (Ohio App. 6 Dist., Ottawa, 05-22-1998) No. OT-97-024, 1998 WL 337901, Unreported.

A woman accused of murdering her abusive live-in boyfriend who asserts self-defense and battered woman syndrome has a common law duty to retreat "to the wall" if possible before killing her co-inhabiter attacker, and a reference to the duty to retreat in the jury instructions without an explanation regarding the extent and limitation of this duty does not constitute plain error. State v. Thomas (Ohio App. 4 Dist., Athens, 07-26-1995) No. 94CA1608, 1995 WL 468183, Unreported, motion to certify appeal granted 1995 WL 542422, motion to certify allowed 74 Ohio St.3d 1445, 656 N.E.2d 345, appeal allowed 74 Ohio St.3d 1446, 656 N.E.2d 346, affirmed in part, reversed in part 77 Ohio St.3d 323, 673 N.E.2d 1339, 67 A.L.R.5th 775, 1997-Ohio-269.

Trial court's mistakenly omitting element of committing aggravated murder during kidnapping from its instruction on felony-murder specification to felony-murder count was not plain error; felony–murder count to which specification was attached was predicated on commission of murder during a kidnapping, and jury was instructed that it had to find defendant guilty of kidnapping to find him guilty of aggravated murder on that felony-murder count. State v. Sanders (Ohio, 07-18-2001) 92 Ohio St.3d 245, 750 N.E.2d 90, 2001-Ohio-189, reconsideration denied 93 Ohio St.3d 1434, 755 N.E.2d 356, stay granted 93 Ohio St.3d 1437, 755 N.E.2d 900, stay revoked 98 Ohio St.3d 1453, 783 N.E.2d 514, 2003-Ohio-651, certiorari denied 122 S.Ct. 1795, 535 U.S. 1036, 152 L.Ed.2d 653, stay granted 98 Ohio St.3d 1506, 786 N.E.2d 57, 2003-Ohio-1573. Criminal Law ⟹ 1038.1(4)

Judge's twice substituting the word "intent" for "attempt" while instructing jury in capital murder prosecution as to felony-murder specification was not plain error; verdict forms correctly stated the elements of the specification, counsel for both parties correctly stated its elements in argument, and evidence supported a finding of the specification. State v. Sanders (Ohio, 07-18-2001) 92 Ohio St.3d 245, 750 N.E.2d 90, 2001-Ohio-189, reconsideration denied 93 Ohio St.3d 1434, 755 N.E.2d 356, stay granted 93 Ohio St.3d 1437, 755 N.E.2d 900, stay revoked 98 Ohio St.3d 1453, 783 N.E.2d 514, 2003-Ohio-651, certiorari denied 122 S.Ct. 1795, 535 U.S. 1036, 152 L.Ed.2d 653, stay granted 98 Ohio St.3d 1506, 786 N.E.2d 57, 2003-Ohio-1573. Criminal Law ⟹ 1038.1(6)

Mere partial nondirection, if such be the case, as to a particular matter or issue, does not of itself constitute reversible error, in the absence of a request for more specific and comprehensive instructions upon the particular point or issue involved. State v. Perry (Athens 1972) 29 Ohio App.2d 33, 278 N.E.2d 50, 58 O.O.2d 25. Criminal Law ⟹ 1038.3

Argument that the state trial court gave an inadequate self-defense instruction, implying that petitioner had to be in fear of death, rather than in fear of other forms of serious bodily harm, in order to use deadly force, had no apparent federal constitutional implications, and thus Court of Appeals, in habeas proceeding, could not question the state appellate court's decision that the instruction accurately reflected Ohio self-defense law. Seymour v. Walker (C.A.6 (Ohio), 08-16-2000) 224 F.3d 542, certiorari denied 121 S.Ct. 1643, 532 U.S. 989, 149 L.Ed.2d 502. Habeas Corpus ⟹ 498

Where there is no evidence on an issue in a state criminal prosecution, the nature of any jury instruction given is generally irrelevant and any error in its formulation is harmless. Melchior v. Jago (C.A.6 (Ohio) 1983) 723 F.2d 486, certiorari denied 104 S.Ct. 2156, 466 U.S. 952, 80 L.Ed.2d 542.

2945.12 When accused may be tried in his absence

A person indicted for a misdemeanor, upon request in writing subscribed by him and entered in the journal, may be tried in his absence by a jury or by the court. No other person shall be tried unless personally present, but if a person indicted escapes or forfeits his recognizance after the jury is sworn, the trial shall proceed and the verdict be received and recorded. If the offense charged is a misdemeanor, judgment and sentence shall be pronounced as if he were personally present. If the offense charged is a felony, the case shall be continued until the accused appears in court, or is retaken.

(1953 H 1, eff. 10–1–53; GC 13442–10)

Historical and Statutory Notes

Pre–1953 H 1 Amendments: 113 v 181, Ch 21, § 10

Cross References

Presence of the defendant at arraignment and trial, Crim R 43

Right of defendant to appear and defend in person, US Const Am 6; O Const Art I §10

Library References

Criminal Law ⟹636.

Westlaw Topic No. 110.

C.J.S. Criminal Law §§ 1161 to 1166.

Research References

Encyclopedias

OH Jur. 3d Criminal Law § 2603, Escape of Accused.

Treatises and Practice Aids

Markus, Trial Handbook for Ohio Lawyers, § 2:3, Presence of Parties and Counsel—Criminal Case.

Carlin, Baldwin's Ohio Practice, Merrick-Rippner Probate Law § 108:10, Juvenile Court—Criminal Jurisdiction—Criminal Trial of Adults: Rules and Procedures.

Hennenberg & Reinhart, Ohio Criminal Defense Motions F 15.03, Motion to Permit the Defendant to be Present at All Proceedings-Miscellaneous Motions.

Gotherman, Babbit and Lang, Baldwin's Ohio Practice, Local Government Law—Municipal, § 28:43, Waiver of Appearance and Bail.

Notes of Decisions

Constitutional issues 1
Presence of defendant required 2
Voluntary absence of defendant 3

1. Constitutional issues

Trial court's administering oath to venire before defendant or his counsel arrived in courtroom was not plain error; defendant was present for every stage of the proceedings except the first swearing in of the potential jury panel, and defendant presented no evidence that his absence thwarted a fair and just hearing. State v. Hawkins (Ohio App. 8 Dist., Cuyahoga, 02-26-2004) No. 82465, 2004-Ohio-855, 2004 WL 351871, Unreported, reversed 104 Ohio St.3d 582, 820 N.E.2d 931, 2004-Ohio-7124. Criminal Law ⚷ 1035(6)

RC 2151.41, RC 2945.12 and O Const Art I, § 10 should be considered and construed together. State v. Walker (Huron 1959) 108 Ohio App. 333, 161 N.E.2d 521, 9 O.O.2d 296.

By virtue of O Const Art I, § 10, and this section, it is the right of a defendant to be present when a jury, during its deliberations in a felony case, returns to the courtroom for further instructions from judge as to the law, where accused is affected by such instructions and giving of such during his absence, without his knowledge and while he is confined in jail, constitutes prejudicial error. State v. Grisafulli (Ohio 1939) 135 Ohio St. 87, 19 N.E.2d 645, 13 O.O. 440. Criminal Law ⚷ 636(7)

Pursuant to RC 2945.12 and O Const Art I, § 10, a defendant is entitled to be present when a court delivers its instructions to the jury and where a court sends tape recorded jury instructions to the jury for use during deliberations over the objections of both counsel and where such tape recorded instructions have not been preserved intact and where there is no written transcript of the recording, the defendant has been denied his right to appear and defend in person and prejudicial error will be found. State v Guice, No. 83AP–883 (10th Dist Ct App, Franklin, 6–28–84).

2. Presence of defendant required

Defendant must be present at every stage of a trial including the imposition of sentence. State v. Welch (Ohio 1978) 53 Ohio St.2d 47, 372 N.E.2d 346, 7 O.O.3d 128.

A person charged on affidavit with a misdemeanor under penalty of imprisonment is entitled to be personally present at the trial, and trial and conviction in his absence are reversible error. State v. Walker (Huron 1959) 108 Ohio App. 333, 161 N.E.2d 521, 9 O.O.2d 296. Criminal Law ⚷ 636(1); Criminal Law ⚷ 1166.14

It is reversible error to impanel the jury during the defendant's involuntary absence. State v Miller, No. CA89–01–001 (12th Dist Ct App, Preble, 8–21–89).

It is prejudicial error for a court to give instructions to a jury while it is deliberating outside the presence of the defendant, defendant's counsel, the prosecutor, and the court reporter. Columbus v Bright, No. 83AP–857 (10th Dist Ct App, Franklin, 6–21–84).

3. Voluntary absence of defendant

During a four-day trial, the defendant's late arrival on the second day does not, without more, warrant a finding that defendant was voluntarily absent on the fourth day of trial. State v. Kirkland (Cuyahoga 1984) 18 Ohio App.3d 1, 480 N.E.2d 85, 18 O.B.R. 25.

RC 2945.12 does not prohibit the trial by the court of one accused of a felony where such accused voluntarily absents himself so that he cannot be found. State v. Phillips (Hamilton 1972) 34 Ohio App.2d 217, 299 N.E.2d 286, 63 O.O.2d 397. Criminal Law ⚷ 636(2)

2945.13 Joint trials in felony cases

When two or more persons are jointly indicted for a felony, except a capital offense, they shall be tried jointly unless the court, for good cause shown on application therefor by the prosecuting attorney or one or more of said defendants, orders one or more of said defendants to be tried separately.

(1953 H 1, eff. 10–1–53; GC 13442–11)

Historical and Statutory Notes

Pre–1953 H 1 Amendments: 113 v 181, Ch 21, § 11

Cross References

Complicity, aiders and abettors, 2923.03
Joinder of offenses and defendants, Crim R 8
Relief from prejudicial joinder, Crim R 14
Trial together of multiple charges, Crim R 13

Library References

Criminal Law ⚷622.
Westlaw Topic No. 110.

C.J.S. Criminal Law §§ 562 to 564.

Research References

Encyclopedias

OH Jur. 3d Criminal Law § 2389, Relief from Prejudicial Joinder of Defendants—Joint or Separate Trials in Felony Cases; Noncapital Cases.

Treatises and Practice Aids

Katz, Giannelli, Blair and Lipton, Baldwin's Ohio Practice, Criminal Law, § 57:4, Consolidation of Indictments and Complaints—Criminal Rule 13.

Katz, Giannelli, Blair and Lipton, Baldwin's Ohio Practice, Criminal Law, § 58:3, Multiple Indictments and Complaints—Criminal Rule 13.

Katz, Giannelli, Blair and Lipton, Baldwin's Ohio Practice, Criminal Law, § 58:4, Severance—Criminal Rule 14.

Katz, Giannelli, Blair and Lipton, Baldwin's Ohio Practice, Criminal Law, § 58:9, Codefendant's Confession (Bruton Rule).

Notes of Decisions

1. Constitutional issues

That the same appointed attorney took part in defending two capital defendants tried separately, and at the trial of each one endeavored to emphasize the blameworthiness of the other, is not a circumstance showing ineffective assistance of counsel or a conflict of interest. Burger v. Kemp (U.S.Ga. 1987) 107 S.Ct. 3114, 483 U.S. 776, 97 L.Ed.2d 638, rehearing denied 108 S.Ct. 32, 483 U.S. 1056, 97 L.Ed.2d 820.

Former GC 13677 (Repealed) held constitutional. Beazell v. Ohio (U.S.Ohio 1925) 46 S.Ct. 68, 269 U.S. 167, 70 L.Ed. 216.

2. Joinder—In general

Evidence adduced at trial demonstrated that defendant and his codefendants participated in the same series of acts, or in the same course of criminal conduct, constituting the charged offense of felony murder, warranting joinder, or joint prosecution, of defendant and codefendants in single trial; evidence showed that each of the three accused participated in jumping and stomping on the victim while he lay motionless on the ground, and medical experts testified that cumulative effect of blows resulted in injuries that ultimately led to victim's death. State v. Jacocks (Ohio App. 5 Dist., Stark, 12-15-2003) No. 2002CA00359, 2003-Ohio-6839, 2003 WL 22956845, Unreported, appeal not allowed 102 Ohio St.3d 1445, 808 N.E.2d 397, 2004-Ohio-2263. Criminal Law ⚷ 622.7(2); Indictment And Information ⚷ 124(4)

A defendant asserting that joinder is improper must make an affirmative showing that his rights will be prejudiced. State v. Thompson (Ohio App. 8 Dist., 05-04-1998) 127 Ohio App.3d 511, 713 N.E.2d 456, appeal not allowed 83 Ohio St.3d 1451, 700 N.E.2d 334. Criminal Law ⚷ 622.7(3)

Where purported confession of codefendant varied only in inconsequential details from other defendants' testimony, and only attempted to recite the movements and conduct of the three defendants up to the time just preceding the alleged rape, trial court's refusal to permit separate trials was not an abuse of discretion. State v. Weil (Cuyahoga 1950) 91 N.E.2d 277, 56 Ohio Law Abs. 136, appeal dismissed 153 Ohio St. 586, 92 N.E.2d 816, 42 O.O. 46. Criminal Law ⚷ 622.7(9)

Two or more persons, jointly indicted for noncapital felony, must be tried jointly, where application for separate trials is made, but good cause therefor is not presented. State v. Fox (Ohio 1938) 133 Ohio St. 154, 12 N.E.2d 413, 10 O.O. 218.

Because an attorney appointed to represent codefendants at trial is in the best position to recognize the risk of conflict of interest, has the responsibility to advise the court of such conflict as soon as it arises, and when so advising the court, his declaration is "virtually under oath," when said attorney makes a timely motion for separate counsel, the motion should generally be granted. Holloway v. Arkansas (U.S.Ark. 1978) 98 S.Ct. 1173, 435 U.S. 475, 55 L.Ed.2d 426.

In a case involving eighty-four counts of criminal activity and three defendants, the denial of a motion for separate trials is not erroneous when the record reflects that confrontation rights are not denied and the jury is able to segregate the evidence. State v Smith, No. 9168 (2d Dist Ct App, Montgomery, 6–5–87).

3. —— Grounds for severance, joinder

Where a defendant was tried jointly with others charged with misdemeanors on individual affidavits, and the jury encounters difficulty in determining which part of the evidence applies to the charges against the defendant, the court committed prejudicial error in refusing him a separate trial. City of Cincinnati v. Reichman (Hamilton 1971) 27 Ohio App.2d 125, 272 N.E.2d 904, 56 O.O.2d 287.

The contemplation of calling a co-defendant to testify without showing any cause to do so, or manner in which such testimony might be beneficial, is not ground for severance, especially where any prejudice resulting from a joint trial is merely speculative. State v. Perod (Ashtabula 1968) 15 Ohio App.2d 115, 239 N.E.2d 100, 44 O.O.2d 249. Criminal Law ⚷ 622.7(10)

4. —— Burden of showing cause, joinder

Denial of defendant's motion, in prosecution for burglary, rape, and other offenses, to sever his trial from those of two codefendants on grounds of antagonistic defenses was not abuse of discretion; defendant failed to demonstrate that codefendants would have provided testimony favorable to his alibi defense, jury chose to believe one victim's testimony identifying defendant as one of the gunmen who broke into house and as the person who raped her, and court gave proper instructions relating to guilt determinations at a trial of multiple defendants. State v. Thompson (Ohio App. 8 Dist., 05-04-1998) 127 Ohio App.3d 511, 713 N.E.2d 456, appeal not allowed 83 Ohio St.3d 1451, 700 N.E.2d 334. Criminal Law ⚷ 622.7(6)

Upon a request by a defendant in a criminal case for a separate trial, the burden of establishing good cause is upon the defendant, and the granting or denial of such separate trial rests within the sound discretion of the trial court. State v. Dingus (Pike 1970) 26 Ohio App.2d 131, 269 N.E.2d 923, 55 O.O.2d 280, affirmed 26 Ohio St.2d 141, 269 N.E.2d 923, 55 O.O.2d 274.

Where two or more persons are jointly indicted for a felony, except a capital offense, the burden is upon the applicant seeking a separate trial to show good cause why a separate trial should be granted. State v. Perod (Ashtabula 1968) 15 Ohio App.2d 115, 239 N.E.2d 100, 44 O.O.2d 249. Criminal Law ⚷ 622.8(4)

Two jointly indicted persons shall be tried together unless the prosecutor or one of the defendants applies for separate trials and shows good cause; the burden of establishing good cause is on the defendant requesting a separate trial and the granting or denial of such separate trial request rests within the sound discretion of the trial court. State v. Fannin (Ohio App. 8 Dist., Cuyahoga, 08-15-2002) No. 80014, 2002-Ohio-4180, 2002 WL 1878860, Unreported, appeal not allowed 98 Ohio St.3d 1412, 781 N.E.2d 1020, 2003-Ohio-60. Criminal Law ⚷ 622.6(3)

5. Discretion of court

The facts of each particular case determine whether the court abused its discretion in not granting a separate trial on motion of a co-defendant; abuse of discretion in refusing a separate trial must affirmatively appear from the record, and a reviewing court will not conjecture abuse of discretion. State v. Perod (Ashtabula 1968) 15 Ohio App.2d 115, 239 N.E.2d 100, 44 O.O.2d 249. Criminal Law ⚷ 622.6(3)

Trial court not guilty of abuse of discretion in denying defendants separate trials where no mention of separate trials was made until after joint trial had been in progress two days and eight witnesses had testified and where request for separate trials was made after the state called a certain witness to whose testimony prosecuting attorney called attention in his opening statement, and where furthermore, the state withdrew such witness after the request for separate trials, and before his testimony. State v. Jones (Ohio 1945) 145 Ohio St. 136, 60 N.E.2d 654, 30 O.O. 337, certiorari denied 66 S.Ct. 469, 326 U.S. 787, 90 L.Ed. 477.

It is not an abuse of discretion for a court to deny a motion for separate trials where the "spillover" effect of evidence against one defendant is minimal and mitigated by cautionary instructions to the jury. State v Brooks, No. 9190 (2d Dist Ct App, Montgomery, 6–4–87).

2945.14 Mistake in charging offense

If it appears during the trial and before submission to the jury or court, that a mistake has been made in charging the proper offense in the indictment or information, the court may order a discontinuance of trial without prejudice to the prosecution. The accused, if there is good cause to detain him, may be recognized to appear at the same or next succeeding term of court, or in default thereof committed to jail. In such case the court shall recognize the witnesses for the state to appear at the same time and testify.

(1953 H 1, eff. 10–1–53; GC 13442–12)

Historical and Statutory Notes

Pre–1953 H 1 Amendments: 113 v 181, Ch 21, § 12

Cross References

Amendment of indictment, information or complaint, Crim R 7(D)

Minor error in indictment, information, or complaint not grounds for new trial, Crim R 33

Pleadings and motions before trial, defenses and objections, Crim R 12

Library References

Criminal Law ⚷303.5.

Westlaw Topic No. 110.

C.J.S. Criminal Law §§ 419 to 424.

Research References

Encyclopedias

OH Jur. 3d Criminal Law § 764, for Mistake in Charging Proper Offense.

OH Jur. 3d Criminal Law § 2189, Trial Discontinued Because of Charging Error.

OH Jur. 3d Criminal Law § 2200, Recognizance of Witness Upon Discontinuance of Trial.

Treatises and Practice Aids

Markus, Trial Handbook for Ohio Lawyers, § 3:7, Involuntary Dismissal.

Notes of Decisions

Lesser included offenses 1

---

1. Lesser included offenses

Where in a prosecution for first degree murder it was discovered after submission of some evidence but before submission of the matter to the jury that the indictment was so defective as to fail to charge first or second degree murder, but that it did charge manslaughter, the defendant has been placed in jeopardy and may not thereafter be tried for murder. State v. McGraw (Ohio Com.Pl. 1961) 177 N.E.2d 697, 86 Ohio Law Abs. 490, 19 O.O.2d 174.

2945.15 Discharge of defendant

When two or more persons are tried jointly, before any of the accused has gone into his defense the trial court may direct one or more of such accused to be discharged that he may be a witness for the state.

An accused person, when there is not sufficient evidence to put him upon his defense, may be discharged by the court, but if not so discharged, shall be entitled to the immediate verdict of the jury in his favor. Such order of discharge, in either case, is a bar to another prosecution for the same offense.

(1953 H 1, eff. 10–1–53; GC 13442–13)

Historical and Statutory Notes

Pre–1953 H 1 Amendments: 113 v 181, Ch 21, § 13

Cross References

Dismissal, Crim R 48

Granting immunity to witness, 2945.44

Motion for acquittal, Crim R 29

Procedure same where two indictments, informations, or complaints tried together, Crim R 13

Library References

Criminal Law ⟹753.2.

Witnesses ⟹304.

Westlaw Topic Nos. 110, 410.

C.J.S. Criminal Law § 1276.

C.J.S. Witnesses §§ 534 to 535, 555 to 558.

Research References

Encyclopedias

OH Jur. 3d Criminal Law § 763, Dismissal for Insufficient Evidence or to Become State's Witness.

OH Jur. 3d Criminal Law § 2825, Discharge to Become Witness for State.

OH Jur. 3d Criminal Law § 3121, Accomplices, Co-Conspirators, and Codefendants.

Treatises and Practice Aids

Markus, Trial Handbook for Ohio Lawyers, § 13:13, Accomplice.

Katz, Giannelli, Blair and Lipton, Baldwin's Ohio Practice, Criminal Law, § 57:4, Consolidation of Indictments and Complaints—Criminal Rule 13.

Katz, Giannelli, Blair and Lipton, Baldwin's Ohio Practice, Criminal Law, § 58:3, Multiple Indictments and Complaints—Criminal Rule 13.

Katz, Giannelli, Blair and Lipton, Baldwin's Ohio Practice, Criminal Law, § 86:6, Motion for Judgment of Acquittal.

Notes of Decisions

1. Motion for acquittal

Judgment of acquittal, untimely postverdict motions, inherent authority of courts. Carlisle v. U.S. (U.S.Mich., 04-29-1996) 116 S.Ct. 1460, 517 U.S. 416, 134 L.Ed.2d 613.

2945.16 View of the premises

When it is proper for the jurors to have a view of the place at which a material fact occurred, the trial court may order them to be conducted in a body, under the charge of the sheriff or other officer, to such place, which shall be shown to them by a person designated by the court. While the jurors are absent on such view no person other than such officer and such person so appointed, shall speak to them on any subject connected with the trial. The accused has the right to attend such view by the jury, but may waive this right.

The expense of such view as approved by the court shall be taxed as other costs in the case.

(129 v 1201, eff. 9–11–61; 1953 H 1; GC 13442–14)

Historical and Statutory Notes

Pre–1953 H 1 Amendments: 113 v 182, Ch 21, § 14

Cross References

Presence of defendant, Crim R 43

Library References

Criminal Law ⚬651.
Westlaw Topic No. 110.
C.J.S. Criminal Law § 1156.

Research References

Encyclopedias

OH Jur. 3d Criminal Law § 390, Viewing Crime Scene by Jury.

OH Jur. 3d Criminal Law § 2671, Premises Subject to View.

OH Jur. 3d Criminal Law § 3968, Items and Amounts Taxable, Generally.

OH Jur. 3d Evidence & Witnesses § 8, View by Jury.

Treatises and Practice Aids

Markus, Trial Handbook for Ohio Lawyers, § 23:1, Right to View Premises.

Markus, Trial Handbook for Ohio Lawyers, § 23:3, Conduct.

Katz, Giannelli, Blair and Lipton, Baldwin's Ohio Practice, Criminal Law, § 67:3, Proceedings Covered.

Katz, Giannelli, Blair and Lipton, Baldwin's Ohio Practice, Criminal Law, § 148:24, Motion for Jury to View Scene.

Katz, Giannelli, Blair and Lipton, Baldwin's Ohio Practice, Criminal Law, § 148:25, Entry Ordering Jury to View Scene.

Giannelli and Snyder, Baldwin's Ohio Practice, Evidence, § 901.21, Jury Views.

1 Giannelli and Snyder, Baldwin's Ohio Practice, Evidence, Index, Index.

Hennenberg & Reinhart, Ohio Criminal Defense Motions F 2.46, Motion to View the Scene-Discovery Demands and Motions.

Notes of Decisions

1. Discretion of court

Trial court did not abuse its discretion by limiting evidence to time period set forth in the city ordinance citation, or in denying defendant's motion to allow jury to view property in trial regarding defendant's construction of a driveway without a permit in violation of ordinance; what happened to property after the citation was issued was not relevant, and the evidence included photographs of the property that aptly illustrated the condition of the property during the time of the citation. Mayfield Hts. v. Barry (Ohio App. 8 Dist., Cuyahoga, 08-21-2003)

No. 82159, 2003-Ohio-4403, 2003 WL 21982909, Unreported, appeal not allowed 100 Ohio St.3d 1546, 800 N.E.2d 752, 2003-Ohio-6879. Criminal Law ⚷ 651(1); Zoning And Planning ⚷ 804

Denial in capital murder prosecution of defense request for jury view of cell in correctional facility where charged killing occurred, to demonstrate how difficult it would have been for defendant to intentionally stab cellmate in the eye, was not abuse of discretion; trial court noted inherent problems of security and possible prejudice to case via other inmates and determined that dimensions and all aspects of cell could be fully presented to jury with aid of diagrams and photographs, and defendant failed to present any diagrams of cell during trial. State v. Hanna (Ohio, 05-22-2002) 95 Ohio St.3d 285, 767 N.E.2d 678, 2002-Ohio-2221, reconsideration denied 96 Ohio St.3d 1441, 770 N.E.2d 1050, 2002-Ohio-3344, certiorari denied 123 S.Ct. 554, 537 U.S. 1036, 154 L.Ed.2d 455. Criminal Law ⚷ 651(1)

Denial of defense request that jury be brought to prison to view the scene of the riot during which corrections officer was killed did not significantly undermine fundamental elements of defendant's defense in capital murder prosecution and, thus, was not an abuse of discretion. State v. Sanders (Ohio, 07-18-2001) 92 Ohio St.3d 245, 750 N.E.2d 90, 2001-Ohio-189, reconsideration denied 93 Ohio St.3d 1434, 755 N.E.2d 356, stay granted 93 Ohio St.3d 1437, 755 N.E.2d 900, stay revoked 98 Ohio St.3d 1453, 783 N.E.2d 514, 2003-Ohio-651, certiorari denied 122 S.Ct. 1795, 535 U.S. 1036, 152 L.Ed.2d 653, stay granted 98 Ohio St.3d 1506, 786 N.E.2d 57, 2003-Ohio-1573. Criminal Law ⚷ 651(1)

Trial court may permit more than one jury view of crime scene. State v. Hopfer (Ohio App. 2 Dist., 07-12-1996) 112 Ohio App.3d 521, 679 N.E.2d 321, dismissed, appeal not allowed 77 Ohio St.3d 1488, 673 N.E.2d 146, reconsideration denied 77 Ohio St.3d 1550, 674 N.E.2d 1187. Criminal Law ⚷ 651(1)

Jury view of crime scene is not considered evidence, nor is it crucial step in criminal proceedings. State v. Hopfer (Ohio App. 2 Dist., 07-12-1996) 112 Ohio App.3d 521, 679 N.E.2d 321, dismissed, appeal not allowed 77 Ohio St.3d 1488, 673 N.E.2d 146, reconsideration denied 77 Ohio St.3d 1550, 674 N.E.2d 1187. Criminal Law ⚷ 651(1)

Trial court has broad discretion in determining whether to authorize jury view of crime scene. State v. Hopfer (Ohio App. 2 Dist., 07-12-1996) 112 Ohio App.3d 521, 679 N.E.2d 321, dismissed, appeal not allowed 77 Ohio St.3d 1488, 673 N.E.2d 146, reconsideration denied 77 Ohio St.3d 1550, 674 N.E.2d 1187. Criminal Law ⚷ 651(1)

Trial court did not abuse its discretion by allowing jury view of defendant's house but forgoing jury view of defendant's bedroom pending further testimony, in prosecution of defendant for murdering her newborn baby and grossly abusing its corpse, where defendant's testimony that she spent part of day of baby's birth lying on her bed and running to bathroom across hall was, at best, ancillary to material facts of case, alleged prejudice against defendant due to mistrust of jury toward her counsel for hiding something from their view was based solely upon speculation and not upon any discernible fact in record, and no aspect of defense depended on anything physically present in bedroom. State v. Hopfer (Ohio App. 2 Dist., 07-12-1996) 112 Ohio App.3d 521, 679 N.E.2d 321, dismissed, appeal not allowed 77 Ohio St.3d 1488, 673 N.E.2d 146, reconsideration denied 77 Ohio St.3d 1550, 674 N.E.2d 1187. Criminal Law ⚷ 651(1)

Trial court did not abuse its discretion in denying defendant's motion to allow jury to view temple prior to sentencing phase in prosecution of defendant, a cult leader, for kidnapping and murder of five of his followers; neither offense nor any material fact occurred at temple and, moreover, jury drove by temple and defendant used temple drawings to illustrate his unsworn statement in which he denied ever planning to take over temple. State v. Lundgren (Ohio, 08-30-1995) 73 Ohio St.3d 474, 653 N.E.2d 304, 1995-Ohio-227, reconsideration denied 74 Ohio St.3d 1422, 655 N.E.2d 742, certiorari denied 116 S.Ct. 1276, 516 U.S. 1178, 134 L.Ed.2d 222, dismissal of post-conviction relief affirmed 1998 WL 964592, dismissed, appeal not allowed 85 Ohio St.3d 1465, 709 N.E.2d 171. Sentencing And Punishment ⚷ 316

Any irregularity in trial court instructing jury, when defendant was absent, prior to jury visit to crime scene was harmless; parties had prior full knowledge about the jury view and court's intention to briefly instruct jury before view and trial court's innocuous comments involved procedures during view and not substantive matters. State v. Hill (Ohio, 08-30-1995) 73 Ohio St.3d 433, 653 N.E.2d 271, 1995-Ohio-287, reconsideration denied 74 Ohio St.3d 1423, 655 N.E.2d 742, certiorari denied 116 S.Ct. 788, 516 U.S. 1079, 133 L.Ed.2d 738, denial of habeas corpus affirmed 400 F.3d 308, rehearing and rehearing en banc denied 140 Fed. Appx. 597, 2005 WL 1683256, petition for certiorari filed 2005 WL 2333459. Criminal Law ⚷ 1166.14

In an action for theft against a building contractor who abandons a construction project after receiving payment, it is within the court's discretion to deny the defendant's motion to view the work sites in question since the premises have been repaired and remodeled since the defendant abandoned them. State v. Karns (Hamilton 1992) 80 Ohio App.3d 199, 608 N.E.2d 1145.

The allowance of a "jury view" is within the discretion of the trial court and will not be disturbed on appeal unless an abuse of discretion is established. State v. Montalvo (Mahoning 1974) 47 Ohio App.2d 296, 353 N.E.2d 855, 1 O.O.3d 357. Criminal Law ⚷ 651(1); Criminal Law ⚷ 1152(1)

Judge's statement, "I went out to the scene. I sat at Kenston. I watched different cars go by. There is no way that the facts could have transpired the way [defendant] testified. There is no way they could have driven partially down the driveway because the driveway isn't that wide," indicated that judge, as trier of fact, violated prohibition against using jury view as an opportunity to insert additional evidence in defendant's trial for criminal damaging, aggravated menacing, and menacing. State v. Eckard (Ohio App. 11 Dist., Geauga, 06-21-2002) No. 2001-G-2336, 2002-Ohio-3127, 2002 WL 1357788, Unreported. Criminal Law ⚿ 254.1

2. Premises subject to view

Statute permitting jury to view place at which material fact in case occurred does not limit jury viewings to scene where crime itself occurred; any number of material facts may occur in variety of places, and it would not violate statute to allow jury to view all such places. State v. Nobles (Ohio App. 2 Dist., 09-01-1995) 106 Ohio App.3d 246, 665 N.E.2d 1137, dismissed, appeal not allowed 74 Ohio St.3d 1510, 659 N.E.2d 1287. Criminal Law ⚿ 651(1)

Trial court properly allowed jury in trial for murder and gross abuse of corpse to view incinerator in which murder victim's body was burned; viewing incinerator assisted jury in understanding trial testimony relating fate of contents of dumpster where defendant confessed she had disposed of victim's body and explained why victim's body had never been recovered, jury was instructed that what it viewed outside courtroom was not evidence and that only purpose of visit was to help jurors understand evidence presented in courtroom, and court personally viewed premises before jury was taken there and found that sight was not unduly prejudicial and that jury would not understand testimony without it. State v. Nobles (Ohio App. 2 Dist., 09-01-1995) 106 Ohio App.3d 246, 665 N.E.2d 1137, dismissed, appeal not allowed 74 Ohio St.3d 1510, 659 N.E.2d 1287. Criminal Law ⚿ 651(1); Criminal Law ⚿ 651(2)

RC 2945.16 does not limit the viewing by jurors of the place where the crime for which the trial is being held occurred; and the trial court may, over objection by the defendant, in the exercise of sound discretion after it has been fully informed of the nature of the evidence to be offered and proper safeguards are taken to protect the rights of the defendant, permit the jurors to view premises where similar acts are alleged to have been committed by the defendant. State v. Pigott (Cuyahoga 1964) 1 Ohio App.2d 22, 197 N.E.2d 911, 94 Ohio Law Abs. 335, 30 O.O.2d 56.

3. Presence of accused

The trial court's adoption of the jail's policy for transporting a defendant to a jury view did not prejudice defendant or deny defendant a fair trial, even though defendant decided not to attend the jury view based on the policies; a jury view was not a critical stage in the proceeding, and defendant failed to suggest any specific prejudice he suffered. State v. Stivender (Ohio App. 2 Dist., Montgomery, 12-13-2002) No. 19094, 2002-Ohio-6864, 2002 WL 31780953, Unreported. Criminal Law ⚿ 636(5)

Trial court's refusal to allow capital murder defendant to be present at jury view of crime scene, defendant's prison cell, did not deprive defendant of due process. State v. Cassano (Ohio, 08-07-2002) 96 Ohio St.3d 94, 772 N.E.2d 81, 2002-Ohio-3751, reconsideration denied 96 Ohio St.3d 1517, 775 N.E.2d 858, 2002-Ohio-4950, certiorari denied 123 S.Ct. 1359, 537 U.S. 1235, 155 L.Ed.2d 201. Constitutional Law ⚿ 268(6); Criminal Law ⚿ 636(5)

Capital murder defendant had statutory right to be present in person during jury view of crime scene, despite expressed concern of court and prison officials with respect to probable duration of the jury view, requirement that prison in which murder had occurred would have been required to be locked down during jury view, and fact that defendant would have been unshackled in his cell during jury view. State v. Cassano (Ohio, 08-07-2002) 96 Ohio St.3d 94, 772 N.E.2d 81, 2002-Ohio-3751, reconsideration denied 96 Ohio St.3d 1517, 775 N.E.2d 858, 2002-Ohio-4950, certiorari denied 123 S.Ct. 1359, 537 U.S. 1235, 155 L.Ed.2d 201. Criminal Law ⚿ 636(5)

Trial court's refusal to allow capital murder defendant to be present at jury view of crime scene, defendant's prison cell, did not materially prejudice defendant, where jury view was neither evidence nor critical stage of proceedings, and court authorized defendant, his counsel, and any agent to view crime scene before trial. State v. Cassano (Ohio, 08-07-2002) 96 Ohio St.3d 94, 772 N.E.2d 81, 2002-Ohio-3751, reconsideration denied 96 Ohio St.3d 1517, 775 N.E.2d 858, 2002-Ohio-4950, certiorari denied 123 S.Ct. 1359, 537 U.S. 1235, 155 L.Ed.2d 201. Criminal Law ⚿ 1166.14

Where, upon such view, counsel for the accused, and the prosecuting attorney, in the presence of the jury, caused measurements to be made, objects to be placed as near as possible in the relative positions they respectively occupied when the alleged crime was committed, and made experiments illustrative of the manner in which it may have been done, the accused, being present, in the company of, and at liberty to communicate freely with, his counsel, indicates no objection to or dissatisfaction with such proceedings, should be deemed to have authorized the same; and a motion made in his behalf, on the return of the jury into court, for its discharge on account of such proceedings, was properly overruled. Jones v. State (Ohio 1894) 51 Ohio St. 331, 32 W.L.B. 241, 38 N.E. 79.

It is not error for the jury to make a view of the place where a felony is claimed to have been committed, under the order of the court and in charge of the sheriff, where the privilege is awarded the accused to accompany the jury, though he may refuse to attend the view. Blythe v. State (Ohio 1890) 47 Ohio St. 234, 23 W.L.B. 352, 24 N.E. 268.

The right of a defendant to be present when a jury views the scene of the crime is fundamental and, absent a waiver of such right, may not be abridged notwithstanding the defendant's incarceration at the time of such viewing. State v DeArmond, No. CA 2282 (2d Dist Ct App, Clark, 5–15–87).

4. Appeal

Abuse of discretion in denying an accused's motion for an order to have the jury view the area where the crime occurred must be raised by appeal and is not cognizable in habeas corpus. Calloway v. Maxwell (Ohio 1965) 2 Ohio St.2d 128, 206 N.E.2d 912, 31 O.O.2d 196. Habeas Corpus ⚷ 294

TRIAL BY JURY

2945.17 Right of trial by jury

(A) At any trial, in any court, for the violation of any statute of this state, or of any ordinance of any municipal corporation, except as provided in divisions (B) and (C) of this section, the accused has the right to be tried by a jury.

(B) The right to be tried by a jury that is granted under division (A) of this section does not apply to a violation of a statute or ordinance that is any of the following:

(1) A violation that is a minor misdemeanor;

(2) A violation for which the potential penalty does not include the possibility of a prison term or jail term and for which the possible fine does not exceed one thousand dollars.

(C) Division (A) of this section does not apply to, and there is no right to a jury trial for, a person who is the subject of a complaint filed under section 2151.27 of the Revised Code against both a child and the parent, guardian, or other person having care of the child.
(2002 H 490, eff. 1–1–04; 2000 S 179, eff. 4–9–01; 1972 H 511, eff. 1–1–74; 1953 H 1; GC 13443)

Historical and Statutory Notes

Pre–1953 H 1 Amendments: 115 v 78

Amendment Note: 2002 H 490 rewrote this section which prior thereto read:

"At any trial, in any court, for the violation of any statute of this state, or of any ordinance of any municipal corporation, except in cases in which the penalty involved does not exceed a fine of one hundred dollars, the accused has the right to be tried by a jury. This section does not apply to, and there is no right to a jury trial for, a person who is the subject of a complaint filed under section 2151.27 of the Revised Code against both a child and the parent, guardian, or other person having care of the child."

Amendment Note: 2000 S 179, § 1, eff. 4–9–01, added the second sentence.

Legislative Service Commission

1973:

This section provides that there is no right to trial by jury when the maximum penalty which may be imposed for the offense charged is no more than a fine of $100. Under former law, the jury limit was a potential penalty of a fine of $50. Since all minor misdemeanors under the new code call for a maximum penalty of a fine of $100, then all such offenses are nonjury matters.

An accused is entitled to a jury if the potential penalty for the offense charged is a fine of more than $100, even if imprisonment isn't imposed, or if the potential penalty includes imprisonment for any length of time no matter how short, even though a fine isn't imposed. It is emphasized that the determining factor is the potential penalty, not the penalty which is actually imposed in a given case.

Cross References

Accused to be informed of, Crim R 5
Effect of plea, accused to be informed of, 2937.02
Jury trial in magistrates court, 2938.04
Right to jury trial, O Const Art I §10
Right to jury trial inviolate, O Const Art I §5
Trial by jury or by the court, waiver of jury, Crim R 23

Library References

Jury ⚷20.
Westlaw Topic No. 230.
C.J.S. Juries §§ 7 to 14, 19 to 20, 138 to 148.

Research References

Encyclopedias

OH Jur. 3d Criminal Law § 432, Nature and Seriousness of Offense as Affecting Right of Accused.

OH Jur. 3d Criminal Law § 1585, Jury and Jury Selection.

OH Jur. 3d Criminal Law § 2609, Computation of Amount of Fine for Jury Trial.

OH Jur. 3d Family Law § 1744, Trial by Jury.

OH Jur. 3d Jury § 36, Other Particular Kinds of Actions and Proceedings.

OH Jur. 3d Schools, Universities, & Colleges § 290, Prosecutions and Criminal Procedure.

OH Jur. 3d Schools, Universities, & Colleges § 291, Prosecutions and Criminal Procedure—Trial and Evidence.

Treatises and Practice Aids

Markus, Trial Handbook for Ohio Lawyers, § 6:2, Selection, Drawing, and Summoning of Jurors.

Markus, Trial Handbook for Ohio Lawyers, § 4:32, Trial by Jury.

Katz, Giannelli, Blair and Lipton, Baldwin's Ohio Practice, Criminal Law, § 62:1, Introduction.

Katz, Giannelli, Blair and Lipton, Baldwin's Ohio Practice, Criminal Law, § 62:3, Ohio Law.

Katz, Giannelli, Blair and Lipton, Baldwin's Ohio Practice, Criminal Law, § 62:5, Contempt Proceedings.

Katz, Giannelli, Blair and Lipton, Baldwin's Ohio Practice, Criminal Law, § 114:4, Indirect Contempt.

Katz, Giannelli, Blair and Lipton, Baldwin's Ohio Practice, Criminal Law, § 148:23, Demand for Jury Trial in Petty Offense Cases.

Law Review and Journal Commentaries

Applicability of the Sixth or Seventh Amendment Right to a Jury Trial in OSHA Penalty Proceedings, Comment. 45 U Cin L Rev 108 (1976).

Nullifying History: Modern–Day Misuse of the Right to Decide the Law, David A. Pepper. 50 Case W Res L Rev 599 (Spring 2000).

The Role of the Jury in Choice of Law, Willis L.M. Reese, Hans Smit and George B. Reese. 25 Case W Res L Rev 82 (Fall 1974).

Notes of Decisions

1. Constitutional issues—In general

The decision of the US Supreme Court in Baldwin v New York, 399 US 66 (1970), holding that "no offense can be deemed "petty" for purposes of the right of trial by jury where imprisonment for more than six months is authorized," insofar as it may be considered applicable to cases of criminal contempt in Ohio courts, should be applied only to those trials commencing on or after the date of that decision, June 22, 1970. State v. Dostal (Ohio 1971) 28 Ohio St.2d 158, 277 N.E.2d 211, 57 O.O.2d 399, certiorari denied 92 S.Ct. 1795, 406 U.S. 931, 32 L.Ed.2d 133. Courts ⚷ 100(1)

The guaranty of a jury trial in criminal cases contained in the state and federal Constitutions is not an absolute and unrestricted right in Ohio with respect to misdemeanors; and a statute, ordinance or authorized rule of court may validly condition the right to a jury trial in such a case on a written demand therefor filed with the court a specified number of days before the date actually set for the trial for the offense charged. City of Mentor v. Giordano (Ohio 1967) 9 Ohio St.2d 140, 224 N.E.2d 343, 38 O.O.2d 366. Jury ⚷ 22(1); Jury ⚷ 25(3)

There is a constitutional right to trial by jury, under O Const Art I, § 5 and O Const Art I, § 10, where imprisonment is a part of the penalty; and the failure to demand a jury does not constitute a waiver thereof. State v. Ferguson (Greene 1955) 100 Ohio App. 191, 135 N.E.2d 884, 60 O.O. 166.

Trial court's placing ceiling on potential penalty, by stating at commencement of menacing trial that it would not sentence defendant to any additional jail time nor would his fine exceed $100, was insufficient to deny defendant his right to a jury trial; charge subjected defendant to a potential penalty of 20 days imprisonment and a fine of $250, such that he had a right to a jury trial. State v. Fisher (Ohio App. 11 Dist., Geauga, 08-02-2002) No. 2001-G-2359, 2002-Ohio-3959, 2002 WL 1803693, Unreported. Jury ⚷ 22(2)

2. —— Burden of proof, constitutional issues

Defendant failed to demonstrate that a jury pool was not assembled on the day of his trial, that this caused the trial to be postponed three days, and that such postponement deprived him of his right to a jury trial; the record did not indicate why the postponement occurred, and the regularity of the trial court proceedings would be presumed. State v. Moore (Ohio App. 7 Dist., Mahoning,

06-17-2004) No. 02CA195, 2004-Ohio-3203, 2004 WL 1376247, Unreported. Jury ⚷ 33(4)

3. —— Fair trial, constitutional issues

Prosecutor's characterization of defendant as having "smirk" on his face asserted opinion about defendant's demeanor which was inappropriate for prosecutor in courtroom, but defendant was not thereby denied right to fair trial, as trial court properly instructed jury to disregard comments. State v. Taniguchi (Ohio App. 10 Dist., 08-30-1994) 96 Ohio App.3d 592, 645 N.E.2d 794. Criminal Law ⚷ 722.3; Criminal Law ⚷ 730(12)

During voir dire examination, the trial court commits reversible error when it refuses the defendant's request to ask the prospective jurors if they could accept the proposition of law that a defendant is presumed to be innocent, has no burden to establish his innocence, and is clothed throughout the trial with this presumption. U. S. v. Blount (C.A.6 (Ohio) 1973) 479 F.2d 650.

4. Duties of court

Trial court is not required to interrogate accused to determine whether accused is fully apprised of his or her right to jury trial. State v. Eley (Ohio, 12-18-1996) 77 Ohio St.3d 174, 672 N.E.2d 640, 1996-Ohio-323, reconsideration denied 77 Ohio St.3d 1549, 674 N.E.2d 1187, certiorari denied 117 S.Ct. 2522, 521 U.S. 1124, 138 L.Ed.2d 1023, dismissal of post-conviction relief affirmed 2001-Ohio-3447, 2001 WL 1497095, appeal not allowed 94 Ohio St.3d 1506, 764 N.E.2d 1036, 2002-Ohio-5738. Jury ⚷ 29(6)

Where a defendant enters a plea of guilty to a crime of sufficient seriousness to warrant a jury trial pursuant to RC 2945.17, compliance with the mandatory requirements of RC 2937.02 will not be presumed from a silent record. City of Fairborn v. Vannicola (Greene 1972) 31 Ohio App.2d 167, 287 N.E.2d 281, 60 O.O.2d 278. Criminal Law ⚷ 1144.4

5. Jury demand—In general

In "serious" offense case, right to jury is automatic, requiring no act by defendant to demand it, and requiring affirmative written document to waive it. State v. Fish (Ohio App. 1 Dist., 05-31-1995) 104 Ohio App.3d 236, 661 N.E.2d 788, dismissed, appeal not allowed 74 Ohio St.3d 1443, 656 N.E.2d 344. Jury ⚷ 22(1); Jury ⚷ 25(3); Jury ⚷ 29(6)

Where charge involved is "petty offense," one with penalty of six months' incarceration or less, defendant must file written jury demand to avoid waiver. State v. Fish (Ohio App. 1 Dist., 05-31-1995) 104 Ohio App.3d 236, 661 N.E.2d 788, dismissed, appeal not allowed 74 Ohio St.3d 1443, 656 N.E.2d 344. Jury ⚷ 25(3)

The filing of a jury request signed only by an attorney in a petty offense case is within the general authority of the attorney to control the procedure for a defendant's defense and is sufficient to require trial by jury. State v. Slack (Scioto 1991) 68 Ohio App.3d 388, 588 N.E.2d 298. Jury ⚷ 25(8)

Where a defendant in a petty offense case has a right to trial by jury and pleads not guilty and demands a jury trial in the manner provided by Crim R 23(A), it must appear of record that such defendant waived this right in writing in the manner provided by RC 2945.05, in order for the trial court to have jurisdiction to try the defendant without a jury. State v. Tate (Ohio 1979) 59 Ohio St.2d 50, 391 N.E.2d 738, 13 O.O.3d 36, certiorari denied 100 S.Ct. 456, 444 U.S. 967, 62 L.Ed.2d 379. Jury ⚷ 29(6)

Where the record on appeal does not reveal a waiver of a jury trial by the defendant, who was convicted of draft evasion after a trial without a jury, the judgment must be reversed and the case remanded for a new trial. U. S. v. Davidson (C.A.6 (Ohio) 1973) 477 F.2d 136.

6. —— Timeliness, jury demand

Defendant's demand for jury trial, which was filed more than ten days prior to trial date set by continuance, was timely in domestic violence prosecution, despite fact that demand was filed after earlier dates which had been set for trial. Garfield Hts. v. Perkins (Ohio App. 8 Dist., 06-13-1994) 95 Ohio App.3d 602, 643 N.E.2d 159, dismissed, appeal not allowed 71 Ohio St.3d 1404, 641 N.E.2d 202. Jury ⚷ 25(6)

It is prejudicial error for court to refuse to allow defendant a jury trial because he failed to file demand for such three days prior to trial, where he filed demand on the day following his receipt of notice of trial date, pursuant to RC 2938.04. City of Cincinnati v. Hill (Hamilton 1971) 29 Ohio App.2d 270, 281 N.E.2d 15, 58 O.O.2d 463. Criminal Law ⚷ 1166.6; Jury ⚷ 25(6)

7. No right to jury

Under RC 2945.17, a defendant is not entitled to a jury trial for a minor misdemeanor speeding charge which has a maximum penalty of a $100 fine. State v Bradley, No. 13606, 1993 WL 125445 (2d Dist Ct App, Montgomery, 4–23–93).

Contempt is not an "offense" within the meaning of the statutory right to a jury trial for every offense if the possible penalty exceeds $100. In re Contemnor Caron (Ohio Com.Pl., 04-27-2000) 110 Ohio Misc.2d 58, 744 N.E.2d 787. Jury ⚷ 24.5

A person accused of a violation of RC 3321.38(A) does not enjoy the right to a jury trial, as the maximum penalty involved is $20. State v. Atwood (Ross 1990) 61 Ohio App.3d 650, 573 N.E.2d 739.

A party charged with a violation of RC 3321.38 is not entitled to a jury trial pursuant to RC 2945.17, as the maximum penalty permitted by RC 3321.99 for a violation of RC 3321.38 is $20 and imprisonment for thirty days. The fact that RC 3321.38(A) permits the court to require a party convicted of violating the statute to post a bond of one hundred dollars to ensure future compliance does not require a jury trial. State v. Levy (Cuyahoga 1988) 55 Ohio App.3d 219, 563 N.E.2d 358.

The right of a defendant to a jury trial is extinguished, and the trial court does not err in failing to secure a written waiver of trial by jury where (1) the accused is charged with two offenses, only one of which carries a right to jury trial; and (2) the charge carrying the jury trial right is nolled after the accused has requested a jury trial. State v. Coyle (Wayne 1984) 14 Ohio App.3d 185, 470 N.E.2d 457, 14 O.B.R. 203.

The right to a jury trial provided for in RC 2945.17 does not extend to the accused in those cases in which the maximum potential penalty involved does not exceed a fine of $50, even though the fine and costs together exceed $50. City of Hilliard v. Miller (Franklin 1972) 31 Ohio App.2d 163, 287 N.E.2d 103, 60 O.O.2d 248. Jury ⚷ 22(1)

In order to subject an accused charged with engaging in common labor on Sunday to imprisonment it is necessary that the affidavit charging such offense aver that the offense charged is a second or subsequent offense, so that a defendant is not entitled to a jury trial under an affidavit which charges merely that the defendant "did unlawfully engage in common labor... on Sunday... contrary to RC 3773.24." State v. Dimacchia (Clark 1962) 116 Ohio App. 319, 188 N.E.2d 69, 22 O.O.2d 153.

In a consolidated trial of two related charges, for only one of which there is a right to a jury trial, the judge may decide that charge himself, and commit only the other charge to the jury for decision. Columbus v Skaggs, No. 84AP–485 (10th Dist Ct App, Franklin, 10–17–85).

When a jury is unable to reach a verdict and is discharged, and the complaint against the defendant is amended to reduce the charge to a minor misdemeanor, the defendant has no right to a jury trial. State v Turner, No. 539 (4th Dist Ct App, Highland, 12–20–84).

8. Waiver of jury—In general

Defendant's jury demand did not act to toll statutory time limit with respect to her misdemeanor prosecution for driving under the influence (DUI), where filing of such request did not require trial court to make a ruling. State v. Delarosa (Ohio App. 11 Dist., Portage, 06-30-2005) No. 2003-P-0129, 2005-Ohio-3399, 2005 WL 1538264, Unreported. Criminal Law ⚷ 577.10(10)

Defendants waived right to jury trial on misdemeanor assault charges, which amounted to petty offenses, by failing to file written demand for jury trial; motion for continuance that made reference to "jury trial" could not reasonably be construed as written demands for jury trial. State v. Singh (Ohio App. 12 Dist., Butler, 08-02-2004) No. CA2003-02-055, No. CA2003-02-056, 2004-Ohio-3995, 2004 WL 1717663, Unreported. Jury ⚷ 25(8)

Defendant did not waive his right to jury trial after filing timely jury demand when he entered plea of no contest, where no written jury waiver, signed by defendant, was made part of record. State v. Fish (Ohio App. 1 Dist., 05-31-1995) 104 Ohio App.3d 236, 661 N.E.2d 788, dismissed, appeal not allowed 74 Ohio St.3d 1443, 656 N.E.2d 344. Jury ⚷ 29(4)

9. —— Mayor's court, waiver of jury

A mayor of a village presiding over a mayor's court may sentence a person to imprisonment for violation of a village ordinance if such person in writing waives a jury and consents to be tried by the mayor as magistrate. OAG 69–117.

2945.171 Verdict in writing

In all criminal cases the verdict of the jury shall be in writing and signed by each of the jurors concurring therein.

(129 v 336, eff. 9–28–61)

Cross References

Verdict, Crim R 31

Library References

Criminal Law ⚷870 to 875.

Westlaw Topic No. 110.

C.J.S. Criminal Law §§ 1395, 1399 to 1403.

Research References

Encyclopedias

OH Jur. 3d Criminal Law § 434, Right to Jury of 12; Necessity of Unanimity in Verdict.

Treatises and Practice Aids

Markus, Trial Handbook for Ohio Lawyers, § 37:9, Returning Verdict.

Katz, Giannelli, Blair and Lipton, Baldwin's Ohio Practice, Criminal Law, § 65:6, Return of Verdict.

Katz, Giannelli, Blair and Lipton, Baldwin's Ohio Practice, Criminal Law, § 148:32, Jury Verdict.

Katz, Giannelli, Blair and Lipton, Baldwin's Ohio Practice, Criminal Law, § 148:33, Verdict of Guilty and Finding of Value of Property.

Katz, Giannelli, Blair and Lipton, Baldwin's Ohio Practice, Criminal Law, § 148:34, Verdict of Guilty on One Count.

Katz, Giannelli, Blair and Lipton, Baldwin's Ohio Practice, Criminal Law, § 148:35, Verdict of

Guilty of Inferior Degree or of Lesser Included Offense.

Katz, Giannelli, Blair and Lipton, Baldwin's Ohio Practice, Criminal Law, § 148:36, Verdict of Guilty of Attempt.

Katz, Giannelli, Blair and Lipton, Baldwin's Ohio Practice, Criminal Law, § 148:37, Verdict of Not Guilty by Reason of Insanity.

Notes of Decisions

1. In general

The requirement imposed under Crim R 31(A) and RC 2945.171 that a jury verdict in a criminal case be in writing is procedural rather than substantive. State v. Carmack (Hamilton 1989) 61 Ohio App.3d 351, 572 N.E.2d 794, dismissed 44 Ohio St.3d 703, 541 N.E.2d 622. Criminal Law ⚷ 1040

2. Verdict form

When trial court submits verdict form containing statutory description of offense, it commits reversible error if the description omits essential elements of that offense. State v. Lampkin (Ohio App. 6 Dist., 12-20-1996) 116 Ohio App.3d 771, 689 N.E.2d 106. Criminal Law ⚷ 798.5; Criminal Law ⚷ 1172.1(3)

Trial court committed plain error when it submitted verdict form containing statutory description of offense of aggravated assault but omitted that offense's essential elements of "knowingly" and "using deadly force" from form. State v. Lampkin (Ohio App. 6 Dist., 12-20-1996) 116 Ohio App.3d 771, 689 N.E.2d 106. Criminal Law ⚷ 1038.1(4)

Because trial court's inclusion of statutory definition of offense on jury verdict form invites confusion and error, Court of Appeals highly disapproves of such practice. State v. Lampkin (Ohio App. 6 Dist., 12-20-1996) 116 Ohio App.3d 771, 689 N.E.2d 106. Criminal Law ⚷ 798.5

Use of a civil verdict form in a criminal proceeding, by means of which the jury returns a verdict finding "in favor of the plaintiff," is not prejudicial to the defendant. City of Lorain v. Lozano (Lorain 1985) 21 Ohio App.3d 173, 486 N.E.2d 1244, 21 O.B.R. 184.

Where a jury is properly instructed on a charge of aggravated burglary but returns a verdict of guilty of burglary because the wrong verdict form was furnished, the trial judge errs by amending the verdict to a finding of guilty of aggravated burglary. State v. English (Hamilton 1985) 21 Ohio App.3d 130, 486 N.E.2d 1212, 21 O.B.R. 138.

3. Poll of jury

A jury verdict in a criminal case is required to be unanimous and in writing; however, if either the prosecutor or defendant calls for a poll of the jury, the trial court may not accept the verdict unless the verdict reflected in the written verdict form is confirmed in open court. State v. Carmack (Hamilton 1989) 61 Ohio App.3d 351, 572 N.E.2d 794, dismissed 44 Ohio St.3d 703, 541 N.E.2d 622. Criminal Law ⚷ 872.5; Criminal Law ⚷ 874; Criminal Law ⚷ 875(1)

Where a jury verdict is signed by only eleven jurors and a poll is requested by the defendant and the defense offers no objection to the verdict form, the deficiency in the form does not constitute plain error. State v. Carmack (Hamilton 1989) 61 Ohio App.3d 351, 572 N.E.2d 794, dismissed 44 Ohio St.3d 703, 541 N.E.2d 622.

2945.18 and 2945.19 Drawing jury in capital cases; obtaining a panel; procedures; conditions—Repealed

(1993 H 41, eff. 9–27–93; 1981 S 1)

Uncodified Law

1993 H 41, § 3, eff. 9–27–93, provides that the provisions of that act, eliminating the special venire in capital cases, apply to any case that is filed on or after the effective date of that act and in which the defendant is charged with the commission of a capital offense, regardless of when the alleged capital offense occurred.

Historical and Statutory Notes

Ed. Note: Former 2945.18 and 2945.19 repealed by 1976 H 133, eff. 6–3–76; 1969 H 424; 131 v S 20; 127 v 847; 1953 H 1; GC 13443–1, 13443–2.

Pre–1953 H 1 Amendments: 113 v 182, Ch 22, § 1, 2

2945.20 Separate trial for capital offense

When two or more persons are jointly indicted for a capital offense, each of such persons shall be tried separately. The court, for good cause shown on application therefor by the prosecuting attorney or one or more of the defendants, may order said defendants to be tried jointly.

(1953 H 1, eff. 10–1–53; GC 13443–3)

Historical and Statutory Notes

Pre–1953 H 1 Amendments: 116 v 301; 113 v 183, Ch 22, § 3

Cross References

Joinder of offenses and defendants, Crim R 8
Relief from prejudicial joinder, Crim R 14
Trial together of multiple charges, Crim R 13
Verdict, where there are several defendants, Crim R 31

Library References

Criminal Law ⚷622.
Westlaw Topic No. 110.
C.J.S. Criminal Law §§ 562 to 564.

Research References

Encyclopedias

OH Jur. 3d Criminal Law § 2390, Relief from Prejudicial Joinder of Defendants—Capital Offenses.

Treatises and Practice Aids

Katz, Giannelli, Blair and Lipton, Baldwin's Ohio Practice, Criminal Law, § 57:4, Consolidation of Indictments and Complaints—Criminal Rule 13.

Katz, Giannelli, Blair and Lipton, Baldwin's Ohio Practice, Criminal Law, § 58:3, Multiple Indictments and Complaints—Criminal Rule 13.

Katz, Giannelli, Blair and Lipton, Baldwin's Ohio Practice, Criminal Law, § 58:4, Severance—Criminal Rule 14.

Katz, Giannelli, Blair and Lipton, Baldwin's Ohio Practice, Criminal Law, § 58:10, Capital Cases.

Notes of Decisions

1. Right to separate trial—In general

A motion for separate trials is required to preserve for appellate review any error in ordering joint trials. State v. Knight (Cuyahoga 1984) 20 Ohio App.3d 289, 485 N.E.2d 1064, 20 O.B.R. 381.

Where two or more persons are jointly indicted for aggravated murder, each of such persons shall be tried separately, unless the trial court orders a joint trial pursuant to the strict mandates set forth in Crim R 14 and RC 2945.20. State v. Henry (Ohio 1983) 4 Ohio St.3d 44, 446 N.E.2d 436, 4 O.B.R. 136, on remand. Criminal Law ⚷ 622.7(1)

Where two or more persons are jointly indicted for a felony, except a capital offense, the burden is upon the applicant seeking a separate trial to show good cause why a separate trial should be granted. State v. Perod (Ashtabula 1968) 15 Ohio App.2d 115, 239 N.E.2d 100, 44 O.O.2d 249. Criminal Law ⚷ 622.8(4)

2. —— Waiver, right to separate trial

A defendant charged with a capital offense may not waive the right to a separate trial provided by RC 2945.20 without the consent of the court, upon a showing of "good cause." State v. Brown (Hamilton 1986) 31 Ohio App.3d 86, 508 N.E.2d 1030, 31 O.B.R. 128.

3. Good cause for joinder

"Good cause" for granting a motion for a joint trial is defined as "some operative factor not present in every case of joint indictments of defendants in capital cases." State v. Brown (Hamilton 1986) 31 Ohio App.3d 86, 508 N.E.2d 1030, 31 O.B.R. 128. Criminal Law ⚷ 622.9

The right to separate trials by one of two or more persons jointly indicted for a capital offense, as granted by RC 2945.20, is a right which may be overcome for good cause shown, the burden of showing the same being upon the state, and such good cause may be shown in any reasonable manner consistent with proof of motions generally, including a showing by the professional statement of counsel; it is not a requirement to submit evidence on the issue of good cause. State v. Fields (Union 1971) 29 Ohio App.2d 154, 279 N.E.2d 616, 58 O.O.2d 212.

4. Discretion of court

The granting or denying of any motion to jointly try defendants in a capital case remains within the sound judgment and discretion of the trial court. State v. Fields (Union 1971) 29 Ohio App.2d 154, 279 N.E.2d 616, 58 O.O.2d 212. Criminal Law ⚷ 622.6(3)

2945.21 Peremptory challenges in capital cases

(A)(1) In criminal cases in which there is only one defendant, each party, in addition to the challenges for cause authorized by law, may peremptorily challenge three of the jurors in misdemeanor cases and four of the jurors in felony cases other than capital cases. If there is more than one defendant, each defendant may peremptorily challenge the same number of jurors as if he were the sole defendant.

(2) Notwithstanding Criminal Rule 24, in capital cases in which there is only one defendant, each party, in addition to the challenges for cause authorized by law, may peremptorily challenge twelve of the jurors. If there is more than one defendant, each defendant may peremptorily challenge the same number of jurors as if he were the sole defendant.

(3) In any case in which there are multiple defendants, the prosecuting attorney may peremptorily challenge a number of jurors equal to the total number of peremptory challenges allowed to all of the defendants.

(B) If any indictments, informations, or complaints are consolidated for trial, the consolidated cases shall be considered, for purposes of exercising peremptory challenges, as though the defendants or offenses had been joined in the same indictment, information, or complaint.

(C) The exercise of peremptory challenges authorized by this section shall be in accordance with the procedures of Criminal Rule 24.

(1981 S 1, eff. 10–19–81; 1953 H 1; GC 13443–4)

Historical and Statutory Notes

Pre–1953 H 1 Amendments: 119 v 594; 113 v 183, Ch 22, § 4

Cross References

Peremptory challenges; number; manner of exercising, Crim R 24

Library References

Jury ⚷33(5.15), 134.

Westlaw Topic No. 230.

C.J.S. Juries §§ 248, 268 to 269, 344, 354 to 355, 367, 421, 423 to 434, 436 to 443, 445 to 446, 450 to 456, 459 to 461.

Research References

Encyclopedias

73 Am. Jur. Proof of Facts 3d 89, Proof of Religion in the Courtroom that Violates the Right to a Fair Trial.

OH Jur. 3d Criminal Law § 2642, Number of Challenges.

OH Jur. 3d Jury § 221, Effect of Error in Granting or Refusing Challenges.

Treatises and Practice Aids

Klein, Darling, & Terez, Baldwin's Ohio Practice Civil Practice § 1:26, Civ. R. 1(C)(1): Upon Appeal to Review Any Judgment, Order, or Ruling--Appeals in Supreme Court--Role of Revised Code Provisions Purporting to Control Application of Civil Rules.

Klein, Darling, & Terez, Baldwin's Ohio Practice Civil Practice § 1:29, Civ. R. 1(C)(1): Upon Appeal to Review Any Judgment, Order, or Ruling--Appeals in Courts of Appeals--Role of Revised Code Provisions Purporting to Control Application of Civil...

Klein, Darling, & Terez, Baldwin's Ohio Practice Civil Practice § 1:32, Civ. R. 1(C)(1): Upon Appeal to Review Any Judgment, Order, or Ruling--Appeals to Common Pleas Courts from Decisions of Governmental Entities--Role of Revised Code Provisions Purporting to...

Katz, Giannelli, Blair and Lipton, Baldwin's Ohio Practice, Criminal Law, § 64:4, Peremptory Challenges.

Hennenberg & Reinhart, Ohio Criminal Defense Motions F 13.27, Motion for Order to Submit Questionnaire to Prospective Jurors-Death Penalty Motions.

Law Review and Journal Commentaries

Deterring the Discriminatory Use of Peremptory Challenges, Comment. 21 Am Crim L Rev 477 (Spring 1984).

A New Peremptory Inclusion to Increase Representativeness and Impartiality in Jury Selection, Note. 45 Case W Res L Rev 251 (Fall 1994).

The Number of Peremptory Challenges Allowed to the state in a Joint Trial of Capital Offense; the Effect of Allowing the State Too Many Peremptory Challenges Upon the Rights of the Defendant, Note. 7 Ohio St L J 80 (December 1940).

The Prosecutor's Exercise of the Peremptory Challenge to Exclude Nonwhite Jurors: A Valued

Common Law Privilege in Conflict with the Equal Protection Clause, Comment. 46 U Cin L Rev 554 (1977).

Prosecutor's Use of Peremptory Challenges to Exclude Racial Minorities from Criminal Juries, Comment. 11 Ohio N U L Rev 767 (1984).

To Waive a Jury?, S. Adele Shank. 1 Crim L J Ohio 1 (July/August 1989).

Notes of Decisions

---

1. Constitutional issues—In general

Exercise of even one peremptory challenge in a purposefully discriminatory manner violates equal protection. State v. Gowdy (Ohio, 04-28-2000) 88 Ohio St.3d 387, 727 N.E.2d 579, 2000-Ohio-355. Constitutional Law ⚷ 250.2(4)

Trial court's finding of no discriminatory intent in using peremptory challenges will not be reversed on appeal absent determination that it was clearly erroneous. State v. Moore (Ohio, 02-04-1998) 81 Ohio St.3d 22, 689 N.E.2d 1, 1998-Ohio-441, dismissal of post-conviction relief affirmed 1998 WL 638353, dismissed, appeal not allowed 84 Ohio St.3d 1472, 704 N.E.2d 579. Criminal Law ⚷ 1158(3)

Prosecutor's use of peremptory challenges to exclude prospective jurors who had expressed reservations about death penalty did not deprive defendant of impartial jury in capital murder prosecution. State v. Dennis (Ohio, 09-24-1997) 79 Ohio St.3d 421, 683 N.E.2d 1096, 1997-Ohio-372, denial of post-conviction relief affirmed 1997 WL 760680, dismissed, appeal not allowed 81 Ohio St.3d 1468, 690 N.E.2d 1287, certiorari denied 118 S.Ct. 1078, 522 U.S. 1128, 140 L.Ed.2d 136, habeas corpus dismissed 68 F.Supp.2d 863, affirmed 354 F.3d 511, certiorari denied 124 S.Ct. 2400, 541 U.S. 1068, 158 L.Ed.2d 971. Jury ⚷ 33(5.15)

Due process did not require that capital defendant be provided more than six peremptory challenges. State v. Garner (Ohio, 11-22-1995) 74 Ohio St.3d 49, 656 N.E.2d 623, 1995-Ohio-168, reconsideration denied 74 Ohio St.3d 1485, 657 N.E.2d 1378, certiorari denied 116 S.Ct. 1444, 517 U.S. 1147, 134 L.Ed.2d 564, rehearing denied 116 S.Ct. 1872, 517 U.S. 1230, 134 L.Ed.2d 969, stay granted 76 Ohio St.3d 1401, 666 N.E.2d 233. Constitutional Law ⚷ 267; Jury ⚷ 136(5)

Court of Appeals may only reverse trial court's decision on *Batson* motion upon finding that trial court's decision was clearly erroneous, that is, so lacking in support of the evidence that to give effect would work that fundamental unfairness which is at war with due process or equal protection; to overturn trial court's finding that there was no discriminatory intent, Court of Appeals must be left with definite and firm conviction that mistake was committed. State v. Belcher (Franklin 1993) 89 Ohio App.3d 24, 623 N.E.2d 583, dismissed, jurisdictional motion overruled 67 Ohio St.3d 1501, 622 N.E.2d 650. Criminal Law ⚷ 1158(3)

The right to peremptorily challenge jurors during voir dire is a substantive right and the numerical limitation imposed by Crim R 24(C) upon the exercise of such right reasonably regulates it. Accordingly, Crim R 24(C) is a rule "governing practice and procedure" under O Const Art IV §5 and RC 2945.21(A)(2), as a law "in conflict with such rule," is "of no further force or effect," pursuant to O Const Art IV §5. State v. Greer (Ohio 1988) 39 Ohio St.3d 236, 530 N.E.2d 382, rehearing denied 40 Ohio St.3d 711, 534 N.E.2d 851, certiorari denied 109 S.Ct. 1766, 490 U.S. 1028, 104 L.Ed.2d 201, stay revoked 75 Ohio St.3d 1444, 663 N.E.2d 326.

The provision by RC 2945.21(A)(2) of twelve peremptory challenges in a capital case, "notwithstanding" the provisions of Crim R 24, is clearly in conflict with the rule, and pursuant to O Const Art IV §5(B), the provisions of Crim R 24(C) take precedence over those of RC 2945.21; as a result, both parties in a capital case are limited to six peremptory challenges. State v. Ruppert (Hancock 1984) 14 Ohio App.3d 74, 470 N.E.2d 239, 14 O.B.R. 86.

Where record in a capital case shows that trial judge gave a general explanation to prospective jurors of their duties under law, asked them if, in view of those duties, they could serve as jurors in the cause, but then restricted them to a total response of "I can" or "I cannot," and prohibited prosecuting attorney and defendant or his counsel from asking them any questions concerning their scruples regarding capital punishment, there has been a failure to establish compliance with requirements of Witherspoon v Illinois, 391 US 510, 88 SCt 1770, 20 LEd(2d) 776 (1968), and execution of death sentence imposed by jury so selected would deprive defendant of his life without due process of law. State v. Anderson (Ohio 1972) 30 Ohio St.2d 66, 282 N.E.2d 568, 59 O.O.2d 85. Constitutional Law ⚷ 267

A prospective juror may be challenged for cause in a capital case where his opinions preclude him from finding the accused guilty of an offense punishable with death. State v. Eaton (Ohio 1969) 19 Ohio St.2d 145, 249 N.E.2d 897, 48 O.O.2d 188, vacated in part 92 S.Ct. 2857, 408 U.S. 935, 33 L.Ed.2d 750.

Criminal defendant is not constitutionally entitled to a jury representative and proportionate of every age group, or ethnic group, or educated, or noneducated, group in the district in which the trial is held, and has no affirmative equal protection right to a jury of a particular racial, gender or age composition. U.S. v. Maxwell (C.A.6 (Ohio), 11-17-1998) 160 F.3d 1071. Constitutional Law ⚷ 221(1); Constitutional Law ⚷ 224(4); Constitutional Law ⚷ 250.2(4); Jury ⚷ 33(1.10); Jury ⚷ 33(1.20)

2. —— Gender discrimination, constitutional issues

The prosecutor's use of peremptory challenges to exclude three women from the jury did not constitute plain error or prejudice defendant; prosecutor provided gender-neutral reasons for challenging the jurors, since first juror knew defendant's sister and recognized several witnesses, second juror stated that the case would be difficult for her because her employer was very busy, and third juror had negative experiences with law enforcement and relied on her husband's opinions and information, and the jury was comprised of eight females and four males, with a male and female alternate. State v. Holder (Ohio App. 11 Dist., Geauga, 12-20-2002) No. 2001-G-2345, No. 2001-G-2350, 2002-Ohio-7124, 2002 WL 31862684, Unreported, appeal not allowed 98 Ohio St.3d 1513, 786 N.E.2d 63, 2003-Ohio-1572, denial of post-conviction relief affirmed 2003-Ohio-5860, 2003 WL 22470862, appeal not allowed 101 Ohio St.3d 1490, 805 N.E.2d 540, 2004-Ohio-1293. Criminal Law ⚷ 1035(5); Criminal Law ⚷ 1166.17

Prosecutors can exercise peremptory challenges for any reason, without inquiry, and without court's control, except that jurors cannot be excluded on basis of race or gender. State v. Reynolds (Ohio, 01-14-1998) 80 Ohio St.3d 670, 687 N.E.2d 1358, 1998-Ohio-171, certiorari denied 118 S.Ct. 2328, 524 U.S. 930, 141 L.Ed.2d 702, denial of post-conviction relief affirmed 1999 WL 980568, dismissed, appeal not allowed 88 Ohio St.3d 1425, 723 N.E.2d 1113. Jury ⚷ 33(5.15)

Striking of one venire member who is member of cognizable racial or gender group without neutral explanation for so doing results in violation of equal protection clause even where neutral explanations are given for striking other members of cognizable racial or gender group. State v. Brock (Ohio App. 3 Dist., 04-26-1996) 110 Ohio App.3d 656, 675 N.E.2d 18, dismissed, appeal not allowed 77 Ohio St.3d 1444, 671 N.E.2d 1283. Constitutional Law ⚷ 221(4); Constitutional Law ⚷ 224(4); Jury ⚷ 33(5.15)

Opponent of peremptory strike who contends that strike was exercised as result of impermissible gender discrimination in violation of equal protection clause must make prima facie showing of intentional gender discrimination before explanation by proponent of strike is required; if opponent makes such a showing, burden shifts to proponent to give nonpretextual explanation for strike, and once proponent tenders gender-neutral explanation, court must decide if opponent has proved purposeful gender discrimination. State v. Brock (Ohio App. 3 Dist., 04-26-1996) 110 Ohio App.3d 656, 675 N.E.2d 18, dismissed, appeal not allowed 77 Ohio St.3d 1444, 671 N.E.2d 1283. Constitutional Law ⚷ 224(4); Jury ⚷ 33(5.15)

Prosecutor failed to establish valid nondiscriminatory reason for use of all seven peremptory strikes against women in capital murder case, and use of strikes violated equal protection clause, where prosecutor stated only that he did not even realize that all of his strikes had been used against women, and that he did not know what to tell court "other than that it was not because of gender that those persons were excused"; mere denial that gender was basis was insufficient to meet prosecutor's burden. State v. Brock (Ohio App. 3 Dist., 04-26-1996) 110 Ohio App.3d 656, 675 N.E.2d 18, dismissed, appeal not allowed 77 Ohio St.3d 1444, 671 N.E.2d 1283. Constitutional Law ⚷ 224(4); Jury ⚷ 33(5.15)

Where prosecutor has been given opportunity to state on record reasons for use of peremptory strikes after prima facie case of intentional discrimination on basis of gender has been established and fails to set forth gender-neutral reasons for use of strikes, defendant is entitled to new trial, but if prosecutor was never given opportunity to defend his use of peremptories, case should be remanded to permit prosecutor to set forth gender-neutral reason, and if prosecutor fails to tender such an explanation, defendant, based on review of all facts and circumstances, should receive new trial. State v. Brock (Ohio App. 3 Dist., 04-26-1996) 110 Ohio App.3d 656, 675 N.E.2d 18, dismissed, appeal not allowed 77 Ohio St.3d 1444, 671 N.E.2d 1283. Criminal Law ⚷ 1166.17; Criminal Law ⚷ 1181.5(3.1)

Failure of prosecutor to provide gender-neutral reason for his exercise of all seven of his peremptory strikes in capital murder case against female jurors after he was given opportunity to do so warranted grant of new trial. State v. Brock (Ohio App. 3 Dist., 04-26-1996) 110 Ohio App.3d 656, 675 N.E.2d 18, dismissed, appeal not allowed 77 Ohio St.3d 1444, 671 N.E.2d 1283. Criminal Law ⚷ 1166.17

3. —— Ineffective assistance of counsel, constitutional issues

Defense counsel did not render ineffective assistance in murder trial by failing to challenge for cause or use peremptory challenge against prospective juror who stated during voir dire that he was worried about losing his job, that he was sponsor for drug and alcohol program at his employment, that his cousin had died as result of cocaine overdose, that his beliefs would prevent him from doing his duty as juror, and that he would have prejudicial attitude towards both sides, where trial court found that there were no grounds to excuse juror for cause, and record did not show reasonable probability that another juror would have decided case differently. State v. Hall (Ohio App. 11 Dist., Lake, 06-18-2004) No. 2001-L-230, 2004-Ohio-3186, 2004 WL 1375752, Unreported, appeal not allowed

103 Ohio St.3d 1494, 816 N.E.2d 1080, 2004-Ohio-5605. Criminal Law ⚷ 641.13(2.1)

Defense counsel did not render ineffective assistance in murder trial by failing to use peremptory challenge against prospective juror who had once been represented by trial judge, where record did not show that juror's relationship with judge caused juror to be biased against defendant. State v. Hall (Ohio App. 11 Dist., Lake, 06-18-2004) No. 2001-L-230, 2004-Ohio-3186, 2004 WL 1375752, Unreported, appeal not allowed 103 Ohio St.3d 1494, 816 N.E.2d 1080, 2004-Ohio-5605. Criminal Law ⚷ 641.13(2.1)

Defense counsel's failure to make a timely challenge to the prosecutor's use of peremptory challenges to remove female venireperson from the jury did not prejudice defendant, and thus could not amount to ineffective assistance; the prosecutor provided race-neutral reasons for all of the challenges, and thus even if counsel had make timely objections the challenges would have been upheld. State v. Holder (Ohio App. 11 Dist., Geauga, 12-20-2002) No. 2001-G-2345, No. 2001-G-2350, 2002-Ohio-7124, 2002 WL 31862684, Unreported, appeal not allowed 98 Ohio St.3d 1513, 786 N.E.2d 63, 2003-Ohio-1572, denial of post-conviction relief affirmed 2003-Ohio-5860, 2003 WL 22470862, appeal not allowed 101 Ohio St.3d 1490, 805 N.E.2d 540, 2004-Ohio-1293. Criminal Law ⚷ 641.13(2.1)

For purposes of ineffective assistance claim, trial counsel's decision in capital case to use peremptory challenge, rather than raise for-cause challenge, to remove prospective juror who said he was biased against defense to some degree but would decide case only on the evidence and would accord defendant the usual presumption of innocence was tactical decision that fell well within range of professionally reasonably judgments. State v. Jones (Ohio, 04-18-2001) 91 Ohio St.3d 335, 744 N.E.2d 1163, 2001-Ohio-57, reconsideration denied 92 Ohio St.3d 1418, 748 N.E.2d 550, stay granted 92 Ohio St.3d 1421, 748 N.E.2d 1142, certiorari denied 122 S.Ct. 483, 534 U.S. 1004, 151 L.Ed.2d 396, denial of post-conviction relief affirmed 2002-Ohio-2074, 2002 WL 737074, appeal not allowed 96 Ohio St.3d 1495, 774 N.E.2d 767, 2002-Ohio-4534, stay revoked 99 Ohio St.3d 1415, 788 N.E.2d 1098, 2003-Ohio-2526, motion to reopen denied 108 Ohio St.3d 1409, 841 N.E.2d 315, 2006-Ohio-179. Criminal Law ⚷ 641.13(2.1)

Defendant failed to show that defense counsel's alleged ineffective assistance in allowing a juror who had been victim of attempted date rape to remain on panel changed outcome of rape prosecution; juror acknowledged that no physical contact was made and she informed counsel that she could set aside her personal feelings and could judge the facts in case fairly, and other jurors who remained on the panel all stated that they would be able to set aside their personal feelings and be objective. State v. Gowdy (Ohio, 04-28-2000) 88 Ohio St.3d 387, 727 N.E.2d 579, 2000-Ohio-355. Criminal Law ⚷ 641.13(2.1)

Capital murder defendant was not prejudiced by trial counsel's alleged ineffectiveness in failing to ask even one question of particular prospective juror, where the juror had indicated that she could not impose the death penalty, so that any attempt to rehabilitate her probably would have been a waste of time. State v. Smith (Ohio, 01-05-2000) 87 Ohio St.3d 424, 721 N.E.2d 93, 2000-Ohio-450, denial of post-conviction relief affirmed 2000 WL 277912, dismissed, appeal not allowed 89 Ohio St.3d 1453, 731 N.E.2d 1140, dismissal of post-conviction relief affirmed 2005-Ohio-2571, 2005 WL 1225931, appeal not allowed 106 Ohio St.3d 1545, 835 N.E.2d 727, 2005-Ohio-5343. Criminal Law ⚷ 641.13(2.1)

Counsel were not ineffective in capital murder case for failing to exercise peremptory challenge on juror who indicated some positive stance towards death penalty and who was dissatisfied that man who had been convicted of crime against his family had not been incarcerated longer, as juror stated he could follow the law and stated his dissatisfaction would have no adverse effect on his ability to serve. State v. Goodwin (Ohio, 01-20-1999) 84 Ohio St.3d 331, 703 N.E.2d 1251, 1999-Ohio-356, reconsideration denied 85 Ohio St.3d 1410, 706 N.E.2d 790, certiorari denied 120 S.Ct. 118, 528 U.S. 846, 145 L.Ed.2d 100, habeas corpus granted in part 2006 WL 753111, supplemented 2006 WL 2056686. Criminal Law ⚷ 641.13(2.1)

4. —— Racial discrimination, constitutional issues

Prosecutor's proffered race-neutral explanation for use of peremptory challenge to exclude only African-American member of jury pool in drug prosecution was valid and nonpretextual, where prospective juror was school teacher for same school district attended by defendant and defendant's roommate and had previously testified for a student in a robbery case, and prosecutor was member of school board in which prospective juror taught. State v. Barker (Ohio App. 7 Dist., Jefferson, 03-27-2006) No. 05-JE-21, 2006-Ohio-1472, 2006 WL 771724, Unreported. Jury ⚷ 33(5.15)

Drug defendant established prima facie case of racial discrimination in state's exercise of peremptory challenges, where state challenged only African-American prospective juror in jury pool. State v. Barker (Ohio App. 7 Dist., Jefferson, 03-27-2006) No. 05-JE-21, 2006-Ohio-1472, 2006 WL 771724, Unreported. Jury ⚷ 33(5.15)

State's proffered reasons for its peremptory challenge of prospective African-American juror, which were that prospective juror indicated that she did not feel police would provide adequate response to her reporting of a crime, and that prospective juror had stated her belief that there was different treatment under law based upon person's race and socioeconomic background, were race-neutral, for purposes of *Batson* challenge raised by defendant, who was African-American, in prosecution for felonious assault and other offenses. State v. Stonestreet (Ohio App. 1 Dist., Hamilton, 08-26-2005) No. C-040264, 2005-Ohio-4416, 2005 WL 2045451, Unreported, appeal allowed 108 Ohio St.3d 1412, 841 N.E.2d 317, 2006-Ohio-179. Jury ⚷ 33(5.15)

The prosecutor's reasons for excluding African-American potential juror were race-neutral and were supported by the evidence, as required by *Batson*; when questioned as to whether she believed that all people were allowed to have equal protection of the laws defendant replied "I believe it is allowed. I don't believe it happens," she further stated that there was different treatment under the law based on "race and economic background," and she indicated that she did not report burglaries to the police because "it would be a waste of time." State v. Terry (Ohio App. 1 Dist., Hamilton, 08-12-2005) No. C-040261, 2005-Ohio-4140, 2005 WL 1923530, Unreported, appeal allowed 107 Ohio St.3d 1422, 837 N.E.2d 1208, 2005-Ohio-6124, reversed in part 109 Ohio St.3d 313, 847 N.E.2d 1174, 2006-Ohio-2109. Jury ⚷ 33(5.15)

Prosecutor provided sufficient race-neutral reasons for using peremptory challenge against African-American prospective juror, even though defendant argued that prosecutor's explanation was self-serving comment not supported by questioning; prosecutor stated that juror's responses indicated that she did not feel that police would provide adequate response to her reporting of a crime and that she had "street justice mentality" and that juror stated her belief that there was different treatment under law based upon a person's race and socioeconomic background, and juror's responses to questions supported prosecutor's explanation. State v. Roberts (Ohio App. 1 Dist., Hamilton, 06-17-2005) No. C-040262, 2005-Ohio-3034, 2005 WL 1413357, Unreported, opinion vacated and superseded 2005-Ohio-4050, 2005 WL 1863401, appeal not allowed 106 Ohio St.3d 1559, 836 N.E.2d 583, 2005-Ohio-5531. Jury ⚷ 33(5.15)

State's representation that African-American juror's body language suggested that he didn't want to be there constituted a race-neutral reason for striking him, rebutting a prima facie case of racial discrimination for purposes of *Batson* challenge. State v. Brown (Ohio App. 8 Dist., Cuyahoga, 12-16-2004) No. 84059, 2004-Ohio-6862, 2004 WL 2914987, Unreported, motion for delayed appeal denied 106 Ohio St.3d 1409, 830 N.E.2d 343, 2005-Ohio-3154. Jury ⚷ 33(5.15)

Defendant established a prima facie case of racial discrimination, for purposes of *Batson* challenge, where 75% of available African-American jurors had been excluded by peremptory challenges. State v. Brown (Ohio App. 8 Dist., Cuyahoga, 12-16-2004) No. 84059, 2004-Ohio-6862, 2004 WL 2914987, Unreported, motion for delayed appeal denied 106 Ohio St.3d 1409, 830 N.E.2d 343, 2005-Ohio-3154. Jury ⚷ 33(5.15)

State's representation that African-American juror acknowledged that he did not want to be a juror because of pressing business matters constituted a race-neutral reason for striking him, rebutting any prima facie case of racial discrimination for purposes of *Batson* challenge. State v. Brown (Ohio App. 8 Dist., Cuyahoga, 12-16-2004) No. 84059, 2004-Ohio-6862, 2004 WL 2914987, Unreported, motion for delayed appeal denied 106 Ohio St.3d 1409, 830 N.E.2d 343, 2005-Ohio-3154. Jury ⚷ 33(5.15)

State's representation that African-American juror had a relative who had been prosecuted by the assistant prosecuting attorney constituted a race-neutral reason for striking him, rebutting any prima facie case of racial discrimination for purposes of *Batson* challenge. State v. Brown (Ohio App. 8 Dist., Cuyahoga, 12-16-2004) No. 84059, 2004-Ohio-6862, 2004 WL 2914987, Unreported, motion for delayed appeal denied 106 Ohio St.3d 1409, 830 N.E.2d 343, 2005-Ohio-3154. Jury ⚷ 33(5.15)

Defense counsel's assertion that prosecutor had "kicked two blacks off the jury" was insufficient to establish a prima facie case of racial discrimination, for purposes of *Batson* challenge. State v. Brown (Ohio App. 8 Dist., Cuyahoga, 12-16-2004) No. 84059, 2004-Ohio-6862, 2004 WL 2914987, Unreported, motion for delayed appeal denied 106 Ohio St.3d 1409, 830 N.E.2d 343, 2005-Ohio-3154. Jury ⚷ 33(5.15)

The state provided race-neutral explanation for using peremptory challenge against African-American prospective juror in prosecution for felony murder, where prosecutor stated that he had excused juror because she had been member of jury in another trial in which jury had acquitted defendant when he thought that conviction was warranted, that he had used another challenge to exclude white prospective juror who had sat on that same jury panel, and that he was concerned that African-American juror could not remember anything about her prior jury service seven years ago. State v. Brundage (Ohio App. 1 Dist., Hamilton, 12-03-2004) No. C-030632, 2004-Ohio-6436, 2004 WL 2757605, Unreported, appeal not allowed 105 Ohio St.3d 1472, 824 N.E.2d 542, 2005-Ohio-1186. Jury ⚷ 33(5.15)

The state had valid race-neutral reasons for exercising peremptory challenge against African American prospective juror, where the state stated that juror was having difficult time comprehending analogy regarding children and truth telling and that juror either did not understand analogy or did not care, and the state was concerned with opinions that juror expressed about amount of credibility that the state's witnesses would need to possess for her to be able to rely on them. State v. Vaughn (Ohio App. 7 Dist., Mahoning, 09-23-2004) No. 03-MA-49, 2004-Ohio-5122, 2004 WL 2334376, Unreported, appeal not allowed 105 Ohio St.3d 1408, 821 N.E.2d 1028, 2005-Ohio-279. Jury ⚷ 33(5.15)

The state had valid race-neutral reasons for exercising peremptory challenge against African American prospective juror, where juror failed to disclose on questionnaire that she had been convicted of domestic violence and had been on probation, and juror was not forthcoming when asked why her husband was no longer employed. State v. Vaughn (Ohio App. 7 Dist., Mahoning, 09-23-2004) No. 03-MA-49, 2004-Ohio-5122, 2004 WL 2334376, Unreported, appeal not allowed 105 Ohio St.3d 1408, 821 N.E.2d 1028, 2005-Ohio-279. Jury ⚷ 33(5.15)

The state had valid race-neutral reasons for exercising peremptory challenge against Hispanic American prospective juror, where juror stated that her son was severely beaten by police officers from certain department, the state stated that officers from that department were involved in case and would be testifying, juror told trial court that she did not know if she would hold incident with her son against officers, and juror stated numerous times that she was nervous about jury process. State v. Vaughn (Ohio App. 7 Dist., Mahoning, 09-23-2004) No. 03-MA-49, 2004-Ohio-5122, 2004 WL 2334376, Unreported, appeal not allowed 105 Ohio St.3d 1408, 821 N.E.2d 1028, 2005-Ohio-279. Jury ⚷ 33(5.15)

Petitioner appealing denial of post-conviction relief failed to establish prima facie case of racially discriminatory exercise of peremptory challenges by prosecution; petitioner failed to provide complete transcript of necessary proceedings, such that appellate court had no record to review *Batson* challenge. State v. Burgess (Ohio App. 11 Dist., Lake, 08-20-2004) No. 2003-L-069, 2004-Ohio-4395, 2004 WL 1872781, Unreported. Criminal Law ⚷ 1115(2)

Defense counsel did not render ineffective assistance in murder trial by failing to challenge for cause or use peremptory challenge against prospective juror whose sister-in-law had terminal illness, even though juror indicated that illness made it difficult for her to concentrate, where record did not show that juror's lack of concentration resulted in prejudice to defendant. State v. Hall (Ohio App. 11 Dist., Lake, 06-18-2004) No. 2001-L-230, 2004-Ohio-3186, 2004 WL 1375752, Unreported, appeal not allowed 103 Ohio St.3d 1494, 816 N.E.2d 1080, 2004-Ohio-5605. Criminal Law ⚷ 641.13(2.1)

For purposes of *Batson*, record supported finding that State provided race-neutral explanation for using three of its peremptory challenges to exclude African-Americans from jury; State claimed that first juror was struck because he had a criminal conviction and was unemployed, that second juror was struck because he worked at the same company as defendant's mother, and that third juror was struck because she knew the alleged victims. State v. Taylor (Ohio App. 1 Dist., Hamilton, 03-26-2004) No. C-020475, 2004-Ohio-1494, 2004 WL 596128, Unreported, appeal not allowed 103 Ohio St.3d 1406, 812 N.E.2d 1289, 2004-Ohio-3980. Jury ⚷ 33(5.15)

Defendant was not required to show a pattern of discriminatory peremptory challenges in order to raise *Batson* challenge to state's exercise of peremptory strike against African-American prospective juror. State v. Graves (Ohio App. 6 Dist., Lucas, 05-09-2003) No. L-02-1053, 2003-Ohio-2359, 2003 WL 21040652, Unreported, appeal not allowed 100 Ohio St.3d 1410, 796 N.E.2d 537, 2003-Ohio-4948. Jury ⚷ 33(5.15)

Attorney's allegedly ineffective failure to use peremptory strike to excuse juror who admitted during voir dire that she would give more weight to police officers' testimony since her son was police officer did not prejudice defendant in prosecution for committing felonious assault, carrying concealed weapon, having a weapon while under disability, and tampering with evidence; no police officer witnessed the shooting, and although the arresting officer testified that he saw defendant holding his hand to his side while running away and that a few minutes later his partner found a gun in the grass nearby, insufficient evidence supported the conviction for carrying a concealed weapon, no reasonable probability existed that the tampering verdict would have been different if attorney had excused the juror. State v. Harris (Ohio App. 6 Dist., Lucas, 08-02-2002) No. L-01-1419, 2002-Ohio-3968, 2002 WL 1781152, Unreported, appeal not allowed 97 Ohio St.3d 1470, 779 N.E.2d 236, 2002-Ohio-6347. Criminal Law ⚷ 641.13(2.1)

Defendant's failure to establish pattern of discrimination in state's exercise of peremptory challenges, even considered together with fact that three African–Americans remained in panel, was not facially valid race-neutral justification for state's exercise of peremptory challenge to remove African–American prospective juror from jury panel, where defendant identified facts and circumstances in prospective juror's voir dire responses sufficient to establish inference that prosecutor's use of peremptory challenge was racially motivated, and both trial court and state proceeded as if defendant had established prima facie case of discriminatory intent. State v. Walker (Ohio App. 1 Dist., 09-01-2000) 139 Ohio App.3d 52, 742 N.E.2d 1173, dismissed, appeal not allowed 90 Ohio St.3d 1490, 739 N.E.2d 815. Jury ⚷ 33(5.15)

Fact that prosecutor allowed another African–American juror to remain on the jury panel did not preclude a holding that the prosecutor's use of peremptory challenge to remove African–American juror was discriminatory. State v. Gowdy (Ohio, 04-28-2000) 88 Ohio St.3d 387, 727 N.E.2d 579, 2000-Ohio-355. Jury ⚷ 33(5.15)

Trial court, who was able to view the cross worn by African–American juror and observe juror's demeanor, did not abuse its discretion in finding that juror's personal appearance was a race-neutral and non-pretextual basis for prosecutor's use of peremptory challenge against juror. State v. Gowdy (Ohio, 04-28-2000) 88 Ohio St.3d 387, 727 N.E.2d 579, 2000-Ohio-355. Jury ⚷ 33(5.15)

African–American juror's strongly held religious beliefs was a race-neutral and non-pretextual basis for prosecutor's peremptory challenge. State v. Gowdy (Ohio, 04-28-2000) 88 Ohio St.3d 387, 727 N.E.2d 579, 2000-Ohio-355. Jury ⚷ 33(5.15)

Prosecution provided race-neutral explanation for peremptory challenge to prospective African–American juror based on her expressed reservations upon death penalty, her expressed belief that there was race problem between police and African–American men, her upcoming plans to close on house, get remarried and take honeymoon, prosecution of her brother by same prosecutor's office, and her having a son about same age as defendant. State v. Johnson (Ohio, 03-01-2000) 88 Ohio St.3d 95, 723 N.E.2d 1054, 2000-Ohio-276, reconsideration denied 88 Ohio St.3d 1489, 727 N.E.2d 596, certiorari denied 121 S.Ct. 212, 531 U.S. 889, 148 L.Ed.2d 149, denial of post-conviction relief affirmed 2000 WL 1760225, appeal not allowed 91 Ohio St.3d 1481, 744 N.E.2d 1194. Jury ⚷ 33(5.15)

Trial court's finding of no discriminatory intent in state's peremptory challenge of African–American member of jury panel was not clearly erroneous in murder prosecution involving African–American defendant; trial court found a facially race-neutral reason for challenging juror in the fact that her son had been prosecuted four years earlier and was still incarcerated, and final make-up of jury included an African–American male. State v. Reaves (Ohio App. 1 Dist., 12-18-1998) 130 Ohio App.3d 776, 721 N.E.2d 424, motion for delayed appeal granted 85 Ohio St.3d 1445, 708 N.E.2d 210, dismissed, appeal not allowed 86 Ohio St.3d 1414, 711 N.E.2d 1010, appeal not allowed 94 Ohio St.3d 1432, 761 N.E.2d 47, 2002-Ohio-5651. Jury ⚷ 33(5.15)

Acceptance by trial court of state's explanation that it used peremptory challenge against juror because juror had "mixed feelings regarding the death penalty" and was single and lived at home with his mother and thereby lacked "a stake in the community" was not clearly erroneous and therefore established that peremptory challenge was exercised for race-neutral reason rather than for discriminatory reasons in violation of equal protection. State v. O'Neal (Ohio, 01-05-2000) 87 Ohio St.3d 402, 721 N.E.2d 73, 2000-Ohio-449, reconsideration denied 88 Ohio St.3d 1428, 723 N.E.2d 1115, denial of post-conviction relief affirmed 88 Ohio St.3d 179, 724 N.E.2d 423, 2000-Ohio-281, certiorari denied 121 S.Ct. 1997, 532 U.S. 1037, 149 L.Ed.2d 1001. Constitutional Law ⚷ 221(4); Jury ⚷ 33(5.15)

Trial court's acceptance of state's explanation that it used peremptory challenge against juror because she was a social worker, which state felt was not a "pro-conviction" occupation, and because she agreed with verdict finding O.J. Simpson not guilty despite her admission she had not followed the case, was not clearly erroneous and therefore established that peremptory challenge was exercised for race-neutral reason rather than for discriminatory reasons in violation of equal protection. State v. O'Neal (Ohio, 01-05-2000) 87 Ohio St.3d 402, 721 N.E.2d 73, 2000-Ohio-449, reconsideration denied 88 Ohio St.3d 1428, 723 N.E.2d 1115, denial of post-conviction relief affirmed 88 Ohio St.3d 179, 724 N.E.2d 423, 2000-Ohio-281, certiorari denied 121 S.Ct. 1997, 532 U.S. 1037, 149 L.Ed.2d 1001. Constitutional Law ⚷ 221(4); Jury ⚷ 33(5.15)

Capital murder defendant failed to establish that prosecutor had impermissible discriminatory motive, in violation of *Batson*, for exercise of peremptory strike against black prospective juror; prosecutor gave race-neutral explanation that juror was stricken because he was opposed to death penalty, prosecutor did not exercise peremptory strikes against any other black jurors, and prosecutor's challenges for cause to two black jurors were well-supported by record and upheld by trial court. State v. White (Ohio, 05-12-1999) 85 Ohio St.3d 433, 709 N.E.2d 140, 1999-Ohio-281, denial of post-conviction relief affirmed 1999 WL 394938, dismissed, appeal not allowed 87 Ohio St.3d 1418, 717 N.E.2d 1105, certiorari denied 120 S.Ct. 345, 528 U.S. 938, 145 L.Ed.2d 270, denial of post-conviction relief affirmed 2005-Ohio-6990, 2005 WL 3556634, appeal allowed 109 Ohio St.3d 1493, 848 N.E.2d 857, 2006-Ohio-2762. Jury ⚷ 33(5.15)

While presence of one or more black persons on a jury certainly does not preclude a finding of discrimination by prosecution in exercise of peremptory strikes against other black prospective jurors, fact may be taken into account as one that suggests that prosecution did not seek to rid the jury of persons of a particular race. State v. White (Ohio, 05-12-1999) 85 Ohio St.3d 433, 709 N.E.2d 140, 1999-Ohio-281, denial of post-conviction relief affirmed 1999 WL 394938, dismissed, appeal not allowed 87 Ohio St.3d 1418, 717 N.E.2d 1105, certiorari denied 120 S.Ct. 345, 528 U.S. 938, 145 L.Ed.2d 270, denial of post-conviction relief affirmed 2005-Ohio-6990, 2005 WL 3556634, appeal allowed 109 Ohio St.3d 1493, 848 N.E.2d 857, 2006-Ohio-2762. Jury ⚷ 33(5.15)

No *Batson* violation arose from prosecutor's exercise of peremptory strike against black prospective juror in aggravated murder case; defendant was drug trafficker accused of killing drug informant, and prosecutor's explanation that he excluded juror because her son was then in prison for drug trafficking was race-neutral on its face. State v. Coleman (Ohio, 03-31-1999) 85 Ohio St.3d 129, 707 N.E.2d 476, 1999-Ohio-258, reconsideration denied 85 Ohio St.3d 1481, 709 N.E.2d 851, certiorari denied 120 S.Ct. 379, 528 U.S. 954, 145 L.Ed.2d 296, denial of post-conviction relief affirmed 2002-Ohio-5377, 2002 WL 31242241, appeal not allowed 98 Ohio St.3d 1478, 784 N.E.2d 711, 2003-Ohio-974, denial of post-conviction relief affirmed 2005-Ohio-3874, 2005 WL 1797040, appeal not allowed 107 Ohio St.3d 1697, 840 N.E.2d 203, 2005-Ohio-6763. Jury ⚷ 33(5.15)

State provided sufficient race-neutral explanations for peremptory challenges to two jurors during capital murder prosecution; state excused first juror because juror did not think she could sign a death verdict, and state excused second juror because of juror's death penalty views and because juror was friend of accomplice's family. State v. Sheppard (Ohio, 12-30-1998) 84 Ohio St.3d 230, 703 N.E.2d 286, 1998-Ohio-323, reconsideration denied 84 Ohio St.3d 1489, 705 N.E.2d 368, stay granted 85 Ohio St.3d 1402, 706 N.E.2d 785, dismissal of post-conviction relief affirmed 1999 WL 162457, appeal not allowed 86 Ohio St.3d 1437, 713 N.E.2d 1049, certiorari denied 120 S.Ct. 1190, 528 U.S. 1168, 145 L.Ed.2d 1095, certiorari denied 119 S.Ct. 2376, 527 U.S. 1026, 144 L.Ed.2d 779, denial of post-conviction relief affirmed 2001 WL 331936, dismissed, appeal not allowed 92 Ohio St.3d 1445, 751 N.E.2d 483, denial of post-conviction relief affirmed 91 Ohio St.3d 329, 744 N.E.2d 770, 2001-Ohio-52. Jury ⚷ 33(5.15)

In absence of complete record of voir dire proceedings, it would be presumed on appeal that prosecutor's questions, and prospective jurors' answers thereto, refuted any inference of racially motivated exclusion of jurors. State v. Tillman (Ohio App. 9 Dist., 05-07-1997) 119 Ohio App.3d 449, 695 N.E.2d 792, motion for delayed appeal denied 90 Ohio St.3d 1471, 738 N.E.2d 382. Criminal Law ⚿ 1144.8

Mere fact that defendant and excluded jurors were of same race did not constitute prima facie showing of discrimination requiring prosecution to state race-neutral reasons for exclusion. State v. Tillman (Ohio App. 9 Dist., 05-07-1997) 119 Ohio App.3d 449, 695 N.E.2d 792, motion for delayed appeal denied 90 Ohio St.3d 1471, 738 N.E.2d 382. Jury ⚿ 33(5.15)

Prosecutors can exercise peremptory challenges for any reason, including opposition to death penalty, but may not exclude jurors based on gender or race. State v. Moore (Ohio, 02-04-1998) 81 Ohio St.3d 22, 689 N.E.2d 1, 1998-Ohio-441, dismissal of post-conviction relief affirmed 1998 WL 638353, dismissed, appeal not allowed 84 Ohio St.3d 1472, 704 N.E.2d 579. Jury ⚿ 33(5.15)

Prosecutor provided race-neutral explanation for using peremptory challenge against African–American prospective juror and lacked discriminatory intent that would violate Fourteenth Amendment, since he noted that juror folded arms during questioning by state and was niece of defense attorney who once served as public defender. State v. Moore (Ohio, 02-04-1998) 81 Ohio St.3d 22, 689 N.E.2d 1, 1998-Ohio-441, dismissal of post-conviction relief affirmed 1998 WL 638353, dismissed, appeal not allowed 84 Ohio St.3d 1472, 704 N.E.2d 579. Jury ⚿ 33(5.15)

To state prima facie case of purposeful discrimination in State's exercise of peremptory challenges, accused must demonstrate that members of recognized racial group were peremptorily challenged, and that facts and circumstances raise inference that prosecutor used peremptory challenges to exclude prospective jurors on account of their race. State v. Dennis (Ohio, 09-24-1997) 79 Ohio St.3d 421, 683 N.E.2d 1096, 1997-Ohio-372, denial of post-conviction relief affirmed 1997 WL 760680, dismissed, appeal not allowed 81 Ohio St.3d 1468, 690 N.E.2d 1287, certiorari denied 118 S.Ct. 1078, 522 U.S. 1128, 140 L.Ed.2d 136, habeas corpus dismissed 68 F.Supp.2d 863, affirmed 354 F.3d 511, certiorari denied 124 S.Ct. 2400, 541 U.S. 1068, 158 L.Ed.2d 971. Jury ⚿ 33(5.15)

Prosecutor did not exercise peremptory challenges in racially discriminatory manner in capital murder prosecution, where prosecutor explained that he challenged jurors who had expressed opposition to death penalty on religious grounds. State v. Dennis (Ohio, 09-24-1997) 79 Ohio St.3d 421, 683 N.E.2d 1096, 1997-Ohio-372, denial of post-conviction relief affirmed 1997 WL 760680, dismissed, appeal not allowed 81 Ohio St.3d 1468, 690 N.E.2d 1287, certiorari denied 118 S.Ct. 1078, 522 U.S. 1128, 140 L.Ed.2d 136, habeas corpus dismissed 68 F.Supp.2d 863, affirmed 354 F.3d 511, certiorari denied 124 S.Ct. 2400, 541 U.S. 1068, 158 L.Ed.2d 971. Jury ⚿ 33(5.15)

Reasons given by prosecutor for exercising peremptory challenges against African–American prospective jurors, that one had son who had been convicted of drug trafficking and that another had prior experience with child support enforcement agency, were race-neutral, as required by *Batson*. State v. McElrath (Ohio App. 9 Dist., 10-02-1996) 114 Ohio App.3d 516, 683 N.E.2d 430, motion for delayed appeal denied 81 Ohio St.3d 1430, 689 N.E.2d 50. Jury ⚿ 33(5.15)

Defendant failed to show that state's peremptory challenge of black potential juror was racially motivated, so as to violate *Batson* state did not challenge two black members of panel, and articulated race-neutral reasons based on challenged juror's employment and former residence. State v. Burns (Ohio App. 8 Dist., 08-19-1996) 113 Ohio App.3d 598, 681 N.E.2d 965, dismissed, appeal not allowed 77 Ohio St.3d 1516, 674 N.E.2d 370, motion to reopen denied 2000 WL 1195673. Jury ⚿ 33(5.15)

Once elements raising inference of purposeful race discrimination in jury selection have been established, prosecutor must articulate race-neutral reasons to excuse potential jurors, and trial court must then determine if accused has proved purposeful discrimination based upon race. State v. Burns (Ohio App. 8 Dist., 08-19-1996) 113 Ohio App.3d 598, 681 N.E.2d 965, dismissed, appeal not allowed 77 Ohio St.3d 1516, 674 N.E.2d 370, motion to reopen denied 2000 WL 1195673. Jury ⚿ 33(5.15)

Criminal defendant can demonstrate violation of his equal protection rights under *Batson* by showing that prosecutor's use of peremptory challenges was used to purposely exclude members of defendant's race. State v. Brock (Ohio App. 3 Dist., 04-26-1996) 110 Ohio App.3d 656, 675 N.E.2d 18, dismissed, appeal not allowed 77 Ohio St.3d 1444, 671 N.E.2d 1283. Constitutional Law ⚿ 221(4); Jury ⚿ 33(5.15)

Trial court's decision on ultimate question of whether intentional racial discrimination motivated use of peremptory strike in violation of *Batson* is finding of fact and is to be afforded great deference by reviewing court, and such a decision will not be overturned unless clearly erroneous. State v. Brock (Ohio App. 3 Dist., 04-26-1996) 110 Ohio App.3d 656, 675 N.E.2d 18, dismissed, appeal not allowed 77 Ohio St.3d 1444, 671 N.E.2d 1283. Criminal Law ⚿ 1158(3)

Prosecutors may assert *Batson* challenge to defendant's exercise of peremptory strikes in racially discriminatory manner. State v. Brock (Ohio App. 3 Dist., 04-26-1996) 110 Ohio App.3d 656, 675 N.E.2d 18, dismissed, appeal not allowed 77 Ohio St.3d 1444, 671 N.E.2d 1283. Jury ⚿ 33(5.15)

Race of defendant is irrelevant to defendant's right to challenge under *Batson* prosecutor's use of peremptory challenges in racially discriminatory manner. State v. Brock (Ohio App. 3 Dist., 04-26-1996) 110 Ohio App.3d 656, 675 N.E.2d 18, dismissed, appeal not allowed 77 Ohio St.3d 1444, 671 N.E.2d 1283. Jury ⚿ 33(5.20)

A trial court's factual finding that state did not exercise its peremptory challenges with racially discriminatory intent largely turns on evaluation of credibility, and thus is to be accorded great deference; such finding will not be disturbed on appeal unless, based on record, it is clearly erroneous. State v. Nobles (Ohio App. 2 Dist., 09-01-1995) 106 Ohio App.3d 246, 665 N.E.2d 1137, dismissed, appeal not allowed 74 Ohio St.3d 1510, 659 N.E.2d 1287. Criminal Law ⚷ 1158(3)

State may not use peremptory challenges against venireman solely on basis of her race. State v. Nobles (Ohio App. 2 Dist., 09-01-1995) 106 Ohio App.3d 246, 665 N.E.2d 1137, dismissed, appeal not allowed 74 Ohio St.3d 1510, 659 N.E.2d 1287. Jury ⚷ 33(5.15)

In analyzing merits of *Batson* challenge, court follows tripartite test articulated in *Batson* as modified by *Powers*: first, defendant must make prima facie showing that prosecutor has exercised peremptory challenges on basis of race; second, if requisite showing has been made, burden shifts to prosecutor to articulate race-neutral explanation for striking jurors in question; finally, trial court must determine whether defendant has carried his burden of proving purposeful discrimination. State v. Nobles (Ohio App. 2 Dist., 09-01-1995) 106 Ohio App.3d 246, 665 N.E.2d 1137, dismissed, appeal not allowed 74 Ohio St.3d 1510, 659 N.E.2d 1287. Jury ⚷ 33(5.15)

Race-neutral explanation offered by prosecutor in response to *Batson* challenge for exercise of peremptory challenge against prospective juror need not rise to level of challenge for cause, nor need it be persuasive, or even plausible; issue is facial validity of prosecutor's explanation, and unless discriminatory intent is inherent in prosecutor's explanation, reason given will be deemed race neutral. State v. Nobles (Ohio App. 2 Dist., 09-01-1995) 106 Ohio App.3d 246, 665 N.E.2d 1137, dismissed, appeal not allowed 74 Ohio St.3d 1510, 659 N.E.2d 1287. Jury ⚷ 33(5.15)

State did not act with unlawful discriminatory intent in exercising peremptory challenge against black venireman, despite fact that defendant was black and stricken venireman was only potential juror who was black; there was no racially discriminatory intent inherent in prosecutor's explanation for exercise of challenge, victim and many of state's important witnesses were black, and veniremen peremptorily challenged by state prior to its challenge against venireman at issue shared several other characteristics with venireman at issue. State v. Nobles (Ohio App. 2 Dist., 09-01-1995) 106 Ohio App.3d 246, 665 N.E.2d 1137, dismissed, appeal not allowed 74 Ohio St.3d 1510, 659 N.E.2d 1287. Jury ⚷ 33(5.15)

Under *Batson* prospective jurors cannot be peremptorily excused based on racial considerations, even if accused does not belong to minority. State v. Wilson (Ohio, 01-24-1996) 74 Ohio St.3d 381, 659 N.E.2d 292, 1996-Ohio-103, reconsideration denied 75 Ohio St.3d 1413, 661 N.E.2d 760, certiorari denied 117 S.Ct. 129, 519 U.S. 845, 136 L.Ed.2d 78, denial of post-conviction relief affirmed 80 Ohio St.3d 132, 684 N.E.2d 1221, 1997-Ohio-303, denial of post-conviction relief affirmed 1998 WL 332940. Jury ⚷ 33(5.15)

One of prosecutor's race-neutral explanations for challenging African–American prospective juror in murder prosecution, that her husband, from whom she was separated, was alcoholic, raising concerns about her ability to fairly and impartially consider intoxication defense, was supported by record and not shown to be pretextual in violation of *Batson*; juror stated that her husband "drinks all the time," and that that fact had played role in their separation. State v. Powers (Ohio App. 10 Dist., 12-07-1993) 92 Ohio App.3d 400, 635 N.E.2d 1298, dismissed, jurisdictional motion overruled 69 Ohio St.3d 1442, 632 N.E.2d 910, certiorari denied 115 S.Ct. 366, 513 U.S. 951, 130 L.Ed.2d 319. Jury ⚷ 33(5.15)

One of prosecutor's race-neutral explanations for challenging African–American prospective juror in murder prosecution, that juror was having difficulty understanding legal concepts, was supported by record and was not shown to be pretext for race discrimination in violation of *Batson*; while juror's initial inclination to place burden of proof on defendant may have suggested juror favorable to state, her responses reflected inability to comprehend basic legal concepts, which would hinder her ability to weigh merits of state's case independent from conclusions of other jurors. State v. Powers (Ohio App. 10 Dist., 12-07-1993) 92 Ohio App.3d 400, 635 N.E.2d 1298, dismissed, jurisdictional motion overruled 69 Ohio St.3d 1442, 632 N.E.2d 910, certiorari denied 115 S.Ct. 366, 513 U.S. 951, 130 L.Ed.2d 319. Jury ⚷ 33(5.15)

Prosecutor's stated reasons for using peremptory challenge to exclude African–American juror, her gun ownership and interest in self-defense, was insufficient to rebut defendant's prima facie case of race discrimination during jury selection in manslaughter prosecution; although prosecutor claimed that juror may have been sympathetic to defendant, who similarly had purchased a gun and was claiming self-defense, prosecutor more reasonably could have determined that juror's interest in guns and self-protection would have made her sympathetic toward victim, and did not strike caucasian juror who admitted owning gun for self-protection. State v. Belcher (Franklin 1993) 89 Ohio App.3d 24, 623 N.E.2d 583, dismissed, jurisdictional motion overruled 67 Ohio St.3d 1501, 622 N.E.2d 650. Jury ⚷ 33(5.15)

Prosecutor's stated reason for using peremptory strike against African–American juror, that juror was too nervous to hear case due to his experiences while in the military and was biased toward defendant, was insufficient to rebut defendant's prima facie case of race discrimination during jury selection in manslaughter prosecution; nothing suggested that juror's military experiences created nervous problem or that he would not be a good juror, and his statement that there were more appropriate means for self-protection than owning a gun suggested he would be a good juror for the state in case involving claim of self-defense. State v. Belcher (Franklin 1993) 89 Ohio App.3d 24, 623 N.E.2d 583, dismissed, jurisdictional motion overruled 67 Ohio St.3d 1501, 622 N.E.2d 650. Jury ⚷ 33(5.15)

Prosecutor's stated reason for striking African–American prospective juror, that she did not appear to be paying attention and appeared to be making comments under her breath, was insufficient to rebut defendant's prima facie case of race discrimination during jury selection; answers given by juror were thoughtful and responsive to questions asked and did not demonstrate casual attitude toward the process. State v. Belcher (Franklin 1993) 89 Ohio App.3d 24, 623 N.E.2d 583, dismissed, jurisdictional motion overruled 67 Ohio St.3d 1501, 622 N.E.2d 650. Jury ⚷ 33(5.15)

Striking of single African–American juror without adequate race-neutral explanation can result in *Batson* violation, even where valid reasons exist for striking other African–American jurors. State v. Belcher (Franklin 1993) 89 Ohio App.3d 24, 623 N.E.2d 583, dismissed, jurisdictional motion overruled 67 Ohio St.3d 1501, 622 N.E.2d 650. Jury ⚷ 33(5.15)

Prosecutor articulated neutral explanation for exercise of peremptory challenge to exclude black prospective juror, despite prosecutor's reference to "basic gut instincts," where prosecutor further explained that juror was giddy, that there was sense of silliness about her, and that she hesitated in answering whether she would hesitate in returning guilty verdict if evidence was produced which convinced her beyond reasonable doubt of defendant's guilt. State v. Hairston (Cuyahoga 1990) 67 Ohio App.3d 341, 586 N.E.2d 1200. Jury ⚷ 33(5.15)

Prosecutor's exercise of peremptory challenge to exclude last black prospective juror did not establish purposeful discrimination, where only other black prospective juror was removed at defendant's request, so that prosecutor was not responsible for removal of all black prospective jurors from jury. State v. Hairston (Cuyahoga 1990) 67 Ohio App.3d 341, 586 N.E.2d 1200. Jury ⚷ 33(5.15)

When defendant makes out prima facie case that prosecutor has used peremptory challenges for racial discrimination, burden is on prosecutor to give neutral explanation related to case. Although explanation need not meet standards of challenges for cause, explanation is insufficient if based on prosecutor's assumption or institution that black jurors will be partial to black defendant, or if it consists of denial of discriminatory motives or in professions of good faith. Batson v. Kentucky (U.S.Ky. 1986) 106 S.Ct. 1712, 476 U.S. 79, 90 L.Ed.2d 69.

Government offered race-neutral explanation for exercising preemptory challenge against African-American prospective juror in narcotics prosecution, as required by *Batson*; juror was challenged based on her age, educational level, single status, and because she resided in neighborhood where the events giving rise to the complaint took place. U.S. v. Campbell (C.A.6 (Ohio), 01-28-2003) 317 F.3d 597. Jury ⚷ 33(5.15)

If the defendant successfully makes a prima facie showing of a *Batson* violation, the burden shifts to the government to come forward with a neutral explanation for its peremptory challenges, which requires a justification for its strikes that does not deny equal protection, but requirements for such a justification are not rigorous. U.S. v. Maxwell (C.A.6 (Ohio), 11-17-1998) 160 F.3d 1071. Jury ⚷ 33(5.15)

Prosecutor's reasons for using peremptory strikes to exclude two African–American veniremembers in defendant's capital murder trial were race-neutral, for purposes of *Batson* analysis; both jurors expressed opposition to death penalty on religious grounds, one juror's son had been convicted of serious crime and other juror was often late and confused about jury procedures. Dennis v. Mitchell (N.D.Ohio, 10-01-1999) 68 F.Supp.2d 863, affirmed 354 F.3d 511, certiorari denied 124 S.Ct. 2400, 541 U.S. 1068, 158 L.Ed.2d 971. Jury ⚷ 33(5.15)

5. Procedure—In general

Any error in trial court's dismissal for cause of juror who stated that he believed drugs should be legalized, without allowing defendant to question juror, was harmless at trial on charges of possession of cocaine and trafficking in cocaine, where state still had a peremptory challenge that it could have exercised to remove juror. State v. Williams (Ohio App. 1 Dist., Hamilton, 12-16-2005) No. C-040747, 2005-Ohio-6772, 2005 WL 3484652, Unreported. Criminal Law ⚷ 1166.17

Juror who formerly lived in neighborhood where murder occurred, who was acquainted with victim, who shopped in victim's store a few times, and who saw defendant around but did not know him was not required to be excused for cause pursuant to defendant's challenge, where juror unequivocally stated his intention to be impartial and decide case only on the facts. State v. Sheppard (Ohio, 12-30-1998) 84 Ohio St.3d 230, 703 N.E.2d 286, 1998-Ohio-323, reconsideration denied 84 Ohio St.3d 1489, 705 N.E.2d 368, stay granted 85 Ohio St.3d 1402, 706 N.E.2d 785, dismissal of post-conviction relief affirmed 1999 WL 162457, appeal not allowed 86 Ohio St.3d 1437, 713 N.E.2d 1049, certiorari denied 120 S.Ct. 1190, 528 U.S. 1168, 145 L.Ed.2d 1095, certiorari denied 119 S.Ct. 2376, 527 U.S. 1026, 144 L.Ed.2d 779, denial of post-conviction relief affirmed 2001 WL 331936, dismissed, appeal not allowed 92 Ohio St.3d 1445, 751 N.E.2d 483, denial of post-conviction relief affirmed 91 Ohio St.3d 329, 744 N.E.2d 770, 2001-Ohio-52. Jury ⚷ 90

Apart from excluding jurors based on race or gender, prosecutors can exercise peremptory challenge for any reason, without inquiry, and without court's control. State v. Biros (Ohio, 05-14-1997) 78 Ohio St.3d 426, 678 N.E.2d 891, 1997-Ohio-204, reconsideration denied 79 Ohio St.3d 1451, 680 N.E.2d 1023, certiorari denied 118 S.Ct. 574, 522 U.S. 1002, 139 L.Ed.2d 413, denial of post-conviction relief affirmed 1999 WL 391090, dismissed, appeal not allowed 87 Ohio St.3d 1406, 716 N.E.2d

1168, denial of post-conviction relief affirmed 93 Ohio St.3d 250, 754 N.E.2d 805, 2001-Ohio-1339, grant of habeas corpus reversed 422 F.3d 379, rehearing and rehearing en banc denied, petition for certiorari filed 2006 WL 1583483. Jury ⚷ 33(5.15); Jury ⚷ 135

Traditionally, peremptory challenges have enabled party to cull from veniremen any person he believed would be more likely to find for his opponent than for him, regardless of his reasons for thinking so. State v. Nobles (Ohio App. 2 Dist., 09-01-1995) 106 Ohio App.3d 246, 665 N.E.2d 1137, dismissed, appeal not allowed 74 Ohio St.3d 1510, 659 N.E.2d 1287. Jury ⚷ 135

Apart from excluding jurors based on race or gender, prosecutors can exercise peremptory challenges to prospective jurors for any reason, without inquiry, and without court's control. State v. Brooks (Ohio, 03-04-1996) 75 Ohio St.3d 148, 661 N.E.2d 1030, 1996-Ohio-134, reconsideration denied 75 Ohio St.3d 1452, 663 N.E.2d 333. Jury ⚷ 33(5.15)

Trial court's refusal to allow defense counsel to ask prospective jurors whether they would consider defendant's youth as mitigating factor in capital prosecution, based on form of question, did not improperly limit defendant's opportunity to exercise peremptory challenges or engage in voir dire, as court allowed jurors to be questioned about whether they would follow instructions court might give, including instruction on youth as mitigating factor, and defendant was not precluded from asking whether prospective jurors would impose death sentence based solely upon finding of aggravated murder and irrespective of facts and circumstances or instructions of court. State v. Garner (Ohio, 11-22-1995) 74 Ohio St.3d 49, 656 N.E.2d 623, 1995-Ohio-168, reconsideration denied 74 Ohio St.3d 1485, 657 N.E.2d 1378, certiorari denied 116 S.Ct. 1444, 517 U.S. 1147, 134 L.Ed.2d 564, rehearing denied 116 S.Ct. 1872, 517 U.S. 1230, 134 L.Ed.2d 969, stay granted 76 Ohio St.3d 1401, 666 N.E.2d 233. Jury ⚷ 131(17)

Under RC 2945.21, a declination in turn to exercise a peremptory challenge to dismiss a juror does not render the state or the defendant unable reasonably to use any remaining peremptory challenges to dismiss a juror seated either before of after the declination (superseded by Crim R 24(D).) State v. Berry (Ohio 1971) 25 Ohio St.2d 255, 267 N.E.2d 775, 54 O.O.2d 374. Jury ⚷ 138(2)

There was no equal protection violation in prosecutor's use of peremptory strikes against prospective jurors who were 18 and 21 years old respectively, though the government conceded that age was a primary reason for its peremptory challenges. U.S. v. Maxwell (C.A.6 (Ohio), 11-17-1998) 160 F.3d 1071. Constitutional Law ⚷ 250.2(4); Jury ⚷ 33(5.15)

6. —— Discretion of court, procedure

Although neither the state nor a defendant may be deprived of any of the challenges by reason of the order of exercising the same, the trial court has the obligation to supervise the peremptory challenge procedure so that the opportunity to challenge is presented to the parties alternately (superseded by Crim R 24(D).) State v. Berry (Ohio 1971) 25 Ohio St.2d 255, 267 N.E.2d 775, 54 O.O.2d 374. Jury ⚷ 138(2)

In a capital case, trial court may determine manner of the exercise of the right of peremptory challenge in absence of a rule fixed by statute governing same (superseded by Crim R 24(D).) Rucker v. State (Ohio 1928) 119 Ohio St. 189, 162 N.E. 802, 6 Ohio Law Abs. 370, 26 Ohio Law Rep. 461. Jury ⚷ 138(1)

Aside from statutory regulations governing peremptory challenges, the order in which they shall be exercised is in the discretion of the court (superseded by Crim R 24(D).) Lyon v. State (Ohio 1927) 116 Ohio St. 265, 155 N.E. 800, 5 Ohio Law Abs. 189, 25 Ohio Law Rep. 68, 25 Ohio Law Rep. 267.

7. —— Juror's aversion to death penalty, procedure

Batson prohibition against peremptory strikes based solely on race does not extend to peremptory strikes against jurors opposed to the death penalty. State v. Mason (Ohio, 06-17-1998) 82 Ohio St.3d 144, 694 N.E.2d 932, 1998-Ohio-370, reconsideration denied 82 Ohio St.3d 1483, 696 N.E.2d 1089, certiorari denied 119 S.Ct. 624, 525 U.S. 1057, 142 L.Ed.2d 562, habeas corpus denied 95 F.Supp.2d 744, affirmed in part, remanded in part 320 F.3d 604, on remand 293 F.Supp.2d 819, on remand 396 F.Supp.2d 837. Jury ⚷ 33(5.15)

Prosecution in capital murder case could properly exercise peremptorily challenges against two prospective jurors who expressed or indicated some aversion to death penalty. State v. Biros (Ohio, 05-14-1997) 78 Ohio St.3d 426, 678 N.E.2d 891, 1997-Ohio-204, reconsideration denied 79 Ohio St.3d 1451, 680 N.E.2d 1023, certiorari denied 118 S.Ct. 574, 522 U.S. 1002, 139 L.Ed.2d 413, denial of post-conviction relief affirmed 1999 WL 391090, dismissed, appeal not allowed 87 Ohio St.3d 1406, 716 N.E.2d 1168, denial of post-conviction relief affirmed 93 Ohio St.3d 250, 754 N.E.2d 805, 2001-Ohio-1339, grant of habeas corpus reversed 422 F.3d 379, rehearing and rehearing en banc denied, petition for certiorari filed 2006 WL 1583483. Jury ⚷ 33(5.15)

Defendant waived issue of peremptory challenges based on jurors' opposition to death penalty by not objecting at trial. State v. Ballew (Ohio, 08-07-1996) 76 Ohio St.3d 244, 667 N.E.2d 369, 1996-Ohio-81, certiorari denied 117 S.Ct. 704, 519 U.S. 1065, 136 L.Ed.2d 625, dismissal of post-conviction relief affirmed 1998 WL 95397, dismissed, appeal not allowed 82 Ohio St.3d 1441, 695 N.E.2d 264, habeas corpus dismissed 2001 WL 242563. Criminal Law ⚷ 1035(5)

Prosecutor in capital murder case could use peremptory challenges to exclude jurors who expressed concerns over capital punishment. State v. Brooks (Ohio, 03-04-1996) 75 Ohio St.3d 148, 661 N.E.2d 1030, 1996-Ohio-134, reconsideration denied 75 Ohio St.3d 1452, 663 N.E.2d 333. Jury ⚷ 33(5.15)

Prospective juror's equivocation about death penalty was proper race-neutral basis for prosecution's exercise of peremptory challenge against prospective juror in capital murder prosecution. State v. Wilson (Ohio, 01-24-1996) 74 Ohio St.3d 381, 659 N.E.2d 292, 1996-Ohio-103, reconsideration denied 75 Ohio St.3d 1413, 661 N.E.2d 760, certiorari denied 117 S.Ct. 129, 519 U.S. 845, 136 L.Ed.2d 78, denial of post-conviction relief affirmed 80 Ohio St.3d 132, 684 N.E.2d 1221, 1997-Ohio-303, denial of post-conviction relief affirmed 1998 WL 332940. Jury ⚷ 33(5.15)

8. —— Race or gender discrimination, procedure

The prosecutor's reasons for excluding African-American potential juror were race-neutral and were supported by the evidence, as required by *Batson*; the State indicated it struck juror after she gave strange responses during voir dire, by stating that she had raised her hand because she was talking to the Lord and by stating, when asked if anyone wanted to respond to any of the questioning that had occurred, that she did not feel that people should be coerced into saying something that they did not want to say, and the prosecutor indicated that she had an overall "negative feeling" about juror. State v. Terry (Ohio App. 1 Dist., Hamilton, 08-12-2005) No. C-040261, 2005-Ohio-4140, 2005 WL 1923530, Unreported, appeal allowed 107 Ohio St.3d 1422, 837 N.E.2d 1208, 2005-Ohio-6124, reversed in part 109 Ohio St.3d 313, 847 N.E.2d 1174, 2006-Ohio-2109. Jury ⚷ 33(5.15)

The prosecutor's reasons for excluding African-American potential juror were race-neutral and were supported by the evidence, as required by *Batson*; the State indicated that it dismissed juror because counsel for co-defendant had represented juror's son two years earlier on a federal charge of possessing a firearm while under a disability, and defendant and second co-defendant were being prosecuted on similar state charges for possessing a firearm while under a disability. State v. Terry (Ohio App. 1 Dist., Hamilton, 08-12-2005) No. C-040261, 2005-Ohio-4140, 2005 WL 1923530, Unreported, appeal allowed 107 Ohio St.3d 1422, 837 N.E.2d 1208, 2005-Ohio-6124, reversed in part 109 Ohio St.3d 313, 847 N.E.2d 1174, 2006-Ohio-2109. Jury ⚷ 33(5.15)

State's facially race-neutral reason for peremptory strike of African-American juror, that juror's initial voir dire silence contradicted his subsequent voir dire testimony, relating to whether he had any relatives with convictions, thus calling into doubt juror's honesty or objectivity, was not pretext for racial discrimination under *Batson*. State v. Williams (Ohio App. 2 Dist., Montgomery, 06-24-2005) No. 19963, 2005-Ohio-3172, 2005 WL 1490140, Unreported, motion for delayed appeal denied 110 Ohio St.3d 1436, 852 N.E.2d 186, 2006-Ohio-3862. Jury ⚷ 33(5.15)

Responses given by African–American juror to questions advanced by State provided adequate race-neutral grounds for State to exercise peremptory challenge, as required under *Batson*; juror indicated that he had unresolved issues with respect to police harassing him and his family and that he probably could not set aside his feelings when weighing the testimony of a police officer. State v. Parsons (Ohio App. 2 Dist., Montgomery, 04-29-2005) No. 20476, 2005-Ohio-2017, 2005 WL 994583, Unreported, motion for delayed appeal denied 110 Ohio St.3d 1437, 852 N.E.2d 186, 2006-Ohio-3862. Jury ⚷ 33(5.15)

Prosecution's proffered race-neutral reasons for exercising peremptory challenge against sole African-American prospective juror in murder prosecution were viable and nonpretextual, and exercise of peremptory challenge did not amount to impermissible discrimination, where prospective juror's nephew had been victim of unsolved murder, and prospective juror was at time of trial commencing treatment for sleep apnea; prospective juror's medical condition could have caused him to be inattentive to proceedings, and crimes of which other prospective jurors or their family members had been victims did not include murder. State v. Herron (Ohio App. 2 Dist., Montgomery, 02-20-2004) No. 19894, 2004-Ohio-773, 2004 WL 315232, Unreported, motion for delayed appeal denied 107 Ohio St.3d 1404, 836 N.E.2d 1226, 2005-Ohio-5859. Jury ⚷ 33(5.15)

Capital murder defendant failed to carry his burden of proving intentional discrimination in prosecutor's use of peremptory challenge to remove African–American juror; defendant offered no evidence of discriminatory intent to counter prosecutor's racially neutral reasons for peremptorily challenging juror, which included reference in her juror questionnaire to story involving a miscarriage of justice and the lynching of an innocent man, her nodding her head in response to question whether jurors felt pressure to return a certain verdict due to community views, and her mannerisms showing she was offended by prosecutor's asking whether she was inconvenienced by jury selection process. State v. Bryan (Ohio, 03-17-2004) 101 Ohio St.3d 272, 804 N.E.2d 433, 2004-Ohio-971, motion granted 102 Ohio St.3d 1437, 807 N.E.2d 937, 2004-Ohio-2226, reconsideration denied 102 Ohio St.3d 1449, 808 N.E.2d 399, 2004-Ohio-2263, motion to reopen denied 103 Ohio St.3d 1490, 816 N.E.2d 1078, 2004-Ohio-5605, reconsideration stricken 103 Ohio St.3d 1529, 817 N.E.2d 891, 2004-Ohio-6040. Jury ⚷ 33(5.15)

Trial court's acceptance of state's impermissible explanation for its exercise of peremptory challenge against African–American juror was clearly erroneous and required reversal of defendant's convictions of murder and felonious assault; defendant was harmed by risk that prejudice that motivated discriminatory selection of jury infected entire proceedings. State v. Walker (Ohio App. 1 Dist., 09-01-2000) 139 Ohio App.3d 52, 742 N.E.2d 1173, dismissed, appeal not allowed 90 Ohio St.3d 1490, 739 N.E.2d 815. Criminal Law ⚷ 1166.17

Fact that other African–American jurors remain on the jury does not exonerate the state for the discriminatory exercise of a peremptory challenge. State v. Walker (Ohio App. 1 Dist., 09-01-2000) 139 Ohio App.3d 52, 742 N.E.2d 1173, dismissed, appeal not allowed 90 Ohio St.3d 1490, 739 N.E.2d 815. Jury ⚷ 33(5.15)

Three-step analysis is applied in determining if racially discriminatory use of peremptory strike under *Batson* has been established: opponent of peremptory challenge must first make out prima facie case of racial discrimination; once such a showing is made, second step of test shifts burden of production to proponent of peremptory challenge to come forward with race-neutral explanation of strike; and if proponent tenders race-neutral explanation, trial court must decide if opponent has proved purposeful racial discrimination. State v. Brock (Ohio App. 3 Dist., 04-26-1996) 110 Ohio App.3d 656, 675 N.E.2d 18, dismissed, appeal not allowed 77 Ohio St.3d 1444, 671 N.E.2d 1283. Jury ⚷ 33(5.15)

Explanation that peremptory strike was exercised by prosecution against sole African–American juror on venire panel in capital murder case because of juror's hesitation about her willingness to consider death penalty and because information provided by juror about her background and her number of children made prosecutor believe that juror might be somewhat reluctant to consider arguments of state provided valid race-neutral basis for exercise of strike under *Batson*. State v. Brock (Ohio App. 3 Dist., 04-26-1996) 110 Ohio App.3d 656, 675 N.E.2d 18, dismissed, appeal not allowed 77 Ohio St.3d 1444, 671 N.E.2d 1283. Jury ⚷ 33(5.15)

Apart from excluding jurors based on race and gender, prosecutor can exercise peremptory challenge for any reason, without inquiry, and without court's control. State v. Ballew (Ohio, 08-07-1996) 76 Ohio St.3d 244, 667 N.E.2d 369, 1996-Ohio-81, certiorari denied 117 S.Ct. 704, 519 U.S. 1065, 136 L.Ed.2d 625, dismissal of post-conviction relief affirmed 1998 WL 95397, dismissed, appeal not allowed 82 Ohio St.3d 1441, 695 N.E.2d 264, habeas corpus dismissed 2001 WL 242563. Jury ⚷ 33(5.15); Jury ⚷ 135

Prosecutor's race-neutral explanations for striking African–American potential juror in murder prosecution, that juror was not in favor of death penalty, and that her prior employment as barmaid would affect her view of anticipated defense of intoxication, were not shown to be pretext for purposeful race discrimination, so as to violate *Batson*, despite similarities between prospective juror and white juror prosecutor did not challenge; stricken juror's statement revealed possible opposition to death penalty, whereas white juror's response revealed only concern that penalty be imposed in most serious cases and when guilt was properly established, and bar in which white juror had been employed did not resemble bar at issue as much as one in which stricken juror had worked. State v. Powers (Ohio App. 10 Dist., 12-07-1993) 92 Ohio App.3d 400, 635 N.E.2d 1298, dismissed, jurisdictional motion overruled 69 Ohio St.3d 1442, 632 N.E.2d 910, certiorari denied 115 S.Ct. 366, 513 U.S. 951, 130 L.Ed.2d 319. Jury ⚷ 33(5.15)

Record supported prosecutor's race-neutral explanation for challenging African–American prospective juror in murder prosecution, that juror would not give him firm commitment on death penalty, and that she was "liberal teacher" who leaned strongly toward rehabilitation as punishment, rather than death penalty; juror stated that she "can't say that I am for the death penalty. I also cannot say that I am not," she responded affirmatively when asked whether emphasis in prison should be on rehabilitation, and she spoke positively about program which sought to teach convicts trade, and for which her husband had been employed as instructor. State v. Powers (Ohio App. 10 Dist., 12-07-1993) 92 Ohio App.3d 400, 635 N.E.2d 1298, dismissed, jurisdictional motion overruled 69 Ohio St.3d 1442, 632 N.E.2d 910, certiorari denied 115 S.Ct. 366, 513 U.S. 951, 130 L.Ed.2d 319. Jury ⚷ 33(5.15)

Prosecutor may not use peremptory challenges to exclude jurors solely because of race, and defendant makes out prima facie discrimination by showing that (1) he is a member of a cognizable racial group, (2) prosecutor used peremptory challenges to exclude members of same group from jury in defendant's case, and (3) these facts and other relevant circumstances raise inference that prosecutor used challenges solely on racial grounds. Batson v. Kentucky (U.S.Ky. 1986) 106 S.Ct. 1712, 476 U.S. 79, 90 L.Ed.2d 69.

Government offered race-neutral explanation for exercising preemptory challenge against African-American prospective juror in narcotics prosecution, as required by *Batson*; juror was challenged based on her age, educational level, single status, and because she resided in neighborhood where the events giving rise to the complaint took place. U.S. v. Campbell (C.A.6 (Ohio), 01-28-2003) 317 F.3d 597. Jury ⚷ 33(5.15)

There was no *Batson* violation in the prosecution's peremptory strike of only remaining black member of jury venire; prosecutor provided race-neutral reasons for strike by noting that venire member was a guidance counselor, and that in his experience, guidance counselors were overly sympathetic with defendants, that venire member stated that she was particularly busy at the time, and the prosecutor noted her "misgivings" about serving, and that she knew one of the defendants' lawyers from his high school days and also knew that lawyer's parents well. U.S. v. Maxwell (C.A.6 (Ohio), 11-17-1998) 160 F.3d 1071. Jury ⚷ 33(5.15)

2945.22 Peremptory challenges—Repealed

(1981 S 1, eff. 10–19–81; 1953 H 1; GC 13443–6)

Historical and Statutory Notes

Pre–1953 H 1 Amendments: 113 v 183, Ch 22, § 6

2945.23 When peremptory challenges required

Except by agreement, neither the state nor the defendant shall be required to exercise any peremptory challenge until twelve jurors have been passed for cause and are in the panel.

(1953 H 1, eff. 10–1–53; GC 13443–7)

Historical and Statutory Notes

Pre–1953 H 1 Amendments: 113 v 183, Ch 22, § 7

Cross References

Trial jurors, Crim R 24

Library References

Jury ⚷134.
Westlaw Topic No. 230.
C.J.S. Juries §§ 344, 421, 423 to 434, 436 to 442.

Research References

Encyclopedias

OH Jur. 3d Family Law § 1744, Trial by Jury.

2945.24 Selecting juries for criminal cases

In all criminal cases, a jury summoned and impaneled under sections 2313.01 to 2313.47 of the Revised Code shall try the accused.

(1993 H 41, eff. 9–27–93; 1981 S 1; 1976 H 133; 1953 H 1; GC 13443–5)

Uncodified Law

1993 H 41, § 3, eff. 9–27–93, provides that the provisions of that act, eliminating the special venire in capital cases, apply to any case that is filed on or after the effective date of that act and in which the defendant is charged with the commission of a capital offense, regardless of when the alleged capital offense occurred.

Historical and Statutory Notes

Pre–1953 H 1 Amendments: 113 v 183, Ch 22, § 5

Amendment Note: 1993 H 41 rewrote this section, which previously read:

"In all criminal cases other than capital cases, a jury summoned and impaneled under sections 2313.01 to 2313.46 of the Revised Code shall try the accused. In capital cases, a jury summoned and impaneled under sections 2945.18 and 2945.19 of the Revised Code shall try the accused."

Library References

Jury ⚷57 to 82.
Westlaw Topic No. 230.
C.J.S. Juries §§ 268, 271 to 272, 279 to 282, 305 to 353, 422, 511.

Research References

Encyclopedias

OH Jur. 3d Jury § 169, Generally; Definitions.

Treatises and Practice Aids

Markus, Trial Handbook for Ohio Lawyers, § 6:2, Selection, Drawing, and Summoning of Jurors.

Law Review and Journal Commentaries

Selecting a Jury in Political Trials, John Van Dyke. 27 Case W Res L Rev 609 (Spring 1977).

Smaller Juries and Non–Unanimity: Analysis and Proposed Revision of the Ohio Jury System, Note. 43 U Cin L Rev 583 (1974).

Notes of Decisions

1. Cross–section of community

Defendant was not denied Sixth Amendment right to fair cross-section of jurors from community in absence of any evidence other than that there were only four African–American jurors in jury pool of 52 prospective jurors. State v. Johnson (Ohio, 03-01-2000) 88 Ohio St.3d 95, 723 N.E.2d 1054, 2000-Ohio-276, reconsideration denied 88 Ohio St.3d 1489, 727 N.E.2d 596, certiorari denied 121 S.Ct. 212, 531 U.S. 889, 148 L.Ed.2d 149, denial of post-conviction relief affirmed 2000 WL 1760225, appeal not allowed 91 Ohio St.3d 1481, 744 N.E.2d 1194. Jury ⚷ 33(1.15)

Jury venire which was created from voter registration rolls and consisted of five African–Americans of fifty members did not entitle defendant to continuance to gather evidence of unfair representation of blacks or fairer representation of blacks by using lists of licensed drivers or Social Security numbers; defendant failed to show violation of fair cross-section requirement of Sixth Amendment. State v. Moore (Ohio, 02-04-1998) 81 Ohio St.3d 22, 689 N.E.2d 1, 1998-Ohio-441, dismissal of post-conviction relief affirmed 1998 WL 638353, dismissed, appeal not allowed 84 Ohio St.3d 1472, 704 N.E.2d 579. Criminal Law ⚷ 589(5)

Jury venire which was created from voter registration rolls and consisted of five African–Americans of fifty members was not shown to violate fair cross-section requirement of Sixth Amendment, even though defendant claimed that large percentage of African–Americans were not registered to vote and lists of licensed drivers or Social Security numbers would attain fairer representation; defendant did not adequately prove unfair representation, but merely alleged that percentage of blacks in jury pool did not equal percentage of blacks in county, and use of voter registration rolls as exclusive sources for jury selection is constitutional. State v. Moore (Ohio, 02-04-1998) 81 Ohio St.3d 22, 689 N.E.2d 1, 1998-Ohio-441, dismissal of post-conviction relief affirmed 1998 WL 638353, dismissed, appeal not allowed 84 Ohio St.3d 1472, 704 N.E.2d 579. Jury ⚷ 33(1.15)

Death qualification of prospective jurors by excluding those opposed to death penalty did not violate fair cross-section requirement of Sixth Amendment; petit juries are not required to reflect composition of community at large, and persons opposed to death penalty do not constitute "distinctive group" for purposes of cross-section claim. State v. Moore (Ohio, 02-04-1998) 81 Ohio St.3d 22, 689 N.E.2d 1, 1998-Ohio-441, dismissal of post-conviction relief affirmed 1998 WL 638353, dismissed, appeal not allowed 84 Ohio St.3d 1472, 704 N.E.2d 579. Jury ⚷ 33(2.15)

Trial court's refusal to grant defendant's motion to supplement annual list of potential jurors with list of licensed drivers did not deprive defendant of impartial jury from a fair cross-section of the community; defendant failed to demonstrate an unfair lack of representation of African–Americans in county juries nor had he shown that such alleged underrepresentation resulted from a systematic exclusion by the state of that particular group. State v. Davie (Ohio, 11-26-1997) 80 Ohio St.3d 311, 686 N.E.2d 245, 1997-Ohio-341, dismissal of post-conviction relief affirmed 1998 WL 684157, dismissed, appeal not allowed 84 Ohio St.3d 1483, 705 N.E.2d 364, reconsideration denied 85 Ohio St.3d 1411, 706 N.E.2d 791, denial of post-conviction relief affirmed 2001-Ohio-8813, 2001 WL 1647193, appeal not allowed 95 Ohio St.3d 1423, 766 N.E.2d 162, 2002-Ohio-1737, habeas corpus denied 291 F.Supp.2d 573, motion to amend denied, certificate of appealability granted in part, denied in part 324 F.Supp.2d 862. Jury ⚷ 33(1.15)

A defendant must demonstrate the following three factors in order to sustain a challenge to a jury-selection procedure on the grounds that the procedure involves a violation of the fair cross-section of the community requirement: (1) the group allegedly excluded constitute a distinctive group in the community, (2) the representation of this group in venires from which juries are selected is not fair and reasonable in relation to the number of such persons in the community, and (3) the underrepresentation is due to a systematic exclusion of the group in the jury selection process. State v. Buell (Butler 1985) 29 Ohio App.3d 215, 504 N.E.2d 1161, 29 O.B.R. 260. Jury ⚷ 33(5.10)

Mere fact that African–American defendant was convicted by all-white jury did not mean that requirement for venire containing fair cross-section of community had been violated; defendant made no showing as to composition of venire, lack of fair and reasonable representation by African–Americans in venire, or systematic exclusion of African–Americans from venire. U.S. v. Anthony (C.A.6 (Ohio), 04-15-2002) No. 00-4118, No. 00-4215, 39 Fed.Appx. 91, 2002 WL 562669, Unreported. Jury ⚷ 33(1.15)

2. Pool from which jurors chosen

Utilization of voter rolls alone to choose prospective jurors is constitutional. State v. Davie (Ohio, 11-26-1997) 80 Ohio St.3d 311, 686 N.E.2d 245, 1997-Ohio-341, dismissal of post-conviction relief affirmed 1998 WL 684157, dismissed, appeal not allowed 84 Ohio St.3d 1483, 705 N.E.2d 364, reconsideration denied 85 Ohio St.3d 1411, 706 N.E.2d 791, denial of post-conviction relief affirmed

2001-Ohio-8813, 2001 WL 1647193, appeal not allowed 95 Ohio St.3d 1423, 766 N.E.2d 162, 2002-Ohio-1737, habeas corpus denied 291 F.Supp.2d 573, motion to amend denied, certificate of appealability granted in part, denied in part 324 F.Supp.2d 862. Jury ⚯ 62(3)

Choosing jurors from a pool of jurors consisting of persons whose last names begin with the letters A through H does not violate a defendant's right to a jury chosen from a fair cross-section of the community. State v. Buell (Butler 1985) 29 Ohio App.3d 215, 504 N.E.2d 1161, 29 O.B.R. 260.

The panel from which jurors are drawn must include electors from eighteen to twenty-one years of age. State v. Willis (Ohio Mun. 1972) 33 Ohio Misc. 159, 293 N.E.2d 895, 62 O.O.2d 288.

2945.25 Causes of challenging of jurors

A person called as a juror in a criminal case may be challenged for the following causes:

(A) That he was a member of the grand jury that found the indictment in the case;

(B) That he is possessed of a state of mind evincing enmity or bias toward the defendant or the state; but no person summoned as a juror shall be disqualified by reason of a previously formed or expressed opinion with reference to the guilt or innocence of the accused, if the court is satisfied, from examination of the juror or from other evidence, that he will render an impartial verdict according to the law and the evidence submitted to the jury at the trial;

(C) In the trial of a capital offense, that he unequivocally states that under no circumstances will he follow the instructions of a trial judge and consider fairly the imposition of a sentence of death in a particular case. A prospective juror's conscientious or religious opposition to the death penalty in and of itself is not grounds for a challenge for cause. All parties shall be given wide latitude in voir dire questioning in this regard.

(D) That he is related by consanguinity or affinity within the fifth degree to the person alleged to be injured or attempted to be injured by the offense charged, or to the person on whose complaint the prosecution was instituted, or to the defendant;

(E) That he served on a petit jury drawn in the same cause against the same defendant, and that jury was discharged after hearing the evidence or rendering a verdict on the evidence that was set aside;

(F) That he served as a juror in a civil case brought against the defendant for the same act;

(G) That he has been subpoenaed in good faith as a witness in the case;

(H) That he is a chronic alcoholic, or drug dependent person;

(I) That he has been convicted of a crime that by law disqualifies him from serving on a jury;

(J) That he has an action pending between him and the state or the defendant;

(K) That he or his spouse is a party to another action then pending in any court in which an attorney in the cause then on trial is an attorney, either for or against him;

(L) That he is the person alleged to be injured or attempted to be injured by the offense charged, or is the person on whose complaint the prosecution was instituted, or the defendant;

(M) That he is the employer or employee, or the spouse, parent, son, or daughter of the employer or employee, or the counselor, agent, or attorney of any person included in division (L) of this section;

(N) That English is not his native language, and his knowledge of English is insufficient to permit him to understand the facts and law in the case;

(O) That he otherwise is unsuitable for any other cause to serve as a juror.

The validity of each challenge listed in this section shall be determined by the court.

(1981 S 1, eff. 10–19–81; 1980 H 965; 1953 H 1; GC 13443–8)

Historical and Statutory Notes

Pre–1953 H 1 Amendments: 118 v 429, § 1; 113 v 183, Ch 22, § 8

Cross References

Challenge for cause, Crim R 24

Library References

Jury ⚖83 to 104.
Westlaw Topic No. 230.

C.J.S. Juries §§ 225, 248, 369 to 403, 415 to 419, 446.

Research References

Encyclopedias

OH Jur. 3d Criminal Law § 448, Statutory Causes for Challenge.

OH Jur. 3d Criminal Law § 449, Statutory Causes for Challenge—Attitude of Juror Toward Capital Punishment as Basis for Challenge.

OH Jur. 3d Criminal Law § 450, Statutory Causes for Challenge—Juror's Preconceived Notion of Guilt or Innocence.

OH Jur. 3d Criminal Law § 2632, Prior Felony Conviction.

OH Jur. 3d Criminal Law § 2633, Interest in Another Case Involving State or Defendant.

OH Jur. 3d Criminal Law § 2634, Enmity or Bias.

OH Jur. 3d Criminal Law § 2635, Enmity or Bias—Prejudice Against Particular Crime.

OH Jur. 3d Criminal Law § 2636, Opposition to Capital Punishment.

OH Jur. 3d Criminal Law § 2637, Relationship to Party or Attorney or Similar Person.

OH Jur. 3d Criminal Law § 2638, Interest in Case.

OH Jur. 3d Criminal Law § 2639, Language Barrier.

OH Jur. 3d Jury § 197, Statutes and Rules Governing Challenges for Cause.

OH Jur. 3d Jury § 198, Physical, Mental, or Other Disability or Handicap.

OH Jur. 3d Jury § 202, Previous Service as Trial or Grand Juror or Talesman.

Treatises and Practice Aids

Markus, Trial Handbook for Ohio Lawyers, § 6:8, Statutory Grounds for Challenge; Civil and Criminal.

Markus, Trial Handbook for Ohio Lawyers, § 6:13, Grounds for Challenge—Family Relationship With Party or Counsel.

Markus, Trial Handbook for Ohio Lawyers, § 6:19, Grounds for Challenge—Opinion as to Guilt or Innocence of Accused.

Markus, Trial Handbook for Ohio Lawyers, § 6:21, Grounds for Challenge—Opposition to Capital Punishment.

Katz, Giannelli, Blair and Lipton, Baldwin's Ohio Practice, Criminal Law, § 64:2, Voir Dire.

Katz, Giannelli, Blair and Lipton, Baldwin's Ohio Practice, Criminal Law, § 118:7, Gun Enhancement.

Giannelli and Snyder, Baldwin's Ohio Practice, Evidence, R 606, Competency of Juror as Witness.

Giannelli and Snyder, Baldwin's Ohio Practice, Evidence, § 606.3, Juror Competency.

Hennenberg & Reinhart, Ohio Criminal Defense Motions F 8.05, Motion for Individual Sequestered Voir Dire-Jury-Related Motions.

Hennenberg & Reinhart, Ohio Criminal Defense Motions F 13.35, Motion for Order Governing Juror Death Qualification Procedure and Memorandum in Support of Proper Death Qualification of Prospective Jurors-Death Penalty Motions.

Hennenberg & Reinhart, Ohio Criminal Defense Motions F 13.50, Motion for Individual Sequestered Voir Dire-Death Penalty Motions.

Law Review and Journal Commentaries

A Doctor's Dilemma: Resolving the Conflict Between Physician Participation in Executions and the AMA's Code of Medical Ethics. 20 U Dayton L Rev 975 (Spring 1995).

Jurors—Challenge for Cause, Lawrence Friedlander. 47 Clev B J 311 (September 1976).

Notes of Decisions

1. Cross–section of community

In order to have a trial by an impartial jury, the array of a veniremen need not reflect an exact cross-section of the community, but the defendant is entitled to a jury panel selected by the best method that thoughtful men who are cognizant of the practicalities of selection and the inherent problems involved have been able to develop; the use of voter registration lists as the source of names of prospective jurors is not unlawful even though it results in the exclusion of nonvoters. State v. Strodes (Ohio 1976) 48 Ohio St.2d 113, 357 N.E.2d 375, 2 O.O.3d 271, vacated 98 S.Ct. 3135, 438 U.S. 911, 57 L.Ed.2d 1154.

Mere fact that African–American defendant was convicted by all-white jury did not mean that requirement for venire containing fair cross-section of community had been violated; defendant made no showing as to composition of venire, lack of fair and reasonable representation by African–Americans in venire, or systematic exclusion of African–Americans from venire. U.S. v. Anthony (C.A.6 (Ohio), 04-15-2002) No. 00-4118, No. 00-4215, 39 Fed.Appx. 91, 2002 WL 562669, Unreported. Jury ⚷ 33(1.15)

2. Bias or enmity—In general

Trial court properly removed for cause juror who stated that he was biased against police officer involved in case because he felt that he had been unfairly treated by that officer in the past, even though defendant did not have opportunity to rehabilitate juror; it was not unreasonable to excuse juror regardless of what may have been elicited by defense counsel since what the witness had already expressed was sufficient for court to exercise its discretion and excuse juror for the purpose of obtaining an unbiased jury. State v. Davis (Ohio App. 3 Dist., Paulding, 05-24-2004) No. 11-03-16, No. 11-03-17, 2004-Ohio-2618, 2004 WL 1146559, Unreported. Jury ⚷ 97(1)

A police sergeant must be dismissed for cause as a prospective juror where the sergeant's working relationship with the police directly involved in the state's charge against the defendant of resisting arrest would cause the sergeant to be biased in deliberating the defendant's fate. State v. Kirkbride (Ohio App. 5 Dist., Muskingum, 04-01-1994) No. C.T. 93-15, 1994 WL 167938, Unreported.

Prospective juror in capital murder prosecution who indicated during voir dire that "maybe" he would feel more strongly about imposing death penalty because one victim was young child was not subject to challenge for cause, where such juror also indicated upon further questioning that he could put victim's age aside and would not feel obligated to return death verdict, and further indicated belief that someone who "lost it" should not be held criminally responsible for his actions. State v. Vrabel (Ohio, 07-02-2003) 99 Ohio St.3d 184, 790 N.E.2d 303, 2003-Ohio-3193, motion granted 102 Ohio St.3d 1465, 809 N.E.2d 672, 2004-Ohio-2829. Jury ⚷ 108

State's use of peremptory challenges to exclude men from jury in prosecution for gross sexual imposition and abduction did not amount to unlawful discrimination on basis of gender, where defense failed to make prima facie showing of discrimination with respect to three of four such challenges, and trial court's acceptance of state's proffered justification for removing fourth prospective juror was not clearly erroneous. State v. Huffman (Ohio App. 11 Dist., 12-20-2002) 151 Ohio App.3d 222, 783 N.E.2d 950, 2002-Ohio-7121. Jury ⚷ 33(5.15)

Trial court's acceptance of state's proffered gender-neutral justification for exercise of peremptory challenge against male prospective juror, in prosecution for gross sexual imposition and abduction, was not abuse of discretion, where proffered reasons included fact that excluded juror did not appear conservative to the state. State v. Huffman (Ohio App. 11 Dist., 12-20-2002) 151 Ohio App.3d 222, 783 N.E.2d 950, 2002-Ohio-7121. Jury ⚷ 33(5.15)

Any deficiency in defense counsel's failure to request trial court to require gender-neutral reasons for prosecution's use of peremptory challenges to exclude male prospective jurors from prosecution for gross sexual imposition and abduction did not prejudice defendant and did not amount to ineffective assistance of counsel, absent any showing that jury containing more males would have rendered different verdict, where defendant's jury was composed of five females and seven males. State v. Huffman (Ohio App. 11 Dist., 12-20-2002) 151 Ohio App.3d 222, 783 N.E.2d 950, 2002-Ohio-7121. Criminal Law ⚷ 641.13(2.1)

Fact that some or all jurors seated in capital murder prosecution had heard of defendant's case prior to trial, without more, did not obviate their stated willingness to function as impartial jurors. State v. Gross (Ohio, 10-30-2002) 97 Ohio St.3d 121, 776 N.E.2d 1061, 2002-Ohio-5524, reconsideration denied 97 Ohio St.3d 1486, 780 N.E.2d 288, 2002-Ohio-6866, certiorari denied 123 S.Ct. 2079, 538 U.S. 1037, 155 L.Ed.2d 1068, rehearing denied 124 S.Ct. 20, 539 U.S. 976, 156 L.Ed.2d 685. Jury ⚷ 100

Trial court's failure sua sponte to excuse for cause a prospective juror who testified during voir dire that he had discussed case with his ex-father-in-law, the former chief of police of city where murder occurred and that prospective juror was biased against the defense to some degree was not error in capital case, where juror also stated that he would try to disregard conversation in question, would decide the case only on the evidence, and would accord defendant the usual presumption of innocence. State v. Jones (Ohio, 04-18-2001) 91 Ohio St.3d 335, 744 N.E.2d 1163, 2001-Ohio-57, reconsideration denied 92 Ohio St.3d 1418, 748 N.E.2d 550, stay granted 92 Ohio St.3d 1421, 748 N.E.2d 1142, certiorari denied 122 S.Ct. 483, 534 U.S. 1004, 151 L.Ed.2d 396, denial of post-conviction relief affirmed 2002-Ohio-2074, 2002 WL 737074, appeal not allowed 96 Ohio St.3d 1495, 774 N.E.2d 767, 2002-Ohio-4534, stay revoked 99 Ohio St.3d 1415, 788 N.E.2d 1098, 2003-Ohio-2526, motion to reopen denied 108 Ohio St.3d 1409, 841 N.E.2d 315, 2006-Ohio-179. Jury ⚷ 103(6); Jury ⚷ 109

Trial court's sua sponte dismissal of a prospective juror from service was not unreasonable or manifestly arbitrary where the juror admitted during questioning by counsel that she had served as a juror in a prior case involving the exact same charge at issue in the instant case, pandering obscenity, involving two employees of exactly the same defendant involved in the instant case, and involving explicit sexual material similar in nature to that at issue in the instant case; trial court could have reasonably determined that allowing juror to serve would have given rise to, at minimum, an appearance of bias or partiality. State v. Midwest Pride IV, Inc. (Ohio App. 12 Dist., 12-28-1998) 131 Ohio App.3d 1, 721 N.E.2d 458, dismissed, appeal not allowed 85 Ohio St.3d 1486, 709 N.E.2d 1214, certiorari denied 120 S.Ct. 400, 528 U.S. 965, 145 L.Ed.2d 312. Jury ⚷ 95; Jury ⚷ 109

Trial court was justified in interrogating prospective jurors concerning apparent conversation with news reporter, given that trial judge had forbidden all prospective jurors from discussing anything about case with anyone, including other prospective jurors. State v. Davie (Ohio, 11-26-1997) 80 Ohio St.3d 311, 686 N.E.2d 245, 1997-Ohio-341, dismissal of post-conviction relief affirmed 1998 WL 684157, dismissed, appeal not allowed 84 Ohio St.3d 1483, 705 N.E.2d 364, reconsideration denied 85 Ohio St.3d 1411, 706 N.E.2d 791, denial of post-conviction relief affirmed 2001-Ohio-8813, 2001 WL 1647193, appeal not allowed 95 Ohio St.3d 1423, 766 N.E.2d 162, 2002-Ohio-1737, habeas corpus denied 291 F.Supp.2d 573, motion to amend denied, certificate of appealability granted in part, denied in part 324 F.Supp.2d 862. Jury ⚷ 131(10)

Unless a juror is challenged for cause, he or she is presumed to be impartial. State v. Williams (Ohio, 06-11-1997) 79 Ohio St.3d 1, 679 N.E.2d 646, 1997-Ohio-407, certiorari denied 118 S.Ct. 703, 522 U.S. 1053, 139 L.Ed.2d 646, denial of post-conviction relief affirmed 1999 WL 1059715, dismissed, appeal not allowed 88 Ohio St.3d 1425, 723 N.E.2d 1113, certiorari denied 121 S.Ct. 109, 531 U.S. 843, 148 L.Ed.2d 66, denial of habeas corpus affirmed 380 F.3d 932, rehearing en banc denied, certiorari denied 125 S.Ct. 1939, 544 U.S. 1003, 161 L.Ed.2d 779. Jury ⚷ 33(2.15)

Trial judge did not abuse his discretion in denying defendant's challenges for cause for prospective juror, who told defense counsel she would automatically vote for death penalty if defendant willfully and intentionally murdered someone, and prospective juror, who told defense counsel that death is always appropriate penalty for intentional murders lacking excuse or justification, given judge's observation of jurors and fact that defense counsel did not explain to those prospective jurors legal meaning of terms "willful," "intentional," "excuse," or "justification." State v. Williams (Ohio, 06-11-1997) 79 Ohio St.3d 1, 679 N.E.2d 646, 1997-Ohio-407, certiorari denied 118 S.Ct. 703, 522 U.S. 1053, 139 L.Ed.2d 646, denial of post-conviction relief affirmed 1999 WL 1059715, dismissed, appeal not allowed 88 Ohio St.3d 1425, 723 N.E.2d 1113, certiorari denied 121 S.Ct. 109, 531 U.S. 843, 148 L.Ed.2d 66, denial of habeas corpus affirmed 380 F.3d 932, rehearing en banc denied, certiorari denied 125 S.Ct. 1939, 544 U.S. 1003, 161 L.Ed.2d 779. Jury ⚷ 108

Trial court did not improperly limit child sexual abuse defendant's questioning of prospective juror, and was not required to excuse that juror for cause after he revealed that he was victim of child abuse and that he could understand why child would take so long to report molestation; trial court determined juror could be fair and impartial, and defense counsel was allowed to question juror at length. State v. Wolfe (Lake 1992) 81 Ohio App.3d 624, 611 N.E.2d 976, dismissed, jurisdictional motion overruled 65 Ohio St.3d 1462, 602 N.E.2d 1171. Jury ⚷ 105(2); Jury ⚷ 131(4)

A trial court in a DUI case does not abuse its discretion in refusing the defendant's challenge for cause of three jurors who opine that it is wrong to drive after drinking, where the jurors go on to state that they could find the defendant not guilty if they believed that his ability to operate his vehicle had not been appreciably impaired by his alcohol consumption. State v. Gleason (Hamilton 1989) 65 Ohio App.3d 206, 583 N.E.2d 975. Jury ⚷ 105(1)

The overruling of a challenge for cause of a venireman who says he will try to be fair but "it could be difficult" is not error given a promise to try to be fair. State v. Tyler (Ohio 1990) 50 Ohio St.3d 24, 553 N.E.2d 576, rehearing denied 51 Ohio St.3d 704, 555 N.E.2d 322, certiorari denied 111 S.Ct. 371, 498 U.S. 951, 112 L.Ed.2d 334, reconsideration denied 75 Ohio St.3d 1474, 663 N.E.2d 1302, stay granted 76 Ohio St.3d 1463, 669 N.E.2d 249.

Exclusion of juror who said he would probably recommend mercy was not error where judge was not satisfied that juror could render an impartial verdict on the evidence on account of the prospective juror's contradictory answers to questions concerning preconceived opinions. State v. Vails (Ohio 1970) 22 Ohio St.2d 103, 258 N.E.2d 225, 51 O.O.2d 133. Jury ⚷ 131(18)

RC 2313.42(E) and RC 2945.25 do not disqualify a state employee from serving as a juror in a criminal case where the state is a party and where actual bias is lacking. State v. Sims (Allen 1969) 20 Ohio App.2d 329, 253 N.E.2d 822, 49 O.O.2d 454.

Trial court does not abuse its discretion when it accepts as a member of jury to try a charge of keeping a room to be used for gambling a person who, on voir dire, says he has a fixed opinion that "numbers game" is gambling but on inquiry by court says that in spite of his opinion he can hear evidence and law and render an impartial verdict and that there is no reason that will prevent him from doing so. State v. Berkman (Lucas 1944) 79 Ohio App. 432, 74 N.E.2d 411, 35 O.O. 228. Jury ⚷ 103(9)

Talesman stating that he knew of case only through newspaper comment and could lay aside opinion as to accused's guilt, and base verdict on facts adduced and law charged *held* properly permitted to sit as juror (Gen. Code, § 13443–8, par. 2). Fry v. State (Coshocton 1932) 43 Ohio App. 154, 182 N.E. 695, 13 Ohio Law Abs. 37. Jury ⚷ 103(14)

A state court finding of a potential juror's bias is to be presumed a correct determination of fact in federal habeas corpus proceedings, and the judge need not draft specific findings or state on the record his conclusion of bias where the transcript shows that the prospective juror was questioned in the presence of counsel and the judge, was challenged by the prosecutor for cause, and that the challenge was sustained. Wainwright v. Witt (U.S.Fla. 1985) 105 S.Ct. 844, 469 U.S. 412, 83 L.Ed.2d 841.

Denial of challenge for cause against juror who had ongoing business relationship with murder victim's parents, had spoken with victim's parents and "listened to them" and did not think he could be fair and impartial juror violated defendant's Sixth Amendment right to impartial jury. Wolfe v. Brigano (C.A.6 (Ohio), 11-17-2000) 232 F.3d 499. Jury ⚷ 33(2.10); Jury ⚷ 90

Denial of challenge for cause against juror who said that she could be fair and impartial, but that she and her husband were "close friends" of murder victim's parents, whom they visited quite a bit, violated defendant's Sixth Amendment right to impartial jury. Wolfe v. Brigano (C.A.6 (Ohio), 11-17-2000) 232 F.3d 499. Jury ⚷ 33(2.10); Jury ⚷ 90

Denial of challenge for cause against juror who had read and heard news accounts of murder, and expressed doubt as to whether she could put aside those reports and decide case solely on evidence presented at trial violated defendant's Sixth Amendment right to impartial jury, in absence of affirmative and believable statement that juror could set aside her opinions and decide case on evidence and in accordance with law. Wolfe v. Brigano (C.A.6 (Ohio), 11-17-2000) 232 F.3d 499. Jury ⚷ 33(2.10); Jury ⚷ 103(14)

Denial of challenge for cause against juror who doubted he would require prosecution to prove its case beyond reasonable doubt violated defendant's Sixth Amendment right to impartial jury, in absence of affirmative and believable statement that juror could set aside his opinions and decide case on evidence and in accordance with law. Wolfe v. Brigano (C.A.6 (Ohio), 11-17-2000) 232 F.3d 499. Jury ⚷ 33(2.10); Jury ⚷ 107

Court's refusal to excuse juror will not be upheld simply because court ultimately elicits from prospective juror a promise that he will be fair and impartial. Wolfe v. Brigano (C.A.6 (Ohio), 11-17-2000) 232 F.3d 499. Jury ⚷ 97(1)

A court does not deny a defendant's right to challenge jurors for cause under RC 2945.25 by denying the challenge of a prospective juror, where such prospective juror, despite doubts, states that she could presume the defendant innocent and fairly judge the case based on the evidence presented. State v Griswold, No. L–85–333 (6th Dist Ct App, Lucas, 3–20–87).

3. —— Ability to render impartial verdict, bias or emnity

Trial court was under no obligation to excuse juror for cause by virtue of juror's apparent anti-drug sentiment and belief that defendant, accused of drug trafficking, should testify on his own behalf if he was not guilty; juror did not state that she would be unable to remain fair and impartial. State v. Freshwater (Ohio App. 11 Dist., Lake, 02-02-2004) No. 2002-L-041, 2004-Ohio-384, 2004 WL 183276, Unreported. Jury ⚷ 105(2); Jury ⚷ 107

Trial court was under no obligation to excuse juror for cause by virtue of her familiarity with family of defendant, in drug trafficking prosecution; juror repeatedly assured trial court and counsel for both parties that she could be fair and impartial and would follow the law as it was given to her by the judge. State v. Freshwater (Ohio App. 11 Dist., Lake, 02-02-2004) No. 2002-L-041, 2004-Ohio-384, 2004 WL 183276, Unreported. Jury ⚷ 90

Prospective juror in capital murder prosecution who stated during voir dire that he did not think "too well" of defendant when he heard of murders with which defendant was charged was not subject to challenge for cause,where prospective juror also asserted that he would listen to defense evidence on insanity, and stated that he could not punish person unable to conform to law or who did not know wrongfulness of his actions and that he would find defendant "not guilty" if he had to decide that day, for lack of solid evidence. State v. Vrabel (Ohio, 07-02-2003) 99 Ohio St.3d 184, 790 N.E.2d 303, 2003-Ohio-3193, motion granted 102 Ohio St.3d 1465, 809 N.E.2d 672, 2004-Ohio-2829. Jury ⚷ 103(6)

Trial courts have discretion in determining a juror's ability to be impartial. State v. Vrabel (Ohio, 07-02-2003) 99 Ohio St.3d 184, 790 N.E.2d 303, 2003-Ohio-3193, motion granted 102 Ohio St.3d 1465, 809 N.E.2d 672, 2004-Ohio-2829. Jury ⚷ 85

Prospective juror in capital murder prosecution who indicated during voir dire that there was "[s]trong possibility" that she would find defendant guilty if he did not present any evidence on his own behalf was not subject to challenge for cause, where such juror also stated that she would put that thinking aside since law required "different way" of thinking, that she could view defendant as innocent and would keep "open mind" during the sentencing phase and with respect to all evidence on insanity, even though one victim was three-and-one-half year-old child. State v. Vrabel (Ohio, 07-02-2003) 99 Ohio St.3d 184, 790 N.E.2d 303, 2003-Ohio-3193, motion granted 102 Ohio St.3d 1465, 809 N.E.2d 672, 2004-Ohio-2829. Jury ⚷ 103(2)

4. Scruples as to death penalty—In general

Trial court properly excluded for cause, in capital murder prosecution, prospective jurors expressing strong views against death penalty, while declining to excuse for cause prospective jurors expressing strong views in favor thereof; excluded jurors all indicated inability to impose the death penalty, retained jurors all indicated their ability to follow the law, instructions and evidence, and those retained jurors specifically challenged never sat on the jury. State v. Stallings (Ohio, 07-19-2000) 89 Ohio St.3d 280, 731 N.E.2d 159, 2000-Ohio-164, stay granted 89 Ohio St.3d 1483, 733 N.E.2d 1184, stay revoked 93 Ohio St.3d 1455, 756 N.E.2d 674, certiorari denied 122 S.Ct. 89, 534 U.S. 836, 151 L.Ed.2d 51, denial of post-conviction relief affirmed 2004-Ohio-4571, 2004 WL 1932869, appeal not allowed 104 Ohio St.3d 1460, 821 N.E.2d 577, 2005-Ohio-204. Jury ⚷ 108

Prospective jurors who clearly and unequivocally indicated during death-qualification process in capital murder prosecution that they would be unable to perform their duties as jurors were properly excused. State v. Johnson (Ohio, 03-01-2000) 88 Ohio St.3d 95, 723 N.E.2d 1054, 2000-Ohio-276, reconsideration denied 88 Ohio St.3d 1489, 727 N.E.2d 596, certiorari denied 121 S.Ct. 212, 531 U.S. 889, 148 L.Ed.2d 149, denial of post-conviction relief affirmed 2000 WL 1760225, appeal not allowed 91 Ohio St.3d 1481, 744 N.E.2d 1194. Jury ⚷ 108

Trial judge did not give favorable treatment to "pro-death penalty" jurors, where the trial judge excused a fair number of prospective jurors who expressed an inability to consider imposing a life sentence. State v. Smith (Ohio, 01-05-2000) 87 Ohio St.3d 424, 721 N.E.2d 93, 2000-Ohio-450, denial of post-conviction relief affirmed 2000 WL 277912, dismissed, appeal not allowed 89 Ohio St.3d 1453, 731 N.E.2d 1140, dismissal of post-conviction relief affirmed 2005-Ohio-2571, 2005 WL 1225931, appeal not allowed 106 Ohio St.3d 1545, 835 N.E.2d 727, 2005-Ohio-5343. Jury ⚷ 108

Capital murder defendant was not entitled to challenge for cause a prospective juror on ground that she was overly concerned about possibility of parole, where prospective juror stated that she could consider all possible penalties and return appropriate verdict when trial judge explained death penalty phase and law involved, and she also stated that she did not think that all murderers should be executed. State v. Williams (Ohio, 06-11-1997) 79 Ohio St.3d 1, 679 N.E.2d 646, 1997-Ohio-407, certiorari denied 118 S.Ct. 703, 522 U.S. 1053, 139 L.Ed.2d 646, denial of post-conviction relief affirmed 1999 WL 1059715, dismissed, appeal not allowed 88 Ohio St.3d 1425, 723 N.E.2d 1113, certiorari denied 121 S.Ct. 109, 531 U.S. 843, 148 L.Ed.2d 66, denial of habeas corpus affirmed 380 F.3d 932, rehearing en banc denied, certiorari denied 125 S.Ct. 1939, 544 U.S. 1003, 161 L.Ed.2d 779. Jury ⚷ 108

Defendant waived issue of peremptory challenges based on jurors' opposition to death penalty by not objecting at trial. State v. Ballew (Ohio, 08-07-1996) 76 Ohio St.3d 244, 667 N.E.2d 369, 1996-Ohio-81, certiorari denied 117 S.Ct. 704, 519 U.S. 1065, 136 L.Ed.2d 625, dismissal of post-conviction relief affirmed 1998 WL 95397, dismissed, appeal not allowed 82 Ohio St.3d 1441, 695 N.E.2d 264, habeas corpus dismissed 2001 WL 242563. Criminal Law ⚷ 1035(5)

The proper standard for determining when a prospective juror may be excluded for cause based on his views on capital punishment is whether the juror's views would prevent or substantially impair the performance of his duties as a juror in accordance with his instructions and oath. (See also State v Rogers, 28 OS(3d) 427, 28 OBR 480, 504 NE(2d) 52 (1986).) State v. Rogers (Ohio 1985) 17 Ohio St.3d 174, 478 N.E.2d 984, 17 O.B.R. 414, vacated 106 S.Ct. 518, 474 U.S. 1002, 88 L.Ed.2d 452, on remand 28 Ohio St.3d 427, 504 N.E.2d 52, 28 O.B.R. 480. Jury ⚷ 108

Upon examination of prospective juror to determine whether he should be disqualified from capital case because of his opposition to capital punishment, the court may properly excuse prospective juror where it appears from his testimony that he could not exercise his own independent judgment in the case but would instead defer to the judgment of his fellow jurors. (See also State v Wilson, 30 OS(2d) 199, 283 NE(2d) 632 (1972).) State v. Wilson (Ohio 1972) 29 Ohio St.2d 203, 280 N.E.2d 915, 58 O.O.2d 409.

Failure of accused to object to exclusion for cause of juror who said he would not vote for death penalty constituted a waiver of such right. State v. Laskey (Ohio 1970) 21 Ohio St.2d 187, 257 N.E.2d 65, 50 O.O.2d 432, vacated in part 92 S.Ct. 2861, 408 U.S. 936, 33 L.Ed.2d 753.

A defendant convicted of murder in the first degree without a recommendation of mercy in a trial conducted prior to the decision of the US Supreme Court in Witherspoon v Illinois, 391 US 510, 88 SCt 1770, 20 LEd(2d) 776 (1968), who did not object when, on the voir dire, some prospective jurors who expressed opinions against capital punishment were excused without a conclusive showing that their opinions would preclude them from finding the accused guilty of an offense punishable by death, as required by Witherspoon, and for which, under RC 2945.25, objection could have been made at that time, is precluded from raising such an issue for the first time in a postconviction remedy proceeding. State v. Duling (Ohio 1970) 21 Ohio St.2d 13, 254 N.E.2d 670, 50 O.O.2d 40, vacated in part 92 S.Ct. 2861, 408 U.S. 936, 33 L.Ed.2d 753.

Permitting the prosecution to secure a jury able to impose a capital penalty does not deny the right to an impartial jury to a defendant against whom that penalty is not sought who is being tried jointly with a codefendant charged with a capital crime. (Ed. note: Kentucky law construed in light of federal constitution.) Buchanan v. Kentucky (U.S.Ky. 1987) 107 S.Ct. 2906, 483 U.S. 402, 97 L.Ed.2d 336, rehearing denied 108 S.Ct. 19, 483 U.S. 1044, 97 L.Ed.2d 807.

In determining whether a prospective juror may be excused for cause because of his views on capital punishment, the standard is whether those views would "prevent or substantially impair the performance of his duties as a juror in accordance with his instructions and oath"; this standard does not require that a juror's bias be proven with "unmistakable clarity." Wainwright v. Witt (U.S.Fla. 1985) 105 S.Ct. 844, 469 U.S. 412, 83 L.Ed.2d 841. Jury ⚷ 108

Allegation that state court misapplied statutory standard for excusal of jurors involved only issue of state law, which was not cognizable in federal habeas corpus proceeding. Frazier v. Mitchell (N.D.Ohio, 01-05-2001) 188 F.Supp.2d 798, reversed in part 343 F.3d 780, opinion supplemented on denial of rehearing 348 F.3d 174, rehearing and suggestion for rehearing en banc denied, certiorari denied 124 S.Ct. 2815, 541 U.S. 1095, 159 L.Ed.2d 261, appeal after new sentencing hearing 2006-Ohio-446, 2006 WL 242476. Habeas Corpus ⚷ 496

5. —— Beliefs preventing impartiality, scruples as to death penalty

Trial court did not abuse its discretion in capital murder trial by excusing for cause prospective juror who stated she did not think that the death penalty was appropriate in any case but that she could consider imposing a death sentence, where juror stated she could not assure the court that her beliefs on death penalty would not have impaired her ability to serve as a juror. State v. Leonard (Ohio, 12-08-2004) 104 Ohio St.3d 54, 818 N.E.2d 229, 2004-Ohio-6235. Jury ⚷ 108

Trial court did not abuse its discretion in capital murder trial by excusing for cause prospective juror who initially stated she could consider imposing death sentence, where juror later stated that she did not feel it was right to "deliberately take the life of another except in self-defense," and that her views against capital punishment were strongly held and that she was opposed to it in all cases, including defendant's case. State v. Leonard (Ohio, 12-08-2004) 104 Ohio St.3d 54, 818 N.E.2d 229, 2004-Ohio-6235. Jury ⚷ 108

Trial court did not abuse its discretion in capital murder trial by failing to excuse for cause prospective juror who stated she strongly favored death penalty in most murder cases with very few exceptions, where upon further questioning, juror stated she could put aside her views and follow the judge's instructions, and stated she could fairly and impartially weigh the mitigation evidence before deciding on appropriate penalty. State v. Leonard (Ohio, 12-08-2004) 104 Ohio St.3d 54, 818 N.E.2d 229, 2004-Ohio-6235. Jury ⚷ 108

Excusing two prospective jurors for cause was not an abuse of discretion in capital murder prosecution, even though defense counsel was able to elicit somewhat contradictory viewpoints from jurors during his examination, where first juror expressed her opposition to the death penalty because of Biblical teachings and indicated she did not want to sign the death-penalty verdict form, and second juror said she could not support the death penalty and doubted if she could sign the death-penalty verdict. State v. Bryan (Ohio, 03-17-2004) 101 Ohio St.3d 272, 804 N.E.2d 433, 2004-Ohio-971, motion granted 102 Ohio St.3d 1437, 807 N.E.2d 937, 2004-Ohio-2226, reconsideration denied 102 Ohio St.3d 1449, 808 N.E.2d 399, 2004-Ohio-2263, motion to reopen denied 103 Ohio St.3d 1490, 816 N.E.2d 1078, 2004-Ohio-5605, reconsideration stricken 103 Ohio St.3d 1529, 817 N.E.2d 891, 2004-Ohio-6040. Jury ⚷ 108

A capital defendant may challenge for cause any prospective juror who, regardless of the evidence of aggravating and mitigating circumstances and in disregard of the jury instructions, will automatically vote for the death penalty. State v. Braden (Ohio, 04-02-2003) 98 Ohio St.3d 354, 785 N.E.2d 439, 2003-Ohio-1325, stay granted 98 Ohio St.3d 1542, 787 N.E.2d 5, 2003-Ohio-2002, denial of post-conviction relief affirmed 2003-Ohio-2949, 2003 WL 21321457, appeal not allowed 100 Ohio St.3d 1431, 797 N.E.2d 511, 2003-Ohio-5396, certiorari denied 124 S.Ct. 182, 540 U.S. 865, 157 L.Ed.2d 119, stay revoked 100 Ohio St.3d 1525, 800 N.E.2d 43, 2003-Ohio-6510. Jury ⚷ 108

Trial court did not act improperly in excusing prospective juror who during voir dire equivocated as to whether she could impose a death sentence, but who indicated several times that her views on death penalty were so strong that they would interfere with her ability to consider imposing death penalty. State v. Smith (Ohio, 01-05-2000) 87 Ohio St.3d 424, 721 N.E.2d 93, 2000-Ohio-450, denial of post-conviction relief affirmed 2000 WL 277912, dismissed, appeal not allowed 89 Ohio St.3d 1453, 731 N.E.2d 1140, dismissal of post-conviction relief affirmed 2005-Ohio-2571, 2005 WL 1225931, appeal not allowed 106 Ohio St.3d 1545, 835 N.E.2d 727, 2005-Ohio-5343. Jury ⚷ 108

Prospective jurors who expressed problems with the death penalty were properly excused in prosecution for aggravated robbery and felony murder; first juror indicated that she had thought about it and did not think she could vote to impose a death sentence, and stated that she could not live with the idea of giving the death penalty to an innocent man, and second juror indicated she did not know if she would be able to vote for the death penalty, but felt she probably could not, and stated that she was bothered by the irrevocability of the death penalty. State v. Madrigal (Ohio, 01-05-2000) 87 Ohio St.3d 378, 721 N.E.2d 52, 2000-Ohio-448, reconsideration denied 88 Ohio St.3d 1428, 723 N.E.2d 1115, certiorari denied 121 S.Ct. 99, 531 U.S. 838, 148 L.Ed.2d 58, habeas corpus granted in part 276 F.Supp.2d 744, affirmed 413 F.3d 548. Jury ⚷ 108

Finding that prospective juror's views regarding death penalty would prevent or substantial impair performance of his duties, thus warranting his removal for cause in capital murder prosecution, was supported by evidence that juror had stated that he opposed capital punishment, that it would be "difficult" for him to follow law as instructed if that would entail recommending death, and that his views would apparently substantially impair his ability to convict, even though juror later appeared to contradict those statements. State v. White (Ohio, 05-12-1999) 85 Ohio St.3d 433, 709 N.E.2d 140, 1999-Ohio-281, denial of post-conviction relief affirmed 1999 WL 394938, dismissed, appeal not allowed 87 Ohio St.3d 1418, 717 N.E.2d 1105, certiorari denied 120 S.Ct. 345, 528 U.S. 938, 145 L.Ed.2d 270, denial of post-conviction relief affirmed 2005-Ohio-6990, 2005 WL 3556634, appeal allowed 109 Ohio St.3d 1493, 848 N.E.2d 857, 2006-Ohio-2762. Jury ⚷ 132

Juror's views on capital punishment would have substantially impaired his ability to follow law, thus warranting his excusal for cause; juror stated that he didn't think he could make decision that would put person to death, and indicated that his views on capital punishment were so strong they would substantially impair his ability to vote for sentence of death. State v. McNeill (Ohio, 10-28-1998) 83 Ohio St.3d 438, 700 N.E.2d 596, 1998-Ohio-293, reconsideration denied 84 Ohio St.3d 1428, 702 N.E.2d 904, certiorari denied 119 S.Ct. 1792, 526 U.S. 1137, 143 L.Ed.2d 1019, denial of post-conviction relief affirmed in part, reversed in part 137 Ohio App.3d 34, 738 N.E.2d 23, dismissed, appeal not allowed 89 Ohio St.3d 1453, 731 N.E.2d 1140, certiorari denied 121 S.Ct. 637, 531 U.S. 1041, 148 L.Ed.2d 543. Jury ⚷ 108

Excusing prospective jurors for cause was permissible in capital murder prosecution since one juror repeatedly said that she would not sign verdict imposing death penalty and that her views were religiously based and since other juror stated that she could not vote for death penalty and indicated that her views would substantially impair ability to follow oath and instructions. State v. Moore (Ohio, 02-04-1998) 81 Ohio St.3d 22, 689 N.E.2d 1, 1998-Ohio-441, dismissal of post-conviction relief affirmed 1998 WL 638353, dismissed, appeal not allowed 84 Ohio St.3d 1472, 704 N.E.2d 579. Jury ⚷ 108

Standard for determining whether prospective juror may be excluded for cause due to his or her views on capital punishment is whether that prospective juror's views would prevent or substantially impair performance of his duties as a juror in accordance with his instructions and oath. State v. Williams (Ohio, 06-11-1997) 79 Ohio St.3d 1, 679 N.E.2d 646, 1997-Ohio-407, certiorari denied 118 S.Ct. 703, 522 U.S. 1053, 139 L.Ed.2d 646, denial of post-conviction relief affirmed 1999 WL 1059715, dismissed, appeal not allowed 88 Ohio St.3d 1425, 723 N.E.2d 1113, certiorari denied 121 S.Ct. 109, 531 U.S. 843, 148 L.Ed.2d 66, denial of habeas corpus affirmed 380 F.3d 932, rehearing en banc denied, certiorari denied 125 S.Ct. 1939, 544 U.S. 1003, 161 L.Ed.2d 779. Jury ⚷ 108

Juror's impartiality in death penalty case is not impaired simply because juror opposes parole for convicted murderers. State v. Williams (Ohio, 06-11-1997) 79 Ohio St.3d 1, 679 N.E.2d 646, 1997-Ohio-407, certiorari denied 118 S.Ct. 703, 522 U.S. 1053, 139 L.Ed.2d 646, denial of post-conviction relief affirmed 1999 WL 1059715, dismissed, appeal not allowed 88 Ohio St.3d 1425, 723 N.E.2d 1113, certiorari denied 121 S.Ct. 109, 531 U.S. 843, 148 L.Ed.2d 66, denial of habeas corpus affirmed 380 F.3d 932, rehearing en banc denied, certiorari denied 125 S.Ct. 1939, 544 U.S. 1003, 161 L.Ed.2d 779. Jury ⚷ 108

Trial court's findings as to whether prospective jury member's views on capital punishment would prevent or substantially impair performance of his duties may not be overturned if supported by substantial testimony. State v. Phillips (Ohio, 11-22-1995) 74 Ohio St.3d 72, 656 N.E.2d 643, 1995-Ohio-171, reconsideration denied 74 Ohio St.3d 1485, 657 N.E.2d 1378, stay granted 74 Ohio St.3d 1503, 659 N.E.2d 795, rehearing granted, opinion recalled 75 Ohio St.3d 1504, 665 N.E.2d 219, certiorari denied 116 S.Ct. 1835, 517 U.S. 1213, 134 L.Ed.2d 938, denial of post-conviction relief affirmed in part, reversed in part 1999 WL 58961, dismissed, appeal not allowed 86 Ohio St.3d 1402, 711 N.E.2d 231, denial of post-conviction relief affirmed 2002-Ohio-823, 2002 WL 274637, appeal not allowed 95 Ohio St.3d 1488, 769 N.E.2d 403, 2002-Ohio-2625. Criminal Law ⚷ 1158(3)

Capital murder defendant did not receive ineffective assistance of counsel when his attorney allegedly failed to challenge for cause prospective jurors favoring death penalty; death penalty views of juror are cause for exclusion only if they prevent or substantially impair his or her ability to follow law, and there was no showing of any such impairment. State v. Phillips (Ohio, 11-22-1995) 74 Ohio St.3d 72, 656 N.E.2d 643, 1995-Ohio-171, reconsideration denied 74 Ohio St.3d 1485, 657 N.E.2d 1378, stay granted 74 Ohio St.3d 1503, 659 N.E.2d 795, rehearing granted, opinion recalled 75 Ohio St.3d 1504, 665 N.E.2d 219, certiorari denied 116 S.Ct. 1835, 517 U.S. 1213, 134 L.Ed.2d 938, denial of post-conviction relief affirmed in part, reversed in part 1999 WL 58961, dismissed, appeal not allowed 86 Ohio St.3d 1402, 711 N.E.2d 231, denial of post-conviction relief affirmed 2002-Ohio-823, 2002 WL 274637, appeal not allowed 95 Ohio St.3d 1488, 769 N.E.2d 403, 2002-Ohio-2625. Criminal Law ⚷ 641.13(2.1)

A juror who originally thinks she "might" be able to subordinate her moral convictions to the law of Ohio but changes her mind when no longer questioned about abstractions and says "I am not sure that what I told you in the beginning was true," is not improperly excused for cause for opposing capital punishment. State v. Tyler (Ohio 1990) 50 Ohio St.3d 24, 553 N.E.2d 576, rehearing denied 51 Ohio St.3d 704, 555 N.E.2d 322, certiorari denied 111 S.Ct. 371, 498 U.S. 951, 112 L.Ed.2d 334, reconsideration denied 75 Ohio St.3d 1474, 663 N.E.2d 1302, stay granted 76 Ohio St.3d 1463, 669 N.E.2d 249.

The criterion for excluding opponents of the death penalty from serving on a jury in a capital case is whether the juror's views would prevent or substantially impair the performance of his duties as a juror in accordance with his instruction and his oath. State v. Scott (Ohio 1986) 26 Ohio St.3d 92, 497 N.E.2d 55, 26 O.B.R. 79, certiorari denied 107 S.Ct. 1386, 480 U.S. 923, 94 L.Ed.2d 699, rehearing denied 107 S.Ct. 1966, 481 U.S. 1034, 95 L.Ed.2d 538, denial of post-conviction relief affirmed in part, reversed in part 63 Ohio App.3d 304, 578 N.E.2d 841, motion to certify denied 47 Ohio St.3d 705, 547 N.E.2d 986.

Prospective jurors in a capital case should be excused for cause if they indicate at voir dire that they could not sign a verdict recommending the death penalty after a mitigation hearing. State ex rel. Miller v. Gillie (Franklin 1986) 24 Ohio App.3d 121, 493 N.E.2d 327, 24 O.B.R. 192.

RC 2945.25(C) allows challenge for cause against a juror irrevocably committed to the death penalty even where there is evidence that mitigation outweighs aggravation. State v. Buell (Ohio 1986) 22 Ohio St.3d 124, 489 N.E.2d 795, 22 O.B.R. 203, certiorari denied 107 S.Ct. 240, 479 U.S. 871, 93 L.Ed.2d 165, rehearing denied 107 S.Ct. 609, 479 U.S. 1000, 93 L.Ed.2d 607, motion to reopen denied 70 Ohio St.3d 1211, 639 N.E.2d 110, reconsideration denied 71 Ohio St.3d 1407, 641 N.E.2d 204, certiorari denied 115 S.Ct. 2252, 515 U.S. 1105, 132 L.Ed.2d 259. Jury ⚿ 31.1

Prospective jurors who indicate during voir dire that they cannot or will not consider imposition of the death penalty may be excluded for cause from a jury in a capital case. State v. Martin (Ohio 1985) 19 Ohio St.3d 122, 483 N.E.2d 1157, 19 O.B.R. 330, certiorari denied 106 S.Ct. 837, 474 U.S. 1073, 88 L.Ed.2d 808, rehearing denied 106 S.Ct. 1253, 475 U.S. 1040, 89 L.Ed.2d 360, dismissal of post-conviction relief affirmed, dismissed, appeal not allowed 72 Ohio St.3d 1548, 650 N.E.2d 1368.

In a bifurcated capital trial, the right to an impartial jury is not denied where potential jurors are excused, pursuant to RC 2945.25(C), before the guilt phase of the trial due to their inability or refusal to impose a death sentence. State v. Jenkins (Ohio 1984) 15 Ohio St.3d 164, 473 N.E.2d 264, 15 O.B.R. 311, certiorari denied 105 S.Ct. 3514, 472 U.S. 1032, 87 L.Ed.2d 643, rehearing denied 106 S.Ct. 19, 473 U.S. 927, 87 L.Ed.2d 697.

It is not reversible error for a trial court to remove jurors for cause where the trial court reasonably believes that the jurors could not determine upon the evidence the guilt or innocence of the accused, but would automatically vote against a verdict which might lead to capital punishment. State v. Roberts (Ohio 1976) 48 Ohio St.2d 221, 358 N.E.2d 530, 2 O.O.3d 399, vacated 98 S.Ct. 3134, 438 U.S. 910, 57 L.Ed.2d 1154.

After venireman has unambiguously stated, on jury voir dire, that he could not vote for the death penalty under any circumstances, a Witherspoon violation cannot be predicated merely upon his ambiguous response to a question of defendant's counsel as to whether there is "anything about the nature of this case that would keep you from listening on the question of the death penalty." State v. Wilson (Ohio 1972) 30 Ohio St.2d 199, 283 N.E.2d 632, 59 O.O.2d 220.

Where a venirewoman indicated that she might be able to listen on the death penalty question, but her prior unambiguous responses showed that she was irrevocably committed before the trial began to vote against the death penalty regardless of the facts and circumstances which might emerge from the proceedings, there was no error in the court's sustaining of the state's challenge for cause. State v. Wilson (Ohio 1972) 30 Ohio St.2d 199, 283 N.E.2d 632, 59 O.O.2d 220.

RC 2945.25(C) authorizes the challenge of a venireman for cause where his opinions regarding capital punishment would preclude him from either finding an accused guilty of an offense for which the death penalty could be imposed or from ever invoking the death penalty in a case where it is authorized. State v. Elliott (Ohio 1971) 25 Ohio St.2d 249, 267 N.E.2d 806, 54 O.O.2d 371, vacated in part 92 S.Ct. 2872, 408 U.S. 939, 33 L.Ed.2d 761.

A state statute may authorize challenge of a prospective juror for cause in a capital case where "his opinions preclude him from finding the accused guilty of an offense punishable with death." (See also State v Pruett, 28 OS(2d) 29, 274 NE(2d) 755 (1971).) State v. Pruett (Ohio 1969) 18 Ohio St.2d 167, 248 N.E.2d 605, 47 O.O.2d 386, reversed 91 S.Ct. 2284, 403 U.S. 946, 29 L.Ed.2d 857, on remand 28 Ohio St.2d 29, 274 N.E.2d 755, 57 O.O.2d 102. Jury ⚿ 84

An impartial jury does not consist of those who will not accept the policy of the state which has declared that death by electrocution is one of the possible penalties of the crime charged. State v. McClellan (Lucas 1967) 12 Ohio App.2d 204, 232 N.E.2d 414, 41 O.O.2d 378, certiorari denied 89 S.Ct. 265, 393 U.S. 929, 21 L.Ed.2d 266. Jury ⚿ 108

6. —— Mere opposition to death penalty, scruples as to death penalty

Trial court did not abuse its discretion in capital murder trial by excusing for cause prospective juror who initially stated she could consider imposing death sentence, where while juror stated after further questioning, that she was not against the death penalty, she stated that she did not feel comfortable being the one to do it and ultimately stated she did not believe she could sign a death verdict. State v. Leonard (Ohio, 12-08-2004) 104 Ohio St.3d 54, 818 N.E.2d 229, 2004-Ohio-6235. Jury ⚿ 108

Juror's ability to perform his duty in accordance with the court's instructions was substantially impaired by his stated inability to impose under any circumstances the death penalty due to his religious beliefs, and thus juror was subject to exclusion for cause, even though juror told defense counsel he could follow instructions; judge properly resolved contradicting statement to defense counsel by inquiring further, and juror reaffirmed that he would follow his religious beliefs even if death sentence was warranted by law. State v. Williams (Ohio, 09-03-2003) 99 Ohio St.3d 493, 794 N.E.2d 27, 2003-Ohio-4396, reconsideration granted 100 Ohio St.3d 1525, 800 N.E.2d 43, 2003-Ohio-6510, on reconsideration 103 Ohio St.3d 112, 814 N.E.2d 818, 2004-Ohio-4747, reconsideration stricken 103 Ohio St.3d 1482, 816 N.E.2d 257, 2004-Ohio-5496. Jury ⚿ 108

Constitutional standard for determining when a prospective juror may be excluded for cause based on his views on capital punishment is whether the juror's views would prevent or substantially impair the performance of his duties as a juror in accordance with his instructions and oath, rather than whether the juror unequivocally states that he would not recommend death under any circumstances. State v. Williams (Ohio, 09-03-2003) 99 Ohio St.3d 493, 794 N.E.2d 27, 2003-Ohio-4396, reconsideration granted 100 Ohio St.3d 1525, 800 N.E.2d 43, 2003-Ohio-6510, on reconsideration 103 Ohio St.3d 112, 814 N.E.2d 818, 2004-Ohio-4747, reconsideration stricken 103 Ohio St.3d 1482, 816 N.E.2d 257, 2004-Ohio-5496. Jury ⚷ 108

Exclusion from capital jury of prospective jurors opposed to the death penalty was not unconstitutional. State v. Lynch (Ohio, 05-14-2003) 98 Ohio St.3d 514, 787 N.E.2d 1185, 2003-Ohio-2284, motion denied 99 Ohio St.3d 1402, 788 N.E.2d 641, 2003-Ohio-2382, certiorari denied 124 S.Ct. 405, 540 U.S. 955, 157 L.Ed.2d 291. Jury ⚷ 33(2.15)

Where one or more of the members of the venire discharged because of opinions regarding the death penalty did not state unambiguously that he would automatically vote against the imposition of the death penalty no matter what the case might reveal, it cannot be presumed that that is his position, and the sentence of death cannot be carried out. State v. Pruett (Ohio 1971) 28 Ohio St.2d 29, 274 N.E.2d 755, 57 O.O.2d 102.

When prospective jurors in a capital case are disqualified for cause simply because of their nonbelief in or opinion against capital punishment, and not because such nonbelief or opinion would unambiguously preclude them from instituting the death sentence in the proper case, the resulting jury is unconstitutional. State v. Watson (Cuyahoga 1969) 20 Ohio App.2d 115, 252 N.E.2d 305, 49 O.O.2d 152, modified 28 Ohio St.2d 15, 275 N.E.2d 153, 57 O.O.2d 95. Criminal Law ⚷ 1134(5)

7. —— Procedure on voir dire, scruples as to death penalty

Trial court did not abuse its discretion during voir dire of capital murder trial by denying trial counsel's request for sequestered voir dire; trial court did permit counsel to individually question prospective jurors, and although jurors were not sequestered, the trial court gave each juror the opportunity to be questioned in private if they were uncomfortable discussing their views in a group setting. State v. Leonard (Ohio, 12-08-2004) 104 Ohio St.3d 54, 818 N.E.2d 229, 2004-Ohio-6235. Jury ⚷ 131(13)

Trial court did not abuse its discretion during voir dire of capital murder trial by precluding trial counsel from using hypothetical question, of whether juror "would impose the death sentence in a case like Timothy McVeigh's" to determine a juror's death-penalty position; trial counsel was permitted to thoroughly explore prospective jurors' views, and defendant failed to show that the trial court unreasonably or arbitrarily restricted counsel's examination. State v. Leonard (Ohio, 12-08-2004) 104 Ohio St.3d 54, 818 N.E.2d 229, 2004-Ohio-6235. Jury ⚷ 131(13)

Rejecting capital murder defendant's challenge for cause against juror who initially said that she could not impose a penalty less severe than death was not an abuse of discretion; although juror was confused by initial questioning, her follow-up responses demonstrated her willingness to follow the law, evaluate mitigating factors, and consider a lesser sentence under appropriate circumstances. State v. Bryan (Ohio, 03-17-2004) 101 Ohio St.3d 272, 804 N.E.2d 433, 2004-Ohio-971, motion granted 102 Ohio St.3d 1437, 807 N.E.2d 937, 2004-Ohio-2226, reconsideration denied 102 Ohio St.3d 1449, 808 N.E.2d 399, 2004-Ohio-2263, motion to reopen denied 103 Ohio St.3d 1490, 816 N.E.2d 1078, 2004-Ohio-5605, reconsideration stricken 103 Ohio St.3d 1529, 817 N.E.2d 891, 2004-Ohio-6040. Jury ⚷ 108

Trial judge has discretion over the scope, length, and manner of voir dire. State v. Williams (Ohio, 09-03-2003) 99 Ohio St.3d 493, 794 N.E.2d 27, 2003-Ohio-4396, reconsideration granted 100 Ohio St.3d 1525, 800 N.E.2d 43, 2003-Ohio-6510, on reconsideration 103 Ohio St.3d 112, 814 N.E.2d 818, 2004-Ohio-4747, reconsideration stricken 103 Ohio St.3d 1482, 816 N.E.2d 257, 2004-Ohio-5496. Jury ⚷ 131(2)

Defense counsel's failure specifically to ask prospective juror in capital murder prosecution whether he would prefer to impose death upon a guilty verdict did not constitute ineffective assistance, where prospective juror's answers in voir dire indicated he would not be "automatic" death penalty juror. State v. Vrabel (Ohio, 07-02-2003) 99 Ohio St.3d 184, 790 N.E.2d 303, 2003-Ohio-3193, motion granted 102 Ohio St.3d 1465, 809 N.E.2d 672, 2004-Ohio-2829. Criminal Law ⚷ 641.13(2.1)

In capital murder trial, court acted within its discretion in refusing to excuse for cause juror who indicated that she favored the death penalty but indicated that she would listen to all the evidence and would require state to prove that aggravating circumstances outweighed mitigating factors. State v. Smith (Ohio, 12-13-2002) 97 Ohio St.3d 367, 780 N.E.2d 221, 2002-Ohio-6659, reconsideration denied 97 Ohio St.3d 1500, 780 N.E.2d 1023, 2002-Ohio-7367, stay granted 98 Ohio St.3d 1417, 782 N.E.2d 73, 2003-Ohio-189, certiorari denied 123 S.Ct. 2255, 539 U.S. 907, 156 L.Ed.2d 118. Jury ⚷ 108

Death qualifying question posed by the prosecutor to prospective jurors as to whether jurors could join in signing a verdict form calling for the imposition of the death penalty did not constitute an inadequate assessment on the juror's view on capital punishment, where two of the prospective jurors indicated a partiality towards imposing death in all cases of murder, and both were excused for cause. State v. Twyford (Ohio, 03-06-2002) 94 Ohio St.3d 340, 763 N.E.2d 122, 2002-Ohio-894, reconsideration denied 95 Ohio St.3d 1423, 766 N.E.2d 163, 2002-Ohio-1737, stay granted 95 Ohio St.3d 1429, 766 N.E.2d 996, 2002-Ohio-1924, certiorari denied 123 S.Ct. 302, 537 U.S. 917, 154 L.Ed.2d 203. Jury ⚷ 131(17)

Denial in capital case of for-cause challenge to prospective juror who testified during voir dire that, according to his religious beliefs, one who takes the life of another should "automatically" lose his own life was not error, where prospective juror further testified that he would follow the law and that he was capable of considering a penalty less than death. State v. Jones (Ohio, 04-18-2001) 91 Ohio St.3d 335, 744 N.E.2d 1163, 2001-Ohio-57, reconsideration denied 92 Ohio St.3d 1418, 748 N.E.2d 550, stay granted 92 Ohio St.3d 1421, 748 N.E.2d 1142, certiorari denied 122 S.Ct. 483, 534 U.S. 1004, 151 L.Ed.2d 396, denial of post-conviction relief affirmed 2002-Ohio-2074, 2002 WL 737074, appeal not allowed 96 Ohio St.3d 1495, 774 N.E.2d 767, 2002-Ohio-4534, stay revoked 99 Ohio St.3d 1415, 788 N.E.2d 1098, 2003-Ohio-2526, motion to reopen denied 108 Ohio St.3d 1409, 841 N.E.2d 315, 2006-Ohio-179. Jury ⚿ 108

Inclusion in capital murder prosecution of juror who initially stated in voir dire that she "believed in" the death penalty because someone who took another person's life should give his life up, and that this principle should apply "in every case," did not violate defendant's right to fair and impartial jury, where juror later stated in voir dire that she had been confused by earlier questions, insisted she would follow the law and the court's directions, and specifically indicated she could consider mitigating circumstances that might warrant a lesser sentence. State v. Treesh (Ohio, 01-03-2001) 90 Ohio St.3d 460, 739 N.E.2d 749, 2001-Ohio-4, stay granted 91 Ohio St.3d 1435, 742 N.E.2d 135, certiorari denied 121 S.Ct. 2247, 533 U.S. 904, 150 L.Ed.2d 234. Jury ⚿ 108

Defendant's counsel in capital murder case was not ineffective in failing to examine prospective jurors during voir dire to determine whether they were capable of considering all mitigating factors; counsel did ask veniremen whether they could consider mitigating circumstances, as opposed to automatically imposing death penalty, and counsel could reasonably decide that it was unnecessary to ask prospective jurors whether they would find specific factors to be mitigating. State v. McGuire (Ohio, 12-10-1997) 80 Ohio St.3d 390, 686 N.E.2d 1112, 1997-Ohio-335, reconsideration denied 81 Ohio St.3d 1433, 689 N.E.2d 52, dismissal of post-conviction relief affirmed 1998 WL 191415, dismissed, appeal not allowed 83 Ohio St.3d 1428, 699 N.E.2d 945, certiorari denied 119 S.Ct. 85, 525 U.S. 831, 142 L.Ed.2d 66, denial of post-conviction relief affirmed 2001 WL 409424, dismissed, appeal not allowed 93 Ohio St.3d 1411, 754 N.E.2d 259. Criminal Law ⚿ 641.13(2.1)

It is duty of trial judge during voir dire of prospective jurors in death penalty case to sort through prospective jurors' responses to questions on their views of death penalty and determine whether prospective jurors will be able to follow the law. State v. Williams (Ohio, 06-11-1997) 79 Ohio St.3d 1, 679 N.E.2d 646, 1997-Ohio-407, certiorari denied 118 S.Ct. 703, 522 U.S. 1053, 139 L.Ed.2d 646, denial of post-conviction relief affirmed 1999 WL 1059715, dismissed, appeal not allowed 88 Ohio St.3d 1425, 723 N.E.2d 1113, certiorari denied 121 S.Ct. 109, 531 U.S. 843, 148 L.Ed.2d 66, denial of habeas corpus affirmed 380 F.3d 932, rehearing en banc denied, certiorari denied 125 S.Ct. 1939, 544 U.S. 1003, 161 L.Ed.2d 779. Jury ⚿ 108

Denial of defendant's challenge for cause of prospective juror was not an abuse of discretion, although juror vacillated in responses to questions concerning death penalty; judge fully explained penalty stage, law of mitigation and aggravation, and corresponding penalties, and by end of voir dire, prospective juror fully understood that automatic death penalty vote was inconsistent with the law, and thus, when she said she could follow law, she was not unaware that maintaining dogmatic beliefs about death penalty would prevent her from doing so. State v. Williams (Ohio, 06-11-1997) 79 Ohio St.3d 1, 679 N.E.2d 646, 1997-Ohio-407, certiorari denied 118 S.Ct. 703, 522 U.S. 1053, 139 L.Ed.2d 646, denial of post-conviction relief affirmed 1999 WL 1059715, dismissed, appeal not allowed 88 Ohio St.3d 1425, 723 N.E.2d 1113, certiorari denied 121 S.Ct. 109, 531 U.S. 843, 148 L.Ed.2d 66, denial of habeas corpus affirmed 380 F.3d 932, rehearing en banc denied, certiorari denied 125 S.Ct. 1939, 544 U.S. 1003, 161 L.Ed.2d 779. Jury ⚿ 108

Trial judge did not abuse his discretion in denying defendant's challenges for cause of prospective jurors who would require defendant to show why he should not receive a death sentence, where after law was more fully explained to them, each prospective juror stated that he or she could follow the law. State v. Williams (Ohio, 06-11-1997) 79 Ohio St.3d 1, 679 N.E.2d 646, 1997-Ohio-407, certiorari denied 118 S.Ct. 703, 522 U.S. 1053, 139 L.Ed.2d 646, denial of post-conviction relief affirmed 1999 WL 1059715, dismissed, appeal not allowed 88 Ohio St.3d 1425, 723 N.E.2d 1113, certiorari denied 121 S.Ct. 109, 531 U.S. 843, 148 L.Ed.2d 66, denial of habeas corpus affirmed 380 F.3d 932, rehearing en banc denied, certiorari denied 125 S.Ct. 1939, 544 U.S. 1003, 161 L.Ed.2d 779. Jury ⚿ 108

Prosecution in capital murder case could properly exercise peremptorily challenges against two prospective jurors who expressed or indicated some aversion to death penalty. State v. Biros (Ohio, 05-14-1997) 78 Ohio St.3d 426, 678 N.E.2d 891, 1997-Ohio-204, reconsideration denied 79 Ohio St.3d 1451, 680 N.E.2d 1023, certiorari denied 118 S.Ct. 574, 522 U.S. 1002, 139 L.Ed.2d 413, denial of post-conviction relief affirmed 1999 WL 391090, dismissed, appeal not allowed 87 Ohio St.3d 1406, 716 N.E.2d 1168, denial of post-conviction relief affirmed 93 Ohio St.3d 250, 754 N.E.2d 805, 2001-Ohio-1339, grant of habeas corpus reversed 422 F.3d 379, rehearing and rehearing en banc denied, petition for certiorari filed 2006 WL 1583483. Jury ⚿ 33(5.15)

Trial court did not abuse discretion, in capital murder case, by interviewing prospective jurors in groups to elicit their views regarding capital punishment, and subsequently questioning individually those persons who had reservations about death penalty. State v. Brooks (Ohio, 03-04-1996) 75 Ohio St.3d 148, 661 N.E.2d 1030, 1996-Ohio-134, reconsideration denied 75 Ohio St.3d 1452, 663 N.E.2d 333. Jury ⚿ 131(13)

Capital murder defendant had not received ineffective assistance of counsel when his counsel allegedly did not probe views of five prospective jurors who indicated they could not or would not vote for death penalty, in order to keep them from being excused for cause; counsel had attempted to rehabilitate some of the individuals but each expressed strong feelings that he or she would be unable to follow law in event death penalty was warranted. State v. Phillips (Ohio, 11-22-1995) 74 Ohio St.3d 72, 656 N.E.2d 643, 1995-Ohio-171, reconsideration denied 74 Ohio St.3d 1485, 657 N.E.2d 1378, stay granted 74 Ohio St.3d 1503, 659 N.E.2d 795, rehearing granted, opinion recalled 75 Ohio St.3d 1504, 665 N.E.2d 219, certiorari denied 116 S.Ct. 1835, 517 U.S. 1213, 134 L.Ed.2d 938, denial of post-conviction relief affirmed in part, reversed in part 1999 WL 58961, dismissed, appeal not allowed 86 Ohio St.3d 1402, 711 N.E.2d 231, denial of post-conviction relief affirmed 2002-Ohio-823, 2002 WL 274637, appeal not allowed 95 Ohio St.3d 1488, 769 N.E.2d 403, 2002-Ohio-2625. Criminal Law ⚿ 641.13(2.1)

Capital murder defendant did not receive ineffective assistance of counsel when his attorneys allegedly failed to question prospective juror regarding specific mitigating factors that might be introduced in penalty phase; defense counsel had posed general questions regarding mitigating factors to some members of each prospective juror group as they were "death-qualified" and it was not essential to ask specific questions in order to provide competent representation. State v. Phillips (Ohio, 11-22-1995) 74 Ohio St.3d 72, 656 N.E.2d 643, 1995-Ohio-171, reconsideration denied 74 Ohio St.3d 1485, 657 N.E.2d 1378, stay granted 74 Ohio St.3d 1503, 659 N.E.2d 795, rehearing granted, opinion recalled 75 Ohio St.3d 1504, 665 N.E.2d 219, certiorari denied 116 S.Ct. 1835, 517 U.S. 1213, 134 L.Ed.2d 938, denial of post-conviction relief affirmed in part, reversed in part 1999 WL 58961, dismissed, appeal not allowed 86 Ohio St.3d 1402, 711 N.E.2d 231, denial of post-conviction relief affirmed 2002-Ohio-823, 2002 WL 274637, appeal not allowed 95 Ohio St.3d 1488, 769 N.E.2d 403, 2002-Ohio-2625. Criminal Law ⚿ 641.13(2.1)

Jurors philosophically opposed to capital punishment were properly excused from venire in capital prosecution, as views would prevent or substantially impair performance of duties as juror in accordance with instructions and oath. State v. Garner (Ohio, 11-22-1995) 74 Ohio St.3d 49, 656 N.E.2d 623, 1995-Ohio-168, reconsideration denied 74 Ohio St.3d 1485, 657 N.E.2d 1378, certiorari denied 116 S.Ct. 1444, 517 U.S. 1147, 134 L.Ed.2d 564, rehearing denied 116 S.Ct. 1872, 517 U.S. 1230, 134 L.Ed.2d 969, stay granted 76 Ohio St.3d 1401, 666 N.E.2d 233. Jury ⚿ 108

Trial court did not improperly restrict capital murder defendant's questioning of venireperson who was stricken from venire after stating that he had could not impose death penalty; while trial court did sustain objections to three defense questions, all three repeated questions judge had already asked. State v. Allen (Ohio, 09-06-1995) 73 Ohio St.3d 626, 653 N.E.2d 675, 1995-Ohio-283, reconsideration denied 74 Ohio St.3d 1422, 655 N.E.2d 742, certiorari denied 116 S.Ct. 1276, 516 U.S. 1178, 134 L.Ed.2d 222, denial of post-conviction relief affirmed 1998 WL 289418, dismissed, appeal not allowed 83 Ohio St.3d 1448, 700 N.E.2d 331. Jury ⚿ 131(4)

Trial court did not err in releasing for cause three jurors who indicated that they could not return death sentence against defendant due to their personal views regarding death penalty. State v. Grant (Ohio 1993) 67 Ohio St.3d 465, 620 N.E.2d 50, rehearing denied 68 Ohio St.3d 1412, 623 N.E.2d 568, certiorari denied 115 S.Ct. 116, 513 U.S. 836, 130 L.Ed.2d 62, rehearing denied 115 S.Ct. 617, 513 U.S. 1033, 130 L.Ed.2d 525. Jury ⚿ 108

It is permissible during voir dire to ask veniremen if they could consider imposing the death penalty "in this case." State v. Tyler (Ohio 1990) 50 Ohio St.3d 24, 553 N.E.2d 576, rehearing denied 51 Ohio St.3d 704, 555 N.E.2d 322, certiorari denied 111 S.Ct. 371, 498 U.S. 951, 112 L.Ed.2d 334, reconsideration denied 75 Ohio St.3d 1474, 663 N.E.2d 1302, stay granted 76 Ohio St.3d 1463, 669 N.E.2d 249. Jury ⚿ 131(8)

When examining prospective jurors, the prosecution has a right to state the nature of the alleged offense and state who is claimed to have been associated with it, to ascertain whether the jurors have read or know of the occurrence. State v. Tyler (Ohio 1990) 50 Ohio St.3d 24, 553 N.E.2d 576, rehearing denied 51 Ohio St.3d 704, 555 N.E.2d 322, certiorari denied 111 S.Ct. 371, 498 U.S. 951, 112 L.Ed.2d 334, reconsideration denied 75 Ohio St.3d 1474, 663 N.E.2d 1302, stay granted 76 Ohio St.3d 1463, 669 N.E.2d 249.

The statement of a judge to veniremen when trying to give them some idea of how the penalty is imposed in a capital trial, that aggravating circumstances are those showing an offense was "heinous," "cruel," "particularly terrible," or "very bad," gives the defendant no basis for objection or for a claim of ineffective assistance of counsel; these general descriptions are not jury instructions. State v. Tyler (Ohio 1990) 50 Ohio St.3d 24, 553 N.E.2d 576, rehearing denied 51 Ohio St.3d 704, 555 N.E.2d 322, certiorari denied 111 S.Ct. 371, 498 U.S. 951, 112 L.Ed.2d 334, reconsideration denied 75 Ohio St.3d 1474, 663 N.E.2d 1302, stay granted 76 Ohio St.3d 1463, 669 N.E.2d 249.

The determination of whether a voir dire in a capital case should be conducted in sequestration is a matter of discretion within the province of the trial judge. State v. Mapes (Ohio 1985) 19 Ohio St.3d 108, 484 N.E.2d 140, 19 O.B.R. 318, certiorari denied 106 S.Ct. 2905, 476 U.S. 1178, 90 L.Ed.2d 991, post-conviction relief denied, dismissed 53 Ohio St.3d 703, 558 N.E.2d 57, rehearing denied 53 Ohio St.3d 718, 560 N.E.2d 779, certiorari denied 111 S.Ct. 504, 498 U.S. 977, 112 L.Ed.2d 433, rehearing denied 56 Ohio St.3d 709, 565 N.E.2d 605. Criminal Law ⚿ 1152(2); Jury ⚿ 131(13)

Since the potential imposition of the death penalty in the trial of an aggravated murder charge with specifications is not within the province of the jury, it is improper, upon voir dire, to question prospective jurors relative to such penalty. State v. Strub (Columbiana 1975) 48 Ohio App.2d 57, 355 N.E.2d 819, 2 O.O.3d 40. Jury ⊂ 131(8)

Procedure during voir dire of a capital case, whereby each prospective juror is initially examined by the court, prosecutor, and defense counsel solely on questions pertaining to capital punishment, before they proceed to examine them on other issues, does not violate constitutional rights. State v. Carver (Ohio 1972) 30 Ohio St.2d 280, 285 N.E.2d 26, 59 O.O.2d 343, certiorari denied 93 S.Ct. 542, 409 U.S. 1044, 34 L.Ed.2d 495. Jury ⊂ 131(13)

RC 2945.25(C) states a cause for which a juror may be challenged in a capital case, and as long as the questions asked on voir dire are intended to and do reveal whether such a cause exists, a reading of the specific language of the statute is not required. State v. Carver (Ohio 1972) 30 Ohio St.2d 280, 285 N.E.2d 26, 59 O.O.2d 343, certiorari denied 93 S.Ct. 542, 409 U.S. 1044, 34 L.Ed.2d 495. Criminal Law ⊂ 1166.16; Jury ⊂ 131(10)

Where record in a capital case shows that trial judge gave a general explanation to prospective jurors of their duties under law, asked them if, in view of those duties, they could serve as jurors in the cause, but then restricted them to a total response of "I can" or "I cannot," and prohibited prosecuting attorney and defendant or his counsel from asking them any questions concerning their scruples regarding capital punishment, there has been a failure to establish compliance with requirements of Witherspoon v Illinois, 391 US 510, 88 SCt 1770, 20 LEd(2d) 776 (1968), and execution of death sentence imposed by jury so selected would deprive defendant of his life without due process of law. State v. Anderson (Ohio 1972) 30 Ohio St.2d 66, 282 N.E.2d 568, 59 O.O.2d 85. Constitutional Law ⊂ 267

Where, before a jury is impaneled, an accused expressly agrees to excuse any and all prospective jurors for cause merely because of their opposition to capital punishment, and at that time such accused has a statutory right to object to excusing any juror because of his opinions with regard to capital punishment unless such opinions preclude him from finding the accused guilty of an offense punishable with death, such accused may not thereafter complain about the excusing of one prospective juror merely because of such juror's opposition to capital punishment, especially where no question was raised at the time by such accused as to the excusing of such juror for that cause. State v. Wigglesworth (Ohio 1969) 18 Ohio St.2d 171, 248 N.E.2d 607, 47 O.O.2d 388, reversed 91 S.Ct. 2284, 403 U.S. 947, 29 L.Ed.2d 857, on remand 28 Ohio St.2d 28, 274 N.E.2d 759, 57 O.O.2d 102. Criminal Law ⊂ 1035(6); Criminal Law ⊂ 1137(1)

Under RC 2945.25(C), a juror in a capital case may be challenged for cause if his views on the death penalty would prevent or substantially impair the performance of his duties as a juror; the state need not show unequivocally that there are no circumstances under which he would follow the court's instructions with regard to the death penalty. State v Orth, No. L–86–260 (6th Dist Ct App, Lucas, 12–11–87).

8. Prior jury service

The prospective juror may be challenged if he has served in two or more trials of criminal cases during or within the three weeks next preceding the trial; however, it is not necessary that the juror shall have actually participated in the trial of criminal cases during the entire three-week-period. State v. Browning (Ohio 1931) 123 Ohio St. 584, 176 N.E. 225, 10 Ohio Law Abs. 158.

9. Prior felony conviction

Person who served penitentiary sentence in another state, where offense was not felony in Ohio, not disqualified as juror. Browning v. State (Ohio 1929) 120 Ohio St. 62, 165 N.E. 566, 7 Ohio Law Abs. 140, 28 Ohio Law Rep. 474.

10. Other causes of unsuitability

Claim that trial court erred in denying motion to have court follow statutory standard for death qualification of venire persons was moot, where defendant was neither convicted of capital murder nor sentenced to death penalty. State v. Gray (Ohio App. 8 Dist., Cuyahoga, 03-25-2004) No. 83097, 2004-Ohio-1454, 2004 WL 584187, Unreported, motion to reopen denied 2004-Ohio-4481, 2004 WL 1902381, motion for delayed appeal denied 103 Ohio St.3d 1476, 816 N.E.2d 252, 2004-Ohio-5405. Criminal Law ⊂ 1134(3)

Trial court's failure to excuse juror for cause after juror disclosed his substantial relationship to defendant's drug trafficking case, thereby forcing defendant to use peremptory challenge, was prejudicial error; in his capacity as prosecutor for neighboring county, juror was currently investigating defendant's brother, and had even spoken to defendant a week earlier regarding defendant's ability to assist in another prosecution, juror's brother was the prosecutor for city from which defendant's case emanated, and during voir dire, rather than outright stating that he could be fair and impartial, juror stated that he might have problem with case, but would "try to be impartial." State v. Freshwater (Ohio App. 11 Dist., Lake, 02-02-2004) No. 2002-L-041, 2004-Ohio-384, 2004 WL 183276, Unreported. Criminal Law ⊂ 1166.18; Jury ⊂ 90; Jury ⊂ 97(2)

Trial court's inquiries as to whether prospective juror had consumed alcohol were legitimate, where both judge and prosecutor thought they smelled alcohol on prospective juror's breath. State v. Davie (Ohio, 11-26-1997) 80 Ohio St.3d 311, 686 N.E.2d 245, 1997-Ohio-341, dismissal of post-conviction relief affirmed 1998 WL 684157, dismissed, appeal not allowed 84 Ohio St.3d 1483, 705 N.E.2d 364, reconsideration denied 85 Ohio St.3d 1411, 706 N.E.2d 791, denial of post-conviction relief affirmed 2001-Ohio-8813, 2001 WL 1647193, appeal not allowed 95 Ohio St.3d 1423, 766 N.E.2d 162, 2002-Ohio-1737, habeas corpus denied 291 F.Supp.2d 573, motion to amend denied, certificate of appealability granted in part, denied in part 324 F.Supp.2d 862. Jury ⊂ 131(10)

Fact that prospective juror in trial for murder and gross abuse of corpse was college student, unemployed, and close in age to defendant was not compelling reason to excuse her from jury and did not correspond to valid for-cause challenge. State v. Nobles (Ohio App. 2 Dist., 09-01-1995) 106 Ohio App.3d 246, 665 N.E.2d 1137, dismissed, appeal not allowed 74 Ohio St.3d 1510, 659 N.E.2d 1287. Jury ⚷ 33(5.15)

Trial court properly denied capital murder defendant's challenge for cause to juror whose murdered brother's alleged killer was acquitted, and who had two friends who were police officers; even though juror admitted to some bitterness, she said she could set aside her feelings and vote solely on evidence, and she answered "no" when asked if her feelings would "impact" on case. State v. Allen (Ohio, 09-06-1995) 73 Ohio St.3d 626, 653 N.E.2d 675, 1995-Ohio-283, reconsideration denied 74 Ohio St.3d 1422, 655 N.E.2d 742, certiorari denied 116 S.Ct. 1276, 516 U.S. 1178, 134 L.Ed.2d 222, denial of post-conviction relief affirmed 1998 WL 289418, dismissed, appeal not allowed 83 Ohio St.3d 1448, 700 N.E.2d 331. Jury ⚷ 97(1); Jury ⚷ 97(2)

In a trespass prosecution of defendants for their participation in an abortion protest, potential jurors are not improperly removed where they expressly state that their views on abortion would prevent them from rendering fair and impartial verdicts. Akron v. Wendell (Summit 1990) 70 Ohio App.3d 35, 590 N.E.2d 380.

A person is not disqualified as a juror in a criminal case because his wife is related to the prosecuting attorney in the degree of first cousin, twice removed, where such person and the prosecuting attorney did not know of the relationship at the time of trial and the defendant did not raise the question until after a verdict had been rendered. State v. Keaton (Pickaway 1967) 9 Ohio App.2d 139, 223 N.E.2d 631, 38 O.O.2d 166, certiorari denied 88 S.Ct. 1092, 390 U.S. 971, 19 L.Ed.2d 1182.

The fact that a person selected to serve as a juror at the trial of one charged with murder in the first degree is acquainted with the sheriff and a deputy sheriff who was a witness for the prosecution and has procured an insurance policy for that witness does not prejudice defendant's right to a fair and impartial trial, where the opportunity was present for defendant's counsel to ascertain this fact, and where there is no evidence that the juror was prejudiced against the defendant by reason of such acquaintance. (See also Woodards v Maxwell, 303 FSupp 690, 24 Misc 157 (SD Ohio 1969).) State v. Woodards (Ohio 1966) 6 Ohio St.2d 14, 215 N.E.2d 568, 35 O.O.2d 8, certiorari denied 87 S.Ct. 289, 385 U.S. 930, 17 L.Ed.2d 212.

No rule exists that prison employees or law enforcement officers must automatically be excluded from juries hearing criminal cases involving prisoners; something more must be shown in order to require a prospective juror's removal. State v. Tucker (Ohio App. 4 Dist., Ross, 04-02-2002) No. 01CA2592, 2002-Ohio-1597, 2002 WL 507529, Unreported. Jury ⚷ 83(3)

Where a special in camera voir dire of a juror elicited her assurance that she would not be influenced by her dream, there was no abuse of discretion in allowing the juror to continue after she informed the court during the penalty deliberations in a capital case that she was a mental patient and that more than twenty years earlier, after receiving shock treatments, she had seen the expert psychiatric witness for the defense in a dream in which he was "fat, carried a briefcase and a clock," and "looked like Satan." State v Montgomery, No. L–86–395 (6th Dist Ct App, Lucas, 8–12–88), affirmed by 61 OS(3d) 410, 575 NE(2d) 167 (1991).

11. Exercising challenges for cause

Court of Appeals would presume in drug prosecution that trial court did not abuse its discretion in denying defendant's challenge for cause to prospective juror who indicated that her judgment might be clouded by fact that her brother-in-law was murdered in drug related incident, where juror's response to court's inquiry as to whether she could lay her personal experiences aside and be fair and impartial juror was inaudible to court reporter and defendant failed to supplement record in order to show how juror answered inquiry. State v. Brock (Ohio App. 2 Dist., Montgomery, 12-27-2002) No. 19291, 2002-Ohio-7292, 2002 WL 31888185, Unreported. Criminal Law ⚷ 1144.8

Trial court in capital murder prosecution was not required to grant challenge for cause to parole officer who stated that a defendant should pay with his life if he took a life in a premeditated act; his occupation did not disqualify him from sitting as a juror, and he expressed his willingness to weigh the aggravating circumstances against mitigating factors, consider sentences other than death, and follow the law even though it might differ from his personal views. State v. Braden (Ohio, 04-02-2003) 98 Ohio St.3d 354, 785 N.E.2d 439, 2003-Ohio-1325, stay granted 98 Ohio St.3d 1542, 787 N.E.2d 5, 2003-Ohio-2002, denial of post-conviction relief affirmed 2003-Ohio-2949, 2003 WL 21321457, appeal not allowed 100 Ohio St.3d 1431, 797 N.E.2d 511, 2003-Ohio-5396, certiorari denied 124 S.Ct. 182, 540 U.S. 865, 157 L.Ed.2d 119, stay revoked 100 Ohio St.3d 1525, 800 N.E.2d 43, 2003-Ohio-6510. Jury ⚷ 83(3); Jury ⚷ 108

Trial court in capital murder prosecution was not required to grant challenge for cause to prospective juror whose brother was a homicide victim and who stated that a life sentence would not be good enough; she told the court that she would follow the law, would not automatically vote for the death penalty, would weigh the aggravating circumstances against the mitigating factors, could put aside her brother's death, would listen to the facts, and could be a fair and impartial juror. State v. Braden (Ohio, 04-02-2003) 98 Ohio St.3d 354, 785 N.E.2d 439, 2003-Ohio-1325, stay granted 98 Ohio St.3d 1542, 787 N.E.2d 5, 2003-Ohio-2002, denial of post-conviction relief affirmed 2003-Ohio-2949, 2003 WL 21321457, appeal not allowed 100 Ohio St.3d

1431, 797 N.E.2d 511, 2003-Ohio-5396, certiorari denied 124 S.Ct. 182, 540 U.S. 865, 157 L.Ed.2d 119, stay revoked 100 Ohio St.3d 1525, 800 N.E.2d 43, 2003-Ohio-6510. Jury ⚿ 97(2); Jury ⚿ 108

Trial court in capital murder prosecution was not required to grant challenge for cause to prospective juror who stated that he would automatically jump to a death sentence upon finding defendant guilty; he agreed that he would have to hear all facts before making a decision, would consider the alternatives, and would weigh the mitigating factors before reaching a sentence, and his other answers showed his commitment to being a fair-minded juror. State v. Braden (Ohio, 04-02-2003) 98 Ohio St.3d 354, 785 N.E.2d 439, 2003-Ohio-1325, stay granted 98 Ohio St.3d 1542, 787 N.E.2d 5, 2003-Ohio-2002, denial of post-conviction relief affirmed 2003-Ohio-2949, 2003 WL 21321457, appeal not allowed 100 Ohio St.3d 1431, 797 N.E.2d 511, 2003-Ohio-5396, certiorari denied 124 S.Ct. 182, 540 U.S. 865, 157 L.Ed.2d 119, stay revoked 100 Ohio St.3d 1525, 800 N.E.2d 43, 2003-Ohio-6510. Jury ⚿ 108

Trial court did not improperly deny challenges for cause, in capital murder prosecution, involving jurors who stated that they could not consider mitigating evidence and would automatically vote to recommend death penalty, and thus did not prejudicially affect defendant's use of peremptory challenges; many jurors challenged on such grounds in fact indicated willingness and ability to follow the law in sentencing phase, trial court excused for cause any prospective juror who did express inability to consider mitigation evidence, and defendant failed to identify any remaining prospective juror against whom he was required to exercise peremptory challenge to his prejudice. State v. Gross (Ohio, 10-30-2002) 97 Ohio St.3d 121, 776 N.E.2d 1061, 2002-Ohio-5524, reconsideration denied 97 Ohio St.3d 1486, 780 N.E.2d 288, 2002-Ohio-6866, certiorari denied 123 S.Ct. 2079, 538 U.S. 1037, 155 L.Ed.2d 1068, rehearing denied 124 S.Ct. 20, 539 U.S. 976, 156 L.Ed.2d 685. Jury ⚿ 108; Jury ⚿ 135

Capital murder defendant who waived his final peremptory challenge had no basis to complain of trial court's refusal to excuse for cause prospective jurors who expressed strong views in favor of imposition of death penalty. State v. Stallings (Ohio, 07-19-2000) 89 Ohio St.3d 280, 731 N.E.2d 159, 2000-Ohio-164, stay granted 89 Ohio St.3d 1483, 733 N.E.2d 1184, stay revoked 93 Ohio St.3d 1455, 756 N.E.2d 674, certiorari denied 122 S.Ct. 89, 534 U.S. 836, 151 L.Ed.2d 51, denial of post-conviction relief affirmed 2004-Ohio-4571, 2004 WL 1932869, appeal not allowed 104 Ohio St.3d 1460, 821 N.E.2d 577, 2005-Ohio-204. Criminal Law ⚿ 1166.18

Time limit on voir dire imposed by trial judge, allotting each side one-half hour to question each prospective juror, did not deprive defendant of the requisite latitude in voir dire questioning so as to amount to an abuse of discretion; defense counsel did not object to the time allotment or request more time to question a juror during voir dire, and trial court's statement to defense counsel that he had fourteen minutes left in questioning that juror was in response to defense counsel's inquiry as to the time. State v. Cornwell (Ohio, 09-22-1999) 86 Ohio St.3d 560, 715 N.E.2d 1144, 1999-Ohio-125, stay granted 87 Ohio St.3d 1414, 717 N.E.2d 714, stay revoked 98 Ohio St.3d 1475, 784 N.E.2d 709, 2003-Ohio-980, certiorari denied 120 S.Ct. 1200, 528 U.S. 1172, 145 L.Ed.2d 1103, denial of post-conviction relief affirmed 2002-Ohio-5177, 2002 WL 31160861, appeal not allowed 98 Ohio St.3d 1413, 781 N.E.2d 1020, 2003-Ohio-60. Jury ⚿ 131(4)

In a first degree murder case a defendant who, on voir dire, passes prospective jurors for cause and stands silently by while each juror is seated, thereby waives any valid objections he might have raised, and cannot raise the question for the first time upon appeal. State v. Carver (Scioto 1971) 30 Ohio App.2d 115, 283 N.E.2d 662, 59 O.O.2d 230, affirmed 30 Ohio St.2d 280, 285 N.E.2d 26, 59 O.O.2d 343, certiorari denied 93 S.Ct. 542, 409 U.S. 1044, 34 L.Ed.2d 495. Criminal Law ⚿ 1035(6)

12. Objection to array

Occupation as a police officer did not disqualify prospective juror from jury duty in capital murder prosecution. State v. Braden (Ohio, 04-02-2003) 98 Ohio St.3d 354, 785 N.E.2d 439, 2003-Ohio-1325, stay granted 98 Ohio St.3d 1542, 787 N.E.2d 5, 2003-Ohio-2002, denial of post-conviction relief affirmed 2003-Ohio-2949, 2003 WL 21321457, appeal not allowed 100 Ohio St.3d 1431, 797 N.E.2d 511, 2003-Ohio-5396, certiorari denied 124 S.Ct. 182, 540 U.S. 865, 157 L.Ed.2d 119, stay revoked 100 Ohio St.3d 1525, 800 N.E.2d 43, 2003-Ohio-6510. Jury ⚿ 83(3)

A claimed error in allowing prosecutor's challenge for cause is not a ground of challenge to the array of the jury, which lies only when the jury is not selected, drawn or summoned, or when the officer who executed the venire did not proceed, as prescribed by law, GC 11419–50 (RC 2313.41), when it was made after the jury was impaneled. State v. Braden (Marion 1936) 56 Ohio App. 19, 9 N.E.2d 999, 23 Ohio Law Abs. 425, 9 O.O. 200. Jury ⚿ 116

2945.26 Challenge for cause

Challenges for cause shall be tried by the court on the oath of the person challenged, or other evidence, and shall be made before the jury is sworn.

(1953 H 1, eff. 10–1–53; GC 13443–9)

Historical and Statutory Notes

Pre–1953 H 1 Amendments: 113 v 184, Ch 22, § 9

Cross References

Challenge for cause, Crim R 24

Library References

Jury ⚷124.
Westlaw Topic No. 230.
C.J.S. Juries §§ 367, 369 to 372, 398 to 399, 411 to 413, 415 to 421, 462 to 488.

Research References

Encyclopedias

OH Jur. 3d Jury § 195, Order and Time of Challenge.

Notes of Decisions

1. Constitutional issues

Defense counsel's failure to challenge for cause a juror who had taken paralegal classes taught by the prosecutor was not ineffective assistance in capital murder prosecution; such a challenge would not likely have succeeded in view of that juror's testimony that her past affiliation with prosecutor's paralegal course would not impair her ability to render a fair and impartial verdict. State v. Treesh (Ohio, 01-03-2001) 90 Ohio St.3d 460, 739 N.E.2d 749, 2001-Ohio-4, stay granted 91 Ohio St.3d 1435, 742 N.E.2d 135, certiorari denied 121 S.Ct. 2247, 533 U.S. 904, 150 L.Ed.2d 234. Criminal Law ⚷ 641.13(2.1)

Defense counsel's failure in capital murder prosecution to challenge for cause a juror who admitted exposure to some newspaper articles about the case and admitted that she favored the death penalty " [w]hen it's warranted" was not ineffective assistance; such a challenge would not likely have been granted in view of juror's additional statements that she had not formed an opinion about the case and that she could fairly and impartially weigh the evidence presented. State v. Treesh (Ohio, 01-03-2001) 90 Ohio St.3d 460, 739 N.E.2d 749, 2001-Ohio-4, stay granted 91 Ohio St.3d 1435, 742 N.E.2d 135, certiorari denied 121 S.Ct. 2247, 533 U.S. 904, 150 L.Ed.2d 234. Criminal Law ⚷ 641.13(2.1)

Trial judge did not apply different standards in ruling upon defense challenges for cause than it did for state's challenges for cause to prospective jurors in capital case, in violation of due process, by excusing for cause prospective jurors that stated that they could not put aside their personal feelings in opposition to death penalty and would not be able to follow the law, but not excluding prospective jurors who stated that death penalty was justifiable punishment for someone who takes another person's life, but would put their personal feelings aside and follow the law, even if that meant they had to impose sentence less than death. State v. Frazier (Ohio, 08-23-1995) 73 Ohio St.3d 323, 652 N.E.2d 1000, 1995-Ohio-235, stay granted 74 Ohio St.3d 1437, 655 N.E.2d 1321, certiorari denied 116 S.Ct. 820, 516 U.S. 1095, 133 L.Ed.2d 763, denial of post-conviction relief affirmed 1997 WL 764810, dismissed, appeal not allowed 81 Ohio St.3d 1496, 691 N.E.2d 1058, habeas corpus denied 188 F.Supp.2d 798, denial of habeas corpus reversed in part 343 F.3d 780, opinion supplemented on denial of rehearing 348 F.3d 174, rehearing and suggestion for rehearing en banc denied, certiorari denied 124 S.Ct. 2815, 541 U.S. 1095, 159 L.Ed.2d 261. Constitutional Law ⚷ 267; Jury ⚷ 108

Prospective juror who gave conflicting answers as to whether he would be able to impose death penalty was properly excused for cause in capital murder case; juror's answers reflected desire to follow court's instructions in the abstract, but made it clear he could not follow Ohio law when required to decide issue of capital punishment. State v. Frazier (Ohio, 08-23-1995) 73 Ohio St.3d 323, 652 N.E.2d 1000, 1995-Ohio-235, stay granted 74 Ohio St.3d 1437, 655 N.E.2d 1321, certiorari denied 116 S.Ct. 820, 516 U.S. 1095, 133 L.Ed.2d 763, denial of post-conviction relief affirmed 1997 WL 764810, dismissed, appeal not allowed 81 Ohio St.3d 1496, 691 N.E.2d 1058, habeas corpus denied 188 F.Supp.2d 798, denial of habeas corpus reversed in part 343 F.3d 780, opinion supplemented on denial of rehearing 348 F.3d 174, rehearing and suggestion for rehearing en banc denied, certiorari denied 124 S.Ct. 2815, 541 U.S. 1095, 159 L.Ed.2d 261. Jury ⚷ 108

Excusing a venireman for cause after confused answers but a final statement of ability to impose the capital penalty necessitates vacation of the sentence even where the trial judge acknowledged he had "cheated" the prosecution earlier in making it exhaust its peremptory challenges by refusing to excuse for cause other veniremen unequivocally opposed to the capital penalty. (Ed. note: Mississippi procedures construed in light of federal constitution.) Gray v. Mississippi (U.S.Miss. 1987) 107 S.Ct. 2045, 481 U.S. 648, 95 L.Ed.2d 622.

Failure to remove biased jurors taints the entire trial, and therefore the resulting conviction must be overturned. Franklin v. Anderson (C.A.6 (Ohio), 01-09-2006) 434 F.3d 412, rehearing and rehearing en banc denied. Criminal Law ⚷ 1166.16; Jury ⚷ 97(1)

The seating of a biased juror who should have been dismissed for cause requires reversal of the conviction. Franklin v. Anderson (C.A.6 (Ohio), 01-09-2006) 434 F.3d 412, rehearing and rehearing en banc denied. Criminal Law ⚷ 1166.16; Jury ⚷ 97(1)

Fact that prosecution in capital murder trial successfully challenged for cause all potential jurors who stated that their beliefs about the death penalty would prevent them from fairly considering death as a penalty, and used its peremptory challenges to remove three potential jurors who had problems with the death penalty, did not deprive defendant of his right to trial by a fair and impartial jury. Mason v. Mitchell (N.D.Ohio, 05-09-2000) 95 F.Supp.2d 744, affirmed in part, remanded in part 320 F.3d 604, on remand 293 F.Supp.2d 819, on remand 396 F.Supp.2d 837. Jury ⚷ 33(2.15)

Trial court's refusal to remove for cause venireperson who indicated that he disapproved of interracial dating did not constitute denial of African–American defendant's right to an impartial jury; venireperson stated that he would convict defendant only if prosecution proved all elements of charged crimes beyond a reasonable doubt, and defendant used one of his peremptory challenges to remove venireperson from panel. Mason v. Mitchell (N.D.Ohio, 05-09-2000) 95 F.Supp.2d 744, affirmed in part, remanded in part 320 F.3d 604, on remand 293 F.Supp.2d 819, on remand 396 F.Supp.2d 837. Jury ⚷ 105(1)

2. Record of ruling on challenge

Trial court, in dismissing juror for cause during voir dire, properly stated its reason for doing so on the record, in prosecution for felonious assault and other offenses; prosecutor, in moving to dismiss juror for cause, explained that she had prosecuted juror's son for aggravated murder, that son had been convicted, that he had been charged with a capital offense but had received a life sentence, and that juror had testified as a witness during mitigation phase of his son's trial, and trial court dismissed juror on this basis, and stressed that it was not going to allow juror to "poison the entire panel." State v. McClanahan (Ohio App. 9 Dist., Summit, 06-15-2005) No. 22277, 2005-Ohio-2975, 2005 WL 1398835, Unreported, appeal allowed 106 Ohio St.3d 1555, 836 N.E.2d 580, 2005-Ohio-5531. Jury ⚷ 91; Jury ⚷ 133

Trial court denial of defendant's two juror challenges for cause was not an abuse of discretion, even though the daughter of one juror was the same age as youngest victim when she was sexually molested; juror stated that she did not find out about her daughter's molestation until her daughter was an adult, her daughter decided not to do anything about the molestation, and that the event would not impair or influence her thinking, and the both jurors stated that even though they had been exposed to pretrial publicity they would be fair, they had not formed an opinion as to guilt, and they would base their decisions solely on what was presented in court. State v. Neal (Ohio App. 2 Dist., Champaign, 12-06-2002) No. 2000 CA 16, No. 2000 CA 18, 2002-Ohio-6786, 2002 WL 31761564, Unreported, appeal not allowed 98 Ohio St.3d 1538, 786 N.E.2d 901, 2003-Ohio-1946, reconsideration denied 99 Ohio St.3d 1438, 789 N.E.2d 1119, 2003-Ohio-2902. Jury ⚷ 97(2); Jury ⚷ 103(14)

Trial court's failure to sustain defense challenge for cause against prospective juror whose husband had been correctional officer at prison where defendant was incarcerated at time of murder, and who favored death penalty, believed justice system was "too slow," and did not think it was "fair" for her to sit on jury, was not abuse of discretion, where juror's husband had been assigned to another facility, and juror stated that her husband's employment would not "taint" her view of evidence, and that she would be fair to both sides, keep open mind, consider all options, and follow the court's instructions, and that she would not automatically vote for death penalty. State v. Cassano (Ohio, 08-07-2002) 96 Ohio St.3d 94, 772 N.E.2d 81, 2002-Ohio-3751, reconsideration denied 96 Ohio St.3d 1517, 775 N.E.2d 858, 2002-Ohio-4950, certiorari denied 123 S.Ct. 1359, 537 U.S. 1235, 155 L.Ed.2d 201. Jury ⚷ 97(2); Jury ⚷ 104.1; Jury ⚷ 108

Trial court's ruling on a challenge for cause will not be disturbed on appeal unless it is manifestly arbitrary and unsupported by substantial testimony, so as to constitute an abuse of discretion. State v. Williams (Ohio, 06-11-1997) 79 Ohio St.3d 1, 679 N.E.2d 646, 1997-Ohio-407, certiorari denied 118 S.Ct. 703, 522 U.S. 1053, 139 L.Ed.2d 646, denial of post-conviction relief affirmed 1999 WL 1059715, dismissed, appeal not allowed 88 Ohio St.3d 1425, 723 N.E.2d 1113, certiorari denied 121 S.Ct. 109, 531 U.S. 843, 148 L.Ed.2d 66, denial of habeas corpus affirmed 380 F.3d 932, rehearing en banc denied, certiorari denied 125 S.Ct. 1939, 544 U.S. 1003, 161 L.Ed.2d 779. Criminal Law ⚷ 1152(2)

A writ of mandamus ordering that a judge dismiss certain prospective jurors for cause will be denied as premature where the trial court's judgment entry states only that the jurors' names will "be retained on the list," and the record does not show that a ruling on a challenge for cause has been made nor that an order has been made having the effect of seating the prospective jurors. State ex rel. Miller v. Gillie (Franklin 1986) 24 Ohio App.3d 121, 493 N.E.2d 327, 24 O.B.R. 192.

A state court finding of a potential juror's bias is to be presumed a correct determination of fact in federal habeas corpus proceedings, and the judge need not draft specific findings or state on the record his conclusion of bias where the transcript shows that the prospective juror was questioned in the presence of counsel and the judge, was challenged by the prosecutor for cause, and that the challenge was sustained. Wainwright v. Witt (U.S.Fla. 1985) 105 S.Ct. 844, 469 U.S. 412, 83 L.Ed.2d 841.

3. Waiver of challenges

This section may be waived since counsel made no request that prospective jurors be sworn. Kidd v. State (Franklin 1933) 15 Ohio Law Abs. 488.

Capital murder defendant's failure to challenge for cause prospective juror who stated during voir dire that he believed that murder in cold blood and murders for hire merited "automatic death sentence" and that those who use gun to commit crime resulting in death should receive death penalty waived appellate review of any issue as to that juror's selection. State v. Stallings (Ohio, 07-19-2000) 89 Ohio St.3d 280, 731 N.E.2d 159, 2000-Ohio-164, stay granted 89 Ohio St.3d 1483, 733 N.E.2d 1184, stay revoked 93 Ohio St.3d 1455, 756 N.E.2d 674, certiorari denied 122 S.Ct. 89, 534 U.S. 836, 151 L.Ed.2d 51, denial of post-conviction relief affirmed 2004-Ohio-4571, 2004 WL 1932869, appeal not allowed 104 Ohio St.3d 1460, 821 N.E.2d 577, 2005-Ohio-204. Criminal Law ⚿ 1166.16

Trial judge did not abuse his discretion in failing to sua sponte excuse four jurors for cause, despite defendant's contention that each one had a personal experience or acquaintance with a victim or investigator in the case that indicated he or she could not be fair and impartial, where neither defense nor prosecution objected to the jurors for cause. State v. Smith (Ohio, 10-15-1997) 80 Ohio St.3d 89, 684 N.E.2d 668, 1997-Ohio-355, reconsideration denied 80 Ohio St.3d 1471, 687 N.E.2d 299, certiorari denied 118 S.Ct. 1811, 523 U.S. 1125, 140 L.Ed.2d 949, dismissal of post conviction relief affirmed 1998 WL 549964, dismissed, appeal not allowed 84 Ohio St.3d 1469, 704 N.E.2d 578, reconsideration denied 85 Ohio St.3d 1410, 706 N.E.2d 791, habeas corpus denied in part 2003 WL 24136073, habeas corpus denied 2005 WL 1969309. Jury ⚿ 90; Jury ⚿ 142

2945.27 Examination of jurors by the court

The judge of the trial court shall examine the prospective jurors under oath or upon affirmation as to their qualifications to serve as fair and impartial jurors, but he shall permit reasonable examination of such jurors by the prosecuting attorney and by the defendant or his counsel.

(127 v 419, eff. 9–9–57; 1953 H 1; GC 13443–10)

Historical and Statutory Notes

Pre–1953 H 1 Amendments: 113 v 184, Ch 22, § 10

Cross References

Voir dire, Crim R 24

Library References

Jury ⚿131.

Westlaw Topic No. 230.

C.J.S. Juries §§ 367, 372, 462 to 488.

Research References

Encyclopedias

OH Jur. 3d Criminal Law § 2621, Oath or Affirmation.

OH Jur. 3d Criminal Law § 2627, Capital Punishment.

OH Jur. 3d Criminal Law § 2634, Enmity or Bias.

OH Jur. 3d Criminal Law § 3982, Convict Witness Expenses.

OH Jur. 3d Jury § 224, Waiver of Challenge for Cause—by Use or Nonuse of Peremptory Challenges.

Treatises and Practice Aids

Markus, Trial Handbook for Ohio Lawyers, § 6:7, Conduct of Voir Dire Examination.

Katz, Giannelli, Blair and Lipton, Baldwin's Ohio Practice, Criminal Law, § 64:2, Voir Dire.

Katz, Giannelli, Blair and Lipton, Baldwin's Ohio Practice, Criminal Law, § 148:26, Oath of Jurors on Examination.

Hennenberg & Reinhart, Ohio Criminal Defense Motions F 8.03, Motion for Alternating Voir Dire-Jury-Related Motions.

Hennenberg & Reinhart, Ohio Criminal Defense Motions F 8.05, Motion for Individual Sequestered Voir Dire-Jury-Related Motions.

Hennenberg & Reinhart, Ohio Criminal Defense Motions F 13.50, Motion for Individual Sequestered Voir Dire-Death Penalty Motions.

Law Review and Journal Commentaries

CRIMINAL PROCEDURE—Voir Dire—The Right to Question Jurors on Racial Prejudice. Ham v. South Carolina, Note. 37 Ohio St L J 412 (1976).

Notes of Decisions

---

1. Oath or affirmation

Where it does not appear that any false answer was given by a juror on the voir dire examination, the mere failure of the trial court to have either oaths or affirmations administered to prospective jurors before such examination cannot be held to have prejudiced a defendant or prevented him from having a fair trial, and a judgment of conviction should not be reversed because of such failure. State v. Glaros (Ohio 1960) 170 Ohio St. 471, 166 N.E.2d 379, 11 O.O.2d 215, on remand 114 Ohio App. 185, 173 N.E.2d 146, 85 Ohio Law Abs. 417, 19 O.O.2d 83. Criminal Law ⚷ 1166.16

Trial court's failure to administer oath to venire panel prior to asking three prospective jurors background questions did not constitute plain error in murder trial; questions to jurors were preliminary in nature, and of three jurors who answered questions, one was excused for cause, one was dismissed after jury panel was fully constituted, and one who was seated as alternate was dismissed before deliberations. State v. Miller (Ohio App. 1 Dist., Hamilton, 06-28-2002) No. C-010543, 2002-Ohio-3296, 2002 WL 1392587, Unreported. Criminal Law ⚷ 1035(6)

2. Examination by court

Trial court's failure to conduct voir dire to determine competency of witness who was approximately 10 years old did not constitute plain error, where it was never established at trial that witness was less than 10 years old, and thus the need for a voir dire of his competency never arose. State v. Miller (Ohio App. 3 Dist., Crawford, 04-19-2004) No. 3-03-26, 2004-Ohio-1947, 2004 WL 829933, Unreported, appeal not allowed 103 Ohio St.3d 1462, 815 N.E.2d 678, 2004-Ohio-5056, appeal not allowed 104 Ohio St.3d 1460, 821 N.E.2d 577, 2005-Ohio-204. Criminal Law ⚷ 1036.2

Trial court abused its discretion in failing to voir dire juror who indicated that she might know a prior alleged victim of defendant, where jury heard testimony regarding the prior alleged victim. State v. McMillin (Ohio App. 3 Dist., Union, 12-22-2003) No. 14-03-25, 2003-Ohio-6989, 2003 WL 22994567, Unreported. Jury ⚷ 149

In context of surrounding circumstances, judge's remarks during voir dire that it is hard to see graphic images involving children and violence and that jury could not turn away from graphic evidence that would be presented at trial was not prejudicial to murder defendant, where judge was questioning prospective juror about concerns that juror might have that would render her unable to give defendant fair and impartial trial. State v. Powe (Ohio App. 9 Dist., Summit, 11-06-2002) No. 21026, 2002-Ohio-6034, 2002 WL 31465826, Unreported. Criminal Law ⚷ 1166.22(2)

Where the court takes very little part in conducting examination on voir dire and no question was raised by counsel nor were any exceptions taken as to the method of impaneling the jury, it does not amount to prejudicial error. Kidd v. State (Franklin 1933) 15 Ohio Law Abs. 488.

Trial court in a capital murder prosecution was not required to conduct sua sponte a further inquiry in response to casual comment by an unknown prospective juror suggesting a preconceived opinion of guilt in a jury-selection waiting room. State v. Adams (Ohio, 11-17-2004) 103 Ohio St.3d 508, 817 N.E.2d 29, 2004-Ohio-5845, reconsideration denied 104 Ohio St.3d 1442, 819 N.E.2d 1124, 2004-Ohio-7033, certiorari denied 125 S.Ct. 2271, 544 U.S. 1040, 161 L.Ed.2d 1072. Jury ⚷ 133

Casual comment by an unknown prospective juror suggesting a preconceived opinion of guilt in a jury-selection waiting room did not prejudice defendant in capital murder prosecution; when this unknown person made the remark, no jury had been seated or sworn, the person and prospective jurors who heard it may not have sat on the jury, and the trial court and counsel conducted thorough and individual voir dire of all prospective jurors in order to uncover any bias, prejudice, or preconceived opinions based on pretrial publicity or out-of-court discussions. State v. Adams (Ohio, 11-17-2004) 103 Ohio St.3d 508, 817 N.E.2d 29, 2004-Ohio-5845, reconsideration denied 104 Ohio St.3d 1442, 819 N.E.2d 1124, 2004-Ohio-7033, certiorari denied 125 S.Ct. 2271, 544 U.S. 1040, 161 L.Ed.2d 1072. Criminal Law ⚷ 1166.16

Trial court's restrictions on and interruptions of voir dire did not impair capital murder defendant's ability to use peremptory challenges effectively to remove prospective jurors or otherwise impair his defense, where trial court was not unduly restrictive, but rather balanced its obligation to control inquiry with according counsel latitude in questioning prospective jurors, and where court's only restrictions on particular areas of inquiry were well within its discretion. State v. Gross (Ohio, 10-30-2002) 97 Ohio St.3d 121, 776 N.E.2d 1061, 2002-Ohio-5524, reconsideration denied 97 Ohio St.3d 1486, 780 N.E.2d 288, 2002-Ohio-6866, certiorari denied 123 S.Ct. 2079, 538 U.S. 1037, 155 L.Ed.2d 1068, rehearing denied 124 S.Ct. 20, 539 U.S. 976, 156 L.Ed.2d 685. Jury ⚷ 131(4)

While statute grants prosecution and defense opportunity to conduct a reasonable examination of prospective jurors, trial court reserves right and responsibility to control proceedings, and must limit trial to relevant and material matters with a view toward expeditious and effective ascertainment of truth. State v. Getsy (Ohio, 12-23-1998) 84 Ohio St.3d 180, 702 N.E.2d 866, 1998-Ohio-533, reconsideration denied 84 Ohio St.3d 1488, 705 N.E.2d 368, certiorari denied 119 S.Ct. 2407, 527 U.S. 1042, 144 L.Ed.2d 805, dismissal of post-conviction relief affirmed 1999 WL 1073682, dismissed, appeal not allowed 88 Ohio St.3d 1425, 723 N.E.2d 1113, habeas corpus granted 456 F.3d 575. Jury ⚿ 131(1)

Trial court did not improperly limit voir dire of prospective jurors during capital murder prosecution; while court attempted to keep voir dire moving, counsel were rarely limited in questioning jurors, and court did not unreasonably or arbitrarily restrict examination of individual jurors. State v. Getsy (Ohio, 12-23-1998) 84 Ohio St.3d 180, 702 N.E.2d 866, 1998-Ohio-533, reconsideration denied 84 Ohio St.3d 1488, 705 N.E.2d 368, certiorari denied 119 S.Ct. 2407, 527 U.S. 1042, 144 L.Ed.2d 805, dismissal of post-conviction relief affirmed 1999 WL 1073682, dismissed, appeal not allowed 88 Ohio St.3d 1425, 723 N.E.2d 1113, habeas corpus granted 456 F.3d 575. Jury ⚿ 131(4)

Defendant accused of interracial murder had an adequate opportunity to question prospective jurors on racial attitudes, where before trial each juror was given a 41–question, case-specific form which asked about background, experiences, and attitudes, the trial court allowed questioning about racial bias during individual voir dire though it wanted to defer extensive questioning until general voir dire, and defense counsel asked about racial attitudes during both individual and general voir dire, which extended into three days. State v. Mason (Ohio, 06-17-1998) 82 Ohio St.3d 144, 694 N.E.2d 932, 1998-Ohio-370, reconsideration denied 82 Ohio St.3d 1483, 696 N.E.2d 1089, certiorari denied 119 S.Ct. 624, 525 U.S. 1057, 142 L.Ed.2d 562, habeas corpus denied 95 F.Supp.2d 744, affirmed in part, remanded in part 320 F.3d 604, on remand 293 F.Supp.2d 819, on remand 396 F.Supp.2d 837. Jury ⚿ 131(6); Jury ⚿ 131(13)

Trial court's introduction of several visiting judges during voir dire in capital murder prosecution was not plain error. State v. Keenan (Ohio, 02-25-1998) 81 Ohio St.3d 133, 689 N.E.2d 929, 1998-Ohio-459, reconsideration denied 81 Ohio St.3d 1503, 691 N.E.2d 1062, certiorari denied 119 S.Ct. 146, 525 U.S. 860, 142 L.Ed.2d 119, rehearing denied 119 S.Ct. 581, 525 U.S. 1035, 142 L.Ed.2d 484, denial of post-conviction relief affirmed 2001 WL 91129, dismissed, appeal not allowed 92 Ohio St.3d 1429, 749 N.E.2d 756, habeas corpus dismissed 262 F.Supp.2d 818, motion to amend denied 262 F.Supp.2d 826, vacated and remanded 400 F.3d 417. Criminal Law ⚿ 1035(6)

Prospective juror's comments during general voir dire, based on his experience as police officer, that detective to be called as witness by state was truthful, and that prosecutor was efficient, did not taint jurors; remarks were tempered by prosecutor's response that the other jurors did not know detective and would have to evaluate his testimony based on what he said in court, and his statement that what happened in the past regarding prosecutor was in the past and this case would have to be decided based on evidence presented. State v. Reynolds (Ohio, 01-14-1998) 80 Ohio St.3d 670, 687 N.E.2d 1358, 1998-Ohio-171, certiorari denied 118 S.Ct. 2328, 524 U.S. 930, 141 L.Ed.2d 702, denial of post-conviction relief affirmed 1999 WL 980568, dismissed, appeal not allowed 88 Ohio St.3d 1425, 723 N.E.2d 1113. Jury ⚿ 133

Trial court did not abuse its discretion by allowing juror to remain on jury in capital murder prosecution, even though court learned during penalty phase that juror had been victim of sexual abuse as child, where court conducted voir dire examination of juror after the discovery, juror explained that she did not mention sexual abuse during original voir dire examination because she did not feel it fit definition of violent crime, and juror maintained that she would be impartial. State v. Dennis (Ohio, 09-24-1997) 79 Ohio St.3d 421, 683 N.E.2d 1096, 1997-Ohio-372, denial of post-conviction relief affirmed 1997 WL 760680, dismissed, appeal not allowed 81 Ohio St.3d 1468, 690 N.E.2d 1287, certiorari denied 118 S.Ct. 1078, 522 U.S. 1128, 140 L.Ed.2d 136, habeas corpus dismissed 68 F.Supp.2d 863, affirmed 354 F.3d 511, certiorari denied 124 S.Ct. 2400, 541 U.S. 1068, 158 L.Ed.2d 971. Jury ⚿ 97(1)

Trial court adequately investigated allegation that victim's friend communicated with jurors in capital murder case, without questioning each juror individually, considering brevity and limited nature of any such contact, which involved friend merely asking single juror whether he or she was a juror. State v. Henness (Ohio, 06-18-1997) 79 Ohio St.3d 53, 679 N.E.2d 686, 1997-Ohio-405, certiorari denied 118 S.Ct. 422, 522 U.S. 971, 139 L.Ed.2d 323, denial of post-conviction relief affirmed 1999 WL 739588, dismissed, appeal not allowed 87 Ohio St.3d 1491, 722 N.E.2d 525, certiorari denied 120 S.Ct. 2669, 530 U.S. 1234, 147 L.Ed.2d 281. Criminal Law ⚿ 868

In give and take of voir dire regarding death penalty in capital murder case, it is often necessary for trial judge to step in and provide some neutral, nonleading instructions and questions in an attempt to determine whether prospective juror can actually be fair and impartial. State v. Williams (Ohio, 06-11-1997) 79 Ohio St.3d 1, 679 N.E.2d 646, 1997-Ohio-407, certiorari denied 118 S.Ct. 703, 522 U.S. 1053, 139 L.Ed.2d 646, denial of post-conviction relief affirmed 1999 WL 1059715, dismissed, appeal not allowed 88 Ohio St.3d 1425, 723 N.E.2d 1113, certiorari denied 121 S.Ct. 109, 531 U.S. 843, 148 L.Ed.2d 66, denial of habeas corpus affirmed 380 F.3d 932, rehearing en banc denied, certiorari denied 125 S.Ct. 1939, 544 U.S. 1003, 161 L.Ed.2d 779. Jury ⚿ 131(10)

Anonymous telephone call informing trial court and defense counsel that caller's wife had heard from juror's mother that juror commented to her either before or during trial that juror wanted to have a baby, together with caller's conjecture that juror might be hostile toward defendant, did not obligate court to conduct voir dire, *in camera* examination of juror, in prosecution of defendant for murdering her newborn baby and grossly abusing its corpse; taken at face value, juror's alleged statement suggested nothing about juror's opinion or partiality toward defendant and did not reflect on her ability fairly to determine whether defendant murdered her baby. State v. Hopfer (Ohio App. 2 Dist., 07-12-1996) 112 Ohio App.3d 521, 679 N.E.2d 321, dismissed, appeal not allowed 77 Ohio St.3d 1488, 673 N.E.2d 146, reconsideration denied 77 Ohio St.3d 1550, 674 N.E.2d 1187. Criminal Law ⚷ 868

Purpose of questioning prospective jurors in voir dire is to determine whether they can render a fair and impartial verdict. Lakewood v. Town (Ohio App. 8 Dist., 09-25-1995) 106 Ohio App.3d 521, 666 N.E.2d 599, dismissed, appeal not allowed 75 Ohio St.3d 1404, 661 N.E.2d 754. Jury ⚷ 131(1)

Scope of voir dire of prospective jurors is within trial court's discretion and varies depending on circumstances of each case, and any limits placed thereon must be reasonable. Lakewood v. Town (Ohio App. 8 Dist., 09-25-1995) 106 Ohio App.3d 521, 666 N.E.2d 599, dismissed, appeal not allowed 75 Ohio St.3d 1404, 661 N.E.2d 754. Jury ⚷ 131(2); Jury ⚷ 131(4)

Trial court did not err, in capital murder case, by conducting voir dire of prospective jurors in groups of six, rather than individually; neither state nor federal law requires individual voir dire. State v. Phillips (Ohio, 11-22-1995) 74 Ohio St.3d 72, 656 N.E.2d 643, 1995-Ohio-171, reconsideration denied 74 Ohio St.3d 1485, 657 N.E.2d 1378, stay granted 74 Ohio St.3d 1503, 659 N.E.2d 795, rehearing granted, opinion recalled 75 Ohio St.3d 1504, 665 N.E.2d 219, certiorari denied 116 S.Ct. 1835, 517 U.S. 1213, 134 L.Ed.2d 938, denial of post-conviction relief affirmed in part, reversed in part 1999 WL 58961, dismissed, appeal not allowed 86 Ohio St.3d 1402, 711 N.E.2d 231, denial of post-conviction relief affirmed 2002-Ohio-823, 2002 WL 274637, appeal not allowed 95 Ohio St.3d 1488, 769 N.E.2d 403, 2002-Ohio-2625. Jury ⚷ 131(13)

In a trespass prosecution of defendants for their participation in an abortion protest, potential jurors are not improperly removed where they expressly state that their views on abortion would prevent them from rendering fair and impartial verdicts. Akron v. Wendell (Summit 1990) 70 Ohio App.3d 35, 590 N.E.2d 380.

The statement of a judge to veniremen when trying to give them some idea of how the penalty is imposed in a capital trial, that aggravating circumstances are those showing an offense was "heinous," "cruel," "particularly terrible," or "very bad," gives the defendant no basis for objection or for a claim of ineffective assistance of counsel; these general descriptions are not jury instructions. State v. Tyler (Ohio 1990) 50 Ohio St.3d 24, 553 N.E.2d 576, rehearing denied 51 Ohio St.3d 704, 555 N.E.2d 322, certiorari denied 111 S.Ct. 371, 498 U.S. 951, 112 L.Ed.2d 334, reconsideration denied 75 Ohio St.3d 1474, 663 N.E.2d 1302, stay granted 76 Ohio St.3d 1463, 669 N.E.2d 249.

Where record in a capital case shows that trial judge gave a general explanation to prospective jurors of their duties under law, asked them if, in view of those duties, they could serve as jurors in the cause, but then restricted them to a total response of "I can" or "I cannot," and prohibited prosecuting attorney and defendant or his counsel from asking them any questions concerning their scruples regarding capital punishment, there has been a failure to establish compliance with requirements of Witherspoon v Illinois, 391 US 510, 88 SCt 1770, 20 LEd(2d) 776 (1968), and execution of death sentence imposed by jury so selected would deprive defendant of his life without due process of law. State v. Anderson (Ohio 1972) 30 Ohio St.2d 66, 282 N.E.2d 568, 59 O.O.2d 85. Constitutional Law ⚷ 267

Interruptions, comments and questions by the trial court during the voir dire examination and either directed to eliciting from the prospective jurors further information as to their qualifications or occasioned by objections raised by the parties or made or asked in the interest of proceeding in an orderly fashion and reasonably directing the conduct of the trial do not constitute error. State v. Ward (Hardin 1957) 105 Ohio App. 1, 150 N.E.2d 465, 5 O.O.2d 130.

Trial court's decision to not dismiss juror constituted manifest error, and his factual finding that juror was not impartial did not merit presumption of correctness on federal habeas review that normally was due trial court factual findings, where record indicated that juror gave definite impression five times that she could not faithfully apply the law concerning burden of proof because she failed to understand it, and she still insisted with her last statement that death penalty defendant had to be proven innocent even after she was corrected by judge three times. Franklin v. Anderson (C.A.6 (Ohio), 01-09-2006) 434 F.3d 412, rehearing and rehearing en banc denied. Habeas Corpus ⚷ 496; Habeas Corpus ⚷ 770

Trial judge's decision, that juror's statement at jury viewing and her subsequent statements in conversation with judge did not indicate bias, was fairly supported by record, and presumed correct on federal habeas review, where juror's statements could have been understood in way that did not indicate bias, juror stated unequivocally that she had not made up her mind about guilt of death penalty defendant, and trial judge specifically stated that he believed that she could be impartial and fair after discussing matter with juror, observing her demeanor, and listening to her responses. Franklin v. Anderson (C.A.6 (Ohio), 01-09-2006) 434 F.3d 412, rehearing and rehearing en banc denied. Habeas Corpus ⚷ 770

Juror was partial or biased, and thus should not have served as juror in death penalty case, where juror's statements at voir dire indicated after she was corrected three times by judge that she so completely misunderstood presumption of innocence and burden of proof that she could not have made fair assessment of evidence of defendant's guilt; although juror assured counsel and judge that she would consider all of evidence before making decision, she also seemed to expect some of that evidence to come from defendant by way of proof of his innocence. Franklin v. Anderson (C.A.6 (Ohio), 01-09-2006) 434 F.3d 412, rehearing and rehearing en banc denied. Jury ⚿ 107

District court's failure to give requested voir dire question on defendant's right not to testify did not create risk of empaneling biased jury, given district court's voir dire questions and jury instructions on presumption of innocence and jury instruction that no inference could be drawn from defendant's election not to testify. U.S. v. Aloi (C.A.6 (Ohio) 1993) 9 F.3d 438, rehearing and suggestion for rehearing en banc denied. Jury ⚿ 131(8)

Trial counsel could reasonably withhold objection to trial court's repeated references during voir dire to murder victim's severed hands because such questioning would illuminate which jurors had been exposed to prejudicial pre-trial publicity. Hartman v. Bagley (N.D.Ohio, 08-31-2004) 333 F.Supp.2d 632. Criminal Law ⚿ 641.13(2.1)

Trial judge's statements during voir dire, admonishing defense counsel not to engage in trickery when questioning prospective jurors about presumption of innocence, were not prejudicial to defendant's right to fair trial; judge specifically stated during its colloquy that defendant should be presumed innocent and later charged jury to disregard anything he might have said that might have given jury a sense of how judge felt about facts of case. Henderson v. Collins (S.D.Ohio, 08-04-1999) 101 F.Supp.2d 866, affirmed in part, vacated in part 262 F.3d 615, rehearing en banc denied, certiorari denied 122 S.Ct. 1572, 535 U.S. 1002, 152 L.Ed.2d 492, on subsequent appeal 2006 WL 1675074. Criminal Law ⚿ 655(5)

If the parties to a criminal action have waived the presence of the judge during voir dire and selection of the jury, and no prejudice is shown to have resulted therefrom, such absence is not ground for a new trial. State v Eberhardt, 32 Misc 39, 282 NE(2d) 62, 60 OO(2d) 395 (CP 1972).

3. Examination by counsel

Trial court abused its discretion in refusing to allow defense counsel to ask potential jurors any supplemental questions on second day of trial in assault prosecution, and thus reversal was required; only trial court questioned potential jurors on second day of trial, and defendant's inability to question these jurors, some of whom were ultimately seated on the jury, was prejudicial. State v. Abuzahrieh (Ohio App. 8 Dist., Cuyahoga, 12-11-2003) No. 82689, 2003-Ohio-6639, 2003 WL 22922995, Unreported. Criminal Law ⚿ 1166.16; Jury ⚿ 131(13)

In medical malpractice and wrongful death action brought by executrix of patient's estate against doctor, counsel for doctor properly was allowed to refer to counsel's status as a physician during voir dire in order to investigate existence of possible bias and determine if any juror had been treated by doctor's counsel or one of the members of counsel's medical group. Kahn v. Moront (Ohio App. 6 Dist., Lucas, 03-14-2003) No. L-02-1202, 2003-Ohio-1410, 2003 WL 1465303, Unreported. Jury ⚿ 131(13)

Because executrix of patient's estate did not object to reference by doctor's counsel to counsel's status as a physician during counsel's voir dire, executrix waived for appeal her claim that trial court erred in denying her motion in limine to preclude any reference to fact that doctor's counsel was a licensed physician during trial of her medical malpractice and wrongful death claims. Kahn v. Moront (Ohio App. 6 Dist., Lucas, 03-14-2003) No. L-02-1202, 2003-Ohio-1410, 2003 WL 1465303, Unreported. Appeal And Error ⚿ 207

Defense counsel's failure to request voir dire on racial bias was not ineffective assistance, in capital murder prosecution, as it did not appear that racial bias permeated case, there were witnesses, including defendant and his brother, who did not mention race as motivating factor in parking-lot fight or in shooting, and, because defendant and person he killed were of same race, defense counsel might have reasonably concluded that race was not an important factor. State v. Conway (Ohio, 03-08-2006) 108 Ohio St.3d 214, 842 N.E.2d 996, 2006-Ohio-791, petition for certiorari filed 2006 WL 1558259. Criminal Law ⚿ 641.13(2.1)

Trial court did not unduly limit defense counsel's opportunity to question prospective jurors during voir dire regarding their views about capital punishment; although court precluded counsel from questioning prospective jurors about their views on specific mitigating factors, it allowed defense counsel to ask prospective jurors whether they would automatically vote for the death penalty, whether they were willing to fairly consider all mitigating factors raised by the defense, as well as all available sentencing options, and whether they would evaluate all evidence before making a sentencing determination. State v. Cunningham (Ohio, 12-29-2004) 105 Ohio St.3d 197, 824 N.E.2d 504, 2004-Ohio-7007, certiorari denied 126 S.Ct. 110, 163 L.Ed.2d 122. Jury ⚿ 131(8)

Defendant could not show prejudice in trial court's decision to limit counsel's opportunity to question prospective jurors during voir dire regarding their views about capital punishment, where he approved the jury selected before exhausting his peremptory challenges. State v. Cunningham (Ohio, 12-29-2004) 105 Ohio St.3d 197, 824 N.E.2d 504, 2004-Ohio-7007, certiorari denied 126 S.Ct. 110, 163 L.Ed.2d 122. Criminal Law ⚿ 1166.18

State's use of peremptory challenges to exclude men from jury in prosecution for gross sexual imposition and abduction did not amount to unlawful discrimination on basis of gender, where defense failed to make prima facie showing of discrimination with respect to three of four such challenges, and trial court's acceptance of state's proffered justification for removing fourth prospective juror was not clearly erroneous. State v. Huffman (Ohio

App. 11 Dist., 12-20-2002) 151 Ohio App.3d 222, 783 N.E.2d 950, 2002-Ohio-7121. Jury ⚿ 33(5.15)

Trial court should have requested that state supply gender-neutral justifications for all four of its uses of peremptory challenges to exclude male prospective jurors from prosecution for gross sexual imposition and abduction, where after originally convincing trial court that *Batson* did not apply to challenges based on gender, state conceded *Batson*'s applicability to such challenges, and after such concession court requested gender-neutral justification for state's final exercise of peremptory challenge against male prospective juror. State v. Huffman (Ohio App. 11 Dist., 12-20-2002) 151 Ohio App.3d 222, 783 N.E.2d 950, 2002-Ohio-7121. Jury ⚿ 33(5.15)

Trial court was not required to ask state to provide gender-neutral reasons for its exercise of peremptory strikes against first three of four male prospective jurors stricken by it in prosecution for gross sexual imposition and abduction, where actions of defense counsel in relation to first three strikes were not sufficient to establish prima facie showing of discrimination; defense counsel did not specifically object until state exercised its final peremptory strike, and did not request that trial court require gender-neutral reasons for first three strikes at time state provided reasons for final strike. State v. Huffman (Ohio App. 11 Dist., 12-20-2002) 151 Ohio App.3d 222, 783 N.E.2d 950, 2002-Ohio-7121. Jury ⚿ 33(5.15); Jury ⚿ 117

Defense counsel's failure, in capital murder prosecution, to object to references during voir dire by prosecutor and court to incorrect standard for weighing aggravating and mitigating factors, did not demonstrate performance below objective standard of reasonable representation, as misquoting of the weighing process was common mistake and did not create reasonable probability that result of trial would have been different were it not for counsel's errors; jury was correctly instructed as to governing legal standard, and its signed verdict form reflected correct legal standard. State v. Stallings (Ohio, 07-19-2000) 89 Ohio St.3d 280, 731 N.E.2d 159, 2000-Ohio-164, stay granted 89 Ohio St.3d 1483, 733 N.E.2d 1184, stay revoked 93 Ohio St.3d 1455, 756 N.E.2d 674, certiorari denied 122 S.Ct. 89, 534 U.S. 836, 151 L.Ed.2d 51, denial of post-conviction relief affirmed 2004-Ohio-4571, 2004 WL 1932869, appeal not allowed 104 Ohio St.3d 1460, 821 N.E.2d 577, 2005-Ohio-204. Criminal Law ⚿ 641.13(2.1)

There is no requirement that counsel, to provide effective assistance, must individually question each juror about his or her views on the death penalty. State v. Goodwin (Ohio, 01-20-1999) 84 Ohio St.3d 331, 703 N.E.2d 1251, 1999-Ohio-356, reconsideration denied 85 Ohio St.3d 1410, 706 N.E.2d 790, certiorari denied 120 S.Ct. 118, 528 U.S. 846, 145 L.Ed.2d 100, habeas corpus granted in part 2006 WL 753111, supplemented 2006 WL 2056686. Criminal Law ⚿ 641.13(2.1)

Counsel were not ineffective in failing to dismiss prospective juror in capital murder case who indicated an aversion to blood, as juror stated she could review evidence of crime scene. State v. Goodwin (Ohio, 01-20-1999) 84 Ohio St.3d 331, 703 N.E.2d 1251, 1999-Ohio-356, reconsideration denied 85 Ohio St.3d 1410, 706 N.E.2d 790, certiorari denied 120 S.Ct. 118, 528 U.S. 846, 145 L.Ed.2d 100, habeas corpus granted in part 2006 WL 753111, supplemented 2006 WL 2056686. Criminal Law ⚿ 641.13(2.1)

Prosecutor did not ask misleading or prejudicial questions during voir dire in capital murder case by prefacing questions with statement that jury should assume that defendant had been found guilty, as questions were properly qualified and were necessary to determine ability of jurors to serve on panel that might consider death penalty. State v. Goodwin (Ohio, 01-20-1999) 84 Ohio St.3d 331, 703 N.E.2d 1251, 1999-Ohio-356, reconsideration denied 85 Ohio St.3d 1410, 706 N.E.2d 790, certiorari denied 120 S.Ct. 118, 528 U.S. 846, 145 L.Ed.2d 100, habeas corpus granted in part 2006 WL 753111, supplemented 2006 WL 2056686. Jury ⚿ 131(17)

Trial court in drug prosecution did not abuse its discretion by limiting voir dire by defendant, who had ignored suggestion to simply ask whether juror could be fair and impartial knowing that defendant had used drugs, and instead asked highly factual question that could not be definitively answered until evidence had been presented, by narrowing inquiry to general questions of bias. State v. Miller (Ohio App. 3 Dist., 07-30-1997) 122 Ohio App.3d 111, 701 N.E.2d 390, appeal after new trial 1999 WL 446592, denial of post-conviction relief affirmed 2000-Ohio-1687, 2000 WL 348994. Jury ⚿ 131(13)

Permitting prosecutor to obtain promises from prospective jurors that they could sign death verdict was not plain error in capital murder prosecution. State v. Moore (Ohio, 02-04-1998) 81 Ohio St.3d 22, 689 N.E.2d 1, 1998-Ohio-441, dismissal of post-conviction relief affirmed 1998 WL 638353, dismissed, appeal not allowed 84 Ohio St.3d 1472, 704 N.E.2d 579. Criminal Law ⚿ 1035(6)

Defense counsel's failure to ask prospective jurors in capital murder prosecution questions about attitudes on race, about whether they could consider the mitigation evidence that would be presented, or questions tailored to fit circumstances of case was not ineffective assistance of counsel. State v. Dennis (Ohio, 09-24-1997) 79 Ohio St.3d 421, 683 N.E.2d 1096, 1997-Ohio-372, denial of post-conviction relief affirmed 1997 WL 760680, dismissed, appeal not allowed 81 Ohio St.3d 1468, 690 N.E.2d 1287, certiorari denied 118 S.Ct. 1078, 522 U.S. 1128, 140 L.Ed.2d 136, habeas corpus dismissed 68 F.Supp.2d 863, affirmed 354 F.3d 511, certiorari denied 124 S.Ct. 2400, 541 U.S. 1068, 158 L.Ed.2d 971. Criminal Law ⚿ 641.13(2.1)

Prosecution did not err when it stated during voir dire that "no matter who killed this child, it's tragic," and questioned potential juror as to whether she understood that job of jury was to make sure that whatever came out of child's death was according to justice. State v. Brown (Ohio App. 12 Dist.,

07-15-1996) 112 Ohio App.3d 583, 679 N.E.2d 361. Jury ⚡ 131(13); Jury ⚡ 131(15.1)

Prosecution did not err when it admonished prospective jurors during voir dire that evidence heard through media might not be reliable and should not be considered, and stated that evidence admitted at trial may be reliable and must be only evidence considered by jury; prosecution did not distinguish between evidence presented by prosecution or defense, or imply that either party would present only reliable evidence. State v. Brown (Ohio App. 12 Dist., 07-15-1996) 112 Ohio App.3d 583, 679 N.E.2d 361. Jury ⚡ 131(13)

Any impropriety in prosecutor's inartful use of terms presume and presuming in connection with guilt, in questioning jurors during voir dire about death penalty, when prosecutor meant to use terms assume and assuming, was waived by defendant's failure to object. State v. Wilson (Ohio, 01-24-1996) 74 Ohio St.3d 381, 659 N.E.2d 292, 1996-Ohio-103, reconsideration denied 75 Ohio St.3d 1413, 661 N.E.2d 760, certiorari denied 117 S.Ct. 129, 519 U.S. 845, 136 L.Ed.2d 78, denial of post-conviction relief affirmed 80 Ohio St.3d 132, 684 N.E.2d 1221, 1997-Ohio-303, denial of post-conviction relief affirmed 1998 WL 332940. Criminal Law ⚡ 1037.1(2)

During voir dire in capital murder prosecution, prosecutor's brief, open-ended and nonjudgmental questions regarding whether prospective jurors had thought about victim's rights involved proper attempt to uncover bias or unsuitable jurors. State v. Wilson (Ohio, 01-24-1996) 74 Ohio St.3d 381, 659 N.E.2d 292, 1996-Ohio-103, reconsideration denied 75 Ohio St.3d 1413, 661 N.E.2d 760, certiorari denied 117 S.Ct. 129, 519 U.S. 845, 136 L.Ed.2d 78, denial of post-conviction relief affirmed 80 Ohio St.3d 132, 684 N.E.2d 1221, 1997-Ohio-303, denial of post-conviction relief affirmed 1998 WL 332940. Jury ⚡ 131(17)

Although counsel must be given opportunity to voir dire prospective jurors or to supplement court's voir dire examination, scope of voir dire falls within trial court's discretion and varies with circumstances. State v. Lundgren (Ohio, 08-30-1995) 73 Ohio St.3d 474, 653 N.E.2d 304, 1995-Ohio-227, reconsideration denied 74 Ohio St.3d 1422, 655 N.E.2d 742, certiorari denied 116 S.Ct. 1276, 516 U.S. 1178, 134 L.Ed.2d 222, dismissal of post-conviction relief affirmed 1998 WL 964592, dismissed, appeal not allowed 85 Ohio St.3d 1465, 709 N.E.2d 171. Jury ⚡ 131(2)

Trial court's refusal to submit defendant's proposed questionnaire to venire prior to voir dire did not deprive defendant of right to meaningfully examine prospective jurors, as court's standard questionnaire, which was given to jurors, was similar to that proffered by defendant, and defense counsel was free to ask additional questions during voir dire. State v. Carter (Ohio, 07-26-1995) 72 Ohio St.3d 545, 651 N.E.2d 965, 1995-Ohio-104, stay granted 73 Ohio St.3d 1469, 654 N.E.2d 1281, certiorari denied 116 S.Ct. 575, 516 U.S. 1014, 133 L.Ed.2d 498, stay dissolved 74 Ohio St.3d 1493, 658 N.E.2d 1063, denial of post-conviction relief affirmed 1997 WL 705487, dismissed, appeal not allowed 81 Ohio St.3d 1467, 690 N.E.2d 1287, certiorari denied 119 S.Ct. 120, 525 U.S. 848, 142 L.Ed.2d 97, denial of post-conviction relief reversed 157 Ohio App.3d 689, 813 N.E.2d 78, 2004-Ohio-3372. Jury ⚡ 131(13)

Defendants who engage in an abortion protest and who are prosecuted for trespass cannot challenge a trial court's failure to permit them to rehabilitate potential jurors who are disqualified, based on their statements that their views on abortion would prevent them from rendering fair and impartial verdicts, by way of a motion for a mistrial where such motion is not raised until after the pertinent veniremen have been excused; defendants were required to call alleged errors to the trial court's attention at the time at which they could be remedied. Akron v. Wendell (Summit 1990) 70 Ohio App.3d 35, 590 N.E.2d 380.

The conduct of voir dire by defense counsel does not have to take a particular form, nor do specific questions have to be asked. State v. Evans (Ohio 1992) 63 Ohio St.3d 231, 586 N.E.2d 1042, rehearing denied 63 Ohio St.3d 1450, 589 N.E.2d 393, certiorari denied 113 S.Ct. 246, 506 U.S. 886, 121 L.Ed.2d 179.

The use of peremptory challenges is permitted as long as they do not purposely exclude an identifiable group; thus, a prosecutor's use in an aggravated murder prosecution of preemptory challenges to excuse jurors opposed to the death penalty is proper since such jurors do not constitute an identifiable group. State v. Evans (Ohio 1992) 63 Ohio St.3d 231, 586 N.E.2d 1042, rehearing denied 63 Ohio St.3d 1450, 589 N.E.2d 393, certiorari denied 113 S.Ct. 246, 506 U.S. 886, 121 L.Ed.2d 179.

Both Crim R 24 and RC 2945.27 require that the trial court "permit" counsel to supplement the court's examination by further inquiry, but only where that opportunity is sought by counsel; they do not place an affirmative duty upon the trial court to invite counsel to participate in the voir dire examination. State v. Jones (Franklin 1982) 2 Ohio App.3d 345, 441 N.E.2d 1121, 2 O.B.R. 390. Jury ⚡ 131(1)

The fact that a person selected to serve as a juror at the trial of one charged with murder in the first degree is acquainted with the sheriff and a deputy sheriff who was a witness for the prosecution and has procured an insurance policy for that witness does not prejudice defendant's right to a fair and impartial trial, where the opportunity was present for defendant's counsel to ascertain this fact, and where there is no evidence that the juror was prejudiced against the defendant by reason of such acquaintance. (See also Woodards v Maxwell, 303 FSupp 690, 24 Misc 157 (SD Ohio 1969).) State v. Woodards (Ohio 1966) 6 Ohio St.2d 14, 215 N.E.2d 568, 35 O.O.2d 8, certiorari denied 87 S.Ct. 289, 385 U.S. 930, 17 L.Ed.2d 212.

That members of a jury had participated in a trial involving the same witnesses and a similar charge and that some jurors did not give an audible answer to counsel's questions on the voir dire did not constitute a ground for reversal where no request was made to the court to require an audible answer. State v. Mays (Montgomery 1956) 139 N.E.2d 639, 74 Ohio Law Abs. 43, appeal dismissed 165 Ohio St. 456, 135 N.E.2d 766, 60 O.O. 100.

4. Sequestered voir dire

Remarks by two prospective jurors in support of capital punishment were not shown to prejudice defendant and did not entitle him to individual sequestered voir dire; remarks were isolated, and effect was purely speculative. State v. Moore (Ohio, 02-04-1998) 81 Ohio St.3d 22, 689 N.E.2d 1, 1998-Ohio-441, dismissal of post-conviction relief affirmed 1998 WL 638353, dismissed, appeal not allowed 84 Ohio St.3d 1472, 704 N.E.2d 579. Jury ⚷ 131(13); Jury ⚷ 133

Determination of whether voir dire in capital case should be conducted in sequestration is matter of discretion within province of trial judge. State v. Soke (Ohio App. 8 Dist., 07-17-1995) 105 Ohio App.3d 226, 663 N.E.2d 986, dismissed, appeal not allowed 74 Ohio St.3d 1475, 657 N.E.2d 783. Criminal Law ⚷ 1152(2)

Trial court did not abuse its discretion in capital murder prosecution by failing to allow individual sequestered voir dire on question of publicity; trial court allowed parties to question prospective jurors who acknowledged hearing or reading news reports concerning trial, defense counsel engaged in full and unlimited questioning concerning pretrial publicity, and parties agreed to remove one prospective juror based on her statement that she could not put aside her exposure to pretrial publicity and render a fair verdict. State v. Soke (Ohio App. 8 Dist., 07-17-1995) 105 Ohio App.3d 226, 663 N.E.2d 986, dismissed, appeal not allowed 74 Ohio St.3d 1475, 657 N.E.2d 783. Jury ⚷ 131(13)

Defendant was not entitled to have voir dire of each prospective juror take place outside hearing of other prospective jurors, absent showing of abuse of discretion or prejudice; sheer repetition of questions asked to members of jury panel, along with effect of others' opinions, was insufficient to prejudice group. State v. Carter (Ohio, 07-26-1995) 72 Ohio St.3d 545, 651 N.E.2d 965, 1995-Ohio-104, stay granted 73 Ohio St.3d 1469, 654 N.E.2d 1281, certiorari denied 116 S.Ct. 575, 516 U.S. 1014, 133 L.Ed.2d 498, stay dissolved 74 Ohio St.3d 1493, 658 N.E.2d 1063, denial of post-conviction relief affirmed 1997 WL 705487, dismissed, appeal not allowed 81 Ohio St.3d 1467, 690 N.E.2d 1287, certiorari denied 119 S.Ct. 120, 525 U.S. 848, 142 L.Ed.2d 97, denial of post-conviction relief reversed 157 Ohio App.3d 689, 813 N.E.2d 78, 2004-Ohio-3372. Jury ⚷ 131(13)

The determination of whether a voir dire in a capital case should be conducted in sequestration is a matter of discretion within the province of the trial court. State v. Brown (Ohio 1988) 38 Ohio St.3d 305, 528 N.E.2d 523, rehearing denied 39 Ohio St.3d 710, 534 N.E.2d 93, certiorari denied 109 S.Ct. 1177, 489 U.S. 1040, 103 L.Ed.2d 239, rehearing denied 109 S.Ct. 1774, 490 U.S. 1032, 104 L.Ed.2d 208. Criminal Law ⚷ 854(6)

The guarantees of open public proceedings in criminal trials cover the voir dire examination of potential jurors. Press–Enterprise Co. v. Superior Court of California, Riverside County (U.S.Cal. 1984) 104 S.Ct. 819, 464 U.S. 501, 78 L.Ed.2d 629. Criminal Law ⚷ 635

5. Pretrial publicity

Defendant charged with aggravated murder was not prejudiced by voir dire of prospective jurors regarding pretrial media publicity regarding his case; although most prospective jurors acknowledged some familiarity with the case, jurors were questioned as to whether they had formed any fixed opinions and whether they could deliberate in a fair and impartial manner based solely on the evidence presented at trial, trial court readily excused members of the venire who had formed fixed opinions due to pretrial publicity, and all jurors empanelled stated that they could set aside any pretrial opinions and render a fair and impartial verdict. State v. Jackson (Ohio, 11-23-2005) 107 Ohio St.3d 53, 836 N.E.2d 1173, 2005-Ohio-5981, reconsideration denied 108 Ohio St.3d 1418, 841 N.E.2d 321, 2006-Ohio-179, certiorari denied 126 S.Ct. 2940, motion to reopen denied 110 Ohio St.3d 1435, 852 N.E.2d 185, 2006-Ohio-3862. Jury ⚷ 103(14); Jury ⚷ 131(7)

Trial court's voir dire of prospective jurors in capital murder prosecution was adequate to permit court to rule on challenges for cause and to ascertain that all seated jurors would serve impartially, despite fact that some or all jurors seated had heard of case prior to trial; trial court conducted probing inquiry that addressed issues of prospective jurors' personal knowledge of individuals involved in case and influence of media reports, and permitted counsel for both sides to question the prospective jurors, and in course of such examination, all empanelled jurors indicated that they would be able to perform their duties as demanded by law. State v. Gross (Ohio, 10-30-2002) 97 Ohio St.3d 121, 776 N.E.2d 1061, 2002-Ohio-5524, reconsideration denied 97 Ohio St.3d 1486, 780 N.E.2d 288, 2002-Ohio-6866, certiorari denied 123 S.Ct. 2079, 538 U.S. 1037, 155 L.Ed.2d 1068, rehearing denied 124 S.Ct. 20, 539 U.S. 976, 156 L.Ed.2d 685. Jury ⚷ 131(7)

Voir dire adequately addressed issue of pretrial publicity in prosecution for aggravated murder of peace officer, and such publicity did not prejudice defendant or violate his right to fair trial, where voir dire covered three days and 450 pages of transcript, involved questioning by court and counsel of prospective jurors who were familiar with case, and resulted in several exclusions. State v. White (Ohio, 05-20-1998) 82 Ohio St.3d 16, 693 N.E.2d 772, 1998-Ohio-363, stay granted 82 Ohio St.3d 1445, 695 N.E.2d 267, stay revoked 85 Ohio St.3d 1453, 708 N.E.2d 1008, reconsideration denied 82 Ohio St.3d 1469, 696 N.E.2d 226, reconsideration denied 82 Ohio St.3d 1470, 696 N.E.2d 226, dismissal of post-conviction relief affirmed 1998 WL 515944, dismissed, appeal not allowed 84 Ohio St.3d 1445, 703 N.E.2d 326, reconsideration denied 84 Ohio St.3d 1489, 705 N.E.2d 368, certiorari denied 119 S.Ct. 623, 525 U.S. 1057, 142 L.Ed.2d 562, denial of habeas corpus affirmed in part, reversed in part 431 F.3d 517, rehearing denied, rehearing and rehearing en banc denied, petition for certiorari filed 2006 WL 2094473. Criminal Law ⚷ 633(1)

Pretrial publicity does not inevitably lead to unfair trial, even if it is pervasive and adverse. State v. White (Ohio, 05-20-1998) 82 Ohio St.3d 16, 693 N.E.2d 772, 1998-Ohio-363, stay granted 82 Ohio St.3d 1445, 695 N.E.2d 267, stay revoked 85 Ohio St.3d 1453, 708 N.E.2d 1008, reconsideration denied 82 Ohio St.3d 1469, 696 N.E.2d 226, reconsideration denied 82 Ohio St.3d 1470, 696 N.E.2d 226, dismissal of post-conviction relief affirmed 1998 WL 515944, dismissed, appeal not allowed 84 Ohio St.3d 1445, 703 N.E.2d 326, reconsideration denied 84 Ohio St.3d 1489, 705 N.E.2d 368, certiorari denied 119 S.Ct. 623, 525 U.S. 1057, 142 L.Ed.2d 562, denial of habeas corpus affirmed in part, reversed in part 431 F.3d 517, rehearing denied, rehearing and rehearing en banc denied, petition for certiorari filed 2006 WL 2094473. Criminal Law ⚷ 633(1)

Fact that prospective jurors have been exposed to pretrial publicity does not, in and of itself, demonstrate prejudice to defendant. State v. White (Ohio, 05-20-1998) 82 Ohio St.3d 16, 693 N.E.2d 772, 1998-Ohio-363, stay granted 82 Ohio St.3d 1445, 695 N.E.2d 267, stay revoked 85 Ohio St.3d 1453, 708 N.E.2d 1008, reconsideration denied 82 Ohio St.3d 1469, 696 N.E.2d 226, reconsideration denied 82 Ohio St.3d 1470, 696 N.E.2d 226, dismissal of post-conviction relief affirmed 1998 WL 515944, dismissed, appeal not allowed 84 Ohio St.3d 1445, 703 N.E.2d 326, reconsideration denied 84 Ohio St.3d 1489, 705 N.E.2d 368, certiorari denied 119 S.Ct. 623, 525 U.S. 1057, 142 L.Ed.2d 562, denial of habeas corpus affirmed in part, reversed in part 431 F.3d 517, rehearing denied, rehearing and rehearing en banc denied, petition for certiorari filed 2006 WL 2094473. Criminal Law ⚷ 1163(2)

If record on voir dire establishes that prospective veniremen have been exposed to pretrial publicity but affirmed they would judge defendant solely on law and evidence presented at trial, it is not error to empanel such veniremen. State v. White (Ohio, 05-20-1998) 82 Ohio St.3d 16, 693 N.E.2d 772, 1998-Ohio-363, stay granted 82 Ohio St.3d 1445, 695 N.E.2d 267, stay revoked 85 Ohio St.3d 1453, 708 N.E.2d 1008, reconsideration denied 82 Ohio St.3d 1469, 696 N.E.2d 226, reconsideration denied 82 Ohio St.3d 1470, 696 N.E.2d 226, dismissal of post-conviction relief affirmed 1998 WL 515944, dismissed, appeal not allowed 84 Ohio St.3d 1445, 703 N.E.2d 326, reconsideration denied 84 Ohio St.3d 1489, 705 N.E.2d 368, certiorari denied 119 S.Ct. 623, 525 U.S. 1057, 142 L.Ed.2d 562, denial of habeas corpus affirmed in part, reversed in part 431 F.3d 517, rehearing denied, rehearing and rehearing en banc denied, petition for certiorari filed 2006 WL 2094473. Jury ⚷ 103(14)

Forum for testing prospective jurors for prejudice from pretrial publicity is voir dire. State v. Brown (Ohio App. 12 Dist., 07-15-1996) 112 Ohio App.3d 583, 679 N.E.2d 361. Jury ⚷ 131(7)

Significant pretrial print and electronic media coverage of aggravated murder, kidnapping, and aggravated robbery did not deprive defendant of fair trial and did not entitle him to change of venue, even though media published his criminal record; the pretrial publicity was not pervasive, trial court took substantial measures to protect right to fair trial by questioning prospective jurors as to impact of pretrial publicity and excusing those in venire who had formed fixed opinions or were otherwise unsuitable, and although sizeable majority of prospective jurors knew at least some details of crime, ten knew nothing, and another eight had only vague, sketchy knowledge. State v. Davis (Ohio, 07-24-1996) 76 Ohio St.3d 107, 666 N.E.2d 1099, 1996-Ohio-414, reconsideration denied 76 Ohio St.3d 1479, 669 N.E.2d 860, denial of post-conviction relief affirmed 1998 WL 703028, dismissed, appeal not allowed 85 Ohio St.3d 1424, 707 N.E.2d 515, habeas corpus denied 110 F.Supp.2d 607, reversed 318 F.3d 682, rehearing and suggestion for rehearing en banc denied, certiorari denied 124 S.Ct. 2902, 542 U.S. 945, 159 L.Ed.2d 827. Criminal Law ⚷ 126(2); Criminal Law ⚷ 633(1)

Pretrial publicity about defendant's criminal record does not create automatic presumption of prejudice. State v. Davis (Ohio, 07-24-1996) 76 Ohio St.3d 107, 666 N.E.2d 1099, 1996-Ohio-414, reconsideration denied 76 Ohio St.3d 1479, 669 N.E.2d 860, denial of post-conviction relief affirmed 1998 WL 703028, dismissed, appeal not allowed 85 Ohio St.3d 1424, 707 N.E.2d 515, habeas corpus denied 110 F.Supp.2d 607, reversed 318 F.3d 682, rehearing and suggestion for rehearing en banc denied, certiorari denied 124 S.Ct. 2902, 542 U.S. 945, 159 L.Ed.2d 827. Criminal Law ⚷ 1163(2)

Where it is possible that media publicity could prejudice a jury, careful voir dire is best test to determine whether jury can be fair and impartial. Lakewood v. Town (Ohio App. 8 Dist., 09-25-1995) 106 Ohio App.3d 521, 666 N.E.2d 599, dismissed, appeal not allowed 75 Ohio St.3d 1404, 661 N.E.2d 754. Jury ⚷ 131(6)

Wide discretion is granted to trial court in conducting voir dire in area of pretrial publicity and other areas of inquiry that might tend to show juror bias. State v. Nobles (Ohio App. 2 Dist., 09-01-1995) 106 Ohio App.3d 246, 665 N.E.2d 1137, dismissed, appeal not allowed 74 Ohio St.3d 1510, 659 N.E.2d 1287. Jury ⚷ 131(2)

Voir dire examination into pretrial publicity is not deficient for failing to uncover details of every article or broadcast to which veniremen have been exposed. State v. Nobles (Ohio App. 2 Dist., 09-01-1995) 106 Ohio App.3d 246, 665 N.E.2d 1137, dismissed, appeal not allowed 74 Ohio St.3d 1510, 659 N.E.2d 1287. Jury ⚷ 131(7)

Voir dire examination on issue of exposure of veniremen to pretrial publicity, whether by court or by counsel, is sufficient if it reveals that veniremen will be able to set aside any impression they formed on basis of pretrial publicity and to decide case solely on law and evidence presented at trial. State v. Nobles (Ohio App. 2 Dist., 09-01-1995) 106 Ohio App.3d 246, 665 N.E.2d 1137, dismissed, appeal not allowed 74 Ohio St.3d 1510, 659 N.E.2d 1287. Jury ⚷ 131(7)

Veniremen impaneled in trial for murder and gross abuse of corpse were examined sufficiently well to enable court to determine whether they could impartially hear case, and defendant was thus not prejudiced by fact that all voir dire on subject of pretrial publicity was conducted by court rather than by counsel; court invited counsel to submit and to file proposed questions, defense counsel submitted questions but did not file them or make them part of record in any way, veniremen were repeatedly told that they were to decide defendant's guilt solely on evidence presented and law instructed during course of trial and had three opportunities to inform court if they could not do so, entire year passed between voir dire examination and last pertinent publicity, and it was likely that any prejudicial effect created by media coverage would have subsided considerably during such time. State v. Nobles (Ohio App. 2 Dist., 09-01-1995) 106 Ohio App.3d 246, 665 N.E.2d 1137, dismissed, appeal not allowed 74 Ohio St.3d 1510, 659 N.E.2d 1287. Jury ⚷ 131(7); Jury ⚷ 131(10)

There was no constitutional error inherent in trial court's not permitting defense counsel to conduct voir dire on issue of adverse pretrial publicity in trial for murder, gross abuse of corpse and inducing panic. State v. Nobles (Ohio App. 2 Dist., 09-01-1995) 106 Ohio App.3d 246, 665 N.E.2d 1137, dismissed, appeal not allowed 74 Ohio St.3d 1510, 659 N.E.2d 1287. Jury ⚷ 131(10)

Criminal defendant has no constitutional right to question prospective jurors individually as to content of news reports to which they had been exposed. State v. Soke (Ohio App. 8 Dist., 07-17-1995) 105 Ohio App.3d 226, 663 N.E.2d 986, dismissed, appeal not allowed 74 Ohio St.3d 1475, 657 N.E.2d 783. Jury ⚷ 131(7); Jury ⚷ 131(13)

No abuse of discretion will be shown in connection with denial of request to question prospective jurors individually as to content of news report to which they were exposed, as long as trial judge is satisfied that prospective jurors can set aside content of such reports and render fair verdict based on evidence. State v. Soke (Ohio App. 8 Dist., 07-17-1995) 105 Ohio App.3d 226, 663 N.E.2d 986, dismissed, appeal not allowed 74 Ohio St.3d 1475, 657 N.E.2d 783. Jury ⚷ 131(7); Jury ⚷ 131(13)

Trial court exercised appropriate discretion in not allowing jurors in murder prosecution to be asked whether they would consider specifically named statutory mitigating factors, despite defendants' claim that, given extensive pretrial publicity, limitation on voir dire prevented him from adequately unearthing juror bias and effectively using his peremptory challenges; defendant had full opportunity to question prospective jurors during eight-day voir dire and individually asked them about their media exposure and their attitudes about death penalty, and jurors could not realistically be asked to weigh specific mitigating factors until they had heard all evidence and been fully instructed on applicable law. State v. Lundgren (Ohio, 08-30-1995) 73 Ohio St.3d 474, 653 N.E.2d 304, 1995-Ohio-227, reconsideration denied 74 Ohio St.3d 1422, 655 N.E.2d 742, certiorari denied 116 S.Ct. 1276, 516 U.S. 1178, 134 L.Ed.2d 222, dismissal of post-conviction relief affirmed 1998 WL 964592, dismissed, appeal not allowed 85 Ohio St.3d 1465, 709 N.E.2d 171. Jury ⚷ 131(4); Jury ⚷ 131(6); Jury ⚷ 131(8)

A defendant, being prosecuted for alleged vaginal and anal rape, is not entitled to have his case dismissed or a sequestered voir dire because his case received unique pretrial publicity when ten days before his trial George Bush, while campaigning for president, met with participants in the county victim-witness program including the alleged victim in his case, resulting in various local newspaper articles in which the alleged victim was identified by name and repeatedly referred to as a "crime victim," "rape victim," and "date-rape victim" since as the defendant did not move for a sequestered voir dire, the trial court had no duty to sequester the veniremen sua sponte and the remedy for pervasive pretrial publicity is a change of venue, not a dismissal; although the trial court treated defendant's motion to dismiss as a motion for a change of venue, it refused to grant a change of venue after the jury was seated and since defense counsel chose not to inquire about the publicity when examining veniremen in voir dire, the record is silent whether any of the jurors or veniremen knew about the alleged victim's meeting with Bush and it can not be assumed that the jurors were or were not exposed to the publicity, despite the extensiveness of the pretrial publicity involved. State v. Lewis (Greene 1990) 66 Ohio App.3d 37, 583 N.E.2d 404, dismissed, jurisdictional motion overruled 55 Ohio St.3d 703, 562 N.E.2d 894.

In a highly publicized case, where there is an absence of presumed prejudice, the trial court, in deciding whether a denial of a change of venue would violate due process, has a responsibility to confront the fact of the publicity and determine if the publicity rises to the level of actual prejudice, and a searching voir dire of the prospective jurors is the primary tool to determine if the impact of the publicity rises to that level. Ritchie v. Rogers (C.A.6 (Ohio), 12-18-2002) 313 F.3d 948, rehearing and suggestion for rehearing en banc denied, certiorari denied 124 S.Ct. 110, 540 U.S. 842, 157 L.Ed.2d 76. Constitutional Law ⚷ 259; Criminal Law ⚷ 126(1); Jury ⚷ 131(7)

State court's rejection of petitioner's due process objections, based on impact of pre-trial publicity, to switch from individual voir dire to group voir dire, and state court's resulting denial of change of venue, did not result in decision that was contrary to, or involved unreasonable application of, clearly established Federal law, or result in decision that was based on unreasonable determination of facts, and thus did not warrant habeas relief, notwithstanding petitioner's argument that prospective jurors, after listening to which answers led to excusal, were conditioned to agree that they could set aside their previously-indicated view that petitioner was guilty. Ritchie v. Rogers (C.A.6 (Ohio), 12-18-2002) 313 F.3d 948, rehearing and suggestion for rehearing en banc denied, certiorari denied 124 S.Ct. 110, 540 U.S. 842, 157 L.Ed.2d 76. Habeas Corpus ⚷ 444; Habeas Corpus ⚷ 496

Pretrial publicity of even the most sensational nature does not necessarily result in an unfair trial; voir dire in some of the most highly publicized criminal prosecutions has revealed the fact that many prospective jurors do not follow such news coverage closely and that juries can be empanelled without inordinate difficulty in such situations. Application of National Broadcasting Co., Inc. (C.A.6 (Ohio) 1987) 828 F.2d 340.

6. Beliefs as to death penalty

Trial court did not improperly deny challenges for cause, in capital murder prosecution, involving jurors who stated that they could not consider mitigating evidence and would automatically vote to recommend death penalty, and thus did not prejudicially affect defendant's use of peremptory challenges; many jurors challenged on such grounds in fact indicated willingness and ability to follow the law in sentencing phase, trial court excused for cause any prospective juror who did express inability to consider mitigation evidence, and defendant failed to identify any remaining prospective juror against whom he was required to exercise peremptory challenge to his prejudice. State v. Gross (Ohio, 10-30-2002) 97 Ohio St.3d 121, 776 N.E.2d 1061, 2002-Ohio-5524, reconsideration denied 97 Ohio St.3d 1486, 780 N.E.2d 288, 2002-Ohio-6866, certiorari denied 123 S.Ct. 2079, 538 U.S. 1037, 155 L.Ed.2d 1068, rehearing denied 124 S.Ct. 20, 539 U.S. 976, 156 L.Ed.2d 685. Jury ⚷ 108; Jury ⚷ 135

Trial court did not abuse its discretion by excusing from capital murder trial prospective juror who opposed the death penalty even for Hitler and juror who was adamant in stating that the death penalty was against his religion and that it was up to God to take a life. State v. Fears (Ohio, 09-08-1999) 86 Ohio St.3d 329, 715 N.E.2d 136, 1999-Ohio-111, reconsideration denied 87 Ohio St.3d 1421, 717 N.E.2d 1107, stay granted 87 Ohio St.3d 1423, 718 N.E.2d 441, denial of post-conviction relief affirmed 1999 WL 1032592, dismissed, appeal not allowed 88 Ohio St.3d 1444, 725 N.E.2d 284, certiorari denied 120 S.Ct. 1535, 529 U.S. 1039, 146 L.Ed.2d 349. Jury ⚷ 108

Trial court did not abuse its discretion in capital murder trial by excusing juror who unequivocally stated she could "never be involved in the decision whether or not someone lives or dies unless it's self-defense," though juror had earlier expressed reservations about serving due to child-care difficulties and had initially felt she could return a death recommendation. State v. Fears (Ohio, 09-08-1999) 86 Ohio St.3d 329, 715 N.E.2d 136, 1999-Ohio-111, reconsideration denied 87 Ohio St.3d 1421, 717 N.E.2d 1107, stay granted 87 Ohio St.3d 1423, 718 N.E.2d 441, denial of post-conviction relief affirmed 1999 WL 1032592, dismissed, appeal not allowed 88 Ohio St.3d 1444, 725 N.E.2d 284, certiorari denied 120 S.Ct. 1535, 529 U.S. 1039, 146 L.Ed.2d 349. Jury ⚷ 108

Trial court took adequate steps to ensure that juror in capital murder prosecution was in fact impartial, where juror, in responding to defense counsel's inquiry whether she could sentence defendant to term of 30 years without parole, stated that her decision would be based on evidence presented during trial, court questioned juror regarding her beliefs on death penalty and instructed juror at length regarding law on guilt and penalty phases, and juror clearly indicated that she would follow and apply law to facts as instructed. State v. Stojetz (Ohio, 02-17-1999) 84 Ohio St.3d 452, 705 N.E.2d 329, 1999-Ohio-464, stay granted 85 Ohio St.3d 1401, 706 N.E.2d 784, reconsideration denied 85 Ohio St.3d 1448, 708 N.E.2d 212, certiorari denied 120 S.Ct. 455, 528 U.S. 999, 145 L.Ed.2d 376, denial of post-conviction relief affirmed 2002-Ohio-6520, 2002 WL 31682231, appeal not allowed 98 Ohio St.3d 1514, 786 N.E.2d 63, 2003-Ohio-1572. Jury ⚷ 108; Jury ⚷ 131(8)

Trial court did not commit plain error, during individual voir dire questioning of capital murder prosecution, by asking each juror if he or she could join in signing verdict form which recommended imposition of death penalty. State v. Goff (Ohio, 06-17-1998) 82 Ohio St.3d 123, 694 N.E.2d 916, 1998-Ohio-369, reconsideration denied 82 Ohio St.3d 1483, 696 N.E.2d 1089, certiorari denied 119 S.Ct. 2402, 527 U.S. 1039, 144 L.Ed.2d 800, dismissal of post-conviction relief affirmed 2001 WL 208845, dismissed, appeal not allowed 92 Ohio St.3d 1430, 749 N.E.2d 756. Criminal Law ⚷ 1035(5)

In capital murder prosecution, prosecutor's questions during voir dire regarding death penalty were not, viewed in context of entire voir dire, attempt to destroy defendant's presumption of innocence and to get jurors to commit themselves to death penalty; questions were proper attempt to discover if prospective jurors could, in actual case and not on abstract level, sign death penalty verdict if they found that aggravated circumstance outweighed mitigating factors. State v. Wilson (Ohio, 01-24-1996) 74 Ohio St.3d 381, 659 N.E.2d 292, 1996-Ohio-103, reconsideration denied 75 Ohio St.3d 1413, 661 N.E.2d 760, certiorari denied 117 S.Ct. 129, 519 U.S. 845, 136 L.Ed.2d 78, denial of post-conviction relief affirmed 80 Ohio St.3d 132, 684 N.E.2d 1221, 1997-Ohio-303, denial of post-conviction relief affirmed 1998 WL 332940. Jury ⚷ 131(13)

Trial court did not commit plain error, in capital murder case, by failing to ask prospective jurors if they would automatically impose death penalty; defense counsel had full opportunity to explore question during his examination of prospects and did so with several of them. State v. Phillips (Ohio, 11-22-1995) 74 Ohio St.3d 72, 656 N.E.2d 643, 1995-Ohio-171, reconsideration denied 74 Ohio St.3d 1485, 657 N.E.2d 1378, stay granted 74 Ohio St.3d 1503, 659 N.E.2d 795, rehearing granted, opinion recalled 75 Ohio St.3d 1504, 665 N.E.2d

219, certiorari denied 116 S.Ct. 1835, 517 U.S. 1213, 134 L.Ed.2d 938, denial of post-conviction relief affirmed in part, reversed in part 1999 WL 58961, dismissed, appeal not allowed 86 Ohio St.3d 1402, 711 N.E.2d 231, denial of post-conviction relief affirmed 2002-Ohio-823, 2002 WL 274637, appeal not allowed 95 Ohio St.3d 1488, 769 N.E.2d 403, 2002-Ohio-2625. Criminal Law ⚷ 1035(5)

Prospective juror who gave conflicting answers as to whether he would be able to impose death penalty was properly excused for cause in capital murder case; juror's answers reflected desire to follow court's instructions in the abstract, but made it clear he could not follow Ohio law when required to decide issue of capital punishment. State v. Frazier (Ohio, 08-23-1995) 73 Ohio St.3d 323, 652 N.E.2d 1000, 1995-Ohio-235, stay granted 74 Ohio St.3d 1437, 655 N.E.2d 1321, certiorari denied 116 S.Ct. 820, 516 U.S. 1095, 133 L.Ed.2d 763, denial of post-conviction relief affirmed 1997 WL 764810, dismissed, appeal not allowed 81 Ohio St.3d 1496, 691 N.E.2d 1058, habeas corpus denied 188 F.Supp.2d 798, denial of habeas corpus reversed in part 343 F.3d 780, opinion supplemented on denial of rehearing 348 F.3d 174, rehearing and suggestion for rehearing en banc denied, certiorari denied 124 S.Ct. 2815, 541 U.S. 1095, 159 L.Ed.2d 261. Jury ⚷ 108

Juror who stated that he could not follow the law and could not vote for death penalty was properly excused for cause. State v. Williams (Ohio, 08-16-1995) 73 Ohio St.3d 153, 652 N.E.2d 721, 1995-Ohio-275, reconsideration denied 74 Ohio St.3d 1409, 655 N.E.2d 188, stay granted 74 Ohio St.3d 1437, 655 N.E.2d 1321, stay terminated 75 Ohio St.3d 1439, 662 N.E.2d 1085, certiorari denied 116 S.Ct. 1047, 516 U.S. 1161, 134 L.Ed.2d 193, denial of post-conviction relief affirmed 1998 WL 330539, dismissed, appeal not allowed 83 Ohio St.3d 1449, 700 N.E.2d 332, reconsideration denied 84 Ohio St.3d 1413, 701 N.E.2d 1021. Jury ⚷ 107; Jury ⚷ 108

Upon examination of a prospective juror to determine whether he should be disqualified from a capital case because of his opposition to capital punishment, the most that can be demanded of a venireman in this regard is that he be willing to consider all of the penalties provided by state law, and that he not be irrevocably committed, before the trial has begun, to vote against the penalty of death regardless of the facts and circumstances which might emerge in the course of the proceedings. State v. Watson (Ohio 1971) 28 Ohio St.2d 15, 275 N.E.2d 153, 57 O.O.2d 95. Jury ⚷ 108

7. Preserving objections for appeal

A statement by counsel that "we aren't waiving any of our rights under the constitution and laws of the state of Ohio in reference to the picking and impaneling of a jury," is not sufficient to constitute prejudicial error by putting the court on notice as to the nature of the objections. City of Columbus v. Burris (Franklin 1958) 151 N.E.2d 690, 78 Ohio Law Abs. 120.

2945.28 Form of oath to jury; effect of form on validity of impanelment

(A) In criminal cases jurors and the jury shall take the following oath to be administered by the trial court or the clerk of the court of common pleas, and the jurors shall respond to the oath "I do swear" or "I do affirm": " Do you swear or affirm that you will diligently inquire into and carefully deliberate all matters between the State of Ohio and the defendant (giving the defendant's name)? Do you swear or affirm you will do this to the best of your skill and understanding, without bias or prejudice? So help you God."

A juror shall be allowed to make affirmation and the words "this you do as you shall answer under the pains and penalties of perjury" shall be substituted for the words, "So help you God."

(B) If, on or after the effective date of this amendment, a court that impanels a jury in a criminal case uses the oath that was in effect prior to the effective date of this amendment instead of the oath set forth in division (A) of this section, the court's use of the former oath does not invalidate or affect the validity of the impanelment of the jury or any action taken by the jury.

(2004 S 71, eff. 5–18–05; 1953 H 1, eff. 10–1–53; GC 13443–11, 13443–12)

Historical and Statutory Notes

Pre–1953 H 1 Amendments: 113 v 184, Ch 22, § 11, 12

Amendment Note: 2004 S 71 rewrote this section, which prior thereto read:

"In criminal cases jurors and the jury shall take the following oath to be administered by the trial court or the clerk of the court of common pleas: 'You shall well and truly try, and true deliverance make between the State of Ohio and the defendant (giving his name). So help you God.'

"A juror shall be allowed to make affirmation and the words 'this you do as you shall answer under the pains and penalties of perjury' shall be substituted for the words, 'So help you God.'"

Cross References

County courts, 1907.29
Grand jury, oath, 2939.06

Library References

Jury ⚷148.
Westlaw Topic No. 230.
C.J.S. Juries § 496.

Research References

Encyclopedias

OH Jur. 3d Criminal Law § 2621, Oath or Affirmation.

OH Jur. 3d Criminal Law § 3561, Statements or Actions of Trial Judge.

OH Jur. 3d Evidence & Witnesses § 783, Requirement that Witness Take Oath or Affirmation—Effect of Failure to Administer Oath or Affirmation.

Treatises and Practice Aids

Markus, Trial Handbook for Ohio Lawyers, § 6:26, Swearing to Oath or Affirmation.

Katz, Giannelli, Blair and Lipton, Baldwin's Ohio Practice, Criminal Law, § 148:27, Oath to Jury (Statutory Form).

Katz, Giannelli, Blair and Lipton, Baldwin's Ohio Practice, Criminal Law, § 148:29, Entry Jury Impaneled and Sworn.

Notes of Decisions

1. Constitutional issues

Defendant failed to show that he was prejudiced by trial counsel's failure to object to oath administered to jury, as required to establish ineffective assistance in prosecution for possession of criminal tools; although defendant argued oath administered to jury was not oath that was customarily administered and that oath given omitted reference to jurors' obligation to render true verdict, jury instructions emphasized jurors' sworn duty to accept instructions given and jurors' role as sole judges of fact and credibility of witnesses, and there was no indication jurors failed to appreciate importance of oath. State v. Boykin (Ohio App. 2 Dist., Montgomery, 04-02-2004) No. 19896, 2004-Ohio-1701, 2004 WL 690799, Unreported. Criminal Law ⚷ 641.13(2.1)

2. Administration of oath

Trial court's alleged failure to comply with statutory provision requiring that oath to jury be administered by the trial court or the clerk of the court did not require reversal, where defendant failed to make an affirmative showing of prejudice and failed to bring the alleged irregularity to the attention of the court at a time when the court could have made correction. State v. Vanblarcome (Ohio App. 10 Dist., Franklin, 02-06-2003) No. 02AP-417, 2003-Ohio-579, 2003 WL 257408, Unreported. Criminal Law ⚷ 1166.19

Administration of oath to jury outside of defendant's presence was not structural error requiring reversal; record failed to show that defendant's absence during that portion of the trial affected the fairness of the proceedings or undermined confidence in the outcome. State v. Vanblarcome (Ohio App. 10 Dist., Franklin, 02-06-2003) No. 02AP-417, 2003-Ohio-579, 2003 WL 257408, Unreported. Criminal Law ⚷ 1166.14

Trial court's failure to strictly comply with statute requiring that trial court or clerk of court of common pleas administer oath to jurors did not require reversal of verdict, absent showing that capital murder defendant had been prejudiced due to fact that bailiff had administered oath to jurors. State v. Conway (Ohio, 03-08-2006) 108 Ohio St.3d 214, 842 N.E.2d 996, 2006-Ohio-791, petition for certiorari filed 2006 WL 1558259. Criminal Law ⚷ 1166.19

Fact that bailiff administered oath to jurors, instead of trial court or clerk of court of common pleas, as required by statute, was at most a statutory violation, not constitutional error, and, as such, no structural error occurred with respect to bailiff administering oath, in capital murder prosecution. State v. Conway (Ohio, 03-08-2006) 108 Ohio St.3d 214, 842 N.E.2d 996, 2006-Ohio-791, petition for certiorari filed 2006 WL 1558259. Jury ⚷ 148(1)

Capital murder defendant waived on appeal all but plain error with respect to whether trial court's having bailiff, rather than clerk of court of common pleas administer oath to jurors prejudiced him, as he did not object at time bailiff administered oath. State v. Conway (Ohio, 03-08-2006) 108 Ohio St.3d 214, 842 N.E.2d 996, 2006-Ohio-791, petition for certiorari filed 2006 WL 1558259. Criminal Law ⚷ 1035(6)

2945.29 Jurors becoming unable to perform duties

If, before the conclusion of the trial, a juror becomes sick, or for other reason is unable to perform his duty, the court may order him to be discharged. In that case, if alternate jurors have been selected, one of them shall be designated to take the place of the juror so discharged. If, after all alternate jurors have been made regular jurors, a juror becomes too incapacitated to perform his duty, and has been discharged by the court, a new juror may be sworn and the trial begin anew, or the jury may be discharged and a new jury then or thereafter impaneled.

(1953 H 1, eff. 10–1–53; GC 13443–13)

Historical and Statutory Notes

Pre–1953 H 1 Amendments: 113 v 184, Ch 22, § 13

Cross References

Trial Jurors, Crim R 24

Library References

Jury ⚷149.
Westlaw Topic No. 230.
C.J.S. Juries §§ 265, 501 to 510.

Research References

Encyclopedias

OH Jur. 3d Criminal Law § 2796, Grounds for Replacing Juror; Discretion of Court.

OH Jur. 3d Jury § 235, Replacement of Regular Juror With Alternate Juror.

Treatises and Practice Aids

Markus, Trial Handbook for Ohio Lawyers, § 37:1, During Deliberations.

Katz, Giannelli, Blair and Lipton, Baldwin's Ohio Practice, Criminal Law, § 63:7, Alternate Jurors.

Katz, Giannelli, Blair and Lipton, Baldwin's Ohio Practice, Criminal Law, § 148:16, Order to Select Alternate Juror.

Katz, Giannelli, Blair and Lipton, Baldwin's Ohio Practice, Criminal Law, § 148:17, Order Directing Alternate Juror to Serve.

Notes of Decisions

1. Constitutional issues

Trial counsel's failure to object to substitution of juror who was reportedly in hospital emergency room did not fall below objective standard of reasonable representation and was not ineffective assistance of counsel in felonious assault prosecution. State v. Owens (Ohio App. 11 Dist., 07-01-1996) 112 Ohio App.3d 334, 678 N.E.2d 956. Criminal Law ⚷ 641.13(2.1)

2. Discharge of juror

Trial court acted within its discretion in replacing two jurors during murder trial with alternate jurors, where first juror informed trial court that he could no longer be impartial but that he had not indicated this to any of the other jurors, and second juror lied to trial court about his ability to attend trial. State v. Miller (Ohio App. 3 Dist., Crawford, 04-19-2004) No. 3-03-26, 2004-Ohio-1947, 2004 WL 829933, Unreported, appeal not allowed 103 Ohio St.3d 1462, 815 N.E.2d 678, 2004-Ohio-5056, appeal not allowed 104 Ohio St.3d 1460, 821 N.E.2d 577, 2005-Ohio-204. Jury ⚷ 149

Trial court acted within its discretion removing juror from jury on the ground that juror's objective participation in the trial had been compromised by her encounter with courtroom spectator; juror was crying as she discussed the encounter, juror became concerned with how parties would react to verdict, and juror was afraid for her safety. State v. Reid (Ohio App. 2 Dist., Montgomery, 08-01-2003) No. 19352, 2003-Ohio-4087, 2003 WL 21771782, Unreported, motion for delayed appeal denied 100 Ohio St.3d 1530, 800 N.E.2d 47, 2003-Ohio-6458, appeal not allowed 101 Ohio St.3d 1491, 805 N.E.2d 541, 2004-Ohio-1293. Criminal Law ⚷ 868

Juror cannot be removed if there is any possibility that fellow jurors' complaints about him or her are rooted in his or her view of the merits of the case. State v. Robb (Ohio, 03-01-2000) 88 Ohio St.3d 59, 723 N.E.2d 1019, 2000-Ohio-275. Jury ⚷ 149

Manifest necessity standard did not apply to trial judge's substitution of alternate juror for reportedly disabled juror. State v. Owens (Ohio App. 11 Dist., 07-01-1996) 112 Ohio App.3d 334, 678 N.E.2d 956. Jury ⚷ 149

Trial court did not abuse its discretion when it substituted alternative juror for juror who was reportedly in emergency room; more extensive inquiry into circumstances surrounding reportedly disabled juror's illness was not required. State v. Owens (Ohio App. 11 Dist., 07-01-1996) 112 Ohio App.3d 334, 678 N.E.2d 956. Jury ⚷ 149

A trial court in a DUI case does not abuse its discretion in replacing a juror who fails to appear for the second day of trial with an alternate juror, where this action avoided a substantial delay of the proceedings. State v. Gleason (Hamilton 1989) 65 Ohio App.3d 206, 583 N.E.2d 975. Jury ⚷ 149

A trial court need not examine a reportedly disabled juror personally, nor must it offer counsel an opportunity to do so before replacing the juror with an alternate. State v. Shields (Cuyahoga 1984) 15 Ohio App.3d 112, 472 N.E.2d 1110, 15 O.B.R. 202.

The discharge of a juror for illness of an immediate member of his family during any stage of a criminal trial is within the sound discretion of the trial court. State v. Sallee (Ashtabula 1966) 8 Ohio App.2d 9, 220 N.E.2d 370, 37 O.O.2d 5. Jury ⚷ 149

3. Excuse for cause after jury sworn

After a jury has been selected and sworn, and after the opening statement by the prosecutor, where a juror states that he recognizes the defendant and that his working relationship with the defendant could affect his decision as a juror, the court may excuse the juror, even though the working relationship might have been disclosed at voir dire had the prosecutor inquired. State v. Hopkins (Lake 1985) 27 Ohio App.3d 196, 500 N.E.2d 323, 27 O.B.R. 235.

2945.30 Medical attendance of juror

In case of sickness of any juror before the conclusion of the trial, the court may order that such juror receive medical attendance and shall order the payment of a reasonable charge for such medical attendance out of the judiciary fund.

(1953 H 1, eff. 10–1–53; GC 13443–14)

Historical and Statutory Notes

Pre–1953 H 1 Amendments: 113 v 184, Ch 22, § 14

Library References

Jury ⚷149.
Westlaw Topic No. 230.
C.J.S. Juries §§ 265, 501 to 510.

Research References

Encyclopedias

OH Jur. 3d Criminal Law § 2791, Care and Comfort of Jurors.

Treatises and Practice Aids

Markus, Trial Handbook for Ohio Lawyers, § 37:1, During Deliberations.

2945.31 Separation of jurors

After the trial has commenced, before or after the jury is sworn, the court may order the jurors to be kept in charge of proper officers, or they may be permitted to separate during the trial. If the jurors are kept in charge of officers of the court, proper arrangements shall be made for their care, maintenance, and comfort, under the orders and direction of the court. In case of necessity the court may permit temporary separation of the jurors.

(1953 H 1, eff. 10–1–53; GC 13443–15)

Historical and Statutory Notes

Pre–1953 H 1 Amendments: 113 v 185, Ch 22, § 15

Cross References

Trial jurors, Crim R 24

Library References

Criminal Law ⚷854.
Westlaw Topic No. 110.
C.J.S. Criminal Law § 1363.

Research References

Encyclopedias

OH Jur. 3d Criminal Law § 2791, Care and Comfort of Jurors.

OH Jur. 3d Criminal Law § 2793, Separation or Segregation of Jury.

Treatises and Practice Aids

Markus, Trial Handbook for Ohio Lawyers, § 37:1, During Deliberations.

Markus, Trial Handbook for Ohio Lawyers, § 37:5, Separation During Trial.

Markus, Trial Handbook for Ohio Lawyers, § 4:32, Trial by Jury.

Katz, Giannelli, Blair and Lipton, Baldwin's Ohio Practice, Criminal Law, § 65:3, Supervision of Sequestration.

Hennenberg & Reinhart, Ohio Criminal Defense Motions F 8.04, Motion for Sequestration of Jurors for Duration of Trial-Jury-Related Motions.

Hennenberg & Reinhart, Ohio Criminal Defense Motions F 13.54, Motion for Sequestration of Jurors for Duration of Trial-Death Penalty Motions.

Notes of Decisions

Pretrial publicity 1

1. Pretrial publicity

Trial court's refusal to sequester jury throughout course of trial did not deprive capital murder defendant of fair trial, where court routinely admonished jury not to discuss case or to read any news accounts related thereto; trial court was in best position to gauge atmosphere of trial proceedings and to evaluate whether its instructions sufficed over sequestration, and pretrial publicity fell well short of justifying change of venue. State v. Gross (Ohio, 10-30-2002) 97 Ohio St.3d 121, 776 N.E.2d 1061, 2002-Ohio-5524, reconsideration denied 97 Ohio St.3d 1486, 780 N.E.2d 288, 2002-Ohio-6866, certiorari denied 123 S.Ct. 2079, 538 U.S. 1037, 155 L.Ed.2d 1068, rehearing denied 124 S.Ct. 20, 539 U.S. 976, 156 L.Ed.2d 685. Criminal Law ⚷ 665(1)

2945.32 Oath to officers if jury sequestered

When an order has been entered by the court of common pleas in any criminal cause, directing the jurors to be kept in charge of the officers of the court, the following oath shall be administered by the clerk of the court of common pleas to said officers: "You do solemnly swear that you will, to the best of your ability, keep the persons sworn as jurors on this trial, from separating from each other; that you will not suffer any communications to be made to them, or any of them, orally or otherwise; that you will not communicate with them, or any of them, orally or otherwise, except by the order of this court, or to ask them if they have agreed on their verdict, until they shall be discharged, and that you will not, before they render their verdict communicate to any person the state of their deliberations or the verdict they have agreed upon, so help you God." Any officer having taken such oath who willfully violates the same, or permits the same to be violated, is guilty of perjury and shall be imprisoned not less than one nor more than ten years.

(1953 H 1, eff. 10–1–53; GC 13443–16; Source—GC 12842)

Historical and Statutory Notes

Pre–1953 H 1 Amendments: 113 v 185, Ch 22, § 16

Cross References

Affirmation in lieu of oath, 3.20

Library References

Criminal Law ⚷851.

Westlaw Topic No. 110.

C.J.S. Criminal Law § 1362.

Research References

Encyclopedias

OH Jur. 3d Criminal Law § 2792, Officers in Charge of Jury.

Treatises and Practice Aids

Markus, Trial Handbook for Ohio Lawyers, § 37:1, During Deliberations.

Markus, Trial Handbook for Ohio Lawyers, § 37:7, Control During Deliberations.

Katz, Giannelli, Blair and Lipton, Baldwin's Ohio Practice, Criminal Law, § 148:30, Oath of Officer in Charge When Jury Sequestered (Statutory Form).

Notes of Decisions

Oath of bailiff or constable 1

1. Oath of bailiff or constable

Statute requiring clerk to administer oath to bailiff or court constable held mandatory. Halsey v. State (Wood 1932) 42 Ohio App. 291, 182 N.E. 127, 11 Ohio Law Abs. 308, error dismissed 125 Ohio St. 628, 185 N.E. 881. Criminal Law ⚷ 851; Oath ⚷ 2; Statutes ⚷ 227

Clerk's failure to administer oath to bailiff or court constable held not to require granting new trial, where counsel sat idly by without objecting and no prejudice was shown. Halsey v. State (Wood 1932) 42 Ohio App. 291, 182 N.E. 127, 11 Ohio Law Abs. 308, error dismissed 125 Ohio St. 628, 185 N.E. 881. Criminal Law ⚷ 918(10); New Trial ⚷ 26

Any failure of clerk to administer oath to bailiff respecting separation of jurors should be shown by judge's certificate, if not appearing in journal entry, and not by supplemental bill of exceptions. Halsey v. State (Wood 1932) 42 Ohio App. 291, 182 N.E. 127, 11 Ohio Law Abs. 308, error dismissed 125 Ohio St. 628, 185 N.E. 881. Appeal And Error ⚷ 541; Criminal Law ⚷ 1092.17; Exceptions, Bill Of ⚷ 59(6)

Failure of clerk to administer oath to bailiff or court constable not being distinctly shown, presumption in favor of regularity of judgment was that clerk performed duty in that respect. Halsey v. State (Wood 1932) 42 Ohio App. 291, 182 N.E. 127, 11 Ohio Law Abs. 308, error dismissed 125 Ohio St. 628, 185 N.E. 881. Criminal Law ⚷ 1144.15

2945.33 Keeping and conduct of jury after case submitted

When a cause is finally submitted the jurors must be kept together in a convenient place under the charge of an officer until they agree upon a verdict, or are discharged by the court. The court, except in cases where the offense charged may be punishable by death, may permit the jurors to separate during the adjournment of court overnight, under proper cautions, or under supervision of an officer. Such officer shall not permit a communication to be made to them, nor make any himself except to ask if they have agreed upon a verdict, unless he does so by order of the court. Such officer shall not communicate to any person, before the verdict is delivered, any matter in relation to their deliberation. Upon the trial of any prosecution for misdemeanor, the court may permit the jury to separate during their deliberation, or upon adjournment of the court overnight.

In cases where the offense charged may be punished by death, after the case is finally submitted to the jury, the jurors shall be kept in charge of the proper officer and proper arrangements for their care and maintenance shall be made as under section 2945.31 of the Revised Code.

(131 v H 708, eff. 11–9–65; 1953 H 1; GC 13448–1)

Historical and Statutory Notes

Pre–1953 H 1 Amendments: 115 v 531; 113 v 194, Ch 27, § 1

Cross References

Trial jurors, Crim R 24

Library References

Criminal Law ⚷854.

Westlaw Topic No. 110.

C.J.S. Criminal Law § 1363.

Research References

Encyclopedias

OH Jur. 3d Criminal Law § 2791, Care and Comfort of Jurors.

OH Jur. 3d Criminal Law § 2792, Officers in Charge of Jury.

OH Jur. 3d Criminal Law § 2793, Separation or Segregation of Jury.

Treatises and Practice Aids

Markus, Trial Handbook for Ohio Lawyers, § 37:1, During Deliberations.

Markus, Trial Handbook for Ohio Lawyers, § 37:7, Control During Deliberations.

Katz, Giannelli, Blair and Lipton, Baldwin's Ohio Practice, Criminal Law, § 65:2, Jury Sequestration.

Katz, Giannelli, Blair and Lipton, Baldwin's Ohio Practice, Criminal Law, § 65:3, Supervision of Sequestration.

Katz, Giannelli, Blair and Lipton, Baldwin's Ohio Practice, Criminal Law, § 125:20, Jury Sequestration.

Giannelli and Snyder, Baldwin's Ohio Practice, Evidence, § 606.5, Impeachment of Verdicts: Evidence Aliunde.

Hennenberg & Reinhart, Ohio Criminal Defense Motions F 8.04, Motion for Sequestration of Jurors for Duration of Trial-Jury-Related Motions.

Hennenberg & Reinhart, Ohio Criminal Defense Motions F 13.54, Motion for Sequestration of Jurors for Duration of Trial-Death Penalty Motions.

Notes of Decisions

---

1. Sequestration

A three judge panel considering a capital murder case on remand for resentencing does not err in separating during sentencing deliberations so as to allow individual consideration of the case over the weekend since the rules pertaining to jury sequestration need not apply to a three-judge panel which is presumed to consider only relevant, competent and admissible evidence in its deliberations. State v. Davis (Ohio 1992) 63 Ohio St.3d 44, 584 N.E.2d 1192, rehearing denied 63 Ohio St.3d 1433, 588 N.E.2d 132, stay granted 63 Ohio St.3d 1444, 589 N.E.2d 388, certiorari denied 113 S.Ct. 172, 506 U.S. 858, 121 L.Ed.2d 119, rehearing denied 66 Ohio St.3d 1489, 612 N.E.2d 1245, dismissal of post-conviction relief affirmed, dismissed, appeal not allowed 77 Ohio St.3d 1520, 674 N.E.2d 372.

It is within the contemplation of the criminal rules that a jury's deliberations may be interrupted without affecting the integrity of the deliberation process or the validity of the verdict; therefore, the criminal rules are not violated by a trial judge's ordering a jury, which had been released from sequestration after the guilt phase of a trial and escorted home, to return to the courthouse for the purpose of continuing deliberations after the judge notices that the jury failed to fill out the verdict form in which the jury was specifically asked to find whether the defendant performed each and every act constituting the offense of aggravated murder; the break in sequestration after the guilt phase did not constitute a discharge of the jury and did not violate the criminal rules and thus, was not prejudicial per se. State v. Sneed (Ohio 1992) 63 Ohio St.3d 3, 584 N.E.2d 1160, rehearing denied 63 Ohio St.3d 1433, 588 N.E.2d 132, stay granted 63 Ohio St.3d 1444, 589 N.E.2d 388, rehearing granted, opinion recalled 66 Ohio St.3d 1449, 609 N.E.2d 1270, certiorari denied 113 S.Ct. 1577, 507 U.S. 983, 123 L.Ed.2d 145, stay granted 66 Ohio St.3d 1504, 613 N.E.2d 1043.

Neither Crim R 24(G)(2)(c) nor RC 2945.33 requires sequestration of a juror throughout a capital trial, as opposed to sequestration during deliberations only. State v. Maurer (Ohio 1984) 15 Ohio St.3d 239, 473 N.E.2d 768, 15 O.B.R. 379, certiorari denied 105 S.Ct. 2714, 472 U.S. 1012, 86 L.Ed.2d 728, rehearing denied 106 S.Ct. 15, 473 U.S. 924, 87 L.Ed.2d 694, stay granted 41 Ohio St.3d 719, 535 N.E.2d 309.

Ohio's statutory framework for imposition of capital punishment neither mandates nor precludes sequestration of the jury following its guilty verdict but prior to the penalty phase. State v. Jenkins (Ohio 1984) 15 Ohio St.3d 164, 473 N.E.2d 264, 15 O.B.R. 311, certiorari denied 105 S.Ct. 3514, 472 U.S. 1032, 87 L.Ed.2d 643, rehearing denied 106 S.Ct. 19, 473 U.S. 927, 87 L.Ed.2d 697. Criminal Law ⚿ 854(8)

Absent a showing of outside influence upon jurors, the discretion of a trial judge in deciding whether sequestration is required under the circumstances existing at the time and place of the trial will not be disturbed. Blackmon v. U. S. (C.A.6 (Ohio) 1973) 474 F.2d 1125, certiorari denied 94 S.Ct. 252, 414 U.S. 912, 38 L.Ed.2d 150. Criminal Law ⚿ 1155

2. Allowing jurors to separate

Trial judge met statutory requirement of keeping jurors together until they agree upon verdict, where, prior to being discharged, jurors agreed on verdict and signed ballots finding defendant guilty and fact that jurors could have changed mind after signing ballots was immaterial. State v. Stewart (Ohio App. 11 Dist., Portage, 12-27-2002) No. 2001-P-0035, 2002-Ohio-7270, 2002 WL 31886657, Unreported, appeal not allowed 98 Ohio St.3d 1567, 787 N.E.2d 1231, 2003-Ohio-2242. Criminal Law ⚿ 872

The substantial rights of a defendant are materially affected due to juror misconduct where two jurors separated themselves from the rest of the panel and went out to smoke cigarettes during deliberations and discussed the case together while outside the presence of the rest of the jury, and even though the jurors indicated that they would recommence deliberations disregarding what occurred when the two men were absent from the jury deliberation room, and the trial court attempted to cure the misconduct by questioning all the jurors, due to the nature of the misconduct the defendant was prejudiced and the trial court should have granted the defendant's motion for a new trial. State v. Fields (Ohio App. 5 Dist., Holmes, 06-30-1998) No. CA584, 1998 WL 430536, Unreported.

Trial court was under no obligation to accommodate juror with smoking breaks; frequent breaks would have prolonged the capital murder trial and disrupted the presentation of evidence, and juror could not take smoking breaks outside the jury room after submission of the case. State v. Sanders (Ohio, 07-18-2001) 92 Ohio St.3d 245, 750 N.E.2d 90, 2001-Ohio-189, reconsideration denied 93 Ohio St.3d 1434, 755 N.E.2d 356, stay granted 93 Ohio St.3d 1437, 755 N.E.2d 900, stay revoked 98 Ohio St.3d 1453, 783 N.E.2d 514, 2003-Ohio-651, certiorari denied 122 S.Ct. 1795, 535 U.S. 1036, 152 L.Ed.2d 653, stay granted 98 Ohio St.3d 1506, 786 N.E.2d 57, 2003-Ohio-1573. Criminal Law ⚷ 848; Criminal Law ⚷ 854(1)

A noncapital felony conviction will not be reversed for error in permitting the jurors to separate for lunch after the case has been submitted to them, where it is not shown that the defendant was thereby prevented from having a fair trial and where the defendant did not object to the separation. State v. Williams (Ohio 1974) 39 Ohio St.2d 20, 313 N.E.2d 859, 72 A.L.R.3d 240, 68 O.O.2d 12. Criminal Law ⚷ 1039; Criminal Law ⚷ 1174(4)

3. Improper communications

Incident in which juror and two other jurors were walking to their car and observed codefendant some distance behind them did not constitute private communication or contact between juror and codefendant, and thus trial court was not required to conduct a voir dire examination of entire jury regarding their ability to remain fair and impartial after juror had shared such incident with other jurors prior to deliberations; juror simply saw codefendant from a distance and reported this incident to the trial court, and no evidence suggested that this juror felt threatened in any way or otherwise feared for her safety so as to detract from her duty to remain fair and impartial. (Per McMonagle, J., with two judges concurring in part.) State v. Johnson (Ohio App. 8 Dist., Cuyahoga, 04-10-2003) No. 80857, 2003-Ohio-1826, 2003 WL 1836675, Unreported, dismissal of post-conviction relief affirmed 2003-Ohio-4954, 2003 WL 22146529, appeal not allowed 101 Ohio St.3d 1423, 802 N.E.2d 154, 2004-Ohio-123. Criminal Law ⚷ 855(8)

Any communications which might have occurred after jury was mistakenly dismissed did not bias jurors and prejudice defendant, where trial transcript revealed that time between when jury left courtroom and time they were called back could only have been few minutes and, when jury was called back into courtroom, each juror affirmed that verdict reached on ballot was indeed his or her verdict. State v. Stewart (Ohio App. 11 Dist., Portage, 12-27-2002) No. 2001-P-0035, 2002-Ohio-7270, 2002 WL 31886657, Unreported, appeal not allowed 98 Ohio St.3d 1567, 787 N.E.2d 1231, 2003-Ohio-2242. Criminal Law ⚷ 1174(5)

Judge's error in communicating with jury outside presence of parties to declaratory judgment action was prejudicial; judge made disparaging remarks regarding counsel, and insured suffered more from disparaging remarks as it had burden of proof. Westfield Cos. v. O.K.L. Can Line (Ohio App. 1 Dist., 12-30-2003) 155 Ohio App.3d 747, 804 N.E.2d 45, 2003-Ohio-7151, appeal not allowed 102 Ohio St.3d 1459, 809 N.E.2d 33, 2004-Ohio-2569. Declaratory Judgment ⚷ 393

Trial court erred in communicating with jury outside presence of parties, after presentation of the evidence to the jury, but before closing argument. Westfield Cos. v. O.K.L. Can Line (Ohio App. 1 Dist., 12-30-2003) 155 Ohio App.3d 747, 804 N.E.2d 45, 2003-Ohio-7151, appeal not allowed 102 Ohio St.3d 1459, 809 N.E.2d 33, 2004-Ohio-2569. Trial ⚷ 18

Communications between court officials and jurors may be grounds for mistrial, new trial, or reversal. State v. Czajka (Ohio App. 8 Dist., 03-06-1995) 101 Ohio App.3d 564, 656 N.E.2d 9. Criminal Law ⚷ 855(7); Criminal Law ⚷ 928; Criminal Law ⚷ 929; Criminal Law ⚷ 1174(5); Criminal Law ⚷ 1174(7)

Communications between bailiff and jury during deliberation process are presumptively prejudicial to defendant who is later found guilty by jury. State v. Czajka (Ohio App. 8 Dist., 03-06-1995) 101 Ohio App.3d 564, 656 N.E.2d 9. Criminal Law ⚷ 1163(6)

State sufficiently rebutted defendant's claim of prejudice with regards to limited communications between jury and bailiff after deliberations; communication of bailiff was strictly of a procedural nature concerning any requirement to find defendant not guilty of count in indictment if jury had unanimously found defendant guilty of a lesser included offense, bailiff was scrupulous in refusing to convey any information that may have compromised the process, any possible prejudice was negated by trial court's subsequent instructions, and fact that jury returned verdicts of lesser included offenses indicated that process was not tainted. State v. Czajka (Ohio App. 8 Dist., 03-06-1995) 101 Ohio App.3d 564, 656 N.E.2d 9. Criminal Law ⚷ 1163(6)

Trial judge may not communicate with jury in defendant's absence; however, if communication is not "substantive," error is harmless. State v. Allen (Ohio, 09-06-1995) 73 Ohio St.3d 626, 653 N.E.2d 675, 1995-Ohio-283, reconsideration denied 74 Ohio St.3d 1422, 655 N.E.2d 742, certiorari denied 116 S.Ct. 1276, 516 U.S. 1178, 134 L.Ed.2d 222, denial of post-conviction relief affirmed 1998 WL 289418, dismissed, appeal not allowed 83 Ohio St.3d 1448, 700 N.E.2d 331. Criminal Law ⚷ 636(7); Criminal Law ⚷ 1166.14

Juror's casually asking testifying detective "how he was feeling" as they passed in hallway did not rise to level of reversible misconduct; requisite prejudice to defendant was absent. State v. Grant (Ohio 1993) 67 Ohio St.3d 465, 620 N.E.2d 50, rehearing denied 68 Ohio St.3d 1412, 623 N.E.2d 568, certiorari denied 115 S.Ct. 116, 513 U.S. 836, 130 L.Ed.2d 62, rehearing denied 115 S.Ct. 617, 513 U.S. 1033, 130 L.Ed.2d 525. Criminal Law ⚷ 1174(5)

During jury deliberations, a trial court may order a radio to be played in the courtroom where the purpose of the music is to preserve the privacy of jury deliberations, especially where one of the plaintiff's attorneys was discovered by a bailiff to be listening to the deliberations and was animated about some responses he heard from the jury room. Costell v. Toledo Hosp. (Lucas 1992) 82 Ohio App.3d 393, 612 N.E.2d 487, motion overruled 66 Ohio St.3d 1413, 607 N.E.2d 12.

Where a party alleges prejudice as a result of improper communication between a juror and members of his family or the public, he must initially demonstrate that such communication was substantive; a mere presumption that communications between jurors and their families in the course of making overnight arrangements during sequestration concerned matters at issue in the present case is insufficient to demonstrate prejudice where the jurors respond to court inquiry that no discussion of the trial occurred. State v. Murphy (Ohio 1992) 65 Ohio St.3d 554, 605 N.E.2d 884, rehearing denied 66 Ohio St.3d 1414, 607 N.E.2d 13, stay granted 66 Ohio St.3d 1427, 608 N.E.2d 757, stay dissolved 67 Ohio St.3d 1492, 621 N.E.2d 1207, certiorari denied 114 S.Ct. 109, 510 U.S. 834, 126 L.Ed.2d 75, stay granted 68 Ohio St.3d 1425, 624 N.E.2d 1063, reconsideration denied 68 Ohio St.3d 1443, 626 N.E.2d 685, denial of post-conviction relief affirmed, dismissed, appeal not allowed 74 Ohio St.3d 1405, 655 N.E.2d 184, reconsideration denied 74 Ohio St.3d 1459, 656 N.E.2d 953.

A bailiff's communication with the jury during deliberations in violation of RC 2945.33 is presumed prejudicial where the defendant is found guilty thereafter by the jury, but forbidding a juror's testimony about the affect of the misconduct on the juror's mind is not an abuse of discretion in view of Evid R 606(B). State v. Lane (Hamilton 1988) 48 Ohio App.3d 172, 549 N.E.2d 193, on reconsideration, opinion modified on reconsideration 49 Ohio App.3d 158, 551 N.E.2d 994.

Where a court bailiff communicates with the jury during its deliberations, such misconduct constitutes a violation of RC 2945.33 and will be presumed to be prejudicial to a defendant where a verdict is returned against such defendant after communication is had with the jury. State v. King (Franklin 1983) 10 Ohio App.3d 93, 460 N.E.2d 1143, 10 O.B.R. 116.

In a criminal case, in the absence of an affirmative showing that the defendant was prejudiced thereby, a judgment of conviction will not be reversed because one of the officers to whose charge the jurors were committed during the night hours between sessions of their deliberations permitted some jurors to make telephone calls in his presence and within his hearing to members of their immediate families. State v. Sheppard (Ohio 1956) 165 Ohio St. 293, 135 N.E.2d 340, 59 O.O. 398, certiorari denied 77 S.Ct. 118, 352 U.S. 910, 1 L.Ed.2d 119, rehearing denied 77 S.Ct. 323, 352 U.S. 955, 1 L.Ed.2d 245. Criminal Law ⚷ 1174(5)

Where court bailiff, on being informed by jury during its deliberations that it could not agree stated to it: "You can't do that. You must reach a decision if you have to stay here for three months," there is violation of this section, which is prejudicial to defendant against whom, following such declaration, verdict is returned by jury. State v. Adams (Ohio 1943) 141 Ohio St. 423, 48 N.E.2d 861, 146 A.L.R. 509, 25 O.O. 570.

Violation by court officer in charge of jury of statute to effect that he shall not communicate with jury in his charge or custody except to inquire whether it has reached verdict, will be presumed to be prejudicial to defendant against whom, after such communication, verdict is returned by such jury. State v. Adams (Ohio 1943) 141 Ohio St. 423, 48 N.E.2d 861, 146 A.L.R. 509, 25 O.O. 570.

Affidavits or testimony of jurors may be received, upon motion for new trial, to prove unlawful communications made to members of the jury by court officers or others, outside the jury room but during the period of the jury's deliberation. Emmert v. State (Ohio 1933) 127 Ohio St. 235, 187 N.E. 862, 90 A.L.R. 242, 39 Ohio Law Rep. 649. Criminal Law ⚷ 957(6)

Due process requires that the accused receive a trial by an impartial jury free from outside influences, and if publicity during the proceedings threatens the fairness of the trial, a new trial should be ordered. Sheppard v. Maxwell (U.S.Ohio 1966) 86 S.Ct. 1507, 384 U.S. 333, 6 Ohio Misc. 231, 16 L.Ed.2d 600, 35 O.O.2d 431.

Allowing federal agent to conduct playback of audiotapes for jury during deliberations was not per se error where jury did not know that playback operator was agent, agent was not connected with defendant's case in any way, and court delegated court reporter to ensure there was no extraneous conversation or conduct and to record it if there was. Mathews v. U.S. (C.A.6 (Ohio) 1993) 11 F.3d 583. Criminal Law ⚷ 859

It is communication's potential to impact upon juror's ability to perform his or her duties impartially, rather than form or source of communication, that dictates necessity for conducting *Remmer* hearing to investigate unauthorized private communication or contact with jury during deliberations. U.S. v. Walker (C.A.6 (Ohio) 1993) 1 F.3d 423, rehearing denied, appeal after new trial 37 F.3d 1500. Criminal Law ⚷ 868

Under prior law, upon exposure of jury to potentially prejudicial communication, it was government's burden to prove that jury had not been biased by communication. U.S. v. Walker (C.A.6 (Ohio) 1993) 1 F.3d 423, rehearing denied, appeal after new trial 37 F.3d 1500. Criminal Law ⚷ 868

Burden of proof rests upon defendant to demonstrate that unauthorized communications with jurors resulted in actual juror partiality; prejudice is not to be presumed. U.S. v. Walker (C.A.6 (Ohio) 1993) 1 F.3d 423, rehearing denied, appeal after new trial 37 F.3d 1500. Criminal Law ⚷ 868; Criminal Law ⚷ 1163(6)

Prejudice to the accused as a matter of law will not be presumed from the fact that some of the jurors, while sequestered, were permitted to telephone their families. Sheppard v. Maxwell (C.A.6 (Ohio) 1965) 346 F.2d 707, certiorari granted 86 S.Ct. 289, 382 U.S. 916, 15 L.Ed.2d 231, remanded 86 S.Ct. 1507, 384 U.S. 333, 6 Ohio Misc. 231, 16 L.Ed.2d 600, 35 O.O.2d 431.

Supplementary charge urging the jurors to continue their deliberations after having reached an impasse, and attempt to reach a verdict on murder charge was not impermissibly coercive; charge was neutral in that it did not single out jurors in the minority, and fact that the jury continued deliberations through half of another day after the charge was given suggested that the jury felt uncoerced in continuing deliberations. Bonnell v. Mitchel (N.D.Ohio, 02-04-2004) 301 F.Supp.2d 698. Criminal Law ⚷ 865(1.5)

Trial court decision to allow the jury to listen to the audiotape of the victim's trial testimony during jury deliberations was not an abuse of discretion, in prosecution for two counts of rape; defendant was aware of exactly what the jury would hear, and the trial judge specifically informed the jury that it could not ask any questions of the court reporter, who played the audiotape to the jury. State v. Maple (Ohio App. 4 Dist., Ross, 04-02-2002) No. 01CA2605, 2002-Ohio-1595, 2002 WL 507530, Unreported, appeal not allowed 96 Ohio St.3d 1470, 772 N.E.2d 1204, 2002-Ohio-3910. Criminal Law ⚷ 859

4. Alternate juror

An alternate juror in a criminal trial who has been excused may not be substituted for a regular juror after the jury has retired to consider its verdict. State v. Locklear (Franklin 1978) 61 Ohio App.2d 231, 401 N.E.2d 457, 15 O.O.3d 369.

2945.34 Admonition if jurors separate during trial

If the jurors are permitted to separate during a trial, they shall be admonished by the court not to converse with, nor permit themselves to be addressed by any person, nor to listen to any conversation on the subject of the trial, nor form or express any opinion thereon, until the case is finally submitted to them.

(1953 H 1, eff. 10–1–53; GC 13443–17)

Historical and Statutory Notes

Pre–1953 H 1 Amendments: 113 v 185, Ch 22, § 17

Cross References

Control of juries, Crim R 24

Library References

Criminal Law ⚷852, 854(4).
Westlaw Topic No. 110.
C.J.S. Criminal Law §§ 1363, 1371.

Research References

Encyclopedias

OH Jur. 3d Criminal Law § 2793, Separation or Segregation of Jury.

Treatises and Practice Aids

Markus, Trial Handbook for Ohio Lawyers, § 37:1, During Deliberations.

Markus, Trial Handbook for Ohio Lawyers, § 37:5, Separation During Trial.

Markus, Trial Handbook for Ohio Lawyers, § 4:32, Trial by Jury.

Katz, Giannelli, Blair and Lipton, Baldwin's Ohio Practice, Criminal Law, § 65:3, Supervision of Sequestration.

Notes of Decisions

1. Sufficiency of admonition

RC 2945.10 is fully complied with if the final arguments of counsel in the case are concluded at the end of a court day, and the court instructs the jury as to its conduct during the adjournment, at which point court is adjourned, and, upon the court convening the next morning, it begins the reading of its charge as the first order of business, which written instruction does not include the instructions given the night before governing conduct of the jury during the adjournment. State v. Sheppard (Cuyahoga 1955) 100 Ohio App. 345, 128 N.E.2d 471, 60 O.O. 298, affirmed 165 Ohio St. 293, 135 N.E.2d 340, 59 O.O. 398, certiorari denied 77 S.Ct. 118, 352 U.S. 910, 1 L.Ed.2d 119, rehearing denied 77 S.Ct. 323, 352 U.S. 955, 1 L.Ed.2d 245.

2. Failure to admonish

The failure by court to perform its statutory duty of admonishing jury concerning conduct while separated during the trial, does not constitute reversible error, where it is not shown that jury was guilty of misconduct or indiscretions. (See also 104 OS 156, 135 NE 544 (1922), Kolotich v State.) Warner v. State (Ohio 1922) 104 Ohio St. 38, 135 N.E. 249, 19 Ohio Law Rep. 550.

The failure by court to admonish jury as prescribed by this section does not constitute reversible error, where it is not shown that jury was guilty of misconduct or indiscretions and where no exception was taken at trial to court's failure to admonish. Warner v. State (Ohio 1922) 104 Ohio St. 38, 135 N.E. 249, 19 Ohio Law Rep. 550.

3. Conversation with others

Juror's casually asking testifying detective "how he was feeling" as they passed in hallway did not rise to level of reversible misconduct; requisite prejudice to defendant was absent. State v. Grant (Ohio 1993) 67 Ohio St.3d 465, 620 N.E.2d 50, rehearing denied 68 Ohio St.3d 1412, 623 N.E.2d 568, certiorari denied 115 S.Ct. 116, 513 U.S. 836, 130 L.Ed.2d 62, rehearing denied 115 S.Ct. 617, 513 U.S. 1033, 130 L.Ed.2d 525. Criminal Law ⚷ 1174(5)

2945.35 Papers the jury may take

Upon retiring for deliberation, the jury, at the discretion of the court, may take with it all papers except depositions, and all articles, photographs, and maps which have been offered in evidence. No article or paper identified but not admitted in evidence shall be taken by the jury upon its retirement.

(1953 H 1, eff. 10–1–53; GC 13444–26)

Historical and Statutory Notes

Pre–1953 H 1 Amendments: 113 v 191, Ch 23, § 26

Library References

Criminal Law ⚷858.

Westlaw Topic No. 110.

C.J.S. Criminal Law §§ 1373 to 1377.

Research References

ALR Library

36 ALR 5th 255, Taking and Use of Trial Notes by Jury.

Encyclopedias

OH Jur. 3d Criminal Law § 2802, Generally; Transcripts; Written Charges and Instructions.

Treatises and Practice Aids

Markus, Trial Handbook for Ohio Lawyers, § 37:6, Items Taken to Jury Room.

Giannelli and Snyder, Baldwin's Ohio Practice, Evidence, § 901.24, Exhibits in Jury Room.

1 Giannelli and Snyder, Baldwin's Ohio Practice, Evidence, Index, Index.

Notes of Decisions

---

1. Items allowed in jury room

Defense counsel's failure to object to the trial court's giving the jury a dictionary to look up word "likely" in prosecution for involuntary manslaughter was harmless, absent presentment of any meaningful basis as to how the definitional meaning of the word could have prejudiced his case. State v. O'Connell (Ohio App. 4 Dist., Washington, 01-21-2003) No. 01CA24, 2003-Ohio-550, 2003 WL 246000, Unreported. Criminal Law ⚷ 641.13(2.1)

Trial court error in allowing the jury to bring a letter, which was purportedly written by defendant and was found in his vehicle, to the jury room at the close of trial was harmless, even though the State admitted that the letter had not been properly authenticated at trial; the State did not mention the letter during closing arguments, and the State presented significant evidence of defendant's guilt. State v. Neal (Ohio App. 2 Dist., Champaign, 12-06-2002) No. 2000 CA 16, No. 2000 CA 18, 2002-Ohio-6786, 2002 WL 31761564, Unreported, appeal not allowed 98 Ohio St.3d 1538, 786 N.E.2d 901, 2003-Ohio-1946, reconsideration denied 99

Ohio St.3d 1438, 789 N.E.2d 1119, 2003-Ohio-2902. Criminal Law ⚷ 1174(6)

Trial court did not deny capital murder defendant fair trial where, in defendant's absence and in response to jury's note asking for copy of psychiatric manual and dictionary, court wrote back that jurors could receive no more exhibits and could not engage in extraneous research; there was no possibility that court's refusal to supply those materials could have influenced jury's conclusion. State v. Allen (Ohio, 09-06-1995) 73 Ohio St.3d 626, 653 N.E.2d 675, 1995-Ohio-283, reconsideration denied 74 Ohio St.3d 1422, 655 N.E.2d 742, certiorari denied 116 S.Ct. 1276, 516 U.S. 1178, 134 L.Ed.2d 222, denial of post-conviction relief affirmed 1998 WL 289418, dismissed, appeal not allowed 83 Ohio St.3d 1448, 700 N.E.2d 331. Criminal Law ⚷ 636(7); Criminal Law ⚷ 858(3); Criminal Law ⚷ 864

Generally, propriety of sending defendant's confession into jury room rests within sound discretion of trial judge. State v. Loza (Ohio, 11-30-1994) 71 Ohio St.3d 61, 641 N.E.2d 1082, 37 A.L.R.5th 841, reconsideration denied 71 Ohio St.3d 1437, 643 N.E.2d 142, certiorari denied 115 S.Ct. 1983, 514 U.S. 1120, 131 L.Ed.2d 871, denial of post-conviction relief affirmed 1997 WL 634348, dismissed, appeal not allowed 81 Ohio St.3d 1429, 689 N.E.2d 49. Criminal Law ⚷ 858(3)

Videotaped exhibit may be replayed during jury deliberations. State v. Loza (Ohio, 11-30-1994) 71 Ohio St.3d 61, 641 N.E.2d 1082, 37 A.L.R.5th 841, reconsideration denied 71 Ohio St.3d 1437, 643 N.E.2d 142, certiorari denied 115 S.Ct. 1983, 514 U.S. 1120, 131 L.Ed.2d 871, denial of post-conviction relief affirmed 1997 WL 634348, dismissed, appeal not allowed 81 Ohio St.3d 1429, 689 N.E.2d 49. Criminal Law ⚷ 859

Sending transcripts of tape-recorded conversations into jury room during deliberations in narcotics prosecution, with no limiting instruction specifically regarding use of transcripts by jury, was error. State v. Rogan (Ohio App. 2 Dist., 03-30-1994) 94 Ohio App.3d 140, 640 N.E.2d 535. Criminal Law ⚷ 858(3)

Error in permitting jury to use transcript of tape-recorded transaction during deliberations was not harmless in narcotics prosecution, where defendant was acquitted on two of three counts supported by transcript evidence, count on which defendant was convicted was supported by transcript that was most specific regarding actual purchase of cocaine, and portions of defendant's tape recorded conversations supporting that count were garbled and substantially inaudible. State v. Rogan (Ohio App. 2 Dist., 03-30-1994) 94 Ohio App.3d 140, 640 N.E.2d 535. Criminal Law ⚷ 1169.1(10)

The trial court has discretion in a criminal case to permit the jury to take the indictment to the jury room. State v. Graven (Ohio 1977) 52 Ohio St.2d 112, 369 N.E.2d 1205, 6 O.O.3d 334.

In a trial for armed bank robbery, it is not prejudicial error to permit the jury to have during its deliberation a map which has been marked for identification only and never introduced or received as evidence. Blackmon v. U. S. (C.A.6 (Ohio) 1973) 474 F.2d 1125, certiorari denied 94 S.Ct. 252, 414 U.S. 912, 38 L.Ed.2d 150.

Where tape recordings as exhibits are admitted into evidence, the jury's use of a tape recorder not admitted into evidence does not violate RC 2945.35 and thus does not constitute error. State v Howland, No. 439 (4th Dist Ct App, Highland, 4–15–82).

2. Depositions

Ordinarily, in a civil action, the trial court acts properly in refusing the request of one of the parties at the close of the trial proper to send to the jury room a deposition which was introduced and read in evidence during the trial. Indianapolis & Southeastern Trailways, Inc. v. Cincinnati St. Ry. Co. (Ohio 1957) 166 Ohio St. 310, 142 N.E.2d 515, 2 O.O.2d 223.

3. Jurors' notes

Absent request of the parties and a chance to object, a trial court errs when it instructs prospective jurors that they are permitted to take notes during the trial and furnishes pads for that purpose even though the court makes it clear that no juror is required to take notes. State v Waddell, No. 94APA03-328, 1994 WL 532065 (10th Dist Ct App, Franklin, 9-29-94).

Trial court has discretion to permit jurors to take notes if warranted under circumstances. State v. Loza (Ohio, 11-30-1994) 71 Ohio St.3d 61, 641 N.E.2d 1082, 37 A.L.R.5th 841, reconsideration denied 71 Ohio St.3d 1437, 643 N.E.2d 142, certiorari denied 115 S.Ct. 1983, 514 U.S. 1120, 131 L.Ed.2d 871, denial of post-conviction relief affirmed 1997 WL 634348, dismissed, appeal not allowed 81 Ohio St.3d 1429, 689 N.E.2d 49. Criminal Law ⚷ 855(1)

Prior to a capital trial, when it is apparent to the trial judge that the proceedings and testimony are going to be complicated and extremely protracted, a trial court does not commit prejudicial error in violation of RC 2945.35 when over the objection of the defendant it permits jurors to make notes during testimony and to take those notes into the jury room during deliberations; the notes need not be preserved for review. State v. Williams (Lorain 1992) 80 Ohio App.3d 648, 610 N.E.2d 545.

4. Evidence, material not admitted into

Even if jury was allowed to take color slides of fire scene and black and white photograph of victims' corpses into jury room despite fact that they were not admitted into evidence, no prejudice resulted; photograph was repetitive, jury had already seen slides, and other evidence as to fire scene was abundant. State v. Grant (Ohio 1993) 67 Ohio St.3d 465, 620 N.E.2d 50, rehearing denied 68 Ohio St.3d 1412, 623 N.E.2d 568, certiorari denied 115 S.Ct. 116, 513 U.S. 836, 130 L.Ed.2d 62, rehearing denied 115 S.Ct. 617, 513 U.S. 1033, 130 L.Ed.2d 525. Criminal Law ⚷ 1174(6)

Defendants' were entitled to inquire into jurors' states of mind to meet burden of proving jurors' actual bias after court discovered that transcripts of videotaped depositions, including highlighted portions which had been deemed inadmissible in drug trial, had been inadvertently sent into jury room along with admitted exhibits, and court's failure to permit inquiry deprived defendants of fair trial. U.S. v. Walker (C.A.6 (Ohio) 1993) 1 F.3d 423, rehearing denied, appeal after new trial 37 F.3d 1500. Criminal Law ⚷ 868; Criminal Law ⚷ 1174(1)

5. Testimony read to jury

All or part of testimony of any witness may be read back to jury upon its request after jurors retire to deliberate. State v. Black (Hamilton 1993) 85 Ohio App.3d 771, 621 N.E.2d 484, dismissed, jurisdictional motion overruled 67 Ohio St.3d 1451, 619 N.E.2d 420. Criminal Law ⚷ 859

Trial court erred in prosecution for contributing to unruliness of a child by failing to read into record question submitted to it by jury during deliberations. State v. Black (Hamilton 1993) 85 Ohio App.3d 771, 621 N.E.2d 484, dismissed, jurisdictional motion overruled 67 Ohio St.3d 1451, 619 N.E.2d 420. Criminal Law ⚷ 863(2)

2945.36 For what cause jury may be discharged

The trial court may discharge a jury without prejudice to the prosecution:

(A) For the sickness or corruption of a juror or other accident or calamity;

(B) Because there is no probability of such jurors agreeing;

(C) If it appears after the jury has been sworn that one of the jurors is a witness in the case;

(D) By the consent of the prosecuting attorney and the defendant.

The reason for such discharge shall be entered on the journal.

(1953 H 1, eff. 10–1–53; GC 13443–18)

Historical and Statutory Notes

Pre–1953 H 1 Amendments: 113 v 185, Ch 22, § 18

Cross References

Trial by jury or by the court, Crim R 23

Verdict, Crim R 31

Library References

Criminal Law ⚷867.

Westlaw Topic No. 110.

C.J.S. Criminal Law §§ 1388 to 1390.

Research References

Encyclopedias

OH Jur. 3d Criminal Law § 769, Mistrial Granted by Trial Judge Sua Sponte.

OH Jur. 3d Criminal Law § 770, Improbability of Jurors Agreeing.

OH Jur. 3d Criminal Law § 771, Sickness, Death, or Corruption of Juror; Illness of Relative of Juror.

OH Jur. 3d Criminal Law § 772, Sickness or Death of Judge.

OH Jur. 3d Criminal Law § 773, Where Juror is Witness.

OH Jur. 3d Criminal Law § 2794, Discharge of Jury Before Verdict.

OH Jur. 3d Family Law § 1744, Trial by Jury.

Treatises and Practice Aids

Markus, Trial Handbook for Ohio Lawyers, § 6:6, Alternate Juror.

Markus, Trial Handbook for Ohio Lawyers, § 37:1, During Deliberations.

Markus, Trial Handbook for Ohio Lawyers, § 37:8, Manner of Conducting Deliberations.

Katz, Giannelli, Blair and Lipton, Baldwin's Ohio Practice, Criminal Law, § 65:5, Hung Juries.

Katz, Giannelli, Blair and Lipton, Baldwin's Ohio Practice, Criminal Law, § 65:8, Multiple Defendant Verdicts.

Katz, Giannelli, Blair and Lipton, Baldwin's Ohio Practice, Criminal Law, § 148:31, Entry Discharging Jury.

Giannelli and Snyder, Baldwin's Ohio Practice, Evidence, R 606, Competency of Juror as Witness.

Giannelli and Snyder, Baldwin's Ohio Practice, Evidence, § 606.3, Juror Competency.

Notes of Decisions

1. Constitutional issues

It is within discretion of trial court to determine which exhibits should be sent to jury room. State v. Crimi (Ohio App. 8 Dist., 08-21-1995) 106 Ohio App.3d 13, 665 N.E.2d 230, dismissed, appeal not allowed 74 Ohio St.3d 1498, 659 N.E.2d 314. Criminal Law ⚷ 858(3)

Decision as to whether jury could view videotape in its deliberations is reviewed under abuse of discretion standard. State v. Crimi (Ohio App. 8 Dist., 08-21-1995) 106 Ohio App.3d 13, 665 N.E.2d 230, dismissed, appeal not allowed 74 Ohio St.3d 1498, 659 N.E.2d 314. Criminal Law ⚷ 1155

Where in a prosecution for first degree murder it was discovered after submission of some evidence but before submission of the matter to the jury that the indictment was so defective as to fail to charge first or second degree murder, but that it did charge manslaughter, the defendant has been placed in jeopardy and may not thereafter be tried for murder. State v. McGraw (Ohio Com.Pl. 1961) 177 N.E.2d 697, 86 Ohio Law Abs. 490, 19 O.O.2d 174.

2. Illness

Trial court did not abuse its discretion in allowing jury to continue deliberating in homicide prosecution after juror arrived 75 minutes late on third day of deliberations because he was ill; there was no evidence in record that anyone coerced him into voting as he did, or that he asked either to be excused from serving or that deliberations be delayed, nor was it even clear that illness persisted after he arrived. State v. Rowe (Ohio App. 10 Dist., 10-26-1993) 92 Ohio App.3d 652, 637 N.E.2d 29, reconsideration denied 1994 WL 41312, dismissed, jurisdictional motion overruled 69 Ohio St.3d 1403, 629 N.E.2d 1365. Criminal Law ⚷ 857(1)

Decision whether to declare mistrial and discharge jury is within sound discretion of trial court, particularly when juror is ill and, thus, Court of Appeals may only reverse decision of trial court to deny motion for mistrial and allow jury verdict to stand where trial court's attitude in rendering decision was arbitrary, unreasonable or unconscionable. State v. Rowe (Ohio App. 10 Dist., 10-26-1993) 92 Ohio App.3d 652, 637 N.E.2d 29, reconsideration denied 1994 WL 41312, dismissed, jurisdictional motion overruled 69 Ohio St.3d 1403, 629 N.E.2d 1365. Criminal Law ⚷ 867; Criminal Law ⚷ 1155

3. Deadlocked jury—In general

Where jury explicitly indicated through message to trial court that, after substantial deliberations, it was evenly deadlocked, that it lacked sufficient evidence upon which to base a verdict, and that any verdict it returned would not be a fair one, trial court was required, sua sponte, to declare a mistrial and discharge jurors, and failure to do so was prejudicial error. State v. Sabbah (Sandusky 1982) 13 Ohio App.3d 124, 468 N.E.2d 718, 13 O.B.R. 155. Criminal Law ⚷ 867; Criminal Law ⚷ 1174(1)

Standing alone, an unguarded statement by trial court to effect that "this jury can reach a verdict if any jury can," under circumstances of case, including fact that jury had explicitly indicated through message to trial court that, after substantial deliberations, it was evenly deadlocked, that it lacked sufficient evidence upon which to base a verdict, and that any verdict it returned would not be a fair one, prejudicially exacerbated potential for coercion of jury. State v. Sabbah (Sandusky 1982) 13 Ohio App.3d 124, 468 N.E.2d 718, 13 O.B.R. 155. Criminal Law ⚷ 865(1.5); Criminal Law ⚷ 1174(1)

4. —— Waiver of jury trial, deadlocked jury

A trial by jury in a criminal case may be waived at any time before it becomes known that the jury is deadlocked in reaching a verdict. City of Columbus v. Voyles (Franklin 1972) 32 Ohio App.2d 309, 291 N.E.2d 536, 61 O.O.2d 435. Jury ⚷ 29(6)

Where the jury in a criminal case is unable to reach a verdict after hearing all of the evidence, and counsel for the defendant thereafter attempts to orally waive the trial by jury and submit the cause to the court, it is not error for the court to declare a mistrial and to refuse to determine the question of guilt or innocence of the defendant. City of Columbus v. Voyles (Franklin 1972) 32 Ohio App.2d 309, 291 N.E.2d 536, 61 O.O.2d 435.

5. Mistrial

Juror's alleged exposure to newspaper article concerning case and dissemination of information to other jurors did not warrant mistrial in murder prosecution, where each of the jurors independently corroborated that the extent of the reference to the article was that defendant's family was not expected to attend trial, and juror who disseminated the information denied any additional knowledge of the article, denied reading the article, and stated that she told her mother, who had initially informed her about the article, not to tell her anything more about the article. State v. Freeman (Ohio App. 8 Dist., Cuyahoga, 06-19-2003) No. 81405, 2003-Ohio-3216, 2003 WL 21419265, Unreported. Criminal Law ⚷ 855(5)

6. Reconvened jury

Trial court's act of reconvening jury to return a second verdict on involuntary manslaughter charge, after jury returned a defective verdict on such charge and was discharged, constituted error. State v. Davis (Ohio App. 2 Dist., Clark, 09-12-2003) No.

2002-CA-43, 2003-Ohio-4839, 2003 WL 22110297, Unreported. Criminal Law ⚷ 889

Defendant's claim, that original jury deliberations concerning involuntary manslaughter charge were improper due to presence of two different verdict forms, was rendered moot, where defendant's conviction and sentence for involuntary manslaughter charge were to be vacated. State v. Davis (Ohio App. 2 Dist., Clark, 09-12-2003) No. 2002-CA-43, 2003-Ohio-4839, 2003 WL 22110297, Unreported. Criminal Law ⚷ 1134(3)

Defendant did not waive claim that trial court erred in reconvening jury to return a second verdict on involuntary manslaughter charge after jury returned a defective verdict on such charge and was discharged, where defendant never consented to the jury's re-deliberating the case after the jury had been discharged, but rather asserted position that defective verdict should be set aside, and that the charge should be dismissed. State v. Davis (Ohio App. 2 Dist., Clark, 09-12-2003) No. 2002-CA-43, 2003-Ohio-4839, 2003 WL 22110297, Unreported. Criminal Law ⚷ 1039

7. Retrial; speedy trial

Where a jury is unable to reach a verdict in a criminal action and is discharged, the re-scheduling of the case for another trial constitutes a reasonable continuance within the meaning of RC 2945.72. State v. Johnson (Franklin 1977) 52 Ohio App.2d 406, 370 N.E.2d 785, 6 O.O.3d 444.

INSANITY

2945.37 Competence to stand trial; raising of issue; procedures; municipal courts

(A) As used in sections 2945.37 to 2945.402 of the Revised Code:

(1) "Prosecutor" means a prosecuting attorney or a city director of law, village solicitor, or similar chief legal officer of a municipal corporation who has authority to prosecute a criminal case that is before the court or the criminal case in which a defendant in a criminal case has been found incompetent to stand trial or not guilty by reason of insanity.

(2) "Examiner" means either of the following:

(a) A psychiatrist or a licensed clinical psychologist who satisfies the criteria of division (I)(1) of section 5122.01 of the Revised Code or is employed by a certified forensic center designated by the department of mental health to conduct examinations or evaluations.

(b) For purposes of a separate mental retardation evaluation that is ordered by a court pursuant to division (H) of section 2945.371 of the Revised Code, a psychologist designated by the director of mental retardation and developmental disabilities pursuant to that section to conduct that separate mental retardation evaluation.

(3) "Nonsecured status" means any unsupervised, off-grounds movement or trial visit from a hospital or institution, or any conditional release, that is granted to a person who is found incompetent to stand trial and is committed pursuant to section 2945.39 of the Revised Code or to a person who is found not guilty by reason of insanity and is committed pursuant to section 2945.40 of the Revised Code.

(4) "Unsupervised, off-grounds movement" includes only off-grounds privileges that are unsupervised and that have an expectation of return to the hospital or institution on a daily basis.

(5) "Trial visit" means a patient privilege of a longer stated duration of unsupervised community contact with an expectation of return to the hospital or institution at designated times.

(6) "Conditional release" means a commitment status under which the trial court at any time may revoke a person's conditional release and order the rehospitalization or reinstitutionalization of the person as described in division (A) of section 2945.402 of the Revised Code and pursuant to which a person who is found incompetent to stand trial or a person who is found not guilty by reason of insanity lives and receives treatment in the community for a period of time that does not exceed the maximum prison term or term of imprisonment that the person could have received for the offense in question had the person been convicted of the offense instead of being found incompetent to stand trial on the charge of the offense or being found not guilty by reason of insanity relative to the offense.

(7) "Licensed clinical psychologist," "mentally ill person subject to hospitalization by court order," and "psychiatrist" have the same meanings as in section 5122.01 of the Revised Code.

(8) "Mentally retarded person subject to institutionalization by court order" has the same meaning as in section 5123.01 of the Revised Code.

(B) In a criminal action in a court of common pleas, a county court, or a municipal court, the court, prosecutor, or defense may raise the issue of the defendant's competence to stand trial. If the issue is raised before the trial has commenced, the court shall hold a hearing on the issue as provided in this section. If the issue is raised after the trial has commenced, the court shall hold a hearing on the issue only for good cause shown or on the court's own motion.

(C) The court shall conduct the hearing required or authorized under division (B) of this section within thirty days after the issue is raised, unless the defendant has been referred for evaluation in which case the court shall conduct the hearing within ten days after the filing of the report of the evaluation or, in the case of a defendant who is ordered by the court pursuant to division (H) of section 2945.371 of the Revised Code to undergo a separate mental retardation evaluation conducted by a psychologist designated by the director of mental retardation and developmental disabilities, within ten days after the filing of the report of the separate mental retardation evaluation under that division. A hearing may be continued for good cause.

(D) The defendant shall be represented by counsel at the hearing conducted under division (C) of this section. If the defendant is unable to obtain counsel, the court shall appoint counsel under Chapter 120. of the Revised Code or under the authority recognized in division (C) of section 120.06, division (E) of section 120.16, division (E) of section 120.26, or section 2941.51 of the Revised Code before proceeding with the hearing.

(E) The prosecutor and defense counsel may submit evidence on the issue of the defendant's competence to stand trial. A written report of the evaluation of the defendant may be admitted into evidence at the hearing by stipulation, but, if either the prosecution or defense objects to its admission, the report may be admitted under sections 2317.36 to 2317.38 of the Revised Code or any other applicable statute or rule.

(F) The court shall not find a defendant incompetent to stand trial solely because the defendant is receiving or has received treatment as a voluntary or involuntary mentally ill patient under Chapter 5122. or a voluntary or involuntary mentally retarded resident under Chapter 5123. of the Revised Code or because the defendant is receiving or has received psychotropic drugs or other medication, even if the defendant might become incompetent to stand trial without the drugs or medication.

(G) A defendant is presumed to be competent to stand trial. If, after a hearing, the court finds by a preponderance of the evidence that, because of the defendant's present mental condition, the defendant is incapable of understanding the nature and objective of the proceedings against the defendant or of assisting in the defendant's defense, the court shall find the defendant incompetent to stand trial and shall enter an order authorized by section 2945.38 of the Revised Code.

(H) Municipal courts shall follow the procedures set forth in sections 2945.37 to 2945.402 of the Revised Code. Except as provided in section 2945.371 of the Revised Code, a municipal court shall not order an evaluation of the defendant's competence to stand trial or the defendant's mental condition at the time of the commission of the offense to be conducted at any hospital operated by the department of mental health. Those evaluations shall be performed through community resources including, but not limited to, certified forensic centers, court probation departments, and community mental health agencies. All expenses of the evaluations shall be borne by the legislative authority of the municipal court, as defined in section 1901.03 of the Revised Code, and shall be taxed as costs in the case. If a defendant is found incompetent to stand trial or not guilty by reason of insanity, a municipal court may commit the defendant as provided in sections 2945.38 to 2945.402 of the Revised Code [1]

(1996 S 285, eff. 7–1–97; 1988 S 156, eff. 7–1–89; 1981 H 694; 1980 S 297; 1978 H 565)

[1] So in original.

Historical and Statutory Notes

Ed. Note: 2945.37 contains provisions analogous to former 2947.25, repealed by 1972 H 511, eff. 1–1–74.

Ed. Note: Former 2945.37 repealed by 1978 H 565, eff. 11–1–78; 1976 S 368; 1953 H 1; GC 13441–1.

Pre–1953 H 1 Amendments: 113 v 177, Ch 19, § 1

Amendment Note: 1996 S 285 rewrote this section, which previously read:

"(A) In a criminal action in a court of common pleas or municipal court, the court, prosecutor, or defense may raise the issue of the defendant's competence to stand trial. If the issue is raised before trial, the court shall hold a hearing on the issue as provided in this section. If the issue is raised after trial has begun, the court shall hold a hearing on the issue only for good cause shown.

"A defendant is presumed competent to stand trial, unless it is proved by a preponderance of the evidence in a hearing under this section that because of his present mental condition he is incapable of understanding the nature and objective of the proceedings against him or of presently assisting in his defense.

"The court shall not find a defendant incompetent to stand trial solely because he is receiving or has received treatment as a voluntary or involuntary mentally ill patient or mentally retarded resident under Chapter 5122. or 5123. of the Revised Code or because he is receiving or has received psychotropic drugs or other medication under medical supervision, even though without the drugs or medication the defendant might become incompetent to stand trial.

"The court shall conduct the hearing within thirty days after the issue is raised, unless the defendant has been referred for examination under section 2945.371 of the Revised Code, in which case the court shall conduct the hearing within ten days after the filing of the report required by that section. A hearing may be continued for good cause shown.

"The defendant shall be represented by counsel at the hearing. If the defendant is unable to obtain counsel, the court shall appoint counsel under Chapter 120. of the Revised Code before proceeding with the hearing.

"The prosecutor and defense counsel may submit evidence on the issue of the defendant's competence to stand trial. A written report made under section 2945.371 of the Revised Code may be admitted into evidence at the hearing by stipulation of the prosecution and defense counsel, but if either objects to its admission, the report may be admitted under sections 2317.36 to 2317.38 of the Revised Code or other applicable statute or rule. A report made under section 2945.37 of the Revised Code is inadmissible into evidence in the criminal action against the defendant, but in such an action the prosecutor or defense counsel may call as witnesses any persons who examined the defendant or prepared a report pursuant to a referral under section 2945.371 of the Revised Code.

"Upon the evidence submitted, the court shall determine the defendant's competence to stand trial and shall make an order under section 2945.38 of the Revised Code.

"(B) As used in sections 2945.37 to 2945.40 of the Revised Code, 'prosecutor' means the prosecuting attorney, village solicitor, city director of law, or similar officer who has the authority to prosecute a criminal case that is before the court or a criminal case in which the person was found incompetent to stand trial or found not guilty by reason of insanity.

"(C) Municipal courts shall follow the procedures set forth in sections 2945.37 to 2945.40 of the Revised Code, except as provided in this division. Notwithstanding sections 2945.371 and 2945.39 of the Revised Code, a municipal court shall not order an evaluation of the defendant's competence to stand trial or the defendant's mental condition at the time of the commission of the offense to be conducted at any hospital operated by the department of mental health. Such evaluations shall be performed through community resources including, but not limited to, certified forensic centers, court probation departments, and community mental health agencies, and all expenses of such evaluations shall be borne by the court and taxed as costs in the case. If a defendant is found incompetent to stand trial or not guilty by reason of insanity, a municipal court may commit him as provided in section 2945.38 or 2945.40 of the Revised Code, whichever is applicable, except that the court shall make no commitment to the Oakwood forensic center."

Cross References

Arrest and detention until warrant can be obtained, 2935.03

Convict sentenced to death, proceedings, if insanity suspected, 2949.28, 2949.29

Department of mental retardation and developmental disabilities, definitions, 5123.01

Hospitalization of mentally ill, applicability of provisions, 5122.011

Institutionalization of person incompetent to stand trial or not guilty by reason of insanity, applicability of provisions, 5123.011

Mentally ill patients absent without leave, applicability, 5122.26

Offenses against justice and public administration; detention, defined, 2921.01

Plea of insanity, Crim R 11

Library References

Criminal Law ⟹623.
Mental Health ⟹432, 434.
Westlaw Topic Nos. 110, 257A.
C.J.S. Criminal Law §§ 549 to 557.

Baldwin's Ohio Legislative Service, 1988 Laws of Ohio, S 156—LSC Analysis, p 5–284

Research References

ALR Library

70 ALR 5th 1, Adequacy of Defense Counsel's Representation of Criminal Client--Issues of Incompetency.

Encyclopedias

OH Jur. 3d Criminal Law § 45, Competency Hearing; Psychiatric Examination.

OH Jur. 3d Criminal Law § 83, Other Actions or Omissions.

OH Jur. 3d Criminal Law § 1029, Mitigating Factors—Waiver of Right to Introduce Mitigating Evidence.

OH Jur. 3d Criminal Law § 2583, Obligations of Trial Court.

OH Jur. 3d Criminal Law § 2584, Right to Hearing on Competency.

OH Jur. 3d Criminal Law § 2585, Conduct of Hearing.

OH Jur. 3d Criminal Law § 2586, Effect of Failure to Hold Hearing.

OH Jur. 3d Criminal Law § 2588, Time and Place of Examination.

OH Jur. 3d Criminal Law § 2590, Examination Report.

OH Jur. 3d Criminal Law § 3259, Right to Counsel.

OH Jur. 3d Family Law § 1637, Order for Social History or Physical or Mental Examination.

Treatises and Practice Aids

Markus, Trial Handbook for Ohio Lawyers, § 4:59, Criminal Case—Defenses—Insanity—Competence to Stand Trial or to be Sentenced.

Klein, Darling, & Terez, Baldwin's Ohio Practice Civil Practice § 1:53, Civ. R. 1(C)(6): Commitment of the Mentally Ill--Proceedings Under RC 2945.38 and RC 2945.40.

Katz, Giannelli, Blair and Lipton, Baldwin's Ohio Practice, Criminal Law, § 54:1, Introduction.

Katz, Giannelli, Blair and Lipton, Baldwin's Ohio Practice, Criminal Law, § 54:2, Right to a Competency Hearing.

Katz, Giannelli, Blair and Lipton, Baldwin's Ohio Practice, Criminal Law, § 54:3, Competency Standard.

Katz, Giannelli, Blair and Lipton, Baldwin's Ohio Practice, Criminal Law, § 54:4, Mental Evaluation.

Katz, Giannelli, Blair and Lipton, Baldwin's Ohio Practice, Criminal Law, § 54:5, Burden of Proof.

Katz, Giannelli, Blair and Lipton, Baldwin's Ohio Practice, Criminal Law, § 54:6, Counsel, Waiver, and Guilty Pleas.

Katz, Giannelli, Blair and Lipton, Baldwin's Ohio Practice, Criminal Law, § 54:7, Competency Hearing.

Katz, Giannelli, Blair and Lipton, Baldwin's Ohio Practice, Criminal Law, § 77:8, Experts—Competency to Stand Trial.

Katz, Giannelli, Blair and Lipton, Baldwin's Ohio Practice, Criminal Law, § 144:4, Plea of Not Guilty by Reason of Insanity at Arraignment.

Katz, Giannelli, Blair and Lipton, Baldwin's Ohio Practice, Criminal Law, § 144:5, Acceptance of Plea of Not Guilty by Reason of Insanity After Arraignment.

Katz, Giannelli, Blair and Lipton, Baldwin's Ohio Practice, Criminal Law, § 144:6, Entry on Plea of Not Guilty by Reason of Insanity.

Katz, Giannelli, Blair and Lipton, Baldwin's Ohio Practice, Criminal Law, § 144:8, Entry Finding Defendant [Competent/Incompetent] to Stand Trial.

Carlin, Baldwin's Ohio Practice, Merrick-Rippner Probate Law § 3:5, Jurisdiction of Probate Court—Subject Matter—Specific Areas—Fiduciaries.

Carlin, Baldwin's Ohio Practice, Merrick-Rippner Probate Law § 3:13, Jurisdiction of Probate Court—Scope—Exclusive and Concurrent Jurisdiction.

Carlin, Baldwin's Ohio Practice, Merrick-Rippner Probate Law § 101:48, Hearings on Nonsecured Status and Termination of Commitment of Persons Found Ngri or Incompetent to Stand Trial.

Carlin, Baldwin's Ohio Practice, Merrick-Rippner Probate Law § 107:53, Adjudicatory Hearings—Mental Competency to Stand Trial.

Hennenberg & Reinhart, Ohio Criminal Defense Motions F 5.20, Motion for Psychiatric Evaluation to Determine Defendant's Competency to Stand Trial-Pretrial Motions.

Hennenberg & Reinhart, Ohio Criminal Defense Motions F 5.21, Motion for Order Permitting Psychiatric Evaluation at State's Expense-Pretrial Motions.

Hennenberg & Reinhart, Ohio Criminal Defense Motions F 13.05, Motion for Order Granting Independent Psychiatric Evaluation at the State's Expense-Death Penalty Motions.

Giannelli & Yeomans, Ohio Juvenile Law § 23:7, Mental Competency.

Law Review and Journal Commentaries

Contesting Incompetency to Stand Trial, Comment. 2 Ohio N U L Rev 739 (1975).

Fit to die: Drug–induced competency for the purpose of execution, Comment. 20 S Ill U L J 149 (Fall 1995).

Insanity as a Defense in Criminal Cases, Frank T. Cullitan. 18 Clev B J 75 (March 1947).

The Insanity Defense, Philip B. Lyons. 9 U Tol L Rev 31 (Fall 1977).

Mens Rea: A New Analysis, Peter H. Karlen. 9 U Tol L Rev 191 (Winter 1978).

Musings Of A Trial Judge—The Ohio "Mentally Handicapped" Criminal Defendant: Should Anybody Care?, Hon. Richard A. Niehaus. 14 Ohio N U L Rev 203 (1987).

Ohio Commitments of the Mentally Ill Offender, James Michael Caulfield. 4 Cap U L Rev 1 (1975).

Sanity: The Psychiatrico–Legal Communicative Gap, James K. L. Lawrence. 27 Ohio St L J 219 (Spring 1966).

State v. Humphries: Who Bears the Burden of Proof for the Defense of Insanity?, Note. 5 Ohio N U L Rev 144 (1978).

Notes of Decisions

Ed. Note: This section contains annotations from former RC 2945.37.

---

1. Constitutional issues—In general

Defendant's alleged mental retardation did not establish his incompetence in criminal proceedings, and thus counsel's failure to assert defendant's mental retardation did not prejudice defendant by denying his federal constitutionally guaranteed right to not be tried while incompetent. State v. Beck (Ohio App. 1 Dist., Hamilton, 10-31-2003) No. C-020432, No. C-020449, No. C-030062, 2003-Ohio-5838, 2003 WL 22459272, Unreported, appeal not allowed 101 Ohio St.3d 1470, 804 N.E.2d 42, 2004-Ohio-819. Criminal Law ⚷ 641.13(2.1)

The right to a competency hearing rises to the level of a constitutional guarantee where the record contains sufficient indicia of incompetence such that an inquiry is necessary to ensure the defendant's right to a fair trial. State v. Skatzes (Ohio, 12-08-2004) 104 Ohio St.3d 195, 819 N.E.2d 215, 2004-Ohio-6391. Criminal Law ⚷ 625.10(2.1)

The right to a competency hearing rises to the level of a constitutional guarantee where the record contains sufficient indicia of incompetence, such that an inquiry into the defendant's competency is necessary to ensure the defendant's right to a fair trial. State v. Ahmed (Ohio, 08-25-2004) 103 Ohio St.3d 27, 813 N.E.2d 637, 2004-Ohio-4190, reconsideration denied 103 Ohio St.3d 1496, 816 N.E.2d 1081, 2004-Ohio-5605, certiorari denied 125 S.Ct. 1703, 544 U.S. 952, 161 L.Ed.2d 531, rehearing denied, rehearing denied 125 S.Ct. 2901, 162 L.Ed.2d 312. Criminal Law ⚷ 625.10(2.1)

Trial court fully protected murder defendant's constitutional rights in determining his competency after defendant waived counsel and actively sought the death penalty; on its own motion, the trial court ordered that defendant undergo two competency evaluations, even though defense counsel disclosed that an independent psychologist had already found defendant competent, defendant stipulated to the two evaluators' findings that he was competent, and trial court conducted a comprehensive inquiry of defendant before finding that he was competent to waive counsel, represent himself, and waive right to jury trial. State v. Mink (Ohio, 04-14-2004) 101 Ohio St.3d 350, 805 N.E.2d 1064, 2004-Ohio-1580, reconsideration denied 102 Ohio St.3d 1473, 809 N.E.2d 1159, 2004-Ohio-2830. Criminal Law ⚷ 641.6(2); Jury ⚷ 29(6)

Right to a competency hearing rises to the level of a constitutional guarantee when the record contains sufficient indicia of incompetency to necessitate inquiry to ensure the defendant's right to a fair trial. State v. Thomas (Ohio, 12-11-2002) 97 Ohio St.3d 309, 779 N.E.2d 1017, 2002-Ohio-6624, reconsideration denied 97 Ohio St.3d 1498, 780 N.E.2d 1022, 2002-Ohio-7248, stay granted 98 Ohio St.3d 1403, 781 N.E.2d 221, 2003-Ohio-40, certiorari denied 123 S.Ct. 2295, 539 U.S. 916, 156 L.Ed.2d 133. Criminal Law ⚷ 625.10(2.1)

Failure to hold competency hearing in capital murder trial was constitutional error requiring reversal of conviction, where defendant asked for hearing on several occasions, defense counsel represented numerous times that they believed defendant was incompetent, counsel filed two separate motions to withdraw based on defendant's bizarre behavior, and defendant filed six pro se motions to dismiss counsel which alleged, among other things, that his attorneys had threatened his life and were conspiring with the prosecution. State v. Were (Ohio, 02-06-2002) 94 Ohio St.3d 173, 761 N.E.2d 591, 2002-Ohio-481, appeal after new trial 2005-Ohio-376, 2005 WL 267671, remanded 106 Ohio St.3d 1529, 835 N.E.2d 379, 2005-Ohio-5146, on remand 2006-Ohio-3511, 2006 WL 1867840. Criminal Law ⚷ 1166(12)

Right to a competency hearing rises to the level of a constitutional guarantee where the record contains sufficient indicia of incompetence, such that an inquiry is necessary to ensure the defendant's right to a fair trial. State v. Smith (Ohio, 07-26-2000) 89 Ohio St.3d 323, 731 N.E.2d 645, 2000-Ohio-166, reconsideration denied 90 Ohio St.3d 1419, 735 N.E.2d 457, certiorari denied 121 S.Ct. 1131, 531 U.S. 1167, 148 L.Ed.2d 997. Criminal Law ⚷ 625.10(1)

Constitutional test under Fourteenth Amendment for competency to stand trial is whether defendant has sufficient present ability to consult with his lawyer with reasonable degree of rational understanding and whether he has rational, as well as factual, understanding of proceedings against him. In re Williams (Ohio App. 2 Dist., 05-23-1997) 116 Ohio App.3d 237, 687 N.E.2d 507, appeal not allowed 80 Ohio St.3d 1415, 684 N.E.2d 706. Constitutional Law ⚷ 268.2(2)

Juvenile's fundamental right not to be tried or convicted of offense while incompetent was not adequately protected, where experts' reports and testimony were irreparably muddled with incorrect standards of law and inappropriate judgments pertaining to moral responsibility. In re Williams (Ohio App. 2 Dist., 05-23-1997) 116 Ohio App.3d 237, 687 N.E.2d 507, appeal not allowed 80 Ohio St.3d 1415, 684 N.E.2d 706. Infants ⚷ 208

The failure to hold a competency hearing is harmless error where the defendant proceeds to participate in the trial, offers his own testimony in defense and is subject to cross-examination, and the record fails to reveal sufficient indicia of incompetency. State v. Bock (Ohio 1986) 28 Ohio St.3d 108, 502 N.E.2d 1016, 28 O.B.R. 207. Criminal Law ⚷ 1166(12)

It is constitutional to place on the defense the burden of proof, by a preponderance of evidence, of the defendant's incompetence to stand trial. State v. Pruitt (Cuyahoga 1984) 18 Ohio App.3d 50, 480 N.E.2d 499, 18 O.B.R. 163.

Petitioner failed to establish entitlement to habeas relief based on his contention that district court made public statement that he was insane by requiring him to undergo psychological evaluation to determine competency to stand trial, absent any showing that petitioner's constitutional rights were violated by such proceedings or any showing as to how this pretrial proceeding denied him a fundamentally fair trial. Norris v. Schotten (C.A.6 (Ohio), 05-26-1998) 146 F.3d 314, certiorari denied 119 S.Ct. 348, 525 U.S. 935, 142 L.Ed.2d 287. Habeas Corpus ⚷ 477

Trial court did not abuse its discretion by failing sua sponte to conduct hearing regarding defendant's competency to stand trial, given that defendant did not act irrational at the trial or the sentencing hearing, there was no indication by defense counsel that defendant was incompetent or unable to assist counsel with her defense, and no prior medical opinions were presented to demonstrate defendant's inability to stand trial. City of Elyria v. Bozman (Ohio App. 9 Dist., Lorain, 05-29-2002) No. 01CA007899, 2002-Ohio-2644, 2002 WL 1263971, Unreported, appeal not allowed 96 Ohio St.3d 1524, 775 N.E.2d 863, 2002-Ohio-5099, certiorari denied 123 S.Ct. 2583, 539 U.S. 931, 156 L.Ed.2d 611. Criminal Law ⚷ 625.10(4)

GC 13441–1 (RC 2945.37) and 13441–4 (RC 2945.40) contemplate as a condition precedent to the action provided therein a formal examination and investigation by the court into the question of the sanity or insanity of the accused, especially where the accused objects to the procedure, and a violation of such sections occurs and an accused is deprived of due process of law where, against his protests, he is committed to the Lima state hospital for observation for a period not exceeding one month, solely upon the unsworn statement of the prosecuting attorney as to his belief, based on hearsay, that the accused is not sane and without any semblance of a formal hearing as to the accused's mental condition and without the presentation of any evidence tending to prove insanity. State ex rel. Smilack v. Bushong (Ohio 1953) 159 Ohio St. 259, 111 N.E.2d 918, 50 O.O. 280.

2. —— Due process, constitutional issues

Defendant's due process rights were not violated by trial court's failure to sua sponte hold a competency hearing during trial; defendant was evaluated four times prior to trial by his own expert who found him competent to stand trial, defendant did not want a court-appointed psychologist and refused a competency hearing, and defendant acted and responded appropriately during trial. State v. Braden (Ohio App. 10 Dist., Franklin, 06-10-2003) No. 02AP-954, 2003-Ohio-2949, 2003 WL 21321457, Unreported, appeal not allowed 100 Ohio St.3d 1431, 797 N.E.2d 511, 2003-Ohio-5396. Constitutional Law ⚷ 268.2(2); Criminal Law ⚷ 625.10(4)

Juvenile court's failure to conduct competency hearing, after issue of juvenile's competency was raised and before adjudication hearing was commenced, in violation of juvenile's right to due process of law, was not harmless error and required reversal of juvenile's adjudication as delinquent on basis of his having committed rape, where court-appointed examiner found juvenile's competency "highly suspect." In re B.M.S. (Ohio App. 2 Dist., 03-03-2006) 165 Ohio App.3d 609, 847 N.E.2d 506, 2006-Ohio-981. Constitutional Law ⚷ 255(4); Infants ⚷ 253

A person who lacks the capacity to understand the nature and object of the proceedings against him, to consult with counsel, and to assist in preparing his defense may not, under due process principles, be subjected to a trial. State v. Skatzes (Ohio, 12-08-2004) 104 Ohio St.3d 195, 819 N.E.2d

215, 2004-Ohio-6391. Constitutional Law ⚷ 268.2(2)

A person who lacks the capacity to understand the nature and object of the proceedings against him, to consult with counsel, and to assist in preparing his defense may not be subjected to a trial; fundamental principles of due process prohibit trial of a criminal defendant who is legally incompetent. State v. Adams (Ohio, 11-17-2004) 103 Ohio St.3d 508, 817 N.E.2d 29, 2004-Ohio-5845, reconsideration denied 104 Ohio St.3d 1442, 819 N.E.2d 1124, 2004-Ohio-7033, certiorari denied 125 S.Ct. 2271, 544 U.S. 1040, 161 L.Ed.2d 1072. Constitutional Law ⚷ 268.2(2); Criminal Law ⚷ 625(1)

Due process principles forbid subjecting a legally incompetent criminal defendant to trial. State v. Braden (Ohio, 04-02-2003) 98 Ohio St.3d 354, 785 N.E.2d 439, 2003-Ohio-1325, stay granted 98 Ohio St.3d 1542, 787 N.E.2d 5, 2003-Ohio-2002, denial of post-conviction relief affirmed 2003-Ohio-2949, 2003 WL 21321457, appeal not allowed 100 Ohio St.3d 1431, 797 N.E.2d 511, 2003-Ohio-5396, certiorari denied 124 S.Ct. 182, 540 U.S. 865, 157 L.Ed.2d 119, stay revoked 100 Ohio St.3d 1525, 800 N.E.2d 43, 2003-Ohio-6510. Constitutional Law ⚷ 268.2(2)

Fundamental principles of due process require that a criminal defendant who is legally incompetent may not be tried. State v. Thomas (Ohio, 12-11-2002) 97 Ohio St.3d 309, 779 N.E.2d 1017, 2002-Ohio-6624, reconsideration denied 97 Ohio St.3d 1498, 780 N.E.2d 1022, 2002-Ohio-7248, stay granted 98 Ohio St.3d 1403, 781 N.E.2d 221, 2003-Ohio-40, certiorari denied 123 S.Ct. 2295, 539 U.S. 916, 156 L.Ed.2d 133. Constitutional Law ⚷ 268.2(2)

Due process principles forbid subjecting a legally incompetent criminal defendant to trial. State v. Tibbetts (Ohio, 07-05-2001) 92 Ohio St.3d 146, 749 N.E.2d 226, 2001-Ohio-132, motion to reopen denied 93 Ohio St.3d 1495, 758 N.E.2d 1147, certiorari denied 122 S.Ct. 1100, 534 U.S. 1144, 151 L.Ed.2d 997. Constitutional Law ⚷ 268.2(2)

To ensure that defendant received due process, trial court was required to conduct hearing on defendant's competency to stand trial where report of court psychiatric clinic indicated that defendant was not competent, report of doctor which allegedly indicated that defendant's competency was restored was not introduced at trial and may have been premised upon incomplete information, and defense counsel apprised court that defendant was unable to assist in his defense. State v. Corethers (Ohio App. 8 Dist., 08-23-1993) 90 Ohio App.3d 428, 629 N.E.2d 1052, dismissed, jurisdictional motion overruled 68 Ohio St.3d 1470, 628 N.E.2d 1389. Constitutional Law ⚷ 268.2(2); Criminal Law ⚷ 625.10(2.1)

Commitment of accused to Lima state hospital by reason of inability to stand trial does not deprive accused of due process where there is a reasonable expectation of recovery. In re Horvath (Ohio 1975) 42 Ohio St.2d 60, 325 N.E.2d 895, 71 O.O.2d 38.

State procedures for criminal prosecutions, including the burden of producing evidence and burden of persuasion, are not proscribed by the Due Process Clause unless they offend some principle of justice so rooted in the public tradition and conscience as to be ranked fundamental; the balancing test for evaluating procedural due process claims set forth in Matthews v Eldridge, 424 US 319 (1976) does not apply to state rules of criminal procedure. Medina v. California (U.S.Cal. 1992) 112 S.Ct. 2572, 505 U.S. 437, 120 L.Ed.2d 353, rehearing denied 113 S.Ct. 19, 505 U.S. 1244, 120 L.Ed.2d 946.

The Due Process Clause does not prevent states from requiring defendants who claim they are incompetent to stand trial to bear the burden of proving incompetence by a preponderance of the evidence. Medina v. California (U.S.Cal. 1992) 112 S.Ct. 2572, 505 U.S. 437, 120 L.Ed.2d 353, rehearing denied 113 S.Ct. 19, 505 U.S. 1244, 120 L.Ed.2d 946.

Due process requires that legally incompetent defendant not stand trial. Franklin v. Francis (S.D.Ohio, 02-27-1998) 997 F.Supp. 916, vacated and remanded 144 F.3d 429, certiorari denied 119 S.Ct. 451, 525 U.S. 985, 142 L.Ed.2d 404, on remand 36 F.Supp.2d 1008. Constitutional Law ⚷ 268.2(2)

RC 2945.37 and 2945.38 create an expectation of protection of competency to stand trial that is protected by the Due Process Clause and whatever procedure is applied by the state to determine competency must be adequate to protect the defendant's due process right to not be convicted if incompetent. Lagway v. Dallman (N.D.Ohio 1992) 806 F.Supp. 1322.

Due process does not require that counsel be permitted at the staffings of indefinite committees at Lima state hospital. Davis v. Balson (N.D.Ohio 1978) 461 F.Supp. 842, 11 O.O.3d 360.

3. —— Habeas corpus, constitutional issues

A conviction upon a plea of guilty of violation of RC 2905.01 is not rendered invalid and subject to collateral attack by habeas corpus merely by reason of the fact that the subsequent examination required by RC 2947.25 resulted in a finding that the defendant was at that time, and for sometime prior thereto, mentally ill as defined by RC 5123.01. Krauter v. Maxwell (Ohio 1965) 3 Ohio St.2d 142, 209 N.E.2d 571, 32 O.O.2d 141.

Defendant's mother and sister presented colorable due process claim, in habeas corpus petition on his behalf, that evidence before state trial court warranted hearing on defendant's competence to stand trial and, thus, they were entitled to stay of defendant's execution; defendant was diagnosed with psychotic and personality disorders, evidenced genetic and organic brain disorders, had long history of mental illness and bizarre behavior, had been institutionalized, had made multiple suicide attempts, and expressed his desire to die when arrested, when interviewed by psychologist, and in prepared statement to jury, and psychologist, who previously found defendant competent, expressed doubt on morning of mitigation phase of trial as to defendant's competence. Franklin v. Francis (S.D.Ohio, 02-27-1998) 997 F.Supp. 916, vacated and remanded 144 F.3d 429, certiorari denied 119 S.Ct. 451, 525 U.S. 985, 142 L.Ed.2d 404, on remand 36 F.Supp.2d 1008. Habeas Corpus ⚷ 679

District court was not bound, in habeas corpus proceeding brought by defendant's mother and sister on his behalf, by state court's determination that defendant was competent to waive further review of his conviction and death sentence, as state court incorrectly interpreted and applied competency standard; standard requires two inquiries, namely, whether defendant is capable of making rational choice with respect to abandoning further litigation and whether he is suffering from mental disorder which "may substantially affect" his capacity, and state court altered second inquiry by reasoning, in effect, that if defendant had capacity to make choice he could not also suffer from mental disorder that could "substantially affect" that capacity. Franklin v. Francis (S.D.Ohio, 02-27-1998) 997 F.Supp. 916, vacated and remanded 144 F.3d 429, certiorari denied 119 S.Ct. 451, 525 U.S. 985, 142 L.Ed.2d 404, on remand 36 F.Supp.2d 1008. Habeas Corpus ⚷ 771

District court was not bound, in habeas corpus proceeding brought by defendant's mother and sister on his behalf, by state court's factual findings, adopting two mental health professionals' opinions, relating to defendant's competency to waive further review of his conviction and death sentence; state court applied incorrect legal standard by holding, in essence, that determining whether defendant had capacity to make rational choice was same inquiry as determining whether mental disorder might substantially affect that capacity, opinions of competency were made under that incorrect legal standard, and failure to inquire into and opine on facts necessary for application of correct standard rendered evidence presented insufficient to determine competency. Franklin v. Francis (S.D.Ohio, 02-27-1998) 997 F.Supp. 916, vacated and remanded 144 F.3d 429, certiorari denied 119 S.Ct. 451, 525 U.S. 985, 142 L.Ed.2d 404, on remand 36 F.Supp.2d 1008. Habeas Corpus ⚷ 771

4. —— Waiver of rights, constitutional issues

Record contained no evidence that defendant was incompetent during time of guilty plea to rape, and thus trial court did not err in allowing defendant to waive constitutional rights; defendant responded clearly and appropriately to judge's questioning and issue of competency was never raised. State v. Rittner (Ohio App. 6 Dist., Fulton, 09-30-2003) No. F-02-034, 2003-Ohio-5201, 2003 WL 22234188, Unreported. Criminal Law ⚷ 273(2)

5. —— Ineffective assistance of counsel, constitutional issues

Defense counsel's failure to insist on second competency evaluation of murder defendant fell within realm of reasonable professional assistance and did not amount to ineffective assistance of counsel, where counsel requested that defendant be evaluated by Court Diagnostic and Treatment Center, and report prepared following such evaluation concluded that defendant was not suffering from emotional disturbance of psychotic proportions, was mildly mentally retarded, was able to understand nature and objectives of proceedings, and was capable of assisting attorney in his own defense. State v. Womack (Ohio App. 6 Dist., Lucas, 05-27-2005) No. L-04-1092, 2005-Ohio-2689, 2005 WL 1283687, Unreported, motion for delayed appeal denied 106 Ohio St.3d 1530, 835 N.E.2d 380, 2005-Ohio-5146. Criminal Law ⚷ 641.13(5)

Defense counsel made strategic decision at competency hearing to not offer evidence of defendant's incompetency to stand trial other than expert testimony, and thus defendant was not denied effective assistance of counsel in prosecution for weapon and drug offenses, even though defendant argued that counsel should have offered his own accounts of interactions with defendant or testimony by defendant's mother; counsel had already secured opinion of expert that defendant was incompetent, and counsel might have risked harm if he chose to place lay people on witness stand to be cross-examined by prosecutors. State v. Mosley (Ohio App. 7 Dist., Mahoning, 09-23-2004) No. 03 MA 52, 2004-Ohio-5187, 2004 WL 2334381, Unreported. Criminal Law ⚷ 641.13(6)

Defendant's trial counsel was not ineffective due to trial counsel's failure to investigate and pursue a possible insanity defense, in prosecution for multiple counts of felonious assault; psychologist report of defendant stated that defendant had no symptoms of mental illness, that he had no history of alcohol or substance abuse, and that the results of defendant's personality inventory test showed that defendant had no significant problems or pathology, and that fact that the drug defendant voluntarily ingested before the police standoff made it difficult for defendant to remember the event clearly did not effect defendant's ability to aid in his own defense. State v. Hedgecoth (Ohio App. 1 Dist., Hamilton, 06-27-2003) No. C-020480, 2003-Ohio-3385, 2003 WL 21473103, Unreported. Criminal Law ⚷ 641.13(6)

Counsel's decision to stipulate to the content of three competency evaluations and not cross-examine these experts or otherwise challenge the competence of defendant was grounded on a reasoned tactical judgment and was not ineffective assistance in capital murder prosecution; the reports were comprehensive and satisfied the statutory requirements, no expert diagnosed any psychosis or mental limitations that would affect the competence to stand trial although all three experts reported that defendant had abused drugs and alcohol, personal requests by defendant demonstrated his understanding of the trial process and his ability to assist his defense, and his complaints about lawyers' tactical decisions established that he understood the trial process and was fully engaged in his defense. State v. Adams (Ohio, 11-17-2004) 103 Ohio St.3d 508, 817 N.E.2d 29, 2004-Ohio-5845, reconsideration denied 104 Ohio St.3d 1442, 819 N.E.2d 1124, 2004-Ohio-7033, certiorari denied 125 S.Ct. 2271,

544 U.S. 1040, 161 L.Ed.2d 1072. Criminal Law ⚷ 641.13(5)

Any deficiency in defense counsel's failure to pursue further psychiatric evaluations of capital murder defendant after defendant was found competent to stand trial did not prejudice defendant and did not amount to ineffective assistance, absent any reasonable probability that result would have been different if further evaluations had been conducted. State v. Williams (Ohio, 08-27-2003) 99 Ohio St.3d 439, 793 N.E.2d 446, 2003-Ohio-4164, stay granted 100 Ohio St.3d 1401, 795 N.E.2d 1245, 2003-Ohio-4882, stay revoked 100 Ohio St.3d 1528, 800 N.E.2d 45, 2003-Ohio-6526, stay granted 101 Ohio St.3d 1418, 802 N.E.2d 151, 2004-Ohio-123. Criminal Law ⚷ 641.13(5)

Defense counsel's decision not to seek further evaluations of capital murder defendant's competence to stand trial reflected reasonable professional judgment and did not amount to deficient performance; counsel knew their client, could best determine if he was able to assist them in his defense or if competency hearing or psychiatric examination was needed, and already had extensive past psychological evaluations of defendant as well as defense expert's recent evaluation concluding that defendant was competent to stand trial. State v. Williams (Ohio, 08-27-2003) 99 Ohio St.3d 439, 793 N.E.2d 446, 2003-Ohio-4164, stay granted 100 Ohio St.3d 1401, 795 N.E.2d 1245, 2003-Ohio-4882, stay revoked 100 Ohio St.3d 1528, 800 N.E.2d 45, 2003-Ohio-6526, stay granted 101 Ohio St.3d 1418, 802 N.E.2d 151, 2004-Ohio-123. Criminal Law ⚷ 641.13(5)

Counsel's failure in capital murder prosecution to request the trial court to order a competency hearing did not constitute deficient performance, as element of ineffective assistance claim, in the absence of sufficient indicia of defendant's incompetence to warrant a competency hearing. State v. Thomas (Ohio, 12-11-2002) 97 Ohio St.3d 309, 779 N.E.2d 1017, 2002-Ohio-6624, reconsideration denied 97 Ohio St.3d 1498, 780 N.E.2d 1022, 2002-Ohio-7248, stay granted 98 Ohio St.3d 1403, 781 N.E.2d 221, 2003-Ohio-40, certiorari denied 123 S.Ct. 2295, 539 U.S. 916, 156 L.Ed.2d 133. Criminal Law ⚷ 641.13(2.1)

Failure of capital murder defendant's attorneys to request competency hearing did not amount to constitutionally ineffective assistance; defendant's competence was not at issue merely because he voluntarily sought psychiatric treatment and took psychotropic medication, possibility that defendant suffered from some form of mental illness did not necessarily imply his legal incompetence, and defendant's attorneys consulted with psychologist and psychiatrist, neither of whom found defendant to be legally incompetent. State v. Tibbetts (Ohio, 07-05-2001) 92 Ohio St.3d 146, 749 N.E.2d 226, 2001-Ohio-132, motion to reopen denied 93 Ohio St.3d 1495, 758 N.E.2d 1147, certiorari denied 122 S.Ct. 1100, 534 U.S. 1144, 151 L.Ed.2d 997. Criminal Law ⚷ 641.13(2.1)

6. Jurisdiction

A court of common pleas has jurisdiction over an accused pursuant to RC 2945.37 and RC 2945.38 when a magistrate's transcript has been filed against the accused. Burton v. Reshetylo (Ohio 1974) 38 Ohio St.2d 35, 309 N.E.2d 907, 67 O.O.2d 53.

A criminal division of a common pleas court lacks jurisdiction to commit a person to the Lima state hospital until restored to reason under RC 2945.37 and RC 2945.38 unless that person has first been indicted by a grand jury. Burton v. Reshetylo (Allen 1973) 35 Ohio App.2d 113, 300 N.E.2d 249, 64 O.O.2d 234, affirmed 38 Ohio St.2d 35, 309 N.E.2d 907, 67 O.O.2d 53.

7. Raising issue of competence—In general

Defendant waived competency hearing before trial court accepted guilty pleas to rape and attempted rape, where, when case was called for competency hearing, parties stipulated as to both contents of medical reports which found defendant competent to stand trial and as to admissibility of reports. State v. O'Neill (Ohio App. 7 Dist., Mahoning, 12-10-2004) No. 03 MA 188, 2004-Ohio-6805, 2004 WL 2913923, Unreported. Criminal Law ⚷ 273(2)

Defendant's conduct during trial did not require trial court to suspend trial proceedings and sua sponte conduct second inquiry relating to defendant's competency to stand trial, where conduct did not indicate change in defendant's mental state, and conduct could be seen as efforts to feign mental illness in order to disrupt trial and avoid conviction; defendant agreed to appear at trial in jail clothing, made obscene hand gestures during trial, revealed after trial had started that he had witnesses he wanted to call, and he took stand against his counsel's advice. State v. Neely (Ohio App. 12 Dist., Madison, 12-23-2002) No. CA2002-02-002, 2002-Ohio-7146, 2002 WL 31859454, Unreported. Criminal Law ⚷ 625(3)

For the purpose of a challenge of a defendant's competence to stand trial, a defendant may be emotionally disturbed or even psychotic and still be capable of understanding the charges against him and of assisting his counsel. State v. Ahmed (Ohio, 08-25-2004) 103 Ohio St.3d 27, 813 N.E.2d 637, 2004-Ohio-4190, reconsideration denied 103 Ohio St.3d 1496, 816 N.E.2d 1081, 2004-Ohio-5605, certiorari denied 125 S.Ct. 1703, 544 U.S. 952, 161 L.Ed.2d 531, rehearing denied, rehearing denied 125 S.Ct. 2901, 162 L.Ed.2d 312. Mental Health ⚷ 432

Capital murder defendant's unsupported assertion that he had been unable to assist his attorneys at trial and had therefore been incompetent to stand trial, without more, was insufficient to overcome presumption of competence; defendant expressed his views throughout proceedings and understood nature of the proceedings and his rights, counsel never questioned defendant's competence, defendant displayed no outrageous, irrational behavior during trial, counsel never complained about any lack of cooperation, and defense psychologist who examined defendant did not question his competency to stand trial and specifically found that he was competent to stand trial. State v. Williams (Ohio, 08-27-2003) 99 Ohio St.3d 439, 793 N.E.2d 446, 2003-Ohio-4164, stay granted 100 Ohio St.3d 1401, 795 N.E.2d 1245, 2003-Ohio-4882, stay revoked 100 Ohio St.3d 1528, 800 N.E.2d 45, 2003-Ohio-6526, stay granted 101 Ohio St.3d 1418, 802 N.E.2d 151, 2004-Ohio-123. Criminal Law ⚷ 625.15

Juvenile court's failure to make determination as to juvenile offender's claim of incompetency violated applicable statute and juvenile's right to due process of law, and required reversal of juvenile's adjudication as delinquent based upon his admission to aggravated robbery with firearm specification, where defense timely raised issue of juvenile's competency before juvenile court, and court held hearing thereon but entered no finding. In re Bailey (Ohio App. 2 Dist., 12-06-2002) 150 Ohio App.3d 664, 782 N.E.2d 1177, 2002-Ohio-6792. Constitutional Law ⚷ 255(4); Infants ⚷ 210; Infants ⚷ 253

Right not to be tried or convicted while incompetent is as fundamental in juvenile proceedings as it is in criminal trials of adults. In re Bailey (Ohio App. 2 Dist., 12-06-2002) 150 Ohio App.3d 664, 782 N.E.2d 1177, 2002-Ohio-6792. Infants ⚷ 153

Juvenile court may order a mental examination in delinquency proceedings where the issue of competency has been raised. In re Bailey (Ohio App. 2 Dist., 12-06-2002) 150 Ohio App.3d 664, 782 N.E.2d 1177, 2002-Ohio-6792. Infants ⚷ 208

Statutory standard for finding an adult defendant incompetent also governs the competency evaluations of juveniles, so long as it is applied in light of juvenile rather than adult norms. In re Bailey (Ohio App. 2 Dist., 12-06-2002) 150 Ohio App.3d 664, 782 N.E.2d 1177, 2002-Ohio-6792. Infants ⚷ 153

While a child may be incompetent to stand trial in adult court, he or she may nevertheless be competent to enter an admission and stand for adjudication in juvenile court, because of the differences in the complexities in adult criminal proceedings versus juvenile proceedings. In re Bailey (Ohio App. 2 Dist., 12-06-2002) 150 Ohio App.3d 664, 782 N.E.2d 1177, 2002-Ohio-6792. Infants ⚷ 153

Juvenile court was not prohibited, as matter of law, from finding that juvenile offender was both competent to stand for adjudication and incompetent to stand trial as adult; juvenile court was entitled to consider differences in complexities in adult criminal proceedings versus juvenile proceedings in determining whether juvenile was competent to enter admission in juvenile court. In re Bailey (Ohio App. 2 Dist., 12-06-2002) 150 Ohio App.3d 664, 782 N.E.2d 1177, 2002-Ohio-6792. Infants ⚷ 153

Under governing statute, decision whether to hold a competency hearing once trial has begun is in the court's discretion. State v. Thomas (Ohio, 12-11-2002) 97 Ohio St.3d 309, 779 N.E.2d 1017, 2002-Ohio-6624, reconsideration denied 97 Ohio St.3d 1498, 780 N.E.2d 1022, 2002-Ohio-7248, stay granted 98 Ohio St.3d 1403, 781 N.E.2d 221, 2003-Ohio-40, certiorari denied 123 S.Ct. 2295, 539 U.S. 916, 156 L.Ed.2d 133. Criminal Law ⚷ 625(2)

Determination of incompetency is not a final appealable order. State v. Stanley (Ohio App. 1 Dist., 06-25-1997) 121 Ohio App.3d 673, 700 N.E.2d 881, dismissed, appeal not allowed 80 Ohio St.3d 1432, 685 N.E.2d 543, denial of post-conviction relief affirmed 82 Fed.Appx. 407, 2003 WL 22290187. Criminal Law ⚷ 1023(3)

On reindictment following dismissal of a prior indictment upon an incompetency finding, the state did not have to prove that defendant was competent. State v. Stanley (Ohio App. 1 Dist., 06-25-1997) 121 Ohio App.3d 673, 700 N.E.2d 881, dismissed, appeal not allowed 80 Ohio St.3d 1432, 685 N.E.2d 543, denial of post-conviction relief affirmed 82 Fed.Appx. 407, 2003 WL 22290187. Criminal Law ⚷ 625.15

For purpose of determining whether sufficient indicia of defendant's incompetence were before trial court at time of capital murder defendant's entry of pleas of no contest to require court sua sponte to conduct hearing as to defendant's competence, trial court's alleged comment to defense counsel that counsel should not request competency hearing did not relieve counsel of responsibility to request hearing if counsel believed defendant to be incompetent. State v. Spivey (Ohio, 04-22-1998) 81 Ohio St.3d 405, 692 N.E.2d 151, 1998-Ohio-437, stay granted 82 Ohio St.3d 1435, 694 N.E.2d 1372, certiorari denied 119 S.Ct. 226, 525 U.S. 898, 142 L.Ed.2d 186. Criminal Law ⚷ 275.3

Risk that defendant will continue to offend if released is wholly irrelevant to issue of his competency to stand trial. In re Williams (Ohio App. 2 Dist., 05-23-1997) 116 Ohio App.3d 237, 687 N.E.2d 507, appeal not allowed 80 Ohio St.3d 1415, 684 N.E.2d 706. Mental Health ⚷ 432

In prosecution in which defendant entered plea of not guilty by reason of insanity to charges of felonious assault and failure to comply with lawful order of police officer, omission from the record of psychological report, evidence of competency hearing, judgment entry as to trial court's findings as to competency or insanity at time of offense, and withdrawal of insanity plea, in conjunction with trial court's failure to follow proper procedures as to competency and insanity plea issues, constituted plain error. State v. Kulp (Ohio App. 6 Dist., 03-29-1996) 110 Ohio App.3d 144, 673 N.E.2d 689. Criminal Law ⚷ 1109(1)

Request for competency hearing between guilt and mitigation phases of capital murder prosecution was made "after trial had begun" within meaning of statute requiring defendant to show good cause in order to obtain midtrial competency hearing, despite defendant's contention that mitigation phase of prosecution was a separate trial. State v. Berry (Ohio, 06-28-1995) 72 Ohio St.3d 354, 650 N.E.2d 433, 1995-Ohio-310, reconsideration denied 73 Ohio St.3d 1428, 652 N.E.2d 801, certiorari denied 116 S.Ct. 823, 516 U.S. 1097, 133 L.Ed.2d 766, stay denied 168 F.3d 261, rehearing and suggestion for rehearing en banc denied, certiorari denied 119 S.Ct. 1022, 525 U.S. 1132, 142 L.Ed.2d 973. Criminal Law ⚷ 625.10(1); Criminal Law ⚷ 625.10(3)

Midtrial competency hearing was not warranted by evidence presented during mitigation phase of capital murder prosecution; such evidence was not before the trial court when competency issue was raised and, further, was offered for sole purpose of mitigation and did not indicate that defendant was incapable of understanding the nature and objective of the proceedings or of assisting in his defense. State v. Berry (Ohio, 06-28-1995) 72 Ohio St.3d 354, 650 N.E.2d 433, 1995-Ohio-310, reconsideration denied 73 Ohio St.3d 1428, 652 N.E.2d 801, certiorari denied 116 S.Ct. 823, 516 U.S. 1097, 133 L.Ed.2d 766, stay denied 168 F.3d 261, rehearing and suggestion for rehearing en banc denied, certiorari denied 119 S.Ct. 1022, 525 U.S. 1132, 142 L.Ed.2d 973. Criminal Law ⚷ 625.10(2.1)

Defendant's failure, until sentencing phase of capital murder prosecution, to disclose to counsel a possible motive for the killing did not amount to good cause to hold midtrial competency hearing; defendant's statements could be viewed as self-serving, last minute attempt by defendant to somehow justify his actions. State v. Berry (Ohio, 06-28-1995) 72 Ohio St.3d 354, 650 N.E.2d 433, 1995-Ohio-310, reconsideration denied 73 Ohio St.3d 1428, 652 N.E.2d 801, certiorari denied 116 S.Ct. 823, 516 U.S. 1097, 133 L.Ed.2d 766, stay denied 168 F.3d 261, rehearing and suggestion for rehearing en banc denied, certiorari denied 119 S.Ct. 1022, 525 U.S. 1132, 142 L.Ed.2d 973. Criminal Law ⚷ 625.10(3)

Defendant was presumed competent until proven otherwise and, thus, her assertion of incompetence at time of deposition of state's witness was not well taken, as she was not found incompetent until some months after deposition was taken. State v. Rowe (Ohio App. 10 Dist., 10-26-1993) 92 Ohio App.3d 652, 637 N.E.2d 29, reconsideration denied 1994 WL 41312, dismissed, jurisdictional motion overruled 69 Ohio St.3d 1403, 629 N.E.2d 1365. Criminal Law ⚷ 311

There is no statutory right of a defendant to a determination of competency before trial; the issue as to the need for a competency hearing may be raised by the court or the defendant and the decision whether to hold such a hearing must be made on a case-by-case basis in the exercise of the trial court's sound discretion. State v. Qualls (Franklin 1988) 50 Ohio App.3d 56, 552 N.E.2d 957. Sentencing And Punishment ⚷ 268

The failure to hold a competency hearing is harmless error where the defendant proceeds to participate in the trial, offers his own testimony in defense and is subject to cross-examination, and the record fails to reveal sufficient indicia of incompetency. State v. Bock (Ohio 1986) 28 Ohio St.3d 108, 502 N.E.2d 1016, 28 O.B.R. 207. Criminal Law ⚷ 1166(12)

A competency hearing is not automatically mandated by virtue of a plea of not guilty by reason of insanity; in order for a competency hearing to take place, a motion for such must be made before the trial commences. State v. Wilcox (Trumbull 1984) 16 Ohio App.3d 273, 475 N.E.2d 516, 16 O.B.R. 298. Criminal Law ⚷ 625.10(4)

The issue of competency to stand trial is not raised by the entry of an order for a psychiatric examination due to a plea of not guilty by reason of insanity. State v. Wilcox (Trumbull 1984) 16 Ohio App.3d 273, 475 N.E.2d 516, 16 O.B.R. 298. Criminal Law ⚷ 625.10(2.1)

A person held under indictment for an indefinite period as incompetent to stand trial has right to a pretrial competency hearing that is a "substantial right," and such hearing is a "special hearing" as those terms are used in statute governing which final orders may be reviewed; thus, order dismissing defendant's motion for a competency hearing in trial court was a final appealable order. State ex rel. Robertson v. Nurre (Hamilton 1981) 3 Ohio App.3d 5, 443 N.E.2d 193, 3 O.B.R. 5. Criminal Law ⚷ 1023(1)

An unqualified suggestion of defendant's incompetency to stand trial by defense counsel during trial without additional objective indications such as, but not limited to, supplemental medical reports, defendant's conduct at trial or specific reference to defendant's irrational behavior or the like does not meet the "good cause shown" standard of RC 2945.37. State v. Chapin (Ohio 1981) 67 Ohio St.2d 437, 424 N.E.2d 317, 21 O.O.3d 273.

The question of the competency to stand trial of the defendant in a criminal prosecution may be raised by the state, and must then be determined before trial. State v. Rand (Ohio Com.Pl. 1969) 20 Ohio Misc. 98, 247 N.E.2d 342, 49 O.O.2d 127.

An inquiry into a defendant's sanity at the time of trial may not be initiated in the absence of some showing that the defendant is insane. State v. Page (Ohio Com.Pl. 1967) 11 Ohio Misc. 31, 228 N.E.2d 686, 40 O.O.2d 173.

Where there has been one trial under the statute before trial on the main issue of guilt and accused has been found sane, he is not entitled to another trial of the question of sanity after conviction but before sentence, in the absence of a showing by certificates of physicians or otherwise that the mental condition of accused has changed since the first trial as to sanity. Rehfeld v. State (Ohio 1921) 102 Ohio St. 431, 131 N.E. 712, 19 Ohio Law Rep. 67, 19 Ohio Law Rep. 68.

Presumption of competence, defendant's burden to establish incompetence by clear and convincing evidence, due process. Cooper v. Oklahoma (U.S.Okla., 04-16-1996) 116 S.Ct. 1373, 517 U.S. 348, 134 L.Ed.2d 498, on remand 924 P.2d 749, on remand 924 P.2d 751.

The Due Process Clause does not prevent states from requiring defendants who claim they are incompetent to stand trial to bear the burden of proving incompetence by a preponderance of the evidence. Medina v. California (U.S.Cal. 1992) 112

S.Ct. 2572, 505 U.S. 437, 120 L.Ed.2d 353, rehearing denied 113 S.Ct. 19, 505 U.S. 1244, 120 L.Ed.2d 946.

State procedures for criminal prosecutions, including the burden of producing evidence and burden of persuasion, are not proscribed by the Due Process Clause unless they offend some principle of justice so rooted in the public tradition and conscience as to be ranked fundamental; the balancing test for evaluating procedural due process claims set forth in Matthews v Eldridge, 424 US 319 (1976) does not apply to state rules of criminal procedure. Medina v. California (U.S.Cal. 1992) 112 S.Ct. 2572, 505 U.S. 437, 120 L.Ed.2d 353, rehearing denied 113 S.Ct. 19, 505 U.S. 1244, 120 L.Ed.2d 946.

Under the law of Ohio, a criminal defendant is presumed to be competent to stand trial. Zuern v. Tate (S.D.Ohio, 03-30-2000) 101 F.Supp.2d 948, affirmed in part, reversed in part 336 F.3d 478, certiorari denied 124 S.Ct. 1456, 540 U.S. 1198, 158 L.Ed.2d 113. Criminal Law ⚿ 625.15

8. —— Duty of court, raising issue of competence

Trial court that accepted defendant's guilty plea to one count of telecommunications harassment and two counts of unlawful possession of dangerous ordnance was not required to inquire into defendant's competency, even though trial court noted at sentencing hearing that defendant was diagnosed as bipolar and that he had no criminal history prior to taking medication for the condition; defendant did not request competency hearing, mental illness was not the equivalent of incompetence, and record did not contain such indicia of incompetence as to necessitate a hearing. State v. Senich (Ohio App. 8 Dist., Cuyahoga, 08-11-2005) No. 85378, 2005-Ohio-4147, 2005 WL 1926036, Unreported. Criminal Law ⚿ 625.10(2.1)

Trial court is not required to refer a defendant for evaluation when the issue of the defendant's competency to stand trial is raised. State v. Burnett (Ohio App. 2 Dist., Darke, 01-07-2005) No. CIV.A. 1638, 2005-Ohio-49, 2005 WL 32797, Unreported. Mental Health ⚿ 434

Denial of request for pretrial competency hearing, made by stalking defendant's counsel on ground defendant had not been taking his psychotropic medications for anxiety and depression, was not reversible error; court inquired extensively of defendant regarding his understanding of procedures, purposes and nature of actions against him, and defendant gave cogent, cohesive and reasonable arguments regarding why he wanted to go to trial. State v. Arnott (Ohio App. 9 Dist., Summit, 01-05-2005) No. 21989, 2005-Ohio-3, 2005 WL 17870, Unreported. Criminal Law ⚿ 1166(12)

Assuming defendant properly raised issue of his competency prior to trial and that hearing on competency prior to guilty plea was mandatory, failing to hold such hearing was harmless error in prosecution for aggravated disorderly conduct, where record failed to reveal sufficient indicia of defendant's incompetency. State v. Hackathorn (Ohio App. 11 Dist., Ashtabula, 12-10-2004) No. 2004-A-0008, 2004-Ohio-6694, 2004 WL 2860898, Unreported. Criminal Law ⚿ 1167(5)

Trial court was under no duty to order competency hearing before accepting guilty plea to aggravated disorderly conduct, where it was clear from transcript of defendant's initial appearance that defendant understood what court explained, defendant asked questions regarding court proceedings, defendant admitted that he was guilty, and defendant was given meaning of pleading guilty or not guilty. State v. Hackathorn (Ohio App. 11 Dist., Ashtabula, 12-10-2004) No. 2004-A-0008, 2004-Ohio-6694, 2004 WL 2860898, Unreported. Criminal Law ⚿ 273(2)

Hearing on defendant's competency before accepting his guilty plea was not mandatory in prosecution for aggravated disorderly conduct, where defendant made no explicit request prior to trial for competency hearing. State v. Hackathorn (Ohio App. 11 Dist., Ashtabula, 12-10-2004) No. 2004-A-0008, 2004-Ohio-6694, 2004 WL 2860898, Unreported. Criminal Law ⚿ 273(2)

Trial court was not under a duty to conduct competency hearing before accepting juvenile's admission to charge of rape, given absence of evidence that juvenile acted irrationally at any stage of the proceedings or exhibited signs of unusual behavior and absence of medical evidence illustrating juvenile's alleged incompetence. In re Wood (Ohio App. 9 Dist., Medina, 12-08-2004) No. 04CA0005-M, 2004-Ohio-6539, 2004 WL 2808913, Unreported, appeal not allowed 105 Ohio St.3d 1518, 826 N.E.2d 315, 2005-Ohio-1880. Infants ⚿ 153

Trial court's failure to conduct pretrial competency hearing to restore defendant's competency prior to retrial in felonious assault prosecution was reversible error; on remand for new trial, trial court committed defendant for treatment upon finding him incompetent to stand trial, but ultimately commenced retrial proceedings without requisite findings to evince the restoration of defendant's competency. State v. Jackson (Ohio App. 8 Dist., Cuyahoga, 07-01-2004) No. 82652, 2004-Ohio-3474, 2004 WL 1472021, Unreported. Criminal Law ⚿ 625(3); Criminal Law ⚿ 1166(12)

Trial court acted within its discretion in denying defendant's motion for competency evaluation in prosecution for aggravated vehicular homicide, even though there was evidence that defendant had difficulty facing up to the possibility that he might be convicted of the charge, where there was no evidence that defendant did not comprehend the nature of the proceedings, no evidence that defendant was unable to counsel with his lawyer, and no evidence that defendant had any previous psychiatric illness. State v. Carson (Ohio App. 2 Dist., Greene, 11-07-2003) No. 2002-CA-73, 2003-Ohio-5958, 2003 WL 22532814, Unreported, appeal not allowed 101 Ohio St.3d 1489, 805 N.E.2d 540, 2004-Ohio-1293, dismissal of post-conviction relief affirmed 2004-Ohio-2741, 2004 WL 1178752. Criminal Law ⚿ 625.10(3)

Trial court was not required to hold competency hearing in prosecution for rape, where issue of defendant's competency was not raised prior to sentencing and nothing in plea or sentencing transcript suggested that defendant was incompetent during proceedings. State v. Rittner (Ohio App. 6 Dist., Fulton, 09-30-2003) No. F-02-034, 2003-Ohio-5201, 2003 WL 22234188, Unreported. Criminal Law ⚷ 625.10(4)

Record did not contain sufficient indicia of incompetence that put the juvenile court on notice that it should have sua sponte held competency hearing following juvenile's guilty plea; record's indication that juvenile had mental illness or was mentally retarded did not, in itself, support claim of incompetence, and statements regarding where he and his father lived did not indicate that juvenile was confused or illogical. In re Adams (Ohio App. 7 Dist., Mahoning, 07-29-2003) No. 01 CA 237, No. 01 CA 238, No. 02 CA 120, 2003-Ohio-4112, 2003 WL 21783682, Unreported. Infants ⚷ 203

Post-conviction relief court did not err in failing to find that defendant was incompetent to stand trial, even though neuropsychologist, who had previously determined that defendant was not incompetent, offered post-sentencing opinion that defendant was not competent to stand trial; demand letter from defendant to his attorney that formed alleged basis for neuropsychologist's change of opinion contained no new information regarding defendant's competency, trial counsel testified that defendant communicated appropriately with counsel during trial, and defendant acted and responded appropriately during trial. State v. Braden (Ohio App. 10 Dist., Franklin, 06-10-2003) No. 02AP-954, 2003-Ohio-2949, 2003 WL 21321457, Unreported, appeal not allowed 100 Ohio St.3d 1431, 797 N.E.2d 511, 2003-Ohio-5396. Criminal Law ⚷ 1618(5)

Trial court was not required to refer defendant for competency evaluation in light of remarks he made to court on day he entered guilty plea to rape, as there was nothing in plea colloquy between court and defendant which indicated that defendant was unable at that time to understand nature of proceedings or was unable to counsel with his lawyer. State v. Scurlock (Ohio App. 2 Dist., Clark, 03-07-2003) No. 2002-CA-34, 2003-Ohio-1052, 2003 WL 864174, Unreported, motion for delayed appeal denied 99 Ohio St.3d 1466, 791 N.E.2d 982, 2003-Ohio-3669, habeas corpus dismissed 2005 WL 1189831. Criminal Law ⚷ 273(2)

Capital murder defendant's decision to limit presentation of mitigating evidence and his suicide attempt nine months before trial did not constitute sufficient indicia to trigger trial court's duty to sua sponte order evaluation of his competence to stand trial; despite defendant's attempted suicide, record did not contain any specific facts suggesting that defendant lacked competency to stand trial, no evidence indicated that defendant was ever treated or hospitalized for mental disorders, or that his friends or family questioned his sanity, and there were no events during trial indicating any lack of competence. State v. Barton (Ohio, 04-05-2006) 108 Ohio St.3d 402, 844 N.E.2d 307, 2006-Ohio-1324. Criminal Law ⚷ 625.10(2.1)

The decision as to whether to hold a competency hearing once trial has commenced is in the trial court's discretion. State v. Skatzes (Ohio, 12-08-2004) 104 Ohio St.3d 195, 819 N.E.2d 215, 2004-Ohio-6391. Criminal Law ⚷ 625.10(1)

Capital murder defendant was not entitled to present rebuttal evidence on the issue of whether he established good cause to a hold a competency hearing; statute governing a request for a competency hearing did not require the court to hold a hearing to determine good cause or allow the presentation of rebuttal testimony, and defendant never made an offer of proof to demonstrate that he had reliable rebuttal evidence. State v. Ahmed (Ohio, 08-25-2004) 103 Ohio St.3d 27, 813 N.E.2d 637, 2004-Ohio-4190, reconsideration denied 103 Ohio St.3d 1496, 816 N.E.2d 1081, 2004-Ohio-5605, certiorari denied 125 S.Ct. 1703, 544 U.S. 952, 161 L.Ed.2d 531, rehearing denied, rehearing denied 125 S.Ct. 2901, 162 L.Ed.2d 312. Criminal Law ⚷ 625.15

The trial court was not required to sua sponte order a competency evaluation for capital murder defendant; defendant made a pro se request for a competency evaluation during trial, jail personnel testified that defendant never complained of any medical, mental, or psychological condition prior to filing his motion, the court noted that defendant used correct legal terms in his pro se motion for a competency evaluation, and defendant assisted counsel subsequent to filing the motion. State v. Ahmed (Ohio, 08-25-2004) 103 Ohio St.3d 27, 813 N.E.2d 637, 2004-Ohio-4190, reconsideration denied 103 Ohio St.3d 1496, 816 N.E.2d 1081, 2004-Ohio-5605, certiorari denied 125 S.Ct. 1703, 544 U.S. 952, 161 L.Ed.2d 531, rehearing denied, rehearing denied 125 S.Ct. 2901, 162 L.Ed.2d 312. Criminal Law ⚷ 625.10(4)

Capital murder defendant's decision to forego presentation of mitigation evidence, without more, did not require trial court to sua sponte inquire into his competence; trial court's assessment that defendant's disruptive conduct, which required his removal from courtroom on several occasions, evidenced pique rather than mental instability, was entitled to deference, defense counsel made no suggestion that defendant might lack competence to waive mitigation, and defendant's behavior did not inherently raise questions concerning his capacity to understand difference between life and death, to fully comprehend ramifications of his decision, or to reason logically. State v. Cowans (Ohio, 10-20-1999) 87 Ohio St.3d 68, 717 N.E.2d 298, 1999-Ohio-250, reconsideration denied 87 Ohio St.3d 1462, 720 N.E.2d 543, certiorari denied 120 S.Ct. 1839, 529 U.S. 1102, 146 L.Ed.2d 782. Sentencing And Punishment ⚷ 1792

Trial judge could use her own observations and opinions of defendant in determining his competency where she did not base her entire finding of competency solely on her observations. State v. Stanley (Ohio App. 1 Dist., 06-25-1997) 121 Ohio

App.3d 673, 700 N.E.2d 881, dismissed, appeal not allowed 80 Ohio St.3d 1432, 685 N.E.2d 543, denial of post-conviction relief affirmed 82 Fed.Appx. 407, 2003 WL 22290187. Criminal Law ⚷ 625.15

Initial finding that defendant was incompetent to stand trial and was not restorable to competency within a year did not preclude any subsequent determination of competency. State v. Stanley (Ohio App. 1 Dist., 06-25-1997) 121 Ohio App.3d 673, 700 N.E.2d 881, dismissed, appeal not allowed 80 Ohio St.3d 1432, 685 N.E.2d 543, denial of post-conviction relief affirmed 82 Fed.Appx. 407, 2003 WL 22290187. Criminal Law ⚷ 625(3)

Trial court was not required sua sponte to conduct hearing on competency of capital murder defendant to enter pleas of no contest, absent any indicia of incompetence at time pleas were entered. State v. Spivey (Ohio, 04-22-1998) 81 Ohio St.3d 405, 692 N.E.2d 151, 1998-Ohio-437, stay granted 82 Ohio St.3d 1435, 694 N.E.2d 1372, certiorari denied 119 S.Ct. 226, 525 U.S. 898, 142 L.Ed.2d 186. Criminal Law ⚷ 275.3

Decision whether to hold midtrial competency hearing is normally a matter committed to the sound discretion of the trial court. State v. Berry (Ohio, 06-28-1995) 72 Ohio St.3d 354, 650 N.E.2d 433, 1995-Ohio-310, reconsideration denied 73 Ohio St.3d 1428, 652 N.E.2d 801, certiorari denied 116 S.Ct. 823, 516 U.S. 1097, 133 L.Ed.2d 766, stay denied 168 F.3d 261, rehearing and suggestion for rehearing en banc denied, certiorari denied 119 S.Ct. 1022, 525 U.S. 1132, 142 L.Ed.2d 973. Criminal Law ⚷ 625.10(1)

Although trial court cannot "punish" counsel by denying competency motion solely on basis of timeliness, timeliness can be issue in determining validity and merits of request. State v. Bailey (Ohio App. 11 Dist., 08-31-1992) 90 Ohio App.3d 58, 627 N.E.2d 1078, motion allowed 65 Ohio St.3d 1498, 605 N.E.2d 951, stay granted 66 Ohio St.3d 1433, 608 N.E.2d 762, appeal dismissed as improvidently allowed 68 Ohio St.3d 1212, 624 N.E.2d 1062, 1994-Ohio-516. Criminal Law ⚷ 625.10(1)

Trial court did not abuse its discretion in not ordering evaluation of defendant's competency to stand trial; trial court conducted interview in which defendant stated that he fully understood court's explanation of charges against him, defendant's responses to court's questions were totally coherent, and, although defendant stated that he was experiencing mental problems, there was no indication that these problems rendered him incapable of assisting counsel. State v. Bailey (Ohio App. 11 Dist., 08-31-1992) 90 Ohio App.3d 58, 627 N.E.2d 1078, motion allowed 65 Ohio St.3d 1498, 605 N.E.2d 951, stay granted 66 Ohio St.3d 1433, 608 N.E.2d 762, appeal dismissed as improvidently allowed 68 Ohio St.3d 1212, 624 N.E.2d 1062, 1994-Ohio-516. Mental Health ⚷ 434

A sua sponte inquiry into a defendant's competency is not required because of a defendant's allegedly irrational behavior of (1) wearing his orange prison jumpsuit at trial; (2) answering a question concerning whether counsel was correct with a response, "More so, yes"; and (3) not informing counsel of a potential alibi witness until several days before trial since such behavior is not irrational to the extent that would require an inquiry into competency; the defendant felt the clothes he wore for trial did not matter, and when the court again sought a response to the question he replied "Yes"; and a medical report signed by a psychiatrist found the defendant competent to stand trial. State v. Draughn (Muskingum 1992) 76 Ohio App.3d 664, 602 N.E.2d 790.

A trial court has no duty to call its own witnesses in mitigation or appoint an independent attorney to do so after a defendant instructs his counsel not to call witnesses whose testimony has been arranged and who decides to present his own unsworn statement; such behavior by the defendant, moreover, does not alone compel the court to conduct a competency hearing, nor is counsel's failure to request such a hearing "ineffective assistance." State v. Tyler (Ohio 1990) 50 Ohio St.3d 24, 553 N.E.2d 576, rehearing denied 51 Ohio St.3d 704, 555 N.E.2d 322, certiorari denied 111 S.Ct. 371, 498 U.S. 951, 112 L.Ed.2d 334, reconsideration denied 75 Ohio St.3d 1474, 663 N.E.2d 1302, stay granted 76 Ohio St.3d 1463, 669 N.E.2d 249.

RC 2945.37(A) requires a trial court to hold a competency hearing if the issue of the defendant's competence to stand trial is raised before trial commences, but after trial begins the court need conduct a hearing on the defendant's competency "only for good cause shown," and the decision to hold a competency hearing once trial has commenced is in the court's discretion; therefore, where there is no evidence of irrational behavior of the defendant before or at trial, no suggestion by his counsel that the defendant was not competent, the trial court does not err by failing to conduct a sua sponte hearing on the defendant's competence to stand trial after he had been determined to be competent and the trial had commenced. State v. Rubenstein (Cuyahoga 1987) 40 Ohio App.3d 57, 531 N.E.2d 732.

Where there is an indication to a trial court that obstructive tactics put forth by the accused may be the result of a lack of mental capacity rather than an intelligent design, it has a duty to protect such accused from his own incapacity to properly defend himself, including the appointment of counsel over his protestations, when appropriate. State v. Jackson (Franklin 1973) 36 Ohio App.2d 164, 303 N.E.2d 903, 65 O.O.2d 253. Criminal Law ⚷ 641.7(1)

Where a defendant in a criminal case has interposed a defense of insanity, has been committed to the Lima state hospital and there is found capable of understanding the nature of the charges against him and of counseling in his own defense, a subsequent suggestion of insanity which does not inform the court that defendant has become insane since the prior determination of sanity was made, does not require the court to make a second examination into the question of the sanity of such defendant. State v. Jemison (Ohio 1968) 14 Ohio St.2d 47, 236

N.E.2d 538, 43 O.O.2d 115, certiorari denied 89 S.Ct. 312, 393 U.S. 943, 21 L.Ed.2d 280.

When an attorney for an accused suggests to the common pleas court that the accused is not then sane, and files a certificate of a reputable physician to that effect, a mandatory duty arises upon the court to proceed to examine into the question pursuant to RC 2945.37. State v. Jemison (Franklin 1967) 9 Ohio App.2d 227, 223 N.E.2d 904, 38 O.O.2d 256, reversed 14 Ohio St.2d 47, 236 N.E.2d 538, 43 O.O.2d 115, certiorari denied 89 S.Ct. 312, 393 U.S. 943, 21 L.Ed.2d 280.

Where a common pleas court receives notice in the manner prescribed by RC 2945.37 or reasonable grounds to believe an accused is not then sane have otherwise come to the attention of the court, a determination of present sanity or capacity of the accused to stand trial is not within the discretion of either counsel or the court and the notice cannot be withdrawn or waived. State v. Jemison (Franklin 1967) 9 Ohio App.2d 227, 223 N.E.2d 904, 38 O.O.2d 256, reversed 14 Ohio St.2d 47, 236 N.E.2d 538, 43 O.O.2d 115, certiorari denied 89 S.Ct. 312, 393 U.S. 943, 21 L.Ed.2d 280.

It is discretionary with the trial court, in a criminal case, to determine whether a jury should be impaneled to inquire into the sanity of the accused. State v. Keaton (Pickaway 1967) 9 Ohio App.2d 139, 223 N.E.2d 631, 38 O.O.2d 166, certiorari denied 88 S.Ct. 1092, 390 U.S. 971, 19 L.Ed.2d 1182.

If suggestion of insanity be made or such notice thereof comes to the court, the court is required either to proceed to examine into the question of sanity of the accused, or to impanel a jury for such purpose; it cannot, in such event, reject defendant's waiver and order defendant placed on trial for the crime charged. State v. Smith (Ohio 1931) 123 Ohio St. 237, 174 N.E. 768, 9 Ohio Law Abs. 286, 34 Ohio Law Rep. 71.

Under this section, if during trial it comes to court's notice that a person accused of crime whose trial is pending in court of common pleas is not then sane, the court is required either forthwith to proceed to examine into the question of sanity of such defendant, or to impanel a jury for such purpose. (See dissenting opinions by Marshal, C. J., and Day, J.) Evans v. State (Ohio 1930) 123 Ohio St. 132, 174 N.E. 348, 9 Ohio Law Abs. 61, 33 Ohio Law Rep. 485.

The word "examine," as used in this section, and the word "investigation," as used in GC 13441–4 (RC 2945.40), each contemplates a judicial inquiry; the word "examination," used in connection with legal proceedings, connotes examination under oath or affirmation. State ex rel. Smilack v. Bushong (Allen 1952) 93 Ohio App. 201, 112 N.E.2d 675, 50 O.O. 499, affirmed 159 Ohio St. 259, 111 N.E.2d 918, 50 O.O. 280.

The failure of a trial court to hold a competency hearing sua sponte during the trial is not error where the defendant's behavior, interrupting a witness's testimony with demands for a copy of the charges and preferring to wait outside during the trial, does not constitute good cause. State v Jackson, No. 52488 (8th Dist Ct App, Cuyahoga, 9–17–87).

9. Psychiatric examination

Refusing to grant rape defendant's request for evaluation as to whether he was competent to stand trial, which was made on morning trial was to begin, was harmless error, where defendant was articulate, understood nature of proceedings, and assisted in his defense and defense counsel stated that he had no reason to doubt defendant's competency. State v. Morales (Ohio App. 10 Dist., Franklin, 06-29-2004) No. 03AP318, No. 03AP319, 2004-Ohio-3391, 2004 WL 1446117, Unreported. Criminal Law ⚷ 1166(12)

Refusing to grant rape defendant's request for evaluation as to whether he was competent to stand trial was error, where request was made on morning trial was to begin. State v. Morales (Ohio App. 10 Dist., Franklin, 06-29-2004) No. 03AP318, No. 03AP319, 2004-Ohio-3391, 2004 WL 1446117, Unreported. Mental Health ⚷ 434

Trial court was not required to consider affidavit of defendant's expert presented with post-conviction petition to challenge competency evaluations conducted prior to and during trial by another expert; permitting expert to challenge prior competency determinations would prevent finality in any case involving psychological examinations, and encourage post-conviction expert shopping. State v. Braden (Ohio App. 10 Dist., Franklin, 06-10-2003) No. 02AP-954, 2003-Ohio-2949, 2003 WL 21321457, Unreported, appeal not allowed 100 Ohio St.3d 1431, 797 N.E.2d 511, 2003-Ohio-5396. Criminal Law ⚷ 1614

Denial of defendant's motion for a psychiatric examination, which defendant alleged that he needed in order to investigate and prepare a motion to suppress evidence, was not error; during hearing on defendant's motion defendant informed the court that he understood the possible sentence he faced, he understood the crimes he was charged with, and he understood the burden of proof, police detective testified that he provided defendant with his *Miranda* rights, defendant seemed attentive during their interview, defendant reviewed and signed his statement, defendant did not exhibit any unusual behavior during the interview, and that he was not suspicious about defendant's mental health, and defendant's confession to police was voluntary. State v. Woodley (Ohio App. 8 Dist., Cuyahoga, 04-17-2003) No. 80732, 2003-Ohio-1950, 2003 WL 1900935, Unreported, appeal not allowed 100 Ohio St.3d 1425, 797 N.E.2d 92, 2003-Ohio-5232. Mental Health ⚷ 434

Denial of pretrial psychological evaluation, based on concern for defendant's "attitude," did not constitute abuse of discretion, in prosecution for assault and conveying weapon into courthouse; counsel made no showing that defendant was unable to understand the nature of proceedings, and evaluation performed prior to sentencing indicated that she did not suffer from any mental illness or defect. State v. Akatova (Ohio App. 8 Dist., Cuyahoga,

01-23-2003) No. 80566, 2003-Ohio-279, 2003 WL 152931, Unreported. Mental Health ⚷ 434

Capital murder defendant's continual erratic behavior prior to and during trial did not compel finding that he was incompetent to stand trial, where at least six mental health examiners, in months prior to trial, found defendant competent to stand trial; neither defendant's emotional outbursts nor his potential for disruption negated findings of competence. State v. Vrabel (Ohio, 07-02-2003) 99 Ohio St.3d 184, 790 N.E.2d 303, 2003-Ohio-3193, motion granted 102 Ohio St.3d 1465, 809 N.E.2d 672, 2004-Ohio-2829. Mental Health ⚷ 432

Fact that court-appointed psychologist recently had developed "some strong feelings" that defendant was not sane enough to proceed with mitigation hearing or to be executed did not amount to good cause for holding midtrial competency hearing; psychologist examined defendant twice before trial and found him to be competent, and psychologist's later hypothesis was based on a series of assumptions and was only as good as the information supplied by defendant and defendant's family. State v. Berry (Ohio, 06-28-1995) 72 Ohio St.3d 354, 650 N.E.2d 433, 1995-Ohio-310, reconsideration denied 73 Ohio St.3d 1428, 652 N.E.2d 801, certiorari denied 116 S.Ct. 823, 516 U.S. 1097, 133 L.Ed.2d 766, stay denied 168 F.3d 261, rehearing and suggestion for rehearing en banc denied, certiorari denied 119 S.Ct. 1022, 525 U.S. 1132, 142 L.Ed.2d 973. Criminal Law ⚷ 625.10(3)

Defendant was not entitled to independent psychiatric evaluation under statutes governing questions of competency to stand trial and sanity at time of offense. State v. Corethers (Ohio App. 8 Dist., 08-23-1993) 90 Ohio App.3d 428, 629 N.E.2d 1052, dismissed, jurisdictional motion overruled 68 Ohio St.3d 1470, 628 N.E.2d 1389. Mental Health ⚷ 434

Trial court is not required to order evaluation of defendant's mental condition every time a defendant raises the issue, but instead is only required to give defendant or his counsel the chance to submit evidence on issue; if evidence raises genuine question as to defendant's competency, court can order that one or more evaluations be performed, and, if it does not, court can find defendant competent and proceed to trial. State v. Bailey (Ohio App. 11 Dist., 08-31-1992) 90 Ohio App.3d 58, 627 N.E.2d 1078, motion allowed 65 Ohio St.3d 1498, 605 N.E.2d 951, stay granted 66 Ohio St.3d 1433, 608 N.E.2d 762, appeal dismissed as improvidently allowed 68 Ohio St.3d 1212, 624 N.E.2d 1062, 1994-Ohio-516. Mental Health ⚷ 434

Defendant was mentally competent to enter guilty plea and trial court did not abuse its discretion in not ordering psychiatric examination sua sponte, despite possibility that defendant may have been suffering from some mental illness such as depression; defendant's concern over treatment did not mean that he was confused or did not comprehend what was occurring in proceeding. State v. Swift (Geauga 1993) 86 Ohio App.3d 407, 621 N.E.2d 513, stay granted 66 Ohio St.3d 1513, 614 N.E.2d 759, motion overruled 67 Ohio St.3d 1410, 615 N.E.2d 1044. Criminal Law ⚷ 273(2); Mental Health ⚷ 434

A defendant motion to set aside a jury verdict and enter a judgment of acquittal, or in the alternative, a new trial will be overruled where it is based on allegedly newly discovered evidence affecting the court's previous determination of the defendant's competency that, prior to trial, because of the defendant's refusal to eat at the jail, the defendant was examined without knowledge of defense counsel at a mental health center pursuant to the probate court's civil commitment procedure, since the examination of the defendant was not done for purposes of determining his competence to stand trial or whether he was not guilty by reason of insanity and the court had three separate reports concluding that the defendant was competent to stand trial. State v. Canton (Ohio Com.Pl. 1990) 61 Ohio Misc.2d 717, 583 N.E.2d 1390, affirmed.

A defendant in a criminal prosecution has no right, by statute or otherwise, to an independent psychiatric evaluation. State v. Marshall (Cuyahoga 1984) 15 Ohio App.3d 105, 472 N.E.2d 1139, 15 O.B.R. 195.

Alleged irregularities in committing defendant for psychiatric examination are not cognizable in habeas corpus where defendant was found sane and subsequently convicted. Grear v. Maxwell (C.A.6 (Ohio) 1966) 8 Ohio Misc. 210, 355 F.2d 991, 35 O.O.2d 333, 37 O.O.2d 268, certiorari denied 86 S.Ct. 1580, 384 U.S. 957, 16 L.Ed.2d 552, rehearing denied 87 S.Ct. 27, 385 U.S. 893, 17 L.Ed.2d 127.

Staff psychiatrist at medical center for federal prisoners at which defendant in bank robbery prosecution was hospitalized after being diagnosed with several disorders by licensed clinical psychologist was not required to discredit the psychologist's conclusions or find fault with his methodology in order to disagree with his conclusions on defendant's competency to stand trial; the psychologist observed defendant for less than two months, while the psychiatrist observed and examined defendant for about six months, the psychiatrist explained his disagreement with the psychologist's reasoning, and attached more significance to the effect defendant's troubled family relationships and his failure to maintain respectable employment had on his depressed mental state than had the psychologist. U.S. v. Hoyt (N.D.Ohio, 04-08-2002) 200 F.Supp.2d 790. Criminal Law ⚷ 625.15

Opinion of staff psychiatrist at medical center for federal prisoners at which defendant in bank robbery prosecution was hospitalized after being diagnosed with several disorders by licensed clinical psychologist, that defendant was competent to stand trial, and was not suffering from major depression, was supported by status reports and testimony of the psychiatrist, who spent substantial amount of time treating defendant over six months and had access to extensive medical history of defendant, and by the district court's observation of defendant's comportment, representations by defense counsel, and defendant's psychiatric history. U.S.

v. Hoyt (N.D.Ohio, 04-08-2002) 200 F.Supp.2d 790. Criminal Law ⚿ 625.15

RC 2945.37 and RC 2945.38 contemplate, as a condition precedent to the commitment of an accused to a hospital for the insane for observation, a formal examination and investigation by the court into the question of the sanity of the accused, especially where the accused objects to the procedure. State ex rel. Smilack v. Bushong (Ohio 1953) 159 Ohio St. 259, 111 N.E.2d 918, 50 O.O. 280.

Where insanity is not pleaded as a defense, the common pleas court is without jurisdiction to commit a person under indictment for crime to the Lima state hospital for observation, without notice to such person that his present insanity is under investigation and without according him the right to be heard and offer evidence in his own behalf. State ex rel. Smilack v. Bushong (Allen 1952) 93 Ohio App. 201, 112 N.E.2d 675, 50 O.O. 499, affirmed 159 Ohio St. 259, 111 N.E.2d 918, 50 O.O. 280.

10. Sufficiency of evidence—In general

Defendant failed to provide evidence that his alleged incompetence to stand trial invalidated his guilty pleas to felonious assault, endangering children, and domestic violence; defendant failed to include on appeal copy of psychiatric reports, on which trial court relied in making its competency determination, and record did not indicate defendant's "rambling" constituted incompetence, as record indicated only that defendant was somewhat hesitant to enter plea. State v. Smith (Ohio App. 8 Dist., Cuyahoga, 01-29-2004) No. 82676, 2004-Ohio-354, 2004 WL 170327, Unreported, motion for delayed appeal denied 103 Ohio St.3d 1403, 812 N.E.2d 1287, 2004-Ohio-3980. Criminal Law ⚿ 273(2)

Res judicata precluded defendant from challenging in post-conviction petition expert's competency evaluations conducted prior to and during trial; there was sufficient information in the record to challenge expert's opinion, such that competency could have been raised on direct appeal, and evidence dehors the record failed to prevent application of res judicata. State v. Braden (Ohio App. 10 Dist., Franklin, 06-10-2003) No. 02AP-954, 2003-Ohio-2949, 2003 WL 21321457, Unreported, appeal not allowed 100 Ohio St.3d 1431, 797 N.E.2d 511, 2003-Ohio-5396. Criminal Law ⚿ 1433(1)

Trial court did not abuse its discretion by not holding competency hearing at time defendant entered guilty plea to felonious assault, aggravated burglary, and domestic violence, even though defendant originally pleaded not guilty by reason of insanity; defendant withdrew not guilty plea, thus waiving right to competency hearing, defendant underwent two sanity evaluations and was deemed sane at time of offense, defendant was thoroughly questioned regarding acceptance of his plea, and defense counsel stated defendant was competent to stand trial. State v. Bellatto (Ohio App. 7 Dist., Mahoning, 03-11-2003) No. 00 CA 141, 2003-Ohio-1214, 2003 WL 1193773, Unreported, appeal not allowed 99 Ohio St.3d 1455, 790 N.E.2d 1219, 2003-Ohio-3396. Criminal Law ⚿ 273(2)

Defendant's decision to exercise his constitutional right to testify on his own behalf did not provide good cause for competency hearing during guilt phase of capital murder trial; defendant attempted to rebut the abundant testimony elicited against him. State v. Skatzes (Ohio, 12-08-2004) 104 Ohio St.3d 195, 819 N.E.2d 215, 2004-Ohio-6391. Criminal Law ⚿ 625.10(2.1)

Allegations that defendant did not understand consequences of answering questions with speculative responses during his trial testimony, that his use of colloquial phrases such as "I reckon" subjected him to ridicule by prosecutor, that he lost a significant amount of weight pending trial, and that he had been suffering from stress and confusion at time of prison takeover by inmates, did not provide good cause for competency hearing during guilt phase of capital murder trial, relating to prison riot and takeover. State v. Skatzes (Ohio, 12-08-2004) 104 Ohio St.3d 195, 819 N.E.2d 215, 2004-Ohio-6391. Criminal Law ⚿ 625.10(3)

Defendant's characterization of himself as "paranoid," fact he was known by the nickname "Crazy George," and his inability during his testimony to remember events from prison riot, did not provide good cause for competency evaluation, during guilt phase of capital murder trial relating to prison riot; such facts were not directly related to defendant's ability to understand nature of proceedings against him and to assist in his own defense. State v. Skatzes (Ohio, 12-08-2004) 104 Ohio St.3d 195, 819 N.E.2d 215, 2004-Ohio-6391. Mental Health ⚿ 434

Clinical psychologists were qualified to determine whether murder defendant's antidepressant medication would have affected his competency, and admission of their reports was not plain error; psychologists' evaluations revealed they were aware that defendant was taking or had taken antidepressant medication and considered its effect, defendant assured trial court that his ability to understand proceedings was not adversely affected by any prescription medication that he was taking, and defendant's taking of antidepressant medications would not have affected trial court's competency findings. State v. Mink (Ohio, 04-14-2004) 101 Ohio St.3d 350, 805 N.E.2d 1064, 2004-Ohio-1580, reconsideration denied 102 Ohio St.3d 1473, 809 N.E.2d 1159, 2004-Ohio-2830. Criminal Law ⚿ 1036.6; Mental Health ⚿ 434

Capital murder defendant's refusal to cooperate with counsel did not compel finding that he was incompetent to stand trial. State v. Vrabel (Ohio, 07-02-2003) 99 Ohio St.3d 184, 790 N.E.2d 303, 2003-Ohio-3193, motion granted 102 Ohio St.3d 1465, 809 N.E.2d 672, 2004-Ohio-2829. Mental Health ⚿ 432

Objective indications such as medical reports, specific references by defense counsel to irrational behavior, or the defendant's demeanor during trial are all relevant in determining whether good cause for a competency hearing was shown after the trial had begun. State v. Thomas (Ohio, 12-11-2002) 97 Ohio St.3d 309, 779 N.E.2d 1017, 2002-Ohio-6624, reconsideration denied 97 Ohio St.3d 1498, 780 N.E.2d 1022, 2002-Ohio-7248, stay granted 98 Ohio St.3d 1403, 781 N.E.2d 221, 2003-Ohio-40, certiorari denied 123 S.Ct. 2295, 539 U.S. 916, 156 L.Ed.2d 133. Criminal Law ⚿ 625.10(2.1)

Defendant was not entitled to competency hearing after commencement of trial; defendant's competency had been considered at pretrial competency hearing, and defendant's erratic behavior at trial, which included belching loudly and interrupting judge, illustrated pattern of rudeness rather than incompetency. State v. Franklin (Ohio, 10-16-2002) 97 Ohio St.3d 1, 776 N.E.2d 26, 2002-Ohio-5304, denial of post-conviction relief affirmed 2002-Ohio-2370, 2002 WL 1000415, appeal not allowed 98 Ohio St.3d 1422, 782 N.E.2d 77, 2003-Ohio-259, reconsideration denied 101 Ohio St.3d 1462, 804 N.E.2d 37, 2004-Ohio-823, appeal not allowed 108 Ohio St.3d 1475, 842 N.E.2d 1054, 2006-Ohio-665, reconsideration denied 97 Ohio St.3d 1486, 780 N.E.2d 288, 2002-Ohio-6866, stay granted 97 Ohio St.3d 1491, 780 N.E.2d 597, 2002-Ohio-7045, certiorari denied 123 S.Ct. 2249, 539 U.S. 905, 156 L.Ed.2d 115, denial of post-conviction relief affirmed 2005-Ohio-1361, 2005 WL 678925, appeal not allowed 106 Ohio St.3d 1464, 830 N.E.2d 1170, 2005-Ohio-3490, certiorari denied 126 S.Ct. 1352, 164 L.Ed.2d 64. Criminal Law ⚿ 625(3); Criminal Law ⚿ 625.10(3)

Capital murder defendant who requested pretrial hearing on competency was entitled to hearing, and thus trial court could not determine competency without hearing, although defendant refused to speak with competency examiners; defendant was found competent, without the benefit of a psychiatric evaluation, based on examiners' opinion that his refusal of examination was part of a deliberate ploy to disrupt trial proceedings and that he was competent, and defendant did not stipulate to that report. State v. Were (Ohio, 02-06-2002) 94 Ohio St.3d 173, 761 N.E.2d 591, 2002-Ohio-481, appeal after new trial 2005-Ohio-376, 2005 WL 267671, remanded 106 Ohio St.3d 1529, 835 N.E.2d 379, 2005-Ohio-5146, on remand 2006-Ohio-3511, 2006 WL 1867840. Criminal Law ⚿ 625.10(1)

Fact that capital murder defendant was foreign national and that English was not his first language did not evidence lack of competency, cultural or otherwise, to stand trial, where defendant was clearly capable of understanding nature and objective of proceedings against him and of assisting in his own defense; defendant's unsworn statement demonstrated that he understood and could speak English well, and defendant had lived in United States for seven years prior to murders and had completed two years of college before emigrating to United States. State v. Issa (Ohio, 08-29-2001) 93 Ohio St.3d 49, 752 N.E.2d 904, 2001-Ohio-1290, stay granted 93 Ohio St.3d 1437, 755 N.E.2d 900, denial of post-conviction relief affirmed 2001-Ohio-3910, 2001 WL 1635592, appeal not allowed 95 Ohio St.3d 1422, 766 N.E.2d 162, 2002-Ohio-1737, certiorari denied 122 S.Ct. 1445, 535 U.S. 974, 152 L.Ed.2d 387. Mental Health ⚿ 432

Trial court did not abuse its discretion by failing to order, sua sponte, a competency examination and competency hearing in capital murder prosecution, where defense counsel had not suggested that defendant lacked competence, defendant merely had been hospitalized several times in the past for mental illness, and defendant was articulate, had superior intelligence with no brain impairment, reported no hallucinations, was oriented as to time and place, and knew why he was in jail. State v. Hessler (Ohio, 09-27-2000) 90 Ohio St.3d 108, 734 N.E.2d 1237, 2000-Ohio-30, reconsideration denied 90 Ohio St.3d 1473, 738 N.E.2d 384, certiorari denied 121 S.Ct. 1662, 532 U.S. 998, 149 L.Ed.2d 643, stay granted 91 Ohio St.3d 1531, 747 N.E.2d 828. Criminal Law ⚿ 625.10(4); Mental Health ⚿ 434

There were insufficient indicia of incompetence to require trial court to conduct a competency hearing sua sponte; while defense psychologist testified that defendant suffered a mental illness, he was not certain how to categorize it and opined that defendant was competent to stand trial, and while defendant may have lacked judgment in rejecting his attorneys' advice, his competence was never an issue. State v. Smith (Ohio, 07-26-2000) 89 Ohio St.3d 323, 731 N.E.2d 645, 2000-Ohio-166, reconsideration denied 90 Ohio St.3d 1419, 735 N.E.2d 457, certiorari denied 121 S.Ct. 1131, 531 U.S. 1167, 148 L.Ed.2d 997. Criminal Law ⚿ 625.10(2.1)

Capital murder defendant did not carry his burden of proving incompetence to stand trial, though doctor wavered on issue of whether defendant was capable of going forward with trial due to his mental/emotional state following incidents in which he was accidentally shocked by stun belt and correctional officers attempted to restrain him, where doctor testified that defendant was competent to stand trial, and defendant still came to trial after stun belt incident and waived his right to jury trial and sat through a half a day of testimony. State v. Filiaggi (Ohio, 07-29-1999) 86 Ohio St.3d 230, 714 N.E.2d 867, 1999-Ohio-99, certiorari denied 120 S.Ct. 821, 528 U.S. 1090, 145 L.Ed.2d 691, denial of post-conviction relief affirmed 445 F.3d 851. Criminal Law ⚿ 625.15

Testimony of attorney regarding capital murder defendant's chances of prevailing in federal habeas corpus proceeding was irrelevant to matters at issue in hearing held to determine if defendant, whose conviction and death sentence had been affirmed on direct appeal, was competent to forego further challenges and submit to execution of sentence; while it was relevant whether defendant was able to listen to and consider attorneys' opinions, whether their opinions were right, wrong, or arguable was not relevant at all. State v. Berry (Ohio, 12-03-1997) 80 Ohio St.3d 371, 686 N.E.2d 1097, 1997-Ohio-336, stay granted 997 F.Supp. 916, vacated and remanded 144 F.3d 429, certiorari denied 119 S.Ct. 451, 525 U.S. 985, 142 L.Ed.2d 404, on remand 36 F.Supp.2d 1008, stay denied 85 Ohio

St.3d 1201, 706 N.E.2d 1273, 1999-Ohio-438. Sentencing And Punishment ⚷ 1793

Test in determining whether defendant is competent to forego further challenges to conviction or sentence is not whether defendant in fact cooperates with counsel, but whether he has sufficient mental capacity to do so. State v. Berry (Ohio, 12-03-1997) 80 Ohio St.3d 371, 686 N.E.2d 1097, 1997-Ohio-336, stay granted 997 F.Supp. 916, vacated and remanded 144 F.3d 429, certiorari denied 119 S.Ct. 451, 525 U.S. 985, 142 L.Ed.2d 404, on remand 36 F.Supp.2d 1008, stay denied 85 Ohio St.3d 1201, 706 N.E.2d 1273, 1999-Ohio-438. Criminal Law ⚷ 981(1); Criminal Law ⚷ 1026.10(1)

There was no evidence of petitioner's incompetence at his guilty plea to warrant inquiry into that matter upon trial court's own initiative, and thus petitioner failed to submit sufficient evidence demonstrating substantive grounds for relief, and therefore was not entitled to evidentiary hearing on his postconviction relief petition claiming that trial court erred in not ordering sua sponte a competency evaluation prior to accepting petitioner's guilty plea. State v. Blankenship (Ohio App. 12 Dist., 11-04-1996) 115 Ohio App.3d 512, 685 N.E.2d 831, dismissed, appeal not allowed 78 Ohio St.3d 1409, 675 N.E.2d 1249. Criminal Law ⚷ 1655(5)

Trial court cannot find defendant incompetent to stand trial solely because he is receiving prescription medication for some mental condition such as depression. State v. Borchers (Ohio App. 2 Dist., 02-10-1995) 101 Ohio App.3d 157, 655 N.E.2d 225, denial of post-conviction relief affirmed 1998 WL 471498. Mental Health ⚷ 432

Defendant may be emotionally disturbed or mentally ill, and yet be competent to stand trial. State v. Borchers (Ohio App. 2 Dist., 02-10-1995) 101 Ohio App.3d 157, 655 N.E.2d 225, denial of post-conviction relief affirmed 1998 WL 471498. Mental Health ⚷ 432

Trial court did not abuse its discretion by proceeding to sentencing phase of capital murder prosecution without holding competency hearing, despite defense counsel's representations that defendant may have withheld information regarding motive for killing, that defendant wanted to die and intended to tell jury so, that defendant had not cooperated in his defense, and that court-appointed psychologist recently had developed "some strong feelings" that defendant was not sane enough to proceed with mitigation hearing or to be executed; none of those matters, taken singularly or together, raised doubt as to defendant's competency to stand trial, and record indicated that at all times defendant understood nature and objective of the proceedings and was perfectly capable of assisting in his own defense if and when he chose to do so. State v. Berry (Ohio, 06-28-1995) 72 Ohio St.3d 354, 650 N.E.2d 433, 1995-Ohio-310, reconsideration denied 73 Ohio St.3d 1428, 652 N.E.2d 801, certiorari denied 116 S.Ct. 823, 516 U.S. 1097, 133 L.Ed.2d 766, stay denied 168 F.3d 261, rehearing and suggestion for rehearing en banc denied, certiorari denied 119 S.Ct. 1022, 525 U.S. 1132, 142 L.Ed.2d 973. Criminal Law ⚷ 625.10(3)

Defendant's failure to cooperate with counsel does not indicate that defendant was incapable of assisting with his defense so as to warrant midtrial competency hearing. State v. Berry (Ohio, 06-28-1995) 72 Ohio St.3d 354, 650 N.E.2d 433, 1995-Ohio-310, reconsideration denied 73 Ohio St.3d 1428, 652 N.E.2d 801, certiorari denied 116 S.Ct. 823, 516 U.S. 1097, 133 L.Ed.2d 766, stay denied 168 F.3d 261, rehearing and suggestion for rehearing en banc denied, certiorari denied 119 S.Ct. 1022, 525 U.S. 1132, 142 L.Ed.2d 973. Criminal Law ⚷ 625.10(3)

Defense counsel's statement that defendant was "sick" for withholding information concerning possible motive for killing did not amount to good cause for holding midtrial competency hearing; defense counsel's statement was not particularly persuasive evidence that defendant was not competent. State v. Berry (Ohio, 06-28-1995) 72 Ohio St.3d 354, 650 N.E.2d 433, 1995-Ohio-310, reconsideration denied 73 Ohio St.3d 1428, 652 N.E.2d 801, certiorari denied 116 S.Ct. 823, 516 U.S. 1097, 133 L.Ed.2d 766, stay denied 168 F.3d 261, rehearing and suggestion for rehearing en banc denied, certiorari denied 119 S.Ct. 1022, 525 U.S. 1132, 142 L.Ed.2d 973. Criminal Law ⚷ 625.10(3)

Defendant's willingness to talk to police about murder did not indicate that defendant was insane or was incompetent to stand trial so as to warrant midtrial competency hearing. State v. Berry (Ohio, 06-28-1995) 72 Ohio St.3d 354, 650 N.E.2d 433, 1995-Ohio-310, reconsideration denied 73 Ohio St.3d 1428, 652 N.E.2d 801, certiorari denied 116 S.Ct. 823, 516 U.S. 1097, 133 L.Ed.2d 766, stay denied 168 F.3d 261, rehearing and suggestion for rehearing en banc denied, certiorari denied 119 S.Ct. 1022, 525 U.S. 1132, 142 L.Ed.2d 973. Criminal Law ⚷ 625.10(3)

Fact that even prosecutor admitted that defendant suffered from mental illness did not amount to good cause to hold midtrial competency hearing; term "mental illness" did not necessarily equate with legal incompetency. State v. Berry (Ohio, 06-28-1995) 72 Ohio St.3d 354, 650 N.E.2d 433, 1995-Ohio-310, reconsideration denied 73 Ohio St.3d 1428, 652 N.E.2d 801, certiorari denied 116 S.Ct. 823, 516 U.S. 1097, 133 L.Ed.2d 766, stay denied 168 F.3d 261, rehearing and suggestion for rehearing en banc denied, certiorari denied 119 S.Ct. 1022, 525 U.S. 1132, 142 L.Ed.2d 973. Criminal Law ⚷ 625.10(3)

Mentally ill defendant may be legally competent to stand trial. State v. Berry (Ohio, 06-28-1995) 72 Ohio St.3d 354, 650 N.E.2d 433, 1995-Ohio-310, reconsideration denied 73 Ohio St.3d 1428, 652 N.E.2d 801, certiorari denied 116 S.Ct. 823, 516 U.S. 1097, 133 L.Ed.2d 766, stay denied 168 F.3d 261, rehearing and suggestion for rehearing en banc denied, certiorari denied 119 S.Ct. 1022, 525 U.S. 1132, 142 L.Ed.2d 973. Mental Health ⚷ 432

Relevant considerations in determining competency of defendant to stand trial include doubts expressed by counsel as to defendant's competence, evidence of irrational behavior, defendant's demeanor at trial, and prior medical opinion relating to competence to stand trial. State v. Corethers (Ohio App. 8 Dist., 08-23-1993) 90 Ohio App.3d 428, 629 N.E.2d 1052, dismissed, jurisdictional motion overruled 68 Ohio St.3d 1470, 628 N.E.2d 1389. Criminal Law ⚿ 625.15

A trial court has no duty to call its own witnesses in mitigation or appoint an independent attorney to do so after a defendant instructs his counsel not to call witnesses whose testimony has been arranged and who decides to present his own unsworn statement; such behavior by the defendant, moreover, does not alone compel the court to conduct a competency hearing, nor is counsel's failure to request such a hearing "ineffective assistance." State v. Tyler (Ohio 1990) 50 Ohio St.3d 24, 553 N.E.2d 576, rehearing denied 51 Ohio St.3d 704, 555 N.E.2d 322, certiorari denied 111 S.Ct. 371, 498 U.S. 951, 112 L.Ed.2d 334, reconsideration denied 75 Ohio St.3d 1474, 663 N.E.2d 1302, stay granted 76 Ohio St.3d 1463, 669 N.E.2d 249.

Psychogenic amnesia, resulting in a defendant's inability to remember events related to the alleged crime, does not alone establish that the defendant is incompetent to stand trial. State v. Brooks (Ohio 1986) 25 Ohio St.3d 144, 495 N.E.2d 407, 25 O.B.R. 190, certiorari denied 107 S.Ct. 1330, 479 U.S. 1101, 94 L.Ed.2d 182, rehearing denied 107 S.Ct. 1915, 481 U.S. 1025, 95 L.Ed.2d 520.

The testimony of an examining psychiatrist that a defendant understands the nature and facts of charges, is capable of assisting in his own defense, and refuses to cooperate by deliberate act rather than because of illness is sufficient to support a finding of competence to stand trial. State v. Marshall (Cuyahoga 1984) 15 Ohio App.3d 105, 472 N.E.2d 1139, 15 O.B.R. 195.

The antics of a defendant during trial do not make additional inquiry into his competency necessary where an examining psychiatrist testified at the competency hearing that the defendant's behavior and refusal to cooperate are intentional acts rather than the results of illness. State v. Marshall (Cuyahoga 1984) 15 Ohio App.3d 105, 472 N.E.2d 1139, 15 O.B.R. 195.

Defendant is not competent to stand trial if he lacks sufficient present ability to consult with his lawyer with reasonable degree of rational understanding and rational as well as factual understanding of proceedings against him. Franklin v. Francis (S.D.Ohio, 02-27-1998) 997 F.Supp. 916, vacated and remanded 144 F.3d 429, certiorari denied 119 S.Ct. 451, 525 U.S. 985, 142 L.Ed.2d 404, on remand 36 F.Supp.2d 1008. Mental Health ⚿ 432

Factors relevant to defendant's competence to stand trial include irrational behavior, demeanor at trial, and any prior medical opinions on competence. Franklin v. Francis (S.D.Ohio, 02-27-1998) 997 F.Supp. 916, vacated and remanded 144 F.3d 429, certiorari denied 119 S.Ct. 451, 525 U.S. 985, 142 L.Ed.2d 404, on remand 36 F.Supp.2d 1008. Mental Health ⚿ 432

A defendant is competent to stand trial if he has sufficient present ability to consult with his lawyer with a reasonable degree of rational understanding, and if he has a rational and factual understanding of the proceedings against him. State v. Bevins (Ohio App. 1 Dist., Hamilton, 03-22-2002) No. C-010316, No. C-010317, 2002-Ohio-1975, 2002 WL 440753, Unreported, appeal not allowed 96 Ohio St.3d 1439, 770 N.E.2d 1048, 2002-Ohio-3344. Mental Health ⚿ 432

Enactment of RC 2945.37 providing that defendant should not be found incompetent to stand trial solely because he is receiving drugs without which he might become incompetent to stand trial, rendered appeal from determination that such a defendant was incompetent moot. State ex rel. Woods v. Kraft (Ohio 1979) 58 Ohio St.2d 251, 389 N.E.2d 860, 12 O.O.3d 245.

Where court of appeals found that a person committed to Lima state hospital was of sufficient soundness of mind to understand and appreciate nature of charge against him, to comprehend his situation and was mentally capable of furnishing his counsel the facts essential to presentation of a proper defense, and the record does not warrant reversal of such finding, then court acted properly in ordering his release from hospital and remanding him to custody of sheriff in proper county for trial. State ex rel. Townsend v. Bushong (Ohio 1946) 146 Ohio St. 271, 65 N.E.2d 407, 32 O.O. 289.

The juvenile court may properly adopt the adult competency to stand trial standard in determining competency for a juvenile delinquency adjudication, so long as the court assesses juveniles by juvenile norms rather than adult norms. In re Johnson, No. 7998 (2d Dist Ct App, Montgomery, 10–25–83).

11. —— Indicia of incompetence, sufficiency of evidence

Term "mental illness" does not necessarily equate with the definition of legal incompetency to stand trial; defendant may be emotionally disturbed or even psychotic and still be capable of understanding the charges against him and of assisting his counsel. State v. Smith (Ohio, 07-26-2000) 89 Ohio St.3d 323, 731 N.E.2d 645, 2000-Ohio-166, reconsideration denied 90 Ohio St.3d 1419, 735 N.E.2d 457, certiorari denied 121 S.Ct. 1131, 531 U.S. 1167, 148 L.Ed.2d 997. Mental Health ⚿ 432

Evidence presented at competency hearing and experts' reports did not support finding that mentally retarded juvenile was competent to stand trial; experts' reports and testimony were irreparably muddled with incorrect standards of law and inappropriate judgments pertaining to moral responsibility, and evidence appeared to establish prima facie case that juvenile did not understand nature of proceedings against him and was incapable of assisting in his own defense. In re Williams (Ohio App. 2 Dist., 05-23-1997) 116 Ohio App.3d 237, 687 N.E.2d 507, appeal not allowed 80 Ohio St.3d 1415, 684 N.E.2d 706. Infants ⚿ 208

Having mental illness is not necessarily equivalent to being legally incompetent to stand trial; incompetency must not be equated with mere mental or emotional instability or even with outright insanity, as defendant may be emotionally disturbed or even psychotic and still be capable of understanding charges against him and of assisting counsel. State v. Blankenship (Ohio App. 12 Dist., 11-04-1996) 115 Ohio App.3d 512, 685 N.E.2d 831, dismissed, appeal not allowed 78 Ohio St.3d 1409, 675 N.E.2d 1249. Mental Health ⚿ 432

12. —— Indicia of competence, sufficiency of evidence

Evidence supported finding that defendant was competent to stand trial on charges of rape, even though he suffered from mild or borderline mental retardation and was incapable of fully comprehending complex legal issues, where defense expert found that defendant understood charges against him and possible penalties associated with those charges, and that he was capable of assisting in planning of legal strategy in close collaboration with his attorney, and, like vast majority of criminal defendants, defendant did not fully understand the legal process, which was precisely the reason why legal counsel was provided to him at state expense. State v. McColgan (Ohio App. 10 Dist., Franklin, 02-15-2005) No. 04AP-120, 2005-Ohio-580, 2005 WL 351758, Unreported. Criminal Law ⚿ 625.15

Credible and reliable evidence supported conclusion that defendant was legally competent to stand trial for capital murder of corrections officer; prison employees who had numerous interactions with defendant testified that his behavior was always responsive and appropriate. State v. Were (Ohio App. 1 Dist., Hamilton, 02-04-2005) No. C-030485, 2005-Ohio-376, 2005 WL 267671, Unreported, remanded 106 Ohio St.3d 1529, 835 N.E.2d 379, 2005-Ohio-5146, on remand 2006-Ohio-3511, 2006 WL 1867840. Criminal Law ⚿ 625.15

Record supported trial court's conclusion that defendant was competent to stand trial, even though one doctor found that defendant was incompetent based on multiple psychiatric disorders, where other doctor found that defendant was competent, testifying that defendant was not impaired in his ability to participate in his defense and understand charges against him and that defendant understood roles of various people in courtroom and knew whether particular act was right or wrong or criminal or not criminal. State v. Mosley (Ohio App. 7 Dist., Mahoning, 09-23-2004) No. 03 MA 52, 2004-Ohio-5187, 2004 WL 2334381, Unreported. Criminal Law ⚿ 625.15

Evidence supported finding that defendant was competent to stand trial, even though defendant suffered from mild mental retardation; expert witness testified that defendant had basic factual knowledge of charges, possible pleas, and potential outcomes, and that he was able to assist his attorney in his defense. State v. Wenzler (Ohio App. 2 Dist., Greene, 04-09-2004) No. 2003-CA-16, 2004-Ohio-1811, 2004 WL 758384, Unreported. Criminal Law ⚿ 625.15

Defendant was not rendered incompetent to enter guilty plea to aggravated murder due to fact that he was taking antidepressant medication, even though defendant stated during plea hearing that medication caused confusion, where defendant also stated that he took medication twice daily but did not take it on morning of hearing and that there was nothing affecting his ability to understand plea proceedings, defendant engaged in lengthy colloquy with trial court, and there was no evidence that medication was causing confusion when defendant pleaded guilty. State v. Doak (Ohio App. 7 Dist., Columbiana, 03-22-2004) No. 03 CO 15, No. 03 CO 31, 2004-Ohio-1548, 2004 WL 614851, Unreported, appeal not allowed 103 Ohio St.3d 1406, 812 N.E.2d 1288, 2004-Ohio-3980. Criminal Law ⚿ 273(2)

Trial judge determination that defendant was competent to stand trial, and thus competent to enter pleas of no contest, was not an abuse of discretion, even though defendant claimed to hear voices and hallucinate; two psychologists opined that defendant's claims of mental illness were false and determined that defendant had intentionally depressed his diagnostic test scores. State v. Johnson (Ohio App. 8 Dist., Cuyahoga, 05-08-2003) No. 81601, 2003-Ohio-2303, 2003 WL 21028319, Unreported. Criminal Law ⚿ 275.3; Mental Health ⚿ 432

Evidence was sufficient to support finding that murder defendant was competent to stand trial; evidence indicated defendant had a good understanding of the legal process and that his misunderstandings were not uncommon, and defendant's depressive attitude and his unwillingness to consider a plea bargain could have been construed as the attitude of one who believes himself innocent. State v. Young (Ohio App. 8 Dist., Cuyahoga, 01-23-2003) No. 80059, 2003-Ohio-272, 2003 WL 152818, Unreported. Criminal Law ⚿ 625.15

Evidence supported trial court's finding that defendant was competent to stand trial on charges of rape and gross sexual imposition (GSI), where expert's testimony at pretrial competency hearing, and his written report stating that defendant was sane and competent to stand for trial, provided trial court with reliable, credible evidence that defendant could understand nature and objective of proceedings against him and assist in his defense. State v. Neely (Ohio App. 12 Dist., Madison, 12-23-2002) No. CA2002-02-002, 2002-Ohio-7146, 2002 WL 31859454, Unreported. Criminal Law ⚿ 625.15

Psychologists adequately considered murder defendant's history of depression, his suicide attempts, and his hospitalization before determining that defendant was competent to stand trial, and trial court's reliance on that finding was not plain error; both psychologists provided trial court with expert advice on defendant's depression before concluding that defendant was competent, they addressed defendant's history of suicide attempts, their evaluations included references to defendant's earlier hospitalizations relayed by defendant himself, and defense stipulated to qualifications of psychologists and their findings that defendant was competent. State v. Mink (Ohio, 04-14-2004) 101 Ohio St.3d 350, 805 N.E.2d 1064, 2004-Ohio-1580, reconsideration denied 102 Ohio St.3d 1473, 809

N.E.2d 1159, 2004-Ohio-2830. Criminal Law ⚷ 1035(2); Mental Health ⚷ 434

Trial court did not abuse its discretion in finding capital murder defendant competent to stand trial, where such determination was supported by some reliable, credible evidence; at least six mental health examiners, in months prior to trial, found defendant competent to stand trial. State v. Vrabel (Ohio, 07-02-2003) 99 Ohio St.3d 184, 790 N.E.2d 303, 2003-Ohio-3193, motion granted 102 Ohio St.3d 1465, 809 N.E.2d 672, 2004-Ohio-2829. Criminal Law ⚷ 625.15

A defendant may be emotionally disturbed or even psychotic and still be capable of understanding the charges against him and of assisting his counsel. State v. Braden (Ohio, 04-02-2003) 98 Ohio St.3d 354, 785 N.E.2d 439, 2003-Ohio-1325, stay granted 98 Ohio St.3d 1542, 787 N.E.2d 5, 2003-Ohio-2002, denial of post-conviction relief affirmed 2003-Ohio-2949, 2003 WL 21321457, appeal not allowed 100 Ohio St.3d 1431, 797 N.E.2d 511, 2003-Ohio-5396, certiorari denied 124 S.Ct. 182, 540 U.S. 865, 157 L.Ed.2d 119, stay revoked 100 Ohio St.3d 1525, 800 N.E.2d 43, 2003-Ohio-6510. Mental Health ⚷ 432

Trial court's failure to find sua sponte that defendant was incompetent to stand trial was not error in capital murder prosecution; defendant showed he understood proceedings by meaningfully responding to court's questions about jury waiver, appointment of a lawyer, and other matters, defense counsel who represented defendant for roughly one year never suggested defendant was incompetent, and no lay or expert opinion indicated defendant was actually incompetent. State v. Thomas (Ohio, 12-11-2002) 97 Ohio St.3d 309, 779 N.E.2d 1017, 2002-Ohio-6624, reconsideration denied 97 Ohio St.3d 1498, 780 N.E.2d 1022, 2002-Ohio-7248, stay granted 98 Ohio St.3d 1403, 781 N.E.2d 221, 2003-Ohio-40, certiorari denied 123 S.Ct. 2295, 539 U.S. 916, 156 L.Ed.2d 133. Criminal Law ⚷ 625.10(4)

A defendant may be emotionally disturbed or even psychotic and still be capable of understanding the charges against him and of assisting his counsel and therefore competent to stand trial. State v. Hessler (Ohio, 09-27-2000) 90 Ohio St.3d 108, 734 N.E.2d 1237, 2000-Ohio-30, reconsideration denied 90 Ohio St.3d 1473, 738 N.E.2d 384, certiorari denied 121 S.Ct. 1662, 532 U.S. 998, 149 L.Ed.2d 643, stay granted 91 Ohio St.3d 1531, 747 N.E.2d 828. Mental Health ⚷ 432

Evidence that defendant attempted suicide while awaiting trial, was unwilling to attend court proceedings, and had apparent disagreements with counsel was insufficient to establish that he was incompetent to stand trial in aggravated murder prosecution, in view of expert testimony indicating that defendant was competent. State v. Carter (Ohio, 09-13-2000) 89 Ohio St.3d 593, 734 N.E.2d 345, 2000-Ohio-172, stay granted 90 Ohio St.3d 1446, 737 N.E.2d 51. Criminal Law ⚷ 625.15

Trial court acted within its discretion, in capital murder case, in denying defense counsel's motion for new trial which was based on claim that defendant was not competent to stand trial; presiding judge considered the additional medical evidence submitted by defendant, and judge's determination that defendant was competent to stand trial was properly based on court's own observations, as well as unrefuted representations of correctional officers who observed defendant showering, eating meals and conversing with other inmates, correctional officers and his attorneys. State v. Filiaggi (Ohio, 07-29-1999) 86 Ohio St.3d 230, 714 N.E.2d 867, 1999-Ohio-99, certiorari denied 120 S.Ct. 821, 528 U.S. 1090, 145 L.Ed.2d 691, denial of post-conviction relief affirmed 445 F.3d 851. Criminal Law ⚷ 913(1)

Capital murder defendant, whose conviction and death sentence had been affirmed on direct appeal, possessed mental capacity to appreciate his position and make rational choice with respect to continuing or abandoning further litigation, and thus was competent to forego further challenges and submit to execution of sentence; while defendant did have mental disorder, it did not substantially affect his ability to make decision, and defendant, while preferring freedom to death, also preferred speedy execution to incarceration during protracted legal struggle and believed that, even if his conviction was overturned, he would be retried and resentenced to death. State v. Berry (Ohio, 12-03-1997) 80 Ohio St.3d 371, 686 N.E.2d 1097, 1997-Ohio-336, stay granted 997 F.Supp. 916, vacated and remanded 144 F.3d 429, certiorari denied 119 S.Ct. 451, 525 U.S. 985, 142 L.Ed.2d 404, on remand 36 F.Supp.2d 1008, stay denied 85 Ohio St.3d 1201, 706 N.E.2d 1273, 1999-Ohio-438. Sentencing And Punishment ⚷ 1641

Defendant was competent to stand trial and enter guilty plea, despite fact that he was taking prescription drug, lithium, for depression, in view of evidence that defendant and his attorney had discussed plea agreement, in view of defendant's expression that he desired to proceed with entry of guilty plea, even though he had attended his father's funeral on that day, and in view of defendant's statement that he entered guilty plea voluntarily and he understood effect of his plea. State v. Borchers (Ohio App. 2 Dist., 02-10-1995) 101 Ohio App.3d 157, 655 N.E.2d 225, denial of post-conviction relief affirmed 1998 WL 471498. Criminal Law ⚷ 273(2)

Although defendant initially expressed lack of understanding regarding his right to compulsory process and how bill of information differed from indictment, following explanation of those matters defendant clearly indicated that he understood them, so that he was competent to stand trial and enter guilty plea. State v. Borchers (Ohio App. 2 Dist., 02-10-1995) 101 Ohio App.3d 157, 655 N.E.2d 225, denial of post-conviction relief affirmed 1998 WL 471498. Criminal Law ⚷ 273(2)

Professed wish for the death penalty, as opposed to life imprisonment, does not, by itself, call defendant's competency into question so as to warrant midtrial competency hearing. State v. Berry (Ohio, 06-28-1995) 72 Ohio St.3d 354, 650 N.E.2d 433,

1995-Ohio-310, reconsideration denied 73 Ohio St.3d 1428, 652 N.E.2d 801, certiorari denied 116 S.Ct. 823, 516 U.S. 1097, 133 L.Ed.2d 766, stay denied 168 F.3d 261, rehearing and suggestion for rehearing en banc denied, certiorari denied 119 S.Ct. 1022, 525 U.S. 1132, 142 L.Ed.2d 973. Criminal Law ⚷ 625.10(3)

Fact that defendant was removed, for disruptive behavior, from the courtroom did not indicate that defendant was incompetent to stand trial and thus did not warrant midtrial competency hearing, where incident was relatively minor and only happened once. State v. Berry (Ohio, 06-28-1995) 72 Ohio St.3d 354, 650 N.E.2d 433, 1995-Ohio-310, reconsideration denied 73 Ohio St.3d 1428, 652 N.E.2d 801, certiorari denied 116 S.Ct. 823, 516 U.S. 1097, 133 L.Ed.2d 766, stay denied 168 F.3d 261, rehearing and suggestion for rehearing en banc denied, certiorari denied 119 S.Ct. 1022, 525 U.S. 1132, 142 L.Ed.2d 973. Criminal Law ⚷ 625.10(3)

Court did not abuse its discretion in denying competency hearing prior to conducting probation revocation proceedings even though there was report indicating that probationer was incompetent to stand trial, where that report indicated that she understood that she was charged with probation violation and could be returned to hospital or reformatory. State v. Bell (Stark 1990) 66 Ohio App.3d 52, 583 N.E.2d 414, dismissed, jurisdictional motion overruled 52 Ohio St.3d 702, 556 N.E.2d 526. Sentencing And Punishment ⚷ 2009

13. Speedy trial

Court-ordered competency examination was not warranted, and defendant was therefore denied a speedy trial, where he did not demonstrate any irrational behavior, there was no prior medical evidence regarding his competency to stand trial, and the only reasons offered for the examination were long plea negotiations and defendant's failure to pay court costs in exchange for a dismissal of the charges. City of Columbus v. Cardinal (Ohio App. 10 Dist., Franklin, 12-09-2004) No. 04AP-229, No. 04AP-232, No. 04AP230, No. 04AP-233, No. 04AP-231, 2004-Ohio-6605, 2004 WL 2830782, Unreported. Criminal Law ⚷ 577.11(6)

Although the time within which an accused must be brought to trial may be tolled during the time when his competence to stand trial is being evaluated, when ten days have elapsed after the filing of the examiner's report and the statutorily mandated hearing has not been held, the time begins to run again. State v. Wilson (Fayette 1982) 7 Ohio App.3d 219, 454 N.E.2d 1348, 7 O.B.R. 281.

When an accused moves the court for an additional evaluation of his mental condition, the statutory period within which he must be brought to trial is tolled from time his motion is granted, and begins to run again on the date when the psychiatrist's report is due to be filed with the court, even if no report is filed on that date. State v. Wilson (Fayette 1982) 7 Ohio App.3d 219, 454 N.E.2d 1348, 7 O.B.R. 281.

The time within which an accused must be brought to trial by virtue of RC 2945.71 is tolled by the accused's plea of not guilty by reason of insanity, whether such plea contemplates insanity at the time of arraignment or insanity at the time the crime was committed. State v. Spratz (Ohio 1979) 58 Ohio St.2d 61, 388 N.E.2d 751, 12 O.O.3d 77. Criminal Law ⚷ 577.11(6)

An accused, committed pursuant to RC 2945.37 and RC 2945.38, can be held only for the period of time reasonably necessary to determine whether it is probable that he will attain the mental competency required to stand trial in the foreseeable future. Burton v. Reshetylo (Ohio 1974) 38 Ohio St.2d 35, 309 N.E.2d 907, 67 O.O.2d 53. Mental Health ⚷ 437

A court's persistent deference to a man who indicates that he is not competent to stand trial, and who is found to be incompetent, does not produce "unjustified delay." State v. Boham (Franklin 1971) 29 Ohio App.2d 142, 279 N.E.2d 609, 58 O.O.2d 205.

14. Insanity defense

Diagnosis of paranoid schizophrenia was not synonymous with incompetence to stand trial in capital murder prosecution. State v. Braden (Ohio, 04-02-2003) 98 Ohio St.3d 354, 785 N.E.2d 439, 2003-Ohio-1325, stay granted 98 Ohio St.3d 1542, 787 N.E.2d 5, 2003-Ohio-2002, denial of post-conviction relief affirmed 2003-Ohio-2949, 2003 WL 21321457, appeal not allowed 100 Ohio St.3d 1431, 797 N.E.2d 511, 2003-Ohio-5396, certiorari denied 124 S.Ct. 182, 540 U.S. 865, 157 L.Ed.2d 119, stay revoked 100 Ohio St.3d 1525, 800 N.E.2d 43, 2003-Ohio-6510. Sentencing And Punishment ⚷ 1793

Defendant's ability to determine right from wrong is appropriate inquiry in legal determination of sanity, not competency to stand trial. In re Williams (Ohio App. 2 Dist., 05-23-1997) 116 Ohio App.3d 237, 687 N.E.2d 507, appeal not allowed 80 Ohio St.3d 1415, 684 N.E.2d 706. Criminal Law ⚷ 48; Mental Health ⚷ 431; Mental Health ⚷ 432

Defendant in capital murder prosecution affirmatively waived his right to previously-requested competency hearing when he withdrew his plea of not guilty by reason of insanity, chose to proceed solely on not guilty plea and filed document acknowledging that he had knowingly and intelligently withdrawn any challenge to his competency to proceed with trial. State v. Eley (Ohio, 12-18-1996) 77 Ohio St.3d 174, 672 N.E.2d 640, 1996-Ohio-323, reconsideration denied 77 Ohio St.3d 1549, 674 N.E.2d 1187, certiorari denied 117 S.Ct. 2522, 521 U.S. 1124, 138 L.Ed.2d 1023, dismissal of post-conviction relief affirmed 2001-Ohio-3447, 2001 WL 1497095, appeal not allowed 94 Ohio St.3d 1506, 764 N.E.2d 1036, 2002-Ohio-5738. Criminal Law ⚷ 625.35

A competency hearing is not mandated by the entry of a not guilty by reason of insanity plea; failure to file a pretrial motion for a competency hearing waives the right to such a hearing. State v. Bekesz (Lake 1991) 75 Ohio App.3d 436, 599

N.E.2d 803, dismissed, jurisdictional motion overruled 62 Ohio St.3d 1494, 583 N.E.2d 966.

The common pleas court has jurisdiction to commit an accused to the Lima state hospital before indictment after an affidavit has been filed against such accused. In re Horvath (Ohio 1975) 42 Ohio St.2d 60, 325 N.E.2d 895, 71 O.O.2d 38. Mental Health ⚷ 436.1

Where a defendant, prior to trial on an indictment, is determined to be insane and is committed to the Lima state hospital until restored to reason, and, subsequent to such confinement, the defendant is found to have been sufficiently restored to reason so that he is capable of standing trial, such latter finding, upon the subsequent determination by the trial court that the defendant is not guilty by reason of insanity, is not sufficient to overcome the statutory presumption of RC 2945.39 that defendant's insanity continues. Fortune v. Reshetylo (Ohio 1973) 33 Ohio St.2d 22, 294 N.E.2d 880, 62 O.O.2d 342. Criminal Law ⚷ 311

In order to establish the defense of insanity where raised by pleas in a criminal proceeding, the accused must establish by a preponderance of the evidence that disease or other defect of his mind had so impaired his reason that, at the time of the criminal act with which he is charged, either he did not know that such act was wrong or he did not have the ability to refrain from doing that act. State v. Jackson (Ohio 1972) 32 Ohio St.2d 203, 291 N.E.2d 432, 61 O.O.2d 433, certiorari denied 93 S.Ct. 1539, 411 U.S. 909, 36 L.Ed.2d 199. Criminal Law ⚷ 570(2)

One accused of criminal conduct is not responsible for such criminal conduct if, at the time of such conduct, as a result of mental illness or defect, he does not have the capacity either to know the wrongfulness of his conduct or to conform his conduct to the requirements of the law. State v. Staten (Ohio 1971) 25 Ohio St.2d 107, 267 N.E.2d 122, 54 O.O.2d 235, vacated in part 92 S.Ct. 2869, 408 U.S. 938, 33 L.Ed.2d 759. Criminal Law ⚷ 48

In order to establish the defense of insanity, the accused must establish by a preponderance of the evidence that disease or other defect of his mind had so impaired his reason that, at the time of the criminal act with which he is charged, either he did not know that such act was wrong or he did not have the ability to refrain from doing that act. State v. Staten (Ohio 1969) 18 Ohio St.2d 13, 247 N.E.2d 293, 47 O.O.2d 82. Criminal Law ⚷ 570(2)

The legal test of insanity, whether the accused's mind was so inflicted with disease as to render him incapable of distinguishing between right and wrong as to the particular act done and as of the time when the act was done, is a test of responsibility rather than a medical test. State v. Colby (Ohio Com.Pl. 1966) 6 Ohio Misc. 19, 215 N.E.2d 65, 35 O.O.2d 61.

A finding by the jury, that defendant in a criminal case is sane, made in a preliminary hearing pursuant to this and next section, between the indictment and trial, is not admissible on behalf of state in trial of the case, in rebuttal of the evidence offered by defendant in support of the defense of insanity. State v. Hagert (Ohio 1944) 144 Ohio St. 316, 58 N.E.2d 764, 29 O.O. 454.

Where a state defendant demonstrates to the trial judge that his sanity at the time of the offense will be a significant issue at trial, the state must provide access to a psychiatrist to examine the defendant and assist him in the evaluation, preparation, and presentation of his defense where the state recognizes a defense of insanity and places the initial burden of producing evidence on the defendant. Ake v. Oklahoma (U.S.Okl. 1985) 105 S.Ct. 1087, 470 U.S. 68, 84 L.Ed.2d 53. Costs ⚷ 302.4

A trial judge having recent psychological reports that a defendant is competent to stand trial has no duty to impose a defense of "not guilty by reason of insanity" on the defendant, particularly where the defendant rejected the advice of three attorneys to offer the defense, said he was able to counsel with his attorney, and understood both the charges and the possible penalties confronting him. Foster v. Marshall (S.D.Ohio 1987) 687 F.Supp. 1174.

Under former GC 13577, 13614 (Repealed) a court of common pleas was authorized to commit to the Lima state hospital an accused person found to be insane upon suggestion of the prosecuting attorney made before trial. State ex rel. Diehlman v. Clark (Ohio 1921) 102 Ohio St. 404, 131 N.E. 734, 19 Ohio Law Rep. 68.

15. Probate court

A person committed to the Lima state hospital under the purported authority of RC 2945.37 and RC 2945.38, but who has not been indicted, is illegally restrained of his liberty and must be released forthwith from that hospital, provided, however, that if his mental condition is such that he is not sane and his release would result in his being dangerous to himself or to society the execution of the order of release will be suspended for a reasonable period of time to permit the probate division of an appropriate common pleas court, having jurisdiction, to cause his commitment to a proper institution. Burton v. Reshetylo (Allen 1973) 35 Ohio App.2d 113, 300 N.E.2d 249, 64 O.O.2d 234, affirmed 38 Ohio St.2d 35, 309 N.E.2d 907, 67 O.O.2d 53.

The mental capacity of one under indictment must be determined under the provisions of this section, and not by the probate judge. State ex rel. Davey v. Owen (Ohio 1937) 133 Ohio St. 96, 12 N.E.2d 144, 114 A.L.R. 686, 10 O.O. 102.

The authority of the common pleas court in a criminal prosecution to determine that the defendant is then insane under RC 2945.37 et seq. is an exception to the exclusiveness of the jurisdiction of the probate court over determinations concerning mental capacity. In re Moser, 19 Misc 81, 246 NE(2d) 626, 47 OO(2d) 420 (CP 1967).

Although the order of a probate court terminating a guardianship was intended as a finding concerning the ward's sanity, it would not deprive the common pleas court which had first determined under RC 2945.37 et seq., that such person was insane, of jurisdiction to consider this issue in a later civil action. In re Moser, 19 Misc 81, 246 NE(2d) 626, 47 OO(2d) 420 (CP 1967).

When a common pleas court which has committed a person to Lima state hospital until he be restored to his reason under RC 2945.37 et seq. is presented with the issue of his mental capacity to have executed a deed on a later date when the probate court had determined that a guardianship was no longer necessary for such person, this intervening order of the probate court does not preclude the consideration by such common pleas court of the issue, nor is such consideration a collateral attack on the action of the probate court, where the finding of the probate court that the guardianship should be terminated could be properly made without a determination of the ward's sanity. In re Moser, 19 Misc 81, 246 NE(2d) 626, 47 OO(2d) 420 (CP 1967).

16. Juvenile proceedings

Trial court's failure to hold competency hearing in delinquency proceeding was not harmless error, even though examiner's written report had concluded that juvenile was competent to proceed, since juvenile's counsel would have had an opportunity at competency hearing to cross-examine that examiner. In re B.M.R. (Ohio App. 2 Dist., Miami, 11-04-2005) No. 2005 CA 1, No. 2005 CA 18, 2005-Ohio-5911, 2005 WL 2978951, Unreported. Infants ⚷ 253

Juvenile's subsequent admission to rape charge did not constitute a waiver of his right to a competency determination in delinquency proceeding. In re B.M.R. (Ohio App. 2 Dist., Miami, 11-04-2005) No. 2005 CA 1, No. 2005 CA 18, 2005-Ohio-5911, 2005 WL 2978951, Unreported. Infants ⚷ 199; Infants ⚷ 203

Trial court's failure to hold competency hearing in delinquency proceeding after juvenile's counsel raised the issue in a timely fashion, and its reliance instead on examiner's written report, violated state statute governing competence to stand trial as well as juvenile's due process rights. In re B.M.R. (Ohio App. 2 Dist., Miami, 11-04-2005) No. 2005 CA 1, No. 2005 CA 18, 2005-Ohio-5911, 2005 WL 2978951, Unreported. Constitutional Law ⚷ 255(4); Infants ⚷ 203

Evidence was sufficient to support finding that juvenile was competent to stand trial in delinquency proceeding, despite juvenile's status as a prior mental health patient; physician found juvenile competent to stand trial in prior delinquency proceeding, same physician again evaluated juvenile and found him competent to stand trial, stating juvenile could understand the nature and objectives of the proceedings against him, and that he was capable of assisting his attorney in his own defense. In re Gooch (Ohio App. 2 Dist., Montgomery, 12-13-2002) No. 19339, 2002-Ohio-6859, 2002 WL 31778051, Unreported. Infants ⚷ 175.1; Infants ⚷ 191

Failure of juvenile's counsel to move for competency evaluation in delinquency proceeding on charge of murder with a gun specification was not ineffective assistance, though psychological evaluation after delinquency adjudication showed juvenile had low IQ, where juvenile's testimony clearly demonstrated his understanding of the charge and of difference between purposefully shooting with intent to kill and acting without purpose, and he testified consistently that he did not intend to discharge gun toward victim. In re York (Ohio App. 8 Dist., 04-12-2001) 142 Ohio App.3d 524, 756 N.E.2d 191, as amended nunc pro tunc. Infants ⚷ 205

Trial court's failure, in delinquency proceeding involving charge of murder with a gun specification, to order sua sponte that a competency hearing be conducted prior to trial, was not error; juvenile demonstrated at trial that he was able to assist effectively in his own defense and clearly understood nature and ramifications of charges against him. In re York (Ohio App. 8 Dist., 04-12-2001) 142 Ohio App.3d 524, 756 N.E.2d 191, as amended nunc pro tunc. Infants ⚷ 253

Statute governing competency evaluations of criminal defendants also governs competency evaluations of juveniles, so long as it is applied in light of juvenile rather than adult norms. In re York (Ohio App. 8 Dist., 04-12-2001) 142 Ohio App.3d 524, 756 N.E.2d 191, as amended nunc pro tunc. Infants ⚷ 200

Adult competency statute applies to juvenile proceedings to determine whether child is competent to face adjudication, provided the court assesses the juvenile by juvenile norms rather than adult norms. In re D.G. (Ohio Com.Pl., 03-24-1998) 91 Ohio Misc.2d 226, 698 N.E.2d 533. Mental Health ⚷ 432

Expert testimony, diagnostic reports, and other evidence established that juvenile's mental condition rendered him incapable of understanding nature and objective of delinquency proceedings or of assisting in his defense, and thus juvenile was not competent to face juvenile delinquency adjudication. In re D.G. (Ohio Com.Pl., 03-24-1998) 91 Ohio Misc.2d 226, 698 N.E.2d 533. Mental Health ⚷ 432

17. Deaf defendant

Defendant, a deaf mute with serious communication difficulties, was incompetent to stand trial for operating a motor vehicle while under the influence of alcohol; although no evidence was presented that a qualified examiner conducted a competency evaluation of defendant, expert witness testified that defendant's limited ability to communicate and understand proceedings rendered him incompetent to assist in his own defense, and trial judge was in a position to observe defendant's competency. State v. Burnett (Ohio App. 2 Dist., Darke, 01-07-2005) No. CIV.A. 1638, 2005-Ohio-49, 2005 WL 32797, Unreported. Mental Health ⚷ 432

Sufficient evidence supported determination that defendant, who was deaf and mentally impaired, was competent to stand trial in murder prosecution, and thus, defendant's habeas claim failed; although there was conflicting expert testimony about defendant's comprehension of the proceedings, expert testimony supported findings that defendant knew he was accused of killing a woman, understood that he could be punished, was able to engage in meaningful communication with his attorney and experts, was able to relate past events, and was able to understand testimony. Stanley v. Lazaroff (C.A.6 (Ohio), 10-03-2003) No. 01-4340, 82 Fed.Appx. 407, 2003 WL 22290187, Unreported. Habeas Corpus ⚷ 718

Deaf defendant was not entitled to videotape a witness's testimony at defendant's competency hearing. State v. Stanley (Ohio App. 1 Dist., 06-25-1997) 121 Ohio App.3d 673, 700 N.E.2d 881, dismissed, appeal not allowed 80 Ohio St.3d 1432, 685 N.E.2d 543, denial of post-conviction relief affirmed 82 Fed.Appx. 407, 2003 WL 22290187. Criminal Law ⚷ 625.20

Deaf defendant's concerns about the accuracy of the sign-language interpreters who assisted in his competency evaluations did not entitle him to have the evaluations videotaped. State v. Stanley (Ohio App. 1 Dist., 06-25-1997) 121 Ohio App.3d 673, 700 N.E.2d 881, dismissed, appeal not allowed 80 Ohio St.3d 1432, 685 N.E.2d 543, denial of post-conviction relief affirmed 82 Fed.Appx. 407, 2003 WL 22290187. Mental Health ⚷ 434

18. Review

Any error committed by trial court in failing to conduct competency hearing during capital murder prosecution was harmless, given that record failed to reveal indicia of defendant's incompetency. State v. Eley (Ohio, 12-18-1996) 77 Ohio St.3d 174, 672 N.E.2d 640, 1996-Ohio-323, reconsideration denied 77 Ohio St.3d 1549, 674 N.E.2d 1187, certiorari denied 117 S.Ct. 2522, 521 U.S. 1124, 138 L.Ed.2d 1023, dismissal of post-conviction relief affirmed 2001-Ohio-3447, 2001 WL 1497095, appeal not allowed 94 Ohio St.3d 1506, 764 N.E.2d 1036, 2002-Ohio-5738. Criminal Law ⚷ 1166(12)

Trial court's failure to conduct pretrial competency hearing was not harmless error; doctor's report which allegedly found that defendant's competency had been restored was apparently based on false information, defendant was not given opportunity to accept and did not accept findings of that report, and, although defendant testified, his conduct and comments presented significant indication of incompetency. State v. Corethers (Ohio App. 8 Dist., 08-23-1993) 90 Ohio App.3d 428, 629 N.E.2d 1052, dismissed, jurisdictional motion overruled 68 Ohio St.3d 1470, 628 N.E.2d 1389. Criminal Law ⚷ 1166(12)

2945.371 Evaluations of mental condition

(A) If the issue of a defendant's competence to stand trial is raised or if a defendant enters a plea of not guilty by reason of insanity, the court may order one or more evaluations of the defendant's present mental condition or, in the case of a plea of not guilty by reason of insanity, of the defendant's mental condition at the time of the offense charged. An examiner shall conduct the evaluation.

(B) If the court orders more than one evaluation under division (A) of this section, the prosecutor and the defendant may recommend to the court an examiner whom each prefers to perform one of the evaluations. If a defendant enters a plea of not guilty by reason of insanity and if the court does not designate an examiner recommended by the defendant, the court shall inform the defendant that the defendant may have independent expert evaluation and that, if the defendant is unable to obtain independent expert evaluation, it will be obtained for the defendant at public expense if the defendant is indigent.

(C) If the court orders an evaluation under division (A) of this section, the defendant shall be available at the times and places established by the examiners who are to conduct the evaluation. The court may order a defendant who has been released on bail or recognizance to submit to an evaluation under this section. If a defendant who has been released on bail or recognizance refuses to submit to a complete evaluation, the court may amend the conditions of bail or recognizance and order the sheriff to take the defendant into custody and deliver the defendant to a center, program, or facility operated or certified by the department of mental health or the department of mental retardation and developmental disabilities where the defendant may be held for evaluation for a reasonable period of time not to exceed twenty days.

(D) A defendant who has not been released on bail or recognizance may be evaluated at the defendant's place of detention. Upon the request of the examiner, the court may order the sheriff to transport the defendant to a program or facility operated by the department of mental health or the department of mental retardation and developmental disabilities, where the defendant may be held for evaluation for a reasonable period of time not to exceed twenty days, and to return the defendant to the place of detention after the evaluation. A municipal court may make an order under this division only upon the request of a certified forensic center examiner.

(E) If a court orders the evaluation to determine a defendant's mental condition at the time of the offense charged, the court shall inform the examiner of the offense with which the defendant is charged.

(F) In conducting an evaluation of a defendant's mental condition at the time of the offense charged, the examiner shall consider all relevant evidence. If the offense charged involves the use of force against another person, the relevant evidence to be considered includes, but is not limited to, any evidence that the defendant suffered, at the time of the commission of the offense, from the "battered woman syndrome."

(G) The examiner shall file a written report with the court within thirty days after entry of a court order for evaluation, and the court shall provide copies of the report to the prosecutor and defense counsel. The report shall include all of the following:

(1) The examiner's findings;

(2) The facts in reasonable detail on which the findings are based;

(3) If the evaluation was ordered to determine the defendant's competence to stand trial, all of the following findings or recommendations that are applicable:

(a) Whether the defendant is capable of understanding the nature and objective of the proceedings against the defendant or of assisting in the defendant's defense;

(b) If the examiner's opinion is that the defendant is incapable of understanding the nature and objective of the proceedings against the defendant or of assisting in the defendant's defense, whether the defendant presently is mentally ill or mentally retarded and, if the examiner's opinion is that the defendant presently is mentally retarded, whether the defendant appears to be a mentally retarded person subject to institutionalization by court order;

(c) If the examiner's opinion is that the defendant is incapable of understanding the nature and objective of the proceedings against the defendant or of assisting in the defendant's defense, the examiner's opinion as to the likelihood of the defendant becoming capable of understanding the nature and objective of the proceedings against the defendant and of assisting in the defendant's defense within one year if the defendant is provided with a course of treatment;

(d) If the examiner's opinion is that the defendant is incapable of understanding the nature and objective of the proceedings against the defendant or of assisting in the defendant's defense and that the defendant presently is mentally ill or mentally retarded, the examiner's recommendation as to the least restrictive treatment alternative, consistent with the defendant's treatment needs for restoration to competency and with the safety of the community.

(4) If the evaluation was ordered to determine the defendant's mental condition at the time of the offense charged, the examiner's findings as to whether the defendant, at the time of the offense charged, did not know, as a result of a severe mental disease or defect, the wrongfulness of the defendant's acts charged.

(H) If the examiner's report filed under division (G) of this section indicates that in the examiner's opinion the defendant is incapable of understanding the nature and objective of the proceedings against the defendant or of assisting in the defendant's defense and that in the examiner's opinion the defendant appears to be a mentally retarded person subject to institutionalization by court order, the court shall order the defendant to undergo a separate mental retardation evaluation conducted by a psychologist designated by the director of mental retardation and developmental disabilities. Divisions (C) to (F) of this section apply in relation to a separate mental retardation evaluation conducted under this division. The psychologist appointed under this division to conduct the separate mental retardation evaluation shall file a written report with the court within thirty days after the entry of the court order requiring the separate mental retardation evaluation, and the court shall provide copies of the report to the prosecutor and defense counsel. The report shall include all of the information described in divisions (G)(1) to (4) of this section. If the court orders a separate mental retardation evaluation of a defendant under this division, the court shall not conduct a hearing under divisions (B) to (H) of section 2945.37 of the Revised Code regarding that defendant until a report of the separate mental retardation evaluation conducted under this division has been filed. Upon the filing of that report, the court shall conduct the hearing within the period of time specified in division (C) of section 2945.37 of the Revised Code.

(I) An examiner appointed under divisions (A) and (B) of this section or under division (H) of this section to evaluate a defendant to determine the defendant's competence to stand trial also may be appointed to evaluate a defendant who has entered a plea of not guilty by reason of insanity, but an examiner of that nature shall prepare separate reports on the issue of competence to stand trial and the defense of not guilty by reason of insanity.

(J) No statement that a defendant makes in an evaluation or hearing under divisions (A) to (H) of this section relating to the defendant's competence to stand trial or to the defendant's mental condition at the time of the offense charged shall be used against the defendant on the issue of guilt in any criminal action or proceeding, but, in a criminal action or proceeding, the prosecutor or defense counsel may call as a witness any person who evaluated the defendant or prepared a report pursuant to a referral under this section. Neither the appointment nor the testimony of an examiner appointed under this section precludes the prosecutor or defense counsel from calling other witnesses or presenting other evidence on competency or insanity issues.

(K) Persons appointed as examiners under divisions (A) and (B) of this section or under division (H) of this section shall be paid a reasonable amount for their services and expenses, as certified by the court. The certified amount shall be paid by the county in the case of county courts and courts of common pleas and by the legislative authority, as defined in section 1901.03 of the Revised Code, in the case of municipal courts.

(2001 S 122, eff. 2–20–02; 1996 S 285, eff. 7–1–97; 1980 H 965, eff. 4–9–81; 1980 H 900, S 297; 1978 H 565)

Historical and Statutory Notes

Amendment Note: 2001 S 122 added new division G(3)(c) and redesignated former division G(3)(c) as new division G(3)(d).

Amendment Note: 1996 S 285 rewrote this section, which previously read:

"(A) If the issue of a defendant's competence to stand trial is raised under section 2945.37 of the Revised Code, the court may order one or more, but not more than three evaluations of the defendant's mental condition. The court shall do either of the following:

"(1) Order that each evaluation be conducted through examination of the defendant by a forensic center designated by the department of mental health to conduct such examinations and make such evaluations in the area in which the court is located or by any other program or facility that is designated by the department of mental health or the department of mental retardation and developmental disabilities to conduct such examinations and make such evaluations provided the center, program, or facility is operated by the appropriate department or is certified by such department as being in compliance with the standards established under division (J) of section 5119.01 or division (C) of section 5123.04 of the Revised Code;

"(2) Designate a center, program, or facility other than one designated by the department to conduct the examination.

"In any case, the court may designate examiners other than the personnel of the center, program, facility, or department to make the examination. If more than one examination is ordered, the prosecutor and the defendant may recommend to the court an examiner whom each prefers to perform one of the examinations.

"(B) If an evaluation is ordered, the defendant shall be available at the times and places established by the center, program, facility, or examiners. The court may order a defendant who has been released on bail or recognizance to submit to an examination under this section. If a defendant who has been released on bail or recognizance refuses to submit to a complete examination, the court may amend the conditions of bail or recognizance and order the sheriff to take the defendant into custody and deliver him to a center, program, or facility operated or certified by the department where he may be held for examination for a reasonable period of time not to exceed twenty days.

"(C) A defendant who has not been released on bail or recognizance may be examined at his place of detention. The court at the request of the examiner may order the sheriff to transport the defendant to a program or facility operated by the department of mental health or the department of mental retardation and developmental disabilities, where he may be held for examination for a reasonable period of time not to exceed twenty days, and to return the defendant to the place of detention after the examination. Such an order may be made by a municipal court only upon the request of a certified forensic center examiner.

"(D) The examiner shall file a written report with the court within thirty days after entry of an order for examination. The court shall provide copies of the report to the prosecutor and defense counsel. The report shall contain the findings of the examiner, the facts in reasonable detail on which the findings are based, and the opinion of the examiner as to the defendant's competence to stand trial. If the examiner reports that in his opinion the defendant is incompetent to stand trial, he shall also state his opinion on the likelihood of the defendant's becoming competent to stand trial within one year and if, in his opinion, the defendant is mentally ill or mentally retarded.

"(E) An examiner appointed under this section may also be appointed under section 2945.39 of the Revised Code to examine a defendant who has entered a plea of not guilty by reason of insanity, but such an examiner shall prepare separate reports on the issue of competence to stand trial and the defense of not guilty by reason of insanity.

"(F) As used in this chapter, 'examiner' means a psychiatrist or licensed clinical psychologist, as defined in section 5122.01 of the Revised Code; provided that a licensed clinical psychologist shall meet the criteria of division (I)(1) of section 5122.01 of the Revised Code or be employed by a certified forensic center designated by the department of mental health to conduct examinations."

Cross References

Arrest and detention until warrant can be obtained, 2935.03

Examiner, defined, 2971.01

Mentally ill patients absent without leave, applicability, 5122.26

Offenses against justice and public administration; detention, defined, 2921.01

Plea of insanity, Crim R 11

Ohio Administrative Code References

Community forensic psychiatric centers, OAC 5122–32–01

Library References

Criminal Law ⚖623.

Mental Health ⚖434.

Westlaw Topic Nos. 110, 257A.

C.J.S. Criminal Law §§ 549 to 557.

Research References

Encyclopedias

OH Jur. 3d Criminal Law § 707, Examiner's Evaluation and Report.

OH Jur. 3d Criminal Law § 708, Use of Statements Against Defendant.

OH Jur. 3d Criminal Law § 2585, Conduct of Hearing.

OH Jur. 3d Criminal Law § 2588, Time and Place of Examination.

OH Jur. 3d Criminal Law § 2589, Conduct of Examination.

OH Jur. 3d Criminal Law § 2590, Examination Report.

OH Jur. 3d Criminal Law § 2592, Initial Disposition of Defendant Found to be Incompetent.

OH Jur. 3d Criminal Law § 2682, Offering Improper Evidence or Asking Improper Question.

OH Jur. 3d Criminal Law § 2923, Insanity.

OH Jur. 3d Criminal Law § 3005, Other Statements or Declarations.

OH Jur. 3d Criminal Law § 3109, Number of Witnesses.

OH Jur. 3d Evidence & Witnesses § 755, Necessity for Existence of Relation of Physician and Patient.

Treatises and Practice Aids

Markus, Trial Handbook for Ohio Lawyers, § 4:59, Criminal Case—Defenses—Insanity—Competence to Stand Trial or to be Sentenced.

Katz, Giannelli, Blair and Lipton, Baldwin's Ohio Practice, Criminal Law, § 54:1, Introduction.

Katz, Giannelli, Blair and Lipton, Baldwin's Ohio Practice, Criminal Law, § 54:4, Mental Evaluation.

Katz, Giannelli, Blair and Lipton, Baldwin's Ohio Practice, Criminal Law, § 54:8, Findings.

Katz, Giannelli, Blair and Lipton, Baldwin's Ohio Practice, Criminal Law, § 54:9, Speedy Trial.

Katz, Giannelli, Blair and Lipton, Baldwin's Ohio Practice, Criminal Law, § 77:6, Experts—Insanity.

Katz, Giannelli, Blair and Lipton, Baldwin's Ohio Practice, Criminal Law, § 77:8, Experts—Competency to Stand Trial.

Katz, Giannelli, Blair and Lipton, Baldwin's Ohio Practice, Criminal Law, § 87:9, Examination of Accused.

Katz, Giannelli, Blair and Lipton, Baldwin's Ohio Practice, Criminal Law, § 144:4, Plea of Not Guilty by Reason of Insanity at Arraignment.

Katz, Giannelli, Blair and Lipton, Baldwin's Ohio Practice, Criminal Law, § 144:5, Acceptance of Plea of Not Guilty by Reason of Insanity After Arraignment.

Katz, Giannelli, Blair and Lipton, Baldwin's Ohio Practice, Criminal Law, § 144:7, Entry Ordering Inquiry Into Insanity of Defendant.

Carlin, Baldwin's Ohio Practice, Merrick-Rippner Probate Law § 101:46, Initial Treatment for Persons Found Incompetent to Stand Trial; Maximum Duration.

Hennenberg & Reinhart, Ohio Criminal Defense Motions F 5.20, Motion for Psychiatric Evaluation to Determine Defendant's Competency to Stand Trial-Pretrial Motions.

Hennenberg & Reinhart, Ohio Criminal Defense Motions F 5.21, Motion for Order Permitting Psychiatric Evaluation at State's Expense-Pretrial Motions.

Hennenberg & Reinhart, Ohio Criminal Defense Motions F 13.05, Motion for Order Granting Independent Psychiatric Evaluation at the State's Expense-Death Penalty Motions.

Law Review and Journal Commentaries

Diminished Capacity and Diminished Responsibility: Irreconcilable Doctrines Confused in State v. Wilcox, Note. 14 U Tol L Rev 1399 (Summer 1983).

Notes of Decisions

---

1. Constitutional issues—In general

Trial court fully protected murder defendant's constitutional rights in determining his competency after defendant waived counsel and actively sought the death penalty; on its own motion, the trial court ordered that defendant undergo two competency evaluations, even though defense counsel disclosed that an independent psychologist had already found defendant competent, defendant stipulated to the two evaluators' findings that he was competent, and trial court conducted a comprehensive inquiry of defendant before finding that he was competent to waive counsel, represent himself, and waive right to jury trial. State v. Mink (Ohio, 04-14-2004) 101 Ohio St.3d 350, 805 N.E.2d 1064, 2004-Ohio-1580, reconsideration denied 102 Ohio St.3d 1473, 809 N.E.2d 1159, 2004-Ohio-2830. Criminal Law ⚷ 641.6(2); Jury ⚷ 29(6)

Capital murder defendant had no constitutional right to examiner of his own choosing and thus, trial court did not need to specifically ask defendant to recommend examiner to evaluate his mental responsibility or condition. State v. Hill (Ohio, 08-30-1995) 73 Ohio St.3d 433, 653 N.E.2d 271, 1995-Ohio-287, reconsideration denied 74 Ohio St.3d 1423, 655 N.E.2d 742, certiorari denied 116 S.Ct. 788, 516 U.S. 1079, 133 L.Ed.2d 738, denial of habeas corpus affirmed 400 F.3d 308, rehearing and rehearing en banc denied 140 Fed.Appx. 597, 2005 WL 1683256, petition for certiorari filed 2005 WL 2333459. Mental Health ⚷ 434

2. —— Ineffective assistance of counsel, constitutional issues

Trial counsel did not provide ineffective assistance to defendant convicted of forgery, uttering, taking the identity of another, and tampering with records by stipulating to defendant's sanity without requesting independent expert evaluation of mental status; defendant failed to show that counsel's actions fell below objective standard of representation or prejudiced her, in that court-appointed psychologist and two experts on dissociative identity disorder examined defendant and found she understood wrongfulness of her actions, and post-trial, court-ordered polygraph examination reported deceptive reactions to questions regarding defendant's subjective belief as to her identity. State v. Roberts (Ohio App. 8 Dist., Cuyahoga, 01-06-2005) No. 84070, 2005-Ohio-28, 2005 WL 23358, Unreported. Criminal Law ⚷ 641.13(5)

3. —— Fair trial, constitutional issues

In prosecution in which defendant entered plea of not guilty by reason of insanity to charges of felonious assault and failure to comply with lawful order of police officer, omission from the record of psychological report, evidence of competency hearing, judgment entry as to trial court's findings as to competency or insanity at time of offense, and withdrawal of insanity plea, in conjunction with trial court's failure to follow proper procedures as to competency and insanity plea issues, constituted plain error. State v. Kulp (Ohio App. 6 Dist., 03-29-1996) 110 Ohio App.3d 144, 673 N.E.2d 689. Criminal Law ⚷ 1109(1)

4. Psychiatric evaluations—In general

Denial of defendant's motion for a psychiatric examination, which defendant alleged that he needed in order to investigate and prepare a motion to suppress evidence, was not error; during hearing on defendant's motion defendant informed the court that he understood the possible sentence he faced, he understood the crimes he was charged with, and he understood the burden of proof, police detective testified that he provided defendant with his *Miranda* rights, defendant seemed attentive during their interview, defendant reviewed and signed his statement, defendant did not exhibit any unusual behavior during the interview, and that he was not suspicious about defendant's mental health, and defendant's confession to police was voluntary. State v. Woodley (Ohio App. 8 Dist., Cuyahoga, 04-17-2003) No. 80732, 2003-Ohio-1950, 2003 WL 1900935, Unreported, appeal not allowed 100 Ohio St.3d 1425, 797 N.E.2d 92, 2003-Ohio-5232. Mental Health ⚷ 434

Reliable, credible evidence supported trial court's findings that murder defendant was competent, even though psychologists failed to examine defendant's medical and mental health treatment records, and such findings were not plain error; psychologists both conducted thorough examinations during which defendant provided detailed information about his medical and psychological problems before filing their written reports, defendant did not contend that his competency evaluations would have been different if psychologists had reviewed his medical and mental health records, and record showed that defendant acted sensibly throughout trial. State v. Mink (Ohio, 04-14-2004) 101 Ohio St.3d 350, 805 N.E.2d 1064, 2004-Ohio-1580, reconsideration denied 102 Ohio St.3d 1473, 809 N.E.2d 1159, 2004-Ohio-2830. Criminal Law ⚷ 625.15; Criminal Law ⚷ 1035(2)

Defendant who had raised level of his competency to stand trial through initial entry of plea of not guilty by reason of insanity could not avoid mental examinations ordered by court pursuant to statute. State v. White (Ohio, 05-12-1999) 85 Ohio St.3d 433, 709 N.E.2d 140, 1999-Ohio-281, denial of post-conviction relief affirmed 1999 WL 394938, dismissed, appeal not allowed 87 Ohio St.3d 1418, 717 N.E.2d 1105, certiorari denied 120 S.Ct. 345, 528 U.S. 938, 145 L.Ed.2d 270, denial of post-conviction relief affirmed 2005-Ohio-6990, 2005 WL 3556634, appeal allowed 109 Ohio St.3d 1493, 848 N.E.2d 857, 2006-Ohio-2762. Mental Health ⚷ 434

Trial court did not err in appointing the same examiners who had evaluated capital murder defendant's mental competency to stand trial to evaluate separately his mental responsibility; appointing the same examiners made sense in view of the myriad complexity of detail involved in mental evaluations and defendant's attempts to fake mental illness had already delayed case and appointing new examiners would necessitate further delay. State v. Hill (Ohio, 08-30-1995) 73 Ohio St.3d 433, 653 N.E.2d 271, 1995-Ohio-287, reconsideration denied 74 Ohio St.3d 1423, 655 N.E.2d 742, certiorari denied 116 S.Ct. 788, 516 U.S. 1079, 133 L.Ed.2d 738, denial of habeas corpus affirmed 400 F.3d 308, rehearing and rehearing en banc denied 140 Fed. Appx. 597, 2005 WL 1683256, petition for certiorari filed 2005 WL 2333459. Mental Health ⚷ 434

Defendant was not entitled to independent psychiatric evaluation under statutes governing questions of competency to stand trial and sanity at time of offense. State v. Corethers (Ohio App. 8 Dist., 08-23-1993) 90 Ohio App.3d 428, 629 N.E.2d 1052, dismissed, jurisdictional motion overruled 68 Ohio St.3d 1470, 628 N.E.2d 1389. Mental Health ⚷ 434

A defendant in a criminal prosecution has no right, by statute or otherwise, to an independent psychiatric evaluation. State v. Marshall (Cuyahoga 1984) 15 Ohio App.3d 105, 472 N.E.2d 1139, 15 O.B.R. 195.

5. —— Duty of court, psychiatric evaluations

Trial court did not abuse its discretion in not ordering evaluation of defendant's competency to stand trial; trial court conducted interview in which defendant stated that he fully understood court's explanation of charges against him, defendant's responses to court's questions were totally coherent, and, although defendant stated that he was experiencing mental problems, there was no indication that these problems rendered him incapable of assisting counsel. State v. Bailey (Ohio App. 11 Dist., 08-31-1992) 90 Ohio App.3d 58, 627 N.E.2d 1078, motion allowed 65 Ohio St.3d 1498, 605 N.E.2d 951, stay granted 66 Ohio St.3d 1433, 608 N.E.2d 762, appeal dismissed as improvidently allowed 68 Ohio St.3d 1212, 624 N.E.2d 1062, 1994-Ohio-516. Mental Health ⚷ 434

Trial court is not required to order evaluation of defendant's mental condition every time a defendant raises the issue, but instead is only required to give defendant or his counsel the chance to submit evidence on issue; if evidence raises genuine question as to defendant's competency, court can order that one or more evaluations be performed, and, if it does not, court can find defendant competent and proceed to trial. State v. Bailey (Ohio App. 11 Dist., 08-31-1992) 90 Ohio App.3d 58, 627 N.E.2d 1078, motion allowed 65 Ohio St.3d 1498, 605 N.E.2d 951, stay granted 66 Ohio St.3d 1433, 608 N.E.2d 762, appeal dismissed as improvidently allowed 68 Ohio St.3d 1212, 624 N.E.2d 1062, 1994-Ohio-516. Mental Health ⚷ 434

6. —— Duty of examiner, psychiatric evaluations

An individual examiner who performs a psychiatric evaluation of a criminal defendant pursuant to RC 2945.371 or RC 2945.39 has a duty to report to law enforcement authorities any information obtained during the evaluation concerning criminal offenses that are felonies. The duty to report also extends to the private organization employing the examiner and to any other employee of the organization who has knowledge of such information. OAG 80–022.

7. Evidence, admissibility

In murder prosecution, any error was harmless in trial court's admission of statements allegedly made by defendant during competency evaluation, where the evidence of defendant's guilt was overwhelming. State v. Taylor (Ohio App. 1 Dist., Hamilton, 03-26-2004) No. C-020475, 2004-Ohio-1494, 2004 WL 596128, Unreported, appeal not allowed 103 Ohio St.3d 1406, 812 N.E.2d 1289, 2004-Ohio-3980. Criminal Law ⚷ 1169.12

Defendant in aggravated murder prosecution waived his physician/patient privilege as to his psychiatric condition when he placed his mental health at issue by entering a plea of not guilty by reason of insanity. State v. Hancock (Ohio App. 12 Dist., Warren, 03-31-2003) No. CA2001-12-115, No. CA2001-12-116, No. CA2002-01-004, 2003-Ohio-1616, 2003 WL 1689612, Unreported, appeal not allowed 99 Ohio St.3d 1513, 792 N.E.2d 200, 2003-Ohio-3957, appeal after new sentencing hearing 108 Ohio St.3d 57, 840 N.E.2d 1032, 2006-Ohio-160, reconsideration denied 108 Ohio St.3d 1513, 844 N.E.2d 857, 2006-Ohio-1329. Witnesses ⚷ 219(5)

Defendant's admission to court-appointed forensic psychiatrist that he "tied [victim] up and strangled him" was not offered as substantive evidence of guilt, but was relevant, in trial for capital murder, to determination of whether defendant had capacity to know wrongfulness of killing victim, for purposes of insanity defense. State v. Hancock (Ohio,

02-01-2006) 108 Ohio St.3d 57, 840 N.E.2d 1032, 2006-Ohio-160, reconsideration denied 108 Ohio St.3d 1513, 844 N.E.2d 857, 2006-Ohio-1329. Homicide ⚷ 1041

Court-appointed forensic psychiatrist's opinion that defendant was not insane but was malingering did not violate psychiatrist-patient privilege based on claim that psychiatrist had relied on information acquired from other mental health care professionals who had examined defendant, in trial for aggravated murder; psychiatrist did not testify as to communications made to him by defendant, and court-appointed psychiatrist was required to consider all relevant evidence in forming opinion. State v. Hancock (Ohio, 02-01-2006) 108 Ohio St.3d 57, 840 N.E.2d 1032, 2006-Ohio-160, reconsideration denied 108 Ohio St.3d 1513, 844 N.E.2d 857, 2006-Ohio-1329. Criminal Law ⚷ 486(6); Witnesses ⚷ 211(2)

Defendant's statements to doctor, who was not court-appointed, during defendant's mental evaluation were inadmissible hearsay with respect to issue of guilt. State v. Franklin (Ohio, 10-16-2002) 97 Ohio St.3d 1, 776 N.E.2d 26, 2002-Ohio-5304, denial of post-conviction relief affirmed 2002-Ohio-2370, 2002 WL 1000415, appeal not allowed 98 Ohio St.3d 1422, 782 N.E.2d 77, 2003-Ohio-259, reconsideration denied 101 Ohio St.3d 1462, 804 N.E.2d 37, 2004-Ohio-823, appeal not allowed 108 Ohio St.3d 1475, 842 N.E.2d 1054, 2006-Ohio-665, reconsideration denied 97 Ohio St.3d 1486, 780 N.E.2d 288, 2002-Ohio-6866, stay granted 97 Ohio St.3d 1491, 780 N.E.2d 597, 2002-Ohio-7045, certiorari denied 123 S.Ct. 2249, 539 U.S. 905, 156 L.Ed.2d 115, denial of post-conviction relief affirmed 2005-Ohio-1361, 2005 WL 678925, appeal not allowed 106 Ohio St.3d 1464, 830 N.E.2d 1170, 2005-Ohio-3490, certiorari denied 126 S.Ct. 1352, 164 L.Ed.2d 64. Criminal Law ⚷ 412(4); Criminal Law ⚷ 419(1.5)

8. Speedy trial

The tolling of the speedy trial time period resulting from a competency motion being filed does not end where an examiner fails to issue a timely report; rather, the time continues to be tolled until a court determines whether the accused is competent to stand trial. State v. Palmer (Ohio, 12-09-1998) 84 Ohio St.3d 103, 702 N.E.2d 72, 1998-Ohio-507. Criminal Law ⚷ 577.11(6)

Where defendant's competency examiner fails to submit report within required 30 days, defendant who desires speedy trial may notify court and ask it to enforce its order. State v. Jones (Ohio App. 11 Dist., 04-04-1997) 119 Ohio App.3d 59, 694 N.E.2d 505. Criminal Law ⚷ 577.11(6)

Defendant's motion for continuance to undergo competency evaluation tolled his statutory speedy-trial period for all 62 days during which motion was pending, even though examiner's report was due after only 30 days. State v. Jones (Ohio App. 11 Dist., 04-04-1997) 119 Ohio App.3d 59, 694 N.E.2d 505. Criminal Law ⚷ 577.11(6)

Where a criminal defendant moves for a psychiatric examination pursuant to RC 2945.39 and 2945.371, the running of the time in which a defendant must be tried is tolled when the motion is granted, not when the motion is made, and the time begins running again immediately after the date the psychiatric report is due where such report is never filed. State v. Bowman (Clermont 1987) 41 Ohio App.3d 318, 535 N.E.2d 730. Criminal Law ⚷ 577.8(2); Criminal Law ⚷ 577.11(6)

Although the time within which an accused must be brought to trial may be tolled during the time when his competence to stand trial is being evaluated, when ten days have elapsed after the filing of the examiner's report and the statutorily mandated hearing has not been held, the time begins to run again. State v. Wilson (Fayette 1982) 7 Ohio App.3d 219, 454 N.E.2d 1348, 7 O.B.R. 281.

When an accused moves the court for an additional evaluation of his mental condition, the statutory period within which he must be brought to trial is tolled from time his motion is granted, and begins to run again on the date when the psychiatrist's report is due to be filed with the court, even if no report is filed on that date. State v. Wilson (Fayette 1982) 7 Ohio App.3d 219, 454 N.E.2d 1348, 7 O.B.R. 281.

Failure to file an evaluation within the thirty-day period established by RC 2945.371 will not toll the time for trial beyond that time. State v. Wilson (Fayette 1982) 7 Ohio App.3d 219, 454 N.E.2d 1348, 7 O.B.R. 281.

9. Probation revocation hearings

Defendant has no right to a hearing to determine his competency to stand trial under RC 2945.371 prior to a hearing on revocation of his probation. State v Blankenship, No. CA86–09–139 (12th Dist Ct App, Butler, 3–2–87).

10. Post–conviction relief

There was no evidence of petitioner's incompetence at his guilty plea to warrant inquiry into that matter upon trial court's own initiative, and thus petitioner failed to submit sufficient evidence demonstrating substantive grounds for relief, and therefore was not entitled to evidentiary hearing on his postconviction relief petition claiming that trial court erred in not ordering sua sponte a competency evaluation prior to accepting petitioner's guilty plea. State v. Blankenship (Ohio App. 12 Dist., 11-04-1996) 115 Ohio App.3d 512, 685 N.E.2d 831, dismissed, appeal not allowed 78 Ohio St.3d 1409, 675 N.E.2d 1249. Criminal Law ⚷ 1655(5)

Petitioner failed to establish entitlement to habeas relief based on his contention that district court made public statement that he was insane by requiring him to undergo psychological evaluation to determine competency to stand trial, absent any showing that petitioner's constitutional rights were violated by such proceedings or any showing as to how this pretrial proceeding denied him a fundamentally fair trial. Norris v. Schotten (C.A.6 (Ohio), 05-26-1998) 146 F.3d 314, certiorari denied 119 S.Ct. 348, 525 U.S. 935, 142 L.Ed.2d 287. Habeas Corpus ⚷ 477

Where a defendant offers expert testimony at a post-conviction relief hearing concerning his sanity at the time of the crime to support the contention that his counsel was ineffective in withdrawing an insanity plea, it is error to bar the expert's testimony. State v Decker, No. 10–181 (11th Dist Ct App, Lake, 12–31–85), reversed by 28 OS(3d) 137, 502 NE(2d) 647 (1986).

2945.38 Effect of findings; treatment or continuing evaluation and treatment of incompetent; medication; disposition of defendant; report; additional hearings; discharge

(A) If the issue of a defendant's competence to stand trial is raised and if the court, upon conducting the hearing provided for in section 2945.37 of the Revised Code, finds that the defendant is competent to stand trial, the defendant shall be proceeded against as provided by law. If the court finds the defendant competent to stand trial and the defendant is receiving psychotropic drugs or other medication, the court may authorize the continued administration of the drugs or medication or other appropriate treatment in order to maintain the defendant's competence to stand trial, unless the defendant's attending physician advises the court against continuation of the drugs, other medication, or treatment.

(B)(1)(a) If, after taking into consideration all relevant reports, information, and other evidence, the court finds that the defendant is incompetent to stand trial and that there is a substantial probability that the defendant will become competent to stand trial within one year if the defendant is provided with a course of treatment, the court shall order the defendant to undergo treatment. If the defendant has been charged with a felony offense and if, after taking into consideration all relevant reports, information, and other evidence, the court finds that the defendant is incompetent to stand trial, but the court is unable at that time to determine whether there is a substantial probability that the defendant will become competent to stand trial within one year if the defendant is provided with a course of treatment, the court shall order continuing evaluation and treatment of the defendant for a period not to exceed four months to determine whether there is a substantial probability that the defendant will become competent to stand trial within one year if the defendant is provided with a course of treatment.

(b) The court order for the defendant to undergo treatment or continuing evaluation and treatment under division (B)(1)(a) of this section shall specify that the treatment or continuing evaluation and treatment shall occur at a facility operated by the department of mental health or the department of mental retardation and developmental disabilities, at a facility certified by either of those departments as being qualified to treat mental illness or mental retardation, at a public or private community mental health or mental retardation facility, or by a psychiatrist or another mental health or mental retardation professional. The order may restrict the defendant's freedom of movement as the court considers necessary. The prosecutor in the defendant's case shall send to the chief clinical officer of the hospital or facility, the managing officer of the institution, the director of the program, or the person to which the defendant is committed copies of relevant police reports and other background information that pertains to the defendant and is available to the prosecutor unless the prosecutor determines that the release of any of the information in the police reports or any of the other background information to unauthorized persons would interfere with the effective prosecution of any person or would create a substantial risk of harm to any person.

In determining placement alternatives, the court shall consider the extent to which the person is a danger to the person and to others, the need for security, and the type of crime involved and shall order the least restrictive alternative available that is consistent with public safety and treatment goals. In weighing these factors, the court shall give preference to protecting public safety.

(c) If the defendant is found incompetent to stand trial, if the chief clinical officer of the hospital or facility, the managing officer of the institution, the director of the program, or the person to which the defendant is committed for treatment or continuing evaluation and treatment under division (B)(1)(b) of this section determines that medication is necessary to restore the defendant's competency to stand trial, and if the defendant lacks the capacity to give informed consent or refuses medication, the chief clinical officer, managing officer, director, or person to which the defendant is committed for treatment or continuing evaluation and treatment may petition the court for authorization for the involuntary administration of medication. The court shall hold a hearing on the petition within five days of the filing of the petition if the petition was filed in a municipal court or a county court regarding an incompetent defendant charged with a misdemeanor or within ten days of the filing of the petition if the petition was filed in a court of common pleas regarding an incompetent defendant charged with a felony offense. Following the hearing, the court may authorize the involuntary administration of medication or may dismiss the petition.

(2) If the court finds that the defendant is incompetent to stand trial and that, even if the defendant is provided with a course of treatment, there is not a substantial probability that the defendant will become competent to stand trial within one year, the court shall order the discharge of the defendant, unless upon motion of the prosecutor or on its own motion, the court either seeks to retain jurisdiction over the defendant pursuant to section 2945.39 of the Revised Code or files an affidavit in the probate court for the civil commitment of the defendant pursuant to Chapter 5122. or 5123. of the Revised Code alleging that the defendant is a mentally ill person subject to hospitalization by court order or a mentally retarded person subject to institutionalization by court order. If an affidavit is filed in the probate court, the trial court shall send to the probate court copies of all written reports of the defendant's mental condition that were prepared pursuant to section 2945.371 of the Revised Code.

The trial court may issue the temporary order of detention that a probate court may issue under section 5122.11 or 5123.71 of the Revised Code, to remain in effect until the probable cause or initial hearing in the probate court. Further proceedings in the probate court are civil proceedings governed by Chapter 5122. or 5123. of the Revised Code.

(C) No defendant shall be required to undergo treatment, including any continuing evaluation and treatment, under division (B)(1) of this section for longer than whichever of the following periods is applicable:

(1) One year, if the most serious offense with which the defendant is charged is one of the following offenses:

(a) Aggravated murder, murder, or an offense of violence for which a sentence of death or life imprisonment may be imposed;

(b) An offense of violence that is a felony of the first or second degree;

(c) A conspiracy to commit, an attempt to commit, or complicity in the commission of an offense described in division (C)(1)(a) or (b) of this section if the conspiracy, attempt, or complicity is a felony of the first or second degree.

(2) Six months, if the most serious offense with which the defendant is charged is a felony other than a felony described in division (C)(1) of this section;

(3) Sixty days, if the most serious offense with which the defendant is charged is a misdemeanor of the first or second degree;

(4) Thirty days, if the most serious offense with which the defendant is charged is a misdemeanor of the third or fourth degree, a minor misdemeanor, or an unclassified misdemeanor.

(D) Any defendant who is committed pursuant to this section shall not voluntarily admit the defendant or be voluntarily admitted to a hospital or institution pursuant to section 5122.02, 5122.15, 5123.69, or 5123.76 of the Revised Code.

(E) Except as otherwise provided in this division, a defendant who is charged with an offense and is committed to a hospital or other institution by the court under this section shall not be granted unsupervised on-grounds movement, supervised off-grounds movement, or nonsecured status. The court may grant a defendant supervised off-grounds movement to obtain medical treatment or specialized habilitation treatment services if the person who supervises the treatment or the continuing evaluation and treatment of the defendant ordered under division (B)(1)(a) of this section informs the court that the treatment or continuing evaluation and treatment cannot be provided at the hospital or the institution to which the defendant is committed. The chief clinical officer of the hospital or the managing officer of the institution to which the defendant is committed or a designee of either of those persons may grant a defendant movement to a medical facility for an emergency medical situation with appropriate supervision to ensure the safety of the defendant, staff, and community during that emergency medical situation. The chief clinical officer of the hospital or the managing officer of the institution shall notify the court within twenty-four hours of the defendant's movement to the medical facility for an emergency medical situation under this division.

(F) The person who supervises the treatment or continuing evaluation and treatment of a defendant ordered to undergo treatment or continuing evaluation and treatment under division (B)(1)(a) of this section shall file a written report with the court at the following times:

(1) Whenever the person believes the defendant is capable of understanding the nature and objective of the proceedings against the defendant and of assisting in the defendant's defense;

(2) For a felony offense, fourteen days before expiration of the maximum time for treatment as specified in division (C) of this section and fourteen days before the expiration of the maximum time for continuing evaluation and treatment as specified in division (B)(1)(a) of this section, and, for a misdemeanor offense, ten days before the expiration of the maximum time for treatment, as specified in division (C) of this section;

(3) At a minimum, after each six months of treatment;

(4) Whenever the person who supervises the treatment or continuing evaluation and treatment of a defendant ordered under division (B)(1)(a) of this section believes that there is not a substantial probability that the defendant will become capable of understanding the nature and objective of the proceedings against the defendant or of assisting in the defendant's defense even if the defendant is provided with a course of treatment.

(G) A report under division (F) of this section shall contain the examiner's findings, the facts in reasonable detail on which the findings are based, and the examiner's opinion as to the defendant's capability of understanding the nature and objective of the proceedings against the defendant and of assisting in the defendant's defense. If, in the examiner's opinion, the defendant remains incapable of understanding the nature and objective of the proceedings against the defendant and of assisting in the defendant's defense and there is a substantial probability that the defendant will become capable of understanding the nature and objective of the proceedings against the defendant and of assisting in the defendant's defense if the defendant is provided with a course of treatment, if in the examiner's opinion the defendant remains mentally ill or mentally retarded, and if the maximum time for treatment as specified in division (C) of this section has not expired, the report also shall contain the examiner's recommendation as to the least restrictive treatment alternative that is consistent with the defendant's treatment needs for restoration to competency and with the safety of the community. The court shall provide copies of the report to the prosecutor and defense counsel.

(H) If a defendant is committed pursuant to division (B)(1) of this section, within ten days after the treating physician of the defendant or the examiner of the defendant who is employed or retained by the treating facility advises that there is not a substantial probability that the defendant will become capable of understanding the nature and objective of the proceedings against the defendant or of assisting in the defendant's defense even if the defendant is provided with a course of treatment, within ten days after the expiration of the maximum time for treatment as specified in division (C) of this section, within ten days after the expiration of the maximum time for continuing evaluation and treatment as specified in division (B)(1)(a) of this section, within thirty days after a defendant's request for a hearing that is made after six months of treatment, or within thirty days after being advised by the treating physician or examiner that the defendant is competent to stand trial, whichever is the earliest, the court shall conduct another hearing to determine if the defendant is competent to stand trial and shall do whichever of the following is applicable:

(1) If the court finds that the defendant is competent to stand trial, the defendant shall be proceeded against as provided by law.

(2) If the court finds that the defendant is incompetent to stand trial, but that there is a substantial probability that the defendant will become competent to stand trial if the defendant is provided with a course of treatment, and the maximum time for treatment as specified in division (C) of this section has not expired, the court, after consideration of the examiner's recommendation, shall order that treatment be continued, may change the facility or program at which the treatment is to be continued, and shall specify whether the treatment is to be continued at the same or a different facility or program.

(3) If the court finds that the defendant is incompetent to stand trial, if the defendant is charged with an offense listed in division (C)(1) of this section, and if the court finds that there is not a substantial probability that the defendant will become competent to stand trial even if the defendant is provided with a course of treatment, or if the maximum time for treatment relative to that offense as specified in division (C) of this section has expired, further proceedings shall be as provided in sections 2945.39, 2945.401, and 2945.402 of the Revised Code.

(4) If the court finds that the defendant is incompetent to stand trial, if the most serious offense with which the defendant is charged is a misdemeanor or a felony other than a felony listed in division (C)(1) of this section, and if the court finds that there is not a substantial probability that the defendant will become competent to stand trial even if the defendant is provided with a course of treatment, or if the maximum time for treatment relative to that offense as specified in division (C) of this section has expired, the court shall dismiss the indictment, information, or complaint against the defendant. A dismissal under this division is not a bar to further prosecution based on the same conduct. The court shall discharge the defendant unless the court or prosecutor files an affidavit in probate court for civil commitment pursuant to Chapter 5122. or 5123. of the Revised Code. If an affidavit for civil commitment is filed, the court may detain the defendant for ten days pending civil commitment. All of the following provisions apply to persons charged with a misdemeanor or a felony other than a felony listed in division (C)(1) of this section who are committed by the probate court subsequent to the court's or prosecutor's filing of an affidavit for civil commitment under authority of this division:

(a) The chief clinical officer of the hospital or facility, the managing officer of the institution, the director of the program, or the person to which the defendant is committed or admitted shall do all of the following:

(i) Notify the prosecutor, in writing, of the discharge of the defendant, send the notice at least ten days prior to the discharge unless the discharge is by the probate court, and state in the notice the date on which the defendant will be discharged;

(ii) Notify the prosecutor, in writing, when the defendant is absent without leave or is granted unsupervised, off-grounds movement, and send this notice promptly after the discovery of the absence without leave or prior to the granting of the unsupervised, off-grounds movement, whichever is applicable;

(iii) Notify the prosecutor, in writing, of the change of the defendant's commitment or admission to voluntary status, send the notice promptly upon learning of the change to voluntary status, and state in the notice the date on which the defendant was committed or admitted on a voluntary status.

(b) Upon receiving notice that the defendant will be granted unsupervised, off-grounds movement, the prosecutor either shall re-indict the defendant or promptly notify the court that the prosecutor does not intend to prosecute the charges against the defendant.

(I) If a defendant is convicted of a crime and sentenced to a jail or workhouse, the defendant's sentence shall be reduced by the total number of days the defendant is confined for evaluation to determine the defendant's competence to stand trial or treatment under this section and sections 2945.37 and 2945.371 of the Revised Code or by the total number of days the defendant is confined for evaluation to determine the defendant's mental condition at the time of the offense charged.

(2001 S 122, eff. 2–20–02; 1996 S 285, eff. 7–1–97; 1996 S 269, eff. 7–1–96; 1988 S 156, eff. 7–1–89; 1980 H 965, H 900, S 297; 1978 H 565; 1975 S 185; 1953 H 1; GC 13441–2)

Uncodified Law

2001 S 122, § 3, eff. 2–20–02, reads:

This act presents section 2945.38 of the Revised Code as it existed prior to its amendment by Am. Sub. S.B. 285 of the 121st General Assembly. The revived version of that section supersedes the version of that section repealed by Section 2 of this act and omits and repeals all changes made to that section by Am. Sub. S.B. 285 of the 121st General Assembly. The omission and repeal of those changes is not intended to have any substantive effect and is intended to present in this act the version of section 2945.38 of the Revised Code that is currently effective. The repeal of section 2945.38 of the Revised Code by Section 2 of this act is to give effect to the holding of the Ohio Supreme Court in *State v. Sullivan* (2001), 90 Ohio St.3d 502, that section 2945.38 of the Revised Code, as amended by Am. Sub. S.B. 285 of the 121st General Assembly, is unconstitutional.

Historical and Statutory Notes

Pre–1953 H 1 Amendments: 113 v 177, Ch 19, § 2

Amendment Note: 2001 S 122 rewrote the section, which prior thereto read:

"(A) If the issue of a defendant's competence to stand trial is raised and if the court, upon conducting the hearing provided for in section 2945.37 of the Revised Code, finds that the defendant is competent to stand trial, the defendant shall be proceeded against as provided by law. If the court finds the defendant competent to stand trial and the defendant is receiving psychotropic drugs or other medication, the court may authorize the continued administration of the drugs or medication or other appropriate treatment in order to maintain the defendant's competence to stand trial, unless the defendant's attending physician advises the court against continuation of the drugs, other medication, or treatment.

"(B) After taking into consideration all relevant reports, information, and other evidence, the court shall order a defendant who is found incompetent to stand trial to undergo treatment at a facility operated by the department of mental health or the department of mental retardation and developmental disabilities, treatment at a facility certified by either of those departments as being qualified to treat mental illness or mental retardation, treatment at a public or private community mental health or mental retardation facility, or private treatment by a psychiatrist or another mental health or mental retardation professional. The order may restrict the defendant's freedom of movement as the court considers necessary. The prosecutor in the defendant's case shall send to the chief clinical officer of the hospital or facility, the managing officer of the institution, the director of the program, or the person to which the defendant is committed copies of relevant police reports and other background information that pertains to the defendant and is available to the prosecutor unless the prosecutor determines that the release of any of the information in the police reports or any of the other background information to unauthorized persons would interfere with the effective prosecution of any person or would create a substantial risk of harm to any person.

"In determining placement alternatives, the court shall consider the extent to which the person is a danger to the person and to others, the need for security, and the type of crime involved and shall order the least restrictive alternative available that is consistent with public safety and treatment goals. In weighing these factors, the court shall give preference to protecting public safety.

"If the defendant is found incompetent to stand trial, if the chief clinical officer of the hospital or facility, the managing officer of the institution, the director of the program, or the person to which the defendant is committed determines that medication is necessary to restore the defendant's competency to stand trial, and if the defendant lacks the capacity to give informed consent or refuses medication, the chief clinical officer, managing officer, director, or person to which the defendant is committed may petition for, and the court may authorize, the involuntary administration of medication.

"(C) No defendant shall be required to undergo treatment under this section for longer than whichever of the following periods is applicable:

"(1) One year, if the most serious offense with which the defendant is charged is one of the following offenses:

"(a) Aggravated murder, murder, or an offense of violence for which a sentence of death or life imprisonment may be imposed;

"(b) An offense of violence that is a felony of the first or second degree;

"(c) A conspiracy to commit, an attempt to commit, or complicity in the commission of an offense described in division (C)(1)(a) or (b) of this section if the conspiracy, attempt, or complicity is a felony of the first or second degree.

"(2) Six months, if the most serious offense with which the defendant is charged is a felony other than a felony described in division (C)(1) of this section;

"(3) Sixty days, if the most serious offense with which the defendant is charged is a misdemeanor.

"(D) Any defendant who is committed pursuant to this section shall not voluntarily admit the defendant or be voluntarily admitted to a hospital or institution pursuant to section 5122.02, 5122.15, 5123.69, or 5123.76 of the Revised Code.

"(E) A defendant charged with an offense and committed to a hospital or other institution by the court under this section shall not be granted unsupervised on-grounds movement, supervised off-grounds movement, or nonsecured status.

"(F) The person who supervises the treatment of a defendant ordered to undergo treatment under division (B) of this section shall file a written report with the court at the following times:

"(1) Whenever the person believes the defendant is capable of understanding the nature and objective of the proceedings against the defendant and of assisting in the defendant's defense;

"(2) For a felony offense, fourteen days before expiration of the maximum time for treatment as specified in division (C) of this section, and, for a misdemeanor offense, ten days before the expiration of the maximum time for treatment as specified in division (C) of this section;

"(3) At a minimum, after each six months of treatment.

"(G) A report under division (F) of this section shall contain the examiner's findings, the facts in reasonable detail on which the findings are based, and the examiner's opinion as to the defendant's capability of understanding the nature and objective of the proceedings against the defendant and of assisting in the defendant's defense. If, in the examiner's opinion, the defendant remains incapable of understanding the nature and objective of the proceedings against the defendant or of assisting in the defendant's defense and also remains mentally ill or mentally retarded, and if the maximum time for treatment as specified in division (C) of this section has not expired, the report also shall contain the examiner's recommendation as to the least restrictive treatment alternative that is consistent with the defendant's treatment needs for restoration to competency and with the safety of the community. The court shall provide copies of the report to the prosecutor and defense counsel.

"(H) Within ten days after the expiration of the maximum time for treatment as specified in division (C) of this section, within thirty days after a defendant's request for a hearing that is made after six months of treatment, or within thirty days after being advised by the treating physician that the defendant is competent to stand trial, whichever is earlier, the court shall conduct another hearing to determine if the defendant is competent to stand trial and shall do whichever of the following is applicable:

"(1) If the court finds that the defendant is competent to stand trial, the defendant shall be proceeded against as provided by law.

"(2) If the court finds that the defendant is incompetent to stand trial and the maximum time for treatment as specified in division (C) of this section has not expired, the court, after consideration of the examiner's recommendation, shall order that treatment be continued until the expiration of the maximum time for treatment, may change the facility or program at which the treatment is to be continued, and shall specify whether the treatment is to be continued at the same or a different facility or program.

"(3) If the court finds that the defendant is incompetent to stand trial, if the defendant is charged with an offense listed in division (C)(1) of this section, and if the maximum time for treatment relative to that offense as specified in that division has expired, further proceedings shall be as provided in sections 2945.39, 2945.401, and 2945.402 of the Revised Code.

"(4) If the court finds that the defendant is incompetent to stand trial, if the most serious offense with which the defendant is charged is a misdemeanor or a felony other than a felony listed in division (C)(1) of this section, and if the maximum time for treatment relative to that offense as specified in division (C) of this section has expired, the court shall dismiss the indictment, information, or complaint against the defendant. A dismissal under this division is not a bar to further prosecution based on the same conduct. The court shall discharge the defendant unless the court or prosecutor files an affidavit in probate court for civil commitment pursuant to Chapter 5122. or 5123. of the Revised Code. If an affidavit for civil commitment is filed, the court may detain the defendant for ten days pending civil commitment. All of the following provisions apply to persons charged with a misdemeanor or a felony other than a felony listed in division (C)(1) of this section who are committed by the probate court subsequent to the court's or prosecutor's filing of an affidavit for civil commitment under authority of this division:

"(a) The chief clinical officer of the hospital or facility, the managing officer of the institution, the director of the program, or the person to which the defendant is committed or admitted shall do all of the following:

"(i) Notify the prosecutor, in writing, of the discharge of the defendant, send the notice at least ten days prior to the discharge unless the discharge is by the probate court, and state in the notice the date on which the defendant will be discharged;

"(ii) Notify the prosecutor, in writing, when the defendant is absent without leave or is granted unsupervised, off-grounds movement, and send this notice promptly after the discovery of the absence without leave or prior to the granting of the unsupervised, off-grounds movement, whichever is applicable;

"(iii) Notify the prosecutor, in writing, of the change of the defendant's commitment or admission to voluntary status, send the notice promptly upon learning of the change to voluntary status, and state in the notice the date on which the defendant was committed or admitted on a voluntary status.

"(b) Upon receiving notice that the defendant will be granted unsupervised, off-grounds movement, the prosecutor either shall re-indict the defendant or promptly notify the court that the prosecutor does not intend to prosecute the charges against the defendant.

"(I) If a defendant is convicted of a crime and sentenced to a jail or workhouse, the defendant's sentence shall be reduced by the total number of days the defendant is confined for evaluation to determine the defendant's competence to stand trial or treatment under this section and sections 2945.37 and 2945.371 of the Revised Code or by the total number of days the defendant is confined for evaluation to determine the defendant's mental condition at the time of the offense charged."

Amendment Note: 1996 S 269 substituted "prison term" for "minimum sentence" and "term of imprisonment" for "maximum sentence" in the second paragraph of division (D); substituted "prison term or term of imprisonment" for "sentence" in division (H)(2); made changes to reflect gender neutral language; and made other nonsubstantive changes.

Amendment Note: 1996 S 285 rewrote this section. See Baldwin's Ohio Legislative Service, 1996, p 12/L–3524, or the OH–LEGIS or OH–LEGIS–OLD database on WESTLAW, for prior version of this section.

Cross References

Arrest and detention until warrant can be obtained, 2935.03

Hospitalization of mentally ill, confidentiality of records, 5122.31

Hospitalization of mentally ill, involuntary confinement, 5122.05

Hospitalization of mentally ill; residence, defined, 5122.01

Mental retardation and developmental disabilities department, treatment of defendants incompetent to stand trial, 5123.04

Mentally ill patients absent without leave, applicability, 5122.26

Mentally retarded person may apply for admission for short-term care, 5123.701

Offenses against justice and public administration; detention, defined, 2921.01

Plea of insanity, Crim R 11

Reimbursement of alcohol, drug addiction, and mental health program expenditures, 5119.62

Library References

Criminal Law ⚷623.

Mental Health ⚷432 to 436.

Westlaw Topic Nos. 110, 257A.

C.J.S. Criminal Law §§ 549 to 557.

C.J.S. Mental Health §§ 235 to 241, 248.

Baldwin's Ohio Legislative Service, 1988 Laws of Ohio, S 156—LSC Analysis, p 5–284

Research References

Encyclopedias

OH Jur. 3d Courts & Judges § 374, Doctrine of Law of Case; Prior Rulings in Same Matter.

OH Jur. 3d Criminal Law § 8, Under the Fourteenth Amendment.

OH Jur. 3d Criminal Law § 2583, Obligations of Trial Court.

OH Jur. 3d Criminal Law § 2584, Right to Hearing on Competency.

OH Jur. 3d Criminal Law § 2592, Initial Disposition of Defendant Found to be Incompetent.

OH Jur. 3d Criminal Law § 2593, Reports Regarding Incompetent Defendant Committed to Treatment.

OH Jur. 3d Criminal Law § 2594, Treatment and Final Disposition of Incompetent Defendant.

OH Jur. 3d Criminal Law § 2595, Treatment and Final Disposition of Incompetent Defendant—Further Proceedings With Respect to Incompetent Defendants Charged With Serious Felony.

OH Jur. 3d Criminal Law § 2596, Treatment and Final Disposition of Incompetent Defendant—Further Proceedings With Respect to Incompetent Defendants Charged With Offenses Other Than Serious Felonies.

OH Jur. 3d Criminal Law § 2585.5, Conduct of Hearing—Evidence.

OH Jur. 3d Incompetent Persons § 40, Admission of Criminal Defendants.

Treatises and Practice Aids

Markus, Trial Handbook for Ohio Lawyers, § 4:59, Criminal Case—Defenses—Insanity—Competence to Stand Trial or to be Sentenced.

Klein, Darling, & Terez, Baldwin's Ohio Practice Civil Practice § 1:53, Civ. R. 1(C)(6): Commitment of the Mentally Ill--Proceedings Under RC 2945.38 and RC 2945.40.

Katz, Giannelli, Blair and Lipton, Baldwin's Ohio Practice, Criminal Law, § 54:1, Introduction.

Katz, Giannelli, Blair and Lipton, Baldwin's Ohio Practice, Criminal Law, § 54:8, Findings.

Katz, Giannelli, Blair and Lipton, Baldwin's Ohio Practice, Criminal Law, § 144:4, Plea of Not Guilty by Reason of Insanity at Arraignment.

Katz, Giannelli, Blair and Lipton, Baldwin's Ohio Practice, Criminal Law, § 144:5, Acceptance of Plea of Not Guilty by Reason of Insanity After Arraignment.

Katz, Giannelli, Blair and Lipton, Baldwin's Ohio Practice, Criminal Law, § 144:7, Entry Ordering Inquiry Into Insanity of Defendant.

Katz, Giannelli, Blair and Lipton, Baldwin's Ohio Practice, Criminal Law, § 144:8, Entry Finding Defendant [Competent/Incompetent] to Stand Trial.

Carlin, Baldwin's Ohio Practice, Merrick-Rippner Probate Law § 101:18, Involuntary Admission—Notice and Assessment Requirements for All Involuntary Patients.

Carlin, Baldwin's Ohio Practice, Merrick-Rippner Probate Law § 101:46, Initial Treatment for Persons Found Incompetent to Stand Trial; Maximum Duration.

Carlin, Baldwin's Ohio Practice, Merrick-Rippner Probate Law § 101:47, Further Commitment of Persons Found Incompetent to Stand Trial.

Carlin, Baldwin's Ohio Practice, Merrick-Rippner Probate Law § 101:58, Consent to Treatment (RC 5122.271)—Psychotropic Medication.

Law Review and Journal Commentaries

Contesting Incompetency to Stand Trial, Comment. 2 Ohio N U L Rev 739 (1975).

Fit to die: Drug–induced competency for the purpose of execution, Comment. 20 S Ill U L J 149 (Fall 1995).

Foucha v. Louisiana: The Danger of Commitment Based on Dangerousness, Note. 44 Case W Res L Rev 157 (Fall 1993).

Informed Consent for Medication in Persons with Mental Retardation and Mental Illness. Joan L. O'Sullivan and Breck G. Borcherding, 12 Health Matrix: J Law-Medicine 63 (Winter 2002).

Ohio's Extra Measure of Procedural Due Process: The Effect of Compliance with Supreme Court Requirements in Criminal and Commitment Proceedings in Jackson v. Indiana. 4 Cap U L Rev 291 (1975).

Notes of Decisions

---

1. Constitutional issues—In general

Burden was on defendant in initial competency hearing to present evidence sufficient for trial court to make finding on whether defendant could be restored to competency within maximum period allowed for charged crime; finding was not required at the first competency hearing by statute or by due process principles. Youngstown v. Ortiz (Ohio App. 7 Dist., 05-01-2003) 153 Ohio App.3d 271, 793 N.E.2d 498, 2003-Ohio-2238, appeal not allowed 99 Ohio St.3d 1545, 795 N.E.2d 683, 2003-Ohio-4671. Criminal Law ⚷ 625.15

When a trial court orders an incompetent defendant to be forcibly medicated with psychotropic drugs in an effort to restore the defendant to competency, that order is final and appealable under statute enumerating various categories of final orders. State v. Muncie (Ohio, 05-23-2001) 91 Ohio St.3d 440, 746 N.E.2d 1092, 2001-Ohio-93. Criminal Law ⚷ 1023(3)

Although statute governing disposition of person found mentally incompetent to stand trial allows for different procedure to be utilized, determination of whether person is subject to hospitalization is still made under standard authorizing judicial hospitalization, and statute authorizing judicial hospitalization provides numerous procedural safeguards which sufficiently satisfy requirements of due process; thus, standard for judicial hospitalization does not violate due process or equal protection as it relates to those persons found incompetent to stand trial. In re Burton (Ohio 1984) 11 Ohio St.3d 147, 464 N.E.2d 530, 11 O.B.R. 465. Constitutional Law ⚷ 242.1(5); Constitutional Law ⚷ 255(5); Mental Health ⚷ 433(1)

Confinement in mental hospital of criminal defendant who has raised insanity defense and has been acquitted on that ground, solely on basis of trial court's finding of insanity by preponderance of evidence, until he has regained his sanity or is no longer dangerous, does not deny due process even if result is to confine acquittee beyond maximum period of incarceration carried by his offense; insanity acquittee is not entitled, at end of confinement period, to civil commitment hearing at which proof of his insanity would have to be established by clear and convincing evidence. Jones v. U.S. (U.S.Dist.Col. 1983) 103 S.Ct. 3043, 463 U.S. 354, 77 L.Ed.2d 694.

2. —— Due process, constitutional issues

Where defendant was deemed incompetent to stand trial and committed to an institution to undergo treatment for an arbitrary period of up to one year, according to RC 2945.38, he was denied due process because the statute, as amended by Senate Bill 285, eliminated the requirement that there be a substantial probability that the defendant would become competent to stand trial after one year of treatment in order to be committed, thereby diluting the requirement that the nature and duration of the commitment bear some reasonable relation to the purpose of the commitment. State v. Sullivan (Ohio App. 2 Dist., Montgomery, 10-08-1999) No. 17509, 1999 WL 812327, Unreported, appeal allowed 88 Ohio St.3d 1436, 724 N.E.2d 811, affirmed and remanded 90 Ohio St.3d 502, 739 N.E.2d 788, 2001-Ohio-6.

Trial court was required to determine if defendant could be restored to competency within one year at initial hearing, rather than if competency could be restored within 60-day maximum period for first degree misdemeanors, and thus trial court acted reasonably and did not violate due process by ordering treatment at first hearing, even though evidence suggested defendant would not be competent within 60-day period; court found at initial hearing that defendant was likely to be competent within one year, defendant failed to prove he would not be competent within maximum period, and statute provided for second hearing to determine if defendant would be restored to competency within 60-days. Youngstown v. Ortiz (Ohio App. 7 Dist., 05-01-2003) 153 Ohio App.3d 271, 793 N.E.2d 498, 2003-Ohio-2238, appeal not allowed 99 Ohio St.3d 1545, 795 N.E.2d 683, 2003-Ohio-4671. Constitutional Law ⚷ 268.2(2); Criminal Law ⚷ 625(3)

Statute's two-tiered review of defendant's competency, under which an initial hearing determined whether defendant could be restored to competency within one year and second hearing determined whether competency would be restored within maximum period allowed for charged committed, did not violate due process. Youngstown v. Ortiz (Ohio App. 7 Dist., 05-01-2003) 153 Ohio App.3d 271, 793 N.E.2d 498, 2003-Ohio-2238, appeal not allowed 99 Ohio St.3d 1545, 795 N.E.2d 683, 2003-Ohio-4671. Constitutional Law ⚷ 268.2(2); Criminal Law ⚷ 625(3)

Fundamental principles of due process require that a criminal defendant who is legally incompetent may not be tried. State v. Thomas (Ohio, 12-11-2002) 97 Ohio St.3d 309, 779 N.E.2d 1017, 2002-Ohio-6624, reconsideration denied 97 Ohio St.3d 1498, 780 N.E.2d 1022, 2002-Ohio-7248, stay granted 98 Ohio St.3d 1403, 781 N.E.2d 221, 2003-Ohio-40, certiorari denied 123 S.Ct. 2295, 539 U.S. 916, 156 L.Ed.2d 133. Constitutional Law ⚷ 268.2(2)

Statute requiring defendants found incompetent to stand trial to undergo mandatory period of treatment to attempt to restore their competency violated due process rights of defendant who was found incompetent to stand trial; mandatory treatment was not rationally related to purpose for treatment, and statute failed to provide for discontinuing treatment if person supervising defendant's treatment reported that treatment was not effective and that defendant would not attain competency to stand trial in foreseeable future. State v. Sullivan (Ohio, 01-03-2001) 90 Ohio St.3d 502, 739 N.E.2d 788, 2001-Ohio-6. Constitutional Law ⚷ 255(5); Mental Health ⚷ 433(1)

Although one year was a reasonable amount of time to hold incompetent defendant to restore him or her to competency to stand trial, if it is determined prior to or during treatment that the defendant cannot be restored to competency, statute requiring treatment of incompetent defendants for mandatory period violates due process requirement that, as soon as it is reliably determined that the defendant will not, in the foreseeable future, attain the mental competence to stand trial, then other procedures must be instituted to either release the person or civilly commit him indefinitely. State v. Sullivan (Ohio, 01-03-2001) 90 Ohio St.3d 502, 739 N.E.2d 788, 2001-Ohio-6. Constitutional Law ⚷ 255(5); Mental Health ⚷ 433(1)

A criminal accused cannot be tried, sentenced, or executed while insane, and an inquiry into the accused's mental state is required if before, during, or after trial, facts brought to the attention of the trial court, either from the court's own observations or upon the suggestion of counsel, raise doubts about the accused's sanity; therefore, it is a deprivation of due process rights for a court to sentence a defendant who begins to exhibit symptoms of mental illness between the time of his conviction and sentencing and then remains incompetent after fifteen months of psychiatric treatment. State v. Phelps (Hamilton 1991) 75 Ohio App.3d 573, 600 N.E.2d 329, dismissed, jurisdictional motion overruled 62 Ohio St.3d 1500, 583 N.E.2d 971.

Commitment of accused to Lima state hospital by reason of inability to stand trial does not deprive accused of due process where there is a reasonable expectation of recovery. In re Horvath (Ohio 1975) 42 Ohio St.2d 60, 325 N.E.2d 895, 71 O.O.2d 38.

RC 2945.37 and 2945.38 create an expectation of protection of competency to stand trial that is protected by the Due Process Clause and whatever procedure is applied by the state to determine competency must be adequate to protect the defendant's due process right to not be convicted if incompetent. Lagway v. Dallman (N.D.Ohio 1992) 806 F.Supp. 1322.

3. —— Equal protection, constitutional issues

Statute allowing for involuntary administration of antipsychotic drugs to mentally ill defendant in order to restore competency to stand trial did not violate equal protection by allegedly failing to provide same procedural safeguards as applicable to persons involuntarily committed who pose imminent threat of harm to themselves or others or lack capacity to give or withhold consent about medical treatment; mentally ill defendant needed to be restored to competency in order to defend himself against charges of rape and assault, which interest was not implicated by individual subject to civil commitment proceedings. State v. Barker (Ohio App. 2 Dist., Montgomery, 01-28-2005) No. 20417, 2005-Ohio-298, 2005 WL 187392, Unreported. Constitutional Law ⚷ 242.1(5); Mental Health ⚷ 433(1)

4. Competency to stand trial—In general

Trial court was not required to hold hearing prior to sentencing to evaluate defendant's competency; defense counsel expressed no concern regarding defendant's competency, trial court was fully aware of defendant's history and his actions during trial, and there was no indication that defendant was unbalanced or incompetent. State v. Roberts (Ohio App. 6 Dist., Sandusky, 12-03-2004) No. S-04-003, 2004-Ohio-6468, 2004 WL 2785424, Unreported. Sentencing And Punishment ⚷ 268

Denying mother's request for continuance of permanent child custody hearing based on mother's alleged temporary incompetency was not abuse of discretion in termination of parental rights proceeding; although mother had previously been found incompetent to stand trial in unrelated criminal case, mother waited until day of hearing to seek continuance, statute under which mother was referred for treatment in criminal case permitted treatment for up to one year such that child could have remained in custodial limbo for additional year if court had granted continuance, mother was represented by two competent attorneys and had guardian ad litem appointed to represent her interests, and mother's alleged incompetence did not affect issue of whether maternal aunt was suitable custodian for child. In re A.U. (Ohio App. 2 Dist., Montgomery, 11-19-2004) No. 20583, No. 20585,

2004-Ohio-6219, 2004 WL 2659137, Unreported. Infants ⟹ 204

Evidence did not support defendant's claim at initial competency hearing that he would not be restored to competency to stand trial on aggravated menacing charge within 60-day maximum period for first-degree misdemeanors so as to require court to dismiss charges against him; doctor testified it would take two or three months to restore competency. Youngstown v. Ortiz (Ohio App. 7 Dist., 05-01-2003) 153 Ohio App.3d 271, 793 N.E.2d 498, 2003-Ohio-2238, appeal not allowed 99 Ohio St.3d 1545, 795 N.E.2d 683, 2003-Ohio-4671. Criminal Law ⟹ 625.15

Applying prior version of statute governing treatment of defendants found to be incompetent to stand trial, after amended version of statute was held unconstitutional, remand to trial court was for a finding as to whether there was a substantial probability that with treatment defendant would attain competency to stand trial on rape and gross sexual imposition charges within one year. State v. Sullivan (Ohio, 01-03-2001) 90 Ohio St.3d 502, 739 N.E.2d 788, 2001-Ohio-6. Criminal Law ⟹ 1181.5(4)

RC 2945.39 does not provide an exclusive method for the release of one acquitted on the sole ground of his insanity at the time of the commission of a criminal act; if such person is declared sane at the time of trial, the presumption that such insanity continues has been overcome, and he may have recourse to the writ of habeas corpus to secure his release from a commitment to the Lima state hospital. Collins v. Campbell (Summit 1965) 4 Ohio App.2d 42, 211 N.E.2d 96, 33 O.O.2d 59.

If upon the issue of insanity the accused be found insane, he is sent to an insane hospital; if found sane, he shall then "be proceeded against as provided by law;" if found sane, the accused is restored to the same rights that any other accused person would have, respecting his right of election to be tried by the court. State v. Smith (Ohio 1931) 123 Ohio St. 237, 174 N.E. 768, 9 Ohio Law Abs. 286, 34 Ohio Law Rep. 71.

Defendant was entitled, at sentencing in homicide case, to credit for the period during which he was confined for a determination of competency to stand trial and for the period, following his release from an involuntary civil commitment as a mentally ill person that did not qualify as pretrial confinement, during which he was held until sentencing. State v. Stafford (Ohio App. 7 Dist., Noble, 09-26-2002) No. 265, 2002-Ohio-5243, 2002 WL 31170127, Unreported, reconsideration denied 2002-Ohio-7184, 2002 WL 31859518, appeal not allowed 98 Ohio St.3d 1477, 784 N.E.2d 710, 2003-Ohio-974, appeal not allowed 98 Ohio St.3d 1515, 786 N.E.2d 64, 2003-Ohio-1572. Sentencing And Punishment ⟹ 1158

Defendant was not prejudiced by fact that grand jury issued re-indictment on murder charge at a time when defendant was civilly committed as a mentally ill person and assertedly had not been restored to competency to stand trial, where defendant was physically and mentally present at his arraignment following discharge from civil commitment and at every stage of the proceedings that followed until his conviction and sentencing. State v. Stafford (Ohio App. 7 Dist., Noble, 09-26-2002) No. 265, 2002-Ohio-5243, 2002 WL 31170127, Unreported, reconsideration denied 2002-Ohio-7184, 2002 WL 31859518, appeal not allowed 98 Ohio St.3d 1477, 784 N.E.2d 710, 2003-Ohio-974, appeal not allowed 98 Ohio St.3d 1515, 786 N.E.2d 64, 2003-Ohio-1572. Criminal Law ⟹ 1167(1); Indictment And Information ⟹ 15(1)

5. —— Administration of medication, competency to stand trial

Defendant adjudicated incompetent to stand trial for rape and assault did not have right to independent psychiatric or psychological evaluation, in proceedings on petition to have antipsychotic drugs involuntarily administered to restore defendant's competency to stand trial. State v. Barker (Ohio App. 2 Dist., Montgomery, 01-28-2005) No. 20417, 2005-Ohio-298, 2005 WL 187392, Unreported. Mental Health ⟹ 436.1

6. —— Admissibility of evidence, competency to stand trial

A finding by jury, that defendant in a criminal case is sane, made in a preliminary hearing, between the indictment and trial, is not admissible on behalf of state in the trial of the criminal case, in rebuttal of the evidence offered by defendant in support of defense of insanity. State v. Hagert (Ohio 1944) 144 Ohio St. 316, 58 N.E.2d 764, 29 O.O. 454.

The physician-patient privilege does not apply to involuntary patients who are confined and receiving treatment by court order. State v Jackson, No. CA–2500 (5th Dist Ct App, Richland, 1–21–88).

Statements made by the defendant during an examination to determine his competency to stand trial which fall short of outright confession of guilt are admissible if they relate to competency. State v Jackson, No. CA–2500 (5th Dist Ct App, Richland, 1–21–88).

7. —— Duty of court, competency to stand trial

Trial court's failure to conduct pretrial competency hearing to restore defendant's competency prior to retrial in felonious assault prosecution was reversible error; on remand for new trial, trial court committed defendant for treatment upon finding him incompetent to stand trial, but ultimately commenced retrial proceedings without requisite findings to evince the restoration of defendant's competency. State v. Jackson (Ohio App. 8 Dist., Cuyahoga, 07-01-2004) No. 82652, 2004-Ohio-3474, 2004 WL 1472021, Unreported. Criminal Law ⟹ 625(3); Criminal Law ⟹ 1166(12)

Trial court had burden under competency statute to make finding that a defendant had a substantial probability of being restored to competency within one year, based on any evidence presented, when the court decided at initial competency hearing to order defendant into treatment. Youngstown v.

Ortiz (Ohio App. 7 Dist., 05-01-2003) 153 Ohio App.3d 271, 793 N.E.2d 498, 2003-Ohio-2238, appeal not allowed 99 Ohio St.3d 1545, 795 N.E.2d 683, 2003-Ohio-4671. Criminal Law ⚿ 625.15; Criminal Law ⚿ 625.30

8. —— Time requirements, competency to stand trial

Statutory ten-day period in which trial court "shall" conduct hearing on petition for involuntary administration of medication to mentally incompetent defendant in order to restore competency to stand trial for rape and assault was directory rather than mandatory, and thus trial court did not lack jurisdiction to conduct hearing on petition after ten-day period had elapsed. State v. Barker (Ohio App. 2 Dist., Montgomery, 01-28-2005) No. 20417, 2005-Ohio-298, 2005 WL 187392, Unreported. Mental Health ⚿ 436.1

9. —— Appeals, competency to stand trial

The determination of a defendant's competency to stand trial made by a trial court pursuant to RC 2945.38 is not a final, appealable order. State v. Scott (Franklin 1984) 20 Ohio App.3d 215, 485 N.E.2d 818, 20 O.B.R. 261. Criminal Law ⚿ 1023(2)

An order dismissing a defendant's motion for a competency hearing in the trial court is a final appealable order. State ex rel. Robertson v. Nurre (Hamilton 1981) 3 Ohio App.3d 5, 443 N.E.2d 193, 3 O.B.R. 5.

10. Jurisdiction to commit

The common pleas court has jurisdiction to commit an accused to the Lima state hospital before indictment after an affidavit has been filed against such accused. In re Horvath (Ohio 1975) 42 Ohio St.2d 60, 325 N.E.2d 895, 71 O.O.2d 38. Mental Health ⚿ 436.1

A court of common pleas has jurisdiction over an accused pursuant to RC 2945.37 and RC 2945.38 when a magistrate's transcript has been filed against the accused. Burton v. Reshetylo (Ohio 1974) 38 Ohio St.2d 35, 309 N.E.2d 907, 67 O.O.2d 53. Mental Health ⚿ 436.1

A criminal division of a common pleas court lacks jurisdiction to commit a person to the Lima state hospital until restored to reason under RC 2945.37 and RC 2945.38 unless that person has first been indicted by a grand jury. Burton v. Reshetylo (Allen 1973) 35 Ohio App.2d 113, 300 N.E.2d 249, 64 O.O.2d 234, affirmed 38 Ohio St.2d 35, 309 N.E.2d 907, 67 O.O.2d 53.

A person committed to the Lima state hospital under the purported authority of RC 2945.37 and RC 2945.38, but who has not been indicted, is illegally restrained of his liberty and must be released forthwith from that hospital, provided, however, that if his mental condition is such that he is not sane and his release would result in his being dangerous to himself or to society the execution of the order of release will be suspended for a reasonable period of time to permit the probate division of an appropriate common pleas court, having jurisdiction, to cause his commitment to a proper institution. Burton v. Reshetylo (Allen 1973) 35 Ohio App.2d 113, 300 N.E.2d 249, 64 O.O.2d 234, affirmed 38 Ohio St.2d 35, 309 N.E.2d 907, 67 O.O.2d 53.

11. Commitment, treatment and release

Trial court's order that side effects from involuntarily administered antipsychotic drugs to mentally incompetent defendant were to be monitored, by itself, did not vitiate trial court's finding that drugs would restore defendant to competency to stand trial for rape and assault. State v. Barker (Ohio App. 2 Dist., Montgomery, 01-28-2005) No. 20417, 2005-Ohio-298, 2005 WL 187392, Unreported. Mental Health ⚿ 436.1

Trial court's failure to make specific written finding that defendant would spend considerable amount of time in institution if not given antipsychotic drugs, in support of order requiring involuntary administration of drugs to make defendant competent to stand trial for rape and assault, was not reversible error; trial court stated that it had considered facts and circumstances of defendant's case and found no special circumstances that would lessen State's interest in bringing defendant to trial, and such finding warranted presumption that trial court considered factor of potentially lengthy commitment. State v. Barker (Ohio App. 2 Dist., Montgomery, 01-28-2005) No. 20417, 2005-Ohio-298, 2005 WL 187392, Unreported. Mental Health ⚿ 436.1

Defendant's improper re-indictment during his civil commitment pending trial was in essence harmless, where defendant was not arraigned in connection with new charges until after doctors discharged him from civil commitment. State v. Stafford (Ohio App. 7 Dist., Noble, 12-18-2002) No. 265, 2002-Ohio-7184, 2002 WL 31859518, Unreported, appeal not allowed 98 Ohio St.3d 1477, 784 N.E.2d 710, 2003-Ohio-974, appeal not allowed 98 Ohio St.3d 1515, 786 N.E.2d 64, 2003-Ohio-1572. Criminal Law ⚿ 1166(3)

Where a defendant is adjudged incompetent to stand trial, not likely to become competent within a year, and mentally ill, and is confined to a hospital pursuant to RC 2945.38(H)(1), the hospital's transfer of the patient to voluntary status is a release within the meaning of RC 2945.38(H)(1) and reindictment is not barred, even though the hospital fails to give the notice of change of status required by RC 5122.21. State v. Davis (Summit 1984) 14 Ohio App.3d 416, 471 N.E.2d 818, 14 O.B.R. 534.

In commitment proceeding for defendant found incompetent to stand trial, one of salient issues to be determined is whether public interest requires institutionalization by court order of defendant. In re Elmore (Franklin 1983) 13 Ohio App.3d 79, 468 N.E.2d 97, 13 O.B.R. 93. Mental Health ⚿ 436.1

A defendant is "released" from a hospital or institution within the meaning of RC 2945.38(H)(1) when he becomes a voluntary patient and is permitted to leave at his pleasure, even though he remains at the institution or hospital. State v. Davis (Summit 1983) 12 Ohio App.3d 84, 466 N.E.2d 572, 12 O.B.R. 283.

The requirement that the notice of RC 2945.38(C) be in writing is not a jurisdictional limitation. State v. Davis (Summit 1983) 12 Ohio App.3d 84, 466 N.E.2d 572, 12 O.B.R. 283.

Evidence was insufficient for trial court to make determination of whether medication should be withheld from patient found incompetent to stand trial in order to establish cause and degree of remission of patient's mental illness, where only one psychiatrist testified to feasibility of drug holiday for patient, and patient's treating physician was not even questioned in that regard. In re Burton (Ohio 1984) 11 Ohio St.3d 147, 464 N.E.2d 530, 11 O.B.R. 465. Mental Health ⚷ 436.1

Under 1978 H 565, § 5, eff. 11–1–78, persons who had been placed in custody as incompetent to stand trial prior to the effective date of the act, must be released on the earlier of two stated deadlines "in the manner specified in divisions (E) and (F) of... 2945.38... as amended by... [the] act"; the determination about the defendant's present incompetence must be made by the trial court, not the probate division. State ex rel. Robertson v. Nurre (Hamilton 1981) 3 Ohio App.3d 5, 443 N.E.2d 193, 3 O.B.R. 5. Mental Health ⚷ 437

Where the accused in a criminal case is found incompetent to stand trial and is committed to Lima state hospital pursuant to RC 2945.38, such finding is not a final order. State v. Hunt (Ohio 1976) 47 Ohio St.2d 170, 351 N.E.2d 106, 1 O.O.3d 99. Criminal Law ⚷ 1023(3)

Where an accused is unlikely to be able to stand trial in the foreseeable future, the common pleas court should release the person into the custody of the probate court pursuant to RC 5122.35. Campbell v. Watkins (Ohio 1974) 38 Ohio St.2d 197, 311 N.E.2d 658, 67 O.O.2d 206.

An accused committed pursuant to RC 2945.37 and RC 2945.38 can be held only for the period of time reasonably necessary to determine whether it is probable that he will attain the mental competency required to stand trial in the foreseeable future. Burton v. Reshetylo (Ohio 1974) 38 Ohio St.2d 35, 309 N.E.2d 907, 67 O.O.2d 53. Mental Health ⚷ 437

The state upon committing an individual "until he regains his sanity" incurs a responsibility to provide such care as is reasonably calculated to achieve that goal. Davis v. Watkins (N.D.Ohio 1974) 384 F.Supp. 1196. Mental Health ⚷ 51.1

12. Dismissal and reindictment

Trial court abused its discretion by dismissing indictment against defendant with prejudice upon finding him incompetent to stand trial and unrestorable within the time frame specified by law, where record was devoid of any finding made by the trial court that defendant was denied a constitutional or statutory right; State was free to seek his re-indictment. State v. Worwell (Ohio App. 8 Dist., Cuyahoga, 12-01-2005) No. 86032, 2005-Ohio-6343, 2005 WL 3219726, Unreported. Criminal Law ⚷ 625.30

On reindictment following dismissal of a prior indictment upon an incompetency finding, the state did not have to prove that defendant was competent. State v. Stanley (Ohio App. 1 Dist., 06-25-1997) 121 Ohio App.3d 673, 700 N.E.2d 881, dismissed, appeal not allowed 80 Ohio St.3d 1432, 685 N.E.2d 543, denial of post-conviction relief affirmed 82 Fed.Appx. 407, 2003 WL 22290187. Criminal Law ⚷ 625.15

Trial court's initial determination of defendant's incompetency, which led to dismissal of the indictment, was not law of the case precluding reindictment, where no reviewing court made any competency determination. State v. Stanley (Ohio App. 1 Dist., 06-25-1997) 121 Ohio App.3d 673, 700 N.E.2d 881, dismissed, appeal not allowed 80 Ohio St.3d 1432, 685 N.E.2d 543, denial of post-conviction relief affirmed 82 Fed.Appx. 407, 2003 WL 22290187. Courts ⚷ 99(6)

Once found incompetent and not restorable within one year, a defendant cannot be reindicted for the same conduct unless he either was institutionalized and later released or was found not to be subject to institutionalization. State v. Stanley (Ohio App. 1 Dist., 06-25-1997) 121 Ohio App.3d 673, 700 N.E.2d 881, dismissed, appeal not allowed 80 Ohio St.3d 1432, 685 N.E.2d 543, denial of post-conviction relief affirmed 82 Fed.Appx. 407, 2003 WL 22290187. Indictment And Information ⚷ 15(1)

Hearsay cannot be used to demonstrate that a defendant whose indictment was dismissed upon an incompetency finding has been released from institutionalization so as to permit reindictment. State v. Stanley (Ohio App. 1 Dist., 06-25-1997) 121 Ohio App.3d 673, 700 N.E.2d 881, dismissed, appeal not allowed 80 Ohio St.3d 1432, 685 N.E.2d 543, denial of post-conviction relief affirmed 82 Fed.Appx. 407, 2003 WL 22290187. Indictment And Information ⚷ 15(1)

Reindictment following dismissal of a prior indictment upon an incompetency finding is not merely a reinstatement of the prior indictment; rather, the state must institute an entirely separate proceeding, starting with obtaining an indictment from the grand jury, as if the prior indictment had not taken place. State v. Stanley (Ohio App. 1 Dist., 06-25-1997) 121 Ohio App.3d 673, 700 N.E.2d 881, dismissed, appeal not allowed 80 Ohio St.3d 1432, 685 N.E.2d 543, denial of post-conviction relief affirmed 82 Fed.Appx. 407, 2003 WL 22290187. Indictment And Information ⚷ 15(1)

A trial court's sentencing of a defendant convicted of aggravated arson is improper where the court sentences the defendant after he had been found incompetent to be sentenced and was committed to psychiatric treatment for more than three-and-one half years, since the trial court, after finding the defendant still incompetent to be sentenced after fifteen months of psychiatric treatment, was required to relinquish jurisdiction to the probate court and to dismiss the indictment against the defendant. State v. Phelps (Hamilton 1991) 75 Ohio App.3d 573, 600 N.E.2d 329, dismissed, jurisdictional motion overruled 62 Ohio St.3d 1500, 583 N.E.2d 971. Sentencing And Punishment ⚷ 250

Determination of a defendant's status for purposes of reindictment under RC 2945.38(H) is erroneous if based on hearsay, and a remand for an evidentiary hearing to determine whether the indictment should have been quashed is proper. State v. Davis (Summit 1983) 12 Ohio App.3d 84, 466 N.E.2d 572, 12 O.B.R. 283.

If a defendant is found to be incompetent to stand trial, the indictment against him must be dismissed pursuant to RC 2945.38(G), and before the defendant can again be prosecuted for the same crime, he must be re-indicted by the grand jury; unless the defendant waives his right to indictment pursuant to Crim R 7(A), the original indictment may not be reinstated against him upon motion to the court. State v. Brown (Hamilton 1981) 2 Ohio App.3d 400, 442 N.E.2d 475, 2 O.B.R. 475.

Grand jury's re-indictment of defendant on murder charge, at a time when he was civilly committed as a mentally ill person and had assertedly not been restored to competency to stand trial, in no way affected the jurisdiction of court of common pleas over the matter. State v. Stafford (Ohio App. 7 Dist., Noble, 09-26-2002) No. 265, 2002-Ohio-5243, 2002 WL 31170127, Unreported, reconsideration denied 2002-Ohio-7184, 2002 WL 31859518, appeal not allowed 98 Ohio St.3d 1477, 784 N.E.2d 710, 2003-Ohio-974, appeal not allowed 98 Ohio St.3d 1515, 786 N.E.2d 64, 2003-Ohio-1572. Criminal Law ⚷ 99

13. Probate court

When a common pleas court which has committed a person to Lima state hospital until he be restored to his reason under RC 2945.37 et seq. is presented with the issue of his mental capacity to have executed a deed on a later date when the probate court had determined that a guardianship was no longer necessary for such person, this intervening order of the probate court does not preclude the consideration by such common pleas court of the issue, nor is such consideration a collateral attack on the action of the probate court, where the finding of the probate court that the guardianship should be terminated could be properly made without a determination of the ward's sanity. In re Moser (Ohio Com.Pl. 1967) 19 Ohio Misc. 81, 246 N.E.2d 626, 47 O.O.2d 420, 48 O.O.2d 253.

In the absence of contrary proof, a condition of lack of mental capacity which has been judicially determined is presumed to continue; an intervening determination of another court on the subject may be given such weight as the court which made the original determination finds proper on a later consideration of the person's present condition. In re Moser (Ohio Com.Pl. 1967) 19 Ohio Misc. 81, 246 N.E.2d 626, 47 O.O.2d 420, 48 O.O.2d 253.

2945.381 Disposition of mentally incompetent persons; hearing—Repealed

(1978 H 565, eff. 11–1–78; 1975 S 185)

2945.39 Civil commitment; expiration of time for treatment; jurisdiction; hearing; reports

(A) If a defendant who is charged with an offense described in division (C)(1) of section 2945.38 of the Revised Code is found incompetent to stand trial, after the expiration of the maximum time for treatment as specified in division (C) of that section or after the court finds that there is not a substantial probability that the defendant will become competent to stand trial even if the defendant is provided with a course of treatment, one of the following applies:

(1) The court or the prosecutor may file an affidavit in probate court for civil commitment of the defendant in the manner provided in Chapter 5122. or 5123. of the Revised Code. If the court or prosecutor files an affidavit for civil commitment, the court may detain the defendant for ten days pending civil commitment. If the probate court commits the defendant subsequent to the court's or prosecutor's filing of an affidavit for civil commitment, the chief clinical officer of the hospital or facility, the managing officer of the institution, the director of the program, or the person to which the defendant is committed or admitted shall send to the prosecutor the notices described in divisions (H)(4)(a)(i) to (iii) of section 2945.38 of the Revised Code within the periods of time and under the circumstances specified in those divisions.

(2) On the motion of the prosecutor or on its own motion, the court may retain jurisdiction over the defendant if, at a hearing, the court finds both of the following by clear and convincing evidence:

(a) The defendant committed the offense with which the defendant is charged.

(b) The defendant is a mentally ill person subject to hospitalization by court order or a mentally retarded person subject to institutionalization by court order.

(B) In making its determination under division (A)(2) of this section as to whether to retain jurisdiction over the defendant, the court may consider all relevant evidence, including, but not limited to, any relevant psychiatric, psychological, or medical testimony or reports, the acts constituting the offense charged, and any history of the defendant that is relevant to the defendant's ability to conform to the law.

(C) If the court conducts a hearing as described in division (A)(2) of this section and if the court does not make both findings described in divisions (A)(2)(a) and (b) of this section by clear and convincing evidence, the court shall dismiss the indictment, information, or complaint against the defendant. Upon the dismissal, the court shall discharge the defendant unless the court or prosecutor files an affidavit in probate court for civil commitment of the defendant pursuant to Chapter 5122. or 5123. of the Revised Code. If the court or prosecutor files an affidavit for civil commitment, the court may order that the defendant be detained for up to ten days pending the civil commitment. If the probate court commits the defendant subsequent to the court's or prosecutor's filing of an affidavit for civil commitment, the chief clinical officer of the hospital or facility, the managing officer of the institution, the director of the program, or the person to which the defendant is committed or admitted shall send to the prosecutor the notices described in divisions (H)(4)(a)(i) to (iii) of section 2945.38 of the Revised Code within the periods of time and under the circumstances specified in those divisions. A dismissal of charges under this division is not a bar to further criminal proceedings based on the same conduct.

(D)(1) If the court conducts a hearing as described in division (A)(2) of this section and if the court makes the findings described in divisions (A)(2)(a) and (b) of this section by clear and convincing evidence, the court shall commit the defendant to a hospital operated by the department of mental health, a facility operated by the department of mental retardation and developmental disabilities, or another medical or psychiatric facility, as appropriate. In determining the place and nature of the commitment, the court shall order the least restrictive commitment alternative available that is consistent with public safety and the welfare of the defendant. In weighing these factors, the court shall give preference to protecting public safety.

(2) If a court makes a commitment of a defendant under division (D)(1) of this section, the prosecutor shall send to the place of commitment all reports of the defendant's current mental condition and, except as otherwise provided in this division, any other relevant information, including, but not limited to, a transcript of the hearing held pursuant to division (A)(2) of this section, copies of relevant police reports, and copies of any prior arrest and conviction records that pertain to the defendant and that the prosecutor possesses. The prosecutor shall send the reports of the defendant's current mental condition in every case of commitment, and, unless the prosecutor determines that the release of any of the other relevant information to unauthorized persons would interfere with the effective prosecution of any person or would create a substantial risk of harm to any person, the prosecutor also shall send the other relevant information. Upon admission of a defendant committed under division (D)(1) of this section, the place of commitment shall send to the board of alcohol, drug addiction, and mental health services or the community mental health board serving the county in which the charges against the defendant were filed a copy of all reports of the defendant's current mental condition and a copy of the other relevant information provided by the prosecutor under this division, including, if provided, a transcript of the hearing held pursuant to division (A)(2) of this section, the relevant police reports, and the prior arrest and conviction records that pertain to the defendant and that the prosecutor possesses.

(3) If a court makes a commitment under division (D)(1) of this section, all further proceedings shall be in accordance with sections 2945.401 and 2945.402 of the Revised Code.

(2001 S 122, eff. 2–20–02; 1996 S 285, eff. 7–1–97)

Historical and Statutory Notes

Ed. Note: Former 2945.39 repealed by 1996 S 285, eff. 7–1–97; 1990 H 484, eff. 11–5–90; 1981 H 1; 1980 H 965, H 736, S 297, H 900; 1978 H 565.

Ed. Note: Prior 2945.39 repealed by 1978 H 565, eff. 11–1–78; 1972 H 511; 132 v S 523; 1953 H 1; GC 13441–3.

Pre–1953 H 1 Amendments: 113 v 177, Ch 19, § 3

Amendment Note: 2001 S 122 inserted "or after the court finds that there is not a substantial probability that the defendant will become competent to stand trial even if the defendant is provided with a course of treatment" in division (A); and made other nonsubstantive changes.

Cross References

Arrest and detention until warrant can be obtained, 2935.03

Department of mental retardation and developmental disabilities, definitions, 5123.01

Department of mental retardation and developmental disabilities, involuntary institutionalization procedures, 5123.71

Department of mental retardation and developmental disabilities, judicial proceedings, procedures, 5123.76

Hospitalization of mentally ill, admission of voluntary patient, 5122.02

Hospitalization of mentally ill, applicability of provisions, 5122.011

Hospitalization of mentally ill, confidentiality of records, 5122.31

Hospitalization of mentally ill, hearings, attorneys, 5122.15

Hospitalization of mentally ill, involuntary confinement, 5122.05

Hospitalization of mentally ill, not guilty by reason of insanity, definitions, 5122.01

Hospitalization of mentally ill, right to writ of habeas corpus, 5122.30

Institutionalization of person incompetent to stand trial or not guilty by reason of insanity, applicability of provisions, 5123.011

Judicial hospitalization of mentally ill, 5122.11

Mental health department, funds for services for persons committed to, 5119.62

Mentally ill patients absent without leave, applicability, 5122.26

Mentally retarded person may apply for admission for short-term care, 5123.701

Offenses against justice and public administration; detention, defined, 2921.01

Plea of insanity, Crim R 11

System for tracking and monitoring persons found not guilty by reason of insanity, 5119.57

Verdict, Crim R 31

Voluntary hospitalization of persons found not guilty by reason of insanity, 5123.69

Ohio Administrative Code References

Community forensic psychiatric centers, OAC 5122–32–01

Library References

Mental Health ⚷434, 436.

Westlaw Topic No. 257A.

C.J.S. Criminal Law §§ 549 to 554.

C.J.S. Mental Health §§ 238 to 240.

Research References

ALR Library

72 ALR 5th 109, Adequacy of Defense Counsel's Representation of Criminal Client--Pretrial Conduct or Conduct at Unspecified Time Regarding Issues of Insanity.

Encyclopedias

OH Jur. 3d Criminal Law § 2592, Initial Disposition of Defendant Found to be Incompetent.

OH Jur. 3d Criminal Law § 2594, Treatment and Final Disposition of Incompetent Defendant.

OH Jur. 3d Criminal Law § 2595, Treatment and Final Disposition of Incompetent Defendant—Further Proceedings With Respect to Incompetent Defendants Charged With Serious Felony.

OH Jur. 3d Habeas Corpus & Post Convict. Remedies § 35, Confinement of Mentally Ill Persons; Mootness.

OH Jur. 3d Habeas Corpus & Post Convict. Remedies § 62, Generally; Discharge of Persons Restrained or Confined.

Treatises and Practice Aids

Markus, Trial Handbook for Ohio Lawyers, § 21:11, Continuance of Condition.

Katz, Giannelli, Blair and Lipton, Baldwin's Ohio Practice, Criminal Law, § 54:8, Findings.

Katz, Giannelli, Blair and Lipton, Baldwin's Ohio Practice, Criminal Law, § 77:6, Experts—Insanity.

Katz, Giannelli, Blair and Lipton, Baldwin's Ohio Practice, Criminal Law, § 87:9, Examination of Accused.

Giannelli and Snyder, Baldwin's Ohio Practice, Evidence, R 702, Testimony by Experts.

Giannelli and Snyder, Baldwin's Ohio Practice, Evidence, § 702.7, Court-Appointed Experts.

Carlin, Baldwin's Ohio Practice, Merrick-Rippner Probate Law § 101:42, Voluntary Status of Persons Committed by Criminal Court.

Carlin, Baldwin's Ohio Practice, Merrick-Rippner Probate Law § 101:43, Commencement of Commitment Proceedings in Criminal Cases.

Carlin, Baldwin's Ohio Practice, Merrick-Rippner Probate Law § 101:47, Further Commitment of Persons Found Incompetent to Stand Trial.

Carlin, Baldwin's Ohio Practice, Merrick-Rippner Probate Law § 101:48, Hearings on Nonsecured Status and Termination of Commitment of Persons Found Ngri or Incompetent to Stand Trial.

Hennenberg & Reinhart, Ohio Criminal Defense Motions F 5.10, Defendant's Written Plea of Not Guilty by Reason of Insanity-Pretrial Motions.

Hennenberg & Reinhart, Ohio Criminal Defense Motions F 5.20, Motion for Psychiatric Evaluation to Determine Defendant's Competency to Stand Trial-Pretrial Motions.

Hennenberg & Reinhart, Ohio Criminal Defense Motions F 5.21, Motion for Order Permitting Psychiatric Evaluation at State's Expense-Pretrial Motions.

Hennenberg & Reinhart, Ohio Criminal Defense Motions F 13.05, Motion for Order Granting Independent Psychiatric Evaluation at the State's Expense-Death Penalty Motions.

Adrine & Ruden, Ohio Domestic Violence Law § 14:17, Presenting Evidence of Domestic Violence—Use of Domestic Violence Experts.

Law Review and Journal Commentaries

Diminished Capacity and Diminished Responsibility: Irreconcilable Doctrines Confused in State v. Wilcox, Note. 14 U Tol L Rev 1399 (Summer 1983).

The Imposition of the Insanity Defense on an Unwilling Defendant, Anne C. Singer. 41 Ohio St L J 637 (1980).

Jones v. United States: Is It Crazy to Plead Crazy?, Note. 11 Ohio N U L Rev 397 (1984).

Ohio's Extra Measure of Procedural Due Process: The Effect of Compliance with Supreme Court Requirements in Criminal and Commitment Proceedings in Jackson v. Indiana, Note. 4 Cap U L Rev 291 (1975).

Release From Confinement of Persons Acquitted by Reason of Insanity in Ohio, Comment. 13 Akron L Rev 582 (Winter 1980).

Notes of Decisions

Ed. Note: *This section contains annotations from former RC 2945.39.*

---

1. Constitutional issues

Defendant was not denied fair trial in assault prosecution by fact that his expert witness on insanity defense could not afford, based on the fee paid to him by court, to change time of his testimony so as to be able to question state expert's methodology; despite disagreements over methodology, defendant's expert agreed with other two experts who testified that defendant was not legally insane at time of offense. State v. Lent (Ohio App. 4 Dist., 09-29-1997) 123 Ohio App.3d 149, 703 N.E.2d 836. Costs ⚩ 302.4

Defense counsel was ineffective for failing to enter plea of not guilty by reason of insanity, where defendant had no recollection of life for period of several days and no recollection of crimes of which he was accused, defendant's last memory was of speaking to his mother whom he believed was buried at service station and defendant recalled need to find shovel so he could properly bury her at cemetery, and defendant then woke up in psychiatric unit of county jail.State v. Brown (Cuyahoga 1992) 84 Ohio App.3d 414, 616 N.E.2d 1179, dismissed, jurisdictional motion overruled 66 Ohio St.3d 1467, 611 N.E.2d 325. Criminal Law ⚩ 641.13(2.1)

Insofar as the provisions of RC 2945.39 permit the imposition of conditions or qualifications upon the release from custody of a person confined to the Lima state hospital under the provisions of said section and found to be sane pursuant to a writ of habeas corpus such provisions are contrary to the Due Process and Equal Protection Clauses of the Ohio and US Constitutions. Holderbaum v. Watkins (Allen 1974) 44 Ohio App.2d 253, 337 N.E.2d 800, 73 O.O.2d 256, affirmed 42 Ohio St.2d 372, 328 N.E.2d 814, 71 O.O.2d 333.

In a trial on a charge of sexual battery to which the defendant pleaded not guilty by reason of insanity, the prosecutor violates the due process clause of US Const Am 14 by stating in closing argument that the soundness of the defendant's reasoning powers is suggested by remarks he made to police that he understood his rights as read and wished to see an attorney; the prosecutor's statement is a forbidden comment on the defendant's "silence" even where the defense did not object earlier to actual testimony on the defendant's words.Wainwright v. Greenfield (U.S.Fla. 1986) 106 S.Ct. 634, 474 U.S. 284, 88 L.Ed.2d 623.

Fact that statements made by defendant during sanity evaluations could be used against defendant in sentencing proceeding in which state sought death penalty did not violate defendant's rights against self-incrimination. Dennis v. Mitchell (N.D.Ohio, 10-01-1999) 68 F.Supp.2d 863, affirmed 354 F.3d 511, certiorari denied 124 S.Ct. 2400, 541 U.S. 1068, 158 L.Ed.2d 971. Criminal Law ⚩ 412.1(1)

A court may not exclude defense experts on the issue of insanity of a defendant as a sanction for the defendant's failure to cooperate with a court-appointed expert when the failure to cooperate is caused by mental illness; such a denial is a violation of the defendant's due process rights.State v Demyan, No. 2519 (2d Dist Ct App, Clark, 5-25-90).

2. Speedy trial

Where a criminal defendant moves for a psychiatric examination pursuant to RC 2945.39 and 2945.371, the running of the time in which a defendant must be tried is tolled when the motion is granted, not when the motion is made, and the time begins running again immediately after the date the psychiatric report is due where such report is never filed.State v. Bowman (Clermont 1987) 41 Ohio App.3d 318, 535 N.E.2d 730.

3. Competency to stand trial

Competency hearing is not automatically mandated when defendant enters plea of not guilty by reason of insanity. State v. Kulp (Ohio App. 6 Dist., 03-29-1996) 110 Ohio App.3d 144, 673 N.E.2d 689. Criminal Law ⚷ 625.10(2.1)

Failure of trial court to hold mandatory hearing when issue of defendant's competence to stand trial is raised may be deemed harmless error where record fails to show sufficient indications of incompetency. State v. Kulp (Ohio App. 6 Dist., 03-29-1996) 110 Ohio App.3d 144, 673 N.E.2d 689. Criminal Law ⚷ 1166(12)

The issue of competency to stand trial is not raised by the entry of an order for a psychiatric examination due to a plea of not guilty by reason of insanity.State v. Wilcox (Trumbull 1984) 16 Ohio App.3d 273, 475 N.E.2d 516, 16 O.B.R. 298.

A competency hearing is not automatically mandated by virtue of a plea of not guilty by reason of insanity; in order for a competency hearing to take place, a motion for such must be made before the trial commences.State v. Wilcox (Trumbull 1984) 16 Ohio App.3d 273, 475 N.E.2d 516, 16 O.B.R. 298. Criminal Law ⚷ 625.10(4)

Although the time within which an accused must be brought to trial may be tolled during the time when his competence to stand trial is being evaluated, when ten days have elapsed after the filing of the examiner's report and the statutorily mandated hearing has not been held, the time begins to run again.State v. Wilson (Fayette 1982) 7 Ohio App.3d 219, 454 N.E.2d 1348, 7 O.B.R. 281.

When an accused moves the court for an additional evaluation of his mental condition, the statutory period within which he must be brought to trial is tolled from time his motion is granted, and begins to run again on the date when the psychiatrist's report is due to be filed with the court, even if no report is filed on that date.State v. Wilson (Fayette 1982) 7 Ohio App.3d 219, 454 N.E.2d 1348, 7 O.B.R. 281.

4. Psychiatric examination

Defendant who had raised level of his competency to stand trial through initial entry of plea of not guilty by reason of insanity could not avoid mental examinations ordered by court pursuant to statute. State v. White (Ohio, 05-12-1999) 85 Ohio St.3d 433, 709 N.E.2d 140, 1999-Ohio-281, denial of post-conviction relief affirmed 1999 WL 394938, dismissed, appeal not allowed 87 Ohio St.3d 1418, 717 N.E.2d 1105, certiorari denied 120 S.Ct. 345, 528 U.S. 938, 145 L.Ed.2d 270, denial of post-conviction relief affirmed 2005-Ohio-6990, 2005 WL 3556634, appeal allowed 109 Ohio St.3d 1493, 848 N.E.2d 857, 2006-Ohio-2762. Mental Health ⚷ 434

Statute providing for court-ordered examinations of defendant's mental state and mandating that examiner complete a report is limited to cases in which insanity plea has been entered and does not apply in any other context, including case in which defendant claims to suffer from battered woman syndrome; in such a case, the state provided defendant with all the documents required by rule when it provided the defense with a copy of all documents which were made in connection with psychologist's examination, including letter indicating that psychologist did not believe defendant suffered from the syndrome, and results of personality test. State v. Daws (Ohio App. 2 Dist., 07-27-1994) 104 Ohio App.3d 448, 662 N.E.2d 805, appeal allowed 71 Ohio St.3d 1406, 641 N.E.2d 203, appeal dismissed as improvidently allowed 74 Ohio St.3d 1284, 659 N.E.2d 1282, 1996-Ohio-281, appeal after new trial 1997 WL 736502, denial of post-conviction relief affirmed 2001-Ohio-1549, 2001 WL 814968. Criminal Law ⚷ 627.6(4); Mental Health ⚷ 434

Defendant was not entitled to independent psychiatric evaluation under statutes governing questions of competency to stand trial and sanity at time of offense.State v. Corethers (Ohio App. 8 Dist., 08-23-1993) 90 Ohio App.3d 428, 629 N.E.2d 1052, dismissed, jurisdictional motion overruled 68 Ohio St.3d 1470, 628 N.E.2d 1389. Mental Health ⚷ 434

A defendant's statements made in the course of a court-ordered psychological examination may be used to refute his assertion of mental incapacity, but may not be used to show that he committed the acts constituting the offense.State v. Cooey (Ohio 1989) 46 Ohio St.3d 20, 544 N.E.2d 895, rehearing denied 46 Ohio St.3d 717, 546 N.E.2d 1335, certiorari denied 111 S.Ct. 1431, 499 U.S. 954, 113 L.Ed.2d 482, rehearing denied 111 S.Ct. 2068, 500 U.S. 938, 114 L.Ed.2d 472, denial of post-conviction relief affirmed, dismissed, appeal not allowed 70 Ohio St.3d 1465, 640 N.E.2d 527, reconsideration denied 71 Ohio St.3d 1424, 642 N.E.2d 389, on subsequent appeal 73 Ohio St.3d 411, 653 N.E.2d 252, reconsideration denied 74 Ohio St.3d 1423, 655 N.E.2d 742. Criminal Law ⚷ 393(1); Criminal Law ⚷ 412(4)

A defendant does not have the right to an independent psychiatric examiner, pursuant to RC 2945.39(C), unless the trial court has ordered more than one psychiatric evaluation and the trial court has refused to appoint an examiner recommended by the defendant. State v. Hix (Ohio 1988) 38 Ohio St.3d 129, 527 N.E.2d 784, certiorari denied 109 S.Ct. 535, 488 U.S. 983, 102 L.Ed.2d 566. Costs ⚷ 302.4

A defendant in a criminal prosecution has no right, by statute or otherwise, to an independent psychiatric evaluation.State v. Marshall (Cuyahoga 1984) 15 Ohio App.3d 105, 472 N.E.2d 1139, 15 O.B.R. 195.

Where a state defendant demonstrates to the trial judge that his sanity at the time of the offense will be a significant issue at trial, the state must provide access to a psychiatrist to examine the defendant and assist him in the evaluation, preparation, and presentation of his defense where the state recognizes a defense of insanity and places the initial burden of producing evidence on the defendant.Ake v. Oklahoma (U.S.Okl. 1985) 105 S.Ct. 1087, 470 U.S. 68, 84 L.Ed.2d 53. Costs ⚯ 302.4

By ordering a third evaluation after the defendant enters his insanity plea, the trial court complies with the requirements of RC 2945.39, and does not abuse its discretion in denying a request for a fourth evaluation.State v Thorne, No. 92–T–4658, 1993 WL 110965 (11th Dist Ct App, Trumbull, 3–12–93).

A court may not exclude defense experts on the issue of insanity of a defendant as a sanction for the defendant's failure to cooperate with a court-appointed expert when the failure to cooperate is caused by mental illness; such a denial is a violation of the defendant's due process rights.State v Demyan, No. 2519 (2d Dist Ct App, Clark, 5–25–90).

In an action for aggravated murder, when an evaluation of a defendant's mental condition is ordered pursuant to RC 2945.39(A), an indigent defendant is entitled to an independent psychiatric examination at state expense, unless he has previously been given the right to an examination by an examiner of his choice under RC 2945.39(A). State v Semenchuk, No. 1036 (4th Dist Ct App, Athens, 3–10–82).

An individual examiner who performs a psychiatric evaluation of a criminal defendant pursuant to RC 2945.371 or RC 2945.39 has a duty to report to law enforcement authorities any information obtained during the evaluation concerning criminal offenses that are felonies. The duty to report also extends to the private organization employing the examiner and to any other employee of the organization who has knowledge of such information.OAG 80–022.

The term "alienist" as used in RC 2945.39 is limited to physicians whose specialty is mental illness; there is no requirement, however, that the alienist appointed be a board certified psychiatrist. OAG 77–080.

5. Insanity defense

Failure to advise defendant about general defense of insanity precluded knowing, voluntary, and intelligent guilty plea to robbery charges, in light of defendant's extensive psychiatric history, including psychiatric hospitalizations within days of alleged offenses; defense attorney and trial court merely correctly noted that, for otherwise sane individual, voluntary ingestion of drugs would not give rise to defense of insanity. State v. Mikulic (Ohio App. 8 Dist., 12-23-1996) 116 Ohio App.3d 787, 689 N.E.2d 116, dismissed, appeal not allowed 78 Ohio St.3d 1452, 677 N.E.2d 813. Criminal Law ⚯ 273.1(4)

Prohibition against offering expert psychiatric testimony, unrelated to insanity defense, to show lack of mental capacity (diminished capacity) to form specific mental state required for particular crime or degree of crime does not apply to evidence disproving element of crime charged.State v. Luff (Lucas 1993) 85 Ohio App.3d 785, 621 N.E.2d 493, dismissed, jurisdictional motion overruled 67 Ohio St.3d 1464, 619 N.E.2d 698, certiorari denied 114 S.Ct. 1116, 510 U.S. 1136, 127 L.Ed.2d 426. Criminal Law ⚯ 474.1

Insanity may be a defense to any crime regardless of whether the particular offense requires that a defendant's conduct be purposeful, knowing, reckless, or negligent.State v. Curry (Ohio 1989) 45 Ohio St.3d 109, 543 N.E.2d 1228. Criminal Law ⚯ 48

The defense of insanity is applicable to negligent vehicular homicide and criminal negligence in general.State v. Curry (Ohio 1989) 45 Ohio St.3d 109, 543 N.E.2d 1228.

The defense of insanity cannot be successfully established simply on the basis that the condition resulted from the use of intoxicants or drugs, where such use is not shown to be habitual or chronic.State v. Mosher (Summit 1987) 37 Ohio App.3d 50, 523 N.E.2d 527. Criminal Law ⚯ 48

Although the law presumes all persons to be sane, this presumption, standing alone, is not necessarily sufficient to preclude a reviewing court from ruling that the trial court's ruling on the issue of insanity is against the manifest weight of the evidence.State v. Conn (Clark 1982) 13 Ohio App.3d 251, 469 N.E.2d 79, 13 O.B.R. 313. Criminal Law ⚯ 324

When a defendant pleads not guilty by reason of insanity, he is not entitled to a jury instruction on the confinement provisions of RC 2945.39.State v. Johnson (Cuyahoga 1978) 57 Ohio App.2d 263, 387 N.E.2d 247, 11 O.O.3d 338. Criminal Law ⚯ 790

A finding of not guilty by reason of insanity is not a final judgment or order appealable to a court of appeals. State v. Janney (Franklin 1977) 55 Ohio App.2d 257, 380 N.E.2d 753, 9 O.O.3d 393. Criminal Law ⚯ 1023(2)

Under RC 2901.05(A), a defendant who pleads an affirmative defense has only the burden of going forward with evidence of a nature and quality sufficient to raise that defense, and does not have the burden of establishing such defense by a preponderance of the evidence. (An affirmative defense must be established by a preponderance of the evidence pursuant to RC 2901.05, as amended by 1978 H 1168, eff. 11–1–78.) State v. Humphries (Ohio 1977) 51 Ohio St.2d 95, 364 N.E.2d 1354, 5 O.O.3d 89. Criminal Law ⚯ 330

Under RC 2901.05(A), when a defendant pleads an affirmative defense, and presents evidence of a nature and quality sufficient to raise that defense, the state bears the burden of persuasion beyond a reasonable doubt upon every issue necessary to convict the defendant. (An affirmative defense must be established by a preponderance of the evidence pursuant to RC 2901.05, as amended by 1978 H 1168, eff. 11–1–78.) State v. Humphries (Ohio 1977) 51 Ohio St.2d 95, 364 N.E.2d 1354, 5 O.O.3d 89.

In order to establish the defense of insanity where raised by pleas in a criminal proceeding, the accused must establish by a preponderance of the evidence that disease or other defect of his mind had so impaired his reason that, at the time of the criminal act with which he is charged, either he did not know that such act was wrong or he did not have the ability to refrain from doing that act. State v. Jackson (Ohio 1972) 32 Ohio St.2d 203, 291 N.E.2d 432, 61 O.O.2d 433, certiorari denied 93 S.Ct. 1539, 411 U.S. 909, 36 L.Ed.2d 199. Criminal Law ⚷ 570(2)

An instruction to the jury on the defense of insanity in a criminal proceeding must contain language from which the jury may conclude that disease or other defect of the defendant's mind had so impaired his reason that, at the time of the criminal act with which he is charged, either he did not know that such act was wrong or he did not have the ability to refrain from doing that act. State v. Anders (Ohio 1972) 29 Ohio St.2d 1, 277 N.E.2d 554, 58 O.O.2d 1. Criminal Law ⚷ 773(2)

One accused of criminal conduct is not responsible for such criminal conduct if, at the time of such conduct, as a result of mental illness or defect, he does not have the capacity either to know the wrongfulness of his conduct or to conform his conduct to the requirements of the law.State v. Staten (Ohio 1971) 25 Ohio St.2d 107, 267 N.E.2d 122, 54 O.O.2d 235, vacated in part 92 S.Ct. 2869, 408 U.S. 938, 33 L.Ed.2d 759. Criminal Law ⚷ 48

In order to establish the defense of insanity where raised by plea in a criminal proceeding, the accused must establish by a preponderance of the evidence that disease or other defect of his mind had so impaired his reason that, at the time of the criminal act with which he is charged, either he did not know that such act was wrong or he did not have the ability to refrain from doing that act. State v. Staten (Ohio 1969) 18 Ohio St.2d 13, 247 N.E.2d 293, 47 O.O.2d 82. Criminal Law ⚷ 570(2)

The legal test of insanity, whether the accused's mind was so afflicted with disease as to render him incapable of distinguishing between right and wrong as to the particular act done and as of the time when the act was done, is a test of responsibility rather than a medical test.State v. Colby (Ohio Com.Pl. 1966) 6 Ohio Misc. 19, 215 N.E.2d 65, 35 O.O.2d 61.

A trial judge having recent psychological reports that a defendant is competent to stand trial has no duty to impose a defense of "not guilty by reason of insanity" on the defendant, particularly where the defendant rejected the advice of three attorneys to offer the defense, said he was able to counsel with his attorney, and understood both the charges and the possible penalties confronting him. Foster v. Marshall (S.D.Ohio 1987) 687 F.Supp. 1174.

6. Evidence

Limiting fee to $2,500 for psychologist chosen by defendant to perform independent evaluation on competency and insanity issues in assault prosecution was not unreasonable, arbitrary, or unconscionable; fee amount was exact amount requested by defendant and the amount to which psychologist had agreed, and psychologist completed evaluation and testified at trial. State v. Lent (Ohio App. 4 Dist., 09-29-1997) 123 Ohio App.3d 149, 703 N.E.2d 836. Costs ⚷ 302.4

In prosecution in which defendant entered plea of not guilty by reason of insanity to charges of felonious assault and failure to comply with lawful order of police officer, omission from the record of psychological report, evidence of competency hearing, judgment entry as to trial court's findings as to competency or insanity at time of offense, and withdrawal of insanity plea, in conjunction with trial court's failure to follow proper procedures as to competency and insanity plea issues, constituted plain error. State v. Kulp (Ohio App. 6 Dist., 03-29-1996) 110 Ohio App.3d 144, 673 N.E.2d 689. Criminal Law ⚷ 1109(1)

Although Court of Appeals found it troublesome that defendant's trial counsel did not seek to question examining psychiatrist as witness when given opportunity by judge to challenge psychiatric report evaluating defendant's sanity at time crimes were committed, Court was unable to hold that this particular failure rose to level of ineffective assistance of counsel since report itself was not included as part of record on appeal.State v. Brown (Cuyahoga 1992) 84 Ohio App.3d 414, 616 N.E.2d 1179, dismissed, jurisdictional motion overruled 66 Ohio St.3d 1467, 611 N.E.2d 325. Criminal Law ⚷ 641.13(6)

Except in the mitigation phase of the trial, a defendant may not offer expert psychiatric testimony, unrelated to the insanity defense, to show that he lacked the mental capacity to form the specific mental state required for a particular crime or degree of crime.State v. Cooey (Ohio 1989) 46 Ohio St.3d 20, 544 N.E.2d 895, rehearing denied 46 Ohio St.3d 717, 546 N.E.2d 1335, certiorari denied 111 S.Ct. 1431, 499 U.S. 954, 113 L.Ed.2d 482, rehearing denied 111 S.Ct. 2068, 500 U.S. 938, 114 L.Ed.2d 472, denial of post-conviction relief affirmed, dismissed, appeal not allowed 70 Ohio St.3d 1465, 640 N.E.2d 527, reconsideration denied 71 Ohio St.3d 1424, 642 N.E.2d 389, on subsequent appeal 73 Ohio St.3d 411, 653 N.E.2d 252, reconsideration denied 74 Ohio St.3d 1423, 655 N.E.2d 742. Criminal Law ⚷ 474

Reports of court-appointed examiners who evaluate the mental condition of a criminal defendant at the time of the commission of an offense must satisfy the requirements of the law of evidence in order to be admissible.State v. Chapin (Ohio 1981) 67 Ohio St.2d 437, 424 N.E.2d 317, 21 O.O.3d 273.

The enactment of RC 2901.05 means that every criminal trial held on and after 1–1–74 is required to be conducted in accordance with the provisions of that statute; after a defendant pleads an affirmative defense and sustains his minimal burden of going forward with it through presentation of evidence of a nature and quality sufficient to raise that defense, the burden of persuasion falls on the state to prove every issue to convict the defendant beyond a reasonable doubt. State v. Humphries (Ohio 1977) 51 Ohio St.2d 95, 364 N.E.2d 1354, 5 O.O.3d 89.

The admission of cross-examination testimony concerning admissions of guilt by the defendant does not raise implications of self-incrimination where the purpose of the examination is to determine the basis for the psychiatrist's conclusions that the defendant was insane at the time of the crime; nor does the failure of the trial court to caution the jury sua sponte in such a situation raise issues of self-incrimination or due process of law.Watters v. Hubbard (C.A.6 (Ohio) 1984) 725 F.2d 381, certiorari denied 105 S.Ct. 133, 469 U.S. 837, 83 L.Ed.2d 74.

"Legal" insanity or that degree of mental illness or disease which will relieve a person of responsibility for crime is included within the term of "medical" insanity, and testimony that a person is not medically insane necessarily requires the conclusion that a person is not insane in the legal meaning of that term. State ex rel. Leeb v. Wilson (Allen 1971) 27 Ohio App.2d 1, 272 N.E.2d 363, 56 O.O.2d 194.

Testimony of lay witnesses as to the insanity of a defendant and mental illness within defendant's family is inadmissible unless there is independent evidence tending to establish insanity of the defendant.State v Semenchuk, No. 1036 (4th Dist Ct App, Athens, 3–10–82).

7. Commitment, treatment and release

Where a person committed to Lima state hospital pursuant to RC 2945.39 is restored to sanity through the use of drugs, but his improved mental state is dependent upon the continued use of such medication, he is not sane within the meaning of the statute so as to qualify for release from the institution under a writ of habeas corpus. Wolonsky v. Balson (Allen 1976) 58 Ohio App.2d 25, 387 N.E.2d 625, 12 O.O.3d 34. Mental Health ⚷ 440

Action of appellate court in finding accused sane and entitled to unconditional release rendered unnecessary determination regarding validity of conditional release provision of RC 2945.39. Holderbaum v. Watkins (Ohio 1975) 42 Ohio St.2d 372, 328 N.E.2d 814, 71 O.O.2d 333.

Where a defendant, prior to trial on an indictment, is determined to be insane and is committed to the Lima state hospital until restored to reason, and, subsequent to such confinement, the defendant is found to have been sufficiently restored to reason so that he is capable of standing trial, such latter finding, upon the subsequent determination by the trial court that the defendant is not guilty by reason of insanity, is not sufficient to overcome the statutory presumption of RC 2945.39 that defendant's insanity continues. Fortune v. Reshetylo (Ohio 1973) 33 Ohio St.2d 22, 294 N.E.2d 880, 62 O.O.2d 342. Criminal Law ⚷ 311

A proceeding under the provisions of RC 2945.39, with reference to a person found "not guilty by reason of insanity" and confined to the Lima state hospital, to determine whether such person has been restored to sanity, and that his release will not be dangerous, is not a judicial proceeding which may result in a judgment which is appealable to the court of appeals. Application of Leeb (Allen 1971) 26 Ohio App.2d 123, 269 N.E.2d 613, 55 O.O.2d 251. Mental Health ⚷ 45

One who pleads "not guilty by reason of insanity," and who has been committed to the Lima state hospital, is not deprived from thereafter seeking a writ of habeas corpus for the purpose of showing that he is sane and, therefore, unlawfully restrained of his liberty. McDonald v. Keiter (Ohio 1971) 25 Ohio St.2d 281, 268 N.E.2d 283, 54 O.O.2d 391. Habeas Corpus ⚷ 538

RC 2945.39 does not provide an exclusive method for the release of one acquitted on the sole ground of his insanity at the time of the commission of a criminal act; if such person is declared sane at the time of trial, the presumption that such insanity continues has been overcome, and he may have recourse to the writ of habeas corpus to secure his release from a commitment to the Lima state hospital. Collins v. Campbell (Summit 1965) 4 Ohio App.2d 42, 211 N.E.2d 96, 33 O.O.2d 59.

The verdict of acquittal on the ground of insanity is prima facie evidence of the inmate's insanity, and presumption of insanity thereafter continues; and in order to obtain his release by writ of habeas corpus, the inmate has burden of removing that presumption and of establishing with reasonable certainty his sanity. Ex parte Remus (Ohio 1928) 119 Ohio St. 166, 162 N.E. 740, 6 Ohio Law Abs. 388, 26 Ohio Law Rep. 562.

Due process, sexually violent offenders, civil commitment, lack of control determination. Kansas v. Crane (U.S.Kan., 01-22-2002) 122 S.Ct. 867, 534 U.S. 407, 151 L.Ed.2d 856.

The state upon committing an individual "until he regains his sanity" incurs a responsibility to provide such care as is reasonably calculated to achieve that goal.Davis v. Watkins (N.D.Ohio 1974) 384 F.Supp. 1196. Mental Health ⚷ 51.1

Where a patient committed to the Lima state hospital under RC 2945.39 as being not guilty by reason of insanity of the crime for which patient stood trial is, in an action in habeas corpus filed in common pleas court, found to be sane and ordered released from the hospital, and is thereupon released without stay of execution of the order of release having been timely applied for and ordered by either common pleas court or by court of appeals, and an appeal is taken by superintendent, Lima state hospital, to court of appeals from order of release, notwithstanding that the order of release is reviewable by court of appeals, issues which would otherwise be presented by appeal have become moot by reason of actual release of patient, and appeal should be dismissed. State ex rel. Colby v. Reshetylo (Allen 1972) 30 Ohio App.2d 183, 284 N.E.2d 188, 59 O.O.2d 306.

2945.391 Applicability of not guilty by reason of insanity plea; impairment of reason not defense

For purposes of sections 2945.371, 2945.40, 2945.401, and 2945.402 and Chapters 5122. and 5123. of the Revised Code, a person is "not guilty by reason of insanity" relative to a charge of an offense only as described in division (A)(14) of section 2901.01 of the Revised Code. Proof that a person's reason, at the time of the commission of an offense, was so impaired that the person did not have the ability to refrain from doing the person's act or acts, does not constitute a defense.

(1996 S 285, eff. 7–1–97; 1996 S 239, eff. 9–6–96; 1990 S 24, eff. 7–24–90)

Historical and Statutory Notes

Amendment Note: 1996 S 239 substituted "(A)(14)" for "(N)"; and made changes to reflect gender neutral language.

Amendment Note: 1996 S 285 substituted "sections 2945.371, 2945.40, 2945.401, and 2945.402" for "section 2945.40" in the first sentence.

Research References

Encyclopedias

OH Jur. 3d Criminal Law § 634, What Constitutes Insanity.

Treatises and Practice Aids

Katz, Giannelli, Blair and Lipton, Baldwin's Ohio Practice, Criminal Law, § 87:7, Ohio Rule.

Katz, Giannelli, Blair and Lipton, Baldwin's Ohio Practice, Criminal Law, § 144:4, Plea of Not Guilty by Reason of Insanity at Arraignment.

Katz, Giannelli, Blair and Lipton, Baldwin's Ohio Practice, Criminal Law, § 144:5, Acceptance of Plea of Not Guilty by Reason of Insanity After Arraignment.

Katz, Giannelli, Blair and Lipton, Baldwin's Ohio Practice, Criminal Law, § 144:7, Entry Ordering Inquiry Into Insanity of Defendant.

Katz, Giannelli, Blair and Lipton, Baldwin's Ohio Practice, Criminal Law, § 124:21, Mitigating Factors—Mental Condition.

Giannelli and Snyder, Baldwin's Ohio Practice, Evidence, § 401.3, Consequential (Material) Facts Defined.

Giannelli and Snyder, Baldwin's Ohio Practice, Evidence, § 702.18, Psychiatric Evidence.

Law Review and Journal Commentaries

The Insanity Defense in the Nineties, Hon. Martin O. Parks. 14 Lake Legal Views 1 (January 1991).

2945.392 Battered woman syndrome

(A) The declarations set forth in division (A) of section 2901.06 of the Revised Code apply in relation to this section.

(B) If a defendant is charged with an offense involving the use of force against another and the defendant enters a plea to the charge of not guilty by reason of insanity, the defendant may introduce expert testimony of the "battered woman syndrome" and expert testimony that the defendant suffered from that syndrome as evidence to establish the requisite impairment of the defendant's reason, at the time of the commission of the offense, that is necessary for a finding that the defendant is not guilty by reason of insanity. The introduction of any expert testimony under this division shall be in accordance with the Ohio Rules of Evidence.

(1996 S 285, eff. 7–1–97; 1990 H 484, eff. 11–5–90)

Historical and Statutory Notes

Amendment Note: 1996 S 285 substituted "defendant" for "person" in division (B).

Cross References

Battered woman syndrome, 2901.06

Library References

Criminal Law ⚖474.4(3).

Westlaw Topic No. 110.

C.J.S. Criminal Law § 1067.

Research References

Treatises and Practice Aids

Katz, Giannelli, Blair and Lipton, Baldwin's Ohio Practice, Criminal Law, § 88:8, Battered Woman Syndrome.

Katz, Giannelli, Blair and Lipton, Baldwin's Ohio Practice, Criminal Law, § 87:11, Evidence Issues.

Giannelli and Snyder, Baldwin's Ohio Practice, Evidence, § 702.21, Battered Woman (Person) Syndrome.

Adrine & Ruden, Ohio Domestic Violence Law § 7:21, Trial Presentation—the Battered Woman Syndrome.

Adrine & Ruden, Ohio Domestic Violence Law § 14:17, Presenting Evidence of Domestic Violence—Use of Domestic Violence Experts.

Law Review and Journal Commentaries

Battered Lesbians: Are They Entitled To A Battered Woman Defense?, Note. 29 J Fam L 879 (August 1991).

Downward Adjustment and the Slippery Slope: The Use of Duress in Defense of Battered Offenders, Laurie Kratky Dore. 56 Ohio St L J 665 (1995).

Ohio Joins the Majority and Allows Expert Testimony on the Battered Woman Syndrome, Note. 60 U Cin L Rev 877 (Winter 1992).

State v. Nemeth—Equal Protection for the Battered Child, Note. 31 Akron L Rev 147 (1997).

2945.40 Verdict of not guilty by reason of insanity; effects; procedures; hearings; rights; commitment

(A) If a person is found not guilty by reason of insanity, the verdict shall state that finding, and the trial court shall conduct a full hearing to determine whether the person is a mentally ill person subject to hospitalization by court order or a mentally retarded person subject to institutionalization by court order. Prior to the hearing, if the trial judge believes that there is probable cause that the person found not guilty by reason of insanity is a mentally ill person subject to hospitalization by court order or mentally retarded person subject to institutionalization by court order, the trial judge may issue a temporary order of detention for that person to remain in effect for ten court days or until the hearing, whichever occurs first.

Any person detained pursuant to a temporary order of detention issued under this division shall be held in a suitable facility, taking into consideration the place and type of confinement prior to and during trial.

(B) The court shall hold the hearing under division (A) of this section to determine whether the person found not guilty by reason of insanity is a mentally ill person subject to hospitalization by court order or a mentally retarded person subject to institutionalization by court order within ten court days after the finding of not guilty by reason of insanity. Failure to conduct the hearing within the ten-day period shall cause the immediate discharge of the respondent, unless the judge grants a continuance for not longer than ten court days for good cause shown or for any period of time upon motion of the respondent.

(C) If a person is found not guilty by reason of insanity, the person has the right to attend all hearings conducted pursuant to sections 2945.37 to 2945.402 of the Revised Code. At any hearing conducted pursuant to one of those sections, the court shall inform the person that the person has all of the following rights:

(1) The right to be represented by counsel and to have that counsel provided at public expense if the person is indigent, with the counsel to be appointed by the court under Chapter 120. of the Revised Code or under the authority recognized in division (C) of section 120.06, division (E) of section 120.16, division (E) of section 120.26, or section 2941.51 of the Revised Code;

(2) The right to have independent expert evaluation and to have that independent expert evaluation provided at public expense if the person is indigent;

(3) The right to subpoena witnesses and documents, to present evidence on the person's behalf, and to cross-examine witnesses against the person;

(4) The right to testify in the person's own behalf and to not be compelled to testify;

(5) The right to have copies of any relevant medical or mental health document in the custody of the state or of any place of commitment other than a document for which the court finds that the release to the person of information contained in the document would create a substantial risk of harm to any person.

(D) The hearing under division (A) of this section shall be open to the public, and the court shall conduct the hearing in accordance with the Rules of Civil Procedure. The court shall make and maintain a full transcript and record of the hearing proceedings. The court may consider all relevant evidence, including, but not limited to, any relevant psychiatric, psychological, or medical testimony or reports, the acts constituting the offense in relation to which the person was found not guilty by reason of insanity, and any history of the person that is relevant to the person's ability to conform to the law.

(E) Upon completion of the hearing under division (A) of this section, if the court finds there is not clear and convincing evidence that the person is a mentally ill person subject to hospitalization by court order or a mentally retarded person subject to institutionalization by court order, the court shall discharge the person, unless a detainer has been placed upon the person by the department of rehabilitation and correction, in which case the person shall be returned to that department.

(F) If, at the hearing under division (A) of this section, the court finds by clear and convincing evidence that the person is a mentally ill person subject to hospitalization by court order or a mentally retarded person subject to institutionalization by court order, it shall commit the person to a hospital operated by the department of mental health, a facility operated by the department of mental retardation and developmental disabilities, or another medical or psychiatric facility, as appropriate, and further proceedings shall be in accordance with sections 2945.401 and 2945.402 of the Revised Code. In determining the place and nature of the commitment, the court shall order the least restrictive commitment alternative available that is consistent with public safety and the welfare of the person. In weighing these factors, the court shall give preference to protecting public safety.

(G) If a court makes a commitment of a person under division (F) of this section, the prosecutor shall send to the place of commitment all reports of the person's current mental condition, and, except as otherwise provided in this division, any other relevant information, including, but not limited to, a transcript of the hearing held pursuant to division (A) of this section, copies of relevant police reports, and copies of any prior arrest and conviction records that pertain to the person and that the prosecutor possesses. The prosecutor shall send the reports of the person's current mental condition in every case of commitment, and, unless the prosecutor determines that the release of any of the other relevant information to unauthorized persons would interfere with the effective prosecution of any person or would create a substantial risk of harm to any person, the prosecutor also shall send the other relevant information. Upon admission of a person committed under division (F) of this section, the place of commitment shall send to the board of alcohol, drug addiction, and mental health services or the community mental health board serving the county in which the charges against the person were filed a copy of all reports of the person's current mental condition and a copy of the other relevant information provided by the prosecutor under this division, including, if provided, a transcript of the hearing held pursuant to division (A) of this section, the relevant police reports, and the prior arrest and conviction records that pertain to the person and that the prosecutor possesses.

(H) A person who is committed pursuant to this section shall not voluntarily admit the person or be voluntarily admitted to a hospital or institution pursuant to sections 5122.02, 5122.15, 5123.69, or 5123.76 of the Revised Code.

(1996 S 285, eff. 7–1–97; 1996 H 567, eff. 10–29–96; 1994 H 571, eff. 10–6–94; 1990 S 24, eff. 7–24–90; 1988 S 156; 1981 H 1; 1980 H 965, S 297; 1978 H 565)

Historical and Statutory Notes

Ed. Note: 2945.40 contains provisions analogous to former 2947.26 to 2947.28, repealed by 1972 H 511, eff. 1–1–74.

Ed. Note: Former 2945.40 repealed by 1978 H 565, eff. 11–1–78; 1953 H 1; GC 13441–4.

Pre–1953 H 1 Amendments: 113 v 178, Ch 19, § 4

Amendment Note: 1996 S 285 rewrote this section. See Baldwin's Ohio Legislative Service, 1996, p 12/L–3532, or the OH–LEGIS or OH–LEGIS–OLD database on WESTLAW, for prior version of this section.

Amendment Note: 1996 H 567 deleted "the attorney general" preceding "and the prosecutor" in the first sentence, and "and attorney general" following "the prosecutor" in the second sentence, of division (D)(4); deleted "to the attorney general and" preceding "to the prosecutor" in division (E); deleted "the attorney general" preceding "and the prosecutor" throughout in the first paragraph of division (F); deleted "and the attorney general" following "give the prosecutor" in the second paragraph of division (F); deleted the final sentence in division (G); and made other changes to reflect gender neutral language. Prior thereto the final sentence in division (G) read:

"An attorney designated by the attorney general shall represent the hospital, facility, program, or institution to which the person was committed, if the person has been committed."

Amendment Note: 1994 H 571 substituted "correctional" for "penal" in division (D)(6).

Legislative Service Commission

1973:

This section provides that when a person is committed to Lima State Hospital after being found not guilty by reason of insanity, his case must be reviewed at least annually to determine whether a release hearing should be held. Former law contained no requirement for the periodic review of such cases. Also, this section provides that when a person committed to Lima State Hospital is released pursuant to a habeas corpus proceeding, his release may be with certain conditions attached. Under former law, only unconditional release was possible. This section is a companion measure to new section 2947.271, dealing with the periodic review of the cases of persons committed as psychopathic offenders. (Ed. note: This comment applied to former RC 2945.39, the tenor of which is now incorporated in RC 2945.40.)

Cross References

Arrest and detention until warrant can be obtained, 2935.03

Department of mental retardation and developmental disabilities, definitions, 5123.01

Department of mental retardation and developmental disabilities, involuntary institutionalization procedures, 5123.71

Department of mental retardation and developmental disabilities, judicial proceedings, notice of hearing, 5123.73

Department of mental retardation and developmental disabilities, judicial proceedings, procedures, 5123.76

Escape, 2921.34

Examination, observation, classification, and assignment to institutions of sentenced persons by department of rehabilitation and correction, AIDS policy, 5120.16

Hospitalization of mentally ill, admission of voluntary patient, 5122.02

Hospitalization of mentally ill, applicability of provisions, 5122.011

Hospitalization of mentally ill, confidentiality of records, 5122.31

Hospitalization of mentally ill, hearings, attorneys, 5122.15

Hospitalization of mentally ill, involuntary confinement, 5122.05

Hospitalization of mentally ill; residence, defined, 5122.01

Hospitalization of mentally ill, right to writ of habeas corpus, 5122.30

Institutionalization of person incompetent to stand trial or not guilty by reason of insanity, applicability of provisions, 5123.011

Judicial hospitalization of mentally ill, 5122.11

Mentally ill patients absent without leave, applicability, 5122.26

Mentally retarded person may apply for admission for short-term care, 5123.701

Offenses against justice and public administration; detention, defined, 2921.01

Reimbursement of alcohol, drug addiction, and mental health program expenditures, 5119.62

System for tracking and monitoring persons found not guilty by reason of insanity, 5119.57

Verdict, Crim R 31

Voluntary hospitalization of persons found not guilty by reason of insanity, 5123.69

Library References

Criminal Law ⚷47.
Mental Health ⚷439.
Westlaw Topic Nos. 110, 257A.
C.J.S. Criminal Law §§ 99 to 108.
C.J.S. Mental Health §§ 241 to 246.

Baldwin's Ohio Legislative Service, 1988 Laws of Ohio, S 156—LSC Analysis, p 5–284

Research References

ALR Library

43 ALR 5th 777, Propriety of Transferring Patient Found Not Guilty by Reason of Insanity to Less Restrictive Confinement.

Encyclopedias

OH Jur. 3d Criminal Law § 3258, Timing of Hearing.

OH Jur. 3d Criminal Law § 3259, Right to Counsel.

OH Jur. 3d Criminal Law § 3260, Discharge of Person.

OH Jur. 3d Criminal Law § 3262, Nature of Commitment.

OH Jur. 3d Habeas Corpus & Post Convict. Remedies § 35, Confinement of Mentally Ill Persons; Mootness.

OH Jur. 3d Incompetent Persons § 40, Admission of Criminal Defendants.

OH Jur. 3d Incompetent Persons § 127, Jurisdiction and Venue.

Treatises and Practice Aids

Markus, Trial Handbook for Ohio Lawyers, § 2:23, Court-Ordered Medical Expert.

Markus, Trial Handbook for Ohio Lawyers, § 4:58, Criminal Case—Defenses—Insanity—as Affirmative Defense.

Klein, Darling, & Terez, Baldwin's Ohio Practice Civil Practice § 1:53, Civ. R. 1(C)(6): Commitment of the Mentally Ill--Proceedings Under RC 2945.38 and RC 2945.40.

Katz, Giannelli, Blair and Lipton, Baldwin's Ohio Practice, Criminal Law, § 65:6, Return of Verdict.

Katz, Giannelli, Blair and Lipton, Baldwin's Ohio Practice, Criminal Law, § 87:7, Ohio Rule.

Katz, Giannelli, Blair and Lipton, Baldwin's Ohio Practice, Criminal Law, § 144:9, Order for Detention and Hearing Following Verdict of Not Guilty by Reason of Insanity.

Katz, Giannelli, Blair and Lipton, Baldwin's Ohio Practice, Criminal Law, § 87:15, Acquittal Consequences.

Katz, Giannelli, Blair and Lipton, Baldwin's Ohio Practice, Criminal Law, § 148:37, Verdict of Not Guilty by Reason of Insanity.

Carlin, Baldwin's Ohio Practice, Merrick-Rippner Probate Law § 101:18, Involuntary Admission—Notice and Assessment Requirements for All Involuntary Patients.

Carlin, Baldwin's Ohio Practice, Merrick-Rippner Probate Law § 101:37, Transfers.

Carlin, Baldwin's Ohio Practice, Merrick-Rippner Probate Law § 101:38, Trial Visits.

Carlin, Baldwin's Ohio Practice, Merrick-Rippner Probate Law § 101:39, Hearing Requirements—Summary.

Carlin, Baldwin's Ohio Practice, Merrick-Rippner Probate Law § 101:41, Jurisdiction Over Commitments in Criminal Cases.

Carlin, Baldwin's Ohio Practice, Merrick-Rippner Probate Law § 101:42, Voluntary Status of Persons Committed by Criminal Court.

Carlin, Baldwin's Ohio Practice, Merrick-Rippner Probate Law § 101:43, Commencement of Commitment Proceedings in Criminal Cases.

Carlin, Baldwin's Ohio Practice, Merrick-Rippner Probate Law § 101:44, Full Hearing for Persons Found Ngri.

Carlin, Baldwin's Ohio Practice, Merrick-Rippner Probate Law § 101:45, Disposition of Persons Committed by Court Order After Finding of Ngri.

Carlin, Baldwin's Ohio Practice, Merrick-Rippner Probate Law § 101:48, Hearings on Nonsecured Status and Termination of Commitment of Persons Found Ngri or Incompetent to Stand Trial.

Law Review and Journal Commentaries

Adopt Guilty But Mentally Ill?—No!, Ann H. Britton and Richard J. Bennett. 15 U Tol L Rev 203 (Fall 1983).

Guilty But Mentally Ill: Broadening the Scope of Criminal Responsibility, Comment. 44 Ohio St L J 797 (1983).

Insanity Defense Reform In Ohio: Does The Court Of Jurisdiction Matter?, Lisa A. Callahan and Henry J. Steadman. 19 Cap U L Rev 809 (Summer 1990).

The Issue—Preclusive Effect Of A Verdict Of Not Guilty By Reason Of Insanity On A Subsequent Prosecution For A Related Offense, Comment. 18 U Dayton L Rev 763 (Spring 1993).

The Judicial Evolution of Ohio's Insanity Defense, Dr. John K. McHenry. 13 U Dayton L Rev 49 (Fall 1987).

The Jurisdictional Implications Of A Mens Rea Approach to Insanity: Plugging The "Detainment Gap" After Foucha v Louisiana, Amy Baker Benjamin. 19 U Dayton L Rev 41 (Fall 1993).

Opinions and Expert Testimony, James L. Young. 6 Cap U L Rev 579 (1977).

A Pleasant Surprise: The Guilty But Mentally Ill Verdict Has Both Succeeded in Its Own Right and Successfully Preserved the Traditional Role of the Insanity Defense, Ira Mickenberg. 55 U Cin L Rev 943 (1987).

Release From Confinement of Persons Acquitted by Reason of Insanity in Ohio, Comment. 13 Akron L Rev 582 (Winter 1980).

Unpacking The Myths: The Symbolism Of Insanity Defense Jurisprudence, Michael L. Perlin. 40 Case W Res L Rev 599 (1988–89).

Notes of Decisions

Ed. Note: This section contains annotations from former RC 2945.40.

---

1. Constitutional issues—In general

The application of the provisions of 1980 S 297, eff. 4–30–80, to a defendant who was found not guilty by reason of insanity prior to that effective date does not constitute ex post facto legislation, nor retroactive legislation in violation of O Const Art II, § 28. State v. Jackson (Franklin 1981) 2 Ohio App.3d 11, 440 N.E.2d 1199, 2 O.B.R. 11.

In the Lima state hospital the staffing of observation committees, subject to automatic judicial review, is not a critical stage in the commitment process to which the right to counsel attaches. Davis v. Balson (N.D.Ohio 1978) 461 F.Supp. 842, 11 O.O.3d 360. Mental Health ⚷ 37.1

GC 13441–1 (RC 2945.37) and this section contemplate as a condition precedent to the action provided therein a formal examination and investigation by the court into the question of the sanity or insanity of the accused, especially where the accused objects to the procedure, and a violation of such sections occurs and an accused is deprived of due process of law where, against his protests, he is committed to the Lima state hospital for observation for a period not exceeding one month, solely upon the unsworn statement of the prosecuting attorney as to his belief, based on hearsay, that the accused is not sane and without any semblance of a formal hearing as to the accused's mental condition and without the presentation of any evidence tending to prove insanity. State ex rel. Smilack v. Bushong (Ohio 1953) 159 Ohio St. 259, 111 N.E.2d 918, 50 O.O. 280.

2. —— Due process, constitutional issues

Confinement in mental hospital of criminal defendant who has raised insanity defense and has been acquitted on that ground, solely on basis of trial court's finding of insanity by preponderance of evidence, until he has regained his sanity or is no longer dangerous, does not deny due process even if result is to confine acquittee beyond maximum period of incarceration carried by his offense; insanity acquittee is not entitled, at end of confinement period, to civil commitment hearing at which proof of his insanity would have to be established by clear and convincing evidence. Jones v. U.S. (U.S.Dist.Col. 1983) 103 S.Ct. 3043, 463 U.S. 354, 77 L.Ed.2d 694.

3. —— Equal protection, constitutional issues

It does not violate equal protection of State or Federal Constitution to allow state hospital to charge and collect from patient for support and maintenance where he was committed to hospital after being found not guilty by reason of insanity. Reid v. Cent. Ohio Psychiatric Hosp. (Ohio Ct.Cl., 07-13-1992) 63 Ohio Misc.2d 332, 629 N.E.2d 1104, 2001-Ohio-146. Constitutional Law ⚷ 243.3; Mental Health ⚷ 73

The differences in the procedure in the involuntary commitment of those committed through civil process and those committed after having been found not guilty by reason of insanity do not amount to a denial of equal protection of the law. State v. Jackson (Franklin 1981) 2 Ohio App.3d 11, 440 N.E.2d 1199, 2 O.B.R. 11. Constitutional Law ⚷ 242.1(5); Mental Health ⚷ 433(1)

4. —— Ineffective assistance of counsel, constitutional issues

Defense counsel's decision to forego insanity defense was reasonably based on fact that neither defense nor court-appointed expert concluded that defendant was legally insane under Ohio law, and thus failure to pursue defense did not support ineffective assistance of counsel claim, even though one expert opined that defendant met first of two criteria for insanity, and other expert found second criterion satisfied; moreover, pursuing defense would have opened door to admission of evidence regarding damaging letter written by defendant. Wong v. Money (C.A.6 (Ohio), 04-16-1998) 142 F.3d 313. Criminal Law ⚷ 641.13(2.1)

Defendant was not prejudiced by defense counsel's failure to waive notice of intent to present insanity defense and to object to remark in prosecution's opening statements contesting defendant's alleged sanity, inasmuch as occurrences at most caused jury to reject defense defendant did not present; defendant thus failed to establish ineffective assistance of counsel claim. Wong v. Money (C.A.6 (Ohio), 04-16-1998) 142 F.3d 313. Criminal Law ⚷ 641.13(2.1)

Failure of defendant's trial counsel to request additional psychiatric examinations of his client falls below the objective standard of reasonable representation where (1) an individual is killed with a fire extinguisher during a three-to-four hour beating, (2) after the beating defendant cuts the victim's brain out of his head and freezes it, believing it could be used to clone the victim, (3) court-ordered experts conclude that defendant was sane when he repeatedly hit the victim with the fire extinguisher for over three hours but then lost his sanity when he removed the victim's brain, concluding the defendant was insane immediately after the killing, and (4) it is probable that a different medical expert could conclude that defendant was also insane a few hours earlier, at the time of the killing. State v. Wortring (Ohio App. 11 Dist., Lake, 12-21-2001) No. 99-L-114, 2001-Ohio-8836, 2001

WL 1647234, Unreported, reconsideration granted, opinion vacated, appeal not allowed 95 Ohio St.3d 1437, 766 N.E.2d 1003, 2002-Ohio-2084, on reconsideration 2003-Ohio-326, 2003 WL 168225, appeal not allowed 99 Ohio St.3d 1452, 790 N.E.2d 1217, 2003-Ohio-3396.

5. Hearing on disposition

Once committed, involuntary patient found not guilty by reason of insanity is entitled to further hearings at specified times on issue of his or her continued commitment. State v. Kinman (Ohio App. 1 Dist., 01-31-1996) 109 Ohio App.3d 95, 671 N.E.2d 1083. Mental Health ⚷ 440

When a defendant is simultaneously found guilty of one or more offenses and not guilty by reason of insanity of other offenses charged within an indictment, it is error for a court to postpone or stay a hearing on hospitalization pursuant to RC 2945.40 until the defendant's release from the sentences imposed on offenses for which the defendant has been found guilty, since the purpose of RC 2945.40(A) is to provide treatment to mentally ill and retarded defendants who are found not guilty by reason of insanity, before or in lieu of punishment. State v. Ware (Hamilton 1988) 44 Ohio App.3d 201, 542 N.E.2d 1115, cause dismissed 43 Ohio St.3d 701, 539 N.E.2d 163. Mental Health ⚷ 439.1

A court's failure to conduct a hearing on the disposition of a person found not guilty by reason of insanity within the time limits of RC 2945.40(F) is not necessarily prejudicial error even though the person's mental condition deteriorated while he was jailed during the delay, if the record does not establish that the delay affected the court's ruling. State v. Bruton (Cuyahoga 1985) 27 Ohio App.3d 362, 501 N.E.2d 651, 27 O.B.R. 457.

Neither RC 5122.15(A) nor 2945.40(I) gives an indigent defendant the right to court-appointed counsel of his choice. State v. Bruton (Cuyahoga 1985) 27 Ohio App.3d 362, 501 N.E.2d 651, 27 O.B.R. 457.

6. Insanity defense

Ohio does not recognize partial defense of diminished capacity; defendant may not offer psychiatric testimony, unrelated to insanity defense, to show that defendant lacked mental capacity to form specific mental state required for conviction of crime. State v. McCray (Ohio App. 9 Dist., 04-19-1995) 103 Ohio App.3d 109, 658 N.E.2d 1076, dismissed, appeal not allowed 73 Ohio St.3d 1450, 654 N.E.2d 986. Criminal Law ⚷ 46; Criminal Law ⚷ 474

A trial court in a capital case is not required to instruct the jury as to the defendant's lawful disposition were he to be found not guilty by reason of insanity. State v. Rogers (Ohio 1985) 17 Ohio St.3d 174, 478 N.E.2d 984, 17 O.B.R. 414, vacated 106 S.Ct. 518, 474 U.S. 1002, 88 L.Ed.2d 452, on remand 28 Ohio St.3d 427, 504 N.E.2d 52, 28 O.B.R. 480. Criminal Law ⚷ 790

The partial defense of diminished capacity is not recognized in Ohio. State v. Wilcox (Ohio 1982) 70 Ohio St.2d 182, 436 N.E.2d 523, 24 O.O.3d 284.

One accused of criminal conduct is not responsible for such criminal conduct if, at the time of such conduct, as a result of mental illness or defect, he does not have the capacity either to know the wrongfulness of his conduct or to conform his conduct to the requirements of law. State v. Staten (Ohio 1971) 25 Ohio St.2d 107, 267 N.E.2d 122, 54 O.O.2d 235, vacated in part 92 S.Ct. 2869, 408 U.S. 938, 33 L.Ed.2d 759. Criminal Law ⚷ 48

In order to establish the defense of insanity, the accused must establish by a preponderance of the evidence that disease or other defect of his mind had so impaired his reason that, at the time of the criminal act with which he is charged, either he did not know that such act was wrong or he did not have the ability to refrain from doing that act. State v. Staten (Ohio 1969) 18 Ohio St.2d 13, 247 N.E.2d 293, 47 O.O.2d 82. Criminal Law ⚷ 570(2)

The legal test of insanity, whether the accused's mind was so afflicted with disease as to render him incapable of distinguishing between right and wrong as to the particular act done and as of the time when the act was done, is a test of responsibility rather than a medical test. State v. Colby (Ohio Com.Pl. 1966) 6 Ohio Misc. 19, 215 N.E.2d 65, 35 O.O.2d 61.

Insanity defense, instructions, consequences of not guilty by reason of insanity verdict. Shannon v. U.S. (U.S.Miss. 1994) 114 S.Ct. 2419, 512 U.S. 573, 129 L.Ed.2d 459.

7. Evidence

Evidence that inmate, who was found not guilty by reason of insanity for two brutal murders and attempted murder, continued to be dangerous after fifteen years of treatment, that he threatened to kill personnel at detention facility, and that he attempted escape at least once was sufficient to warrant finding that public safety required inmate to be placed in more secure facility. State v. Kinman (Ohio App. 1 Dist., 01-31-1996) 109 Ohio App.3d 95, 671 N.E.2d 1083. Mental Health ⚷ 439.1

A criminal defendant who is found not guilty by reason of insanity is properly found to be a mentally ill person subject to court ordered hospitalization where a three-panel report indicates that he suffers from organic hallucinosis, narcissistic personality disorder, and opines that he is suffering from a substantial disorder of thought in full remission. State v. Traywick (Cuyahoga 1991) 72 Ohio App.3d 674, 595 N.E.2d 986. Mental Health ⚷ 439.1

Facts or data upon which an expert bases an opinion concerning mental status of a defendant must be perceived by expert or admitted in evidence at hearing. State v. Jones (Ohio 1984) 9 Ohio St.3d 123, 459 N.E.2d 526, 9 O.B.R. 347. Evidence ⚷ 555.3

RC 2945.40(C) imposes a clear and convincing standard of proof upon the determination of whether a person is a mentally ill or a mentally retarded person subject to hospitalization or institutionalization; however, the general assembly has not imposed the clear and convincing evidence standard upon the court's decision under RC 2945.40(D)(1) to implement "the least restrictive commitment alternative available consistent with the public safety and the welfare of the person," i.e., the standard of proof under amended RC 2945.40(D)(1) is by a preponderance of the evidence. State v. Jackson (Franklin 1981) 2 Ohio App.3d 11, 440 N.E.2d 1199, 2 O.B.R. 11. Mental Health ⚷ 439.1

Where an accused interposes insanity as a defense for a criminal act, the expert opinion of a physician relative to the mental condition of the accused at the time of the crime is competent, although the observations upon which that opinion is based were obtained in part during the course of an examination called for by the court for an entirely different purpose. State v. Henley (Ohio 1968) 15 Ohio St.2d 86, 238 N.E.2d 773, 44 O.O.2d 61, certiorari denied 89 S.Ct. 500, 393 U.S. 1006, 21 L.Ed.2d 471. Criminal Law ⚷ 474; Criminal Law ⚷ 486(6)

8. Commitment, treatment and release

A court seeking to order the conditional release of a person acquitted of a criminal charge by reason of insanity under RC 2945.40(D) pursuant to RC 5122.15(B) must first make a finding that this individual is a mentally ill person subject to hospitalization under RC 2945.40(C). State v. Engleman (Ohio App. 6 Dist., Ottawa, 09-30-1994) No. 94OT013, 1994 WL 530839, Unreported.

Nature and conditions of insanity acquittee's confinement are a determination which lies within sound discretion of trial court; accordingly, trial court may reject recommendations of the state, the acquittee, and the hospital caring for acquittee. State v. Crossan (Ohio App. 4 Dist., 09-10-1997) 122 Ohio App.3d 511, 702 N.E.2d 157. Mental Health ⚷ 439.1

Imposition of nightly house arrest, as one condition of release from psychiatric hospitalization of defendant found not guilty by reason of insanity on breaking and entering charges, was not abuse of discretion; although psychologist testified house arrest was not necessary for safety of community or defendant, he testified it might be appropriate measure for addressing certain personality problems. State v. Crossan (Ohio App. 4 Dist., 09-10-1997) 122 Ohio App.3d 511, 702 N.E.2d 157. Mental Health ⚷ 440

Finding that least restrictive commitment for mental health patient consistent with public safety and welfare of patient was maximum security forensic unit of psychiatric center was not abuse of discretion, even though sole testifying witness specifically indicated that patient no longer met criteria for maximum security hospital environment; witness had met with patient for only three one-hour sessions, and his conclusion that patient's condition appeared to have stabilized had been reached at least three times in past by mental health professionals, each time being followed by periods of patient's regression. State v. Green (Ohio App. 7 Dist., 09-18-1996) 116 Ohio App.3d 56, 686 N.E.2d 1138. Mental Health ⚷ 439.1

A trial court ordering commitment of a criminal defendant found not guilty by reason of insanity errs in restricting the defendant's daughter's visitation since once a trial court has ordered commitment of a criminal defendant found not guilty by reason of insanity, the court's continuing jurisdiction is limited to decisions regarding a discharge, a conditional release, a trial visit, or a transfer; the court has no supervisory powers over the details of a patient's confinement or treatment and no jurisdiction to regulate general visitation, as opposed to trial visitation. State v. Traywick (Cuyahoga 1991) 72 Ohio App.3d 674, 595 N.E.2d 986.

A trial court's refusal to order the conditional release of a defendant found not guilty by reason of insanity to a less restrictive facility does not constitute an abuse of discretion even though a letter from the acting director of the facility where the defendant is housed asserts that the defendant derived maximum benefit from his hospitalization since the record reflected that he was functioning at a very high level at his current housing facility and that he would not be functioning at such a level were he transferred to the less restrictive facility and on cross-examination, another physician admitted that there was not much structural difference between the less restrictive facility and the one the defendant was currently at. State v. Traywick (Cuyahoga 1991) 72 Ohio App.3d 674, 595 N.E.2d 986. Mental Health ⚷ 439.1

A trial court's awareness, when considering whether a defendant found not guilty by reason of insanity should be released to a less restrictive facility, of the possible criminal sentence which could have been imposed on the defendant had he been found guilty of killing his stepson, is not a manifest abuse of discretion since RC 2945.40(D)(6) indicates that conditional release must terminate no later than on the expiration of the maximum criminal sentence the patient would have served. State v. Traywick (Cuyahoga 1991) 72 Ohio App.3d 674, 595 N.E.2d 986. Mental Health ⚷ 439.1

Parties to commitment proceeding have duty to present relevant, competent evidence to aid court in choosing treatment facility, and once trial court has considered the evidence it must order the implementation of the least restrictive alternative available as set forth in statute; trial court is not required to follow recommendation of state or defendant and has discretion to choose appropriate facility. State v. Gladding (Lake 1991) 72 Ohio App.3d 16, 593 N.E.2d 415, dismissed, jurisdictional motion overruled 60 Ohio St.3d 708, 573 N.E.2d 667. Mental Health ⚷ 439.1

A trial court has continuing jurisdiction to terminate an individual's conditional release from a state psychiatric hospital and to return him to confinement where that individual was committed under RC 5122.01(B) and 2945.45 after being found not guilty by reason of insanity of the charges of carrying a concealed weapon and having a weapon under a disability and had several conditional releases before the trial judge acted to terminate the then-current conditional release; habeas corpus cannot be used as a substitute for appeal and will not lie where the trial court's actions are within its jurisdiction. Reid v. Morris (Franklin 1990) 70 Ohio App.3d 807, 592 N.E.2d 875.

Involuntary committee is entitled to full hearing on continued commitment when he has not had such a hearing within the last 180 days, and he is not required to file an affidavit setting forth good cause for the hearing. State v. Rine (Licking 1991) 68 Ohio App.3d 460, 588 N.E.2d 981. Mental Health ⚷ 60

A trial court errs by denying a discharge to a defendant who was found not guilty by reason of insanity for the stabbing death of his girlfriend and who was committed to a psychiatric institution for less than a year and then placed on conditional release, where the court hears psychiatric testimony that (1) the defendant is not mentally ill at present and poses no threat of physical harm to himself or society in general, (2) he understands what his problem is and the need to follow doctor's instructions, (3) his wife indicated that she was capable of seeking professional assistance for her husband if symptoms of his schizophreniform psychosis reappear, and (4) the state fails to present any evidence, much less prove by clear and convincing evidence that the defendant is mentally ill and a threat to himself and others. State v. McNeal (Cuyahoga 1989) 64 Ohio App.3d 447, 581 N.E.2d 1148.

The authority to transfer a person found not guilty of a criminal offense by reason of insanity from a maximum security facility to a less restrictive setting necessarily and implicitly includes the authority to place conditions on the patient's confinement. Any conditions placed on the patient's confinement by the court should be consistent with the welfare of the patient and the safety of the public. The determination that a transfer is warranted, and the conditions placed thereon, are within the sound discretion of the trial court. State v. Lanzy (Ohio 1991) 58 Ohio St.3d 154, 569 N.E.2d 468, rehearing denied 59 Ohio St.3d 721, 572 N.E.2d 697. Mental Health ⚷ 439.1

Statutory provisions empowering court to place a not guilty by reason of insanity defendant and to regulate nature of his commitment did not grant court supervisory powers over details of defendant's treatment decisions. State v. Lake (Franklin 1986) 33 Ohio App.3d 275, 515 N.E.2d 960. Mental Health ⚷ 439.1

Where the sole determination to be made is whether an insanity acquittee, already established as being a mentally ill person subject to hospitalization by court order, should be transferred to a less restrictive treatment setting, no party has the burden of proof. Rather, the parties have a duty to present relevant, competent evidence to aid the court in its determination of whether the proposed less restrictive commitment alternative is appropriate considering the treatment needs of the person and the safety of the public. The determination of whether the person should be transferred from his current commitment setting to a less restrictive placement is within the sound discretion of the trial court. State v. Johnson (Ohio 1987) 32 Ohio St.3d 109, 512 N.E.2d 652. Mental Health ⚷ 439.1

The continuing jurisdiction of a court over a defendant committed after being found not guilty by reason of insanity is limited to decisions regarding the discharge, release, trial visit, or transfer of defendant; consequently, a court order which sets forth a treatment schedule and requires the supervision of defendant by a private security guard within the place of commitment is invalid. State v. Lanzy (Cuyahoga 1985) 29 Ohio App.3d 244, 504 N.E.2d 1150, 29 O.B.R. 306.

The clear and convincing standard of proof must be satisfied in all subsequent recommitment hearings, as well as the original commitment hearing, even when the only issue consists of ascertaining which controlled environment, among the available alternatives, is most appropriate to the patient's mental health, physical well-being, and treatment needs, as well as the imperatives of public safety. State v. Shepard (Wood 1984) 13 Ohio App.3d 389, 469 N.E.2d 1040, 13 O.B.R. 473.

In a recommitment proceeding, the trial court is required, automatically, to order placement in the least restrictive setting unless the prosecution shows by clear and convincing evidence that such less restrictive confinement would jeopardize the patient's welfare or the public safety. State v. Shepard (Wood 1984) 13 Ohio App.3d 389, 469 N.E.2d 1040, 13 O.B.R. 473. Mental Health ⚷ 439.1

Defendant who was found not guilty by reason of insanity and was thereafter committed to state hospital was not denied equal protection of the laws by fact that statute permitted state to charge and collect from defendant's estate for his support and maintenance while confined in the state facility even though those who had been convicted of a crime or had been committed to such a facility until they became competent to stand trial were exempted from payment. State ex rel. Dept. of Mental Health and Mental Retardation, Section of Reimbursement Services v. Talikka (Lake 1983) 13 Ohio App.3d 420, 469 N.E.2d 888, 13 O.B.R. 507, appeal dismissed 105 S.Ct. 56, 469 U.S. 801, 83 L.Ed.2d 7. Constitutional Law ⚷ 243.3

The trial court has jurisdiction to decide questions relating to the continued commitment of a person committed pursuant to RC 2945.40 after being found not guilty by reason of insanity, and such jurisdiction continues after the ninety-day period of RC 5122.15(H) until the time of lawful discharge. Townsend v. McAvoy (Ohio 1984) 12 Ohio St.3d 314, 466 N.E.2d 555, 12 O.B.R. 385. Mental Health ⚷ 439.1

It is held a violation of the Due Process Clause for a state statute to allow a criminal defendant found not guilty by reason of insanity to be committed to a mental institution until he demonstrates that he is not dangerous to himself or others even though he no longer suffers from any mental illness; due process requires that the nature of a commitment bear some reasonable relation to the purpose for which the individual is committed. (Ed. note: Louisiana statute construed in light of federal constitution.) Foucha v. Louisiana (U.S.La. 1992) 112 S.Ct. 1780, 504 U.S. 71, 118 L.Ed.2d 437.

Although the continuing jurisdiction of a court over a defendant committed after being found not guilty by reason of insanity is limited, an order of transfer to a civil hospital specifying "extremely limited on-grounds privileges" and requiring prior court approval of supervised off-grounds privileges is within the jurisdiction of the court because such an order is predominantly related to the "nature of the commitment" and does not amount to an extra-jurisdictional interference with treatment decisions. State v Lanzy, No. 55970 (8th Dist Ct App, Cuyahoga, 11–16–89), affirmed by 58 OS(3d) 154, 569 NE(2d) 468 (1991).

Where a person committed to and granted conditional release from a minimum security hospital pursuant to RC 2945.40(D)(2), violates the terms of the release, the court errs when it orders commitment to a maximum security hospital as this issue is not before the court. State v Gladding, No. 12–209 (11th Dist Ct App, Lake, 1–20–89).

Decisions of treating personnel to grant passes to and permit college attendance by a person committed under RC 2945.40, while possibly related to "treatment," change the nature of court-ordered commitment and require judicial approval. State v Dixon, Nos. 48253 and 48254 (8th Dist Ct App, Cuyahoga, 12–27–84).

9. Competence to stand trial

Where a defendant in a criminal case has interposed a defense of insanity, has been committed to the Lima state hospital and there is found capable of understanding the nature of the charges against him and of counseling in his own defense, a subsequent suggestion of insanity which does not inform the court that defendant has become insane since the prior determination of insanity was made, does not require the court to make a second examination into the question of the sanity of such defendant. State v. Jemison (Ohio 1968) 14 Ohio St.2d 47, 236 N.E.2d 538, 43 O.O.2d 115, certiorari denied 89 S.Ct. 312, 393 U.S. 943, 21 L.Ed.2d 280.

Where a common pleas court receives notice in the manner prescribed by RC 2945.37 or reasonable grounds to believe an accused is not then sane have otherwise come to the attention of the court, a determination of present sanity or capacity of the accused to stand trial is not within the discretion of either counsel or the court and the notice cannot be withdrawn or waived. State v. Jemison (Franklin 1967) 9 Ohio App.2d 227, 223 N.E.2d 904, 38 O.O.2d 256, reversed 14 Ohio St.2d 47, 236 N.E.2d 538, 43 O.O.2d 115, certiorari denied 89 S.Ct. 312, 393 U.S. 943, 21 L.Ed.2d 280.

When an attorney for an accused suggests to the common pleas court that the accused is not then sane, and files a certificate of a reputable physician to that effect, a mandatory duty arises upon the court to proceed to examine into the question pursuant to RC 2945.37. State v. Jemison (Franklin 1967) 9 Ohio App.2d 227, 223 N.E.2d 904, 38 O.O.2d 256, reversed 14 Ohio St.2d 47, 236 N.E.2d 538, 43 O.O.2d 115, certiorari denied 89 S.Ct. 312, 393 U.S. 943, 21 L.Ed.2d 280.

10. Psychiatric examination

A patient acquitted of murder by reason of insanity has the right to an independent psychiatric evaluation before being transferred to a more restrictive institution. State v. Dixon (Cuyahoga 1991) 77 Ohio App.3d 777, 603 N.E.2d 1056.

A court may refuse to grant a prosecutor's request that defendant be sent to the Lima state hospital where such request is not made until four days before the trial date where local psychiatric facilities are available. State v. Page (Ohio Com. Pl. 1967) 11 Ohio Misc. 31, 228 N.E.2d 686, 40 O.O.2d 173.

The number of specialists on mental diseases the court appoints to investigate and examine into the mental condition of a defendant in a criminal case is discretionary with the trial court, as long as the statutory minimum and maximum number provided for is observed. State v. Keaton (Pickaway 1967) 9 Ohio App.2d 139, 223 N.E.2d 631, 38 O.O.2d 166, certiorari denied 88 S.Ct. 1092, 390 U.S. 971, 19 L.Ed.2d 1182.

In any case in which insanity is set up as a defense the court may commit the defendant to a local hospital for the mentally ill or the Lima state hospital, where the defendant shall remain under observation for such time as the court directs, not exceeding one month, and its jurisdiction is not affected by a previous consideration of the defendant's sanity in a proceeding in the probate court. In re Fisher (Ohio 1958) 167 Ohio St. 296, 148 N.E.2d 227, 4 O.O.2d 343.

Alleged irregularities in committing defendant for psychiatric examination are not cognizable in habeas corpus where defendant was found sane and subsequently convicted. Grear v. Maxwell (C.A.6 (Ohio) 1966) 8 Ohio Misc. 210, 355 F.2d 991, 35 O.O.2d 333, 37 O.O.2d 268, certiorari denied 86 S.Ct. 1580, 384 U.S. 957, 16 L.Ed.2d 552, rehearing denied 87 S.Ct. 27, 385 U.S. 893, 17 L.Ed.2d 127.

The commitment of a fifteen-year-old to a state institution pursuant to RC 2151.26 for the purpose of examination is not an act for which a writ of prohibition will issue. State ex rel. Harris v. Common Pleas Court, Division of Probate and Juvenile (Ross 1970) 25 Ohio App.2d 78, 266 N.E.2d 589, 54 O.O.2d 115.

The term "alienist" as used in RC 2945.39 is limited to physicians whose specialty is mental illness; there is no requirement, however, that the alienist appointed be a board certified psychiatrist. OAG 77–080.

2945.401 Nonsecured status or termination of commitment; reports on competence; jurisdiction; hearing

(A) A defendant found incompetent to stand trial and committed pursuant to section 2945.39 of the Revised Code or a person found not guilty by reason of insanity and committed pursuant to section 2945.40 of the Revised Code shall remain subject to the jurisdiction of the trial court pursuant to that commitment, and to the provisions of this section, until the final termination of the commitment as described in division (J)(1) of this section. If the jurisdiction is terminated under this division because of the final termination of the commitment resulting from the expiration of the maximum prison term or term of imprisonment described in division (J)(1)(b) of this section, the court or prosecutor may file an affidavit for the civil commitment of the defendant or person pursuant to Chapter 5122. or 5123. of the Revised Code.

(B) A hearing conducted under any provision of sections 2945.37 to 2945.402 of the Revised Code shall not be conducted in accordance with Chapters 5122. and 5123. of the Revised Code. Any person who is committed pursuant to section 2945.39 or 2945.40 of the Revised Code shall not voluntarily admit the person or be voluntarily admitted to a hospital or institution pursuant to section 5122.02, 5122.15, 5123.69, or 5123.76 of the Revised Code. All other provisions of Chapters 5122. and 5123. of the Revised Code regarding hospitalization or institutionalization shall apply to the extent they are not in conflict with this chapter. A commitment under section 2945.39 or 2945.40 of the Revised Code shall not be terminated and the conditions of the commitment shall not be changed except as otherwise provided in division (D)(2) of this section with respect to a mentally retarded person subject to institutionalization by court order or except by order of the trial court.

(C) The hospital, facility, or program to which a defendant or person has been committed under section 2945.39 or 2945.40 of the Revised Code shall report in writing to the trial court, at the times specified in this division, as to whether the defendant or person remains a mentally ill person subject to hospitalization by court order or a mentally retarded person subject to institutionalization by court order and, in the case of a defendant committed under section 2945.39 of the Revised Code, as to whether the defendant remains incompetent to stand trial. The hospital, facility, or program shall make the reports after the initial six months of treatment and every two years after the initial report is made. The trial court shall provide copies of the reports to the prosecutor and to the counsel for the defendant or person. Within thirty days after its receipt pursuant to this division of a report from a hospital, facility, or program, the trial court shall hold a hearing on the continued commitment of the defendant or person or on any changes in the conditions of the commitment of the defendant or person. The defendant or person may request a change in the conditions of confinement, and the trial court shall conduct a hearing on that request if six months or more have elapsed since the most recent hearing was conducted under this section.

(D)(1) Except as otherwise provided in division (D)(2) of this section, when a defendant or person has been committed under section 2945.39 or 2945.40 of the Revised Code, at any time after evaluating the risks to public safety and the welfare of the defendant or person, the chief clinical officer of the hospital, facility, or program to which the defendant or person is committed may recommend a termination of the defendant's or person's commitment or a change in the conditions of the defendant's or person's commitment.

Except as otherwise provided in division (D)(2) of this section, if the chief clinical officer recommends on-grounds unsupervised movement, off-grounds supervised movement, or nonsecured status for the defendant or person or termination of the defendant's or person's commitment, the following provisions apply:

(a) If the chief clinical officer recommends on-grounds unsupervised movement or off-grounds supervised movement, the chief clinical officer shall file with the trial court an application for approval of the movement and shall send a copy of the application to the prosecutor. Within fifteen days after receiving the application, the prosecutor may request a hearing on the application and, if a hearing is requested, shall so inform the chief clinical officer. If the prosecutor does not request a hearing within the fifteen-day period, the trial court shall approve the application by entering its order approving the requested movement or, within five days after the expiration of the fifteen-day period, shall set a date for a hearing on the application. If the prosecutor requests a hearing on the application within the fifteen-day period, the trial court shall hold a hearing on the application within thirty days after the hearing is requested. If the trial court, within five days after the expiration of the fifteen-day period, sets a date for a hearing on the application, the trial court shall hold the hearing within thirty days after setting the hearing date. At least fifteen days before any hearing is held under this division, the trial court shall give the prosecutor written notice of the date, time, and place of the hearing. At the conclusion of each hearing conducted under this division, the trial court either shall approve or disapprove the application and shall enter its order accordingly.

(b) If the chief clinical officer recommends termination of the defendant's or person's commitment at any time or if the chief clinical officer recommends the first of any nonsecured status for the defendant or person, the chief clinical officer shall send written notice of this recommendation to the trial court and to the local forensic center. The local forensic center shall evaluate the committed defendant or person and, within thirty days after its receipt of the written notice, shall submit to the trial court and the chief clinical officer a written report of the evaluation. The trial court shall provide a copy of the chief clinical officer's written notice and of the local forensic center's written report to the prosecutor and to the counsel for the defendant or person. Upon the local forensic center's submission of the report to the trial court and the chief clinical officer, all of the following apply:

(i) If the forensic center disagrees with the recommendation of the chief clinical officer, it shall inform the chief clinical officer and the trial court of its decision and the reasons for the decision. The chief clinical officer, after consideration of the forensic center's decision, shall either withdraw, proceed with, or modify and proceed with the recommendation. If the chief clinical officer proceeds with, or modifies and proceeds with, the recommendation, the chief clinical officer shall proceed in accordance with division (D)(1)(b)(iii) of this section.

(ii) If the forensic center agrees with the recommendation of the chief clinical officer, it shall inform the chief clinical officer and the trial court of its decision and the reasons for the decision, and the chief clinical officer shall proceed in accordance with division (D)(1)(b)(iii) of this section.

(iii) If the forensic center disagrees with the recommendation of the chief clinical officer and the chief clinical officer proceeds with, or modifies and proceeds with, the recommendation or if the forensic center agrees with the recommendation of the chief clinical officer, the chief clinical officer shall work with the board of alcohol, drug addiction, and mental health services or community mental health board serving the area, as appropriate, to develop a plan to implement the recommendation. If the defendant or person is on medication, the plan shall include, but shall not be limited to, a system to monitor the defendant's or person's compliance with the prescribed medication treatment plan. The system shall include a schedule that clearly states when the defendant or person shall report for a medication compliance check. The medication compliance checks shall be based upon the effective duration of the prescribed medication, taking into account the route by which it is taken, and shall be scheduled at intervals sufficiently close together to detect a potential increase in mental illness symptoms that the medication is intended to prevent.

The chief clinical officer, after consultation with the board of alcohol, drug addiction, and mental health services or the community mental health board serving the area, shall send the recommendation and plan developed under division (D)(1)(b)(iii) of this section, in writing, to the trial court, the prosecutor and the counsel for the committed defendant or person. The trial court shall conduct a hearing on the recommendation and plan developed under division (D)(1)(b)(iii) of this section. Divisions (D)(1)(c) and (d) and (E) to (J) of this section apply regarding the hearing.

(c) If the chief clinical officer's recommendation is for nonsecured status or termination of commitment, the prosecutor may obtain an independent expert evaluation of the defendant's or person's mental condition, and the trial court may continue the hearing on the recommendation for a period of not more than thirty days to permit time for the evaluation.

The prosecutor may introduce the evaluation report or present other evidence at the hearing in accordance with the Rules of Evidence.

(d) The trial court shall schedule the hearing on a chief clinical officer's recommendation for nonsecured status or termination of commitment and shall give reasonable notice to the prosecutor and the counsel for the defendant or person. Unless continued for independent evaluation at the prosecutor's request or for other good cause, the hearing shall be held within thirty days after the trial court's receipt of the recommendation and plan.

(2)(a) Division (D)(1) of this section does not apply to on-grounds unsupervised movement of a defendant or person who has been committed under section 2945.39 or 2945.40 of the

Revised Code, who is a mentally retarded person subject to institutionalization by court order, and who is being provided residential habilitation, care, and treatment in a facility operated by the department of mental retardation and developmental disabilities.

(b) If, pursuant to section 2945.39 of the Revised Code, the trial court commits a defendant who is found incompetent to stand trial and who is a mentally retarded person subject to institutionalization by court order, if the defendant is being provided residential habilitation, care, and treatment in a facility operated by the department of mental retardation and developmental disabilities, if an individual who is conducting a survey for the department of health to determine the facility's compliance with the certification requirements of the medicaid program under Chapter 5111. of the Revised Code and Title XIX of the "Social Security Act," 49 Stat. 620 (1935), 42 U.S.C.A. 301, as amended, cites the defendant's receipt of the residential habilitation, care, and treatment in the facility as being inappropriate under the certification requirements, if the defendant's receipt of the residential habilitation, care, and treatment in the facility potentially jeopardizes the facility's continued receipt of federal medicaid moneys, and if as a result of the citation the chief clinical officer of the facility determines that the conditions of the defendant's commitment should be changed, the department of mental retardation and developmental disabilities may cause the defendant to be removed from the particular facility and, after evaluating the risks to public safety and the welfare of the defendant and after determining whether another type of placement is consistent with the certification requirements, may place the defendant in another facility that the department selects as an appropriate facility for the defendant's continued receipt of residential habilitation, care, and treatment and that is a no less secure setting than the facility in which the defendant had been placed at the time of the citation. Within three days after the defendant's removal and alternative placement under the circumstances described in division (D)(2)(b) of this section, the department of mental retardation and developmental disabilities shall notify the trial court and the prosecutor in writing of the removal and alternative placement.

The trial court shall set a date for a hearing on the removal and alternative placement, and the hearing shall be held within twenty-one days after the trial court's receipt of the notice from the department of mental retardation and developmental disabilities. At least ten-days before the hearing is held, the trial court shall give the prosecutor, the department of mental retardation and developmental disabilities, and the counsel for the defendant written notice of the date, time, and place of the hearing. At the hearing, the trial court shall consider the citation issued by the individual who conducted the survey for the department of health to be prima-facie evidence of the fact that the defendant's commitment to the particular facility was inappropriate under the certification requirements of the medicaid program under chapter 5111. of the Revised Code and Title XIX of the "Social Security Act," 49 Stat. 620 (1935), 42 U.S.C.A. 301, as amended, and potentially jeopardizes the particular facility's continued receipt of federal medicaid moneys. At the conclusion of the hearing, the trial court may approve or disapprove the defendant's removal and alternative placement. If the trial court approves the defendant's removal and alternative placement, the department of mental retardation and developmental disabilities may continue the defendant's alternative placement. If the trial court disapproves the defendant's removal and alternative placement, it shall enter an order modifying the defendant's removal and alternative placement, but that order shall not require the department of mental retardation and developmental disabilities to replace the defendant for purposes of continued residential habilitation, care, and treatment in the facility associated with the citation issued by the individual who conducted the survey for the department of health.

(E) In making a determination under this section regarding nonsecured status or termination of commitment, the trial court shall consider all relevant factors, including, but not limited to, all of the following:

(1) Whether, in the trial court's view, the defendant or person currently represents a substantial risk of physical harm to the defendant or person or others;

(2) Psychiatric and medical testimony as to the current mental and physical condition of the defendant or person;

(3) Whether the defendant or person has insight into the dependant's or person's condition so that the defendant or person will continue treatment as prescribed or seek professional assistance as needed;

(4) The grounds upon which the state relies for the proposed commitment;

(5) Any past history that is relevant to establish the defendant's or person's degree of conformity to the laws, rules, regulations, and values of society;

(6) If there is evidence that the defendant's or person's mental illness is in a state of remission, the medically suggested cause and degree of the remission and the probability that the defendant or person will continue treatment to maintain the remissive state of the defendant's or person's illness should the defendant's or person's commitment conditions be altered.

(F) At any hearing held pursuant to division (C) or (D)(1) or (2) of this section, the defendant or the person shall have all the rights of a defendant or person at a commitment hearing as described in section 2945.40 of the Revised Code.

(G) In a hearing held pursuant to division (C) or (D)(1) of this section, the prosecutor has the burden of proof as follows:

(1) For a recommendation of termination of commitment, to show by clear and convincing evidence that the defendant or person remains a mentally ill person subject to hospitalization by court order or a mentally retarded person subject to institutionalization by court order;

(2) For a recommendation for a change in the conditions of the commitment to a less restrictive status, to show by clear and convincing evidence that the proposed change represents a threat to public safety or a threat to the safety of any person.

(H) In a hearing held pursuant to division (C) or (D)(1) or (2) of this section, the prosecutor shall represent the state or the public interest.

(I) At the conclusion of a hearing conducted under division (D)(1) of this section regarding a recommendation from the chief clinical officer of a hospital, program, or facility, the trial court may approve, disapprove, or modify the recommendation and shall enter an order accordingly.

(J)(1) A defendant or person who has been committed pursuant to section 2945.39 or 2945.40 of the Revised Code continues to be under the jurisdiction of the trial court until the final termination of the commitment. For purposes of division (J) of this section, the final termination of a commitment occurs upon the earlier of one of the following:

(a) The defendant or person no longer is a mentally ill person subject to hospitalization by court order or a mentally retarded person subject to institutionalization by court order, as determined by the trial court;

(b) The expiration of the maximum prison term or term of imprisonment that the defendant or person could have received if the defendant or person had been convicted of the most serious offense with which the defendant or person is charged or in relation to which the defendant or person was found not guilty by reason of insanity;

(c) The trial court enters an order terminating the commitment under the circumstances described in division (J)(2)(a)(ii) of this section.

(2)(a) If a defendant is found incompetent to stand trial and committed pursuant to section 2945.39 of the Revised Code, if neither of the circumstances described in divisions (J)(1)(a) and (b) of this section applies to that defendant, and if a report filed with the trial court pursuant to division (C) of this section indicates that the defendant presently is competent to stand trial or if, at any other time during the period of the defendant's commitment, the prosecutor, the counsel for the defendant, or the chief clinical officer of the hospital, facility, or program to which the defendant is committed files an application with the trial court alleging that the defendant presently is competent to stand trial and requesting a hearing on the competency issue or the trial court otherwise has reasonable cause to believe that the defendant presently is competent to stand trial and determines on its own motion to hold a hearing on the competency issue, the trial court shall schedule a hearing on the competency of the defendant to stand trial, shall give the prosecutor, the counsel for the defendant, and the chief clinical officer notice of the date, time, and place of the hearing at least fifteen days before the hearing, and shall conduct the hearing within thirty days of the filing of the application or of its own motion. If, at the conclusion of the hearing, the trial court determines that the defendant presently is capable of understanding the nature and objective of the proceedings against the defendant and of assisting in the defendant's defense, the trial court shall order that the defendant is competent to stand trial and shall be proceeded against as provided by law with respect to the applicable offenses described in division (C)(1) of section 2945.38 of the Revised Code and shall enter whichever of the following additional orders is appropriate:

(i) If the trial court determines that the defendant remains a mentally ill person subject to hospitalization by court order or a mentally retarded person subject to institutionalization by court order, the trial court shall order that the defendant's commitment to the hospital, facility, or program be continued during the pendency of the trial on the applicable offenses described in division (C)(1) of section 2945.38 of the Revised Code.

(ii) If the trial court determines that the defendant no longer is a mentally ill person subject to hospitalization by court order or a mentally retarded person subject to institutionalization by court order, the trial court shall order that the defendant's commitment to the hospital, facility, or program shall not be continued during the pendency of the trial on the applicable offenses described in division (C)(1) of section 2945.38 of the Revised Code. This order shall be a final termination of the commitment for purposes of division (J)(1)(c) of this section.

(b) If, at the conclusion of the hearing described in division (J)(2)(a) of this section, the trial court determines that the defendant remains incapable of understanding the nature and objective of the proceedings against the defendant or of assisting in the defendant's defense, the trial court shall order that the defendant continues to be incompetent to stand trial, that the defendant's commitment to the hospital, facility, or program shall be continued, and that the defendant remains subject to the jurisdiction of the trial court pursuant to that commitment, and to the provisions of this section, until the final termination of the commitment as described in division (J)(1) of this section.

(1996 S 285, eff. 7–1–97)

Cross References

Arrest and detention until warrant can be obtained, 2935.03

Department of mental retardation and developmental disabilities, definitions, 5123.01

Department of mental retardation and developmental disabilities, involuntary institutionalization procedures, 5123.71

Department of mental retardation and developmental disabilities, judicial proceedings, procedures, 5123.76

Examination, observation, classification, and assignment to institutions of sentenced persons by department of rehabilitation and correction, 5120.16

Hospitalization of mentally ill, admission of voluntary patient, 5122.02

Hospitalization of mentally ill, applicability of provisions, 5122.011

Hospitalization of mentally ill, confidentiality of records, 5122.31

Hospitalization of mentally ill, hearings, attorneys, 5122.15

Hospitalization of mentally ill, involuntary confinement, 5122.05

Hospitalization of mentally ill, not guilty by reason of insanity, definitions, 5122.01

Hospitalization of mentally ill, right to writ of habeas corpus, 5122.30

Institutionalization of person incompetent to stand trial or not guilty by reason of insanity, applicability of provisions, 5123.011

Judicial hospitalization of mentally ill, 5122.11

Mental health department, funds for services for persons committed to, 5119.62

Mentally ill patients absent without leave, applicability, 5122.26

Mentally retarded person may apply for admission for short-term care, 5123.701

Offenses against justice and public administration, detention defined, 2921.01

Offenses against justice and public administration, escape, 2921.34

Voluntary hospitalization of persons found not guilty by reason of insanity, 5123.69

Library References

Mental Health ⟾439.

Westlaw Topic No. 257A.

C.J.S. Mental Health §§ 241 to 246.

Research References

Encyclopedias

OH Jur. 3d Criminal Law § 2594, Treatment and Final Disposition of Incompetent Defendant.

OH Jur. 3d Criminal Law § 2595, Treatment and Final Disposition of Incompetent Defendant—Further Proceedings With Respect to Incompetent Defendants Charged With Serious Felony.

OH Jur. 3d Criminal Law § 3263, Conditional Release.

OH Jur. 3d Criminal Law § 3265, Continued Commitment; Termination.

OH Jur. 3d Habeas Corpus & Post Convict. Remedies § 35, Confinement of Mentally Ill Persons; Mootness.

OH Jur. 3d Incompetent Persons § 68, Consent to Treatment.

Treatises and Practice Aids

Markus, Trial Handbook for Ohio Lawyers, § 4:58, Criminal Case—Defenses—Insanity—as Affirmative Defense.

Katz, Giannelli, Blair and Lipton, Baldwin's Ohio Practice, Criminal Law, § 83:3, Ex Post Facto.

Katz, Giannelli, Blair and Lipton, Baldwin's Ohio Practice, Criminal Law, § 87:15, Acquittal Consequences.

Carlin, Baldwin's Ohio Practice, Merrick-Rippner Probate Law § 101:41, Jurisdiction Over Commitments in Criminal Cases.

Carlin, Baldwin's Ohio Practice, Merrick-Rippner Probate Law § 101:42, Voluntary Status of Persons Committed by Criminal Court.

Carlin, Baldwin's Ohio Practice, Merrick-Rippner Probate Law § 101:43, Commencement of Commitment Proceedings in Criminal Cases.

Carlin, Baldwin's Ohio Practice, Merrick-Rippner Probate Law § 101:48, Hearings on Nonsecured Status and Termination of Commitment of Persons Found Ngri or Incompetent to Stand Trial.

Carlin, Baldwin's Ohio Practice, Merrick-Rippner Probate Law § 101:49, Conditional Release.

Carlin, Baldwin's Ohio Practice, Merrick-Rippner Probate Law § 101:50, Review Hearings—Review Process for Persons Found Incompetent and Ngri.

Carlin, Baldwin's Ohio Practice, Merrick-Rippner Probate Law § 101:51, Discharge for Persons Found Incompetent or Ngri.

Notes of Decisions

---

1. Continuing jurisdiction over committed person

In order to retain jurisdiction over a defendant found not guilty by reason of mental illness and subject to hospitalization, the trial court must continue to find, at periodic hearings, that there is clear and convincing evidence that the defendant remains a mentally ill person subject to hospitalization by court order. State v. Bowen (Ohio App. 1 Dist., 07-28-2000) 139 Ohio App.3d 41, 742 N.E.2d 1166. Mental Health ⚷ 440

Defendant, an insanity acquittee who was committed to treatment facility, received required statutory notice of request by facility's chief clinical officer for authorization to medicate defendant forcibly, where defendant's attorney received notice of the written request and defendant appeared at hearing on that request. State v. Jung (Ohio App. 6 Dist., 03-31-1999) 132 Ohio App.3d 369, 724 N.E.2d 1262. Mental Health ⚷ 436.1

Trial court order, authorizing psychiatrists at treatment facility to which defendant had been committed following insanity acquittal to use reasonable force to administer prescribed antipsychotic medication to him, was not abuse of discretion, where it was undisputed defendant was mentally ill and all psychiatrists who treated or evaluated him concluded that proper medication would help to control his mental illness. State v. Jung (Ohio App. 6 Dist., 03-31-1999) 132 Ohio App.3d 369, 724 N.E.2d 1262. Mental Health ⚷ 436.1

Defendant was not entitled to personal notice for hearing on authorization to forcibly medicate him and thus trial court had jurisdiction over the proceeding as notice given to his attorney satisfied the statutory notice requirements. State v. Jung (Ohio App. 6 Dist., 03-31-1999) 132 Ohio App.3d 369, 724 N.E.2d 1262.

Statute requiring discharge of person who was found not guilty by reason of insanity upon expiration of maximum term for most serious offense charged applied prospectively to recommitment hearing that arose subsequent to statute's effective date. State v. Hawkins (Ohio, 12-22-1999) 87 Ohio St.3d 311, 720 N.E.2d 521, 1999-Ohio-70. Mental Health ⚷ 433(1)

2. Less restrictive status—In general

At hearing on continued commitment, state failed to produce some competent, credible evidence that granting insanity acquitee's request for increased movement privileges would represent a threat to the public safety or to the safety of any person, and thus, request should have been granted; acquitee's psychologist and psychiatrist recommended the increase in privileges, but state did not present any evidence contrary to those recommendations. State v. Mahaffey (Ohio App. 4 Dist., 11-28-2000) 140 Ohio App.3d 396, 747 N.E.2d 872, 2000-Ohio-1940. Mental Health ⚷ 439.1

3. —— Burden of proof, less restrictive status

Upon insanity acquittee's motion to increase his level of movement at state psychiatric institution, prosecutor had the burden of proof to show by clear and convincing evidence that the proposed change represented a threat to public safety or a threat to the safety of any person. State v. Northcutt (Ohio App. 5 Dist., Morgan, 11-15-2004) No. CA04-003, 2004-Ohio-6135, 2004 WL 2635597, Unreported. Mental Health ⚷ 439.1

At hearing on continued commitment, mental health providers' recommendation that insanity acquitee should receive increased movement privileges was a recommendation for a "less restrictive status" under commitment statute, and thus, state had burden to prove by clear and convincing evidence that recommendation should not be granted because it would represent a threat to the public safety or the safety of any person. State v. Mahaffey (Ohio App. 4 Dist., 11-28-2000) 140 Ohio App.3d 396, 747 N.E.2d 872, 2000-Ohio-1940. Mental Health ⚷ 439.1

4. Termination of commitment—In general

Because any evaluation of the mental state of a defendant found not guilty by reason of mental illness and subject to hospitalization is a factor relevant to the court's decision regarding termination of commitment, the court may, and should for public-safety purposes, consider any mental evaluation brought to the court's attention. State v. Bowen (Ohio App. 1 Dist., 07-28-2000) 139 Ohio App.3d 41, 742 N.E.2d 1166. Mental Health ⚷ 440

5. —— Evaluation report, termination of commitment

Evaluation report is to be considered separately from all other evidence presented at hearing on motion for termination of commitment of person originally found mentally ill and subject to hospitalization. State v. Bowen (Ohio App. 1 Dist., 07-28-2000) 139 Ohio App.3d 41, 742 N.E.2d 1166. Mental Health ⚷ 440

State was entitled to submit mental health evaluation prepared by defendant's expert, over defendant's objection, in proceedings on motion for termination of commitment filed by defendant originally found not guilty by reason of mental illness and subject to hospitalization. State v. Bowen (Ohio App. 1 Dist., 07-28-2000) 139 Ohio App.3d 41, 742 N.E.2d 1166. Mental Health ⚷ 440

6. —— Denial, termination of commitment

Clear and convincing evidence supported finding that commitment to less restrictive status of mental health patient, who was committed in forensic unit at psychiatric institution, represented threat to public safety or to any person, where state presented evidence about patient's degree of paranoid at time he murdered his father, and patient's current paranoid pattern of thinking, psychiatrists testified that patient still harbored unrealistic goals and expectations for himself, placed blame on others, had paranoid delusional disorder, and was suspicious person. State v. Hilton (Ohio App. 10 Dist., Franklin, 01-14-2003) No. 02AP-518, 2003-Ohio-87, 2003 WL 116145, Unreported. Mental Health ⚷ 439.1

Evidence clearly supported trial court's denial of motion for termination of commitment filed by defendant originally found not guilty by reason of mental illness and found to be subject to hospitalization; treating physician's report indicated that defendant would have to take psychotropic medications indefinitely and would be at risk of rapid decompensation should he fail to do so, medical evaluation prepared by forensic center's clinical psychologist indicated that defendant occasionally intentionally skipped his medication and had history of rapid decompensation, and defendant's expert concluded that defendant was not ready to control his own treatment. State v. Bowen (Ohio App. 1 Dist., 07-28-2000) 139 Ohio App.3d 41, 742 N.E.2d 1166. Mental Health ⚷ 440

7. "Credit for time served"

Patient, who was found not guilty of receiving stolen property by reason of insanity, was entitled to credit for time served after his arrest and before was committed to mental hospital; felony sentencing laws determine the length of time the court has jurisdiction over a defendant found not guilty by reason of insanity, and thus the same criminal statutes that pertain to reduce of criminal sentence apply for reduction of the length of commitment for defendants committed to a mental hospital after being found not guilty by reason of insanity. State v. Tuomala (Ohio App. 11 Dist., Ashtabula, 12-13-2002) No. 2001-A-0088, 2002-Ohio-6936, 2002 WL 31813031, Unreported, motion for delayed appeal granted 98 Ohio St.3d 1473, 784 N.E.2d 707, 2003-Ohio-904, appeal allowed 98 Ohio St.3d 1563, 787 N.E.2d 1229, 2003-Ohio-2242, reversed 104 Ohio St.3d 93, 818 N.E.2d 272, 2004-Ohio-6239. Mental Health ⚷ 440

2945.402 Conditional release

(A) In approving a conditional release, the trial court may set any conditions on the release with respect to the treatment, evaluation, counseling, or control of the defendant or person that the court considers necessary to protect the public safety and the welfare of the defendant or person. The trial court may revoke a defendant's or person's conditional release and order rehospitalization or reinstitutionalization at any time the conditions of the release have not been satisfied, provided that the revocation shall be in accordance with this section.

(B) A conditional release is a commitment. The hearings on continued commitment as described in section 2945.401 of the Revised Code apply to a defendant or person on conditional release.

(C) A person, agency, or facility that is assigned to monitor a defendant or person on conditional release immediately shall notify the trial court on learning that the defendant or person being monitored has violated the terms of the conditional release. Upon learning of any violation of the terms of the conditional release, the trial court may issue a temporary order of detention or, if necessary, an arrest warrant for the defendant or person. Within ten court days after the defendant's or person's detention or arrest, the trial court shall conduct a hearing to determine whether the conditional release should be modified or terminated. At the hearing, the defendant or person shall have the same rights as are described in division (C) of section 2945.40 of the Revised Code. The trial court may order a continuance of the ten-court-day period for no longer than ten days for good cause shown or for any period on motion of the defendant or person. If the trial court fails to conduct the hearing within the ten-court-day period and does not order a continuance in accordance with this division, the defendant or person shall be restored to the prior conditional release status.

(D) The trial court shall give all parties reasonable notice of a hearing conducted under this section. At the hearing, the prosecutor shall present the case demonstrating that the defendant or person violated the terms of the conditional release. If the court finds by a preponderance of the evidence that the defendant or person violated the terms of the conditional release, the court may continue, modify, or terminate the conditional release and shall enter its order accordingly.

(1996 S 285, eff. 7–1–97)

Cross References

Arrest and detention until warrant can be obtained, 2935.03

Department of mental retardation and developmental disabilities, definitions, 5123.01

Department of mental retardation and developmental disabilities, involuntary institutionalization procedures, 5123.71

Department of mental retardation and developmental disabilities, judicial proceedings, procedures, 5123.76

Examination, observation, classification, and assignment to institutions of sentenced persons by department of rehabilitation and correction, 5120.16

Hospitalization of mentally ill, admission of voluntary patient, 5122.02

Hospitalization of mentally ill, applicability of provisions, 5122.011

Hospitalization of mentally ill, confidentiality of records, 5122.31

Hospitalization of mentally ill, hearings, attorneys, 5122.15

Hospitalization of mentally ill, involuntary confinement, 5122.05

Hospitalization of mentally ill, right to writ of habeas corpus, 5122.30

Institutionalization of person incompetent to stand trial or not guilty by reason of insanity, applicability of provisions, 5123.011

Judicial hospitalization of mentally ill, 5122.11

Mental health department, funds for services for persons committed to, 5119.62

Mentally ill patients absent without leave, applicability, 5122.26

Mentally retarded person may apply for admission for short-term care, 5123.701

Offenses against justice and public administration, detention defined, 2921.01

Offenses against justice and public administration, escape, 2921.34

Voluntary hospitalization of persons found not guilty by reason of insanity, 5123.69

Library References

Mental Health ⟹439.

Westlaw Topic No. 257A.

C.J.S. Mental Health §§ 241 to 246.

Research References

Encyclopedias

OH Jur. 3d Criminal Law § 2594, Treatment and Final Disposition of Incompetent Defendant.

OH Jur. 3d Criminal Law § 2595, Treatment and Final Disposition of Incompetent Defendant—Further Proceedings With Respect to Incompetent Defendants Charged With Serious Felony.

OH Jur. 3d Criminal Law § 3259, Right to Counsel.

OH Jur. 3d Criminal Law § 3263, Conditional Release.

OH Jur. 3d Criminal Law § 3264, Conditional Release—Violation of Terms; Hearing.

OH Jur. 3d Habeas Corpus & Post Convict. Remedies § 35, Confinement of Mentally Ill Persons; Mootness.

Treatises and Practice Aids

Carlin, Baldwin's Ohio Practice, Merrick-Rippner Probate Law § 101:42, Voluntary Status of Persons Committed by Criminal Court.

Carlin, Baldwin's Ohio Practice, Merrick-Rippner Probate Law § 101:49, Conditional Release.

WITNESSES

2945.41 Rules applicable in criminal cases

The rules of evidence in civil causes, where applicable, govern in all criminal causes.

(1953 H 1, eff. 10–1–53; GC 13444–1)

Historical and Statutory Notes

Pre–1953 H 1 Amendments: 113 v 185, Ch 23, § 1

Cross References

Evidence rules, applicability, Evid R 101

Proof of official records provisions of Civ R 44.1 apply in criminal cases, Crim R 27

Library References

Criminal Law ⚷661.

Westlaw Topic No. 110.

C.J.S. Criminal Law §§ 656, 751, 1202.

Research References

Encyclopedias

OH Jur. 3d Criminal Law § 2859, Civil Rules of Evidence; Applicability in Criminal Cases.

Forms

Ohio Jurisprudence Pleading and Practice Forms § 57:1, Introduction.

Treatises and Practice Aids

Giannelli and Snyder, Baldwin's Ohio Practice, Evidence, R 101, Scope of Rules: Applicability; Privileges; Exceptions.

Giannelli and Snyder, Baldwin's Ohio Practice, Evidence, R 601, General Rule of Competency.

Giannelli and Snyder, Baldwin's Ohio Practice, Evidence, § 101.1, Introduction.

1 Giannelli and Snyder, Baldwin's Ohio Practice, Evidence, Index, Index.

Law Review and Journal Commentaries

The Admissibility of Hypnotically Influenced Testimony, Neil J. Dilloff. 4 Ohio N U L Rev 1 (1977).

The Game Plan: Drafting the Ohio Rules of Evidence, Norman B. Miller. 6 Cap U L Rev 549 (1977).

A Guide to the Proposed Ohio Rules of Evidence, Kurt A. Phillips, Jr. 5 Ohio N U L Rev 28 (1978).

The Ohio and Federal Rules of Evidence, Jack B. Weinstein. 6 Cap U L Rev 517 (1977).

The Ohio Evidence Rules: 105 Years of Heritage and Dilemma, Josiah H. Blackmore II. 6 Cap U L Rev 533 (1977).

Our Witness: Testimony at Trial, Norman B. Miller. 6 Cap U L Rev 555 (1977).

The Proposed Ohio Rules of Evidence: The General Assembly, Evidence, and Rulemaking, Paul C. Giannelli. 29 Case W Res L Rev 16 (Fall 1978).

Some Things about Hearsay: Article VIII, Josiah H. Blackmore II. 6 Cap U L Rev 597 (1977).

Notes of Decisions

1. In general

General rules of evidence are usually same in civil and criminal cases under provisions of this section. State v. Nevius (Ohio 1947) 147 Ohio St. 263, 71 N.E.2d 258, 34 O.O. 210, certiorari denied 67 S.Ct. 1521, 331 U.S. 839, 91 L.Ed. 1851.

2. Discovery—In general

Prior to the trial of a criminal case a court may properly refuse an application by defendant or his attorney to require a prosecuting attorney to submit for his inspection and examination a statement made by the defendant respecting the crime involved, reduced to writing and in the possession of the prosecuting attorney. State v. Corkran (Ohio 1965) 3 Ohio St.2d 125, 209 N.E.2d 437, 32 O.O.2d 132.

The denial to an accused in a criminal case of access to papers and documents in the possession of the prosecutor pertaining to the case is not an abuse of discretion, where the record does not reflect any demand therefor and such documents were neither offered in evidence nor used in the examination of witnesses. City of Dayton v. Thomas (Montgomery 1963) 118 Ohio App. 165, 193 N.E.2d 521, 25 O.O.2d 19, appeal dismissed 175 Ohio St. 179, 191 N.E.2d 806.

Defendant in criminal case who alleged he could not remember contents of statements given by him to prosecuting attorney due to emotional disturbance and intoxication at the time of the giving of such statements was entitled to copies of notes and transcriptions thereof. State v. Hill (Ohio Com.Pl. 1963) 191 N.E.2d 235, 91 Ohio Law Abs. 125, 23 O.O.2d 255.

It was not an abuse of discretion for a court in a criminal case to deny the defendant the right to inspect and copy a hospital report of a blood test of the defendant regarding the alcoholic content of his blood or the right to interview the technician who prepared such reports. State v. Regedanz (Ohio Com.Pl. 1953) 120 N.E.2d 480, 68 Ohio Law Abs. 81, 54 O.O. 76.

3. —— Hospital records, discovery

The business records as evidence act is not applicable to criminal proceedings so as to allow the admission into evidence under such act of hospital records showing the results of a physical examination of an alleged rape victim. State v. Tims (Ohio 1967) 9 Ohio St.2d 136, 224 N.E.2d 348, 38 O.O.2d 328. Criminal Law ⚷ 662.40

4. Attorney–client privilege

If the defendant in a criminal case voluntarily testifies, his attorney may be compelled to testify on the same subject unless barred by constitutional rights of the defendant. State v. Crissman (Columbiana 1971) 31 Ohio App.2d 170, 287 N.E.2d 642, 60 O.O.2d 279. Witnesses ⚷ 219(3)

2945.42 Competency of witnesses

No person is disqualified as a witness in a criminal prosecution by reason of the person's interest in the prosecution as a party or otherwise or by reason of the person's conviction of crime. Husband and wife are competent witnesses to testify in behalf of each other in all criminal prosecutions and to testify against each other in all actions, prosecutions, and proceedings for personal injury of either by the other, bigamy, or failure to provide for, neglect of, or cruelty to their children under eighteen years of age or their physically or mentally handicapped child under twenty-one years of age. A spouse may testify against his or her spouse in a prosecution under a provision of sections 2903.11 to 2903.13, 2919.21, 2919.22, or 2919.25 of the Revised Code for cruelty to, neglect of, or abandonment of such spouse, in a prosecution against his or her spouse under section 2903.211 or 2911.211, of the Revised Code for the commission of the offense against the spouse who is testifying, in a prosecution under section 2919.27 of the Revised Code involving a protection order issued or consent agreement approved pursuant to section 2919.26 or 3113.31 of the Revised Code for the commission of the offense against the spouse who is testifying, or in a prosecution under section 2907.02 of the Revised Code for the commission of rape or under former section 2907.12 of the Revised Code for felonious sexual penetration against such spouse in a case in which the offense can be committed against a spouse. Such interest, conviction, or relationship may be shown for the purpose of affecting the credibility of the witness. Husband or wife shall not testify concerning a communication made by one to the other, or act done by either in the presence of the other, during coverture, unless the communication was made or act done in the known presence or hearing of a third person competent to be a witness, or in case of personal injury by either the husband or wife to the other, or rape or the former offense of felonious sexual penetration in a case in which the offense can be committed against a spouse, or bigamy, or failure to provide for, or neglect or cruelty of either to their children under eighteen years of age or their physically or mentally handicapped child under twenty-one years of age, violation of a protection order or consent agreement, or neglect or abandonment of a spouse under a provision of those sections. The presence or whereabouts of the husband or wife is not an act under this section. The rule is the same if the marital relation has ceased to exist.
(1996 H 445, eff. 9–3–96; 1995 S 2, eff. 7–1–96; 1992 H 536, eff. 11–5–92; 1985 H 475; 1980 H 920; 1975 H 1; 1971 S 312; 1953 H 1; GC 13444–2)

Historical and Statutory Notes

Pre–1953 H 1 Amendments: 113 v 186, Ch 23, § 2

Amendment Note: 1996 H 445 changed a reference to section 2907.12 to the reference to former section 2907.12 in the third sentence; and made other nonsubstantive changes.

Amendment Note: 1995 S 2 inserted "involving a protection order issued or consent agreement approved pursuant to section 2919.26 or 3113.31 of the Revised Code for the commission of the offense against the spouse who is testifying" in the third sentence; and made changes to reflect gender neutral language and other nonsubstantive changes.

Cross References

Competent witnesses, 2317.01

General rule of competency, Evid R 601

Reciprocal enforcement of support, husband-wife privilege inapplicable, 3115.20

Library References

Witnesses ⚷35 to 223.

Westlaw Topic No. 410.

C.J.S. Criminal Law §§ 641 to 644.

C.J.S. Federal Civil Procedure § 584.

C.J.S. Witnesses §§ 87 to 389.

Research References

Encyclopedias

OH Jur. 3d Criminal Law § 2961, Cross-Examination of Testifying Defendant as to Other Crimes.

OH Jur. 3d Criminal Law § 3011, Statements of Persons Not Available as Witnesses—Statements Against Interest; Statements of Third Persons.

OH Jur. 3d Criminal Law § 3118, Conviction of Crime or Guilty Plea.

OH Jur. 3d Criminal Law § 3119, Interest in Action.

OH Jur. 3d Criminal Law § 3126, Husband and Wife.

OH Jur. 3d Criminal Law § 3143, Interest in Result of Case.

OH Jur. 3d Evidence & Witnesses § 746, Actions for Wrongs to Marital Relation, Spouse, or Child.

OH Jur. 3d Evidence & Witnesses § 748, Generally; Effect of Presence of Third Person.

OH Jur. 3d Evidence & Witnesses § 854, Proof of Conviction of Crime.

OH Jur. 3d Evidence & Witnesses § 917, Relationship to Parties.

Forms

Ohio Jurisprudence Pleading and Practice Forms § 61:2, Privileges.

Ohio Jurisprudence Pleading and Practice Forms § 61:3, General Rule of Competency.

Treatises and Practice Aids

Markus, Trial Handbook for Ohio Lawyers, § 12:4, Bias or Prejudice.

Markus, Trial Handbook for Ohio Lawyers, § 13:3, Person Convicted of Crime.

Markus, Trial Handbook for Ohio Lawyers, § 13:5, Spouse.

Markus, Trial Handbook for Ohio Lawyers, § 19:1, Nature and Scope.

Markus, Trial Handbook for Ohio Lawyers, § 19:2, Communications Between Husband and Wife.

Markus, Trial Handbook for Ohio Lawyers, § 19:4, Communications Between Husband and Wife—Requirements for Spousal Privilege—Existence of Marital Relationship.

Markus, Trial Handbook for Ohio Lawyers, § 13:13, Accomplice.

Sowald & Morganstern, Baldwin's Ohio Practice Domestic Relations Law § 2:73, Cohabitation Agreements—Limitations.

Giannelli and Snyder, Baldwin's Ohio Practice, Evidence, R 501, General Rule.

Giannelli and Snyder, Baldwin's Ohio Practice, Evidence, R 601, General Rule of Competency.

Giannelli and Snyder, Baldwin's Ohio Practice, Evidence, R 607, Impeachment.

Giannelli and Snyder, Baldwin's Ohio Practice, Evidence, R 609, Impeachment by Evidence of Conviction of Crime.

Giannelli and Snyder, Baldwin's Ohio Practice, Evidence, R 616, Methods of Impeachment.

Giannelli and Snyder, Baldwin's Ohio Practice, Evidence, § 601.3, Competency Rules Defined.

Giannelli and Snyder, Baldwin's Ohio Practice, Evidence, § 609.4, Prior Ohio Law.

Giannelli and Snyder, Baldwin's Ohio Practice, Evidence, § 616.3, Impeachment: Bias.

Giannelli and Snyder, Baldwin's Ohio Practice, Evidence, § 501.23, Spousal Privilege: in General.

Giannelli and Snyder, Baldwin's Ohio Practice, Evidence, § 501.26, Spousal Privilege: Exceptions.

Giannelli and Snyder, Baldwin's Ohio Practice, Evidence, § 601.12, Spousal Competency & Privilege Distinguished.

Giannelli and Snyder, Baldwin's Ohio Practice, Evidence, § 601.16, Statutes; Dead Man Rule.

1 Giannelli and Snyder, Baldwin's Ohio Practice, Evidence, Index, Index.

Law Review and Journal Commentaries

Admissibility of Hypnotic Statements: Is the Law of Evidence Susceptible?, Robert S. Spector and Teree E. Foster. 38 Ohio St L J 567 (1977).

The Admissibility of Hypnotically Influenced Testimony, Neil J. Dilloff. 4 Ohio N U L Rev 1 (1977).

Criminal Law—Evidence—Spouse Shall Not Testify, Alan Belkin and Lawrence Friedlander. 46 Clev B J 106 (March 1975).

Impeachment by Bias, Paul C. Giannelli. 3 Crim L J Ohio 1 (January/February 1991).

Interviewing Child Victims/Witnesses, Mary A. Lentz. 9 Baldwin's Ohio Sch L J 25 (July/August 1997).

Interviewing the child witness: Do's and don't's, how's and why's, Nancy E. Walker and Matthew Nguyen. 29 Creighton L Rev 1587 (1996).

Privileged Communications in Ohio and What's New on the Horizon: Ohio House Bill 52 Accountant–Client Privilege, Note. 31 Akron L Rev 505 (1998).

Shield a Prosecution Sword—rape laws can protect accuser who has reason to lie, John Gibeaut. 83 A B A J 36 (December 1997).

Spousal privilege and the meanings of marriage, Milton C. Regan, Jr. 81 Va L Rev 2045 (1995).

Notes of Decisions

---

1. Testimony before grand jury

Defendant was denied due process when she executed warranty deed transferring real property to county board of commissioners outside of review of any court in violation of statute setting forth procedural requirements in criminal forfeiture proceeding, and when she was thereby denied opportunity for court assessment of whether forfeiture constituted excessive fine. Rice v. Logan Cty. Bd. of Commrs. (Ohio App. 3 Dist., 10-09-1996) 114 Ohio App.3d 198, 682 N.E.2d 1106. Constitutional Law ⚷ 303; Forfeitures ⚷ 5

An indictment and subsequent proceedings based thereon are not rendered invalid on the ground that illegal and incompetent testimony was heard by the grand jury which voted such indictment, inasmuch as the grand jury does not exercise a judicial function. Wickline v. Alvis (Franklin 1957) 103 Ohio App. 1, 144 N.E.2d 207, 3 O.O.2d 105. Indictment And Information ⚷ 10.2(2)

2. Impeachment of witness—In general

The housemate of a defendant charged with gross sexual imposition on his nine-year-old grandnephew can be impeached on cross-examination where he has testified that the defendant's relationship with the victim was "normal," while on cross-examination the housemate admits to a homosexual relationship with the defendant and being in love with him, thereby showing bias toward the defendant; it is not necessary to lay a foundation before impeaching a witness by showing bias or prejudice during cross-examination the way a foundation is necessary before impeaching a witness by prior inconsistent statement. State v. Eben (Meigs 1992) 81 Ohio App.3d 341, 610 N.E.2d 1109.

Under RC 2945.42, the defendant in a criminal prosecution may be cross-examined as to his convictions of crime under state or federal laws. State v. Peoples (Mahoning 1971) 28 Ohio App.2d 162, 275 N.E.2d 626, 57 O.O.2d 226. Witnesses ⚷ 337(7)

In prosecution by affidavit for driving a motor vehicle while under the influence of intoxicating liquor in violation of RC 4511.19 the defendant testifying in his own behalf may properly be asked on cross-examination and required to answer whether he has previously been convicted of such an offense, where such offense is cognizable by statute and it does not appear that the former conviction was not under such statute. State v. Murdock (Ohio 1961) 172 Ohio St. 221, 174 N.E.2d 543, 15 O.O.2d 372. Witnesses ⚷ 337(27)

The disqualification as a witness of one convicted of crime is removed by RC 2945.42, but the conviction of a witness for an offense under state laws may be shown for the purpose of affecting his credibility. State v. Murdock (Ohio 1961) 172 Ohio St. 221, 174 N.E.2d 543, 15 O.O.2d 372.

Where a defendant in a criminal case admits on cross-examination that he has been convicted of other state and federal crimes, it is not prejudicial to permit further cross-examination which is limited to an attempt to get from the witness the specific names of the offenses of which he has been convicted. State v. Hill (Hamilton 1959) 111 Ohio App. 257, 165 N.E.2d 241, 12 O.O.2d 447.

In the trial of an accused for murder, it is prejudicial error for the prosecution to ask the accused, on cross-examination, about a prior "murder charge" and, following the accused's answer, "never convicted of anything else in my life," to ask him, "you weren't convicted of murder in 1927?" State v. Cole (Hamilton 1958) 107 Ohio App. 444, 155 N.E.2d 507, 8 O.O.2d 427.

For the purpose of reflecting upon the credibility of the accused, he may be asked on cross-examination whether he has ever been convicted of a crime that comes within the designation of the crimen falsi of the common law, but he may not be cross-examined as to a former conviction for violating a city ordinance. State v. Hickman (Erie 1956) 102

Ohio App. 78, 141 N.E.2d 202, 2 O.O.2d 70. Witnesses ⚷ 337(15)

Where a party offers himself as a witness it has always been competent in Ohio to ask him, for the purpose of reflecting upon his credibility, whether he has been convicted of treason, a felony or any other crime that came within the designation of the crimen falsi of the common law. Kornreich v. Industrial Fire Ins. Co. (Ohio 1936) 132 Ohio St. 78, 5 N.E.2d 153, 7 O.O. 198. Witnesses ⚷ 345(2)

Such inquiries upon cross-examination touching former convictions of crime are not collateral to the inquiry, but directly affect the credibility of the witness. Harper v. State (Ohio 1922) 106 Ohio St. 481, 140 N.E. 364, 1 Ohio Law Abs. 80, 20 Ohio Law Rep. 497, 20 Ohio Law Rep. 500. Witnesses ⚷ 337(7)

Under the statute, the defendant in a criminal prosecution may be cross-examined as to his conviction of crime under state or federal laws, but not as to his conviction under a city ordinance. Harper v. State (Ohio 1922) 106 Ohio St. 481, 140 N.E. 364, 1 Ohio Law Abs. 80, 20 Ohio Law Rep. 497, 20 Ohio Law Rep. 500. Witnesses ⚷ 337(7)

If upon cross-examination defendant denies his conviction of crime, the proper record of conviction, duly authenticated, may be offered by the state in rebuttal, as bearing upon his credibility; and such record, unmodified and unreversed, may neither be impeached nor contradicted by defendant, or other witness in his behalf, in a collateral proceeding. Harper v. State (Ohio 1922) 106 Ohio St. 481, 140 N.E. 364, 1 Ohio Law Abs. 80, 20 Ohio Law Rep. 497, 20 Ohio Law Rep. 500. Judgment ⚷ 751; Witnesses ⚷ 360

3. —— Spouses testifying against one another, impeachment of witness

Testimony regarding a pending divorce and custody dispute involving the defendant and his estranged wife, threats by the defendant he would "blow her away," and previous domestic violence the defendant allegedly committed as a result of the divorce and custody dispute is admissible in a prosecution for the aggravated murder of the defendant's mother-in-law and attempted aggravated murder of his estranged wife a few days before the final divorce and custody hearing since the evidence is probative of motive and intent. State v. Sandella (Ohio App. 11 Dist., Ashtabula, 12-30-1993) No. 91-A-1677, 1993 WL 548441, Unreported, appeal not allowed 70 Ohio St.3d 1414, 637 N.E.2d 11.

Although a communication from one spouse to another made in the presence of a third party is not privileged under RC 2317.02 or RC 2945.42, a spouse is not rendered competent to testify to the non-privileged information and the admission of a spouse's testimony in such a case is reversible error. State v Dawson, No. 62182, 1993 WL 226436 (8th Dist Ct App, Cuyahoga, 6–24–93).

Where evidence shows that incidents of coverture have been relinquished, no legitimate purpose would be served by exclusion of spousal testimony, and therefore spousal communication privilege does not apply. State v. Shaffer (Ohio App. 3 Dist., 09-16-1996) 114 Ohio App.3d 97, 682 N.E.2d 1040, dismissed, appeal not allowed 77 Ohio St.3d 1543, 674 N.E.2d 1183. Witnesses ⚷ 189

Spousal incompetency to testify is separate from spousal privilege. State v. Phelps (Ohio App. 8 Dist., 01-17-1995) 100 Ohio App.3d 187, 652 N.E.2d 1032. Witnesses ⚷ 52(1); Witnesses ⚷ 188

Eliciting wife's testimony without informing her of her right to not testify against her husband was "plain error," where defendant's story that he accidentally stabbed victim during scuffle which occurred when victim startled him was contradicted in key respects by wife's testimony that defendant had "words" with victim and pulled victim out of his automobile before stabbing occurred. State v. Adamson (Ohio, 07-05-1995) 72 Ohio St.3d 431, 650 N.E.2d 875, 1995-Ohio-199. Criminal Law ⚷ 1036.2; Witnesses ⚷ 52(7)

Even when spousal privilege does not apply because another person witnessed acts or communications, spouse still is not competent to testify about those acts or communications unless she specifically elects to testify. State v. Adamson (Ohio, 07-05-1995) 72 Ohio St.3d 431, 650 N.E.2d 875, 1995-Ohio-199. Witnesses ⚷ 52(1)

If accused commits acts in known presence of third person, accused may not assert spousal privilege; that is case even if third person is unable to testify. State v. Adamson (Ohio, 07-05-1995) 72 Ohio St.3d 431, 650 N.E.2d 875, 1995-Ohio-199. Witnesses ⚷ 193

Since defendant performed his acts in presence of murder victim, he could not assert that those acts were protected by spousal privilege. State v. Adamson (Ohio, 07-05-1995) 72 Ohio St.3d 431, 650 N.E.2d 875, 1995-Ohio-199. Witnesses ⚷ 193

In criminal trial, spousal privilege exists under which defendant can seek to have his wife's testimony excluded. State v. Jaschik (Trumbull 1993) 85 Ohio App.3d 589, 620 N.E.2d 883, dismissed, jurisdictional motion overruled 67 Ohio St.3d 1450, 619 N.E.2d 419. Witnesses ⚷ 188

Evidentiary rule of procedure prescribed by Supreme Court supersedes conflicting portions of separate statute on issue of spouse's competency to testify against other spouse charged with crime, but spousal privilege portions of statute remain applicable. State v. Carpenter (Clermont 1992) 83 Ohio App.3d 842, 615 N.E.2d 1103. Courts ⚷ 85(1)

Defendant's involvement of his minor girlfriend, whom he later married, in theft of money from her employer, resulting in defendant's indictment for contributing to delinquency of a minor, was crime against spouse as contemplated by Rule of Evidence making spouse competent to testify about crime committed against him or her; wife was thus competent to testify against defendant at trial on contributing charge, as well as related theft charge arising from same criminal event. State v. Ellis (Hardin 1992) 83 Ohio App.3d 362, 614 N.E.2d 1126, dismissed, jurisdictional motion overruled 66 Ohio St.3d 1444, 609 N.E.2d 170. Witnesses ⚷ 190

Where a husband kidnaps his wife and threatens her life with a firearm, such acts and threats are not confidential communications; therefore, the husband cannot assert the privilege embodied in RC 2945.42 to prevent the wife from testifying in a criminal prosecution stemming from the incident. State v. Bryant (Wood 1988) 56 Ohio App.3d 20, 564 N.E.2d 709.

The spousal privilege for confidential communications does not apply when the spouses are separated and not living as husband and wife. State v. Bradley (Cuyahoga 1986) 30 Ohio App.3d 181, 507 N.E.2d 396, 30 O.B.R. 323.

Where the record is silent as to the presence of a third person during an act or communication between spouses, there is a presumption of admissibility of the spousal testimony. State v. Bradley (Cuyahoga 1986) 30 Ohio App.3d 181, 507 N.E.2d 396, 30 O.B.R. 323. Witnesses 🔑 222

Where a defendant, in a single continuous transaction, commits crimes against his spouse, his child, and another, the spouse is competent to testify as to the entire transaction. State v. Fewerwerker (Cuyahoga 1985) 24 Ohio App.3d 27, 492 N.E.2d 873, 24 O.B.R. 49.

Evid R 601 governs competency of witnesses and does not supersede RC 2945.42 as to spousal privilege, which privilege is preserved by Evid R 501. State v. Rahman (Ohio 1986) 23 Ohio St.3d 146, 492 N.E.2d 401, 23 O.B.R. 315.

Identification of a defendant's clothes by his spouse is not within the spousal privilege of RC 2945.42. State v. Rahman (Ohio 1986) 23 Ohio St.3d 146, 492 N.E.2d 401, 23 O.B.R. 315.

RC 2945.42 and Evid R 601 do not render the spouse of an accused incompetent to testify against the accused with respect to a crime committed against a third person, when such crime is part of one continuous transaction or happening which culminates in offenses against the third party and the spouse. State v. Mowery (Ohio 1982) 1 Ohio St.3d 192, 438 N.E.2d 897, 1 O.B.R. 219, certiorari denied 104 S.Ct. 1916, 466 U.S. 940, 80 L.Ed.2d 464.

An accused may not assert a privilege under RC 2945.42 to preclude a spouse from testifying with respect to a crime committed against a third person, where the crime is committed in the known presence of such third person, as well as in the presence of the testifying spouse. State v. Mowery (Ohio 1982) 1 Ohio St.3d 192, 438 N.E.2d 897, 1 O.B.R. 219, certiorari denied 104 S.Ct. 1916, 466 U.S. 940, 80 L.Ed.2d 464.

The prosecution of a person for the alleged commission of petit larceny of the property of a woman whom he thereafter marries does not constitute a prosecution for "personal injury of either by the other," as required by RC 2945.42 to permit the testimony of one spouse against the other; therefore the wife may not testify concerning such alleged crime. City of Dayton v. Patton (Ohio Mun. 1970) 24 Ohio Misc. 151, 259 N.E.2d 763, 53 O.O.2d 113, 53 O.O.2d 169.

The spouse of an accused may testify at the accused's trial as to the whereabouts of the accused at the time the accused claims an alibi. State v. Sprouse (Jackson 1968) 13 Ohio App.2d 170, 234 N.E.2d 922, 42 O.O.2d 296.

Where a wife is made a competent witness against her husband, it is not optional with the wife to testify; if presented as a witness she may be compelled to testify. State v. Antill (Ohio 1964) 176 Ohio St. 61, 197 N.E.2d 548, 26 O.O.2d 366.

Where an indictment is returned against a husband for an assault upon his wife with a dangerous weapon or instrument likely to produce death or great bodily harm, and the wife is in fact injured, the wife is a competent witness against her husband at the trial on such indictment. State v. Antill (Ohio 1964) 176 Ohio St. 61, 197 N.E.2d 548, 26 O.O.2d 366.

In a prosecution for child stealing, where the child was the accused's stepson who was living with his mother who had been divorced from the child's father, testimony by the mother that she had been given custody of the child at the divorce hearing is not objectionable and in no way prejudicial to the accused, and the mother may testify against her accused husband. State v. White (Montgomery 1962) 116 Ohio App. 522, 189 N.E.2d 160, 22 O.O.2d 398.

Where a wife was present when defendant husband shot the deceased, it is error to permit the wife to testify for the prosecution, where timely objection is made to such testimony. State v. Rodriguez (Fulton 1959) 110 Ohio App. 307, 169 N.E.2d 444, 13 O.O.2d 79.

Admission of testimony by the wife against her husband, upon his trial for crime, without objection by his counsel at any stage of the proceedings, does not constitute reversible error. Ruch v. State (Ohio 1924) 111 Ohio St. 580, 146 N.E. 67, 22 Ohio Law Rep. 669.

The spousal privilege set forth in RC 2945.42 does not apply to the aggravated murder of a defendant's mother-in-law in the presence of his estranged wife and the attempted aggravated murder of his estranged wife; therefore, the admission of the estranged wife's testimony is proper. State v Sandella, No. 91–A–1677, 1993 WL 548441 (11th Dist Ct App, Ashtabula, 12–30–93).

An excited utterance to a third party implicating one's spouse, admissible as a hearsay exception, does not constitute testimony against one's spouse and hence is not excludable by reason of Evid R 601(B). State v Johnson, No. 86–CA–47 (2d Dist Ct App, Miami, 7–20–87).

In a prosecution for aggravated assault, a wife may testify that her husband forced her to have sex with him against her will even though he is not being prosecuted for rape because the spousal exception to rape was in force when the offense was committed. State v Saunders, No. 52091 (8th Dist Ct App, Cuyahoga, 5–7–87).

Letters written by a defendant that are voluntarily provided to the police by the defendant's spouse are properly admitted into evidence. State v Ward, No. 413 (4th Dist Ct App, Vinton, 6–24–85).

4. Privileged communications between spouses

Arson defendant's statements to estranged spouse were not protected by spousal communication privilege, where defendant and estranged spouse were separated and not living as husband and wife when spouse recorded defendant's statements. State v. Sparkman (Ohio App. 6 Dist., Huron, 03-19-2004) No. H-03-017, 2004-Ohio-1338, 2004 WL 541816, Unreported. Witnesses ⚷ 189

Domestic violence defendant was not entitled to appellate relief with respect to claim that alleged victim was denied effective assistance of counsel in that alleged victim was unable to successfully assert spousal privilege and privilege against self-incrimination, where defendant was attempting to argue issues affecting another person, and defendant's claim was simply a collateral attack on alleged victim's testimony, which was properly found to be admissible. State v. Smith (Ohio App. 3 Dist., Seneca, 10-14-2003) No. 13-03-25, 2003-Ohio-5461, 2003 WL 22336098, Unreported. Criminal Law ⚷ 1136

Record supported finding that spousal privilege was not applicable to wife's testimony in prosecution for domestic violence, even though wife and defendant husband were still legally married, where wife was the alleged victim of the crime, and wife and husband were not living together at time of alleged offense. State v. Smith (Ohio App. 3 Dist., Seneca, 10-14-2003) No. 13-03-25, 2003-Ohio-5461, 2003 WL 22336098, Unreported. Witnesses ⚷ 61(1)

Class of cases in which wife is a competent witness against husband is limited to those specific cases mentioned in the statute; provision that husband or wife shall not testify to a communication made by one to the other, or act done by one in presence of the other during coverture, unless in presence of a third person, does not enlarge the class of cases in which husband or wife is made competent to testify. Rosser v. State (Athens 1931) 10 Ohio Law Abs. 69. Witnesses ⚷ 53(1)

Murder-for-hire mastermind's hearsay statement to his spouse that he had paid $5,000 to a hit-man to have an informant killed was against the mastermind's penal interest, even though the marital privilege would have prevented the spouse from testifying about the statement in a prosecution of the mastermind; by telling his wife that he had paid for the murder, the mastermind placed himself at serious risk of arrest and prosecution. State v. Yarbrough (Ohio, 05-15-2002) 95 Ohio St.3d 227, 767 N.E.2d 216, 2002-Ohio-2126, reconsideration denied 96 Ohio St.3d 1441, 770 N.E.2d 1050, 2002-Ohio-3344, certiorari denied 123 S.Ct. 533, 537 U.S. 1023, 154 L.Ed.2d 433. Criminal Law ⚷ 422(5)

Communications between defendant and his former wife on day after he had allegedly been involved in criminal activity were not made during coverture, and thus were not protected by spousal privilege, where defendant and wife had been divorced over ten years earlier and had never remarried, and while defendant and wife were living together at time in question, they were both involved in relationships with others. State v. Baker (Ohio App. 12 Dist., 04-03-2000) 137 Ohio App.3d 628, 739 N.E.2d 819, dismissed, appeal not allowed 90 Ohio St.3d 1402, 734 N.E.2d 834, denial of post-conviction relief affirmed 2001 WL 1218888. Witnesses ⚷ 189; Witnesses ⚷ 195

Statutes providing privilege for communications between husband and wife did not apply to corrections officer's testimony regarding content of inmate's monitored telephone conversations with his wife; such statutes prevented only spouses from testifying. State v. Smith (Ohio App. 8 Dist., 02-24-1997) 117 Ohio App.3d 656, 691 N.E.2d 324, dismissed, appeal not allowed 79 Ohio St.3d 1418, 680 N.E.2d 156, certiorari denied 118 S.Ct. 424, 522 U.S. 972, 139 L.Ed.2d 325. Witnesses ⚷ 193

Spouses must be living as husband and wife in order for spousal communication privilege to apply. State v. Shaffer (Ohio App. 3 Dist., 09-16-1996) 114 Ohio App.3d 97, 682 N.E.2d 1040, dismissed, appeal not allowed 77 Ohio St.3d 1543, 674 N.E.2d 1183. Witnesses ⚷ 189

Spousal communication privilege did not apply to tape-recordings of telephone conversations between defendant and his former spouse which had occurred at time they were still legally married, given that parties had been separated and living apart at time of conversations. State v. Shaffer (Ohio App. 3 Dist., 09-16-1996) 114 Ohio App.3d 97, 682 N.E.2d 1040, dismissed, appeal not allowed 77 Ohio St.3d 1543, 674 N.E.2d 1183. Witnesses ⚷ 189

Because existence of marital privilege turned on specific circumstances surrounding each allegedly privileged communication, namely whether third party was present, continuing objection was inadequate to preserve error in admission of allegedly privileged testimony in capital murder case. State v. Henness (Ohio, 06-18-1997) 79 Ohio St.3d 53, 679 N.E.2d 686, 1997-Ohio-405, certiorari denied 118 S.Ct. 422, 522 U.S. 971, 139 L.Ed.2d 323, denial of post-conviction relief affirmed 1999 WL 739588, dismissed, appeal not allowed 87 Ohio St.3d 1491, 722 N.E.2d 525, certiorari denied 120 S.Ct. 2669, 530 U.S. 1234, 147 L.Ed.2d 281. Criminal Law ⚷ 1043(1)

Marital privilege did not attach to communication made within hearing of third person. State v. Henness (Ohio, 06-18-1997) 79 Ohio St.3d 53, 679 N.E.2d 686, 1997-Ohio-405, certiorari denied 118 S.Ct. 422, 522 U.S. 971, 139 L.Ed.2d 323, denial of post-conviction relief affirmed 1999 WL 739588, dismissed, appeal not allowed 87 Ohio St.3d 1491, 722 N.E.2d 525, certiorari denied 120 S.Ct. 2669, 530 U.S. 1234, 147 L.Ed.2d 281. Witnesses ⚷ 193

Absent coverture, communication between spouses is not privileged. Bentleyville v. Pisani (Ohio App. 8 Dist., 01-30-1995) 100 Ohio App.3d 515, 654 N.E.2d 394. Witnesses ⚷ 189

Spousal communication privilege did not apply to communications made during marriage, but while parties were separated and living apart with divorce proceedings pending; spouses were not living in coverture at time of communication. Bentleyville

v. Pisani (Ohio App. 8 Dist., 01-30-1995) 100 Ohio App.3d 515, 654 N.E.2d 394. Witnesses ⚷ 195

Spousal privilege and spousal competency are distinct legal concepts which interrelate and provide two difference levels of protection for communications between spouses. State v. Adamson (Ohio, 07-05-1995) 72 Ohio St.3d 431, 650 N.E.2d 875, 1995-Ohio-199. Witnesses ⚷ 52(1); Witnesses ⚷ 188

Hearsay statements of accused's wife may be properly relied upon to form basis of probable cause under which search warrant is issued; use of hearsay statements concerning confidential spousal communications does not violate statute prohibiting testimony of spouse. State v. Jaschik (Trumbull 1993) 85 Ohio App.3d 589, 620 N.E.2d 883, dismissed, jurisdictional motion overruled 67 Ohio St.3d 1450, 619 N.E.2d 419. Searches And Seizures ⚷ 116

Ohio's spousal privilege statutes protect oral communications with one's spouse intended to be private, but do not protect written communications with one's spouse, even though it is reasonably expected that the communication will remain confidential. State v. Howard (Clark 1990) 62 Ohio App.3d 910, 577 N.E.2d 749, dismissed 58 Ohio St.3d 713, 570 N.E.2d 277. Witnesses ⚷ 191

A conversation between spouses is not privileged and is admissible in a criminal trial where the conversation was conducted in the presence or hearing of third parties. State v. Howard (Clark 1990) 62 Ohio App.3d 910, 577 N.E.2d 749, dismissed 58 Ohio St.3d 713, 570 N.E.2d 277.

A witness may testify as to statements of her spouse made in the presence of her two minor children. State v. Muenick (Summit 1985) 26 Ohio App.3d 3, 498 N.E.2d 171, 26 O.B.R. 171.

Although a spouse may be competent to testify in a criminal trial, RC 2945.42 confers a substantive right upon the accused to exclude privileged spousal testimony concerning a confidential communication made or act done during coverture unless a third person was present or one of the other specifically enumerated exceptions contained in the statute is applicable. State v. Rahman (Ohio 1986) 23 Ohio St.3d 146, 492 N.E.2d 401, 23 O.B.R. 315. Witnesses ⚷ 188

In action in which plaintiff claimed there had been common-law marriage after previous divorce, excluding evidence regarding conversations between the parties tending to show agreement of marriage on ground that it would constitute personal communication between husband and wife was error, since they had been previously divorced and no common-law marriage would exist until after agreement was made. Holmes v. Pere Marquette R. Co. (Lucas 1927) 28 Ohio App. 297, 162 N.E. 675, 6 Ohio Law Abs. 628.

Defendant waived appellate review of admissibility of his wife's testimony under statutory privilege for confidential spousal communications or acts, where at trial in the prosecution for theft, defendant merely objected to wife's testimony on the basis of competency under the rules of evidence. State v. Elswick (Ohio App. 11 Dist., Ashtabula, 06-28-2002) No. 2001-A-0035, 2002-Ohio-3365, 2002 WL 1400218, Unreported. Criminal Law ⚷ 1043(3)

5. Defense counsel as witness

A defendant in a criminal case is denied fair trial when his trial attorney is called by state as prosecution witness, over objection and without previous notice, and gives testimony that tends to prove one of essential elements of crime charged. State v. Livingston (Summit 1972) 30 Ohio App.2d 232, 285 N.E.2d 75, 59 O.O.2d 364. Criminal Law ⚷ 641.13(2.1)

6. Convicted felon as witness

The testimony of convicted felons is competent in a disbarment proceeding. In re Lieberman (Ohio 1955) 163 Ohio St. 35, 125 N.E.2d 328, 56 O.O. 23.

7. Common law marriage

Grand jury indictment was not rendered invalid by fact that grand jury had considered testimony of his "common-law" wife, which defendant claimed had resulted in violation of spousal privilege, where indictment was valid on its face, and testimony in question was only a part of overall testimony presented to grand jury. State v. Baker (Ohio App. 12 Dist., 04-03-2000) 137 Ohio App.3d 628, 739 N.E.2d 819, dismissed, appeal not allowed 90 Ohio St.3d 1402, 734 N.E.2d 834, denial of post-conviction relief affirmed 2001 WL 1218888. Indictment And Information ⚷ 10.2(2)

Trial court's conclusion that common-law marriage existed between defendant and alleged wife, so as to have rendered wife incompetent to testify against defendant, was supported by sufficient evidence, including defendant's testimony that they were married in Islamic ceremony, Islamic marriage certificate signed by witnesses, checking and savings accounts established in both of their names, bills addressed to both parties, and representing themselves in community as husband and wife. State v. Phelps (Ohio App. 8 Dist., 01-17-1995) 100 Ohio App.3d 187, 652 N.E.2d 1032. Marriage ⚷ 50(2); Marriage ⚷ 50(3); Marriage ⚷ 50(5); Witnesses ⚷ 78

Spousal privilege is available to spouses in common-law marriage. State v. Burkitt (Clark 1993) 89 Ohio App.3d 214, 624 N.E.2d 210, dismissed, jurisdictional motion overruled 67 Ohio St.3d 1501, 622 N.E.2d 650. Witnesses ⚷ 63

8. Hypnotized witnesses

Prosecutors' failure to tell capital murder defendant's attorneys that three witnesses had been hypnotized, and to disclose information regarding a witness's mental capacity, was not material evidence, as would render prosecutors' withholding such evidence a *Brady* violation, where there was sufficient evidence to constitute overwhelming proof of defendant's guilt regardless of disclosure or suppression of hypnotically refreshed testimony and witness's brief treatment at a mental health center. Buell v. Mitchell (C.A.6 (Ohio), 12-04-2001) 274 F.3d 337. Criminal Law ⚷ 700(3); Criminal Law ⚷ 700(4)

2945.43 Defendant may testify

On the trial of a criminal cause, a person charged with an offense may, at his own request, be a witness, but not otherwise. The failure of such person to testify may be considered by the court and jury and may be made the subject of comment by counsel.

(1953 H 1, eff. 10–1–53; GC 13444–3)

Historical and Statutory Notes

Ed. Note: In 1965, the United States Supreme Court, in *Griffin v California*, 380 US 609, 85 SCt 1229, 14 LEd(2d) 106 (1965), held that a defendant's failure to testify in a state criminal trial cannot be commented upon by the prosecutor or be considered by the jury in reaching its verdict.

Pre–1953 H 1 Amendments: 113 v 186, Ch 23, § 3

Cross References

Preliminary matter, testimony by accused regarding not subjecting accused to cross-examination as to other issues in the case, Evid R 104

Right against compulsory self-incrimination, US Const Am 5; O Const Art I §10

Library References

Witnesses ⚷87.

Westlaw Topic No. 410.

C.J.S. Criminal Law §§ 641 to 644.

C.J.S. Witnesses § 207.

Research References

Encyclopedias

OH Jur. 3d Criminal Law § 488, Ohio Constitutional and Statutory Bases.

OH Jur. 3d Criminal Law § 493, Necessity of Compulsion—Effect of Accused Offering to Testify at Trial.

OH Jur. 3d Criminal Law § 498, Failure or Refusal to Testify.

Treatises and Practice Aids

Markus, Trial Handbook for Ohio Lawyers, § 14:7, Privilege Against Self-Incrimination—When Lost.

Markus, Trial Handbook for Ohio Lawyers, § 35:15, Criminal Case.

Katz, Giannelli, Blair and Lipton, Baldwin's Ohio Practice, Criminal Law, § 68:5, Accused's Right to Testify.

Hennenberg & Reinhart, Ohio Criminal Defense Motions F 4.05, Motion to Prohibit the Filming, Photographing or Videotaping of the Defendant While in the Courtroom-Administrative Motions.

Law Review and Journal Commentaries

Constitutional Law—Criminal Procedure—Self–Incrimination—California Constitution Prohibits the Use of Illegally Obtained Statements for Impeachment Purposes.—People v. Disbrow, Note. 45 U Cin L Rev 724 (1976).

The Dilemma of the Perjurious Defendant: Resolution, Not Avoidance, Dan Aaron Polster. 28 Case W Res L Rev 3 (Fall 1977).

Impeaching A Defendant's Testimony By Proof Of Post–Arrest Silence: Doyle v. Ohio, Note. 25 Clev St L Rev 261 (1976).

Recorded Statement of Defendant, Alan Belkin and Lawrence Friedlander. 46 Clev B J 225 (July 1975).

Notes of Decisions

1. Constitutional issues

Trial court was not required to apprise defendant of his right to remain silent and not to testify, where defendant took advantage of his constitutional right to testify in his own defense, and there was no indication that he was compelled to testify against himself. State v. Seibert (Ohio App. 10 Dist., Franklin, 06-13-2003) No. WD-02-017, 2003-Ohio-3107, 2003 WL 21386293, Unreported. Witnesses ⚷ 302

US Const Am 5, in its bearing on the states by reason of the Fourteenth Amendment, forbids either comment by the prosecution in a criminal case on the failure of the defendant to testify or instructions by the court that such silence is evidence of guilt. (See also Broeckel v Green, 298 FSupp 249, 22 Misc 165 (1967).) State v. Broeckel (Cuyahoga 1966) 8 Ohio App.2d 330, 222 N.E.2d 443, 37 O.O.2d 390, certiorari denied 87 S.Ct. 2140, 388 U.S. 920, 18 L.Ed.2d 1365. Constitutional Law ⚷ 268(8)

Comment by the trial court or by the prosecutor upon the failure of an accused to testify in a criminal proceeding against him violates the Self-Incrimination Clause of the Fifth Amendment made applicable to the states by the Fourteenth Amendment (US Supreme Court in Griffin v California), and this doctrine is applicable to cases pending on appeal at the time of its pronouncement. State v. Lynn (Ohio 1966) 5 Ohio St.2d 106, 214 N.E.2d 226, 34 O.O.2d 226.

The rule, enunciated first in Griffin v California, 380 US 609, 85 SCt 1229, 14 LEd(2d) 106 (1965) that it is improper for either the prosecuting attorney or the court to comment on the fact that the accused did not testify, should not be given effect retrospectively. Pinch v. Maxwell (Ohio 1965) 3 Ohio St.2d 212, 210 N.E.2d 883, 32 O.O.2d 504, certiorari denied 86 S.Ct. 1072, 383 U.S. 938, 15 L.Ed.2d 855.

An accused in a bastardy case may be called by counsel for complainant, and, over defendant's objection, be compelled to testify under cross-examination, either orally or by deposition, but cannot be forced to testify nor to give evidence in such proceeding, when to do so would tend to incriminate him. Taylor v. Mosley (Ohio Juv. 1961) 178 N.E.2d 55, 87 Ohio Law Abs. 335, 17 O.O.2d 439.

A defense attorney remarking during his closing statement that the federal authorities "never gave [the defendant] a chance to explain" opens the door for the prosecutor to note in his statement that the defendant "could have taken the stand and explained it to you." U.S. v. Robinson (U.S.Tenn. 1988) 108 S.Ct. 864, 485 U.S. 25, 99 L.Ed.2d 23, on remand 846 F.2d 1047.

A cautionary instruction to the jury that it is not to draw any adverse inference from defendant's refusal to testify on his behalf does not violate defendant's Fifth Amendment right against self-incrimination. Lakeside v. Oregon (U.S.Or. 1978) 98 S.Ct. 1091, 435 U.S. 333, 55 L.Ed.2d 319. Criminal Law ⚷ 787(1)

Failure to object in the state court to the prosecutor's comment that the petitioner failed to testify during his trial cannot bar the petitioner from asserting his federal right, where petitioner's conviction was not final when the US Supreme Court announced the constitutional rule in Griffin v California, 380 US 609, 85 SCt 1229, 14 LEd(2d) 106 (1965). O'Connor v. Ohio (U.S.Ohio 1966) 87 S.Ct. 252, 385 U.S. 92, 9 Ohio Misc. 59, 17 L.Ed.2d 189, 37 O.O.2d 374, 38 O.O.2d 91.

The rule adopted in 380 US 609, 85 SCt 1229, 14 LEd(2d) 106 (1965), Griffin v California, that adverse comment by a prosecutor or trial judge upon a defendant's failure to testify in a state criminal trial violates the federal privilege against compulsory self-incrimination will not be given retrospective application. Tehan v. U. S. ex rel. Shott (U.S.Ohio 1966) 86 S.Ct. 459, 382 U.S. 406, 8 Ohio Misc. 81, 15 L.Ed.2d 453, 35 O.O.2d 391, rehearing denied 86 S.Ct. 925, 383 U.S. 931, 15 L.Ed.2d 850. Courts ⚷ 100(1)

Under US Const Am 5, in its direct application to the federal government and its bearing on the states by reason of the Fourteenth Amendment, forbids either comment by the prosecution on the accused's silence or instructions by the court that such silence is evidence of guilt. Griffin v. California (U.S.Cal. 1965) 85 S.Ct. 1229, 380 U.S. 609, 5 Ohio Misc. 127, 14 L.Ed.2d 106, 32 O.O.2d 437, rehearing denied 85 S.Ct. 1797, 381 U.S. 957, 14 L.Ed.2d 730. Constitutional Law ⚷ 268(8)

References by the prosecutor to the fact that a defendant's codefendant did not testify are constitutionally impermissible. Scott v. Perini (C.A.6 (Ohio) 1971) 439 F.2d 1066.

The protection against self-incrimination under the Fifth Amendment includes not only the right to refuse incriminating questions, but also the right that such refusal shall not be commented upon by counsel for the prosecution. U. S. ex rel. Shott v. Tehan (C.A.6 (Ohio) 1964) 3 Ohio Misc. 131, 337 F.2d 990, 31 O.O.2d 182, certiorari granted 85 S.Ct. 1560, 381 U.S. 923, 14 L.Ed.2d 683, vacated 86 S.Ct. 459, 382 U.S. 406, 8 Ohio Misc. 81, 15 L.Ed.2d 453, 35 O.O.2d 391, rehearing denied 86 S.Ct. 925, 383 U.S. 931, 15 L.Ed.2d 850.

2. Comment on defendant's silence

Prosecutor's statement in final argument that only defendant and victim were present at time of crime and that " [victim] can't talk, [defendant] won't," in context of discussion of element of aggravated murder charges requiring state to prove that defendant had purposely caused victim's death, was improper direct and adverse comment on defendant's refusal to testify. State v. Clark (Hamilton 1991) 74 Ohio App.3d 151, 598 N.E.2d 740, dismissed, jurisdictional motion overruled 62 Ohio St.3d 1431, 578 N.E.2d 823. Criminal Law ⚷ 721(3)

A prosecutor's improper comments on defendant's failure to testify do not require automatic reversal; conviction must be affirmed if it is concluded, based on the whole record, that prosecutor's comments were harmless beyond any reasonable doubt. State v. Zimmerman (Ohio 1985) 18 Ohio St.3d 43, 479 N.E.2d 862, 18 O.B.R. 79. Criminal Law ⚷ 1171.5

Reference by prosecutor in closing argument to fact that state's evidence was uncontradicted was not improper comment on defendant's failure to testify, given that comment was directed to strength of the state's evidence and not to silence of defendant, and jury was instructed not to consider accused's failure to testify for any purpose. State v. Ferguson (Ohio 1983) 5 Ohio St.3d 160, 450 N.E.2d 265, 5 O.B.R. 380. Criminal Law ⚷ 730(10)

In the trial of a criminal case, reference by the prosecutor in his final argument to the jury to defendant's previously asserted silence at any stage of the accusatorial process, or to implications drawn therefrom, is not permissible unless the record clearly demonstrates by the action or testimony of the defendant that he has waived the privilege against self-incrimination previously invoked. State v. Stephens (Ohio 1970) 24 Ohio St.2d 76, 263

N.E.2d 773, 53 O.O.2d 182. Criminal Law ⚷ 720(6)

A bastardy action is essentially civil in nature, and the failure of the defendant in such action to testify may be the subject of comment to the jury. Smith v. Lautenslager (Hamilton 1968) 15 Ohio App.2d 212, 240 N.E.2d 109, 44 O.O.2d 371.

In a criminal prosecution a prosecuting attorney may not testify as to or comment upon the refusal of the accused to testify before the grand jury. State v. Minamyer (Ohio 1967) 12 Ohio St.2d 67, 232 N.E.2d 401, 41 O.O.2d 282. Criminal Law ⚷ 721(1)

It is error for the trial court in a criminal case not to declare a mistrial where the prosecution, in argument to the jury, says that defendant "never took the stand to tell you that." State v. Smith (Hamilton 1967) 10 Ohio App.2d 186, 226 N.E.2d 807, 39 O.O.2d 342.

Comment by prosecuting attorney that defendant had failed to testify at preliminary hearing was improper. State v. Davis (Ohio 1967) 10 Ohio St.2d 136, 226 N.E.2d 736, 39 O.O.2d 122.

The admission of testimony pertaining to a defendant's refusal to submit to a polygraph test constitutes prejudicial error. State v. Hegel (Montgomery 1964) 9 Ohio App.2d 12, 222 N.E.2d 666, 38 O.O.2d 25.

Comment by the prosecuting attorney on the defendant's failure to testify necessitates a reversal of a conviction. State v. Howell (Ohio 1965) 4 Ohio St.2d 11, 211 N.E.2d 56, 33 O.O.2d 43.

A defense attorney remarking during his closing statement that the federal authorities "never gave [the defendant] a chance to explain" opens the door for the prosecutor to note in his statement that the defendant "could have taken the stand and explained it to you." U.S. v. Robinson (U.S.Tenn. 1988) 108 S.Ct. 864, 485 U.S. 25, 99 L.Ed.2d 23, on remand 846 F.2d 1047.

In a trial on a charge of sexual battery to which the defendant pleaded not guilty by reason of insanity, the prosecutor violates the due process clause of US Const Am 14 by stating in closing argument that the soundness of the defendant's reasoning powers is suggested by remarks he made to police that he understood his rights as read and wished to see an attorney; the prosecutor's statement is a forbidden comment on the defendant's "silence" even where the defense did not object earlier to actual testimony on the defendant's words. Wainwright v. Greenfield (U.S.Fla. 1986) 106 S.Ct. 634, 474 U.S. 284, 88 L.Ed.2d 623.

Failure to object to the prosecutor's comments on the failure of the defendant in a criminal proceeding to testify, does not bar the defendant from claiming error if the decision in the case was not final at the time of the decision in Griffin v California. O'Connor v. Ohio (U.S.Ohio 1966) 87 S.Ct. 252, 385 U.S. 92, 9 Ohio Misc. 59, 17 L.Ed.2d 189, 37 O.O.2d 374, 38 O.O.2d 91.

A closing statement by the prosecutor, in which he refers to defense counsel's forthcoming closing argument and says "I think you are entitled to hear from the defendants" about certain inconsistencies in the testimony of defense witnesses, is obviously directed to the defense attorney, not to the defendants themselves and is not a comment on the fact they did not take the stand. Hollbrook v. U. S. (C.A.6 (Ohio) 1971) 441 F.2d 371.

Closing remarks of a prosecutor, that an accomplice in the crime with which the defendant is charged reached "the depths" when he took part in the crime, but has since admitted his guilt and testified under subpoena in the defendant's prosecution, and that the accomplice "is on his way back up. Not Wells [the defendant]. He is still down there," are ambiguous and not manifestly meant to be taken as a comment on the defendant's refusal to take the stand. U. S. v. Wells (C.A.6 (Ohio) 1970) 431 F.2d 434, certiorari denied 91 S.Ct. 475, 400 U.S. 997, 27 L.Ed.2d 448.

Where defendant was tried for rape and codefendant for aiding and abetting defendant, comment on codefendant's failure to testify was prejudicial to defendant. Kinser v. Cooper (C.A.6 (Ohio) 1969) 24 Ohio Misc. 141, 413 F.2d 730, 51 O.O.2d 206, 53 O.O.2d 169.

3. Jury instructions

Defendant was not entitled to jury instruction as to reasons defendant may decide not to testify; court instructed jury, in accordance with standard instructions, that defendant had constitutional right not to testify and that fact that defendant did not testify could not be considered for any purpose. State v. Grant (Ohio 1993) 67 Ohio St.3d 465, 620 N.E.2d 50, rehearing denied 68 Ohio St.3d 1412, 623 N.E.2d 568, certiorari denied 115 S.Ct. 116, 513 U.S. 836, 130 L.Ed.2d 62, rehearing denied 115 S.Ct. 617, 513 U.S. 1033, 130 L.Ed.2d 525. Criminal Law ⚷ 787(2)

Trial court need not instruct jury on defendant's right not to testify in exact language requested by defendant. State v. Grant (Ohio 1993) 67 Ohio St.3d 465, 620 N.E.2d 50, rehearing denied 68 Ohio St.3d 1412, 623 N.E.2d 568, certiorari denied 115 S.Ct. 116, 513 U.S. 836, 130 L.Ed.2d 62, rehearing denied 115 S.Ct. 617, 513 U.S. 1033, 130 L.Ed.2d 525. Criminal Law ⚷ 834(2)

There is no provision in the Ohio Constitution or in the Ohio Revised Code which entitles a defendant in a criminal case to have the jury instructed that his failure to testify must not be considered for any purpose, and so it is discretionary with the trial court whether to charge on the defendant's right to elect not to testify. State v. Nelson (Ohio 1973) 36 Ohio St.2d 79, 303 N.E.2d 865, 65 O.O.2d 222. Criminal Law ⚷ 787(1)

A court must upon request charge that it is not evidence of guilt when a defendant maintains his silence. State v. Wade (Cuyahoga 1972) 31 Ohio App.2d 33, 285 N.E.2d 898, 60 O.O.2d 138.

In a postconviction relief proceeding the court may find that the distribution to the prospective jurors of a handbook which contained the statement that the jury in a criminal case in which the defendant failed to testify could take that fact into consideration was harmless error where the record discloses that the court instructed the jury correctly on this subject, there was no comment by counsel on the failure to testify, and the three jurors presented as witnesses by the petitioner all testified substantially alike on cross-examination, to the effect that the handbook was not relied upon by them in this regard, that they applied the law as given to them in the court's instruction, and did not consider the defendant's silence. Thomas v. State (Ohio Com.Pl. 1968) 16 Ohio Misc. 199, 241 N.E.2d 760, 45 O.O.2d 149, 45 O.O.2d 171.

On voir dire examination of the jury panel in a criminal prosecution, defendant's counsel does not have the right to tell the panel that the court will instruct them that they cannot take into consideration, in arriving at a verdict, the fact that a defendant does not testify. (See also Broeckel v Green, 298 FSupp 249, 22 Misc 165 (1967).) State v. Broeckel (Cuyahoga 1966) 8 Ohio App.2d 330, 222 N.E.2d 443, 37 O.O.2d 390, certiorari denied 87 S.Ct. 2140, 388 U.S. 920, 18 L.Ed.2d 1365.

Where, in response to a jury request for further instructions on the law as to whether the state could have called or caused the defendant to take the witness stand, the court, by agreement of and with consent of counsel, fulfills its mandatory duty to answer such query by reading to the jury that provision of the Ohio Constitution which states that "no person shall be compelled, in any criminal case, to be witness against himself," and the state statute to the same effect, such reading does not constitute a "comment" violative of the defendant's constitutional rights. State v. McRae (Cuyahoga 1965) 4 Ohio App.2d 217, 211 N.E.2d 875, 33 O.O.2d 271.

4. Appeal

The Ohio Supreme Court may properly refuse to consider a claim of error that was not raised in any way in the trial court or in the court of appeals and was not considered or decided by the court of appeals. State v. O'Connor (Ohio 1966) 6 Ohio St.2d 169, 217 N.E.2d 685, 35 O.O.2d 295, certiorari granted, opinion reversed 87 S.Ct. 252, 385 U.S. 92, 9 Ohio Misc. 59, 17 L.Ed.2d 189, 37 O.O.2d 374, 38 O.O.2d 91. Criminal Law ⚷ 1037.1(2); Criminal Law ⚷ 1038.1(5)

Where a codefendant in a criminal proceeding exercises his constitutional privilege of refusing to take the witness stand during the course of his trial, and the prosecuting attorney comments upon this refusal, a codefendant who did testify cannot later contend that error was committed as to him, where such codefendant did not object to such comment at the trial and present his contention in the court of appeals. State v. Lynn (Ohio 1966) 5 Ohio St.2d 106, 214 N.E.2d 226, 34 O.O.2d 226.

State court determination that any error resulting from claimed violation of defendant's right to testify in his own defense was harmless was not contrary to, or an unreasonable application of, clearly established federal law, and thus could not provide basis for habeas corpus relief. Skeens v. Haskins (C.A.6 (Ohio), 02-06-2001) No. 99-4250, 4 Fed.Appx. 236, 2001 WL 128432, Unreported. Habeas Corpus ⚷ 495

2945.44 Court of common pleas to grant transactional immunity; procedure; exceptions

(A) In any criminal proceeding in this state or in any criminal or civil proceeding brought pursuant to sections 2923.31 to 2923.36 of the Revised Code, if a witness refuses to answer or produce information on the basis of his privilege against self-incrimination, the court of common pleas of the county in which the proceeding is being held, unless it finds that to do so would not further the administration of justice, shall compel the witness to answer or produce the information, if both of the following apply:

(1) The prosecuting attorney of the county in which the proceedings are being held makes a written request to the court of common pleas to order the witness to answer or produce the information, notwithstanding his claim of privilege;

(2) The court of common pleas informs the witness that by answering, or producing the information he will receive immunity under division (B) of this section.

(B) If, but for this section, the witness would have been privileged to withhold an answer or any information given in any criminal proceeding, and he complies with an order under division (A) of this section compelling him to give an answer or produce any information, he shall not be prosecuted or subjected to any criminal penalty in the courts of this state for or on account of any transaction or matter concerning which, in compliance with the order, he gave an answer or produced any information.

(C) A witness granted immunity under this section may be subjected to a criminal penalty for any violation of section 2921.11, 2921.12, or 2921.13 of the Revised Code, or for contempt committed in answering, failing to answer, or failing to produce information in compliance with the order.

(1985 H 5, eff. 1–1–86; 1978 H 491)

Historical and Statutory Notes

Ed. Note: 2945.44 contains provisions analogous to former 2901.17 and 2917.04, repealed by 1972 H 511, eff. 1–1–74.

Ed. Note: Former 2945.44 repealed by 1978 H 491, eff. 5–30–78; 1976 S 234; 1972 H 511; prior 2945.44 repealed by 1972 H 511, eff. 1–1–74; 126 v 168; 1953 H 1; GC 13444–4.

Pre–1953 H 1 Amendments: 113 v 186, Ch 23, § 4

Legislative Service Commission

1973:

This section is a general immunity provision replacing a former, limited provision permitting courts to grant witnesses immunity from prosecution in return for their testimony only in gambling and liquor violations cases. Under this section, immunity may be granted in any criminal case in the interests of justice, when a person's testimony or other evidence in his possession is necessary not only to a successful prosecution, but to a full investigation of the criminal conduct under scrutiny. Immunity may be granted only by a common pleas or appeals court judge, or by a Supreme Court Justice. When granted, immunity extends to any and all prosecutions based on the testimony or other evidence given by the person granted immunity, other than prosecutions for perjury or tampering with evidence (applicable to section prior to amendment by 1978 H 491).

Cross References

Paternity proceedings, self-incrimination, immunity, admissibility of genetic test results or DNA records, jury trial, 3111.12

Reciprocal enforcement of support proceedings, self-incrimination, immunity, 3115.19

Right against compulsory self-incrimination, US Const Am 5; O Const Art I §10

Testimony regarding witness credibility, not waiver of privilege against self-incrimination, Evid R 608

Library References

Criminal Law ⚷42.

Westlaw Topic No. 110.

C.J.S. Criminal Law §§ 78 to 86.

Research References

ALR Library

29 ALR 5th 1, Propriety, Under State Constitutional Provisions, of Granting Use or Transactional Immunity for Compelled Incriminating Testimony--Post-Kastigar Cases.

Encyclopedias

OH Jur. 3d Contempt § 21, Refusal to be Sworn or to Testify.

OH Jur. 3d Criminal Law § 667, Examination of Witnesses Concerning Felony.

OH Jur. 3d Criminal Law § 719, Retrial.

OH Jur. 3d Criminal Law § 720, Effect in Federal Prosecution.

OH Jur. 3d Criminal Law § 1424, Effect of Perjury While Testifying Under Grant of Immunity.

OH Jur. 3d Criminal Law § 3115, Granting of Immunity.

OH Jur. 3d Criminal Law § 3547, Necessity and Sufficiency of Objection or Equivalent, Generally.

OH Jur. 3d Evidence & Witnesses § 685, Particular Statutes.

Treatises and Practice Aids

Markus, Trial Handbook for Ohio Lawyers, § 4:1, Criminal Procedure; in General.

Markus, Trial Handbook for Ohio Lawyers, § 14:7, Privilege Against Self-Incrimination—When Lost.

Katz, Giannelli, Blair and Lipton, Baldwin's Ohio Practice, Criminal Law, § 41:6, Self-Incrimination—Immunity.

Katz, Giannelli, Blair and Lipton, Baldwin's Ohio Practice, Criminal Law, § 69:6, Limits on Cross-Examination.

Katz, Giannelli, Blair and Lipton, Baldwin's Ohio Practice, Criminal Law, § 70:5, Immunity.

Katz, Giannelli, Blair and Lipton, Baldwin's Ohio Practice, Criminal Law, § 79:8, Newly Discovered Evidence.

Katz, Giannelli, Blair and Lipton, Baldwin's Ohio Practice, Criminal Law, § 82:5, Rules of Construction.

Katz, Giannelli, Blair and Lipton, Baldwin's Ohio Practice, Criminal Law, § 102:7, Coercion.

Katz, Giannelli, Blair and Lipton, Baldwin's Ohio Practice, Criminal Law, § 141:12, Motion for an Immunity Order.

Giannelli and Snyder, Baldwin's Ohio Practice, Evidence, R 501, General Rule.

Giannelli and Snyder, Baldwin's Ohio Practice, Evidence, § 501.4, Ohio Statutory Privileges.

Giannelli and Snyder, Baldwin's Ohio Practice, Evidence, § 611.8, Cross-Examination: Limits.

Carlin, Baldwin's Ohio Practice, Merrick-Rippner Probate Law § 107:127, Contempt of Court in Juvenile Proceedings.

Adrine & Ruden, Ohio Domestic Violence Law § 13:6, Law Enforcement Policies and Procedures.

Giannelli & Yeomans, Ohio Juvenile Law § 33:8, Contempt.

Law Review and Journal Commentaries

Immunity, Note. 19 Am Crim L Rev 238 (Fall 1981).

Manipulated by *Miranda*: A Critical Analysis of Bright Lines and Voluntary Confessions Under *United States v. Dickerson*, Casenote. 68 U Cin L Rev 555 (Winter 2000).

The Right to Remain Silent: The Use of Pre–Arrest Silence in *United States v. Oplinger*, 150 F.3d 1061 (5th Cir. 1998), Casenote. 68 U Cin L Rev 505 (Winter 2000).

Summary Contempt May Properly Be Applied to the Orderly Refusal of Witnesses to Testify at Trial After Grant of Immunity—United States v Wilson, Note. 13 Am Crim L Rev 271 (1975).

Notes of Decisions

Ed. Note: *This section contains annotations from former RC 2945.44.*

---

1. Constitutional issues

Trial court acted within its discretion in compelling alleged victim to testify in prosecution for domestic violence, where prosecuting attorney filed motion to grant immunity to alleged victim, and trial court subsequently granted alleged victim immunity from prosecution. State v. Smith (Ohio App. 3 Dist., Seneca, 10-14-2003) No. 13-03-25, 2003-Ohio-5461, 2003 WL 22336098, Unreported. Witnesses ⚷ 304(1)

Trial court was within its authority to hold witness in criminal contempt for failure to testify at her husband's domestic violence trial, where, by reason of grant of immunity under both Fifth Amendment and state's immunity statute, witness could not have been prosecuted for perjury for prior statements because of her grand jury testimony nor could she have been prosecuted for perjury for her testimony before grand jury solely because of inconsistent prior statements. State v. Adams (Ohio App. 7 Dist., 06-09-2003) 153 Ohio App.3d 134, 791 N.E.2d 1045, 2003-Ohio-3086. Witnesses ⚷ 21

Claim by defendant that trial court had improperly granted transactional immunity to witness who refused to testify, because witness did not have valid Fifth Amendment privilege against self-incrimination, was sufficiently preserved for appellate review when defendant objected to grant of immunity during hearing held by court to determine whether grant of immunity would further the administration of justice. State v. Reiner (Ohio, 07-26-2000) 89 Ohio St.3d 342, 731 N.E.2d 662, 2000-Ohio-190, reconsideration denied 90 Ohio St.3d 1419, 735 N.E.2d 457, certiorari granted, reversed 121 S.Ct. 1252, 532 U.S. 17, 149 L.Ed.2d 158, on remand 93 Ohio St.3d 601, 757 N.E.2d 1143, 2001-Ohio-1800. Criminal Law ⚷ 1036.2

Wrongful grant of transactional immunity to witness, who had provided day care for child who died as result of shaken baby syndrome, but who had no valid Fifth Amendment privilege against self-incrimination because she denied any involvement in abuse which led to child's death, was prejudicial to father of child in manslaughter prosecution arising from child's death, and required reversal; grant of immunity essentially told jury that witness did not cause child's injuries, and jury should have been able to hear and evaluate all the evidence to decide whether someone other than father was responsible for child's death. State v. Reiner (Ohio, 07-26-2000) 89 Ohio St.3d 342, 731 N.E.2d 662, 2000-Ohio-190, reconsideration denied 90 Ohio St.3d 1419, 735 N.E.2d 457, certiorari granted, reversed 121 S.Ct. 1252, 532 U.S. 17, 149 L.Ed.2d 158, on remand 93 Ohio St.3d 601, 757 N.E.2d 1143, 2001-Ohio-1800. Criminal Law ⚷ 1170.5(1); Witnesses ⚷ 304(4)

Before a court may exercise its authority to grant transactional immunity, it is implicit that the person has validly asserted Fifth Amendment privilege against self-incrimination. State v. Reiner (Ohio, 07-26-2000) 89 Ohio St.3d 342, 731 N.E.2d 662, 2000-Ohio-190, reconsideration denied 90 Ohio St.3d 1419, 735 N.E.2d 457, certiorari granted, reversed 121 S.Ct. 1252, 532 U.S. 17, 149 L.Ed.2d 158, on remand 93 Ohio St.3d 601, 757 N.E.2d 1143, 2001-Ohio-1800. Witnesses ⚷ 304(1)

Defendant had standing to challenge grant of transactional immunity to witness who did not have valid Fifth Amendment privilege against self-incrimination, and thus was ineligible for immunity. State v. Reiner (Ohio, 07-26-2000) 89 Ohio St.3d 342, 731 N.E.2d 662, 2000-Ohio-190, reconsideration denied 90 Ohio St.3d 1419, 735 N.E.2d 457, certiorari granted, reversed 121 S.Ct. 1252, 532 U.S. 17, 149 L.Ed.2d 158, on remand 93 Ohio St.3d 601, 757 N.E.2d 1143, 2001-Ohio-1800. Witnesses ⚷ 304(1)

Witness who had provided day care for defendant's child, and had refused to testify, did not have valid Fifth Amendment privilege against self-incrimination in prosecution of defendant brought after child died of shaken baby syndrome, and thus could not be granted transactional immunity, where witness asserted only her fear that she would be focus of defense asserted by defendant, and denied any involvement in the child abuse which led to child's death. State v. Reiner (Ohio, 07-26-2000) 89 Ohio St.3d 342, 731 N.E.2d 662, 2000-Ohio-190, reconsideration denied 90 Ohio St.3d 1419, 735 N.E.2d 457, certiorari granted, reversed 121 S.Ct. 1252, 532 U.S. 17, 149 L.Ed.2d 158, on remand 93 Ohio St.3d 601, 757 N.E.2d 1143, 2001-Ohio-1800. Witnesses ⚷ 304(4)

Requirements for compelling the testimony of witness who had asserted Fifth Amendment privilege against self-incrimination were met where, upon the special prosecutor's written motion, the court informed witness that by answering he would receive immunity, and where court also found that granting witness immunity would further the administration of justice. State v. Tomlinson (Ohio App. 11 Dist., 12-15-1997) 125 Ohio App.3d 13, 707 N.E.2d 955. Witnesses ⚷ 304(1)

Revocation of immunity for state witness in vehicular homicide prosecution was not abuse of discretion, where witness continued to assert Fifth Amendment privilege, witness made no incriminating statements before or after grant of immunity, defendant made no showing that witness would have provided any exculpatory evidence, and there was possibility that with continued immunity witness might give testimony incriminating himself but favorable to defendant, thus defeating purpose of allowing state to make case against defendant. State v. Tomlinson (Ohio App. 11 Dist., 12-15-1997) 125 Ohio App.3d 13, 707 N.E.2d 955. Witnesses ⚷ 304(1)

Witness who was granted transactional immunity and compelled to testify at first trial of her husband on aggravated murder charge, but invoked Fifth Amendment right against self-incrimination and refused to testify at husband's retrial, remained immune from prosecution for her own role in murder; witness complied with applicable statute by testifying at first trial, and immunity attached upon compliance. State v. Adamson (Ohio, 09-30-1998) 83 Ohio St.3d 248, 699 N.E.2d 478, 1998-Ohio-284. Criminal Law ⚷ 42.6

Immunity may not be granted to witness unless witness refuses to answer on basis of his privilege against self-incrimination, prosecuting attorney makes written request to order witness to answer, and court informs witness he will receive transactional immunity. State ex rel. Koren v. Grogan (Ohio 1994) 68 Ohio St.3d 590, 629 N.E.2d 446. Witnesses ⚷ 304(1)

Although a witness may claim a privilege against self-incrimination, courts may compel testimony in exchange for transactional, not limited use, immunity, since under RC 2945.44 he cannot be prosecuted for any matter about which he testifies. State v. Thompson (Ohio Com.Pl. 1992) 62 Ohio Misc.2d 555, 607 N.E.2d 118.

A trial court may not exclude a person who has previously asserted his right against self-incrimination from appearing as a witness on behalf of a criminal defendant at trial. State v. Ellis (Ohio 1991) 62 Ohio St.3d 106, 579 N.E.2d 701, rehearing denied 62 Ohio St.3d 1479, 581 N.E.2d 1100. Witnesses ⚷ 2(1); Witnesses ⚷ 307

The different treatment of witnesses afforded under RC 2939.17 and 2945.44, whereby one class of witnesses may be offered full transactional immunity upon being compelled to testify and another class may only be offered limited use and derivative use immunity, does not violate the Equal Protection Clause. In re Special Grand Jury Investigating Medicaid Fraud & Nursing Homes (Franklin 1987) 38 Ohio App.3d 161, 528 N.E.2d 598.

A decision to prosecute one or more individuals involved in criminal activity, upon the testimony of others also involved in that activity, and to grant immunity from prosecution to those in the latter group in exchange for their testimony, does not violate the right of those in the former group to equal protection of the laws, absent a showing that the selection of those to be prosecuted was deliberately based upon an unjustifiable standard such as race, religion, or other arbitrary classification (decided prior to amendment of RC 2945.44 by 1978 H 491, eff. 5–30–78). State v. Wolery (Ohio 1976) 46 Ohio St.2d 316, 348 N.E.2d 351, 75 O.O.2d 366, certiorari denied 97 S.Ct. 339, 429 U.S. 932, 50 L.Ed.2d 301.

2. Procedures—In general

Trial court's observation that grand jury transcript demonstrated that immunity had been granted to witness was both inadequate and incorrect. State v. Asher (Ohio App. 1 Dist., 07-17-1996) 112 Ohio App.3d 646, 679 N.E.2d 1147, appeal not allowed 77 Ohio St.3d 1492, 673 N.E.2d 148. Witnesses ⚷ 304(1)

A juvenile court has authority to grant immunity under RC 2945.44, even though there was not any criminal proceeding pending against the "grantee" of the immunity, and even though the grantee was not a witness at the time of the grant. In re Poth (Huron 1981) 2 Ohio App.3d 361, 442 N.E.2d 105, 2 O.B.R. 417.

Immunity is erroneously granted to a witness when the witness has not refused to answer on the basis of his privilege against self-incrimination, and the prosecuting attorney has not requested the court to order the witness to answer. State, ex rel. Leis v. Outcalt (Ohio 1982) 1 Ohio St.3d 147, 438 N.E.2d 443, 1 O.B.R. 181.

While RC 2945.44 provides for the granting to a witness of immunity from prosecution, other than for perjury, based upon his testimony where such granting of immunity to obtain the testimony of the witness is in the interests of justice, such immunity is not immunity from prosecution for a crime (decided prior to amendment of RC 2945.44 by 1978 H 491, eff. 5–30–78). State v. Broady (Franklin 1974) 41 Ohio App.2d 17, 321 N.E.2d 890, 70 O.O.2d 18.

Where the defendant in a criminal case seeks, pursuant to RC 2945.44, testimonial use immunity for a witness whose testimony is vital for the defendant's defense, and there is no indication that any prosecution of the witness will be thwarted by the granting of such limited immunity, such immunity should be granted in the interests of justice so as to afford the defendant the benefit of the testimony (decided prior to amendment of RC 2945.44 by 1978 H 491, eff. 5–30–78). State v. Broady (Franklin 1974) 41 Ohio App.2d 17, 321 N.E.2d 890, 70 O.O.2d 18.

Immunity pursuant to RC 2945.44 may be granted either upon the request of the defendant or the prosecutor in a criminal case and should not be denied solely because the testimony of the witness would tend to exonerate rather than convict the defendant (decided prior to amendment of RC 2945.44 by 1978 H 491, eff. 5–30–78). State v. Broady (Franklin 1974) 41 Ohio App.2d 17, 321 N.E.2d 890, 70 O.O.2d 18.

This section, as amended by 1978 H 491, eff. 5–30–78, allows immunity only at the written request of the prosecutor, and it is not error for a court to refuse a request made by the defendant only. State v Marshall, No. 3–83–13 (3d Dist Ct App, Crawford, 4–11–84).

3. —— Prosecutorial discretion, procedures

Subpoenaing of domestic violence victim to appear before grand jury and ostensible grant of immunity to her were apparently used to force her testimony concerning her alleged dispute with defendant, her husband, which was inappropriate use of prosecutorial discretion. State v. Asher (Ohio App. 1 Dist., 07-17-1996) 112 Ohio App.3d 646, 679 N.E.2d 1147, appeal not allowed 77 Ohio St.3d 1492, 673 N.E.2d 148. Grand Jury ⚷ 36.4(2)

4. —— Duty of court, procedures

Where witness is testifying in municipal court proceeding, municipal court judge personally must determine whether statutory procedure for granting immunity to witness has been properly followed, and must ensure that some competent evidence of its existence, such as common pleas entry granting immunity, is included in municipal court records; trial court cannot presume grant of immunity, nor will reviewing court. State v. Asher (Ohio App. 1 Dist., 07-17-1996) 112 Ohio App.3d 646, 679 N.E.2d 1147, appeal not allowed 77 Ohio St.3d 1492, 673 N.E.2d 148. Witnesses ⚷ 304(1)

Trial court erred in relying on prosecutor's verbal assurances that immunity had been granted to witness; it was trial judge's job to personally make independent determination that immunity had been granted and granted properly. State v. Asher (Ohio App. 1 Dist., 07-17-1996) 112 Ohio App.3d 646, 679 N.E.2d 1147, appeal not allowed 77 Ohio St.3d 1492, 673 N.E.2d 148. Witnesses ⚷ 304(1)

A grant or denial of transactional immunity pursuant to RC 2945.44 is within the sound discretion of the trial court; consequently, a writ of mandamus to compel the grant of transactional immunity to a specific witness must be denied. State ex rel. Ney v. Niehaus (Ohio 1987) 33 Ohio St.3d 118, 515 N.E.2d 914.

5. —— Revocation of immunity, procedures

When a witness has not made any self-incriminating statements after the grant of immunity, a trial court's revocation of immunity will not be disturbed on appeal in the absence of an abuse of discretion. State v. Tomlinson (Ohio App. 11 Dist., 12-15-1997) 125 Ohio App.3d 13, 707 N.E.2d 955. Criminal Law ⚷ 1153(4)

6. Transactional or use immunity

Trial court did not abuse its discretion at drug trial by refusing to grant defense witness, who testified that defendant was not involved in his sale of drugs to undercover police officer and then invoked his Fifth Amendment rights before he could be cross-examined, immunity from prosecution; trial court lacked authority to grant immunity at defendant's request, immunity for witnesses turning state's evidence typically required testimony implicating, rather than exculpating, defendant, prosecution had no advance knowledge of witness's identity or what his testimony would be, and prosecution did not coerce witness into invoking Fifth Amendment. State v. Perry (Ohio App. 8 Dist., Cuyahoga, 01-06-2005) No. 84397, 2005-Ohio-27, 2005 WL 23357, Unreported, appeal not allowed 105 Ohio St.3d 1564, 828 N.E.2d 118, 2005-Ohio-2447. Witnesses ⚷ 304(4)

Trial court acted within its discretion in finding that compelling alleged victim to testify in prosecution for domestic violence furthered administration of justice, where act of domestic violence may have gone unpunished if trial court had not compelled testimony. State v. Smith (Ohio App. 3 Dist., Seneca, 10-14-2003) No. 13-03-25, 2003-Ohio-5461, 2003 WL 22336098, Unreported. Witnesses ⚷ 4

Granting immunity to babysitter called as witness in involuntary manslaughter prosecution of father of baby who had died of shaken-baby syndrome resulted in serious prejudice to father and did not further the administration of justice. State v. Reiner (Ohio, 11-28-2001) 93 Ohio St.3d 601, 757 N.E.2d 1143, 2001-Ohio-1800, reconsideration denied 94 Ohio St.3d 1434, 761 N.E.2d 49, 2002-Ohio-5651, certiorari denied 122 S.Ct. 2621, 536 U.S. 940, 153 L.Ed.2d 804. Criminal Law ⚷ 1170.5(1)

On state's appeal from trial court's refusal to compel an essential witness to testify after immunity was granted, Court of Appeals would presume that state's immunity request was properly made in writing and in full compliance with statute, where request was not part of record on appeal, and no objections were made with respect to this issue at time court stated its intention to grant immunity. State v. Neff (Ohio App. 3 Dist., 09-23-1999) 135 Ohio App.3d 7, 732 N.E.2d 1008, 1999-Ohio-875. Criminal Law ⚷ 1144.1

Trial court could not refuse to order a witness to testify, subsequent to a grant of immunity pursuant to state statute, based upon witness' expressed concern that the state immunity might not bind federal government; witness' fear that she would still be subject to federal prosecution was unfounded, in light of ruling of United States Supreme Court that grant of immunity under state statute was binding on federal government to the extent that it could not use the testimony elicited in state action or the fruits thereof. State v. Neff (Ohio App. 3 Dist., 09-23-1999) 135 Ohio App.3d 7, 732 N.E.2d 1008, 1999-Ohio-875. Witnesses ⚷ 304(3)

There is no need for a grant of immunity where the witness denies all culpability. State v. Reiner (Ohio, 07-26-2000) 89 Ohio St.3d 342, 731 N.E.2d 662, 2000-Ohio-190, reconsideration denied 90 Ohio St.3d 1419, 735 N.E.2d 457, certiorari granted, reversed 121 S.Ct. 1252, 532 U.S. 17, 149 L.Ed.2d 158, on remand 93 Ohio St.3d 601, 757 N.E.2d 1143, 2001-Ohio-1800. Witnesses ⚷ 304(1)

In situations where an admission of guilt by one person would completely exonerate any possible guilt of another person, a grant of immunity is unnecessary and improper. State v. Reiner (Ohio, 07-26-2000) 89 Ohio St.3d 342, 731 N.E.2d 662, 2000-Ohio-190, reconsideration denied 90 Ohio St.3d 1419, 735 N.E.2d 457, certiorari granted, reversed 121 S.Ct. 1252, 532 U.S. 17, 149 L.Ed.2d 158, on remand 93 Ohio St.3d 601, 757 N.E.2d 1143, 2001-Ohio-1800. Witnesses ⚷ 304(1)

Ohio courts may only grant "transactional immunity," which protects the witness from prosecution for any criminal activity about which he testified within the limits of the grant. State v. Tomlinson (Ohio App. 11 Dist., 12-15-1997) 125 Ohio App.3d 13, 707 N.E.2d 955. Criminal Law ⚷ 42.3(2)

"Transactional immunity" protects witness from prosecution for any criminal activity about which he testified within limits of grant, whereas "use immunity" protects witness only from having specific compelled testimony or information directly or indirectly derived from compelled testimony used as evidence against him in later prosecution. State ex rel. Koren v. Grogan (Ohio 1994) 68 Ohio St.3d 590, 629 N.E.2d 446. Criminal Law ⚷ 42.3(2); Criminal Law ⚷ 42.3(3)

Transactional immunity statute patently and unambiguously divested municipal court of its general jurisdiction to proceed in prosecution of defendant who had been granted transactional immunity, thus justifying allowance of writ of prohibition despite municipal court's general jurisdiction. State ex rel. Koren v. Grogan (Ohio 1994) 68 Ohio St.3d 590, 629 N.E.2d 446. Prohibition ⚷ 10(3)

Witness who testified in criminal prosecution was not deprived of transactional immunity by fact that common pleas court, in informing defendant of transactional immunity, erroneously added use immunity instruction. State ex rel. Koren v. Grogan (Ohio 1994) 68 Ohio St.3d 590, 629 N.E.2d 446. Witnesses ⚷ 304(1)

Ohio courts may grant only transactional immunity and not use immunity. State ex rel. Koren v. Grogan (Ohio 1994) 68 Ohio St.3d 590, 629 N.E.2d 446. Criminal Law ⚷ 42.3(2); Criminal Law ⚷ 42.3(3)

A court does not have inherent authority to grant nonstatutory use immunity to a defense witness at an accused's request. State v. Landrum (Ohio 1990) 53 Ohio St.3d 107, 559 N.E.2d 710, rehearing denied 54 Ohio St.3d 710, 561 N.E.2d 945, certiorari denied 111 S.Ct. 1092, 498 U.S. 1127, 112 L.Ed.2d 1196, rehearing denied 111 S.Ct. 1612, 499 U.S. 971, 113 L.Ed.2d 673. Witnesses ⚷ 304(1)

The different treatment of witnesses afforded under RC 2939.17 and 2945.44, whereby one class of witnesses may be offered full transactional immunity upon being compelled to testify and another class may only be offered limited use and derivative use immunity, does not violate the Equal Protection Clause. In re Special Grand Jury Investigating Medicaid Fraud & Nursing Homes (Franklin 1987) 38 Ohio App.3d 161, 528 N.E.2d 598.

RC 2945.44 provides both use and derivative use immunity (decided prior to amendment of RC 2945.44 by 1978 H 491, eff. 5–30–78). State v. Sinito (Ohio 1975) 43 Ohio St.2d 98, 330 N.E.2d 896, 72 O.O.2d 54.

Immunity pursuant to RC 2945.44 is "transactional" immunity which can only be granted only upon the written request of the prosecutor; the trial court is without authority to grant immunity upon the request of the defendant. State v Berry, No. 83AP–874 (10th Dist Ct App, Franklin, 5–10–84).

7. Agreement not to prosecute

Where agreement not to prosecute is conditioned upon defendant's agreement to "fully cooperate" or otherwise disclose truthful information to authorities, and it is later determined that defendant has not fulfilled terms of agreement, defendant's failure to comply with his obligation nullifies government's promise not to prosecute. State v. Small (Cuyahoga 1987) 41 Ohio App.3d 252, 535 N.E.2d 352. Criminal Law ⚷ 42.5(3)

Police officer's statements during internal investigation were protected by the carte blanc promise of immunity given by the investigators, and thus the statements were to be suppressed in trial for falsification and obstructing official business; although a person may be prosecuted for falsification during an internal affairs interview and investigation, the investigators' promise that "the Division of Police will not use any of the answers or information gained from the interview in any criminal proceeding against you" assured the police officer that he could speak freely without threat of criminal prosecution, and the officer's answers were predicated on that promise of unconditional immunity. State v. McKinley (Ohio App. 5 Dist., Richland, 06-25-2002) No. 01CA98, 2002-Ohio-3825, 2002 WL 1732136, Unreported. Criminal Law ⚷ 42.6

8. Waiver of self-incrimination rights

Defendant waived all but plain error regarding his claim that trial court erred by failing to offer victim transactional immunity when victim stated that she wanted to claim privilege against self-incrimination, where defendant failed to object to failure to grant victim transactional immunity. State v. Scarl (Ohio App. 11 Dist., Portage, 06-30-2003) No. 2002-P-0091, 2003-Ohio-3493, 2003 WL 21511161, Unreported, appeal not allowed 100 Ohio St.3d 1434, 797 N.E.2d 513, 2003-Ohio-5396. Criminal Law ⚷ 1036.2

Trial court was not authorized to grant witness transactional immunity based on witness's statement that she wanted to claim privilege against self-incrimination, where prosecutor made no written request to have the witness answer the question. State v. Scarl (Ohio App. 11 Dist., Portage, 06-30-2003) No. 2002-P-0091, 2003-Ohio-3493, 2003 WL 21511161, Unreported, appeal not allowed 100 Ohio St.3d 1434, 797 N.E.2d 513, 2003-Ohio-5396. Witnesses ⚷ 304(1)

Defendant was not prejudiced by trial court's failure to offer victim transactional immunity when victim stated that she wanted to claim privilege against self-incrimination; there was nothing in victim's testimony to suggest what her testimony would have been if she were forced to testify, and defendant never proffered at trial what her testimony would have been. State v. Scarl (Ohio App. 11 Dist., Portage, 06-30-2003) No. 2002-P-0091, 2003-Ohio-3493, 2003 WL 21511161, Unreported, appeal not allowed 100 Ohio St.3d 1434, 797 N.E.2d 513, 2003-Ohio-5396. Criminal Law ⚷ 1170.5(1)

Defendant's waiver of her Fifth Amendment right to remain silent before grand jury did not waive statutory immunity for compelled testimony given before legislative committee and, thus, use of compelled testimony before grand jury tainted indictment. State v. Conrad (Ohio 1990) 50 Ohio St.3d 1, 552 N.E.2d 214. Criminal Law ⚷ 42.7(1); Indictment And Information ⚷ 10.2(2)

2945.45 Subpoenas to issue to any county

In all criminal cases, the clerk of the court of common pleas, upon a praecipe being filed, shall issue writs of subpoena for the witnesses named therein, directed to the sheriff of such county, or the county where such witnesses reside or are found, which shall be served and returned as in other cases. Such sheriff, by writing indorsed on the writs, may depute a disinterested person to serve and return them. The person so deputed to serve such subpoenas shall make a return of the service made, and make oath thereto before a person competent to administer oaths, which shall be indorsed on the writ. The return may be forwarded through the post office, or otherwise.

(1953 H 1, eff. 10–1–53; GC 13444–5)

Historical and Statutory Notes

Pre–1953 H 1 Amendments: 113 v 187, Ch 23, § 5

Cross References

Right to compulsory process to obtain witnesses, O Const Art I §10

Serving and filing papers, Crim R 49

Subpoenas, Crim R 17

Library References

Witnesses ⚷6, 7.

Westlaw Topic No. 410.

C.J.S. Witnesses §§ 2, 14 to 31.

Research References

Encyclopedias

OH Jur. 3d Criminal Law § 459, Generally; Constitutional Basis.

OH Jur. 3d Criminal Law § 3113, Compelling Attendance.

Treatises and Practice Aids

Markus, Trial Handbook for Ohio Lawyers, § 11:1, Compelling Attendance.

Notes of Decisions

1. Discovery

In a criminal case, the overruling of defendant's motion to examine evidence in the possession of the state is not an abuse of discretion, where it appears that the evidence requested had been returned by the state to the owner thereof prior to the filing of the motion, and there is no showing that such evidence was returned to the owner with the idea of defeating any attempt by the defendant to inspect it. State v. Bostic (Franklin 1961) 115 Ohio App. 214, 184 N.E.2d 597, 20 O.O.2d 301, appeal dismissed 173 Ohio St. 176, 180 N.E.2d 582, 18 O.O.2d 441, certiorari denied 82 S.Ct. 1249, 370

U.S. 903, 8 L.Ed.2d 400. Criminal Law ⚷ 627.5(5)

2. Service of subpoena

In a contempt action based on a defendant's failure to comply with a subpoena, the admission of a praecipe for subpoena with return into evidence as an exhibit constitutes error where the person serving the subpoena testifies he did not personally make the return of service, but rather left the task to an "office lady," in violation of RC 2945.45 and Crim R 17(D). State v Wright, No. 92AP090070, 1993 WL 221268 (5th Dist Ct App, Tuscarawas, 6–8–93).

2945.451 Employee's attendance at proceeding in criminal case under subpoena; employer may not penalize

No employer shall discharge or terminate from employment, threaten to discharge or terminate from employment, or otherwise punish or penalize any employee because of time lost from regular employment as a result of the employee's attendance at any proceeding in a criminal case pursuant to a subpoena. This section generally does not require and shall not be construed to require an employer to pay an employee for time lost as a result of attendance at any criminal proceeding. However, if an employee is subpoenaed to appear at a criminal proceeding and the proceeding pertains to an offense against the employer or an offense involving the employee during the course of his employment, the employer shall not decrease or withhold the employee's pay for any time lost as a result of compliance with the subpoena. Any employer who knowingly violates this section is in contempt of court.

(1984 S 172, eff. 9–26–84)

Cross References

Contempt proceedings, Ch 2705

Knowingly, defined, 2901.22

Victims' rights pamphlet, publication and distribution, 109.42

Victims' rights, retaliation by employer prohibited, 2930.18

Research References

Treatises and Practice Aids

Employment Coordinator Benefits § 14:37, Ohio.

Notes of Decisions

Punishment of employee who is charged or indicted, distinguished 1

1. Punishment of employee who is charged or indicted, distinguished

Even assuming Ohio law evidenced clear public policy against employers terminating employee based upon fact that employee had been charged but not convicted of crime, employer did not violate any public policy by terminating truck driver who was arrested for driving under the influence (DUI), even though he was later acquitted of charges, and thus truck driver failed to support claim of public policy wrongful discharge under Ohio law. Roberts v. Alan Ritchey, Inc. (S.D.Ohio, 04-17-1997) 962 F.Supp. 1028. Labor And Employment ⚷ 767

2945.46 Attendance of witness enforced

Civil procedure relative to compelling the attendance and testimony of witnesses, their examination, the administering of oaths and affirmations, and proceedings for contempt to enforce the remedies and protect the rights of parties, extend to criminal cases as far as applicable.

(1953 H 1, eff. 10–1–53; GC 13444–6)

Historical and Statutory Notes

Pre–1953 H 1 Amendments: 113 v 187, Ch 23, § 6

Cross References

Discovery and inspection, Crim R 16

Right to compulsory process to obtain witnesses, O Const Art I §10

Subpoenas, Crim R 17

Library References

Witnesses ⚷1 to 34.
Westlaw Topic No. 410.
C.J.S. Criminal Law §§ 469 to 485.
C.J.S. Federal Civil Procedure § 585.
C.J.S. Witnesses §§ 1 to 86.

Research References

Encyclopedias

OH Jur. 3d Criminal Law § 3113, Compelling Attendance.

OH Jur. 3d Criminal Law § 3128, Generally; Calling and Interrogation of Witness by Court.

Treatises and Practice Aids

Markus, Trial Handbook for Ohio Lawyers, § 11:4, Subpoena and Subpoena Duces Tecum.

Markus, Trial Handbook for Ohio Lawyers, § 11:7, Swearing to Oath or Affirmation.

Katz, Giannelli, Blair and Lipton, Baldwin's Ohio Practice, Criminal Law, § 61:9, Contempt.

Katz, Giannelli, Blair and Lipton, Baldwin's Ohio Practice, Criminal Law, § 149:8, Entry of Order on Witness Served at Residence.

Katz, Giannelli, Blair and Lipton, Baldwin's Ohio Practice, Criminal Law, § 149:9, Witness Served at Residence to Show Cause.

Katz, Giannelli, Blair and Lipton, Baldwin's Ohio Practice, Criminal Law, § 148:28, Oath of Witness.

Katz, Giannelli, Blair and Lipton, Baldwin's Ohio Practice, Criminal Law, § 149:10, Order as for Contempt When Witness Personally Served.

Katz, Giannelli, Blair and Lipton, Baldwin's Ohio Practice, Criminal Law, § 149:11, Writ of Commitment.

Katz, Giannelli, Blair and Lipton, Baldwin's Ohio Practice, Criminal Law, § 149:12, Return of Writ of Commitment.

Katz, Giannelli, Blair and Lipton, Baldwin's Ohio Practice, Criminal Law, § 149:13, Witness Not Guilty of Contempt.

Katz, Giannelli, Blair and Lipton, Baldwin's Ohio Practice, Criminal Law, § 149:14, Witness Guilty of Contempt.

Katz, Giannelli, Blair and Lipton, Baldwin's Ohio Practice, Criminal Law, § 149:15, Application to Release Witness Held for Contempt.

Giannelli and Snyder, Baldwin's Ohio Practice, Evidence, R 603, Oath or Affirmation.

Law Review and Journal Commentaries

Contempt of Court: Eliminating the Confusion Between Civil and Criminal Contempt, Robert J. Martineau. 50 U Cin L Rev 677 (1981).

Notes of Decisions

In general 1
Discovery 2

1. In general

Trial court was not obligated to compel witness's appearance at trial, where record did not demonstrate that witness had actual knowledge of subpoena, and thus valid service of subpoena was not completed. State v. Juenger (Ohio App. 12 Dist., Butler, 02-23-2004) No. CA2003-02-049, 2004-Ohio-796, 2004 WL 323155, Unreported, appeal not allowed 102 Ohio St.3d 1485, 810 N.E.2d 968, 2004-Ohio-3069. Witnesses ⚷ 13

The right of a criminal defendant to secure the attendance of witnesses is not violated where the witness is properly subpoenaed but leaves the court's jurisdiction for military service and does not appear in court and where although the defense was aware of the witness' plans it makes no effort prior to the final day of trial to secure the witness. State v. Mayhew (Jackson 1991) 71 Ohio App.3d 622, 594 N.E.2d 1133, motion overruled 62 Ohio St.3d 1409, 577 N.E.2d 361, appeal not allowed 70 Ohio St.3d 1441, 638 N.E.2d 1044, motion for delayed appeal denied 81 Ohio St.3d 1514, 692 N.E.2d 619.

Cited with reference to the compelling of attendance of witnesses and the taking of their testimony. State v. Rhoads (Ohio 1910) 81 Ohio St. 397, 91 N.E. 186, 7 Ohio Law Rep. 614, 18 Am.Ann.Cas. 415.

2. Discovery

A trial court's denial in a child endangering and felonious assault case of a defendant's request that the three year old child victim be subject to a pretrial, out-of-court interview by a clinical psychologist proposed as a defense expert witness is not erroneous since a prospective witness for the prosecution in a criminal action has the right to refuse to speak to or to be interviewed by the defense prior to trial, and except under certain carefully delineated circumstances, he cannot be compelled to do so. State v. Barton (Hamilton 1991) 71 Ohio App.3d 455, 594 N.E.2d 702, dismissed, jurisdictional motion overruled 61 Ohio St.3d 1427, 575 N.E.2d 215, rehearing denied 62 Ohio St.3d 1419, 577 N.E.2d 664, certiorari denied 112 S.Ct. 1209, 502 U.S. 1109, 117 L.Ed.2d 448, denial of habeas corpus affirmed

91 F.3d 143, certiorari denied 117 S.Ct. 529, 136 L.Ed.2d 415.

When the state's principal witness admits in open court that her testimony is inconsistent with some or all of her prior statements to the police, and that these statements are inconsistent with each other, the trial court must grant a request by defense counsel to inspect such statements. State v. White (Ohio 1968) 15 Ohio St.2d 146, 239 N.E.2d 65, 44 O.O.2d 132. Criminal Law ⚷ 627.7(3)

A defendant in a felony case does not have the right to inspect and copy or examine written statements or confessions of his or of other witnesses and documents or property in the possession of the prosecution, unless upon the trial on the merits such evidence is used by the prosecution in such a way as to make such statement or property an issue in the case or unless such evidence or property is of such a character that to keep it from the knowledge of the defendant would constitute the denial of a fair trial. State v. White (Cuyahoga 1967) 9 Ohio App.2d 271, 224 N.E.2d 377, 38 O.O.2d 330, reversed 15 Ohio St.2d 146, 239 N.E.2d 65, 44 O.O.2d 132.

In a criminal case, the refusal of a trial court to allow defendant to take the deposition of a witness is not an abuse of discretion, where the court had done all it could to make the witness available at the trial and the request to take the deposition was made after the case had been concluded and at the conclusion of defendant's argument on a motion for a new trial. State v. Blanton (Lawrence 1960) 111 Ohio App. 111, 170 N.E.2d 754, 14 O.O.2d 13.

2945.47 Testimony of prisoners in criminal proceedings

(A)(1) As used in this section, "detention facility" has the same meaning as in section 2921.01 of the Revised Code.

(2) If it is necessary in a criminal proceeding before the court to procure the testimony of a person who is imprisoned in a detention facility or state correctional institution within this state, or who is in the custody of the department of youth services, the court may require that the person's testimony be taken by deposition pursuant to Criminal Rule 15 at the place of the person's confinement, if the person is not a defendant in the case and if the court determines that the interests of justice do not demand that the person be brought before the court for the presentation of the person's testimony. All witnesses for the prosecution shall be brought before the court. The defendant may waive any right to compel the appearance of a person brought before the court pursuant to this division.

(B) Subject to division (C) of this section, if it is necessary in a criminal proceeding before the court to procure the testimony of a person who is imprisoned in a detention facility within this state, the court may order a subpoena to be issued, directed to the keeper of the institution, commanding the keeper to bring the prisoner named in the subpoena before the court.

The keeper, upon receiving the subpoena, shall take the witness before the court at the time and place named in the subpoena, and hold the witness until the witness is discharged by the court. When discharged, the witness shall be returned in the custody of such officer to the place of imprisonment from which the witness was taken, and the officer may command any assistance that the officer considers proper for the transportation of the witness.

(C) If it is necessary in a criminal proceeding before the court to procure the testimony of a person who is imprisoned in a state correctional institution within this state, or who is in the custody of the department of youth services, the court may order a subpoena to be issued directed to the sheriff of the county in which the indictment or grand jury proceeding is pending. When a copy of the subpoena is presented by the sheriff to the warden or superintendent of a state correctional institution, or to the person in charge of the facility in which a juvenile is confined, the witness shall be delivered at the institution or facility to the sheriff who shall take the witness before the court at the time and place named in the subpoena and hold the witness until the witness is discharged by the court. When discharged, the witness shall be returned in the custody of the sheriff to the place of imprisonment from which the witness was taken.

(D) The court, in the manner provided in Chapter 120. of the Revised Code, shall either assign counsel or designate a public defender to represent a juvenile subpoenaed as a witness under this section. Compensation for assigned counsel shall be made pursuant to section 2941.51 of the Revised Code.

(E) When a person's testimony is taken by deposition pursuant to division (A) of this section, the deposition shall be upon oral examination if either the prosecuting authority or the defendant who is taking the deposition requests that the deposition be upon oral examination, and may be videotaped if either the prosecuting authority or the defendant who is taking the deposition requests that it be recorded by means of videotape.

The person requesting the testimony of the person whose deposition is taken pursuant to division (A) of this section shall pay the expense of taking the deposition, except that the court may tax the expense as court costs in appropriate cases.

(1998 H 293, eff. 3–17–98; 1994 H 571, eff. 10–6–94; 1981 H 440, eff. 11–23–81; 1981 H 145; 1976 S 393; 129 v 322; 1953 H 1; GC 13444–7, 13444–8)

Historical and Statutory Notes

Pre–1953 H 1 Amendments: 113 v 187, Ch 23, § 7, 8

Amendment Note: 1998 H 293 added division (A)(1); designated division (A)(2); deleted "workhouse, juvenile" before "detention facility" and ", jail," following "detention facility" in division (A)(2); inserted "Subject to division (C) of this section," and deleted "workhouse, a juvenile" before "detention facility" and ", or a jail" following "detention facility" in the first paragraph in division (B); and made changes reflecting gender neutral language and other nonsubstantive changes.

Amendment Note: 1994 H 571 changed references to the penitentiary and reformatories to references to state correctional institutions.

Cross References

Evidence, proving testimony of absent witness, prisoners, 2317.06

Right to compulsory process to obtain witnesses, O Const Art I §10

Library References

Criminal Law ⚷627.2.

Witnesses ⚷7.

Westlaw Topic Nos. 110, 410.

C.J.S. Criminal Law § 468.

C.J.S. Witnesses §§ 2, 20 to 31.

Research References

Encyclopedias

OH Jur. 3d Criminal Law § 2519, Place of Deposition.

OH Jur. 3d Jury § 148, Compelling Attendance and Testimony of Witnesses.

OH Jur. 3d Penal & Correctional Institutions § 36, Officers and Employees—Warden.

Treatises and Practice Aids

Markus, Trial Handbook for Ohio Lawyers, § 11:2, Prisoners.

Katz, Giannelli, Blair and Lipton, Baldwin's Ohio Practice, Criminal Law, § 61:10, Out-Of-State Witnesses.

Katz, Giannelli, Blair and Lipton, Baldwin's Ohio Practice, Criminal Law, § 61:11, Prisoners.

Katz, Giannelli, Blair and Lipton, Baldwin's Ohio Practice, Criminal Law, § 149:16, Motion for an Order to Bring Incarcerated Witness Into Court to Testify.

Katz, Giannelli, Blair and Lipton, Baldwin's Ohio Practice, Criminal Law, § 149:17, Order to Bring Prisoner Into Court to Testify.

Katz, Giannelli, Blair and Lipton, Baldwin's Ohio Practice, Criminal Law, § 149:18, Motion to Compel the Appearance of a Witness Residing Outside the State of Ohio.

Giannelli and Snyder, Baldwin's Ohio Practice, Evidence, § 804.8, Unavailability: Unable to Procure Testimony.

Notes of Decisions

1. Authority to order subpoena—In general

A municipal court may, pursuant to RC 2317.06(B), when the interests of justice demand, order a subpoena issued directing the sheriff of the county in which the municipal court is located to deliver an individual in the custody of the rehabilitation and correction department or the youth services department to the court for the purpose of procuring the individual's testimony in a civil proceeding before the court. OAG 90–054.

A municipal court, pursuant to RC 2945.47(C), may order a subpoena issued directing the sheriff of the county in which the court is located to deliver an individual in the custody of the rehabilitation and correction department or the youth services department to the court for the purpose of obtaining the individual's testimony in any trial conducted under RC Ch 2938. OAG 90–009.

2. —— Discretion of court, authority to order subpoena

A trial court has discretion to issue or not issue a subpoena under RC 2945.47(B) to cause a jailed witness to appear in court; where the witness is a belligerent felon, it is not an abuse of discretion for the court to permit the videotaping in the jail of a deposition at which the opposing party may thoroughly examine the witness. State v. Donnelly (Ohio Com.Pl. 1984) 17 Ohio Misc.2d 1, 477 N.E.2d 1243, 17 O.B.R. 129.

2945.48 Witness may be placed in jail

When a witness mentioned in section 2945.47 of the Revised Code is in attendance upon a court he may be placed in the jail of the county. The expenses of the officer in transporting him to and from such court, including compensation for the guard or attendant of such prisoner not exceeding the per diem salary of such guard for the time he is away from said institution, shall be allowed by the court and taxed and paid as other costs against the state.

(1953 H 1, eff. 10–1–53; GC 13444–9)

Historical and Statutory Notes

Pre–1953 H 1 Amendments: 113 v 188, Ch 23, § 9

Library References

Witnesses ⇨20.

Westlaw Topic No. 410.

C.J.S. Witnesses §§ 2, 69.

Research References

Encyclopedias

OH Jur. 3d Criminal Law § 3110, Compensation of Witnesses.

OH Jur. 3d Criminal Law § 3982, Convict Witness Expenses.

Treatises and Practice Aids

Markus, Trial Handbook for Ohio Lawyers, § 11:2, Prisoners.

2945.481 Deposition of child sex offense victim; presence of defendant; additional depositions; videotaped deposition; admissibility of deposition; televised or recorded testimony

(A)(1) As used in this section, "victim" includes any person who was a victim of a violation identified in division (A)(2) of this section or an offense of violence or against whom was directed any conduct that constitutes, or that is an element of, a violation identified in division (A)(2) of this section or an offense of violence.

(2) In any proceeding in the prosecution of a charge of a violation of section 2905.03, 2905.05, 2907.02, 2907.03, 2907.04, 2907.05, 2907.06, 2907.07, 2907.09, 2907.21, 2907.23, 2907.24, 2907.31, 2907.32, 2907.321, 2907.322, 2907.323, or 2919.22 of the Revised Code or an offense of violence and in which an alleged victim of the violation or offense was a child who was less than thirteen years of age when the complaint, indictment, or information was filed, whichever occurred earlier, the judge of the court in which the prosecution is being conducted, upon motion of an attorney for the prosecution, shall order that the testimony of the child victim be taken by deposition. The prosecution also may request that the deposition be videotaped in accordance with division (A)(3) of this section. The judge shall notify the child victim whose deposition is to be taken, the prosecution, and the defense of the date, time, and place for taking the deposition. The notice shall identify the child victim who is to be examined and shall indicate whether a request that the deposition be videotaped has been made. The defendant shall have the right to attend the deposition and the right to be represented by counsel. Depositions shall be taken in the manner provided in civil cases, except that the judge shall preside at the taking of the deposition and shall rule at that time on any objections of the prosecution or the attorney for the defense. The prosecution and the attorney for the defense shall have the right, as at trial, to full examination and cross-examination of the child victim whose deposition is to be taken. If a deposition taken under this division is intended to be offered as evidence in the proceeding, it shall be filed in the court in which the action is pending and is admissible in the manner described in division (B) of this section. If a deposition of a child victim taken under this division is admitted as

evidence at the proceeding under division (B) of this section, the child victim shall not be required to testify in person at the proceeding. However, at any time before the conclusion of the proceeding, the attorney for the defense may file a motion with the judge requesting that another deposition of the child victim be taken because new evidence material to the defense has been discovered that the attorney for the defense could not with reasonable diligence have discovered prior to the taking of the admitted deposition. A motion for another deposition shall be accompanied by supporting affidavits. Upon the filing of a motion for another deposition and affidavits, the court may order that additional testimony of the child victim relative to the new evidence be taken by another deposition. If the court orders the taking of another deposition under this provision, the deposition shall be taken in accordance with this division; if the admitted deposition was a videotaped deposition taken in accordance with division (A)(3) of this section, the new deposition also shall be videotaped in accordance with that division and in other cases, the new deposition may be videotaped in accordance with that division.

(3) If the prosecution requests that a deposition to be taken under division (A)(2) of this section be videotaped, the judge shall order that the deposition be videotaped in accordance with this division. If a judge issues an order that the deposition be videotaped, the judge shall exclude from the room in which the deposition is to be taken every person except the child victim giving the testimony, the judge, one or more interpreters if needed, the attorneys for the prosecution and the defense, any person needed to operate the equipment to be used, one person chosen by the child victim giving the deposition, and any person whose presence the judge determines would contribute to the welfare and well-being of the child victim giving the deposition. The person chosen by the child victim shall not be a witness in the proceeding and, both before and during the deposition, shall not discuss the testimony of the child victim with any other witness in the proceeding. To the extent feasible, any person operating the recording equipment shall be restricted to a room adjacent to the room in which the deposition is being taken, or to a location in the room in which the deposition is being taken that is behind a screen or mirror, so that the person operating the recording equipment can see and hear, but cannot be seen or heard by, the child victim giving the deposition during the deposition. The defendant shall be permitted to observe and hear the testimony of the child victim giving the deposition on a monitor, shall be provided with an electronic means of immediate communication with the defendant's attorney during the testimony, and shall be restricted to a location from which the defendant cannot be seen or heard by the child victim giving the deposition, except on a monitor provided for that purpose. The child victim giving the deposition shall be provided with a monitor on which the child victim can observe, during the testimony, the defendant. The judge, at the judge's discretion, may preside at the deposition by electronic means from outside the room in which the deposition is to be taken; if the judge presides by electronic means, the judge shall be provided with monitors on which the judge can see each person in the room in which the deposition is to be taken and with an electronic means of communication with each person, and each person in the room shall be provided with a monitor on which that person can see the judge and with an electronic means of communication with the judge. A deposition that is videotaped under this division shall be taken and filed in the manner described in division (A)(2) of this section and is admissible in the manner described in this division and division (B) of this section, and, if a deposition that is videotaped under this division is admitted as evidence at the proceeding, the child victim shall not be required to testify in person at the proceeding. No deposition videotaped under this division shall be admitted as evidence at any proceeding unless division (B) of this section is satisfied relative to the deposition and all of the following apply relative to the recording:

(a) The recording is both aural and visual and is recorded on film or videotape, or by other electronic means.

(b) The recording is authenticated under the Rules of Evidence and the Rules of Criminal Procedure as a fair and accurate representation of what occurred, and the recording is not altered other than at the direction and under the supervision of the judge in the proceeding.

(c) Each voice on the recording that is material to the testimony on the recording or the making of the recording, as determined by the judge, is identified.

(d) Both the prosecution and the defendant are afforded an opportunity to view the recording before it is shown in the proceeding.

(B)(1) At any proceeding in a prosecution in relation to which a deposition was taken under division (A) of this section, the deposition or a part of it is admissible in evidence upon motion of the prosecution if the testimony in the deposition or the part to be admitted is not excluded by the hearsay rule and if the deposition or the part to be admitted otherwise is admissible under the Rules of Evidence. For purposes of this division, testimony is not excluded by the hearsay rule if the testimony is not hearsay under Evidence Rule 801; if the testimony is within an exception to the hearsay rule set forth in Evidence Rule 803; if the child victim who gave the testimony is unavailable as a witness, as defined in Evidence Rule 804, and the testimony is admissible under that rule; or if both of the following apply:

(a) The defendant had an opportunity and similar motive at the time of the taking of the deposition to develop the testimony by direct, cross, or redirect examination.

(b) The judge determines that there is reasonable cause to believe that, if the child victim who gave the testimony in the deposition were to testify in person at the proceeding, the child victim would experience serious emotional trauma as a result of the child victim's participation at the proceeding.

(2) Objections to receiving in evidence a deposition or a part of it under division (B) of this section shall be made as provided in civil actions.

(3) The provisions of divisions (A) and (B) of this section are in addition to any other provisions of the Revised Code, the Rules of Criminal Procedure, or the Rules of Evidence that pertain to the taking or admission of depositions in a criminal proceeding and do not limit the admissibility under any of those other provisions of any deposition taken under division (A) of this section or otherwise taken.

(C) In any proceeding in the prosecution of any charge of a violation listed in division (A)(2) of this section or an offense of violence and in which an alleged victim of the violation or offense was a child who was less than thirteen years of age when the complaint, indictment, or information was filed, whichever occurred earlier, the prosecution may file a motion with the judge requesting the judge to order the testimony of the child victim to be taken in a room other than the room in which the proceeding is being conducted and be televised, by closed circuit equipment, into the room in which the proceeding is being conducted to be viewed by the jury, if applicable, the defendant, and any other persons who are not permitted in the room in which the testimony is to be taken but who would have been present during the testimony of the child victim had it been given in the room in which the proceeding is being conducted. Except for good cause shown, the prosecution shall file a motion under this division at least seven days before the date of the proceeding. The judge may issue the order upon the motion of the prosecution filed under this section, if the judge determines that the child victim is unavailable to testify in the room in which the proceeding is being conducted in the physical presence of the defendant, for one or more of the reasons set forth in division (E) of this section. If a judge issues an order of that nature, the judge shall exclude from the room in which the testimony is to be taken every person except a person described in division (A)(3) of this section. The judge, at the judge's discretion, may preside during the giving of the testimony by electronic means from outside the room in which it is being given, subject to the limitations set forth in division (A)(3) of this section. To the extent feasible, any person operating the televising equipment shall be hidden from the sight and hearing of the child victim giving the testimony, in a manner similar to that described in division (A)(3) of this section. The defendant shall be permitted to observe and hear the testimony of the child victim giving the testimony on a monitor, shall be provided with an electronic means of immediate communication with the defendant's attorney during the testimony, and shall be restricted to a location from which the defendant cannot be seen or heard by the child victim giving the testimony, except on a monitor provided for that purpose. The child victim giving the testimony shall be provided with a monitor on which the child victim can observe, during the testimony, the defendant.

(D) In any proceeding in the prosecution of any charge of a violation listed in division (A)(2) of this section or an offense of violence and in which an alleged victim of the violation or offense was a child who was less than thirteen years of age when the complaint, indictment, or information was filed, whichever occurred earlier, the prosecution may file a motion with the judge requesting the judge to order the testimony of the child victim to be taken outside of the room in which the proceeding is being conducted and be recorded for showing in the room in which the proceeding is being conducted before the judge, the jury, if applicable, the defendant, and any other persons who would have been present during the testimony of the child victim had it been given in the room in which the proceeding is being conducted. Except for good cause shown, the prosecution shall file a motion under this division at least seven days before the date of the proceeding. The judge may issue the order upon the motion of the prosecution filed under this division, if the judge determines that the child victim is unavailable to testify in the room in which the proceeding is being conducted in the physical presence of the defendant, for one or more of the reasons set forth in division (E) of this section. If a judge issues an order of that nature, the judge shall exclude from the room in which the testimony is to be taken every person except a person described in division (A)(3) of this section. To the extent feasible, any person operating the recording equipment shall be hidden from the sight and hearing of the child victim giving the testimony, in a manner similar to that described in division (A)(3) of this section. The defendant shall be permitted to observe and hear the testimony of the child victim who is giving the testimony on a monitor, shall be provided with an electronic means of immediate communication with the defendant's attorney during the testimony, and shall be restricted to a location from which the defendant cannot be seen or heard by the child victim giving the testimony, except on a monitor provided for that purpose. The child victim giving the testimony shall be provided with a monitor on which the child victim can observe, during the testimony, the defendant. No order for the taking of testimony by recording shall be issued under this division unless the provisions set forth in divisions (A)(3)(a), (b), (c), and (d) of this section apply to the recording of the testimony.

(E) For purposes of divisions (C) and (D) of this section, a judge may order the testimony of a child victim to be taken outside the room in which the proceeding is being conducted if the judge determines that the child victim is unavailable to testify in the room in the physical presence of the defendant due to one or more of the following:

(1) The persistent refusal of the child victim to testify despite judicial requests to do so;

(2) The inability of the child victim to communicate about the alleged violation or offense because of extreme fear, failure of memory, or another similar reason;

(3) The substantial likelihood that the child victim will suffer serious emotional trauma from so testifying.

(F)(1) If a judge issues an order pursuant to division (C) or (D) of this section that requires the testimony of a child victim in a criminal proceeding to be taken outside of the room in which the proceeding is being conducted, the order shall specifically identify the child victim to whose testimony it applies, the order applies only during the testimony of the specified child victim, and the child victim giving the testimony shall not be required to testify at the proceeding other than in accordance with the order.

(2) A judge who makes any determination regarding the admissibility of a deposition under divisions (A) and (B) of this section, the videotaping of a deposition under division (A)(3) of this section, or the taking of testimony outside of the room in which a proceeding is being conducted under division (C) or (D) of this section, shall enter the determination and findings on the record in the proceeding.

(1997 S 53, eff. 10–14–97)

Uncodified Law

1996 H 445, § 3: See Uncodified Law under RC 2907.11.

Historical and Statutory Notes

Ed. Note: 2945.481 is former 2907.41, amended and recodified by 1997 S 53, eff. 10–14–97; 1996 H 445, eff. 9–3–96; 1986 H 108, eff. 10–14–86.

Amendment Note: 1997 S 53 added division (A)(1); redesignated former division (A)(2) as division (A)(3); designated division (A)(2); inserted references to Revised Code sections 2905.03, 2905.05, 2907.07, 2907.09, 2907.23, and 2907.24 in division (A)(2); inserted "or an offense of violence and" following "Revised Code" in division (A)(2); substituted "less than thirteen" for "under eleven" in divisions (A)(2), (C) and (D); substituted references to division (A)(2) with references to division (A)(3) throughout; inserted "or an offense of violence and" before "in which an alleged victim" in division (D); and made changes to reflect gender neutral language an other nonsubstantive changes.

Amendment Note: 1996 H 445 removed a reference to section 2907.12 from the first sentence in division (A)(1); and made changes to reflect gender neutral language and other nonsubstantive changes.

Cross References

Bureau of criminal identification and investigation, recording and televising equipment for child sex offense victims, 109.54

Library References

Criminal Law ⚷627.2.

Westlaw Topic No. 110.

C.J.S. Criminal Law § 468.

Research References

Encyclopedias

OH Jur. 3d Criminal Law § 478, Depositions.

OH Jur. 3d Criminal Law § 1134, Child Victim's Testimony.

OH Jur. 3d Criminal Law § 1154, Evidence—Child Victim's Testimony.

OH Jur. 3d Criminal Law § 1200, Confrontation of Child Victim.

OH Jur. 3d Criminal Law § 2515, Deposition of Child Victim of Sexual Offense.

Treatises and Practice Aids

Giannelli and Snyder, Baldwin's Ohio Practice, Evidence, § 601.6, Child Competency: in General.

1 Giannelli and Snyder, Baldwin's Ohio Practice, Evidence, Index, Index.

Law Review and Journal Commentaries

Child Sex Abuse Evidence Problems—Update 1988, Robert P. Ringland. 14 U Dayton L Rev 147 (Fall 1988).

Coy v Iowa: Should Children Be Heard and Not Seen?, Comment. 50 U Pitt L Rev 1187 (Summer 1989).

Idaho v. Wright: A Confrontation Clause Escape Hatch for Defendants in Child Sex Abuse Cases, Note. 18 Ohio N U L Rev 693 (1991).

A Model Statute to Provide Foreign-Language Interpreters in the Ohio Courts, Alice J. Baker. 30 U Tol L Rev 593 (Summer 1999).

Navigating Between Scylla and Charybdis: Ohio's Efforts to Protect Children Without Eviscerating the Rights of Criminal Defendants–Evidentiary Considerations and the Rebirth of Confrontation Clause Analysis in Child Abuse Cases, Myrna S. Raeder. 25 U Tol L Rev 43 (1994).

Protecting the Innocent: Confrontation, Coy v. Iowa, and Televised Testimony in Child Sexual Abuse Cases, Comment. 78 Ky L J 803 (1989–90).

The Uses of Technology, Stanley B. Kent. 62 Clev B J 220 (April 1991).

Videotaped Child Testimony And The Confrontation Clause: Are They Reconcilable?, Comment. 14 U Dayton L Rev 361 (Winter 1989).

Notes of Decisions

Ed. Note: *This section contains annotations from former RC 2907.41.*

1. Right to call witnesses

RC 2907.41 does not infringe on a defendant's constitutional right to call witnesses as the defendant is free to call a child victim to the stand unless and until the prosecution chooses to use the procedure for closed circuit testimony set out in the statute. State v Hardway, Nos. 92–CA–4 and 92–CA–6 (5th Dist Ct App, Licking, 9–14–92).

2. Right to confront witnesses—In general

Physical setup of closed circuit television system to allow child witness to testify outside presence of defendant complied with statutory requirements for such testimony, where defendant could adequately communicate privately with his attorney; defendant was not prejudiced by having video camera focused on him, since during every trial, defendant sits in front of jury throughout proceeding and witnesses are given opportunity to observe and identify him. State v. Sibert (Ohio App. 4 Dist., 11-04-1994) 98 Ohio App.3d 412, 648 N.E.2d 861, motion for delayed appeal denied 71 Ohio St.3d 1479, 645 N.E.2d 1258, denial of post-conviction relief affirmed 74 Ohio St.3d 342, 658 N.E.2d 772, 1996-Ohio-15. Witnesses ⚷ 228

Before a court denies a defendant the right to confront a child witness in a sex offense prosecution by positioning the witness so that the defendant is unable to view the child while testifying, the court must make a particularized finding concerning the emotional well-being of the child and the necessity of the seating arrangement. State v. Bean (Sandusky 1990) 62 Ohio App.3d 881, 577 N.E.2d 732.

O Const Art I §10 provides no greater right of confrontation than US Const Am 6; further, the use, in accord with RC 2907.41(A) and 2907.41(B), of a child sexual abuse victim's videotaped deposition at trial in place of live testimony does not violate a defendant's constitutional right of confrontation. State v. Self (Ohio 1990) 56 Ohio St.3d 73, 564 N.E.2d 446.

A state statute providing that a one-way mirror or screen must shield a child on the stand from seeing the defendant while testifying at a trial for child molesting violates the defendant's right to "confront" the witnesses against him guaranteed by US Const Am 6. (Ed. note: Iowa law construed in light of federal constitution.) Coy v. Iowa (U.S.Iowa 1988) 108 S.Ct. 2798, 487 U.S. 1012, 101 L.Ed.2d 857, on remand 433 N.W.2d 714.

The failure to allow objections to a videotape deposition of a six-year-old rape victim during the taping of the deposition is not prejudicial to a defendant where a viewing of the deposition, at which time objections were ruled on, was held subsequent to the taping and where the defendant had waived his right to a trial by jury. State v Lipp, No. E–86–74 (6th Dist Ct App, Erie, 1–29–88).

In a prosecution for rape, where the victim is the defendant's six-year-old stepdaughter, the testimony of the victim may be taken in a room outside the presence of the defendant where the defendant can observe the proceedings by video camera and communicate with counsel by telephone pursuant to RC 2907.41, notwithstanding this section had not been enacted at the time the offense was committed. State v Eastham, No. 86–CA–51 (2d Dist Ct App, Miami 7–28–87), reversed by 39 OS(3d) 307, 530 NE(2d) 409 (1988).

3. —— Emotional harm to victim, right to confront witnesses

Permitting child victim to testify outside physical presence of defendant without satisfying statutory requirements for such procedure did not constitute plain error in rape prosecution, where defendant failed to demonstrate that, but for such error, outcome of proceeding would have been different. State v. McConnell (Ohio App. 2 Dist., Montgomery, 08-13-2004) No. 19993, 2004-Ohio-4263, 2004 WL 1802142, Unreported, appeal not allowed 104 Ohio St.3d 1427, 819 N.E.2d 710, 2004-Ohio-6585. Criminal Law ⚷ 1036.2

Claim that trial court improperly permitted child victim to testify outside physical presence of rape defendant without satisfying statutory requirements for such procedure could only be reviewed on appeal for plain error, where, at trial, defendant failed to object to victim testifying outside presence of defendant. State v. McConnell (Ohio App. 2 Dist., Montgomery, 08-13-2004) No. 19993, 2004-Ohio-4263, 2004 WL 1802142, Unreported, appeal not allowed 104 Ohio St.3d 1427, 819 N.E.2d 710, 2004-Ohio-6585. Criminal Law ⚷ 1036.2

Statutory requirements for permitting child victim to testify outside room in which proceeding is being conducted, that child is unable to communicate about offense because of extreme fear and that there is substantial likelihood that child victim will suffer serious emotional trauma from testifying in physical presence of defendant, were not satisfied in rape prosecution, where child testified that she was scared to see defendant, which made her feel sad, and psychologist testified that if would be difficult for child to testify in front of defendant and that child would suffer emotional trauma if required to testify, but psychologist did not indicate that child would suffer serious emotional trauma. State v. McConnell (Ohio App. 2 Dist., Montgomery, 08-13-2004) No. 19993, 2004-Ohio-4263, 2004 WL 1802142, Unreported, appeal not allowed 104 Ohio St.3d 1427, 819 N.E.2d 710, 2004-Ohio-6585. Witnesses ⚷ 228

Social worker's opinion testimony can support a trial court's finding of serious emotional trauma so that a child's videotaped testimony may be admitted in lieu of live testimony, even without the social worker's qualification as an expert. State v. Cooper (Ohio App. 12 Dist., 07-24-2000) 139 Ohio App.3d 149, 743 N.E.2d 427, dismissed, appeal not allowed 90 Ohio St.3d 1468, 738 N.E.2d 381. Criminal Law ⚷ 456

To admit a child victim's videotaped deposition, the trial court must make a finding that the child would experience serious emotional trauma if required to testify in open court. State v. Cooper (Ohio App. 12 Dist., 07-24-2000) 139 Ohio App.3d 149, 743 N.E.2d 427, dismissed, appeal not allowed 90 Ohio St.3d 1468, 738 N.E.2d 381. Criminal Law ⚷ 627.2

Testimony of licensed social worker, who had been seeing eight-year-old child victim on a weekly basis for 13 months preceding mother's rape prosecution and who had access to his clinical evaluations, that there was a substantial likelihood that child would suffer serious emotional trauma if forced to testify supported admission of videotape of child's testimony into evidence in lieu of requiring child to testify live at trial. State v. Cooper (Ohio App. 12 Dist., 07-24-2000) 139 Ohio App.3d 149, 743 N.E.2d 427, dismissed, appeal not allowed 90 Ohio St.3d 1468, 738 N.E.2d 381. Witnesses ⚷ 228

Trial court was not obligated to conduct a sua sponte competency hearing before allowing 12–year–old victim to testify in her mother's rape prosecution via videotape, even if child had been committed to a mental facility on several different occasions, had been in restraints in a mental facility for much of the two weeks preceding her testimony, and she was taking several psychotropic medications, where child never testified in such a way as to place her competency into question. State v. Cooper (Ohio App. 12 Dist., 07-24-2000) 139 Ohio App.3d 149, 743 N.E.2d 427, dismissed, appeal not allowed 90 Ohio St.3d 1468, 738 N.E.2d 381. Witnesses ⚷ 77

Psychologist who testified that child victims of sexual abuse would suffer serious emotional distress if they were to testify in presence of defendant and that they should be permitted to testify by closed circuit television gave facts and data underlying his opinion, where he testified that he administered a variety of assessment measures to children, that he and his assistant met with each child three times, he described visits, and he explained his experience in working with sexually abused children. State v. Sibert (Ohio App. 4 Dist., 11-04-1994) 98 Ohio App.3d 412, 648 N.E.2d 861, motion for delayed appeal denied 71 Ohio St.3d 1479, 645 N.E.2d 1258, denial of post-conviction relief affirmed 74 Ohio St.3d 342, 658 N.E.2d 772, 1996-Ohio-15. Criminal Law ⚷ 486(5)

To admit a child-victim's videotaped deposition under RC 2907.41(B)(1)(b), a finding must be made that the child would experience serious emotional trauma if required to testify in open court. Permanent injury need not be proven to establish serious emotional trauma. State v. Self (Ohio 1990) 56 Ohio St.3d 73, 564 N.E.2d 446. Criminal Law ⚷ 627.2

A "case-specific" finding of necessity is required for the introduction of videotaped testimony of children authorized by RC 2907.41(A)(2) and 2907.41(B)(1); a psychologist's finding that "I feel it would be damaging for them to appear in court" is insufficient and the introduction of videotaped evidence under such circumstances is violative of O Const Art I §10 and US Const Am 6. State v Kreitzer, No. 2492 (2d Dist Ct App, Clark, 11–3–89).

A mother's testimony that a child/victim "might be traumatized" and that she would not permit the child to testify in an open courtroom, because it would not be in the child's best interests, is insufficient for a court to find a "substantial likelihood that the child victim will suffer serious emotional trauma" from testifying in open court where the child does not appear to be a reluctant witness and specifically states he was not scared during his testimony at the competency hearing; consequently, the admission of the child victim's videotape deposition at trial, in violation of the prerequisites set forth in RC 2907.41, constitutes a violation of a defendant's confrontation rights pursuant to O Const Art I §10. State v Butts, No. 88AP–764 (10th Dist Ct App, Franklin, 6–29–89).

2945.482 Testimony of mentally retarded or developmentally disabled victim

(A) As used in this section:

(1) "Mentally retarded person" and "developmentally disabled person" have the same meanings as in section 5123.01 of the Revised Code.

(2) "Mentally retarded or developmentally disabled victim" includes a mentally retarded or developmentally disabled person who was a victim of a violation identified in division (B)(1) of this section or an offense of violence or against whom was directed any conduct that constitutes, or that is an element of, a violation identified in division (B)(1) of this section or an offense of violence.

(B)(1) In any proceeding in the prosecution of a charge of a violation of section 2903.16, 2903.34, 2903.341, 2905.03, 2907.02, 2907.03, 2907.05, 2907.06, 2907.09, 2907.21, 2907.23, 2907.24, 2907.32, 2907.321, 2907.322, or 2907.323 of the Revised Code or an offense of violence and in which an alleged victim of the violation or offense was a mentally retarded or developmentally disabled person, the judge of the court in which the prosecution is being conducted, upon motion of an attorney for the prosecution, shall order that the testimony of the mentally retarded or developmentally disabled victim be taken by deposition. The prosecution also may request that the deposition be videotaped in accordance with division (B)(2) of this section. The judge shall notify the mentally retarded or developmentally disabled victim whose deposition is to be taken, the prosecution, and the defense of the date, time, and place for taking the deposition. The notice shall identify the mentally retarded or developmentally disabled victim who is to be examined and shall indicate whether a request that the deposition be videotaped has been made. The defendant shall have the right to attend the deposition and the right to be represented by counsel. Depositions shall be taken in the manner provided in civil cases, except that the judge shall preside at the taking of the deposition and shall rule at the time on any objections of the prosecution or the attorney for the defense. The prosecution and the attorney for the defense shall have the right, as at trial, to full examination and cross-examination of the mentally retarded or developmentally disabled victim whose deposition is to be taken. If a deposition taken under this division is intended to be offered as evidence in the proceeding, it shall be filed in the court in which the action is pending and is admissible in the manner described in division (C) of this section.

If a deposition of a mentally retarded or developmentally disabled victim taken under this division is admitted as evidence at the proceeding under division (C) of this section, the mentally retarded or developmentally disabled victim shall not be required to testify in person at the proceeding.

At any time before the conclusion of the proceeding, the attorney for the defense may file a motion with the judge requesting that another deposition of the mentally retarded or developmentally disabled victim be taken because new evidence material to the defense has been discovered that the attorney for the defense could not with reasonable diligence have discovered prior to the taking of the admitted deposition. If the court orders the taking of another deposition under this provision, the deposition shall be taken in accordance with this division. If the admitted deposition was a videotaped deposition taken in accordance with division (B)(2) of this section, the new deposition shall be videotaped in accordance with that division. In other cases, the new deposition may be videotaped in accordance with that division.

(2) If the prosecution requests that a deposition to be taken under division (B)(2) of this section be videotaped, the judge shall order that the deposition be videotaped in accordance with this division. If a judge issues an order that the deposition be videotaped, the judge shall exclude from the room in which the deposition is to be taken every person except the mentally retarded or developmentally disabled victim giving the testimony, the judge, one or more interpreters if needed, the attorneys for the prosecution and the defense, any person needed to operate the equipment to be used, one person chosen by the mentally retarded or developmentally disabled victim giving the deposition, and any person whose presence the judge determines would contribute to the welfare and well-being of the mentally retarded or developmentally disabled victim giving the deposition. The person chosen by the mentally retarded or developmentally disabled victim shall not be a witness in the proceeding and, both before and during the deposition, shall not discuss the testimony of the mentally retarded or developmentally disabled victim with any other witness in the proceeding. To the extent feasible, any person operating the recording equipment shall be restricted to a room adjacent to the room in which the deposition is being taken, or to a location in the room in which the deposition is being taken that is behind a screen or mirror, so that the person operating the recording equipment can see and hear, but cannot be seen or heard by, the mentally retarded or developmentally disabled victim giving the deposition during the deposition.

The defendant shall be permitted to observe and hear the testimony of the mentally retarded or developmentally disabled victim giving the deposition on a monitor, shall be provided with an electronic means of immediate communication with the defendant's attorney during the testimony, and shall be restricted to a location from which the defendant cannot be seen or heard by the mentally retarded or developmentally disabled victim giving the deposition, except on a monitor provided for that purpose. The mentally retarded or developmentally disabled victim giving the deposition shall be provided with a monitor on which the victim can observe, during the testimony, the defendant. The judge, at the judge's discretion, may preside at the deposition by electronic means from outside the room in which the deposition is to be taken. If the judge presides by electronic means, the judge shall be provided with monitors on which the judge can see each person in the room in which the deposition is to be taken and with an electronic means of communication with each person, and each person in the room shall be provided with a monitor on which that person can see the judge and with an electronic means of communication with the judge. A deposition that is videotaped under this division shall be taken and filed in the manner described in division (B)(1) of this section and is admissible in the manner described in this division and division (C) of this section, and, if a deposition that is videotaped under this division is admitted as evidence at the proceeding, the mentally retarded or developmentally disabled victim shall not be required to testify in person at the proceeding. No deposition videotaped under this division shall be admitted as evidence at any proceeding unless division (C) of this section is satisfied relative to the deposition and all of the following apply relative to the recording:

(a) The recording is both aural and visual and is recorded on film or videotape, or by other electronic means.

(b) The recording is authenticated under the Rules of Evidence and the Rules of Criminal Procedure as a fair and accurate representation of what occurred, and the recording is not altered other than at the direction and under the supervision of the judge in the proceeding.

(c) Each voice on the recording that is material to the testimony on the recording or the making of the recording, as determined by the judge, is identified.

(d) Both the prosecution and the defendant are afforded an opportunity to view the recording before it is shown in the proceeding.

(C)(1) At any proceeding in a prosecution in relation to which a deposition was taken under division (B) of this section, the deposition or a part of it is admissible in evidence upon motion of the prosecution if the testimony in the deposition or the part to be admitted is not excluded by the hearsay rule and if the deposition or the part to be admitted otherwise is admissible under the Rules of Evidence. For purposes of this division, testimony is not excluded by the hearsay rule if the testimony is not hearsay under Evidence Rule 801; the testimony is within an exception to the hearsay rule set forth in Evidence Rule 803; the mentally retarded or developmentally disabled victim who gave the testimony is unavailable as a witness, as defined in Evidence Rule 804, and the testimony is admissible under that rule; or both of the following apply:

(a) The defendant had an opportunity and similar motive at the time of the taking of the deposition to develop the testimony by direct, cross, or redirect examination.

(b) The judge determines that there is reasonable cause to believe that, if the mentally retarded or developmentally disabled victim who gave the testimony in the deposition were to testify in person at the proceeding, the mentally retarded or developmentally disabled victim would experience serious emotional trauma as a result of the mentally retarded or developmentally disabled victim's participation at the proceeding.

(2) Objections to receiving in evidence a deposition or a part of it under division (C) of this section shall be made as provided in civil actions.

(3) The provisions of divisions (B) and (C) of this section are in addition to any other provisions of the Revised Code, the Rules of Criminal Procedure, or the Rules of Evidence that pertain to the taking or admission of depositions in a criminal proceeding and do not limit the admissibility under any of those other provisions of any deposition taken under division (B) of this section or otherwise taken.

(D) In any proceeding in the prosecution of any charge of a violation listed in division (B)(1) of this section or an offense of violence and in which an alleged victim of the violation or offense was a mentally retarded or developmentally disabled person, the prosecution may file a motion with the judge requesting the judge to order the testimony of the mentally retarded or developmentally disabled victim to be taken in a room other than the room in which the proceeding is being conducted and be televised, by closed circuit equipment, into the room in which the proceeding is being conducted to be viewed by the jury, if applicable, the defendant, and any other persons who are not permitted in the room in which the testimony is to be taken but who would have been present during the testimony of the mentally retarded or developmentally disabled victim had it been given in the room in which the proceeding is being conducted. Except for good cause shown, the prosecution shall file a motion under this division at least seven days before the date of the proceeding. The judge may issue the order upon the motion of the prosecution filed under this section, if the judge determines that the mentally retarded or developmentally disabled victim is unavailable to testify in the room in which the proceeding is being conducted in the physical presence of the defendant for one or more of the reasons set forth in division (F) of this section. If a judge issues an order of that nature, the judge shall exclude from the room in which the testimony is to be taken every person except a person described in division (B)(2) of this section. The judge, at the judge's discretion, may preside during the giving of the testimony by electronic means from outside the room in which it is being given, subject to the limitations set forth in division (B)(2) of this section. To the extent feasible, any person operating the televising equipment shall be hidden from the sight and hearing of the mentally retarded or developmentally disabled victim giving the testimony, in a manner similar to that described in division (B)(2) of this section. The defendant shall be permitted to observe and hear the testimony of the mentally retarded or developmentally disabled victim giving the testimony on a monitor, shall be provided with an electronic means of immediate communication with the defendant's attorney during the testimony, and shall be restricted to a location from which the defendant cannot be seen or heard by the mentally retarded or developmentally disabled victim giving the testimony, except on a monitor provided for that purpose. The mentally retarded or developmentally disabled victim giving the testimony shall be provided with a monitor on which the mentally retarded or developmentally disabled victim can observe, during the testimony, the defendant.

(E) In any proceeding in the prosecution of any charge of a violation listed in division (B)(1) of this section or an offense of violence and in which an alleged victim of the violation or offense was a mentally retarded or developmentally disabled victim, the prosecution may file a motion with the judge requesting the judge to order the testimony of the mentally retarded or developmentally disabled victim to be taken outside of the room in which the proceeding is being conducted and be recorded for showing in the room in which the proceeding is being conducted before the judge, the jury, if applicable, the defendant, and any other persons who would have been present during the testimony of the mentally retarded or developmentally disabled victim had it been given in the room in which the proceeding is being conducted. Except for good cause shown, the prosecution shall file a motion under this division at least seven days before the date of the proceeding. The judge may issue the order upon the motion of the prosecution filed under this division, if the judge determines that the mentally retarded or developmentally disabled victim is unavailable to testify in the room in which the proceeding is being conducted in the physical presence of the defendant, for one or more of the reasons set forth in division (F) of this section. If a judge issues an order of that nature, the judge shall exclude from the room in which the testimony is to be taken every person except a person described in division (B)(2) of this section. To the extent feasible, any person operating the recording equipment shall be hidden from the sight and hearing of the mentally retarded or developmentally disabled victim giving the testimony, in a manner similar to that described in division (B)(2) of this section. The defendant shall be permitted to observe and hear the testimony of the mentally retarded or developmentally disabled victim who is giving the testimony on a monitor, shall be provided with an electronic means of immediate communication with the defendant's attorney during the testimony, and shall be restricted to a location from which the defendant cannot be seen or heard by the mentally retarded or developmentally disabled victim giving the testimony, except on a monitor provided for that purpose. The mentally retarded or developmentally disabled victim giving the testimony shall be provided with a monitor on which the victim can observe, during the testimony, the defendant. No order for the taking of testimony by recording shall be issued under this division unless the provisions set forth in divisions (B)(2)(a), (b), (c), and (d) of this section apply to the recording of the testimony.

(F) For purposes of divisions (D) and (E) of this section, a judge may order the testimony of a mentally retarded or developmentally disabled victim to be taken outside the room in which the proceeding is being conducted if the judge determines that the mentally retarded or developmentally disabled victim is unavailable to testify in the room in the physical presence of the defendant due to one or more of the following:

(1) The persistent refusal of the mentally retarded or developmentally disabled victim to testify despite judicial requests to do so;

(2) The inability of the mentally retarded or developmentally disabled victim to communicate about the alleged violation or offense because of extreme fear, failure of memory, or another similar reason;

(3) The substantial likelihood that the mentally retarded or developmentally disabled victim will suffer serious emotional trauma from so testifying.

(G)(1) If a judge issues an order pursuant to division (D) or (E) of this section that requires the testimony of a mentally retarded or developmentally disabled victim in a criminal proceeding to be taken outside of the room in which the proceeding is being conducted, the order shall specifically identify the mentally retarded or developmentally disabled victim to whose testimony it applies, the order applies only during the testimony of the specified mentally retarded or developmentally disabled victim, and the mentally retarded or developmentally disabled victim giving the testimony shall not be required to testify at the proceeding other than in accordance with the order.

(2) A judge who makes any determination regarding the admissibility of a deposition under divisions (B) and (C) of this section, the videotaping of a deposition under division (B)(2) of this section, or the taking of testimony outside of the room in which a proceeding is being

conducted under division (D) or (E) of this section shall enter the determination and findings on the record in the proceeding.

(2004 S 178, eff. 1–30–04)

Library References

Criminal Law ⇐627.2.
Witnesses ⇐228.
Westlaw Topic Nos. 110, 410.
C.J.S. Criminal Law § 468.
C.J.S. Witnesses §§ 396 to 398, 404 to 405.

Research References

Encyclopedias

OH Jur. 3d Criminal Law § 2525, Particular Uses of Depositions.

Treatises and Practice Aids

1 Giannelli and Snyder, Baldwin's Ohio Practice, Evidence, Index, Index.

2945.49 Testimony of deceased or absent witness; videotaped testimony of child victim

(A)(1) As used in this section, "victim" includes any person who was a victim of a felony violation identified in division (B)(1) of this section or a felony offense of violence or against whom was directed any conduct that constitutes, or that is an element of, a felony violation identified in division (B)(1) of this section or a felony offense of violence.

(2) Testimony taken at an examination or a preliminary hearing at which the defendant is present, or at a former trial of the cause, or taken by deposition at the instance of the defendant or the state, may be used whenever the witness giving the testimony dies or cannot for any reason be produced at the trial or whenever the witness has, since giving that testimony, become incapacitated to testify. If the former testimony is contained within an authenticated transcript of the testimony, it shall be proven by the transcript, otherwise by other testimony.

(B)(1) At a trial on a charge of a felony violation of section 2905.05, 2907.02, 2907.03, 2907.04, 2907.05, 2907.21, 2907.24, 2907.31, 2907.32, 2907.321, 2907.322, 2907.323, or 2919.22 of the Revised Code or a felony offense of violence and in which an alleged victim of the alleged violation or offense was less than thirteen years of age when the complaint or information was filed, whichever occurred earlier, the court, upon motion of the prosecutor in the case, may admit videotaped preliminary hearing testimony of the child victim as evidence at the trial, in lieu of the child victim appearing as a witness and testifying at the trial, if all of the following apply:

(a) The videotape of the testimony was made at the preliminary hearing at which probable cause of the violation charged was found;

(b) The videotape of the testimony was made in accordance with division (C) of section 2937.11 of the Revised Code;

(c) The testimony in the videotape is not excluded by the hearsay rule and otherwise is admissible under the Rules of Evidence. For purposes of this division, testimony is not excluded by the hearsay rule if the testimony is not hearsay under Evidence Rule 801, if the testimony is within an exception to the hearsay rule set forth in Evidence Rule 803, if the child victim who gave the testimony is unavailable as a witness, as defined in Evidence Rule 804, and the testimony is admissible under that rule, or if both of the following apply:

(i) The accused had an opportunity and similar motive at the preliminary hearing to develop the testimony of the child victim by direct, cross, or redirect examination;

(ii) The court determines that there is reasonable cause to believe that if the child victim who gave the testimony at the preliminary hearing were to testify in person at the trial, the child victim would experience serious emotional trauma as a result of the child victim's participation at the trial.

(2) If a child victim of an alleged felony violation of section 2905.05, 2907.02, 2907.03, 2907.04, 2907.05, 2907.21, 2907.24, 2907.31, 2907.32, 2907.321, 2907.322, 2907.323, or 2919.22 of the Revised Code or an alleged felony offense of violence testifies at the preliminary hearing in the case, if the testimony of the child victim at the preliminary hearing was videotaped

pursuant to division (C) of section 2937.11 of the Revised Code, and if the defendant in the case files a written objection to the use, pursuant to division (B)(1) of this section, of the videotaped testimony at the trial, the court, immediately after the filing of the objection, shall hold a hearing to determine whether the videotaped testimony of the child victim should be admissible at trial under division (B)(1) of this section and, if it is admissible, whether the child victim should be required to provide limited additional testimony of the type described in this division. At the hearing held pursuant to this division, the defendant and the prosecutor in the case may present any evidence that is relevant to the issues to be determined at the hearing, but the child victim shall not be required to testify at the hearing.

After the hearing, the court shall not require the child victim to testify at the trial, unless it determines that both of the following apply:

(a) That the testimony of the child victim at trial is necessary for one or more of the following reasons:

(i) Evidence that was not available at the time of the testimony of the child victim at the preliminary hearing has been discovered;

(ii) The circumstances surrounding the case have changed sufficiently to necessitate that the child victim testify at the trial.

(b) That the testimony of the child victim at the trial is necessary to protect the right of the defendant to a fair trial.

The court shall enter its finding and the reasons for it in the journal. If the court requires the child victim to testify at the trial, the testimony of the victim shall be limited to the new evidence and changed circumstances, and the child victim shall not otherwise be required to testify at the trial. The required testimony of the child victim may be given in person or, upon motion of the prosecution, may be taken by deposition in accordance with division (A) of section 2945.481 of the Revised Code provided the deposition is admitted as evidence under division (B) of that section, may be taken outside of the courtroom and televised into the courtroom in accordance with division (C) of that section, or may be taken outside of the courtroom and recorded for showing in the courtroom in accordance with division (D) of that section.

(3) If videotaped testimony of a child victim is admitted at trial in accordance with division (B)(1) of this section, the child victim shall not be compelled in any way to appear as a witness at the trial, except as provided in division (B)(2) of this section.

(C) An order issued pursuant to division (B) of this section shall specifically identify the child victim concerning whose testimony it pertains. The order shall apply only during the testimony of the child victim it specifically identifies.

(D) As used in this section, "prosecutor" has the same meaning as in section 2935.01 of the Revised Code.

(1997 S 53, eff. 10–14–97; 1996 H 445, eff. 9–3–96; 1986 H 108, eff. 10–14–86; 1953 H 1; GC 13444–10)

Uncodified Law

1996 H 445, § 3, eff. 9–3–96, reads:

(A) When a complaint is filed alleging that a child is a delinquent child for committing felonious sexual penetration in violation of former section 2907.12 of the Revised Code and the arresting authority, a court, or a probation officer discovers that the child or a person whom the child caused to engage in sexual activity has a communicable disease, the arresting authority, court, or probation officer shall notify the victim of the delinquent act of the nature of the disease in accordance with division (C) of section 2151.14 of the Revised Code.

As used in division (A) of Section 3 of this act:

(1) "Child" has the same meaning as in section 2151.011 of the Revised Code.

(2) "Delinquent child" has the same meaning as in section 2151.02 of the Revised Code.

(3) "Sexual activity" has the same meaning as in section 2907.01 of the Revised Code.

(B) If a child is adjudicated a delinquent child for violating any provision of former section 2907.12 of the Revised Code other than division (A)(1)(b) of that section when the insertion involved was consensual and when the victim of the violation of division (A)(1)(b) of that section was older than the delinquent child, was the same age as the delinquent child, or was less that three years younger than the delinquent child, the juvenile court with jurisdiction over the child may commit the child to the legal custody of the department of youth services pursuant to division (A)(5)(a) of section 2151.355 of the Revised Code, as amended by this act, and all provisions of the Revised Code that apply to a disposition otherwise imposed pursuant to division (A)(5)(a) of section 2151.355 of the Revised Code, as amended by this act, apply to a disposition imposed in accordance with division (B) of Section 3 of this act.

As used in division (B) of Section 3 of this act:

(1) "Child" and "legal custody" have the same meanings as in section 2151.011 of the Revised Code.

(2) "Delinquent child" has the same meaning as in section 2151.02 of the Revised Code.

(C) Section 2151.3511 of the Revised Code, as amended by this act, applies to a proceeding in juvenile court involving a complaint in which a child is charged with committing an act that if committed by an adult would be felonious sexual penetration in violation of former section 2907.12 of the Revised Code and in which an alleged victim of the act was a child who was under eleven years of age when the complaint was filed.

As used in division (C) of Section 3 of this act, "child" has the same meaning as in section 2151.011 of the Revised Code.

(D) Division (E) of section 2743.62 of the Revised Code applies to a claim for an award of reparations arising out of the commission of felonious sexual penetration in violation of former section 2907.12 of the Revised Code.

(E) Section 2907.11 of the Revised Code, as amended by this act, applies to a prosecution for felonious sexual penetration committed in violation of former section 2907.12 of the Revised Code.

(F) Division (A) of section 2907.28 and sections 2907.29 and 2907.30 of the Revised Code, as amended by this act, apply to a victim of felonious sexual penetration committed in violation of former section 2907.12 of the Revised Code.

(G) Sections 2907.41 and 2945.49 of the Revised Code, as amended by this act, apply to a trial or other proceeding involving a charge of felonious sexual penetration in violation of former section 2907.12 of the Revised Code in which an alleged victim of the offense was a child who was under eleven years of age when the complaint, indictment, or information was filed relative to the trial or other proceeding.

(H) Divisions (B) and (C) of section 2937.11 of the Revised Code, as amended by this act, apply to a case involving an alleged commission of the offense of felonious sexual penetration in violation of former section 2907.12 of the Revised Code.

(I) Notwithstanding section 2967.13 of the Revised Code, as amended by this act, a prisoner serving a term of imprisonment for life for committing the offense of felonious sexual penetration in violation of former section 2907.12 of the Revised Code becomes eligible for parole after serving a term of ten full years' imprisonment.

(J) Notwithstanding section 2967.18 of the Revised Code, as amended by this act, no reduction of sentence pursuant to division (B)(1) of section 2967.18 of the Revised Code shall be given to a person who is serving a term of imprisonment for the commission of felonious sexual penetration in violation of former section 2907.12 of the Revised Code.

Historical and Statutory Notes

Pre–1953 H 1 Amendments: 113 v 188, Ch 23, § 10

Amendment Note: 1997 S 53 added division (A)(1); designated division (A)(2); inserted references to Revised Code sections 2909.05, 2907.21, 2907.24, 2907.31, 2907.32, 2907.321, 2907.322, 2907.323 and 2919.22 in division (B)(1); inserted "or a felony offense of violence and" following "Revised Code" in division (B)(1); substituted "less than thirteen" for "under eleven" in division (B)(1); deleted "2907.06" in division (B)(2); inserted references to Revised Code sections 2909.05 and 2907.24 in division (B)(2); inserted "or an alleged felony offense of violence" before "testifies" in division (B)(2); substituted "2945.481" for "2907.41" in division (B)(2)(b); and made other changes to reflect gender neutral language and other nonsubstantive changes.

Amendment Note: 1996 H 445 removed references to section 2907.12 from the first paragraph in division (B)(1) and from the first paragraph in division (B)(2); and made changes to reflect gender neutral language and other nonsubstantive changes.

Cross References

Deposition, Crim R 15

General assembly may provide for depositions in criminal cases, O Const Art I §10

Library References

Criminal Law ⇐539 to 548.

Witnesses ⇐228.

Westlaw Topic Nos. 110, 410.

C.J.S. Criminal Law §§ 858, 1089 to 1093.

C.J.S. Witnesses §§ 396 to 398, 404 to 405.

Research References

Encyclopedias

OH Jur. 3d Criminal Law § 3043, Admissibility, Generally.

OH Jur. 3d Criminal Law § 3045, Method of Proving Former Testimony.

Treatises and Practice Aids

Giannelli and Snyder, Baldwin's Ohio Practice, Evidence, R 801, Definitions.

Giannelli and Snyder, Baldwin's Ohio Practice, Evidence, R 802, Hearsay Rule.

Giannelli and Snyder, Baldwin's Ohio Practice, Evidence, R 803, Hearsay Exceptions; Availability of Declarant Immaterial.

Giannelli and Snyder, Baldwin's Ohio Practice, Evidence, R 804, Hearsay Exceptions; Declarant Unavailable.

Giannelli and Snyder, Baldwin's Ohio Practice, Evidence, § 802.5, Ohio Statutes.

Giannelli and Snyder, Baldwin's Ohio Practice, Evidence, § 804.7, Unavailability: Death or Illness.

Giannelli and Snyder, Baldwin's Ohio Practice, Evidence, § 804.8, Unavailability: Unable to Procure Testimony.

Giannelli and Snyder, Baldwin's Ohio Practice, Evidence, § 804.9, Former Testimony: in General.

Giannelli and Snyder, Baldwin's Ohio Practice, Evidence, § 804.14, Former Testimony: Method of Proof.

1 Giannelli and Snyder, Baldwin's Ohio Practice, Evidence, Index, Index.

Law Review and Journal Commentaries

Evidence—Constitutional Law—Criminal Procedure—Defendant's Right of Confrontation Is Not Denied by Admission of Evidence of Out-of-Court Declarations of His Co-conspirators—Park v. Huff, Note. 44 U Cin L Rev 622 (1975).

Navigating Between Scylla and Charybdis: Ohio's Efforts to Protect Children Without Eviscerating the Rights of Criminal Defendants–Evidentiary Considerations and the Rebirth of Confrontation Clause Analysis in Child Abuse Cases, Myrna S. Raeder. 25 U Tol L Rev 43 (1994).

Sixth Amendment, Right of Confrontation, Unavailable Witness (State v Roberts), Note. 12 Akron L Rev 572 (Winter 1979).

Notes of Decisions

---

1. Constitutional issues

Where a witness, who testified against the defendant at preliminary hearing and was not cross-examined, is later shown to be unavailable to testify at the trial, US Const Am 6, precludes the state's use of the witness' recorded testimony, notwithstanding RC 2945.49. State v. Roberts (Ohio 1978) 55 Ohio St.2d 191, 378 N.E.2d 492, 9 O.O.3d 143, certiorari granted 99 S.Ct. 1990, 441 U.S. 904, 60 L.Ed.2d 372, reversed 100 S.Ct. 2531, 448 U.S. 56, 65 L.Ed.2d 597, 17 O.O.3d 240. Criminal Law ⚷ 662.60

Evidence of the preliminary hearing testimony of a witness who is unavailable at trial may be introduced if the earlier testimony has sufficient indicia of reliability. Ohio v. Roberts (U.S.Ohio 1980) 100 S.Ct. 2531, 448 U.S. 56, 65 L.Ed.2d 597, 17 O.O.3d 240.

2. Admissibility of prior recorded statement—In general

Prosecutor made good-faith effort to secure presence of out-of-state witness at new trial ordered after remand, even though prosecutor failed to use Uniform Act to Secure the Attendance of Witnesses from Without the State, RC 2939.25 et seq., 2939.29, where out-of-state witness at first appeared very willing to cooperate and then refused to appear to testify four days after start of trial; witness' testimony from prior trial was thus admissible pursuant to exception to the confrontation requirement of the Sixth Amendment. State v. Young (Cuyahoga 1984) 20 Ohio App.3d 269, 485 N.E.2d 814, 20 O.B.R. 332. Criminal Law ⚷ 662.60

Under Evid R 804(A)(5), prior testimony of a witness may be utilized where the witness is unavailable if it is demonstrated that the witness is not at the trial, and the party offering the statement has been unable to procure attendance of that witness by process or other reasonable means. State v. Bragg (Franklin 1981) 2 Ohio App.3d 193, 441 N.E.2d 272, 2 O.B.R. 211. Criminal Law ⚷ 543(1)

RC 2945.49 permits the admissibility at trial of prior recorded testimony taken at a preliminary hearing upon a showing that, despite a good faith effort to secure the witness' presence at trial, the witness was unavailable, and that the witness' prior recorded testimony bears an "adequate indicia of reliability." State v. Madison (Ohio 1980) 64 Ohio St.2d 322, 415 N.E.2d 272, 18 O.O.3d 491.

In order to use the testimony of a complaining witness at a preliminary hearing at the trial of the matter, the state must prove the witness was unavailable and could not be produced at trial by diligent effort. State v. Smith (Ohio 1979) 58 Ohio St.2d 344, 390 N.E.2d 778, 12 O.O.3d 313, vacated 100 S.Ct. 3041, 448 U.S. 902, 65 L.Ed.2d 1132.

Where witness for state in homicide case, whose testimony at preliminary hearing state desired to read under GC 13444–10, had merely gone out of state on two weeks vacation, several days of which had elapsed at time of trial, and there was every reason to believe witness would desire to be present as witness for state and he knew nothing as to date of trial when he went on vacation, and there was no suggestion of absence by collusion, state presented merely an "excuse" and not a "reason" for presenting such previous testimony, and since a week's postponement would probably have enabled state to produce him at the trial, it was prejudicial error to admit his testimony taken at the former hearing over defendant's objection. Mitchell v. State (Butler 1931) 40 Ohio App. 367, 178 N.E. 325, 10 Ohio Law Abs. 262, 35 Ohio Law Rep. 96. Criminal Law ⚿ 543(1)

3. —— Child victims, admissibility of prior recorded statement

Psychologist who testified that child victims of sexual abuse would suffer serious emotional distress if they were to testify in presence of defendant and that they should be permitted to testify by closed circuit television gave facts and data underlying his opinion, where he testified that he administered a variety of assessment measures to children, that he and his assistant met with each child three times, he described visits, and he explained his experience in working with sexually abused children. State v. Sibert (Ohio App. 4 Dist., 11-04-1994) 98 Ohio App.3d 412, 648 N.E.2d 861, motion for delayed appeal denied 71 Ohio St.3d 1479, 645 N.E.2d 1258, denial of post-conviction relief affirmed 74 Ohio St.3d 342, 658 N.E.2d 772, 1996-Ohio-15. Criminal Law ⚿ 486(5)

Testimony of child psychologist that he recommended allowing victims to testify by closed circuit television because forcing them to testify in defendant's presence would cause serious emotional trauma was properly admitted, though testimony was not relevant to any issue at trial, where defense counsel elicited from psychologist on cross-examination that he had written letter to prosecution following only one examination of children, giving prosecution the right to attempt to rehabilitate psychologist by allowing him to explain purpose of earlier letter. State v. Sibert (Ohio App. 4 Dist., 11-04-1994) 98 Ohio App.3d 412, 648 N.E.2d 861, motion for delayed appeal denied 71 Ohio St.3d 1479, 645 N.E.2d 1258, denial of post-conviction relief affirmed 74 Ohio St.3d 342, 658 N.E.2d 772, 1996-Ohio-15. Criminal Law ⚿ 490

4. Opportunity to cross-examine; impeachment

When, in an adjudicatory hearing held pursuant to Juv R 29, the only evidence of guilt utilized by the court is testimony presented at the preliminary hearing, where the accused exercised adequate rights of cross-examination, he is denied no constitutional right. Matter of Gantt (Wood 1978) 61 Ohio App.2d 44, 398 N.E.2d 800, 15 O.O.3d 67.

Where a witness testifies unfavorably against an accused at a preliminary hearing and such testimony is allowed at trial because of the absence of the witness, the defendant is entitled to introduce, for impeachment purposes, written evidence originating after the preliminary hearing which refutes the testimony. Crim R 15(F) is complementary to RC 2945.49, does not conflict, and was not intended to disturb the rules on prior testimony. State v. Earley (Guernsey 1975) 49 Ohio App.2d 377, 361 N.E.2d 254, 3 O.O.3d 447. Constitutional Law ⚿ 268(10)

RC 2945.49 does not require the state to show why a witness is absent, and the fact that his whereabouts are unknown is sufficient to allow the introduction of his deposition into evidence, if the accused was present at the time of its taking. State v. Gaines (Hamilton 1974) 40 Ohio App.2d 224, 318 N.E.2d 857, 69 O.O.2d 210.

It is not error, in the trial of a criminal case, to transfer the court and jury and the parties to the home of a witness for the state, who is too ill to attend court, where, during the proceedings in such witness's home, the defendant is within a few feet of the witness who is cross-examined in depth, and in detail, and where the trial judge is in the presence of the witness, the attorneys involved, and the court reporter. State v. Lamonge (Trumbull 1962) 117 Ohio App. 143, 191 N.E.2d 207, 23 O.O.2d 314, appeal dismissed 174 Ohio St. 545, 190 N.E.2d 691, 23 O.O.2d 210, certiorari denied 84 S.Ct. 346, 375 U.S. 942, 11 L.Ed.2d 272.

2945.491 Testimony of mentally retarded or developmentally disabled victim; videotaped testimony

(A) As used in this section:

(1) "Mentally retarded person" and "developmentally disabled person" have the same meanings as in section 5123.01 of the Revised Code.

(2) "Mentally retarded or developmentally disabled victim" includes a mentally retarded or developmentally disabled person who was a victim of a felony violation identified in division (B)(1) of this section or a felony offense of violence or against whom was directed any conduct that constitutes, or that is an element of, a felony violation identified in division (B)(1) of this section or a felony offense of violence.

(B)(1) At a trial on a charge of a felony violation of section 2903.16, 2903.34, 2903.341, 2907.02, 2907.03, 2907.05, 2907.21, 2907.23, 2907.24, 2907.32, 2907.321, 2907.322, or 2907.323 of the Revised Code or an offense of violence and in which an alleged victim of the violation or offense was a mentally retarded or developmentally disabled person, the court, upon motion of the prosecutor in the case, may admit videotaped preliminary hearing testimony of the mentally retarded or developmentally disabled victim as evidence at the trial, in lieu of the mentally retarded or developmentally disabled victim appearing as a witness and testifying at trial, if all of the following apply:

(a) The videotape of the testimony was made at the preliminary hearing at which probable cause of the violation charged was found.

(b) The videotape of the testimony was made in accordance with division (C) of section 2937.11 of the Revised Code.

(c) The testimony in the videotape is not excluded by the hearsay rule and otherwise is admissible under the Rules of Evidence. For purposes of this division, testimony is not excluded by the hearsay rule if the testimony is not hearsay under Evidence Rule 801, the testimony is within an exception to the hearsay rule set forth in Evidence Rule 803, the mentally retarded or developmentally disabled victim who gave the testimony is unavailable as a witness, as defined in Evidence Rule 804, and the testimony is admissible under that rule, or both of the following apply:

(i) The accused had an opportunity and similar motive at the preliminary hearing to develop the testimony of the mentally retarded or developmentally disabled victim by direct, cross, or redirect examination.

(ii) The court determines that there is reasonable cause to believe that if the mentally retarded or developmentally disabled victim who gave the testimony at the preliminary hearing were to testify in person at the trial, the mentally retarded or developmentally disabled victim would experience serious emotional trauma as a result of the victim's participation at the trial.

(2) If a mentally retarded or developmentally disabled victim of an alleged felony violation of section 2903.16, 2903.34, 2903.341, 2907.02, 2907.03, 2907.05, 2907.21, 2907.23, 2907.24, 2907.32, 2907.321, 2907.322, or 2907.323 of the Revised Code or an alleged felony offense of violence testifies at the preliminary hearing in the case, if the testimony of the mentally retarded or developmentally disabled victim at the preliminary hearing was videotaped pursuant to division (C) of section 2937.11 of the Revised Code, and if the defendant in the case files a written objection to the use, pursuant to division (B)(1) of this section, of the videotaped testimony at the trial, the court, immediately after the filing of the objection, shall hold a hearing to determine whether the videotaped testimony of the mentally retarded or developmentally disabled victim should be admissible at trial under division (B)(1) of this section and, if it is admissible, whether the mentally retarded or developmentally disabled victim should be required to provide limited additional testimony of the type described in this division. At the hearing held pursuant to this division, the defendant and the prosecutor in the case may present any evidence that is relevant to the issues to be determined at the hearing, but the mentally retarded or developmentally disabled victim shall not be required to testify at the hearing.

After the hearing, the court shall not require the mentally retarded or developmentally disabled victim to testify at the trial, unless it determines that both of the following apply:

(a) That the testimony of the mentally retarded or developmentally disabled victim at trial is necessary for one or more of the following reasons:

(i) Evidence that was not available at the time of the testimony of the mentally retarded or developmentally disabled victim at the preliminary hearing has been discovered.

(ii) The circumstances surrounding the case have changed sufficiently to necessitate that the mentally retarded or developmentally disabled victim testify at the trial.

(b) That the testimony of the mentally retarded or developmentally disabled victim at the trial is necessary to protect the right of the defendant to a fair trial.

The court shall enter its finding and the reasons for it in the journal. If the court requires the mentally retarded or developmentally disabled victim to testify at the trial, the testimony of the victim shall be limited to the new evidence and changed circumstances, and the mentally retarded or developmentally disabled victim shall not otherwise be required to testify at the trial. The required testimony of the mentally retarded or developmentally disabled victim may be given in person or, upon motion of the prosecution, may be taken by deposition in accordance with division (B) of section 2945.482 of the Revised Code provided the deposition is admitted as evidence under division (C) of that section, may be taken outside of the courtroom and televised into the courtroom in accordance with division (D) of that section, or may be taken outside of the courtroom and recorded for showing in the courtroom in accordance with division (E) of that section.

(3) If videotaped testimony of a mentally retarded or developmentally disabled victim is admitted at trial in accordance with division (B)(1) of this section, the mentally retarded or developmentally disabled victim shall not be compelled in any way to appear as a witness at the trial, except as provided in division (B)(2) of this section.

(C) An order issued pursuant to division (B) of this section shall specifically identify the mentally retarded or developmentally disabled victim concerning whose testimony it pertains. The order shall apply only during the testimony of the mentally retarded or developmentally disabled victim it specifically identifies.

(2004 S 178, eff. 1–30–04)

Library References

Criminal Law ⚷539 to 548.
Witnesses ⚷228.
Westlaw Topic Nos. 110, 410.
C.J.S. Criminal Law §§ 858, 1089 to 1093.
C.J.S. Witnesses §§ 396 to 398, 404 to 405.

Research References

Encyclopedias

OH Jur. 3d Criminal Law § 2525, Particular Uses of Depositions.

Treatises and Practice Aids

1 Giannelli and Snyder, Baldwin's Ohio Practice, Evidence, Index, Index.

2945.50 Deposition in criminal cases

At any time after an issue of fact is joined upon an indictment, information, or an affidavit, the prosecution or the defendant may apply in writing to the court in which such indictment, information, or affidavit is pending for a commission to take the depositions of any witness. The court or a judge thereof may grant such commission and make an order stating in what manner and for what length of time notice shall be given to the prosecution or to the defendant, before such witness shall be examined.

(131 v H 153, eff. 10–13–65; 1953 H 1; GC 13444–11)

Historical and Statutory Notes

Pre–1953 H 1 Amendments: 113 v 188, Ch 23, § 11

Cross References

Deposition, Crim R 15
Deposition in civil cases, Civ R 26 to 32
Depositions, Juv R 25
General assembly may provide for depositions in criminal cases, O Const Art I §10
Military court, depositions in, 5924.49

Library References

Criminal Law ⚷627.2.
Westlaw Topic No. 110.
C.J.S. Criminal Law § 468.

Research References

Encyclopedias

OH Jur. 3d Criminal Law § 101, Appointment of Cocounsel or Counsel at Deposition.

OH Jur. 3d Criminal Law § 2514, Motion to Permit the Taking of a Deposition.

Treatises and Practice Aids

Katz, Giannelli, Blair and Lipton, Baldwin's Ohio Practice, Criminal Law, § 53:1, Introduction.

Katz, Giannelli, Blair and Lipton, Baldwin's Ohio Practice, Criminal Law, § 53:3, Deposition Order.

Katz, Giannelli, Blair and Lipton, Baldwin's Ohio Practice, Criminal Law, § 49:13, Witnesses—Protecting Identity.

Katz, Giannelli, Blair and Lipton, Baldwin's Ohio Practice, Criminal Law, § 145:12, Motion for Deposition.

Giannelli and Snyder, Baldwin's Ohio Practice, Evidence, R 804, Hearsay Exceptions; Declarant Unavailable.

Giannelli and Snyder, Baldwin's Ohio Practice, Evidence, § 804.10, Former Testimony: Type of Proceeding.

Notes of Decisions

---

1. Constitutional issues

RC 2945.50 is constitutional. State ex rel. Jackman v. Court of Common Pleas of Cuyahoga County (Ohio 1967) 9 Ohio St.2d 159, 224 N.E.2d 906, 38 O.O.2d 404.

RC 2945.50, authorizing the taking of testimony by deposition of specified witnesses in a criminal case, which provides that the granting or withholding of such right is at the discretion of the court, without setting out guidelines for the exercise of such discretion, is unenforceable and unconstitutional. State ex rel. Jackman v. Court of Common Pleas of Cuyahoga County (Cuyahoga 1966) 6 Ohio App.2d 182, 217 N.E.2d 251, 35 O.O.2d 346, reversed 9 Ohio St.2d 159, 224 N.E.2d 906, 38 O.O.2d 404.

2. Discretion of court—In general

Trial court's decision to deny defendant's request to depose child victims was not an abuse of discretion in prosecution for gross sexual imposition and rape, despite defendant's claim that absent more definite times for the alleged offenses, he was unable to develop alibi evidence supporting his innocence; in hindsight, given the victims' trial testimony, it did not appear that such questioning would have resulted in the information defendant sought, and even without hindsight, it was clear that at the time defendant requested authority to depose the victims, the exercise presented a substantial potential for abuse. State v. Adams (Ohio App. 6 Dist., Erie, 09-03-2004) No. E-03-042, 2004-Ohio-4673, 2004 WL 1949422, Unreported. Criminal Law ⚷ 627.2

A court is not required to grant a commission to take depositions under RC 2945.50, but may exercise its discretion in this area. State v. Conley (Marion 1971) 32 Ohio App.2d 54, 288 N.E.2d 296, 61 O.O.2d 50. Criminal Law ⚷ 627.2

The allowance or overruling under RC 2945.50 of a motion to appoint a commissioner to take pretrial depositions in a criminal case rests within the sound discretion of the court, and, unless a plain abuse of that discretion is shown, no prejudicial error occurs. State v. Hill (Ohio 1967) 12 Ohio St.2d 88, 232 N.E.2d 394, 41 O.O.2d 369. Criminal Law ⚷ 1148; Criminal Law ⚷ 627.2

In a criminal case, the refusal of a trial court to allow defendant to take the deposition of a witness is not an abuse of discretion, where the court had done all it could to make the witness available at the trial and the request to take the deposition was made after the case had been concluded and at the conclusion of defendant's argument on a motion for a new trial. State v. Blanton (Lawrence 1960) 111 Ohio App. 111, 170 N.E.2d 754, 14 O.O.2d 13.

The granting, under statute, of a commission to take the deposition of one confined in jail, rests in the trial court's sound discretion. State v. Anthoulis (Mahoning 1939) 62 Ohio App. 113, 23 N.E.2d 312, 29 Ohio Law Abs. 615, 15 O.O. 349, appeal dismissed 135 Ohio St. 631, 22 N.E.2d 84, 15 O.O. 283. Pretrial Procedure ⚷ 92

The standards of discretionary review by the Supreme Court of Ohio of nonconstitutional matters on direct appeal in a criminal case are not a violation of constitutional due process where such limited discretionary review may deprive a convicted offender of the possible benefits of a favorable decision rendered after the accused has lost his direct appeal as a matter of right to the court of appeals. Klein v. Cardwell (C.A.6 (Ohio) 1971) 448 F.2d 407, 63 O.O.2d 416.

3. —— Representation of defendant, discretion of court

In granting a commission for the taking of the deposition in a criminal case of a material witness for an indigent defendant, which witness is in the military service outside the United States and not amenable to the ordinary subpoena procedures, a trial court may assign different counsel to represent defendant before the deposition commissioner than assigned to represent him at the ultimate trial of the case and provide reasonable compensation and expenses for such counsel. State v. Stark (Hamilton 1966) 9 Ohio App.2d 42, 222 N.E.2d 794, 37 O.O.2d 370, 38 O.O.2d 46. Criminal Law ⚷ 627.2

4. Appeals

The denial of a defendant's application in a criminal case to take the deposition of a witness is a final order, where such witness is material and is in the military service outside the United States and not amenable to the ordinary subpoena procedures. State v. Stark (Hamilton 1966) 9 Ohio App.2d 42, 222 N.E.2d 794, 37 O.O.2d 370, 38 O.O.2d 46. Criminal Law ⚷ 627.2

2945.51 When deposition may be taken; expenses

When a deposition is to be taken in this state, and a commission is granted under section 2945.50 of the Revised Code while the defendant is confined in jail, the sheriff or deputy or other person having custody of the defendant shall be ordered by the court to take the defendant to the place of the taking of the deposition, and have him before the officer at the time of taking such deposition. Such sheriff or deputy or other person having custody of the defendant shall be reimbursed for actual reasonable traveling expenses for himself and the defendant, the bills for the same, upon the approval of the board of county commissioners, to be paid from the county treasury on the warrant of the county auditor. Such sheriff shall receive as fees therefor, one dollar for each day in attendance thereat. Such fees and traveling expenses shall be taxed and collected as other fees and costs in the case.

(131 v H 153, eff. 10–13–65; 1953 H 1; GC 13444–12)

Historical and Statutory Notes

Pre–1953 H 1 Amendments: 113 v 188, Ch 23, § 12

Cross References

Deposition, Crim R 15

General assembly may provide for depositions in criminal cases, O Const Art I §10

Library References

Criminal Law ⚡627.2.

Westlaw Topic No. 110.

C.J.S. Criminal Law § 468.

Research References

Encyclopedias

OH Jur. 3d Criminal Law § 3968, Items and Amounts Taxable, Generally.

OH Jur. 3d Police, Sheriffs, & Related Officers § 47, Other Sheriff's Fees.

Treatises and Practice Aids

Giannelli and Snyder, Baldwin's Ohio Practice, Evidence, § 804.10, Former Testimony: Type of Proceeding.

2945.52 Counsel appointed shall represent the defendant

Counsel assigned by the court to represent the defendant may attend upon and represent the defendant at the taking of a deposition under section 2945.50 of the Revised Code, and said counsel shall be paid a reasonable fee for his services in taking such deposition, in addition to the compensation allowed for defending such defendant, to be fixed by the court. He shall also be allowed his actual expenses incurred in going to and from the place of taking the deposition.

(1953 H 1, eff. 10–1–53; GC 13444–13)

Historical and Statutory Notes

Pre–1953 H 1 Amendments: 113 v 189, Ch 23, § 13

Cross References

Deposition, Crim R 15

General assembly may provide for depositions in criminal cases; right to counsel, O Const Art I §10

Library References

Criminal Law ⚡641.3(4).

Westlaw Topic No. 110.

C.J.S. Criminal Law §§ 277, 282 to 283, 289, 293.

Research References

Encyclopedias

OH Jur. 3d Criminal Law § 2521, Right to Counsel at Deposition.

Notes of Decisions

Different counsel 1

1. Different counsel

In granting a commission for the taking of the deposition in a criminal case of a material witness for an indigent defendant, which witness is in the military service outside the United States and not amenable to the ordinary subpoena procedures, a trial court may assign different counsel to represent defendant before the deposition commissioner than assigned to represent him at the ultimate trial of the case and provide reasonable compensation and expenses for such counsel. State v. Stark (Hamilton 1966) 9 Ohio App.2d 42, 222 N.E.2d 794, 37 O.O.2d 370, 38 O.O.2d 46. Criminal Law ⚷ 627.2

2945.53 Right of accused to examine witness

In all cases in which depositions are taken by the state or the accused, to be used by or against the accused, as provided in sections 2945.50 to 2945.52, inclusive, of the Revised Code, the court shall by proper order provide and secure to the accused the means and opportunity to be present in person and with counsel at the taking of such deposition, and to examine the witness face to face, as fully and in the same manner as if in court. All expenses necessarily incurred in the securing of such means and opportunity, and the expenses of the prosecuting attorney in attending the taking of such deposition, shall be paid out of the county treasury upon the certificate of the court making such order.

(1953 H 1, eff. 10–1–53; GC 13444–14)

Historical and Statutory Notes

Pre–1953 H 1 Amendments: 113 v 189, Ch 23, § 14

Cross References

Deposition, Crim R 15

General assembly may provide for depositions in criminal cases, O Const Art I §10

Library References

Criminal Law ⚷627.2.

Westlaw Topic No. 110.

C.J.S. Criminal Law § 468.

Research References

Encyclopedias

OH Jur. 3d Cvl. Servants & Pub. Officers & Employ. § 464, Expense Allowance—Particular Expenses.

2945.54 Conduct of examination

The examination of witnesses by deposition in criminal cases shall be taken and certified, and the return thereof to the court made as for taking depositions under sections 2319.05 to 2319.31, inclusive, of the Revised Code. The commissioners appointed under section 2945.50 of the Revised Code to take depositions shall receive such compensation as the court directs, to be paid out of the county treasury and taxed as part of the costs in the case.

(1953 H 1, eff. 10–1–53; GC 13444–15)

Historical and Statutory Notes

Pre–1953 H 1 Amendments: 113 v 189, Ch 23, § 15

Cross References

Deposition, Crim R 15

General assembly may provide for depositions in criminal cases, O Const Art I §10

Library References

Criminal Law ⚷627.2.

Westlaw Topic No. 110.

C.J.S. Criminal Law § 468.

Research References

Treatises and Practice Aids

Katz, Giannelli, Blair and Lipton, Baldwin's Ohio Practice, Criminal Law, § 53:1, Introduction.

Katz, Giannelli, Blair and Lipton, Baldwin's Ohio Practice, Criminal Law, § 145:19, Heading of Deposition.

Katz, Giannelli, Blair and Lipton, Baldwin's Ohio Practice, Criminal Law, § 145:20, Certificate of Officer to Deposition.

2945.55 Testimony of previous identification

When identification of the defendant is an issue, a witness who has on previous occasion identified such person may testify to such previous identification. Such identification may be proved by other witnesses.

(1953 H 1, eff. 10–1–53; GC 13444–16)

Historical and Statutory Notes

Pre–1953 H 1 Amendments: 113 v 189, Ch 23, § 16

Library References

Criminal Law ⚷339, 421(6).

Westlaw Topic No. 110.

C.J.S. Criminal Law §§ 799, 858, 861.

Research References

ALR Library

23 ALR 5th 672, Admissibility in Evidence of Composite Picture or Sketch Produced by Police to Identify Offender.

Encyclopedias

OH Jur. 3d Criminal Law § 2941, Generally; Testimony by Eyewitness or Others.

Treatises and Practice Aids

Markus, Trial Handbook for Ohio Lawyers, § 29:40, Identification of Accused—Drawing, Photograph, or Voiceprint Identifying Accused at Trial.

Katz, Giannelli, Blair and Lipton, Baldwin's Ohio Practice, Criminal Law, § 28:6, Hearsay.

Katz, Giannelli, Blair and Lipton, Baldwin's Ohio Practice, Criminal Law, § 137:3, Motion to Suppress—Suggestive Pretrial Identification.

Giannelli and Snyder, Baldwin's Ohio Practice, Evidence, R 801, Definitions.

Giannelli and Snyder, Baldwin's Ohio Practice, Evidence, § 801.16, Statements of Identification: Related Issues.

1 Giannelli and Snyder, Baldwin's Ohio Practice, Evidence, Index, Index.

Katz, Ohio Arrest, Search & Seizure § 25:2, Hearsay.

Law Review and Journal Commentaries

Criminal Procedure: Admissibility of In-court Identifications, Unnecessarily Suggestive Out-of-court Identifications, Due Process, Note. 11 Akron L Rev 763 (Spring 1978).

Impeaching Credibility Through Evidence of Prior Convictions: Federal Rule of Evidence 609(a), Comment. 3 U Dayton L Rev 459 (Summer 1978).

Proof of Authentication Under the New Ohio Rules of Evidence, Randolph C. Wiseman. 6 Cap U L Rev 625 (1977).

Notes of Decisions

1. Constitutional issues—Due process

Trial court committed reversible error during hearing on defendant's motion to suppress pretrial and in-court identifications of him by denying his request to present testimony from witnesses to whom photo array had been shown; trial court's actions denied defendant a full and fair hearing regarding the photo array and identification procedures used by police. State v. Glover (Ohio App. 8 Dist., Cuyahoga, 04-28-2005) No. 84413, 2005-Ohio-1984, 2005 WL 991904, Unreported. Criminal Law ⚷ 339.11(4); Criminal Law ⚷ 1169.1(5)

Officer's in-court identification of defendant was credible and reliable, and thus admission of such identification was not unconstitutional; although defendant claimed a mix-up between him and the driver of another car in which police discovered cocaine following traffic accident, defendant did not give notice of an alibi defense and did not dispute that he was transported to the hospital from scene of accident, only one car was discovered at accident scene, and there was no evidence that anyone other than defendant was involved in the accident. State v. Taylor (Ohio App. 8 Dist., Cuyahoga, 08-26-2004) No. 83551, 2004-Ohio-4468, 2004 WL 1900333, Unreported, appeal not allowed 105 Ohio St.3d 1406, 821 N.E.2d 1027, 2005-Ohio-279. Criminal Law ⚷ 339.9(1)

Photographic array presented to eyewitnesses was not unduly suggestive in violation of due process, and thus witnesses' identification of defendant from array was not subject to suppression; six photographs in array all depicted similar black males roughly the same age with short hair, normal complexions, and facial hair. State v. Perry (Ohio App. 11 Dist., Trumbull, 12-31-2003) No. 2002-T-0035, 2003-Ohio-7204, 2003 WL 23096545, Unreported, appeal not allowed 102 Ohio St.3d 1422, 807 N.E.2d 367, 2004-Ohio-2003, dismissal of post-conviction relief affirmed 2004-Ohio-3334, 2004 WL 1433644, appeal after new sentencing hearing 2005-Ohio-4653, 2005 WL 2133706, appeal allowed 108 Ohio St.3d 1435, 842 N.E.2d 61, 2006-Ohio-421. Constitutional Law ⚷ 266(3.1); Criminal Law ⚷ 339.7(4)

Though suggestive, one-man "show-up" procedure by which robbery victim identified defendant was reliable and thus comported with due process; victim had ample opportunity to view suspect on night in question, scuffle that ensued between victim and the two perpetrators caused him to focus his attention on them as well as the knife wielded by one of them, victim indicated he had no question about defendant's identity as one of the perpetrators and noted defendant's facial injuries and bent glasses from the altercation, and identification occurred within 24 hours of the incident. State v. Elliott (Ohio App. 7 Dist., Columbiana, 03-21-2003) No. 01 CO 24, 2003-Ohio-1426, 2003 WL 1463903, Unreported, stay denied 99 Ohio St.3d 1433, 789 N.E.2d 1115, 2003-Ohio-2902, appeal not allowed 99 Ohio St.3d 1469, 791 N.E.2d 984, 2003-Ohio-3669. Constitutional Law ⚷ 266(3.2); Criminal Law ⚷ 339.8(6)

When a witness has been confronted with a suspect before trial, due process requires a court to suppress the witness's identification of the suspect if the confrontation was unnecessarily suggestive of the suspect's guilt and the identification was unreliable under all the circumstances. State v. Duncan (Ohio App. 1 Dist., 09-05-2003) 154 Ohio App.3d 254, 796 N.E.2d 1006, 2003-Ohio-4695, appeal not allowed 100 Ohio St.3d 1532, 800 N.E.2d 48, 2003-Ohio-6458. Constitutional Law ⚷ 266(3.2)

There is no due process violation in an identification that is the result of observations at the time of the crime, even where a pretrial identification procedure is improperly conducted. State v. Norman (Ohio App. 1 Dist., 12-03-1999) 137 Ohio App.3d 184, 738 N.E.2d 403. Constitutional Law ⚷ 266(3.2)

Witnesses' in-court identifications of robbery defendant and their testimony that they had identified him at pretrial lineup were admissible at trial, where defendant's Sixth Amendment right to counsel had not attached at time of lineup. State v. Norman (Ohio App. 1 Dist., 12-03-1999) 137 Ohio App.3d 184, 738 N.E.2d 403. Criminal Law ⚷ 339.8(7); Criminal Law ⚷ 641.3(10)

State appellate court did not unreasonably apply due process analysis in rejecting murder defendant's challenge to admissibility of witness' out-of-court identification, foreclosing federal habeas relief; even though identification was made more than 20 years after offense, only one of two photographs shown to witness depicted man with hairstyle matching witness' description of offender, and witness was allowed to watch first day of trial, witness had opportunity to observe offender for approximately three hours prior to offense, under relaxed conditions, and was certain that his identification was correct. Wilson v. Mitchell (C.A.6 (Ohio), 05-14-2001) 250 F.3d 388, rehearing en banc denied. Habeas Corpus ⚷ 490(2)

2. —— Effective assistance of counsel, constitutional issues

Defense counsel did not render ineffective assistance in robbery prosecution by failing to move to suppress victims' pretrial identifications of defendant, even though defendant argued that identifications were unreliable; defendant did not argue that photographic lineup was unduly suggestive, nothing suggested that photographic lineup was unduly suggestive, in that photographs were of young black males with roughly same build, clothing, and haircuts, and victims positively identified defendant at trial. State v. Harris (Ohio App. 2 Dist., Montgomery, 06-30-2004) No. CIV.A. 19796, 2004-Ohio-3570, 2004 WL 1506227, Unreported, appeal not allowed 110 Ohio St.3d 1443, 852 N.E.2d 190, 2006-Ohio-3862. Criminal Law ⚷ 641.13(6)

Assuming trial counsel's failure to challenge pretrial identification of defendant as perpetrator constituted deficient performance, defendant failed to show prejudice, as required to establish ineffective assistance, where defendant failed to establish that there existed reasonable probability that, but for this error, result of trial would have been different. State v. Marbury (Ohio App. 10 Dist., Franklin, 06-29-2004) No. 03AP-233, 2004-Ohio-3373, 2004 WL 1445224, Unreported, appeal not allowed 103 Ohio St.3d 1493, 816 N.E.2d 1080, 2004-Ohio-5605. Criminal Law ⚷ 641.13(6)

Defense counsel was not ineffective in electing not to object to sentencing court's statement that defendant had shown no genuine remorse, where defendant maintained his innocence throughout the proceedings. State v. White (Ohio App. 8 Dist., Cuyahoga, 05-27-2004) No. 83562, 2004-Ohio-2702, 2004 WL 1172085, Unreported, appeal not allowed 103 Ohio St.3d 1493, 816 N.E.2d 1080, 2004-Ohio-5605. Criminal Law ⚷ 641.13(7)

Defense counsel was not ineffective in advising felonious assault defendant to waive presentence investigation report (PSI); record indicated that defendant had prior felony convictions and a juvenile record, and thus waiving PSI represented a strategic tactic. State v. White (Ohio App. 8 Dist., Cuyahoga, 05-27-2004) No. 83562, 2004-Ohio-2702, 2004 WL 1172085, Unreported, appeal not allowed 103 Ohio St.3d 1493, 816 N.E.2d 1080, 2004-Ohio-5605. Criminal Law ⚷ 641.13(7)

3. Identification procedure generally

Admission of evidence of victim's identification of defendant as one perpetrator of kidnapping and aggravated robbery was not plain error, where victim gave clear description of clothing worn by perpetrators and direction in which they fled, defendant and three other individuals were found in that direction, wearing the described clothing, victim pointed out each individual and described his role during "cold stand," and victim was wearing his glasses on night in question. State v. Vinson (Ohio App. 8 Dist., Cuyahoga, 07-21-2005) No. 85321, 2005-Ohio-3714, 2005 WL 1707002, Unreported. Criminal Law ⚷ 1036.2

Victim's identification of defendant as her attacker after defendant was apprehended by police was reliable and admissible at trial; victim observed defendant as he followed her and then again during attack, victim's description of defendant's appearance and clothing matched defendant's characteristics and clothing when he was apprehended a short time after attack, victim stated that she was "positively sure" of her identification of defendant, and victim identified defendant approximately ten to fifteen minutes after officers responded to the scene. State v. Breeden (Ohio App. 8 Dist., Cuyahoga, 02-10-2005) No. 84663, 2005-Ohio-510, 2005 WL 315370, Unreported. Criminal Law ⚷ 339.8(6)

Juvenile, who was adjudicated a delinquent child, waived for appellate review claim that his conviction for breaking and entering was against the manifest weight of the evidence and not supported by sufficient evidence, where juvenile failed to file objections to the magistrate's decision adjudicating him a delinquent child. In re Carter (Ohio App. 4 Dist., Jackson, 12-30-2004) No. 04CA15, No. 04CA16, 2004-Ohio-7285, 2004 WL 3090250, Unreported. Infants ⚷ 243

Victim's pretrial identifications of defendant and codefendants as perpetrators of aggravated burglary were reliable; although identifications were made several months after crime occurred, victim had good look at codefendant when he was standing inside victim's laundry room with gun, victim saw codefendant again when he was running down driveway, victim saw second codefendant open door of van so that codefendant could get in, victim had good look at defendant when he pointed gun at her, descriptions of defendant and codefendants given by victim were similar to appearances of defendant and codefendants, and victim was certain of her identifications. State v. West (Ohio App. 8 Dist., Cuyahoga, 09-30-2004) No. 83779, 2004-Ohio-5212, 2004 WL 2340180, Unreported, motion for delayed appeal denied 105 Ohio St.3d 1437, 822 N.E.2d 809, 2005-Ohio-531, motion for delayed appeal denied 106 Ohio St.3d 1480, 832 N.E.2d 734, 2005-Ohio-3978. Criminal Law ⚷ 339.10(11)

Identification process was no more suggestive that typical photographic lineup, and thus, trial court properly declined to suppress first witness's identification testimony in murder prosecution, where police officer's testimony offered no evidence that she purposely left case folder on table when she left room to entice witnesses to view photographs and first witness testified that she joined second witness in squad room after being individually interviewed at police station, that she spotted "lineup pictures" on table nearby after police officer left room, that witnesses were "nosy" and looked through photographs, and that she identified defendant as person she observed on night of shooting. State v. Nix (Ohio App. 1 Dist., Hamilton, 10-15-2004) No. C-030696, 2004-Ohio-5502, 2004 WL 2315035, Unreported, motion for delayed appeal denied 105 Ohio St.3d 1496, 825 N.E.2d 621, 2005-Ohio-1666. Criminal Law ⚷ 339.10(2)

Victim's out-of-court identification of defendant in "cold stand," or one-on-one show up, was reliable, and thus was admissible in prosecution for aggravated robbery, kidnapping, and having weapon while under disability; victim had sufficient opportunity to view attacker at time of crime, victim's attention was not diverted, his description of man who robbed him was consistent with appearance of defendant at cold stand, victim was certain defendant and his assailant were one and same person, and victim's identification arose from his unaided earlier identification that helped police find defendant. State v. Dowdell (Ohio App. 8 Dist., Cuyahoga, 10-14-2004) No. 83829, 2004-Ohio-5487, 2004 WL 2306678, Unreported, appeal not allowed 105 Ohio St.3d 1441, 822 N.E.2d 812, 2005-Ohio-531. Criminal Law ⚷ 339.8(5)

Admitting evidence of pretrial identification did not constitute plain error in assault prosecution; given overwhelming evidence of guilt, including positive in-court identification of defendant, outcome of trial would not have been different but for admission of evidence of pretrial identification. State v. Scott (Ohio App. 5 Dist., Richland, 09-24-2004) No. 03 CA 119, 2004-Ohio-5292, 2004 WL 2260702, Unreported. Criminal Law ⚷ 1036.1(7)

Victim's "cold stand" identification of defendant as perpetrator, which was conducted approximately one hour after robbery, was reliable, where victim had sufficient opportunity to view perpetrator at time of robbery, victim's attention was not diverted, victim's description of perpetrator was consistent with defendant's appearance during such show-up identification procedure, and victim was certain that defendant was perpetrator. State v. Lowe (Ohio App. 8 Dist., Cuyahoga, 09-02-2004) No. 82997, 2004-Ohio-4622, 2004 WL 1944785, Unreported, appeal not allowed 104 Ohio St.3d 1461, 821 N.E.2d 578, 2005-Ohio-204, motion to reopen denied 2005-Ohio-5986, 2005 WL 3007146. Criminal Law ⚷ 339.8(6)

State was not required to inform defendant before trial that officer on witness list would make in-court identification of defendant, where defendant did not request notification of identification witnesses, and defendant was aware that police officers observed him at the scene. State v. Taylor (Ohio App. 8 Dist., Cuyahoga, 08-26-2004) No. 83551, 2004-Ohio-4468, 2004 WL 1900333, Unreported, appeal not allowed 105 Ohio St.3d 1406, 821 N.E.2d 1027, 2005-Ohio-279. Criminal Law ⚷ 629(10)

Alleged victim's in-court identification of defendant was admissible, even if photo array shown to alleged victim prior to trial was unnecessarily suggestive; alleged victim had known defendant for some time and interacted with him on a daily basis, and thus alleged victim had an independent basis for identifying defendant. State v. White (Ohio App. 8 Dist., Cuyahoga, 05-27-2004) No. 83562, 2004-Ohio-2702, 2004 WL 1172085, Unreported, appeal not allowed 103 Ohio St.3d 1493, 816 N.E.2d 1080, 2004-Ohio-5605. Criminal Law ⚷ 339.10(7)

Although procedures used resulting in a show-up identification were inherently suggestive, two eyewitness identifications of defendant were not so unreliable as to give rise to a substantial likelihood of misidentification; both witnesses viewed the defendant at a very short distance, both witnesses were involved in circumstances which presumably demanded their full attention, both witnesses were certain of their identification of defendant, and the time between the crime and the confrontation was two hours or less. U.S. v. Goist (C.A.6 (Ohio), 03-07-2003) No. 01-4211, 59 Fed.Appx. 757, 2003 WL 1194254, Unreported, habeas corpus dismissed 2005 WL 2406152. Criminal Law ⚷ 339.8(5)

Identification of defendant as he sat in the back of a patrol car was reliable, where victim had the opportunity to view appellant during the robbery and a few seconds after the robbery, defendant was not wearing a full mask over his face, and identification was conducted within approximately 45 minutes to an hour of the incident. State v. Walker (Ohio App. 10 Dist., Franklin, 03-06-2003) No. 02AP-679, 2003-Ohio-986, 2003 WL 757525, Unreported, appeal not allowed 99 Ohio St.3d 1455, 790 N.E.2d 1218, 2003-Ohio-3396. Criminal Law ⚷ 339.8(6)

Victim's identification of defendant as the burglar was sufficient to support defendant's conviction for burglary, where victim testified that he chased burglar from his home, threw his camera at burglar, who then turned around and met him face-to-face in fairly well lit area. State v. Pesci (Ohio App. 11 Dist., Lake, 12-20-2002) No. 2001-L-026, 2002-Ohio-7131, 2002 WL 31866167, Unreported, appeal not allowed 98 Ohio St.3d 1566, 787 N.E.2d 1231, 2003-Ohio-2242. Burglary ⚷ 41(6)

Investigating officer's comment to eyewitnesses that one of subjects in photographic lineup could possibly be suspect and request that they identify, if they could, person they saw at victim's residence, did not render photographic lineup unduly suggestive, and thus, trial counsel was not ineffective for failing to object to pretrial identification, in trial for burglary, attempted burglary and theft of firearm; same photographic lineup was used with both witnesses, witnesses had gotten good look at person breaking into victim's home, and both witnesses positively identified defendant as person they saw from both photographic lineup and at trial. State v. Hanning (Ohio App. 5 Dist., Perry, 11-20-2002) No. 01CA8, 2002-Ohio-6342, 2002 WL 31626898, Unreported. Criminal Law ⚷ 641.13(6)

In a rape prosecution, the use of a "one-man showup" is not so suggestive as to create a possibility of misidentification where the witness gives an accurate description of the defendant prior to the showup, the showup occurs only two days after the night of the rape, the witness is able to view the defendant closely for a period of fifteen minutes on the night of the rape, and the witness is able to identify the clothing worn by the defendant on that night. State v. Davidson (Ohio App. 12 Dist., Clermont, 08-15-1994) No. CA93-10-074, 1994 WL 424115, Unreported.

Victim's identification of defendant was reliable and thus admissible in prosecution for robbery, although police used one-person show-up; victim had ample opportunity to view robber from a distance and up close, victim's attention was drawn to robber because of his suspicious behavior and tug of war with purse, victim identified defendant less than hour after robbery, officer took care not to bias victim during drive by, and officer specifically noted victim's reactions to make sure that victim was being honest. State v. Wilson (Ohio App. 6 Dist., 04-29-2005) 162 Ohio App.3d 119, 832 N.E.2d 1220, 2005-Ohio-2108. Criminal Law ⚷ 339.8(6)

Although defense counsel's failure to object to identification made after store clerk was shown a single photograph of defendant the night before trial commenced and his failure to move to suppress that identification was deficient performance, given that defendant made statements to police implicating himself in incident at store, prejudice resulting from counsel's omission was not shown. State v. Ruby (Ohio App. 2 Dist., 10-04-2002) 149 Ohio App.3d 541, 778 N.E.2d 101, 2002-Ohio-5381. Criminal Law ⚷ 641.13(6)

Store clerk's identification of defendant at show-up procedure was reliable, where quick-change scheme between defendant and clerk lasted several minutes, clerk realized that defendant had swindled her after he drove away, officer stopped defendant a short distance from store, clerk could see that police had stopped defendant down the street, just minutes after defendant left store he was returned there by officer, clerk then identified defendant as the perpetrator, saying she remembered his face, and before defendant was returned to store by police he admitted he had been there shortly before and had been given too much change by the clerk. State v. Ruby (Ohio App. 2 Dist., 10-04-2002) 149 Ohio App.3d 541, 778 N.E.2d 101, 2002-Ohio-5381. Criminal Law ⚷ 339.8(6)

Any prejudice to defendant arising from prosecutor's conduct in showing store clerk a single photograph depicting only defendant the night before trial to aid her in-court identification was not plain error, although procedure was suggestive and could have created a substantial likelihood of misidentification, as defendant made statements to officer implicating himself in the incident at store, and thus court could not say that, but for clerk's identification of defendant after seeing a single photograph, outcome of trial would clearly have been different. State v. Ruby (Ohio App. 2 Dist., 10-04-2002) 149 Ohio App.3d 541, 778 N.E.2d 101, 2002-Ohio-5381. Criminal Law ⚷ 1036.1(7)

Circumstances of show-up identifications of capital murder defendant by two witnesses, in which witnesses, sitting in separate police cars, identified defendant as he stood with his hands behind his back between two officers, although suggestive, were not so suggestive as to create very substantial likelihood of irreparable misidentification, where both witnesses had time to view defendant during commission of crimes, focused their attention on him, described him prior to show-up identification, were confident in their respective identifications, and identified defendant mere hours after witnessing crime. State v. Gross (Ohio, 10-30-2002) 97 Ohio St.3d 121, 776 N.E.2d 1061, 2002-Ohio-5524, reconsideration denied 97 Ohio St.3d 1486, 780 N.E.2d 288, 2002-Ohio-6866, certiorari denied 123 S.Ct. 2079, 538 U.S. 1037, 155 L.Ed.2d 1068, rehearing denied 124 S.Ct. 20, 539 U.S. 976, 156 L.Ed.2d 685. Criminal Law ⚷ 339.8(5)

Defendant has the burden to show the court that challenged identification procedures were unnecessarily suggestive. State v. Thompson (Ohio App. 8 Dist., 05-04-1998) 127 Ohio App.3d 511, 713 N.E.2d 456, appeal not allowed 83 Ohio St.3d 1451, 700 N.E.2d 334. Criminal Law ⚷ 339.11(3)

Totality of circumstances indicated that identification procedures were reliable; witness testified that defendant stared at her for about 15 seconds from a short distance away on a clear, sunny morning, that same morning witness chose defendant's photo from an array in only about 30 seconds as man she saw getting out of truck, witness' degree of attention at time she saw defendant on morning of murders was high, and witness again chose defendant's photograph from array one week later. State v. Davie (Ohio, 11-26-1997) 80 Ohio St.3d 311, 686 N.E.2d 245, 1997-Ohio-341, dismissal of post-conviction relief affirmed 1998 WL 684157, dismissed, appeal not allowed 84 Ohio St.3d 1483, 705 N.E.2d 364, reconsideration denied 85 Ohio St.3d 1411, 706 N.E.2d 791, denial of post-conviction relief affirmed 2001-Ohio-8813, 2001 WL 1647193, appeal not allowed 95 Ohio St.3d 1423, 766 N.E.2d 162, 2002-Ohio-1737, habeas corpus denied 291 F.Supp.2d 573, motion to amend denied, certificate of appealability granted in part, denied in part 324 F.Supp.2d 862. Criminal Law ⚷ 339.7(1)

Victim's identification of defendant as her attacker after observing him in jail clothes, handcuffs, and leg irons was inadmissible in prosecution for unrelated sexual offenses against separate victim; during attack defendant was disguised by dark hooded sweatshirt pulled to eyebrows and wore bandanna covering his face, and inherently prejudicial and suggestive effect of defendant's attire as well as circumstances surrounding the confrontation diminished reliability of identification. State v. Pearson (Ohio App. 3 Dist., 10-04-1996) 114 Ohio App.3d 168, 682 N.E.2d 1086. Criminal Law ⚷ 369.8

Fact that detective allegedly contacted witness on several occasions prior to interview with witness, at which she reaffirmed her identification of defendant, did not render witness' identification of photograph of defendant unreliable; detective spoke to witness only regarding her physical condition, to inform her of upcoming court dates, and, on one occasion, to ask her if she was positive about her earlier tentative identification of defendant. State v. Ayala (Ohio App. 10 Dist., 06-11-1996) 111 Ohio App.3d 627, 676 N.E.2d 1201. Criminal Law ⚷ 339.7(1)

Identifications made subsequent to impermissibly suggestive procedure are admissible where identification itself is nevertheless deemed reliable; central question is whether under totality of circumstances identification is reliable even though confrontation procedure was suggestive. State v. Garner (Ohio, 11-22-1995) 74 Ohio St.3d 49, 656 N.E.2d 623, 1995-Ohio-168, reconsideration denied 74 Ohio St.3d 1485, 657 N.E.2d 1378, certiorari denied 116 S.Ct. 1444, 517 U.S. 1147, 134 L.Ed.2d 564, rehearing denied 116 S.Ct. 1872, 517 U.S. 1230, 134 L.Ed.2d 969, stay granted 76 Ohio St.3d 1401, 666 N.E.2d 233. Criminal Law ⚿ 339.10(1)

Arresting officer's testimony that defendant told police he had come back from California, where he had been in trouble for auto theft, tended to confirm convenience store employees' identification of defendant as person who told them he had recently come from California and had juvenile record, and thus testimony was admissible to prove identification. State v. Williams (Ohio, 08-16-1995) 73 Ohio St.3d 153, 652 N.E.2d 721, 1995-Ohio-275, reconsideration denied 74 Ohio St.3d 1409, 655 N.E.2d 188, stay granted 74 Ohio St.3d 1437, 655 N.E.2d 1321, stay terminated 75 Ohio St.3d 1439, 662 N.E.2d 1085, certiorari denied 116 S.Ct. 1047, 516 U.S. 1161, 134 L.Ed.2d 193, denial of post-conviction relief affirmed 1998 WL 330539, dismissed, appeal not allowed 83 Ohio St.3d 1449, 700 N.E.2d 332, reconsideration denied 84 Ohio St.3d 1413, 701 N.E.2d 1021. Criminal Law ⚿ 369.15

A drawing of an alleged assailant sketched by a police artist, a poster reproduction of that drawing, a "mug shot" of the accused taken after arrest, and the testimony of police officers as to statements describing the accused made to them by a prosecuting witness, are admissible solely to indicate the process by which the accused was identified, where that process is under attack, and to corroborate that identification. State v. Lancaster (Ohio 1971) 25 Ohio St.2d 83, 267 N.E.2d 291, 54 O.O.2d 222. Witnesses ⚿ 414(1); Witnesses ⚿ 414(2)

Victim's identification of defendant as aggravated robbery perpetrator through cold stand or one-on-one show-up identification procedure was reliable, and thus, such identification was not subject to suppression; victim had the opportunity to view defendant immediately prior to and during robbery, robbery occurred during broad daylight, defendant was not wearing a mask or other covering at time of robbery, victim testified that he stared at the defendant during the robbery so that he could get a good look at him, victim provided police with an accurate description of defendant prior to identification procedure that included race, height, facial hair and clothing, victim. State v. Thompson (Ohio App. 8 Dist., Cuyahoga, 05-16-2002) No. 79938, 2002-Ohio-2390, 2002 WL 999312, Unreported. Criminal Law ⚿ 339.8(6)

4. "Impermissibly suggestive" test

One-man showup, conducted with defendant in back of police cruiser did not give rise to substantial likelihood of misidentification, where showup was conducted shortly after incident, in which victim was robbed at gunpoint, and victim's identification was certain. State v. Isaac (Ohio App. 2 Dist., Montgomery, 07-15-2005) No. 20662, 2005-Ohio-3733, 2005 WL 1707019, Unreported. Criminal Law ⚿ 339.8(6)

Cold stand identification procedure was not so impermissibly suggestive as to create substantial likelihood of irreparable misidentification, in trial for aggravated robbery, kidnapping, and theft; victim had ample opportunity to view defendant over course of more than one hour both prior to and during time victim was forced to drive defendant at gunpoint, victim turned and looked at defendant throughout ordeal, victim's description of defendant to police was accurate, victim was 100% positive in his identification, and length of time between crime and show up was less than two hours. State v. Freeman (Ohio App. 8 Dist., Cuyahoga, 07-07-2005) No. 85137, 2005-Ohio-3480, 2005 WL 1581105, Unreported, motion for delayed appeal granted 107 Ohio St.3d 1404, 836 N.E.2d 1226, 2005-Ohio-5859. Criminal Law ⚿ 339.10(11)

Single-photograph identification system used by arresting officer to identify defendant was so impermissibly suggestive as to give rise to substantial likelihood of irreparable misidentification, where officer had limited opportunity to view suspect and was unable to identify his clothing, facial features, or characteristics, and officer's identification of defendant was unreliable under totality of circumstances. State v. Bates (Ohio App. 8 Dist., Cuyahoga, 06-30-2005) No. 84654, 2005-Ohio-3411, 2005 WL 1541008, Unreported. Criminal Law ⚿ 339.7(4)

Pretrial identification procedure using photographic lineup, even if impermissibly suggestive, did not pose substantial likelihood of irreparable misidentification, even though victim had already been shot when defendant approached within a few feet of his face before shooting him again; victim was aware enough to notice specific details about defendant, including that defendant had two different colored eyes, and victim identified defendant as shooter by writing across defendant's photograph, "he shot me." State v. Merriman (Ohio App. 10 Dist., Franklin, 06-30-2005) No. 04AP-463, No. 04AP-464, 2005-Ohio-3376, 2005 WL 1532418, Unreported. Criminal Law ⚿ 339.7(1)

Pretrial identification procedure using photographic lineup was not suggestive; lineup contained six photographs of African-American males with similar features, including short hair and facial hair, and detective who showed lineup to victim made no suggestion as to who should be picked from lineup. State v. Merriman (Ohio App. 10 Dist., Franklin, 06-30-2005) No. 04AP-463, No. 04AP-464, 2005-Ohio-3376, 2005 WL 1532418, Unreported. Criminal Law ⚿ 339.7(3); Criminal Law ⚿ 339.7(4)

Identification procedures through which surviving victims and witnesses identified defendant as perpetrator of offenses including of aggravated murder, attempted aggravated murder, aggravated robbery, and kidnapping, including photographic lineups and through personal knowledge of defendant, were not unduly suggestive. State v. Whitfield (Ohio App. 2 Dist., Montgomery, 05-13-2005) No. 20742, 2005-Ohio-2530, 2005 WL 1206898, Unreported. Criminal Law ⚿ 339.6

Victim's identification of defendant as one of passengers he saw in vehicle leaving scene of robbery was not unreliable, so as to warrant suppression, even though there was almost two-year delay between robbery and identification; victim indicated that maroon car that approached vehicle victim had entered in attempt to escape was no more than four or five feet away, that car stopped "long enough for me to look at this guy," and that he "could see real good," identification took about one second, victim was sure he would be able to identify passenger if he saw him again, and victim had identified individual whose fingerprint was on weapon used in robbery. State v. Howard (Ohio App. 2 Dist., Clark, 05-06-2005) No. 2004CA29, 2005-Ohio-2237, 2005 WL 1060621, Unreported, appeal allowed 106 Ohio St.3d 1543, 835 N.E.2d 725, 2005-Ohio-5343. Criminal Law ⚷ 339.8(2.1)

Photographic lineup was not impermissibly suggestive so as to give rise to substantial likelihood of irreparable misidentification; all six photographs contained suspects with similar build and appearance, defendant's hair was not significantly longer than that of other suspects, and each suspect had substantially similar, though not identical, facial hair. State v. Howard (Ohio App. 2 Dist., Clark, 05-06-2005) No. 2004CA29, 2005-Ohio-2237, 2005 WL 1060621, Unreported, appeal allowed 106 Ohio St.3d 1543, 835 N.E.2d 725, 2005-Ohio-5343. Criminal Law ⚷ 339.7(4)

Photographic array consisting of five photographs from which victim identified defendant was not impermissibly suggestive; victim had no problem identifying defendant, victim's testimony reflected she was certain she had made a proper identification, victim did not say she selected defendant's photograph for any of the reasons articulated by defendant, i.e., lack of moustache, cocked head, or age, and each of individuals in array had some unique characteristics but all also shared similar features. State v. Page (Ohio App. 8 Dist., Cuyahoga, 03-31-2005) No. 84341, 2005-Ohio-1493, 2005 WL 730057, Unreported, appeal not allowed 106 Ohio St.3d 1487, 832 N.E.2d 739, 2005-Ohio-3978. Criminal Law ⚷ 339.7(4)

Pretrial identification procedure using photographic array was not unduly suggestive; all six photographs in array were of young African-American males with roughly the same build and with very similar short hair styles, nothing made any one photograph stand out from the others, police read standard photographic array instructions to witnesses, and witnesses did not speak to each other about array during interval between their two identifications of defendant. State v. Mitchell (Ohio App. 2 Dist., Montgomery, 03-04-2005) No. 20372, 2005-Ohio-912, 2005 WL 498250, Unreported, appeal after new sentencing hearing 2006-Ohio-1602, 2006 WL 827389. Criminal Law ⚷ 339.7(4)

Photographic lineups used by police officer were not unduly suggestive; lineup was generated by a computer, computer generated five photographs of individuals who had similar features to defendant, witnesses were shown the lineup in separate identification rooms, when complaining witness reviewed the lineup at a later date all of the photographs that were used in the initial lineup were reused and the photographs were rearranged, and all of the men depicted in the lineup were white males with short dark hair and some facial hair. State v. White (Ohio App. 2 Dist., Montgomery, 01-21-2005) No. 20324, 2005-Ohio-212, 2005 WL 120059, Unreported. Criminal Law ⚷ 339.7(3); Criminal Law ⚷ 339.7(4)

Out-of-court photograph lineup procedure was not unduly suggestive, despite defendant's claim that the witness did not initially identify his photograph, but rather, the witness identified him only after the witness covered the top portion of the subjects' heads; witness testified that he observed defendant for three or four minutes from a 30-foot distance, this observation occurred under the glare of vehicle headlights, and witness explained that at the time of the event, the suspect wore a bandanna and that covering the top portion of the subject's heads in the photo array helped him to make a correct identification. State v. Trego (Ohio App. 4 Dist., Ross, 12-27-2004) No. 04CA2763, 2004-Ohio-7287, 2004 WL 3090202, Unreported, motion for delayed appeal denied 106 Ohio St.3d 1501, 833 N.E.2d 1245, 2005-Ohio-4605. Criminal Law ⚷ 339.7(3)

Photographic array from which murder defendant was identified was not impermissibly suggestive or likely to cause irreparable misidentification, even though defendant was the only person in array who was present at scene of fatal shooting; each of four witnesses testified that they observed shooting and the shooter, witnesses described defendant's appearance, three of four witnesses identified defendant by name, and witness's identified defendant's photograph immediately and unequivocally. State v. Cheers (Ohio App. 9 Dist., Lorain, 12-08-2004) No. 04CA008465, 2004-Ohio-6533, 2004 WL 2806345, Unreported, appeal not allowed 105 Ohio St.3d 1501, 825 N.E.2d 624, 2005-Ohio-1666. Criminal Law ⚷ 339.7(3)

Inclusion in photographic lineup from which witness identified burglary defendant of only one individual with reddish blond hair did not render lineup impermissibly suggestive, where two other individuals in lineup had blond hair, and witness further testified that hair color was not basis of his identification of defendant. State v. Elersic (Ohio App. 11 Dist., Lake, 09-30-2004) No. 2002-L-172, 2004-Ohio-5301, 2004 WL 2804809, Unreported, appeal not allowed 105 Ohio St.3d 1407, 821 N.E.2d 1027, 2005-Ohio-279. Criminal Law ⚷ 339.7(4)

Assuming that photographic lineup from which witness identified burglary defendant was rendered unduly suggestive by inclusion therein of only one individual with reddish blond hair, such suggestiveness did not render identification inadmissible, where witness' identification of defendant was otherwise reliable; witness had opportunity to speak face to face with defendant when defendant attempted to purchase remote control for stolen stereo system from him, witness had been notified by police to be on lookout for individual inquiring about such a remote control, witness' description of defendant was accurate, and witness testified that he was 100 percent certain of his identification. State v. Elersic (Ohio App. 11 Dist., Lake, 09-30-2004) No. 2002-L-172, 2004-Ohio-5301, 2004 WL 2804809, Unreported, appeal not allowed 105

Ohio St.3d 1407, 821 N.E.2d 1027, 2005-Ohio-279. Criminal Law ⚿ 339.7(4)

Photographic array containing six pictures of African-American men with similar facial features and similar skin tone was not unduly suggestive, even though defendant clearly had long hair; three other men clearly had hair long enough to be braided, the other two men had hair of an indeterminate length, and all men had facial hair. State v. Hayes (Ohio App. 6 Dist., Lucas, 12-03-2004) No. L-03-1221, No. L-03-1222, 2004-Ohio-6460, 2004 WL 2785290, Unreported, appeal not allowed 105 Ohio St.3d 1516, 826 N.E.2d 314, 2005-Ohio-1880. Criminal Law ⚿ 339.7(4)

Witness's identification of defendant from photographic identification array several months after alleged shooting did not constitute unduly suggestive identification procedure, as would require determination of reliability. State v. Kemper (Ohio App. 2 Dist., Clark, 11-12-2004) No. 2002-CA-101, No. 2002-CA-102, 2004-Ohio-6055, 2004 WL 2588313, Unreported. Criminal Law ⚿ 339.7(1)

Eight-man photo array used by police to obtain witness's identification of defendant was not unduly suggestive; the eight photographs in the array all depicted eight similar black males, who were roughly the same age, with short hair, unremarkable complexions, and facial hair. State v. Armstrong (Ohio App. 11 Dist., Trumbull, 10-22-2004) No. 2001-T-0120, No. 2002-T-0071, 2004-Ohio-5635, 2004 WL 2376467, Unreported, stay granted 104 Ohio St.3d 1438, 819 N.E.2d 1122, 2004-Ohio-7033, appeal not allowed 105 Ohio St.3d 1463, 824 N.E.2d 91, 2005-Ohio-1024. Criminal Law ⚿ 339.7(4)

Photographic array from which victim identified defendant was not impermissibly suggestive, even though defendant argued that other five black males depicted in array differed in complexion and hairstyle; defendant did not stand out as unique in array, and differences in complexion and hairstyle were not so drastic as to render array impermissibly suggestive. State v. Jennings (Ohio App. 9 Dist., Summit, 10-13-2004) No. 22016, 2004-Ohio-5447, 2004 WL 2292776, Unreported, appeal not allowed 105 Ohio St.3d 1441, 822 N.E.2d 812, 2005-Ohio-531. Criminal Law ⚿ 339.7(4)

Claim that photographic array used in pretrial identification procedure was impermissibly suggestive could only be reviewed on appeal for plain error, where defendant failed at trial to file pretrial motion to suppress identification, as required by rule. State v. Scott (Ohio App. 5 Dist., Richland, 09-24-2004) No. 03 CA 119, 2004-Ohio-5292, 2004 WL 2260702, Unreported. Criminal Law ⚿ 1044.1(6)

Pretrial photographic identification procedure was not unduly suggestive and did not unnecessarily suggest robbery defendant's guilt; cashiers on duty during store robberies were shown photo arrays of possible suspects, each array contained six pictures, including the suspect and five other men who had similar physical characteristics, and both cashiers identified defendant as the person who had committed the robberies. State v. Fletcher (Ohio App. 2 Dist., Clark, 08-27-2004) No. 2003-CA-62, 2004-Ohio-4517, 2004 WL 1908336, Unreported. Criminal Law ⚿ 339.7(4)

Murder defendant, an African-American male who wore a mustache and goatee, failed to demonstrate that photographic array was impermissibly suggestive, where array contained photographs of African-American men of approximately the same age with varying styles of short to medium length hair, at least four of the individuals appeared to have some facial hair, and police did not indicate to any of the witnesses whether the suspected killer was included in the array. State v. Taylor (Ohio App. 1 Dist., Hamilton, 03-26-2004) No. C-020475, 2004-Ohio-1494, 2004 WL 596128, Unreported, appeal not allowed 103 Ohio St.3d 1406, 812 N.E.2d 1289, 2004-Ohio-3980. Criminal Law ⚿ 339.7(4)

Eyewitness identifications of murder defendant were not result of impermissibly suggestive practices, despite investigating detectives' use of "loose" photo of defendant, where eyewitnesses to murder included victim's teen-aged sons, defense counsel had ample opportunity to cross-examine these witnesses, at least one witness stated he was familiar with defendant from the neighborhood and knew him by his "street name," witnesses were able to identify defendant when presented with his picture in addition to describing his general appearance on night in question, and two witnesses testified that they had seen defendant in neighborhood prior to the night of the murder. State v. Crosby (Ohio App. 8 Dist., Cuyahoga, 12-31-2003) No. 81779, 2003-Ohio-7236, 2003 WL 23095998, Unreported, appeal not allowed 103 Ohio St.3d 1404, 812 N.E.2d 1287, 2004-Ohio-3980. Criminal Law ⚿ 339.7(3)

Pretrial identification procedure was not so impermissibly suggestive as to give rise to a very substantial likelihood of irreparable misidentification, and thus identification was not subject to suppression, even though law enforcement officer showed victim only three photographs, two of the photographs were suspects and the other was defendant, and defendant did not resemble other suspects, where victim had ample opportunity to view defendant during crime, victim was sufficiently aware to describe circumstances of crime, and only three days elapsed between crime and identification. State v. Carroll (Ohio App. 1 Dist., Hamilton, 10-03-2003) No. C-020777, 2003-Ohio-5260, 2003 WL 22267147, Unreported. Criminal Law ⚿ 339.7(4)

Photo line-up by which robbery victims identified defendant was not overly suggestive, and thus, supported admissibility of photo array, even though defendant's name appeared on sheet of paper containing his picture used in photo array, while no other photo sheets contained the names of the persons depicted, where detective testified that he independently showed each victim the photo array, each identified defendant's picture as the photograph of one of the assailants, the victims did not know the name of the suspect at the time they viewed the array, and each victim became visibly shaken upon seeing the photograph of defendant. State v. Ingram (Ohio App. 9 Dist., Summit, 01-29-2003) No. 21041, 2003-Ohio-357, 2003 WL 187572, Unreported. Criminal Law ⚷ 339.7(4)

Victim's pretrial identification of defendant as burglar he chased from his home was not unnecessarily suggestive and prejudicial, even though confrontation was at night, victim could not identify object burglar carried, and his description to police did not mention facial stubble and indicated that burglar's age was 12 years younger than defendant's age, considering that victim had face-to-face encounter under streetlight, victim's description matched defendant's height, weight, clothing, and hair color, identification occurred without any encouragement from officers and within two hours of crime, and victim stated he was "100% sure" defendant was burglar. State v. Pesci (Ohio App. 11 Dist., Lake, 12-20-2002) No. 2001-L-026, 2002-Ohio-7131, 2002 WL 31866167, Unreported, appeal not allowed 98 Ohio St.3d 1566, 787 N.E.2d 1231, 2003-Ohio-2242. Criminal Law ⚷ 339.8(6)

In-court identification of defendant was not highly prejudicial, unreliable, and unnecessarily suggestive of defendant's guilt, even though trial court suppressed pretrial identification arising from a show-up following crime on grounds that officer's comments to witness were too suggestive, where witness stated comments were not unduly suggestive, and at time of show-up he had no discussions with other witnesses concerning identification of defendant, only basis for witness's in-court identification was defendant's hands, his hands were not visible during show-up identification, thus show-up could not have influenced in-court identification, witness consistently stated that during robbery his attention was focused on perpetrator's weapon, and hands holding the weapon, and jury had other evidence to neutralize allegedly suggestive nature of the in-court identification. State v. Savage (Ohio App. 10 Dist., Franklin, 12-12-2002) No. 02AP-202, 2002-Ohio-6837, 2002 WL 31771245, Unreported. Criminal Law ⚷ 339.10(1)

Even if trial court erred by denying defendant's motion to suppress identification testimony, upon the ground that it was based upon an unduly suggestive show-up procedure at crime scene, that error was harmless, since witness never definitely identified defendant as the perpetrator. State v. Leroy (Ohio App. 2 Dist., Montgomery, 10-04-2002) No. 18623, 2002-Ohio-5379, 2002 WL 31243532, Unreported. Criminal Law ⚷ 1169.1(5)

Photographic array from which one of victims identified defendant charged with robbery was not unduly suggestive, so that admission of identification testimony did not violate due process clause, even though defendant's photograph was only one of six photographs used which did not contain horizontal lines denoting the height of the person photographed. State v. Sanders (Ohio App. 1 Dist., 09-25-1998) 130 Ohio App.3d 92, 719 N.E.2d 619, dismissed, appeal not allowed 84 Ohio St.3d 1472, 704 N.E.2d 579. Constitutional Law ⚷ 266(3.1); Criminal Law ⚷ 339.7(3)

Physical reactions of one of group of complaining witnesses who simultaneously viewed line-up did not make line-up so impermissibly suggestive as to give rise to very substantial likelihood of irreparable misidentification; while one witness stated that upon seeing defendant in line-up she began shaking, started breathing heavily, and put her head between her legs, no other witness testified that her reaction influenced their determination, it was unclear from record whether all witnesses even noticed her reaction, and three witnesses specifically testified that they were given no assistance by anyone in their identification of defendant. State v. Echols (Ohio App. 1 Dist., 06-26-1998) 128 Ohio App.3d 677, 716 N.E.2d 728, appeal not allowed 83 Ohio St.3d 1472, 701 N.E.2d 380, appeal after new trial 146 Ohio App.3d 81, 765 N.E.2d 379, appeal not allowed 94 Ohio St.3d 1430, 761 N.E.2d 47, 2002-Ohio-5651, habeas corpus denied 2005 WL 1745475. Criminal Law ⚷ 339.8(2.1)

Complaining witness' viewing of defendant while he sat in back of police cruiser was not so impermissibly suggestive as to give rise to very substantial likelihood of irreparable misidentification, where witness had previously provided police with description of robber, had identified defendant in photographic array, and had viewed two other men brought to her by police before she identified defendant. State v. Echols (Ohio App. 1 Dist., 06-26-1998) 128 Ohio App.3d 677, 716 N.E.2d 728, appeal not allowed 83 Ohio St.3d 1472, 701 N.E.2d 380, appeal after new trial 146 Ohio App.3d 81, 765 N.E.2d 379, appeal not allowed 94 Ohio St.3d 1430, 761 N.E.2d 47, 2002-Ohio-5651, habeas corpus denied 2005 WL 1745475. Criminal Law ⚷ 339.8(6)

Reliability of victim show-up identification procedure that occurred within ten minutes of robbery was insufficient to overcome its suggestive nature, such that victim's identification was inadmissible, where there was no evidence that victim had opportunity to see perpetrator's face, victim gave police only description of perpetrator's clothing, victim heard police radio broadcasts prior to show-up indicating that they had caught perpetrator, and victim was unusually susceptible to police suggestion. State v. Martin (Ohio App. 2 Dist., 04-17-1998) 127 Ohio App.3d 272, 712 N.E.2d 795. Criminal Law ⚷ 339.8(6)

Pretrial photographic identification procedure was not unduly suggestive; while police could have done better job of blacking out age, weight, and height information on mug shots, men shown were not so disparate in age as to indicate that defendant was the culprit, and alleged size difference between men did not make it likelier that witnesses would choose defendant. State v. Wills (Ohio App. 8 Dist., 06-16-1997) 120 Ohio App.3d 320, 697 N.E.2d 1072, dismissed, appeal not allowed 80 Ohio St.3d 1409, 684 N.E.2d 703. Criminal Law ⚷ 339.7(4)

Though arranging photographic lineup in which defendant was only one with distinctive "box" haircut may have been unnecessarily suggestive, particularly since victim described person who stole her vehicle at gunpoint as having such haircut, any error in admitting victim's identification testimony was harmless, where defendant confessed to stealing a vehicle, another witness saw the theft, defendant was actually in victim's vehicle when he was arrested, and vehicle's license plates had been switched with plates from another vehicle defendant had stolen. State v. Keene (Ohio, 05-13-1998) 81 Ohio St.3d 646, 693 N.E.2d 246, 1998-Ohio-342, motion stricken 82 Ohio St.3d 1437, 694 N.E.2d 1373, stay granted 82 Ohio St.3d 1445, 695 N.E.2d 267, certiorari denied 119 S.Ct. 350, 525 U.S. 936, 142 L.Ed.2d 288, denial of post-conviction relief affirmed 1999 WL 55711, dismissed, appeal not allowed 85 Ohio St.3d 1496, 710 N.E.2d 716, habeas corpus dismissed 2004 WL 3325797. Criminal Law ⚷ 1169.1(5)

Even if robbery victim's identification of defendant in one-on-one showup shortly after the crime was unnecessarily suggestive, there was no substantial likelihood of misidentification; victim had seen robber's face as he pointed gun at him and demanded money, and although victim could not initially identify defendant, when officer shined light on defendant, victim expressed high degree of certainty in identifying defendant. State v. Wilson (Ohio App. 1 Dist., 12-24-1996) 117 Ohio App.3d 290, 690 N.E.2d 574. Criminal Law ⚷ 339.10(9)

Factors to consider in determining whether identification is reliable even though confrontation procedure was unnecessarily suggestive include: (1) opportunity of witness to view criminal at time of crime, (2) witness's degree of attention, (3) accuracy of witness's prior description of criminal, (4) level of certainty demonstrated by witness at confrontation, and (5) length of time between crime and confrontation. State v. Wilson (Ohio App. 1 Dist., 12-24-1996) 117 Ohio App.3d 290, 690 N.E.2d 574. Criminal Law ⚷ 339.8(2.1)

Generally, identification will be suppressed only when alleged suggestive methods used by police have rendered identification unreliable under totality of circumstances. State v. Ayala (Ohio App. 10 Dist., 06-11-1996) 111 Ohio App.3d 627, 676 N.E.2d 1201. Criminal Law ⚷ 339.6

Pretrial identification procedure in which witness identified defendant as person he had seen near area where victim's body was found was not unnecessarily suggestive, although witness was unable to identify defendant from photo array shortly after victim's body was discovered, identified defendant's picture but expressed some reservation when shown different photo array almost a year later, and positively identified defendant only when shown single black and white photograph of him. State v. Wogenstahl (Ohio, 03-06-1996) 75 Ohio St.3d 344, 662 N.E.2d 311, 1996-Ohio-219, reconsideration denied 75 Ohio St.3d 1453, 663 N.E.2d 333, certiorari denied 117 S.Ct. 240, 519 U.S. 895, 136 L.Ed.2d 169, denial of post-conviction relief affirmed 2004-Ohio-5994, 2004 WL 2567655, appeal not allowed 105 Ohio St.3d 1465, 824 N.E.2d 93, 2005-Ohio-1024. Criminal Law ⚷ 339.7(3)

Factors to be considered in determining whether, under totality of circumstances, identification was reliable, even though confrontation procedure was suggestive, include: opportunity of witness to view criminal at time of crime; witness' degree of attention; accuracy of witness' prior description of criminal; level of certainty demonstrated by witness at the confrontation; and length of time between crime and confrontation. State v. Williams (Ohio, 08-16-1995) 73 Ohio St.3d 153, 652 N.E.2d 721, 1995-Ohio-275, reconsideration denied 74 Ohio St.3d 1409, 655 N.E.2d 188, stay granted 74 Ohio St.3d 1437, 655 N.E.2d 1321, stay terminated 75 Ohio St.3d 1439, 662 N.E.2d 1085, certiorari denied 116 S.Ct. 1047, 516 U.S. 1161, 134 L.Ed.2d 193, denial of post-conviction relief affirmed 1998 WL 330539, dismissed, appeal not allowed 83 Ohio St.3d 1449, 700 N.E.2d 332, reconsideration denied 84 Ohio St.3d 1413, 701 N.E.2d 1021. Criminal Law ⚷ 339.10(3)

Assuming that photographic array out of which robbery defendant was selected by victims was suggestive, on grounds that defendant's photograph was larger and darker than other photographs, pretrial identifications were nonetheless reliable and identification did not violate defendant's due process rights; all victims had been able to get clear and unobstructed view of defendant's face while they were being robbed, each victim gave police identification of assailant which matched defendant's actual appearance with high degree of accuracy, and detail of description indicated that each victim was highly attentive during robbery. State v. Wells (Ohio App. 10 Dist., 03-24-1994) 94 Ohio App.3d 48, 640 N.E.2d 217, motion for delayed appeal denied 76 Ohio St.3d 1407, 666 N.E.2d 567. Constitutional Law ⚷ 266(3.1); Criminal Law ⚷ 339.7(4)

Victim's identification of defendant from 55–person photo array approximately 10 hours after attack was reliable and admissible, even if earlier smaller array from which victim did not make identification was somehow impermissibly suggestive, where victim had opportunity to view and converse with defendant on two occasions prior to crime, viewed defendant during crime and was positive in her identification. State v. Halley (Ohio App. 10 Dist., 01-20-1994) 93 Ohio App.3d 71, 637 N.E.2d 937, dismissed, jurisdictional motion overruled 69 Ohio St.3d 1476, 634 N.E.2d 1023. Criminal Law ⚷ 339.7(3); Criminal Law ⚷ 339.7(4)

Where a defendant claims that the identification procedure at trial was unnecessarily and impermissibly suggestive, the trial court must balance the suggestiveness of the identification procedure against (1) the opportunity of the witness to view the criminal at the time of the crime, (2) the witness' degree of attention, (3) the accuracy of the witness' prior description of the criminal, (4) the level of certainty demonstrated by the witness at the confrontation, and (5) the length of elapsed time between the crime and the confrontation. State v. Green (Cuyahoga 1990) 67 Ohio App.3d 72, 585 N.E.2d 990. Criminal Law ⚷ 339.8(2.1)

A victim's identification of defendant is reliable and overcomes any questions of the photographic arrays being tainted or suggestive when the testimony of the victim at trial established that the victim viewed the defendant during the entire criminal episode, the victim's degree of attention was acute during the episode, the victim provided a positive description of the defendant and, upon viewing the second set of photographs, the victim immediately recognized the defendant as her assailant, and that the victim made a positive identification of the defendant only four days after the criminal episode. State v. Green (Cuyahoga 1990) 67 Ohio App.3d 72, 585 N.E.2d 990. Criminal Law ⚷ 339.10(10)

Even if pretrial identification procedures were unduly suggestive, witnesses' identifications of defendant bore sufficient indicia of reliability to be admissible; witnesses each had unobstructed opportunity to view and speak directly to assailant during underlying robberies, each witness indicated that he or she attentively watched assailant either upon entry to store robbed or during robbery, and each witness viewed challenged lineup within one to four months after robbery in which he or she was involved. Jamison v. Collins (S.D.Ohio, 05-10-2000) 100 F.Supp.2d 647, affirmed 291 F.3d 380, amended on denial of rehearing. Criminal Law ⚷ 339.8(3)

5. Police line-up

Eyewitness identifications of robbery defendant were sufficiently reliable to be admissible, despite possibility that conversations among witnesses tainted lineup in which multiple witnesses viewed and identified defendant, where lineup occurred approximately 11 days after robbery, and any discrepancy between descriptions provided by the two witnesses went to weight of their testimony, not admissibility of identifications. State v. Norman (Ohio App. 1 Dist., 12-03-1999) 137 Ohio App.3d 184, 738 N.E.2d 403. Criminal Law ⚷ 339.8(3)

Even though a procedure employed by police to identify a defendant is unnecessarily suggestive when only one black male suspect is shown to a rape victim and she is told that the defendant had been involved in a similar attack, the identification is still reliable and admissible where the victim testifies that she had more than ten seconds to observe the defendant and that the sergeant's statement that the defendant "had done this kind of thing before" did not influence her, and where her description to the police is thorough, and she identifies the defendant within ten minutes of the attack. State v. Jones (Lorain 1990) 67 Ohio App.3d 542, 587 N.E.2d 886, motion overruled 54 Ohio St.3d 705, 561 N.E.2d 944. Criminal Law ⚷ 339.8(5)

There are five factors to consider in assessing the reliability of a witness identification: (1) the opportunity of the witness to view the criminal at the time of the crime, (2) the witness' degree of attention at the time of observation, (3) the accuracy of the witness' prior description of the criminal, (4) the level of certainty demonstrated by the witness when confronting the defendant, and (5) the length of time between the crime and the confrontation. Jamison v. Collins (S.D.Ohio, 05-10-2000) 100 F.Supp.2d 647, affirmed 291 F.3d 380, amended on denial of rehearing. Criminal Law ⚷ 339.8(1)

That robbery victim was told that there was suspect in lineup and was shown jewelry which was stolen during robbery did not render lineup unduly suggestive; arranging of lineup itself gave rise to inference that suspect was present, and while showing victim jewelry indicated that suspect was more likely than not the robber, it did not create substantial likelihood of misidentification. Jamison v. Collins (S.D.Ohio, 05-10-2000) 100 F.Supp.2d 647, affirmed 291 F.3d 380, amended on denial of rehearing. Criminal Law ⚷ 339.8(3)

Defendant failed to show that lineup was rendered unduly suggestive because multiple witnesses viewed lineup simultaneously, given absence of showing as to whether witnesses viewing same lineup were connected to same or different crimes and whether witnesses stated their identification of defendant in front of other witnesses, and given that two witnesses testified that they were instructed not to talk to other witnesses during identification process. Jamison v. Collins (S.D.Ohio, 05-10-2000) 100 F.Supp.2d 647, affirmed 291 F.3d 380, amended on denial of rehearing. Criminal Law ⚷ 339.8(3)

That witness gave varying descriptions of suspect prior to identifying defendant went to weight of credibility of identification. Jamison v. Collins (S.D.Ohio, 05-10-2000) 100 F.Supp.2d 647, affirmed 291 F.3d 380, amended on denial of rehearing. Criminal Law ⚷ 339.6

6. Photo array

For purposes of determining admissibility of out-of-court identification of defendant by arresting officer, officer's identification of defendant through single-photograph identification system was unreliable, where officer failed to identify defendant in their first face-to-face encounter, prior to out-of-court identification at issue, and was in possession of additional information suggesting that defendant was perpetrator at time of out-of-court identification, defendant and his identical twin brother were depicted in photograph found in vehicle allegedly abandoned by defendant, officer did not testify that defendant resembled his twin, two black males were observed in vehicle, and less suggestive identification procedure was available. State v. Bates (Ohio App. 8 Dist., Cuyahoga, 06-30-2005) No. 84654, 2005-Ohio-3411, 2005 WL 1541008, Unreported. Criminal Law ⚷ 339.7(4)

For purposes of determining admissibility of out-of-court identification of defendant by arresting officer, single-photograph identification system used by officer to identify defendant was unduly suggestive; officer testified that he had had limited opportunity to observe suspect, suspect escaped, and there were two black males in vehicle chased by him, and that at time suspect exited vehicle, officer was 25 to 35 feet away from him and could not identify his clothing, facial features, or characteristics. State v. Bates (Ohio App. 8 Dist., Cuyahoga, 06-30-2005) No. 84654, 2005-Ohio-3411, 2005 WL 1541008, Unreported. Criminal Law ⚷ 339.7(4)

Evidence was sufficient to support defendant's conviction for aggravated robbery; eyewitness identified defendant before trial in photographic array, eyewitness testified at trial that she saw defendant walking on sidewalk outside store, that she then saw defendant enter store and walk to the end of the service counter, during which time eyewitness was able to see defendant's face for about 20 to 30 seconds without any obstructions, and eyewitness testified that defendant pulled gun and ordered eyewitness to get on the ground, at which point eyewitness heard defendant open two cash drawers and complain about how little money was there. State v. Tonn (Ohio App. 2 Dist., Greene, 04-29-2005) No. 204-CA-36, No. 2004-CA-37, 2005-Ohio-2021, 2005 WL 994692, Unreported. Robbery ⇨ 24.40

That eyewitness to robbery misidentified defendant's eye color and erroneously stated that defendant had freckles on her forehead did not render her pretrial identification of defendant from photographic array unreliable, where eyewitness testified at trial that she had an unobstructed view of defendant at the crime scene for 20 to 30 seconds and was "one hundred and twenty percent" sure defendant had robbed her. State v. Tonn (Ohio App. 2 Dist., Greene, 04-29-2005) No. 204-CA-36, No. 2004-CA-37, 2005-Ohio-2021, 2005 WL 994692, Unreported. Criminal Law ⇨ 339.7(1)

Evidence in prosecution for aggravated robbery, robbery, two counts of felonious assault, and accompanying firearms specifications, was sufficient to identify defendant as one of the men who robbed and attacked cab driver; ID card with defendant's name and social security number was found in the cab, and cab driver immediately identified defendant as one of his attackers during a photographic lineup. State v. Smith (Ohio App. 1 Dist., Hamilton, 03-25-2005) No. C-040348, 2005-Ohio-1325, 2005 WL 678532, Unreported, motion for delayed appeal denied 106 Ohio St.3d 1502, 833 N.E.2d 1246, 2005-Ohio-4605, appeal not allowed 107 Ohio St.3d 1701, 840 N.E.2d 205, 2005-Ohio-6763, appeal not allowed 108 Ohio St.3d 1509, 844 N.E.2d 855, 2006-Ohio-1329. Criminal Law ⇨ 566; Robbery ⇨ 24.40

Defendant's conviction for felonious assault was not against the manifest weight of the evidence, even though complaining witness was unsure of his identification of defendant; companion of complaining witness identified defendant from a photographic lineup as the perpetrator, the perpetrator drove a red hatchback vehicle, a red hatchback vehicle was found at defendant's residence at the time of his arrest, and defendant's friend testified that defendant admitted that he committed the assault and then warned friend not to tell anyone about the incident. State v. White (Ohio App. 2 Dist., Montgomery, 01-21-2005) No. 20324, 2005-Ohio-212, 2005 WL 120059, Unreported. Criminal Law ⇨ 566

Evidence was sufficient to establish that defendant was the perpetrator of assault, in support of conviction for felonious assault; companion of complaining witness identified defendant from a photographic lineup as the perpetrator, the perpetrator drove a red hatchback vehicle, a red hatchback vehicle was found at defendant's residence at the time of his arrest, and defendant's friend testified that defendant admitted that he committed the assault and then warned friend not to tell anyone about the incident. State v. White (Ohio App. 2 Dist., Montgomery, 01-21-2005) No. 20324, 2005-Ohio-212, 2005 WL 120059, Unreported. Criminal Law ⇨ 566

Victim's pretrial identification of defendant from an allegedly suggestive photographic array was reliable, even though victim was not able to see robber's entire face during robbery and four months had elapsed between time of robbery and the identification; victim looked at robber during entire holdup, which lasted 30 to 60 seconds, victim described robber as a large African-American man with long hair, which accurately described defendant, victim was very certain that defendant was robber, and victim identified defendant in under 30 seconds. State v. Hayes (Ohio App. 6 Dist., Lucas, 12-03-2004) No. L-03-1221, No. L-03-1222, 2004-Ohio-6460, 2004 WL 2785290, Unreported, appeal not allowed 105 Ohio St.3d 1516, 826 N.E.2d 314, 2005-Ohio-1880. Criminal Law ⇨ 339.7(3)

Evidence supported defendant's convictions for aggravated murder and complicity of murder; although witness failed to identify defendant in photographic array immediately following shooting, witness identified defendant from photographic array several months after shooting as person holding gun at time of murder, eyewitness made positive identification of defendant's codefendant shortly after shooting, and defendant testified he was with codefendant on night of shooting. State v. Sailor (Ohio App. 8 Dist., Cuyahoga, 09-30-2004) No. 83552, 2004-Ohio-5207, 2004 WL 2340113, Unreported, appeal not allowed 105 Ohio St.3d 1464, 824 N.E.2d 92, 2005-Ohio-1024. Homicide ⇨ 1181

Witness's in-court identification of defendant as shooter was reliable and admissible in murder prosecution; although witness failed to identify defendant in photographic array immediately following shooting, witness had opportunity to view defendant at time of shooting, witness accurately described defendant to police, witness identified defendant from photographic array several months after shooting, and witness spoke to detective upon seeing defendant in courtroom to identify defendant as the shooter. State v. Sailor (Ohio App. 8 Dist., Cuyahoga, 09-30-2004) No. 83552, 2004-Ohio-5207, 2004 WL 2340113, Unreported, appeal not allowed 105 Ohio St.3d 1464, 824 N.E.2d 92, 2005-Ohio-1024. Criminal Law ⇨ 339.9(3)

Identification of defendant by victim using photographic array was reliable and thus admissible in trial for failure to stop after accident even presuming that array was unduly suggestive, where defendant turned and faced victim as defendant entered vehicle, area of vehicle was lit by streetlights, victim immediately chose defendant from array when it was presented, and very short time passed between accident and presentation of array. State v. Jennings (Ohio App. 9 Dist., Summit, 10-13-2004) No. 22004, 2004-Ohio-5446, 2004 WL 2292931, Unreported. Criminal Law ⇨ 339.7(3)

Identification of defendant by victim from photographic array was not so unreliable as to give rise to very substantial likelihood of irreparable misidentification, as required for reversal based on allegedly impermissibly suggestive identification procedure given that victim identified defendant at trial; victim had ample opportunity to view defendant both during and after attack, victim provided police with accurate description of defendant's race, height, weight, age, hair length, hair color, skin tone, and complexion, victim identified defendant from array within seconds, and only four days had passed between attack and presentation of array. State v. Jennings (Ohio App. 9 Dist., Summit, 10-13-2004) No. 22016, 2004-Ohio-5447, 2004 WL 2292776, Unreported, appeal not allowed 105 Ohio St.3d 1441, 822 N.E.2d 812, 2005-Ohio-531. Criminal Law ⚿ 339.10(8); Criminal Law ⚿ 339.10(10)

Victim's identification of defendant was reliable under totality of circumstances, in prosecution for aggravated robbery, kidnapping, and having a weapon while under a disability; witness had ample amount of time to view suspect during commission of crime in well illuminated bedroom at close proximity, victim's prior description of second perpetrator accurately matched co-defendant, only discrepancy in victim's description of accomplice was estimating his height, and victim identified defendant in photo array 10 months after commission of crime. State v. Anderson (Ohio App. 8 Dist., Cuyahoga, 08-19-2004) No. 83381, 2004-Ohio-4349, 2004 WL 1846142, Unreported. Criminal Law ⚿ 339.7(1)

Out of court identification of defendant by victim was not unnecessarily suggestive, even though victim looked at Bureau of Motor Vehicle photographs on a computer screen that depicted the subject's height and weight; victim testified that he had ample opportunity to clearly see his assailant's face, he claimed that he was familiar with defendant because he had seen him before, he dismissed the first photograph he was shown by police and immediately identified the second as his assailant, and he stated that he did not look at the subject's height and weight information when viewing the photographs. State v. Pondexter (Ohio App. 8 Dist., Cuyahoga, 07-22-2004) No. 83576, 2004-Ohio-3869, 2004 WL 1631126, Unreported. Criminal Law ⚿ 339.7(3)

Under totality of circumstances, photographic identification procedure was reliable; although defendant complained that victims at same time were given stack of photographs to review, victims were placed at different ends of room so that they could not see which photographs each other were viewing, and, although police station's entire collection of photographs was given to victims, misidentification was unlikely as victims gave similar description of suspect noting suspect's unusual scar, and victims were certain of their identification. State v. Charley (Ohio App. 8 Dist., Cuyahoga, 07-01-2004) No. 82944, 2004-Ohio-3463, 2004 WL 1472745, Unreported. Criminal Law ⚿ 339.7(3)

Store employee's identification of defendant as perpetrator after reviewing photographic array was reliable, where employee engaged in conversation with perpetrator during robbery, employee had high degree of attention during robbery, employee described perpetrator following robbery, and defendant did not contend that he did not possess physical characteristics described by employee. State v. Marbury (Ohio App. 10 Dist., Franklin, 06-29-2004) No. 03AP-233, 2004-Ohio-3373, 2004 WL 1445224, Unreported, appeal not allowed 103 Ohio St.3d 1493, 816 N.E.2d 1080, 2004-Ohio-5605. Criminal Law ⚿ 339.7(1)

Defendant failed to demonstrate that photo array was unnecessarily suggestive, even though defendant was the only suspect wearing a bright yellow jogging suit; alleged victim was first shown a set of four photographs depicting only the head and shoulders of each suspect and identified defendant as the person who shot him, and alleged victim was later shown a photo array which did not contain a photograph of defendant, and alleged victim indicated that the person who shot him was not depicted in the array. State v. White (Ohio App. 8 Dist., Cuyahoga, 05-27-2004) No. 83562, 2004-Ohio-2702, 2004 WL 1172085, Unreported, appeal not allowed 103 Ohio St.3d 1493, 816 N.E.2d 1080, 2004-Ohio-5605. Criminal Law ⚿ 339.7(4)

Even if photographic array, in which defendant's picture had different background than other pictures and defendant, unlike other individuals in array, was depicted wearing orange jumpsuit typically issued as jail clothing, was unfairly suggestive, such error was harmless in burglary prosecution, in light of other evidence and victim's prior identification of defendant on the night of offense. State v. Davis (Ohio App. 8 Dist., Cuyahoga, 04-15-2004) No. 83033, 2004-Ohio-1908, 2004 WL 802768, Unreported. Criminal Law ⚿ 1169.1(5)

Photographic array used for identification of defendant was not unduly suggestive; police showed witness a six-photograph array after reading to her standard photographic show-up instructions, and officer who exhibited photographic array to witness expressly stated that he did not influence witness's selection of defendant's photograph from array. State v. Staley (Ohio App. 2 Dist., Montgomery, 04-25-2003) No. 19415, 2003-Ohio-2090, 2003 WL 1949800, Unreported. Criminal Law ⚿ 339.7(4)

Robbery defendant was not entitled to a mistrial based on in-court identification by victim who had been unable to identify defendant from a photograph array shown to him at the police station, even though victim based identification on his recognition of defendant's voice during exchange between judge and defendant that he witnessed in violation of separation order; separation order violation occurred early in the proceedings before any testimony in the case-in-chief was taken, and defendant failed to show that he suffered any material prejudice as a result of the separation order violation. State v. Walker (Ohio App. 10 Dist., Franklin, 03-06-2003) No. 02AP-679, 2003-Ohio-986, 2003 WL 757525, Unreported, appeal not allowed 99 Ohio St.3d 1455, 790 N.E.2d 1218, 2003-Ohio-3396. Criminal Law ⚿ 665(4)

Eyewitness's accidental exposure to newspaper headline indicating that individual picked out murder suspect's photograph and accompanying photograph of suspect prior to eyewitness's out-of-court identification of defendant did not require exclusion of eyewitness's in-court identification of defendant, where witness's exposure to newspaper was chance event not caused by state and witness was thoroughly cross-examined as to quality of his observation of defendant and procedures used by police during out-of-court identification. State v. Roper (Ohio App. 9 Dist., Summit, 12-31-2002) No. 20836, 2002-Ohio-7321, 2002 WL 31890116, Unreported, appeal not allowed 98 Ohio St.3d 1567, 787 N.E.2d 1231, 2003-Ohio-2242. Criminal Law ⚷ 339.10(1)

Competent evidence supported trial court finding that witnesses' identification testimony was not tainted by suggestiveness, in prosecution for murder; witness testified that a week after the shooting she was shown a photo array, that she identified defendant as the shooter, that no other witnesses were in the room when she made the identification, and that police officer did not say anything to her prior to her identification. State v. Duncan (Ohio App. 1 Dist., 09-05-2003) 154 Ohio App.3d 254, 796 N.E.2d 1006, 2003-Ohio-4695, appeal not allowed 100 Ohio St.3d 1532, 800 N.E.2d 48, 2003-Ohio-6458. Criminal Law ⚷ 339.7(3)

Victim's identification of defendant from photographs numbered one though six as the person who held gun on him during robbery was sufficiently reliable; while police officer told victim that person suspected of being the assailant was in one of the photographs, defendant's photograph was only one with a circle around number, and identification took place 24 days after the crime, victim testified at suppression hearing that he had "good" opportunity over course of about one full minute to view defendant under lit sky and from close distance, and victim's identification both at photographic lineup and in court was unequivocal. State v. Kiner (Ohio App. 1 Dist., 10-18-2002) 149 Ohio App.3d 599, 778 N.E.2d 144, 2002-Ohio-5578, appeal not allowed 99 Ohio St.3d 1412, 788 N.E.2d 648, 2003-Ohio-2454. Criminal Law ⚷ 339.7(3)

Circumstances of out-of-court identifications of capital murder defendant by juvenile eyewitnesses were not unduly suggestive, despite defendant's contention that state subjected juveniles to numerous viewings of defendant or defendant's photograph before photographic arrays and in-court identifications; investigators showed juveniles between 30 and 100 photographs, made no suggestions or comments to juveniles, did not rush them, and did not tell them whether they had chosen defendant's photograph, and any encounters juveniles might have had with media reports or with defendant in courtroom went to weight to be given identifications rather than their admissibility. State v. Gross (Ohio, 10-30-2002) 97 Ohio St.3d 121, 776 N.E.2d 1061, 2002-Ohio-5524, reconsideration denied 97 Ohio St.3d 1486, 780 N.E.2d 288, 2002-Ohio-6866, certiorari denied 123 S.Ct. 2079, 538 U.S. 1037, 155 L.Ed.2d 1068, rehearing denied 124 S.Ct. 20, 539 U.S. 976, 156 L.Ed.2d 685. Criminal Law ⚷ 339.7(4)

Trial court committed reversible error, during burglary and theft trial, in admitting into evidence the photo array which contained mug shot photo of defendant with police identification number hanging from placard around his neck and in allowing detective to testify that he specifically chose to include defendant's photo based on prior contacts with him; photo array, when coupled with detective's testimony, impermissibly suggested to jury that defendant had prior criminal involvement. State v. Yarbrough (Ohio App. 8 Dist., 08-17-1998) 129 Ohio App.3d 437, 717 N.E.2d 1173. Criminal Law ⚷ 374; Criminal Law ⚷ 1169.11

Photo array showing 15 males who were comparable to general descriptions of intruders given by victims of charged burglary, robbery, kidnapping, and rape was not impermissibly suggestive, even though pictures of defendant and codefendant were the only single shots with a measuring wall background, where witnesses gave corroborating description of defendant at scene of crime, had opportunity to see defendant's face and were attentive when viewing him, and were certain their identifications were correct. State v. Thompson (Ohio App. 8 Dist., 05-04-1998) 127 Ohio App.3d 511, 713 N.E.2d 456, appeal not allowed 83 Ohio St.3d 1451, 700 N.E.2d 334. Criminal Law ⚷ 339.7(4)

Witness' in-court identification of defendant was not product of impermissible police investigatory tactics, where witness had identified defendant from photo array as person she had seen parked outside store in which she was working on night of victim's disappearance and testified that she had focused her attention on defendant because she thought defendant was about to rob her. State v. Wogenstahl (Ohio, 03-06-1996) 75 Ohio St.3d 344, 662 N.E.2d 311, 1996-Ohio-219, reconsideration denied 75 Ohio St.3d 1453, 663 N.E.2d 333, certiorari denied 117 S.Ct. 240, 519 U.S. 895, 136 L.Ed.2d 169, denial of post-conviction relief affirmed 2004-Ohio-5994, 2004 WL 2567655, appeal not allowed 105 Ohio St.3d 1465, 824 N.E.2d 93, 2005-Ohio-1024. Criminal Law ⚷ 339.10(2)

Cab driver's in-court identification of defendant as driver's fare from apartment in which fires were set and caused death of sleeping children was reliable, despite claim that defendant's was only photograph to appear in both photographic lineups and that defendant was only person in lineup matching height description given by driver, as driver initially refused to identify anyone in lineup in which defendant's photograph was not present, recognized defendant in convenience store's surveillance tape by clothing only, and immediately recognized defendant in lineup including defendant's photograph, and because others pictured in photographs were close to driver's height description, and driver observed defendant for extended period of time. State v. Garner (Ohio, 11-22-1995) 74 Ohio St.3d 49, 656 N.E.2d 623, 1995-Ohio-168, reconsideration denied 74 Ohio St.3d 1485, 657 N.E.2d 1378, certiorari denied 116 S.Ct. 1444, 517 U.S. 1147, 134 L.Ed.2d 564, rehearing denied 116 S.Ct. 1872, 517

U.S. 1230, 134 L.Ed.2d 969, stay granted 76 Ohio St.3d 1401, 666 N.E.2d 233. Criminal Law ⚩ 339.7(4); Criminal Law ⚩ 339.9(2)

Out-of-court identification of defendant by victim who, while in the hospital, saw newspaper photograph of defendant following his arrest in connection with murder, and selected defendant's photograph from photo array thereafter, was reliable, where victim had ample opportunity to observe defendant while defendant was passenger in his truck, and only two days passed between assault and identification in newspaper. State v. Williams (Ohio, 08-16-1995) 73 Ohio St.3d 153, 652 N.E.2d 721, 1995-Ohio-275, reconsideration denied 74 Ohio St.3d 1409, 655 N.E.2d 188, stay granted 74 Ohio St.3d 1437, 655 N.E.2d 1321, stay terminated 75 Ohio St.3d 1439, 662 N.E.2d 1085, certiorari denied 116 S.Ct. 1047, 516 U.S. 1161, 134 L.Ed.2d 193, denial of post-conviction relief affirmed 1998 WL 330539, dismissed, appeal not allowed 83 Ohio St.3d 1449, 700 N.E.2d 332, reconsideration denied 84 Ohio St.3d 1413, 701 N.E.2d 1021. Criminal Law ⚩ 339.7(1)

Identification of defendant from photo array, by convenience store employees who spoke with defendant for approximately 20 to 45 minutes while he waited for cab, was reliable. State v. Williams (Ohio, 08-16-1995) 73 Ohio St.3d 153, 652 N.E.2d 721, 1995-Ohio-275, reconsideration denied 74 Ohio St.3d 1409, 655 N.E.2d 188, stay granted 74 Ohio St.3d 1437, 655 N.E.2d 1321, stay terminated 75 Ohio St.3d 1439, 662 N.E.2d 1085, certiorari denied 116 S.Ct. 1047, 516 U.S. 1161, 134 L.Ed.2d 193, denial of post-conviction relief affirmed 1998 WL 330539, dismissed, appeal not allowed 83 Ohio St.3d 1449, 700 N.E.2d 332, reconsideration denied 84 Ohio St.3d 1413, 701 N.E.2d 1021. Criminal Law ⚩ 339.7(1)

Victim's subsequent out-of-court identification of defendant from photo array of 55 persons was not rendered impermissibly suggestive by earlier viewing of smaller "photo album" that did not contain defendant's picture and from which victim did not identify her assailant. State v. Halley (Ohio App. 10 Dist., 01-20-1994) 93 Ohio App.3d 71, 637 N.E.2d 937, dismissed, jurisdictional motion overruled 69 Ohio St.3d 1476, 634 N.E.2d 1023. Criminal Law ⚩ 339.7(3)

Trial court did not err in allowing identification testimony based on photo array that did not comply with standard police procedures, where defendant, not prosecution, elicited testimony at trial. State v. Wooden (Summit 1993) 86 Ohio App.3d 23, 619 N.E.2d 1132, motion for delayed appeal denied 84 Ohio St.3d 1410, 701 N.E.2d 1020, dismissed, appeal not allowed 85 Ohio St.3d 1487, 709 N.E.2d 1215. Criminal Law ⚩ 339.7(3)

Horizontal "height" lines in the background of each photograph used in an out-of-court identification do not provide the trier of fact with the reasonable inference of prior criminal involvement necessary to ban their use at trial where the police identification numbers are obscured and only the faces of the individuals are visible on the photographs. State v. Tolbert (Hamilton 1990) 70 Ohio App.3d 372, 591 N.E.2d 325, dismissed 58 Ohio St.3d 701, 569 N.E.2d 504, rehearing granted 59 Ohio St.3d 715, 572 N.E.2d 697.

It is not a requirement for the use of photo arrays that all pictures shown must be of the same type nor that they bear no differing marks or blemishes, nor is it required that only one photo of an accused be used; the only inquiry is whether the photo or procedure used is so impermissibly suggestive as to give rise to a very substantial likelihood of irreparable misidentification. State v. Green (Cuyahoga 1990) 67 Ohio App.3d 72, 585 N.E.2d 990. Criminal Law ⚩ 339.7(4)

Photographic arrays are not impermissibly suggestive as defendant contends when photographs in the first photo array show all persons in a typical "mug shot" except for the defendant, who is shown in a wallet-type photo which was darker and had a scratched surface, and in the second array in which defendant appeared in a mug shot with a physical description information card; these points of distinction do not rise to the level of mistake contemplated by Simmons. State v. Green (Cuyahoga 1990) 67 Ohio App.3d 72, 585 N.E.2d 990.

On direct examination, evidence of the identification of the defendant from a selection of photographs, using photographs from police files with police identification numerals thereon which provide the finder of facts with the reasonable inference that defendant has had prior criminal involvement, may not be used for the purpose of proving defendant's identity. (See also 26 OS(2d) 185, 271 NE(2d) 242 (1971), State v Wilkinson.) State v. Breedlove (Ohio 1971) 26 Ohio St.2d 178, 271 N.E.2d 238, 55 O.O.2d 441.

Under RC 2945.55, where identification of the defendant is in issue, a witness who on a previous occasion has selected, or observed another select, defendant's photograph from a number of photographs, may testify to such previous photographic identification if the photographs, or the photographs coupled with other testimony given on direct examination, do not provide the finder of facts with the reasonable inference that defendant has had prior criminal involvement, and if the procedure of identification does not violate defendant's constitutional rights. State v. Breedlove (Ohio 1971) 26 Ohio St.2d 178, 271 N.E.2d 238, 55 O.O.2d 441.

Even if second photo array shown to abduction victim who identified defendant's clean-shaven face was unduly suggestive, on grounds police had told victim following first array that photograph depicting defendant with a beard was their suspect, there was no substantial likelihood of misidentification, where victim had unimpeded opportunity to view defendant at time of crime, devoted her full attention to defendant's face as she stared at it from close range, and expressed certainty at first array that her abductor had not been bearded and identified unbearded face of defendant in less than 90 seconds during second array. Ledbetter v. Edwards (C.A.6 (Ohio), 09-21-1994) 35 F.3d 1062, certiorari denied 115 S.Ct. 2584, 515 U.S. 1145, 132 L.Ed.2d 833. Criminal Law ⚩ 339.7(3); Criminal Law ⚩ 339.7(4)

Photo arrays from which witness identified petitioner as person she had seen chasing intended third victim from scene of double murder were not impermissibly suggestive; mere fact that petitioner's photo contained writing in different colored ink than other photos was immaterial, depiction of petitioner in two different arrays was not impermissible, since different photos were used, and variations in age and facial hair were not so great that witness's attention necessarily and unavoidably would have been focused on petitioner's photo. Davie v. Mitchell (N.D.Ohio, 08-06-2003) 291 F.Supp.2d 573, motion to amend denied, certificate of appealability granted in part, denied in part 324 F.Supp.2d 862. Criminal Law ⚷ 339.7(4)

2945.56 Rebuttal of defendant's character evidence

When the defendant offers evidence of his character or reputation, the prosecution may offer, in rebuttal thereof, proof of his previous conviction of a crime involving moral turpitude, in addition to other competent evidence.

(1953 H 1, eff. 10–1–53; GC 13444–17)

Historical and Statutory Notes

Pre–1953 H 1 Amendments: 113 v 189, Ch 23, § 17

Cross References

Witnesses, impeachment by evidence of conviction of crime, Evid R 609

Library References

Criminal Law ⚷378.

Westlaw Topic No. 110.

C.J.S. Criminal Law §§ 816 to 817.

Research References

Encyclopedias

OH Jur. 3d Criminal Law § 2950, Rebuttal by State of Evidence of Defendant's Character and Reputation.

Treatises and Practice Aids

Giannelli and Snyder, Baldwin's Ohio Practice, Evidence, R 404, Character Evidence Not Admissible to Prove Conduct; Exceptions; Other Crimes.

Giannelli and Snyder, Baldwin's Ohio Practice, Evidence, § 404.5, Accused's Character: Prosecution Rebuttal.

Giannelli and Snyder, Baldwin's Ohio Practice, Evidence, § 405.5, Specific Instances: in General.

1 Giannelli and Snyder, Baldwin's Ohio Practice, Evidence, Index, Index.

Notes of Decisions

---

1. Foundation for questioning

It is reversible error, in the trial of an accused for robbery, for the prosecution to ask the defendant on cross-examination whether "you have ever been tried of attempted theft in 1964," where the prosecution makes no attempt to show that defendant was ever tried for an attempted theft in 1964 and produces no evidence of any conviction of an "attempted theft in 1964." State v. Crawford (Hamilton 1969) 17 Ohio App.2d 141, 244 N.E.2d 774, 46 O.O.2d 175. Criminal Law ⚷ 706(5); Criminal Law ⚷ 1171.8(2)

2. Prior juvenile record

Where the defense introduces character evidence to the effect that the defendant had never been in any kind of trouble, and where the trial court disallows cross-examination of defendant's witnesses on the subject of prior juvenile court involvement, the introduction of a juvenile record to rebut such evidence is not prejudicial error. State v. Hale (Franklin 1969) 21 Ohio App.2d 207, 256 N.E.2d 239, 50 O.O.2d 340.

Although Ohio law generally protects a minor from the exposure of his acts in another judicial forum, RC 2151.35(G) does not prohibit the cross-examination, in a criminal trial, of a defendant, or defendant's witnesses, concerning a prior juvenile record, where the defendant's evidence attempts to establish his good character. State v. Hale (Franklin 1969) 21 Ohio App.2d 207, 256 N.E.2d 239, 50 O.O.2d 340.

2945.57 Number of witnesses to character

The number of witnesses who are expected to testify upon the subject of character or reputation, for whom subpoenas are issued, shall be designated upon the praecipe and, except in cases of murder in the first and second degree, manslaughter, rape, assault with intent to commit rape, or selling intoxicating liquor to a person in the habit of becoming intoxicated, shall not exceed ten upon each side, unless a deposit of at least one per diem and mileage fee for each of such additional witnesses is first made with the clerk of the court of common pleas. Not more than ten witnesses upon each side shall be permitted to testify upon the question of character or reputation in a criminal cause unless their full per diem and mileage fees have been deposited or paid by the party in whose behalf they are sworn, and the clerk shall not issue a certificate for compensation to be paid out of the county treasury to a witness who has testified upon the subject of character or reputation, except as provided in this section.

(1953 H 1, eff. 10–1–53; GC 13444–18)

Historical and Statutory Notes

Pre–1953 H 1 Amendments: 113 v 189, Ch 23, § 18

Cross References

Character evidence, Evid R 404, 405

Subpoenas, Crim R 17

Library References

Criminal Law ⚷676.

Witnesses ⚷23.

Westlaw Topic Nos. 110, 410.

C.J.S. Criminal Law § 1213.

C.J.S. Federal Civil Procedure § 585.

C.J.S. Witnesses §§ 2, 70 to 86.

Research References

Encyclopedias

OH Jur. 3d Criminal Law § 461, Limitations on Right.

OH Jur. 3d Criminal Law § 3109, Number of Witnesses.

OH Jur. 3d Criminal Law § 3110, Compensation of Witnesses.

Treatises and Practice Aids

Markus, Trial Handbook for Ohio Lawyers, § 11:5, Compensation.

Markus, Trial Handbook for Ohio Lawyers, § 2:18, Limiting Number of Witnesses.

Giannelli and Snyder, Baldwin's Ohio Practice, Evidence, R 403, Exclusion of Relevant Evidence on Grounds of Prejudice, Confusion, or Undue Delay.

Giannelli and Snyder, Baldwin's Ohio Practice, Evidence, § 403.8, Undue Delay; Cumulative Evidence.

1 Giannelli and Snyder, Baldwin's Ohio Practice, Evidence, Index, Index.

Notes of Decisions

1. Limiting number of witnesses

Where court, upon refusing counsel for accused the right to call three more character witnesses after five such witnesses have testified, states that "nothing is added by parade of witnesses, all of whom will say he had a good reputation," error is committed prejudicial to accused in that the value of such evidence is minimized and jury is misled in its consideration thereof. State v. Carter (Cuyahoga 1944) 75 Ohio App. 545, 58 N.E.2d 794, 41 Ohio Law Abs. 545, 31 O.O. 322.

A trial court in a criminal case has no authority to limit unreasonably the number of witnesses called to give character or reputation testimony, in view of GC 13444–18 (RC 2945.57). State v. Carter (Cuyahoga 1944) 75 Ohio App. 545, 58 N.E.2d 794, 41 Ohio Law Abs. 545, 31 O.O. 322. Criminal Law ⚷ 676

ALIBI

2945.58 Alibi

Whenever a defendant in a criminal cause proposes to offer in his defense, testimony to establish an alibi on his behalf, such defendant shall, not less than three days before the trial of such cause, file and serve upon the prosecuting attorney a notice in writing of his intention to claim such alibi. Notice shall include specific information as to the place at which the defendant claims to have been at the time of the alleged offense. If the defendant fails to file such written notice, the court may exclude evidence offered by the defendant for the purpose of proving such alibi.

(1953 H 1, eff. 10–1–53; GC 13444–20)

Historical and Statutory Notes

Pre–1953 H 1 Amendments: 113 v 190, Ch 23, § 20

Cross References

Computation of time, 1.14

Notice of alibi, Crim R 12.1

Time, Crim R 45

Library References

Criminal Law ⚷629(9), 629.5(6).

Westlaw Topic No. 110.

C.J.S. Criminal Law §§ 451 to 452, 463.

Research References

Encyclopedias

OH Jur. 3d Criminal Law § 724, Alibi.

Treatises and Practice Aids

Katz, Giannelli, Blair and Lipton, Baldwin's Ohio Practice, Criminal Law, § 52:2, Constitutionality.

Katz, Giannelli, Blair and Lipton, Baldwin's Ohio Practice, Criminal Law, § 52:3, Time Limit and Service.

Katz, Giannelli, Blair and Lipton, Baldwin's Ohio Practice, Criminal Law, § 52:4, Content and Form of Notice.

Katz, Giannelli, Blair and Lipton, Baldwin's Ohio Practice, Criminal Law, § 52:5, Sanctions—Exclusion.

Katz, Giannelli, Blair and Lipton, Baldwin's Ohio Practice, Criminal Law, § 143:35, Notice of Alibi.

Law Review and Journal Commentaries

Criminal Discovery, Albert C. Garber. 15 W Reserve U L Rev 495 (June 1964).

Criminal Law—Pretrial Notice of Alibi—Preclusion Sanction—Trial Court's Exclusion of Alibi Testimony Pursuant to Ohio R Crim P. 12.1 Constitutes an Abuse of Discretion Where Admission of Such Evidence Is Necessary to Insure a Fair Trial and There Is No Showing of Bad Faith by Defendant or Prejudice to the Prosecution.—State v. Smith, Note. 46 U Cin L Rev 1020 (1977).

State v. Smith: Abuse of Discretion for Notice of Alibi, Note. 4 Ohio N U L Rev 850 (1977).

Notes of Decisions

1. Constitutional issues

RC 2945.58 is constitutional. State v. Cunningham (Columbiana 1961) 185 N.E.2d 327, 89 Ohio Law Abs. 206.

The Supreme Court of Ohio did not concur with the court of appeals in the reasons assigned by court of appeals to sustain the unconstitutionality of former GC 13444–20 (RC 2945.58). State v. Thayer (Ohio 1931) 124 Ohio St. 1, 176 N.E. 656, 75 A.L.R. 48, 9 Ohio Law Abs. 734, 34 Ohio Law Rep. 429.

In a habeas corpus proceeding based on an armed robbery conviction, the trial court's refusal to order the prosecutor to locate and produce alibi witnesses for an indigent defendant does not deprive the defendant of any constitutional rights. Cox v. Cardwell (C.A.6 (Ohio) 1972) 464 F.2d 639, 65 O.O.2d 353. Criminal Law ⚷ 629(9)

Where a defendant's attorney fails to thoroughly investigate his client's claimed alibi, which is his client's only defense, such failure results in the deprivation of defendant's constitutional right to effective assistance of counsel. Johns v. Perini (C.A.6 (Ohio) 1972) 462 F.2d 1308, 66 O.O.2d 69, certiorari denied 93 S.Ct. 519, 409 U.S. 1049, 34 L.Ed.2d 501.

2. Mandatory nature of section

RC 2945.58 is mandatory. State v. Payne (Franklin 1957) 104 Ohio App. 410, 149 N.E.2d 583, 77 Ohio Law Abs. 558, 5 O.O.2d 87.

3. False and fraudulent claims

Statute gives the state some protection against false and fraudulent claims of alibi often presented by accused so near the close of the trial as to make it quite impossible for state to ascertain any facts as to the credibility of the witnesses called by accused, who may reside at some point far distant from the place of trial. State v. Thayer (Ohio 1931) 124 Ohio St. 1, 176 N.E. 656, 75 A.L.R. 48, 9 Ohio Law Abs. 734, 34 Ohio Law Rep. 429.

4. Failure to file notice

Indictment which charged defendant with committing three counts of rape of a child under the age of 13 but failed to specify the exact date on which the rapes allegedly occurred did not deprive defendant of due process; defendant was charged with raping his step-daughter, defendant lived with victim for 16 months, indictment alleged that the rapes occurred in the family home on occasions when mother was running errands or was otherwise out of the house, defendant failed to file notice of an alibi defense, and the victim testified to generalized dates and times at trial. State v. Alicea (Ohio App. 7 Dist., Mahoning, 12-11-2002) No. 99 CA 36, 2002-Ohio-6907, 2002 WL 31813090, Unreported, appeal not allowed 98 Ohio St.3d 1515, 786 N.E.2d 64, 2003-Ohio-1572, habeas corpus denied 2005 WL 2280281. Indictment And Information ⚷ 87(7)

Although no notice of alibi is filed by the defendant, as required under Crim R 12.1, in the interest of justice, work records and witnesses' testimony relative thereto should be admitted at trial to establish an alibi when the question of credibility of such evidence and witnesses is at a minimum. State v. Edwards (Lucas 1975) 52 Ohio App.2d 120, 368 N.E.2d 302, 6 O.O.3d 91. Criminal Law ⚷ 629.5(6)

Appellate court could not say that trial court abused its discretion in excluding the testimony of supporting alibi witnesses where defendant neither filed a notice of alibi prior to trial nor sought a continuance. State v. Focht (Ohio 1974) 37 Ohio St.2d 173, 309 N.E.2d 922, 66 O.O.2d 359.

Upon trial of persons jointly indicted for grand larceny, a verdict of guilty will not be disturbed where no abuse of discretion appears in trial court excluding testimony offered by accused for purpose of proving an alibi, no notice of which has been given the state as provided in the statute, such proffered testimony being "for the purpose of showing the whereabouts of said defendant and to disprove the testimony of witness for the prosecution," it not appearing that such proffer went to any other subject than that of alibi. State v. Nooks (Ohio 1930) 123 Ohio St. 190, 174 N.E. 743, 9 Ohio Law Abs. 59, 33 Ohio Law Rep. 441.

Under RC 2945.58, even a defendant's own alibi testimony may be excluded if inadequate notice is given of the intent to rely upon an alibi. Johns v. Perini (C.A.6 (Ohio) 1971) 440 F.2d 577, 59 O.O.2d 71.

5. Jury instructions

Error by trial court in failing to give requested alibi instruction was not prejudicial in aggravated robbery prosecution. State v. Frost (Ohio App. 2 Dist., 10-14-2005) 164 Ohio App.3d 61, 841 N.E.2d 336, 2005-Ohio-5510. Criminal Law ⚷ 1173.2(3)

Where a defendant files a timely notice of alibi, presents evidence to support the contention, and relies on alibi as his sole defense, the trial court has a statutory duty to charge the jury on alibi; however, the trial court is not required to give such instruction in the exact form requested by the defendant and may, instead, frame the instructions in the court's own words. State v. Frost (Ohio App. 2 Dist., 10-14-2005) 164 Ohio App.3d 61, 841 N.E.2d 336, 2005-Ohio-5510. Criminal Law ⚷ 775(1); Criminal Law ⚷ 834(3)

A trial court's jury instruction that a defendant is required to prove his alibi by a preponderance of the evidence constitutes harmless and nonprejudicial error where given the overwhelming evidence of the defendant's guilt, the instruction could not have misled the jury and therefore, even if a correct instruction on the issue of alibi were given the outcome of the trial would not have been any different; the testimony of the alibi witnesses that the defendant was with them when the crime was committed was incredible and contradictory, both to each other's testimony and to that of the defendant, and an alibi witness damaged the defendant's case by admitting that on the morning of the crime the defendant told him he was going to steal a dairy truck, which corroborated the victim's testimony that the defendant put her in a a dairy truck, and defendant's own statement to the police contradicted his alibi. State v. Gladding (Lake 1990) 66 Ohio App.3d 502, 585 N.E.2d 838, dismissed, jurisdictional motion overruled 52 Ohio St.3d 706, 557 N.E.2d 1212.

Failure to give defendant's requested instruction on alibi was harmless error, where evidence, including that of defendant's own witnesses, tended to contradict alibi, and evidence clearly supported guilty verdict beyond reasonable doubt. State v. Mitchell (Cuyahoga 1989) 60 Ohio App.3d 106, 574 N.E.2d 573, cause dismissed 49 Ohio St.3d 709, 551 N.E.2d 1306. Criminal Law ⚷ 1173.2(3)

A trial judge commits plain error by telling a jury that the facts are not in controversy where the defendant asserts the defenses of alibi and mistaken identity. State v. Gover (Hamilton 1989) 61 Ohio App.3d 330, 572 N.E.2d 781, dismissed 43 Ohio St.3d 710, 540 N.E.2d 725.

Where the defense offers no direct evidence contradicting the commission of the crimes charged, and relies solely on the defense of alibi, the defendant's failure to refute the claim that the crimes were committed does not warrant the trial court's omission in its instructions to the jury of the elements of the crimes charged, including their specifications, and such omission may be noticed as plain error affecting the defendant's substantial rights to a trial by jury and to a fair trial, notwithstanding defense counsel's failure to request such instructions as provided by Crim R 30. State v. Bridgeman (Cuyahoga 1977) 51 Ohio App.2d 105, 366 N.E.2d 1378, 5 O.O.3d 275. Criminal Law ⚿ 772(1)

Where the accused has seasonably filed a notice of alibi, presented testimony at trial in its support, and relies on alibi as his sole defense, and the trial court does not instruct on the defense of alibi, the court has failed to instruct on "all matters of law necessary for the information of the jury in giving its verdict" as provided by RC 2945.11, and this omission may be noticed as plain error affecting the substantial rights of the accused, notwithstanding defense counsel's failure to request an instruction on alibi as provided by Crim R 30. State v. Bridgeman (Cuyahoga 1977) 51 Ohio App.2d 105, 366 N.E.2d 1378, 5 O.O.3d 275. Criminal Law ⚿ 775(2)

Language in alibi instructions directing the jury to acquit if all the evidence in the case raises a reasonable doubt of guilt, does not erroneously shift the burden of proof from the state where other language in the charge clearly explains that the burden remains upon the state. State v. Childs (Ohio 1968) 14 Ohio St.2d 56, 236 N.E.2d 545, 43 O.O.2d 119, certiorari denied 89 S.Ct. 1596, 394 U.S. 1002, 22 L.Ed.2d 779. Criminal Law ⚿ 778(5)

The failure of the trial court, in a criminal case, to charge the jury on the law regarding alibi is not prejudicial to the defendant where no request for such an instruction was made, and the testimony of defendant's alibi witnesses, even if believed by the jury, would not necessarily preclude his involvement in the offense charged or establish the defense of alibi. State v. Goode (Greene 1962) 118 Ohio App. 479, 195 N.E.2d 581, 25 O.O.2d 395, appeal dismissed 174 Ohio St. 232, 188 N.E.2d 421, 22 O.O.2d 224.

Unless there is some evidence, at least a scintilla, establishing or tending to establish an alibi, there is no duty on the part of the court to charge on the question. State v. Payne (Franklin 1957) 104 Ohio App. 410, 149 N.E.2d 583, 77 Ohio Law Abs. 558, 5 O.O.2d 87. Criminal Law ⚿ 775(2)

A charge to the jury that the defense of alibi must be proved by a preponderance of the evidence and if so proved the defendant must be acquitted but that if the defendant fails to prove the alibi by a preponderance of the evidence the burden is still on the state to prove the defendant's guilt beyond a reasonable doubt, is erroneous; but such incorrect charge cannot be said to have misled the jury and is not prejudicial where there is no evidence on the subject. State v. Payne (Franklin 1957) 104 Ohio App. 410, 149 N.E.2d 583, 77 Ohio Law Abs. 558, 5 O.O.2d 87.

6. Failure of defense

A trial court's definition of "on or about" to mean "a reasonable time" does not prejudice a defendant who presents an alibi for the date on which the indictment alleges the offense occurred but the victim testifies that the offense occurred approximately two weeks before the date alleged in the indictment. State v. Price (Crawford 1992) 80 Ohio App.3d 35, 608 N.E.2d 818.

PROOF

2945.59 Proof of defendant's motive

In any criminal case in which the defendant's motive or intent, the absence of mistake or accident on his part, or the defendant's scheme, plan, or system in doing an act is material, any acts of the defendant which tend to show his motive or intent, the absence of mistake or accident on his part, or the defendant's scheme, plan, or system in doing the act in question may be proved, whether they are contemporaneous with or prior or subsequent thereto, notwithstanding that such proof may show or tend to show the commission of another crime by the defendant.

(1953 H 1, eff. 10–1–53; GC 13444–19)

Historical and Statutory Notes

Pre–1953 H 1 Amendments: 113 v 190, Ch 23, § 19

Cross References

Gross sexual imposition, evidence, 2907.05

Rape, evidence, marriage or cohabitation not defense to rape charges, 2907.02

Library References

Criminal Law ⚿342, 369 to 374.

Homicide ⚿1000.

Westlaw Topic Nos. 110, 203.

C.J.S. Criminal Law §§ 454, 726, 825 to 830, 832.

Research References

ALR Library

86 ALR 5th 59, Admissibility, in Rape Case, of Evidence that Accused Raped or Attempted to Rape Person Other Than Prosecutrix--Prior Offenses.

Encyclopedias

OH Jur. 3d Appellate Review § 164, Objection to Admission of Evidence.

OH Jur. 3d Criminal Law § 990, Acts and Threats of Violence by Accused Against Third Persons.

OH Jur. 3d Criminal Law § 2768, Evidence of Other Acts of Defendant.

OH Jur. 3d Criminal Law § 2770, Evidence of Other Acts of Defendant—Propriety of Reference to "Other Offenses".

OH Jur. 3d Criminal Law § 2914, Evidence of Motive; Intent.

OH Jur. 3d Criminal Law § 2958, Evidence of Other Crimes to Show Defendant's Propensity or Predisposition for Crime.

OH Jur. 3d Criminal Law § 2966, Harmless Error as to Admission of Evidence of Other Crimes or Acts.

OH Jur. 3d Criminal Law § 2967, Generally; Proof of Motive, Opportunity, Intent, Preparation, Plan, Knowledge, Identity, or Absence of Mistake or Accident.

OH Jur. 3d Criminal Law § 2968, Necessity of Similarity of Other Crimes With Crime Charged.

OH Jur. 3d Criminal Law § 2969, Necessity of Relevancy of Other Crimes or Acts.

OH Jur. 3d Criminal Law § 2970, Necessity of Materiality of Other Crimes or Acts.

OH Jur. 3d Criminal Law § 2973, Showing Identity of Accused.

OH Jur. 3d Criminal Law § 2974, Showing Intent of Accused.

OH Jur. 3d Criminal Law § 2977, Showing Motive of Accused.

OH Jur. 3d Criminal Law § 2978, Showing Scheme, Plan, Habit, or System of Accused.

OH Jur. 3d Criminal Law § 2979, Showing Absence of Mistake or Accident.

OH Jur. 3d Criminal Law § 2981, Sexual Crimes.

OH Jur. 3d Criminal Law § 3083, Photographs.

Forms

Ohio Jurisprudence Pleading and Practice Forms § 60:6, Character Evidence.

Treatises and Practice Aids

Markus, Trial Handbook for Ohio Lawyers, § 15:7, Admissibility of Evidence of Similar Act or Occurrence in Criminal Case.

Markus, Trial Handbook for Ohio Lawyers, § 9:13, Criminal Case—Party Having Burden of Proof—Identity of Accused.

Markus, Trial Handbook for Ohio Lawyers, § 15:24, Other Crimes, Wrongs, or Acts.

Giannelli and Snyder, Baldwin's Ohio Practice, Evidence, R 404, Character Evidence Not Admissible to Prove Conduct; Exceptions; Other Crimes.

Giannelli and Snyder, Baldwin's Ohio Practice, Evidence, § 404.7, Rape Shield Law: in General.

Giannelli and Snyder, Baldwin's Ohio Practice, Evidence, § 404.12, Other-Acts Evidence: "Similar Acts" Statute Compared.

Giannelli and Snyder, Baldwin's Ohio Practice, Evidence, § 404.13, Other-Acts Evidence: Common Misconceptions.

Giannelli and Snyder, Baldwin's Ohio Practice, Evidence, § 404.14, Determining Admissibility; Rule 403.

Giannelli and Snyder, Baldwin's Ohio Practice, Evidence, § 404.18, Proof of Mens Rea: Lack of Mistake or Accident.

Giannelli and Snyder, Baldwin's Ohio Practice, Evidence, § 404.28, Other-Acts Evidence: Civil Cases.

1 Giannelli and Snyder, Baldwin's Ohio Practice, Evidence, Index, Index.

Hennenberg & Reinhart, Ohio Criminal Defense Motions F 7.01, Motion in Limine to Prohibit the State from Introducing Evidence of Uncharged Misconduct-Motions in Limine.

Hennenberg & Reinhart, Ohio Criminal Defense Motions F 7.02, Motion in Limine to Prohibit Use of Uncharged Misconduct Evidence and Request for Notice of Intention to Use Evidence-Motions in Limine.

Adrine & Ruden, Ohio Domestic Violence Law § 3:6, Elements and Penalties—Menacing by Stalking Under RC 2903.211.

Adrine & Ruden, Ohio Domestic Violence Law § 5:23, Case Preparation—Prior Bad Acts.

Law Review and Journal Commentaries

Evidence—Evidence of Prior Similar Incidents Is Admissible to Show the Corpus Delecti of Murder.—United States v. Woods, Note. 43 U Cin L Rev 437 (1974).

Navigating Between Scylla and Charybdis: Ohio's Efforts to Protect Children Without Eviscerating the Rights of Criminal Defendants–Evidentiary Considerations and the Rebirth of Confrontation Clause Analysis in Child Abuse Cases, Myrna S. Raeder. 25 U Tol L Rev 43 (1994).

Ohio's "Similar Acts Statute": Its Uses and Abuses, David L. Herbert and Dick W. Mount, Jr. 9 Akron L Rev 301 (Fall 1975).

Notes of Decisions

---

1. Constitutional issues

Defense counsel's failure to sever two burglary prosecutions into two trials was not ineffective assistance of counsel, as similar nature of alleged multiple offenses warranted joinder of cases into one trial. State v. Hobbs (Ohio App. 8 Dist., Cuyahoga, 08-14-2003) No. 81533, 2003-Ohio-4338, 2003 WL 21954778, Unreported, appeal not allowed 100 Ohio St.3d 1545, 800 N.E.2d 751, 2003-Ohio-6879. Criminal Law ⚿ 641.13(2.1)

Defendant did not comply with rules of appellate procedure in alleging, on appeal of felonious assault convictions, that state improperly used "other incidents and an alleged threat to prove that [she] shot into victim's house" and that trial counsel rendered ineffective assistance by not objecting to that "other acts" evidence, where defendant did not specify by reference to the record the "incidents" or "threat" to which she was referring. State v. Ivey (Ohio App. 8 Dist., Cuyahoga, 04-10-2003) No. 80812, 2003-Ohio-1825, 2003 WL 1835513, Unreported, appeal not allowed 99 Ohio St.3d 1470, 791 N.E.2d 984, 2003-Ohio-3669. Criminal Law ⚿ 1130(2)

The collateral estoppel component of the double jeopardy clauses does not bar admission of "other acts" solicitation testimony in a retrial of defendant for arson and insurance fraud. State v. Pence (Ohio App. 12 Dist., Butler, 08-14-1995) No. CA94-11-210, 1995 WL 476196, Unreported, dismissed, appeal not allowed 74 Ohio St.3d 1482, 657 N.E.2d 1376.

Testimony of one witness that defendant "was hateful," that his personality would change when he drank alcohol and that defendant told her he had once had sexual contact with a horse, and testimony of another witness that defendant started giving her "strange looks" during month before murder and that he had graphically expressed to her his desire to have sex did not deny defendant fair trial in capital murder prosecution. State v. Gumm (Ohio, 08-30-1995) 73 Ohio St.3d 413, 653 N.E.2d 253, 1995-Ohio-24, reconsideration denied 74 Ohio St.3d 1423, 655 N.E.2d 742, certiorari denied 116 S.Ct. 1275, 516 U.S. 1177, 134 L.Ed.2d 221, rehearing denied 116 S.Ct. 1707, 517 U.S. 1204, 134 L.Ed.2d 806, denial of post-conviction relief affirmed 1997 WL 752608, dismissed, appeal not allowed 81 Ohio St.3d 1495, 691 N.E.2d 1057, certiorari denied 119 S.Ct. 195, 525 U.S. 884, 142 L.Ed.2d 159, denial of post-conviction relief affirmed 103 Ohio St.3d 162, 814 N.E.2d 861, 2004-Ohio-4755, reconsideration denied 104 Ohio St.3d 1411, 818 N.E.2d 712, 2004-Ohio-6364. Criminal Law ⚿ 338(7)

Court of Appeals would decline to engage in gratuitous discussion of constitutional implications concerning admission of other acts testimony in murder prosecution, where defendant only mentioned in passing State Constitution and made no mention of Federal Constitution. State v. Elliott (Ohio App. 3 Dist., 11-05-1993) 91 Ohio App.3d 763, 633 N.E.2d 1144, dismissed, jurisdictional motion overruled 69 Ohio St.3d 1422, 631 N.E.2d 162. Criminal Law ⚿ 1134(3)

RC 2945.59 is constitutional. State v. Pack (Montgomery 1968) 18 Ohio App.2d 76, 246 N.E.2d 912, 47 O.O.2d 113.

Statute, permitting the introduction in evidence of similar acts which may tend to show motive or intent, is merely declaratory of the common law and is constitutional. State v. Hahn (Hamilton 1938) 59 Ohio App. 178, 17 N.E.2d 392, 27 Ohio Law Abs. 27, 11 O.O. 560, appeal dismissed 133 Ohio St. 440, 14 N.E.2d 354, 11 O.O. 106, appeal dismissed 59 S.Ct. 75, 305 U.S. 557, 83 L.Ed. 351.

Defendant was not denied due process of law by state's introduction of evidence of other acts, including murder, in capital murder prosecution, where the other acts evidence was relevant because it showed that the methodology the killer used in the case on trial closely resembled that used in other crimes committed by defendant and thus tended to show that defendant was the killer in the instant case. Coleman v. Mitchell (C.A.6 (Ohio), 03-26-2001) 244 F.3d 533, rehearing and rehearing en banc denied, certiorari denied 122 S.Ct. 405, 534 U.S. 977, 151 L.Ed.2d 307. Constitutional Law ⚷ 266(4); Criminal Law ⚷ 372(4)

2. In general

Admissibility of other-acts evidence is carefully limited, particularly in prosecutions for sexual offenses. State v. Decker (Hamilton 1993) 88 Ohio App.3d 544, 624 N.E.2d 350. Criminal Law ⚷ 369.2(5); Criminal Law ⚷ 369.8

Generally, evidence of previous or subsequent criminal acts wholly independent from offense for which defendant is on trial are inadmissible in criminal trial with exception of specified instances where probative value of evidence is sufficient to allow its admission. State v. Covrett (Franklin 1993) 87 Ohio App.3d 534, 622 N.E.2d 712, dismissed, jurisdictional motion overruled 67 Ohio St.3d 1479, 620 N.E.2d 852. Criminal Law ⚷ 369.1; Criminal Law ⚷ 369.2(1)

Other acts of defendant may or may not be similar to crime charged, but to be admissible they must tend to show by substantial proof one or more of elements enumerated in rule or statute providing that other crimes evidence is admissible to prove intent, motive, plan or absence of mistake or accident. State v. Smith (Greene 1992) 84 Ohio App.3d 647, 617 N.E.2d 1160, motion to certify denied 66 Ohio St.3d 1488, 612 N.E.2d 1244. Criminal Law ⚷ 369.2(1)

3. Construction with other laws

Evidence of acts by a defendant, which is otherwise admissible under RC 2945.59 and which does not constitute part of a disposition or evidence given in court, is not barred by RC 2151.358, even though the evidence tends to show the commission of another crime by the defendant when a juvenile. State v. Bayless (Ohio 1976) 48 Ohio St.2d 73, 357 N.E.2d 1035, 2 O.O.3d 249, vacated 98 S.Ct. 3135, 438 U.S. 911, 57 L.Ed.2d 1155.

4. Strict construction

Evidence rule and statute permitting introduction of other crimes evidence for purposes other than proving that defendant acted in conformity with character are exceptions to general rule which excludes evidence of previous or subsequent acts by defendant which are wholly independent from the charges for which defendant is on trial; because they are exceptions, rule and statute are strictly construed against admissibility. State v. Goines (Ohio App. 8 Dist., 06-24-1996) 111 Ohio App.3d 840, 677 N.E.2d 412, appeal not allowed 77 Ohio St.3d 1482, 673 N.E.2d 143. Criminal Law ⚷ 369.2(1)

Statute and rule permitting evidence of other acts under certain circumstances are both exceptions to common-law rule that evidence of other acts is inadmissible to prove any element of crime for which defendant stands trial, and, as such, both rule and statute must be strictly construed against admissibility. State v. Clemons (Ohio App. 12 Dist., 05-02-1994) 94 Ohio App.3d 701, 641 N.E.2d 778, dismissed, appeal not allowed 70 Ohio St.3d 1454, 639 N.E.2d 793. Criminal Law ⚷ 369.1

Both rule and statute permitting admission of other crimes evidence to prove intent, motive, plan or absence of mistake or accident must be strictly construed against admissibility of evidence of other acts of wrongdoing since they codify an exception to the common law. State v. Smith (Greene 1992) 84 Ohio App.3d 647, 617 N.E.2d 1160, motion to certify denied 66 Ohio St.3d 1488, 612 N.E.2d 1244. Criminal Law ⚷ 370; Criminal Law ⚷ 371(1); Criminal Law ⚷ 371(12)

5. Rule of evidence

Testimony of forensic dental expert that murder defendant was likely source of bite marks found on victim was relevant to prove defendant's intent to harm victim, absence of mistake or accident, and defendant's identity as perpetrator; bite marks on and near victim's buttocks contradicted defendant's claims that fatal injuries were accidental and that he had only punished victim with spankings given while victim was clothed, bites occurred proximately in time to fatal shaking, and location of bite marks suggested that both biting and fatal shaking could have occurred in course of toilet training victim. State v. Smith (Ohio App. 4 Dist., Ross, 10-08-2003) No. 02CA2687, 2003-Ohio-5524, 2003 WL 22369273, Unreported. Criminal Law ⚷ 475.7

In prosecution for gross sexual imposition (GSI), erroneous admission of victim's testimony that defendant had previously struck his ex-girlfriend and his then-girlfriend, victim's stepsister, was harmless; properly admitted evidence included victim's testimony that defendant kissed her and fondled her breasts, buttocks, and pubic area, and testimony of pediatric nurse practitioner that victim reported the same unwanted sexual approaches when examined for sexual abuse. State v. Watkins (Ohio App. 9 Dist., Lorain, 03-19-2003) No. 02CA008087, 2003-Ohio-1308, 2003 WL 1240469, Unreported. Criminal Law ⚷ 1169.11

Rule and statute governing admission of other acts evidence codify common law respecting evidence of other acts of wrongdoing, and are construed against admissibility. State v. Lowe (Ohio, 07-06-1994) 69 Ohio St.3d 527, 634 N.E.2d 616, 1994-Ohio-345. Criminal Law ⚷ 369.2(1)

Evidence of prior rapes and expressions of desire of engaging in sexual acts with juvenile males is properly admitted in an aggravated murder prosecution where (1) the victim, a juvenile male, is sexually assaulted, rectally impaled, and his genitalia exhibit human teeth marks and the witnesses testify as to the defendant's rape in the area where the victim was raped and murdered; (2) another witness testifies as to her rape by the defendant in which he bit her and threatened to rectally impale her; and (3) a third witness testifies to the defendant's expression of desire to engage in sexual activity with him while they were both minors. State v. Hill (Ohio 1992) 64 Ohio St.3d 313, 595 N.E.2d 884, rehearing denied 65 Ohio St.3d 1421, 598 N.E.2d 1172, certiorari denied 113 S.Ct. 1651, 507 U.S. 1007, 123 L.Ed.2d 272, denial of post-conviction relief affirmed, dismissed, jurisdictional motion overruled 74 Ohio St.3d 1456, 656 N.E.2d 951.

In a prosecution for the rape of a child under the age of thirteen, evidence admitted at trial of other prior specific instances of the defendant's sexual activity with the child victim is material to show that the defendant purposely compelled the child to submit to sexual conduct by force or threat of force, and its probative value outweighed any inflammatory or prejudicial effect. State v. Fenton (Ottawa 1990) 68 Ohio App.3d 412, 588 N.E.2d 951, dismissed, jurisdictional motion overruled 56 Ohio St.3d 702, 564 N.E.2d 704.

Because RC 2945.59 and Evid R 404(B) codify an exception to the common law with respect to evidence of other acts of wrongdoing, they must be construed against admissibility, and the standard for determining admissibility of such evidence is strict. The rule and the statute contemplate acts which may or may not be similar to the crime at issue; thus, if the other act does in fact "tend to show" by substantial proof any of those things enumerated, such as proof of motive, opportunity, intent, preparation, plan, knowledge, identity, or absence of mistake or accident, then evidence of the other act may be admissible. State v. Broom (Ohio 1988) 40 Ohio St.3d 277, 533 N.E.2d 682, certiorari denied 109 S.Ct. 2089, 490 U.S. 1075, 104 L.Ed.2d 653, stay granted 49 Ohio St.3d 710, 551 N.E.2d 1302, stay revoked 83 Ohio St.3d 1458, 700 N.E.2d 876, denial of post-conviction relief affirmed, dismissed, appeal not allowed 83 Ohio St.3d 1430, 699 N.E.2d 946.

Evidence of other acts of a defendant is admissible pursuant to RC 2945.59 only when it tends to show one of the matters enumerated in that statute and when it is relevant to prove the defendant's guilt of the offense in question. State v. DeMarco (Ohio 1987) 31 Ohio St.3d 191, 509 N.E.2d 1256, 31 O.B.R. 390. Criminal Law ⚿ 369.2(1)

Prior to taking testimony or receiving evidence of any "collateral acts" of a sexual nature of the victim or the defendant, RC 2907.02(D) and 2907.02(E) require a trial court in a rape offense proceeding to conduct an in camera hearing to resolve the materiality and admissibility of the evidence and to determine whether the probative value of the evidence is greater than its prejudicial effect, and where the witnesses' testimony is merely corroborative or cumulative to that which has been given by other witnesses, a failure to conduct such in camera hearing upon such evidence may in certain instances be found to be nonprejudicial. State v. Acre (Ohio 1983) 6 Ohio St.3d 140, 451 N.E.2d 802, 6 O.B.R. 197.

Evidence of prior crimes cannot be shown in the trial of a defendant; only evidence bearing on a particular charge on which defendant is brought to trial may be introduced at trial unless evidence of other criminal acts falls within those acts enumerated in RC 2945.59. State v. Sampson (Belmont 1982) 4 Ohio App.3d 287, 448 N.E.2d 467, 4 O.B.R. 536. Criminal Law ⚿ 369.1

Evidence of other acts of a criminal defendant is admissible, pursuant to RC 2945.59, only if one or more of the matters enumerated in the statute is a material issue at trial and only if such evidence tends to show the material enumerated matter. State v. Curry (Ohio 1975) 43 Ohio St.2d 66, 330 N.E.2d 720, 72 O.O.2d 37. Criminal Law ⚿ 369.1

RC 2945.59 does not require that the trial court limit the effect of evidence introduced under this section, either with or without objection or motion of defendant. State v. Carver (Scioto 1971) 30 Ohio App.2d 115, 283 N.E.2d 662, 59 O.O.2d 230, affirmed 30 Ohio St.2d 280, 285 N.E.2d 26, 59 O.O.2d 343, certiorari denied 93 S.Ct. 542, 409 U.S. 1044, 34 L.Ed.2d 495.

Acts of an accused which have no relation to or logical connection with and do not tend to disclose a motive or purpose for the commission of the offense for which the accused is on trial are not admissible under RC 2945.59. State v. Williams (Clermont 1969) 21 Ohio App.2d 184, 255 N.E.2d 639, 50 O.O.2d 280.

RC 2945.59 must be strictly construed against the state. State v. Watson (Cuyahoga 1969) 20 Ohio App.2d 115, 252 N.E.2d 305, 49 O.O.2d 152, modified 28 Ohio St.2d 15, 275 N.E.2d 153, 57 O.O.2d 95.

RC 2945.59 is merely expressive of the common law and is a rule of evidence and not a rule of substantive law; testimony of witnesses as to acts of an accused similar to that for which he is on trial is admissible as bearing on the issue of such accused's intent, where such evidence is relevant and material as bearing on the intent of the accused and shows a similar plan of proceeding on his part, the offenses attributed to the accused are not too remote in point of time to the offense for which he is being tried, the jury is properly instructed that such testimony is to be considered for such limited purpose, and there is no reason to believe that the jury was probably misled or confused unfairly by such testimony. State v. Pack (Montgomery 1968) 18 Ohio App.2d 76, 246 N.E.2d 912, 47 O.O.2d 113.

RC 2945.59 is a rule of evidence and not a rule of substantive law. State v. Pigott (Cuyahoga 1964) 1 Ohio App.2d 22, 197 N.E.2d 911, 94 Ohio Law Abs. 335, 30 O.O.2d 56.

Evidence of similar offenses may not be admitted where there is no issue of defendant's motive or intent, the absence of mistake or accident on his part, or his scheme, play or system in committing an act. State v. Hirsch (Cuyahoga 1956) 101 Ohio App. 425, 131 N.E.2d 419, 75 Ohio Law Abs. 57, 1 O.O.2d 349.

The admission of evidence of an abortion, other than that named in the indictment, is competent because it was admissible in common law, and this section is a rule of evidence and not a rule of substantive law. Clyne v. State (Ohio 1931) 123 Ohio St. 234, 174 N.E. 767, 9 Ohio Law Abs. 445, appeal dismissed 51 S.Ct. 653, 283 U.S. 810, 75 L.Ed. 1428.

Defendant failed to demonstrate that admission of evidence that defendant in prosecution for gross sexual imposition molested victim's juvenile female cousin was plain error, where, given remaining evidence of guilt, there was nothing to suggest that, but for error, result of trial would have clearly been different. State v. Griffin (Ohio App. 8 Dist., Cuyahoga, 08-22-2002) No. 80499, 2002-Ohio-4288, 2002 WL 1938250, Unreported, appeal not allowed 98 Ohio St.3d 1422, 782 N.E.2d 77, 2003-Ohio-259. Criminal Law ⚷ 1036.1(8)

RC 2945.59 operates in contravention of the rule prohibiting the introduction of evidence of prior offenses and should be construed against the state in doubtful cases. State v Wilson, No. CA–8362 (2d Dist Ct App, Montgomery, 4–5–84).

This section merely writes into statutory law what long has been law of this state under adjudicated cases. (See also State v Hahn, 25 Abs 449 (CP, Putnam 1937).) State v Hahn, 25 Abs 258 (CP, Hamilton 1937), affirmed by 59 App 178, 17 NE(2d) 392 (1938).

6. Indictment

The purpose of a bill of particulars is not to disclose the state's evidence, but to state specifically the nature of the offense charged, and the statutes do not require that an indictment contain an allegation as to any like act or similar offense and therefore under this section, fact that bill of exception contains no such allegation does not make evidence as to like acts or similar offenses inadmissible. State v. De Righter (Ohio 1945) 145 Ohio St. 552, 62 N.E.2d 332, 31 O.O. 194.

7. Joinder of cases

Similar nature of defendant's alleged multiple burglary offenses warranted joinder of cases into one trial; both burglaries involved residences in same neighborhood and entry was made through a window, both burglaries involved intruder escaping by diving head first out of window, both burglaries involved intruder returning to residence within short period of time after committing offenses while police were still on scene, and both burglaries involved suspect telling police that he was in area of burglarized homes after his vehicle had been carjacked by man similar in appearance to him. State v. Hobbs (Ohio App. 8 Dist., Cuyahoga, 08-14-2003) No. 81533, 2003-Ohio-4338, 2003 WL 21954778, Unreported, appeal not allowed 100 Ohio St.3d 1545, 800 N.E.2d 751, 2003-Ohio-6879. Criminal Law ⚷ 620(1)

8. Credibility of defendant's testimony

Prosecution may not impugn the accused's character until the accused presents evidence of his good character; but, evidence of drug paraphernalia in accused's home is admissible to prove knowing possession of heroin and cocaine. State v. Gibson (Cuyahoga 1980) 69 Ohio App.2d 91, 430 N.E.2d 954, 23 O.O.3d 130.

Where, in a criminal action, evidence of other acts of the defendant is sought to be presented, as provided for by RC 2945.59, the defendant as well as his attorney has a right to be present at an in camera hearing regarding the admissibility of testimony. State v. Howard (Hamilton 1978) 57 Ohio App.2d 1, 385 N.E.2d 308, 11 O.O.3d 3. Criminal Law ⚷ 636(3)

Appellant's admission that, concerning homicide, he lied to the police is singularly relevant and admissible as bearing upon his credibility in a homicide case. State v. Osborne (Ohio 1977) 50 Ohio St.2d 211, 364 N.E.2d 216, 4 O.O.3d 406, vacated 98 S.Ct. 3137, 438 U.S. 911, 57 L.Ed.2d 1157.

Where an accused takes the stand in his own behalf, his credibility as a witness becomes a proper subject for cross-examination, and the limitation on such cross-examination rests within the sound discretion of the trial court. State v. Tharp (Marion 1976) 49 Ohio App.2d 291, 361 N.E.2d 469, 3 O.O.3d 340.

Where there is a joint trial on various alleged frauds arising out of the operation of a business, it is prejudicial error for the trial court to exclude evidence of other acts and transactions during the same period of time, offered by the defense to rebut evidence introduced by the state on the question of fraudulent intent. State v. Marinos (Summit 1975) 45 Ohio App.2d 312, 345 N.E.2d 76, 74 O.O.2d 483.

Where an accused is properly cross-examined concerning a previous offense having no relationship to the one for which he is standing trial, for the purpose of attacking the credibility of his testimony on direct examination, it is not improper to allow rebuttal witnesses to appear and impeach his answers given during such cross-examination, as long as their testimony does not, in the discretion of the court, pertain to the guilt of the accused, and the court adequately instructs the jury that the testimony should be considered only for the purpose of testing his veracity. State v. Patterson (Hamilton 1974) 43 Ohio App.2d 63, 332 N.E.2d 770, 72 O.O.2d 208.

Where plaintiff, in action on fire insurance policy, defended by the insurer on the grounds of misrepresentation, conspiracy and incendiarism, offers himself as a witness and upon cross-examination is asked the question, "You went to the police department and made a confession of your part in the plot to destroy the Middle West Hat Company," such question is competent as reflecting upon credibility of the witness, and the sustaining of an objection to such question by trial court constitutes prejudicial error. Kornreich v. Industrial Fire Ins. Co. (Ohio 1936) 132 Ohio St. 78, 5 N.E.2d 153, 7 O.O. 198.

9. Admissibility of prior acts—In general

Evidence of other criminal acts by a defendant is admissible only when it tends to show one of the matters enumerated in the statute and evidence rule codifying an exception to general prohibition against such evidence, and only when the evidence offered is relevant to prove that the defendant is guilty of the offense in question. State v. Wilkins (Ohio App. 9 Dist., 09-29-1999) 135 Ohio App.3d

26, 732 N.E.2d 1021, dismissed, appeal not allowed 88 Ohio St.3d 1412, 723 N.E.2d 118. Criminal Law ⚷ 369.2(1)

Rule and statute providing for admission of other acts evidence codify an exception to common law and, accordingly, are construed against admissibility of other acts evidence. State v. Smith (Ohio App. 3 Dist., 11-20-1996) 115 Ohio App.3d 419, 685 N.E.2d 595.

If other act tends to show by substantial proof any of the items enumerated by rule and statute providing for admissibility of other acts evidence, such as proof of motive, opportunity, intent, preparation, plan, knowledge, identity, or absence of mistake or accident, then evidence of other act may be admissible. State v. Goines (Ohio App. 8 Dist., 06-24-1996) 111 Ohio App.3d 840, 677 N.E.2d 412, appeal not allowed 77 Ohio St.3d 1482, 673 N.E.2d 143. Criminal Law ⚷ 369.2(1)

To be relevant on issue of motive or intent, other act testimony must have such temporal, modal, and situational relationship with acts constituting the crimes charged that evidence of other acts discloses purposeful action in commission of offense in question. State v. Clemons (Ohio App. 12 Dist., 05-02-1994) 94 Ohio App.3d 701, 641 N.E.2d 778, dismissed, appeal not allowed 70 Ohio St.3d 1454, 639 N.E.2d 793. Criminal Law ⚷ 371(1); Criminal Law ⚷ 371(12)

When using other acts evidence to show defendant's intent, offense for which defendant is being tried and other act must have occurred reasonably near to each other and similar scheme, plan, or system must have been utilized to commit offense at issue and other offenses. State v. Elliott (Ohio App. 3 Dist., 11-05-1993) 91 Ohio App.3d 763, 633 N.E.2d 1144, dismissed, jurisdictional motion overruled 69 Ohio St.3d 1422, 631 N.E.2d 162. Criminal Law ⚷ 371(1)

Before admitting other acts evidence, trial court must determine that evidence is relevant to crime charged and to issue placed in question by conduct of present trial, and consider other factors, such as time of other act, defendant's modus operandi, nature of other act, and location of other act. State v. McCornell (Ohio App. 8 Dist., 10-12-1993) 91 Ohio App.3d 141, 631 N.E.2d 1110. Criminal Law ⚷ 369.2(1)

The like acts or other acts which may be shown against a defendant, within the contemplation of the statute, are acts of a character so related to the offense for which defendant is on trial that they have a logical connection therewith and may reasonably disclose a motive or purpose for the commission of such offense. State v. Moore (Ohio 1948) 149 Ohio St. 226, 78 N.E.2d 365, 36 O.O. 566. Criminal Law ⚷ 371(1); Criminal Law ⚷ 371(12)

10. —— Identity, admissibility of prior acts

Evidence that defendant and his companion had broken into a church and received traffic tickets a week before the charged offenses, involving theft of a van and break-in at school concession stand, was admissible as proof of defendant's identity as the perpetrator of charged offenses; issue of defendant's identity was in dispute, prior events were inextricably related to, and formed part of the immediate background of, the break-in at the school and the theft of the van, and prior events helped establish that defendant and his companion were partners in crime. State v. Siney (Ohio App. 12 Dist., Warren, 03-14-2005) No. CA2004-04-044, 2005-Ohio-1081, 2005 WL 578986, Unreported, denial of post-conviction relief affirmed 2005-Ohio-3449, 2005 WL 1545793. Criminal Law ⚷ 369.15

Testimony by victim of rape committed by defendant 12 years prior to charged rape was not admissible as similar-acts evidence for purpose of establishing identity; factual dispute at trial focused on defendant's conduct with present victim rather than his identity, and the two crimes were not factually similar except in their most general description. State v. Wilkins (Ohio App. 9 Dist., 09-29-1999) 135 Ohio App.3d 26, 732 N.E.2d 1021, dismissed, appeal not allowed 88 Ohio St.3d 1412, 723 N.E.2d 118. Criminal Law ⚷ 369.8

Evidence of prior rape was admissible to show defendant's identity in prosecution for rape, gross sexual imposition, felonious sexual penetration, aggravated burglary, and abduction committed approximately three months later; both rapes were committed in same area of city, both victims were alone in the dark when attacked from behind and threatened, perpetrator covered victims' faces with glove, began same series of sexual offenses, and became apologetic and warned victims against contacting police, and these similarities provided behavioral fingerprint to identify defendant as perpetrator. State v. Pearson (Ohio App. 3 Dist., 10-04-1996) 114 Ohio App.3d 168, 682 N.E.2d 1086. Criminal Law ⚷ 369.15

In penalty phase of capital murder trial, evidence of shooting of another victim, which would have been admissible as probative of defendant's identity even if charges had not been joined, was relevant as tending to prove aggravating circumstances. State v. Williams (Ohio, 08-16-1995) 73 Ohio St.3d 153, 652 N.E.2d 721, 1995-Ohio-275, reconsideration denied 74 Ohio St.3d 1409, 655 N.E.2d 188, stay granted 74 Ohio St.3d 1437, 655 N.E.2d 1321, stay terminated 75 Ohio St.3d 1439, 662 N.E.2d 1085, certiorari denied 116 S.Ct. 1047, 516 U.S. 1161, 134 L.Ed.2d 193, denial of post-conviction relief affirmed 1998 WL 330539, dismissed, appeal not allowed 83 Ohio St.3d 1449, 700 N.E.2d 332, reconsideration denied 84 Ohio St.3d 1413, 701 N.E.2d 1021. Sentencing And Punishment ⚷ 1762

Other acts can be evidence of identity, so as to render evidence of other acts admissible, when they form part of immediate background of alleged act which forms foundation of crime charged in indictment and which are inextricably related to alleged criminal act. State v. Lowe (Ohio, 07-06-1994) 69 Ohio St.3d 527, 634 N.E.2d 616, 1994-Ohio-345. Criminal Law ⚷ 369.15

Other acts can prove identity, so as to render evidence of other acts admissible, by establishing modus operandi applicable to crime with which defendant is charged. State v. Lowe (Ohio, 07-06-1994) 69 Ohio St.3d 527, 634 N.E.2d 616, 1994-Ohio-345. Criminal Law ⚷ 369.15

While other acts need not be the same as or similar to crime charged in order to be admissible to show modus operandi so as to prove identity, acts should show modus operandi identifiable with defendant. State v. Lowe (Ohio, 07-06-1994) 69 Ohio St.3d 527, 634 N.E.2d 616, 1994-Ohio-345. Criminal Law ⚷ 369.15; Criminal Law ⚷ 372(1)

Certain modus operandi is admissible through other acts evidence not because it labels defendant as criminal, but because it provides behavioral fingerprint which, when compared to behavioral fingerprints associated with crime in question, can be used to identify defendant as perpetrator. State v. Lowe (Ohio, 07-06-1994) 69 Ohio St.3d 527, 634 N.E.2d 616, 1994-Ohio-345. Criminal Law ⚷ 369.15; Criminal Law ⚷ 372(1)

Other acts evidence is admissible to prove identity through characteristics of acts, rather than through person's character. State v. Lowe (Ohio, 07-06-1994) 69 Ohio St.3d 527, 634 N.E.2d 616, 1994-Ohio-345. Criminal Law ⚷ 369.15

To be admissible to prove identity through certain modus operandi, other acts evidence must be related to and share common features with crime in question. State v. Lowe (Ohio, 07-06-1994) 69 Ohio St.3d 527, 634 N.E.2d 616, 1994-Ohio-345. Criminal Law ⚷ 369.15

Other acts testimony that murder defendant had previously participated in beating witness was admissible to establish identity or intent respecting murder, where murder victim was beaten severely about the head, chest, and stomach, defendant told fellow inmate that defendant had done so to victim, and witness was beaten in same way by defendant and accomplice. State v. Elliott (Ohio App. 3 Dist., 11-05-1993) 91 Ohio App.3d 763, 633 N.E.2d 1144, dismissed, jurisdictional motion overruled 69 Ohio St.3d 1422, 631 N.E.2d 162. Criminal Law ⚷ 369.15; Criminal Law ⚷ 371(4)

When other acts evidence is used to establish defendant's identity as perpetrator of crime in question, prosecution must demonstrate that defendant utilized identifiable scheme, plan, or system in commission of crimes. State v. Elliott (Ohio App. 3 Dist., 11-05-1993) 91 Ohio App.3d 763, 633 N.E.2d 1144, dismissed, jurisdictional motion overruled 69 Ohio St.3d 1422, 631 N.E.2d 162. Criminal Law ⚷ 369.15

In prosecution for aggravated robbery, kidnapping and theft, defendant's previous conviction for aggravated robbery did not consist of other acts forming unique, identifiable plan of criminal activity so as to be admissible under other crimes rule; evidence merely showed that both crimes involved homosexual victims, both offenses occurred in home of victim, victims were tied with cords found inside their homes and, in both cases, defendant was primarily interested in stealing cash. State v. Covrett (Franklin 1993) 87 Ohio App.3d 534, 622 N.E.2d 712, dismissed, jurisdictional motion overruled 67 Ohio St.3d 1479, 620 N.E.2d 852. Criminal Law ⚷ 372(5); Criminal Law ⚷ 372(14)

In a criminal prosecution for rape and aggravated murder, where the identity of the perpetrator is at issue, there is sufficient commonality to permit evidence of a prior rape to be admitted as "other act" evidence under Evid R 404(B) and RC 2945.59 where both victims were thirteen-year-old girls who, upon just returning home, were both vaginally and anally raped in the same manner by having their pants pulled down and turned inside out and who were then stabbed in the neck with a pair of scissors. State v. Shedrick (Ohio 1991) 61 Ohio St.3d 331, 574 N.E.2d 1065.

Evidence of defendant's rapes as juvenile were inadmissible to identify defendant as perpetrator of subsequent rape offense, where prior rapes occurred two years before and in different part of city than charged offense and characteristics shared by all three offenses were common to rape cases generally. State v. Hall (Cuyahoga 1989) 57 Ohio App.3d 144, 567 N.E.2d 305, motion overruled 42 Ohio St.3d 714, 538 N.E.2d 1065. Criminal Law ⚷ 369.15

Evidence of other robberies committed by defendant was sufficiently probative as to identity to warrant its admission as other acts evidence in prosecution for aggravated robbery and felony-murder, even though differences between charged robbery and other robberies existed as to type of business robbed, whether robber acted alone or with accomplice, whether firearm was observable, and whether robber escaped on foot or by bicycle; robberies occurred within four-month period in general downtown area of one city and usually on weekday afternoons, places robbed were all first floor, on-the-street, walk-in businesses, and in all cases defendant physically took or attempted to take money from register, forced, threw, or knocked victims to the floor, and directed violence at victims' heads. State v. Jamison (Ohio 1990) 49 Ohio St.3d 182, 552 N.E.2d 180, rehearing denied 50 Ohio St.3d 712, 553 N.E.2d 1368, certiorari denied 111 S.Ct. 228, 498 U.S. 881, 112 L.Ed.2d 183, denial of habeas corpus affirmed, motion overruled 66 Ohio St.3d 1459, 610 N.E.2d 423, rehearing denied 66 Ohio St.3d 1490, 612 N.E.2d 1245. Criminal Law ⚷ 369.15

Under RC 2945.59 and Evid R 404(B), evidence of "other acts" to prove intent to commit a crime and the identity of the perpetrator is admissible where two deaths occur under almost identical circumstances. State v. Smith (Ohio 1990) 49 Ohio St.3d 137, 551 N.E.2d 190.

Evidence that a defendant charged with a crime committed a similar act in the past is admissible to prove identity under Evid R 404(B) where both crimes share unusual or peculiar characteristics; the earlier crime need not have been committed near, in both place and time, to the present offense. State v. DePina (Medina 1984) 21 Ohio App.3d 91, 486 N.E.2d 1155, 21 O.B.R. 97.

In a trial for rape, testimony regarding a rape committed by the defendant seven years earlier may be admissible to prove identity by the showing of an idiosyncratic pattern of conduct; the key to the probative value of such conduct lies in its peculiar character rather than its proximity to the event at issue. State v. DePina (Medina 1984) 21 Ohio App.3d 91, 486 N.E.2d 1155, 21 O.B.R. 97. Criminal Law ⚿ 372(1)

Under RC 2945.55, where identification of the defendant is in issue, a witness who on a previous occasion has selected, or observed another select, defendant's photograph from a number of photographs, may testify to such previous photographic identification if the photographs, or the photographs coupled with other testimony given on direct examination, do not provide the finder of facts with the reasonable inference that defendant has had prior criminal involvement, and if the procedure of identification does not violate defendant's constitutional rights. (See also State v Wilkinson, 26 OS(2d) 185, 271 NE(2d) 242 (1971). State v. Breedlove (Ohio 1971) 26 Ohio St.2d 178, 271 N.E.2d 238, 55 O.O.2d 441.

On direct examination, evidence of the identification of the defendant from a selection of photographs, using photographs from police files with police identification numerals thereon which provide the finder of facts with the reasonable inference that defendant has had prior criminal involvement, may not be used for the purpose of proving defendant's identity. (See also State v Wilkinson, 26 OS(2d) 185, 271 NE(2d) 242 (1971). State v. Breedlove (Ohio 1971) 26 Ohio St.2d 178, 271 N.E.2d 238, 55 O.O.2d 441.

Where evidence, tending to prove the commission of a similar act by an accused, is offered by the state under RC 2945.59, it is not necessary for the state to establish the identity of the accused as the perpetrator of the similar act by proof beyond a reasonable doubt, but is sufficient that it offers substantial proof that the alleged similar act was committed by the defendant. State v. Carter (Ohio 1971) 26 Ohio St.2d 79, 269 N.E.2d 115, 55 O.O.2d 130. Criminal Law ⚿ 374

Testimony of other offenses similar to robbery charged, committed by same persons, in same locality, under same system, reasonably near time of offense charged, held relevant to issue of identity. Whiteman v. State (Ohio 1928) 119 Ohio St. 285, 164 N.E. 51, 63 A.L.R. 595, 6 Ohio Law Abs. 695, 27 Ohio Law Rep. 642. Criminal Law ⚿ 372(14); Robbery ⚿ 23(1)

Property which was taken from victim's vehicle was direct evidence relevant to charge of attempted theft of a motor vehicle, and its admission was not dependent upon meeting the identity exception to general rule prohibiting other crimes evidence or identity exception to statute enumerating identity as one of the purposes for using other acts evidence, and thus, this evidence was admissible as it served as direct evidence connecting defendant to the attempted theft of the vehicle; it was not "other acts" evidence. State v. Hardman (Ohio App. 5 Dist., Delaware, 07-12-2002) No. 01CA-A-12-069, 2002-Ohio-3698, 2002 WL 1575019, Unreported. Criminal Law ⚿ 374; Criminal Law ⚿ 404.75

Anonymous handwritten notes, letters, and pictures admittedly sent by the defendant to one victim are not relevant to a charge of attempted rape and gross sexual imposition against another victim, and the admission of such other acts evidence is prejudicial because the relationship between time, location, and method is tenuous at best; first, the letters and photographs were sent anonymously while the defendant accosted the attempted rape and gross sexual imposition victim in person and in broad daylight, second, the notes and letters did not threaten to compel sexual conduct with the use of force, and third, over fifteen months separated the acts. State v Hannah, No. 2902 (2d Dist Ct App, Clark, 1–8–93).

Anonymous handwritten letters and photographs admittedly sent to a victim during the same period of time as alleged harassing telephone calls are admissible in a prosecution for telephone harassment, where the letters, photographs, and telephone calls are (1) made anonymously to the same victim, (2) sexual in nature, and (3) express a keen interest in the victim's panties, because such other acts evidence is probative of both the identity and purpose of the anonymous caller and its probative value is not outweighed by the danger of unfair prejudice. State v Hannah, No. 2902 (2d Dist Ct App, Clark, 1–8–93).

11. —— Propensity, admissibility of prior acts

Admission of relevant, other-acts evidence is permitted, not for proving the defendant's propensity for criminal behavior but to prove motive, opportunity, intent, preparation, plan, knowledge, identity, or absence of mistake or accident. State v. McIntosh (Ohio App. 1 Dist., 08-31-2001) 145 Ohio App.3d 567, 763 N.E.2d 704, appeal not allowed 94 Ohio St.3d 1411, 759 N.E.2d 787, appeal not allowed 96 Ohio St.3d 1488, 774 N.E.2d 763, 2002-Ohio-4478, denial of post-conviction relief affirmed in part, reversed in part 2003-Ohio-3824, 2003 WL 21673323. Criminal Law ⚿ 369.2(1); Criminal Law ⚿ 369.15; Criminal Law ⚿ 371(1); Criminal Law ⚿ 371(12); Criminal Law ⚿ 372(1)

Admissibility of other-acts evidence is carefully limited because of substantial danger that jury will convict defendant solely because it assumes that defendant has propensity to commit criminal acts, or deserves punishment regardless of whether he or she committed crimes charged in indictment. State v. Cotton (Ohio App. 1 Dist., 06-26-1996) 113 Ohio App.3d 125, 680 N.E.2d 657. Criminal Law ⚿ 369.1

Other-acts evidence is never admissible when its only purpose is to establish that defendant committed act alleged in indictment. State v. Cotton (Ohio App. 1 Dist., 06-26-1996) 113 Ohio App.3d 125, 680 N.E.2d 657. Criminal Law ⚿ 369.1

Other acts evidence, as used for purposes other than to show defendant acted in conformity with character, may or may not be similar to crime at issue. State v. Goines (Ohio App. 8 Dist., 06-24-1996) 111 Ohio App.3d 840, 677 N.E.2d 412, appeal not allowed 77 Ohio St.3d 1482, 673 N.E.2d 143. Criminal Law ⚿ 369.2(1)

Evidence of prior acts may not be used to prove inference that, in committing alleged crime, defendant acted in conformity with his other acts or that he has propensity to act in such a manner. State v. Goines (Ohio App. 8 Dist., 06-24-1996) 111 Ohio App.3d 840, 677 N.E.2d 412, appeal not allowed 77 Ohio St.3d 1482, 673 N.E.2d 143. Criminal Law ⚷ 369.1

Defendant cannot be convicted of one crime by proving he committed other crimes or is a bad person. State v. Goines (Ohio App. 8 Dist., 06-24-1996) 111 Ohio App.3d 840, 677 N.E.2d 412, appeal not allowed 77 Ohio St.3d 1482, 673 N.E.2d 143. Criminal Law ⚷ 369.1

Other acts evidence is never admissible when its only purpose is to establish that defendant committed the act alleged in the indictment. State v. Clemons (Ohio App. 12 Dist., 05-02-1994) 94 Ohio App.3d 701, 641 N.E.2d 778, dismissed, appeal not allowed 70 Ohio St.3d 1454, 639 N.E.2d 793. Criminal Law ⚷ 369.1

Other crimes evidence is never admissible when its sole purpose is to establish that defendant committed act alleged of him in indictment. State v. Smith (Greene 1992) 84 Ohio App.3d 647, 617 N.E.2d 1160, motion to certify denied 66 Ohio St.3d 1488, 612 N.E.2d 1244. Criminal Law ⚷ 369.1

Where a defendant, after the state has rested its case-in-chief, affirmatively pursues the defense of entrapment, he concedes that he committed the crime and he puts in issue whether he had a predisposition to commit the crime and state's rebuttal on the predisposition issue may include other crimes or "other acts" evidence. State v. Savage (Muskingum 1980) 1 Ohio App.3d 13, 437 N.E.2d 1202, 1 O.B.R. 15. Criminal Law ⚷ 369.2(1)

Where evidence has been admitted for a limited purpose, which the state claims shows that defendant did certain "other acts" which show motive or intent of accused or absence of mistake or accident on his part or defendant's scheme, plan or system in doing the act alleged in indictment, such evidence must not be considered by the jury as any proof whatsoever that accused did any act alleged in indictment. State v. Flonnory (Ohio 1972) 31 Ohio St.2d 124, 285 N.E.2d 726, 60 O.O.2d 95. Criminal Law ⚷ 673(5)

12. —— Remoteness, admissibility of prior acts

Prior crimes evidence cannot be too remote and must be closely related in nature, time, and place to the offense charged. State v. Goines (Ohio App. 8 Dist., 06-24-1996) 111 Ohio App.3d 840, 677 N.E.2d 412, appeal not allowed 77 Ohio St.3d 1482, 673 N.E.2d 143. Criminal Law ⚷ 369.2(1)

Where evidence of prior similar acts, offered to show motive under RC 2945.59, occurred more than ten years previously, it is too remote in time for consideration; however, the admission of such evidence by the trial court constitutes harmless error. State v Siegenthaler, No. 184 (7th Dist Ct App, Noble, 7–18–84).

13. —— Absence of mistake or accident, admissibility of prior acts

Probative value of prior bad acts evidence that witness regularly purchased bricks of cocaine from defendant was not outweighed by its prejudicial effect in prosecution for possession of cocaine; witness's testimony was probative of defendant's opportunity to possess drugs, his plan to sell drugs, his knowledge that he possessed drugs, and to show the absence of any accidental appearance of the drugs in his truck. State v. Martinez (Ohio App. 3 Dist., Marion, 04-10-2003) No. 9-02-57, 2003-Ohio-1821, 2003 WL 1836672, Unreported. Criminal Law ⚷ 370; Criminal Law ⚷ 371(1); Criminal Law ⚷ 372(13)

Evidence of past fires and insurance claims at the last church a pastor was associated with is admissible to prove absence of accident, motive and identity in the present prosecution of the pastor for fires and insurance claims at his current church. State v. Patton (Ohio App. 9 Dist., Summit, 05-10-1995) No. 16475, No. 16634, 1995 WL 283767, Unreported, dismissed, appeal not allowed 74 Ohio St.3d 1417, 655 N.E.2d 737, reconsideration denied 74 Ohio St.3d 1464, 656 N.E.2d 1300.

Statute providing that, where absence of mistake or accident "on defendant's part" is material, any acts of defendant which tend to show absence of mistake or accident "on his part" may be proved does not permit evidence of other acts of defendant to rebut suggestions raised in cross-examination of state's witnesses that "they" are mistaken; only absence of mistake or accident on part of defendant may be so shown and only when it is fact in issue. State v. Smith (Greene 1992) 84 Ohio App.3d 647, 617 N.E.2d 1160, motion to certify denied 66 Ohio St.3d 1488, 612 N.E.2d 1244. Criminal Law ⚷ 370; Criminal Law ⚷ 371(9)

In prosecution for gross sexual imposition, testimony concerning other sexual acts of defendant, offered to prove absence of mistake or accident, should have been excluded; facts to which victims testified demonstrated conduct that was unquestionably knowing and intentional and therefore, mistake or accident were not material issues in defense or in state's case. State v. Smith (Greene 1992) 84 Ohio App.3d 647, 617 N.E.2d 1160, motion to certify denied 66 Ohio St.3d 1488, 612 N.E.2d 1244. Criminal Law ⚷ 370; Criminal Law ⚷ 371(9)

In gross sexual imposition prosecution, testimony of state's witness that defendant asserted theory of accident when he told her that "my hand could have went anywhere" when he slept with victim was insufficient basis to permit state to rebut it with testimony of another witness showing other acts of wrongdoing by defendant pursuant to statute providing that acts of defendant which tend to show absence of mistake or accident are admissible provided absence of mistake or accident on defendant's part is material; statute was to be strictly construed against admissibility and witness' testimony was uncorroborated, was denied by defendant and was inconsistent with operative facts of offense related by alleged victim, who denied that he and defendant had slept in same bed. State v. Smith (Greene 1992) 84 Ohio App.3d 647, 617 N.E.2d 1160, motion to certify denied 66 Ohio St.3d 1488, 612 N.E.2d 1244. Criminal Law ⚿ 371(9)

Improper admission of drugs and drug paraphernalia that were found in vacant house owned by house where charged crimes allegedly occurred and that served only to prove defendant's bad character was not plain error in prosecution for murder, rape, and kidnapping in light of overwhelming physical evidence against defendant. State v. Satta (Ohio App. 3 Dist., Marion, 09-25-2002) No. 9-01-38, 2002-Ohio-5049, 2002 WL 31114690, Unreported, appeal not allowed 98 Ohio St.3d 1461, 783 N.E.2d 520, 2003-Ohio-644, reconsideration denied 98 Ohio St.3d 1516, 786 N.E.2d 64, 2003-Ohio-1572, motion for delayed appeal denied 98 Ohio St.3d 1509, 786 N.E.2d 60, 2003-Ohio-1572, appeal not allowed 99 Ohio St.3d 1437, 789 N.E.2d 1118, 2003-Ohio-2902. Criminal Law ⚿ 1036.1(8)

Evidence that the defendant found the body of her twenty-month-old son in a heating duct two days after the defendant had discovered that her son could remove the grates over the heating duct and did nothing to secure them is sufficient to meet the negligence standard, which is the culpable mental state described in RC 2919.22(A); evidence that the defendant previously left her son at home alone, leaving a baby monitor with the neighbor, shows absence of mistake or accident. State v McGee, No. 8–94–38, 1995 WL 737664 (3d Dist Ct App, Logan, 12–12–95), reversed by 79 OS(3d) 193 (1997).

The "accident" referred to in Evid R 404 and in RC 2945.59 is an accidental act on the part of the defendant that results in a consequence, and is more or less a matter of the defendant's "confession" of involvement in an act causing injury or a crime and "avoidance" on the ground that the defendant's act was purely accidental and not intentional; where the defendant's defense, on the other hand, is that the victim had an accident independent of the defendant, this "accident" is not what the rule and statute are about, and rebuttal evidence of the defendant's other acts and wrongs is not admissible. State v Davis, No. 94–CD–12, 1995 WL 569191 (7th Dist Ct App, Columbiana, 9–26–95).

Where a woman, reacting to an altercation involving her children, put her hand in her purse and shot a woman in the leg, it is not error at her resultant trial for felonious assault to admit testimony about an earlier incident where she reacted to an altercation involving her son by reaching into her purse, putting her hand on her gun, and intentionally firing in the direction of a door being opened by a man, even though charges based on the earlier incident were dismissed; the evidence regarding the earlier altercation is relevant to absence of mistake or accident under Evid R 404(B). State v Hartfield, No. L–87–323 (6th Dist Ct App, Lucas, 11–18–88).

14. —— Scheme, plan or system, admissibility of prior acts

Acts committed shortly subsequent to time of the offense charged are competent for purpose of showing a conspiracy if they appear to be so connected as to authorize the inference that they were all part of a single conspiracy to commit several crimes. (See also 122 OS 443, 5 NE(2d) 482 (1930), Beckman v State.) Jackson v. State (Ohio 1883) 38 Ohio St. 585.

Where in a trial upon an indictment it becomes material for the state to prove that a conspiracy existed between the persons jointly indicted, evidence that the same persons were, shortly prior to the time of the alleged crime, engaged in a conspiracy to commit crimes of a similar nature, is competent. Tarbox v. State (Ohio 1883) 38 Ohio St. 581, 9 W.L.B. 24. Conspiracy ⚿ 45; Criminal Law ⚿ 427(4)

Witness's testimony, regarding alleged other acts of sexual imposition committed by defendant, was admissible to prove defendant's motive, plan, scheme or opportunity to commit gross sexual imposition and sexual imposition against victim; witness's testimony was reasonably offered to prove defendant's motive to inappropriately touch younger woman for purpose of sexual gratification, defendant's touchings of witness and victim were both accompanied by comments about women's breasts, and witness's testimony served to prove defendant's plan and opportunity. State v. Guenther (Ohio App. 9 Dist., Lorain, 02-22-2006) No. 05CA008663, 2006-Ohio-767, 2006 WL 401309, Unreported, appeal not allowed 110 Ohio St.3d 1412, 850 N.E.2d 73, 2006-Ohio-3306. Criminal Law ⚿ 371(9)

Extraneous offense or other acts evidence showing that defendant had drank alcohol or made debit card purchases at bars and restaurants was admissible as relevant to defendant's intent and plan to take customers' money to spend for his own purposes, i.e., bar-restaurant bills, child support payments, and not for the customers or subcontractors, in prosecution for theft by deception, money laundering, and engaging in a pattern of corrupt activity. State v. Piesciuk (Ohio App. 12 Dist., Butler, 10-31-2005) No. CA2004-03-055, 2005-Ohio-5767, 2005 WL 2840637, Unreported, motion to certify allowed 108 Ohio St.3d 1470, 842 N.E.2d 1051, 2006-Ohio-665, appeal allowed 108 Ohio St.3d 1472, 842 N.E.2d 1052, 2006-Ohio-665, reversed in part 109 Ohio St.3d 313, 847 N.E.2d 1174, 2006-Ohio-2109. Criminal Law ⚿ 371(1)

Evidence of prior criminal acts, consisting of testimony that drug courier arrested out-of-state was carrying receipt containing defendant's name and signature, that defendant flew to that state, and that airline coupon defendant used was commonly used by drug couriers, was admissible in drug prosecution under statutory exception permitting other acts testimony to prove defendant's scheme, plan or system in doing the act in question; other acts evidence established modus operandi that shared common features with crimes for which defendant was charged, along with pattern of travel, and was significant since it established that defendant utilized same methods in both instances. State v. Conner (Ohio App. 8 Dist., Cuyahoga, 04-28-2005) No. 84073, 2005-Ohio-1971, 2005 WL 977670, Unreported, motion to reopen denied 2005-Ohio-6354, 2005 WL 3219717. Criminal Law ⚷ 372(13)

Extraneous offense or collateral crimes evidence of defendant's bar fight that occurred one week prior to the similar incident that gave rise to charges of attempted murder, robbery, and two counts of assault was admissible, not only to identify defendant as one of the persons involved in the incident forming the basis of the facts underlying defendant's trial, but also to indicate a similar plan or scheme to attack patrons exiting from the same bar. State v. Perdue (Ohio App. 5 Dist., Richland, 03-02-2005) No. 04-CA-46, 2005-Ohio-1051, 2005 WL 567453, Unreported, appeal not allowed 106 Ohio St.3d 1463, 830 N.E.2d 1170, 2005-Ohio-3490. Criminal Law ⚷ 369.15; Criminal Law ⚷ 372(4); Criminal Law ⚷ 372(14)

Other acts evidence was admissible in prosecution for gross sexual imposition to prove identity, where other act shared significant common features sufficient to establish modus operandi identifying defendant as perpetrator of charged offenses; both victims of charged offenses and other acts witness were young girls who testified that defendant took them to room in his house, placed them on his lap, kissed them, and pushed them back and forth on his lap. State v. Sharp (Ohio App. 8 Dist., Cuyahoga, 02-03-2005) No. 84346, 2005-Ohio-390, 2005 WL 272998, Unreported, appeal allowed 106 Ohio St.3d 1411, 830 N.E.2d 345, 2005-Ohio-3154, reversed in part, appeal dismissed in part 109 Ohio St.3d 313, 847 N.E.2d 1174, 2006-Ohio-2109. Criminal Law ⚷ 369.15

Witness's testimony regarding defendant's "staking out" of women in order to break into their homes and steal their undergarments, two pairs of women's underwear recovered from defendant's person at police department, four pairs of women's underwear recovered from defendant's vehicle, and 806 women's undergarments recovered from defendant's apartment were admissible in burglary prosecution involving defendant climbing through window of female college student's apartment to show common scheme, plan, design, and identity. State v. Entze (Ohio App. 11 Dist., Portage, 09-30-2004) No. 2003-P-0018, 2004-Ohio-5321, 2004 WL 2801699, Unreported. Criminal Law ⚷ 369.15; Criminal Law ⚷ 372(10)

Probative value of evidence that defendant sexually abused his biological daughters, which was relevant to prove pattern of conduct, was not substantially outweighed by possibility of unfair prejudice in rape prosecution in which step-daughter was victim. State v. Russell (Ohio App. 8 Dist., Cuyahoga, 09-23-2004) No. 83699, 2004-Ohio-5031, 2004 WL 2340125, Unreported, appeal not allowed 105 Ohio St.3d 1452, 823 N.E.2d 457, 2005-Ohio-763, motion to reopen denied 2005-Ohio-2998, 2005 WL 1406347, appeal not allowed 106 Ohio St.3d 1537, 835 N.E.2d 384, 2005-Ohio-5146. Criminal Law ⚷ 338(7)

Evidence that defendant sexually abused his biological daughters was admissible in rape prosecution in which step-daughter was victim to prove defendant's pattern of conduct, where state showed that defendant chose females of filial position to him who were under age of 12 and that defendant began touching them in progressively sexual manner. State v. Russell (Ohio App. 8 Dist., Cuyahoga, 09-23-2004) No. 83699, 2004-Ohio-5031, 2004 WL 2340125, Unreported, appeal not allowed 105 Ohio St.3d 1452, 823 N.E.2d 457, 2005-Ohio-763, motion to reopen denied 2005-Ohio-2998, 2005 WL 1406347, appeal not allowed 106 Ohio St.3d 1537, 835 N.E.2d 384, 2005-Ohio-5146. Criminal Law ⚷ 372(7)

Extraneous offense or other act evidence of photographs depicting child molestation victim, who was defendant's biological daughter, in various stages of undress in sexually provocative poses with defendant was admissible for purpose of showing sequence of events leading up to, and part of, sexual abuse. State v. Burris (Ohio App. 5 Dist., Licking, 08-26-2004) No. 2004CA00016, 2004-Ohio-4531, 2004 WL 1921091, Unreported, motion for delayed appeal denied 106 Ohio St.3d 1530, 835 N.E.2d 380, 2005-Ohio-5146. Criminal Law ⚷ 369.2(5)

Evidence that defendant, a high school teacher, inquired into a student's "dating life" and came to her place of employment was not improper "other acts" evidence in prosecution for sexual imposition; evidence tended to support a pattern of inappropriate inquiry and pattern of conduct with teenage girls. State v. Shanklin (Ohio App. 5 Dist., Stark, 06-01-2004) No. 2003CA00317, 2004-Ohio-2910, 2004 WL 1240414, Unreported. Criminal Law ⚷ 374

Evidence of defendant's prior acts of sexual abuse against three other young girls was admissible in prosecution for gross sexual imposition to establish scheme, plan, or system; all acts were committed against girls between 10 and 12 years old, acts occurred when girls were babysitting at defendant's residence, and defendant had romantic relationship with the mothers of the girls. State v. Leadingham (Ohio App. 5 Dist., Stark, 04-19-2004) No. 2003CA00194, 2004-Ohio-1990, 2004 WL 844591, Unreported. Criminal Law ⚷ 372(7)

Probative value of evidence of letters previously written by defendant to victim was not substantially outweighed by danger of unfair prejudice in prosecution for felony menacing by stalking; evidence tended to show the existence of scheme, plan or system, and jury was given limiting instruction on use of evidence. State v. Werfel (Ohio App. 11 Dist., Lake, 12-22-2003) No. 2002-L-101, No. 2002-L-102, 2003-Ohio-6958, 2003 WL 22994981, Unreported. Criminal Law ⚷ 372(14)

Defendant's alleged attempted robbery of restaurant constituted part of common scheme or plan that ultimately led to his alleged commission of robbery and homicide at nearby motel 45 minutes later, thus warranting joinder of all charges stemming from apparent inextricably related crimes in one trial; inasmuch as evidence from both crimes would have been admissible in both trials whether or not cases were tried separately or jointly, defendant failed to show that he was prejudiced by trial court's refusal to sever counts. State v. Hodge (Ohio App. 10 Dist., Franklin, 10-16-2003) No. 02AP-1358, 2003-Ohio-5492, 2003 WL 22351122, Unreported. Criminal Law ⚷ 620(6)

Evidence that defendant had, while possessing a firearm, robbed a restaurant 45 minutes prior to committing robbery and homicide at nearby motel was admissible as relevant to showing common scheme, plan, or system in committing offenses; witness testified that defendant, using another person's money, had been ripped off in cocaine deal, rendering defendant desperate to find more money and cocaine, precipitating apparent inextricably related crimes. State v. Hodge (Ohio App. 10 Dist., Franklin, 10-16-2003) No. 02AP-1358, 2003-Ohio-5492, 2003 WL 22351122, Unreported. Criminal Law ⚷ 372(4); Criminal Law ⚷ 372(14)

Trial court's admission of burglary defendant's prior burglary convictions, which were admitted for limited purpose of showing intent, preparation, or plan, did not result in undue prejudice so as to deny defendant a fair trial, where convictions showed similar mode of operation, and jury was given a limiting instruction. State v. Douglas (Ohio App. 5 Dist., Stark, 07-28-2003) No. 2002CA00240, 2003-Ohio-4259, 2003 WL 21910659, Unreported, motion for delayed appeal denied 100 Ohio St.3d 1543, 800 N.E.2d 749, 2003-Ohio-6879. Criminal Law ⚷ 1169.11

Testimony that officer first observed defendant in front of a "dope house" was admissible under the "scheme, plan, or system" exception to rule governing admissibility of "other acts" evidence; testimony provided inextricably related background information necessary to give a complete picture of the charged offense of possession of crack cocaine. State v. Draper (Ohio App. 10 Dist., Franklin, 07-15-2003) No. 02AP-1371, 2003-Ohio-3751, 2003 WL 21652187, Unreported. Criminal Law ⚷ 372(13)

Probative value of prior bad acts evidence that defendant, who was charged with possession of cocaine, had been previously apprehended transporting over 100 pounds of marijuana was not outweighed by its prejudicial effect; material issue at trial was whether defendant knew the drugs were inside of the tool box in his truck, and thus, it was reasonable for the trial court to determine that witness's testimony regarding a prior incident in which defendant was found with drugs in his car was directly probative as to what defendant knew, his opportunity to obtain drugs, his common scheme or plan and whether the cocaine was mistakenly or accidentally placed in his truck. State v. Martinez (Ohio App. 3 Dist., Marion, 04-10-2003) No. 9-02-57, 2003-Ohio-1821, 2003 WL 1836672, Unreported. Criminal Law ⚷ 370; Criminal Law ⚷ 371(1)

Codefendant's videotaped statement, in which codefendant referred to sexual misconduct involving other individuals that included defendant, was admissible in rape prosecution, even though defendant claimed statement was objectionable under the Rape Shield Act; rules of evidence favored admission of such evidence, and statements demonstrated that the rape defendant was charged with was part of a pattern of behavior, scheme, or modus operandi. State v. Robinson (Ohio App. 7 Dist., Mahoning, 12-04-2002) No. 00 CA 190, 2002-Ohio-6734, 2002 WL 31750204, Unreported, appeal not allowed 98 Ohio St.3d 1538, 786 N.E.2d 900, 2003-Ohio-1946. Criminal Law ⚷ 372(7)

Trial court did not abuse its discretion in drug prosecution by admitting evidence of defendant's prior involvement with drugs as evidence of a " common scheme or plan," where a defense strategy was to question whether detective focused a drug investigation on defendant only because detective previously had attempted unsuccessfully to have defendant prosecuted. State v. Washington (Ohio App. 8 Dist., Cuyahoga, 10-24-2002) No. 80418, 2002-Ohio-5834, 2002 WL 31401558, Unreported, appeal not allowed 98 Ohio St.3d 1491, 785 N.E.2d 473, 2003-Ohio-1189, dismissal of habeas corpus affirmed 101 Ohio St.3d 131, 802 N.E.2d 655, 2004-Ohio-298, appeal not allowed 102 Ohio St.3d 1413, 806 N.E.2d 564, 2004-Ohio-1763. Criminal Law ⚷ 372(13)

Circumstantial evidence supports a jury's finding that an amount taken by a cashier from a cash register exceeds $500 where a "customer" with some clothing items gives what appears to be three twenty dollar bills to the cashier who rings up the transaction and gives as change money that is in the left side of the drawer where the fifty and hundred dollar bills are kept and records indicate the register is $1500 short on the day that a videotape depicts the cashier handing the money over to the person in the tape; in addition, evidence of three other occasions that the cash register was short of cash is admissible to show a scheme or plan regarding the theft of $1500 and that the shortage was not a mistake or accident on the cashier's part. State v. Egler (Ohio App. 8 Dist., Cuyahoga, 04-05-2001) No. 77982, 2001 WL 328558, Unreported.

Evidence a defendant invited children to his house, gave them beer, transported them in a pickup truck which was equipped with a loaded gun, and took another child to West Virginia without anyone's permission were not relevant to a charge of statutory rape because there is no indication these other acts were intertwined with the charged offense, some of the other acts did not involve the rape victim in any way, and there is no evidence as to when the other acts occurred, i.e. before or after the rape; therefore, the failure of defense counsel to object to the admission of such evidence constituted ineffective assistance of counsel and the conviction was reversed and remanded. State v Miller, No. 92-CA-496, 1993 WL 415306 (4th Dist Ct App, Meigs, 10-13-93).

Inmate's testimony that he had purchased large quantities of drugs from defendant on numerous previous occasions was not admissible, in prosecution for trafficking in drugs, under rule of evidence or statute which permitted admission of evidence of other crimes to prove motive, intent, absence of mistake, accident or defendant's scheme, plan or system. State v. Agner (Ohio App. 3 Dist., 10-29-1999) 135 Ohio App.3d 286, 733 N.E.2d 676, 1999-Ohio-918. Criminal Law ⚷ 371(1); Criminal Law ⚷ 371(12); Criminal Law ⚷ 372(13)

Evidence that defendant, who was charged with bribery and sexual battery based on his actions in allegedly coercing victim to provide sexual favors while acting in his official capacity as police officer, had engaged in similar actions with respect to three other victims, was relevant to show "behavioral fingerprint," or modus operandi associated with officer, and thus was admissible evidence of prior acts in prosecution for bribery and sexual battery, in which court had determined that separate trials would be held for charges relating to each of four victims. State v. Knight (Ohio App. 1 Dist., 06-05-1998) 131 Ohio App.3d 349, 722 N.E.2d 568, dismissed, appeal not allowed 83 Ohio St.3d 1432, 699 N.E.2d 947. Criminal Law ⚷ 372(7)

Evidence as to defendant's actions and demeanor during first encounter with cashier, in which he stole beer and flagrantly defied cashier's command to put beer back, was admissible in robbery prosecution to establish that defendant used or threatened to use force against cashier when he reentered store 30 minutes later and stole money and more beer, even though criminal charges relating to first encounter were dismissed. State v. Bush (Ohio App. 2 Dist., 04-11-1997) 119 Ohio App.3d 146, 694 N.E.2d 984, appeal not allowed 79 Ohio St.3d 1460, 681 N.E.2d 442. Criminal Law ⚷ 369.2(6)

For other acts testimony regarding scheme, plan, or system to be admissible under governing statute, it must be inextricably related to crime and form immediate background that serves as foundation of crime; where inflammatory prior-act testimony does not serve these purposes, conviction must be reversed unless there is no reasonable possibility that such testimony contributed to conviction. State v. Cotton (Ohio App. 1 Dist., 06-26-1996) 113 Ohio App.3d 125, 680 N.E.2d 657. Criminal Law ⚷ 372(1); Criminal Law ⚷ 1169.11

Evidence of defendant's prior aggravated burglary conviction was admissible in capital murder case to establish prior aggravated felony specifications in connection with burglary and kidnapping charges and to show defendant's scheme, plan or system in perpetrating offense; both prior burglary and charged burglary involved persons defendant had been with or visited with day before, involved defendant's utilization of ruse to get occupant out of home so he could commit burglary, and defendant had used same alibi in both cases. State v. Wogenstahl (Ohio, 03-06-1996) 75 Ohio St.3d 344, 662 N.E.2d 311, 1996-Ohio-219, reconsideration denied 75 Ohio St.3d 1453, 663 N.E.2d 333, certiorari denied 117 S.Ct. 240, 519 U.S. 895, 136 L.Ed.2d 169, denial of post-conviction relief affirmed 2004-Ohio-5994, 2004 WL 2567655, appeal not allowed 105 Ohio St.3d 1465, 824 N.E.2d 93, 2005-Ohio-1024. Criminal Law ⚷ 369.2(4); Criminal Law ⚷ 372(4)

Testimony about defendant's participation in prior burglary for which he had been prosecuted and convicted was admissible as evidence of "purpose, motive, scheme, plan or system, or absence of mistake or accident" in defendant's trial for burglary, where testimony demonstrated that he had committed similar burglary in same neighborhood, where both previous burglary and current burglaries were committed at night, and where defendant had entered home he previously burglarized by going through window and one of houses he was accused of burglarizing in present action was entered through window. State v. Lopez (Ohio App. 9 Dist., 09-29-1993) 90 Ohio App.3d 566, 630 N.E.2d 32. Criminal Law ⚷ 371(6); Criminal Law ⚷ 371(12); Criminal Law ⚷ 372(10)

When other acts demonstrate criminal conduct they should be so blended or connected with act on trial that proof of one incidentally involves the other, explains the circumstances thereof, or tends logically to prove any element of crime charged and absent that nexus, the other criminal act, whether like or unlike the act charged or similar or dissimilar to it, cannot be used to prove scheme, plan or system employed by accused to commit offense for which he or she is on trial. State v. Smith (Greene 1992) 84 Ohio App.3d 647, 617 N.E.2d 1160, motion to certify denied 66 Ohio St.3d 1488, 612 N.E.2d 1244. Criminal Law ⚷ 369.1; Criminal Law ⚷ 369.2(2)

Extrinsic evidence of scheme, plan or system leading to crime charged is admissible when acts constituting scheme, plan or system are part of immediate background of crime and inextricably related to it and in that event, extrinsic acts must rationally constitute same transaction that is object of proof, that is, crime charged. State v. Smith (Greene 1992) 84 Ohio App.3d 647, 617 N.E.2d 1160, motion to certify denied 66 Ohio St.3d 1488, 612 N.E.2d 1244. Criminal Law ⚷ 369.2(2)

Defendant's prior behavior with two alleged child victims, such as taking them to sporting events and out to eat, demonstrated creation of relationship that culminated in their sleeping over at defendant's home, enabling him to engage in sexual imposition crimes charged, and these acts, although extrinsic to crimes charged, constituted defendant's scheme, plan or system leading to charged crimes and, therefore, were admissible for this limited purpose. State v. Smith (Greene 1992) 84 Ohio App.3d 647, 617 N.E.2d 1160, motion to certify denied 66 Ohio St.3d 1488, 612 N.E.2d 1244. Criminal Law ⚷ 372(7)

Sexual acts to which victim testified, though they occurred during same period as those alleged in indictment for gross sexual imposition, were wholly separate from offenses charged, factually and chronologically, such that they were not part of immediate background of crimes alleged and therefore, they could not be used to show defendant's scheme, plan or system in doing them. State v. Smith (Greene 1992) 84 Ohio App.3d 647, 617 N.E.2d 1160, motion to certify denied 66 Ohio St.3d 1488, 612 N.E.2d 1244. Criminal Law ⚷ 372(7)

Evidence in a rape trial that the defendant used drugs, frequented taverns, spent time in jail, intended to go over to the victim's house with a gun on a night sometime subsequent to the rape, had a bad attitude, and was a "real creep," as well as evidence of bruises on the victim, could be admitted as other acts evidence under RC 2945.59 or Evid R 404(B) to show a plan or scheme of intimidation and a motive of sexual subjugation of the victim. State v. Soke (Geauga 1989) 65 Ohio App.3d 590, 584 N.E.2d 1273, motion overruled 50 Ohio St.3d 715, 553 N.E.2d 1367, rehearing denied 51 Ohio St.3d 710, 555 N.E.2d 647.

The "scheme, plan, or system" provision contained within RC 2945.59 permits the introduction in evidence of testimony concerning other acts which "form part of the immediate background of the alleged act which forms the foundation of the crime charged in the indictment." State v. Wilkinson (Ohio 1980) 64 Ohio St.2d 308, 415 N.E.2d 261, 18 O.O.3d 482. Criminal Law ⚿ 372(1)

In a first degree murder case, where the evidence shows that defendant, while participating in an attempted motel robbery, shot and killed the motel owner with a shotgun which was found in his possession shortly thereafter, evidence that defendant participated in a similar motel robbery three hours earlier in the same general area, in which incident defendant fired a shot at the motel manager from the same weapon, is admissible under RC 2945.59 as tending to show defendant's scheme, plan, or system in doing the act for which he is being tried. State v. Moorehead (Ohio 1970) 24 Ohio St.2d 166, 265 N.E.2d 551, 53 O.O.2d 379, vacated in part 92 S.Ct. 2869, 408 U.S. 938, 33 L.Ed.2d 759.

The legal determination, by comparison of the plan, system or method employed in a prior crime with the plan, system or method employed in the crime in question, of whether the former is relevant to the issue of identity of the perpetrator of the latter, must be made without consideration of the fact that eye witnesses have identified the same person as the perpetrator of both crimes. State v. Hector (Ohio 1969) 19 Ohio St.2d 167, 249 N.E.2d 912, 48 O.O.2d 199. Criminal Law ⚿ 369.15

In a prosecution for the crime of pocket picking, testimony by a police officer, from his own knowledge of a prior investigation, concerning similar acts of defendant is admissible where no reference is made to a prior conviction or to the disposition of any prior offense and where the court carefully limits the purpose of such testimony, both during the course of the trial and in the general charge to the jury. State v. Haines (Montgomery 1960) 112 Ohio App. 487, 176 N.E.2d 446, 16 O.O.2d 376.

In a prosecution for sodomy any act of the defendant which, either directly or by reasonable inference, tends to show a course of lascivious conduct, degeneracy and sexual perversion is admissible to show such qualities of character and moral disposition. State v. Shively (Jackson 1960) 176 N.E.2d 436, 86 Ohio Law Abs. 71, affirmed 172 Ohio St. 128, 174 N.E.2d 104, 15 O.O.2d 211. Sodomy ⚿ 6

Where separate and distinct offenses are sought to be shown by the state as having some relation to the offense on trial, showing motive, scienter, etc., testimony tending to prove the offense charged is not rendered incompetent because it also tends to prove such separate offenses (Brown v State, 26 OS 176 (1875)); this rule of competency is also applicable when such other offenses are the result of a common scheme embracing the commission of two or more crimes, including the crime charged, and which are so related that proof of one tends to establish the others. (See also Tarbox v State, 38 OS 581 (1883); Jackson v State, 38 OS 585 (1883), and Reed v State, 15 O 217 (1846).) Beckman v. State (Ohio 1930) 122 Ohio St. 443, 5 N.E.2d 482, 8 Ohio Law Abs. 353, 32 Ohio Law Rep. 111.

Where there is evidence tending to show commission of similar crimes subsequent to crime charged, which crimes are carried out under a common agreement between joint defendants to engage in such criminal transactions, such evidence is competent to show the existence of a conspiracy to commit crime charged as well as to commit the crimes referred to in the evidence. Beckman v. State (Ohio 1930) 122 Ohio St. 443, 5 N.E.2d 482, 8 Ohio Law Abs. 353, 32 Ohio Law Rep. 111.

Upon trial of the accused for larceny of W's automobile, where state relies for conviction upon proof of such criminal plan to steal various automobiles, belonging to W, C, and others, and offers evidence of such plan and the larcenies of cars other than charged in the indictment, the fact that accused at a former trial had been acquitted of the larceny of C's car does not conclude the state from proving that such plan embraced the larceny of C's car, although the evidence offered at such second trial was substantially the same as that produced by the state on the former trial which resulted in a verdict of acquittal. Patterson v. State (Ohio 1917) 96 Ohio St. 90, 117 N.E. 169, 15 Ohio Law Rep. 84, 15 Ohio Law Rep. 104.

"Other acts" evidence consisting of sexual lotions, pornographic magazines, and pornographic videotapes that were found in vacant house owned by defendant where charged offenses allegedly occurred were relevant to issue of preparation in prosecution on murder, kidnapping, and rape charges involving seven-year-old victim. State v. Satta (Ohio App. 3 Dist., Marion, 09-25-2002) No. 9-01-38, 2002-Ohio-5049, 2002 WL 31114690, Unreported, appeal not allowed 98 Ohio St.3d 1461, 783 N.E.2d 520, 2003-Ohio-644, reconsideration denied 98 Ohio St.3d 1516, 786 N.E.2d 64, 2003-Ohio-1572, motion for delayed appeal denied 98 Ohio St.3d 1509, 786 N.E.2d 60, 2003-Ohio-1572, appeal not allowed 99 Ohio St.3d 1437, 789 N.E.2d 1118, 2003-Ohio-2902. Criminal Law ⚿ 369.2(4); Criminal Law ⚿ 369.2(5)

Store security guard's testimony as to events that occurred approximately six weeks before the incident for which defendant was convicted of receiving stolen property was not admissible under the scheme, plan or system exception to general rule prohibiting admission of other crimes evidence; security guard testified to events that were not inextricably related to the crimes charged, but, rather, were chronologically and factually separate occurrences. State v. Colon (Ohio App. 9 Dist., Summit, 08-07-2002) No. 20949, 2002-Ohio-3985, 2002 WL 1800274, Unreported. Criminal Law ⚷ 372(14)

Defendant was not prejudiced, as element of ineffective assistance claim, when defense counsel during opening statement in child sexual abuse prosecution conceded that victims had been molested but argued that defendant was not perpetrator; while trial court later admitted "other acts" evidence to prove a plan or scheme on part of defendant, it did not find defendant had "opened the door" to such evidence, it did not limit defense counsel from presenting evidence that attempted to show victims' stories were fabricated, and it ruled prior to opening statements that the "other acts" evidence was admissible. State v. Adkins (Ohio App. 5 Dist., Morrow, 07-24-2002) No. CA-906, 2002-Ohio-3942, 2002 WL 1773153, Unreported. Criminal Law ⚷ 641.13(2.1)

Introduction of testimony that defendant shot another victim two hours after his murder spree is admissible under RC 2945.59 where that testimony is inextricably related to the facts surrounding the first murders and provides the jury with the setting and background of the case as well as defendant's scheme or plan. State v Howard, No. 62191 (8th Dist Ct App, Cuyahoga, 4–8–93).

Evidence of prior incidents of sexual contact between a teacher and students is admissible in a prosecution for gross sexual imposition by a teacher upon a student to prove scheme, plan, or system. State v Cobb, No. 61676 (8th Dist Ct App, Cuyahoga, 3–18–93).

In order to introduce evidence of other acts against a defendant to show a common scheme, plan, or system pursuant to Evid R 404(B), the defendant must be sufficiently identified as the perpetrator of the other acts. State v Nelson; appeal dismissed by 39 OS(3d) 605, 530 NE(2d) 916 (1988), No. 87 CA 12 (2d Dist Ct App, Greene, 7-29-87).

15. —— Defendant's testimony, admissibility of prior acts

Testimony from co-defendants that defendant had sold drugs on occasions not covered in the indictment for trafficking in, and possession of, marijuana, and that defendant and a co-defendant had participated in theft from another marijuana dealer, was illustrative of defendant's predisposition to commit the charged offenses and, thus, admissible for other purposes than to show defendant's propensity for criminal behavior. State v. McIntosh (Ohio App. 1 Dist., 08-31-2001) 145 Ohio App.3d 567, 763 N.E.2d 704, appeal not allowed 94 Ohio St.3d 1411, 759 N.E.2d 787, appeal not allowed 96 Ohio St.3d 1488, 774 N.E.2d 763, 2002-Ohio-4478, denial of post-conviction relief affirmed in part, reversed in part 2003-Ohio-3824, 2003 WL 21673323. Criminal Law ⚷ 369.2(7)

Trial court acted within its discretion in admitting character and other acts evidence of murder defendant's homosexuality, his prior domestic abuse of his wife, and his alleged use of racist remarks; such evidence was relevant in that it provided a full context for defendant's written confession, in which defendant stated that he killed 11-week-old child because of problems that defendant and his wife were having in their relationship as well as defendant's difficulty in coping with a biracial child. State v. Smith (Ohio App. 3 Dist., 11-20-1996) 115 Ohio App.3d 419, 685 N.E.2d 595.

Evidence of prior report to police by defendant's wife that he stabbed her was admissible in trial on charge of felonious assault arising out of defendant's shooting of wife to impeach wife's credibility as witness and to refute defendant's testimony that shooting was accidental; stabbing took place seven months before shooting, wife recanted her story of stabbing, stating that it was accident that was her fault and that she would not prosecute, wife told detective and paramedic that defendant shot her and that it was not accident, wife later informed police that shooting was accident and that she did not wish to prosecute, and wife testified at trial that shooting was accidental. State v. McCornell (Ohio App. 8 Dist., 10-12-1993) 91 Ohio App.3d 141, 631 N.E.2d 1110. Criminal Law ⚷ 371(1); Witnesses ⚷ 406

In a trial for rape and gross sexual imposition involving the defendant's minor daughter, a trial court properly permits the state to call two rebuttal witnesses to testify to prior instances of alleged sexual conduct of the defendant where (1) the defendant repeatedly testified as a witness on his own behalf that he never had any sexual contact or related activities with his daughter or any minor child, thus opening the door to the issue of past sexual conduct and waiving statutory limitations under the Rape Shield Law; (2) the defense called a witness on direct examination to testify that the defendant had no perversion or strangeness and the witness had not known the defendant to engage in such conduct with female children; and (3) the witnesses, the defendant's daughter by a previous marriage and the daughter of one of the defendant's former girlfriends, testified that the defendant had engaged in sexual conduct with them while they were four or five years old. State v. Banks (Seneca 1991) 71 Ohio App.3d 214, 593 N.E.2d 346.

Only where an accused specifically places his particularized intent to commit the crime with which he is charged in issue, either by directly denying such intent, or asserting accident or mistake, is it material and admissible to introduce otherwise relevant evidence of other acts of a similar nature. State v. Snowden (Clermont 1976) 49 Ohio App.2d 7, 359 N.E.2d 87, 3 O.O.3d 92. Criminal Law ⚷ 371(1)

The defendant cannot complain about the prosecutor cross-examining him concerning his past convictions under state law of Ohio and other states where he volunteered this information upon direct examination by his own counsel. State v. Pollard (Ohio 1970) 21 Ohio St.2d 171, 256 N.E.2d 620, 50 O.O.2d 394. Criminal Law ⚷ 1137(5)

The failure of the trial court in a criminal prosecution to admonish the jury, at the time evidence of "similar acts" is introduced that such evidence is not to be considered as substantive evidence or proof of the crime charged and to limit the purpose for which such evidence is received, is not prejudicial error, where defendant makes no request for such admonition and limitation and the court's general charge to the jury adequately covers the situation, and the trial court's comments in its charge to the jury, that evidence of "similar acts is evidence that the defendant may have committed other crimes" and that "there is evidence that this defendant may have committed other crimes," constitute error; but such error is cured where the defendant testifies in his own behalf and admits committing the "other crimes" involved. State v. Pigott (Cuyahoga 1964) 1 Ohio App.2d 22, 197 N.E.2d 911, 94 Ohio Law Abs. 335, 30 O.O.2d 56.

In a prosecution for arson in the burning of a barn and its contents, it is not error to admit in evidence defendant's confessions to setting other fires and his method and reason, and evidence of other barn fires and of an attempt to burn a bridge is admissible, where the actions disclosed by such evidence are closely related, in nature, time and place, to the offense charged. State v. Hopkins (Greene 1962) 117 Ohio App. 48, 189 N.E.2d 636, 23 O.O.2d 11.

Where the defendant in a criminal prosecution places in issue his character and reputation, the admission into evidence of testimony of a prior identical offense by defendant is not error prejudicial to him, where the trial court exercises caution in the admission of such evidence and limits its application solely to the question of the credibility of such witness. State v. Deboard (Highland 1962) 116 Ohio App. 108, 187 N.E.2d 83, 21 O.O.2d 398.

16. —— Judicial admissions, admissibility of prior acts

Testimony by a deputy clerk of courts, in a trial for forgery, that the defendant, while accompanied by his attorney, had previously entered a plea of guilty to an earlier charge of forgery, is admissible under RC 2945.59 as a judicial admission of defendant tending to show his intent, motive, habit or state of mind at the time he is alleged to have committed the offense for which he is on trial. State v. Murphy (Clark 1967) 13 Ohio App.2d 159, 234 N.E.2d 619, 42 O.O.2d 273. Criminal Law ⚷ 371(5); Criminal Law ⚷ 371(12)

17. Admissibility of subsequent acts

It was not error for trial court to admit evidence of a subsequent similar crime, which was committed three months after instant crime, for which defendant was incarcerated at time of investigation, indictment and trial in present case where material was offered to show motive, intent or absence of mistake or accident on defendant's part as well as identity of defendant as perpetrator. State v. Harvill (Hamilton 1984) 15 Ohio App.3d 94, 472 N.E.2d 743, 15 O.B.R. 123. Criminal Law ⚷ 369.15; Criminal Law ⚷ 371(1); Criminal Law ⚷ 371(12)

On a charge of a "second or subsequent" offense, it is necessary that the indictment charge such prior offense as an element of the crime and prove it as a matter of fact. State v. Gordon (Ohio 1971) 28 Ohio St.2d 45, 276 N.E.2d 243, 57 O.O.2d 180.

In the trial of a person for violating a municipal ordinance prohibiting drunkenness, evidence of such person's subsequent similar acts (drunkenness) is permissible. City of Cincinnati v. Billman (Hamilton 1968) 14 Ohio App.2d 161, 237 N.E.2d 403, 43 O.O.2d 347.

In a prosecution for abortion, evidence of an abortion allegedly performed on another person subsequent to that charged in the indictment is admissible. State v. Brown (Montgomery 1955) 137 N.E.2d 609, 73 Ohio Law Abs. 349.

18. Prior acts admissible—In general

"Other acts" evidence that alleged victim's clothes were scattered on ground and that her tires were slashed was admissible in prosecution for aggravated arson and intimidation of a witness because that evidence formed part of the immediate background of crimes charged and was inextricably related to them. State v. Jackson (Ohio App. 10 Dist., Franklin, 11-20-2003) No. 02AP-867, 2003-Ohio-6183, 2003 WL 22725287, Unreported, appeal not allowed 102 Ohio St.3d 1411, 806 N.E.2d 562, 2004-Ohio-1763. Criminal Law ⚷ 369.2(3.1)

Trial court acted within its discretion in playing audiotape of defendant's oral confession in its entirety, even though confession contained statement in which defendant referred to his cellmate as "colored." State v. Smith (Ohio App. 3 Dist., 11-20-1996) 115 Ohio App.3d 419, 685 N.E.2d 595.

Evidence that arson defendant previously threatened his former girlfriend's life was relevant and material to show motive and intent in prosecution for throwing Molotov cocktail into girlfriend's house, despite contention that evidence was prohibited "other acts" testimony. State v. Billings (Ohio App. 8 Dist., 04-06-1995) 103 Ohio App.3d 343, 659 N.E.2d 799, belated appeal granted 73 Ohio St.3d 1412, 651 N.E.2d 1310, dismissed, jurisdictional motion overruled 74 Ohio St.3d 1455, 656 N.E.2d 950, subsequent mandamus proceeding 1999 WL 754508, affirmed 88 Ohio St.3d 237, 724 N.E.2d 1151, 2000-Ohio-317. Criminal Law ⚷ 371(7); Criminal Law ⚷ 371(12)

Scheme, plan, or system testimony of other acts is admissible to establish motive or intent where the similarities in the crimes indicate there is a strong likelihood that the offender in the solved crime also committed the unsolved crime. State v. Coleman (Ohio 1988) 37 Ohio St.3d 286, 525 N.E.2d 792, stay granted 38 Ohio St.3d 720, 533 N.E.2d 1061, rehearing granted, opinion recalled 41 Ohio St.3d 710, 534 N.E.2d 1208, certiorari denied 109 S.Ct. 250, 488 U.S. 900, 102 L.Ed.2d 238, stay granted 41 Ohio St.3d 711, 534 N.E.2d 1209, rehearing denied 41 Ohio St.3d 726, 536 N.E.2d 385. Criminal Law ⚷ 372(1)

In an action for a malicious prosecution alleging the arrest of a plaintiff on a false charge of uttering a check against insufficient funds, it is proper to admit in evidence bank statements of the plaintiff offered by the defense to prove such plaintiff's intent to give a bad check. Faranda v. King Tire Co. (Hamilton 1971) 31 Ohio App.2d 196, 287 N.E.2d 283, 60 O.O.2d 294.

In the trial of a criminal case pursuant to an indictment charging the defendant with making repeated telephone calls to a person for the sole purpose of harassing or molesting such person or his family, motive of intent is an essential element of the offense charged, and evidence of prior similar acts of the defendant closely related in point of time to the offense charged is admissible to show the motive or intent prompting the defendant's alleged commission of the offense charged in the indictment. State v. Goode (Greene 1962) 118 Ohio App. 479, 195 N.E.2d 581, 25 O.O.2d 395, appeal dismissed 174 Ohio St. 232, 188 N.E.2d 421, 22 O.O.2d 224.

In a prosecution for child stealing, evidence regarding sexual acts by the accused with the child is admissible to show motive or intent as well as evidence of previous more sordid acts with another boy. State v. White (Montgomery 1962) 116 Ohio App. 522, 189 N.E.2d 160, 22 O.O.2d 398.

In prosecution for practicing medicine without a license, where accused claims that he merely performed some "back rubbing" and taping and sold some pills, evidence of prior convictions of practicing medicine without a license is admissible to show the motive, intent and plan of the accused, and absence of mistake or accident, in doing the acts in question. State v. Ensminger (Ohio 1948) 149 Ohio St. 289, 77 N.E.2d 79, 37 O.O. 6. Criminal Law ⚷ 371(1); Criminal Law ⚷ 371(12); Criminal Law ⚷ 372(14)

In prosecution of sheriff for receiving a bribe with intent to protect gambling in certain tavern, evidence concerning alleged gambling operations at another place in county was properly admitted as tending to show that sheriff knew of gambling operations there but failed to act. State v. Young (Clark 1946) 70 N.E.2d 458, 48 Ohio Law Abs. 22. Bribery ⚷ 10; Criminal Law ⚷ 370

Trial court did not abuse its discretion when it admitted evidence of the surveillance of the defendant and prior arrest as other acts of defendant; such evidence was admissible for the purpose of proof of motive, opportunity, intent, preparation, plan, knowledge, identity, or absence of mistake or accident, and court provided the jury with a corrective instruction to disregard the question as to whether a scale was found in the defendant's vehicle. State v. Fannin (Ohio App. 8 Dist., Cuyahoga, 08-15-2002) No. 80014, 2002-Ohio-4180, 2002 WL 1878860, Unreported, appeal not allowed 98 Ohio St.3d 1412, 781 N.E.2d 1020, 2003-Ohio-60. Criminal Law ⚷ 369.2(1)

19. —— Makeup, prior acts admissible

Questioning of the arresting officers by the prosecution on the issue of whether defendants were wearing makeup at the time of their arrest does not constitute testimony concerning other criminal acts in violation of Evid R 404(B) or RC 2945.59. State v Doles, No. L–81–176 (6th Dist Ct App, Lucas, 3–5–82).

Prosecution's questions concerning whether or not defendant was wearing makeup do not constitute testimony concerning other criminal acts in violation of Evid R 404(B) or RC 2945.59 where defense counsel has questioned witnesses extensively concerning the defendant's complexion. State v Jordan, No. L–81–177 (6th Dist Ct App, Lucas, 3–5–82).

20. —— Assault, prior acts admissible

Testimony that a child's mother was assaulted by defendant and that he had previously taken the child is admissible to show intent in an action for child stealing. State v. Armstrong (Montgomery 1991) 74 Ohio App.3d 732, 600 N.E.2d 690.

21. —— Burglary and robbery, prior acts admissible

Defendant's other acts of telling different "stories" at each location to justify his presence at the locations, and entering school without anyone's knowledge, being escorted out, and then re-entering school were admissible in burglary prosecution to establish pattern of behavior and his intent to steal money or commit other offenses in places he visited; "other acts" were part of continuous course of conduct, which included actions which were close together in time and location, and carried out in a highly similar manner. State v. DeBoe (Ohio App. 6 Dist., Huron, 01-30-2004) No. H-02-057, 2004-Ohio-403, 2004 WL 190068, Unreported, motion for delayed appeal denied 103 Ohio St.3d 1424, 814 N.E.2d 488, 2004-Ohio-4524. Criminal Law ⚷ 372(10)

Where sole issue was whether defendant was at scene of robbery committed by his brother and another man by design or by circumstance, evidence that defendant had joined same persons in other robberies was properly admitted. State v. Martin (Montgomery 1961) 191 N.E.2d 581, 91 Ohio Law Abs. 139, 91 Ohio Law Abs. 147. Criminal Law ⚷ 369.2(7)

Other acts evidence that defendant, who was charged with aggravated robbery and attempted murder, was a passenger in the automobile that crashed during the police chase on the night at issue properly was admitted to show that defendant was near the scene of the crime. State v. Tucker (Ohio App. 8 Dist., Cuyahoga, 09-19-2002) No. 80221, 2002-Ohio-4902, 2002 WL 31087511, Unreported, appeal not allowed 98 Ohio St.3d 1477, 784 N.E.2d 711, 2003-Ohio-974, denial of post-conviction relief affirmed 2005-Ohio-109, 2005 WL 77051, appeal not allowed 106 Ohio St.3d 1413, 830 N.E.2d 346, 2005-Ohio-3154. Criminal Law ⚷ 369.2(6)

In an action for aggravated robbery, evidence of an uncharged attempted robbery is admissible under RC 2945.59 and Evid R 404(B) where such evidence is probative of defendant's intent and both the attempted and aggravated robbery were committed in a similar fashion, in the same locality, within a close period of time. State v Porter, No. 43825 (8th Dist Ct App, Cuyahoga, 3–11–82).

22. —— **Drug offenses, prior acts admissible**

Other-acts evidence of defendant's drug activities and prostitution and her behavior toward her child was admissible in trial for aggravated vehicular homicide and child endangerment to show intent, motive, and plan; defendant's theory at trial was that she was victim of carjacking while visiting certain area to visit friend, the state's theory was that offenses arose out of defendant's attempt to scam victim out of drugs, and other-acts evidence demonstrated that defendant went to area to buy drugs and not to visit friend and was indicative of defendant's system of buying drugs in area with her son in back seat of vehicle. State v. Atkins-Boozer (Ohio App. 8 Dist., Cuyahoga, 05-31-2005) No. 84151, 2005-Ohio-2666, 2005 WL 1274215, Unreported, appeal allowed 107 Ohio St.3d 1406, 836 N.E.2d 1227, 2005-Ohio-5859. Criminal Law ⚩ 371(1); Criminal Law ⚩ 371(12); Criminal Law ⚩ 372(14)

Other-crimes evidence that defendant was sought by police for distributing crack cocaine and that he had pellet gun and cell phone in his vehicle did not mislead jury in trial for possession of cocaine, even though defendant argued that evidence implied that he was drug dealer and that there was no evidence that he distributed or intended to sell cocaine; the state asserted that evidence was presented only to explain why police were looking for defendant's vehicle, defendant was never charged with weapons offense or possession of criminal tools, and the state never presented evidence that defendant possessed or used pellet gun. State v. Edwards (Ohio App. 5 Dist., Stark, 11-15-2004) No. 2004-CA-00060, 2004-Ohio-6139, 2004 WL 2616423, Unreported. Criminal Law ⚩ 369.2(7)

Other-acts evidence of defendant's prior arrests for possession of methamphetamine and lab equipment was admissible to show intent, in trial for illegal assembly or possession of chemicals for manufacture of drugs. State v. Kolvek (Ohio App. 9 Dist., Summit, 07-14-2004) No. 21752, 2004-Ohio-3706, 2004 WL 1562573, Unreported, appeal not allowed 103 Ohio St.3d 1528, 817 N.E.2d 410, 2004-Ohio-5852, appeal not allowed 104 Ohio St.3d 1441, 819 N.E.2d 1124, 2004-Ohio-7033. Criminal Law ⚩ 371(1)

Evidence of defendant's prior drug arrest was admissible as proof of intent, motive, plan, and absence of mistake, despite defendant's claim that such evidence constituted improper "other crimes" evidence; in the instant case, defendant was arrested with the same person on almost the same block where he was previously arrested for trafficking drugs, and defendant's level of participation and interaction in each instance were also similar. State v. McCuller (Ohio App. 8 Dist., Cuyahoga, 07-08-2004) No. 83379, 2004-Ohio-3615, 2004 WL 1533248, Unreported. Criminal Law ⚩ 371(1); Criminal Law ⚩ 371(12)

Evidence of defendant's home detention and her federal drug case was admissible "other acts" evidence in prosecution for attempted murder to show defendant's motive and intent to murder victim; evidence showed that defendant intended to feign her own death using victim's body, and thereby avoid prosecution in drug case. State v. Jenksin (Ohio App. 8 Dist., Cuyahoga, 01-15-2004) No. 82622, 2004-Ohio-136, 2004 WL 63937, Unreported. Criminal Law ⚩ 371(4); Criminal Law ⚩ 371(12)

Other acts evidence, including defendant's admission that he wrote prescriptions to friends and others for Percocet and other painkillers and took some of the pills from the filled prescriptions to medicate himself, was admissible to provide motive behind defendant's conduct, in aggravated drug trafficking case, of writing and paying for a prescription for Percocet for an individual he recently met socially and had never treated, and taking some of the prescription for himself. State v. Dinozzi (Ohio App. 12 Dist., Clermont, 04-21-2003) No. CA2002-02-014, 2003-Ohio-2012, 2003 WL 1906737, Unreported, appeal not allowed 99 Ohio St.3d 1543, 795 N.E.2d 682, 2003-Ohio-4671. Criminal Law ⚩ 371(12)

Evidence that defendant purchased crack cocaine, sold crack to three individuals, and used scale to weigh the crack in his motel room on same day that police searched motel room was admissible, in prosecution for possession of cocaine, to show the immediate background of facts supporting the charge and to prove motive, opportunity, intent, preparation, plan, and knowledge. State v. Elam (Ohio App. 3 Dist., Hancock, 03-31-2003) No. 5-02-57, 2003-Ohio-1577, 2003 WL 1617996, Unreported, motion for delayed appeal denied 99 Ohio St.3d 1540, 795 N.E.2d 680, 2003-Ohio-4671. Criminal Law ⚩ 369.2(7); Criminal Law ⚩ 371(1); Criminal Law ⚩ 371(12)

Because "other acts" evidence is admissible where relevant to some issue involving proof of guilt, testimony concerning the defendant's participation in drug sales is admissible in a murder trial to prove that the defendant killed the victim to avenge a theft of drug money. State v. Bobo (Cuyahoga 1989) 65 Ohio App.3d 685, 585 N.E.2d 429, dismissed, jurisdictional motion overruled 50 Ohio St.3d 714, 553 N.E.2d 1363.

Evidence of defendant's past drug dealing was admissible in prosecution for murder in order to show that defendant lived in lifestyle beyond his legitimate means and that defendant's motive for the killing was a theft of drugs from him by the victim. State v. Hill (Hamilton 1987) 37 Ohio App.3d 72, 523 N.E.2d 894. Criminal Law ⚩ 371(4); Criminal Law ⚩ 371(12)

23. —— **Insurance offenses, prior acts admissible**

Evidence that an automobile leased by the insured's girlfriend was damaged in an incendiary fire two days before the insured's warehouse was damaged by another fire was admissible as evidence of other wrongful acts in the insured's suit seeking coverage for the warehouse fire, where the insured had procured insurance coverage on the automobile, both the automobile and the warehouse were lockable but unlocked when the fires occurred, both had evidence of a liquid accelerant, and the insured had a financial motive to set the warehouse fire. Ragone v. Sentry Ins. Co. (Ohio App. 8 Dist., 06-09-1997) 121 Ohio App.3d 362, 700 N.E.2d 48, appeal not allowed 80 Ohio St.3d 1425, 685 N.E.2d 238. Evidence ⚷ 134

24. —— Murder, prior acts admissible

"Other acts" evidence was relevant and admissible in kidnapping and murder prosecution for the purpose of proving motive, where according to the state's theory, victim was killed because he witnessed a shooting that involved defendant and his companion, and victim's murder was part of an overall scheme that involved killing witnesses that could potentially implicate companion in criminal activities. State v. Horton (Ohio App. 10 Dist., Franklin, 02-08-2005) No. 03AP-665, 2005-Ohio-458, 2005 WL 289466, Unreported, appeal not allowed 106 Ohio St.3d 1415, 830 N.E.2d 347, 2005-Ohio-3154, appeal not allowed 108 Ohio St.3d 1490, 843 N.E.2d 795, 2006-Ohio-962. Criminal Law ⚷ 371(12)

In prosecution for complicity to commit murder, trial court acted within its discretion in admitting evidence of a fight involving defendant, defendant's cousin, and alleged victim which allegedly occurred prior to murder, despite defendant's claim that such evidence constituted improper "other crimes" evidence; record revealed that State introduced the evidence of the fight to demonstrate defendant's motive or intent regarding alleged victim's murder. State v. Moore (Ohio App. 7 Dist., Mahoning, 05-03-2004) No. 02CA152, 2004-Ohio-2320, 2004 WL 1043223, Unreported, appeal not allowed 103 Ohio St.3d 1463, 815 N.E.2d 678, 2004-Ohio-5056. Criminal Law ⚷ 371(4); Criminal Law ⚷ 371(12)

In prosecution for conspiracy to commit murder, evidence that defendant had previously been convicted of murdering alleged victim's sister was admissible to demonstrate motive, despite defendant's claim that such evidence constituted improper "other acts" evidence; testimony was presented that defendant plotted to have alleged victim murdered in the same manner as sister, so as to permit defendant to show that he had been wrongfully convicted for the murder of sister. State v. Bloomfield (Ohio App. 4 Dist., Ross, 02-17-2004) No. 03CA2720, 2004-Ohio-749, 2004 WL 307467, Unreported. Criminal Law ⚷ 371(12)

Evidence of defendant's probation violation was properly admitted as other crimes evidence in murder prosecution; such evidence was offered to show motive. State v. Young (Ohio App. 8 Dist., Cuyahoga, 01-23-2003) No. 80059, 2003-Ohio-272, 2003 WL 152818, Unreported. Criminal Law ⚷ 371(12)

Evidence that defendant did not deny killing his daughter in jailhouse conversation, was admissible in murder prosecution as other crimes evidence, where defendant had declined to talk about whether he had killed his daughter. State v. Young (Ohio App. 8 Dist., Cuyahoga, 01-23-2003) No. 80059, 2003-Ohio-272, 2003 WL 152818, Unreported. Criminal Law ⚷ 369.2(4)

Evidence that defendant threatened to kill victim's mother, that he planned to hide if he killed someone, that he offered money to another to beat up victim's mother, was admissible as other crimes evidence in murder prosecution; evidence showed motive, the absence of mistake, and defendant's plan. State v. Young (Ohio App. 8 Dist., Cuyahoga, 01-23-2003) No. 80059, 2003-Ohio-272, 2003 WL 152818, Unreported. Criminal Law ⚷ 369.2(4); Criminal Law ⚷ 371(12); Criminal Law ⚷ 372(4)

Trial court, in murder prosecution, did not abuse its discretion in admitting as other crimes evidence, testimony from witnesses concerning prior acts of violence and threats defendant directed toward victim and victim's former girlfriends; dispute existed over whether defendant acted out of fear when she stabbed victim or whether defendant's conduct was indicative of her desire to inflict physical harm, and since State contended victim's motive in stabbing victim was driven by her loss of control over her relationship with victim, nature of defendant's relationship with victim bore directly on whether defendant had a motive to harm victim. State v. Brown (Ohio App. 3 Dist., Marion, 12-11-2002) No. 9-02-02, 2002-Ohio-6765, 2002 WL 31758593, Unreported, motion for delayed appeal granted 98 Ohio St.3d 1509, 786 N.E.2d 60, 2003-Ohio-1572, appeal not allowed 99 Ohio St.3d 1467, 791 N.E.2d 983, 2003-Ohio-3669. Criminal Law ⚷ 371(12)

Where a defendant in a prosecution for murder testifies that he loves his wife and would never do anything to harm his spouse or his unborn child, it is not error to allow testimony concerning defendant's prior acts of violence against the victim/spouse since the acts are relevant to the issues of intent, purpose, and the defendant's capacity for violence against the victim. State v. Banks (Franklin 1986) 31 Ohio App.3d 57, 508 N.E.2d 986, 31 O.B.R. 97.

In trial of defendant on two counts of first degree murder arising out of a single death, one count alleging premeditation and one count alleging a killing while perpetrating robbery, where evidence shows that accused was a gunman and had two accomplices, other evidence that he participated in two other armed robberies as a gunman with the same two accomplices, one such incident being approximately two months earlier and another being two days after the crime charged, in which later robbery accused killed another man, tends to show intent on the part of accused to rob and intent to kill, and is admissible, with proper limiting instructions, for those purposes, irrespective of whether the other circumstances involved in those other acts comprise substantial probative evidence that the accused participated in the crime for which he is standing trial. State v. Flonnory (Ohio 1972) 31 Ohio St.2d 124, 285 N.E.2d 726, 60 O.O.2d 95. Criminal Law ⚷ 371(4); Criminal Law ⚷ 673(5)

Where state is required to show possession of murder weapon by defendant to establish its case, it is permissible to allow in evidence proof of other criminal acts committed by defendant which tend to establish such possession, even though such evidence incidentally tends to prove commission of crimes other than the one with which defendant is charged. State v. Watson (Ohio 1971) 28 Ohio St.2d 15, 275 N.E.2d 153, 57 O.O.2d 95. Criminal Law ⚷ 369.2(4)

"Other acts" evidence that before the murder, defendant had been involved with murderer and a youth in shoplifting and breaking into homes was admissible in prosecution for obstructing justice, relating to defendant's statements to police during investigation of the murder; the evidence was relevant to defendant's knowledge of murderer's and youth's criminal propensities and his motive to conceal information regarding their criminal activities. State v. Terry (Ohio App. 12 Dist., Fayette, 08-26-2002) No. CA2001-07-012, 2002-Ohio-4378, 2002 WL 1964694, Unreported. Criminal Law ⚷ 370; Criminal Law ⚷ 371(12)

25. —— Sexual offenses, prior acts admissible

Trial court acted within its discretion in trial for domestic violence and rape in admitting prior-acts evidence of defendant's acts of violence against women to show motive, intent, purpose, and absence of mistake or accident, given defendant's contentions that he accidentally caused victim's injuries by pushing her by shoulders, causing her to stumble into her toilet, which caused articles on overhead shelves to fall on her head, in addition to striking her face accidentally while trying to knock a lit crack pipe out of her mouth. State v. Roper (Ohio App. 9 Dist., Summit, 11-30-2005) No. 22566, 2005-Ohio-6327, 2005 WL 3190966, Unreported. Criminal Law ⚷ 371(9); Criminal Law ⚷ 371(12); Criminal Law ⚷ 372(7)

Witness' testimony regarding defendant's prior sexual acts properly was admitted in rape prosecution pursuant to statute and rule providing that evidence of other crimes is admissible as proof of motive, preparation, plan, identity, or absence of mistake; in her testimony, witness identified defendant as the person who committed unlawful sex acts against her as a child similar to the ones committed by defendant against the victim in this case, and the prior acts that witness testified to proved a modus operandi applicable to defendant. State v. Ristich (Ohio App. 9 Dist., Summit, 06-16-2004) No. 21701, 2004-Ohio-3086, 2004 WL 1344853, Unreported, appeal not allowed 103 Ohio St.3d 1494, 816 N.E.2d 1080, 2004-Ohio-5605. Criminal Law ⚷ 372(7)

Other acts evidence of defendant's prior sexual acts and convictions for rape and gross sexual imposition were admissible during rape prosecution to establish modus operandi and identity; in three prior cases defendant befriended young girls, isolated them, and then performed forced intercourse with them, just as he had done with victim. State v. McAdory (Ohio App. 9 Dist., Summit, 03-17-2004) No. 21454, 2004-Ohio-1234, 2004 WL 510186, Unreported. Criminal Law ⚷ 369.15; Criminal Law ⚷ 372(7)

In the absence of any physical resistance by alleged rape victim, the probative value of evidence of prior abuse of victim by defendant outweighs the possibility of unfair prejudice and such other act evidence is admissible to prove the element of force. State v Scholz, No. 92-L-062, 1993 WL 346443 (11th Dist Ct App, Lake, 9-3-93).

Evidence that defendant took child victim and his brother to an "all gay" church and to a gay-friendly church was not unfairly prejudicial and was admissible in prosecution for kidnapping with a sexual-motivation specification and gross sexual imposition to show attempt to condition victim and brothers to accept pedophilia as appropriate conduct; testimony that the defendant took the children to allegedly homosexual churches did not lead so inexorably to the conclusion that he was homosexual that its admission was an abuse of discretion. State v. Crotts (Ohio, 12-15-2004) 104 Ohio St.3d 432, 820 N.E.2d 302, 2004-Ohio-6550, reconsideration denied 105 Ohio St.3d 1441, 822 N.E.2d 812, 2005-Ohio-531, certiorari denied 125 S.Ct. 2978, 162 L.Ed.2d 890, on remand 2005-Ohio-3435, 2005 WL 1541077. Criminal Law ⚷ 369.2(5)

Evidence of photographs of nude juveniles and adults on defendant's computer, his acts of taking child victim and his brother to an "all gay" church and a church catering to the gay community, a photograph of victim's older brother and a male friend with a caption "Sisters for Life," and a photograph with a lewd caption of the same friend unclothed were admissible in prosecution for kidnapping with a sexual-motivation specification and gross sexual imposition to show attempt to condition victim and brothers to accept pedophilia as appropriate conduct; even though the defendant denied committing the acts, his motive was material to the specification. State v. Crotts (Ohio, 12-15-2004) 104 Ohio St.3d 432, 820 N.E.2d 302, 2004-Ohio-6550, reconsideration denied 105 Ohio St.3d 1441, 822 N.E.2d 812, 2005-Ohio-531, certiorari denied 125 S.Ct. 2978, 162 L.Ed.2d 890, on remand 2005-Ohio-3435, 2005 WL 1541077. Criminal Law ⚷ 371(12)

Where evidence of defendant's sexual activity does not involve origin of semen, pregnancy or disease, or defendant's past sexual activity with victim, jury can hear such evidence only if its inflammatory nature does not outweigh its probative value, and if it is admissible against defendant under statute providing for proof of acts of defendant tending to show his motive or intent, absence of mistake or accident, or scheme, plan or system. State v. Cotton (Ohio App. 1 Dist., 06-26-1996) 113 Ohio App.3d 125, 680 N.E.2d 657. Criminal Law ⚷ 369.2(5)

When evidence of defendant's sexual activity does not involve origin of semen, pregnancy, or disease, or defendant's past sexual activity with victim, such evidence may come in only if it is admissible against defendant under statute on other acts evidence, and only to extent that its inflammatory nature does not outweigh its probative value. State v. Clemons (Ohio App. 12 Dist., 05-02-1994) 94 Ohio App.3d 701, 641 N.E.2d 778, dismissed, appeal not allowed 70 Ohio St.3d 1454, 639 N.E.2d 793. Criminal Law ⚷ 369.2(5)

Testimony in a rape case regarding salacious statements spoken to an inmate-victim by the defendant, a corrections officer, prior to the first incident, are admissible to establish intent to commit the sexual act. State v. Patton (Union 1991) 74 Ohio App.3d 224, 598 N.E.2d 777, dismissed, jurisdictional motion overruled 62 Ohio St.3d 1439, 579 N.E.2d 212, rehearing denied 62 Ohio St.3d 1466, 580 N.E.2d 786.

In a rape prosecution, evidence that (1) the child victim was not unhappy that the defendant, her father, had left because he had hurt her mother; and (2) the defendant had physically beaten the child's mother, is admissible to establish the time frame in which the victim came forward with an account that the defendant had sexually abused her and to show why the victim reported the sexual abuse after the defendant had threatened to hurt her mother. State v. Stokes (Franklin 1991) 72 Ohio App.3d 735, 596 N.E.2d 480, dismissed, jurisdictional motion overruled 61 Ohio St.3d 1419, 574 N.E.2d 1090, denial of post-conviction relief affirmed, dismissed, appeal not allowed 82 Ohio St.3d 1473, 696 N.E.2d 602. Criminal Law ⚷ 369.2(5); Rape ⚷ 49.2

In a prosecution for rape and assault a witness' testimony that she saw the defendant while in a convenience store near the scene of the rape, that he had blood on his shirt, and that he exposed himself and masturbated while watching her through the window of the store is properly admitted; evidence of other crimes is admissible when evidence of the other crime is so blended or connected with the crime on trial that the proof of one crime incidentally involves the other crime, explains the circumstances, or tends logically to prove any element of the crime charged. State v. Long (Summit 1989) 64 Ohio App.3d 615, 582 N.E.2d 626.

Trial court did not abuse discretion by admitting defendant's statement that he had engaged in sexual activity with his two year old daughter previously and that when he hit her in the chest it was his intent to engage in sexual activity with her again and that is why he asked daughter to "love on daddy" as other acts evidence in defendant's trial for raping and murdering his two year old daughter; defendant's statement regarding prior sexual encounters related directly to his state of mind and his intent at the time of the offenses, and any unfair prejudice was outweighed by the probative value of the statement. State v. Fuller (Ohio App. 12 Dist., Butler, 08-12-2002) No. CA2000-11-217, No. CA2001-03-048, No. CA2001-03-061, 2002-Ohio-4110, 2002 WL 1832858, Unreported. Criminal Law ⚷ 369.2(4)

Evidence of physical, emotional, and verbal abuse that transpired in the house between appellant and his children was relevant to and probative of the method of control used by appellant to force sex upon his son. State v Martin, No. 58648 (8th Dist Ct App, Cuyahoga, 12–6–90).

26. Prior acts inadmissible—In general

Other-acts evidence that defendant had at least 12 previous encounters with police was irrelevant and inadmissible under other-acts rule in trial for aggravated vehicular homicide and child endangerment; evidence served no purpose but to imply that defendant had bad character. State v. Atkins-Boozer (Ohio App. 8 Dist., Cuyahoga, 05-31-2005) No. 84151, 2005-Ohio-2666, 2005 WL 1274215, Unreported, appeal allowed 107 Ohio St.3d 1406, 836 N.E.2d 1227, 2005-Ohio-5859. Criminal Law ⚷ 369.1

Evidence of defendant's prior conviction for driving under the influence (DUI) was not admissible in DUI prosecution; prior conviction could only serve to enhance potential sentence following conviction and was not an element of present offense. State v. Ferrell (Ohio App. 7 Dist., Mahoning, 02-09-2004) No. 02 CA 172, 2004-Ohio-803, 2004 WL 324839, Unreported. Automobiles ⚷ 359; Criminal Law ⚷ 369.1

Evidence that defendant urinated in back of police cruiser after he was arrested was not relevant to any proper purpose in prosecution for aggravated arson and intimidation of a witness. State v. Jackson (Ohio App. 10 Dist., Franklin, 11-20-2003) No. 02AP-867, 2003-Ohio-6183, 2003 WL 22725287, Unreported, appeal not allowed 102 Ohio St.3d 1411, 806 N.E.2d 562, 2004-Ohio-1763. Criminal Law ⚷ 351(2)

Admission of defendant's prior act of domestic violence is reversible error where a case evolves into an issue of credibility of the defendant and his live-in girlfriend whose severe problems with depression frequently cause her to strike her head and fists against hard objects with enough force to make her head and fists bleed. State v. Deyling (Ohio App. 9 Dist., Medina, 01-28-1998) No. 2672-M, 1998 WL 46753, Unreported.

A tape-recorded conversation of defendant is not admissible under the similar acts statute as part of the prosecution's case-in-chief where the evidence is not directed at showing defendant's motive or intent, the absence of mistake or accident on his part, or his plan in committing the acts in question but, instead is intended to negate a defense of which the jury is not to be made aware until the defendant's case. City of Columbus v. Corne (Franklin 1982) 7 Ohio App.3d 344, 455 N.E.2d 696, 7 O.B.R. 443. Criminal Law ⚷ 680(1); Criminal Law ⚷ 1168(1)

Evidence which shows only that an accused was an intemperate and violent individual and not that a connection in the mind of the defendant must have existed between the offense in question and the other acts of a similar nature is not admissible under RC 2945.59. State v. Burson (Ohio 1974) 38 Ohio St.2d 157, 311 N.E.2d 526, 67 O.O.2d 174.

In a trial for embezzlement, testimony and prosecuting attorney's remarks at salient points throughout the trial suggesting that defendant might have committed arson in an attempt to destroy the evidence of embezzlement, when such testimony and remarks have no probative value as to any issue in the case, are inflammatory, and prejudicial to the defendant. State v. Doll (Ohio 1970) 24 Ohio St.2d 130, 265 N.E.2d 279, 53 O.O.2d 324.

In prosecution for breaking and entering, trial court should not have admitted other acts evidence of three break-ins in a neighboring jurisdiction, as there was no substantial proof that defendant committed the alleged other acts; police officers were permitted to testify about the type of buildings that were broken into and about the fact that the break-ins all involved a large object being thrown through a glass window, but there was no evidence presented that defendant committed those offenses. State v. Burns (Ohio App. 11 Dist., Lake, 07-12-2002) No. 2000-L-189, 2002-Ohio-3585, 2002 WL 1488917, Unreported. Criminal Law ⚟ 374

In prosecution for breaking and entering, trial court should not have admitted other acts evidence that defendant was arrested for trespassing after he was found standing outside of a business holding a large piece of concrete and wearing a camouflage jacket; while the arrest was substantial evidence that defendant committed the alleged other acts, modus operandi required to use the other acts to prove identity was not established, even though defendant allegedly used a large rock and wore a camouflage jacket when committing the charged offenses. State v. Burns (Ohio App. 11 Dist., Lake, 07-12-2002) No. 2000-L-189, 2002-Ohio-3585, 2002 WL 1488917, Unreported. Criminal Law ⚟ 369.15

In a prosecution for theft of gasoline from a school bus garage, extrinsic evidence of previous instances of theft of gasoline by the defendant is inadmissible under RC 2945.59 because the offense did not involve an elaborate scheme or plan and because the identity of the defendant was not in question. State v Powell, No. 467 (4th Dist Ct App, Meigs, 3–2–93).

27. —— Intoxication, prior acts inadmissible

Photographs that purportedly showed defendant's intoxication on night of arrest were improper "other acts" evidence, as offered by state in prosecution for carrying a concealed weapon; photographs did not satisfy any of the permissible uses of "other acts" evidence, but were used for sole purpose of showing defendant to be a person of bad character who acted in conformity with that character in committing charged offenses. State v. Penland (Ohio App. 1 Dist., 12-31-1998) 132 Ohio App.3d 176, 724 N.E.2d 841. Criminal Law ⚟ 374

Evidence of an accused's intoxication, belligerence and profanity are not relevant to a charge of felonious assault in connection with the discharge of a firearm from a vehicle. State v. Renner (Ohio App. 2 Dist., 01-16-1998) 125 Ohio App.3d 383, 708 N.E.2d 765.

28. —— Assault, prior acts inadmissible

Probative value of evidence that witness had observed a prior altercation involving defendant was substantially outweighed by danger of unfair prejudice to defendant, and, as such, was inadmissible, in prosecution for felonious assault; evidence was irrelevant to charge at issue, there was plethora of other evidence establishing that defendant was perpetrator of crimes at issue, and evidence had possibility of inferring that defendant was a violent person and had acted in same way in instant matter. State v. Frazier (Ohio App. 8 Dist., Cuyahoga, 08-04-2005) No. 85588, 2005-Ohio-4015, 2005 WL 1846999, Unreported. Criminal Law ⚟ 369.13

29. —— Burglary and robbery, prior acts inadmissible

Evidence that defendant committed two burglaries prior to present charges of vandalism and breaking and entering arising from defendant's forced entry into his former apartment was improperly admitted; although defendant had broken doors to gain entrance in all three instances, earlier incidents involved other persons' homes and were insufficiently similar to present incident to show common scheme, defendant's identity was not an issue, prior offenses occurred more than a year before incident in question, and prosecution used prior acts evidence to prove defendant was a bad person who had acted in conformity with his character. State v. Goines (Ohio App. 8 Dist., 06-24-1996) 111 Ohio App.3d 840, 677 N.E.2d 412, appeal not allowed 77 Ohio St.3d 1482, 673 N.E.2d 143. Criminal Law ⚟ 369.7

Admission of evidence that defendant committed two burglaries of other persons' residence prior to present incident, involving forced entry into defendant's own former residence, was plain error requiring new trial on charges of vandalism and breaking and entering; it could not be concluded, based on entire record, that the other acts evidence did not substantially affect outcome, as it was not clear defendant would have been convicted without that evidence. State v. Goines (Ohio App. 8 Dist., 06-24-1996) 111 Ohio App.3d 840, 677 N.E.2d 412, appeal not allowed 77 Ohio St.3d 1482, 673 N.E.2d 143. Criminal Law ⚟ 369.7; Criminal Law ⚟ 1036.1(8); Criminal Law ⚟ 1169.11

30. —— Drug offenses, prior acts inadmissible

Extraneous offense or collateral crimes evidence of defendant's purported chemical dependency was inadmissible character evidence to show that defendant, on the night in which he allegedly committed involuntary manslaughter, acted in conformity therewith; evidence of officer's previous contacts with defendant, during which he was drunk or disorderly, was admitted for sole purpose of showing that defendant had character trait of drinking to excess, and 24 such observations of intoxication spanning an 11-year period were of insufficient regularity to rise to the level of "habit" evidence. State v. Worthington (Ohio App. 5 Dist., Richland, 09-01-2005) No. 2004-CA-0083, 2005-Ohio-4719, 2005 WL 2175135, Unreported, appeal allowed 108 Ohio St.3d 1413, 841 N.E.2d 318, 2006-Ohio-179, appeal dismissed as improvidently granted 109 Ohio St.3d 313, 847 N.E.2d 1174, 2006-Ohio-2109. Criminal Law ⚟ 369.3

Testimony relating to alleged third controlled buy, for which defendant was not charged, was not relevant to prove defendant's guilt with respect to counts for which defendant was charged, in drug prosecution; attempted third buy took place about two weeks after second controlled buy, which resulted in second count, substance that defendant sold was not cocaine, and even if alleged sale was minimally probative to show motive, opportunity, intent, preparation, plan, knowledge, identity, or absence of mistake or accident, sale of a counterfeit substance was in no way relevant in proving defendant's guilt to other counts for which he was charged. State v. Pietrangelo (Ohio App. 11 Dist., Lake, 04-08-2005) No. 2003-L-125, 2005-Ohio-1686, 2005 WL 820526, Unreported. Criminal Law ⚷ 369.1

Evidence of defendant's prior drug transactions was inadmissible in prosecution for aggravated murder, in absence of any relevant relationship between drug transactions and murder; while defendant's drug transactions in house in which murder occurred arguably explained presence of some of the witnesses, they were not part of scheme or plan to commit murder or part of immediate background or foundation of the murder, and no evidence suggested that argument between defendant and victim which led to shooting was related to defendant's use or sale of drugs. State v. Mardis (Ohio App. 10 Dist., 08-19-1999) 134 Ohio App.3d 6, 729 N.E.2d 1272, motion for delayed appeal denied 93 Ohio St.3d 1431, 755 N.E.2d 354. Criminal Law ⚷ 369.3

Although evidence of defendant's prior drug conviction was admissible to establish the element of previous conviction of felony drug offense in prosecution for felony trafficking and drugs, it was prejudicial to introduce details surrounding commission of prior offense. State v. Sutherland (Ohio App. 3 Dist., 02-01-1994) 92 Ohio App.3d 840, 637 N.E.2d 366. Criminal Law ⚷ 374

Drugs and drug paraphernalia that were found in vacant house owned by defendant where charged crimes allegedly occurred were not relevant in prosecution for murder, rape, and kidnapping to prove any issue other than defendant's bad character and were thus inadmissible. State v. Satta (Ohio App. 3 Dist., Marion, 09-25-2002) No. 9-01-38, 2002-Ohio-5049, 2002 WL 31114690, Unreported, appeal not allowed 98 Ohio St.3d 1461, 783 N.E.2d 520, 2003-Ohio-644, reconsideration denied 98 Ohio St.3d 1516, 786 N.E.2d 64, 2003-Ohio-1572, motion for delayed appeal denied 98 Ohio St.3d 1509, 786 N.E.2d 60, 2003-Ohio-1572, appeal not allowed 99 Ohio St.3d 1437, 789 N.E.2d 1118, 2003-Ohio-2902. Criminal Law ⚷ 369.1; Criminal Law ⚷ 369.3; Criminal Law ⚷ 369.8

Details of a prior drug-related conviction are irrelevant to a present charge of possessing marijuana where (1) the defendant has a prior conviction for distributing marijuana which he purchased for personal use to his friends, while seated in his own vehicle, and (2) in the present incident, the defendant is a passenger in a friend's truck and the friend has concealed marijuana under the hood of his own truck and the defendant is charged with knowingly possessing bulk amounts of marijuana; the prior incident has no relevance to whether the defendant knew there was marijuana hidden under the hood of his friend's car in the present case. State v Sutherland, No. 2-93-10, 1994 WL 29870 (3rd Dist Ct App, Auglaize, 2-1-94).

31. —— Insurance offenses, prior acts inadmissible

In a prosecution for defrauding an insurance company, evidence concerning defendant's delinquency in loan payments to a bank does not tend to establish guilt in the offense charged and its admission is error. State v. DeMarco (Ohio 1987) 31 Ohio St.3d 191, 509 N.E.2d 1256, 31 O.B.R. 390.

32. —— Murder, prior acts inadmissible

For the purpose of proving a scheme, plan, or system in a prosecution for aggravated murder with specifications, it is error for the trial court to admit testimony concerning other crimes not inextricably related to the crime charged. State v. Lytle (Ohio 1976) 48 Ohio St.2d 391, 358 N.E.2d 623, 2 O.O.3d 495, vacated 98 S.Ct. 3135, 438 U.S. 910, 57 L.Ed.2d 1154. Criminal Law ⚷ 372(1)

In a first degree murder trial the admission of evidence of previous crimes, presented for the purpose of showing possession of the murder weapon, is reversible error when other substantial evidence of the possession of the weapon has been adduced, the possession has not been disputed by the defense, and the admission of the evidence of other crimes does not qualify under any of the conditions of RC 2945.59 (similar acts). State v. Watson (Cuyahoga 1969) 20 Ohio App.2d 115, 252 N.E.2d 305, 49 O.O.2d 152, modified 28 Ohio St.2d 15, 275 N.E.2d 153, 57 O.O.2d 95.

In prosecution for felonious homicide, testimony as to threats made by defendant against third person sometime prior to the killing, with which former incident deceased had no connection and which formed no part of affair in which deceased was killed, is not, over objection, admissible in evidence against defendant. State v. Moore (Ohio 1948) 149 Ohio St. 226, 78 N.E.2d 365, 36 O.O. 566. Homicide ⚷ 970; Criminal Law ⚷ 1169.1(7)

33. —— Sexual offenses, prior acts inadmissible

Testimony by mother of two alleged victims in prosecution for rape and gross sexual imposition, that mother wanted to get back from defendant a van she had purchased in his name because she had heard he went out to fairgrounds on a particular date and supposedly had two young girls in van with him, was improper "other acts" evidence and was not relevant or probative to any of the charges against defendant. State v. Smith (Ohio App. 2 Dist., Clark, 02-13-2004) No. 2003-CA-23, 2004-Ohio-665, 2004 WL 259246, Unreported. Criminal Law ⚷ 369.8

Testimony by victim of rape committed by defendant 12 years prior to charged rape was not admissible to show a common scheme, plan, or system. State v. Wilkins (Ohio App. 9 Dist., 09-29-1999) 135 Ohio App.3d 26, 732 N.E.2d 1021, dismissed, appeal not allowed 88 Ohio St.3d 1412, 723 N.E.2d 118. Criminal Law ⚷ 372(7)

Error in rape prosecution in admitting testimony by prior rape victim that did not meet exception to general prohibition against propensity evidence was not curable by limiting instruction, in view of inflammatory nature of prior victim's testimony concerning the facts of prior offense. State v. Wilkins (Ohio App. 9 Dist., 09-29-1999) 135 Ohio App.3d 26, 732 N.E.2d 1021, dismissed, appeal not allowed 88 Ohio St.3d 1412, 723 N.E.2d 118. Criminal Law ⚷ 1169.5(3)

Defendant was prejudiced in rape prosecution by improper admission of testimony by prior rape victim that did not meet any exceptions to general prohibition against propensity evidence, and thus reversal of conviction was required, in view of inflammatory nature of prior victim's testimony. State v. Wilkins (Ohio App. 9 Dist., 09-29-1999) 135 Ohio App.3d 26, 732 N.E.2d 1021, dismissed, appeal not allowed 88 Ohio St.3d 1412, 723 N.E.2d 118. Criminal Law ⚷ 1169.11

Testimony of police sergeant and officer detailing past allegations of sexual misconduct by defendant did not serve purposes of statute providing for admissibility of act tending to show motive or intent, absence of mistake or accident, or defendant's scheme, plan or system, and was improperly admitted in prosecution for rape and gross sexual imposition; evidence of prior accusations by people unrelated to issues for resolution at trial only added to ease with which jury might have made forbidden inference that, because defendant may have been involved in misconduct with other patients at psychiatric center, it had to have been defendant who attacked complaining witnesses. State v. Cotton (Ohio App. 1 Dist., 06-26-1996) 113 Ohio App.3d 125, 680 N.E.2d 657. Criminal Law ⚷ 369.8

Prior-act testimony regarding alleged instances of sexual misconduct by defendant with psychiatric patients permitted jury to make forbidden inference that because defendant may have been involved in misconduct with other patients, it had to have been defendant who attacked patients alleged to be victims of felonious sexual penetration. State v. Cotton (Ohio App. 1 Dist., 06-26-1996) 113 Ohio App.3d 125, 680 N.E.2d 657. Criminal Law ⚷ 374

Testimony of witness that, when she heard televised news reports that worker at psychiatric center was under investigation for sexual activity with adolescent female patients, she knew it had to be defendant, and recounting for jury report heard from former patient, that defendant was having sex with patients, did not tend to show scheme or opportunity and was inadmissible; in essence, witness made forbidden inference that because defendant may have been involved in misconduct with other patients, it had to have been defendant who attacked complaining witnesses, which was precisely type of testimony that evidentiary rule and rape-shield statutes were designed to prevent. State v. Cotton (Ohio App. 1 Dist., 06-26-1996) 113 Ohio App.3d 125, 680 N.E.2d 657. Criminal Law ⚷ 369.2(5); Criminal Law ⚷ 372(7)

Evidence of defendant's "problem" with masturbation was not substantial proof of, and did not tend to show, any of enumerated purposes for which such "other acts" evidence is admissible, and thus should have been excluded in prosecution for rape and gross sexual imposition arising from two separate incidents involving his girlfriend's seven-year-old daughter; state presented no evidence closely connecting alleged acts of masturbation while watching pornographic movies to charges involving victim, as there was no indication that children were present during masturbation. State v. Clemons (Ohio App. 12 Dist., 05-02-1994) 94 Ohio App.3d 701, 641 N.E.2d 778, dismissed, appeal not allowed 70 Ohio St.3d 1454, 639 N.E.2d 793. Criminal Law ⚷ 369.8

Evidence of defendant's prior sexual acts is not admissible if they are too remote, and not closely related in nature, time, and place to the offense charged. State v. Clemons (Ohio App. 12 Dist., 05-02-1994) 94 Ohio App.3d 701, 641 N.E.2d 778, dismissed, appeal not allowed 70 Ohio St.3d 1454, 639 N.E.2d 793. Criminal Law ⚷ 369.8

Other acts evidence respecting defendant's activities with girls, including victim's daughters, which included dissemination of sexually explicit material, was inadmissible to prove defendant's identity in aggravated murder prosecution, where other acts were separate from planning, carrying out, and aftermath of murders, defendant's activities with girls established no modus operandi applicable to murders, and evidence did not inextricably tie defendant to murders. State v. Lowe (Ohio, 07-06-1994) 69 Ohio St.3d 527, 634 N.E.2d 616, 1994-Ohio-345. Criminal Law ⚷ 369.15

Evidence of defendants other acts would not have been admissible if defendant had had separate trials on charges of gross sexual imposition involving two young girls and charges of rape, sexual battery and gross sexual imposition involving his son where defendant denied his involvement in the acts. State v. Decker (Hamilton 1993) 88 Ohio App.3d 544, 624 N.E.2d 350. Criminal Law ⚷ 369.8

In prosecution for gross sexual imposition, evidence of defendant's other sexual acts was inadmissible to prove his motive or intent to commit crimes charged; motive and intent of defendant remained that of sexual gratification and that fact was apparent from charges and was not material issue. State v. Smith (Greene 1992) 84 Ohio App.3d 647, 617 N.E.2d 1160, motion to certify denied 66 Ohio St.3d 1488, 612 N.E.2d 1244. Criminal Law ⚷ 371(9); Criminal Law ⚷ 371(12)

Evidence of a defendant's sexual activity with the sister of a sexual assault victim offered to prove the character of the defendant and that in sexually assaulting the victim he acted in conformity therewith is inadmissible and prejudicial. State v. Price (Crawford 1992) 80 Ohio App.3d 35, 608 N.E.2d 818.

In a gross sexual imposition prosecution of a father for acts committed against his thirteen-year-old daughter, evidence of an alleged act of sexual misconduct which occurred seven or eight years prior is improperly admitted since it is (1) too remote in time to be admissible to show the element of force, and (2) was uncorroborated and unsubstantiated since the victim never told anyone about the incident at the time and the victim's young age of five or six probably would have precluded her from testifying. State v. Henderson (Clermont 1991) 76 Ohio App.3d 290, 601 N.E.2d 596, dismissed, jurisdictional motion overruled 63 Ohio St.3d 1445, 589 N.E.2d 389.

The general rule of evidence regarding the admissibility of "other acts" testimony under Evid R 404(B) is not applicable to rape cases; therefore, in a prosecution for vaginal and anal rape, the admission of testimony from the defendant's former lover that the defendant anally raped her four years earlier is erroneous since (1) the victim did not allege pregnancy or that she had contracted a disease (2) the defendant admitted intercourse so there was no question as to the origin of semen and (3) the testimony was too temporally remote to have probative value as to the defendant's intent. State v. Lewis (Greene 1990) 66 Ohio App.3d 37, 583 N.E.2d 404, dismissed, jurisdictional motion overruled 55 Ohio St.3d 703, 562 N.E.2d 894.

In a prosecution for vaginal and anal rape, a trial court's failure to give a limiting instruction to the jury as to "other acts" testimony at the time a defendant's former lover testifies as to the defendant's alleged anal rape of her four years earlier is not cured later by the court in its general instructions where the court merely reads to the jury RC 2945.59, the statute on admissibility of acts tending to show the defendant's motive or intent, absence of mistake, plan, or system in doing an act, without explaining the meaning of the statute or telling the jurors that the statute is applicable to the witness' testimony; to be effective, a limiting instruction on "other acts" testimony should specifically say that this evidence is not to be used as substantive evidence that the defendant committed the crime charged, a proposition which is not contained in the text of RC 2945.59. State v. Lewis (Greene 1990) 66 Ohio App.3d 37, 583 N.E.2d 404, dismissed, jurisdictional motion overruled 55 Ohio St.3d 703, 562 N.E.2d 894.

Testimony excluded in limine from the state's case in chief regarding remote prior instances of sexual activity by the defendant are not admissible as rebuttal evidence where the defendant does not introduce the issue of prior acts, nor does testimony from the defendant elicited by the prosecutor on cross-examination serve to open the door to rebuttal testimony; it would also be error to admit such testimony under the similar acts exception of RC 2945.59 and Evid R 608(B) to show motive or intent where the testimony alleges acts twenty-six and thirteen years prior to the time of trial. State v. Strobel (Henry 1988) 51 Ohio App.3d 31, 554 N.E.2d 916.

Testimony as to defendant's sexual contact with his daughter following her thirteenth birthday was inadmissible in prosecution for violation of RC 2907.05(A)(3). State v. Thompson (Ohio 1981) 66 Ohio St.2d 496, 422 N.E.2d 855, 20 O.O.3d 411.

In a prosecution for first degree murder, testimony as to boasts made by the defendant to third persons of having committed other offenses such as arson and sex deviation which have no connection with and form no part of the affair in which the deceased was killed, is not, over objection, admissible in evidence against the defendant. State v. Strong (Stark 1963) 119 Ohio App. 31, 196 N.E.2d 801, 26 O.O.2d 134.

Evidence of defendant's arrest, conviction, lazy habits, or slovenly housekeeping was impermissible in prosecution for child rape where defendant had not placed his character in issue, and the evidence had no relevance to the charges or to motive, opportunity, intent, preparation, plan, knowledge, identity, or absence of mistake or accident. State v. Bronner (Ohio App. 9 Dist., Summit, 08-21-2002) No. 20753, 2002-Ohio-4248, 2002 WL 1906507, Unreported, appeal not allowed 98 Ohio St.3d 1411, 781 N.E.2d 1019, 2003-Ohio-60. Criminal Law ⚷ 369.8; Criminal Law ⚷ 380

Testimony concerning other acts of sexual activity with boys is irrelevant in a prosecution for rape where the defendant denies engaging in any sexual activity, never claims "accident or mistake," and the alleged other acts testified to are not inextricably related to the criminal activity alleged in the case at bar; the admission of such testimony at trial constitutes plain error where, absent the inadmissible testimony, the prosecution's case rests almost entirely on the testimony of the victim whose credibility is subject to attack on various grounds. State v Russell, No. 88AP–457 (10th Dist Ct App, Franklin, 12–30–88).

34. Culpable mental state

Testimony regarding defendant's alleged prior act of assaulting his estranged wife victim was admissible to prove not only victim's state of mind during her alleged rape, and whether she consented to defendant's actions, but also defendant's plan, motive, and intent regarding aggravated burglary, subsequent kidnapping, rapes, and domestic violence defendant allegedly inflicted upon victim; prior incident was not used to show defendant's bad character and that he acted in conformity therewith, but rather, was used to demonstrate his plan to rape his victim wife and motive behind it as well, so as to discredit his testimony that he went to her home simply to work things out between them. State v. Weatherholtz (Ohio App. 3 Dist., Wyandot, 07-09-2003) No. 16-02-15, 2003-Ohio-3633, 2003 WL 21543813, Unreported. Criminal Law ⚷ 371(9); Criminal Law ⚷ 371(12); Criminal Law ⚷ 372(10)

Where two defendants engage in an automobile drag race and there is testimony that one defendant attempted to avoid a collision with an oncoming car whose driver was killed, the evidence of an intent and purpose to maliciously kill does not attain the high degree of probative force required to sustain a verdict of murder in the second degree. State v. Butler (Ohio 1967) 11 Ohio St.2d 23, 227 N.E.2d 627, 21 A.L.R.2d 102, 40 O.O.2d 43.

In a prosecution charging murder in the second degree, where there is evidence from which a jury could find beyond reasonable doubt that, pursuant to an agreement, two defendants jointly indicted were operating their automobiles on the public highway with such reckless, willful and intentional violation of laws of this state applying to the use and regulation of traffic that the natural and probable consequence of their voluntary acts would be to produce death, and that death was caused thereby, an intent and purpose to kill may be presumed from such voluntary acts, unless the circumstances are such as to indicate the absence of such intent; and if the fact of killing, with intent and purpose to kill, is proved, malice is to be presumed and all the circumstances of justification, excuse or extenuation must be made out by the accused, unless they appear from the evidence adduced against him, and if the jury finds beyond reasonable doubt that the accused as principal or as an aider and abettor purposely and maliciously killed another, then the accused may be found guilty of murder in the second degree. State v. Butler (Stark 1966) 6 Ohio App.2d 193, 217 N.E.2d 237, 35 O.O.2d 353, reversed 11 Ohio St.2d 23, 227 N.E.2d 627, 21 A.L.R.2d 102, 40 O.O.2d 43.

35. Jury instructions

Trial court's limiting instruction, which told jury to disregard question and answer that revealed defendant's prior conviction for driving under the influence (DUI), was inadequate to remedy effect of improperly disclosed evidence on jury in DUI prosecution; there appeared to be insufficient independent evidence that, if believed by jury, supported conviction, and scant evidence supporting conviction failed to overcome prejudicial effect of inappropriate evidence. State v. Ferrell (Ohio App. 7 Dist., Mahoning, 02-09-2004) No. 02 CA 172, 2004-Ohio-803, 2004 WL 324839, Unreported. Criminal Law ⚿ 783(1)

Trial court's failure to admonish jury to disregard any evidence pertaining to defendant's alleged prior domestic abuse conviction, upon dismissing allegation for insufficient evidence, did not amount to plain error; informing jury that it was to disregard testimony and comments regarding prior conviction, and to not consider any such testimony in its deliberations, may have been advisable, but failure to do so did not constitute obvious defect in proceedings affecting substantial right of defendant, given testimony and other evidence presented at trial, in which defendant stood accused of rape, kidnapping, aggravated burglary, and domestic abuse. State v. Weatherholtz (Ohio App. 3 Dist., Wyandot, 07-09-2003) No. 16-02-15, 2003-Ohio-3633, 2003 WL 21543813, Unreported. Criminal Law ⚿ 1035(10)

By failing to specifically state grounds at trial for his objection to general charge to jury, murder defendant failed to preserve for appeal contention that portion of instruction respecting other acts evidence should not have been omitted. State v. Elliott (Ohio App. 3 Dist., 11-05-1993) 91 Ohio App.3d 763, 633 N.E.2d 1144, dismissed, jurisdictional motion overruled 69 Ohio St.3d 1422, 631 N.E.2d 162. Criminal Law ⚿ 1043(2)

Any error was harmless in murder prosecution in omission from general jury charge of portion of other acts evidence instruction, stating that such evidence could not be considered as proof that defendant did act alleged, where limiting instruction given at time of other acts witness' testimony included that portion. State v. Elliott (Ohio App. 3 Dist., 11-05-1993) 91 Ohio App.3d 763, 633 N.E.2d 1144, dismissed, jurisdictional motion overruled 69 Ohio St.3d 1422, 631 N.E.2d 162. Criminal Law ⚿ 1172.2

Where evidence of similar offenses is admitted under RC 2945.59 and the trial court does not instruct the jury either at the time of the reception of such evidence or in its general charge that the reception is under such statute and upon the limited purpose for which it is received and is to be considered by the jury, failure of the trial court to so instruct the jury is reversible error, even though no request for such instruction is ever made. State v. Crafton (Guernsey 1968) 15 Ohio App.2d 160, 239 N.E.2d 571, 44 O.O.2d 295.

36. Enhanced punishment

It is not necessary to submit issue of prior conviction to jury in situation where fact of prior conviction for identical type of offense is relevant only for purpose of enhanced punishment for subsequent offense and is not element of offense for which accused is being tried, and under such circumstances, such issue should be submitted to court for determination in connection with punishment rather than to jury. State v. Gordon (Franklin 1971) 26 Ohio App.2d 270, 271 N.E.2d 300, 55 O.O.2d 421, reversed 28 Ohio St.2d 45, 276 N.E.2d 243, 57 O.O.2d 180. Sentencing And Punishment ⚿ 1382

37. Review—Standard

The standards of discretionary review by the Supreme Court of Ohio of nonconstitutional matters on direct appeal in a criminal case are not a violation of constitutional due process where such limited discretionary review may deprive a convicted offender of the possible benefits of a favorable decision rendered after the accused has lost his direct appeal as a matter of right to the court of appeals. Klein v. Cardwell (C.A.6 (Ohio) 1971) 448 F.2d 407, 63 O.O.2d 416.

38. —— Plain errors, review

Any error in admission of testimony that officer first observed drug defendant in front of a "dope house" did not rise to level of plain error, where evidence established that drugs were found in defendant's truck and that defendant fled from the scene. State v. Draper (Ohio App. 10 Dist., Franklin, 07-15-2003) No. 02AP-1371, 2003-Ohio-3751, 2003 WL 21652187, Unreported. Criminal Law ⚿ 1036.1(8)

Admission of prior bad acts evidence that witness regularly purchased bricks of cocaine from defendant was not plain error in prosecution for possession of cocaine, where jury heard evidence regarding the amount of cash found in defendant's possession and the discovery of electronic scales inside of the truck, both of which could lead to a reasonable inference of habitual drug dealing, and defendant did not present any form of defense other than opening remarks, closing remarks, and cross-examination. State v. Martinez (Ohio App. 3 Dist., Marion, 04-10-2003) No. 9-02-57,

2003-Ohio-1821, 2003 WL 1836672, Unreported. Criminal Law ⚷ 1036.1(8)

Trial court's error in admitting, as other crimes evidence, evidence that defendant threatened to kill a man over a compact disc, would not have affected outcome of trial and thus, did not constitute plain error. State v. Young (Ohio App. 8 Dist., Cuyahoga, 01-23-2003) No. 80059, 2003-Ohio-272, 2003 WL 152818, Unreported. Criminal Law ⚷ 1036.1(8)

39. —— Prejudice, review

Where other acts evidence is relevant to prove motive or intent, absence of mistake or accident, or scheme or plan, its admission is proper, even though evidence may show or tend to show commission of another crime by defendant, unless prejudice is shown. State v. McCornell (Ohio App. 8 Dist., 10-12-1993) 91 Ohio App.3d 141, 631 N.E.2d 1110. Criminal Law ⚷ 369.2(1)

Where the state presents testimony, without limitation, against an accused pertaining to his commission of other crimes, for which he has not been indicted, and the crimes bear no relevance to an element of the offense with which he is charged, the court's admission of such evidence is prejudicial error. State v. Smith (Muskingum 1977) 59 Ohio App.2d 194, 392 N.E.2d 1264, 13 O.O.3d 213. Criminal Law ⚷ 369.1; Criminal Law ⚷ 1169.11

Admission of evidence of defendant's sexual activities with third parties was not prejudicial error. State v. Gardner (Ohio 1979) 59 Ohio St.2d 14, 391 N.E.2d 337, 13 O.O.3d 8.

Where prosecuting attorney in his opening statement improperly and repeatedly refers to prior conviction and prior imprisonment for identical type of offense, indictment containing allegations of prior conviction is read twice to jury and is sent with exhibits to jury, evidence of prior conviction is admitted, trial court neither submits issue of prior conviction to jury nor explains purpose for which such evidence is admitted, and court appointed defense counsel does not request such instruction although calling to attention of court limited purpose for which evidence is admissible, there is prejudicial error necessitating new trial. State v. Gordon (Franklin 1971) 26 Ohio App.2d 270, 271 N.E.2d 300, 55 O.O.2d 421, reversed 28 Ohio St.2d 45, 276 N.E.2d 243, 57 O.O.2d 180. Criminal Law ⚷ 369.1; Criminal Law ⚷ 673(5); Criminal Law ⚷ 1169.11

References to other "offenses," in that part of the charge to the jury in such case relating to the admission of evidence "tending to show the commission of an offense or offenses by the defendant other than that for which" he is on trial, are not prejudicially erroneous, where such charge clearly explains the restricted purpose for which the testimony was introduced and based upon evidence of similar acts of defendant; and, in such case, the use of the term, "offense," rather than the term, "acts," is not prejudicial. State v. Haines (Montgomery 1960) 112 Ohio App. 487, 176 N.E.2d 446, 16 O.O.2d 376. Criminal Law ⚷ 1172.2

On the evidence testimony regarding prior unusual or immoral acts or strange conduct of defendant in sodomy prosecution was not prejudicial error. State v. Shively (Ohio 1961) 172 Ohio St. 128, 174 N.E.2d 104, 15 O.O.2d 211.

In a prosecution for rape and incest it was prejudicial error to admit testimony by the prosecuting witness's sister that defendant father had sexual relations with her twice at a date eight years prior thereto. State v. Chapman (Franklin 1959) 111 Ohio App. 441, 168 N.E.2d 14, 83 Ohio Law Abs. 135, 15 O.O.2d 19.

It is prejudicial error, in a civil action, to admit evidence of prior convictions of the defendant for traffic violations; and such error is not cured by the court's charge to the jury that such evidence be disregarded. Chambers v. Robert (Franklin 1959) 110 Ohio App. 472, 166 N.E.2d 530, 82 Ohio Law Abs. 513, 13 O.O.2d 224.

Where accused charged with murder defended on ground of self-defense, and accused had not placed his character or reputation for peace and quietude or his reputation for veracity in issue, cross-examination consisting of effort to prove certain incidents of violence in accused's life over a period of more than 20 years, which was not accompanied by effort to prove conviction of any crime or to show motive or plan of accused to do act in question, was prejudicial error. State v. Kennedy (Butler 1943) 72 Ohio App. 462, 52 N.E.2d 873, 40 Ohio Law Abs. 224, 27 O.O. 389. Criminal Law ⚷ 1170.5(5)

Where, upon trial of a case on an indictment containing a count that defendant burned certain personal property of his own, with intent to defraud insurance company, testimony as to two previous fires was introduced, objected to, objections overruled and exceptions saved by defendant's counsel, and later, during progress of the case, a written statement made by accused, in which there was reference to two previous fires in property occupied by him, was offered, admitted without objection and sent to jury as an exhibit, no error can be predicated upon its admission, notwithstanding the statement might have contained infirmities that would have rendered it inadmissible, as there was no objection or exception; the failure to object and except to the admission of the written statement in evidence was not cured by fact that the testimony with reference to other fires, adduced from other witnesses, was objected to, objections overruled by the court and exceptions duly saved. Russo v. State (Ohio 1933) 126 Ohio St. 114, 184 N.E. 241, 37 Ohio Law Rep. 421.

40. —— Reversible errors, review

It is reversible error, in the trial of an accused for robbery, for the prosecution to ask the defendant on cross-examination whether "you have ever been tried of attempted theft in 1964," where the prosecution makes no attempt to show that defendant was ever tried for an attempted theft in 1964 and produces no evidence of any conviction of an "attempted theft in 1964." State v. Crawford (Hamilton 1969) 17 Ohio App.2d 141, 244 N.E.2d 774, 46

O.O.2d 175. Criminal Law ⚷ 706(5); Criminal Law ⚷ 1171.8(2)

41. —— Harmless errors, review

Error in trial court's admission of other-acts evidence that defendant had at least 12 previous encounters with police, which was irrelevant and inadmissible under other-acts rule, was harmless, in trial for aggravated vehicular homicide and child endangerment; there was other overwhelming evidence of defendant's guilt, including undisputed evidence that defendant dragged victim while he was hanging from her car and testimony that she sideswiped parked car after failing to dislodge victim from her car by weaving back and forth. State v. Atkins-Boozer (Ohio App. 8 Dist., Cuyahoga, 05-31-2005) No. 84151, 2005-Ohio-2666, 2005 WL 1274215, Unreported, appeal allowed 107 Ohio St.3d 1406, 836 N.E.2d 1227, 2005-Ohio-5859. Criminal Law ⚷ 1169.11

Erroneous admission of evidence of prior allegations of sexual misconduct by defendant was not harmless in prosecution for rape and gross sexual imposition committed against female adolescent psychiatric patients; evidence did not overwhelmingly support conviction, particularly considering absence of physical evidence, number of years between alleged acts and trial, effect of cross-examination of complaining witnesses, and testimony of one patient that she and complaining witness plotted against defendant in search for attention. State v. Cotton (Ohio App. 1 Dist., 06-26-1996) 113 Ohio App.3d 125, 680 N.E.2d 657. Criminal Law ⚷ 1169.11

If there is no reasonable possibility that improperly admitted testimony concerning other acts contributed to defendant's conviction, then admission constitutes harmless error. State v. Elliott (Ohio App. 3 Dist., 11-05-1993) 91 Ohio App.3d 763, 633 N.E.2d 1144, dismissed, jurisdictional motion overruled 69 Ohio St.3d 1422, 631 N.E.2d 162. Criminal Law ⚷ 1169.11

In a prosecution for gross sexual imposition, admission of testimony regarding other sexual acts of defendant was harmless error. State v. Eubank (Ohio 1979) 60 Ohio St.2d 183, 398 N.E.2d 567, 14 O.O.3d 416.

Where evidence of prior similar acts, offered to show motive under RC 2945.59, occurred more than ten years previously, it is too remote in time for consideration; however, the admission of such evidence by the trial court constitutes harmless error. State v Siegenthaler, No. 184 (7th Dist Ct App, Noble, 7–18–84).

2945.60 to 2945.63 Proof in cases of treason, unauthorized military expedition, perjury, and seduction—Repealed

(1972 H 511, eff. 1–1–74; 1953 H 1; GC 13444–21 to 13444–23)

Historical and Statutory Notes

Ed. Note: See now 2921.11 and 2907.03 for provisions analogous to former 2945.62 and 2945.63, respectively.

Pre–1953 H 1 Amendments: 113 v 190, Ch 23, § 21, 22, 23

2945.64 Prima–facie evidence of embezzlement

Failure or refusal to pay over or produce public money by a person charged with the collection, receipt, transfer, disbursement, or safekeeping of such money, whether belonging to this state, a county, township, municipal corporation, or board of education, or other public money, or to account to or make settlement with a legal authority of the official accounts of such person, is prima-facie evidence of the embezzlement thereof. Upon the trial of such person for the embezzlement of public money, it is sufficient evidence for the purpose of showing a balance against him, to produce a transcript from the records of the auditor of state, director of budget and management, county auditor, or board of county commissioners. The refusal of such person, whether in or out of office, to pay a draft, order, or warrant drawn upon him by an authorized officer, for public money in his hands, or a refusal by a person promptly to pay over to his successor public money or securities on the legal requirement of an authorized officer of the state or county, on the trial of an indictment against him for embezzlement, is prima-facie evidence thereof.

(1985 H 201, eff. 7–1–85; 1953 H 1; GC 13444–25)

Historical and Statutory Notes

Pre–1953 H 1 Amendments: 113 v 191, Ch 23, § 25

Cross References

Presumptions, Evid R 301

Theft, 2913.02

Library References

Embezzlement ⚷36, 44.
Westlaw Topic No. 146.
C.J.S. Embezzlement §§ 41, 46.

Research References

Encyclopedias

OH Jur. 3d Criminal Law § 1893, Prima Facie Evidence of Embezzlement.

OH Jur. 3d Schools, Universities, & Colleges § 418, Fiscal Duties of Treasurer of Board of Education.

Treatises and Practice Aids

Princehorn, Baldwin's Ohio Practice, Local Government Law—Township, § 6:15, Offenses.

Notes of Decisions

1. Failure to pay money

Failure of mayor to pay money received in payment of a fine into the city treasury as provided by statute constitutes prima facie evidence of embezzlement. Koppe v. State (Hocking 1926) 21 Ohio App. 33, 153 N.E. 109, 4 Ohio Law Abs. 715.

2. Jury instructions

In prosecution of mayor for embezzlement of money received in payment of fines and not paid into the city treasury, it is not error to instruct jury that if the embezzlement has been shown beyond a reasonable doubt, it is not material that defendant afterwards replaced the money. Koppe v. State (Hocking 1926) 21 Ohio App. 33, 153 N.E. 109, 4 Ohio Law Abs. 715.

BILL OF EXCEPTIONS

2945.65 and 2945.66 Bill of exceptions; proceedings on filing—Repealed

(1986 H 412, eff. 3–17–87; 1977 H 219; 131 v H 231; 129 v 1398; 128 v 141; 125 v 39; 1953 H 1; GC 13445–1, 13445–2)

Historical and Statutory Notes

Pre–1953 H 1 Amendments: 113 v 191, 192, Ch 24, § 1, 2

Annotations Under Repealed Sections

SECTION 2945.65

Notes of Decisions

1. Bill of exceptions

Under RC 2945.65 a defendant has "filed a bill of exceptions" when he files the bill with the clerk of the trial court for further proceeding as required by RC 2945.66. City of Cincinnati v. Acme Barrel & Drum Co. (Ohio 1971) 27 Ohio St.2d 212, 271 N.E.2d 766, 56 O.O.2d 128.

In municipal courts the procedure with respect to the filing of bills of exceptions in criminal cases is governed by RC 2945.65 and not by RC 1913.32. City of Cincinnati v. Parker (Ohio 1970) 22 Ohio St.2d 209, 259 N.E.2d 114, 51 O.O.2d 284.

In municipal courts, the procedure with respect to the filing of bills of exceptions in criminal cases is governed by RC 2945.65. City of Cincinnati v. Brooks (Ohio 1970) 21 Ohio St.2d 73, 255 N.E.2d 251, 50 O.O.2d 165, vacated 22 Ohio St.2d 153, 258 N.E.2d 439, 51 O.O.2d 224.

The amendment to RC 1901.30 by 131 v 606, eff. 11–1–65, incorporating by reference the procedure for filing bills of exceptions contained in RC 2945.65 to RC 2945.70 is so irreconcilable with the amendment to RC 1901.21 by 129 v 423, eff. 10–19–61, incorporating by reference the procedure for filing bills of exceptions contained in RC 1913.31 to RC 1913.34, that RC 1901.21 must be considered as having been repealed by implication, insofar as it pertains to the procedure for filing bills of exceptions. City of Cincinnati v. Brooks (Ohio 1970) 21 Ohio St.2d 73, 255 N.E.2d 251, 50 O.O.2d 165, vacated 22 Ohio St.2d 153, 258 N.E.2d 439, 51 O.O.2d 224. Municipal Corporations ⚷ 642(3)

Where a bill of exceptions has been properly filed in the court of common pleas and the appellants, within the time for filing such bill in the court of appeals, filed their brief and assignment of errors but by mistake or inadvertence failed to request the clerk to also file the bill of exceptions in the court of appeals, such failure does not constitute grounds for the dismissal of the appeal for lack of a bill of exceptions. Ordway v. Motor Exp., Inc. (Ohio 1967) 11 Ohio St.2d 70, 227 N.E.2d 607, 40 O.O.2d 72. Appeal And Error ⚷ 554(2)

Where there was nothing in the record before the court of appeals other than the statements of the appellant that his failure to file a bill of exceptions was due to a lack of funds, it cannot be held that the court abused its discretion in overruling his motion for leave to appeal. State v. Forsythe (Ohio 1967) 10 Ohio St.2d 224, 226 N.E.2d 756, 39 O.O.2d 323. Criminal Law ⚷ 1072

This section and GC 13459–4 (RC 2953.05) are in pari materia, and where, in a criminal case, the trial court overrules a motion for a new trial filed by a convicted accused, the journalization of such overruling must be contemporaneous with or subsequent to the journalization of the judgment of sentence of such accused; any other journalization of the overruling is a nullity. State v. Nickles (Ohio 1953) 159 Ohio St. 353, 112 N.E.2d 531, 50 O.O. 322.

GC 1579–440a (Repealed) was not repealed by implication by this section prescribing time within which to file bills of exceptions in criminal cases generally. Henrich v. Hoffman (Ohio 1947) 148 Ohio St. 23, 72 N.E.2d 458, 34 O.O. 473.

Former GC 13680 (Repealed), as amended by 110 v 301, eff. 4–5–23 limited the time for filing a bill of exceptions in all criminal cases without exception to thirty days from the date of overruling of the motion for a new trial, and the proviso in that section related solely to the procedure whereby a bill of exceptions was prepared, signed and allowed, and had no relation to the filing of the same. Luff v. State (Ohio 1927) 117 Ohio St. 102, 157 N.E. 388, 5 Ohio Law Abs. 403, 25 Ohio Law Rep. 377.

The statute applies only to trial courts. Boone v. State (Ohio 1923) 109 Ohio St. 1, 141 N.E. 841, 1 Ohio Law Abs. 861, 21 Ohio Law Rep. 329. Criminal Law ⚷ 1106(2)

It will be presumed that notice and formal preliminaries of bill, certified to contain all the evidence, found to be true, allowed and signed of record were complied with. State v. Wirick (Ohio 1910) 81 Ohio St. 343, 90 N.E. 937, 7 Ohio Law Rep. 577.

By virtue of the amendment in 1965 to RC 1901.30, the legislature repealed by necessary implication the reference in RC 1901.21 to bills of exceptions, and thereby changed the method of presenting and processing bills of exceptions in municipal court criminal cases to that set forth in RC 2945.65 to 2945.70 so that the time for filing a bill of exceptions in criminal cases in a municipal court is now governed by the thirty-day time limitation prescribed by RC 2945.65, and not by the ten-day limitation prescribed by RC 1913.32. State v. Huffman (Hancock 1969) 20 Ohio App.2d 263, 253 N.E.2d 812, 49 O.O.2d 357.

In determining what part of the evidence should be included in a bill of exceptions requested by an indigent defendant in a felony case, it should be noted that under RC 2945.65 if the assignments of error are other than to the weight and sufficiency of the evidence, the bill of exceptions need contain only so much of the evidence as is necessary to present the errors, and that the reviewing court may order a full transcript if necessary. State v. Armstrong (Mahoning 1969) 18 Ohio App.2d 249, 248 N.E.2d 212, 47 O.O.2d 370. Criminal Law ⚷ 1077.2(2)

Where a defendant in a criminal case files notice of appeal to the court of appeals on questions of law and fact and a bill of exceptions, but no assignments of error or brief is filed within time, such appeal will be dismissed. State v. Genovese (Lake 1964) 120 Ohio App. 391, 202 N.E.2d 714, 29 O.O.2d 272, appeal dismissed 177 Ohio St. 7, 201 N.E.2d 522, 28 O.O.2d 411, appeal dismissed, certiorari denied 85 S.Ct. 954, 380 U.S. 261, 13 L.Ed.2d 960. Criminal Law ⚷ 1129(8); Criminal Law ⚷ 1130(4)

Failure of counsel, upon an appeal as of right in a criminal case, to file the bill of exceptions within time because he was not familiar with the statutes of Ohio, is not a showing of "good cause" for sustaining a motion for leave to appeal. State v. Candy (Hamilton 1959) 113 Ohio App. 334, 175 N.E.2d 191, 17 O.O.2d 361.

An appellant in a criminal case is not entitled to an allowance of a motion for leave to withdraw his appeal filed as of right and for leave to appeal, and there is no provision in the law for the conversion of an appeal filed as of right into an appeal instituted by the granting of leave to appeal. State v. Dench (Hamilton 1959) 113 Ohio App. 329, 175 N.E.2d 188, 17 O.O.2d 358.

Where no motion for new trial in a criminal case is filed, the thirty-day period provided in RC 2945.65 for the filing of the bill of exceptions in the trial court, begins to run from the date of sentencing; and where a bill of exceptions is filed in the court of appeals the same day it is allowed by the trial court, there is a compliance with the provisions of Rule VII, D of the Rules of the courts of appeals for the filing of a bill of exceptions. State v. Waymire (Darke 1957) 105 Ohio App. 177, 152 N.E.2d 686, 5 O.O.2d 458.

Where in a criminal case a notice of appeal and precipe for a transcript of the docket and journal entries are timely filed in the common pleas court but through inadvertence are not docketed in the court of appeals until more than ninety days thereafter, the court of appeals may, in its discretion, waive the time requirements for filing an assignment of errors, bill of exceptions and briefs. State v. Payne (Franklin 1957) 104 Ohio App. 405, 149 N.E.2d 579, 5 O.O.2d 84. Criminal Law ⚷ 1092.8; Criminal Law ⚷ 1129(8); Criminal Law ⚷ 1130(4)

An applicant must file his bill of exceptions in a criminal case in a municipal court in accordance with RC 2945.65. State v. De Camillo (Ohio Com. Pl. 1961) 176 N.E.2d 352, 86 Ohio Law Abs. 429, 16 O.O.2d 364.

2. Effect of late filing

Under RC 2945.65 it is not essential that a motion to extend the period for filing a bill of exceptions be filed in the trial court within the time fixed for the filing of such bill; and, after expiration of an original extension of such period, the trial court may, in the exercise of sound discretion and for good cause shown, grant a further extension thereof. State v. Holt (Ohio 1967) 9 Ohio St.2d 147, 224 N.E.2d 525, 38 O.O.2d 370.

Where a bill of exceptions is not filed in the trial court within the prescribed time, and the errors charged are such as can be disclosed only by a bill of exceptions, the judgment must be affirmed. Luff v. State (Ohio 1925) 112 Ohio St. 102, 146 N.E. 892, 3 Ohio Law Abs. 164, 23 Ohio Law Rep. 88.

A bill of exceptions was not available unless filed within the time fixed by the court, which, under former GC 13680 (Repealed), as amended by 110 v 301, eff. 4–5–23, could not be more than thirty days from the overruling of the motion for a new trial. Luff v. State (Ohio 1925) 112 Ohio St. 102, 146 N.E. 892, 3 Ohio Law Abs. 164, 23 Ohio Law Rep. 88.

The court of common pleas is without authority to extend the time for filing a bill of exceptions in an appeal from a municipal court in a criminal case. City of Cincinnati v. Nunnelley (Hamilton 1969) 20 Ohio App.2d 163, 252 N.E.2d 295, 49 O.O.2d 196.

An application for extension of time for filing a bill of exceptions and brief in an appeal to the court of appeals by a defendant in a criminal case, which is filed more than five days after "requesting transcript in the trial court," as provided by Rule VII, C(1)(c), of the rules of the courts of appeals is not timely filed and will be denied. City of Kettering v. Slothower (Montgomery 1960) 112 Ohio App. 313, 176 N.E.2d 449, 16 O.O.2d 223.

An appellate court has no authority to extend the time for filing a bill of exceptions. State v. Leighly (Greene 1957) 161 N.E.2d 509, 81 Ohio Law Abs. 317.

2945.67 When prosecutor may appeal; when public defender to oppose

(A) A prosecuting attorney, village solicitor, city director of law, or the attorney general may appeal as a matter of right any decision of a trial court in a criminal case, or any decision of a juvenile court in a delinquency case, which decision grants a motion to dismiss all or any part of an indictment, complaint, or information, a motion to suppress evidence, or a motion for the return of seized property or grants post conviction relief pursuant to sections 2953.21 to 2953.24 of the Revised Code, and may appeal by leave of the court to which the appeal is taken any other decision, except the final verdict, of the trial court in a criminal case or of the juvenile court in a delinquency case. In addition to any other right to appeal under this section or any other provision of law, a prosecuting attorney, city director of law, village solicitor, or similar chief legal officer of a municipal corporation, or the attorney general may appeal, in accordance with section 2953.08 of the Revised Code, a sentence imposed upon a person who is convicted of or pleads guilty to a felony.

(B) In any proceeding brought pursuant to division (A) of this section, the court, in accordance with Chapter 120. of the Revised Code, shall appoint the county public defender, joint county public defender, or other counsel to represent any person who is indigent, is not represented by counsel, and does not waive the person's right to counsel.

(1995 S 2, eff. 7–1–96; 1978 H 1168, eff. 11–1–78)

Historical and Statutory Notes

Ed. Note: Former 2945.67 repealed by 1978 H 1168, eff. 11–1–78; 1977 H 219; 131 v H 231; 1953 H 1; GC 13446–1.

Pre–1953 H 1 Amendments: 113 v 192, Ch 25, § 1

Amendment Note: 1995 S 2 added the second sentence in division (A); and made other changes to reflect gender neutral language.

Legislative Service Commission

1973:

This section permits the state to appeal an adverse decision on a motion to suppress evidence in a criminal case, on the merits of the particular case. Under former law, the state could appeal motions to quash, pleas in abatement, demurrers, and motions in arrest of judgment on the merits, but an appeal on a motion to quash was permitted only to determine the law to govern in future cases and could not affect the case at bar. See *State v. Collins*, 24 Ohio St. 2nd 107 (1970). (Ed. note: This comment applied to former RC 2945.70, the tenor of which is no incorporated in RC 2945.67.)

Cross References

Appeal as of right from judgments and orders of court of record, how taken, App R 3

Appeal as of right from judgments and orders of court of record, when taken, App R 4

Appeals by leave of court in criminal cases, App R 5

Library References

Criminal Law ⚷1024, 1077.

Infants ⚷242.

Westlaw Topic Nos. 110, 211.

C.J.S. Criminal Law §§ 1675, 1689 to 1694, 1752 to 1757.

C.J.S. Infants §§ 100 to 101, 104.

Research References

Encyclopedias

OH Jur. 3d Criminal Law § 2423, Amendment that Changes Substance of Offense.

OH Jur. 3d Criminal Law § 2839, Pretrial Appeal.

OH Jur. 3d Criminal Law § 2937, Polygraph and Truth Serum Tests.

OH Jur. 3d Criminal Law § 3511, Court of Appeals; Mayor's Courts.

OH Jur. 3d Criminal Law § 3521, Order Relating to Indictment, Information, or Plea.

OH Jur. 3d Criminal Law § 3528, Miscellaneous Nonfinal Orders.

OH Jur. 3d Criminal Law § 3532, Granting of Motion to Suppress Evidence or Motion for Return of Seized Property.

OH Jur. 3d Criminal Law § 3533, Granting of Motion to Suppress Evidence or Motion for Return of Seized Property—Construction of Rule.

OH Jur. 3d Criminal Law § 3534, Judgment or Directed Verdict of Acquittal.

OH Jur. 3d Criminal Law § 3537, Granting of Post-Conviction Relief.

OH Jur. 3d Criminal Law § 3538, Other Appealable or Nonappealable Orders.

OH Jur. 3d Criminal Law § 3580, Notice of Appeal as of Right.

OH Jur. 3d Family Law § 1626, Right Under Juvenile Court Law and Rules.

OH Jur. 3d Family Law § 1727, State's Right of Appeal.

OH Jur. 3d Family Law § 1728, State's Right of Appeal—Where Evidence Suppressed.

OH Jur. 3d Family Law § 1732, Stay of Execution Pending Appeal.

OH Jur. 3d Habeas Corpus & Post Convict. Remedies § 84, Counsel for Indigent Petitioners.

OH Jur. 3d Habeas Corpus & Post Convict. Remedies § 89, Appeal.

Treatises and Practice Aids

Markus, Trial Handbook for Ohio Lawyers, § 38:5, Criminal Case—Power of Court After Verdict.

Klein, Darling, & Terez, Baldwin's Ohio Practice Civil Practice § 1:26, Civ. R. 1(C)(1): Upon Appeal to Review Any Judgment, Order, or Ruling--Appeals in Supreme Court--Role of Revised Code Provisions Purporting to Control Application of Civil Rules.

Klein, Darling, & Terez, Baldwin's Ohio Practice Civil Practice § 1:29, Civ. R. 1(C)(1): Upon Appeal to Review Any Judgment, Order, or Ruling--Appeals in Courts of Appeals--Role of Revised Code Provisions Purporting to Control Application of Civil...

Klein, Darling, & Terez, Baldwin's Ohio Practice Civil Practice § 1:32, Civ. R. 1(C)(1): Upon Appeal to Review Any Judgment, Order, or Ruling--Appeals to Common Pleas Courts from Decisions of Governmental Entities--Role of Revised Code Provisions Purporting to...

Klein, Darling, & Terez, Baldwin's Ohio Practice Civil Practice § 1:100, Modern Courts Amendment of 1968 as Limiting Scope of Application of Civil Rules.

Katz, Giannelli, Blair and Lipton, Baldwin's Ohio Practice, Criminal Law, § 152:1, Table of Final Appealable Orders.

Katz, Giannelli, Blair and Lipton, Baldwin's Ohio Practice, Criminal Law, § 152:4, State's Notice of Appeal of Order Granting Suppression of Evidence.

Katz, Giannelli, Blair and Lipton, Baldwin's Ohio Practice, Criminal Law, § 152:5, Prosecuting Attorney's Certification in Appeal of Order Granting Suppression of Evidence.

Katz, Giannelli, Blair and Lipton, Baldwin's Ohio Practice, Criminal Law, § 47:12, Prosecution Appeals.

Katz, Giannelli, Blair and Lipton, Baldwin's Ohio Practice, Criminal Law, § 74:20, Prosecution Appeals.

Katz, Giannelli, Blair and Lipton, Baldwin's Ohio Practice, Criminal Law, § 80:24, Prosecution Appeals.

Giannelli and Snyder, Baldwin's Ohio Practice, Evidence, § 103.8, Motions in Limine.

Carlin, Baldwin's Ohio Practice, Merrick-Rippner Probate Law § 104:7, Juvenile Court—Constitutional Issues—Double Jeopardy in Juvenile Proceedings.

Carlin, Baldwin's Ohio Practice, Merrick-Rippner Probate Law § 108:2, Juvenile Court—Criminal Jurisdiction—Contributing to Dependency, Neglect, Unruliness, or Delinquency.

Carlin, Baldwin's Ohio Practice, Merrick-Rippner Probate Law § 107:71, Appealability of Bindover Order.

Carlin, Baldwin's Ohio Practice, Merrick-Rippner Probate Law § 107:122, Appeals—Juvenile Court Judgments—Determination of Neglect, Dependency, Unruliness, Abuse, or Delinquency.

Painter & Dennis, Ohio Appellate Practice § 1:8, Courts of Appeals-Appellate Jurisdiction.

Painter & Dennis, Ohio Appellate Practice § 3:6, Time for Filing Notice of Appeal-Appeal by State in Criminal Case.

Painter & Dennis, Ohio Appellate Practice § 1:26, Right to Appeal-Government's Right to Appeal in Criminal Case.

Painter & Dennis, Ohio Appellate Practice § 12:7, State's Motion for Leave to Appeal in Criminal Case.

Painter & Dennis, Ohio Appellate Practice § 12:8, Prosecuting Attorney's Certificate in Appeal from Order Suppressing Evidence or Requiring Return of Seized Property.

Painter & Dennis, Ohio Appellate Practice § 3:23, Appeal by State in Criminal Case.

Hennenberg & Reinhart, Ohio Criminal Defense Motions F 10.04, Motion to Set Aside Jury Verdict and to Enter Judgment of Acquittal (Defense of Consent)-Post-Trial Motions.

Painter, Ohio Driving Under the Influence § 8:22, Appellate Review—State's Appeal.

Giannelli & Yeomans, Ohio Juvenile Law § 14:2, Exclusionary Rule.

Giannelli & Yeomans, Ohio Juvenile Law § 34:8, State Appeals.

Giannelli & Yeomans, Ohio Juvenile Law § 34:10, Right to Counsel.

Gotherman, Babbit and Lang, Baldwin's Ohio Practice, Local Government Law—Municipal, § 33:9, Mandamus.

Gotherman, Babbit and Lang, Baldwin's Ohio Practice, Local Government Law—Municipal, § 28:16, Drunk Driving.

Law Review and Journal Commentaries

Perfecting a Criminal Appeal in the Eighth Appellate District, Randi Marie Ostry. 68 Clev B J 14 (February 1997).

Notes of Decisions

Ed. Note: This section contains annotations from former RC 2945.67.

---

1. Constitutional issues

The Double Jeopardy Clause does not bar reprosecution where a criminal prosecution is dismissed for failure to prosecute after the trial court has erroneously required the state to proceed with trial despite the state's properly filed Crim R 12(J) appeal. State v. Malinovsky (Ohio 1991) 60 Ohio St.3d 20, 573 N.E.2d 22, on remand 81 Ohio App.3d 170, 610 N.E.2d 529, certiorari denied 112 S.Ct. 582, 502 U.S. 980, 116 L.Ed.2d 607. Double Jeopardy ⚿ 92

An appeal by the state is forbidden when a court finds a defendant guilty of a lesser offense than that to which he entered a plea of no contest; the judgment of guilty to the lesser offense is an implicit acquittal on the greater offense. State v. Conti (Cuyahoga 1989) 57 Ohio App.3d 36, 565 N.E.2d 1286.

RC 2945.67(A) may forbid appeal by the state even when reversal of the trial court's judgment would not result in a double jeopardy violation. State v. Conti (Cuyahoga 1989) 57 Ohio App.3d 36, 565 N.E.2d 1286. Criminal Law ⚿ 1024(1)

After a directed verdict of acquittal, the state may appeal adverse evidentiary rulings, with leave of court, even though retrial is barred by the constitutional double jeopardy protections, and even though appeal of the acquittal itself is barred by RC 2945.67(A). State v. Keeton (Ohio 1985) 18 Ohio St.3d 379, 481 N.E.2d 629, 18 O.B.R. 434.

A defendant is put in jeopardy where, after the jury had been sworn and evidence presented by the state, the trial court dismisses three counts of the indictment on defendant's motion for acquittal and an appeal by the state does not lie from the entry of such dismissals. State v. Lewis (Union 1982) 4 Ohio App.3d 275, 448 N.E.2d 487, 4 O.B.R. 494.

Insofar as App R 4(B), permitting the prosecution as of right to appeal judgments of trial courts, enlarges the statutory right of appeal provided by RC 2945.67 through RC 2945.70 and abridges the right of appellate courts to exercise their discretion in allowing appeals provided by these same sections, such rule is invalid under the provisions of O Const Art IV §5, and an appeal filed by the state pursuant to App R 4(B) is properly dismissed where the provisions of RC 2945.68 have not been complied with. State v. Hughes (Ohio 1975) 41 Ohio St.2d 208, 324 N.E.2d 731, 70 O.O.2d 395.

RC 2945.67 to RC 2945.70 are unconstitutional insofar as they permit the prosecutor in a criminal case to institute proceedings to review a judgment of the trial court, except where the judgment of such court decides "a motion to quash, a plea in abatement, a demurrer, or a motion in arrest of judgment," or the equivalent thereof. City of Euclid v. Heaton (Ohio 1968) 15 Ohio St.2d 65, 238 N.E.2d 790, 44 O.O.2d 50. Criminal Law ⚷ 1005

The state may appeal from an interlocutory order in a criminal case filed prior to the time defendant was placed in jeopardy, and such appeal, if valid, will not have the effect of a dismissal or an acquittal where such defendant was not placed in jeopardy. State v. Doyle (Hamilton 1967) 11 Ohio App.2d 97, 228 N.E.2d 863, 40 O.O.2d 251. Double Jeopardy ⚷ 60.1; Criminal Law ⚷ 1024(2)

The erroneous granting of a motion to dismiss a criminal charge on the constitutional ground of an alleged denial of a speedy trial does not result in an acquittal of the accused, nor is it a bar to further proceedings on the indictment against such accused. State v. Doyle (Hamilton 1967) 11 Ohio App.2d 97, 228 N.E.2d 863, 40 O.O.2d 251. Double Jeopardy ⚷ 92

RC 2945.67 to RC 2945.70 are in pari materia, and, insofar as they provide a proceeding for and prescribe a decision of a court of appeals, upon questions determined by a trial court in a criminal case where jeopardy has attached presented by the prosecuting attorney to the court of appeals by a bill of exceptions filed in that court by leave, which shall not affect the judgment of the trial court in such cause but merely shall determine the law to govern in a similar case, such sections constitute an attempt to enlarge the jurisdiction, as well as the judicial power, of the courts of appeals beyond that prescribed by O Const Art IV, § 6, and are void. State v. Dodge (Hancock 1967) 10 Ohio App.2d 92, 226 N.E.2d 156, 39 O.O.2d 174, affirmed 15 Ohio St.2d 65, 238 N.E.2d 790, 44 O.O.2d 50.

The provisions of former GC 13446–2 and GC 13446–4 (repealed) attempt to enlarge the judicial power of the Ohio Supreme Court and to abridge that of the Court of Appeals, and are therefore void by reason of conflict with O Const Art IV, § 2 and O Const Art IV §6. Eastman v. State (Ohio 1936) 131 Ohio St. 1, 1 N.E.2d 140, 5 O.O. 248, appeal dismissed 57 S.Ct. 21, 299 U.S. 505, 81 L.Ed. 374.

Without violating the protection against double jeopardy, the government may appeal an acquittal based on insufficiency of evidence which is granted by the court after a guilty verdict from a jury; and if the acquittal is found on appeal to have been erroneously granted, the guilty verdict may be reinstated. State v Dunn, Nos. 11745 and 11746 (9th Dist Ct App, Summit, 4–3–85).

2. In general

Statute governing appeals by prosecuting attorneys enumerates four trial court decisions from which State may appeal as a matter of right; all other appeals are by leave at discretion of court of appeals, except, of course, that State may not appeal final verdict. State v. Matthews (Ohio, 04-15-1998) 81 Ohio St.3d 375, 691 N.E.2d 1041, 1998-Ohio-433, on remand 1999 WL 135264. Criminal Law ⚷ 1024(1); Criminal Law ⚷ 1072

The state has an absolute right to appeal a judgment granting a motion to seal criminal records. State v. Netter (Ross 1989) 64 Ohio App.3d 322, 581 N.E.2d 597. Criminal Law ⚷ 1024(1)

The state cannot bring an appeal from the trial court's reasons for its decision under RC 2945.67(A); it may only appeal from the decision itself. State v. Dotson (Cuyahoga 1987) 31 Ohio App.3d 200, 510 N.E.2d 817, 31 O.B.R. 469. Criminal Law ⚷ 1023(1)

Trial court order compelling government to disclose identity of confidential informant was a final appealable order. State v. Port Clinton Fisheries, Inc. (Ohio 1984) 12 Ohio St.3d 114, 465 N.E.2d 865, 12 O.B.R. 157, on remand. Appeal And Error ⚷ 78(1)

State could appeal, as a matter of right, trial court's decision to strike one of three prior convictions for driving under the influence (DUI) in prosecution for DUI, as prior conviction enhanced current DUI violation from a first degree misdemeanor to a fourth degree felony, such that striking prior conviction affected an essential element of the current charge. State v. Skala (Ohio App. 8 Dist., Cuyahoga, 06-13-2002) No. 80331, 2002-Ohio-2962, 2002 WL 1308629, Unreported. Criminal Law ⚷ 1024(1)

3. Construction with other laws

RC 2945.67 is inapplicable to the state's right of direct appeal in expungement cases, as expungement under RC 2953.32 is a post-conviction relief proceeding governed by the Ohio Rules of Appellate Procedure as applicable to civil actions. State v. Bissantz (Ohio 1987) 30 Ohio St.3d 120, 507 N.E.2d 1117, 30 O.B.R. 434, on remand.

4. Criminal cases

Statute governing appeals by prosecuting attorneys is unique to criminal cases, dealing with procedural aspects that occur only in criminal cases, and draws distinction between appeal as of right and appeal by leave of court. State v. Matthews (Ohio, 04-15-1998) 81 Ohio St.3d 375, 691 N.E.2d 1041, 1998-Ohio-433, on remand 1999 WL 135264. Criminal Law ⚷ 1024(1); Criminal Law ⚷ 1072

State may appeal in criminal case only when statute gives express authority to do so. State v. Rogers (Ohio App. 4 Dist., 03-28-1996) 110 Ohio App.3d 106, 673 N.E.2d 666. Criminal Law ⚷ 1024(1)

State's appeal from trial court order which applied Financial Responsibility Act to suspend defendant's driver's license, but granted her occupational driving privileges, after she entered no-contest plea to charge of operating motor vehicle with breath-alcohol concentration in excess of lawful limit, was criminal appeal controlled by provisions of statute governing state's right to appeal decisions of trial court in criminal case; had defendant never been charged with underlying traffic offense and had she not pleaded guilty or been found guilty of the offense, her suspension of driving privileges under Act could not have been legally imposed. State v. Williams (Hamilton 1993) 85 Ohio App.3d 542, 620 N.E.2d 171. Criminal Law ⚷ 1024(1)

5. Juvenile court

State had right to appeal from juvenile court's probable cause findings in mandatory-bindover hearing in delinquency adjudication proceedings. In re S.J. (Ohio, 07-13-2005) 106 Ohio St.3d 11, 829 N.E.2d 1207, 2005-Ohio-3215, on remand 2005-Ohio-6353, 2005 WL 3215227. Infants ⚷ 68.8

State's filing of notice of appeal from juvenile court's probable-cause rulings in mandatory-bindover hearing divested juvenile court of any jurisdiction to proceed with delinquency adjudication during pendency of appeal. In re S.J. (Ohio, 07-13-2005) 106 Ohio St.3d 11, 829 N.E.2d 1207, 2005-Ohio-3215, on remand 2005-Ohio-6353, 2005 WL 3215227. Infants ⚷ 68.8

6. Dismissal of charges or indictment

State could challenge trial court's denial of forfeiture specification of indictment for possession of drugs via cross-assignment of error upon defendant's appeal from underlying convictions and without seeking leave to appeal; state could appeal as a matter of right any decision granting motion to dismiss all or part of indictment, and trial court's denial of forfeiture specification essentially constituted dismissal of part of indictment. State v. Kish (Ohio App. 9 Dist., Lorain, 05-14-2003) No. 02CA008146, 2003-Ohio-2426, 2003 WL 21078099, Unreported, appeal not allowed 100 Ohio St.3d 1410, 796 N.E.2d 538, 2003-Ohio-4948, habeas corpus denied 2005 WL 2849049. Criminal Law ⚷ 1023(8)

Decision of trial court granting defendant's motion to dismiss indictment for failure to state offense was appealable. State v. Larabee (Ohio, 05-25-1994) 69 Ohio St.3d 357, 632 N.E.2d 511, 1994-Ohio-318. Criminal Law ⚷ 1023(8)

Dismissal of an indictment because of a prosecutor's failure to honor a "plea bargain" arranged by a police officer is improper where the defendant has not demonstrated prejudice as there is no evidence that the defendant provided information in reliance on the agreement or that the prosecutor was involved in the police officer's improper conduct. State v. Fulton (Seneca 1990) 66 Ohio App.3d 215, 583 N.E.2d 1088, dismissed, jurisdictional motion overruled 52 Ohio St.3d 706, 557 N.E.2d 1212.

Where a trial court dismisses criminal charges on its own motion for failure of the prosecution to elect between charges under RC 4511.19(A)(1) and 4511.19(A)(3), the decision is a final order and is a grant of a motion within the meaning of RC 2945.67(A); hence the state may appeal the dismissal. State v. Ryan (Hamilton 1984) 17 Ohio App.3d 150, 478 N.E.2d 257, 17 O.B.R. 250.

7. Motion for continuance

Order denying prosecution's motion for continuance, which motion was filed on basis that defendant was unavailable for trial due to federal case pending against him, was not final, appealable order; order did not affect substantial right of State and did not determine action or prevent judgment since, even if trial court proceeded to trial, any judgment would be void, defendant would not be able to claim double jeopardy since court had no jurisdiction to convict him, unavailable defendant could not claim he was not brought to trial within statutory time limit, and indictment tolled statute of limitations. State v. Yee (Erie 1989) 55 Ohio App.3d 88, 563 N.E.2d 54. Criminal Law ⚷ 1023(3)

8. Evidence—Admissibility

Court of Appeals had jurisdiction over state's appeal, pursuant to statute allowing prosecuting attorney to appeal as a matter of right a trial court's substantive law rulings made in a criminal case which results in a judgment of acquittal, from decision of the trial court to permit the defendant to use grand jury testimony for purposes of cross-examination during felonious assault trial, where defendant was convicted of lesser included offense of felonious assault, and state did not challenge conviction itself. State v. Burroughs (Ohio App. 3 Dist., 12-05-2005) 165 Ohio App.3d 172, 845 N.E.2d 540, 2005-Ohio-6411, appeal not allowed 109 Ohio St.3d 1424, 846 N.E.2d 534, 2006-Ohio-1967. Criminal Law ⚷ 1024(1)

Court of Appeals did not have jurisdiction to hear the state's appeal of evidentiary rulings refusing to compel defendants to produce videotape, and allowing defendants to present evidence of alternative methods to commit a crime, in environmental prosecution; state could appeal only motion to dismiss, motion to suppress evidence, motion for the return of seized property, or grant of post-conviction relief. State v. Steiner (Ohio App. 8 Dist., Cuyahoga, 08-08-2002) No. 80488, No. 80489, No. 80490, 2002-Ohio-4019, 2002 WL 1821748, Unreported, appeal not allowed 98 Ohio St.3d 1410, 781 N.E.2d 1019, 2003-Ohio-60. Criminal Law ⚷ 1023(3)

Pursuant to RC 2945.67, a prosecutor may appeal the granting of a motion for a new trial due to error in the admission of evidence where it appears the defendant was not prejudiced by such admission. State v Weaver, No. 84AP–937 (10th Dist Ct App, Franklin, 1–15–85).

9. —— Suppression, evidence

Trial court's decision granting defendants' motions to suppress evidence did not trigger commencement of seven-day period for filing notice of appeal from judgment or order granting motion to suppress evidence, where trial court's decision was not unequivocally intended to be trial court's final judgment entry on defendants' motions to suppress, but instead was merely intended to be announcement of trial court's decision on defendants' suppression motions. State v. Pilot (Ohio App. 12 Dist., Clermont, 07-12-2004) No. CA2003-03-023,

No. CA2003-03-24, 2004-Ohio-3669, 2004 WL 1551517, Unreported. Criminal Law ⚷ 1024(1)

In prosecution for operating a motor vehicle under the influence of alcohol (OMVI), it was error for trial court to indirectly rule on admissibility of State's evidence by granting motion for dismissal, where trial court had not ruled on motion to suppress brought by defendant. State v. Francis (Ohio App. 3 Dist., Hardin, 02-07-2003) No. 6-02-09, 2003-Ohio-568, 2003 WL 255747, Unreported. Criminal Law ⚷ 394.6(5); Criminal Law ⚷ 752.5

Trial court's order granting defendant's pretrial motion to suppress in prosecution for driving under the influence of alcohol (DUI) clearly stated that arresting officer's observations, and defendant's blood alcohol content (BAC) results, were suppressed, thereby destroying State's ability to prosecute the case, and thus, the seven-day period for State's appeal was not tolled by State's motion for clarification. State v. Bassham (Ohio, 02-27-2002) 94 Ohio St.3d 269, 762 N.E.2d 963, 2002-Ohio-797. Criminal Law ⚷ 1069(5)

A motion for clarification of a final order suppressing evidence does not affect the time requirements for the State's filing of a notice of appeal from the order. State v. Bassham (Ohio, 02-27-2002) 94 Ohio St.3d 269, 762 N.E.2d 963, 2002-Ohio-797. Criminal Law ⚷ 1081(6)

The state has an appeal as of right from an order granting a motion to suppress. State v. Hartikainen (Ohio App. 6 Dist., 04-12-2000) 137 Ohio App.3d 421, 738 N.E.2d 881, appeal not allowed 90 Ohio St.3d 1406, 734 N.E.2d 836. Criminal Law ⚷ 1024(1)

State's appeal of the granting of motion to suppress, certifying that granting of suppression motion has so weakened proof on pending charge as to destroy any reasonable probability of effective prosecution, is not a discretionary appeal but rather an appeal as of right. State v. Bertram (Ohio, 11-19-1997) 80 Ohio St.3d 281, 685 N.E.2d 1239, 1997-Ohio-114. Criminal Law ⚷ 1024(1)

Appellate court is without authority to review reasonableness of prosecutor's certification that granting of motion to suppress has rendered state's proof on pending charge so weak in its entirety that any reasonable possibility of effective prosecution has been destroyed; appellate court may not therefore dismiss prosecutor's appeal for want of a final appealable order based on merits of prosecutor's certification. State v. Bertram (Ohio, 11-19-1997) 80 Ohio St.3d 281, 685 N.E.2d 1239, 1997-Ohio-114. Criminal Law ⚷ 1024(1)

In reviewing trial court's decision on motion to suppress, it is not appellate court's task to reevaluate evidence or witness' credibility, but to determine whether trial court's application of law to facts was appropriate. State v. Woods (Ohio App. 2 Dist., 08-02-1996) 113 Ohio App.3d 240, 680 N.E.2d 729. Criminal Law ⚷ 1158(4)

Trial court did not have authority to grant final verdict by dismissing charges in juvenile delinquency proceeding so as to defeat state's right to appeal granting of juveniles' motion to suppress evidence granted during trial; state could appeal from granting of motion to suppress as matter of right. In re Mojica (Ohio App. 8 Dist., 11-20-1995) 107 Ohio App.3d 461, 669 N.E.2d 35. Infants ⚷ 202; Infants ⚷ 242

Important characteristic of motion to suppress is that finality attaches so that ruling of court at suppression hearing prevails at trial and is, therefore, automatically appealable by the state. State v. French (Ohio, 07-05-1995) 72 Ohio St.3d 446, 650 N.E.2d 887, 1995-Ohio-32. Criminal Law ⚷ 394.6(5); Criminal Law ⚷ 1024(1)

In prosecution for transporting loaded firearm in motor vehicle, it was error for trial court to indirectly rule on admissibility of state's evidence by granting final judgment of acquittal; no motion to suppress was ever filed with or granted by trial court, and court in substance sua sponte suppressed evidence found in defendant's van and characterized its ruling as judgment of acquittal. State v. Hamilton (Ohio App. 3 Dist., 10-18-1994) 97 Ohio App.3d 648, 647 N.E.2d 238. Criminal Law ⚷ 753.2(2)

When motion to suppress is granted, it is not for trial court to determine sufficiency of state's evidence to proceed with prosecution and hence enter judgment of acquittal, but rather, state must be permitted to determine whether it will seek stay of proceedings in order to exercise its right of appeal, or alternatively to proceed to final judgment or verdict; choice is that of prosecution. State v. Hamilton (Ohio App. 3 Dist., 10-18-1994) 97 Ohio App.3d 648, 647 N.E.2d 238. Criminal Law ⚷ 394.6(5); Criminal Law ⚷ 753.2(3.1); Criminal Law ⚷ 1024(1)

Trial court properly classified motions for pretrial ruling under which assault victim's prior testimony was excluded, as motions to suppress evidence, so as to permit immediate appeal, where challenges were sustained, seriously weakening state's case. State v. Jackson (Ohio App. 1 Dist., 04-28-1993) 92 Ohio App.3d 467, 636 N.E.2d 332, motion allowed 67 Ohio St.3d 1454, 619 N.E.2d 422, appeal dismissed as improvidently granted 69 Ohio St.3d 1214, 633 N.E.2d 1136, 1994-Ohio-406. Criminal Law ⚷ 632(3.1); Criminal Law ⚷ 1024(1)

State was entitled to seven days in which to perfect its appeal before trial court dismissed case after suppressing evidence; judge was required to state on the record its findings of fact and reasons for sua sponte dismissal. State v. Newell (Lucas 1990) 68 Ohio App.3d 623, 589 N.E.2d 412. Criminal Law ⚷ 1069(1)

At a suppression hearing, a trial court's refusal to permit the state the opportunity to present evidence on the defendant's motion to suppress is reversible error where the prosecutor is prepared to bear his burden of going forward with evidence on the issue of whether probable cause existed for the arrest. State v. Hooker (Lucas 1989) 64 Ohio App.3d 631, 582 N.E.2d 636. Criminal Law ⚷ 394.6(4); Criminal Law ⚷ 1168(2)

Under RC 2945.67 and Crim R 12(J), the state may appeal as of right the granting of a motion to suppress evidence in a prosecution for drunk driving; the failure of Traf R 11(I) to enumerate Traf R 13(B)(2) does not deprive the state of a statutory right. City of Toledo v. Fogel (Lucas 1985) 20 Ohio App.3d 146, 485 N.E.2d 302, 20 O.B.R. 180.

An order which restricts the state in the presentation of certain evidence and, thereby, renders the state's proof with respect to the pending charge so weak in its entirety that any reasonable possibility of effective prosecution has been destroyed, is, in effect, a suppression order and is appealable pursuant to RC 2945.67 and Crim R 12(J), notwithstanding the labeling of the order as merely an order in limine. State v. Davidson (Ohio 1985) 17 Ohio St.3d 132, 477 N.E.2d 1141, 17 O.B.R. 277.

Where a trial court sustains a portion of defendant's motion to suppress and the state fails to appeal that ruling pursuant to Crim R 12(J), RC 2945.67, and App R 4(B), the state is precluded from contesting that portion of the suppression ruling unfavorable to it in an appeal by defendant from his conviction based upon the evidence which was not suppressed. State v. Felty (Hamilton 1981) 2 Ohio App.3d 62, 440 N.E.2d 803, 2 O.B.R. 69. Criminal Law ⚿ 1136

A court of appeals has jurisdiction to entertain the state's appeal from a trial court decision in a criminal case granting defendant's pretrial motion to suppress evidence only where the state has complied with Crim R 12(J). State v. Buckingham (Ohio 1980) 62 Ohio St.2d 14, 402 N.E.2d 536, 16 O.O.3d 8.

Where a motion to suppress is made and granted after the commencement of trial, a trial court shall not proceed to enter judgment of acquittal so as to defeat the state's right of appeal pursuant to Crim R 12(J). State v. Fraternal Order of Eagles Aerie 0337 Buckeye (Ohio 1991) 58 Ohio St.3d 166, 569 N.E.2d 478.

10. Leave of court

State's failure to seek leave to appeal from trial court's determination that it lacked jurisdiction over issue of forfeiture of defendant's property after criminal case with which forfeiture action was merged was dismissed precluded appellate jurisdiction to consider issue. State v. Mitchell (Ohio App. 6 Dist., Lucas, 05-14-2004) No. L-03-1270, 2004-Ohio-2460, 2004 WL 1088380, Unreported. Criminal Law ⚿ 1072

Court of Appeals validly exercised jurisdiction over State's appeal, pursuant to statute allowing prosecuting attorney to appeal as a matter of right, in allowing state to appeal substantive legal issue concerning amount of defendant's theft of welfare benefits, as judgment, itself, was not appealed, and thus, case was properly certified to Supreme Court, after Court of Appeals' decision on the legal issue revealed an actual conflict between appellate judicial districts on rule of law. State v. Edmondson (Ohio, 07-25-2001) 92 Ohio St.3d 393, 750 N.E.2d 587, 2001-Ohio-210. Criminal Law ⚿ 1020.5; Criminal Law ⚿ 1024(1)

State's failure, in certifying interlocutory appeal from order suppressing breathalyzer results in separate prosecutions in which each defendant was charged with driving while intoxicated (DWI) and other traffic-related offenses, to identify which of the multiple offenses charged to each defendant was adversely affected by the suppression order did not deprive Court of Appeals of jurisdiction over appeal. State v. Melms (Ohio App. 3 Dist., 03-09-1999) 131 Ohio App.3d 246, 722 N.E.2d 159. Criminal Law ⚿ 1024(1)

Trial court's order granting defendant new trial in criminal case is final appealable order, which State may appeal by leave of court to which appeal is taken; abrogating *State v Huntsman*, 18 Ohio St.2d 206, 47 O.O.2d 440, 249 N.E.2d 40. State v. Matthews (Ohio, 04-15-1998) 81 Ohio St.3d 375, 691 N.E.2d 1041, 1998-Ohio-433, on remand 1999 WL 135264. Criminal Law ⚿ 1024(7)

State has right to appeal even interlocutory orders in criminal case by leave of Court of Appeals. State ex rel. Heck v. Kessler (Ohio, 04-26-1995) 72 Ohio St.3d 98, 647 N.E.2d 792, 1995-Ohio-304. Criminal Law ⚿ 1023(3); Criminal Law ⚿ 1072

Under statute governing state's right to appeal decisions of trial court in criminal case, state did not possess right to appeal trial court's order which suspended defendant's driver's license, but granted her occupational driving privileges, for operating motor vehicle while failing to maintain proof of financial responsibility in violation of Financial Responsibility Act after she entered no contest plea to charge of operating motor vehicle with breath-alcohol concentration in excess of lawful limit; action did not fall under any of categories giving state appeal by right and, therefore, state's only course was to file motion for leave to appeal, which it did not do. State v. Williams (Hamilton 1993) 85 Ohio App.3d 542, 620 N.E.2d 171. Automobiles ⚿ 144.2(5.1)

A state's motion for leave to appeal a trial court's rulings on matters of substantive law made in a criminal case which result in a judgment of acquittal will be denied by an appellate court in the exercise of its discretion on the grounds that the duty of the court is to decide actual controversies between the parties and to enter judgments capable of enforcement and not to give mere advisory opinions or to rule on questions of law which cannot affect the matters in issue in the case; the criminal statute applicable to the case was substantially amended and thus, an advisory opinion on it as it was at the time of trial and prior to amendment would serve no purpose and would constitute a waste of judicial time. State v. Bistricky (Cuyahoga 1990) 66 Ohio App.3d 395, 584 N.E.2d 75.

Where trial court amends an indictment for involuntary manslaughter to one for negligent homicide, there has been no final action concerning the substantive elements of the offense; thus, the state may not appeal such amendment as a matter of right pursuant to RC 2945.67(A); however, the state may seek to appeal the ruling by filing a motion for leave to appeal in the court to which the appeal is taken. State v. Cook (Butler 1987) 35 Ohio App.3d 20, 519 N.E.2d 419.

The state may appeal from an order granting shock probation only by leave of court, pursuant to RC 2945.67(A). State v. Fisher (Ohio 1988) 35 Ohio St.3d 22, 517 N.E.2d 911. Criminal Law ⚷ 1072

The decision to grant or deny a motion for leave to appeal by the state in a criminal case is solely within the discretion of the court of appeals. State v. Fisher (Ohio 1988) 35 Ohio St.3d 22, 517 N.E.2d 911. Criminal Law ⚷ 1072

Where a prosecution for conspiracy to commit murder results in an acquittal, the state's motion for leave to appeal the issue of alleged prejudice to the state resulting from a question which was asked in the presence of the jury but was never completed or answered will be denied since the issue in question is not one of admissibility of the evidence. State v. Bireley (Clinton 1986) 31 Ohio App.3d 234, 510 N.E.2d 830, 31 O.B.R. 518.

After a criminal conviction, the state should be granted leave to cross-appeal an order based on a pretrial motion, where the defendant has also appealed, since, in case of reversal of the conviction, a decision on the state's cross-appeal would not be merely an advisory opinion. State v. Dotson (Franklin 1986) 31 Ohio App.3d 199, 510 N.E.2d 815, 31 O.B.R. 468.

Where a trial court grants a motion to dismiss a single-count indictment "to the extent that" the court finds the statute under which the indictment charges to be unconstitutional in part, the state may immediately appeal the order under RC 2945.67(A), since the order in effect dismisses part of the indictment. State v. Hayes (Ohio 1986) 25 Ohio St.3d 173, 495 N.E.2d 578, 25 O.B.R. 214, on remand 31 Ohio App.3d 40, 507 N.E.2d 1176, 31 O.B.R. 56.

Pursuant to RC 2945.67(A), a court of appeals has jurisdiction to grant the state leave to appeal from a decision of the trial court on the admissibility of evidence, notwithstanding the acquittal of the defendant. State v. Arnett (Ohio 1986) 22 Ohio St.3d 186, 489 N.E.2d 284, 22 O.B.R. 272. Criminal Law ⚷ 1024(1)

In order to review errors of law leading to an acquittal pursuant to Crim R 29(A), a court of appeals may grant the state leave to appeal, even though the judgment of acquittal cannot be affected by the appeal. State v. Ulrich (Wood 1983) 17 Ohio App.3d 179, 478 N.E.2d 809, 17 O.B.R. 368, appeal decided 17 Ohio App.3d 182, 478 N.E.2d 812, 17 O.B.R. 372.

Entry of a final verdict does not render unappealable orders which would otherwise be appealable by leave of court pursuant to RC 2945.67(A). State v. Owen (Williams 1983) 16 Ohio App.3d 384, 476 N.E.2d 358, 16 O.B.R. 452.

After an acquittal, by leave of court pursuant to App R 5, the state may appeal the sustaining of a defendant's objection to the admission of certain evidence. State v. Burkhart (Franklin 1984) 14 Ohio App.3d 446, 472 N.E.2d 52, 14 O.B.R. 565.

The denial of a state motion for leave to appeal under RC 2945.67 by a court of appeals is appealable to the supreme court; thus, a writ of mandamus to compel the court of appeals to vacate an order of a court of common pleas must be denied. State ex rel. Corrigan v. Lawther (Ohio 1988) 39 Ohio St.3d 157, 529 N.E.2d 1377.

A judgment of acquittal by the trial judge, based upon Crim R 29(C), is a final verdict within the meaning of RC 2945.67(A) and is not appealable by the state as a matter of right or by leave to appeal pursuant to that statute. State ex rel. Yates v. Court of Appeals for Montgomery County (Ohio 1987) 32 Ohio St.3d 30, 512 N.E.2d 343.

The granting of an accused's motion for a polygraphic test at state expense in a criminal case is a "final order" within the meaning of O Const Art IV §3(B)(2), and is therefore appealable by leave of court under RC 2945.67(A). State ex rel. Leis v. Kraft (Ohio 1984) 10 Ohio St.3d 34, 460 N.E.2d 1372, 10 O.B.R. 237.

11. Mistrial

Great deference is given to the exercise of discretion by a trial court in declaring a mistrial based on misconduct of defense counsel in closing argument; such a mistrial is properly declared where the jurors' impartiality may have been affected by improper comments regarding the punishment required for the charged offense. State v. Abboud (Cuyahoga 1983) 13 Ohio App.3d 62, 468 N.E.2d 155, 13 O.B.R. 66.

12. Speedy trial

The state's appeal from a judgment to dismiss tax fraud indictments in a case involving an individual defendant has no relation to a case involving a corporate defendant, and its pendency could not, for that reason alone, extend the speedy trial time in the case against the corporate defendant. State v. Perry (Allen 1990) 67 Ohio App.3d 775, 588 N.E.2d 897. Criminal Law ⚷ 577.10(5)

State's appeal from order on motion to dismiss that was taken only in case involving individual defendant had no relation to case involving corporate defendant and its pendency could not, for that reason alone, extend speedy trial time in case against corporate defendant. State v. Perry (Allen 1990) 67 Ohio App.3d 775, 588 N.E.2d 897. Criminal Law ⚷ 577.10(5)

State's abortive appeal from order on motion to dismiss could not extend speedy trial time, where state never met either jurisdictional or procedural requirements for appeal to Court of Appeals under relevant provisions, or for any appeal derivative thereto to the Supreme Court. State v. Perry (Allen 1990) 67 Ohio App.3d 775, 588 N.E.2d 897. Criminal Law ⚷ 577.13

A 197–day delay resulting from Court of Appeals' granting leave and accepting State's appeal of trial court's order to disclose informer identity was not attributable to State for purposes of speedy trial statute; speedy trial time period was tolled during pendency of appeal pursuant to statute setting forth allowable extensions of time for bringing a criminal defendant to trial. State v. DeLeon (Ohio App. 2 Dist., Montgomery, 06-28-2002) No. 18114,

2002-Ohio-3286, 2002 WL 1393665, Unreported, appeal not allowed 98 Ohio St.3d 1424, 782 N.E.2d 78, 2003-Ohio-259. Criminal Law ⚿ 577.10(7)

The state may appeal as a matter of right the discharge of a defendant for violation of the speedy trial requirements under RC 2945.71. State v Davis, No. 1885 (11th Dist Ct App, Portage, 11–14–88).

13. Final verdict

Judgment of acquittal in prosecution for attempted felonious assault was not appealable; judgment of acquittal is final verdict and question raised on appeal as to whether gun was pointed at alleged victim was question of fact, rather than question of law over which Court of Appeals has discretionary authority to review if question is capable of repetition. State v. Davis (Ohio App. 5 Dist., Delaware, 05-26-2004) No. 03 CA-A-07038, 2004-Ohio-2804, 2004 WL 1194064, Unreported. Criminal Law ⚿ 1024(5)

Assuming challenge to judgment of acquittal in prosecution for attempted felonious assault raised question of law as to sufficiency of evidence presented, Court of Appeals would decline to exercise its discretion to hear appeal, where case involved complex set of facts which was not likely to recur. State v. Davis (Ohio App. 5 Dist., Delaware, 05-26-2004) No. 03 CA-A-07038, 2004-Ohio-2804, 2004 WL 1194064, Unreported. Criminal Law ⚿ 1024(5)

State was statutorily precluded from appealing verdict that acquitted defendant after defendant had entered no contest plea, where statute barred State from appealing final verdict in criminal case, and acquittal was final verdict in case. State v. Mayfield (Ohio App. 8 Dist., Cuyahoga, 05-08-2003) No. 81924, 2003-Ohio-2312, 2003 WL 21028352, Unreported, appeal allowed 100 Ohio St.3d 1423, 797 N.E.2d 91, 2003-Ohio-5232, appeal dismissed as improvidently allowed 102 Ohio St.3d 1240, 811 N.E.2d 81, 2004-Ohio-3440. Criminal Law ⚿ 1024(5)

Court of Appeals lacked subject-matter jurisdiction to accept state's appeal from denial of its motion to amend indictment charging defendant with aggravated murder to include capital specification, where motion was denied after three-judge panel of trial court which heard the case entered findings and order denominated by it as its "verdicts," which findings and order included a not guilty finding as to murder count to which only capital specification included in indictment was attached, and state's appeal thus amounted to collateral attack on a final verdict. State v. Lomax (Ohio, 09-11-2002) 96 Ohio St.3d 318, 774 N.E.2d 249, 2002-Ohio-4453. Criminal Law ⚿ 1024(1)

State was statutorily precluded from appealing final verdict of Juvenile Court providing that juvenile was not delinquent of rape and assault. In re Lee (Ohio App. 8 Dist., 08-06-2001) 145 Ohio App.3d 167, 762 N.E.2d 396. Infants ⚿ 242

Judgment of acquittal is final verdict and is not appealable by state as matter of right or by leave to appeal. State v. Schiewe (Ohio App. 6 Dist., 03-29-1996) 110 Ohio App.3d 170, 673 N.E.2d 941. Criminal Law ⚿ 1024(5); Criminal Law ⚿ 1072

Statute did not provide basis for state's appeal from not guilty verdict on ground that it was against manifest weight of the evidence; while statute provides for appeal as of right by state with regard to certain rulings, final verdict is not expressly enumerated as judgment that can be appealed by state. State v. Rogers (Ohio App. 4 Dist., 03-28-1996) 110 Ohio App.3d 106, 673 N.E.2d 666. Criminal Law ⚿ 1024(5)

New trial order after guilt phase, but before penalty phase, of capital murder prosecution was final and appealable by state, even though order did not vacate or set aside judgment. State v. Rudge (Trumbull 1993) 89 Ohio App.3d 429, 624 N.E.2d 1069, dismissed, jurisdictional motion overruled 67 Ohio St.3d 1502, 622 N.E.2d 651. Criminal Law ⚿ 1024(7)

An appeal by the state is forbidden when a court finds a defendant guilty of a lesser offense than that to which he entered a plea of no contest; the judgment of guilty to the lesser offense is an implicit acquittal on the greater offense. State v. Conti (Cuyahoga 1989) 57 Ohio App.3d 36, 565 N.E.2d 1286.

An acquittal in a criminal prosecution constitutes a final verdict which may not be appealed by the state. State v. Dotson (Cuyahoga 1987) 31 Ohio App.3d 200, 510 N.E.2d 817, 31 O.B.R. 469.

A court of appeals has no jurisdiction to consider the state's appeal from a verdict of not guilty regarding a violation of RC 4511.21 since the offense of which the defendant could have been convicted constitutes a criminal offense pursuant to RC 2901.03. State v. Huxtable (Preble 1983) 13 Ohio App.3d 371, 469 N.E.2d 931, 13 O.B.R. 453.

A judgment of acquittal is a "final verdict," and a municipality may not appeal such a decision pursuant to RC 2945.67. Village of Northwood v. Volschow (Wood 1980) 68 Ohio App.2d 187, 428 N.E.2d 466, 22 O.O.3d 283. Criminal Law ⚿ 1024(5)

A judgment of acquittal by the trial judge, based upon Crim R 29(C), is a final verdict within the meaning of RC 2945.67(A) and is not appealable by the state as a matter of right or by leave to appeal pursuant to that statute. State ex rel. Yates v. Court of Appeals for Montgomery County (Ohio 1987) 32 Ohio St.3d 30, 512 N.E.2d 343.

The state has no right to appeal an adverse verdict under RC 2945.67 in a forfeiture proceeding involving a boat allegedly used in the unlawful taking of wild animals where such forfeiture proceedings are governed by the Rules of Criminal Procedure pursuant to RC 1531.21. State v Boger, No. OT–86–60 (6th Dist Ct App, Ottawa, 3–27–87).

14. Correction of sentence

Statutory bar against appeal by state of sentence imposed for aggravated murder did not preclude appellate court from reviewing state's claims that trial court failed to follow proper procedure at penalty phase of capital case when it imposed sentence of life without parole and that trial court made incorrect evidentiary rulings at penalty phase. State v. Hancock (Ohio App. 12 Dist., Warren, 03-31-2003) No. CA2001-12-115, No. CA2001-12-116, No. CA2002-01-004, 2003-Ohio-1616, 2003 WL 1689612, Unreported, appeal not allowed 99 Ohio St.3d 1513, 792 N.E.2d 200, 2003-Ohio-3957, appeal after new sentencing hearing 108 Ohio St.3d 57, 840 N.E.2d 1032, 2006-Ohio-160, reconsideration denied 108 Ohio St.3d 1513, 844 N.E.2d 857, 2006-Ohio-1329. Criminal Law ⚷ 1023(11)

The correction of an invalid sentence does not violate constitutional prohibitions against double jeopardy, and although the Home Rule Amendment permits municipalities to enforce police regulations within their limits, the trial courts of the state do not have the inherent power to suspend execution of a sentence in a criminal case and may order such suspension only as authorized by statute; therefore, where a city council has explicitly declared a fine for keeping a pit bull terrier to be "mandatory" and "nonsuspendable," this specific and unequivocal language supersedes the general authorization to modify sentencing requirements. Akron v. Smith (Summit 1992) 82 Ohio App.3d 57, 611 N.E.2d 435, dismissed, jurisdictional motion overruled 65 Ohio St.3d 1463, 602 N.E.2d 1171.

Although a trial court errs in vacating a mandatory sentence imposed under RC 4511.19 due to the unavailability of jail space until more than three years after the end of the probation period imposed for a drunk driving conviction, the state has no right of appeal of the vacation as the defendant alleged neither constitutional violations nor filed a postconviction relief action, but alleged a violation of RC 2951.09. State v. Medley (Seneca 1991) 75 Ohio App.3d 728, 600 N.E.2d 789.

The state is permitted to appeal a trial court's termination of probation without hearing and imposition of new probation. State v. Conti (Cuyahoga 1989) 57 Ohio App.3d 36, 565 N.E.2d 1286.

Trial court's error in finding defendant guilty of lesser included offenses upon his plea of no contest to charges in indictment could not be corrected; case involved felonies, when no-contest plea was offered and accepted defendant had subjected herself to jeopardy, which precluded any and all subsequent procedures addressing defendant's guilt or innocence, and thus remand for further procedures would violate constitutional provisions against double jeopardy. State v. Rader (Hamilton 1988) 55 Ohio App.3d 102, 563 N.E.2d 304. Double Jeopardy ⚷ 165

Trial court's correction of a statutorily incorrect sentence, which was void and to which jeopardy did not attach, did not violate defendant's right to be free from double jeopardy. State v. Beasley (Ohio 1984) 14 Ohio St.3d 74, 471 N.E.2d 774, 14 O.B.R. 511. Double Jeopardy ⚷ 114.1

15. Extraordinary writs in lieu of appeal

Mandamus will not lie to compel a court to impose a mandatory ten-day imprisonment on a defendant convicted of soliciting under a city ordinance. State ex rel. City of Cleveland v. Calandra (Ohio 1980) 62 Ohio St.2d 121, 403 N.E.2d 989, 16 O.O.3d 143.

The denial of a state motion for leave to appeal under RC 2945.67 by a court of appeals is appealable to the Supreme Court; thus, a writ of mandamus to compel the court of appeals to vacate an order of a court of common pleas must be denied. State ex rel. Corrigan v. Lawther (Ohio 1988) 39 Ohio St.3d 157, 529 N.E.2d 1377.

A writ of prohibition does not lie against a trial court which has ordered pretrial disclosure under Crim R 16 of potential witnesses' written statements; instead, appeal may be taken under RC 2945.67 even where no sanctions have yet been imposed for disobedience to the order. State ex rel. Lighttiser v. Spahr (Ohio 1985) 18 Ohio St.3d 234, 480 N.E.2d 779, 18 O.B.R. 292.

The availability of appeal of a discovery order by leave of court pursuant to RC 2945.67 is an adequate remedy at law for a prosecutor, which precludes a challenge of such order by the prosecutor by a writ of prohibition. State ex rel. Corrigan v. Griffin (Ohio 1984) 14 Ohio St.3d 26, 470 N.E.2d 894, 14 O.B.R. 328.

Where a municipal judge has disregarded the mandatory sentencing provisions of RC 4511.19, the city law director has standing to maintain an action in mandamus to compel compliance therewith, but may not maintain such action because of the appeal available through RC 2945.67. State ex rel. Zoller v. Talbert (Ohio 1980) 62 Ohio St.2d 329, 405 N.E.2d 724, 16 O.O.3d 391.

16. Interlocutory appeals

State had no basis for appeal as of right from trial court's order denying its motion to amend indictment charging defendant with aggravated murder to include capital specification charging defendant as principal offender, where order denying motion was not dismissal of all or any part of the indictment, but merely ruled on language contained in indictment, and did not involve any other statutory circumstances for appeal as of right. State v. Lomax (Ohio, 09-11-2002) 96 Ohio St.3d 318, 774 N.E.2d 249, 2002-Ohio-4453. Criminal Law ⚷ 1024(1)

Order granting defendant access to grand jury minutes was interlocutory order, was not entered in special proceeding, and could not be foundation of independent appeal; relief sought was made pursuant to ordinary motion filed in pending criminal action, defendant did not file special petition seeking remedy that was conferred upon him by statute, and proceeding did not represent independent judicial inquiry. State v. Myers (Ohio App. 2 Dist., 01-19-1994) 92 Ohio App.3d 750, 637 N.E.2d 92, motion overruled 69 Ohio St.3d 1452, 633 N.E.2d 545. Criminal Law ⚷ 1023(3)

Because of the procedural safeguards provided by certification, Crim R 12(J) allows for expedited appeals from evidentiary rulings during trial without impermissibly infringing upon a defendant's interest in an uninterrupted trial. State v. Malinovsky (Ohio 1991) 60 Ohio St.3d 20, 573 N.E.2d 22, on remand 81 Ohio App.3d 170, 610 N.E.2d 529, certiorari denied 112 S.Ct. 582, 502 U.S. 980, 116 L.Ed.2d 607.

17. Substantive review

Court of Appeals had jurisdiction over state's appeal, pursuant to statute allowing prosecuting attorney to appeal as a matter of right a trial court's substantive law rulings made in a criminal case which results in a judgment of acquittal, from decision of the trial court to permit the defendant to use grand jury testimony for purposes of cross-examination during felonious assault trial, where defendant was convicted of lesser included offense of felonious assault, and state did not challenge conviction itself. State v. Burroughs (Ohio App. 3 Dist., 12-05-2005) 165 Ohio App.3d 172, 845 N.E.2d 540, 2005-Ohio-6411, appeal not allowed 109 Ohio St.3d 1424, 846 N.E.2d 534, 2006-Ohio-1967. Criminal Law ⚿ 1024(1)

Court of Appeals' decision on substantive law ruling made by trial court which resulted in judgment of acquittal cannot disturb judgment. State v. Squires (Ohio App. 2 Dist., 01-24-1996) 108 Ohio App.3d 716, 671 N.E.2d 627. Criminal Law ⚿ 1024(5)

A court of appeals has discretionary authority pursuant to RC 2945.67(A) to review substantive law rulings made in a criminal case which result in a judgment of acquittal so long as the judgment itself is not appealed. State v. Bistricky (Ohio 1990) 51 Ohio St.3d 157, 555 N.E.2d 644, on remand 66 Ohio App.3d 395, 584 N.E.2d 75. Criminal Law ⚿ 1024(1); Criminal Law ⚿ 1134(6)

The purpose of the statute is not to obtain a reversal of the judgment, but to determine what the law is in fact. State v. Granville (Ohio 1887) 45 Ohio St. 264, 18 W.L.B. 86, 12 N.E. 803.

Where a trial court sua sponte suppresses evidence on the grounds that the police had no right to search a defendant's vehicle incident to a routine traffic stop and acquits the defendant who pled no contest to a charge of knowingly transporting a loaded firearm the reviewing court has discretion pursuant to RC 2945.67(A) to review substantive law issues, such as whether the evidence was properly suppressed, which result in a judgment of acquittal so long as the verdict itself is not appealed. State v Hamilton, No. 8–94–6, 1994 WL 581547 (3d Dist Ct App, Logan, 10–18–94).

2945.68 Application by prosecutor, solicitor, or attorney general to file bill of exceptions—Repealed

(1995 S 2, eff. 7–1–96; 1978 H 1168, eff. 11–1–78; 1977 H 219; 131 v H 231; 1953 H 1; GC 13446–2)

Historical and Statutory Notes

Publisher's Note: Although 1995 S 2, eff. 7–1–96, repealed 2945.68, this section was previously repealed by 1978 H 1168, eff. 11–1–78.

Pre–1953 H 1 Amendments: 113 v 192, Ch 25, § 2

2945.69 and 2945.70 Appointment of attorney by trial judge; decision of the court; appeal by the state—Repealed

(1978 H 1168, eff. 11–1–78; 1977 H 219; 1972 H 511; 131 v H 231; 1953 H 1; GC 13446–3, 13446–4)

Historical and Statutory Notes

Pre–1953 H 1 Amendments: 113 v 192, § 3; 113 v 193, § 4

SCHEDULE OF TRIAL AND HEARINGS

2945.71 Time within which hearing or trial must be held

(A) Subject to division (D) of this section, a person against whom a charge is pending in a court not of record, or against whom a charge of minor misdemeanor is pending in a court of record, shall be brought to trial within thirty days after the person's arrest or the service of summons.

(B) Subject to division (D) of this section, a person against whom a charge of misdemeanor, other than a minor misdemeanor, is pending in a court of record, shall be brought to trial as follows:

(1) Within forty-five days after the person's arrest or the service of summons, if the offense charged is a misdemeanor of the third or fourth degree, or other misdemeanor for which the maximum penalty is imprisonment for not more than sixty days;

(2) Within ninety days after the person's arrest or the service of summons, if the offense charged is a misdemeanor of the first or second degree, or other misdemeanor for which the maximum penalty is imprisonment for more than sixty days.

(C) A person against whom a charge of felony is pending:

(1) Notwithstanding any provisions to the contrary in Criminal Rule 5(B), shall be accorded a preliminary hearing within fifteen consecutive days after the person's arrest if the accused is not held in jail in lieu of bail on the pending charge or within ten consecutive days after the person's arrest if the accused is held in jail in lieu of bail on the pending charge;

(2) Shall be brought to trial within two hundred seventy days after the person's arrest.

(D) A person against whom one or more charges of different degrees, whether felonies, misdemeanors, or combinations of felonies and misdemeanors, all of which arose out of the same act or transaction, are pending shall be brought to trial on all of the charges within the time period required for the highest degree of offense charged, as determined under divisions (A), (B), and (C) of this section.

(E) For purposes of computing time under divisions (A), (B), (C)(2), and (D) of this section, each day during which the accused is held in jail in lieu of bail on the pending charge shall be counted as three days. This division does not apply for purposes of computing time under division (C)(1) of this section.

(F) This section shall not be construed to modify in any way section 2941.401 or sections 2963.30 to 2963.35 of the Revised Code.

(1999 S 49, eff. 10–29–99; 1981 S 119, eff. 3–17–82; 1980 S 288; 1975 S 83; 1973 H 716; 1972 H 511)

Uncodified Law

1981 S 119, § 3, eff. 3–17–82, reads: The provisions of Sections 1 and 2 of this act apply in relation to all persons who commit any felony offense on or after the effective date of this act and to all persons who commit any felony offense prior to the effective date of this act who are not arrested in relation to the offense until a time on or after the effective date of this act.

Historical and Statutory Notes

Ed. Note: Former 2945.71 repealed by 1972 H 511, eff. 1–1–74; 1953 H 1; GC 13447–1; see now 2945.73 for provisions analogous to former 2945.71.

Pre–1953 H 1 Amendments: 113 v 193, § 1

Amendment Note: 1999 S 49 inserted "Subject to division (D) of this section," in divisions (A) and (B); rewrote division (D); and made changes to reflect gender neutral language and other nonsubstantive changes. Prior to amendment, division (D) read:

"(D) A person against whom one or more charges of minor misdemeanor and one or more charges of misdemeanor other than minor misdemeanor, all of which arose out of the same act or transaction, are pending, or against whom charges of misdemeanors of different degrees, other than minor misdemeanors, all of which arose out of the same act or transaction, are pending shall be brought to trial within the time period required for the highest degree of misdemeanor charged, as determined under division (B) of this section."

Legislative Service Commission

1973:

This section requires preliminary hearings and trials to be held within the following times after arrest or the service of summons in criminal cases:

Type of Hearing or Trial	Time Limit Generally	Time Limit when accused Confined in lieu of Bail
Trials in mayors' or police courts (regardless of offense)	15 days	5 days
Trials for minor misdemeanors (regardless of court)	15 days	5 days
Trials for 3rd and 4th degree misdemeanors or misdemeanors for which maximum penalty does not exceed 60 days (regardless of court)	45 days	15 days
Trials for 1st and 2nd degree misdemeanors or misdemeanors for which maximum penalty exceeds 60 days (regardless of court)	90 days	30 days
Preliminary hearings in felony cases	15 days	5 days
Trials for felony	270 days	90 days

It is emphasized that in each of the cases above, the time limit when an accused is held in jail in lieu of bail on the pending charge is 1/3 the general time limit.

The time limits given in this section do not apply to the time limits applicable to the interstate agreement on detainers or to its complementary intrastate provision. See, sections 2941.401 and 2963.30 to 2963.35. Also, the time limits in this section may be extended as provided in section 2945.72.

Cross References

Classification of offenses, 2901.02

Court calendars; precedence of criminal cases, Crim R 50

Court not of record; mayor's court, Ch 1905

Criminal case time limits, Sup R 39

Dismissal, Crim R 48

First day excluded and last day included in computing time, 1.14

Right to speedy trial, O Const Art I §10

Standard time, official legal proceedings to be governed by, 1.04

Time, Crim R 45

Library References

Criminal Law ⚷577.1 to 577.16.

Westlaw Topic No. 110.

C.J.S. Criminal Law §§ 578 to 621.

Research References

Encyclopedias

7 Am. Jur. Proof of Facts 2d 477, Prejudice Resulting from Unreasonable Delay in Trial.

OH Jur. 3d Criminal Law § 396, Ohio Constitutional and Statutory Bases.

OH Jur. 3d Criminal Law § 399, Determination of Denial of Right; Necessity of Prejudice.

OH Jur. 3d Criminal Law § 403, Applicability to Defendant Imprisoned for Another Offense; Imprisonment in Ohio.

OH Jur. 3d Criminal Law § 409, Extension of Time for Hearing or Trial.

OH Jur. 3d Criminal Law § 411, Delay Attributable to Postponement of Trial.

OH Jur. 3d Criminal Law § 413, Delay Attributable to Mistrial.

OH Jur. 3d Criminal Law § 2063, Time for Hearing.

OH Jur. 3d Criminal Law § 2256, Generally; Applicability of Speedy Trial Provisions.

OH Jur. 3d Criminal Law § 2597, Continuances, Generally.

OH Jur. 3d Criminal Law § 2602, Lack of Time to Try Case.

OH Jur. 3d Criminal Law § 2829, Effect of Incarceration on Time Requirement.

OH Jur. 3d Criminal Law § 2830, Proceedings to Which Requirement is Applicable.

OH Jur. 3d Criminal Law § 2831, Waiver.

OH Jur. 3d Criminal Law § 2832, When Time Begins to Run.

OH Jur. 3d Criminal Law § 2833, When Time Begins to Run—Charges Against Juveniles.

OH Jur. 3d Criminal Law § 2834, Generally; Unavailability of Defendant.

OH Jur. 3d Criminal Law § 2835, Defendant's Physical Incapacity or Mental Incompetency, or Pendency of Proceedings to Determine Competency.

OH Jur. 3d Criminal Law § 2836, Defendant's Lack of Counsel.

OH Jur. 3d Criminal Law § 2839, Pretrial Appeal.

OH Jur. 3d Criminal Law § 2840, Retrials.

OH Jur. 3d Criminal Law § 2849, Effect of Dismissal.

OH Jur. 3d Criminal Law § 2853, Rules of Superintendence as to Prompt Trial.

OH Jur. 3d Criminal Law § 3547, Necessity and Sufficiency of Objection or Equivalent, Generally.

OH Jur. 3d Criminal Law § 3636, Unnecessary or Immaterial Matter; Moot Questions.

OH Jur. 3d Criminal Law § 3675, Continuance.

OH Jur. 3d Criminal Law § 2839.5, State's Response to Discovery.

OH Jur. 3d Habeas Corpus & Post Convict. Remedies § 16, Lack of or Defect in Preliminary Hearing.

Treatises and Practice Aids

Markus, Trial Handbook for Ohio Lawyers, § 4:6, Speedy Trial—Statutory Time Limits.

Markus, Trial Handbook for Ohio Lawyers, § 4:10, Speedy Trial—Statutory Time Limits—Procedures to Challenge Unlawful Delay.

Markus, Trial Handbook for Ohio Lawyers, § 4:13, Speedy Trial—Statutory Time Limits—Extension—by Defendant's Request.

Katz, Giannelli, Blair and Lipton, Baldwin's Ohio Practice, Criminal Law, § 36:5, Rule 5(A) Violations.

Katz, Giannelli, Blair and Lipton, Baldwin's Ohio Practice, Criminal Law, § 38:5, Time Limits.

Katz, Giannelli, Blair and Lipton, Baldwin's Ohio Practice, Criminal Law, § 38:6, Intervening Indictment.

Katz, Giannelli, Blair and Lipton, Baldwin's Ohio Practice, Criminal Law, § 60:2, Speedy Trial Statutes.

Katz, Giannelli, Blair and Lipton, Baldwin's Ohio Practice, Criminal Law, § 60:3, Constitutional Challenges to Statute.

Katz, Giannelli, Blair and Lipton, Baldwin's Ohio Practice, Criminal Law, § 60:4, Applicability of Statute.

Katz, Giannelli, Blair and Lipton, Baldwin's Ohio Practice, Criminal Law, § 60:5, Statutory Time Limits.

Katz, Giannelli, Blair and Lipton, Baldwin's Ohio Practice, Criminal Law, § 60:6, Time Limits—Felony and Misdemeanor Charges in the Same Indictment.

Katz, Giannelli, Blair and Lipton, Baldwin's Ohio Practice, Criminal Law, § 60:7, Counting Time.

Katz, Giannelli, Blair and Lipton, Baldwin's Ohio Practice, Criminal Law, § 60:8, Time Extensions—in General.

Katz, Giannelli, Blair and Lipton, Baldwin's Ohio Practice, Criminal Law, § 114:4, Indirect Contempt.

Katz, Giannelli, Blair and Lipton, Baldwin's Ohio Practice, Criminal Law, § 140:1, Waiver of Preliminary Hearing in Felony Case.

Katz, Giannelli, Blair and Lipton, Baldwin's Ohio Practice, Criminal Law, § 140:6, Motion for Extension of Time for Preliminary Hearing.

Katz, Giannelli, Blair and Lipton, Baldwin's Ohio Practice, Criminal Law, § 140:7, Time Limit Extension for Preliminary Hearing.

Katz, Giannelli, Blair and Lipton, Baldwin's Ohio Practice, Criminal Law, § 140:8, Time Limit Extension for Preliminary Hearing (Additional Form).

Katz, Giannelli, Blair and Lipton, Baldwin's Ohio Practice, Criminal Law, § 147:1, Motion to Dismiss Felony Charge for Delay of Preliminary Hearing.

Katz, Giannelli, Blair and Lipton, Baldwin's Ohio Practice, Criminal Law, § 147:2, Dismissal of Felony Charge for Delay of Preliminary Hearing.

Katz, Giannelli, Blair and Lipton, Baldwin's Ohio Practice, Criminal Law, § 147:3, Motion to Dismiss Felony Charge for Delay of Trial.

Katz, Giannelli, Blair and Lipton, Baldwin's Ohio Practice, Criminal Law, § 147:4, Dismissal of Felony Charge Delay in Trial.

Katz, Giannelli, Blair and Lipton, Baldwin's Ohio Practice, Criminal Law, § 147:5, Motion to Dismiss Misdemeanor Charge for Delay in Trial.

Katz, Giannelli, Blair and Lipton, Baldwin's Ohio Practice, Criminal Law, § 147:6, Dismissal of Misdemeanor Charge for Delay in Trial.

Katz, Giannelli, Blair and Lipton, Baldwin's Ohio Practice, Criminal Law, § 147:7, Waiver of Time for Preliminary Hearing or Trial.

Katz, Giannelli, Blair and Lipton, Baldwin's Ohio Practice, Criminal Law, § 59:14, Rules of Superintendence.

Katz, Giannelli, Blair and Lipton, Baldwin's Ohio Practice, Criminal Law, § 60:16, Extension—Continuances.

Katz, Giannelli, Blair and Lipton, Baldwin's Ohio Practice, Criminal Law, § 60:17, Extension—Change in Charge.

Katz, Giannelli, Blair and Lipton, Baldwin's Ohio Practice, Criminal Law, § 60:19, Remedies for Unexcused Delay.

Katz, Giannelli, Blair and Lipton, Baldwin's Ohio Practice, Criminal Law, § 60:20, Appellate Review.

Katz, Giannelli, Blair and Lipton, Baldwin's Ohio Practice, Criminal Law, § 60:21, Common Errors.

Carlin, Baldwin's Ohio Practice, Merrick-Rippner Probate Law § 108:9, Juvenile Court—Criminal Jurisdiction—Assignment of Case for Disposition.

Carlin, Baldwin's Ohio Practice, Merrick-Rippner Probate Law § 107:43, Scheduling Juvenile Court Hearing.

Carlin, Baldwin's Ohio Practice, Merrick-Rippner Probate Law § 107:70, Authority of Criminal Court Over Children.

Painter & Dennis, Ohio Appellate Practice § 10:34, Habeas Corpus-Nonavailability-Criminal Cases-Availability of Appeal.

Hennenberg & Reinhart, Ohio Criminal Defense Motions F 5.02, Waiver of Right to Speedy Trial and Request for Indefinite Continuance-Pretrial Motions.

Hennenberg & Reinhart, Ohio Criminal Defense Motions F 5.35, Motion to Quash the Venire-Pretrial Motions-Improperly Selected Venire.

Hennenberg & Reinhart, Ohio Criminal Defense Motions F 11.01, Motion for a Discharge for Delay in Trial (Right to Speedy Trial).

Adrine & Ruden, Ohio Domestic Violence Law § 4:2, Distinctions Between a Criminal Protection Order and a Civil Protection Order.

Painter, Ohio Driving Under the Influence § 2:7, Service of Citation.

Painter, Ohio Driving Under the Influence § 10:1, Motion to Dismiss—Grounds for Motion to Dismiss.

Painter, Ohio Driving Under the Influence § 10:4, Failure to State an Offense—Procedure for Motion.

Painter, Ohio Driving Under the Influence § 10:5, Speedy Trial—First Degree Misdemeanor Cases.

Giannelli & Yeomans, Ohio Juvenile Law § 15:3, Diversion, Youth Services Grant.

Giannelli & Yeomans, Ohio Juvenile Law § 23:29, Speedy Trial.

Law Review and Journal Commentaries

An Analysis of the Judicial Interpretation of the 1974 Ohio Speedy Trial Act: The First Five Years, Comment. 40 Ohio St L J 363 (1979).

Criminal Law—Speedy Trial—Criminal Procedure, Lawrence Friedlander. 47 Clev B J 185 (March 1976).

Criminal Procedure—Appeal and Error—The State Has No Right to Appeal a Trial Court's

Dismissal of Criminal Charges Pursuant to the Ohio Speedy Trial Act.—State v. Sonnie, Note. 45 U Cin L Rev 680 (1976).

The Right to a Speedy Trial: Ohio Follows The Trend, Note. 43 U Cin L Rev 610 (1974).

Speedy Trial—Misdemeanor, Richard Aynes. 47 Clev B J 124 (March 1976).

State v. Singer: The State Alone Guards The Speedy Trial Right, Note. 4 Ohio N U L Rev 692 (1977).

Notes of Decisions

---

1. Constitutional issues—In general

"Law of the case doctrine" prohibited further review of defendant's double jeopardy claim on appeal of his convictions for sexual battery and attempted sexual battery, which claim was based on his prior acquittal on charges of rape and attempted rape, where Court of Appeals court had previously considered and rejected same claim on its merits during prior appeal in case. State v. Morris (Ohio App. 2 Dist., Montgomery, 03-07-2003) No. 19283, 2003-Ohio-1049, 2003 WL 862656, Unreported. Criminal Law ⚷ 1180

Incarcerated defendant's constitutional right to a speedy trial was adequately protected by speedy trial statute. State v. Pesci (Ohio App. 11 Dist.,

Lake, 12-20-2002) No. 2001-L-026, 2002-Ohio-7131, 2002 WL 31866167, Unreported, appeal not allowed 98 Ohio St.3d 1566, 787 N.E.2d 1231, 2003-Ohio-2242. Criminal Law ⚷ 577.4

Sixth Amendment to the United States Constitution and the equivalent provision of the state constitution guarantee a criminal defendant the right to a speedy trial, with such right being implemented by the state statutory scheme imposing specific time limits. State v. Kerby (Ohio App. 2 Dist., 07-15-2005) 162 Ohio App.3d 353, 833 N.E.2d 757, 2005-Ohio-3734, appeal not allowed 107 Ohio St.3d 1682, 839 N.E.2d 403, 2005-Ohio-6480. Criminal Law ⚷ 577.4

Statutory speedy trial provisions are coextensive with speedy trial rights guaranteed by the United States and Ohio Constitutions. State v. Grinnell (Ohio App. 10 Dist., 06-27-1996) 112 Ohio App.3d 124, 678 N.E.2d 231, appeal not allowed 77 Ohio St.3d 1474, 673 N.E.2d 138, appeal not allowed 77 Ohio St.3d 1475, 673 N.E.2d 138, denial of habeas corpus affirmed 215 F.3d 1326, certiorari denied 121 S.Ct. 232, 531 U.S. 898, 148 L.Ed.2d 166. Criminal Law ⚷ 577.5

Statutory speedy trial provisions are coextensive with constitutional speedy trial provisions. State v. Mays (Ohio App. 8 Dist., 01-11-1996) 108 Ohio App.3d 598, 671 N.E.2d 553, dismissed, appeal not allowed 75 Ohio St.3d 1509, 665 N.E.2d 679. Criminal Law ⚷ 577.5

Continuance on charge of operating motor vehicle with certain concentration of alcohol in urine, due to defendant's motion to suppress, would not be excluded from speedy trial calculation for separate charge of operating motor vehicle while under influence of alcohol, which arose from same incident, as offenses were separate for double jeopardy purposes. State v. Jacot (Ohio App. 9 Dist., 04-07-1993) 97 Ohio App.3d 415, 646 N.E.2d 1128, motion allowed 68 Ohio St.3d 1409, 623 N.E.2d 566, appeal dismissed as improvidently allowed 71 Ohio St.3d 1217, 644 N.E.2d 1383. Criminal Law ⚷ 577.10(5); Criminal Law ⚷ 577.10(8)

Insofar as the constitutional right, as distinguished from the statutory right, to a speedy trial is concerned, affirmative action on the part of the accused in the nature of a demand to be tried is necessary to invoke the constitutional protection. State v. Gettys (Seneca 1976) 49 Ohio App.2d 241, 360 N.E.2d 735, 3 O.O.3d 286. Criminal Law ⚷ 577.10(10)

2. —— Due process or equal protection, constitutional issues

Consistent with the Equal Protection Clause of US Const Am 14, persons who committed an offense prior to January 1, 1974, and were indicted and held in jail in lieu of bail on a felony charge after that date must be tried within two terms after the term of the indictment, or within ninety days of January 1, 1974, whichever is earlier. State v. Perkins (Cuyahoga 1974) 40 Ohio App.2d 406, 320 N.E.2d 698, 69 O.O.2d 365. Criminal Law ⚷ 577.15(5)

Where Ohio courts have determined that delay in the commencement of a criminal trial caused by the attempts of television stations to obtain an order allowing televising of the trial does not violate rights secured by the Ohio speedy trial statute, the criminal defendant cannot seek federal habeas corpus relief on grounds of denial of equal protection or deprivation of liberty without due process of law. Hutchison v. Marshall (C.A.6 (Ohio) 1984) 744 F.2d 44, certiorari denied 105 S.Ct. 1208, 469 U.S. 1221, 84 L.Ed.2d 350.

3. —— Effective assistance of counsel, constitutional issues

Trial counsel's failure to pursue a statutory speedy trial claim did not fall below an objective standard of reasonableness, and therefore did not constitute ineffective assistance, even though defendant was not brought to trial within 270 days after his arrest; a month after his arrest defendant was sentenced to serve two years on a federal charge, and while serving that sentence defendant was unavailable for trial. State v. Jordan (Ohio App. 5 Dist., Muskingum, 11-09-2005) No. CT2003-0029, 2005-Ohio-6064, 2005 WL 3047527, Unreported, appeal not allowed 108 Ohio St.3d 1511, 844 N.E.2d 856, 2006-Ohio-1329. Criminal Law ⚷ 641.13(2.1)

Delay of 62 days on three-to-one basis under triple count provision, for total of 186 days between arrest for aggravated robbery and trial, did not violate defendant's right to speedy trial, and thus, counsel's failure to move to dismiss charge on speedy trial grounds did not constitute ineffective assistance. State v. Knight (Ohio App. 2 Dist., Greene, 06-24-2005) No. 03-CA-014, 2005-Ohio-3179, 2005 WL 1490364, Unreported. Criminal Law ⚷ 577.8(1); Criminal Law ⚷ 577.15(3); Criminal Law ⚷ 641.13(2.1)

Delay of 121 days, which under triple count provision totaled 363 days, plus two days counted on one-to-one basis, for total of 365 days between arrest for aggravated robbery, which delay was mostly attributable to State, violated defendant's right to speedy trial, and thus, counsel's failure to file motion to dismiss constituted deficient performance that prejudiced defendant, as required to support claim for ineffective assistance of counsel. State v. Knight (Ohio App. 2 Dist., Greene, 06-24-2005) No. 03-CA-014, 2005-Ohio-3179, 2005 WL 1490364, Unreported. Criminal Law ⚷ 577.8(1); Criminal Law ⚷ 577.12(1); Criminal Law ⚷ 577.15(3); Criminal Law ⚷ 641.13(2.1)

Defendant was not prejudiced by defense counsel's failure to move to dismiss charges based on trial court's failure to provide him with preliminary hearing on charges, and thus defendant was not denied effective assistance of counsel in prosecution for failure to comply with order or signal of police officer, reckless operation of motor vehicle, and speeding; earliest time that motion could have been filed was one day before defendant was indicted, and thus it did not appear reasonably likely that motion, after providing time for a response, would have been ruled on before filing of indictment.

State v. Leach (Ohio App. 9 Dist., Summit, 05-25-2005) No. 22369, 2005-Ohio-2569, 2005 WL 1225755, Unreported, appeal not allowed 106 Ohio St.3d 1547, 835 N.E.2d 728, 2005-Ohio-5343. Criminal Law ⚷ 641.13(2.1)

Defense counsel's failure to file motion to dismiss theft charge based upon alleged speedy trial violation was not ineffective assistance of counsel, since delay in bringing defendant to trial was due to newly-appointed counsel's unavailability for a pretrial, and delay was not presumptively prejudicial, with trial occurring within one year of his arrest. State v. Ross (Ohio App. 4 Dist., Ross, 04-15-2005) No. 04CA2780, 2005-Ohio-1888, 2005 WL 928531, Unreported. Criminal Law ⚷ 641.13(2.1)

Defendant was not entitled to reopening of direct appeal from convictions for murder on grounds that appellate counsel was ineffective for failing to argue that his case should have been dismissed due to speedy trial violation, since defendant waived speedy trial issue when he pleaded guilty following remand for retrial. State v. Carley (Ohio App. 8 Dist., Cuyahoga, 10-08-2004) No. 81001, 2004-Ohio-5479, 2004 WL 2335805, Unreported, appeal not allowed 104 Ohio St.3d 1463, 821 N.E.2d 578, 2005-Ohio-204. Criminal Law ⚷ 1133

Defense counsel's failure to pursue speedy trial issues was reasonable trial strategy, during murder prosecution, and therefore was not ineffective assistance; defendant's speedy trial argument lacked merit. State v. Parker (Ohio App. 8 Dist., Cuyahoga, 06-10-2004) No. 82687, 2004-Ohio-2976, 2004 WL 1277243, Unreported, appeal not allowed 103 Ohio St.3d 1493, 816 N.E.2d 1080, 2004-Ohio-5605. Criminal Law ⚷ 641.13(2.1)

Defense counsel's failure to file motion to dismiss all charges against defendant based upon supposed violation of his speedy trial rights was not ineffective assistance of counsel, at trial in which defendant was convicted of complicity to commit aggravated murder and kidnapping; language contained in defendant's written waiver of his speedy trial rights did not contain limiting language as to period in which trial was to commence, and waiver was therefore unlimited in duration, and defendant never reinvoked his speedy trial rights, but rather filed three motions for continuances. State v. Green (Ohio App. 7 Dist., Mahoning, 06-13-2003) No. 01 CA 54, 2003-Ohio-3074, 2003 WL 21373172, Unreported, motion for delayed appeal granted 100 Ohio St.3d 1407, 796 N.E.2d 535, 2003-Ohio-4948, dismissal of post-conviction relief affirmed 2003-Ohio-5142, 2003 WL 22231592, motion to reopen denied 2003-Ohio-5442, 2003 WL 22332000, appeal not allowed 100 Ohio St.3d 1544, 800 N.E.2d 750, 2003-Ohio-6879, denial of post-conviction relief reversed 2006-Ohio-3097, 2006 WL 1680044. Criminal Law ⚷ 641.13(2.1)

Defendant was not denied his right to counsel when, after trial court dismissed defendant's original counsel based on improper conduct toward prosecutor, court obtained defendant's waiver of speedy trial rights in order to enable defendant to hire new attorney; court went to great lengths to confer with defendant and explain reasons for removal of original counsel, it appointed county public defender's office to represent defendant, and defendant subsequently obtained new counsel. State v. Madhobe (Ohio App. 5 Dist., Stark, 04-07-2003) No. 2002CA00230, 2003-Ohio-1793, 2003 WL 1818928, Unreported. Criminal Law ⚷ 641.10(2)

Statute requiring that an accused incarcerated on pending charge be tried within 90 days did not apply to defendant who was in custody pending resolution of unrelated criminal charges, and thus, trial counsel's failure to raise alleged speedy trial violation did not constitute deficient performance as required to support claim of ineffective assistance of counsel, in trial for felonious assault and improper discharge of firearm into occupied structure. State v. Dubose (Ohio App. 7 Dist., Mahoning, 11-26-2002) No. 00-C.A.-60, 2002-Ohio-6613, 2002 WL 31718806, Unreported, appeal not allowed 98 Ohio St.3d 1475, 784 N.E.2d 708, 2003-Ohio-904. Criminal Law ⚷ 577.6

Defendant could not demonstrate that his counsel was ineffective for failing to move to dismiss charges against him for failure to provide him with a speedy trial because appellate court, on the record before it, could not determine when the speedy trial time began to run. State v. Thompson (Ohio App. 8 Dist., Cuyahoga, 10-31-2002) No. 79334, 2002-Ohio-5957, 2002 WL 31426356, Unreported, dismissal of post-conviction relief affirmed 2002-Ohio-6845, 2002 WL 31771437, appeal not allowed 100 Ohio St.3d 1506, 799 N.E.2d 186, 2003-Ohio-6161, appeal not allowed 98 Ohio St.3d 1512, 786 N.E.2d 62, 2003-Ohio-1572, reconsideration denied 99 Ohio St.3d 1414, 788 N.E.2d 649, 2003-Ohio-2454, motion to reopen denied 2003-Ohio-4336, 2003 WL 21954760, as amended nunc pro tunc, appeal not allowed 100 Ohio St.3d 1509, 799 N.E.2d 187, 2003-Ohio-6161. Criminal Law ⚷ 1119(1)

4. Construction with other laws

The ten-day period of limitations in Juv R 29(A) is procedural only and such rule confers no substantive right upon an accused to have his case dismissed if he is not tried within the designated time. In re Therklidsen (Franklin 1977) 54 Ohio App.2d 195, 376 N.E.2d 970, 8 O.O.3d 335.

RC 2945.71 is a constitutional enactment which prescribes the time within which criminal cases must be brought to trial and Sup R 8(B) does not conflict with such statute, but rather complements its functions and works in harmony therewith. State v. Smith (Cuyahoga 1976) 47 Ohio App.2d 317, 354 N.E.2d 699, 1 O.O.3d 385. Criminal Law ⚷ 573

Since RC 2945.71 to RC 2945.73 confer substantive rights upon an accused, they take precedence over procedural or superintendent rules of the Ohio Supreme Court, including Sup R 8(B). State v. Westbrook (Franklin 1975) 47 Ohio App.2d 211, 353 N.E.2d 637, 1 O.O.3d 284.

O Const Art IV, § 5, paragraph (A)(1) is independent of paragraph (B) of such section, and the Ohio Supreme Court Rules of Superintendence do not invalidate any existing statute. State v. Lacy (Belmont 1975) 46 Ohio App.2d 215, 348 N.E.2d 381, 75 O.O.2d 376.

Where a petitioner brings an action seeking federal habeas corpus relief alleging a federal constitutional question or federal law violation, such claim precludes any contention that the state violated its own Speedy Trial Act. Hutchinson v. Casey (S.D.Ohio 1981) 507 F.Supp. 521. Habeas Corpus ⚷ 479

When a defendant is incarcerated on other charges, statute governing requests by a prisoner for trial on pending charges prevails over the general speedy trial statutes, governing the time within which the defendant must be brought to trial. State v. Cox (Ohio App. 4 Dist., Jackson, 05-14-2002) No. 01CA10, 2002-Ohio-2382, 2002 WL 1083897, Unreported. Criminal Law ⚷ 577.11(3)

An appeal from a finding of guilty by a mayor's court to a county or municipal court pursuant to RC 1905.22, is governed by the speedy trial statute, RC 2945.71, and a delay in excess of forty-five days from the date of docketing is prima facie unreasonable. Bethel v Fiscus, Nos. CA89–05–037 and CA89–05–038 (12th Dist Ct App, Clermont, 12–26–89).

5. Strict construction

Speedy trial statutes are to be strictly construed against state. State v. Miller (Ohio App. 11 Dist., 08-19-1996) 113 Ohio App.3d 606, 681 N.E.2d 970. Criminal Law ⚷ 577.5

Ohio speedy trial statute is constitutional and mandatory and must be strictly construed against state. State v. Wirtanen (Ohio App. 6 Dist., 04-26-1996) 110 Ohio App.3d 604, 674 N.E.2d 1245. Criminal Law ⚷ 577.2; Criminal Law ⚷ 577.5

Ohio speedy trial statute is constitutional, mandatory, and must be strictly construed against state. State v. Mays (Ohio App. 8 Dist., 01-11-1996) 108 Ohio App.3d 598, 671 N.E.2d 553, dismissed, appeal not allowed 75 Ohio St.3d 1509, 665 N.E.2d 679. Criminal Law ⚷ 577.2; Criminal Law ⚷ 577.4

Availability of speedy trial is fundamental and must be strictly enforced by courts. State v. Clark (Ohio App. 2 Dist., 10-27-1995) 107 Ohio App.3d 141, 667 N.E.2d 1262. Criminal Law ⚷ 577.3

Person arrested on first-degree misdemeanor charge generally must be brought to trial within 90 days following arrest, and courts are to strictly enforce speedy trial provision. State v. Jacot (Ohio App. 9 Dist., 04-07-1993) 97 Ohio App.3d 415, 646 N.E.2d 1128, motion allowed 68 Ohio St.3d 1409, 623 N.E.2d 566, appeal dismissed as improvidently allowed 71 Ohio St.3d 1217, 644 N.E.2d 1383. Criminal Law ⚷ 577.5

Under Ohio's speedy trial requirements, which are mandatory and require strict adherence, a person accused of a minor misdemeanor must be brought to trial within thirty days from the date of arrest or service of summons. Boston Hts. v. Weikle (Summit 1991) 81 Ohio App.3d 165, 610 N.E.2d 526.

The statutory speedy trial provisions, RC 2945.71 et seq., constitute a rational effort to enforce the constitutional right to a public speedy trial of an accused charged with the commission of a felony or a misdemeanor and shall be strictly enforced by the courts of this state. State v. Pachay (Ohio 1980) 64 Ohio St.2d 218, 416 N.E.2d 589, 18 O.O.3d 427. Criminal Law ⚷ 577.5

6. Purpose

Purpose of speedy-trial statute is to prevent inexcusable delays caused by indolence within the judicial system. State v. Sanchez (Ohio App. 6 Dist., 04-29-2005) 162 Ohio App.3d 113, 832 N.E.2d 1215, 2005-Ohio-2093, reversed 2009 WL 676, appeal allowed 106 Ohio St.3d 1532, 835 N.E.2d 381, 2005-Ohio-5146. Criminal Law ⚷ 577.5

Speedy trial guarantee is important safeguard to prevent undue and oppressive incarceration prior to trial, to minimize anxiety and concern accompanying public accusation and to limit possibilities that long delay will impair ability of accused to defend himself. State v. Clark (Ohio App. 2 Dist., 10-27-1995) 107 Ohio App.3d 141, 667 N.E.2d 1262. Criminal Law ⚷ 577.5

7. Retroactive effect

RC 2945.71 through RC 2945.73, enacted by 1972 H 511, eff. 1–1–74, are not applied retroactively; computation of the time limit derived from these sections is from January 1, 1974, for actions then pending, rather than from the actual earlier date of arrest. State v. MacDonald (Ohio 1976) 48 Ohio St.2d 66, 357 N.E.2d 40, 2 O.O.3d 219.

RC 2945.71 to RC 2945.73, effective on and after January 1, 1974, do not have retroactive application. State v. Walker (Ohio 1976) 46 Ohio St.2d 157, 346 N.E.2d 687, 75 O.O.2d 201.

The time limitations of RC 2945.71 to RC 2945.73, enacted by 1972 H 511, eff. 1–1–74, are to be computed from January 1, 1974, rather than from the actual earlier date of arrest, with respect to criminal prosecutions pending on January 1, 1974. City of Columbus v. Vest (Franklin 1974) 42 Ohio App.2d 83, 330 N.E.2d 726, 71 O.O.2d 520. Criminal Law ⚷ 577.2

RC 2945.71 to RC 2945.73, enacted by 1972 H 511, eff. 1–1–74, apply to criminal prosecutions pending on that date, the arrests for which were made prior to such date. City of Columbus v. Vest (Franklin 1974) 42 Ohio App.2d 83, 330 N.E.2d 726, 71 O.O.2d 520.

RC 2945.71, RC 2945.72 and RC 2945.73, enacted by 1972 H 511, eff. 1–1–74, are not applicable to arrests made prior to January 1, 1974. City of Reynoldsburg v. Wesley (Ohio Mun. 1974) 39 Ohio Misc. 166, 316 N.E.2d 926.

8. Mandatory nature of section

Speedy-trial statutes are mandatory and strictly enforced. State v. Sanchez (Ohio App. 6 Dist., 04-29-2005) 162 Ohio App.3d 113, 832 N.E.2d 1215, 2005-Ohio-2093, reversed 2009 WL 676, appeal allowed 106 Ohio St.3d 1532, 835 N.E.2d 381, 2005-Ohio-5146. Criminal Law ⚿ 577.5

9. Held in jail

RC 2945.71(D) is applicable only to those defendants held in jail in lieu of bail solely on the pending charge. State v. MacDonald (Ohio 1976) 48 Ohio St.2d 66, 357 N.E.2d 40, 2 O.O.3d 219; State v. Kaiser (Ohio 1978) 56 Ohio St.2d 29, 381 N.E.2d 633, 10 O.O.3d 75; State v. Ladd (Ohio 1978) 56 Ohio St.2d 197, 383 N.E.2d 579, 10 O.O.3d 363, certiorari denied 99 S.Ct. 2038, 441 U.S. 926, 60 L.Ed.2d 400.

If court chooses to continue bond for defendant pending sentence for one conviction, even while awaiting trial on remaining charges, accused who remains in jail is still being held "in lieu of bail" for speedy trial computation purposes. State v. Collins (Ohio App. 6 Dist., 09-30-1993) 91 Ohio App.3d 10, 631 N.E.2d 666, dismissed, jurisdictional motion overruled 68 Ohio St.3d 1470, 628 N.E.2d 1389. Criminal Law ⚿ 577.11(3)

After defendant pled guilty to one count of indictment, defendant's days in jail in lieu of bond, for purposes of computing speedy trial time as to remaining counts, continued until date he was sentenced and committed to prison for count to which he pled guilty, where trial court continued bail between conviction and date of sentencing. State v. Collins (Ohio App. 6 Dist., 09-30-1993) 91 Ohio App.3d 10, 631 N.E.2d 666, dismissed, jurisdictional motion overruled 68 Ohio St.3d 1470, 628 N.E.2d 1389. Criminal Law ⚿ 577.8(1)

If a defendant is held in jail or released on bail pursuant to Crim R 12(I), such time in jail or on bail must be included in the computation of time for speedy trial. State v. Stephens (Cuyahoga 1977) 52 Ohio App.2d 361, 370 N.E.2d 759, 6 O.O.3d 404.

10. Evidentiary hearing

Trial court was not required to conduct evidentiary hearing on motion to dismiss on speedy trial grounds, where trial court was able to determine speedy trial issue from record. State v. Freeman (Ohio App. 8 Dist., Cuyahoga, 07-07-2005) No. 85137, 2005-Ohio-3480, 2005 WL 1581105, Unreported, motion for delayed appeal granted 107 Ohio St.3d 1404, 836 N.E.2d 1226, 2005-Ohio-5859. Criminal Law ⚿ 577.16(10)

11. Burden of proof

Defendant presented a prima facie case for discharge of felony driving while under the influence of alcohol (DUI) charge based upon a violation of speedy trial limitations, and thus, burden shifted to State to demonstrate that limitations had not expired, where defendant alleged in his motion to dismiss that State held him solely on pending charge and that more than 270 days elapsed since his arrest. State v. Eldridge (Ohio App. 4 Dist., Scioto, 03-10-2003) No. 02CA2842, 2003-Ohio-1198, 2003 WL 1145442, Unreported. Criminal Law ⚿ 577.16(8)

Once defendant has established prima facie case that he was denied his right to speedy trial, burden of production of evidence shifts to state to prove that sufficient time was extended under speedy trial statute within which to bring defendant to trial. State v. Price (Ohio App. 10 Dist., 07-31-1997) 122 Ohio App.3d 65, 701 N.E.2d 41, dismissed, appeal not allowed 80 Ohio St.3d 1466, 687 N.E.2d 295. Criminal Law ⚿ 577.16(8)

Defendant set forth a prima facie case that his right to speedy trial on first-degree misdemeanor charge was violated by asserting that more than 90 days had passed between his initial arrest and trial; burden then shifted to state to show what time was tolled during that period so as to extend speedy trial time limitation. N. Olmsted v. Cipiti (Ohio App. 8 Dist., 09-09-1996) 114 Ohio App.3d 549, 683 N.E.2d 795, dismissed, appeal not allowed 77 Ohio St.3d 1518, 674 N.E.2d 372. Criminal Law ⚿ 577.16(8)

12. Presumption of prejudice

Delay of 153 days between arrest for robbery and filing of motion to dismiss for speedy trial violation demonstrated prima facie violation of right to speedy trial within 90 days. State v. Waits (Ohio App. 3 Dist., Marion, 02-22-2005) No. 9-04-50, 2005-Ohio-672, 2005 WL 405717, Unreported. Criminal Law ⚿ 577.15(3)

Sixteen-month delay was sufficiently long to be "presumptively prejudicial," thus triggering *Barker* inquiry to determine whether the post-indictment delay violated defendant's right to a speedy trial. State v. Smith (Ohio App. 8 Dist., Cuyahoga, 07-03-2003) No. 81808, 2003-Ohio-3524, 2003 WL 21512796, Unreported. Criminal Law ⚿ 577.16(8)

Delay in bringing defendant to trial on charges of rape, and improperly discharging firearm at, or into, habitation, was not presumptively prejudicial, where defendant's withdrawal of his waiver of speedy trial right meant state was required to bring defendant to trial within reasonable amount of time of defendant's written demand for trial and, while defendant did not make written demand, he was brought to trial eight months after his arrest, and less than six months after he withdrew his waiver of right to speedy trial, with most delays in bringing defendant to trial being attributable to defendant. State v. Boles (Ohio App. 2 Dist., Montgomery, 05-23-2003) No. 18762, 2003-Ohio-2693, 2003 WL 21213383, Unreported, appeal not allowed 100 Ohio St.3d 1411, 796 N.E.2d 538, 2003-Ohio-4948. Criminal Law ⚿ 577.10(10); Criminal Law ⚿ 577.16(4); Criminal Law ⚿ 577.16(8)

Defendant presented prima facie case of a violation of his speedy trial rights, where defendant was not brought to trial until after expiration of what would ordinarily be the 270-day speedy trial period as calculated by counting each day he was held in jail in lieu of bail following his arrest as three days. State v. Curtis (Ohio App. 3 Dist., Marion, 10-08-2002) No. 9-02-11, 2002-Ohio-5409, 2002 WL 31250286, Unreported, appeal not allowed 98 Ohio St.3d 1478, 784 N.E.2d 711, 2003-Ohio-974. Criminal Law ⚿ 577.15(3)

Defendant was denied his right to speedy trial where he presented prima facie case that he was not brought to trial within limits imposed by triple-count provision of speedy trial statute, and state failed to produce any evidence to rebut defendant's prima facie case. State v. Price (Ohio App. 10 Dist., 07-31-1997) 122 Ohio App.3d 65, 701 N.E.2d 41, dismissed, appeal not allowed 80 Ohio St.3d 1466, 687 N.E.2d 295. Criminal Law ⚷ 577.16(9)

Defendant is not required to show that he was prejudiced by delay beyond time limits provided in speedy trial statute. State v. Clark (Ohio App. 2 Dist., 10-27-1995) 107 Ohio App.3d 141, 667 N.E.2d 1262. Criminal Law ⚷ 577.16(4)

13. Felonies and misdemeanors

Where a single indictment contains felony and misdemeanor counts, the shorter statutory speedy trial provisions governing misdemeanors must be applied to the misdemeanor counts, rather than the longer, 270–day provision applicable to felonies. State v. Hughes (Ohio, 09-15-1999) 86 Ohio St.3d 424, 715 N.E.2d 540, 1999-Ohio-118. Criminal Law ⚷ 577.10(5)

Days between date on which misdemeanor charges against defendant for driving while under the influence (DUI) and for having passenger on outside of vehicle were dismissed and date on which grand jury returned no bill on felony vehicular homicide charge against defendant, during which defendant was bound over to grand jury on felony charge, were chargeable to state for constitutional speedy trial purposes under statutory 90–day trial deadline for misdemeanor charges, in proceeding in which misdemeanor charges were subsequently refiled, where all three charged offenses arose out of same event. City of Oregon v. Kohne (Ohio App. 6 Dist., 01-10-1997) 117 Ohio App.3d 179, 690 N.E.2d 66. Criminal Law ⚷ 577.12(1)

Financial institution's conviction for wrongful conveyance under statute prohibiting wrongful or culpable withholding or concealing of estate assets could not be characterized as misdemeanor or felony and, therefore, institution could not prove violation of either constitutional or statutory right to speedy trial. In re Estate of Popp (Ohio App. 8 Dist., 04-18-1994) 94 Ohio App.3d 640, 641 N.E.2d 739, dismissed 70 Ohio St.3d 1446, 639 N.E.2d 114, certiorari denied 115 S.Ct. 1256, 513 U.S. 1192, 131 L.Ed.2d 136. Action ⚷ 18

Village public affairs board president's speedy trial right was not violated by state's failure to try president on second-degree misdemeanor charge of dereliction of duty within 90 days of charging her with third-degree felony of theft in office; state had 270 days from indictment on felony count to bring president to trial on both counts. State v. Metheney (Medina 1993) 87 Ohio App.3d 562, 622 N.E.2d 730, motion overruled 67 Ohio St.3d 1471, 619 N.E.2d 1028. Criminal Law ⚷ 577.10(5)

If person is held on both misdemeanor and felony charges, time period for speedy trial which applies to felony charge is also applicable to misdemeanor charge. State v. Metheney (Medina 1993) 87 Ohio App.3d 562, 622 N.E.2d 730, motion overruled 67 Ohio St.3d 1471, 619 N.E.2d 1028. Criminal Law ⚷ 577.10(5)

Even though the ninety-day speedy trial limit for misdemeanors must still apply when a defendant is also charged in the same proceeding with a felony that has a 270–day speedy trial limit, a defendant convicted of driving while under the influence of drugs, a misdemeanor, and aggravated vehicular homicide, a felony, is not denied her right to a speedy trial on the misdemeanor charge when there were only sixty-six counted days between the arrest and a plea of no contest. State v. Walton (Cuyahoga 1991) 77 Ohio App.3d 706, 603 N.E.2d 294.

When both felony and misdemeanor charges are pending against a person, the state must bring the person to trial on the misdemeanor charges within ninety days, even though it has two hundred seventy days to bring the felony charges. State v. Doane (Trumbull 1990) 69 Ohio App.3d 638, 591 N.E.2d 735, dismissed, jurisdictional motion overruled 58 Ohio St.3d 701, 569 N.E.2d 504.

The statutory time limitations respecting a misdemeanor shall apply, subject to the requirement that the time for trial shall not exceed the statutory period which would have applied to an original felony charge, where: (1) a felony complaint is filed, (2) the accused is bound over to a grand jury, and (3) an indictment charging only a misdemeanor is returned. State v. Cattee (Scioto 1983) 14 Ohio App.3d 239, 470 N.E.2d 421, 14 O.B.R. 268.

When a defendant is arrested on a felony complaint, which is subsequently reduced to a misdemeanor by the action of a grand jury, the applicable time period for the misdemeanor charge under the Ohio Speedy Trial Act, RC 2945.71(B), runs from the date of arrest or service of summons on the misdemeanor charge and not from the date of the original arrest on the felony complaint. State v. Sauers (Ohio Mun. 1977) 52 Ohio Misc. 19, 368 N.E.2d 342, 6 O.O.3d 104, affirmed 52 Ohio App.2d 113, 368 N.E.2d 334, 6 O.O.3d 87. Criminal Law ⚷ 577.8(2)

The ninety-day time limit applicable to first degree misdemeanors commences with the filing of a judgment entry reducing a felony theft charge to a misdemeanor theft charge. State v Branham, No. 11–85–9 (3d Dist Ct App, Paulding, 10–8–87).

A misdemeanor must be brought to trial within ninety days of arrest regardless of the existence of additional felony offenses in the same indictment. State v Walton, No. 59165 (8th Dist Ct App, Cuyahoga, 10–3–91).

Where an indictment returns multiple counts of felonies and misdemeanors, the misdemeanors shall be brought to trial within ninety days. State v Leadingham, No. 1749 (4th Dist Ct App, Scioto, 6–1–89).

14. Juvenile or delinquency proceedings

Juvenile proceedings involving juvenile traffic offenders are not criminal proceedings and do not try the alleged juvenile offender for any crime, either misdemeanor or felony; thus, RC 2945.71 to 2945.73 does not apply to juvenile traffic offense proceedings. In re Washburn (Wyandot 1990) 70 Ohio App.3d 178, 590 N.E.2d 855.

The speedy trial provisions of RC 2945.71(C) do not apply to delinquency proceedings. In re Corcoran (Geauga 1990) 68 Ohio App.3d 213, 587 N.E.2d 957, dismissed 56 Ohio St.3d 702, 564 N.E.2d 703. Infants ⚷ 204

The ninety-day time requirement of RC 2945.71 applies only from the time that the juvenile court relinquishes jurisdiction and transfers the defendant to be tried as an adult, which relinquishment does not occur until a journal entry determining to transfer the defendant to the general division for trial as an adult is filed in the juvenile court. State v. Steele (Franklin 1982) 8 Ohio App.3d 137, 456 N.E.2d 513, 8 O.B.R. 194.

The statutory speedy trial provisions of RC 2945.71 et seq. do not apply to juvenile traffic offenders. State v. Reed (Coshocton 1977) 54 Ohio App.2d 193, 376 N.E.2d 609, 8 O.O.3d 333. Infants ⚷ 204

If a juvenile is accused of committing a felony, the ninety-day period established by RC 2945.71(C)(2) and RC 2945.71(D) for commencing trial does not begin to run until the juvenile court relinquishes jurisdiction and transfers the accused to the "adult" court. State ex rel. Williams v. Court of Common Pleas of Lucas County (Ohio 1975) 42 Ohio St.2d 433, 329 N.E.2d 680, 71 O.O.2d 410.

15. Municipal ordinances

Forty-five day speedy trial period applicable to fourth degree misdemeanor charges applied to charges that property owner violated zoning ordinance and flood damage prevention ordinance, rather than 30 day speedy trial period applicable to minor misdemeanor charges; although violations of zoning ordinance were minor misdemeanors, applicable speedy trial limits are those for time limit required with respect to highest degree of offense, and violations of flood damage prevention ordinance were fourth degree misdemeanors. Village of Versailles v. Poly (Ohio App. 2 Dist., Darke, 03-26-2004) No. 1627, 2004-Ohio-1485, 2004 WL 596079, Unreported. Criminal Law ⚷ 577.6

Speedy trial rights are violated where a motorist is charged with violating municipal ordinances regarding speeding and failing to wear a seat belt and (1) is not tried in mayor's court within the thirty-day statutory period, (2) the case is not transferred to the municipal court within the time requirement, (3) the record does not reflect any continuance or other disposition, and (4) a waiver of speedy trial time is not executed by the accused. City of Brooklyn v. Blake (Ohio App. 8 Dist., Cuyahoga, 10-08-1998) No. 73354, 1998 WL 703262, Unreported.

Defendant who was charged with speeding under city ordinance was not entitled to trial within 30 days of citation, though the offense as defined by state law was minor misdemeanor requiring trial within 30 days; under city ordinance, which was found to be constitutional, the offense was a fourth degree misdemeanor, for which state law required trial within 45 days of arrest or summons. Cleveland Hts. v. Wood (Ohio App. 8 Dist., 12-04-1995) 107 Ohio App.3d 616, 669 N.E.2d 281. Criminal Law ⚷ 577.6

16. Extradition proceedings

Ohio's speedy trial statutes do not apply to extradition proceedings. State v. Hirsch (Ohio App. 1 Dist., 08-07-1998) 129 Ohio App.3d 294, 717 N.E.2d 789, dismissed, appeal not allowed 84 Ohio St.3d 1436, 702 N.E.2d 1213, denial of habeas corpus affirmed 74 Fed.Appx. 486, 2003 WL 21949184. Criminal Law ⚷ 577.11(1)

Trial court did not abuse its discretion in finding that county prosecutor did not actually receive Interstate Agreement on Detainers (IAD) speedy trial request that was misdelivered to city attorney's office, although customary mail-handling practices of city attorney's office made it likely that request was actually delivered to county prosecutor; testimony of employee who processed IAD requests for county prosecutor, of supervisor of front desk of city attorney's office, and of receptionist who signed for delivery at city attorney's office was competent, credible evidence that county prosecutor did not actually receive IAD request. State v. Wells (Ohio App. 10 Dist., 04-04-1996) 110 Ohio App.3d 275, 673 N.E.2d 1008, dismissed, appeal not allowed 77 Ohio St.3d 1413, 670 N.E.2d 1002. Evidence ⚷ 111; Extradition And Detainers ⚷ 59

Under the interstate agreement on detainers, RC 2963.30, a defendant who is imprisoned in a sister state and has an indictment pending in Ohio may make a request to appropriate Ohio authorities to be tried within 180 days; however, when such defendant is discharged from custody in the sister state prior to the expiration of 180 days, he loses the right to be tried by Ohio within 180 days, and thereafter his right to a speedy trial on the charges pending in Ohio is governed by RC 2945.71. State v. Thompson (Cuyahoga 1984) 19 Ohio App.3d 261, 483 N.E.2d 1207, 19 O.B.R. 414.

RC 2945.71 to RC 2945.73, do not apply to persons incarcerated pending the outcome of extradition proceedings. State v. Haynes (Cuyahoga 1982) 8 Ohio App.3d 119, 456 N.E.2d 1279, 8 O.B.R. 174. Criminal Law ⚷ 577.11(1)

Where a defendant is arrested in another state on a fugitive from justice warrant, and waives extradition and is transported to Ohio, the speedy trial requirements of RC 2945.71 et seq. do not begin to run until the defendant is in Ohio and arrested under an Ohio charge. State v. Adkins (Shelby 1982) 4 Ohio App.3d 231, 447 N.E.2d 1314, 4 O.B.R. 422. Criminal Law ⚷ 577.11(5)

Ohio court would not determine whether Missouri courts violated defendant's speedy trial rights regarding the prosecution of defendant in Missouri, where defendant was arrested and charged in Ohio for aiding or abetting aggravated robbery with a gun specification, but was extradited to Missouri to face outstanding charges there before his trial in Ohio. State v. Davis (Ohio App. 5 Dist., Richland, 05-15-2002) No. 01 CA 67, 2002-Ohio-2502, 2002 WL 999322, Unreported, appeal not allowed 99 Ohio St.3d 1438, 789 N.E.2d 1118, 2003-Ohio-2902. Criminal Law ⚷ 577.11(4)

17. Contempt proceedings

An accused contemnor does not have the statutory right to a speedy trial; contempt is neither a misdemeanor nor a felony governed by the speedy trial statute. In re Contemnor Caron (Ohio Com. Pl., 04-27-2000) 110 Ohio Misc.2d 58, 744 N.E.2d 787. Contempt ⚷ 61(1)

Contempt proceedings are not subject to the legislative strictures of RC 2945.71, and a trial court's failure to immediately enforce its sentence does not involve an unconstitutional imposition of sentence and therefore does not prejudice constitutional rights of a defendant. Cleveland v. Anderson (Cuyahoga 1992) 82 Ohio App.3d 63, 611 N.E.2d 439.

Contempt proceedings are not subject to the speedy trial limits of RC 2945.71, but are subject to the constitutional right to a speedy trial. State v. Khong (Cuyahoga 1985) 29 Ohio App.3d 19, 502 N.E.2d 682, 29 O.B.R. 20.

18. Ethics violations

RC 2945.71 does not apply to proceedings before the Ohio ethics commission. OAG 81–063.

19. Transfer of cases

Where defendant is issued a citation and summons in mayor's court and the case is subsequently transferred to municipal court, only that period of time from certification by the mayor's court to docketing in the municipal court is excluded when applying the speedy trial statute. City of Brecksville v. Cook (Ohio App. 8 Dist., Cuyahoga, 08-11-1994) No. 65766, 1994 WL 422267, Unreported, motion to certify allowed 70 Ohio St.3d 1466, 640 N.E.2d 528, reversed 75 Ohio St.3d 53, 661 N.E.2d 706, 1996-Ohio-171, reconsideration denied 75 Ohio St.3d 1452, 663 N.E.2d 333.

Time during which assault charge against defendant was pending in municipal court, prior to state's dismissal, must be added to time same charge was pending in mayor's court for purposes of calculating defendant's speedy trial rights in mayor's court. State v. Jarvis (Ohio App. 10 Dist., 06-10-1997) 121 Ohio App.3d 105, 699 N.E.2d 101, dismissed, appeal not allowed 80 Ohio St.3d 1424, 685 N.E.2d 237. Criminal Law ⚷ 577.14

Transfer of case from mayor's court to municipal court is "removal" within meaning of speedy trial statute, as word "removal" as used therein refers to transfer of case from one state court to another. Brecksville v. Cook (Ohio, 03-04-1996) 75 Ohio St.3d 53, 661 N.E.2d 706, 1996-Ohio-171, reconsideration denied 75 Ohio St.3d 1452, 663 N.E.2d 333. Criminal Law ⚷ 577.10(7)

Where a person charged with a misdemeanor is served with a summons by the common pleas court and the case is subsequently transferred to the municipal court, which serves a summons on the defendant on the same charge, the time within which the defendant must be brought to trial under RC 2945.71(B)(2) commences at the time of the initial service of summons. City of Cleveland v. Selvia (Cuyahoga 1988) 58 Ohio App.3d 1, 567 N.E.2d 1310.

Where a defendant charged with a misdemeanor set for trial at a mayor's court demands a jury trial, thereby necessitating transfer to the municipal court, this "removal" extends the time within which the defendant must be brought to trial; the removal is deemed to take place when the case is certified by the mayor's court, not when it is docketed by the municipal court. City of Gahanna v. Partlow (Franklin 1985) 27 Ohio App.3d 267, 501 N.E.2d 51, 27 O.B.R. 311.

20. Trial de novo

Statute establishing 30–day speedy trial period for minor misdemeanor charges in a court of record did not apply to defendant's trial de novo in municipal court following his conviction on speeding charges in mayor's court. Amberley v. Mize (Ohio Mun., 04-14-2000) 106 Ohio Misc.2d 32, 733 N.E.2d 337. Criminal Law ⚷ 577.6

21. Retrials

Time between mistrial, which was necessitated because state sought to amend date in indictment, and new trial was to be counted against defendant's speedy trial time, as state waited to amend date in indictment until trial had already begun, which meant that defendant could no longer present his alibi as planned, and state had notice of alibi beforehand. State v. Brown (Ohio App. 7 Dist., Mahoning, 06-07-2005) No. 03-MA-32, 2005-Ohio-2939, 2005 WL 1385715, Unreported, appeal not allowed 106 Ohio St.3d 1558, 836 N.E.2d 582, 2005-Ohio-5531. Criminal Law ⚷ 577.14

Defendant's speedy trial rights were not violated, even though it took the State 149 days to bring defendant to trial after defendant's no contest plea to driving under the influence (DUI) was vacated and the case was remanded for trial; defendant was required to be brought to trial on remand within a reasonable period of time, and less than one year was not presumptively prejudicial. State v. Hull (Ohio App. 7 Dist., Mahoning, 03-30-2005) No. 04 MA 2, 2005-Ohio-1659, 2005 WL 775885, Unreported, motion to certify allowed 106 Ohio St.3d 1479, 832 N.E.2d 733, 2005-Ohio-3978, appeal allowed 106 Ohio St.3d 1482, 832 N.E.2d 736, 2005-Ohio-3978, affirmed 110 Ohio St.3d 183, 2006-Ohio-4252. Criminal Law ⚷ 577.14; Criminal Law ⚷ 577.15(1)

The speedy-trial statute does not apply to retrials, but it nevertheless serves to provide useful guidelines to evaluate what constitutes a reasonable time for constitutional speedy-trial purposes, as to a retrial. State v. Echols (Ohio App. 1 Dist., 09-14-2001) 146 Ohio App.3d 81, 765 N.E.2d 379, appeal not allowed 94 Ohio St.3d 1430, 761 N.E.2d 47, 2002-Ohio-5651, habeas corpus denied 2005 WL 1745475. Criminal Law ⚷ 577.14

Retrial on robbery charge, 22 months after reversal of defendant's conviction at his first trial, did not violate defendant's constitutional right to speedy trial; 109–day delay was primarily result of withdrawal of defendant's trial counsel and appointment of new counsel, another 55–day delay occurred because State requested continuance to secure the appearance of two police officers as witnesses, and defendant never made a demand for speedy trial. State v. Echols (Ohio App. 1 Dist., 09-14-2001) 146 Ohio App.3d 81, 765 N.E.2d 379, appeal not allowed 94 Ohio St.3d 1430, 761 N.E.2d 47, 2002-Ohio-5651, habeas corpus denied 2005 WL 1745475. Criminal Law ⚿ 577.14

Speedy trial statutes have no application where verdict has been reversed on appeal and new trial has been ordered. State v. Pearson (Ohio App. 3 Dist., 11-23-1998) 130 Ohio App.3d 577, 720 N.E.2d 924, dismissed, appeal not allowed 85 Ohio St.3d 1441, 708 N.E.2d 208, dismissal of post-conviction relief affirmed 2000 WL 1132575, dismissed, appeal not allowed 90 Ohio St.3d 1489, 739 N.E.2d 815. Criminal Law ⚿ 577.14

Statutory speedy trial protections pertain only to original trial and have no obligation to retrial following mistrial because of hung jury; standard to be applied in that situation is one of reasonableness under United States and Ohio Constitutions. State v. McElrath (Ohio App. 9 Dist., 10-02-1996) 114 Ohio App.3d 516, 683 N.E.2d 430, motion for delayed appeal denied 81 Ohio St.3d 1430, 689 N.E.2d 50. Criminal Law ⚿ 577.14

Statutory speedy trial limitations periods are inapplicable to retrials, and a one-year delay between the declaration of a mistrial and a retrial is not an unreasonable delay where numerous pretrial motions are made and counsel requests a continuance for trial preparation. State v. Fields (Hamilton 1991) 75 Ohio App.3d 123, 598 N.E.2d 1264, dismissed, jurisdictional motion overruled 62 Ohio St.3d 1493, 583 N.E.2d 966.

RC 2945.71 is not applicable to retrials, the time for which is limited by standards of reasonableness under the Ohio and US Constitutions. State v. Saunders (Franklin 1984) 23 Ohio App.3d 69, 491 N.E.2d 313, 23 O.B.R. 132. Criminal Law ⚿ 577.14

Where a case is remanded to the trial court after a successful interlocutory pretrial appeal by the prosecution, the prosecutor's duty to diligently prosecute the case and bring the defendant to trial resumes. State v. Geraldo (Lucas 1983) 13 Ohio App.3d 27, 468 N.E.2d 328, 13 O.B.R. 29. Criminal Law ⚿ 577.8(2)

RC 2945.71 et seq., the speedy trial statutes, do not apply to retrials ordered upon reversal of conviction and remand; instead, constitutional requirements are applicable. State v. Turner (Medina 1982) 4 Ohio App.3d 305, 448 N.E.2d 516, 4 O.B.R. 556. Criminal Law ⚿ 577.14

RC 2945.71 is not applicable to retrials. State v. Fanning (Ohio 1982) 1 Ohio St.3d 19, 437 N.E.2d 583, 1 O.B.R. 57.

Where an appellate court reverses an erroneous dismissal and remands a criminal case for trial, Ohio's speedy trial statutes apply. State v. Willis (Cuyahoga 1980) 69 Ohio App.2d 128, 432 N.E.2d 219, 23 O.O.3d 332.

RC 2945.71 et seq., pertaining to time for trial, is not applicable to a situation where, trial having been timely commenced, a mistrial is properly declared and the time limit for the second trial is that provided by the constitutional guarantees for a speedy trial. State v. Workman (Hancock 1977) 60 Ohio App.2d 204, 396 N.E.2d 777, 14 O.O.3d 181.

The provisions of Ohio's speedy trial statutes are directed solely to an original trial following the arrest of a defendant, and have no application to the time within which a defendant must be tried following the vacation of a no contest plea on his own motion. State v. McAllister (Cuyahoga 1977) 53 Ohio App.2d 176, 372 N.E.2d 1341, 7 O.O.3d 247. Criminal Law ⚿ 577.6

Where a jury is unable to reach a verdict in a criminal action and is discharged, the re-scheduling of the case for another trial constitutes a reasonable continuance within the meaning of RC 2945.72. State v. Johnson (Franklin 1977) 52 Ohio App.2d 406, 370 N.E.2d 785, 6 O.O.3d 444.

The requirements set forth in RC 2945.71 et seq. pertaining to time for trial have no application to the time for trial of a cause in which an original conviction has been reversed and the matter remanded for retrial. State v. Gettys (Seneca 1976) 49 Ohio App.2d 241, 360 N.E.2d 735, 3 O.O.3d 286.

The speedy trial time limits do not apply to a retrial after a mistrial; a delay of 156 days is not unreasonable. State v Delong, No. 5–86–34 (3d Dist Ct App, Hancock, 5–4–88).

22. Commitment proceedings

A person committed to the Lima state hospital under the purported authority of RC 2945.37 and RC 2945.38, but who has not been indicted, is illegally restrained of his liberty and must be released forthwith from that hospital, provided, however, that if his mental condition is such that he is not sane and his release would result in his being dangerous to himself or to society the execution of the order of release will be suspended for a reasonable period of time to permit the probate division of an appropriate common pleas court, having jurisdiction, to cause his commitment to a proper institution. Burton v. Reshetylo (Allen 1973) 35 Ohio App.2d 113, 300 N.E.2d 249, 64 O.O.2d 234, affirmed 38 Ohio St.2d 35, 309 N.E.2d 907, 67 O.O.2d 53.

23. When time begins to run

Trial court's finding that speedy trial period in prosecution for illegal conveyance did not begin to run on date defendant, incarcerated in connection with another matter, claimed to have been was taken from his prison cell and placed in isolation was supported by some competent, credible evidence, where evidence established subsequent dates that defendant was indicted by grand jury, that warrant on indictment issued, and that defendant was arrested. State v. Hughes (Ohio App. 9 Dist., Lorain, 09-24-2003) No. 02CA008206, 2003-Ohio-5045, 2003 WL 22187441, Unreported. Criminal Law ⚿ 577.8(2)

Statutory speedy trial clock began to run with respect to theft charge against defendant on date he was charged and matter was bound over for trial, and not on earlier date detainer was allegedly placed against him during his incarceration on other charges. State v. Randazzo (Ohio App. 8 Dist., Cuyahoga, 05-09-2002) No. 79667, 2002-Ohio-2250, 2002 WL 973083, Unreported. Criminal Law ⚷ 577.8(2)

When a defendant is apprehended for the commission of certain offenses and imprisoned because such arrest establishes a violation of his parole, the speedy trial period will not begin to run until he specifically requests disposition of the charges for which he was arrested. State v Adams, No. 86 CA 174 (7th Dist Ct App, Mahoning, 11–23–88).

24. Computing time generally—In general

Trial court's setting of trial date on misdemeanor charge of driving under the influence (DUI) which was 18 days after end of statutory speedy trial period did not violate defendant's statutory right to speedy trial, where defendant's motion to suppress, filed within statutory speedy trial limit, tolled speedy trial clock, and speedy trial calculation was based upon date defendant was actually brought to trial, not upon scheduled trial date. State v. Delarosa (Ohio App. 11 Dist., Portage, 06-30-2005) No. 2003-P-0129, 2005-Ohio-3399, 2005 WL 1538264, Unreported. Criminal Law ⚷ 577.8(1); Criminal Law ⚷ 577.10(8)

In determining whether defendant's statutory speedy trial time period was violated, defendant was entitled to have each day spent in jail count as three days, where defendant remained in jail in lieu of bail. State v. Saxon (Ohio App. 8 Dist., Cuyahoga, 09-23-2004) No. 83889, 2004-Ohio-5017, 2004 WL 2340106, Unreported, appeal dismissed 104 Ohio St.3d 1421, 819 N.E.2d 299, 2004-Ohio-6675, stay denied 104 Ohio St.3d 1424, 819 N.E.2d 708, 2004-Ohio-6585, appeal allowed 105 Ohio St.3d 1437, 822 N.E.2d 810, 2005-Ohio-531, reversed 109 Ohio St.3d 176, 846 N.E.2d 824, 2006-Ohio-1245. Criminal Law ⚷ 577.11(1)

For speedy trial purposes, the holding of defendant in jail for 38 days in lieu of bond was the equivalent of 114 days in prison at the time defendant's motion to dismiss was filed, and thus defendant was held the equivalent of 24 days longer from the date of his arrest than permitted by speedy trial statute. State v. Vera (Ohio App. 3 Dist., Logan, 03-01-2004) No. 8-03-15, No. 8-03-16, 2004-Ohio-921, 2004 WL 370213, Unreported. Criminal Law ⚷ 577.11(1); Criminal Law ⚷ 577.15(3)

Where there is conflicting evidence as to filing dates of motions and their resolution, a calculation of the number of days which had passed before the start of trial using only the dates time-stamped on the motions and entries as they appear on the court's journal will be used and where such calculation shows a defendant was not brought to trial within the speedy trial provisions, a conviction will be reversed and the defendant discharged. State v Cayse, No. 803, 1993 WL 271339 (4th Dist Ct App, Highland, 6–29–93).

Period between date on which defendant withdrew his motion to suppress, and later date on which defendant's attorney signed entry extending time provisions, was attributable to State for purposes of speedy trial statute. State v. Stamps (Ohio App. 1 Dist., 04-03-1998) 127 Ohio App.3d 219, 712 N.E.2d 762. Criminal Law ⚷ 577.12(1)

Defendant's right to speedy trial was not violated, even though his trial began day after statutory speedy trial period expired; date on which period ended was Sunday, and, thus, defendant's speedy trial date was automatically extended to next day. State v. McCornell (Ohio App. 8 Dist., 10-12-1993) 91 Ohio App.3d 141, 631 N.E.2d 1110. Criminal Law ⚷ 577.10(3)

The time limits in the speedy trial statutes apply to the trial date, not to the date of the judgment entry. Blanchester v McLaren, No. CA87–08–018 (12th Dist Ct App, Clinton, 5–16–88).

25. —— Notice, computing time generally

State had 270 days from date of arrest to bring defendant to trial on charges of illegal conveyance, where neither state nor trial court ever received required notice that defendant wished to be tried within 180 days of his arrest. State v. Salyers (Ohio App. 3 Dist., Marion, 09-26-2005) No. 9-05-04, 2005-Ohio-5037, 2005 WL 2335061, Unreported. Criminal Law ⚷ 577.15(3)

Defendant's failure to deliver to either prosecuting attorney or trial court the requisite notice of his imprisonment and request for final disposition tolled speedy trial period, on pending charges of escape. State v. Milner (Ohio App. 5 Dist., Morgan, 07-06-2005) No. 04 CA 5, 2005-Ohio-3467, 2005 WL 1580816, Unreported. Criminal Law ⚷ 577.11(5)

Statute which applies when charges are pending against a prisoner does not require state to exercise reasonable diligence in locating an incarcerated defendant against whom charges are pending; rather, the statute requires the state to bring the defendant to trial within 180 days after he causes to be delivered to the prosecuting attorney and the appropriate court written notice of the place of his imprisonment and a request for a final disposition. State v. Milner (Ohio App. 5 Dist., Morgan, 07-06-2005) No. 04 CA 5, 2005-Ohio-3467, 2005 WL 1580816, Unreported. Criminal Law ⚷ 577.11(5)

26. —— Arrest, computing time generally

Defendant's statutory speedy trial right began to run upon his initial arrest for misdemeanor drug charges, and State's failure to bring defendant to trial on more serious drug charges stemming from same incident within 270 days, or approximately 13 months after his arrest and over a year after he pleaded no contest to misdemeanor drug charges, violated defendant's statutory speedy trial rights; second indictment was not based upon new facts or discovered evidence that would have allowed for patent violation of defendant's speedy trial rights. State v. Rutkowski (Ohio App. 8 Dist., Cuyahoga, 03-09-2006) No. 86289, 2006-Ohio-1087, 2006 WL 562160, Unreported. Criminal Law ⚷ 577.8(2); Criminal Law ⚷ 577.15(3)

Date of defendant's first arrest was triggering event that started running of speedy trial time, for purposes of computing how much time has run under speedy trial statute, in prosecution for deception to obtain drugs. State v. Azbell (Ohio App. 5 Dist., Richland, 08-23-2005) No. 2005CA0004, 2005-Ohio-4405, 2005 WL 2045024, Unreported, appeal allowed 108 Ohio St.3d 1412, 841 N.E.2d 317, 2006-Ohio-179. Criminal Law ⚷ 577.8(2)

Speedy trial statute, providing that person charged with a felony must be brought to trial within 270 days after person's arrest, began to run on date of defendant's arrest for possession of cocaine, not on date on which he was taken into custody, detained for six hours, and released without any charges pending and without any restraints on his liberty. State v. Evans (Ohio App. 11 Dist., Trumbull, 04-15-2005) No. 2003-T-0132, 2005-Ohio-1787, 2005 WL 879401, Unreported, appeal not allowed 106 Ohio St.3d 1509, 833 N.E.2d 1250, 2005-Ohio-4605. Criminal Law ⚷ 577.8(2)

State was required to bring defendant, charged with felonies and incarcerated from date of arrest to entry of pleas, to trial within 90 days of his arrest. State v. Smith (Ohio App. 2 Dist., Clark, 11-12-2004) No. 2003 CA 93, 2004-Ohio-6062, 2004 WL 2588269, Unreported, motion for delayed appeal denied 105 Ohio St.3d 1450, 823 N.E.2d 455, 2005-Ohio-763, motion for delayed appeal denied 105 Ohio St.3d 1496, 825 N.E.2d 621, 2005-Ohio-1666. Criminal Law ⚷ 577.11(1); Criminal Law ⚷ 577.15(3)

Statutory speedy trial time period began to run on date defendant was arrested. State v. Saxon (Ohio App. 8 Dist., Cuyahoga, 09-23-2004) No. 83889, 2004-Ohio-5017, 2004 WL 2340106, Unreported, appeal dismissed 104 Ohio St.3d 1421, 819 N.E.2d 299, 2004-Ohio-6675, stay denied 104 Ohio St.3d 1424, 819 N.E.2d 708, 2004-Ohio-6585, appeal allowed 105 Ohio St.3d 1437, 822 N.E.2d 810, 2005-Ohio-531, reversed 109 Ohio St.3d 176, 846 N.E.2d 824, 2006-Ohio-1245. Criminal Law ⚷ 577.8(2)

Day of arrest does not count against the state for purposes of speedy trial claim. State v. Burgess (Ohio App. 11 Dist., Lake, 08-20-2004) No. 2003-L-069, 2004-Ohio-4395, 2004 WL 1872781, Unreported. Criminal Law ⚷ 577.8(2)

Arrest of defendant, under a reindictment which is premised on the same underlying facts alleged in a previous indictment, is the proper point at which to resume running of the speedy-trial period. State v. Burgess (Ohio App. 11 Dist., Lake, 08-20-2004) No. 2003-L-069, 2004-Ohio-4395, 2004 WL 1872781, Unreported. Criminal Law ⚷ 577.14

Detainer placed on drug defendant was not the functional equivalent of an arrest, so as to commence speedy trial period, where defendant was not "held in jail in lieu of bail on the pending charge" while he was serving his sentence on a separate misdemeanor charge. State v. Fowler (Ohio App. 5 Dist., Muskingum, 12-23-2003) No. CT2003-0026, 2003-Ohio-7099, 2003 WL 23016045, Unreported, appeal not allowed 102 Ohio St.3d 1424, 807 N.E.2d 368, 2004-Ohio-2003. Criminal Law ⚷ 577.8(2)

Statutory speedy trial period began to run, in prosecution for illegal conveyance, on day after defendant's arrest on such charge. State v. Hughes (Ohio App. 9 Dist., Lorain, 09-24-2003) No. 02CA008206, 2003-Ohio-5045, 2003 WL 22187441, Unreported. Criminal Law ⚷ 577.8(2)

Finding that speedy trial period did not commence on date defendant alleged he was arrested for illegal conveyance was supported by competent, credible evidence, as record was devoid of any evidence that demonstrated defendant was arrested on that date, and in fact revealed that a warrant on indictment was not issued, nor was defendant arrested, until several months after date defendant alleged he was arrested. State v. Szorady (Ohio App. 9 Dist., Lorain, 05-28-2003) No. 02CA008159, 2003-Ohio-2716, 2003 WL 21222139, Unreported. Criminal Law ⚷ 577.8(2)

The date which the time for a speedy trial began to run from was the date charges were originally filed, rather than from the date defendant was arrested, and thus defendant's right to a speedy trial was not violated. State v. Fallat (Ohio App. 8 Dist., Cuyahoga, 01-16-2003) No. 81073, 2003-Ohio-169, 2003 WL 125261, Unreported, appeal not allowed 99 Ohio St.3d 1412, 788 N.E.2d 648, 2003-Ohio-2454. Criminal Law ⚷ 577.8(2)

Defendant became an accused, and thus right to speedy trial within 90 days began to run, when defendant was arrested for operating a motor vehicle while under the influence of alcohol (OMVI), not when defendant was formally served with citations for OMVI and for speeding, failure to control, and reckless operation; officer confronted defendant at time of arrest with form stating that defendant was under arrest, and all evidence pertaining to charges stemmed from night of arrest. City of Shaker Heights v. Kissee (Ohio App. 8 Dist., Cuyahoga, 12-26-2002) No. 81301, 2002-Ohio-7255, 2002 WL 31883358, Unreported. Criminal Law ⚷ 577.8(2)

Defendant's neglectful or improper action, or his unavailability for trial due to other criminal proceedings or confinement, operated to extend speedy trial period as measured from date of defendant's arrest. State v. Robison (Ohio App. 5 Dist., Licking, 12-19-2002) No. 02CA00015, 2002-Ohio-7216, 2002 WL 31875016, Unreported, motion for delayed appeal denied 98 Ohio St.3d 1473, 784 N.E.2d 707, 2003-Ohio-904, appeal not allowed 98 Ohio St.3d 1565, 787 N.E.2d 1230, 2003-Ohio-2242. Criminal Law ⚷ 577.10(8)

Record did not show date of defendant's re-arrest after he absconded before original trial date on charges of aggravated robbery and kidnapping, and thus date he was brought to jail was proper date to use to calculate defendant's speedy trial time. State v. Weimer (Ohio App. 2 Dist., Darke, 12-20-2002) No. 1586, 2002-Ohio-7099, 2002 WL 31846296, Unreported. Criminal Law ⚷ 577.8(2)

Commencement of time calculated under RC 2945.71(C) and 2945.71(E), RC 1.14, and Crim R

45 provide that day of arrest may be excluded. State v Wright, No. 93 CA 2110, 1993 WL 248262 (4th Dist Ct App, Scioto, 7–8–93).

Particular rights that the speedy trial statutory scheme confers attach when a defendant is arrested on criminal charges, and continue so long as those charges remain pending, until his criminal liability is determined by trial or a plea of guilty or no contest. State v. Kerby (Ohio App. 2 Dist., 07-15-2005) 162 Ohio App.3d 353, 833 N.E.2d 757, 2005-Ohio-3734, appeal not allowed 107 Ohio St.3d 1682, 839 N.E.2d 403, 2005-Ohio-6480. Criminal Law ⚷ 577.8(2)

Time period for bringing defendant to trial under speedy trial statute begins with the arrest of defendant. State v. Stamps (Ohio App. 1 Dist., 04-03-1998) 127 Ohio App.3d 219, 712 N.E.2d 762. Criminal Law ⚷ 577.8(2)

Day of defendant's arrest does not count against the State, for purposes of speedy trial statute. State v. Stamps (Ohio App. 1 Dist., 04-03-1998) 127 Ohio App.3d 219, 712 N.E.2d 762. Time ⚷ 9(11)

Speedy trial period for charge of driving with a prohibited blood-alcohol content, based on results of blood test taken after defendant was involved in automobile accident, commenced when defendant was originally arrested on charge of driving under the influence of alcohol, not when he was served with prohibited blood-alcohol-content charge over two months later, although state did not charge defendant earlier because of testing laboratory's delay in processing blood test. State v. Cooney (Ohio App. 1 Dist., 12-26-1997) 124 Ohio App.3d 570, 706 N.E.2d 854. Criminal Law ⚷ 577.8(2)

Day of arrest is not included when computing time within which defendant must be brought to trial under speedy-trial statute. State v. Jones (Ohio App. 11 Dist., 04-04-1997) 119 Ohio App.3d 59, 694 N.E.2d 505. Criminal Law ⚷ 577.8(1)

Administrative detention in prison was not the equivalent of "arrest" for purposes of starting time for speedy trial computation. State v. Grinnell (Ohio App. 10 Dist., 06-27-1996) 112 Ohio App.3d 124, 678 N.E.2d 231, appeal not allowed 77 Ohio St.3d 1474, 673 N.E.2d 138, appeal not allowed 77 Ohio St.3d 1475, 673 N.E.2d 138, denial of habeas corpus affirmed 215 F.3d 1326, certiorari denied 121 S.Ct. 232, 531 U.S. 898, 148 L.Ed.2d 166. Criminal Law ⚷ 577.8(2)

In determining the time within which defendant must be brought to trial, use of rule, under which day of arrest is disregarded when counting days elapsed before trial, did not abridge defendant's right to speedy trial. State v. Lautenslager (Ohio App. 3 Dist., 06-28-1996) 112 Ohio App.3d 108, 677 N.E.2d 1263. Criminal Law ⚷ 577.8(1)

If accused is arrested and in jail when charged with another unrelated offense, arrest date for second offense, for purposes of speedy trial statute, occurs on date warrant was issued. State v. Collins (Ohio App. 6 Dist., 09-30-1993) 91 Ohio App.3d 10, 631 N.E.2d 666, dismissed, jurisdictional motion overruled 68 Ohio St.3d 1470, 628 N.E.2d 1389. Criminal Law ⚷ 577.8(1)

In sentencing following a defendant's conviction for trafficking in marijuana, a court properly denies the defendant's motion to dismiss for failure to commence trial within the mandatory period (ninety days, since RC 2945.71(E) sets forth that each day that the accused spends in jail in lieu of bail shall be counted as three days) specified in RC 2945.71 where the defendant was held in jail in lieu of bail from his arrest on May 18, 1990 through the beginning of the trial on August 16, 1990; the day of arrest is not to be counted in computing the statutory time period. State v. Steiner (Summit 1991) 71 Ohio App.3d 249, 593 N.E.2d 368.

The right to a speedy trial, under O Const Art I, § 10, and US Const Am 6, does not accrue until arrest or detention on a charge. State v. Cross (Lorain 1975) 48 Ohio App.2d 357, 357 N.E.2d 1103, 2 O.O.3d 356.

Where an accused is placed in jail for a parole violation, at which time he is interviewed by officers investigating another crime, his arrest for such crime occurs, for the purpose of RC 2945.71, on the date the warrant is issued, and not at the time he was incarcerated. State v. Kelly (Montgomery 1974) 44 Ohio App.2d 40, 335 N.E.2d 729, 73 O.O.2d 24. Criminal Law ⚷ 573

Ninety day speedy trial period commenced on date that misdemeanor charges were filed against defendant and she was served with a summons, instead of on earlier date when defendant was arrested, and since only 76 days had elapsed since charges were filed and defendant was served a summons and date trial began, trial was well within the 90 day speedy trial period. Cleveland v. Baker (Ohio App. 8 Dist., Cuyahoga, 08-15-2002) No. 80955, 2002-Ohio-4171, 2002 WL 1878897, Unreported. Criminal Law ⚷ 577.15(4)

Where the original counts of an indictment are severed to eliminate potential prejudice, the time for bringing an accused to trial begins to run with the initial arrest; thus, the time for bringing an accused to trial under the Ohio Speedy Trial statute does not begin anew following the severance of the indictment. State v. DeLeon (Ohio App. 2 Dist., Montgomery, 06-28-2002) No. 18114, 2002-Ohio-3286, 2002 WL 1393665, Unreported, appeal not allowed 98 Ohio St.3d 1424, 782 N.E.2d 78, 2003-Ohio-259. Criminal Law ⚷ 577.14

Taking a defendant's blood sample after advising her of her rights under the implied consent law, RC 4511.191, and Miranda do not constitute an arrest which causes time to run under the speedy trial provisions of RC 2945.71(B)(2); instead, time runs after the defendant is served with a citation for driving under the influence of alcohol. State v Vickrey, No. C–880336 (1st Dist Ct App, Hamilton, 7–5–89).

Taking a blood sample from an unconscious person suspected of driving under the influence of alcohol, following a motor vehicle accident, does not constitute an arrest for purposes of the speedy trial statute despite the language in RC 4511.191(A) which requires an arrest prior to the taking of blood, breath, or urine sample. State v

Mapes, No. C–880089 (1st Dist Ct App, Hamilton, 12–21–88).

The 270–day period provided in the Ohio Speedy Trial Act (RC 2945.71 et seq.) does not commence until defendant actually has been arrested. State v Lewis, No. 43987 (8th Dist Ct App, Cuyahoga, 5–6–82).

27. —— Service of summons, computing time generally

Speedy trial period applicable to defendant charged with operation of a vehicle under the influence of alcohol and endangering children did not begin to run until date defendant was served with warrant issued with respect to those charges, even though State's complaint was filed over six months earlier. State v. Pyle (Ohio App. 5 Dist., Coshocton, 11-18-2004) No. 04CA12, 2004-Ohio-6201, 2004 WL 2650270, Unreported. Criminal Law ⚷ 577.8(2)

Starting date for speedy trial purposes was date that defendant admitted receiving summons, not one day after issuance; no evidence indicated that summons was served one day after it was issued. State v. Stewart (Ohio App. 2 Dist., Montgomery, 08-15-2003) No. CIV.A. 19663, 2003-Ohio-4329, 2003 WL 21949751, Unreported. Criminal Law ⚷ 577.8(2)

The date from which the speedy trial provisions of RC 2945.71 begin to run for an accused whose original felony charge has been reduced to a misdemeanor is the date the summons was served for the lesser offense. State v. Sauers (Summit 1977) 52 Ohio App.2d 113, 368 N.E.2d 334, 6 O.O.3d 87. Criminal Law ⚷ 577.8(2)

28. —— Arraignment or indictment, computing time generally

Statutory speedy trial period began to run, with respect to defendant already incarcerated for prior conviction, on date of indictment. State v. Salyers (Ohio App. 3 Dist., Marion, 09-26-2005) No. 9-05-04, 2005-Ohio-5037, 2005 WL 2335061, Unreported. Criminal Law ⚷ 577.8(2)

Date on which defendant was arraigned would be date of arrest for purposes of calculating whether defendant's statutory right to speedy trial was violated; although defendant was already in custody at time indictment was filed, there was no indication of when defendant was served with indictment or notified of proceeding. State v. Griffin (Ohio App. 8 Dist., Cuyahoga, 08-19-2004) No. 83724, 2004-Ohio-4344, 2004 WL 1846121, Unreported. Criminal Law ⚷ 577.8(2); Criminal Law ⚷ 577.15(3)

Speedy-trial time began to run on date defendants were served with indictments, in prosecution for felony theft. State v. Riley (Ohio App. 12 Dist., 08-22-2005) 162 Ohio App.3d 730, 834 N.E.2d 887, 2005-Ohio-4337. Criminal Law ⚷ 577.8(2)

The time for a speedy trial, for a convict already in prison, does not begin to run when he is placed in some form of administrative detention, but instead commences when he is indicted. State v. Grinnell (Ohio App. 10 Dist., 06-27-1996) 112 Ohio App.3d 124, 678 N.E.2d 231, appeal not allowed 77 Ohio St.3d 1474, 673 N.E.2d 138, appeal not allowed 77 Ohio St.3d 1475, 673 N.E.2d 138, denial of habeas corpus affirmed 215 F.3d 1326, certiorari denied 121 S.Ct. 232, 531 U.S. 898, 148 L.Ed.2d 166.

29. —— Voir dire, computing time generally

For purposes of State speedy trial statute, a trial commences when voir dire begins. State v. Knight (Ohio App. 2 Dist., Greene, 04-16-2004) No. 2003CA14, 2004-Ohio-1941, 2004 WL 830043, Unreported, appeal not allowed 103 Ohio St.3d 1427, 814 N.E.2d 490, 2004-Ohio-4524. Criminal Law ⚷ 577.8(1)

30. —— Additional charges or refiling of indictment, computing time generally

Statutory speedy trial time period applicable to first indictment also applied to second indictment, where state knew all relevant facts at time of first indictment. State v. Thompson (Ohio App. 2 Dist., Montgomery, 03-19-2004) No. 20114, 2004-Ohio-1320, 2004 WL 541165, Unreported, on subsequent appeal 161 Ohio App.3d 334, 830 N.E.2d 394, 2005-Ohio-2508. Criminal Law ⚷ 577.14

Computation of speedy trial time for any subsequently indicted offenses begins on the date the warrant was served on the later offenses, not from the date of arrest, if the offenses charged in the later indictment do not stem from the same occurrence as the previously indicted offenses. State v. Garrett (Ohio App. 6 Dist., Erie, 09-30-2003) No. E-02-015, 2003-Ohio-5185, 2003 WL 22233542, Unreported. Criminal Law ⚷ 577.14

Statutory speedy trial time applicable to sexual battery and attempted sexual battery charges against defendant ran from date of second indictment, rather than upon reversal of his convictions for rape and attempted rape. State v. Morris (Ohio App. 2 Dist., Montgomery, 03-07-2003) No. 19283, 2003-Ohio-1049, 2003 WL 862656, Unreported. Criminal Law ⚷ 577.10(5)

Although defendant was in jail during most of the time between nolle prosequi and his reindictment for aggravated murder, his imprisonment would not be counted for purposes of computing the speedy trial time period; defendant's imprisonment resulted from his conviction on 11 counts of forgery in a wholly unrelated matter, and nolle prosequi was entered by the state in part based on defense arguments that there was insufficient proof and that further investigation of other suspects was necessary. State v. Myers (Ohio, 12-13-2002) 97 Ohio St.3d 335, 780 N.E.2d 186, 2002-Ohio-6658, reconsideration denied 97 Ohio St.3d 1500, 780 N.E.2d 1023, 2002-Ohio-7367, certiorari denied 123 S.Ct. 2254, 539 U.S. 906, 156 L.Ed.2d 116, motion to reopen denied 100 Ohio St.3d 1505, 799 N.E.2d 184, 2003-Ohio-6161. Criminal Law ⚷ 577.14

For purposes of speedy trial statute, time period between dismissal without prejudice of an original indictment, and the filing of a subsequent indictment, premised on same facts as alleged in original indictment, is not chargeable to State unless defendant is held in jail or released on bail. State v. Stamps (Ohio App. 1 Dist., 04-03-1998) 127 Ohio App.3d 219, 712 N.E.2d 762. Criminal Law ⚷ 577.14

Period between refiling of indictment against defendant after original indictment was dismissed without prejudice, and defendant's arraignment, was chargeable to State for purposes of speedy trial statute. State v. Stamps (Ohio App. 1 Dist., 04-03-1998) 127 Ohio App.3d 219, 712 N.E.2d 762. Criminal Law ⚷ 577.14

Time period between nolle prosequi of a felony charge and re-indictment is excluded in computing speedy trial time. State v. Jarvis (Ohio App. 10 Dist., 06-10-1997) 121 Ohio App.3d 105, 699 N.E.2d 101, dismissed, appeal not allowed 80 Ohio St.3d 1424, 685 N.E.2d 237. Criminal Law ⚷ 577.14

In issuing subsequent indictment, state is not subject to speedy-trial timetable of initial indictment, where additional criminal charges arise from facts different from original charges, or state did not know of these facts at time of initial indictment. State v. Baker (Ohio, 04-02-1997) 78 Ohio St.3d 108, 676 N.E.2d 883, 1997-Ohio-229, reconsideration denied 78 Ohio St.3d 1517, 679 N.E.2d 312. Criminal Law ⚷ 577.14

In computing the time within which a defendant must be brought to trial, the period after a dismissal nolle prosequi and before service of a second summons should be excluded. City of Westlake v. Cougill (Ohio 1978) 56 Ohio St.2d 230, 383 N.E.2d 599, 10 O.O.3d 382.

Where a nolle prosequi has been entered on an indictment or where a dismissal premised on the fault of the prosecution has been entered on an indictment and the defendant is subsequently reindicted, the proper method of computing time pursuant to RC 2945.71 is to include the time incarcerated pending trial under the original indictment in addition to the time spent pending trial under the reindictment; where the defendant is released without bail upon dismissal of the original indictment, the defendant is not entitled to have time between the dismissal and the reindictment included pursuant to RC 2945.71, because during such period no charge is pending; however, if upon dismissal, the defendant is held in jail or on bail pursuant to Crim R 12(I), such time in jail or on bail will be included in the computation of time under RC 2945.71. State v. Stephens (Cuyahoga 1977) 52 Ohio App.2d 361, 370 N.E.2d 759, 6 O.O.3d 404. Criminal Law ⚷ 577.14

In determining whether defendant's Sixth Amendment right to a speedy trial has been violated, the time period between dismissal of criminal charges and institution of new charges is not to be considered. U. S. v. MacDonald (U.S.N.C. 1982) 102 S.Ct. 1497, 456 U.S. 1, 71 L.Ed.2d 696, on remand 688 F.2d 224.

Thirty-day clock under Speedy Trial Act, which requires that defendant be indicted within 30 days of his arrest, is reset by the dismissal of an outstanding indictment by the government where no further restraint on the defendant's freedom remains after that dismissal. U.S. v. DeJohn (C.A.6 (Ohio), 05-13-2004) 368 F.3d 533, rehearing en banc denied, certiorari denied 125 S.Ct. 510, 543 U.S. 988, 160 L.Ed.2d 373. Criminal Law ⚷ 577.14; Indictment And Information ⚷ 7

Thirty-day period under Speedy Trial Act in which to indict defendant after his arrest did not continue to run after dismissal of indictment against defendants, where no restraints were thereafter placed on their freedom, and thus reindictment 45 days after dismissal of initial indictment did not violate Speedy Trial Act. U.S. v. DeJohn (C.A.6 (Ohio), 05-13-2004) 368 F.3d 533, rehearing en banc denied, certiorari denied 125 S.Ct. 510, 543 U.S. 988, 160 L.Ed.2d 373. Indictment And Information ⚷ 7

31. —— Sentencing, computing time generally

Two-year gap between when defendant was placed on community control, following his conviction for passing bad checks, and his sentencing following termination of his community control, did not violate speedy trial statute; speedy trial statute guaranteed trial within 270 days of arrest on felony charge, but defendant's trial ended when he pled guilty to passing bad checks, just over three months after his indictment, and well within limits established by speedy trial statute. State v. Keeble (Ohio App. 2 Dist., Greene, 07-09-2004) No. CIV.A. 03CA84, 2004-Ohio-3785, 2004 WL 1588286, Unreported. Criminal Law ⚷ 577.6

32. —— Sundays and holidays, computing time generally

For purposes of calculating the speedy trial time requirement applicable to a defendant, the sixteen days that elapsed while the defendant's motions were pending are not included; thus, the defendant was timely brought to trial. State v. Parker (Marion 1991) 72 Ohio App.3d 456, 594 N.E.2d 1033, dismissed, jurisdictional motion overruled 61 Ohio St.3d 1418, 574 N.E.2d 1090.

33. Tolling—In general

On charges of rape and assault, the state's assertion, based on the affidavit of a state's witness, that the defendant suborned perjury and intimidated witnesses testifying before the grand jury and that this misconduct impeded the issuance of the indictment against the defendant and thus tolled the statute of limitations under RC 2945.71, extending the time within which the state could bring the defendant to trial, is without merit where (1) the witness' affidavit sheds no light on the mental processes of the grand jurors in refusing to indict the defendant at an earlier opportunity, and more than just her testimony presumably was considered by the jurors; (2) the witness' allegations while under oath were not subject to cross-examination and therefore do not establish misconduct as an irrefutable fact; and (3) the court below appeared to give little if any credence to this evidence, which was improperly before it. State v. Lewis (Lawrence 1990) 70 Ohio App.3d 624, 591 N.E.2d 854, cause dismissed 58 Ohio St.3d 716, 570 N.E.2d 277, rehearing denied 59 Ohio St.3d 715, 572 N.E.2d 697, dismissal of post-conviction relief affirmed, dismissed, appeal not allowed 78 Ohio St.3d 1490, 678 N.E.2d 1227.

Failure to file an evaluation within the thirty-day period established by RC 2945.371 will not toll the time for trial beyond that time. State v. Wilson (Fayette 1982) 7 Ohio App.3d 219, 454 N.E.2d 1348, 7 O.B.R. 281.

RC 2945.71 was tolled by defendant's actions where he: (1) made three requests for a change of counsel; (2) made a request for a polygraph test; (3) made a request for a transcript of proceedings from prior hearings; and (4) made a series of other motions to the court. State v Charlton, No. 82 CA 71 (7th Dist Ct App, Mahoning, 3–1–84).

34. —— Probation or parole violations, tolling

Where state shows that there is valid parole or probation holder, the pertinent speedy trial statutory time frame is tolled so long as defendant is not being held "solely" on the charge in question. State v. Hubbard (Ohio App. 11 Dist., 06-12-1995) 104 Ohio App.3d 443, 662 N.E.2d 394, dismissed, jurisdictional motion overruled 74 Ohio St.3d 1456, 656 N.E.2d 950. Criminal Law ⚷ 577.11(3)

35. —— Failure to appear, tolling

Where a defendant fails to show up for his arraignment on a misdemeanor charge and also fails to appear at his second trial date, those delays caused by defendant will toll the running of the speedy trial deadline. Boston Hts. v. Weikle (Summit 1991) 81 Ohio App.3d 165, 610 N.E.2d 526.

36. —— Severance of trials, tolling

The speedy trial time period under RC 2945.71 is tolled by the defendant's motion to sever his trial from that of a codefendant. State v Floyd, No. CA87–11–150 (12th Dist Ct App, Butler, 12–30–88).

37. —— Pleas, tolling

The time within which an accused must be brought to trial by virtue of RC 2945.71 is tolled by the accused's plea of not guilty by reason of insanity, whether such plea contemplates insanity at the time of arraignment or insanity at the time the crime was committed. State v. Spratz (Ohio 1979) 58 Ohio St.2d 61, 388 N.E.2d 751, 12 O.O.3d 77. Criminal Law ⚷ 577.11(6)

38. —— Notice by defendant, tolling

Statutory speedy trial time was tolled with respect to pending forgery charge against defendant until he was released from prison, as defendant failed to meet his initial duty to provide written notice requesting final disposition and to notify state of his whereabouts, under statute governing request by a prisoner for trial on pending charges. (Per Kline, J., with two judges concurring in judgment only.) State v. Roulette (Ohio App. 4 Dist., 10-04-2005) 163 Ohio App.3d 775, 840 N.E.2d 645, 2005-Ohio-5435. Criminal Law ⚷ 577.8(2); Criminal Law ⚷ 577.11(1)

When a defendant who is imprisoned is aware of pending charges against him and fails to file a written notice requesting final disposition and notifying the state of his whereabouts, as permitted by statute governing request by a prisoner for trial on pending charges, the statutory speedy trial time period tolls until his release from prison; while statute governing extension of time for hearing or trial places a duty of reasonable diligence to secure a defendant's availability on the state, that duty is not triggered if the defendant is aware of the pending charges and fails to exercise his duty under statute governing request by a prisoner for trial on pending charges, and the state is not aware of his whereabouts. (Per Kline, J., with two judges concurring in judgment only.) State v. Roulette (Ohio App. 4 Dist., 10-04-2005) 163 Ohio App.3d 775, 840 N.E.2d 645, 2005-Ohio-5435. Criminal Law ⚷ 577.8(2); Criminal Law ⚷ 577.11(1)

39. —— Transfer of case, tolling

Period of delay necessary to removal of case from mayor's court to municipal court, during which time speedy trial statute is tolled, is time from arrest or summons to date on which mayor's court certifies case to municipal court; it is not time from certification in mayor's court to docketing in municipal court. Brecksville v. Cook (Ohio, 03-04-1996) 75 Ohio St.3d 53, 661 N.E.2d 706, 1996-Ohio-171, reconsideration denied 75 Ohio St.3d 1452, 663 N.E.2d 333. Criminal Law ⚷ 577.10(7)

In accordance with Ohio's speedy trial requirements, the running of the deadline in a misdemeanor prosecution for a speeding violation is tolled during the delay where the case is transferred from mayor's court to municipal court, and the time period to be excluded is from the date of arrest until the date the mayor's court certifies the case to the municipal court. Boston Hts. v. Weikle (Summit 1991) 81 Ohio App.3d 165, 610 N.E.2d 526.

40. —— Retention or withdrawal of counsel, tolling

Defendant's statutory right to speedy trial on charge of trafficking in cocaine was not violated, where period of at least 30 days, between date defendant told trial court he would retain private counsel, and date private counsel entered his appearance, tolled speedy trial clock. State v. Seward (Ohio App. 4 Dist., Ross, 03-03-2005) No. 04CA2784, 2005-Ohio-934, 2005 WL 503973, Unreported. Criminal Law ⚷ 577.13

Defendant's agreement to retain counsel after he was informed that counsel could not proceed to trial on scheduled date due to scheduling conflict, together with defendant's subsequent request for substitution of counsel, tolled 90-day speedy trial period. State v. Waits (Ohio App. 3 Dist., Marion, 02-22-2005) No. 9-04-50, 2005-Ohio-672, 2005 WL 405717, Unreported. Criminal Law ⚷ 577.10(8)

Defendant's statutory speedy trial time was tolled during delay caused by defense counsel's motion to withdraw as counsel. State v. Kemper (Ohio App. 2 Dist., Clark, 11-12-2004) No. 2002-CA-101, No. 2002-CA-102, 2004-Ohio-6055, 2004 WL 2588313, Unreported. Criminal Law ⚷ 577.10(8)

Defense counsel's filing of motion to withdraw tolled speedy trial time limit in drug case until trial court granted the motion. State v. Ward (Ohio App. 5 Dist., Richland, 05-10-2004) No. 03 CA 60, 2004-Ohio-2323, 2004 WL 1044137, Unreported. Criminal Law ⚷ 577.10(7)

Defense counsel's motion to withdraw and request that trial court appoint new counsel tolled statutory speedy trial period. State v. Blessing (Ohio App. 5 Dist., Morgan, 01-15-2004) No. 02 CA 13, 2004-Ohio-190, 2004 WL 77872, Unreported. Criminal Law ⚷ 577.10(8)

In general, delay for purposes of securing counsel tolls operation of speedy trial statute. State v. Hiatt (Ohio App. 4 Dist., 03-26-1997) 120 Ohio App.3d 247, 697 N.E.2d 1025. Criminal Law ⚷ 577.10(4)

41. —— Continuances, tolling

State's motion for continuance did not toll running of 270-day speedy trial period based on claims that defendant failed to comply with discovery, that prolonged plea negotiations would likely be unsuccessful, and that defendant acquiesced to continuance; defendant had in fact fully complied with discovery in timely manner, prolonged plea negotiations did not preclude State's obligation to prepare for trial, and defendant's failure to object to continuance did not constitute waiver of speedy trial right or motion for continuance for which delay would have been charged to defendant. State v. Knight (Ohio App. 2 Dist., Greene, 06-24-2005) No. 03-CA-014, 2005-Ohio-3179, 2005 WL 1490364, Unreported. Criminal Law ⚷ 577.10(8)

Delay of 283 days between defendant's arrest and his first trial did not violate his statutory right to a speedy trial; the 191 days of continuances from the originally scheduled trial date until the first trial date were agreed to by defense counsel, and defendant's motion for a bill of particulars tolled the speedy trial clock for an additional 16 days. State v. Miller (Ohio App. 10 Dist., Franklin, 02-10-2005) No. 04AP-285, 2005-Ohio-518, 2005 WL 314695, Unreported. Criminal Law ⚷ 577.10(8); Criminal Law ⚷ 577.10(9)

Period of continuances granted at defendant's request tolled statutory speedy trial time period. State v. Donald (Ohio App. 8 Dist., Cuyahoga, 12-16-2004) No. 81570, No. 83947, 2004-Ohio-6848, 2004 WL 2914928, Unreported, appeal not allowed 105 Ohio St.3d 1562, 828 N.E.2d 117, 2005-Ohio-2447. Criminal Law ⚷ 577.13

Continuances granted at defendant's request tolled statutory speedy trial time period. State v. Saxon (Ohio App. 8 Dist., Cuyahoga, 09-23-2004) No. 83889, 2004-Ohio-5017, 2004 WL 2340106, Unreported, appeal dismissed 104 Ohio St.3d 1421, 819 N.E.2d 299, 2004-Ohio-6675, stay denied 104 Ohio St.3d 1424, 819 N.E.2d 708, 2004-Ohio-6585, appeal allowed 105 Ohio St.3d 1437, 822 N.E.2d 810, 2005-Ohio-531, reversed 109 Ohio St.3d 176, 846 N.E.2d 824, 2006-Ohio-1245. Criminal Law ⚷ 577.10(8)

Defense counsel's request for continuance did not violate any essential duty defense counsel had with respect to defendant in terms of ensuring defendant's speedy trial right, in prosecution for driving while intoxicated and other offenses; even if period at issue had not been tolled due to trial continuance at defense counsel's request, result would still have been under statutory 90-day requirement for purposes of speedy trial analysis. State v. Rector (Ohio App. 5 Dist., Delaware, 08-27-2004) No. 04 CA C 03022, 2004-Ohio-4549, 2004 WL 1926116, Unreported. Criminal Law ⚷ 641.13(2.1)

Time period during which trial court granted continuance due to trial schedule conflict involving counsel for burglary defendant tolled constitutional and statutory speedy trial time periods. State v. Ossman (Ohio App. 5 Dist., Licking, 08-16-2004) No. 03 CA 92, 2004-Ohio-4302, 2004 WL 1827813, Unreported, appeal reopened 2006-Ohio-720, 2006 WL 367122, appeal not allowed 109 Ohio St.3d 1506, 849 N.E.2d 1028, 2006-Ohio-2998. Criminal Law ⚷ 577.10(7)

Counsel's request for continuance because of schedule conflict tolled running of 270-day speedy trial period, even if defendant objected to continuance. State v. Wade (Ohio App. 10 Dist., Franklin, 07-29-2004) No. 03AP-774, 2004-Ohio-3974, 2004 WL 1688434, Unreported, stay granted 103 Ohio St.3d 1476, 816 N.E.2d 253, 2004-Ohio-5405, appeal not allowed 104 Ohio St.3d 1427, 819 N.E.2d 709, 2004-Ohio-6585, appeal not allowed 104 Ohio St.3d 1462, 821 N.E.2d 578, 2005-Ohio-204. Criminal Law ⚷ 577.10(8)

Defendant's requests for discovery on two occasions, together with request for bill of particulars and agreement with State to continue trial for rape and gross sexual imposition, tolled running of 270-day speedy trial period. State v. Benman (Ohio App. 10 Dist., Franklin, 07-27-2004) No. 03AP-1012, 2004-Ohio-3935, 2004 WL 1663497, Unreported. Criminal Law ⚷ 577.10(8)

Any delay in bringing defendant to trial on drug-related charges did not violate his speedy trial rights; delay beyond 270-day speedy trial period was attributable to defendant's five motions for continuance, a motion to suppress evidence, and defense counsel's motion to withdraw, which motions served to toll limitations period. State v. Kolvek (Ohio App. 9 Dist., Summit, 05-19-2004) No. 21808, 2004-Ohio-2515, 2004 WL 1103994, Unreported. Criminal Law ⚷ 577.10(8)

Speedy trial time limit was not tolled in drug case where trial court failed to journalize its decision to grant defendant's request for a continuance. State v. Ward (Ohio App. 5 Dist., Richland, 05-10-2004) No. 03 CA 60, 2004-Ohio-2323, 2004 WL 1044137, Unreported. Criminal Law ⚷ 577.13

Defendant who was charged with operating a motor vehicle under the influence (OMVI) while underage tolled her speedy trial time by expressly agreeing to set second pretrial proceeding and vacate initial trial date, which action was sufficient to demonstrate continuance by way of agreement to post-statutory trial date; although defendant was not involved in setting actual date for second pretrial, defense counsel admitted that he actively participated in scheduling a second pretrial and vacating initial trial date, which necessarily placed trial date outside 45-day speedy trial limit. State v. Steinke (Ohio App. 3 Dist., 03-15-2004) 158 Ohio App.3d 241, 814 N.E.2d 1230, 2004-Ohio-1201. Criminal Law ⚷ 577.10(9)

Defense counsel's request for continuance and defendant's filing of suggestion of incompetence and not guilty by reason of insanity plea, requesting sanity evaluation, tolled statutory speedy trial period. State v. Blessing (Ohio App. 5 Dist., Morgan, 01-15-2004) No. 02 CA 13, 2004-Ohio-190, 2004 WL 77872, Unreported. Criminal Law ⚷ 577.10(8)

Violation of defendant's statutory right to speedy trial was not negated by her subsequent filing of request for continuance tolling statutory speedy trial period. State v. Blessing (Ohio App. 5 Dist., Morgan, 01-15-2004) No. 02 CA 13, 2004-Ohio-190, 2004 WL 77872, Unreported. Criminal Law ⚷ 577.10(8)

Time between defendant's arrest and date when trial was supposed to have begun, in order to comport with speedy trial requirements, was tolled by state's motion for continuance, which was reasonable, and by defendant's motion to dismiss indictment or to suppress results of traffic stop. State v. Cano (Ohio App. 10 Dist., Franklin, 09-18-2003) No. 03AP-58, 2003-Ohio-4957, 2003 WL 22149336, Unreported. Criminal Law ⚷ 577.10(3); Criminal Law ⚷ 577.10(8)

Murder defendant's exclusion from pretrial proceedings in which his counsel sought and obtained continuances neither rendered such continuances ineffective to toll speedy trial period nor deprived defendant of his right to be present at critical stages of trial. State v. Chapman (Ohio App. 8 Dist., Cuyahoga, 08-07-2003) No. 73609, 2003-Ohio-4163, 2003 WL 21805616, Unreported. Criminal Law ⚷ 577.10(8); Criminal Law ⚷ 636(3)

Defendant's speedy trial rights were not violated; speedy trial time period was tolled for 20 days between time defense counsel requested continuance to time state requested a second continuance, thereby reducing period from arrest to trial to 82 days, within the 90 day period a defendant is to be brought to trial. State v. Jackson (Ohio App. 10 Dist., Franklin, 03-31-2003) No. 02AP-468, 2003-Ohio-1653, 2003 WL 1701188, Unreported, appeal not allowed 99 Ohio St.3d 1469, 791 N.E.2d 984, 2003-Ohio-3669, appeal not allowed 100 Ohio St.3d 1546, 800 N.E.2d 751, 2003-Ohio-6879. Criminal Law ⚷ 577.10(8)

Defendant's motion to suppress prior convictions, request for hearing on such motion, and motions for continuances tolled speedy trial period. State v. Davis (Ohio App. 7 Dist., Mahoning, 05-30-2002) No. 01 CA 171, 2002-Ohio-2789, 2002 WL 32806896, Unreported. Criminal Law ⚷ 577.13

270-day speedy trial period was tolled by numerous continuances granted at defendant's request, and thus, fact that entry of defendant's guilty pleas to robbery charges occurred 567 days after arrest did not violate his speedy trial rights. State v. Brown (Ohio App. 1 Dist., Hamilton, 10-25-2002) No. C-010755, 2002-Ohio-5813, 2002 WL 31398564, Unreported, motion for delayed appeal denied 98 Ohio St.3d 1487, 785 N.E.2d 471, 2003-Ohio-1189. Criminal Law ⚷ 577.13

Defendant was not denied the right to a speedy trial when he was brought to trial one hundred thirteen days after his arrest, since the continuance necessitated by defendant's hospitalization and motion to suppress tolled the time pursuant to RC 2945.71 such that defendant was brought to trial within the statutorily required time period. State v Oliver, No. 15994, 1993 WL 175536 (9th Dist Ct App, Summit, 5–26–93).

While a defendant's mere failure to object to a state-scheduled original trial date outside of the speedy-trial time limit does not constitute a continuance that would toll the speedy trial period, an agreement by all parties to a post-statutory trial date will be treated as a continuance. State v. Steinke (Ohio App. 3 Dist., 03-15-2004) 158 Ohio App.3d 241, 814 N.E.2d 1230, 2004-Ohio-1201. Criminal Law ⚷ 577.10(9)

Defendant's request for continuance of trial tolled the running of the speedy trial period. State v. McDonald (Ohio App. 8 Dist., 08-14-2003) 153 Ohio App.3d 679, 795 N.E.2d 701, 2003-Ohio-4342, stay granted 100 Ohio St.3d 1480, 798 N.E.2d 615, 2003-Ohio-5993, appeal not allowed 100 Ohio St.3d 1531, 800 N.E.2d 48, 2003-Ohio-6458. Criminal Law ⚷ 577.10(8)

Defendant's request for continuance of trial tolled the running of the speedy trial period. State v. McDonald (Ohio App. 8 Dist., 08-14-2003) 153 Ohio App.3d 679, 795 N.E.2d 701, 2003-Ohio-4342, stay granted 100 Ohio St.3d 1480, 798 N.E.2d 615, 2003-Ohio-5993, appeal not allowed 100 Ohio St.3d 1531, 800 N.E.2d 48, 2003-Ohio-6458. Criminal Law ⚷ 577.10(8)

Defendant was brought to trial for driving under the influence (DUI) within 90–day statutory period after arrest; continuance requested by defendant and one due to absence of police officer tolled speedy-trial statute. State v. Campbell (Ohio App. 1 Dist., 11-08-2002) 150 Ohio App.3d 90, 779 N.E.2d 811, 2002-Ohio-6064, motion to certify allowed 98 Ohio St.3d 1459, 783 N.E.2d 519, 2003-Ohio-644, affirmed 100 Ohio St.3d 361, 800 N.E.2d 356, 2003-Ohio-6804, reconsideration denied 101 Ohio St.3d 1470, 804 N.E.2d 43, 2004-Ohio-819. Criminal Law ⚷ 577.10(6); Criminal Law ⚷ 577.10(8)

Statutory speedy trial period in rape prosecution was tolled by continuances pursuant to or necessitated by defendant's own motions, where defendant filed his first motion to continue within same reasonable extension of speedy trial period granted on state's motion, and filed each of his subsequent motions prior to expiration of extension granted by the immediately preceding motion. State v. High (Ohio App. 7 Dist., 01-24-2001) 143 Ohio App.3d 232, 757 N.E.2d 1176, 2001-Ohio-3530. Criminal Law ⚷ 577.10(8)

Defendant's right to trial within 90 days on first-degree misdemeanor charge was not violated; timely journal entry tolled running of speedy trial period for two days based on continuance requested by defendant in order to obtain counsel, another timely entry tolled period for 30 days based on a continuance resulting from defendant's contempt of court, and remaining period of 27 days, multiplied by three to reflect fact that defendant was incarcerated for the duration, counted as 81 days. N. Olmsted v. Cipiti (Ohio App. 8 Dist., 09-09-1996) 114 Ohio App.3d 549, 683 N.E.2d 795, dismissed, appeal not allowed 77 Ohio St.3d 1518, 674 N.E.2d 372. Criminal Law ⚷ 577.10(8); Criminal Law ⚷ 577.15(1)

Running of statutory speedy trial period was not tolled by sua sponte continuance, where trial court did not journalize entry of continuance prior to expiration of speedy trial period. State v. Stamper (Ohio App. 11 Dist., 04-10-1995) 102 Ohio App.3d 431, 657 N.E.2d 365. Criminal Law ⚷ 577.10(7)

Defendant's trial took place within statutory speedy trial requirements, though statutory period was 90 days and defendant's trial did not commence until 291 days after arrest; 221 days before trial were tolled from speedy trial requirements by defendant's requests for continuances, time that defendant was hospitalized, delay for locating civilian clothing for defendant to wear at trial, and trial judge's sua sponte continuance for time that judge was to appear as witness at different trial. State v. Baker (Ohio App. 8 Dist., 12-20-1993) 92 Ohio App.3d 516, 636 N.E.2d 363. Criminal Law ⚷ 577.10(8); Criminal Law ⚷ 577.15(3)

Two week continuance, to allow defendant charged with driving under influence to engage counsel, did not toll running of speedy trial period, absent journal entry prior to expiration of statutory time limit. State v. Fry (Ohio App. 2 Dist., Darke, 07-05-2002) No. 1572, 2002-Ohio-3489, 2002 WL 1438626, Unreported. Criminal Law ⚷ 577.10(8)

The speedy trial period is tolled by defense counsel's request for discovery, and his telephone authorization of a motion for continuance. State v Roquemore, No. 92AP–356 (10th Dist Ct App, Franklin, 3–16–93).

42. —— Discovery, tolling

Defendant's motion to compel discovery did not toll running of 270-day speedy trial period, in prosecution for aggravated robbery, where motion to compel was necessitated by State's failure to fully comply with prior discovery request. State v. Knight (Ohio App. 2 Dist., Greene, 06-24-2005) No. 03-CA-014, 2005-Ohio-3179, 2005 WL 1490364, Unreported. Criminal Law ⚷ 577.10(8)

Defendant's request for discovery did not toll running of 270-day speedy trial period in case where State had already provided discovery. State v. Knight (Ohio App. 2 Dist., Greene, 06-24-2005) No. 03-CA-014, 2005-Ohio-3179, 2005 WL 1490364, Unreported. Criminal Law ⚷ 577.10(8)

State's demand for discovery prior to defendant's request for discovery did not toll running of 270-day speedy trial period, in prosecution for aggravated robbery; State's right to request and receive discovery did not accrue until after defendant had both requested and obtained discovery from State. State v. Knight (Ohio App. 2 Dist., Greene, 06-24-2005) No. 03-CA-014, 2005-Ohio-3179, 2005 WL 1490364, Unreported. Criminal Law ⚷ 577.10(7)

Defendant's statutory speedy trial time was tolled during delay caused by defendant's discovery request. State v. Kemper (Ohio App. 2 Dist., Clark, 11-12-2004) No. 2002-CA-101, No. 2002-CA-102, 2004-Ohio-6055, 2004 WL 2588313, Unreported. Criminal Law ⚷ 577.10(8)

Time period during which burglary defendant's discovery request was pending tolled constitutional and statutory speedy trial time periods. State v. Ossman (Ohio App. 5 Dist., Licking, 08-16-2004) No. 03 CA 92, 2004-Ohio-4302, 2004 WL 1827813, Unreported, appeal reopened 2006-Ohio-720, 2006 WL 367122, appeal not allowed 109 Ohio St.3d 1506, 849 N.E.2d 1028, 2006-Ohio-2998. Criminal Law ⚷ 577.10(8)

Defendant's filing of a demand for discovery, in prosecution for trafficking in cocaine, corrupting another with drugs, and possessing criminal tools, tolled the running of the statutory speedy trial deadline, and thus defendant's right to a speedy trial was not violated. State v. Risner (Ohio App. 3 Dist., Seneca, 01-20-2004) No. 13-03-40, 2004-Ohio-186, 2004 WL 77885, Unreported. Criminal Law ⚷ 577.10(8)

Speedy trial period was tolled by defendant's request for discovery until the state responded to it. State v. Dunston (Ohio App. 12 Dist., Fayette, 10-07-2002) No. CA2002-03-008, 2002-Ohio-5454, 2002 WL 31261594, Unreported. Criminal Law ⚷ 577.10(8)

Upon defendant's request for bill of particulars and demand for discovery, State's response to requests after more than 11 months had passed was unreasonable and did not toll the running of the speedy trial period for the full 11 months. State v. McDonald (Ohio App. 8 Dist., 08-14-2003) 153 Ohio App.3d 679, 795 N.E.2d 701, 2003-Ohio-4342, stay granted 100 Ohio St.3d 1480, 798 N.E.2d 615, 2003-Ohio-5993, appeal not allowed 100 Ohio St.3d 1531, 800 N.E.2d 48, 2003-Ohio-6458. Criminal Law ⚷ 577.13

Record showed defendant was brought to trial within the 90 days required by RC 2945.71 (B)(2) where a period of 10 days was tolled as result of his request for pretrial conference and subsequent trial and period of 24 days was tolled due to his motions demanding bill of particulars and discovery. Linndale v Anthony, No. 62326 (8th Dist Ct App, Cuyahoga, 4–8–93).

43. —— Motions, tolling

A motion to dismiss acts to toll the time in which a defendant must be brought to trial under speedy trial statute, and such a motion tolls the statutory time until the trial court issues its decision on the motion. State v. Evans (Ohio App. 11 Dist., Trumbull, 04-15-2005) No. 2003-T-0132, 2005-Ohio-1787, 2005 WL 879401, Unreported, appeal not allowed 106 Ohio St.3d 1509, 833 N.E.2d 1250, 2005-Ohio-4605. Criminal Law ⚷ 577.8(1)

Defendant's right to trial within 30 days on citation issued against him for speeding and failing to maintain an assured clear distance ahead (ACDA) was not violated, even though defendant's trial occurred more than 30 days after citation was issued, as defendant's motions for dismissal and discovery tolled running of speedy trial period. State v. Wiest (Ohio App. 1 Dist., Hamilton, 05-21-2004) No. C-030674, 2004-Ohio-2577, 2004 WL 1124594, Unreported. Criminal Law ⚷ 577.10(8)

Forty-five day speedy trial period applicable to charges that property owner violated zoning ordinance and flood damage prevention ordinance was tolled from date owner filed motion to dismiss charges until date trial court denied motion. Village of Versailles v. Poly (Ohio App. 2 Dist., Darke, 03-26-2004) No. 1627, 2004-Ohio-1485, 2004 WL 596079, Unreported. Criminal Law ⚷ 577.10(8)

Statutory speedy trial time period was tolled while defendant's motion to dismiss complaint on speedy trial ground was pending. City of Maple Heights v. Pinkney (Ohio App. 8 Dist., Cuyahoga, 03-18-2004) No. 81514, 2004-Ohio-1256, 2004 WL 536195, Unreported. Criminal Law ⚷ 577.10(8)

Defendant's filing of motion to dismiss for failure to convene a speedy trial tolled speedy trial period from the filing of motion until the date that trial court denied motion. State v. Armstrong (Ohio App. 9 Dist., Medina, 02-18-2004) No. 03CA0064-M, 2004-Ohio-726, 2004 WL 298685, Unreported. Criminal Law ⚷ 577.13

Defendant's motion to dismiss indictment tolled statutory speedy trial period. State v. Blessing (Ohio App. 5 Dist., Morgan, 01-15-2004) No. 02 CA 13, 2004-Ohio-190, 2004 WL 77872, Unreported. Criminal Law ⚷ 577.10(8)

Defendant's right to speedy trial on charges of rape and improper discharge of firearm at, or into, habitation, was not violated under statute that required trial within 90 days of arrest, where computation of time established that total of only 83 days of speedy trial period had run against state; time for speedy trial purposes was tolled from time defendant executed waiver of right to speedy trial until he withdrew waiver, time was tolled when defendant filed motions to dismiss, trial court took reasonable amount of time to decide motions, and trial court granted state reasonable continuance of five days for purposes of motion to suppress hearing. State v. Boles (Ohio App. 2 Dist., Montgomery, 05-23-2003) No. 18762, 2003-Ohio-2693, 2003 WL 21213383, Unreported, appeal not allowed 100 Ohio St.3d 1411, 796 N.E.2d 538, 2003-Ohio-4948. Criminal Law ⚷ 577.10(7); Criminal Law ⚷ 577.10(8)

Defendant's filing of motion to dismiss indictments based on speedy trial violation tolled speedy trial time until trial court ruled on motion. State v. Hawkins (Ohio App. 11 Dist., Portage, 12-31-2002) No. 2001-P-0060, 2002-Ohio-7347, 2002 WL 31895118, Unreported, appeal not allowed 98 Ohio St.3d 1567, 787 N.E.2d 1231, 2003-Ohio-2242. Criminal Law ⚷ 577.13

Defendant's filing of motion to suppress evidence tolled speedy trial time until trial court ruled on motion. State v. Hawkins (Ohio App. 11 Dist., Portage, 12-31-2002) No. 2001-P-0060, 2002-Ohio-7347, 2002 WL 31895118, Unreported, appeal not allowed 98 Ohio St.3d 1567, 787 N.E.2d 1231, 2003-Ohio-2242. Criminal Law ⚷ 577.13

Filing of defendant's motion in limine, which sought to prevent disclosure of defendant's citizenship status during trial, did not toll speedy-trial time period in prosecution for money laundering and possession of criminal tools; motion did not cause any delays in proceeding since motion required only simple discretionary evidentiary ruling by trial court and did not require extensive research or response by state. State v. Sanchez (Ohio App. 6 Dist., 04-29-2005) 162 Ohio App.3d 113, 832 N.E.2d 1215, 2005-Ohio-2093, reversed 2009 WL 676, appeal allowed 106 Ohio St.3d 1532, 835 N.E.2d 381, 2005-Ohio-5146. Criminal Law ⚷ 577.10(8)

Defendant's filing of pretrial motion to suppress evidence relating to driving under the influence (DUI) charge did not toll statutory speedy trial period in which defendant had to be brought to trial on child endangering charge, which was filed subsequent to filing of the motion to suppress. State v. Homan (Ohio, 08-16-2000) 89 Ohio St.3d 421, 732 N.E.2d 952, 2000-Ohio-212, reconsideration denied 90 Ohio St.3d 1431, 736 N.E.2d 27. Criminal Law ⚷ 577.14

Defendant who was held in jail 97 days between court-ordered bindover for trial as an adult and start of trial was not denied right to speedy trial, though each day he was held in jail in lieu of bail would normally have counted as three days for purposes of 270–day speedy trial period for persons accused of felony; period was tolled for eleven days between defendant's filing of pretrial motions and trial court's ruling on those motions, reducing period between bindover as adult and trial to 86 days. State v. Michael (Ohio App. 7 Dist., 10-02-1996) 114 Ohio App.3d 523, 683 N.E.2d 435, cause dismissed 77 Ohio St.3d 1452, 672 N.E.2d 176, dismissed, appeal not allowed 77 Ohio St.3d 1520, 674 N.E.2d 372. Criminal Law ⚷ 577.10(8); Criminal Law ⚷ 577.11(1)

A defendant's filing of a motion to (1) suppress evidence, (2) preserve and produce substance for independent laboratory analysis, (3) continue her case, and (4) dismiss, all toll the time period for speedy trial purposes resulting in extending the time within which she must be brought to trial. State v. Brownlow (Allen 1991) 75 Ohio App.3d 88, 598 N.E.2d 888.

Even though a plea of no contest in an attempted domestic violence action will not act to toll the speedy trial time limit, since the court must still determine the accused's guilt or innocence within the statutory time limit, the defendant's act of filing a motion to dismiss will act to toll the time until the motion is ruled upon. State v. Mintz (Wood 1991) 74 Ohio App.3d 62, 598 N.E.2d 52, dismissed, jurisdictional motion overruled 62 Ohio St.3d 1431, 578 N.E.2d 823.

The filing of a motion to dismiss an indictment tolls the time under which a defendant must be brought to trial pursuant to RC 2945.71. State v. Bunyan (Auglaize 1988) 51 Ohio App.3d 190, 555 N.E.2d 980. Criminal Law ⚷ 577.10(8)

Where a criminal defendant moves for a psychiatric examination pursuant to RC 2945.39 and 2945.371, the running of the time in which a defendant must be tried is tolled when the motion is granted, not when the motion is made, and the time begins running again immediately after the date the psychiatric report is due where such report is never filed. State v. Bowman (Clermont 1987) 41 Ohio App.3d 318, 535 N.E.2d 730. Criminal Law ⚷ 577.8(2); Criminal Law ⚷ 577.11(6)

When an accused files a motion for discharge for delay of trial, the statutory period within which the accused must be brought to trial is tolled while the court considers the motion, and, although seventy-eight of the ninety days have already expired, it is not unreasonable for the court to take twenty-one days to respond to the motion. State v. Wilson (Fayette 1982) 7 Ohio App.3d 219, 454 N.E.2d 1348, 7 O.B.R. 281.

The statutory provisions for speedy trial run from the date of arrest but are tolled from the date of defendant's request for a delay until a new date is set, and upon the filing of a motion to dismiss. City of Willoughby v. Hoffman (Ohio Mun. 1980) 64 Ohio Misc. 15, 409 N.E.2d 1387, 18 O.O.3d 71.

A defendant's continuances and motion to dismiss toll the running of the ninety-day period within which the defendant must be brought to trial for a misdemeanor. State v Walton, No. 59165 (8th Dist Ct App, Cuyahoga, 10–3–91).

44. —— Refiling of charges, tolling

Speedy trial statute is tolled during time period between original dismissal of charges and subsequent refiling of new charges based upon same underlying facts as original charges, unless defendant is being held in jail or released on bail. State v. DePue (Ohio App. 4 Dist., 06-29-1994) 96 Ohio App.3d 513, 645 N.E.2d 745. Criminal Law ⚷ 577.14

45. —— Appeals, tolling

Constitutional and statutory speedy trial time periods were tolled from time Court of Appeals issued decision in first appeal, which reversed trial court's decision, until time expired for parties to appeal to Supreme Court. State v. Ossman (Ohio App. 5 Dist., Licking, 08-16-2004) No. 03 CA 92, 2004-Ohio-4302, 2004 WL 1827813, Unreported, appeal reopened 2006-Ohio-720, 2006 WL 367122, appeal not allowed 109 Ohio St.3d 1506, 849 N.E.2d 1028, 2006-Ohio-2998. Criminal Law ⚷ 577.14

Where defendant, charged with a felony, files a petition for certiorari to the US Supreme Court, such filing does not toll the running of the speedy trial statute. State v. Geraldo (Lucas 1983) 13 Ohio App.3d 27, 468 N.E.2d 328, 13 O.B.R. 29.

A 197–day delay resulting from Court of Appeals' granting leave and accepting State's appeal of trial court's order to disclose informer identity was not attributable to State for purposes of speedy trial statute; speedy trial time period was tolled during pendency of appeal pursuant to statute setting forth allowable extensions of time for bringing a criminal defendant to trial. State v. DeLeon (Ohio App. 2 Dist., Montgomery, 06-28-2002) No. 18114, 2002-Ohio-3286, 2002 WL 1393665, Unreported, appeal not allowed 98 Ohio St.3d 1424, 782 N.E.2d 78, 2003-Ohio-259. Criminal Law ⚷ 577.10(7)

Where a defendant moves to withdraw his guilty plea, the motion is denied, and that denial is reversed on appeal, it is error for a court to dismiss the indictment against the defendant pursuant to RC 2945.71 on speedy trial grounds due to the state's appeal of the appellate court's decision to grant the defendant's motion to the Supreme Court because the speedy trial time was stayed until the expiration of all appeals on defendant's motion to withdraw his guilty plea. State v Arden, No. 93–CA–567, 1994 WL 534898 (4th Dist Ct App, Adams, 9–28–94).

46. Revised or additional charges generally—In general

Speedy trial right of defendant who was a prisoner at the time of his indictment, but who was released from prison and held in county jail, was violated when he was not brought to trial within 90 days of his release from prison, where defendant was held in jail in lieu of bond solely on the pending charge, and there was no valid holder related to any other charge. State v. Beverly (Ohio App. 4 Dist., Ross, 09-13-2005) No. 04CA2809, 2005-Ohio-4954, 2005 WL 2293581, Unreported. Criminal Law ⚷ 577.11(1)

Six-month speedy trial period to bring defendant incarcerated on unrelated offense to trial on pending charges of assault, kidnapping and escape began to run from date that defendant was first brought before trial court and informed of charges. State ex rel. Jackson v. Wilson (Ohio App. 11 Dist., Trumbull, 01-17-2003) No. 2002-T-0169, 2003-Ohio-196, 2003 WL 139282, Unreported, affirmed 100 Ohio St.3d 315, 798 N.E.2d 1086, 2003-Ohio-6112. Criminal Law ⚷ 577.8(2)

Statute setting 180–day period for bringing to trial defendant who was already incarcerated, rather than statute setting forth 270–day speedy trial period, governed prosecution of defendant who was incarcerated for other offenses after he failed to appear for arraignment on instant charges. State v. Smith (Ohio App. 3 Dist., 09-29-2000) 140 Ohio App.3d 81, 746 N.E.2d 678, 2000-Ohio-1777. Criminal Law ⚷ 577.5

An incarcerated defendant arrested on a domestic violence charge, who is then charged with child endangering three days later, must be brought to trial within ninety days of the filing of the last charge, not the initial charge. State v. Rockwell (Franklin 1992) 80 Ohio App.3d 157, 608 N.E.2d 1118, dismissed, jurisdictional motion overruled 65 Ohio St.3d 1440, 600 N.E.2d 683.

A trial court errs in dismissing an assault count in an indictment for lack of a speedy trial where (1) the alleged assault occurred on December 18, 1976; (2) no indictment was returned against the defendant although it was considered twice by a grand jury, once in late 1976 and once in early 1977; and (3) the defendant was arrested on the assault charge and other charges on February 24, 1989, in Tennessee; since there was no pending criminal charge against the defendant after some time in early 1977, the 270–day time period under RC 2945.71(C)(2) stopped running and did not recommence until the arrest on the indictment in 1989. State v. Lewis (Lawrence 1990) 70 Ohio App.3d 624, 591 N.E.2d 854, cause dismissed 58 Ohio St.3d 716, 570 N.E.2d 277, rehearing denied 59 Ohio St.3d 715, 572 N.E.2d 697, dismissal of post-conviction relief affirmed, dismissed, appeal not allowed 78 Ohio St.3d 1490, 678 N.E.2d 1227.

Provisions of statute governing time within which preliminary hearing or trial must be held did not preclude State from bringing additional charges against defendant at a time subsequent to charges contained in original indictment. State v. Davis (Medina 1982) 4 Ohio App.3d 199, 447 N.E.2d 139, 4 O.B.R. 303. Criminal Law ⚿ 228; Criminal Law ⚿ 577.5

Where a defendant is charged with violating RC 4511.31, a minor misdemeanor, and the traffic ticket does not specifically allege a previous violation within the previous twelve months which would render the offense a misdemeanor of the fourth degree, the defendant must be brought to trial within the thirty-day period mandated for minor misdemeanors under RC 2945.71(A). State v Hutchinson, No. CA–3251 (5th Dist Ct App, Licking, 5–4–87).

When a defendant is charged with violating RC 4511.19, irrespective of the subsection or sections charged, a RC 4511.19 charge is "pending" within the meaning of RC 2945.71(A) and any additional charges filed against the accused under other subsections must be tried within the time limits statutorily mandated for the initial charge. State v Puckett, No. 1516 (4th Dist Ct App, Scioto, 6–14–85).

47. —— Amendment or reduction of charges, revised or additional charges generally

Amendment of original charge of resisting arrest to charge of prohibition against resisting an officer did not create an additional charge, and thus, defendant's speedy trial time waivers and extensions applicable to the original charge applied as well to the amended charge. City of Cleveland v. Robinson (Ohio App. 8 Dist., Cuyahoga, 02-20-2003) No. 81659, 2003-Ohio-771, 2003 WL 361296, Unreported. Criminal Law ⚿ 577.14

When an original charge is reduced to a lesser charge that carries a shorter time limit under speedy trial statute, the speedy trial deadline will be the earlier of (1) the speedy trial deadline for the original charge, applied from the date of the original charge, or (2) the speedy trial deadline for the lesser charge, applied from the date that the original charge was reduced to the lesser charge. State v. Gasnik (Ohio App. 1 Dist., 09-25-1998) 132 Ohio App.3d 612, 725 N.E.2d 1162. Criminal Law ⚿ 577.8(2)

48. —— Different or same facts, revised or additional charges generally

State was required, under speedy trial statute, to bring defendant to trial within 270 days after his arrest under the original indictment on charge of unauthorized use of a computer in the second indictment, which was a new and additional charge arising from the same facts as did the original charge of unauthorized use of telecommunication property, where State knew of facts underlying new charge at the time of the original indictment. State v. Templin (Ohio App. 12 Dist., Fayette, 11-22-2004) No. CA2003-12-014, 2004 WL 3154959, Unreported. Criminal Law ⚿ 577.14

Speedy trial period applicable to minor misdemeanor charge filed when original fourth-degree misdemeanor charge was dismissed was the same period applicable to original charge, where both charges stemmed from the original set of facts and circumstances. Akron v. Hicks (Ohio App. 9 Dist., Summit, 10-27-2004) No. 21961, 2004-Ohio-5685, 2004 WL 2390123, Unreported. Criminal Law ⚿ 577.14

When issuing second indictment against defendant, State was not subject to speedy trial time limits of original arrest, where the subsequent charges were based on additional facts revealed through further investigation. State v. Armstrong (Ohio App. 9 Dist., Medina, 02-18-2004) No. 03CA0064-M, 2004-Ohio-726, 2004 WL 298685, Unreported. Criminal Law ⚿ 577.14

Forgery defendant failed to demonstrate that speedy trial time limits applicable to charges in prior case were also applicable to instant charges and that he was thus denied his statutory right to a speedy trial, where the two indictments were the result of separate facts and occurrences which transpired on different dates and which constituted separate and distinct criminal offense. State v. Hughes (Ohio App. 2 Dist., Montgomery, 08-08-2003) No. 19568, 2003-Ohio-4203, 2003 WL 21839150, Unreported. Criminal Law ⚿ 577.10(5)

Defendant was entitled, for purposes of computing statutory speedy trial time on charges of sexual battery and attempted sexual battery, to benefit of time applicable to prior charges of rape and attempted rape arising from same misconduct, convictions for which were dismissed, commencing when he was arrested until he was brought to trial on those prior charges; so long as State knew of facts supporting both set of charges, statutory speedy trial time applicable to earlier charges attaches as well to later charges. State v. Morris (Ohio App. 2 Dist., Montgomery, 03-07-2003) No. 19283, 2003-Ohio-1049, 2003 WL 862656, Unreported. Criminal Law ⚿ 577.10(5)

For speedy trial purposes, only those charges that related to the sexual battery charges occurring between October 12-14 related back to the date that defendant was initially arrested and charged with singular count of sexual battery for acts occurring between October 12-14, and with respect to sexual battery charges involving incidents which occurred on different dates and involved different acts than those initially charged, those charges would not be considered as arising from the same sequence of events for purposes of speedy trial computation. State v. Brady (Ohio App. 5 Dist., Tuscarawas, 01-06-2003) No. 02 AP 04 0025, 2003-Ohio-138, 2003 WL 124289, Unreported, appeal not allowed 98 Ohio St.3d 1567, 787 N.E.2d 1231, 2003-Ohio-2242. Criminal Law ⚩ 577.8(2)

Time accumulated against the state during the pendency of a first complaint must be added to the time charged against the state during the pendency of a second complaint where the subsequent indictment is premised on the same underlying facts alleged in the previous indictment. State v. Penwell (Ohio App. 4 Dist., Highland, 02-24-1994) No. 821, 1994 WL 63051, Unreported.

Indictment charging defendant, a pharmacist indicted for drug trafficking, with additional drug trafficking charges after audit of defendant's pharmacy disclosed additional offenses was not subject to speedy trial time limits of original indictment, since subsequent charges were based on new additional facts which state had no knowledge of at time of original indictment. State v. Baker (Ohio, 04-02-1997) 78 Ohio St.3d 108, 676 N.E.2d 883, 1997-Ohio-229, reconsideration denied 78 Ohio St.3d 1517, 679 N.E.2d 312. Criminal Law ⚩ 577.14

Additional crimes based on different facts should not be considered as arising from same sequence of events for purposes of speedy-trial computation for second indictment. State v. Baker (Ohio, 04-02-1997) 78 Ohio St.3d 108, 676 N.E.2d 883, 1997-Ohio-229, reconsideration denied 78 Ohio St.3d 1517, 679 N.E.2d 312. Criminal Law ⚩ 577.14

When new and additional charges arise from same facts as did original charge, for which defendant waived his right to speedy trial, and state knew of such facts at time of initial indictment, time within which trial is to begin on additional charge is subject to same statutory limitations period that is applied to original charge. State v. Clark (Ohio App. 2 Dist., 10-27-1995) 107 Ohio App.3d 141, 667 N.E.2d 1262. Criminal Law ⚩ 577.10(5)

The arrest of a defendant under a subsequent indictment which is premised on the same underlying facts alleged in a previous indictment is the proper point at which to resume the running of the speedy-trial period. State v. Broughton (Ohio 1991) 62 Ohio St.3d 253, 581 N.E.2d 541. Criminal Law ⚩ 577.8(2); Criminal Law ⚩ 577.14

For purposes of computing how much time has run against the state under RC 2945.71 et seq., the time period between the dismissal without prejudice of an original indictment and the filing of a subsequent indictment, premised upon the same facts as alleged in the original indictment, shall not be counted unless the defendant is held in jail or released on bail pursuant to Crim R 12(I). State v. Broughton (Ohio 1991) 62 Ohio St.3d 253, 581 N.E.2d 541. Criminal Law ⚩ 577.14

Where the dismissal of a felony charge is followed by a misdemeanor charge arising from the same conduct, time pending the trial of the felony charge is not counted against the time for the misdemeanor trial, which time begins to run only from service of summons. State v. Phillips (Franklin 1984) 19 Ohio App.3d 85, 482 N.E.2d 1337, 19 O.B.R. 169.

Where indictments are brought against a defendant at separate times but arising out of the same conduct, the time within which trial must be brought runs from the date of the first indictment; however, all extensions applicable to the original indictment are also applicable to the subsequent indictment. State v Bickerstaff, No. 1141 (9th Dist Ct App, Medina, 11-17-82), affirmed by 10 OS(3d) 62, 10 OBR 352, 461 NE(2d) 892 (1984).

Where the state knew of new and additional charges arising from the same facts as the original charge at the time of the initial indictment, the computation of speedy trial time on the additional charges is the same as that applied to the original charge. State v. Clay (Trumbull 1983) 9 Ohio App.3d 216, 459 N.E.2d 609, 9 O.B.R. 366.

Where a prosecutor obtains a felony indictment, based upon the same conduct as was a previously nolled, lesser-included misdemeanor charge, the time within which the accused shall be brought to trial pursuant to RC 2945.71 et seq. consists of whatever residue remains from the 270–day period set forth in RC 2945.71(C) after deducting the speedy trial time expended prior to the nolle prosequi. State v. Bonarrigo (Ohio 1980) 62 Ohio St.2d 7, 402 N.E.2d 530, 16 O.O.3d 4. Criminal Law ⚩ 577.14

Where an accused is held pursuant to a charge which must be tried pursuant to RC 2945.71(B)(2) and which is based on facts which are identical to those in a charge previously dismissed for want of prosecution, if no continuance has been granted pursuant to RC 2945.72(H), the accused must be brought to trial within ninety days after his first arrest or service of summons. State v. Justice (Hamilton 1976) 49 Ohio App.2d 46, 358 N.E.2d 1382, 3 O.O.3d 109. Criminal Law ⚩ 577.14

49. —— Probation or parole violations, revised or additional charges generally

Statutory speedy trial period in prosecution for aggravated robbery, kidnapping, and assault was not subject to acceleration due to defendant's pre-trial incarceration, where defendant was not held in jail in lieu of bail solely on pending charges, but also on parole violation which amounted to separate charge. State v. Butler (Ohio App. 8 Dist., Cuyahoga, 08-11-2005) No. 85366, 2005-Ohio-4122, 2005 WL 1907279, Unreported. Criminal Law ⚩ 577.11(1); Criminal Law ⚩ 577.11(3)

Evidence was sufficient to support trial court's finding, in ruling on defendant's motion to dismiss for speedy trial violation, that valid probation holder had existed at time defendant was being held prior to trial, despite state's failure to give defendant written notice of such a holder, where written notice was not required; defendant's probation officer and administrative warden of county correctional center testified that no written notice was generated when person was detained on capias. State v. Canales (Ohio App. 8 Dist., Cuyahoga, 03-10-2005) No. 84351, 2005-Ohio-1006, 2005 WL 563827, Unreported. Criminal Law ⚷ 577.16(5.1); Criminal Law ⚷ 577.16(9)

Evidence that defendant was held prior to trial both on pending charges and on outstanding probation violation capias was sufficient to support trial court's finding that statutory accelerated speedy trial requirements did not apply, despite state's failure to give defendant written notice that he was being so held, where valid probation holder existed and defendant was orally informed that he was being held both on pending charges and on outstanding probation violation capias. State v. Canales (Ohio App. 8 Dist., Cuyahoga, 03-10-2005) No. 84351, 2005-Ohio-1006, 2005 WL 563827, Unreported. Criminal Law ⚷ 577.11(3)

Ninety-day statutory speedy trial time period did not apply to defendant, where defendant was not being held in jail in lieu of bond solely on pending charges as he had five arrest warrants and parole detainer outstanding. State v. Murray (Ohio App. 9 Dist., Lorain, 09-22-2004) No. 03CA008330, 2004-Ohio-4966, 2004 WL 2244444, Unreported. Criminal Law ⚷ 577.11(3)

State's failure to bring defendant to trial within the statutorily prescribed time limit did not violate defendant's statutory speedy trial rights; prosecutor informed trial court that defendant was also being held in jail on a parole holder for other charges in a different jurisdiction, and defense counsel did not dispute existence of parole holder. State v. Brown (Ohio App. 11 Dist., Trumbull, 12-31-2003) No. 2002-T-0077, 2003-Ohio-7183, 2003 WL 23100331, Unreported. Criminal Law ⚷ 577.11(4)

Statutory triple count provisions did not apply to require trial of defendant within 90 days after his arrest, where defendant was also being held prior to trial pursuant to valid parole holder. State v. Stadmire (Ohio App. 8 Dist., Cuyahoga, 02-27-2003) No. 81188, 2003-Ohio-873, 2003 WL 549912, Unreported. Criminal Law ⚷ 577.11(3)

Documents indicating that post-conviction petitioner's parole holder had become inactive during his pretrial incarceration did not amount to new evidence entitling petitioner to hearing on otherwise untimely petition alleging speedy trial violation, where parole officer's testimony admitted that parole holder had become inactive. State v. Davis (Ohio App. 7 Dist., Mahoning, 05-30-2002) No. 01 CA 171, 2002-Ohio-2789, 2002 WL 32806896, Unreported. Criminal Law ⚷ 1655(1)

Absent motion to dismiss for violation of speedy trial statute filed at or prior to commencement of trial, prosecutor had no duty to produce evidence of parole or probation "holder" relieving prosecutor of obligation to bring defendant to trial within 90 days of arrest. State v. Thompson (Ohio App. 6 Dist., 09-16-1994) 97 Ohio App.3d 183, 646 N.E.2d 499, dismissed, appeal not allowed 71 Ohio St.3d 1456, 644 N.E.2d 1029. Criminal Law ⚷ 577.16(7); Criminal Law ⚷ 577.16(8)

If defendant is held for parole or probation violation in addition to pending charges, 90–day period of speedy trial statute is not triggered. State v. Thompson (Ohio App. 6 Dist., 09-16-1994) 97 Ohio App.3d 183, 646 N.E.2d 499, dismissed, appeal not allowed 71 Ohio St.3d 1456, 644 N.E.2d 1029. Criminal Law ⚷ 577.11(3)

There was evidence to support existence of valid parole holder on defendant, where trial transcript reflected that defense counsel entered into stipulation establishing existence of parole holder, preventing application of triple-count provisions of statute guaranteeing accused's right to be tried without inordinate delay. State v. Mann (Ohio App. 8 Dist., 11-15-1993) 93 Ohio App.3d 301, 638 N.E.2d 585, dismissed, appeal not allowed 70 Ohio St.3d 1412, 637 N.E.2d 9. Criminal Law ⚷ 577.8(1)

Where a defendant is arrested on a robbery charge and a parole violation holder is issued on the day he is arrested, RC 2945.71 does not apply since the defendant is not being held solely on a criminal charge where he remains in jail after the robbery charge is dismissed. State v. Jones (Portage 1992) 81 Ohio App.3d 348, 611 N.E.2d 329, dismissed, jurisdictional motion overruled 65 Ohio St.3d 1441, 600 N.E.2d 684.

RC 2945.71(D) is not applicable where a defendant is held on both pending criminal charges and for probation violation. State v. Martin (Ohio 1978) 56 Ohio St.2d 207, 383 N.E.2d 585, 10 O.O.3d 369.

When a defendant is apprehended for the commission of certain offenses and imprisoned because such arrest establishes a violation of his parole, the speedy trial period will not begin to run until he specifically requests disposition of the charges for which he was arrested. State v Adams, No. 86 CA 174 (7th Dist Ct App, Mahoning, 11–23–88).

Where defendant is arrested pursuant to an "order to hold" by the Ohio parole authority and defendant is subsequently charged with another offense, the statutory time for speedy trial for the second offense begins to run from the time of the charge for that offense. State v Martin, No. 10629 (9th Dist Ct App, Summit, 10–13–82).

50. Triple-count mechanism—In general

Statute that requires each day accused is held in jail in lieu of bail pending trial be counted as three days for purposes of computing time in which accused must be brought to trial does not require that each day of jail credit be credited as three for purposes of reducing sentence imposed. State v. Lomack (Ohio App. 10 Dist., Franklin, 06-02-2005) No. 04AP-648, 2005-Ohio-2716, 2005 WL 1303190, Unreported. Sentencing And Punishment ⚷ 1158

Defendant was not denied statutory right to speedy trial in prosecution for aggravated robbery; defendant was not entitled to triple count provision for several of the days he was held in jail in lieu of bail, since for part of the time a parole hold was placed on him and he was therefore held for separate offenses, and defendant then filed several motions which tolled the statutory speedy trial period, including motions requesting discovery, bill of particulars, preliminary hearing, withdrawal of previous not guilty plea, treatment in lieu of conviction, multiple continuances, dismissal based on speedy trial violations, and proceedings related to his insanity plea. State v. Turner (Ohio App. 7 Dist., Mahoning, 03-19-2004) No. 93 CA 91, 2004-Ohio-1545, 2004 WL 614808, Unreported, habeas corpus granted 401 F.3d 718. Criminal Law ⚿ 577.10(8); Criminal Law ⚿ 577.11(1)

Defendant was denied his right to speedy trial because he was not brought to trial within limits imposed by triple-count provision of speedy trial statute and record did not demonstrate that defendant was not entitled to be brought to trial within those limits. State v. McDonald (Ohio App. 8 Dist., 08-14-2003) 153 Ohio App.3d 679, 795 N.E.2d 701, 2003-Ohio-4342, stay granted 100 Ohio St.3d 1480, 798 N.E.2d 615, 2003-Ohio-5993, appeal not allowed 100 Ohio St.3d 1531, 800 N.E.2d 48, 2003-Ohio-6458. Criminal Law ⚿ 577.8(1)

Defendant was denied his right to speedy trial because he was not brought to trial within limits imposed by triple-count provision of speedy trial statute and record did not demonstrate that defendant was not entitled to be brought to trial within those limits. State v. McDonald (Ohio App. 8 Dist., 08-14-2003) 153 Ohio App.3d 679, 795 N.E.2d 701, 2003-Ohio-4342, stay granted 100 Ohio St.3d 1480, 798 N.E.2d 615, 2003-Ohio-5993, appeal not allowed 100 Ohio St.3d 1531, 800 N.E.2d 48, 2003-Ohio-6458. Criminal Law ⚿ 577.8(1)

Defendant was not being held in jail in lieu of bond on misdemeanor charges, and was not entitled to application of triple-count provision of speedy trial statute under which each day held in jail in lieu of bail is counted as three days in determining date by which trial must be held, where after defendant was charged with two misdemeanors and felony arising out of same conduct he was released on own recognizance on misdemeanor charges but remained in jail in lieu of bond on felony charge after bond was set at $50,000 and misdemeanors and felony followed different paths to litigation, notwithstanding fact that defendant had been in jail for over five months since his arrest. State v. Fielder (Ohio Mun., 10-28-1994) 66 Ohio Misc.2d 163, 643 N.E.2d 633. Criminal Law ⚿ 577.8(1); Criminal Law ⚿ 577.11(1)

RC 2945.71(C) is the appropriate time limit for felony trials in cases in which the accused is not entitled to the triple-count provision of RC 2945.71(D). State v. MacDonald (Ohio 1976) 48 Ohio St.2d 66, 357 N.E.2d 40, 2 O.O.3d 219.

An accused in a court of common pleas who has been bound over from a juvenile court is entitled to have his "jail time," service while under the jurisdiction of the latter, deducted from his sentence. State v. Young (Franklin 1975) 44 Ohio App.2d 387, 339 N.E.2d 668, 73 O.O.2d 462.

51. —— Single indictment and single trial, triple-count mechanism

Triple-count provision of speedy trial statute, under which each day accused is held in jail in lieu of bail is counted as three days in determining date before which trial must occur, applies to defendant held on multiple counts on same indictment if all counts are to be heard at same trial. State v. Fielder (Ohio Mun., 10-28-1994) 66 Ohio Misc.2d 163, 643 N.E.2d 633. Criminal Law ⚿ 577.8(1); Criminal Law ⚿ 577.11(1)

Triple-count provision of speedy trial statute, under which each day accused is held in jail is counted as three days, applies to criminal defendant in jail in lieu of bail and charged with multiple counts under single indictment, if all counts are to be tried in single trial. State v. Collins (Ohio App. 6 Dist., 09-30-1993) 91 Ohio App.3d 10, 631 N.E.2d 666, dismissed, jurisdictional motion overruled 68 Ohio St.3d 1470, 628 N.E.2d 1389. Criminal Law ⚿ 577.8(1)

RC 2945.71(E) applies to a defendant held in jail in lieu of bail on multiple counts in a single indictment and tried in a single trial. State v. Bowman (Clermont 1987) 41 Ohio App.3d 318, 535 N.E.2d 730. Criminal Law ⚿ 577.10(5)

The triple-count provision of RC 2945.71(E) applies where a defendant is held on multiple charges based on the same incident and such charges are raised in a single indictment to be tried jointly. State v Crouse, Nos. CA 87–05–042 and CA 87–06–047 (12th Dist Ct App, Clermont, 4–11–88).

52. —— Pending charges, triple-count mechanism

Appropriate speedy-trial period for felony defendant was within 270 days of arrest, as opposed to 90 days that would apply if defendant were held in jail in lieu of bail solely on pending charges, given triple-count statute providing that each day that a defendant is held in jail in lieu of bail on pending charges is counted as three days; defendant was not in jail solely on pending charges, in that he was served with valid holder for separate charges, and thus triple-count statute did not apply. State v. Wright (Ohio App. 12 Dist., Clermont, 08-01-2005) No. CA2004-08-061, 2005-Ohio-3907, 2005 WL 1799296, Unreported, appeal allowed 107 Ohio St.3d 1696, 840 N.E.2d 202, 2005-Ohio-6763, reversed 109 Ohio St.3d 313, 847 N.E.2d 1174, 2006-Ohio-2109. Criminal Law ⚿ 577.11(3); Criminal Law ⚿ 577.15(3)

Defendant was not entitled to application of triple count provision with respect to statutory 270-day speedy trial period, in trial for aggravated robbery, kidnapping, and theft, where defendant was not being held in jail solely on pending charges but was also being held on other, unrelated charges. State v. Freeman (Ohio App. 8 Dist., Cuyahoga, 07-07-2005) No. 85137, 2005-Ohio-3480, 2005 WL 1581105, Unreported, motion for delayed appeal granted 107 Ohio St.3d 1404, 836 N.E.2d 1226, 2005-Ohio-5859. Criminal Law ⚿ 577.8(1)

Defendant who remained in jail pending trial on drug and other charges, and against whom probation officer placed a holder, was not held solely on the pending charges, and thus State's failure to bring defendant to trial within 90 days did not violate defendant's speedy trial rights pursuant to speedy trial provision triple counting days for which a defendant is held solely on the pending charges, even though the holder was also based on the pending charges; placement of holder meant that defendant would not have been released from jail if he posted bail, and probation violation was separate cause with different scope of inquiry. State v. McGhee (Ohio App. 4 Dist., Lawrence, 03-30-2005) No. 04CA15, 2005-Ohio-1585, 2005 WL 737581, Unreported. Criminal Law ⚷ 577.11(1)

Triple-count provision of speedy trial rule did not apply to defendant who was not held solely on pending burglary charges, but also for a parole violation. State v. Miller (Ohio App. 11 Dist., Lake, 11-26-2004) No. 2002-L-162, 2004-Ohio-6342, 2004 WL 2697264, Unreported. Criminal Law ⚷ 577.10(5)

Defendant was entitled to triple-counting of days held in jail in lieu of bail on pending charges raised in second indictment until date he was committed to prison on charge raised in initial indictment, for purpose of determining whether defendant's statutory speedy trial right was violated; defendant was no longer jailed in lieu of bail after he was committed to prison as he no longer had ability to post bond or be released on bond. State v. Thompson (Ohio App. 2 Dist., Montgomery, 03-19-2004) No. 20114, 2004-Ohio-1320, 2004 WL 541165, Unreported, on subsequent appeal 161 Ohio App.3d 334, 830 N.E.2d 394, 2005-Ohio-2508. Criminal Law ⚷ 577.8(2)

Statute authorizing triple count for days spent incarcerated in lieu of bail on pending charges did not apply to defendant incarcerated on unrelated offense, for purposes of speedy trial analysis. State v. Monroe (Ohio App. 4 Dist., Hocking, 03-25-2003) No. 02CA23, 2003-Ohio-1709, 2003 WL 1756702, Unreported. Criminal Law ⚷ 577.11(3)

The "triple-count" provision of RC 2945.71(E) applies only to defendants held in jail in lieu of bail solely on the pending charge; it does not apply to a defendant who, in addition to a pending charge, also faces a parole violation. State v. Smith (Ohio App. 8 Dist., Cuyahoga, 04-27-1995) No. 66497, 1995 WL 248532, Unreported, motion for delayed appeal denied 73 Ohio St.3d 1424, 652 N.E.2d 798, reconsideration denied 74 Ohio St.3d 1423, 655 N.E.2d 742, certiorari denied 116 S.Ct. 1272, 516 U.S. 1176, 134 L.Ed.2d 218.

Where a defendant was indicted on a second unrelated charge while being held in jail on the first charge, the triple count provision of RC 2945.71 is inapplicable since the defendant was being held on two pending charges. State v. Mack (Ohio App. 8 Dist., Cuyahoga, 01-27-1994) No. 65819, 1994 WL 24260, Unreported, dismissed, appeal not allowed 70 Ohio St.3d 1412, 637 N.E.2d 9.

Triple-count provision, which counts each day held in jail in lieu of bail as three days for speedy-trial purposes, applies only when the person is being held in jail solely on the pending case. State v. Sanchez (Ohio App. 6 Dist., 04-29-2005) 162 Ohio App.3d 113, 832 N.E.2d 1215, 2005-Ohio-2093, reversed 2009 WL 676, appeal allowed 106 Ohio St.3d 1532, 835 N.E.2d 381, 2005-Ohio-5146. Criminal Law ⚷ 577.11(1)

Because defendant was serving sentence of 25 years on conviction for aggravated robbery, he was being held on more than pending charges and was not entitled to benefit of triple count provisions of the speedy trial statute. State v. Grinnell (Ohio App. 10 Dist., 06-27-1996) 112 Ohio App.3d 124, 678 N.E.2d 231, appeal not allowed 77 Ohio St.3d 1474, 673 N.E.2d 138, appeal not allowed 77 Ohio St.3d 1475, 673 N.E.2d 138, denial of habeas corpus affirmed 215 F.3d 1326, certiorari denied 121 S.Ct. 232, 531 U.S. 898, 148 L.Ed.2d 166. Criminal Law ⚷ 577.8(1); Criminal Law ⚷ 577.11(3)

Issue of speedy trial and triple-count provision, stating that for purposes of computing time within which defendant shall be brought to trial, each day during which accused is held in jail in lieu of bail on pending charge shall be counted as three days, is raised when defendant alleges in motion to dismiss that the only cause of incarceration is the pending charge and that time requirements of triple-count provision have not been met and once this is accomplished, burden of producing evidence demonstrating that defendant is not entitled to be brought to trial under limits of the triple-count provision falls upon state. State v. Hubbard (Ohio App. 11 Dist., 06-12-1995) 104 Ohio App.3d 443, 662 N.E.2d 394, dismissed, jurisdictional motion overruled 74 Ohio St.3d 1456, 656 N.E.2d 950. Criminal Law ⚷ 577.16(6); Criminal Law ⚷ 577.16(8)

State failed to establish that defendant was held in jail in lieu of bail on charges in addition to pending charge, and thus, defendant was entitled to application of triple-count provision of speedy trial statute; although state maintained at oral hearing that two cases were pending against defendant, and trial court responded that such records would be made available on appeal, records were not submitted on appeal. State v. Baker (Ohio App. 8 Dist., 12-20-1993) 92 Ohio App.3d 516, 636 N.E.2d 363. Criminal Law ⚷ 577.8(1)

State has responsibility to demonstrate that defendant is being held in jail in lieu of bail on additional charges and not solely on pending charge where defendant asserts entitlement to triple-count provision of speedy trial statute which applies where defendant is held in jail in lieu of bail on pending charge only. State v. Baker (Ohio App. 8 Dist., 12-20-1993) 92 Ohio App.3d 516, 636 N.E.2d 363. Criminal Law ⚷ 577.16(8)

Where a defendant is charged with both domestic violence and assault arising from a single transaction, incarceration on both charges will be considered incarceration on the "pending charge" for purposes of RC 2945.71(E) to trigger the three-for-one provisions of that section; thus, the case will be dismissed where the defendant is not brought to trial within thirty days of his arrest. State v. Parsley

(Franklin 1993) 82 Ohio App.3d 567, 612 N.E.2d 813.

When a defendant's motion for discharge, based on the triple-count provisions of RC 2945.71(E), alleges that he is incarcerated solely on the pending charge, the burden of production of evidence shifts to the prosecutor to establish that other charges are pending and that the triple-count provisions are therefore inapplicable. State v. Butcher (Ohio 1986) 27 Ohio St.3d 28, 500 N.E.2d 1368, 27 O.B.R. 445.

The triple count provisions of RC 2945.71(D) do not apply in favor of a defendant held on a pending charge and also on a parole detainer predicated on that charge. State v. Jones (Ohio Com.Pl. 1983) 12 Ohio Misc.2d 15, 467 N.E.2d 577, 12 O.B.R. 424.

The placement of a defendant in holding facilities during the post-arraignment processing incidental to release on bail does not constitute detention as defined by RC 2921.01(E), and therefore may not be counted as a day served in lieu of bail on the pending charge for speedy trial purposes. State v. Wolos (Cuyahoga 1983) 8 Ohio App.3d 361, 457 N.E.2d 358, 8 O.B.R. 473. Criminal Law ⚷ 577.8(2)

RC 2945.71(C)(2) and RC 2945.71(D) provide that a person against whom a felony charge is pending shall be brought to trial within ninety days after his arrest, where such person has been held in jail in lieu of bail on the pending charge, unless such time is extended by RC 2945.72. State v. Walker (Jefferson 1974) 42 Ohio App.2d 41, 327 N.E.2d 796, 71 O.O.2d 238.

Evidence was insufficient to show that triple-count provision of speedy trial statute, which demanded that a defendant held in jail in lieu of bail solely on pending charges be brought to trial within 90 days instead of usual 270 days, applied to defendant, and thus, trial court's refusal to dismiss on speedy trial grounds was not plain error, where no evidence of a valid parole holder existed in record, as prosecution was not afforded opportunity to produce evidence of such holder. State v. Duvall (Ohio App. 8 Dist., Cuyahoga, 09-05-2002) No. 80316, 2002-Ohio-4574, 2002 WL 2027318, Unreported, appeal not allowed 98 Ohio St.3d 1461, 783 N.E.2d 520, 2003-Ohio-644. Criminal Law ⚷ 1035(1)

Evidence supported finding that defendant was held solely on pending charges, and thus triple count provision, which required that, when accused remained in jail in lieu of bail solely on pending charges, each day was counted as three days for purposes of statute requiring that those accused of felonies be brought to trial within 270 days, applied, where state failed to introduce evidence that sheriff's department received parole holder, held defendant on it, or that parole holder was still effective, parole holder bore no sign or stamp to indicate that sheriff's office received it, and parole holder was not authenticated or certified. State v. Green (Ohio App. 4 Dist., Ross, 07-02-2002) No. 01CA2641, 2002-Ohio-3403, 2002 WL 1436032, Unreported. Criminal Law ⚷ 577.11(1)

Following arrest, defendant was not held in jail in lieu of bail on the pending charge, as required for application of "triple-count" provision of speedy trial statute, where defendant was incarcerated not only on the pending criminal charges, but also under a valid parole holder. State v. DeLeon (Ohio App. 2 Dist., Montgomery, 06-28-2002) No. 18114, 2002-Ohio-3286, 2002 WL 1393665, Unreported, appeal not allowed 98 Ohio St.3d 1424, 782 N.E.2d 78, 2003-Ohio-259. Criminal Law ⚷ 577.11(3)

RC 2945.71(E), which requires that each day an accused is held in jail in lieu of bail pending trial be counted as three days for purposes of computing the time in which the accused must be brought to trial, has no relation to and does not apply to the adult parole authority's reduction of a defendant's sentence by the total number of days that the prisoner was confined before trial pursuant to RC 2967.191. State ex rel. Freshour v. State (Ohio 1988) 39 Ohio St.3d 41, 528 N.E.2d 1259.

The triple-count provisions of RC 2945.71(D) apply only when the defendant is detained solely on the pending charge, and do not apply if he is also detained on a parole detainer. State v Hunter, No. 47551 (8th Dist Ct App, Cuyahoga, 6–21–84).

53. —— Additional or unrelated charges, triple-count mechanism

Defendant convicted of aggravated murder, murder, and aggravated robbery was not entitled, under speedy-trial law, to be brought to trial within 270-days of original indictment charging him with burglary arising out of the same events, where murder and robbery charges arose out of additional facts discovered by police after the burglary indictment. State v. Burrell (Ohio App. 1 Dist., Hamilton, 01-07-2005) No. C-030803, 2005-Ohio-34, 2005 WL 27469, Unreported, appeal not allowed 105 Ohio St.3d 1546, 827 N.E.2d 328, 2005-Ohio-2188. Criminal Law ⚷ 577.10(5); Criminal Law ⚷ 577.14

In calculating whether defendant's statutory speedy trial right was violated, defendant was entitled to straight-time credit, rather than triple-time credit, for time defendant was subject to Clark County holder on theft charges while he was incarcerated in Green County jail on unrelated charges. State v. Phillips (Ohio App. 2 Dist., Clark, 09-03-2004) No. 2003-CA-15, 2004-Ohio-4688, 2004 WL 1949470, Unreported. Criminal Law ⚷ 577.11(4)

Triple-count provision of speedy trial statute, pursuant to which each day that the accused is held in jail in lieu of bail counts as three days, did not apply to time defendant spent in jail, where record contained a holder from another state, and defendant was wanted on open warrants in other jurisdictions. State v. Brewster (Ohio App. 1 Dist., Hamilton, 06-11-2004) No. C-030024, No. C-030025, 2004-Ohio-2993, 2004 WL 1284008, Unreported, motion for delayed appeal denied 103 Ohio St.3d 1490, 816 N.E.2d 1078, 2004-Ohio-5605. Criminal Law ⚷ 577.11(1); Criminal Law ⚷ 577.11(3)

Competent, credible evidence supported finding that defendant was not being held in county jail solely on underlying charges arising out of robbery and failure to comply with the order or signal of a police officer offenses committed in that county, for purposes of determining whether triple-county provision of speedy trial statute, which provided that each day spent in jail count as three days, applied, but was also being held on charges in another county and in another state; defendant's suggestion that he could be released on bone to await trial in other county and state were speculative at best. State v. Tyler (Ohio App. 5 Dist., Fairfield, 10-08-2003) No. 02 CA 85, 2003-Ohio-5420, 2003 WL 22319420, Unreported. Criminal Law ⚷ 577.11(1)

Defendant's right to a speedy trial was not violated; statutory provision providing that each day during which defendant is held in jail in lieu of bail on pending charges is counted as three days for speedy trial purposes, was not applicable to defendant, as defendant was in jail on separate unrelated charges following arrest for current charges, and defendant's cases went to trial within 270 days from date of first indictment. State v. Johnson (Ohio App. 8 Dist., Cuyahoga, 06-19-2003) No. 81692, No. 81693, 2003-Ohio-3241, 2003 WL 21419631, Unreported, appeal not allowed 100 Ohio St.3d 1433, 797 N.E.2d 513, 2003-Ohio-5396. Criminal Law ⚷ 577.11(3)

Time spent by defendant in county jail was not subject to the triple-counting provision of speedy trial rules in determining whether defendant was brought to trial on the state charges within 270 days of his arrest; defendant was not being held solely on charges in one county, but also on separate charges in other counties. State v. Tyler (Ohio App. 5 Dist., Fairfield, 06-09-2003) No. 02CA67, 2003-Ohio-3014, 2003 WL 21357355, Unreported. Criminal Law ⚷ 577.8(1)

For purposes of statutory 270-day time period for bringing an accused arrested and charged with a felony to trial, defendant was not entitled to triple-count provision between time of arrest on felony driving under the influence of alcohol (DUI) and other misdemeanor charges and date municipal court disposed of misdemeanor charges, where misdemeanor and felony counts did not share common litigation history, and if defendant wanted to be released from jail prior to court's disposition of misdemeanor charges, he would have had to post bond in both common pleas court and municipal court. State v. Eldridge (Ohio App. 4 Dist., Scioto, 03-10-2003) No. 02CA2842, 2003-Ohio-1198, 2003 WL 1145442, Unreported. Criminal Law ⚷ 577.11(3)

Triple count provision of speedy trial statute, providing that "each day during which the accused is held in jail in lieu of bail on the pending charge shall be counted as three days," did not apply to the period of time defendant, who was charged with felonious assault and domestic violence, was serving time in jail on an unrelated municipal court case. State v. Will (Ohio App. 2 Dist., Montgomery, 08-30-2002) No. 18792, 2002-Ohio-4462, 2002 WL 1998210, Unreported. Criminal Law ⚷ 577.11(3)

Where an accused, while legally incarcerated, commits a crime, the triple-count provisions of RC 2945.71(C) and RC 2945.71(D) are suspended as to the first offense while he is also held in jail in lieu of bail pursuant to arrest on the second charge. State v. Thieshen (Marion 1977) 55 Ohio App.2d 99, 379 N.E.2d 622, 9 O.O.3d 259. Criminal Law ⚷ 577.11(3)

Triple count provision of speedy trial statute, providing that "each day during which the accused is held in jail in lieu of bail on the pending charge shall be counted as three days," did not apply to the period of time defendant, who was charged with felonious assault and domestic violence, was serving time in jail on an unrelated municipal court case. State v. Will (Ohio App. 2 Dist., Montgomery, 08-30-2002) No. 18792, 2002-Ohio-4462, 2002 WL 1998210, Unreported. Criminal Law ⚷ 577.11(3)

The triple-count provision of RC 2945.71(E) is not tolled when a defendant who does not post bond is not served with a valid holder on an unrelated charge until after the expiration of the statutory period. State v Rembert, No. 55654 (8th Dist Ct App, Cuyahoga, 10–19–89).

Where a defendant is held for two separate offenses and is ordered to post bond on one but allowed to sign a recognizance bond on the second, and where the defendant fails to post bond, the triple count provision will only apply to the first count, and time served in jail due to failure to post bond will not be tripled as applied to the second count. State v Sowards, No. 1599 (4th Dist Ct App, Scioto, 9–4–87).

Where defendant is held in jail in lieu of bail on two separate felony offenses, the triple-count provision of RC 2945.71(E) is inapplicable, and incarceration of one hundred eleven days before trial does not violate defendant's right to a speedy trial as explained in RC 2945.71(C)(2). State v Rudd, No. CA86–05–036 (12th Dist Ct App, Clermont, 3–2–87).

54. —— Probation or parole violations, triple-count mechanism

Triple-count provision of speedy trial statute did not apply to defendant incarcerated on separate parole violation at time he was indicted on new charges. State v. Dixon (Ohio App. 5 Dist., Richland, 06-03-2005) No. 2004-CA-90, 2005-Ohio-2846, 2005 WL 1364615, Unreported, appeal not allowed 106 Ohio St.3d 1556, 836 N.E.2d 581, 2005-Ohio-5531. Criminal Law ⚷ 577.11(3)

Statutory "triple count" speedy trial provision, which requires person charged with felony to be brought to trial within 90 days, did not apply to defendant, despite contention that provision applied to defendant as he was not properly served with notice of federal holder for parole violation, where defendant was being held in jail in lieu of bail for both state charges and federal holder for parole violation and requirement that detainee be served with notice of charge is inapplicable to parole holder situation. State v. Donald (Ohio

App. 8 Dist., Cuyahoga, 12-16-2004) No. 81570, No. 83947, 2004-Ohio-6848, 2004 WL 2914928, Unreported, appeal not allowed 105 Ohio St.3d 1562, 828 N.E.2d 117, 2005-Ohio-2447. Criminal Law ⚷ 577.11(3)

Defendant's entitlement to triple counting of days held in jail, for purposes of 270-day speedy trial period, ceased from date of probation holder. State v. Wade (Ohio App. 10 Dist., Franklin, 07-29-2004) No. 03AP-774, 2004-Ohio-3974, 2004 WL 1688434, Unreported, stay granted 103 Ohio St.3d 1476, 816 N.E.2d 253, 2004-Ohio-5405, appeal not allowed 104 Ohio St.3d 1427, 819 N.E.2d 709, 2004-Ohio-6585, appeal not allowed 104 Ohio St.3d 1462, 821 N.E.2d 578, 2005-Ohio-204. Criminal Law ⚷ 577.8(1)

Triple-count provision of statute establishing speedy trial time period did not apply to defendant such that state had 270 days in which to bring defendant to trial following arrest, where defendant was held in jail in lieu of bail on both pending aggravated assault charge and parole violation. State v. Reed (Ohio App. 8 Dist., Cuyahoga, 06-17-2004) No. 83434, 2004-Ohio-3124, 2004 WL 1354063, Unreported, appeal not allowed 103 Ohio St.3d 1527, 817 N.E.2d 409, 2004-Ohio-5852. Criminal Law ⚷ 577.11(1)

A valid parole holder was placed on defendant, and thus the "triple-count" provision of the speedy trial statute did not apply and defendant's right to a speedy trial was not violated. State v. Myers (Ohio App. 5 Dist., Richland, 06-09-2004) No. 03-CA-61, 2004-Ohio-3052, 2004 WL 1327929, Unreported, appeal not allowed 103 Ohio St.3d 1479, 816 N.E.2d 255, 2004-Ohio-5405. Criminal Law ⚷ 577.11(1)

Defendant was not entitled to triple credit for time served in jail in lieu of bail, under triple-count provision of speedy-trial statute, where defendant was on parole holder. State v. Olverson (Ohio App. 10 Dist., Franklin, 03-18-2003) No. 02AP-554, 2003-Ohio-1274, 2003 WL 1227597, Unreported, motion for delayed appeal denied 99 Ohio St.3d 1457, 790 N.E.2d 1220, 2003-Ohio-3514. Sentencing And Punishment ⚷ 1157

Valid parole holder that was executed against defendant the day after his arrest on present charges rendered inapplicable the provisions of speedy-trial statute under which each day during which an accused is held in jail in lieu of bail is counted as three days. State v. Garrett (Ohio App. 8 Dist., Cuyahoga, 01-23-2003) No. 80172, 2003-Ohio-274, 2003 WL 152820, Unreported, appeal not allowed 99 Ohio St.3d 1437, 789 N.E.2d 1118, 2003-Ohio-2902, appeal not allowed 101 Ohio St.3d 1491, 805 N.E.2d 541, 2004-Ohio-1293. Criminal Law ⚷ 577.11(1)

Assuming lack of valid parole holder during defendant's pretrial incarceration, triple-count provision of speedy trial statute was inapplicable, where defendant had already been recommitted for parole violation and was not being held on pending charge alone. State v. Davis (Ohio App. 7 Dist., Mahoning, 05-30-2002) No. 01 CA 171, 2002-Ohio-2789, 2002 WL 32806896, Unreported. Criminal Law ⚷ 577.11(1)

In computing the time in capital murder prosecution in conformity with the speedy trial statute, defendant was not entitled to the triple-count provision of speedy trial statute for the time he was held in jail, where probation detainer was placed against defendant the day after his arrest. State v. Myers (Ohio, 12-13-2002) 97 Ohio St.3d 335, 780 N.E.2d 186, 2002-Ohio-6658, reconsideration denied 97 Ohio St.3d 1500, 780 N.E.2d 1023, 2002-Ohio-7367, certiorari denied 123 S.Ct. 2254, 539 U.S. 906, 156 L.Ed.2d 116, motion to reopen denied 100 Ohio St.3d 1505, 799 N.E.2d 184, 2003-Ohio-6161. Criminal Law ⚷ 577.8(1); Criminal Law ⚷ 577.11(3)

One method of excusing triple-count provision, stating that, for purposes of computing time within which defendant must be brought to trial, each day during which accused is held in jail in lieu of bail on the pending charge shall be counted as three days, is to produce proof that defendant is being held on a parole or probation violation holder. State v. Hubbard (Ohio App. 11 Dist., 06-12-1995) 104 Ohio App.3d 443, 662 N.E.2d 394, dismissed, jurisdictional motion overruled 74 Ohio St.3d 1456, 656 N.E.2d 950. Criminal Law ⚷ 577.8(1); Criminal Law ⚷ 577.11(3)

Existence of valid probation violation holder serves to prevent triggering of the triple-count provision stating that, for purposes of computing time within which defendant must be brought to trial, each day during which accused is held in jail in lieu of bail on the pending charge shall be counted as three days. State v. Hubbard (Ohio App. 11 Dist., 06-12-1995) 104 Ohio App.3d 443, 662 N.E.2d 394, dismissed, jurisdictional motion overruled 74 Ohio St.3d 1456, 656 N.E.2d 950. Criminal Law ⚷ 577.8(1); Criminal Law ⚷ 577.11(3)

Because there was probation holder on defendant, defendant was not being held "solely" on the pending charge so as to trigger triple-count provision stating that, for purposes of computing time within which defendant must be brought to trial, each day during which accused is held in jail in lieu of bail on the pending charge shall be counted as three days and thus, trial court erred in dismissing case pursuant to triple-count provision. State v. Hubbard (Ohio App. 11 Dist., 06-12-1995) 104 Ohio App.3d 443, 662 N.E.2d 394, dismissed, jurisdictional motion overruled 74 Ohio St.3d 1456, 656 N.E.2d 950. Criminal Law ⚷ 577.11(3)

Ninety-day, three-for-one speedy trial provisions did not apply, and state was required only to meet 270–day limit for bringing defendant to trial, where during time between arrest and trial defendant was in custody on parole holder. State v. Fields (Ohio App. 1 Dist., 09-28-1994) 97 Ohio App.3d 337, 646 N.E.2d 866, motion for delayed appeal denied 84 Ohio St.3d 1427, 702 N.E.2d 903. Criminal Law ⚷ 577.11(3)

Existence of valid parole holder prevents application of triple-count provision of speedy trial statute requiring each day to be counted as three days if accused is in jail in lieu of bail on pending charge. State v. Brown (Ohio 1992) 64 Ohio St.3d 476, 597 N.E.2d 97. Criminal Law ⚷ 577.8(1); Criminal Law ⚷ 577.11(1)

Transcripts of hearing on motion to dismiss on speedy trial grounds and in-chambers conference established that there was valid parole holder on defendant and, therefore, that he was not entitled to triple-count provision of speedy trial statute requiring each day to be counted as three days, if accused is held in jail in lieu of bail on pending charge, even though trial court made no findings of fact supporting denial of speedy trial motion; defendant never requested findings of fact, and trial counsel could acknowledge the parole holder had been placed on defendant. State v. Brown (Ohio 1992) 64 Ohio St.3d 476, 597 N.E.2d 97. Criminal Law ⚷ 577.16(9); Criminal Law ⚷ 577.16(10)

The triple count provision of RC 2945.71 does not entitle a defendant to have charges against him prosecuted within ninety days of his arrest where he faces a charge of probation or parole violation in addition to pending charges; such a defendant charged with felony violations is subject to the time limitation of 270 days under RC 2945.71(C). State v. Phillips (Hamilton 1990) 69 Ohio App.3d 379, 590 N.E.2d 1281, motion overruled 57 Ohio St.3d 725, 568 N.E.2d 1229.

The triple-count provision of RC 2945.71(E) does not apply where a defendant is held in jail under a parole holder, even if additional criminal charges are pending. State v. Dunkins (Summit 1983) 10 Ohio App.3d 72, 460 N.E.2d 688, 10 O.B.R. 82.

Existence of a valid parole holder prevents application of the triple-count provision of speedy trial statute, which demands that a defendant incarcerated in lieu of bail solely on pending charges be brought to trial within 90 days instead of usual 270 days. State v. Duvall (Ohio App. 8 Dist., Cuyahoga, 09-05-2002) No. 80316, 2002-Ohio-4574, 2002 WL 2027318, Unreported, appeal not allowed 98 Ohio St.3d 1461, 783 N.E.2d 520, 2003-Ohio-644. Criminal Law ⚷ 577.8(1)

55. —— Home arrest, triple-count mechanism

Time spent under a home arrest program after a defendant has posted bond does not constitute jail time for speedy trial purposes since the restraints placed on a defendant under a home arrest program are not considered "detention" which would entitled a defendant to count each day as three days under RC 2945.71(E). State v. Brownlow (Allen 1991) 75 Ohio App.3d 88, 598 N.E.2d 888.

56. Delays generally—Trial date schedule

Neither defendant's statutory nor constitutional rights to a speedy trial were violated in prosecution for non-support of dependents; defendant's motion for recusal tolled the speedy trial time, and while his motion for recusal remained pending, defendant requested that the trial date be rescheduled and sought a stay of the proceedings pending the outcome of his federal litigation. State v. Galluzzo (Ohio App. 2 Dist., Champaign, 01-20-2006) No. 2004 CA 25, 2006-Ohio-309, 2006 WL 202599, Unreported, appeal not allowed 109 Ohio St.3d 1482, 847 N.E.2d 1227, 2006-Ohio-2466. Criminal Law ⚷ 577.10(8)

Defendant's pre-trial motions to suppress, for discovery, and for bill of particulars, filed after trial court erroneously scheduled trial date beyond statutory speedy trial period, tolled running of speedy trial period, where speedy trial calculation was based upon date defendant was actually brought to trial, and not upon scheduled trial date. State v. Delarosa (Ohio App. 11 Dist., Portage, 06-30-2005) No. 2003-P-0129, 2005-Ohio-3399, 2005 WL 1538264, Unreported. Criminal Law ⚷ 577.10(8)

Trial court complied with its duties with respect to its sua sponte continuance, which tolled defendant's speedy trial date for first-degree misdemeanor operating motor vehicle under the influence (OMVI), where trial court filed journal entry prior to expiration of speedy trial date and indicated in journal entry that its reason for continuance was due to specific scheduling conflict in its docket. State v. Glass (Ohio App. 3 Dist., Auglaize, 08-23-2004) No. 2-04-01, 2004-Ohio-4402, 2004 WL 1874574, Unreported, appeal not allowed 104 Ohio St.3d 1460, 821 N.E.2d 577, 2005-Ohio-204. Criminal Law ⚷ 577.10(7)

Trial court's sua sponte continuance was reasonable and, thus, tolled defendant's speedy trial date for first-degree misdemeanor operating motor vehicle under the influence (OMVI); trial court continued trial due to scheduling conflicts within trial court's docket for previously scheduled trial date, trial court noted difficulty of impaneling jury on previously scheduled trial date because of lack of potential jurors due to approaching holidays and to illness, and trial court continued trial to earliest possible date within trial court's docket. State v. Glass (Ohio App. 3 Dist., Auglaize, 08-23-2004) No. 2-04-01, 2004-Ohio-4402, 2004 WL 1874574, Unreported, appeal not allowed 104 Ohio St.3d 1460, 821 N.E.2d 577, 2005-Ohio-204. Criminal Law ⚷ 577.10(7)

Trial court has the discretion to extend time limits of speedy trial statute when counsel for the accused voluntarily agrees to a trial date beyond the statutory time limits. State v. Huckaby (Ohio Mun., 08-05-1997) 91 Ohio Misc.2d 16, 696 N.E.2d 1116. Criminal Law ⚷ 577.13

Defendant's delay in filing motion for competency evaluation until week in which trial was originally scheduled, which purportedly left state unable to arrange jury trial in timely manner under speedy-trial statute once defendant was found competent, did not preclude dismissal on speedy-trial grounds. State v. Jones (Ohio App. 11 Dist., 04-04-1997) 119 Ohio App.3d 59, 694 N.E.2d 505. Criminal Law ⚷ 577.11(6); Criminal Law ⚷ 577.16(2)

Scheduling of pretrial conference or hearing does not automatically extend speedy trial time requirements; however, where pretrial conference was granted upon defendant's own request and there is nothing facially unreasonable about amount of time taken to permit pretrial and subsequent trial, time is tolled in calculating whether speedy trial requirements were satisfied. State v. Wirtanen (Ohio

App. 6 Dist., 04-26-1996) 110 Ohio App.3d 604, 674 N.E.2d 1245. Criminal Law ⚷ 577.10(7); Criminal Law ⚷ 577.10(8)

Although crowded docket may be sound reason to extend time period for speedy trial, practices that undercut implementation of speedy trial provisions must not be employed to extend requisite time periods. State v. Daugherty (Ohio App. 3 Dist., 03-28-1996) 110 Ohio App.3d 103, 673 N.E.2d 664. Criminal Law ⚷ 577.10(7)

Defendant was accountable for delay of trial date of more than 100 days caused by defendant's motions for continuances in determining whether defendant was tried within statutory speedy-trial limits. State v. Fields (Ohio App. 1 Dist., 09-28-1994) 97 Ohio App.3d 337, 646 N.E.2d 866, motion for delayed appeal denied 84 Ohio St.3d 1427, 702 N.E.2d 903. Criminal Law ⚷ 577.10(8)

A sua sponte continuance based on docket congestion will not be found reasonable absent a showing that the continued criminal case will take precedence over pending civil matters. State v. Terra (Franklin 1991) 74 Ohio App.3d 189, 598 N.E.2d 753, dismissed, jurisdictional motion overruled 62 Ohio St.3d 1452, 579 N.E.2d 1391.

Where the record on appeal does not reflect a reason for a fourteen-day delay between the date a case is set for trial and the date of trial or to whom it is attributable, such a fourteen-day delay is chargeable to the state for speedy trial purposes. State v. Collura (Cuyahoga 1991) 72 Ohio App.3d 364, 594 N.E.2d 975, dismissed, jurisdictional motion overruled 60 Ohio St.3d 718, 574 N.E.2d 1079.

The mere setting of an original trial date beyond the time limits of RC 2945.71 does not constitute a continuance "other than upon the accused's own motion" pursuant to RC 2945.72(H). State v. Cutcher (Ohio 1978) 56 Ohio St.2d 383, 384 N.E.2d 275, 10 O.O.3d 502. Criminal Law ⚷ 577.13

Failure of the accused to object to his trial assignment, announced within rule, for a trial date commencing after the time provided for trial in RC 2945.71 constitutes a "delay occasioned by the neglect... of the accused," within the meaning of RC 2945.72(H), and so extends the time within which an accused must be brought to trial. State v. Wentz (Stark 1975) 49 Ohio App.2d 96, 359 N.E.2d 446, 3 O.O.3d 157.

Where a case has been set for trial on a date beyond the period required by RC 2945.71 and the accused has ample notice thereof, he may not sit idly by and let the time within which he should be brought to trial expire in order to take advantage of the provisions of RC 2945.73. State v. Westbrook (Franklin 1975) 47 Ohio App.2d 211, 353 N.E.2d 637, 1 O.O.3d 284. Criminal Law ⚷ 577.10(10)

Where trial court failed to set date for trial for first degree misdemeanor within ninety-day period and thereafter ruled sua sponte that the presence of a crowded docket warranted a continuance, defendant was entitled to discharge. State v. Pudlock (Ohio 1975) 44 Ohio St.2d 104, 338 N.E.2d 524, 73 O.O.2d 357.

Since the burden is on the state, not the accused, to bring the defendant to trial within the statutory period, and the Supreme Court of Ohio has decided that a defendant's failure to object to a trial date unilaterally set by the court on a day beyond the 90–day time limit of RC 2945.71(C)(2) and 2945.71(E) does not amount to acquiescence in the trial date and defendant's silence does not constitute a "continuance" under RC 2945.72(H), the lower court's decision is reversed and the defendant is discharged. State v Kavish, No. C–920568 (1st Dist Ct App, Hamilton, 6–16–93).

57. —— Defendant's fault, delays generally

Defendant's right to a speedy trial was not violated, where the vast majority of the delay in his case was due to the motions, proceedings, or action made or instituted by defendant. State v. Ruse (Ohio App. 5 Dist., Tuscarawas, 02-15-2005) No. 2004-AP-07-0054, 2005-Ohio-734, 2005 WL 427993, Unreported. Criminal Law ⚷ 577.10(8)

Neither defendant's statutory nor constitutional rights to a speedy trial were violated in prosecution for attempted murder, rape, and aggravated burglary, despite fact that he spent over two years in jail before pleading no contest to charged offenses; defendant's defense revolved around specialized and complex neurological and psychiatric testing and reports, which took time to procure, complete, and verify, defendant filed for multiple continuances, and he expressly and repeatedly waived his speedy trial rights for a period of approximately two years, and thereafter, he caused other delays, and the State was granted a reasonable continuance. State v. Stanley (Ohio App. 7 Dist., Mahoning, 12-07-2004) No. 03 MA 42, 2004-Ohio-6801, 2004 WL 2913912, Unreported, appeal not allowed 105 Ohio St.3d 1516, 826 N.E.2d 314, 2005-Ohio-1880. Criminal Law ⚷ 577.10(8); Criminal Law ⚷ 577.10(9); Criminal Law ⚷ 577.13

Time spent resolving defendant's motion for bill of particulars, motion for discovery, motion for transcript, and motion to dismiss for speedy trial violation was chargeable to defendant in determining whether his statutory 270-day speedy trial time period was violated. State v. Murray (Ohio App. 9 Dist., Lorain, 09-22-2004) No. 03CA008330, 2004-Ohio-4966, 2004 WL 2244444, Unreported. Criminal Law ⚷ 577.10(8)

Trial delays caused by defendant's attorney's pretrial motions and requests for pretrial hearings were attributable to defendant for purposes of statutory speedy trial claim. State v. Griffin (Ohio App. 8 Dist., Cuyahoga, 08-19-2004) No. 83724, 2004-Ohio-4344, 2004 WL 1846121, Unreported. Criminal Law ⚷ 577.10(8)

Time spent determining motions filed by defendant would be counted against defendant for purposes of speedy trial statute. State v. Brewster (Ohio App. 1 Dist., Hamilton, 06-11-2004) No. C-030024, No. C-030025, 2004-Ohio-2993, 2004 WL 1284008, Unreported, motion for delayed appeal denied 103 Ohio St.3d 1490, 816 N.E.2d 1078, 2004-Ohio-5605. Criminal Law ⚷ 577.10(8)

Delay of more than a year before defendant was brought to trial, although length was presumptively prejudicial and defendant adequately asserted speedy trial right, did not violate defendant of his constitutional right to speedy trial in prosecution for aggravated robbery; much of delay was attributable to defendant through numerous continuances and motions he and his counsel filed, and since large amount of delay was attributable to defendant, rather than state, any prejudice defendant suffered was a result of his own actions. State v. Turner (Ohio App. 7 Dist., Mahoning, 03-19-2004) No. 93 CA 91, 2004-Ohio-1545, 2004 WL 614808, Unreported, habeas corpus granted 401 F.3d 718. Criminal Law ⚷ 577.10(8); Criminal Law ⚷ 577.16(4)

Time period between defendant's initial appearance and pretrial hearing was not attributable to defendant, for purpose of determining whether his statutory speedy trial right was violated, where record failed to show that delay was due to defendant's failure to have attorney at initial appearance, date on which pretrial hearing was set complied with local rules, and there was no indication pretrial hearing would have been scheduled earlier if defendant was represented by counsel at initial appearance. City of Maple Heights v. Pinkney (Ohio App. 8 Dist., Cuyahoga, 03-18-2004) No. 81514, 2004-Ohio-1256, 2004 WL 536195, Unreported. Criminal Law ⚷ 577.10(8)

Delay of 391 days from date defendant was arrested until date of guilty plea did not violate his constitutional and statutory speedy trial rights; defendant filed multiple motions for continuance and numerous other motions, including two motions to suppress, a motion to withdraw counsel, several discovery motions, and a motion for a transcript at State's expense. State v. Crayton (Ohio App. 8 Dist., Cuyahoga, 05-08-2003) No. 81257, 2003-Ohio-2299, 2003 WL 21027500, Unreported, as amended nunc pro tunc, appeal not allowed 100 Ohio St.3d 1411, 796 N.E.2d 538, 2003-Ohio-4948, motion to reopen denied 2004-Ohio-6293, 2004 WL 2677641. Criminal Law ⚷ 577.15(3)

Period from defendant's filing of motion to dismiss on speedy trial grounds to date on which defendant entered no contest plea and was found guilty, three weeks prior to judgment entry overruling motion to dismiss, was chargeable to defendant. State v. Dunston (Ohio App. 12 Dist., Fayette, 10-07-2002) No. CA2002-03-008, 2002-Ohio-5454, 2002 WL 31261594, Unreported. Criminal Law ⚷ 577.10(8)

Period of 96 days, from state's filing of request for discovery to defendant's response to that request, was chargeable to defendant for speedy trial purposes in view of length of delay in responding to state's simple discovery motion. State v. Dunston (Ohio App. 12 Dist., Fayette, 10-07-2002) No. CA2002-03-008, 2002-Ohio-5454, 2002 WL 31261594, Unreported. Criminal Law ⚷ 577.10(8)

Defendant's constitutional right to speedy trial was not violated by 54–month delay between her indictment and trial, though state could have done more to apprehend defendant, where defendant precipitated delay by failing to accept certified mail informing her of her indictment at address which she had given to police at time of her arrest, defendant claimed that she had been completely ignorant of charges against her during interim period, and issue of speedy trial was first raised sua sponte by trial judge at hearing in which defendant's plea agreement was being read into record. State v. Triplett (Ohio, 06-11-1997) 78 Ohio St.3d 566, 679 N.E.2d 290, 1997-Ohio-182. Criminal Law ⚷ 577.10(10); Criminal Law ⚷ 577.11(2); Criminal Law ⚷ 577.15(4)

58. —— Competency examinations, delays generally

Statutory 270-day speedy trial period was extended by 60 days for period of time from when defendant was referred to psychiatric clinic for competency determination to competency hearing. State v. Freeman (Ohio App. 8 Dist., Cuyahoga, 07-07-2005) No. 85137, 2005-Ohio-3480, 2005 WL 1581105, Unreported, motion for delayed appeal granted 107 Ohio St.3d 1404, 836 N.E.2d 1226, 2005-Ohio-5859. Criminal Law ⚷ 577.11(6)

Court-ordered competency examination was not warranted, and defendant was therefore denied a speedy trial, where he did not demonstrate any irrational behavior, there was no prior medical evidence regarding his competency to stand trial, and the only reasons offered for the examination were long plea negotiations and defendant's failure to pay court costs in exchange for a dismissal of the charges. City of Columbus v. Cardinal (Ohio App. 10 Dist., Franklin, 12-09-2004) No. 04AP-229, No. 04AP-232, No. 04AP230, No. 04AP-233, No. 04AP-231, 2004-Ohio-6605, 2004 WL 2830782, Unreported. Criminal Law ⚷ 577.11(6)

Defendant's motion to determine his competency in child rape case tolled the 270-day speedy trial period, and such statutory extension was not limited to a specific time period. State v. Thomas (Ohio App. 12 Dist., Brown, 01-13-2003) No. CA2002-01-001, 2003-Ohio-74, 2003 WL 103411, Unreported. Criminal Law ⚷ 577.11(6)

The time elapsing between the tendering of a plea of "not guilty by reason of insanity" and a finding of mental competency to stand trial directly resulting from such plea shall not be included in computing days under RC 2945.71. State v. Walker (Ohio 1976) 46 Ohio St.2d 157, 346 N.E.2d 687, 75 O.O.2d 201. Criminal Law ⚷ 577.11(6)

59. —— Suppression of evidence, delays generally

The time within which to try the defendant is not extended by defense counsel's representation at the pretrial conference that he intends to file a motion to suppress where the judgment entry expressing defense counsel's intention is not filed by the last possible day to try the defendant. State v. Moore (Ohio App. 5 Dist., Delaware, 06-15-1995) No. 95CAC03010, 1995 WL 495544, Unreported.

Defendant's right to speedy trial was violated by 635-day period between his motion to suppress evidence and trial court's ruling on the motion; trial court did not explain reason for delay, and total of

832 days elapsed between defendant's arraignment and filing of motion to dismiss. State v. Mullins (Ohio App. 3 Dist., 02-03-2003) 152 Ohio App.3d 83, 786 N.E.2d 911, 2003-Ohio-477. Criminal Law ⚷ 577.10(3); Criminal Law ⚷ 577.15(1)

Scheduling of trial on charge of operating motor vehicle while under influence of alcohol beyond 90–day statutory time period was violation of speedy trial limitation, notwithstanding defendant's motion to suppress in connection with charge of operating motor vehicle with certain concentration of alcohol in urine, which arose from same incident; there was no evidence that state and defendant agreed to try charges together, suppression motion applied only to latter charge, no defense delays tolled time limit, and state did not argue that trial court granted continuance as to charge of operating motor vehicle while under influence of alcohol sua sponte. State v. Jacot (Ohio App. 9 Dist., 04-07-1993) 97 Ohio App.3d 415, 646 N.E.2d 1128, motion allowed 68 Ohio St.3d 1409, 623 N.E.2d 566, appeal dismissed as improvidently allowed 71 Ohio St.3d 1217, 644 N.E.2d 1383. Criminal Law ⚷ 577.10(5)

Where a criminal defendant made a motion to certify the record on a motion to suppress, and the Ohio Supreme Court overruled defendant's motion, the running of defendant's speedy trial time recommenced on the date the Supreme Court's decision was journalized, rather than on the date its decision to overrule was announced. City of Cleveland Heights v. Richardson (Cuyahoga 1983) 9 Ohio App.3d 152, 458 N.E.2d 901, 9 O.B.R. 218.

Failure to bring defendant charged with driving motor vehicle while under the influence (DUI), a second degree misdemeanor, to trial within 90 days after arrest or service of summons violated defendant's speedy trial rights, even though defendant filed motion to suppress evidence and speedy trial motion, where at least 41 days elapsed during first prosecution, which was dismissed when troopers failed to appear, 19 days expired between service of new charges until filing of suppression motion, 54 days expired between overruling of suppression motion and filing of motion to dismiss, and no days expired between overruling of motion to dismiss and start of trial, which totaled 114 days. State v. Davis (Ohio App. 4 Dist., Ross, 05-22-2002) No. 01CA2610, 2002-Ohio-2554, 2002 WL 1293055, Unreported. Criminal Law ⚷ 577.14

60. —— Disqualification of judge, delays generally

Delay resulting from suspension of capital murder proceedings, after defendant filed an affidavit of disqualification against the trial court judge, which automatically divested judge of jurisdiction to proceed until the matter was resolved by Supreme Court, was not chargeable to the state, for speedy trial purposes. State v. Myers (Ohio, 12-13-2002) 97 Ohio St.3d 335, 780 N.E.2d 186, 2002-Ohio-6658, reconsideration denied 97 Ohio St.3d 1500, 780 N.E.2d 1023, 2002-Ohio-7367, certiorari denied 123 S.Ct. 2254, 539 U.S. 906, 156 L.Ed.2d 116, motion to reopen denied 100 Ohio St.3d 1505, 799 N.E.2d 184, 2003-Ohio-6161. Criminal Law ⚷ 577.10(8)

61. —— Justified, delays generally

Delay of approximately one year from the time defendant was arrested for murder until the time he was brought to trial did not violate his statutory right to a speedy trial; time period during which defendant's mental competence to stand trial was being determined was tolled, and the trial began 136 days after defendant withdrew his waiver of speedy trial time. State v. Florence (Ohio App. 2 Dist., Montgomery, 08-19-2005) No. 20439, 2005-Ohio-4508, 2005 WL 2083079, Unreported, appeal not allowed 107 Ohio St.3d 1700, 840 N.E.2d 205, 2005-Ohio-6763, appeal not allowed 109 Ohio St.3d 1427, 846 N.E.2d 535, 2006-Ohio-1967. Criminal Law ⚷ 577.11(6); Criminal Law ⚷ 577.15(3)

Delay of approximately five months from date of defendant's arrest until date trial court found him guilty of operating a vehicle under the influence of alcohol or drugs (OVI), pursuant to no contest plea, did not violate his statutory speedy trial rights; defendant's desire to retain private counsel and have his public defender withdraw necessitated a period of delay. State v. Madden (Ohio App. 10 Dist., Franklin, 08-18-2005) No. 04AP-1228, 2005-Ohio-4281, 2005 WL 1983376, Unreported, appeal not allowed 108 Ohio St.3d 1415, 841 N.E.2d 319, 2006-Ohio-179. Criminal Law ⚷ 577.10(8); Criminal Law ⚷ 577.15(3)

Defendant's statutory right to speedy trial on murder charge was not violated; delay that resulted from defendant's filing of motion to suppress and motion to dismiss was attributable to defendant and tolled speedy trial time, only 255 days elapsed between defendant's arrest and trial, stated reasons for delay were valid and any delays were incurred by both sides, defendant failed to assert alleged speedy trial violation during trial proceedings, and no prejudice was suffered by defendant as result of delayed trial. State v. Ziegler (Ohio App. 11 Dist., Trumbull, 03-11-2005) No. 2003-T-0168, 2005-Ohio-1099, 2005 WL 583795, Unreported. Criminal Law ⚷ 577.10(8); Criminal Law ⚷ 577.10(10); Criminal Law ⚷ 577.16(4)

Delays in bringing drug trafficking defendant to trial caused by his change of counsel and original counsel's filing of suppression motion, which was subsequently withdrawn by his new counsel, were chargeable to defendant rather than state for purposes of speedy trial computation. State v. Meridy (Ohio App. 12 Dist., Clermont, 01-24-2005) No. CA2003-11-091, 2005-Ohio-241, 2005 WL 123993, Unreported. Criminal Law ⚷ 577.10(8)

Defendant was not deprived of statutory right to speedy trial for misdemeanor operating motor vehicle while intoxicated; 90-day speedy trial period was tolled for defendant's motion to suppress, motion to dismiss, and motion for reconsideration, which left 27 net speedy trial days utilized when defendant entered plea. State v. Hall (Ohio App. 5 Dist., Licking, 12-27-2004) No. 2004CA00038,

2004-Ohio-7262, 2004 WL 3090201, Unreported. Criminal Law ⚷ 577.10(8)

Delay of three years in issuing indictment charging defendant with burglary with firearm specification did not implicate defendant's constitutional right to speedy trial, despite fact that prior charge against defendant of receiving stolen property, which also carried firearm specification, involved same gun and some of the same witnesses, where charges stemmed from separate acts, defendant suffered no actual prejudice as result of delay, indictment issued within applicable statute of limitations, and defendant was tried within statutory speedy trial period. State v. Elersic (Ohio App. 11 Dist., Lake, 09-30-2004) No. 2002-L-172, 2004-Ohio-5301, 2004 WL 2804809, Unreported, appeal not allowed 105 Ohio St.3d 1407, 821 N.E.2d 1027, 2005-Ohio-279. Indictment And Information ⚷ 7

Defendant's right to speedy trial on assault charge was not violated, even though it took almost two years for case to proceed to trial; speedy trial period was tolled from time defendant failed to appear at pretrial, and until he was arrested, and record contained valid written waiver of speedy trial limitations. State v. Tate (Ohio App. 7 Dist., Mahoning, 09-27-2004) No. 03 MA 97, 2004-Ohio-5358, 2004 WL 2334321, Unreported. Criminal Law ⚷ 577.10(9); Criminal Law ⚷ 577.11(2)

Defendant's constitutional and statutory right to speedy trial was not violated; after time was excluded from speedy trial calculation due to defendant's waiver of his right to speedy trial, his filing of request for bill of particulars, his filing of various motions, and his request for a continuance, total time counted against State was 73 days, which was within the 90 days State was required to bring defendant to trial. State v. McKinney (Ohio App. 3 Dist., Defiance, 10-18-2004) No. 4-04-12, 2004-Ohio-5518, 2004 WL 2334318, Unreported, motion for delayed appeal granted 104 Ohio St.3d 1459, 821 N.E.2d 576, 2005-Ohio-204, appeal not allowed 105 Ohio St.3d 1561, 828 N.E.2d 116, 2005-Ohio-2447, reconsideration denied 106 Ohio St.3d 1488, 832 N.E.2d 740, 2005-Ohio-3978. Criminal Law ⚷ 577.15(1)

Defendant was not entitled to dismissal of the misdemeanor escape charges against her based on an alleged violation of defendant's right to a speedy trial; only 53 days were chargeable against the State, for speedy trial purposes, since time defendant was incarcerated on the escape charges and on a probation violation counted only as single count days, time was tolled while the court ruled on defendant's motions, and time stopped running after defendant's request for a continuance was granted. State v. Baumgartner (Ohio App. 6 Dist., Ottawa, 07-23-2004) No. OT-03-013, 2004-Ohio-3907, 2004 WL 1662193, Unreported. Criminal Law ⚷ 577.10(7); Criminal Law ⚷ 577.10(8); Criminal Law ⚷ 577.11(1); Criminal Law ⚷ 577.16(11)

Defendant's right to speedy trial under state and federal constitutions was not violated; although over 500 days elapsed between defendant's arrest and no contest plea to possession of cocaine, most of delay was attributable to defendant's filing of motions, defendant did not assert constitutional right to speedy trial until well after statutory speedy time trial period expired, and defendant failed to show prejudice. State v. Gaines (Ohio App. 9 Dist., Lorain, 06-30-2004) No. 00CA008298, 2004-Ohio-3407, 2004 WL 1461524, Unreported. Criminal Law ⚷ 577.10(8); Criminal Law ⚷ 577.10(10)

Defendant charged with driving under the influence of alcohol (DUI), a first degree misdemeanor, was brought to trial within 90-day statutory speedy trial period; delay in the case was attributable to defendant, time attributable to the State was 68 days, and defendant was not incarcerated during this time. State v. Snyder (Ohio App. 7 Dist., Belmont, 06-15-2004) No. 03BE15, 2004-Ohio-3200, 2004 WL 1376229, Unreported. Criminal Law ⚷ 577.10(8)

Misdemeanor defendant was not denied his right to a speedy trial, where original trial date was set within statutory timeframe, defendant then made demand for jury trial, and the new trial date was merely a month after defendant's speedy trial time would have expired, which was reasonable. State v. Herbst (Ohio App. 6 Dist., Lucas, 06-18-2004) No. L-03-1238, 2004-Ohio-3157, 2004 WL 1368210, Unreported. Criminal Law ⚷ 577.10(8); Criminal Law ⚷ 577.15(1)

Period of 11 days between hearing on defendant's motion to suppress and trial court's ruling on motion was reasonable, and thus time for bringing defendant to trial for felony drug possession under speedy trial statute was tolled for entire period that motion was pending, even though defendant argued that trial court should have ruled on motion in seven days. State v. Jackson (Ohio App. 11 Dist., Ashtabula, 06-04-2004) No. 2003-A-0005, 2004-Ohio-2920, 2004 WL 1238392, Unreported, appeal not allowed 103 Ohio St.3d 1480, 816 N.E.2d 255, 2004-Ohio-5405. Criminal Law ⚷ 577.10(8)

Delay of 58 days in bringing defendant to trial on charge of murder, kidnapping, and robbery was not presumptively prejudicial so as to require Court of Appeals to apply *Barker* factors in determining whether delay violated defendant's speedy trial rights; 200-day delay in bringing defendant to trial after Court of Appeals finding that defendant could withdraw his initial plea was, for the most part, attributable to period during which State could appeal Court's finding and subsequent continuance to which defendant consented, minus which tolling period left 58 days in which State brought defendant to trial. State v. Yuen (Ohio App. 10 Dist., Franklin, 03-18-2004) No. 03AP-513, 2004-Ohio-1276, 2004 WL 540280, Unreported. Criminal Law ⚷ 577.10(7); Criminal Law ⚷ 577.10(9); Criminal Law ⚷ 577.15(1)

Jailed defendant's right to speedy trial on charges of domestic violence and assault was not violated, since his motions for bill of particulars, a discovery request, intent to use evidence, and dismissal tolled running of speedy trial period. City of Cleveland v.

Sheldon (Ohio App. 8 Dist., Cuyahoga, 11-26-2003) No. 82319, 2003-Ohio-6331, 2003 WL 22804364, Unreported. Criminal Law ⚷ 577.10(8)

Defendant was not entitled to motion to dismiss based on State's failure to bring defendant to trial within statutorily prescribed time limit; defendant's filing motion for bill of particulars tolled speedy trial time, State's delay in complying with bill of particulars was reasonable, and on day trial was to begin, defendant filed a waiver of his right to speedy trial. State v. Gibson (Ohio App. 11 Dist., Trumbull, 10-24-2003) No. 2002-T-0055, 2003-Ohio-5695, 2003 WL 22427821, Unreported. Criminal Law ⚷ 577.10(8); Criminal Law ⚷ 577.10(9)

Ninety-day speedy trial limit to bring incarcerated defendant to trial on charges related to harassment and stalking were tolled by time for extradition from another state, appointment of counsel, and various requests and motions of defense, which rendered time from defendant's arrest to date of trial well within speedy trial limitation; untolled time from date of arrest to trial was 69 days, date of arrest was not counted as day of incarceration, and defense requested leave to file plea of not guilty by reason of insanity, moved for continuance and to suppress evidence. State v. Cline (Ohio App. 2 Dist., Champaign, 09-05-2003) No. 2002-CA-05, 2003-Ohio-4712, 2003 WL 22064118, Unreported, stay granted 100 Ohio St.3d 1529, 800 N.E.2d 47, 2003-Ohio-6458, motion to certify allowed 100 Ohio St.3d 1543, 800 N.E.2d 749, 2003-Ohio-6879, appeal not allowed 100 Ohio St.3d 1547, 800 N.E.2d 752, 2003-Ohio-6879, stay granted 101 Ohio St.3d 1461, 804 N.E.2d 36, 2004-Ohio-814, reversed 103 Ohio St.3d 471, 816 N.E.2d 1069, 2004-Ohio-5701, on remand 164 Ohio App.3d 228, 841 N.E.2d 846, 2005-Ohio-5779. Criminal Law ⚷ 577.10(8); Criminal Law ⚷ 577.11(4)

Defendant failed to demonstrate that his statutory right to speedy trial was violated; total time charged to State before State dismissed case without prejudice was 61 days, total time charged to State after defendant was re-indicted based on the same underlying facts was 69 days, and thus total time charged to State of 133 days did not exceed statutory period of 270 days. State v. Hess (Ohio App. 8 Dist., Cuyahoga, 07-10-2003) No. 82254, 2003-Ohio-3676, 2003 WL 21555478, Unreported, appeal after new sentencing hearing 2004-Ohio-5214, 2004 WL 2340641. Criminal Law ⚷ 577.14

Sixteen-month post-indictment delay did not violate defendant's right to a speedy trial, even though delay was the result of state's negligence; defendant's periodic incarceration during delay period resulted from unrelated charges, defendant was unaware of pending charges against him, and defendant failed to allege that delay prevented him from mounting a defense. State v. Smith (Ohio App. 8 Dist., Cuyahoga, 07-03-2003) No. 81808, 2003-Ohio-3524, 2003 WL 21512796, Unreported. Criminal Law ⚷ 577.15(4)

Defendant was brought to trial well within the 270-day speedy trial period for persons charged with felonies; defendant spent seven days in jail before trial, which constituted 21 days under the triple credit rule, and an additional 137 days expired before defendant was brought to trial, totaling 158 days. State v. Humphrey (Ohio App. 2 Dist., Clark, 05-30-2003) No. CIV.A. 02CA0025, 2003-Ohio-2825, 2003 WL 21267255, Unreported, motion for delayed appeal denied 101 Ohio St.3d 1485, 805 N.E.2d 537, 2004-Ohio-1293, appeal not allowed 102 Ohio St.3d 1533, 811 N.E.2d 1152, 2004-Ohio-3580. Criminal Law ⚷ 577.8(1); Criminal Law ⚷ 577.15(1)

Defendant's right to speedy trial on minor misdemeanor speeding charge was not violated under statute that required trial within 30 days of arrest or service of summons, even though trial occurred 44 days after defendant received summons, and 33 days after her initial court appearance in Mayor's Court, where transfer of case from Mayor's Court to Municipal Court constituted "removal" and extended time for trial until 30 days after Mayor's Court certified case, and two-day continuance beyond speedy trial limit, in order to allow citing officer to be subpoenaed, was reasonable. City of Brecksville v. Carothers (Ohio App. 8 Dist., Cuyahoga, 05-01-2003) No. 81907, 2003-Ohio-2198, 2003 WL 1995624, Unreported. Criminal Law ⚷ 577.13

Defendant was afforded speedy trial after his arrest for receiving stolen property, failure to comply with order or signal of police officer, vandalism, and felonious assault, where first day of trial was on 90th day following arrest, not including day of arrest and Sunday before trial, in compliance with speedy trial statute and criminal rule. State v. Ray (Ohio App. 9 Dist., Summit, 04-30-2003) No. 21233, 2003-Ohio-2159, 2003 WL 1984349, Unreported, appeal not allowed 99 Ohio St.3d 1515, 792 N.E.2d 201, 2003-Ohio-3957, appeal not allowed 100 Ohio St.3d 1509, 799 N.E.2d 187, 2003-Ohio-6161. Criminal Law ⚷ 577.15(3)

For purposes of speedy trial calculation for defendant who was unable to post bond and remained in jail pending trial, 89 days elapsed between the date of defendant's arrest and the date on which trial began, and thus defendant was brought to trial within the 90-day statutory period. State v. Brownlow (Ohio App. 3 Dist., Allen, 04-10-2003) No. 1-02-73, 2003-Ohio-1819, 2003 WL 1834504, Unreported, appeal not allowed 105 Ohio St.3d 1472, 824 N.E.2d 541, 2005-Ohio-1186. Criminal Law ⚷ 577.15(3)

Even if alleged date of defendant's re-arrest after he absconded before original trial date on charges of aggravated robbery and kidnapping were used to calculate speedy trial requirements, trial could have been rescheduled because of evidence that state had failed to disclose within 25 days without violating speedy trial right, and thus trial judge abused its discretion in dismissing charges rather than continuing case; trial judge recognized that state's discovery violation was not at all willful, and expressed that he did not want to dismiss the case, but felt he had no other choice because of speedy trial requirements. State v. Weimer (Ohio App. 2 Dist., Darke,

12-20-2002) No. 1586, 2002-Ohio-7099, 2002 WL 31846296, Unreported. Criminal Law ⚿ 577.16(2)

In calculating defendant's speedy trial time on charges of aggravated robbery and kidnapping, state should not have been charged with any time between defendant's arrest and the original trial date, since defendant absconded and did not appear for original trial. State v. Weimer (Ohio App. 2 Dist., Darke, 12-20-2002) No. 1586, 2002-Ohio-7099, 2002 WL 31846296, Unreported. Criminal Law ⚿ 577.11(2)

Defendant's right to a speedy trial was not violated, even though defendant claimed his new trial following remand was held beyond applicable time limit; although approximately two months passed after reversal of defendant's original convictions, defendant had not requested any action in the meantime, and defendant's newly-assigned counsel almost immediately took steps to familiarize himself with his client's cases. State v. Washington (Ohio App. 8 Dist., Cuyahoga, 10-24-2002) No. 80418, 2002-Ohio-5834, 2002 WL 31401558, Unreported, appeal not allowed 98 Ohio St.3d 1491, 785 N.E.2d 473, 2003-Ohio-1189, dismissal of habeas corpus affirmed 101 Ohio St.3d 131, 802 N.E.2d 655, 2004-Ohio-298, appeal not allowed 102 Ohio St.3d 1413, 806 N.E.2d 564, 2004-Ohio-1763. Criminal Law ⚿ 577.14

Even if 10-month delay between filing of formal charges against defendant, that were subsequently dismissed, and his indictment following dismissal of charges, crossed threshold for presuming prejudice as to his constitutional right to speedy trial, defendant did not suffer prejudice as result of delay in prosecution for drug trafficking, where defendant remained employed, he was not subjected to lengthy pretrial incarceration, he was free of any public accusation or humiliation, and there was no evidence delay had impact on defendant's ability to recall events sufficiently to advance his case. State v. Bayless (Ohio App. 10 Dist., Franklin, 10-24-2002) No. 02AP-215, 2002-Ohio-5791, 2002 WL 31388972, Unreported, appeal not allowed 98 Ohio St.3d 1480, 784 N.E.2d 712, 2003-Ohio-974. Criminal Law ⚿ 577.16(4)

Defendant's constitutional right to speedy trial on drug trafficking charges was not violated by 10-month delay between filing of formal charges against defendant, which were eventually dismissed, and his subsequent indictment arising out of same transactions, where delay did not cross threshold for presuming prejudice because delay was broken by defendant's arrest and charge in municipal court, and there was no evidence state failed to exercise reasonable diligence during time between dismissal of original charges, and subsequent indictment; analysis of drugs confiscated from defendant took time, and existence of co-defendants suggested that state's investigation was more time-consuming than that for ordinary street crime. State v. Bayless (Ohio App. 10 Dist., Franklin, 10-24-2002) No. 02AP-215, 2002-Ohio-5791, 2002 WL 31388972, Unreported, appeal not allowed 98 Ohio St.3d 1480, 784 N.E.2d 712, 2003-Ohio-974. Criminal Law ⚿ 577.14; Criminal Law ⚿ 577.15(4)

Even if municipal court had continued defendant's bail under former rule after drug trafficking case against defendant had been dismissed without prejudice, bail would not have continued for period of time greater than 14 days, and thus defendant's statutory right to speedy trial would not have been violated, where only 98 days, of allowable 270-day statutory period following arrest in which defendant is to be brought to trial, would have elapsed before defendant was tried on subsequent indictment based on same transactions as dismissed case. State v. Bayless (Ohio App. 10 Dist., Franklin, 10-24-2002) No. 02AP-215, 2002-Ohio-5791, 2002 WL 31388972, Unreported, appeal not allowed 98 Ohio St.3d 1480, 784 N.E.2d 712, 2003-Ohio-974. Criminal Law ⚿ 577.8(1)

Defendant's statutory right to speedy trial on drug trafficking charges was not violated, where time between municipal court's dismissal of case without prejudice, and defendant's subsequent indictment resulting from same transactions as original complaint, was excluded from calculation of speedy trial time, and defendant was prosecuted within 270-day statutory period. State v. Bayless (Ohio App. 10 Dist., Franklin, 10-24-2002) No. 02AP-215, 2002-Ohio-5791, 2002 WL 31388972, Unreported, appeal not allowed 98 Ohio St.3d 1480, 784 N.E.2d 712, 2003-Ohio-974. Criminal Law ⚿ 577.14

A defendant indicted for welfare fraud is not denied a speedy trial where the length of the post-indictment delay is six months and the reason for the delay is difficulty in obtaining service due to defendant's several changes of address. State v. Ellis (Ohio App. 2 Dist., Montgomery, 05-30-1997) No. 15963, 1997 WL 282313, Unreported, appeal not allowed 80 Ohio St.3d 1415, 684 N.E.2d 706.

Defendants' failure to file motion to compel discovery, or to request trial court to prohibit state from introducing evidence it failed to timely disclose, pursuant to rule, constituted acquiescence in state's failure to provide discovery in a timely manner, for purposes of speedy trial analysis, in prosecution for felony theft; first and only time defendants objected to state's timeliness in providing discovery was on date they filed their motions to dismiss on speedy trial grounds. State v. Riley (Ohio App. 12 Dist., 08-22-2005) 162 Ohio App.3d 730, 834 N.E.2d 887, 2005-Ohio-4337. Criminal Law ⚿ 577.10(10)

State's response time to defendants' discovery requests in excess of three months was reasonable, for purposes of statutory speedy trial analysis, in prosecution for felony theft; even if state were granted only three months to respond to requests, trial date still fell within 270-day statutory limit. State v. Riley (Ohio App. 12 Dist., 08-22-2005) 162 Ohio App.3d 730, 834 N.E.2d 887, 2005-Ohio-4337. Criminal Law ⚿ 577.15(1)

Immigration and Customs Enforcement Agency (ICE) detainer did not nullify triple-count requirement, which counts each day held in jail in lieu of bail as three days for speedy-trial purposes if defendant is being held in jail solely for pending case, while defendant was in custody for money laundering and possession of criminal tools; ICE detainer did not act as independent charge but rather served only as notice to local law enforcement officials of potential immigration proceedings. State v. Sanchez (Ohio App. 6 Dist., 04-29-2005) 162 Ohio App.3d 113, 832 N.E.2d 1215, 2005-Ohio-2093, reversed 2009 WL 676, appeal allowed 106 Ohio St.3d 1532, 835 N.E.2d 381, 2005-Ohio-5146. Criminal Law ⚷ 577.11(1)

The 65 days that elapsed to resolve defendant's motion to suppress statements that she made to authorities were chargeable to defendant, for purposes of determining whether she was deprived of her statutory right to a speedy trial on charge of complicity to commit aggravated murder; period was reasonable, as motion was extremely important in that state would have to decide whether it could proceed if statements were suppressed, and it resulted in a lengthy hearing with complex constitutional considerations. State v. Santini (Ohio App. 7 Dist., 06-27-2001) 144 Ohio App.3d 396, 760 N.E.2d 442, 2001-Ohio-3313, dismissed, appeal not allowed 93 Ohio St.3d 1459, 756 N.E.2d 1236. Criminal Law ⚷ 577.10(8)

The seven days that elapsed to resolve defendant's motion to dismiss were chargeable to defendant, for purposes of determining whether she was deprived of her statutory right to a speedy trial on charge of complicity to commit aggravated murder, as that time was a reasonable and necessary period of delay. State v. Santini (Ohio App. 7 Dist., 06-27-2001) 144 Ohio App.3d 396, 760 N.E.2d 442, 2001-Ohio-3313, dismissed, appeal not allowed 93 Ohio St.3d 1459, 756 N.E.2d 1236. Criminal Law ⚷ 577.10(8)

Three-month delay in rape defendant's retrial was not unreasonable and did not prejudice defendant; defendant filed series of motions following his mistrial, raising several difficult issues for trial court to consider, and after ruling on defendant's motions trial court continued trial for additional month because of unanticipated medical incapacitation of the prosecuting attorney. State v. Roughton (Ohio App. 6 Dist., 02-12-1999) 132 Ohio App.3d 268, 724 N.E.2d 1193, appeal not allowed 86 Ohio St.3d 1406, 711 N.E.2d 234. Criminal Law ⚷ 577.14

Trial in aggravated theft prosecution was stayed pursuant to "express statutory requirement," thus tolling 270–day speedy trial period, during ten months that state's affidavit of disqualification of trial judge was pending with Ohio Supreme Court, even though no formal stay was issued; trial judge was powerless to proceed with trial of case until Supreme Court resolved disqualification matter. State v. Mays (Ohio App. 8 Dist., 01-11-1996) 108 Ohio App.3d 598, 671 N.E.2d 553, dismissed, appeal not allowed 75 Ohio St.3d 1509, 665 N.E.2d 679. Criminal Law ⚷ 577.10(7)

For purposes of determining whether defendant was denied his statutory right to speedy trial, period of 27 days between defendant's filing of motion for leave to file motion to suppress and filing of motion to suppress was attributable to defendant, despite defendant's contention that delay was caused by failure of state to provide timely discovery, where defendant did not serve his request for discovery on the state until 22 days after he had been arraigned at his initial appearance. State v. Stamper (Ohio App. 11 Dist., 04-10-1995) 102 Ohio App.3d 431, 657 N.E.2d 365. Criminal Law ⚷ 577.10(8)

Trial delay caused by defendant's motion to suppress in second driving under the influence of alcohol (DUI) prosecution, which was identical to defendant's motion to suppress in first DUI prosecution, which was dismissed because of state witness' failure to appear for trial, was chargeable to defendant, for speedy trial purposes; second prosecution was de novo. State v. Wyde (Ohio App. 1 Dist., 09-22-1993) 90 Ohio App.3d 471, 629 N.E.2d 1079, dismissed, jurisdictional motion overruled 68 Ohio St.3d 1445, 626 N.E.2d 687. Criminal Law ⚷ 577.10(8); Criminal Law ⚷ 577.14

A defendant is not denied his statutory right to a speedy trial even though he is brought to trial more than 270–days after his initial arrest since only 249 days actually elapsed after permissible extensions of time are considered; the defendant's initial trial date was scheduled within the 270–day time period but was continued on the defendant's own motion and then in order to allow proper trial preparation due to a substitution of defense counsel added to the failure of the defendant to appear for hearings and to stay in contact with his attorney or the court, and the defendant's escape from the jurisdiction, waived his right to a speedy trial until he was subsequently rearrested. State v. Gibson (Logan 1992) 75 Ohio App.3d 388, 599 N.E.2d 438.

A five-year delay in indicting a defendant after the commission of acts alleged to constitute a crime is not prejudicial or a denial of speedy trial rights where the indictment is handed down less than fifty days after the crime charged in the indictment was discovered. State v. Tillman (Lorain 1990) 66 Ohio App.3d 464, 585 N.E.2d 550, appeal after new trial 119 Ohio App.3d 449, 695 N.E.2d 792.

Failure to commence defendant's trial within statutory 70–day period did not violate Speedy Trial Act, where government was required to overcome series of logistical and legal problems, not of its own making, in taking depositions of important witnesses in Japan and continuing trial from May 2, 1990 to April 29, 1991 was necessary because witnesses were absent or unavailable for trial so that periods of delay were excludable in computing time under Speedy Trial Act. U.S. v. Walker (C.A.6 (Ohio) 1993) 1 F.3d 423, rehearing denied, appeal after new trial 37 F.3d 1500. Criminal Law ⚷ 577.10(4); Criminal Law ⚷ 577.10(6)

Although a little over a year had elapsed between the time of defendant's arrest for driving under the influence and his trial, there was no speedy trial violation since only 231 of these days counted against the State, and thus, defendant was brought to trial well within the 270 day speedy trial period for persons charged with felonies; defendant's waiver of time requirements for purposes of grand jury tolled 60 day period between when he filed waiver and was indicted, 13 days were tolled due to State's request for continuance, and defendant's motion to suppress and suppression hearing tolled another 15 days. State v. Dunckleman (Ohio App. 2 Dist., Montgomery, 08-30-2002) No. 19233, 2002-Ohio-4463, 2002 WL 1998439, Unreported, appeal not allowed 98 Ohio St.3d 1411, 781 N.E.2d 1019, 2003-Ohio-60. Criminal Law ⚷ 577.10(7); Criminal Law ⚷ 577.10(8)

Defendant was not prejudiced by 44–day delay in bringing him to trial, which he claimed resulted in patrolman forgetting details of defendant's arrest for failure to wear safety belt, and thus delay did not violate his speedy trial rights, where defendant properly refreshed patrolman's memory in accordance with rules of evidence, thereby enabling patrolman to testify regarding events. State v. Bigley (Ohio App. 9 Dist., Medina, 08-14-2002) No. 02CA0017-M, 2002-Ohio-4149, 2002 WL 1842409, Unreported. Criminal Law ⚷ 577.16(4)

A delay in trying a defendant beyond the period prescribed by RC 2945.71(C)(2) is justified where such delay is caused by the defendant constantly changing his place of residence, thus preventing earlier service of a summons. State v Goetz, No. CA86–09–059 (12th Dist Ct App, Clermont, 2–9–87).

Request by defendant in a misdemeanor case to extend the trial date may be construed as having been made upon her "own motion" pursuant to RC 2945.72(H) and, therefore, there was no violation of the forty-five-day speedy trial requirement of RC 2945.71. State v Cooper, No. 43765 (8th Dist Ct App, Cuyahoga, 3–18–82).

Although time from when felony indictment was filed to when defendant was brought to trial, including triple count for time incarcerated, exceeds 270 days, when days that defendant was on fugitive status are subtracted defendant was brought to trial within the time limitation of RC 2945.71. State v Van Johnson, No. 13152 (2d Dist Ct App, Montgomery, 3–31–93).

62. —— Unjustified, delays generally

Delay in bringing defendant to trial on felony drug charges, approximately 13 months after his initial arrest, violated his constitutional right to speedy trial, when only justification for delay was delayed receipt of laboratory results on confiscated pills and a backload of paperwork. State v. Rutkowski (Ohio App. 8 Dist., Cuyahoga, 03-09-2006) No. 86289, 2006-Ohio-1087, 2006 WL 562160, Unreported. Criminal Law ⚷ 577.15(3)

Trial court's 311-day delay in ruling on defendant's motion to suppress evidence was unreasonable and thus that period of unreasonable and unnecessary delay did not toll the running of the 90-day statutory speedy trial period; 120 days would have been a reasonable amount of time within which to rule on defendant's motion. State v. Fields (Ohio App. 5 Dist., Guernsey, 01-20-2006) No. 05-CA-17, 2006-Ohio-223, 2006 WL 163563, Unreported. Criminal Law ⚷ 577.10(7); Criminal Law ⚷ 577.15(1)

Defendant's failure to respond to State's discovery request did not toll period between date State filed its motion for reciprocal discovery and date defendant filed his response, and thus, defendant's statutory right to speedy trial was violated; there was no evidence presented that State was prejudiced in any way, nor did they avail themselves of a motion to compel as facilitated by criminal rules. State v. Palmer (Ohio App. 11 Dist., Portage, 12-16-2005) No. 2004-P-0106, 2005-Ohio-6710, 2005 WL 3476650, Unreported, stay granted 108 Ohio St.3d 1435, 842 N.E.2d 61, 2006-Ohio-421, motion to certify allowed 109 Ohio St.3d 1403, 845 N.E.2d 521, 2006-Ohio-1703, appeal allowed 109 Ohio St.3d 1405, 845 N.E.2d 522, 2006-Ohio-1703. Criminal Law ⚷ 577.10(8)

Defendant's speedy trial rights were violated in prosecution for violating temporary protection order, where there was no valid waiver of speedy trial time limits in record, and defendant was not brought to trial within 90 days of his arrest. State v. Zeger (Ohio App. 5 Dist., Richland, 09-01-2005) No. 2003-CA-109, 2005-Ohio-4717, 2005 WL 2175129, Unreported. Criminal Law ⚷ 577.10(9); Criminal Law ⚷ 577.15(3)

Defendant's right to a speedy trial was violated, thus requiring reversal of his conviction for felonious assault, where defendant's trial was conducted 13 days beyond speedy trial deadline, state failed to show that deadline was extended, and there was no affirmative demonstration of waiver of defendant's right to speedy trial. State v. Henry (Ohio App. 5 Dist., Licking, 06-23-2005) No. 04 CA 00062, 2005-Ohio-3191, 2005 WL 1491462, Unreported, appeal not allowed 107 Ohio St.3d 1423, 837 N.E.2d 1208, 2005-Ohio-6124. Criminal Law ⚷ 577.15(1); Criminal Law ⚷ 1166(7)

Failure to bring defendant to trial within 270 days of his re-arrest for assault on a peace officer violated his statutory right to a speedy trial. State v. Campbell (Ohio App. 11 Dist., Ashtabula, 06-17-2005) No. 2003-A-0056, 2005-Ohio-3091, 2005 WL 1423499, Unreported, appeal not allowed 107 Ohio St.3d 1410, 836 N.E.2d 1229, 2005-Ohio-5859. Criminal Law ⚷ 577.15(3)

State's delay of 41 days in sending DNA samples to laboratory for testing was unreasonable, and, as such, 41 days were to be counted against defendant's speedy trial time; in its motion to continue, state represented to trial court that it had requested a "rush" on the DNA testing, and thus state should have sent DNA sample out within days of filing its motion. State v. Brown (Ohio App. 7 Dist., Mahoning, 06-07-2005) No. 03-MA-32, 2005-Ohio-2939, 2005 WL 1385715, Unreported, appeal not allowed 106 Ohio St.3d 1558, 836 N.E.2d 582, 2005-Ohio-5531. Criminal Law ⚷ 577.12(1)

Wildlife Division violated defendant's right to speedy trial by delaying its prosecution of defendant on charge that he unlawfully took a deer out of season, where deer out of season case arose from same set of facts as Wildlife Division's original charge against defendant for illegal possession of deer parts, and Wildlife Division knew of such facts at time of the original charge. State, Div. of Wildlife v. Brumley (Ohio App. 4 Dist., Adams, 05-04-2005) No. 04CA785, 2005-Ohio-2226, 2005

WL 1060563, Unreported. Criminal Law ⚷ 577.14

Defendant's constitutional right to speedy trial on charges of obstructing official business, and resisting arrest, was violated; defendant was not tried within 90 days of arrest, and trial court's entry, which continued trial until next scheduled jury date, was never journalized. State v. Nichols (Ohio App. 5 Dist., Richland, 04-13-2005) No. 04CA56, 2005-Ohio-1771, 2005 WL 858161, Unreported. Criminal Law ⚷ 577.15(3)

Defendant's statutory right to speedy trial on assault charge was violated; in calculating time under speedy trial statute, there was no evidence in record to substantiate that period of nearly nine months in which defendant was not brought to trial should be attributed to defendant, there was nothing in record to support delay, and there was no evidence in record to establish that trial court's delay in appointing new counsel for defendant was due to anything other than lack of diligence, or that nine month continuance was reasonable. State v. Easley (Ohio App. 4 Dist., Scioto, 02-22-2005) No. 03CA2910, 2005-Ohio-767, 2005 WL 433431, Unreported. Criminal Law ⚷ 577.16(9)

Defendant made prima facie showing that his statutory speedy trial right was violated, where over 500 days elapsed between defendant's arrest and no contest plea to possession of cocaine. State v. Gaines (Ohio App. 9 Dist., Lorain, 06-30-2004) No. 00CA008298, 2004-Ohio-3407, 2004 WL 1461524, Unreported. Criminal Law ⚷ 577.15(3)

Trial court's 265-day delay in ruling on defendant's motion to suppress was unreasonable and thus that period of unreasonable and unnecessary delay did not toll the running of the speedy trial time; defendant was required to be brought to trial within 90 days of his arrest for driving while under the influence of alcohol (DWI), and within 120 days would have been a reasonable amount of time within which to rule on defendant's motion. State v. Edwards (Ohio App. 5 Dist., Tuscarawas, 01-17-2003) No. 2002 AP 08 0065, 2003-Ohio-334, 2003 WL 169952, Unreported. Criminal Law ⚷ 577.10(7)

Indictment for aggravated robbery nearly 10 years after complaint was filed did not violate defendant's right to speedy trial, as delay was caused by defendant's flight from jurisdiction in order to evade arrest. State v. Bennett (Ohio App. 9 Dist., Summit, 01-22-2003) No. 21121, 2003-Ohio-238, 2003 WL 150086, Unreported, motion for delayed appeal denied 98 Ohio St.3d 1473, 784 N.E.2d 707, 2003-Ohio-904, appeal not allowed 98 Ohio St.3d 1565, 787 N.E.2d 1230, 2003-Ohio-2242. Indictment And Information ⚷ 7

State was statutorily required to bring defendant to trial on charges of aggravated murder with a firearm specification, murder, aggravated robbery, felonious assault, and tampering with evidence within 90 days of his arrest, exclusive of extensions pursuant to statute, where defendant was held in jail in lieu of bail solely on such charges from date of his arrest. State v. Kerby (Ohio App. 2 Dist., 07-15-2005) 162 Ohio App.3d 353, 833 N.E.2d 757, 2005-Ohio-3734, appeal not allowed 107 Ohio St.3d 1682, 839 N.E.2d 403, 2005-Ohio-6480. Criminal Law ⚷ 577.11(1)

Upon defendant's request for bill of particulars and demand for discovery, State's response to requests after more than 11 months had passed was unreasonable and did not toll the running of the speedy trial period for the full 11 months. State v. McDonald (Ohio App. 8 Dist., 08-14-2003) 153 Ohio App.3d 679, 795 N.E.2d 701, 2003-Ohio-4342, stay granted 100 Ohio St.3d 1480, 798 N.E.2d 615, 2003-Ohio-5993, appeal not allowed 100 Ohio St.3d 1531, 800 N.E.2d 48, 2003-Ohio-6458. Criminal Law ⚷ 577.13

Filing of detainer, without more, was insufficient to establish that state exercised reasonable diligence in securing availability of defendant, who was held on unrelated charges in another county, and thus delay in excess of 270–day statutory period in bringing defendant to trial required dismissal. State v. Bailey (Ohio App. 2 Dist., 09-15-2000) 141 Ohio App.3d 144, 750 N.E.2d 603, appeal not allowed 91 Ohio St.3d 1431, 741 N.E.2d 895. Criminal Law ⚷ 577.11(4)

Where defendant fled jurisdiction in order to evade prosecution on instant charges, he could not claim that his right to a speedy trial was violated prior to his request, filed while he was incarcerated for other offenses, that those untried indictments pending against him be disposed of. State v. Smith (Ohio App. 3 Dist., 09-29-2000) 140 Ohio App.3d 81, 746 N.E.2d 678, 2000-Ohio-1777. Criminal Law ⚷ 577.11(2)

Delay of 19 months between indictment and commencement of trial was not unreasonable, for speedy trial purposes; because overriding factor preventing defendant's trial was his decision to flee jurisdiction, delay was solely within his control. State v. Smith (Ohio App. 3 Dist., 09-29-2000) 140 Ohio App.3d 81, 746 N.E.2d 678, 2000-Ohio-1777. Criminal Law ⚷ 577.11(2); Criminal Law ⚷ 577.15(4)

Defendant's statutory right to trial within 90 days of arrest or summons on misdemeanor charge was violated by 592–day delay in bringing him to trial where at least two delays, of 109 days and 62 days, were chargeable to state. State v. Wirtanen (Ohio App. 6 Dist., 04-26-1996) 110 Ohio App.3d 604, 674 N.E.2d 1245. Criminal Law ⚷ 577.12(1); Criminal Law ⚷ 577.15(1)

Defendant's knowledge of possibility that state would bring aggravated burglary charges and prior violent offense specifications against him, in addition to pending felonious assault charges for which defendant waived his speedy trial rights, did not alter state's obligation to bring such additional charges within 90–day period prescribed by speedy trial statute, and therefore conviction for aggravated burglary charge and prior violent offense specifications which were brought to trial after 90–day period violated speedy trial statute. State v. Clark (Ohio App. 2 Dist., 10-27-1995) 107 Ohio App.3d

141, 667 N.E.2d 1262. Criminal Law ⚷ 577.10(5); Criminal Law ⚷ 577.10(9)

Improper handling of firearm charge against defendant had to be dismissed on speedy trial grounds; state did not bring him to trial within 90 days as required by speedy trial statute. State v. DePue (Ohio App. 4 Dist., 06-29-1994) 96 Ohio App.3d 513, 645 N.E.2d 745. Criminal Law ⚷ 577.16(1)

Case on appeal from mayor's court would be dismissed on basis of 96–day delay in filing original documents in county municipal court by clerk of mayor's court, which violated speedy trial statute, and also due to failure of clerk of mayor's court to prepare certified transcript of proceedings. Johnstown v. Tullos (Ohio Mun. 1993) 63 Ohio Misc.2d 155, 620 N.E.2d 278. Municipal Corporations ⚷ 642(3)

State could not avoid statutory speedy trial limitations period by bringing additional charges that arose from same facts as did earlier charge when state knew of facts at time of initial indictment, even though state claimed that Supreme Court had rendered new decision that improved prospects for prosecution for later charge. State v. Wood (Greene 1992) 81 Ohio App.3d 489, 611 N.E.2d 418, dismissed, jurisdictional motion overruled 65 Ohio St.3d 1417, 598 N.E.2d 1168. Criminal Law ⚷ 577.14

A delay before a defendant's arrest for possession of marijuana and cocaine of more than two years after indictment is filed is "unjustifiable" and denies the defendant a fair and speedy trial where he lived in the county during that period and worked at a tavern where he had regular contact with local police. State v. Behymer (Clermont 1992) 80 Ohio App.3d 791, 610 N.E.2d 1126, dismissed, jurisdictional motion overruled 66 Ohio St.3d 1419, 607 N.E.2d 842.

Where there is a delay in the commencement of trial on a speeding violation due to the assignment of a referee to hear the case in municipal court, to which the defendant had not consented and requested a judge, this delay does not toll the running of the speedy trial deadline, as Traf R 14 prohibits contested cases from being assigned to a referee unless the defendant gives his written consent. Boston Hts. v. Weikle (Summit 1991) 81 Ohio App.3d 165, 610 N.E.2d 526.

A defendant's right to a speedy trial is violated when he remains in jail, unable to post bond, for ninety-six speedy trial days (thirty–two actual days) after the expiration of the statutory limit due to the court granting two sua sponte continuances merely stating that the court and judge were in trial without sufficient further explanation. State v. Terra (Franklin 1991) 74 Ohio App.3d 189, 598 N.E.2d 753, dismissed, jurisdictional motion overruled 62 Ohio St.3d 1452, 579 N.E.2d 1391.

A seventy-five-month delay between the filing of a warrant on an indictment and its execution and trial is presumptively prejudicial and violates the defendant's speedy trial right, even though it is only possible that the defendant was prejudiced. State v. Looper (Montgomery 1988) 61 Ohio App.3d 448, 573 N.E.2d 123, motion allowed 38 Ohio St.3d 721, 533 N.E.2d 1062, appeal dismissed 44 Ohio St.3d 601, 540 N.E.2d 1380.

A defendant's request at arraignment for a pretrial conference does not extend the time for trial allowed under RC 2945.71. State v. Reuschling (Ashtabula 1986) 30 Ohio App.3d 81, 506 N.E.2d 558, 30 O.B.R. 138.

Defendant's constitutional guaranty of speedy trial was denied by delay of 22 months between date of his alleged assault of baseball umpire, who had forfeited game in which defendant's son was pitching to the other team, and date of filing of complaint, where one year of the delay was due to umpire's attempt to obtain civil relief, nine months' delay was due to prosecutor's investigation, defendant asserted his speedy trial right in timely fashion after complaint was filed, and delay prejudiced defense. City of Bowling Green v. Dickinson (Ohio Mun. 1984) 19 Ohio Misc.2d 9, 483 N.E.2d 500, 19 O.B.R. 251. Indictment And Information ⚷ 42

The state is not barred from prosecution following an unsuccessful appeal from the sustaining of a motion to suppress so long as the state's certification upon appeal pursuant to Juv R 22(F) or Crim R 12(J), that the evidence suppressed was of such nature that the prosecution could not be successful without it, was made in good faith; if such certification were not made in good faith, the time consumed in determining the appeal from the motion to suppress must be charged to the state as undue delay in prosecution of the accused with respect to a determination of whether there has been a violation of the accused's right to a speedy trial. In re Hester (Franklin 1982) 3 Ohio App.3d 458, 446 N.E.2d 202, 3 O.B.R. 539. Criminal Law ⚷ 577.12(1)

Where a trial court orders counsel to be appointed for a defendant, but neglects to implement such order until the date of trial, any delay occasioned by a continuance to permit appointed counsel to prepare for trial is not a "reasonable continuance" and shall not be effective to extend the time requirements of RC 2945.71. City of Columbus v. Bonner (Franklin 1981) 2 Ohio App.3d 34, 440 N.E.2d 606, 2 O.B.R. 37. Criminal Law ⚷ 577.13

On the evidence, it was unreasonable for the trial court to have extended accused's date of trial four days beyond the statutory time limit. State v. Reeser (Ohio 1980) 63 Ohio St.2d 189, 407 N.E.2d 25, 17 O.O.3d 117.

The fact that a comparatively large number of witnesses was expected to be called to testify at trial does not indicate such an exceptional circumstance as to justify the postponement of the trial date approximately four months beyond the prescribed time period. Village of Elmwood Place v. Denike (Ohio 1978) 56 Ohio St.2d 427, 384 N.E.2d 707, 10 O.O.3d 528. Criminal Law ⚷ 577.13

An order, although entered within the ninety-day time period prescribed for trial by RC 2945.71(B)(2), continuing a case for trial to a date more than double such ninety-day period and stating the continuance was necessary for the reason of a crowded docket, without further explication of such reason appearing in the record, is insufficient to extend the RC 2945.71(B)(2) time limitation for trial as a "reasonable continuance granted other than upon the accused's own motion" pursuant to RC 2945.72(H). State v. Wentworth (Ohio 1978) 54 Ohio St.2d 171, 375 N.E.2d 424, 8 O.O.3d 162.

Appellant tried ninety-three days after arrest was entitled to discharge. State v. Tope (Ohio 1978) 53 Ohio St.2d 250, 374 N.E.2d 152, 7 O.O.3d 408.

It is the mandatory duty of the state to try an accused within the time prescribed by RC 2945.71 and RC 2945.73 and the failure of defense counsel to indicate to the trial court that a guilty plea would not be forthcoming does not constitute a period of delay occasioned by the neglect or improper act of the accused as provided in RC 2945.72(D). State v. Smith (Cuyahoga 1976) 47 Ohio App.2d 317, 354 N.E.2d 699, 1 O.O.3d 385.

A defendant to a criminal charge is denied a speedy trial and entitled to discharge of the indictment when approximately seventeen months elapses from the date of indictment to date of service thereof, approximately two years and four months elapses between the date of indictment and the date of trial, during which period the only delay occasioned by the defendant has been created by his failure to enter his plea of not guilty by reason of insanity in writing resulting in a delay of some thirty days for pretrial observation, and during which period the defendant has on at least five separate occasions moved to dismiss the proceedings against him or quash the indictment because of the denial of a speedy trial. State v. Stapleton (Allen 1974) 41 Ohio App.2d 219, 325 N.E.2d 243, 70 O.O.2d 440.

The Sixth Amendment right to speedy trial is violated where the federal government indicted an individual on drug charges and, after he fled the country, asked that he be expelled back to the United States by Panama but never followed up until arresting him eight and one-half years after his indictment, during which time he had married, completed college, found a career as a computer operations manager, lived openly under his own name, and stayed within the law; the government's negligent delay also presumptively prejudiced his ability to prepare an adequate defense. Doggett v. U.S. (U.S.Fla. 1992) 112 S.Ct. 2686, 505 U.S. 647, 120 L.Ed.2d 520, on remand 972 F.2d 1258.

A delay of six and one-half months between arrest and trial is not clearly excessive for purposes of the US Constitution. Takacs v. Engle (C.A.6 (Ohio) 1985) 768 F.2d 122.

Where an error by a sending state which has adopted the interstate agreement on detainers causes a delay which results in a failure to provide a defendant a speedy trial, such delay will be charged to a receiving state which has also adopted the interstate agreement on detainers, and the case shall be dismissed. State v Mourey, No. 90AP–1199 (10th Dist Ct App, Franklin, 5–9–91), affirmed by 64 OS(3d) 482 (1992).

Where charges against a defendant are pending in a court not of record, an appeal filed by that defendant in a municipal court does not extend the thirty day time for trial established by RC 2945.71. Mount Healthy v Sellins, No. C–830811 (1st Dist Ct App, Hamilton, 7–3–84).

Where the accused was tried ninety-three days after his arrest and was being held solely upon the pending charge, that a parole violation holder was filed against the defendant based on the same charges will not be considered an exception to the ninety day rule. State v Sisco, No. 2–CA–82 (5th Dist Ct App, Fairfield, 6–28–82).

63. Continuances generally—In general

Where a defendant is arrested for various traffic offenses and approximately 142 days pass before defendant moves for dismissal of the complaints against him under RC 2945.71, it is error for a court to deny the motion where the request for a continuance is not in writing and does not state the grounds as required by Traf R 18. State v. Brogan (Ohio App. 2 Dist., Montgomery, 08-24-1994) No. 14462, 1994 WL 461752, Unreported.

Indictment of defendant, who was incarcerated on separate conviction at time of indictment, should have been dismissed on speedy trial grounds, where state failed to notify warden of indictment, warden did not notify defendant of indictment or of right to make request for final disposition pursuant to speedy trial statute, and record did not reflect that trial court's order continuing case past speedy trial limit due to number of cases on its docket was entered in open court with either defendant or counsel present. State v. Miller (Ohio App. 11 Dist., 08-19-1996) 113 Ohio App.3d 606, 681 N.E.2d 970. Criminal Law ⚿ 577.11(3); Criminal Law ⚿ 577.16(2)

Representations made to the trial court by defense counsel that he was unable to proceed with the case until a later time do not extend the time for trial pursuant to RC 2945.72 unless the trial court grants a continuance by entry prior to the expiration of time limit provided by RC 2945.71. State v. Siler (Ohio 1979) 57 Ohio St.2d 1, 384 N.E.2d 710, 11 O.O.3d 1.

Where a case is set for trial only two days following pretrial, and a defendant is unable to subpoena a necessary witness within the two-day period prior to trial because of the sporadic nature of the witness' work hours, the denial of a continuance requested by the defense in order to secure the appearance of the witness constitutes an abuse of discretion. State v Mularkey, Nos. 90AP–1377 and 90AP–1378 (10th Dist Ct App, Franklin, 5–30–91).

64. —— Journal entries, continuances generally

Trial court's failure to journalize defendant's request for continuance to retain counsel did not require that prosecution for trafficking in cocaine be dismissed under speedy trial statute; trial court was only required to state on record reason for continuance when trial court or some party other than defendant requested continuance, so delay resulting from continuance requested by defendant could be attributed to defendant for speedy trial purposes. State v. Seward (Ohio App. 4 Dist., Ross, 03-03-2005) No. 04CA2784, 2005-Ohio-934, 2005 WL 503973, Unreported. Criminal Law ⚷ 577.13

Unjournalized continuance granted at defendant's own request extended the time provided by state's speedy trial statute for bringing defendant to trial. State v. Richardson (Ohio App. 2 Dist., Clark, 10-22-2004) No. 03CA92, 2004-Ohio-5815, 2004 WL 2445347, Unreported, appeal not allowed 105 Ohio St.3d 1464, 824 N.E.2d 92, 2005-Ohio-1024, appeal not allowed 108 Ohio St.3d 1473, 842 N.E.2d 1053, 2006-Ohio-665. Criminal Law ⚷ 577.13

Trial court's grant of several continuances, mostly requested by and for the benefit of defendant, did not violate defendant's speedy trial right, even though trial court did not place in its journal entries the reasons for continuances; rationale of court was not required when continuance was requested by defendant, and statutory time limitation would not have been exceeded but for defendant's requested continuances. State v. Phillips (Ohio App. 8 Dist., Cuyahoga, 02-05-2004) No. 82886, 2004-Ohio-484, 2004 WL 226120, Unreported, appeal not allowed 103 Ohio St.3d 1404, 812 N.E.2d 1287, 2004-Ohio-3980. Criminal Law ⚷ 577.10(8)

For purposes of defendant's motion to dismiss assault indictments due to violation of right to speedy trial, Court of Appeals would not attempt to determine whether the journal entries accurately reflected which party requested the continuances of trial, where review of record indicated that various continuances were made at the request of defense counsel as reflected in the journal entries, and the docket and journal entries did not indicate any obvious error. State v. Barnett (Ohio App. 8 Dist., Cuyahoga, 11-27-2002) No. 81101, 2002-Ohio-6506, 2002 WL 31667667, Unreported, appeal not allowed 98 Ohio St.3d 1514, 786 N.E.2d 64, 2003-Ohio-1572, motion to reopen denied 2003-Ohio-3938, 2003 WL 21710610. Criminal Law ⚷ 1118

A seventy-eight-day sua sponte continuance containing no reasons specifying its institution in the journal entry and no reflection that it is attributable to the defendant, may not be used to extend the speedy trial time period, and a defendant served with an indictment fourteen months before he is brought to trial is denied his right to a speedy trial. State v. Shough (Ohio App. 2 Dist., Montgomery, 08-02-1995) No. 14849, 1995 WL 461260, Unreported, appeal not allowed 74 Ohio St.3d 1485, 657 N.E.2d 1378.

Continuances of trial for menacing, due to vacation of prosecution witness and upon sua sponte journal entry by court attributed to court's vacation and to jammed docket, did not suffice to toll time within which to commence trial pursuant to speedy trial statute; form journal entry incorrectly attributed continuance to defendant and failed to state purpose for continuance, and sua sponte journal entry failed to set forth with specificity reasonableness of continuance in light of its necessity or purpose. Cleveland v. Jones (Ohio App. 8 Dist., 05-06-1996) 110 Ohio App.3d 791, 675 N.E.2d 498. Criminal Law ⚷ 577.13

Trial court, in sua sponte continuing trial beyond statutory speedy trial time limit, was at minimum required to enter order of continuance and reason therefor by journal entry prior to expiration of time limit. State v. King (Ohio, 08-31-1994) 70 Ohio St.3d 158, 637 N.E.2d 903, 1994-Ohio-412. Criminal Law ⚷ 577.13

When extending time for criminal trial, court must enter order of continuance and reasons therefor by journal entry, prior to expiration of time limits for trial prescribed in speedy trial statute. State v. Collins (Ohio App. 6 Dist., 09-30-1993) 91 Ohio App.3d 10, 631 N.E.2d 666, dismissed, jurisdictional motion overruled 68 Ohio St.3d 1470, 628 N.E.2d 1389. Criminal Law ⚷ 577.13

In journal entry meeting minimum requirements for continuance to toll speedy trial time, trial court must record such continuance, must identify party to whom continuance is chargeable, and must indicate briefly underlying reasons necessitating continuance. State v. Collins (Ohio App. 6 Dist., 09-30-1993) 91 Ohio App.3d 10, 631 N.E.2d 666, dismissed, jurisdictional motion overruled 68 Ohio St.3d 1470, 628 N.E.2d 1389. Criminal Law ⚷ 577.13

Sua sponte continuance granted by trial court when public defender moved for leave to withdraw as counsel on ground of conflict of interest was not excludable from speedy trial time period although continuance may have been to give defendant time to prepare a defense, where trial court's journal entry failed to indicate any reason to justify sua sponte continuance and did not identify party to whom it was chargeable. State v. Wagner (Ross 1993) 88 Ohio App.3d 398, 623 N.E.2d 1338. Criminal Law ⚷ 577.10(4)

Speedy trial limits were not extended, as trial court did not journalize continuance of trial or reason for continuance. State v. Miller (Highland 1990) 70 Ohio App.3d 727, 591 N.E.2d 1355. Criminal Law ⚷ 577.13

Failure to journalize the reasons for numerous continuances following pretrials prior to the expiration of the statutory speedy trial period requires dismissal of the charges as the time must be charged against the state. State v. Ball (Cuyahoga 1990) 66 Ohio App.3d 224, 583 N.E.2d 1094.

Defendant did not waive right under statute to trial within 90 days on misdemeanor charge by filing motion for continuance where no journal entry granting motion was made by trial court within statutory time limitations for speedy trial. State v. Doane (Ohio Mun. 1987) 41 Ohio Misc.2d 9, 535 N.E.2d 762. Criminal Law ⚷ 577.10(9)

Unjournalized continuances do not extend the time for speedy trial. State v. Benson (Cuyahoga 1985) 29 Ohio App.3d 321, 505 N.E.2d 987, 29 O.B.R. 448.

Where a trial court grants a continuance before trial, the court, through its journal entry (1) must record the continuance, (2) must identify the party chargeable with the continuance, (3) must briefly indicate the reasons for granting the continuance, and (4) must indicate whether the court is acting sua sponte, and the reasons for such action; any period elapsed during which such record is not kept will be charged against the state in computing time under RC 2945.71 et seq. State v. Geraldo (Lucas 1983) 13 Ohio App.3d 27, 468 N.E.2d 328, 13 O.B.R. 29.

When sua sponte granting a continuance under RC 2945.72(H), the trial court must enter the order of continuance and the reasons therefor by journal entry prior to the expiration of the time limit prescribed in RC 2945.71 for bringing a defendant to trial. State v. Mincy (Ohio 1982) 2 Ohio St.3d 6, 441 N.E.2d 571, 2 O.B.R. 282. Criminal Law ⚷ 577.13; Criminal Law ⚷ 1166(7)

A standardized entry form completed by the trial court indicating a crowded court docket is alone insufficient to support a sua sponte continuance order substantially extending the date of trial beyond the mandatory time limitations of RC 2945.71(B)(2). Village of Elmwood Place v. Denike (Ohio 1978) 56 Ohio St.2d 427, 384 N.E.2d 707, 10 O.O.3d 528.

Where a court, pursuant to RC 2945.72(H), continues the date of trial of a criminal case by entry made prior to the expiration of the time limit derived from RC 2945.71 to a date two days in excess of that time limit, gives as the reason therefor "crowded docket & judge's conference," and notifies the defendant and his counsel of the court's action, entry and reasons, the reasonableness of the extension is satisfactorily evidenced by the failure of the defendant to object and to assert persuasively his basis for a contrary conclusion. State v. Lee (Ohio 1976) 48 Ohio St.2d 208, 357 N.E.2d 1095, 2 O.O.3d 392.

The granting of a sua sponte continuance may not be implied from the fact that the trial court originally set an accused's trial for a date beyond that permitted by RC 2945.71, and where the court's journal does not reflect that a continuance has been granted on or before the last day for trial permitted by RC 2945.71, the state may not rely upon RC 2945.72(H) to justify a delay in bringing the accused to trial. Village of Oakwood v. Ferrante (Cuyahoga 1975) 44 Ohio App.2d 318, 338 N.E.2d 767, 73 O.O.2d 374.

Continuance of DUI trial date could not be excluded from statutory speedy trial period, even though it appeared from transcript that continuance was necessary due to ill judge, where trial court failed to make journal entry providing reason for continuance. State v. Webb (Ohio App. 4 Dist., Washington, 07-12-2002) No. 01CA32, 2002-Ohio-3552, 2002 WL 1565686, Unreported. Criminal Law ⚷ 577.10(4)

The right to a speedy trial is violated in a misdemeanor case where the elapsed time between service of summons and trial is beyond ninety days and journal entries indicate the trial court did record several continuances, but failed to indicate which party made the requests and or the reasons necessitating the continuances. Cleveland v Saah, No. 68043, 1995 WL 328440 (8th Dist Ct App, Cuyahoga, 6–1–95).

A trial court may not wait until after the expiration of the statutory time within which a trial must be commenced to file journal entries which purport to toll the statutory time. State v Burks, No. 55271 (8th Dist Ct App, Cuyahoga, 5–4–89).

Where a court grants the prosecution's motion for a continuance because of the unavailability of a witness, but fails to properly journalize the entry, the ninety-day time period is not extended. State v Crosby, No. 1330 (11th Dist Ct App, Ashtabula, 4–29–88).

Where a continuance has been granted beyond the speedy trial limits allegedly at the defendant's request, failure of the trial judge to make a journal entry timely filed reflecting a basis for the granting of the continuance constitutes reversible error. Greenfield v Mallow, No. 454 (4th Dist Ct App, Highland, 11–15–82).

65. —— Withdrawal of counsel, continuances generally

Trial court did not violate defendant's statutory right to a speedy trial when it allowed his trial counsel to withdraw just prior to trial and then continued the matter so that defendant could acquire new counsel; defendant agreed that he wanted to have counsel represent him at trial. State v. Mustard (Ohio App. 4 Dist., Pike, 09-14-2004) No. 04CA724, 2004-Ohio-4917, 2004 WL 2072454, Unreported, appeal not allowed 105 Ohio St.3d 1438, 822 N.E.2d 810, 2005-Ohio-531, habeas corpus dismissed 2006 WL 783452. Criminal Law ⚷ 577.10(8)

66. —— Reasonableness, continuances generally

Reasonableness of continuance beyond speedy trial deadline, granted in rape prosecution in connection with genetic testing, was apparent from the record; total continuance amounted to only 11 days, defendant consented to testing upon which continuance was based, testing would have been a vain act if results had not been obtained, and consent to testing would have been in vain without additional time to prepare for trial or to bring any additional motions necessitated by results. State v. High (Ohio App. 7 Dist., 01-24-2001) 143 Ohio App.3d 232, 757 N.E.2d 1176, 2001-Ohio-3530. Criminal Law ⚷ 1086.11

In a misdemeanor speeding case, the length of a continuance is unreasonable and violates speedy trial provisions where (1) the next open trial date is used as the length of the continuance, (2) the date is thirty plus days after the initial thirty-day speedy trial period, and (3) it is caused by the court's practice of hearing traffic trials only on two Tuesdays of each month. State v. Daugherty (Ohio App. 3 Dist., 03-28-1996) 110 Ohio App.3d 103, 673 N.E.2d 664.

Reasonableness of continuance depends upon facts and circumstances of case; however, in determining reasonableness, statute permitting reasonable continuances must not be interpreted too broadly as to render speedy-trial statutes meaningless. State v. Daugherty (Ohio App. 3 Dist., 03-28-1996) 110 Ohio App.3d 103, 673 N.E.2d 664. Criminal Law ⚿ 577.13

Upon granting continuance, it is not per se unreasonable extension of time to schedule trial on "next available date" or to extend time for trial a specific number of days past statutory speedy trial limitation. State v. Daugherty (Ohio App. 3 Dist., 03-28-1996) 110 Ohio App.3d 103, 673 N.E.2d 664. Criminal Law ⚿ 577.13

Where a defendant filed more than thirty pretrial motions pro se, and their dispositions or lack of same were insufficiently established, the commencement of trial four days beyond the period provided by RC 2945.71 may be excused either as due to the defendant's own actions or based on the "reasonable continuance" provisions of RC 2945.72(H). State v. Pruitt (Cuyahoga 1984) 18 Ohio App.3d 50, 480 N.E.2d 499, 18 O.B.R. 163.

Trial court's order rescheduling defendant's trial on minor misdemeanor charge eighteen days following the expiration of the speedy trial time limit due to a pending jury trial was not unreasonable, and thus speedy trial statute was tolled during period of continuance. State v. Berner (Ohio App. 9 Dist., Medina, 06-19-2002) No. 3275-M, 2002-Ohio-3024, 2002 WL 1363686, Unreported. Criminal Law ⚿ 577.10(7)

For purposes of tolling speedy trial statute, reasonableness of continuance requested by the state on basis that necessary witness was unavailable for trial was satisfactorily evidenced by defendant's failure to object when the continuance was granted. State v. Berner (Ohio App. 9 Dist., Medina, 06-19-2002) No. 3275-M, 2002-Ohio-3024, 2002 WL 1363686, Unreported. Criminal Law ⚿ 577.10(6)

Trial court's action in twice setting case for trial past statutory time limit due to "judge's schedule," without further explanation, did not constitute "reasonable continuance" pursuant to statutory provision tolling statute of limitations in prosecution for failure to correct a nuisance. City of Toledo v. Pack (Ohio App. 6 Dist., Lucas, 03-29-2002) No. L-01-1019, 2002-Ohio-1517, 2002 WL 471743, Unreported. Criminal Law ⚿ 577.13

While the provisions of RC 2945.71, with respect to the periods of time within which trials in criminal cases must be held, apply to violations of traffic laws, the judge presiding over such cases may, however, pursuant to RC 2945.72, grant a continuance which extends the period upon a reasonable showing that there is insufficient time in which to try the case. OAG 74–062.

A continuance which extends the accused's date of trial beyond the speedy trial limitation because of a crowded docket and judges' conference is not an unreasonable extension. State v Renicker, Nos. CA–1638, CA–1656, CA–1648, and CA–1647 (5th Dist Ct App, Tuscarawas, 9–23–82).

67. —— Calculation, continuances generally

Time period during which trial court granted continuance due to burglary defendant's failure to appear in court was included in calculating whether defendant's constitutional and statutory speedy trial rights were violated. State v. Ossman (Ohio App. 5 Dist., Licking, 08-16-2004) No. 03 CA 92, 2004-Ohio-4302, 2004 WL 1827813, Unreported, appeal reopened 2006-Ohio-720, 2006 WL 367122, appeal not allowed 109 Ohio St.3d 1506, 849 N.E.2d 1028, 2006-Ohio-2998. Criminal Law ⚿ 577.11(2)

For purposes of statutory speedy trial calculation, period of time which elapsed between filing of defendant's notice for continuance and the new trial date set by trial court was excluded from speedy trial period. State v. Humphrey (Ohio App. 2 Dist., Clark, 06-27-2003) No. 2002 CA 30, 2003-Ohio-3401, 2003 WL 21487780, Unreported, motion for delayed appeal denied 103 Ohio St.3d 1490, 816 N.E.2d 1078, 2004-Ohio-5605. Criminal Law ⚿ 577.10(8)

An exclusion from the statutory 270–day speedy trial period should be made for the period between the date a defendant moves for a continuance and an additional pretrial and the date the defendant's motion is granted and the pretrial set. State v. Collura (Cuyahoga 1991) 72 Ohio App.3d 364, 594 N.E.2d 975, dismissed, jurisdictional motion overruled 60 Ohio St.3d 718, 574 N.E.2d 1079.

68. —— Allowed, continuances generally

Trial court did not abuse its discretion in prosecution for operating a motor vehicle under the influence and failing to maintain reasonable control of a motor vehicle by granting State an ex parte continuance of the trial date due to the arresting police officer being on vacation and unavailable to testify. State v. Williamson (Ohio App. 5 Dist., Licking, 11-18-2005) No. 2005 CA 00046, 2005-Ohio-6198, 2005 WL 3112873, Unreported. Criminal Law ⚿ 594(1)

Continuances of trial date which were granted at State's request in prosecution for operating a motor vehicle under the influence and failing to maintain reasonable control of a motor vehicle were reasonable and necessary, and thus running of the 90-day speedy trial period following defendant's arrest within which State was required to bring defendant to trial was tolled during such continuances; first continuance was due to a sudden death in prosecutor's family, and second was due to the arresting police officer being on vacation and unable to testify on the rescheduled trial date. State v. Williamson (Ohio App. 5 Dist., Licking, 11-18-2005) No. 2005 CA 00046, 2005-Ohio-6198, 2005 WL 3112873, Unreported. Criminal Law ⚿ 577.13

Defendant's speedy trial rights were not violated, though 1,520 days had passed between date of defendant's arrest and date of trial; there had been 27 motions for continuance filed, the majority of which had been filed by defense counsel, and, by these continuances alone, without including any time tolled due to defendant's discovery demands, defendant waived 1,363 days, which meant that state had additional 113 days to bring defendant to trial within 270 days specified by statute. State v. Barnes (Ohio App. 10 Dist., Franklin, 06-28-2005) No. 04AP-1133, 2005-Ohio-3279, 2005 WL 1515325, Unreported. Criminal Law ⚷ 577.10(8); Criminal Law ⚷ 577.15(3)

Delay of approximately one year between arrest and trial did not violate right to speedy trial; continuances were warranted due to scheduling conflicts and delay was not unreasonable. State v. Wade (Ohio App. 10 Dist., Franklin, 07-29-2004) No. 03AP-774, 2004-Ohio-3974, 2004 WL 1688434, Unreported, stay granted 103 Ohio St.3d 1476, 816 N.E.2d 253, 2004-Ohio-5405, appeal not allowed 104 Ohio St.3d 1427, 819 N.E.2d 709, 2004-Ohio-6585, appeal not allowed 104 Ohio St.3d 1462, 821 N.E.2d 578, 2005-Ohio-204. Criminal Law ⚷ 577.15(3)

Continuance in felony drug prosecution based on unavailability of law enforcement officer was reasonable and necessary, and thus time for bringing defendant to trial under speedy trial statute was tolled for period of continuance; officer effectuated initial traffic stop that resulted in discovery of drugs and was thus crucial prosecution witness. State v. Jackson (Ohio App. 11 Dist., Ashtabula, 06-04-2004) No. 2003-A-0005, 2004-Ohio-2920, 2004 WL 1238392, Unreported, appeal not allowed 103 Ohio St.3d 1480, 816 N.E.2d 255, 2004-Ohio-5405. Criminal Law ⚷ 577.10(6); Criminal Law ⚷ 594(1)

Continuance granted to state was reasonable for speedy trial purposes even though trial court stated that the case was continued "at a time outside the normal time limits" and failed to set new trial date, as an order setting a new trial date was filed three days after the journalization of the continuance entry. State v. Lee (Ohio App. 2 Dist., Montgomery, 02-13-2004) No. 20012, 2004-Ohio-668, 2004 WL 259274, Unreported. Criminal Law ⚷ 577.13

Defendant was not denied right to speedy trial on misdemeanor assault charge, although trial began two days after 90-day time limit for trial had elapsed, as state had been granted reasonable continuance to obtain presence of two witnesses. State v. Lee (Ohio App. 2 Dist., Montgomery, 02-13-2004) No. 20012, 2004-Ohio-668, 2004 WL 259274, Unreported. Criminal Law ⚷ 577.13

State did not violate defendant's right to a speedy trial; defendant's original trial date was within 90 days of his arrest, and the additional delay was occasioned by defense counsel's request for a continuance and did not count against State for speedy trial purposes. State v. Perez (Ohio App. 2 Dist., Clark, 06-13-2003) No. 2002 CA 28, 2003-Ohio-3055, 2003 WL 21361006, Unreported. Criminal Law ⚷ 577.10(8)

Trial court's judgment entry granting defendant's motion to continue pre-trial adequately continued the criminal proceedings and extended the speedy trial time period. State v. Pierson (Ohio App. 11 Dist., 08-30-2002) 149 Ohio App.3d 318, 777 N.E.2d 296, 2002-Ohio-4515. Criminal Law ⚷ 577.13

Trial court's grant of continuance 11 days beyond speedy trial deadline in rape prosecution, pursuant to state's motion for genetic testing, was reasonable under the circumstances, where defendant specifically consented to collection of samples for testing, and defendant himself later sought continuance for further DNA testing and testing results; only apparent reason for defendant's consent was his expectation of discovering exculpatory evidence, and defendant's later motions reflected his belief that testing would exculpate him. State v. High (Ohio App. 7 Dist., 01-24-2001) 143 Ohio App.3d 232, 757 N.E.2d 1176, 2001-Ohio-3530. Criminal Law ⚷ 577.10(9); Criminal Law ⚷ 577.13

Continuance that was granted in rape prosecution to allow performance of DNA testing was both a reasonable and proper exercise of the court's own initiative, especially since results could have been either inculpatory or exculpatory for defendant, and was thus excludable from statutory speedy trial period. State v. Austin (Ohio App. 1 Dist., 05-15-1998) 131 Ohio App.3d 329, 722 N.E.2d 555, dismissed, appeal not allowed 83 Ohio St.3d 1431, 699 N.E.2d 946. Criminal Law ⚷ 577.13

A continuance granted by a trial court is both necessary and reasonable to protect a defendant's due process rights where the defendant decides to represent herself only shortly before the preliminary hearing, the discovery process was not completed until the day of the preliminary hearing, and the case was such that even a qualified attorney would have faced serious difficulties in attempting to prepare a defense in three days; therefore, the running of the ninety-day time limit for bringing the defendant to trial on misdemeanor charges is tolled during the period of the continuance. State v. Doane (Trumbull 1990) 69 Ohio App.3d 638, 591 N.E.2d 735, dismissed, jurisdictional motion overruled 58 Ohio St.3d 701, 569 N.E.2d 504. Criminal Law ⚷ 577.10(8)

The statement "judge ill" in support of a continuance is a sufficient and specific enough reason for continuing a case beyond the speedy trial limit. Columbus v Browning, No. 82AP–293 (10th Dist Ct App, Franklin, 7–13–82).

69. —— Not allowed, continuances generally

Trial court did not abuse its discretion in denying defense counsel's motion for continuance, made immediately before trial, in prosecution for telecommunications harassment; state had 90 days to bring defendant to trial, pursuant to statute, trial court was concerned about defendant's speedy trial rights being violated, defense counsel did not attempt to alleviate trial court's concerns at time it was making its decision, and witnesses were present and ready to testify. State v. Cossack (Ohio App. 7 Dist., Mahoning, 06-02-2005) No. 03 MA 110, 2005-Ohio-2784, 2005 WL 1324757, Unreported. Criminal Law ⚷ 590(2)

Where trial court did not journalize trial date continuance and the record does not disclose any basis for continuance or any other delay of defendant's trial date beyond the 45–day speedy trial limit, dismissal for lack of speedy trial was proper.

Cleveland v McDonough, No. 64935, 1993 WL 302375 (8th Dist Ct App, Cuyahoga, 8–5–93).

Denial of defendant's motion to dismiss, which was brought on speedy trial grounds, was warranted, even though trial court stated erroneous reason for denial, where defendant requested and was granted a continuance which extended speedy trial time period. State v. Pierson (Ohio App. 11 Dist., 08-30-2002) 149 Ohio App.3d 318, 777 N.E.2d 296, 2002-Ohio-4515. Criminal Law ⚷ 577.16(11)

Trial court did not abuse its discretion by denying defendant's request for continuance, which was sought on day of trial, and after defendant's motion to dismiss under speedy trial statute was denied, where defendant had previously requested and received a continuance, defendant should have been aware, even though he was proceeding pro se, that motion to dismiss might not be granted, and State had several witnesses present, two of whom would have been inconvenienced by delay. State v. Gasnik (Ohio App. 1 Dist., 09-25-1998) 132 Ohio App.3d 612, 725 N.E.2d 1162. Criminal Law ⚷ 587

Trial court did not abuse its discretion in denying the defense motion for a continuance which resulted in trial commencing within eleven days of arraignment for robbery. State v. Sowders (Ohio 1983) 4 Ohio St.3d 143, 447 N.E.2d 118, 4 O.B.R. 386.

70. —— Chargeable against defendant, continuances generally

Defendant's speedy trial rights were not violated, even though defendant was not brought to trial within 90 days after arrest; defendant requested numerous continuances prior to trial and engaged in significant motion practice. State v. Melton (Ohio App. 8 Dist., Cuyahoga, 10-14-2004) No. 82765, 2004-Ohio-5483, 2004 WL 2306565, Unreported, motion to reopen denied 2005-Ohio-6235, 2005 WL 3120219. Criminal Law ⚷ 577.10(8)

Sixty-three days of defendant's 145-day wait between arrest and first day of trial were attributable to defendant's requests for continuances, and thus defendant's speedy trial rights were not violated. State v. Barker (Ohio App. 6 Dist., Lucas, 10-10-2003) No. L-01-1290, 2003-Ohio-5417, 2003 WL 22319572, Unreported, appeal not allowed 101 Ohio St.3d 1469, 804 N.E.2d 42, 2004-Ohio-819. Criminal Law ⚷ 577.10(8); Criminal Law ⚷ 577.15(3)

Robbery defendant was not denied speedy trial; delays were attributable to continuances requested or consented to by defendant. State v. Olverson (Ohio App. 10 Dist., Franklin, 03-18-2003) No. 02AP-554, 2003-Ohio-1274, 2003 WL 1227597, Unreported, motion for delayed appeal denied 99 Ohio St.3d 1457, 790 N.E.2d 1220, 2003-Ohio-3514. Criminal Law ⚷ 577.10(8); Criminal Law ⚷ 577.10(9)

Defendant's right to speedy trial was not violated, where defendant was not held in jail in lieu of bail, and was brought to trial within 247 days, well within time limit of 270 days, considering defendant and his counsel's numerous requests for continuances, which were granted by the trial court, and period that jury was unavailable due to holidays. State v. Barnett (Ohio App. 8 Dist., Cuyahoga, 11-27-2002) No. 81101, 2002-Ohio-6506, 2002 WL 31667667, Unreported, appeal not allowed 98 Ohio St.3d 1514, 786 N.E.2d 64, 2003-Ohio-1572, motion to reopen denied 2003-Ohio-3938, 2003 WL 21710610. Criminal Law ⚷ 577.10(8); Criminal Law ⚷ 577.15(1)

Defendant's requests for continuances extended the 30–day time period in which he was required to be brought to trial in mayor's court on speeding charges. Amberley v. Mize (Ohio Mun., 04-14-2000) 106 Ohio Misc.2d 32, 733 N.E.2d 337. Criminal Law ⚷ 577.10(8)

Continuance which was granted by trial court after defendant notified court of witness's unavailability, and set date for trial which was within 90–day limit in light of extension granted following defendant's earlier motion for continuance, was attributable to defendant for purposes of speedy trial statute. State v. Nelson (Ohio App. 5 Dist., 08-06-1996) 122 Ohio App.3d 309, 701 N.E.2d 747, appeal allowed 77 Ohio St.3d 1523, 674 N.E.2d 374, appeal dismissed as improvidently allowed 82 Ohio St.3d 1207, 693 N.E.2d 804, 1998-Ohio-415. Criminal Law ⚷ 577.10(8)

Fact that there was scheduling conflict on part of defendant and his attorney did not provide justification for charging the resulting continuance to state, in determining whether defendant's statutory speedy trial rights were violated, where it was undisputed that continuance was granted upon defendant's own motion. State v. Soto (Ohio App. 9 Dist., 09-07-1994) 96 Ohio App.3d 743, 645 N.E.2d 1307. Criminal Law ⚷ 577.10(9); Criminal Law ⚷ 577.12(1)

Defendant was properly charged with continuance he requested four days prior to trial to secure presence of out-of-state witness at trial and, accordingly, trial date did not exceed statutory time limit; trial court had issued delayed judgment entry. State v. Ebright (Clinton 1992) 83 Ohio App.3d 846, 615 N.E.2d 1105. Criminal Law ⚷ 577.10(8)

Defendant's speedy trial rights were not violated, where defendant was brought to trial within 90 day time limit permitted by statute, and defendant's motion for continuance justified extension of 90 day limit. State v. Murray (Ohio App. 5 Dist., Licking, 05-03-2002) No. 01 CA 00108, 2002-Ohio-2500, 2002 WL 925264, Unreported. Criminal Law ⚷ 577.10(8)

71. —— Chargeable against state, continuances generally

Error in trial court's journal entry, in which trial court indicated continuance was at state's request, could not be corrected to indicate that continuance was sua sponte continuance, once statutory speedy trial period had expired, and thus continuance was chargeable against state for purposes of defendant's motion to dismiss, on speedy trial grounds, charges of aggravated robbery with gun specification, robbery, and carrying concealed weapon. State v. Williams (Ohio App. 1 Dist., Hamilton, 08-12-2005)

No. C-040685, 2005-Ohio-4142, 2005 WL 1923531, Unreported. Criminal Law ⚷ 577.12(1); Criminal Law ⚷ 1110(5)

State's request for continuance, due to absence of key prosecution witness, was chargeable against state for purposes of defendant's motion to dismiss on statutory speedy trial grounds, in prosecution for aggravated robbery with gun specification, robbery, and carrying a concealed weapon, where state was given opportunity to go forward with trial as scheduled, and to continue case in progress to secure missing witness, but state declined and chose not to go forward with trial. State v. Williams (Ohio App. 1 Dist., Hamilton, 08-12-2005) No. C-040685, 2005-Ohio-4142, 2005 WL 1923531, Unreported. Criminal Law ⚷ 577.12(1)

Continuances at request of the parties, continuance for purposes of determining defendant's mental competency to stand trial, and continuances at request of court were not attributable to the State for purposes of determining speedy trial time period. State v. Tullis (Ohio App. 10 Dist., Franklin, 05-05-2005) No. 04AP-333, 2005-Ohio-2205, 2005 WL 1055977, Unreported, appeal not allowed 106 Ohio St.3d 1510, 833 N.E.2d 1250, 2005-Ohio-4605. Criminal Law ⚷ 577.10(7); Criminal Law ⚷ 577.10(8)

Period between granting of state's motion for continuance to respond to defendant's motion to dismiss on speedy trial grounds and defendant's entry of no contest plea was not chargeable to state under speedy trial statute, though failure of entry granting state's motion to identify party to whom continuance was chargeable would normally have required that it be charged against state, where trial had been scheduled for day on which court granted continuance and state's sole purpose in seeking continuance was to respond to motion to dismiss. State v. Dunston (Ohio App. 12 Dist., Fayette, 10-07-2002) No. CA2002-03-008, 2002-Ohio-5454, 2002 WL 31261594, Unreported. Criminal Law ⚷ 577.10(8)

Period between granting of state's motion for continuance to respond to defendant's motion to dismiss on speedy trial grounds and defendant's entry of no contest plea was not chargeable to state under speedy trial statute, though failure of entry granting state's motion to identify party to whom continuance was chargeable would normally have required that it be charged against state, where trial had been scheduled for day on which court granted continuance and state's sole purpose in seeking continuance was to respond to motion to dismiss. State v. Dunston (Ohio App. 12 Dist., Fayette, 10-07-2002) No. CA2002-03-008, 2002-Ohio-5454, 2002 WL 31261594, Unreported. Criminal Law ⚷ 577.10(8)

The delay resulting from defense counsel's request to continue the trial in order to consider motions filed on defendant's behalf should not be charged against the state for speedy trial purposes. State v. Taylor (Ohio, 12-20-2002) 98 Ohio St.3d 27, 781 N.E.2d 72, 2002-Ohio-7017, stay granted 98 Ohio St.3d 1402, 781 N.E.2d 221, 2003-Ohio-40, certiorari denied 123 S.Ct. 2227, 538 U.S. 1062, 155 L.Ed.2d 1115. Criminal Law ⚷ 577.10(8)

Fifteen-day delay from date capital murder trial was scheduled to commence and actual start of trial would be charged to the state, for speedy trial purposes, where it was not clear who requested continuance or reason behind it. State v. Myers (Ohio, 12-13-2002) 97 Ohio St.3d 335, 780 N.E.2d 186, 2002-Ohio-6658, reconsideration denied 97 Ohio St.3d 1500, 780 N.E.2d 1023, 2002-Ohio-7367, certiorari denied 123 S.Ct. 2254, 539 U.S. 906, 156 L.Ed.2d 116, motion to reopen denied 100 Ohio St.3d 1505, 799 N.E.2d 184, 2003-Ohio-6161. Criminal Law ⚷ 577.12(1)

For continuance granted to State, or ordered sua sponte by trial court, to be deemed as "reasonable," so that resulting delay will not be charged against State for purposes of speedy trial statute, court must journalize continuance before expiration of time limit set forth in statute and must state the reason for continuance. State v. Stamps (Ohio App. 1 Dist., 04-03-1998) 127 Ohio App.3d 219, 712 N.E.2d 762. Criminal Law ⚷ 577.10(7); Criminal Law ⚷ 577.12(1)

Delay resulting from continuance requested by defendant was not chargeable to State for purposes of speedy trial statute, even though journal entry gave no reason for continuance. State v. Stamps (Ohio App. 1 Dist., 04-03-1998) 127 Ohio App.3d 219, 712 N.E.2d 762. Criminal Law ⚷ 577.10(8)

Four-day delay resulting from grant of continuance requested by defendant while his motion to suppress was pending was not attributable to State for purposes of speedy trial statute. State v. Stamps (Ohio App. 1 Dist., 04-03-1998) 127 Ohio App.3d 219, 712 N.E.2d 762. Criminal Law ⚷ 577.10(8)

Journal entry from date of defendant's arraignment, which included date four weeks in future and symbol representing defendant, when read in conjunction with hearing transcript indicating that defendant had asked for four-week continuance, was sufficient to indicate that granted continuance had been requested by defendant, so that resulting delay was not chargeable to State for purposes of speedy trial statute. State v. Stamps (Ohio App. 1 Dist., 04-03-1998) 127 Ohio App.3d 219, 712 N.E.2d 762. Criminal Law ⚷ 577.16(9)

Sua sponte continuance by trial court, for which trial court has failed to make journal entry stating reasons for continuance and identifying party to whom it is chargeable, must be counted against the state for speedy trial purposes. State v. Wagner (Ross 1993) 88 Ohio App.3d 398, 623 N.E.2d 1338. Criminal Law ⚷ 577.12(1)

Where no continuance is on record extending a state's deadline to file a brief in opposition to a defendant's motion to suppress evidence, the period between the date the state was supposed to file its brief in opposition and the date the state in fact filed its brief is chargeable to the state for speedy trial purposes. State v. Collura (Cuyahoga 1991) 72 Ohio App.3d 364, 594 N.E.2d 975, dismissed, jurisdictional motion overruled 60 Ohio St.3d 718, 574 N.E.2d 1079.

72. —— Sua sponte, continuances generally

Defendant's statutory right to speedy trial was not violated by trial court's decision to continue defendant's trial, sua sponte, without explanation, where 90-day time limit prescribed in speedy trial statute had not yet expired, and trial was commenced and completed prior to expiration of time allowed. Cleveland v. Jovanovic (Ohio App. 8 Dist., 06-05-2003) 153 Ohio App.3d 37, 790 N.E.2d 824, 2003-Ohio-2875. Criminal Law ⚷ 577.10(7)

Defendant's statutory right to speedy trial was not violated by trial court's decision to continue defendant's trial, sua sponte, without explanation, where 90-day time limit prescribed in speedy trial statute had not yet expired, and trial was commenced and completed prior to expiration of time allowed. Cleveland v. Jovanovic (Ohio App. 8 Dist., 06-05-2003) 153 Ohio App.3d 37, 790 N.E.2d 824, 2003-Ohio-2875. Criminal Law ⚷ 577.10(7)

Resolution of issue of reasonableness of trial court's sua sponte continuance of trial for minor misdemeanor beyond statutory 30–day limit depends upon peculiar facts and circumstances of particular case; it is difficult, if not unwise, to establish *per se* rule of what constitutes "reasonableness" beyond statutory limit. State v. King (Ohio App. 9 Dist., 10-23-1996) 114 Ohio App.3d 669, 683 N.E.2d 870. Criminal Law ⚷ 577.13

Court could not sua sponte continue trial date beyond period prescribed in RC 2945.71(C)(2) on ground of inclement weather where such action was taken after expiration of the period. State v. Montgomery (Ohio 1980) 61 Ohio St.2d 78, 399 N.E.2d 552, 15 O.O.3d 119.

Where an almost three-month delay in obtaining an indictment results in a trial date being set with only five days' notice, and where defense counsel is unavailable on the day of trial, leaving a defendant with an unprepared stand-in appointed counsel, a sua sponte continuance for purposes of ensuring that the defendant receives a fair trial is not reasonable absent an explanation for the substantial lapse of time between the arrest and indictment. State v Jordan, No. 90AP–660 (10th Dist Ct App, Franklin, 2–21–91).

Where a court sua sponte orders a continuance for which there are no reasonable grounds the speedy trial period will not be tolled. State v Breedlove, No. C–880175 (1st Dist Ct App, Hamilton, 4–12–89).

A sua sponte continuance of a drunk-driving prosecution by a trial court due to docket congestion to a date seven days beyond the trial date prescribed by RC 2945.71(B)(2) is a reasonable extension of time under RC 2945.72(H) and does not deny the defendant his right to a speedy trial. State v Richardson, No. CA86–07–108 (12th Dist Ct App, Butler, 2–17–87).

73. Preliminary hearing

Habeas corpus is an available remedy to challenge the time parameters of a Crim R 5(B) preliminary hearing if filed prior to that hearing; there is no adequate remedy at law available to prevent what may constitute unlawful incarceration under the statutory framework of RC 2945.71 to 2945.73. Styer v. Brichta (Wood 1990) 69 Ohio App.3d 738, 591 N.E.2d 1255.

An automatic extension of the time requirements of RC 2945.71 does not result from a request for a pretrial hearing, but a defendant is not denied a speedy trial where: (1) the defendant requests the pretrial hearing, and (2) the amount of time taken to provide the pretrial hearing and trial is not unreasonable on its face. State v. Gowe (Medina 1983) 13 Ohio App.3d 358, 469 N.E.2d 909, 13 O.B.R. 439.

An accused convicted after trial cannot obtain discharge upon the ground that he was not afforded a preliminary hearing or indicted within fifteen days after his arrest. State v. Pugh (Ohio 1978) 53 Ohio St.2d 153, 372 N.E.2d 1351, 7 O.O.3d 238.

A motion to dismiss for failure to hold a preliminary hearing within five days, pursuant to Crim R 5(B)(1) and RC 2945.71, is filed too late where a preliminary hearing has been conducted in another court, in which no such motion was made, and a grand jury finds probable cause to hand down an indictment. State v. Grim (Hamilton 1975) 44 Ohio App.2d 152, 336 N.E.2d 458, 73 O.O.2d 141. Criminal Law ⚷ 245

Confinement in violation of RC 2945.71(C)(1) and 2945.71(C)(2) is directly in violation of the mandatory provision of RC 2945.73(A) and 2945.73(B). Styer v Brichta, No. 90WD072 (6th Dist Ct App, Wood, 10–10–90).

74. Waiver by defendant—In general

Trial delay following defendant's waiver of speedy trial rights was not counted against State for purposes of speedy trial statute. State v. Williams (Ohio App. 2 Dist., Montgomery, 09-30-2004) No. 20104, 2004-Ohio-5273, 2004 WL 2245101, Unreported. Criminal Law ⚷ 577.10(9)

Record did not support claim that trial court pressured defendant into waiving speedy trial rights; date on which trial court removed defendant's original counsel from case based on improper conduct toward prosecutor was last day on which case could be timely tried, court explained to defendant that it would not allow trial to go forward on that day because defendant was not represented by counsel, and defendant agreed after being told he could seek new counsel or have public defender appointed that he would waive speedy trial rights in order to have time to hire another attorney. State v. Madhobe (Ohio App. 5 Dist., Stark, 04-07-2003) No. 2002CA00230, 2003-Ohio-1793, 2003 WL 1818928, Unreported. Criminal Law ⚷ 577.10(9)

Post-conviction petitioner was not entitled to hearing on his untimely filed petition for relief, especially where petition was not supported by new evidence, petitioner failed to establish that he was unavoidably prevented from discovering evidence submitted in support of petition, evidence submitted in support of petition failed to establish violation of petitioner's right to speedy trial, petitioner had waived his right to speedy trial, and petitioner was brought to trial within speedy trial period. State v. Davis (Ohio App. 7 Dist., Mahoning, 05-30-2002) No. 01 CA 171, 2002-Ohio-2789, 2002 WL 32806896, Unreported. Criminal Law ⚷ 1655(1)

Defendants' waiver of speedy trial time on date of hearing on state's motion to join, from date of hearing until next pretrial hearing, a period of 232 days, was valid, as waivers were made on record in open court. State v. Riley (Ohio App. 12 Dist., 08-22-2005) 162 Ohio App.3d 730, 834 N.E.2d 887, 2005-Ohio-4337. Criminal Law ⚷ 577.10(9)

Criminal defendant may waive his speedy trial right. State v. Clark (Ohio App. 2 Dist., 10-27-1995) 107 Ohio App.3d 141, 667 N.E.2d 1262. Criminal Law ⚷ 577.10(9)

Criminal defendant may waive his right to be tried within 270–day period prescribed by statute. State v. Vaughn (Ohio App. 12 Dist., 10-16-1995) 106 Ohio App.3d 775, 667 N.E.2d 82, denial of post-conviction relief affirmed 1997 WL 133526, dismissed, appeal not allowed 79 Ohio St.3d 1419, 680 N.E.2d 156, denial of post-conviction relief affirmed 1999 WL 1142922. Criminal Law ⚷ 577.10(9)

Defendant's right to speedy trial was violated when court requested and received waivers of right to speedy trial with less than 30 days left on speedy trial period, to permit review of possibly applicable state Supreme Court decision, and over two years elapsed without further activity. State v. Scolaro (Tuscarawas 1992) 73 Ohio App.3d 555, 597 N.E.2d 1184, dismissed, jurisdictional motion overruled 64 Ohio St.3d 1429, 594 N.E.2d 970. Criminal Law ⚷ 577.10(9); Criminal Law ⚷ 577.15(1)

Petitioner who had instituted action to dismiss indictments pending against him and who had unsuccessfully taken an appeal could not be held to have slept on his constitutional right to a speedy trial, and unwarranted delay by state in prosecuting charges contained in indictments brought in 1952 and 1953 entitled petitioner to dismissal thereof on the ground that he had been denied speedy trial. State ex rel. Lotz v. Hover (Ohio 1962) 174 Ohio St. 68, 186 N.E.2d 841, 21 O.O.2d 332, on rehearing 174 Ohio St. 380, 189 N.E.2d 433, 22 O.O.2d 443. Criminal Law ⚷ 576(1)

Commencement of defendant's trial for obstructing justice ten months after his arrest was reasonable, under the Sixth Amendment, where defendant's waiver of right to speedy trial had not specified a time limit for trial. State v. Terry (Ohio App. 12 Dist., Fayette, 08-26-2002) No. CA2001-07-012, 2002-Ohio-4378, 2002 WL 1964694, Unreported. Criminal Law ⚷ 577.15(3)

75. —— Conditional or limited, waiver by defendant

Defendant was not denied speedy trial rights in prosecution for domestic violence, felonious assault, and disrupting public services, as defendant had originally signed waiver of speedy trial rights which, although reputedly marked "limited waiver," did not give date certain for beginning and ending points for tolling purposes and was thus unlimited in duration, and trial began 20 days after defendant formally reasserted right to speedy trial. State v. Bray (Ohio App. 9 Dist., Lorain, 03-10-2004) No. 03CA008241, 2004-Ohio-1067, 2004 WL 432265, Unreported. Criminal Law ⚷ 577.10(9)

Court of Appeals strongly disapproves of conditioning continuances requested by a defendant on a waiver of his speedy-trial rights; not only is that generally unnecessary because of the extension of time resulting from the continuance, but as a practice it undermines the purpose of the statutory speedy-trial scheme. State v. Kerby (Ohio App. 2 Dist., 07-15-2005) 162 Ohio App.3d 353, 833 N.E.2d 757, 2005-Ohio-3734, appeal not allowed 107 Ohio St.3d 1682, 839 N.E.2d 403, 2005-Ohio-6480. Criminal Law ⚷ 612

76. —— Counsel's waiver, waiver by defendant

Scheduling error on part of trial court in prosecution for misdemeanor driving under the influence (DUI), resulting in setting of trial date outside statutory speedy trial period, did not prejudice defendant and was harmless, where speedy trial period was tolled within statutory period by defendant's filing of motion to suppress and defense counsel was aware that trial would not be held on date scheduled due to filing of suppression motion. State v. Delarosa (Ohio App. 11 Dist., Portage, 06-30-2005) No. 2003-P-0129, 2005-Ohio-3399, 2005 WL 1538264, Unreported. Criminal Law ⚷ 577.16(4)

Defense counsel's filing of time waiver which did not specify a time limit for trial operated to waive defendant's statutory right to speedy trial, even if waiver was executed without defendant's consent. State v. Collins (Ohio App. 5 Dist., Tuscarawas, 11-20-2003) No. 2003AP030019, 2003-Ohio-6407, 2003 WL 22843915, Unreported. Attorney And Client ⚷ 88; Criminal Law ⚷ 577.10(9)

Defendant was bound by his counsel's waiver of his right to speedy trial. State v. Davis (Ohio App. 7 Dist., Mahoning, 05-30-2002) No. 01 CA 171, 2002-Ohio-2789, 2002 WL 32806896, Unreported. Criminal Law ⚷ 577.10(9)

If an attorney moves for a continuance in one case due to a prior commitment, it is logical that he will be unavailable for another case against the defendant, which is scheduled for the same date, and this circumstance serves as a waiver of the defendant's speedy trial rights. State v. Conkle (Ohio App. 5 Dist., Tuscarawas, 03-09-1994) No. 93 AP 070049, 1994 WL 112205, Unreported.

Defense counsel's waiver of defendant's speedy trial right was sound trial strategy, and as such did not constitute ineffective assistance of counsel, where defendant pled guilty to reduced charges on date on which trial would have commenced had his speedy trial right not been waived. State v. Patterson (Ohio App. 7 Dist., 09-24-1997) 123 Ohio App.3d 237, 704 N.E.2d 14. Criminal Law ⚷ 641.13(2.1)

Defense counsel's signing of docket and journal entry which contained waiver of speedy trial requirement in consideration of continuance of trial constituted waiver of defendant's speedy trial rights, despite defense counsel's contention that he had signed docket and journal entry merely to acknowledge his receipt thereof; there was no language on the entry to support defense counsel's contention. State v. Hughey (Ohio App. 7 Dist., 11-20-1996) 115 Ohio App.3d 664, 685 N.E.2d 1318. Criminal Law ⚷ 577.10(9)

Fact that defendant did not consent to defense counsel's waiver of defendant's right to speedy trial did not render speedy trial waiver invalid; defense counsel may waive right to speedy trial for reasons of trial preparation and defendant is bound by such waiver. State v. Vaughn (Ohio App. 12 Dist., 10-16-1995) 106 Ohio App.3d 775, 667 N.E.2d 82, denial of post-conviction relief affirmed 1997 WL 133526, dismissed, appeal not allowed 79 Ohio St.3d 1419, 680 N.E.2d 156, denial of post-conviction relief affirmed 1999 WL 1142922. Criminal Law ⚷ 577.10(9)

Counsel may waive defendant's statutory right to speedy trial even when defendant is not aware of waiver. State v. Wood (Greene 1992) 81 Ohio App.3d 489, 611 N.E.2d 418, dismissed, jurisdictional motion overruled 65 Ohio St.3d 1417, 598 N.E.2d 1168. Attorney And Client ⚷ 88

A defense counsel has the power to waive a defendant's right to a speedy trial and the defendant will be bound by the waiver; thus, where a defense attorney participates in the reassignment of a defendant's case and in the waiving of the defendant's rights to a speedy trial after the time for trial has run, his actions constitute an effective waiver of the right to a speedy trial which is binding on the defendant. State v. Dumas (Franklin 1990) 68 Ohio App.3d 174, 587 N.E.2d 932, dismissed, jurisdictional motion overruled 56 Ohio St.3d 712, 565 N.E.2d 835.

A defendant's right to a speedy trial is waived by defense counsel's consent to continuances. State v. Saunders (Franklin 1984) 23 Ohio App.3d 69, 491 N.E.2d 313, 23 O.B.R. 132.

The right of a defendant to a speedy trial, as implemented by RC 2945.71 to RC 2945.73, can be waived by the attorney for the accused even though the accused is neither aware of nor informed about the waiver. State v. McRae (Hamilton 1977) 56 Ohio App.2d 72, 381 N.E.2d 946, 10 O.O.3d 98, affirmed 55 Ohio St.2d 149, 378 N.E.2d 476, 9 O.O.3d 118.

The constitutional right to a speedy trial, as implemented by RC 2945.71 to RC 2945.73, can be waived by the attorney of an accused even if the accused is not aware of or informed of the waiver. State v. McRae (Ohio 1978) 55 Ohio St.2d 149, 378 N.E.2d 476, 9 O.O.3d 118.

A defendant's right to be brought to trial within the time limits expressed in RC 2945.71 may be waived by his counsel for reasons of trial preparation, and the defendant is bound by the waiver even though the waiver is executed without his consent. State v. McBreen (Ohio 1978) 54 Ohio St.2d 315, 376 N.E.2d 593, 8 O.O.3d 302, certiorari denied 99 S.Ct. 287, 439 U.S. 914, 58 L.Ed.2d 261. Attorney And Client ⚷ 88

Where the privately retained counsel of a defendant agrees to an extension of a trial date beyond ninety days from the date of arrest, in the absence of the personal consent of the accused, there is no violation of the defendant's constitutional or statutory rights. State v. Davis (Hamilton 1975) 44 Ohio App.2d 95, 335 N.E.2d 874, 73 O.O.2d 89.

A trial court has discretion to extend the time limit set out in RC 2945.71(B)(2), where counsel for the accused voluntarily agrees to a trial date ninety days beyond the date of arrest. State v. Davis (Hamilton 1975) 44 Ohio App.2d 95, 335 N.E.2d 874, 73 O.O.2d 89.

An agreed entry setting the date of trial outside the applicable time limits of RC 2945.71 acts as a waiver of speedy-trial rights, notwithstanding the fact that the defense attorney places an addendum at the bottom of the entry limiting its effective dates. State v Lockett, No. C–880298 (1st Dist Ct App, Hamilton, 5–17–89).

77. —— Knowingly, intelligently and voluntarily, waiver by defendant

Defendant did not knowingly, intelligently, and voluntarily waive his right to a speedy trial, where waiver of speedy trial was contained on pre-printed form without explanation of its meaning or consequence of its waiver; however, there was no speedy trial violation, where trial court found all continuances were reasonable. State v. Baloh (Ohio App. 9 Dist., Medina, 06-30-2004) No. 04CA0010-M, 2004-Ohio-3421, 2004 WL 1462825, Unreported. Criminal Law ⚷ 577.10(9); Criminal Law ⚷ 577.13

Defendant pled guilty to charges of felonious assault, aggravated burglary, and domestic violence, and thus waived right to challenge convictions on statutory speedy trial grounds; defendant did not challenge knowingness or voluntariness of plea, and although he sent letter to trial court addressing right to speedy trial, he did so only after he had pleaded guilty to all counts. State v. Bellatto (Ohio App. 7 Dist., Mahoning, 03-11-2003) No. 00 CA 141, 2003-Ohio-1214, 2003 WL 1193773, Unreported, appeal not allowed 99 Ohio St.3d 1455, 790 N.E.2d 1219, 2003-Ohio-3396. Criminal Law ⚷ 273.4(1)

Speedy trial period was tolled during period in which case was continued at defendant's request, despite defendant's claim that his waiver of time, as noted in trial court's journalized entry, was not knowingly and voluntarily made. State v. Hirsch (Ohio App. 1 Dist., 08-07-1998) 129 Ohio App.3d 294, 717 N.E.2d 789, dismissed, appeal not allowed 84 Ohio St.3d 1436, 702 N.E.2d 1213, denial of habeas corpus affirmed 74 Fed.Appx. 486, 2003 WL 21949184. Criminal Law ⚷ 577.10(8)

Defendant who made decision 96 days after his initial court appearance not to file motion to dismiss, but rather to request that case be referred and set for trial five weeks later, made knowing, voluntary, and intelligent waiver of his constitutional right to speedy trial. State v. Huckaby (Ohio Mun.,

08-05-1997) 91 Ohio Misc.2d 16, 696 N.E.2d 1116. Criminal Law ⚷ 577.10(9)

Only requirement to criminal defendant waiving his speedy trial right is that such waiver be made knowingly, intelligently, and voluntarily. State v. Clark (Ohio App. 2 Dist., 10-27-1995) 107 Ohio App.3d 141, 667 N.E.2d 1262. Criminal Law ⚷ 577.10(9)

Capital murder defendant's waiver of speedy trial rights was valid, even though trial court had not explained to defendant purpose, functions or protections of right which he was waiving; trial court need not enumerate all possible implications of waiver of constitutional rights in order for waiver to be knowing and voluntary. State v. Phillips (Ohio, 11-22-1995) 74 Ohio St.3d 72, 656 N.E.2d 643, 1995-Ohio-171, reconsideration denied 74 Ohio St.3d 1485, 657 N.E.2d 1378, stay granted 74 Ohio St.3d 1503, 659 N.E.2d 795, rehearing granted, opinion recalled 75 Ohio St.3d 1504, 665 N.E.2d 219, certiorari denied 116 S.Ct. 1835, 517 U.S. 1213, 134 L.Ed.2d 938, denial of post-conviction relief affirmed in part, reversed in part 1999 WL 58961, dismissed, appeal not allowed 86 Ohio St.3d 1402, 711 N.E.2d 231, denial of post-conviction relief affirmed 2002-Ohio-823, 2002 WL 274637, appeal not allowed 95 Ohio St.3d 1488, 769 N.E.2d 403, 2002-Ohio-2625. Criminal Law ⚷ 577.10(9)

Any claim by defendant that waivers of his right to speedy trial were not knowingly or voluntarily made on the record would involve consideration of evidence outside record and should be tested by postconviction proceedings. State v. Clary (Franklin 1991) 73 Ohio App.3d 42, 596 N.E.2d 554, dismissed, jurisdictional motion overruled 62 Ohio St.3d 1405, 577 N.E.2d 358. Criminal Law ⚷ 1134(3)

Defendant who waived statutory right to trial within 90 days by signing knowing and voluntary waiver was not prejudiced when her case could not go forward until approximately nine months after her arrest, where she did not specify time limit for trial in waiver. State v. Doane (Ohio Mun. 1987) 41 Ohio Misc.2d 9, 535 N.E.2d 762. Criminal Law ⚷ 577.10(9); Criminal Law ⚷ 577.15(3)

An accused's express written waiver of his statutory rights to a speedy trial as provided in RC 2945.71 et seq., if knowingly and voluntarily made, may also constitute a waiver of the coextensive speedy trial rights guaranteed by the United States and Ohio Constitutions. State v. O'Brien (Ohio 1987) 34 Ohio St.3d 7, 516 N.E.2d 218. Criminal Law ⚷ 577.10(9)

An accused's express written waiver of his statutory rights to a speedy trial as provided in RC 2945.71 et seq., if knowingly and voluntarily made, may also constitute a waiver of the coextensive speedy trial rights guaranteed by the United States and Ohio Constitutions. State v. O'Brien (Ohio 1987) 34 Ohio St.3d 7, 516 N.E.2d 218. Criminal Law ⚷ 577.10(9)

Where a defendant knowingly and voluntarily signs a waiver of his right to be brought to trial within the time period specified in RC 2945.71, and the waiver states no time period after which it would expire, his rights are not infringed upon as long as he is tried within a reasonable time. State v. Kidd (Hamilton 1978) 60 Ohio App.2d 374, 397 N.E.2d 768, 14 O.O.3d 326. Criminal Law ⚷ 577.10(9)

Trial court was not required to ascertain that defendant understood he was waiving right to present an arguable motion for discharge of charges against him when he plead guilty to attempted rape and aggravated burglary; motion for discharge was remedy for right to speedy trial, which had already been violated, and thus, trial court was only required to ascertain that defendant understood, and knowingly, intelligently, and voluntarily agreed to waive those rights that had not yet been violated before accepting his guilty plea. State v. Kitchens (Ohio App. 2 Dist., Clark, 08-23-2002) No. 2001-CA-92, 2002-Ohio-4335, 2002 WL 1941154, Unreported, appeal not allowed 98 Ohio St.3d 1411, 781 N.E.2d 1019, 2003-Ohio-60, appeal not allowed 105 Ohio St.3d 1519, 826 N.E.2d 316, 2005-Ohio-1880. Criminal Law ⚷ 273.1(4)

78. —— Failure to raise claim, waiver by defendant

Speedy trial statute did not apply to defendant whose first conviction for felonious assault had resulted in reversal and remand on appeal and who was awaiting a new trial; furthermore, defendant failed to raise issue of speedy trial on appeal with respect to first conviction, and did not raise issue of speedy trial rights in second trial until trial was set to begin, thus waiving any error. State v. Richards (Ohio App. 8 Dist., Cuyahoga, 10-02-2003) No. 81452, 2003-Ohio-5235, 2003 WL 22251431, Unreported, motion for delayed appeal denied 101 Ohio St.3d 1466, 804 N.E.2d 40, 2004-Ohio-819. Criminal Law ⚷ 577.14; Criminal Law ⚷ 1180

For purposes of appellate review, murder defendant waived claim that he was denied speedy trial, where defendant failed to raise claim in trial court. State v. Shakoor (Ohio App. 7 Dist., Mahoning, 09-23-2003) No. 01CA121, 2003-Ohio-5140, 2003 WL 22231582, Unreported. Criminal Law ⚷ 1035(1)

Defendant was precluded from raising speedy trial issue on appeal, where he failed to move for dismissal or discharge for a violation of his speedy trial rights, either orally or in writing, during or prior to trial. State v. Humphrey (Ohio App. 2 Dist., Clark, 05-30-2003) No. CIV.A. 02CA0025, 2003-Ohio-2825, 2003 WL 21267255, Unreported, motion for delayed appeal denied 101 Ohio St.3d 1485, 805 N.E.2d 537, 2004-Ohio-1293, appeal not allowed 102 Ohio St.3d 1533, 811 N.E.2d 1152, 2004-Ohio-3580. Criminal Law ⚷ 1044.1(1)

Speedy trial provisions are not self-executing but must be asserted by defendant in timely fashion to avoid such rights being waived. State v. Trummer (Ohio App. 7 Dist., 09-30-1996) 114 Ohio App.3d 456, 683 N.E.2d 392, dismissed, appeal not allowed 78 Ohio St.3d 1409, 675 N.E.2d 1249, denial of post-conviction relief affirmed 1998 WL 896457, dismissed, appeal not allowed 85 Ohio St.3d 1464,

709 N.E.2d 171, motion for delayed appeal denied 2000 WL 1476604. Criminal Law ⚷ 577.10(10)

Defendant's speedy trial right was not violated, although defendant objected to one continuance, where defendant waived right to speedy trial shortly after arrest, defendant never objected to other continuances and in some instances instigated them, and defendant at no time demanded trial or revoked or attempted to revoke waiver. Village of Glenwillow v. Tomsick (Ohio App. 8 Dist., 06-17-1996) 111 Ohio App.3d 718, 676 N.E.2d 1259. Criminal Law ⚷ 577.10(8); Criminal Law ⚷ 577.10(9); Criminal Law ⚷ 577.10(10)

Where a defendant's failure to object to an alleged erroneous journal entry permits the prosecution and the court to believe that a motion to suppress will be filed and where defendant fails to indicate that a scheduled hearing on motion to suppress was not requested, a court's tolling of speedy trial time pursuant to RC 2945.71 is proper, and the defendant waived any objection he may have had regarding the court's findings. State v. Kasarda (Marion 1992) 82 Ohio App.3d 388, 612 N.E.2d 484.

Misdemeanor defendant did not waive her statutory right to speedy trial by failing to file jury demand until after passage of statutory 90–day period for bringing her to trial; defendant's exercise of constitutional right to trial by jury neither explicitly nor implicitly waived constitutional right to speedy trial. State v. Doane (Ohio Mun. 1987) 41 Ohio Misc.2d 9, 535 N.E.2d 762. Criminal Law ⚷ 577.10(9)

A defendant's failure to object to a trial date scheduled outside the ninety-day limitation period of RC 2945.71(C)(2) and RC 2945.71(D), before the expiration of that period, does not amount to acquiescence in the trial date. State v. Singer (Ohio 1977) 50 Ohio St.2d 103, 362 N.E.2d 1216, 4 O.O.3d 237. Criminal Law ⚷ 577.10(9)

79. —— Failure to appear, waiver by defendant

Defendant's failure to appear at scheduled trial and whose trial was therefore rescheduled for later date, waived his right to assert statutory speedy trial rights for that period of time which elapsed from his initial arrest to date of subsequent rearrest. State v. Nethers (Ohio App. 5 Dist., Licking, 06-05-2003) No. 02CA00110, 2003-Ohio-2896, 2003 WL 21290928, Unreported. Criminal Law ⚷ 577.10(9)

Defendant who failed to appear at scheduled change of plea hearing waived his right to assert statutory speedy trial rights for the period of time which elapsed from his initial arrest to date of subsequent re-arrest. State v. Bishop (Ohio App. 4 Dist., Vinton, 03-12-2003) No. 02CA573, 2003-Ohio-1385, 2003 WL 1422469, Unreported. Criminal Law ⚷ 577.11(2)

Defendant waived his right to assert a statutory speedy trial violation for the period between his initial arrest for felony driving under the influence of alcohol (DUI) and his subsequent arrest on outstanding warrants for felony and misdemeanor charges, where defendant failed to appear for his felony arraignment after posting a surety bond. State v. Eldridge (Ohio App. 4 Dist., Scioto, 03-10-2003) No. 02CA2842, 2003-Ohio-1198, 2003 WL 1145442, Unreported. Criminal Law ⚷ 577.11(2)

A defendant who fails to appear at a scheduled trial, and whose trial must therefore be rescheduled for a later date, waives his right to assert the provisions of RC 2945.71 to RC 2945.73 for that period of time which elapses from his initial arrest to the date he is subsequently rearrested. State v. Bauer (Ohio 1980) 61 Ohio St.2d 83, 399 N.E.2d 555, 15 O.O.3d 122. Criminal Law ⚷ 577.10(8)

Failure by the accused to appear for his scheduled arraignment waives the right to trial within the periods established by RC 2945.71. State v Owens, No. CA–3076 (5th Dist Ct App, Licking, 12–10–84).

80. —— Failure to comply with order or request, waiver by defendant

Speedy trial waiver entered by defendant in prior case applied in defendant's subsequent prosecution for violation of city ordinance by failing to comply with order served by city conservation specialist, where prior and subsequent misdemeanor charges were both founded on defendant's alleged failure to comply with same underlying order issued pursuant to substantive prohibitions of city ordinance, and no defense applied with respect to charge in subsequent case that did not likewise apply in prior case. City of Dayton v. Mitman (Ohio App. 2 Dist., Montgomery, 08-26-2005) No. 20714, 2005-Ohio-4530, 2005 WL 2087477, Unreported. Criminal Law ⚷ 577.10(9)

Ten-month delay in ruling on defendant's motion to discharge indictment charging various sex offenses involving a minor did not violate defendant's speedy trial rights; defendant's failure to comply with State's discovery request and her motion for leave to file motion to suppress evidence tolled speedy trial time. State v. Brummett (Ohio App. 4 Dist., Highland, 01-28-2004) No. 03CA5, 2004-Ohio-431, 2004 WL 193872, Unreported. Criminal Law ⚷ 577.10(8)

81. —— Continuances, waiver by defendant

A defendant's request for continuance waives his speedy trial rights in reference to the requested continuance and is not a waiver of unlimited duration and it tolls the speedy trial time from the scheduled trial date to the rescheduled date. State v. Corfias (Ohio App. 4 Dist., Gallia, 08-30-1994) No. 93 CA 03, 1994 WL 501766, Unreported.

Delays caused by the state's motions do not toll the speedy trial deadline where the court does not journalize the reason continuance is granted or to whom the continuance will be charged. State v. Corfias (Ohio App. 4 Dist., Gallia, 08-30-1994) No. 93 CA 03, 1994 WL 501766, Unreported.

A defendant who moves the court for a continuance and "further waives time limits by making this motion" waives his speedy trial rights only during the pendency of his requested continuance and does not execute a waiver of unlimited duration. State v. Corfias (Ohio App. 4 Dist., Gallia,

08-30-1994) No. 93 CA 03, 1994 WL 501766, Unreported.

Where the state breaches its agreement not to request any more continuances in exchange for the defendant's waiver of speedy trial rights in connection with the state's second request for a continuance, the time is charged to the state, and the failure to bring the defendant to trial within the speedy trial time limits requires the conviction be reversed and the defendant discharged. State v Bitzer, No. CA93-04-032, 1993 WL 471497 (12th Dist Ct App, Clermont, 11-15-93).

An oral waiver of speedy trial noted on a file jacket by a court administrative assistant is not effective where a trial court does not journalize a continuance and the reasons for the continuance prior to the expiration of the time in which a defendant must be brought to trial and a judgment of conviction and sentence must be vacated. State v King, No. CA 9131, 1993 WL 135345 (5th Dist Ct App, Stark, 4–19–93), affirmed by 70 Ohio St.3d 158 (1994).

In a trial for murder and abuse of a corpse, a trial court does not err in continuing a trial twice for a total of 111 days at the state's request where the defense initially moved for a continuance on the ground of inability to prepare adequately for trial having received discovery evidence only a few weeks before trial and expressly waived the right to be brought to trial within the time period specified by Ohio law, and where the state requested and was granted, over the verbal objection of the defense counsel, two continuances on the grounds of (1) newly discovered technical evidence which required scientific (DNA) analysis, and (2) the eleventh-hour disability of the lead counsel who was familiar with the technical nature of the evidence and the likely witnesses, without which whose expertise the county prosecutor opined that the case should not go forward. State v. Blair (Clark 1990) 70 Ohio App.3d 774, 592 N.E.2d 854, motion for delayed appeal denied 75 Ohio St.3d 1476, 663 N.E.2d 1303.

82. —— Writing, waiver by defendant

Trial court violated defendant's right to a speedy trial when defendant was not brought to trial on fourth degree misdemeanor charges of parking in a no parking zone and having a firearm in a motor vehicle until 81 chargeable days following his arrest; defendant did not expressly waive his right to a speedy trial in writing or by statement made in open court, no delay was occasioned by defendant's request for counsel since counsel was appointed for defendant the day it was requested, and the trial court did not grant a continuance by journal entry or explain the reason for the delay. State v. McLean (Ohio App. 11 Dist., Trumbull, 03-04-2005) No. 2003-T-0115, No. 2003-T-0116, 2005-Ohio-954, 2005 WL 517455, Unreported. Criminal Law ⚩ 577.10(8); Criminal Law ⚩ 577.10(9)

Waiver of statutory right to speedy trial was invalid; although waiver of rights form was signed by defendant and "yes" next to waiver of speedy trial category on form was circled, there was no transcript indicating defendant was notified by court of his speedy trial right, defendant was only instructed to sign form such that question existed as to who circled "yes" on form, and witness did not sign form. City of Maple Heights v. Pinkney (Ohio App. 8 Dist., Cuyahoga, 03-18-2004) No. 81514, 2004-Ohio-1256, 2004 WL 536195, Unreported. Criminal Law ⚩ 577.10(9)

Murder defendant failed to demonstrate that he was denied his right to speedy trial, even though time between arrest and trial was one and one-half years, where defendant signed unlimited waiver of speedy trial rights and did not later file written objection and demand for trial. State v. Shakoor (Ohio App. 7 Dist., Mahoning, 09-23-2003) No. 01CA121, 2003-Ohio-5140, 2003 WL 22231582, Unreported. Criminal Law ⚩ 577.10(9); Criminal Law ⚩ 577.10(10); Criminal Law ⚩ 577.15(3)

State had to comply with requirements of speedy trial statute as to charges that had not yet been brought at time defendant executed waiver of right to speedy trial, where waiver, which purported to be applicable to all charges that could be brought against defendant relating to factual situation of original charges, applied only to charges that had been brought against defendant at time waiver was signed, and thus withdrawal of waiver applied only to charges that had been brought as of time waiver had been executed. State v. Boles (Ohio App. 2 Dist., Montgomery, 05-23-2003) No. 18762, 2003-Ohio-2693, 2003 WL 21213383, Unreported, appeal not allowed 100 Ohio St.3d 1411, 796 N.E.2d 538, 2003-Ohio-4948. Criminal Law ⚩ 577.10(9)

Defendant's waiver of right to speedy trial, executed when he had been charged only with rape and improperly discharging firearm at, or into, habitation, which purported to be applicable to all charges that could be brought against defendant relating to factual situation of original charges, was applicable only to charges that had been brought against defendant at time waiver was signed, and waiver did not apply to charges brought subsequent to waiver, and subsequent to defendant's withdrawal of waiver. State v. Boles (Ohio App. 2 Dist., Montgomery, 05-23-2003) No. 18762, 2003-Ohio-2693, 2003 WL 21213383, Unreported, appeal not allowed 100 Ohio St.3d 1411, 796 N.E.2d 538, 2003-Ohio-4948. Criminal Law ⚩ 577.10(9); Criminal Law ⚩ 577.14

Defendant waived his right to a speedy trial, where defendant signed a form which waived his right to a speedy trial, and the waiver was filed with the trial court. State v. Woodley (Ohio App. 8 Dist., Cuyahoga, 04-17-2003) No. 80732, 2003-Ohio-1950, 2003 WL 1900935, Unreported, appeal not allowed 100 Ohio St.3d 1425, 797 N.E.2d 92, 2003-Ohio-5232. Criminal Law ⚩ 577.10(9)

To be effective, defendant's waiver of his or her constitutional and statutory rights to a speedy trial must be expressed in writing or made in open court on the record. State v. Stamps (Ohio App. 1 Dist., 04-03-1998) 127 Ohio App.3d 219, 712 N.E.2d 762. Criminal Law ⚩ 577.10(9)

Form for requesting hearing to contest parking tickets was invalid insofar as it was structured in such a manner that hearing could be requested only if statutory speedy trial rights were waived; granting hearing to contest charges could not constitutionally be conditioned upon waiver of statutory speedy trial rights. Warren v. Granitto (Ohio App. 11 Dist., 03-28-1994) 93 Ohio App.3d 723, 639 N.E.2d 865. Criminal Law ⚷ 577.4; Criminal Law ⚷ 577.10(9)

Defendant did not waive her statutory or constitutional rights to speedy trial, despite alleged oral waiver by trial counsel; neither defendant nor counsel made express written waiver or waived her right to speedy trial in open court on record. State v. King (Ohio, 08-31-1994) 70 Ohio St.3d 158, 637 N.E.2d 903, 1994-Ohio-412. Criminal Law ⚷ 577.10(9)

Following an express written waiver of unlimited duration by an accused of his right to a speedy trial, the accused is not entitled to a discharge for delay in bringing him to trial unless the accused files a formal written objection and demand for trial, following which the state must bring the accused to trial within a reasonable time. State v. O'Brien (Ohio 1987) 34 Ohio St.3d 7, 516 N.E.2d 218. Criminal Law ⚷ 577.10(10)

Following an express written waiver of unlimited duration by an accused of his right to a speedy trial, the accused is not entitled to a discharge for delay in bringing him to trial unless the accused files a formal written objection and demand for trial, following which the state must bring the accused to trial within a reasonable time. State v. O'Brien (Ohio 1987) 34 Ohio St.3d 7, 516 N.E.2d 218. Criminal Law ⚷ 577.10(10)

As long as a defendant is tried within a reasonable time, his constitutional and statutory rights to a speedy trial are not violated where (1) the defendant signed a waiver of his rights to a speedy trial, (2) defendant's counsel witnessed the waiver, and (3) the waiver stated that the case would be "continued indefinitely." State v. Johnson (Cuyahoga 1984) 13 Ohio App.3d 271, 469 N.E.2d 559, 13 O.B.R. 335.

Execution of a waiver form by a defendant purporting to waive the defendant's speedy trial rights removes the case from the operation of the speedy trial statutes. City of Westlake v. Cougill (Ohio 1978) 56 Ohio St.2d 230, 383 N.E.2d 599, 10 O.O.3d 382.

83. —— Plea, waiver by defendant

Entry of *Alford* plea to rape and gross sexual imposition resulted in waiver of right to appeal denial of motion to dismiss based on speedy trial grounds. State v. Benman (Ohio App. 10 Dist., Franklin, 07-27-2004) No. 03AP-1012, 2004-Ohio-3935, 2004 WL 1663497, Unreported. Criminal Law ⚷ 1026.10(4)

Violation of defendant's right to speedy trial as to charges brought after defendant had executed, and then withdrawn, waiver of right to speedy trial, was not rendered harmless by fact defendant pled no contest to original charges of rape and improperly discharging weapon at, or into, habitation, brought against him, and all additional charges were dismissed, where it appeared defendant's plea was influenced by potential sentences associated with charges that should have been dismissed under speedy trial statute because waiver of right to speedy trial did not apply to charges brought after waiver was executed. State v. Boles (Ohio App. 2 Dist., Montgomery, 05-23-2003) No. 18762, 2003-Ohio-2693, 2003 WL 21213383, Unreported, appeal not allowed 100 Ohio St.3d 1411, 796 N.E.2d 538, 2003-Ohio-4948. Criminal Law ⚷ 1166(7)

A plea of guilty waives a defendant's right to challenge his or her conviction on statutory speedy trial grounds pursuant to RC 2945.71(B)(2). State v. Kelley (Ohio 1991) 57 Ohio St.3d 127, 566 N.E.2d 658. Criminal Law ⚷ 273.4(1)

A plea of no contest does not constitute a waiver of a defendant's right to a speedy trial. State v. McCormick (Cuyahoga 1988) 41 Ohio App.3d 158, 534 N.E.2d 942, cause dismissed 38 Ohio St.3d 709, 533 N.E.2d 359.

Defendant's guilty plea waived his right to raise statutory right to speedy trial on appeal. Village of Montpelier v. Greeno (Ohio 1986) 25 Ohio St.3d 170, 495 N.E.2d 581, 25 O.B.R. 212. Criminal Law ⚷ 1026.10(4)

Where a defendant bases his claim to a speedy trial solely on his statutory right thereto, pursuant to RC 2945.71, he waives such right by entering a plea of guilty. State v. Branch (Cuyahoga 1983) 9 Ohio App.3d 160, 458 N.E.2d 1287, 9 O.B.R. 226.

84. —— Additional charges or refiling of indictment, waiver by defendant

Defendant's speedy trial waiver for first indictment charging defendant with murder was applicable to second indictment that charged defendant with involuntary manslaughter, and thus trial court's refusal to dismiss second indictment, which was filed 158 days following arrest, did not constitute violation of defendant's speedy trial rights; involuntary manslaughter was a lesser-included offense of murder and therefore manslaughter charge would not have involved considerations of defense that would not have been contemplated in defending against murder charge. State v. Davis (Ohio App. 2 Dist., Clark, 09-12-2003) No. 2002-CA-43, 2003-Ohio-4839, 2003 WL 22110297, Unreported, cause dismissed 100 Ohio St.3d 1480, 798 N.E.2d 616, 2003-Ohio-5993. Criminal Law ⚷ 577.10(9)

Conviction for felonious assault under second indictment which added aggravated burglary charge and two prior violent offense specifications to sole felonious assault charge in first indictment did not violate speedy trial statute, though trial on second indictment was brought after statutory 90–day period, where defendant waived his right to speedy trial as to felonious assault charge in first indictment and, after aggravated burglary charge and prior violent offense specifications dismissed, first and second indictment differed only in case number. State v. Clark (Ohio App. 2 Dist., 10-27-1995) 107

Ohio App.3d 141, 667 N.E.2d 1262. Criminal Law ⚷ 577.10(9); Criminal Law ⚷ 577.14

Waiver of right to speedy trial in case based on initial indictment applied to case based upon second indictment which became identical when trial court dismissed one charge and one death penalty specification. State v. Luff (Lucas 1993) 85 Ohio App.3d 785, 621 N.E.2d 493, dismissed, jurisdictional motion overruled 67 Ohio St.3d 1464, 619 N.E.2d 698, certiorari denied 114 S.Ct. 1116, 510 U.S. 1136, 127 L.Ed.2d 426. Criminal Law ⚷ 577.14

When defendant waives right to speedy trial as to initial charge, waiver is not applicable to additional charges arising from same set of circumstances that are brought subsequent to execution of waiver. State v. Wood (Greene 1992) 81 Ohio App.3d 489, 611 N.E.2d 418, dismissed, jurisdictional motion overruled 65 Ohio St.3d 1417, 598 N.E.2d 1168. Criminal Law ⚷ 577.10(9)

A defendant's waiver of his speedy trial rights on a charge of indecent exposure does not constitute a waiver of his speedy trial rights on a subsequent charge of disorderly conduct arising out of the same set of circumstances. State v. Warf (Seneca 1991) 72 Ohio App.3d 604, 595 N.E.2d 537.

When an accused waives the right to a speedy trial as to an initial charge, this waiver is not applicable to additional charges arising from the same set of circumstances that are brought subsequent to the execution of the waiver. State v. Adams (Ohio 1989) 43 Ohio St.3d 67, 538 N.E.2d 1025. Criminal Law ⚷ 577.10(9)

Defendant's waiver of speedy trial regarding charges brought against him in original indictment did not apply to additional charges brought against him in subsequent indictment filed while original charges were pending on appeal. State v. DeLeon (Ohio App. 2 Dist., Montgomery, 06-28-2002) No. 18114, 2002-Ohio-3286, 2002 WL 1393665, Unreported, appeal not allowed 98 Ohio St.3d 1424, 782 N.E.2d 78, 2003-Ohio-259. Criminal Law ⚷ 577.10(9); Criminal Law ⚷ 577.14

85. Dismissal of charges or discharge

Defendant was entitled to dismissal, on statutory speedy trial grounds, of charge of complicity to commit aggravated robbery, where defendant's motion to dismiss presented prima facie case for discharge under speedy trial statute, but trial court never scheduled hearing on defendant's motion, and state failed to respond to motion by showing that speedy trial time limitations had not expired. State v. Whitt (Ohio App. 4 Dist., Scioto, 09-26-2005) No. 04CA2962, 2005-Ohio-5154, 2005 WL 2389891, Unreported, stay denied 107 Ohio St.3d 1680, 839 N.E.2d 401, 2005-Ohio-6480, appeal not allowed 108 Ohio St.3d 1474, 842 N.E.2d 1054, 2006-Ohio-665. Criminal Law ⚷ 577.16(2)

Dismissal of criminal charges was warranted, where rescheduling of trial date following withdrawal of counsel occurred after speedy trial time limit had expired. State v. Ward (Ohio App. 5 Dist., Richland, 05-10-2004) No. 03 CA 60, 2004-Ohio-2323, 2004 WL 1044137, Unreported. Criminal Law ⚷ 577.16(1)

Motion to dismiss for violation of defendant's right to speedy trial, filed approximately 16 days before expiration of statutory speedy trial period, was properly denied as premature. State v. Hughes (Ohio App. 9 Dist., Lorain, 09-24-2003) No. 02CA008206, 2003-Ohio-5045, 2003 WL 22187441, Unreported. Criminal Law ⚷ 577.16(7)

Defendant's motion to dismiss illegal conveyance charges for violation of right to speedy trial was premature, as it was filed approximately 80 days before date speedy trial period expired. State v. Szorady (Ohio App. 9 Dist., Lorain, 05-28-2003) No. 02CA008159, 2003-Ohio-2716, 2003 WL 21222139, Unreported. Criminal Law ⚷ 577.16(7)

Statutory 270-day time frame for bringing defendant arrested and charged with felony driving under the influence of alcohol (DUI) to trial had not expired at time defendant filed motion to dismiss charge for alleged speedy trial violation, and thus, defendant was not entitled to dismissal; defendant was only entitled to 183 statutory days credit at time defendant filed motion and court disposed of defendant's case in 197 statutory days. State v. Eldridge (Ohio App. 4 Dist., Scioto, 03-10-2003) No. 02CA2842, 2003-Ohio-1198, 2003 WL 1145442, Unreported. Criminal Law ⚷ 577.8(1)

The speedy trial statute, RC 2945.71, is violated where more than 200 days pass from the date of arrest to the date of the jury trial and the city fails to demonstrate any reasonable diligence to secure defendant's availability for trial, despite notice by defendant of his incarceration in an adjoining county. City of Newark v. Barcus (Ohio App. 5 Dist., Licking, 09-09-1994) No. 94 CA 00015, 1994 WL 590498, Unreported.

Accused presents prima facie case for discharge based upon violation of limitations created by speedy trial statute by charging in motion to dismiss that he or she was held solely on pending charge and for time exceeding statutory time limits; burden then shifts to State to show that limits have not been exceeded by demonstrating that time limit had been properly extended. State v. Hiatt (Ohio App. 4 Dist., 03-26-1997) 120 Ohio App.3d 247, 697 N.E.2d 1025. Criminal Law ⚷ 577.16(6); Criminal Law ⚷ 577.16(8)

State's failure to discharge defendant pending trial did not violate defendant's statutory right to speedy trial, where defendant did not raise matter of speedy trial with trial judge. State v. Trummer (Ohio App. 7 Dist., 09-30-1996) 114 Ohio App.3d 456, 683 N.E.2d 392, dismissed, appeal not allowed 78 Ohio St.3d 1409, 675 N.E.2d 1249, denial of post-conviction relief affirmed 1998 WL 896457, dismissed, appeal not allowed 85 Ohio St.3d 1464, 709 N.E.2d 171, motion for delayed appeal denied 2000 WL 1476604. Criminal Law ⚷ 577.16(6)

Any extensions of time that are tolled pursuant to speedy trial statute must be strictly construed against the state and, once defendant has shown that 270 days have elapsed, prima facie case for discharge has been established and state bears burden to show that defendant was timely tried. State v. Grinnell (Ohio App. 10 Dist., 06-27-1996) 112

Ohio App.3d 124, 678 N.E.2d 231, appeal not allowed 77 Ohio St.3d 1474, 673 N.E.2d 138, appeal not allowed 77 Ohio St.3d 1475, 673 N.E.2d 138, denial of habeas corpus affirmed 215 F.3d 1326, certiorari denied 121 S.Ct. 232, 531 U.S. 898, 148 L.Ed.2d 166. Criminal Law ⚷ 577.13; Criminal Law ⚷ 577.16(8)

Extension of trial due to absence of prosecution witness was unreasonable, and thus, speedy trial rights of motorist charged with speeding were violated, requiring discharge of motorist; due to absence of state's witness (highway patrol trooper), trial court granted continuance, and earliest available date for rescheduled trial was 30 plus days after initial 30–day speedy trial period. State v. Daugherty (Ohio App. 3 Dist., 03-28-1996) 110 Ohio App.3d 103, 673 N.E.2d 664. Criminal Law ⚷ 577.13; Criminal Law ⚷ 577.15(4); Criminal Law ⚷ 577.16(2)

Once 270–day statutory speedy trial limit has expired, defendant has established prima facie case for dismissal; at that point, burden is on state to demonstrate any tolling or extension of time limit. State v. Mays (Ohio App. 8 Dist., 01-11-1996) 108 Ohio App.3d 598, 671 N.E.2d 553, dismissed, appeal not allowed 75 Ohio St.3d 1509, 665 N.E.2d 679. Criminal Law ⚷ 577.15(1); Criminal Law ⚷ 577.16(8); Criminal Law ⚷ 577.16(9)

State's failure to comply with mandates of Ohio speedy trial statute requires defendant's discharge. State v. Mays (Ohio App. 8 Dist., 01-11-1996) 108 Ohio App.3d 598, 671 N.E.2d 553, dismissed, appeal not allowed 75 Ohio St.3d 1509, 665 N.E.2d 679. Criminal Law ⚷ 577.16(1)

Where defendant has established prima facie case that defendant should be discharged due to violation of speedy trial rule, state is obligated to produce evidence demonstrating that defendant was not entitled to be brought to trial within speedy trial period. State v. Baker (Ohio App. 8 Dist., 12-20-1993) 92 Ohio App.3d 516, 636 N.E.2d 363. Criminal Law ⚷ 577.16(8)

Where criminal defendant alleges, in motion for discharge due to speedy trial violation, that defendant was incarcerated solely on pending charge and demonstrates that he was not brought to trial within limits imposed by statutory triple-count provision, defendant presents prima facie case for discharge. State v. Baker (Ohio App. 8 Dist., 12-20-1993) 92 Ohio App.3d 516, 636 N.E.2d 363. Criminal Law ⚷ 577.16(9)

Where a defendant is not brought to trial within the time set forth in RC 2945.71 and there are no journal entries establishing continuances allegedly granted at defendant's request, the defendant is entitled to a discharge under RC 2945.73. State v. Benson (Cuyahoga 1985) 29 Ohio App.3d 321, 505 N.E.2d 987, 29 O.B.R. 448.

Trial court was required, upon defendant's request, to state essential findings of fact in support of its denial of motion to discharge for failure to comply with speedy trial provisions. City of Bryan v. Knapp (Ohio 1986) 21 Ohio St.3d 64, 488 N.E.2d 142, 21 O.B.R. 363. Criminal Law ⚷ 577.16(10)

A defendant is not required to request a trial within the time provided for in RC 2945.71, and is not required to show he was prejudiced by the delay. State v. Coatoam (Lake 1975) 45 Ohio App.2d 183, 341 N.E.2d 635, 74 O.O.2d 229. Criminal Law ⚷ 577.16(5.1)

The language of RC 2945.71 is pre-emptory and mandatory, directing that an accused be brought to trial within the time specified, and it is not necessary for a defendant to object to the setting of a trial date forty-five days beyond the time of his arrest before requesting a discharge pursuant to RC 2945.73. City of Cincinnati v. Williams (Hamilton 1975) 44 Ohio App.2d 143, 336 N.E.2d 464, 73 O.O.2d 137. Criminal Law ⚷ 577.15(5); Criminal Law ⚷ 577.10(10)

Defendant accused of violation of RC 4511.20 whose trial is not held within fifteen days after arrest or service of summons must be discharged if defendant took no action which delayed proceedings. State v. Sells (Ohio Co. 1974) 41 Ohio Misc. 49, 322 N.E.2d 378, 70 O.O.2d 109.

A trial court errs in denying a defendant's motion to dismiss under RC 2945.73 for the failure of the state to bring the defendant to trial within the time required by RC 2945.71. State v Croop, No. CA–9163 (5th Dist Ct App, Stark, 5–10–93).

86. Appeals generally

Any error in post-conviction court's finding that petitioner's claim of violation of his statutory right to speedy trial was barred by res judicata did not prejudice petitioner and was harmless, where petitioner failed to state valid claim of violation of his statutory right to speedy trial. State v. Dixon (Ohio App. 5 Dist., Richland, 06-03-2005) No. 2004-CA-90, 2005-Ohio-2846, 2005 WL 1364615, Unreported, appeal not allowed 106 Ohio St.3d 1556, 836 N.E.2d 581, 2005-Ohio-5531. Criminal Law ⚷ 1177

Defendant's claim that he raised in his motion for correction of jail-time credit, that trial court made an erroneous legal determination in affording him merely 115 days of jail-time credit, was barred by operation of res judicata, having failed to raise claim on direct appeal; had defendant claimed that error resulted from mathematical mistake, rather than an erroneous legal determination, issue could have been reviewed on the merits. State v. Lomack (Ohio App. 10 Dist., Franklin, 06-02-2005) No. 04AP-648, 2005-Ohio-2716, 2005 WL 1303190, Unreported. Criminal Law ⚷ 1433(2)

Defendant waived appellate review of his claim that he was not brought to trial on felony charges within time provided by speedy trial statute and, therefore, should have been discharged, where record did not indicate that issue of speedy trial was raised to trial court. State v. Kolvek (Ohio App. 9 Dist., Summit, 07-14-2004) No. 21752, 2004-Ohio-3706, 2004 WL 1562573, Unreported, appeal not allowed 103 Ohio St.3d 1528, 817 N.E.2d 410, 2004-Ohio-5852, appeal not allowed 104 Ohio St.3d 1441, 819 N.E.2d 1124, 2004-Ohio-7033. Criminal Law ⚷ 1035(1)

Res judicata barred defendant's appellate argument that alleged that his speedy trial rights were violated, during second appeal of murder conviction; defendant could have brought up the issue of whether his speedy trial rights were denied on the first appeal of his case. State v. Parker (Ohio App. 8 Dist., Cuyahoga, 06-10-2004) No. 82687, 2004-Ohio-2976, 2004 WL 1277243, Unreported, appeal not allowed 103 Ohio St.3d 1493, 816 N.E.2d 1080, 2004-Ohio-5605. Judgment ⚷ 751

Complaint for a writ of mandamus could not be employed to challenge denial of a relator's right to speedy trial; rather, speedy trial issues could only be addressed through a direct appeal following trial. Gales v. State (Ohio App. 8 Dist., Cuyahoga, 04-30-2004) No. 84300, 2004-Ohio-2327, 2004 WL 1045894, Unreported. Mandamus ⚷ 4(1)

Defendant waived for appellate review his claim that he was denied his right to speedy trial under State speedy trial rule, where defendant failed to file a motion for discharge prior to voir dire. State v. Knight (Ohio App. 2 Dist., Greene, 04-16-2004) No. 2003CA14, 2004-Ohio-1941, 2004 WL 830043, Unreported, appeal not allowed 103 Ohio St.3d 1427, 814 N.E.2d 490, 2004-Ohio-4524. Criminal Law ⚷ 1044.1(1)

Criminal defendant had adequate remedy at law, through a direct appeal if he was convicted of murder, and thus, defendant was not entitled to mandamus relief, as to trial court's alleged violation of his statutory speedy trial rights while he was being held in county jail as he awaited trial. Hamilton v. Collins (Ohio App. 11 Dist., Lake, 10-24-2003) No. 2003-L-106, 2003-Ohio-5703, 2003 WL 22427933, Unreported. Mandamus ⚷ 4(1)

Petitioner had adequate remedy of law through appellate process for issues regarding speedy trial violations, sealing of motion to dismiss based upon speedy trial violations, or issues regarding findings of fact, and thus was not entitled to mandamus seeking an order to compel state to release and unseal speedy trial motion and to issue findings of fact as to why motion was denied. State v. Ross (Ohio App. 7 Dist., Mahoning, 09-10-2003) No. 96 CA 247, No. 96 CA 251, 2003-Ohio-4889, 2003 WL 22120715, Unreported, affirmed 102 Ohio St.3d 73, 806 N.E.2d 553, 2004-Ohio-1827. Mandamus ⚷ 4(4)

Mandamus petitioner never filed request for findings of fact in his motion for speedy trial, and thus petitioner had no legal right to mandamus seeking order to compel state to issue findings of fact as to why motion was denied, and state was under no legal duty to perform act requested. State v. Ross (Ohio App. 7 Dist., Mahoning, 09-10-2003) No. 96 CA 247, No. 96 CA 251, 2003-Ohio-4889, 2003 WL 22120715, Unreported, affirmed 102 Ohio St.3d 73, 806 N.E.2d 553, 2004-Ohio-1827. Criminal Law ⚷ 577.16(10)

Prisoner's claim that his right to speedy trial was violated failed to meet fundamental requirement of jurisdictional error for habeas corpus relief; claim could be addressed on direct appeal. Elersic v. Wilson (Ohio App. 11 Dist., Trumbull, 08-08-2003) No. 2003-T-0070, 2003-Ohio-4229, 2003 WL 21892758, Unreported, affirmed 101 Ohio St.3d 417, 805 N.E.2d 1127, 2004-Ohio-1501, reconsideration denied 102 Ohio St.3d 1474, 809 N.E.2d 1160, 2004-Ohio-2830. Habeas Corpus ⚷ 291; Habeas Corpus ⚷ 479

Defendant waived for appellate review question as to whether his speedy trial rights were violated, where defendant failed to raise issue at trial, in which he was ultimately convicted of complicity to commit aggravated murder and kidnapping. State v. Green (Ohio App. 7 Dist., Mahoning, 06-13-2003) No. 01 CA 54, 2003-Ohio-3074, 2003 WL 21373172, Unreported, motion for delayed appeal granted 100 Ohio St.3d 1407, 796 N.E.2d 535, 2003-Ohio-4948, dismissal of post-conviction relief affirmed 2003-Ohio-5142, 2003 WL 22231592, motion to reopen denied 2003-Ohio-5442, 2003 WL 22332000, appeal not allowed 100 Ohio St.3d 1544, 800 N.E.2d 750, 2003-Ohio-6879, denial of post-conviction relief reversed 2006-Ohio-3097, 2006 WL 1680044. Criminal Law ⚷ 1035(1)

Alleged violation of speedy trial statutes could not form the basis of a habeas corpus claim, because petitioner had an adequate legal remedy through a direct appeal from the conviction. State ex rel. Davis v. Wilson (Ohio App. 11 Dist., Trumbull, 05-23-2003) No. 2003-T-0049, 2003-Ohio-2840, 2003 WL 21267817, Unreported, affirmed 100 Ohio St.3d 269, 798 N.E.2d 379, 2003-Ohio-5898, motion denied 100 Ohio St.3d 1505, 799 N.E.2d 185, 2003-Ohio-6161, reconsideration denied 101 Ohio St.3d 1425, 802 N.E.2d 155, 2004-Ohio-123, certiorari denied 125 S.Ct. 77, 543 U.S. 830, 160 L.Ed.2d 47, rehearing denied, rehearing denied 125 S.Ct. 645, 543 U.S. 1016, 160 L.Ed.2d 487. Habeas Corpus ⚷ 291

Assault defendant failed to file pre-trial motion to dismiss based on failure to provide speedy trial and thus waived the contention on appeal. State v. Culpepper (Ohio App. 2 Dist., Montgomery, 05-09-2003) No. 19077, 2003-Ohio-2395, 2003 WL 21060738, Unreported. Criminal Law ⚷ 1044.1(1)

When reviewing a ruling on a speedy trial issue, Court of Appeals gives deference to trial judge's factual findings, but reviews the application of those facts to the law de novo. Cleveland v. Adkins (Ohio App. 8 Dist., 03-11-2004) 156 Ohio App.3d 482, 806 N.E.2d 1007, 2004-Ohio-1118. Criminal Law ⚷ 1139; Criminal Law ⚷ 1158(1)

Claimed violation of criminal defendant's right to a speedy trial was not cognizable in habeas corpus; instead, an appeal was proper remedy for alleged violation of speed trial right. Travis v. Bagley (Ohio, 07-18-2001) 92 Ohio St.3d 322, 750 N.E.2d 166, 2001-Ohio-198. Habeas Corpus ⚷ 291

Murder defendant's failure, after case was first continued at state's request due to unavailability of key witness, to raise matter again did not eliminate need for Court of Appeals to make further inquiry into speedy trial issue. State v. Hirsch (Ohio App. 1 Dist., 08-07-1998) 129 Ohio App.3d 294, 717 N.E.2d 789, dismissed, appeal not allowed 84 Ohio St.3d 1436, 702 N.E.2d 1213, denial of habeas corpus affirmed 74 Fed.Appx. 486, 2003 WL 21949184. Criminal Law ⚷ 1035(1)

Reviewing court may look behind the journal entry to the transcript to determine whether defendant in fact requested a continuance, so that delay resulting from continuance is not chargeable to State for purposes of speedy trial statute. State v. Stamps (Ohio App. 1 Dist., 04-03-1998) 127 Ohio App.3d 219, 712 N.E.2d 762. Criminal Law ⚷ 1134(2)

Petitioner, whose conviction had been affirmed on direct appeal, had adequate legal remedy through appeal and postconviction relief to raise his claim concerning trial court's alleged failure to journalize decisions relating to statutory speedy trial provisions, and thus was not entitled to writ of mandamus compelling common pleas court judge, clerk of courts, and county prosecutor, to journalize those decisions in order to allow him to establish speedy trial claim. State ex rel. Arnold v. Reid (Ohio, 03-31-1999) 85 Ohio St.3d 147, 707 N.E.2d 492, 1999-Ohio-442. Mandamus ⚷ 3(3); Mandamus ⚷ 4(4)

Defendant was prejudiced by trial court's error in refusing to accept his no-contest plea pursuant to blanket policy of not accepting such pleas, where defendant then decided to enter guilty plea pursuant to prosecutor's proposed settlement, and such plea resulted in waiver of defendant's right to appeal denial of his speedy trial motion. State v. Carter (Ohio App. 2 Dist., 12-12-1997) 124 Ohio App.3d 423, 706 N.E.2d 409. Criminal Law ⚷ 1167(5)

A plea of guilty waives the defendant's right to appeal from his conviction based on a purported violation of his statutory right to a speedy trial. State v. Carter (Ohio App. 2 Dist., 12-12-1997) 124 Ohio App.3d 423, 706 N.E.2d 409. Criminal Law ⚷ 1026.10(4)

Entries for continuances filed both in the original case, which was later "nol-prossed," and case that resulted in conviction could not be considered on appeal to rebut defendant's prima facie case that he was denied his right to speedy trial, where such entries were not presented to trial court. State v. Price (Ohio App. 10 Dist., 07-31-1997) 122 Ohio App.3d 65, 701 N.E.2d 41, dismissed, appeal not allowed 80 Ohio St.3d 1466, 687 N.E.2d 295. Criminal Law ⚷ 1128(4)

Delay of 87 days between Supreme Court's denial of further review of decision of Court of Appeals, which reversed defendant's murder conviction on basis that trial court should have granted mistrial, and date on which defendant moved to dismiss indictment in connection with retrial, was not unreasonable, and thus did not violate defendant's speedy trial rights; delay stemmed in part from time needed to reassign matter to new judge, defendant filed several pretrial motions which caused delay, and defendant's ability to prepare his defense was not prejudiced by delay. State v. Girts (Ohio App. 8 Dist., 07-24-1997) 121 Ohio App.3d 539, 700 N.E.2d 395, dismissed, appeal not allowed 80 Ohio St.3d 1424, 685 N.E.2d 237, reconsideration denied 80 Ohio St.3d 1472, 687 N.E.2d 299, denial of post-conviction relief affirmed 2000 WL 1739293, appeal not allowed 91 Ohio St.3d 1481, 744 N.E.2d 1194, habeas corpus denied 2005 WL 1637862. Criminal Law ⚷ 577.14

Time for computing reasonableness of delay in commencing retrial of defendant, whose murder conviction was reversed by Court of Appeals on ground that trial court should have granted mistrial, commenced from time Supreme Court refused further appeal, rather than time of reversal; while Court of Appeals had reversed unanimously, that fact did not prevent state from exercising its right to seek further review. State v. Girts (Ohio App. 8 Dist., 07-24-1997) 121 Ohio App.3d 539, 700 N.E.2d 395, dismissed, appeal not allowed 80 Ohio St.3d 1424, 685 N.E.2d 237, reconsideration denied 80 Ohio St.3d 1472, 687 N.E.2d 299, denial of post-conviction relief affirmed 2000 WL 1739293, appeal not allowed 91 Ohio St.3d 1481, 744 N.E.2d 1194, habeas corpus denied 2005 WL 1637862. Criminal Law ⚷ 577.14

In reviewing speedy trial claim, appellate court merely counts days chargeable to either side and determines whether case was tried within time limits set by statute governing time within which hearing or trial must be held. City of Oregon v. Kohne (Ohio App. 6 Dist., 01-10-1997) 117 Ohio App.3d 179, 690 N.E.2d 66. Criminal Law ⚷ 1134(3)

While it is state's responsibility to produce evidence demonstrating that defendant was not entitled to be brought to trial within limits of speedy trial statute, reviewing court will not reverse trial court's decision overruling motion to dismiss for lack of speedy trial where defendant does not request and trial court does not state its findings of fact, if there is sufficient evidence demonstrating that trial court's decision is legally justified and supported by record. State v. Baker (Ohio App. 8 Dist., 12-20-1993) 92 Ohio App.3d 516, 636 N.E.2d 363. Criminal Law ⚷ 1166(7)

The speedy trial time period is tolled in an aggravated vehicular homicide prosecution during the state's appeal from an order suppressing the defendant's blood test results where the appeal was made in good faith, even where the prosecutor indicates his intention to pursue the case regardless of the outcome of the suppression issue. State v. Comstock (Lucas 1992) 79 Ohio App.3d 414, 607 N.E.2d 520, motion overruled 65 Ohio St.3d 1435, 600 N.E.2d 678.

Where an appellate court remands a case for further proceedings subsequent to a defendant's appeal of a trial court judgment overruling his motion to dismiss the charges, the speedy trial time limits set forth in RC 2945.71(B) commence running. State v. McCormick (Cuyahoga 1988) 41 Ohio App.3d 158, 534 N.E.2d 942, cause dismissed 38 Ohio St.3d 709, 533 N.E.2d 359. Criminal Law ⚷ 577.8(1)

An appeal rather than a writ of habeas corpus is the proper remedy to challenge alleged violations of the right to a speedy trial. In re Jackson (Ohio

1988) 36 Ohio St.3d 189, 522 N.E.2d 540. Habeas Corpus ⚩ 291

An appeal rather than a writ of habeas corpus is the proper remedy to challenge alleged violations of the right to a speedy trial. In re Jackson (Ohio 1988) 36 Ohio St.3d 189, 522 N.E.2d 540. Habeas Corpus ⚩ 291

It is not a final appealable order where a motion to dismiss upon the issue of speedy trial is denied without being followed by a nolle prosequi. City of Middletown v. Jackson (Butler 1983) 8 Ohio App.3d 431, 457 N.E.2d 898, 8 O.B.R. 556.

A defendant is allowed to raise the issue of "speedy trial" on appeal from a plea of guilty. State v. Berry (Brown 1983) 8 Ohio App.3d 379, 457 N.E.2d 371, 8 O.B.R. 493.

A mayor's court is not a court of record and need not keep a journal; therefore a certified copy of its criminal docket sheet may be sufficient evidence of a record of its official proceedings. City of Blue Ash v. Madden (Hamilton 1982) 8 Ohio App.3d 312, 456 N.E.2d 1277, 8 O.B.R. 421.

An appellant cannot for the first time raise the issue of the denial of a speedy trial in the court of appeals. City of Worthington v. Ogilby (Franklin 1982) 8 Ohio App.3d 25, 455 N.E.2d 1022, 8 O.B.R. 26. Criminal Law ⚩ 1035(1)

The denial of a motion to dismiss a criminal charge, made pursuant to RC 2945.73, is not a final appealable order. State v. Cinema X Bookstore (Montgomery 1976) 49 Ohio App.2d 164, 359 N.E.2d 1382, 3 O.O.3d 218. Criminal Law ⚩ 1023(1)

Delay in the preliminary hearing or of the trial itself cannot ordinarily be urged as a ground for relief in habeas corpus after the accused has pleaded guilty or been convicted of the crime charged, since the delay no longer exists. Bolus v. Engle (Ohio 1976) 48 Ohio St.2d 3, 355 N.E.2d 493, 2 O.O.3d 2, certiorari denied 97 S.Ct. 1183, 430 U.S. 909, 51 L.Ed.2d 586. Habeas Corpus ⚩ 472; Habeas Corpus ⚩ 479

Under RC 2945.71 through RC 2945.73, a trial court has discretion to extend the time limit for trial prescribed therein, and, where the trial court dismisses an indictment and discharges an accused on the basis that it lacks discretion to consider an extension, upon appeal thereof the cause will be remanded to the trial court for an exercise of that court's discretion. State v. Davis (Ohio 1976) 46 Ohio St.2d 444, 349 N.E.2d 315, 75 O.O.2d 498. Criminal Law ⚩ 577.16(3); Criminal Law ⚩ 1181.5(3.1)

Habeas corpus is not a proper remedy to test an appellant's allegation that he was not tried within the time mandated by RC 2945.71, there being an adequate remedy at law by way of appeal. In re Singer (Ohio 1976) 45 Ohio St.2d 130, 341 N.E.2d 849, 74 O.O.2d 253.

Mandamus will not lie to test whether an accused has been denied a speedy trial since a remedy by appeal is available. State ex rel. Racine v. Dull (Ohio 1975) 44 Ohio St.2d 72, 337 N.E.2d 776, 73 O.O.2d 320.

The failure of the trial court to comply with Crim R 48(B) when dismissing an indictment for lack of a speedy trial requires a remand to the trial court, on appeal by the state, for such findings of fact and reasons for the dismissal that will enable the reviewing court to pass upon the assignments of error. State v. Bound (Cuyahoga 1975) 43 Ohio App.2d 44, 332 N.E.2d 366, 72 O.O.2d 197.

The overruling of a motion in a criminal case to dismiss a charge of misdemeanor of the first degree because the accused was not brought to trial within ninety days after his arrest or service of summons, pursuant to RC 2945.71(B)(2), is interlocutory and is not a final, appealable order. State v. Lile (Mahoning 1974) 42 Ohio App.2d 89, 330 N.E.2d 452, 71 O.O.2d 524. Criminal Law ⚩ 1023(3)

Even assuming Ohio legislature created liberty interest in requiring that petitioner be tried within 90 days of his arrest, and assuming that state trial court acted arbitrarily and deviated from proper procedures in denying petitioner's motion to discharge, any insufficiency in procedural due process was cured through appellate review process that was available to petitioner and which he took advantage of, thus defeating petitioner's claim for federal habeas relief based on alleged violation of his state statutory speedy trial rights. Norris v. Schotten (C.A.6 (Ohio), 05-26-1998) 146 F.3d 314, certiorari denied 119 S.Ct. 348, 525 U.S. 935, 142 L.Ed.2d 287. Habeas Corpus ⚩ 479

An appeal from a finding of guilty by a mayor's court to a county or municipal court pursuant to RC 1905.22, is governed by the speedy trial statute, RC 2945.71, and a delay in excess of forty-five days from the date of docketing is prima facie unreasonable. Bethel v Fiscus, Nos. CA89–05–037 and CA89–05–038 (12th Dist Ct App, Clermont, 12–26–89).

The state may appeal as a matter of right the discharge of a defendant for violation of the speedy trial requirements under RC 2945.71. State v Davis, No. 1885 (11th Dist Ct App, Portage, 11–14–88).

87. Mandamus

Mandamus would not lie to compel correctional institution to recompute jail credit time to which inmate was entitled pursuant to order of sentencing court, where declaratory judgment provided inmate plain and adequate remedy in ordinary course of the law through which to challenge administration of sentence reduction for related days of confinement, and where correctional institution had no statutory duty to apply jail time credit, such responsibility being solely with Department of Rehabilitation and Correction (DRC). Nicholson v. North Cent. Corr. Inst. (Ohio App. 3 Dist., Marion, 01-24-2003) No. 9-02-44, 2003-Ohio-303, 2003 WL 161463, Unreported. Mandamus ⚩ 3(1); Mandamus ⚩ 73(1)

2945.72 Extension of time for hearing or trial

The time within which an accused must be brought to trial, or, in the case of felony, to preliminary hearing and trial, may be extended only by the following:

(A) Any period during which the accused is unavailable for hearing or trial, by reason of other criminal proceedings against him, within or outside the state, by reason of his confinement in another state, or by reason of the pendency of extradition proceedings, provided that the prosecution exercises reasonable diligence to secure his availability;

(B) Any period during which the accused is mentally incompetent to stand trial or during which his mental competence to stand trial is being determined, or any period during which the accused is physically incapable of standing trial;

(C) Any period of delay necessitated by the accused's lack of counsel, provided that such delay is not occasioned by any lack of diligence in providing counsel to an indigent accused upon his request as required by law;

(D) Any period of delay occasioned by the neglect or improper act of the accused;

(E) Any period of delay necessitated by reason of a plea in bar or abatement, motion, proceeding, or action made or instituted by the accused;

(F) Any period of delay necessitated by a removal or change of venue pursuant to law;

(G) Any period during which trial is stayed pursuant to an express statutory requirement, or pursuant to an order of another court competent to issue such order;

(H) The period of any continuance granted on the accused's own motion, and the period of any reasonable continuance granted other than upon the accused's own motion;

(I) Any period during which an appeal filed pursuant to section 2945.67 of the Revised Code is pending.

(1978 H 1168, eff. 11–1–78; 1976 S 368; 1975 H 164; 1972 H 511)

Historical and Statutory Notes

Ed. Note: Former 2945.72 repealed by 1972 H 511, eff. 1–1–74; 1953 H 1; GC 13447–2; see now 2945.73 for provisions analogous to former 2945.72.

Pre–1953 H 1 Amendments: 113 v 193, Ch 26, § 2

Legislative Service Commission

1973:

This section specifies the reasons for which the limits stated in section 2945.71 for according an accused a hearing or trial may be extended. The reasons include: the accused's unavailability; the accused's mental incompetence or physical incapacity; the accused's lack of counsel (provided the court is not dilatory in assigning him counsel as required by law); the neglect or improper act of the accused; a stay necessitated by preliminary or collateral proceedings; delay caused by a removal or change of venue; a stay pursuant to the order of another court; a continuance granted on the accused's own motion; and a reasonable continuance granted on other than the accused's own motion. In each of the above cases, the applicable time limit is not tolled absolutely, but merely extended by the time necessary in light of the reason for the delay.

Cross References

Assignment of counsel, Crim R 44

Dismissal, Crim R 48

Extradition, Ch 2963

Pleadings and motions before trial, defenses and objections, Crim R 12

Right to speedy trial, O Const Art I §10

Venue, 2901.12

Venue and change of venue, Crim R 18

Library References

Criminal Law ⚷577.10 to 577.13.

Westlaw Topic No. 110.

C.J.S. Criminal Law §§ 583 to 591, 593, 600 to 604, 607 to 609.

Research References

Encyclopedias

OH Jur. 3d Criminal Law § 396, Ohio Constitutional and Statutory Bases.

OH Jur. 3d Criminal Law § 399, Determination of Denial of Right; Necessity of Prejudice.

OH Jur. 3d Criminal Law § 409, Extension of Time for Hearing or Trial.

OH Jur. 3d Criminal Law § 411, Delay Attributable to Postponement of Trial.

OH Jur. 3d Criminal Law § 2063, Time for Hearing.

OH Jur. 3d Criminal Law § 2064, Time for Hearing—Extension of Time for Hearing.

OH Jur. 3d Criminal Law § 2597, Continuances, Generally.

OH Jur. 3d Criminal Law § 2602, Lack of Time to Try Case.

OH Jur. 3d Criminal Law § 2605, Absence of Witness.

OH Jur. 3d Criminal Law § 2606, to Secure Counsel and Prepare Case.

OH Jur. 3d Criminal Law § 2830, Proceedings to Which Requirement is Applicable.

OH Jur. 3d Criminal Law § 2831, Waiver.

OH Jur. 3d Criminal Law § 2832, When Time Begins to Run.

OH Jur. 3d Criminal Law § 2834, Generally; Unavailability of Defendant.

OH Jur. 3d Criminal Law § 2835, Defendant's Physical Incapacity or Mental Incompetency, or Pendency of Proceedings to Determine Competency.

OH Jur. 3d Criminal Law § 2836, Defendant's Lack of Counsel.

OH Jur. 3d Criminal Law § 2837, Defendant's Neglect or Improper Act.

OH Jur. 3d Criminal Law § 2838, Removal or Change of Venue.

OH Jur. 3d Criminal Law § 2839, Pretrial Appeal.

OH Jur. 3d Criminal Law § 2845, Reasonable Continuance Other Than on Defendant's Motion.

OH Jur. 3d Criminal Law § 2849, Effect of Dismissal.

Treatises and Practice Aids

Markus, Trial Handbook for Ohio Lawyers, § 4:6, Speedy Trial—Statutory Time Limits.

Markus, Trial Handbook for Ohio Lawyers, § 4:13, Speedy Trial—Statutory Time Limits—Extension—by Defendant's Request.

Markus, Trial Handbook for Ohio Lawyers, § 4:14, Speedy Trial—Statutory Time Limits—Extension—by State's Request.

Katz, Giannelli, Blair and Lipton, Baldwin's Ohio Practice, Criminal Law, § 38:5, Time Limits.

Katz, Giannelli, Blair and Lipton, Baldwin's Ohio Practice, Criminal Law, § 54:9, Speedy Trial.

Katz, Giannelli, Blair and Lipton, Baldwin's Ohio Practice, Criminal Law, § 60:2, Speedy Trial Statutes.

Katz, Giannelli, Blair and Lipton, Baldwin's Ohio Practice, Criminal Law, § 60:5, Statutory Time Limits.

Katz, Giannelli, Blair and Lipton, Baldwin's Ohio Practice, Criminal Law, § 60:8, Time Extensions—in General.

Katz, Giannelli, Blair and Lipton, Baldwin's Ohio Practice, Criminal Law, § 60:9, Extension—Unavailability of Accused.

Katz, Giannelli, Blair and Lipton, Baldwin's Ohio Practice, Criminal Law, § 140:1, Waiver of Preliminary Hearing in Felony Case.

Katz, Giannelli, Blair and Lipton, Baldwin's Ohio Practice, Criminal Law, § 140:6, Motion for Extension of Time for Preliminary Hearing.

Katz, Giannelli, Blair and Lipton, Baldwin's Ohio Practice, Criminal Law, § 140:7, Time Limit Extension for Preliminary Hearing.

Katz, Giannelli, Blair and Lipton, Baldwin's Ohio Practice, Criminal Law, § 140:8, Time Limit Extension for Preliminary Hearing (Additional Form).

Katz, Giannelli, Blair and Lipton, Baldwin's Ohio Practice, Criminal Law, § 147:2, Dismissal of Felony Charge for Delay of Preliminary Hearing.

Katz, Giannelli, Blair and Lipton, Baldwin's Ohio Practice, Criminal Law, § 147:4, Dismissal of Felony Charge Delay in Trial.

Katz, Giannelli, Blair and Lipton, Baldwin's Ohio Practice, Criminal Law, § 147:6, Dismissal of Misdemeanor Charge for Delay in Trial.

Katz, Giannelli, Blair and Lipton, Baldwin's Ohio Practice, Criminal Law, § 60:10, Extension—Accused's Mental-Physical Incapacity.

Katz, Giannelli, Blair and Lipton, Baldwin's Ohio Practice, Criminal Law, § 60:11, Extension—Delay to Obtain Counsel.

Katz, Giannelli, Blair and Lipton, Baldwin's Ohio Practice, Criminal Law, § 60:12, Extension—Delay Due to Accused's Conduct.

Katz, Giannelli, Blair and Lipton, Baldwin's Ohio Practice, Criminal Law, § 60:13, Extension—Defense Motions or Other Action.

Katz, Giannelli, Blair and Lipton, Baldwin's Ohio Practice, Criminal Law, § 60:14, Extension—Removal or Change of Venue.

Katz, Giannelli, Blair and Lipton, Baldwin's Ohio Practice, Criminal Law, § 60:15, Extension—Stay of Proceedings.

Katz, Giannelli, Blair and Lipton, Baldwin's Ohio Practice, Criminal Law, § 60:16, Extension—Continuances.

Katz, Giannelli, Blair and Lipton, Baldwin's Ohio Practice, Criminal Law, § 60:17, Extension—Change in Charge.

Katz, Giannelli, Blair and Lipton, Baldwin's Ohio Practice, Criminal Law, § 60:19, Remedies for Unexcused Delay.

Katz, Giannelli, Blair and Lipton, Baldwin's Ohio Practice, Criminal Law, § 60:21, Common Errors.

Carlin, Baldwin's Ohio Practice, Merrick-Rippner Probate Law § 108:9, Juvenile Court—Criminal Jurisdiction—Assignment of Case for Disposition.

Hennenberg & Reinhart, Ohio Criminal Defense Motions F 5.02, Waiver of Right to Speedy Trial and Request for Indefinite Continuance-Pretrial Motions.

Adrine & Ruden, Ohio Domestic Violence Law § 4:2, Distinctions Between a Criminal Protection Order and a Civil Protection Order.

Adrine & Ruden, Ohio Domestic Violence Law § 4:6, Violation of a Protection Order.

Painter, Ohio Driving Under the Influence § 10:5, Speedy Trial—First Degree Misdemeanor Cases.

Painter, Ohio Driving Under the Influence § 8:12, Filing the Motion.

Law Review and Journal Commentaries

An Analysis of the Judicial Interpretation of the 1974 Ohio Speedy Trial Act: The First Five Years, Comment. 40 Ohio St L J 363 (1979).

The Right to a Speedy Trial: Ohio Follows the Trend, Note. 43 U Cin L Rev 610 (1974).

Notes of Decisions

1. Constitutional issues

Defendant's speedy trial rights were not violated, though 1,520 days had passed between date of defendant's arrest and date of trial; there had been 27 motions for continuance filed, the majority of which had been filed by defense counsel, and, by these continuances alone, without including any time tolled due to defendant's discovery demands, defendant waived 1,363 days, which meant that state had additional 113 days to bring defendant to trial within 270 days specified by statute. State v. Barnes (Ohio App. 10 Dist., Franklin, 06-28-2005) No. 04AP-1133, 2005-Ohio-3279, 2005 WL 1515325, Unreported. Criminal Law ⚷ 577.10(8); Criminal Law ⚷ 577.15(3)

Defense counsel's failure to file motion to dismiss theft charge based upon alleged speedy trial violation was not ineffective assistance of counsel, since delay in bringing defendant to trial was due to newly-appointed counsel's unavailability for a pretrial, and delay was not presumptively prejudicial, with trial occurring within one year of his arrest. State v. Ross (Ohio App. 4 Dist., Ross, 04-15-2005) No. 04CA2780, 2005-Ohio-1888, 2005 WL 928531, Unreported. Criminal Law ⚷ 641.13(2.1)

Court-ordered competency examination was not warranted, and defendant was therefore denied a speedy trial, where he did not demonstrate any irrational behavior, there was no prior medical evidence regarding his competency to stand trial, and the only reasons offered for the examination were long plea negotiations and defendant's failure to pay court costs in exchange for a dismissal of the charges. City of Columbus v. Cardinal (Ohio App. 10 Dist., Franklin, 12-09-2004) No. 04AP-229, No. 04AP-232, No. 04AP230, No. 04AP-233, No. 04AP-231, 2004-Ohio-6605, 2004 WL 2830782, Unreported. Criminal Law ⚷ 577.11(6)

Misdemeanor defendant was not denied his right to a speedy trial, where original trial date was set within statutory timeframe, defendant then made demand for jury trial, and the new trial date was merely a month after defendant's speedy trial time would have expired, which was reasonable. State v. Herbst (Ohio App. 6 Dist., Lucas, 06-18-2004) No. L-03-1238, 2004-Ohio-3157, 2004 WL 1368210, Unreported. Criminal Law ⚷ 577.10(8); Criminal Law ⚷ 577.15(1)

Trial court's grant of several continuances, mostly requested by and for the benefit of defendant, did not violate defendant's speedy trial right, even though trial court did not place in its journal entries the reasons for continuances; rationale of court was not required when continuance was requested by defendant, and statutory time limitation would not have been exceeded but for defendant's requested continuances. State v. Phillips (Ohio App. 8 Dist., Cuyahoga, 02-05-2004) No. 82886, 2004-Ohio-484, 2004 WL 226120, Unreported, appeal not allowed 103 Ohio St.3d 1404, 812 N.E.2d 1287, 2004-Ohio-3980. Criminal Law ⚷ 577.10(8)

Defendant could not complain that his speedy trial rights were violated, where defense counsel represented to the court he would enter a plea and that he would file a formal motion for continuance but no such motion was filed and no plea entered which resulted in delay in bringing defendant to trial. State v. Minshall (Ohio App. 2 Dist., Greene, 05-30-2003) No. CIV.A. 2002 CA 111, 2003-Ohio-2830, 2003 WL 21267272, Unreported. Criminal Law ⚷ 577.10(8)

The extensions of time for trial pursuant to RC 2945.72 do not apply to an appeal of an administrative license suspension (ALS) because the ALS appeal is a separate civil proceeding that is not part of the criminal case involving a charge of operating a motor vehicle while under the influence; accordingly, the motions by defendant to appeal the ALS and to continue the ALS hearing do not toll the speedy trial deadline and where the state fails to bring the defendant to trial for the OMVI within the required ninety days, defendant's statutory right to speedy trial is violated and the defendant is discharged. State v. Rozell (Ohio App. 4 Dist., Pickaway, 06-20-1996) No. 95CA17, 1996 WL 344034, Unreported.

A seventy-eight-day sua sponte continuance containing no reasons specifying its institution in the journal entry and no reflection that it is attributable to the defendant, may not be used to extend the speedy trial time period, and a defendant served with an indictment fourteen months before he is brought to trial is denied his right to a speedy trial. State v. Shough (Ohio App. 2 Dist., Montgomery, 08-02-1995) No. 14849, 1995 WL 461260, Unreported, appeal not allowed 74 Ohio St.3d 1485, 657 N.E.2d 1378.

A trial court entry continuing a defendant's trial that is not journalized until after expiration of time limits prescribed by RC 2945.71 does not extend the time limit for bringing the defendant to trial and he is discharged for failure of the trial court to comply with the mandatory provisions of the Ohio speedy trial statute. State v. Brooks (Ohio App. 8 Dist., Cuyahoga, 11-23-1994) No. 65853, 1994 WL 663408, Unreported.

Defendant's right to speedy trial was violated by 635-day period between his motion to suppress evidence and trial court's ruling on the motion; trial court did not explain reason for delay, and total of 832 days elapsed between defendant's arraignment and filing of motion to dismiss. State v. Mullins (Ohio App. 3 Dist., 02-03-2003) 152 Ohio App.3d 83, 786 N.E.2d 911, 2003-Ohio-477. Criminal Law ⚷ 577.10(3); Criminal Law ⚷ 577.15(1)

No reasonable basis existed to grant continuance of date for trial of defendant on misdemeanor speeding charge after she appeared in village mayor's court on date specified for trial, but witness was absent and prosecution was unable to proceed, and thus, grant of continuance under which trial date was extended beyond statutory speedy trial period required dismissal of case, even though defendant had failed to make telephone call to clerk of court indicating that she would be appearing to plead not guilty; village could not place burden of providing a timely trial on defendants by making them "register" not guilty pleas. Amberley v. Levine (Ohio Mun., 03-03-2000) 108 Ohio Misc.2d 13, 738 N.E.2d 487. Criminal Law ⚷ 577.16(1)

Motion for bill of particulars and motion for change of venue both tolled time for speedy trial. State v. Grinnell (Ohio App. 10 Dist., 06-27-1996) 112 Ohio App.3d 124, 678 N.E.2d 231, appeal not allowed 77 Ohio St.3d 1474, 673 N.E.2d 138, appeal not allowed 77 Ohio St.3d 1475, 673 N.E.2d 138, denial of habeas corpus affirmed 215 F.3d 1326, certiorari denied 121 S.Ct. 232, 531 U.S. 898, 148 L.Ed.2d 166. Criminal Law ⚷ 577.10(8)

In a misdemeanor speeding case, the length of a continuance is unreasonable and violates speedy trial provisions where (1) the next open trial date is used as the length of the continuance, (2) the date is thirty plus days after the initial thirty-day speedy trial period, and (3) it is caused by the court's practice of hearing traffic trials only on two Tuesdays of each month. State v. Daugherty (Ohio App. 3 Dist., 03-28-1996) 110 Ohio App.3d 103, 673 N.E.2d 664.

A court need not journalize the reasons for a continuance prior to expiration of the speedy trial limits of RC 2945.71 where the delay is necessitated by motions of the defendant to review a license suspension and jury trial demand and the defendant is aware of the reasons for the continuance. State v. Sharp (Marion 1991) 71 Ohio App.3d 336, 594 N.E.2d 19.

Habeas corpus is an available remedy to challenge the time parameters of a Crim R 5(B) preliminary hearing if filed prior to that hearing; there is no adequate remedy at law available to prevent what may constitute unlawful incarceration under the statutory framework of RC 2945.71 to 2945.73. Styer v. Brichta (Wood 1990) 69 Ohio App.3d 738, 591 N.E.2d 1255.

Since RC 2945.71 to RC 2945.73 confer substantive rights upon an accused, they take precedence over procedural or superintendent rules of the Ohio Supreme Court, including Sup R 8(B). State v. Westbrook (Franklin 1975) 47 Ohio App.2d 211, 353 N.E.2d 637, 1 O.O.3d 284.

O Const Art IV, § 5, paragraph (A)(1) is independent of paragraph (B) of such section, and the Ohio Supreme Court Rules of Superintendence do not invalidate any existing statute. State v. Lacy (Belmont 1975) 46 Ohio App.2d 215, 348 N.E.2d 381, 75 O.O.2d 376.

In determining whether defendant's Sixth Amendment right to a speedy trial has been violated, the time period between dismissal of criminal charges and institution of new charges is not to be considered. U. S. v. MacDonald (U.S.N.C. 1982)

102 S.Ct. 1497, 456 U.S. 1, 71 L.Ed.2d 696, on remand 688 F.2d 224.

Where Ohio courts have determined that delay in the commencement of a criminal trial caused by the attempts of television stations to obtain an order allowing televising of the trial does not violate rights secured by the Ohio speedy trial statute, the criminal defendant cannot seek federal habeas corpus relief on grounds of denial of equal protection or deprivation of liberty without due process of law. Hutchison v. Marshall (C.A.6 (Ohio) 1984) 744 F.2d 44, certiorari denied 105 S.Ct. 1208, 469 U.S. 1221, 84 L.Ed.2d 350.

No federal due process violation occurred when defendant was given notice and an opportunity to object to a continuance within a short time following expiration of the time for trial. Johnson v. Overberg (C.A.6 (Ohio) 1981) 639 F.2d 326, 22 O.O.3d 326.

Agreement pursuant to which driver released any and all claims against village, village police officers, and any other village law enforcement officer arising from stop of his vehicle and citation in exchange for a dismissal, without prejudice, of traffic offense against driver barred driver's claims that he was denied due process on the ground that mayor served as both executive officer of village and judge in village mayor's court and that Ohio statute setting period of time in which misdemeanor defendants had to be brought to trial was unconstitutional where the only evidence presented showed that execution of release was completely voluntary, there was no indicia of any prosecutorial overreaching, and enforcement of release did not adversely affect any relevant public interest. Rose v. Village of Peninsula (N.D.Ohio, 01-27-1995) 875 F.Supp. 442. Release ⚷ 38

Failure to bring defendant charged with driving motor vehicle while under the influence (DUI), a second degree misdemeanor, to trial within 90 days after arrest or service of summons violated defendant's speedy trial rights, even though defendant filed motion to suppress evidence and speedy trial motion, where at least 41 days elapsed during first prosecution, which was dismissed when troopers failed to appear, 19 days expired between service of new charges until filing of suppression motion, 54 days expired between overruling of suppression motion and filing of motion to dismiss, and no days expired between overruling of motion to dismiss and start of trial, which totaled 114 days. State v. Davis (Ohio App. 4 Dist., Ross, 05-22-2002) No. 01CA2610, 2002-Ohio-2554, 2002 WL 1293055, Unreported. Criminal Law ⚷ 577.14

2. In general

Forty-five day speedy trial period applicable to fourth degree misdemeanor charges applied to charges that property owner violated zoning ordinance and flood damage prevention ordinance, rather than 30 day speedy trial period applicable to minor misdemeanor charges; although violations of zoning ordinance were minor misdemeanors, applicable speedy trial limits are those for time limit required with respect to highest degree of offense, and violations of flood damage prevention ordinance were fourth degree misdemeanors. Village of Versailles v. Poly (Ohio App. 2 Dist., Darke, 03-26-2004) No. 1627, 2004-Ohio-1485, 2004 WL 596079, Unreported. Criminal Law ⚷ 577.6

Although crowded docket may be sound reason to extend time period for speedy trial, practices that undercut implementation of speedy trial provisions must not be employed to extend requisite time periods. State v. Daugherty (Ohio App. 3 Dist., 03-28-1996) 110 Ohio App.3d 103, 673 N.E.2d 664. Criminal Law ⚷ 577.10(7)

3. Strict construction

Statutory provision extending the statutory speedy trial period for any delay resulting from motion filed by defendant is strictly construed in favor of defendant. State v. Homan (Ohio, 08-16-2000) 89 Ohio St.3d 421, 732 N.E.2d 952, 2000-Ohio-212, reconsideration denied 90 Ohio St.3d 1431, 736 N.E.2d 27. Criminal Law ⚷ 577.10(8)

Extensions of time under speedy trial statute are to be strictly construed against state. Cleveland v. Jones (Ohio App. 8 Dist., 05-06-1996) 110 Ohio App.3d 791, 675 N.E.2d 498. Criminal Law ⚷ 577.13

Statutory extensions on the speedy trial deadline, outlined in RC 2945.72, must be strictly construed against the state. Boston Hts. v. Weikle (Summit 1991) 81 Ohio App.3d 165, 610 N.E.2d 526. Criminal Law ⚷ 577.13

The provisions of RC 2945.72 that delineate various contingencies for extending the time within which an accused must be brought to trial are to be strictly construed against the state. State v. Geraldo (Lucas 1983) 13 Ohio App.3d 27, 468 N.E.2d 328, 13 O.B.R. 29.

The statutory speedy trial provisions, RC 2945.71 et seq., constitute a rational effort to enforce the constitutional right to a public speedy trial of an accused charged with the commission of a felony or a misdemeanor and shall be strictly enforced by the courts of this state. State v. Pachay (Ohio 1980) 64 Ohio St.2d 218, 416 N.E.2d 589, 18 O.O.3d 427. Criminal Law ⚷ 577.5

4. Retroactive effect

RC 2945.71 through RC 2945.73, enacted by 1972 H 511, eff. 1–1–74, are not applied retroactively; computation of the time limit derived from these sections is from January 1, 1974, for actions then pending, rather than from the actual earlier date of arrest. State v. MacDonald (Ohio 1976) 48 Ohio St.2d 66, 357 N.E.2d 40, 2 O.O.3d 219.

RC 2945.71 to RC 2945.73, effective on and after January 1, 1974, do not have retroactive application. State v. Walker (Ohio 1976) 46 Ohio St.2d 157, 346 N.E.2d 687, 75 O.O.2d 201.

The time limitations of RC 2945.71 to RC 2945.73, enacted by 1972 H 511, eff. 1–1–74, are to be computed from January 1, 1974, rather than from the actual earlier date of arrest, with respect to criminal prosecutions pending on January 1, 1974. City of Columbus v. Vest (Franklin 1974) 42

Ohio App.2d 83, 330 N.E.2d 726, 71 O.O.2d 520. Criminal Law ⚷ 577.2

RC 2945.71 to RC 2945.73, enacted by 1972 H 511, eff. 1–1–74, apply to criminal prosecutions pending on that date, the arrests for which were made prior to such date. City of Columbus v. Vest (Franklin 1974) 42 Ohio App.2d 83, 330 N.E.2d 726, 71 O.O.2d 520.

RC 2945.71, RC 2945.72 and RC 2945.73, enacted by 1972 H 511, eff. 1–1–74, are not applicable to arrests made prior to January 1, 1974. City of Reynoldsburg v. Wesley (Ohio Mun. 1974) 39 Ohio Misc. 166, 316 N.E.2d 926.

5. Extradition proceedings

Time period between defendant's arrest in Missouri and arraignment on assault and attempted murder charges was not attributable to the State under speedy trial statute, absent evidence that prosecution failed to exercise diligence in seeking custody of defendant. State v. Tullis (Ohio App. 10 Dist., Franklin, 05-05-2005) No. 04AP-333, 2005-Ohio-2205, 2005 WL 1055977, Unreported, appeal not allowed 106 Ohio St.3d 1510, 833 N.E.2d 1250, 2005-Ohio-4605. Criminal Law ⚷ 577.11(5)

Ohio's speedy trial statutes do not apply to extradition proceedings. State v. Hirsch (Ohio App. 1 Dist., 08-07-1998) 129 Ohio App.3d 294, 717 N.E.2d 789, dismissed, appeal not allowed 84 Ohio St.3d 1436, 702 N.E.2d 1213, denial of habeas corpus affirmed 74 Fed.Appx. 486, 2003 WL 21949184. Criminal Law ⚷ 577.11(1)

6. Running of time period

Defendant's statutory speedy trial right began to run upon his initial arrest for misdemeanor drug charges, and State's failure to bring defendant to trial on more serious drug charges stemming from same incident within 270 days, or approximately 13 months after his arrest and over a year after he pleaded no contest to misdemeanor drug charges, violated defendant's statutory speedy trial rights; second indictment was not based upon new facts or discovered evidence that would have allowed for patent violation of defendant's speedy trial rights. State v. Rutkowski (Ohio App. 8 Dist., Cuyahoga, 03-09-2006) No. 86289, 2006-Ohio-1087, 2006 WL 562160, Unreported. Criminal Law ⚷ 577.8(2); Criminal Law ⚷ 577.15(3)

Defendant's right to speedy trial was not implicated by delay of over one year between his arrest and entry of his no-contest plea to felony charges, where all but 68 days of such period was tolled for speedy trial purposes. State v. Smith (Ohio App. 2 Dist., Clark, 11-12-2004) No. 2003 CA 93, 2004-Ohio-6062, 2004 WL 2588269, Unreported, motion for delayed appeal denied 105 Ohio St.3d 1450, 823 N.E.2d 455, 2005-Ohio-763, motion for delayed appeal denied 105 Ohio St.3d 1496, 825 N.E.2d 621, 2005-Ohio-1666. Criminal Law ⚷ 577.10(8)

Defendant's right to speedy trial on charges of rape and improper discharge of firearm at, or into, habitation, was not violated under statute that required trial within 90 days of arrest, where computation of time established that total of only 83 days of speedy trial period had run against state; time for speedy trial purposes was tolled from time defendant executed waiver of right to speedy trial until he withdrew waiver, time was tolled when defendant filed motions to dismiss, trial court took reasonable amount of time to decide motions, and trial court granted state reasonable continuance of five days for purposes of motion to suppress hearing. State v. Boles (Ohio App. 2 Dist., Montgomery, 05-23-2003) No. 18762, 2003-Ohio-2693, 2003 WL 21213383, Unreported, appeal not allowed 100 Ohio St.3d 1411, 796 N.E.2d 538, 2003-Ohio-4948. Criminal Law ⚷ 577.10(7); Criminal Law ⚷ 577.10(8)

State was statutorily required to bring defendant to trial on charges of aggravated murder with a firearm specification, murder, aggravated robbery, felonious assault, and tampering with evidence within 90 days of his arrest, exclusive of extensions pursuant to statute, where defendant was held in jail in lieu of bail solely on such charges from date of his arrest. State v. Kerby (Ohio App. 2 Dist., 07-15-2005) 162 Ohio App.3d 353, 833 N.E.2d 757, 2005-Ohio-3734, appeal not allowed 107 Ohio St.3d 1682, 839 N.E.2d 403, 2005-Ohio-6480. Criminal Law ⚷ 577.11(1)

Detainer issued against defendant, who was arrested in another county on unrelated charges, was functional equivalent of arrest, and consequently running of 270–day period for trial was triggered on day when he was both under arrest for unrelated charges and subject of active arrest warrant on robbery charge. State v. Bailey (Ohio App. 2 Dist., 09-15-2000) 141 Ohio App.3d 144, 750 N.E.2d 603, appeal not allowed 91 Ohio St.3d 1431, 741 N.E.2d 895. Criminal Law ⚷ 577.11(4)

Where an accused is held pursuant to a charge which must be tried pursuant to RC 2945.71(B)(2) and which is based on facts which are identical to those in a charge previously dismissed for want of prosecution, if no continuance has been granted pursuant to RC 2945.72(H), the accused must be brought to trial within ninety days after his first arrest or service of summons. State v. Justice (Hamilton 1976) 49 Ohio App.2d 46, 358 N.E.2d 1382, 3 O.O.3d 109. Criminal Law ⚷ 577.14

The time limits in the speedy trial statutes apply to the trial date, not to the date of the judgment entry. Blanchester v McLaren, No. CA87–08–018 (12th Dist Ct App, Clinton, 5–16–88).

A trial is commenced in compliance with RC 2945.72 when the jury is sworn, notwithstanding an indefinite continuance immediately following commencement. State v Page, Nos. CA 6326 and CA 6334 (5th Dist Ct App, Stark, 6–25–84).

7. Triple-count mechanism

Statements of defense counsel at hearing on defendant's motion to dismiss constituted acknowledgement that defendant was being held on both pending rape charges and a parole holder, and, as such, defendant was not entitled to invoke triple-count provision of speedy trial statute requiring each day to be counted as three days, if accused was being held in jail in lieu of bail on pending charge, even though trial court made no findings of fact supporting denial of speedy trial motion, as defendant never requested findings of fact. State v. Brown (Ohio App. 7 Dist., Mahoning, 06-07-2005) No. 03-MA-32, 2005-Ohio-2939, 2005 WL 1385715, Unreported, appeal not allowed 106 Ohio St.3d 1558, 836 N.E.2d 582, 2005-Ohio-5531. Criminal Law ⚷ 577.11(1); Criminal Law ⚷ 577.16(10)

A valid parole holder was placed on defendant, and thus the "triple-count" provision of the speedy trial statute did not apply and defendant's right to a speedy trial was not violated. State v. Myers (Ohio App. 5 Dist., Richland, 06-09-2004) No. 03-CA-61, 2004-Ohio-3052, 2004 WL 1327929, Unreported, appeal not allowed 103 Ohio St.3d 1479, 816 N.E.2d 255, 2004-Ohio-5405. Criminal Law ⚷ 577.11(1)

Defendant's right to a speedy trial was not violated; statutory provision providing that each day during which defendant is held in jail in lieu of bail on pending charges is counted as three days for speedy trial purposes, was not applicable to defendant, as defendant was in jail on separate unrelated charges following arrest for current charges, and defendant's cases went to trial within 270 days from date of first indictment. State v. Johnson (Ohio App. 8 Dist., Cuyahoga, 06-19-2003) No. 81692, No. 81693, 2003-Ohio-3241, 2003 WL 21419631, Unreported, appeal not allowed 100 Ohio St.3d 1433, 797 N.E.2d 513, 2003-Ohio-5396. Criminal Law ⚷ 577.11(3)

Valid parole holder that was executed against defendant the day after his arrest on present charges rendered inapplicable the provisions of speedy-trial statute under which each day during which an accused is held in jail in lieu of bail is counted as three days. State v. Garrett (Ohio App. 8 Dist., Cuyahoga, 01-23-2003) No. 80172, 2003-Ohio-274, 2003 WL 152820, Unreported, appeal not allowed 99 Ohio St.3d 1437, 789 N.E.2d 1118, 2003-Ohio-2902, appeal not allowed 101 Ohio St.3d 1491, 805 N.E.2d 541, 2004-Ohio-1293. Criminal Law ⚷ 577.11(1)

Triple-count provision of speedy trial statute, under which days spent in jail awaiting trial on pending charge each count as three days, was inapplicable to defendant who was serving sentence on separate convictions during time he was being held prior to trial in instant case. State v. Hiatt (Ohio App. 4 Dist., 03-26-1997) 120 Ohio App.3d 247, 697 N.E.2d 1025. Criminal Law ⚷ 577.8(1)

Defendant who was held in jail 97 days between court-ordered bindover for trial as an adult and start of trial was not denied right to speedy trial, though each day he was held in jail in lieu of bail would normally have counted as three days for purposes of 270–day speedy trial period for persons accused of felony; period was tolled for eleven days between defendant's filing of pretrial motions and trial court's ruling on those motions, reducing period between bindover as adult and trial to 86 days. State v. Michael (Ohio App. 7 Dist., 10-02-1996) 114 Ohio App.3d 523, 683 N.E.2d 435, cause dismissed 77 Ohio St.3d 1452, 672 N.E.2d 176, dismissed, appeal not allowed 77 Ohio St.3d 1520, 674 N.E.2d 372. Criminal Law ⚷ 577.10(8); Criminal Law ⚷ 577.11(1)

Triple-count provision, whereby for purposes of computing speedy trial time, each day during which accused is held in jail in lieu of bail on pending charge is to be counted as three days, was inapplicable where defendant was held in jail under parole holder, even where there were additional criminal charges pending; hence, 270–day period was applicable for bringing defendant to trial. State v. Dunkins (Summit 1983) 10 Ohio App.3d 72, 460 N.E.2d 688, 10 O.B.R. 82. Criminal Law ⚷ 577.11(1)

RC 2945.71(D) is applicable only to those defendants held in jail in lieu of bail solely on the pending charge. State v. Ladd (Ohio 1978) 56 Ohio St.2d 197, 383 N.E.2d 579, 10 O.O.3d 363, certiorari denied 99 S.Ct. 2038, 441 U.S. 926, 60 L.Ed.2d 400.

Where a person against whom a felony charge is pending is held in jail in lieu of bail, such person must be brought to trial within ninety days after arrest unless the time for trial is extended by one or more provisions of RC 2945.72(A) to RC 2945.72(H). State v. Eberhardt (Cuyahoga 1978) 56 Ohio App.2d 193, 381 N.E.2d 1357, 10 O.O.3d 197. Criminal Law ⚷ 577.11(1)

RC 2945.71(C)(2) and RC 2945.71(D) provide that a person against whom a felony charge is pending shall be brought to trial within ninety days after his arrest, where such person has been held in jail in lieu of bail on the pending charge, unless such time is extended by RC 2945.72. State v. Walker (Jefferson 1974) 42 Ohio App.2d 41, 327 N.E.2d 796, 71 O.O.2d 238.

8. Unavailability of accused

Defendant's neglectful or improper action, or his unavailability for trial due to other criminal proceedings or confinement, operated to extend speedy trial period as measured from date of defendant's arrest. State v. Robison (Ohio App. 5 Dist., Licking, 12-19-2002) No. 02CA00015, 2002-Ohio-7216, 2002 WL 31875016, Unreported, motion for delayed appeal denied 98 Ohio St.3d 1473, 784 N.E.2d 707, 2003-Ohio-904, appeal not allowed 98 Ohio St.3d 1565, 787 N.E.2d 1230, 2003-Ohio-2242. Criminal Law ⚷ 577.10(8)

The speedy trial statute, RC 2945.71, is violated where more than 200 days pass from the date of arrest to the date of the jury trial and the city fails to demonstrate any reasonable diligence to secure defendant's availability for trial, despite notice by defendant of his incarceration in an adjoining county. City of Newark v. Barcus (Ohio App. 5 Dist., Licking, 09-09-1994) No. 94 CA 00015, 1994 WL 590498, Unreported.

Where trial of defendant who was already incarcerated for other offenses was rescheduled because trial court learned three days before originally scheduled trial date that defendant would not be available because he was being tried for separate charges in another county on same day, 180–day speedy trial period was tolled for 75 days between original trial date and rescheduled trial date. State v. Smith (Ohio App. 3 Dist., 09-29-2000) 140 Ohio App.3d 81, 746 N.E.2d 678, 2000-Ohio-1777. Criminal Law ⚷ 577.11(2)

Period under speedy trial statute in which defendant was to be brought to trial did not begin to run until date that county received custody of defendant, after defendant was arrested in another state and fought extradition. State v. Hirsch (Ohio App. 1 Dist., 08-07-1998) 129 Ohio App.3d 294, 717 N.E.2d 789, dismissed, appeal not allowed 84 Ohio St.3d 1436, 702 N.E.2d 1213, denial of habeas corpus affirmed 74 Fed.Appx. 486, 2003 WL 21949184. Criminal Law ⚷ 577.8(2)

Under Crim R 4(E), defendants are required to be brought before the court in the county in which they were arrested before being made available to authorities in the nonadjacent county which issued the arrest warrant; this requirement constitutes "other criminal proceedings" under RC 2945.72 and thus, the ten-day time limitation for the preliminary hearing does not begin until the date the defendants are taken into custody by the nonadjacent county. Styer v. Brichta (Wood 1990) 69 Ohio App.3d 738, 591 N.E.2d 1255. Criminal Law ⚷ 228

Evidence was insufficient to support trial court's finding that law enforcement authorities failed to exercise reasonable diligence in trying to bring defendant to arrest and trial on charges of possession of illegal drugs, even though authorities did not arrest defendant until 38 months after warrant was issued, where authorities, immediately upon receiving indictment, summons and warrant against defendant did what was required of them by sending copy of warrant to sheriff of county in which defendant resided and transmitting information over teletype network. State v. Packard (Clermont 1988) 52 Ohio App.3d 99, 557 N.E.2d 808, cause dismissed 40 Ohio St.3d 708, 534 N.E.2d 843. Arrest ⚷ 67

The 270–day period, within which criminal defendant charged with felony must be tried, is tolled when defendant is unavailable for trial because he is incarcerated in another jurisdiction. State v. Reitz (Summit 1984) 26 Ohio App.3d 1, 498 N.E.2d 163, 26 O.B.R. 168. Criminal Law ⚷ 577.11(4)

Proceedings to extradite defendant to another state were "pending," though defendant signed a waiver of extradition, and thus, the time for bringing defendant to trial in Ohio on charge of aiding or abetting aggravated robbery with a gun specification, for speedy trial purposes, was extended while defendant was unavailable for trial. State v. Davis (Ohio App. 5 Dist., Richland, 05-15-2002) No. 01 CA 67, 2002-Ohio-2502, 2002 WL 999322, Unreported, appeal not allowed 99 Ohio St.3d 1438, 789 N.E.2d 1118, 2003-Ohio-2902. Criminal Law ⚷ 577.11(4)

Where a defendant is arrested and makes an initial appearance on a charge based on another county's arrest warrant under Crim R 4(E), such appearance constitutes "other criminal proceeding" pursuant to RC 2945.72, thereby extending the time for the preliminary hearing on the charge. Styer v Brichta, No. 90WD072 (6th Dist Ct App, Wood, 10–10–90).

9. Mental or physical disabilities

Delay of approximately one year from the time defendant was arrested for murder until the time he was brought to trial did not violate his statutory right to a speedy trial; time period during which defendant's mental competence to stand trial was being determined was tolled, and the trial began 136 days after defendant withdrew his waiver of speedy trial time. State v. Florence (Ohio App. 2 Dist., Montgomery, 08-19-2005) No. 20439, 2005-Ohio-4508, 2005 WL 2083079, Unreported, appeal not allowed 107 Ohio St.3d 1700, 840 N.E.2d 205, 2005-Ohio-6763, appeal not allowed 109 Ohio St.3d 1427, 846 N.E.2d 535, 2006-Ohio-1967. Criminal Law ⚷ 577.11(6); Criminal Law ⚷ 577.15(3)

Trial court did not abuse its discretion by referring defendant, over defendant's objections, to court psychiatric clinic for competency and sanity evaluation, and thereby tolling time limit for trial under speedy trial statute, where defendant had still refused, without explanation, to waive his speedy trial right after his counsel withdrew because counsel lacked adequate time to prepare a defense, and defendant had asserted he had killed the victim after reading biblical passage. State v. Prim (Ohio App. 8 Dist., 09-07-1999) 134 Ohio App.3d 142, 730 N.E.2d 455, motion for delayed appeal denied 88 Ohio St.3d 1436, 724 N.E.2d 811. Criminal Law ⚷ 577.11(6)

The time within which an accused must be brought to trial is tolled from the date the accused files a motion challenging his or her competency to stand trial; abrogating *State v Wilson*, 7 Ohio App.3d 219, 7 OBR 281, 454 N.E.2d 1348, and *State v. Bowman*, 41 Ohio App.3d 318, 535 N.E.2d 730. State v. Palmer (Ohio, 12-09-1998) 84 Ohio St.3d 103, 702 N.E.2d 72, 1998-Ohio-507. Criminal Law ⚷ 577.11(6)

The tolling of the speedy trial time period resulting from a competency motion being filed does not end where an examiner fails to issue a timely report; rather, the time continues to be tolled until a court determines whether the accused is competent to stand trial. State v. Palmer (Ohio, 12-09-1998) 84 Ohio St.3d 103, 702 N.E.2d 72, 1998-Ohio-507. Criminal Law ⚷ 577.11(6)

Defendant's delay in filing motion for competency evaluation until week in which trial was originally scheduled, which purportedly left state unable to arrange jury trial in timely manner under speedy-trial statute once defendant was found competent, did not preclude dismissal on speedy-trial grounds. State v. Jones (Ohio App. 11 Dist., 04-04-1997) 119 Ohio App.3d 59, 694 N.E.2d 505. Criminal Law ⚷ 577.11(6); Criminal Law ⚷ 577.16(2)

Where defendant's competency examiner fails to submit report within required 30 days, defendant who desires speedy trial may notify court and ask it to enforce its order. State v. Jones (Ohio App. 11 Dist., 04-04-1997) 119 Ohio App.3d 59, 694 N.E.2d 505. Criminal Law ⚷ 577.11(6)

Although the time within which an accused must be brought to trial may be tolled during the time when his competence to stand trial is being evaluated, when ten days have elapsed after the filing of the examiner's report and the statutorily mandated hearing has not been held, the time begins to run again. State v. Wilson (Fayette 1982) 7 Ohio App.3d 219, 454 N.E.2d 1348, 7 O.B.R. 281.

When an accused moves the court for an additional evaluation of his mental condition, the statutory period within which he must be brought to trial is tolled from time his motion is granted, and begins to run again on the date when the psychiatrist's report is due to be filed with the court, even if no report is filed on that date. State v. Wilson (Fayette 1982) 7 Ohio App.3d 219, 454 N.E.2d 1348, 7 O.B.R. 281.

Where the trial court makes a proper journal entry within the time allowed for trial by statutory speedy trial limits, those limits are extended by (1) the period of a reasonable continuance granted to the state because of the temporary absence of a critical witness reported by the prosecutor in good faith, (2) the reasonable period necessary to determine defendant's mental competence to stand trial after that issue has been raised by the court or counsel, (3) the reasonable period necessary to rule on defendant's motion to transfer the defendant from jail for medical or psychiatric treatment, and (4) the reasonable period necessary to rule on defendant's motion to discharge him for failure to begin the trial within statutory speedy trial limits. State v. Smith (Cuyahoga 1981) 3 Ohio App.3d 115, 444 N.E.2d 85, 3 O.B.R. 130. Criminal Law ⚿ 577.10(6); Criminal Law ⚿ 577.10(8); Criminal Law ⚿ 577.11(6)

Speedy trial period was required to be tolled during period that defendant underwent court-ordered mental competency evaluation, upon state's motion, and subsequent residential treatment, where evaluation was conducted within seven days of trial court's order and defendant was treated and restored to competency within 60 days thereafter. State v. Sanabria (Ohio App. 1 Dist., Hamilton, 08-02-2002) No. C-020052, 2002-Ohio-3929, 2002 WL 1769441, Unreported. Criminal Law ⚿ 577.11(6)

The running of the speedy trial time period will be tolled between the time the defendant requests a determination on his competency to stand trial and the time he is found to be competent. State v Kramer, No. 1779 (11th Dist Ct App, Portage, 8–12–88).

Under RC 2945.72, the time within which an accused must be brought to trial is tolled from the time the accused enters a plea of not guilty by reason of insanity until the accused is evaluated. State v Gillenwater, No. 651 (4th Dist Ct App, Highland, 11–11–87).

10. Lack of counsel

Defendant's agreement to retain counsel after he was informed that counsel could not proceed to trial on scheduled date due to scheduling conflict, together with defendant's subsequent request for substitution of counsel, tolled 90-day speedy trial period. State v. Waits (Ohio App. 3 Dist., Marion, 02-22-2005) No. 9-04-50, 2005-Ohio-672, 2005 WL 405717, Unreported. Criminal Law ⚿ 577.10(8)

Defendant's statutory speedy trial time was tolled during delay caused by defense counsel's motion to withdraw as counsel. State v. Kemper (Ohio App. 2 Dist., Clark, 11-12-2004) No. 2002-CA-101, No. 2002-CA-102, 2004-Ohio-6055, 2004 WL 2588313, Unreported. Criminal Law ⚿ 577.10(8)

Speedy trial period was not tolled following state's discovery requests to defendant, where, due to state's failure to exercise diligence in providing counsel to defendant, he was not represented by counsel when state's discovery request was pending. (Per Karpinski, P.J., with two judges concurring in judgment only.) State v. Borrero (Ohio App. 8 Dist., Cuyahoga, 08-26-2004) No. 82595, 2004-Ohio-4488, 2004 WL 1902530, Unreported. Criminal Law ⚿ 577.10(8)

Even if defendant was acting as his own counsel, his motions to waive counsel and represent himself would have tolled the running of the statutory speedy trial period. State v. Taylor (Ohio, 12-20-2002) 98 Ohio St.3d 27, 781 N.E.2d 72, 2002-Ohio-7017, stay granted 98 Ohio St.3d 1402, 781 N.E.2d 221, 2003-Ohio-40, certiorari denied 123 S.Ct. 2227, 538 U.S. 1062, 155 L.Ed.2d 1115. Criminal Law ⚿ 577.10(8)

Pretrial delay resulting from death of defendant's original counsel tolled the speedy trial period established by statute. State v. Morton (Ohio App. 8 Dist., 03-29-2002) 147 Ohio App.3d 43, 768 N.E.2d 730, 2002-Ohio-813, appeal not allowed 96 Ohio St.3d 1469, 772 N.E.2d 1204, 2002-Ohio-3910, appeal after new sentencing hearing 2003-Ohio-4063, 2003 WL 21757725, appeal not allowed 100 Ohio St.3d 1531, 800 N.E.2d 48, 2003-Ohio-6458. Criminal Law ⚿ 577.10(4)

There is no fixed time standard by which court's alleged lack of diligence in appointing counsel for indigent defendant can be measured, for purposes of determining whether operation of speedy trial statute has been tolled; on the contrary, each case must be decided in light of its own unique facts, and generally, substantial delay in appointing counsel will not result in finding that speedy trial statute was tolled during delay. State v. Hiatt (Ohio App. 4 Dist., 03-26-1997) 120 Ohio App.3d 247, 697 N.E.2d 1025. Criminal Law ⚿ 577.10(4)

Defendant's request to discharge his first appointed counsel, coupled with his request for continuance in order to retain counsel, tolled operation of speedy trial statute. State v. Hiatt (Ohio App. 4 Dist., 03-26-1997) 120 Ohio App.3d 247, 697 N.E.2d 1025. Criminal Law ⚿ 577.10(8)

There is no lack of diligence when counsel is appointed by the court on the same day that the defendant makes the request, even though counsel is not notified until two days later, three days before the trial, even if the evidence is strictly construed against the state. State v. Rockwell (Franklin 1992) 80 Ohio App.3d 157, 608 N.E.2d

1118, dismissed, jurisdictional motion overruled 65 Ohio St.3d 1440, 600 N.E.2d 683.

Where a trial court orders counsel to be appointed for a defendant, but neglects to implement such order until the date of trial, any delay occasioned by a continuance to permit appointed counsel to prepare for trial is not a "reasonable continuance" and shall not be effective to extend the time requirements of RC 2945.71. City of Columbus v. Bonner (Franklin 1981) 2 Ohio App.3d 34, 440 N.E.2d 606, 2 O.B.R. 37. Criminal Law ⚷ 577.13

The unavailability of assigned counsel for a pretrial hearing does not constitute "any period of delay necessitated by the accused's lack of counsel..." within the meaning of RC 2945.72(C), when such counsel's unavailability is due to his engagement in another trial and when substitute counsel appears at the pre-trial hearing on behalf of the accused and in place of the accused's assigned counsel. State v. Smith (Cuyahoga 1976) 47 Ohio App.2d 317, 354 N.E.2d 699, 1 O.O.3d 385.

Where a defendant is arrested, incarcerated and arraigned and a pretrial hearing in her case is scheduled, all while the defendant is without counsel, a trial court cannot claim that the time requirement for a speedy trial in RC 2945.71 is extended by RC 2945.72(C), and a defendant whose trial date came over 300 days after her arrest will be discharged upon appeal. State v Henry, No. 93–C–26 (7th Dist Ct App, Columbiana, 8–10–94).

11. Motions or requests of accused—In general

Motions to dismiss, motion for new attorney, motion amending suppression motion, motion for change of venue, motion for independent analysis of seized contraband, and motion requesting trial court to order laboratory technician who tested contraband to appear and testify at trial tolled statutory speedy trial period in prosecution for possession of cocaine. State v. Gaines (Ohio App. 9 Dist., Lorain, 06-30-2004) No. 00CA008298, 2004-Ohio-3407, 2004 WL 1461524, Unreported. Criminal Law ⚷ 577.10(8)

Ninety-day speedy trial limit to bring incarcerated defendant to trial on charges related to harassment and stalking were tolled by time for extradition from another state, appointment of counsel, and various requests and motions of defense, which rendered time from defendant's arrest to date of trial well within speedy trial limitation; untolled time from date of arrest to trial was 69 days, date of arrest was not counted as day of incarceration, and defense requested leave to file plea of not guilty by reason of insanity, moved for continuance and to suppress evidence. State v. Cline (Ohio App. 2 Dist., Champaign, 09-05-2003) No. 2002-CA-05, 2003-Ohio-4712, 2003 WL 22064118, Unreported, stay granted 100 Ohio St.3d 1529, 800 N.E.2d 47, 2003-Ohio-6458, motion to certify allowed 100 Ohio St.3d 1543, 800 N.E.2d 749, 2003-Ohio-6879, appeal not allowed 100 Ohio St.3d 1547, 800 N.E.2d 752, 2003-Ohio-6879, stay granted 101 Ohio St.3d 1461, 804 N.E.2d 36, 2004-Ohio-814, reversed 103 Ohio St.3d 471, 816 N.E.2d 1069, 2004-Ohio-5701, on remand 164 Ohio App.3d 228, 841 N.E.2d 846, 2005-Ohio-5779. Criminal Law ⚷ 577.10(8); Criminal Law ⚷ 577.11(4)

Defendant's motion to suppress prior convictions, request for hearing on such motion, and motions for continuances tolled speedy trial period. State v. Davis (Ohio App. 7 Dist., Mahoning, 05-30-2002) No. 01 CA 171, 2002-Ohio-2789, 2002 WL 32806896, Unreported. Criminal Law ⚷ 577.13

Ninety-day speedy trial period from defendant's arrest until time of trial was tolled for defendant arrested for menacing by stalking, where defendant brought two continuances and a motion to dismiss; journal entries indicated, and defendant admitted, that he requested continuances. Cleveland v. Kittrell (Ohio App. 8 Dist., Cuyahoga, 10-10-2002) No. 80954, 2002-Ohio-5456, 2002 WL 31260440, Unreported. Criminal Law ⚷ 577.10(8)

When a criminal defendant files a pretrial motion and the state later files against defendant additional, related criminal charges, the defendant's filing of the pretrial motion does not extend the time within which he or she must be brought to trial on those additional charges. State v. Homan (Ohio, 08-16-2000) 89 Ohio St.3d 421, 732 N.E.2d 952, 2000-Ohio-212, reconsideration denied 90 Ohio St.3d 1431, 736 N.E.2d 27. Criminal Law ⚷ 577.14

Delay occasioned by defendant's filing of pleadings entitled "Legal notice of Revocation of Unauthorized Plea" and "Dilatory plea to quash" was chargeable to defendant under speedy trial statute. State v. Keith (Ohio App. 12 Dist., 11-09-1998) 130 Ohio App.3d 456, 720 N.E.2d 216. Criminal Law ⚷ 577.10(8)

Where defense counsel would not proceed to trial until civilian clothing for defendant could be obtained, delay was attributable to defendant and tolled speedy trial statute. State v. Baker (Ohio App. 8 Dist., 12-20-1993) 92 Ohio App.3d 516, 636 N.E.2d 363. Criminal Law ⚷ 577.10(8)

In a prosecution for aggravated robbery with a firearms specification and breaking and entering, a defendant's speedy trial rights are not violated for failure to bring him to trial within 180 days of his demand for final disposition where (1) the defendant requested final disposition January 16, 1990; (2) the defendant's counsel agreed on March 26 to a continuance for purposes of preparing for trial; (3) the defendant, on September 10, 1990, moved to dismiss the indictment; and (4) the trial was held on October 22, 1990; the defendant's motion to dismiss tolled the 180–day period through the date of trial and the agreement of counsel to the continuance bound the defendant and waived his speedy trial right for a period of sixty-four days until he again requested final disposition, regardless of whether the defendant consented to the waiver. State v. Logan (Franklin 1991) 71 Ohio App.3d 292, 593 N.E.2d 395, dismissed, jurisdictional motion overruled 62 Ohio St.3d 1463, 580 N.E.2d 784, cause dismissed 75 Ohio St.3d 1427, 662 N.E.2d 376.

RC 2945.72(E) provides that a motion filed by accused may extend the time within which such accused may be brought to trial. State v. Walker (Jefferson 1974) 42 Ohio App.2d 41, 327 N.E.2d 796, 71 O.O.2d 238.

Request by defendant in a misdemeanor case to extend the trial date may be construed as having been made upon her "own motion" pursuant to RC 2945.72(H) and, therefore, there was no violation of the forty-five-day speedy trial requirement of RC 2945.71. State v Cooper, No. 43765 (8th Dist Ct App, Cuyahoga, 3–18–82).

12. —— Competency evaluation, motions or requests of accused

Defendant's motion to determine his competency in child rape case tolled the 270-day speedy trial period, and such statutory extension was not limited to a specific time period. State v. Thomas (Ohio App. 12 Dist., Brown, 01-13-2003) No. CA2002-01-001, 2003-Ohio-74, 2003 WL 103411, Unreported. Criminal Law ⚷ 577.11(6)

Pretrial delay resulting from trial court's grant of defendant's request for a psychiatric examination tolled statutory speedy-trial period. State v. Morton (Ohio App. 8 Dist., 03-29-2002) 147 Ohio App.3d 43, 768 N.E.2d 730, 2002-Ohio-813, appeal not allowed 96 Ohio St.3d 1469, 772 N.E.2d 1204, 2002-Ohio-3910, appeal after new sentencing hearing 2003-Ohio-4063, 2003 WL 21757725, appeal not allowed 100 Ohio St.3d 1531, 800 N.E.2d 48, 2003-Ohio-6458. Criminal Law ⚷ 577.11(6)

A continuance for a competency evaluation granted upon the accused's own motion extends the time within which trial must be had only for the actual period of the continuance; other delay, even delay attributable to completion of the evaluation, which elapsed beyond the specific period for which the continuance was granted is charged against the state. State v Jarrett, No. CA88–03–004 (12th Dist Ct App, Fayette, 9–12–88).

13. —— Discovery, motions or requests of accused

Defendant's statutory speedy trial time was tolled during delay caused by defendant's discovery request. State v. Kemper (Ohio App. 2 Dist., Clark, 11-12-2004) No. 2002-CA-101, No. 2002-CA-102, 2004-Ohio-6055, 2004 WL 2588313, Unreported. Criminal Law ⚷ 577.10(8)

Statutory speedy trial time period was tolled from date state filed its responses to defendant's discovery request and also filed its own motion for reciprocal discovery until time of trial, where defendant never responded to state's reciprocal discovery request, as required by rule. State v. Saxon (Ohio App. 8 Dist., Cuyahoga, 09-23-2004) No. 83889, 2004-Ohio-5017, 2004 WL 2340106, Unreported, appeal dismissed 104 Ohio St.3d 1421, 819 N.E.2d 299, 2004-Ohio-6675, stay denied 104 Ohio St.3d 1424, 819 N.E.2d 708, 2004-Ohio-6585, appeal allowed 105 Ohio St.3d 1437, 822 N.E.2d 810, 2005-Ohio-531, reversed 109 Ohio St.3d 176, 846 N.E.2d 824, 2006-Ohio-1245. Criminal Law ⚷ 577.10(8)

Defendant's discovery request tolled speedy-trial time until state reasonably complied with request, in prosecution for rape, kidnapping, and felonious assault. State v. Barnett (Ohio App. 12 Dist., Fayette, 04-21-2003) No. CA2002-06-011, 2003-Ohio-2014, 2003 WL 1906768, Unreported, appeal not allowed 99 Ohio St.3d 1544, 795 N.E.2d 682, 2003-Ohio-4671. Criminal Law ⚷ 577.10(8)

A demand for discovery or a bill of particulars is a tolling event pursuant to speedy trial statute permitting extension of speedy trial period by any period of delay necessitated by reason of a motion, proceeding, or action made or instituted by the accused; abrogating *State v Spicer*, 1998 WL 226411. State v. Brown (Ohio, 12-23-2002) 98 Ohio St.3d 121, 781 N.E.2d 159, 2002-Ohio-7040. Criminal Law ⚷ 577.10(8)

The speedy trial period is tolled by defense counsel's request for discovery, and his telephone authorization of a motion for continuance. State v Roquemore, No. 92AP–356 (10th Dist Ct App, Franklin, 3–16–93).

14. —— Continuance, motions or requests of accused

Speedy trial time was tolled during interval resulting from grant of defendant's request for continuance. City of Cleveland v. Pavarini (Ohio App. 8 Dist., Cuyahoga, 07-14-2005) No. 85185, 2005-Ohio-3552, 2005 WL 1648691, Unreported, appeal not allowed 108 Ohio St.3d 1414, 841 N.E.2d 319, 2006-Ohio-179. Criminal Law ⚷ 577.10(8)

Period of continuances granted on defendant's own motion tolled speedy trial time, in rape prosecution. State v. Brown (Ohio App. 7 Dist., Mahoning, 06-07-2005) No. 03-MA-32, 2005-Ohio-2939, 2005 WL 1385715, Unreported, appeal not allowed 106 Ohio St.3d 1558, 836 N.E.2d 582, 2005-Ohio-5531. Criminal Law ⚷ 577.10(8)

Statutory speedy trial period was tolled, in prosecution for grand theft of a motor vehicle, aggravated robbery, having weapon while under disability, carrying concealed weapon, and failure to comply with signal of police officer, during continuance of trial date on joint motion of defendant and co-defendant after co-defendant was involved in automobile accident. State v. Smith (Ohio App. 2 Dist., Clark, 11-12-2004) No. 2003 CA 93, 2004-Ohio-6062, 2004 WL 2588269, Unreported, motion for delayed appeal denied 105 Ohio St.3d 1450, 823 N.E.2d 455, 2005-Ohio-763, motion for delayed appeal denied 105 Ohio St.3d 1496, 825 N.E.2d 621, 2005-Ohio-1666. Criminal Law ⚷ 577.10(5)

Statutory speedy trial period was tolled, in prosecution for grand theft of a motor vehicle, aggravated robbery, having weapon while under disability, carrying concealed weapon, and failure to comply with signal of police officer, during continuance of trial date on motion filed by counsel for defendant, despite defendant's claim that he did not concur in such motion and that speedy trial clock therefore should not have been tolled; defense counsel, appointed three weeks before first scheduled trial date, was entitled to request continuance in order to obtain more time to prepare for trial without defendant's agreement, and defendant was bound thereby. State v. Smith (Ohio App. 2 Dist., Clark, 11-12-2004) No. 2003 CA 93, 2004-Ohio-6062, 2004 WL 2588269, Unreported, motion for delayed appeal denied 105 Ohio St.3d 1450, 823 N.E.2d 455, 2005-Ohio-763, motion for delayed appeal denied 105 Ohio St.3d 1496, 825 N.E.2d 621, 2005-Ohio-1666. Criminal Law ⚿ 577.10(8)

Continuances granted at defendant's own request tolled statutory speedy trial period. State v. Williams (Ohio App. 2 Dist., Montgomery, 09-30-2004) No. 20104, 2004-Ohio-5273, 2004 WL 2245101, Unreported. Criminal Law ⚿ 577.10(8)

Defendant was not entitled to dismissal of the misdemeanor escape charges against her based on an alleged violation of defendant's right to a speedy trial; only 53 days were chargeable against the State, for speedy trial purposes, since time defendant was incarcerated on the escape charges and on a probation violation counted only as single count days, time was tolled while the court ruled on defendant's motions, and time stopped running after defendant's request for a continuance was granted. State v. Baumgartner (Ohio App. 6 Dist., Ottawa, 07-23-2004) No. OT-03-013, 2004-Ohio-3907, 2004 WL 1662193, Unreported. Criminal Law ⚿ 577.10(7); Criminal Law ⚿ 577.10(8); Criminal Law ⚿ 577.11(1); Criminal Law ⚿ 577.16(11)

Defendant's request for continuance of trial for disorderly conduct in order to obtain new counsel, together with State's reasonable request for continuance because key witness was unavailable, to which request defendant acquiesced, and defendant's motion to dismiss, tolled 90-day speedy trial period, and thus, delay of 134 days between arrest and trial for disorderly conduct did not violate defendant's right to speedy trial. State v. Elliott (Ohio App. 10 Dist., Franklin, 04-27-2004) No. 03AP-605, 2004-Ohio-2134, 2004 WL 886831, Unreported. Criminal Law ⚿ 577.10(8); Criminal Law ⚿ 577.10(9)

Defendant who was charged with operating a motor vehicle under the influence (OMVI) while underage tolled her speedy trial time by expressly agreeing to set second pretrial proceeding and vacate initial trial date, which action was sufficient to demonstrate continuance by way of agreement to post-statutory trial date; although defendant was not involved in setting actual date for second pretrial, defense counsel admitted that he actively participated in scheduling a second pretrial and vacating initial trial date, which necessarily placed trial date outside 45-day speedy trial limit. State v. Steinke (Ohio App. 3 Dist., 03-15-2004) 158 Ohio App.3d 241, 814 N.E.2d 1230, 2004-Ohio-1201. Criminal Law ⚿ 577.10(9)

For speedy trial purposes, one-week continuance would be charged against defendant, even though trial court's journal entry did not indicate that defendant requested continuance, where transcript clearly indicated that defendant requested continuance. State v. Garries (Ohio App. 2 Dist., Montgomery, 12-19-2003) No. 19825, 2003-Ohio-6895, 2003 WL 22973460, Unreported. Criminal Law ⚿ 577.10(8)

Trial court did not abuse its discretion in prosecution for rape and gross sexual imposition by denying defendant's request for continuance on date trial was scheduled to begin due to co-counsel's illness; defendant was represented by counsel on date trial was scheduled to begin who indicated that he was prepared and wished to proceed despite the court's willingness to delay the taking of evidence until the following day, and granting continuance could have resulted in harm to victim, who was ready to testify. State v. Galloway (Ohio App. 6 Dist., Lucas, 10-24-2003) No. L-00-1362, No. L-00-1328, 2003-Ohio-5681, 2003 WL 22417142, Unreported. Criminal Law ⚿ 589(2)

Period between original date of pretrial conference and the rescheduled pretrial date was chargeable to defendant so as to stop the speedy trial clock during that period, even though the rescheduling order was entered only a few days before the new date; the defendant moved for the continuance, and the rescheduling entry was prompted by the motion almost one month earlier. State v. Stewart (Ohio App. 2 Dist., Montgomery, 08-15-2003) No. CIV.A. 19663, 2003-Ohio-4329, 2003 WL 21949751, Unreported. Criminal Law ⚿ 577.10(8)

For purposes of statutory speedy trial calculation, period of time which elapsed between filing of defendant's notice for continuance and the new trial date set by trial court was excluded from speedy trial period. State v. Humphrey (Ohio App. 2 Dist., Clark, 06-27-2003) No. 2002 CA 30, 2003-Ohio-3401, 2003 WL 21487780, Unreported, motion for delayed appeal denied 103 Ohio St.3d 1490, 816 N.E.2d 1078, 2004-Ohio-5605. Criminal Law ⚿ 577.10(8)

State did not violate defendant's right to a speedy trial; defendant's original trial date was within 90 days of his arrest, and the additional delay was occasioned by defense counsel's request for a continuance and did not count against State for speedy trial purposes. State v. Perez (Ohio App. 2 Dist., Clark, 06-13-2003) No. 2002 CA 28, 2003-Ohio-3055, 2003 WL 21361006, Unreported. Criminal Law ⚿ 577.10(8)

Pretrial motions to continue trial on original charges, filed by defendant prior to issuance of amended indictment, did not extend time within which defendant had to be tried on charges brought by amended indictment, where new and additional charges arose from same facts as did original charges, and state knew of such facts at time of initial indictment, so time within which trial was to begin on additional charges was subject to same statutory limitations period that applied to original charges. State v. Taylor (Ohio App. 11 Dist., Portage, 12-20-2002) No. 2000-P-0121, 2002-Ohio-7120, 2002 WL 31862688, Unreported. Criminal Law ⚿ 577.14

Defendant's right to speedy trial was not violated, where defendant was not held in jail in lieu of bail, and was brought to trial within 247 days, well within time limit of 270 days, considering defendant and his counsel's numerous requests for continuances, which were granted by the trial court, and period that jury was unavailable due to holidays. State v. Barnett (Ohio App. 8 Dist., Cuyahoga, 11-27-2002) No. 81101, 2002-Ohio-6506, 2002 WL 31667667, Unreported, appeal not allowed 98 Ohio St.3d 1514, 786 N.E.2d 64, 2003-Ohio-1572, motion to reopen denied 2003-Ohio-3938, 2003 WL 21710610. Criminal Law 🔑 577.10(8); Criminal Law 🔑 577.15(1)

270-day speedy trial period was tolled by numerous continuances granted at defendant's request, and thus, fact that entry of defendant's guilty pleas to robbery charges occurred 567 days after arrest did not violate his speedy trial rights. State v. Brown (Ohio App. 1 Dist., Hamilton, 10-25-2002) No. C-010755, 2002-Ohio-5813, 2002 WL 31398564, Unreported, motion for delayed appeal denied 98 Ohio St.3d 1487, 785 N.E.2d 471, 2003-Ohio-1189. Criminal Law 🔑 577.13

Trial within a year of the murders was not presumptively prejudicial and did not violate constitutional right to speedy trial; even though the defendant had verbally asserted his right to a speedy trial early in the process, he never filed a motion to dismiss his case on speedy trial grounds and in fact successfully moved for a continuance later on. State v. Taylor (Ohio, 12-20-2002) 98 Ohio St.3d 27, 781 N.E.2d 72, 2002-Ohio-7017, stay granted 98 Ohio St.3d 1402, 781 N.E.2d 221, 2003-Ohio-40, certiorari denied 123 S.Ct. 2227, 538 U.S. 1062, 155 L.Ed.2d 1115. Criminal Law 🔑 577.15(1); Criminal Law 🔑 577.16(8)

Trial court's judgment entry granting defendant's motion to continue pre-trial adequately continued the criminal proceedings and extended the speedy trial time period. State v. Pierson (Ohio App. 11 Dist., 08-30-2002) 149 Ohio App.3d 318, 777 N.E.2d 296, 2002-Ohio-4515. Criminal Law 🔑 577.13

Defendant's requests for continuances extended the 30–day time period in which he was required to be brought to trial in mayor's court on speeding charges. Amberley v. Mize (Ohio Mun., 04-14-2000) 106 Ohio Misc.2d 32, 733 N.E.2d 337. Criminal Law 🔑 577.10(8)

Journal entry from date of defendant's arraignment, which included date four weeks in future and symbol representing defendant, when read in conjunction with hearing transcript indicating that defendant had asked for four-week continuance, was sufficient to indicate that granted continuance had been requested by defendant, so that resulting delay was not chargeable to State for purposes of speedy trial statute. State v. Stamps (Ohio App. 1 Dist., 04-03-1998) 127 Ohio App.3d 219, 712 N.E.2d 762. Criminal Law 🔑 577.16(9)

Defendant's motion for continuance to undergo competency evaluation tolled his statutory speedy-trial period for all 62 days during which motion was pending, even though examiner's report was due after only 30 days. State v. Jones (Ohio App. 11 Dist., 04-04-1997) 119 Ohio App.3d 59, 694 N.E.2d 505. Criminal Law 🔑 577.11(6)

Fact that there was scheduling conflict on part of defendant and his attorney did not provide justification for charging the resulting continuance to state, in determining whether defendant's statutory speedy trial rights were violated, where it was undisputed that continuance was granted upon defendant's own motion. State v. Soto (Ohio App. 9 Dist., 09-07-1994) 96 Ohio App.3d 743, 645 N.E.2d 1307. Criminal Law 🔑 577.10(9); Criminal Law 🔑 577.12(1)

Defendant's trial took place within statutory speedy trial requirements, though statutory period was 90 days and defendant's trial did not commence until 291 days after arrest; 221 days before trial were tolled from speedy trial requirements by defendant's requests for continuances, time that defendant was hospitalized, delay for locating civilian clothing for defendant to wear at trial, and trial judge's sua sponte continuance for time that judge was to appear as witness at different trial. State v. Baker (Ohio App. 8 Dist., 12-20-1993) 92 Ohio App.3d 516, 636 N.E.2d 363. Criminal Law 🔑 577.10(8); Criminal Law 🔑 577.15(3)

When record clearly indicates that continuance is attributable to defendant, delay occasioned by continuance will be assessed to defendant, for purpose of speedy trial statute, even in absence of court's journal entry. State v. Baker (Ohio App. 8 Dist., 12-20-1993) 92 Ohio App.3d 516, 636 N.E.2d 363. Criminal Law 🔑 577.10(8)

Representations made to the trial court by defense counsel that he was unable to proceed with the case until a later time do not extend the time for trial pursuant to RC 2945.72 unless the trial court grants a continuance by entry prior to the expiration of time limit provided by RC 2945.71. State v. Siler (Ohio 1979) 57 Ohio St.2d 1, 384 N.E.2d 710, 11 O.O.3d 1.

When, at the request of defendant's counsel, a judge extends the time for a preliminary hearing pursuant to Crim R 5(B)(1), this continuance extends the time the defendant is required to be brought to both a preliminary hearing and trial pursuant to RC 2945.72(H). State v. Martin (Ohio 1978) 56 Ohio St.2d 289, 384 N.E.2d 239, 10 O.O.3d 415. Criminal Law 🔑 228; Criminal Law 🔑 577.13

RC 2945.72(H) does not give the trial court blanket discretion to extend the time in which an accused must be brought to trial, but rather provides for an extension of the time for trial during the period of any continuance granted on the accused's own motion and during the period of any reasonable continuance granted on other than the accused's motion, and before this provision is applicable, the court by journal entry must have granted such continuance prior to the expiration of the statutory time limitations for trial. State v. Eberhardt (Cuyahoga 1978) 56 Ohio App.2d 193, 381 N.E.2d 1357, 10 O.O.3d 197. Criminal Law 🔑 577.13

Defendant who requested five continuances and filed total of 38 motions was not denied speedy trial, where state neither requested nor caused any continuances. State v. Lawless (Ohio App. 5 Dist., Muskingum, 07-12-2002) No. CT2000-0037, 2002-Ohio-3686, 2002 WL 1585846, Unreported, appeal not allowed 97 Ohio St.3d 1470, 779 N.E.2d 236, 2002-Ohio-6347. Criminal Law ⚷ 577.10(8)

A 98–day continuance granted by trial court in response to defense counsel's statement in pretrial scheduling conference in open court that presently approaching trial date was problematic was a continuance granted at request of defendant, and thus such delay, from grant of continuance to new trial date, was attributable to defendant for purposes of speedy trial statute. State v. DeLeon (Ohio App. 2 Dist., Montgomery, 06-28-2002) No. 18114, 2002-Ohio-3286, 2002 WL 1393665, Unreported, appeal not allowed 98 Ohio St.3d 1424, 782 N.E.2d 78, 2003-Ohio-259. Criminal Law ⚷ 577.10(8)

A defendant's request for a continuance on the morning of the trial for a subpoena that is not timely requested is a continuance attributable to the defendant under RC 2945.72 and a motion to dismiss is denied. State v Lawson, No. 92–CA–66 (5th Dist Ct App, Licking, 3–31–93).

Continuances allegedly requested by a defendant will extend the statutory speedy trial time limits only if they are represented by timely written journal entries. State v Page, No. 54252 (8th Dist Ct App, Cuyahoga, 8–18–88).

15. —— Suppression of evidence, motions or requests of accused

Defendant's filing of pretrial motion to suppress evidence relating to driving under the influence (DUI) charge did not toll statutory speedy trial period in which defendant had to be brought to trial on child endangering charge, which was filed subsequent to filing of the motion to suppress. State v. Homan (Ohio, 08-16-2000) 89 Ohio St.3d 421, 732 N.E.2d 952, 2000-Ohio-212, reconsideration denied 90 Ohio St.3d 1431, 736 N.E.2d 27. Criminal Law ⚷ 577.14

A defendant filing a motion to suppress evidence of a breath alcohol concentration test will be charged with the time between the motion and the hearing on that request for purposes of the speedy trial requirements, even where the court neglected to journalize an entry giving a reason for the continuance. State v. Bumbalough (Summit 1992) 81 Ohio App.3d 408, 611 N.E.2d 367.

The right to a speedy trial is not denied when the defendant filed a motion to suppress fifty-four days after arrest, and the trial commenced 109 days later, since the municipal court rules require that motions be ruled upon within 120 days of filing, thereby setting an outer limit on reasonableness; furthermore, the effective delay was only seventy-three days since there remained a thirty-six-day surplus under the ninety-day requirement of the statute. State v. Beam (Lake 1991) 77 Ohio App.3d 200, 601 N.E.2d 547, dismissed, jurisdictional motion overruled 62 Ohio St.3d 1500, 583 N.E.2d 971.

Speedy trial statute was tolled in aggravated robbery case for the 71 days that elapsed from when defendant filed his motion to suppress until date decision was rendered, where codefendant joined motion, state filed its opposition, a two day hearing was held, and court was also presiding over an aggravated murder trial that lasted in excess of a week. State v. Littlefield (Ohio App. 3 Dist., Marion, 06-28-2002) No. 9-02-03, 2002-Ohio-3399, 2002 WL 1433772, Unreported. Criminal Law ⚷ 577.10(7); Criminal Law ⚷ 577.10(8)

16. —— Dismissal, motions or requests of accused

Forty-five day speedy trial period applicable to charges that property owner violated zoning ordinance and flood damage prevention ordinance was tolled from date owner filed motion to dismiss charges until date trial court denied motion. Village of Versailles v. Poly (Ohio App. 2 Dist., Darke, 03-26-2004) No. 1627, 2004-Ohio-1485, 2004 WL 596079, Unreported. Criminal Law ⚷ 577.10(8)

Defendant's motion to dismiss charges of illegal conveyance for violation of right to speedy trial, which was filed before speedy trial period had expired, tolled speedy trial period until date motion to dismiss was denied. State v. Szorady (Ohio App. 9 Dist., Lorain, 05-28-2003) No. 02CA008159, 2003-Ohio-2716, 2003 WL 21222139, Unreported. Criminal Law ⚷ 577.10(8)

For purposes of defendant's motion to dismiss assault indictments due to violation of right to speedy trial, Court of Appeals would not attempt to determine whether the journal entries accurately reflected which party requested the continuances of trial, where review of record indicated that various continuances were made at the request of defense counsel as reflected in the journal entries, and the docket and journal entries did not indicate any obvious error. State v. Barnett (Ohio App. 8 Dist., Cuyahoga, 11-27-2002) No. 81101, 2002-Ohio-6506, 2002 WL 31667667, Unreported, appeal not allowed 98 Ohio St.3d 1514, 786 N.E.2d 64, 2003-Ohio-1572, motion to reopen denied 2003-Ohio-3938, 2003 WL 21710610. Criminal Law ⚷ 1118

Denial of defendant's motion to dismiss, which was brought on speedy trial grounds, was warranted, even though trial court stated erroneous reason for denial, where defendant requested and was granted a continuance which extended speedy trial time period. State v. Pierson (Ohio App. 11 Dist., 08-30-2002) 149 Ohio App.3d 318, 777 N.E.2d 296, 2002-Ohio-4515. Criminal Law ⚷ 577.16(11)

Period between date on which defendant filed affidavit and demand for a hearing or dismissal, in which he challenged trial court's jurisdiction and sought to dismiss case for lack of proper complaint, and date on which trial court denied such demand was chargeable to defendant under speedy trial statute. State v. Keith (Ohio App. 12 Dist., 11-09-1998) 130 Ohio App.3d 456, 720 N.E.2d 216. Criminal Law ⚷ 577.10(8)

Motion to dismiss indictment tolls time for speedy trial. State v. Grinnell (Ohio App. 10 Dist.,

06-27-1996) 112 Ohio App.3d 124, 678 N.E.2d 231, appeal not allowed 77 Ohio St.3d 1474, 673 N.E.2d 138, appeal not allowed 77 Ohio St.3d 1475, 673 N.E.2d 138, denial of habeas corpus affirmed 215 F.3d 1326, certiorari denied 121 S.Ct. 232, 531 U.S. 898, 148 L.Ed.2d 166. Criminal Law ⚷ 577.10(8)

A defendant's motion to dismiss bad check charges against her for violation of the speedy trial statutes is properly denied where the time period for bringing her to trial was extended by the period during which she was in federal custody and unavailable for trial, and by the time consumed by numerous continuances granted at her request. State v. Howard (Cuyahoga 1992) 79 Ohio App.3d 705, 607 N.E.2d 1121, dismissed, jurisdictional motion overruled 65 Ohio St.3d 1416, 598 N.E.2d 1168.

Where an indictment is dismissed on defendant's motion for failure to state all of the elements of the crime, the indictment is a nullity, and the elapsed time from arrest to dismissal is not tacked onto a subsequent indictment to aggregate elapsed time for the application of RC 2945.73. State v. Lyons (Medina 1978) 60 Ohio App.2d 228, 401 N.E.2d 452, 15 O.O.3d 367. Criminal Law ⚷ 577.14

17. Motions of court or prosecutor—In general

Continuance which was granted by trial court after defendant notified court of witness's unavailability, and set date for trial which was within 90–day limit in light of extension granted following defendant's earlier motion for continuance, was attributable to defendant for purposes of speedy trial statute. State v. Nelson (Ohio App. 5 Dist., 08-06-1996) 122 Ohio App.3d 309, 701 N.E.2d 747, appeal allowed 77 Ohio St.3d 1523, 674 N.E.2d 374, appeal dismissed as improvidently allowed 82 Ohio St.3d 1207, 693 N.E.2d 804, 1998-Ohio-415. Criminal Law ⚷ 577.10(8)

Agreement by all parties to a poststatutory trial date constitutes limited exception to general *Singer* rule that continuance pursuant to speedy trial statute must actually take form of a continuance in order to be effective. State v. Huckaby (Ohio Mun., 08-05-1997) 91 Ohio Misc.2d 16, 696 N.E.2d 1116. Criminal Law ⚷ 577.13

Period of 21 days resulting from continuance requested by state because of unavailability of arresting officer on date scheduled for trial was not chargeable to state in computing speedy trial time limit where defendant then asked for continuance and, in any event, trial court assigned new trial date that fell within statutory time limit for bringing defendant to trial. State v. Wirtanen (Ohio App. 6 Dist., 04-26-1996) 110 Ohio App.3d 604, 674 N.E.2d 1245. Criminal Law ⚷ 577.11(1)

State was chargeable with delay caused by continuance of hearing on defendant's motion to dismiss in calculating speedy trial limit, where record did not contain reason for continuance. State v. Wirtanen (Ohio App. 6 Dist., 04-26-1996) 110 Ohio App.3d 604, 674 N.E.2d 1245. Criminal Law ⚷ 577.12(1)

The mere setting of an original trial date beyond the time limits of RC 2945.71 does not constitute a continuance "other than upon the accused's own motion" pursuant to RC 2945.72(H). State v. Cutcher (Ohio 1978) 56 Ohio St.2d 383, 384 N.E.2d 275, 10 O.O.3d 502. Criminal Law ⚷ 577.13

RC 2945.72(H) does not give the trial court blanket discretion to extend the time in which an accused must be brought to trial, but rather provides for an extension of the time for trial during the period of any continuance granted on the accused's own motion and during the period of any reasonable continuance granted on other than the accused's motion, and before this provision is applicable, the court by journal entry must have granted such continuance prior to the expiration of the statutory time limitations for trial. State v. Eberhardt (Cuyahoga 1978) 56 Ohio App.2d 193, 381 N.E.2d 1357, 10 O.O.3d 197. Criminal Law ⚷ 577.13

A court's scheduling a trial for a date beyond the speedy trial deadline constitutes a "continuance granted other than upon the accused's own motion" pursuant to RC 2945.72(H) when that trial date is one which the accused's attorney specifically agrees to in a pretrial conference in which the judge and the attorneys for both sides participate. State v. McRae (Ohio 1978) 55 Ohio St.2d 149, 378 N.E.2d 476, 9 O.O.3d 118.

Delay in defendant's trial resulting from trial court's continuance, which was not based on defendant's request, and for which the trial court failed to state a reason, was attributable to the State for purposes of speedy trial statute, even if continuance was reasonable. State v. DeLeon (Ohio App. 2 Dist., Montgomery, 06-28-2002) No. 18114, 2002-Ohio-3286, 2002 WL 1393665, Unreported, appeal not allowed 98 Ohio St.3d 1424, 782 N.E.2d 78, 2003-Ohio-259. Criminal Law ⚷ 577.12(1)

18. —— Procedural requirements, motions of court or prosecutor

Trial court's failure to journalize two orders setting new trial dates until after previous dates had passed did not result in statutory speedy trial clock continuing to run. State v. Smith (Ohio App. 2 Dist., Clark, 11-12-2004) No. 2003 CA 93, 2004-Ohio-6062, 2004 WL 2588269, Unreported, motion for delayed appeal denied 105 Ohio St.3d 1450, 823 N.E.2d 455, 2005-Ohio-763, motion for delayed appeal denied 105 Ohio St.3d 1496, 825 N.E.2d 621, 2005-Ohio-1666. Criminal Law ⚷ 577.10(7)

Trial court complied with its duties with respect to its sua sponte continuance, which tolled defendant's speedy trial date for first-degree misdemeanor operating motor vehicle under the influence (OMVI), where trial court filed journal entry prior to expiration of speedy trial date and indicated in journal entry that its reason for continuance was due to specific scheduling conflict in its docket. State v. Glass (Ohio App. 3 Dist., Auglaize, 08-23-2004) No. 2-04-01, 2004-Ohio-4402, 2004 WL 1874574, Unreported, appeal not allowed 104 Ohio St.3d 1460, 821 N.E.2d 577, 2005-Ohio-204. Criminal Law ⚷ 577.10(7)

In granting a continuance under provision of statute permitting extension of speedy trial period for any reasonable continuance other than upon the accused's own motion, the court must journalize an entry stating the reasons therefor before the expiration of the time limit within which the defendant must be brought to trial. State v. Hirsch (Ohio App. 1 Dist., 08-07-1998) 129 Ohio App.3d 294, 717 N.E.2d 789, dismissed, appeal not allowed 84 Ohio St.3d 1436, 702 N.E.2d 1213, denial of habeas corpus affirmed 74 Fed.Appx. 486, 2003 WL 21949184. Criminal Law ⚷ 577.13

Under speedy trial statute, continuance will not extend time to try defendant unless court records continuance through its journal entry prior to expiration of speedy trial requirements, identifies party to be charged with continuance, and briefly indicates reasons requiring continuance. Cleveland v. Jones (Ohio App. 8 Dist., 05-06-1996) 110 Ohio App.3d 791, 675 N.E.2d 498. Criminal Law ⚷ 577.13

In order for continuance to toll speedy trial time, trial court must record continuance, identify party to whom continuance is chargeable and indicate underlying reason for continuance. State v. Wirtanen (Ohio App. 6 Dist., 04-26-1996) 110 Ohio App.3d 604, 674 N.E.2d 1245. Criminal Law ⚷ 577.13

Trial court, in sua sponte continuing trial beyond statutory speedy trial time limit, was at minimum required to enter order of continuance and reason therefor by journal entry prior to expiration of time limit. State v. King (Ohio, 08-31-1994) 70 Ohio St.3d 158, 637 N.E.2d 903, 1994-Ohio-412. Criminal Law ⚷ 577.13

For purpose of tolling speedy trial statute, granting of continuance must be recorded by trial court in its journal, journal entry must identify party to whom continuance is chargeable, and if trial court is acting sua sponte, journal entry must so indicate and must set forth reasons justifying continuance; trial court need not set forth reasons for granting continuance at defendant's request. State v. Baker (Ohio App. 8 Dist., 12-20-1993) 92 Ohio App.3d 516, 636 N.E.2d 363. Criminal Law ⚷ 577.13

In journal entry meeting minimum requirements for continuance to toll speedy trial time, trial court must record such continuance, must identify party to whom continuance is chargeable, and must indicate briefly underlying reasons necessitating continuance. State v. Collins (Ohio App. 6 Dist., 09-30-1993) 91 Ohio App.3d 10, 631 N.E.2d 666, dismissed, jurisdictional motion overruled 68 Ohio St.3d 1470, 628 N.E.2d 1389. Criminal Law ⚷ 577.13

When extending time for criminal trial, court must enter order of continuance and reasons therefor by journal entry, prior to expiration of time limits for trial prescribed in speedy trial statute. State v. Collins (Ohio App. 6 Dist., 09-30-1993) 91 Ohio App.3d 10, 631 N.E.2d 666, dismissed, jurisdictional motion overruled 68 Ohio St.3d 1470, 628 N.E.2d 1389. Criminal Law ⚷ 577.13

For a continuance of a trial to extend beyond the speedy trial time limits the trial court is required to record the continuance through a journal entry before the speedy trial time limits expire, indicate which party will be charged with the continuance, and indicate why the continuance is required. State v. Harr (Medina 1992) 81 Ohio App.3d 244, 610 N.E.2d 1049.

A trial court's journal entry for a sua sponte continuance in a case where the charge is driving under a suspended license meets the requirements of RC 2945.72(H) where the journal entry was timely, the case was reset to the next available open jury date, the delay was not charged to the defendant, and the reason given which necessitated the continuance was that another case proceeded to jury trial on the date the case was originally scheduled; it was not unreasonable for the court to reset to the next available open jury date as the court cannot be expected to anticipate possible earlier dates which occur due to subsequent docket changes. State v. Harr (Medina 1992) 81 Ohio App.3d 244, 610 N.E.2d 1049.

Failure to journalize the reason for a continuance necessitated by a conflict in the prosecutor's schedule does not extend the speedy trial limit. State v. Miller (Highland 1990) 70 Ohio App.3d 727, 591 N.E.2d 1355.

A defendant's conviction and sentence for DUI is reversed where the trial court grants a continuance on its own motion pursuant to RC 2945.72(H), but fails to make a journal entry concerning the continuance order and the reasons for it before the expiration of the statutorily prescribed time within which the defendant could be brought to trial. State v. Orrill (Clark 1990) 66 Ohio App.3d 259, 583 N.E.2d 1116.

Unjournalized continuances do not extend the time for speedy trial. State v. Benson (Cuyahoga 1985) 29 Ohio App.3d 321, 505 N.E.2d 987, 29 O.B.R. 448.

Where a trial court grants a continuance before trial, the court, through its journal entry (1) must record the continuance, (2) must identify the party chargeable with the continuance, (3) must briefly indicate the reasons for granting the continuance, and (4) must indicate whether the court is acting sua sponte, and the reasons for such action; any period elapsed during which such record is not kept will be charged against the state in computing time under RC 2945.71 et seq. State v. Geraldo (Lucas 1983) 13 Ohio App.3d 27, 468 N.E.2d 328, 13 O.B.R. 29.

When sua sponte granting a continuance under RC 2945.72(H), the trial court must enter the order of continuance and the reasons therefor by journal entry prior to the expiration of the time limit prescribed in RC 2945.71 for bringing a defendant to trial. State v. Mincy (Ohio 1982) 2 Ohio St.3d 6, 441 N.E.2d 571, 2 O.B.R. 282. Criminal Law ⚷ 577.13; Criminal Law ⚷ 1166(7)

Court could not sua sponte continue trial date beyond period prescribed in RC 2945.71(C)(2) on ground of inclement weather where such action was taken after expiration of the period. State v. Montgomery (Ohio 1980) 61 Ohio St.2d 78, 399 N.E.2d 552, 15 O.O.3d 119.

RC 2945.72(H) does not give the trial court blanket discretion to extend the time in which an accused must be brought to trial, but rather provides for an extension of the time for trial during the period of any continuance granted on the accused's own motion and during the period of any reasonable continuance granted on other than the accused's motion, and before this provision is applicable, the court by journal entry must have granted such continuance prior to the expiration of the statutory time limitations for trial. State v. Eberhardt (Cuyahoga 1978) 56 Ohio App.2d 193, 381 N.E.2d 1357, 10 O.O.3d 197. Criminal Law ⚷ 577.13

The granting of a sua sponte continuance may not be implied from the fact that the trial court originally set an accused's trial for a date beyond that permitted by RC 2945.71, and where the court's journal does not reflect that a continuance has been granted on or before the last day for trial permitted by RC 2945.71, the state may not rely upon RC 2945.72(H) to justify a delay in bringing the accused to trial. Village of Oakwood v. Ferrante (Cuyahoga 1975) 44 Ohio App.2d 318, 338 N.E.2d 767, 73 O.O.2d 374.

A defendant is denied a speedy trial where: (1) a motion by the defendant is denied on a hearing held on the final day on which trial would be timely; (2) a trial date is set for the first time on the last day on which trial would be timely; and (3) there is no journal entry indicating that motions by the accused necessitated the delay. State v Marshall, No. 3–83–13 (3d Dist Ct App, Crawford, 4–11–84).

A trial court may not wait until after the expiration of the statutory time within which a trial must be commenced to file journal entries which purport to toll the statutory time. State v Burks, No. 55271 (8th Dist Ct App, Cuyahoga, 5–4–89).

19. —— Reasonable continuances, motions of court or prosecutor

Continuances of trial date which were granted at State's request in prosecution for operating a motor vehicle under the influence and failing to maintain reasonable control of a motor vehicle were reasonable and necessary, and thus running of the 90-day speedy trial period following defendant's arrest within which State was required to bring defendant to trial was tolled during such continuances; first continuance was due to a sudden death in prosecutor's family, and second was due to the arresting police officer being on vacation and unable to testify on the rescheduled trial date. State v. Williamson (Ohio App. 5 Dist., Licking, 11-18-2005) No. 2005 CA 00046, 2005-Ohio-6198, 2005 WL 3112873, Unreported. Criminal Law ⚷ 577.13

Trial court did not abuse its discretion in prosecution for operating a motor vehicle under the influence and failing to maintain reasonable control of a motor vehicle by granting State an ex parte continuance of the trial date due to the arresting police officer being on vacation and unavailable to testify. State v. Williamson (Ohio App. 5 Dist., Licking, 11-18-2005) No. 2005 CA 00046, 2005-Ohio-6198, 2005 WL 3112873, Unreported. Criminal Law ⚷ 594(1)

Speedy trial time resumed its countdown, following defendant's motion to determine competency in prosecution for assault on a peace officer, on the date the trial court found him competent to stand trial. State v. Campbell (Ohio App. 11 Dist., Ashtabula, 06-17-2005) No. 2003-A-0056, 2005-Ohio-3091, 2005 WL 1423499, Unreported, appeal not allowed 107 Ohio St.3d 1410, 836 N.E.2d 1229, 2005-Ohio-5859. Criminal Law ⚷ 577.11(6)

Defendant's statutory right to a speedy trial was not violated, even though she was not brought to trial within 180 days after she caused delivery of written notice of the place of her imprisonment and a request for a final disposition; time was tolled while defendant was incarcerated as a result of other criminal charges, and the State exercised reasonable diligence in attempting to secure her attendance in the case. State v. Ray (Ohio App. 2 Dist., Greene, 05-27-2005) No. 2004-CA-64, 2005-Ohio-2771, 2005 WL 1322723, Unreported. Criminal Law ⚷ 577.11(3)

Continuance of trial on State's request, due to DNA testing and the unavailability of a complaining witness due to pregnancy complications, were not attributable to the State for purposes of speedy trial, given that reasons for continuance were reasonable in light of necessity. State v. Hess (Ohio App. 5 Dist., Stark, 12-13-2004) No. 2003CA00348, 2004-Ohio-6820, 2004 WL 2913569, Unreported. Criminal Law ⚷ 594(1)

Trial court did not violate defendant's statutory right to a speedy trial when it allowed his trial counsel to withdraw just prior to trial and then continued the matter so that defendant could acquire new counsel; defendant agreed that he wanted to have counsel represent him at trial. State v. Mustard (Ohio App. 4 Dist., Pike, 09-14-2004) No. 04CA724, 2004-Ohio-4917, 2004 WL 2072454, Unreported, appeal not allowed 105 Ohio St.3d 1438, 822 N.E.2d 810, 2005-Ohio-531, habeas corpus dismissed 2006 WL 783452. Criminal Law ⚷ 577.10(8)

Trial court's sua sponte continuance was reasonable and, thus, tolled defendant's speedy trial date for first-degree misdemeanor operating motor vehicle under the influence (OMVI); trial court continued trial due to scheduling conflicts within trial court's docket for previously scheduled trial date, trial court noted difficulty of impaneling jury on previously scheduled trial date because of lack of potential jurors due to approaching holidays and to illness, and trial court continued trial to earliest possible date within trial court's docket. State v. Glass (Ohio App. 3 Dist., Auglaize, 08-23-2004) No. 2-04-01, 2004-Ohio-4402, 2004 WL 1874574, Unreported, appeal not allowed 104 Ohio St.3d 1460, 821 N.E.2d 577, 2005-Ohio-204. Criminal Law ⚷ 577.10(7)

Granting state continuance due to absence of victim was not abuse of discretion in prosecution for felonious assault with peace officer specification; although defendant argued continuance was inconvenient, continuance was only for one week and reason for continuance was legitimate. State v. Chandler (Ohio App. 8 Dist., Cuyahoga, 11-13-2003) No. 81817, 2003-Ohio-6037, 2003 WL 22671580, Unreported. Criminal Law ⚷ 594(1); Criminal Law ⚷ 613

Time between defendant's arrest and date when trial was supposed to have begun, in order to comport with speedy trial requirements, was tolled by state's motion for continuance, which was reasonable, and by defendant's motion to dismiss indictment or to suppress results of traffic stop. State v. Cano (Ohio App. 10 Dist., Franklin, 09-18-2003) No. 03AP-58, 2003-Ohio-4957, 2003 WL 22149336, Unreported. Criminal Law ⚷ 577.10(3); Criminal Law ⚷ 577.10(8)

Defendant's speedy trial rights, on charges of aiding and abetting aggravated robbery and aiding and abetting murder, were not violated; a properly granted continuance to conduct DNA testing extended the time for bringing defendant to trial, as the testing was critical to determining whether to exonerate defendant and the delay was not unduly lengthy. State v. Terrell (Ohio App. 1 Dist., Hamilton, 06-13-2003) No. C-020194, 2003-Ohio-3044, 2003 WL 21360278, Unreported, motion for delayed appeal denied 100 Ohio St.3d 1530, 800 N.E.2d 47, 2003-Ohio-6458. Criminal Law ⚷ 577.10(2)

Defendant's right to speedy trial on charges of rape and improper discharge of firearm at, or into, habitation, was not violated under statute that required trial within 90 days of arrest, where computation of time established that total of only 83 days of speedy trial period had run against state; time for speedy trial purposes was tolled from time defendant executed waiver of right to speedy trial until he withdrew waiver, time was tolled when defendant filed motions to dismiss, trial court took reasonable amount of time to decide motions, and trial court granted state reasonable continuance of five days for purposes of motion to suppress hearing. State v. Boles (Ohio App. 2 Dist., Montgomery, 05-23-2003) No. 18762, 2003-Ohio-2693, 2003 WL 21213383, Unreported, appeal not allowed 100 Ohio St.3d 1411, 796 N.E.2d 538, 2003-Ohio-4948. Criminal Law ⚷ 577.10(7); Criminal Law ⚷ 577.10(8)

Continuance granted to state tolled speedy-trial time in prosecution for rape, kidnapping, and felonious assault, since absence of one of state's key witnesses and lack of completion of DNA testing provided reasonable grounds for granting of continuance. State v. Barnett (Ohio App. 12 Dist., Fayette, 04-21-2003) No. CA2002-06-011, 2003-Ohio-2014, 2003 WL 1906768, Unreported, appeal not allowed 99 Ohio St.3d 1544, 795 N.E.2d 682, 2003-Ohio-4671. Criminal Law ⚷ 577.13

Trial court's sua sponte continuance of trial to a date four days beyond statutory speedy trial time period was reasonable; date in question was earliest date on which defense counsel, prosecuting attorney, and court were available, an entry providing reasons for continuance was issued before expiration of speed trial time period, and defendant failed to demonstrate any prejudice resulting from continuance. State v. Curtis (Ohio App. 3 Dist., Marion, 10-08-2002) No. 9-02-11, 2002-Ohio-5409, 2002 WL 31250286, Unreported, appeal not allowed 98 Ohio St.3d 1478, 784 N.E.2d 711, 2003-Ohio-974. Criminal Law ⚷ 577.10(7); Criminal Law ⚷ 577.16(4)

Prosecution's request for continuance following unexpected delay in DNA testing of hair sample and failure of defense to respond to discovery requests was not unreasonable and could not be charged against the state, for speedy trial purposes. State v. Myers (Ohio, 12-13-2002) 97 Ohio St.3d 335, 780 N.E.2d 186, 2002-Ohio-6658, reconsideration denied 97 Ohio St.3d 1500, 780 N.E.2d 1023, 2002-Ohio-7367, certiorari denied 123 S.Ct. 2254, 539 U.S. 906, 156 L.Ed.2d 116, motion to reopen denied 100 Ohio St.3d 1505, 799 N.E.2d 184, 2003-Ohio-6161. Criminal Law ⚷ 577.10(4)

Prosecution's request for continuance to permit expert with immovable 12–week backlog of cases to test foreign hair found on murder victim's body was not unreasonable and could not be charged against the state, for speedy trial purposes. State v. Myers (Ohio, 12-13-2002) 97 Ohio St.3d 335, 780 N.E.2d 186, 2002-Ohio-6658, reconsideration denied 97 Ohio St.3d 1500, 780 N.E.2d 1023, 2002-Ohio-7367, certiorari denied 123 S.Ct. 2254, 539 U.S. 906, 156 L.Ed.2d 116, motion to reopen denied 100 Ohio St.3d 1505, 799 N.E.2d 184, 2003-Ohio-6161. Criminal Law ⚷ 577.10(6)

Trial court's continuance of domestic violence trial, due to former wife's failure to appear, was reasonable, and thus did not violate defendant's right to a speedy trial; former wife was the main witness against defendant, wife had been properly subpoenaed, and prosecutor used due diligence to attempt to secure her presence. State v. Adkins (Ohio App. 12 Dist., 07-16-2001) 144 Ohio App.3d 633, 761 N.E.2d 94. Criminal Law ⚷ 577.13

Continuance that was granted in rape prosecution to allow performance of DNA testing was both a reasonable and proper exercise of the court's own initiative, especially since results could have been either inculpatory or exculpatory for defendant, and was thus excludable from statutory speedy trial period. State v. Austin (Ohio App. 1 Dist., 05-15-1998) 131 Ohio App.3d 329, 722 N.E.2d 555, dismissed, appeal not allowed 83 Ohio St.3d 1431, 699 N.E.2d 946. Criminal Law ⚷ 577.13

Speedy trial period was tolled during period in which case was continued at state's request due to unavailability of one of its major witnesses, who was incarcerated in another state immediately before trial was scheduled; continuance was reasonable, and record indicated that defendant and his agents were responsible for witness' incarceration. State v. Hirsch (Ohio App. 1 Dist., 08-07-1998) 129 Ohio App.3d 294, 717 N.E.2d 789, dismissed, appeal not allowed 84 Ohio St.3d 1436, 702 N.E.2d 1213, denial of habeas corpus affirmed 74 Fed.Appx. 486, 2003 WL 21949184. Criminal Law ⚷ 577.10(8)

For continuance granted to State, or ordered sua sponte by trial court, to be deemed as "reasonable," so that resulting delay will not be charged against State for purposes of speedy trial statute, court must journalize continuance before expiration of time limit set forth in statute and must state the reason for continuance. State v. Stamps (Ohio App. 1 Dist., 04-03-1998) 127 Ohio App.3d 219, 712 N.E.2d 762. Criminal Law ⚷ 577.10(7); Criminal Law ⚷ 577.12(1)

Continuance entered sua sponte by trial court due to congested trial docket was reasonable and, thus, extended time within which defendant had to be brought to trial pursuant to speedy trial statute. State v. Webb (Ohio App. 5 Dist., 03-25-1998) 126 Ohio App.3d 808, 711 N.E.2d 711. Criminal Law ⚷ 577.10(4); Criminal Law ⚷ 603.1

Continuance entered sua sponte by trial judge due to fact he was assigned by Supreme Court to preside over another case was reasonable and, thus, extended time within which defendant had to be brought to trial pursuant to speedy trial statute, though case over which trial judge was appointed to preside did not ultimately proceed to jury trial; record did not reflect that trial judge was aware that case was not going to proceed to trial at time the entry continuing defendant's case was filed. State v. Webb (Ohio App. 5 Dist., 03-25-1998) 126 Ohio App.3d 808, 711 N.E.2d 711. Criminal Law ⚷ 577.10(4); Criminal Law ⚷ 603.1

Court's continuance of defendant's burglary trial for 35 days so it could proceed with unrelated aggravated murder trial was reasonable, and thus tolled time within which defendant had to be brought to trial under speedy-trial statute. State v. Jones (Ohio App. 11 Dist., 04-04-1997) 119 Ohio App.3d 59, 694 N.E.2d 505. Criminal Law ⚷ 577.10(7)

Trial court's sua sponte continuance, beyond statutory 30–day speedy trial limit, of defendant's trial on minor misdemeanor charge of disobeying signal device giving warning of approach of train was reasonable; defendant was in court on original trial date on two unrelated matters, first trial was completed after close of business, trial court was unable to get to second case until 4:55 p.m. on Friday and therefore continued second case, and defendant demonstrated no prejudice resulting from continuance. State v. King (Ohio App. 9 Dist., 10-23-1996) 114 Ohio App.3d 669, 683 N.E.2d 870. Criminal Law ⚷ 577.13

Delay of 109 days following state's second motion for continuance in trial date due to unavailability of arresting officer did not extend time for trial, for purposes of determining whether speedy trial statute was satisfied where, although officer's vacation constituted basis for reasonable continuance, there was no indication why trial could not be scheduled within statutory speedy trial limit of 90 days. State v. Wirtanen (Ohio App. 6 Dist., 04-26-1996) 110 Ohio App.3d 604, 674 N.E.2d 1245. Criminal Law ⚷ 577.10(7); Criminal Law ⚷ 577.11(1)

Reasonableness of continuance depends upon facts and circumstances of case; however, in determining reasonableness, statute permitting reasonable continuances must not be interpreted too broadly as to render speedy-trial statutes meaningless. State v. Daugherty (Ohio App. 3 Dist., 03-28-1996) 110 Ohio App.3d 103, 673 N.E.2d 664. Criminal Law ⚷ 577.13

Upon granting continuance, it is not per se unreasonable extension of time to schedule trial on "next available date" or to extend time for trial a specific number of days past statutory speedy trial limitation. State v. Daugherty (Ohio App. 3 Dist., 03-28-1996) 110 Ohio App.3d 103, 673 N.E.2d 664. Criminal Law ⚷ 577.13

Trial court's sua sponte continuance due to trial judge's appearance as witness in another proceeding tolled speedy trial statute; defendant did not object to continuance, and four-day delay was not unreasonable. State v. Baker (Ohio App. 8 Dist., 12-20-1993) 92 Ohio App.3d 516, 636 N.E.2d 363. Criminal Law ⚷ 577.10(4)

For speedy trial purposes, trial court may extend time for trial as long as continuance is reasonable. State v. Collins (Ohio App. 6 Dist., 09-30-1993) 91 Ohio App.3d 10, 631 N.E.2d 666, dismissed, jurisdictional motion overruled 68 Ohio St.3d 1470, 628 N.E.2d 1389. Criminal Law ⚷ 577.13

A trial court's sua sponte continuance of a trial on a charge of driving under a suspended license to a date which exceeds the limit permitted under the speedy trial statute is permissible if the court can show the need for a continuance and its reasonableness. State v. Harr (Medina 1992) 81 Ohio App.3d 244, 610 N.E.2d 1049.

If a continuance is granted upon a motion by the accused so that the defense counsel can complete discovery, there is no requirement that the extension be reasonable as it would for a sua sponte one week continuance granted due to the judge's illness, which would meet the requirement under RC 2925.72(H) that the purpose and duration of the continuance be reasonable. State v. Rockwell (Franklin 1992) 80 Ohio App.3d 157, 608 N.E.2d 1118, dismissed, jurisdictional motion overruled 65 Ohio St.3d 1440, 600 N.E.2d 683.

A continuance granted by a trial court is both necessary and reasonable to protect a defendant's due process rights where the defendant decides to represent herself only shortly before the preliminary hearing, the discovery process was not completed until the day of the preliminary hearing, and the case was such that even a qualified attorney would have faced serious difficulties in attempting to prepare a defense in three days; therefore, the running of the ninety-day time limit for bringing the defendant to trial on misdemeanor charges is tolled during the period of the continuance. State v. Doane (Trumbull 1990) 69 Ohio App.3d 638, 591 N.E.2d 735, dismissed, jurisdictional motion overruled 58 Ohio St.3d 701, 569 N.E.2d 504. Criminal Law ⚷ 577.10(8)

A continuance granted to the state based on the fact that the arresting officer would be on vacation at the time of the originally scheduled trial date is reasonable and extends the time for bringing an accused to trial. State v. Saffell (Ohio 1988) 35 Ohio St.3d 90, 518 N.E.2d 934.

An extension of eleven days beyond the statutory speedy trial period was reasonable under RC 2945.72 where there was a clear indication on the record that the trial court was engaged in the trial of another case, and therefore could not begin defendant's trial within the required time. State v. Hudson (Cuyahoga 1983) 10 Ohio App.3d 52, 460 N.E.2d 668, 10 O.B.R. 62.

Where the trial court makes a proper journal entry within the time allowed for trial by statutory speedy trial limits, those limits are extended by (1) the period of a reasonable continuance granted to the state because of the temporary absence of a critical witness reported by the prosecutor in good faith, (2) the reasonable period necessary to determine defendant's mental competence to stand trial after that issue has been raised by the court or counsel, (3) the reasonable period necessary to rule on defendant's motion to transfer the defendant from jail for medical or psychiatric treatment, and (4) the reasonable period necessary to rule on defendant's motion to discharge him for failure to begin the trial within statutory speedy trial limits. State v. Smith (Cuyahoga 1981) 3 Ohio App.3d 115, 444 N.E.2d 85, 3 O.B.R. 130. Criminal Law ⚷ 577.10(6); Criminal Law ⚷ 577.10(8); Criminal Law ⚷ 577.11(6)

Where a trial was set for the ninetieth day after the arrest and then continued because such day was a holiday until the ninety-ninth day, such extension was not unreasonable. City of Aurora v. Patrick (Ohio 1980) 61 Ohio St.2d 107, 399 N.E.2d 1220, 15 O.O.3d 150.

Where a jury is unable to reach a verdict in a criminal action and is discharged, the re-scheduling of the case for another trial constitutes a reasonable continuance within the meaning of RC 2945.72. State v. Johnson (Franklin 1977) 52 Ohio App.2d 406, 370 N.E.2d 785, 6 O.O.3d 444.

Where a court, pursuant to RC 2945.72(H), continues the date of trial of a criminal case by entry made prior to the expiration of the time limit derived from RC 2945.71 to a date two days in excess of that time limit, gives as the reason therefor "crowded docket & judge's conference," and notifies the defendant and his counsel of the court's action, entry and reasons, the reasonableness of the extension is satisfactorily evidenced by the failure of the defendant to object and to assert persuasively his basis for a contrary conclusion. State v. Lee (Ohio 1976) 48 Ohio St.2d 208, 357 N.E.2d 1095, 2 O.O.3d 392.

An agreement between defense counsel, the prosecutor and an officer of the court made at a pre-trial hearing (held within sixty days after arrest) to set the trial date beyond ninety days after defendant's arrest is valid and binding upon the defendant, and is a continuance pursuant to RC 2945.72(H) which will bar defendant's discharge. State v. Taylor (Lorain 1975) 47 Ohio App.2d 171, 352 N.E.2d 604, 1 O.O.3d 259. Criminal Law ⚷ 577.10(9)

A trial court has discretion to extend the time limit set out in RC 2945.71(B)(2), where counsel for the accused voluntarily agrees to a trial date ninety days beyond the date of arrest. State v. Davis (Hamilton 1975) 44 Ohio App.2d 95, 335 N.E.2d 874, 73 O.O.2d 89.

DUI defendant's statutory right to speedy trial was not violated by fact that 186 days passed from arrest to trial; continuances were granted due to crowded court docket and defendant's motions to suppress. State v. Webb (Ohio App. 4 Dist., Washington, 07-12-2002) No. 01CA32, 2002-Ohio-3552, 2002 WL 1565686, Unreported. Criminal Law ⚷ 577.10(7); Criminal Law ⚷ 577.10(8)

Trial court's order rescheduling defendant's trial on minor misdemeanor charge eighteen days following the expiration of the speedy trial time limit due to a pending jury trial was not unreasonable, and thus speedy trial statute was tolled during period of continuance. State v. Berner (Ohio App. 9 Dist., Medina, 06-19-2002) No. 3275-M, 2002-Ohio-3024, 2002 WL 1363686, Unreported. Criminal Law ⚷ 577.10(7)

For purposes of tolling speedy trial statute, reasonableness of continuance requested by the state on basis that necessary witness was unavailable for trial was satisfactorily evidenced by defendant's failure to object when the continuance was granted. State v. Berner (Ohio App. 9 Dist., Medina, 06-19-2002) No. 3275-M, 2002-Ohio-3024, 2002 WL 1363686, Unreported. Criminal Law ⚷ 577.10(6)

Where a case is set for trial only two days following pretrial, and a defendant is unable to subpoena a necessary witness within the two-day period prior to trial because of the sporadic nature of the witness' work hours, the denial of a continuance requested by the defense in order to secure the appearance of the witness constitutes an abuse of discretion. State v Mularkey, Nos. 90AP–1377 and 90AP–1378 (10th Dist Ct App, Franklin, 5–30–91).

Pursuant to RC 2745.72, a trial court has discretion to extend the time limits for purposes of the speedy trial statute where a necessary witness is not available on the originally scheduled trial date. State v Menke, No. 10735 (2d Dist Ct App, Montgomery, 5–18–88).

A sua sponte continuance of a drunk-driving prosecution by a trial court due to docket congestion to a date seven days beyond the trial date prescribed by RC 2945.71(B)(2) is a reasonable extension of time under RC 2945.72(H) and does not deny the defendant his right to a speedy trial. State v Richardson, No. CA86–07–108 (12th Dist Ct App, Butler, 2–17–87).

While the provisions of RC 2945.71, with respect to the periods of time within which trials in criminal cases must be held, apply to violations of traffic laws, the judge presiding over such cases may, however, pursuant to RC 2945.72, grant a continuance which extends the period upon a reasonable showing that there is insufficient time in which to try the case. OAG 74–062.

20. —— Unreasonable continuances, motions of court or prosecutor

Trial court's 311-day delay in ruling on defendant's motion to suppress evidence was unreasonable and thus that period of unreasonable and unnecessary delay did not toll the running of the 90-day statutory speedy trial period; 120 days would have been a reasonable amount of time within which to rule on defendant's motion. State v. Fields (Ohio App. 5 Dist., Guernsey, 01-20-2006) No. 05-CA-17, 2006-Ohio-223, 2006 WL 163563, Unreported. Criminal Law ⚷ 577.10(7); Criminal Law ⚷ 577.15(1)

Extension of trial due to absence of prosecution witness was unreasonable, and thus, speedy trial rights of motorist charged with speeding were violated, requiring discharge of motorist; due to absence of state's witness (highway patrol trooper), trial court granted continuance, and earliest available date for rescheduled trial was 30 plus days after initial 30–day speedy trial period. State v. Daugherty (Ohio App. 3 Dist., 03-28-1996) 110 Ohio App.3d 103, 673 N.E.2d 664. Criminal Law ⚷ 577.13; Criminal Law ⚷ 577.15(4); Criminal Law ⚷ 577.16(2)

A sua sponte continuance based on docket congestion will not be found reasonable absent a showing that the continued criminal case will take precedence over pending civil matters. State v. Terra (Franklin 1991) 74 Ohio App.3d 189, 598 N.E.2d 753, dismissed, jurisdictional motion overruled 62 Ohio St.3d 1452, 579 N.E.2d 1391.

Indefinite term waivers of defendants' speedy trial rights which are given at the request of the trial court to permit the court to assess recent Ohio Supreme Court decisions are express waivers of limited and reasonable duration; thus, where the waivers are obtained with less than thirty days remaining on the defendants' speedy trial period, a delay of over two years during which the defendants are still not called or scheduled for trial is unreasonable and violates the defendants' speedy trial rights warranting dismissal of pending criminal charges. State v. Scolaro (Tuscarawas 1992) 73 Ohio App.3d 555, 597 N.E.2d 1184, dismissed, jurisdictional motion overruled 64 Ohio St.3d 1429, 594 N.E.2d 970.

On the evidence, it was unreasonable for the trial court to have extended accused's date of trial four days beyond the statutory time limit. State v. Reeser (Ohio 1980) 63 Ohio St.2d 189, 407 N.E.2d 25, 17 O.O.3d 117.

The fact that a comparatively large number of witnesses was expected to be called to testify at trial does not indicate such an exceptional circumstance as to justify the postponement of the trial date approximately four months beyond the prescribed time period. Village of Elmwood Place v. Denike (Ohio 1978) 56 Ohio St.2d 427, 384 N.E.2d 707, 10 O.O.3d 528. Criminal Law ⚷ 577.13

A standardized entry form completed by the trial court indicating a crowded court docket is alone insufficient to support a sua sponte continuance order substantially extending the date of trial beyond the mandatory time limitations of RC 2945.71(B)(2). Village of Elmwood Place v. Denike (Ohio 1978) 56 Ohio St.2d 427, 384 N.E.2d 707, 10 O.O.3d 528.

An order, although entered within the ninety-day time period prescribed for trial by RC 2945.71(B)(2), continuing a case for trial to a date more than double such ninety-day period and stating the continuance was necessary for the reason of a crowded docket, without further explication of such reason appearing in the record, is insufficient to extend the RC 2945.71(B)(2) time limitation for trial as a "reasonable continuance granted other than upon the accused's own motion" pursuant to RC 2945.72(H). State v. Wentworth (Ohio 1978) 54 Ohio St.2d 171, 375 N.E.2d 424, 8 O.O.3d 162.

Appellant tried ninety-three days after arrest was entitled to discharge. State v. Tope (Ohio 1978) 53 Ohio St.2d 250, 374 N.E.2d 152, 7 O.O.3d 408.

Trial court's action in twice setting case for trial past statutory time limit due to "judge's schedule," without further explanation, did not constitute "reasonable continuance" pursuant to statutory provision tolling statute of limitations in prosecution for failure to correct a nuisance. City of Toledo v. Pack (Ohio App. 6 Dist., Lucas, 03-29-2002) No. L-01-1019, 2002-Ohio-1517, 2002 WL 471743, Unreported. Criminal Law ⚷ 577.13

Where an almost three-month delay in obtaining an indictment results in a trial date being set with only five days' notice, and where defense counsel is unavailable on the day of trial, leaving a defendant with an unprepared stand-in appointed counsel, a sua sponte continuance for purposes of ensuring that the defendant receives a fair trial is not reasonable absent an explanation for the substantial lapse of time between the arrest and indictment. State v Jordan, No. 90AP–660 (10th Dist Ct App, Franklin, 2–21–91).

Where a court sua sponte orders a continuance for which there are no reasonable grounds the speedy trial period will not be tolled. State v Breedlove, No. C–880175 (1st Dist Ct App, Hamilton, 4–12–89).

A defendant is denied a speedy trial where: (1) a motion by the defendant is denied on a hearing held on the final day on which trial would be timely; (2) a trial date is set for the first time on the last day on which trial would be timely; and (3) there is no journal entry indicating that motions by the accused necessitated the delay. State v Marshall, No. 3–83–13 (3d Dist Ct App, Crawford, 4–11–84).

Where the accused was tried ninety-three days after his arrest and was being held solely upon the pending charge, that a parole violation holder was filed against the defendant based on the same charges will not be considered an exception to the ninety day rule. State v Sisco, No. 2–CA–82 (5th Dist Ct App, Fairfield, 6–28–82).

21. Proceedings instituted by accused

Delay of approximately five months from date of defendant's arrest until date trial court found him guilty of operating a vehicle under the influence of alcohol or drugs (OVI), pursuant to no contest plea, did not violate his statutory speedy trial rights; defendant's desire to retain private counsel and have his public defender withdraw necessitated a period of delay. State v. Madden (Ohio App. 10 Dist., Franklin, 08-18-2005) No. 04AP-1228, 2005-Ohio-4281, 2005 WL 1983376, Unreported, appeal not allowed 108 Ohio St.3d 1415, 841 N.E.2d 319, 2006-Ohio-179. Criminal Law ⚷ 577.10(8); Criminal Law ⚷ 577.15(3)

Holding of *State v. Brown*, that requests for discovery toll running of speedy trial clock, applied to defendant's case, though *Brown* was decided after defendant's motion for discovery was filed, as appellate court had applied tolling rule of *Brown* to requests for discovery and bills of particulars that had been filed before *Brown* was decided. State v. Brown (Ohio App. 7 Dist., Mahoning, 06-07-2005) No. 03-MA-32, 2005-Ohio-2939, 2005 WL 1385715, Unreported, appeal not allowed 106 Ohio St.3d 1558, 836 N.E.2d 582, 2005-Ohio-5531. Courts ⚷ 100(1)

Statutory speedy trial period was tolled, in prosecution for grand theft of a motor vehicle, aggravated robbery, having weapon while under disability, carrying concealed weapon, and failure to comply with signal of police officer, during pendency of defendant's numerous pre-trial motions. State v. Smith (Ohio App. 2 Dist., Clark, 11-12-2004) No. 2003 CA 93, 2004-Ohio-6062, 2004 WL 2588269, Unreported, motion for delayed appeal denied 105 Ohio St.3d 1450, 823 N.E.2d 455, 2005-Ohio-763, motion for delayed appeal denied 105 Ohio St.3d 1496, 825 N.E.2d 621, 2005-Ohio-1666. Criminal Law ⚷ 577.10(8)

Statutory 180-day period under speedy trial statute was tolled as result of conduct attributable to defendant, and thus defendant's right to speedy trial on charges of breaking and entering, and receiving stolen property, was not violated; defendant filed motion for evidentiary hearing which tolled statutory period for 22 days, defendant filed request for counsel, which resulted in tolling of period for 16 days until counsel was appointed, and defendant filed motion to dismiss which tolled period for 45 days until trial court ruled on motion and dismissed indictment. State v. Roberts (Ohio App. 6 Dist., Wood, 10-15-2004) No. WD-04-028, 2004-Ohio-5509, 2004 WL 2320338, Unreported. Criminal Law ⚷ 577.10(8)

Trial delay attributable to defendant's motion to suppress evidence was not counted against the State for purposes of defendant's statutory speedy trial rights. State v. Williams (Ohio App. 2 Dist., Montgomery, 09-30-2004) No. 20104, 2004-Ohio-5273, 2004 WL 2245101, Unreported. Criminal Law ⚷ 577.10(8)

Time spent resolving defendant's motion for bill of particulars, motion for discovery, motion for transcript, and motion to dismiss for speedy trial violation was chargeable to defendant in determining whether his statutory 270-day speedy trial time period was violated. State v. Murray (Ohio App. 9 Dist., Lorain, 09-22-2004) No. 03CA008330, 2004-Ohio-4966, 2004 WL 2244444, Unreported. Criminal Law ⚷ 577.10(8)

Defendant's right to trial within 30 days on citation issued against him for speeding and failing to maintain an assured clear distance ahead (ACDA) was not violated, even though defendant's trial occurred more than 30 days after citation was issued, as defendant's motions for dismissal and discovery tolled running of speedy trial period. State v. Wiest (Ohio App. 1 Dist., Hamilton, 05-21-2004) No. C-030674, 2004-Ohio-2577, 2004 WL 1124594, Unreported. Criminal Law ⚷ 577.10(8)

Defendant was not denied statutory right to speedy trial in prosecution for aggravated robbery; defendant was not entitled to triple count provision for several of the days he was held in jail in lieu of bail, since for part of the time a parole hold was placed on him and he was therefore held for separate offenses, and defendant then filed several motions which tolled the statutory speedy trial period, including motions requesting discovery, bill of particulars, preliminary hearing, withdrawal of previous not guilty plea, treatment in lieu of conviction, multiple continuances, dismissal based on speedy trial violations, and proceedings related to his insanity plea. State v. Turner (Ohio App. 7 Dist., Mahoning, 03-19-2004) No. 93 CA 91, 2004-Ohio-1545, 2004 WL 614808, Unreported, habeas corpus granted 401 F.3d 718. Criminal Law ⚷ 577.10(8); Criminal Law ⚷ 577.11(1)

For speedy trial purposes, delay caused by defendant's failure to respond to State's request for discovery was properly charged to defendant. State v. Borrero (Ohio App. 8 Dist., Cuyahoga, 02-19-2004) No. 82595, 2004-Ohio-739, 2004 WL 308138, Unreported, superseded 2004-Ohio-4488, 2004 WL 1902530. Criminal Law ⚷ 577.10(8)

Defendant was not entitled to motion to dismiss based on State's failure to bring defendant to trial within statutorily prescribed time limit; defendant's filing motion for bill of particulars tolled speedy trial time, State's delay in complying with bill of particulars was reasonable, and on day trial was to begin, defendant filed a waiver of his right to speedy trial. State v. Gibson (Ohio App. 11 Dist., Trumbull, 10-24-2003) No. 2002-T-0055, 2003-Ohio-5695, 2003 WL 22427821, Unreported. Criminal Law ⚷ 577.10(8); Criminal Law ⚷ 577.10(9)

Time during which discovery motion filed by defendant was pending tolled speedy trial clock, regardless of whether discovery motion caused an actual delay in bringing the defendant to trial. State v. Cook (Ohio App. 5 Dist., Licking, 10-16-2003) No. 03-CA-0019, 2003-Ohio-5589, 2003 WL 22391252, Unreported. Criminal Law ⚷ 577.10(8)

Delay in trial caused by defendant's motion to sever counts against him was attributable to defendant for purposes of speedy trial statute. State v. Garrett (Ohio App. 6 Dist., Erie, 09-30-2003) No. E-02-015, 2003-Ohio-5185, 2003 WL 22233542, Unreported. Criminal Law ⚷ 577.10(8)

Twenty-four day delay in deciding defendant's motion to suppress following a hearing on that motion was reasonable, such that speedy trial clock was tolled during that period, especially in consideration of fact that same court was presiding over a lengthy aggravated murder case contemporaneously with defendant's case. State v. Curtis (Ohio App. 3 Dist., Marion, 10-08-2002) No. 9-02-11, 2002-Ohio-5409, 2002 WL 31250286, Unreported, appeal not allowed 98 Ohio St.3d 1478, 784 N.E.2d 711, 2003-Ohio-974. Criminal Law ⚷ 577.10(7)

Murder defendant's request for continuance, for express purpose of obtaining additional time to prepare for trial, tolled time within which speedy trial statutes required state to bring defendant to trial to new trial date. State v. Kerby (Ohio App. 2 Dist., 07-15-2005) 162 Ohio App.3d 353, 833 N.E.2d 757, 2005-Ohio-3734, appeal not allowed 107 Ohio St.3d 1682, 839 N.E.2d 403, 2005-Ohio-6480. Criminal Law ⚷ 577.10(8)

Murder defendant's demand for discovery tolled or extended speedy trial time from date of filing thereof until state provided requested discovery. State v. Kerby (Ohio App. 2 Dist., 07-15-2005) 162 Ohio App.3d 353, 833 N.E.2d 757, 2005-Ohio-3734, appeal not allowed 107 Ohio St.3d 1682, 839 N.E.2d 403, 2005-Ohio-6480. Criminal Law ⚷ 577.10(8)

The 65 days that elapsed to resolve defendant's motion to suppress statements that she made to authorities were chargeable to defendant, for purposes of determining whether she was deprived of her statutory right to a speedy trial on charge of complicity to commit aggravated murder; period was reasonable, as motion was extremely important in that state would have to decide whether it could proceed if statements were suppressed, and it resulted in a lengthy hearing with complex constitutional considerations. State v. Santini (Ohio App. 7 Dist., 06-27-2001) 144 Ohio App.3d 396, 760 N.E.2d 442, 2001-Ohio-3313, dismissed, appeal not allowed 93 Ohio St.3d 1459, 756 N.E.2d 1236. Criminal Law ⚷ 577.10(8)

The seven days that elapsed to resolve defendant's motion to dismiss were chargeable to defendant, for purposes of determining whether she was deprived of her statutory right to a speedy trial on charge of complicity to commit aggravated murder, as that time was a reasonable and necessary period of delay. State v. Santini (Ohio App. 7 Dist., 06-27-2001) 144 Ohio App.3d 396, 760 N.E.2d 442, 2001-Ohio-3313, dismissed, appeal not allowed 93 Ohio St.3d 1459, 756 N.E.2d 1236. Criminal Law ⚷ 577.10(8)

Statutory speedy trial period was tolled by defendant's request for bill of particulars until state responded to it. State v. Keith (Ohio App. 12 Dist., 11-09-1998) 130 Ohio App.3d 456, 720 N.E.2d 216. Criminal Law ⚷ 577.8(1)

Scheduling of pretrial conference or hearing does not automatically extend speedy trial time requirements; however, where pretrial conference was granted upon defendant's own request and there is nothing facially unreasonable about amount of time taken to permit pretrial and subsequent trial, time is tolled in calculating whether speedy trial requirements were satisfied. State v. Wirtanen (Ohio App. 6 Dist., 04-26-1996) 110 Ohio App.3d 604, 674 N.E.2d 1245. Criminal Law ⚷ 577.10(7); Criminal Law ⚷ 577.10(8)

Scheduling of trial on charge of operating motor vehicle while under influence of alcohol beyond 90–day statutory time period was violation of speedy trial limitation, notwithstanding defendant's motion to suppress in connection with charge of operating motor vehicle with certain concentration of alcohol in urine, which arose from same incident; there was no evidence that state and defendant agreed to try charges together, suppression motion applied only to latter charge, no defense delays tolled time limit, and state did not argue that trial court granted continuance as to charge of operating motor vehicle while under influence of alcohol sua sponte. State v. Jacot (Ohio App. 9 Dist., 04-07-1993) 97 Ohio App.3d 415, 646 N.E.2d 1128, motion allowed 68 Ohio St.3d 1409, 623 N.E.2d 566, appeal dismissed as improvidently allowed 71 Ohio St.3d 1217, 644 N.E.2d 1383. Criminal Law ⚷ 577.10(5)

Trial delay caused by defendant's motion to suppress in second driving under the influence of alcohol (DUI) prosecution, which was identical to defendant's motion to suppress in first DUI prosecution, which was dismissed because of state witness' failure to appear for trial, was chargeable to defendant, for speedy trial purposes; second prosecution was de novo. State v. Wyde (Ohio App. 1 Dist., 09-22-1993) 90 Ohio App.3d 471, 629 N.E.2d 1079, dismissed, jurisdictional motion overruled 68 Ohio St.3d 1445, 626 N.E.2d 687. Criminal Law ⚷ 577.10(8); Criminal Law ⚷ 577.14

Defense counsel's demand for discovery required some continuance of trial and, thus, defendant's speedy trial rights were not violated, even though no entry had been journalized at that time appointing him as counsel; prosecutor, defense counsel and trial court had assumed that defense counsel was attorney of record because he so acted. State v. Roquemore (Franklin 1993) 85 Ohio App.3d 448, 620 N.E.2d 110. Criminal Law ⚷ 577.10(8)

A suppression motion filed by a defendant in a criminal prosecution tolls the speedy trial period only to the extent of the reasonable time necessary for the court to rule on the motion; a seven-month delay between the filing and the disposition of the motion in an OMVI case is unreasonable, and the ninety-day speedy trial period will be deemed lapsed and the defendant will be discharged. State v. Arrizola (Henry 1992) 79 Ohio App.3d 72, 606 N.E.2d 1020.

Even though a plea of no contest in an attempted domestic violence action will not act to toll the speedy trial time limit, since the court must still determine the accused's guilt or innocence within the statutory time limit, the defendant's act of filing a motion to dismiss will act to toll the time until the motion is ruled upon. State v. Mintz (Wood 1991) 74 Ohio App.3d 62, 598 N.E.2d 52, dismissed, jurisdictional motion overruled 62 Ohio St.3d 1431, 578 N.E.2d 823.

For purposes of calculating the speedy trial time requirement applicable to a defendant, the sixteen days that elapsed while the defendant's motions were pending are not included; thus, the defendant was timely brought to trial. State v. Parker (Marion 1991) 72 Ohio App.3d 456, 594 N.E.2d 1033, dismissed, jurisdictional motion overruled 61 Ohio St.3d 1418, 574 N.E.2d 1090.

Period between date state was supposed to file brief in opposition to defendant's suppression motion and date state in fact filed its brief was chargeable to state for speedy trial purposes, where no continuance was on record extending state's deadline. State v. Collura (Cuyahoga 1991) 72 Ohio App.3d 364, 594 N.E.2d 975, dismissed, jurisdictional motion overruled 60 Ohio St.3d 718, 574 N.E.2d 1079. Criminal Law ⚷ 577.12(1)

A court need not journalize the reasons for a continuance prior to expiration of the speedy trial limits of RC 2945.71 where the delay is necessitated by motions of the defendant to review a license suspension and jury trial demand and the defendant is aware of the reasons for the continuance. State v. Sharp (Marion 1991) 71 Ohio App.3d 336, 594 N.E.2d 19.

The appeal of a driver's license suspension imposed pursuant to RC 4511.191(K) must take place in the criminal case arising from the alleged RC 4511.19 violation, not a separate civil action; thus, any delay necessitated by the defendant's request for a hearing on his refusal to submit to an alcohol test must be charged to the defendant requesting the hearing under the provisions of RC 2945.72(E). State v. Sharp (Marion 1991) 71 Ohio App.3d 336, 594 N.E.2d 19.

In a DUI case involving a defendant with a prior DUI and earlier participation in a diversion program, it is error for the trial court to deny the defendant's motion for discharge on speedy trial grounds without making findings of fact on the necessity for the delay even though the delay results from her own motion for consideration for the diversion program in which she is ultimately denied participation because she was in a diversion program the previous year despite no allegations of a prior offense in the form of complaint filed by the arresting officer or on the computer printout of her driving offense record. State v. Long (Miami 1990) 70 Ohio App.3d 810, 592 N.E.2d 877.

A trial date required for speedy trial purposes is to be extended by the nine days it takes between the filing and disposition of a defendant's speedy trial dismissal motion, and an additional one day for each day that the state's appeal from that dismissal order has been pending and remains pending before trial is commenced. State v. Perry (Allen 1990) 67 Ohio App.3d 775, 588 N.E.2d 897. Criminal Law ⚷ 577.13

Motion by defendant to dismiss indictment acts to toll time within which defendant must be brought to trial. State v. Bunyan (Auglaize 1988) 51 Ohio App.3d 190, 555 N.E.2d 980. Criminal Law ⚷ 577.10(8)

When criminal defendant moves for psychiatric examination, running of time limit for trial is tolled when motion is granted, not when it is made; if report of psychiatric examination is not filed when due, time begins to run again, for speedy trial purposes, after due date. State v. Bowman (Clermont 1987) 41 Ohio App.3d 318, 535 N.E.2d 730. Criminal Law ⚷ 577.8(2); Criminal Law ⚷ 577.11(6)

A defendant's request at arraignment for a pretrial conference does not extend the time for trial allowed under RC 2945.71. State v. Reuschling (Ashtabula 1986) 30 Ohio App.3d 81, 506 N.E.2d 558, 30 O.B.R. 138.

Pursuant to RC 2945.72(E), the time for trial is tolled during consideration of the defendant's jury demand. City of University Heights v. Dachman (Cuyahoga 1984) 20 Ohio App.3d 26, 484 N.E.2d 199, 20 O.B.R. 27.

Where a defendant filed more than thirty pretrial motions pro se, and their dispositions or lack of same were insufficiently established, the commencement of trial four days beyond the period provided by RC 2945.71 may be excused either as due to the defendant's own actions or based on the "reasonable continuance" provisions of RC 2945.72(H). State v. Pruitt (Cuyahoga 1984) 18 Ohio App.3d 50, 480 N.E.2d 499, 18 O.B.R. 163.

Defendant, charged with the traffic offense of failure to yield at an intersection while turning left, was not denied a speedy trial by a 23–day period necessitated by his request for a pretrial hearing, which resulted in the extension of his trial date by eight days. State v. Gowe (Medina 1983) 13 Ohio App.3d 358, 469 N.E.2d 909, 13 O.B.R. 439. Criminal Law ⚷ 577.10(8)

When an accused files a motion for discharge for delay of trial, the statutory period within which the accused must be brought to trial is tolled while the court considers the motion, and, although seventy-eight of the ninety days have already expired, it is not unreasonable for the court to take twenty-one days to respond to the motion. State v. Wilson (Fayette 1982) 7 Ohio App.3d 219, 454 N.E.2d 1348, 7 O.B.R. 281.

Where the trial court makes a proper journal entry within the time allowed for trial by statutory speedy trial limits, those limits are extended by (1) the period of a reasonable continuance granted to the state because of the temporary absence of a critical witness reported by the prosecutor in good faith, (2) the reasonable period necessary to determine defendant's mental competence to stand trial after that issue has been raised by the court or counsel, (3) the reasonable period necessary to rule on defendant's motion to transfer the defendant from jail for medical or psychiatric treatment, and (4) the reasonable period necessary to rule on defendant's motion to discharge him for failure to begin the trial within statutory speedy trial limits. State v. Smith (Cuyahoga 1981) 3 Ohio App.3d 115, 444 N.E.2d 85, 3 O.B.R. 130. Criminal Law ⚷

577.10(6); Criminal Law ⚷ 577.10(8); Criminal Law ⚷ 577.11(6)

As the state is obligated to furnish discovery within the statutory speedy trial time period, a motion by a defendant pertaining to discovery does not constitute "action of the accused" within the meaning of RC 2945.72(E) and does not toll the running of the speedy trial time period. State v Cox, No. CA–367 (5th Dist Ct App, Holmes, 4–1–87).

A defendant is denied a speedy trial where: (1) a motion by the defendant is denied on a hearing held on the final day on which trial would be timely; (2) a trial date is set for the first time on the last day on which trial would be timely; and (3) there is no journal entry indicating that motions by the accused necessitated the delay. State v Marshall, No. 3–83–13 (3d Dist Ct App, Crawford, 4–11–84).

22. Neglect or improper acts of accused

Defendant's failure to respond to State's discovery request did not toll period between date State filed its motion for reciprocal discovery and date defendant filed his response, and thus, defendant's statutory right to speedy trial was violated; there was no evidence presented that State was prejudiced in any way, nor did they avail themselves of a motion to compel as facilitated by criminal rules. State v. Palmer (Ohio App. 11 Dist., Portage, 12-16-2005) No. 2004-P-0106, 2005-Ohio-6710, 2005 WL 3476650, Unreported, stay granted 108 Ohio St.3d 1435, 842 N.E.2d 61, 2006-Ohio-421, motion to certify allowed 109 Ohio St.3d 1403, 845 N.E.2d 521, 2006-Ohio-1703, appeal allowed 109 Ohio St.3d 1405, 845 N.E.2d 522, 2006-Ohio-1703. Criminal Law ⚷ 577.10(8)

Statutory speedy trial period began to run, in prosecution for assault on a peace officer, on the date of defendant's re-arrest, where defendant failed to appear at his preliminary hearing. State v. Campbell (Ohio App. 11 Dist., Ashtabula, 06-17-2005) No. 2003-A-0056, 2005-Ohio-3091, 2005 WL 1423499, Unreported, appeal not allowed 107 Ohio St.3d 1410, 836 N.E.2d 1229, 2005-Ohio-5859. Criminal Law ⚷ 577.8(2)

Defendant charged with driving under the influence of alcohol (DUI), a first degree misdemeanor, was brought to trial within 90-day statutory speedy trial period; delay in the case was attributable to defendant, time attributable to the State was 68 days, and defendant was not incarcerated during this time. State v. Snyder (Ohio App. 7 Dist., Belmont, 06-15-2004) No. 03BE15, 2004-Ohio-3200, 2004 WL 1376229, Unreported. Criminal Law ⚷ 577.10(8)

Statutory speedy trial time was tolled with respect to pending forgery charge against defendant until he was released from prison, as defendant failed to meet his initial duty to provide written notice requesting final disposition and to notify state of his whereabouts, under statute governing request by a prisoner for trial on pending charges. (Per Kline, J., with two judges concurring in judgment only.) State v. Roulette (Ohio App. 4 Dist., 10-04-2005) 163 Ohio App.3d 775, 840 N.E.2d 645, 2005-Ohio-5435. Criminal Law ⚷ 577.8(2); Criminal Law ⚷ 577.11(1)

When a defendant who is imprisoned is aware of pending charges against him and fails to file a written notice requesting final disposition and notifying the state of his whereabouts, as permitted by statute governing request by a prisoner for trial on pending charges, the statutory speedy trial time period tolls until his release from prison; while statute governing extension of time for hearing or trial places a duty of reasonable diligence to secure a defendant's availability on the state, that duty is not triggered if the defendant is aware of the pending charges and fails to exercise his duty under statute governing request by a prisoner for trial on pending charges, and the state is not aware of his whereabouts. (Per Kline, J., with two judges concurring in judgment only.) State v. Roulette (Ohio App. 4 Dist., 10-04-2005) 163 Ohio App.3d 775, 840 N.E.2d 645, 2005-Ohio-5435. Criminal Law ⚷ 577.8(2); Criminal Law ⚷ 577.11(1)

Five-day period between when trial court issued bench warrant for defendant's arrest, upon his failure to appear at arraignment, and when trial court cancelled the bench warrant was chargeable to defendant under speedy trial statute. State v. Keith (Ohio App. 12 Dist., 11-09-1998) 130 Ohio App.3d 456, 720 N.E.2d 216. Criminal Law ⚷ 577.10(8)

Seven-day period between date of defendant's originally scheduled arraignment, on which he failed to appear, and date on which he was subsequently ordered to again appear for arraignment was chargeable to defendant under speedy trial statute. State v. Keith (Ohio App. 12 Dist., 11-09-1998) 130 Ohio App.3d 456, 720 N.E.2d 216. Criminal Law ⚷ 577.10(8)

For purposes of determining whether defendant was denied his statutory right to speedy trial, period of 27 days between defendant's filing of motion for leave to file motion to suppress and filing of motion to suppress was attributable to defendant, despite defendant's contention that delay was caused by failure of state to provide timely discovery, where defendant did not serve his request for discovery on the state until 22 days after he had been arraigned at his initial appearance. State v. Stamper (Ohio App. 11 Dist., 04-10-1995) 102 Ohio App.3d 431, 657 N.E.2d 365. Criminal Law ⚷ 577.10(8)

Failure of counsel or defendant to attend a scheduled pretrial conference does not warrant the rescheduling of the pretrial beyond the statutory speedy trial period absent circumstances demonstrating that the failure to appear at the pretrial resulted in delay requiring a trial date beyond the required time. State v. Hengstler (Logan 1991) 75 Ohio App.3d 400, 599 N.E.2d 780, motion overruled 62 Ohio St.3d 1478, 581 N.E.2d 1099.

A defendant is not denied his statutory right to a speedy trial even though he is brought to trial more than 270–days after his initial arrest since only 249 days actually elapsed after permissible extensions of time are considered; the defendant's initial trial date was scheduled within the 270–day time period but was continued on the defendant's own motion and then in order to allow proper trial preparation due to a substitution of defense counsel added to the failure of the defendant to appear for hearings and to stay in contact with his attorney or the court, and the defendant's escape from the jurisdiction, waived his right to a speedy trial until he was subsequently rearrested. State v. Gibson (Logan 1992) 75 Ohio App.3d 388, 599 N.E.2d 438.

On charges of rape and assault, the state's assertion, based on the affidavit of a state's witness, that the defendant suborned perjury and intimidated witnesses testifying before the grand jury and that this misconduct impeded the issuance of the indictment against the defendant and thus tolled the statute of limitations under RC 2945.71, extending the time within which the state could bring the defendant to trial, is without merit where (1) the witness' affidavit sheds no light on the mental processes of the grand jurors in refusing to indict the defendant at an earlier opportunity, and more than just her testimony presumably was considered by the jurors; (2) the witness' allegations while under oath were not subject to cross-examination and therefore do not establish misconduct as an irrefutable fact; and (3) the court below appeared to give little if any credence to this evidence, which was improperly before it. State v. Lewis (Lawrence 1990) 70 Ohio App.3d 624, 591 N.E.2d 854, cause dismissed 58 Ohio St.3d 716, 570 N.E.2d 277, rehearing denied 59 Ohio St.3d 715, 572 N.E.2d 697, dismissal of post-conviction relief affirmed, dismissed, appeal not allowed 78 Ohio St.3d 1490, 678 N.E.2d 1227.

Failure of the accused to object to his trial assignment, announced within rule, for a trial date commencing after the time provided for trial in RC 2945.71 constitutes a "delay occasioned by the neglect... of the accused," within the meaning of RC 2945.72(H), and so extends the time within which an accused must be brought to trial. State v. Wentz (Stark 1975) 49 Ohio App.2d 96, 359 N.E.2d 446, 3 O.O.3d 157.

It is the mandatory duty of the state to try an accused within the time prescribed by RC 2945.71 and RC 2945.73 and the failure of defense counsel to indicate to the trial court that a guilty plea would not be forthcoming does not constitute a period of delay occasioned by the neglect or improper act of the accused as provided in RC 2945.72(D). State v. Smith (Cuyahoga 1976) 47 Ohio App.2d 317, 354 N.E.2d 699, 1 O.O.3d 385.

An extension of time for trying defendant beyond the period prescribed by RC 2945.71(C)(2) is allowed under RC 2945.72(D) where such extension is required because of the defendant constantly changing his place of residence, thus preventing earlier service of a summons. State v Goetz, No. CA86–09–059 (12th Dist Ct App, Clermont, 2–9–87).

While the interstate flight of the defendant before arraignment is improper conduct under RC 2945.72(D), time for trial is not extended thereby, unless it is shown that this conduct caused any delay. State v McBride, No. 10–055 (11th Dist Ct App, Lake, 6–15–84).

23. Burden of proof

The state bears the burden to show that actions or events chargeable to the defendant have tolled enough time so that the defendant is tried within the speedy-trial period. State v. Brewster (Ohio App. 1 Dist., 05-28-2004) 157 Ohio App.3d 342, 811 N.E.2d 162, 2004-Ohio-2722, appeal not allowed 103 Ohio St.3d 1480, 816 N.E.2d 255, 2004-Ohio-5405. Criminal Law ⚷ 577.16(8)

Once defendant has established prima facie case that he was denied his right to speedy trial, burden of production of evidence shifts to state to prove that sufficient time was extended under speedy trial statute within which to bring defendant to trial. State v. Price (Ohio App. 10 Dist., 07-31-1997) 122 Ohio App.3d 65, 701 N.E.2d 41, dismissed, appeal not allowed 80 Ohio St.3d 1466, 687 N.E.2d 295. Criminal Law ⚷ 577.16(8)

A defendant is not required to request a trial within the time provided for in RC 2945.71, and is not required to show he was prejudiced by the delay. State v. Coatoam (Lake 1975) 45 Ohio App.2d 183, 341 N.E.2d 635, 74 O.O.2d 229. Criminal Law ⚷ 577.16(5.1)

24. Agreement by parties

While a defendant's mere failure to object to a state-scheduled original trial date outside of the speedy-trial time limit does not constitute a continuance that would toll the speedy trial period, an agreement by all parties to a post-statutory trial date will be treated as a continuance. State v. Steinke (Ohio App. 3 Dist., 03-15-2004) 158 Ohio App.3d 241, 814 N.E.2d 1230, 2004-Ohio-1201. Criminal Law ⚷ 577.10(9)

Where prosecution of defendant who was already incarcerated on other charges was continued after first pretrial conference because parties needed more time to discuss case, 35 days between first and second pretrial conferences were tolled, for speedy trial purposes. State v. Smith (Ohio App. 3 Dist., 09-29-2000) 140 Ohio App.3d 81, 746 N.E.2d 678, 2000-Ohio-1777. Criminal Law ⚷ 577.10(4)

25. Change of venue or removal

Defendant's right to speedy trial on minor misdemeanor speeding charge was not violated under statute that required trial within 30 days of arrest or service of summons, even though trial occurred 44 days after defendant received summons, and 33 days after her initial court appearance in Mayor's Court, where transfer of case from Mayor's Court to Municipal Court constituted "removal" and extended time for trial until 30 days after Mayor's Court certified case, and two-day continuance beyond speedy trial limit, in order to allowing citing officer to be subpoenaed, was reasonable. City of Brecksville v. Carothers (Ohio App. 8 Dist., Cuyahoga, 05-01-2003) No. 81907, 2003-Ohio-2198, 2003 WL 1995624, Unreported. Criminal Law ⚷ 577.13

Transfer of case from mayor's court to municipal court is "removal" within meaning of statute that permits speedy trial period to be extended by any delay resulting from removal. Portage v. Belcher (Ohio App. 6 Dist., 12-30-1996) 117 Ohio App.3d 90, 689 N.E.2d 1032. Criminal Law ⚷ 577.10(7)

Transfer of case from mayor's court to municipal court is "removal" within meaning of speedy trial statute, as word "removal" as used therein refers to transfer of case from one state court to another. Brecksville v. Cook (Ohio, 03-04-1996) 75 Ohio St.3d 53, 661 N.E.2d 706, 1996-Ohio-171, reconsideration denied 75 Ohio St.3d 1452, 663 N.E.2d 333. Criminal Law ⚷ 577.10(7)

Period of delay necessary to removal of case from mayor's court to municipal court, during which time speedy trial statute is tolled, is time from arrest or summons to date on which mayor's court certifies case to municipal court; it is not time from certification in mayor's court to docketing in municipal court. Brecksville v. Cook (Ohio, 03-04-1996) 75 Ohio St.3d 53, 661 N.E.2d 706, 1996-Ohio-171, reconsideration denied 75 Ohio St.3d 1452, 663 N.E.2d 333. Criminal Law ⚷ 577.10(7)

Where a defendant charged with a misdemeanor set for trial at a mayor's court demands a jury trial, thereby necessitating transfer to the municipal court, this "removal" extends the time within which the defendant must be brought to trial; the removal is deemed to take place when the case is certified by the mayor's court, not when it is docketed by the municipal court. City of Gahanna v. Partlow (Franklin 1985) 27 Ohio App.3d 267, 501 N.E.2d 51, 27 O.B.R. 311.

Time for speedy trial of defendant over whom juvenile court relinquishes jurisdiction commences to run the day after the juvenile court relinquishes jurisdiction. State v. Bickerstaff (Ohio 1984) 10 Ohio St.3d 62, 461 N.E.2d 892, 10 O.B.R. 352. Criminal Law ⚷ 577.8(2)

A motion for change of venue is a motion that extends the time for trial under RC 2945.72(E). State v. Willey (Guernsey 1981) 5 Ohio App.3d 86, 449 N.E.2d 471, 5 O.B.R. 200. Criminal Law ⚷ 577.10(8)

The reassignment of a case due to the recusal of the municipal court judge is not a removal within the meaning of RC 2945.72(F). Eastlake v Parsons, No. 89–L–14–021 (11th Dist Ct App, Lake, 9–8–89).

Transfer of a drunk driving prosecution from a mayor's court to a county court is a removal within the meaning of RC 2945.72(F), which tolls the running of the ninety-day speedy trial period. Bellaire v Tennat, No. 86–B–16 (7th Dist Ct App, Belmont, 5–20–87).

26. Delay pending appeal by state

The time for bringing a murder case to trial is extended by the state's appeal of the denial of its motion in limine to exclude the testimony of an expert on the battered woman syndrome. State v. Spinks (Cuyahoga 1992) 79 Ohio App.3d 720, 607 N.E.2d 1130, dismissed, jurisdictional motion overruled 65 Ohio St.3d 1440, 600 N.E.2d 683, denial of habeas corpus affirmed 59 F.3d 171.

State's abortive appeal from order on motion to dismiss could not extend speedy trial time, where state never met either jurisdictional or procedural requirements for appeal to Court of Appeals under relevant provisions, or for any appeal derivative thereto to the Supreme Court. State v. Perry (Allen 1990) 67 Ohio App.3d 775, 588 N.E.2d 897. Criminal Law ⚷ 577.13

The state's appeal from a judgment to dismiss tax fraud indictments in a case involving an individual defendant has no relation to a case involving a corporate defendant, and its pendency could not, for that reason alone, extend the speedy trial time in the case against the corporate defendant. State v. Perry (Allen 1990) 67 Ohio App.3d 775, 588 N.E.2d 897. Criminal Law ⚷ 577.10(5)

For speedy trial purposes, stay of proceedings "pending the resolution of this appeal" ordered by the Supreme Court extended until the Supreme Court entered order overruling motion for rehearing, and did not terminate at time of earlier journal entry of dismissal. State v. Perry (Allen 1990) 67 Ohio App.3d 775, 588 N.E.2d 897. Criminal Law ⚷ 577.8(1)

Once the statute is tolled by an appeal, time does not begin to run again until the expiration of time for notice of further appeal or motion for rehearing. City of Akron v. Downey (Summit 1984) 24 Ohio App.3d 225, 495 N.E.2d 28, 24 O.B.R. 435.

A dismissal order tolls the statute until after the state has appealed and the time for filing for further appeal or rehearing has expired. City of Akron v. Downey (Summit 1984) 24 Ohio App.3d 225, 495 N.E.2d 28, 24 O.B.R. 435.

27. Stay

Trial in aggravated theft prosecution was stayed pursuant to "express statutory requirement," thus tolling 270–day speedy trial period, during ten months that state's affidavit of disqualification of trial judge was pending with Ohio Supreme Court, even though no formal stay was issued; trial judge was powerless to proceed with trial of case until Supreme Court resolved disqualification matter. State v. Mays (Ohio App. 8 Dist., 01-11-1996) 108 Ohio App.3d 598, 671 N.E.2d 553, dismissed, appeal not allowed 75 Ohio St.3d 1509, 665 N.E.2d 679. Criminal Law ⚷ 577.10(7)

For the purposes of a speedy trial, the supreme court's staying of all proceedings in the trial court "pending the resolution of this appeal" does not terminate at the time of an earlier journal entry of dismissal but extends until the supreme court enters an order overruling the motion for rehearing. State v. Perry (Allen 1990) 67 Ohio App.3d 775, 588 N.E.2d 897.

A petition for certiorari filed with the US Supreme Court only addresses that court's discretionary jurisdiction to review the case; therefore, until and unless the court specifically directs otherwise, the mere filing of such a petition and the time elapsing while it is pending do not divest the trial court of its jurisdiction, nor do they suspend or stay the trial court's power to proceed with the case. State v. Geraldo (Lucas 1983) 13 Ohio App.3d 27,

468 N.E.2d 328, 13 O.B.R. 29. Federal Courts ⚷ 501

Defendant's speedy trial rights were not violated, where defendant was brought to trial within 90 day time limit permitted by statute, and defendant's motion for continuance justified extension of 90 day limit. State v. Murray (Ohio App. 5 Dist., Licking, 05-03-2002) No. 01 CA 00108, 2002-Ohio-2500, 2002 WL 925264, Unreported. Criminal Law ⚷ 577.10(8)

28. Dismissal or discharge generally

Defendant's motion to dismiss indictment did not extend speedy trial period, where trial date had been set beyond the time limits initially and remained unchanged by any motion filed by defendant. State v. Derrico (Ohio App. 12 Dist., Warren, 12-16-2002) No. CA2002-07-067, 2002-Ohio-6946, 2002 WL 31819166, Unreported. Criminal Law ⚷ 577.10(8)

Accused presents prima facie case for discharge based upon violation of limitations created by speedy trial statute by charging in motion to dismiss that he or she was held solely on pending charge and for time exceeding statutory time limits; burden then shifts to State to show that limits have not been exceeded by demonstrating that time limit had been properly extended. State v. Hiatt (Ohio App. 4 Dist., 03-26-1997) 120 Ohio App.3d 247, 697 N.E.2d 1025. Criminal Law ⚷ 577.16(6); Criminal Law ⚷ 577.16(8)

Any extensions of time that are tolled pursuant to speedy trial statute must be strictly construed against the state and, once defendant has shown that 270 days have elapsed, prima facie case for discharge has been established and state bears burden to show that defendant was timely tried. State v. Grinnell (Ohio App. 10 Dist., 06-27-1996) 112 Ohio App.3d 124, 678 N.E.2d 231, appeal not allowed 77 Ohio St.3d 1474, 673 N.E.2d 138, appeal not allowed 77 Ohio St.3d 1475, 673 N.E.2d 138, denial of habeas corpus affirmed 215 F.3d 1326, certiorari denied 121 S.Ct. 232, 531 U.S. 898, 148 L.Ed.2d 166. Criminal Law ⚷ 577.13; Criminal Law ⚷ 577.16(8)

Once accused has established prima facie case for discharge upon showing that statutory speedy trial period has elapsed, state bears burden of demonstrating that any statutory factor extended time for bringing defendant to trial. Cleveland v. Jones (Ohio App. 8 Dist., 05-06-1996) 110 Ohio App.3d 791, 675 N.E.2d 498. Criminal Law ⚷ 577.16(8)

Once statutory limit of 90 days for bringing defendant to trial on misdemeanor has expired, prima facie case for dismissal is made, and burden is on state to demonstrate that sufficient time was tolled to leave fewer than 90 days chargeable to state. State v. Wirtanen (Ohio App. 6 Dist., 04-26-1996) 110 Ohio App.3d 604, 674 N.E.2d 1245. Criminal Law ⚷ 577.16(8)

A per se rule that would require a defendant's trial counsel to file a motion to dismiss on speedy trial grounds in every case not tried within the statutory period, regardless of the merits of the defense is expressly rejected; any rule of law that mandates the filing of obviously fruitless and time consuming motions, or requires the utilization of procedure which has reliably and professionally been determined to be futile, should be discouraged so the courts use their valuable time to deal with matters of arguable merit and such a rule would practically encourage defense counsel to strategically fail to file such motions, knowing that their client would automatically obtain a new trial. State v. Clary (Franklin 1991) 73 Ohio App.3d 42, 596 N.E.2d 554, dismissed, jurisdictional motion overruled 62 Ohio St.3d 1405, 577 N.E.2d 358.

Where a defendant is not brought to trial within the time set forth in RC 2945.71 and there are no journal entries establishing continuances allegedly granted at defendant's request, the defendant is entitled to a discharge under RC 2945.73. State v. Benson (Cuyahoga 1985) 29 Ohio App.3d 321, 505 N.E.2d 987, 29 O.B.R. 448.

Where an accused has been incarcerated since his arrest and due to clerical error the statutory time period for bringing him to trial has been allowed to expire and where none of the provisions of RC 2945.72 is applicable to extend the time for trial, then pursuant to RC 2945.73, the accused is, as a matter of law, entitled to be discharged and any further criminal proceedings against him based upon the same conduct are barred. State v. Eberhardt (Cuyahoga 1978) 56 Ohio App.2d 193, 381 N.E.2d 1357, 10 O.O.3d 197. Criminal Law ⚷ 577.16(2)

Defendant accused of violation of RC 4511.20 whose trial is not held within fifteen days after arrest or service of summons must be discharged if defendant took no action which delayed proceedings. State v. Sells (Ohio Co. 1974) 41 Ohio Misc. 49, 322 N.E.2d 378, 70 O.O.2d 109.

Where an error by a sending state which has adopted the interstate agreement on detainers causes a delay which results in a failure to provide a defendant a speedy trial, such delay will be charged to a receiving state which has also adopted the interstate agreement on detainers, and the case shall be dismissed. State v Mourey, No. 90AP–1199 (10th Dist Ct App, Franklin, 5–9–91), affirmed by 64 OS(3d) 482 (1992).

29. Mistrial

The speedy trial time limits do not apply to a retrial after a mistrial; a delay of 156 days is not unreasonable. State v Delong, No. 5–86–34 (3d Dist Ct App, Hancock, 5–4–88).

30. Waiver of speedy trial

Defendant's right to a speedy trial was violated, thus requiring reversal of his conviction for felonious assault, where defendant's trial was conducted 13 days beyond speedy trial deadline, state failed to show that deadline was extended, and there was no affirmative demonstration of waiver of defendant's right to speedy trial. State v. Henry (Ohio App. 5 Dist., Licking, 06-23-2005) No. 04 CA 00062, 2005-Ohio-3191, 2005 WL 1491462, Unreported, appeal not allowed 107 Ohio St.3d 1423, 837 N.E.2d 1208, 2005-Ohio-6124. Criminal Law ⚷ 577.15(1); Criminal Law ⚷ 1166(7)

Trial court violated defendant's right to a speedy trial when defendant was not brought to trial on fourth degree misdemeanor charges of parking in a no parking zone and having a firearm in a motor vehicle until 81 chargeable days following his arrest; defendant did not expressly waive his right to a speedy trial in writing or by statement made in open court, no delay was occasioned by defendant's request for counsel since counsel was appointed for defendant the day it was requested, and the trial court did not grant a continuance by journal entry or explain the reason for the delay. State v. McLean (Ohio App. 11 Dist., Trumbull, 03-04-2005) No. 2003-T-0115, No. 2003-T-0116, 2005-Ohio-954, 2005 WL 517455, Unreported. Criminal Law ⚷ 577.10(8); Criminal Law ⚷ 577.10(9)

Defendant did not knowingly, intelligently, and voluntarily waive his right to a speedy trial, where waiver of speedy trial was contained on pre-printed form without explanation of its meaning or consequence of its waiver; however, there was no speedy trial violation, where trial court found all continuances were reasonable. State v. Baloh (Ohio App. 9 Dist., Medina, 06-30-2004) No. 04CA0010-M, 2004-Ohio-3421, 2004 WL 1462825, Unreported. Criminal Law ⚷ 577.10(9); Criminal Law ⚷ 577.13

Any delay in bringing defendant to trial on drug-related charges did not violate his speedy trial rights; delay beyond 270-day speedy trial period was attributable to defendant's five motions for continuance, a motion to suppress evidence, and defense counsel's motion to withdraw, which motions served to toll limitations period. State v. Kolvek (Ohio App. 9 Dist., Summit, 05-19-2004) No. 21808, 2004-Ohio-2515, 2004 WL 1103994, Unreported. Criminal Law ⚷ 577.10(8)

Post-conviction petitioner was not entitled to hearing on his untimely filed petition for relief, especially where petition was not supported by new evidence, petitioner failed to establish that he was unavoidably prevented from discovering evidence submitted in support of petition, evidence submitted in support of petition failed to establish violation of petitioner's right to speedy trial, petitioner had waived his right to speedy trial, and petitioner was brought to trial within speedy trial period. State v. Davis (Ohio App. 7 Dist., Mahoning, 05-30-2002) No. 01 CA 171, 2002-Ohio-2789, 2002 WL 32806896, Unreported. Criminal Law ⚷ 1655(1)

Defendant waived his right to right to speedy trial, where record indicated that court repeatedly informed defendant as to effect of his requesting a change of counsel on his right to speedy trial, and defendant stated he understood. State v. Seldon (Ohio App. 8 Dist., Cuyahoga, 10-24-2002) No. 80130, No. 80129, 2002-Ohio-5825, 2002 WL 31398708, Unreported, motion to reopen denied 2003-Ohio-1947, 2003 WL 1894562, appeal not allowed 99 Ohio St.3d 1543, 795 N.E.2d 682, 2003-Ohio-4671. Criminal Law ⚷ 577.10(9)

If an attorney moves for a continuance in one case due to a prior commitment, it is logical that he will be unavailable for another case against the defendant, which is scheduled for the same date, and this circumstance serves as a waiver of the defendant's speedy trial rights. State v. Conkle (Ohio App. 5 Dist., Tuscarawas, 03-09-1994) No. 93 AP 070049, 1994 WL 112205, Unreported.

Trial court's written finding that murder defendant waived his speedy trial rights, signed by defendant and his counsel, without more, did not demonstrate that defendant's waiver of his speedy trial rights was knowing, intelligent, and voluntary. State v. Kerby (Ohio App. 2 Dist., 07-15-2005) 162 Ohio App.3d 353, 833 N.E.2d 757, 2005-Ohio-3734, appeal not allowed 107 Ohio St.3d 1682, 839 N.E.2d 403, 2005-Ohio-6480. Criminal Law ⚷ 577.10(9)

Waiver of speedy-trial rights must be knowing, intelligent, and voluntary, which includes an understanding of both the effect of the waiver and the duration and extent of that waiver. State v. Kerby (Ohio App. 2 Dist., 07-15-2005) 162 Ohio App.3d 353, 833 N.E.2d 757, 2005-Ohio-3734, appeal not allowed 107 Ohio St.3d 1682, 839 N.E.2d 403, 2005-Ohio-6480. Criminal Law ⚷ 577.10(9)

Speedy-trial waivers are distinct from the statutory provisions that extend the statutory speedy-trial time by tolling it: a waiver relinquishes the right, at least until the waiver is withdrawn; tolling, however, does not waive the speedy-trial right, and, in most circumstances, allows sufficient time to avoid any prejudice the underlying request or order might create. State v. Kerby (Ohio App. 2 Dist., 07-15-2005) 162 Ohio App.3d 353, 833 N.E.2d 757, 2005-Ohio-3734, appeal not allowed 107 Ohio St.3d 1682, 839 N.E.2d 403, 2005-Ohio-6480. Criminal Law ⚷ 577.10(9)

Murder defendant's waiver of his right to speedy trial was knowing, intelligent, and voluntary, and of unlimited duration, despite trial court's confusion, in questioning defendant concerning his knowledge and understanding of effects of speedy-trial waiver, of effects of speedy-trial waiver with tolling of speedy trial period resulting from continuance defendant requested, where trial court never expanded upon its suggestion that defendant's waiver was "limited," other than by explaining that waiver would extend defendant's speedy-trial time beyond statutory 90-day period. State v. Kerby (Ohio App. 2 Dist., 07-15-2005) 162 Ohio App.3d 353, 833 N.E.2d 757, 2005-Ohio-3734, appeal not allowed 107 Ohio St.3d 1682, 839 N.E.2d 403, 2005-Ohio-6480. Criminal Law ⚷ 577.10(9)

Speedy trial period was tolled during period in which case was continued at defendant's request, despite defendant's claim that his waiver of time, as noted in trial court's journalized entry, was not knowingly and voluntarily made. State v. Hirsch (Ohio App. 1 Dist., 08-07-1998) 129 Ohio App.3d 294, 717 N.E.2d 789, dismissed, appeal not allowed 84 Ohio St.3d 1436, 702 N.E.2d 1213, denial of habeas corpus affirmed 74 Fed.Appx. 486, 2003 WL 21949184. Criminal Law ⚷ 577.10(8)

Defense counsel's signing of docket and journal entry which contained waiver of speedy trial requirement in consideration of continuance of trial constituted waiver of defendant's speedy trial rights, despite defense counsel's contention that he had signed docket and journal entry merely to acknowledge his receipt thereof; there was no language on the entry to support defense counsel's contention. State v. Hughey (Ohio App. 7 Dist., 11-20-1996) 115 Ohio App.3d 664, 685 N.E.2d 1318. Criminal Law ⚿ 577.10(9)

Speedy trial provisions are not self-executing but must be asserted by defendant in timely fashion to avoid such rights being waived. State v. Trummer (Ohio App. 7 Dist., 09-30-1996) 114 Ohio App.3d 456, 683 N.E.2d 392, dismissed, appeal not allowed 78 Ohio St.3d 1409, 675 N.E.2d 1249, denial of post-conviction relief affirmed 1998 WL 896457, dismissed, appeal not allowed 85 Ohio St.3d 1464, 709 N.E.2d 171, motion for delayed appeal denied 2000 WL 1476604. Criminal Law ⚿ 577.10(10)

Motion filed by defendant is not required to assert waiver of speedy trial time for purposes of deciding motion in order for that motion to be found to have tolled time for speedy trial, as act of filing most motions by defendant in and of itself tolls the time. State v. Grinnell (Ohio App. 10 Dist., 06-27-1996) 112 Ohio App.3d 124, 678 N.E.2d 231, appeal not allowed 77 Ohio St.3d 1474, 673 N.E.2d 138, appeal not allowed 77 Ohio St.3d 1475, 673 N.E.2d 138, denial of habeas corpus affirmed 215 F.3d 1326, certiorari denied 121 S.Ct. 232, 531 U.S. 898, 148 L.Ed.2d 166. Criminal Law ⚿ 577.10(8)

Entry stating that cause came to be heard on arraignment of defendant, that plea of not guilty was entered for defendant, and that his rights were either explained to him or were waived did not establish that defendant had waived speedy trial rights. State v. Grinnell (Ohio App. 10 Dist., 06-27-1996) 112 Ohio App.3d 124, 678 N.E.2d 231, appeal not allowed 77 Ohio St.3d 1474, 673 N.E.2d 138, appeal not allowed 77 Ohio St.3d 1475, 673 N.E.2d 138, denial of habeas corpus affirmed 215 F.3d 1326, certiorari denied 121 S.Ct. 232, 531 U.S. 898, 148 L.Ed.2d 166. Criminal Law ⚿ 577.10(9)

A defendant is not denied effective assistance of counsel because his appointed attorney failed to file a motion to dismiss on speedy trial grounds due to continuances granted on account of court administration difficulties which prevented the defendant from being brought to trial within ninety days of his arrest where the trial court's entries continuing the defendant's trial included language stating that the defendant waived his right to a speedy trial for the period of the continuances. State v. Clary (Franklin 1991) 73 Ohio App.3d 42, 596 N.E.2d 554, dismissed, jurisdictional motion overruled 62 Ohio St.3d 1405, 577 N.E.2d 358.

A defense counsel does not substantially violate any essential duty to his client by allowing him to accept a waiver of his speedy trial right since there are many legitimate as well as good tactical reasons to waive a defense or to acquiesce in delay. State v. Clary (Franklin 1991) 73 Ohio App.3d 42, 596 N.E.2d 554, dismissed, jurisdictional motion overruled 62 Ohio St.3d 1405, 577 N.E.2d 358.

Defense counsel's participation in reassignment of case and in waiving of defendant's rights to speedy trial, after time for trial had run, was effective and bound defendant to waiver. State v. Dumas (Franklin 1990) 68 Ohio App.3d 174, 587 N.E.2d 932, dismissed, jurisdictional motion overruled 56 Ohio St.3d 712, 565 N.E.2d 835. Criminal Law ⚿ 577.10(9)

Where a defendant signs a waiver of speedy trial rights, which waiver is witnessed by his attorney, and by which waiver defendant consents to case being "continued indefinitely," defendant's statutory and constitutional rights to a speedy trial are not violated so long as he is tried within a reasonable time. State v. Johnson (Cuyahoga 1984) 13 Ohio App.3d 271, 469 N.E.2d 559, 13 O.B.R. 335. Criminal Law ⚿ 577.10(9)

A defendant who fails to appear at a scheduled trial, and whose trial must therefore be rescheduled for a later date, waives his right to assert the provisions of RC 2945.71 to RC 2945.73 for that period of time which elapses from his initial arrest to the date he is subsequently rearrested. State v. Bauer (Ohio 1980) 61 Ohio St.2d 83, 399 N.E.2d 555, 15 O.O.3d 122. Criminal Law ⚿ 577.10(8)

The right of a defendant to a speedy trial, as implemented by RC 2945.71 to RC 2945.73, can be waived by the attorney for the accused even though the accused is neither aware of nor informed about the waiver. State v. McRae (Hamilton 1977) 56 Ohio App.2d 72, 381 N.E.2d 946, 10 O.O.3d 98, affirmed 55 Ohio St.2d 149, 378 N.E.2d 476, 9 O.O.3d 118.

The constitutional right to a speedy trial, as implemented by RC 2945.71 to RC 2945.73, can be waived by the attorney of an accused even if the accused is not aware of or informed of the waiver. State v. McRae (Ohio 1978) 55 Ohio St.2d 149, 378 N.E.2d 476, 9 O.O.3d 118.

A defendant's right to be brought to trial within the time limits expressed in RC 2945.71 may be waived by his counsel for reasons of trial preparation, and the defendant is bound by the waiver even though the waiver is executed without his consent. State v. McBreen (Ohio 1978) 54 Ohio St.2d 315, 376 N.E.2d 593, 8 O.O.3d 302, certiorari denied 99 S.Ct. 287, 439 U.S. 914, 58 L.Ed.2d 261. Attorney And Client ⚿ 88

A defendant's failure to object to a trial date scheduled outside the ninety-day limitation period of RC 2945.71(C)(2) and RC 2945.71(D), before the expiration of that period, does not amount to acquiescence in the trial date. State v. Singer (Ohio 1977) 50 Ohio St.2d 103, 362 N.E.2d 1216, 4 O.O.3d 237. Criminal Law ⚿ 577.10(9)

Where the privately retained counsel of a defendant agrees to an extension of a trial date beyond ninety days from the date of arrest, in the absence of the personal consent of the accused, there is no violation of the defendant's constitutional or statutory rights. State v. Davis (Hamilton 1975) 44 Ohio App.2d 95, 335 N.E.2d 874, 73 O.O.2d 89.

Since the burden is on the state, not the accused, to bring the defendant to trial within the statutory period, and the Supreme Court of Ohio has decided that a defendant's failure to object to a trial date unilaterally set by the court on a day beyond the 90–day time limit of RC 2945.71(C)(2) and 2945.71(E) does not amount to acquiescence in the trial date and defendant's silence does not constitute a "continuance" under RC 2945.72(H), the lower court's decision is reversed and the defendant is discharged. State v Kavish, No. C–920568 (1st Dist Ct App, Hamilton, 6–16–93).

A handwritten note filed with a court the day before a scheduled arraignment, stating that the accused "had to go out of the state for a week or more" need not be treated as a motion for a continuance for purposes of determining whether the defendant's failure to appear at arraignment waives the right to a speedy trial. State v Owens, No. CA–3076 (5th Dist Ct App, Licking, 12–10–84).

31. Appeal

Criminal defendant had adequate remedy at law, through a direct appeal if he was convicted of murder, and thus, defendant was not entitled to mandamus relief, as to trial court's alleged violation of his statutory speedy trial rights while he was being held in county jail as he awaited trial. Hamilton v. Collins (Ohio App. 11 Dist., Lake, 10-24-2003) No. 2003-L-106, 2003-Ohio-5703, 2003 WL 22427933, Unreported. Mandamus ⚿ 4(1)

Speedy trial statutes have no application where verdict has been reversed on appeal and new trial has been ordered. State v. Pearson (Ohio App. 3 Dist., 11-23-1998) 130 Ohio App.3d 577, 720 N.E.2d 924, dismissed, appeal not allowed 85 Ohio St.3d 1441, 708 N.E.2d 208, dismissal of post-conviction relief affirmed 2000 WL 1132575, dismissed, appeal not allowed 90 Ohio St.3d 1489, 739 N.E.2d 815. Criminal Law ⚿ 577.14

Murder defendant's failure, after case was first continued at state's request due to unavailability of key witness, to raise matter again did not eliminate need for Court of Appeals to make further inquiry into speedy trial issue. State v. Hirsch (Ohio App. 1 Dist., 08-07-1998) 129 Ohio App.3d 294, 717 N.E.2d 789, dismissed, appeal not allowed 84 Ohio St.3d 1436, 702 N.E.2d 1213, denial of habeas corpus affirmed 74 Fed.Appx. 486, 2003 WL 21949184. Criminal Law ⚿ 1035(1)

The requirements set forth in RC 2945.71 et seq. pertaining to time for trial have no application to the time for trial of a cause in which an original conviction has been reversed and the matter remanded for retrial. State v. Gettys (Seneca 1976) 49 Ohio App.2d 241, 360 N.E.2d 735, 3 O.O.3d 286.

Under RC 2945.71 through RC 2945.73, a trial court has discretion to extend the time limit for trial prescribed therein, and, where the trial court dismisses an indictment and discharges an accused on the basis that it lacks discretion to consider an extension, upon appeal thereof the cause will be remanded to the trial court for an exercise of that court's discretion. State v. Davis (Ohio 1976) 46 Ohio St.2d 444, 349 N.E.2d 315, 75 O.O.2d 498. Criminal Law ⚿ 577.16(3); Criminal Law ⚿ 1181.5(3.1)

The failure of the trial court to comply with Crim R 48(B) when dismissing an indictment for lack of a speedy trial requires a remand to the trial court, on appeal by the state, for such findings of fact and reasons for the dismissal that will enable the reviewing court to pass upon the assignments of error. State v. Bound (Cuyahoga 1975) 43 Ohio App.2d 44, 332 N.E.2d 366, 72 O.O.2d 197.

Mandamus will not lie to compel relator's discharge on the ground he was denied a speedy trial for the reason that an adequate remedy by way of appeal is available. State ex rel. Wentz v. Correll (Ohio 1975) 41 Ohio St.2d 101, 322 N.E.2d 889, 70 O.O.2d 196.

2945.73 Discharge for delay in trial

(A) A charge of felony shall be dismissed if the accused is not accorded a preliminary hearing within the time required by sections 2945.71 and 2945.72 of the Revised Code.

(B) Upon motion made at or prior to the commencement of trial, a person charged with an offense shall be discharged if he is not brought to trial within the time required by sections 2945.71 and 2945.72 of the Revised Code.

(C) Regardless of whether a longer time limit may be provided by sections 2945.71 and 2945.72 of the Revised Code, a person charged with misdemeanor shall be discharged if he is held in jail in lieu of bond awaiting trial on the pending charge:

(1) For a total period equal to the maximum term of imprisonment which may be imposed for the most serious misdemeanor charged;

(2) For a total period equal to the term of imprisonment allowed in lieu of payment of the maximum fine which may be imposed for the most serious misdemeanor charged, when the offense or offenses charged constitute minor misdemeanors.

(D) When a charge of felony is dismissed pursuant to division (A) of this section, such dismissal has the same effect as a nolle prosequi. When an accused is discharged pursuant to division (B) or (C) of this section, such discharge is a bar to any further criminal proceedings against him based on the same conduct.

(1972 H 511, eff. 1–1–74)

Historical and Statutory Notes

Ed. Note: 2945.73 contains provisions analogous to former 2945.71 and 2945.72, repealed by 1972 H 511, eff. 1–1–74.

Ed. Note: Former 2945.73 repealed by 1972 H 511, eff. 1–1–74; 1953 H 1; GC 13447–3.

Pre–1953 H 1 Amendments: 113 v 193, Ch 26, § 3

Legislative Service Commission

1973:

This section states the effect of a failure to bring an accused to preliminary hearing or trial within the time allowed by section 2945.71 as extended pursuant to section 2945.72.

Failure to bring a person accused of felony to preliminary hearing within the proper time requires that the case be dismissed as on a nolle prosequi. Failure to bring an accused to trial (for misdemeanor or felony) within the proper time requires that the case against him be dismissed with prejudice to the state as to any future prosecutions based on the same conduct.

Regardless of whether a longer time limit may otherwise apply, a case must be dismissed with prejudice to the state when the accused is held in jail awaiting trial for a period equal to the maximum jail sentence which could be imposed, or, in minor misdemeanor cases, for a period equal to the time during which he could work off the maximum fine which could be imposed. For example, if a person is charged with an offense for which the maximum penalty is 10 days in jail, he must be brought to trial within 10 days after his arrest if he is held in lieu of bond, even though an extension of time might otherwise be applicable to his case under section 2945.72. As another example, a person jailed on a misdemeanor charge carrying a maximum penalty of a fine of $50 must be brought to trial within 5 days of his arrest. See, section 2947.20, which establishes a $10 daily jail time credit toward payment of a fine.

Cross References

Computation of time, 1.14
Criminal case time limits, Sup R 39
Dismissal, Crim R 48
Motions, Crim R 47
Pleadings and motions before trial, defenses and objections, Crim R 12
Right to speedy trial, O Const Art I §10

Library References

Criminal Law ⚷228, 577.16.
Westlaw Topic No. 110.
C.J.S. Criminal Law §§ 340, 344, 583, 610 to 621.

Research References

Encyclopedias

OH Jur. 3d Criminal Law § 396, Ohio Constitutional and Statutory Bases.

OH Jur. 3d Criminal Law § 2063, Time for Hearing.

OH Jur. 3d Criminal Law § 2256, Generally; Applicability of Speedy Trial Provisions.

OH Jur. 3d Criminal Law § 2849, Effect of Dismissal.

OH Jur. 3d Criminal Law § 2850, Review.

OH Jur. 3d Criminal Law § 2853, Rules of Superintendence as to Prompt Trial.

OH Jur. 3d Habeas Corpus & Post Convict. Remedies § 16, Lack of or Defect in Preliminary Hearing.

Treatises and Practice Aids

Markus, Trial Handbook for Ohio Lawyers, § 4:6, Speedy Trial—Statutory Time Limits.

Katz, Giannelli, Blair and Lipton, Baldwin's Ohio Practice, Criminal Law, § 38:5, Time Limits.

Katz, Giannelli, Blair and Lipton, Baldwin's Ohio Practice, Criminal Law, § 60:2, Speedy Trial Statutes.

Katz, Giannelli, Blair and Lipton, Baldwin's Ohio Practice, Criminal Law, § 60:4, Applicability of Statute.

Katz, Giannelli, Blair and Lipton, Baldwin's Ohio Practice, Criminal Law, § 140:1, Waiver of Preliminary Hearing in Felony Case.

Katz, Giannelli, Blair and Lipton, Baldwin's Ohio Practice, Criminal Law, § 147:1, Motion to Dismiss Felony Charge for Delay of Preliminary Hearing.

Katz, Giannelli, Blair and Lipton, Baldwin's Ohio Practice, Criminal Law, § 147:2, Dismissal of Felony Charge for Delay of Preliminary Hearing.

Katz, Giannelli, Blair and Lipton, Baldwin's Ohio Practice, Criminal Law, § 147:3, Motion to Dismiss Felony Charge for Delay of Trial.

Katz, Giannelli, Blair and Lipton, Baldwin's Ohio Practice, Criminal Law, § 147:4, Dismissal of Felony Charge Delay in Trial.

Katz, Giannelli, Blair and Lipton, Baldwin's Ohio Practice, Criminal Law, § 147:5, Motion to Dismiss Misdemeanor Charge for Delay in Trial.

Katz, Giannelli, Blair and Lipton, Baldwin's Ohio Practice, Criminal Law, § 147:6, Dismissal of Misdemeanor Charge for Delay in Trial.

Katz, Giannelli, Blair and Lipton, Baldwin's Ohio Practice, Criminal Law, § 59:14, Rules of Superintendence.

Katz, Giannelli, Blair and Lipton, Baldwin's Ohio Practice, Criminal Law, § 60:17, Extension—Change in Charge.

Katz, Giannelli, Blair and Lipton, Baldwin's Ohio Practice, Criminal Law, § 60:19, Remedies for Unexcused Delay.

Katz, Giannelli, Blair and Lipton, Baldwin's Ohio Practice, Criminal Law, § 60:20, Appellate Review.

Painter & Dennis, Ohio Appellate Practice § 10:34, Habeas Corpus-Nonavailability-Criminal Cases-Availability of Appeal.

Hennenberg & Reinhart, Ohio Criminal Defense Motions F 5.02, Waiver of Right to Speedy Trial and Request for Indefinite Continuance-Pretrial Motions.

Hennenberg & Reinhart, Ohio Criminal Defense Motions F 11.01, Motion for a Discharge for Delay in Trial (Right to Speedy Trial).

Law Review and Journal Commentaries

An Analysis of the Judicial Interpretation of the 1974 Ohio Speedy Trial Act: The First Five Years, Comment. 40 Ohio St L J 363 (1979).

The Right to a Speedy Trial: Ohio Follows the Trend, Note. 43 U Cin L Rev 610 (1974).

Notes of Decisions

1. Constitutional issues

Defendant was entitled to dismissal, on statutory speedy trial grounds, of charge of complicity to commit aggravated robbery, where defendant's motion to dismiss presented prima facie case for discharge under speedy trial statute, but trial court never scheduled hearing on defendant's motion, and state failed to respond to motion by showing that speedy trial time limitations had not expired. State v. Whitt (Ohio App. 4 Dist., Scioto, 09-26-2005) No. 04CA2962, 2005-Ohio-5154, 2005 WL 2389891, Unreported, stay denied 107 Ohio St.3d 1680, 839 N.E.2d 401, 2005-Ohio-6480, appeal not allowed 108 Ohio St.3d 1474, 842 N.E.2d 1054, 2006-Ohio-665. Criminal Law ⚷ 577.16(2)

Defendant's speedy trial rights were not violated, though 1,520 days had passed between date of defendant's arrest and date of trial; there had been 27 motions for continuance filed, the majority of which had been filed by defense counsel, and, by these continuances alone, without including any time tolled due to defendant's discovery demands, defendant waived 1,363 days, which meant that state had additional 113 days to bring defendant to trial within 270 days specified by statute. State v. Barnes (Ohio App. 10 Dist., Franklin, 06-28-2005) No. 04AP-1133, 2005-Ohio-3279, 2005 WL 1515325, Unreported. Criminal Law ⚷ 577.10(8); Criminal Law ⚷ 577.15(3)

The trial court's failure to provide defendant with a preliminary hearing did not entitle defendant to a dismissal of the murder charges against him; defendant failed to file a motion to dismiss before the grand jury returned an indictment against him, and defendant failed to assert that the denial of a preliminary hearing violated equal protection until four months after the indictment was issued. State v. Zaffino (Ohio App. 9 Dist., Summit, 12-31-2003) No. 21514, 2003-Ohio-7202, 2003 WL 23095392, Unreported, appeal not allowed 102 Ohio St.3d 1459, 809 N.E.2d 32, 2004-Ohio-2569, habeas corpus dismissed 2006 WL 2360902. Criminal Law ⚷ 223

Under double jeopardy clause of United States and of Ohio Constitutions, dismissal of criminal complaint for speedy trial violations amounts to dismissal with prejudice, or an acquittal, and bars any further punitive actions by state based on same act or omission. State v. Adams (Ohio App. 2 Dist., 08-04-1995) 105 Ohio App.3d 492, 664 N.E.2d 588. Double Jeopardy ⚷ 104

Habeas corpus is an available remedy to challenge the time parameters of a Crim R 5(B) preliminary hearing if filed prior to that hearing; there is no adequate remedy at law available to prevent what may constitute unlawful incarceration under the statutory framework of RC 2945.71 to 2945.73. Styer v. Brichta (Wood 1990) 69 Ohio App.3d 738, 591 N.E.2d 1255.

Since RC 2945.71 to RC 2945.73 confer substantive rights upon an accused, they take precedence over procedural or superintendent rules of the Ohio Supreme Court, including Sup R 8(B). State v. Westbrook (Franklin 1975) 47 Ohio App.2d 211, 353 N.E.2d 637, 1 O.O.3d 284.

In determining whether defendant's Sixth Amendment right to a speedy trial has been violated, the time period between dismissal of criminal charges and institution of new charges is not to be considered. U. S. v. MacDonald (U.S.N.C. 1982) 102 S.Ct. 1497, 456 U.S. 1, 71 L.Ed.2d 696, on remand 688 F.2d 224.

2. In general

Defendant's right to preliminary hearing on charges against him was extinguished when he was indicted by grand jury before any steps were taken by him to secure dismissal of charges. State v. Leach (Ohio App. 9 Dist., Summit, 05-25-2005) No. 22369, 2005-Ohio-2569, 2005 WL 1225755, Unreported, appeal not allowed 106 Ohio St.3d 1547, 835 N.E.2d 728, 2005-Ohio-5343. Criminal Law ⚷ 224

Continuances at request of the parties, continuance for purposes of determining defendant's mental competency to stand trial, and continuances at request of court were not attributable to the State for purposes of determining speedy trial time period. State v. Tullis (Ohio App. 10 Dist., Franklin, 05-05-2005) No. 04AP-333, 2005-Ohio-2205, 2005 WL 1055977, Unreported, appeal not allowed 106 Ohio St.3d 1510, 833 N.E.2d 1250, 2005-Ohio-4605. Criminal Law ⚷ 577.10(7); Criminal Law ⚷ 577.10(8)

A trial court errs in denying a defendant's motion to dismiss under RC 2945.73 for the failure of the state to bring the defendant to trial within the time required by RC 2945.71. State v Croop, No. CA–9163 (5th Dist Ct App, Stark, 5–10–93).

The dismissal of a complaint charging a violation of RC 4511.19(A)(1) for failure to bring the defendant to trial within the time required by law constitutes a discharge and is a bar to subsequent prosecution under RC 4511.19(A)(4) based on the same conduct. State v Barkie, No. 1231 (4th Dist Ct App, Athens, 6–12–85).

3. Construction with other law

The ten-day period of limitations in Juv R 29(A) is procedural only and such rule confers no substantive right upon an accused to have his case dismissed if he is not tried within the designated time. In re Therklidsen (Franklin 1977) 54 Ohio App.2d 195, 376 N.E.2d 970, 8 O.O.3d 335.

4. Strict construction

Any extensions of time that are tolled pursuant to speedy trial statute must be strictly construed against the state and, once defendant has shown that 270 days have elapsed, prima facie case for discharge has been established and state bears burden to show that defendant was timely tried. State v. Grinnell (Ohio App. 10 Dist., 06-27-1996) 112 Ohio App.3d 124, 678 N.E.2d 231, appeal not allowed 77 Ohio St.3d 1474, 673 N.E.2d 138, appeal not allowed 77 Ohio St.3d 1475, 673 N.E.2d 138, denial of habeas corpus affirmed 215 F.3d 1326, certiorari denied 121 S.Ct. 232, 531 U.S. 898, 148 L.Ed.2d 166. Criminal Law ⚷ 577.13; Criminal Law ⚷ 577.16(8)

The statutory speedy trial provisions, RC 2945.71 et seq., constitute a rational effort to enforce the constitutional right to a public speedy trial of an accused charged with the commission of a felony or a misdemeanor and shall be strictly enforced by the courts of this state. State v. Pachay (Ohio 1980) 64 Ohio St.2d 218, 416 N.E.2d 589, 18 O.O.3d 427. Criminal Law ⚷ 577.5

5. Retroactive effect

RC 2945.71 through RC 2945.73, enacted by 1972 H 511, eff. 1–1–74, are not applied retroactively; computation of the time limit derived from these sections is from January 1, 1974, for actions then pending, rather than from the actual earlier date of arrest. State v. MacDonald (Ohio 1976) 48 Ohio St.2d 66, 357 N.E.2d 40, 2 O.O.3d 219.

RC 2945.71 to RC 2945.73, effective on and after January 1, 1974, do not have retroactive application. State v. Walker (Ohio 1976) 46 Ohio St.2d 157, 346 N.E.2d 687, 75 O.O.2d 201.

The time limitations of RC 2945.71 to RC 2945.73, enacted by 1972 H 511, eff. 1–1–74, are to be computed from January 1, 1974, rather than from the actual earlier date of arrest, with respect to criminal prosecutions pending on January 1, 1974. City of Columbus v. Vest (Franklin 1974) 42 Ohio App.2d 83, 330 N.E.2d 726, 71 O.O.2d 520. Criminal Law ⚷ 577.2

RC 2945.71 to RC 2945.73, enacted by 1972 H 511, eff. 1–1–74, apply to criminal prosecutions pending on that date, the arrests for which were made prior to such date. City of Columbus v. Vest (Franklin 1974) 42 Ohio App.2d 83, 330 N.E.2d 726, 71 O.O.2d 520.

RC 2945.71, RC 2945.72 and RC 2945.73, enacted by 1972 H 511, eff. 1–1–74, are not applicable to arrests made prior to January 1, 1974. City of Reynoldsburg v. Wesley (Ohio Mun. 1974) 39 Ohio Misc. 166, 316 N.E.2d 926.

6. Mandatory nature of section

It is the mandatory duty of the state to try an accused within the time prescribed by RC 2945.71 and RC 2945.73 and the failure of defense counsel to indicate to the trial court that a guilty plea would not be forthcoming does not constitute a period of delay occasioned by the neglect or improper act of the accused as provided in RC 2945.72(D). State v. Smith (Cuyahoga 1976) 47 Ohio App.2d 317, 354 N.E.2d 699, 1 O.O.3d 385.

The language of RC 2945.71 is pre-emptory and mandatory, directing that an accused be brought to trial within the time specified, and it is not necessary for a defendant to object to the setting of a trial date forty-five days beyond the time of his arrest before requesting a discharge pursuant to RC 2945.73. City of Cincinnati v. Williams (Hamilton 1975) 44 Ohio App.2d 143, 336 N.E.2d 464, 73 O.O.2d 137. Criminal Law ⚷ 577.15(5); Criminal Law ⚷ 577.10(10)

Confinement in violation of RC 2945.71(C)(1) and 2945.71(C)(2) is directly in violation of the mandatory provision of RC 2945.73(A) and

2945.73(B). Styer v Brichta, No. 90WD072 (6th Dist Ct App, Wood, 10–10–90).

When a defendant is charged with violating RC 4511.19, irrespective of the subsection or sections charged, a RC 4511.19 charge is "pending" within the meaning of RC 2945.71(A) and any additional charges filed against the accused under other subsections must be tried within the time limits statutorily mandated for the initial charge. State v Puckett, No. 1516 (4th Dist Ct App, Scioto, 6–14–85).

7. Felonies and misdemeanors

Speedy trial statute provision, that person charged with misdemeanor shall be discharged if he is held in jail in lieu of bond awaiting trial on the pending charge, applies only to offenses that are classified as misdemeanors, and does not apply to fifth degree felony offenses. State v. Williams (Ohio App. 2 Dist., Montgomery, 09-30-2004) No. 20104, 2004-Ohio-5273, 2004 WL 2245101, Unreported. Criminal Law ⚷ 577.5

8. Parole or probation violations

There was evidence to support existence of valid parole holder on defendant, where trial transcript reflected that defense counsel entered into stipulation establishing existence of parole holder, preventing application of triple-count provisions of statute guaranteeing accused's right to be tried without inordinate delay. State v. Mann (Ohio App. 8 Dist., 11-15-1993) 93 Ohio App.3d 301, 638 N.E.2d 585, dismissed, appeal not allowed 70 Ohio St.3d 1412, 637 N.E.2d 9. Criminal Law ⚷ 577.8(1)

RC 2945.71(D) is not applicable where a defendant is held on both pending criminal charges and for probation violation. State v. Martin (Ohio 1978) 56 Ohio St.2d 207, 383 N.E.2d 585, 10 O.O.3d 369.

9. Juvenile offenders

The statutory speedy trial provisions of RC 2945.71 et seq. do not apply to juvenile traffic offenders. State v. Reed (Coshocton 1977) 54 Ohio App.2d 193, 376 N.E.2d 609, 8 O.O.3d 333. Infants ⚷ 204

10. Running of time period

Defendant became an accused, and thus right to speedy trial within 90 days began to run, when defendant was arrested for operating a motor vehicle while under the influence of alcohol (OMVI), not when defendant was formally served with citations for OMVI and for speeding, failure to control, and reckless operation; officer confronted defendant at time of arrest with form stating that defendant was under arrest, and all evidence pertaining to charges stemmed from night of arrest. City of Shaker Heights v. Kissee (Ohio App. 8 Dist., Cuyahoga, 12-26-2002) No. 81301, 2002-Ohio-7255, 2002 WL 31883358, Unreported. Criminal Law ⚷ 577.8(2)

Where an indictment is dismissed on defendant's motion for failure to state all of the elements of the crime, the indictment is a nullity, and the elapsed time from arrest to dismissal is not tacked onto a subsequent indictment to aggregate elapsed time for the application of RC 2945.73. State v. Lyons (Medina 1978) 60 Ohio App.2d 228, 401 N.E.2d 452, 15 O.O.3d 367. Criminal Law ⚷ 577.14

11. Extension of time

While the provisions of RC 2945.71, with respect to the periods of time within which trials in criminal cases must be held, apply to violations of traffic laws, the judge presiding over such cases may, however, pursuant to RC 2945.72, grant a continuance which extends the period upon a reasonable showing that there is insufficient time in which to try the case. OAG 74–062.

12. Burden of proof

Absent motion to dismiss for violation of speedy trial statute filed at or prior to commencement of trial, prosecutor had no duty to produce evidence of parole or probation "holder" relieving prosecutor of obligation to bring defendant to trial within 90 days of arrest. State v. Thompson (Ohio App. 6 Dist., 09-16-1994) 97 Ohio App.3d 183, 646 N.E.2d 499, dismissed, appeal not allowed 71 Ohio St.3d 1456, 644 N.E.2d 1029. Criminal Law ⚷ 577.16(7); Criminal Law ⚷ 577.16(8)

When a defendant moves for discharge on the basis that he has not been brought to trial within the time limits of RC 2945.71, and he presents a prima facie case entitling him to discharge, the burden of production of evidence shifts to the prosecution and the discharge is required if the prosecution fails to produce evidence in rebuttal. State v. Butcher (Ohio 1986) 27 Ohio St.3d 28, 500 N.E.2d 1368, 27 O.B.R. 445.

A prima facie case for discharge pursuant to RC 2945.73(B) is established where a felony defendant shows that 270 days have elapsed without a trial; the burden then falls on the prosecution to prove that sufficient time was extended under RC 2945.72 to leave fewer than 270 days remaining at the time the motion to dismiss is filed. State v. Geraldo (Lucas 1983) 13 Ohio App.3d 27, 468 N.E.2d 328, 13 O.B.R. 29. Criminal Law ⚷ 577.16(8); Criminal Law ⚷ 577.16(9)

13. Right to speedy trial denied

Defendant's failure to respond to State's discovery request did not toll period between date State filed its motion for reciprocal discovery and date defendant filed his response, and thus, defendant's statutory right to speedy trial was violated; there was no evidence presented that State was prejudiced in any way, nor did they avail themselves of a motion to compel as facilitated by criminal rules. State v. Palmer (Ohio App. 11 Dist., Portage, 12-16-2005) No. 2004-P-0106, 2005-Ohio-6710, 2005 WL 3476650, Unreported, stay granted 108 Ohio St.3d 1435, 842 N.E.2d 61, 2006-Ohio-421, motion to certify allowed 109 Ohio St.3d 1403, 845 N.E.2d 521, 2006-Ohio-1703, appeal allowed 109 Ohio St.3d 1405, 845 N.E.2d 522, 2006-Ohio-1703. Criminal Law ⚷ 577.10(8)

Trial court denied defendant his statutory right to a speedy trial, thus rendering his conviction for operating his vehicle at an excessive speed improper; defendant was not brought to trial within 45 days of transfer of his case to municipal court, and although court informed defendant village's most important witness was unavailable when defendant appeared for trial as scheduled on docket, village had not filed motion for continuance, as required. Oakwood v. Frailey (Ohio App. 8 Dist., Cuyahoga, 11-03-2005) No. 85973, 2005-Ohio-5856, 2005 WL 2885952, Unreported. Criminal Law ⚷ 577.12(1)

Defendant's right to a speedy trial was violated, thus requiring reversal of his conviction for felonious assault, where defendant's trial was conducted 13 days beyond speedy trial deadline, state failed to show that deadline was extended, and there was no affirmative demonstration of waiver of defendant's right to speedy trial. State v. Henry (Ohio App. 5 Dist., Licking, 06-23-2005) No. 04 CA 00062, 2005-Ohio-3191, 2005 WL 1491462, Unreported, appeal not allowed 107 Ohio St.3d 1423, 837 N.E.2d 1208, 2005-Ohio-6124. Criminal Law ⚷ 577.15(1); Criminal Law ⚷ 1166(7)

Failure to bring defendant to trial within 270 days of his re-arrest for assault on a peace officer violated his statutory right to a speedy trial. State v. Campbell (Ohio App. 11 Dist., Ashtabula, 06-17-2005) No. 2003-A-0056, 2005-Ohio-3091, 2005 WL 1423499, Unreported, appeal not allowed 107 Ohio St.3d 1410, 836 N.E.2d 1229, 2005-Ohio-5859. Criminal Law ⚷ 577.15(3)

Defendant held in lieu of bond on pending charge of criminal trespass for total period equal to maximum term for charge was entitled to dismissal of charge; criminal trespass charge carried maximum term of imprisonment of 30 days, and defendant had been held in lieu of bond for 30 days. City of Columbus v. Bryan (Ohio App. 10 Dist., Franklin, 07-22-2004) No. 03AP-1136, 2004-Ohio-3885, 2004 WL 1631739, Unreported. Criminal Law ⚷ 303.30(1)

If State does not comply with requirements of speedy trial statute, trial court must discharge defendant upon defendant's motion. State v. Stamps (Ohio App. 1 Dist., 04-03-1998) 127 Ohio App.3d 219, 712 N.E.2d 762. Criminal Law ⚷ 577.16(2)

State's failure to discharge defendant pending trial did not violate defendant's statutory right to speedy trial, where defendant did not raise matter of speedy trial with trial judge. State v. Trummer (Ohio App. 7 Dist., 09-30-1996) 114 Ohio App.3d 456, 683 N.E.2d 392, dismissed, appeal not allowed 78 Ohio St.3d 1409, 675 N.E.2d 1249, denial of post-conviction relief affirmed 1998 WL 896457, dismissed, appeal not allowed 85 Ohio St.3d 1464, 709 N.E.2d 171, motion for delayed appeal denied 2000 WL 1476604. Criminal Law ⚷ 577.16(6)

Failure of state to comply with mandates of Ohio speedy trial statute requires discharge of defendant. State v. Wirtanen (Ohio App. 6 Dist., 04-26-1996) 110 Ohio App.3d 604, 674 N.E.2d 1245. Criminal Law ⚷ 577.16(2)

When defendant demonstrates that either 270 days, or 90 triple-count days for days held in jail in lieu of bail, have elapsed following arrest, he has established prima facie case for dismissal under speedy trial statutes. State v. Collins (Ohio App. 6 Dist., 09-30-1993) 91 Ohio App.3d 10, 631 N.E.2d 666, dismissed, jurisdictional motion overruled 68 Ohio St.3d 1470, 628 N.E.2d 1389. Criminal Law ⚷ 577.15(3)

Defense counsel's demand for discovery required some continuance of trial and, thus, defendant's speedy trial rights were not violated, even though no entry had been journalized at that time appointing him as counsel; prosecutor, defense counsel and trial court had assumed that defense counsel was attorney of record because he so acted. State v. Roquemore (Franklin 1993) 85 Ohio App.3d 448, 620 N.E.2d 110. Criminal Law ⚷ 577.10(8)

A suppression motion filed by a defendant in a criminal prosecution tolls the speedy trial period only to the extent of the reasonable time necessary for the court to rule on the motion; a seven-month delay between the filing and the disposition of the motion in an OMVI case is unreasonable, and the ninety-day speedy trial period will be deemed lapsed and the defendant will be discharged. State v. Arrizola (Henry 1992) 79 Ohio App.3d 72, 606 N.E.2d 1020.

Where a defendant is not brought to trial within the time set forth in RC 2945.71 and there are no journal entries establishing continuances allegedly granted at defendant's request, the defendant is entitled to a discharge under RC 2945.73. State v. Benson (Cuyahoga 1985) 29 Ohio App.3d 321, 505 N.E.2d 987, 29 O.B.R. 448.

The trial court errs in vacating its order discharging the defendant on speedy trial grounds because the entry discharging the defendant was tantamount to a dismissal with prejudice, and thus acted as a bar to any further criminal proceedings based on the same conduct, especially a reinstatement, where the facts of the case lack a clear showing of delay occasioned by an act of the defendant that would extend the time in which he must be brought to trial. State v. England (Cuyahoga 1982) 8 Ohio App.3d 149, 456 N.E.2d 544, 8 O.B.R. 207.

Where an accused has been incarcerated since his arrest and due to clerical error the statutory time period for bringing him to trial has been allowed to expire and where none of the provisions of RC 2945.72 is applicable to extend the time for trial, then pursuant to RC 2945.73, the accused is, as a matter of law, entitled to be discharged and any further criminal proceedings against him based upon the same conduct are barred. State v. Eberhardt (Cuyahoga 1978) 56 Ohio App.2d 193, 381 N.E.2d 1357, 10 O.O.3d 197. Criminal Law ⚷ 577.16(2)

Appellant tried ninety-three days after arrest was entitled to discharge. State v. Tope (Ohio 1978) 53 Ohio St.2d 250, 374 N.E.2d 152, 7 O.O.3d 408.

An accused convicted after trial cannot obtain discharge upon the ground that he was not afforded a preliminary hearing or indicted within fifteen days after his arrest. State v. Pugh (Ohio 1978) 53 Ohio St.2d 153, 372 N.E.2d 1351, 7 O.O.3d 238.

Where trial court failed to set date for trial for first degree misdemeanor within ninety-day period and thereafter ruled sua sponte that the presence of a crowded docket warranted a continuance, defendant was entitled to discharge. State v. Pudlock (Ohio 1975) 44 Ohio St.2d 104, 338 N.E.2d 524, 73 O.O.2d 357.

Defendant accused of violation of RC 4511.20 whose trial is not held within fifteen days after arrest or service of summons must be discharged if defendant took no action which delayed proceedings. State v. Sells (Ohio Co. 1974) 41 Ohio Misc. 49, 322 N.E.2d 378, 70 O.O.2d 109.

Defendant who was charged with second-degree felony of abduction and was found guilty of third-degree misdemeanor of unlawful restraint was not entitled to discharge under speedy trial statute, though he was held in jail pending trial for longer than maximum allowable sentence for a third-degree misdemeanor; discharge under speedy trial statute required that original charge also be a misdemeanor. State v. Andujar (Ohio App. 10 Dist., Franklin, 06-27-2002) No. 01AP-1219, 2002-Ohio-3325, 2002 WL 1379984, Unreported. Criminal Law ⚷ 577.16(1)

RC 2945.73 mandates the dismissal of charges against a defendant denied a timely preliminary hearing; the dismissal of the original charge has the effect of a nolle prosequi. Styer v Brichta, No. 90WD072 (6th Dist Ct App, Wood, 10–10–90).

14. Judgement and findings

Trial judge possessed no duty to issue findings of fact and conclusions of law with regard to denial of motion to dismiss as based upon a lack of speedy trial. Gales v. State (Ohio App. 8 Dist., Cuyahoga, 04-30-2004) No. 84300, 2004-Ohio-2327, 2004 WL 1045894, Unreported. Criminal Law ⚷ 577.16(10)

A trial court must, upon the defendant's request, state essential findings of fact in support of its denial of a motion to discharge for failure to comply with the speedy trial provisions of RC 2945.71. City of Bryan v. Knapp (Ohio 1986) 21 Ohio St.3d 64, 488 N.E.2d 142, 21 O.B.R. 363. Criminal Law ⚷ 577.16(10)

A judge's notation on the jacket of a criminal case file does not constitute a judgment entry. City of Columbus v. McCreary (Franklin 1981) 3 Ohio App.3d 216, 444 N.E.2d 436, 3 O.B.R. 245, reconsideration overruled. Criminal Law ⚷ 994(1)

15. Sentence

Where an accused is originally charged with an offense within the category of felony, and is entitled to have his period of incarceration deducted from any future sentence, pursuant to RC 2967.191, a subsequent amendment of the complaint changing the offense to one within the category of misdemeanor does not affect his right to the benefits of the statute. Haddox v. Houser (Franklin 1975) 44 Ohio App.2d 389, 339 N.E.2d 666, 73 O.O.2d 464.

16. Appeal

Defendant waived appellate review of his claim that he was not brought to trial on felony charges within time provided by speedy trial statute and, therefore, should have been discharged, where record did not indicate that issue of speedy trial was raised to trial court. State v. Kolvek (Ohio App. 9 Dist., Summit, 07-14-2004) No. 21752, 2004-Ohio-3706, 2004 WL 1562573, Unreported, appeal not allowed 103 Ohio St.3d 1528, 817 N.E.2d 410, 2004-Ohio-5852, appeal not allowed 104 Ohio St.3d 1441, 819 N.E.2d 1124, 2004-Ohio-7033. Criminal Law ⚷ 1035(1)

Complaint for a writ of mandamus could not be employed to challenge denial of a relator's right to speedy trial; rather, speedy trial issues could only be addressed through a direct appeal following trial. Gales v. State (Ohio App. 8 Dist., Cuyahoga, 04-30-2004) No. 84300, 2004-Ohio-2327, 2004 WL 1045894, Unreported. Mandamus ⚷ 4(1)

Criminal defendant could not use mandamus to obtain dismissal of charges against him on speedy trial grounds; claim of lack of speedy trial had to be addressed through direct appeal. State ex rel. Dunn v. Callahan (Ohio App. 8 Dist., Cuyahoga, 11-18-2003) No. 83451, 2003-Ohio-6182, 2003 WL 22725087, Unreported. Mandamus ⚷ 4(4)

Criminal defendant had adequate remedy at law, through a direct appeal if he was convicted of murder, and thus, defendant was not entitled to mandamus relief, as to trial court's alleged violation of his statutory speedy trial rights while he was being held in county jail as he awaited trial. Hamilton v. Collins (Ohio App. 11 Dist., Lake, 10-24-2003) No. 2003-L-106, 2003-Ohio-5703, 2003 WL 22427933, Unreported. Mandamus ⚷ 4(1)

Failure to file a motion to dismiss on speedy trial grounds prior to trial prevented defendant from raising speedy trial issue on appeal. State v. Taylor (Ohio, 12-20-2002) 98 Ohio St.3d 27, 781 N.E.2d 72, 2002-Ohio-7017, stay granted 98 Ohio St.3d 1402, 781 N.E.2d 221, 2003-Ohio-40, certiorari denied 123 S.Ct. 2227, 538 U.S. 1062, 155 L.Ed.2d 1115. Criminal Law ⚷ 1044.1(1)

An appeal rather than a writ of habeas corpus is the appropriate remedy when challenging violations of the right to speedy trial. Russell v. Tate (Ohio 1992) 64 Ohio St.3d 444, 596 N.E.2d 1039, rehearing denied 65 Ohio St.3d 1436, 600 N.E.2d 680. Habeas Corpus ⚷ 479

Mandamus is not available to compel a judge to dismiss an indictment on speedy trial grounds, as the defendant has an adequate remedy at law by way of a post-trial appeal. State ex rel. Dix v. Angelotta (Ohio 1985) 18 Ohio St.3d 115, 480 N.E.2d 407, 18 O.B.R. 146.

The state is not barred from prosecution following an unsuccessful appeal from the sustaining of a motion to suppress so long as the state's certification upon appeal pursuant to Juv R 22(F) or Crim R 12(J), that the evidence suppressed was of such nature that the prosecution could not be successful without it, was made in good faith; if such certification were not made in good faith, the time consumed in determining the appeal from the motion to suppress must be charged to the state as undue delay in prosecution of the accused with respect to a determination of whether there has been a violation of the accused's right to a speedy trial. In re Hester (Franklin 1982) 3 Ohio App.3d 458, 446

N.E.2d 202, 3 O.B.R. 539. Criminal Law ⇔ 577.12(1)

The denial of a motion to dismiss a criminal charge, made pursuant to RC 2945.73, is not a final appealable order. State v. Cinema X Bookstore (Montgomery 1976) 49 Ohio App.2d 164, 359 N.E.2d 1382, 3 O.O.3d 218. Criminal Law ⇔ 1023(1)

Under RC 2945.71 through RC 2945.73, a trial court has discretion to extend the time limit for trial prescribed therein, and, where the trial court dismisses an indictment and discharges an accused on the basis that it lacks discretion to consider an extension, upon appeal thereof the cause will be remanded to the trial court for an exercise of that court's discretion. State v. Davis (Ohio 1976) 46 Ohio St.2d 444, 349 N.E.2d 315, 75 O.O.2d 498. Criminal Law ⇔ 577.16(3); Criminal Law ⇔ 1181.5(3.1)

The granting of a motion to dismiss a charge against an accused for delaying trial, made pursuant to RC 2945.73, may not be appealed by the state. State v. Sonnie (Lake 1975) 46 Ohio App.2d 164, 346 N.E.2d 791, 75 O.O.2d 254. Criminal Law ⇔ 1024(2)

The failure of the trial court to comply with Crim R 48(B) when dismissing an indictment for lack of a speedy trial requires a remand to the trial court, on appeal by the state, for such findings of fact and reasons for the dismissal that will enable the reviewing court to pass upon the assignments of error. State v. Bound (Cuyahoga 1975) 43 Ohio App.2d 44, 332 N.E.2d 366, 72 O.O.2d 197.

Mandamus will not lie to compel relator's discharge on the ground he was denied a speedy trial for the reason that an adequate remedy by way of appeal is available. State ex rel. Wentz v. Correll (Ohio 1975) 41 Ohio St.2d 101, 322 N.E.2d 889, 70 O.O.2d 196.

Mandamus will not lie to compel authorities to dismiss pending criminal charges due to an alleged denial of a speedy trial. State ex rel. Woodbury v. Spitler (Ohio 1974) 40 Ohio St.2d 1, 318 N.E.2d 165, 69 O.O.2d 42.

17. Waiver

Trial court violated defendant's right to a speedy trial when defendant was not brought to trial on fourth degree misdemeanor charges of parking in a no parking zone and having a firearm in a motor vehicle until 81 chargeable days following his arrest; defendant did not expressly waive his right to a speedy trial in writing or by statement made in open court, no delay was occasioned by defendant's request for counsel since counsel was appointed for defendant the day it was requested, and the trial court did not grant a continuance by journal entry or explain the reason for the delay. State v. McLean (Ohio App. 11 Dist., Trumbull, 03-04-2005) No. 2003-T-0115, No. 2003-T-0116, 2005-Ohio-954, 2005 WL 517455, Unreported. Criminal Law ⇔ 577.10(8); Criminal Law ⇔ 577.10(9)

Defendant was precluded from raising speedy trial issue on appeal, where he failed to move for dismissal or discharge for a violation of his speedy trial rights, either orally or in writing, during or prior to trial. State v. Humphrey (Ohio App. 2 Dist., Clark, 05-30-2003) No. CIV.A. 02CA0025, 2003-Ohio-2825, 2003 WL 21267255, Unreported, motion for delayed appeal denied 101 Ohio St.3d 1485, 805 N.E.2d 537, 2004-Ohio-1293, appeal not allowed 102 Ohio St.3d 1533, 811 N.E.2d 1152, 2004-Ohio-3580. Criminal Law ⇔ 1044.1(1)

Right to a speedy trial is denied defendant when she is brought to trial on a charge of child endangering nearly eight months after her arrest for driving under the influence involving the same set of circumstances; a waiver of speedy trial as to the DUI charge is not applicable to the child endangering charge. State v. Homan (Ohio App. 6 Dist., Erie, 05-14-1999) No. E-97-100, 1999 WL 300229, Unreported, stay granted 86 Ohio St.3d 1423, 712 N.E.2d 124, dismissed, appeal not allowed 86 Ohio St.3d 1487, 716 N.E.2d 720, appeal allowed 87 Ohio St.3d 1443, 719 N.E.2d 7, affirmed 89 Ohio St.3d 421, 732 N.E.2d 952, 2000-Ohio-212, reconsideration denied 90 Ohio St.3d 1431, 736 N.E.2d 27.

Defense counsel's signing of docket and journal entry which contained waiver of speedy trial requirement in consideration of continuance of trial constituted waiver of defendant's speedy trial rights, despite defense counsel's contention that he had signed docket and journal entry merely to acknowledge his receipt thereof; there was no language on the entry to support defense counsel's contention. State v. Hughey (Ohio App. 7 Dist., 11-20-1996) 115 Ohio App.3d 664, 685 N.E.2d 1318. Criminal Law ⇔ 577.10(9)

Speedy trial provisions are not self-executing but must be asserted by defendant in timely fashion to avoid such rights being waived. State v. Trummer (Ohio App. 7 Dist., 09-30-1996) 114 Ohio App.3d 456, 683 N.E.2d 392, dismissed, appeal not allowed 78 Ohio St.3d 1409, 675 N.E.2d 1249, denial of post-conviction relief affirmed 1998 WL 896457, dismissed, appeal not allowed 85 Ohio St.3d 1464, 709 N.E.2d 171, motion for delayed appeal denied 2000 WL 1476604. Criminal Law ⇔ 577.10(10)

Defendant did not waive her statutory or constitutional rights to speedy trial, despite alleged oral waiver by trial counsel; neither defendant nor counsel made express written waiver or waived her right to speedy trial in open court on record. State v. King (Ohio, 08-31-1994) 70 Ohio St.3d 158, 637 N.E.2d 903, 1994-Ohio-412. Criminal Law ⇔ 577.10(9)

An attorney's failure to move for discharge based on a speedy trial violation does not render a guilty plea unknowing and involuntary or constitute ineffective assistance of counsel. State v. Barnett (Montgomery 1991) 73 Ohio App.3d 244, 596 N.E.2d 1101.

By pleading guilty, a defendant waives the right to appeal his conviction on the ground that his trial was not begun within the time required by RC 2945.71 et seq. Village of Montpelier v. Greeno (Ohio 1986) 25 Ohio St.3d 170, 495 N.E.2d 581, 25 O.B.R. 212.

A defendant who fails to appear at a scheduled trial, and whose trial must therefore be rescheduled for a later date, waives his right to assert the provisions of RC 2945.71 to RC 2945.73 for that period of time which elapses from his initial arrest to the date he is subsequently rearrested. State v. Bauer (Ohio 1980) 61 Ohio St.2d 83, 399 N.E.2d 555, 15 O.O.3d 122. Criminal Law ⚷ 577.10(8)

Execution of a waiver form by a defendant purporting to waive the defendant's speedy trial rights removes the case from the operation of the speedy trial statutes. City of Westlake v. Cougill (Ohio 1978) 56 Ohio St.2d 230, 383 N.E.2d 599, 10 O.O.3d 382.

A defendant's failure to object to a trial date scheduled outside the ninety-day limitation period of RC 2945.71(C)(2) and RC 2945.71(D), before the expiration of that period, does not amount to acquiescence in the trial date. State v. Singer (Ohio 1977) 50 Ohio St.2d 103, 362 N.E.2d 1216, 4 O.O.3d 237. Criminal Law ⚷ 577.10(9)

Where a case has been set for trial on a date beyond the period required by RC 2945.71 and the accused has ample notice thereof, he may not sit idly by and let the time within which he should be brought to trial expire in order to take advantage of the provisions of RC 2945.73. State v. Westbrook (Franklin 1975) 47 Ohio App.2d 211, 353 N.E.2d 637, 1 O.O.3d 284. Criminal Law ⚷ 577.10(10)

An agreement between defense counsel, the prosecutor and an officer of the court made at a pre-trial hearing (held within sixty days after arrest) to set the trial date beyond ninety days after defendant's arrest is valid and binding upon the defendant, and is a continuance pursuant to RC 2945.72(H) which will bar defendant's discharge. State v. Taylor (Lorain 1975) 47 Ohio App.2d 171, 352 N.E.2d 604, 1 O.O.3d 259. Criminal Law ⚷ 577.10(9)

Trial court was not required to ascertain that defendant understood he was waiving right to present an arguable motion for discharge of charges against him when he plead guilty to attempted rape and aggravated burglary; motion for discharge was remedy for right to speedy trial, which had already been violated, and thus, trial court was only required to ascertain that defendant understood, and knowingly, intelligently, and voluntarily agreed to waive those rights that had not yet been violated before accepting his guilty plea. State v. Kitchens (Ohio App. 2 Dist., Clark, 08-23-2002) No. 2001-CA-92, 2002-Ohio-4335, 2002 WL 1941154, Unreported, appeal not allowed 98 Ohio St.3d 1411, 781 N.E.2d 1019, 2003-Ohio-60, appeal not allowed 105 Ohio St.3d 1519, 826 N.E.2d 316, 2005-Ohio-1880. Criminal Law ⚷ 273.1(4)

Trial counsel was not ineffective in having permitted defendant to enter into a plea agreement wherein his possibility of obtaining a speedy trial discharge was exchanged for dismissal of serious charges of kidnapping and felonious assault, and the State's waiver of any objection to an aggregate sentence of 18 years, upon entering plea to attempted rape and aggravated burglary, and likelihood of obtaining relief under the speedy trial statute was not so great as to render the plea bargain unattractive. State v. Kitchens (Ohio App. 2 Dist., Clark, 08-23-2002) No. 2001-CA-92, 2002-Ohio-4335, 2002 WL 1941154, Unreported, appeal not allowed 98 Ohio St.3d 1411, 781 N.E.2d 1019, 2003-Ohio-60, appeal not allowed 105 Ohio St.3d 1519, 826 N.E.2d 316, 2005-Ohio-1880. Criminal Law ⚷ 641.13(5)

DEGREE OF OFFENSE

2945.74 Defendant may be convicted of lesser offense

The jury may find the defendant not guilty of the offense charged, but guilty of an attempt to commit it if such attempt is an offense at law. When the indictment or information charges an offense, including different degrees, or if other offenses are included within the offense charged, the jury may find the defendant not guilty of the degree charged but guilty of an inferior degree thereof or lesser included offense.

If the offense charged is murder and the accused is convicted by confession in open court, the court shall examine the witnesses, determine the degree of the crime, and pronounce sentence accordingly.

(1953 H 1, eff. 10–1–53; GC 13448–2)

Historical and Statutory Notes

Pre–1953 H 1 Amendments: 113 v 194, Ch 27, § 2

Cross References

Code of military justice, conviction of lesser included offense by person subject to, 5924.79

Judge may reduce conviction to lesser degree or offense, Crim R 33

Trial for crimes; witness, O Const Art I §10

Verdict, Crim R 31

Library References

Criminal Law ⚩878, 883.

Indictment and Information ⚩189 to 192.

Westlaw Topic Nos. 110, 210.

C.J.S. Criminal Law §§ 1406, 1409.

Research References

Encyclopedias

OH Jur. 3d Criminal Law § 609, Lesser Included Offenses.

OH Jur. 3d Criminal Law § 610, Inferior Degrees of Crime.

OH Jur. 3d Criminal Law § 650, Trial; Jury Charge.

OH Jur. 3d Criminal Law § 1015, Upon Confession in Open Court.

OH Jur. 3d Criminal Law § 2343, Lesser Degrees, Lesser Included Offenses, and Attempts to Commit Crime Charged.

Treatises and Practice Aids

Katz, Giannelli, Blair and Lipton, Baldwin's Ohio Practice, Criminal Law, § 40:5, Nature and Contents.

Katz, Giannelli, Blair and Lipton, Baldwin's Ohio Practice, Criminal Law, § 148:32, Jury Verdict.

Katz, Giannelli, Blair and Lipton, Baldwin's Ohio Practice, Criminal Law, § 148:34, Verdict of Guilty on One Count.

Katz, Giannelli, Blair and Lipton, Baldwin's Ohio Practice, Criminal Law, § 148:35, Verdict of Guilty of Inferior Degree or of Lesser Included Offense.

Katz, Giannelli, Blair and Lipton, Baldwin's Ohio Practice, Criminal Law, § 148:36, Verdict of Guilty of Attempt.

Hennenberg & Reinhart, Ohio Criminal Defense Motions F 13.49, Memorandum in Support of Charge to Jury of Lesser Included Offenses to Aggravated Murder-Death Penalty Motions.

Law Review and Journal Commentaries

Constitutional Limitations on the Lesser Included Offense Doctrine, Christen R. Blair. 21 Am Crim L Rev 445 (Spring 1984).

State v. Ikner: Examining the Merger Doctrine and Double Jeopardy in Terms of Auto Theft, Note. 4 Ohio N U L Rev 111 (1977).

Notes of Decisions

---

1. Constitutional issues

To determine whether a subsequent prosecution is barred by the Double Jeopardy Clause of the Fifth Amendment, a court must first apply the Blockburger test; if application of the test reveals that the offenses have identical statutory elements or one that is a lesser included offense of the other, the subsequent prosecution is barred. State v. Tolbert (Ohio 1991) 60 Ohio St.3d 89, 573 N.E.2d 617, certiorari denied 112 S.Ct. 1215, 502 U.S. 1111, 117 L.Ed.2d 453. Double Jeopardy ⚩ 132.1; Double Jeopardy ⚩ 161

Trial court's error in finding defendant guilty of lesser included offenses upon his plea of no contest to charges in indictment could not be corrected; case involved felonies, when no-contest plea was offered and accepted defendant had subjected herself to jeopardy, which precluded any and all subsequent procedures addressing defendant's guilt or innocence, and thus remand for further procedures would violate constitutional provisions against double jeopardy. State v. Rader (Hamilton 1988) 55 Ohio App.3d 102, 563 N.E.2d 304. Double Jeopardy ⚩ 165

The rule as to former jeopardy under the US Const Am 5, is that, where the same act or transaction constitutes a violation of a distinct provision of an Ohio statute and a distinct provision of a city ordinance, the test to be applied to determine whether there are two offenses or only one is whether each provision requires proof of a fact which the other does not; a single act may be an offense against both the ordinance and the statute, and, if the statute requires proof of an additional fact which the ordinance does not, an acquittal or conviction under the ordinance does not exempt the defendant from prosecution and punishment under the statute. State v. Ikner (Ohio 1975) 44 Ohio St.2d 132, 339 N.E.2d 633, 73 O.O.2d 444. Double Jeopardy ⚩ 135

RC 2945.06 and RC 2945.74 are in pari materia, so that to the extent that an open-court confession, i.e., a plea to homicide generally, supersedes an in-custody confession, the alleged failure to comply with Miranda criteria is waived and is not prejudicial. State v. Place (Lucas 1971) 25 Ohio App.2d 158, 267 N.E.2d 832, 54 O.O.2d 337.

The general rule against attacks on inconsistent verdicts does not except cases in which a jury acquits of a predicate felony while convicting on a compound felony; thus, a conviction of a defendant for use of a telephone to facilitate both a conspiracy to possess cocaine and possession of cocaine need not be reversed merely because it cannot be reconciled with an acquittal of the defendant by the jury at the same trial on conspiracy and possession charges. U.S. v. Powell (U.S.Cal. 1984) 105 S.Ct. 471, 469 U.S. 57, 83 L.Ed.2d 461.

Where defendant pleads guilty to first degree murder, neither failure of the court to appoint counsel nor failure to obtain a written waiver of the right to jury trial from such defendant is grounds for issuance of a writ of habeas corpus. Sims v. Alvis (C.A.6 (Ohio) 1958) 253 F.2d 114, 16 O.O.2d 185, certiorari denied 79 S.Ct. 67, 358 U.S. 844, 3 L.Ed.2d 78.

2. In general

Offense may be lesser included offense of another if (i) offense carries lesser penalty than other; (ii) greater offense cannot, as statutorily defined, ever be committed without lesser, as statutorily defined, also being committed; and (iii) some element of greater offense is not required to prove commission of lesser offense. State v. Fleming (Ohio App. 2 Dist., 09-27-1996) 114 Ohio App.3d 294, 683 N.E.2d 79. Indictment And Information ⚿ 191(.5)

Where it would be possible for the same evidence to prove both a greater offense and a lesser offense depending solely on the culpable mental state of the accused, the lesser offense is a lesser included offense of the greater offense even though it might be possible in a different case to prove commission of the greater offense without proving commission of the lesser. State v. Banks (Franklin 1986) 31 Ohio App.3d 57, 508 N.E.2d 986, 31 O.B.R. 97. Indictment And Information ⚿ 191(.5)

"Lesser included offense" relates only to an offense of the same general character and not to a distinct and independent offense of a different class. State v. Stover (Cuyahoga 1982) 8 Ohio App.3d 179, 456 N.E.2d 833, 8 O.B.R. 239. Indictment And Information ⚿ 191(.5)

The doctrine of "inferior degrees" or "included offenses," whereby an accused may be found not guilty of the offense charged but guilty of a lesser included offense, relates only to offenses of the same general character and not to distinct and independent offenses of different classes, and a jury may not lawfully find an accused, indicted with assault with intent to kill, not guilty of that crime, but guilty of the crime of assault with intent to maim. State v. Kuchmak (Ohio 1953) 159 Ohio St. 363, 112 N.E.2d 371, 50 O.O. 327.

3. Included elements

Offense may be lesser included offense of another if offense carries lesser penalty than other, greater offense cannot, if statutorily defined, ever be committed without lesser offense also being committed, and some element of greater offense is not required to prove commission of lesser offense. State v. Sibert (Ohio App. 4 Dist., 11-04-1994) 98 Ohio App.3d 412, 648 N.E.2d 861, motion for delayed appeal denied 71 Ohio St.3d 1479, 645 N.E.2d 1258, denial of post-conviction relief affirmed 74 Ohio St.3d 342, 658 N.E.2d 772, 1996-Ohio-15. Indictment And Information ⚿ 191(.5)

Aggravated assault, RC 2903.12, contains elements which are identical to the elements defining felonious assault, RC 2903.11, except for the additional mitigating element of serious provocation; thus, in a trial for felonious assault, where the defendant presents sufficient evidence of serious provocation, an instruction on aggravated assault must be given to the jury. State v. Deem (Ohio 1988) 40 Ohio St.3d 205, 533 N.E.2d 294.

An offense is an "inferior degree" of the indicted offense where its elements are identical to or contained within the indicted offense, except for one or more additional mitigating elements. State v. Deem (Ohio 1988) 40 Ohio St.3d 205, 533 N.E.2d 294. Indictment And Information ⚿ 189(1)

An offense may be a lesser included offense of another only if (1) the offense is a crime of lesser degree than the other, (2) the offense of the greater degree cannot, as statutorily defined, ever be committed without the offense of the lesser degree, as statutorily defined, also being committed, and (3) some element of the greater offense is not required to prove the commission of the lesser offense. State v. Kidder (Ohio 1987) 32 Ohio St.3d 279, 513 N.E.2d 311. Indictment And Information ⚿ 191(.5)

Separate charges for operating a gambling house and possession of criminal tools may be prosecuted separately as "each provision requires proof of an additional fact which the other does not." State v. Stover (Cuyahoga 1982) 8 Ohio App.3d 179, 456 N.E.2d 833, 8 O.B.R. 239.

"Lesser included offense" relates only to an offense of the same general character and not to a distinct and independent offense of a different class. State v. Stover (Cuyahoga 1982) 8 Ohio App.3d 179, 456 N.E.2d 833, 8 O.B.R. 239. Indictment And Information ⚿ 191(.5)

Where an indictment issued by a grand jury charges an accused with a theft offense while having a deadly weapon on his person contrary to RC 2911.01(A)(1), a subsequent amendment of such indictment by the court which eliminates any reference to the weapon but substitutes words indicating the defendant threatened the use of immediate force contrary to RC 2911.02 changes the offense to one unrelated to the original crime charged and is invalid. State v. Washington (Montgomery 1978) 56 Ohio App.2d 129, 381 N.E.2d 1142, 10 O.O.3d 150.

The rule as to former jeopardy under the US Const Am 5, is that, where the same act or transaction constitutes a violation of a distinct provision of an Ohio statute and a distinct provision of a city ordinance, the test to be applied to determine whether there are two offenses or only one is whether each provision requires proof of a fact which the other does not; a single act may be an offense against both the ordinance and the statute, and, if the statute requires proof of an additional fact which the ordinance does not, an acquittal or conviction under the ordinance does not exempt the defendant from prosecution and punishment under the statute. State v. Ikner (Ohio 1975) 44 Ohio St.2d 132, 339 N.E.2d 633, 73 O.O.2d 444. Double Jeopardy ⚿ 135

Where the proper averments of an indictment for the aggravated degree of rape specified in RC 2905.02 set forth or indicate with reasonable certainty all the essential elements of the crime of statutory rape described in RC 2905.03, such indictment will support a conviction for the latter crime. State v. Daniels (Ohio 1959) 169 Ohio St. 87, 157 N.E.2d 736, 76 A.L.R.2d 468, 8 O.O.2d 56.

An indictment of an accused over eighteen for carnally knowing and abusing a female person under sixteen with her consent has the effect also of charging the accused with an attempt to rape a female person under sixteen with her consent, and sufficiently informs the accused that he is charged with committing rape and also with attempting to commit rape and conforms to all constitutional requirements as to the manner in which a person should be charged with the commission of an offense. State v. Ross (Paulding 1954) 96 Ohio App. 157, 121 N.E.2d 289, 54 O.O. 230, appeal dismissed 161 Ohio St. 408, 119 N.E.2d 618, 53 O.O. 310, certiorari denied 75 S.Ct. 68, 348 U.S. 846, 99 L.Ed. 666.

4. Evidence of lesser offenses

Defendant charged with domestic violence by threats could be convicted of minor misdemeanor of disorderly conduct, where disorderly conduct was lesser included offense of domestic violence by threats; "knowingly" state of mind required for greater offense of domestic violence by threats encompassed reckless state of mind required for disorderly conduct. State v. Stewart (Ohio App. 2 Dist., Montgomery, 01-17-2003) No. 19309, 2003-Ohio-214, 2003 WL 139971, Unreported. Indictment And Information ⚿ 191(.5)

Charge on lesser included offense is required only when evidence presented at trial would reasonably support both an acquittal on crime charged and a conviction upon lesser included offense. State v. Braxton (Ohio App. 8 Dist., 03-21-1995) 102 Ohio App.3d 28, 656 N.E.2d 970, dismissed, appeal not allowed 73 Ohio St.3d 1425, 652 N.E.2d 798. Criminal Law ⚿ 795(2.1)

A jury instruction of the lesser included offense of sexual battery in a rape trial is not necessary where the defendant presents no evidence to substantiate his claim that force was not involved. State v. Patton (Union 1991) 74 Ohio App.3d 224, 598 N.E.2d 777, dismissed, jurisdictional motion overruled 62 Ohio St.3d 1439, 579 N.E.2d 212, rehearing denied 62 Ohio St.3d 1466, 580 N.E.2d 786.

Aggravated assault, RC 2903.12, contains elements which are identical to the elements defining felonious assault, RC 2903.11, except for the additional mitigating element of serious provocation; thus, in a trial for felonious assault, where the defendant presents sufficient evidence of serious provocation, an instruction on aggravated assault must be given to the jury. State v. Deem (Ohio 1988) 40 Ohio St.3d 205, 533 N.E.2d 294.

An offense may be a lesser included offense of another if (1) the offense carries a lesser penalty than the other; (2) the greater offense cannot, as statutorily defined, ever be committed without the lesser offense, as statutorily defined, also being committed; and (3) some element of the greater offense is not required to prove the commission of the lesser offense. State v. Deem (Ohio 1988) 40 Ohio St.3d 205, 533 N.E.2d 294. Indictment And Information ⚿ 191(.5)

Even though an offense may be statutorily defined as a lesser included offense of another, a charge on such lesser included offense is required only where the evidence presented at trial would reasonably support both an acquittal on the crime charged and a conviction upon the lesser included offense. State v. Thomas (Ohio 1988) 40 Ohio St.3d 213, 533 N.E.2d 286, certiorari denied 110 S.Ct. 89, 493 U.S. 826, 107 L.Ed.2d 54. Criminal Law ⚿ 795(2.1)

A defendant charged with felonious assault may be found guilty of the lesser included offense of aggravated assault where there is evidence of provocation, as the legislature, in enacting RC 2903.12, the aggravated assault statute, provided for a reduction in penalty for an assault provoked by the victim. State v. Whitt (Hamilton 1987) 31 Ohio App.3d 92, 508 N.E.2d 1041, 31 O.B.R. 134.

Involuntary manslaughter does not constitute a lesser included offense of murder where there is no evidence that an underlying misdemeanor such as aggravated menacing was being committed at the time of the shooting, and a court's refusal to instruct the jury on the lesser included offense of involuntary manslaughter is proper. State v. Hill (Hamilton 1987) 31 Ohio App.3d 65, 508 N.E.2d 1038, 31 O.B.R. 105.

In a prosecution for murder where it is undisputed that the death was caused by means of a deadly weapon, and there is evidence, which if believed, could support a finding that the death was a result of negligence, negligent homicide constitutes a lesser included offense of murder, and a court's failure to so instruct a jury is error. State v. Banks (Franklin 1986) 31 Ohio App.3d 57, 508 N.E.2d 986, 31 O.B.R. 97.

In the trial of a defendant for aggravated burglary, it would be unreasonable for the trier of the fact to conclude that a confrontation between the defendant and some resident of the burglarized house or legitimate visitor therein was unlikely solely because the defendant had observed one of the residents playing cards at a neighboring house, and a requested charge to the jury on the lesser-included offense of burglary is properly refused. State v. Kilby

(Ohio 1977) 50 Ohio St.2d 21, 361 N.E.2d 1336, 4 O.O.3d 80.

In a criminal prosecution, instructions to the jury on lesser included offenses to the crime charged are not automatically given; there must first be some basis for them arising from the law and the evidence in the case; the general rule is that, where the evidence in a criminal case would support a finding by the jury of guilt of a lesser included offense to the offense for which the defendant was indicted and tried, a charge on such lesser included offense must be given; the refusal of a trial court to charge upon such a required lesser included offense is error prejudicial to the rights of the defendant. State v. Jones (Cuyahoga 1975) 47 Ohio App.2d 8, 351 N.E.2d 798, 1 O.O.3d 156.

No charge as to a lesser-included offense need be given unless, in view of evidence introduced at trial, there are elements of principal charge which could reasonably be found for the state, and against defendant, which elements would sustain only a conviction on such lesser-included offense. State v. Carver (Ohio 1972) 30 Ohio St.2d 280, 285 N.E.2d 26, 59 O.O.2d 343, certiorari denied 93 S.Ct. 542, 409 U.S. 1044, 34 L.Ed.2d 495. Criminal Law ⚷ 795(2.20)

Where the record of a trial for shooting with intent to wound shows that the undisputed use of a pistol is the only element differentiating the lesser included offense of assault with a dangerous weapon from assault and battery, the accused is not entitled to a jury instruction on the latter offense. State v. Mastel (Ohio 1971) 26 Ohio St.2d 170, 270 N.E.2d 650, 55 O.O.2d 378.

Where an accused is indicted and tried upon a charge of murder in the second degree, if the evidence raises a jury issue as to whether the killing was intentional or unintentional and the testimony tends to show and is such that the jury may find beyond reasonable doubt an unlawful and unintentional killing caused by the accused while violating a law or laws of this state applying to the use or regulation of traffic, the jury should consider, and it is the duty of the court to charge upon, the lesser included offense of manslaughter in the second degree. State v. Butler (Stark 1966) 6 Ohio App.2d 193, 217 N.E.2d 237, 35 O.O.2d 353, reversed 11 Ohio St.2d 23, 227 N.E.2d 627, 21 A.L.R.2d 102, 40 O.O.2d 43. Automobiles ⚷ 357

Murder in the second degree, literally considered, necessarily includes manslaughter, and depends not merely upon whether it is literally included in the formal charge, but upon whether there is any evidence tending to support a charge of manslaughter. State v. Loudermill (Lucas 1963) 2 Ohio App.2d 311, 208 N.E.2d 156, 31 O.O.2d 466, affirmed 2 Ohio St.2d 79, 206 N.E.2d 198, 31 O.O.2d 60.

Where the evidence in a criminal case would support a finding by the jury of guilt of a lesser offense included in the offense for which defendant was indicted and tried, the refusal of the trial court to charge upon that lesser included offense is error prejudicial to the rights of defendant. State v. Loudermill (Ohio 1965) 2 Ohio St.2d 79, 206 N.E.2d 198, 31 O.O.2d 60.

Where defendant was present when the front door was forced open and while others ransacked the house and he admitted that he possessed jewelry, defendant was not entitled to an instruction of criminal trespass, a lesser offense of aggravated burglary. State v Mann, No. 1074 (11th Dist Ct App, Ashtabula, 5–28–82).

Although defendant charged with aggravated murder is entitled to jury instructions as to the lesser included offenses of murder and involuntary manslaughter even though defendant asserts a complete defense of alibi, defendant is not entitled to such instruction where defendant's evidence does not tend to prove either lesser offense. State v Lewis, No. 43987 (8th Dist Ct App, Cuyahoga, 5–6–82).

Trial court did not abuse its discretion in failing to instruct the jury on assault as a lesser included offense of robbery where the jury could not reasonably find the evidence to support a conviction of assault. State v Howell, No. 1078 (4th Dist Ct App, Athens, 2–18–82).

5. Assertion of complete defense

If evidence adduced on behalf of defense is such that if accepted by trier of fact, it would constitute complete defense to all substantive elements of crime charged, trier of fact will not be permitted to consider lesser included offense. State v. Braxton (Ohio App. 8 Dist., 03-21-1995) 102 Ohio App.3d 28, 656 N.E.2d 970, dismissed, appeal not allowed 73 Ohio St.3d 1425, 652 N.E.2d 798. Criminal Law ⚷ 748

The assertion that a death was the result of a mutual suicide pact is a complete defense to any crime by the survivor to the pact; thus, given such assertion, the trial court in an aggravated murder case does not commit reversible error by refusing to charge on lesser included offenses. State v. Sage (Ohio 1987) 31 Ohio St.3d 173, 510 N.E.2d 343, 31 O.B.R. 375.

Where a defendant in a murder prosecution asserts an accident defense throughout the entire trial, a request for jury instructions on the lesser included offense of negligent homicide must be denied where the theory of negligent homicide is not asserted until the instruction is requested, and the evidence is insufficient to demonstrate criminal negligence. State v. Hill (Hamilton 1987) 31 Ohio App.3d 65, 508 N.E.2d 1038, 31 O.B.R. 105.

Where the evidence adduced on behalf of the defendant constitutes a complete defense to the substantive elements of the crime charged, an instruction on a lesser included offense should be given to the trier of fact only if, based on the evidence adduced by the state, the trier of fact can find for the defendant and against the state on some element of the greater offense which is not required to prove the commission of the lesser offense and for the state on the elements required to prove the commission of the lesser offense. State v. Solomon (Ohio 1981) 66 Ohio St.2d 214,

421 N.E.2d 139, 20 O.O.3d 213. Criminal Law ⚷ 795(2.1)

Where an accused is charged with murder and pleads self-defense, the refusal of the court to charge the jury on the lesser included offense of negligent homicide is not error. State v. Grace (Lucas 1976) 50 Ohio App.2d 259, 362 N.E.2d 1237, 4 O.O.3d 223.

A refinement of the general rule on when a trial court should instruct a jury on a lesser included offense occurs in cases where the defendant presents a defense, such as accident, alibi, or self defense, which if accepted by the trier of the facts would constitute a complete defense to all substantive elements of the crime charged, and it would be reasonable for the trier to find against the state on one or more elements of the crime charged but for the state on a lesser included offense; under the foregoing circumstances a charge on the lesser included offense is both warranted and required. State v. Jones (Cuyahoga 1975) 47 Ohio App.2d 8, 351 N.E.2d 798, 1 O.O.3d 156.

If in a criminal case the evidence adduced on behalf of the defense is such that if accepted by the trier of the facts it would constitute a complete defense to all substantive elements of the crime charged, the trier will not be permitted to consider a lesser included offense. State v. Nolton (Ohio 1969) 19 Ohio St.2d 133, 249 N.E.2d 797, 48 O.O.2d 119. Criminal Law ⚷ 748

A defendant charged with murder is entitled to a jury instruction on involuntary manslaughter where the defendant stabs and kills an aggressor with one wound and testifies that he did not intend to kill and the assertion of an "accident" defense does not preclude such instruction. State v Hughes, No. 1463 (4th Dist Ct App, Ross, 11–29–88).

Although defendant charged with aggravated murder is entitled to jury instructions as to the lesser included offenses of murder and involuntary manslaughter even though defendant asserts a complete defense of alibi, defendant is not entitled to such instruction where defendant's evidence does not tend to prove either lesser offense. State v Lewis, No. 43987 (8th Dist Ct App, Cuyahoga, 5–6–82).

6. Plea bargains

It is not improper for the court to accept a plea of guilty to homicide generally when the accused was indicted for second degree murder. Gallagher v. Maxwell (Ohio 1964) 175 Ohio St. 440, 195 N.E.2d 810, 25 O.O.2d 449.

A defendant charged with assault to commit rape who pleads guilty to an amended charge of assault with intent to commit robbery waives prosecution by indictment. Stacy v Van Curen, 432 F(2d) 970 (6th Cir Ohio 1970).

7. Jury—Duties

A jury must unanimously agree that the defendant is guilty of a particular criminal offense before returning a verdict of guilty on that offense; however, if a jury is unable to agree unanimously that a defendant is guilty of a particular offense, it may proceed to consider a lesser included offense upon which evidence has been presented, since the jury is not required to determine unanimously that the defendant is not guilty of the crime charged before it may consider a lesser included offense. State v. Thomas (Ohio 1988) 40 Ohio St.3d 213, 533 N.E.2d 286, certiorari denied 110 S.Ct. 89, 493 U.S. 826, 107 L.Ed.2d 54. Criminal Law ⚷ 872.5

8. —— Instructions, jury

Evidence did not warrant giving of jury instruction on lesser included offense of unauthorized use of motor vehicle, in prosecution for theft of motor vehicle, where fact defendant abandoned van after being chased by police was not evidence of lack of intent to permanently deprive van owner of possession of van. State v. Mayle (Ohio App. 7 Dist., Carroll, 03-15-2005) No. 04 CA 808, 2005-Ohio-1346, 2005 WL 678579, Unreported. Criminal Law ⚷ 795(2.40)

Defendant did not present evidence of serious provocation occasioned by victims and, thus, was not entitled in trial for felonious assault to jury instruction on lesser-included offense of aggravated assault, even though victim allegedly threw coins in defendant's face; defendant testified that he was not in fit of rage, was not angry, and was cool, calm, and collected. State v. Crim (Ohio App. 8 Dist., Cuyahoga, 05-20-2004) No. 82347, 2004-Ohio-2553, 2004 WL 1118719, Unreported, appeal after new sentencing hearing 2005-Ohio-4129, 2005 WL 1910669, appeal allowed 107 Ohio St.3d 1696, 840 N.E.2d 202, 2005-Ohio-6763, reversed 109 Ohio St.3d 450, 849 N.E.2d 1, 2006-Ohio-2626, habeas corpus denied 2006 WL 2164673. Assault And Battery ⚷ 96(1)

Conviction for misdemeanor intimidation of witness was not invalidated by trial court's failure to give instruction, in trial for felony intimidation of witness; misdemeanor intimidation of witness was lesser included offense of felony intimidation of witness, in that felony offense contained all elements required to find misdemeanor offense. State v. Mayle (Ohio App. 5 Dist., Muskingum, 04-09-2003) No. CT 2002-0043, 2003-Ohio-1898, 2003 WL 1875573, Unreported. Criminal Law ⚷ 1173.2(4); Indictment And Information ⚷ 189(1)

Jury instruction informing jury that it could consider lesser included offense of reckless homicide only if it first found the defendant not guilty of murder was not plain error; while the better practice would have been to include the preferred "inability to agree" language, the instructions did not expressly require the jury to agree unanimously that defendant was not guilty of murder. State v. Crowley (Ohio App. 10 Dist., 12-31-2002) 151 Ohio App.3d 249, 783 N.E.2d 970, 2002-Ohio-7366, appeal allowed 98 Ohio St.3d 1564, 787 N.E.2d 1229, 2003-Ohio-2242, affirmed 99 Ohio St.3d 146, 789 N.E.2d 238, 2003-Ohio-2766. Criminal Law ⚷ 1038.1(3.1)

Jury is instructed to consider lesser included offense only if it is unable to agree unanimously that defendant is guilty of a particular offense and if there has been evidence presented relative to lesser included offense. State v. Trummer (Ohio App. 7 Dist., 09-30-1996) 114 Ohio App.3d 456, 683 N.E.2d 392, dismissed, appeal not allowed 78 Ohio St.3d 1409, 675 N.E.2d 1249, denial of post-conviction relief affirmed 1998 WL 896457, dismissed, appeal not allowed 85 Ohio St.3d 1464, 709 N.E.2d 171, motion for delayed appeal denied 2000 WL 1476604. Criminal Law ⚿ 798(.6)

Instruction on lesser offense is required only where evidence presented at trial would reasonably support both acquittal on crime charged and conviction upon lesser offense. State v. Hopfer (Ohio App. 2 Dist., 07-12-1996) 112 Ohio App.3d 521, 679 N.E.2d 321, dismissed, appeal not allowed 77 Ohio St.3d 1488, 673 N.E.2d 146, reconsideration denied 77 Ohio St.3d 1550, 674 N.E.2d 1187. Criminal Law ⚿ 795(1)

Defendant charged with receiving automobile as stolen property was not entitled to an instruction on lesser included offense of receiving stolen property limited to luggage rack from automobile, which was found in his house; defense to charge of receiving stolen automobile was that defendant lacked any knowledge of its existence, and his lack of knowledge would constitute complete defense to crime charged as well as lesser included offense, and jury charge on receiving stolen property for luggage rack would have been inappropriate as inviting jury to reach compromise verdict. State v. Braxton (Ohio App. 8 Dist., 03-21-1995) 102 Ohio App.3d 28, 656 N.E.2d 970, dismissed, appeal not allowed 73 Ohio St.3d 1425, 652 N.E.2d 798. Criminal Law ⚿ 795(2.40)

Trial court's instruction on lesser included offense over objection of defendant does not threaten defendant's constitutional right to have notice of charges against him, because when one crime is lesser included offense of another crime, the other crime constitutes sufficient notice of not only crime charged, but also that defendant can be convicted of any of lesser included offenses of crime charged. State v. Schmidt (Ohio App. 3 Dist., 01-13-1995) 100 Ohio App.3d 167, 652 N.E.2d 254. Constitutional Law ⚿ 268(11); Criminal Law ⚿ 795(2.90)

Defendant did not have state or federal constitutional right to prevent giving of instruction on lesser included offense of abduction after indictment charged defendant with kidnapping; trial court was required to give instruction on lesser included offense and defendant had sufficient notice that he could be convicted of kidnapping or any lesser included offense of kidnapping, including abduction. State v. Schmidt (Ohio App. 3 Dist., 01-13-1995) 100 Ohio App.3d 167, 652 N.E.2d 254. Criminal Law ⚿ 795(2.60)

Although defendant can waive jury instruction on lesser included offense, that does not mean that defendant can prevent instruction on lesser included offense. State v. Schmidt (Ohio App. 3 Dist., 01-13-1995) 100 Ohio App.3d 167, 652 N.E.2d 254. Criminal Law ⚿ 795(2.90)

Jury must be instructed on three groups of lesser offenses when supported by evidence at trial: (1) attempts to commit crime charged, if attempt is offense at law; (2) inferior degrees of indicted offense; or (3) lesser included offenses. State v. Sibert (Ohio App. 4 Dist., 11-04-1994) 98 Ohio App.3d 412, 648 N.E.2d 861, motion for delayed appeal denied 71 Ohio St.3d 1479, 645 N.E.2d 1258, denial of post-conviction relief affirmed 74 Ohio St.3d 342, 658 N.E.2d 772, 1996-Ohio-15. Criminal Law ⚿ 795(1)

Instruction to jury on lesser offense is required only where evidence presented at trial would reasonably support both acquittal on crime charged and conviction upon lesser offense. State v. Sibert (Ohio App. 4 Dist., 11-04-1994) 98 Ohio App.3d 412, 648 N.E.2d 861, motion for delayed appeal denied 71 Ohio St.3d 1479, 645 N.E.2d 1258, denial of post-conviction relief affirmed 74 Ohio St.3d 342, 658 N.E.2d 772, 1996-Ohio-15. Criminal Law ⚿ 795(2.1)

Instruction to jury on lesser offense is not required unless evidence presented at trial reasonably supports both acquittal on crime charged and conviction of lesser offense. State v. Wong (Ohio App. 4 Dist., 05-12-1994) 95 Ohio App.3d 39, 641 N.E.2d 1137, reconsideration denied 97 Ohio App.3d 244, 646 N.E.2d 538, dismissed, appeal not allowed 70 Ohio St.3d 1455, 639 N.E.2d 793. Criminal Law ⚿ 795(2.5)

Jury was erroneously instructed in assault prosecution that it could not consider defendant's guilt or innocence on lesser included offense of assault until after it had arrived at verdict of not guilty on felonious assault charge; jury should have been permitted to consider lesser-included offense even in event that it had not been able to reach unanimous verdict with respect to greater offense. State v. Shaw (Clark 1990) 65 Ohio App.3d 821, 585 N.E.2d 515. Criminal Law ⚿ 798(.6)

Pursuant to RC 2945.74 and Crim R 31(C), a jury may consider three groups of lesser offenses on which, when supported by the evidence at trial, it must be charged and on which it may reach a verdict: (1) attempts to commit the crime charged, if such an attempt is an offense at law; (2) inferior degrees of the indicted offense; or (3) lesser included offenses. State v. Deem (Ohio 1988) 40 Ohio St.3d 205, 533 N.E.2d 294.

In a criminal prosecution, instructions to the jury on lesser included offenses to the crime charged are not automatically given; there must first be some basis for them arising from the law and the evidence in the case; the general rule is that, where the evidence in a criminal case would support a finding by the jury of guilt of a lesser included offense to the offense for which the defendant was indicted and tried, a charge on such lesser included offense must be given; the refusal of a trial court to charge upon such a required lesser included offense is error prejudicial to the rights of the defendant. State v. Jones (Cuyahoga 1975) 47 Ohio App.2d 8, 351 N.E.2d 798, 1 O.O.3d 156.

Defendant, who was charged with kidnapping, was not entitled to jury instruction on the lesser included offense of abduction; after defendant approached the victims he asked them whether they carried any money, and after defendant made victims accompany him to a house, he marched them to a dark alley and forced them to strip down whereupon defendant proceeded to go through the pockets of victim's clothes, taking a tape recorder. State v. Ogletree (Ohio App. 8 Dist., Cuyahoga, 08-08-2002) No. 79882, 2002-Ohio-4070, 2002 WL 1821958, Unreported, appeal not allowed 97 Ohio St.3d 1483, 780 N.E.2d 287, 2002-Ohio-6866, denial of habeas corpus affirmed 2004-Ohio-7100, 2004 WL 2988426. Criminal Law ⚷ 795(2.60)

9. Merger of convictions

Effect of statutes which permit a defendant to be acquitted of charged offense but convicted of a lesser included offense and which provide that a defendant who is convicted, acquitted or put in jeopardy may not be further indicted for that offense or for a necessarily included offense is to merge into a conviction all lesser degrees of the offense charged. State v. Rogers (Ohio Com.Pl. 1976) 346 N.E.2d 352. Criminal Law ⚷ 30

10. Sentencing

Following trial court's grant of defendant's motion to vacate perjury conviction and find defendant guilty of lesser-included offense of falsification, trial court was authorized to impose sentence for falsification, where motion to vacate was filed before the sentence for perjury was journalized, and sentence for falsification was within misdemeanor sentencing scheme. State v. Knight (Ohio App. 6 Dist., Sandusky, 08-19-2005) No. S-05-007, 2005-Ohio-4347, 2005 WL 2008144, Unreported. Criminal Law ⚷ 1663

11. Specific offenses—In general

Disorderly conduct is not a lesser included offense of domestic violence and a trial court errs in finding defendant not guilty of domestic violence but convicting him of disorderly conduct as a lesser included offense. State v. Schaefer (Ohio App. 2 Dist., Greene, 04-28-2000) No. 99 CA 88, 2000 WL 492094, Unreported.

Offense of attempted patient abuse was lesser included offense of patient abuse, permitting state to amend indictment charging patient abuse during trial to charge of attempted patient abuse. State v. Briscoe (Cuyahoga 1992) 84 Ohio App.3d 569, 617 N.E.2d 747, dismissed, jurisdictional motion overruled 66 Ohio St.3d 1485, 612 N.E.2d 1242. Indictment And Information ⚷ 189(1)

Disorderly conduct by fighting is not lesser included offense of domestic violence, in that greater offense of domestic violence can be committed without lesser offense also being committed. City of Bucyrus v. Fawley (Crawford 1988) 50 Ohio App.3d 25, 552 N.E.2d 676. Indictment And Information ⚷ 191(.5)

Crime of obstructing official business is lesser included offense of obstructing justice. State v. Gordon (Hamilton 1983) 9 Ohio App.3d 184, 458 N.E.2d 1277, 9 O.B.R. 294. Indictment And Information ⚷ 191(7)

12. —— Drugs, specific offenses

Trial court had no power or authority to find defendant, who pleaded no contest to sale of cocaine in an amount in excess of three times bulk amount and sale of cocaine in excess of bulk amount, guilty of lesser included offense of sale of cocaine in less than bulk amount, where trial court had no "evidence" before it to support conclusion that sales involved less than bulk amount, in that prosecutor recited facts sufficient to support charges of sale of cocaine in excess of bulk amount and in excess of three times bulk amount, and upon completion of prosecutor's statement, and without intervention by defense counsel and without questions from court, court found defendant guilty of lesser included offenses. State v. Rader (Hamilton 1988) 55 Ohio App.3d 102, 563 N.E.2d 304. Criminal Law ⚷ 275.3

Where a defendant is indicted for an offense constituting aggravated drug trafficking with the specification of a prior conviction for a felony drug abuse offense and the verdict form finds the defendant guilty of trafficking in drugs with a prior conviction for trafficking in drugs, the discrepancy between the indictment and the verdict form is sufficient to cast doubt upon the jury's verdict and create the need for a new trial, because, under the facts of the case on review, trafficking in drugs cannot be a lesser included offense of aggravated trafficking. State v. Whiting (Hamilton 1987) 41 Ohio App.3d 107, 534 N.E.2d 904.

The general rule against attacks on inconsistent verdicts does not except cases in which a jury acquits of a predicate felony while convicting on a compound felony; thus, a conviction of a defendant for use of a telephone to facilitate both a conspiracy to possess cocaine and possession of cocaine need not be reversed merely because it cannot be reconciled with an acquittal of the defendant by the jury at the same trial on conspiracy and possession charges. U.S. v. Powell (U.S.Cal. 1984) 105 S.Ct. 471, 469 U.S. 57, 83 L.Ed.2d 461.

13. —— Gambling, specific offenses

Separate charges for operating a gambling house and possession of criminal tools may be prosecuted separately as "each provision requires proof of an additional fact which the other does not." State v. Stover (Cuyahoga 1982) 8 Ohio App.3d 179, 456 N.E.2d 833, 8 O.B.R. 239.

Separate charges for operating a gambling house and possession of criminal tools may be prosecuted separately as "each provision requires proof of an additional fact which the other does not." State v. Stover (Cuyahoga 1982) 8 Ohio App.3d 179, 456 N.E.2d 833, 8 O.B.R. 239.

14. —— Homicide and assault, specific offenses

Trial court was not required to convene three-judge panel when it accepted defendant's guilty pleas to murder, kidnapping, aggravated burglary, and two counts of felonious assault; statute requiring convening of three-judge panel if defendant has been charged with crime punishable by death or has pleaded guilty to aggravated murder did not apply in defendant's case, as defendant was no longer charged with offense punishable by death at time he entered his guilty pleas. State v. West (Ohio App. 9 Dist., Lorain, 03-09-2005) No. 04CA008554, 2005-Ohio-990, 2005 WL 544820, Unreported, appeal not allowed 106 Ohio St.3d 1484, 832 N.E.2d 737, 2005-Ohio-3978. Criminal Law ⚷ 273(4.1)

If a defendant charged with murder testifies that he did not intend to kill the victim during a fight but was angered by the victim's attack on him, a reasonable jury could conclude that he intended to inflict serious physical harm or that his fatal stabbing of the victim was the result of a sudden, provoked rage; the defendant is entitled to a jury instruction concerning involuntary and voluntary manslaughter. State v. Ledbetter (Ohio App. 2 Dist., Greene, 10-14-1994) No. 93-CA-54, 1994 WL 558996, Unreported, appeal not allowed 71 Ohio St.3d 1493, 646 N.E.2d 468.

Assault was not lesser-included offense of domestic violence as applied to defendant, and thus, notice of charge by means of new charging instrument was necessary to support conviction; although all of the elements required to prove assault were required to prove domestic violence, defendant had no previous convictions for domestic violence, meaning that both offenses carried an identical maximum penalty, of six months in jail and a $1,000 fine. State v. Daugherty (Ohio App. 2 Dist., 03-10-2006) 166 Ohio App.3d 551, 852 N.E.2d 202, 2006-Ohio-1133. Indictment And Information ⚷ 191(.5)

If felony or misdemeanor underlying offense of involuntary manslaughter constitutes act in direct violation of physical integrity of victim, involuntary manslaughter is lesser included offense of murder. State v. Campbell (Hamilton 1991) 74 Ohio App.3d 352, 598 N.E.2d 1244, dismissed, jurisdictional motion overruled 62 Ohio St.3d 1431, 578 N.E.2d 823. Indictment And Information ⚷ 191(4)

Failure to include jury instruction concerning aggravated assault in prosecution for felonious assault was not plain error where evidence did not establish that outcome of trial would clearly have been otherwise had jury been given aggravated assault instruction. State v. Shaw (Clark 1990) 65 Ohio App.3d 821, 585 N.E.2d 515. Criminal Law ⚷ 1038.2

Aggravated assault, RC 2903.12, contains elements which are identical to the elements defining felonious assault, RC 2903.11, except for the additional mitigating element of serious provocation; thus, in a trial for felonious assault, where the defendant presents sufficient evidence of serious provocation, an instruction on aggravated assault must be given to the jury. State v. Deem (Ohio 1988) 40 Ohio St.3d 205, 533 N.E.2d 294.

Involuntary manslaughter, RC 2903.04, is, as statutorily defined, a lesser included offense of aggravated murder, RC 2903.01(A). State v. Thomas (Ohio 1988) 40 Ohio St.3d 213, 533 N.E.2d 286, certiorari denied 110 S.Ct. 89, 493 U.S. 826, 107 L.Ed.2d 54. Indictment And Information ⚷ 191(4)

Negligent homicide is not a lesser included offense of murder. State v. Eubank (Lucas 1987) 38 Ohio App.3d 141, 528 N.E.2d 1294. Indictment And Information ⚷ 189(8)

Aggravated menacing, RC 2903.21, is not a lesser included offense of attempted murder, RC 2923.02 and 2903.02. State v. Kidder (Ohio 1987) 32 Ohio St.3d 279, 513 N.E.2d 311.

A defendant charged with felonious assault may be found guilty of the lesser included offense of aggravated assault where there is evidence of provocation, as the legislature, in enacting RC 2903.12, the aggravated assault statute, provided for a reduction in penalty for an assault provoked by the victim. State v. Whitt (Hamilton 1987) 31 Ohio App.3d 92, 508 N.E.2d 1041, 31 O.B.R. 134.

Negligent homicide is not a lesser included offense of murder regardless of whether the offense is committed with a deadly weapon. State v. Hill (Hamilton 1987) 31 Ohio App.3d 65, 508 N.E.2d 1038, 31 O.B.R. 105. Indictment And Information ⚷ 191(4)

Involuntary manslaughter by aggravated menacing may be a lesser included offense of murder where the evidence in a particular case is such that the trier of fact could reasonably find that the greater offense could not have been committed without the other offense also being committed. State v. Rohdes (Ohio 1986) 23 Ohio St.3d 225, 492 N.E.2d 430, 23 O.B.R. 382. Indictment And Information ⚷ 191(.5)

This cause on appeal from the court of appeals is reversed on authority of State v Rohdes, 23 OS(3d) 225, 23 OBR 382, 492 NE(2d) 430 (1986). State v. Berry (Ohio 1986) 23 Ohio St.3d 231, 492 N.E.2d 164, 23 O.B.R. 387.

Aggravated menacing and menacing are not lesser included offenses of felonious assault or attempted murder because menacing offenses contain additional element of causing apprehension which is not contained in the other offenses. State v. Gray (Cuyahoga 1984) 20 Ohio App.3d 318, 486 N.E.2d 159, 20 O.B.R. 420. Indictment And Information ⚷ 191(.5)

It was not error for trial court to instruct jury on offense of a felonious assault and its lesser included offense of aggravated assault, while refusing to give instruction on lesser included offense of assault, in light of record containing substantial credible evidence of probative value from which trial court could reasonably conclude that trier of fact could not possibly find defendant not guilty of one of the greater offenses and guilty of the lesser included offense. State v. Daniels (Hamilton 1984) 14 Ohio App.3d 41, 469 N.E.2d 1338, 14 O.B.R. 45. Assault And Battery ⚷ 96(1)

Negligent homicide is not a lesser included offense of murder regardless of whether offense is in fact committed with a deadly weapon. State v. Jenkins (Hamilton 1983) 13 Ohio App.3d 122, 468 N.E.2d 387, 13 O.B.R. 141. Indictment And Information ⚷ 189(8)

In prosecution for aggravated murder, instruction directing jury to disregard lesser offense of voluntary manslaughter until after it had decided defendant's lack of guilt on charge of murder was error, as it precluded jury from considering mitigating circumstances of acting under extreme emotional distress while considering offenses of murder and aggravated murder; however, absent any evidence of defendant's extreme emotional stress, defendant was not entitled to voluntary manslaughter jury instruction in any event and, hence, was not prejudiced by the instruction given. State v. Osburn (Medina 1983) 9 Ohio App.3d 343, 460 N.E.2d 314, 9 O.B.R. 611. Criminal Law ⚷ 798(.6)

Disorderly conduct is a lesser included offense of assault. State v. Roberts (Hamilton 1982) 7 Ohio App.3d 253, 455 N.E.2d 508, 7 O.B.R. 333. Indictment And Information ⚷ 191(.5)

In prosecution which resulted in conviction of aggravated murder and other offenses, trial court should have charged jury on lesser included offense of involuntary manslaughter since jury might have found that defendant lacked purpose to kill victim as required for aggravated murder, but nevertheless in committing robbery, caused his death. State v. Mabry (Cuyahoga 1982) 5 Ohio App.3d 13, 449 N.E.2d 16, 5 O.B.R. 14. Homicide ⚷ 1458

In prosecution which resulted in conviction of attempted murder and other offenses, trial court should have instructed jury on felonious assault, since jury could have reasonably found that defendant did not have purpose to kill victim, and reasonably could have inferred that defendant knowingly caused serious physical harm to victim. State v. Mabry (Cuyahoga 1982) 5 Ohio App.3d 13, 449 N.E.2d 16, 5 O.B.R. 14. Assault And Battery ⚷ 96(1)

In prosecution which resulted in conviction of attempted murder, trial court did not err in refusing instruction on aggravated assault, where testimony did not support inference of serious provocation. State v. Mabry (Cuyahoga 1982) 5 Ohio App.3d 13, 449 N.E.2d 16, 5 O.B.R. 14. Assault And Battery ⚷ 96(7)

A person charged with first degree murder may be convicted of second degree murder as a lesser included offense even though capital punishment has been abolished. Vargas v. Metzger (Ohio 1973) 35 Ohio St.2d 116, 298 N.E.2d 600, 64 O.O.2d 70, certiorari denied 94 S.Ct. 1431, 415 U.S. 925, 39 L.Ed.2d 482.

Where an accused is indicted and tried upon a charge of murder in the second degree, if the evidence raises a jury issue as to whether the killing was intentional or unintentional and the testimony tends to show and is such that the jury may find beyond reasonable doubt an unlawful and unintentional killing caused by the accused while violating a law or laws of this state applying to the use or regulation of traffic, the jury should consider, and it is the duty of the court to charge upon, the lesser included offense of manslaughter in the second degree. State v. Butler (Stark 1966) 6 Ohio App.2d 193, 217 N.E.2d 237, 35 O.O.2d 353, reversed 11 Ohio St.2d 23, 227 N.E.2d 627, 21 A.L.R.2d 102, 40 O.O.2d 43. Automobiles ⚷ 357

Murder in the second degree, literally considered, necessarily includes manslaughter, and depends not merely upon whether it is literally included in the formal charge, but upon whether there is any evidence tending to support a charge of manslaughter. State v. Loudermill (Lucas 1963) 2 Ohio App.2d 311, 208 N.E.2d 156, 31 O.O.2d 466, affirmed 2 Ohio St.2d 79, 206 N.E.2d 198, 31 O.O.2d 60.

It is not improper for the court to accept a plea of guilty to homicide generally when the accused was indicted for second degree murder. Gallagher v. Maxwell (Ohio 1964) 175 Ohio St. 440, 195 N.E.2d 810, 25 O.O.2d 449.

A person charged with first degree murder may be convicted of second degree murder. Lamos v. Sacks (Ohio 1961) 172 Ohio St. 295, 175 N.E.2d 177, 16 O.O.2d 37, certiorari denied 82 S.Ct. 182, 368 U.S. 904, 7 L.Ed.2d 98. Indictment And Information ⚷ 189(8)

The offenses of pointing firearms in violation of RC 3773.04 and discharging firearms in violation of RC 3773.21 are not lesser included offenses in the crime of maliciously shooting with intent to wound. State v. Fleming (Lorain 1957) 102 Ohio App. 244, 142 N.E.2d 546, 2 O.O.2d 268. Indictment And Information ⚷ 189(6)

The offenses of intentionally and without malice pointing or aiming a firearm at or toward a person, and of intentionally and without malice discharging a firearm so pointed or aimed, are lesser included offenses of the offense of maliciously shooting at another person with intent to kill, wound or maim. State v. Hreno (Ohio 1954) 162 Ohio St. 193, 122 N.E.2d 681, 55 O.O. 97.

A defendant charged with murder is entitled to a jury instruction on involuntary manslaughter where the defendant stabs and kills an aggressor with one wound and testifies that he did not intend to kill and the assertion of an "accident" defense does not preclude such instruction. State v Hughes, No. 1463 (4th Dist Ct App, Ross, 11–29–88).

In a prosecution for aggravated murder, the defendant is entitled to a jury instruction on the lesser included offense of involuntary manslaughter, where there is evidence of the defendant's intoxication while committing an armed robbery and homicide, as the defendant's intoxicated state might lead a jury to conclude that she did not act with a purposeful intent to kill. State v Young, No. C–830757 (1st Dist Ct App, Hamilton, 5–14–86).

Although defendant charged with aggravated murder is entitled to jury instructions as to the lesser included offenses of murder and involuntary manslaughter even though defendant asserts a complete defense of alibi, defendant is not entitled to such instruction where defendant's evidence does not tend to prove either lesser offense. State v Lewis, No. 43987 (8th Dist Ct App, Cuyahoga, 5–6–82).

15. —— Robbery, burglary and trespass, specific offenses

Defendant charged with attempted burglary based on his act of knocking on residence door was not entitled to jury instruction on lesser included offense of criminal trespass, given absence of evidence to indicate defendant's motive for being at the residence. State v. Miller (Ohio App. 11 Dist., Lake, 11-26-2004) No. 2002-L-162, 2004-Ohio-6342, 2004 WL 2697264, Unreported. Criminal Law ⚷ 795(2.35)

Theft is not a lesser included offense of aggravated robbery since theft carries a lesser penalty than aggravated robbery whose element of having a deadly weapon on or about the accused's person or under his or her control is not necessary to prove theft; as a result, aggravated robbery can be committed without theft and where an offense is not a lesser included offense but may be reasonably supported by evidence the offense should be set out separately in the indictment. State v. Bozeman (Ohio App. 2 Dist., Montgomery, 04-20-1994) No. 13741, 1994 WL 147791, Unreported, dismissed, appeal not allowed 71 Ohio St.3d 1404, 641 N.E.2d 202.

A trial court does not err in refusing to instruct the jury on the lesser offense of attempted breaking and entering on an attempted aggravated burglary charge when the defendant had been placed at the scene of a home that was temporarily unoccupied due to fire damage because the evidence clearly showed that the structure was a permanent dwelling. State v. Adams (Lorain 1991) 74 Ohio App.3d 140, 598 N.E.2d 719, dismissed, jurisdictional motion overruled 62 Ohio St.3d 1431, 578 N.E.2d 823.

Where evidence did not show beyond a reasonable doubt that defendant knowingly inflicted, or attempted to inflict serious physical harm on another, then, under such circumstances, felonious assault was not a lesser included offense of aggravated robbery. State v. Crawford (Hamilton 1983) 10 Ohio App.3d 207, 461 N.E.2d 312, 10 O.B.R. 280. Indictment And Information ⚷ 191(9)

In robbery prosecution, evidence, including testimony that defendant held his hand under his clothes as if carrying a weapon, made it possible for jury to find that defendant did not threaten immediate use of force, but employed threat of lesser degree, and thus, trial court was required to give instruction on lesser included offense of theft by threat. State v. Davis (Ohio 1983) 6 Ohio St.3d 91, 451 N.E.2d 772, 6 O.B.R. 131. Robbery ⚷ 27(5)

In prosecution for robbery of convenience food store, it would have been possible for jury to find that defendant's conduct did not constitute a threat of immediate use of force but, instead, amounted only to a threat which did not involve immediate use of force and therefore trial court was required to give instruction on attempted theft by threat as a lesser included offense of robbery. State v. Gates (Franklin 1981) 2 Ohio App.3d 485, 442 N.E.2d 1321, 2 O.B.R. 611. Robbery ⚷ 27(5)

Where an indictment issued by a grand jury charges an accused with a theft offense while having a deadly weapon on his person contrary to RC 2911.01(A)(1), a subsequent amendment of such indictment by the court which eliminates any reference to the weapon but substitutes words indicating the defendant threatened the use of immediate force contrary to RC 2911.02 changes the offense to one unrelated to the original crime charged and is invalid. State v. Washington (Montgomery 1978) 56 Ohio App.2d 129, 381 N.E.2d 1142, 10 O.O.3d 150.

Robbery is a lesser included offense of armed robbery. Curry v. Maxwell (Ohio 1965) 3 Ohio St.2d 107, 209 N.E.2d 202, 32 O.O.2d 71.

Assault with intent to commit robbery is included within the offense of armed robbery and is an offense at law. State v. Curtis (Ohio 1948) 149 Ohio St. 153, 78 N.E.2d 46, 36 O.O. 500. Indictment And Information ⚷ 189(11)

Because defendant did not plead guilty to, and therefore was not actually convicted of, aggravated burglary charge contained in state court indictment charging him with aggravated burglary of a residence, but instead pleaded guilty to lesser included offense of burglary, indictment alone was insufficient to meet government's burden of proving that defendant was previously convicted of burglary of a dwelling, which would qualify as a crime of violence for purposes of 16-level enhancement under sentencing guidelines of defendant's base offense level for illegally reentering United States following deportation. U.S. v. Bernal-Aveja (C.A.6 (Ohio), 07-21-2005) 414 F.3d 625. Sentencing And Punishment ⚷ 793; Sentencing And Punishment ⚷ 963

Trial court did not abuse its discretion in failing to instruct the jury on assault as a lesser included offense of robbery where the jury could not reasonably find the evidence to support a conviction of assault. State v Howell, No. 1078 (4th Dist Ct App, Athens, 2–18–82).

Assault with intent to commit robbery is not an included offense within the offense of assault with intent to commit rape. Stacy v Van Curen, 432 F(2d) 970 (6th Cir Ohio 1970).

16. —— Sex offenses, specific offenses

Defendant was not entitled to instruction on sexual battery as a lesser included offense of rape, where there was no evidence presented at trial that coercion other than force was used. State v. Trummer (Ohio App. 7 Dist., 09-30-1996) 114 Ohio App.3d 456, 683 N.E.2d 392, dismissed, appeal not allowed 78 Ohio St.3d 1409, 675 N.E.2d 1249, denial of post-conviction relief affirmed 1998 WL 896457, dismissed, appeal not allowed 85 Ohio St.3d 1464, 709 N.E.2d 171, motion for delayed appeal denied 2000 WL 1476604. Rape ⚷ 59(20.1)

In a rape prosecution a jury instruction on the lesser included offense of gross sexual imposition is not required where (1) the state chooses to prosecute solely for the one charge of rape, (2) the defendant's defense is that the charged act never occurred, and (3) the testimony of the victim fit clearly within the definition of sexual conduct as required by RC 2907.02, and not sexual contact as required by RC 2907.05. State v. Fenton (Ottawa 1990) 68 Ohio App.3d 412, 588 N.E.2d 951, dismissed, jurisdictional motion overruled 56 Ohio St.3d 702, 564 N.E.2d 704. Rape ⚷ 59(20.1)

A criminal defendant is not entitled to a jury instruction on gross sexual imposition as a lesser included offense of rape where the defendant has denied participation in the alleged offense, and the jury, considering such defense, could not reasonably disbelieve the victim's testimony as to "sexual conduct," RC 2907.01(A), and, at the same time, consistently and reasonably believe her testimony on the contrary theory of mere "sexual contact," RC 2907.01(B). (See also State v Kidder, 32 OS(3d) 279, 513 NE(2d) 311 (1987); and State v Wilkins, 64 OS(2d) 382, 415 NE(2d) 303 (1980).) State v. Johnson (Ohio 1988) 36 Ohio St.3d 224, 522 N.E.2d 1082. Criminal Law ⚷ 795(2.80)

Gross sexual imposition, RC 2907.05(A)(3), is a lesser included offense of rape under former RC 2907.02(A)(3) (now RC 2907.02(A)(1)(b)). (See also State v Kidder, 32 OS(3d) 279, 513 NE(2d) 311 (1987).) State v. Johnson (Ohio 1988) 36 Ohio St.3d 224, 522 N.E.2d 1082.

Sexual battery, as defined in RC 2907.03(A)(1), may be a lesser included offense of rape, as defined in RC 2907.02(A)(1). State v. Wilkins (Ohio 1980) 64 Ohio St.2d 382, 415 N.E.2d 303, 18 O.O.3d 528. Indictment And Information ⚷ 189(10)

The crimes of gross sexual imposition and contributing to the delinquency of a child are separate and distinct crimes, and the latter is not a lesser offense included within the former. State v. Moore (Fulton 1978) 62 Ohio App.2d 86, 404 N.E.2d 174, 16 O.O.3d 183. Indictment And Information ⚷ 191(8)

The crimes of gross sexual imposition and contributing to the delinquency of a child are separate and distinct crimes, and the latter is not a lesser offense included within the former. State v. Moore (Fulton 1978) 62 Ohio App.2d 86, 404 N.E.2d 174, 16 O.O.3d 183. Indictment And Information ⚷ 191(8)

Assault with intent to rape is a lesser included offense of rape, and one indicted for rape may be convicted of assault with intent to rape. Daniel v. Maxwell (Ohio 1964) 176 Ohio St. 207, 198 N.E.2d 657, 27 O.O.2d 90. Indictment And Information ⚷ 189(10)

Where the proper averments of an indictment for the aggravated degree of rape specified in RC 2905.02 set forth or indicate with reasonable certainty all the essential elements of the crime of statutory rape described in RC 2905.03, such indictment will support a conviction for the latter crime. State v. Daniels (Ohio 1959) 169 Ohio St. 87, 157 N.E.2d 736, 76 A.L.R.2d 468, 8 O.O.2d 56.

An indictment of an accused over eighteen for carnally knowing and abusing a female person under sixteen with her consent has the effect also of charging the accused with an attempt to rape a female person under sixteen with her consent, and sufficiently informs the accused that he is charged with committing rape and also with attempting to commit rape and conforms to all constitutional requirements as to the manner in which a person should be charged with the commission of an offense. State v. Ross (Paulding 1954) 96 Ohio App. 157, 121 N.E.2d 289, 54 O.O. 230, appeal dismissed 161 Ohio St. 408, 119 N.E.2d 618, 53 O.O. 310, certiorari denied 75 S.Ct. 68, 348 U.S. 846, 99 L.Ed. 666.

Assault with intent to commit robbery is not an included offense within the offense of assault with intent to commit rape. Stacy v Van Curen, 432 F(2d) 970 (6th Cir Ohio 1970).

17. —— Weapons, specific offenses

An automobile may be so used as to constitute a deadly weapon. State v. Orlett (Ohio Mun. 1975) 44 Ohio Misc. 7, 335 N.E.2d 894, 73 O.O.2d 30.

The offenses of pointing firearms in violation of RC 3773.04 and discharging firearms in violation of RC 3773.21 are not lesser included offenses in the crime of maliciously shooting with intent to wound. State v. Fleming (Lorain 1957) 102 Ohio App. 244, 142 N.E.2d 546, 2 O.O.2d 268. Indictment And Information ⚷ 189(6)

The offenses of intentionally and without malice pointing or aiming a firearm at or toward a person, and of intentionally and without malice discharging a firearm so pointed or aimed, are lesser included offenses of the offense of maliciously shooting at another person with intent to kill, wound or maim. State v. Hreno (Ohio 1954) 162 Ohio St. 193, 122 N.E.2d 681, 55 O.O. 97.

2945.75 Degree of offense; charge and verdict; prior convictions

(A) When the presence of one or more additional elements makes an offense one of more serious degree:

(1) The affidavit, complaint, indictment, or information either shall state the degree of the offense which the accused is alleged to have committed, or shall allege such additional element or elements. Otherwise, such affidavit, complaint, indictment, or information is effective to charge only the least degree of the offense.

(2) A guilty verdict shall state either the degree of the offense of which the offender is found guilty, or that such additional element or elements are present. Otherwise, a guilty verdict constitutes a finding of guilty of the least degree of the offense charged.

(B) Whenever in any case it is necessary to prove a prior conviction, a certified copy of the entry of judgment in such prior conviction together with evidence sufficient to identify the defendant named in the entry as the offender in the case at bar, is sufficient to prove such prior conviction.

(1972 H 511, eff. 1–1–74)

Historical and Statutory Notes

Ed. Note: Former 2945.75 repealed by 1972 H 511, eff. 1–1–74; 1953 H 1; GC 13448–3; see now 2913.61 for provisions analogous to former 2945.75.

Pre–1953 H 1 Amendments: 113 v 194, Ch 27, § 3

Legislative Service Commission

1973:

This section provides that when an additional element or elements operate to increase the severity of the penalty for an offense, then the charge must either allege the additional elements or allege the higher degree. Similarly, in such cases, a guilty verdict must specify whether such additional elements are found or that the verdict is guilty of the higher degree. If a charge omits to specify the additional elements or to specify the degree, it is effective to charge only the lowest degree of the offense. In the same way, a verdict of guilty which specifies neither that additional elements nor the higher degree constitutes a verdict of guilty of the lowest degree of the offense.

For example, suppose that a person accused of theft has a prior theft offense conviction, which under section 2913.02 makes the offense grand theft (4th degree felony) regardless of the value of the stolen property. Section 2945.75 requires the complaint to state that the accused's crime is a 4th degree felony or, alternatively, to allege that the accused has a prior theft offense conviction. In the absence of either of these, the complaint is sufficient to charge only petty theft, a 1st degree misdemeanor. Assuming the complaint specifies 4th degree felony or alleges the prior conviction, then the guilty verdict must also state either that the verdict is guilty of a 4th degree felony or that the offender has a prior conviction of a theft offense. Otherwise, the verdict constitutes a verdict of guilty only of petty theft.

This section also provides that when it is necessary to prove a prior conviction in any case, a certified copy of the judgment entry coupled with evidence sufficient to identify the offender in the case at bar as the offender named in the entry, is sufficient to prove the prior conviction. In essence, this codifies existing practice.

Cross References

Determination of amount of property damage or physical harm, 2909.11

Verdict, Crim R 31

Library References

Criminal Law ⚷883, 893.

Indictment and Information ⚷185 to 192.

Westlaw Topic Nos. 110, 210.

C.J.S. Criminal Law §§ 1409 to 1410.

Research References

Encyclopedias

OH Jur. 3d Criminal Law § 1228, Determining Amount of Damage.

OH Jur. 3d Criminal Law § 2021, Municipal Court—Specific Offenses.

OH Jur. 3d Criminal Law § 2344, Stating Degree of Offense.

OH Jur. 3d Criminal Law § 2873, Elements of Offense—Prior Conviction.

OH Jur. 3d Criminal Law § 3267, Specification as Prerequisite to Enhanced Penalty; State's Burden of Proof; Proof of Prior Conviction.

Treatises and Practice Aids

Markus, Trial Handbook for Ohio Lawyers, § 37:9, Returning Verdict.

Klein, Darling, & Terez, Baldwin's Ohio Practice Civil Practice § 44:3, Authentication of Official Record or Entry Under Civ. R. 44(A)--Domestic Record or Entry.

Klein, Darling, & Terez, Baldwin's Ohio Practice Civil Practice § 44:8, Proof by Any Other Method Authorized by Law--Revised Code Provisions.

Katz, Giannelli, Blair and Lipton, Baldwin's Ohio Practice, Criminal Law, § 40:5, Nature and Contents.

Katz, Giannelli, Blair and Lipton, Baldwin's Ohio Practice, Criminal Law, § 65:7, Lesser Included Offenses.

Katz, Giannelli, Blair and Lipton, Baldwin's Ohio Practice, Criminal Law, § 148:32, Jury Verdict.

Katz, Giannelli, Blair and Lipton, Baldwin's Ohio Practice, Criminal Law, § 148:33, Verdict of Guilty and Finding of Value of Property.

Katz, Giannelli, Blair and Lipton, Baldwin's Ohio Practice, Criminal Law, § 148:34, Verdict of Guilty on One Count.

Katz, Giannelli, Blair and Lipton, Baldwin's Ohio Practice, Criminal Law, § 148:35, Verdict of Guilty of Inferior Degree or of Lesser Included Offense.

Giannelli and Snyder, Baldwin's Ohio Practice, Evidence, R 609, Impeachment by Evidence of Conviction of Crime.

Giannelli and Snyder, Baldwin's Ohio Practice, Evidence, R 802, Hearsay Rule.

Giannelli and Snyder, Baldwin's Ohio Practice, Evidence, § 802.5, Ohio Statutes.

Giannelli and Snyder, Baldwin's Ohio Practice, Evidence, § 609.15, Methods of Proof.

Adrine & Ruden, Ohio Domestic Violence Law § 2:7, Felony Violations.

Adrine & Ruden, Ohio Domestic Violence Law § 5:20, Case Preparation—Hearsay Exceptions—Judgment of Previous Conviction.

Adrine & Ruden, Ohio Domestic Violence Law § 15:18, Hearsay Exceptions—Judgment of Previous Conviction.

Painter, Ohio Driving Under the Influence § 2:3, Sufficiency of Citation—Application to Ovi.

Painter, Ohio Driving Under the Influence § 12:33, Prior Convictions—Proof—Misdemeanors.

Giannelli & Yeomans, Ohio Juvenile Law § 16:8, Delinquency Complaints.

Law Review and Journal Commentaries

The Disparate Sentencing Provision of Ohio's Organized Crime Statute, Comment. 46 U Cin L Rev 583 (1977).

Notes of Decisions

1. Constitutional issues

Presentation at sexual predator determination proceeding of certified copies of rape defendant's prior convictions for sexual battery and kidnapping satisfied requirements of due process, where defendant did not challenge his identity as defendant in those convictions, and did not present witnesses to challenge prior convictions despite having had opportunity to do so. State v. High (Ohio App. 7 Dist., 01-24-2001) 143 Ohio App.3d 232, 757 N.E.2d 1176, 2001-Ohio-3530. Constitutional Law ⚷ 255(5); Mental Health ⚷ 460(1)

2. In general

Judgment entry met statutory requirement by designating attempted aggravated arson offense as felony such that trial court was not required to meet alternative statutory requirement of stating element of offense that made offense felony, rather than misdemeanor. State v. Heap (Ohio App. 1 Dist., Hamilton, 11-05-2004) No. C-040007, 2004-Ohio-5850, 2004 WL 2480703, Unreported, appeal not allowed 105 Ohio St.3d 1465, 824 N.E.2d 92, 2005-Ohio-1024. Criminal Law ⚷ 990.1

While defendant ordinarily is required to call to attention of trial court error in proceedings, there is also duty upon prosecutor to call error to attention of trial court where error affects degree of offense, and verdict form indicates finding of guilt only of least degree of offense charged; if prosecution desires that guilty verdict be of higher degree than would be permitted by verdict form, it is incumbent upon prosecution to call error to attention of trial court. State v. Breaston (Franklin 1993) 83 Ohio App.3d 410, 614 N.E.2d 1156. Criminal Law ⚷ 798.5; Criminal Law ⚷ 839

3. Indictment generally

Indictment charging defendant with possession of marijuana as a third degree felony was sufficient, even though indictment failed to specify the amount of marijuana defendant was charged with possessing; notice to defendant was adequate, given that defendant needed only to consult the statute to find the specific amount or quantity of marijuana necessary to constitute a third degree felony. State v. Chamblin (Ohio App. 4 Dist., Adams, 05-03-2004) No. 02CA753, 2004-Ohio-2252, 2004 WL 958079, Unreported, appeal not allowed 103 Ohio St.3d 1463, 815 N.E.2d 678, 2004-Ohio-5056. Controlled Substances ⚷ 65

Indictment charging aggravated murder was not required to state the degree of the charged offense, where offense of aggravated murder was not classified by degree of felony. State v. Wiley (Ohio App. 10 Dist., Franklin, 03-04-2004) No. 03AP-340, 2004-Ohio-1008, 2004 WL 396767, Unreported, appeal not allowed 102 Ohio St.3d 1533, 811 N.E.2d 1151, 2004-Ohio-3580, habeas corpus dismissed 2006 WL 1132960. Homicide ⚷ 831

4. Jury verdict generally

In prosecution for failure to provide for functionally impaired person, trial court substantially complied with statute requiring guilty verdict to state degree of offense for which defendant was found guilty; although verdict form did not include specification of degree of offense, jury instructions covered only fourth degree offense, and jury was at no time instructed that defendant could be convicted of different degree of offense. State v. Davis (Ohio App. 9 Dist., Summit, 06-23-2004) No. 21794, 2004-Ohio-3246, 2004 WL 1397607, Unreported. Criminal Law ⚷ 798.5

Jury verdict forms in prosecution for 12 counts of possession of criminal tools failed to comply with statutory requirements, warranting guilty verdicts on least degree of each offense charged, where jury verdict forms failed to contain degree of offenses, to provide additional elements making offenses more serious degree, or to include language of indictment. State v. Boykin (Ohio App. 2 Dist., Montgomery, 04-02-2004) No. 19896, 2004-Ohio-1701, 2004 WL 690799, Unreported. Criminal Law ⚷ 798.5

Verdict form finding defendant guilty of murder was not required to state the degree of the offense, where offense of murder was not classified by degree of felony. State v. Wiley (Ohio App. 10 Dist., Franklin, 03-04-2004) No. 03AP-340, 2004-Ohio-1008, 2004 WL 396767, Unreported, appeal not allowed 102 Ohio St.3d 1533, 811 N.E.2d 1151, 2004-Ohio-3580, habeas corpus dismissed 2006 WL 1132960. Homicide ⚷ 1551

Trial court's failure to state degree of offense of possession of criminal tools or that criminal tools were intended to be used in commission of felony, as required to elevate offense to felony, was not reversible error; trial court found that defendant possessed cable-signal converter to avail himself of signal without paying for it, evidence showed overwhelmingly that converter was intended to be used in commission of felony, and defendant did not object to verdict at trial. State v. Sullivan (Ohio App. 8 Dist., Cuyahoga, 11-06-2003) No. 82816, 2003-Ohio-5930, 2003 WL 22510808, Unreported. Criminal Law ⚷ 1040

Defendant did not waive challenge to verdict form by failing to object in trial court, where error in verdict form was structural in nature. State v. Woullard (Ohio App. 2 Dist., 06-25-2004) 158 Ohio App.3d 31, 813 N.E.2d 964, 2004-Ohio-3395. Criminal Law ⚷ 1038.1(3.1)

Verdict form, which failed to contain specific finding as to whether defendant was previously convicted of domestic violence, was improper, warranting reversal of conviction for felony domestic violence, which required such finding, and remand for entry of judgment convicting defendant of misdemeanor domestic violence. State v. Woullard (Ohio App. 2 Dist., 06-25-2004) 158 Ohio App.3d 31, 813 N.E.2d 964, 2004-Ohio-3395. Criminal Law ⚷ 798.5; Criminal Law ⚷ 1172.1(2)

Sentencing defendant to 14 months' incarceration for the felony version of carrying a concealed weapon was plain error after court gave jury a meaningful opportunity to find defendant guilty only of misdemeanor offense of carrying a concealed weapon; even though felony-enhancement language of indictment properly supplied enhancement element and trial court read indictment to jury, court did not further instruct jury on felony-enhancement element, and form returned by jury did not contain degree of offense or include felony-enhancement language. State v. Burrow (Ohio App. 1 Dist., 11-09-2000) 140 Ohio App.3d 466, 748 N.E.2d 95. Criminal Law ⚷ 1042

Guilty verdicts on two counts of disseminating matter harmful to juveniles constituted finding of guilty on misdemeanor of first degree, least degree of offense charged, where verdict form did not state degree of offense or require finding that material distributed was "obscene," but merely stated only that material disseminated was "harmful." State v. Gleason (Ohio App. 9 Dist., 04-03-1996) 110 Ohio App.3d 240, 673 N.E.2d 985, appeal not allowed 77 Ohio St.3d 1416, 670 N.E.2d 1004. Criminal Law ⚷ 893

State had responsibility to call to court's attention errors in verdict form which prejudiced state, and defendant had no duty to inform state that verdict form, as drawn, charged him with disseminating matter harmful to juveniles as misdemeanor of first degree, rather than as felony. State v. Gleason (Ohio App. 9 Dist., 04-03-1996) 110 Ohio App.3d 240, 673 N.E.2d 985, appeal not allowed 77 Ohio St.3d 1416, 670 N.E.2d 1004. Criminal Law ⚷ 1038.1(3.1)

Jury's verdict finding defendant guilty of receiving stolen property, but finding that value of property received was not $100,000 or more, as alleged in indictment, permitted trial court to sentence defendant for misdemeanor offense of receiving stolen property worth less than $300. State v. Wright (Ohio App. 3 Dist., 08-10-1993) 91 Ohio App.3d 71, 631 N.E.2d 1066, dismissed, jurisdictional motion overruled 69 Ohio St.3d 1408, 629 N.E.2d 1370. Receiving Stolen Goods ⚷ 10

Where verdict form asked jury to determine whether defendant was guilty of carrying concealed weapon, but did not ask whether weapon was loaded or whether ammunition was ready at hand, as required to enhance offense from misdemeanor to felony, defendant could be convicted only of misdemeanor offense. State v. Breaston (Franklin 1993) 83 Ohio App.3d 410, 614 N.E.2d 1156. Criminal Law ⚷ 798.5

Jury verdict was sufficient to convict defendants of first-degree felony of theft of drugs, even though it included specification that offense was committed with "firearm," instead of including statutory language that offense was committed with "deadly weapon or dangerous ordnance"; form, in essence, stated presence of aggravating element of possession or control of deadly weapon. State v. Lundy (Hamilton 1987) 41 Ohio App.3d 163, 535 N.E.2d 664. Criminal Law ⚷ 875(1)

A jury's general verdict of guilty in a prosecution for gross sexual imposition under RC 2907.05(A)(3) need not specify the additional element of the victim's age or the degree of the offense in order to constitute a conviction for a third degree felony so long as the jury concludes in its deliberations that the state has proved the age of the victim beyond a reasonable doubt. State v. Heidelburg (Sandusky 1986) 30 Ohio App.3d 265, 507 N.E.2d 1149, 30 O.B.R. 462.

RC 2945.75 does not apply to guilty verdicts that do not contain an "essential" element indicating the offense committed, inasmuch as such verdicts are void. State v. Reed (Hamilton 1985) 23 Ohio App.3d 119, 491 N.E.2d 723, 23 O.B.R. 230.

A jury verdict that finds a defendant guilty of gross sexual imposition without specifying the presence of the additional element of the victim's age or the degree of the offense constitutes a finding of guilt on the least degree of such offense, a fourth degree felony, and the defendant can only be sentenced for a fourth degree felony. State v. Prater (Wood 1983) 13 Ohio App.3d 98, 468 N.E.2d 356, 13 O.B.R. 114. Rape ⚿ 60

The failure of verdict forms to comply strictly with RC 2945.75(A)(2) does not constitute reversible error, when the verdicts incorporate the language of the indictments, the evidence overwhelmingly shows the presence of the aggravating circumstances, and defendants never objected at trial to the form of the verdicts. State v. Woods (Cuyahoga 1982) 8 Ohio App.3d 56, 455 N.E.2d 1289, 8 O.B.R. 87.

Trial court's failure to state in the verdict and judgment entry the degree of the crime charged for the offense of theft resulted in a conviction for the least degree of the crime charged, a first degree misdemeanor. State v. Lantz (Ohio App. 5 Dist., Fairfield, 07-15-2002) No. 01 CA 38, 2002-Ohio-3838, 2002 WL 1729910, Unreported. Criminal Law ⚿ 255.4

Trial court was precluded from sentencing defendant for anything other than least degree of offense of speeding, where the guilty verdict failed to state degree of the offense of which defendant was convicted. Cleveland v. Benn (Ohio App. 8 Dist., Cuyahoga, 07-25-2002) No. 80674, 2002-Ohio-3796, 2002 WL 1728553, Unreported. Sentencing And Punishment ⚿ 1000

Where a guilty verdict in a prosecution for carrying a concealed weapon carries no finding that the weapon was a firearm either loaded or with ammunition ready at hand, a sentence for a third-degree felony is improper as this factual finding is necessary to enhance the offense to a third-degree felony; the cause will be remanded for sentencing for a first-degree misdemeanor. State v Breaston, No. 92AP–1448 (10th Dist Ct App, Franklin, 3–30–93).

A jury verdict finding a defendant guilty of gross sexual imposition without specifying the degree of the offense or the victim's age, may support a conviction on a charge of third degree felony, where the indictment states the victim's age is under thirteen and the jury instructions clearly require proof the defendant had sexual contact with a person less than thirteen years old. State v Kuhn, No. 1377 (4th Dist Ct App, Athens, 10–30–89).

A verdict form finding a defendant guilty of "aggravated trafficking in cocaine," which fails to specify the quantity of the drug involved or to refer to the appropriate count in the indictment, is defective and requires the court to find the defendant guilty of the least degree of the offense charged. State v McGuire, No. 10224 (2d Dist Ct App, Montgomery, 9–23–88).

5. Sentencing generally

Trial court was precluded from sentencing defendant for anything other than least degree of offense of speeding, where the guilty verdict failed to state degree of the offense of which defendant was convicted. Cleveland v. Benn (Ohio App. 8 Dist., Cuyahoga, 07-25-2002) No. 80674, 2002-Ohio-3796, 2002 WL 1728553, Unreported. Sentencing And Punishment ⚿ 1000

Where a defendant is convicted of an enhanced degree of an offense, an enhanced sentence may be imposed even where the verdict fails to specifically indicate the enhanced degree, provided the verdict indicates a finding of the essential element distinguishing the enhanced offense from the lesser offense in accordance with the provisions of RC 2945.75(A)(2). Fairborn v Ashmore, No. 86–CA–48 (2d Dist Ct App, Greene, 3–10–87).

6. Prior convictions—In general

Trial court was prohibited from enhancing defendant's speeding offense to a fourth-degree misdemeanor based on its sua sponte discovery of the existence of defendant's prior speeding conviction, where citation charging defendant with instant speeding offense did not reflect that it was charged as fourth-degree second offense. State v. Carr (Ohio App. 7 Dist., Mahoning, 01-24-2003) No. 01 CA 162, 2003-Ohio-331, 2003 WL 169962, Unreported. Automobiles ⚿ 359

Municipal Court had jurisdiction over misdemeanor driving while under the influence of alcohol (DUI) charge, even though traffic ticket noted "4th offense DUI," which was a felony offense; the ticket notation was insufficient under charging statute to indicate offense was being prosecuted as a felony, as it did not allege the degree of the offense or the additional element, i.e., that defendant had three prior DUI convictions within six years. State v. Tamburin (Ohio App. 9 Dist., 09-12-2001) 145 Ohio App.3d 774, 764 N.E.2d 503, appeal not allowed 94 Ohio St.3d 1430, 761 N.E.2d 47, 2002-Ohio-5651. Automobiles ⚿ 351.1; Criminal Law ⚿ 93

Where earlier conviction merely affects penalty imposed for subsequent offense, and is not element of subsequent offense, defendant may request that trial court determine evidence of prior conviction at sentencing hearing. State v. Day (Ohio App. 12 Dist., 12-27-1994) 99 Ohio App.3d 514, 651 N.E.2d 52, dismissed, appeal not allowed 72 Ohio St.3d 1518, 649 N.E.2d 278, denial of habeas corpus affirmed 142 F.3d 433, certiorari denied 118 S.Ct. 2355, 524 U.S. 944, 141 L.Ed.2d 724. Sentencing And Punishment ⚿ 325

It is proper to submit the question of a previous conviction to a jury for their determination. State v. Alexander (Lorain 1975) 50 Ohio App.2d 55, 361 N.E.2d 459, 4 O.O.3d 39.

Where the existence of a prior conviction elevates the degree of the offense charged, the prior conviction is a material element of the offense charged, and, as such, bifurcation of the prior conviction specification and the crime charged is not permitted. State v Tolle, No. 755 (4th Dist Ct App, Highland, 4–23–91).

7. —— Indictment, prior convictions

Where indictment complies with criminal rule providing that indictments need not contain any technical averments or any allegations not essential to be proved, and gives defendant adequate notice that state will seek to prove that defendant previously had been convicted of theft offenses, indictment does not need to allege that defendant was, at a certain stated time, in a certain stated court, convicted of a certain stated offense. State v. Larsen (Lawrence 1993) 89 Ohio App.3d 371, 624 N.E.2d 766. Larceny ⚷ 28(4)

Allegation of prior offense is essential element of crime which must be proven beyond reasonable doubt, where allegation of prior offense in indictment elevates degree of crime charged as opposed to merely enhancing penalty to be imposed. State v. Mosley (Hamilton 1993) 88 Ohio App.3d 461, 624 N.E.2d 297. Sentencing And Punishment ⚷ 1351; Sentencing And Punishment ⚷ 1380(2)

An indictment stating that on a specified date the accused caused the death of a named person as the proximate result of committing a felony in violation of RC 2903.04(A) complies with the requirements of Crim R 7(B) and RC 2945.75. State v. Mineer (Ohio Com.Pl. 1983) 8 Ohio Misc.2d 11, 456 N.E.2d 590, 8 O.B.R. 70. Indictment And Information ⚷ 71.4(5)

8. —— Lack of counsel, prior convictions

If after an evidentiary hearing the trial judge determines that the prior convictions for theft used to enhance the degree of the charged offense of defrauding a livery were uncounselled and that there was no valid waiver of counsel, the trial judge should suppress that evidence; the court may not sua sponte amend the indictment to conform to the evidence. State v. Daniels (Lorain 1988) 61 Ohio App.3d 17, 572 N.E.2d 129, motion overruled 46 Ohio St.3d 716, 546 N.E.2d 1334.

Where a defendant alleges that prior convictions for theft used to enhance the charged offense of defrauding a livery were uncounselled, the court must allow the prosecution the opportunity to rebut the defendant's claims prior to dismissing the charge. State v. Daniels (Lorain 1988) 61 Ohio App.3d 17, 572 N.E.2d 129, motion overruled 46 Ohio St.3d 716, 546 N.E.2d 1334.

Defendant's testimony that he had two prior petty theft convictions was insufficient to demonstrate that prior convictions were uncounseled so as to preclude use of those convictions for enhancement. State v. Brandon (Ohio 1989) 45 Ohio St.3d 85, 543 N.E.2d 501. Sentencing And Punishment ⚷ 1381(5)

Although an uncounseled prior conviction cannot ordinarily serve to enhance a penalty for a later conviction, a defendant has the burden of challenging an apparently constitutional prior conviction with some evidence that he was not afforded his right to counsel and the defendant may not rely on a silent record; however, once the defendant has presented some evidence that the earlier conviction was without benefit of counsel, the burden to show the constitutional validity of the prior conviction shifts to the state. State v. Maynard (Cuyahoga 1987) 38 Ohio App.3d 50, 526 N.E.2d 316.

In order to sustain a conviction for grand theft under RC 2913.02(A)(1), the state must do more than merely comply with the requirements of RC 2945.75(B); the state must affirmatively prove that in relation to the previous conviction, defendant either had the benefit of counsel or made a knowing, intelligent waiver of counsel. State v. Elling (Ohio Com.Pl. 1983) 11 Ohio Misc.2d 13, 463 N.E.2d 668, 11 O.B.R. 108.

Where a prior conviction's constitutionality is challenged and the record is silent as to whether the right to counsel was waived or the defendant was represented by counsel, the burden of proof on the issue is shifted to the state. State v McKinley, No. 50016 (8th Dist Ct App, Cuyahoga, 2–6–86).

Once the state has proved the existence of a prior conviction and identified the defendant as the person previously convicted, the defendant has the burden of going forward with evidence of a lack of counsel in the first prosecution. State v Wang, No. C–830287 (1st Dist Ct App, Hamilton, 1–25–84).

Where no imprisonment, probation, or other restriction of liberty was imposed on a defendant in an earlier conviction, such conviction may be used to enhance the penalty for a subsequent conviction, regardless of whether the defendant had assistance of counsel, or waived such assistance, in the first prosecution. State v Wang, No. C–830287 (1st Dist Ct App, Hamilton, 1–25–84).

9. —— Burden of proof, prior convictions

As an element of having a weapon while under disability, the state must prove the defendant had a prior conviction for an "offense involving the illegal possession, use, sale, administration, distribution, or trafficking in any drug of abuse" pursuant to RC 2923.13, and where the state, pursuant to RC 2945.75(B) (1) presents testimony of a deputy clerk of court through whom the state offers the indictment, entry of waiver and plea, and termination entry from the defendant's prior aggravated trafficking conviction, and (2) to establish that the defendant is the person identified in the termination entry, the state presents testimony of an undercover narcotics detective concerning his prior encounter with the defendant as "sitting on a couch with a plate of crack cocaine on his lap and a 32–automatic just to the left of him on the couch," the trial court errs in its refusal to strike and to instruct the jury to disregard the detective's objectionable testimony. State v. Owens (Ohio App. 2 Dist., Montgomery, 11-30-1994) No. 14068, No. 93-CR-214, 1994 WL 683395, Unreported.

Where existence of prior offense is element of subsequent crime, state must prove prior conviction beyond reasonable doubt, just as it must prove any other element, and jury must find that previous conviction has been established in order to find defendant guilty on second offense. State v. Day (Ohio App. 12 Dist., 12-27-1994) 99 Ohio App.3d 514, 651 N.E.2d 52, dismissed, appeal not allowed 72 Ohio St.3d 1518, 649 N.E.2d 278, denial of habeas corpus affirmed 142 F.3d 433, certiorari denied 118 S.Ct. 2355, 524 U.S. 944, 141 L.Ed.2d 724. Criminal Law ⚷ 328; Criminal Law ⚷ 561(1)

10. —— Instructions, prior convictions

Trial court's failure to instruct jury, concerning how to consider stipulation to certified copy of driving under influence (DUI) defendant's prior felony DUI in final instruction, did not constitute plain error, where court noted in preliminary instructions that if attorneys agreed to any facts such agreement would be brought to the jurors' attention, and they could then regard such fact as conclusively proved without necessity of further evidence of such fact, and defendant testified that he had previously been convicted of a felony DUI offense upon a plea of guilty. State v. McMannis (Ohio App. 5 Dist., Stark, 04-14-2003) No. 2002CA00258, 2003-Ohio-1901, 2003 WL 1874723, Unreported, motion for delayed appeal denied 107 Ohio St.3d 1405, 836 N.E.2d 1226, 2005-Ohio-5859, reconsideration denied 108 Ohio St.3d 1419, 841 N.E.2d 322, 2006-Ohio-179. Criminal Law ⚷ 1042.5

Trial court's alleged failure to properly inform jury of the level of the offense, when defining driving under the influence (DUI) defendant's prior DUI conviction to the jury, did not constitute plain error, where court properly instructed jurors that they must make a finding that defendant had been previously convicted of a felony DUI offense. State v. McMannis (Ohio App. 5 Dist., Stark, 04-14-2003) No. 2002CA00258, 2003-Ohio-1901, 2003 WL 1874723, Unreported, motion for delayed appeal denied 107 Ohio St.3d 1405, 836 N.E.2d 1226, 2005-Ohio-5859, reconsideration denied 108 Ohio St.3d 1419, 841 N.E.2d 322, 2006-Ohio-179. Criminal Law ⚷ 1042.5

11. —— Verdict form, prior convictions

Failure of verdict form, on which jury made additional finding of prior driving under the influence (DUI) conviction, to contain the word "felony" or phrase "as previously charged in the indictment," did not prevent DUI defendant from being convicted of greater third-degree felony offense, where verdict form stated defendant was found guilty of DUI offense as charged in indictment, evidence was undisputed that prior conviction was felony DUI, state introduced a certified copy of prior conviction, defendant testified that he pleaded guilty to prior felony DUI, and trial court instructed jurors that they must find beyond reasonable doubt that defendant had been convicted of felony DUI. State v. McMannis (Ohio App. 5 Dist., Stark, 04-14-2003) No. 2002CA00258, 2003-Ohio-1901, 2003 WL 1874723, Unreported, motion for delayed appeal denied 107 Ohio St.3d 1405, 836 N.E.2d 1226, 2005-Ohio-5859, reconsideration denied 108 Ohio St.3d 1419, 841 N.E.2d 322, 2006-Ohio-179. Automobiles ⚷ 358

12. —— Admissibility of evidence, prior convictions

In a prosecution for felony domestic violence, the trial court errs in ruling that, in view of the defendant's stipulation to a prior domestic violence conviction, Evid R 403 and the interests of judicial economy preclude the state from presenting any evidence to the jury of the conviction; the previous conviction is an essential element of the offense which the state must be able to prove to the jury, and the state cannot be precluded from informing the jury that a defendant has stipulated to one element of the offense charged, that he admits a prior conviction. State v. Arnold (Ohio App. 8 Dist., Cuyahoga, 01-24-2002) No. 79280, 2002 WL 93423, Unreported, appeal not allowed 95 Ohio St.3d 1474, 768 N.E.2d 1182, 2002-Ohio-2444.

Certified copy of letter from municipal court which contained journal entries related to defendant's prior convictions for driving under the influence (DUI) did not comply with requirements for admissibility of prior conviction, and thus was inadmissible in prosecution for possession of weapon by person who is disabled from doing so by reason of chronic alcoholism. State v. Semenchuk (Ohio App. 8 Dist., 07-24-1997) 122 Ohio App.3d 30, 701 N.E.2d 19, appeal not allowed 80 Ohio St.3d 1425, 685 N.E.2d 238, dismissed, appeal not allowed 80 Ohio St.3d 1446, 686 N.E.2d 274. Criminal Law ⚷ 374

Certified copy of municipal court docket pertaining to defendant's prior conviction for driving under the influence (DUI) did not comply with requirements for admissibility of prior conviction, and thus was inadmissible in prosecution for possession of weapon by person who is disabled from doing so by reason of chronic alcoholism. State v. Semenchuk (Ohio App. 8 Dist., 07-24-1997) 122 Ohio App.3d 30, 701 N.E.2d 19, appeal not allowed 80 Ohio St.3d 1425, 685 N.E.2d 238, dismissed, appeal not allowed 80 Ohio St.3d 1446, 686 N.E.2d 274. Criminal Law ⚷ 374

Evidence of prior drug conviction could be introduced, for purpose of increasing degree of defendant's offense in present case, despite rule providing for exclusion when prejudicial effect of evidence outweighed its probative value; once limiting instruction had been given, probative value outweighed prejudicial effect. State v. Rivera (Ohio App. 11 Dist., 08-15-1994) 99 Ohio App.3d 325, 650 N.E.2d 906, dismissed, appeal not allowed 71 Ohio St.3d 1435, 643 N.E.2d 141. Criminal Law ⚷ 338(7); Criminal Law ⚷ 673(5)

Trial court did not err by admitting evidence that defendant charged with drug abuse had been previously convicted of a drug-related offense, even though defendant's counsel had stipulated to existence of prior conviction and to fact that defendant was the defendant in prior conviction; proof of prior conviction was required to be introduced in order to achieve state's objective of obtaining conviction for a third degree rather than fourth degree felony, and court had given a limiting instruction regarding purpose of prior conviction evidence. State v. Rivera (Ohio App. 11 Dist., 08-15-1994) 99 Ohio App.3d 325, 650 N.E.2d 906, dismissed, appeal not allowed 71 Ohio St.3d 1435, 643 N.E.2d 141. Criminal Law ⚷ 369.2(7); Criminal Law ⚷ 673(5)

Statute requiring that evidence of other drug convictions be introduced in order to increase degree of offense for which defendant could be convicted in present case did not conflict with evidence rule providing that other crime evidence was not admissible to prove character of person to show he acted in conformity therewith, even though rule further provided that evidence could be admissible for other purposes, listing examples, and enhancement of offense degree was not an enumerated purpose. State v. Rivera (Ohio App. 11 Dist., 08-15-1994) 99 Ohio App.3d 325, 650 N.E.2d 906, dismissed, appeal not allowed 71 Ohio St.3d 1435, 643 N.E.2d 141. Controlled Substances ⚿ 69

Defendant could not be heard to complain that entries from his prior convictions were admitted into evidence when defendant had refused to stipulate to those prior convictions, which state was required to prove in order to elevate conviction for receiving stolen property to third degree felony; absent such stipulation, it was necessary for prosecutor to prove those convictions by other means and, as provided by statute, certified copy of prior judgment entries and evidence identifying defendant as offender sufficed to prove those prior convictions. State v. Taniguchi (Ohio App. 10 Dist., 08-30-1994) 96 Ohio App.3d 592, 645 N.E.2d 794. Receiving Stolen Goods ⚿ 8(2)

Testimony from arresting police officers from prior offenses that led to conviction for violation of a protection order and menacing by stalking and from victim of those offenses was not properly admissible to prove prior convictions in subsequent prosecution for violation of a protection order and menacing by stalking that sought felony convictions on each offense due to prior convictions, since evidence of prior convictions had already been presented, and testimony of officers and victim, which concerned underlying facts of those offenses, went beyond establishing existence of prior convictions. State v. Moissis (Ohio App. 11 Dist., Lake, 09-20-2002) No. 2000-L-187, 2002-Ohio-4955, 2002 WL 31101605, Unreported. Sentencing And Punishment ⚿ 1379(2)

13. —— Sufficiency of evidence, prior convictions

Jury's finding with respect to charge of possessing firearm while under a disability, that defendant had prior conviction involving illegal possession, use, sale, administration, distribution, or trafficking in any drug of abuse, was not against manifest weight of evidence; defendant stipulated to the identification of him as the person named in certified copy of judgment entry of conviction and sentence for trafficking in cocaine and possession of cocaine, and trial court instructed jury in accordance with that stipulation. State v. Smith (Ohio App. 9 Dist., Summit, 03-19-2003) No. 21069, 2003-Ohio-1306, 2003 WL 1240403, Unreported, appeal not allowed 99 Ohio St.3d 1455, 790 N.E.2d 1219, 2003-Ohio-3396, appeal not allowed 100 Ohio St.3d 1412, 796 N.E.2d 539, 2003-Ohio-4948, habeas corpus dismissed 2006 WL 2233211. Weapons ⚿ 17(4)

Use of evidence of rape defendant's prior convictions in sexual predator determination proceeding was not barred by fact that such convictions were more than 10 years old, or by court's failure to make express determination that probative value of prior convictions outweighed their prejudicial effect, where prior convictions were proved by certified copies of defendant's prior convictions for sexual battery and kidnapping; Rules of Evidence did not strictly apply to sexual predator determination hearing. State v. High (Ohio App. 7 Dist., 01-24-2001) 143 Ohio App.3d 232, 757 N.E.2d 1176, 2001-Ohio-3530. Mental Health ⚿ 460(1)

Prior convictions referred to in indictment could be used to elevate the instant offenses into fourth degree felonies, even though the prior convictions were on appeal and had not yet been affirmed; certified copy of the entry of judgment in such prior conviction together with evidence sufficient to identify the defendant named in the entry as the offender in the case at bar, was all that was required. State v. Midwest Pride IV, Inc. (Ohio App. 12 Dist., 12-28-1998) 131 Ohio App.3d 1, 721 N.E.2d 458, dismissed, appeal not allowed 85 Ohio St.3d 1486, 709 N.E.2d 1214, certiorari denied 120 S.Ct. 400, 528 U.S. 965, 145 L.Ed.2d 312. Criminal Law ⚿ 28

State must present more than piece of paper evidencing defendant's prior conviction to satisfy its burden of proving prior conviction as element of later offense beyond reasonable doubt; additional evidence, besides certified copy of judgment entry, must be presented. State v. Blonski (Ohio App. 9 Dist., 12-31-1997) 125 Ohio App.3d 103, 707 N.E.2d 1168, dismissed, appeal not allowed 81 Ohio St.3d 1521, 692 N.E.2d 1023. Criminal Law ⚿ 374

Identical names in defendant's booking sheet and certified judgment entry were insufficient to establish beyond reasonable doubt that defendant was individual whose conviction was established in certified judgment entry and, thus, state failed to prove prior offense specification; while eight-digit number appeared on booking sheet, and same eight-digit number was written by hand at top of page on certified copy of journal entry, nothing in record indicated nature of connection between those numbers. State v. O'Neil (Ohio App. 6 Dist., 12-01-1995) 107 Ohio App.3d 557, 669 N.E.2d 95. Sentencing And Punishment ⚿ 1381(6)

Method used to prove defendant's prior domestic violence conviction, during prosecution for domestic violence as second offense, did not prejudice jury and cause jury to find defendant guilty based upon past conduct rather than on direct evidence, where prosecuting attorney limited evidence of defendant's prior conviction to certified copy of judgment entry and identification testimony, thereby eliminating surplus evidence which could unduly emphasize defendant's prior conduct to jury. State v. Day (Ohio App. 12 Dist., 12-27-1994) 99 Ohio App.3d 514, 651 N.E.2d 52, dismissed, appeal not allowed 72 Ohio St.3d 1518, 649 N.E.2d 278, denial of habeas corpus affirmed 142 F.3d 433, certiorari denied 118 S.Ct. 2355, 524 U.S. 944, 141 L.Ed.2d 724. Criminal Law ⚿ 374

Additional evidence, besides certified copy of judgment entry, must be presented to prove prior conviction of accused beyond reasonable doubt and, without such evidence, there can be no enhancement. State v. McCoy (Franklin 1993) 89 Ohio

App.3d 479, 624 N.E.2d 1102. Sentencing And Punishment ⚷ 1380(2); Sentencing And Punishment ⚷ 1381(2)

State failed to prove that defendant was previously convicted of theft offense, despite submission to jury of documents relating to prior convictions which contained signatures purporting to be defendant's; no foundation was laid that any of signatures in exhibits contained defendant's signature, which was not authenticated by any witness, jurors were not instructed to determine whether signatures were defendant's, and instruction that jurors were to make whatever comparisons they could from documents was so broad that it was mere speculation whether jurors conducted any handwriting comparison. State v. McCoy (Franklin 1993) 89 Ohio App.3d 479, 624 N.E.2d 1102. Sentencing And Punishment ⚷ 1381(3)

A defendant is not shown to have been convicted of prior drug abuse, for purposes of establishing guilt for aggravated trafficking in drugs and permitting drug abuse with prior drug abuse, where the record in the previous cases indicates that the defendant only pleaded guilty to two counts in the indictment without indicating what the indictment charged. State v. Velez (Defiance 1991) 72 Ohio App.3d 836, 596 N.E.2d 545. Controlled Substances ⚷ 33; Controlled Substances ⚷ 34

Evidence was insufficient to prove defendant's prior conviction for menacing by stalking, and thus was insufficient to support conviction for menacing by stalking as a fourth degree felony; judgment entry of prior conviction was incomplete because it did not contain jury's verdict of guilt or court's findings, and complaining party in prior case did not make an in-court identification of defendant. State v. Harrington (Ohio App. 3 Dist., Logan, 05-03-2002) No. 8-01-20, 2002-Ohio-2190, 2002 WL 987836, Unreported. Extortion And Threats ⚷ 32

Where the prosecution, seeking to prove a prior conviction for the charge of felony theft, offers the testimony of the defendant's probation officer and a certified copy of a conviction, the jury's conclusion that the prior conviction exists beyond a reasonable doubt is reasonable. State v Mobley, No. 9856 (2d Dist Ct App, Montgomery, 6–8–87).

Where the prosecution, seeking to prove a prior conviction, offers no evidence beyond the similarity of names to identify John Eugene Newton in the case at bar as the John or James Eugene Newton named in the prior judgment entry, reasonable doubt exists as a matter of law concerning the identity of the person being tried with the person previously convicted, and the element of prior conviction is not established. State v Newton, No. 2–83–20 (3d Dist Ct App, Auglaize, 6–19–84).

14. —— Sentence, prior convictions

Where an accused has entered a plea of guilty to a theft offense but has not been sentenced by the court on that charge, such offender has not been previously convicted of a theft offense within the meaning of RC 2913.02(B). State v. Henderson (Ohio 1979) 58 Ohio St.2d 171, 389 N.E.2d 494, 12 O.O.3d 177.

2945.76 Circumstances for acquittal for carrying concealed weapon—Repealed

(1972 H 511, eff. 1–1–74; 1969 H 288; 1953 H 1; GC 13448–4)

Historical and Statutory Notes

Ed. Note: See now 2923.12 for provisions analogous to former 2945.76.

Pre–1953 H 1 Amendments: 113 v 194, Ch 27, § 4

POST TRIAL PROCEDURE

2945.77 Polling jury

When the jurors agree upon their verdict, they must be conducted into court by the officer having them in charge.

Before the verdict is accepted, the jury may be polled at the request of either the prosecuting attorney or the defendant. If one of the jurors upon being polled declares that said verdict is not his verdict, the jury must further deliberate upon the case.

(1953 H 1, eff. 10–1–53; GC 13448–5)

Historical and Statutory Notes

Pre–1953 H 1 Amendments: 113 v 195, Ch 27, § 5

Cross References

Verdict, poll of jury, Crim R 31

Library References

Criminal Law ⚷874.

Westlaw Topic No. 110.

C.J.S. Criminal Law § 1399.

Research References

Encyclopedias

OH Jur. 3d Criminal Law § 2796, Grounds for Replacing Juror; Discretion of Court.

OH Jur. 3d Criminal Law § 2812, Rendition and Reception of Verdict.

OH Jur. 3d Criminal Law § 2813, Polling the Jury.

Treatises and Practice Aids

Katz, Giannelli, Blair and Lipton, Baldwin's Ohio Practice, Criminal Law, § 65:10, Polling the Jury.

Notes of Decisions

---

1. In general

A jury verdict in a criminal case is required to be unanimous and in writing; however, if either the prosecutor or defendant calls for a poll of the jury, the trial court may not accept the verdict unless the verdict reflected in the written verdict form is confirmed in open court. State v. Carmack (Hamilton 1989) 61 Ohio App.3d 351, 572 N.E.2d 794, dismissed 44 Ohio St.3d 703, 541 N.E.2d 622. Criminal Law ⚷ 872.5; Criminal Law ⚷ 874; Criminal Law ⚷ 875(1)

2. Disagreements

Trial court's acceptance of jury's verdict during robbery prosecution was not arbitrary, unreasonable, or unconscionable, despite defendant's claim that the statements of the fourth juror during juror polling indicated that the verdict was not his own; when the trial court asked the fourth juror to confirm the guilty verdict several times, the juror did confirm the verdict. State v. Boyd (Ohio App. 9 Dist., Summit, 01-12-2005) No. 22151, 2005-Ohio-73, 2005 WL 53431, Unreported. Criminal Law ⚷ 874

Trial court acted within its discretion in denying defendant's motion for mistrial and, instead, ordering further deliberations upon discovering, when polling jury, that guilty verdict was not unanimous. State v. Williams (Ohio App. 8 Dist., Cuyahoga, 10-21-2004) No. 83423, 2004-Ohio-5592, 2004 WL 2361981, Unreported, appeal not allowed 105 Ohio St.3d 1470, 824 N.E.2d 540, 2005-Ohio-1186. Criminal Law ⚷ 867

Once a poll of the jurors had been completed and all had assented to criminal verdict, a juror could not thereafter rescind or modify his or her vote, and thus, juror who indicated to judge that she did not believe murder defendant raped victim after she had been polled, but before guilty verdict was journalized and entered, could not repudiate her initial guilty vote. State v. Williams (Ohio, 09-03-2003) 99 Ohio St.3d 493, 794 N.E.2d 27, 2003-Ohio-4396, reconsideration granted 100 Ohio St.3d 1525, 800 N.E.2d 43, 2003-Ohio-6510, on reconsideration 103 Ohio St.3d 112, 814 N.E.2d 818, 2004-Ohio-4747, reconsideration stricken 103 Ohio St.3d 1482, 816 N.E.2d 257, 2004-Ohio-5496. Criminal Law ⚷ 957(2)

Juror, when polled, did not express hesitancy that necessitated further interrogation when jury reached its verdict after initially expressing that it was at a stalemate. State v. Williams (Ohio, 08-16-1995) 73 Ohio St.3d 153, 652 N.E.2d 721, 1995-Ohio-275, reconsideration denied 74 Ohio St.3d 1409, 655 N.E.2d 188, stay granted 74 Ohio St.3d 1437, 655 N.E.2d 1321, stay terminated 75 Ohio St.3d 1439, 662 N.E.2d 1085, certiorari denied 116 S.Ct. 1047, 516 U.S. 1161, 134 L.Ed.2d 193, denial of post-conviction relief affirmed 1998 WL 330539, dismissed, appeal not allowed 83 Ohio St.3d 1449, 700 N.E.2d 332, reconsideration denied 84 Ohio St.3d 1413, 701 N.E.2d 1021. Criminal Law ⚷ 874

A juror may, after coming into court, change his vote and so express himself when a poll of the jury is taken; although it is proper not to allow a juror to explain or give reasons for his or her vote, it is not wrong for the trial court to interrogate the juror to make clear such juror's answer, when, upon poll, there is doubt as to the vote being given. State v. Brown (Summit 1953) 110 Ohio App. 57, 168 N.E.2d 419, 12 O.O.2d 227.

3. Remedies

Ambiguity in juror's response to trial court's poll following entry of verdict finding defendant guilty of assault on a peace officer obligated trial court, in the exercise of its discretion, to either direct jurors to deliberate further or to discharge them and declare mistrial; while confirming her signature on verdict form, juror revealed then-existing doubt about defendant's guilt. State v. Pheanis (Ohio App. 2 Dist., Montgomery, 03-25-2005) No. 20667, 2005-Ohio-1372, 2005 WL 678991, Unreported. Criminal Law ⚷ 874

After jury informed trial judge that wrong verdict had been delivered and that they had unanimously found defendant not guilty of menacing by stalking, reasonable course of action for trial court would have been to direct jury to resolve the apparent clerical/procedural error, and there was no manifest necessity to justify court's grant of mistrial. Cleveland v. Walters (Ohio App. 8 Dist., 10-24-1994) 98 Ohio App.3d 165, 648 N.E.2d 37. Criminal Law ⚷ 867; Criminal Law ⚷ 889

Where a poll of the jury establishes that one juror did not concur in the jury verdict, the court properly orders the jurors to continue deliberating, and the judge is not required to reinstruct them. State v. Green (Cuyahoga 1990) 67 Ohio App.3d 72, 585 N.E.2d 990. Criminal Law ⚷ 863(1)

4. Verdict forms

Defendant was not denied his right to poll the jury when trial court read one or more of the verdict forms incorrectly when jury was polled after receipt of the verdict; as soon as court became aware that it might have made a mistake, all of the jurors were recalled, and the parties and counsel were also recalled, and the court did not ask jurors to reconsider their verdict, but instead, only asked whether or not each of the jurors had, in fact, signed the verdict form that the court then, at that time, correctly read in open court. State v. Draughon (Ohio App. 10 Dist., Franklin, 05-29-2003) No. 02AP-895, 2003-Ohio-2727, 2003 WL 21234913, Unreported, appeal not allowed 100 Ohio St.3d 1412, 796 N.E.2d 538, 2003-Ohio-4948, motion to reopen denied 2004-Ohio-320, 2004 WL 117632, appeal not allowed 102 Ohio St.3d 1461, 809 N.E.2d 34, 2004-Ohio-2569. Criminal Law ⚷ 874

Where a jury verdict is signed by only eleven jurors and a poll is requested by the defendant and the defense offers no objection to the verdict form, the deficiency in the form does not constitute plain error. State v. Carmack (Hamilton 1989) 61 Ohio App.3d 351, 572 N.E.2d 794, dismissed 44 Ohio St.3d 703, 541 N.E.2d 622.

5. Record

Defendant was not prejudiced by court reporter's failure to record actual polling of jury at conclusion of guilt phase. State v. Williams (Ohio, 08-16-1995) 73 Ohio St.3d 153, 652 N.E.2d 721, 1995-Ohio-275, reconsideration denied 74 Ohio St.3d 1409, 655 N.E.2d 188, stay granted 74 Ohio St.3d 1437, 655 N.E.2d 1321, stay terminated 75 Ohio St.3d 1439, 662 N.E.2d 1085, certiorari denied 116 S.Ct. 1047, 516 U.S. 1161, 134 L.Ed.2d 193, denial of post-conviction relief affirmed 1998 WL 330539, dismissed, appeal not allowed 83 Ohio St.3d 1449, 700 N.E.2d 332, reconsideration denied 84 Ohio St.3d 1413, 701 N.E.2d 1021. Criminal Law ⚷ 1166.13

6. Review

Lack of a voir dire of the entire jury, to ascertain whether there was intimidation of one juror who had indicated to court during deliberations that the other jurors had "jumped all over" her for thinking that defendant was innocent, was not plain error, even though juror ultimately changed her opinion during further deliberations and found defendant guilty, where defendant did not present evidence that juror was pressured or intimidated into changing her opinion or that her decision was not of her own free will, after verdict was returned the jurors were polled and juror clearly stated that it was her verdict, juror had not presented any further complaints regarding the deliberation process to the court, and although juror was suffering from depression, nothing showed that she was not capable of continuing deliberations due to her mental state. State v. Edge (Ohio App. 8 Dist., Cuyahoga, 01-30-2003) No. 80919, 2003-Ohio-424, 2003 WL 194854, Unreported. Criminal Law ⚷ 1039

In deciding whether there has been an abuse of discretion by a trial court in determining whether to grant a mistrial when a juror states that his or her verdict was compromised, Supreme Court will not second-guess that determination absent an abuse of discretion. State v. Brown (Ohio, 10-08-2003) 100 Ohio St.3d 51, 796 N.E.2d 506, 2003-Ohio-5059, stay granted 798 N.E.2d 615, 2003-Ohio-5993, certiorari denied 124 S.Ct. 1516, 540 U.S. 1224, 158 L.Ed.2d 162, habeas corpus denied 2006 WL 533405. Criminal Law ⚷ 1155

The failure of the court in a criminal action to poll the jury when so requested by the defendant is reversible error. City of Dayton v. Allen (Ohio Com.Pl. 1959) 200 N.E.2d 356, 94 Ohio Law Abs. 129, 27 O.O.2d 179.

7. Waiver

Defendant waived all but plain error claim to the lack of voir dire of the entire jury to ascertain whether a juror had been intimidated, where defendant did not object when the trial court permitted juror to continue with deliberations, defendant did not request that the entire panel be subject to examination, and did not object when the trial court examined only the juror in question. State v. Edge (Ohio App. 8 Dist., Cuyahoga, 01-30-2003) No. 80919, 2003-Ohio-424, 2003 WL 194854, Unreported. Criminal Law ⚷ 1039

2945.78 Recording the verdict

When the verdict given is such as the court may receive, it must be immediately entered in full upon the minutes.

(1953 H 1, eff. 10–1–53; GC 13448–6)

Historical and Statutory Notes

Pre–1953 H 1 Amendments: 113 v 195, Ch 27, § 6

Library References

Criminal Law ⚷892.
Westlaw Topic No. 110.
C.J.S. Criminal Law § 1395.

Research References

Encyclopedias

OH Jur. 3d Criminal Law § 2814, Entry.

2945.79 Causes for new trial

A new trial, after a verdict of conviction, may be granted on the application of the defendant for any of the following causes affecting materially his substantial rights:

(A) Irregularity in the proceedings of the court, jury, prosecuting attorney, or the witnesses for the state, or for any order of the court, or abuse of discretion by which the defendant was prevented from having a fair trial;

(B) Misconduct of the jury, prosecuting attorney, or the witnesses for the state;

(C) Accident or surprise which ordinary prudence could not have guarded against;

(D) That the verdict is not sustained by sufficient evidence or is contrary to law; but if the evidence shows the defendant is not guilty of the degree of crime for which he was convicted, but guilty of a lesser degree thereof, or of a lesser crime included therein, the court may modify the verdict or finding accordingly, without granting or ordering a new trial, and pass sentence on such verdict or finding as modified, provided that this power extends to any court to which the cause may be taken on appeal;

(E) Error of law occurring at the trial;

(F) When new evidence is discovered material to the defendant, which he could not with reasonable diligence have discovered and produced at the trial. When a motion for a new trial is made upon the ground of newly discovered evidence, the defendant must produce at the hearing of said motion, in support thereof, the affidavits of the witnesses by whom such evidence is expected to be given, and if time is required by the defendant to procure such affidavits, the court may postpone the hearing of the motion for such length of time as under all the circumstances of the case is reasonable. The prosecuting attorney may produce affidavits or other evidence to impeach the affidavits of such witnesses.

(1953 H 1, eff. 10–1–53; GC 13449–1)

Historical and Statutory Notes

Pre–1953 H 1 Amendments: 113 v 195, Ch 28, § 1

Cross References

New trial, 2931.15; Crim R 33

Library References

Criminal Law ⚷905 to 965.
Westlaw Topic No. 110.
C.J.S. Criminal Law §§ 1415 to 1419, 1423 to 1428, 1430 to 1447.

Research References

Encyclopedias

OH Jur. 3d Criminal Law § 2811, Explanation, Amendment, or Correction of Verdict.

OH Jur. 3d Criminal Law § 3169, Prosecutions in Magistrates' Courts.

OH Jur. 3d Criminal Law § 3172, Right of State to New Trial.

OH Jur. 3d Criminal Law § 3175, Irregularity in Course or Conduct of Trial; Generally.

OH Jur. 3d Criminal Law § 3180, Errors of Law Occurring at Trial; Erroneous Instructions and Admission of Evidence.

OH Jur. 3d Criminal Law § 3182, Verdict Contrary to Law or Not Sustained by Evidence; Modification of Verdict.

OH Jur. 3d Criminal Law § 3183, Accident or Surprise.

OH Jur. 3d Criminal Law § 3184, Misconduct of Prosecuting Attorney; Suppression of Evidence.

OH Jur. 3d Criminal Law § 3187, Misconduct of Witnesses for State.

OH Jur. 3d Criminal Law § 3204, Necessity of Diligence.

OH Jur. 3d Criminal Law § 3213, Affidavits and Other Proof.

OH Jur. 3d Criminal Law § 3215, Hearing and Determination of Motion.

Treatises and Practice Aids

Katz, Giannelli, Blair and Lipton, Baldwin's Ohio Practice, Criminal Law, § 79:2, Grounds for New Trial.

Giannelli and Snyder, Baldwin's Ohio Practice, Evidence, R 606, Competency of Juror as Witness.

Giannelli and Snyder, Baldwin's Ohio Practice, Evidence, § 606.6, Juror Misconduct; Substantive Grounds.

Law Review and Journal Commentaries

Constitutional Law—Criminal Law—Due Process—Right to Counsel—The Test in Ohio for Effectiveness of Counsel Is Whether the Accused Had a Fair Trial and Whether Substantial Justice Was Done.—State v. Hester, Note. 45 U Cin L Rev 514 (1976).

A Quest for Justice in the Conversion of Security Interests, Russell A. Hakes. 82 Ky L J 837 (1993–94).

Symposium on Post–Conviction Remedies: Foreward and Afterword, Lawrence Herman. 27 Ohio St L J 237 (Spring 1966).

Notes of Decisions

---

1. Constitutional issues

Trial court's decision to sua sponte declare mistrial, over defendant's objection, in prosecution for aggravated robbery and aggravated burglary was based on manifest necessity, so that retrial of defendant was not barred by double jeopardy clause; terrorist attacks of September 11, 2001, occurred on second day of trial, courthouse was evacuated and closed that day, judge was concerned about jurors' ability to concentrate on serious charges against defendant in light of breaking national news and, while judge considered instructing jurors to return next day, he did not do so because he did not know if courthouse would be open and he remained concerned about jurors' ability to concentrate. State v. Walls (Ohio App. 6 Dist., Lucas, 01-31-2003) No. L-01-1492, 2003-Ohio-493, 2003 WL 220460, Unreported, appeal not allowed 99 Ohio St.3d 1435, 789 N.E.2d 1117, 2003-Ohio-2902, habeas corpus granted 418 F.Supp.2d 962. Double Jeopardy ⚿ 99

Prosecutor's improper comments during closing arguments, in which prosecutor referred to defendant's post-arrest silence, constituted harmless error; improper comments were only a small portion of the closing argument, an inference of guilt was not stressed to jury when viewing the context of entire closing argument, and evidence of guilt was overwhelming. State v. Thomas (Ohio App. 1 Dist., Hamilton, 12-31-2002) No. C-010724, 2002-Ohio-7333, 2002 WL 31894850, Unreported, appeal not allowed 98 Ohio St.3d 1515, 786 N.E.2d 64, 2003-Ohio-1572. Criminal Law ⚿ 1171.3

Prosecutor did not improperly vouch for state witness's testimony by telling her that she was doing a good job; prosecutor was simply reassuring witness in the midst of her difficult testimony. State v. Smith (Ohio, 12-13-2002) 97 Ohio St.3d 367, 780 N.E.2d 221, 2002-Ohio-6659, reconsideration denied 97 Ohio St.3d 1500, 780 N.E.2d 1023, 2002-Ohio-7367, stay granted 98 Ohio St.3d 1417, 782 N.E.2d 73, 2003-Ohio-189, certiorari denied 123 S.Ct. 2255, 539 U.S. 907, 156 L.Ed.2d 118. Criminal Law ⚿ 720(5)

Prosecutor's question during closing argument, "Did he claim accident, that he didn't do this on purpose?", was not an improper comment on defendant's failure to testify; comment showed how evidence supported fact that defendant purposely committed crimes in question. State v. Smith (Ohio, 12-13-2002) 97 Ohio St.3d 367, 780 N.E.2d 221, 2002-Ohio-6659, reconsideration denied 97 Ohio St.3d 1500, 780 N.E.2d 1023, 2002-Ohio-7367, stay granted 98 Ohio St.3d 1417, 782 N.E.2d 73, 2003-Ohio-189, certiorari denied 123 S.Ct. 2255, 539 U.S. 907, 156 L.Ed.2d 118. Criminal Law ⚷ 721(3)

Prosecutor's statement during closing argument that murder defendant was "seated right over there next to his counsel" was not an improper attempt to denigrate defendant and his trial counsel; prosecutor was merely pointing out defendant to jury as a means of emphasizing that it was he who committed the crimes. State v. Smith (Ohio, 12-13-2002) 97 Ohio St.3d 367, 780 N.E.2d 221, 2002-Ohio-6659, reconsideration denied 97 Ohio St.3d 1500, 780 N.E.2d 1023, 2002-Ohio-7367, stay granted 98 Ohio St.3d 1417, 782 N.E.2d 73, 2003-Ohio-189, certiorari denied 123 S.Ct. 2255, 539 U.S. 907, 156 L.Ed.2d 118. Criminal Law ⚷ 722.3

Prosecution's repeated discovery violations in rape trial, while evidencing woeful lack of comprehension of purpose behind discovery rules, were not intended to goad defendant into requesting mistrial, and defendant was therefore not placed in double jeopardy when he was retried. State v. Roughton (Ohio App. 6 Dist., 02-12-1999) 132 Ohio App.3d 268, 724 N.E.2d 1193, appeal not allowed 86 Ohio St.3d 1406, 711 N.E.2d 234. Double Jeopardy ⚷ 97

In determining whether double jeopardy prohibits retrial following the declaration of a mistrial, the journal entry of the trial court, or the record itself, must indicate the trial court's basis for ordering the mistrial. State v. Morgan (Ohio App. 8 Dist., 09-21-1998) 129 Ohio App.3d 838, 719 N.E.2d 102, appeal not allowed 84 Ohio St.3d 1475, 704 N.E.2d 581. Double Jeopardy ⚷ 95.1

Trial court abused its discretion in sua sponte declaring mistrial based on possibility that jury would be irreparably tainted by evidence that should not have been before it, and thus double jeopardy barred retrial, where record did not indicate what the evidence improperly before the jury was or the significance of such evidence, and trial court made no attempts to cure or otherwise determine effect of the purportedly tainted evidence. State v. Morgan (Ohio App. 8 Dist., 09-21-1998) 129 Ohio App.3d 838, 719 N.E.2d 102, appeal not allowed 84 Ohio St.3d 1475, 704 N.E.2d 581. Double Jeopardy ⚷ 99

When mistrial has been declared prior to verdict, conclusion that jeopardy has attached begins, rather than ends, inquiry as to whether Double Jeopardy Clause bars retrial; whether subsequent prosecution can proceed depends on whether exception to double jeopardy bar applies. City of Sidney v. Little (Ohio App. 3 Dist., 04-15-1997) 119 Ohio App.3d 193, 694 N.E.2d 1386. Double Jeopardy ⚷ 95.1

Psychologist's testimony that defendant's biological father was violent and was stabbed to death when she was seven years old, that defendant's mother and stepfather physically abused her, and that defendant was not close to her mother or stepfather was not so egregious that it was impossible for defendant to have had fair trial after testimony was given, and therefore, trial court did not abuse its discretion in sustaining defendant's objection but denying her motion for mistrial. State v. Stewart (Ohio App. 9 Dist., 06-05-1996) 111 Ohio App.3d 525, 676 N.E.2d 912. Criminal Law ⚷ 867

A defendant is not entitled to a new trial on the ground that she was effectively denied her right to counsel and a fair trial where she specifically states her desire to represent herself, and even though the trial court does not follow the technically correct procedure in accepting the waiver, there is nothing in the record showing that the defendant is not as competent as any other layman who chooses to represent himself. State v. Doane (Trumbull 1990) 69 Ohio App.3d 638, 591 N.E.2d 735, dismissed, jurisdictional motion overruled 58 Ohio St.3d 701, 569 N.E.2d 504. Criminal Law ⚷ 1166.10(2)

Double jeopardy principles do not bar retrial where an appellate court reverses a conviction based upon prosecutorial misconduct when such conduct was not calculated to goad the defense into seeking a mistrial. State v. Sage (Ohio 1987) 31 Ohio St.3d 173, 510 N.E.2d 343, 31 O.B.R. 375. Double Jeopardy ⚷ 108

Statute regulating the right to a new trial of a person convicted of crime is not in violation of either O Const Art I, § 1, or of US Const Am 14. Luff v. State (Ohio 1927) 117 Ohio St. 102, 157 N.E. 388, 5 Ohio Law Abs. 403, 25 Ohio Law Rep. 377.

The federal constitution makes no mention of new trials and they were not granted in England until the end of the seventeenth century; even then, new trials were granted only in misdemeanor cases, although a writ of error coram nobis was issued for some errors of fact in felony cases. Herrera v. Collins (U.S.Tex. 1993) 113 S.Ct. 853, 506 U.S. 390, 122 L.Ed.2d 203, rehearing denied 113 S.Ct. 1628, 507 U.S. 1001, 123 L.Ed.2d 186.

Where the reviewing court has found the evidence insufficient to sustain the jury's verdict of guilty, the Fifth Amendment will bar a second trial. Burks v. U. S. (U.S.Tenn. 1978) 98 S.Ct. 2141, 437 U.S. 1, 57 L.Ed.2d 1, on remand 579 F.2d 1013.

In determining whether prosecutorial misconduct rises to level of due process violation, federal habeas court must bear in mind that the touchstone of due process analysis is the fairness of the trial, not the culpability of the prosecutor. Byrd v. Collins (C.A.6 (Ohio), 04-06-2000) 209 F.3d 486, rehearing en banc denied 227 F.3d 756, certiorari denied 121 S.Ct. 786, 531 U.S. 1082, 148 L.Ed.2d 682, rehearing denied 121 S.Ct. 1176, 531 U.S. 1186, 148 L.Ed.2d 1034. Constitutional Law ⚷ 268(8); Habeas Corpus ⚷ 497

Prosecutor's statements speculating about whether defendant had previously seen store clerk killed during robbery and whereabouts of missing evidence did not rise to level of due process violation, even if they were impermissible comments on facts not in evidence, given that statements were qualified with language suggesting their speculative nature, and thus did not mislead jury, remarks were relatively isolated, other evidence of guilt was strong, and defense counsel did not object or seek curative instruction. Byrd v. Collins (C.A.6 (Ohio), 04-06-2000) 209 F.3d 486, rehearing en banc denied 227 F.3d 756, certiorari denied 121 S.Ct. 786, 531 U.S. 1082, 148 L.Ed.2d 682, rehearing denied 121 S.Ct. 1176, 531 U.S. 1186, 148 L.Ed.2d 1034. Constitutional Law ⚷ 268(8); Criminal Law ⚷ 719(1); Criminal Law ⚷ 728(2)

State trial court's refusal to grant mistrial after juror mentioned to bailiff some concern about precautions that were being taken as jurors entered and exited courtroom for aggravated murder trial did not deny petitioner a fair trial, in violation of due process; petitioner's counsel opposed any questioning of jurors as to whether any concerns prevented them from being fair and impartial, and court noted that juror in question had raised no specific incidents or circumstances, but was simply inquiring as to better way for jurors to enter and leave courtroom. Benge v. Johnson (S.D.Ohio, 03-31-2004) 312 F.Supp.2d 978. Constitutional Law ⚷ 268(2.1); Criminal Law ⚷ 867

State trial court's refusal to grant mistrial after victim's son attempted to assault petitioner in hallway outside courtroom during lunch recess at aggravated murder trial did not deny petitioner a fair trial, in violation of due process; no juror witnessed incident, and only juror who had any awareness of it expressly indicated that his ability to be fair and impartial had not been impaired. Benge v. Johnson (S.D.Ohio, 03-31-2004) 312 F.Supp.2d 978. Constitutional Law ⚷ 268(2.1); Criminal Law ⚷ 867

State trial court's refusal to grant mistrial after member of victim's family left courtroom in tears during police officer's testimony did not deny petitioner a fair trial, in violation of due process; trial necessarily involved testimony describing victim's brutal death, a matter which was not in dispute, and fact that family member became upset during testimony describing circumstances of victim's death would not necessarily have prejudiced jury. Benge v. Johnson (S.D.Ohio, 03-31-2004) 312 F.Supp.2d 978. Constitutional Law ⚷ 268(2.1); Criminal Law ⚷ 867

2. Mistrials—In general

Defendant was not prejudiced by trial court's refusal to grant mistrial in robbery prosecution after juror reported to other jurors that defendant had approached him and told him to "look out for" defendant, where trial court replaced two jurors with alternates and admonished jury with limiting instruction, and other jurors indicated they could disregard the incident and render decision based solely upon facts and law presented; there was no evidence suggesting that remaining jurors were biased or that they considered any inappropriate information in reaching their decision. State v. Jordan (Ohio App. 10 Dist., Franklin, 02-20-2003) No. 02AP-370, 2003-Ohio-755, 2003 WL 360953, Unreported. Criminal Law ⚷ 855(1)

Juror's disclosure to jury foreperson day after entry of the guilty verdict that he was familiar with the bar at which defendant worked as bouncer and that he was familiar with fact that defendant had body slammed other patrons, causing them physical injuries, did not warrant mistrial, in trial for felonious assault; there was no showing that juror exercised undue influence or otherwise committed misconduct during deliberations, or that juror was not impartial, and disclosure was not inconsistent with response during voir dire that juror was familiar with the bar. State v. Mohammad (Ohio App. 8 Dist., Cuyahoga, 10-24-2002) No. 80867, 2002-Ohio-5850, 2002 WL 31401708, Unreported, appeal not allowed 98 Ohio St.3d 1490, 785 N.E.2d 473, 2003-Ohio-1189. Criminal Law ⚷ 862; Jury ⚷ 131(18)

Admission of defendant's short tape recorded statement to police that he had previously been imprisoned did not warrant mistrial; evidence of defendant's guilt, including his acknowledgement of his involvement in many of the charged crimes, was overwhelming, and there was nothing in the record to indicate defendant was prejudiced by statement's admission. State v. McCain (Ohio App. 4 Dist., Pickaway, 09-27-2002) No. 01CA22, 2002-Ohio-5342, 2002 WL 31194332, Unreported, appeal not allowed 98 Ohio St.3d 1461, 783 N.E.2d 520, 2003-Ohio-644, appeal from denial of post-conviction relief dismissed 2005-Ohio-4952, 2005 WL 2293583, appeal not allowed 108 Ohio St.3d 1440, 842 N.E.2d 64, 2006-Ohio-421. Criminal Law ⚷ 1169.12

Motion for mistrial is untimely prior to jury being impaneled; correct method for correcting any irregularities prior to jury being sworn is a motion to dismiss entire jury panel. State v. Trummer (Ohio App. 7 Dist., 09-30-1996) 114 Ohio App.3d 456, 683 N.E.2d 392, dismissed, appeal not allowed 78 Ohio St.3d 1409, 675 N.E.2d 1249, denial of post-conviction relief affirmed 1998 WL 896457, dismissed, appeal not allowed 85 Ohio St.3d 1464, 709 N.E.2d 171, motion for delayed appeal denied 2000 WL 1476604. Jury ⚷ 115

Although state violated *Brady* by failing to disclose state's promise not to pursue criminal charges against its witness in prosecution for violation of hazardous waste laws, mistrial was not warranted; defendant had ample opportunity to use information at trial, trier of fact learned of inducement and could use it in judging witness' credibility, and evidence, even if revealed to defendant prior to trial, would not have changed outcome. State v. Barzacchini (Ohio App. 6 Dist., 08-19-1994) 96 Ohio App.3d 440, 645 N.E.2d 137. Criminal Law ⚷ 700(5); Criminal Law ⚷ 867

When mistrial is declared at behest of prosecutor or on court's own motion, valued right of defendant to have his trial completed by particular tribunal summoned to sit in judgment on him is balanced against public interest in ensuring that justice is meted out to offenders. Malinovsky v. Court of Common Pleas of Lorain County (C.A.6 (Ohio) 1993) 7 F.3d 1263, certiorari denied 114 S.Ct. 1300, 510 U.S. 1194, 127 L.Ed.2d 652. Double Jeopardy ⚷ 95.1

3. —— Fair trial, mistrials

Mistrials need be declared only when ends of justice so require and fair trial is no longer possible. State v. Ayala (Ohio App. 10 Dist., 06-11-1996) 111 Ohio App.3d 627, 676 N.E.2d 1201. Criminal Law ⚷ 867

Mistrial should be declared only when fair trial is no longer possible. State v. Stewart (Ohio App. 9 Dist., 06-05-1996) 111 Ohio App.3d 525, 676 N.E.2d 912. Criminal Law ⚷ 867

Mistrials need be declared only when ends of justice so require and fair trial is no longer possible. State v. Williams (Ohio App. 8 Dist., 07-31-1995) 105 Ohio App.3d 471, 664 N.E.2d 576, cause dismissed 74 Ohio St.3d 1442, 656 N.E.2d 343, dismissed, appeal not allowed 74 Ohio St.3d 1444, 656 N.E.2d 345. Criminal Law ⚷ 867

Granting of a mistrial is only necessary where fair trial is no longer possible. State v. Blankenship (Ohio App. 12 Dist., 04-17-1995) 102 Ohio App.3d 534, 657 N.E.2d 559, dismissed, appeal not allowed 73 Ohio St.3d 1426, 652 N.E.2d 799, denial of post-conviction relief affirmed 1995 WL 746232, dismissed, appeal not allowed 75 Ohio St.3d 1484, 664 N.E.2d 536, denial of post-conviction relief affirmed 74 Ohio St.3d 522, 660 N.E.2d 448, 1996-Ohio-58, denial of post-conviction relief affirmed 1997 WL 700073, dismissed, appeal not allowed 81 Ohio St.3d 1466, 690 N.E.2d 1287. Criminal Law ⚷ 867

4. —— Manifest necessity, mistrials

A declaration of mistrial may be found justified by manifest necessity where jurors were exposed to news reports about the judge's handling of another criminal matter and where the judge believed assignment of another judge would not protect the integrity of the judicial process. U.S. v. Cameron (C.A.6 (Ohio) 1992) 953 F.2d 240. Double Jeopardy ⚷ 99

A trial judge has no duty before granting a mistrial to inquire sua sponte each time there are included offenses where there is no suggestion that the jury may have reached a partial verdict; whether "manifest necessity" dictated a declaration of mistrial must be addressed at the time a mistrial is declared. Fitzgerald v. Lile (N.D.Ohio 1990) 732 F.Supp. 784, affirmed 918 F.2d 178.

5. —— Prejudicial errors, mistrials

When, in absence of judge, error occurs which prejudicially affects merits of case and substantial rights of party, mistrial should be ordered. State v. Paxton (Ohio App. 6 Dist., 05-19-1995) 110 Ohio App.3d 305, 674 N.E.2d 379, appeal dismissed as improvidently allowed 72 Ohio St.3d 485, 650 N.E.2d 1359, 1995-Ohio-74, reconsideration denied 73 Ohio St.3d 1454, 654 N.E.2d 989, appeal dismissed 73 Ohio St.3d 1441, 654 N.E.2d 352, reconsideration denied 74 Ohio St.3d 1411, 655 N.E.2d 409, appeal allowed 74 Ohio St.3d 1458, 656 N.E.2d 952, appeal dismissed as improvidently allowed 77 Ohio St.3d 1204, 670 N.E.2d 1359, 1996-Ohio-341. Criminal Law ⚷ 867

Mistrial should not be granted merely because some minor error or irregularity has arisen. State v. Blankenship (Ohio App. 12 Dist., 04-17-1995) 102 Ohio App.3d 534, 657 N.E.2d 559, dismissed, appeal not allowed 73 Ohio St.3d 1426, 652 N.E.2d 799, denial of post-conviction relief affirmed 1995 WL 746232, dismissed, appeal not allowed 75 Ohio St.3d 1484, 664 N.E.2d 536, denial of post-conviction relief affirmed 74 Ohio St.3d 522, 660 N.E.2d 448, 1996-Ohio-58, denial of post-conviction relief affirmed 1997 WL 700073, dismissed, appeal not allowed 81 Ohio St.3d 1466, 690 N.E.2d 1287. Criminal Law ⚷ 867

Mistrial should not be ordered in criminal case merely because some error or irregularity has intervened, unless substantial rights of accused are adversely affected. State v. Nichols (Pike 1993) 85 Ohio App.3d 65, 619 N.E.2d 80. Criminal Law ⚷ 867

"Mistrial" is defined as trial which has been terminated prior to its normal conclusion because of some extraordinary event, prejudicial error that cannot be corrected at trial, or deadlocked jury. Malinovsky v. Court of Common Pleas of Lorain County (C.A.6 (Ohio) 1993) 7 F.3d 1263, certiorari denied 114 S.Ct. 1300, 510 U.S. 1194, 127 L.Ed.2d 652. Criminal Law ⚷ 867

6. —— Handcuffs or shackles, mistrials

Assuming that two jurors in prosecution for trafficking in marijuana, resisting arrest, possession of drug abuse paraphernalia, and obstructing official business saw defendant sitting in courthouse hallway in handcuffs, such sighting did not prejudice defendant and did not warrant mistrial, where defense counsel admitted that he was not certain jurors saw defendant in handcuffs, any observation which did occur would have been brief, and defense counsel declined limiting instruction. State v. Vactor (Ohio App. 9 Dist., Lorain, 12-31-2003) No. 02CA008068, 2003-Ohio-7195, 2003 WL 23095277, Unreported. Criminal Law ⚷ 867

Defendant's right to fair trial is not prejudiced by the use of handcuffs or shackles where jurors' view of defendant in custody is brief, inadvertent, and outside of the courtroom. State v. Blankenship (Ohio App. 12 Dist., 04-17-1995) 102 Ohio App.3d 534, 657 N.E.2d 559, dismissed, appeal not allowed 73 Ohio St.3d 1426, 652 N.E.2d 799, denial of post-conviction relief affirmed 1995 WL 746232, dismissed, appeal not allowed 75 Ohio St.3d 1484, 664 N.E.2d 536, denial of post-conviction relief affirmed 74 Ohio St.3d 522, 660 N.E.2d 448, 1996-Ohio-58, denial of post-conviction relief affirmed 1997 WL 700073, dismissed, appeal not allowed 81 Ohio St.3d 1466, 690 N.E.2d 1287. Criminal Law ⚷ 637

Defendant was not entitled to mistrial on ground that several members of the jury saw him in handcuffs and shackles as he was being led into courthouse; any glimpse of defendant in restraints by members of the jury was brief and inadvertent and occurred outside of the courtroom and there was no evidence that these circumstances unduly prejudiced defendant's right to fair trial or contributed to guilty verdict. State v. Blankenship (Ohio App. 12 Dist., 04-17-1995) 102 Ohio App.3d 534, 657 N.E.2d 559, dismissed, appeal not allowed 73 Ohio St.3d 1426, 652 N.E.2d 799, denial of post-conviction relief affirmed 1995 WL 746232, dismissed, appeal not allowed 75 Ohio St.3d 1484, 664 N.E.2d 536, denial of post-conviction relief affirmed 74 Ohio St.3d 522, 660 N.E.2d 448, 1996-Ohio-58, denial of post-conviction relief affirmed 1997 WL 700073, dismissed, appeal not allowed 81 Ohio St.3d 1466, 690 N.E.2d 1287. Criminal Law ⚷ 637

7. —— Testimony, mistrials

Defendant was not entitled to a mistrial in drug possession prosecution based on officer testimony that defendant had been arrested on an outstanding warrant for allegedly robbing a bank; jury was instructed to disregard the underlying reason for the outstanding warrant. State v. Colbert (Ohio App. 8 Dist., Cuyahoga, 11-10-2004) No. 84189, 2004-Ohio-6012, 2004 WL 2578861, Unreported. Criminal Law ⚷ 783(1)

Witness's testimony that defendant was convicted felon did not warrant mistrial in assault prosecution, where curative instruction was given providing that testimony should not be considered and evidence of guilt was overwhelming. State v. Elko (Ohio App. 8 Dist., Cuyahoga, 09-30-2004) No. 83641, 2004-Ohio-5209, 2004 WL 2340258, Unreported, appeal not allowed 105 Ohio St.3d 1441, 822 N.E.2d 811, 2005-Ohio-540. Criminal Law ⚷ 867

Prosecutor's questioning of state witness, which elicited testimony that murder defendant said he "got that M.F.er," did not warrant mistrial, where witness's name was provided on original witness list, defendant received copy of tape recorded interview in which individual discussed defendant's alleged confession to witness, defendant interviewed witness prior to trial, and court instructed jury to disregard witness's testimony. State v. Woodward (Ohio App. 10 Dist., Franklin, 08-24-2004) No. 03AP-398, 2004-Ohio-4418, 2004 WL 1879037, Unreported, cause dismissed 103 Ohio St.3d 1489, 816 N.E.2d 1077, 2004-Ohio-5606, reconsideration denied 104 Ohio St.3d 1428, 819 N.E.2d 710, 2004-Ohio-6585. Criminal Law ⚷ 867

Testimony regarding defendant's prior incarceration did not require mistrial, where trial court instructed jury to disregard the testimony, and defendant offered no evidence that the jury disregarded that instruction. State v. Pruiett (Ohio App. 9 Dist., Summit, 06-23-2004) No. 21796, 2003-Ohio-3256, 2004 WL 1397974, Unreported. Criminal Law ⚷ 867

Detective's reference to knowing certain gang members did not warrant mistrial in murder prosecution, where detective's reference was non-responsive to any question posed and did not indicate that defendant was part of gang, and trial court cured any prejudice by sustaining defendant's objection, instructing the jury to disregard the reference, and admonishing the detective in the presence of the jury. State v. Freeman (Ohio App. 8 Dist., Cuyahoga, 06-19-2003) No. 81405, 2003-Ohio-3216, 2003 WL 21419265, Unreported. Criminal Law ⚷ 1169.5(3)

Improper admission of testimony of murder defendant's live-in girlfriend, referencing prison in which defendant had previously been confined, did not so damage fairness of proceedings to warrant mistrial in and of itself, where reference was brief and was not highlighted by prosecution, and where defense counsel declined court's offer to give limiting or cautionary instruction. State v. Moulder (Ohio App. 8 Dist., Cuyahoga, 10-03-2002) No. 80266, 2002-Ohio-5327, 2002 WL 31195391, Unreported, appeal not allowed 98 Ohio St.3d 1512, 786 N.E.2d 62, 2003-Ohio-1572. Criminal Law ⚷ 867

Witness's testimony in capital murder prosecution that, on night victim was murdered, she did not go inside victim's home after dropping victim off from work because defendant was home, did not violate court order that precluded witness from testifying about why she felt victim had fear of defendant, and thus defendant was not entitled to mistrial based on such testimony; witness's testimony did not reasonably relate to victim's fear, but rather, the most likely inference was simply that victim felt that inviting witness inside would be awkward because defendant was there, and at trial, prosecutor recognized that witness was somebody who was avoiding defendant. State v. Brinkley (Ohio, 04-13-2005) 105 Ohio St.3d 231, 824 N.E.2d 959, 2005-Ohio-1507, motion to reopen denied 106 Ohio St.3d 1529, 835 N.E.2d 379, 2005-Ohio-5146. Criminal Law ⚷ 867

Mistrial was not warranted in murder trial when head and leg of doll came off as coroner demonstrated way in which young victim was injured; incident was accidental, and prosecutor in no way tried to inflame passions of jury. State v. Smith (Ohio, 12-13-2002) 97 Ohio St.3d 367, 780 N.E.2d 221, 2002-Ohio-6659, reconsideration denied 97 Ohio St.3d 1500, 780 N.E.2d 1023, 2002-Ohio-7367, stay granted 98 Ohio St.3d 1417, 782 N.E.2d 73, 2003-Ohio-189, certiorari denied 123 S.Ct. 2255, 539 U.S. 907, 156 L.Ed.2d 118. Criminal Law ⚷ 867

Police officer's testimony explaining that a "96 Move" is a technique in which drug traffickers hollow out a car battery to transport illegal narcotics did not require a mistrial on racketeering and money laundering charges, where the state was attempting to elicit evidence of the condition of a battery removed from a van used by defendant and her group and there was other evidence that some members of the group were involved with drug trafficking. State v. Duncan (Ohio App. 1 Dist., 09-25-1998) 130 Ohio App.3d 77, 719 N.E.2d 608. Criminal Law ⚷ 867

Mistrial was not required in narcotics case when prosecution witness testified during cross-examination that he was willing to take a polygraph test to prove he was telling the truth, where trial court struck answer as unresponsive, gave curative instruction, and instructed jury on manner in which they were to test credibility of witnesses. State v. Bereschik (Ohio App. 7 Dist., 12-19-1996) 116 Ohio App.3d 829, 689 N.E.2d 589, dismissed, appeal not allowed 78 Ohio St.3d 1464, 678 N.E.2d 221. Criminal Law ⚿ 867

Trial court did not abuse its discretion by denying defendant's motion for mistrial when prosecutor asked state's witness, who was a police officer, whether defendant was present in the courtroom and then motioned to table where defendant was seated and witness testified that defendant resembled man she had arrested, but she was unable to identify defendant with absolute certainty; there was nothing in the record to suggest that form of prosecutor's question was designed to improperly coax or prod witness into identifying defendant and issue of whether defendant was the man arrested by witness was not subject to serious dispute at trial. State v. Blankenship (Ohio App. 12 Dist., 04-17-1995) 102 Ohio App.3d 534, 657 N.E.2d 559, dismissed, appeal not allowed 73 Ohio St.3d 1426, 652 N.E.2d 799, denial of post-conviction relief affirmed 1995 WL 746232, dismissed, appeal not allowed 75 Ohio St.3d 1484, 664 N.E.2d 536, denial of post-conviction relief affirmed 74 Ohio St.3d 522, 660 N.E.2d 448, 1996-Ohio-58, denial of post-conviction relief affirmed 1997 WL 700073, dismissed, appeal not allowed 81 Ohio St.3d 1466, 690 N.E.2d 1287. Criminal Law ⚿ 706(3); Criminal Law ⚿ 867

Trial court did not abuse discretion by declining to order mistrial, after police officer testified that he had been advised to approach defendant with caution, as defendant had been previously observed with weapon; trial court gave extensive curative instruction that jury was to disregard statement and that there was no evidence that defendant had ever possessed weapon. State v. Rivera (Ohio App. 11 Dist., 08-15-1994) 99 Ohio App.3d 325, 650 N.E.2d 906, dismissed, appeal not allowed 71 Ohio St.3d 1435, 643 N.E.2d 141. Criminal Law ⚿ 867

8. —— Outside evidence, mistrials

Juror's overhearing of question from nonparticipating attorney to bailiff on second day of deliberations as to how long it took jury to convict defendant did not warrant mistrial, in prosecution for complicity to commit aggravated robbery; bailiff immediately notified trial court, trial court questioned juror, bailiff and attorney involved, juror had not discussed comment with any other juror, and juror assured trial court that he could put matter out of his mind. State v. Gordon (Ohio App. 5 Dist., Stark, 07-18-2005) No. 2005CA00031, 2005-Ohio-3638, 2005 WL 1682658, Unreported, motion for delayed appeal granted 107 Ohio St.3d 1420, 837 N.E.2d 1206, 2005-Ohio-6124, appeal not allowed 108 Ohio St.3d 1509, 844 N.E.2d 855, 2006-Ohio-1329, appeal not allowed 109 Ohio St.3d 1408, 845 N.E.2d 524, 2006-Ohio-1703. Criminal Law ⚿ 855(7)

Juror's personal investigation of murder scene during jury deliberations did not require mistrial, where all jurors had previously been allowed to view the crime scene in person under court supervision, and juror indicated to trial court that his personal investigation did not add any new material information or discussion to jury deliberations. State v. Miller (Ohio App. 3 Dist., Crawford, 04-19-2004) No. 3-03-26, 2004-Ohio-1947, 2004 WL 829933, Unreported, appeal not allowed 103 Ohio St.3d 1462, 815 N.E.2d 678, 2004-Ohio-5056, appeal not allowed 104 Ohio St.3d 1460, 821 N.E.2d 577, 2005-Ohio-204. Criminal Law ⚿ 855(9)

Juror's alleged exposure to newspaper article concerning case and dissemination of information to other jurors did not warrant mistrial in murder prosecution, where each of the jurors independently corroborated that the extent of the reference to the article was that defendant's family was not expected to attend trial, and juror who disseminated the information denied any additional knowledge of the article, denied reading the article, and stated that she told her mother, who had initially informed her about the article, not to tell her anything more about the article. State v. Freeman (Ohio App. 8 Dist., Cuyahoga, 06-19-2003) No. 81405, 2003-Ohio-3216, 2003 WL 21419265, Unreported. Criminal Law ⚿ 855(5)

Defendant was entitled to mistrial when seven of twelve jurors became aware of prior charges against defendant through media reports, even though trial court received assurances from jurors that they were not influenced by the information; trial court had already determined that evidence of prior charges was inadmissible, jurors were not initially instructed that they were not to view, read or listen to any media reports concerning the case, reports erroneously stated that previous charges were for same offense as defendant faced at trial, and information was highly prejudicial. State v. Dute (Ohio App. 1 Dist., Hamilton, 05-30-2003) No. C-020709, 2003-Ohio-2774, 2003 WL 21242199, Unreported, appeal not allowed 100 Ohio St.3d 1411, 796 N.E.2d 538, 2003-Ohio-4948. Criminal Law ⚿ 867

Trial court acted within its discretion in refusing to declare mistrial and refusing to grant defense motion to set aside jury panel, even though one prospective juror mentioned that she had heard that there were two victims; prospective juror who indicated that there were two victims was dismissed from panel, and trial judge conscientiously and extensively inquired of remaining prospective jurors as to their ability to sit fairly and impartially. State v. Trummer (Ohio App. 7 Dist., 09-30-1996) 114 Ohio App.3d 456, 683 N.E.2d 392, dismissed, appeal not allowed 78 Ohio St.3d 1409, 675 N.E.2d 1249, denial of post-conviction relief affirmed 1998 WL 896457, dismissed, appeal not allowed 85 Ohio St.3d 1464, 709 N.E.2d 171, motion for delayed appeal denied 2000 WL 1476604. Jury ⚿ 133

9. —— Failure to produce evidence, mistrials

State's failure to produce photographs and videotaped interview of white male who also went by same nickname "Shorty Mack" as defendant did not warrant mistrial based on defendant's claim that photographs and videotape would have established that he was not individual that co-defendant had asserted had forced him to commit crimes, in trial for aggravated robbery, rape and other crimes; nondisclosure of photographs and videotape was inadvertent mistake, in that they were labeled with individual's proper name and not nickname also used by defendant, defendant was not prevented from arguing that police did poor investigation in locating individual by name of "Shorty Mack" who looked nothing like defendant, and there was overwhelming, independent evidence of defendant's participation in crimes. State v. Bunch (Ohio App. 7 Dist., Mahoning, 06-24-2005) No. 02 CA 196, 2005-Ohio-3309, 2005 WL 1523844, Unreported, appeal allowed 107 Ohio St.3d 1680, 839 N.E.2d 401, 2005-Ohio-6480. Criminal Law ⚷ 867

Mistrial was not warranted due to State's failure to provide to defendant copies of photographs taken of murder scene before loaded gun found near victim's body was moved away from body, in prosecution for felony murder; photographs of gun near victim's body would not have suggested defense, namely that victim shot herself, that defendant would not have asserted otherwise at trial, and defendant in fact elicited testimony from two prosecution witnesses and from his own expert that gun found near victim's body was consistent with self-inflicted shot. State v. Thacker (Ohio App. 2 Dist., Greene, 05-06-2005) No. 2004-CA-38, No. 2004-CA-57, 2005-Ohio-2230, 2005 WL 1060616, Unreported, appeal not allowed 106 Ohio St.3d 1544, 835 N.E.2d 726, 2005-Ohio-5343. Criminal Law ⚷ 627.8(6)

Prosecution's failure to disclose until trial existence of audiotaped discussion in which sergeant told detective that individual said specific person was in area when shots were fired did not warrant mistrial in murder prosecution, where disclosure was made toward beginning of trial, court ordered prosecution to immediately provide defendant with audiotape, court recessed so that defendant could locate and interview individual, and court granted defendant leave to place individual on witness list, but defendant failed to do so. State v. Woodward (Ohio App. 10 Dist., Franklin, 08-24-2004) No. 03AP-398, 2004-Ohio-4418, 2004 WL 1879037, Unreported, cause dismissed 103 Ohio St.3d 1489, 816 N.E.2d 1077, 2004-Ohio-5606, reconsideration denied 104 Ohio St.3d 1428, 819 N.E.2d 710, 2004-Ohio-6585. Criminal Law ⚷ 627.8(6)

Defendant failed to demonstrate that trial court abused its discretion, during prosecution for trafficking in drugs, in refusing to declare mistrial based on prosecution's alleged discovery violation in refusing to provide defendant with copies of tape-recordings of underlying drug transaction, and instead permitting defendant and his counsel to listen to tapes on listening equipment of alleged poor quality; Court of Appeals was not provided with the machines on which defense counsel listened to tapes and, thus, could not compare the alleged poor sound quality. State v. Agner (Ohio App. 3 Dist., 10-29-1999) 135 Ohio App.3d 286, 733 N.E.2d 676, 1999-Ohio-918. Criminal Law ⚷ 1115(1)

10. —— Prosecutorial comments, mistrials

Prosecutor's comments during closing argument, that it was defendant, and not other witnesses, who mentioned lipstick being on his shirt, and suggesting that photocopy of receipt from automobile supply store was forgery, did not entitle defendant to mistrial in prosecution for rape, attempted rape, and gross sexual imposition; review of transcript indicated that it was defendant's attorney who claimed that defendant's shirt had lipstick on it, and defense made much of exculpatory nature of photocopied receipt prior to prosecutor's remarks. State v. Starcher (Ohio App. 9 Dist., Medina, 12-10-2003) No. 03CA0014-M, 2003-Ohio-6588, 2003 WL 22900642, Unreported, motion for delayed appeal denied 103 Ohio St.3d 1403, 812 N.E.2d 1287, 2004-Ohio-3980, habeas corpus dismissed 2006 WL 1515659. Criminal Law ⚷ 730(7)

Defendant's motion for mistrial at conclusion of state's initial closing argument during penalty phase of capital murder case, based upon prosecutor's alleged improper comments, did not preserve for review defendant's claims regarding comments, where defendant did not object at time comments were made. State v. Wogenstahl (Ohio, 03-06-1996) 75 Ohio St.3d 344, 662 N.E.2d 311, 1996-Ohio-219, reconsideration denied 75 Ohio St.3d 1453, 663 N.E.2d 333, certiorari denied 117 S.Ct. 240, 519 U.S. 895, 136 L.Ed.2d 169, denial of post-conviction relief affirmed 2004-Ohio-5994, 2004 WL 2567655, appeal not allowed 105 Ohio St.3d 1465, 824 N.E.2d 93, 2005-Ohio-1024. Criminal Law ⚷ 1037.1(4); Criminal Law ⚷ 1044.2(1)

11. —— Jurors sleeping, mistrials

Trial court did not abuse its discretion in failing to grant a mistrial based claim that juror was sleeping during trial, where defendant withdrew his motion for mistrial. State v. Windham (Ohio App. 6 Dist., Erie, 01-24-2003) No. E-01-015, 2003-Ohio-305, 2003 WL 164796, Unreported. Criminal Law ⚷ 867

Trial court did not have a sua sponte duty to declare a mistrial based on claim on juror slept during trial, where portion of testimony juror slept through was tape recording that had previously been played to jury. State v. Windham (Ohio App. 6 Dist., Erie, 01-24-2003) No. E-01-015, 2003-Ohio-305, 2003 WL 164796, Unreported. Criminal Law ⚷ 855(1)

12. —— Request, mistrials

For purposes of appellate review, defendant waived claim that alleged juror misconduct required mistrial, where defendant failed to request mistrial until after the verdict was read. State v. Miller (Ohio App. 3 Dist., Crawford, 04-19-2004) No. 3-03-26, 2004-Ohio-1947, 2004 WL 829933, Unreported, appeal not allowed 103 Ohio St.3d 1462, 815 N.E.2d 678, 2004-Ohio-5056, appeal not allowed 104 Ohio St.3d 1460, 821 N.E.2d 577, 2005-Ohio-204. Criminal Law ⚷ 1044.2(1)

Fact that victim's father entered jury room and poured himself cup of coffee on second day of aggravated murder trial did not require that trial court grant mistrial, or conduct individual voir dire of each juror; trial court questioned five jurors who explained that, at first, they thought father was another juror, and that father did not try to discuss case, none of jurors questioned felt that incident would interfere with his or her ability to serve as fair and impartial juror, and, after trial court said it was satisfied that nothing had occurred to cause jury to be prejudiced, defendant did not request that trial court interview remaining jurors. State v. Early (Ohio App. 6 Dist., Lucas, 02-06-2004) No. L-01-1454, 2004-Ohio-471, 2004 WL 226096, Unreported, appeal not allowed 102 Ohio St.3d 1483, 810 N.E.2d 967, 2004-Ohio-3069. Criminal Law ⚷ 868

Defendant waived right to argue on appeal that mistrial should have been granted as he was prejudiced by failure of subpoenaed defense witness to appear and/or trial court's refusal to issue arrest warrant for witness, where defendant did not ask trial court for mistrial. State v. Brock (Ohio App. 2 Dist., Montgomery, 12-27-2002) No. 19291, 2002-Ohio-7292, 2002 WL 31888185, Unreported. Criminal Law ⚷ 1039

13. —— Discretion of court, mistrials

Trial court denial of defendant's motion for a mistrial, based on a previously undisclosed witness testifying at trial, was not an abuse of discretion; State learned of witness after trial had commenced, State subpoenaed the witness immediately, and defense counsel was provided several days to prepare and review the witnesses and testimony. State v. Wooden (Ohio App. 9 Dist., Summit, 04-16-2003) No. 21138, 2003-Ohio-1917, 2003 WL 1877631, Unreported, motion for delayed appeal denied 100 Ohio St.3d 1543, 800 N.E.2d 750, 2003-Ohio-6879. Criminal Law ⚷ 629.5(1)

Denial of defendant's motion for a mistrial, after the victim's father verbally assaulted defendant in the presence of the jury, was not an abuse of discretion; each juror assured the court during individual voir dire that their opinions would not be affected by the verbal assault they witnessed. State v. Rucker (Ohio App. 5 Dist., Richland, 03-12-2003) No. 02-CA35-2, 2003-Ohio-1193, 2003 WL 1145450, Unreported. Criminal Law ⚷ 855(4); Criminal Law ⚷ 867

Order of trial judge declaring mistrial during course of criminal trial, on motion of State, is error and contrary to law, constituting failure to exercise sound discretion, where, taking all circumstances under consideration, there is no manifest necessity for mistrial, no extraordinary and striking circumstances and no end of public justice served by mistrial, and where judge has not made scrupulous search for alternatives to deal with problem. City of Sidney v. Little (Ohio App. 3 Dist., 04-15-1997) 119 Ohio App.3d 193, 694 N.E.2d 1386. Criminal Law ⚷ 1155

Decision whether to grant mistrial lies within sound discretion of trial court. State v. Stewart (Ohio App. 9 Dist., 06-05-1996) 111 Ohio App.3d 525, 676 N.E.2d 912. Criminal Law ⚷ 867

Granting or denying motion for mistrial rests within sound discretion of trial court. State v. Nichols (Pike 1993) 85 Ohio App.3d 65, 619 N.E.2d 80. Criminal Law ⚷ 867

The grant or denial of a motion for mistrial is within the sound discretion of the trial court; a motion for mistrial can be granted only where the defendant's right to a fair trial has been prejudiced by the complaint of misconduct or irregularity. State v. Green (Cuyahoga 1990) 67 Ohio App.3d 72, 585 N.E.2d 990. Criminal Law ⚷ 867

Great deference is given trial judges as having the best position to determine whether a situation warrants the declaration of a mistrial. State v. Simmons (Summit 1989) 61 Ohio App.3d 514, 573 N.E.2d 165, dismissed 58 Ohio St.3d 713, 570 N.E.2d 277. Criminal Law ⚷ 1155

14. —— Journal entries, mistrials

Trial judge's mistaken oral declaration of mistrial did not result in mistrial, and accordingly, judge was not prevented from correcting error and accepting jury's verdict, where judge's oral declaration was never journalized. State v. Stewart (Ohio App. 11 Dist., Portage, 12-27-2002) No. 2001-P-0035, 2002-Ohio-7270, 2002 WL 31886657, Unreported, appeal not allowed 98 Ohio St.3d 1567, 787 N.E.2d 1231, 2003-Ohio-2242. Criminal Law ⚷ 867

While statute requires that the trial court enter on the journal its reasons for mistrial, it is sufficient if the record supports the trial court's reasons for doing so. State v. Morgan (Ohio App. 8 Dist., 09-21-1998) 129 Ohio App.3d 838, 719 N.E.2d 102, appeal not allowed 84 Ohio St.3d 1475, 704 N.E.2d 581. Criminal Law ⚷ 867

15. —— Retrials, mistrials

If defendant successfully seeks to avoid his trial prior to its conclusion by motion for mistrial, retrial may still be had. Malinovsky v. Court of Common Pleas of Lorain County (C.A.6 (Ohio) 1993) 7 F.3d 1263, certiorari denied 114 S.Ct. 1300, 510 U.S. 1194, 127 L.Ed.2d 652. Double Jeopardy ⚷ 96

16. —— Review, mistrials

Appellate court will not reverse decision on motion for mistrial unless that decision constitutes abuse of discretion. State v. Powers (Ohio App. 9 Dist., 10-04-1995) 106 Ohio App.3d 696, 667 N.E.2d 32. Criminal Law ⚷ 1155

Court of Appeals reviews ruling on motion for mistrial for abuse of discretion. State v. Williams (Ohio App. 8 Dist., 07-31-1995) 105 Ohio App.3d 471, 664 N.E.2d 576, cause dismissed 74 Ohio St.3d 1442, 656 N.E.2d 343, dismissed, appeal not allowed 74 Ohio St.3d 1444, 656 N.E.2d 345. Criminal Law ⚷ 1155

17. Motion

Petitioner could not request new trial, where he was convicted on plea of no contest, and never had a trial in the first instance. State v. Coleman (Ohio App. 10 Dist., Franklin, 12-31-2003) No. 03AP-219, No. 03AP-220, 2003-Ohio-7234, 2003 WL 23096039, Unreported. Criminal Law ⚷ 275.2

Denying new trial motion based on testimony of reluctant witness was not abuse of discretion in prosecution for assault with peace officer specification, where defense counsel made tactical decision at trial not to call such unreliable witness to stand. State v. Jones (Ohio App. 8 Dist., Cuyahoga, 06-12-2003) No. 81112, 2003-Ohio-3004, 2003 WL 21356758, Unreported. Criminal Law ⚷ 939(2)

Appeal pertaining to allegedly erroneous denial of new trial motion was premature, where motion for new trial was pending in trial court. State v. Jones (Ohio App. 8 Dist., Cuyahoga, 06-12-2003) No. 81112, 2003-Ohio-3004, 2003 WL 21356758, Unreported. Criminal Law ⚷ 1065

Admission of question from the State, asking defendant if he had ever previously engaged in sexual contact with a person who was initially asleep when defendant began his contact with the person, did not deny defendant his right to a fair trial or violate the rape shield statute or the statute regarding proof of a defendant's motive; trial court specifically found that the probative value of the question outweighed its prejudicial effect. State v. Rucker (Ohio App. 5 Dist., Richland, 03-12-2003) No. 02-CA35-2, 2003-Ohio-1193, 2003 WL 1145450, Unreported. Criminal Law ⚷ 338(7); Rape ⚷ 42

Affidavits of alleged victims of rape, recanting their trial testimony, were not so strong on their face as to render trial court's decision to overrule defendant's motion for new trial an abuse of discretion, although evidentiary hearing should have been held on motion for new trial. State v. Monk (Ohio App. 5 Dist., Knox, 12-03-2002) No. 02CA000026, 2002-Ohio-6602, 2002 WL 31713825, Unreported. Criminal Law ⚷ 942(2)

Even if jury would have believed testimony of defendant's friend, as corroborated by eyewitness, that he had placed cocaine in footpegs of defendant's motorcycle while defendant was asleep, such testimony did not raise probability that result of trial would be different, so as to warrant new trial for trafficking of cocaine by possessing cocaine in amount exceeding bulk, but less than three times bulk amount; defendant had actual possession of cocaine that was found in footpegs, in that he owned footpegs and motorcycle, he purchased footpegs for express purpose of transporting cocaine, and police, during execution of search warrant on defendant's home, discovered scales, razor blades, and plastic bag containing cocaine residue, which provided circumstantial evidence of cocaine possession. State v. Callihan (Ohio App. 4 Dist., Scioto, 10-23-2002) No. 01CA2815, 2002-Ohio-5878, 2002 WL 31415353, Unreported. Criminal Law ⚷ 945(2)

Eyewitness' testimony at hearing on motion for new trial, that he observed defendant's friend put cocaine in footpegs of defendant's motorcycle while defendant was asleep, was merely cumulative of other identical evidence at trial, and thus, did not entitle defendant to new trial for trafficking of cocaine by possessing cocaine in amount exceeding bulk amount. State v. Callihan (Ohio App. 4 Dist., Scioto, 10-23-2002) No. 01CA2815, 2002-Ohio-5878, 2002 WL 31415353, Unreported. Criminal Law ⚷ 941(2)

Determination that informant's trial testimony was not false was not abuse of discretion, and thus, informant's recantation of trial testimony did not warrant new trial for aggravated trafficking in cocaine; trial testimony was sworn, while evidence that informant recanted was introduced via attorney to whom informant gave unsworn statement. State v. Callihan (Ohio App. 4 Dist., Scioto, 10-23-2002) No. 01CA2815, 2002-Ohio-5878, 2002 WL 31415353, Unreported. Criminal Law ⚷ 942(2)

Where a prosecutor urges the jury to convict the defendant of operating a motor vehicle without a valid operator's license to keep the defendant from becoming involved in automobile accidents, even though defendant is not involved in an accident in this case, the defendant is denied a fair trial. State v. Kleve (Ohio App. 1 Dist., Hamilton, 04-06-1994) No. C-930375, 1994 WL 114306, Unreported.

Trial court did not abuse its discretion in narcotics case when it denied motion for mistrial and motion for new trial after two jurors revealed that they had viewed television news report concerning case; jurors stated during questioning by court that they had viewed only portion of report and that it would not affect their ability to be impartial, and defense counsel did not object when they were allowed to rejoin panel and claimed that they had not answered truthfully and that other jurors had seen report only after jury returned guilty verdict. State v. Bereschik (Ohio App. 7 Dist., 12-19-1996) 116 Ohio App.3d 829, 689 N.E.2d 589, dismissed, appeal not allowed 78 Ohio St.3d 1464, 678 N.E.2d 221. Criminal Law ⚷ 867; Criminal Law ⚷ 925.5(1)

Rulings on motions for new trials are within sound discretion of trial court, and appellate court may not disturb them on appeal absent clear showing that trial court abused its discretion; "abuse of discretion" connotes more than error of law or judgment, and implies that court's attitude was unreasonable, arbitrary, or unconscionable. State v. Miller (Ohio App. 4 Dist., 08-11-1995) 105 Ohio App.3d 679, 664 N.E.2d 1309. Criminal Law ⚷ 911; Criminal Law ⚷ 1156(1)

Where an accused fails to raise an objection as to venue prior to trial, and his motion for new trial is made on specified grounds which do not include an objection that the state failed to prove venue, the accused's right to raise an objection that the state did not prove venue is waived and the question of venue may not be raised for the first time in the court of appeals. State v. Loucks (Gallia 1971) 28 Ohio App.2d 77, 274 N.E.2d 773, 57 O.O.2d 160.

A defendant in a criminal case has the right to file a motion for a new trial, and it is reversible error for a court to strike such motion from the files. State v. O'Banion (Butler 1970) 26 Ohio App.2d 285, 271 N.E.2d 312, 55 O.O.2d 503. Criminal Law ⚷ 964; Criminal Law ⚷ 1176

18. Irregularities

Trial court's failure in capital murder case to conduct a hearing or issue curative instruction upon learning that several jurors saw defendant in shackles just before closing arguments in mitigation phase did not deny defendant a fair trial; defendant simply asserted he was prejudiced by that incident without demonstrating prejudice, and risk of prejudice was slight in any event, considering that jurors' view of defendant in custody was brief, inadvertent, and outside the courtroom. State v. Nields (Ohio, 08-29-2001) 93 Ohio St.3d 6, 752 N.E.2d 859, 2001-Ohio-1291, reconsideration denied 93 Ohio St.3d 1452, 756 N.E.2d 116. Criminal Law ⚿ 1166.8

Even if state withholds evidence, mere failure to disclose evidence does not by itself warrant new trial, and the contested evidence claimed to be withheld must also be found to be material to the outcome of the trial, specifically, there must be reasonable probability that, had the evidence been disclosed, results of proceeding would have been different; "reasonable probability" is a probability sufficient to undermine confidence in the outcome. State v. Self (Ohio App. 12 Dist., 07-22-1996) 112 Ohio App.3d 688, 679 N.E.2d 1173. Criminal Law ⚿ 1166(10.10)

If the court conducts a voir dire and concludes that the jurors did not read about a prior theft conviction reference in a full transcript of a post-conviction statement while a redacted version of it played in court, the court may deny a request for mistrial. State v. Burge (Franklin 1992) 82 Ohio App.3d 244, 611 N.E.2d 866, dismissed, jurisdictional motion overruled 65 Ohio St.3d 1495, 605 N.E.2d 949, reconsideration denied 88 Ohio App.3d 91, 623 N.E.2d 146, dismissed, jurisdictional motion overruled 67 Ohio St.3d 1479, 620 N.E.2d 852.

In a sentencing hearing on an aggravated murder case, a trial court did not commit prejudicial error by sustaining a prosecutor's objection to a defense witness' expression of opinion that because of the defendant's character he could not be guilty of killing anyone, where although a defendant in a capital sentencing proceeding is entitled to wide latitude in the presentation of mitigation evidence, the defense witness was permitted to testify at length about his relationship with the defendant and his general opinion of the defendant's character and the jury was permitted to consider that testimony when it recommended the death penalty. State v. Franklin (Ohio 1991) 62 Ohio St.3d 118, 580 N.E.2d 1, rehearing denied 62 Ohio St.3d 1497, 583 N.E.2d 968, certiorari denied 112 S.Ct. 2315, 504 U.S. 960, 119 L.Ed.2d 235, reconsideration denied 70 Ohio St.3d 1437, 638 N.E.2d 1041, dismissal of post-conviction relief affirmed, dismissed, appeal not allowed 72 Ohio St.3d 1538, 650 N.E.2d 479, reconsideration denied 73 Ohio St.3d 1429, 652 N.E.2d 801, certiorari denied 116 S.Ct. 394, 516 U.S. 950, 133 L.Ed.2d 315.

Where a trial judge during a sentencing hearing in an aggravated murder case sustains a prosecutor's objection to the testimony made by a defense witness that because of the defendant's character he could not be guilty of killing anyone, and then remarks to the jury that the defense witness was present throughout the trial and could have testified about that during the trial, the court's remark to the jury did not constitute prejudicial error requiring a mistrial to be declared since the witness' presence in the courtroom during the guilt phase of the trial was evident to the jury and could have been explored on cross-examination and although the judge did delay in giving a curative instruction, it was given before the jury deliberated on the sentencing and the judge clearly eliminated any inference that the defendant was required to present evidence on his own behalf. State v. Franklin (Ohio 1991) 62 Ohio St.3d 118, 580 N.E.2d 1, rehearing denied 62 Ohio St.3d 1497, 583 N.E.2d 968, certiorari denied 112 S.Ct. 2315, 504 U.S. 960, 119 L.Ed.2d 235, reconsideration denied 70 Ohio St.3d 1437, 638 N.E.2d 1041, dismissal of post-conviction relief affirmed, dismissed, appeal not allowed 72 Ohio St.3d 1538, 650 N.E.2d 479, reconsideration denied 73 Ohio St.3d 1429, 652 N.E.2d 801, certiorari denied 116 S.Ct. 394, 516 U.S. 950, 133 L.Ed.2d 315.

While ordinarily precise times and dates are not essential elements of offenses and temporal information is generally irrelevant in preparing a defense, the state must, in response to a bill of particulars or demand for discovery, supply specific dates and times with regard to an alleged offense where it possesses such information; adherence to this rule will ensure that no constitutional right of an accused to due process or a fair trial will be transgressed. State v. Sellards (Ohio 1985) 17 Ohio St.3d 169, 478 N.E.2d 781, 17 O.B.R. 410.

Where a paragraph in a general charge, by itself, is improper and misleading, but when the court's entire charge is considered it is apparent that no prejudicial error resulted, the judgment will not be reversed. State v. Porter (Ohio 1968) 14 Ohio St.2d 10, 235 N.E.2d 520, 43 O.O.2d 5. Criminal Law ⚿ 822(1)

Where a trial court's answer to a request from the jury for supplemental instructions is incomplete, confusing or misleading, but does not prejudice the accused, a judgment of conviction will not be reversed. State v. Porter (Ohio 1968) 14 Ohio St.2d 10, 235 N.E.2d 520, 43 O.O.2d 5.

Where evidence was not equally applicable to both defendants, and there was joint verdict of guilty, it was not error as matter of law to grant new trial as to one defendant only. Marcoguiseppe v. State (Ohio 1926) 114 Ohio St. 299, 151 N.E. 182, 4 Ohio Law Abs. 194, 24 Ohio Law Rep. 312. Criminal Law ⚿ 910

Irregularities on part of ministerial officers in summoning and impaneling jurors will be disregarded by reviewing courts, and also by trial courts after verdict rendered, unless it is shown that one or more of the accepted jurors did not possess the requisite qualifications to act as juror. Long v. State (Ohio 1923) 109 Ohio St. 77, 141 N.E. 691, 1 Ohio Law Abs. 861, 21 Ohio Law Rep. 331.

Where counsel employed by defendant and counsel appointed by the state to assist in his defense were unable to agree as to the line of defense to be adopted, and engaged in continuous wrangling in the presence of the jury, each charging the other with withholding information, and each giving contradictory advice to the client, held, that a new trial will be awarded. Cornwell v. State (Ohio 1922) 106 Ohio St. 626, 140 N.E. 363, 1 Ohio Law Abs. 876, 20 Ohio Law Rep. 501. Criminal Law ⚷ 920

Allowing juror to ask detective about the discrepancy between testimony of victim's friend that there were two robbers and detective's testimony mentioning three names, and allowing detective to answer that the third person acted as a lookout, was not plain error, in prosecution for aggravated robbery; the question and answer did not relate to defendant, and thus, the question and answer did not affect the outcome of the trial. State v. Davis (Ohio App. 8 Dist., Cuyahoga, 06-20-2002) No. 80364, 2002-Ohio-3104, 2002 WL 1348136, Unreported, affirmed 99 Ohio St.3d 142, 789 N.E.2d 235, 2003-Ohio-2770, certiorari denied 124 S.Ct. 575, 540 U.S. 1021, 157 L.Ed.2d 438. Criminal Law ⚷ 1036.2

19. Misconduct generally—In general

Police officer's reference to defendant's prior police record did not warrant mistrial, as reference was fleeting and was promptly followed by curative instruction. State v. Garner (Ohio, 11-22-1995) 74 Ohio St.3d 49, 656 N.E.2d 623, 1995-Ohio-168, reconsideration denied 74 Ohio St.3d 1485, 657 N.E.2d 1378, certiorari denied 116 S.Ct. 1444, 517 U.S. 1147, 134 L.Ed.2d 564, rehearing denied 116 S.Ct. 1872, 517 U.S. 1230, 134 L.Ed.2d 969, stay granted 76 Ohio St.3d 1401, 666 N.E.2d 233. Criminal Law ⚷ 867

Although reliance upon victim-impact evidence in arguing for death penalty is improper and constitutes error in sentencing phase of capital murder, same evidence may be admissible, relevant evidence in guilt phase of proceedings. State v. Loza (Ohio, 11-30-1994) 71 Ohio St.3d 61, 641 N.E.2d 1082, 37 A.L.R.5th 841, reconsideration denied 71 Ohio St.3d 1437, 643 N.E.2d 142, certiorari denied 115 S.Ct. 1983, 514 U.S. 1120, 131 L.Ed.2d 871, denial of post-conviction relief affirmed 1997 WL 634348, dismissed, appeal not allowed 81 Ohio St.3d 1429, 689 N.E.2d 49. Homicide ⚷ 997; Sentencing And Punishment ⚷ 1763

Ignorance of rules of evidence does not render otherwise improper questioning by attorney allowable, even though attorney's lack of familiarity with rules of evidence may affect question of whether misconduct was intentional or inadvertent. State v. Smidi (Wood 1993) 88 Ohio App.3d 177, 623 N.E.2d 655. Criminal Law ⚷ 705.1

Where a mistrial is the result of governmental misconduct calculated to deprive an accused of his constitutional right to defend himself, double jeopardy bars a subsequent criminal prosecution. State v Sellards, No. CA-1814 (5th Dist Ct App, Tuscarawas, 6-7-84), reversed by 17 OS(3d) 169, 17 OBR 410, 478 NE(2d) 781 (1985).

20. —— False or misleading testimony, misconduct generally

Proper remedy for defendant who sustained material prejudice, in drug trial, from law-enforcement officer's false and misleading testimony at suppression hearing was remand for new trial, rather than dismissal of charges against defendant. State v. Williams (Ohio App. 12 Dist., Butler, 08-04-2003) No. CA2002-09-233, 2003-Ohio-4114, 2003 WL 21783683, Unreported. Criminal Law ⚷ 1181.5(7)

Defendant was materially prejudiced and, thus, denied fair trial, in prosecution for trafficking in cocaine, by law-enforcement officer's false and misleading testimony at suppression hearing that confidential informant had not been searched prior to controlled drug buy; the testimony created impression that defense counsel could have shown reasonable doubt simply by establishing that the state lacked proof that informant did not already possess cocaine at time of the drug buy, another officer stated during trial that he carefully searched informant prior to the drug buy, and the false testimony might have caused defendant to reject favorable plea bargain. State v. Williams (Ohio App. 12 Dist., Butler, 08-04-2003) No. CA2002-09-233, 2003-Ohio-4114, 2003 WL 21783683, Unreported. Criminal Law ⚷ 1168(2)

Defendant was materially prejudiced and, thus, denied fair trial, in prosecution for trafficking in cocaine, by law-enforcement officer's attempt at suppression hearing to mislead defense counsel by making it appear that two confidential informants had been used during controlled drug buy; counsel was left with impression that neither informant would testify at trial and, thus, might have believed that this gave him opportunity to argue reasonable doubt, opportunity disappeared when it became clear at trial that second informant to which officer had referred was another officer, who testified, and the misleading testimony might have caused defendant to reject favorable plea bargain. State v. Williams (Ohio App. 12 Dist., Butler, 08-04-2003) No. CA2002-09-233, 2003-Ohio-4114, 2003 WL 21783683, Unreported. Criminal Law ⚷ 1168(2)

Conviction obtained by the knowing use of perjured testimony is fundamentally unfair, and must be set aside if there is any reasonable likelihood that the false testimony could have affected the judgment of the jury. Byrd v. Collins (C.A.6 (Ohio), 04-06-2000) 209 F.3d 486, rehearing en banc denied 227 F.3d 756, certiorari denied 121 S.Ct. 786, 531 U.S. 1082, 148 L.Ed.2d 682, rehearing denied 121 S.Ct. 1176, 531 U.S. 1186, 148 L.Ed.2d 1034. Criminal Law ⚷ 706(2)

21. —— Jurors, misconduct generally

Denial of motion for new trial, based on presence of someone who was not member of jury in jury room, was not abuse of discretion in prosecution for domestic violence, violation of protection order, intimidation, and retaliation, where, by immediately inquiring into whether there had been any misconduct on part of jurors, and by determining that incident had been mistake and that unknown individual had not talked to any of jurors, trial court satisfied its duty to inquire into matter. State v. Solomon (Ohio App. 3 Dist., Marion, 06-01-2004) No. 9-03-58, 2004-Ohio-2795, 2004 WL 1191966, Unreported, appeal not allowed 105 Ohio St.3d 1466, 824 N.E.2d 93, 2005-Ohio-1024. Criminal Law ⚷ 868

District Court's finding that it could not conclude that the jury reached its verdict on the basis of evidence that it properly could consider, without regard to evidence having no bearing on the limited issues it was asked to decide, was sufficient ground to warrant new trial, in prosecution for filing false tax returns. U.S. v. Costin (C.A.6 (Ohio), 03-05-2003) No. 00-3287, No. 00-3288, No. 00-3289, 59 Fed.Appx. 726, 2003 WL 839236, Unreported. Criminal Law ⚷ 921

Capital murder defendant's allegation of guilt phase juror's out-of-court misconduct was insufficient to warrant or require replacement of allegedly offending juror with alternate; defendant's nephew testified that he overheard juror, from distance of 25 to 30 feet away at crowded public event, respond to question concerning trial by saying that "it shouldn't be much longer because I think he's guilty," juror at issue testified that he had done no more than confirm that he was a juror in defendant's trial and specifically denied that he had told anyone that he had made up his mind about the case, and ultimate issue for the court was one of credibility. State v. Gross (Ohio, 10-30-2002) 97 Ohio St.3d 121, 776 N.E.2d 1061, 2002-Ohio-5524, reconsideration denied 97 Ohio St.3d 1486, 780 N.E.2d 288, 2002-Ohio-6866, certiorari denied 123 S.Ct. 2079, 538 U.S. 1037, 155 L.Ed.2d 1068, rehearing denied 124 S.Ct. 20, 539 U.S. 976, 156 L.Ed.2d 685. Criminal Law ⚷ 855(8)

Trial court may not examine alternate jurors following receipt of a verdict in order to determine existence, extent, or effect of juror or alternate misconduct. State v. Gross (Ohio, 10-30-2002) 97 Ohio St.3d 121, 776 N.E.2d 1061, 2002-Ohio-5524, reconsideration denied 97 Ohio St.3d 1486, 780 N.E.2d 288, 2002-Ohio-6866, certiorari denied 123 S.Ct. 2079, 538 U.S. 1037, 155 L.Ed.2d 1068, rehearing denied 124 S.Ct. 20, 539 U.S. 976, 156 L.Ed.2d 685. Criminal Law ⚷ 874

There was no juror misconduct as to jury's recommendations of death sentences for multiple aggravated murders, though one juror told the judge, after the jury had reached its sentencing recommendations but before they were announced in open court, that other jurors were "mean" and "rude" and she wanted to go home, where juror was given the chance to declare in open court her assent to or dissent from the recommendations and, when individually polled, she answered that she agreed with the recommendations. State v. Hessler (Ohio, 09-27-2000) 90 Ohio St.3d 108, 734 N.E.2d 1237, 2000-Ohio-30, reconsideration denied 90 Ohio St.3d 1473, 738 N.E.2d 384, certiorari denied 121 S.Ct. 1662, 532 U.S. 998, 149 L.Ed.2d 643, stay granted 91 Ohio St.3d 1531, 747 N.E.2d 828. Sentencing And Punishment ⚷ 1779(1)

Brief encounter between three jurors and material witness in capital murder prosecution outside courtroom did not require mistrial or replacement of jurors involved, absent any showing of prejudice to defendant resulting from encounter; incident was momentary, witness' comment to jurors was his personal opinion as to appropriateness of the death penalty, not fact, only two jurors heard the remark, and each of the three jurors declared unequivocally that they would not be affected by the event. State v. Stallings (Ohio, 07-19-2000) 89 Ohio St.3d 280, 731 N.E.2d 159, 2000-Ohio-164, stay granted 89 Ohio St.3d 1483, 733 N.E.2d 1184, stay revoked 93 Ohio St.3d 1455, 756 N.E.2d 674, certiorari denied 122 S.Ct. 89, 534 U.S. 836, 151 L.Ed.2d 51, denial of post-conviction relief affirmed 2004-Ohio-4571, 2004 WL 1932869, appeal not allowed 104 Ohio St.3d 1460, 821 N.E.2d 577, 2005-Ohio-204. Criminal Law ⚷ 855(8); Jury ⚷ 149

Juror's decision, before jury deliberations in penalty phase of capital murder prosecution, to ask his psychologist friend for outside opinion of definition of paranoid schizophrenia constituted "juror misconduct." State v. Sheppard (Ohio, 12-30-1998) 84 Ohio St.3d 230, 703 N.E.2d 286, 1998-Ohio-323, reconsideration denied 84 Ohio St.3d 1489, 705 N.E.2d 368, stay granted 85 Ohio St.3d 1402, 706 N.E.2d 785, dismissal of post-conviction relief affirmed 1999 WL 162457, appeal not allowed 86 Ohio St.3d 1437, 713 N.E.2d 1049, certiorari denied 120 S.Ct. 1190, 528 U.S. 1168, 145 L.Ed.2d 1095, certiorari denied 119 S.Ct. 2376, 527 U.S. 1026, 144 L.Ed.2d 779, denial of post-conviction relief affirmed 2001 WL 331936, dismissed, appeal not allowed 92 Ohio St.3d 1445, 751 N.E.2d 483, denial of post-conviction relief affirmed 91 Ohio St.3d 329, 744 N.E.2d 770, 2001-Ohio-52. Criminal Law ⚷ 855(8)

In reviewing circumstances suggesting juror misconduct, court must employ two-tier analysis: (1) determine whether there was juror misconduct, and (2) if juror misconduct is found, determine whether it materially affected defendant's substantial rights. State v. Hopfer (Ohio App. 2 Dist., 07-12-1996) 112 Ohio App.3d 521, 679 N.E.2d 321, dismissed, appeal not allowed 77 Ohio St.3d 1488, 673 N.E.2d 146, reconsideration denied 77 Ohio St.3d 1550, 674 N.E.2d 1187. Criminal Law ⚷ 855(1)

One form of juror misconduct is "bias" or "prejudice," that is, refusal to consider evidence or forming of opinion of guilt or innocence before all evidence is presented. State v. Hopfer (Ohio App. 2 Dist., 07-12-1996) 112 Ohio App.3d 521, 679 N.E.2d 321, dismissed, appeal not allowed 77 Ohio St.3d 1488, 673 N.E.2d 146, reconsideration denied 77 Ohio St.3d 1550, 674 N.E.2d 1187. Criminal Law ⚷ 855(1)

In cases involving outside influences on jurors, trial courts have broad discretion in dealing with contact and determining whether to declare mistrial or replace affected juror. State v. Phillips (Ohio, 11-22-1995) 74 Ohio St.3d 72, 656 N.E.2d 643, 1995-Ohio-171, reconsideration denied 74 Ohio St.3d 1485, 657 N.E.2d 1378, stay granted 74 Ohio St.3d 1503, 659 N.E.2d 795, rehearing granted, opinion recalled 75 Ohio St.3d 1504, 665 N.E.2d 219, certiorari denied 116 S.Ct. 1835, 517 U.S. 1213, 134 L.Ed.2d 938, denial of post-conviction relief affirmed in part, reversed in part 1999 WL 58961, dismissed, appeal not allowed 86 Ohio St.3d 1402, 711 N.E.2d 231, denial of post-conviction relief affirmed 2002-Ohio-823, 2002 WL 274637, appeal not allowed 95 Ohio St.3d 1488, 769 N.E.2d 403,

2002-Ohio-2625. Criminal Law ⚷ 867; Jury ⚷ 149

Trial court could continue capital murder trial after five jurors reported that member of a grand jury panel had approached them during break and had apparently told them she hoped defendant "gets it," or "gets whatever he deserves" in heated and agitated tone; jurors had shown that they were aware of impropriety of comments by leaving area immediately and reporting to bailiff, and jurors had stated they were not affected by remarks. State v. Phillips (Ohio, 11-22-1995) 74 Ohio St.3d 72, 656 N.E.2d 643, 1995-Ohio-171, reconsideration denied 74 Ohio St.3d 1485, 657 N.E.2d 1378, stay granted 74 Ohio St.3d 1503, 659 N.E.2d 795, rehearing granted, opinion recalled 75 Ohio St.3d 1504, 665 N.E.2d 219, certiorari denied 116 S.Ct. 1835, 517 U.S. 1213, 134 L.Ed.2d 938, denial of post-conviction relief affirmed in part, reversed in part 1999 WL 58961, dismissed, appeal not allowed 86 Ohio St.3d 1402, 711 N.E.2d 231, denial of post-conviction relief affirmed 2002-Ohio-823, 2002 WL 274637, appeal not allowed 95 Ohio St.3d 1488, 769 N.E.2d 403, 2002-Ohio-2625. Criminal Law ⚷ 867

When trial court learns of an improper outside communication with juror, it must hold hearing to determine whether communication biased juror. State v. Phillips (Ohio, 11-22-1995) 74 Ohio St.3d 72, 656 N.E.2d 643, 1995-Ohio-171, reconsideration denied 74 Ohio St.3d 1485, 657 N.E.2d 1378, stay granted 74 Ohio St.3d 1503, 659 N.E.2d 795, rehearing granted, opinion recalled 75 Ohio St.3d 1504, 665 N.E.2d 219, certiorari denied 116 S.Ct. 1835, 517 U.S. 1213, 134 L.Ed.2d 938, denial of post-conviction relief affirmed in part, reversed in part 1999 WL 58961, dismissed, appeal not allowed 86 Ohio St.3d 1402, 711 N.E.2d 231, denial of post-conviction relief affirmed 2002-Ohio-823, 2002 WL 274637, appeal not allowed 95 Ohio St.3d 1488, 769 N.E.2d 403, 2002-Ohio-2625. Criminal Law ⚷ 868

Juror's statement, "we should hang him now," which was made between guilt and penalty phases entitled defendant to mistrial as to both guilt and penalty phases of capital murder prosecution; statement evidenced partial juror predisposed to guilty verdict and death penalty. State v. Rudge (Trumbull 1993) 89 Ohio App.3d 429, 624 N.E.2d 1069, dismissed, jurisdictional motion overruled 67 Ohio St.3d 1502, 622 N.E.2d 651. Criminal Law ⚷ 855(1)

A defendant does not make a prima facie case of jury misconduct which would prejudice his rights and entitle him to a new trial where (1) the only evidence of jury misconduct is an uncorroborated allegation by a defense witness who later marries the defendant and who had testified that a juror approached her and indicated that the jurors had made up their minds on the case before deliberation had begun; or (2) a juror expresses sympathy to a defense witness. State v. Jones (Portage 1992) 81 Ohio App.3d 348, 611 N.E.2d 329, dismissed, jurisdictional motion overruled 65 Ohio St.3d 1441, 600 N.E.2d 684.

A defendant who claims that she was denied a fair trial because of misconduct of witnesses, a juror, and a spectator, fails to show any prejudice resulting from the misconduct; thus, a trial court does not err in denying her motion for a new trial. State v. Brownlow (Allen 1991) 75 Ohio App.3d 88, 598 N.E.2d 888.

Substantial evidence exists to support a trial court's finding that no juror misconduct was committed for purposes of a defendant's motion for a new trial, despite a defendant's claim that a juror had a conversation with other members of the jury during a recess where he stated that he had formed an opinion as to the guilt or innocence of the defendant, where during a trial court's hearing on the matter the juror testifies that (1) he did not remember stating that he had his mind made up, (2) he listened to the trial court's instructions as to the law, and (3) his mind was still open at the end of the case. State v. Taylor (Pike 1991) 73 Ohio App.3d 827, 598 N.E.2d 818, dismissed, jurisdictional motion overruled 62 Ohio St.3d 1453, 579 N.E.2d 1392.

Two jurors do not commit juror misconduct when they speak to a defense witness during a recess concerning the witness' current and former employment since the conversations did not involve matters related to the defendant's trial and there is nothing indicating that the jurors' verdicts were influenced by their brief conversations with the defense witness. State v. Taylor (Pike 1991) 73 Ohio App.3d 827, 598 N.E.2d 818, dismissed, jurisdictional motion overruled 62 Ohio St.3d 1453, 579 N.E.2d 1392.

A jury is not guilty of misconduct in an aggravated murder trial where they play cards during a suspension of deliberations while waiting for written instructions; the jurors did not play cards during deliberations and waiting for written instructions indicates conscientiousness, not carelessness. State v. Waddy (Ohio 1992) 63 Ohio St.3d 424, 588 N.E.2d 819, rehearing denied 63 Ohio St.3d 1470, 590 N.E.2d 1269, stay granted 64 Ohio St.3d 1424, 594 N.E.2d 625, certiorari denied 113 S.Ct. 338, 506 U.S. 921, 121 L.Ed.2d 255, rehearing granted, opinion recalled 71 Ohio St.3d 1418, 642 N.E.2d 384, dismissal of habeas corpus affirmed, dismissed, appeal not allowed 80 Ohio St.3d 1423, 685 N.E.2d 237, stay denied 80 Ohio St.3d 1479, 687 N.E.2d 474, certiorari denied 118 S.Ct. 1198, 140 L.Ed.2d 327.

A brief hallway conversation between a spectator and a juror, standing by itself, does not raise a presumption of misconduct sufficient to require a new trial, and where a trial court concludes that there was no misconduct after a recorded interview with the spectator, a reviewing court will not disturb the determination of the trial court absent a demonstration of prejudice to the defendants even though no interview of the juror took place. State v. Loshin (Hamilton 1986) 34 Ohio App.3d 62, 517 N.E.2d 229.

Permitting a government witness to serve as a custodian for the jury does not per se constitute reversible error. State v. Cooper (Ohio 1977) 52 Ohio St.2d 163, 370 N.E.2d 725, 6 O.O.3d 377, vacated 98 S.Ct. 3137, 438 U.S. 911, 57 L.Ed.2d 1157. Criminal Law ⚷ 1174(1)

Affidavits or testimony of jurors may be received, upon motion for new trial, to prove unlawful communications made to members of jury by court officers or others, outside the jury room but during period of jury's deliberation. Emmert v. State (Ohio 1933) 127 Ohio St. 235, 187 N.E. 862, 90 A.L.R. 242, 39 Ohio Law Rep. 649. Criminal Law ⚷ 957(6)

Where a juror is excused before the taking of evidence for an alleged statement of opinion that the defendant "looks guilty," the defendant is entitled to a hearing to determine the effect of the remark on other jurors; it is for the state court to determine whether an evidentiary hearing conducted two years after the conviction will suffice to show that the jury was impartial, thereby rendering retrial unnecessary. Hook v. Berkemer (S.D.Ohio 1984) 606 F.Supp. 73, vacated 772 F.2d 907.

22. Prosecutorial misconduct—In general

In a prosecution for drug trafficking, where a defendant alleges an individual posing as a Bureau of Criminal Identification and Investigation (BCI) employee enlisted her help in convicting suspected drug dealers through the sale of "fake" LSD, and the BCI identification card used to obtain the defendant's cooperation is introduced into evidence, a prosecutor's failure to inform the defense a handwriting analysis proves the defendant did not forge the fake BCI identification card constitutes withholding of exculpatory evidence and a trial court's denial of a motion for a new trial will be reversed. State v Swartz, Nos. 479+, 1993 WL 97727 (4th Dist Ct App, Meigs, 4–5–93).

Cumulative effect of prosecutorial misconduct, in voicing prosecutor's personal opinion as to guilt of defendant charged with gross sexual imposition, of improper admission of expert testimony vouching for credibility of child victim, and of inadequacy of curative instruction given with respect to expert testimony improperly impugning credibility of criminal defendants in general, was to deprive defendant of fair trial. State v. Coffman (Ohio App. 3 Dist., 11-06-1998) 130 Ohio App.3d 467, 720 N.E.2d 545. Criminal Law ⚷ 1186.1

Prosecutor engaged in misconduct by informing jury that defendant charged with receiving stolen property was suspected of running a "chop shop"; prosecutor improperly drew inference on matters not supported by record, as there was no evidence that other automobile parts found in home, not associated with stolen vehicle, were themselves stolen. State v. Braxton (Ohio App. 8 Dist., 03-21-1995) 102 Ohio App.3d 28, 656 N.E.2d 970, dismissed, appeal not allowed 73 Ohio St.3d 1425, 652 N.E.2d 798. Criminal Law ⚷ 720(7.1)

New trial is required if prosecutor has misstated facts, put words into witnesses' mouths, spoke as if from personal knowledge, assumed prejudicial facts not in evidence, bullied witnesses, and conducted himself in thoroughly indecorous and improper manner. State v. Smidi (Wood 1993) 88 Ohio App.3d 177, 623 N.E.2d 655. Criminal Law ⚷ 700(1); Criminal Law ⚷ 706(3); Criminal Law ⚷ 719(1); Criminal Law ⚷ 719(3)

The prosecutor's primary interest in a criminal prosecution is that justice shall be done; thus, while he may strike hard blows, he is not at liberty to strike foul ones. Lorraine v. Coyle (C.A.6 (Ohio), 05-23-2002) 291 F.3d 416, opinion corrected on denial of rehearing 307 F.3d 459, certiorari denied 123 S.Ct. 1621, 538 U.S. 947, 155 L.Ed.2d 489, rehearing denied 123 S.Ct. 2243, 538 U.S. 1069, 155 L.Ed.2d 1128. Criminal Law ⚷ 700(1)

Prosecutor improperly drew attention to defense counsel when he implied that their job required them to raise doubts about defendant's guilt even where none existed. Jamison v. Collins (S.D.Ohio, 05-10-2000) 100 F.Supp.2d 647, affirmed 291 F.3d 380, amended on denial of rehearing. Criminal Law ⚷ 723(1)

23. —— Test, prosecutorial misconduct

The test for determining whether prosecutorial failure to reveal evidence favorable to the accused constitutes reversible error is whether there is a reasonable probability that, had the evidence been disclosed to the defense, the result of the proceeding would have been different; therefore, in a prosecution of an on-site supervisor of a hazardous waste facility for illegally disposing of hazardous waste and other related charges, a trial court does not abuse its discretion in denying the supervisor's motion for a new trial on the ground that the state did not reveal until after the supervisor had rested that the test results on a certain water sample were not as accurate as they originally had been presented, where the trial court does not need to rely solely on the results of the sample at issue to find the supervisor guilty of the offenses with which he was charged since other tests revealed the presence of other chemicals, and the state presents evidence regarding the mixture rule so that the results of the trial would not have been different had the information been presented by the state prior to, rather than after, the supervisor's decision to rest his case. State v. Stirnkorb (Clermont 1990) 63 Ohio App.3d 778, 580 N.E.2d 69, dismissed, jurisdictional motion overruled 57 Ohio St.3d 718, 568 N.E.2d 690.

24. —— Threats, coercion or intimidation, prosecutorial misconduct

Prosecutor's statement to capital murder defendant's accomplice, indicating that accomplice's plea bargain could be set aside if he failed to cooperate as provided for therein, did not amount to improper threats, coercion or intimidation causing accomplice to refuse to testify on defendant's behalf, where accomplice refused to talk to defendant's counsel and indicated that he would invoke the Fifth Amendment if called to testify, and prosecutor's statement merely reiterated terms of accomplice's plea agreement. State v. Jackson (Ohio, 08-15-2001) 92 Ohio St.3d 436, 751 N.E.2d 946, 2001-Ohio-1266, reconsideration denied 93 Ohio St.3d 1453, 756 N.E.2d 116, motion to reopen denied 94 Ohio St.3d 1426, 761 N.E.2d 44, denial of post-conviction relief affirmed 2002-Ohio-3330, 2002 WL 1379001. Criminal Law ⚷ 700(10)

25. —— Comments, prosecutorial misconduct

Prosecutor's references to defendant, during trial phase of capital murder case, as a "mean-spirited derelict" and an "unemployed killer" represented fair comment. State v. Nields (Ohio, 08-29-2001) 93 Ohio St.3d 6, 752 N.E.2d 859, 2001-Ohio-1291, reconsideration denied 93 Ohio St.3d 1452, 756 N.E.2d 116. Criminal Law ⚷ 720(9)

A prosecutor's response during voir dire to a question posed by a prospective juror regarding a co-defendant's involvement in the case is not improper and therefore, does not amount to reversible error where the prosecutor's response is merely a remark about what the evidence at trial will show. State v. Sneed (Ohio 1992) 63 Ohio St.3d 3, 584 N.E.2d 1160, rehearing denied 63 Ohio St.3d 1433, 588 N.E.2d 132, stay granted 63 Ohio St.3d 1444, 589 N.E.2d 388, rehearing granted, opinion recalled 66 Ohio St.3d 1449, 609 N.E.2d 1270, certiorari denied 113 S.Ct. 1577, 507 U.S. 983, 123 L.Ed.2d 145, stay granted 66 Ohio St.3d 1504, 613 N.E.2d 1043.

A prosecutor may not make statements designed to arouse the passions or prejudice of the jury. Lorraine v. Coyle (C.A.6 (Ohio), 05-23-2002) 291 F.3d 416, opinion corrected on denial of rehearing 307 F.3d 459, certiorari denied 123 S.Ct. 1621, 538 U.S. 947, 155 L.Ed.2d 489, rehearing denied 123 S.Ct. 2243, 538 U.S. 1069, 155 L.Ed.2d 1128. Criminal Law ⚷ 723(1)

Prosecutor's use of term "predator" to describe murder defendant did not deprive defendant of fair trial. Byrd v. Collins (C.A.6 (Ohio), 04-06-2000) 209 F.3d 486, rehearing en banc denied 227 F.3d 756, certiorari denied 121 S.Ct. 786, 531 U.S. 1082, 148 L.Ed.2d 682, rehearing denied 121 S.Ct. 1176, 531 U.S. 1186, 148 L.Ed.2d 1034. Criminal Law ⚷ 724(1)

Prosecutor's overzealous remarks in capital case about the murder victim, the victim's suffering prior to death, and the victim's right to a fair trial were inappropriate. Jamison v. Collins (S.D.Ohio, 05-10-2000) 100 F.Supp.2d 647, affirmed 291 F.3d 380, amended on denial of rehearing. Criminal Law ⚷ 723(1)

Under Ohio law, neither the trial court nor the prosecutor may comment on the statutory mitigating factors that a capital defendant does not raise during the penalty phase of trial. Jamison v. Collins (S.D.Ohio, 05-10-2000) 100 F.Supp.2d 647, affirmed 291 F.3d 380, amended on denial of rehearing. Sentencing And Punishment ⚷ 1780(2); Sentencing And Punishment ⚷ 1781

When a prosecutor comments on a defendant's failure to testify in his own defense at his trial, and the key issue is the defendant's credibility, the prosecutor's comments are not harmless beyond a reasonable doubt and the admission of the statements requires a reversal. State v Perry, No. 91–CA–97 (2d Dist Ct App, Greene, 3–15–93).

26. —— Evidence, prosecutorial misconduct

Submission, as state's exhibit, of paper which consisted of photocopy of two separate documents was not false or misleading, and did not rise to level of prosecutorial misconduct, by allegedly creating false impression that documents were related, given clarifying testimony provided by custodian of documents in question. State v. Brumback (Ohio App. 9 Dist., 01-31-1996) 109 Ohio App.3d 65, 671 N.E.2d 1064. Criminal Law ⚷ 706(2)

Any error arising from prosecutor's introduction, in capital murder case, of videotape of television interview with victim and his family did not rise to level of due process violation, given key witness' testimony that defendant confessed to murder while watching interview in jail; any prejudice resulting from showing of videotape stemmed not from tape itself, but from admissible testimony regarding confession and defendant's callous remarks about victim. Byrd v. Collins (C.A.6 (Ohio), 04-06-2000) 209 F.3d 486, rehearing en banc denied 227 F.3d 756, certiorari denied 121 S.Ct. 786, 531 U.S. 1082, 148 L.Ed.2d 682, rehearing denied 121 S.Ct. 1176, 531 U.S. 1186, 148 L.Ed.2d 1034. Constitutional Law ⚷ 266(1); Criminal Law ⚷ 438(8)

27. —— Testimony, prosecutorial misconduct

State did not commit prosecutorial misconduct, much less promote plain error, by asking police officers, as witnesses to shooting of fellow police officer, questions that led to their emotional display of crying on the witness stand, where State did nothing to prompt or elicit emotional displays, and reactions by witnesses was expected in light of their close professional relationship with permanently injured officer. State v. Twitty (Ohio App. 2 Dist., Montgomery, 10-18-2002) No. 18749, 2002-Ohio-5595, 2002 WL 31341561, Unreported, appeal not allowed 98 Ohio St.3d 1475, 784 N.E.2d 708, 2003-Ohio-904, appeal not allowed 98 Ohio St.3d 1478, 784 N.E.2d 711, 2003-Ohio-974. Criminal Law ⚷ 1037.1(2)

Prosecutor's questions to state's firearms expert in capital murder prosecution, asking whether expert's ballistics work could be double-checked by other experts should the need arise, were permissible to show that expert's opinion was unchallenged, and did not amount to improper bolstering of expert's opinion. State v. Jackson (Ohio, 08-15-2001) 92 Ohio St.3d 436, 751 N.E.2d 946, 2001-Ohio-1266, reconsideration denied 93 Ohio St.3d 1453, 756 N.E.2d 116, motion to reopen denied 94 Ohio St.3d 1426, 761 N.E.2d 44, denial of post-conviction relief affirmed 2002-Ohio-3330, 2002 WL 1379001. Criminal Law ⚷ 720(5)

State's direct examination of capital murder defendant's accomplice, and of police detective, eliciting testimony that accomplice's plea agreement required him to provide truthful testimony, was not improper prosecutorial vouching for credibility of accomplice; rather, prosecutor was attempting to establish existence of plea agreement and fact that, as part of such agreement, accomplice had agreed to tell the truth. State v. Jackson (Ohio, 08-15-2001) 92 Ohio St.3d 436, 751 N.E.2d 946, 2001-Ohio-1266, reconsideration denied 93 Ohio St.3d 1453, 756 N.E.2d 116, motion to reopen denied 94 Ohio St.3d 1426, 761 N.E.2d 44, denial of post-conviction relief affirmed 2002-Ohio-3330, 2002 WL 1379001. Criminal Law ⚷ 720(5)

In a trial for murder and abuse of a corpse, a trial court does not err when it refuses to grant the defendant's request for a mistrial after the prosecutor elicits from a witness testimony that the defendant had previously been in jail where (1) the jury heard only that the defendant had been in jail, (2) the trial court immediately instructed the jury to disregard that information, (3) there is no indication that the jury did not so disregard it, and (4) the prosecutor was instructed not to ask the witness questions which, if answered truthfully, would elicit a response revealing that the defendant had been in the penitentiary. State v. Blair (Clark 1990) 70 Ohio App.3d 774, 592 N.E.2d 854, motion for delayed appeal denied 75 Ohio St.3d 1476, 663 N.E.2d 1303.

A defendant who is prosecuted for allegedly engaging in sexual intercourse with a child when she was sixteen years old is not entitled to a mistrial based on a prosecutor's repeated attempts to interject inadmissible testimony inferring that the defendant engaged in improper activity with the child when she was only thirteen years old where the references to the prior incident are not the result of a deliberate attempt by the state to prejudice the defendant and any possible prejudice thereby would not warrant the granting of a mistrial. State v. Lukens (Franklin 1990) 66 Ohio App.3d 794, 586 N.E.2d 1099, motion to certify overruled 55 Ohio St.3d 713, 563 N.E.2d 722.

The actions of a prosecuting attorney constitute prosecutorial misconduct where (1) he fails to disclose what he knows to be the truth about incorrect and misleading testimony given by his witness, and (2) he relies on the mistaken impression given by such testimony to draw a favorable inference in his opening and closing statements to the jury; the result of such prosecutorial misconduct is an unfair trial violative of US Const Am 6 where there is a reasonable possibility that the misleading and incorrect testimony might have affected the jury's judgment. State v. Staten (Miami 1984) 14 Ohio App.3d 78, 470 N.E.2d 249, 14 O.B.R. 91. Criminal Law ⚷ 700(3)

Defendant must show that the statement in question was indisputably false, rather than merely misleading, to establish a claim of prosecutorial misconduct or denial of due process based on knowing use of false or perjured testimony. Byrd v. Collins (C.A.6 (Ohio), 04-06-2000) 209 F.3d 486, rehearing en banc denied 227 F.3d 756, certiorari denied 121 S.Ct. 786, 531 U.S. 1082, 148 L.Ed.2d 682, rehearing denied 121 S.Ct. 1176, 531 U.S. 1186, 148 L.Ed.2d 1034. Constitutional Law ⚷ 268(9); Criminal Law ⚷ 706(2)

Witness' testimony that he had no pending charges against him at time of defendant's trial was not indisputably false, as required to support claim of prosecutorial misconduct or denial of due process based on state's alleged knowing use of false or perjured testimony, given that witness was not facing any criminal charges when he testified and that the record suggested that he, and the prosecutor, interpreted question raising issue as not encompassing parole revocation proceedings which witness faced at completion of workhouse sentence he was then serving. Byrd v. Collins (C.A.6 (Ohio), 04-06-2000) 209 F.3d 486, rehearing en banc denied 227 F.3d 756, certiorari denied 121 S.Ct. 786, 531 U.S. 1082, 148 L.Ed.2d 682, rehearing denied 121 S.Ct. 1176, 531 U.S. 1186, 148 L.Ed.2d 1034. Constitutional Law ⚷ 268(9); Criminal Law ⚷ 706(2)

Given extensive impeachment information elicited during defendant's cross-examination, witness' allegedly false testimony that he had no pending charges against him at time of defendant's trial was not "material," as required to support claim of prosecutorial misconduct or denial of due process based on state's alleged knowing use of witness' false or perjured testimony, even though witness faced parole revocation proceedings following completion of workhouse sentence he was then serving. Byrd v. Collins (C.A.6 (Ohio), 04-06-2000) 209 F.3d 486, rehearing en banc denied 227 F.3d 756, certiorari denied 121 S.Ct. 786, 531 U.S. 1082, 148 L.Ed.2d 682, rehearing denied 121 S.Ct. 1176, 531 U.S. 1186, 148 L.Ed.2d 1034. Constitutional Law ⚷ 268(9); Criminal Law ⚷ 706(2)

Denial of a motion for mistrial is reversible error where the prosecution, in a rape case, asks the defendant step-father if he performed a charged act in front of "other children"; the sustaining of an objection to the question is not sufficient to prevent possible prejudice. State v Harris, No. CA84–10–073 (12th Dist Ct App, Clermont, 6–17–85).

28. —— Opening or closing arguments, prosecutorial misconduct

Any error in prosecutor's crying during opening statement, in prosecution for kidnapping and rape, did not rise to level of prejudicial error necessary to require finding that defendant was deprived of fair trial, where jury clearly was not swayed or influenced by prosecutor's action. State v. Flannery (Ohio App. 5 Dist., Richland, 04-01-2005) No. 03-CA-24, 2005-Ohio-1614, 2005 WL 750077, Unreported, appeal not allowed 106 Ohio St.3d 1486, 832 N.E.2d 738, 2005-Ohio-3978. Criminal Law ⚷ 1171.2

Prosecutor's comments during closing arguments of aggravated murder prosecution, in which prosecutor told the jury that defendant had left the victim to die, was not improper; comment was fair statement of evidence presented. State v. Tenace (Ohio App. 6 Dist., Lucas, 06-30-2003) No. L-00-1002, 2003-Ohio-3458, 2003 WL 21500249, Unreported, dismissal of post-conviction relief affirmed 2006-Ohio-1226, 2006 WL 664327, affirmed in part, reversed in part 109 Ohio St.3d 255, 847 N.E.2d 386, 2006-Ohio-2417, denial of post-conviction relief affirmed 109 Ohio St.3d 451, 849 N.E.2d 1, 2006-Ohio-2987. Criminal Law ⚷ 720(2)

Even if prosecutor's statements during opening and closing statements of aggravated murder prosecution, in which prosecutor stated that victim had massive damage, and that only reason massive damage was inflicted upon victim was to cause victim's death, constituted an exaggeration of evidence, such statements did not rise to level of plain error; evidence indicated that defendant intended to kill victim and amount of damage defendant inflicted upon victim would not have been the only evidence needed to prove defendant's intent to kill. State v. Tenace (Ohio App. 6 Dist., Lucas, 06-30-2003) No. L-00-1002, 2003-Ohio-3458, 2003 WL 21500249, Unreported, dismissal of post-conviction relief affirmed 2006-Ohio-1226, 2006 WL 664327, affirmed in part, reversed in part 109 Ohio St.3d 255, 847 N.E.2d 386, 2006-Ohio-2417, denial of post-conviction relief affirmed 109 Ohio St.3d 451, 849 N.E.2d 1, 2006-Ohio-2987. Criminal Law ⚿ 1037.1(2)

Prosecutor's statements during opening and closing statements of aggravated murder prosecution, in which prosecutor stated that victim had massive damage, and that only reason massive damage was inflicted upon victim was to cause victim's death, was not improper, even though coroner never testified that amount of injury suffered by victim was inflicted for purpose of causing death; fact that it may not have taken much force to cause victim's death did not minimize consequence of victim's various injuries. State v. Tenace (Ohio App. 6 Dist., Lucas, 06-30-2003) No. L-00-1002, 2003-Ohio-3458, 2003 WL 21500249, Unreported, dismissal of post-conviction relief affirmed 2006-Ohio-1226, 2006 WL 664327, affirmed in part, reversed in part 109 Ohio St.3d 255, 847 N.E.2d 386, 2006-Ohio-2417, denial of post-conviction relief affirmed 109 Ohio St.3d 451, 849 N.E.2d 1, 2006-Ohio-2987. Criminal Law ⚿ 720(9)

Prosecuting attorney did not vouch for the credibility of witnesses in drug prosecution; prosecutor used the facts that were introduced into evidence to argue that certain witnesses were believable. State v. Windham (Ohio App. 6 Dist., Erie, 01-24-2003) No. E-01-015, 2003-Ohio-305, 2003 WL 164796, Unreported. Criminal Law ⚿ 720(5)

A prosecutor's remarks during closing argument in a trial of a pastor for insurance fraud and deliberate fires at his church, likening the pastor and his parishioners to the Waco and Jonestown fanatics are overly dramatic comments but are still within the latitude allowed. State v. Patton (Ohio App. 9 Dist., Summit, 05-10-1995) No. 16475, No. 16634, 1995 WL 283767, Unreported, dismissed, appeal not allowed 74 Ohio St.3d 1417, 655 N.E.2d 737, reconsideration denied 74 Ohio St.3d 1464, 656 N.E.2d 1300.

During the guilt determination phase of a murder trial where (1) the strongest evidence linking the defendant to the convenience store shooting is a set of his palm prints on a meat case which was routinely cleaned daily, (2) the prosecutor asserts during closing argument that there is "not one shred of evidence" that the defendant was in the store within one month before the shooting, and (3) where it later appears through the testimony of a witness during the mitigation phase that the defendant was in the store twice the day before the shooting, testimony corroborated by the store's videotape, this potentially exculpatory testimony constitutes newly discovered evidence warranting a new trial; moreover, assuming the prosecutor knowingly failed to disclose the nature of this testimony to defense counsel, the failure to disclose constitutes a denial of due process, and even assuming a disclosure before trial, the prosecutor's closing argument constitutes serious misconduct warranting a new trial. State v. Hairston (Ohio App. 10 Dist., Franklin, 12-30-1994) No. 94APA02-205, 1994 WL 723316, Unreported.

In a prosecution for soliciting drug sales, where police officers set up a meet and sale with a defendant, a prosecutor's arguments that the defendant was selling drugs rather than buying drugs, that the defendant did not care about her children, and that an invitation to the jury to let defendant sell drugs in their neighborhood if they choose to find defendant not guilty are clearly inflammatory and flagrant because the comments concern matters clearly outside the facts and law of the case and such comments are of such an egregious nature as to warrant a reversal of defendant's conviction and remand for a new trial. City of Canton v Lerario, No. CA-9147, 1993 WL 364888 (5th Dist Ct App, Stark, 8-16-93).

Prosecutor's statements that murder victim was "actually speaking to you through the evidence in this case" and that victim was "crying out to you" were within the wide latitude allowed by a prosecutor in closing argument. State v. Smith (Ohio, 12-13-2002) 97 Ohio St.3d 367, 780 N.E.2d 221, 2002-Ohio-6659, reconsideration denied 97 Ohio St.3d 1500, 780 N.E.2d 1023, 2002-Ohio-7367, stay granted 98 Ohio St.3d 1417, 782 N.E.2d 73, 2003-Ohio-189, certiorari denied 123 S.Ct. 2255, 539 U.S. 907, 156 L.Ed.2d 118. Criminal Law ⚿ 723(1)

Prosecutor's comment during closing argument that murder defendant "gets happiness out of molesting, raping a six-month old baby" was a permissible comment addressing sexual motivation specification. State v. Smith (Ohio, 12-13-2002) 97 Ohio St.3d 367, 780 N.E.2d 221, 2002-Ohio-6659, reconsideration denied 97 Ohio St.3d 1500, 780 N.E.2d 1023, 2002-Ohio-7367, stay granted 98 Ohio St.3d 1417, 782 N.E.2d 73, 2003-Ohio-189, certiorari denied 123 S.Ct. 2255, 539 U.S. 907, 156 L.Ed.2d 118. Criminal Law ⚿ 723(2)

Prosecutor did not commit misconduct during closing argument by characterizing murder as a ten- to thirty-minute beating; expert testified that the attack lasted that long. State v. Smith (Ohio, 12-13-2002) 97 Ohio St.3d 367, 780 N.E.2d 221, 2002-Ohio-6659, reconsideration denied 97 Ohio St.3d 1500, 780 N.E.2d 1023, 2002-Ohio-7367, stay granted 98 Ohio St.3d 1417, 782 N.E.2d 73, 2003-Ohio-189, certiorari denied 123 S.Ct. 2255, 539 U.S. 907, 156 L.Ed.2d 118. Criminal Law ⚿ 723(2)

Prosecutor's references to murder defendant in opening statement as a "baby murderer" and a "baby molester" were not improper comments; evidence supported such characterization. State v. Smith (Ohio, 12-13-2002) 97 Ohio St.3d 367, 780 N.E.2d 221, 2002-Ohio-6659, reconsideration denied 97 Ohio St.3d 1500, 780 N.E.2d 1023,

2002-Ohio-7367, stay granted 98 Ohio St.3d 1417, 782 N.E.2d 73, 2003-Ohio-189, certiorari denied 123 S.Ct. 2255, 539 U.S. 907, 156 L.Ed.2d 118. Criminal Law ⚷ 724(2)

Prosecutor's comment during trial phase of capital murder case, that it was humorous to him that defense counsel argued that alcohol had nothing to do with the murder but then asserted that defendant was acting in a bizarre manner and under the influence of the demons of alcohol on night of murder, improperly denigrated defense counsel. State v. Nields (Ohio, 08-29-2001) 93 Ohio St.3d 6, 752 N.E.2d 859, 2001-Ohio-1291, reconsideration denied 93 Ohio St.3d 1452, 756 N.E.2d 116. Criminal Law ⚷ 723(1)

Prosecutor's improper comment during trial phase of capital murder case, that it was humorous that defense counsel argued that alcohol had nothing to do with the murder but then asserted that defendant was acting strange and was under the influence of the demons of alcohol on night of murder, was neither outcome determinative nor unduly prejudicial. State v. Nields (Ohio, 08-29-2001) 93 Ohio St.3d 6, 752 N.E.2d 859, 2001-Ohio-1291, reconsideration denied 93 Ohio St.3d 1452, 756 N.E.2d 116. Criminal Law ⚷ 723(1)

Prosecutorial misconduct in rape prosecution did not require reversal, where properly admitted testimony and forensic evidence made it clear beyond reasonable doubt that jury would have found defendant guilty even absent comments amounting to misconduct; misconduct consisted of prosecutor's reference, during rebuttal closing argument and in violation of in limine rulings, to witness's testimony that defendant said he should have killed the victim. State v. Roughton (Ohio App. 6 Dist., 02-12-1999) 132 Ohio App.3d 268, 724 N.E.2d 1193, appeal not allowed 86 Ohio St.3d 1406, 711 N.E.2d 234. Criminal Law ⚷ 1171.3

In burglary prosecution, in which there was evidence that defendant, in attempting to gain entry into home, stated that he wanted occupant in his "personal world" and would kill everyone in house to get to her, prosecutor did not commit misconduct in arguing that defendant was romantically obsessed with occupant and that his actions may have been those of an "egomaniac." State v. Sweeney (Ohio App. 2 Dist., 01-08-1999) 131 Ohio App.3d 765, 723 N.E.2d 655. Criminal Law ⚷ 720(8)

Prosecutor's improper remarks during closing argument in prosecution for gross sexual imposition, indicating prosecutor's personal opinion regarding defendant's guilt, were not invited by defense counsel's remarks allegedly impugning prosecutor; defense counsel's remarks were addressed to validity of state's investigation of defendant rather than to prosecutor's integrity, prosecutor did not object to defense counsel's remarks, and prosecutor's response was not proportional. State v. Coffman (Ohio App. 3 Dist., 11-06-1998) 130 Ohio App.3d 467, 720 N.E.2d 545. Criminal Law ⚷ 726

Prosecutor's repeated misconduct during domestic violence trial, including badgering witnesses, arguing with court in front of jury, and repeatedly referring to past instances of defendant's misconduct in direct contravention of court's ruling, was not harmless and required mistrial, though court sustained defendant's objections and gave several cautionary instructions to jury, where prosecutor was not strongly admonished to end his inappropriate conduct, and case hinged solely on credibility of eyewitnesses, who were all close friends of either defendant or victim. State v. Gardner (Ohio App. 5 Dist., 05-11-1998) 127 Ohio App.3d 538, 713 N.E.2d 473. Criminal Law ⚷ 700(1); Criminal Law ⚷ 1171.1(1)

Prosecutor's comment on defendant's prior drug trafficking convictions, while making closing argument in trial for aggravated drug trafficking with specification of prior felony drug abuse conviction, was improper, but did not require mistrial, where trial court immediately sustained defense counsel's objection to comment and instructed jury to disregard comment. State v. Henton (Ohio App. 11 Dist., 07-14-1997) 121 Ohio App.3d 501, 700 N.E.2d 371, dismissed, appeal not allowed 80 Ohio St.3d 1445, 686 N.E.2d 273. Criminal Law ⚷ 722.5; Criminal Law ⚷ 730(13)

Test for prosecutorial misconduct in closing argument is whether remarks were improper and, if so, whether they prejudicially affected defendant's substantial rights. State v. White (Ohio, 05-20-1998) 82 Ohio St.3d 16, 693 N.E.2d 772, 1998-Ohio-363, stay granted 82 Ohio St.3d 1445, 695 N.E.2d 267, stay revoked 85 Ohio St.3d 1453, 708 N.E.2d 1008, reconsideration denied 82 Ohio St.3d 1469, 696 N.E.2d 226, reconsideration denied 82 Ohio St.3d 1470, 696 N.E.2d 226, dismissal of post-conviction relief affirmed 1998 WL 515944, dismissed, appeal not allowed 84 Ohio St.3d 1445, 703 N.E.2d 326, reconsideration denied 84 Ohio St.3d 1489, 705 N.E.2d 368, certiorari denied 119 S.Ct. 623, 525 U.S. 1057, 142 L.Ed.2d 562, denial of habeas corpus affirmed in part, reversed in part 431 F.3d 517, rehearing denied, rehearing and rehearing en banc denied, petition for certiorari filed 2006 WL 2094473. Criminal Law ⚷ 709

Prosecutor did not commit misconduct in closing argument, in stating that stepson of defendant accused of receiving stolen property was "terrified" by defendant; remark was drawn from testimony of stepson, in which he stated that defendant was "terrorizing" him and his mother. State v. Braxton (Ohio App. 8 Dist., 03-21-1995) 102 Ohio App.3d 28, 656 N.E.2d 970, dismissed, appeal not allowed 73 Ohio St.3d 1425, 652 N.E.2d 798. Criminal Law ⚷ 720(7.1)

Prosecutor engaged in misconduct in closing argument, by rendering opinion that defendant charged with receiving stolen property was setting up and hiding behind "smoke screen"; remark improperly intimated that defense counsel had suborned perjury by manufacturing, conceiving and fashioning lies. State v. Braxton (Ohio App. 8 Dist., 03-21-1995) 102 Ohio App.3d 28, 656 N.E.2d

970, dismissed, appeal not allowed 73 Ohio St.3d 1425, 652 N.E.2d 798. Criminal Law ⚩ 723(1)

In making determination as to whether prosecutorial misconduct in closing argument is prejudicial, court is to consider (1) nature of remarks, (2) whether objection was made by counsel, (3) whether corrective instructions were given by court, and (4) strength of evidence against defendant. State v. Braxton (Ohio App. 8 Dist., 03-21-1995) 102 Ohio App.3d 28, 656 N.E.2d 970, dismissed, appeal not allowed 73 Ohio St.3d 1425, 652 N.E.2d 798. Criminal Law ⚩ 1171.1(2.1)

In determining whether prosecutorial misconduct in closing argument was prejudicial, appellate court should consider whether misconduct was an isolated incident in an otherwise properly tried case. State v. Braxton (Ohio App. 8 Dist., 03-21-1995) 102 Ohio App.3d 28, 656 N.E.2d 970, dismissed, appeal not allowed 73 Ohio St.3d 1425, 652 N.E.2d 798. Criminal Law ⚩ 1171.1(2.1)

Improper prosecutorial closing argument, that defendant accused of receiving stolen goods was operating "chop shop" and that he had hidden behind a "smoke screen" did not deprive defendant of fair trial; evidence left no doubt that defendant had knowingly received stolen automobile, and stepson who had given only exculpatory evidence had been thoroughly discredited on cross-examination. State v. Braxton (Ohio App. 8 Dist., 03-21-1995) 102 Ohio App.3d 28, 656 N.E.2d 970, dismissed, appeal not allowed 73 Ohio St.3d 1425, 652 N.E.2d 798. Criminal Law ⚩ 1171.1(3)

Mistrial was warranted by trial court's express finding that misconduct of prosecutor was close to, if not beyond, point of requiring mistrial, together with additional acts of misconduct not identified by trial court; prosecutor presented alleged facts to jury in guise of asking witnesses questions that were not supported by evidence, implied that he possessed additional evidence to rebut defendant's testimony and which attacked defendant's character, and made closing argument that played on jury's sympathies and personal interests. State v. Smidi (Wood 1993) 88 Ohio App.3d 177, 623 N.E.2d 655. Criminal Law ⚩ 706(3); Criminal Law ⚩ 719(3); Criminal Law ⚩ 723(1)

Prosecutor engaged in misconduct requiring new trial in closing argument that encouraged jury to convict defendant improperly either on basis of bad character and associations with drug dealers or to serve public demand by ridding community of one manifestation of problem posed by drug trafficking; prosecutor suggested that law was "putting a lot of unfair things on you" to jury, encouraging jury to ignore law by insinuating that law unfairly hindered search for truth in fact-finding process; trial judge, instead of making meaningful effort to cure prejudice by issuance of cautionary instruction, effectively endorsed errors by stating to jury that prosecutor "is not telling you anything you don't know." State v. Hudson (Hamilton 1993) 86 Ohio App.3d 113, 619 N.E.2d 1190. Criminal Law ⚩ 722.3; Criminal Law ⚩ 723(1); Criminal Law ⚩ 730(12); Criminal Law ⚩ 730(14); Criminal Law ⚩ 1171.1(6); Criminal Law ⚩ 1171.6

References made by prosecutor during closing argument of child sexual abuse case concerning "the last sexual conduct" between the parties did not require mistrial, despite defendant's contention that reference to "last" sexual conduct tended to suggest there had been multiple incidents of such conduct even though no such evidence had been introduced; trial court gave cautionary instruction which mandated that jury disregard the comments, and court pointed out to jury that there was no evidence of any prior sexual contact between defendant and victim; moreover, prosecutor, upon resuming closing argument after objection, admitted to jury that his reference to "last" sexual conduct had been a misstatement. State v. Nichols (Pike 1993) 85 Ohio App.3d 65, 619 N.E.2d 80. Criminal Law ⚩ 730(13)

In an aggravated drug trafficking prosecution, a prosecutor's statements in his rebuttal argument that urges the jurors to convict the defendant to aid in the war on drugs are not invited by the defense counsel's argument and are improper, and the trial court abuses its discretion in overruling the defendant's motion for mistrial based on such improper statements since the statements are so prejudicial that a cautionary instruction is insufficient to cure the error. State v. Draughn (Muskingum 1992) 76 Ohio App.3d 664, 602 N.E.2d 790.

In a prosecution for cruelty to animals, a prosecutor's misstatements made during his opening statement does not constitute plain error or deny the defendant a fair trial since the defendant did not object to any of the statements and the trial court properly instructed the jury that opening and closing statements are not evidence and should not be so regarded; likewise, the prosecutor's remarks during closing arguments that the defendant's defense witness is his girlfriend and that her videotape seems rehearsed, which is challenged by the defendant as improper personal opinion, does not constitute plain error. State v. Lapping (Trumbull 1991) 75 Ohio App.3d 354, 599 N.E.2d 416, dismissed, jurisdictional motion overruled 63 Ohio St.3d 1441, 589 N.E.2d 45.

In a prosecution for aggravated assault, a prosecutor's remarks during closing arguments that the defendant's defense is "baloney" and "garbage" and that the defendant is "trying every trick in the book," address the quality of the expert testimony presented by the defense and the weight of the evidence and, although imprudent, do not rise to the exceptional level necessary to constitute plain error so as to warrant reversal of the trial court's judgment. State v. Underwood (Washington 1991) 73 Ohio App.3d 834, 598 N.E.2d 822.

A trial court's jury instructions in a capital murder prosecution that closing arguments are simply the attorneys' opinions about what they think the evidence has already shown and their opinions as to how the jury should apply the law to the evidence obviates any prejudice which may have occurred as a result of a prosecutor's closing statements. State v. Parrish (Franklin 1991) 71 Ohio App.3d 659, 595 N.E.2d 354, dismissed, jurisdictional motion overruled 60 Ohio St.3d 718, 574 N.E.2d 1079.

A prosecutor's comments during closing argument in a child endangering and felonious assault case that the defendant was "probably" responsible for the bruises on a child victim's buttocks which were inflicted during a prior incident, and that if the child's burns had been left untreated for "maybe another four or five hours, his would be an aggravated murder case" did not deprive the defendant of his right to a fair trial since the result of the trial would not have been changed in the absence of the prosecutor's remarks. State v. Barton (Hamilton 1991) 71 Ohio App.3d 455, 594 N.E.2d 702, dismissed, jurisdictional motion overruled 61 Ohio St.3d 1427, 575 N.E.2d 215, rehearing denied 62 Ohio St.3d 1419, 577 N.E.2d 664, certiorari denied 112 S.Ct. 1209, 502 U.S. 1109, 117 L.Ed.2d 448, denial of habeas corpus affirmed 91 F.3d 143, certiorari denied 117 S.Ct. 529, 136 L.Ed.2d 415.

A prosecutor in a rape trial is guilty of prosecutorial misconduct where, during closing argument, the prosecutor improperly characterized opposing counsel as seeking to mislead the jury through trickery; there was no evidence to substantiate the prosecutor's accusations so that his conduct was well beyond the normal latitude allowed in closing arguments and other evidence presented at trial was not sufficient to find it clear beyond a reasonable doubt that, absent the prosecutor's comments, the jury would have found the defendant guilty. State v. Cantlebarry (Franklin 1990) 69 Ohio App.3d 216, 590 N.E.2d 342.

Generally, a prosecutor is entitled to a certain degree of latitude during closing argument; prosecutorial misconduct may result if the remarks were improper and if they prejudicially affected substantial rights of the defendant. State v. Cantlebarry (Franklin 1990) 69 Ohio App.3d 216, 590 N.E.2d 342.

A prosecutor's statement in an aggravated murder trial that the defense counsel's argument to the jury that another person might be the killer is "a standard defense" is improper since it suggests that such defenses are common and implies that they are usually bogus, thereby inviting the jury to substitute the prosecutor's experience for its own evaluation; however, it does not constitute reversible error since it did not rob the defendant of a fair trial where the prosecutor's statement was not repeated and the prosecutor's argument concentrated on the evidence. State v. Waddy (Ohio 1992) 63 Ohio St.3d 424, 588 N.E.2d 819, rehearing denied 63 Ohio St.3d 1470, 590 N.E.2d 1269, stay granted 64 Ohio St.3d 1424, 594 N.E.2d 625, certiorari denied 113 S.Ct. 338, 506 U.S. 921, 121 L.Ed.2d 255, rehearing granted, opinion recalled 71 Ohio St.3d 1418, 642 N.E.2d 384, dismissal of habeas corpus affirmed, dismissed, appeal not allowed 80 Ohio St.3d 1423, 685 N.E.2d 237, stay denied 80 Ohio St.3d 1479, 687 N.E.2d 474, certiorari denied 118 S.Ct. 1198, 140 L.Ed.2d 327.

Reversal is not the remedy for every trivial factual error in a prosecutor's argument; thus, where a prosecutor makes incorrect statements in an aggravated murder trial, such mistakes do not constitute reversible error where the errors are corrected by the trial court's instruction to the jurors to rely on their own memories, and the prosecutor's mistakes do not render the trial fundamentally unfair. State v. Waddy (Ohio 1992) 63 Ohio St.3d 424, 588 N.E.2d 819, rehearing denied 63 Ohio St.3d 1470, 590 N.E.2d 1269, stay granted 64 Ohio St.3d 1424, 594 N.E.2d 625, certiorari denied 113 S.Ct. 338, 506 U.S. 921, 121 L.Ed.2d 255, rehearing granted, opinion recalled 71 Ohio St.3d 1418, 642 N.E.2d 384, dismissal of habeas corpus affirmed, dismissed, appeal not allowed 80 Ohio St.3d 1423, 685 N.E.2d 237, stay denied 80 Ohio St.3d 1479, 687 N.E.2d 474, certiorari denied 118 S.Ct. 1198, 140 L.Ed.2d 327.

A death sentence need not be vacated because of a prosecutor's improper comments concerning the possibility of escape, commutation, and pardon; the trial judge's admonition to the jury is sufficient to correct any prejudice induced by the prosecutor's inappropriate response to the argument of the defense. State v. Evans (Ohio 1992) 63 Ohio St.3d 231, 586 N.E.2d 1042, rehearing denied 63 Ohio St.3d 1450, 589 N.E.2d 393, certiorari denied 113 S.Ct. 246, 506 U.S. 886, 121 L.Ed.2d 179. Criminal Law ⚷ 730(1)

A prosecutor's reference to "justice" during both the guilt and penalty phases of an aggravated murder trial does not deprive the defendant of a fair trial since there is nothing inherently erroneous in calling for justice; thus, the argument was proper. State v. Evans (Ohio 1992) 63 Ohio St.3d 231, 586 N.E.2d 1042, rehearing denied 63 Ohio St.3d 1450, 589 N.E.2d 393, certiorari denied 113 S.Ct. 246, 506 U.S. 886, 121 L.Ed.2d 179.

Although, in an aggravated murder case, a prosecutor's sentencing comments which focus on the victims' anguish and suffering prior to their being shot in the head by the defendant were erroneous since the prosecutor engaged in gross speculation and improperly injected nonstatutory aggravated circumstances, the prosecutor's comments do not rise to the level of plain error since the prosecutor could legitimately refer to the nature and circumstances of the offense, both to refute any suggestion that they were mitigating and to explain why the specified aggravating circumstance, a course of conduct to kill two or more persons, outweighed mitigating factors; the prosecutor's argument made no crucial difference and the defendant received a fair trial. State v. Combs (Ohio 1991) 62 Ohio St.3d 278, 581 N.E.2d 1071, rehearing denied 62 Ohio St.3d 1503, 583 N.E.2d 974, certiorari denied 112 S.Ct. 2950, 504 U.S. 977, 119 L.Ed.2d 573, stay granted 65 Ohio St.3d 1446, 600 N.E.2d 1077, stay granted 66 Ohio St.3d 1470, 611 N.E.2d 328, stay granted 66 Ohio St.3d 1475, 611 N.E.2d 837, denial of post-conviction relief affirmed 100 Ohio App.3d 90, 652 N.E.2d 205, dismissed, appeal not allowed 71 Ohio St.3d 1472, 645 N.E.2d 735, reconsideration denied 71 Ohio St.3d 1494, 646 N.E.2d 469.

A prosecutor's reference to the defendant as a "maggot" during closing argument is inflammatory and improper but is not grounds for reversal of a rape conviction. State v. Chandler (Cuyahoga

1984) 19 Ohio App.3d 109, 483 N.E.2d 192, 19 O.B.R. 197.

A prosecutor's unsubstantiated references in closing argument to defense evidence as "lies," "a smoke screen," and "a well conceived and well rehearsed lie," constitute prejudicial misconduct warranting reversal of conviction and remand for a new trial. State v. Smith (Ohio 1984) 14 Ohio St.3d 13, 470 N.E.2d 883, 14 O.B.R. 317.

Prosecutor's appeals to community sentiment in voir dire and closing argument, in state capital murder prosecution, even if erroneous, constituted only harmless error, and thus did not warrant federal habeas relief; most of remarks were permissible, and there was neither showing that remarks violated federal law, nor showing that state court's finding that remarks were harmless violated federal law. Lorraine v. Coyle (C.A.6 (Ohio), 05-23-2002) 291 F.3d 416, opinion corrected on denial of rehearing 307 F.3d 459, certiorari denied 123 S.Ct. 1621, 538 U.S. 947, 155 L.Ed.2d 489, rehearing denied 123 S.Ct. 2243, 538 U.S. 1069, 155 L.Ed.2d 1128. Habeas Corpus ⚷ 497

Prosecutor's comment during closing argument of penalty phase of state capital murder trial, which criticized petitioner's apology as being an unsworn statement, did not prejudice petitioner, and thus did not warrant federal habeas relief; rather, comment was a fair response to petitioner's statement to the jury, remark was isolated, and there was extensive mitigating evidence before the jury. Lorraine v. Coyle (C.A.6 (Ohio), 05-23-2002) 291 F.3d 416, opinion corrected on denial of rehearing 307 F.3d 459, certiorari denied 123 S.Ct. 1621, 538 U.S. 947, 155 L.Ed.2d 489, rehearing denied 123 S.Ct. 2243, 538 U.S. 1069, 155 L.Ed.2d 1128. Habeas Corpus ⚷ 508

Prosecutor's suggestion that defense counsel was trying to hide something about source of blood found on sweater alleged to have been worn by accomplice was suggestion of reasonable inference to be drawn from defense counsel's presentation of evidence and argument, and did not rise to level of due process violation. Byrd v. Collins (C.A.6 (Ohio), 04-06-2000) 209 F.3d 486, rehearing en banc denied 227 F.3d 756, certiorari denied 121 S.Ct. 786, 531 U.S. 1082, 148 L.Ed.2d 682, rehearing denied 121 S.Ct. 1176, 531 U.S. 1186, 148 L.Ed.2d 1034. Constitutional Law ⚷ 268(8); Criminal Law ⚷ 720(9)

Prosecutor's conduct in vouching for credibility of witness did not rise to level of due process violation, and thus did not warrant federal habeas relief; remarks did not mislead jury, which was told by prosecutor that his remarks were not evidence, trial court instructed jury immediately after arguments that arguments were not evidence, witness' testimony was reread at jury's request following initial deliberation, jury returned guilty verdict soon after again hearing witness' testimony, which was not complicated, and trial court instructed jury as to factors to consider in evaluating weight of witnesses' testimony. Byrd v. Collins (C.A.6 (Ohio), 04-06-2000) 209 F.3d 486, rehearing en banc denied 227 F.3d 756, certiorari denied 121 S.Ct. 786, 531 U.S. 1082, 148 L.Ed.2d 682, rehearing denied 121 S.Ct. 1176, 531 U.S. 1186, 148 L.Ed.2d 1034. Constitutional Law ⚷ 268(8); Criminal Law ⚷ 730(8); Habeas Corpus ⚷ 497

Statements in which prosecutor speculated as to whether defendant had previously seen store clerk who was killed during robbery due to store's close proximity to defendant's childhood home, as to whether witness had faulty recall as to color of one perpetrator's pants, and as to location of missing evidence were arguably reasonable inferences from the evidence presented at trial that prosecutor was allowed to draw. Byrd v. Collins (C.A.6 (Ohio), 04-06-2000) 209 F.3d 486, rehearing en banc denied 227 F.3d 756, certiorari denied 121 S.Ct. 786, 531 U.S. 1082, 148 L.Ed.2d 682, rehearing denied 121 S.Ct. 1176, 531 U.S. 1186, 148 L.Ed.2d 1034. Criminal Law ⚷ 720(9)

Prosecutor's remark in closing argument of Hobbs Act prosecution insinuating that defendants kept money they received from sale of honorary deputy sheriff commissions was not so pronounced and persistent that it permeated entire atmosphere of trial nor so gross as probably to prejudice defendants; challenged conduct of prosecutor was isolated statement, where money actually ended up was somewhat of a mystery and, while there was no direct evidence indicating that defendants personally benefitted from solicitation of contributions, there was evidence that, with one exception, none of contributions were reflected in official campaign records of sheriff. U.S. v. Farley (C.A.6 (Ohio) 1993) 2 F.3d 645, rehearing and suggestion for rehearing en banc denied, certiorari denied 114 S.Ct. 649, 510 U.S. 1030, 126 L.Ed.2d 607. Criminal Law ⚷ 1171.3

Prosecutor's comments during closing arguments, which implied that defense counsel was making unfounded argument because he was being paid to do so, was not plain error sufficient to deprive defendant of fair trial. State v. Wilks (Ohio App. 5 Dist., Richland, 07-24-2002) No. 01-CA-81, 2002-Ohio-3835, 2002 WL 1729923, Unreported, appeal not allowed 97 Ohio St.3d 1471, 779 N.E.2d 237, 2002-Ohio-6347. Criminal Law ⚷ 1037.1(2)

29. —— Plain errors, prosecutorial misconduct

State did not commit prosecutorial misconduct, much less promote plain error, by virtue of fact that the courtroom was packed with police officers at time defendant's shooting victim, a police officer, testified to events surrounding her shooting and resulting permanent paralysis; eyewitness testimony that defendant shot officer was such compelling direct evidence that such display of police solidarity added little to it, and record failed to demonstrate that State had anything to do with it. State v. Twitty (Ohio App. 2 Dist., Montgomery, 10-18-2002) No. 18749, 2002-Ohio-5595, 2002 WL 31341561, Unreported, appeal not allowed 98 Ohio St.3d 1475, 784 N.E.2d 708, 2003-Ohio-904, appeal not allowed 98 Ohio St.3d 1478, 784 N.E.2d 711, 2003-Ohio-974. Criminal Law ⚷ 1037.1(1)

Trial judge's apparent act of wiping tear from her eye at conclusion of testimony of shooting victim, a police officer, wherein officer described shooting and her resulting permanent paralysis, did not constitute prosecutorial misconduct, much less plain error, where judge's conduct did not implicate any misconduct on part of State, and, even if judge did wipe tear from her eye, she instructed jury to disregard anything the court might have said or done that they believed reflected the court's opinion about the case. State v. Twitty (Ohio App. 2 Dist., Montgomery, 10-18-2002) No. 18749, 2002-Ohio-5595, 2002 WL 31341561, Unreported, appeal not allowed 98 Ohio St.3d 1475, 784 N.E.2d 708, 2003-Ohio-904, appeal not allowed 98 Ohio St.3d 1478, 784 N.E.2d 711, 2003-Ohio-974. Criminal Law ⚷ 1037.1(1)

Prosecutor's so-called "theatrics" of displaying large photograph of slain police officer in uniform on easel in full view of jury, hanging officer's blood-soaked and tattered uniform on witness stand, and demonstrating disgust toward defendant by using latex gloves to handle defendant's clothing were not plain error in aggravated murder prosecution, particularly since these events were not reflected in transcript and defendant's motion to correct record was overruled. State v. White (Ohio, 05-20-1998) 82 Ohio St.3d 16, 693 N.E.2d 772, 1998-Ohio-363, stay granted 82 Ohio St.3d 1445, 695 N.E.2d 267, stay revoked 85 Ohio St.3d 1453, 708 N.E.2d 1008, reconsideration denied 82 Ohio St.3d 1469, 696 N.E.2d 226, reconsideration denied 82 Ohio St.3d 1470, 696 N.E.2d 226, dismissal of post-conviction relief affirmed 1998 WL 515944, dismissed, appeal not allowed 84 Ohio St.3d 1445, 703 N.E.2d 326, reconsideration denied 84 Ohio St.3d 1489, 705 N.E.2d 368, certiorari denied 119 S.Ct. 623, 525 U.S. 1057, 142 L.Ed.2d 562, denial of habeas corpus affirmed in part, reversed in part 431 F.3d 517, rehearing denied, rehearing and rehearing en banc denied, petition for certiorari filed 2006 WL 2094473. Criminal Law ⚷ 1037.1(2); Criminal Law ⚷ 1037.1(3)

Alleged instances of prosecutorial misconduct could be reviewed only for plain error where defense counsel made no objections at trial. State v. White (Ohio, 05-20-1998) 82 Ohio St.3d 16, 693 N.E.2d 772, 1998-Ohio-363, stay granted 82 Ohio St.3d 1445, 695 N.E.2d 267, stay revoked 85 Ohio St.3d 1453, 708 N.E.2d 1008, reconsideration denied 82 Ohio St.3d 1469, 696 N.E.2d 226, reconsideration denied 82 Ohio St.3d 1470, 696 N.E.2d 226, dismissal of post-conviction relief affirmed 1998 WL 515944, dismissed, appeal not allowed 84 Ohio St.3d 1445, 703 N.E.2d 326, reconsideration denied 84 Ohio St.3d 1489, 705 N.E.2d 368, certiorari denied 119 S.Ct. 623, 525 U.S. 1057, 142 L.Ed.2d 562, denial of habeas corpus affirmed in part, reversed in part 431 F.3d 517, rehearing denied, rehearing and rehearing en banc denied, petition for certiorari filed 2006 WL 2094473. Criminal Law ⚷ 1037.1(1)

Finding of plain error was required to reverse capital murder conviction based on defendant's contention that prosecutor's sentencing remarks denied him fair penalty determination, since defendant did not object to these remarks at trial. State v. Loza (Ohio, 11-30-1994) 71 Ohio St.3d 61, 641 N.E.2d 1082, 37 A.L.R.5th 841, reconsideration denied 71 Ohio St.3d 1437, 643 N.E.2d 142, certiorari denied 115 S.Ct. 1983, 514 U.S. 1120, 131 L.Ed.2d 871, denial of post-conviction relief affirmed 1997 WL 634348, dismissed, appeal not allowed 81 Ohio St.3d 1429, 689 N.E.2d 49. Criminal Law ⚷ 1037.1(1)

30. Errors of law

A claim that perjured testimony was admitted during trial is not cognizable in habeas corpus. O'Bannon v. Haskins (Ohio 1965) 1 Ohio St.2d 110, 205 N.E.2d 16, 30 O.O.2d 430.

Denying the request of a foreman of a jury to make a statement after the verdict is announced does not constitute prejudicial error. State v. Baldridge (Fayette 1956) 144 N.E.2d 656, 75 Ohio Law Abs. 549, 75 Ohio Law Abs. 554.

31. Newly discovered evidence

Defendant's claim that witness lied in testifying against him in prosecution for rape, felonious sexual penetration, and gross sexual imposition did not constitute newly-discovered evidence that would permit untimely filing of motion for new trial; fact should have been apparent to defendant at time witness testified, and defendant did not submit any newly discovered evidence to indicate that prosecutor's office induced perjured testimony, or knew witness was lying. State v. Ferrell (Ohio App. 5 Dist., Stark, 06-16-2003) No. 2002-CA-00272, 2003-Ohio-3134, 2003 WL 21384851, Unreported, appeal not allowed 100 Ohio St.3d 1425, 797 N.E.2d 92, 2003-Ohio-5232. Criminal Law ⚷ 951(1)

Defendant convicted of murder with firearm specification, aggravated murder with firearm specification, kidnaping with firearm specification, aggravated robbery with a firearm specification, tampering with evidence, and obstruction of justice was not entitled to evidentiary hearing on motion for new trial, since defendant failed to present any new evidence in support of motion for new trial. State v. Blalock (Ohio App. 8 Dist., Cuyahoga, 06-12-2003) No. 82080, No. 82081, 2003-Ohio-3026, 2003 WL 21360467, Unreported, appeal not allowed 100 Ohio St.3d 1485, 798 N.E.2d 1093, 2003-Ohio-5992. Criminal Law ⚷ 959

Assuming defendant was permitted to request new trial when he pled no contest to felonious assault and endangering children, defendant was not entitled to file delayed motion for new trial following convictions, since defendant could not explain how he had been unable to discover potentially favorable information, coming from woman he was living with at time of incident, within time required to file motion for new trial. State v. Carr (Ohio App. 10 Dist., Franklin, 06-10-2003) No. 02AP-1240, 2003-Ohio-2947, 2003 WL 21321453, Unreported, motion for delayed appeal denied 100 Ohio St.3d 1421, 797 N.E.2d 90, 2003-Ohio-5232. Criminal Law ⚷ 951(1)

Trial court abused its discretion in holding that defendant was not unavoidably prevented, prior to deadline imposed by rule, from discovering evidence that defendant offered in support of motion for new trial; record showed fingerprint report prepared by Bureau of Crime Investigation (BCI) did not surface until discovery was ordered in habeas corpus action and, once defendant received report, he quickly filed his motion for new trial. State v. Hoffman (Ohio App. 11 Dist., Lake, 11-29-2002) No. 2001-L-022, 2002-Ohio-6576, 2002 WL 31716684, Unreported, appeal not allowed 98 Ohio St.3d 1514, 786 N.E.2d 63, 2003-Ohio-1572. Criminal Law ⚷ 951(1)

Hearing was not required on defendant's motion for new trial based on newly discovered evidence, where only affidavit included in defendant's motion was his own, and State did not file response to defendant's motion. State v. Hoffman (Ohio App. 11 Dist., Lake, 11-29-2002) No. 2001-L-022, 2002-Ohio-6576, 2002 WL 31716684, Unreported, appeal not allowed 98 Ohio St.3d 1514, 786 N.E.2d 63, 2003-Ohio-1572. Criminal Law ⚷ 959

Fingerprint report allegedly suppressed by prosecution in murder trial, that showed that fingerprints of defendant's wife were found in home of defendant's parents, where parents were murdered, was not sufficient to warrant new trial in light of overwhelming evidence of defendant's guilt; wife had visited home on various occasions, no other evidence linked wife to crimes, record showed murders matched plan discussed by defendant, defendant admitted to hollowing out bullets used in crime, and hair evidence linked defendant to crimes. State v. Hoffman (Ohio App. 11 Dist., Lake, 11-29-2002) No. 2001-L-022, 2002-Ohio-6576, 2002 WL 31716684, Unreported, appeal not allowed 98 Ohio St.3d 1514, 786 N.E.2d 63, 2003-Ohio-1572. Criminal Law ⚷ 945(2)

Evidentiary hearing was required on defendant's motion for new trial on grounds of newly discovered evidence and witness misconduct in rape prosecution, where defendant offered affidavits of victims recanting their trial testimony, even though trial court found trial testimony was more credible that affidavits; recanted testimony would, if believed, prove defendant's innocence, and testimony would have been difficult to procure at time of trial because victims were then living in situation which they claim caused them to lie about defendant's actions. State v. Monk (Ohio App. 5 Dist., Knox, 12-03-2002) No. 02CA000026, 2002-Ohio-6602, 2002 WL 31713825, Unreported. Criminal Law ⚷ 959

Juror statements and exposure to media reports are not evidence. State v. Gross (Ohio, 10-30-2002) 97 Ohio St.3d 121, 776 N.E.2d 1061, 2002-Ohio-5524, reconsideration denied 97 Ohio St.3d 1486, 780 N.E.2d 288, 2002-Ohio-6866, certiorari denied 123 S.Ct. 2079, 538 U.S. 1037, 155 L.Ed.2d 1068, rehearing denied 124 S.Ct. 20, 539 U.S. 976, 156 L.Ed.2d 685.

Failure of trial court to grant new trial was abuse of discretion, report of clinical psychologist, who was appointed to conduct psychological examination of defendant for purposes of use at mitigation hearing in murder trial, indicating that defendant was suffering from transient mental disorder which rendered him incapable of knowing right from wrong, was material, newly discovered evidence which could not have been discovered with reasonable diligence prior to trial and should have entitled defendant to new trial given arguments of defense counsel that had they been aware of psychologist's findings prior to trial, representation of defendant may have been totally different and may have included additional evidence in support of insanity defense. State v. King (Lucas 1989) 63 Ohio App.3d 183, 578 N.E.2d 501, appeal dismissed 46 Ohio St.3d 712, 546 N.E.2d 948, rehearing denied 47 Ohio St.3d 708, 547 N.E.2d 993, motion overruled 46 Ohio St.3d 717, 546 N.E.2d 1334. Criminal Law ⚷ 945(2)

The denial of a motion for a new trial on the grounds of newly discovered evidence is within the competence and discretion of the trial court, and, in the absence of a clear showing of abuse, such decision will not be disturbed. State v. Lane (Ohio 1976) 49 Ohio St.2d 77, 358 N.E.2d 1081, 3 O.O.3d 45, vacated 98 S.Ct. 3148, 438 U.S. 911, 57 L.Ed.2d 1155.

Where on a motion for a new trial based on newly discovered evidence, movant seeks to introduce hearsay evidence which purports to be within the declaration-against-penal-interest exception to the hearsay rule, he must first establish the unavailability of the declarant. State v. Williams (Ohio 1975) 43 Ohio St.2d 88, 330 N.E.2d 891, 72 O.O.2d 49.

In a motion for a new trial, a polygraph test is not such newly discovered evidence as contemplated by RC 2945.80. State v. Jaroszyk (Carroll 1973) 39 Ohio App.2d 35, 315 N.E.2d 521, 68 O.O.2d 175.

Upon application for leave to file a motion for new trial in a criminal case, defendant must set forth the allegedly newly discovered evidence for the court to determine first, whether it is new evidence, second, whether it is newly discovered evidence which defendant was unavoidably prevented from discovering within 120 days after verdict, and third, whether there is reasonable probability that such evidence is based on fact and is not being proffered in bad faith. State v. Hall (Ohio Com.Pl. 1971) 27 Ohio Misc. 49, 267 N.E.2d 445, 55 O.O.2d 330, 56 O.O.2d 260.

RC 2945.80, as amended, relative to application for leave to file motion for new trial on account of newly discovered evidence, does not in any way restrict or limit the broad discretion invested in the trial court, on such an application, to resort to any legally acceptable evidence, be it oral testimony under oath, affidavit, or deposition. State v. Hall (Ohio Com.Pl. 1971) 27 Ohio Misc. 49, 267 N.E.2d 445, 55 O.O.2d 330, 56 O.O.2d 260. Criminal Law ⚷ 956(1)

Generally, a court will not grant a new trial on statements made by a witness after a criminal trial tending to show that his testimony at the trial was perjured, even though such after statements were made under oath. State v. Hall (Ohio Com.Pl. 1971) 27 Ohio Misc. 49, 267 N.E.2d 445, 55 O.O.2d 330, 56 O.O.2d 260.

A common pleas court does not have jurisdiction after conviction in a criminal case to entertain a motion for new trial filed at a subsequent term upon grounds of newly discovered evidence. State v. Westlake (Ohio Com.Pl. 1957) 145 N.E.2d 501, 76 Ohio Law Abs. 102.

The sole purpose of an affidavit supporting a motion for a new trial on the ground of newly discovered evidence is to inform the trial court of the substance of the evidence claimed to be newly discovered; it is never intended as a method of reconsidering the evidence introduced at the trial of the case for the purpose of impugning the soundness of the verdict brought by a jury. State v. Sheppard (Cuyahoga 1955) 100 Ohio App. 399, 128 N.E.2d 504, 60 O.O. 332, appeal dismissed 164 Ohio St. 428, 131 N.E.2d 837, 58 O.O. 247. Criminal Law ⚷ 958(1)

Where experiments conducted after trial could just as well have been prepared for presentation at the trial, had due diligence and reasonable foresight been exercised, their results are not "newly discovered evidence" and do not constitute grounds for the allowance of a new trial. State v. Sheppard (Cuyahoga 1955) 100 Ohio App. 399, 128 N.E.2d 504, 60 O.O. 332, appeal dismissed 164 Ohio St. 428, 131 N.E.2d 837, 58 O.O. 247. Criminal Law ⚷ 939(1)

Refusal to grant new trial for newly discovered evidence, where defendant's admissions would sustain murder conviction, if all other evidence were disregarded, held not error. Ralls v. State (Crawford 1931) 43 Ohio App. 129, 182 N.E. 691, 11 Ohio Law Abs. 141, 35 Ohio Law Rep. 80. Criminal Law ⚷ 945(1)

Under former GC 13746 (Repealed), trial courts were without jurisdiction to grant a new trial on the ground of newly discovered evidence when the motion therefor was filed at a term subsequent to the one at which the verdict was rendered. Weaver v. State (Ohio 1929) 120 Ohio St. 44, 165 N.E. 573.

Defendant could not obtain new trial for newly discovered evidence upon motion supported by affidavit of witness whom he had had opportunity to cross-examine, with knowledge of facts which might have developed matters stated in witness' affidavit. State v. Lopa (Ohio 1917) 96 Ohio St. 410, 117 N.E. 319, 15 Ohio Law Rep. 191. Criminal Law ⚷ 939(3); New Trial ⚷ 102(5)

32. Consent

Defendant's consent to mistrial is implied only if there is some positive indication from record of defendant's willingness to consent to declaration of mistrial. Malinovsky v. Court of Common Pleas of Lorain County (C.A.6 (Ohio) 1993) 7 F.3d 1263, certiorari denied 114 S.Ct. 1300, 510 U.S. 1194, 127 L.Ed.2d 652. Double Jeopardy ⚷ 96

33. Modification of verdict

In order to sustain a charge of assault with intent to kill in violation of RC 2901.24, the state must prove that the accused intended to kill at the time of the alleged assault. State v. Kinnemore (Montgomery 1972) 34 Ohio App.2d 39, 295 N.E.2d 680, 63 O.O.2d 62. Homicide ⚷ 727

Where evidence of deliberate and premeditated malice is insufficient for a jury to reach a verdict of guilty of first degree murder beyond a reasonable doubt, but the total evidence is sufficient to sustain a verdict of guilty as to the included offense of second degree murder, a reviewing court may modify the judgment of first degree murder and enter final judgment of guilty of second degree murder. State v. Esherick (Lake 1969) 19 Ohio App.2d 40, 249 N.E.2d 78, 48 O.O.2d 35.

Where the Supreme Court has held that a verdict of second degree murder is sustained by sufficient evidence and a court of appeals determines that the verdict is against the weight of the evidence, it cannot reduce the verdict to manslaughter, but can only order a new trial. State v. Robinson (Ohio 1955) 162 Ohio St. 486, 124 N.E.2d 148, 55 O.O. 388.

If there is no evidence to establish beyond a reasonable doubt the guilt of an accused of murder in the second degree, the court of appeals, on review, may modify a conviction of such offense by reducing it, where the evidence warrants, to one of manslaughter in the first degree. State v. Robinson (Ohio 1954) 161 Ohio St. 213, 118 N.E.2d 517, 53 O.O. 96.

34. Lesser included offenses

An offense is a lesser included offense where all the elements of such offense are present with others in the offense charged in the indictment. State v. Shoe (Miami 1969) 20 Ohio App.2d 344, 254 N.E.2d 382, 49 O.O.2d 485.

The factual situation in each criminal case determines the necessity of instructing the jury on lesser included offenses rather than the fact that certain offenses are literally included in the crime formally charged in the indictment. State v. Patterson (Ohio 1961) 172 Ohio St. 319, 175 N.E.2d 741, 16 O.O.2d 106. Criminal Law ⚷ 795(2.1)

Where the proper averments of an indictment for the aggravated degree of rape specified in RC 2905.02 set forth or indicate with reasonable certainty all the essential elements of the crime of statutory rape described in RC 2905.03, such indictment will support a conviction for the latter crime. State v. Daniels (Ohio 1959) 169 Ohio St. 87, 157 N.E.2d 736, 76 A.L.R.2d 468, 8 O.O.2d 56.

In an instance where an indictment for the crime of rape of a daughter does not contain an averment that the victim was known by the defendant to be his daughter, the crime of incest will not be either "a lesser degree" of or "a lesser crime included" in such crime of rape. State v. Daniels (Ohio 1959) 169 Ohio St. 87, 157 N.E.2d 736, 76 A.L.R.2d 468, 8 O.O.2d 56.

2945.80 Application for new trial

Application for a new trial shall be made by motion upon written grounds, and except for the cause of newly discovered evidence material for the person applying, which he could not with reasonable diligence have discovered and produced at the trial, shall be filed within three days after the verdict was rendered, or the decision of the court where a trial by jury has been waived, unless it is made to appear by clear and convincing proof that the defendant was unavoidably prevented from filing his motion for new trial in which case it shall be filed within three days from the order of the court finding that he was unavoidably prevented from filing such motion within the time provided herein.

Motions for new trial on account of newly discovered evidence shall be filed within one hundred twenty days following the day upon which the verdict was rendered, or the decision of the court where trial by jury has been waived. If it is made to appear by clear and convincing proof that the defendant was unavoidably prevented from the discovery of the evidence upon which he must rely, such motion shall be filed within three days from an order of the court finding that he was unavoidably prevented from discovering the evidence within the one hundred twenty day period.

(131 v S 389, eff. 11–1–65; 128 v 141; 1953 H 1; GC 13449–2)

Historical and Statutory Notes

Pre–1953 H 1 Amendments: 113 v 196, Ch 28, § 2

Cross References

Computation of time, 1.14; Crim R 45

Motions, Crim R 47

New trial, Crim R 33

Library References

Criminal Law ⚷948.

Westlaw Topic No. 110.

C.J.S. Criminal Law §§ 1415 to 1419.

Research References

Encyclopedias

OH Jur. 3d Criminal Law § 3210, Generally; Application by Motion Upon Written Grounds.

OH Jur. 3d Criminal Law § 3211, Time Within Which Motion Must be Filed.

OH Jur. 3d Criminal Law § 3212, Where Application is Made After Prescribed Period; Clear and Convincing Proof Required.

Forms

Am. Jur. Pl. & Pr. Forms New Trial § 14, Introductory Comments.

Treatises and Practice Aids

Katz, Giannelli, Blair and Lipton, Baldwin's Ohio Practice, Criminal Law, § 79:9, Motion for New Trial.

Law Review and Journal Commentaries

The Courtroom Status of the Polygraph, Comment. 14 Akron L Rev 133 (Summer 1980).

Notes of Decisions

1. In general

A defendant in a criminal case has the right to file a motion for a new trial, and it is reversible error for a court to strike such motion from the files. State v. O'Banion (Butler 1970) 26 Ohio App.2d 285, 271 N.E.2d 312, 55 O.O.2d 503. Criminal Law ⚷ 964; Criminal Law ⚷ 1176

A common pleas court does not have jurisdiction after conviction in a criminal case to entertain a motion for new trial filed at a subsequent term upon grounds of newly discovered evidence. State v. Westlake (Ohio Com.Pl. 1957) 145 N.E.2d 501, 76 Ohio Law Abs. 102.

2. Newly discovered evidence

Defendant's claim that witness lied in testifying against him in prosecution for rape, felonious sexual penetration, and gross sexual imposition did not constitute newly-discovered evidence that would permit untimely filing of motion for new trial; fact should have been apparent to defendant at time witness testified, and defendant did not submit any newly discovered evidence to indicate that prosecutor's office induced perjured testimony, or knew witness was lying. State v. Ferrell (Ohio App. 5 Dist., Stark, 06-16-2003) No. 2002-CA-00272, 2003-Ohio-3134, 2003 WL 21384851, Unreported, appeal not allowed 100 Ohio St.3d 1425, 797 N.E.2d 92, 2003-Ohio-5232. Criminal Law ⚷ 951(1)

Assuming defendant was permitted to request new trial when he pled no contest to felonious assault and endangering children, defendant was not entitled to file delayed motion for new trial following convictions, since defendant could not explain how he had been unable to discover potentially favorable information, coming from woman he was living with at time of incident, within time required to file motion for new trial. State v. Carr (Ohio App. 10 Dist., Franklin, 06-10-2003) No. 02AP-1240, 2003-Ohio-2947, 2003 WL 21321453, Unreported, motion for delayed appeal denied 100 Ohio St.3d 1421, 797 N.E.2d 90, 2003-Ohio-5232. Criminal Law ⚷ 951(1)

Defendant failed to establish a reasonable probability that if the State had produced a blood culture report showing the possible existence of infection in newborn baby's blood, thereby, supporting defendant's theory that infection, not asphyxiation, was the cause of newborn baby's death, that the outcome of the proceedings, finding defendant guilty of involuntary manslaughter pursuant to R.C. 2919.22, would have been different, as both theories would support a finding of creating a substantial risk to the health or safety of the child, and, as a result, new trial would not be granted. State v. Iacona (Ohio App. 9 Dist., Medina, 03-15-2000) No. CA 2891-M, 2000 WL 277911, Unreported, stay granted 88 Ohio St.3d 1458, 726 N.E.2d 501, on reconsideration 88 Ohio St.3d 1235, 727 N.E.2d 594, 2000-Ohio-362, appeal allowed 89 Ohio St.3d 1469, 732 N.E.2d 1000, affirmed 93 Ohio St.3d 83, 752 N.E.2d 937, 2001-Ohio-1292, on remand 2002 WL 208073.

Trial court's failure to issue order explicitly stating that defendant was unavoidably prevented from discovering new evidence, although error, did not defeat court's jurisdiction to grant defendant a new trial, based on newly discovered evidence, beyond 120 days after verdict convicting him of child endangering and involuntary manslaughter, and thus judgment granting defendant new trial was not void, but merely voidable, and state was precluded from challenging judgment collaterally, by motion to strike, instead of by direct appeal. State v. Blankenship (Ohio App. 9 Dist., 05-22-1996) 111 Ohio App.3d 198, 675 N.E.2d 1303, appeal not allowed 77 Ohio St.3d 1481, 673 N.E.2d 142. Criminal Law ⚷ 961; Criminal Law ⚷ 951(1)

In a motion for a new trial, a polygraph test is not such newly discovered evidence as contemplated by RC 2945.80. State v. Jaroszyk (Carroll 1973) 39 Ohio App.2d 35, 315 N.E.2d 521, 68 O.O.2d 175.

RC 2945.80, as amended, relative to application for leave to file motion for new trial on account of newly discovered evidence, does not in any way restrict or limit the broad discretion invested in the trial court, on such an application, to resort to any legally acceptable evidence, be it oral testimony under oath, affidavit, or deposition. State v. Hall (Ohio Com.Pl. 1971) 27 Ohio Misc. 49, 267 N.E.2d 445, 55 O.O.2d 330, 56 O.O.2d 260. Criminal Law ⚷ 956(1)

Upon application for leave to file a motion for new trial in a criminal case, defendant must set forth the allegedly newly discovered evidence for the court to determine first, whether it is new evidence, second, whether it is newly discovered evidence which defendant was unavoidably prevented from discovering within 120 days after verdict, and third, whether there is reasonable probability that such evidence is based on fact and is not being proffered in bad faith. State v. Hall (Ohio Com.Pl. 1971) 27 Ohio Misc. 49, 267 N.E.2d 445, 55 O.O.2d 330, 56 O.O.2d 260.

RC 2945.80 grants an extender only to within 120 days after the return of the verdict; and where such time has elapsed there is no procedure by which a new trial may be granted, and the granting thereof is an abuse of discretion. State v. Dean (Franklin 1958) 107 Ohio App. 219, 158 N.E.2d 217, 80 Ohio Law Abs. 328, 80 Ohio Law Abs. 333, 8 O.O.2d 103, certiorari denied 81 S.Ct. 1662, 366 U.S. 937, 6 L.Ed.2d 848.

2945.81 Causes to be sustained by affidavits

The causes enumerated in divisions (B) and (C) of section 2945.79 of the Revised Code must be sustained by affidavit showing their truth, and may be controverted by affidavits.

(1953 H 1, eff. 10–1–53; GC 13449–3)

Historical and Statutory Notes

Pre–1953 H 1 Amendments: 113 v 196, Ch 28, § 3

Cross References

Affidavits required when certain grounds for new trial alleged, Crim R 33

Motions, Crim R 47

Library References

Criminal Law ⚩956.
Westlaw Topic No. 110.
C.J.S. Criminal Law § 1419.

Research References

Encyclopedias

OH Jur. 3d Criminal Law § 3213, Affidavits and Other Proof.

Forms

Am. Jur. Pl. & Pr. Forms New Trial § 80, Introductory Comments.

Treatises and Practice Aids

Katz, Giannelli, Blair and Lipton, Baldwin's Ohio Practice, Criminal Law, § 79:9, Motion for New Trial.

Giannelli and Snyder, Baldwin's Ohio Practice, Evidence, § 606.6, Juror Misconduct; Substantive Grounds.

Notes of Decisions

1. Sufficiency

Affidavit supporting motion for new trial for juror's misconduct, which failed to state that defendant or his attorney did not have information of act complained of prior to qualification of juror, held incomplete. Lyon v. State (Huron 1926) 23 Ohio App. 237, 155 N.E. 569, 4 Ohio Law Abs. 546, affirmed 116 Ohio St. 265, 155 N.E. 800, 5 Ohio Law Abs. 189, 25 Ohio Law Rep. 68, 25 Ohio Law Rep. 267. Criminal Law ⚩ 956(13); New Trial ⚩ 140(1)

2945.82 New trial

When a new trial is granted by the trial court, or when a new trial is awarded on appeal, the accused shall stand for trial upon the indictment or information as though there had been no previous trial thereof.

(1953 H 1, eff. 10–1–53; GC 13449–4)

Historical and Statutory Notes

Pre–1953 H 1 Amendments: 113 v 196, Ch 28, § 4

Cross References

New trial, Crim R 33

Library References

Criminal Law ⚩965.
Westlaw Topic No. 110.

Research References

Encyclopedias

OH Jur. 3d Criminal Law § 3216, Effect of Filing and of Granting Motion on Judgment and Sentence.

Treatises and Practice Aids

Katz, Giannelli, Blair and Lipton, Baldwin's Ohio Practice, Criminal Law, § 79:9, Motion for New Trial.

Notes of Decisions

1. Constitutional issues

RC 2945.82 does not contravene the double jeopardy provisions of O Const Art I §10. State v. Robinson (Mahoning 1956) 100 Ohio App. 466, 137 N.E.2d 141, 60 O.O. 373.

2. Mention of previous trial at retrial

Statute providing that accused, upon being awarded new trial on appeal, shall stand for trial as though there had been no previous trial, does not preclude any mention of previous trial at new trial; rather, it means simply that there is no requirement for new indictment or information when case is remanded for retrial. State v. Keenan (Ohio, 02-25-1998) 81 Ohio St.3d 133, 689 N.E.2d 929, 1998-Ohio-459, reconsideration denied 81 Ohio

St.3d 1503, 691 N.E.2d 1062, certiorari denied 119 S.Ct. 146, 525 U.S. 860, 142 L.Ed.2d 119, rehearing denied 119 S.Ct. 581, 525 U.S. 1035, 142 L.Ed.2d 484, denial of post-conviction relief affirmed 2001 WL 91129, dismissed, appeal not allowed 92 Ohio St.3d 1429, 749 N.E.2d 756, habeas corpus dismissed 262 F.Supp.2d 818, motion to amend denied 262 F.Supp.2d 826, vacated and remanded 400 F.3d 417. Criminal Law ⚷ 965; Criminal Law ⚷ 1192

2945.83 When new trial shall not be granted

No motion for a new trial shall be granted or verdict set aside, nor shall any judgment of conviction be reversed in any court because of:

(A) An inaccuracy or imperfection in the indictment, information, or warrant, provided that the charge is sufficient to fairly and reasonably inform the accused of the nature and cause of the accusation against him;

(B) A variance between the allegations and the proof thereof unless the accused is misled or prejudiced thereby;

(C) The admission or rejection of any evidence offered against or for the accused unless it affirmatively appears on the record that the accused was or may have been prejudiced thereby;

(D) A misdirection of the jury unless the accused was or may have been prejudiced thereby;

(E) Any other cause unless it appears affirmatively from the record that the accused was prejudiced thereby or was prevented from having a fair trial.

(1953 H 1, eff. 10–1–53; GC 13449–5)

Historical and Statutory Notes

Pre–1953 H 1 Amendments: 113 v 196, Ch 28, § 5

Cross References

Harmless error and plain error, Crim R 52

New trial, Crim R 33

Library References

Criminal Law ⚷915, 921, 922, 932.

Westlaw Topic No. 110.

C.J.S. Criminal Law §§ 1432, 1436 to 1437.

Research References

Encyclopedias

OH Jur. 3d Criminal Law § 2414, Variance.

OH Jur. 3d Criminal Law § 2966, Harmless Error as to Admission of Evidence of Other Crimes or Acts.

OH Jur. 3d Criminal Law § 3169, Prosecutions in Magistrates' Courts.

OH Jur. 3d Criminal Law § 3174, Prerequisite of Prejudice to Defendant.

OH Jur. 3d Criminal Law § 3180, Errors of Law Occurring at Trial; Erroneous Instructions and Admission of Evidence.

OH Jur. 3d Criminal Law § 3670, Prejudicial Error, Generally—Statutory Provisions.

OH Jur. 3d Criminal Law § 3678, Consolidation and Severance of Cases.

OH Jur. 3d Criminal Law § 3681, Generally; Adequacy of the Indictment, Information, Complaint.

OH Jur. 3d Criminal Law § 3739, Reply to Improper Evidence; Provocation.

OH Jur. 3d Criminal Law § 3746, Criticism or Sanctioning of Counsel or Witness.

OH Jur. 3d Criminal Law § 3748, Exposing Jury to Inappropriate Information.

OH Jur. 3d Criminal Law § 3751, Independent Investigation of Case.

OH Jur. 3d Criminal Law § 3756, as to Role of Jury Regarding Punishment.

OH Jur. 3d Criminal Law § 3761, on Lesser Included Offenses.

OH Jur. 3d Criminal Law § 3765, Instructions as to Evidence, Generally.

OH Jur. 3d Criminal Law § 3769, Assuming or Determining as Fact a Disputed Matter.

OH Jur. 3d Criminal Law § 3774, Instructions as to Lesser Included Offenses.

OH Jur. 3d Criminal Law § 3777, Additional Instructions or Review of Evidence Upon Return of Jury.

OH Jur. 3d Criminal Law § 3784, Special Verdict.

Treatises and Practice Aids

Katz, Giannelli, Blair and Lipton, Baldwin's Ohio Practice, Criminal Law, § 79:10, Invalid Grounds for New Trial.

Katz, Giannelli, Blair and Lipton, Baldwin's Ohio Practice, Criminal Law, § 80:25, Judgments on Appeal.

Notes of Decisions

1. Constitutional issues

While it is technically incorrect to have an affidavit for a search warrant acknowledged by the clerk of a court rather than a judge, where the affiant is sworn in the presence of a judge and the judge hears the affiant swear to the affidavit's truthfulness, such error is not of constitutional proportion and is not prejudicial to the substantial rights of a defendant. State v. Kuykendall (Wayne 1977) 51 Ohio App.2d 215, 367 N.E.2d 905, 5 O.O.3d 354. Searches And Seizures ⚷ 107

Where the constitutional error complained of in a particular case is so unimportant and insignificant that it may, consistent with the state and federal constitutions, be deemed harmless, such error does not require the automatic reversal of the conviction. State v. Vaughn (Mahoning 1969) 19 Ohio App.2d 76, 249 N.E.2d 844, 48 O.O.2d 132. Criminal Law ⚷ 1186.4(1)

The statute may not be invoked in a case which discloses the clear disregard of a constitutional prerogative. State v. Grisafulli (Ohio 1939) 135 Ohio St. 87, 19 N.E.2d 645, 13 O.O. 440.

2. Indictment

Indictment for attempted promoting prostitution was sufficient to reasonably inform defendant of nature of charge, even though subdivision of statute under which defendant was charged was not specified; language of indictment mirrored language set forth in subdivision, and indictment identified name of victim and date of alleged crime. State v. Sullivan (Ohio App. 8 Dist., Cuyahoga, 11-06-2003) No. 82816, 2003-Ohio-5930, 2003 WL 22510808, Unreported. Indictment And Information ⚷ 108

It was not prejudicial error that defendants in a criminal proceeding were identified in the indictment by aliases where no evidence was offered of a claimed use of an alias. State v. Senzarino (Ohio Com.Pl. 1967) 10 Ohio Misc. 241, 224 N.E.2d 389, 39 O.O.2d 383.

Where an indictment, framed under RC 2907.30, charges defendant with knowingly receiving and concealing stolen personal property, viz., "beer and wine," of a value of less than $60, a misdemeanor, and at the trial the evidence shows such articles to be a case of beer and a bottle of champagne, no prejudicial error occurs to defendant by the state's failure to introduce evidence of the actual value of such articles nor in the return of a verdict finding the defendant guilty of "receiving stolen property and concealing stolen property," where such articles obviously possess some value and there is no express objection to the form of verdict submitted and returned. State v. Corkran (Ohio 1965) 3 Ohio St.2d 125, 209 N.E.2d 437, 32 O.O.2d 132.

Where the indictment set out the value of the goods allegedly stolen by defendant as $300, and defendant, through his counsel, conceded, during the course of the trial, that the goods alleged to have been stolen were worth $300, a jury verdict finding defendant guilty of the offense of "grand larceny" as charged in the indictment was not prejudicial. State v. Park (Ohio 1962) 174 Ohio St. 81, 186 N.E.2d 736, 21 O.O.2d 339.

On trial upon an indictment for obtaining currency by trick, evidence that the transaction upon which the indictment was based involved the issuance of a cashier's check to the prosecuting witness, that the check was cashed and that the proceeds, whether immediately delivered to the defendant or to the prosecuting witness, ultimately found their way into the hands of the defendant, does not constitute a variance prejudicial to the defendant, and defendant's motion for leave to appeal on that ground will be overruled. State v. Candy (Hamilton 1959) 113 Ohio App. 334, 175 N.E.2d 191, 17 O.O.2d 361.

An indictment which charged that defendant "published and offered to sell" a medical diploma whereas the statute used the language "publish or sell" was not defective. State v. Broadwell (Cuyahoga 1956) 104 Ohio App. 37, 136 N.E.2d 72, 75 Ohio Law Abs. 47, 3 O.O.2d 217, certiorari denied 77 S.Ct. 668, 353 U.S. 911, 1 L.Ed.2d 665, rehearing denied 77 S.Ct. 1281, 353 U.S. 989, 1 L.Ed.2d 1147.

The practice of signing the name of an arresting officer by another arresting officer to an affidavit charging an offense is to be condemned, but if the affidavit is actually executed by the latter officer and is sufficient to apprise defendant of the offense with which he is charged, the false signature is surplusage and such irregularity is not prejudicial to defendant. City of Toledo v. Miscikowski (Lucas 1955) 99 Ohio App. 189, 132 N.E.2d 231, 58 O.O. 331.

Amendment of an indictment to correct a misdescription of the victim's name does not infringe upon defendant's constitutional rights. (See also In Re Dye, 170 OS 97, 162 NE(2d) 520 (1959).) Dye v. Sacks (C.A.6 (Ohio) 1960) 279 F.2d 834, 14 A.L.R.3d 1352, 86 Ohio Law Abs. 476, 13 O.O.2d 301.

3. Evidence

Defendant was prejudiced in rape prosecution by improper admission of testimony by prior rape victim that did not meet any exceptions to general prohibition against propensity evidence, and thus reversal of conviction was required, in view of inflammatory nature of prior victim's testimony. State v. Wilkins (Ohio App. 9 Dist., 09-29-1999) 135 Ohio App.3d 26, 732 N.E.2d 1021, dismissed, appeal not allowed 88 Ohio St.3d 1412, 723 N.E.2d 118. Criminal Law ⚿ 1169.11

The allowance of a motion for a new trial on the grounds of newly discovered evidence is within the competence and discretion of the trial judge; and in the absence of a clear showing of abuse such decision will not be disturbed. State v. Williams (Ohio 1975) 43 Ohio St.2d 88, 330 N.E.2d 891, 72 O.O.2d 49. Criminal Law ⚿ 938(1); Criminal Law ⚿ 1156(3)

Although error in admitting evidence may be harmless where the facts intended to be proved thereby are fully shown by other evidence which is competent, which is admitted without objection, or which is adduced by the accused, nevertheless, such other evidence must be substantially uncontradicted or not susceptible of other reasonable explanation to the contrary for such error to be held harmless and not prejudicial to the defendant in a criminal case. State v. Miracle (Mercer 1973) 33 Ohio App.2d 289, 294 N.E.2d 903, 62 O.O.2d 440.

Where an indictment under RC 2921.14 for conspiracy to defraud specifies the manner of defrauding relied upon as the defrauding part of that conspiracy, the proof of a manner of defrauding that is not suggested by any allegations of the indictment or by any bill of particulars thereunder will necessarily prejudice the accused. State v. Lewis (Ohio 1970) 21 Ohio St.2d 203, 257 N.E.2d 59, 50 O.O.2d 441. Conspiracy ⚿ 43(12)

A reviewing court may not reverse a judgment of conviction in a criminal case in a trial court, where the record shows that a verdict of guilty was returned by a jury on sufficient evidence and where no prejudicial error occurred in the actual trial of the case or in the instructions given the jury by the court. State v. DeHass (Ohio 1967) 10 Ohio St.2d 230, 227 N.E.2d 212, 39 O.O.2d 366.

Where the trial court has admitted into evidence testimony relating to a confession obtained in violation of the federal constitution, RC 2945.83 is inapplicable and such error is prejudicial if "there is a reasonable possibility that the evidence complained of might have contributed to the conviction." State v. Cowans (Ohio 1967) 10 Ohio St.2d 96, 227 N.E.2d 201, 39 O.O.2d 97.

A court of appeals, in weighing the evidence in a review of the issue of self-defense in a homicide case, when the evidence on that issue is so conflicting that that court is unable to determine from the record wherein the truth lies, will adopt the conclusion of the jury and the trial court, they being in a better situation to judge of the truth by reason of their opportunity to see the witnesses and observe their conduct. State v. Reid (Allen 1965) 3 Ohio App.2d 215, 210 N.E.2d 142, 32 O.O.2d 316.

Where evidence has been found as a result of an illegal search, has not been suppressed on request and has been erroneously admitted against a defendant, such defendant's conviction should not be set aside if it does not appear that there is a reasonable possibility that the admission of such evidence may have contributed to the conviction. State v. Waldbillig (Ohio 1964) 1 Ohio St.2d 50, 203 N.E.2d 361, 30 O.O.2d 28.

A conviction for the offense of contributing to the delinquency of a minor will not be disturbed on appeal, where competent evidence was introduced at the trial showing that the defendant, a married man, twenty-nine years of age and with a family, persistently associated with a sixteen-year old girl in such a way as to disrupt her life and morals. State ex rel. Meng v. Todaro (Ohio 1954) 161 Ohio St. 348, 119 N.E.2d 281, 53 O.O. 252.

On appeal from a judgment of conviction, where defendant on trial for robbery was asked on cross-examination whether he had committed certain similar offenses, to which questions he objected but on instruction to answer did so in the negative, and trial court later withdrew such testimony from the jury, it is error, under this section, relating to reversal for improper admission of evidence, for a reviewing court stating its belief that defendant's guilt was established beyond a reasonable doubt irrespective of such excluded evidence, to reverse the judgment because of misconduct of the prosecuting attorney in asking such questions. State v. Witsel (Ohio 1944) 144 Ohio St. 190, 58 N.E.2d 212, 29 O.O. 374.

4. Misdirection of jury

Any error associated with trial court's failure to instruct jury on statutory definition of "counterfeit controlled substance" in prosecution for selling or offering to sell counterfeit controlled substance was harmless in absence of evidence that instruction given prejudiced defense. State v. Kimbro (Ohio App. 9 Dist., 03-13-1996) 109 Ohio App.3d 802, 673 N.E.2d 192. Criminal Law ⚿ 1173.2(2)

With regard to jury charge, reversible error will not lie unless defense was prejudiced. State v. Shue (Ohio App. 9 Dist., 09-21-1994) 97 Ohio App.3d 459, 646 N.E.2d 1156, dismissed, appeal not allowed 71 Ohio St.3d 1476, 645 N.E.2d 1257. Criminal Law ⚿ 1172.1(1)

Where a defendant who is charged with operating a vehicle while under the influence of alcohol refuses to submit to a breathalyzer test, and the trial court instructs the jury on the presumptions in RC 4511.19 concerning the alcohol content which is determined by such a test, that instruction is inapplicable to the case which the evidence tends to establish and is prejudicial to the defendant. State v. Sargent (Ohio 1975) 41 Ohio St.2d 85, 322 N.E.2d 634, 70 O.O.2d 169.

In a criminal case, it is not mandatory upon a trial court to give requested instructions to the jury verbatim, but if the requested instructions contain a correct, pertinent statement of the law and are appropriate to the facts they must be included, at least in substance, in the court's charge to the jury. State v. Nelson (Ohio 1973) 36 Ohio St.2d 79, 303 N.E.2d 865, 65 O.O.2d 222. Criminal Law ⚿ 834(2)

Where a paragraph in a general charge, by itself, is improper and misleading, but when the court's entire charge is considered it is apparent that no prejudicial error resulted, the judgment will not be reversed. State v. Porter (Ohio 1968) 14 Ohio St.2d 10, 235 N.E.2d 520, 43 O.O.2d 5. Criminal Law ⚷ 822(1)

Where a trial court's answer to a request from the jury for supplemental instructions is incomplete, confusing or misleading, but does not prejudice the accused, a judgment of conviction will not be reversed. State v. Porter (Ohio 1968) 14 Ohio St.2d 10, 235 N.E.2d 520, 43 O.O.2d 5.

Where the value of property concerned in a prosecution for fraud is found to be $250, a charge that $60 rather than $35 was the dividing line between a felony and a misdemeanor was harmless error. State v. Kollar (Wayne 1952) 128 N.E.2d 669, 70 Ohio Law Abs. 353.

Explanation of the possibility of parole in the event of conviction of second degree murder was not prejudicial where the defendant was convicted of first degree murder without a recommendation of mercy. State v. Meyer (Ohio 1955) 163 Ohio St. 279, 126 N.E.2d 585, 56 O.O. 256.

In a first degree murder case the court may, although it is better practice not to, explain the possibilities of pardon, commutation or parole in connection with a sentence of life imprisonment. State v. Meyer (Ohio 1955) 163 Ohio St. 279, 126 N.E.2d 585, 56 O.O. 256.

Judgment of conviction, based on a verdict of guilty, in prosecution for murder in first degree, should not be reversed for failure of trial court to submit to jury, with other forms of verdict, a form of not guilty, where accused, upon formal arraignment, had entered a plea of not guilty, had not waived jury trial, and during such trial his counsel, in argument to jury, for purpose of the record, had entered a plea of guilty, and every element of offense had been established not only by testimony of witnesses for the state but by a full confession by accused, since such action of the trial court did not deprive defendant of any substantial right under the constitution or the law and was not prejudicial error. State v. Wells (Ohio 1938) 134 Ohio St. 404, 17 N.E.2d 658, 13 O.O. 12. Constitutional Law ⚷ 268(11)

Where defendant is charged with and convicted of aggravated robbery and aggravated murder, trial court erred in instructing the jury on the matters of theft by deception, theft of services and aiding and abetting, where such matters are unsupported by the evidence; however, where it appears that such instructions could not possibly have contributed to the conviction of the defendant such instructions constitute harmless error. State v Lewis, No. 43987 (8th Dist Ct App, Cuyahoga, 5–6–82).

Although a trial court's supplemental definition of reasonable doubt beyond the statutory definition prescribed by RC 2901.05 is unnecessary and inappropriate, such definition does not constitute prejudicial error absent a showing that the jury was misled or confused. State v Lewis, No. 43987 (8th Dist Ct App, Cuyahoga, 5–6–82).

Failure to instruct the jury on the statutory definition of "sexual activity" as used in RC 2907.01 does not constitute plain error. Cleveland v Leisinger, No. 43902 (8th Dist Ct App, Cuyahoga, 4–8–82).

5. Statements of counsel

Where the prosecuting attorney makes a statement to the jury on closing argument expressing his personal opinion or belief in the guilt of the accused based solely on the evidence presented in the case, an examination of the entire record in the case, including the closing argument of the counsel for accused, must be made to determine whether such statement is prejudicial. State v. Conrad (Monroe 1969) 19 Ohio App.2d 82, 249 N.E.2d 854, 48 O.O.2d 135. Criminal Law ⚷ 1134(2)

Where counsel for state in argument to jury expresses his personal opinion of guilt of accused and no objection is made thereto, it is too late to raise question for first time in an appellate court; where court does not have before it arguments to jury of defendant and his counsel as well as argument of which complaint is made for first time in court of appeals, appellate court is not in position to say that it affirmatively appears from record that accused was prejudiced thereby or was prevented from having a fair trial under this section. State v. Nevius (Ohio 1947) 147 Ohio St. 263, 71 N.E.2d 258, 34 O.O. 210, certiorari denied 67 S.Ct. 1521, 331 U.S. 839, 91 L.Ed. 1851.

Prosecutor's remarks during closing argument implying that defendant's witnesses were testifying falsely for money where such implications were not supported by evidence, although improper, were not of such prejudicial effect as to deny defendant a fair trial. State v Howland, No. 439 (4th Dist Ct App, Highland, 4–15–82).

Where the prosecution sought to create an impermissible inference in the minds of the jurors that the defendant either refused to take or failed to pass a polygraph test, such error is not harmless beyond a reasonable doubt and is grounds for reversal. State v Bates, No. 43904 (8th Dist Ct App, Cuyahoga, 4–1–82).

6. Irregularities or misconduct

Defendant was not entitled to a new trial based on his submission of affidavits from inmates who asserted that prosecution witness admitted to them that he lied during defendant's murder trial; the State filed witness' affidavit in which he affirmed his trial testimony and denied that he lied. State v. Neal (Ohio App. 2 Dist., Champaign, 12-06-2002) No. 2000 CA 16, No. 2000 CA 18, 2002-Ohio-6786, 2002 WL 31761564, Unreported, appeal not allowed 98 Ohio St.3d 1538, 786 N.E.2d 901, 2003-Ohio-1946, reconsideration denied 99 Ohio St.3d 1438, 789 N.E.2d 1119, 2003-Ohio-2902. Criminal Law ⚷ 942(2)

Mistrial was not warranted by detective's actions, during jury view, of attempting to say something to one of the jurors; before detective said anything of consequence, bailiff apprised detective that he was not to speak to jurors. State v. Ayala (Ohio App. 10 Dist., 06-11-1996) 111 Ohio App.3d 627, 676 N.E.2d 1201. Criminal Law ⚷ 855(4)

Mistrial was not warranted by prosecutor's actions, during jury view, of pointing out two bullet holes for bailiff, asking bailiff to show jurors a vacant lot that was allegedly not on written list, or moving object to show bullet hole to bailiff. State v. Ayala (Ohio App. 10 Dist., 06-11-1996) 111 Ohio App.3d 627, 676 N.E.2d 1201. Criminal Law ⚷ 867

Mistrial was not required after trial court reprimanded defense counsel for allowing witnesses to leave for day prior to conclusion of day's proceedings in prosecution for contributing to unruliness of a child. State v. Black (Hamilton 1993) 85 Ohio App.3d 771, 621 N.E.2d 484, dismissed, jurisdictional motion overruled 67 Ohio St.3d 1451, 619 N.E.2d 420. Criminal Law ⚷ 867

In grand theft prosecution in which state witness testified that he and defendant entered camera store by kicking in the doors and that they grabbed some cameras, judge's ordering of witness' arrest, in presence of jury, for having committed a crime violated defendant's right to fair trial. State v. Kish (Jefferson 1981) 4 Ohio App.3d 252, 448 N.E.2d 455, 4 O.B.R. 468. Criminal Law ⚷ 658

Permitting a government witness to serve as a custodian for the jury does not per se constitute reversible error. State v. Cooper (Ohio 1977) 52 Ohio St.2d 163, 370 N.E.2d 725, 6 O.O.3d 377, vacated 98 S.Ct. 3137, 438 U.S. 911, 57 L.Ed.2d 1157. Criminal Law ⚷ 1174(1)

Where, in a criminal case, the credibility of an informer-witness is central to the determination of guilt or innocence of the defendant, comments by the trial court in the presence of the jury which may enhance the credibility of such witness will justify a reversal of the judgment of conviction under RC 2945.83. State v. Thomas (Ohio 1973) 36 Ohio St.2d 68, 303 N.E.2d 882, 65 O.O.2d 216.

Whether an emotional demonstration in the courtroom during the course of a murder trial by a spectator related to the victim improperly influences the jury against the accused; and whether a gift by the jury to the prosecuting attorneys, inspired by their repeated remarks to none of which the accused made objection, conceived in part during the trial but not connected with any part of the deliberations of the jury and presented after sentence of the accused and discharge of the jury, constitute misconduct so as to deprive the accused of a fair trial are questions of fact to be resolved by the trial court, whose determination thereon will not be disturbed on review in the absence of evidence contrary to that determination clearly and affirmatively appearing on the face of the record. State v. Bradley (Ohio 1965) 3 Ohio St.2d 38, 209 N.E.2d 215, 32 O.O.2d 21.

Where it does not appear that any false answer was given by a juror in the voir dire examination, the mere failure of the trial court to have either oaths or affirmations administered to prospective jurors before such examination cannot be held to have prejudiced a defendant or prevented him from having a fair trial, and a judgment of conviction should not be reversed because of such failure. State v. Glaros (Ohio 1960) 170 Ohio St. 471, 166 N.E.2d 379, 11 O.O.2d 215, on remand 114 Ohio App. 185, 173 N.E.2d 146, 85 Ohio Law Abs. 417, 19 O.O.2d 83. Criminal Law ⚷ 1166.16

In a criminal case, in the absence of an affirmative showing that the defendant was prejudiced thereby, a judgment of conviction will not be reversed because one of the officers to whose charge the jurors were committed during the night hours between sessions of their deliberations permitted some jurors to make telephone calls in his presence and within his hearing to members of their immediate families. State v. Sheppard (Ohio 1956) 165 Ohio St. 293, 135 N.E.2d 340, 59 O.O. 398, certiorari denied 77 S.Ct. 118, 352 U.S. 910, 1 L.Ed.2d 119, rehearing denied 77 S.Ct. 323, 352 U.S. 955, 1 L.Ed.2d 245. Criminal Law ⚷ 1174(5)

Statutory presumption that court officer's communication with jury in his charge or custody will be presumed to be prejudicial may be overcome by evidence and attendant facts and circumstances. State v. Weil (Cuyahoga 1950) 91 N.E.2d 277, 56 Ohio Law Abs. 136, appeal dismissed 153 Ohio St. 586, 92 N.E.2d 816, 42 O.O. 46. Criminal Law ⚷ 1163(6)

A trial court must protect defendants from inherently prejudicial publicity in the community and from disruptive influences in the courtroom, and its failure to do so prevents defendants from having a fair trial and denies them due process of law, entitling them to a new trial. Sheppard v. Maxwell (U.S.Ohio 1966) 86 S.Ct. 1507, 384 U.S. 333, 6 Ohio Misc. 231, 16 L.Ed.2d 600, 35 O.O.2d 431.

Presence of alternate juror in jury room for forty-five minutes did not require reversal of guilty verdict on constitutional grounds. Potter v. Perini (C.A.6 (Ohio) 1976) 545 F.2d 1048, 4 O.O.3d 110.

Prejudice to the accused as a matter of law will not be presumed from the fact that some of the jurors, while sequestered, were permitted to telephone their families. Sheppard v. Maxwell (C.A.6 (Ohio) 1965) 346 F.2d 707, certiorari granted 86 S.Ct. 289, 382 U.S. 916, 15 L.Ed.2d 231, remanded 86 S.Ct. 1507, 384 U.S. 333, 6 Ohio Misc. 231, 16 L.Ed.2d 600, 35 O.O.2d 431.

2945.831 Motion not necessary for appellate review

A motion for a new trial is not a necessary prerequisite to obtain appellate review of the sufficiency or weight of the evidence in the trial of a criminal case.

(128 v 141, eff. 1–1–60)

Cross References

Motion for new trial not prerequisite for appellate review, Crim R 33

Library References

Criminal Law ⚷1063(4).
Westlaw Topic No. 110.

Research References

Encyclopedias

OH Jur. 3d Criminal Law § 3549, Motion for New Trial Unnecessary.

Treatises and Practice Aids

Katz, Giannelli, Blair and Lipton, Baldwin's Ohio Practice, Criminal Law, § 80:9, Appellate Procedure.

Notes of Decisions

Waiver, failure to raise objections 1

1. Waiver, failure to raise objections

Where an accused fails to raise an objection as to venue prior to trial, and his motion for new trial is made on specified grounds which do not include an objection that the state failed to prove venue, the accused's right to raise an objection that the state did not prove venue is waived and the question of venue may not be raised for the first time in the court of appeals. State v. Loucks (Gallia 1971) 28 Ohio App.2d 77, 274 N.E.2d 773, 57 O.O.2d 160.

2945.832 Taking and recording exceptions—Repealed

(1986 H 412, eff. 3–17–87; 128 v 141)

CHAPTER 2947

JUDGMENT; SENTENCE

MAGISTRATE DEFINED

2947.01 Definition of magistrate

The definition of "magistrate" set forth in section 2931.01 of the Revised Code applies to Chapter 2947. of the Revised Code.

(1953 H 1, eff. 10–1–53)

ARREST OF JUDGMENT

2947.02 Motion in arrest

A judgment may be arrested by the court upon motion of the defendant, or upon the court's own motion, for either of the following causes:

(A) The offense charged is not within the jurisdiction of the court;

(B) The facts stated in the indictment or information do not constitute an offense.

(1953 H 1, eff. 10–1–53; GC 13450–1)

Historical and Statutory Notes

Pre–1953 H 1 Amendments: 113 v 196, Ch 29, § 1

Cross References

Arrest of judgment, Crim R 34
Motion for acquittal, Crim R 29
Motions, Crim R 47
Municipal court, grant by, 1901.13

Library References

Criminal Law ⚩966 to 976.
Westlaw Topic No. 110.
C.J.S. Criminal Law §§ 1453 to 1456.

Research References

Encyclopedias

OH Jur. 3d Criminal Law § 3217, Allowance or Denial in Particular Instances.

Treatises and Practice Aids

Katz, Giannelli, Blair and Lipton, Baldwin's Ohio Practice, Criminal Law, § 78:1, Introduction.

Katz, Giannelli, Blair and Lipton, Baldwin's Ohio Practice, Criminal Law, § 78:4, Procedural Requirements.

Katz, Giannelli, Blair and Lipton, Baldwin's Ohio Practice, Criminal Law, § 78:5, Alternative Remedies.

Katz, Giannelli, Blair and Lipton, Baldwin's Ohio Practice, Criminal Law, § 86:6, Motion for Judgment of Acquittal.

Law Review and Journal Commentaries

Symposium on Post–Conviction Remedies: Forward and Afterword, Lawrence Herman. 27 Ohio St L J 237 (Spring 1966).

Notes of Decisions

Limitation of actions 1

1. Limitation of actions

Where an affidavit charging a misdemeanor is filed after the expiration of the time of prosecution provided by a statute of limitations, the trial court is without jurisdiction to entertain such action; a plea of guilty to the offense is a nullity. City of Akron v. Akins (Summit 1968) 15 Ohio App.2d 168, 239 N.E.2d 430, 44 O.O.2d 299. Municipal Corporations ⚩ 636

2947.03 When judgment not arrested

A judgment shall not be arrested for a defect in form. Motions in arrest of judgment shall be made within three days after the verdict is rendered.

(1953 H 1, eff. 10–1–53; GC 13450–2)

Historical and Statutory Notes

Pre–1953 H 1 Amendments: 113 v 197, Ch 29, § 2

Cross References

Arrest of judgment, Crim R 34

Library References

Criminal Law ⚩967, 974(2).
Westlaw Topic No. 110.
C.J.S. Criminal Law §§ 1454 to 1456.

Research References

Encyclopedias

OH Jur. 3d Criminal Law § 3218, Time Within Which Motion Must be Made.

Treatises and Practice Aids

Katz, Giannelli, Blair and Lipton, Baldwin's Ohio Practice, Criminal Law, § 78:1, Introduction.

Katz, Giannelli, Blair and Lipton, Baldwin's Ohio Practice, Criminal Law, § 78:5, Alternative Remedies.

Notes of Decisions

Grounds for motion 1

---

1. Grounds for motion

Arrest of judgment when available as provided by this section, may be asserted upon two grounds stated under GC 13450–1 (RC 2947.02). State v. Burton (Clark 1939) 30 Ohio Law Abs. 165. Criminal Law ⚷ 968(1)

2947.04 Effect of arrest of judgment

When a judgment is arrested, it places the defendant in a like position with respect to the prosecution as before the indictment or information was found. If, from the evidence at the trial, there is reason to believe that the defendant is guilty of an offense, the trial court shall order him to enter into a recognizance with sufficient surety for his appearance at the first day of the next term of such court, or the court having jurisdiction of the offense if within this state, otherwise the defendant shall be discharged.

(1953 H 1, eff. 10–1–53; GC 13450–3)

Historical and Statutory Notes

Pre–1953 H 1 Amendments: 113 v 197, Ch 29, § 3

Cross References

Arrest of judgment, Crim R 34

Library References

Criminal Law ⚷976.

Westlaw Topic No. 110.

Research References

Encyclopedias

OH Jur. 3d Criminal Law § 2191, Arrest of Judgment.

OH Jur. 3d Criminal Law § 3219, Effect of Arrest of Judgment.

Treatises and Practice Aids

Katz, Giannelli, Blair and Lipton, Baldwin's Ohio Practice, Criminal Law, § 78:1, Introduction.

Katz, Giannelli, Blair and Lipton, Baldwin's Ohio Practice, Criminal Law, § 78:6, Effect of Arrest of Judgment.

SENTENCING

2947.05 Defendant's and victim's rights before sentence—Repealed

(1995 S 2, eff. 7–1–96; 1994 S 186, eff. 10–12–94; 1953 H 1, eff. 10–1–53; GC 13451–1)

Historical and Statutory Notes

Ed. Note: See now Crim R 32 for provisions somewhat analogous to former 2947.05.

Pre–1953 H 1 Amendments: 113 v 197, Ch 30, § 1

2947.051 Victim impact statement for use in sentencing

(A) In all criminal cases in which a person is convicted of or pleads guilty to a felony, if the offender, in committing the offense, caused, attempted to cause, threatened to cause, or created a risk of physical harm to the victim of the offense, the court, prior to sentencing the offender, shall order the preparation of a victim impact statement by the department of probation of the county in which the victim of the offense resides, by the court's own regular probation officer, or by a victim assistance program that is operated by the state, any county or municipal corporation, or any other governmental entity. The court, in accordance with sections 2929.13 and 2929.19 of the Revised Code, shall consider the victim impact statement in determining the sentence to be imposed upon the offender.

(B) Each victim impact statement prepared under this section shall identify the victim of the offense, itemize any economic loss suffered by the victim as a result of the offense, identify any physical injury suffered by the victim as a result of the offense and the seriousness and permanence of the injury, identify any change in the victim's personal welfare or familial relationships as a result of the offense and any psychological impact experienced by the victim or the victim's family as a result of the offense, and contain any other information related to the impact of the offense upon the victim that the court requires. Each victim impact statement prepared under this section shall include any statement made by the victim pursuant to section 2930.13 of the Revised Code.

(C) A victim impact statement prepared under this section shall be kept confidential and is not a public record as defined in section 149.43 of the Revised Code. However, the court may furnish copies of the statement to both the defendant or the defendant's counsel and the prosecuting attorney. Immediately following the imposition of sentence upon the defendant, the defendant, the defendant's counsel, and the prosecuting attorney shall return to the court the copies of the victim impact statement that were made available to the defendant, the counsel, or the prosecuting attorney.

(1995 S 2, eff. 7–1–96; 1994 S 186, eff. 10–12–94; 1982 H 269, § 4, eff. 7–1–83; 1982 S 199; 1980 S 384)

Uncodified Law

1982 H 269, § 4, eff. 1–5–83, amended 1982 S 199, § 10, eff. 1–5–83, to read, in part: " [2947.051], as amended by [1982 S 199],... shall take effect on July 1, 1983, and shall apply only to offenses committed on or after July 1, 1983."

Historical and Statutory Notes

Amendment Note: 1995 S 2 rewrote this section, which previously read:

"(A) In all criminal cases in which a person is convicted of, pleads guilty to and the plea is accepted to, or pleads no contest to and is found guilty of a felony, the court, prior to sentencing the offender, shall order the preparation of a victim impact statement by the department of probation of the county in which the victim of the offense resides, by the court's own regular probation officer, or by a victim assistance program that is operated by the state, any county or municipal corporation, or any other governmental entity if the offender caused, attempted to cause, threatened to cause, or created the risk of physical harm to the victim of the offense. The court, in accordance with sections 2929.12 and 2929.14 of the Revised Code, shall consider the victim impact statement in determining the sentence to be imposed upon the offender.

"(B) Each victim impact statement shall identify the victim of the offense, itemize any economic loss suffered by the victim as a result of the offense, identify any physical injury suffered by the victim as a result of the offense and the seriousness and permanence of the injury, identify any change in the victim's personal welfare or familial relationships as a result of the offense and any psychological impact experienced by the victim or the victim's family as a result of the offense, and contain any other information related to the impact of the offense upon the victim that the court requires. Each victim impact statement prepared under this section shall include any statement made by the victim pursuant to section 2930.13 of the Revised Code.

"(C) A victim impact statement shall be kept confidential and is not a public record as defined in section 149.43 of the Revised Code. However, the court may furnish copies of the statement to both the defendant or his counsel and the prosecuting attorney. Any copies of a victim impact statement that are made available to the defendant or his counsel or to the prosecuting attorney shall be returned by the person to whom they were made available to the court immediately following the imposition of sentence upon the defendant."

Amendment Note: 1994 S 186 added the final sentence in division (B).

Cross References

Sentencing, Crim R 32

Victims' rights, identification of person preparing victim impact statement, 2930.12

Victims' rights, statement prior to judicial release, 2930.17

Library References

Records ⚷32.

Sentencing and Punishment ⚷286, 310, 361.

Westlaw Topic Nos. 326, 350H.

C.J.S. Criminal Law §§ 1460, 1472, 1479 to 1480, 1492, 1506, 1508, 1510, 1530, 1534 to 1538, 1779.

C.J.S. Records §§ 65, 67 to 75.

Research References

ALR Library

79 ALR 5th 33, Victim Impact Evidence in Capital Sentencing Hearings--Post-Payne v. Tennessee.

Encyclopedias

OH Jur. 3d Criminal Law § 11, Right to Equal Protection.

OH Jur. 3d Criminal Law § 3296, Victim Impact Statement.

Treatises and Practice Aids

Hennenberg & Reinhart, Ohio Criminal Defense Motions F 13.18, Motion in Limine-Victim Impact Statement-Death Penalty Motions.

Adrine & Ruden, Ohio Domestic Violence Law § 12:16, Victim Impact Statement.

Law Review and Journal Commentaries

Admitting Victim Impact Evidence in Capital Cases, Victor L. Streib. 3 Crim L J Ohio 149 (October 1991).

Do the Victims of Crime Have a Role to Play in Criminal Justice After Booth v Maryland?, Charles O. Monk. 59 Clev B J 9 (November 1987).

From Botany Bay to Booth: Defendants, Victims and Justice, George E. Burns Jr. 59 Clev B J 8 (November 1987).

Sentencing criminals: The constitutionality of victim impact statements. 60 Mo L Rev 731 (1995).

State v. Huertas—The Final Indignity: The Reluctance of Courts to Allow Victim Impact Statements in Death Penalty Cases, Note. 17 Ohio N U L Rev 211 (1990).

Notes of Decisions

---

1. Constitutional issues

Presence of defendant, who was convicted of corruption of a minor, was not constitutionally or statutorily required when unsworn oral victim impact statements were presented to trial court during sentencing proceedings; statements did not constitute a critical stage of the sentencing procedure, oral statements were comparable to written victim impact statements, defendant never objected to presentation of testimony, and defendant relied on testimony. State v. Wallace (Ohio App. 5 Dist., Richland, 07-30-2003) No. 2002CA0072, 2003-Ohio-4119, 2003 WL 21787573, Unreported. Sentencing And Punishment ⚷ 342

Defendant failed to demonstrate that counsel was ineffective in not ensuring that a victim impact statement was prepared in prosecution for aggravated burglary and misdemeanor assault; counsel's decision may have been a strategic choice based on the belief that such a statement would have done more harm than good, and defendant failed to demonstrate that he was prejudiced by the lack of a victim impact statement. State v. Shaffner (Ohio App. 12 Dist., Madison, 07-21-2003) No. CA2002-07-012, 2003-Ohio-3872, 2003 WL 21687821, Unreported. Criminal Law ⚷ 641.13(7)

Defendant was given adequate notice and opportunity to respond to victim impact evidence where defendant responded in the negative when asked if he wanted to speak prior to imposition of sentence and court asked defendant after reading one of the victim impact letters if there was any reason why sentence should not be imposed at that time. State v. Patterson (Ohio App. 10 Dist., 04-04-1996) 110 Ohio App.3d 264, 673 N.E.2d 1001, dismissed, appeal not allowed 76 Ohio St.3d 1493, 670 N.E.2d 240. Sentencing And Punishment ⚷ 359

Closing remarks by the prosecutor during the sentencing hearing for a convicted murderer and sex offender, in which the prosecutor recites from religious tracts carried by the victim and notes that the victim's voter registration card, thrown to the ground with the tracts by the murderer, showed that the victim was involved in his community and believed people have a right to sit in a public park without being beaten and killed, are comments about the victim's character that are held unnecessary to the jury's understanding of the circumstances of the crime; as with a "victim impact statement," the prosecutor's extensive comments could cause the jury to impose a capital penalty because of circumstances the murderer was unaware of, and that were "irrelevant to the decision to kill"; consequently, the comments violated the murderer's rights under the Eighth Amendment. South Carolina v. Gathers (U.S.S.C. 1989) 109 S.Ct. 2207, 490 U.S. 805, 104 L.Ed.2d 876, rehearing denied 110 S.Ct. 24, 492 U.S. 938, 106 L.Ed.2d 636.

2. Victim impact evidence

Victim impact statements by victim and victim's father were permissible under statute allowing for impact statements from victim and victim's family. State v. Bunch (Ohio App. 7 Dist., Mahoning, 06-24-2005) No. 02 CA 196, 2005-Ohio-3309, 2005 WL 1523844, Unreported, appeal allowed 107 Ohio St.3d 1680, 839 N.E.2d 401, 2005-Ohio-6480. Sentencing And Punishment ⚿ 361

Introduction of testimony of the long-range effects of aggravated robbery on victim in the state's case-in-chief did not deny defendant his constitutional right to a fair trial; testimony was necessary to prove serious physical harm element of offense. State v. Ridgeway (Ohio App. 8 Dist., Cuyahoga, 02-05-2004) No. 82713, 2004-Ohio-497, 2004 WL 229520, Unreported, appeal not allowed 102 Ohio St.3d 1484, 810 N.E.2d 967, 2004-Ohio-3069. Robbery ⚿ 23(2)

In prosecution for multiple sex offenses involving young teenage victims, trial court's failure to permit defendant to view victim impact statements did not constitute plain error, where trial court placed on the record those aspects of the victim impact statements on which it relied to impose sentence, and thus court in effect advised defendant of the content of the statements and further gave defendant the opportunity to respond. State v. Randlett (Ohio App. 10 Dist., Franklin, 12-18-2003) No. 03AP-385, No. 03AP-388, No. 03AP-386, No. 03AP-387, 2003-Ohio-6934, 2003 WL 22976553, Unreported, appeal not allowed 102 Ohio St.3d 1447, 808 N.E.2d 398, 2004-Ohio-2263, habeas corpus dismissed 2006 WL 1805937, appeal not allowed 110 Ohio St.3d 1443, 852 N.E.2d 190, 2006-Ohio-3862. Criminal Law ⚿ 1042

Trial court acted within its discretion in electing not to order victim impact statements prior to sentencing in prosecution for multiple counts of attempted murder and felonious assault, where the interested victims appeared and testified at trial, and thus trial court had knowledge of the type of information which would have been presented in victim impact statements. State v. Sealey (Ohio App. 11 Dist., Lake, 12-12-2003) No. 2002-L-100, 2003-Ohio-6697, 2003 WL 22931376, Unreported. Sentencing And Punishment ⚿ 361

In imposing maximum five-year sentence on defendant following conviction for aggravated vehicular assault, trial court was permitted to consider alleged victim's statements as reported in victim impact statement, even though such statements did not have evidentiary support. State v. Leonard (Ohio App. 11 Dist., Ashtabula, 11-21-2003) No. 2002-A-0073, 2003-Ohio-6226, 2003 WL 22763577, Unreported. Sentencing And Punishment ⚿ 361

Trial court's failure to order preparation of victim impact statement in prosecution for aggravated burglary and misdemeanor assault did not amount to plain error, despite defendant's claims that victim impact statement would have revealed that alleged victims, defendant's former girlfriend and the couple's minor child, would suffer economically and socially during defendant's incarceration; defendant failed to demonstrate that he was prejudiced by the lack of a victim impact statement, and all of the information which defendant claimed would have been brought out in a victim impact statement was within defendant's knowledge and could have been raised at trial. State v. Shaffner (Ohio App. 12 Dist., Madison, 07-21-2003) No. CA2002-07-012, 2003-Ohio-3872, 2003 WL 21687821, Unreported. Criminal Law ⚿ 1042

Trial court error, if any, in considering victim impact statement regarding a boy defendant was alleged to have molested, but from which no charges were filed, was harmless; there was no evidence the court considered the statements about the impact of the molestation on the boy when it imposed sentence, there was no evidence that the court imposed a harsher sentence based on statements about the boy, and the court could consider the "the history, character, and condition of the offender and his need for correctional or rehabilitative treatment" when imposing sentence. State v. Byrd (Ohio App. 12 Dist., Warren, 02-03-2003) No. CA2001-02-012, No. CA86-03-020, 2003-Ohio-511, 2003 WL 231301, Unreported. Criminal Law ⚿ 1177

Record supported finding that trial court did not consider and weigh victim-impact statements in determining sentence in capital murder trial; record indicated that trial court had already accepted the jury's penalty verdict and had sentenced defendant to death before hearing any victim-impact statements. State v. Leonard (Ohio, 12-08-2004) 104 Ohio St.3d 54, 818 N.E.2d 229, 2004-Ohio-6235. Sentencing And Punishment ⚿ 1763

To extent that incidental mention, in capital murder prosecution, of fact that victim's son, like victim a police officer, had arrived at murder scene shortly after shooting, could be said to constitute victim impact evidence, its admission did not prejudice defendant, where reference to victim's son was not detailed, not inflammatory, and not focus of witness' testimony. State v. Gross (Ohio, 10-30-2002) 97 Ohio St.3d 121, 776 N.E.2d 1061, 2002-Ohio-5524, reconsideration denied 97 Ohio St.3d 1486, 780 N.E.2d 288, 2002-Ohio-6866, certiorari denied 123 S.Ct. 2079, 538 U.S. 1037, 155 L.Ed.2d 1068, rehearing denied 124 S.Ct. 20, 539 U.S. 976, 156 L.Ed.2d 685. Criminal Law ⚿ 1169.1(3)

Emotional responses of witnesses in guilt phase of capital murder prosecution did not amount to improper victim impact evidence. State v. Gross (Ohio, 10-30-2002) 97 Ohio St.3d 121, 776 N.E.2d 1061, 2002-Ohio-5524, reconsideration denied 97 Ohio St.3d 1486, 780 N.E.2d 288, 2002-Ohio-6866, certiorari denied 123 S.Ct. 2079, 538 U.S. 1037, 155 L.Ed.2d 1068, rehearing denied 124 S.Ct. 20, 539 U.S. 976, 156 L.Ed.2d 685. Homicide ⚿ 984

Autopsy photographs, eyewitness' testimony to effect that upon her arrival at murder scene, victim had rolled over and looked at her before he died, and victim's clothes and personal belongings were all admissible in both guilt and penalty phases of capital murder prosecution, despite defendant's contention that they amounted to impermissible victim impact evidence, where all such evidence and testimony established circumstances of the crime. State v. Gross (Ohio, 10-30-2002) 97 Ohio St.3d 121, 776 N.E.2d 1061, 2002-Ohio-5524, reconsideration denied 97 Ohio St.3d 1486, 780 N.E.2d 288, 2002-Ohio-6866, certiorari denied 123 S.Ct. 2079, 538 U.S. 1037, 155 L.Ed.2d 1068, rehearing denied 124 S.Ct. 20, 539 U.S. 976, 156 L.Ed.2d 685. Homicide ⚷ 997; Homicide ⚷ 998; Sentencing And Punishment ⚷ 1759

Just because a victim impact statement is included in a presentence investigation report (PSI) does not mean that a defendant will have access to it, and thus statutes governing victim impact statements and PSIs do not violate a defendant's right to equal protection of the laws on the ground that statutes can produce a classification between defendants who receive sentencing information and those that do not because some victim impact statements are opted out of PSI. State v. Stewart (Ohio App. 12 Dist., 08-12-2002) 149 Ohio App.3d 1, 775 N.E.2d 563, 2002-Ohio-4124, appeal not allowed 98 Ohio St.3d 1409, 781 N.E.2d 1018, 2003-Ohio-60. Constitutional Law ⚷ 250.3(1); Sentencing And Punishment ⚷ 206

Trial court's refusal to allow defendant access to victim impact statements did not violate due process. State v. Stewart (Ohio App. 12 Dist., 08-12-2002) 149 Ohio App.3d 1, 775 N.E.2d 563, 2002-Ohio-4124, appeal not allowed 98 Ohio St.3d 1409, 781 N.E.2d 1018, 2003-Ohio-60. Constitutional Law ⚷ 270(1); Sentencing And Punishment ⚷ 244

Defendant was not entitled to access to victim impact statements, although trial court considered those statements, as the facts ultimately relied upon by the trial court in sentencing defendant were otherwise reflected in the psychological evaluations and the presentence investigation report (PSI). State v. Stewart (Ohio App. 12 Dist., 08-12-2002) 149 Ohio App.3d 1, 775 N.E.2d 563, 2002-Ohio-4124, appeal not allowed 98 Ohio St.3d 1409, 781 N.E.2d 1018, 2003-Ohio-60. Sentencing And Punishment ⚷ 244

Trial court erred in failing to order preparation of victim-impact statement for purposes of sentencing defendant convicted of robbery and abduction, but such error was harmless given that trial testimony provided trial court with information about economic harm and physical injury suffered by victims and that defendant did not point to any other information that would have been set forth in victim-impact statement that could have worked to his advantage. State v. Garrison (Ohio App. 2 Dist., 09-19-1997) 123 Ohio App.3d 11, 702 N.E.2d 1222. Sentencing And Punishment ⚷ 361; Criminal Law ⚷ 1177

Admitting evidence that murder victim's friend had close relationship with victim and that they borrowed each other's clothes did not violate rule precluding guilt-phase "victim impact" evidence, where it was relevant for another purpose, namely, to explain why victim was wearing friend's jacket when she was killed and jacket taken from her. State v. Keene (Ohio, 05-13-1998) 81 Ohio St.3d 646, 693 N.E.2d 246, 1998-Ohio-342, motion stricken 82 Ohio St.3d 1437, 694 N.E.2d 1373, stay granted 82 Ohio St.3d 1445, 695 N.E.2d 267, certiorari denied 119 S.Ct. 350, 525 U.S. 936, 142 L.Ed.2d 288, denial of post-conviction relief affirmed 1999 WL 55711, dismissed, appeal not allowed 85 Ohio St.3d 1496, 710 N.E.2d 716, habeas corpus dismissed 2004 WL 3325797. Sentencing And Punishment ⚷ 310

Trial court abused its discretion by finding criminal defense attorney to be in contempt when attorney attempted to make objection during recitation of victim impact statement to protect client's interests, as attorney's behavior was not a substantial disruption of judicial process. In re Contempt of Morris (Ohio App. 8 Dist., 04-22-1996) 110 Ohio App.3d 475, 674 N.E.2d 761. Contempt ⚷ 10

Trial court erred in failing to comply with requirement that victim impact statement be prepared prior to sentencing. State v. Patterson (Ohio App. 10 Dist., 04-04-1996) 110 Ohio App.3d 264, 673 N.E.2d 1001, dismissed, appeal not allowed 76 Ohio St.3d 1493, 670 N.E.2d 240. Sentencing And Punishment ⚷ 361

Defendant was not prejudiced by court's failure to prepare victim impact statement where there was no objection during sentencing or request that victim impact statement be prepared, and where victim testified at trial and his mother made oral statement to the court at sentencing. State v. Patterson (Ohio App. 10 Dist., 04-04-1996) 110 Ohio App.3d 264, 673 N.E.2d 1001, dismissed, appeal not allowed 76 Ohio St.3d 1493, 670 N.E.2d 240. Criminal Law ⚷ 1177

Where maximum sentence was imposed, reviewing court could not determine that defendant was not prejudiced by court's error in considering victim impact letter which related to charge on which defendant was acquitted. State v. Patterson (Ohio App. 10 Dist., 04-04-1996) 110 Ohio App.3d 264, 673 N.E.2d 1001, dismissed, appeal not allowed 76 Ohio St.3d 1493, 670 N.E.2d 240. Criminal Law ⚷ 1177

Although record did not affirmatively demonstrate that trial court in sentencing defendant for attempted murder considered statement of mother of victim of murder of which defendant was acquitted, fact that it did so could be inferred from court's statement at sentencing hearing that it had considered the letter to be a victim impact statement, and consideration of that statement was improper. State v. Patterson (Ohio App. 10 Dist., 04-04-1996) 110 Ohio App.3d 264, 673 N.E.2d 1001, dismissed, appeal not allowed 76 Ohio St.3d 1493, 670 N.E.2d 240. Sentencing And Punishment ⚷ 310

True victim-impact evidence shall be considered by trial court prior to imposing sentence on defendant, not during guilt phase of proceedings. State v. Fautenberry (Ohio, 07-05-1995) 72 Ohio St.3d 435, 650 N.E.2d 878, 1995-Ohio-209, certiorari denied 116 S.Ct. 534, 516 U.S. 996, 133 L.Ed.2d 439, reconsideration denied 75 Ohio St.3d 1475, 663 N.E.2d 1302, dismissal of post-conviction relief affirmed 1998 WL 906395, dismissed, appeal not allowed 85 Ohio St.3d 1477, 709 N.E.2d 849, reconsideration denied 86 Ohio St.3d 1422, 711 N.E.2d 1015. Sentencing And Punishment ⚷ 1763

Evidence which depicts both circumstances surrounding commission of murder and also impact of murder on victim's family may be admissible during both guilt and sentencing phases. State v. Fautenberry (Ohio, 07-05-1995) 72 Ohio St.3d 435, 650 N.E.2d 878, 1995-Ohio-209, certiorari denied 116 S.Ct. 534, 516 U.S. 996, 133 L.Ed.2d 439, reconsideration denied 75 Ohio St.3d 1475, 663 N.E.2d 1302, dismissal of post-conviction relief affirmed 1998 WL 906395, dismissed, appeal not allowed 85 Ohio St.3d 1477, 709 N.E.2d 849, reconsideration denied 86 Ohio St.3d 1422, 711 N.E.2d 1015. Homicide ⚷ 975; Sentencing And Punishment ⚷ 309; Sentencing And Punishment ⚷ 310

Although portion of victim-impact statements relating to sentencing recommendations should not have been permitted in capital murder prosecution, such error did not warrant reversal, particularly as three-judge panel's decision did not demonstrate that they contemplated or relied upon victim-impact evidence which was available to them. State v. Fautenberry (Ohio, 07-05-1995) 72 Ohio St.3d 435, 650 N.E.2d 878, 1995-Ohio-209, certiorari denied 116 S.Ct. 534, 516 U.S. 996, 133 L.Ed.2d 439, reconsideration denied 75 Ohio St.3d 1475, 663 N.E.2d 1302, dismissal of post-conviction relief affirmed 1998 WL 906395, dismissed, appeal not allowed 85 Ohio St.3d 1477, 709 N.E.2d 849, reconsideration denied 86 Ohio St.3d 1422, 711 N.E.2d 1015. Sentencing And Punishment ⚷ 1789(9)

Victim impact evidence is not improperly considered in sentencing a defendant on aggravated murder and aggravated robbery charges since (1) the trial judge did not state that he considered such evidence as to the aggravated murder sentence; (2) the judge was required to consider such evidence for purposes of the aggravated robbery sentence; (3) RC 2945.07, which requires a victim impact statement in most felony convictions, does not prohibit such evidence in a capital offense where the death penalty is not sought; and (4) Evid R 404 does not apply to sentencing hearings. State v. Griffin (Coshocton 1992) 73 Ohio App.3d 546, 597 N.E.2d 1178, dismissed, jurisdictional motion overruled 64 Ohio St.3d 1428, 594 N.E.2d 970.

A prosecutor's closing remark during the guilt phase of an aggravated murder prosecution regarding the impact of the death of one of the victims on her son because he watched as his mother was being stabbed constitutes a recitation of the facts brought out during trial rather than a victim-impact statement. State v. Evans (Ohio 1992) 63 Ohio St.3d 231, 586 N.E.2d 1042, rehearing denied 63 Ohio St.3d 1450, 589 N.E.2d 393, certiorari denied 113 S.Ct. 246, 506 U.S. 886, 121 L.Ed.2d 179.

Defendant, who entered negotiated plea of guilty to aggravated vehicular homicide, should not have been ordered to make restitution in the amount of $10,000; there was no due process ascertainment that amount of restitution bore reasonable relationship to loss suffered but, rather, trial court relied on figures presented in victim impact statement prepared by county probation department to arrive at restitution amount and that statement merely estimated hospital, medical and funeral expenses incurred by victim's family and did not itemize economic loss suffered as a result of offense. State v. Williams (Clark 1986) 34 Ohio App.3d 33, 516 N.E.2d 1270. Sentencing And Punishment ⚷ 2188(4)

A state may properly conclude that for the jury to assess meaningfully the defendant's moral culpability and blameworthiness, it should have before it at the sentencing phase evidence of the specific harm caused by the defendant; there is nothing unfair about allowing the jury to bear in mind that harm at the same time it considers the mitigating evidence introduced by the defendant; therefore, a state may legitimately conclude that victim impact evidence is relevant to the jury's decision whether to impose the death penalty. Payne v. Tennessee (U.S.Tenn. 1991) 111 S.Ct. 2597, 501 U.S. 808, 115 L.Ed.2d 720, rehearing denied 112 S.Ct. 28, 501 U.S. 1277, 115 L.Ed.2d 1110.

Victims' testimony regarding the fear they experienced as defendant fired a gun into their home after threatening to kill them and their children was not improper victim-impact testimony, at guilt phase of prosecution for one count of improperly discharging a firearm into an occupied structure and two counts of felonious assault. State v. Dubose (Ohio App. 7 Dist., Mahoning, 06-06-2002) No. 00-C.A.-60, 2002-Ohio-3020, 2002 WL 1376248, Unreported, appeal not allowed 96 Ohio St.3d 1525, 775 N.E.2d 864, 2002-Ohio-5099, motion to reopen denied 2002-Ohio-6613, 2002 WL 31718806, appeal not allowed 98 Ohio St.3d 1475, 784 N.E.2d 708, 2003-Ohio-904. Criminal Law ⚷ 338(7)

3. Presentence report

It is within the trial court's discretion whether to make a presentence report and a victim impact statement available to the defendant. State v. Bayless (Wayne 1982) 4 Ohio App.3d 301, 448 N.E.2d 511, 4 O.B.R. 552. Constitutional Law ⚷ 270(2); Sentencing And Punishment ⚷ 294

4. Deceased victim generally

Admission in capital murder trial of victim's dying declarations, pursuant to firmly rooted hearsay exception for dying declarations, did not violate defendant's rights under Confrontation Clause. Byrd v. Collins (C.A.6 (Ohio), 04-06-2000) 209 F.3d 486, rehearing en banc denied 227 F.3d 756, certiorari denied 121 S.Ct. 786, 531 U.S. 1082, 148 L.Ed.2d 682, rehearing denied 121 S.Ct. 1176, 531 U.S. 1186, 148 L.Ed.2d 1034. Criminal Law ⚷ 662.8

2947.052 Victim or family member to be notified of electronically monitored early release—Repealed

(1994 S 186, eff. 10–12–94; 1992 H 725, eff. 4–16–93)

2947.06 Testimony after verdict to mitigate penalty; reports confidential

(A)(1) The trial court may hear testimony in mitigation of a sentence at the term of conviction or plea or at the next term. The prosecuting attorney may offer testimony on behalf of the state to give the court a true understanding of the case. The court shall determine whether sentence should immediately be imposed. The court on its own motion may direct the department of probation of the county in which the defendant resides, or its own regular probation officer, to make any inquiries and presentence investigation reports that the court requires concerning the defendant.

(2) The provisions of section 2951.03 of the Revised Code shall govern the preparation of, the provision, receipt, and retention of copies of, the use of, and the confidentiality, nonpublic record character, and sealing of a presentence investigation report prepared pursuant to division (A)(1) of this section.

(B) The court may appoint not more than two psychologists or psychiatrists to make any reports concerning the defendant that the court requires for the purpose of determining the disposition of the case. Each psychologist or psychiatrist shall receive a fee to be fixed by the court and taxed in the costs of the case. The psychologist's or psychiatrist's reports shall be made in writing, in open court, and in the presence of the defendant, except in misdemeanor cases in which sentence may be pronounced in the absence of the defendant. A copy of each report of a psychologist or psychiatrist may be furnished to the defendant, if present, who may examine the persons making the report, under oath, as to any matter or thing contained in the report.

(2002 H 490, eff. 1–1–04; 1996 S 269, eff. 7–1–96; 1995 S 2, eff. 7–1–96; 1987 H 73, § 5, eff. 10–1–89; 1987 H 73, § 1; 1982 H 269, § 4, S 199; 130 v H 686; 1953 H 1; GC 13451–2)

Historical and Statutory Notes

Ed. Note: The repeal of this section by 1982 S 199, eff. 1–5–83, was rescinded by 1982 H 269, § 4, eff. 1–5–83. See *Baldwin's Ohio Legislative Service*, 1982 Laws of Ohio, pages 5–363 and 5–539.

Pre–1953 H 1 Amendments: 113 v 197, Ch 30, § 2

Amendment Note: 2002 H 490 substituted "should" for "ought" before "immediately", and deleted "or whether, if the offense is a misdemeanor, to place the defendant on probation" in division (A)(1); and made other nonsubstantive changes.

Amendment Note: 1996 S 269 designated divisions (A)(1) and (B); added division (A)(2); and deleted the fifth and sixth sentences in division (A)(1), which prior thereto read:

"The presentence investigation reports shall be confidential. The court shall permit the prosecuting attorney and the defendant or the defendant's counsel, as provided in section 2951.03 of the Revised Code, to read the presentence investigation report."

Amendment Note: 1995 S 2 inserted "whether, if the offense is a misdemeanor," in the first paragraph; deleted "and do not have to be furnished to the defendant or his counsel or to the prosecuting attorney unless the court in its discretion so orders" after "confidential" in the first paragraph; added the sixth sentence in the first paragraph; and made other nonsubstantive changes.

Cross References

Appeals based on felony sentencing guidelines, 2953.08

Appointments by court of common pleas, 2301.12

Delinquency adjudications or dispositions, court records of, availability, 2152.71

Imposing sentence for a capital offense, 2929.03

Offender background investigation and report in lieu of presentence investigation report, AIDS policy, 5120.16

Presentence investigation report, Crim R 32.2

Presentence investigation report, right of defendant or counsel to read; confidentiality, 2951.03

Probation department records, availability, 2151.14

Sentence, Crim R 32

Sentencing, Ch 2929

Victim impact statement, availability, 2152.19

Victim impact statement, presentence investigation report, 2930.13

Youth services department records, availability, 2152.18

Library References

Records ⚷32.
Sentencing and Punishment ⚷275 to 301.
Westlaw Topic Nos. 326, 350H.
C.J.S. Criminal Law §§ 1488, 1491, 1506 to 1510, 1544, 1554, 1564.
C.J.S. Records §§ 65, 67 to 75.

Research References

Encyclopedias

OH Jur. 3d Criminal Law § 3968, Items and Amounts Taxable, Generally.

Treatises and Practice Aids

Katz, Giannelli, Blair and Lipton, Baldwin's Ohio Practice, Criminal Law, § 77:4, Experts—Capital Cases.

Katz, Giannelli, Blair and Lipton, Baldwin's Ohio Practice, Criminal Law, § 115:7, Presentence Investigation and Report.

Katz, Giannelli, Blair and Lipton, Baldwin's Ohio Practice, Criminal Law, § 125:10, Expert Witnesses.

Katz, Giannelli, Blair and Lipton, Baldwin's Ohio Practice, Criminal Law, § 125:13, Mental Examination.

Giannelli and Snyder, Baldwin's Ohio Practice, Evidence, R 702, Testimony by Experts.

Giannelli and Snyder, Baldwin's Ohio Practice, Evidence, § 702.7, Court-Appointed Experts.

Notes of Decisions

1. Constitutional issues

RC 2929.024 and 2929.03(D)(1) are wholly independent provisions. A court, when requested by a defendant to order a presentence investigation or to appoint a psychologist or psychiatrist to conduct a mental examination pursuant to RC 2929.03(D)(1) and 2947.06, is not required by the constitution or the provisions of RC 2929.024 to appoint a psychiatrist or psychologist of the defendant's own choosing. Rather, additional expert services must be provided to an indigent defendant only if the court determines, within its sound discretion, that such services "are reasonably necessary for the proper representation of a defendant" at the sentencing hearing, pursuant to RC 2929.024. State v. Esparza (Ohio 1988) 39 Ohio St.3d 8, 529 N.E.2d 192, rehearing denied 39 Ohio St.3d 725, 534 N.E.2d 359, certiorari denied 109 S.Ct. 1657, 490 U.S. 1012, 104 L.Ed.2d 171.

In conducting a mitigation hearing, under RC 2929.03(D), a court, having appointed a psychiatrist and a psychologist pursuant to RC 2947.06, is not constitutionally required to appoint at state expense an additional psychiatrist of the defendant's choosing. State v. Downs (Ohio 1977) 51 Ohio St.2d 47, 364 N.E.2d 1140, 5 O.O.3d 30, vacated 98 S.Ct. 3133, 438 U.S. 909, 57 L.Ed.2d 1153.

Where statute on probation revocation, such as RC 2947.06, before amendment, requires notice to criminal defendant that an investigation of his conduct has been made, report submitted, and report's content made available for examination—all as precondition to the use of report on hearing—and statutory notice has not been given, it is an abuse of discretion amounting to a denial of due process and prejudicial error for trial court to allow use of report at the hearing on revocation. State v. Smith (Cuyahoga 1972) 29 Ohio App.2d 241, 281 N.E.2d 17, 58 O.O.2d 447.

2. Presentence investigation

Any error committed in including prosecutor's death penalty recommendation in presentence investigation report for defendant convicted of capital murder constituted harmless error, as it did not appear that trial court placed any reliance on prosecutor's recommendation. State v. Eley (Ohio, 12-18-1996) 77 Ohio St.3d 174, 672 N.E.2d 640, 1996-Ohio-323, reconsideration denied 77 Ohio St.3d 1549, 674 N.E.2d 1187, certiorari denied 117 S.Ct. 2522, 521 U.S. 1124, 138 L.Ed.2d 1023, dismissal of post-conviction relief affirmed 2001-Ohio-3447, 2001 WL 1497095, appeal not allowed 94 Ohio St.3d 1506, 764 N.E.2d 1036, 2002-Ohio-5738. Sentencing And Punishment ⚷ 1789(9)

Presentence investigation report for defendant convicted of capital murder properly included information regarding former charges brought against defendant that were dismissed. State v. Eley (Ohio, 12-18-1996) 77 Ohio St.3d 174, 672 N.E.2d 640, 1996-Ohio-323, reconsideration denied 77 Ohio St.3d 1549, 674 N.E.2d 1187, certiorari denied 117 S.Ct. 2522, 521 U.S. 1124, 138 L.Ed.2d 1023, dismissal of post-conviction relief affirmed 2001-Ohio-3447, 2001 WL 1497095, appeal not allowed 94 Ohio St.3d 1506, 764 N.E.2d 1036, 2002-Ohio-5738. Sentencing And Punishment ⚷ 288

Under RC 2929.03(D), RC 2929.03(E) and RC 2929.04(B), the court is required to order a presentence investigation and a psychiatric examination to be made, and to be submitted to the court pursuant to RC 2947.06. State v. Downs (Ohio 1977) 51 Ohio St.2d 47, 364 N.E.2d 1140, 5 O.O.3d 30, vacated 98 S.Ct. 3133, 438 U.S. 909, 57 L.Ed.2d 1153.

Suspension of imposition of sentence is a matter entirely within the discretion of the trial judge, and for that purpose he may conduct an examination of witnesses, with or without the help of counsel; call witnesses other than those presented by the prosecutor, or counsel for the defendant; and make an independent probation inquiry of such scope as he deems necessary in addition to that required to be furnished to him by RC 2951.03. In re Reed (Summit 1969) 21 Ohio App.2d 1, 254 N.E.2d 384, 50 O.O.2d 7.

3. Probation hearing

A probation hearing under RC 2951.20 is not adversary in character; such hearing is conducted by the trial judge who, through his control of an investigation and inquiry, is to determine whether he should immediately sentence the defendant or suspend the imposition of sentence. In re Reed (Summit 1969) 21 Ohio App.2d 1, 254 N.E.2d 384, 50 O.O.2d 7.

Under RC 2947.061 a defendant, who has filed a motion to suspend further execution of sentence and requesting probation, is not entitled to a hearing on the motion, as there is no clear statutory expression in that section conferring upon the defendant the right to such a hearing. State v. Poffenbaugh (Wood 1968) 14 Ohio App.2d 59, 237 N.E.2d 147, 43 O.O.2d 191.

4. Mitigating factors

To the extent that trial court's initial colloquy with defendant concerning waiver of right to present mitigating evidence at penalty phase of capital case did not establish defendant's understanding of use of mitigating evidence to offset aggravating circumstances, written waiver that defendant subsequently signed satisfied that requirement for a knowing, voluntary, and intelligent waiver. State v. Jordan (Ohio, 03-10-2004) 101 Ohio St.3d 216, 804 N.E.2d 1, 2004-Ohio-783, stay granted 101 Ohio St.3d 1492, 805 N.E.2d 542, 2004-Ohio-1444, reconsideration denied 102 Ohio St.3d 1425, 807 N.E.2d 368, 2004-Ohio-2003, motion to reopen denied 103 Ohio St.3d 1423, 814 N.E.2d 488, 2004-Ohio-4524, certiorari dismissed 125 S.Ct. 439, 543 U.S. 952, 160 L.Ed.2d 314. Sentencing And Punishment 🔑 1782

Commitment of a mental defective to an institution in lieu of a sentence for the crime of which he has been convicted will not support a subsequent sentence of the defendant to the penitentiary as a parole violator after his release from the institution. Petition of Oponowicz (Franklin 1955) 100 Ohio App. 531, 135 N.E.2d 778, 72 Ohio Law Abs. 516, 60 O.O. 409.

A court will not reduce the sentence of a foreign businesswoman convicted of illegal drug transactions where the request is based on the fact she will be imprisoned here thousands of miles from her children; while it is regrettable these children must suffer for their mother's crime, they are not the only victims of drug importation, since vast numbers of American children suffer because of readily available drugs. U.S. v. Adeymi (S.D.Ohio 1987) 687 F.Supp. 1173.

2947.061 Probation after serving thirty days of sentence; hearing; exception; limitations—Repealed

(1996 S 269, eff. 7–1–96; 1995 S 2, eff. 7–1–96; 1995 H 4, eff. 11–9–95; 1994 S 186, eff. 10–12–94; 1994 H 571, eff. 10–6–94; 1982 H 269, eff. 7–1–83; 1982 S 199; 1976 H 837; 1969 H 686; 131 v H 781)

Uncodified Law

1996 S 269, § 12, eff. 6–28–96, reads: The repeal by this act of section 2947.061 of the Revised Code is intended to confirm the result intended by the General Assembly in enacting Am. Sub. S.B. 2 and Sub. H.B. 4 of the 121st General Assembly. Both acts passed on June 29, 1995. Am. Sub. S.B. 2 repealed the section while Sub. H.B. 4 amended it. The existence of the section is therefore uncertain. The intention of the General Assembly was for the section to be neither continued nor revived as the result of its amendment by Sub. H.B. 4, but rather for the section to be repealed as provided in Am. Sub. S.B. 2.

1995 H 4, § 3, eff. 11–9–95, reads: Sections 2151.02, 2151.022, 2151.355, 2151.411, 2913.02, 2913.51, 2913.71, 2921.13, 2923.21, 2947.061, 2951.02, 2967.01, and 2967.15 of the Revised Code, as amended by this act, and sections 2923.211 and 2967.131 of the Revised Code, as enacted by this act, apply to any offense, delinquent act, or unruly act committed on or after the effective date of this act. Sections 2151.02, 2151.022, 2151.355, 2151.411, 2913.02, 2913.51, 2913.71, 2921.13, 2923.21, 2947.061, 2951.02, 2967.01, and 2967.15 of the Revised Code, as they existed immediately prior to the effective date of this act, apply to any offense, delinquent act, or unruly act committed before the effective date of this act.

Notes of Decisions

Constitutional issues 1
Eligibility 3
Granting or denying shock probation 6
Hearing; presence of convict 5
Other forms of probation; parole 7
Revocation of probation 8
Shock probation; authority to grant 2
Time limits 4

---

1. Constitutional issues

Defendant did not have legitimate expectation of finality in discretionary allowance or withdrawal of various conditions of incarceration and, thus, trial court's conclusive removal of defendant's eligibility for such conditions, following revocation of shock probation, by reinstating his sentence of four to ten years for attempted burglary and additionally ordering that reinstated term be one of actual incarceration did not impose a new and more severe sentence constituting multiple punishments for the same offense in violation of double jeopardy clauses of United States and Ohio Constitutions. State v. Meyer (Ohio App. 3 Dist., 09-29-1994) 98 Ohio App.3d 4, 647 N.E.2d 818, dismissed, appeal not allowed 71 Ohio St.3d 1477, 645 N.E.2d 1257. Double Jeopardy ⚷ 117

Denial of motion for shock probation is made in special proceeding and is order that affects substantial right, i.e., right of offender to have trial court exercise its discretion in ruling upon motion for shock probation in nonarbitrary, and rationale manner, in short, right of offender to procedural due process. State v. Brandon (Greene 1993) 86 Ohio App.3d 671, 621 N.E.2d 776. Criminal Law ⚷ 1023(16)

If denial of motion for shock probation is not appealable, then reviewing court has no power to find violation of constitutional or statutory standard in denial, and imprisoned movant for probation is ipso facto denied his substantive right to due process. State v. Brandon (Greene 1993) 86 Ohio App.3d 671, 621 N.E.2d 776. Criminal Law ⚷ 1023(16)

Sufficient probability of error is shown in a trial court's grant of super shock probation to a defendant who enters a guilty plea to a charge including possession of a firearm, but not a firearm specification, to warrant an appellate court to grant the prosecution's motion for leave to appeal, notwithstanding the fact that the defendant has served a portion of his sentence; double jeopardy is not violated by an appeal of an improperly imposed sentence. State v. Ellis (Franklin 1992) 78 Ohio App.3d 221, 604 N.E.2d 229.

2. Shock probation; authority to grant

Eligibility for probation is prerequisite to eligibility for shock probation. State v. Bistarkey (Ohio, 03-01-1996) 75 Ohio St.3d 7, 661 N.E.2d 167, 1996-Ohio-185. Sentencing And Punishment ⚷ 1936

Defendant convicted of felonious assault was not eligible for shock probation where he was ineligible for regular probation because of his use of firearm in commission of crime. State v. Bistarkey (Ohio, 03-01-1996) 75 Ohio St.3d 7, 661 N.E.2d 167, 1996-Ohio-185. Sentencing And Punishment ⚷ 1843

The restrictions upon the granting of probation at the time of sentencing contained in RC 2951.02(F) do not limit the discretion of the trial court in granting "shock probation" pursuant to RC 2947.061. State ex rel. Corrigan v. Court of Common Pleas (Ohio 1976) 45 Ohio St.2d 187, 343 N.E.2d 94, 74 O.O.2d 300.

A party lacks standing to invoke the jurisdiction of the court unless he has, in an individual or representative capacity, some real interest in the subject matter of the action. State ex rel. Dallman v. Court of Common Pleas, Franklin County (Ohio 1973) 35 Ohio St.2d 176, 298 N.E.2d 515, 64 O.O.2d 103. Parties ⚷ 6(1)

Order denying defendant's motion for super shock probation was not final, appealable order, and thus Court of Appeals lacked jurisdiction to consider it. State v. Singh (Ohio App. 11 Dist., 09-24-2001) 146 Ohio App.3d 38, 764 N.E.2d 1096. Criminal Law ⚷ 1023(16)

Prisoner could be considered for "shock probation" (probation with close supervision and waiver of search protest rights) after he had served six months of sentence, even though presentence investigation had not been ordered prior to announcement of sentence in his case and statute and criminal rule required that court review presentence report before granting or denying probation; because prisoner would not be eligible to apply for probation until he had been incarcerated for at least 30 days, literal compliance with statutory requirements would necessitate preparation of investigative report for every case, and under circumstances report could be compiled after conviction, as long as it was read by judge before probation decision was made. State v. Digrino (Ohio App. 9 Dist., 11-08-1995) 107 Ohio App.3d 336, 668 N.E.2d 965. Sentencing And Punishment ⚷ 1894; Sentencing And Punishment ⚷ 276

Once a judge leaves his position on a court of common pleas and his docket is assigned to a new judge, the original judge becomes unable to act as defined by RC 2947.061(C); even though a judge resumes his former position by his reappointment to the court of common pleas, he has not retained his former docket. State ex rel. Solowitch v. Cleary (Cuyahoga 1989) 59 Ohio App.3d 8, 569 N.E.2d 1076.

RC 5143.03 does not require that a convicted youthful offender serve the entire period of incarceration called for by the minimum range of his indefinite sentence before he has served a sentence; therefore, a youthful offender whose first sentence was shortened by shock probation or parole may be sentenced to the penitentiary instead of the reformatory. State v. Smith (Franklin 1982) 8 Ohio App.3d 142, 456 N.E.2d 535, 8 O.B.R. 199. Infants ⚷ 69(4)

A trial court has jurisdiction over a motion for shock probation and may proceed to dispose of such while an appeal of the judgment is pending. State v. Lett (Hamilton 1978) 58 Ohio App.2d 45, 388 N.E.2d 1386, 12 O.O.3d 131.

While probation generally refers to action taken at the time of sentencing or at any time before the offender is delivered into the custody of the institution in which he is to serve his sentence, the legislature can provide for exceptions to this general rule such as shock probation. State v. Stevens (Cuyahoga 1978) 58 Ohio App.2d 6, 387 N.E.2d 654, 12 O.O.3d 23. Sentencing And Punishment ⚷ 1894

A trial court lacks jurisdiction to reconsider its final decision overruling a motion for super shock probation under RC 2947.061(B). State v Kean,

No. 89AP–152 (10th Dist Ct App, Franklin, 1–25–90).

Once an offender has been delivered into the custody of the institution in which he is to serve his sentence, a trial court's power to suspend execution of the sentence imposed is limited to "shock" probation. State v. Wheeler (Ohio Com.Pl. 1976) 49 Ohio Misc. 41, 361 N.E.2d 564, 2 O.O.3d 210, 3 O.O.3d 346. Sentencing And Punishment ⚷ 1894

RC 2951.04 cannot be utilized to suspend execution of sentence after an offender has been delivered into the custody of the institution in which he is to serve his sentence. State v. Wheeler (Ohio Com.Pl. 1976) 49 Ohio Misc. 41, 361 N.E.2d 564, 2 O.O.3d 210, 3 O.O.3d 346. Sentencing And Punishment ⚷ 1894

RC 2947.061 has been made subject only to RC 2951.03 to 2951.09, and no reading of those sections requires the court to act under the new section only if there is a misapprehension of the facts. State v. Head (Ohio Com.Pl. 1966) 6 Ohio Misc. 157, 217 N.E.2d 56, 35 O.O.2d 288.

3. Eligibility

Statute prohibiting granting of probation to persons who committed their offenses with firearms applies to trial court's decision as to whether to grant motions for shock probation or super shock probation. State v. Brandon (Greene 1993) 86 Ohio App.3d 671, 621 N.E.2d 776. Sentencing And Punishment ⚷ 1840

A person who is convicted of complicity to armed robbery where the evidence supports the conclusion that the gun involved was procured from the accused and delivered to the robber for use during the actual robbery is not eligible for shock probation. State v Moore, No. CA 2912 (5th Dist Ct App, Licking, 2–1–83).

4. Time limits

A defendant who is sentenced to an initial three-year term of actual incarceration on a firearm specification, plus two concurrent indefinite terms on aggravated robbery charges, is eligible to file for super shock probation on the aggravated robbery charges under RC 2947.061(B) six months from the date on which he begins serving his entire sentence, i.e. the beginning of the firearm specification sentence, not six months from the date on which he begins serving the sentences which he is seeking to have suspended, i.e. the aggravated robbery sentences, which do not begin to run until after the firearm specification sentence is completed; the defendant is eligible to file only one such motion, however; thus, a timely filed initial motion bars consideration of a second motion. State v. Reid (Cuyahoga 1989) 65 Ohio App.3d 330, 583 N.E.2d 1336, motion overruled 49 Ohio St.3d 713, 552 N.E.2d 950.

The imposition of consecutive sentences does not relieve a defendant applying for shock probation from the requirement that he apply for shock probation within thirty days of his initial delivery to the penal institution; a defendant serving consecutive sentences may not apply for shock probation after the commencement of each of his consecutive sentences. State v. Hatfield (Montgomery 1990) 61 Ohio App.3d 427, 572 N.E.2d 842.

It is not sufficient for the court to announce its decision on a motion for shock probation within the time provided by RC 2947.061(B), it must journalize its ruling as well; if the judge in his discretion elects not to hold a hearing on a motion for shock probation and does not rule on the motion within sixty days after its filing, the court loses jurisdiction over the motion. State v. Ellington (Lorain 1987) 36 Ohio App.3d 76, 521 N.E.2d 504.

Where the trial judge chooses not to hold a hearing on a motion for shock probation, he should rule on the motion within sixty days after it is filed; if the judge does not hold a hearing or rule on a motion within such sixty-day period, he loses jurisdiction to grant the motion. State v. Delaney (Cuyahoga 1983) 9 Ohio App.3d 47, 458 N.E.2d 462, 9 O.B.R. 50. Sentencing And Punishment ⚷ 1905

After a finding of inability due to illness, the presumption of regularity attending proceedings under RC 2947.061 and Sup R 8(D) is effective to support a substitution in the absence of evidence by the movant that the disabled judge will be available within the time frame established by the statute and rule. State v. Blythewood (Cuyahoga 1978) 60 Ohio App.2d 300, 396 N.E.2d 1068, 14 O.O.3d 262.

Where a defendant files a motion for shock probation pursuant to RC 2947.061, and a hearing is held, the ruling of the court must be entered within ten days of the hearing, and although the trial court does have the power to grant certain limited reconsideration, the act of reconsideration must be taken within time limits equal to those applicable to the original motion, so that if the trial court does not dispose of the motion for reconsideration within ten days after the hearing, it is without authority to proceed, and a writ of prohibition will lie to prevent it from exercising jurisdiction. State ex rel. Corrigan v. White (Cuyahoga 1976) 55 Ohio App.2d 11, 378 N.E.2d 743, 9 O.O.3d 174.

A court has no jurisdiction to consider the probation of a convicted person, pursuant to RC 2947.061, where the motion requesting the suspension of the sentence is not made before the sixty-day time limit specified by the statute has expired. State v. Crawford (Hamilton 1973) 34 Ohio App.2d 137, 296 N.E.2d 578, 63 O.O.2d 213.

At the expiration of the ten-day period for granting probation prescribed by RC 2947.061, the trial court loses its jurisdiction over the subject matter and over the person of the defendant and any attempt by the trial court thereafter by virtue of that statute to suspend execution of sentence, grant probation or order the defendant's release from his penal custodian is wholly void and no legal effect; in such circumstances prohibition will lie to prohibit such attempted judicial act. State ex rel. Dallman v. Court of Common Pleas, Hardin County (Hardin 1972) 32 Ohio App.2d 102, 288 N.E.2d 303, 61 O.O.2d 97.

Repealed

The time period for granting "shock" probation is mandatory and it may not be granted by a trial court beyond the ten-day period following a hearing on a motion for same. State ex rel. Dallman v. Court of Common Pleas, Hardin County (Hardin 1972) 32 Ohio App.2d 102, 288 N.E.2d 303, 61 O.O.2d 97. Sentencing And Punishment ⚷ 1893

Under RC 2947.061 the legislature has prescribed by mandatory words (1) that the period of time for filing a motion for "shock" probation begins not earlier than thirty days and expires not later than sixty days after the sentenced defendant is delivered into the custody of the keeper of the institution in which he is to begin serving his sentence, (2) that the period of time for hearing the motion begins on the date of filing and expires sixty days thereafter, and (3) that the period of time for a ruling thereon (when hearing has been had) begins on the date of hearing and expires ten days thereafter. State ex rel. Dallman v. Court of Common Pleas, Hardin County (Hardin 1972) 32 Ohio App.2d 102, 288 N.E.2d 303, 61 O.O.2d 97.

RC 2947.061 does not limit or restrict the plenary discretion of the common pleas court; and a ruling on a motion timely filed under the provisions of such section some six months after the filing thereof is not an abuse of discretion, nor is such ruling made in an unreasonable time, or impinge on or usurp the authority vested in the Ohio adult parole authority. State v. Allison (Wood 1968) 14 Ohio App.2d 55, 237 N.E.2d 145, 43 O.O.2d 189.

Time constraints of former RC 2947.061 are mandatory so failure of the trial court to journalize its decision within ten days of any hearing or, if no hearing is held, within sixty days of the filing of the motion, divests the trial court of its jurisdiction and, even if the trial court makes its entry nunc pro tunc, thereby attempting to relate back its decision, with nothing on the record to indicate that the trial court had considered the motion during the statutory period, the motion is automatically denied. State v Brill, No. CA99–06–016, 2000 WL 190004 (12th Dist Ct App, Fayette, 2–14–00).

An inmate is not constructively redelivered into the custody of the keeper of the institution upon the commencement of his second, successive term of imprisonment, thus his motion for shock probation after serving thirty days of his second consecutive term is untimely. State v Deibel, No. 94AP120092, 1995 WL 498719 (5th Dist Ct App, Tuscarawas, 7–12–95).

Where a trial court fails to rule on a defendant's motion for shock probation within thirty days pursuant to RC 2947.061, the motion is deemed denied, and no final appealable order exists. State v Alexander, No. 88AP–495 (10th Dist Ct App, Franklin, 3–16–89).

The trial court has jurisdiction to consider, reconsider, or consider anew an application for shock probation provided the motion is made within the thirty-day period between the thirtieth and the sixtieth day after sentencing. State v Moore, No. CA 2912 (5th Dist Ct App, Licking, 2–1–83).

Under RC 2947.061, the trial court must grant or deny a motion for "shock" probation within the ten-day period imposed, and may not continue such motion beyond such period. OAG 73–070.

After the expiration of the ten-day time period imposed by RC 2947.061, the trial court loses jurisdiction over the subject matter and over the person of the defendant and may neither vacate nor set aside its ruling granting or denying a motion for "shock" probation under that section. OAG 73–070.

5. Hearing; presence of convict

The failure of a trial court to hold an oral hearing on a prisoner's motion for shock probation does not constitute an abuse of discretion despite the defendant's claim that the court failed to consider statutory factors required to be considered, since (1) a hearing is not required under RC 2947.062, or under general due process guarantees so that it is doubtful that the court's refusal to hold an oral hearing is subject to review; (2) the record does not exemplify the defendant's claimed error that the trial court failed to consider required statutory sentencing criteria and does not demonstrate that these factors actually militate in favor of the defendant; and (3) the silent record present in the case raises the presumption that the court did in fact consider all salient criteria. State v. Hatcher (Cuyahoga 1991) 71 Ohio App.3d 823, 595 N.E.2d 457.

The holding of a hearing on a motion for probation after thirty days of sentence has been served pursuant to RC 2947.061 is discretionary with the trial court, and failure to conduct an oral hearing upon such a motion is not a denial of due process of law, the only mandatory requirement of RC 2947.061 being that the disposition of the motion be within certain specified time limits. State v. Orris (Delaware 1971) 26 Ohio App.2d 87, 269 N.E.2d 623, 55 O.O.2d 211.

Under RC 2947.061 a defendant, who has filed a motion to suspend further execution of sentence and requesting probation, is not entitled to a hearing on the motion, as there is no clear statutory expression in that section conferring upon the defendant the right to such a hearing. State v. Pofenbaugh (Wood 1968) 14 Ohio App.2d 59, 237 N.E.2d 147, 43 O.O.2d 191.

If the court by RC 2947.061 determines that a formal hearing is required to decide whether the relief sought is to be granted or denied, such hearing may be conducted in any manner including ex parte which the court determines will enable the court to reach a sound decision, and in such hearing it is necessary for the defendant to be present only if the court determines that his presence is necessary to ascertain facts and/or to receive his probationary sentence; if the presence of the defendant is so required, the cost of transporting him from the penal institution should be assessed in accordance with RC 2949.14 to 2949.19. OAG 70–089.

6. Granting or denying shock probation

A trial court's order granting shock probation is reinstated by the Ohio Supreme Court's use of its equitable powers in a case where a woman was convicted of aggravated robbery while armed with a toy gun, which is not a "firearm" for purposes of the probation statute. State v. West (Ohio 1993) 66 Ohio St.3d 508, 613 N.E.2d 622.

A trial court lacks jurisdiction to grant shock probation under RC 2947.061 unless and until it has considered a written investigation report prepared as required by RC 2951.03; the fact that shock probation is a post-sentence proceeding and the report is termed a presentence investigation report is irrelevant, since the statutory scheme plainly contemplates and mandates consideration of such a report prior to granting shock probation. State v. Harris (Ohio 1993) 66 Ohio St.3d 89, 609 N.E.2d 162.

The state may appeal from an order granting shock probation only by leave of court, pursuant to RC 2945.67(A). State v. Fisher (Ohio 1988) 35 Ohio St.3d 22, 517 N.E.2d 911. Criminal Law ⚷ 1072

Under shock probation statute which provides that, if probation is terminated, court may impose any sentence which might originally have been imposed, jurisdiction of sentencing court does not cease until end or termination of probation period. State v. Meyer (Ohio App. 3 Dist., 09-29-1994) 98 Ohio App.3d 4, 647 N.E.2d 818, dismissed, appeal not allowed 71 Ohio St.3d 1477, 645 N.E.2d 1257. Sentencing And Punishment ⚷ 2010

Denial of motion for shock probation is final appealable order. State v. Brandon (Greene 1993) 86 Ohio App.3d 671, 621 N.E.2d 776. Criminal Law ⚷ 1023(16)

The trial court has exclusive discretion to grant or deny shock probation, and no one convicted of a crime has any right or entitlement to be granted shock probation, regardless of the circumstances of his case. State v. Hawk (Summit 1992) 81 Ohio App.3d 296, 610 N.E.2d 1082. Sentencing And Punishment ⚷ 1936

A defendant whose sentence includes a six month term of actual incarceration may not be placed on shock probation by a trial court after he has served his six month term of incarceration in contravention of RC 2947.061(A) and 2951.02(F), despite the defendant's argument that the modifying phrase in RC 2929.01(C), "until after the expiration of his term of actual incarceration" pertains to the portion of RC 2929.01(C) relating to the trial court's authority to suspend the offender's sentence or grant probation or shock probation, since it has previously been implicitly decided by the Ohio Supreme Court that the modifying phrase relied on by the defendant only applies to the portion of RC 2929.01(C) referring to the rehabilitation and correction department's or the adult parole authority's ability to grant an offender a furlough or parole following the expiration of his term of actual incarceration. State v. Sparks (Ross 1990) 66 Ohio App.3d 348, 584 N.E.2d 45.

A defendant who is sentenced to a term of actual incarceration on a firearm specification and two concurrent indefinite terms on aggravated robbery charges is not eligible for super shock probation under RC 2947.061(B) on the aggravated robbery sentences, as the defendant would not be eligible for probation under RC 2951.02(F)(5) since his sentence included a term of actual incarceration, thus also barring probation on the nonactual incarceration terms, and since the defendant pled guilty to having a firearm on his person or under his control during the robbery, and was thus armed with a firearm within the meaning of the probation bar of RC 2951.02(F)(3). State v. Reid (Cuyahoga 1989) 65 Ohio App.3d 330, 583 N.E.2d 1336, motion overruled 49 Ohio St.3d 713, 552 N.E.2d 950.

A defendant convicted of trafficking in drugs and sentenced to a mandatory term of actual incarceration of eighteen months pursuant to RC 2925.03(C)(4) is not eligible for shock probation under RC 2947.061, despite the trial court's use of the phrase "mandatory eighteen months," rather than the phrase "actual incarceration," in sentencing the defendant. State v. Milano (Cuyahoga 1989) 65 Ohio App.3d 284, 583 N.E.2d 1025.

Condition of shock probation which prohibited all contact by defendant, a prisoners' rights activist, with Department of Rehabilitation and Correction or its agencies or institutions on behalf of any prisoner or releasee other than herself was invalid; there was no indication that defendant's prisoner rights activities or contacts with the Department played a role in her criminal conduct in assisting her husband in evading the police, the condition bore no relationship to the crime committed or to future criminal conduct, and the prohibited conduct did not involve illegal activity. State v. Maynard (Wood 1988) 47 Ohio App.3d 76, 547 N.E.2d 409. Sentencing And Punishment ⚷ 1971(2)

Although the disposition of a motion for shock probation made while the convicted person is serving a sentence pursuant to a judgment is a "special proceeding," the denial of a motion for shock probation is not a final appealable order because the decision to deny such a motion rests exclusively in the discretion of the trial court and thus does not affect any substantial right of the movant. State v. Jones (Hamilton 1987) 40 Ohio App.3d 123, 532 N.E.2d 153.

"Shock probation" under RC 2947.061 (B) of felons convicted of aggravated crimes of the first, second, or third degree is available only where the offense was committed before July 1, 1983. State v. Meacham (Ottawa 1985) 30 Ohio App.3d 38, 506 N.E.2d 234, 30 O.B.R. 92.

Unless a constitutional or statutory standard has been violated, the decision of the trial court to grant or deny shock probation is not subject to review. State v. Delaney (Cuyahoga 1983) 9 Ohio App.3d 47, 458 N.E.2d 462, 9 O.B.R. 50.

The order of the court granting or denying a motion of a defendant under RC 2947.061 is not reviewable. State v. Poffenbaugh (Wood 1968) 14 Ohio App.2d 59, 237 N.E.2d 147, 43 O.O.2d 191.

A guilty plea is not knowingly entered where defendant understands that he is not eligible for probation during the three-year actual incarceration for a firearm specification and does not know that he is ineligible for super-shock probation after serving three years of actual incarceration on a gun specification. State v. Brigham (Ohio App. 10 Dist., Franklin, 02-27-1997) No. 96APA07-964, No. 96APA07-970, 1997 WL 84650, Unreported.

After the denial of a defendant's motion for super shock probation, a motion for reconsideration again requesting super shock probation in effect constitutes a second motion for super shock probation and therefore violates RC 2947.061(B). State v Garcia, No. 94APA11–1646, 1995 WL 259168 (10th Dist Ct App, Franklin, 5–2–95).

A trial court lacks jurisdiction to reconsider its final decision overruling a motion for super shock probation under RC 2947.061(B). State v Kean, No. 89AP–152 (10th Dist Ct App, Franklin, 1–25–90).

The consecutive sentencing requirement for escape convictions under RC 2921.34(C) does not preclude a court from granting a defendant convicted of escape shock probation pursuant to RC 2947.061. State v Reese, No. CA–2467 (5th Dist Ct App, Richland, 7–22–87).

A motion for probation under RC 2947.061 may be denied where the length of the defendant's criminal record causes the court to doubt that this method will serve a useful purpose in such case. State v. Scruggs (Ohio Com.Pl. 1969) 20 Ohio Misc. 291, 254 N.E.2d 394, 49 O.O.2d 496.

In considering a motion of a defendant serving a penitentiary sentence for delayed probation pursuant to RC 2947.061, the court should apply the test of RC 2951.02, which indicates that probation should be granted only when it appears to the satisfaction of the judge that the character of the defendant and the circumstances of the case are such that the defendant is not likely again to engage in an offensive course of conduct. State v. Scruggs (Ohio Com.Pl. 1969) 20 Ohio Misc. 291, 254 N.E.2d 394, 49 O.O.2d 496.

In making a determination on a motion to suspend further execution of sentence after term and place the defendant on probation, the defendant's good conduct in the penal institution after his incarceration is not of primary concern to the court, and it should not modify its original sentence on such a motion unless it can be shown that it acted under a misapprehension of the facts in passing sentence. State v Viegel, 5 Misc 45, 213 NE(2d) 751, 34 OO(2d) 96 (CP 1965).

7. Other forms of probation; parole

The authority of the trial court to suspend the execution of sentence imposed on a drug-dependent convict under RC 3719.51 must be invoked before the offender is delivered into the custody of the institution in which he is to serve his sentence. State v. Ramey (Ottawa 1975) 46 Ohio App.2d 184, 348 N.E.2d 371, 75 O.O.2d 311. Sentencing And Punishment ⚿ 1894

Where a defendant, pursuant to RC 3719.51, files a motion for a medical examination more than thirteen months after he has commenced serving his sentence, the jurisdiction of the trial court to grant probation under such section has expired. State v. Armstrong (Franklin 1973) 40 Ohio App.2d 46, 317 N.E.2d 253, 69 O.O.2d 26.

Prisoners in the custody of the department of rehabilitation and correction on January 1, 1974, are eligible for early release on parole under the terms of RC 2967.31. OAG 74–005.

The filing of a motion for "shock" probation subsequent to sentencing does not limit the jurisdiction of the adult parole authority over the defendant. OAG 73–070.

8. Revocation of probation

While RC 2951.09 authorizes a trial court to revoke shock probation granted an offender pursuant to RC 2929.51(B) and 2947.061 for violation of the terms thereof, the court may not impose a term of incarceration in excess of the original sentence. State v. Draper (Ohio 1991) 60 Ohio St.3d 81, 573 N.E.2d 602.

Trial court committed plain and prejudicial error by increasing defendant's sentence to 18 months upon revocation of his shock probation from 12 month sentence imposed initially upon plea of guilty. State v. Hylton (Gallia 1991) 75 Ohio App.3d 778, 600 N.E.2d 821. Sentencing And Punishment ⚿ 2036; Criminal Law ⚿ 1042

A trial court errs in increasing a defendant's sentence following the revocation of shock probation, where the defendant has already served a portion of the initial sentence prior to the grant of shock probation. State v Sharp, No. CA90–03–022 (12th Dist Ct App, Clermont, 11–26–90).

2947.062 Attendance of prisoner at probation hearing; transportation—Repealed

(1995 S 2, eff. 7–1–96; 1994 H 571, eff. 10–6–94; 1983 H 291, eff. 7–1–83; 1970 H 1136)

2947.07 When court to pronounce judgment

If a convicted defendant does not show sufficient cause as to why judgment should not be pronounced, the court shall pronounce the judgment.

(1953 H 1, eff. 10–1–53; GC 13451–4)

Historical and Statutory Notes

Pre–1953 H 1 Amendments: 113 v 198, Ch 30, § 4

Cross References

Journalization of judgment, App R 4

Library References

Criminal Law ⚩977, 996.
Westlaw Topic No. 110.

C.J.S. Criminal Law §§ 1420 to 1422, 1458, 1480, 1483 to 1484, 1511, 1544 to 1545.

Notes of Decisions

Ed. Note: *This section contains annotations from former RC 2937.10.*

Erroneous judgment 2
Judgment or journal entry 1

---

1. Judgment or journal entry

Trial court did not err in sua sponte ordering judgment entry of sentence to conform to transcript of sentencing hearing. State v. Turner (Ohio App. 8 Dist., Cuyahoga, 09-18-2003) No. 81449, 2003-Ohio-4933, 2003 WL 22145816, Unreported, appeal not allowed 101 Ohio St.3d 1422, 802 N.E.2d 154, 2004-Ohio-123. Criminal Law ⚩ 996(1); Sentencing And Punishment ⚩ 1138

A sentence pronounced in open court, though not formalized by journal entry, may not be vacated or amended, even though the defendant has not satisfied or suffered any part of the punishment thereunder, unless the revocation or amendment is formalized by journal entry. State v. Butler (Allen 1974) 44 Ohio App.2d 177, 337 N.E.2d 633, 73 O.O.2d 196. Sentencing And Punishment ⚩ 2315; Criminal Law ⚩ 1663

The pronouncement of sentence in open court upon conviction is then and there an act of court which needs no formalization by journal entry before appeal may be perfected therefrom. State v. Boyd (Ohio 1972) 30 Ohio St.2d 64, 282 N.E.2d 366, 59 O.O.2d 84, on remand 35 Ohio App.2d 147, 300 N.E.2d 752, 64 O.O.2d 260. Criminal Law ⚩ 1023(10)

The sentence in a criminal case constitutes the judgment. State v. Curtis (Miami 1965) 2 Ohio App.2d 31, 206 N.E.2d 217, 31 O.O.2d 72. Criminal Law ⚩ 994(1)

The obligation of the trial judge to inform an indigent defendant of his right to appointment of counsel to represent him is prior to and different from the obligation to determine the propriety of accepting a plea of guilty and pronouncing sentence. State v. Cartwright (Fayette 1957) 161 N.E.2d 456, 81 Ohio Law Abs. 226.

A judgment may "pronounce" sentence without signing a written instrument. Foglio v. Alvis (Ohio Com.Pl. 1957) 143 N.E.2d 641, 75 Ohio Law Abs. 228.

2. Erroneous judgment

Final judgment rendered erroneously by a magistrate is voidable but not void, and the magistrate is not civilly liable for his error. Stahl v. Currey (Ohio 1939) 135 Ohio St. 253, 20 N.E.2d 529, 14 O.O. 112.

If final judgment be rendered erroneously by the magistrate, he acts in excess of his jurisdiction. Stahl v. Currey (Ohio 1939) 135 Ohio St. 253, 20 N.E.2d 529, 14 O.O. 112.

2947.08 Time of execution in capital cases

In cases where the death sentence is imposed, at least one hundred twenty days shall intervene between the day of sentence and the day appointed for the execution thereof.

(131 v H 24, eff. 8–10–65; 1953 H 1; GC 13451–5)

Historical and Statutory Notes

Pre–1953 H 1 Amendments: 113 v 198, Ch 30, § 5

Cross References

Execution of death sentence, 2949.22, 2949.24 to 2949.29, 2949.31

Resentencing after death sentence vacated, 2929.06

Library References

Sentencing and Punishment ⚷1795.
Westlaw Topic No. 350H.
C.J.S. Criminal Law §§ 1591, 1605 to 1609.

Research References

Encyclopedias

OH Jur. 3d Criminal Law § 3429, Time, Place, and Method of Execution.

Treatises and Practice Aids

Katz, Giannelli, Blair and Lipton, Baldwin's Ohio Practice, Criminal Law, § 153:26, Death Sentence.

Katz, Giannelli, Blair and Lipton, Baldwin's Ohio Practice, Criminal Law, § 153:27, Death Sentence (Additional Form).

2947.09 to 2947.13 Fines and sentences—Repealed

(1972 H 511, eff. 1–1–74; 1971 H 139; 1970 S 460; 1953 H 1; GC 13451–6 to 13451–8b)

Historical and Statutory Notes

Ed. Note: See now parenthetical references for provisions analogous to former sections: 2947.09 (2929.22); 2947.10 (2929.21, 2929.22); 2947.11 (2951.02); 2947.13 (2951.02).

Pre–1953 H 1 Amendments: 115 v 542; 113 v 198, Ch 30, § 6, 7, 8

2947.14 Satisfaction of fine and costs; determination of ability to pay must precede commitment; hearing on change of circumstances

(A) If a fine is imposed as a sentence or a part of a sentence, the court or magistrate that imposed the fine may order that the offender be committed to the jail or workhouse until the fine is paid or secured to be paid, or the offender is otherwise legally discharged, if the court or magistrate determines at a hearing that the offender is able, at that time, to pay the fine but refuses to do so. The hearing required by this section shall be conducted at the time of sentencing.

(B) At the hearing, the offender has the right to be represented by counsel and to testify and present evidence as to the offender's ability to pay the fine. If a court or magistrate determines after considering the evidence presented by an offender, that the offender is able to pay a fine, the determination shall be supported by findings of fact set forth in a judgment entry that indicate the offender's income, assets, and debts, as presented by the offender, and the offender's ability to pay.

(C) If the court or magistrate has found the offender able to pay a fine at a hearing conducted in compliance with divisions (A) and (B) of this section, and the offender fails to pay the fine, a warrant may be issued for the arrest of the offender. Any offender held in custody pursuant to such an arrest shall be entitled to a hearing on the first regularly scheduled court day following the date of arrest in order to inform the court or magistrate of any change of circumstances that has occurred since the time of sentencing and that affects the offender's ability to pay the fine. The right to the hearing on any change of circumstances may be waived by the offender.

At the hearing to determine any change of circumstances, the offender has the right to testify and present evidence as to any portion of the offender's income, assets, or debts that has changed in such a manner as to affect the offender's ability to pay the fine. If a court or magistrate determines, after considering any evidence presented by the offender, that the offender remains able to pay the fine, that determination shall be supported by a judgment entry that includes findings of fact upon which such a determination is based.

(D) No person shall be ordered to be committed to a jail or workhouse or otherwise be held in custody in satisfaction of a fine imposed as the whole or a part of a sentence except as provided in this section. Any person imprisoned pursuant to this section shall receive credit upon the fine at the rate of fifty dollars per day or fraction of a day. If the unpaid fine is less than fifty dollars, the person shall be imprisoned one day.

(E) No commitment pursuant to this section shall exceed six months.

(2002 H 170, eff. 9–6–02; 1984 H 113, eff. 1–8–85; 1984 H 277; 1970 S 460; 1953 H 1; GC 13451–9)

Historical and Statutory Notes

Ed. Note: 2947.14 contains provisions analogous to former 2947.20, repealed by 1984 H 113, eff. 1–8–85.

Pre–1953 H 1 Amendments: 120 v 320; 113 v 199, Ch 30, § 9

Amendment Note: 2002 H 170 substituted "fifty" for "thirty" throughout division (D); and made changes to reflect gender neutral language throughout the section.

Cross References

Excessive fines, imposition of prohibited, O Const Art I §9

Fines, ability to pay determination in felony cases, 2929.14

Fines, ability to pay determination in misdemeanor cases, 2929.22

Library References

Fines ⚷9 to 19.

Westlaw Topic No. 174.

C.J.S. Fines §§ 4 to 5, 13 to 14, 18, 20 to 22.

Research References

Encyclopedias

OH Jur. 3d Criminal Law § 521, Imprisonment for Nonpayment of Fine or Costs.

OH Jur. 3d Criminal Law § 2075, Who May be Arrested.

OH Jur. 3d Criminal Law § 3415, Hearing Required.

OH Jur. 3d Criminal Law § 3416, Imprisonment for Failure to Pay Fine.

OH Jur. 3d Criminal Law § 3417, Imprisonment for Failure to Pay Fine—Community Service.

OH Jur. 3d Criminal Law § 3418, Credit Upon the Fine.

OH Jur. 3d Criminal Law § 3419, Maximum Period of Confinement for Unpaid Fine.

OH Jur. 3d Intoxicating Liquors § 346, Imprisonment Until Fine is Paid.

Treatises and Practice Aids

Katz, Giannelli, Blair and Lipton, Baldwin's Ohio Practice, Criminal Law, § 115:3, Equal Protection in Sentencing.

Katz, Giannelli, Blair and Lipton, Baldwin's Ohio Practice, Criminal Law, § 119:6, Financial Sanctions.

Katz, Giannelli, Blair and Lipton, Baldwin's Ohio Practice, Criminal Law, § 153:14, Sentencing Imposing Fine.

Katz, Giannelli, Blair and Lipton, Baldwin's Ohio Practice, Criminal Law, § 153:16, Sentence Imposing Fine and Ordering Commitment Until Paid.

Katz, Giannelli, Blair and Lipton, Baldwin's Ohio Practice, Criminal Law, § 153:17, Sentence Sending to Jail or Workhouse.

Painter, Ohio Driving Under the Influence § 12:42, Credit for Time Served.

Gotherman, Babbit and Lang, Baldwin's Ohio Practice, Local Government Law—Municipal, § 27:13, Municipal Liability for Damage Caused by Riotous Conduct.

Gotherman, Babbit and Lang, Baldwin's Ohio Practice, Local Government Law—Municipal, § 28:44, Fines for Traffic Violations.

Notes of Decisions

---

1. Commitment for failure to pay fine

Warrant fees constituted court costs rather than fines for the purposes of determining the number of days of incarceration that defendant could be sentenced for failing to pay fine; warrant fees were nothing other than administrative costs and were not punitive in nature. State v. Swift (Ohio App. 2 Dist., Montgomery, 04-01-2005) No. 20543, 2005-Ohio-1595, 2005 WL 742496, Unreported. Fines ⚷ 11

Trial court was not authorized to incarcerate defendant for failure to pay fines, where trial court failed to inform defendant of the right to counsel, trial court did not take evidence on defendant's ability to pay, and trial court made no findings about credit defendant would receive for time served. State v. Self (Ohio App. 2 Dist., Montgomery, 03-14-2005) No. 20370, 2005-Ohio-1120, 2005 WL 589887, Unreported. Fines ⚷ 11

Before revoking suspended sentence due to defendant's failure to pay ordered fees and costs following conviction for driving under suspension (DUS) and failure to stop at a red light, trial court was required to give notice to defendant and prosecutor, inform defendant of his right to be represented by counsel, and give defendant an opportunity to present evidence. State v. Self (Ohio App. 2 Dist., Montgomery, 03-14-2005) No. 20370, 2005-Ohio-1120, 2005 WL 589887, Unreported. Sentencing And Punishment ⚩ 2013; Sentencing And Punishment ⚩ 2014; Sentencing And Punishment ⚩ 2024

Trial court could not incarcerate defendant for failure to pay court costs and fines without first holding hearing as to his ability to pay. State v. Perkins (Ohio App. 2 Dist., 09-26-2003) 154 Ohio App.3d 631, 798 N.E.2d 646, 2003-Ohio-5092. Costs ⚩ 322; Fines ⚩ 11

Statute providing that, if fine is imposed as part of sentence and if court determines that offender is able to pay but refuses to do so, court may order offender confined until the fine is paid supplies courts with mechanism for collecting fines from offenders who refuse to pay. State v. James (Ohio App. 9 Dist., 10-04-1995) 106 Ohio App.3d 686, 666 N.E.2d 1185. Fines ⚩ 11

In a case where abortion protestors refuse to pay a fine for disorderly conduct because of religious and philosophical beliefs but are willing to serve time in the county workhouse to satisfy the fine, such defendants have a statutory right to refuse to perform community service as a condition of probation in lieu of paying fines pursuant to RC 2947.14, and such refusal is based on a correct interpretation of law so that a finding of contempt is invalid. Cleveland v. Anderson (Cuyahoga 1992) 82 Ohio App.3d 63, 611 N.E.2d 439.

Jailing as a sanction for contempt for failure to pay a court-imposed fine without first determining ability to pay and compliance with other procedural requirements of RC 2947.14 constitutes reversible error. City of Alliance v. Kelly (Stark 1988) 48 Ohio App.3d 133, 548 N.E.2d 952.

In the enactment of RC 2947.20, the general assembly has provided a method for collecting a fine from one who is unwilling or unable to pay. Strattman v. Studt (Ohio 1969) 20 Ohio St.2d 95, 253 N.E.2d 749, 49 O.O.2d 428. Fines ⚩ 11

Petitioner who had been fined $1,000 and sentenced to imprisonment for one year, is not entitled to release after six months under provision of GC 13451–9 (RC 2947.14) that "no commitment under this section shall exceed six months", since it applies only to sentence necessary to pay off fine and not to sentence of a term solely as punishment. In re Benedict (Ohio 1944) 142 Ohio St. 632, 53 N.E.2d 646, 27 O.O. 541.

2. Court costs

An arrest warrant issued after a defendant fails to attend a hearing for failure to pay costs is defective because failure to pay court costs is a civil liability, not an obligation, such as a fine, that subjects a debtor to arrest. Strongsville v. Waiwood (Cuyahoga 1989) 62 Ohio App.3d 521, 577 N.E.2d 63, motion overruled 46 Ohio St.3d 714, 546 N.E.2d 1331.

While the state may constitutionally order expenditures made to counsel appointed to defend indigent defendants charged with felony charged as costs and enter judgment therefor upon which execution may issue as in civil cases, the state cannot imprison such defendant for failure to pay the state money expended to assigned counsels until such amount has been paid or he has been held in servitude until the debt is discharged at the rate of $3 per day. Ex parte Wilson (Cuyahoga 1962) 183 N.E.2d 625, 89 Ohio Law Abs. 575. Costs ⚩ 308; Costs ⚩ 322

3. Motion to vacate fine

Defendant was not entitled to grant of motion to vacate payment of court fines on grounds that he was unable to pay, where defendant failed to demonstrate any attempt to enforce the fine and costs. State v. Chaney (Ohio App. 5 Dist., Delaware, 12-13-2004) No. 2004-CAC-07057, 2004-Ohio-6712, 2004 WL 2892017, Unreported. Costs ⚩ 319

Defendant preserved issue of his ability to pay fine by filing motion to vacate fine after it was imposed, notwithstanding his failure to object or to move for hearing at time of sentencing. State v. Horton (Franklin 1993) 85 Ohio App.3d 268, 619 N.E.2d 527. Criminal Law ⚩ 1042; Criminal Law ⚩ 1044.2(1)

4. Hearing

Trial court was not required to hold a hearing to consider defendant's ability to pay before imposing fine as condition of probation. State v. Meyer (Ohio App. 1 Dist., 12-05-1997) 124 Ohio App.3d 373, 706 N.E.2d 378. Sentencing And Punishment ⚩ 1906

A hearing is not required by statute whenever a fine is merely imposed; rather, the hearing requirement does not arise until the trial court decides to incarcerate the offender for failure to pay. State v. Meyer (Ohio App. 1 Dist., 12-05-1997) 124 Ohio App.3d 373, 706 N.E.2d 378. Fines ⚩ 1.5; Fines ⚩ 11

Question of whether trial court erred by imposing fine without first holding a hearing to consider defendant's ability to pay was ripe for review, though defendant had not been penalized for failing to pay fine. State v. Horton (Franklin 1993) 85 Ohio App.3d 268, 619 N.E.2d 527. Criminal Law ⚩ 1134(3)

Prior to imposing fine on defendant who had filed affidavit of indigency, and for whom counsel had been appointed, trial court should have held hearing to determine defendant's ability to pay fine. State v. Horton (Franklin 1993) 85 Ohio App.3d 268, 619 N.E.2d 527. Fines ⚩ 1.5

5. Credit for pretrial detention

Enforcement of collection of monies owed by defendant to trial court, in form of fines and court costs, was required to be had pursuant to statute, and could not be accomplished through summarily finding defendant in contempt, where summary procedure employed by court did not include informing defendant of his right to counsel, and court did not take evidence or make findings of fact with respect to defendant's ability to pay his fines, and made no findings with respect to credit to which defendant was entitled for time served as result of his numerous arrests for failure to appear at scheduled hearings. State v. Swift (Ohio App. 2 Dist., Montgomery, 04-01-2005) No. 20544, 2005-Ohio-1599, 2005 WL 742503, Unreported. Contempt ⚷ 51.1; Costs ⚷ 320; Fines ⚷ 2

Trial court failed to follow the legal requirements for collecting unpaid fine from defendant prior to incarcerating him for contempt for 10 days, where defendant was not informed of his right to counsel, the court did not take evidence or make findings of fact with respect to his ability to pay his fines, and the court made no findings regarding the credit defendant should have received for time served as a result of his numerous arrests for failure to appear at scheduled hearings. State v. Swift (Ohio App. 2 Dist., Montgomery, 04-01-2005) No. 20543, 2005-Ohio-1595, 2005 WL 742496, Unreported. Contempt ⚷ 61(1); Contempt ⚷ 61(6)

The trial court lacked authority to convert fines owed by defendant to community service; defendant served at least part of two days in jail in each of two cases for the non-payment of fines, statute provided that nonindigent defendants who failed to pay fines could be jailed for non-payment but they were entitled to a credit of $50 per day against their fines, and if the court had credited defendant with time served for nonpayment of fines the fines would have been completely satisfied. State v. Lamb (Ohio App. 2 Dist., 09-09-2005) 163 Ohio App.3d 290, 837 N.E.2d 833, 2005-Ohio-4741. Fines ⚷ 1.5; Fines ⚷ 11

Unless defendant was explicitly imprisoned for the purpose of satisfying his fine, he was not entitled to the corresponding $30 per day credit pursuant to statute providing that any person imprisoned for failure to pay fine shall receive credit upon the fine at the rate of $30 per day. State v. James (Ohio App. 9 Dist., 10-04-1995) 106 Ohio App.3d 686, 666 N.E.2d 1185. Fines ⚷ 12

Defendant was not entitled to $30 per day credit towards his fine since defendant was not confined pursuant to statute providing that, if fine is imposed as part of sentence and if court determines that offender is able to pay but refuses to do so, court may order offender confined until fine is paid; time that defendant served in juvenile detention facility was prior to sentencing and, thus, he was not ordered to serve this time in satisfaction of his fine and even at time of sentencing, there was no issue raised as to defendant's ability or willingness to pay the $1,000 fine. State v. James (Ohio App. 9 Dist., 10-04-1995) 106 Ohio App.3d 686, 666 N.E.2d 1185. Fines ⚷ 12

Where defendant was held in lieu of bond, solely on charges on which his convictions for reckless operation and possession of marijuana were based, which offenses were punishable only by fine, defendant more than served sufficient time to absolve him from further liability on sentence, and was entitled to credit of up to $720 against his fines and costs. State v. Sparks (Franklin 1990) 69 Ohio App.3d 400, 590 N.E.2d 1294. Costs ⚷ 292; Fines ⚷ 1.5

Arrestee had no due process or equal protection rights to receive, pursuant to Ohio law, dollar amount credit for jail time served, and thus, claim that he was deprived of credit toward his fines and court costs failed to state a constitutional violation, for purposes of §§ 1983 claim against county, county court judge, county court, and sheriff. Alkire v. Irving (C.A.6 (Ohio), 06-02-2003) 330 F.3d 802. Constitutional Law ⚷ 250.3(1); Constitutional Law ⚷ 270(1); Fines ⚷ 1.5

MISCELLANEOUS PROVISIONS

2947.15 Jail limits and proceeds of convict labor; rehabilitation of prisoners

Persons committed to jail by a judge or magistrate for nonpayment of fine, or convicts sentenced to hard labor in the county jail, shall perform labor under the direction of the board of county commissioners within or outside the jail, within the county, and the board shall adopt orders and rules in relation to the performance of labor and the sheriff or other officer having the custody of the persons or convicts shall be governed by the orders and rules. The sheriff of the county shall collect the proceeds of the labor of the persons or convicts, pay it into the county treasury, take the county treasurer's duplicate receipts for the amount paid, and forthwith deposit one of them with the county auditor. The sheriff, with the approval of the board, may provide for the vocational training and rehabilitation of prisoners confined in the county jail.

This section does not apply to prisoners participating in a county jail industry program established under section 5147.30 of the Revised Code.

(1990 H 51, eff. 11–8–90; 1990 H 588; 1970 S 460; 125 v 385; 1953 H 1; GC 13451–10)

Historical and Statutory Notes

Ed. Note: The amendment of this section by 1990 H 51, eff. 11–8–90, was identical to its amendment by 1990 H 588, eff. 10–31–90.

Pre–1953 H 1 Amendments: 113 v 199, Ch 30, § 10

Library References

Convicts ⚷7 to 10, 13.
Fines ⚷14.
Westlaw Topic Nos. 174, 98.
C.J.S. Convicts §§ 13 to 19.
C.J.S. Fines § 18.

Research References

Encyclopedias

OH Jur. 3d Penal & Correctional Institutions § 107, Generally; Prisoners in State Correctional Institutions—Prisoners in County Jails, County and Municipal Workhouses; County Jail Industry Program.

OH Jur. 3d Penal & Correctional Institutions § 119, Revenues; Services and Agricultural Fund.

Law Review and Journal Commentaries

Criminal Law: A Reappraisal of Treating the Criminal Offender, Alexander B. Smith and Louis Berlin. 3 U Dayton L Rev 59 (Winter 1978).

Notes of Decisions

Commitment for failure to pay fine 1
Work release 2

---

1. Commitment for failure to pay fine

In the enactment of RC 2947.20, the general assembly has provided a method for collecting a fine from one who is unwilling or unable to pay. Strattman v. Studt (Ohio 1969) 20 Ohio St.2d 95, 253 N.E.2d 749, 49 O.O.2d 428. Fines ⚷ 11

2. Work release

The common pleas courts, municipal courts, and county courts do not have the power to grant to persons convicted in their courts as part of their sentence to the county jail, the privilege of working at their regular employment away from the jail. OAG 65–204.

The common pleas court does not have the power to establish rules and regulations to provide for county jail inmates leaving the jail daily to continue their regular employment. OAG 65–204.

2947.151 Reduction of jail sentence

The sheriff in charge of a county jail may, upon a consideration of the quality and amount of work done in the kitchen, in the jail offices, on the jail premises, or elsewhere, allow reductions of inmates' sentences as follows:

(A) On sentences of ninety days or less, up to three days for each thirty days of sentence;

(B) On sentences longer than ninety days but not longer than six months, up to four days for each thirty days of sentence;

(C) On sentences longer than six months, up to five days for each thirty days of sentence.

The reduction of the inmate's sentence, shall become effective only upon the written concurrence of the presiding or sentencing judge or magistrate of the court where the sentence was imposed.

This section shall in no way restrict any other powers vested in the presiding or sentencing judge or magistrate of the court where the sentence was imposed.

(128 v 595, eff. 10–1–59)

Cross References

Prisoners, deduction from sentence for participation in prison industries, 2967.193

Library References

Prisons ⚷15.
Westlaw Topic No. 310.

C.J.S. Prisons and Rights of Prisoners §§ 144 to 154.

Research References

Encyclopedias

OH Jur. 3d Penal & Correctional Institutions § 129, Diminution of Sentence for Good Behavior or Services Rendered.

Notes of Decisions

1. Discretion of sheriff

OAC 5120:1–8–15(G), guaranteeing that prisoners in administrative segregation have the same rights and privileges as the general prison population, does not concern or in any way relate to prisoners' rights to earn credits for work performed, a right that is governed by RC 2947.151; the sheriff has complete discretion in recommending a sentence reduction, and segregated homosexual convicts have no protected liberty interest in the right to sentence reduction. Hansard v. Barrett (C.A.6 (Ohio) 1992) 980 F.2d 1059.

2. Concurrence of judge

Although a hearing is the preferable prelude to the discharge of the judicial duty imposed by RC 2947.151, and in some circumstances may be essential, lack of hearing is not necessarily harmful error. Skapura v. McFaul (Cuyahoga 1977) 57 Ohio App.2d 128, 385 N.E.2d 1078, 11 O.O.3d 123, affirmed 54 Ohio St.2d 348, 376 N.E.2d 1339, 8 O.O.3d 356.

Where a sheriff allows a reduction of an inmate's sentence pursuant to RC 2947.151, the sentencing judge, in determining whether to concur in the reduction of sentence, is not required to conduct an evidentiary hearing in the matter or to state reasons for a refusal to concur in such reduction. Skapura v. McFaul (Ohio 1978) 54 Ohio St.2d 348, 376 N.E.2d 1339, 8 O.O.3d 356. Prisons ⚿ 15(7)

3. Good time credit—Constitutional issues

Statute providing that person confined in state correctional institution is entitled to a deduction from his minimum sentence of 30% of the sentence prorated for each month of the sentence during which he faithfully has observed rules of the institution does not violate equal protection or due process because General Assembly had rational basis for treating certain classes of prisoners differently from others for purposes of good time credit; General Assembly could reasonably conclude that most misdemeanants require less rehabilitation than inmates confined to state prison and that misdemeanants should not be granted good time credit. Adkins v. McFaul (Ohio, 08-21-1996) 76 Ohio St.3d 350, 667 N.E.2d 1171, 1996-Ohio-388. Constitutional Law ⚿ 250.3(2); Constitutional Law ⚿ 272(2); Prisons ⚿ 15(2)

4. —— Appeal, good time credit

Although defendant's jail term had been completed, Supreme Court would consider merits of his appeal from dismissal of habeas corpus petition, rather than dismiss it as moot, because issue of whether inmates serving sentences in county jails are entitled to good time credit comparable to that received under statute for confinement in state correctional institutions was matter of public importance which had never been addressed by Court and was capable of repetition yet evading review. Adkins v. McFaul (Ohio, 08-21-1996) 76 Ohio St.3d 350, 667 N.E.2d 1171, 1996-Ohio-388. Habeas Corpus ⚿ 826(4)

5. —— General assembly authority, good time credit

It is within province of the General Assembly to determine applicability of good time credit to various categories of crime. Adkins v. McFaul (Ohio, 08-21-1996) 76 Ohio St.3d 350, 667 N.E.2d 1171, 1996-Ohio-388. Prisons ⚿ 15(1)

2947.16 Recognizance

A person convicted of a misdemeanor may be required by the judge or magistrate to enter into a recognizance, with sufficient surety, in such sum as the judge or magistrate finds proper, to keep the peace and be of good behavior for such time, not exceeding two years, as the court directs. The court may order such person to stand committed until such order is complied with or he is discharged by law, but the court may discharge such person at any time of [1] his own recognizance, or cancel such recognizance.

(1953 H 1, eff. 10–1–53; GC 13451–11)

[1] So in original; should this read "on"?

Historical and Statutory Notes

Pre–1953 H 1 Amendments: 113 v 199, Ch 30, § 11

Cross References

Bail, Crim R 46

Peace warrants, 2933.01 to 2933.16

Library References

Breach of the Peace ⚿15.

Westlaw Topic No. 62.

C.J.S. Breach of the Peace §§ 14 to 19, 21 to 25.

C.J.S. Domestic Abuse and Violence §§ 2 to 23.

Research References

Treatises and Practice Aids

Katz, Giannelli, Blair and Lipton, Baldwin's Ohio Practice, Criminal Law, § 153:28, Entry Ordering Defendant Convicted of Misdemeanor to Enter Into Recognizance to Keep Peace.

Notes of Decisions

1. Bond for good behavior

The bond required of a person convicted of violating the compulsory education laws must be set pursuant to RC 3321.38(A). State v. Hershberger (Hardin 1955) 103 Ohio App. 188, 144 N.E.2d 693, 3 O.O.2d 249.

When a recognizance bond posted in a municipal court under RC 2947.16 is ordered forfeited by the court, such recognizance bond is subject to RC 1901.31(F) and 2937.36, and required to be distributed to the county treasury after deduction of municipal court costs. 1964 OAG 1410.

2. Work release

The common pleas courts, municipal courts, and county courts do not have the power to grant to persons convicted in their courts as part of their sentence to the county jail, the privilege of working at their regular employment away from the jail. OAG 65–204.

The common pleas court does not have the power to establish rules and regulations to provide for county jail inmates leaving the jail daily to continue their regular employment. OAG 65–204.

2947.17 Breach of a condition of a recognizance

In case of a breach of the condition of any recognizance given under section 2947.16 of the Revised Code, the same proceedings shall be had as are prescribed in relation to forfeiture of other recognizances.

(1980 H 736, eff. 10–16–80; 1969 H 228; 1953 H 1; GC 13451–12)

Historical and Statutory Notes

Pre–1953 H 1 Amendments: 113 v 199, Ch 30, § 12

Cross References

Bail, Crim R 46

Peace warrants, 2933.01 to 2933.16

Library References

Breach of the Peace ⚿15.

Westlaw Topic No. 62.

C.J.S. Breach of the Peace §§ 14 to 19, 21 to 25.

C.J.S. Domestic Abuse and Violence §§ 2 to 23.

Research References

Encyclopedias

OH Jur. 3d Criminal Law § 2228, Recognizance to Keep the Peace.

2947.18 Sentence to workhouse for jail offense

Where the board of county commissioners of a county, or legislative authority of a municipal corporation having no workhouse, has made provisions for receiving prisoners into the workhouse of a city in any other county or district in the state, a court or magistrate, where imprisonment in jail may lawfully be imposed in such case, may sentence persons convicted of a misdemeanor, including a violation of a municipal ordinance, to such workhouse.

(1970 S 460, eff. 9–3–70; 1953 H 1; GC 13451–13)

Historical and Statutory Notes

Pre–1953 H 1 Amendments: 113 v 199, Ch 30, § 13

Cross References

Imprisoned, defined, 1.05

Misdemeanor as a class of offense, 2901.02

Municipal corporations, commitment of offender to workhouse, reimbursement by prisoner, 753.04

Place of imprisonment, 2929.221

Library References

Prisons ⚷13.3.

Westlaw Topic No. 310.

Research References

Encyclopedias

OH Jur. 3d Criminal Law § 3356, Sentence to Workhouse.

Notes of Decisions

Commitment to workhouse 1

1. Commitment to workhouse

Imprisonment at "hard labor" in the workhouse for violation of GC 1654 (Repealed) does not make the conviction one for a felony, and it remains only a conviction of a misdemeanor. Stockum v. State (Ohio 1922) 106 Ohio St. 249, 139 N.E. 855, 1 Ohio Law Abs. 72, 20 Ohio Law Rep. 470, 20 Ohio Law Rep. 471.

A county sheriff may not transfer persons sentenced to incarceration in the county jail to a city workhouse without a specific order from the sentencing judge providing for workhouse incarceration. OAG 82–077.

2947.19 Maintenance of prisoners; reimbursement by prisoner; testing for contagious diseases

(A) In a county that has no workhouse but in which is located a city that has a workhouse maintained by the city, the board of county commissioners may agree with the proper authorities of that city upon terms under which persons convicted of misdemeanors shall be maintained in the city workhouse at the expense of the county. In the case of persons committed to the city workhouse for the violation of a law of this state, whether the commitment is from the court of common pleas, magistrate's court, or other court, the cost of maintaining those persons committed shall be paid out of the general fund of the county, on the allowance of the board of county commissioners, provided that all persons committed to the city workhouse for the violation of ordinances of the city shall be maintained in that workhouse at the sole cost of the city.

(B) Pursuant to section 2929.37 of the Revised Code, the board of county commissioners or the legislative authority of the city may require a person who was convicted of an offense and who is confined in the city workhouse as provided in division (A) of this section to reimburse the county or the city, as the case may be, for its expenses incurred by reason of the person's confinement. If a person is convicted of or pleads guilty to a felony and the court imposes a sanction that requires the offender to serve a term in a city workhouse, sections 341.23, 753.02, 753.04, and 753.16 of the Revised Code govern the determination of whether the court may impose a sanction under section 2929.18 of the Revised Code that requires the offender to reimburse the expenses of confinement.

(C) Notwithstanding any contrary provision in this section or section 2929.18, 2929.28, or 2929.37 of the Revised Code, the board of county commissioners or the legislative authority of the city may establish a policy that complies with section 2929.38 of the Revised Code and that requires any person who is not indigent and who is confined in the city workhouse to pay a reception fee or a fee for any medical treatment or service requested by and provided to that person.

(D) If a person who has been convicted of or pleaded guilty to an offense is confined in the workhouse as provided in division (A) of this section, at the time of reception and at other times the person in charge of the operation of the workhouse determines to be appropriate, the person in charge of the operation of the workhouse may cause the convicted offender to be examined and tested for tuberculosis, HIV infection, hepatitis, including but not limited to hepatitis A, B, and C, and other contagious diseases. The person in charge of the operation of the workhouse may cause a convicted offender in the workhouse who refuses to be tested or treated for tuberculosis, HIV infection, hepatitis, including but not limited to hepatitis A, B, and C, or another contagious disease to be tested and treated involuntarily.

(2002 H 490, eff. 1–1–04; 2002 H 170, eff. 9–6–02; 1997 S 111, eff. 3–17–98; 1996 H 480, eff. 10–16–96; 1996 S 269, eff. 7–1–96; 1995 S 2, eff. 7–1–96; 1984 H 363, eff. 9–26–84; 1975 H 205; 1953 H 1; GC 13451–14)

Historical and Statutory Notes

Pre–1953 H 1 Amendments: 113 v 200, Ch 30, § 14

Amendment Note: 2002 H 490 substituted "2929.28" for "2929.21, 2929.36" in division (C).

Amendment Note: 2002 H 170 rewrote the section, which prior thereto read:

"(A) In a county that has no workhouse but in which is located a city that has a workhouse maintained by the city, the board of county commissioners may agree with the proper authorities of that city upon terms under which persons convicted of misdemeanors shall be maintained in the city workhouse at the expense of the county. In the case of persons committed to the city workhouse for the violation of a law of this state, whether the commitment is from the court of common pleas, magistrate's court, or other court, the cost of maintaining those persons committed shall be paid out of the general fund of the county, on the allowance of the board of county commissioners, provided that all persons committed to the city workhouse for the violation of ordinances of the city shall be maintained in that workhouse at the sole cost of the city.

"(B)(1) The board of county commissioners or the legislative authority of the city may require a person who was convicted of an offense and who is confined in the city workhouse as provided in division (A) of this section to reimburse the county or the city, as the case may be, for its expenses incurred by reason of the person's confinement, including, but not limited to, the expenses relating to the provision of food, clothing, shelter, medical care, personal hygiene products, including, but not limited to, toothpaste, toothbrushes, and feminine hygiene items, and up to two hours of overtime costs the sheriff or municipal corporation incurred relating to the trial of the person. The amount of reimbursement may be the actual cost of the prisoner's confinement plus the authorized trial overtime costs or a lesser amount determined by the board of county commissioners for the county or the legislative authority of the city, provided that the lesser amount shall be determined by a formula that is uniformly applied to persons incarcerated in the workhouse. The court shall determine the amount of reimbursement at a hearing held pursuant to section 2929.18 of the Revised Code if the person is confined for a felony or section 2929.223 of the Revised Code if the person is confined for a misdemeanor. The amount or amounts paid in reimbursement by a prisoner confined for a misdemeanor or the amount recovered from a prisoner confined for a misdemeanor by executing upon the judgment obtained pursuant to section 2929.223 of the Revised Code shall be paid into the treasury of the county or city that incurred the expenses. If a person is convicted of or pleads guilty to a felony and the court imposes a sanction that requires the offender to serve a term in a city workhouse, sections 341.23, 753.02, 753.04, and 753.16 of the Revised Code govern the determination of whether the court may impose a sanction under section 2929.18 of the Revised Code that requires the offender to reimburse the expenses of confinement. If a person is confined for a felony and the court imposes a sanction under section 2929.18 of the Revised Code that requires the offender to reimburse the costs of confinement, the prosecuting attorney of the county or city director of law shall bring an action to recover the expenses of confinement in accordance with section 2929.18 of the Revised Code.

"(2) The board of county commissioners or the legislative authority of the city may adopt a resolution or ordinance specifying that a person who is convicted of a felony and who is confined in the city workhouse as provided in division (A) of this section is not required to reimburse the county or city, as the case may be, for its expenses incurred by reason of the person's confinement, including the expenses listed in division (B)(1) of this section. If the board or legislative authority adopts a resolution or ordinance of that nature, the court that sentences a person convicted of a felony shall not impose a sanction under section 2929.18 of the Revised Code that requires the person to reimburse the costs of the confinement.

"(C) In lieu of requiring offenders to reimburse the county or the city for expenses incurred by reason of the person's confinement under division (A) of this section, the board of county commissioners or the legislative authority of the city may adopt a prisoner reimbursement policy for the city workhouse under this division. The workhouse administrator may appoint a reimbursement coordinator to administer the prisoner reimbursement policy. A prisoner reimbursement policy adopted under this division is a policy that requires a person confined to the workhouse to reimburse the county or city for any expenses it incurs by reason of the person's confinement in the workhouse, which expenses may include, but are not limited to, the following:

"(1) A per diem fee for room and board of not more than sixty dollars per day or the actual per diem cost, whichever is less for the entire period of time the person is confined to the workhouse;

"(2) Actual charges for medical and dental treatment;

"(3) Reimbursement for government property damaged by the person while confined to the workhouse.

"Rates charged shall be on a sliding scale determined by the board of county commissioners or the legislative authority of the city, based on the ability of the person confined in the workhouse to pay and on consideration of any legal obligation of the person to support a spouse, minor children, or other dependents and any moral obligation to support dependents to whom the person is providing or has in fact provided support.

"The reimbursement coordinator or another person designated by the workhouse administrator may investigate the financial status of the confined person and obtain information necessary to investigate that status, by means that may include contacting employers and reviewing income tax records. The coordinator may work with the confined person to create a repayment plan to be implemented upon the person's release. At the end of the person's incarceration, the person shall be presented with a billing statement.

"The reimbursement coordinator or another person designated by the workhouse administrator may collect, or the board of county commissioners or the legislative authority of the city may enter into a contract with one or more public agencies or private vendors to collect, any amounts remaining unpaid. Within twelve months after the date of the confined person's release, the prosecuting attorney or city director of law may file a civil action to seek reimbursement from that person for any billing amount that remains unpaid. The county or city shall not enforce any judgment obtained under this section by means of execution against the person's homestead. For purposes of this section, 'homestead' has the same meaning as in division (A) of section 323.151 of the Revised Code. Any reimbursement received under this section shall be credited to the general fund of the county or city that bore the expense, to be used for general fund purposes.

"(D)(1) Notwithstanding any contrary provision in this section or section 2929.18 or 2929.223 of the Revised Code, the board of county commissioners or the legislative authority of the city may establish a policy that requires any person who is not indigent and who is confined in the city workhouse to pay a reasonable fee for any medical treatment or service requested by and provided to that person. This fee shall not exceed the actual cost of the treatment or service provided. No person confined to a city workhouse who is indigent shall be required to pay those fees, and no person confined to a city workhouse shall be denied any necessary medical care because of inability to pay those fees.

"Upon provision of the requested medical treatment or service, payment of the required fee may be automatically deducted from a person's account record in the workhouse's business office. If the person has no funds in the person's account, a deduction may be made at a later date during the person's confinement in the workhouse if funds later become available in the person's account. If the person is released from the workhouse and has an unpaid balance of these fees, the board of county commissioners or the legislative authority may bill the person for payment of the remaining unpaid fees. Fees received for medical treatment or services shall be paid into the commissary fund, if one has been created for the workhouse, or if no commissary fund exists, into the county or city treasury.

"(2) If a person confined to a city workhouse is required under division (B) of this section or section 2929.18 or 2929.223 of the Revised Code to reimburse the county or city for expenses incurred by reason of the person's confinement to the workhouse, any fees paid by the person under division (D)(1) of this section shall be deducted from the expenses required to be reimbursed under division (b) of this section or section 2929.18 or 2929.223 of the Revised Code.

"(E) If a person who has been convicted of or pleaded guilty to an offense is confined in the workhouse as provided in division (A) of this section, at the time of reception and at other times the person in charge of the operation of the workhouse determines to be appropriate, the person in charge of the operation of the workhouse may cause the convicted offender to be examined and tested for tuberculosis, HIV infection, hepatitis, including but not limited to hepatitis A, B, and C, and other contagious diseases. The person in charge of the operation of the workhouse may cause a convicted offender in the workhouse who refuses to be tested or treated for tuberculosis, HIV infection, hepatitis, including but not limited to hepatitis A, B, and C, or another contagious disease to be tested and treated involuntarily."

Amendment Note: 1997 S 111 deleted "for the person convicted of the misdemeanor" before "at a hearing" and made a corrective change in division (B)(1); and added division (E).

Amendment Note: 1996 S 269 designated division (B)(1); substituted "an offense" for "a misdemeanor" and "section 2929.18 of the Revised Code if the person is confined for a felony or section 2929.223 of the Revised Code if the person is confined for a misdemeanor" for "section 2929.223 of the Revised Code" in the first paragraph of division (B)(1); inserted "confined for a misdemeanor" and the fourth sentence in the second paragraph of division (B)(1); added division (B)(2); and made other nonsubstantive changes.

Amendment Note: 1996 H 480 rewrote the section, which prior thereto read:

"(A) In a county that has no workhouse but in which is located a city that has a workhouse maintained by the city, the board of county commissioners may agree with the proper authorities of that city upon terms under which persons convicted of misdemeanors shall be maintained in the city workhouse at the expense of the county. In the case of persons committed to the city workhouse for the violation of a law of this state, whether the commitment is from the court of common pleas, magistrate's court, or other court, the cost of maintaining those persons committed shall be paid out of the general fund of the county, on the allowance of the board of county commissioners, provided that all persons committed to the city workhouse for the violation of ordinances of the city shall be maintained in that workhouse at the sole cost of the city.

"(B)(1) The board of county commissioners or the legislative authority of the city may require a person who was convicted of a misdemeanor other than a minor misdemeanor and who is confined in the city workhouse as provided in division (A) of this section to reimburse the county or the city, as the case may be, for its expenses incurred by reason of the person's confinement, including, but not limited to, the expenses relating to the provision of food, clothing, and shelter. The court shall determine the amount of reimbursement at a hearing held pursuant to section 2929.223 of the Revised Code.

"Upon the authorization of the board of county commissioners or of the legislative authority of the city, the prosecuting attorney of the county or the city director of law may institute an appropriate civil action in the name of the state if instituted by the county or in the name of the city in the court of common pleas of the county in which the workhouse is located to recover from a person confined for a misdemeanor the reimbursement for the expenses of the person's confinement in the city workhouse, as determined by a court pursuant to section 2929.223 of the Revised Code. The prosecuting attorney or city director of law shall bring the action within one year after the person is released from incarceration. The amount recovered shall be paid into the treasury of the county or city that incurred the expenses.

Amendment Note: 1995 S 2 substituted "a misdemeanor" for "an offense" and "2929.223" for "2929.15" in the first paragraph in division (B); substituted "person" for "convict" before "the reimbursement" and "2929.223" for "2929.15" and inserted "prosecuting attorney or city director of law" in the second paragraph in division (B); and made changes to reflect gender neutral language and other nonsubstantive changes.

Cross References

Confinement, judgment for costs of, 2929.19, 2929.21

Confinement, reimbursement of costs, authority of board of county commissioners, 2929.37

Insurance coverage of confined beneficiary; confinement, defined, 3924.53

Sentencing, financial sanctions, 2929.18

Library References

Prisons ⚷17, 18.

Westlaw Topic No. 310.

C.J.S. Prisons and Rights of Prisoners §§ 6, 55, 59, 63 to 66, 68 to 72, 76 to 90, 124 to 125, 129, 138.

Research References

Encyclopedias

OH Jur. 3d Penal & Correctional Institutions § 68, Use of City Workhouse by County.

OH Jur. 3d Penal & Correctional Institutions § 83, Contribution by Inmates Toward Cost of Confinement.

Treatises and Practice Aids

Katz, Giannelli, Blair and Lipton, Baldwin's Ohio Practice, Criminal Law, § 123:6, Misdemeanor Jail Terms.

Notes of Decisions

1. Contract for maintenance of prisoners

Where county prisoners are incarcerated in the workhouse of a city, whether inside or outside the county, the board of county commissioners is not bound to expend county funds for the payment of expenses incurred in connection with such incarceration in the absence of a written contract between the county and the proper authority of the jurisdiction receiving and housing such prisoners. OAG 81–042.

A contract, between county and city therein, relating to the maintenance of county prisoners by the city is properly authorized under this section, although the county agrees to reimburse the city for any occurrence causing extra expense to city, including medical treatment of prisoners. 1937 OAG 1424.

2947.20 Health insurance claims of persons confined in city workhouse

(A) For each person who is confined in a city workhouse as provided in section 2947.19 of the Revised Code, the county or the city, as the case may be, may make a determination as to whether the person is covered under a health insurance or health care policy, contract, or plan and, if the person has such coverage, what terms and conditions are imposed by it for the filing and payment of claims.

(B) If, pursuant to division (A) of this section, it is determined that the person is covered under a policy, contract, or plan and, while that coverage is in force, the workhouse renders or arranges for the rendering of health care services to the person in accordance with the terms and conditions of the policy, contract, or plan, then the person, county, city, or provider of the health care services, as appropriate under the terms and conditions of the policy, contract, or plan, shall promptly submit a claim for payment for the health care services to the appropriate third-party payer and shall designate, or make any other arrangement necessary to ensure, that payment of any amount due on the claim be made to the county, city, or provider, as the case may be.

(C) Any payment made to the county or the city pursuant to division (B) of this section shall be paid into the treasury of the governmental entity that incurred the expenses.

(D) This section also applies to any person who is under the custody of a law enforcement officer, as defined in section 2901.01 of the Revised Code, prior to the person's confinement in the workhouse.

(1996 S 163, eff. 10–16–96)

Historical and Statutory Notes

Ed. Note: Former 2947.20 repealed by 1984 H 113, eff. 1–8–85; 1984 H 277; 1972 H 511; 1970 S 460; 1953 H 1; GC 13451–15; see now 2947.14 for provisions analogous to former 2947.20.

Pre–1953 H 1 Amendments: 120 v 320; 113 v 200, Ch 30, § 15

Library References

Prisons ⚖17.
Westlaw Topic No. 310.
C.J.S. Prisons and Rights of Prisoners §§ 55, 59, 63 to 66, 68 to 72, 76 to 90, 124 to 125, 129, 138.

Research References

Treatises and Practice Aids

Katz, Giannelli, Blair and Lipton, Baldwin's Ohio Practice, Criminal Law, § 115:3, Equal Protection in Sentencing.

2947.21 Commitment to workhouse

When a person is sentenced to a workhouse by the court of common pleas, the clerk of the court of common pleas shall make and deliver to the sheriff a certified copy of the judgment. The copy shall describe the crime charged and the sentence of the court. The sheriff shall deliver the copy to the officer in charge of the workhouse, and the copy shall be that officer's warrant for detaining the person in custody. In case of such a conviction by any other court or magistrate, the court or magistrate shall make a certified transcript of the docket in the case, which, in like manner, shall be delivered to the marshal, constable, or sheriff to be delivered by the marshal, constable, or sheriff to the proper officer in charge of the workhouse and be that officer's warrant for detaining the person in custody.

When a person is sentenced to a jail or workhouse under section 2929.24 of the Revised Code, the court shall certify a transcript of the docket in the case, and the court shall deliver the certified transcript to the proper officer in charge of the workhouse or jail, and the certified transcript is the officer's warrant for detaining the person in custody during the prescribed period or periods.

(2002 H 490, eff. 1–1–04; 1995 S 2, eff. 7–1–96; 1980 H 736, eff. 10–16–80; 1969 H 228; 1953 H 1; GC 13451–16)

Historical and Statutory Notes

Pre–1953 H 1 Amendments: 113 v 200, Ch 30, § 16

Amendment Note: 2002 H 490 deleted "division (A)(3) of" after "or workhouse under" and substituted "2929.24" for "2929.51" in the second paragraph of the section.

Amendment Note: 1995 S 2 substituted "(A)(3)" for "(C)(2)" in the second paragraph; and made changes to reflect gender neutral language and other nonsubstantive changes.

Cross References

Municipal corporations, commitment of offender to workhouse, reimbursement by prisoner, 753.04

Place of imprisonment, 2929.221

Library References

Sentencing and Punishment ⚷461.

Westlaw Topic No. 350H.

Research References

Encyclopedias

OH Jur. 3d Criminal Law § 3422, Commitment to Workhouse.

2947.22 Person may be confined in jail temporarily

A person sentenced to a workhouse may be confined in the jail of the county in which he was convicted, for such period as is necessary to procure the papers and make arrangements to transport him to the workhouse.

(1953 H 1, eff. 10–1–53; GC 13451–17)

Historical and Statutory Notes

Pre–1953 H 1 Amendments: 113 v 200, Ch 30, § 17

Cross References

Place of imprisonment, 2929.221

Library References

Prisons ⚷13.3, 13.5(1).

Westlaw Topic No. 310.

C.J.S. Prisons and Rights of Prisoners §§ 130 to 138.

Research References

Encyclopedias

OH Jur. 3d Criminal Law § 3422, Commitment to Workhouse.

2947.23 Judgment for costs and jury fees; community service upon failure to pay

(A)(1) In all criminal cases, including violations of ordinances, the judge or magistrate shall include in the sentence the costs of prosecution and render a judgment against the defendant for such costs. At the time the judge or magistrate imposes sentence, the judge or magistrate shall notify the defendant of both of the following:

(a) If the defendant fails to pay that judgment or fails to timely make payments towards that judgment under a payment schedule approved by the court, the court may order the defendant to perform community service in an amount of not more than forty hours per month until the judgment is paid or until the court is satisfied that the defendant is in compliance with the approved payment schedule.

(b) If the court orders the defendant to perform the community service, the defendant will receive credit upon the judgment at the specified hourly credit rate per hour of community service performed, and each hour of community service performed will reduce the judgment by that amount.

(2) The following shall apply in all criminal cases:

(a) If a jury has been sworn at the trial of a case, the fees of the jurors shall be included in the costs, which shall be paid to the public treasury from which the jurors were paid.

(b) If a jury has not been sworn at the trial of a case because of a defendant's failure to appear without good cause, the costs incurred in summoning jurors for that particular trial may be included in the costs of prosecution. If the costs incurred in summoning jurors are assessed against the defendant, those costs shall be paid to the public treasury from which the jurors were paid.

(B) If a judge or magistrate has reason to believe that a defendant has failed to pay the judgment described in division (A) of this section or has failed to timely make payments towards that judgment under a payment schedule approved by the judge or magistrate, the judge or magistrate shall hold a hearing to determine whether to order the offender to perform community service for that failure. The judge or magistrate shall notify both the defendant and the prosecuting attorney of the place, time, and date of the hearing and shall give each an opportunity to present evidence. If, after the hearing, the judge or magistrate determines that the defendant has failed to pay the judgment or to timely make payments under the payment schedule and that imposition of community service for the failure is appropriate, the judge or magistrate may order the offender to perform community service in an amount of not more than forty hours per month until the judgment is paid or until the judge or magistrate is satisfied that the offender is in compliance with the approved payment schedule. If the judge or magistrate orders the defendant to perform community service under this division, the defendant shall receive credit upon the judgment at the specified hourly credit rate per hour of community service performed, and each hour of community service performed shall reduce the judgment by that amount. Except for the credit and reduction provided in this division, ordering an offender to perform community service under this division does not lessen the amount of the judgment and does not preclude the state from taking any other action to execute the judgment.

(C) As used in this section, "specified hourly credit rate" means the wage rate that is specified in 26 U.S.C.A. 206(a)(1) under the federal Fair Labor Standards Act of 1938, that then is in effect, and that an employer subject to that provision must pay per hour to each of the employer's employees who is subject to that provision.

(2004 S 71, eff. 5–18–05; 2002 H 271, eff. 3–24–03; 1953 H 1, eff. 10–1–53; GC 13451–18)

Historical and Statutory Notes

Pre–1953 H 1 Amendments: 120 v 320; 113 v 201, Ch 30, § 18

Amendment Note: 2004 S 71 inserted "The following shall apply in all criminal cases:" in division (A)(2); designated division (A)(2)(a); and added division (A)(2)(b).

Amendment Note: 2002 H 271 rewrote this section, which prior thereto read:

"In all criminal cases, including violations of ordinances, the judge or magistrate shall include in the sentence the costs of prosecution and render a judgment against the defendant for such costs. If a jury has been sworn at the trial of a case, the fees of the jurors shall be included in the costs, which shall be paid to the public treasury from which the jurors were paid."

Cross References

Sentencing, financial sanctions, 2929.18

Library References

Costs ⚩292, 304, 311, 320.
Westlaw Topic No. 102.
C.J.S. Criminal Law §§ 1740, 1743.

Research References

Encyclopedias

OH Jur. 3d Costs in Civil Actions § 65, Methods of Collection.

OH Jur. 3d Criminal Law § 103, Payment of Assigned Counsel.

OH Jur. 3d Criminal Law § 104, Payment of Assigned Counsel—Reimbursement by Accused.

OH Jur. 3d Criminal Law § 3329, Costs and Jury Fees, Generally.

OH Jur. 3d Criminal Law § 3817, for Resentence.

OH Jur. 3d Criminal Law § 3969, Judgment for Costs and Jury Fees.

OH Jur. 3d Criminal Law § 3984, Liability of Defendant.

OH Jur. 3d Mandamus, Procedendo, & Prohibition § 183, Effect of Patent and Unambiguous Lack of Jurisdiction.

Treatises and Practice Aids

Katz, Giannelli, Blair and Lipton, Baldwin's Ohio Practice, Criminal Law, § 61:5, Indigent Defendants.

Katz, Giannelli, Blair and Lipton, Baldwin's Ohio Practice, Criminal Law, § 119:6, Financial Sanctions.

Katz, Giannelli, Blair and Lipton, Baldwin's Ohio Practice, Criminal Law, § 123:10, Financial Sanctions.

Notes of Decisions

Ability to pay 5
Appointed counsel costs 2
Execution on defendant's property 4
Jury costs 1
Miscellaneous court costs 3

1. Jury costs

Defendant who failed to appear on contingency trial date could not be required to pay jury costs for that date, as there was no evidence that jury was sworn and began to serve in his case on that date. State v. Galbreath (Ohio App. 6 Dist., 08-04-2000) 138 Ohio App.3d 559, 741 N.E.2d 936. Costs ⚩ 311

A defendant incurs no jury costs unless and until the jury is sworn and begins to serve. State v. Galbreath (Ohio App. 6 Dist., 08-04-2000) 138 Ohio App.3d 559, 741 N.E.2d 936. Costs ⚩ 311

Where jurors were never sworn or impanelled prior to a defendant's waiver of her right to a jury trial, it is error for the court to assess costs of the jury against the defendant. State v Alderton, No. 91–CA–2 (5th Dist Ct App, Coshocton, 10–4–91).

In a municipal court criminal action involving a violation of state law the fees of jurors and witnesses are to be taxed as costs and paid out of the county treasury which is to be reimbursed by the clerk of courts when the costs have been paid. OAG 74–077.

A defendant acquitted by a jury of a charge is entitled to the return of costs posted by him before the trial. OAG 69–801.

The costs of prosecution, including jury fees, arising out of a mistrial and subsequent trial and conviction, must be assessed against the defendant pursuant to RC 2947.23, and where, in the subsequent trial, he pleads "guilty" before the jury is impanelled, the fees of that jury may not properly be included in the costs of prosecution; the court has no discretion in the taxing of jury fees in the case where a mistrial is declared resulting in a subsequent trial and conviction. OAG 69–058.

2. Appointed counsel costs

Trial court abused its discretion in assessing jury fees and indigent counsel fees to State upon retrial of defendant on charges of forgery, theft, and grand theft, despite trial court's finding that actions of police officer resulted in mistrial in initial trial; there was no indication that mistrial was intentionally caused by State, trial court had other remedies to express its displeasure with officer's actions, and jury fees and indigent counsel fees were specifically provided for by statute and payable through the county treasury. State v. Songer (Ohio App. 5 Dist., Ashland, 03-17-2004) No. 03COA051, 2004-Ohio-1281, 2004 WL 540305, Unreported, motion for delayed appeal denied 102 Ohio St.3d 1470, 809 N.E.2d 1157, 2004-Ohio-2830, appeal not allowed 103 Ohio St.3d 1477, 816 N.E.2d 254, 2004-Ohio-5405. Costs ⚩ 308; Costs ⚩ 311

The purpose of determining before or during trial whether a defendant is indigent is to protect his or her constitutional rights, such as the right to counsel, from infringement caused by a defendant's indigency; thus, that protection does not shelter a convicted defendant from other burdens, such as court costs. State v. Threatt (Ohio, 03-15-2006) 108 Ohio St.3d 277, 843 N.E.2d 164, 2006-Ohio-905. Costs ⚷ 302; Criminal Law ⚷ 641.6(3)

Attorney fees and court costs could not be assessed against indigent defendant convicted of involuntary manslaughter in absence of court determination that defendant had, or reasonably may be expected to have, the means to pay all or some part of the cost of the legal services rendered to him. State v. Cooper (Ohio App. 12 Dist., 02-19-2002) 147 Ohio App.3d 116, 768 N.E.2d 1223, 2002-Ohio-617. Costs ⚷ 314

The auditor of state is required, upon certification to him of the statement of costs of a criminal conviction pursuant to RC 2949.19, to pay an amount equal to the moneys expended for fees and expenses of court-appointed counsel, approved and taxed as a part of the costs under RC 2941.51, provided there are sufficient funds in the state treasury appropriated for that purpose. State ex rel. Clifford v. Cloud (Ohio 1966) 7 Ohio St.2d 55, 218 N.E.2d 605, 36 O.O.2d 46.

3. Miscellaneous court costs

Trial court had the authority to order indigent defendant, convicted of sexual battery, to pay costs. State v. Cloud (Ohio App. 7 Dist., Columbiana, 03-18-2005) No. 01 CO 64, 2005-Ohio-1331, 2005 WL 678767, Unreported, appeal allowed 106 Ohio St.3d 1482, 832 N.E.2d 736, 2005-Ohio-3978. Costs ⚷ 302

Trial court was authorized to impose fine of $300 on defendant convicted of menacing and resisting arrest, in addition to imposing jail time. State v. Harpster (Ohio App. 5 Dist., Ashland, 03-09-2005) No. 04COA061, 2005-Ohio-1046, 2005 WL 567319, Unreported. Fines ⚷ 1.5

Statutory scheme for assessment of juror fees in criminal cases did not authorize trial court sua sponte to assess juror fees against state, following continuance of trial on joint motion of state and defense. State v. Christian (Ohio App. 7 Dist., Jefferson, 02-10-2005) No. 04 JE 20, 2005-Ohio-905, 2005 WL 497285, Unreported. Costs ⚷ 314

Sentencing court's assessment of court costs against indigent felony defendant was within its statutory discretion. State v. Cole (Ohio App. 6 Dist., Lucas, 02-04-2005) No. L-03-1163, No. L-03-1162, 2005-Ohio-408, 2005 WL 280223, Unreported. Costs ⚷ 302

Defendant, who was convicted of driving under suspension and failure to stop at a red light, and who was given a suspended sentence of 30 days and ordered to pay fines and costs, could be ordered to serve previously suspended 30-day sentence, where defendant failed to pay fines and costs despite his acknowledged employment, defendant failed to appear in court numerous times as ordered, and defendant failed twice to report for community service that was ordered in lieu of the fines and costs. State v. Self (Ohio App. 2 Dist., Montgomery, 01-28-2005) No. 20370, 2005-Ohio-310, 2005 WL 187465, Unreported, judgment vacated on reconsideration 2005-Ohio-1120, 2005 WL 589887. Sentencing And Punishment ⚷ 2003; Sentencing And Punishment ⚷ 2034

Term "costs of prosecution" in statute providing that a sentencing court shall include in sentence costs of prosecution and render a judgment against defendant for costs means court costs in a criminal case, which are those directly related to court proceedings and identified by a specific statutory authorization, and since no statute authorized as costs of proceeding towing and storage of defendant's vehicle, they could not be imposed on defendant who pleaded no contest to aggravated vehicular homicide. State v. Christy (Ohio App. 3 Dist., Wyandot, 12-20-2004) No. 16-04-04, 2004-Ohio-6963, 2004 WL 2940888, Unreported. Costs ⚷ 304

Since trial court was required to include costs as part of its sentence following conviction for possession of drugs, it was not required to orally order defendant to pay the costs of his prosecution. State v. Ward (Ohio App. 3 Dist., Logan, 12-20-2004) No. 8-04-27, 2004-Ohio-6959, 2004 WL 2940878, Unreported. Costs ⚷ 314

Trial court was statutorily required to include in sentence costs of prosecution and render judgment against defendant for such costs, in prosecution for robbery. State v. Hart (Ohio App. 6 Dist., Lucas, 10-15-2004) No. L-03-1073, 2004-Ohio-5511, 2004 WL 2320334, Unreported, appeal not allowed 105 Ohio St.3d 1408, 821 N.E.2d 1028, 2005-Ohio-279, habeas corpus denied 2006 WL 1348434. Costs ⚷ 314

Trial court had jurisdiction to enforce collection of court costs and fees associated with petitioner's conviction for driving under the influence (DUI), even though petitioner's probationary period had ended, and thus writ of prohibition would not lie to compel trial court to take no further action to enforce collection of costs and fees; action to collect unpaid court costs was wholly independent and divorced from other proceedings, and trial court's authority to collect costs and fees was in no way contingent on petitioner's probationary period after conviction. State ex rel. Logue v. Fregiato (Ohio App. 7 Dist., Belmont, 08-11-2004) No. 04-BE-26, 2004-Ohio-4289, 2004 WL 1812833, Unreported, subsequent mandamus proceeding 2005-Ohio-2941, 2005 WL 1385725. Costs ⚷ 320

Statute requiring a convicted defendant to pay costs of prosecution was applicable to defendant despite his indigent status; costs would be collected when defendant ceased to be indigent. State v. Hall (Ohio App. 11 Dist., Lake, 06-18-2004) No. 2001-L-230, 2004-Ohio-3186, 2004 WL 1375752, Unreported, appeal not allowed 103 Ohio St.3d 1494, 816 N.E.2d 1080, 2004-Ohio-5605. Costs ⚷ 302

Trial court was required by statute to include, in sentence for possession of crack cocaine, and tampering with evidence, costs of prosecution, and to render judgment against defendant for such costs. State v. Fuller (Ohio App. 6 Dist., Lucas, 05-07-2004) No. L-02-1387, No. L-02-1390, No. L-02-1388, No. L-02-1389, 2004-Ohio-2675, 2004 WL 1171056, Unreported. Costs ⚷ 292

Defendant's claim that trial court erred in denying his motion to waive court costs was not ripe for appellate review, where no attempt had been made to collect the costs assessed to defendant. State v. Chambers (Ohio App. 5 Dist., Stark, 03-15-2004) No. 2003CA00337, 2004-Ohio-1279, 2004 WL 539997, Unreported. Criminal Law ⚷ 1134(3)

Trial court did not err in assessing costs of murder prosecution against defendant; statute provided that judge in criminal cases would include in sentence costs of prosecution and render judgment against defendant for such costs. State v. Anderson (Ohio App. 6 Dist., Lucas, 03-12-2004) No. L-01-1239, No. L-01-1248, 2004-Ohio-1188, 2004 WL 485568, Unreported. Costs ⚷ 292

Trial court properly charged defendant with the prosecution costs. State v. Peoples (Ohio App. 6 Dist., Lucas, 05-30-2003) No. L-02-1048, 2003-Ohio-2794, 2003 WL 21255943, Unreported. Costs ⚷ 292

Trial court was authorized to assess costs of prosecution against defendant following trial for rape, aggravated robbery, felonious assault, and aggravated burglary; statute on taxing costs against litigants was intended to lighten burden on taxpayers of financing court system, and statutory provisions for payment of court costs were not enacted to serve punitive, retributive, or rehabilitative purpose, as were fines. State v. Jones (Ohio App. 6 Dist., Lucas, 04-11-2003) No. L-02-1047, 2003-Ohio-1865, 2003 WL 1861033, Unreported, appeal not allowed 100 Ohio St.3d 1409, 796 N.E.2d 537, 2003-Ohio-4948, habeas corpus denied 2006 WL 903199. Costs ⚷ 292

A judgment ordering defendant to pay "costs of prosecution" does not include the defendant's attorney fees but, rather, orders payment of the court costs incurred in the prosecution of the case. State v. Holmes (Ohio App. 6 Dist., Lucas, 11-08-2002) No. L-01-1459, 2002-Ohio-6185, 2002 WL 31521456, Unreported. Costs ⚷ 304; Costs ⚷ 308

Trial court has authority to impose court costs upon indigent defendant; statute requires court to include costs as part of sentence and, while second statute provides collection mechanism only for non-indigent defendants, nothing in second statute prohibits court from collecting costs from indigent defendant. State v. Haynie (Ohio App. 3 Dist., 05-17-2004) 157 Ohio App.3d 708, 813 N.E.2d 686, 2004-Ohio-2452, appeal allowed 103 Ohio St.3d 1477, 816 N.E.2d 253, 2004-Ohio-5405, reconsideration denied 104 Ohio St.3d 1428, 819 N.E.2d 710, 2004-Ohio-6585, affirmed 105 Ohio St.3d 133, 823 N.E.2d 448, 2005-Ohio-785. Costs ⚷ 302

A trial court's failure to specify amount of costs assessed in its sentencing entry does not defeat finality of sentencing entry as to costs for purposes of appeal; courts have authority to assess costs against convicted criminal defendants, and assessment of costs is merely a ministerial task. State v. Threatt (Ohio, 03-15-2006) 108 Ohio St.3d 277, 843 N.E.2d 164, 2006-Ohio-905. Criminal Law ⚷ 1023(11)

Clerk of courts could attempt collection of court costs that had been assessed against indigent defendant who had been convicted of a felony as part of his sentence; statutory scheme at issue was silent as to indigent defendants, from which it could be inferred that collection of court costs from indigent defendants was merely permissive. State v. White (Ohio, 11-24-2004) 103 Ohio St.3d 580, 817 N.E.2d 393, 2004-Ohio-5989. Costs ⚷ 320

Trial court may order an indigent defendant to pay court costs as part of his sentence. State v. Roux (Ohio App. 7 Dist., 09-11-2003) 154 Ohio App.3d 296, 797 N.E.2d 112, 2003-Ohio-4876, motion to certify allowed 101 Ohio St.3d 1419, 802 N.E.2d 151, 2004-Ohio-123, appeal allowed 101 Ohio St.3d 1420, 802 N.E.2d 152, 2004-Ohio-123, affirmed 105 Ohio St.3d 126, 823 N.E.2d 443, 2005-Ohio-783. Costs ⚷ 302

Statutes providing that sentence includes costs of prosecution and that specific dollar amount be imposed as part of costs when offender has been convicted or pled guilty were intended by legislature to authorize assessment of costs against defendant, including jury fees, only when state has been successful. State v. Powers (Ohio App. 6 Dist., 12-30-1996) 117 Ohio App.3d 124, 690 N.E.2d 32. Costs ⚷ 288; Costs ⚷ 311

After conviction on misdemeanor charge of reckless operation of motor vehicle and acquittals on charges of assault and menacing, sentencing court could assess against defendant only those costs associated with bench trial of misdemeanor charge and not those incurred as result of jury trial on charges of assault and menacing. State v. Powers (Ohio App. 6 Dist., 12-30-1996) 117 Ohio App.3d 124, 690 N.E.2d 32. Costs ⚷ 290

Defendants' potential liability for "costs of prosecution" does not include costs of probation and, thus, court may not order defendant to pay expenses incurred in preparing presentence investigation. State v. Watkins (Ohio App. 1 Dist., 07-20-1994) 96 Ohio App.3d 195, 644 N.E.2d 1049. Costs ⚷ 304

Trial court lacked authority to assess court costs against defendant after prosecutor dismissed criminal charge; defendant was not proven or otherwise found to be guilty, and was not sentenced. Cuyahoga Falls v. Coup–Peterson (Ohio App. 9 Dist. 1997) 124 Ohio App.3d 716, 707 N.E.2d 545.

Absent a plea agreement an accused who is never found guilty of failing to wear a seatbelt is not responsible for the forty dollar court costs assessed by the trial court. Willoughby v Sapina, Nos. 2000–L–138+, 2001 WL 1602651 (11th Dist Ct App, Lake, 12–14–01).

A county prosecuting attorney is not required to pay court costs when a criminal prosecution brought in the court of common pleas does not result in a defendant being convicted of, or pleading guilty to, an offense. OAG 05–014.

The cost of a breathalyzer test used to secure the criminal conviction of a defendant pursuant to RC 4511.19 may not be taxed as costs of prosecution and assessed against the defendant. OAG 84–088.

The reasonable costs of transporting an out-of-state prisoner into the state of Ohio as a necessary witness in a criminal prosecution for violation of state law is taxable as a criminal cost and payable by the auditor of state under the criminal cost subsidy program. OAG 74–101.

4. Execution on defendant's property

Money that an accused has in his possession at the time he is taken into custody, and which is turned over to and remains in the possession of law enforcement officers, is subject to execution for the payment of the costs of the prosecution. Witherspoon v. Belt (Ohio 1964) 177 Ohio St. 1, 201 N.E.2d 590, 28 O.O.2d 407.

Trial court did not patently and unambiguously lack jurisdiction to issue order reviving judgment for collection of court costs from inmate, and thus, prohibition was unavailable to stop garnishment of funds from his prison account in order to satisfy that judgment. State ex rel. Pless v. McMonagle (Ohio App. 8 Dist. 2000) 139 Ohio App.3d 503, 744 N.E.2d 274.

5. Ability to pay

Trial court was required by statute to impose court costs upon defendant, on his conviction for obstructing official business, despite his claim of indigency; statute at issue, stating that, in all criminal cases, judge had to include in sentence costs of prosecution and render judgment against defendant for such costs, did not prohibit trial court from assessing costs against indigent defendants, but, rather, required trial court to assess costs against all convicted defendants. State v. Hayes (Ohio App. 11 Dist., Ashtabula, 06-10-2005) No. 2004-A-0024, 2005-Ohio-2881, 2005 WL 1383959, Unreported. Costs ⚷ 302

Trial court was required to order defendant to pay restitution upon convictions for breaking and entering and grand theft, regardless of defendant's indigent status. State v. Terrell (Ohio App. 3 Dist., Wyandot, 05-09-2005) No. 16-04-16, 2005-Ohio-2253, 2005 WL 1074813, Unreported. Sentencing And Punishment ⚷ 2135

Trial court was not required to determine defendant's ability to pay before ordering defendant to pay costs of prosecution for unlawful sexual contact. State v. Bulgakov (Ohio App. 6 Dist., Wood, 04-08-2005) No. WD-03-096, 2005-Ohio-1675, 2005 WL 791403, Unreported. Costs ⚷ 292

Although the trial court was not required to make a determination as to defendant's ability to pay the costs of prosecution, the court did not err in making such a finding prior to assessing such costs. State v. Hawthorne (Ohio App. 6 Dist., Lucas, 03-31-2005) No. L-03-1120, No. L-03-1127, 2005-Ohio-1553, 2005 WL 736994, Unreported. Costs ⚷ 314

Trial court abused its discretion in not granting defendant a waiver for payment of imposed court costs and costs of prosecution after he was sentenced to prison for felonies, even though defendant might have had potential for prison earnings; it was highly probable that defendant would be unable to pay costs, given his extremely poor health, lack of any employment history, lack of education, and 18-year aggregated sentence. State v. John (Ohio App. 6 Dist., Lucas, 03-18-2005) No. L-03-1261, 2005-Ohio-1218, 2005 WL 635026, Unreported, appeal allowed 106 Ohio St.3d 1482, 832 N.E.2d 736, 2005-Ohio-3978, appeal not allowed 107 Ohio St.3d 1685, 839 N.E.2d 404, 2005-Ohio-6480, reversed in part 109 Ohio St.3d 313, 847 N.E.2d 1174, 2006-Ohio-2109. Costs ⚷ 319

Trial court had authority to assess court costs against indigent defendant who had been convicted of felonious assault; statute governing assessment of court costs did not prohibit assessment of costs against indigent defendants but, rather, required assessment of costs against all convicted defendants. State v. Clifford (Ohio App. 3 Dist., Paulding, 03-07-2005) No. 11-04-06, 2005-Ohio-958, 2005 WL 517514, Unreported, appeal allowed 106 Ohio St.3d 1460, 830 N.E.2d 1168, 2005-Ohio-3490, reversed 109 Ohio St.3d 313, 847 N.E.2d 1174, 2006-Ohio-2109. Costs ⚷ 302

Defendant's right to be present at imposition of sentence was not violated when trial court, in judgment entry of sentencing and not at sentencing hearing, ordered defendant to pay court costs; imposition of court costs was mandatory and not at discretion of trial court, and statute governing assessment of court costs did not require imposition of costs to be made on record at sentencing hearing. State v. Clifford (Ohio App. 3 Dist., Paulding, 03-07-2005) No. 11-04-06, 2005-Ohio-958, 2005 WL 517514, Unreported, appeal allowed 106 Ohio St.3d 1460, 830 N.E.2d 1168, 2005-Ohio-3490, reversed 109 Ohio St.3d 313, 847 N.E.2d 1174, 2006-Ohio-2109. Sentencing And Punishment ⚷ 341

Defendant's indigent status did not preclude assessment against him of court costs, or prevent garnishment of his inmate stipend with respect thereto, where trial court was statutorily required to impose costs of prosecution irrespective of defendant's indigent status. State v. Felder (Ohio App. 3 Dist., Marion, 02-14-2005) No. 9-04-51, 2005-Ohio-546, 2005 WL 335977, Unreported. Costs ⚷ 302; Costs ⚷ 320

Trial court was not required to waive imposition of costs of prosecution as part of sentencing for aggravated murder simply because defendant was indigent. State v. Morgan (Ohio App. 3 Dist., Shelby, 02-07-2005) No. 17-04-14, 2005-Ohio-426, 2005 WL 280448, Unreported. Costs ⚷ 302

Sentencing court's imposition of statutory fees was supported by sufficient evidence of defendant's future ability to pay, where sentencing court reviewed defendant's pre-sentence investigation report, which contained information about defendant's family history, employment history, educational history, and his physical and mental health. State v. Cole (Ohio App. 6 Dist., Lucas, 02-04-2005) No. L-03-1163, No. L-03-1162, 2005-Ohio-408, 2005 WL 280223, Unreported. Costs ⚷ 314

Trial court was required to impose costs of prosecution for sexual battery, regardless of defendant's indigency status. State v. Dickinson (Ohio App. 7 Dist., Columbiana, 11-26-2004) No. 03 CO 52, 2004-Ohio-6373, 2004 WL 2726057, Unreported, appeal not allowed 105 Ohio St.3d 1499, 825 N.E.2d 623, 2005-Ohio-1666. Costs ⚷ 292

Trial court was not required to determine defendant's ability to pay before ordering defendant to pay court costs following his guilty plea to charge of harassment by inmate. State v. Brunson (Ohio App. 7 Dist., Belmont, 11-17-2004) No. 03-BE-26, 2004-Ohio-6211, 2004 WL 2659243, Unreported. Costs ⚷ 292

In the absence of transcript of sentencing hearing, Court of Appeals was unable to review hearing to determine if court committed any error in assessing court costs and attorney fees or if court considered any additional evidence regarding defendant's ability to pay costs and fees, and thus, Court had to presume regularity of proceeding. State v. Call (Ohio App. 3 Dist., Marion, 10-25-2004) No. 9-04-29, 2004-Ohio-5645, 2004 WL 2377822, Unreported, appeal not allowed 105 Ohio St.3d 1453, 823 N.E.2d 457, 2005-Ohio-763. Criminal Law ⚷ 1144.17

Trial court is not required to hold hearing or otherwise determine offender's ability to pay before ordering him to pay court costs. State v. Robinson (Ohio App. 3 Dist., Hancock, 10-04-2004) No. 5-04-12, 2004-Ohio-5346, 2004 WL 2260101, Unreported. Costs ⚷ 314

Trial court possessed authority to order indigent defendant to pay court costs; clerk of court's inability to collect costs from indigent party did not prevent trial court from ordering payment of such costs. State v. Dobbins (Ohio App. 5 Dist., Muskingum, 09-02-2004) No. 03 CA 58, 2004-Ohio-4715, 2004 WL 1969137, Unreported. Costs ⚷ 302

Statute governing trial court's authority to impose costs on defendant convicted of felony did not prohibit court from assessing costs to indigent defendant as part of sentence. State v. Vasquez (Ohio App. 10 Dist., Franklin, 07-22-2004) No. 03AP-460, 2004-Ohio-3880, 2004 WL 1631610, Unreported, affirmed 104 Ohio St.3d 507, 820 N.E.2d 370, 2004-Ohio-7016. Costs ⚷ 302

Record reflected that trial court had considered defendant's present and future ability to pay costs, court-appointed counsel fees, and restitution to victim; before imposing community control, trial court indicated it had reviewed defendant's confidential presentence investigation (PSI) report that described defendant's criminal record, family history, living arrangements, educational background, physical and mental health, and defendant's employment history, and trial court explicitly stated on record that defendant had, or could reasonably be expected to have, means to pay costs of restitution, costs of supervision and prosecution, and cost of counsel fee. State v. Riegsecker (Ohio App. 6 Dist., Fulton, 07-16-2004) No. F-03-022, 2004-Ohio-3808, 2004 WL 1595723, Unreported. Costs ⚷ 314; Sentencing And Punishment ⚷ 2134

Statute governing assessment of court costs and jury fees applied to both indigent and nonindigent defendants. State v. Cantwell (Ohio App. 5 Dist., Stark, 06-07-2004) No. 2003CA00367, 2004-Ohio-2964, 2004 WL 1267101, Unreported, appeal allowed 103 Ohio St.3d 1491, 816 N.E.2d 1078, 2004-Ohio-5605, motion to certify allowed 105 Ohio St.3d 1495, 825 N.E.2d 620, 2005-Ohio-1666, reversed 108 Ohio St.3d 528, 844 N.E.2d 1190, 2006-Ohio-1706. Costs ⚷ 304; Costs ⚷ 311

Trial court appropriately considered defendant's present and future ability to pay unspecified court costs, fees, and restitution following defendant's conviction by no contest plea to robbery; trial court noted that it had considered defendant's presentence investigation report (PSI), which indicated that defendant had earned approximately $60,000 per year for the past seven years as a sub-contractor laying carpet for retailers. State v. Loofbourrow (Ohio App. 6 Dist., Lucas, 05-07-2004) No. L-03-1002, 2004-Ohio-2678, 2004 WL 1171147, Unreported, appeal not allowed 103 Ohio St.3d 1464, 815 N.E.2d 679, 2004-Ohio-5056. Costs ⚷ 314; Sentencing And Punishment ⚷ 2134

Record did not support trial court's finding of indigency, and thus trial court erred in waiving court costs in sentencing defendant; record did not show that finding was based on defendant's financial condition or that court considered any other relevant circumstances from which the court could reasonably find indigency. City of Cleveland v. Lockwood (Ohio App. 8 Dist., Cuyahoga, 05-06-2004) No. 83165, 2004-Ohio-2349, 2004 WL 1047923, Unreported. Costs ⚷ 314

Trial court's finding of indigency, for purposes of determining whether court costs may be suspended in criminal case, should be clear from the record and be based on a reasonable consideration of the circumstances in existence at the time of the finding, including the individual's financial condition. City of Cleveland v. Lockwood (Ohio App. 8 Dist., Cuyahoga, 05-06-2004) No. 83165, 2004-Ohio-2349, 2004 WL 1047923, Unreported. Costs ⚷ 314

Imposition of court costs as part of sentence in criminal cases is mandatory, absent finding of indigency. City of Cleveland v. Lockwood (Ohio App. 8 Dist., Cuyahoga, 05-06-2004) No. 83165, 2004-Ohio-2349, 2004 WL 1047923, Unreported. Costs ⚷ 292

Issue as to collection of court costs assessed to defendant, who was allegedly indigent, was not ripe for review either when defendant filed his motion to waive with trial court or when trial court denied the same. State v. Durenda (Ohio App. 5 Dist., Stark, 03-15-2004) No. 2003CA00336, 2004-Ohio-1292, 2004 WL 540923, Unreported. Criminal Law ⚷ 1134(3)

Nothing prevented trial court from assessing defendant court costs by virtue of his indigent status, upon his conviction for multiple theft-related offenses and engaging in corrupt activity; imposition of court costs was not an infringement of defendant's rights nor did it violate any statute. State v. Glavic (Ohio App. 11 Dist., Lake, 12-22-2003) No. 2001-L-177, No. 2001-L-179, 2003-Ohio-6961, 2003 WL 22994557, Unreported, motion for delayed appeal granted 102 Ohio St.3d 1444, 808 N.E.2d 396, 2004-Ohio-2263, appeal allowed 103 Ohio St.3d 1442, 814 N.E.2d 869, 2004-Ohio-4626, appeal not allowed 104 Ohio St.3d 1411, 818 N.E.2d 711, 2004-Ohio-6364, affirmed 105 Ohio St.3d 131, 823 N.E.2d 447, 2005-Ohio-31, appeal not allowed 107 Ohio St.3d 1411, 836 N.E.2d 1230, 2005-Ohio-5859. Costs ⚷ 302

Defendant was required to pay court costs that had been imposed as part of sentence for driving under the influence conviction, even though defendant was indigent at time of conviction; statute providing that a court include costs as part of a defendant's sentence made no distinction between indigent and non-indigent defendants, and no State law prohibited a judge from including court costs as part of the sentence of an indigent defendant. State v. May (Ohio App. 11 Dist., Ashtabula, 12-22-2003) No. 2001-A-0037, 2003-Ohio-6979, 2003 WL 22994542, Unreported, appeal allowed 102 Ohio St.3d 1408, 806 N.E.2d 560, 2004-Ohio-1763, affirmed 105 Ohio St.3d 131, 823 N.E.2d 446, 2005-Ohio-789. Costs ⚷ 302

Criminal statute requiring convicted defendant to pay costs of prosecution was applicable to drug defendant, despite his indigent status; costs would be collected when defendant ceased to be indigent. State v. Peacock (Ohio App. 11 Dist., Lake, 12-12-2003) No. 2002-L-115, 2003-Ohio-6772, 2003 WL 22952755, Unreported. Costs ⚷ 302

Trial court lacked statutory authority to impose court costs on indigent defendant as part of sentencing for domestic violence. State v. Schofield (Ohio App. 4 Dist., Washington, 12-05-2003) No. 01CA36, No. 02CA13, 2003-Ohio-6553, 2003 WL 22889403, Unreported. Costs ⚷ 292

Imposition of costs of prosecution on defendant convicted of robbery and theft was required by law, even though defendant was indigent; statute required imposition of costs on all defendants, and statute on collection of costs from nonindigent defendants did not prohibit imposition of costs on indigent defendants, but simply detailed procedure for collecting costs from defendants able to pay them. State v. Barlow (Ohio App. 2 Dist., Montgomery, 11-26-2003) No. 19628, 2003-Ohio-6530, 2003 WL 22887903, Unreported, appeal allowed 102 Ohio St.3d 1408, 806 N.E.2d 561, 2004-Ohio-1763, affirmed 105 Ohio St.3d 130, 823 N.E.2d 446, 2005-Ohio-790. Costs ⚷ 302

Inmate could not use mandamus claim to collaterally attack order imposing court costs in his underlying criminal case, as he could have raised that issue in his original direct appeal. State of Ohio ex rel. Biros v. Logan (Ohio App. 11 Dist., Trumbull, 10-10-2003) No. 2003-T-0016, 2003-Ohio-5425, 2003 WL 22326666, Unreported. Mandamus ⚷ 4(4)

Inmate had adequate legal remedy for challenging imposition of court costs at sentencing, and thus he was not entitled to writ of prohibition to prevent garnishment of court costs from his prison account, where inmate could have challenged order imposing court costs on direct appeal from sentence. State of Ohio ex rel. Biros v. Logan (Ohio App. 11 Dist., Trumbull, 10-10-2003) No. 2003-T-0016, 2003-Ohio-5425, 2003 WL 22326666, Unreported. Prohibition ⚷ 3(4)

Decision to impose court costs on indigent defendant could only be contested on direct appeal from sentencing judgment; consequently, res judicata barred inmate from collaterally attacking that order in original action in prohibition and mandamus. State of Ohio ex rel. Biros v. Logan (Ohio App. 11 Dist., Trumbull, 10-10-2003) No. 2003-T-0016, 2003-Ohio-5425, 2003 WL 22326666, Unreported. Judgment ⚷ 479; Judgment ⚷ 648

Record demonstrated that trial court properly considered whether defendant had or reasonably could be expected to have means to pay all or part of costs of legal services rendered to him before ordering him to pay costs; trial court asked defendant if defendant owned an interest in any real estate, defendant informed court that he owned a house which he intended to sell as soon as possible, and court noted that defendant had been gainfully employed his entire adult life. State v. Estes (Ohio App. 12 Dist., Preble, 10-06-2003) No. CA2002-05-008, 2003-Ohio-5283, 2003 WL 22283503, Unreported, denial of post-conviction relief affirmed 2005-Ohio-5478, 2005 WL 2626194, appeal not allowed 108 Ohio St.3d 1488, 843 N.E.2d 794, 2006-Ohio-962. Costs ⚷ 314

Trial court was not required to consider defendant's ability to pay costs of prosecution before ordering defendant to pay such costs. State v. Estes (Ohio App. 12 Dist., Preble, 10-06-2003) No. CA2002-05-008, 2003-Ohio-5283, 2003 WL 22283503, Unreported, denial of post-conviction relief affirmed 2005-Ohio-5478, 2005 WL 2626194, appeal not allowed 108 Ohio St.3d 1488, 843 N.E.2d 794, 2006-Ohio-962. Costs ⚷ 292

Defendant's sentence to more than 200 community service hours, for driving without a license and disorderly conduct, was lawful, where defendant was ordered to serve 160 hours as a condition of probation on one conviction, 80 hours for cost of prosecution, and 20 hours in lieu of a fine for second offense. City of Toledo v. Kelley (Ohio App. 6 Dist., Lucas, 10-03-2003) No. L-02-1266, 2003-Ohio-5269, 2003 WL 22272078, Unreported. Sentencing And Punishment ⚷ 1982(3)

Statute governing trial court's authority to impose costs on a defendant convicted of a felony did not prohibit court from assessing costs to an indigent defendant as part of a sentence; in the event indigent defendant at some point ceased to be indigent, clerk could then collect costs pursuant to statutory procedure. State v. White (Ohio App. 5 Dist., Guernsey, 04-30-2003) No. 02CA23, 2003-Ohio-2289, 2003 WL 21025839, Unreported, motion to certify allowed 100 Ohio St.3d 1406, 796 N.E.2d 534, 2003-Ohio-4948, appeal allowed 100 Ohio St.3d 1409, 796 N.E.2d 536, 2003-Ohio-4948, motion granted 101 Ohio St.3d 1461, 804 N.E.2d 36, 2004-Ohio-814. Costs ⚷ 302

Trial court did not err by ordering defendant convicted of aggravated robbery to pay costs of prosecution without first determining his ability to pay. State v. Robinson (Ohio App. 6 Dist., Lucas, 03-31-2003) No. L-02-1061, 2003-Ohio-1627, 2003 WL 1700570, Unreported. Costs ⚷ 314

That defendant was declared indigent at time of trial for attempted murder and felonious assault did not preclude Department of Rehabilitation and Correction from withdrawing amounts from prison account to pay court costs. State v. Morrison (Ohio App. 10 Dist., Franklin, 03-27-2003) No. 02AP-651, 2003-Ohio-1517, 2003 WL 1564303, Unreported. Costs ⚷ 320

Trial court was not required to consider defendant's ability to pay before ordering in sentencing entry that he pay costs of prosecution. State v. Willis (Ohio App. 12 Dist., Butler, 11-12-2002) No. CA2002-02-028, 2002-Ohio-6303, 2002 WL 31564561, Unreported. Costs ⚷ 292

A motion by an indigent criminal defendant for waiver of payment of costs must be made at the time of sentencing. State v. Threatt (Ohio, 03-15-2006) 108 Ohio St.3d 277, 843 N.E.2d 164, 2006-Ohio-905. Costs ⚷ 319

When collecting court costs from an indigent criminal defendant, the state may use any collection method that is available to collect a civil money judgment or may collect from a prisoner's account; an indigent criminal defendant is not different from any other indigent who owes a debt. State v. Threatt (Ohio, 03-15-2006) 108 Ohio St.3d 277, 843 N.E.2d 164, 2006-Ohio-905. Costs ⚷ 320

Trial court had authority to assess court costs against indigent defendant who had been convicted of a felony as part of his sentence; statutes at issue did not prohibit trial court from assessing costs against indigent defendants, but instead required trial court to assess costs against all convicted defendants; abrogating, *State v. Clark*, 2002 WL 31742999. State v. White (Ohio, 11-24-2004) 103 Ohio St.3d 580, 817 N.E.2d 393, 2004-Ohio-5989. Costs ⚷ 302

Trial court's finding that defendant was unemployed was insufficient basis to conclude that defendant was indigent, and thus trial court was required to conduct a further inquiry on remand to determine whether defendant's indigent status permitted suspension of court costs arising from defendant's conviction for parking in a handicap zone. Cleveland v. King (Ohio App. 8 Dist., 07-17-2003) 153 Ohio App.3d 326, 794 N.E.2d 88, 2003-Ohio-3807. Costs ⚷ 302; Criminal Law ⚷ 1181.5(8)

Trial court was entitled to order defendant to pay the costs of prosecution without considering his present and future ability to pay them. State v Willis, No. CA2001–05–119, 2002–Ohio–4868, 2002 WL 31060278 (12th Dist Ct App, 9–16–02).

MENTALLY DEFICIENT AND PSYCHOPATHIC OFFENDERS

2947.24 to 2947.29 Mentally deficient and psychopathic offenders—Repealed

(1978 H 565, eff. 11–1–78; 1977 H 1; 1976 H 244; 1975 H 1; 1972 H 494, H 511; 1970 S 272; 1969 H 688; 132 v S 316, H 1; 130 v H 430; 129 v 1448; 126 v 392; 125 v 823; 1953 H 1; GC 13451–19 to 13451–23)

Historical and Statutory Notes

Ed. Note: See now parenthetical references for provisions analogous to former sections: 2947.24 (5122.01); 2947.25 (2945.37, 5122.141); 2947.26 to 2947.28 (2945.40, 5122.15).

Pre–1953 H 1 Amendments: 124 v S 265; 121 v 443; 118 v 686, § 1

2947.30 and 2947.31 Possession of firearms while committing certain crimes; periodic sentences—Repealed

(1972 H 511, eff. 1–1–74; 1972 H 143; 1969 H 228; 132 v H 996)

Historical and Statutory Notes

Ed. Note: See now 2917.02 for provisions analogous to former 2947.30.

CHAPTER 2949

EXECUTION OF SENTENCE

MAGISTRATE DEFINED

2949.01 Definition of magistrate

The definition of "magistrate" set forth in section 2931.01 of the Revised Code applies to Chapter 2949. of the Revised Code.

(1953 H 1, eff. 10–1–53)

SUSPENSION OF SENTENCE

2949.02 Suspension of execution of sentence or judgment pending appeal to court of appeals; bail; exceptions

(A) If a person is convicted of any bailable offense, including, but not limited to, a violation of an ordinance of a municipal corporation, in a municipal or county court or in a court of common pleas and if the person gives to the trial judge or magistrate a written notice of the person's intention to file or apply for leave to file an appeal to the court of appeals, the trial judge or magistrate may suspend, subject to division (A)(2)(b) of section 2953.09 of the Revised Code, execution of the sentence or judgment imposed for any fixed time that will give the person time either to prepare and file, or to apply for leave to file, the appeal. In all bailable cases, except as provided in division (B) of this section, the trial judge or magistrate may release the person on bail in accordance with Criminal Rule 46, and the bail shall at least be conditioned that the person will appeal without delay and abide by the judgment and sentence of the court.

(B) Notwithstanding any provision of Criminal Rule 46 to the contrary, a trial judge of a court of common pleas shall not release on bail pursuant to division (A) of this section a person who is convicted of a bailable offense if the person is sentenced to imprisonment for life or if that offense is a violation of section 2903.01, 2903.02, 2903.03, 2903.04, 2903.11, 2905.01, 2905.02, 2905.11, 2907.02, 2909.02, 2911.01, 2911.02, or 2911.11 of the Revised Code or is felonious sexual penetration in violation of former section 2907.12 of the Revised Code.

(C) If a trial judge of a court of common pleas is prohibited by division (B) of this section from releasing on bail pursuant to division (A) of this section a person who is convicted of a bailable offense and not sentenced to imprisonment for life, the appropriate court of appeals or two judges of it, upon motion of such a person and for good cause shown, may release the person on bail in accordance with Appellate Rule 8 and Criminal Rule 46, and the bail shall at least be conditioned as described in division (A) of this section.

(1996 H 445, eff. 9–3–96; 1986 H 412, eff. 3–17–87; 1982 H 269, § 4, S 199; 1953 H 1; GC 13453–1)

Uncodified Law

1982 H 269, § 4, eff. 1–5–83, amended 1982 S 199, § 10, eff. 1–5–83, to read, in part: " [2949.02], as amended by [1982 S 199],... shall take effect on July 1, 1983, and shall apply only to offenses committed on or after July 1, 1983."

Historical and Statutory Notes

Pre–1953 H 1 Amendments: 113 v 203, Ch 32, § 1

Amendment Note: 1996 H 445 changed the designation of division (A)(1) to division (A); removed a reference to section 2907.12 from, and inserted "or is felonious sexual penetration in violation of former section 2907.12 of the Revised Code" in, division (B); and made changes to reflect gender neutral language and other nonsubstantive changes.

Cross References

Bail, Crim R 46

Bail on appeal, suspension of execution of sentence, App R 8

Bailable offenses, O Const Art I §9

Effects of appeal to supreme court, bail, recognizance, exception, 2953.09

Life imprisonment, 2907.02, 2929.02

Probation, Ch 2951

Transmission of recognizance, 2937.28

Library References

Bail ⚷44.

Sentencing and Punishment ⚷475 to 480.

Westlaw Topic Nos. 350H, 49.

C.J.S. Bail; Release and Detention Pending Proceedings §§ 6, 9, 14, 30 to 32, 34 to 37.

C.J.S. Criminal Law §§ 1525, 1547, 1552, 1688.

Research References

Encyclopedias

OH Jur. 3d Criminal Law § 1969, Power of Ohio Supreme Court to Prescribe Rules.

OH Jur. 3d Criminal Law § 2195, After Conviction of Bailable Offense.

OH Jur. 3d Criminal Law § 3360, Suspension of Sentence for Purpose of Appeal.

Treatises and Practice Aids

Katz, Giannelli, Blair and Lipton, Baldwin's Ohio Practice, Criminal Law, § 80:15, Bail and Stay of Sentence.

Katz, Giannelli, Blair and Lipton, Baldwin's Ohio Practice, Criminal Law, § 153:29, Entry for Sentence Suspended and Bail Given.

Katz, Giannelli, Blair and Lipton, Baldwin's Ohio Practice, Criminal Law, § 153:30, Entry for Sentence Suspended and Bail Not Given.

Katz, Giannelli, Blair and Lipton, Baldwin's Ohio Practice, Criminal Law, § 153:31, Bond on Suspension of Execution of Sentence and Entry.

Katz, Giannelli, Blair and Lipton, Baldwin's Ohio Practice, Criminal Law, § 153:32, Entry Increasing Recognizance.

Painter & Dennis, Ohio Appellate Practice § 1:20, Effect of Appeal on Jurisdiction of Court Below-Stays Pending Appeal-Criminal Cases.

Painter & Dennis, Ohio Appellate Practice § 1:40, Basic Steps in Appeal to Court of Appeals-Checklist.

Hennenberg & Reinhart, Ohio Criminal Defense Motions F 12.22, Appellant's Motion for Order Suspending Execution of Sentence Pending Appeal to Court of Appeals-Appeal/Appellate Motions.

Hennenberg & Reinhart, Ohio Criminal Defense Motions F 12.23, Appeal/Appellate Motion-Stay of Execution Pending Appeal-Direct Appeal from Trial Court.

Notes of Decisions

1. Constitutional issues

There is no constitutional right to bail after conviction and pending appeal, and the granting of bail on appeal is within the sound discretion of the court. Coleman v. McGettrick (Ohio 1965) 2 Ohio St.2d 177, 207 N.E.2d 552, 31 O.O.2d 326, certiorari denied 86 S.Ct. 78, 382 U.S. 834, 15 L.Ed.2d 77. Bail ⚷ 44(1)

There is no constitutional provision assuring person sentenced the right to have a bail bond fixed on an appeal from such sentence. State v. Fullmer (Montgomery 1945) 76 Ohio App. 335, 62 N.E.2d 268, 43 Ohio Law Abs. 193, 32 O.O. 53.

Former GC 13453–1 (RC 2949.02) (113 v 203) denying accused persons right to bail after judgment in trial court where the punishment is imprisonment for life is not unconstitutional. Ex parte Halsey (Ohio 1931) 124 Ohio St. 318, 178 N.E. 271, 77 A.L.R. 1232, 10 Ohio Law Abs. 670, 35 Ohio Law Rep. 291. Bail ⚷ 42

The conflict between App R 8 and Crim R 46 on the one hand, and RC 2949.02 and 2953.09 on the other, is one involving procedural matters; App R 8 and Crim R 46 prevail over the conflicting statutes, because O Const Art IV §5 commits matters of practice and procedure to the Ohio Supreme Court's rulemaking authority. State ex rel. Silcott v. Spahr (Ohio 1990) 50 Ohio St.3d 110, 552 N.E.2d 926.

2. Authority to suspend sentence or admit to bail

Absent an appeal on behalf of a defendant, there is no authority by which the trial court may suspend the execution of a sentence except upon the granting of probation or parole. State v. Kraguljac (Lorain 1988) 39 Ohio App.3d 167, 530 N.E.2d 970.

The punishment of one convicted of murder in the second degree is not life imprisonment, and such imprisonment is only "until legally released," and upon appeal of such conviction any judge of the court of appeals may admit such defendant to bail. (But see State v Sheppard, 97 App 489, 123 NE(2d) 544 (1955) and 97 App 493, 124 NE(2d) 730 (1955).) State v. Hawkins (Belmont 1954) 97 Ohio App. 477, 124 N.E.2d 453, 56 O.O. 127.

The statutory law of the state prohibits either the trial court or the reviewing court to which an appeal is taken from extending the privilege of bail pending appeal to one found guilty of a crime for which the punishment is life imprisonment. State v. Sheppard (Cuyahoga 1955) 97 Ohio App. 489, 123 N.E.2d 544, 69 Ohio Law Abs. 286, 56 O.O. 425, motion denied 97 Ohio App. 493, 124 N.E.2d 730, 56 O.O. 451.

When a defendant has been found guilty of a crime for which the punishment is life imprisonment, neither the trial court nor a reviewing court can admit him to bail pending appeal. (But see State v Hawkins, 97 App 477, 124 NE(2d) 453 (1954).) State v. Sheppard (Cuyahoga 1955) 97 Ohio App. 489, 123 N.E.2d 544, 69 Ohio Law Abs. 286, 56 O.O. 425, motion denied 97 Ohio App. 493, 124 N.E.2d 730, 56 O.O. 451. Bail ⚷ 44(2)

This section is directed toward trial court and not toward reviewing courts. State v. Cook (Stark 1942) 70 Ohio App. 1, 44 N.E.2d 474, 24 O.O. 304.

Court of common pleas has no authority to suspend execution of sentence duly imposed following conviction for felony, except for such period of time as will give accused opportunity to prosecute appeal proceedings. State v. Parks (Summit 1941) 67 Ohio App. 96, 36 N.E.2d 42, 21 O.O. 120. Sentencing And Punishment ⚷ 1806

Where court has suspended execution of sentence without lawful authority so to do, order of suspension may be treated as nullity and void, and original sentence carried into execution, even after the term in which order suspending execution of sentence was made; court does not lose jurisdiction to enforce sentence in criminal case by unauthorized attempt to suspend it. State v. Parks (Summit 1941) 67 Ohio App. 96, 36 N.E.2d 42, 21 O.O. 120. Sentencing And Punishment ⚩ 2010

By statute, authority is conferred upon trial judges to suspend imposition of sentence and place defendant upon probation; also discretionary power is conferred upon trial judges in this section as to bailable offenses; also provision is made for conditional sentence in misdemeanors. Municipal Court of Toledo v. State (Ohio 1933) 126 Ohio St. 103, 184 N.E. 1, 37 Ohio Law Rep. 382.

Ohio trial courts may order suspension of execution of criminal case sentence only as authorized by statute. Municipal Court of Toledo v. State (Ohio 1933) 126 Ohio St. 103, 184 N.E. 1, 37 Ohio Law Rep. 382.

3. Discretion of court

Denial of bail pending appeal of a conviction of theft in office is not an abuse of discretion where (1) the strength of the case on appeal cannot be determined from the pleadings, (2) the absence of a threat to the community is not established by the pleadings, and (3) only the fact that no flight from trial took place is offered as proof that no likelihood exists of flight pending appeal. Christopher v. McFaul (Ohio 1985) 18 Ohio St.3d 233, 480 N.E.2d 484, 18 O.B.R. 291.

Where two courts of appeals are not in agreement as to the court's power to grant bail at its discretion to a defendant after conviction in a criminal action upon appeal, such conflict of opinion cannot be certified to the Supreme Court for the reason that such order granting or denying bail is not a "judgment" within the meaning of O Const Art IV §6. State v. Sheppard (Cuyahoga 1955) 97 Ohio App. 493, 124 N.E.2d 730, 56 O.O. 451.

The suspension of the execution of sentence and admission to bail after conviction rest in the sound discretion of the judge, and strong consideration should be accorded the principle that an accused should not suffer the penalty for a crime until he has exhausted the appeals avenues open to him. State v. Hawkins (Belmont 1954) 97 Ohio App. 477, 124 N.E.2d 453, 56 O.O. 127.

Where a juvenile court finds a child to be a delinquent child and commits her to an industrial school, refusal to allow bail bond, pending an appeal, is not prejudicial, where there is no showing of abuse of discretion. State v. Fullmer (Montgomery 1945) 76 Ohio App. 335, 62 N.E.2d 268, 43 Ohio Law Abs. 193, 32 O.O. 53.

One convicted of felony is not entitled as a matter of right to be admitted to bail or to have execution of sentence suspended pending appeal of such judgment of conviction in a reviewing court; but trial court may under this section suspend execution of sentence and release defendant upon approved recognizance pending appeal. Ex parte Thorpe (Ohio 1936) 132 Ohio St. 119, 5 N.E.2d 333, 7 O.O. 224. Bail ⚩ 44(2)

4. Moot appeal

A defendant convicted of a criminal offense must, where practicable, seek a stay of sentence in order to defeat a claim of mootness. Middletown v. Allen (Butler 1989) 63 Ohio App.3d 443, 579 N.E.2d 254. Criminal Law ⚩ 1134(3)

A defendant's appeal of a petty theft conviction is not rendered moot simply because he has completed his sentence where it would have been impracticable for him to seek a stay of sentence since it could have nearly doubled the amount of actual jail time he would have to serve; defendant was ordered to serve time on an unrelated charge which was to run concurrent to his petty theft sentence and had he sought a stay of his petty theft sentence, he would still have served the sentence arising from a bench warrant. Middletown v. Allen (Butler 1989) 63 Ohio App.3d 443, 579 N.E.2d 254.

5. Mandamus

Mandamus will not lie to compel the common pleas court to act on a motion to suspend sentence where the court has denied the motion. State ex rel. Breaux v. Court of Common Pleas of Cuyahoga County (Ohio 1977) 50 Ohio St.2d 164, 363 N.E.2d 743, 4 O.O.3d 352.

Where a court has made an unlawful order of suspension of execution of a sentence in a criminal case, mandamus is a proper remedy for ordering court to set aside and vacate such order and compel execution of the original sentence. Municipal Court of Toledo v. State (Ohio 1933) 126 Ohio St. 103, 184 N.E. 1, 37 Ohio Law Rep. 382.

2949.03 Suspension of execution of sentence or judgment pending appeal to supreme court

If a judgment of conviction by a court of common pleas, municipal court, or county court is affirmed by a court of appeals and remanded to the trial court for execution of the sentence or judgment imposed, and the person so convicted gives notice of his intention to file a notice of appeal to the supreme court, the trial court, on the filing of a motion by such person within three days after the rendition by the court of appeals of the judgment of affirmation, may further suspend, subject to division (A)(2)(b) of section 2953.09 of the Revised Code, the execution of the sentence or judgment imposed for a time sufficient to give such person an opportunity to file a notice of appeal to the supreme court, but the sentence or judgment imposed shall not be suspended more than thirty days for that purpose.

(1986 H 412, eff. 3–17–87; 1953 H 1; GC 13453–2)

Historical and Statutory Notes

Pre–1953 H 1 Amendments: 113 v 204, Ch 32, § 2

Cross References

Bail, Crim R 46

Bail on appeal, suspension of execution of sentence, App R 8

Library References

Sentencing and Punishment ⚷475 to 480.

Westlaw Topic No. 350H.

C.J.S. Criminal Law §§ 1525, 1547, 1552, 1688.

Research References

Treatises and Practice Aids

Katz, Giannelli, Blair and Lipton, Baldwin's Ohio Practice, Criminal Law, § 80:15, Bail and Stay of Sentence.

Notes of Decisions

Modification of sentence 1

1. Modification of sentence

After the denial of an appeal in the court of appeals, the Supreme Court of Ohio and the US Supreme Court, a court cannot modify a legal sentence subsequent to the term at which it was rendered. State v. Markos (Ohio Com.Pl. 1961) 179 N.E.2d 397, 88 Ohio Law Abs. 26, 18 O.O.2d 75. Sentencing And Punishment ⚷ 2281

2949.04 Increase or decrease of bail

When bail is fixed pursuant to division (B) of section 2953.03 or section 2949.02 or 2953.09 of the Revised Code in connection with an appeal, a reduction or increase in the amount of that bail or other change in that bail shall not be required of the accused during the pendency of the appeal unless the trial judge or magistrate, or the court in which the appeal is being prosecuted, finds that there is good cause to reduce or increase the amount of that bail or good cause for any other change in that bail. If the court in which the appeal is being prosecuted finds there is good cause to reduce or increase the amount of that bail or good cause for any other change in that bail, it shall order the reduction, increase, or other change in accordance with Criminal Rule 46, and the new bail shall be in the amount and form so ordered and otherwise be to the approval of and filed with the clerk of the court in which the appeal is being prosecuted.

(1986 H 412, eff. 3–17–87; 129 v 423; 1953 H 1; GC 13453–3)

Historical and Statutory Notes

Pre–1953 H 1 Amendments: 113 v 204, Ch 32, § 3

Cross References

Bail, Crim R 46

Bail on appeal, suspension of execution of sentence, App R 8

Library References

Bail ⚷53.

Westlaw Topic No. 49.

C.J.S. Bail; Release and Detention Pending Proceedings §§ 66, 68, 70.

Research References

Encyclopedias

OH Jur. 3d Criminal Law § 2195, After Conviction of Bailable Offense.

Treatises and Practice Aids

Katz, Giannelli, Blair and Lipton, Baldwin's Ohio Practice, Criminal Law, § 80:15, Bail and Stay of Sentence.

Katz, Giannelli, Blair and Lipton, Baldwin's Ohio Practice, Criminal Law, § 153:31, Bond on Suspension of Execution of Sentence and Entry.

Katz, Giannelli, Blair and Lipton, Baldwin's Ohio Practice, Criminal Law, § 153:32, Entry Increasing Recognizance.

EXECUTION OF SENTENCE GENERALLY

2949.05 Execution of sentence or judgment

If no appeal is filed, if leave to file an appeal or certification of a case is denied, if the judgment of the trial court is affirmed on appeal, or if post-conviction relief under section 2953.21 of the Revised Code is denied, the trial court or magistrate shall carry into execution the sentence or judgment which had been pronounced against the defendant.

(1986 H 412, eff. 3–17–87; 1969 S 354; 129 v 423; 1953 H 1; GC 13453–4)

Historical and Statutory Notes

Pre–1953 H 1 Amendments: 113 v 204, Ch 32, § 4

Library References

Sentencing and Punishment ⚩460.

Westlaw Topic No. 350H.

C.J.S. Criminal Law §§ 1420 to 1422, 1458, 1471, 1480 to 1481, 1484, 1504 to 1505, 1511.

Research References

Encyclopedias

OH Jur. 3d Criminal Law § 3403, Void Sentencing Orders.

OH Jur. 3d Criminal Law § 3413, When Sentence Will be Executed, Generally.

Treatises and Practice Aids

Katz, Giannelli, Blair and Lipton, Baldwin's Ohio Practice, Criminal Law, § 153:33, Entry Carrying Suspended Sentence Into Execution.

Notes of Decisions

1. Execution of sentence

Trial court did not have authority or jurisdiction to resentence defendant after Court of Appeals rendered decision upholding validity of trial court's original sentencing decision and defendant was transferred to penal institution of executive branch. State v. Harrold (Ohio App. 9 Dist., Summit, 06-30-2004) No. 21797, 2004-Ohio-3423, 2004 WL 1462991, Unreported. Sentencing And Punishment ⚩ 2282

Releasing convicted criminals due to overcrowding with instructions to return to jail at a later date to serve their sentences is proper. Ruth v Leis, No. C-930117, 1994 WL 79587 (1st Dist Ct App, Hamilton, 3-16-94).

Former statute regarding deduction from sentence for faithful observance of rules did not entitle inmate to release from prison before he served maximum term of his sentence. Rollins v. Haviland (Ohio 2001) 93 Ohio St.3d 590, 757 N.E.2d 769, 2001 –Ohio- 1884. Prisons ⚩ 15(3)

Once the trial court has carried into execution a valid sentence, it may no longer amend or modify that sentence. State v. Garretson (Ohio App. 12 Dist., 06-30-2000) 140 Ohio App.3d 554, 748 N.E.2d 560, appeal allowed 90 Ohio St.3d 1451, 737 N.E.2d 55, appeal dismissed as improvidently allowed 91 Ohio St.3d 1267, 746 N.E.2d 1127, 2001-Ohio-94. Sentencing And Punishment ⚩ 2282

Trial court lacked subject matter jurisdiction to order defendant returned to prison after he had been released by Department of Rehabilitation and Corrections, even if Department had miscalculated his time spent in prison and mistakenly given him good time credit under old sentencing laws; original sentencing order was valid, as trial court was authorized to sentence defendant to term set forth therein, and thus, judicial branch's authority over sentence ended when defendant was delivered to permanent detention facility. State v. Garretson (Ohio App. 12 Dist., 06-30-2000) 140 Ohio App.3d 554, 748 N.E.2d 560, appeal allowed 90 Ohio St.3d 1451, 737 N.E.2d 55, appeal dismissed as improvidently allowed 91 Ohio St.3d 1267, 746 N.E.2d 1127, 2001-Ohio-94. Sentencing And Punishment ⚷ 2282

After finding a probation violation and reimposing a suspended sentence, the court has no power to stay execution until the defendant gets his GED, and thus no jurisdiction to grant additional probation in lieu of execution of the sentence or subsequently determine that the defendant violated the additional probation. State v. Sanders (Hamilton 1992) 78 Ohio App.3d 672, 605 N.E.2d 1265, dismissed, jurisdictional motion overruled 64 Ohio St.3d 1428, 594 N.E.2d 970.

Absent parole or probation, trial court is without authority to stay execution of sentence unless defendant perfects appeal from conviction. State v. Kraguljac (Lorain 1988) 39 Ohio App.3d 167, 530 N.E.2d 970. Sentencing And Punishment ⚷ 476

Where a defendant does not report to serve his sentence following the affirmance of his conviction, but instead continues to reside at his previous address until arrested on a capias four years later, the state does not forfeit its jurisdiction to enforce that sentence, and does not thereby violate the defendant's constitutional rights. State v Dawley, No. 50974 (8th Dist Ct App, Cuyahoga, 9–25–86).

2. Modification of sentence

Trial court lacked jurisdiction to modify defendant's sentence for felonious assault once her incarceration had begun, where defendant's motion for modification of sentence did not allege that sentencing order was void or contained clerical mistake. State v. Longmire (Ohio App. 11 Dist., Portage, 12-20-2002) No. 2001-P-0014, 2002-Ohio-7153, 2002 WL 31862676, Unreported. Sentencing And Punishment ⚷ 2277

A trial court has the authority to correct void sentencing orders; for these purposes, a sentence is rendered void when there is an attempt by the court to disregard statutory requirements when imposing a sentence. State v. Garretson (Ohio App. 12 Dist., 06-30-2000) 140 Ohio App.3d 554, 748 N.E.2d 560, appeal allowed 90 Ohio St.3d 1451, 737 N.E.2d 55, appeal dismissed as improvidently allowed 91 Ohio St.3d 1267, 746 N.E.2d 1127, 2001-Ohio-94. Sentencing And Punishment ⚷ 2254

After the denial of an appeal in the court of appeals, the Supreme Court of Ohio and the US Supreme Court, a court cannot modify a legal sentence subsequent to the term at which it was rendered. State v. Markos (Ohio Com.Pl. 1961) 179 N.E.2d 397, 88 Ohio Law Abs. 26, 18 O.O.2d 75. Sentencing And Punishment ⚷ 2281

2949.06 Recapture after escape

If a person escapes after sentence and before confinement in a state correctional institution or jail, the clerk of the trial court, upon application of the prosecuting attorney or by order of the court, shall issue a warrant stating the conviction and sentence and commanding the sheriff to pursue the person into any county of this state. The sheriff shall take into custody the person so escaping and shall make return of the warrant to the court if it is in session, and if it is not in session he shall commit the accused to the jail of the county and bring him before the court at the next session of the court. The court shall set aside the former sentence and again pronounce judgment upon the verdict.

(1994 H 571, eff. 10–6–94; 1953 H 1, eff. 10–1–53; GC 13453–5)

Historical and Statutory Notes

Pre–1953 H 1 Amendments: 113 v 204, Ch 32, § 5

Amendment Note: 1994 H 571 substituted "a state correctional institution" for "the penitentiary".

Cross References

Escape, 2921.34

Library References

Arrest ⚷72, 73.

Westlaw Topic No. 35.

C.J.S. Arrest § 50.

Research References

Encyclopedias

OH Jur. 3d Criminal Law § 3410, After Escape.

Treatises and Practice Aids

Katz, Giannelli, Blair and Lipton, Baldwin's Ohio Practice, Criminal Law, § 153:34, Entry for Sentence of Accused Upon Recapture.

2949.07 Computing time served

If a convict escapes from a state correctional institution, the time the convict is absent from the institution because of his escape shall not be credited as a part of the time for which he was sentenced.

(1994 H 571, eff. 10–6–94; 1953 H 1, eff. 10–1–53; GC 13453–6)

Historical and Statutory Notes

Pre–1953 H 1 Amendments: 113 v 204, Ch 32, § 6

Amendment Note: 1994 H 571 substituted "a state correctional institution" for "the penitentiary or reformatory".

Cross References

Escape, 2921.34

Parole eligibility, 2967.13

Library References

Sentencing and Punishment ⚷1176.

Westlaw Topic No. 350H.

C.J.S. Criminal Law §§ 1570 to 1574, 1577 to 1581.

Research References

Encyclopedias

OH Jur. 3d Criminal Law § 1435, Effect of Escape on Prior Conviction and Sentence.

OH Jur. 3d Penal & Correctional Institutions § 130, Extension of Sentence; Effect of Escape.

Notes of Decisions

Dead time 1

---

1. Dead time

Where a convict is absent from the Ohio penitentiary by reason of his escape therefrom, the time of such absence shall not be credited as a part of the time for which he was sentenced, even though during a portion of the time of such absence the convict was imprisoned in the penitentiary of another state for an offense in that state. In re Pullins (Franklin 1952) 94 Ohio App. 364, 115 N.E.2d 398, 52 O.O. 31. Sentencing And Punishment ⚷ 1182

2949.08 Confinement of convicts; reduction of sentence for confinement prior to conviction

(A) When a person who is convicted of or pleads guilty to a felony is sentenced to a community residential sanction in a community-based correctional facility pursuant to section 2929.16 of the Revised Code or when a person who is convicted of or pleads guilty to a felony or a misdemeanor is sentenced to a term of imprisonment in a jail, the judge or magistrate shall order the person into the custody of the sheriff or constable, and the sheriff or constable shall deliver the person with the record of the person's conviction to the jailer, administrator, or keeper, in whose custody the person shall remain until the term of imprisonment expires or the person is otherwise legally discharged.

(B) The record of the person's conviction shall specify the total number of days, if any, that the person was confined for any reason arising out of the offense for which the person was convicted and sentenced prior to delivery to the jailer, administrator, or keeper under this section. The record shall be used to determine any reduction of sentence under division (C) of this section.

(C) (1) If the person is sentenced to a jail for a felony or a misdemeanor, the jailer in charge of a jail shall reduce the sentence of a person delivered into the jailer's custody pursuant to division (A) of this section by the total number of days the person was confined for any reason arising out of the offense for which the person was convicted and sentenced, including confinement in lieu of bail while awaiting trial, confinement for examination to determine the person's competence to stand trial or to determine sanity, and confinement while awaiting transportation to the place where the person is to serve the sentence.

(2) If the person is sentenced to a community-based correctional facility for a felony, the total amount of time that a person shall be confined in a community-based correctional facility, in a jail, and for any reason arising out of the offense for which the person was convicted and sentenced prior to delivery to the jailer, administrator, or keeper shall not exceed the maximum prison term available for that offense. Any term in a jail shall be reduced first pursuant to division (C)(1) of this section by the total number of days the person was confined prior to delivery to the jailer, administrator, or keeper. Only after the term in a jail has been entirely reduced may the term in a community-based correctional facility be reduced pursuant to this division. This division does not affect the limitations placed on the duration of a term in a jail or a community-based correctional facility under divisions (A)(1), (2), and (3) of section 2929.16 of the Revised Code.

(D) For purposes of divisions (B) and (C) of this section, a person shall be considered to have been confined for a day if the person was confined for any period or periods of time totaling more than eight hours during that day.

(E) As used in this section, "Community–based correctional facility" and "jail" have the same meanings as in section 2929.01 of the Revised Code.

(1999 S 107, eff. 3–23–00; 1979 S 23, eff. 3–27–80; 1953 H 1; GC 13454–1)

Historical and Statutory Notes

Pre–1953 H 1 Amendments: 113 v 205, Ch 33, § 1

Amendment Note: 1999 S 107 rewrote this section, which prior thereto read:

"(A) When a person convicted of a misdemeanor is sentenced to imprisonment in jail or the workhouse, the judge or magistrate shall order him into the custody of the sheriff or constable, who shall deliver him with the record of his conviction, to the jailer or keeper, in whose custody he shall remain until the term of his imprisonment expires or he is otherwise legally discharged.

"(B) The record of the person's conviction shall specify the total number of days, if any, that the person was confined for any reason arising out of the offense for which he was convicted and sentenced prior to delivery to the jailer or keeper under this section. The record shall be used to determine any reduction of sentence under division (C) of this section.

"(C) The jailer, administrator, or keeper in charge of a jail or workhouse shall reduce the sentence of a person delivered into his custody pursuant to division (A) of this section by the total number of days the prisoner was confined for any reason arising out of the offense for which the prisoner was convicted and sentenced, including confinement in lieu of bail while awaiting trial, confinement for examination to determine his competence to stand trial or to determine sanity, and confinement while awaiting transportation to the place where he is to serve his sentence.

"(D) For purposes of divisions (B) and (C) of this section, a person shall be considered to have been confined for a day if the person was confined for any period or periods of time totaling more than eight hours during that day."

Cross References

Endangering children, reduction of sentence, 2919.22

Library References

Sentencing and Punishment ⚷1156.

Time ⚷11.

Westlaw Topic Nos. 350H, 378.

C.J.S. Criminal Law §§ 1571 to 1576, 1578, 1580.

C.J.S. Time §§ 8, 11.

Research References

Encyclopedias

OH Jur. 3d Criminal Law § 3420, Confinement Upon Conviction.

OH Jur. 3d Criminal Law § 3421, Credit for Time Served.

OH Jur. 3d Criminal Law § 3423, Delivery of Convict to Reception Facility.

OH Jur. 3d Criminal Law § 3425, Credit for Time Served.

Treatises and Practice Aids

Katz, Giannelli, Blair and Lipton, Baldwin's Ohio Practice, Criminal Law, § 115:3, Equal Protection in Sentencing.

Katz, Giannelli, Blair and Lipton, Baldwin's Ohio Practice, Criminal Law, § 119:8, Violations of Community Control Sanctions.

Painter, Ohio Driving Under the Influence § 12:42, Credit for Time Served.

Notes of Decisions

---

1. Credit for jail time

Evidence was insufficient to establish that defendant was under detention at time he allegedly violated condition of electronic home monitoring, thus requiring reversal of his escape conviction; although evidence showed that defendant, while released on pretrial bond pending his burglary and felonious assault prosecution, removed his electronic monitoring ankle bracelet and left his home without permission of monitoring department, defendant's electronic monitoring was not a sentence condition, but rather a pretrial condition of bond, which did not constitute detention. State v. Sutton (Ohio App. 6 Dist., Lucas, 05-07-2004) No. L-03-1104, 2004-Ohio-2679, 2004 WL 1171149, Unreported, appeal allowed 103 Ohio St.3d 1461, 815 N.E.2d 677, 2004-Ohio-5056, affirmed 104 Ohio St.3d 264, 819 N.E.2d 284, 2004-Ohio-6558. Escape ⚷ 1

Where multiple sentences run consecutively, jail-time credit is credited to one charge. State v. Altenbaugh (Ohio App. 6 Dist., Lucas, 05-30-2003) No. L-02-1357, 2003-Ohio-2787, 2003 WL 21255923, Unreported. Sentencing And Punishment ⚷ 1157

Defendant was entitled to six additional days of credit for time served, where there was no indication that defendant received credit for time between his arrest and his subsequent release on bond. State v. Altenbaugh (Ohio App. 6 Dist., Lucas, 05-30-2003) No. L-02-1357, 2003-Ohio-2787, 2003 WL 21255923, Unreported. Sentencing And Punishment ⚷ 1158

Inmate was not entitled to have sentencing credit from time served on prior attempted rape conviction counted towards parole consideration for rape conviction for rape occurring several years later; sentence for later conviction was entirely independent of his earlier conviction. State ex rel. Hayden v. Ohio Adult Parole Authority (Ohio App. 10 Dist., Franklin, 05-08-2003) No. 02AP-1157, 2003-Ohio-2316, 2003 WL 21027905, Unreported. Pardon And Parole ⚷ 49

Even if petitioner was legally entitled to double credit on length of prison sentence due to time served in county jail before convictions for possession of cocaine, any alleged error in calculation of petitioner's credit could not be reviewed in context of habeas corpus action, because determination of jail-time credit lied within province of sentencing court, and any error by sentencing court could have been contested only in direct appeal from sentencing judgment. Tillis v. Gansheimer (Ohio App. 11 Dist., Ashtabula, 03-07-2003) No. 2002-A-0099, 2003-Ohio-1097, 2003 WL 943790, Unreported. Habeas Corpus ⚷ 296

Defendant, who filed motion for correction of jail credit time, was entitled to correction, where there was no evidence in record that trial court had given defendant credit for time he spent in jail prior to trial and until his subsequent transportation to prison on sexual battery charge; record indicated that only credit for jail time defendant had received was for time spent in jail while awaiting probation violation hearing. State v. Camp (Ohio App. 12 Dist., Clinton, 11-25-2002) No. CA2002-03-013, 2002-Ohio-6393, 2002 WL 31647909, Unreported. Sentencing And Punishment ⚷ 2334

Inmate's 30 days of jail-time credit could not be used to shorten 30-month aggregate term for second county convictions, and thus, such credit would not alter inmate's release date from prison; in two cases in which inmate did receive 30-day credit, he was originally sentenced to concurrent terms of 24 and six months under first county convictions and inmate started to serve such sentences approximately three weeks before aggregate term for second county convictions was even imposed, and two first county sentences were to be completely served before conclusion of 30-month aggregate term for second county convictions. Engelhart v. Warran (Ohio App. 11 Dist., Ashtabula, 10-25-2002) No. 2002-A-0037, 2002-Ohio-5867, 2002 WL 31411067, Unreported. Sentencing And Punishment ⚷ 1160

Defendant was not entitled to have jail term reduced for days he spent on his own recognizance following date bail was set and before trial; being released on one's own recognizance with condition of returning to court for disposition was not confinement, for jail credit purposes. State v. Sullivan (Ohio App. 7 Dist., Columbiana, 09-26-2002) No. 01 CO 66, 2002-Ohio-5225, 2002 WL 31169164, Unreported. Sentencing And Punishment ⚷ 1157

Complaint for a writ of mandamus seeking an order from requiring grant of jail-time credit in underlying cases was moot since relator had been granted jail-time credit in both cases. S/O ex rel. Lewis v. Fuerst (Ohio App. 8 Dist., Cuyahoga, 02-21-2002) No. 80666, 2002-Ohio-657, 2002 WL 253917, Unreported. Mandamus ⚷ 16(1)

Where an indigent misdemeanor defendant is not advised of his right to or provided with counsel, the court may not sentence that defendant to incarceration; this is true even if the defendant need not report to jail due to the credit he is given for time served. State v. O'Neill (Ohio App. 7 Dist., 09-13-2000) 140 Ohio App.3d 48, 746 N.E.2d 654, 2000-Ohio-2656. Criminal Law ⚷ 641.2(4)

Time spent by defendant in "Pathfinder" halfway house program as condition of probation following his conviction for domestic violence did not constitute "confinement," and thus, defendant was not entitled to credit for that time against previously suspended sentence of imprisonment which was reimposed following revocation of probation; halfway house did not have bars, and participants in program, who maintained outside employment while residing at halfway house, were free to come and go from building with permission. State v.

Combs (Ohio App. 2 Dist., 09-10-1999) 134 Ohio App.3d 566, 731 N.E.2d 750.

Appeal of a 30–day jail sentence which was suspended on condition of one year of probation, in which defendant argued that trial court improperly failed to give him credit for 59 days spent in jail prior to sentencing, was not premature, even though defendant had received stay of execution pending appeal and had not yet been transmitted to jailer. N. Olmsted v. Cipiti (Ohio App. 8 Dist., 09-09-1996) 114 Ohio App.3d 549, 683 N.E.2d 795, dismissed, appeal not allowed 77 Ohio St.3d 1518, 674 N.E.2d 372. Criminal Law ⚷ 1134(3)

Sentence of 30 days in jail for fourth-degree misdemeanor, suspended on condition of one year of probation, was void and defendant was entitled to release, where defendant had spent 59 days in jail prior to sentencing, thus exceeding the maximum 30 days of incarceration that could be imposed for violation of probation. N. Olmsted v. Cipiti (Ohio App. 8 Dist., 09-09-1996) 114 Ohio App.3d 549, 683 N.E.2d 795, dismissed, appeal not allowed 77 Ohio St.3d 1518, 674 N.E.2d 372. Sentencing And Punishment ⚷ 1162

Trial court committed reversible error by failing to specify in defendant's record of conviction that he had served 179 days in juvenile detention facility or to order that defendant's sentence be reduced by the number of days he served in that facility. State v. James (Ohio App. 9 Dist., 10-04-1995) 106 Ohio App.3d 686, 666 N.E.2d 1185. Criminal Law ⚷ 1177

Statute stating that jailor shall reduce sentence of prisoner by the total number of days prisoner was "confined for any reason" arising out of offense for which prisoner was sentenced focuses on "confinement," which is followed by the broad modifier "for any reason," and, thus, statute is intended to encompass a wide range of situations and facilities. State v. James (Ohio App. 9 Dist., 10-04-1995) 106 Ohio App.3d 686, 666 N.E.2d 1185. Sentencing And Punishment ⚷ 1157

Since defendant was unable to leave juvenile detention facility of his own volition, he was "confined" within meaning of statute stating that jailor shall reduce sentence of prisoner by the total number of days prisoner was "confined" for any reason, and, thus, defendant should have received credit for the 179 days that he served in juvenile detention facility. State v. James (Ohio App. 9 Dist., 10-04-1995) 106 Ohio App.3d 686, 666 N.E.2d 1185. Sentencing And Punishment ⚷ 1157

Under RC 2949.08 the number of days an individual is confined in the juvenile detention center are to be included in the record of conviction. State v. James (Ohio App. 9 Dist., 10-04-1995) 106 Ohio App.3d 686, 666 N.E.2d 1185.

Any pretrial confinement of a defendant on charges which ultimately are concluded by a conviction for a charge which constitutes a minor misdemeanor must be credited against any fine or costs imposed by the sentencing trial court. State v. Sparks (Franklin 1990) 69 Ohio App.3d 400, 590 N.E.2d 1294.

Where a defendant remains in jail for any reason before trial, the period of actual confinement must be credited against the sentence ultimately imposed by statute; failure to credit the period of confinement is plain error. State v. Piersall (Hamilton 1984) 20 Ohio App.3d 110, 485 N.E.2d 276, 20 O.B.R. 142.

Credit for pretrial confinement pursuant to RC 2949.08 must be given against the minimum three-day sentence required by RC 4511.99(A)(1). State v. Dixon (Clark 1984) 18 Ohio App.3d 86, 481 N.E.2d 1197, 18 O.B.R. 402.

RC 2949.08 clearly requires a trial court to certify to a jailer the number of days that a defendant was confined while awaiting bail, and the jailer must give the defendant credit for that time in determining the date of release from confinement following conviction. State v. Ward (Butler 1984) 16 Ohio App.3d 276, 475 N.E.2d 802, 16 O.B.R. 301. Sentencing And Punishment ⚷ 1159

Defendant was entitled, at sentencing in homicide case, to credit for the period during which he was confined for a determination of competency to stand trial and for the period, following his release from an involuntary civil commitment as a mentally ill person that did not qualify as pretrial confinement, during which he was held until sentencing. State v. Stafford (Ohio App. 7 Dist., Noble, 09-26-2002) No. 265, 2002-Ohio-5243, 2002 WL 31170127, Unreported, reconsideration denied 2002-Ohio-7184, 2002 WL 31859518, appeal not allowed 98 Ohio St.3d 1477, 784 N.E.2d 710, 2003-Ohio-974, appeal not allowed 98 Ohio St.3d 1515, 786 N.E.2d 64, 2003-Ohio-1572. Sentencing And Punishment ⚷ 1158

Where a defendant, incarcerated and unable to make bond under multiple felony and misdemeanor charges and multiple bonds, is given concurrent sentences in county jail and a state reformatory, the question of which bond defendant is unable to post is irrelevant; the court's judgment entry should give credit for all time served. State v Starcher, Nos. 2082 and 2113 (9th Dist Ct App, Wayne, 11–20–85).

2. Time in rehabilitation

Insufficiency of record on nature of treatment facility necessitated remand for determination of whether nature of facility warranted that defendant be given jail time credit for time he was at facility. State v. Glancy (Ohio App. 5 Dist., Licking, 07-07-2003) No. 03-CA-23, 2003-Ohio-3580, 2003 WL 21525480, Unreported. Criminal Law ⚷ 1181.5(8)

Time served in a correctional institution as a condition of probation must be credited to defendant's original sentence where the primary purpose of the confinement is correction rather than rehabilitation. State v. Giles (Ohio App. 6 Dist., Erie, 03-29-1996) No. E-95-047, 1996 WL 139518, Unreported, dismissed, appeal not allowed 77 Ohio St.3d 1412, 670 N.E.2d 1001.

In determining whether defendant is entitled to jail-time credit for time spent in a treatment facility while on probation, court must review the nature of the rehabilitation program to determine whether the restrictions on the participants are so stringent as to constitute "confinement" as contemplated by the legislature. State v. Jones (Ohio App. 5 Dist., 08-08-1997) 122 Ohio App.3d 430, 702 N.E.2d 106. Sentencing And Punishment ⚷ 2041

When a defendant's sentence has been suspended and he has been placed on conditional probation pursuant to RC 2951.04 and later violates the terms of such probation, the trial court is not required to credit time spent in a rehabilitation facility against any sentence originally imposed. State v. Nagle (Ohio 1986) 23 Ohio St.3d 185, 492 N.E.2d 158, 23 O.B.R. 348. Sentencing And Punishment ⚷ 2041

3. Mandamus to compel sentence reduction

Proper remedy for inmate challenging trial court's determination of jail time credit was appeal, not mandamus. State v. Sherman (Ohio App. 8 Dist., Cuyahoga, 11-19-2003) No. 83158, 2003-Ohio-6166, 2003 WL 22724735, Unreported. Mandamus ⚷ 4(4)

Mandamus would not lie to compel correctional institution to recompute jail credit time to which inmate was entitled pursuant to order of sentencing court, where declaratory judgment provided inmate plain and adequate remedy in ordinary course of the law through which to challenge administration of sentence reduction for related days of confinement, and where correctional institution had no statutory duty to apply jail time credit, such responsibility being solely with Department of Rehabilitation and Correction (DRC). Nicholson v. North Cent. Corr. Inst. (Ohio App. 3 Dist., Marion, 01-24-2003) No. 9-02-44, 2003-Ohio-303, 2003 WL 161463, Unreported. Mandamus ⚷ 3(1); Mandamus ⚷ 73(1)

Trial court's apparent rationale for dismissing inmate's petition for writ of mandamus seeking to compel recalculation of his release date, namely, inmate's failure to allege lack of jurisdiction in sentencing court, was improper, where inmate was not challenging sentencing court's factual determination as to length of his confinement, but rather sought to compel correctional institution to follow sentencing court's order with respect to jail time credit. Nicholson v. North Cent. Corr. Inst. (Ohio App. 3 Dist., Marion, 01-24-2003) No. 9-02-44, 2003-Ohio-303, 2003 WL 161463, Unreported. Mandamus ⚷ 169

Clerk of Courts for County Court of Common Pleas possessed no legal duty to grant jail-time credit; such duty strictly lay with the trial judge that originally imposed the sentence; therefore, writ of mandamus could not issue compelling him to grant jail-time credit. S/O ex rel. Lewis v. Fuerst (Ohio App. 8 Dist., Cuyahoga, 02-21-2002) No. 80666, 2002-Ohio-657, 2002 WL 253917, Unreported. Sentencing And Punishment ⚷ 1155

A writ of mandamus for double jail-time credit will not be issued for offenses committed in different jurisdictions. State ex rel. Moss v. Subora (Ohio 1987) 29 Ohio St.3d 66, 505 N.E.2d 965, 29 O.B.R. 447.

The trial court has the duty to enter into a misdemeanant's record of conviction the number of days that the misdemeanant was confined prior to his conviction, and the jailer has the duty to reduce the misdemeanant's sentence in accordance with that record of conviction. Mandamus is the remedy for enforcing the misdemeanant's right to have his sentence so reduced. State v. Berger (Lucas 1984) 17 Ohio App.3d 8, 477 N.E.2d 473, 17 O.B.R. 54.

4. Work release

The common pleas courts, municipal courts, and county courts do not have the power to grant to persons convicted in their courts as part of their sentence to the county jail, the privilege of working at their regular employment away from the jail. OAG 65–204.

The common pleas court does not have the power to establish rules and regulations to provide for county jail inmates leaving the jail daily to continue their regular employment. OAG 65–204.

5. Transportation of prisoner

A county sheriff has no duty to transport prisoners from the jail to the municipal court before the prisoners have been convicted and sentenced. OAG 87–091.

Where it is necessary to transport a prisoner between the county jail and a municipal court (in which court he is accused), the bailiff or deputy bailiff of the court has the duty to transport the prisoner as necessary; except that the court may designate police officers and constables to provide the transportation; and except that the transportation of a prisoner convicted of a misdemeanor and sentenced to imprisonment in jail or a workhouse should be provided by the sheriff or constable. 1962 OAG 3420, approved and followed by OAG 04–024.

2949.09 Execution for fine

When a judge or magistrate renders judgment for a fine, an execution may issue for such judgment and costs of prosecution, to be levied on the property, or in default thereof, upon the body of the defendant for nonpayment of the fine. The officer holding such writ may arrest such defendant in any county and commit him to the jail of the county in which such writ issued, until such fine is paid or secured to be paid or he is otherwise legally discharged.

(1970 S 460, eff. 9–3–70; 1953 H 1; GC 13454–2)

Historical and Statutory Notes

Pre–1953 H 1 Amendments: 113 v 205, Ch 33, § 2

Library References

Fines ⚖6, 9.
Westlaw Topic No. 174.
C.J.S. Fines § 16.

Research References

Encyclopedias

OH Jur. 3d Criminal Law § 3991, Collection of Costs in Misdemeanor Cases; Fines.

Notes of Decisions

Execution on defendant's property 1
Payment to secure release 2

1. Execution on defendant's property

Where money, found in the possession of a person charged with, and subsequently convicted of, armed robbery and placed in the possession of the prosecuting attorney for use as evidence in the criminal action, is attached by a creditor of the accused, such attachment, vitalized by a judgment in favor of the creditor, takes precedence over a subsequent execution issued against the fund for court costs in the criminal action. Scharfenberger v. Hover (Hamilton 1961) 113 Ohio App. 393, 174 N.E.2d 112, 17 O.O.2d 467.

A constable serving a writ of execution issued under GC 13454–2 (RC 2949.09) is a public officer and is presumed to act in accordance with law and duty. In re Weber (Butler 1945) 75 Ohio App. 206, 61 N.E.2d 502, 43 Ohio Law Abs. 377, 30 O.O. 521. Evidence ⚖ 83(7)

2. Payment to secure release

Where a person is convicted of a misdemeanor in a municipal or county court, is committed to the county jail for failure to pay the fine and costs, and wishes to pay the amount of the unpaid fine and costs in order to be released, such payment must be paid to the appropriate clerk of court before the prisoner may be released; and the county sheriff is without authority to collect the amount and release the prisoner without an appropriate authorization from the clerk. 1961 OAG 2384.

2949.091 Fees and costs

(A)(1) The court, in which any person is convicted of or pleads guilty to any offense other than a traffic offense that is not a moving violation, shall impose the sum of fifteen dollars as costs in the case in addition to any other court costs that the court is required by law to impose upon the offender. All such moneys collected during a month shall be transmitted on or before the twentieth day of the following month by the clerk of the court to the treasurer of state and deposited by the treasurer of state into the general revenue fund. The court shall not waive the payment of the additional fifteen dollars court costs, unless the court determines that the offender is indigent and waives the payment of all court costs imposed upon the indigent offender.

(2) The juvenile court, in which a child is found to be a delinquent child or a juvenile traffic offender for an act which, if committed by an adult, would be an offense other than a traffic offense that is not a moving violation, shall impose the sum of fifteen dollars as costs in the case in addition to any other court costs that the court is required or permitted by law to impose upon the delinquent child or juvenile traffic offender. All such moneys collected during a month shall be transmitted on or before the twentieth day of the following month by the clerk of the court to the treasurer of state and deposited by the treasurer of state into the general revenue fund. The fifteen dollars court costs shall be collected in all cases unless the court determines the juvenile is indigent and waives the payment of all court costs, or enters an order on its journal stating that it has determined that the juvenile is indigent, that no other court costs are to be taxed in the case, and that the payment of the fifteen dollars court costs is waived.

(B) Whenever a person is charged with any offense other than a traffic offense that is not a moving violation and posts bail, the court shall add to the amount of the bail the fifteen dollars required to be paid by division (A)(1) of this section. The fifteen dollars shall be retained by the clerk of the court until the person is convicted, pleads guilty, forfeits bail, is found not guilty, or has the charges dismissed. If the person is convicted, pleads guilty, or forfeits bail, the clerk shall transmit the fifteen dollars on or before the twentieth day of the month following the month in which the person was convicted, pleaded guilty, or forfeited bail to the treasurer of state, who shall deposit it into the general revenue fund. If the person is found not guilty or the charges are dismissed, the clerk shall return the fifteen dollars to the person.

(C) No person shall be placed or held in a detention facility for failing to pay the additional fifteen dollars court costs or bail that are required to be paid by this section.

(D) As used in this section:

(1) "Moving violation" and "bail" have the same meanings as in section 2743.70 of the Revised Code.

(2) "Detention facility" has the same meaning as in section 2921.01 of the Revised Code.

(2003 H 95, eff. 9–26–03; 1998 H 426, eff. 7–22–98; 1991 H 298, eff. 7–26–91; 1990 S 131; 1989 H 111; 1987 H 171; 1983 H 291)

Historical and Statutory Notes

Amendment Note: 2003 H 95 substituted "fifteen" for "eleven" throughout the section.

Amendment Note: 1998 H 426 substituted "moneys collected during a month shall be transmitted on or before the twentieth day of the following month" for "moneys shall be transmitted on the first business day of each month" in divisions (A)(1) and (A)(2); inserted "on or before the twentieth day of the month following the month in which the person was convicted, pleaded guilty, or forfeited bail" in division (B); and made changes to reflect gender neutral language.

Cross References

Fees and costs allowed in juvenile court cases, 2151.54

Library References

Costs ⚡304, 319.

Infants ⚡212.

Westlaw Topic Nos. 102, 211.

C.J.S. Infants §§ 43, 71 to 95.

Baldwin's Ohio Legislative Service, 1990 Laws of Ohio, S 131—LSC Analysis, p 5–623

Research References

Encyclopedias

OH Jur. 3d Courts & Judges § 109, Generally; Acts Within Scope of Jurisdiction.

OH Jur. 3d Criminal Law § 3974, Additional Court Costs or Bail.

Notes of Decisions

Costs assessed per case 1
Indigency 3
Juvenile court costs 5
Moving violation, defined 4
Violations bureau 2

1. Costs assessed per case

Statutes providing that sentence includes costs of prosecution and that specific dollar amount be imposed as part of costs when offender has been convicted or pled guilty were intended by legislature to authorize assessment of costs against defendant, including jury fees, only when state has been successful. State v. Powers (Ohio App. 6 Dist., 12-30-1996) 117 Ohio App.3d 124, 690 N.E.2d 32. Costs ⚡ 288; Costs ⚡ 311

After conviction on misdemeanor charge of reckless operation of motor vehicle and acquittals on charges of assault and menacing, sentencing court could assess against defendant only those costs associated with bench trial of misdemeanor charge and not those incurred as result of jury trial on charges of assault and menacing. State v. Powers (Ohio App. 6 Dist., 12-30-1996) 117 Ohio App.3d 124, 690 N.E.2d 32. Costs ⚡ 290

If an individual is charged with more than one misdemeanor arising from the same act or transaction or series of acts or transactions, and a municipal court or a county court assigns a single case number with respect to the prosecution of these misdemeanors, while simultaneously distinguishing between each misdemeanor charged within that case number by attaching an additional identifier, each misdemeanor charged within that case number is not considered a "case" for purposes of assessing the court costs mandated by RC 2743.70 and 2949.091. OAG 91–039.

The court costs imposed by RC 2743.70(A)(1) and 2949.091(A)(1) are to be charged per case, and not per offense. OAG 91–022; affirmed by OAG 91–039.

2. Violations bureau

Except when a mayor's court determines that an individual is indigent and waives the payment of all court costs imposed upon the indigent individual, a traffic violations bureau established by a mayor's court pursuant to Traf R 13, in which an individual appears in person to pay the total amount of the fine and costs or mails the ticket and a check or money order for the total amount of the fines and costs to the traffic violations bureau, is required to impose the mandatory court costs of RC 2743.70 and 2949.091. OAG 93–009.

3. Indigency

Probationer who filed uncontested affidavit of indigency upon revocation of probation was entitled to waiver of costs and vacation of order of garnishment. State v. Massey (Ohio App. 5 Dist., Stark, 06-21-2004) No. 2003CA00373, 2004-Ohio-3257, 2004 WL 1397529, Unreported, appeal allowed 103 Ohio St.3d 1491, 816 N.E.2d 1079, 2004-Ohio-5605, motion to certify allowed 104 Ohio St.3d 1445, 820 N.E.2d 383, 2004-Ohio-7156, reversed 108 Ohio St.3d 530, 844 N.E.2d 1191, 2006-Ohio-1708. Costs ⚷ 319

A "blanket waiver of indigency" that determines, without regard to the individual's financial condition, that an individual is indigent because that individual is a member of a specified group or class of individuals is impermissible. OAG 93–009.

4. Moving violation, defined

As used in RC 2743.70 and 2949.091, "moving violation" means any violation of any statute or ordinance (other than RC 4513.263, an ordinance that is substantially equivalent to that section, or a statute or ordinance that regulates pedestrians or the parking of vehicles) that regulates the operation of vehicles, streetcars, or trackless trolleys on highways or streets or that regulates size or load limitations or fitness requirements of vehicles. OAG 94–050.

5. Juvenile court costs

In juvenile court cases in which the Ohio Rules of Juvenile Procedure apply, Juv R 17(B) grants a juvenile court the authority to tax as costs and collect from a party the fees of the county sheriff in serving subpoenas issued by the court and the fees of witnesses subpoenaed by the court; however, pursuant to RC 2151.54, such fees may not be taxed as costs and collected by a juvenile court in cases of delinquent, unruly, dependent, abused, or neglected children except when specifically ordered by the court. OAG 98–021.

Except in cases of delinquent, unruly, dependent, abused, or neglected children, RC 2151.54 grants a juvenile court the authority to tax and collect the same fees and costs as are allowed the clerk of the court of common pleas for similar services. No fees or costs shall be taxed by the juvenile court in cases of delinquent, unruly, dependent, abused, or neglected children except as required by RC 2743.70 or RC 2949.091 or when specifically ordered by the court. OAG 97–024, approved and followed by OAG 98–021.

Pursuant to RC 2151.54, no fees or costs shall be taxed by the Trumbull county court of common pleas, domestic relations/juvenile division in cases filed by the Trumbull county children services board in which a particular child is alleged to be delinquent, unruly, abused, neglected, or dependent, or in which the board seeks to obtain custody of such a child, except as required by RC 2743.70 or RC 2949.091 or when specifically ordered by the court. OAG 97–024, approved and followed by OAG 98–021.

2949.092 Waiver of additional court costs

If a person is convicted of or pleads guilty to an offense and the court specifically is required, pursuant to section 2743.70, 2949.091, or 2949.093 of the Revised Code or pursuant to any other section of the Revised Code to impose a specified sum of money as costs in the case in addition to any other costs that the court is required or permitted by law to impose in the case, the court shall not waive the payment of the specified additional court costs that the section of the Revised Code specifically requires the court to impose unless the court determines that the offender is indigent and the court waives the payment of all court costs imposed upon the offender.

(2005 H 66, eff. 9–29–05; 1990 S 131, eff. 7–25–90)

Historical and Statutory Notes

Amendment Note: 2005 H 66 deleted "or" and inserted ", or 2949.093"; and made other nonsubstantive changes.

Library References

Costs ⚷304, 319.
Westlaw Topic No. 102.

Baldwin's Ohio Legislative Service, 1990 Laws of Ohio, S 131—LSC Analysis, p 5–623

Research References

Encyclopedias

OH Jur. 3d Criminal Law § 3975, Additional Court Costs or Bail—Condition for Waiver of Additional Court Costs.

Notes of Decisions

1. No authority to waive

Trial court did not have the authority to waive mandatory court costs for defendant convicted of persistent disorderly conduct, a fourth-degree misdemeanor, absent a finding of indigency even though the trial court wanted to give a break to defendant because he had already spent a substantial sum on the action. City of Cleveland v. Tighe (Ohio App. 8 Dist., Cuyahoga, 04-10-2003) No. 81767, No. 81795, 2003-Ohio-1845, 2003 WL 1849217, Unreported. Costs ⚬ 319

2. Discretion

Sentencing court's assessment of court costs against indigent felony defendant was within its statutory discretion. State v. Cole (Ohio App. 6 Dist., Lucas, 02-04-2005) No. L-03-1163, No. L-03-1162, 2005-Ohio-408, 2005 WL 280223, Unreported. Costs ⚬ 302

2949.093 Participation in criminal justice regional information system; requirements; funding

(A) A board of county commissioners of any county containing fifty-five or more law enforcement agencies by resolution may elect to participate in a criminal justice regional information system, either by creating and maintaining a new criminal justice regional information system or by participating in an existing criminal justice regional information system.

(B) A county is not eligible to participate in any criminal justice regional information system unless it creates in its county treasury, pursuant to section 305.28 of the Revised Code, a criminal justice regional information fund.

(C) A county that elects to participate in a criminal justice regional information system shall obtain revenues to fund its participation by establishing an additional court cost not exceeding five dollars to be imposed for moving violations that occur in that county. The board of county commissioners of that county shall establish the amount of the additional court cost by resolution. The board shall give written notice to all courts located in that county that adjudicate or otherwise process moving violations that occur in that county of the county's election to participate in the system and of the amount of the additional court cost. Upon receipt of such notice, each recipient court shall impose that amount as an additional court cost for all moving violations the court adjudicates or otherwise processes, in accordance with divisions (D) and (E) of this section.

(D)(1) The court in which any person is convicted of or pleads guilty to any moving violation that occurs in a county that has elected to participate in a criminal justice regional information system shall impose the sum established by the board pursuant to division (C) of this section as costs in the case in addition to any other court costs that the court is required by law to impose upon the offender. The court shall not waive the payment of the additional court cost established by the board pursuant to division (C) of this section unless the court determines that the offender is indigent and waives the payment of all court costs imposed upon the indigent offender.

All such money collected during a month shall be transmitted on the first business day of the following month by the clerk of the court to the county treasurer of the county in which the court is located and thereafter the county treasurer shall deposit the money in that county's criminal justice regional information fund.

(2) The juvenile court in which a child is found to be a juvenile traffic offender for an act that is a moving violation occurring in a county participating in a criminal justice regional information system shall impose the sum established by the board pursuant to division (C) of this section as costs in the case in addition to any other court costs that the court is required by law to impose upon the juvenile traffic offender. The juvenile court shall not waive the

payment of the additional court cost established by the board pursuant to division (C) of this section unless the court determines that the juvenile is indigent and waives the payment of all court costs imposed upon the indigent offender.

All such money collected during a month shall be transmitted on the first business day of the following month by the clerk of the court to the county treasurer of the county in which the juvenile court is located and thereafter the county treasurer shall deposit the money in that county's criminal justice regional information fund.

(E) Whenever a person is charged with any offense that is a moving violation and posts bail, the court shall add to the amount of the bail the set sum required to be paid by division (D)(1) of this section. The clerk of the court shall retain that set sum until the person is convicted, pleads guilty, forfeits bail, is found not guilty, or has the charges dismissed. If the person is convicted, pleads guilty, or forfeits bail, the clerk shall transmit the set sum to the county treasurer, who shall deposit it in the county criminal justice regional information fund. If the person is found not guilty or the charges are dismissed, the clerk shall return the set sum to the person.

(F) No person shall be placed or held in a detention facility as defined in section 2921.01 of the Revised Code for failing to pay the court cost or bail that is required to be paid by this section.

(G)(1) Except as provided in division (G)(2) of this section, all funds collected by a county under this section shall be used by that county only to pay the costs it incurs in creating and maintaining a new criminal justice regional information system or to pay the costs it incurs in participating in an existing criminal justice regional information system.

(2) If the board of county commissioners of a county determines that the funds in that county's criminal justice regional information fund are more than sufficient to satisfy the purpose for which the additional court cost described in division (C) of this section was imposed, the board may declare a surplus in the fund. The county may expend the surplus only to pay the costs it incurs in improving the law enforcement computer technology of local law enforcement agencies located in that county.

(H) As used in this section:

(1) "Moving violation" means any violation of any statute or ordinance, other than section 4513.263 of the Revised Code or an ordinance that is substantially equivalent to that section, that regulates the operation of vehicles, streetcars, or trackless trolleys on highways or streets or that regulates size or load limitations or fitness requirements of vehicles. "Moving violation" does not include the violation of any statute or ordinance that regulates pedestrians or the parking of vehicles.

(2) "Bail" means cash, a check, a money order, a credit card, or any other form of money that is posted by or for an offender pursuant to sections 2937.22 to 2937.46 of the Revised Code, Criminal Rule 46, or Traffic Rule 4 to prevent the offender from being placed or held in a detention facility, as defined in section 2921.01 of the Revised Code.

(3) "Criminal justice regional information system" means a governmental computer system that serves as a cooperative between political subdivisions in a particular region for the purpose of providing a consolidated computerized information system for criminal justice agencies in that region.

(2005 H 66, eff. 9–29–05)

Cross References

Criminal justice regional information fund, 305.28

Library References

Automobiles ⚩361.

Westlaw Topic No. 48A.

C.J.S. Motor Vehicles § 1337.

2949.10 Execution for fine to issue to other county

An execution under section 2949.09 of the Revised Code may issue to the sheriff of any county in which the defendant resides, is found, or has property, and the sheriff shall execute the writ. If the defendant is taken, the sheriff shall commit him to the jail of the county in which the writ issued and deliver a certified copy of the writ to the sheriff of such county, who shall detain the offender until he is discharged as provided in such section.

(1953 H 1, eff. 10–1–53; GC 13454–3)

Historical and Statutory Notes

Pre–1953 H 1 Amendments: 113 v 205, Ch 33, § 3

Library References

Fines ⚷6, 9.
Westlaw Topic No. 174.
C.J.S. Fines § 16.

Research References

Encyclopedias

OH Jur. 3d Criminal Law § 3991, Collection of Costs in Misdemeanor Cases; Fines.

2949.11 Fines paid into county treasury

Unless otherwise required in the Revised Code, an officer who collects a fine shall pay it into the treasury of the county in which such fine was assessed, within twenty days after the receipt of the fine, to the credit of the county general fund. The county treasurer shall issue duplicate receipts for the fine, and the officer making the collection shall deposit one of these receipts with the county auditor.

(1986 S 54, eff. 5–6–86; 125 v 903; 1953 H 1; GC 13454–4)

Historical and Statutory Notes

Pre–1953 H 1 Amendments: 113 v 205, Ch 33, § 4

Library References

Fines ⚷19, 20.
Westlaw Topic No. 174.
C.J.S. Fines §§ 4, 6, 13, 20.

Research References

Encyclopedias

OH Jur. 3d Criminal Law § 3997, Payment Into County Treasury.

Notes of Decisions

Disposition of fines 1
Payment of fine to obtain release 2

1. Disposition of fines

Trial court's imposition of $1,000 fine on defendant, who was convicted of misdemeanor vehicular homicide, for purpose of reimbursing Ohio Highway Patrol for costs of its investigation in case was plain error; trial court had no statutory authority to impose such fine, and statute did not allow any payments on fine collected from defendant to be passed on to Ohio Highway Patrol. State v. Johnson (Ohio App. 2 Dist., 12-23-2005) 164 Ohio App.3d 792, 844 N.E.2d 372, 2005-Ohio-6826. Criminal Law ⚷ 1042

Trial court had no statutory authority to impose $1,000 fine on defendant, who was convicted of misdemeanor vehicular homicide, for purpose of reimbursing Ohio Highway Patrol for costs of its investigation in case; statute specifying types of financial sanctions that trial court could impose in misdemeanor cases did not provide authorization of a financial sanction as reimbursement to a law enforcement agency for costs of its investigation. State v. Johnson (Ohio App. 2 Dist., 12-23-2005) 164 Ohio App.3d 792, 844 N.E.2d 372, 2005-Ohio-6826. Costs ⚷ 304

Under statute mandating that all fines be paid into county treasury, a trial court does not have the statutory authority to direct payment of a fine to a charitable organization. State v. Cooper (Ohio App. 8 Dist., 06-18-2001) 144 Ohio App.3d 316, 760 N.E.2d 34. Fines ⚷ 20

Fines imposed upon juvenile traffic offenders pursuant to RC 2151.356(A) must be paid to the general fund of the county treasury pursuant to RC 2949.11 rather than to the county law library association pursuant to RC 3375.52 or RC 3375.53. OAG 82–062; overruled on other grounds to the extent that it is inconsistent with OAG 87–023.

The provisions of RC 1907.101, 2931.08, and 2949.11 as to the distribution of fines do not render inoperative the provisions of RC 5503.04 and 4513.35; and fines collected in county courts from persons arrested by state highway patrolmen should be distributed as provided in RC 5503.04. 1961 OAG 2332.

Where a jury trial case involving a violation of a municipal ordinance is certified to the court of common pleas of the county, and said court imposes a fine for the violation, the amount of the fine collected should be paid into the treasury of the county, and the treasurer of the municipal corporation is not authorized to demand and receive such fine. 1961 OAG 2309.

2. Payment of fine to obtain release

Where a person is convicted of a misdemeanor in a municipal or county court, is committed to the county jail for failure to pay the fine and costs, and wishes to pay the amount of the unpaid fine and costs in order to be released, such payment must be paid to the appropriate clerk of court before the prisoner may be released; and the county sheriff is without authority to collect the amount and release the prisoner without an appropriate authorization from the clerk. 1961 OAG 2384.

2949.111 Priority of assignment of payments to satisfaction of costs, restitution, fines, and probation fees

(A) As used in this section:

(1) "Court costs" means any assessment that the court requires an offender to pay to defray the costs of operating the court.

(2) "State fines or costs" means any costs imposed or forfeited bail collected by the court under section 2743.70 of the Revised Code for deposit into the reparations fund or under section 2949.091 of the Revised Code for deposit into the general revenue fund and all fines, penalties, and forfeited bail collected by the court and paid to a law library association under sections 3375.50 to 3375.53 of the Revised Code.

(3) "Reimbursement" means any reimbursement for the costs of confinement that the court orders an offender to pay pursuant to section 2929.28 of the Revised Code, any supervision fee, any fee for the costs of house arrest with electronic monitoring that an offender agrees to pay, any reimbursement for the costs of an investigation or prosecution that the court orders an offender to pay pursuant to section 2929.71 of the Revised Code, or any other costs that the court orders an offender to pay.

(4) "Supervision fees" means any fees that a court, pursuant to sections 2929.18, 2929.28, and 2951.021 of the Revised Code, requires an offender who is under a community control sanction to pay for supervision services.

(5) "Community control sanction" has the same meaning as in section 2929.01 of the Revised Code.

(B) Unless the court, in accordance with division (C) of this section, enters in the record of the case a different method of assigning payments, if a person who is charged with a misdemeanor is convicted of or pleads guilty to the offense, if the court orders the offender to pay any combination of court costs, state fines or costs, restitution, a conventional fine, or any reimbursement, and if the offender makes any payment of any of them to a clerk of court, the clerk shall assign the offender's payment in the following manner:

(1) If the court ordered the offender to pay any court costs, the offender's payment shall be assigned toward the satisfaction of those court costs until they have been entirely paid.

(2) If the court ordered the offender to pay any state fines or costs and if all of the court costs that the court ordered the offender to pay have been paid, the remainder of the offender's payment shall be assigned on a pro rata basis toward the satisfaction of the state fines or costs until they have been entirely paid.

(3) If the court ordered the offender to pay any restitution and if all of the court costs and state fines or costs that the court ordered the offender to pay have been paid, the remainder of the offender's payment shall be assigned toward the satisfaction of the restitution until it has been entirely paid.

(4) If the court ordered the offender to pay any fine and if all of the court costs, state fines or costs, and restitution that the court ordered the offender to pay have been paid, the remainder of the offender's payment shall be assigned toward the satisfaction of the fine until it has been entirely paid.

(5) If the court ordered the offender to pay any reimbursement and if all of the court costs, state fines or costs, restitution, and fines that the court ordered the offender to pay have been paid, the remainder of the offender's payment shall be assigned toward the satisfaction of the reimbursements until they have been entirely paid.

(C) If a person who is charged with a misdemeanor is convicted of or pleads guilty to the offense and if the court orders the offender to pay any combination of court costs, state fines or costs, restitution, fines, or reimbursements, the court, at the time it orders the offender to make those payments, may prescribe an order of payments that differs from the order set forth in division (B) of this section by entering in the record of the case the order so prescribed. If a different order is entered in the record, on receipt of any payment, the clerk of the court shall assign the payment in the manner prescribed by the court.

(2002 H 490, eff. 1–1–04; 2002 H 170, eff. 9–6–02; 1995 S 2, eff. 7–1–96; 1994 H 406, eff. 11–11–94)

Historical and Statutory Notes

Amendment Note: 2002 H 490 rewrote this section which prior thereto read:

"(A) As used in this section:

"(1) 'Costs' means any court costs that the court requires an offender to pay, any reimbursement for the costs of confinement that the court orders an offender to pay pursuant to section 2929.28 of the Revised Code, any fee for the costs of electronically monitored house arrest that an offender agrees to pay pursuant to section 2929.23 of the Revised Code, any reimbursement for the costs of an investigation or prosecution that the court orders an offender to pay pursuant to section 2929.28 of the Revised Code, or any other costs that the court orders an offender to pay.

"(2) 'Supervision fees' means any fees that a court, pursuant to section 2951.021 of the Revised Code and as a condition of probation, requires an offender who is placed on probation to pay for probation services or that a court, pursuant to section 2929.18 of the Revised Code, requires an offender who is under a community control sanction to pay for supervision services.

"(3) 'Community control sanction' has the same meaning as in section 2929.01 of the Revised Code.

"(B) Unless the court, in accordance with division (C) of this section, enters in the record of the case a different method of assigning a payment toward the satisfaction of costs, restitution, a fine, or supervision fees, if a person who is charged with a misdemeanor is convicted of or pleads guilty to the offense, if the court orders the offender to pay any combination of costs, restitution, a fine, or supervision fees, and if the offender makes any payment to a clerk of court toward the satisfaction of the costs, restitution, fine, or supervision fees, the clerk of the court shall assign the offender's payment so made toward the satisfaction of the costs, restitution, fine, or supervision fees in the following manner:

"(1) If the court ordered the offender to pay any costs, the offender's payment shall be assigned toward the satisfaction of the costs until the court costs have been entirely paid.

"(2) If the court ordered the offender to pay any restitution and if all of the costs that the court ordered the offender to pay, if any, have been paid, the remainder of the offender's payment after any assignment required under division (B)(1) of this section shall be assigned toward the satisfaction of the restitution until the restitution has been entirely paid.

"(3) If the court ordered the offender to pay any fine and if all of the costs and restitution that the court ordered the offender to pay, if any, have been paid, the remainder of the offender's payment after any assignments required under divisions (B)(1) and (2) of this section shall be assigned toward the satisfaction of the fine until the fine has been entirely paid.

"(4) If the court ordered the offender to pay any supervision fees and if all of the costs, restitution, and fine that the court ordered the offender to pay, if any, have been paid, the remainder of the offender's payment after any assignments required under divisions (B)(1), (2), and (3) of this section shall be assigned toward the satisfaction of the supervision fees until the supervision fees have been entirely paid.

"(C) If a person who is charged with a misdemeanor is convicted of or pleads guilty to the offense and if the court orders the offender to pay any combination of costs, restitution, a fine, or supervision fees, the court, at the time it orders the offender to pay the combination of costs, restitution, a fine, or supervision fees, may prescribe a method of assigning payments that the person makes toward the satisfaction of the costs, restitution, fine, or supervision fees that differs from the method set forth in division (B) of this section. If the court prescribes a method of assigning payments under this division, the court shall enter in the record of the case the method so prescribed. Upon the entry in the record of the case of the method of assigning payments prescribed pursuant to this division, if the offender makes any payment to a clerk of court for the costs, restitution, fine, or supervision fees, the clerk of the court shall assign the payment so made toward the satisfaction of the costs, restitution, fine, or supervision fees in the manner prescribed by the court and entered in the record of the case instead of in the manner set forth in division (B) of this section."

Amendment Note: 2002 H 170 substituted "2929.28" for "2929.223" in the second clause of division (A)(1).

Amendment Note: 1995 S 2 substituted "2929.223" for "2929.15" in division (A)(1); substituted "supervision fees" for "probation fees" throughout; inserted "or that a court, pursuant to section 2929.18 of the Revised Code, requires an offender who is under a community control sanction to pay for supervision services" in division (A)(2); added division (A)(3); and substituted "misdemeanor" for "criminal offense" in the first paragraph in division (B) and in division (C).

Cross References

Financial sanctions, 2929.18, 2929.28

Library References

Costs ⚷304.

Fines ⚷20.

Sentencing and Punishment ⚷2210.

Westlaw Topic Nos. 102, 174, 350H.

C.J.S. Criminal Law §§ 1771 to 1786.

C.J.S. Fines § 6.

Research References

Encyclopedias

OH Jur. 3d Criminal Law § 3984, Liability of Defendant.

Notes of Decisions

Contempt 1

---

1. Contempt

Warrant fees assessed against defendant at time he was found in contempt counted as costs, requiring sentencing court to follow statutory procedure before holding defendant in contempt for failure to pay such fees, where fees were nothing other than administrative costs and were not punitive in nature. State v. Swift (Ohio App. 2 Dist., Montgomery, 04-01-2005) No. 20544, 2005-Ohio-1599, 2005 WL 742503, Unreported. Costs ⚷ 320

COSTS AND TRANSPORTATION OF CONVICTS

2949.12 Conveying convicted felon to reception facility

Unless the execution of sentence is suspended, a convicted felon who is sentenced to serve a term of imprisonment in a state correctional institution shall be conveyed, within five days after sentencing, excluding Saturdays, Sundays, and legal holidays, by the sheriff of the county in which the conviction was had to the facility that is designated by the department of rehabilitation and correction for the reception of convicted felons. The sheriff shall deliver the convicted felon into the custody of the managing officer of the reception facility and, at that time, shall present the managing officer with a copy of the convicted felon's sentence that clearly describes each offense for which the felon was sentenced to a correctional institution, designates each section of the Revised Code that the felon violated and that resulted in the felon's conviction and sentence to a correctional institution, designates the sentence imposed for each offense for which the felon was sentenced to a correctional institution, and, pursuant to section 2967.191 of the Revised Code, specifies the total number of days, if any, that the felon was confined for any reason prior to conviction and sentence. The sheriff, at that time, also shall present the managing officer with a copy of the indictment. The clerk of the court of common pleas shall furnish the copies of the sentence and indictment. In the case of a person under the age of eighteen years who is certified to the court of common pleas by the juvenile court, the clerk of the court of common pleas also shall attach a copy of the certification to the copy of the indictment.

The convicted felon shall be assigned to an institution or designated to be housed in a county, multicounty, municipal, municipal-county, or multicounty-municipal jail or workhouse, if authorized pursuant to section 5120.161 of the Revised Code, shall be conveyed to the institution, jail, or workhouse, and shall be kept within the institution, jail, or workhouse until the term of the felon's imprisonment expires, the felon is pardoned, paroled, or placed under a post-release control sanction, or the felon is transferred under laws permitting the transfer of prisoners. If the execution of the felon's sentence is suspended, and the judgment thereafter affirmed, the felon shall be conveyed, in the same manner as if the execution of the felon's sentence had not been suspended, to the reception facility as soon as practicable after the judge directs the execution of sentence. The trial judge or other judge of the court, in the judge's discretion and for good cause shown, may extend the time of the conveyance.
(1995 S 2, eff. 7–1–96; 1994 H 571, eff. 10–6–94; 1988 H 708, eff. 4–19–88; 1987 H 261, H 455, S 6, § 3; 1984 S 172, § 1, 3; 1983 S 210; 1982 H 269, § 4, S 199; 1976 H 685; 1973 S 254; 1953 H 1; GC 13455–1)

Uncodified Law

1982 H 269, § 4, eff. 1–5–83, amended 1982 S 199, § 10, eff. 1–5–83, to read, in part: " [2949.12], as amended by [1982 S 199],... shall take effect on July 1, 1983, and shall apply only to offenses committed on or after July 1, 1983."

Historical and Statutory Notes

Pre–1953 H 1 Amendments: 120 v 628; 113 v 205, Ch 34, § 1

Amendment Note: 1995 S 2 deleted "If the record in the convicted felon's case includes a notation entered pursuant to division (A) of section 2943.041 or division (A) of section 2945.07 of the Revised Code that indicates that a victim or a representative member of a victim's family was present at a proceeding of a type described in that division and that identifies the victim or the representative member by name, a copy of the notation also shall be attached to the copy of the sentence." before and ", and of the notation of appearance by the victim or a representative member of the victim's family" after "The clerk of the court of common pleas shall furnish the copies of the sentence and indictment" in the first paragraph; added a reference to post-release control sanctions in the second paragraph; and made changes to reflect gender neutral language and other nonsubstantive changes.

Amendment Note: 1994 H 571 substituted "correctional" for "penal" throughout the first paragraph.

Cross References

Credit for confinement awaiting trial and commitment, 2967.191

Pardon and parole, Ch 2967

Payment by prisoner of costs of confinement, 2929.15

Suspension of sentence before and after delivery to institution, 2929.51

Ohio Administrative Code References

Reduction of minimum and maximum or definite sentence for jail-time credit, OAC 5120–2–04

Library References

Prisons ⚷13.5.

Sentencing and Punishment ⚷1156.

Sheriffs and Constables ⚷86.

Westlaw Topic Nos. 310, 350H, 353.

C.J.S. Criminal Law §§ 1571 to 1576, 1578, 1580.

C.J.S. Prisons and Rights of Prisoners §§ 130 to 143.

C.J.S. Sheriffs and Constables §§ 66 to 79.

Research References

Encyclopedias

OH Jur. 3d Criminal Law § 3423, Delivery of Convict to Reception Facility.

OH Jur. 3d Criminal Law § 3424, Assignment to Local Jail or Workhouse.

OH Jur. 3d Criminal Law § 3425, Credit for Time Served.

OH Jur. 3d Mandamus, Procedendo, & Prohibition § 60, State and Local Administrative Bodies.

OH Jur. 3d Penal & Correctional Institutions § 36, Officers and Employees—Warden.

Treatises and Practice Aids

Hennenberg & Reinhart, Ohio Criminal Defense Motions F 10.25, Motion for Order Granting

Defendant Credit for Time Served-Post-Trial Motions.

Notes of Decisions

---

1. Mittimus paper regarding prisoner's conveyance to confinement and welcome by jailor

Where an accused is properly indicted, convicted and sentenced by a court of competent jurisdiction, errors in the mittimus delivered to the warden of the penitentiary are not grounds for release of the accused by habeas corpus. Orr v. Maxwell (Ohio 1963) 174 Ohio St. 344, 189 N.E.2d 77, 22 O.O.2d 391. Habeas Corpus ⚷ 505

A failure to include the section number in the mittimus is merely an irregularity which in no way affects the jurisdiction of the trial court or petitioner's conviction, and is not a matter which is cognizable in a habeas corpus action. Foutty v. Maxwell (Ohio 1962) 174 Ohio St. 35, 186 N.E.2d 623, 21 O.O.2d 288. Habeas Corpus ⚷ 474

2. Sheriff's duties

The trial court, upon motion by the county prosecutor, may issue an order to the county sheriff to execute a reinstated sentence, where a defendant's probation was revoked and the original sentence was reinstated, but for undisclosed reasons the county sheriff did not deliver the defendant to the designated penal institution; in so doing, the trial court does not modify or otherwise affect that sentence, since a court has inherent authority to direct the officers of such court to perform their duties, including the duty imposed on the county sheriff by RC 2949.12 to execute such sentences. State v. Wobler (Paulding 1983) 10 Ohio App.3d 155, 461 N.E.2d 927, 10 O.B.R. 207.

There is a presumption that a sheriff has delivered a felon to the institution to which he was committed. State ex rel. Snyder v. Hayes (Fayette 1958) 153 N.E.2d 171, 78 Ohio Law Abs. 448. Habeas Corpus ⚷ 701.1

The only papers which the law prescribes to be delivered to the head of a penal institution are those required by RC 2949.12, which are furnished by the clerk of courts, and the signature of the sentencing judge is not required thereon. Foglio v. Alvis (Ohio Com.Pl. 1957) 143 N.E.2d 641, 75 Ohio Law Abs. 228.

Provisions of this section are directory. Ex parte Silverman (Hamilton 1942) 69 Ohio App. 128, 42 N.E.2d 87, 37 Ohio Law Abs. 199, 23 O.O. 555, appeal dismissed 140 Ohio St. 335, 43 N.E.2d 238, 23 O.O. 547.

3. Journal entry of sentence

Certified copy of journal entry of sentence complied with RC 2949.12. Orr v. Maxwell (Ohio 1963) 174 Ohio St. 344, 189 N.E.2d 77, 22 O.O.2d 391.

In a criminal action the trial judge is not required to sign a written journal entry in sentencing a prisoner, for the judgment is complete when the judge orally pronounces sentence in open court and the clerk enters such sentence in the journal, and where the journal record needs to be completed or corrected so as to show the actual sentence pronounced previously, it is not essential that the prisoner be present. Stewart v. Alvis (Ohio Com. Pl. 1957) 144 N.E.2d 907, 75 Ohio Law Abs. 283.

That no signed entry was issued to the clerk ordering that the sentence pronounced in court be journalized does not constitute a ground for the issuance of a writ of habeas corpus where the judgment was in fact journalized. Reiter v. Alvis (Franklin 1957) 144 N.E.2d 902, 80 Ohio Law Abs. 479.

4. Time for transporting prisoner

Fact that defendant was not conveyed into custody of corrections department within five days after his sentence was imposed as required by statute did not render defendant's life sentence invalid; statute was merely directory and could not be used to invalidate defendant's sentence or prevent its enforcement. State v. Vaughn (Ohio App. 12 Dist., 10-16-1995) 106 Ohio App.3d 775, 667 N.E.2d 82, denial of post-conviction relief affirmed 1997 WL 133526, dismissed, appeal not allowed 79 Ohio St.3d 1419, 680 N.E.2d 156, denial of post-conviction relief affirmed 1999 WL 1142922. Sentencing And Punishment ⚷ 1155

A failure to comply with the five-day provisions of GC 13455–1 (RC 2949.12) is not an irregularity for which habeas corpus will lie. Norton v. Green (Ohio 1962) 173 Ohio St. 531, 184 N.E.2d 401, 20 O.O.2d 148.

Failure of sheriff to lodge therein a person sentenced to penitentiary within five days in absence of a suspension, does not invalidate sentence or prevent its subsequent enforcement. Ex parte Silverman (Hamilton 1942) 69 Ohio App. 128, 42 N.E.2d 87, 37 Ohio Law Abs. 199, 23 O.O. 555, appeal dismissed 140 Ohio St. 335, 43 N.E.2d 238, 23 O.O. 547.

5. Jail time credit

Relator, seeking writ of mandamus to compel Clerk of Courts to send copy of order granting relator 128 days jail time credit to prison officials, failed to establish clerk's office possessed duty to forward copy of order, where journal entry indicated copy of order was provided to sheriff's office which was responsible for presenting copy of sentence to managing officer. State ex rel. Weaver v. Common Pleas Clerk of Courts (Ohio App. 8 Dist.,

Cuyahoga, 08-04-2004) No. 84847, 2004-Ohio-4075, 2004 WL 1752915, Unreported. Mandamus ⚷ 73(1)

Defendant convicted of unlawful sexual conduct with minor was entitled to 99 days of jail time credit for days defendant spent in custody prior to conviction and sentence. State v. Young (Ohio App. 5 Dist., Delaware, 07-30-2004) No. 03-CAA-10051, 2004-Ohio-4002, 2004 WL 1717601, Unreported. Sentencing And Punishment ⚷ 1159; Sentencing And Punishment ⚷ 1160

Sentencing court fulfilled its duty to notify adult parole authority of defendant's credit for time served prior to sentencing him, even though court did not set forth credit for time served in its sentencing entry, as court filed separate entry crediting defendant with time served. State v. Moore (Ohio App. 12 Dist., Butler, 11-24-2003) No. CA2002-12-307, 2003-Ohio-6255, 2003 WL 22764143, Unreported. Sentencing And Punishment ⚷ 1160

Trial court's failure to properly calculate credit to which defendant was entitled for time served in pretrial or presentencing detention, and to include such credit in body of its sentencing order, was plain error, where such calculation and inclusion were mandatory. State v. Cook (Ohio App. 7 Dist., Mahoning, 12-18-2002) No. 00CA184, 2002-Ohio-7170, 2002 WL 31859442, Unreported. Criminal Law ⚷ 1042

Defendant's challenge of trial court's award of credit for time served for robbery sentence, but not for felonious assault sentence, was not cognizable in mandamus petition against Adult Parole Authority (APA), but rather by way of direct appeal of criminal case; APA had no authority to alter sentence and was required to adhere to trial court's determination of jail-time credit. State ex rel. Rankin v. Ohio Adult Parole Auth. (Ohio, 05-07-2003) 98 Ohio St.3d 476, 786 N.E.2d 1286, 2003-Ohio-2061. Mandamus ⚷ 4(4)

In sentencing a defendant on a plea of guilty to a reduced charge of breaking and entering, a trial court properly refuses to give jail time credit for time that the prisoner was confined for an unrelated prior misdemeanor; a defendant is not entitled to jail time credit for any period of incarceration which arose from facts separate and apart from those on which his current sentence is based. State v. Smith (Franklin 1992) 71 Ohio App.3d 302, 593 N.E.2d 402.

Defendant was entitled, at sentencing in homicide case, to credit for the period during which he was confined for a determination of competency to stand trial and for the period, following his release from an involuntary civil commitment as a mentally ill person that did not qualify as pretrial confinement, during which he was held until sentencing. State v. Stafford (Ohio App. 7 Dist., Noble, 09-26-2002) No. 265, 2002-Ohio-5243, 2002 WL 31170127, Unreported, reconsideration denied 2002-Ohio-7184, 2002 WL 31859518, appeal not allowed 98 Ohio St.3d 1477, 784 N.E.2d 710, 2003-Ohio-974, appeal not allowed 98 Ohio St.3d 1515, 786 N.E.2d 64, 2003-Ohio-1572. Sentencing And Punishment ⚷ 1158

Communication from a sheriff indicating the number of days that a prisoner was confined in a particular institution is not the copy of the sentence contemplated by RC 2949.12 or the certification by the trial court in the journal entry of sentence as required by Crim R 32.2. State, ex rel. Corder v. Wilson (Franklin 1991) 68 Ohio App.3d 567, 589 N.E.2d 113, motion to certify overruled 62 Ohio St.3d 1484, 581 N.E.2d 1391.

6. Public defender's costs

Imprisonment of indigents is a prerequisite to the payment of criminal costs by the Ohio public defender commission pursuant to RC 2949.12 et seq., and 1977 H 191, eff. 6–30–77. OAG 78–004.

2949.13 Sheriff may require assistance

During the time the sheriff is conveying a convicted felon to an institution for imprisonment therein, he may secure him in a jail and demand the assistance of a sheriff, jailer, or other person in keeping such prisoner, as if he were in his own county. Such sheriff, jailer, or other person is liable, on refusal, to like penalties as if the sheriff making the demand were in his own county.

(1953 H 1, eff. 10–1–53; GC 13455–2)

Historical and Statutory Notes

Pre–1953 H 1 Amendments: 113 v 206, Ch 34, § 2

Library References

Sheriffs and Constables ⚷99.

Westlaw Topic No. 353.

C.J.S. Sheriffs and Constables §§ 107 to 113.

2949.14 Cost bill in case of felony

Upon conviction of a nonindigent person for a felony, the clerk of the court of common pleas shall make and certify under his hand and seal of the court, a complete itemized bill of the costs made in such prosecution, including the sum paid by the board of county commissioners, certified by the county auditor, for the arrest and return of the person on the requisition of the governor, or on the request of the governor to the president of the United States, or on the return of the fugitive by a designated agent pursuant to a waiver of extradition except in cases of parole violation. Such bill of costs shall be presented by such clerk to the prosecuting attorney, who shall examine each item therein charged and certify to it if correct and legal. Upon certification by the prosecuting attorney, the clerk shall attempt to collect the costs from the person convicted.

(1983 H 291, eff. 7–1–83; 132 v S 447; 1953 H 1; GC 13455–3)

Historical and Statutory Notes

Pre–1953 H 1 Amendments: 113 v 206, Ch 34, § 3

Library References

Costs ⚬284 to 325.

Westlaw Topic No. 102.

C.J.S. Criminal Law §§ 1738 to 1751.

Research References

Encyclopedias

OH Jur. 3d Cvl. Servants & Pub. Officers & Employ. § 491, Postconviction Responsibilities.

OH Jur. 3d Costs in Civil Actions § 65, Methods of Collection.

OH Jur. 3d Courts & Judges § 213, Seal.

OH Jur. 3d Criminal Law § 3971, Extradition; Cost Bill in Case of Felony.

OH Jur. 3d Criminal Law § 3984, Liability of Defendant.

OH Jur. 3d Criminal Law § 3990, Collection of Costs in Felony Cases; Payment by State.

Treatises and Practice Aids

Katz, Giannelli, Blair and Lipton, Baldwin's Ohio Practice, Criminal Law, § 119:6, Financial Sanctions.

Notes of Decisions

1. Cost items

Cost bill provided to defendant being assessed court costs was not required to list statutory reference for each cost itemized therein. State v. Heft (Ohio App. 5 Dist., Knox, 06-17-2005) No. 04 CA 28, 2005-Ohio-3253, 2005 WL 1503594, Unreported. Costs ⚬ 314

Statute governing cost bill in a felony case permits collection and garnishment for court costs against nonindigent felons only. State v. Williams (Ohio App. 5 Dist., Stark, 06-28-2004) No. 2003CA00369, 2004-Ohio-3525, 2004 WL 1486308, Unreported, appeal allowed 103 Ohio St.3d 1492, 816 N.E.2d 1079, 2004-Ohio-5605, motion to certify allowed 105 Ohio St.3d 1495, 825 N.E.2d 620, 2005-Ohio-1666, reversed 108 Ohio St.3d 532, 844 N.E.2d 1192, 2006-Ohio-1710. Costs ⚬ 320

Statute governing cost bill in a felony case does not prohibit clerk of courts from preparing an itemized bill of costs for indigent defendants. State v. Williams (Ohio App. 5 Dist., Stark, 06-28-2004) No. 2003CA00369, 2004-Ohio-3525, 2004 WL 1486308, Unreported, appeal allowed 103 Ohio St.3d 1492, 816 N.E.2d 1079, 2004-Ohio-5605, motion to certify allowed 105 Ohio St.3d 1495, 825 N.E.2d 620, 2005-Ohio-1666, reversed 108 Ohio St.3d 532, 844 N.E.2d 1192, 2006-Ohio-1710. Costs ⚬ 314

Statute governing cost bill in a felony case permits collection and garnishment for court costs against nonindigent felons only. State v. Carter (Ohio App. 5 Dist., Stark, 06-28-2004) No. 2003-CA-00372, 2004-Ohio-3523, 2004 WL 1486157, Unreported, appeal allowed 103 Ohio St.3d 1492, 816 N.E.2d 1079, 2004-Ohio-5605, motion to certify allowed 105 Ohio St.3d 1495, 825 N.E.2d 620, 2005-Ohio-1666, reversed 108 Ohio St.3d 532, 844 N.E.2d 1193, 2006-Ohio-1711. Costs ⚬ 320

Statute governing cost bill in a felony case does not prohibit clerk of courts from preparing an itemized bill of costs for indigent defendants. State v. Carter (Ohio App. 5 Dist., Stark, 06-28-2004) No. 2003-CA-00372, 2004-Ohio-3523, 2004 WL 1486157, Unreported, appeal allowed 103 Ohio St.3d 1492, 816 N.E.2d 1079, 2004-Ohio-5605, motion to certify allowed 105 Ohio St.3d 1495, 825 N.E.2d 620, 2005-Ohio-1666, reversed 108 Ohio St.3d 532, 844 N.E.2d 1193, 2006-Ohio-1711. Costs ⚬ 314

Statute requiring a convicted defendant to pay costs of prosecution was applicable to defendant despite his indigent status; costs would be collected when defendant ceased to be indigent. State v.

Hall (Ohio App. 11 Dist., Lake, 06-18-2004) No. 2001-L-230, 2004-Ohio-3186, 2004 WL 1375752, Unreported, appeal not allowed 103 Ohio St.3d 1494, 816 N.E.2d 1080, 2004-Ohio-5605. Costs ⚯ 302

Issue as to collection of court costs assessed to defendant, who was allegedly indigent, was not ripe for review either when defendant filed his motion to waive with trial court or when trial court denied the same. State v. Durenda (Ohio App. 5 Dist., Stark, 03-15-2004) No. 2003CA00336, 2004-Ohio-1292, 2004 WL 540923, Unreported. Criminal Law ⚯ 1134(3)

Defendant's claim that trial court erred in denying his motion to waive court costs was not ripe for appellate review, where no attempt had been made to collect the costs assessed to defendant. State v. Chambers (Ohio App. 5 Dist., Stark, 03-15-2004) No. 2003CA00337, 2004-Ohio-1279, 2004 WL 539997, Unreported. Criminal Law ⚯ 1134(3)

Nothing prevented trial court from assessing defendant court costs by virtue of his indigent status, upon his conviction for multiple theft-related offenses and engaging in corrupt activity; imposition of court costs was not an infringement of defendant's rights nor did it violate any statute. State v. Glavic (Ohio App. 11 Dist., Lake, 12-22-2003) No. 2001-L-177, No. 2001-L-179, 2003-Ohio-6961, 2003 WL 22994557, Unreported, motion for delayed appeal granted 102 Ohio St.3d 1444, 808 N.E.2d 396, 2004-Ohio-2263, appeal allowed 103 Ohio St.3d 1442, 814 N.E.2d 869, 2004-Ohio-4626, appeal not allowed 104 Ohio St.3d 1411, 818 N.E.2d 711, 2004-Ohio-6364, affirmed 105 Ohio St.3d 131, 823 N.E.2d 447, 2005-Ohio-31, appeal not allowed 107 Ohio St.3d 1411, 836 N.E.2d 1230, 2005-Ohio-5859. Costs ⚯ 302

Defendant was required to pay court costs that had been imposed as part of sentence for driving under the influence conviction, even though defendant was indigent at time of conviction; statute providing that a court include costs as part of a defendant's sentence made no distinction between indigent and non-indigent defendants, and no State law prohibited a judge from including court costs as part of the sentence of an indigent defendant. State v. May (Ohio App. 11 Dist., Ashtabula, 12-22-2003) No. 2001-A-0037, 2003-Ohio-6979, 2003 WL 22994542, Unreported, appeal allowed 102 Ohio St.3d 1408, 806 N.E.2d 560, 2004-Ohio-1763, affirmed 105 Ohio St.3d 131, 823 N.E.2d 446, 2005-Ohio-789. Costs ⚯ 302

Criminal statute requiring convicted defendant to pay costs of prosecution was applicable to drug defendant, despite his indigent status; costs would be collected when defendant ceased to be indigent. State v. Peacock (Ohio App. 11 Dist., Lake, 12-12-2003) No. 2002-L-115, 2003-Ohio-6772, 2003 WL 22952755, Unreported. Costs ⚯ 302

Trial court lacked statutory authority to impose court costs on indigent defendant as part of sentencing for domestic violence. State v. Schofield (Ohio App. 4 Dist., Washington, 12-05-2003) No. 01CA36, No. 02CA13, 2003-Ohio-6553, 2003 WL 22889403, Unreported. Costs ⚯ 292

Trial court lacked statutory authority to assess costs of plea proceeding and sentencing for felonious assault against indigent defendant. State v. Clark (Ohio App. 4 Dist., Pickaway, 11-27-2002) No. 02CA12, 2002-Ohio-6684, 2002 WL 31742999, Unreported, as amended nunc pro tunc. Costs ⚯ 292

Trial court has authority to impose court costs upon indigent defendant; statute requires court to include costs as part of sentence and, while second statute provides collection mechanism only for non-indigent defendants, nothing in second statute prohibits court from collecting costs from indigent defendant. State v. Haynie (Ohio App. 3 Dist., 05-17-2004) 157 Ohio App.3d 708, 813 N.E.2d 686, 2004-Ohio-2452, appeal allowed 103 Ohio St.3d 1477, 816 N.E.2d 253, 2004-Ohio-5405, reconsideration denied 104 Ohio St.3d 1428, 819 N.E.2d 710, 2004-Ohio-6585, affirmed 105 Ohio St.3d 133, 823 N.E.2d 448, 2005-Ohio-785. Costs ⚯ 302

Inclusion by the court of compensation of an expert in the bill of costs, and certificate by the prosecuting attorney of its correctness and legality, and its allowance by the warden, do not authorize the state auditor to draw a warrant therefor. Under RS 1302–1 (See GC 2494), compensation of an expert is not costs authorized to be paid from the state treasury. State ex rel. Franklin County Com'rs v. Guilbert (Ohio 1907) 77 Ohio St. 333, 83 N.E. 80, 5 Ohio Law Rep. 522. Costs ⚯ 310; Witnesses ⚯ 28(1)

Trial court is required under governing statute to assess cost of prosecution against a convicted defendant, and separate statute allowing court to waive payment of certain "additional costs" by an indigent defendant does not supercede or conflict with that requirement. State v. Satta (Ohio App. 3 Dist., Marion, 09-25-2002) No. 9-01-38, 2002-Ohio-5049, 2002 WL 31114690, Unreported, appeal not allowed 98 Ohio St.3d 1461, 783 N.E.2d 520, 2003-Ohio-644, reconsideration denied 98 Ohio St.3d 1516, 786 N.E.2d 64, 2003-Ohio-1572, motion for delayed appeal denied 98 Ohio St.3d 1509, 786 N.E.2d 60, 2003-Ohio-1572, appeal not allowed 99 Ohio St.3d 1437, 789 N.E.2d 1118, 2003-Ohio-2902. Costs ⚯ 292; Costs ⚯ 319

The reasonable costs of transporting an out-of-state prisoner into the state of Ohio as a necessary witness in a criminal prosecution for violation of state law is taxable as a criminal cost and payable by the auditor of state under the criminal cost subsidy program. OAG 74–101.

The costs of prosecution, including jury fees, arising out of a mistrial and subsequent trial and conviction, must be assessed against the defendant pursuant to RC 2947.23, and where, in the subsequent trial, he pleads "guilty" before the jury is impanelled, the fees of that jury may not properly be included in the costs of prosecution; the court has no discretion in the taxing of jury fees in the case where a mistrial is declared resulting in a subsequent trial and conviction. OAG 69–058.

Expenditures for medical and hospital services for convicted prisoners while awaiting transfer to a penal institution, should not be included as costs of the prosecution of such prisoners and should not be included as costs to be paid by the treasurer of state. 1960 OAG 1642.

2. Execution

Trial court had jurisdiction to enforce collection of court costs and fees associated with petitioner's conviction for driving under the influence (DUI), even though petitioner's probationary period had ended, and thus writ of prohibition would not lie to compel trial court to take no further action to enforce collection of costs and fees; action to collect unpaid court costs was wholly independent and divorced from other proceedings, and trial court's authority to collect costs and fees was in no way contingent on petitioner's probationary period after conviction. State ex rel. Logue v. Fregiato (Ohio App. 7 Dist., Belmont, 08-11-2004) No. 04-BE-26, 2004-Ohio-4289, 2004 WL 1812833, Unreported, subsequent mandamus proceeding 2005-Ohio-2941, 2005 WL 1385725. Costs ⚷ 320

Trial court was required to allow State to respond to defendant's affidavit of indigency before ruling on issue, as basis for order imposing and collecting costs. State v. Olson (Ohio App. 5 Dist., Stark, 06-07-2004) No. 2003CA00371, 2004-Ohio-2965, 2004 WL 1265726, Unreported, appeal allowed 103 Ohio St.3d 1491, 816 N.E.2d 1078, 2004-Ohio-5605, reversed 108 Ohio St.3d 527, 844 N.E.2d 1189, 2006-Ohio-1704. Costs ⚷ 314

Statute governing imposition and collection of costs of prosecution applied only to nonindigent defendants. State v. Olson (Ohio App. 5 Dist., Stark, 06-07-2004) No. 2003CA00371, 2004-Ohio-2965, 2004 WL 1265726, Unreported, appeal allowed 103 Ohio St.3d 1491, 816 N.E.2d 1078, 2004-Ohio-5605, reversed 108 Ohio St.3d 527, 844 N.E.2d 1189, 2006-Ohio-1704. Costs ⚷ 292; Costs ⚷ 320

When collecting court costs from an indigent criminal defendant, the state may use any collection method that is available to collect a civil money judgment or may collect from a prisoner's account; an indigent criminal defendant is not different from any other indigent who owes a debt. State v. Threatt (Ohio, 03-15-2006) 108 Ohio St.3d 277, 843 N.E.2d 164, 2006-Ohio-905. Costs ⚷ 320

Money that an accused has in his possession at the time he is taken into custody, and which is turned over to and remains in the possession of law enforcement officers, is subject to execution for the payment of the costs of the prosecution. Witherspoon v. Belt (Ohio 1964) 177 Ohio St. 1, 201 N.E.2d 590, 28 O.O.2d 407.

A county prosecuting attorney has a duty, pursuant to RC 2949.14, to examine each item charged in a bill of costs to a nonindigent individual convicted of a felony and to certify to it if correct and legal, and a duty, under RC 309.08(A), in every case of conviction to cause execution to be issued for the costs, to faithfully urge collection of such costs, and to pay all collected costs in his possession to the county treasurer. OAG 90–109.

3. Ability to pay

Trial court was required to impose costs of prosecution for sexual battery, regardless of defendant's indigency status. State v. Dickinson (Ohio App. 7 Dist., Columbiana, 11-26-2004) No. 03 CO 52, 2004-Ohio-6373, 2004 WL 2726057, Unreported, appeal not allowed 105 Ohio St.3d 1499, 825 N.E.2d 623, 2005-Ohio-1666. Costs ⚷ 292

Trial court possessed authority to order indigent defendant to pay court costs; clerk of court's inability to collect costs from indigent party did not prevent trial court from ordering payment of such costs. State v. Dobbins (Ohio App. 5 Dist., Muskingum, 09-02-2004) No. 03 CA 58, 2004-Ohio-4715, 2004 WL 1969137, Unreported. Costs ⚷ 302

Imposition of costs of prosecution on defendant convicted of robbery and theft was required by law, even though defendant was indigent; statute required imposition of costs on all defendants, and statute on collection of costs from nonindigent defendants did not prohibit imposition of costs on indigent defendants, but simply detailed procedure for collecting costs from defendants able to pay them. State v. Barlow (Ohio App. 2 Dist., Montgomery, 11-26-2003) No. 19628, 2003-Ohio-6530, 2003 WL 22887903, Unreported, appeal allowed 102 Ohio St.3d 1408, 806 N.E.2d 561, 2004-Ohio-1763, affirmed 105 Ohio St.3d 130, 823 N.E.2d 446, 2005-Ohio-790. Costs ⚷ 302

Clerk of courts could attempt collection of court costs that had been assessed against indigent defendant who had been convicted of a felony as part of his sentence; statutory scheme at issue was silent as to indigent defendants, from which it could be inferred that collection of court costs from indigent defendants was merely permissive. State v. White (Ohio, 11-24-2004) 103 Ohio St.3d 580, 817 N.E.2d 393, 2004-Ohio-5989. Costs ⚷ 320

Trial court had authority to assess court costs against indigent defendant who had been convicted of a felony as part of his sentence; statutes at issue did not prohibit trial court from assessing costs against indigent defendants, but instead required trial court to assess costs against all convicted defendants; abrogating, *State v. Clark*, 2002 WL 31742999. State v. White (Ohio, 11-24-2004) 103 Ohio St.3d 580, 817 N.E.2d 393, 2004-Ohio-5989. Costs ⚷ 302

4. Appellate procedure

Defendant's time for appeal of order assessing court costs began to run when trial court ordered garnishment, rather than at time of actual sentencing entry; itemized cost bill was prepared by clerk of courts and specific amount due was not included in judgment entry. State v. Williams (Ohio App. 5 Dist., Stark, 06-28-2004) No. 2003CA00369, 2004-Ohio-3525, 2004 WL 1486308, Unreported, appeal allowed 103 Ohio St.3d 1492, 816 N.E.2d 1079, 2004-Ohio-5605, motion to certify allowed 105 Ohio St.3d 1495, 825 N.E.2d 620, 2005-Ohio-1666, reversed 108 Ohio St.3d 532, 844

N.E.2d 1192, 2006-Ohio-1710. Criminal Law ⚷ 1069(5)

Defendant's time for appeal of order assessing court costs began to run when trial court ordered garnishment, rather than at time of actual sentencing entry; itemized cost bill was prepared by clerk of courts and specific amount due was not included in judgment entry. State v. Carter (Ohio App. 5 Dist., Stark, 06-28-2004) No. 2003-CA-00372, 2004-Ohio-3523, 2004 WL 1486157, Unreported, appeal allowed 103 Ohio St.3d 1492, 816 N.E.2d 1079, 2004-Ohio-5605, motion to certify allowed 105 Ohio St.3d 1495, 825 N.E.2d 620, 2005-Ohio-1666, reversed 108 Ohio St.3d 532, 844 N.E.2d 1193, 2006-Ohio-1711. Criminal Law ⚷ 1069(5)

Appeal time to challenge imposition of court costs as part of sentence for driving under influence did not begin to run until there was attempt to levy or garnish. State v. Cantwell (Ohio App. 5 Dist., Stark, 06-07-2004) No. 2003CA00367, 2004-Ohio-2964, 2004 WL 1267101, Unreported, appeal allowed 103 Ohio St.3d 1491, 816 N.E.2d 1078, 2004-Ohio-5605, motion to certify allowed 105 Ohio St.3d 1495, 825 N.E.2d 620, 2005-Ohio-1666, reversed 108 Ohio St.3d 528, 844 N.E.2d 1190, 2006-Ohio-1706. Criminal Law ⚷ 1069(5)

2949.15 Writs of execution to issue

If a nonindigent person convicted of a felony fails to pay the costs of prosecution pursuant to section 2949.14 of the Revised Code, the clerk of the court of common pleas shall forthwith issue to the sheriff of the county in which the indictment was found, and to the sheriff of any other county in which the person has property, executions against his property for fines and the costs of prosecution, which shall be served and returned within ten days, with the proceedings of such sheriff or the certification that there is no property upon which to levy, indorsed thereon.

When a levy is made upon property under such execution, a writ shall forthwith be issued by the clerk for the sale thereof, and such sheriff shall sell the property and make return thereof, and after paying the costs of conviction, execution, and sale, pay the balance to the person authorized to receive it.

(1983 H 291, eff. 7–1–83; 1953 H 1; GC 13455–4)

Historical and Statutory Notes

Pre–1953 H 1 Amendments: 113 v 206, Ch 34, § 4

Library References

Costs ⚷320 to 325.
Westlaw Topic No. 102.
C.J.S. Criminal Law § 1743.

Research References

Encyclopedias

OH Jur. 3d Criminal Law § 3990, Collection of Costs in Felony Cases; Payment by State.

Notes of Decisions

Cost items 1
Execution 2
Indigent defendant 4
Payment of fine to obtain release 3

1. Cost items

When the court deems it necessary to appoint counsel for a juvenile, pursuant to RC 2151.351, such counsel's services shall be paid for by the county as is stated therein. OAG 69–110.

Fees and expenses of counsel assigned by the court to an accused under RC 2941.50 are required to be paid by the county and should not be paid by the state. OAG 65–219.

2. Execution

Trial court had jurisdiction to enforce collection of court costs and fees associated with petitioner's conviction for driving under the influence (DUI), even though petitioner's probationary period had ended, and thus writ of prohibition would not lie to compel trial court to take no further action to enforce collection of costs and fees; action to collect unpaid court costs was wholly independent and divorced from other proceedings, and trial court's authority to collect costs and fees was in no way contingent on petitioner's probationary period after conviction. State ex rel. Logue v. Fregiato (Ohio App. 7 Dist., Belmont, 08-11-2004) No. 04-BE-26, 2004-Ohio-4289, 2004 WL 1812833, Unreported, subsequent mandamus proceeding 2005-Ohio-2941, 2005 WL 1385725. Costs ⚿ 320

Money that an accused has in his possession at the time he is taken into custody, and which is turned over to and remains in the possession of law enforcement officers, is subject to execution for the payment of the costs of the prosecution. Witherspoon v. Belt (Ohio 1964) 177 Ohio St. 1, 201 N.E.2d 590, 28 O.O.2d 407.

RC 2933.43(B)(2) precludes execution, pursuant to RC 2949.15, against contraband seized pursuant to RC 2933.43(A), pending a forfeiture hearing held pursuant to RC 2933.43(C). OAG 89–078.

3. Payment of fine to obtain release

Where a person is convicted of a misdemeanor in a municipal or county court, is committed to the county jail for failure to pay the fine and costs, and wishes to pay the amount of the unpaid fine and costs in order to be released, such payment must be paid to the appropriate clerk of court before the prisoner may be released; and the county sheriff is without authority to collect the amount and release the prisoner without an appropriate authorization from the clerk. 1961 OAG 2384.

4. Indigent defendant

Trial court was precluded by statute from collecting court costs against defendant, where defendant was indigent. State v. Lawless (Ohio App. 5 Dist., Muskingum, 09-28-2004) No. 03 CA 30, 2004-Ohio-5344, 2004 WL 2260699, Unreported. Costs ⚿ 320

2949.16 Costs on execution for felony—Repealed

(1983 H 291, eff. 7–1–83; 1953 H 1; GC 13455–5)

Historical and Statutory Notes

Pre–1953 H 1 Amendments: 113 v 206, Ch 34, § 5

2949.17 Transportation of prisoners; expenses

(A) The sheriff may take one guard for every two convicted felons to be transported to a correctional institution. The trial judge may authorize a larger number of guards upon written application of the sheriff, in which case a transcript of the order of the judge shall be certified by the clerk of the court of common pleas under the seal of the court, and the sheriff shall deliver the order with the convict to the person in charge of the correctional institution.

(B) In order to obtain reimbursement for the county for the expenses of transportation for indigent convicted felons, the clerk of the court of common pleas shall prepare a transportation cost bill for each indigent convicted felon transported pursuant to this section for an amount equal to ten cents a mile from the county seat to the state correctional institution and return for the sheriff and each of the guards and five cents a mile from the county seat to the state correctional institution for each prisoner. The number of miles shall be computed by the usual route of travel. The clerk's duties under this division are subject to division (B) of section 2949.19 of the Revised Code.

(1999 H 283, eff. 9–29–99; 1994 H 571, eff. 10–6–94; 1983 H 291, eff. 7–1–83; 1981 H 694; 1979 H 204; 128 v 542; 1953 H 1; GC 13455–6)

Historical and Statutory Notes

Pre–1953 H 1 Amendments: 113 v 207, Ch 34, § 6

Amendment Note: 1999 H 283 designated divisions (A) and (B); and added the final sentence in division (B).

Amendment Note: 1994 H 571 substituted "correctional" for "penal" throughout.

Library References

Counties ⚿135, 139.
Westlaw Topic No. 104.
C.J.S. Counties § 175.

Research References

Encyclopedias

OH Jur. 3d Cvl. Servants & Pub. Officers & Employ. § 504, Duties Regarding Reimbursement of Costs.

OH Jur. 3d Criminal Law § 3973, Transportation of Indigent Prisoners.

OH Jur. 3d Police, Sheriffs, & Related Officers § 47, Other Sheriff's Fees.

Notes of Decisions

Transporting prisoner to federal proceeding 1

1. Transporting prisoner to federal proceeding

No rule prevents a federal court from ordering the custodian of a prisoner to transport him to court proceedings at the custodian's own expense, including federal habeas corpus proceedings commenced by the prisoner himself; similarly, nothing in 28 USC 1920 permits federal courts to tax as costs against a losing party the custodian's expense of complying with a prisoner's writ of habeas corpus ad testificandum. Sales v. Marshall (C.A.6 (Ohio) 1989) 873 F.2d 115.

2949.18 Certification and payment of cost bill—Repealed

(1983 H 291, eff. 7–1–83; 1981 H 694; 1979 H 204; 1953 H 1; GC 13455–7)

Historical and Statutory Notes

Pre–1953 H 1 Amendments: 113 v 207, Ch 34, § 7

2949.19 Subsidy by state for certain costs

(A) Subject to division (B) of this section, the clerk of the court of common pleas shall report to the state public defender all cases in which an indigent person was convicted of a felony, all cases in which reimbursement is required by section 2949.20 of the Revised Code, and all cost bills for transportation that are prepared pursuant to section 2949.17 of the Revised Code. The reports shall be filed for each fiscal quarter within thirty days after the end of the quarter on a form prescribed by the state public defender and shall be accompanied by a certification of a judge of the court that in all cases listed in the report the defendant was determined to be indigent and convicted of a felony or that the case is reported pursuant to section 2949.20 of the Revised Code and that for each transportation cost bill submitted pursuant to section 2949.17 of the Revised Code that the convicted felon was determined to be indigent. The state public defender shall review the reports received under this division and prepare a transportation cost voucher and a quarterly subsidy voucher for each county for the amounts the state public defender finds to be correct. To compute the quarterly subsidy, the state public defender first shall subtract the total of all transportation cost vouchers that the state public defender approves for payment for the quarter from one-fourth of the state public defender's total appropriation for criminal costs subsidy for the fiscal year of which the quarter is part. The state public defender then shall compute a base subsidy amount per case by dividing the remainder by the total number of cases from all counties the state public defender approves for subsidy for the quarter. The quarterly subsidy voucher for each county shall then be the product of the base subsidy amount times the number of cases submitted by the county and approved for subsidy for the quarter. Payment shall be made to the clerk.

The clerk shall keep a record of all cases submitted for the subsidy in which the defendant was bound over to the court of common pleas from the municipal court. Upon receipt of the quarterly subsidy, the clerk shall pay to the clerk of the municipal court, for municipal court costs in such cases, an amount that does not exceed fifteen dollars per case, shall pay foreign sheriffs for their services, and shall deposit the remainder of the subsidy to the credit of the general fund of the county. The clerk of the court of common pleas then shall stamp the clerk's records subsidy costs satisfied.

(B) If notified by the state public defender under section 2949.201 of the Revised Code that, for a specified state fiscal year, the general assembly has not appropriated funding for reimbursement payments pursuant to division (A) of this section, the clerk of the court of common pleas is exempt for that state fiscal year from the duties imposed upon the clerk by division (A) of this section and by sections 2949.17 and 2949.20 of the Revised Code. Upon providing the notice described in this division, the state public defender is exempt for that state fiscal year from the duties imposed upon the state public defender by division (A) of this section.

(1999 H 283, eff. 9–29–99; 1987 H 171, eff. 7–1–87; 1985 H 201; 1984 H 462; 1983 H 291; 1981 H 694; 1979 H 204; 130 v S 342; 1953 H 1; GC 13455–8)

Historical and Statutory Notes

Pre–1953 H 1 Amendments: 113 v 207, Ch 34, § 8

Amendment Note: 1999 H 283 designated division (A) and inserted "Subject to division (B) of this section," and "received under this division" therein; added division (B); and made changes to reflect gender neutral language and other nonsubstantive changes.

Cross References

Powers and duties of state public defender, funds, 120.04

Library References

States ⚿123.

Westlaw Topic No. 360.

C.J.S. States §§ 377 to 380.

Research References

Encyclopedias

OH Jur. 3d Cvl. Servants & Pub. Officers & Employ. § 504, Duties Regarding Reimbursement of Costs.

OH Jur. 3d Criminal Law § 3973, Transportation of Indigent Prisoners.

OH Jur. 3d Criminal Law § 3986, State Payment of Criminal Costs.

Treatises and Practice Aids

Katz, Giannelli, Blair and Lipton, Baldwin's Ohio Practice, Criminal Law, § 61:5, Indigent Defendants.

Notes of Decisions

1. Constitutional issues

Defendant waived appellate review of constitutionality of indigency statute by failing to raise alleged equal protection violation at the trial court level. State v. Pasqualone (Ohio App. 11 Dist., 09-18-2000) 140 Ohio App.3d 650, 748 N.E.2d 1153. Criminal Law ⚿ 1030(2)

Appellate review of constitutionality of indigency statute on appeal from denial of post-conviction relief was barred by res judicata, where post-conviction movant could have raised alleged equal protection violation on his direct appeal from conviction and sentence but failed to do so. State v. Pasqualone (Ohio App. 11 Dist., 09-18-2000) 140 Ohio App.3d 650, 748 N.E.2d 1153. Criminal Law ⚿ 1180

2. Transcripts

The cost of preparing transcripts for indigent defendants in felony cases is to be treated as part of the overall cost of providing such indigents with local level legal representation pursuant to the Ohio Public Defender Commission Act. Under the Act, the counties must initially bear the cost of such legal services, but the state is required to reimburse the counties for fifty per cent of the total cost, subject to the limitation that in cases where an indigent is provided with legal representation through a public defender's officer or a county-appointed counsel system, the total amount of reimbursement shall not exceed the amount appropriated for the fiscal year by the general assembly for that purpose. OAG 80–099.

3. Transporting prisoner or witness

Statute governing collection of costs for transporting felons applied only to nonindigent defendants, and thus, remand was required for trial court to make finding regarding defendant's indigent status. State v. Cantwell (Ohio App. 5 Dist., Stark, 06-07-2004) No. 2003CA00367, 2004-Ohio-2964, 2004 WL 1267101, Unreported, appeal allowed 103 Ohio St.3d 1491, 816 N.E.2d 1078, 2004-Ohio-5605, motion to certify allowed 105 Ohio St.3d 1495, 825 N.E.2d 620, 2005-Ohio-1666, reversed 108 Ohio St.3d 528, 844 N.E.2d 1190, 2006-Ohio-1706. Costs ⚿ 320

The reasonable costs of transporting an out-of-state prisoner into the state of Ohio as a necessary witness in a criminal prosecution for violation of state law is taxable as a criminal cost and payable by the auditor of state under the criminal cost subsidy program. OAG 74–101.

4. Payment of costs by public defender commission

Imprisonment of indigents is a prerequisite to the payment of criminal costs by the Ohio public defender commission pursuant to RC 2949.12 et seq., and 1977 H 191, eff. 6–30–77. OAG 78–004.

5. Assigned counsel

Counsel appointed as assigned counsel under RC 2941.50 to conduct appeals were entitled to a writ of mandamus ordering auditor to issue warrants in payment of their fees, ordering commissioners to create a fund if necessary for payment, and ordering the treasurer to pay such warrants. State ex rel. Giuliani v. Perk (Ohio 1968) 14 Ohio St.2d 235, 237 N.E.2d 397, 43 O.O.2d 366.

The auditor of state is required, upon certification to him of the statement of costs of a criminal conviction pursuant to RC 2949.19, to pay an amount equal to the moneys expended for fees and expenses of court-appointed counsel, approved and taxed as a part of the costs under RC 2941.51, provided there are sufficient funds in the state treasury appropriated for that purpose. State ex rel. Clifford v. Cloud (Ohio 1966) 7 Ohio St.2d 55, 218 N.E.2d 605, 36 O.O.2d 46.

When the court deems it necessary to appoint counsel for a juvenile, pursuant to RC 2151.351, such counsel's services shall be paid for by the county as is stated therein. OAG 69–110.

RC 2949.19 requires that the state of Ohio must bear the costs as provided in RC 2953.03 and counsel fees as provided in RC 2941.51 of an indigent defendant on appeal whether or not he has been committed prior to his appeal. OAG 68–098; overruled to the extent that it is inconsistent with OAG 80–099.

Fees and expense of counsel assigned by the court to an accused under RC 2941.50 are required to be paid by the county and should not be paid by the state. OAG 65–219.

2949.20 Reimbursement in case of reversal

In any case of final judgment of reversal as provided in section 2953.07 of the Revised Code, whenever the state of Ohio is the appellee, the clerk of the court of common pleas of the county in which sentence was imposed shall certify the case to the state public defender for reimbursement in the report required by section 2949.19 of the Revised Code, subject to division (B) of section 2949.19 of the Revised Code.

(1999 H 283, eff. 9–29–99; 1983 H 291, eff. 7–1–83; 1981 H 694; 1979 H 204; 1953 H 1; GC 13455–9)

Historical and Statutory Notes

Pre–1953 H 1 Amendments: 115 v 532

Amendment Note: 1999 H 283 inserted ", subject to division (B) of section 2949.19 of the Revised Code".

Library References

Costs ⚷294, 319.

Westlaw Topic No. 102.

Research References

Encyclopedias

OH Jur. 3d Criminal Law § 3976, Costs on Appellate Review.

OH Jur. 3d Criminal Law § 3986, State Payment of Criminal Costs.

Notes of Decisions

1. Payment of assigned counsel

RC 2949.19 requires that the state of Ohio must bear the costs as provided in RC 2953.03 and counsel fees as provided in RC 2941.51 of an indigent defendant on appeal whether or not he has been committed prior to his appeal. OAG 68–098; overruled to the extent that it is inconsistent with OAG 80–099.

RC 2941.51(C) requires the state of Ohio to pay as costs, in addition to the counsel fees received for representation at the trial as provided in RC 2941.51(B), any counsel fees up to $300 resulting from an appeal as approved by the court of appeals. OAG 68–098; overruled to the extent that it is inconsistent with OAG 80–099.

2. Cost of transcripts

The cost of preparing transcripts for indigent defendants in felony cases is to be treated as part of the overall cost of providing such indigents with local level legal representation pursuant to the Ohio Public Defender Commission Act. Under the Act, the counties must initially bear the cost of such legal services, but the state is required to reimburse the counties for fifty per cent of the total cost, subject to the limitation that in cases where an indigent is provided with legal representation through a public defender's officer or a county-appointed counsel system, the total amount of reimbursement shall not exceed the amount appropriated for the fiscal year by the general assembly for that purpose. OAG 80–099.

2949.201 State public defender to provide notification regarding reimbursements

(A) On or before the date specified in division (B) of this section, in each state fiscal year, the state public defender shall notify the clerk of the court of common pleas of each county whether the general assembly has, or has not, appropriated funding for that state fiscal year for reimbursement payments pursuant to division (A) of section 2949.19 of the Revised Code.

(B) The state public defender shall provide the notification required by division (A) of this section on or before whichever of the following dates is applicable:

(1) If, on the first day of July of the fiscal year in question, the main operating appropriations act that covers that fiscal year is in effect, on or before the thirty-first day of July;

(2) If, on the first day of July of the fiscal year in question, the main operating appropriations act that covers that fiscal year is not in effect, on or before the day that is thirty days after the effective date of the main operating appropriations act that covers that fiscal year.

(1999 H 283, eff. 9–29–99; 1983 H 291, eff. 7–1–83; 1981 H 694)

Historical and Statutory Notes

Amendment Note: 1999 H 283 rewrote the section, which prior thereto read:

"On or before the first day of February of even-numbered years, the state public defender shall report to the speaker and minority leader of the house of representatives, the president and minority leader of the senate, the office of budget and management, and the legislative budget office of the legislative service commission an estimate of the amount of money that will be required for the next fiscal biennium to make the payments required by section 2949.19 of the Revised Code."

Cross References

Public defender, duties, 120.04

Library References

Costs ⟹294, 319.
Westlaw Topic No. 102.

2949.21 Conveyance to correctional institution

A writ for the execution of the death penalty shall be directed to the sheriff by the court issuing it, and the sheriff, within thirty days and in a private manner, shall convey the prisoner to the facility designated by the director of rehabilitation and correction for the reception of the prisoner. For conducting the prisoner to the facility, the sheriff shall receive like fees and mileage as in other cases, when approved by the warden of the facility. After the procedures performed at the reception facility are completed, the prisoner shall be assigned to an appropriate correctional institution, conveyed to the institution, and kept within the institution until the execution of his sentence.

(1994 H 571, eff. 10–6–94; 1992 S 359, eff. 12–22–92; 1953 H 1; GC 13456–1)

Historical and Statutory Notes

Pre–1953 H 1 Amendments: 113 v 207, Ch 35, § 1

Amendment Note: 1994 H 571 substituted "correctional" for "penal".

Ohio Administrative Code References

Inmates sentenced to death, OAC 5120–9–12

Library References

Sentencing and Punishment ⟹1795.
Westlaw Topic No. 350H.
C.J.S. Criminal Law §§ 1591, 1605 to 1609.

DEATH SENTENCE

2949.22 Execution of death sentence

(A) Except as provided in division (C) of this section, a death sentence shall be executed by causing the application to the person, upon whom the sentence was imposed, of a lethal injection of a drug or combination of drugs of sufficient dosage to quickly and painlessly cause death. The application of the drug or combination of drugs shall be continued until the person is dead. The warden of the correctional institution in which the sentence is to be executed or another person selected by the director of rehabilitation and correction shall ensure that the death sentence is executed.

(B) A death sentence shall be executed within the walls of the state correctional institution designated by the director of rehabilitation and correction as the location for executions, within an enclosure to be prepared for that purpose, under the direction of the warden of the institution or, in the warden's absence, a deputy warden, and on the day designated by the judge passing sentence or otherwise designated by a court in the course of any appellate or postconviction proceedings. The enclosure shall exclude public view.

(C) If a person is sentenced to death, and if the execution of a death sentence by lethal injection has been determined to be unconstitutional, the death sentence shall be executed by using any different manner of execution prescribed by law subsequent to the effective date of this amendment instead of by causing the application to the person of a lethal injection of a drug or combination of drugs of sufficient dosage to quickly and painlessly cause death, provided that the subsequently prescribed different manner of execution has not been determined to be unconstitutional. The use of the subsequently prescribed different manner of execution shall be continued until the person is dead. The warden of the state correctional institution in which the sentence is to be executed or another person selected by the director of rehabilitation and correction shall ensure that the sentence of death is executed.

(D) No change in the law made by the amendment to this section that took effect on October 1, 1993, or by this amendment constitutes a declaration by or belief of the general assembly that execution of a death sentence by electrocution is a cruel and unusual punishment proscribed by the Ohio Constitution or the United States Constitution.

(2001 H 362, eff. 11–21–01; 1994 H 571, eff. 10–6–94; 1993 H 11, eff. 10–1–93; 1992 S 359; 1953 H 1; GC 13456–2)

Historical and Statutory Notes

Pre–1953 H 1 Amendments: 113 v 208, Ch 35, § 2

Amendment Note: 2001 H 362 rewrote the section, which prior thereto read:

"(A) Except as provided in division (B)(1) of this section, a death sentence shall be executed by causing a current of electricity, of sufficient intensity to cause death, to pass through the body of the person upon whom the sentence was imposed. The application of the current shall be continued until the person upon whom the sentence was imposed is dead. The warden of the correctional institution in which the sentence is to be executed or another person selected by the director of rehabilitation and correction shall ensure that the death sentence is executed.

"(B)(1) Any person sentenced to death may elect to be executed by lethal injection instead of by electrocution as described in division (A) of this section. The election shall be made no later than one week prior to the scheduled date of execution of the person by filing a written notice of the election with the department of rehabilitation and correction. If a person sentenced to death timely files with the department a written notice of an election to be executed by lethal injection, the person's death sentence shall be executed by causing the application to the person of a lethal injection of a drug or combination of drugs of sufficient dosage to quickly and painlessly cause death instead of by electrocution as described in division (A) of this section. The application of the drug or combination of drugs shall be continued until the person is dead. The warden of the correctional institution in which the sentence is to be executed or another person selected by the director of rehabilitation and correction shall ensure that the death sentence is executed.

"If a person sentenced to death does not timely file with the department a written notice of election to be executed by lethal injection, his death sentence shall be executed by electrocution in accordance with division (A) of this section.

"(2) Neither a person's timely filing of a written notice of election under division (B)(1) of this section nor a person's failure to file or timely file a written notice of election under that division shall affect or waive any right of appeal or postconviction relief that may be available under the laws of this state or the United States relative to the conviction for which the sentence of death was imposed upon the person or relative to the imposition or execution of that sentence of death.

"(C) A death sentence shall be executed within the walls of the state correctional institution designated by the director of rehabilitation and correction as the location for executions, within an enclosure to be prepared for that purpose, under the direction of the warden of the institution or, in his absence, a deputy warden, and on the day designated by the judge passing sentence or otherwise designated by a court in the course of any appellate or postconviction proceedings. The enclosure shall exclude public view.

"(D) If a death sentence is required to be executed by lethal injection because the person sentenced to death elected to be executed by lethal injection pursuant to division (B)(1) of this section and if the execution of a death sentence by lethal injection is determined to be unconstitutional, the death sentence shall be executed by causing a current of electricity, of sufficient intensity to cause death, to pass through the body of the person upon whom the sentence was imposed. The application of the current shall be continued until the person is dead. The warden of the state correctional institution in which the sentence is to be executed or another person selected by the director of rehabilitation and correction shall ensure that the death sentence is executed.

"(E) No change in the law made by this amendment constitutes a declaration by or belief of the general assembly that execution of a death sentence by electrocution is a cruel and unusual punishment proscribed by the Ohio Constitution or the United States Constitution."

Amendment Note: 1994 H 571 substituted "correctional" for "penal" in divisions (A) and (B)(1); and substituted "state correctional" for "penal" in divisions (C) and (D).

Amendment Note: 1993 H 11 designated division (A); added "Except as provided in division (B)(1) of this section," at the beginning of, and inserted "in which the sentence is to be executed" in, division (A); added division (B); designated division (C); inserted "of the institution" in division (C); and added divisions (D) and (E).

Cross References

Capital case status reports, 109.97

Death penalty, 2929.02

Library References

Sentencing and Punishment ⚿1796.

Westlaw Topic No. 350H.

C.J.S. Criminal Law §§ 1591, 1605 to 1609.

Research References

Encyclopedias

OH Jur. 3d Criminal Law § 3223, Generally; Proportionality of Penalty to Crime.

OH Jur. 3d Criminal Law § 3249, Delay in Sentencing—Delay in Execution of Sentence.

OH Jur. 3d Criminal Law § 3429, Time, Place, and Method of Execution.

OH Jur. 3d Criminal Law § 3430, Persons Authorized to Attend.

Treatises and Practice Aids

Katz, Giannelli, Blair and Lipton, Baldwin's Ohio Practice, Criminal Law, § 126:13, Method of Execution.

Katz, Giannelli, Blair and Lipton, Baldwin's Ohio Practice, Criminal Law, § 153:26, Death Sentence.

Katz, Giannelli, Blair and Lipton, Baldwin's Ohio Practice, Criminal Law, § 153:27, Death Sentence (Additional Form).

Law Review and Journal Commentaries

Gardner v. Florida: Pre–sentence Reports in Capital Sentencing Procedures, Note. 5 Ohio N U L Rev 175 (1978).

Killing me softly: Is the gas chamber, or any other method of execution, "cruel and unusual punishment?" 22 Hastings Const L Q 815 (1995).

Methodology of death: Reexamining deterrence rationale, Jonathan S. Abernethy. 27 Colum Hum Rts L Rev 379 (1996).

Ohio's Death Penalty: History and Current Developments, Comment. 31 Cap U L Rev 659 (2003).

Pro-death, self-fulfilling constitutional construct: Supreme Court's evolving standard of decency for the death penalty, Susan Raeker–Jordan. 23 Hastings Const L Q 455 (1996).

"Unusual" Punishment: The Domestic Effects of International Norms Restricting the Application of the Death Penalty, Joan F. Hartman. 52 U Cin L Rev 655 (1983).

When judges impose the death penalty after the jury recommends life: *Harris v. Alabama* as the excision of the tympanic membrane in an augmentedly death-biased procedure, Amy D. Ronner. 23 Hastings Const L Q 217 (1995).

Witherspoon Revisited: Exploring the Tension Between Witherspoon and Furman, Welsh S. White. 45 U Cin L Rev 19 (1976).

Notes of Decisions

1. Constitutional issues

Execution by lethal injection does not run afoul of Eighth Amendment's proscription against cruel and unusual punishment. State v. Fitzpatrick (Ohio App. 1 Dist., Hamilton, 10-22-2004) No. C-030804, 2004-Ohio-5615, 2004 WL 2367987, Unreported, appeal not allowed 105 Ohio St.3d 1499, 825 N.E.2d 623, 2005-Ohio-1666. Sentencing And Punishment ⚿ 1796

Appellate counsel in appeal of capital case did not provide deficient assistance in failing to argue that death penalty statute violates international law or that postconviction petition procedure provides capital defendants with insufficient constitutional safeguards; appellate counsel could reasonably conclude that such arguments would detract from other attacks on state's death penalty scheme. State v. Mack (Ohio App. 8 Dist., Cuyahoga, 05-19-2003) No. 62366, 2003-Ohio-2605, 2003 WL 21185786, Unreported, affirmed 101 Ohio St.3d 397, 805 N.E.2d 1108, 2004-Ohio-1526. Criminal Law ⚿ 641.13(7)

Issue of whether defense counsel was entitled to argue in closing arguments of punishment phase of capital trial regarding the cruelty of electrocution as a means of execution was moot when raised in application for reopening, given that statute governing method of execution had been amended since trial to eliminate electrocution as the means of execution. State v. Mack (Ohio App. 8 Dist., Cuyahoga, 05-19-2003) No. 62366, 2003-Ohio-2605, 2003 WL 21185786, Unreported, affirmed 101 Ohio St.3d 397, 805 N.E.2d 1108, 2004-Ohio-1526. Criminal Law ⚿ 1133

Challenge to electrocution was moot because electrocution was no longer authorized to carry out the death penalty. State v. Adams (Ohio, 11-17-2004) 103 Ohio St.3d 508, 817 N.E.2d 29, 2004-Ohio-5845, reconsideration denied 104 Ohio St.3d 1442, 819 N.E.2d 1124, 2004-Ohio-7033, certiorari denied 125 S.Ct. 2271, 544 U.S. 1040, 161 L.Ed.2d 1072. Criminal Law ⚿ 1134(3)

The carrying out of the death penalty, imposed by a court having jurisdiction of the matter, by electrocution, is neither a cruel nor unusual punishment for the condemned person. State v. Wallen (Stark 1969) 21 Ohio App.2d 27, 254 N.E.2d 716, 50 O.O.2d 50, affirmed 25 Ohio St.2d 45, 266 N.E.2d 561, 54 O.O.2d 172.

Capital murder defendant's sentence to death by electrocution was not unconstitutional as cruel and unusual punishment, and habeas relief from sentence was not warranted regardless since Ohio statute allowed defendant option of choosing between death by electrocution or death by lethal injection, a form of execution that he did not argue was cruel and unusual. Buell v. Mitchell (C.A.6 (Ohio), 12-04-2001) 274 F.3d 337. Habeas Corpus ⚿ 408; Sentencing And Punishment ⚿ 1796

Habeas petitioner was procedurally barred from claiming that execution by electric chair was cruel and unusual punishment where he failed to raise claim on direct appeal to state appellate court; failure to raise on appeal claim that appeared on face of record constituted procedural default under Ohio's doctrine of res judicata. Smith v. Anderson (S.D.Ohio, 02-22-2000) 104 F.Supp.2d 773, affirmed 348 F.3d 177, rehearing and rehearing en banc denied, certiorari denied 125 S.Ct. 278, 543 U.S. 841, 160 L.Ed.2d 65, rehearing denied, rehearing denied 125 S.Ct. 646, 543 U.S. 1016, 160 L.Ed.2d 488. Habeas Corpus ⚿ 366

Ohio practice of execution via electric chair, especially in light of defendant's option of choosing death by lethal injection, did not violate constitutional prohibition against cruel and unusual punishment. Smith v. Anderson (S.D.Ohio, 02-22-2000) 104 F.Supp.2d 773, affirmed 348 F.3d 177, rehearing and rehearing en banc denied, certiorari denied 125 S.Ct. 278, 543 U.S. 841, 160 L.Ed.2d 65, rehearing denied, rehearing denied 125 S.Ct. 646, 543 U.S. 1016, 160 L.Ed.2d 488. Sentencing And Punishment ⚿ 1796

Imposition of death penalty under Ohio's death penalty statute for murder with aggravating circumstance of rape was not disproportionate punishment, as would violate the Eighth Amendment, absent evidence of substantial mitigating factors. Mason v. Mitchell (N.D.Ohio, 05-09-2000) 95 F.Supp.2d 744, affirmed in part, remanded in part 320 F.3d 604, on remand 293 F.Supp.2d 819, on remand 396 F.Supp.2d 837. Sentencing And Punishment ⚿ 1681

2. Lethal injection option

Trial judge's order of "death by electrocution" did not preclude capital murder defendant's statutory right to elect lethal injection, especially considering the trial judge's express statement that defendant's execution comply with statute affording defendant the lethal injection option. State v. Bey (Ohio, 05-19-1999) 85 Ohio St.3d 487, 709 N.E.2d 484, 1999-Ohio-283, reconsideration denied 86 Ohio St.3d 1421, 711 N.E.2d 1014, certiorari denied 120 S.Ct. 587, 528 U.S. 1049, 145 L.Ed.2d 488. Sentencing And Punishment ⚿ 1796

Challenge to Ohio's former reliance on electrocution as the statutorily-defined method of execution was moot where Ohio law designated lethal injection as the sole means of execution. Williams v. Bagley (C.A.6 (Ohio), 08-13-2004) 380 F.3d 932, rehearing en banc denied, certiorari denied 125 S.Ct. 1939, 544 U.S. 1003, 161 L.Ed.2d 779. Habeas Corpus ⚿ 223

Ohio's capital punishment scheme was not unconstitutional, even if death by electrocution was cruel and unusual punishment, in that death-sentenced defendant had option of choosing execution by lethal injection. Scott v. Anderson (N.D.Ohio, 09-30-1998) 58 F.Supp.2d 767, reversed 209 F.3d 854, rehearing and suggestion for rehearing en banc denied, certiorari denied 121 S.Ct. 588, 531 U.S.

1021, 148 L.Ed.2d 503. Sentencing And Punishment ⚷ 1796

2949.23 Time of execution—Repealed

(1992 S 359, eff. 12–22–92; 1953 H 1; GC 13456–3)

Historical and Statutory Notes

Pre–1953 H 1 Amendments: 113 v 208, Ch 35, § 3

2949.24 Execution and return of warrant

Unless a suspension of execution is ordered by the court of appeals in which the cause is pending on appeal or the supreme court for a case in which a sentence of death is imposed for an offense committed before January 1, 1995, or by the supreme court for a case in which a sentence of death is imposed for an offense committed on or after January 1, 1995, or is ordered by two judges or four justices of that court, the warden or another person selected by the director of rehabilitation and correction shall proceed at the time and place named in the warrant to ensure that the death sentence of the prisoner under death sentence is executed in accordance with section 2949.22 of the Revised Code. The warden shall make the return to the clerk of the court of common pleas of the county immediately from which the prisoner was sentenced of the manner of the execution of the warrant. The clerk shall record the warrant and the return in the records of the case.

(1995 S 4, eff. 9–21–95; 1992 S 359, eff. 12–22–92; 1953 H 1; GC 13456–4)

Historical and Statutory Notes

Pre–1953 H 1 Amendments: 113 v 208, Ch 35, § 4

Amendment Note: 1995 S 4 rewrote this section, which previously read:

"Unless a suspension of execution is ordered by the court in which the cause is pending on appeal, or by two judges of that court, the warden or another person selected by the director of rehabilitation and correction shall proceed at the time and place named in the warrant to ensure that the death sentence of the prisoner under death sentence is executed in accordance with section 2949.22 of the Revised Code. The warden forthwith shall make the return to the clerk of the court of common pleas of the county from which the prisoner was sentenced of the manner of the execution of the warrant. The clerk shall record the warrant and the return in the records of the case."

Library References

Sentencing and Punishment ⚷1795.

Westlaw Topic No. 350H.

C.J.S. Criminal Law §§ 1591, 1605 to 1609.

Research References

Encyclopedias

OH Jur. 3d Courts & Judges § 205, Records of Court Judgments and Proceedings, and Miscellaneous Records Prescribed by Statute.

OH Jur. 3d Criminal Law § 3431, Execution and Return of Warrant.

2949.25 Attendance at execution

(A) At the execution of a death sentence, only the following persons may be present:

(1) The warden of the state correctional institution in which the sentence is executed or a deputy warden, any other person selected by the director of rehabilitation and correction to ensure that the death sentence is executed, any persons necessary to execute the death sentence by lethal injection, and the number of correction officers that the warden thinks necessary;

(2) The sheriff of the county in which the prisoner was tried and convicted;

(3) The director of rehabilitation and correction, or the director's agent;

(4) Physicians of the state correctional institution in which the sentence is executed;

(5) The clergyperson in attendance upon the prisoner, and not more than three other persons, to be designated by the prisoner, who are not confined in any state institution;

(6) Not more than three persons to be designated by the immediate family of the victim;

(7) Representatives of the news media as authorized by the director of rehabilitation and correction.

(B) The director shall authorize at least one representative of a newspaper, at least one representative of a television station, and at least one representative of a radio station to be present at the execution of the sentence under division (A)(7) of this section.

(2001 H 362, eff. 11–21–01; 1994 H 571, eff. 10–6–94; 1993 H 11, eff. 10–1–93; 1992 S 359; 1972 H 494; 125 v 823; 1953 H 1; GC 13456–5)

Historical and Statutory Notes

Pre–1953 H 1 Amendments: 113 v 208, Ch 35, § 5

Amendment Note: 2001 H 362 deleted "electrocution or" before "lethal injection" in division (A)(1); and made changes to reflect gender-neutral language.

Amendment Note: 1994 H 571 substituted "state correctional" for "penal" throughout.

Amendment Note: 1993 H 11 designated division (A); redesignated former divisions (A) through (E) as divisions (A)(1) through (5), respectively; inserted "of the penal institution in which the sentence is executed" and "or lethal injection" in division (A)(1); added "in which the sentence is executed" in division (A)(4); added division (A)(6); redesignated former division (F) as division (A)(7); rewrote division (A)(7); and added division (B). Prior to amendment, division (A)(7) read:

"(F) Representatives of not exceeding three newspapers in the county where the crime was committed, one reporter for each of the daily newspapers published in the city of Columbus, and such other representatives of the news media as the director of rehabilitation and correction authorizes."

Library References

Sentencing and Punishment ⚷1797.
Westlaw Topic No. 350H.
C.J.S. Criminal Law §§ 1591, 1605 to 1609.

Research References

ALR Library

107 ALR 5th 291, Validity of Rules and Regulations Concerning Viewing of Execution of Death Penalty.

Encyclopedias

OH Jur. 3d Criminal Law § 3430, Persons Authorized to Attend.

Notes of Decisions

---

1. Broadcasting of event

Allegedly improper statement of trial court judge, authorizing authorities in charge of executing death sentence to permit media representatives to broadcast execution, was of no force, where it was not incorporated into trial court's journal entries. State v. Keenan (Ohio, 02-25-1998) 81 Ohio St.3d 133, 689 N.E.2d 929, 1998-Ohio-459, reconsideration denied 81 Ohio St.3d 1503, 691 N.E.2d 1062, certiorari denied 119 S.Ct. 146, 525 U.S. 860, 142 L.Ed.2d 119, rehearing denied 119 S.Ct. 581, 525 U.S. 1035, 142 L.Ed.2d 484, denial of post-conviction relief affirmed 2001 WL 91129, dismissed, appeal not allowed 92 Ohio St.3d 1429, 749 N.E.2d 756, habeas corpus dismissed 262 F.Supp.2d 818, motion to amend denied 262 F.Supp.2d 826, vacated and remanded 400 F.3d 417. Criminal Law ⚷ 655(1)

2. Victim's family members allowed

Prisoner who was sentenced to death was not entitled to a temporary restraining order on allegation that officials intended to violate his rights to privacy and due process by permitting excessive number of victim family members to view execution and by improperly allowing recording equipment in execution chamber, as prisoner did not show a strong or substantial likelihood of success on underlying 1983 claim. Coleman v. Wilkinson (Ohio App. 10 Dist., 04-25-2002) 147 Ohio App.3d 357, 770 N.E.2d 637, 2002-Ohio-2021. Civil Rights ⚷ 1457(5)

2949.26 Disposition of body of executed convict

The body of an executed convict shall be returned for burial in any county of the state, to friends who made written request therefor, if made to the warden the day before or on the morning of the execution. The warden may pay the transportation and other funeral expenses, not to exceed fifty dollars.

If no request is made by such friends therefor, such body shall be disposed of as provided by section 1713.34 of the Revised Code and the rules of the director of job and family services.
(1999 H 471, eff. 7–1–00; 1985 H 201, eff. 7–1–85; 1953 H 1; GC 13456–6)

Historical and Statutory Notes

Pre–1953 H 1 Amendments: 113 v 208, Ch 35, § 6

Amendment Note: 1999 H 471 substituted "director of job and family services" for "department of human services" in the second paragraph.

Library References

Sentencing and Punishment ⚷1797.
Westlaw Topic No. 350H.
C.J.S. Criminal Law §§ 1591, 1605 to 1609.

Research References

Encyclopedias

OH Jur. 3d Criminal Law § 3432, Disposition of Body of Executed Convict.

2949.27 Escape, rearrest, and execution

If a convicted felon escapes after sentence of death, and is not retaken before the time fixed for his execution, any sheriff may rearrest and commit him to the county jail, and make return thereof to the court in which the sentence was passed. Such court shall again fix the time for execution, which shall be carried into effect as provided in sections 2949.21 to 2949.26, inclusive, of the Revised Code.
(1953 H 1, eff. 10–1–53; GC 13456–7)

Historical and Statutory Notes

Pre–1953 H 1 Amendments: 113 v 209, Ch 35, § 7

Library References

Sentencing and Punishment ⚷1799.
Westlaw Topic No. 350H.

Research References

Encyclopedias

OH Jur. 3d Criminal Law § 3433, Escape Before Execution.

2949.28 Inquiry on sanity of convict

(A) As used in this section and section 2949.29 of the Revised Code, "insane" means that the convict in question does not have the mental capacity to understand the nature of the death penalty and why it was imposed upon the convict.

(B)(1) If a convict sentenced to death appears to be insane, the warden or the sheriff having custody of the convict, the convict's counsel, or a psychiatrist or psychologist who has examined the convict shall give notice of the apparent insanity to whichever of the following is applicable:

(a) If the convict was tried by a jury, to the judge who imposed the sentence upon the convict or, if that judge is unavailable, to another judge of the same court of common pleas;

(b) If the convict was tried by a three-judge panel, to any of the three judges who imposed the sentence upon the convict or, if each of those judges is unavailable, to another judge of the same court of common pleas.

(2) Upon receiving a notice pursuant to division (B)(1) of this section, a judge shall determine, based on the notice and any supporting information, any information submitted by the prosecuting attorney, and the record in the case, including previous hearings and orders, whether probable cause exists to believe that the convict is insane. If the judge finds that probable cause exists to believe that the convict is insane, the judge shall hold a hearing to determine whether the convict is insane. If the judge does not find that probable cause of that nature exists, the judge may dismiss the matter without a hearing.

(3) If the judge who is given notice under division (B)(1) of this section finds probable cause to believe that the convict is insane, the judge shall inquire into the convict's insanity at a time and place to be fixed by the judge and shall give immediate notice of the inquiry to the prosecuting attorney who prosecuted the case, or that prosecuting attorney's successor, and to the convict and the convict's counsel. The judge may hold the inquiry at the place at which the convict is confined. If the convict does not have counsel, the court shall appoint an attorney to represent the convict in the inquiry. The court may appoint one or more psychiatrists or psychologists to examine the convict. The court shall not appoint a psychiatrist or psychologist who is an employee of the department of rehabilitation and correction to examine the convict. The court shall conduct any hearing under this section and section 2949.29 of the Revised Code and issue any ruling in the matter no later than sixty days from the date of the notice given under division (B)(1) of this section.

(4) Execution of the sentence shall be suspended pending completion of the inquiry only upon an order of the supreme court. If the supreme court issues an order granting a stay of execution, the supreme court in that order also may authorize the court of common pleas to continue the stay of execution or to set a new date for execution as provided in this section or section 2949.29 of the Revised Code.

(C) If the court appoints a psychiatrist or psychologist to examine the convict, the court shall inform the psychiatrist or psychologist of the location of the convict and of the purpose of the examination. The examiner shall have access to any available psychiatric or psychological report previously submitted to the court with respect to the mental condition of the convict, including, if applicable, a report regarding the convict's competency to stand trial or the convict's plea of not guilty by reason of insanity. The examiner also shall have access to any available current mental health and medical records of the convict.

The examiner shall conduct a thorough examination of the convict and shall submit a report to the court within thirty days of the examiner's appointment. The report shall contain the examiner's findings as to whether the convict has the mental capacity to understand the nature of the death penalty and why it was imposed upon the convict and the facts, in reasonable detail, upon which the findings are based.

(1998 S 107, eff. 7–29–98; 1969 S 354, eff. 11–18–69; 1953 H 1; GC 13456–8)

Historical and Statutory Notes

Pre–1953 H 1 Amendments: 113 v 209, Ch 35, § 8

Amendment Note: 1998 S 107 rewrote this section, which previously read:

"If a convict sentenced to death appears to be insane, the warden or the sheriff having custody of such convict shall give notice thereof to a judge of the court of common pleas of the county in which the prisoner is confined. Said judge shall inquire into such insanity at a time and place to be fixed by said judge, or impanel a jury for that purpose and shall give immediate notice thereof to the prosecuting attorney of the county in which the prisoner was convicted. Execution of the sentence shall be suspended pending completion of the inquiry."

Cross References

Competence to stand trial, 2945.37 to 2945.38
Not guility by reason of insanity plea; verdict, 2945.39, 2945.40
Plea of not guilty by reason of insanity, verdict, Crim R 11

Library References

Sentencing and Punishment ⚖1791 to 1794.
Westlaw Topic No. 350H.
C.J.S. Criminal Law §§ 1486, 1547, 1605 to 1609.

Research References

Encyclopedias

OH Jur. 3d Criminal Law § 3230, Federal Constitutional Restrictions on Imposition of Death Penalty, Generally.

OH Jur. 3d Criminal Law § 3232, Ohio's Constitutional Requirements.

OH Jur. 3d Criminal Law § 3428, Proceedings Where Defendant Appears to be Pregnant.

OH Jur. 3d Criminal Law § 3435, Execution of Sentence.

OH Jur. 3d Criminal Law § 3436, Examination by Court-Appointed Psychiatrist or Psychologist.

OH Jur. 3d Criminal Law § 3437, Conduct of Proceedings; Limitations.

Treatises and Practice Aids

Katz, Giannelli, Blair and Lipton, Baldwin's Ohio Practice, Criminal Law, § 126:11, Executions of Insane and Retarded Convicts.

Katz, Giannelli, Blair and Lipton, Baldwin's Ohio Practice, Criminal Law, § 153:35, Entry for Inquest When Condemned Prisoner Reported Insane—Insanity Found and Execution Suspended.

Katz, Giannelli, Blair and Lipton, Baldwin's Ohio Practice, Criminal Law, § 153:36, Entry for Inquest When Condemned Prisoner Reported Insane—No Insanity Found.

Law Review and Journal Commentaries

Ford v. Wainwright, Statutory Changes and a New Test for Sanity: You Can't Execute Me, I'm Crazy!, Note. 35 Clev St L Rev 515 (1986–87).

Ohio's Death Penalty: History and Current Developments, Comment. 31 Cap U L Rev 659 (2003).

Notes of Decisions

1. Constitutional issues

Convict under sentence of death had burden of showing that he was incompetent to be executed. State v. Scott (Ohio, 05-11-2001) 92 Ohio St.3d 1, 748 N.E.2d 11, 111 A.L.R.5th 777, 2001-Ohio-148, certiorari denied 121 S.Ct. 1996, 532 U.S. 1034, 149 L.Ed.2d 780. Sentencing And Punishment ⚷ 1754

Placing burden of proof on convict under sentence of death to prove probable cause or to prove by preponderance of evidence that he was incompetent to be executed did not violate his due process protections. State v. Scott (Ohio, 05-11-2001) 92 Ohio St.3d 1, 748 N.E.2d 11, 111 A.L.R.5th 777, 2001-Ohio-148, certiorari denied 121 S.Ct. 1996, 532 U.S. 1034, 149 L.Ed.2d 780. Constitutional Law ⚷ 272(1); Sentencing And Punishment ⚷ 1754

Court of appeals would grant state's motion to expand record to include an affidavit from a neuroradiologist who reviewed petitioner's MRI results, for purposes of petitioner's motion for relief from judgment of denial of habeas petition alleging that counsel's failure to present evidence of organic brain impairment in death penalty prosecution was ineffective assistance of counsel; the state acted diligently in informing the district court of the MRI and in attempting to present the relevant materials to the district court, and, the MRI results were plainly relevant to the court's determination of whether a stay of execution was warranted. Smith v. Anderson (C.A.6 (Ohio), 03-06-2005) 402 F.3d 718, rehearing en banc denied, certiorari denied 125 S.Ct. 1609, 161 L.Ed.2d 293. Habeas Corpus ⚷ 823

Ohio statute providing that inmate is competent to be executed unless he "does not have the mental capacity to understand the nature of the death penalty and why it was imposed upon the convict" did not violate Eighth Amendment and due process rights of death row inmate suffering from schizophrenia. Scott v. Mitchell (C.A.6 (Ohio), 05-15-2001) 250 F.3d 1011, rehearing and suggestion for rehearing en banc denied, petition for certiorari filed 2001 WL 687422, certiorari denied 121 S.Ct. 2266, 533 U.S. 912, 150 L.Ed.2d 250. Constitutional Law ⚷ 272(1); Sentencing And Punishment ⚷ 1628

Ohio's failure to grant death row inmate evidentiary hearing on question of whether he was competent to be executed did not violate inmate's due process rights, where inmate was permitted to present live expert testimony, but expert did not state that inmate could not understand nature of death penalty and why it was imposed on him. Scott v. Mitchell (C.A.6 (Ohio), 05-15-2001) 250 F.3d 1011, rehearing and suggestion for rehearing en banc denied, petition for certiorari filed 2001 WL 687422, certiorari denied 121 S.Ct. 2266, 533 U.S. 912, 150 L.Ed.2d 250. Constitutional Law ⚷ 272(1); Sentencing And Punishment ⚷ 1794

2. Test of insanity

Convict was competent to be executed, even if he suffered from chronic undifferentiated schizophrenia; he presented no medical or psychiatric testimony, or expert testimony of any nature showing that he was insane, as defined, or that further proceedings were warranted to consider that issue. State v. Scott (Ohio, 05-11-2001) 92 Ohio St.3d 1, 748 N.E.2d 11, 111 A.L.R.5th 777, 2001-Ohio-148, certiorari denied 121 S.Ct. 1996, 532 U.S. 1034, 149 L.Ed.2d 780. Sentencing And Punishment ⚷ 1772

The test of whether a convict awaiting execution is "insane" within the meaning of RC 2949.28, RC 2949.29, and RC 2949.30 is not whether he is "mentally ill," but whether he has sufficient intelligence to understand the nature of the proceedings against him, what he was tried for, the purpose of his punishment, the impending fate that awaits him, a sufficient understanding to know any fact which might exist which would make his punishment unjust or unlawful, and the intelligence to convey such information to his attorney or the court, and a judge, having the power to grant a stay of execution pending such "inquiry," has the inherent power in the event of a finding that such convict is "not insane" to terminate such stay of execution and set a date when the sentence shall be carried into execution. In re Keaton (Franklin 1969) 19 Ohio App.2d 254, 250 N.E.2d 901, 48 O.O.2d 376, vacated in part 92 S.Ct. 2860, 408 U.S. 936, 33 L.Ed.2d 752.

2949.29 Proceedings on the insanity inquiry

(A) The prosecuting attorney, the convict, and the convict's counsel shall attend an inquiry commenced as provided in section 2949.28 of the Revised Code. The prosecuting attorney and the convict or the convict's counsel may produce, examine, and cross-examine witnesses, and all findings shall be in writing signed by the judge. If it is found that the convict is not insane, the sentence shall be executed at the time previously appointed, unless that time has passed pending completion of the inquiry, in which case the judge conducting the inquiry, if authorized by the supreme court, shall appoint a time for execution of the sentence to be effective fifteen days from the date of the entry of the judge's findings in the inquiry.

(B) If it is found that the convict is insane and if authorized by the supreme court, the judge shall continue any stay of execution of the sentence previously issued, order the convict to be confined in the area at which other convicts sentenced to death are confined or in a maximum security medical or psychiatric facility operated by the department of rehabilitation and correction, and order treatment of the convict. Thereafter, the court at any time may conduct and, on motion of the prosecuting attorney, shall conduct a hearing pursuant to division (A) of this section to continue the inquiry into the convict's insanity and, as provided in section 2949.28 of the Revised Code, may appoint one or more psychiatrists or psychologists to make a further examination of the convict and to submit a report to the court. If the court finds at the hearing that the convict is not insane and if the time previously appointed for execution of the sentence has not passed, the sentence shall be executed at the previously appointed time. If the court finds at the hearing that the convict is not insane and if the time previously appointed for execution of the sentence has passed, the judge who conducts the hearing, if authorized by the supreme court, shall appoint a new time for execution of the sentence to be effective fifteen days from the date of the entry of the judge's findings in the hearing.

(C) In all proceedings under this section, the convict is presumed not to be insane, and the court shall find that the convict is not insane unless the court finds by a preponderance of the evidence that the convict is insane.

(D) Proceedings for inquiry into the insanity of any convict sentenced to death shall be exclusively pursuant to this section, section 2949.28 of the Revised Code, and the Rules of Evidence. Neither Chapter 5122. or 5123. of the Revised Code nor any other provision of the Revised Code nor any other rule concerning mentally ill persons, mentally retarded persons, or insane persons applies to any proceeding for inquiry into the insanity of any convict sentenced to death.

(1998 S 107, eff. 7–29–98; 1969 S 354, eff. 11–18–69; 1953 H 1; GC 13456–9)

Historical and Statutory Notes

Pre–1953 H 1 Amendments: 113 v 209, Ch 35, § 9

Amendment Note: 1998 S 107 rewrote this section, which previously read:

"In addition to the warden or sheriff, the judge of the court of common pleas, clerk of the court of common pleas, and prosecuting attorney shall attend the inquiry commenced as provided in section 2949.28 of the Revised Code. Witnesses may be produced and examined before the judge or jury, and all findings shall be in writing signed by the judge or jury. If it is found that the convict is not insane, the sentence shall be executed at the time previously appointed, unless such time has passed pending completion of the inquiry, in which case the judge conducting the inquiry shall appoint a time for execution. If it is found that the convict is insane, the judge shall suspend the execution until the warden or sheriff receives a warrant from the governor directing such execution as provided in section 2949.30 of the Revised Code. The finding, and the order of such judge, certified by him, shall be entered on the journal of the court by the clerk."

Library References

Sentencing and Punishment ⚷1791 to 1794.
Westlaw Topic No. 350H.
C.J.S. Criminal Law §§ 1486, 1547, 1605 to 1609.

Research References

Encyclopedias

OH Jur. 3d Cvl. Servants & Pub. Officers & Employ. § 491, Postconviction Responsibilities.

OH Jur. 3d Criminal Law § 3428, Proceedings Where Defendant Appears to be Pregnant.

OH Jur. 3d Criminal Law § 3437, Conduct of Proceedings; Limitations.

Treatises and Practice Aids

Katz, Giannelli, Blair and Lipton, Baldwin's Ohio Practice, Criminal Law, § 126:11, Executions of Insane and Retarded Convicts.

Katz, Giannelli, Blair and Lipton, Baldwin's Ohio Practice, Criminal Law, § 153:35, Entry for Inquest When Condemned Prisoner Reported Insane—Insanity Found and Execution Suspended.

Katz, Giannelli, Blair and Lipton, Baldwin's Ohio Practice, Criminal Law, § 153:36, Entry for Inquest When Condemned Prisoner Reported Insane—No Insanity Found.

Notes of Decisions

Constitutional issues 1
Nature of proceeding 2
Test of insanity 3

---

1. Constitutional issues

Convict under sentence of death had burden of showing that he was incompetent to be executed. State v. Scott (Ohio, 05-11-2001) 92 Ohio St.3d 1, 748 N.E.2d 11, 111 A.L.R.5th 777, 2001-Ohio-148, certiorari denied 121 S.Ct. 1996, 532 U.S. 1034, 149 L.Ed.2d 780. Sentencing And Punishment ⚷ 1754

Placing burden of proof on convict under sentence of death to prove probable cause or to prove by preponderance of evidence that he was incompetent to be executed did not violate his due process protections. State v. Scott (Ohio, 05-11-2001) 92 Ohio St.3d 1, 748 N.E.2d 11, 111 A.L.R.5th 777, 2001-Ohio-148, certiorari denied 121 S.Ct. 1996, 532 U.S. 1034, 149 L.Ed.2d 780. Constitutional Law ⚷ 272(1); Sentencing And Punishment ⚷ 1754

The prohibition by US Const Am 8 of federal infliction of cruel and unusual punishments is extended to forbid state execution of a capital sentence upon an insane prisoner, notwithstanding that the common or statute law of all fifty states has always proscribed such punishment anyway; now that this substantive federal right has been created, where a state prisoner seeks a federal writ of habeas corpus and alleges present incapacity the US district court must grant a hearing de novo on the issue where the state decision on present capacity was not by a court, or was inadequate; a governor's commission of three experts conducting an objective examination without advocacy is "inadequate." (Ed. note: Florida statute construed in light of federal constitution.) Ford v. Wainwright (U.S.Fla. 1986) 106 S.Ct. 2595, 477 U.S. 399, 91 L.Ed.2d 335.

2. Nature of proceeding

Where a statutory procedure has been provided for suspending an execution upon notice by the warden to a judge of the common pleas court of the county in which the prisoner is confined that such convict "appears to be insane," the "inquiry" by the court "into such sanity" is not an adversary proceeding, the convict is not a "party" thereto, the determination of the question of present insanity is not subject to judicial review, and such convict has no right of appeal from a factual determination by the judge of the common pleas court that the convict is "not insane." In re Keaton (Franklin 1969) 19 Ohio App.2d 254, 250 N.E.2d 901, 48 O.O.2d 376, vacated in part 92 S.Ct. 2860, 408 U.S. 936, 33 L.Ed.2d 752.

3. Test of insanity

The test of whether a convict awaiting execution is "insane" within the meaning of RC 2949.28, RC 2949.29, and RC 2949.30 is not whether he is "mentally ill," but whether he has sufficient intelligence to understand the nature of the proceedings against him, what he was tried for, the purpose of his punishment, the impending fate that awaits him, a sufficient understanding to know any fact which might exist which would make his punishment unjust or unlawful, and the intelligence to convey such information to his attorney or the court, and a judge, having the power to grant a stay of execution pending such "inquiry," has the inherent power in the event of a finding that such convict is "not insane" to terminate such stay of execution and set a date when the sentence shall be carried into execution. In re Keaton (Franklin 1969) 19 Ohio App.2d 254, 250 N.E.2d 901, 48 O.O.2d 376, vacated in part 92 S.Ct. 2860, 408 U.S. 936, 33 L.Ed.2d 752.

2949.30 When convict restored, governor to order execution—Repealed

(1998 S 107, eff. 7–29–98; 130 v H 428, eff. 9–27–63; 1953 H 1; GC 13456–10)

Historical and Statutory Notes

Pre–1953 H 1 Amendments: 113 v 209, Ch 35, § 10

2949.31 Pregnant prisoners

If a female convict sentenced to death appears to be pregnant, the warden or sheriff having custody of the convict, her counsel, or a physician who has examined the convict shall give notice of the apparent pregnancy to the appropriate judge of the appropriate court of common pleas as determined in the same manner as is provided in divisions (B)(1)(a) and (b) of section 2949.28 of the Revised Code, and like proceedings shall be had as are provided under sections 2949.28 and 2949.29 of the Revised Code in case of an insane convict sentenced to death, except to the extent that they by their nature clearly would be inapplicable.

If it is found at the inquiry held in accordance with sections 2949.28 and 2949.29 of the Revised Code that the convict is not pregnant, the sentence shall be executed at the time previously appointed, unless that time has passed pending completion of the inquiry, in which case the judge conducting the inquiry, if authorized by the supreme court, shall appoint a new time for execution of the sentence to be effective fifteen days from the date of the entry of the judge's ruling in the inquiry.

If it is found at the inquiry that the convict is pregnant, the judge shall suspend execution of the sentence and order the convict to be confined in the area at which other convicts sentenced to death are confined or in an appropriate medical facility. When the court finds that the convict no longer is pregnant, if the time previously appointed for execution of the sentence has not passed, the sentence shall be executed at the previously appointed time. When the court finds that the convict no longer is pregnant, if the time previously appointed for execution of the sentence has passed, the judge who conducts the inquiry, if authorized by the supreme court, shall appoint a new time for execution of the sentence to be effective fifteen days from the date of the entry of the judge's ruling in the inquiry.

(1998 S 107, eff. 7–29–98; 1953 H 1, eff. 10–1–53; GC 13456–11)

Historical and Statutory Notes

Pre–1953 H 1 Amendments: 113 v 209, Ch 35, § 11

Amendment Note: 1998 S 107 rewrote this section, which previously read:

"If a female convict sentenced to death appears to be pregnant, the warden or sheriff having custody of such convict shall give notice thereof to a judge of the court of common pleas of the county in which the prisoner is confined, and like proceedings shall be had as are provided under sections 2949.28 and 2949.29 of the Revised Code in case of an insane convict sentenced to death."

Library References

Sentencing and Punishment ⚷1798.

Westlaw Topic No. 350H.

C.J.S. Criminal Law §§ 1547, 1687.

Research References

Encyclopedias

OH Jur. 3d Cvl. Servants & Pub. Officers & Employ. § 491, Postconviction Responsibilities.

OH Jur. 3d Criminal Law § 3428, Proceedings Where Defendant Appears to be Pregnant.

Law Review and Journal Commentaries

Nine Months to Life—The Law and the Pregnant Inmate, Note. 20 J Fam L 523 (1981–82).

2949.32 When execution to be ordered—Repealed

(1998 S 107, eff. 7–29–98; 1969 S 354, eff. 11–18–69; 1953 H 1; GC 13456–12)

Historical and Statutory Notes

Pre–1953 H 1 Amendments: 113 v 209, Ch 35, § 12

2949.33 to 2949.36 Habitual offenders; cumulative sentences; parole from workhouse—Repealed

(1973 H 716, eff. 1–1–74; 1972 H 511; 1970 S 460; 1953 H 1; GC 13457–1 to 13457–4)

Historical and Statutory Notes

Ed. Note: See now parenthetical references for provisions analogous to former statutes: 2949.33 (2929.41); 2949.34 (2929.11, 2929.12, 2929.41); 2949.35 (2967.04); 2949.36 (2941.46, 2967.02).

Pre–1953 H 1 Amendments: 113 v 210, Ch 36, § 1 to 4

INDEX

See volume containing end of Title 29, Crimes—Procedure.

END OF VOLUME

2015 Pocket Part

BALDWIN'S

ANNOTATED

Replacing the 2014 Pocket Part
Supplementing the 2006 main volume

Includes all laws through December 31, 2014

For changes after 12-31-14, please consult
Baldwin's Ohio Legislative Service Annotated, 2015.

Title 29

Crimes—Procedure

Chapters 2935 to 2949

Mat# 41793086

PREFACE

The 2015 Pocket Parts, for use in 2015, bring the text of Baldwin's™ Ohio Revised Code Annotated to date through December 31, 2014, with legislative histories, uncodified law, and historical and statutory notes. Annotations are provided covering constructions and interpretations by state and federal courts, opinions of the attorney general, selected decisions from state agencies, and law review and journal commentaries. Uniform laws, cross references, Ohio Administrative Code references, and Research References are also updated.

State and federal court decisions that have not yet been assigned a Reporter citation (i.e., pre-reported cases) have a Westlaw citation. The Reporter citation will appear in future publications when available. Unreported decisions appear with a Westlaw citation and the designation "unreported." The official WebCite citation for State court decisions is given as available.

Notes of decisions of State and Federal courts include cases received through February 23, 2015. Opinions of the attorney general are current through February 23, 2015.

The General Index provides subject access to the Ohio Statutes, United States and Ohio Constitutions, and State Rules of Court and is complete through December 31, 2014. The index is replaced annually to assure complete and current access to the law in a convenient format.

For changes in the law after December 31, 2014, and additional annotations, please consult 2015 issues of Baldwin's Ohio Legislative Service Annotated™. These later laws and annotations will be published in subsequent pamphlets and annual cumulative pocket parts.

All material from the 2014 issues of Baldwin's Ohio Legislative Service Annotated (OLS) is now incorporated within the 2015 Pocket Parts. The 2014 OLS issues and 2014 ORC Pocket Parts may now be archived, recycled or discarded.

Please consult the Main Volume of Baldwin's ORC for a list of frequently used abbreviations.

For additional information or research assistance call the West reference attorneys at 1-800-REF-ATTY (1-800-733-2889). Contact West's editorial department directly with your questions and suggestions by e-mail at west.editor@thomson.com.

BALDWIN'S OHIO REVISED CODE ANNOTATED

Title XXIX

CRIMES—PROCEDURE

(Chapters 2935 to 2949)

CHAPTER 2935

ARREST, CITATION, AND DISPOSITION ALTERNATIVES

DEFINITIONS

2935.01 Definitions

As used in this chapter:

(A) "Magistrate" has the same meaning as in section 2931.01 of the Revised Code.

(B) "Peace officer" includes, except as provided in section 2935.081 of the Revised Code, a sheriff; deputy sheriff; marshal; deputy marshal; member of the organized police department of any municipal corporation, including a member of the organized police department of a municipal corporation in an adjoining state serving in Ohio under a contract pursuant to section 737.04 of the Revised Code; member of a police force employed by a metropolitan housing authority under division (D) of section 3735.31 of the Revised Code; member of a police force employed by a regional transit authority under division (Y) of section 306.05 of the Revised Code; state university law enforcement officer appointed under section 3345.04 of the Revised Code; enforcement agent of the department of public safety designated under section 5502.14 of the Revised Code; employee of the department of taxation to whom investigation powers have been delegated under section 5743.45 of the Revised Code; employee of the department of natural resources who is a natural resources law enforcement staff officer designated pursuant to section 1501.013 of the Revised Code, a forest officer designated pursuant to section 1503.29 of the Revised Code, a preserve officer designated pursuant to section 1517.10 of the Revised Code, a wildlife officer designated pursuant to section 1531.13 of the Revised Code, a park officer designated pursuant to section 1541.10 of the Revised Code, or a state watercraft officer designated pursuant to section 1547.521 of the Revised Code; individual designated to perform law enforcement duties under section 511.232, 1545.13, or 6101.75 of the Revised Code; veterans' home police officer appointed under section 5907.02 of the Revised Code; special police officer employed by a port authority under section 4582.04 or 4582.28 of the Revised Code; police constable of any township; police officer of a township or joint police district; a special police officer employed by a municipal corporation at a municipal airport, or other municipal air navigation facility, that has scheduled operations, as defined in section 119.3 of Title 14 of the Code of Federal Regulations, 14 C.F.R. 119.3, as amended, and that is required to be under a security program and is governed by aviation security rules of the transportation security administration of the United States department of transportation as provided in Parts 1542. and 1544. of Title 49 of the Code of Federal Regulations, as amended; the house of representatives sergeant at arms if the house of representatives sergeant at arms has arrest authority pursuant to division (E)(1) of section 101.311 of the Revised Code; an assistant house of representatives sergeant at arms; the senate sergeant at arms; an assistant senate sergeant at arms; officer or employee of the bureau of criminal identification and investigation established pursuant to section 109.51 of the Revised Code who has been awarded a certificate by the executive director of the Ohio peace officer training commission attesting to the officer's or employee's satisfactory completion of an approved state, county, municipal, or department of natural resources peace officer basic training program and who is providing assistance upon request to a law enforcement officer or emergency assistance to a peace officer pursuant to section 109.54 or 109.541 of the Revised Code; a state fire marshal law enforcement officer described in division (A)(23) of section 109.71 of the Revised Code; and, for the purpose of arrests within those areas, for the purposes of Chapter 5503. of the Revised Code, and the filing of and service of process relating to those offenses witnessed or investigated by them, the superintendent and troopers of the state highway patrol.

(C) "Prosecutor" includes the county prosecuting attorney and any assistant prosecutor designated to assist the county prosecuting attorney, and, in the case of courts inferior to courts of common pleas, includes the village solicitor, city director of law, or similar chief legal officer of a municipal corporation, any such officer's assistants, or any attorney designated by the prosecuting attorney of the county to appear for the prosecution of a given case.

(D) "Offense," except where the context specifically indicates otherwise, includes felonies, misdemeanors, and violations of ordinances of municipal corporations and other public bodies authorized by law to adopt penal regulations.

(2012 H 487, eff. 9-10-12; 2011 H 153, eff. 9-29-11; 2008 H 562, eff. 9–23–08; 2002 H 675, eff. 3–14–03; 2002 H 545, eff. 3–19–03; 2002 H 427, eff. 8–29–02; 2002 S 200, eff. 9–6–02; 2000 S 317, eff. 3–22–01; 2000 S 137, eff. 5–17–00; 1999 H 163, eff. 6–30–99; 1998 S 187, eff. 3–18–99; 1996 H 72, eff. 3–18–97; 1995 S 162, eff. 10–29–95; 1995 S 2, eff. 7–1–96; 1991 S 144, eff. 8–8–91; 1991 H 77; 1988 H 708, § 1)

Historical and Statutory Notes

Amendment Note: 2012 H 487, in division (B), inserted "the senate sergeant at arms; an assistant senate sergeant at arms;" following "an assistant house of representatives sergeant at arms;"; and made other nonsubstantive changes.

Amendment Note: 2011 H 153, in division (B) deleted "township" following "police officer of a township or joint"

Amendment Note: 2008 H 562 inserted "of representatives" following "house" in three instances and inserted "a state fire marshal law enforcement officer described in division (A)(23) of section 109.71 of the Revised Code;" in division (B).

Cross References

Polygraph examination of sex offense victims prohibited, see 2907.10

Sanctions for commission of felony while serving in position of honor, trust or profit, see 2929.192

Ohio Administrative Code References

Adult protective services definitions, see OAC 5101:2–20–01

Contingent registration, see OAC 1501:47–1–07.1

Required experience, see OAC 4501:5–1–06

Restrictions on warrantless administrative inspections, see OAC 4301:1–1–79

Uniforms, see OAC 4501:5–1–12

Research References

ALR Library

70 ALR 6th 1, Judicial Expunction of Criminal Record of Convicted Adult Under Statute-Expunction Under Statutes Addressing "First Offenders" and "Innocent Persons," Where Conviction was for Minor Drug or Other Offense, Where...

Encyclopedias

OH Jur. 3d Acknowledgments, Affidavits, Oaths, and Notaries § 13, Peace Officers.

OH Jur. 3d Civil Servants and Other Public Officers and Employees § 176, Eligibility for Promotion.

OH Jur. 3d Civil Servants and Other Public Officers and Employees § 490, Who is Prosecuting Attorney in Magistrates' Courts.

OH Jur. 3d Criminal Law: Procedure § 677, Generally; Peace Officers.

OH Jur. 3d Criminal Law: Procedure § 1891, Seven-Year Term.

OH Jur. 3d Criminal Law: Procedure § 1917, Offenses for Which Prison Term Must Not be Reduced.

OH Jur. 3d Criminal Law: Procedure § 1926, Misdemeanor Jail Terms.

OH Jur. 3d Criminal Law: Procedure § 2715, Requirements for Eligibility--Requirements Pertaining to Charged Offense.

OH Jur. 3d Criminal Law: Substantive Principles and Offenses § 334, Offense and Punishment.

OH Jur. 3d Criminal Law: Substantive Principles and Offenses § 338, Offense and Punishment.

OH Jur. 3d Criminal Law: Substantive Principles and Offenses § 340, Offense and Punishment.

OH Jur. 3d Hotels, Motels, and Restaurants § 53, Prosecution and Remedies.

OH Jur. 3d Police, Sheriffs, and Related Officers § 3, Police Officers Within Various Agencies and Organizations--"Peace Officer".

OH Jur. 3d Railroads § 418, Bylaws, Rules, and Regulations.

OH Jur. 3d Schools, Universities, and Colleges § 343, Free Tuition.

Treatises and Practice Aids

Katz & Giannelli, Baldwin's Ohio Practice Criminal Law § 6:2, Arrest Defined.

Katz & Giannelli, Baldwin's Ohio Practice Criminal Law § 7:6, Authority to Execute Arrest Warrants.

Katz & Giannelli, Baldwin's Ohio Practice Criminal Law § 97:3, Assault.

Katz & Giannelli, Baldwin's Ohio Practice Criminal Law § 97:4, Felonious Assault.

Katz & Giannelli, Baldwin's Ohio Practice Criminal Law § 97:5, Aggravated Assault.

Katz & Giannelli, Baldwin's Ohio Practice Criminal Law § 103:4, Aggravated Arson.

Katz & Giannelli, Baldwin's Ohio Practice Criminal Law § 110:10, False Allegation of Police Officer Misconduct.

Katz & Giannelli, Baldwin's Ohio Practice Criminal Law § 110:14, Disclosure of Confidential Information.

Katz & Giannelli, Baldwin's Ohio Practice Criminal Law § 113:13, Illegal Collection of Bodily Substance.

Katz & Giannelli, Baldwin's Ohio Practice Criminal Law § 118:13, Shooting at a Police Officer.

Painter & Pollis, Ohio Appellate Practice App. M, Local Appellate Rules.

Painter & Pollis, Ohio Appellate Practice App. P, Ohio Revised Code.

Katz, Ohio Arrest, Search & Seizure § 3:2, Defining Arrest.

Adrine & Ruden, Ohio Domestic Violence Law § 3:3, Elements and Penalties--Felonious Assault Under RC 2903.11.

Adrine & Ruden, Ohio Domestic Violence Law § 3:4, Elements and Penalties--Aggravated Assault Under RC 2903.12.

Adrine & Ruden, Ohio Domestic Violence Law § 3:5, Elements and Penalties--Assault Under RC 2903.13.

Adrine & Ruden, Ohio Domestic Violence Law App. A, Ohio Revised Code (Selected Provisions).

Adrine & Ruden, Ohio Domestic Violence Law § 5:14, Case Preparation--Hearsay Exceptions--Generally.

Weiler & Weiler, Ohio Driving Under the Influence App. A, Ohio Revised Code--Selected Provisions.

Princehorn, Ohio Township Law § 11:15, Special Constables.

Notes of Decisions

1. Peace officers generally

Evidence of each necessary element of aggravated murder, aggravated robbery, and having a weapon under disability was sufficient to support defendant's convictions thereof, as well as related specifications; eyewitness testimony and forensic and documentary evidence, including DNA tests, autopsy results, and defendant's prior criminal record, indicated that victim, a deputy sheriff in performance of his duties, interrupted defendant's robbery of gas station, and that defendant repeatedly shot victim with victim's own gun, more than once in the head as victim lay prone, fled in his car, and went to residence of acquaintance, where he traded victim's gun for crack cocaine. State v. Gross (Ohio, 10-30-2002) 97 Ohio St.3d 121, 776 N.E.2d 1061, 2002-Ohio-5524, reconsideration denied 97 Ohio St.3d 1486, 780 N.E.2d 288, 2002-Ohio-6866, certiorari denied 123 S.Ct. 2079, 538 U.S. 1037, 155 L.Ed.2d 1068, rehearing denied 124 S.Ct. 20, 539 U.S. 976, 156 L.Ed.2d 685, denial of post-conviction relief affirmed 2003-Ohio-6295, 2003 WL 22765845, appeal not allowed 102 Ohio St.3d 1410, 806 N.E.2d 562, 2004-Ohio-1763, certiorari denied 125 S.Ct. 165, 543 U.S. 888, 160 L.Ed.2d 149, dismissal of post-conviction relief affirmed 2006-Ohio-6941, 2006 WL 3804532, appeal not allowed 113 Ohio St.3d 1468, 864 N.E.2d 654, 2007-Ohio-1722, habeas corpus dismissed 2008 WL 4702181, motion to amend denied 2008 WL 4889626, certificate of appealability denied 2008 WL 5190017, affirmed 426 Fed.Appx. 349, 2011 WL 1597659. Homicide ⚷ 1139; Robbery ⚷ 24.15(2); Weapons ⚷ 293(3); Weapons ⚷ 293(4)

ARREST

2935.03 Arrest and detention until warrant can be obtained

(A)(1) A sheriff, deputy sheriff, marshal, deputy marshal, municipal police officer, township constable, police officer of a township or joint police district, member of a police force employed by a metropolitan housing authority under division (D) of section 3735.31 of the Revised Code, member of a police force employed by a regional transit authority under division (Y) of section 306.35 of the Revised Code, state university law enforcement officer appointed under section 3345.04 of the Revised Code, veterans' home police officer appointed under section 5907.02 of the Revised Code, special police officer employed by a port authority under section 4582.04 or 4582.28 of the Revised Code, or a special police officer employed by a municipal corporation at a municipal airport, or other municipal air navigation facility, that has scheduled operations, as defined in section 119.3 of Title 14 of the Code of Federal Regulations, 14 C.F.R. 119.3, as amended, and that is required to be under a security program and is governed by aviation security rules of the transportation security administration of the United States department of transportation as provided in Parts 1542. and 1544. of Title 49 of the Code of Federal Regulations, as amended, shall arrest and detain, until a warrant can be obtained, a person found violating, within the limits of the political subdivision, metropolitan housing authority housing project, regional transit authority facilities or areas of a municipal corporation that have been agreed to by a regional transit authority and a municipal corporation located within its territorial jurisdiction, college, university, veterans' home operated under Chapter 5907. of the Revised Code, port authority, or municipal airport or other municipal air navigation facility, in which the peace officer is appointed, employed, or elected, a law of this state, an ordinance of a municipal corporation, or a resolution of a township.

(2) A peace officer of the department of natural resources, a state fire marshal law enforcement officer described in division (A)(23) of section 109.71 of the Revised Code, or an individual designated to perform law enforcement duties under section 511.232, 1545.13, or 6101.75 of the Revised Code shall arrest and detain, until a warrant can be obtained, a person found violating, within the limits of the peace officer's, state fire marshal law enforcement officer's, or individual's territorial jurisdiction, a law of this state.

(3) The house sergeant at arms, if the house sergeant at arms has arrest authority pursuant to division (E)(1) of section 101.311 of the Revised Code, and an assistant house sergeant at

arms shall arrest and detain, until a warrant can be obtained, a person found violating, within the limits of the sergeant at arms's or assistant sergeant at arms's territorial jurisdiction specified in division (D)(1)(a) of section 101.311 of the Revised Code or while providing security pursuant to division (D)(1)(f) of section 101.311 of the Revised Code, a law of this state, an ordinance of a municipal corporation, or a resolution of a township.

(4) The senate sergeant at arms and an assistant senate sergeant at arms shall arrest and detain, until a warrant can be obtained, a person found violating, within the limits of the sergeant at arms's or assistant sergeant at arms's territorial jurisdiction specified in division (B) of section 101.312 of the Revised Code, a law of this state, an ordinance of a municipal corporation, or a resolution of a township.

(B)(1) When there is reasonable ground to believe that an offense of violence, the offense of criminal child enticement as defined in section 2905.05 of the Revised Code, the offense of public indecency as defined in section 2907.09 of the Revised Code, the offense of domestic violence as defined in section 2919.25 of the Revised Code, the offense of violating a protection order as defined in section 2919.27 of the Revised Code, the offense of menacing by stalking as defined in section 2903.211 of the Revised Code, the offense of aggravated trespass as defined in section 2911.211 of the Revised Code, a theft offense as defined in section 2913.01 of the Revised Code, or a felony drug abuse offense as defined in section 2925.01 of the Revised Code, has been committed within the limits of the political subdivision, metropolitan housing authority housing project, regional transit authority facilities or those areas of a municipal corporation that have been agreed to by a regional transit authority and a municipal corporation located within its territorial jurisdiction, college, university, veterans' home operated under Chapter 5907. of the Revised Code, port authority, or municipal airport or other municipal air navigation facility, in which the peace officer is appointed, employed, or elected or within the limits of the territorial jurisdiction of the peace officer, a peace officer described in division (A) of this section may arrest and detain until a warrant can be obtained any person who the peace officer has reasonable cause to believe is guilty of the violation.

(2) For purposes of division (B)(1) of this section, the execution of any of the following constitutes reasonable ground to believe that the offense alleged in the statement was committed and reasonable cause to believe that the person alleged in the statement to have committed the offense is guilty of the violation:

(a) A written statement by a person alleging that an alleged offender has committed the offense of menacing by stalking or aggravated trespass;

(b) A written statement by the administrator of the interstate compact on mental health appointed under section 5119.71 of the Revised Code alleging that a person who had been hospitalized, institutionalized, or confined in any facility under an order made pursuant to or under authority of section 2945.37, 2945.371, 2945.38, 2945.39, 2945.40, 2945.401, or 2945.402 of the Revised Code has escaped from the facility, from confinement in a vehicle for transportation to or from the facility, or from supervision by an employee of the facility that is incidental to hospitalization, institutionalization, or confinement in the facility and that occurs outside of the facility, in violation of section 2921.34 of the Revised Code;

(c) A written statement by the administrator of any facility in which a person has been hospitalized, institutionalized, or confined under an order made pursuant to or under authority of section 2945.37, 2945.371, 2945.38, 2945.39, 2945.40, 2945.401, or 2945.402 of the Revised Code alleging that the person has escaped from the facility, from confinement in a vehicle for transportation to or from the facility, or from supervision by an employee of the facility that is incidental to hospitalization, institutionalization, or confinement in the facility and that occurs outside of the facility, in violation of section 2921.34 of the Revised Code.

(3)(a) For purposes of division (B)(1) of this section, a peace officer described in division (A) of this section has reasonable grounds to believe that the offense of domestic violence or the offense of violating a protection order has been committed and reasonable cause to believe that a particular person is guilty of committing the offense if any of the following occurs:

(i) A person executes a written statement alleging that the person in question has committed the offense of domestic violence or the offense of violating a protection order against the person who executes the statement or against a child of the person who executes the statement.

(ii) No written statement of the type described in division (B)(3)(a)(i) of this section is executed, but the peace officer, based upon the peace officer's own knowledge and observation of the facts and circumstances of the alleged incident of the offense of domestic violence or the alleged incident of the offense of violating a protection order or based upon any other information, including, but not limited to, any reasonably trustworthy information given to the peace officer by the alleged victim of the alleged incident of the offense or any witness of the alleged incident of the offense, concludes that there are reasonable grounds to believe that the offense of domestic violence or the offense of violating a protection order has been committed and reasonable cause to believe that the person in question is guilty of committing the offense.

(iii) No written statement of the type described in division (B)(3)(a)(i) of this section is executed, but the peace officer witnessed the person in question commit the offense of domestic violence or the offense of violating a protection order.

(b) If pursuant to division (B)(3)(a) of this section a peace officer has reasonable grounds to believe that the offense of domestic violence or the offense of violating a protection order has been committed and reasonable cause to believe that a particular person is guilty of committing the offense, it is the preferred course of action in this state that the officer arrest and detain that person pursuant to division (B)(1) of this section until a warrant can be obtained.

If pursuant to division (B)(3)(a) of this section a peace officer has reasonable grounds to believe that the offense of domestic violence or the offense of violating a protection order has been committed and reasonable cause to believe that family or household members have committed the offense against each other, it is the preferred course of action in this state that the officer, pursuant to division (B)(1) of this section, arrest and detain until a warrant can be obtained the family or household member who committed the offense and whom the officer has reasonable cause to believe is the primary physical aggressor. There is no preferred course of action in this state regarding any other family or household member who committed the offense and whom the officer does not have reasonable cause to believe is the primary physical aggressor, but, pursuant to division (B)(1) of this section, the peace officer may arrest and detain until a warrant can be obtained any other family or household member who committed the offense and whom the officer does not have reasonable cause to believe is the primary physical aggressor.

(c) If a peace officer described in division (A) of this section does not arrest and detain a person whom the officer has reasonable cause to believe committed the offense of domestic violence or the offense of violating a protection order when it is the preferred course of action in this state pursuant to division (B)(3)(b) of this section that the officer arrest that person, the officer shall articulate in the written report of the incident required by section 2935.032 of the Revised Code a clear statement of the officer's reasons for not arresting and detaining that person until a warrant can be obtained.

(d) In determining for purposes of division (B)(3)(b) of this section which family or household member is the primary physical aggressor in a situation in which family or household members have committed the offense of domestic violence or the offense of violating a protection order against each other, a peace officer described in division (A) of this section, in addition to any other relevant circumstances, should consider all of the following:

(i) Any history of domestic violence or of any other violent acts by either person involved in the alleged offense that the officer reasonably can ascertain;

(ii) If violence is alleged, whether the alleged violence was caused by a person acting in self-defense;

(iii) Each person's fear of physical harm, if any, resulting from the other person's threatened use of force against any person or resulting from the other person's use or history of the use of force against any person, and the reasonableness of that fear;

(iv) The comparative severity of any injuries suffered by the persons involved in the alleged offense.

(e)(i) A peace officer described in division (A) of this section shall not require, as a prerequisite to arresting or charging a person who has committed the offense of domestic violence or the offense of violating a protection order, that the victim of the offense specifically consent to the filing of charges against the person who has committed the offense or sign a complaint against the person who has committed the offense.

(ii) If a person is arrested for or charged with committing the offense of domestic violence or the offense of violating a protection order and if the victim of the offense does not cooperate with the involved law enforcement or prosecuting authorities in the prosecution of the offense or, subsequent to the arrest or the filing of the charges, informs the involved law enforcement or prosecuting authorities that the victim does not wish the prosecution of the offense to continue or wishes to drop charges against the alleged offender relative to the offense, the involved prosecuting authorities, in determining whether to continue with the prosecution of the offense or whether to dismiss charges against the alleged offender relative to the offense and notwithstanding the victim's failure to cooperate or the victim's wishes, shall consider all facts and circumstances that are relevant to the offense, including, but not limited to, the statements and observations of the peace officers who responded to the incident that resulted in the arrest or filing of the charges and of all witnesses to that incident.

(f) In determining pursuant to divisions (B)(3)(a) to (g) of this section whether to arrest a person pursuant to division (B)(1) of this section, a peace officer described in division (A) of this section shall not consider as a factor any possible shortage of cell space at the detention facility to which the person will be taken subsequent to the person's arrest or any possibility that the person's arrest might cause, contribute to, or exacerbate overcrowding at that detention facility or at any other detention facility.

(g) If a peace officer described in division (A) of this section intends pursuant to divisions (B)(3)(a) to (g) of this section to arrest a person pursuant to division (B)(1) of this section and if the officer is unable to do so because the person is not present, the officer promptly shall seek a warrant for the arrest of the person.

(h) If a peace officer described in division (A) of this section responds to a report of an alleged incident of the offense of domestic violence or an alleged incident of the offense of violating a protection order and if the circumstances of the incident involved the use or threatened use of a deadly weapon or any person involved in the incident brandished a deadly weapon during or in relation to the incident, the deadly weapon that was used, threatened to be used, or brandished constitutes contraband, and, to the extent possible, the officer shall seize the deadly weapon as contraband pursuant to Chapter 2981. of the Revised Code. Upon the seizure of a deadly weapon pursuant to division (B)(3)(h) of this section, section 2981.12 of the Revised Code shall apply regarding the treatment and disposition of the deadly weapon. For purposes of that section, the "underlying criminal offense" that was the basis of the seizure of a deadly weapon under division (B)(3)(h) of this section and to which the deadly weapon had a relationship is any of the following that is applicable:

(i) The alleged incident of the offense of domestic violence or the alleged incident of the offense of violating a protection order to which the officer who seized the deadly weapon responded;

(ii) Any offense that arose out of the same facts and circumstances as the report of the alleged incident of the offense of domestic violence or the alleged incident of the offense of violating a protection order to which the officer who seized the deadly weapon responded.

(4) If, in the circumstances described in divisions (B)(3)(a) to (g) of this section, a peace officer described in division (A) of this section arrests and detains a person pursuant to division (B)(1) of this section, or if, pursuant to division (B)(3)(h) of this section, a peace officer described in division (A) of this section seizes a deadly weapon, the officer, to the extent described in and in accordance with section 9.86 or 2744.03 of the Revised Code, is immune in any civil action for damages for injury, death, or loss to person or property that arises from or is related to the arrest and detention or the seizure.

(C) When there is reasonable ground to believe that a violation of division (A)(1), (2), (3), (4), or (5) of section 4506.15 or a violation of section 4511.19 of the Revised Code has been committed by a person operating a motor vehicle subject to regulation by the public utilities commission of Ohio under Title XLIX of the Revised Code, a peace officer with authority to enforce that provision of law may stop or detain the person whom the officer has reasonable cause to believe was operating the motor vehicle in violation of the division or section and, after investigating the circumstances surrounding the operation of the vehicle, may arrest and detain the person.

(D) If a sheriff, deputy sheriff, marshal, deputy marshal, municipal police officer, member of a police force employed by a metropolitan housing authority under division (D) of section 3735.31 of the Revised Code, member of a police force employed by a regional transit authority under division (Y) of section 306.35 of the Revised Code, special police officer employed by a port authority under section 4582.04 or 4582.28 of the Revised Code, special police officer employed by a municipal corporation at a municipal airport or other municipal air navigation facility described in division (A) of this section, township constable, police officer of a township or joint police district, state university law enforcement officer appointed under section 3345.04 of the Revised Code, peace officer of the department of natural resources, individual designated to perform law enforcement duties under section 511.232, 1545.13, or 6101.75 of the Revised Code, the house sergeant at arms if the house sergeant at arms has arrest authority pursuant to division (E)(1) of section 101.311 of the Revised Code, or an assistant house sergeant at arms is authorized by division (A) or (B) of this section to arrest and detain, within the limits of the political subdivision, metropolitan housing authority housing project, regional transit authority facilities or those areas of a municipal corporation that have been agreed to by a regional transit authority and a municipal corporation located within its territorial jurisdiction, port authority, municipal airport or other municipal air navigation facility, college, or university in which the officer is appointed, employed, or elected or within the limits of the territorial jurisdiction of the peace officer, a person until a warrant can be obtained, the peace officer, outside the limits of that territory, may pursue, arrest, and detain that person until a warrant can be obtained if all of the following apply:

(1) The pursuit takes place without unreasonable delay after the offense is committed;

(2) The pursuit is initiated within the limits of the political subdivision, metropolitan housing authority housing project, regional transit authority facilities or those areas of a municipal corporation that have been agreed to by a regional transit authority and a municipal corporation located within its territorial jurisdiction, port authority, municipal airport or other municipal air navigation facility, college, or university in which the peace officer is appointed, employed, or elected or within the limits of the territorial jurisdiction of the peace officer;

(3) The offense involved is a felony, a misdemeanor of the first degree or a substantially equivalent municipal ordinance, a misdemeanor of the second degree or a substantially equivalent municipal ordinance, or any offense for which points are chargeable pursuant to section 4510.036 of the Revised Code.

(E) In addition to the authority granted under division (A) or (B) of this section:

(1) A sheriff or deputy sheriff may arrest and detain, until a warrant can be obtained, any person found violating section 4503.11, 4503.21, or 4549.01, sections 4549.08 to 4549.12, section 4549.62, or Chapter 4511. or 4513. of the Revised Code on the portion of any street or highway that is located immediately adjacent to the boundaries of the county in which the sheriff or deputy sheriff is elected or appointed.

(2) A member of the police force of a township police district created under section 505.48 of the Revised Code, a member of the police force of a joint police district created under section 505.482 of the Revised Code, or a township constable appointed in accordance with section 509.01 of the Revised Code, who has received a certificate from the Ohio peace officer training commission under section 109.75 of the Revised Code, may arrest and detain, until a warrant can be obtained, any person found violating any section or chapter of the Revised Code listed in division (E)(1) of this section, other than sections 4513.33 and 4513.34 of the Revised Code, on the portion of any street or highway that is located immediately adjacent to the boundaries of the township police district or joint police district, in the case of a member of a township police district or joint police district police force, or the unincorporated territory of the township, in the case of a township constable. However, if the population of the township that created the township police district served by the member's police force, or the townships and municipal corporations that created the joint police district served by the member's police force, or the township that is served by the township constable, is sixty thousand or less, the member of the township police district or joint police district police force or the township

constable may not make an arrest under division (E)(2) of this section on a state highway that is included as part of the interstate system.

(3) A police officer or village marshal appointed, elected, or employed by a municipal corporation may arrest and detain, until a warrant can be obtained, any person found violating any section or chapter of the Revised Code listed in division (E)(1) of this section on the portion of any street or highway that is located immediately adjacent to the boundaries of the municipal corporation in which the police officer or village marshal is appointed, elected, or employed.

(4) A peace officer of the department of natural resources, a state fire marshal law enforcement officer described in division (A)(23) of section 109.71 of the Revised Code, or an individual designated to perform law enforcement duties under section 511.232, 1545.13, or 6101.75 of the Revised Code may arrest and detain, until a warrant can be obtained, any person found violating any section or chapter of the Revised Code listed in division (E)(1) of this section, other than sections 4513.33 and 4513.34 of the Revised Code, on the portion of any street or highway that is located immediately adjacent to the boundaries of the lands and waters that constitute the territorial jurisdiction of the peace officer or state fire marshal law enforcement officer.

(F)(1) A department of mental health and addiction services special police officer or a department of developmental disabilities special police officer may arrest without a warrant and detain until a warrant can be obtained any person found committing on the premises of any institution under the jurisdiction of the particular department a misdemeanor under a law of the state.

A department of mental health and addiction services special police officer or a department of developmental disabilities special police officer may arrest without a warrant and detain until a warrant can be obtained any person who has been hospitalized, institutionalized, or confined in an institution under the jurisdiction of the particular department pursuant to or under authority of section 2945.37, 2945.371, 2945.38, 2945.39, 2945.40, 2945.401, or 2945.402 of the Revised Code and who is found committing on the premises of any institution under the jurisdiction of the particular department a violation of section 2921.34 of the Revised Code that involves an escape from the premises of the institution.

(2)(a) If a department of mental health and addiction services special police officer or a department of developmental disabilities special police officer finds any person who has been hospitalized, institutionalized, or confined in an institution under the jurisdiction of the particular department pursuant to or under authority of section 2945.37, 2945.371, 2945.38, 2945.39, 2945.40, 2945.401, or 2945.402 of the Revised Code committing a violation of section 2921.34 of the Revised Code that involves an escape from the premises of the institution, or if there is reasonable ground to believe that a violation of section 2921.34 of the Revised Code has been committed that involves an escape from the premises of an institution under the jurisdiction of the department of mental health and addiction services or the department of developmental disabilities and if a department of mental health and addiction services special police officer or a department of developmental disabilities special police officer has reasonable cause to believe that a particular person who has been hospitalized, institutionalized, or confined in the institution pursuant to or under authority of section 2945.37, 2945.371, 2945.38, 2945.39, 2945.40, 2945.401, or 2945.402 of the Revised Code is guilty of the violation, the special police officer, outside of the premises of the institution, may pursue, arrest, and detain that person for that violation of section 2921.34 of the Revised Code, until a warrant can be obtained, if both of the following apply:

(i) The pursuit takes place without unreasonable delay after the offense is committed;

(ii) The pursuit is initiated within the premises of the institution from which the violation of section 2921.34 of the Revised Code occurred.

(b) For purposes of division (F)(2)(a) of this section, the execution of a written statement by the administrator of the institution in which a person had been hospitalized, institutionalized, or confined pursuant to or under authority of section 2945.37, 2945.371, 2945.38, 2945.39, 2945.40, 2945.401, or 2945.402 of the Revised Code alleging that the person has escaped from the premises of the institution in violation of section 2921.34 of the Revised Code constitutes reasonable ground to believe that the violation was committed and reasonable cause to believe that the person alleged in the statement to have committed the offense is guilty of the violation.

(G) As used in this section:

(1) A "department of mental health and addiction services special police officer" means a special police officer of the department of mental health and addiction services designated under section 5119.08 of the Revised Code who is certified by the Ohio peace officer training commission under section 109.77 of the Revised Code as having successfully completed an approved peace officer basic training program.

(2) A "department of developmental disabilities special police officer" means a special police officer of the department of developmental disabilities designated under section 5123.13 of the Revised Code who is certified by the Ohio peace officer training council under section 109.77 of the Revised Code as having successfully completed an approved peace officer basic training program.

(3) "Deadly weapon" has the same meaning as in section 2923.11 of the Revised Code.

(4) "Family or household member" has the same meaning as in section 2919.25 of the Revised Code.

(5) "Street" or "highway" has the same meaning as in section 4511.01 of the Revised Code.

(6) "Interstate system" has the same meaning as in section 5516.01 of the Revised Code.

(7) "Peace officer of the department of natural resources" means an employee of the department of natural resources who is a natural resources law enforcement staff officer designated pursuant to section 1501.013 of the Revised Code, a forest officer designated pursuant to section 1503.29 of the Revised Code, a preserve officer designated pursuant to section 1517.10 of the Revised Code, a wildlife officer designated pursuant to section 1531.13 of the Revised Code, a park officer designated pursuant to section 1541.10 of the Revised Code, or a state watercraft officer designated pursuant to section 1547.521 of the Revised Code.

(8) "Portion of any street or highway" means all lanes of the street or highway irrespective of direction of travel, including designated turn lanes, and any berm, median, or shoulder.

(2013 H 59, eff. 9-29-13; 2012 H 487, eff. 9-10-12; 2011 H 153, eff. 9-29-11; 2009 S 79, eff. 10-6-09; 2008 H 562, eff. 9–23–08; 2007 H 119, eff. 9–29–07; 2006 H 241, eff. 7–1–07; 2005 H 68, eff. 6–29–05; 2002 H 675, § 1.04, eff. 1–1–04; 2002 H 675, § 1.01, eff. 3–14–03; 2002 H 545, eff. 3–19–03; 2002 S 123, eff. 1–1–04; 2000 S 317, eff. 3–22–01; 2000 S 137, eff. 5–17–00; 1998 S 187, eff. 3–18–99; 1997 S 1, eff. 10–21–97; 1996 S 285, eff. 7–1–97; 1996 H 670, eff. 12–2–96; 1996 S 269, eff. 7–1–96; 1995 S 2, eff. 7–1–96; 1994 H 335, eff. 12–9–94; 1994 S 82, eff. 5–4–94; 1993 H 42, eff. 2–9–94; 1992 H 536; 1991 H 77; 1990 H 669, H 88; 1988 H 708, § 1)

Historical and Statutory Notes

Amendment Note: 2013 H 59 substituted "5119.71" for "5119.51" in division (B)(2)(b); substituted "mental health and addiction services" for "mental health" in division (F)(1) and (F)(2)(a); and substituted "mental health and addiction services" for "mental health" and "5119.08" for "5119.14" in division (G)(1).

Amendment Note: 2012 H 487 added division (A)(4).

Amendment Note: 2011 H 153 deleted "township" before "police district" in divisions (A)(1) and (D); rewrote division (E)(2); and made other nonsubstantive changes. Prior to amendment, division (E)(2) read:

"(2) A member of the police force of a township police district created under section 505.48 of the Revised Code, a member of the police force of a joint township police district created under section 505.481 of the Revised Code, or a township constable appointed in accordance with section 509.01 of the Revised Code, who has received a certificate from the Ohio peace officer training commission under section 109.75 of the Revised Code, may arrest and detain, until a warrant can be obtained, any person found violating any section or chapter of the Revised Code listed in division (E)(1) of this section, other than sections 4513.33 and 4513.34 of the Revised Code, on the portion of any street or highway that is located immediately adjacent to the boundaries of the township police district or joint township police district, in the case of a member of a township police district or joint township police district police force, or the unincorporated territory of the township, in the case of a township constable. However, if the population of the township that created the township police district served by the member's police force, or the townships that created the joint township police district served by the member's police force, or the township that is served by the township constable, is sixty thousand or less, the member of the township police district or joint police district police force or the township constable may not make an arrest under division (E)(2) of this section on a state highway that is included as part of the interstate system."

Amendment Note: 2009 S 79 deleted "mental retardation and" from "department of mental retardation and developmental disabilities" throughout.

Amendment Note: 2008 H 562 inserted "a state fire marshal law enforcement officer described in division (A)(23) of section 109.71 of the Revised Code," and inserted ", state fire marshal law enforcement officer's," in division (A)(2); and inserted "a state fire marshal law enforcement officer described in division (A)(23) of section 109.71 of the Revised Code," and inserted "or state fire marshal law enforcement officer" in division (E)(4).

Amendment Note: 2007 H 119 added division (G)(8); and made nonsubstantive changes.

Cross References

Mental health and addiction services department, appointment and qualification of special police, see 5119.08

Sergeant at arms of senate, see 101.312

Ohio Administrative Code References

Authority of forest officer, see OAC 1501:3–7–01

Research References

ALR Library

18 ALR 6th 519, Authority of Public Official, Whose Duties or Functions Generally Do Not Entail Traffic Stops, to Effectuate Traffic Stop of Vehicle.

Encyclopedias

OH Jur. 3d Criminal Law: Procedure § 671, Territorial Power to Arrest Without Warrant.

OH Jur. 3d Criminal Law: Procedure § 673, Violations Involving Alcohol.

OH Jur. 3d Criminal Law: Procedure § 677, Generally; Peace Officers.

OH Jur. 3d Criminal Law: Procedure § 679, Special Police Officers Under Jurisdiction of Department of Mental Retardation and Developmental Disabilities.

OH Jur. 3d Criminal Law: Procedure § 692, Duty to Investigate.

OH Jur. 3d Criminal Law: Substantive Principles and Offenses § 373, Filing of Complaint and Motion; Bail.

OH Jur. 3d Fish and Game § 67, Process and Arrest; Bond or Confinement Prior to Appearance.

Forms

Ohio Jurisprudence Pleading and Practice Forms § 61:3, General Rule of Competency.

Treatises and Practice Aids

Katz & Giannelli, Baldwin's Ohio Practice Criminal Law § 6:6, Warrantless Misdemeanor Arrests--"In Presence" Rule.

Katz & Giannelli, Baldwin's Ohio Practice Criminal Law § 6:7, Warrantless Misdemeanor Arrests--"In Presence" Rule--DUI Cases.

Katz & Giannelli, Baldwin's Ohio Practice Criminal Law § 6:9, Extraterritorial Misdemeanor Arrests.

Katz & Giannelli, Baldwin's Ohio Practice Criminal Law § 7:6, Authority to Execute Arrest Warrants.

Katz & Giannelli, Baldwin's Ohio Practice Criminal Law § 29:5, Exclusionary Rule--Statutes.

Katz & Giannelli, Baldwin's Ohio Practice Criminal Law § 5:21, Statutory Designation of Probable Cause in Domestic Violence Cases.

Katz & Giannelli, Baldwin's Ohio Practice Criminal Law § 89:2, Use of Force--Police Arrest.

Katz & Giannelli, Baldwin's Ohio Practice Criminal Law § 109:15, Domestic Violence.

Sowald & Morganstern, Baldwin's Ohio Practice Domestic Relations Law § 5:3, Criminal Domestic Violence--Practice and Procedure.

Katz, Ohio Arrest, Search & Seizure § 4:3, Nature of the Offense--Misdemeanors.

Katz, Ohio Arrest, Search & Seizure § 4:4, Misdemeanors: Exceptions to the "In Presence" Requirement.

Katz, Ohio Arrest, Search & Seizure § 4:5, Extraterritorial Misdemeanor Arrests.

Katz, Ohio Arrest, Search & Seizure App. A, Arrest Provisions: Checklist.

Katz, Ohio Arrest, Search & Seizure § 2:25, Statutory Designation of Probable Cause in Domestic Violence Cases.

Katz, Ohio Arrest, Search & Seizure § 28:3, Exclusion for Violation of State Law.

Adrine & Ruden, Ohio Domestic Violence Law § 3:7, Elements and Penalties--Aggravated Trespass Under RC 2911.211.

Adrine & Ruden, Ohio Domestic Violence Law § 4:7, Enforcement of a Protection Order.

Adrine & Ruden, Ohio Domestic Violence Law § 5:3, Prosecutorial Discretion.

Adrine & Ruden, Ohio Domestic Violence Law § 5:4, Case Triage.

Adrine & Ruden, Ohio Domestic Violence Law § 7:4, Arrest Considerations; Determining the Primary Physical Aggressor.

Adrine & Ruden, Ohio Domestic Violence Law § 7:5, Pretrial Detention and Initial Appearance Issues.
Adrine & Ruden, Ohio Domestic Violence Law § 8:6, Parents and Children.
Adrine & Ruden, Ohio Domestic Violence Law App. A, Ohio Revised Code (Selected Provisions).
Adrine & Ruden, Ohio Domestic Violence Law § 12:3, Full Hearing--Participation of the Parties.
Adrine & Ruden, Ohio Domestic Violence Law § 13:2, Court Enforcement of Civil Protection Orders--Generally.
Adrine & Ruden, Ohio Domestic Violence Law § 13:3, Court Enforcement of Civil Protection Orders--Criminal Prosecution.
Adrine & Ruden, Ohio Domestic Violence Law § 14:2, Ohio Statutory Procedure.
Adrine & Ruden, Ohio Domestic Violence Law § 14:3, Arrest of the Perpetrator.
Adrine & Ruden, Ohio Domestic Violence Law § 14:4, Determination of Primary Physical Aggressor.
Adrine & Ruden, Ohio Domestic Violence Law § 14:5, False Arrest, Warrantless Arrests and Searches, and Weapons Confiscation.
Adrine & Ruden, Ohio Domestic Violence Law § 14:6, Law Enforcement Policies and Procedures.
Adrine & Ruden, Ohio Domestic Violence Law § 15:6, Ohio's Judicial Response to Domestic Violence.
Adrine & Ruden, Ohio Domestic Violence Law § 5:12, Case Preparation--Physical Evidence.
Adrine & Ruden, Ohio Domestic Violence Law § 10:11, Parties Authorized to File for Civil Protection Orders.
Adrine & Ruden, Ohio Domestic Violence Law § 11:19, Ex Parte Protection Orders--Available Relief--Property Division.
Adrine & Ruden, Ohio Domestic Violence Law § 11:22, Ex Parte Protection Orders--Miscellaneous Issues.
Adrine & Ruden, Ohio Domestic Violence Law § 12:21, Remedies--Miscellaneous Issues.
Adrine & Ruden, Ohio Domestic Violence Law § 12:28, Mutual Protection Orders.
Adrine & Ruden, Ohio Domestic Violence Law § 14:12, Police Liability for Failing to Protect Victims of Domestic Violence--Legal Theories for Recovery--State Duty to Protect.
Adrine & Ruden, Ohio Domestic Violence Law § 14:14, Significant Cases Involving Police Officer Action or Inaction.
Adrine & Ruden, Ohio Domestic Violence Law § 14:15, Potential Police Liability in the Enforcement of Protection Orders.
Adrine & Ruden, Ohio Domestic Violence Law § 18:11, Firearm Offenses Under VAWA.
Weiler & Weiler, Ohio Driving Under the Influence § 9:5, Requirement of Motion--To Challenge Illegally Obtained Evidence.
Weiler & Weiler, Ohio Driving Under the Influence App. A, Ohio Revised Code--Selected Provisions.
Weiler & Weiler, Ohio Driving Under the Influence § 12:8, Authority to Stop, Detain and Arrest.
Weiler & Weiler, Ohio Driving Under the Influence § 12:9, Authority to Stop, Detain and Arrest--Extraterritorial Detention and Arrest.
Weiler & Weiler, Ohio Driving Under the Influence § 9:16, Grounds for Motion--The Stop--Constitutional Implications.
Weiler & Weiler, Ohio Driving Under the Influence § 9:40, Grounds for Motion--The Arrest--Probable Cause--Overview.
Weiler & Weiler, Ohio Driving Under the Influence § 9:47, Grounds for Motion--The Arrest--Probable Cause--View Requirement.
Weiler & Weiler, Ohio Driving Under the Influence § 9:79, Motion Hearing--Burden of Proof--Search and Seizure Issues.
Giannelli & Yeomans Salvador, Ohio Juvenile Law § 9:3, Custody, Arrests and Stops.
Lang, Gotherman & Babbit, Ohio Municipal Law § 26:4, Metropolitan Housing Authorities.
Lang, Gotherman & Babbit, Ohio Municipal Law § 8:23, Safety Forces.
Lang, Gotherman & Babbit, Ohio Municipal Law § 8:31, Arrest Powers.
Lang, Gotherman & Babbit, Ohio Municipal Law § 23:16, Extraterritorial Exercise of Municipal Power.
Lang, Gotherman & Babbit, Ohio Municipal Law § 28:41, Arrest of Violators.
Princehorn, Ohio Township Law § 5:1, Regional Councils.
Princehorn, Ohio Township Law § 11:9, Territorial Jurisdiction.
Princehorn, Ohio Township Law § 49:4, Enforcement.
Princehorn, Ohio Township Law § 52:1, Contract for Police Protection.
Princehorn, Ohio Township Law § 52:6, Authority to Arrest and Detain Until Warrant Can be Obtained.
Princehorn, Ohio Township Law § 52:7, Power to Make Arrests for Traffic Violations.
Princehorn, Ohio Township Law § 57:2, Authority to Make Arrests.
Princehorn, Ohio Township Law § 11:11, Duties of Constable--Criminal.
Princehorn, Ohio Township Law § 11:39, Police Officers--Territorial Jurisdiction.
Princehorn, Ohio Township Law § 11:40, Police Officers--Duties.
Princehorn, Ohio Township Law § 11:43, Police Officers--Authority to Arrest and Detain Until Warrant Can be Obtained.

Notes of Decisions

Duty to respond 32

---

2. —— Warrantless arrest or pursuit to arrest, constitutional issue

Exigent circumstances did not justify warrantless entry into defendant's residence by police officer, who had been called to residence because of alleged incidence of domestic violence, absent any evidence that any danger existed to either alleged victim or her daughters who were not in defendant's vicinity when officers arrived, and where nothing suggested that evidence was in danger of being destroyed. State v. DeLong (Ohio App. 4 Dist., Ross, 05-11-2007) No. 06CA2920, 2007-Ohio-2330, 2007 WL 1413394, Unreported. Arrest ⚷ 68.2(5)

Statute providing for arrest and detention of suspect who police have reasonable cause to believe has committed domestic violence did not justify warrantless entry of defendant's residence when police did not observe any act of domestic violence, and alleged victim expressly told police that defendant never struck her. State v. DeLong (Ohio App. 4 Dist., Ross, 05-11-2007) No. 06CA2920, 2007-Ohio-2330, 2007 WL 1413394, Unreported. Arrest ⚷ 68.2(9)

Counsel's failure to file motion to suppress based on warrantless arrest did not constitute deficient performance, as required to support claim of ineffective assistance of counsel, in trial for felonious assault; domestic violence complaint executed by defendant's girlfriend was sufficient to justify defendant's warrantless arrest and detention for that offense. State v. Christian (Ohio App. 7 Dist., Mahoning, 03-21-2005) No. 02 CA 170, 2005-Ohio-1440, 2005 WL 704866, Unreported, denial of post-conviction relief affirmed 2007-Ohio-3336, 2007 WL 1879984, dismissal of habeas corpus affirmed 118 Ohio St.3d 235, 887 N.E.2d 1175, 2008-Ohio-2219, certiorari denied 129 S.Ct. 275, 555 U.S. 917, 172 L.Ed.2d 203, habeas corpus dismissed 2009 WL 2256956. Criminal Law ⚷ 1926

3. —— Probable cause, constitutional issues

Police officers, who had been called to residence because of alleged incidence of domestic violence, lacked probable cause to make warrantless entry into defendant's residence, where alleged victim told officers that defendant had calmed down and did not hit her, and no demonstrative physical evidence indicated that defendant assaulted her and officers could point to nothing specific why they should disbelieve her statement. State v. DeLong (Ohio App. 4 Dist., Ross, 05-11-2007) No. 06CA2920, 2007-Ohio-2330, 2007 WL 1413394, Unreported. Arrest ⚷ 68.2(9)

Even if warrantless arrest of defendant based on admissions that he hit gas station pole and fled scene without intention of reporting incident was illegal, exclusionary rule would not bar admission of items seized from defendant's person upon his arrest in trial for drug possession and trafficking, since probable cause existed and defendant's constitutional rights were not violated by seizure; officers were aware of incident, defendant was identified as driver of vehicle, and defendant admitted to accident and that he intended not to report it. State v. Brown (Ohio App. 5 Dist., 06-09-2014) 14 N.E.3d 465, 2014-Ohio-2493. Criminal Law ⚷ 392.17(2)

Searches and seizures, reasonableness, driving with suspended license, nonarrestable offense under state law. Virginia v. Moore, 2008, 128 S.Ct. 1598, 170 L.Ed.2d 559.

7. Arrest or detention

The general assembly has not identified in RC 2935.03(B) the reasons a peace officer may consider for not arresting and detaining a person the officer has reasonable grounds to believe committed the offense of domestic violence. Rather, pursuant to RC 2935.032, the policy adopted by an agency, instrumentality, or subdivision to implement the domestic violence arrest provisions must set forth examples of reasons a peace officer may consider for not arresting and detaining a person in that situation. OAG 01–039, 2001 WL 1172828.

8. Warrantless arrest

Defendant's admissions to hitting pole at gas station and leaving scene without any intention of reporting incident led to reasonable conclusion that defendant violated statute governing duty to stop after accident occurring on property other than public highways in police officer's presence, such that warrantless arrest was proper and it was not necessary to wait 24 hours to see if defendant was going to report accident prior to arrest. State v. Brown (Ohio App. 5 Dist., 06-09-2014) 14 N.E.3d 465, 2014-Ohio-2493. Arrest ⚷ 63.4(13)

10. Officer's presence—element of offense observed by officer

The general rule is that a police officer may not make a warrantless arrest for a misdemeanor unless the offense is committed in the presence of the officer. State v. Filchock (Ohio App. 11 Dist., 05-05-2006) 166 Ohio App.3d 611, 852 N.E.2d 759, 2006-Ohio-2242, appeal after new sentencing hearing 2007-Ohio-2574, 2007 WL 1532969, appeal not allowed 115 Ohio St.3d 1423, 874 N.E.2d 539, 2007-Ohio-5056, certiorari denied 128 S.Ct. 1664, 552 U.S. 1265, 170 L.Ed.2d 367, denial of post-conviction relief affirmed 2007-Ohio-5779, 2007 WL 3133801. Arrest ⚷ 63.3

11. —— Offense committed in, officer's presence

Under Ohio statute providing that an officer had the authority to arrest and detain individuals found violating the laws of the state until a warrant could be obtained, police officer had legal authority to arrest and detain the arrestee for committing the offense of falsification, and thus, officer was not liable to arrestee under Ohio law for false arrest; officer was on duty and was patrolling the area near a bar when he encountered a disturbance at the bar involving the arrestee, and when officer asked arrestee for her name and Social Security number, she responded with a false name and Social Security number. Gill v. Kovach (N.D.Ohio, 07-27-2010) 729 F.Supp.2d 925. False Imprisonment ⚷ 7(3)

12. Traffic offenses

Offense of trafficking in drugs and possession of same drugs were not allied offenses of similar import; drug trafficking required an element of sale, while possession of drugs required that a person obtain, possess, or use a controlled substance. State v. Hudson (Ohio App. 8 Dist., Cuyahoga, 03-28-2002) No. 79010, 2002-Ohio-1408, 2002 WL 472304, Unreported, appeal after new sentencing hearing 2004-Ohio-1452, 2004 WL 583925. Criminal Law ⚷ 29(8)

Having an individual sit in a police cruiser for a short time to answer a few questions does not necessarily elevate the situation to something greater than an ordinary traffic stop, and this is true whether the individual is being requested to stay while an accident report is completed or relevant facts are ascertained; individual may also be temporarily restrained either for his own safety or that of the officer. State v. Kelly (Ohio App. 12 Dist., 08-02-2010) 188 Ohio App.3d 842, 937 N.E.2d 149, 2010-Ohio-3560, habeas corpus dismissed 2012 WL 2890878, appeal not allowed 133 Ohio St.3d 1493, 978 N.E.2d 911, 2012-Ohio-5459, denial of post-conviction relief affirmed 997 N.E.2d 215, 2013-Ohio-3675. Automobiles ⚷ 349(17); Automobiles ⚷ 349(18)

14. Probable cause

Canine sniff occurred well within the 10 to 15 minutes officer normally took to perform a traffic stop and within the time period necessary to effectuate the original purpose of the stop, and fact that the officers neither contacted the dispatcher to verify defendant's license and registration information nor issued a traffic citation was irrelevant when they had probable cause to initiate the lawful traffic stop. State v. Kelly (Ohio App. 12 Dist., 08-02-2010) 188 Ohio App.3d 842, 937 N.E.2d 149, 2010-Ohio-3560, habeas corpus dismissed 2012 WL 2890878, appeal not allowed 133 Ohio St.3d 1493, 978 N.E.2d 911, 2012-Ohio-5459, denial of post-conviction relief affirmed 997 N.E.2d 215, 2013-Ohio-3675. Automobiles ⚷ 349(17)

Officers, who stopped defendant for traffic violation, were justified in placing defendant in the back of the cruiser as law enforcement continued to gather facts, and that placement did not constitute an arrest that required probable cause; officers placed defendant, without handcuffs, in the back of their cruiser and then continued to gather facts, and while defendant was in the cruiser, the other officers and canine units were on the scene performing their normal fact-finding and investigatory duties. State v. Kelly (Ohio App. 12 Dist., 08-02-2010) 188 Ohio App.3d 842, 937 N.E.2d 149, 2010-Ohio-3560, habeas corpus dismissed 2012 WL 2890878, appeal not allowed 133 Ohio St.3d 1493, 978 N.E.2d 911, 2012-Ohio-5459, denial of post-conviction relief affirmed 997 N.E.2d 215, 2013-Ohio-3675. Automobiles ⚷ 349(10); Automobiles ⚷ 349(14.1)

15. Extraterritorial arrest

Exclusionary rule could not be invoked in case in which officer had probable cause to make traffic stop, even though stop was invalid under statute because officer did not have the authority to stop defendant outside of his jurisdiction for misdemeanor traffic violations for following too closely and crossing marked lanes. State v. Jones (Ohio App. 6 Dist., 04-09-2010) 187 Ohio App.3d 478, 932 N.E.2d 904, 2010-Ohio-1600, motion for delayed appeal granted 126 Ohio St.3d 1511, 930 N.E.2d 330, 2010-Ohio-3331, stay denied 126 Ohio St.3d 1578, 934 N.E.2d 352, 2010-Ohio-4542, appeal not allowed 126 Ohio St.3d 1616, 935 N.E.2d 854, 2010-Ohio-5101. Criminal Law ⚷ 394.4(9)

Police officer had probable cause to make traffic stop of defendants outside his territorial jurisdiction, after observing defendant driver driving without headlights, and thus stop was not unreasonable under Fourth Amendment, even though stop violated statute governing territorial jurisdiction in which a police officer may make an arrest; fact that officer was outside his jurisdiction was irrelevant to Fourth Amendment analysis. State v. Jones (Ohio, 02-04-2009) 121 Ohio St.3d 103, 902 N.E.2d 464, 2009-Ohio-316, certiorari denied 130 S.Ct. 235, 558 U.S. 876, 175 L.Ed.2d 129. Automobiles ⚷ 349(12)

18. —— Conduct of officer, arresting officer

Police officers' use of force to arrest suspect after they reported to a dwelling in response to a domestic violence call, including using stun gun, was reasonable under the Fourth Amendment, and thus did not constitute excessive force; suspect had just slashed his girlfriend's car tires with a kitchen knife and assaulted her in front of her children, fought with a private citizen, resisted arrest, kicked and punched the officers, and tried to gain control of one officer's loaded gun. Carnahan v. McClure (N.D.Ohio, 06-11-2014) 29 F.Supp.3d 1044. Arrest ⚷ 68.1(4)

27. Law enforcement agencies

Statute that allowed a state university law enforcement officer to arrest a person without a warrant if they are "found violating" the law within the limits of the university was not irreconcilable with subsequently enacted statute providing that a state university and a municipality could enter into a mutual aid agreement allowing the university police to perform any police function, exercise any police power, or render any police service on behalf of the municipality. State v. Littlejohn (Ohio App. 7 Dist., Mahoning, 09-28-2012) No. 11 MA 106, 2012-Ohio-4554, 2012 WL 4712383, Unreported. Education ⚷ 1025

In the event of a conflict, statute providing that a state university and a municipality could enter into a mutual aid agreement allowing the university police to perform any police function, exercise any police power, or render any police service on behalf of the municipality would prevail, as a special provision, over general provision that existed at time of special provision's enactment and allowed a state university law enforcement officer to arrest a person without a warrant who was "found violating" the law within the limits of the university. State v. Littlejohn (Ohio App. 7 Dist., Mahoning, 09-28-2012) No. 11 MA 106, 2012-Ohio-4554, 2012 WL 4712383, Unreported. Education ⚷ 1025

32. Duty to respond

A police officer's authority to make an arrest is different from a police officer's professional obligation to respond to a request for assistance, and a responding officer may provide assistance to another law-enforcement officer absent the authority to arrest. Smith v. McBride (Ohio, 09-20-2011) 130 Ohio St.3d 51, 955 N.E.2d 954, 2011-Ohio-4674. Municipal Corporations ⚷ 189(1)

The county sheriff's office and a municipal corporation police department are required to respond to calls for law enforcement assistance on county property that is located within the municipal corporation. OAG 09-008, 2009 WL 637116.

2935.032 Domestic violence arrest policies

Notes of Decisions

2.4. Use of force

Police officers' use of force to arrest suspect after they reported to a dwelling in response to a domestic violence call, including using stun gun, was reasonable under the Fourth Amendment, and thus did not constitute excessive force; suspect had just slashed his girlfriend's car tires with a kitchen knife and assaulted her in front of her children, fought with a private citizen, resisted arrest, kicked and punched the officers, and tried to gain control of one officer's loaded gun. Carnahan v. McClure (N.D.Ohio, 06-11-2014) 29 F.Supp.3d 1044. Arrest ⚷ 68.1(4)

4. Nonarrest or detention

The general assembly has not identified in RC 2935.03(B) the reasons a peace officer may consider for not arresting and detaining a person the officer has reasonable grounds to believe committed the offense of domestic violence. Rather, pursuant to RC 2935.032, the policy adopted by an agency, instrumentality, or subdivision to implement the domestic violence arrest provisions must set forth examples of reasons a peace officer may consider for not arresting and detaining a person in that situation. OAG 01–039, 2001 WL 1172828.

5. Constitutional issues

City prosecutor had probable cause to initiate proceedings against arrestee for charges of domestic violence and violating protective order, as negated arrestee's claims against prosecutor for malicious prosecution under § 1983 and Ohio law. Wiley v. Oberlin Police Dept. (C.A.6 (Ohio), 05-15-2009) No. 07-4441, 330 Fed.Appx. 524, 2009 WL 1391532, Unreported. Civil Rights ⚷ 1088(5); Malicious Prosecution ⚷ 18(1)

City police officers had probable cause to arrest girlfriend for domestic violence; after receiving emergency call from boyfriend that his girlfriend was attacking him, officer responded to boyfriend's residence, boyfriend told officer that girlfriend had hit him in chest where he had recently received pacemaker, showed him redness in area of alleged attack, and requested charges against girlfriend for domestic violence and temporary restraining order, and another officer took written statement from boyfriend, confirming statements made to responding officer. Wiley v. Oberlin Police Dept. (C.A.6 (Ohio), 05-15-2009) No. 07-4441, 330 Fed.Appx. 524, 2009 WL 1391532, Unreported. Arrest ⚷ 63.4(7.1)

Exigent circumstances did not justify warrantless entry into defendant's residence by police officer, who had been called to residence because of alleged incidence of domestic violence, absent any evidence that any danger existed to either alleged victim or her daughters who were not in defendant's vicinity when officers arrived, and where nothing suggested that evidence was in danger of being destroyed. State v. DeLong (Ohio App. 4 Dist., Ross, 05-11-2007) No. 06CA2920, 2007-Ohio-2330, 2007 WL 1413394, Unreported. Arrest ⚷ 68.2(5)

Police officers, who had been called to residence because of alleged incidence of domestic violence, lacked probable cause to make warrantless entry into defendant's resident, where alleged victim told officers that defendant had calmed down and did not hit her, and no demonstrative physical evidence indicated that defendant assaulted her and officers could point to nothing specific why they should disbelieve her statement. State v. DeLong (Ohio App. 4 Dist., Ross, 05-11-2007) No. 06CA2920, 2007-Ohio-2330, 2007 WL 1413394, Unreported. Arrest ⚷ 68.2(9)

Statute providing for arrest and detention of suspect who police have reasonable cause to believe has committed domestic violence did not justify warrantless entry of defendant's residence when police did not observe any act of domestic violence, and alleged victim expressly told police that defendant never struck her. State v. DeLong (Ohio App. 4 Dist., Ross, 05-11-2007) No. 06CA2920, 2007-Ohio-2330, 2007 WL 1413394, Unreported. Arrest ⚷ 68.2(9)

2935.04 When any person may arrest

Notes of Decisions

7. —— Test, "Reasonable" cause or probable cause

Under statute permitting warrantless detention of suspected felony offender until a warrant can be obtained, a reasonably prudent person must, at the time of arrest, believe that the person placed under arrest was committing or had committed a criminal offense. State v. Brown (Ohio, 10-03-2007) 115 Ohio St.3d 55, 873 N.E.2d 858, 2007-Ohio-4837, reconsideration denied 116 Ohio St.3d 1442, 877 N.E.2d 992, 2007-Ohio-6518, appeal after new trial 2010-Ohio-2460, 2010 WL 2202962, appeal not allowed 126 Ohio St.3d 1601, 935 N.E.2d 47, 2010-Ohio-4928. Arrest ⚿ 63.4(2)

8. —— Source of information, "Reasonable" cause or probable cause

Warrantless arrest following vehicle stop for drug trafficking crimes committed several months prior to arrest, after period of surveillance of defendant's activities, was illegal; officer's concern over confidential informant's identity was not exigent circumstance that made obtaining arrest warrant impracticable. State v. VanNoy (Ohio App. 2 Dist., 06-18-2010) 188 Ohio App.3d 89, 934 N.E.2d 413, 2010-Ohio-2845, appeal not allowed 126 Ohio St.3d 1618, 935 N.E.2d 855, 2010-Ohio-5101. Arrest ⚿ 63.1

2935.041 Detention of shoplifters; rights of museums and libraries; rights of motion picture facility owner or lessee

(A) A merchant, or an employee or agent of a merchant, who has probable cause to believe that items offered for sale by a mercantile establishment have been unlawfully taken by a person, may, for the purposes set forth in division (C) of this section, detain the person in a reasonable manner for a reasonable length of time within the mercantile establishment or its immediate vicinity.

(B) Any officer, employee, or agent of a library, museum, or archival institution may, for the purposes set forth in division (C) of this section or for the purpose of conducting a reasonable investigation of a belief that the person has acted in a manner described in divisions (B)(1) and (2) of this section, detain a person in a reasonable manner for a reasonable length of time within, or in the immediate vicinity of, the library, museum, or archival institution, if the officer, employee, or agent has probable cause to believe that the person has either:

(1) Without privilege to do so, knowingly moved, defaced, damaged, destroyed, or otherwise improperly tampered with property owned by or in the custody of the library, museum, or archival institution; or

(2) With purpose to deprive the library, museum, or archival institution of property owned by it or in its custody, knowingly obtained or exerted control over the property without the consent of the owner or person authorized to give consent, beyond the scope of the express or implied consent of the owner or person authorized to give consent, by deception, or by threat.

(C) An officer, agent, or employee of a library, museum, or archival institution pursuant to division (B) of this section or a merchant or employee or agent of a merchant pursuant to division (A) of this section may detain another person for any of the following purposes:

(1) To recover the property that is the subject of the unlawful taking, criminal mischief, or theft;

(2) To cause an arrest to be made by a peace officer;

(3) To obtain a warrant of arrest;

(4) To offer the person, if the person is suspected of the unlawful taking, criminal mischief, or theft and notwithstanding any other provision of the Revised Code, an opportunity to complete a pretrial diversion program and to inform the person of the other legal remedies available to the library, museum, archival institution, or merchant.

(D) The owner or lessee of a facility in which a motion picture is being shown, or the owner's or lessee's employee or agent, who has probable cause to believe that a person is or has been operating an audiovisual recording function of a device in violation of section 2913.07 of the Revised Code may, for the purpose of causing an arrest to be made by a peace officer or of obtaining an arrest warrant, detain the person in a reasonable manner for a reasonable length of time within the facility or its immediate vicinity.

(E) The officer, agent, or employee of the library, museum, or archival institution, the merchant or employee or agent of a merchant, or the owner, lessee, employee, or agent of the facility acting under division (A), (B), or (D) of this section shall not search the person detained, search or seize any property belonging to the person detained without the person's consent, or use undue restraint upon the person detained.

(F) Any peace officer may arrest without a warrant any person that the officer has probable cause to believe has committed any act described in division (B)(1) or (2) of this section, that the officer has probable cause to believe has committed an unlawful taking in a mercantile establishment, or that the officer has reasonable cause to believe has committed an act prohibited by section 2913.07 of the Revised Code. An arrest under this division shall be made within a reasonable time after the commission of the act or unlawful taking.

(G) As used in this section:

(1) "Archival institution" means any public or private building, structure, or shelter in which are stored historical documents, devices, records, manuscripts, or items of public interest, which historical materials are stored to preserve the materials or the information in the materials, to disseminate the information contained in the materials, or to make the materials available for public inspection or for inspection by certain persons who have a particular interest in, use for, or knowledge concerning the materials.

(2) "Museum" means any public or private nonprofit institution that is permanently organized for primarily educational or aesthetic purposes, owns or borrows objects or items of public interest, and cares for and exhibits to the public the objects or items.

(3) "Audiovisual recording function" and "facility" have the same meaning as in section 2913.07 of the Revised Code.

(4) "Pretrial diversion program" means a rehabilitative, educational program designed to reduce recidivism and promote personal responsibility that is at least four hours in length and that has been approved by any court in this state.

(2011 H 86, eff. 9-30-11; 2003 H 179, eff. 3-9-04; 1978 H 403, eff. 7-4-78; 1969 H 49; 131 v H 395; 127 v 765)

Historical and Statutory Notes

Amendment Note: 2011 H 86 substituted "tampered" for "tempered" in division (B)(1); added divisions (C)(4) and (G)(4); and made other nonsubstantive changes.

Research References

Encyclopedias

OH Jur. 3d Criminal Law: Procedure § 675, Misdemeanors and Other Minor Offenses--Shoplifting.

OH Jur. 3d Criminal Law: Procedure § 676, Misdemeanors and Other Minor Offenses--Tampering and Like Interference With Property of Library, Museum, or Archival Institution.

OH Jur. 3d False Imprisonment and Malicious Prosecution § 16, by Private Individual, Generally.

OH Jur. 3d False Imprisonment and Malicious Prosecution § 17, by Merchants or Employees Thereof; Shoplifting.

OH Jur. 3d False Imprisonment and Malicious Prosecution § 119, Principal or Employer for Act of Agent or Employee.

Treatises and Practice Aids

Katz & Giannelli, Baldwin's Ohio Practice Criminal Law § 3:6, Private Security Guards.

Katz & Giannelli, Baldwin's Ohio Practice Criminal Law § 6:6, Warrantless Misdemeanor Arrests--"In Presence" Rule.

Katz & Giannelli, Baldwin's Ohio Practice Criminal Law § 6:10, Arrests by Private Citizens.

Katz, Ohio Arrest, Search & Seizure § 4:3, Nature of the Offense--Misdemeanors.

Katz, Ohio Arrest, Search & Seizure § 4:4, Misdemeanors: Exceptions to the "In Presence" Requirement.

Katz, Ohio Arrest, Search & Seizure § 28:14, Searches by Private Persons.

Siegel & Stephen, Ohio Employment Practices Law § 5:19, False Imprisonment and False Arrest.

Lang, Gotherman & Babbit, Ohio Municipal Law § 8:31, Arrest Powers.

Lang, Gotherman & Babbit, Ohio Municipal Law § 28:41, Arrest of Violators.

Notes of Decisions

1. Constitutional issues

City ordinance and police department directive, authorizing impoundment of a vehicle when the vehicle is left unattended due to the removal of an arrested operator, did not authorize police to impound defendant's vehicle, left in store parking lot following defendant's arrest in store for shoplifting; although defendant's arrest and transport to police station left vehicle unattended in the parking lot for an uncertain period of time, defendant was not in or near the vehicle when arrested. State v. Huddleston (Ohio App. 10 Dist., 08-30-2007) 173 Ohio App.3d 17, 877 N.E.2d 354, 2007-Ohio-4455. Searches And Seizures ⚿ 66

2. Authority to detain or arrest

Grocery store owner could raise self-defense as an affirmative defense to undue restraint claim in wrongful-death action brought by mother of store patron who was killed in a struggle with store employees, since employees acted within their statutory rights to pursue and detain patron, and then merely responded to patron's violent attacks until he was subdued; patron threw first punch and continued to fight against being restrained, and employees believed that the only way to end the fight was by restraining patron. Niskanen v. Giant Eagle, Inc. (Ohio, 07-30-2009) 122 Ohio St.3d 486, 912 N.E.2d 595, 2009-Ohio-3626. False Imprisonment ⚿ 10

2935.09 Accusation by affidavit to cause arrest or prosecution

Law Review and Journal Commentaries

Survey of Ohio law, 2011 Supreme Court of Ohio decisions, State v. Mbodji. Joshua A. Brown, 38 Ohio N.U. L. Rev. 1139. (2012).

Notes of Decisions

4. Knowledge of facts

Affiant failed to establish probable cause to support criminal charge of theft in office against judge who in separate criminal case ordered return of funds allegedly in control of county to alleged victims, where affiant failed to appear at probable cause hearing, and, as a result, no evidence was offered in support of the affidavit. In re Charging Affidavit of Demis (Ohio App. 5 Dist., Stark, 12-16-2013) No. 2013 CA 00098, 2013-Ohio-5520, 2013 WL 6671837, Unreported. Criminal Law ⚿ 238(4)

Prosecutor who signed and filed complaint against traffic defendant was not required to withdraw and was not subject to separation of witnesses order, where prosecutor had no factual knowledge of the offense, prosecutor was not subpoenaed as a witness, prosecutor signed and filed complaint in his official capacity, and prosecutor's testimony was not relevant to trial issues. State v. Donkers (Ohio App. 11 Dist., 03-30-2007) 170 Ohio App.3d 509, 867 N.E.2d 903, 2007-Ohio-1557. Criminal Law ⚿ 665(3); Criminal Law ⚿ 1694

5. Issuance of complaint or warrant

Complaint was insufficient to provide probable cause for an arrest warrant for defendant based on selling alcohol to an underage person; the officer swore that the defendant committed the offense on a specified date at a specified location and named the type of beer, but did not disclose what the source of his belief was. State v. Jones (Ohio App. 7 Dist., Mahoning, 03-20-2012) No. 11 MA 60, 2012-Ohio-1301, 2012 WL 1035017, Unreported. Criminal Law ⚿ 211(4)

Defendant waived any defense or objection to victim's private citizen complaint for domestic violence on the basis that it was not submitted to reviewing official as required by statute that allowed private citizen to file an affidavit with a reviewing official charging the offense committed for the purpose of review to determine if a complaint should be filed by the prosecuting attorney; statute did not create a jurisdiction barrier, and any defect could have been remedied through a motion to dismiss or to grant appropriate relief. State v. Mbodji (Ohio, 06-21-2011) 129 Ohio St.3d 325, 951 N.E.2d 1025, 2011-Ohio-2880, reconsideration denied 129 Ohio St.3d 1454, 951 N.E.2d 1049, 2011-Ohio-4217. Indictment and Information ⚿ 196(1)

Although a private citizen may file with a judge, clerk of court, or magistrate an affidavit charging an offense committed in order to cause the arrest or prosecution of the person charged, the private citizen must follow the applicable statutory procedure in order to do so. State ex rel. Dominguez v. State (Ohio, 06-29-2011) 129 Ohio St.3d 203, 951 N.E.2d 77, 2011-Ohio-3091. Criminal Law ⚿ 208.1; Criminal Law ⚿ 210

Claimed perjury charges against prosecuting attorney allegedly occurred outside of the six-year statute of limitations, and therefore private citizen was not entitled to writ of mandamus to compel clerk of courts to file criminal complaint and affidavit charging prosecuting attorney with perjury; claimed perjury occurred more than 15 years prior to filing of petition for writ of mandamus, thus, writ would not have resulted in the issuance of an arrest warrant or prosecution of the claimed offense. State ex rel. Dominguez v. State (Ohio, 06-29-2011) 129 Ohio St.3d 203, 951 N.E.2d 77, 2011-Ohio-3091. Criminal Law ⚿ 147; Mandamus ⚿ 16(1)

2935.10 Procedure upon filing of affidavit or complaint; withdrawal of unexecuted warrants

Notes of Decisions

3. Sufficiency of affidavit or complaint

Affiant failed to establish probable cause to support criminal charge of theft in office against judge who in separate criminal case ordered return of funds allegedly in control of county to alleged victims, where affiant failed to appear at probable cause hearing, and, as a result, no evidence was offered in support of the affidavit. In re Charging Affidavit of Demis (Ohio App. 5 Dist., Stark, 12-16-2013) No. 2013 CA 00098, 2013-Ohio-5520, 2013 WL 6671837, Unreported. Criminal Law ⇔ 238(4)

Complaint was insufficient to provide probable cause for an arrest warrant for defendant based on selling alcohol to an underage person; the officer swore that the defendant committed the offense on a specified date at a specified location and named the type of beer, but did not disclose what the source of his belief was. State v. Jones (Ohio App. 7 Dist., Mahoning, 03-20-2012) No. 11 MA 60, 2012-Ohio-1301, 2012 WL 1035017, Unreported. Criminal Law ⇔ 211(4)

5. Issuance of warrant or summons

Although a private citizen may file with a judge, clerk of court, or magistrate an affidavit charging an offense committed in order to cause the arrest or prosecution of the person charged, the private citizen must follow the applicable statutory procedure in order to do so. State ex rel. Dominguez v. State (Ohio, 06-29-2011) 129 Ohio St.3d 203, 951 N.E.2d 77, 2011-Ohio-3091. Criminal Law ⇔ 208.1; Criminal Law ⇔ 210

Claimed perjury charges against prosecuting attorney allegedly occurred outside of the six-year statute of limitations, and therefore private citizen was not entitled to writ of mandamus to compel clerk of courts to file criminal complaint and affidavit charging prosecuting attorney with perjury; claimed perjury occurred more than 15 years prior to filing of petition for writ of mandamus, thus, writ would not have resulted in the issuance of an arrest warrant or prosecution of the claimed offense. State ex rel. Dominguez v. State (Ohio, 06-29-2011) 129 Ohio St.3d 203, 951 N.E.2d 77, 2011-Ohio-3091. Criminal Law ⇔ 147; Mandamus ⇔ 16(1)

2935.12 Forcible entry in making arrest; execution of search warrant

Law Review and Journal Commentaries

Reviving the knock and announce rule and constructively abolishing no-knock entries by giving the people a ground they can stand on. Amanda M. Yeaples–Coleman, 37 U. Dayton L. Rev. 381 (2012).

Taking advice from the doctors in the wake of Hudson V. Michigan: Modeling a remedy for knock and announce violations after the Indiana Medical Malpractice Act. K. Robert Schalburg, 34 Ohio N.U. L. Rev. 267.

Notes of Decisions

1. Constitutional issues

Exigent circumstances did not authorize police officers' "no knock" entry into apartment, even though confidential informant informed officers immediately before the search that the occupants of apartment possessed a weapon and were under the influence of LSD; the officers did not act on the exigent circumstances and had planned to conduct a "no knock" search before they received the information from informant, and officer testified that the special response team, which executed the warrant, followed their standard procedure when executing the warrant and that information from the informant did not alter their plans or cause the team to fear for their safety. State v. Winfield (Ohio App. 6 Dist., Huron, 03-24-2006) No. H-04-043, 2006-Ohio-1392, 2006 WL 751367, Unreported. Controlled Substances ⇔ 153

3. Knock and announce rule

Police officers failed to comply with knock and announce statute in executing search warrant of residence, thus requiring suppression of evidence seized during search of residence, in drug prosecution; police broke into residence without first having been refused admittance, in violation of statute, and none of the occupants of residence, including defendant, were sufficiently alerted to have refused admittance. State v. Oliver (Ohio App. 8 Dist., Cuyahoga, 08-25-2005) No. 85606, 2005-Ohio-4411, 2005 WL 2045792, Unreported, appeal allowed 108 Ohio St.3d 1435, 842 N.E.2d 61, 2006-Ohio-421, remanded 112 Ohio St.3d 447, 860 N.E.2d 1002, 2007-Ohio-372. Criminal Law ⇔ 392.16(6)

No exigent circumstances existed to justify police officers' entry into residence to execute search warrant, which entry violated knock and announce statute; officers were able to observe occupants of house through picture window, and, as such, they would have been able to observe any attempt at destroying evidence, but no such attempt was observed, and officer testified that one of the men was lying on a couch, while the other was sitting on a chair with his back towards the window, and that neither man moved. State v. Oliver (Ohio App. 8

Dist., Cuyahoga, 08-25-2005) No. 85606, 2005-Ohio-4411, 2005 WL 2045792, Unreported, appeal allowed 108 Ohio St.3d 1435, 842 N.E.2d 61, 2006-Ohio-421, remanded 112 Ohio St.3d 447, 860 N.E.2d 1002, 2007-Ohio-372. Searches And Seizures ⚷ 143.1

Failure of police officers to knock and announce their presence before entering apartment to execute search warrant did not deprive defendant of notice of officers' presence, or opportunity to allow officers to enter apartment peaceably; man police saw standing in doorway of apartment went in and slammed door closed when police began approaching thereby demonstrating his intent not to allow officers into apartment, and exigent circumstances existed because, if officers had delayed, defendant would have had time to conceal or destroy evidence, secure weapon, or flee apartment. State v. Varner (Ohio App. 9 Dist., Summit, 02-19-2003) No. 21056, 2003-Ohio-719, 2003 WL 357526, Unreported, appeal not allowed 99 Ohio St.3d 1438, 789 N.E.2d 1118, 2003-Ohio-2902, appeal not allowed 101 Ohio St.3d 1424, 802 N.E.2d 155, 2004-Ohio-123, denial of post-conviction relief affirmed 180 Ohio App.3d 684, 906 N.E.2d 1191, 2009-Ohio-335. Searches And Seizures ⚷ 143.1

Waiver of knock-and-announce requirements in warrant for search of defendant's residence was invalid, since there was insufficient basis at time of issuance of warrant to believe that a risk of serious physical harm existed for sheriff's officers executing warrant; affidavit supporting warrant asserted that another person living at residence owned and had recently discharged a firearm there, but failed to present facts or relationship on which to assert that a risk existed that that person would be present at defendant's apartment. State v. Nunez (Ohio App. 6 Dist., 12-19-2008) 180 Ohio App.3d 189, 904 N.E.2d 924, 2008-Ohio-6806. Searches and Seizures ⚷ 143.1

Evidence seized during search of defendant's residence was not required to be excluded in prosecution of defendant for possession of cocaine, even though warrant for search of residence contained an invalid waiver of knock-and-announce requirements; defendant failed to present any evidence how entry into the apartment was secured to conduct the search, and exclusionary rule did not apply in all circumstances to violations of the knock-and-announce rule. State v. Nunez (Ohio App. 6 Dist., 12-19-2008) 180 Ohio App.3d 189, 904 N.E.2d 924, 2008-Ohio-6806. Criminal Law ⚷ 392.16(6); Criminal Law ⚷ 392.49(7)

Exceptions exist, but the "knock and announce" rule directs police officers executing a search warrant at a residence to first knock on the door, announce their purpose, and identity themselves before they forcibly enter the home. State v. Oliver (Ohio, 02-14-2007) 112 Ohio St.3d 447, 860 N.E.2d 1002, 2007-Ohio-372. Searches And Seizures ⚷ 143.1

In executing a warrant to search a home, the police are expected to comply with the "knock and announce" rule, which predates the United States Constitution but is reflected in the Fourth Amendment, and which is codified in federal and state statutes. State v. Oliver (Ohio, 02-14-2007) 112 Ohio St.3d 447, 860 N.E.2d 1002, 2007-Ohio-372. Searches And Seizures ⚷ 143.1

6. Effective assistance of counsel

Defendant was not entitled to evidentiary hearing on postconviction motion based on alleged claims of ineffective assistance of counsel for failure to pursue motions to dismiss arising from police officers' failure to give notice of intent to execute search warrant prior to breaking down door and for counsel's failure to pursue motion to suppress before trial court when he entered plea agreement, where defendant failed to submit evidentiary documents, other than his own self-serving affidavit, to support his claim. State v. Williams (Ohio App. 9 Dist., Summit, 08-06-2003) No. 21395, 2003-Ohio-4154, 2003 WL 21804750, Unreported, appeal not allowed 100 Ohio St.3d 1509, 799 N.E.2d 187, 2003-Ohio-6161, post-conviction relief denied 2006 WL 3742667. Criminal Law ⚷ 1655(6)

2935.13 Proceedings upon arrest

Notes of Decisions

2. Detention or arrest

There was no evidence that railroad police officers' two hour delay in transporting arrestee to county justice center violated Ohio law, as required for arrestee's claims alleging that officers failed to promptly present him to judicial officer following arrest. Nerswick v. CSX Transp., Inc. (C.A.6 (Ohio), 09-14-2011) No. 10-3328, 441 Fed.Appx. 320, 2011 WL 4119153, Unreported. Arrest ⚷ 70(2)

Under Ohio law, railroad police officers who arrested arrestee for receiving stolen property did not commit abuse of process by taking arrestee to railroad's police facility for questioning following his arrest before eventually taking him to county jail, a ten-minute drive; delay in bringing arrestee to jail was brief, and there was no evidence to support finding that the officers' questioning at railroad facility was an attempt to accomplish an ulterior purpose outside of the legal proceedings. Nerswick v. CSX Transp., Inc. (S.D.Ohio, 02-19-2010) 692 F.Supp.2d 866, affirmed 441 Fed.Appx. 320, 2011 WL 4119153. Process ⚷ 192

WARRANT AND GENERAL PROVISIONS

2935.20 Right of one in custody to be visited by attorney

Notes of Decisions

4. —— Statutory right, affording opportunity to contact attorney

Application of exclusionary rule was not an available remedy, in prosecution for operating a motor vehicle under the influence of alcohol (OVI), for police officer's alleged violation of defendant's statutory right to counsel upon being arrested and transported to police station for breath test. State v. Turner (Ohio App. 11 Dist., Portage, 08-01-2008) No. 2007-P-0090, 2008-Ohio-3898, 2008 WL 2955396, Unreported, appeal not allowed 120 Ohio St.3d 1489, 900 N.E.2d 199, 2009-Ohio-278. Automobiles ⚷ 421; Criminal Law ⚷ 392.27

6. DWI and sobriety test

Defendant at trial for operating a motor vehicle under the influence of alcohol (OVI) was not prejudiced by any error in trial court's failure to instruct jury that defendant's refusal to submit to blood testing was not evidence of a consciousness of guilt because it had conditioned upon his statutory right to seek the advice of counsel, since a large amount of other evidence showed defendant's guilt, including that police officer observed defendant commit several traffic violations, detected a strong odor of alcohol from defendant, and observed that defendant had glassy bloodshot eyes, and that defendant admitted to having consumed alcohol prior to driving. State v. Simin (Ohio App. 9 Dist., 09-26-2012) 977 N.E.2d 714, 2012-Ohio-4389. Criminal Law ⚷ 1173.2(5)

A violation by police of statute entitling a defendant to have an attorney present before submitting to chemical testing to determine his blood alcohol content will not bar the admission of any results obtained from an otherwise admissible test; the exclusionary rule does not apply when the police violate an accused's statutory right to counsel. State v. Simin (Ohio App. 9 Dist., 09-26-2012) 977 N.E.2d 714, 2012-Ohio-4389. Automobiles ⚷ 421; Criminal Law ⚷ 392.22

2935.26 When citation must be used rather than arrest; exceptions; procedures

Law Review and Journal Commentaries

Factoring the seriousness of the offense into fourth amendment equations: Strip searches in detention facilities—Atwater strikes again. William A. Schroeder, 46 Akron L. Rev. 331 (2013).

Notes of Decisions

1. Constitutional issues

Police officers had probable cause to arrest motorist for speeding, turning without signaling, and failing to use a seat belt and, thus, motorist's arrest was not a wrongful arrest in violation of § 1983, even if state statute prohibited officers from arresting motorist for such minor misdemeanors; state law protection from arrest did not govern the scope of Fourth Amendment protection. Bodager v. Campbell (Ohio App. 4 Dist., Pike, 10-07-2013) No. 12CA828, 2013-Ohio-4650, 2013 WL 5741005, Unreported, appeal not allowed 138 Ohio St.3d 1434, 4 N.E.3d 1051, 2014-Ohio-889. Automobiles ⚷ 349(2.1); Automobiles ⚷ 349(5.3)

As investigative stop progressed, officer, who had received information from an identified citizen informant that "there was a male in [a] parking lot in a white van possibly dealing drugs," developed probable cause to arrest defendant for obstruction of official business, given that defendant's initial refusal to exit his van impeded the officer's investigation; as such, under the Fourth Amendment, officers had authority to search defendant incident to his arrest. State v. Carrocce (Ohio App. 10 Dist., Franklin, 12-05-2006) No. 06AP-101, 2006-Ohio-6376, 2006 WL 3491740, Unreported, on subsequent appeal 2008-Ohio-1517, 2008 WL 852603. Arrest ⚷ 63.4(12); Arrest ⚷ 63.4(15)

2. Arrest for minor misdemeanor

The general rule is that an offender cannot be arrested for a minor misdemeanor. State v. Habel (Ohio App. 2 Dist., 08-20-2010) 190 Ohio App.3d 393, 942 N.E.2d 389, 2010-Ohio-3907. Arrest ⚷ 63.4(5)

A county dog warden is required by RC 2935.26(A) to issue citations for failure to register a dog, a violation of RC 955.21, when the offense is a first offense and thus a minor misdemeanor pursuant to RC 955.99(E)(1) and RC 2901.02(G)(2). For subsequent violations of RC 955.21, the offense is an unclassified misdemeanor, for which there is no statutory authority for a county dog warden to issue a citation in lieu of an arrest. OAG 2014-025, 2014 WL 4471238.

3. Search incident to citation or arrest

Following traffic stop, defendant who could not or would not provide identification could be detained and searched incident to arrest for minor misdemeanor. State v. Bush (Ohio App. 8 Dist., Cuyahoga, 11-17-2011) No. 96495, 2011-Ohio-5925, 2011 WL 5589564, Unreported. Automobiles ⚷

349.5(1); Automobiles ⚿ 349(8); Automobiles ⚿ 349(17)

Police officer's frisk of bicyclist he had stopped for minor misdemeanor of riding her bicycle on the sidewalk, and his placement of bicyclist in back seat of cruiser following frisk, were not justified; officer avowed that bicyclist's clothing was tight and that he did not see any bulges indicating a weapon, while bicyclist was unable to produce any identification when asked, she was not given opportunity to prove whether she could provide satisfactory evidence of her identity before she was frisked and placed in cruiser, given that she was on a bicycle and the officers were in a cruiser, she could not evade them, and there was no indication that she was not cooperative, and bicyclist's mere presence in high-drug area, by itself, was insufficient to justify the frisk. State v. Habel (Ohio App. 2 Dist., 08-20-2010) 190 Ohio App.3d 393, 942 N.E.2d 389, 2010-Ohio-3907. Automobiles ⚿ 349.5(10); Automobiles ⚿ 349(17)

5. Content of citation

On appeal of conviction in Mayor's Court for allowing his dogs to run loose, defendant failed to timely object in pretrial motion that the citation he had been issued did not contain required statutory language informing him that he could have signed plea of guilty and paid fine rather than appearing for trial before Mayor's Court, and thus trial court did not err in failing to dismiss defendant's charge based on apparent lack of required statutory language on the citation. Blue Ash v. Hensley (Ohio App. 1 Dist., 08-08-2014) 17 N.E.3d 1180, 2014-Ohio-3428. Municipal Corporations ⚿ 642(1)

2935.27 Alternatives for security for appearance

Cross References

Driving under suspension, see 4510.111

2935.29 Definition of fresh pursuit and state

Comparative Laws

Ariz.—A.R.S. §§ 13–3831 to 13–3834.
Ark.—A.C.A. §§ 16–81–401 to 16–81–407.
Cal.—West's Ann.Cal.Penal Code, §§ 852 to 852.4.
Colo.—West's C.R.S.A. § 16–3–104.
Conn.—C.G.S.A. § 54–156.
Del.—11 Del.C. §§ 1931 to 1935.
D.C.—D.C. Official Code, 2001 Ed. §§ 23–901 to 23–903.
Fla.—West's F.S.A. §§ 941.31 to 941.37.
Idaho—I.C. §§ 19–701 to 19–707.
Ill.—S.H.A. 725 ILCS 5/107–4.
Ind.—West's A.I.C. 35–33–3–1 to 35–33–3–7.
Iowa—I.C.A. §§ 806.1 to 806.6.
Kan.—K.S.A. 22–2404.
La.—LSA–C.Cr.P. arts. 231, 232.
Maine—15 M.R.S.A. §§ 151 to 155.
Md.—Code, Criminal Procedure, §§ 2–304 to 2–309.
Mass.—M.G.L.A. c. 276, §§ 10A to 10D.
Mich.—M.C.L.A. §§ 780.101 to 780.108.
Minn.—M.S.A. §§ 626.65 to 626.72.
Mo.—V.A.M.S. § 544.155.
Mt.—M.C.A. 46–6–411.
Neb.—R.R.S. 1943, §§ 29–416 to 29–421.
Nev.—N.R.S. 171.154 to 171.164, 171.166 to 171.176.
N.H.—RSA 614:1 to 614:6.
N.J.—N.J.S.A. 2A:155–1 to 2A:155–7.
N.M.—NMSA 1978, §§ 31–2–1 to 31–2–8.
N.Y.—McKinney's CPL, § 140.55.
N.C.—G.S. § 15A–403.
N.D.—NDCC 29–06–05 to 29–06–07.
Ohio—R.C. §§ 2935.29 to 2935.31.
Okl.—22 Okl.St.Ann. §§ 221 to 228.
Ore.—ORS 133.410 to 133.440.
Pa.—42 Pa.C.S.A. §§ 8921 to 8924.
R.I.—Gen.Laws. 1956, §§ 12–8–1 to 12–8–6.
S.C.—Code 1976, § 25–3–180.
S.D.—SDCL 23A–3–10 to 23A–3–14.
Tenn.—T.C.A. §§ 40–7–201 to 40–7–205.
Tex.—Vernon's Ann.C.C.P. art. 14.051.
Utah—U.C.A. 1953, 77–9–1 to 77–9–3.
Vt.—13 V.S.A. §§ 5041 to 5045.
Wash.—West's RCWA 10.89.010 to 10.89.080.
W.Va.—Code, 62–11–1 to 62–11–7.
Wis.—W.S.A. 976.04.

2935.33 Commitment of alcoholics and intoxicated persons

(A) If a person charged with a misdemeanor is taken before a judge of a court of record and if it appears to the judge that the person is an alcoholic or is suffering from acute alcohol intoxication and that the person would benefit from services provided by a community addiction services provider certified under Chapter 5119. of the Revised Code, the judge may place the person temporarily in a services provider certified under that chapter in the area in which the court has jurisdiction for inpatient care and treatment for an indefinite period not exceeding five days. The commitment does not limit the right to release on bail. The judge may dismiss a charge of a violation of division (B) of section 2917.11 of the Revised Code or of a municipal ordinance substantially equivalent to that division if the defendant complies with all the conditions of treatment ordered by the court.

The court may order that any fines or court costs collected by the court from defendants who have received inpatient care from a community addiction services provider be paid, for the benefit of the program, to the board of alcohol, drug addiction, and mental health services of the alcohol, drug addiction, and mental health service district in which the services provider is located or to the director of mental health and addiction services.

(B) If a person is being sentenced for a violation of division (B) of section 2917.11 or section 4511.19 of the Revised Code, a misdemeanor violation of section 2919.25 of the Revised Code, a misdemeanor violation of section 2919.27 of the Revised Code involving a protection order issued or consent agreement approved pursuant to section 2919.26 or 3113.31 of the Revised Code, or a violation of a municipal ordinance substantially equivalent to that division or any of those sections and if it appears to the judge at the time of sentencing that the person is an alcoholic or is suffering from acute alcohol intoxication and that, in lieu of imprisonment, the person would benefit from services provided by a community addiction services provider certified under Chapter 5119. of the Revised Code, the court may commit the person to close supervision in any facility in the area in which the court has jurisdiction that is, or is operated by, such a services provider. Such close supervision may include outpatient services and part-time release, except that a person convicted of a violation of division (A) of section 4511.19 of the Revised Code shall be confined to the facility for at least three days and except that a person convicted of a misdemeanor violation of section 2919.25 of the Revised Code, a misdemeanor violation of section 2919.27 of the Revised Code involving a protection order issued or consent agreement approved pursuant to section 2919.26 or 3113.31 of the Revised Code, or a violation of a substantially equivalent municipal ordinance shall be confined to the facility in accordance with the order of commitment. A commitment of a person to a facility for purposes of close supervision shall not exceed the maximum term for which the person could be imprisoned.

(C) A law enforcement officer who finds a person subject to prosecution for violation of division (B) of section 2917.11 of the Revised Code or a municipal ordinance substantially equivalent to that division and who has reasonable cause to believe that the person is an alcoholic or is suffering from acute alcohol intoxication and would benefit from immediate treatment immediately may place the person in a community addiction services provider certified under Chapter 5119. of the Revised Code in the area in which the person is found, for emergency treatment, in lieu of other arrest procedures, for a maximum period of forty-eight hours. During that time, if the person desires to leave such custody, the person shall be released forthwith.

(D) As used in this section:

(1) "Alcoholic" has the same meaning as in section 5119.01 of the Revised Code;

(2) "Acute alcohol intoxication" means a heavy consumption of alcohol over a relatively short period of time, resulting in dysfunction of the brain centers controlling behavior, speech, and memory and causing characteristic withdrawal symptoms.

(2013 H 59, eff. 9-29-13; 2002 H 490, eff. 1-1-04; 1995 S 2, eff. 7-1-96; 1994 S 82, eff. 5-4-94; 1989 H 317, eff. 10-10-89; 1985 H 475; 1984 H 37; 1976 H 907; 1975 H 1; 1972 H 240)

Historical and Statutory Notes

Amendment Note: 2013 H 59 substituted "a community addiction services provider" for "an alcohol and drug addiction program", "5119" for "3793", and "services provider" for "program" throughout the section; substituted "mental health and addiction services" for "alcohol and drug addiction services" in division (A); substituted "5119.01" for "3793.01" in division (D)(1); and made other nonsubstantive changes.

Research References

Encyclopedias

OH Jur. 3d Incompetent Persons § 194, Short-Term Commitment of Alcoholics and Intoxicated Persons.

2935.36 Pre–trial diversion programs for adult offenders; limits; procedure

(A) The prosecuting attorney may establish pre-trial diversion programs for adults who are accused of committing criminal offenses and whom the prosecuting attorney believes probably will not offend again. The prosecuting attorney may require, as a condition of an accused's participation in the program, the accused to pay a reasonable fee for supervision services that include, but are not limited to, monitoring and drug testing. The programs shall be operated pursuant to written standards approved by journal entry by the presiding judge or, in courts with only one judge, the judge of the court of common pleas and shall not be applicable to any of the following:

(1) Repeat offenders or dangerous offenders;

(2) Persons accused of an offense of violence, of a violation of section 2903.06, 2907.04, 2907.05, 2907.21, 2907.22, 2907.31, 2907.32, 2907.34, 2911.31, 2919.12, 2919.13, 2919.22, 2921.02, 2921.11, 2921.12, 2921.32, or 2923.20 of the Revised Code, or of a violation of section 2905.01, 2905.02, or 2919.23 of the Revised Code that, had it occurred prior to July 1, 1996, would have been a violation of section 2905.04 of the Revised Code as it existed prior to that date, with the exception that the prosecuting attorney may permit persons accused of any such offense to enter a pre-trial diversion program, if the prosecuting attorney finds any of the following:

(a) The accused did not cause, threaten, or intend serious physical harm to any person;

(b) The offense was the result of circumstances not likely to recur;

(c) The accused has no history of prior delinquency or criminal activity;

(d) The accused has led a law-abiding life for a substantial time before commission of the alleged offense;

(e) Substantial grounds tending to excuse or justify the alleged offense.

(3) Persons accused of a violation of Chapter 2925. or 3719. of the Revised Code;

(4) Persons accused of a violation of section 4511.19 of the Revised Code or a violation of any substantially similar municipal ordinance;

(5)(a) Persons who are accused of an offense while operating a commercial motor vehicle or persons who hold a commercial driver's license and are accused of any offense, if conviction of the offense would disqualify the person from operating a commercial motor vehicle under Chapter 4506. of the Revised Code or would subject the person to any other sanction under that chapter;

(b) As used in division (A)(5) of this section, "commercial driver's license" and "commercial motor vehicle" have the same meanings as in section 4506.01 of the Revised Code.

(B) An accused who enters a diversion program shall do all of the following:

(1) Waive, in writing and contingent upon the accused's successful completion of the program, the accused's right to a speedy trial, the preliminary hearing, the time period within which the grand jury may consider an indictment against the accused, and arraignment, unless the hearing, indictment, or arraignment has already occurred;

(2) Agree, in writing, to the tolling while in the program of all periods of limitation established by statutes or rules of court, that are applicable to the offense with which the accused is charged and to the conditions of the diversion program established by the prosecuting attorney;

(3) Agree, in writing, to pay any reasonable fee for supervision services established by the prosecuting attorney.

(C) The trial court, upon the application of the prosecuting attorney, shall order the release from confinement of any accused who has agreed to enter a pre-trial diversion program and shall discharge and release any existing bail and release any sureties on recognizances and shall release the accused on a recognizance bond conditioned upon the accused's compliance with the terms of the diversion program. The prosecuting attorney shall notify every victim of the crime and the arresting officers of the prosecuting attorney's intent to permit the accused to enter a pre-trial diversion program. The victim of the crime and the arresting officers shall have the opportunity to file written objections with the prosecuting attorney prior to the commencement of the pre-trial diversion program.

(D) If the accused satisfactorily completes the diversion program, the prosecuting attorney shall recommend to the trial court that the charges against the accused be dismissed, and the court, upon the recommendation of the prosecuting attorney, shall dismiss the charges. If the accused chooses not to enter the prosecuting attorney's diversion program, or if the accused violates the conditions of the agreement pursuant to which the accused has been released, the accused may be brought to trial upon the charges in the manner provided by law, and the waiver executed pursuant to division (B)(1) of this section shall be void on the date the accused is removed from the program for the violation.

(E) As used in this section:

(1) "Repeat offender" means a person who has a history of persistent criminal activity and whose character and condition reveal a substantial risk that the person will commit another offense. It is prima-facie evidence that a person is a repeat offender if any of the following applies:

(a) Having been convicted of one or more offenses of violence and having been imprisoned pursuant to sentence for any such offense, the person commits a subsequent offense of violence;

(b) Having been convicted of one or more sexually oriented offenses or child-victim oriented offenses, both as defined in section 2950.01 of the Revised Code, and having been imprisoned pursuant to sentence for one or more of those offenses, the person commits a subsequent sexually oriented offense or child-victim oriented offense;

(c) Having been convicted of one or more theft offenses as defined in section 2913.01 of the Revised Code and having been imprisoned pursuant to sentence for one or more of those theft offenses, the person commits a subsequent theft offense;

(d) Having been convicted of one or more felony drug abuse offenses as defined in section 2925.01 of the Revised Code and having been imprisoned pursuant to sentence for one or more of those felony drug abuse offenses, the person commits a subsequent felony drug abuse offense;

(e) Having been convicted of two or more felonies and having been imprisoned pursuant to sentence for one or more felonies, the person commits a subsequent offense;

(f) Having been convicted of three or more offenses of any type or degree other than traffic offenses, alcoholic intoxication offenses, or minor misdemeanors and having been imprisoned pursuant to sentence for any such offense, the person commits a subsequent offense.

(2) "Dangerous offender" means a person who has committed an offense, whose history, character, and condition reveal a substantial risk that the person will be a danger to others, and whose conduct has been characterized by a pattern of repetitive, compulsive, or aggressive behavior with heedless indifference to the consequences.

(2012 H 337, eff. 1-27-12; 2008 H 130, eff. 4-7-09; 2003 S 5, eff. 7-31-03; 2003 H 95, eff. 9-26-03; 1999 S 107, eff. 3-23-00; 1996 H 180, eff. 7-1-97; 1995 S 2, eff. 7-1-96; 1994 S 82, eff. 5-4-94; 1986 S 262, eff. 3-20-87; 1978 H 473)

Uncodified Law

2008 H 130, § 5, eff. 4-7-09, reads:

The items of law contained in this act, and their applications, are severable. If any item of law contained in this act, or if any application of any item of law contained in this act, is held invalid, the invalidity does not affect other items of law contained in this act and their applications that can be given effect without the invalid item of law or application.

Historical and Statutory Notes

Amendment Note: 2012 H 337 added division (A)(5), and made other nonsubstantive changes.

Amendment Note: 2008 H 130 deleted former division (A)(4) and redesignated former division (A)(5) as new division (A)(4).

Cross References

Expungement of sealed records, see 2151.358
Unprofessional conduct procedures, college-preparatory boarding schools, see 3328.19

Ohio Administrative Code References

Employment of individuals in positions that require a license and licensure of individuals with certain criminal convictions or other alternative dispositions, see OAC 3301–20–01

Research References

Encyclopedias

OH Jur. 3d Criminal Law: Procedure § 857, Establishment of Pretrial Diversion Program.
OH Jur. 3d Criminal Law: Procedure § 858, Notice to Victims of Crime of Accused's Entry in Program.
OH Jur. 3d Criminal Law: Procedure § 859, Operation of Programs.
OH Jur. 3d Criminal Law: Procedure § 861, Repeat or Dangerous Offenders.
OH Jur. 3d Criminal Law: Procedure § 862, Persons Accused of Specific Offenses.
OH Jur. 3d Criminal Law: Procedure § 863, Persons Accused of Specific Offenses--Exceptions.
OH Jur. 3d Criminal Law: Procedure § 864, Drug-Dependent Persons.
OH Jur. 3d Criminal Law: Procedure § 865, Persons Driving While Under the Influence of Alcohol.
OH Jur. 3d Criminal Law: Procedure § 866, Waiver and Agreement by Person Entering Program.
OH Jur. 3d Criminal Law: Procedure § 867, Release of Person, Bail, and Sureties Upon Entering Program.
OH Jur. 3d Criminal Law: Procedure § 868, Dismissal of Charges; Effect of Successful Completion of Charges.
OH Jur. 3d Criminal Law: Procedure § 869, Dismissal of Charges; Effect of Successful Completion of Charges--Proceedings Upon Refusal of Accused to Participate in Program or Violation of Agreement.
OH Jur. 3d Criminal Law: Procedure § 2645, Inspection of Record Subsequent to Sealing--By Prosecutor, Attorney General, or Law Enforcement Officer or Agency.
OH Jur. 3d Criminal Law: Procedure § 2669, Maintenance of Index; Availability of Records.

Treatises and Practice Aids

Katz & Giannelli, Baldwin's Ohio Practice Criminal Law § 35:10, Pretrial Diversion.
Katz & Giannelli, Baldwin's Ohio Practice Criminal Law § 143:35, Motion for Pre-Trial Diversion.
Katz & Giannelli, Baldwin's Ohio Practice Criminal Law § 143:36, Prosecutor's Consent to Place Defendant on Pre-Trial Diversion Program.
Hennenberg & Reinhart, Ohio Criminal Defense Motions F 5:13, Treatment in Lieu of Conviction--Pretrial Motions.
Hennenberg & Reinhart, Ohio Criminal Defense Motions F 5:14, Motion for Intervention in Lieu of Conviction.
Giannelli & Yeomans Salvador, Ohio Juvenile Law App. A, Ohio Revised Code--Selected Provisions.

Law Review and Journal Commentaries

The unified "sealed" theory: Updating Ohio's record-sealing statute for the twenty-first century, Michael H. Jagunic. 59 Clev St L Rev 161(2011).

Notes of Decisions

1. Constitutional issues

Pretrial diversion program did not violate pretrial diversion statute because the program, established by the court rather than the prosecutor, was not governed by the statute, and thus college students' rights to equal protection and due process were not violated when the court did not produce written standards for the program, standards were not approved in a journal entry by the presiding judge, and students were ordered to pay fees and donations that were not allowed under statute. Lane v. Phillabaum (Ohio App. 12 Dist., 05-27-2008) 182

Ohio App.3d 145, 912 N.E.2d 113, 2008-Ohio-2502, appeal not allowed 119 Ohio St.3d 1503, 895 N.E.2d 566, 2008-Ohio-5467. Sentencing and Punishment ⚿ 2054

2. Diversionary programs

Defendant's establishing a diversion program that could only be established by a prosecuting attorney did not support conviction for dereliction of duty, where statute governing establishment of diversion program did not impose an express duty on police officer to refrain from creating a diversion program. State v. Martin (Ohio App. 11 Dist., Trumbull, 11-24-2006) No. 2005-T-0041, 2006-Ohio-6202, 2006 WL 3393472, Unreported, stay granted 112 Ohio St.3d 1468, 861 N.E.2d 143, 2007-Ohio-388, appeal not allowed 113 Ohio St.3d 1489, 865 N.E.2d 913, 2007-Ohio-1986. Municipal Corporations ⚿ 190

Pretrial diversion program for adult offenders statute did not deprive trial court of the power to establish pretrial diversion program by vesting exclusive authority to establish such programs in the prosecuting attorneys; while statute stated that a prosecuting attorney may establish a pretrial diversion program, it did not state that only a prosecuting attorney could do so. Lane v. Phillabaum (Ohio App. 12 Dist., 05-27-2008) 182 Ohio App.3d 145, 912 N.E.2d 113, 2008-Ohio-2502, appeal not allowed 119 Ohio St.3d 1503, 895 N.E.2d 566, 2008-Ohio-5467. Sentencing and Punishment ⚿ 2054

Defendant's prior participation in prosecutor's pretrial diversion program did not render her ineligible for intervention in lieu of conviction (ILC); no such restriction was contained in statute governing ILC, and diversion program was not a regimen similar to ILC. State v. Leisten (Ohio App. 2 Dist., 05-12-2006) 166 Ohio App.3d 805, 853 N.E.2d 673, 2006-Ohio-2362. Chemical Dependents ⚿ 12

R.C. 5705.10(D) requires fees paid by persons participating in a pre-trial diversion program established pursuant to R.C. 2935.36 to be deposited into a special fund created under R.C. 5705.09(F) for use in defraying the costs of supervising persons participating in the program. (2003 Op. Att'y Gen. No. 2003-005, 2003 WL 343225 overruled on the basis of statutory amendment.). OAG 2011-017, 2011 WL 2177384.

CHAPTER 2937

PRELIMINARY EXAMINATION; BAIL

PRELIMINARY EXAMINATION

PRELIMINARY EXAMINATION

2937.02 Announcement of charge and rights of accused by court

(A) When, after arrest, the accused is taken before a court or magistrate, or when the accused appears pursuant to terms of summons or notice, the affidavit or complaint being first filed, the court or magistrate shall, before proceeding further:

(1) Inform the accused of the nature of the charge and the identity of the complainant and permit the accused or counsel for the accused to see and read the affidavit or complaint or a copy of the affidavit or complaint;

(2) Inform the accused of the right to have counsel and the right to a continuance in the proceedings to secure counsel;

(3) Inform the accused of the effect of pleas of guilty, not guilty, and no contest, of the right to trial by jury, and the necessity of making written demand for trial by jury;

(4) If the charge is a felony, inform the accused of the nature and extent of possible punishment on conviction and of the right to preliminary hearing;

(5) If the charge is a violation of section 2907.02 or 2907.03 of the Revised Code, inform the accused that a conviction of or plea of guilty to the violation may result in the following:

(a) In accordance with sections 3109.50 to 3109.507 of the Revised Code, the termination, denial, or limitation, as applicable, of the following:

(i) The accused's parental rights with respect to a child conceived as a result of the violation;

(ii) The rights of a relative of the accused with respect to a child conceived as a result of the violation.

(b) The granting of a petition to adopt a child conceived as a result of the violation without the accused's consent as described in division (F) of section 3107.07 of the Revised Code;

(c) The termination of the accused's, and the accused's relative's, eligibility to inherit from a child conceived as a result of the violation or the child's lineal descendants pursuant to section 2105.062 of the Revised Code.

(B) The court or magistrate may give the information provided pursuant to division (A) of this section to each accused individually, or, if at any time there exists any substantial number of defendants to be arraigned at the same session, the judge or magistrate may, by general announcement or by distribution of printed matter, advise all those accused concerning those rights general in their nature and informing as to individual matters at arraignment.

(2014 S 207, eff. 3-23-15; 128 v 97, eff. 1-1-60)

Historical and Statutory Notes

Amendment Note: 2014 S 207 rewrote this section, which prior thereto read:

"When, after arrest, the accused is taken before a court or magistrate, or when the accused appears pursuant to terms of summons or notice, the affidavit or complaint being first filed, the court or magistrate shall, before proceeding further:

"(A) Inform the accused of the nature of the charge against him and the identity of the complainant and permit the accused or his counsel to see and read the affidavit or complaint or a copy thereof;

"(B) Inform the accused of his right to have counsel and the right to a continuance in the proceedings to secure counsel;

"(C) Inform the accused of the effect of pleas of guilty, not guilty, and no contest, of his right to trial by jury, and the necessity of making written demand therefor;

"(D) If the charge be a felony, inform the accused of the nature and extent of possible punishment on conviction and of the right to preliminary hearing. Such information may be given to each accused individually or, if at any time there exists any substantial number of defendants to be arraigned at the same session, the judge or magistrate may, by general announcement or by distribution of printed matter, advise all those accused concerning those rights general in their nature, and informing as to individual matters at arraignment."

Research References

Encyclopedias

OH Jur. 3d Criminal Law: Procedure § 34, Informing Accused of Right to Attorney.

OH Jur. 3d Criminal Law: Procedure § 1194, Securing Counsel.

Treatises and Practice Aids

Katz & Giannelli, Baldwin's Ohio Practice Criminal Law § 36:1, Introduction.

Katz & Giannelli, Baldwin's Ohio Practice Criminal Law § 36:2, Procedure.

Katz & Giannelli, Baldwin's Ohio Practice Criminal Law § 36:3, Pleas.

Katz & Giannelli, Baldwin's Ohio Practice Criminal Law § 36:5, Rule 5(A) Violations.

Katz & Giannelli, Baldwin's Ohio Practice Criminal Law § 38:1, Introduction.

Katz & Giannelli, Baldwin's Ohio Practice Criminal Law § 43:2, Right to Counsel.

Katz & Giannelli, Baldwin's Ohio Practice Criminal Law § 43:13, Understanding the Waiver of Rights.

Katz & Giannelli, Baldwin's Ohio Practice Criminal Law § 75:14, Waiver of Right.

Weiler & Weiler, Ohio Driving Under the Influence § 5:7, Pleas.

Notes of Decisions

2. Right to counsel

Right to counsel, effective assistance, plea negotiations, motion to vacate and dismiss with prejudice, moot claims, see Arave v. Hoffman, 2008, 128 S.Ct. 749.

Right to counsel, effective assistance, plea hearing, appearance via speaker phone, habeas corpus relief, see Wright v. Van Patten, 2008, 128 S.Ct. 743.

2937.03 Arraignment; counsel; bail

Notes of Decisions

Right to counsel, constitutional issues 3

---

1. Constitutional issues—in general

Even if defendant was never formally arraigned, he waived right to arraignment by first entering pleas of not guilty, then not guilty by reason of insanity, and finally of no contest to rape of person under age 13. Palmer v. Wilson (Ohio App. 5 Dist., Richland, 05-12-2005) No. 2005-CA-2, 2005-Ohio-2346, 2005 WL 1125336, Unreported, appeal not allowed 106 Ohio St.3d 1534, 835 N.E.2d 383, 2005-Ohio-5146. Criminal Law ⚖ 262

2. —— Bail, constitutional issues

Right to counsel, effective assistance, plea negotiations, motion to vacate and dismiss with prejudice, moot claims, see Arave v. Hoffman, 2008, 128 S.Ct. 749.

3. —— Right to counsel, constitutional issues

Right to counsel, effective assistance, plea hearing, appearance via speaker phone, habeas corpus relief, see Wright v. Van Patten, 2008, 128 S.Ct. 743.

2937.06 Pleas

Notes of Decisions

3. Failure to follow procedure

Trial court failed to inform defendant of his right to compulsory process, and thus his guilty pleas to three separate charges of robbery required vacation. State v. Cummings (Ohio App. 8 Dist., Cuyahoga, 08-26-2004) No. 83759, 2004-Ohio-4470, 2004 WL 1902119, Unreported, appeal allowed 104 Ohio St.3d 1459, 821 N.E.2d 576, 2005-Ohio-204, appeal dismissed as improvidently granted 107 Ohio St.3d 1206, 839 N.E.2d 27, 2005-Ohio-6506, reconsideration denied 108 Ohio St.3d 1476, 842 N.E.2d 1055, 2006-Ohio-665. Criminal Law ⚖ 273.1(4); Criminal Law ⚖ 1167(5)

2937.07 Action on pleas of "guilty" and "no contest" in misdemeanor cases

If the offense is a misdemeanor and the accused pleads guilty to the offense, the court or magistrate shall receive and enter the plea unless the court or magistrate believes that it was made through fraud, collusion, or mistake. If the court or magistrate believes that it was made through fraud, collusion, or mistake, the court or magistrate shall enter a plea of not guilty and set the matter for trial pursuant to Chapter 2938. of the Revised Code. Upon receiving a plea of guilty, the court or magistrate shall call for an explanation of the circumstances of the offense from the affiant or complainant or the affiant's or complainant's representatives unless the offense to which the accused is pleading is a minor misdemeanor in which case the court or magistrate is not required to call for an explanation of the circumstances of the offense. After hearing the explanation of circumstances, together with any statement of the accused or after receiving the plea of guilty if an explanation of the circumstances of the offense is not required, the court or magistrate shall proceed to pronounce the sentence or shall continue the matter for the purpose of imposing the sentence.

A plea to a misdemeanor offense of "no contest" or words of similar import shall constitute an admission of the truth of the facts alleged in the complaint and that the judge or magistrate may make a finding of guilty or not guilty from the explanation of the circumstances of the offense. If the offense to which the accused is entering a plea of "no contest" is a minor misdemeanor, the judge or magistrate is not required to call for an explanation of the circumstances of the offense, and the judge or magistrate may base a finding on the facts alleged in the complaint. If a finding of guilty is made, the judge or magistrate shall impose the sentence or continue the case for sentencing accordingly. A plea of "no contest" or words of similar import shall not be construed as an admission of any fact at issue in the criminal charge in any subsequent civil or criminal action or proceeding.

(2010 H 338, eff. 9-17-10; 2002 H 490, eff. 1-1-04; 128 v 97, eff. 1-1-60)

Historical and Statutory Notes

Amendment Note: 2010 H 338 rewrote this section, which prior thereto read:

"If the offense is a misdemeanor and the accused pleads guilty to the offense, the court or magistrate shall receive and enter the plea unless the court or magistrate believes that it was made through fraud, collusion, or mistake. If the court or magistrate so believes, the court or magistrate shall enter a plea of not guilty and set the matter for trial pursuant to Chapter 2938. of the Revised Code. Upon receiving a plea of guilty, the court or magistrate shall call for an explanation of the circumstances of the offense from the affiant or complainant or the affiant's or complainant's representatives. After hearing the explanation of circumstances, together with any statement of the accused, the court or magistrate shall proceed to pronounce the sentence or shall continue the matter for the purpose of imposing the sentence.

"A plea to a misdemeanor offense of "no contest" or words of similar import shall constitute a stipulation that the judge or magistrate may make a finding of guilty or not guilty from the explanation of the circumstances of the offense. If a finding of guilty is made, the judge or magistrate shall impose the sentence or continue the case for sentencing accordingly. A plea of "no contest" or words of similar import shall not be construed as an admission of any fact at issue in the criminal charge in any subsequent civil or criminal action or proceeding."

Research References

Encyclopedias

OH Jur. 3d Criminal Law: Procedure § 1024, Cases Involving Serious Offenses.

OH Jur. 3d Criminal Law: Procedure § 1035, Misdemeanor Cases; Explanation of Circumstances.

Treatises and Practice Aids

Klein, Darling, & Terez, Baldwin's Ohio Practice Civil Practice § 1:100, Modern Courts Amendment of 1968 as Limiting Scope of Application of Civil Rules.

Katz & Giannelli, Baldwin's Ohio Practice Criminal Law § 36:5, Rule 5(A) Violations.

Katz & Giannelli, Baldwin's Ohio Practice Criminal Law § 43:7, Refusing to Accept Guilty Plea.

Katz & Giannelli, Baldwin's Ohio Practice Criminal Law § 45:2, Guilty Pleas Distinguished.

Katz & Giannelli, Baldwin's Ohio Practice Criminal Law § 43:19, Misdemeanor Cases.

Katz & Giannelli, Baldwin's Ohio Practice Criminal Law § 80:21, Appeal After No Contest Plea.

Weiler & Weiler, Ohio Driving Under the Influence § 5:7, Pleas.

Lang, Gotherman & Babbit, Ohio Municipal Law § 28:43, Waiver of Appearance and Bail.

Notes of Decisions

1. Plea of no contest—in general

Evidence was insufficient to allow the trial court to make a finding that defendant was guilty of reckless operation; police officer's written report made no mention of defendant's manner of driving, and the trial court's recitation of the facts did not include anything regarding defendant's driving. State v. Jasper (Ohio App. 2 Dist., Greene, 06-23-2006) No. 2005 CA 98, 2006-Ohio-3197, 2006 WL 1719751, Unreported. Automobiles ⚿ 355(4)

Under Ohio law, fact that judge makes finding of guilty or not guilty after explanation of circumstances does not elevate taking of no contest plea to level of adjudication of guilt after not guilty plea. Bailey v. City of Broadview Heights, Ohio (N.D.Ohio, 06-14-2010) 721 F.Supp.2d 653, affirmed 674 F.3d 499. Criminal Law ⚿ 275.3

Mayor's adjudication and sentencing of individual on traffic misdemeanor and contempt charges, in mayor's court, did not violate due process, even if mayor had pecuniary interest in case, where plaintiff voluntarily entered plea of no contest on misdemeanor traffic citation and plea of guilty to failure to appear charge, failure to appear citation was issued by mayor's court clerk, not mayor, and mayor merely performed ministerial function. Bailey v. City of Broadview Heights, Ohio (N.D.Ohio, 06-14-2010) 721 F.Supp.2d 653, affirmed 674 F.3d 499. Constitutional Law ⚿ 4494; Constitutional Law ⚿ 4621; Constitutional Law ⚿ 4720; Municipal Corporations ⚿ 641

2. —— Explanation of circumstances, plea of no contest

Trial court's terse explanation of circumstances when finding defendant guilty pursuant to defendant's no-contest plea to 18 misdemeanor violations of city ordinance requiring a party selling real property to furnish the purchaser with a certificate of disclosure regarding the condition of the property, which explanation stated that certificates of disclosure had not been filed, was sufficient, for purposes of statute providing that a no-contest plea to a misdemeanor offense constitutes a stipulation that the judge or magistrate may make a finding of guilty or not guilty from the explanation of the circumstances of the offense, where the city ordinance was a strict liability ordinance; defendant's failure to furnish any type of certificate of disclosure, whether proper or not, constituted a violation of the ordinance. Cleveland v. Go Invest Wisely, L.L.C. (Ohio App. 8 Dist., Cuyahoga, 07-07-2011) No. 95189, No. 95192, No. 95195, No. 95190, No. 95193, No. 95196, No. 95191, No. 95194, No. 95197, 2011-Ohio-3410, 2011 WL 2671927, Unreported. Criminal Law ⚷ 275.3

Municipal court, in entering no contest plea for corporate defendant that had been charged with multiple petty misdemeanor offenses involving violations of building and health codes, failed to comply with statute and rule governing pleas, thus rendering defendant's no contest plea invalid; not only did the court failed to take a plea of no contest, but it also failed to inform defendant of the effect of the plea, or to elicit an explanation of circumstances before it found defendant guilty. Cleveland v. Paramount Land Holdings, L.L.C. (Ohio App. 8 Dist., Cuyahoga, 07-07-2011) No. 95448, 2011-Ohio-3383, 2011 WL 2640236, Unreported, on subsequent appeal 2011-Ohio-4270, 2011 WL 3793517, opinion vacated on reconsideration 2011-Ohio-4270, 2011 WL 4978480. Criminal Law ⚷ 275.3; Municipal Corporations ⚷ 635

3. —— Basis for finding of guilt, plea of no contest

The record contained sufficient facts for the court to find defendant guilty of driving under financial responsibility law suspension or cancellation upon his no contest plea; defendant was found in the driver's seat of vehicle, the keys were in the ignition, and the vehicle's motor was running. State v. Cochran (Ohio App. 2 Dist., Montgomery, 07-18-2008) No. 22240, 2008-Ohio-3612, 2008 WL 2809220, Unreported. Criminal Law ⚷ 275.3

2937.08 Action on pleas of "not guilty" or "once in jeopardy" in misdemeanor cases

Law Review and Journal Commentaries

Nothing but trouble: The Ohio Legislature's failed attempts to abolish mayor's courts, Paul Revelson. 35 U Dayton L Rev 223 (Winter 2010).

2937.11 Presentation of state's case; videotaped, recorded, or remote testimony of certain victims

(A)(1) As used in divisions (B) and (C) of this section, "victim" includes any person who was a victim of a felony violation identified in division (B) of this section or a felony offense of violence or against whom was directed any conduct that constitutes, or that is an element of, a felony violation identified in division (B) of this section or a felony offense of violence.

(2) As used in division (D) of this section, "victim" means any person who is less than sixteen years of age and who was a victim of a violation of section 2905.32 of the Revised Code or against whom was directed any conduct that constitutes, or is an element of, a violation of section 2905.32 of the Revised Code.

(3) At the preliminary hearing set pursuant to section 2937.10 of the Revised Code and the Criminal Rules, the prosecutor may state, but is not required to state, orally the case for the state and shall then proceed to examine witnesses and introduce exhibits for the state. The accused and the magistrate have full right of cross examination, and the accused has the right of inspection of exhibits prior to their introduction. The hearing shall be conducted under the rules of evidence prevailing in criminal trials generally. On motion of either the state or the accused, witnesses shall be separated and not permitted in the hearing room except when called to testify.

(B) In a case involving an alleged felony violation of section 2905.05, 2905.32, 2907.02, 2907.03, 2907.04, 2907.05, 2907.21, 2907.24, 2907.31, 2907.32, 2907.321, 2907.322, 2907.323, or 2919.22 of the Revised Code or an alleged felony offense of violence and in which an alleged victim of the alleged violation or offense was less than thirteen years of age when the complaint or information was filed, whichever occurred earlier, upon motion of the prosecution, the testimony of the child victim at the preliminary hearing may be taken in a room other than the room in which the preliminary hearing is being conducted and be televised, by closed circuit equipment, into the room in which the preliminary hearing is being conducted, in accordance with division (C) of section 2945.481 of the Revised Code.

(C) In a case involving an alleged felony violation listed in division (B) of this section or an alleged felony offense of violence and in which an alleged victim of the alleged violation or offense was less than thirteen years of age when the complaint or information was filed, whichever occurred earlier, the court, on written motion of the prosecutor in the case filed at least three days prior to the hearing, shall order that all testimony of the child victim be recorded and preserved on videotape, in addition to being recorded for purposes of the transcript of the proceeding. If such an order is issued, it shall specifically identify the child victim concerning whose testimony it pertains, apply only during the testimony of the child victim it specifically identifies, and apply to all testimony of the child victim presented at the hearing, regardless of whether the child victim is called as a witness by the prosecution or by the defense.

(D)(1)(a) In a case involving an alleged violation of section 2905.32 of the Revised Code, upon motion of the prosecution, the testimony of the victim at the preliminary hearing may be taken in a place or room other than the room in which the preliminary hearing is being conducted and be televised, by closed circuit equipment, into the room in which the preliminary hearing is being conducted, to be viewed by the accused and any other persons who are not permitted in the room in which the testimony is to be taken but who would have been present during the testimony of the victim had it been given in the room in which the preliminary hearing is being conducted. Except for good cause shown, the prosecution shall file a motion under this division at least seven days before the date of the preliminary hearing.

(b) Upon the motion of the prosecution filed under division (D)(1)(a) of this section and if the judge or magistrate determines that the victim is unavailable to testify in the room in which the preliminary hearing is being conducted in the physical presence of the accused for one or more of the reasons set forth in division (D)(2) of this section, the judge or magistrate may issue an order for the testimony of the victim to be taken in a place or room other than the room in which the preliminary hearing is being conducted and televised, by closed circuit equipment, into the room in which the preliminary hearing is being conducted. If a judge or magistrate issues an order of that nature, the judge or magistrate shall exclude from the room in which the testimony of the victim is to be taken every person except the following:

(i) The victim giving the testimony;

(ii) The judge or magistrate;

(iii) One or more interpreters if needed;

(iv) The attorneys for the prosecution and the defense;

(v) Any person needed to operate the equipment to be used;

(vi) One person chosen by the victim giving the testimony;

(vii) Any person whose presence the judge or magistrate determines would contribute to the welfare and well-being of the victim giving the testimony.

(c) The person chosen by the victim under division (D)(1)(b)(vi) of this section shall not be a witness in the preliminary hearing and, both before and during the testimony, shall not discuss the testimony of the victim with any other witness in the preliminary hearing.

(d) The judge or magistrate, at the judge's or magistrate's discretion, may preside during the giving of the testimony by electronic means from outside the room in which it is being given, subject to the limitations set forth in this division. If the judge or magistrate presides by electronic means, the judge or magistrate shall be provided with monitors on which the judge or magistrate can see each person in the room in which the testimony is to be taken and with an electronic means of communication with each person, and each person in the room shall be provided with a monitor on which that person can see the judge or magistrate and with an electronic means of communication with the judge or magistrate. To the extent feasible, any person operating the televising equipment shall be restricted to a room adjacent to the room in which the testimony is being taken, or to a location in the room in which the testimony is being taken that is behind a screen or mirror, so that the person operating the televising equipment can see and hear, but cannot be seen or heard by, the victim giving the testimony during the testimony. The accused shall be permitted to observe and hear the testimony of the victim giving the testimony on a monitor, shall be provided with an electronic means of immediate communication with the attorney of the accused during the testimony, and shall be restricted to a location from which the accused cannot be seen or heard by the victim giving the testimony, except on a monitor provided for that purpose. The accused and the judge or magistrate have full right of cross examination, and the accused has the right of inspection of exhibits prior to their introduction. The victim giving the testimony shall be provided with a monitor on which the victim can observe the accused during the testimony.

(2) For purposes of division (D)(1) of this section, a judge or magistrate may order the testimony of a victim to be taken at a place or room outside the room in which the preliminary hearing is being conducted if the judge or magistrate determines that the victim is unavailable to testify in the room in the physical presence of the accused due to one or more of the following:

(a) The inability of the victim to communicate about the alleged offense because of extreme fear, severe trauma, or another similar reason;

(b) The substantial likelihood that the victim will suffer serious emotional trauma from so testifying;

(c) The victim is at a hospital for care and treatment for any physical, mental, or emotional injury suffered by reason of the alleged offense.

(2014 H 130, eff. 6-20-14; 1997 S 53, eff. 10–14–97; 1996 H 445, eff. 9–3–96; 1986 H 108, eff. 10–14–86; 128 v 97)

Historical and Statutory Notes

Amendment Note: 2014 H 130 inserted "divisions (B) and (C) of" after "As used in" in division (A)(1); added new division (A)(2); redesignated former division (A)(2) as division (A)(3); inserted "2905.32," after "2905.05," in division (B); and added division (D).

Research References

Treatises and Practice Aids

Katz & Giannelli, Baldwin's Ohio Practice Criminal Law § 38:9, Rules of Evidence.

Katz & Giannelli, Baldwin's Ohio Practice Criminal Law § 38:10, Illegally Obtained Evidence.

Giannelli & Yeomans Salvador, Ohio Juvenile Law App. A, Ohio Revised Code--Selected Provisions.

2937.16 When witnesses shall be recognized to appear

Law Review and Journal Commentaries

A reasonable detention? Rethinking the material witness statute's probable cause standard after Al-Kidd. Hallie T. Damon, 44 Colum. Hum. Rts. L. Rev. 537 (2013).

2937.17 Recognizance for minor

Law Review and Journal Commentaries

A reasonable detention? Rethinking the material witness statute's probable cause standard after Al-Kidd. Hallie T. Damon, 44 Colum. Hum. Rts. L. Rev. 537 (2013).

2937.18 Detention of material witnesses

Law Review and Journal Commentaries

A reasonable detention? Rethinking the material witness statute's probable cause standard after Al-Kidd. Hallie T. Damon, 44 Colum. Hum. Rts. L. Rev. 537 (2013).

BAIL

2937.22 Forms of bail; surcharge; receipt

(A) Bail is security for the appearance of an accused to appear and answer to a specific criminal or quasi-criminal charge in any court or before any magistrate at a specific time or at any time to which a case may be continued, and not depart without leave. It may take any of the following forms:

(1) The deposit of cash by the accused or by some other person for the accused;

(2) The deposit by the accused or by some other person for the accused in form of bonds of the United States, this state, or any political subdivision thereof in a face amount equal to the sum set by the court or magistrate. In case of bonds not negotiable by delivery such bonds shall be properly endorsed for transfer.

(3) The written undertaking by one or more persons to forfeit the sum of money set by the court or magistrate, if the accused is in default for appearance, which shall be known as a recognizance.

(B) Whenever a person is charged with any offense other than a traffic offense that is not a moving violation and posts bail, the person shall pay a surcharge of twenty-five dollars. The clerk of the court shall retain the twenty-five dollars until the person is convicted, pleads guilty, forfeits bail, is found not guilty, or has the charges dismissed. If the person is convicted, pleads guilty, or forfeits bail, the clerk shall transmit the twenty-five dollars on or before the twentieth day of the month following the month in which the person was convicted, pleaded guilty, or forfeited bail to the treasurer of state, and the treasurer of state shall deposit it into the indigent defense support fund created under section 120.08 of the Revised Code. If the person is found not guilty or the charges are dismissed, the clerk shall return the twenty-five dollars to the person.

(C) All bail shall be received by the clerk of the court, deputy clerk of court, or by the magistrate, or by a special referee appointed by the supreme court pursuant to section 2937.46 of the Revised Code, and, except in cases of recognizances, receipt shall be given therefor.

(D) As used in this section, "moving violation" has the same meaning as in section 2743.70 of the Revised Code.

(2009 H 1, eff. 10-16-09; 128 v 97, eff. 1–1–60)

Historical and Statutory Notes

Amendment Note: 2009 H 1 designated divisions (A) and (C); redesignated former divisions (A) through (C) as divisions (A)(1) through (A)(3); added divisions (B) and (D); and made other nonsubstantive changes.

Research References

Encyclopedias

OH Jur. 3d Criminal Law: Procedure § 728, Definitions.

OH Jur. 3d Criminal Law: Procedure § 729, Purpose and Effect.

OH Jur. 3d Criminal Law: Procedure § 743, Generally; Upon Arrest or Appearance.

OH Jur. 3d Criminal Law: Procedure § 761, Receipt of Bail and Recognizance; Who Authorized.

OH Jur. 3d Criminal Law: Procedure § 767, Forms of Bail, Generally.

OH Jur. 3d Criminal Law: Procedure § 778, Generally; Requirements of Bonds.

OH Jur. 3d Criminal Law: Procedure § 788, Bases of Forfeiture.

Treatises and Practice Aids

Katz & Giannelli, Baldwin's Ohio Practice Criminal Law § 37:1, Introduction.

Katz & Giannelli, Baldwin's Ohio Practice Criminal Law § 37:6, Types of Pretrial Release.

Notes of Decisions

Purpose 1.3

1.3. Purpose

Bail ensures appearance; therefore, the conditions placed on it must relate to appearance and the reasons for forfeiture to nonappearance. State ex rel. Sylvester v. Neal (Ohio, 07-08-2014) 140 Ohio St.3d 47, 14 N.E.3d 1024, 2014-Ohio-2926. Bail ⚷ 42.5; Bail ⚷ 75.2(1)

2937.221 Use of driver's or commercial driver's license as bond in certain traffic violation arrests

(A) A person arrested without warrant for any violation listed in division (B) of this section, and having a current valid Ohio driver's or commercial driver's license, if the person has been notified of the possible consequences of the person's actions as required by division (C) of this section, may post bond by depositing the license with the arresting officer if the officer and person so choose, or with the local court having jurisdiction if the court and person so choose. The license may be used as bond only during the period for which it is valid.

When an arresting officer accepts the driver's or commercial driver's license as bond, the officer shall note the date, time, and place of the court appearance on "the violator's notice to appear," and the notice shall serve as a valid Ohio driver's or commercial driver's license until the date and time appearing thereon. The arresting officer immediately shall forward the license to the appropriate court.

When a local court accepts the license as bond or continues the case to another date and time, it shall provide the person with a card in a form approved by the registrar of motor vehicles setting forth the license number, name, address, the date and time of the court appearance, and a statement that the license is being held as bond. The card shall serve as a valid license until the date and time contained in the card.

The court may accept other bond at any time and return the license to the person. The court shall return the license to the person when judgment is satisfied, including, but not limited to, compliance with any court orders, unless a suspension or cancellation is part of the penalty imposed.

Neither "the violator's notice to appear" nor a court- granted card shall continue driving privileges beyond the expiration date of the license.

If the person arrested fails to appear in court at the date and time set by the court or fails to satisfy the judgment of the court, including, but not limited to, compliance with all court orders within the time allowed by the court, the court may declare the forfeiture of the person's license. Thirty days after the declaration of the forfeiture, the court shall forward the person's license to the registrar. The court also shall enter information relative to the forfeiture on a form approved and furnished by the registrar and send the form to the registrar. The registrar shall suspend the person's license and send written notification of the suspension to the person at the person's last known address. No valid driver's or commercial driver's license shall be granted to the person until the court having jurisdiction orders that the forfeiture be terminated. The court shall inform the registrar of the termination of the forfeiture by entering information relative to the termination on a form approved and furnished by the registrar and sending the form to the registrar. Upon the termination, the person shall pay to the bureau of motor vehicles a reinstatement fee of fifteen dollars to cover the costs of the bureau in administering this section. The registrar shall deposit the fees so paid into the state bureau of motor vehicles fund created by section 4501.25 of the Revised Code.

In addition, upon receipt from the court of the copy of the declaration of forfeiture, neither the registrar nor any deputy registrar shall accept any application for the registration or transfer of registration of any motor vehicle owned by or leased in the name of the person named in the declaration of forfeiture until the court having jurisdiction over the offense that led to the suspension issues an order terminating the forfeiture. However, for a motor vehicle leased in the name of a person named in a declaration of forfeiture, the registrar shall not implement the preceding sentence until the registrar adopts procedures for that implementation under section 4503.39 of the Revised Code. Upon receipt by the registrar of such an order, the registrar also shall take the measures necessary to permit the person to register a motor vehicle the person owns or leases or to transfer the registration of a motor vehicle the person owns or leases if the person later makes a proper application and otherwise is eligible to be issued or to transfer a motor vehicle registration.

(B) Division (A) of this section applies to persons arrested for violation of:

(1) Any of the provisions of Chapter 4511. or 4513. of the Revised Code, except sections 4511.19, 4511.20, 4511.251, and 4513.36 of the Revised Code;

(2) Any municipal ordinance substantially similar to a section included in division (B)(1) of this section;

(3) Any bylaw, rule, or regulation of the Ohio turnpike and infrastructure commission substantially similar to a section included in division (B)(1) of this section.

Division (A) of this section does not apply to those persons issued a citation for the commission of a minor misdemeanor under section 2935.26 of the Revised Code.

(C) No license shall be accepted as bond by an arresting officer or by a court under this section until the officer or court has notified the person that, if the person deposits the license with the officer or court and either does not appear on the date and at the time set by the officer or the court, if the court sets a time, or does not satisfy any judgment rendered, including, but not limited to, compliance with all court orders, the license will be suspended, and the person will not be eligible for reissuance of the license or issuance of a new license, or the issuance of a certificate of registration for a motor vehicle owned or leased by the person until the person appears and complies with any order issued by the court. The person also is subject to any criminal penalties that may apply to the person.

(D) The registrar shall not restore the person's driving or vehicle registration privileges until the person pays the reinstatement fee as provided in this section.

(2013 H 51, eff. 7-1-13; 2004 H 230, eff. 9–16–04; 2002 S 123, eff. 1–1–04; 1997 S 85, eff. 5–15–97; 1996 S 121, eff. 11–19–96; 1996 H 353, eff. 9–17–96; 1994 H 687, eff. 10–12–94; 1989 S 49, eff. 11–3–89; 1989 H 381; 1986 S 356; 1978 S 351; 1975 H 1; 1973 H 234)

Historical and Statutory Notes

Amendment Note: 2013 H 51 inserted "and infrastructure" in division (B)(3).

Research References

Encyclopedias

OH Jur. 3d Criminal Law: Procedure § 767, Forms of Bail, Generally.

OH Jur. 3d Criminal Law: Procedure § 771, Notice or Card as Temporary License.

OH Jur. 3d Criminal Law: Procedure § 772, Failure to Appear or Satisfy Judgment.

OH Jur. 3d Criminal Law: Substantive Principles and Offenses § 1295, Bail and Security.

Treatises and Practice Aids

Katz & Giannelli, Baldwin's Ohio Practice Criminal Law § 37:6, Types of Pretrial Release.

Weiler & Weiler, Ohio Driving Under the Influence App. C, Ohio Traffic Rules.

2937.27 Duties of county recorder

The county recorder of the county in which the property of a surety on a recognizance is located, shall keep and file in the official records all notices of lien and notices of discharge that are filed with the county recorder pursuant to section 2937.26 of the Revised Code. When a lien has been released or discharged for a period of one year, the county recorder may destroy all notices of such lien. The county recorder may use any nonpaper electronic or magnetic medium specified in section 9.01 of the Revised Code to record the notices of lien and the notices of discharge. If the county recorder wishes to dispose of paper versions of the notices because they are no longer needed in that format, the county recorder shall request the county records commission to revise the county's schedule of records retention and disposal in accordance with section 149.38 of the Revised Code to provide for the disposal of those paper records.

(2013 H 72, eff. 1-30-14; 129 v 1033, eff. 10–26–61; 1953 H 1; GC 13435–7)

Historical and Statutory Notes

Amendment Note: 2013 H 72 rewrote this section, which prior thereto read:

"The county recorder of the county in which the property of a surety on a recognizance is located, shall keep and file all notices of lien and notices of discharge which are filed with him pursuant to section 2937.26 of the Revised Code, and shall keep in addition thereto, a book or record in which he shall index notice of liens and notice of discharges, as they are filed with him. When a lien has been released or discharged for a period of one year, the county recorder may destroy all notices of such lien."

Research References

Encyclopedias

OH Jur. 3d Criminal Law: Procedure § 786, Lien.

Treatises and Practice Aids

Painter & Pollis, Ohio Appellate Practice App. P, Ohio Revised Code.

Kuehnle & Levey, Ohio Real Estate Law and Practice § 10:29, Recognizance Bonds.

Kuehnle & Levey, Ohio Real Estate Law and Practice § 10:31, Supersedeas Bonds on Appeal.

2937.35 Forfeit of bail

Notes of Decisions

1. Forfeiture proceedings; grounds

Bond surety's appeal was not from nonfinal order forfeiting accused's bail in form of surety bond, but from judgment against surety to remit payment on bond following forfeiture, for purposes of time for filing appeal. Dept. of Liquor Control v. Calvert (Ohio App. 6 Dist., 09-02-2011) 195 Ohio App.3d 627, 961 N.E.2d 247, 2011-Ohio-4735. Criminal Law ⚿ 1023(3)

Even if trial court's initial forfeiture determination as to defendant's bail bond in the amount of $10,000.00 was correct, upon defendant's failure to appear for final pretrial hearing, entry of judgment against defendant after the court sua sponte advanced show cause hearing was erroneous, where defendant was never given actual notice of the change in dates, and minimal delay resulted, the defendant having appealed and entered a plea to the drug charges 18 days after the judgment forfeiting the bond was filed by the trial court. State v. Bryson (Ohio App. 5 Dist., Stark, 01-22-2008) No. 2007-CA-00108, No. 2007-CA-00132, 2008-Ohio-193, 2008 WL 188118, Unreported. Bail ⚿ 77(2)

Trial court did not abuse its discretion at bond-forfeiture hearing in failing to grant surety additional time to secure criminal defendant's attendance, though defendant was arrested within the time-frame of continuance requested by surety, where defendant had previously failed to appear for scheduled trial on multicount felony indictment, and surety presented no evidence at bond-forfeiture hearing of defendant's whereabouts or surety's efforts to locate him. State v. Slider (Ohio App. 4 Dist., 08-12-2009) 184 Ohio App.3d 68, 919 N.E.2d 775, 2009-Ohio-4179. Bail ⚿ 79(2)

2937.36 Forfeiture proceedings

Upon declaration of forfeiture, the magistrate or clerk of the court adjudging forfeiture shall proceed as follows:

(A) As to each bail, the magistrate or clerk shall proceed forthwith to deal with the sum deposited as if the same were imposed as a fine for the offense charged and distribute and account for the same accordingly provided that prior to so doing, the magistrate or clerk may satisfy accrued costs in the case out of the fund.

(B) As to any securities deposited, the magistrate or clerk shall proceed to sell the same, either at public sale advertised in the same manner as sale on chattel execution, or through any state or national bank performing such service upon the over the counter securities market and shall apply proceeds of sale, less costs or brokerage thereof as in cases of forfeited cash bail. Prior to such sale, the clerk shall give notices by ordinary mail to the depositor, at the depositor's address listed of record, if any, of the intention so to do, and such sale shall not proceed if the depositor, within ten days of mailing of such notice appears, and redeems said securities by either producing the body of the defendant in open court or posting the amount set in the recognizance in cash, to be dealt with as forfeited cash bail.

(C) As to recognizances the magistrate or clerk shall notify the accused and each surety within fifteen days after the declaration of the forfeiture by ordinary mail at the address shown by them in their affidavits of qualification or on the record of the case, of the default of the accused and the adjudication of forfeiture and require each of them to show cause on or before a date certain to be stated in the notice, and which shall be not less than forty-five nor more than sixty days from the date of mailing notice, why judgment should not be entered against each of them for the penalty stated in the recognizance. If good cause by production of the body of the accused or otherwise is not shown, the court or magistrate shall thereupon enter judgment against the sureties or either of them, so notified, in such amount, not exceeding the penalty of the bond, as has been set in the adjudication of forfeiture, and shall award execution therefor as in civil cases. The proceeds of sale shall be received by the clerk or magistrate and distributed as on forfeiture of cash bail.

(2011 H 86, eff. 9-30-11; 128 v 97, eff. 1-1-60)

Historical and Statutory Notes

Amendment Note: 2011 H 86 inserted "within fifteen days after the declaration of the forfeiture" in division (C); substituted "forty-five" for "twenty" and "sixty" for "thirty" in division (C); made changes to reflect gender neutral language; and made other nonsubstantive changes.

Research References

Encyclopedias

OH Jur. 3d Criminal Law: Procedure § 788, Bases of Forfeiture.

OH Jur. 3d Criminal Law: Procedure § 789, Adjudication of Forfeiture on Cash Bail and 10% Bonds; Disposition of Funds.

OH Jur. 3d Criminal Law: Procedure § 790, Proceedings for Forfeiture of Securities.

OH Jur. 3d Criminal Law: Procedure § 791, Proceedings for Forfeiture of Recognizances.

OH Jur. 3d Criminal Law: Procedure § 793, Discharge or Exoneration of Sureties; Defenses.

OH Jur. 3d Criminal Law: Procedure § 2192, Orders Pertaining to Arrest and Bail.

Treatises and Practice Aids

Katz & Giannelli, Baldwin's Ohio Practice Criminal Law § 37:18, Financial Responsibility of Sureties.

Katz & Giannelli, Baldwin's Ohio Practice Criminal Law § 139:14, Entry for Recognizance Forfeited.

Katz & Giannelli, Baldwin's Ohio Practice Criminal Law § 139:15, Notice to Defendant Upon Forfeiture of Bond.

Katz & Giannelli, Baldwin's Ohio Practice Criminal Law § 139:16, Entry of Judgment Against Surety.

Notes of Decisions

Bond conditions 6

---

1. Forfeiture proceedings; grounds

Judgment against bond surety for forfeiture of bond after accused failed to appear for sentencing was not abuse of discretion due to trial court's failure to strictly comply with requirement that hearing on bond forfeiture be held not less than 20 nor more than 30 days from date notice was mailed and requirement that notice also be mailed to accused; surety did not argue that she did not receive notice or that she was prejudiced by noncompliance, and she failed to show good cause for accused's nonappearance as reason why bond should not be forfeited. Dept. of Liquor Control v. Calvert (Ohio App. 6 Dist., 09-02-2011) 195 Ohio App.3d 627, 961 N.E.2d 247, 2011-Ohio-4735. Bail ⚿ 77(1)

In judgment against bond surety for forfeiture of bond after accused failed to appear for sentencing hearing, trial court had to specify amount of bond forfeited. Dept. of Liquor Control v. Calvert (Ohio App. 6 Dist., 09-02-2011) 195 Ohio App.3d 627, 961 N.E.2d 247, 2011-Ohio-4735. Bail ⚿ 77(2)

Notice to surety of show-cause hearing 35 days prior to hearing, rather than statutorily mandated 45 to 60 days, did not prejudice surety, and therefore did not preclude forfeiture of recognizance bonds, where surety received notice and filed a written response, surety appeared at hearing and informed court that she was unable to produce the defendant due to defendant's incarceration in a different state, and providing surety with additional time would not have permitted surety to produce defendant. State v. Lott (Ohio App. 1 Dist., 08-06-2014) 17 N.E.3d 1167, 2014-Ohio-3404. Bail ⚿ 79(1)

The trial court's failure to provide surety with the statutorily required notice of at least 20 days before conducting bond forfeiture hearing did not prejudice surety, where surety and defendant both appeared at the bond forfeiture hearing. Toledo v. Floyd (Ohio App. 6 Dist., 10-16-2009) 185 Ohio App.3d 27, 923 N.E.2d 159, 2009-Ohio-5507. Bail ⚿ 77(1)

Trial court erred when it ordered the forfeiture of bonds, where defendant appeared with surety at bond forfeiture hearing. Toledo v. Floyd (Ohio App. 6 Dist., 10-16-2009) 185 Ohio App.3d 27, 923 N.E.2d 159, 2009-Ohio-5507. Bail ⚿ 75.2(1)

4. Remission of forfeiture

Bond surety's appeal was not from nonfinal order forfeiting accused's bail in form of surety bond, but from judgment against surety to remit payment on bond following forfeiture, for purposes of time for filing appeal. Dept. of Liquor Control v. Calvert (Ohio App. 6 Dist., 09-02-2011) 195 Ohio App.3d 627, 961 N.E.2d 247, 2011-Ohio-4735. Criminal Law ⚿ 1023(3)

Surety was entitled to full remission of $2500 bond that was forfeited for defendant's failure to appear at court hearing; although defendant's reappearance occurred after rearrest and surety did not contribute to the reappearance, defendant was arrested only one day after court sent it notice of defendant's nonappearance, and defendant had already appeared and pleaded guilty prior to surety's show cause hearing, reappearance occurred less than two weeks after the failure to appear, defendant asserted he was unable to appear due to death in family, and the absence did not cause inconvenience or expense to the state. Youngstown v. Durrett (Ohio App. 7 Dist., Mahoning, 03-26-2010) No. 09 MA 57, 2010-Ohio-1313, 2010 WL 1208300, Unreported. Bail ⚷ 79(1)

6. Bond conditions

The impossibility of performance of a condition of bond must have been unforeseeable at the time the surety entered into the contract in order to exonerate the surety. State v. Lott (Ohio App. 1 Dist., 08-06-2014) 17 N.E.3d 1167, 2014-Ohio-3404. Bail ⚷ 79(1)

A surety may be exonerated of breach of a condition of bond where performance of the conditions in the bond is rendered impossible by an act of law. State v. Lott (Ohio App. 1 Dist., 08-06-2014) 17 N.E.3d 1167, 2014-Ohio-3404. Bail ⚷ 79(1)

Defendant's subsequent incarceration in a different state for a probation violation warranted forfeiture of recognizance bonds posted in Ohio, where trial court did not permit defendant to leave the jurisdiction, defendant left Ohio to report to his probation officer without seeking the trial court's permission, and defendant violated condition of his bond by leaving Ohio. State v. Lott (Ohio App. 1 Dist., 08-06-2014) 17 N.E.3d 1167, 2014-Ohio-3404. Bail ⚷ 75.1

2937.39 Remission of penalty

Notes of Decisions

2. Judicial discretion

Trial court denial of bail bond company's motion for remittitur was not an abuse of discretion; it took company eight months to recapture defendant, the State was delayed and inconvenienced by defendant's disappearance, the trial court noted that company assisted defendant with bond even though he had no ties to the community, he was a two-time convicted felon, and he had different felonies pending, and that the information company took from defendant only stated that he was a black male and was 22 years old and did not include a description of defendant, a photograph, an address, or a telephone number, and the court could consider company's bonding practices in rendering its decision. State v. Smith (Ohio App. 7 Dist., Jefferson, 09-01-2006) No. 05 JE 49, 2006-Ohio-4614, 2006 WL 2574582, Unreported. Bail ⚷ 79(1)

2937.40 Release of bail and sureties; use to satisfy fine or costs only when deposited by accused

Notes of Decisions

1. Use of deposit

Request for writ of prohibition preventing juvenile court judges from applying appearance bond funds to child-support arrearages was moot, where court had changed policy to require release of funds to the person posting the bond if a defendant appeared in court. Denton v. Bedinghaus (Ohio App. 1 Dist., Hamilton, 06-28-2002) No. C-000819, 2002-Ohio-3273, 2002 WL 1393563, Unreported, affirmed 98 Ohio St.3d 298, 784 N.E.2d 99, 2003-Ohio-861. Prohibition ⚷ 13

2. Defenses to forfeiture

Surety was not entitled to remission of forfeiture of bail bond; after failing to appear at trial and forfeiture hearing, defendant did not subsequently appear, did not surrender, and was not re-arrested. Toledo v. Gaston (Ohio App. 6 Dist., 07-09-2010) 188 Ohio App.3d 241, 935 N.E.2d 92, 2010-Ohio-3217. Judgment ⚷ 343

4. Payment into court after default

Under statute governing release of bail and sureties, payment of sums ordered in order of forfeiture of bail bond, not court's declaration of forfeiture, is the event triggering release and discharge of obligations of a surety under a bail bond. Toledo v. Gaston (Ohio App. 6 Dist., 07-09-2010) 188 Ohio App.3d 241, 935 N.E.2d 92, 2010-Ohio-3217. Bail ⚷ 74(1)

Order requiring payment of forfeited bail bond to clerk of court within 30 days did not result in discharge of bond, and thus bond remained in effect at the time defendant failed to appear for trial; payment of sums ordered in order of forfeiture was event triggering release and discharge of surety's obligations, and order was vacated before payment was made. Toledo v. Gaston (Ohio App. 6 Dist., 07-09-2010) 188 Ohio App.3d 241, 935 N.E.2d 92, 2010-Ohio-3217. Bail ⚷ 74(1)

2937.41 Return of bail; notice of discharge of recognizance

Notes of Decisions

1. Forfeiture proceedings

Surety was not entitled to remission of forfeiture of bail bond; after failing to appear at trial and forfeiture hearing, defendant did not subsequently appear, did not surrender, and was not re-arrested. Toledo v. Gaston (Ohio App. 6 Dist., 07-09-2010) 188 Ohio App.3d 241, 935 N.E.2d 92, 2010-Ohio-3217. Judgment ⚯ 343

CHAPTER 2938

TRIAL—MAGISTRATE COURTS

PRELIMINARY PROVISIONS

PRELIMINARY PROVISIONS

2938.03 Setting and continuing cases; assignment of additional judges

Notes of Decisions

2. Continuances

Trial court denial of defendant's second request for a continuance was not an abuse of discretion, during prosecution for aggravated murder; when the trial court granted defendant's first request for a continuance it impressed upon the parties the date scheduled for trial, defendant filed her second request for continuance on the day trial was scheduled to begin based on counsel and witnesses being on vacation and the need for additional time to prepare expert witness, the trial court noted that the first continuance had been granted in part because expert was not available for trial and to provide additional time for expert to prepare for trial, and the court found that additional delay would substantially interrupt the court's docket and would inconvenience the 60 jurors waiting to be impaneled and the numerous witnesses subpoenaed for trial. State v. Prom (Ohio App. 12 Dist., Butler, 05-09-2005) No. CA2004-07-174, 2005-Ohio-2272, 2005 WL 1077238, Unreported, appeal not allowed 106 Ohio St.3d 1536, 835 N.E.2d 384, 2005-Ohio-5146, reconsideration denied 107 Ohio St.3d 1686, 839 N.E.2d 405, 2005-Ohio-6480, habeas corpus denied 2009 WL 1270463. Criminal Law ⚯ 614(1)

Trial court acted within its discretion in denying defendant's request for continuance to secure the appearance of two witnesses, where there was no indication that any additional time would have produced the desired witnesses. State v. Braddy (Ohio App. 8 Dist., Cuyahoga, 06-17-2004) No. 83462, 2004-Ohio-3128, 2004 WL 1364730, Unreported, motion to reopen denied 2005-Ohio-282, 2005 WL 174771, motion for delayed appeal denied 106 Ohio St.3d 1458, 830 N.E.2d 1167, 2005-Ohio-3490, denial of post-conviction relief affirmed 2012-Ohio-4720, 2012 WL 4848992, appeal not allowed 134 Ohio St.3d 1453, 982 N.E.2d 729, 2013-Ohio-347, habeas corpus denied 2014 WL 4285632. Criminal Law ⚯ 594(3)

JURIES

2938.04 Jury trial

Notes of Decisions

2. Jury demand; waiver of jury trial

Defendant validly waived his right to jury trial, even though waiver was not signed in open court and waiver may not have been filed until trial was over; trial court conducted lengthy colloquy with defendant regarding his waiver of jury trial at forefront of trial, and waiver was in writing, signed by defendant, filed and journalized in the case, and made a part of the record. State v. Kiriazis (Ohio App. 8 Dist., Cuyahoga, 02-05-2004) No. 82887, 2004-Ohio-502, 2004 WL 231478, Unreported, appeal not allowed 102 Ohio St.3d 1485, 810 N.E.2d 968, 2004-Ohio-3069, habeas corpus denied 2007 WL 4355355, affirmed 410 Fed.Appx. 958, 2011 WL 504191. Jury ⚷ 29(6)

Defendant's waiver of his right to a jury trial was voluntary and intelligent; defendant signed a written jury waiver form, which was filed and journalized, when trial court accepted the written waiver, defendant affirmed that his decision was voluntary, he also affirmed that his counsel had reviewed the waiver form with him and that he had discussed his decision with them, and his decision to waive a jury trial followed from his decision to plead guilty. State v. Fitzpatrick (Ohio, 07-07-2004) 102 Ohio St.3d 321, 810 N.E.2d 927, 2004-Ohio-3167, reconsideration denied 103 Ohio St.3d 1429, 814 N.E.2d 491, 2004-Ohio-4524, denial of post-conviction relief affirmed 2004-Ohio-5615, 2004 WL 2367987, appeal not allowed 105 Ohio St.3d 1499, 825 N.E.2d 623, 2005-Ohio-1666, motion to reopen denied 105 Ohio St.3d 1436, 822 N.E.2d 808, 2005-Ohio-531, certiorari denied 125 S.Ct. 2930, 545 U.S. 1130, 162 L.Ed.2d 869, habeas corpus denied 2009 WL 3734143, certificate of appealability granted in part, denied in part 2010 WL 2761578, affirmed 723 F.3d 624, certiorari denied 134 S.Ct. 1939, 188 L.Ed.2d 965. Jury ⚷ 29(6)

Petitioner intelligently consented to waiver of jury, in favor of three-judge panel, for capital murder trial; counsel did not promise, or state as matter of law, that petitioner would not be sentenced to death by panel, and despite petitioner's intellectual limitations, he understood risks involved. Sowell v. Bradshaw (C.A.6 (Ohio), 06-23-2004) 372 F.3d 821, rehearing en banc denied, certiorari denied 125 S.Ct. 1645, 544 U.S. 925, 161 L.Ed.2d 485, on remand 557 F.Supp.2d 843. Jury ⚷ 29(6)

State courts were not required to look beyond trial court's colloquy with petitioner, and petitioner's written waiver, in determining that petitioner intelligently consented to waive jury for capital murder trial, since petitioner presented no evidence to rebut presumption that proceeding on record was valid. Sowell v. Bradshaw (C.A.6 (Ohio), 06-23-2004) 372 F.3d 821, rehearing en banc denied, certiorari denied 125 S.Ct. 1645, 544 U.S. 925, 161 L.Ed.2d 485, on remand 557 F.Supp.2d 843. Jury ⚷ 29(6)

While defendant may be deemed sufficiently informed to make intelligent waiver of right to jury trial if he is aware that jury is composed of 12 members of community, he may participate in their selection, verdict must be unanimous, and that judge alone will decide guilt or innocence upon waiver of jury, such elements are not constitutionally required. Sowell v. Bradshaw (C.A.6 (Ohio), 06-23-2004) 372 F.3d 821, rehearing en banc denied, certiorari denied 125 S.Ct. 1645, 544 U.S. 925, 161 L.Ed.2d 485, on remand 557 F.Supp.2d 843. Jury ⚷ 29(6)

State trial court's failure, during colloquy on petitioner's waiver of jury for capital murder trial, to question petitioner on his understanding of his right to participate in jury selection and requirement of unanimity of recommendation to impose death sentence, or whether anyone had induced him to waive jury, did not render waiver unknowing. Sowell v. Bradshaw (C.A.6 (Ohio), 06-23-2004) 372 F.3d 821, rehearing en banc denied, certiorari denied 125 S.Ct. 1645, 544 U.S. 925, 161 L.Ed.2d 485, on remand 557 F.Supp.2d 843. Jury ⚷ 29(6)

2938.05 Withdrawal of claim of jury

Claim of jury, once made, may be withdrawn by written waiver of jury but in such case the court may, if a jury has been summoned, require accused to pay all costs of mileage and fees of the summoned jurors for one day's service, notwithstanding the outcome of the case. No withdrawal of claim for jury shall effect any re-transfer of a case, once it has been certified to a court of record.

(2012 H 268, eff. 5-22-12; 128 v 97, eff. 1-1-60)

Historical and Statutory Notes

Amendment Note: 2012 H 268 substituted "the summoned jurors" for "members of the venire".

2938.06 Number of jurors; challenges

Notes of Decisions

1. Peremptory challenges

Doctor and clinic gave legitimate, race-neutral bases for exercising peremptory challenge to remove African-American prospective juror from venire in medical malpractice action, which was brought by African-American patient and which arose from alleged negligence during delivery of patient, and thus peremptory challenge was not racially discriminatory; prospective juror was single mother like patient's mother had been at time of patient's birth, prospective juror testified that she had family member or friend who had suffered an injury, and defense counsel did not view prospective juror's occupation as car salesperson as one of the more traditional, conservative occupations. Thompson v. Capaldo (Ohio App. 5 Dist., Richland, 12-03-2008) No. 08 CA 1, 2008-Ohio-6329, 2008 WL 5104760, Unreported, appeal not allowed 121 Ohio St.3d 1452, 904 N.E.2d 901, 2009-Ohio-1820. Jury ⚡ 33(5.15)

Murder defendant failed to prove purposeful discrimination with regard to state's use of peremptory challenges on two black potential jurors, and thus, trial court properly denied defendant's *Batson* objections; state exercised its challenge with respect to jurors on ground that jurors had attitudes that state believed favored defense, at time of state's challenge to second juror, there were four black potential jurors seated, and next replacement juror to take second juror's seat was black. State v. Melvin (Ohio App. 8 Dist., Cuyahoga, 05-12-2005) No. 84471, 2005-Ohio-2329, 2005 WL 1119959, Unreported, motion for delayed appeal granted 106 Ohio St.3d 1530, 835 N.E.2d 380, 2005-Ohio-5146, appeal not allowed 108 Ohio St.3d 1473, 842 N.E.2d 1053, 2006-Ohio-665, habeas corpus dismissed 2008 WL 3166182. Jury ⚡ 33(5.15)

Prosecutor provided sufficient race-neutral explanations for striking two African-American prospective jurors in prosecution for robbery, assault, and receiving stolen property; State removed first juror because he had previously been convicted of theft, a crime of dishonesty, and State removed second juror because of his hypertechnicality. State v. Thomas (Ohio App. 1 Dist., Hamilton, 12-31-2002) No. C-010724, 2002-Ohio-7333, 2002 WL 31894850, Unreported, appeal not allowed 98 Ohio St.3d 1515, 786 N.E.2d 64, 2003-Ohio-1572, on reconsideration 2009-Ohio-971, 2009 WL 565511, stay granted 123 Ohio St.3d 1469, 915 N.E.2d 1252, 2009-Ohio-5704, vacated 124 Ohio St.3d 412, 922 N.E.2d 964, 2010-Ohio-577. Jury ⚡ 33(5.15)

Habeas corpus, peremptory challenge, demeanor based explanation for challenge. Thaler v. Haynes, (U.S., 02-22-2010) 130 S.Ct. 1171.

PRACTICE AND PROCEDURE

2938.08 Presumption of innocence

Notes of Decisions

2. Burden of proof

Argument that residual doubt was not a mitigating factor because all guilt issues had already been decided was a correct statement of Ohio law. Bonnell v. Mitchel (N.D.Ohio, 02-04-2004) 301 F.Supp.2d 698, affirmed 212 Fed.Appx. 517, 2007 WL 62628, certiorari denied 128 S.Ct. 710, 552 U.S. 1064, 169 L.Ed.2d 558. Sentencing And Punishment ⚡ 1780(2)

2938.11 Order of proceedings of trial

Law Review and Journal Commentaries

The use of secret evidence by government lawyers: balancing defendants' rights with national security concerns. Comment, 52 Clev St L Rev 571 (2004–05).

Notes of Decisions

Evidence 1.5

---

1. Procedural statutes as guidelines

Statute providing that any finding by trial court judge or magistrate in criminal proceeding shall be announced in open court not more than 48 hours after submission of the case to him is directory, not mandatory. State ex rel. Martin v. Mannen (Ohio, 05-16-2007) 113 Ohio St.3d 373, 865 N.E.2d 898, 2007-Ohio-2078. Criminal Law ⚡ 255.4

1.5. Evidence

Witness's testimony about what defendant allegedly told her about shooting was not proper rebuttal evidence, where the evidence the State called witness to rebut was not new facts introduced by defendant in her case-in-chief, but testimony elicited by the State in its cross-examination of defendant. State v. Carrasquillo (Ohio App. 9 Dist., Lorain, 10-18-2010) No. 09CA009639, 2010-Ohio-5063, 2010 WL 4056127, Unreported. Criminal Law ⚯ 683(1)

By letting witness testify about what defendant allegedly told her about shooting, a matter defendant had not raised in her case-in-chief, trial court essentially let the State reopen its case, and thus trial court should have let defendant reopen her case-in-chief to call two witnesses to challenge the new evidence. State v. Carrasquillo (Ohio App. 9 Dist., Lorain, 10-18-2010) No. 09CA009639, 2010-Ohio-5063, 2010 WL 4056127, Unreported. Criminal Law ⚯ 686(2)

Trial court's error, in refusing to let two witnesses testify to challenge new evidence offered when State reopened its case-in-chief, affected defendant's substantial rights, warranting reversal of conviction and retrial. State v. Carrasquillo (Ohio App. 9 Dist., Lorain, 10-18-2010) No. 09CA009639, 2010-Ohio-5063, 2010 WL 4056127, Unreported. Criminal Law ⚯ 1168(2)

2. Jury instructions

Instructing jury that it must accept stipulated facts as true did not constitute plain error, where defendant could not have been prejudiced by instruction as defendant testified that he was present at crime scene and only question was whether defendant committed certain crimes at scene. State v. McSwain (Ohio App. 8 Dist., Cuyahoga, 06-24-2004) No. 83394, 2004-Ohio-3292, 2004 WL 1402700, Unreported, appeal not allowed 104 Ohio St.3d 1425, 819 N.E.2d 709, 2004-Ohio-6585, certiorari denied 125 S.Ct. 2269, 544 U.S. 1040, 161 L.Ed.2d 1072, on subsequent appeal 2008-Ohio-3661, 2008 WL 2833937, appeal not allowed 120 Ohio St.3d 1457, 898 N.E.2d 970, 2008-Ohio-6813, habeas corpus denied 2011 WL 3490152. Criminal Law ⚯ 1038.1(5)

Claim that trial court deprived defendant of right to jury trial by instructing jury that it must accept stipulated facts as true could only be reviewed for plain error, where defendant failed at trial to object to instruction on stipulations. State v. McSwain (Ohio App. 8 Dist., Cuyahoga, 06-24-2004) No. 83394, 2004-Ohio-3292, 2004 WL 1402700, Unreported, appeal not allowed 104 Ohio St.3d 1425, 819 N.E.2d 709, 2004-Ohio-6585, certiorari denied 125 S.Ct. 2269, 544 U.S. 1040, 161 L.Ed.2d 1072, on subsequent appeal 2008-Ohio-3661, 2008 WL 2833937, appeal not allowed 120 Ohio St.3d 1457, 898 N.E.2d 970, 2008-Ohio-6813, habeas corpus denied 2011 WL 3490152. Criminal Law ⚯ 1038.1(5)

4. Opening and closing statements

Prosecutor's comment during closing argument in a prosecution for possession with intent to distribute pseudoephedrine, asserting that defendant testified he was selling to "buying groups," and that there was no evidence other than from defendant's lips that there were buying groups, was supported by the evidence at trial, and thus, was not improper; defendant was the only person at trial who used the words "buying groups" when testifying, and the records showed no evidence of buying groups. U.S. v. Merkosky (C.A.6 (Ohio), 06-14-2005) No. 02-4332, 135 Fed.Appx. 828, 2005 WL 1400201, Unreported, appeal after new sentencing hearing 237 Fed.Appx. 66, 2007 WL 1880595, post-conviction relief denied 2008 WL 5169640. Criminal Law ⚯ 2111

Prosecutor's comment during rebuttal closing argument that, under defense counsel's own argument to effect that inconsistencies between eyewitness' testimony indicated that they were liars, defense counsel's misspelling of word would make him a liar, did not constitute impermissible denigration of defense counsel, in trial for aggravated murder, murder, and aggravated robbery; rather, prosecutor's comment was in response to defense counsel's assertion that eyewitnesses were liars and to expose weakness in counsel's argument, and prosecutor quickly pointed out that defense counsel was not liar but had simply made mistake. State v. Huges (Ohio App. 1 Dist., Hamilton, 05-20-2005) No. C-030489, 2005-Ohio-2453, 2005 WL 1190715, Unreported, habeas corpus dismissed 2014 WL 4704585. Criminal Law ⚯ 2179

Murder defendant failed to establish ineffective assistance based on trial counsel's failure to give opening statement, where decision to waive opening statement is matter of trial strategy. State v. Fayne (Ohio App. 8 Dist., Cuyahoga, 09-02-2004) No. 83267, 2004-Ohio-4625, 2004 WL 1944793, Unreported, motion for delayed appeal denied 106 Ohio St.3d 1502, 833 N.E.2d 1246, 2005-Ohio-4605, habeas corpus denied 2007 WL 1485812. Criminal Law ⚯ 1942

Prosecutor's closing argument comment that only jury could correct injustices done to victims, when viewed in context of entire argument, was not prejudicial to defendant, who was convicted of kidnapping, aggravated robbery, aggravated burglary, and felonious assault, where such appeal to jury's sympathies was modest and prosecutor asked jury to use reason and common sense. State v. McSwain (Ohio App. 8 Dist., Cuyahoga, 06-24-2004) No. 83394, 2004-Ohio-3292, 2004 WL 1402700, Unreported, appeal not allowed 104 Ohio St.3d 1425, 819 N.E.2d 709, 2004-Ohio-6585, certiorari denied 125 S.Ct. 2269, 544 U.S. 1040, 161 L.Ed.2d 1072, on subsequent appeal 2008-Ohio-3661, 2008 WL 2833937, appeal not allowed 120 Ohio St.3d 1457, 898 N.E.2d 970, 2008-Ohio-6813, habeas corpus denied 2011 WL 3490152. Criminal Law ⚯ 2146

Claim that prosecutor's closing argument comment that only jury could correct injustices done to victims was improper could only be reviewed for plain error, where defendant failed at trial to object to such comment. State v. McSwain (Ohio App. 8 Dist., Cuyahoga, 06-24-2004) No. 83394, 2004-Ohio-3292, 2004 WL 1402700, Unreported, appeal not allowed 104 Ohio St.3d 1425, 819 N.E.2d 709, 2004-Ohio-6585, certiorari denied 125 S.Ct. 2269, 544 U.S. 1040, 161 L.Ed.2d 1072, on subsequent appeal 2008-Ohio-3661, 2008 WL

2833937, appeal not allowed 120 Ohio St.3d 1457, 898 N.E.2d 970, 2008-Ohio-6813, habeas corpus denied 2011 WL 3490152. Criminal Law ⚷ 1037.1(2)

Assuming Fifth Amendment right not to put forth any evidence in corroboration of defendant's testimony exists, prosecutor's closing argument comment that defendant offered version of events that was completely unsupported by anything else did not violate such right, where prosecutor did not comment on defendant's failure to offer corroborating testimony, but simply indicated that defendant's testimony was not consistent with other testimony. State v. McSwain (Ohio App. 8 Dist., Cuyahoga, 06-24-2004) No. 83394, 2004-Ohio-3292, 2004 WL 1402700, Unreported, appeal not allowed 104 Ohio St.3d 1425, 819 N.E.2d 709, 2004-Ohio-6585, certiorari denied 125 S.Ct. 2269, 544 U.S. 1040, 161 L.Ed.2d 1072, on subsequent appeal 2008-Ohio-3661, 2008 WL 2833937, appeal not allowed 120 Ohio St.3d 1457, 898 N.E.2d 970, 2008-Ohio-6813, habeas corpus denied 2011 WL 3490152. Criminal Law ⚷ 2136

Once robbery defendant waived his right against self-incrimination by testifying, his credibility was at issue and could properly be challenged by charge of recent fabrication. State v. McSwain (Ohio App. 8 Dist., Cuyahoga, 06-24-2004) No. 83394, 2004-Ohio-3292, 2004 WL 1402700, Unreported, appeal not allowed 104 Ohio St.3d 1425, 819 N.E.2d 709, 2004-Ohio-6585, certiorari denied 125 S.Ct. 2269, 544 U.S. 1040, 161 L.Ed.2d 1072, on subsequent appeal 2008-Ohio-3661, 2008 WL 2833937, appeal not allowed 120 Ohio St.3d 1457, 898 N.E.2d 970, 2008-Ohio-6813, habeas corpus denied 2011 WL 3490152. Witnesses ⚷ 337(1)

Prosecutor's comments during closing argument of murder trial that defendant should not have escaped punishment for aggravated murder by alleging sudden passion or fit of rage and words alone were not enough to allow someone to escape their punishment for aggravated murder were not prejudicial, where defense counsel objected, trial court sustained objection, and trial court gave a curative instruction. State v. Brandy (Ohio App. 10 Dist., Franklin, 04-10-2003) No. 02AP-832, 2003-Ohio-1836, 2003 WL 1848761, Unreported, appeal not allowed 99 Ohio St.3d 1515, 792 N.E.2d 201, 2003-Ohio-3957, denial of post-conviction relief affirmed 2007-Ohio-1505, 2007 WL 949439, appeal not allowed 114 Ohio St.3d 1511, 872 N.E.2d 952, 2007-Ohio-4285. Criminal Law ⚷ 2209

Prosecutor's characterization of murder defendant as a "drug dealer extraordinaire" was not plain error, where characterization was based on evidence presented at trial during which defendant admitted to a life of drug dealing. State v. Brandy (Ohio App. 10 Dist., Franklin, 04-10-2003) No. 02AP-832, 2003-Ohio-1836, 2003 WL 1848761, Unreported, appeal not allowed 99 Ohio St.3d 1515, 792 N.E.2d 201, 2003-Ohio-3957, denial of post-conviction relief affirmed 2007-Ohio-1505, 2007 WL 949439, appeal not allowed 114 Ohio St.3d 1511, 872 N.E.2d 952, 2007-Ohio-4285. Criminal Law ⚷ 1037.1(2)

Prosecutor's comment during closing argument of murder trial comparing defendant's actions in shooting victim to that of a dog hunting someone or something down, while it may have been a bit harsh, was merely an attempt by the prosecutor to explain to the jury defendant's actions and fell into the latitude afforded counsel during closing argument. State v. Brandy (Ohio App. 10 Dist., Franklin, 04-10-2003) No. 02AP-832, 2003-Ohio-1836, 2003 WL 1848761, Unreported, appeal not allowed 99 Ohio St.3d 1515, 792 N.E.2d 201, 2003-Ohio-3957, denial of post-conviction relief affirmed 2007-Ohio-1505, 2007 WL 949439, appeal not allowed 114 Ohio St.3d 1511, 872 N.E.2d 952, 2007-Ohio-4285. Criminal Law ⚷ 2149

Three comments made by prosecutor during closing arguments, when read in full context, were neither materially prejudicial nor did they deny defendant convicted of murder and possession of cocaine a fair trial, but were an attempt by prosecutor to convince jury that defendant's defense of voluntary manslaughter must be rejected; prosecutor asked jury what else could defendant have said but that his actions were merely voluntary manslaughter, and prosecutor stated that defendant's claim that victim and his wife who were attempting to buy drugs from defendant had time to hide drugs and money on their person or in body cavities was "ridiculous." State v. Brandy (Ohio App. 10 Dist., Franklin, 04-10-2003) No. 02AP-832, 2003-Ohio-1836, 2003 WL 1848761, Unreported, appeal not allowed 99 Ohio St.3d 1515, 792 N.E.2d 201, 2003-Ohio-3957, denial of post-conviction relief affirmed 2007-Ohio-1505, 2007 WL 949439, appeal not allowed 114 Ohio St.3d 1511, 872 N.E.2d 952, 2007-Ohio-4285. Criminal Law ⚷ 1171.1(3)

Defendant failed to object to prosecutor's remarks during closing argument of murder trial and thus waived all but plain error. State v. Brandy (Ohio App. 10 Dist., Franklin, 04-10-2003) No. 02AP-832, 2003-Ohio-1836, 2003 WL 1848761, Unreported, appeal not allowed 99 Ohio St.3d 1515, 792 N.E.2d 201, 2003-Ohio-3957, denial of post-conviction relief affirmed 2007-Ohio-1505, 2007 WL 949439, appeal not allowed 114 Ohio St.3d 1511, 872 N.E.2d 952, 2007-Ohio-4285. Criminal Law ⚷ 1037.1(1)

Prosecutor during closing argument of rape trial did not interject her personal beliefs about the veracity of victim's testimony, but rather merely argued that the evidence supported the theory that victim did not lie or concoct her story of abuse by her father, the defendant, and thus prosecutor did not commit misconduct. State v. Geboy (Ohio App. 3 Dist., 08-30-2001) 145 Ohio App.3d 706, 764 N.E.2d 451, 2001-Ohio-2214, appeal not allowed 94 Ohio St.3d 1410, 759 N.E.2d 787, appeal after new trial 2003-Ohio-343, 2003 WL 178616, appeal not allowed 99 Ohio St.3d 1412, 788 N.E.2d 648, 2003-Ohio-2454, grant of habeas corpus reversed in part 489 F.3d 752. Criminal Law ⚷ 2098(3)

Statement by prosecutor during closing argument in murder prosecution that, while it is fundamental that law be upheld and rights of defendant be recognized, "On the other side of the coin it's just as important to all of us" that victim "did have a right to live," and that "no one has a right to extinguish the lives of others," was proper; comment did not constitute victim impact evidence, but merely pointed out that persons have a right to live and that murder takes away that right. State v. Getsy (Ohio, 12-23-1998) 84 Ohio St.3d 180, 702 N.E.2d 866, 1998-Ohio-533, reconsideration denied 84 Ohio St.3d 1488, 705 N.E.2d 368, certiorari denied 119 S.Ct. 2407, 527 U.S. 1042, 144 L.Ed.2d 805, dismissal of post-conviction relief affirmed 1999 WL 1073682, dismissed, appeal not allowed 88 Ohio St.3d 1425, 723 N.E.2d 1113, habeas corpus granted 456 F.3d 575, rehearing granted, opinion vacated, denial of habeas corpus affirmed 495 F.3d 295. Criminal Law ⚷ 2146

2938.14 Drawing and summoning of jurors in inferior courts

Jurors in courts of record inferior to the court of common pleas shall be drawn and summoned in the manner provided in the various acts creating such courts. But no challenge to the array shall be sustained in any case for the reason that some of the jurors are not residents of the territory of the court, if it appears that the jurors were regularly drawn and certified by the jury commissioners of county or municipality as the case may be.

(2012 H 268, eff. 5-22-12; 129 v 582, eff. 1–10–61; 128 v 97)

Historical and Statutory Notes

Amendment Note: 2012 H 268 substituted "Jurors" for "Venires for juries", "some of the jurors" for "some of the venire", and "jurors were" for "venire was".

Research References

Encyclopedias

OH Jur. 3d Jury § 192, Challenge in Inferior Courts.

Notes of Decisions

1. Constitutional issues

Defendant failed to establish claim that African–Americans were unfairly and systematically underrepresented in jury venires relative to their numbers in the community in violation of Sixth Amendment's fair-cross-section requirement; there was no evidence that juries in the county had traditionally been void of African–Americans, and there was no evidence of systematic exclusion of African–Americans. State v. Jackson (Ohio, 11-23-2005) 107 Ohio St.3d 53, 836 N.E.2d 1173, 2005-Ohio-5981, reconsideration denied 108 Ohio St.3d 1418, 841 N.E.2d 321, 2006-Ohio-179, certiorari denied 126 S.Ct. 2940, 548 U.S. 912, 165 L.Ed.2d 964, motion to reopen denied 110 Ohio St.3d 1435, 852 N.E.2d 185, 2006-Ohio-3862, habeas corpus denied 2008 WL 1946790, affirmed 687 F.3d 723, certiorari denied 133 S.Ct. 1243, 185 L.Ed.2d 190. Jury ⚷ 33(1.15)

Jury selection, peremptory challenges, race discrimination, pretext, prospective juror's student teaching status, see Snyder v. Louisiana, 2008, 128 S.Ct. 1203.

2. Challenge

Defendant's contention that his trial was rendered unfair by fact that he was required to move for dismissal of tainted juror following denial of his motion for mistrial, resulting in loss of only African-American juror and leaving defendant as "only African-American in the courtroom" for remainder of trial, amounted to untimely challenge to composition of venire, where motion for dismissal was made after commencement of trial and defendant did not provide district court with good cause to permit untimely challenge. U.S. v. Robertson (C.A.6 (Ohio), 06-30-2006) No. 04-3056, 187 Fed. Appx. 547, 2006 WL 1878337, Unreported. Jury ⚷ 117

5. Voir dire in capital case

Jury pool was not tainted in murder prosecution by potential juror's remarks describing his prior experience as a juror in a murder case, including his remark that, in the other case, he believed the defendant was guilty, but he had voted not guilty because all of the other jurors believed that the defendant was not guilty; trial court and counsel repeatedly questioned jury pool regarding their ability to assert their views during deliberations and stand by their opinions, trial court repeatedly informed potential jurors that defendant was presumed innocent, and that state bore burden of proving his guilt beyond a reasonable doubt, and potential juror did not sit on panel. State v. Myers (Ohio App. 2 Dist., Darke, 03-31-2006) No. 1643, 2006-Ohio-1604, 2006 WL 827341, Unreported, appeal not allowed 110 Ohio St.3d 1465, 852 N.E.2d 1214, 2006-Ohio-4288. Jury ⚷ 133

CHAPTER 2939

GRAND JURIES

GRAND JURORS

GRAND JURORS

2939.01 Definition of magistrate

Law Review and Journal Commentaries

Bullies in a wired world: The impact of cyberspace victimization on adolescent mental health and the need for cyberbullying legislation in Ohio. Kelly A. Albin, 25 J.L. & Health 155 (2012).

2939.02 Selection of grand jury

Grand juries shall consist of fifteen persons who satisfy the qualifications of a juror specified in section 2313.17 of the Revised Code. Persons to serve as grand jurors in the court of common pleas of each county shall be selected from the persons whose names are contained in the annual jury list.

At the time of the selection of the persons who are to constitute the grand jury, the commissioners of jurors shall randomly draw from the annual jury list the names of not fewer than twenty-five persons. The first fifteen persons whose names are drawn shall constitute the grand jury, if they can be located and served by the sheriff, and if they are not excused by the court or a judge of the court. If any of the first fifteen persons whose names are so drawn are not located or are unable to serve and are for that reason excused by the court or by a judge of the court, whose duty it is to supervise the impaneling of the grand jury, the judge shall then designate the person whose name next appears on the list of persons drawn, to serve in the place of the person not found or excused and shall so continue to substitute the names of the persons drawn in the order in which they were drawn, to fill all vacancies resulting from persons not being found or having been excused by the court or the judge of the court, until the necessary fifteen persons are selected to make up the grand jury. If all of the names appearing on the list of persons drawn are exhausted before the grand jury is complete, the judge shall order the commissioners of jurors to draw such additional names as the judge determines, and shall proceed to fill the vacancies from those names in the order in which they are drawn.

The judge of the court of common pleas may select any person who satisfies the qualifications of a juror and whose name is not included in the annual jury list to preside as foreperson of the grand jury, in which event the grand jury shall consist of the foreperson so selected and fourteen additional grand jurors selected from the annual jury list.

(2012 H 268, eff. 5-22-12; 1984 H 183, eff. 10–1–84; 1969 H 424; 131 v S 20; 130 v S 103; 1953 H 1; GC 11419–34)

Historical and Statutory Notes

Amendment Note: 2012 H 268 rewrote this section, which prior thereto read:

"Grand juries shall consist of fifteen persons who satisfy the qualifications of a juror specified in section 2313.42 of the Revised Code. Persons to serve as grand jurors in the court of common pleas of each county shall be selected from the persons whose names are contained in the annual jury list and from the ballots deposited in the jury wheel, or in the automation data processing storage drawer, or from the names contained in an automated data processing information storage device as prescribed by sections 2313.07, 2313.08, and 2313.35 of the Revised Code.

"At the time of the selection of the persons who are to constitute the grand jury, the commissioners of jurors shall draw from the jury wheel, or draw by utilizing the automation data processing equipment and procedures described in section 2313.07 of the Revised Code, ballots containing the names of not less than twenty-five persons. The first fifteen persons whose names are drawn shall constitute the grand jury, if they can be located and served by the sheriff, and if they are not excused by the court or a judge of the court. If any of the first fifteen persons whose names are so drawn are not located or are unable to serve and are for that reason excused by the court or by a judge of the court, whose duty it is to supervise the impaneling of the grand jury, the judge shall then designate the person whose name next appears on the list of persons drawn, to serve in the place of the person not found or excused and shall so continue to substitute the names of the persons drawn in the order in which they were drawn, to fill all vacancies resulting from persons not being found or having been excused by the court or the judge of the court, until the necessary fifteen persons are selected to make up the grand jury. If all of the names appearing on the list of persons drawn are exhausted before the grand jury is complete, the judge shall order the commissioners of jurors to draw such additional names as the judge determines, and shall proceed to fill the vacancies from those names in the order in which they are drawn.

"The judge of the court of common pleas may select any person who satisfies the qualifications of a juror and whose name is not included in the annual jury list or on a ballot deposited in the jury wheel or automation data processing storage drawer, or whose name is not contained in an automated data processing information storage device, to preside as foreman of the grand jury, in which event the grand jury shall consist of the foreman so selected and fourteen additional grand jurors selected from the jury wheel or by use of the automation data processing equipment and procedures in the manner provided in this section."

Research References

Encyclopedias

OH Jur. 3d Jury § 61, Number of Grand Jurors.
OH Jur. 3d Jury § 70, Selection; General Procedure.
OH Jur. 3d Jury § 100, Requirement that Jurors be Electors.
OH Jur. 3d Jury § 116, Foreperson of Grand Jury; Deputy Foreperson.
OH Jur. 3d Jury § 168, Number of Jurors Required for Indictment.

Treatises and Practice Aids

Katz & Giannelli, Baldwin's Ohio Practice Criminal Law § 39:5, Selection Procedure.
Katz & Giannelli, Baldwin's Ohio Practice Criminal Law § 39:6, Composition.
Katz & Giannelli, Baldwin's Ohio Practice Criminal Law § 39:7, Foreman and Deputy Foreman.
Katz & Giannelli, Baldwin's Ohio Practice Criminal Law § 39:8, Alternate Grand Jurors.
Katz & Giannelli, Baldwin's Ohio Practice Criminal Law § 141:2, Order to Summon Grand Jury.
Katz & Giannelli, Baldwin's Ohio Practice Criminal Law § 141:3, Summons for Grand Juror.
Katz & Giannelli, Baldwin's Ohio Practice Criminal Law § 143:1, Motion to Dismiss Indictment--Challenge to Panel [Or Individual Grand Juror].
Katz & Giannelli, Baldwin's Ohio Practice Criminal Law § 148:3, Order to Draw Jurors.
Katz & Giannelli, Baldwin's Ohio Practice Criminal Law § 39:20, Findings and Return of Indictment.
Hennenberg & Reinhart, Ohio Criminal Defense Motions F 5:40, Motion to Quash the Venire-Pretrial Motions-Improperly Selected Venire.

Law Review and Journal Commentaries

Appointed but (nearly) prevented from serving: My experiences as a grand jury foreperson. Phyllis L. Crocker, 2 Ohio St. J. Crim. L. 289 (2004).

Notes of Decisions

1. Constitutional issues

Trial court's error in relying on its own personal knowledge of the procedure used by the county court in appointing the grand jury foreperson when it denied defendant's claim of racial discrimination in appointment of the foreperson was harmless; trial court's dismissal of the racial discrimination claims were properly based upon either that fact that the claims were barred by res judicata or that defendant's evidentiary materials were insufficient to raise a prima facie showing of discrimination. State v. Jackson (Ohio App. 11 Dist., Trumbull, 03-03-2006) No. 2004-T-0089, 2006-Ohio-1007, 2006 WL 532105, Unreported, opinion superseded on reconsideration 2006-Ohio-2651, 2006 WL 1459757, cause dismissed 110 Ohio St.3d 1407, 850 N.E.2d 69, 2006-Ohio-3306, appeal not allowed 111 Ohio St.3d 1469, 855 N.E.2d 1258, 2006-Ohio-5625. Criminal Law ⚿ 1166(2)

Trial court improperly relied on its own personal knowledge of the procedure used by the county court in appointing the grand jury foreperson when it denied defendant's claim of racial discrimination in appointment of the foreperson; any proceeding before the grand jury was distinct from the petit trial, the trial judge was not permitted to take judicial notice of any action separate from the proceeding before him, and the trial judge's own knowledge of county grand jury proceedings in general did not encompass all possible information on that topic. State v. Jackson (Ohio App. 11 Dist., Trumbull, 03-03-2006) No. 2004-T-0089, 2006-Ohio-1007, 2006 WL 532105, Unreported, opinion superseded on reconsideration 2006-Ohio-2651, 2006 WL 1459757, cause dismissed 110 Ohio St.3d 1407, 850 N.E.2d 69, 2006-Ohio-3306, appeal not allowed 111 Ohio St.3d 1469, 855 N.E.2d 1258, 2006-Ohio-5625. Grand Jury ⚿ 21

Defendant's assertion that the county court selected a grand jury foreperson in a racially discriminatory manner was barred by res judicata in postconviction relief proceeding; evidence as to the manner by which the grand jury foreperson was chosen could have been sought prior to defendant's actual trial. State v. Jackson (Ohio App. 11 Dist., Trumbull, 03-03-2006) No. 2004-T-0089, 2006-Ohio-1007, 2006 WL 532105, Unreported, opinion superseded on reconsideration 2006-Ohio-2651, 2006 WL 1459757, cause dismissed 110 Ohio St.3d 1407, 850 N.E.2d 69, 2006-Ohio-3306, appeal not allowed 111 Ohio St.3d 1469, 855 N.E.2d 1258, 2006-Ohio-5625. Criminal Law ⚿ 1433(2)

No evidence supported capital defendant's claim in postconviction relief proceedings that the county grand jury that indicted him contained an underrepresentation of African-Americans, where defendant presented no evidence of an intentional exclusion of African–Americans from the grand jury. State v. Jackson (Ohio App. 11 Dist., Trumbull, 03-03-2006) No. 2004-T-0089, 2006-Ohio-1007, 2006 WL 532105, Unreported, opinion superseded on reconsideration 2006-Ohio-2651, 2006 WL 1459757, cause dismissed 110 Ohio St.3d 1407, 850 N.E.2d 69, 2006-Ohio-3306, appeal not allowed 111 Ohio St.3d 1469, 855 N.E.2d 1258, 2006-Ohio-5625. Criminal Law ⚿ 1477

2939.03 Grand jurors subject to same provisions and regulations as other jurors

Except for a foreperson selected by the judge of the court of common pleas under section 2939.02 of the Revised Code, a grand jury is drawn and notified in the same manner as other jurors are drawn and notified under Chapter 2313. of the Revised Code. Grand jurors so drawn and notified are not entitled to an exemption for any reason but may be excused from service or have their service postponed for the same reasons and in the same manner as other jurors under that chapter and not otherwise. Grand jurors are subject to the same fines and penalties for nonattendance and otherwise as are other jurors under that chapter. The duties and the powers of courts of common pleas, clerks of courts of common pleas, and commissioners of jurors in regard to grand jurors in all respects are the same as in regard to other jurors.

(2012 H 268, eff. 5-22-12; 1998 S 69, eff. 4–16–98; 1969 H 424, eff. 11–25–69; 131 v S 20; 1953 H 1; GC 11419–35)

Historical and Statutory Notes

Amendment Note: 2012 H 268 rewrote this section, which prior thereto read:

"A grand jury is drawn and notified by the same persons, from the same jury wheel, automation data processing storage drawer, or automated data processing information storage device, and in the same manner as other jurors are drawn and notified under sections 2939.02 to 2939.04 and 2313.01 to 2313.46 of the Revised Code. Grand jurors so drawn and notified are not entitled to an exemption for any reason but may be excused from service or have their service postponed for the same reasons and in the same manner as other jurors under those sections and not otherwise. Grand jurors are subject to the same fines and penalties for nonattendance and otherwise as are other jurors under those sections. The duties and the powers of courts of common pleas, clerks of courts of common pleas, and commissioners of jurors in regard to grand jurors in all respects are the same as in regard to other jurors."

Research References

Encyclopedias

OH Jur. 3d Jury § 6, Applicability to Grand Juries of Statutes Relating to Petit Juries.

OH Jur. 3d Jury § 70, Selection; General Procedure.

OH Jur. 3d Jury § 72, Notification and Summoning.

Treatises and Practice Aids

Katz & Giannelli, Baldwin's Ohio Practice Criminal Law § 39:5, Selection Procedure.

Katz & Giannelli, Baldwin's Ohio Practice Criminal Law § 148:3, Order to Draw Jurors.

Katz & Giannelli, Baldwin's Ohio Practice Criminal Law § 141:17, Entry for Formation of New Grand Jury.

Katz & Giannelli, Baldwin's Ohio Practice Criminal Law § 141:18, Entry for Formation of Special Grand Jury.

Hennenberg & Reinhart, Ohio Criminal Defense Motions F 10:20, Motion for New Trial--Rule 33--Irregularity in Venue.

Hennenberg & Reinhart, Ohio Criminal Defense Motions F 10:21, Motion for a New Trial-Improper Selection of the Venire-Discriminatory Exclusion of Jurors from Jury Wheel.

OFFICIALS

2939.10 Who shall have access to grand jury

Notes of Decisions

4. Access to grand jury

Pursuant to R.C. 2939.10 and Ohio R. Crim. P. 6(D), a deputy sheriff may not be present in the grand jury room during the testimony of an inmate who has been subpoenaed to provide testimony to the grand jury. OAG 2011-004, 2011 WL 675016.

The unauthorized presence of a deputy sheriff during the testimony of an inmate who has been subpoenaed to testify before the grand jury is not sufficient to set aside an indictment unless prejudice to the accused is shown. OAG 2011-004, 2011 WL 675016.

5. Access to record of testimony

Defendant charged with abduction, assault and intimidation was not entitled to production of grand jury minutes to determine whether charges against him in a second indictment were the result of undue law enforcement influence upon victim, defendant's girlfriend; defendant's claim was speculative, victim attested to the validity of her allegations by signing her statement, defendant was free to cross-examine police officers at trial as to whether they pressured victim into making complaints, and victim's reluctance to come forward with all allegations of abuse was consistent with charges of abuse. State v. Kelly (Ohio App. 8 Dist., Cuyahoga, 11-09-2006) No. 85662, 2006-Ohio-5902, 2006 WL 3233895, Unreported, appeal not allowed 113 Ohio St.3d 1416, 862 N.E.2d 844, 2007-Ohio-1036, appeal after new sentencing hearing 2007-Ohio-6838, 2007 WL 4445405, motion for delayed appeal denied 117 Ohio St.3d 1496, 885 N.E.2d 953, 2008-Ohio-2028. Criminal Law ⚿ 627.9(2.1)

2939.11 Official reporters

The official reporter of the county, or any reporter designated by the court of common pleas, at the request of the prosecuting attorney, or any such reporter designated by the attorney general in investigations conducted by the attorney general, may take notes of or electronically record testimony before the grand jury, and furnish a transcript to the prosecuting attorney or the attorney general, and to no other person. The reporter shall withdraw from the jury room before the jurors begin to express their views or take their vote on the matter before them. Such reporter shall take an oath to be administered by the judge after the grand jury is sworn, imposing an obligation of secrecy to not disclose any testimony taken or heard except to the grand jury, prosecuting attorney, or attorney general, unless called upon in court to make disclosures.

(2012 H 487, eff. 9-10-12; 1953 H 1, eff. 10–1–53; GC 13436–8)

Historical and Statutory Notes

Amendment Note: 2012 H 487 deleted all occurrences of "shorthand" preceding ""reporter" or "notes"; substituted "the attorney general" for "him" following "investigations conducted by"; and inserted "or electronically record" preceding "testimony before the grand jury".

Research References

Encyclopedias

OH Jur. 3d Jury § 139, Who May be Present at Session of Grand Jury--Shorthand Reporter, Stenographer, or Operator of Recording Device.
OH Jur. 3d Jury § 155, Persons Subject to Secrecy Requirements.
OH Jur. 3d State of Ohio § 150, Overall Function; Grand Jury.

Treatises and Practice Aids

Katz & Giannelli, Baldwin's Ohio Practice Criminal Law § 39:13, Presence in Jury Room.
Katz & Giannelli, Baldwin's Ohio Practice Criminal Law § 39:22, Grand Jury Secrecy.

Notes of Decisions

2. Access to record of testimony

Defendant in capital murder prosecution failed to show particularized need for transcript of grand jury testimony by accomplice in robbery during which charged killing of security guard occurred, where accomplice never testified at trial. State v. Treesh (Ohio, 01-03-2001) 90 Ohio St.3d 460, 739 N.E.2d 749, 2001-Ohio-4, stay granted 91 Ohio St.3d 1435, 742 N.E.2d 135, certiorari denied 121 S.Ct. 2247, 533 U.S. 904, 150 L.Ed.2d 234, habeas corpus denied 2007 WL 1039081. Criminal Law ⚷ 627.9(2.1)

2939.12 Clerk to issue subpoenas for witnesses

Law Review and Journal Commentaries

The new abridged reporter's privilege: Policies, principles, and pathological perspectives. Erik Ugland, 71 Ohio St. L.J. 1 (2010).

Notes of Decisions

Student records 2

2. Student records

Grand jury subpoena for production of documents that might have been student records was lawfully issued to dean of students of university; student was given notice of subpoena, filed no motion to quash or modify or other motion to bar production of the records, and some of the records could have been considered law enforcement unit records. In re Subpoena Issued to Smith (Ohio Com.Pl., 09-04-2009) 155 Ohio Misc.2d 46, 921 N.E.2d 731, 2009-Ohio-7086. Grand Jury ⚷ 36.4(1)

GENERAL PROVISIONS

2939.18 Fact of indictment shall be kept secret

Notes of Decisions

1. Secrecy of proceedings

Defendant failed to show particularized need for disclosure of grand jury minutes for second indictment, and thus defendant was not entitled to production of grand jury minutes in prosecution for abduction, felonious assault, intimidation, and assault, although defendant stated that he could only assure himself of the "legality of the proceedings" if he saw minutes to determine whether any undue influence had been exerted on victim; claimed right of access was so marginal as to be nothing more than fishing expedition, and defendant was fully able to cross-examine police officers at trial regarding whether police officers had pressured victim. State v. Kelly (Ohio App. 8 Dist., 09-21-2006) 970 N.E.2d 986, 2006-Ohio-4879, superseded 2006-Ohio-5902, 2006 WL 3233895, appeal not allowed 113 Ohio St.3d 1416, 862 N.E.2d 844, 2007-Ohio-1036, appeal after new sentencing hearing 2007-Ohio-6838, 2007 WL 4445405, motion for delayed appeal denied 117 Ohio St.3d 1496, 885 N.E.2d 953, 2008-Ohio-2028. Criminal Law ⚷ 627.9(2.1)

2939.20 Indictment by twelve jurors

Notes of Decisions

2. Endorsement and signature on true bill

Defendant was barred from raising, in a habeas corpus action, his assertion that his indictment was void as a result of grand jury foreman's failure to write "a true bill" above his signature in longhand, rather than in type; direct appeal was the proper vehicle by which defendant could challenge the validity or sufficiency of the indictment. Lucas v. Richland Correctional Inst. (Ohio App. 5 Dist., Richland, 10-06-2005) No. 05CA0017, 2005-Ohio-5328, 2005 WL 2462279, Unreported. Criminal Law ⚷ 1134.36; Habeas Corpus ⚷ 292

Defendant's indictment was not void as a result of grand jury foreman's failure to write "a true bill" above his signature in longhand, rather than in type, where the indictment did contain the words "a true bill." Lucas v. Richland Correctional Inst. (Ohio App. 5 Dist., Richland, 10-06-2005) No. 05CA0017, 2005-Ohio-5328, 2005 WL 2462279, Unreported. Indictment and Information ⚷ 34(2)

Fact that indictment charging defendant with menacing by stalking was initialed by the foreperson of the grand jury, rather than signed, did not invalidate the indictment or defendant's resulting conviction. State v. Payne (Ohio App. 9 Dist., 10-22-2008) 178 Ohio App.3d 617, 899 N.E.2d 1011, 2008-Ohio-5447. Criminal Law ⚷ 99; Indictment and Information ⚷ 33(4)

Claim attacking validity and sufficiency of indictment, by alleging that indictment did not satisfy statutory requirement that foreman of grand jury must indorse on the indictment the words "A true bill" and subscribe his name as foreman, should have been raised on direct appeal from the criminal conviction and sentence, rather than in habeas corpus. Payne v. Jeffreys (Ohio, 05-24-2006) 109 Ohio St.3d 239, 846 N.E.2d 1248, 2006-Ohio-2288. Habeas Corpus ⚷ 292

OUT–OF–STATE WITNESS

Comparative Laws

Uniform Act to Secure the Attendance of Witnesses from Without a State in Criminal Proceedings

Table of Jurisdictions Wherein Act Has Been Adopted.

For text of Uniform Act, and variation notes and annotation materials for adopting jurisdictions, see Uniform Laws Annotated, Master Edition, Volume 11.

Jurisdiction	Laws	Effective Date	Statutory Citation
Alabama	1977, No. 638, p. 1084		Code 1975, §§ 12–21–280 to 12–21–285.
Alaska	1962, c. 34	3–23–1962*	AS 12.50.010 to 12.50.080.
Arizona	1937, c. 74	3–25–1937*	A.R.S. §§ 13–4091 to 13–4096.
Arkansas	1935, No. 65	2–20–1935*	A.C.A. §§ 16–43–402 to 16–43–409.
California	1937, p. 562	8–27–1937	West's Ann.Cal.Penal Code, §§ 1334 to 1334.6.
Colorado	1939, c. 99	4–10–1939	West's C.R.S.A. §§ 16–9–201 to 16–9–205.
Connecticut	1937, c. 333	4–16–1937	C.G.S.A. § 54–82i.
Delaware	1937, c. 214	4–7–1937	11 Del.C. §§ 3521 to 3526.
District of Columbia	1952, Stat. 15	3–5–1952	D.C. Official Code, 2001 Ed. §§ 23–1501 to 23–1504.
Florida	1941, c. 20458	5–26–1941*	West's F.S.A. §§ 942.01 to 942.06.
Georgia	1976, No. 1351	3–31–1976	O.C.G.A. §§ 24–10–90 to 24–10–97.
Hawaii	1972, c. 9	1–1–1973	HRS §§ 836–1 to 836–6.
Idaho	1935, c. 10	2–11–1935*	I.C. § 19–3005.
Illinois	1959, p. 2147	7–23–1959	S.H.A. 725 ILCS 220/1 to 220/6.
Indiana	1935, c. 21	7–1–1935	West's A.I.C. 35–37–5–1 to 35–37–5–9.
Iowa			I.C.A. §§ 819.1 to 819.5.
Kansas	1951, c. 354	3–31–1951*	K.S.A. 22–4201 to 22–4206.
Kentucky	1952, c. 132	6–19–1952	KRS 421.230 to 421.270.
Louisiana	1936, No. 285	7–9–1936*	LSA–C.Cr.P. arts. 741 to 745.
Maine	1939, c. 9	2–21–1939*	15 M.R.S.A. §§ 1411 to 1415.
Maryland	1955, c. 333	6–1–1955	Code, Courts and Judicial Proceedings, §§ 9–301 to 9–306.
Massachusetts	1937, c. 210	4–16–1937*	M.G.L.A. c. 233, §§ 13A to 13D.

Jurisdiction	Laws	Effective Date	Statutory Citation
Michigan	1970, No. 232	12-3-1970	M.C.L.A. §§ 767.91 to 767.95.
Minnesota	1935, c. 140	4-11-1935*	M.S.A. §§ 634.06 to 634.09.
Mississippi	1938, c. 261	4-7-1938	Code 1972, §§ 99-9-27 to 99-9-35.
Missouri	1959, H.B. 295	6-12-1959*	V.A.M.S. §§ 491.400 to 491.450.
Montana	1937, c. 188	3-18-1937	MCA 46-15-112, 46-15-113, 46-15-120.
Nebraska	1937, c. 71	5-13-1937*	R.R.S.1943, §§ 29-1906 to 29-1911.
Nevada	1957, c. 41	2-18-1951	N.R.S. 174.395 to 174.445.
New Hampshire	1937, c. 65	4-15-1937	RSA 613:1 to 613:6.
New Jersey	1941, c. 88	4-28-1941	N.J.S.A. 2A:81-18 to 2A:81-23.
New Mexico	1937, c. 66	3-5-1937*	NMSA 1978, §§ 31-8-1 to 31-8-6.
New York	1936, c. 387	5-1-1936	McKinney's CPL § 640.10.
North Carolina	1937, c. 217	3-17-1937	G.S. §§ 15A-811 to 15A-816.
Ohio	1937, p. 668	8-23-1937	R.C. §§ 2939.25 to 2939.29.
Oklahoma	1949, p. 205	4-21-1949	22 Okl.St.Ann. §§ 721 to 727.
Oregon	1937, c. 124	2-26-1937*	ORS 136.623 to 136.637.
Pennsylvania	1941, P.L. 147	6-23-1941	42 Pa.C.S.A. §§ 5961 to 5965.
Rhode Island	1936, c. 2382	5-1-1936*	Gen.Laws 1956, §§ 12-16-1 to 12-16-13.
South Carolina	1948, p. 1810	4-8-1948	Code 1976, §§ 19-9-10 to 19-9-130.
South Dakota	1937, c. 259	3-6-1937*	SDCL 23A-14-1 et seq.
Tennessee	1939, c. 148	3-7-1939*	T.C.A. §§ 40-17-201 to 40-17-212.
Texas	1951, c. 441	6-15-1951	Vernon's Ann.Texas C.C.P. art. 24.28.
Utah	1937, c. 147	3-17-1937	U.C.A.1953, 77-21-1 to 77-21-5.
Vermont	1937, No. 46	3-9-1937	13 V.S.A. §§ 6641 to 6649.
Virgin Islands	1957, No. 160	9-1-1957	5 V.I.C. §§ 3861 to 3865.
Virginia	1938, c. 397	4-1-1938*	Code 1950, §§ 19.2-272 to 19.2-282.
Washington	1943, c. 218	3-20-1943*	West's RCWA 10.55.010 to 10.55.130.
West Virginia	1937, c. 41	3-12-1937*	Code, 62-6A-1 to 62-6A-6.
Wisconsin	1969, c. 255	7-1-1970	W.S.A. 976.02.
Wyoming	1935, c. 120	2-20-1935	Wyo.Stat.Ann. §§ 7-11-404 to 7-11-406.

* Date of approval.

CHAPTER 2941

INDICTMENT

MAGISTRATE DEFINED

INDICTMENTS AND INFORMATIONS

PLEADING, AVERMENTS, AND ALLEGATIONS

MAGISTRATE DEFINED

2941.01 Definition of magistrate

Cross References

Release of prisoner in imminent danger of death, return to institution from which released, see 2967.05

INDICTMENTS AND INFORMATIONS

2941.021 Prosecution by information

Notes of Decisions

2. In general

R.C. 2941.021 and Ohio R. Crim. P. 7(A) prohibit a county prosecuting attorney from filing an information to prosecute a felony case before the accused waives in writing and in open court his right to indictment by a grand jury. (1949 Op. Att'y Gen. No. 801, p. 465 and 1933 Op. Att'y Gen. No. 969, vol. II, p. 926, overruled). OAG 2012-042, 2012 WL 7857309.

4. —— Knowing, intelligent, voluntary waiver, waiver of indictment

Defendant validly waived presentment to grand jury of charge of engaging in a pattern of corrupt activity, and thus plea agreement, in which defendant pleaded guilty to unpresented charge, was valid; at plea hearing defendant was represented by counsel, was fully aware of charges against him, and waived a new indictment after trial court explained the corrupt-activity charge to defendant, and plea agreement itself contained an express waiver. State v. Owens (Ohio App. 7 Dist., 03-26-2009) 181 Ohio App.3d 725, 910 N.E.2d 1059, 2009-Ohio-1508, appeal from denial of habeas corpus 2009-Ohio-2637, 2009 WL 1581189, appeal dismissed 123 Ohio St.3d 1204, 914 N.E.2d 407, 2009-Ohio-4086. Indictment and Information ⚷ 5

2941.03 Sufficiency of indictments or informations

Notes of Decisions

1. Sufficiency of indictment

Indictment of defendant for rape and gross sexual imposition was properly filed and alleged sufficient facts to apprise defendant of charges; indictment recited definition of rape and gross sexual imposition as defined in relevant statutes, and indictment was not rendered invalid for failure to state exact date that offenses were committed, as range of years in indictment supported fact that victim was under age of 13. State v. Bogan (Ohio App. 8 Dist., Cuyahoga, 06-30-2005) No. 84468, 2005-Ohio-3412, 2005 WL 1541014, Unreported, appeal after new sentencing hearing 2006-Ohio-3842, 2006 WL 2100111. Indictment And Information ⚷ 87(7); Indictment And Information ⚷ 110(3); Indictment And Information ⚷ 110(6)

In prosecution for multiple sex offenses, trial court's instruction to jury that it was not necessary for State to prove that the offenses were committed on the exact day as charged in indictment did not improperly open the door to "guesswork of the jury"; specificity as to the date and time of offenses was not required. State v. Braddy (Ohio App. 8 Dist., Cuyahoga, 06-17-2004) No. 83462, 2004-Ohio-3128, 2004 WL 1364730, Unreported, motion to reopen denied 2005-Ohio-282, 2005 WL 174771, motion for delayed appeal denied 106 Ohio St.3d 1458, 830 N.E.2d 1167, 2005-Ohio-3490, denial of post-conviction relief affirmed 2012-Ohio-4720, 2012 WL 4848992, appeal not allowed 134 Ohio St.3d 1453, 982 N.E.2d 729, 2013-Ohio-347, habeas corpus denied 2014 WL 4285632. Rape ⚷ 35(4); Rape ⚷ 59(4)

Amendment of indictment to expand by approximately sixteen months the time frame of alleged rapes of child under age thirteen did not violate state constitutional requirement to try defendant on the same essential facts on which the grand jury found probable cause; the grand jury had found probable cause of sexual conduct with child under thirteen years and could easily have found probable cause of rape at a later time, and time was not an element. State v. Shafer (Ohio App. 8 Dist., Cuyahoga, 12-05-2002) No. 79758, 2002-Ohio-6632, 2002 WL 31722127, Unreported, appeal not allowed 98 Ohio St.3d 1540, 786 N.E.2d 902, 2003-Ohio-1946, appeal after new sentencing hearing 2004-Ohio-2555, 2004 WL 1118805, appeal not allowed 103 Ohio St.3d 1480, 816 N.E.2d 255, 2004-Ohio-5405, certiorari denied 125 S.Ct. 1663, 544 U.S. 928, 161 L.Ed.2d 491, rehearing denied, rehearing denied 125 S.Ct. 2249, 544 U.S. 1045, 161 L.Ed.2d 1083, habeas corpus denied 2007 WL 315760, certificate of appealability granted in part, denied in part 2007 WL 789579, denial of habeas corpus affirmed 364 Fed.Appx. 940, 2010 WL 395914. Indictment And Information ⚷ 159(3)

Indictment was not invalid or insufficient because it did not describe the specific dates on which the crimes allegedly occurred; specificity as to the date and time of the offense was not required in the indictment. State v. Thompson (Ohio App. 8 Dist., Cuyahoga, 10-31-2002) No. 79334, 2002-Ohio-5957, 2002 WL 31426356, Unreported, dismissal of post-conviction relief affirmed 2002-Ohio-6845, 2002 WL 31771437, appeal not allowed 100 Ohio St.3d 1506, 799 N.E.2d 186, 2003-Ohio-6161, appeal not allowed 98 Ohio St.3d 1512, 786 N.E.2d 62, 2003-Ohio-1572, reconsideration denied 99 Ohio St.3d 1414, 788 N.E.2d 649, 2003-Ohio-2454, motion to reopen denied 2003-Ohio-4336, 2003 WL 21954760, as amended nunc pro tunc, appeal not allowed 100 Ohio St.3d 1509, 799 N.E.2d 187, 2003-Ohio-6161, habeas corpus denied 2007 WL 2080454. Indictment And Information ⚷ 87(2)

Indictment charging defendant with 14 counts of rape, four which included a specification that the victim was under ten years old and 13 counts of gross sexual imposition was sufficiently specific to provide defendant with notice of alleged offenses, and thus did not violate double jeopardy or due process; the indictment did distinguish the various counts by providing month the alleged offense occurred, the victim, and the age of the victim, the bill of particulars provided distinguishing details about the crimes, such as the type of sexual contact, how the contact was started, and how long the contact lasted, and the evidence presented at trial demonstrated that there were more instances of the crimes than were charged, not less. State v. Stefka (Ohio App. 7 Dist., 06-27-2012) 973 N.E.2d 786, 2012-Ohio-3004. Assault and Battery ⚷ 74; Constitutional Law ⚷ 4581; Double Jeopardy ⚷ 148; Infants ⚷ 1658; Rape ⚷ 20

Where crimes alleged in the indictment constitute sexual offenses against children, they need not state with specificity the dates of the alleged abuse, so long as the state establishes that the offense was committed within the time frame alleged. State v. Blankenburg (Ohio App. 12 Dist., 03-26-2012) 197 Ohio App.3d 201, 966 N.E.2d 958, 2012-Ohio-1289, appeal not allowed 132 Ohio St.3d 1514, 974 N.E.2d 112, 2012-Ohio-4021, denial of post-conviction relief reversed 2012-Ohio-6175, 2012 WL 6738255. Infants ⚷ 1654

Indictment was not "duplicitous" in prosecution for gross sexual imposition against two victims, corruption of a minor, and compelling prostitution in connection with allegations that defendant molested his pediatric patients, where case involved a continuing course of conduct charged as separate offenses differentiated by certain time frames, counts involved allegations of conduct toward victims who were children or teenagers when the alleged acts occurred, and possibility of one conviction, rather than many, was to defendant's advantage. State v. Blankenburg (Ohio App. 12 Dist., 03-26-2012) 197 Ohio App.3d 201, 966 N.E.2d 958, 2012-Ohio-1289, appeal not allowed 132 Ohio St.3d

1514, 974 N.E.2d 112, 2012-Ohio-4021, denial of post-conviction relief reversed 2012-Ohio-6175, 2012 WL 6738255. Indictment And Information ⚿ 125(4.1)

Where the inability to produce in an indictment a specific time or date when the criminal conduct occurred is without material detriment to the preparation of a defense, the omission is without prejudice and without constitutional consequence. State v. Blankenburg (Ohio App. 12 Dist., 03-26-2012) 197 Ohio App.3d 201, 966 N.E.2d 958, 2012-Ohio-1289, appeal not allowed 132 Ohio St.3d 1514, 974 N.E.2d 112, 2012-Ohio-4021, denial of post-conviction relief reversed 2012-Ohio-6175, 2012 WL 6738255. Criminal Law ⚿ 1167(1)

A common situation resulting in prejudice from state's failure to provide specific dates and times in an indictment is where the defendant was indisputably elsewhere during part, but not all, of the intervals of time set out in the indictment. State v. Blankenburg (Ohio App. 12 Dist., 03-26-2012) 197 Ohio App.3d 201, 966 N.E.2d 958, 2012-Ohio-1289, appeal not allowed 132 Ohio St.3d 1514, 974 N.E.2d 112, 2012-Ohio-4021, denial of post-conviction relief reversed 2012-Ohio-6175, 2012 WL 6738255. Criminal Law ⚿ 1167(1)

The state's failure to provide specific dates and times in an indictment is more likely to prejudice an accused in cases in which the age of the victim is an element of the crime charged and the victim bordered on the age required to make the conduct criminal. State v. Blankenburg (Ohio App. 12 Dist., 03-26-2012) 197 Ohio App.3d 201, 966 N.E.2d 958, 2012-Ohio-1289, appeal not allowed 132 Ohio St.3d 1514, 974 N.E.2d 112, 2012-Ohio-4021, denial of post-conviction relief reversed 2012-Ohio-6175, 2012 WL 6738255. Criminal Law ⚿ 1167(1)

Any failure by State to provide specific dates and times in indictment was not plain error in prosecution for corruption of a minor on the basis of sexual conduct with a person who was 13 years of age or older but less than 16 years of age and compelling prostitution on the basis that defendant induced, procured, solicited, or requested a minor to engage in sexual activity for hire, where victim testified that he was able to identify the date once he reviewed his old medical records and remembered the context within which the events occurred, and lack of specific dates did not serve as a material detriment to defendant, who appeared to maintain that no sexual activity ever occurred during the time frame when any victim was a minor. State v. Blankenburg (Ohio App. 12 Dist., 03-26-2012) 197 Ohio App.3d 201, 966 N.E.2d 958, 2012-Ohio-1289, appeal not allowed 132 Ohio St.3d 1514, 974 N.E.2d 112, 2012-Ohio-4021, denial of post-conviction relief reversed 2012-Ohio-6175, 2012 WL 6738255. Criminal Law ⚿ 1032(5)

Indictment for armed bank robbery was constitutionally adequate, though indictment omitted the initials "N.A." when naming the bank, which initials were part of bank's legal name and were an abbreviation for "National Association," where indictment specified the address of the bank. U.S. v. Tunstall (S.D.Ohio, 10-17-2006) 456 F.Supp.2d 940. Indictment And Information ⚿ 101

2. Jurisdiction and venue

Trial court was vested with jurisdiction over prosecution of defendant for gross sexual imposition, where defendant had been charged with offenses via a valid indictment. State v. Bogan (Ohio App. 8 Dist., Cuyahoga, 06-30-2005) No. 84468, 2005-Ohio-3412, 2005 WL 1541014, Unreported, appeal after new sentencing hearing 2006-Ohio-3842, 2006 WL 2100111. Criminal Law ⚿ 99

3. Name of defendant

The manner by which an accused is charged with a crime is procedural rather than jurisdictional, and after a conviction for crimes charged in an indictment, the judgment binds the defendant for the crime for which he was convicted. Gotel v. Gansheimer (Ohio, 12-13-2007) 116 Ohio St.3d 316, 878 N.E.2d 1041, 2007-Ohio-6437. Criminal Law ⚿ 977(1); Indictment And Information ⚿ 4

4. Bill of particulars

Although defendant claimed the bill of particulars led him to believe that the State alleged all three crimes occurred on the same night, he did not claim that his ability to defend himself was prejudiced by this fact, and thus, defendant did not show that the date of the offenses was material to his defense, such that the indictment was invalid because it did not describe the specific dates on which the crimes allegedly occurred. State v. Thompson (Ohio App. 8 Dist., Cuyahoga, 10-31-2002) No. 79334, 2002-Ohio-5957, 2002 WL 31426356, Unreported, dismissal of post-conviction relief affirmed 2002-Ohio-6845, 2002 WL 31771437, appeal not allowed 100 Ohio St.3d 1506, 799 N.E.2d 186, 2003-Ohio-6161, appeal not allowed 98 Ohio St.3d 1512, 786 N.E.2d 62, 2003-Ohio-1572, reconsideration denied 99 Ohio St.3d 1414, 788 N.E.2d 649, 2003-Ohio-2454, motion to reopen denied 2003-Ohio-4336, 2003 WL 21954760, as amended nunc pro tunc, appeal not allowed 100 Ohio St.3d 1509, 799 N.E.2d 187, 2003-Ohio-6161, habeas corpus denied 2007 WL 2080454. Indictment And Information ⚿ 87(2)

A precise time and date of an alleged offense are ordinarily not essential elements of an indictment, information, complaint or bill of particulars. State v. Blankenburg (Ohio App. 12 Dist., 03-26-2012) 197 Ohio App.3d 201, 966 N.E.2d 958, 2012-Ohio-1289, appeal not allowed 132 Ohio St.3d 1514, 974 N.E.2d 112, 2012-Ohio-4021, denial of post-conviction relief reversed 2012-Ohio-6175, 2012 WL 6738255. Indictment And Information ⚿ 87(7); Indictment And Information ⚿ 121.1(6.1)

2941.04 Two or more offenses in one indictment

Notes of Decisions

3. Multiple counts

Indictment was not "duplicitous" in prosecution for gross sexual imposition against two victims, corruption of a minor, and compelling prostitution in connection with allegations that defendant molested his pediatric patients, where case involved a continuing course of conduct charged as separate offenses differentiated by certain time frames, counts involved allegations of conduct toward victims who were children or teenagers when the alleged acts occurred, and possibility of one conviction, rather than many, was to defendant's advantage. State v. Blankenburg (Ohio App. 12 Dist., 03-26-2012) 197 Ohio App.3d 201, 966 N.E.2d 958, 2012-Ohio-1289, appeal not allowed 132 Ohio St.3d 1514, 974 N.E.2d 112, 2012-Ohio-4021, denial of post-conviction relief reversed 2012-Ohio-6175, 2012 WL 6738255. Indictment And Information ⚷ 125(4.1)

2941.05 Statement charging an offense

Notes of Decisions

1. Sufficiency of indictment

Indictment was not "duplicitous" in prosecution for gross sexual imposition against two victims, corruption of a minor, and compelling prostitution in connection with allegations that defendant molested his pediatric patients, where case involved a continuing course of conduct charged as separate offenses differentiated by certain time frames, counts involved allegations of conduct toward victims who were children or teenagers when the alleged acts occurred, and possibility of one conviction, rather than many, was to defendant's advantage. State v. Blankenburg (Ohio App. 12 Dist., 03-26-2012) 197 Ohio App.3d 201, 966 N.E.2d 958, 2012-Ohio-1289, appeal not allowed 132 Ohio St.3d 1514, 974 N.E.2d 112, 2012-Ohio-4021, denial of post-conviction relief reversed 2012-Ohio-6175, 2012 WL 6738255. Indictment And Information ⚷ 125(4.1)

2941.07 Bill of particulars

Notes of Decisions

2. Sufficiency of charge

Bill of particulars provided by state in rape prosecution was sufficient to fulfill its intended purpose, as it set out date of alleged offenses, general nature of alleged conduct, and applicable statute. State v. Brown (Ohio App. 7 Dist., Mahoning, 06-07-2005) No. 03-MA-32, 2005-Ohio-2939, 2005 WL 1385715, Unreported, appeal not allowed 106 Ohio St.3d 1558, 836 N.E.2d 582, 2005-Ohio-5531, habeas corpus denied 2007 WL 3342717, affirmed 656 F.3d 325, rehearing and rehearing en banc denied, certiorari denied 133 S.Ct. 1452, 185 L.Ed.2d 360. Indictment And Information ⚷ 121.4

3. Right to bill of particulars—in general

State's delay in providing defendant with bill of particulars, while not to be condoned, did not prejudice defendant, in rape prosecution; county in which defendant was prosecuted had somewhat unique policy of "open discovery" in prosecutor's office, and, thus, all of state's evidence was available for defendant and his counsel to examine in preparation for trial, including police reports and witness statements, and thus defendant would have been able to determine what time of day alleged crimes occurred and what type of sexual conduct was alleged, as long as state had this information. State v. Brown (Ohio App. 7 Dist., Mahoning, 06-07-2005) No. 03-MA-32, 2005-Ohio-2939, 2005 WL 1385715, Unreported, appeal not allowed 106 Ohio St.3d 1558, 836 N.E.2d 582, 2005-Ohio-5531, habeas corpus denied 2007 WL 3342717, affirmed 656 F.3d 325, rehearing and rehearing en banc denied, certiorari denied 133 S.Ct. 1452, 185 L.Ed.2d 360. Criminal Law ⚷ 1167(1); Indictment And Information ⚷ 121.4

9. Specificity of bill of particulars

More detailed bill of particulars than that provided in capital murder prosecution was unnecessary, where defendant's original trial counsel filed motion for bill of particulars, defendant's second counsel obtained trial court order for state to supply bill, and state complied, and where counsel was conducting extensive discovery during process of obtaining bill of particulars. State v. Gross (Ohio, 10-30-2002) 97 Ohio St.3d 121, 776 N.E.2d 1061, 2002-Ohio-5524, reconsideration denied 97 Ohio St.3d 1486, 780 N.E.2d 288, 2002-Ohio-6866, certiorari denied 123 S.Ct. 2079, 538 U.S. 1037, 155 L.Ed.2d 1068, rehearing denied 124 S.Ct. 20, 539 U.S. 976, 156 L.Ed.2d 685, denial of post-conviction relief affirmed 2003-Ohio-6295, 2003 WL 22765845, appeal not allowed 102 Ohio St.3d 1410, 806 N.E.2d 562, 2004-Ohio-1763, certiorari denied 125 S.Ct. 165, 543 U.S. 888, 160 L.Ed.2d 149, dismissal of post-conviction relief affirmed 2006-Ohio-6941, 2006 WL 3804532, appeal not allowed 113 Ohio St.3d 1468, 864 N.E.2d 654, 2007-Ohio-1722, habeas corpus dismissed 2008 WL 4702181, motion to amend denied 2008 WL 4889626, certificate of appealability denied 2008 WL 5190017, affirmed

426 Fed.Appx. 349, 2011 WL 1597659. Indictment And Information ⚯ 121.4

2941.08 Certain defects do not render indictment invalid

Notes of Decisions

Location 5.5

---

3. Fatal defects

Although defendant claimed the bill of particulars led him to believe that the State alleged all three crimes occurred on the same night, he did not claim that his ability to defend himself was prejudiced by this fact, and thus, defendant did not show that the date of the offenses was material to his defense, such that the indictment was invalid because it did not describe the specific dates on which the crimes allegedly occurred. State v. Thompson (Ohio App. 8 Dist., Cuyahoga, 10-31-2002) No. 79334, 2002-Ohio-5957, 2002 WL 31426356, Unreported, dismissal of post-conviction relief affirmed 2002-Ohio-6845, 2002 WL 31771437, appeal not allowed 100 Ohio St.3d 1506, 799 N.E.2d 186, 2003-Ohio-6161, appeal not allowed 98 Ohio St.3d 1512, 786 N.E.2d 62, 2003-Ohio-1572, reconsideration denied 99 Ohio St.3d 1414, 788 N.E.2d 649, 2003-Ohio-2454, motion to reopen denied 2003-Ohio-4336, 2003 WL 21954760, as amended nunc pro tunc, appeal not allowed 100 Ohio St.3d 1509, 799 N.E.2d 187, 2003-Ohio-6161, habeas corpus denied 2007 WL 2080454. Indictment And Information ⚯ 87(2)

5. Time

Indictment charging defendant with 47 counts related to child sex abuse contained sufficient information to allow defendant to mount a defense and bar future prosecutions for the same offenses, even though the specific dates the offenses allegedly took place were not always specified; all of defendant's victims were young girls under the age of ten and may have been unable to remember specific dates, narrow time frames were provided for some of the victims, defendant did not dispute the charges against him, and he did not allege that not knowing specific dates would prejudice him in any way. State v. Thompson (Ohio App. 8 Dist., Cuyahoga, 04-13-2006) No. 86357, 2006-Ohio-1836, 2006 WL 951447, Unreported, motion denied 113 Ohio St.3d 1511, 866 N.E.2d 510, 2007-Ohio-2208. Indictment And Information ⚯ 87(7)

Where the inability to produce in an indictment a specific time or date when the criminal conduct occurred is without material detriment to the preparation of a defense, the omission is without prejudice and without constitutional consequence. State v. Blankenburg (Ohio App. 12 Dist., 03-26-2012) 197 Ohio App.3d 201, 966 N.E.2d 958, 2012-Ohio-1289, appeal not allowed 132 Ohio St.3d 1514, 974 N.E.2d 112, 2012-Ohio-4021, denial of post-conviction relief reversed 2012-Ohio-6175, 2012 WL 6738255. Criminal Law ⚯ 1167(1)

A common situation resulting in prejudice from state's failure to provide specific dates and times in an indictment is where the defendant was indisputably elsewhere during part, but not all, of the intervals of time set out in the indictment. State v. Blankenburg (Ohio App. 12 Dist., 03-26-2012) 197 Ohio App.3d 201, 966 N.E.2d 958, 2012-Ohio-1289, appeal not allowed 132 Ohio St.3d 1514, 974 N.E.2d 112, 2012-Ohio-4021, denial of post-conviction relief reversed 2012-Ohio-6175, 2012 WL 6738255. Criminal Law ⚯ 1167(1)

The state's failure to provide specific dates and times in an indictment is more likely to prejudice an accused in cases in which the age of the victim is an element of the crime charged and the victim bordered on the age required to make the conduct criminal. State v. Blankenburg (Ohio App. 12 Dist., 03-26-2012) 197 Ohio App.3d 201, 966 N.E.2d 958, 2012-Ohio-1289, appeal not allowed 132 Ohio St.3d 1514, 974 N.E.2d 112, 2012-Ohio-4021, denial of post-conviction relief reversed 2012-Ohio-6175, 2012 WL 6738255. Criminal Law ⚯ 1167(1)

Any failure by State to provide specific dates and times in indictment was not plain error in prosecution for corruption of a minor on the basis of sexual conduct with a person who was 13 years of age or older but less than 16 years of age and compelling prostitution on the basis that defendant induced, procured, solicited, or requested a minor to engage in sexual activity for hire, where victim testified that he was able to identify the date once he reviewed his old medical records and remembered the context within which the events occurred, and lack of specific dates did not serve as a material detriment to defendant, who appeared to maintain that no sexual activity ever occurred during the time frame when any victim was a minor. State v. Blankenburg (Ohio App. 12 Dist., 03-26-2012) 197 Ohio App.3d 201, 966 N.E.2d 958, 2012-Ohio-1289, appeal not allowed 132 Ohio St.3d 1514, 974 N.E.2d 112, 2012-Ohio-4021, denial of post-conviction relief reversed 2012-Ohio-6175, 2012 WL 6738255. Criminal Law ⚯ 1032(5)

A precise time and date of an alleged offense are ordinarily not essential elements of an indictment, information, complaint or bill of particulars. State v. Blankenburg (Ohio App. 12 Dist., 03-26-2012) 197 Ohio App.3d 201, 966 N.E.2d 958, 2012-Ohio-1289, appeal not allowed 132 Ohio St.3d 1514, 974 N.E.2d 112, 2012-Ohio-4021, denial of post-conviction relief reversed 2012-Ohio-6175, 2012 WL 6738255. Indictment And Information ⚯ 87(7); Indictment And Information ⚯ 121.1(6.1)

Where crimes alleged in the indictment constitute sexual offenses against children, they need not state with specificity the dates of the alleged abuse, so long as the state establishes that the offense was committed within the time frame alleged. State v. Blankenburg (Ohio App. 12 Dist., 03-26-2012) 197 Ohio App.3d 201, 966 N.E.2d 958, 2012-Ohio-1289, appeal not allowed 132 Ohio St.3d 1514, 974 N.E.2d 112, 2012-Ohio-4021, denial of post-conviction relief reversed 2012-Ohio-6175, 2012 WL 6738255. Infants ⇨ 1654

5.5. Location

Failure of indictment to state at least once that crimes occurred in particular counties was not plain error in prosecution for aggravated murder and other felonies committed in three counties, where the State provided a detailed bill of particulars that set out the location of the offenses. State v. Jackson (Ohio, 09-02-2014) 141 Ohio St.3d 171, 23 N.E.3d 1023, 2014-Ohio-3707. Criminal Law ⇨ 1032(5)

6. Surplusage

Indictment was not "duplicitous" in prosecution for gross sexual imposition against two victims, corruption of a minor, and compelling prostitution in connection with allegations that defendant molested his pediatric patients, where case involved a continuing course of conduct charged as separate offenses differentiated by certain time frames, counts involved allegations of conduct toward victims who were children or teenagers when the alleged acts occurred, and possibility of one conviction, rather than many, was to defendant's advantage. State v. Blankenburg (Ohio App. 12 Dist., 03-26-2012) 197 Ohio App.3d 201, 966 N.E.2d 958, 2012-Ohio-1289, appeal not allowed 132 Ohio St.3d 1514, 974 N.E.2d 112, 2012-Ohio-4021, denial of post-conviction relief reversed 2012-Ohio-6175, 2012 WL 6738255. Indictment And Information ⇨ 125(4.1)

2941.10 Indictment complete

Notes of Decisions

1. Sufficiency of indictment

Under Ohio law, once an indictment has been returned by a grand jury, plaintiff in a malicious prosecution action has the burden of producing substantial evidence to establish lack of probable cause; plaintiff must produce evidence to the effect that the return of the indictment resulted from perjured testimony or that the grand jury proceedings were otherwise significantly irregular. Reynolds v. Guerra (N.D.Ohio, 11-04-2009) 670 F.Supp.2d 633. Malicious Prosecution ⇨ 24(7)

PLEADING, AVERMENTS, AND ALLEGATIONS

2941.14 Allegations in homicide indictment

Notes of Decisions

1. In general

State's felony murder indictment did not need to specify the underlying felony; statute provided that, in an indictment for aggravated murder, murder, or voluntary or involuntary manslaughter, the manner in which, or the means by which, the death was caused need not be set forth, and defendant did not cite any authority that required the State to specify the underlying felony in his indictment of murder. State v. Jones (Ohio App. 8 Dist., Cuyahoga, 11-07-2002) No. 80737, 2002-Ohio-6045, 2002 WL 31478933, Unreported, motion for delayed appeal denied 98 Ohio St.3d 1509, 786 N.E.2d 60, 2003-Ohio-1572, appeal not allowed 98 Ohio St.3d 1513, 786 N.E.2d 63, 2003-Ohio-1572, motion to reopen denied 2003-Ohio-4397, 2003 WL 21981989, appeal not allowed 100 Ohio St.3d 1532, 800 N.E.2d 48, 2003-Ohio-6458, denial of post-conviction relief affirmed 2004-Ohio-3868, 2004 WL 1631122, habeas corpus denied 2006 WL 2849766. Homicide ⇨ 850

2. Multiple specifications in same count

Indictment for murder and involuntary manslaughter for causing a death during the commission of a felony did not need to specify the predicate felony offenses underlying the charges. State v. Talley (Ohio App. 8 Dist., Cuyahoga, 06-03-2004) No. 83237, 2004-Ohio-2846, 2004 WL 1234291, Unreported, appeal not allowed 103 Ohio St.3d 1494, 816 N.E.2d 1080, 2004-Ohio-5605, certiorari denied 125 S.Ct. 2548, 545 U.S. 1107, 162 L.Ed.2d 280, habeas corpus denied 619 F.Supp.2d 407. Homicide ⇨ 850

5. Aggravating circumstances

Aggregate sentence of 43 years in prison for attempted murder with a firearm specification, aggravated robbery, aggravated burglary, and kidnapping did not violate the Eighth Amendment's prohibition of cruel and unusual punishment in violation of the Eighth Amendment; defendant called victim, told him to exit his apartment, shot him in the abdomen, and went into the apartment, defendant and codefendant, who had shot victim several more times, ransacked the apartment, threatened a woman inside, and then tried to stuff victim in the trunk of a car, and defendant had an extensive and violent criminal and juvenile history. State v. Love (Ohio App. 1 Dist., 05-11-2011) 194 Ohio App.3d

16, 954 N.E.2d 202, 2011-Ohio-2224, appeal not allowed 129 Ohio St.3d 1490, 954 N.E.2d 663, 2011-Ohio-5129. Sentencing and Punishment ⚷ 645; Sentencing and Punishment ⚷ 1508

Trial court's error in giving instruction on aggravating circumstances at penalty phase of capital murder trial, describing defendant as causing victim's death with prior calculation and design "and" as principal offender in the aggravated murder, without requiring additional finding that the murder was committed while defendant was committing, attempting to commit, or fleeing immediately after committing or attempting to commit kidnapping, rape, aggravated arson, aggravated robbery, or aggravated burglary, and improperly using conjunctive "and" rather than disjunctive "or,", did not require reversal of death sentence; indictment accurately reflected statutory language for aggravating circumstance, instructions on alternative aggravating circumstances properly referred to kidnapping and aggravating robbery, jury unanimously found existence of alternative aggravating circumstances, there was dearth of mitigation evidence while overwhelming evidence established aggravating circumstances, and jury's conviction of defendant for aggravated murder, at guilt phase, constituted a specific finding of prior calculation and design. State v. Dixon (Ohio, 04-14-2004) 101 Ohio St.3d 328, 805 N.E.2d 1042, 2004-Ohio-1585, reconsideration denied 102 Ohio St.3d 1473, 809 N.E.2d 1159, 2004-Ohio-2830, certiorari denied 125 S.Ct. 875, 543 U.S. 1060, 160 L.Ed.2d 787, denial of habeas corpus reversed 627 F.3d 553, certiorari granted, reversed 132 S.Ct. 26, 181 L.Ed.2d 328, on remand 731 F.3d 539, withdrawn from bound volume. Sentencing And Punishment ⚷ 1789(9)

Although death penalty was never available as a sentencing option for 16-year-old defendant, due to his age, prosecution charging defendant with aggravated murder and aggravated robbery with specifications that would have made him eligible for the death penalty had he been an adult was required to be heard by a three-judge panel, as jurisdictional matter that could not be waived. State v. Koger (Ohio App. 6 Dist., 02-07-2003) 151 Ohio App.3d 534, 784 N.E.2d 780, 2003-Ohio-576, appeal allowed 99 Ohio St.3d 1451, 790 N.E.2d 1217, 2003-Ohio-3396, affirmed 102 Ohio St.3d 263, 809 N.E.2d 661, 2004-Ohio-2824, appeal after new trial 2007-Ohio-2398, 2007 WL 1452796. Criminal Law ⚷ 250; Sentencing And Punishment ⚷ 1643

Capital specifications in state indictment charging capital murder defendant both as being principal offender in commission of aggravated murder and as committing aggravated murder with prior calculation and design did not prejudice defendant, as required to obtain federal habeas corpus relief, where state trial court deleted reference to prior calculation and design from jury instructions, and jury was instructed to consider only whether defendant was principal offender. Brinkley v. Houk (N.D.Ohio, 12-05-2011) 866 F.Supp.2d 747, amended in part 2012 WL 1537661. Habeas Corpus ⚷ 474

2941.141 Specification concerning possession of firearm essential to affect sentence

(A) Imposition of a one-year mandatory prison term upon an offender under division (B)(1)(a) of section 2929.14 of the Revised Code is precluded unless the indictment, count in the indictment, or information charging the offense specifies that the offender had a firearm on or about the offender's person or under the offender's control while committing the offense. The specification shall be stated at the end of the body of the indictment, count, or information, and shall be in substantially the following form:

"SPECIFICATION (or, SPECIFICATION TO THE FIRST COUNT). The Grand Jurors (or insert the person's or the prosecuting attorney's name when appropriate) further find and specify that (set forth that the offender had a firearm on or about the offender's person or under the offender's control while committing the offense.)"

(B) Imposition of a one-year mandatory prison term upon an offender under division (B)(1)(a) of section 2929.14 of the Revised Code is precluded if a court imposes a three-year or six-year mandatory prison term on the offender under that division relative to the same felony.

(C) The specification described in division (A) of this section may be used in a delinquent child proceeding in the manner and for the purpose described in section 2152.17 of the Revised Code.

(D) As used in this section, "firearm" has the same meaning as in section 2923.11 of the Revised Code.

(2011 H 86, eff. 9-30-11; 2000 S 179, § 3, eff. 1-1-02; 1999 S 107, eff. 3-23-00; 1995 S 2, eff. 7-1-96; 1990 H 669, eff. 1-10-91; 1990 S 258; 1982 H 269, § 4, S 199)

Historical and Statutory Notes

Amendment Note: 2011 H 86 substituted "(B)(1)(a)" for "(D)(1)(a)" throughout.

Cross References

Felony specifications, see 2152.17

Research References

Encyclopedias

OH Jur. 3d Criminal Law: Procedure § 922, Firearms.

OH Jur. 3d Criminal Law: Procedure § 1873, Specification as Prerequisite to Enhanced Penalty; State's Burden of Proof; Proof of Prior Conviction.

OH Jur. 3d Criminal Law: Procedure § 1895, One-Year Term; Operability of Firearm.

OH Jur. 3d Criminal Law: Procedure § 1897, Role in Offense; Accomplice Liability.

OH Jur. 3d Criminal Law: Procedure § 1898, Applicability to Deadly Weapon.

OH Jur. 3d Habeas Corpus and Post Conviction Remedies § 39, Duration and Extent of Sentence and Punishment.

Treatises and Practice Aids

Katz & Giannelli, Baldwin's Ohio Practice Criminal Law § 40:5, Nature and Contents.

Katz & Giannelli, Baldwin's Ohio Practice Criminal Law § 106:5, Deadly Weapon or Ordnance on School Premises.

Katz & Giannelli, Baldwin's Ohio Practice Criminal Law § 118:8, Gun Enhancement.

Katz & Giannelli, Baldwin's Ohio Practice Criminal Law § 142:1, Skeleton Indictment--Single Count.

Katz & Giannelli, Baldwin's Ohio Practice Criminal Law § 142:2, Skeleton Indictment--Multiple Counts.

Katz & Giannelli, Baldwin's Ohio Practice Criminal Law § 80:22, Appellate Review of Sentencing.

Katz & Giannelli, Baldwin's Ohio Practice Criminal Law § 106:11, Discharging Firearm Into a School or Home.

Katz & Giannelli, Baldwin's Ohio Practice Criminal Law § 118:12, Drive-By Shooting.

Carlin, Baldwin's Ohio Prac. Merrick-Rippner Probate Law § 109:87, Enhanced Dispositions Due to Felony Specifications, Effective January 1, 2002.

Weiler & Weiler, Ohio Driving Under the Influence App. A, Ohio Revised Code--Selected Provisions.

Giannelli & Yeomans Salvador, Ohio Juvenile Law App. A, Ohio Revised Code--Selected Provisions.

Giannelli & Yeomans Salvador, Ohio Juvenile Law § 22:3, Department of Youth Services Commitment.

Notes of Decisions

1. Constitutional issues

In prosecution of defendant for using a firearm during and in relation to any drug trafficking offense, failure of indictment to specify particular drug trafficking offenses involved did not undermine its sufficiency, where indictment tracked statutory language, properly gave defendant notice of charges that he would be facing at trial, and was sufficiently specific to provide protection against double jeopardy, inasmuch as it specified particular dates on which drug trafficking offenses occurred and type of drugs which were involved in each transaction. U.S. v. Kuehne (C.A.6 (Ohio), 10-28-2008) 547 F.3d 667, rehearing and rehearing en banc denied, habeas corpus dismissed 2009 WL 1045897, certiorari dismissed 130 S.Ct. 21, 557 U.S. 947, 174 L.Ed.2d 605, certiorari denied 130 S.Ct. 342, 558 U.S. 928, 175 L.Ed.2d 227, post-conviction relief dismissed 2011 WL 5521245, reconsideration denied 2012 WL 1424994. Indictment And Information ⚷ 110(38); Weapons ⚷ 230

Sentencing guidelines, notice of departure, variance from recommended range. Irizarry v. U.S., 2008, 128 S.Ct. 2198, 171 L.Ed.2d 28.

2. Penalty enhancement

Sentence of 77 months' imprisonment, imposed upon defendant who pled guilty to being a felon in possession of a firearm, was procedurally reasonable, where sentence was within properly calculated advisory guidelines range and sentencing court adequately explained its reasoning; court referenced arguments of counsel, presentence report, relevant sentencing factors, recognized its duty to impose sentence sufficient, but not greater than necessary, to comply with statutory sentencing purposes, summarized such purposes, and explicitly discussed both applicable statutory factors and defendant's arguments in mitigation. U.S. v. Pettie (C.A.6 (Ohio), 06-19-2007) No. 06-3458, 242 Fed.Appx. 313, 2007 WL 1786821, Unreported. Sentencing And Punishment ⚷ 996; Weapons ⚷ 343

Evidence in rape prosecution did not support imposition of one-year mandatory sentence for a firearm specification; although victim believed defendant had a gun in his coat pocket because he kept his hand in his pocket, there was no evidence that defendant threatened victim with a gun, or that victim felt an object or saw a shape which could be construed as a gun. State v. Evans (Ohio App. 8 Dist., Cuyahoga, 07-28-2005) No. 85396, 2005-Ohio-3847, 2005 WL 1792351, Unreported, appeal allowed 108 Ohio St.3d 1411, 841 N.E.2d 317, 2006-Ohio-179, remanded 113 Ohio St.3d 100, 863 N.E.2d 113, 2007-Ohio-861, on remand

2007-Ohio-3278, 2007 WL 1848719. Sentencing And Punishment ⚿ 323

Trial court properly sentenced defendant for three-year and five-year firearms specifications attached to charged offenses of aggravated murder and attempted murder, even though defendant claimed both enhancements were based on same act; legislature required enhancements to be served consecutively to one another and to the prison terms for the base offense. State v. Gresham (Ohio App. 8 Dist., Cuyahoga, 02-20-2003) No. 81250, 2003-Ohio-744, 2003 WL 360922, Unreported, dismissal of post-conviction relief affirmed 2008-Ohio-4248, 2008 WL 3870612. Sentencing And Punishment ⚿ 144

Defendant possessed sawed-off shotgun that police officers found on top of his trash can while investigating burglary at his residence, as required to support enhancement of his sentence on a felon-in-possession-of-ammunition charge; although defendant's girlfriend stated that she had not seen the shotgun in the house before the burglary, the officers recovered the shotgun from the residence and defendant admitted on two separate occasions that he owned the gun. U.S. v. Conway (C.A.6 (Ohio), 01-23-2008) 513 F.3d 640. Sentencing And Punishment ⚿ 980

Defendant's possession of sawed-off shotgun could be treated as "relevant conduct" when sentencing him for being a felon in possession of nine-millimeter and assault-rifle ammunition; relevant conduct bore considerable similarity to the offense of conviction, in addition to the nine-millimeter and assault-rifle ammunition, police also discovered shotgun ammunition in defendant's house, and the offenses occurred at the same time and at the same place. U.S. v. Conway (C.A.6 (Ohio), 01-23-2008) 513 F.3d 640. Sentencing And Punishment ⚿ 726(3)

Criminal law, sentencing, armed career offenders, prior convictions for serious drug offenses, maximum term of imprisonment, required recidivist enhancements for prior offense. U.S. v. Rodriquez, 2008, 128 S.Ct. 1783, 170 L.Ed.2d 719.

5. Deadly weapon; firearm

Habeas petitioner's purported newly-discovered evidence failed to establish that it was more likely than not that no reasonable juror would have found him guilty beyond reasonable doubt of aggravated murder with a firearm specification, as required to excuse untimely habeas petition and allow review of petitioner's procedurally defaulted claims based on actual innocence; post-trial affidavits, which stated that there was second shooter and that gunfight ensued, contained contradictions and inconsistencies, fact that bullet hole in petitioner's car was made using same gun that fired bullet that killed victim suggested, at very least, that petitioner was at scene of murder, and while affiants' statements that second shooter was shooting from hood of car provided explanation as to why bullet hole was later found in roof of petitioner's car, reasonable juror could easily conclude that bullet hole was made later in order to frustrate evidence. Chavis-Tucker v. Hudson (C.A.6 (Ohio), 10-09-2009) No. 07-4537, 348 Fed.Appx. 125, 2009 WL 3232068, Unreported, certiorari denied 130 S.Ct. 1712, 559 U.S. 982, 176 L.Ed.2d 198. Habeas Corpus ⚿ 401; Habeas Corpus ⚿ 407

6. Procedural issues

Defendant convicted of being felon in possession of firearm was not entitled to six-level downward departure on ground that weapon at issue was antique and was not used for any criminal purpose, where defendant's predicate offense was controlled substance offense. U.S. v. Fuson (C.A.6 (Ohio), 11-16-2004) No. 04-3050, 116 Fed.Appx. 588, 2004 WL 2590566, Unreported, appeal after new sentencing hearing 215 Fed.Appx. 468, 2007 WL 414265. Sentencing And Punishment ⚿ 855

7. Weapon "on person" or "under control"

Finding of defendant's possession of firearm, as element for firearm specification carrying one-year mandatory prison sentence, was against manifest weight of evidence, in prosecution for two counts of complicity to commit aggravated robbery and one count of complicity to commit felonious assault; while gun on kitchen table in apartment had distinctive characteristics of defendant's gun, there was no evidence defendant had been in the kitchen during the crimes. State v. Jackson (Ohio App. 6 Dist., 11-17-2006) 169 Ohio App.3d 440, 863 N.E.2d 223, 2006-Ohio-6059. Sentencing And Punishment ⚿ 323

8. Firearm specification; lesser included offense

Evidence, including victim's testimony as corroborated by investigating officer, as to number, types, and operability of firearms stolen from victim's home, was sufficient to support conviction of burglary with firearm specification. State v. Elersic (Ohio App. 11 Dist., Lake, 09-30-2004) No. 2002-L-172, 2004-Ohio-5301, 2004 WL 2804809, Unreported, appeal not allowed 105 Ohio St.3d 1407, 821 N.E.2d 1027, 2005-Ohio-279, habeas corpus denied 2008 WL 618647, denial of post-conviction relief affirmed 2008-Ohio-2121, 2008 WL 1932109. Burglary ⚿ 41(1)

State may use circumstantial evidence to establish that the defendant possessed an operable firearm, as required to prove firearm specification. State v. Dickess (Ohio App. 4 Dist., 01-03-2008) 174 Ohio App.3d 658, 884 N.E.2d 92, 2008-Ohio-39, appeal not allowed 118 Ohio St.3d 1434, 887 N.E.2d 1203, 2008-Ohio-2595, habeas corpus denied 2010 WL 5276992. Sentencing And Punishment ⚿ 323

There was sufficient circumstantial evidence that defendant possessed a firearm to support conviction for firearm specification; victim saw gun, defendant told victim that he would kill him if he did not cooperate, and victim obviously took these threats seriously. State v. Dickess (Ohio App. 4 Dist., 01-03-2008) 174 Ohio App.3d 658, 884 N.E.2d 92, 2008-Ohio-39, appeal not allowed 118 Ohio St.3d 1434, 887 N.E.2d 1203, 2008-Ohio-2595, habeas corpus denied 2010 WL 5276992. Sentencing And Punishment ⚯ 323

Fact that first of two guns in apartment, which gun was not in possession of defendant or robber/assailant, was operable, and that robber/assailant possessed another gun, which other gun was inoperable, could not be "blended" so as to impute to defendant the possession of an operable gun, as basis for firearm specification carrying one-year mandatory prison sentence, in prosecution for two counts of complicity to commit aggravated robbery and one count of complicity to commit felonious assault. State v. Jackson (Ohio App. 6 Dist., 11-17-2006) 169 Ohio App.3d 440, 863 N.E.2d 223, 2006-Ohio-6059. Sentencing And Punishment ⚯ 79

Evidence of postseizure test firing may prove operability of a firearm, as element for firearm specification which carries one-year mandatory prison term. State v. Jackson (Ohio App. 6 Dist., 11-17-2006) 169 Ohio App.3d 440, 863 N.E.2d 223, 2006-Ohio-6059. Sentencing And Punishment ⚯ 323

2941.142 Specification concerning offense of violence while participating in criminal gang activity

(A) Imposition of a mandatory prison term of one, two, or three years pursuant to division (G) of section 2929.14 of the Revised Code upon an offender who committed a felony that is an offense of violence while participating in a criminal gang is precluded unless the indictment, count in the indictment, or information charging the felony specifies that the offender committed the felony that is an offense of violence while participating in a criminal gang. The specification shall be stated at the end of the body of the indictment, count, or information, and shall be in substantially the following form:

"SPECIFICATION (or, SPECIFICATION TO THE FIRST COUNT). The grand jurors (or insert the person's or the prosecuting attorney's name when appropriate) further find and specify that (set forth that the offender committed the felony that is an offense of violence while participating in a criminal gang.)"

(B) The specification described in division (A) of this section may be used in a delinquent child proceeding in the manner and for the purpose described in section 2152.17 of the Revised Code.

(C) As used in this section, "criminal gang" has the same meaning as in section 2923.41 of the Revised Code.

(2011 H 86, eff. 9-30-11; 2000 S 179, § 3, eff. 1-1-02; 1998 H 2, eff. 1-1-99)

Historical and Statutory Notes

Amendment Note: 2011 H 86 substituted "(G)" for "(I)" in division (A).

Research References

Encyclopedias

OH Jur. 3d Criminal Law: Procedure § 924, Violence, Generally.

OH Jur. 3d Criminal Law: Procedure § 1900, Participation in Criminal Gang Activity.

Treatises and Practice Aids

Katz & Giannelli, Baldwin's Ohio Practice Criminal Law § 40:5, Nature and Contents.

Katz & Giannelli, Baldwin's Ohio Practice Criminal Law § 118:8, Gun Enhancement.

Katz & Giannelli, Baldwin's Ohio Practice Criminal Law § 80:22, Appellate Review of Sentencing.

Katz & Giannelli, Baldwin's Ohio Practice Criminal Law § 118:10, Criminal Gang Add-Ons.

Carlin, Baldwin's Ohio Prac. Merrick-Rippner Probate Law § 109:87, Enhanced Dispositions Due to Felony Specifications, Effective January 1, 2002.

Weiler & Weiler, Ohio Driving Under the Influence App. A, Ohio Revised Code--Selected Provisions.

Giannelli & Yeomans Salvador, Ohio Juvenile Law App. A, Ohio Revised Code--Selected Provisions.

Giannelli & Yeomans Salvador, Ohio Juvenile Law § 22:3, Department of Youth Services Commitment.

2941.143 Specification concerning school safety zone

Imposition of a sentence by a court pursuant to division (H) of section 2929.14 of the Revised Code is precluded unless the indictment, count in the indictment, or information charging aggravated murder, murder, or a felony of the first, second, or third degree that is an offense of violence specifies that the offender committed the offense in a school safety zone or towards a person in a school safety zone. The specification shall be stated at the end of the body of the indictment, count, or information and shall be in substantially the following form:

"SPECIFICATION (or, SPECIFICATION TO THE FIRST COUNT). The grand jurors (or insert the person's or the prosecuting attorney's name when appropriate) further find and specify that (set forth that the offender committed aggravated murder, murder, or the felony of the first, second, or third degree that is an offense of violence in a school safety zone or towards a person in a school safety zone)."

(2011 H 86, eff. 9-30-11; 1999 S 1, eff. 8–6–99)

Historical and Statutory Notes

Amendment Note: 2011 H 86 substituted "(H)" for "(J)" in the first paragraph; and made other nonsubstantive changes.

Research References

Encyclopedias

OH Jur. 3d Criminal Law: Procedure § 924, Violence, Generally.

OH Jur. 3d Criminal Law: Procedure § 1901, Offense Within School Safety Zone; Violation Within Proximity to School.

Treatises and Practice Aids

Katz & Giannelli, Baldwin's Ohio Practice Criminal Law § 40:5, Nature and Contents.

Katz & Giannelli, Baldwin's Ohio Practice Criminal Law § 40:7, Amendments to the Indictment.

Katz & Giannelli, Baldwin's Ohio Practice Criminal Law § 62:10, Waiver of Jury Trial.

Katz & Giannelli, Baldwin's Ohio Practice Criminal Law § 80:22, Appellate Review of Sentencing.

Katz & Giannelli, Baldwin's Ohio Practice Criminal Law § 118:11, School Safety Zone Add-on.

Adrine & Ruden, Ohio Domestic Violence Law § 2:7, Felony Violations.

Weiler & Weiler, Ohio Driving Under the Influence App. A, Ohio Revised Code--Selected Provisions.

2941.144 Specification concerning possession of automatic firearm or firearm with suppressor

(A) Imposition of a six-year mandatory prison term upon an offender under division (B)(1)(a) of section 2929.14 of the Revised Code is precluded unless the indictment, count in the indictment, or information charging the offense specifies that the offender had a firearm that is an automatic firearm or that was equipped with a firearm muffler or suppressor on or about the offender's person or under the offender's control while committing the offense. The specification shall be stated at the end of the body of the indictment, count, or information and shall be stated in substantially the following form:

"SPECIFICATION (or, SPECIFICATION TO THE FIRST COUNT). The Grand Jurors (or insert the person's or the prosecuting attorney's name when appropriate) further find and specify that (set forth that the offender had a firearm that is an automatic firearm or that was equipped with a firearm muffler or suppressor on or about the offender's person or under the offender's control while committing the offense)."

(B) Imposition of a six-year mandatory prison term upon an offender under division (B)(1)(a) of section 2929.14 of the Revised Code is precluded if a court imposes a three-year or one-year mandatory prison term on the offender under that division relative to the same felony.

(C) The specification described in division (A) of this section may be used in a delinquent child proceeding in the manner and for the purpose described in section 2152.17 of the Revised Code.

(D) As used in this section, "firearm" and "automatic firearm" have the same meanings as in section 2923.11 of the Revised Code.

(2014 H 234, eff. 3-23-15; 2011 H 86, eff. 9-30-11; 2000 S 179, § 3, eff. 1–1–02; 1999 S 107, eff. 3–23–00; 1995 S 2, eff. 7–1–96; 1990 S 258, eff. 11–20–90)

Historical and Statutory Notes

Amendment Note: 2014 H 234 twice substituted "suppressor" for "silencer" in division (A).

Amendment Note: 2011 H 86 substituted "(B)(1)(a)" for "(D)(1)(a)" throughout.

Cross References

Felony specifications, see 2152.17

Research References

Encyclopedias

OH Jur. 3d Criminal Law: Procedure § 922, Firearms.

OH Jur. 3d Criminal Law: Procedure § 1892, Six-Year Term.

Treatises and Practice Aids

Katz & Giannelli, Baldwin's Ohio Practice Criminal Law § 40:5, Nature and Contents.

Katz & Giannelli, Baldwin's Ohio Practice Criminal Law § 106:5, Deadly Weapon or Ordnance on School Premises.

Katz & Giannelli, Baldwin's Ohio Practice Criminal Law § 118:8, Gun Enhancement.

Katz & Giannelli, Baldwin's Ohio Practice Criminal Law § 80:22, Appellate Review of Sentencing.

Katz & Giannelli, Baldwin's Ohio Practice Criminal Law § 106:11, Discharging Firearm Into a School or Home.

Katz & Giannelli, Baldwin's Ohio Practice Criminal Law § 106:13, Unlawful Possession of Dangerous Ordnance.

Carlin, Baldwin's Ohio Prac. Merrick-Rippner Probate Law § 109:87, Enhanced Dispositions Due to Felony Specifications, Effective January 1, 2002.

Weiler & Weiler, Ohio Driving Under the Influence App. A, Ohio Revised Code--Selected Provisions.

Giannelli & Yeomans Salvador, Ohio Juvenile Law App. A, Ohio Revised Code--Selected Provisions.

Giannelli & Yeomans Salvador, Ohio Juvenile Law § 22:3, Department of Youth Services Commitment.

Notes of Decisions

Indictment 1

1. Indictment

Indictment charging defendant with illegal possession of machinegun was not deficient for failing to allege that defendant possessed a mechanical trigger; defendant was charged with possessing frame or receiver of a machinegun and parts designed and intended for use in converting weapon into machinegun, and testimony established that weapon could actually be fired manually. U.S. v. Carter (C.A.6 (Ohio), 10-17-2006) 465 F.3d 658, certiorari denied 127 S.Ct. 2444, 550 U.S. 964, 167 L.Ed.2d 1142. Internal Revenue ⚷ 5265; Internal Revenue ⚷ 5295

2941.145 Specification concerning use of firearm to facilitate offense

(A) Imposition of a three-year mandatory prison term upon an offender under division (B)(1)(a) of section 2929.14 of the Revised Code is precluded unless the indictment, count in the indictment, or information charging the offense specifies that the offender had a firearm on or about the offender's person or under the offender's control while committing the offense and displayed the firearm, brandished the firearm, indicated that the offender possessed the firearm, or used it to facilitate the offense. The specification shall be stated at the end of the body of the indictment, count, or information, and shall be stated in substantially the following form:

"SPECIFICATION (or, SPECIFICATION TO THE FIRST COUNT). The Grand Jurors (or insert the person's or the prosecuting attorney's name when appropriate) further find and specify that (set forth that the offender had a firearm on or about the offender's person or under the offender's control while committing the offense and displayed the firearm, brandished the firearm, indicated that the offender possessed the firearm, or used it to facilitate the offense)."

(B) Imposition of a three-year mandatory prison term upon an offender under division (B)(1)(a) of section 2929.14 of the Revised Code is precluded if a court imposes a one-year or six-year mandatory prison term on the offender under that division relative to the same felony.

(C) The specification described in division (A) of this section may be used in a delinquent child proceeding in the manner and for the purpose described in section 2152.17 of the Revised Code.

(D) As used in this section, "firearm" has the same meaning as in section 2923.11 of the Revised Code.

(2011 H 86, eff. 9-30-11; 2000 S 179, § 3, eff. 1-1-02; 1999 S 107, eff. 3-23-00; 1995 S 2, eff. 7-1-96)

Historical and Statutory Notes

Amendment Note: 2011 H 86 substituted "(B)(1)(a)" for "(D)(1)(a)" throughout.

Cross References

Felony specifications, see 2152.17

Research References

ALR Library

76 ALR 468, Illegal or Erroneous Sentence as Ground for Habeas Corpus.

Encyclopedias

OH Jur. 3d Criminal Law: Procedure § 922, Firearms.

OH Jur. 3d Criminal Law: Procedure § 1894, Three-Year Term.

OH Jur. 3d Criminal Law: Procedure § 1896, Double Jeopardy Considerations.

OH Jur. 3d Criminal Law: Procedure § 1897, Role in Offense; Accomplice Liability.

OH Jur. 3d Habeas Corpus and Post Conviction Remedies § 39, Duration and Extent of Sentence and Punishment.

Treatises and Practice Aids

Katz & Giannelli, Baldwin's Ohio Practice Criminal Law § 40:5, Nature and Contents.

Katz & Giannelli, Baldwin's Ohio Practice Criminal Law § 106:5, Deadly Weapon or Ordnance on School Premises.

Katz & Giannelli, Baldwin's Ohio Practice Criminal Law § 118:8, Gun Enhancement.

Katz & Giannelli, Baldwin's Ohio Practice Criminal Law § 152:9, Motion to Correct Improper Sentence--Firearm Specifications as Part of One Transaction.

Katz & Giannelli, Baldwin's Ohio Practice Criminal Law § 73:10, Allied Offenses of Similar Import.

Katz & Giannelli, Baldwin's Ohio Practice Criminal Law § 80:22, Appellate Review of Sentencing.

Katz & Giannelli, Baldwin's Ohio Practice Criminal Law § 106:11, Discharging Firearm Into a School or Home.

Carlin, Baldwin's Ohio Prac. Merrick-Rippner Probate Law § 109:87, Enhanced Dispositions Due to Felony Specifications, Effective January 1, 2002.

Weiler & Weiler, Ohio Driving Under the Influence App. A, Ohio Revised Code--Selected Provisions.

Giannelli & Yeomans Salvador, Ohio Juvenile Law App. A, Ohio Revised Code--Selected Provisions.

Giannelli & Yeomans Salvador, Ohio Juvenile Law § 22:3, Department of Youth Services Commitment.

Notes of Decisions

Allied offenses of similar import 9
Applicability 10
Constitutional issues 1–3.5
Failure to raise issue 3.5

---

2. —— Double jeopardy, constitutional issues

Imposition of sentences on both underlying charge of theft of a firearm and on concomitant firearm specification did not violate double jeopardy principles, where firearm specification required finding that defendant either displayed firearm, brandished it, indicated that he possessed it, or used it to facilitate offense, and jury specifically found that defendant not only possessed firearm but indicated that he possessed it. State v. Mosley (Ohio App. 5 Dist., 04-04-2006) 166 Ohio App.3d 71, 849 N.E.2d 73, 2006-Ohio-1756. Double Jeopardy ⚷ 30

3.5. —— Failure to raise issue, constitutional issues

Although constitutionality of firearm specification statute as it applied to conviction of police officer for felonious assault based on use of his service weapon was not raised in the trial court, appellate court would consider the issue; the issue was raised and argued in the parties' briefs, and it touched on the rights and interests of any Ohio peace officer who, under similarly hurried conditions during an on-duty encounter, may have to draw, point and fire his gun at a criminal suspect, and thereby subject himself to a felony charge and the imposition of the specification. State v. White (Ohio App. 6 Dist., 01-11-2013) 988 N.E.2d 595, 2013-Ohio-51, stay granted 134 Ohio St.3d 1483, 984 N.E.2d 27, 2013-Ohio-902, appeal allowed 135 Ohio St.3d 1447, 987 N.E.2d 703, 2013-Ohio-2062. Criminal Law ⚷ 1042.3(1)

Firearm specification statute, which enhanced penalty when firearm was used in criminal offense, was unconstitutional as applied to defendant police officer, who was prosecuted for felonious assault based on his shooting of a suspect whom he believed had a weapon; to convict the officer of the firearm specification for an act he unambiguously took in the good-faith performance of a law enforcement function, using a firearm he was compelled to carry, violated his due process rights. State v. White (Ohio App. 6 Dist., 01-11-2013) 988 N.E.2d 595, 2013-Ohio-51, stay granted 134 Ohio St.3d 1483, 984 N.E.2d 27, 2013-Ohio-902, appeal allowed 135 Ohio St.3d 1447, 987 N.E.2d 703, 2013-Ohio-2062. Constitutional Law ⚷ 4509(25); Sentencing and Punishment ⚷ 8

4. Stolen gun

Firearm that was object of defendant's theft from deputy sheriff also supported firearm specification for aggravated robbery charge arising from that theft, where defendant used firearm immediately after the theft to facilitate his flight by committing carjacking. State v. Campbell (Ohio, 12-20-2000) 90 Ohio St.3d 320, 738 N.E.2d 1178, 2000-Ohio-183, reconsideration denied 91 Ohio St.3d 1433, 741 N.E.2d 896, certiorari denied 121 S.Ct. 2606, 533 U.S. 956, 150 L.Ed.2d 762, dismissal of post-conviction relief affirmed 2003-Ohio-6305, 2003 WL 22783857, appeal not allowed 102 Ohio St.3d 1470, 809 N.E.2d 1158, 2004-Ohio-2830, habeas corpus denied in part 2008 WL 657536, habeas corpus denied 2009 WL 773866. Robbery ⚷ 24.15(2)

5. Evidence

Evidence was sufficient to support trial court finding that juvenile committed acts that, if he was an adult, would have constituted aggravated robbery with a firearm specification, warranting adjudication of delinquency; victim testified that a perpetrator grabbed her car door and demanded her purse while sticking handgun in her face, and fingerprints taken from victim's car matched defendant's, and victim later identified the defendant as the perpetrator, despite fact that he wore a bandana over face, based on distinctive eyes and stature. In re Wallace (Ohio App. 5 Dist., Stark, 03-24-2008) No. 2007CA00156, 2008-Ohio-1389, 2008 WL 786870, Unreported. Infants ⚷ 2640(8)

Defendant's conviction for complicity to murder with a gun specification was not against the manifest weight or the sufficiency of the evidence; defendant suspected that victim had broken into his car, and, rather than involve the police, he went out searching for victim, defendant testified that he fired a loaded semi-automatic weapon at victim, but no bullets discharged, and further evidence indicated that defendant supplied accomplice with a second gun used to kill victim. State v. Alexander (Ohio App. 9 Dist., Summit, 05-18-2005) No. 22295, 2005-Ohio-2393, 2005 WL 1162984, Unreported, motion for delayed appeal denied 107 Ohio St.3d 1405, 836 N.E.2d 1226, 2005-Ohio-5859, habeas corpus denied 2007 WL 1989597, objections overruled 2007 WL 2153275. Homicide ⚷ 1207

Conviction for aggravated robbery with gun specification was not against manifest weight of evidence; defendant intended to rob victim at apartment and, during that attempt, aimed gun at victim's girlfriend, victim heard voice tell girlfriend to get down, heard girlfriend crying, jumped from apartment window and went for help, and saw flash of handgun toward apartment when he glanced back. State v. Dillard (Ohio App. 7 Dist., Jefferson, 03-28-2005) No. 03 JE 32, 2005-Ohio-1656, 2005 WL 775888, Unreported, appeal after new sentencing hearing 2006-Ohio-3524, 2006 WL 1868318, appeal after new sentencing hearing 2010-Ohio-1407, 2010 WL 1237102, denial of post-conviction relief affirmed 2014-Ohio-439, 2014 WL 539153. Robbery ⚷ 24.15(2)

Defendant's convictions for first-degree aggravated robbery with a firearm specification and second-degree robbery were not against the manifest weight of the evidence, even if teenage victim was only able to observe robber for less than a minute, robber had a sock pulled over much of his face, and defendant did not confess; victim was able to see bottom portion of robber's face, victim noticed details such as robber's long hair, leather coat, and black gun, victim readily identified defendant as robber after viewing photo array for no longer than 30 seconds, there was testimony that defendant "pitched" his black gun around time of robbery, defendant owned a black leather coat around time of robbery, and defendant had in his possession at time of robbery the approximate amount of cash taken in robbery. State v. Hayes (Ohio App. 6 Dist., Lucas, 12-03-2004) No. L-03-1221, No. L-03-1222, 2004-Ohio-6460, 2004 WL 2785290, Unreported, appeal not allowed 105 Ohio St.3d 1516, 826 N.E.2d 314, 2005-Ohio-1880, habeas corpus denied 2008 WL 596097. Robbery ⚷ 24.40

Conviction for aggravated murder with firearm specification was supported by sufficient evidence and was not against manifest weight of evidence, even though inconsistencies in testimonies of eyewitnesses raised questions as to credibility of some parts of testimonies; unarmed victim and defendant, who was armed with gun, were engaged in progressively escalating argument, eyewitnesses heard gunshot, one eyewitness looked to find defendant standing over victim holding gun, bullets and bullet fragments recovered from scene and from victim were consistent with being fired from gun that defendant was known to own, and eyewitnesses corroborated each other in significant aspects. State v. Towler (Ohio App. 10 Dist., Franklin, 12-02-2004) No. 04AP-141, 2004-Ohio-6445, 2004 WL 2757849, Unreported, appeal not allowed 105 Ohio St.3d 1499, 825 N.E.2d 623, 2005-Ohio-1666, dismissal of post-conviction relief affirmed 2006-Ohio-2441, 2006 WL 1351605, appeal not allowed 111 Ohio St.3d 1414, 854 N.E.2d 1093, 2006-Ohio-5083. Homicide ⚷ 1139

Defendant could be convicted of firearm specification with respect to offense of felonious assault, where felonious assault did not require use of firearm. State v. Elko (Ohio App. 8 Dist., Cuyahoga, 09-30-2004) No. 83641, 2004-Ohio-5209, 2004 WL 2340258, Unreported, appeal not allowed 105

Ohio St.3d 1441, 822 N.E.2d 811, 2005-Ohio-540, denial of post-conviction relief affirmed 2007-Ohio-2638, 2007 WL 1559297, habeas corpus dismissed 2008 WL 728367. Sentencing And Punishment ⚯ 139

Defendant could not be convicted of firearm specification with respect to offense of improperly discharging firearm at or into habitation, where use of firearm was element of offense of improperly discharging firearm. State v. Elko (Ohio App. 8 Dist., Cuyahoga, 09-30-2004) No. 83641, 2004-Ohio-5209, 2004 WL 2340258, Unreported, appeal not allowed 105 Ohio St.3d 1441, 822 N.E.2d 811, 2005-Ohio-540, denial of post-conviction relief affirmed 2007-Ohio-2638, 2007 WL 1559297, habeas corpus dismissed 2008 WL 728367. Sentencing And Punishment ⚯ 139

Convictions for murder with firearm specification, attempted murder with firearm specification, felonious assault with firearm specification, and kidnapping with firearm specification were not against manifest weight of evidence; although defendant claimed testimony of attempted murder victim and witness was not credible, credibility was issue for jury to resolve, and victim testified that defendant shot him and forced him out of vehicle with gun. State v. Fayne (Ohio App. 8 Dist., Cuyahoga, 09-02-2004) No. 83267, 2004-Ohio-4625, 2004 WL 1944793, Unreported, motion for delayed appeal denied 106 Ohio St.3d 1502, 833 N.E.2d 1246, 2005-Ohio-4605, habeas corpus denied 2007 WL 1485812. Homicide ⚯ 1184; Kidnapping ⚯ 36; Sentencing And Punishment ⚯ 323

Evidence was sufficient to support conviction for murder with firearm specification; police officer testified that defendant said he shot victim and that shooting involved gang dispute and detective testified that defendant admitted that he shot victim. State v. Fayne (Ohio App. 8 Dist., Cuyahoga, 09-02-2004) No. 83267, 2004-Ohio-4625, 2004 WL 1944793, Unreported, motion for delayed appeal denied 106 Ohio St.3d 1502, 833 N.E.2d 1246, 2005-Ohio-4605, habeas corpus denied 2007 WL 1485812. Homicide ⚯ 1186

Evidence was sufficient to support conviction for felonious assault with firearm specification; victim testified that defendant and another gang member force victim out of vehicle and that defendant shot victim as victim fled. State v. Fayne (Ohio App. 8 Dist., Cuyahoga, 09-02-2004) No. 83267, 2004-Ohio-4625, 2004 WL 1944793, Unreported, motion for delayed appeal denied 106 Ohio St.3d 1502, 833 N.E.2d 1246, 2005-Ohio-4605, habeas corpus denied 2007 WL 1485812. Assault And Battery ⚯ 91.6(3)

Evidence was sufficient to support conviction for attempted murder with firearm specification; victim testified that defendant and another gang member forced victim out of vehicle, that gang member hit victim, and that defendant shot victim as victim fled. State v. Fayne (Ohio App. 8 Dist., Cuyahoga, 09-02-2004) No. 83267, 2004-Ohio-4625, 2004 WL 1944793, Unreported, motion for delayed appeal denied 106 Ohio St.3d 1502, 833 N.E.2d 1246, 2005-Ohio-4605, habeas corpus denied 2007 WL 1485812. Homicide ⚯ 1181

Evidence was sufficient to support conviction for kidnapping with firearm specification; victim testified that defendant and another gang member ran up to vehicle, that defendant put gun in victim's face and told victim to get out of vehicle or defendant would kill victim, and that victim got out of vehicle. State v. Fayne (Ohio App. 8 Dist., Cuyahoga, 09-02-2004) No. 83267, 2004-Ohio-4625, 2004 WL 1944793, Unreported, motion for delayed appeal denied 106 Ohio St.3d 1502, 833 N.E.2d 1246, 2005-Ohio-4605, habeas corpus denied 2007 WL 1485812. Kidnapping ⚯ 36

Evidence was sufficient to establish that defendant, in process of committing kidnapping, rape, aggravated robbery, felonious assault, and attempted murder, brandished a firearm that was operable, or could readily have been rendered operable, thus supporting his convictions for such offenses with firearm specification, where defendant threatened to kill victim, victim had ample opportunity to observe firearm, which was used to strike victim twice, and was described in victim's testimony as a shotgun with a wooden stock. State v. Axson (Ohio App. 8 Dist., Cuyahoga, 05-01-2003) No. 81231, 2003-Ohio-2182, 2003 WL 1994490, Unreported, appeal dismissed 99 Ohio St.3d 1517, 792 N.E.2d 730, 2003-Ohio-4009, appeal allowed 100 Ohio St.3d 1408, 796 N.E.2d 536, 2003-Ohio-4948, motion to dismiss appeal denied 100 Ohio St.3d 1425, 797 N.E.2d 92, 2003-Ohio-5232, reversed 104 Ohio St.3d 248, 819 N.E.2d 271, 2004-Ohio-6396, subsequent determination 2005-Ohio-4396, 2005 WL 2038692, appeal after new sentencing hearing 2005-Ohio-6342, 2005 WL 3219727, appeal allowed, reversed 109 Ohio St.3d 509, 849 N.E.2d 284, 2006-Ohio-2721, reconsideration denied 110 Ohio St.3d 1444, 852 N.E.2d 191, 2006-Ohio-3862, appeal after new sentencing hearing 2007-Ohio-2892, 2007 WL 1695108, appeal after new sentencing hearing 2007-Ohio-3126, 2007 WL 1805041, motion for delayed appeal denied 116 Ohio St.3d 1436, 877 N.E.2d 988, 2007-Ohio-6518, habeas corpus dismissed 2010 WL 750176, appeal after new sentencing hearing 2007-Ohio-5811, 2007 WL 3171233, appeal not allowed 117 Ohio St.3d 1426, 882 N.E.2d 446, 2008-Ohio-969, appeal after new sentencing hearing 2011-Ohio-3187, 2011 WL 2569789. Sentencing And Punishment ⚯ 78

Defendant knowingly, intelligently, and voluntarily entered guilty plea to complicity to commit murder and to a firearm specification; colloquy with defendant strictly complied with requirements regarding advisements of constitutional rights being waived, defendant responded "yes" when asked whether he understood he would be giving up nonconstitutional appeal rights, and trial court gave defendant opportunity to withdraw plea when defendant, on being asked whether there had been any promises or threats to secure his plea, vented frustration with a prosecutor in contemporaneous federal case. State v. Pough (Ohio App. 11 Dist.,

Trumbull, 12-13-2002) No. 2000-T-0151, 2002-Ohio-6927, 2002 WL 31813100, Unreported, appeal not allowed 98 Ohio St.3d 1538, 786 N.E.2d 901, 2003-Ohio-1946, dismissal of post-conviction relief affirmed 2004-Ohio-3933, 2004 WL 1663519, habeas corpus dismissed 2006 WL 3241791, denial of post-conviction relief affirmed 2011-Ohio-3630, 2011 WL 2982332. Criminal Law ⇔ 273.1(4)

State adequately proved that defendant utilized a firearm in commission of aggravated robbery, and thus conviction was not against the weight of the evidence, even though firearm was not found on defendant's person; police officers observed defendant flee in victim's vehicle through a field where firearm was recovered and officer observed him open the vehicle's driver's side door, victim testified that driver's side window was inoperable, firearm trigger contained defendant's DNA, and during his arrest defendant stated that he could not be charged with aggravated robbery without a gun. State v. Ervin-Williams (Ohio App. 11 Dist., 12-15-2014) 2014-Ohio-5473, 2014 WL 7014601. Robbery ⇔ 24.15(2)

Jury verdict that defendant was guilty of felonious assault but not guilty of firearms specification for having firearm on or about his person or under his control while committing offense, was inconsistent, and because jury acquitted defendant of firearms specification, State could not re-try defendant for that offense on remand for new trial on felonious assault. State v. Wright (Ohio App. 7 Dist., 03-26-2013) 990 N.E.2d 615, 2013-Ohio-1424, appeal after new sentencing hearing 2013-Ohio-4445, 2013 WL 5569271, appeal not allowed 137 Ohio St.3d 1410, 998 N.E.2d 510, 2013-Ohio-5096. Criminal Law ⇔ 878(4); Criminal Law ⇔ 1192; Double Jeopardy ⇔ 100.1

Firearm specification was inapplicable to defendant's conviction for having a weapon while under a disability, absent any evidence that defendant had previously been convicted of aggravated murder, murder, or any felony of first or second degree, or that less than five years had passed since he was released from prison or postrelease control for prior offense. State v. Mosley (Ohio App. 5 Dist., 04-04-2006) 166 Ohio App.3d 71, 849 N.E.2d 73, 2006-Ohio-1756. Sentencing And Punishment ⇔ 77

Defendant's conviction for aggravated robbery and accompanying firearm specification was not against the manifest weight of the evidence; inconsistencies in testimony of state's witnesses were minor and did not render testimony inherently unworthy of belief, defendant's version of events was far from plausible since in order to believe it, jury would have had to believe that victims invited defendant into their home, robbed him, and then called police to have them come and arrest him, and police found victim's wallet, money, and birth certificate in defendant's pocket, and defendant was unable to explain how wallet got in his pocket. State v. Berry (Ohio App. 12 Dist., 11-15-2004) 159 Ohio App.3d 476, 824 N.E.2d 543, 2004-Ohio-6027, appeal not allowed 106 Ohio St.3d 1488, 832 N.E.2d 739, 2005-Ohio-3978, reconsideration denied 106 Ohio St.3d 1537, 835 N.E.2d 385, 2005-Ohio-5146. Robbery ⇔ 24.15(2); Sentencing And Punishment ⇔ 323

Conviction for aggravated murder with a firearm specification was not against the manifest weight of the evidence and thus was sufficient as a matter of law, in regard to a victim who was shot six times; state presented testimony that defendant, a police officer, had motive to kill victim, who was his ex-wife, due to financial and personal problems, two eyewitnesses testified that they saw defendant at the scene of the crime immediately before and after the murder, testimony established that defendant was proficient in shooting with both of his hands, and state's expert, a forensic odontologist, established that the bite mark left on victim was made by defendant. State v. Prade (Ohio App. 9 Dist., 08-23-2000) 139 Ohio App.3d 676, 745 N.E.2d 475, dismissed, appeal not allowed 90 Ohio St.3d 1490, 739 N.E.2d 816, denial of post-conviction relief affirmed 2009-Ohio-704, 2009 WL 388217, appeal allowed 122 Ohio St.3d 1409, 907 N.E.2d 1193, 2009-Ohio-2751. Homicide ⇔ 1184; Homicide ⇔ 1185

6. Jury instructions

Defendant failed to object to, and thus waived for appellate review, trial court's jury instruction defining "deadly weapon" as "any instrument, device or thing capable of inflicting death or designed or specifically adapted for use as a weapon, or possessed, carried or used as a weapon," which instruction was relevant to firearm specification attached to charges of kidnapping, rape, aggravated robbery, felonious assault, and attempted murder. State v. Axson (Ohio App. 8 Dist., Cuyahoga, 05-01-2003) No. 81231, 2003-Ohio-2182, 2003 WL 1994490, Unreported, appeal dismissed 99 Ohio St.3d 1517, 792 N.E.2d 730, 2003-Ohio-4009, appeal allowed 100 Ohio St.3d 1408, 796 N.E.2d 536, 2003-Ohio-4948, motion to dismiss appeal denied 100 Ohio St.3d 1425, 797 N.E.2d 92, 2003-Ohio-5232, reversed 104 Ohio St.3d 248, 819 N.E.2d 271, 2004-Ohio-6396, subsequent determination 2005-Ohio-4396, 2005 WL 2038692, appeal after new sentencing hearing 2005-Ohio-6342, 2005 WL 3219727, appeal allowed, reversed 109 Ohio St.3d 509, 849 N.E.2d 284, 2006-Ohio-2721, reconsideration denied 110 Ohio St.3d 1444, 852 N.E.2d 191, 2006-Ohio-3862, appeal after new sentencing hearing 2007-Ohio-2892, 2007 WL 1695108, appeal after new sentencing hearing 2007-Ohio-3126, 2007 WL 1805041, motion for delayed appeal denied 116 Ohio St.3d 1436, 877 N.E.2d 988, 2007-Ohio-6518, habeas corpus dismissed 2010 WL 750176, appeal after new sentencing hearing 2007-Ohio-5811, 2007 WL 3171233, appeal not allowed 117 Ohio St.3d 1426, 882 N.E.2d 446, 2008-Ohio-969, appeal after new sentencing hearing 2011-Ohio-3187, 2011 WL 2569789. Criminal Law ⇔ 1038.1(4)

Trial court's instruction in aggravated robbery prosecution, when considered as a whole, substantially comported with instruction in *Howard*, which set forth charge given to jury that became deadlocked; language seized upon by defendant to demonstrate error appeared to be one of several mistakes that were made in transcribing court's statements, and slight difference in wording, which was use of "in" rather than "and," would not have caused jurors to disregard their oaths and decide case based upon views of other jurors rather than their own views. State v. Berry (Ohio App. 12 Dist., 11-15-2004) 159 Ohio App.3d 476, 824 N.E.2d 543, 2004-Ohio-6027, appeal not allowed 106 Ohio St.3d 1488, 832 N.E.2d 739, 2005-Ohio-3978, reconsideration denied 106 Ohio St.3d 1537, 835 N.E.2d 385, 2005-Ohio-5146. Criminal Law ⚷ 865(1.5)

Trial court's issuance of *Howard* charge, which was charge given to jury that became deadlocked, did not improperly coerce jury into convicting defendant of aggravated robbery; although defendant suggested that fact that jury deliberated for less than a half-hour after being given charge militated in favor finding that instruction was coercive, evidence of defendant's guilt was overwhelming, and his claim that he was the one who was actually robbed lacked credibility. State v. Berry (Ohio App. 12 Dist., 11-15-2004) 159 Ohio App.3d 476, 824 N.E.2d 543, 2004-Ohio-6027, appeal not allowed 106 Ohio St.3d 1488, 832 N.E.2d 739, 2005-Ohio-3978, reconsideration denied 106 Ohio St.3d 1537, 835 N.E.2d 385, 2005-Ohio-5146. Criminal Law ⚷ 865(1.5)

Trial court was not required in aggravated robbery prosecution to inquire of jury "whether further deliberations would result in a verdict" before giving them *Howard* charge, which was charge given to jury that became deadlocked. State v. Berry (Ohio App. 12 Dist., 11-15-2004) 159 Ohio App.3d 476, 824 N.E.2d 543, 2004-Ohio-6027, appeal not allowed 106 Ohio St.3d 1488, 832 N.E.2d 739, 2005-Ohio-3978, reconsideration denied 106 Ohio St.3d 1537, 835 N.E.2d 385, 2005-Ohio-5146. Criminal Law ⚷ 865(1.5)

7. Prison term

Trial court erred when it failed to merge all of the firearm specifications at sentencing for aggravated murder and aggravated robbery; the aggravated murders and aggravated robbery did not have separate purposes so as to support two separate gun specifications. State v. Like (Ohio App. 2 Dist., Montgomery, 04-18-2008) No. 21991, 2008-Ohio-1873, 2008 WL 1759080, Unreported, appeal not allowed 119 Ohio St.3d 1449, 893 N.E.2d 518, 2008-Ohio-4487. Sentencing And Punishment ⚷ 145

A 188-month sentence was substantively reasonable for defendant convicted of use of a firearm during a crime of violence and involvement in the robbery of a credit union; the sentence reflected the mitigating circumstances of his offense and his criminal history, as the district court granted him a greater departure for substantial assistance than that requested by the government, producing a significantly lower advisory range, and defendant was then sentenced at the very bottom of that already-reduced guidelines range. U.S. v. Harden (C.A.6 (Ohio), 08-16-2006) No. 05-4079, 195 Fed. Appx. 382, 2006 WL 2373259, Unreported, post-conviction relief denied 2007 WL 1544789. Sentencing And Punishment ⚷ 94; Sentencing And Punishment ⚷ 645; Sentencing And Punishment ⚷ 861

Record supported imposition of ten-year total sentence for aggravated robbery, aggravated burglary, and firearm specification, even though defendant argued that his codefendant had extensive role in offense and received only a four-year prison term; trial court explained that codefendant's sentence had been jointly recommended by the parties, and more important, defendant had a more extensive record of prior convictions than codefendant had, on which basis trial court found that defendant posed greater risk of recidivism and danger to community than codefendant. State v. Parrish (Ohio App. 2 Dist., Montgomery, 08-11-2006) No. 21206, 2006-Ohio-4161, 2006 WL 2336529, Unreported, motion for delayed appeal denied 112 Ohio St.3d 1417, 859 N.E.2d 557, 2006-Ohio-6712, habeas corpus denied 2008 WL 471543. Sentencing And Punishment ⚷ 56; Sentencing And Punishment ⚷ 94; Sentencing And Punishment ⚷ 645

Firearm specifications for displaying, brandishing, indicating possession of or using a firearm in the commission of an offense, and for discharging a firearm from a motor vehicle, did not merge prior to sentencing, where underlying felony of murder was one which included element of purposely causing the death of another. State v. Bates (Ohio App. 10 Dist., Franklin, 08-10-2004) No. 03AP-893, 2004-Ohio-4224, 2004 WL 1790068, Unreported, habeas corpus dismissed 2010 WL 100990, motion to proceed in forma pauperis denied 2010 WL 2471691. Sentencing And Punishment ⚷ 144

Trial court properly sentenced defendant for three-year and five-year firearms specifications attached to charged offenses of aggravated murder and attempted murder, even though defendant claimed both enhancements were based on same act; legislature required enhancements to be served consecutively to one another and to the prison terms for the base offense. State v. Gresham (Ohio App. 8 Dist., Cuyahoga, 02-20-2003) No. 81250, 2003-Ohio-744, 2003 WL 360922, Unreported, dismissal of post-conviction relief affirmed 2008-Ohio-4248, 2008 WL 3870612. Sentencing And Punishment ⚷ 144

Defendant convicted of aggravated robbery used firearm in commission of such offense, within scope of such sentence enhancement, warranting three-year sentence. State v. Stadmire (Ohio Com.Pl., 03-26-2002) No. CR-410305, 2002 WL 32066755, Unreported, affirmed 2003-Ohio-873, 2003 WL 549912, motion for delayed appeal denied 114 Ohio St.3d 1408, 867 N.E.2d 842, 2007-Ohio-2632. Sentencing And Punishment ⚷ 80

If a defendant is convicted of a firearms specification, the sentencing court is required to impose a three-year mandatory prison term; however, the court is not permitted to impose more than one such term for multiple firearms specification convictions, if the underlying felonies were committed as part of the same act or transaction. State v. Stevens (Ohio App. 2 Dist., 11-03-2008) 2008 -Ohio-5775, 2008 WL 4823364. Sentencing and Punishment ⚿ 77; Sentencing and Punishment ⚿ 509

Trial court was required to sentence defendant, who had been convicted of multiple felony charges, including two convictions for felonious assault, as well as three firearm specifications, to a three-year prison term for each of the two most serious specifications of which defendant was convicted, and also to consider whether a third three-year prison term should be imposed for his third firearm specification conviction, as sentencing statute so mandated. State v. Carson (Ohio App. 10 Dist., 09-28-2012) 978 N.E.2d 621, 2012-Ohio-4501. Assault and Battery ⚿ 100; Sentencing and Punishment ⚿ 77

Even if State's promise, in plea agreement for three felony offenses with firearms specifications, not to pursue sentencing enhancements could be construed as encompassing a promise by State to recommend treatment of the offenses as a single offense, so that State breached the plea agreement by recommending maximum, consecutive sentences, there was no manifest miscarriage of justice, as would warrant the noticing of plain error, where the sentence imposed by trial court, i.e., consecutive three-year sentences for firearms enhancements in two separate cases plus three-year and four-year consecutive sentences for two felonies, for total sentence of 13 years, was within the maximum permissible sentence if the sentences for the felonies were concurrent, i.e., maximum felony sentence was ten years, which, when added to three-year firearm specification, the imposition of which was mandatory even if the specifications were merged, equaled 13 years. State v. Byrd (Ohio App. 2 Dist., 10-24-2008) 178 Ohio App.3d 646, 899 N.E.2d 1033, 2008-Ohio-5515. Criminal Law ⚿ 1031(4)

Trial court's imposition of five-year prison term on defendant for aggravated robbery, rather than three-year minimum term, was not plain error; although defendant argued that under the Supreme Court's *Blakely v. Washington* decision, which decided defendant had right to have jury decide factual issues that would increase his sentence, court was obligated to sentence him to no more than statutory minimum sentence of three years, *Blakely* did not apply to state's indeterminate sentencing scheme, and to extent that *Blakely* did apply, court's imposition of sentence did not violate that decision, since five-year sentence was within range authorized by law. State v. Berry (Ohio App. 12 Dist., 11-15-2004) 159 Ohio App.3d 476, 824 N.E.2d 543, 2004-Ohio-6027, appeal not allowed 106 Ohio St.3d 1488, 832 N.E.2d 739, 2005-Ohio-3978, reconsideration denied 106 Ohio St.3d 1537, 835 N.E.2d 385, 2005-Ohio-5146. Criminal Law ⚿ 1042.3(3)

8. Display of firearm

State may use circumstantial evidence to establish that the defendant possessed an operable firearm, as required to prove firearm specification. State v. Dickess (Ohio App. 4 Dist., 01-03-2008) 174 Ohio App.3d 658, 884 N.E.2d 92, 2008-Ohio-39, appeal not allowed 118 Ohio St.3d 1434, 887 N.E.2d 1203, 2008-Ohio-2595, habeas corpus denied 2010 WL 5276992. Sentencing And Punishment ⚿ 323

There was sufficient circumstantial evidence that defendant possessed a firearm to support conviction for firearm specification; victim saw gun, defendant told victim that he would kill him if he did not cooperate, and victim obviously took these threats seriously. State v. Dickess (Ohio App. 4 Dist., 01-03-2008) 174 Ohio App.3d 658, 884 N.E.2d 92, 2008-Ohio-39, appeal not allowed 118 Ohio St.3d 1434, 887 N.E.2d 1203, 2008-Ohio-2595, habeas corpus denied 2010 WL 5276992. Sentencing And Punishment ⚿ 323

Ohio Court of Appeals's determination upholding application of firearm specification for committing aggravated robbery and attempted murder offenses while displaying or brandishing firearm was not unreasonable application of clearly established law, as required to grant federal habeas relief; while legitimate argument could be advanced that the momentary, accidental viewing of the firearm in victim's apartment when the gun fell to the floor did not constitute either "display" or "brandishing," it was equally plausible that the victim's viewing of the weapon facilitated the offense by emphasizing to victim the futility of resistance. Brown v. Konteh (C.A.6 (Ohio), 06-02-2009) 567 F.3d 191, rehearing and rehearing en banc denied, certiorari denied 130 S.Ct. 1081, 558 U.S. 1114, 175 L.Ed.2d 888. Habeas Corpus ⚿ 503.1

9. Allied offenses of similar import

Trial court's alleged failure to merge firearm specifications into single mandatory three-year term did not result in void sentence, but rather, was plain error warranting remand for correction, if necessary. State v. Moore (Ohio App. 7 Dist., 03-27-2013) 990 N.E.2d 165, 2013-Ohio-1431, appeal not allowed 137 Ohio St.3d 1421, 998 N.E.2d 1177, 2013-Ohio-5285. Criminal Law ⚿ 1042.3(1); Criminal Law ⚿ 1181.5(8); Sentencing and Punishment ⚿ 539

Firearms specification statute creates a penalty enhancement, not a separate criminal offense, and consequently it does not merge with the underlying felony at sentencing. State v. White (Ohio App. 6 Dist., 01-11-2013) 988 N.E.2d 595, 2013-Ohio-51, stay granted 134 Ohio St.3d 1483, 984 N.E.2d 27, 2013-Ohio-902, appeal allowed 135 Ohio St.3d 1447, 987 N.E.2d 703, 2013-Ohio-2062. Criminal Law ⚿ 30; Sentencing and Punishment ⚿ 77

For purposes of statute providing that defendant may be convicted of only one allied offense of similar import, firearm specification for use of firearm to facilitate a felony is sentence enhancement, not separate criminal offense, and thus firearm specification and offense of discharging a firearm at or into a habitation are not allied offenses of similar import; abrogating *State v. Elko*, 2004-Ohio-5209, 2004 WL 2340258. R.C. State v. Ford (Ohio, 02-24-2011) 128 Ohio St.3d 398, 945 N.E.2d 498, 2011-Ohio-765. Criminal Law ⇨ 29(15)

10. Applicability

Firearm specification did not apply to prosecution of a police officer for felonious assault stemming from the officer's shooting of a suspect; given the need for hurried judgments without the chance for reflection, and given the extensive training that causes officers to act reflexively when encountering potentially dangerous situations, it was neither just nor reasonable to apply a firearm specification to a police officer involved in an on-duty shooting based only on a showing of poor judgment or negligence in using force. State v. White (Ohio, 02-18-2015) 2015-Ohio-492, 2015 WL 687461. Sentencing and Punishment ⇨ 80

2941.146 Specification concerning discharge of firearm from motor vehicle

(A) Imposition of a mandatory five-year prison term upon an offender under division (B)(1)(c) of section 2929.14 of the Revised Code for committing a violation of section 2923.161 of the Revised Code or for committing a felony that includes, as an essential element, purposely or knowingly causing or attempting to cause the death of or physical harm to another and that was committed by discharging a firearm from a motor vehicle other than a manufactured home is precluded unless the indictment, count in the indictment, or information charging the offender specifies that the offender committed the offense by discharging a firearm from a motor vehicle other than a manufactured home. The specification shall be stated at the end of the body of the indictment, count, or information, and shall be stated in substantially the following form:

"SPECIFICATION (or, SPECIFICATION TO THE FIRST COUNT). The Grand Jurors (or insert the person's or prosecuting attorney's name when appropriate) further find and specify that (set forth that the offender committed the violation of section 2923.161 of the Revised Code or the felony that includes, as an essential element, purposely or knowingly causing or attempting to cause the death of or physical harm to another and that was committed by discharging a firearm from a motor vehicle other than a manufactured home)."

(B) The specification described in division (A) of this section may be used in a delinquent child proceeding in the manner and for the purpose described in section 2152.17 of the Revised Code.

(C) As used in this section:

(1) "Firearm" has the same meaning as in section 2923.11 of the Revised Code;

(2) "Motor vehicle" and "manufactured home" have the same meanings as in section 4501.01 of the Revised Code.

(2011 H 86, eff. 9-30-11; 2000 S 179, § 3, eff. 1-1-02; 1999 S 107, eff. 3-23-00; 1995 S 2, eff. 7-1-96)

Historical and Statutory Notes

Amendment Note: 2011 H 86 substituted "(B)(1)(c)" for "(D)(1)(c)" in division (A).

Cross References

Felony specifications, see 2152.17

Research References

Encyclopedias

OH Jur. 3d Criminal Law: Procedure § 922, Firearms.

OH Jur. 3d Criminal Law: Procedure § 1893, Five-Year Term.

OH Jur. 3d Criminal Law: Substantive Principles and Offenses § 1538, Discharging Firearm.

OH Jur. 3d Criminal Law: Substantive Principles and Offenses § 1551, Discharging Firearms at or Into Occupied Structure or School Safety Zone.

Treatises and Practice Aids

Katz & Giannelli, Baldwin's Ohio Practice Criminal Law § 40:5, Nature and Contents.

Katz & Giannelli, Baldwin's Ohio Practice Criminal Law § 118:8, Gun Enhancement.

Katz & Giannelli, Baldwin's Ohio Practice Criminal Law § 152:9, Motion to Correct Improper Sentence--Firearm Specifications as Part of One Transaction.

Katz & Giannelli, Baldwin's Ohio Practice Criminal Law § 80:22, Appellate Review of Sentencing.
Katz & Giannelli, Baldwin's Ohio Practice Criminal Law § 106:11, Discharging Firearm Into a School or Home.
Katz & Giannelli, Baldwin's Ohio Practice Criminal Law § 118:12, Drive-By Shooting.
Carlin, Baldwin's Ohio Prac. Merrick-Rippner Probate Law § 109:87, Enhanced Dispositions Due to Felony Specifications, Effective January 1, 2002.
Weiler & Weiler, Ohio Driving Under the Influence App. A, Ohio Revised Code--Selected Provisions.
Giannelli & Yeomans Salvador, Ohio Juvenile Law App. A, Ohio Revised Code--Selected Provisions.
Giannelli & Yeomans Salvador, Ohio Juvenile Law § 22:3, Department of Youth Services Commitment.

Notes of Decisions

3. Sentencing

Defendant, who was convicted of four counts of felonious assault, was properly given only one five year prison term pursuant to firearm specification addressing offender who discharges firearm from motor vehicle, where assaults stemmed from same act or transaction and involved four victim. State v. Dixson (Ohio App. 1 Dist., Hamilton, 05-21-2004) No. C-030227, 2004-Ohio-2575, 2004 WL 1124524, Unreported, appeal not allowed 103 Ohio St.3d 1479, 816 N.E.2d 254, 2004-Ohio-5405, habeas corpus dismissed 2010 WL 60905. Sentencing And Punishment ⚿ 80

4. Evidence

State was permitted to used the analogy of a drive-by shooting to demonstrate the rationale of the doctrine of transferred intent during murder prosecution, where it did not attempt to attribute such a crime to defendant. State v. Villa (Ohio App. 9 Dist., Lorain, 09-05-2006) No. 05CA008773, 2006-Ohio-4529, 2006 WL 2527964, Unreported, appeal not allowed 112 Ohio St.3d 1445, 860 N.E.2d 768, 2007-Ohio-152, certiorari denied 127 S.Ct. 2885, 550 U.S. 973, 167 L.Ed.2d 1159, appeal not allowed 114 Ohio St.3d 1428, 868 N.E.2d 681, 2007-Ohio-2904, dismissal of post-conviction relief affirmed 2009-Ohio-5055, 2009 WL 3068397, habeas corpus denied 2012 WL 1435725. Criminal Law ⚿ 2086

Statutory provision that imposed a mandatory five-year prison term upon an offender who purposely or knowingly caused or attempted to cause the death of or physical harm to another and that was committed by discharging a firearm from a motor vehicle other than a manufactured home, was not applicable to defendant who fired a weapon while standing with both feet planted on the ground with no substantial physical connection with the motor vehicle, regardless of whether the motor vehicle was the starting point from which defendant staged his attack when he retrieved a gun from under the motor vehicle's seat. State v. Swidas (Ohio, 10-11-2012) 133 Ohio St.3d 460, 979 N.E.2d 254, 2012-Ohio-4638. Weapons ⚿ 342

Without a substantial physical connection to the vehicle, a shooter cannot be said to have fired a shot that commenced from the motor vehicle, for purposes of statutory provision that mandates a five-year prison term upon a shooter who attempts to cause physical harm to another by discharging a firearm from a motor vehicle. State v. Swidas (Ohio, 10-11-2012) 133 Ohio St.3d 460, 979 N.E.2d 254, 2012-Ohio-4638. Weapons ⚿ 342

For the locus of the discharge of a weapon to be the motor vehicle, for purposes of statutory provision that mandates a five-year prison term upon a person who attempts to cause physical harm to another by discharging a firearm from a motor vehicle, then, the person discharging the weapon must have a substantial physical connection to the vehicle; if a person were in or on a vehicle to the extent that the vehicle was providing substantial support to the person, the locus of that person's firing of the weapon would be the motor vehicle. State v. Swidas (Ohio, 10-11-2012) 133 Ohio St.3d 460, 979 N.E.2d 254, 2012-Ohio-4638. Weapons ⚿ 342

2941.147 Sexual motivation specification

Cross References

Notice of incarceration or release of defendant or custody of alleged juvenile offender, see 2930.16

2941.148 Sexually violent predator specification

(A)(1) The application of Chapter 2971. of the Revised Code to an offender is precluded unless one of the following applies:

(a) The offender is charged with a violent sex offense, and the indictment, count in the indictment, or information charging the violent sex offense also includes a specification that the offender is a sexually violent predator, or the offender is charged with a designated homicide, assault, or kidnapping offense, and the indictment, count in the indictment, or information charging the designated homicide, assault, or kidnapping offense also includes both a specification of the type described in section 2941.147 of the Revised Code and a specification that the offender is a sexually violent predator.

(b) The offender is convicted of or pleads guilty to a violation of division (A)(1)(b) of section 2907.02 of the Revised Code committed on or after January 2, 2007, and division (B) of section 2907.02 of the Revised Code does not prohibit the court from sentencing the offender pursuant to section 2971.03 of the Revised Code.

(c) The offender is convicted of or pleads guilty to attempted rape committed on or after January 2, 2007, and to a specification of the type described in section 2941.1418, 2941.1419, or 2941.1420 of the Revised Code.

(d) The offender is convicted of or pleads guilty to a violation of section 2905.01 of the Revised Code and to a specification of the type described in section 2941.147 of the Revised Code, and section 2905.01 of the Revised Code requires a court to sentence the offender pursuant to section 2971.03 of the Revised Code.

(e) The offender is convicted of or pleads guilty to aggravated murder and to a specification of the type described in section 2941.147 of the Revised Code, and division (A)(2)(b)(ii) of section 2929.022, division (A)(1)(e), (C)(1)(a)(v), (C)(2)(a)(ii), (D)(2)(b), (D)(3)(a)(iv), or (E)(1)(d) of section 2929.03, or division (A) or (B) of section 2929.06 of the Revised Code requires a court to sentence the offender pursuant to division (B)(3) of section 2971.03 of the Revised Code.

(f) The offender is convicted of or pleads guilty to murder and to a specification of the type described in section 2941.147 of the Revised Code, and division (B)(2) of section 2929.02 of the Revised Code requires a court to sentence the offender pursuant to section 2971.03 of the Revised Code.

(2) A specification required under division (A)(1)(a) of this section that an offender is a sexually violent predator shall be stated at the end of the body of the indictment, count, or information and shall be stated in substantially the following form:

"Specification (or, specification to the first count). The grand jury (or insert the person's or prosecuting attorney's name when appropriate) further find and specify that the offender is a sexually violent predator."

(B) In determining for purposes of this section whether a person is a sexually violent predator, all of the factors set forth in divisions (H)(1) to (6) of section 2971.01 of the Revised Code that apply regarding the person may be considered as evidence tending to indicate that it is likely that the person will engage in the future in one or more sexually violent offenses.

(C) As used in this section, "designated homicide, assault, or kidnapping offense," "violent sex offense," and "sexually violent predator" have the same meanings as in section 2971.01 of the Revised Code.

(2007 S 10, eff. 1-1-08; 2006 S 260, eff. 1-2-07; 2004 H 473, eff. 4-29-05; 1996 H 180, eff. 1-1-97)

Historical and Statutory Notes

Amendment Note: 2007 S 10 substituted "January 2, 2007," for "the effective date of this amendment" in divisions (A)(1)(b) and (A)(1)(c); and added new divisions (A)(1)(d), (A)(1)(e), and (A)(1)(f).

Amendment Note: 2006 S 260 rewrote division (A), which prior thereto read:

"(A) The application of Chapter 2971. of the Revised Code to an offender is precluded unless the indictment, count in the indictment, or information charging the violent sex offense also includes a specification that the offender is a sexually violent predator, or the indictment, count in the indictment, or information charging the designated homicide, assault, or kidnapping offense also includes both a specification of the type described in section 2941.147 of the Revised Code and a specification that the offender is a sexually violent predator. The specification that the offender is a sexually violent predator shall be stated at the end of the body of the indictment, count, or information and shall be stated in substantially the following form:

"'Specification (or, specification to the first count). The grand jury (or insert the person's or prosecuting attorney's name when appropriate) further find and specify that the offender is a sexually violent predator.'"

Ohio Administrative Code References

Life sentences, see OAC 5120–2–10

Research References

Encyclopedias

OH Jur. 3d Criminal Law: Procedure § 925, Sexual Motivation and Sexual Predator.

OH Jur. 3d Criminal Law: Procedure § 1873, Specification as Prerequisite to Enhanced Penalty; State's Burden of Proof; Proof of Prior Conviction.

Treatises and Practice Aids

Katz & Giannelli, Baldwin's Ohio Practice Criminal Law § 40:5, Nature and Contents.

Katz & Giannelli, Baldwin's Ohio Practice Criminal Law § 121:2, Sentencing Violent Sexual Predators.

Katz & Giannelli, Baldwin's Ohio Practice Criminal Law § 121:3.10, Sexual Offender Classifications--Pre-2008 Law.

Painter & Pollis, Ohio Appellate Practice App. P, Ohio Revised Code.

Weiler & Weiler, Ohio Driving Under the Influence App. A, Ohio Revised Code--Selected Provisions.

Notes of Decisions

2. Charged offense

Defendant's prior rape conviction was improperly used as basis for sexually violent predator specifications, in prosecution for rape, gross sexual imposition, and compelling prostitution, because it occurred some ten years prior to the enactment of statute which governs sexually violent predator specifications. State v. Robinson (Ohio App. 8 Dist., Cuyahoga, 09-29-2005) No. 85207, 2005-Ohio-5132, 2005 WL 2386608, Unreported, appeal not allowed 108 Ohio St.3d 1488, 843 N.E.2d 794, 2006-Ohio-962, habeas corpus denied 2015-Ohio-68, 2015 WL 139101. Sentencing And Punishment ⚿ 99

For purposes of sexually violent predator specification in prosecution for rape and kidnapping, charged offense of rape could not be used to establish that defendant had been "convicted" of a sexually violent offense, and thus evidence was insufficient to support sexually violent predator specification. State v. Smith (Ohio App. 5 Dist., Morrow, 06-19-2003) No. CA-957, 2003-Ohio-3416, 2003 WL 21489929, Unreported, appeal allowed 100 Ohio St.3d 1430, 797 N.E.2d 511, 2003-Ohio-5396, affirmed 104 Ohio St.3d 106, 818 N.E.2d 283, 2004-Ohio-6238, appeal after new sentencing hearing 2006-Ohio-5276, 2006 WL 2847421, appeal after new sentencing hearing 2008-Ohio-2772, 2008 WL 2572657, appeal not allowed 120 Ohio St.3d 1418, 897 N.E.2d 653, 2008-Ohio-6166, habeas corpus denied 2011 WL 3652692. Mental Health ⚿ 454

3. Conviction on underlying offense

Defendant need not have a prior conviction for a sexually violent offense at the time of indictment in order for a sexually violent predator specification to attach; rather, a conviction on the underlying offense is enough. State v. Haven (Ohio App. 9 Dist., Wayne, 05-19-2004) No. 02CA0069, 2004-Ohio-2512, 2004 WL 1103957, Unreported, motion to certify allowed 103 Ohio St.3d 1459, 815 N.E.2d 676, 2004-Ohio-5056, appeal allowed 103 Ohio St.3d 1461, 815 N.E.2d 677, 2004-Ohio-5056, reversed 105 Ohio St.3d 418, 827 N.E.2d 319, 2005-Ohio-2286, appeal after new sentencing hearing 2006-Ohio-3283, 2006 WL 1751048. Mental Health ⚿ 469(2)

2941.149 Specification concerning repeat violent offenders

Validity

For validity of this section, see State v. Payne, 2005 WL 3610429, 2005-Ohio-7043 (Ohio App. 11 Dist.).

Notes of Decisions

1. Constitutional issues

Defendant was constitutionally entitled to jury trial on facts relied upon by sentencing court in adjudicating him a repeat violent offender (RVO), and enhancing his sentence beyond statutory maximum for underlying offenses on basis of such finding, where such adjudication required additional findings with respect to defendant's prior felony convictions not apparent from face thereof, namely, whether prior convictions for conspiracy to aggravated robbery, conspiracy to aggravated burglary, and conspiracy to kidnapping resulted in death, serious harm, or physical harm to a person, and enhancement required additional findings as to seriousness and recidivism factors. State v. Payne (Ohio App. 11 Dist., Lake, 12-29-2005) No. 2004-L-118, 2005-Ohio-7043, 2005 WL 3610429,

Unreported, appeal after new sentencing hearing 2007-Ohio-6740, 2007 WL 4395051, appeal not allowed 118 Ohio St.3d 1408, 886 N.E.2d 872, 2008-Ohio-2340, denial of post-conviction relief affirmed 2011-Ohio-4698, 2011 WL 4346509. Jury ⚷ 21.4

2. Separate animus for each offense

Imposition of consecutive sentences for two repeat violent offender specifications, one of which was alleged in connection with charge of attempted murder and the other in connection with charge of aggravated robbery, was not improper; defendant had distinct, separate animus for each charged crime, such that they did not constitute allied offenses of similar import, and, therefore, defendant could be separately sentenced on repeat violent offender specifications pertaining to each charged crime. State v. Dodson (Ohio App. 3 Dist., 12-03-2012) 983 N.E.2d 797, 2012-Ohio-5576. Sentencing and Punishment ⚷ 606

2941.1410 Specification concerning major drug offender

Notes of Decisions

Sentencing 3

2. Law governing

Trial court properly sentenced defendant as a major drug offender following convictions for complicity in trafficking of drugs and complicity in the possession of drugs, where trial court submitted question of whether defendant was a major drug offender to jury when it asked the jury to determine whether the amount of drugs defendant was complicit in possessing and selling exceeded 1,000 grams, and jury answered such question in the affirmative. State v. McDermott (Ohio App. 6 Dist., Lucas, 04-29-2005) No. L-03-1110, 2005-Ohio-2095, 2005 WL 1007133, Unreported, motion for delayed appeal granted 106 Ohio St.3d 1480, 832 N.E.2d 735, 2005-Ohio-3978, appeal not allowed 107 Ohio St.3d 1697, 840 N.E.2d 203, 2005-Ohio-6763, habeas corpus dismissed 2008 WL 2600008, habeas corpus denied 2011 WL 590225. Jury ⚷ 34(8)

Sentence enhancement based on major drug offender specification did not violate *Apprendi v. New Jersey,* where specification was expressly dependent on a jury finding that the amount of drug possessed or sold by defendant was in excess of a certain amount. State v. Graves (Ohio App. 6 Dist., Lucas, 05-09-2003) No. L-02-1053, 2003-Ohio-2359, 2003 WL 21040652, Unreported, appeal not allowed 100 Ohio St.3d 1410, 796 N.E.2d 537, 2003-Ohio-4948, denial of post-conviction relief affirmed 2007-Ohio-4713, 2007 WL 2683569, appeal not allowed 116 Ohio St.3d 1479, 879 N.E.2d 786, 2008-Ohio-153. Jury ⚷ 34(8)

Sentencing guidelines, appellate review, non-guidelines sentence, abuse of discretion standard, see Gall v. U.S., 2007, 128 S.Ct. 586.

3. Sentencing

Once jury determined that quantity of cocaine involved exceeded 100 grams, defendant's designation as major drug offender, which subjected defendant to enhanced sentences for possession of cocaine and trafficking in cocaine, was automatic. State v. Dues (Ohio App. 8 Dist., 11-26-2014) 24 N.E.3d 751, 2014-Ohio-5276. Controlled Substances ⚷ 100(1)

2941.1411 Specification concerning use of body armor

(A) Imposition of a two-year mandatory prison term upon an offender under division (B)(1)(d) of section 2929.14 of the Revised Code is precluded unless the indictment, count in the indictment, or information charging the offense specifies that the offender wore or carried body armor while committing the offense and that the offense is an offense of violence that is a felony. The specification shall be stated at the end of the body of the indictment, count, or information and shall be stated in substantially the following form:

"SPECIFICATION (or, SPECIFICATION TO THE FIRST COUNT). The Grand Jurors (or insert the person's or the prosecuting attorney's name when appropriate) further find and specify that (set forth that the offender wore or carried body armor while committing the specified offense and that the specified offense is an offense of violence that is a felony)."

(B) As used in this section, "body armor" means any vest, helmet, shield, or similar item that is designed or specifically carried to diminish the impact of a bullet or projectile upon the offender's body.

(2011 H 86, eff. 9-30-11; 2000 S 222, eff. 3-22-01)

Historical and Statutory Notes

Amendment Note: 2011 H 86 substituted "(B)(1)(d)" for "(D)(1)(d)" in division (A).

Research References

Encyclopedias

OH Jur. 3d Criminal Law: Procedure § 928, Body Armor.

OH Jur. 3d Criminal Law: Procedure § 1902, Offense While Carrying or Wearing Body Armor.

Treatises and Practice Aids

Katz & Giannelli, Baldwin's Ohio Practice Criminal Law § 40:5, Nature and Contents.

Katz & Giannelli, Baldwin's Ohio Practice Criminal Law § 118:9, Body Armor.

Katz & Giannelli, Baldwin's Ohio Practice Criminal Law § 80:22, Appellate Review of Sentencing.

Weiler & Weiler, Ohio Driving Under the Influence App. A, Ohio Revised Code--Selected Provisions.

Giannelli & Yeomans Salvador, Ohio Juvenile Law App. A, Ohio Revised Code--Selected Provisions.

2941.1412 Discharging firearm at peace officer or corrections officer

(A) Imposition of a seven-year mandatory prison term upon an offender under division (B)(1)(f) of section 2929.14 of the Revised Code is precluded unless the indictment, count in the indictment, or information charging the offense specifies that the offender discharged a firearm at a peace officer or a corrections officer while committing the offense. The specification shall be stated at the end of the body of the indictment, count, or information and shall be in substantially the following form:

"SPECIFICATION (or, SPECIFICATION TO THE FIRST COUNT).

The Grand Jurors (or insert the person's or the prosecuting attorney's name when appropriate) further find and specify that (set forth that the offender discharged a firearm at a peace officer or a corrections officer while committing the offense)."

(B) As used in this section:

(1) "Firearm" has the same meaning as in section 2923.11 of the Revised Code.

(2) "Peace officer" has the same meaning as in section 2935.01 of the Revised Code.

(3) "Corrections officer" means a person employed by a detention facility as a corrections officer.

(4) "Detention facility" has the same meaning as in section 2921.01 of the Revised Code.

(2011 H 86, eff. 9-30-11; 2002 H 130, eff. 4-7-03)

Historical and Statutory Notes

Amendment Note: 2011 H 86 substituted "(B)(1)(f)" for "(D)(1)(f)" in division (A).

Research References

Encyclopedias

OH Jur. 3d Criminal Law: Procedure § 923, Firearms--Discharging Firearm at Peace Officer or Corrections Officer.

OH Jur. 3d Criminal Law: Procedure § 1873, Specification as Prerequisite to Enhanced Penalty; State's Burden of Proof; Proof of Prior Conviction.

OH Jur. 3d Criminal Law: Procedure § 1891, Seven-Year Term.

Treatises and Practice Aids

Katz & Giannelli, Baldwin's Ohio Practice Criminal Law § 80:22, Appellate Review of Sentencing.

Katz & Giannelli, Baldwin's Ohio Practice Criminal Law § 118:13, Shooting at a Police Officer.

Carlin, Baldwin's Ohio Prac. Merrick-Rippner Probate Law § 109:87, Enhanced Dispositions Due to Felony Specifications, Effective January 1, 2002.

Weiler & Weiler, Ohio Driving Under the Influence App. A, Ohio Revised Code--Selected Provisions.

Giannelli & Yeomans Salvador, Ohio Juvenile Law App. A, Ohio Revised Code--Selected Provisions.

Giannelli & Yeomans Salvador, Ohio Juvenile Law § 22:3, Department of Youth Services Commitment.

2941.1413 Specification concerning prior felony OVI offenses

Validity

For validity of this section, see State v. Klembus, 17 N.E.3d 603, 2014 WL 3697685, 2014 -Ohio- 3227 (8th Dist. Ct. App. 2014).

Notes of Decisions

1/2. Constitutional issues

Enhanced sentence of 24 months defendant received for repeat operating a vehicle while intoxicated (OVI) offender specification did not violate double jeopardy protections against cumulative punishment, despite contention that, because his penalty had already been enhanced due to prior OVI convictions when underlying OVI offense was elevated from misdemeanor to felony, specification punished him twice for prior convictions; trial court had discretion to impose sentence for underlying OVI charge in addition to mandatory prison term for specification, and sentence was within limits established by legislature. State v. Hartsook (Ohio App. 12 Dist., 10-13-2014) 21 N.E.3d 617, 2014-Ohio-4528. Double Jeopardy ⚿ 30

Appropriate level of scrutiny under which to analyze defendant's claim that state's discretion under repeat operating a vehicle while intoxicated (OVI) offender specification to either include or omit specification from indictment violated equal protection was rational basis review; repeat OVI offenders were not suspect class, individual did not have fundamental constitutional right to operate vehicle on multiple occasions under the influence of alcohol or drugs, and OVI statutes did not involve classifications based on sex or illegitimacy. State v. Hartsook (Ohio App. 12 Dist., 10-13-2014) 21 N.E.3d 617, 2014-Ohio-4528. Automobiles ⚿ 359.6; Constitutional Law ⚿ 3809

State's discretion under statute governing repeat operating a vehicle while intoxicated (OVI) offender specification to either omit or include specification in indictment charging defendant did not violate constitutional equal protection guarantee, despite contention that state's sole discretion to include or omit specification permitted arbitrary and unequal operation of OVI sentencing provisions on similarly situated OVI offenders; defendant failed to show that cumulative punishment that legislature sought to impose under specification and OVI statute did not serve legitimate government interest and that there was no rational basis that justified challenged statute. State v. Hartsook (Ohio App. 12 Dist., 10-13-2014) 21 N.E.3d 617, 2014-Ohio-4528. Automobiles ⚿ 359.6; Constitutional Law ⚿ 3809

Repeat operating a vehicle under the influence of alcohol (OVI) offender specification is not rationally related to a legitimate state interest and, thus, violates equal protection; the increased penalty under the specification depends solely on a prosecutor's decision on whether to present the specification to the grand jury, and there is no logical rationale for the increased penalty imposed on some repeat OVI offenders and not others without requiring proof of some additional element to justify the enhancement. State v. Klembus (Ohio App. 8 Dist., 07-24-2014) 17 N.E.3d 603, 2014-Ohio-3227. Automobiles ⚿ 359.6; Constitutional Law ⚿ 3809

1. Mandatory jail term construed

Trial court failed to substantially comply with requirement of advising defendant, before accepting his negotiated guilty plea to fourth-degree felony driving under the influence (DUI), of maximum penalty applicable to his offense, and thus, plea was not knowing, intelligent, and voluntary; trial court advised defendant only of maximum 30-month sentence for underlying offense, and did not advise him of additional, consecutive mandatory sentence of up to five years, relating to specification of five prior DUI offenses within the last 20 years. State v. Eckles (Ohio App. 7 Dist., 11-14-2007) 173 Ohio App.3d 606, 879 N.E.2d 829, 2007-Ohio-6220. Criminal Law ⚿ 273.1(4)

Application of statute governing specification regarding prior felony operating a motor vehicle while intoxicated (OVI) offenses and imposing mandatory additional prison terms is not limited to offenses that are specifically entitled "OVI" offenses. State v. Norris (Ohio App. 12 Dist., 08-21-2006) 168 Ohio App.3d 572, 861 N.E.2d 148, 2006-Ohio-4325. Automobiles ⚿ 359.6

2. Equivalent offense

An "equivalent offense," for purposes of statute governing specification concerning prior felony operating a vehicle while intoxicated (OVI) offenses, can be either a felony or a misdemeanor. State ex rel. Beechler v. Rastatter (Ohio, 09-25-2014) 140 Ohio St.3d 343, 18 N.E.3d 433, 2014-Ohio-4061. Automobiles ⚿ 359.6

Defendant, who was convicted of operating a vehicle while intoxicated (OVI), could be found guilty of specification concerning prior felony OVI offenses based on his non-felony equivalent offenses, despite defendant's argument that he could not have been found guilty because he did not have at least five felony OVI convictions in the last 20 years, as equivalent offenses required for conviction could be misdemeanors or felonies. State ex rel. Beechler v. Rastatter (Ohio, 09-25-2014) 140 Ohio

St.3d 343, 18 N.E.3d 433, 2014-Ohio-4061. Automobiles ⚯ 359.6

2941.1414 Specifications concerning drug or alcohol related vehicular homicide of peace officer or BCII investigator in construction zone

(A) Imposition of a five-year mandatory prison term upon an offender under division (B)(5) of section 2929.14 of the Revised Code is precluded unless the offender is convicted of or pleads guilty to violating division (A)(1) or (2) of section 2903.06 of the Revised Code and unless the indictment, count in the indictment, or information charging the offense specifies that the victim of the offense is a peace officer or an investigator of the bureau of criminal identification and investigation. The specification shall be stated at the end of the body of the indictment, count, or information and shall be stated in substantially the following form:

"SPECIFICATION (or, SPECIFICATION TO THE FIRST COUNT). The Grand Jurors (or insert the person's or the prosecuting attorney's name when appropriate) further find and specify that (set forth that the victim of the offense is a peace officer or an investigator of the bureau of criminal identification and investigation)."

(B) The specification described in division (A) of this section may be used in a delinquent child proceeding in the manner and for the purpose described in section 2152.17 of the Revised Code.

(C) As used in this section:

(1) "Peace officer" has the same meaning as in section 2935.01 of the Revised Code.

(2) "Investigator of the bureau of criminal identification and investigation" has the same meaning as in section 2903.11 of the Revised Code.

(2011 H 86, eff. 9-30-11; 2006 S 281, eff. 4-5-07; 2004 H 52, eff. 6-1-04)

Historical and Statutory Notes

Amendment Note: 2011 H 86 substituted "(B)(5)" for "(D)(5)" in division (A).

Amendment Note: 2006 S 281 inserted "or an investigator of the bureau of criminal identification and investigation" at the end of the first sentence of division (A); inserted "or an investigator of the bureau of criminal identification and investigation" at the end of the second paragraph in division (A); substituted ": (1) Peace" for ", peace" between "section" and "officer" in division (C); and added a new division (C)(2).

Research References

Encyclopedias

OH Jur. 3d Criminal Law: Procedure § 930, Certain Crimes Arising from Use of Vehicle.

OH Jur. 3d Criminal Law: Procedure § 1873, Specification as Prerequisite to Enhanced Penalty; State's Burden of Proof; Proof of Prior Conviction.

OH Jur. 3d Criminal Law: Substantive Principles and Offenses § 501, Aggravated Vehicular Homicide or Vehicular Homicide--Mandatory Prison or Jail Term.

Treatises and Practice Aids

Katz & Giannelli, Baldwin's Ohio Practice Criminal Law § 80:22, Appellate Review of Sentencing.

Carlin, Baldwin's Ohio Prac. Merrick-Rippner Probate Law § 109:87, Enhanced Dispositions Due to Felony Specifications, Effective January 1, 2002.

Weiler & Weiler, Ohio Driving Under the Influence App. A, Ohio Revised Code--Selected Provisions.

Giannelli & Yeomans Salvador, Ohio Juvenile Law App. A, Ohio Revised Code--Selected Provisions.

2941.1415 Specifications concerning drug or alcohol related vehicular homicide of peace officer in construction zone and prior convictions

(A) Imposition of a three-year mandatory prison term upon an offender under division (B)(6) of section 2929.14 of the Revised Code is precluded unless the offender is convicted of or pleads guilty to violating division (A)(1) or (2) of section 2903.06 of the Revised Code and unless the indictment, count in the indictment, or information charging the offense specifies that the offender previously has been convicted of or pleaded guilty to three or more violations of division (A) or (B) of section 4511.19 of the Revised Code or an equivalent offense, or three or more violations of any combination of those divisions and offenses. The specification shall be stated at the end of the body of the indictment, count, or information and shall be stated in substantially the following form:

"SPECIFICATION (or, SPECIFICATION TO THE FIRST COUNT). The Grand Jurors (or insert the person's or the prosecuting attorney's name when appropriate) further find and specify that (set forth that the offender previously has been convicted of or pleaded guilty to three or more violations of division (A) or (B) of section 4511.19 of the Revised Code or an equivalent offense, or three or more violations of any combination of those divisions and offenses)."

(B) The specification described in division (A) of this section may be used in a delinquent child proceeding in the manner and for the purpose described in section 2152.17 of the Revised Code.

(C) As used in this section, "equivalent offense" has the same meaning as in section 4511.181 of the Revised Code.

(2011 H 86, eff. 9-30-11; 2004 H 52, eff. 6–1–04)

Historical and Statutory Notes

Amendment Note: 2011 H 86 substituted "(B)(6)" for "(D)(6)" in division (A).

Research References

Encyclopedias

OH Jur. 3d Criminal Law: Procedure § 930, Certain Crimes Arising from Use of Vehicle.

OH Jur. 3d Criminal Law: Procedure § 1873, Specification as Prerequisite to Enhanced Penalty; State's Burden of Proof; Proof of Prior Conviction.

OH Jur. 3d Criminal Law: Procedure § 1917, Offenses for Which Prison Term Must Not be Reduced.

Treatises and Practice Aids

Katz & Giannelli, Baldwin's Ohio Practice Criminal Law § 80:22, Appellate Review of Sentencing.

Weiler & Weiler, Ohio Driving Under the Influence App. A, Ohio Revised Code--Selected Provisions.

Giannelli & Yeomans Salvador, Ohio Juvenile Law App. A, Ohio Revised Code--Selected Provisions.

2941.1417 Specification concerning forfeiture of property

(A) Property is not subject to forfeiture in a criminal case unless the indictment, count in the indictment, or information charging the offense specifies, to the extent it is reasonably known at the time of filing, the nature and extent of the alleged offender's interest in the property, a description of the property, and, if the property is alleged to be an instrumentality, the alleged use or intended use of the property in the commission or facilitation of the offense. The specification shall be stated at the end of the body of the indictment, count, or information and shall be in substantially the following form:

"SPECIFICATION (or SPECIFICATION TO THE FIRST COUNT). The grand jurors (or insert the person's or prosecuting attorney's name when appropriate) further find and specify that (set forth the alleged offender's interest in the property, a description of the property subject to forfeiture, and any alleged use or intended use of the property in the commission or facilitation of the offense)."

(B) The trier of fact shall determine whether the property is subject to forfeiture.

(C) The specification described in division (A) of this section may be used in a delinquent child proceeding.

(2006 H 241, eff. 7–1–07)

Research References

Encyclopedias

OH Jur. 3d Criminal Law: Procedure § 931, Forfeiture of Property.

OH Jur. 3d Criminal Law: Procedure § 1823, Fines, Penalties, and Forfeitures Defined and Distinguished.

OH Jur. 3d Forfeitures and Penalties § 24, Criminal Forfeiture.
OH Jur. 3d Forfeitures and Penalties § 29, Right to Jury Trial.

Treatises and Practice Aids

Katz & Giannelli, Baldwin's Ohio Practice Criminal Law § 129:7, Criminal Forfeiture.

Katz & Giannelli, Baldwin's Ohio Practice Criminal Law § 142:3, Petition for Forfeiture.

Notes of Decisions

Firearms 1
Instructions 2
Waiver 3

1. Firearms

Defendant's firearms that defendant had been required to turn over to police while he was under indictment for rape could not, as part of sentence after defendant was convicted, be ordered destroyed as instrumentalities of the crime, without compliance with statutory forfeiture process, including inclusion of a forfeiture specification in the indictment, notice being furnished to defendant that firearms were being made subject to forfeiture, and initiation of either civil or criminal forfeiture proceedings. State v. Brimacombe (Ohio App. 6 Dist., 09-30-2011) 195 Ohio App.3d 524, 960 N.E.2d 1042, 2011-Ohio-5032. Forfeitures ⚷ 51

2. Instructions

The trial court erred when it issued an order of forfeiture as a matter of law; the trial court failed to instruct the jury on the necessary law relating to the forfeiture specification, and thus the jury did not enter a finding on the specification. State v. Taylor (Ohio App. 11 Dist., 08-27-2012) 974 N.E.2d 175, 2012-Ohio-3890. Forfeitures ⚷ 115

3. Waiver

The failure to raise any objections based on defects in the indictment prior to trial results in a waiver of these defenses or objections. State v. Schmidt (Ohio App. 3 Dist., 03-03-2014) 9 N.E.3d 458, 2014-Ohio-758, appeal not allowed 139 Ohio St.3d 1430, 11 N.E.3d 285, 2014-Ohio-2725. Indictment and Information ⚷ 196(1)

Defendant who had been charged with receiving stolen property and possessing criminal tools waived for appellate review assertion that forfeiture specification in indictment was statutorily insufficient, in challenge to forfeiture order related to vehicle allegedly used in commission of an offense, where defendant failed to object to indictment's specification at trial, alleged defect did not deprive trial court of jurisdiction, and indictment did not fail to charge an offense. State v. Schmidt (Ohio App. 3 Dist., 03-03-2014) 9 N.E.3d 458, 2014-Ohio-758, appeal not allowed 139 Ohio St.3d 1430, 11 N.E.3d 285, 2014-Ohio-2725. Forfeitures ⚷ 124

2941.1418 Attempted rape specification

(A) Imposition of a mandatory indefinite prison term consisting of a minimum term of five years and a maximum term of twenty-five years upon an offender pursuant to division (A)(3)(e)(ii) or (B)(2)(a) of section 2971.03 of the Revised Code is precluded unless the offender is convicted of or pleads guilty to attempted rape and unless the indictment, count in the indictment, or information charging the offense specifies that the offender was sixteen years of age or older at the time of the commission of the offense and that, had the offender completed the rape that was attempted, the offender would have been guilty of rape in violation of division (A)(1)(b) of section 2907.02 of the Revised Code.

(B) The specification shall be stated at the end of the body of the indictment, count, or information and shall be stated in substantially the following form:

"SPECIFICATION (or, SPECIFICATION TO THE FIRST COUNT). The Grand Jurors (or insert the person's or the prosecuting attorney's name when appropriate) further find and specify that (set forth that the offender was sixteen years of age or older at the time of the commission of the offense and that, had the offender completed the rape that was attempted, the offender would have been guilty of a violation of division (A)(1)(b) of section 2907.02 of the Revised Code)."

(2006 S 260, eff. 1–2–07)

Cross References

Application of chapter, searches authorized, see 2971.07

Attempt, see 2923.02

Community notification of sex offender registration, see 2950.11
Definitions, see 2929.01
Escape, see 2921.34
Factors to be considered in certain of court's sentencing decisions, see 2929.13
Factors to be considered in determining whether to impose a fine for a felony, see 2929.14
Internet database of inmates, see 5120.66
Notice of incarceration or release of defendant, see 2930.16
Parole board standards and guidelines for termination of control over violent sex offender's service of prison term, see 5120.49
Reparations fund, procedures for payment of awards by commissioners, publicity expenses, see 2743.191
Sentence for offender convicted of violent sex offense and sexually violent predator specification, sentence for offender convicted of designated homicide, assault, or kidnapping offense and both a sexual motivation and sexually violent predator specification, see 2971.03
Sentencing hearing. 2929.19
Sexually violent predator specification, see 2941.148
Standards for assessing offender convicted of violent sex offense or designated homicide, assault, or kidnapping offense and adjudicated a sexually violent predator, risk assessment report, see 5120.61
Victims' rights pamphlet, publication and distribution, costs, see 109.42

Research References

Encyclopedias

OH Jur. 3d Criminal Law: Procedure § 926, Attempted Rape.
OH Jur. 3d Criminal Law: Procedure § 1850, Inclusion of Finding in Sentence.
OH Jur. 3d Criminal Law: Substantive Principles and Offenses § 137, Classification of Crime.

Treatises and Practice Aids

Katz & Giannelli, Baldwin's Ohio Practice Criminal Law § 93:11, Punishment.
Weiler & Weiler, Ohio Driving Under the Influence App. A, Ohio Revised Code--Selected Provisions.

2941.1419 Attempted rape specification; victim under ten years of age

Imposition of a mandatory indefinite prison term consisting of a minimum term of ten years and a maximum term of life imprisonment upon an offender pursuant to division (A)(3)(e)(iii) or (B)(2)(b) of section 2971.03 of the Revised Code is precluded unless the offender is convicted of or pleads guilty to attempted rape and unless the indictment, count in the indictment, or information charging the offense specifies that, had the offender completed the rape that was attempted, the offender would have been guilty of rape in violation of division (A)(1)(b) of section 2907.02 of the Revised Code and specifies that one of the following applies:

(A) The victim was under ten years of age.

(B) The offender attempted to commit rape by purposely compelling the victim to submit by force or threat of force, and the offender was sixteen years of age or older at the time of the commission of the offense.

The specification shall be stated at the end of the body of the indictment, count, or information and shall be stated in substantially the following form:

"SPECIFICATION (or, SPECIFICATION TO THE FIRST COUNT). The Grand Jurors (or insert the person's or the prosecuting attorney's name when appropriate) further find and specify that (set forth that, had the offender completed the rape that was attempted, the offender would have been guilty of a violation of division (A)(1)(b) of section 2907.02 of the Revised Code, and the victim was under ten years of age or the offender attempted to commit rape by purposely compelling the victim to submit by force or threat of force, and the offender was sixteen years of age or older at the time of the commission of the offense)."

(2006 S 260, eff. 1–2–07)

Cross References

Application of chapter, searches authorized, see 2971.07
Attempt, see 2923.02
Community notification of sex offender registration, see 2950.11
Definitions, see 2929.01
Escape, see 2921.34
Factors to be considered in certain of court's sentencing decisions, see 2929.13
Factors to be considered in determining whether to impose a fine for a felony, see 2929.14
Internet database of inmates, see 5120.66

Notice of incarceration or release of defendant, see 2930.16
Parole board standards and guidelines for termination of control over violent sex offender's service of prison term, see 5120.49
Reparations fund, procedures for payment of awards by commissioners, publicity expenses, see 2743.191
Sentence for offender convicted of violent sex offense and sexually violent predator specification, sentence for offender convicted of designated homicide, assault, or kidnapping offense and both a sexual motivation and sexually violent predator specification, see 2971.03
Sentencing hearing. 2929.19
Sexually violent predator specification, see 2941.148
Standards for assessing offender convicted of violent sex offense or designated homicide, assault, or kidnapping offense and adjudicated a sexually violent predator, risk assessment report, see 5120.61
Victims' rights pamphlet, publication and distribution, costs, see 109.42

Ohio Administrative Code References

Life sentences, see OAC 5120–2–10

Research References

Encyclopedias

OH Jur. 3d Criminal Law: Procedure § 926, Attempted Rape.
OH Jur. 3d Criminal Law: Procedure § 1850, Inclusion of Finding in Sentence.
OH Jur. 3d Criminal Law: Substantive Principles and Offenses § 137, Classification of Crime.

Treatises and Practice Aids

Katz & Giannelli, Baldwin's Ohio Practice Criminal Law § 93:11, Punishment.
Weiler & Weiler, Ohio Driving Under the Influence App. A, Ohio Revised Code--Selected Provisions.

2941.1420 Attempted rape specification; repeat offenders

(A) Imposition of a mandatory indefinite prison term consisting of a minimum term of fifteen years and a maximum term of life imprisonment upon an offender pursuant to division (A)(3)(e)(iv) or (B)(2)(c) of section 2971.03 of the Revised Code is precluded unless the offender is convicted of or pleads guilty to attempted rape and unless the indictment, count in the indictment, or information charging the offense specifies that, had the offender completed the rape that was attempted, the offender would have been guilty of rape in violation of division (A)(1)(b) of section 2907.02 of the Revised Code, and any of the following apply:

(1) The offender previously has been convicted of or pleaded guilty to one of the following:

(a) Attempted rape and previously has been convicted of or pleaded guilty to a specification of the type described in this section or section 2941.1418 or 2941.1419 of the Revised Code;

(b) Attempted rape under circumstances that are substantially similar to the circumstances described in this section or section 2941.1419 or 2941.1420 of the Revised Code;

(c) A violation of an existing or former law of this state, another state, or the United States that is substantially similar to any of the offenses described in divisions (A)(1)(a) and (b) of this section.

(2) The offender previously has been convicted of or pleaded guilty to violating division (A)(1)(b) of section 2907.02 of the Revised Code or to violating a substantially similar existing or former law of this state, another state, or the United States.

(3) The offender during or immediately after the commission of the offense caused serious physical harm to the victim.

(B) The specification shall be stated at the end of the body of the indictment, count, or information and shall be stated in substantially the following form:

"SPECIFICATION (or, SPECIFICATION TO THE FIRST COUNT). The Grand Jurors (or insert the person's or the prosecuting attorney's name when appropriate) further find and specify that (set forth that, had the offender completed the rape that was attempted, the offender would have been guilty of a violation of division (A)(1)(b) of section 2907.02 of the Revised Code, and the offender previously has been convicted of or pleaded guilty to attempted rape and previously has been convicted of or pleaded guilty to a specification of the type described in this section or section 2941.1418 or 2941.1419 of the Revised Code, previously has been convicted of or pleaded guilty to attempted rape under circumstances that are substantially similar to the circumstances described in this section or section 2941.1419 or 2941.1420 of the Revised Code, or previously has been convicted of or pleaded guilty to violating a substantially similar existing or former law of this state, another state, or the United States; previously has been convicted of or pleaded guilty to violating division (A)(1)(b) of section 2907.02 of the Revised Code or to violating a substantially similar existing or former law of this state, another state, or the United States; or the offender during or immediately after the commission of the offense caused serious physical harm to the victim)."

(2006 S 260, eff. 1–2–07)

Cross References

Application of chapter, searches authorized, see 2971.07

Attempt, see 2923.02

Community notification of sex offender registration, see 2950.11

Definitions, see 2929.01

Escape, see 2921.34

Factors to be considered in certain of court's sentencing decisions, see 2929.13

Factors to be considered in determining whether to impose a fine for a felony, see 2929.14

Internet database of inmates, see 5120.66

Notice of incarceration or release of defendant, see 2930.16

Parole board standards and guidelines for termination of control over violent sex offender's service of prison term, see 5120.49

Reparations fund, procedures for payment of awards by commissioners, publicity expenses, see 2743.191

Sentence for offender convicted of violent sex offense and sexually violent predator specification, sentence for offender convicted of designated homicide, assault, or kidnapping offense and both a sexual motivation and sexually violent predator specification, see 2971.03

Sentencing hearing. 2929.19

Sexually violent predator specification, see 2941.148

Standards for assessing offender convicted of violent sex offense or designated homicide, assault, or kidnapping offense and adjudicated a sexually violent predator, risk assessment report, see 5120.61

Victims' rights pamphlet, publication and distribution, costs, see 109.42

Ohio Administrative Code References

Life sentences, see OAC 5120–2–10

Research References

Encyclopedias

OH Jur. 3d Criminal Law: Procedure § 926, Attempted Rape.

OH Jur. 3d Criminal Law: Procedure § 1850, Inclusion of Finding in Sentence.

OH Jur. 3d Criminal Law: Substantive Principles and Offenses § 137, Classification of Crime.

Treatises and Practice Aids

Katz & Giannelli, Baldwin's Ohio Practice Criminal Law § 93:11, Punishment.

Weiler & Weiler, Ohio Driving Under the Influence App. A, Ohio Revised Code--Selected Provisions.

2941.1421 Additional term precluded; exception

(A) Imposition of an additional prison term of one, two, three, four, five, or six months under division (H)(2)(a)(i) of section 2929.14 of the Revised Code, an additional prison term of one, two, three, four, five, six, seven, eight, nine, ten, eleven, or twelve months under division (H)(2)(a)(ii) of section 2929.14 of the Revised Code, an additional definite jail term of not more than sixty days under division (F)(1)(a) of section 2929.24 of the Revised Code, or an additional definite jail term of not more than one hundred twenty days under division (F)(1)(b) of section 2929.24 of the Revised Code is precluded unless the indictment, count in the indictment, or information charging a felony violation of section 2907.22, 2907.24, 2907.241, or 2907.25 of the Revised Code or a misdemeanor violation of section 2907.23, 2907.24, 2907.241, or 2907.25 of the Revised Code, whichever is applicable, specifies that the violation was committed in proximity to a school. The specification shall be stated at the end of the body of the indictment, count, or information and shall be in substantially the following form:

"SPECIFICATION (or, SPECIFICATION TO THE FIRST COUNT). The Grand Jurors (or insert the person's or the prosecuting attorney's name when appropriate) further find and specify that (set forth that the specified offense was committed in proximity to a school).

(B) As used in this section, "committed in proximity to a school" has the same meaning as in section 2929.01 of the Revised Code.

(2011 H 86, eff. 9-30-11; 2008 S 220, eff. 9–30–08)

Historical and Statutory Notes

Amendment Note: 2011 H 86 substituted "(H)(2)(a)(i)" for "(J)(2)(a)(i)" and "(H)(2)(a)(ii)" for "(J)(2)(a)(ii)" in division (A).

Cross References

Fees and costs, all courts, criminal cases, juvenile cases, and some civil actions related to criminal cases, see 2746.02

Misdemeanor jail terms, see 2929.24

Prison terms, see 2929.14

Research References

Encyclopedias

OH Jur. 3d Criminal Law: Procedure § 932, Proximity to School.

OH Jur. 3d Criminal Law: Procedure § 1901, Offense Within School Safety Zone; Violation Within Proximity to School.

OH Jur. 3d Criminal Law: Procedure § 1927, Misdemeanor Jail Terms--Additional Jail Terms.

Treatises and Practice Aids

Katz & Giannelli, Baldwin's Ohio Practice Criminal Law § 80:22, Appellate Review of Sentencing.

Katz & Giannelli, Baldwin's Ohio Practice Criminal Law § 118:11, School Safety Zone Add-on.

Weiler & Weiler, Ohio Driving Under the Influence App. A, Ohio Revised Code--Selected Provisions.

2941.1422 Additional term; human trafficking specification

(A) Imposition of a mandatory prison term under division (B)(7) of section 2929.14 of the Revised Code is precluded unless the offender is convicted of or pleads guilty to a felony violation of section 2905.01, 2905.02, 2907.21, 2907.22, or 2923.32, division (A)(1) or (2) of section 2907.323, or division (B)(1), (2), (3), (4), or (5) of section 2919.22 of the Revised Code and unless the indictment, count in the indictment, or information charging the offense specifies that the offender knowingly committed the offense in furtherance of human trafficking. The specification shall be stated at the end of the body of the indictment, count, or information and shall be stated in substantially the following form:

"SPECIFICATION (or, SPECIFICATION TO THE FIRST COUNT). The Grand Jurors (or insert the person's or the prosecuting attorney's name when appropriate) further find and specify that (set forth that the defendant knowingly committed the offense in furtherance of human trafficking)."

(B) As used in this section, "human trafficking" has the same meaning as in section 2929.01 of the Revised Code.

(2011 H 86, eff. 9-30-11; 2008 H 280, eff. 4-7-09)

Historical and Statutory Notes

Amendment Note: 2011 H 86 substituted "(B)(7)" for "(D)(7)" in division (A).

Cross References

Abduction, see 2905.02

Compelling prostitution, see 2907.21

Endangering children, see 2919.22

Engaging in a pattern of corrupt activity, fines, penalties, forfeiture, records and reports, third–party claims to property subject to forfeiture, see 2923.32

Financial sanctions, see 2929.18

Illegal use of a minor in nudity–oriented material or performance, see 2907.323

Kidnapping, see 2905.01

Prison terms, see 2929.14

Promoting prostitution, see 2907.22

Sentencing guidelines for various specific offenses and degrees of offenses, see 2929.13

United States Code Annotated

Crimes, peonage, slavery and trafficking in persons, benefitting financially from peonage, slavery, and trafficking in persons, see 18 USCA 1593A

Crimes, peonage, slavery and trafficking in persons, enforcement, additional jurisdiction on certain trafficking offenses, see 18 USCA 1596

Crimes, peonage, slavery and trafficking in persons, enticement into slavery, see 18 USCA 1583

Crimes, peonage, slavery and trafficking in persons, forced labor, see 18 USCA 1589

Research References

Encyclopedias

OH Jur. 3d Criminal Law: Procedure § 933, Human Trafficking.

OH Jur. 3d Criminal Law: Procedure § 1873, Specification as Prerequisite to Enhanced Penalty; State's Burden of Proof; Proof of Prior Conviction.

OH Jur. 3d Criminal Law: Procedure § 1917, Offenses for Which Prison Term Must Not be Reduced.

OH Jur. 3d Criminal Law: Procedure § 1921, Restitution.

OH Jur. 3d Criminal Law: Substantive Principles and Offenses § 300, Offense and Punishment.

OH Jur. 3d Criminal Law: Substantive Principles and Offenses § 392, Violations Based on Omission by a Parent or on the Action of Any Person.

OH Jur. 3d Criminal Law: Substantive Principles and Offenses § 673, Degrees of Offense.

OH Jur. 3d Criminal Law: Substantive Principles and Offenses § 696, Compelling Prostitution.

OH Jur. 3d Criminal Law: Substantive Principles and Offenses § 697, Promoting Prostitution.

Treatises and Practice Aids

Katz & Giannelli, Baldwin's Ohio Practice Criminal Law § 105:4, Compelling Prostitution.

Katz & Giannelli, Baldwin's Ohio Practice Criminal Law § 105:5, Promoting Prostitution.

Katz & Giannelli, Baldwin's Ohio Practice Criminal Law § 80:22, Appellate Review of Sentencing.

Katz & Giannelli, Baldwin's Ohio Practice Criminal Law § 105:16, Illegal Use of a Minor in Nudity-Oriented Material.

Adrine & Ruden, Ohio Domestic Violence Law App. A, Ohio Revised Code (Selected Provisions).

Weiler & Weiler, Ohio Driving Under the Influence App. A, Ohio Revised Code--Selected Provisions.

Law Review and Journal Commentaries

Our backyard slave trade: The result of Ohio's failure to enact comprehensive state-level human-sex-trafficking legislation. Priscila A. Rocha, 25 J.L. & Health 415 (2012).

2941.1423 Additional term; pregnant victim specification

Imposition of a mandatory prison term under division (B)(8) of section 2929.14 of the Revised Code or a mandatory jail term under division (F) of section 2929.24 of the Revised Code is precluded unless the offender is convicted of or pleads guilty to a violation of section 2903.11, 2903.12, or 2903.13 of the Revised Code and unless the indictment, count in the indictment, or information charging the offense specifies the victim of the offense was a woman whom the offender knew was pregnant at the time of the offense. The specification shall be stated at the end of the body of the indictment, count, or information and shall be stated in substantially the following form:

"SPECIFICATION (or, SPECIFICATION TO THE FIRST COUNT). The Grand Jurors (or insert the person's or prosecuting attorney's name when appropriate) further find and specify that (set forth that the victim of the offense was a woman whom the defendant knew was pregnant at the time of the offense)."

(2011 H 86, eff. 9-30-11; 2008 H 280, eff. 4-7-09)

Historical and Statutory Notes

Amendment Note: 2011 H 86 substituted "(B)(8)" for "(D)(8)" in division (A).

Cross References

Aggravated assault, see 2903.12

Assault, see 2903.13

Felonious assault, see 2903.11

Misdemeanor jail terms, see 2929.24

Research References

Encyclopedias

OH Jur. 3d Criminal Law: Procedure § 927, Pregnant Victim Specification.

OH Jur. 3d Criminal Law: Procedure § 1873, Specification as Prerequisite to Enhanced Penalty; State's Burden of Proof; Proof of Prior Conviction.

OH Jur. 3d Criminal Law: Procedure § 1926, Misdemeanor Jail Terms.

OH Jur. 3d Criminal Law: Substantive Principles and Offenses § 334, Offense and Punishment.

OH Jur. 3d Criminal Law: Substantive Principles and Offenses § 338, Offense and Punishment.

Treatises and Practice Aids

Katz & Giannelli, Baldwin's Ohio Practice Criminal Law § 80:22, Appellate Review of Sentencing.

Adrine & Ruden, Ohio Domestic Violence Law § 3:3, Elements and Penalties--Felonious Assault Under RC 2903.11.

Adrine & Ruden, Ohio Domestic Violence Law § 3:4, Elements and Penalties--Aggravated Assault Under RC 2903.12.

Adrine & Ruden, Ohio Domestic Violence Law § 3:5, Elements and Penalties--Assault Under RC 2903.13.

Adrine & Ruden, Ohio Domestic Violence Law App. A, Ohio Revised Code (Selected Provisions).

Weiler & Weiler, Ohio Driving Under the Influence App. A, Ohio Revised Code--Selected Provisions.

2941.25 Multiple counts

Cross References

Texting while driving, see 4511.204

Trafficking in persons, see 2905.32

Using electronic wireless communications device while driving, see 4511.205

Law Review and Journal Commentaries

Punish Once, Punish Twice: Ohio's Inconsistent Interpretation of its Multiple Counts Statute. Richard R. Parsons, 36 Cap. U. L. Rev. 809 (Spring 2008).

State v. Johnson, Matthew M. Mitchell. 37 Ohio N U L Rev 853 (2011).

State v. Whitfield, Amy A. Jeffries. 37 Ohio N U L Rev 869 (2011).

Notes of Decisions

1. Constitutional issues

Ohio supreme court's decision in *State v. Johnson*, overruling its prior decision in *State v. Rance* and stating new test for double jeopardy claims based on Ohio's allied offenses statute, did not apply retroactively in state inmate's habeas proceeding. Walters v. Warden, Ross Correctional Inst. (C.A.6 (Ohio), 04-02-2013) No. 12-3202, 521 Fed.Appx. 375, 2013 WL 1296249, Unreported, certiorari denied 134 S.Ct. 640, 187 L.Ed.2d 424. Courts ⚷ 100(1)

Receiving stolen property and criminal damaging charges against sole proprietorship, a lumber company owned by defendant, were allied offenses of similar import as charges against defendant, and thus sole proprietorship could not be subject to criminal liability for charges without violating defendant's rights against double jeopardy, in prosecution arising from defendant's purchase of lumber wrongfully removed from victim's land; sole proprietorship and defendant were both charged together in the same counts of the indictment for the same acts. State v. Lowman Lumber Co. (Ohio App. 2 Dist., Montgomery, 01-09-2009) No. 22398, 2009-Ohio-63, 2009 WL 50613, Unreported. Double Jeopardy ⚷ 188

Defendant's kidnapping of victim was not merely incidental to his rapes of victim, but rather was committed separately or with a separate animus, and thus defendant's convictions of both kidnapping and rape did not violate multiple count statute; defendant's confinement of victim was secretive, as he carried her away from an area where other partygoers were present to an isolated area in the woods, and defendant's movement of victim was substantial and subjected her to an increase in the risk of harm, as he threw victim into a truck several times while moving her and choked her when she resisted. State v. Swank (Ohio App. 11 Dist., Lake, 11-21-2008) No. 2008-L-019, 2008-Ohio-6059, 2008 WL 4964659, Unreported, appeal allowed in part 121 Ohio St.3d 1439, 903 N.E.2d 1222, 2009-Ohio-1638, reversed 130 Ohio St.3d 254, 957 N.E.2d 289, 2011-Ohio-5348, reconsideration denied 130 Ohio St.3d 1499, 958 N.E.2d 960, 2011-Ohio-6556, on remand 2012-Ohio-98, 2012 WL 114271, on remand 2012-Ohio-153, 2012 WL 171016. Criminal Law ⚷ 29(13)

Rape and kidnapping offenses for which defendant was convicted were not allied offenses of similar import in manner as to render imposition of separate sentences for each violative of defendant's right of protection against double jeopardy. State v. Hardges (Ohio App. 9 Dist., Summit, 10-29-2008) No. 24175, 2008-Ohio-5567, 2008 WL 4724692, Unreported, appeal not allowed 121 Ohio St.3d 1427, 903 N.E.2d 326, 2009-Ohio-1296. Double Jeopardy ⚿ 149

Felonious assault and attempted murder offenses for which defendant was convicted were not allied offenses of similar import in manner as to render separate sentences for each violative of defendant's right of protection against double jeopardy. State v. Hardges (Ohio App. 9 Dist., Summit, 10-29-2008) No. 24175, 2008-Ohio-5567, 2008 WL 4724692, Unreported, appeal not allowed 121 Ohio St.3d 1427, 903 N.E.2d 326, 2009-Ohio-1296. Double Jeopardy ⚿ 150(1)

Given state appellate court's holding that multiple punishments for robbery and aggravated robbery were permissible under Ohio law, state trial court did not violate defendant's federal right against double jeopardy by sentencing him for both offenses. Palmer v. Haviland (C.A.6 (Ohio), 04-09-2008) No. 06-3857, 273 Fed.Appx. 480, 2008 WL 961640, Unreported. Double Jeopardy ⚿ 145

In deciding petitioner's double jeopardy claim, federal habeas court was bound by state courts' interpretation of Ohio statutes as permitting a defendant convicted of both robbery and aggravated robbery to be punished for both offenses. Palmer v. Haviland (C.A.6 (Ohio), 04-09-2008) No. 06-3857, 273 Fed.Appx. 480, 2008 WL 961640, Unreported. Habeas Corpus ⚿ 770

Defendant's two convictions for aggravated assault were improper and in violation of double jeopardy safeguards; defendant committed only one act of aggravated assault. State v. Brown (Ohio App. 8 Dist., Cuyahoga, 11-30-2006) No. 87651, 2006-Ohio-6267, 2006 WL 3446238, Unreported, appeal allowed 114 Ohio St.3d 1409, 867 N.E.2d 843, 2007-Ohio-2632, affirmed on other grounds 119 Ohio St.3d 447, 895 N.E.2d 149, 2008-Ohio-4569, certiorari denied 129 S.Ct. 1356, 555 U.S. 1190, 173 L.Ed.2d 618. Double Jeopardy ⚿ 141

Trial counsel's failure to raise in trial court claim that three kidnapping convictions merged with two rape convictions and one attempted rape conviction as they were allied offenses of similar import, which resulted in waiver of right to raise claim on appeal, did not constitute ineffective assistance, where record revealed that counsel was well-prepared and zealous advocate for defendant in face of overwhelming evidence of guilt and counsel could have decided as matter of trial strategy to be considerate of both jury's and court's patience. State v. Russell (Ohio App. 8 Dist., Cuyahoga, 09-23-2004) No. 83699, 2004-Ohio-5031, 2004 WL 2340125, Unreported, appeal not allowed 105 Ohio St.3d 1452, 823 N.E.2d 457, 2005-Ohio-763, motion to reopen denied 2005-Ohio-2998, 2005 WL 1406347, appeal not allowed 106 Ohio St.3d 1537, 835 N.E.2d 384, 2005-Ohio-5146, habeas corpus dismissed 2008 WL 2600006. Criminal Law ⚿ 1909

Appellate court would decline to review defendant's claim on appeal, that statute governing multiple counts was unconstitutionally vague, where defendant did not challenge constitutionality of statute before trial court. State v. Haller (Ohio App. 3 Dist., 11-13-2012) 982 N.E.2d 111, 2012-Ohio-5233, appeal not allowed 134 Ohio St.3d 1508, 984 N.E.2d 1102, 2013-Ohio-1123. Criminal Law ⚿ 1030(2)

It was plain error to sentence defendant for two counts of aggravated theft and two counts of theft that were allied offenses of similar import, although, if defendant was only sentenced for one count of each type, his sentence would have been the same length, and defendant agreed to sentence; defendant was prejudiced by having more convictions than were authorized by law, and nothing in record demonstrated that defendant was informed that he was agreeing to be convicted of allied offenses, thereby waiving his constitutional right to be free from double jeopardy. State v. Underwood (Ohio, 01-05-2010) 124 Ohio St.3d 365, 922 N.E.2d 923, 2010-Ohio-1, reconsideration denied 124 Ohio St.3d 1494, 922 N.E.2d 229, 2010-Ohio-670. Criminal Law ⚿ 1042.3(1)

Statute that prohibited appellate review of sentence if it was authorized by law, recommended jointly by the defendant and the prosecution, and imposed by court did not prohibit appellate review of sentence for two counts of aggravated theft that were allied offenses of similar import and two counts of theft that were allied offenses of similar import, although sentence was jointly recommended by the parties and imposed by the court; Double Jeopardy Clause and statute governing sentencing for multiple counts prohibited multiple sentences for the same conduct. State v. Underwood (Ohio, 01-05-2010) 124 Ohio St.3d 365, 922 N.E.2d 923, 2010-Ohio-1, reconsideration denied 124 Ohio St.3d 1494, 922 N.E.2d 229, 2010-Ohio-670. Criminal Law ⚿ 1023(11); Double Jeopardy ⚿ 143; Sentencing and Punishment ⚿ 509

Where a court of appeals finds reversible error in the imposition of multiple punishments for allied offenses, the State is not precluded as a matter of double jeopardy from pursuing any of the allied offenses upon a remand for a new sentencing hearing. State v. Whitfield (Ohio, 01-05-2010) 124 Ohio St.3d 319, 922 N.E.2d 182, 2010-Ohio-2. Criminal Law ⚿ 1192; Double Jeopardy ⚿ 108

To avoid punishing a defendant twice for the same offense, when two or more allied offenses of similar import are charged and guilty verdicts for two or more are returned, multiple guilty verdicts are required to be merged into a single judgment of conviction, not a merger of sentences upon multiple judgments of conviction. State v. Fritz (Ohio App. 2 Dist., 05-08-2009) 182 Ohio App.3d 299, 912 N.E.2d 650, 2009-Ohio-2175. Criminal Law ⚿ 30; Sentencing and Punishment ⚿ 501

Charged crimes of complicity to commit robbery and receiving stolen property were not allied offenses of similar import, but rather were offenses of dissimilar import, and thus defendant's convictions for the crimes did not violate statutory double jeopardy; defendant could commit a robbery by inflicting, attempting to inflict, or threatening to inflict physical harm in the course of attempting to commit a theft offense without necessarily receiving, retaining, or disposing of property he had reasonable cause to believe was obtained through commission of a theft offense, while defendant could receive, retain, or dispose of property he had reasonable cause to believe had been obtained through commission of a theft offense without necessarily aiding another person in inflicting, attempting to inflict, or threatening to inflict physical harm during the course of the theft offense. State v. Stevenson (Ohio App. 2 Dist., 02-27-2009) 181 Ohio App.3d 292, 908 N.E.2d 1005, 2009-Ohio-901, appeal not allowed 122 Ohio St.3d 1478, 910 N.E.2d 478, 2009-Ohio-3625, habeas corpus dismissed 2011 WL 3678670. Double Jeopardy ⚿ 145

Kidnapping and aggravated robbery, when analyzed in the abstract, are allied offenses of similar import, and thus cumulative punishment of a defendant for both offenses stemming from the same conduct would violate double jeopardy; presence of a weapon that has been shown or used, or whose possession has been made known to the victim during the commission of a theft offense, as required to support aggravated robbery conviction, necessarily also forcibly restrains the liberty of another, as required to support kidnapping conviction. State v. Winn (Ohio, 03-17-2009) 121 Ohio St.3d 413, 905 N.E.2d 154, 2009-Ohio-1059. Double Jeopardy ⚿ 29.1; Double Jeopardy ⚿ 149

Just as there must be an initial attachment of jeopardy before double-jeopardy concerns arise, there must also be a conviction on one offense before court can conduct an allied-offense-of-similar-import analysis concerning a second conviction. State v. Baranski (Ohio App. 4 Dist., 08-07-2007) 173 Ohio App.3d 410, 878 N.E.2d 1058, 2007-Ohio-4072. Double Jeopardy ⚿ 132.1

Defendant could not be convicted of both kidnapping and aggravated robbery; kidnapping and aggravated robbery were allied offenses of similar import, and since victim was held in her bedroom in furtherance of aggravated robbery, there was not a separate animus for kidnapping and aggravated robbery, and thus, convictions for both offenses would violate double jeopardy. State v. Winn (Ohio App. 2 Dist., 08-24-2007) 173 Ohio App.3d 202, 877 N.E.2d 1020, 2007-Ohio-4327, appeal allowed 117 Ohio St.3d 1405, 881 N.E.2d 273, 2008-Ohio-565, affirmed 121 Ohio St.3d 413, 905 N.E.2d 154, 2009-Ohio-1059. Double Jeopardy ⚿ 149

Convictions for tampering with evidence and gross abuse of a corpse were not allied offenses of similar import and did not violate the Double Jeopardy Clause; the offense of tampering with evidence could be committed without committing gross abuse of a corpse, as the offense did not have to involve the use of a corpse, and a person could abuse a corpse without tampering with the evidence. State v. Gabriel (Ohio App. 2 Dist., 02-23-2007) 170 Ohio App.3d 393, 867 N.E.2d 474, 2007-Ohio-794, motion to certify allowed 114 Ohio St.3d 1423, 868 N.E.2d 678, 2007-Ohio-2904, appeal not allowed 114 Ohio St.3d 1428, 868 N.E.2d 681, 2007-Ohio-2904, certified question answered and reversed 116 Ohio St.3d 31, 876 N.E.2d 528, 2007-Ohio-5551, habeas corpus denied 2009 WL 1212262, appeal from denial of post-conviction relief dismissed 2009-Ohio-2082, 2009 WL 1175623, denial of post-conviction relief affirmed 2009-Ohio-2161, 2009 WL 1263653, appeal not allowed 122 Ohio St.3d 1505, 912 N.E.2d 109, 2009-Ohio-4233, habeas corpus dismissed 2009 WL 2058591, habeas corpus dismissed 2009 WL 2591676, certificate of appealability denied 2009 WL 4283207, habeas corpus dismissed 2010 WL 1416992, habeas corpus dismissed 2010 WL 3258395, habeas corpus dismissed 2012 WL 2562428, certificate of appealability denied 2012 WL 4442740. Double Jeopardy ⚿ 139.1

Separate convictions for engaging in corrupt activity, conspiracy to engage in corrupt activity, and multiple counts of tampering with evidence did not unconstitutionally subject defendant to cumulative punishment, based on claim that tampering with evidence provided predicate for corruption offenses; General Assembly provided for separate conviction for engaging in pattern of corrupt activity if jury found two or more predicate offenses. State v. DeMastry (Ohio App. 5 Dist., 10-17-2003) 155 Ohio App.3d 110, 799 N.E.2d 229, 2003-Ohio-5588, appeal not allowed 101 Ohio St.3d 1488, 805 N.E.2d 539, 2004-Ohio-1293, appeal not allowed 103 Ohio St.3d 1495, 816 N.E.2d 1081, 2004-Ohio-5605, denial of post-conviction relief affirmed 2005-Ohio-4962, 2005 WL 2300288, appeal not allowed 108 Ohio St.3d 1440, 842 N.E.2d 64, 2006-Ohio-421, habeas corpus dismissed 2007 WL 869695. Sentencing And Punishment ⚿ 520(1)

Defendant's acquittal on one count of possession of crack cocaine did not raise double jeopardy bar to his subsequent prosecution for trafficking in crack cocaine, or to prosecution on other counts of possession of crack cocaine, where subsequent prosecutions did not involve allied offenses of similar import; trafficking and possession each required proof of additional fact, and elements of each did not correspond to such degree that commission of one would result in commission of the other. State v. Gonzales (Ohio App. 1 Dist., 09-20-2002) 151 Ohio App.3d 160, 783 N.E.2d 903, 2002-Ohio-4937, appeal not allowed 98 Ohio St.3d 1423, 782 N.E.2d 78, 2003-Ohio-259, habeas corpus dismissed 2006 WL 2792162, certificate of appealability 2006 WL 3716792, affirmed 290 Fed.Appx. 799, 2008 WL 3889866, certiorari denied 129 S.Ct. 1016, 555 U.S. 1144, 173 L.Ed.2d 306. Double Jeopardy ⚿ 146

Defendant's convictions and sentence did not violate double jeopardy or due process, where the trial court merged the three murder convictions into a single offense, the trial jury verdict referred to one death penalty, and the trial court imposed only a single death penalty. State v. Coley (Ohio, 10-03-2001) 93 Ohio St.3d 253, 754 N.E.2d 1129, 2001-Ohio-1340, habeas corpus denied 2010 WL 1375217. Constitutional Law ⚩ 4563; Double Jeopardy ⚩ 28; Double Jeopardy ⚩ 182

Ohio Court of Appeals adjudicated petitioner's claim that consecutive sentences imposed on his Ohio convictions for aggravated robbery and attempted kidnapping violated the Double Jeopardy Clause's ban on multiple punishments for the same offense "on the merits," and thus, federal habeas court would review state court's decision under heightened standards imposed by the Antiterrorism and Effective Death Penalty Act (AEDPA), even though the Ohio Court of Appeals' analysis of the double jeopardy claim was limited to an application of Ohio's allied offenses statute as interpreted by the Ohio Supreme Court; that analysis was entirely dispositive of the federal double jeopardy claim, as the Ohio Supreme Court had recognized in prior case explaining that the allied offenses analysis answered the constitutional and state statutory inquiries. Jackson v. Smith (C.A.6 (Ohio), 03-07-2014) 745 F.3d 206, certiorari denied 135 S.Ct. 118, 190 L.Ed.2d 90. Habeas Corpus ⚩ 766

New test in Ohio for allied offenses was inapplicable to state prisoner's petition for writ of habeas corpus alleging that her convictions for operating vehicle while under the influence and aggravated vehicular homicide as proximate result of operating vehicle while under the influence violated Double Jeopardy, since new test became available two years after prisoner's conviction became final and judicial development of allied-offenses concept was little different from development of judicially-announced law because legislature had left it to courts to give life to concept. Volpe v. Trim (C.A.6 (Ohio), 01-08-2013) 708 F.3d 688, amended on denial of rehearing. Courts ⚩ 100(1)

Habeas petitioner procedurally defaulted his allied offense/double jeopardy claims where he failed to raise them on his first state court appeal challenging the imposition of consecutive sentences; while he raised the issue in a subsequent appeal, he had already presented and lost the prior appeal on the consecutive nature of his sentences, thereby precluding his claim. Scuba v. Brigano (C.A.6 (Ohio), 12-27-2007) 527 F.3d 479, certiorari denied 129 S.Ct. 269, 555 U.S. 915, 172 L.Ed.2d 199. Habeas Corpus ⚩ 366

Defendant was punished multiple times for same offense in violation of double jeopardy when trial court failed to merge two counts of having weapons while under disability at sentencing in accordance with Ohio's multiple-count statute. Render v. Warden, Southern Ohio Correctional Facility (S.D.Ohio, 08-22-2012) 889 F.Supp.2d 1014. Double Jeopardy ⚩ 140

Ohio state courts did not violate defendant's double jeopardy rights by not merging three kidnapping charges with defendant's aggravated robbery convictions for purposes of sentencing, precluding federal habeas corpus relief; state courts based decision on reasonable finding that evidence reflected separate criminal acts due to prolonged restraint and movement of victims. Spence v. Sheets (S.D.Ohio, 12-18-2009) 675 F.Supp.2d 792. Double Jeopardy ⚩ 149

Double Jeopardy Clause barred re-prosecution of a defendant on a kidnapping charge where the defendant had been was acquitted of rape charges which arose from the same conduct as the kidnapping charge; it was the alleged rape that constituted the restraint, and thus the restraint element of kidnapping was a critical issue of ultimate fact shared by the rape charges. Madsen v. McFaul (N.D.Ohio, 08-13-2009) 643 F.Supp.2d 962. Double Jeopardy ⚩ 149

Money laundering, prohibition on international transportation of proceeds of unlawful activity, appearance of legitimate wealth requirement. Cuellar v. U.S., 2008, 128 S.Ct. 1994, 170 L.Ed.2d 942.

1.5. Legislative intent

In deciding whether to afford a defendant the protections of the multiple count statute, the intent of the General Assembly is controlling. State v. Anderson (Ohio App. 1 Dist., 07-27-2012) 974 N.E.2d 1236, 2012-Ohio-3347, appeal not allowed 133 Ohio St.3d 1492, 978 N.E.2d 911, 2012-Ohio-5459. Criminal Law ⚩ 29(1)

Petitioner was not entitled to habeas relief on basis that state court's assessment of its legislature's intent for aggravated robbery and attempted kidnapping to be punished cumulatively was wrong; the state court's decision was not contrary to or an unreasonable application of clearly established federal law that the legislature's intent controlled, rather, at worst, the state court incorrectly applied allied offenses statute to determine legislature's intent. Jackson v. Smith (C.A.6 (Ohio), 03-07-2014) 745 F.3d 206, certiorari denied 135 S.Ct. 118, 190 L.Ed.2d 90. Habeas Corpus ⚩ 466

Ohio legislature intended to authorize cumulative punishments for aggravated vehicular homicide (AVH) and operating vehicle while under the influence (OVI), and thus cumulative punishments did not violate Double Jeopardy clause, since they did not correspond to such degree that commission of one crime would result in commission of the other; one could drive under the influence of alcohol, a drug of abuse, or a combination of them and not cause the death of another, and one could drive recklessly or negligently and cause the death of another and not drive under the influence of alcohol, a drug of abuse, or a combination of them. Volpe v. Trim (C.A.6 (Ohio), 01-08-2013) 708 F.3d 688, amended on denial of rehearing. Double Jeopardy ⚩ 29.1

3. Test for allied offenses of similar import

Remand was required in prosecution for felonious assault and having weapons while under a disability for trial court to analyze whether offenses were allied offenses of similar import, such that merger of convictions was required, where trial court had not performed this analysis in the first instance. State v. Wilson (Ohio App. 9 Dist., Summit, 02-05-2014) No. 26683, 2014-Ohio-376, 2014 WL 467499, Unreported, appeal not allowed 139 Ohio St.3d 1406, 9 N.E.3d 1064, 2014-Ohio-2245. Criminal Law ⚷ 1181.5(3.1)

Doctrine of law of the case precluded common pleas court from vacating post-conviction movant's sentences for rape and kidnapping on ground that such offenses were allied offenses of similar import, where claim was addressed on movant's reopened direct appeal. State v. Lawson (Ohio App. 1 Dist., Hamilton, 11-16-2012) No. C-120077, No. C-120067, 2012-Ohio-5281, 2012 WL 5830593, Unreported. Criminal Law ⚷ 1433(2)

Each of defendant's four kidnapping offenses involved a different victim, and thus offenses were not allied offenses of similar import for purpose of imposing separate and consecutive sentences. State v. Blackford (Ohio App. 5 Dist., Perry, 10-16-2012) No. 12 CA 3, 2012-Ohio-4956, 2012 WL 5288320, Unreported. Criminal Law ⚷ 29(13)

Aggravated robbery and two counts of kidnapping were not allied offenses of similar import under multiple-count statute, and thus defendant could be convicted of and sentenced for all three offenses; defendant's acts with respect to each offense were separate and had different animi, in that defendant's acts in entering bank, brandishing knife, and ordering tellers to put money in bag that he had brought provided basis for aggravated robbery charge, defendant's acts in grabbing teller and threatening to kill her provided basis for one kidnapping charge, and defendant's acts of holding knife against other teller and threatening to kill her provided basis for second kidnapping charge. State v. Bright (Ohio App. 3 Dist., Marion, 05-09-2005) No. 9-04-61, 2005-Ohio-2247, 2005 WL 1077539, Unreported, denial of post-conviction relief affirmed 2008-Ohio-1341, 2008 WL 755505. Criminal Law ⚷ 29(13)

Offenses of trafficking in crack cocaine and possession of crack cocaine were not allied offenses of similar import such that it was impossible to commit one without committing the other, and thus defendant's conviction of both offenses did not violate double jeopardy; it was possible to obtain, possess, or use crack cocaine without preparing it for shipment or distributing it, and it was possible to distribute crack cocaine, or prepare it for distribution, without actually possessing it, such as by directing its transportation or serving as middle man in a drug sale. State v. McGhee (Ohio App. 4 Dist., Lawrence, 03-30-2005) No. 04CA15, 2005-Ohio-1585, 2005 WL 737581, Unreported, appeal after new sentencing hearing 2006-Ohio-6623, 2006 WL 3691664. Double Jeopardy ⚷ 146

Aggravated robbery and having weapon while under disability are not of similar import, and thus, defendant could be convicted of both offenses; although defendant argued he could not have committed aggravated robbery without firearm, commission of having weapon under disability does not result in commission of aggravated robbery, and element of aggravated robbery is commission of or attempt to commit theft. State v. Nelson (Ohio App. 8 Dist., Cuyahoga, 06-03-2004) No. 83553, 2004-Ohio-2849, 2004 WL 1232155, Unreported, appeal not allowed 103 Ohio St.3d 1494, 816 N.E.2d 1080, 2004-Ohio-5605, habeas corpus denied in part, dismissed in part 2008 WL 1901392. Criminal Law ⚷ 29(15)

Offenses of felonious assault and attempted murder committed by defendant who, in addition thereto, allegedly committed kidnapping, rape, and aggravated robbery were not allied offenses of similar import, and thus, defendant was properly sentenced separately for both offenses upon his conviction by jury trial; elements of each offense did not correspond to such a degree that the commission of one offense would result in commission of the other. State v. Axson (Ohio App. 8 Dist., Cuyahoga, 05-01-2003) No. 81231, 2003-Ohio-2182, 2003 WL 1994490, Unreported, appeal dismissed 99 Ohio St.3d 1517, 792 N.E.2d 730, 2003-Ohio-4009, appeal allowed 100 Ohio St.3d 1408, 796 N.E.2d 536, 2003-Ohio-4948, motion to dismiss appeal denied 100 Ohio St.3d 1425, 797 N.E.2d 92, 2003-Ohio-5232, reversed 104 Ohio St.3d 248, 819 N.E.2d 271, 2004-Ohio-6396, subsequent determination 2005-Ohio-4396, 2005 WL 2038692, appeal after new sentencing hearing 2005-Ohio-6342, 2005 WL 3219727, appeal allowed, reversed 109 Ohio St.3d 509, 849 N.E.2d 284, 2006-Ohio-2721, reconsideration denied 110 Ohio St.3d 1444, 852 N.E.2d 191, 2006-Ohio-3862, appeal after new sentencing hearing 2007-Ohio-2892, 2007 WL 1695108, appeal after new sentencing hearing 2007-Ohio-3126, 2007 WL 1805041, motion for delayed appeal denied 116 Ohio St.3d 1436, 877 N.E.2d 988, 2007-Ohio-6518, habeas corpus dismissed 2010 WL 750176, appeal after new sentencing hearing 2007-Ohio-5811, 2007 WL 3171233, appeal not allowed 117 Ohio St.3d 1426, 882 N.E.2d 446, 2008-Ohio-969, appeal after new sentencing hearing 2011-Ohio-3187, 2011 WL 2569789. Sentencing And Punishment ⚷ 537

If multiple offenses can be committed by the same conduct, then the court must determine whether the offenses were committed by the same conduct, or a single act, committed with a single state of mind; if the answer to both questions is yes, then the offenses are allied offenses of similar import and will be merged for sentencing purposes. State v. Earley (Ohio App. 8 Dist., 06-19-2014) 15 N.E.3d 357, 2014-Ohio-2643, motion to certify allowed 140 Ohio St.3d 1450, 17 N.E.3d 597, 2014-Ohio-4414, appeal allowed 140 Ohio St.3d 1451, 17 N.E.3d 598, 2014-Ohio-4414. Sentencing and Punishment ⚷ 501

Defendant's conduct of discharging a firearm into a habitation was committed with same animus as felonious assaults and murder, and thus was allied offense of similar import with each of the other offenses for purposes of sentencing merger analysis; defendant shot into house he had just vacated and in direction of group of individuals including persons with whom he had been fighting or arguing and one person who had just threatened him, indicating that defendant's intent was to injure or kill and that shooting into habitation was merely ancillary to that goal. State v. Jackson (Ohio App. 9 Dist., 12-18-2013) 5 N.E.3d 116, 2013-Ohio-5557, appeal not allowed 139 Ohio St.3d 1404, 9 N.E.3d 1062, 2014-Ohio-2245. Sentencing and Punishment ⚿ 539

When determining whether two offenses are allied offenses of similar import subject to merger for sentencing purposes, the conduct of the accused must be considered. State v. Jackson (Ohio App. 9 Dist., 12-18-2013) 5 N.E.3d 116, 2013-Ohio-5557, appeal not allowed 139 Ohio St.3d 1404, 9 N.E.3d 1062, 2014-Ohio-2245. Sentencing and Punishment ⚿ 501

In determining whether an offender's sentences should merge for sentencing purposes, the first prong of the test looks to the import of the offenses and requires a comparison of their elements. State v. Jackson (Ohio App. 9 Dist., 12-18-2013) 5 N.E.3d 116, 2013-Ohio-5557, appeal not allowed 139 Ohio St.3d 1404, 9 N.E.3d 1062, 2014-Ohio-2245. Sentencing and Punishment ⚿ 501

A two-part test is utilized for determining whether offenses are allied offenses of similar import, for the purposes of merger: the first inquiry focuses on whether it is possible to commit one offense and commit the other with the same conduct, and if it is possible to commit both offenses with the same conduct, the court must next determine whether the offenses were in fact committed by a single act, performed with a single state of mind; if so, the offenses are allied offenses of similar import, and must be merged. State v. Clay (Ohio App. 12 Dist., 10-03-2011) 196 Ohio App.3d 305, 963 N.E.2d 220, 2011-Ohio-5086, appeal after new sentencing hearing 2012-Ohio-5011, 2012 WL 5306150, appeal not allowed 134 Ohio St.3d 1471, 983 N.E.2d 370, 2013-Ohio-553, appeal after new sentencing hearing 2013-Ohio-4984, 2013 WL 6021228. Criminal Law ⚿ 30

Robbery and possession of criminal tools were allied offenses of similar import, and thus, merged for purposes of sentencing; defendant used note threatening to kill everyone in bank to commit robbery, and State relied upon same conduct, namely, defendant's possession of note to support both convictions. State v. Clay (Ohio App. 12 Dist., 10-03-2011) 196 Ohio App.3d 305, 963 N.E.2d 220, 2011-Ohio-5086, appeal after new sentencing hearing 2012-Ohio-5011, 2012 WL 5306150, appeal not allowed 134 Ohio St.3d 1471, 983 N.E.2d 370, 2013-Ohio-553, appeal after new sentencing hearing 2013-Ohio-4984, 2013 WL 6021228. Sentencing and Punishment ⚿ 537

When determining whether two offenses are of similar import subject to merger under double jeopardy principles and state multiple-count statute, the conduct of the accused must be considered. State v. Grube (Ohio App. 4 Dist., 02-07-2013) 987 N.E.2d 287, 2013-Ohio-692, appeal not allowed 135 Ohio St.3d 1459, 988 N.E.2d 579, 2013-Ohio-2285. Criminal Law ⚿ 30; Double Jeopardy ⚿ 132.1

Violation of protective order and felonious assault were allied offenses of similar import, and thus, convictions on two counts of felony violations of protective order merged with convictions on two counts of felonious assault arising out of two separate incidents in which defendant drove his vehicle at victim, where conduct that formed basis of each count of felonious assault also formed basis of each count of violation of protection order, and both offenses were committed with same animus. State v. O'Brien (Ohio App. 11 Dist., 01-07-2013) 986 N.E.2d 531, 2013-Ohio-13. Criminal Law ⚿ 30

Defendant's convictions for reckless homicide of victim and reckless homicide of her unborn child were not allied offenses of similar import, and thus, trial court properly imposed separate sentences for offenses; although defendant's offenses arose from a single course of conduct, each offense involved a separate victim. State v. Feller (Ohio App. 1 Dist., 12-21-2012) 985 N.E.2d 210, 2012-Ohio-6016. Sentencing and Punishment ⚿ 529

Appellate courts apply the law to the facts of individual cases to make a legal determination as to the application of statute prohibiting separate sentencing for allied offenses of similar import; that facts are involved in the analysis does not make the issue a question of fact deserving of deference to a trial court. State v. Williams (Ohio, 12-06-2012) 134 Ohio St.3d 482, 983 N.E.2d 1245, 2012-Ohio-5699. Criminal Law ⚿ 1134.75

In making an allied-offenses determination, a court should not employ an abstract analysis, but instead should consider the statutory elements of each offense in the context of the defendant's conduct. State v. Williams (Ohio, 12-06-2012) 134 Ohio St.3d 482, 983 N.E.2d 1245, 2012-Ohio-5699. Criminal Law ⚿ 29(1)

Offense of complicity to commit burglary and offense of complicity to commit grand theft were committed by two separate acts, and thus, offenses were not allied offenses of similar import subject to merger. State v. Haller (Ohio App. 3 Dist., 11-13-2012) 982 N.E.2d 111, 2012-Ohio-5233, appeal not allowed 134 Ohio St.3d 1508, 984 N.E.2d 1102, 2013-Ohio-1123. Criminal Law ⚿ 30

Receiving stolen property and complicity to commit grand theft were allied offenses of similar import subject to merger; it was possible to commit theft and receiving stolen property with the same conduct, and counts both related to accomplice's act of stealing guns fro residence. State v. Haller (Ohio App. 3 Dist., 11-13-2012) 982 N.E.2d 111, 2012-Ohio-5233, appeal not allowed 134 Ohio St.3d 1508, 984 N.E.2d 1102, 2013-Ohio-1123. Criminal Law ⚿ 30

Offense of complicity to commit burglary and offense of complicity to commit grand theft were not committed with the same conduct, and thus, offenses were not allied offenses of similar import subject to merger; burglary was complete upon entering residence, and it was not until accomplice exerted control over victim's guns, an act which occurred apart from unlawful entry into residence, that accomplice committed grand theft. State v. Haller (Ohio App. 3 Dist., 11-13-2012) 982 N.E.2d 111, 2012-Ohio-5233, appeal not allowed 134 Ohio St.3d 1508, 984 N.E.2d 1102, 2013-Ohio-1123. Criminal Law ⚷ 30

A sentence may be imposed for only one of multiple allied offenses of similar import if the record shows that the state relied upon the same conduct to prove the offenses, and that the offenses were committed neither separately nor with a separate animus as to each. State v. Campbell (Ohio App. 1 Dist., 09-19-2012) 978 N.E.2d 970, 2012-Ohio-4231, appeal not allowed 134 Ohio St.3d 1452, 982 N.E.2d 729, 2013-Ohio-347. Sentencing and Punishment ⚷ 509; Sentencing and Punishment ⚷ 513

In determining whether offenses are allied offenses of similar import subject to merger, if the offenses can be committed by the same conduct, then the court must determine whether the offenses were committed by the same conduct, i.e., a single act, committed with a single state of mind, and if the answer to both questions is yes, then the offenses are allied offenses of similar import and will be merged; conversely, if the court determines that the commission of one offense will never result in the commission of the other, or if the offenses are committed separately, or if the defendant has separate animus for each offense, then the offenses will not merge. State v. Carson (Ohio App. 10 Dist., 09-28-2012) 978 N.E.2d 621, 2012-Ohio-4501. Criminal Law ⚷ 30

Trial court committed plain error in failing to merge, for purposes of sentencing, defendant's convictions for possession of marijuana, illegal cultivation of marijuana, and possession of criminal tools; offenses were allied offenses of similar import, committed at same time and with same animus. State v. Luong (Ohio App. 12 Dist., 10-01-2012) 977 N.E.2d 1075, 2012-Ohio-4519. Criminal Law ⚷ 1042.3(1); Sentencing and Punishment ⚷ 524

When determining whether two offenses are allied offenses of similar import subject to merger, court must ask: (1) whether it is possible to commit one offense and commit the other with the same conduct, and, if the multiple offenses can be committed by the same conduct, (2) whether the offenses were committed by the same conduct; if the answer to both questions is yes, then the offenses are allied offenses of similar import and will be merged. State v. Luong (Ohio App. 12 Dist., 10-01-2012) 977 N.E.2d 1075, 2012-Ohio-4519. Criminal Law ⚷ 30

Trial court's failure to merge defendant's convictions for aggravated robbery and kidnapping as allied offenses of similar import under the multiple-count statute was plain error, as the offenses were committed in a single course of conduct with a single animus. State v. Anderson (Ohio App. 1 Dist., 07-27-2012) 974 N.E.2d 1236, 2012-Ohio-3347, appeal not allowed 133 Ohio St.3d 1492, 978 N.E.2d 911, 2012-Ohio-5459. Criminal Law ⚷ 1042.3(1)

Court of appeals, when determining whether two offenses are allied offenses of similar import subject to merger, looks to the evidence adduced below, and if that evidence reveals that the state relied upon the same conduct to prove the two offenses, and that the offenses were committed neither separately nor with a separate animus as to each, then the defendant is afforded the protections of the multiple-count statute and the trial court errs by imposing separate sentences for the offenses. State v. Anderson (Ohio App. 1 Dist., 07-27-2012) 974 N.E.2d 1236, 2012-Ohio-3347, appeal not allowed 133 Ohio St.3d 1492, 978 N.E.2d 911, 2012-Ohio-5459. Sentencing and Punishment ⚷ 509

Under the multiple-count statute, a trial court, in a single proceeding, may convict a defendant for two or more offenses having as their genesis the same criminal conduct or transaction, if the offenses (1) were not allied offenses of similar import, (2) were committed separately, or (3) were committed with a separate animus as to each offense. State v. Anderson (Ohio App. 1 Dist., 07-27-2012) 974 N.E.2d 1236, 2012-Ohio-3347, appeal not allowed 133 Ohio St.3d 1492, 978 N.E.2d 911, 2012-Ohio-5459. Criminal Law ⚷ 29(1)

Defendant waived all but plain error on appeal of his convictions for aggravated robbery and kidnapping on issue of whether his offenses were allied offenses of similar import subject to merger, where he failed to raise any objection to the imposition of multiple punishments on his convictions at his sentencing hearing. State v. Anderson (Ohio App. 1 Dist., 07-27-2012) 974 N.E.2d 1236, 2012-Ohio-3347, appeal not allowed 133 Ohio St.3d 1492, 978 N.E.2d 911, 2012-Ohio-5459. Criminal Law ⚷ 1030(3)

If multiple offenses can be committed by the same conduct, then the court must determine whether the offenses were committed by the same conduct, meaning a single act, committed with a single state of mind; if the answer to both questions is yes, then the offenses are allied offenses of similar import and will be merged, otherwise, if the court determines that the commission of one offense will never result in the commission of the other, or if the offenses are committed separately, or if the defendant has separate animus for each offense, then the offenses will not merge. State v. Moore (Ohio App. 8 Dist., 05-03-2012) 970 N.E.2d 1098, 2012-Ohio-1958, appeal not allowed 133 Ohio St.3d 1413, 975 N.E.2d 1030, 2012-Ohio-4650, appeal after new sentencing hearing 24 N.E.3d 1197, 2014-Ohio-5135, cause dismissed 141 Ohio St.3d 1433, 23 N.E.3d 1178, 2015-Ohio-168, stay denied 141 Ohio St.3d 1452, 23 N.E.3d 1195, 2015-Ohio-239. Criminal Law ⚷ 30

Felony murder offense based upon child endangering involving abuse of a child that resulted in serious physical harm to the child, and the offense of child endangering involving abuse of a child that results in serious physical harm to the child, which were not committed separately or with a separate animus as to each, were allied offenses of similar import and, thus, were required to be merged for purposes of sentence. State v. Cook (Ohio App. 2 Dist., 12-17-2010) 970 N.E.2d 1020, 2010-Ohio-6222. Sentencing and Punishment ⚿ 529

Because statute that states that defendant can be convicted of only one offense based upon the same conduct that could be construed to be two or more allied offenses of similar import protects a defendant only from being punished for allied offenses, the determination of the defendant's guilt for committing allied offenses remains intact, both before and after the merger of allied offenses for sentencing. State v. Thomas (Ohio App. 8 Dist., 11-23-2011) 197 Ohio App.3d 176, 966 N.E.2d 939, 2011-Ohio-6073, appeal not allowed 132 Ohio St.3d 1425, 969 N.E.2d 272, 2012-Ohio-2729, appeal after new sentencing hearing 2013-Ohio-1804, 2013 WL 1858890, appeal after new sentencing hearing 2014-Ohio-2410, 2014 WL 2566106, appeal not allowed 141 Ohio St.3d 1422, 21 N.E.3d 1115, 2014-Ohio-5567. Sentencing and Punishment ⚿ 509

Defendant was not prejudiced by trial court's failure to inform him in plea colloquy that it could impose consecutive terms for thirty sexual offenses, six counts of endangering children, and one count of possession of criminal tools, even if he did not understand that some of his offenses could be considered allied offenses for which he could only be punished once; rule of criminal procedure governing entry of pleas contained no requirement for court to present such information, trial court was required to convict him of any allied offenses, and knowledge of the allied-offense issue would have given defendant even more of an incentive to plead guilty. State v. Thomas (Ohio App. 8 Dist., 11-23-2011) 197 Ohio App.3d 176, 966 N.E.2d 939, 2011-Ohio-6073, appeal not allowed 132 Ohio St.3d 1425, 969 N.E.2d 272, 2012-Ohio-2729, appeal after new sentencing hearing 2013-Ohio-1804, 2013 WL 1858890, appeal after new sentencing hearing 2014-Ohio-2410, 2014 WL 2566106, appeal not allowed 141 Ohio St.3d 1422, 21 N.E.3d 1115, 2014-Ohio-5567. Criminal Law ⚿ 1167(5)

Supreme Court decision of *State v. Johnson*, announcing new standard for determining appropriateness of the merger of allied offenses of similar import for sentencing purposes, applied to defendant's appeal of his sentences on his convictions for kidnapping, rape, and other offenses, though defendant was sentenced ten months before *Johnson* was decided, as *Johnson* was decided while defendant's appeal was pending, such that his convictions had not yet become final. State v. Swiergosz (Ohio App. 6 Dist., 03-02-2012) 197 Ohio App.3d 40, 965 N.E.2d 1070, 2012-Ohio-830, appeal not allowed 133 Ohio St.3d 1493, 978 N.E.2d 911, 2012-Ohio-5459, appeal after new sentencing hearing 2013-Ohio-4625, 2013 WL 5728349, appeal not allowed 138 Ohio St.3d 1435, 4 N.E.3d 1051, 2014-Ohio-889. Courts ⚿ 100(1)

Imposing multiple sentences for allied offenses constitutes plain error. State v. Swiergosz (Ohio App. 6 Dist., 03-02-2012) 197 Ohio App.3d 40, 965 N.E.2d 1070, 2012-Ohio-830, appeal not allowed 133 Ohio St.3d 1493, 978 N.E.2d 911, 2012-Ohio-5459, appeal after new sentencing hearing 2013-Ohio-4625, 2013 WL 5728349, appeal not allowed 138 Ohio St.3d 1435, 4 N.E.3d 1051, 2014-Ohio-889. Criminal Law ⚿ 1042.3(1)

First question for court to answer in determining whether offenses are allied offenses of similar import such that they merge for sentencing is whether it is possible to commit one offense and commit the other with the same conduct, not whether it is possible to commit one without committing the other. State v. Swiergosz (Ohio App. 6 Dist., 03-02-2012) 197 Ohio App.3d 40, 965 N.E.2d 1070, 2012-Ohio-830, appeal not allowed 133 Ohio St.3d 1493, 978 N.E.2d 911, 2012-Ohio-5459, appeal after new sentencing hearing 2013-Ohio-4625, 2013 WL 5728349, appeal not allowed 138 Ohio St.3d 1435, 4 N.E.3d 1051, 2014-Ohio-889. Sentencing and Punishment ⚿ 501

A sentence that contains an allied-offenses error is contrary to law. State v. Swiergosz (Ohio App. 6 Dist., 03-02-2012) 197 Ohio App.3d 40, 965 N.E.2d 1070, 2012-Ohio-830, appeal not allowed 133 Ohio St.3d 1493, 978 N.E.2d 911, 2012-Ohio-5459, appeal after new sentencing hearing 2013-Ohio-4625, 2013 WL 5728349, appeal not allowed 138 Ohio St.3d 1435, 4 N.E.3d 1051, 2014-Ohio-889. Sentencing and Punishment ⚿ 509

Charge of tampering with evidence and charge of tampering with records were not allied offenses of similar import, and thus prohibition on double jeopardy was not violated by defendant's convictions on both charges for falsely informing attorney that he had found person who was the real owner of cocaine found in defendant's car and having attorney prepare a statement to be sent to prosecutor's office, and for escorting the alleged owner of the cocaine to prosecutor's office to give a false statement there, since a separate animus existed for each distinct act committed. State v. Johnson (Ohio App. 5 Dist., 05-31-2011) 196 Ohio App.3d 338, 963 N.E.2d 828, 2011-Ohio-2653, appeal not allowed 130 Ohio St.3d 1416, 956 N.E.2d 308, 2011-Ohio-5605. Double Jeopardy ⚿ 139.1

Offenses of theft of a firearm by deception and tampering with records were not "allied offenses of similar import," and, thus, defendant could be convicted and sentenced for both offenses; conduct, or animus, for the theft of a firearm by deception charge occurred when defendant physically removed the firearm from his employer's store, and animus for the tampering with records charge occurred when he manipulated his employer's sales records to show canceled class registrations followed by deposits made to his lay-away account. State v. Leach (Ohio App. 5 Dist., 09-16-2011) 195

Ohio App.3d 433, 960 N.E.2d 531, 2011-Ohio-4745. Criminal Law ⚷ 29(10)

The issue in determining whether two offenses are "allied offenses of similar import" so that defendant may be charged with both, but convicted of only one, is whether the offenses were committed by the same conduct i.e., a single act, committed with a single state of mind. State v. Leach (Ohio App. 5 Dist., 09-16-2011) 195 Ohio App.3d 433, 960 N.E.2d 531, 2011-Ohio-4745. Criminal Law ⚷ 29(1)

If the court determines that the commission of one offense will never result in the commission of the other, or if the offenses are committed separately, or if the defendant has separate animus for each offense, then, the offenses will not merge as "allied offenses of similar import." State v. Leach (Ohio App. 5 Dist., 09-16-2011) 195 Ohio App.3d 433, 960 N.E.2d 531, 2011-Ohio-4745. Criminal Law ⚷ 29(1)

If the offenses correspond to such a degree that the conduct of the defendant constituting commission of one offense constitutes commission of the other, then the offenses are allied offenses of similar import such that both offenses may be charged, but the defendant may be convicted of only one. State v. Leach (Ohio App. 5 Dist., 09-16-2011) 195 Ohio App.3d 433, 960 N.E.2d 531, 2011-Ohio-4745. Criminal Law ⚷ 29(1)

When determining whether two offenses are allied offenses of similar import subject to merger under statute that allows indictment or information to contain counts for all such offenses, but states that defendant may be convicted of only one, the question is whether it is possible to commit one offense and commit the other with the same conduct, not whether it is possible to commit one without committing the other. State v. Leach (Ohio App. 5 Dist., 09-16-2011) 195 Ohio App.3d 433, 960 N.E.2d 531, 2011-Ohio-4745. Criminal Law ⚷ 29(1)

Defendant was precluded from arguing on appeal of denial of his postconviction motion seeking a new sentencing hearing, that the trial court erred in imposing prison terms on both felonious-assault charges, on grounds that they were allied offenses, because defendant failed to present that challenge as a ground for relief in his motion, which only asserted that his sentence was void because the trial court had failed to adequately notify him concerning postrelease control. State v. Gonzalez (Ohio App. 1 Dist., 08-24-2011) 195 Ohio App.3d 262, 959 N.E.2d 596, 2011-Ohio-4219. Criminal Law ⚷ 1042.7(2)

If the evidence adduced at trial reveals that the state relied upon the same conduct to support two offenses and that the offenses were committed neither separately nor with a separate animus as to each, then the defendant is afforded the protection of statute that allows the conviction of two or more offenses having as their genesis the same criminal conduct or transaction, if they are not allied offenses of similar import, were committed separately, or were committed with a separate animus as to each offense. State v. Johnson (Ohio App. 1 Dist., 06-29-2011) 195 Ohio App.3d 59, 958 N.E.2d 977, 2011-Ohio-3143, motion for delayed appeal granted 129 Ohio St.3d 1487, 954 N.E.2d 661, 2011-Ohio-5129, appeal not allowed 131 Ohio St.3d 1437, 960 N.E.2d 987, 2012-Ohio-331. Criminal Law ⚷ 29(1)

Felony murder and felonious assault of victim were allied offenses of similar import, and, thus, defendant could not be sentenced for both crimes, where defendant committed the felony murder and felonious assault with the same conduct of firing in rapid succession shots from .45 caliber handgun at victim's truck with the purpose to cause him physical harm and which resulted in victim's death, and defendant's motive was the same and was exhibited in a continuous sequence intended to inflict serious injury upon victim. State v. Johnson (Ohio App. 1 Dist., 06-29-2011) 195 Ohio App.3d 59, 958 N.E.2d 977, 2011-Ohio-3143, motion for delayed appeal granted 129 Ohio St.3d 1487, 954 N.E.2d 661, 2011-Ohio-5129, appeal not allowed 131 Ohio St.3d 1437, 960 N.E.2d 987, 2012-Ohio-331. Sentencing and Punishment ⚷ 568

Attempted murder, felonious assault based on knowingly causing serious physical harm to another, and felonious assault based on causing or attempting to cause physical harm to another by means of deadly weapon or dangerous ordinance were not committed separately or with a separate animus as to each, and therefore were allied offenses of similar import that, under codified double jeopardy principles, merged for sentencing in prosecution arising from defendant's firing at same victim with the same gun at the same location in rapid succession without pausing or reloading gun. State v. Lanier (Ohio App. 1 Dist., 03-02-2011) 192 Ohio App.3d 762, 950 N.E.2d 600, 2011-Ohio-898, appeal not allowed 128 Ohio St.3d 1515, 948 N.E.2d 451, 2011-Ohio-2686. Double Jeopardy ⚷ 150(1); Sentencing and Punishment ⚷ 529

Under codified double jeopardy test for allied offenses of similar import, it is possible to commit, by the same conduct, attempted murder, felonious assault based on knowingly causing serious physical harm to another, and felonious assault based on causing or attempting to cause physical harm to another by means of deadly weapon or dangerous ordinance; when a defendant shoots another person with a gun and succeeds in injuring the other person but not in killing him, the defendant has attempted to and has caused physical harm with a deadly weapon and has engaged in conduct that, if successful, would have resulted in the victim's death. State v. Lanier (Ohio App. 1 Dist., 03-02-2011) 192 Ohio App.3d 762, 950 N.E.2d 600, 2011-Ohio-898, appeal not allowed 128 Ohio St.3d 1515, 948 N.E.2d 451, 2011-Ohio-2686. Double Jeopardy ⚷ 150(1)

If the commission of one offense will never result in the commission of the other, the offenses will not merge as allied offenses of similar import under codified double jeopardy principles. State v. Lanier (Ohio App. 1 Dist., 03-02-2011) 192 Ohio App.3d 762, 950 N.E.2d 600, 2011-Ohio-898, appeal not allowed 128 Ohio St.3d 1515, 948 N.E.2d 451, 2011-Ohio-2686. Criminal Law ⚷ 30; Double Jeopardy ⚷ 134

Under two-part test for determining whether offenses are allied offenses of similar import under codified double jeopardy principles, the first inquiry focuses on whether it is possible to commit both offenses with the same conduct; if it is possible to do so, the court must next determine whether the offenses were in fact committed by a single act, performed with a single state of mind; if so, offenses are allied offenses of similar import and must be merged for sentencing, but if the offenses are committed separately or with a separate animus, the offenses will not merge. State v. Lanier (Ohio App. 1 Dist., 03-02-2011) 192 Ohio App.3d 762, 950 N.E.2d 600, 2011-Ohio-898, appeal not allowed 128 Ohio St.3d 1515, 948 N.E.2d 451, 2011-Ohio-2686. Double Jeopardy ⚷ 134; Sentencing and Punishment ⚷ 501

Two offenses are allied offenses of similar import, such that a defendant may not be convicted of both, if, in comparing the elements of the offenses in the abstract, the offenses are so similar that the commission of one offense will necessarily result in commission of the other. State v. Barker (Ohio App. 2 Dist., 11-24-2010) 191 Ohio App.3d 293, 945 N.E.2d 1107, 2010-Ohio-5744. Criminal Law ⚷ 29(1)

For purposes of statute providing that defendant may be convicted of only one allied offense of similar import, firearm specification for use of firearm to facilitate a felony is sentence enhancement, not separate criminal offense, and thus firearm specification and offense of discharging a firearm at or into a habitation are not allied offenses of similar import; abrogating *State v. Elko*, 2004-Ohio-5209, 2004 WL 2340258. R.C. State v. Ford (Ohio, 02-24-2011) 128 Ohio St.3d 398, 945 N.E.2d 498, 2011-Ohio-765. Criminal Law ⚷ 29(15)

When determining whether two offenses are allied offenses of similar import subject to merger, court must ask: (1) whether it is possible to commit one offense and commit the other with the same conduct, and, if the multiple offenses can be committed by the same conduct, (2) whether the offenses were committed by the same conduct; if the answer to both questions is yes, then the offenses are allied offenses of similar import and will be merged. State v. Johnson (Ohio, 12-29-2010) 128 Ohio St.3d 153, 942 N.E.2d 1061, 2010-Ohio-6314. Criminal Law ⚷ 30

When determining whether two offenses are allied offenses of similar import subject to merger statute, the conduct of the accused must be considered; overruling *State v. Rance*, 85 Ohio St.3d 632, 710 N.E.2d 699. (Per Brown, C.J., with two justices concurring and four justices concurring in result.) R.C. State v. Johnson (Ohio, 12-29-2010) 128 Ohio St.3d 153, 942 N.E.2d 1061, 2010-Ohio-6314. Criminal Law ⚷ 30

In determining whether two offenses are allied offenses of similar import, the statutorily defined elements of offenses that are claimed to be of similar import are compared in the abstract. State v. Afshari (Ohio App. 12 Dist., 02-01-2010) 187 Ohio App.3d 151, 931 N.E.2d 596, 2010-Ohio-325. Criminal Law ⚷ 29(1)

When considering whether offenses are of similar import, a court must compare the statutorily defined elements of the offenses and determine whether they correspond to such a degree that the commission of one crime will result in the commission of the other. State v. Afshari (Ohio App. 12 Dist., 02-01-2010) 187 Ohio App.3d 151, 931 N.E.2d 596, 2010-Ohio-325. Criminal Law ⚷ 29(1)

Only aggravating circumstances that are allied offenses of similar import, within meaning of rule providing that defendant can be convicted of only one such offense, are duplicative for purposes of principle that, where two or more aggravating circumstances arise from same act or indivisible course of conduct and are thus duplicative, the duplicative aggravating circumstances will be merged for purposes of sentencing. State v. Reynolds (Ohio, 01-14-1998) 80 Ohio St.3d 670, 687 N.E.2d 1358, 1998-Ohio-171, certiorari denied 118 S.Ct. 2328, 524 U.S. 930, 141 L.Ed.2d 702, denial of post-conviction relief affirmed 1999 WL 980568, dismissed, appeal not allowed 88 Ohio St.3d 1425, 723 N.E.2d 1113, denial of habeas corpus affirmed 2007 WL 2323850. Sentencing And Punishment ⚷ 146

Allied offenses of similar import do not merge until sentencing, since "conviction" consists of verdict and sentence. State v. McGuire (Ohio, 12-10-1997) 80 Ohio St.3d 390, 686 N.E.2d 1112, 1997-Ohio-335, reconsideration denied 81 Ohio St.3d 1433, 689 N.E.2d 52, dismissal of post-conviction relief affirmed 1998 WL 191415, dismissed, appeal not allowed 83 Ohio St.3d 1428, 699 N.E.2d 945, certiorari denied 119 S.Ct. 85, 525 U.S. 831, 142 L.Ed.2d 66, denial of post-conviction relief affirmed 2001 WL 409424, dismissed, appeal not allowed 93 Ohio St.3d 1411, 754 N.E.2d 259, habeas corpus denied 2007 WL 1893902. Criminal Law ⚷ 30

When determining whether two offenses are allied offenses of similar import subject to merger Ohio's multiple-count statute, the conduct of the accused must be considered. Render v. Warden, Southern Ohio Correctional Facility (S.D.Ohio, 08-22-2012) 889 F.Supp.2d 1014. Criminal Law ⚷ 30

4. Single conviction or sentence

Trial court committed plain error by entering convictions on two kidnapping counts arising from same incident, where there was only one "restraint" of victim's liberty, and thus, there was only one kidnapping. State v. Haines (Ohio App. 11 Dist., Lake, 04-08-2005) No. 2003-L-035, 2005-Ohio-1692,

2005 WL 820539, Unreported, motion to certify allowed 106 Ohio St.3d 1479, 832 N.E.2d 733, 2005-Ohio-3978, appeal allowed 106 Ohio St.3d 1483, 832 N.E.2d 736, 2005-Ohio-3978, affirmed in part, reversed in part 112 Ohio St.3d 393, 860 N.E.2d 91, 2006-Ohio-6711. Criminal Law ⚷ 1030(3)

Defendant's convictions of kidnapping and rape did not merge for sentencing purposes, despite fact that kidnapping and rape were offenses of similar import for merging purposes, where kidnapping and rape were committed separately and with separate, different animus; victims were abducted, confined and forced to ride in car with defendant and his two co-defendants for significant period of time before and after rapes, during which time victims were subjected to risk of harm from operation of automobile separate and distinct from rape injuries. State v. Flannery (Ohio App. 5 Dist., Richland, 04-01-2005) No. 03-CA-24, 2005-Ohio-1614, 2005 WL 750077, Unreported, appeal not allowed 106 Ohio St.3d 1486, 832 N.E.2d 738, 2005-Ohio-3978, habeas corpus denied 2008 WL 1787155, affirmed 397 Fed.Appx. 189, 2010 WL 3927075. Sentencing And Punishment ⚷ 501

Defendant's two burglary convictions were not subject to merger for sentencing, where convictions arose out of entirely separate incidents. State v. Hillman (Ohio App. 10 Dist., 12-30-2014) 2014-Ohio-5760, 2014 WL 7462995. Sentencing and Punishment ⚷ 519

A defendant can be convicted and sentenced on more than one offense if the evidence shows that the defendant's conduct satisfies the elements of two or more disparate offenses; but if the conduct satisfies elements of offenses of similar import, then a defendant can be convicted and sentenced on only one, unless they were committed with separate intent. State v. Earley (Ohio App. 8 Dist., 06-19-2014) 15 N.E.3d 357, 2014-Ohio-2643, motion to certify allowed 140 Ohio St.3d 1450, 17 N.E.3d 597, 2014-Ohio-4414, appeal allowed 140 Ohio St.3d 1451, 17 N.E.3d 598, 2014-Ohio-4414. Criminal Law ⚷ 29(1); Sentencing and Punishment ⚷ 509

Two or more offenses arising from the same conduct and of similar import may result in only one conviction; however, two or more offenses may result in multiple convictions if they are offenses of dissimilar import, they are separately committed, or the defendant possesses a separate animus as to each. State v. Jackson (Ohio App. 9 Dist., 12-18-2013) 5 N.E.3d 116, 2013-Ohio-5557, appeal not allowed 139 Ohio St.3d 1404, 9 N.E.3d 1062, 2014-Ohio-2245. Criminal Law ⚷ 29(1)

Trial court was required to determine whether offenses of aggravated burglary and rape, to which defendant pled guilty, were committed by the same conduct in order to determine whether offenses merged for sentencing purposes. State v. Bryant (Ohio App. 10 Dist., 11-19-2013) 1 N.E.3d 878, 2013-Ohio-5105. Sentencing and Punishment ⚷ 522

A "conviction" within the meaning of the merger statute consists of a guilty verdict and the imposition of a sentence or penalty. State v. Clay (Ohio App. 12 Dist., 10-03-2011) 196 Ohio App.3d 305, 963 N.E.2d 220, 2011-Ohio-5086, appeal after new sentencing hearing 2012-Ohio-5011, 2012 WL 5306150, appeal not allowed 134 Ohio St.3d 1471, 983 N.E.2d 370, 2013-Ohio-553, appeal after new sentencing hearing 2013-Ohio-4984, 2013 WL 6021228. Criminal Law ⚷ 30

Aggravated vehicular homicide based on operating motor vehicle while under influence of alcohol and recklessness-based aggravated vehicular homicide were allied offenses of similar import, and thus, defendant could only be sentenced on one count, where both convictions were predicated upon same conduct, namely that defendant's drunk driving caused him to speed, run stop sign, and collide into building, killing his passenger. State v. Campbell (Ohio App. 1 Dist., 09-19-2012) 978 N.E.2d 970, 2012-Ohio-4231, appeal not allowed 134 Ohio St.3d 1452, 982 N.E.2d 729, 2013-Ohio-347. Sentencing and Punishment ⚷ 534

In a case involving charges for multiple offenses, when in substance and effect but one offense has been committed, the defendant may be convicted of only one offense. State v. Anderson (Ohio App. 1 Dist., 07-27-2012) 974 N.E.2d 1236, 2012-Ohio-3347, appeal not allowed 133 Ohio St.3d 1492, 978 N.E.2d 911, 2012-Ohio-5459. Criminal Law ⚷ 29(1)

For purposes of statute barring multiple convictions for allied offenses of similar import, a "conviction" consists of a guilty verdict and the imposition of a sentence or penalty. State v. Swiergosz (Ohio App. 6 Dist., 03-02-2012) 197 Ohio App.3d 40, 965 N.E.2d 1070, 2012-Ohio-830, appeal not allowed 133 Ohio St.3d 1493, 978 N.E.2d 911, 2012-Ohio-5459, appeal after new sentencing hearing 2013-Ohio-4625, 2013 WL 5728349, appeal not allowed 138 Ohio St.3d 1435, 4 N.E.3d 1051, 2014-Ohio-889. Criminal Law ⚷ 29(1)

The statutory mandate that only one "conviction" result from allied offenses is a restriction against sentencing a defendant for more than one allied offense. State v. Swiergosz (Ohio App. 6 Dist., 03-02-2012) 197 Ohio App.3d 40, 965 N.E.2d 1070, 2012-Ohio-830, appeal not allowed 133 Ohio St.3d 1493, 978 N.E.2d 911, 2012-Ohio-5459, appeal after new sentencing hearing 2013-Ohio-4625, 2013 WL 5728349, appeal not allowed 138 Ohio St.3d 1435, 4 N.E.3d 1051, 2014-Ohio-889. Criminal Law ⚷ 29(1)

6. Separate animus, in general

Murder and having a weapon while under a disability were not allied offenses of similar import subject to merger for sentencing purposes, as offenses were committed with a separate animus in that the offense of murder required that defendant have the specific purpose to kill, whereas offense of having a weapon while under disability did not require a similar purposeful intent. State v. Jones

(Ohio App. 1 Dist., Hamilton, 12-23-2011) No. C-110059, 2011-Ohio-6633, 2011 WL 6826417, Unreported, motion for delayed appeal denied 131 Ohio St.3d 1552, 967 N.E.2d 763, 2012-Ohio-2263. Sentencing And Punishment ⚷ 539

Aggravated robbery by inflicting or attempting to inflict serious bodily harm during a theft and felonious assault by knowingly causing serious physical harm were committed separately and with separate animus, such that the offenses did not merge even if they were allied offenses of similar import; facts indicated that the felonious assault was committed with the purpose to debilitate victim and render her immobile, while the aggravated robbery was completed when victim, after being dragged to her kitchen, was punched several times with a closed fist while defendants demanded to know where money, drugs, and her purse were located. State v. Lee (Ohio App. 3 Dist., 11-22-2010) 190 Ohio App.3d 581, 943 N.E.2d 602, 2010-Ohio-5672, appeal allowed, vac 128 Ohio St.3d 501, 946 N.E.2d 756, 2011-Ohio-1960, on remand 2011-Ohio-5733, 2011 WL 5353506, appeal not allowed 137 Ohio St.3d 1476, 2 N.E.3d 270, 2014-Ohio-176. Double Jeopardy ⚷ 145

Restraint and movement of victim were merely incidental to aggravated robbery, such that there existed no separate animus sufficient to sustain separate convictions for kidnapping and aggravated robbery; defendant dragged victim from her porch over a step into her kitchen and then taped her mouth, defendant and codefendants then began asking victim for the location of money and drugs, and when victim would not respond, she was hit with a closed fist. State v. Lee (Ohio App. 3 Dist., 11-22-2010) 190 Ohio App.3d 581, 943 N.E.2d 602, 2010-Ohio-5672, appeal allowed, vac 128 Ohio St.3d 501, 946 N.E.2d 756, 2011-Ohio-1960, on remand 2011-Ohio-5733, 2011 WL 5353506, appeal not allowed 137 Ohio St.3d 1476, 2 N.E.3d 270, 2014-Ohio-176. Kidnapping ⚷ 22

Under two-step analysis for determining whether offenses should be merged as allied offense of similar import, the court must first compare the elements of the crimes, and if the elements of the offenses correspond to such a degree that the commission of one will result in the commission of the other, the crimes are allied offenses of similar import; the second step then calls for reviewing the defendant's conduct in order to determine whether the defendant can be convicted of both offenses, and if the court finds either that the crimes were committed separately or that there was a separate animus for each crime, the defendant may be convicted of both offenses. State v. Lee (Ohio App. 3 Dist., 11-22-2010) 190 Ohio App.3d 581, 943 N.E.2d 602, 2010-Ohio-5672, appeal allowed, vac 128 Ohio St.3d 501, 946 N.E.2d 756, 2011-Ohio-1960, on remand 2011-Ohio-5733, 2011 WL 5353506, appeal not allowed 137 Ohio St.3d 1476, 2 N.E.3d 270, 2014-Ohio-176. Double Jeopardy ⚷ 145

Greater and lesser child endangering offenses are not allied offense of similar import, and thus, defendant may be convicted of both offenses, where greater offense, which may be committed by anyone, may be committed without committing lesser offense, which may only be committed by certain defined group of people. State v. Garcia (Ohio App. 10 Dist., Franklin, 03-23-2004) No. 03AP-384, 2004-Ohio-1409, 2004 WL 557343, Unreported, appeal not allowed 103 Ohio St.3d 1406, 812 N.E.2d 1288, 2004-Ohio-3980, habeas corpus conditionally granted 2007 WL 1028528, affirmed 599 F.3d 529, rehearing denied. Criminal Law ⚷ 29(1)

Defendant failed to produce clear and convincing evidence that trial court erred in imposing consecutive sentences for two counts of gross sexual imposition, where counts were based on separate and distinct acts, including touching victim's bare breast and then massaging her genitalia through her underwear, and each count had its own independent animus. State v. While (Ohio App. 11 Dist., Trumbull, 08-29-2003) No. 2001-T-0051, 2003-Ohio-4594, 2003 WL 22040803, Unreported, appeal not allowed 106 Ohio St.3d 1510, 833 N.E.2d 1250, 2005-Ohio-4605, habeas corpus dismissed 2007 WL 2840406. Sentencing And Punishment ⚷ 561; Sentencing And Punishment ⚷ 591

Defendant's felonious assault and attempted murder offenses, though committed against the same victim, were the result of separate acts, and thus, defendant was properly sentenced separately for both offenses upon his conviction by jury trial; felonious assault offense was complete when defendant struck victim in her head with a shotgun, whereas attempted murder offense was complete when defendant kidnapped victim by putting her into the trunk of her own vehicle and threatened to kill her with the shotgun. State v. Axson (Ohio App. 8 Dist., Cuyahoga, 05-01-2003) No. 81231, 2003-Ohio-2182, 2003 WL 1994490, Unreported, appeal dismissed 99 Ohio St.3d 1517, 792 N.E.2d 730, 2003-Ohio-4009, appeal allowed 100 Ohio St.3d 1408, 796 N.E.2d 536, 2003-Ohio-4948, motion to dismiss appeal denied 100 Ohio St.3d 1425, 797 N.E.2d 92, 2003-Ohio-5232, reversed 104 Ohio St.3d 248, 819 N.E.2d 271, 2004-Ohio-6396, subsequent determination 2005-Ohio-4396, 2005 WL 2038692, appeal after new sentencing hearing 2005-Ohio-6342, 2005 WL 3219727, appeal allowed, reversed 109 Ohio St.3d 509, 849 N.E.2d 284, 2006-Ohio-2721, reconsideration denied 110 Ohio St.3d 1444, 852 N.E.2d 191, 2006-Ohio-3862, appeal after new sentencing hearing 2007-Ohio-2892, 2007 WL 1695108, appeal after new sentencing hearing 2007-Ohio-3126, 2007 WL 1805041, motion for delayed appeal denied 116 Ohio St.3d 1436, 877 N.E.2d 988, 2007-Ohio-6518, habeas corpus dismissed 2010 WL 750176, appeal after new sentencing hearing 2007-Ohio-5811, 2007 WL 3171233, appeal not allowed 117 Ohio St.3d 1426, 882 N.E.2d 446, 2008-Ohio-969, appeal after new sentencing hearing 2011-Ohio-3187, 2011 WL 2569789. Sentencing And Punishment ⚷ 529

If multiple offenses are committed separately or with a separate animus, the offenses will not merge. State v. Clay (Ohio App. 12 Dist., 10-03-2011) 196

Ohio App.3d 305, 963 N.E.2d 220, 2011-Ohio-5086, appeal after new sentencing hearing 2012-Ohio-5011, 2012 WL 5306150, appeal not allowed 134 Ohio St.3d 1471, 983 N.E.2d 370, 2013-Ohio-553, appeal after new sentencing hearing 2013-Ohio-4984, 2013 WL 6021228. Criminal Law ⚿ 30

Imposition of consecutive sentences for two repeat violent offender specifications, one of which was alleged in connection with charge of attempted murder and the other in connection with charge of aggravated robbery, was not improper; defendant had distinct, separate animus for each charged crime, such that they did not constitute allied offenses of similar import, and, therefore, defendant could be separately sentenced on repeat violent offender specifications pertaining to each charged crime. State v. Dodson (Ohio App. 3 Dist., 12-03-2012) 983 N.E.2d 797, 2012-Ohio-5576. Sentencing and Punishment ⚿ 606

A defendant may, in a single proceeding, be sentenced for two or more offenses, having as their genesis the same criminal conduct or transaction, only if the offenses (1) are not allied offenses of similar import, (2) were committed separately, or (3) were committed with a separate animus as to each offense. State v. Campbell (Ohio App. 1 Dist., 09-19-2012) 978 N.E.2d 970, 2012-Ohio-4231, appeal not allowed 134 Ohio St.3d 1452, 982 N.E.2d 729, 2013-Ohio-347. Sentencing and Punishment ⚿ 509; Sentencing and Punishment ⚿ 513

If offenses were committed separately or with a separate animus, the offenses will not merge. State v. Luong (Ohio App. 12 Dist., 10-01-2012) 977 N.E.2d 1075, 2012-Ohio-4519. Criminal Law ⚿ 30

Trial court on remand for resentencing was bound, under the doctrine of the law of the case, by a prior legal determination of the Court of Appeals in the same case that trial court had properly imposed multiple sentences for aggravated robbery and kidnapping as alleged, even though the Supreme Court in the same case had reversed a determination of the Court of Appeals that felonious assault and attempted murder were not allied offenses of similar import; Supreme Court took no action affecting the determination of the Court of Appeals that aggravated robbery and kidnapping were committed with a separate animus. State v. Love (Ohio App. 1 Dist., 05-11-2011) 194 Ohio App.3d 16, 954 N.E.2d 202, 2011-Ohio-2224, appeal not allowed 129 Ohio St.3d 1490, 954 N.E.2d 663, 2011-Ohio-5129. Criminal Law ⚿ 1192

Restraint and movement of victim were merely incidental to aggravated robbery, such that there existed no separate animus sufficient to sustain separate convictions for kidnapping and aggravated robbery; defendant dragged victim from her porch over a step into her kitchen and then taped her mouth, defendant and codefendants then began asking victim for the location of money and drugs, and when victim would not respond, she was hit with a closed fist. State v. Lee (Ohio App. 3 Dist., 11-22-2010) 190 Ohio App.3d 581, 943 N.E.2d 602, 2010-Ohio-5672, appeal allowed, vac 128 Ohio St.3d 501, 946 N.E.2d 756, 2011-Ohio-1960, on remand 2011-Ohio-5733, 2011 WL 5353506, appeal not allowed 137 Ohio St.3d 1476, 2 N.E.3d 270, 2014-Ohio-176. Kidnapping ⚿ 22

When a kidnapping is committed during another crime, there exists no separate animus, as would allow separate convictions for kidnapping and the other crime, where the restraint or movement of the victim is merely incidental to the underlying crime. State v. Lee (Ohio App. 3 Dist., 11-22-2010) 190 Ohio App.3d 581, 943 N.E.2d 602, 2010-Ohio-5672, appeal allowed, vac 128 Ohio St.3d 501, 946 N.E.2d 756, 2011-Ohio-1960, on remand 2011-Ohio-5733, 2011 WL 5353506, appeal not allowed 137 Ohio St.3d 1476, 2 N.E.3d 270, 2014-Ohio-176. Kidnapping ⚿ 22

Defendant had separate animus to both feloniously assault and attempt to murder his live-in girlfriend, and thus could be convicted of both offenses; defendant began attacking girlfriend with steak knife and stabbed her until blade broke from handle, and defendant then obtained butcher knife from kitchen, chased girlfriend down hallway, and continued to stab her. State v. Roberts (Ohio App. 3 Dist., 01-26-2009) 180 Ohio App.3d 666, 906 N.E.2d 1177, 2009-Ohio-298. Criminal Law ⚿ 29(14)

Aggravated murder and kidnapping are not allied offenses of similar import, for double jeopardy purposes. State v. Coley (Ohio, 10-03-2001) 93 Ohio St.3d 253, 754 N.E.2d 1129, 2001-Ohio-1340, habeas corpus denied 2010 WL 1375217. Double Jeopardy ⚿ 150(2)

Defendant did not commit rape and kidnapping separately or with separate animus, and therefore convictions of those offenses merged, where after victim let defendant into apartment where she was staying, defendant took victim by the hand from bathroom to living room, where he forced her to have sexual intercourse on the couch. State v. Williams (Ohio App. 10 Dist., Franklin, 09-03-2002) No. 02AP-35, 2002-Ohio-4503, 2002 WL 2005815, Unreported, appeal not allowed 98 Ohio St.3d 1412, 781 N.E.2d 1020, 2003-Ohio-60, denial of post-conviction relief affirmed 2006-Ohio-2197, 2006 WL 1174504, appeal not allowed 111 Ohio St.3d 1414, 854 N.E.2d 1092, 2006-Ohio-5083, habeas corpus dismissed 2009 WL 773902. Criminal Law ⚿ 30

Defendant did not commit rape and kidnapping separately or with separate animus, and therefore convictions of those offenses merged, where victim was sleeping on a couch in apartment where she was staying when defendant forced himself on her and held her hands down as he had sexual intercourse with her. State v. Williams (Ohio App. 10 Dist., Franklin, 09-03-2002) No. 02AP-35, 2002-Ohio-4503, 2002 WL 2005815, Unreported, appeal not allowed 98 Ohio St.3d 1412, 781 N.E.2d 1020, 2003-Ohio-60, denial of post-conviction relief affirmed 2006-Ohio-2197, 2006 WL 1174504, appeal not allowed 111 Ohio St.3d 1414, 854 N.E.2d 1092, 2006-Ohio-5083, habeas corpus dismissed 2009 WL 773902. Criminal Law ⚷ 30

Sufficient evidence of a separate animus supported independent convictions and sentences for kidnapping and rape in prosecution that also resulted in felony murder convictions for victim's death at defendant's apartment; testimony of neighbor who heard victim screaming and heard defendant threatening to tie her up, as well as timing of other events culminating in arrival of defendant's half-brother at scene, suggested fairly long period of restraint, and binding of victim's hands and feet not only facilitated rape, but substantially increased risk of asphyxiation separate and apart from rape. State v. Haynes (Ohio App. 10 Dist., Franklin, 08-27-2002) No. 01AP-430, 2002-Ohio-4389, 2002 WL 1969636, Unreported, appeal not allowed 97 Ohio St.3d 1484, 780 N.E.2d 287, 2002-Ohio-6866, appeal not allowed 98 Ohio St.3d 1463, 783 N.E.2d 521, 2003-Ohio-644, denial of post-conviction relief affirmed 2004-Ohio-591, 2004 WL 240011, appeal not allowed 102 Ohio St.3d 1473, 809 N.E.2d 1159, 2004-Ohio-2830, appeal not allowed 109 Ohio St.3d 1482, 847 N.E.2d 1226, 2006-Ohio-2466, dismissal of habeas corpus affirmed 110 Ohio St.3d 243, 852 N.E.2d 1198, 2006-Ohio-4355, denial of post-conviction relief affirmed 2007-Ohio-6540, 2007 WL 4285139, appeal not allowed 117 Ohio St.3d 1460, 884 N.E.2d 68, 2008-Ohio-1635, denial of habeas corpus affirmed 267 Fed.Appx. 422, 2008 WL 538497, certiorari denied 129 S.Ct. 122, 555 U.S. 855, 172 L.Ed.2d 94. Kidnapping ⚷ 36; Rape ⚷ 51(4)

7. Common elements, in general

Trial court may, in a single proceeding, sentence a defendant for two or more offenses having as their genesis the same criminal conduct or transaction, if the offenses: (1) are not allied offenses of similar import; (2) were committed separately; or (3) were committed with a separate animus as to each offense. State v. Whipple (Ohio App. 1 Dist., 06-29-2012) 972 N.E.2d 1141, 2012-Ohio-2938, appeal not allowed 133 Ohio St.3d 1467, 977 N.E.2d 694, 2012-Ohio-5149. Sentencing and Punishment ⚷ 509

If multiple offenses can be committed by the same conduct, then the court must determine whether the offenses were committed by the same conduct, i.e., a single act committed with a single state of mind. State v. Thomas (Ohio App. 8 Dist., 11-23-2011) 197 Ohio App.3d 176, 966 N.E.2d 939, 2011-Ohio-6073, appeal not allowed 132 Ohio St.3d 1425, 969 N.E.2d 272, 2012-Ohio-2729, appeal after new sentencing hearing 2013-Ohio-1804, 2013 WL 1858890, appeal after new sentencing hearing 2014-Ohio-2410, 2014 WL 2566106, appeal not allowed 141 Ohio St.3d 1422, 21 N.E.3d 1115, 2014-Ohio-5567. Criminal Law ⚷ 29(1)

Felonious assault causing serious bodily harm and felony murder with the underlying felony of felonious assault were allied offenses of similar import, such that defendant could not be convicted of both offenses; felony murder required the causing of the death of another as a proximate result of committing or attempting to commit an offense of violence, felonious assault was an act of violence, the commission of felony murder necessarily resulted from the commission of an offense of violence, which in defendant's case was felonious assault, and victim's death was a proximate result of the felonious assault. State v. Barker (Ohio App. 2 Dist., 11-24-2010) 191 Ohio App.3d 293, 945 N.E.2d 1107, 2010-Ohio-5744. Criminal Law ⚷ 29(14)

8. Complicity

Trial court's imposition on defendants of sentence on charges of complicity in operating a mobile tire shredding facility without a license, to which defendants did not object in the trial court, was not plain error, even though defendants were also convicted and sentenced on the principal offense of operating facility without a license; offenses were committed with separate animus, in that the charge for operating facility alleged that tires were shredded on two particular dates, and the charge for complicity alleged solicitation or aiding and abetting the offense during a four-month period. State v. Elyria Acquisition Co. No. 1, Inc. (Ohio App. 3 Dist., Crawford, 03-27-2006) No. 3-04-36, No. 3-04-37, No. 3-04-38, 2006-Ohio-1415, 2006 WL 758548, Unreported. Criminal Law ⚷ 1042.3(1)

For purposes of sentencing, defendant failed to demonstrate that his convictions for complicity to commit aggravated murder and complicity to commit felonious assault constituted allied offenses of similar import; record revealed that defendant conspired to unlawfully terminate alleged victim's pregnancy, and thus the intent to harm separately extended to defendant's complicity in the contemporaneous assault on alleged victim's physical person. State v. Tarver (Ohio App. 5 Dist., Stark, 12-15-2003) No. 2002CA00394, 2003-Ohio-6840, 2003 WL 22958400, Unreported, appeal after new sentencing hearing 2004-Ohio-5508, 2004 WL 2315192, appeal not allowed 105 Ohio St.3d 1452, 823 N.E.2d 457, 2005-Ohio-763, denial of post-conviction relief affirmed 2005-Ohio-3119, 2005 WL 1463240, appeal not allowed 107 Ohio St.3d 1409, 836 N.E.2d 1229, 2005-Ohio-5859, habeas corpus denied 2007 WL 927951. Double Jeopardy ⚷ 150(1)

To determine whether offenses are "allied offenses of similar import" that must merge, courts must compare the elements of offenses in the abstract, i.e., without considering the evidence in the case; the elements need not, however, be identical for the offenses to constitute allied offenses of similar import. State v. Creech (Ohio App. 4 Dist., 06-01-2010) 188 Ohio App.3d 513, 936 N.E.2d 79, 2010-Ohio-2553, appeal not allowed 126 Ohio St.3d 1600, 935 N.E.2d 46, 2010-Ohio-4928. Criminal Law ⚷ 30

Offenses constitute "allied offenses of similar import" that must merge if, in comparing the elements of the offenses in the abstract, the offenses are so similar that the commission of one offense will necessarily result in commission of the other. State v. Creech (Ohio App. 4 Dist., 06-01-2010) 188 Ohio App.3d 513, 936 N.E.2d 79, 2010-Ohio-2553, appeal not allowed 126 Ohio St.3d 1600, 935 N.E.2d 46, 2010-Ohio-4928. Criminal Law ⚷ 30

9.5. Merger of offenses

Trial court was required to determine whether defendant committed robbery and grand theft separately or with separate animus, for purposes of determining whether offenses were allied offenses of similar import, and therefore, whether offenses merged. State v. Reives-Bey (Ohio App. 9 Dist., Summit, 04-13-2011) No. 25138, 2011-Ohio-1778, 2011 WL 1378939, Unreported, appeal not allowed 129 Ohio St.3d 1454, 951 N.E.2d 1049, 2011-Ohio-4217. Criminal Law ⚷ 30

Felonious assault, child endangering, and domestic violence were allied offenses of similar import under multiple-count statute, and thus were subject to merger; state relied upon same conduct to prove offenses, and convictions for all offenses were generally based on series of events which resulted in injuries of victims. State v. Craycraft (Ohio App. 12 Dist., 01-31-2011) 193 Ohio App.3d 594, 953 N.E.2d 337, 2011-Ohio-413, appeal after new sentencing hearing 2012-Ohio-884, 2012 WL 699577, appeal not allowed 132 Ohio St.3d 1463, 969 N.E.2d 1231, 2012-Ohio-3054. Criminal Law ⚷ 29(5.5); Criminal Law ⚷ 29(12)

Crimes of domestic violence and second-degree child endangering, as related to defendant's conduct, were allied offenses and thus subject to merger, where defendant's conviction for both offenses arose out of single act of shaking his wife's child. State v. Blanda (Ohio App. 12 Dist., Butler, 01-31-2011) No. CA2010-03-050, 2011-Ohio-411, 2011 WL 332725, Unreported, stay denied 132 Ohio St.3d 1422, 969 N.E.2d 270, 2012-Ohio-2729, appeal not allowed 132 Ohio St.3d 1514, 974 N.E.2d 112, 2012-Ohio-4021, on subsequent appeal 2014-Ohio-2234, 2014 WL 2211386. Criminal Law ⚷ 30

Defendant's offenses of failure to provide adequate support to person's child under age of 18 and failure to provide support as established by court order, with regard to his failure to support his minor children, were of allied offenses of similar import, such that merger of offenses was required; offenses were committed by same conduct. State v. Smith (Ohio App. 6 Dist., Ottawa, 01-14-2011) No. OT-10-001, 2011-Ohio-138, 2011 WL 281139, Unreported. Criminal Law ⚷ 30

Error in imposing concurrent sentences for convictions of allied offenses of similar import of failure to provide adequate support to person's child under age of 18 and failure to provide support as established by court order, with regard to his failure to support his minor children, was not harmless error. State v. Smith (Ohio App. 6 Dist., Ottawa, 01-14-2011) No. OT-10-001, 2011-Ohio-138, 2011 WL 281139, Unreported. Criminal Law ⚷ 1165(1)

Defendant's movement and restraint of victim was merely incidental to the attempted rape, and thus, kidnapping and attempted rape offenses were allied offenses of similar import that were subject to merger for sentencing purposes; the force by which defendant moved victim from the alley to under the porch to attempt to engage in sexual conduct was indistinguishable from the force by which defendant restrained victim of her liberty, and there was no act of asportation distinct from the attempted rape either in time or in function. State v. Johnson (Ohio App. 3 Dist., 10-27-2014) 22 N.E.3d 249, 2014-Ohio-4750. Criminal Law ⚷ 30

Three counts of having weapons while under disability were subject to merger as arising from defendant's simultaneous, undifferentiated possession of all three weapons that were stored together in the closet in defendant's master bedroom. State v. Mitchell (Ohio App. 2 Dist., 11-14-2014) 21 N.E.3d 1124, 2014-Ohio-5070. Criminal Law ⚷ 30

Felonious assault and abduction, as offenses to which defendant pled guilty, were not allied offenses of similar import subject to merger, even though it was possible to commit felonious assault in process of abduction, since offenses were committed at different times and with separate animus; defendant beat and choked victim into unconsciousness and physically prevented victim from leaving house when she regained consciousness. State v. McCormick (Ohio App. 6 Dist., 06-06-2014) 13 N.E.3d 740, 2014-Ohio-2433. Criminal Law ⚷ 30

In determining whether an offender's conduct involved separate acts or a separate animus, and thus, whether the offenses charged from those acts were allied offenses of similar import, for purposes of merger, the court must consider whether the acts were separated by time or conduct. State v. Mooty (Ohio App. 2 Dist., 02-28-2014) 9 N.E.3d 443, 2014-Ohio-733. Criminal Law ⚷ 30

Endangering children based on defendant's animus in violating her duty of care, protection, and support of child victim, which resulted in serious physical harm to victim at hands of boyfriend, was separated in time from and was completed prior to offenses of complicity to commit felonious assault and permitting child abuse, and thus, offenses were not allied offenses of similar import, as required for offenses to merge; child endangering began in July when family members expressed concerns about child's injuries to defendant, defendant was instructed by Children Services not to allow boyfriend access to child yet she continued to leave child in boyfriend's care unsupervised, and latter two offenses were based on conduct that occurred in December in days just prior to child's death. State v. Mooty (Ohio App. 2 Dist., 02-28-2014) 9 N.E.3d 443, 2014-Ohio-733. Criminal Law ⚷ 30

Defendant's violation of Ohio's Racketeer Influenced and Corrupt Organizations Act (RICO) did not merge with his predicate offenses for purposes of sentencing, and thus, defendant could be sentenced for both his RICO offense and for trafficking in marijuana. State v. Miranda (Ohio,

02-12-2014) 138 Ohio St.3d 184, 5 N.E.3d 603, 2014-Ohio-451. Sentencing and Punishment ⚷ 501

For purposes of sentence merger analysis, if two offenses of conviction are of similar import, a court must review the entire record, including arguments and information presented at the sentencing hearing, to determine whether the offenses were committed separately or with a separate animus; if the offenses were committed by the same conduct and with a single animus, the offenses merge. State v. Jackson (Ohio App. 9 Dist., 12-18-2013) 5 N.E.3d 116, 2013-Ohio-5557, appeal not allowed 139 Ohio St.3d 1404, 9 N.E.3d 1062, 2014-Ohio-2245. Sentencing and Punishment ⚷ 501

When determining whether offenses are allied offenses of similar import subject to merger at sentencing, the court considers whether the two offenses can be committed by the same conduct and, if so, whether the two offenses were committed by the same conduct as a single act with a single state of mind. State v. Shaw (Ohio App. 7 Dist., 10-31-2013) 4 N.E.3d 406, 2013-Ohio-5292, appeal not allowed 138 Ohio St.3d 1436, 4 N.E.3d 1052, 2014-Ohio-889, dismissal of post-conviction relief affirmed 2014-Ohio-5633, 2014 WL 7275311. Sentencing and Punishment ⚷ 501; Sentencing and Punishment ⚷ 509

When the issue of allied offenses is before the court, the question is not whether a particular sentence is justified, but whether the defendant may be sentenced upon all the offenses. State v. Shaw (Ohio App. 7 Dist., 10-31-2013) 4 N.E.3d 406, 2013-Ohio-5292, appeal not allowed 138 Ohio St.3d 1436, 4 N.E.3d 1052, 2014-Ohio-889, dismissal of post-conviction relief affirmed 2014-Ohio-5633, 2014 WL 7275311. Sentencing and Punishment ⚷ 509

Merger statute prohibiting multiple sentences for allied offense of similar import codifies the state and federal constitutional prohibition against double jeopardy. State v. Shaw (Ohio App. 7 Dist., 10-31-2013) 4 N.E.3d 406, 2013-Ohio-5292, appeal not allowed 138 Ohio St.3d 1436, 4 N.E.3d 1052, 2014-Ohio-889, dismissal of post-conviction relief affirmed 2014-Ohio-5633, 2014 WL 7275311. Sentencing and Punishment ⚷ 501

Fourth-degree felony theft by deception and 25 counts of third-degree felony tampering with government records were not allied offenses of similar import and, therefore, did not merge; defendant's conduct of receiving and cashing checks from a county for services that were not provided, on which the theft charge was based, and defendant's conduct of signing contracts and invoices, on which the tampering charges were based, were significantly separated in time. State v. Trammell (Ohio App. 2 Dist., 10-18-2013) 3 N.E.3d 260, 2013-Ohio-4615, appeal not allowed 138 Ohio St.3d 1435, 4 N.E.3d 1052, 2014-Ohio-889. Criminal Law ⚷ 30

Defendant was not convicted of allied offenses of similar import and trial court properly sentenced him on each count of intimidation; defendant was charged with 23 separate counts of intimidation, defendant, for each count, drafted and printed separate documents purporting to state legal demand for money, separately addressed each set of documents to each of 23 victims, and paid separate postage, and although defendant may have been motivated by same animus in each instance, each offense involved distinct actions, targeted different victims, and violated the same statute. State v. Kinstle (Ohio App. 3 Dist., 12-17-2012) 985 N.E.2d 184, 2012-Ohio-5952, appeal from denial of post-conviction relief dismissed 2013-Ohio-850, 2013 WL 937747, motion for delayed appeal denied 984 N.E.2d 1101, 2013-Ohio-1123. Sentencing and Punishment ⚷ 536

Offense of discharge of firearm on or near prohibited premises and the offense of felonious assaults were allied offenses of similar import and, thus, should have merged; it was possible to commit felonious assault by means of deadly weapon and discharge of a firearm on or near prohibited premises, the offenses were committed by the same conduct, the fight and shooting were one continuous act and the assaults and discharge of the firearm on or near prohibited premises were committed by the same conduct. State v. Melton (Ohio App. 8 Dist., Cuyahoga, 11-21-2012) No. 97675, 2012-Ohio-5413, 2012 WL 5875609, Unreported, opinion vacated and superseded on reconsideration 984 N.E.2d 1112, 2013-Ohio-257. Criminal Law ⚷ 30

Courts must determine whether it is possible to commit one offense and commit the other with the same conduct, and if multiple offenses can be committed by the same conduct, then the court must determine whether the offenses were committed by the same conduct, i .e., a single act, committed with a single state of mind, and if the answer to both questions is yes, then the offenses are allied offenses of similar import and will be merged. State v. Melton (Ohio App. 8 Dist., Cuyahoga, 11-21-2012) No. 97675, 2012-Ohio-5413, 2012 WL 5875609, Unreported, opinion vacated and superseded on reconsideration 984 N.E.2d 1112, 2013-Ohio-257. Criminal Law ⚷ 30

Aggravated robbery and tampering with evidence involved separate conduct and different property and, thus, were not allied offenses and defendant could be separately sentenced on each conviction; defendant tampered with evidence when he removed a cup and the long gun from the victim's home and concealed them in bushes, and committed other conduct supporting aggravated robbery conviction when he stole victims' wallet and jewelry. State v. Wesson (Ohio, 10-23-2013) 137 Ohio St.3d 309, 999 N.E.2d 557, 2013-Ohio-4575, motion to stay mandate denied, reconsideration denied 137 Ohio St.3d 1444, 999 N.E.2d 698, 2013-Ohio-5678, certiorari denied 134 S.Ct. 2311, 189 L.Ed.2d 191. Sentencing and Punishment ⚷ 537

Courts must determine whether it is possible to commit one offense and commit the other with the same conduct, and if multiple offenses can be committed by the same conduct, then the court must determine whether the offenses were committed by the same conduct, i.e., a single act, committed with a single state of mind, and if the answer to both questions is yes, then the offenses are allied offenses of similar import and will be merged. State v. Melton (Ohio App. 8 Dist., 01-31-2013) 984 N.E.2d 1112, 2013-Ohio-257. Criminal Law ⚿ 30

To ensure compliance with both Double Jeopardy Clause and merger statute prohibiting punishment for allied offenses of similar import, a trial court is required to merge allied offenses of similar import at sentencing; thus, when the issue of allied offenses is before the court, the question is not whether a particular sentence is justified, but whether the defendant may be sentenced upon all the offenses. State v. Williams (Ohio, 12-06-2012) 134 Ohio St.3d 482, 983 N.E.2d 1245, 2012-Ohio-5699. Double Jeopardy ⚿ 134; Sentencing and Punishment ⚿ 501

"Merger" is the penal philosophy that a major crime often includes as inherent therein the component elements of other crimes and that these component elements, in legal effect, are merged in the major crime. State v. Williams (Ohio, 12-06-2012) 134 Ohio St.3d 482, 983 N.E.2d 1245, 2012-Ohio-5699. Criminal Law ⚿ 30

Attempted murder and aggravated robbery were each committed with a separate animus, and, therefore, were not allied offenses of similar import that should have merged at sentencing; the 27 stab wounds inflicted on victim while she was on her knees or low to the ground demonstrated a purpose to cause death that was separate and apart from defendant's immediate motive of robbing restaurant where victim was employed. State v. Dodson (Ohio App. 3 Dist., 12-03-2012) 983 N.E.2d 797, 2012-Ohio-5576. Sentencing and Punishment ⚿ 537

Appellate court was required to determine whether attempted murder and aggravated robbery were allied offenses of similar import that should have merged at sentencing, though defendant did not raise merger issue at sentencing, as imposition of multiple sentences for allied offenses of similar import would constitute plain error. State v. Dodson (Ohio App. 3 Dist., 12-03-2012) 983 N.E.2d 797, 2012-Ohio-5576. Criminal Law ⚿ 1042.3(1)

In determining whether offenses are allied offenses of similar import subject to merger, the question is whether it is possible to commit one offense and commit the other with the same conduct, not whether it is possible to commit one without committing the other; if the offenses correspond to such a degree that the conduct of the defendant constituting commission of one offense constitutes commission of the other, then the offenses are of similar import. State v. Carson (Ohio App. 10 Dist., 09-28-2012) 978 N.E.2d 621, 2012-Ohio-4501. Criminal Law ⚿ 30

Allied offenses statute protects against multiple punishments for the same criminal conduct and is a codification of the common law doctrine of merger. State v. Carson (Ohio App. 10 Dist., 09-28-2012) 978 N.E.2d 621, 2012-Ohio-4501. Criminal Law ⚿ 30

Cases involving a failure to merge allied offenses of similar import, which constitutes plain error even where a defendant's sentences are run concurrently because a defendant is prejudiced by having more convictions than are authorized by law, are remanded for a limited resentencing hearing so that the prosecution can select which of the merged offenses for which it wishes the court to enter a conviction and sentence the defendant. State v. Tapscott (Ohio App. 7 Dist., 09-14-2012) 978 N.E.2d 210, 2012-Ohio-4213, appeal not allowed 134 Ohio St.3d 1451, 982 N.E.2d 729, 2013-Ohio-347. Criminal Law ⚿ 1181.5(8)

Failure to merge allied offenses of similar import constitutes plain error even where a defendant's sentences are run concurrently because a defendant is prejudiced by having more convictions than are authorized by law. State v. Tapscott (Ohio App. 7 Dist., 09-14-2012) 978 N.E.2d 210, 2012-Ohio-4213, appeal not allowed 134 Ohio St.3d 1451, 982 N.E.2d 729, 2013-Ohio-347. Criminal Law ⚿ 1030(3)

Sentencing concurrently on merged counts does not satisfy the merger doctrine, as no sentence at all should be entered on one of the two merged counts. State v. Tapscott (Ohio App. 7 Dist., 09-14-2012) 978 N.E.2d 210, 2012-Ohio-4213, appeal not allowed 134 Ohio St.3d 1451, 982 N.E.2d 729, 2013-Ohio-347. Sentencing and Punishment ⚿ 500

When a court merges offenses, it cannot run the sentences for the merged offenses concurrently; rather, the court must refrain from entering a sentence on one of the merged offenses. State v. Tapscott (Ohio App. 7 Dist., 09-14-2012) 978 N.E.2d 210, 2012-Ohio-4213, appeal not allowed 134 Ohio St.3d 1451, 982 N.E.2d 729, 2013-Ohio-347. Sentencing and Punishment ⚿ 500

Defendant's convictions for aggravated robbery and kidnapping were allied offenses of similar import that were not committed with a separate animus for each offense, and thus convictions were subject to merger under the multiple-count statute; state relied on the same conduct to demonstrate both offenses, based upon defendant's actions in jumping over bank counter and taking bank's money, while co-defendant brandished a handgun to move victims to a common area in the bank, and co-defendant's conduct in moving and restraining victim with a handgun so that all defendants could take bank's money satisfied the elements of both the aggravated robbery and the kidnapping offenses. State v. Anderson (Ohio App. 1 Dist., 07-27-2012) 974 N.E.2d 1236, 2012-Ohio-3347, appeal not allowed 133 Ohio St.3d 1492, 978 N.E.2d 911, 2012-Ohio-5459. Criminal Law ⚿ 30

Unless committed separately or with a separate animus, allied offenses must be merged for purposes of sentencing following the state's election of which offense should survive. State v. Anderson (Ohio App. 1 Dist., 07-27-2012) 974 N.E.2d 1236, 2012-Ohio-3347, appeal not allowed 133 Ohio St.3d 1492, 978 N.E.2d 911, 2012-Ohio-5459. Sentencing and Punishment ⚿ 501

Absence of any facts in record demonstrating that child pornography counts to which defendant pled guilty should merge as allied offenses ruled out any finding of plain error on appeal; defendant did not have any discussion or reach agreement with state on whether counts were allied, and failed to raise issue of allied offenses at sentencing, and although defendant stated in sentencing memorandum that he had "images" depicting minors in state of nudity, which along with multiple counts indicated that more than one picture was involved, images were not in record on appeal and there was nothing in record that would indicate that offenses were allied.(Per Stewart, P.J., with one judge concurring in the result.) R.C. State v. Barrett (Ohio App. 8 Dist., 08-30-2012) 974 N.E.2d 185, 2012-Ohio-3948. Criminal Law ⚿ 1030(3)

Offenses are "allied" and must be merged for sentencing if the defendant's conduct is such that a single act could lead to the commission of separately defined offenses, but those separate offenses were committed with a state of mind to commit only one act. State v. Barrett (Ohio App. 8 Dist., 08-30-2012) 974 N.E.2d 185, 2012-Ohio-3948. Sentencing and Punishment ⚿ 501

Line of distinction that enables a trier of fact considering a claim of merger for sentencing purposes to reasonably conclude separate and distinct crimes were committed can be drawn either horizontally or vertically: court makes a horizontal line of distinction when it considers the amount of time between the commissions of the offenses; a vertical line of distinction is made when considering the severity of the conduct, that is, the conduct so exceeds the degree required to commit the one offense that a separate animus is demonstrated as to a second offense. State v. Whipple (Ohio App. 1 Dist., 06-29-2012) 972 N.E.2d 1141, 2012-Ohio-2938, appeal not allowed 133 Ohio St.3d 1467, 977 N.E.2d 694, 2012-Ohio-5149. Criminal Law ⚿ 30

Court considering a claim of merger for sentencing purposes should consider whether facts appear in the record that distinguish the circumstances or draw a line of distinction that enables a trier of fact to reasonably conclude separate and distinct crimes were committed. State v. Whipple (Ohio App. 1 Dist., 06-29-2012) 972 N.E.2d 1141, 2012-Ohio-2938, appeal not allowed 133 Ohio St.3d 1467, 977 N.E.2d 694, 2012-Ohio-5149. Criminal Law ⚿ 30

Charges of improperly discharging a firearm and three counts of felonious assault did not merge for sentencing purposes, where defendant committed each crime at issue with a separate animus; police recovered 28 shell casings from crime scene, in street spread across length of property, on sidewalk, in driveway, in yard, on porch, and three actually inside home, most of the windows of victims' van were shot out, and one victim testified that she had heard footsteps on porch during shooting, and that afterward house had been filled with smoke and dust. State v. Whipple (Ohio App. 1 Dist., 06-29-2012) 972 N.E.2d 1141, 2012-Ohio-2938, appeal not allowed 133 Ohio St.3d 1467, 977 N.E.2d 694, 2012-Ohio-5149. Criminal Law ⚿ 30

There is no presumption that offenses merge for sentencing purposes, as each case must be individually considered, given that the statute instructs courts to examine a defendant's conduct, an inherently subjective determination. State v. Whipple (Ohio App. 1 Dist., 06-29-2012) 972 N.E.2d 1141, 2012-Ohio-2938, appeal not allowed 133 Ohio St.3d 1467, 977 N.E.2d 694, 2012-Ohio-5149. Criminal Law ⚿ 30

Criminal defendant has the burden of establishing his entitlement to merger of offenses pursuant to the allied-offense statute. State v. Whipple (Ohio App. 1 Dist., 06-29-2012) 972 N.E.2d 1141, 2012-Ohio-2938, appeal not allowed 133 Ohio St.3d 1467, 977 N.E.2d 694, 2012-Ohio-5149. Criminal Law ⚿ 30

Felony murder offense based upon felonious assault by causing serious physical harm, and the predicate offense of felonious assault by causing serious physical harm, which were not committed separately or with a separate animus as to each, were allied offenses of similar import and, thus, were required to be merged for purposes of sentence. State v. Cook (Ohio App. 2 Dist., 12-17-2010) 970 N.E.2d 1020, 2010-Ohio-6222. Sentencing and Punishment ⚿ 529

Where multiple allied counts exist, the trial court's duty to merge these counts for sentencing is mandatory, not discretionary. State v. Swiergosz (Ohio App. 6 Dist., 03-02-2012) 197 Ohio App.3d 40, 965 N.E.2d 1070, 2012-Ohio-830, appeal not allowed 133 Ohio St.3d 1493, 978 N.E.2d 911, 2012-Ohio-5459, appeal after new sentencing hearing 2013-Ohio-4625, 2013 WL 5728349, appeal not allowed 138 Ohio St.3d 1435, 4 N.E.3d 1051, 2014-Ohio-889. Sentencing and Punishment ⚿ 501

Imposing concurrent sentences for multiple offenses does not cure the failure to determine whether offenses are allied offenses of similar import such that they merge for sentencing, as the concept operates to preclude multiple sentences for conduct giving rise to allied offenses. State v. Swiergosz (Ohio App. 6 Dist., 03-02-2012) 197 Ohio App.3d 40, 965 N.E.2d 1070, 2012-Ohio-830, appeal not allowed 133 Ohio St.3d 1493, 978 N.E.2d 911, 2012-Ohio-5459, appeal after new sentencing hearing 2013-Ohio-4625, 2013 WL 5728349, appeal not allowed 138 Ohio St.3d 1435, 4 N.E.3d 1051, 2014-Ohio-889. Criminal Law ⚿ 1177.3(1)

Defendant was prejudiced by sentencing court's failure to conduct required determination prior to sentencing as to whether his multiple convictions for kidnapping, rape, and other offenses were allied offenses of similar import such that they merged for sentencing purposes, even though defendant received mostly concurrent sentences, and thus remand was required for sentencing court to conduct a merger analysis and to resentence defendant; imposition of concurrent sentences did not cure the failure to determine merger, as the concept operated to preclude multiple sentences for conduct giving rise to allied offenses. State v. Swiergosz (Ohio App. 6 Dist., 03-02-2012) 197 Ohio App.3d 40, 965 N.E.2d 1070, 2012-Ohio-830, appeal not allowed 133 Ohio St.3d 1493, 978 N.E.2d 911, 2012-Ohio-5459, appeal after new sentencing hearing 2013-Ohio-4625, 2013 WL 5728349, appeal not allowed 138 Ohio St.3d 1435, 4 N.E.3d 1051, 2014-Ohio-889. Criminal Law ⚷ 1177.3(1); Criminal Law ⚷ 1181.5(8)

For purposes of determining whether offenses are allied offenses of similar import such that they merge for sentencing, if the sentencing court determines that the commission of one offense will never result in the commission of the other, or if the offenses are committed separately, or if the defendant has separate animus for each offense, then the offenses will not merge. State v. Swiergosz (Ohio App. 6 Dist., 03-02-2012) 197 Ohio App.3d 40, 965 N.E.2d 1070, 2012-Ohio-830, appeal not allowed 133 Ohio St.3d 1493, 978 N.E.2d 911, 2012-Ohio-5459, appeal after new sentencing hearing 2013-Ohio-4625, 2013 WL 5728349, appeal not allowed 138 Ohio St.3d 1435, 4 N.E.3d 1051, 2014-Ohio-889. Sentencing and Punishment ⚷ 501; Sentencing and Punishment ⚷ 509

For purposes of determining whether offenses are allied offenses of similar import that merge for sentencing, if the multiple offenses can be committed by the same conduct, then the court must determine whether the offenses were committed by the same conduct, i.e., a single act, committed with a single state of mind; this question is a fact-based inquiry into what the defendant intended to do, i.e., animus or immediate motive, and did do, in committing the offenses. State v. Swiergosz (Ohio App. 6 Dist., 03-02-2012) 197 Ohio App.3d 40, 965 N.E.2d 1070, 2012-Ohio-830, appeal not allowed 133 Ohio St.3d 1493, 978 N.E.2d 911, 2012-Ohio-5459, appeal after new sentencing hearing 2013-Ohio-4625, 2013 WL 5728349, appeal not allowed 138 Ohio St.3d 1435, 4 N.E.3d 1051, 2014-Ohio-889. Sentencing and Punishment ⚷ 501; Sentencing and Punishment ⚷ 509

Trial court's determination as to whether offenses are allied offenses of similar import that merge for sentencing must be made prior to sentencing. State v. Swiergosz (Ohio App. 6 Dist., 03-02-2012) 197 Ohio App.3d 40, 965 N.E.2d 1070, 2012-Ohio-830, appeal not allowed 133 Ohio St.3d 1493, 978 N.E.2d 911, 2012-Ohio-5459, appeal after new sentencing hearing 2013-Ohio-4625, 2013 WL 5728349, appeal not allowed 138 Ohio St.3d 1435, 4 N.E.3d 1051, 2014-Ohio-889. Sentencing and Punishment ⚷ 501

The trial court, in determining whether offenses are allied offenses of similar import that merge for sentencing, has a statutory duty in the first instance to determine whether offenses are allied, and if they are, to convict the defendant of only one offense. State v. Swiergosz (Ohio App. 6 Dist., 03-02-2012) 197 Ohio App.3d 40, 965 N.E.2d 1070, 2012-Ohio-830, appeal not allowed 133 Ohio St.3d 1493, 978 N.E.2d 911, 2012-Ohio-5459, appeal after new sentencing hearing 2013-Ohio-4625, 2013 WL 5728349, appeal not allowed 138 Ohio St.3d 1435, 4 N.E.3d 1051, 2014-Ohio-889. Criminal Law ⚷ 29(1); Sentencing and Punishment ⚷ 501

Court of Appeals was authorized to vacate felony sentences that were affected by an allied-offenses sentencing error and remand the matter for a new sentencing hearing. State v. Wilson (Ohio, 06-08-2011) 129 Ohio St.3d 214, 951 N.E.2d 381, 2011-Ohio-2669, appeal after new sentencing hearing 2012-Ohio-4159, 2012 WL 4018909, appeal after new sentencing hearing 2013-Ohio-4035, 2013 WL 5310444, appeal after new sentencing hearing 2014-Ohio-4686, 2014 WL 5409112. Criminal Law ⚷ 1177.3(1); Criminal Law ⚷ 1181.5(8)

If multiple offenses can be committed by the same conduct, then the court must determine whether the offenses were committed by the same conduct, i.e., a single act, committed with a single state of mind; if so, then the offenses are allied offenses of similar import and will be merged. State v. Sidibeh (Ohio App. 10 Dist., 02-17-2011) 192 Ohio App.3d 256, 948 N.E.2d 995, 2011-Ohio-712, appeal not allowed 128 Ohio St.3d 1558, 949 N.E.2d 44, 2011-Ohio-2905, habeas corpus dismissed 2013 WL 80362, denial of post-conviction relief affirmed 2013-Ohio-2309, 2013 WL 2444627, appeal not allowed 137 Ohio St.3d 1411, 998 N.E.2d 510, 2013-Ohio-5096. Criminal Law ⚷ 30

Defendant's restraint of two victims during home invasion was incidental to, and stemmed from the same conduct as, aggravated robbery, and thus the kidnapping offense pertaining to each victim would merge with the aggravated robbery offense pertaining to that victim; restraint lasted no longer than the time it took for the commission of the aggravated robbery, and defendant's movement of the victims to a common area of the home was not so substantial as to demonstrate significance independent of the aggravated robbery. State v. Sidibeh (Ohio App. 10 Dist., 02-17-2011) 192 Ohio App.3d 256, 948 N.E.2d 995, 2011-Ohio-712, appeal not allowed 128 Ohio St.3d 1558, 949 N.E.2d 44, 2011-Ohio-2905, habeas corpus dismissed 2013 WL 80362, denial of post-conviction relief affirmed 2013-Ohio-2309, 2013 WL 2444627, appeal not allowed 137 Ohio St.3d 1411, 998 N.E.2d 510, 2013-Ohio-5096. Criminal Law ⚷ 30; Kidnapping ⚷ 22

When in substance and effect but one offense has been committed, the defendant may be convicted of only one offense, pursuant to merger statute. State v. Johnson (Ohio, 12-29-2010) 128 Ohio St.3d 153, 942 N.E.2d 1061, 2010-Ohio-6314. Criminal Law ⚷ 30

In determining whether two offenses are allied offenses of similar import required to be merged, court first compares the elements of offenses in the abstract without considering the evidence in the case; offenses are allied if they are so similar that the commission of one offense will necessarily result in commission of the other, and if the offenses satisfy this first step, the court must then consider whether the offenses were committed separately or with a separate animus. State v. Marriott (Ohio App. 2 Dist., 07-02-2010) 189 Ohio App.3d 98, 937 N.E.2d 614, 2010-Ohio-3115, appeal not allowed 127 Ohio St.3d 1461, 938 N.E.2d 363, 2010-Ohio-6008. Criminal Law ⚷ 29(11)

Illegal assembly or possession of chemicals for the manufacture of drugs and illegal manufacture of drugs were not allied offenses of similar import that were required to be merged; elements of the offenses were not so similar that the commission of one crime necessarily resulted in the commission of the other, as a defendant could have knowingly assembled or possessed chemicals without knowingly manufacturing them, and a defendant could have manufactured drugs without assembling or possessing a chemical used to make the substance. State v. Creech (Ohio App. 4 Dist., 06-01-2010) 188 Ohio App.3d 513, 936 N.E.2d 79, 2010-Ohio-2553, appeal not allowed 126 Ohio St.3d 1600, 935 N.E.2d 46, 2010-Ohio-4928. Criminal Law ⚷ 30

Having a weapon while under disability and unlawful possession of dangerous ordnance were not allied offenses of similar import that had to be merged; one who committed the crime of unlawful possession of dangerous ordnance did not also necessarily commit the crime of having a weapon while under a disability, as a person could acquire, have, carry, or use any dangerous ordnance without also acquiring, having, carrying, or using any firearm or dangerous ordnance while under a disability, and two statutes protected different societal interests as one applied only to persons legislature deemed deserved punishment for possessing a weapon, while the other applied to the public at large. State v. Creech (Ohio App. 4 Dist., 06-01-2010) 188 Ohio App.3d 513, 936 N.E.2d 79, 2010-Ohio-2553, appeal not allowed 126 Ohio St.3d 1600, 935 N.E.2d 46, 2010-Ohio-4928. Criminal Law ⚷ 30

10. Specific offenses construed—animals and hunting

Ten counts of cruelty against a companion animal were not allied offenses, and thus, were not subject to merger; defendant's omittance and neglect resulted in 10 different injuries to 10 different cats, and even if defendant committed offenses through same conduct, a separate animus existed for each animal defendant harmed by his conduct. State v. Helmbright (Ohio App. 10 Dist., 03-26-2013) 990 N.E.2d 154, 2013-Ohio-1143. Criminal Law ⚷ 30

11. —— Murder; homicide, specific offenses construed

Crimes of felony murder and second-degree child endangering, as related to defendant's conduct, were allied offenses and thus subject to merger, in prosecution arising out of child's death, where defendant's shaking of child served as the basis for the offense of child endangering, which in turn served as the predicate offense for defendant's felony murder conviction. State v. Blanda (Ohio App. 12 Dist., Butler, 01-31-2011) No. CA2010-03-050, 2011-Ohio-411, 2011 WL 332725, Unreported, stay denied 132 Ohio St.3d 1422, 969 N.E.2d 270, 2012-Ohio-2729, appeal not allowed 132 Ohio St.3d 1514, 974 N.E.2d 112, 2012-Ohio-4021, on subsequent appeal 2014-Ohio-2234, 2014 WL 2211386. Criminal Law ⚷ 30

Crimes of felony murder and misdemeanor domestic violence, as related to defendant's conduct, were not allied offenses subject to merger, in prosecution arising out of child's death from shaking incident, because commission of misdemeanor domestic violence could never result in the commission of felony murder. State v. Blanda (Ohio App. 12 Dist., Butler, 01-31-2011) No. CA2010-03-050, 2011-Ohio-411, 2011 WL 332725, Unreported, stay denied 132 Ohio St.3d 1422, 969 N.E.2d 270, 2012-Ohio-2729, appeal not allowed 132 Ohio St.3d 1514, 974 N.E.2d 112, 2012-Ohio-4021, on subsequent appeal 2014-Ohio-2234, 2014 WL 2211386. Criminal Law ⚷ 30

Defendant could not be convicted of two counts of felony murder arising out of the beating death of his girlfriend's son; the two counts did not involve separate murders, but rather were alternate theories of liability for a single murder, one of which was based on the predicate offense of child endangering and the other of which was based on the predicate offense of felonious assault. State v. Johnson (Ohio App. 1 Dist., Hamilton, 06-05-2009) No. C-080156, No. C-080158, 2009-Ohio-2568, 2009 WL 1576644, Unreported, appeal not allowed 123 Ohio St.3d 1409, 914 N.E.2d 206, 2009-Ohio-5031, motion to certify allowed 123 Ohio St.3d 1405, 914 N.E.2d 203, 2009-Ohio-5031, reversed 128 Ohio St.3d 153, 942 N.E.2d 1061, 2010-Ohio-6314. Criminal Law ⚷ 29(14)

Aggravated murder was not an allied offense of similar import to aggravated robbery, and thus the offenses did not merge for sentencing purposes. State v. Walker (Ohio App. 9 Dist., Summit, 12-31-2008) No. 24240, 2008-Ohio-6929, 2008 WL 5412372, Unreported. Sentencing and Punishment ⚷ 537

The two crimes of which defendant was convicted, vehicular homicide and aggravated vehicular homicide, were allied offenses of similar import that were not committed separately and had no separate animus, and thus, defendant could be convicted of only one of those offenses; statutes of conviction proscribed identical conduct, except that required culpable mental state was recklessness for aggravated vehicular homicide and negligence for vehicular homicide, under statutory definitions, a person could not act recklessly without also acting negligently, both of defendant's convictions resulted from same vehicle collision, and defendant could not have logically committed aggravated vehicular homicide and vehicular homicide with separate purpose or different immediate motive. State v. Hatfield (Ohio App. 11 Dist., Ashtabula, 12-28-2007) No. 2006-A-0033, 2007-Ohio-7130, 2007 WL 4564868, Unreported, stay granted 116 Ohio St.3d 1505, 880 N.E.2d 482, 2008-Ohio-381, appeal allowed 118 Ohio St.3d 1407, 886 N.E.2d 871, 2008-Ohio-2340, appeal dismissed as improvidently allowed 121 Ohio St.3d 1201, 901 N.E.2d 813, 2009-Ohio-353, reconsideration denied 121 Ohio St.3d 1429, 903 N.E.2d 327, 2009-Ohio-1296. Criminal Law ⚷ 29(14)

Offense of child endangering and offense of felony murder were not allied offenses of similar import as would require merging of convictions for purposes of sentencing; commission of one offense would not automatically result in the commission of the other. State v. Hoover-Moore (Ohio App. 10 Dist., Franklin, 10-19-2004) No. 03AP-1186, 2004-Ohio-5541, 2004 WL 2341691, Unreported, appeal not allowed 105 Ohio St.3d 1453, 823 N.E.2d 457, 2005-Ohio-763, denial of post-conviction relief affirmed 2008-Ohio-2020, 2008 WL 1886310, appeal not allowed 119 Ohio St.3d 1475, 894 N.E.2d 333, 2008-Ohio-4911. Criminal Law ⚷ 30

Convictions for murder and felonious assault involving separate victims did not merge for sentencing purposes, as each shooting was undertaken with separate animus. State v. Jackson (Ohio App. 9 Dist., 12-18-2013) 5 N.E.3d 116, 2013-Ohio-5557, appeal not allowed 139 Ohio St.3d 1404, 9 N.E.3d 1062, 2014-Ohio-2245. Sentencing and Punishment ⚷ 529

Attempted murder and felonious assault offenses were allied offenses of similar import, committed with a separate animus, and thus were separately punishable; defendant fired two shots at victim, intending to either purposely cause her death or physical harm through the use of a deadly weapon. State v. Monford (Ohio App. 10 Dist., 09-30-2010) 190 Ohio App.3d 35, 940 N.E.2d 634, 2010-Ohio-4732, motion to certify denied 2010-Ohio-5624, 2010 WL 4702362, appeal allowed in part 127 Ohio St.3d 1531, 940 N.E.2d 985, 2011-Ohio-376, appeal dismissed as improvidently allowed 131 Ohio St.3d 40, 960 N.E.2d 440, 2011-Ohio-6398, motion to reopen denied 2012-Ohio-5247, 2012 WL 5497871. Sentencing and Punishment ⚷ 529

Crimes of felony murder and child endangering, as related to defendant's conduct, were allied offenses and thus subject to merger, in prosecution arising out of child's death from beating; beating of child was discrete act resulting in simultaneous commission of child abuse and felony murder. State v. Johnson (Ohio, 12-29-2010) 128 Ohio St.3d 153, 942 N.E.2d 1061, 2010-Ohio-6314. Criminal Law ⚷ 30

Offense of attempted murder by engaging in conduct which, if successful, would result in purposely causing the death of another, and offense of felonious assault by causing or attempting to cause physical harm to another by means of a deadly weapon, are allied offenses of similar import, as a consideration in determining whether merger is required; although assault contains a weapon requirement while attempted murder offense does not, a defendant committing each offense must be proved to have engaged in conduct which, if successful, would have resulted in the death of the victim. State v. Williams (Ohio, 01-27-2010) 124 Ohio St.3d 381, 922 N.E.2d 937, 2010-Ohio-147. Criminal Law ⚷ 30

Capital murder defendant's right to not be convicted of more than one offense based on same conduct was not violated, given that, trial court, in imposing sentence, merged separate murder counts relating to each victim. State v. Gapen (Ohio, 12-15-2004) 104 Ohio St.3d 358, 819 N.E.2d 1047, 2004-Ohio-6548, dismissal of post-conviction relief reversed 2005-Ohio-441, 2005 WL 281171, appeal not allowed 106 Ohio St.3d 1483, 832 N.E.2d 737, 2005-Ohio-3978, reconsideration denied 105 Ohio St.3d 1441, 822 N.E.2d 812, 2005-Ohio-531, certiorari denied 126 S.Ct. 97, 546 U.S. 846, 163 L.Ed.2d 112, denial of post-conviction relief affirmed 2007-Ohio-4333, 2007 WL 2405719, appeal not allowed 117 Ohio St.3d 1423, 882 N.E.2d 444, 2008-Ohio-969. Sentencing And Punishment ⚷ 501

Aggravated murder and kidnapping are not allied offenses of similar import, so as to permit conviction of only one of them upon an indictment charging both, since kidnapping can take place without aggravated murder, and vice versa. State v. Keenan (Ohio, 02-25-1998) 81 Ohio St.3d 133, 689 N.E.2d 929, 1998-Ohio-459, reconsideration denied 81 Ohio St.3d 1503, 691 N.E.2d 1062, certiorari denied 119 S.Ct. 146, 525 U.S. 860, 142 L.Ed.2d 119, rehearing denied 119 S.Ct. 581, 525 U.S. 1035, 142 L.Ed.2d 484, denial of post-conviction relief affirmed 2001 WL 91129, dismissed, appeal not allowed 92 Ohio St.3d 1429, 749 N.E.2d 756, habeas corpus dismissed 262 F.Supp.2d 818, motion to amend denied 262 F.Supp.2d 826, vacated and remanded 400 F.3d 417, on remand 2007 WL 838923, dismissal of post-conviction relief affirmed 2006-Ohio-6031, 2006 WL 3317922, appeal not allowed 114 Ohio St.3d 1508, 872 N.E.2d 950, 2007-Ohio-4285. Criminal Law ⚷ 29(14)

Indictment could properly charge multiple counts of murder in connection with death of same victim, even though those charges may have merged at sentencing. State v. Blalock (Ohio App. 8 Dist., Cuyahoga, 09-05-2002) No. 80419, No. 80420, 2002-Ohio-4580, 2002 WL 2027520, Unreported, appeal not allowed 98 Ohio St.3d 1461, 783 N.E.2d 520, 2003-Ohio-644, denial of post-conviction relief affirmed 2003-Ohio-3026, 2003 WL 21360467, appeal not allowed 100 Ohio St.3d 1485, 798 N.E.2d 1093, 2003-Ohio-5992, appeal after new sentencing hearing 2003-Ohio-6627, 2003 WL 22922426, appeal not allowed 102 Ohio St.3d 1448, 808 N.E.2d 399, 2004-Ohio-2263, habeas corpus dismissed 2006 WL 1866666, affirmed 320 Fed.Appx. 396, 2009 WL 938700, certiorari denied 130 S.Ct. 1052, 175

L.Ed.2d 892, denial of post-conviction relief affirmed 2010-Ohio-4494, 2010 WL 3722545, appeal not allowed 127 Ohio St.3d 1548, 941 N.E.2d 804, 2011-Ohio-647. Indictment And Information ⚿ 125(29)

13. —— Assault, specific offenses construed

The crime of felonious assault by knowingly causing serious physical harm to another, and the crime of felonious assault by causing or attempting to cause physical harm to another by means of a deadly weapon, were allied offenses of similar import in prosecution of defendant, and thus should have been merged rather than sentenced concurrently; although the offenses were not aligned in the abstract, they were nonetheless so similar that commission of one offense necessarily resulted in commission of the other, and the record indicated not that defendant committed two separate acts or committed them with a separate animus but, instead, pointed to a single gunshot wound. State v. Minifee (Ohio App. 8 Dist., Cuyahoga, 06-25-2009) No. 91017, 2009-Ohio-3089, 2009 WL 1819493, Unreported, appeal not allowed 123 Ohio St.3d 1426, 914 N.E.2d 1065, 2009-Ohio-5340. Sentencing and Punishment ⚿ 501

Felonious assault and child endangering are not allied offense of similar import, and thus, defendant may be convicted of both offense; although offenses both have causation and resultant serious physical harm in common, conviction for felonious assault requires proof that defendant acted knowingly, while child endangering conviction only requires proof that defendant acted recklessly. State v. Garcia (Ohio App. 10 Dist., Franklin, 03-23-2004) No. 03AP-384, 2004-Ohio-1409, 2004 WL 557343, Unreported, appeal not allowed 103 Ohio St.3d 1406, 812 N.E.2d 1288, 2004-Ohio-3980, habeas corpus conditionally granted 2007 WL 1028528, affirmed 599 F.3d 529, rehearing denied. Criminal Law ⚿ 29(9)

Defendant could commit felonious assault without committing kidnapping, and thus two offenses were not allied offenses, but rather were of dissimilar import, such that defendant could be convicted and sentenced for both. State v. Brown (Ohio App. 2 Dist., Montgomery, 11-22-2002) No. 19113, 2002-Ohio-6370, 2002 WL 31641092, Unreported, appeal not allowed 98 Ohio St.3d 1491, 785 N.E.2d 473, 2003-Ohio-1189, denial of post-conviction relief affirmed 2003-Ohio-5738, 2003 WL 22429289, appeal not allowed 101 Ohio St.3d 1469, 804 N.E.2d 42, 2004-Ohio-819, habeas corpus denied 2007 WL 2156275. Criminal Law ⚿ 29(13); Sentencing And Punishment ⚿ 531

Felonious assault convictions and attempted murder conviction arose from allied offenses of similar import and thus were subject to merger for sentencing purposes; a although surviving victim was shot twice, the shots were fired in rapid succession with no delay in between, there was no evidence to suggest that defendant continued to follow victim or did any other act that showed a separate animus or separate state of mind, and the single purpose as to surviving victim was to injure or kill him. State v. Shaw (Ohio App. 7 Dist., 10-31-2013) 4 N.E.3d 406, 2013-Ohio-5292, appeal not allowed 138 Ohio St.3d 1436, 4 N.E.3d 1052, 2014-Ohio-889, dismissal of post-conviction relief affirmed 2014-Ohio-5633, 2014 WL 7275311. Sentencing and Punishment ⚿ 529

Two felonious assault offenses involved the same victim and thus constituted allied offenses of similar import such that convictions should have been merged for sentencing purposes. State v. Shaw (Ohio App. 7 Dist., 10-31-2013) 4 N.E.3d 406, 2013-Ohio-5292, appeal not allowed 138 Ohio St.3d 1436, 4 N.E.3d 1052, 2014-Ohio-889, dismissal of post-conviction relief affirmed 2014-Ohio-5633, 2014 WL 7275311. Sentencing and Punishment ⚿ 518

Defendant's two felonious assaults were committed separately and he had a separate animus, and thus were not subject to merger; although both shootings occurred while defendant and victim were together in vehicle, there was a significant delay between the first and second shooting, defendant's "immediate motive" for the first shooting was anger over his belief that victim might have taken his gun and refused money, and defendant later shot victim a second time in response to victim's attempt to grab the steering wheel. State v. Hudson (Ohio App. 2 Dist., 06-07-2013) 993 N.E.2d 443, 2013-Ohio-2351, appeal not allowed 138 Ohio St.3d 1471, 6 N.E.3d 1206, 2014-Ohio-1674, appeal reopened 2014-Ohio-1977, 2014 WL 1887835, denial of post-conviction relief affirmed in part, reversed in part 2014-Ohio-5363, 2014 WL 6852131. Criminal Law ⚿ 30

Offense of discharge of firearm on or near prohibited premises and the offense of felonious assaults were allied offenses of similar import and, thus, should have merged; it was possible to commit felonious assault by means of deadly weapon and discharge of a firearm on or near prohibited premises, the offenses were committed by the same conduct, the fight and shooting were one continuous act and the assaults and discharge of the firearm on or near prohibited premises were committed by the same conduct. State v. Melton (Ohio App. 8 Dist., 01-31-2013) 984 N.E.2d 1112, 2013-Ohio-257. Criminal Law ⚿ 30

Defendant who struck a police officer with his car and then rammed car into an undercover police vehicle committed the allied offenses of simple assault and felonious assault by means of deadly weapon with the same act and with the same animus towards the same victims, and thus defendant could not be convicted of both offenses; events happened one after the other, in the same location, after defendant accelerated his car, against multiple police officers' warnings, in an attempt to flee from the authorities without concern for who or what was in his way. State v. Anderson (Ohio App. 8 Dist., 08-06-2009) 183 Ohio App.3d 522, 917 N.E.2d 843, 2009-Ohio-3900, reversed 124 Ohio St.3d 513, 924 N.E.2d 366, 2010-Ohio-1109. Criminal Law ⚿ 29(9)

Offenses of felonious assault by causing serious physical harm to another, and felonious assault by causing physical harm by means of a deadly weapon or dangerous ordnance, were allied offenses of similar import, and thus defendant could not be convicted of both offenses when both offenses were committed with the same animus against the same victim. State v. Harris (Ohio, 07-07-2009) 122 Ohio St.3d 373, 911 N.E.2d 882, 2009-Ohio-3323. Criminal Law ⚷ 29(9)

Attempted murder and felonious assault, pursuant to statute prohibiting a person from causing or attempting to cause physical harm to another by means of a deadly weapon or dangerous ordnance, were allied offenses of similar import, as first step of test to determine whether defendant's convictions for both offenses were required to be merged for sentencing; committing an attempted murder and engaging in conduct that, if successful, would result in the victim's death, was necessarily attempting to cause the victim physical harm. State v. Lanier (Ohio App. 1 Dist., 12-31-2008) 180 Ohio App.3d 376, 905 N.E.2d 687, 2008-Ohio-6906, motion to certify allowed 121 Ohio St.3d 1448, 904 N.E.2d 899, 2009-Ohio-1820, appeal allowed 121 Ohio St.3d 1449, 904 N.E.2d 900, 2009-Ohio-1820, vacated in part 128 Ohio St.3d 339, 944 N.E.2d 221, 2011-Ohio-5. Criminal Law ⚷ 29(14)

Defendant's separate convictions for aggravated assault by causing serious physical harm to another and aggravated assault by causing physical harm by means of a deadly weapon or dangerous ordnance, which arose out of a single act, one stab wound to one victim, were allied offenses of similar import committed with a single animus, even though, comparing the elements of the offenses in the abstract, the commission of one would not necessarily result in commission of the other, and thus defendant could be convicted of and sentenced only for one offense of aggravated assault; in each form of the offense of aggravated assault, legislature manifested its intent to serve the same interest, preventing physical harm to persons. State v. Brown (Ohio, 09-17-2008) 119 Ohio St.3d 447, 895 N.E.2d 149, 2008-Ohio-4569, certiorari denied 129 S.Ct. 1356, 555 U.S. 1190, 173 L.Ed.2d 618. Criminal Law ⚷ 29(9); Sentencing And Punishment ⚷ 510

Upon remand for merger and resentencing, following Supreme Court's determination that defendant's convictions for aggravated assault involved allied offenses of similar import committed with a single animus, State had to elect which of defendant's two aggravated assault charges would merge into the other for purposes of her conviction and sentence. State v. Brown (Ohio, 09-17-2008) 119 Ohio St.3d 447, 895 N.E.2d 149, 2008-Ohio-4569, certiorari denied 129 S.Ct. 1356, 555 U.S. 1190, 173 L.Ed.2d 618. Criminal Law ⚷ 30; Sentencing And Punishment ⚷ 501

14. —— Kidnapping, specific offenses construed

Kidnapping and aggravated robbery offenses arising out of defendant's robbery of video store were allied offenses of similar import, and thus kidnapping conviction merged into aggravated robbery conviction; although defendant stood between victim employee and the exit, forcing her back to cash register, the incident lasted no more than a few minutes, and victim's movement was incidental to the separate underlying crime of aggravated robbery. State v. Dzelajlija (Ohio App. 8 Dist., Cuyahoga, 05-01-2008) No. 89912, 2008-Ohio-2039, 2008 WL 1903995, Unreported. Criminal Law ⚷ 30

Defendant waived right to claim on appeal that his three kidnapping convictions merged with two rape convictions and one attempted rape conviction as they were allied offenses of similar import, where defendant failed to raise claim in trial court. State v. Russell (Ohio App. 8 Dist., Cuyahoga, 09-23-2004) No. 83699, 2004-Ohio-5031, 2004 WL 2340125, Unreported, appeal not allowed 105 Ohio St.3d 1452, 823 N.E.2d 457, 2005-Ohio-763, motion to reopen denied 2005-Ohio-2998, 2005 WL 1406347, appeal not allowed 106 Ohio St.3d 1537, 835 N.E.2d 384, 2005-Ohio-5146, habeas corpus dismissed 2008 WL 2600006. Criminal Law ⚷ 1030(3)

Crime of aggravated robbery and crime of kidnapping required proof of element not included in other crime, and thus offenses were not allied offenses and did not merge in prosecution for aggravated robbery, kidnapping, and having weapon while under disability; aggravated robbery required proof that defendant brandished deadly weapon in order to facilitate theft offense, and kidnapping required proof that defendant restrained victim's liberty. State v. Dowdell (Ohio App. 8 Dist., Cuyahoga, 10-14-2004) No. 83829, 2004-Ohio-5487, 2004 WL 2306678, Unreported, appeal not allowed 105 Ohio St.3d 1441, 822 N.E.2d 812, 2005-Ohio-531, habeas corpus denied 2007 WL 1299269. Criminal Law ⚷ 30

Aggravated burglary and kidnapping were not allied offenses of similar import, and thus defendant was properly convicted and sentenced for both such offenses; burglary offense required commission of felony in connection with a trespass, and such elements were not required to commit kidnapping. State v. Johnson (Ohio App. 8 Dist., Cuyahoga, 06-19-2003) No. 81692, No. 81693, 2003-Ohio-3241, 2003 WL 21419631, Unreported, appeal not allowed 100 Ohio St.3d 1433, 797 N.E.2d 513, 2003-Ohio-5396, denial of habeas corpus affirmed 493 Fed.Appx. 666, 2012 WL 3241545. Criminal Law ⚷ 29(13)

Defendant was not entitled to merger of offenses of aggravated robbery and kidnapping, despite his assertion that conviction for both offenses subjected him to unconstitutional multiple punishments, where restraint and movement of the victim in this case was not merely incidental to the robbery but had a significance independent of the robbery, defendant and co-defendant forcibly restrained victim in her car for over four hours, drove to several locations while she was duct-taped, bound, and buried under blankets in back seat, extended detention satisfied requirements of prolonged restraint and substantial movement, confinement was secretive because she was buried under yoga mat and blankets in back seat, defendant also sexually assaulted victim after her movement was restrained . State v. Stadmire (Ohio App. 8 Dist., Cuyahoga, 02-27-2003) No. 81188, 2003-Ohio-873, 2003 WL 549912, Unreported, motion for delayed appeal denied 114 Ohio St.3d 1408, 867 N.E.2d 842, 2007-Ohio-2632. Criminal Law ⚷ 30

Kidnapping of victim was not incidental to defendant's felonious assault on victim, and therefore the crimes were not committed by a single act, as could require merging of allied offenses, in prosecution arising out of attack on victim in her apartment, where kidnapping offense included dragging victim from living room to balcony, and dragging of victim was not connected to assault since defendant punched victim three times before dragging her. State v. Long (Ohio App. 11 Dist., 10-06-2014) 19 N.E.3d 981, 2014-Ohio-4416. Criminal Law ⚷ 30

Aggravated robbery and kidnapping offenses were not allied offenses of similar import as to require merger; facts supporting defendant's kidnapping conviction were committed subsequent to the actual commission of the aggravated robbery. State v. Moore (Ohio App. 8 Dist., 05-03-2012) 970 N.E.2d 1098, 2012-Ohio-1958, appeal not allowed 133 Ohio St.3d 1413, 975 N.E.2d 1030, 2012-Ohio-4650, appeal after new sentencing hearing 24 N.E.3d 1197, 2014-Ohio-5135, cause dismissed 141 Ohio St.3d 1433, 23 N.E.3d 1178, 2015-Ohio-168, stay denied 141 Ohio St.3d 1452, 23 N.E.3d 1195, 2015-Ohio-239. Criminal Law ⚷ 30

For purposes of statute allowing only one conviction for allied offenses of similar import, offenses of domestic violence and kidnapping are not allied offenses of similar import. State v. Mosley (Ohio App. 8 Dist., 10-23-2008) 178 Ohio App.3d 631, 899 N.E.2d 1021, 2008-Ohio-5483, appeal not allowed 121 Ohio St.3d 1427, 903 N.E.2d 326, 2009-Ohio-1296, habeas corpus denied 2011 WL 4944024. Criminal Law ⚷ 29(13)

Defendant's kidnapping of victim had a significance and an animus independent of victim's murder, as would support convictions for both offenses; even if victim lived only for a few minutes after defendant hogtied him, sufficient evidence existed for jury to find that defendant intended to prevent victim from getting assistance for his injuries, had he regained consciousness, and sufficient evidence existed for jury to infer that defendant carried victim, while victim still lived, to basement in order to confine him and prevent anyone from finding him and rendering aid. State v. Johnson (Ohio, 12-13-2006) 112 Ohio St.3d 210, 858 N.E.2d 1144, 2006-Ohio-6404, reconsideration denied 112 Ohio St.3d 1472, 861 N.E.2d 145, 2007-Ohio-388, denial of post-conviction relief affirmed 2007-Ohio-1685, 2007 WL 1098106, appeal not allowed 115 Ohio St.3d 1439, 875 N.E.2d 101, 2007-Ohio-5567, certiorari denied 128 S.Ct. 74, 552 U.S. 836, 169 L.Ed.2d 55, habeas corpus dismissed in part 2009 WL 3124423, application for writ of habeas corpus held in abeyance 2012 WL 628507, denial of post-conviction relief affirmed 2013-Ohio-1398, 2013 WL 1400607. Criminal Law ⚷ 29(14)

Trial court's failure to properly merge conviction for kidnapping with conviction for aggravated robbery constituted plain error, where defendant was sentenced to consecutive prison term on kidnapping offense. State v. Taogaga (Ohio App. 8 Dist., 02-16-2006) 165 Ohio App.3d 775, 848 N.E.2d 861, 2006-Ohio-692. Criminal Law ⚷ 1030(3)

Conviction for kidnapping merged with conviction for aggravated robbery, where the holding of victims at gunpoint was inherent to the offense of robbery, and robbers did not move victims or subject them to greater risk of harm beyond that related to the commission of aggravated robbery and aggravated burglary offenses. State v. Taogaga (Ohio App. 8 Dist., 02-16-2006) 165 Ohio App.3d 775, 848 N.E.2d 861, 2006-Ohio-692. Criminal Law ⚷ 30

Kidnapping is separate and distinct from the crime of aggravated robbery, and does not constitute an allied offenses of similar import, when the kidnapping protrudes from the facts of the case, such that a separate animus is established. State v. Taogaga (Ohio App. 8 Dist., 02-16-2006) 165 Ohio App.3d 775, 848 N.E.2d 861, 2006-Ohio-692. Criminal Law ⚷ 29(13); Kidnapping ⚷ 22

Kidnapping and robbery are allied offenses of similar import when the restraint of the victim is merely incidental to the crime of robbery. State v. Taogaga (Ohio App. 8 Dist., 02-16-2006) 165 Ohio App.3d 775, 848 N.E.2d 861, 2006-Ohio-692. Criminal Law ⚷ 29(13); Kidnapping ⚷ 22

Double jeopardy principles did not preclude punishing capital defendant for both felony-murder and underlying kidnapping in case in which state relied upon victim's murder to satisfy the "serious physical harm" element of kidnapping; felony–murder was not an allied offense of similar import to the underlying felony. State v. Campbell (Ohio, 12-20-2000) 90 Ohio St.3d 320, 738 N.E.2d 1178, 2000-Ohio-183, reconsideration denied 91 Ohio St.3d 1433, 741 N.E.2d 896, certiorari denied 121 S.Ct. 2606, 533 U.S. 956, 150 L.Ed.2d 762, dismissal of post-conviction relief affirmed 2003-Ohio-6305, 2003 WL 22783857, appeal not allowed 102 Ohio St.3d 1470, 809 N.E.2d 1158, 2004-Ohio-2830, habeas corpus denied in part 2008 WL 657536, habeas corpus denied 2009 WL 773866. Double Jeopardy ⚷ 150(2)

When a kidnapping is committed during another crime, there exists no separate animus where the restraint or movement of the victim is merely incidental to the underlying crime, and the kidnapping specification thus merges with the other crime, but where the restraint is prolonged, the confinement is secretive, or the movement is substantial, there exists a separate animus as to each offense and merger does not occur. State v. Fears (Ohio, 09-08-1999) 86 Ohio St.3d 329, 715 N.E.2d 136, 1999-Ohio-111, reconsideration denied 87 Ohio St.3d 1421, 717 N.E.2d 1107, stay granted 87 Ohio St.3d 1423, 718 N.E.2d 441, denial of post-conviction relief affirmed 1999 WL 1032592, dismissed, appeal not allowed 88 Ohio St.3d 1444, 725 N.E.2d 284, certiorari denied 120 S.Ct. 1535, 529 U.S. 1039, 146 L.Ed.2d 349, habeas corpus denied 2008 WL 2782888. Criminal Law ⚷ 30

Resentencing was not required after appellate court determined in capital murder case that the offenses of kidnapping and aggravated robbery were committed with no separate animus and therefore should have merged as aggravating circumstances at death sentencing, where the jury's consideration of duplicative aggravating circumstances did not affect the outcome of the penalty phase and the remaining aggravating circumstances outweighed the mitigating circumstances. State v. Fears (Ohio, 09-08-1999) 86 Ohio St.3d 329, 715 N.E.2d 136, 1999-Ohio-111, reconsideration denied 87 Ohio St.3d 1421, 717 N.E.2d 1107, stay granted 87 Ohio St.3d 1423, 718 N.E.2d 441, denial of post-conviction relief affirmed 1999 WL 1032592, dismissed, appeal not allowed 88 Ohio St.3d 1444, 725 N.E.2d 284, certiorari denied 120 S.Ct. 1535, 529 U.S. 1039, 146 L.Ed.2d 349, habeas corpus denied 2008 WL 2782888. Sentencing And Punishment ⚷ 1788(11)

Aggravated burglary and kidnapping were not "allied offenses of similar import," for purposes of rule providing that defendant could be convicted of only one such offense; even if restraint were element of burglary, defendant imposed further restraint on victim, beyond that involved in burglary, by tying her up. State v. Reynolds (Ohio, 01-14-1998) 80 Ohio St.3d 670, 687 N.E.2d 1358, 1998-Ohio-171, certiorari denied 118 S.Ct. 2328, 524 U.S. 930, 141 L.Ed.2d 702, denial of post-conviction relief affirmed 1999 WL 980568, dismissed, appeal not allowed 88 Ohio St.3d 1425, 723 N.E.2d 1113, denial of habeas corpus affirmed 2007 WL 2323850. Criminal Law ⚷ 29(13)

Kidnapping constituted separate offense from murder, attempted rape, and robbery charges, and defendant's kidnapping charge thus would not be merged into any of those other felonies, where defendant was in process of robbing victim when he noticed she was attempting to use the phone and struck her, then tied her hands behind her back, and killed her only after he had restrained her for a period of time. State v. Reynolds (Ohio, 01-14-1998) 80 Ohio St.3d 670, 687 N.E.2d 1358, 1998-Ohio-171, certiorari denied 118 S.Ct. 2328, 524 U.S. 930, 141 L.Ed.2d 702, denial of post-conviction relief affirmed 1999 WL 980568, dismissed, appeal not allowed 88 Ohio St.3d 1425, 723 N.E.2d 1113, denial of habeas corpus affirmed 2007 WL 2323850. Criminal Law ⚷ 30

In determining whether a kidnapping offense was committed with a separate animus from rape, as required for a defendant to be convicted of both offenses under Ohio law, courts must consider whether the restraint or movement of the victim is merely incidental to a separate underlying crime or, instead, whether it has significance independent of the other offense. Madsen v. McFaul (N.D.Ohio, 08-13-2009) 643 F.Supp.2d 962. Criminal Law ⚷ 29(13)

Sufficient circumstantial evidence supported Ohio Supreme Court's finding that the State established that the restraint associated with the kidnapping specification and charge was distinguishable from the restraint associated with aggravated murder of victim; petitioner's tying of victim's leg to bed significantly increased her risk of harm of assault and rape but only marginally increased her risk of murder by strangulation and a slit throat. Hartman v. Bagley (N.D.Ohio, 08-31-2004) 333 F.Supp.2d 632, affirmed 492 F.3d 347, rehearing and rehearing en banc denied, certiorari denied 128 S.Ct. 2971, 554 U.S. 924, 171 L.Ed.2d 897, motion for relief from judgment denied 2012 WL 5290292. Sentencing And Punishment ⚷ 1660

15. —— Gambling and alcohol, specific offenses construed

Charges arising from same conduct of operating a motor vehicle with a prohibited breath-alcohol concentration (OVI per se) and operating a motor vehicle while impaired (OVI impaired) should have been merged for purposes of sentencing, and defendant should have been sentenced on one of the two charges as elected by the prosecution. Columbus v. Aleshire (Ohio App. 10 Dist., 06-17-2010) 187 Ohio App.3d 660, 933 N.E.2d 317, 2010-Ohio-2773, appeal not allowed 126 Ohio St.3d 1617, 935 N.E.2d 855, 2010-Ohio-5101. Sentencing and Punishment ⚷ 534

16. —— Sex offenses, specific offenses construed

Rape and felonious assault were not allied offenses of similar import, and thus, trial court could impose separate sentence for each offense; rape did not require serious physical harm, a deadly weapon, or dangerous ordnance, as did felonious assault, and, in any event, defendant's act of hitting the victim in the head was not related to the rape, in that it occurred while the victim slept, and defendant then waited for the victim to regain consciousness before raping her. State v. Singleton (Ohio App. 8 Dist., Cuyahoga, 11-18-2010) No. 94877, 2010-Ohio-5612, 2010 WL 4684909, Unreported, appeal not allowed 128 Ohio St.3d 1428, 943 N.E.2d 574, 2011-Ohio-1049. Sentencing and Punishment ⚷ 522

Rape and gross sexual imposition counts against defendant merged for purposes of sentencing; victim's testimony indicated that defendant was touching her at the same time he was orally assaulting her, and it appeared as though any touching was to assist in committing the rape. State v. Younger (Ohio App. 8 Dist., Cuyahoga, 01-26-2006) No. 86235, 2006-Ohio-296, 2006 WL 181914, Unreported, appeal allowed, reversed in part 110 Ohio St.3d 70, 850 N.E.2d 1168, 2006-Ohio-3663, on remand 2006 WL 4782046, appeal after new sentencing hearing 2007-Ohio-5547, 2007 WL 3026942. Sentencing And Punishment ⚷ 501

Multiple counts of pandering sexually oriented matter involving a minor had separate animi, and thus defendant could be convicted on each count under multiple-count statute; children depicted in photographs with respect to each count appeared to be different individuals, and even assuming that some photographs were of identical children, photographs depicted children in separate positions and against different backgrounds. State v. Smith (Ohio App. 10 Dist., Franklin, 05-24-2005) No. 04AP-859, 2005-Ohio-2560, 2005 WL 1220742, Unreported, appeal not allowed 106 Ohio St.3d 1556, 836 N.E.2d 581, 2005-Ohio-5531, appeal after new sentencing hearing 196 Ohio App.3d 431, 964 N.E.2d 3, 2011-Ohio-3786, appeal not allowed 131 Ohio St.3d 1412, 959 N.E.2d 1056, 2012-Ohio-136. Criminal Law ⚿ 29(12)

Gross sexual imposition and rape were not allied offenses of similar import, and thus defendant could be convicted of both charges; according to victim's testimony, the sexual contact necessary for the gross sexual imposition conviction was completed before the sexual conduct necessary for the rape convictions started, and sexual contact element of the gross sexual imposition offenses was not incidental to the sexual conduct element of the rapes because the rapes could have been committed without the preceding sexual contact. State v. Reid (Ohio App. 8 Dist., Cuyahoga, 04-22-2004) No. 83206, 2004-Ohio-2018, 2004 WL 859172, Unreported, appeal not allowed 103 Ohio St.3d 1428, 814 N.E.2d 491, 2004-Ohio-4524, reconsideration denied 103 Ohio St.3d 1496, 816 N.E.2d 1081, 2004-Ohio-5605, appeal after new sentencing hearing 2006-Ohio-3978, 2006 WL 2192039, appeal after new sentencing hearing 2007-Ohio-5858, 2007 WL 3203061. Criminal Law ⚿ 29(12)

Evidence was sufficient to support finding that defendant raped victim while she was under 13 years of age, as required to support convictions for two counts of rape; victim testified that defendant raped her both before and after her thirteenth birthday. State v. Reid (Ohio App. 8 Dist., Cuyahoga, 04-22-2004) No. 83206, 2004-Ohio-2018, 2004 WL 859172, Unreported, appeal not allowed 103 Ohio St.3d 1428, 814 N.E.2d 491, 2004-Ohio-4524, reconsideration denied 103 Ohio St.3d 1496, 816 N.E.2d 1081, 2004-Ohio-5605, appeal after new sentencing hearing 2006-Ohio-3978, 2006 WL 2192039, appeal after new sentencing hearing 2007-Ohio-5858, 2007 WL 3203061. Infants ⚿ 1755; Rape ⚿ 52(4)

Defendant's two sexual assault convictions, arising from defendant's conduct against his daughter on different occasions, were not for the same conduct, and thus two sexual battery counts would not merge. State v. Wilson (Ohio App. 5 Dist., Coshocton, 03-30-2004) No. 02CA030, 2004-Ohio-1692, 2004 WL 690176, Unreported, appeal not allowed 103 Ohio St.3d 1407, 812 N.E.2d 1289, 2004-Ohio-3980, habeas corpus dismissed 2007 WL 3307765. Criminal Law ⚿ 30

Each instance of rape defendant committed against victim was done with a separate animus and, as a result, permitted imposition of consecutive sentences; each of defendant's actions that victim testified to at trial formed a separate basis for the crime of rape when defendant used his hands, mouth, and penis in a systematic order to penetrate her vagina to see if she was sleeping with someone else, and when each of defendant's "tests" yielded no results, he raped her a different way. State v. Madsen (Ohio App. 8 Dist., Cuyahoga, 10-30-2003) No. 82399, 2003-Ohio-5822, 2003 WL 22457002, Unreported, appeal not allowed 101 Ohio St.3d 1489, 805 N.E.2d 540, 2004-Ohio-1293, motion to reopen denied 2004-Ohio-4895, 2004 WL 2065653, appeal not allowed 104 Ohio St.3d 1427, 819 N.E.2d 710, 2004-Ohio-6585, dismissal of post-conviction relief affirmed 2005-Ohio-3850, 2005 WL 1792337, appeal not allowed 107 Ohio St.3d 1425, 837 N.E.2d 1209, 2005-Ohio-6124, habeas corpus granted 2007 WL 2510030, habeas corpus granted 643 F.Supp.2d 962. Sentencing And Punishment ⚿ 561; Sentencing And Punishment ⚿ 605

Assuming crimes of rape, unlawful sexual conduct with a minor and gross sexual imposition, when compared in the abstract, were allied of similar import under the *Rance* test, separate animus existed for each crime, which warranted sentencing defendant on each count; charges were based on events that occurred over period of time and involved different types of conduct. State v. Waters (Ohio App. 5 Dist., Ashland, 08-28-2003) No. 03-COA-002, 2003-Ohio-4624, 2003 WL 22039441, Unreported, appeal not allowed 100 Ohio St.3d 1545, 800 N.E.2d 751, 2003-Ohio-6879, denial of post-conviction relief affirmed 2006-Ohio-5528, 2006 WL 3020297, appeal not allowed 113 Ohio St.3d 1415, 862 N.E.2d 844, 2007-Ohio-1036. Sentencing And Punishment ⚿ 522

The multiple counts of gross sexual imposition that defendant pled guilty to were not allied offenses of similar import, for sentencing purposes; defendant groomed his four-year-old granddaughter to engage in various sexual acts, he had her touch his penis on multiple occasions, he rubbed his penis on her face, he put his penis in her mouth, he had her kiss the head of his penis, he had her lay her face on his penis at least six times, and he ejaculated on her face about six times. State v. Devai (Ohio App. 11 Dist., 12-02-2013) 2 N.E.3d 993, 2013-Ohio-5264. Sentencing and Punishment ⚿ 522

Merger was required of defendant's convictions for child endangering and transferring any material or performance that showed a minor in a state of nudity, where defendant's solicitation for minors to transfer nude photographs of themselves to him and his transfer of the photographs from his personal digital assistant (PDA) to his computer were the same actions that led to both charges. State v. Thomas (Ohio App. 8 Dist., 11-23-2011) 197 Ohio App.3d 176, 966 N.E.2d 939, 2011-Ohio-6073, appeal not allowed 132 Ohio St.3d 1425, 969 N.E.2d 272, 2012-Ohio-2729, appeal after new sentencing hearing 2013-Ohio-1804, 2013 WL 1858890, appeal after new sentencing hearing 2014-Ohio-2410, 2014 WL 2566106, appeal not allowed 141 Ohio St.3d 1422, 21 N.E.3d 1115, 2014-Ohio-5567. Criminal Law ⚿ 30

In sentencing defendant for sexual battery regarding his 16-year-old student, count arising from digital penetration of student's vagina and count arising from cunnilingus involved different, distinct types of sexual activity and thus constituted separate crimes, and therefore merger of counts for sentencing purposes was not required by statute governing allied offenses of similar import. State v. Parker (Ohio App. 2 Dist., 03-25-2011) 193 Ohio App.3d 506, 952 N.E.2d 1159, 2011-Ohio-1418, appeal not allowed 129 Ohio St.3d 1452, 951 N.E.2d 1048, 2011-Ohio-4217. Sentencing and Punishment ⚿ 522

In sentencing defendant for four counts of sexual battery regarding his 16-year-old student, acts committed during first encounter were committed separately from acts committed during second encounter, which occurred eight days later, and thus counts arising from first encounter and counts arising from second encounter were not allied offenses of similar import and could not be merged. State v. Parker (Ohio App. 2 Dist., 03-25-2011) 193 Ohio App.3d 506, 952 N.E.2d 1159, 2011-Ohio-1418, appeal not allowed 129 Ohio St.3d 1452, 951 N.E.2d 1048, 2011-Ohio-4217. Sentencing and Punishment ⚿ 522

Rape by fellatio and vaginal rape are separate offenses, even when one is followed immediately by the other. State v. Adams (Ohio, 11-17-2004) 103 Ohio St.3d 508, 817 N.E.2d 29, 2004-Ohio-5845, reconsideration denied 104 Ohio St.3d 1442, 819 N.E.2d 1124, 2004-Ohio-7033, certiorari denied 125 S.Ct. 2271, 544 U.S. 1040, 161 L.Ed.2d 1072, habeas corpus denied 2007 WL 671296, habeas corpus denied 484 F.Supp.2d 753, opinion after remand from court of appeals 2009 WL 2922042, stay granted, motion to certify appeal granted 2010 WL 816532, subsequent determination 2010 WL 1964904, affirmed 644 F.3d 481, on remand 2013 WL 3991867. Criminal Law ⚿ 29(12)

Defendant's two convictions for rape were not allied offenses of similar import, for the purpose of imposing multiple convictions and sentences for defendant's actions; each count of rape in the indictment referred to a separate incident or occurrence, defendant provided a written statement that indicated that he vaginally raped his daughter on two separate occasions, and defendant admitted to physician that he raped his daughter on two separate occasions. State v. Gopp (Ohio App. 9 Dist., 09-17-2003) 154 Ohio App.3d 385, 797 N.E.2d 531, 2003-Ohio-4908, denial of post-conviction relief affirmed 2006-Ohio-5477, 2006 WL 2993343, appeal not allowed 113 Ohio St.3d 1415, 862 N.E.2d 844, 2007-Ohio-1036, certiorari denied 128 S.Ct. 183, 552 U.S. 875, 169 L.Ed.2d 124. Double Jeopardy ⚿ 148

Defendant's animus to rape victim was separate from his animus to commit burglary, robbery, kidnapping, and murder, and his attempted rape charge thus would not be merged into any of those other felonies. State v. Reynolds (Ohio, 01-14-1998) 80 Ohio St.3d 670, 687 N.E.2d 1358, 1998-Ohio-171, certiorari denied 118 S.Ct. 2328, 524 U.S. 930, 141 L.Ed.2d 702, denial of post-conviction relief affirmed 1999 WL 980568, dismissed, appeal not allowed 88 Ohio St.3d 1425, 723 N.E.2d 1113, denial of habeas corpus affirmed 2007 WL 2323850. Criminal Law ⚿ 30

17. —— Drug offenses, specific offenses construed

Trafficking in cocaine and possession of cocaine are not allied offenses of similar import, and thus, offenses do not merge; statute proscribing possession does not include element of sale or offer to sell, while trafficking statute does not require actual possession or use of controlled substance. State v. Sanders (Ohio App. 11 Dist., Portage, 10-22-2004) No. 2003-P-0072, 2004-Ohio-5629, 2004 WL 2376014, Unreported, appeal not allowed 105 Ohio St.3d 1441, 822 N.E.2d 812, 2005-Ohio-531, appeal after new sentencing hearing 2006-Ohio-2147, 2006 WL 1133192, appeal after new sentencing hearing 2007-Ohio-5613, 2007 WL 3052570, appeal not allowed 117 Ohio St.3d 1426, 882 N.E.2d 446, 2008-Ohio-969, habeas corpus denied 2012 WL 2568186. Criminal Law ⚿ 30

Offense of trafficking in drugs and possession of same drugs were not allied offenses of similar import; drug trafficking required an element of sale, while possession of drugs required that a person obtain, possess, or use a controlled substance. State v. Hudson (Ohio App. 8 Dist., Cuyahoga, 03-28-2002) No. 79010, 2002-Ohio-1408, 2002 WL 472304, Unreported, appeal after new sentencing hearing 2004-Ohio-1452, 2004 WL 583925. Criminal Law ⚿ 29(8)

Defendant's convictions for drug possession and trafficking were allied offenses of similar import subject to merger, absent sufficient evidence to establish that defendant's conduct resulted in two separate acts or was committed with separate animus; investigating officer testified that defendant stated he had drug problem and purchased drugs to sell to support his drug habit. State v. Brown (Ohio App. 5 Dist., 06-09-2014) 14 N.E.3d 465, 2014-Ohio-2493. Criminal Law ⚿ 30

Defendant's two convictions for possession of cocaine arose out of the same conduct, committed with the same criminal animus, and thus were required to be merged as arising from allied offenses of similar import; defendant's possession of one portion of cocaine that he had been videotaped smoking prior to arrest, and his possession of unused portion of cocaine at time of his arrest, were performed with same animus of smoking cocaine. State v. Brown (Ohio App. 12 Dist., 02-01-2010) 2010 -Ohio- 324, 2010 WL 339810. Criminal Law ⚿ 30

Offenses of drug possession and drug trafficking are allied offenses of similar import for which multiple punishments are barred. State v. Whitfield (Ohio, 01-05-2010) 124 Ohio St.3d 319, 922 N.E.2d 182, 2010-Ohio-2. Double Jeopardy ⚿ 146

Convictions for trafficking in powder cocaine and trafficking in crack cocaine were not allied offenses of similar import, and thus, did not merge; legislature specifically intended that crack cocaine offenses be treated more severely than powder cocaine offenses, and defendant treated the powder cocaine transactions and crack cocaine transactions separately. State v. Ligon (Ohio App. 3 Dist., 11-24-2008) 179 Ohio App.3d 544, 902 N.E.2d 1011, 2008-Ohio-6085. Criminal Law ⚷ 30

Offense of possessing a controlled substance, committed by knowingly obtaining, possessing, or using a controlled substance, and offense of trafficking in a controlled substance, committed by knowingly selling or offering to sell a controlled substance, are not allied offenses of similar import, and thus merger is not required; trafficking offense requires an intent to sell, but the offender need not possess the controlled substance in order to offer to sell it, while possession offense requires no intent to sell. State v. Cabrales (Ohio, 04-09-2008) 118 Ohio St.3d 54, 886 N.E.2d 181, 2008-Ohio-1625. Criminal Law ⚷ 29(8)

Offense of possessing a controlled substance, committed by knowingly obtaining, possessing, or using a controlled substance, and offense of trafficking in a controlled substance, committed by knowingly preparing for shipment, shipping, transporting, delivering, preparing for distribution, or distributing a controlled substance, knowing, or having reason to know, that the substance is intended for sale, are allied offenses of similar import, and thus merger is required; in order to ship a controlled substance, deliver it, distribute it, or prepare it for shipping, the offender must have control over it. State v. Cabrales (Ohio, 04-09-2008) 118 Ohio St.3d 54, 886 N.E.2d 181, 2008-Ohio-1625. Criminal Law ⚷ 29(8); Criminal Law ⚷ 30

Offense of trafficking a controlled substance by selling or offering to sell a controlled substance, and offense of trafficking in a controlled substance by knowingly preparing for shipment, shipping, transporting, delivering, preparing for distribution, or distributing a controlled substance, knowing, or having reason to know, that the substance is intended for sale, are not allied offenses of similar import, and thus merger is not required. State v. Cabrales (Ohio, 04-09-2008) 118 Ohio St.3d 54, 886 N.E.2d 181, 2008-Ohio-1625. Criminal Law ⚷ 29(8)

Convictions for trafficking in cocaine and possession of cocaine are not allied offenses of similar import and therefore do not merge, since trafficking imposes the additional element that possession of the controlled substance is incident to preparation for shipment, transportation, delivery or distribution of the drug through a sale. State v. Bridges (Ohio App. 8 Dist., Cuyahoga, 07-25-2002) No. 80171, 2002-Ohio-3771, 2002 WL 1728602, Unreported, appeal not allowed 97 Ohio St.3d 1484, 780 N.E.2d 287, 2002-Ohio-6866, habeas corpus denied 2007 WL 2571931. Criminal Law ⚷ 30

18. —— Robbery and burglary, specific offenses construed

Defendant's convictions for robbery and aggravated robbery constituted allied offenses of similar import, and thus multiple sentences could not be imposed for the convictions; the commission of aggravated robbery necessarily resulted in the commission of robbery; overruling *State v. Palmer*, 148 Ohio App.3d 246, 772 N.E.2d 726. State v. Madaris (Ohio App. 1 Dist., Hamilton, 05-23-2008) No. C-070287, 2008-Ohio-2470, 2008 WL 2152691, Unreported, appeal allowed 119 Ohio St.3d 1444, 893 N.E.2d 515, 2008-Ohio-4487, appeal not allowed 119 Ohio St.3d 1445, 893 N.E.2d 516, 2008-Ohio-4487, affirmed 123 Ohio St.3d 127, 914 N.E.2d 405, 2009-Ohio-4903. Criminal Law ⚷ 29(11)

Defendant's act of committing aggravated robbery of flower shop and aggravated robbery of employees at flower show were committed with a separate animus, and thus defendant was properly convicted and sentenced on each robbery; each offense was perpetrated against different victim and each victim was forced to relinquish their property to defendant. State v. Payne (Ohio App. 10 Dist., Franklin, 09-16-2003) No. 02AP-723, No. 02AP-725, 2003-Ohio-4891, 2003 WL 22128810, Unreported, appeal not allowed 101 Ohio St.3d 1421, 802 N.E.2d 153, 2004-Ohio-123, appeal not allowed 107 Ohio St.3d 1411, 836 N.E.2d 1230, 2005-Ohio-5859, habeas corpus dismissed 2006 WL 2583380, certificate of appealability denied 2006 WL 2903933, denial of post-conviction relief affirmed 2007-Ohio-4594, 2007 WL 2505486. Criminal Law ⚷ 29(11)

Defendant's act of committing aggravated robbery of credit union and aggravated robbery of individual at credit union were committed with a separate animus, and thus defendant was properly convicted and sentenced on for each robbery; each offense was perpetrated against different victim and each victim was forced to relinquish their property to defendant. State v. Payne (Ohio App. 10 Dist., Franklin, 09-16-2003) No. 02AP-723, No. 02AP-725, 2003-Ohio-4891, 2003 WL 22128810, Unreported, appeal not allowed 101 Ohio St.3d 1421, 802 N.E.2d 153, 2004-Ohio-123, appeal not allowed 107 Ohio St.3d 1411, 836 N.E.2d 1230, 2005-Ohio-5859, habeas corpus dismissed 2006 WL 2583380, certificate of appealability denied 2006 WL 2903933, denial of post-conviction relief affirmed 2007-Ohio-4594, 2007 WL 2505486. Criminal Law ⚷ 29(11)

Aggravated burglary and theft were not allied offenses of similar import, and thus defendant was properly convicted and sentenced for both such offenses; completion of theft was not a necessary element of burglary because purpose to commit any felony will suffice to supply requisite intent for burglary offense. State v. Johnson (Ohio App. 8 Dist., Cuyahoga, 06-19-2003) No. 81692, No. 81693, 2003-Ohio-3241, 2003 WL 21419631, Unreported, appeal not allowed 100 Ohio St.3d 1433, 797 N.E.2d 513, 2003-Ohio-5396, denial of habeas corpus affirmed 493 Fed.Appx. 666, 2012 WL 3241545. Criminal Law ⚷ 29(11)

Defendant's convictions for aggravated robbery and aggravated burglary were not allied offenses of similar import subject to merger, since offenses were separate acts committed with separate animus; although it was possible to commit offenses with same conduct, crime of aggravated burglary occurred when defendant broke into victim's home, with deadly weapon in his possession, intending to commit burglary on premises, and crime of aggravated robbery occurred later in time when, as defendant was committing burglary, victim came out of hiding and was attacked by defendant. State v. Santamaria (Ohio App. 9 Dist., 10-29-2014) 22 N.E.3d 288, 2014-Ohio-4787. Criminal Law ⚷ 30

Defendant's aggravated robbery convictions did not merge because he committed three offenses of the same kind separately against three individual victims; defendant entered the establishment with the intent of committing a theft offense, he brandished a weapon in the presence of each victim, and he indicated an intention to use that weapon on each discrete person. State v. May (Ohio App. 11 Dist., 09-30-2014) 20 N.E.3d 396, 2014-Ohio-4286. Criminal Law ⚷ 30

Aggravated robbery and robbery were not allied offenses of similar import, and thus, separate convictions for each arising from same criminal episode did not violate prohibition against double jeopardy, since robbery did not require proof that defendant brandished firearm. State v. Jones (Ohio App. 6 Dist., 04-10-2009) 182 Ohio App.3d 183, 912 N.E.2d 142, 2009-Ohio-1742, reversed 123 Ohio St.3d 146, 914 N.E.2d 1037, 2009-Ohio-4689, on remand 2010-Ohio-6973, 2009 WL 5174145. Double Jeopardy ⚷ 145

Offenses of robbery committed while inflicting, attempting to inflict, or threatening to inflict physical harm, and aggravated robbery using a deadly weapon, were allied offenses of similar import, and thus defendant could not be convicted of both offenses when both offenses were committed with the same animus against the same victim; possession of a deadly weapon, used, shown, brandished, or made known to victim during a theft also constituted a threat to inflict physical harm on victim. State v. Harris (Ohio, 07-07-2009) 122 Ohio St.3d 373, 911 N.E.2d 882, 2009-Ohio-3323. Criminal Law ⚷ 29(11)

Aggravated burglary specification for death penalty did not merge with aggravated robbery specification; as soon as defendant entered the apartment by force armed with a deadly weapon with the intent to commit a theft, the aggravated burglary was completed. State v. Fears (Ohio, 09-08-1999) 86 Ohio St.3d 329, 715 N.E.2d 136, 1999-Ohio-111, reconsideration denied 87 Ohio St.3d 1421, 717 N.E.2d 1107, stay granted 87 Ohio St.3d 1423, 718 N.E.2d 441, denial of post-conviction relief affirmed 1999 WL 1032592, dismissed, appeal not allowed 88 Ohio St.3d 1444, 725 N.E.2d 284, certiorari denied 120 S.Ct. 1535, 529 U.S. 1039, 146 L.Ed.2d 349, habeas corpus denied 2008 WL 2782888. Criminal Law ⚷ 30

Aggravated burglary and aggravated robbery were not "allied offenses of similar import," for purposes of rule providing that defendant could be convicted of only one such offense; defendant committed aggravated burglary by using deception to obtain entry into victim's home and used force to complete that entry in order to take her property, but committed aggravated robbery when he subjected victim to further injury in order to take her property. State v. Reynolds (Ohio, 01-14-1998) 80 Ohio St.3d 670, 687 N.E.2d 1358, 1998-Ohio-171, certiorari denied 118 S.Ct. 2328, 524 U.S. 930, 141 L.Ed.2d 702, denial of post-conviction relief affirmed 1999 WL 980568, dismissed, appeal not allowed 88 Ohio St.3d 1425, 723 N.E.2d 1113, denial of habeas corpus affirmed 2007 WL 2323850. Criminal Law ⚷ 29(11)

Aggravated robbery and aggravated murder are not "allied offenses of similar import," for purposes of rule providing that, where conduct of defendant can be construed as constituting two or more allied offenses of similar import, indictment may contain counts for all such offenses, but defendant may be convicted of only one. State v. Reynolds (Ohio, 01-14-1998) 80 Ohio St.3d 670, 687 N.E.2d 1358, 1998-Ohio-171, certiorari denied 118 S.Ct. 2328, 524 U.S. 930, 141 L.Ed.2d 702, denial of post-conviction relief affirmed 1999 WL 980568, dismissed, appeal not allowed 88 Ohio St.3d 1425, 723 N.E.2d 1113, denial of habeas corpus affirmed 2007 WL 2323850. Criminal Law ⚷ 29(14)

Aggravated burglary and aggravated murder are not "allied offenses of similar import," for purposes of rule providing that, where conduct of defendant can be construed as constituting two or more allied offenses of similar import, indictment may contain counts for all such offenses, but defendant may be convicted of only one. State v. Reynolds (Ohio, 01-14-1998) 80 Ohio St.3d 670, 687 N.E.2d 1358, 1998-Ohio-171, certiorari denied 118 S.Ct. 2328, 524 U.S. 930, 141 L.Ed.2d 702, denial of post-conviction relief affirmed 1999 WL 980568, dismissed, appeal not allowed 88 Ohio St.3d 1425, 723 N.E.2d 1113, denial of habeas corpus affirmed 2007 WL 2323850. Criminal Law ⚷ 29(14)

19. —— Theft and other offenses, specific offenses construed

Two counts of burglary for which defendant was convicted should have been merged for sentencing purposes; but for the addition of two different victim names, the two counts were precisely the same. State v. Powers (Ohio App. 8 Dist., Cuyahoga, 05-18-2006) No. 86365, 2006-Ohio-2458, 2006 WL 1351661, Unreported. Sentencing And Punishment ⚷ 519

Defendant's convictions for money laundering and theft in office, as well as his convictions for theft in office and tempering with records, were not allied offenses of similar import; theft in office required a theft offense, by a public official, involving property owned by a government entity, neither money laundering or tampering with records had those same requirements, money laundering required either an intent to conceal the nature, location, source, or ownership of the proceeds from some unlawful activity, or a purpose to promote, manage, establish or carry on a corrupt activity, theft in office and tampering with records did not require those same purposes or intent, and tampering with records required falsification, destruction, removal, concealment, or alteration of some record, and theft in office and money laundering did not have that requirement. State v. Gray (Ohio App. 2 Dist., Greene, 01-06-2006) No. 04CA129, 2006-Ohio-40, 2006 WL 38282, Unreported, motion for delayed appeal granted 109 Ohio St.3d 1422, 846 N.E.2d 532, 2006-Ohio-1967, appeal not allowed 110 Ohio St.3d 1464, 852 N.E.2d 1213, 2006-Ohio-4288, on subsequent appeal 2007-Ohio-5173, 2007 WL 2812964. Criminal Law ⚷ 29(10)

Two counts of grand theft of firearms were not allied offenses of similar import for sentencing purposes merely because both subject firearms were stolen in course of single theft, where theft of each firearm was separate offense. State v. Helton (Ohio App. 3 Dist., Logan, 08-15-2005) No. 8-05-06, 2005-Ohio-4184, 2005 WL 1939437, Unreported, appeal not allowed 108 Ohio St.3d 1415, 841 N.E.2d 319, 2006-Ohio-179, denial of post-conviction relief affirmed 2008-Ohio-3601, 2008 WL 2789542, appeal not allowed 120 Ohio St.3d 1487, 900 N.E.2d 198, 2009-Ohio-278, appeal not allowed 119 Ohio St.3d 1473, 894 N.E.2d 332, 2008-Ohio-4911. Sentencing And Punishment ⚷ 532

Two counts of receiving stolen property, arising from single occurrence of defendant's possession of stolen car stereo, wallet, and credit cards, were required to be merged as allied offense of similar import, even though one offense involved a credit card and was subject to enhancement, since it was impossible to commit offense of receiving a stolen credit card without also violating general offense of receiving stolen property. State v. Afshari (Ohio App. 12 Dist., 02-01-2010) 2010 -Ohio- 325, 2010 WL 339808. Criminal Law ⚷ 30

Defendant failed to establish on appeal that trial court committed plain error by failing to merge for sentencing two counts of receiving stolen property; although defendant argued that receiving stolen property counts related to stolen pickup truck and tires and rims from that same truck, indictment identified truck that defendant received, retained, or tried to dispose of, and count relating to tires and rims made no connection to them being a part of stolen truck. State v. Rogers (Ohio App. 8 Dist., 03-21-2013) 990 N.E.2d 1085, 2013-Ohio-1027, on reconsideration 994 N.E.2d 499, 2013-Ohio-3235, motion to certify allowed 136 Ohio St.3d 1508, 995 N.E.2d 1212, 2013-Ohio-4657, also published at 137 Ohio St.3d 1458, 1 N.E.3d 424, 2013-Ohio-4657, motion to certify allowed 137 Ohio St.3d 1456, 1 N.E.3d 423, 2013-Ohio-4657, appeal not allowed 137 Ohio St.3d 1475, 2 N.E.3d 270, 2014-Ohio-176. Criminal Law ⚷ 1042.3(1)

Aggravated robbery and grand theft were not "allied offenses of similar import," and, thus, capital defendant could be convicted of both offenses, under statute providing that, where same conduct by defendant can be construed to constitute two or more allied offenses of similar import, indictment may contain counts for all such offenses, but defendant may be convicted of only one, as defendant committed aggravated robbery by taking victim's purse before he killed her, but he committed grand theft after he left house and drove off in victim's car, such that theft of purse was committed separately from theft of car. State v. Elmore (Ohio, 12-13-2006) 111 Ohio St.3d 515, 857 N.E.2d 547, 2006-Ohio-6207, certiorari denied 127 S.Ct. 2974, 551 U.S. 1133, 168 L.Ed.2d 707, appeal after new sentencing hearing 122 Ohio St.3d 472, 912 N.E.2d 582, 2009-Ohio-3478, certiorari denied 130 S.Ct. 1025, 558 U.S. 1096, 175 L.Ed.2d 627, motion to reopen denied 124 Ohio St.3d 1439, 920 N.E.2d 370, 2010-Ohio-188, denial of post-conviction relief affirmed 2014-Ohio-3674, 2014 WL 4180275. Criminal Law ⚷ 29(11)

Although receiving stolen property is technically not a lesser included offense of theft, receiving stolen property and theft of the same property are allied offenses of similar import, for purposes of statute allowing a conviction for only one of the offenses, if the indictment or information contains counts for allied offenses of similar import. State v. Yarbrough (Ohio, 12-01-2004) 104 Ohio St.3d 1, 817 N.E.2d 845, 2004-Ohio-6087, overturned due to legislative action, reconsideration denied 104 Ohio St.3d 1437, 819 N.E.2d 1121, 2004-Ohio-7079. Receiving Stolen Goods ⚷ 6

20. —— Multiple theft, specific offenses construed

Breaking and entering with intent to commit theft and attempted theft of firearm were allied offenses of similar import so as to require merger; trespass into unoccupied structure with purpose to steal firearm was substantial affirmative act towards commission of theft of firearm and constituted attempt to steal firearm, there was no separate animus, in that defendant admitted that he entered premises with intent to steal firearm, and both were completed by same act. State v. Allen (Ohio App. 3 Dist., 12-15-2014) 2014-Ohio-5483, 2014 WL 7014738. Criminal Law ⚷ 30

21. —— Forgery and uttering, specific offenses construed

Defendant's convictions for one count of possessing criminal tools, one count of tampering with evidence, and thirty counts of forgery were not allied offenses of similar import, for purposes of sentencing statute, and defendant was properly sentenced for all three offenses; when compared in the abstract, offenses did not correspond to the degree that the commission of one would result in the commission of the others, and multiple violations of the same statute are not allied offenses of similar import. State v. Brewster (Ohio App. 1 Dist., Hamilton, 06-11-2004) No. C-030024, No. C-030025, 2004-Ohio-2993, 2004 WL 1284008, Unreported, motion for delayed appeal denied 103 Ohio St.3d 1490, 816 N.E.2d 1078, 2004-Ohio-5605, habeas corpus denied 2007 WL 2688425. Sentencing And Punishment ⚷ 536

Sentence of sixteen years' imprisonment was warranted for defendant convicted of one count of possessing criminal tools, one count of tampering with evidence, and thirty counts of forgery; sentence was within statutory limits, trial court made proper findings to justify sentences imposed and properly stated its reasons for those findings, evidence revealed that defendant and his brother conducted extensive check-forging operation, defendant had a lengthy criminal record for similar offenses, and sentence was less than half of maximum time that he could have received. State v. Brewster (Ohio App. 1 Dist., Hamilton, 06-11-2004) No. C-030024, No. C-030025, 2004-Ohio-2993, 2004 WL 1284008, Unreported, motion for delayed appeal denied 103 Ohio St.3d 1490, 816 N.E.2d 1078, 2004-Ohio-5605, habeas corpus denied 2007 WL 2688425. Sentencing And Punishment ⚷ 645

22. —— Weapons violations and other offenses, specific offenses construed

Trial court improperly imposed three consecutive three-year terms of actual incarceration for firearm specifications on underlying counts of felonious assault and improperly discharging a firearm at or into a habitation; evidence established that defendant fired two shots in rapid succession at an inhabited dwelling in response to inhabitants' verbal attempts at thwarting an attempted burglary, and three felony convictions arose from a single transaction, and thus, defendant could be sentenced to only one three-year term of actual incarceration. State v. Gray (Ohio App. 10 Dist., Franklin, 09-01-2005) No. 04AP-938, 2005-Ohio-4563, 2005 WL 2100595, Unreported, appeal after new sentencing hearing 2006-Ohio-4595, 2006 WL 2567830. Sentencing And Punishment ⚷ 604

For purposes of merger analysis, the discharge of multiple gunshots in quick succession is generally identified as the "same conduct" under the multiple-count statute. State v. Jackson (Ohio App. 9 Dist., 12-18-2013) 5 N.E.3d 116, 2013-Ohio-5557, appeal not allowed 139 Ohio St.3d 1404, 9 N.E.3d 1062, 2014-Ohio-2245. Criminal Law ⚷ 30

Whether improperly discharging a firearm into a habitation merges with other offenses for sentencing purposes is a fact-specific inquiry. State v. Jackson (Ohio App. 9 Dist., 12-18-2013) 5 N.E.3d 116, 2013-Ohio-5557, appeal not allowed 139 Ohio St.3d 1404, 9 N.E.3d 1062, 2014-Ohio-2245. Sentencing and Punishment ⚷ 539

Defendant committed a single act with a single state of mind when he possessed the two guns, and thus, two counts of having weapons while under disability represented allied offenses of similar import that should have been merged for sentencing purposes; defendant's continued possession of the second weapon beyond his initial apprehension was due solely to the police officer's failure to discover the second weapon during the initial pat down at the site of defendant's arrest and the subsequent pat down at the police department. State v. King (Ohio App. 2 Dist., 05-17-2013) 992 N.E.2d 491, 2013-Ohio-2021. Sentencing and Punishment ⚷ 539

Defendant's convictions for possession of criminal tools and dangerous ordnance based on defendant's possession of firebombs, which merged for sentencing purposes, were separate and distinct from defendant's subsequent act of transporting and throwing firebombs into residence and committing crimes of attempted murder and aggravated arson, and thus, defendant's convictions for possession of dangerous tools and dangerous ordinance did not merge into any other of defendant's convictions. State v. Piscura (Ohio App. 8 Dist., 05-02-2013) 991 N.E.2d 709, 2013-Ohio-1793, appeal not allowed 136 Ohio St.3d 1510, 995 N.E.2d 1213, 2013-Ohio-4657, also published at 137 Ohio St.3d 1460, 1 N.E.3d 426, 2013-Ohio-4657. Sentencing and Punishment ⚷ 539

Defendant's convictions for possession of a dangerous ordnance and possessing criminal tools were allied offenses and merged for sentencing purposes, as defendant's conduct of possessing a firebomb was sufficient to support a charge and conviction of both possession of a dangerous ordnance and possessing criminal tools, and state identified under the indictment that the firebomb was both the dangerous ordnance and a criminal tool. State v. Piscura (Ohio App. 8 Dist., 05-02-2013) 991 N.E.2d 709, 2013-Ohio-1793, appeal not allowed 136 Ohio St.3d 1510, 995 N.E.2d 1213, 2013-Ohio-4657, also published at 137 Ohio St.3d 1460, 1 N.E.3d 426, 2013-Ohio-4657. Sentencing and Punishment ⚷ 539

A firearms specification is not "allied" to the underlying crime, for purposes of statute barring multiple convictions for allied offenses of similar import, because the specification is a penalty enhancement, not a criminal offense. State v. Swiergosz (Ohio App. 6 Dist., 03-02-2012) 197 Ohio App.3d 40, 965 N.E.2d 1070, 2012-Ohio-830, appeal not allowed 133 Ohio St.3d 1493, 978 N.E.2d 911, 2012-Ohio-5459, appeal after new sentencing hearing 2013-Ohio-4625, 2013 WL 5728349, appeal not allowed 138 Ohio St.3d 1435, 4 N.E.3d 1051, 2014-Ohio-889. Criminal Law ⚷ 29(15)

23. —— Arson, specific offenses construed

Defendant's conviction for aggravated arson for creating substantial risk of serious physical harm to a person, and conviction for aggravated arson for causing physical harm to an occupied structure were of dissimilar import, such that separate sentences were permissible; although the two counts involved the same fire set by defendant, each offense required proof of an element that the other did not. State v. Campbell (Ohio App. 1 Dist., Hamilton, 12-30-2003) No. C-020822, 2003-Ohio-7149, 2003 WL 23022038, Unreported, appeal not allowed 102 Ohio St.3d 1412, 806 N.E.2d 563, 2004-Ohio-1763, habeas corpus denied 2010 WL 2465374. Sentencing And Punishment ⚷ 517

Convictions for three counts of attempted murder and aggravated arson did not merge for sentencing purposes, where there were three people in the house at the time of the fire, each victim corresponded to one count of attempted murder, and with resect to the aggravated arson conviction, this was for knowingly causing physical harm to house owned by landlords that they leased to attempted murder victims that was separate and apart from attempting to cause the death of the three attempted murder victims. State v. Piscura (Ohio App. 8 Dist., 05-02-2013) 991 N.E.2d 709, 2013-Ohio-1793, appeal not allowed 136 Ohio St.3d 1510, 995 N.E.2d 1213, 2013-Ohio-4657, also published at 137 Ohio St.3d 1460, 1 N.E.3d 426, 2013-Ohio-4657. Sentencing and Punishment ⚿ 529; Sentencing and Punishment ⚿ 540

Three counts of aggravated arson with which defendant was charged were not "allied offenses of similar import," and therefore were not subject to merger, where indictment alleged conduct against two different victims and an occupied structure, and further indicated that only one victim had been bound prior to fire. State v. Garcia (Ohio App. 8 Dist., Cuyahoga, 08-15-2002) No. 79917, 2002-Ohio-4179, 2002 WL 1874535, Unreported, appeal not allowed 98 Ohio St.3d 1411, 781 N.E.2d 1019, 2003-Ohio-60, denial of habeas corpus affirmed 488 F.3d 370, certiorari denied 128 S.Ct. 493, 552 U.S. 994, 169 L.Ed.2d 346. Criminal Law ⚿ 30

26. Miscellaneous offenses

Offenses of driving truck with a tandem axle overload and driving truck with a gross weight overload were allied offenses of similar import, and thus defendant who drove overweight truck could not be convicted of both offenses arising out of a single traffic stop; offenses were both violations of same municipal ordinance and, accordingly, had the same elements. State v. Hassel (Ohio App. 9 Dist., Lorain, 06-07-2006) No. 05CA008760, 2006-Ohio-2849, 2006 WL 1541050, Unreported, appeal not allowed 111 Ohio St.3d 1469, 855 N.E.2d 1258, 2006-Ohio-5625. Criminal Law ⚿ 29(7)

Even if offenses to which defendant pled guilty, aggravated vehicular assault and operating a vehicle while under the influence (OVI), were allied offenses of similar import, sentencing statute specifically permitted cumulative punishments for these crimes such that they were not subject to merger for sentencing purposes, and doing so did not violate defendant's right of protection against double jeopardy. State v. Earley (Ohio App. 8 Dist., 06-19-2014) 15 N.E.3d 357, 2014-Ohio-2643, motion to certify allowed 140 Ohio St.3d 1450, 17 N.E.3d 597, 2014-Ohio-4414, appeal allowed 140 Ohio St.3d 1451, 17 N.E.3d 598, 2014-Ohio-4414. Sentencing and Punishment ⚿ 501

Defendant's convictions for breaking and entering and vandalism were not allied offenses of similar import, as argued by defendant; a conviction for breaking and entering will not necessarily result in a conviction for vandalism, which required physical harm to limited types of property and with a value restriction, and a conviction for vandalism would not necessarily result in a conviction for breaking and entering as the offense of vandalism could be committed on one's own land or on land the offender was privileged to enter. State v. Parker (Ohio App. 3 Dist., 07-27-2009) 2009 -Ohio- 3667, 2009 WL 2231707. Criminal Law ⚿ 29(11)

Trial court was not required to merge convictions for engaging in pattern of corrupt activity and conspiracy to engage in pattern of corrupt activity for purposes of sentencing; General Assembly had specifically provided for separate punishments. State v. DeMastry (Ohio App. 5 Dist., 10-17-2003) 155 Ohio App.3d 110, 799 N.E.2d 229, 2003-Ohio-5588, appeal not allowed 101 Ohio St.3d 1488, 805 N.E.2d 539, 2004-Ohio-1293, appeal not allowed 103 Ohio St.3d 1495, 816 N.E.2d 1081, 2004-Ohio-5605, denial of post-conviction relief affirmed 2005-Ohio-4962, 2005 WL 2300288, appeal not allowed 108 Ohio St.3d 1440, 842 N.E.2d 64, 2006-Ohio-421, habeas corpus dismissed 2007 WL 869695. Conspiracy ⚿ 37

27.5. Evidence

Finding that defendant charged with murder, felonious assault, and shooting into a habitation was one of several shooters was not against manifest weight of the evidence, where defendant was identified by multiple eyewitnesses, forensic evidence established that multiple weapons, including weapon of caliber and manufacturer one witness testified defendant owned, were fired during incident, and questions of credibility, including inconsistencies between and within identification testimony of various eyewitnesses and evidence of plea deal received by one eyewitness, were for resolution by trier of fact. State v. Jackson (Ohio App. 9 Dist., 12-18-2013) 5 N.E.3d 116, 2013-Ohio-5557, appeal not allowed 139 Ohio St.3d 1404, 9 N.E.3d 1062, 2014-Ohio-2245. Criminal Law ⚿ 566; Homicide ⚿ 1181; Homicide ⚿ 1184

28. Appeal

Court of Appeals, on review of trial court's decision that defendant's convictions for failure to comply with a police officer and obstruction of official business did not merge for sentencing purposes, was required to review the entire record, including arguments and information presented at the resentencing hearing, to determine whether the offenses were committed separately or with a separate animus, not merely what it perceived as the state's theory of the case at trial, without consideration of information presented at sentencing hearing. State v. Washington (Ohio, 11-14-2013) 137 Ohio St.3d 427, 999 N.E.2d 661, 2013-Ohio-4982, on remand 2014-Ohio-1876, 2014 WL 1800410. Criminal Law ⚿ 30; Criminal Law ⚿ 1180

Doctrine of judicial estoppel did not apply to prohibit the state from arguing against merger of defendant's convictions for failure to comply with a police officer and obstruction of official business for sentencing purposes at defendant's resentencing hearing, as state's argument at trial was not inconsistent with its argument at resentencing hearing; at trial, state never argued that police car chase was the basis for both the failure-to-comply and obstructing-official-business offenses, but, rather, presented evidence of both the car chase and the subsequent police foot chase of defendant, and it repeatedly referred to both chases during opening statement and closing argument, and, at best, it was unclear whether the state relied on the foot chase to support the obstructing-official-business count. State v. Washington (Ohio, 11-14-2013) 137 Ohio St.3d 427, 999 N.E.2d 661, 2013-Ohio-4982, on remand 2014-Ohio-1876, 2014 WL 1800410. Estoppel ⚷ 68(2)

Sentencing court's failure to determine whether offenses of aggravated burglary and rape, to which defendant had pled guilty, were committed by the same conduct, as required to determine whether offenses merged, was plain error. State v. Bryant (Ohio App. 10 Dist., 11-19-2013) 1 N.E.3d 878, 2013-Ohio-5105. Criminal Law ⚷ 1042.3(1)

Defendant failed to establish on appeal that trial court committed plain error by failing to merge for sentencing two counts of receiving stolen property, where it was unclear from transcript whether two counts were committed with state of mind to commit only one act. State v. Rogers (Ohio App. 8 Dist., 03-21-2013) 990 N.E.2d 1085, 2013-Ohio-1027, on reconsideration 994 N.E.2d 499, 2013-Ohio-3235, motion to certify allowed 136 Ohio St.3d 1508, 995 N.E.2d 1212, 2013-Ohio-4657, also published at 137 Ohio St.3d 1458, 1 N.E.3d 424, 2013-Ohio-4657, motion to certify allowed 137 Ohio St.3d 1456, 1 N.E.3d 423, 2013-Ohio-4657, appeal not allowed 137 Ohio St.3d 1475, 2 N.E.3d 270, 2014-Ohio-176. Criminal Law ⚷ 1042.3(1)

If a defendant who pleads guilty wishes to make an allied offenses argument at sentencing, that defendant has the responsibility in the first instance to ensure that the record contains facts to support that argument; if the defendant fails to do so, any argument on appeal is waived. State v. Rogers (Ohio App. 8 Dist., 03-21-2013) 990 N.E.2d 1085, 2013-Ohio-1027, on reconsideration 994 N.E.2d 499, 2013-Ohio-3235, motion to certify allowed 136 Ohio St.3d 1508, 995 N.E.2d 1212, 2013-Ohio-4657, also published at 137 Ohio St.3d 1458, 1 N.E.3d 424, 2013-Ohio-4657, motion to certify allowed 137 Ohio St.3d 1456, 1 N.E.3d 423, 2013-Ohio-4657, appeal not allowed 137 Ohio St.3d 1475, 2 N.E.3d 270, 2014-Ohio-176. Criminal Law ⚷ 1086.4; Criminal Law ⚷ 1114.1(1)

Trial court's application of merger statute in determining that rape and kidnapping offenses were allied offenses of similar import was subject to de novo standard of review; trial court's determination addressed specific conduct of defendant, which did not give rise to an abuse-of-discretion standard, and while Court of Appeals owed deference to jury's factual determinations, it owed no deference to trial court's application of the law to those facts, and because the decision involved interpretation of merger statute, independent review was necessary to maintain control of, and to clarify, the legal principles embodied in statute. State v. Williams (Ohio, 12-06-2012) 134 Ohio St.3d 482, 983 N.E.2d 1245, 2012-Ohio-5699. Criminal Law ⚷ 1139

At a new sentencing hearing on remand for correction of an allied-offenses sentencing error, the trial court must accept the state's choice among allied offenses, merge the crimes into a single conviction for sentencing, and impose a sentence that is appropriate for the merged offense. State v. Wilson (Ohio, 06-08-2011) 129 Ohio St.3d 214, 951 N.E.2d 381, 2011-Ohio-2669, appeal after new sentencing hearing 2012-Ohio-4159, 2012 WL 4018909, appeal after new sentencing hearing 2013-Ohio-4035, 2013 WL 5310444, appeal after new sentencing hearing 2014-Ohio-4686, 2014 WL 5409112. Criminal Law ⚷ 1192; Sentencing And Punishment ⚷ 501

29. Remand

Remand was required for trial court consideration of whether child endangering count, of which defendant was convicted, was not committed separately and with a separate animus from the aggravated murder charge of which defendant was also committed, as would require merger of defendant's convictions under double jeopardy principles and state multiple-count statute. State v. Grube (Ohio App. 4 Dist., 02-07-2013) 987 N.E.2d 287, 2013-Ohio-692, appeal not allowed 135 Ohio St.3d 1459, 988 N.E.2d 579, 2013-Ohio-2285. Criminal Law ⚷ 30; Criminal Law ⚷ 1181.5(3.1); Double Jeopardy ⚷ 150(1)

Remedy for plain error in trial court's imposition of concurrent sentences for aggravated burglary and two counts of aggravated robbery, where trial court had merged the aggravated burglary with the aggravated robberies, was a remand for a limited resentencing hearing so the prosecution could select whether it wished defendant to be sentenced on the two aggravated robberies but not the aggravated burglary or on the aggravated burglary and one of the aggravated robbery counts. State v. Tapscott (Ohio App. 7 Dist., 09-14-2012) 978 N.E.2d 210, 2012-Ohio-4213, appeal not allowed 134 Ohio St.3d 1451, 982 N.E.2d 729, 2013-Ohio-347. Criminal Law ⚷ 1181.5(8)

Remand court, which merged defendant's convictions for possession of marijuana and trafficking in marijuana, exceeded appellate court's mandate, where appellate court had determined that only the part of defendant's sentence relating to postrelease control was void because it did not specify the duration of postrelease-control supervision and had affirmed the remainder of the sentence. State v. Truitt (Ohio App. 1 Dist., 02-10-2012) 197 Ohio App.3d 758, 968 N.E.2d 637, 2012-Ohio-461, motion for delayed appeal denied 132 Ohio St.3d 1422, 969 N.E.2d 270, 2012-Ohio-2729. Criminal Law ⚷ 1192

In a remand for a new sentencing hearing based only on an allied-offenses sentencing error, the guilty verdicts underlying a defendant's sentences remain the law of the case and are not subject to review. State v. Wilson (Ohio, 06-08-2011) 129 Ohio St.3d 214, 951 N.E.2d 381, 2011-Ohio-2669, appeal after new sentencing hearing 2012-Ohio-4159, 2012 WL 4018909, appeal after new sentencing hearing 2013-Ohio-4035, 2013 WL 5310444, appeal after new sentencing hearing 2014-Ohio-4686, 2014 WL 5409112. Criminal Law ⚷ 1192

PROCEDURE

2941.26 Variance

Notes of Decisions

Federal provisions 4

4. Federal provisions

In prosecution for conspiracy to obstruct justice, trial evidence demonstrated a single conspiracy to obstruct justice, as was alleged in indictment, and thus, no variance occurred; as National Association of Securities Dealers (NASD) launched investigation into insider trading by defendants and coconspirator, coconspirator received list from NASD of suspicious purchasers, including defendants and other coconspirators, within a three-day period that month, coconspirator used his telephone calling card to make calls to defendants and other coconspirators, coconspirator kept track of who was being subpoenaed by Securities and Exchange Commission (SEC), defendant talked with other coconspirators about their subpoenas, and all persons who testified before SEC essentially made same statement. U.S. v. Hughes (C.A.6 (Ohio), 10-26-2007) 505 F.3d 578. Conspiracy ⚷ 43(12)

In prosecution of two defendants for conspiracy to engage in insider trading, even though a variance occurred between the indictment charging defendants with a single conspiracy and trial evidence demonstrating multiple unrelated conspiracies, defendants did not suffer substantial prejudice so as to justify new trial; conspiracy involving defendants was contained within indictment, those claims substantially corresponded to trial evidence, so that defendants would not have been misled by indictment, indictment put them on notice about evidence that would be produced at trial, and although indictment alleged 11 conspirators, only six were tried together, three of whom were part of defendants' conspiracy, and jury instructions adequately protected defendants from guilt transference. U.S. v. Hughes (C.A.6 (Ohio), 10-26-2007) 505 F.3d 578. Criminal Law ⚷ 1167(1)

In prosecution of two defendants for conspiracy to engage in insider trading, the trial evidence demonstrated multiple unrelated conspiracies, resulting in a variance from the indictment charging defendants with a single conspiracy; there was no basis for a reasonable juror to conclude that defendants knew or should have known that coconspirator who provided them with inside information had provided inside information to anyone else, and although government presented evidence of social connections among some conspirators, it did not demonstrate that those individuals discussed the stock market, and there was no evidence that there was any sort of agreement amongst all those named in the conspiracy count of the indictment. U.S. v. Hughes (C.A.6 (Ohio), 10-26-2007) 505 F.3d 578. Conspiracy ⚷ 43(12)

If an indictment alleges one conspiracy, but the evidence can reasonably be construed only as supporting a finding of multiple conspiracies, the resulting variance between the indictment and the proof is reversible error if the appellant can show that he was prejudiced thereby. U.S. v. Hughes (C.A.6 (Ohio), 10-26-2007) 505 F.3d 578. Conspiracy ⚷ 43(12); Criminal Law ⚷ 1167(1)

2941.28 Misjoinder of parties or offenses

Notes of Decisions

Dates 2

1. Misjoinder of offenses

A precise time and date of an alleged offense are ordinarily not essential elements of an indictment, information, complaint or bill of particulars. State v. Blankenburg (Ohio App. 12 Dist., 03-26-2012) 197 Ohio App.3d 201, 966 N.E.2d 958, 2012-Ohio-1289, appeal not allowed 132 Ohio St.3d 1514, 974 N.E.2d 112, 2012-Ohio-4021, denial of post-conviction relief reversed 2012-Ohio-6175, 2012 WL 6738255. Indictment And Information ⚷ 87(7); Indictment And Information ⚷ 121.1(6.1)

Where crimes alleged in the indictment constitute sexual offenses against children, they need not state with specificity the dates of the alleged abuse, so long as the state establishes that the offense was committed within the time frame alleged. State v. Blankenburg (Ohio App. 12 Dist., 03-26-2012) 197 Ohio App.3d 201, 966 N.E.2d 958, 2012-Ohio-1289, appeal not allowed 132 Ohio St.3d 1514, 974 N.E.2d 112, 2012-Ohio-4021, denial of post-conviction relief reversed 2012-Ohio-6175, 2012 WL 6738255. Infants ⚷ 1654

2. Dates

Where the inability to produce in an indictment a specific time or date when the criminal conduct occurred is without material detriment to the preparation of a defense, the omission is without prejudice and without constitutional consequence. State v. Blankenburg (Ohio App. 12 Dist., 03-26-2012) 197 Ohio App.3d 201, 966 N.E.2d 958, 2012-Ohio-1289, appeal not allowed 132 Ohio St.3d 1514, 974 N.E.2d 112, 2012-Ohio-4021, denial of post-conviction relief reversed 2012-Ohio-6175, 2012 WL 6738255. Criminal Law ⇐ 1167(1)

A common situation resulting in prejudice from state's failure to provide specific dates and times in an indictment is where the defendant was indisputably elsewhere during part, but not all, of the intervals of time set out in the indictment. State v. Blankenburg (Ohio App. 12 Dist., 03-26-2012) 197 Ohio App.3d 201, 966 N.E.2d 958, 2012-Ohio-1289, appeal not allowed 132 Ohio St.3d 1514, 974 N.E.2d 112, 2012-Ohio-4021, denial of post-conviction relief reversed 2012-Ohio-6175, 2012 WL 6738255. Criminal Law ⇐ 1167(1)

The state's failure to provide specific dates and times in an indictment is more likely to prejudice an accused in cases in which the age of the victim is an element of the crime charged and the victim bordered on the age required to make the conduct criminal. State v. Blankenburg (Ohio App. 12 Dist., 03-26-2012) 197 Ohio App.3d 201, 966 N.E.2d 958, 2012-Ohio-1289, appeal not allowed 132 Ohio St.3d 1514, 974 N.E.2d 112, 2012-Ohio-4021, denial of post-conviction relief reversed 2012-Ohio-6175, 2012 WL 6738255. Criminal Law ⇐ 1167(1)

Any failure by State to provide specific dates and times in indictment was not plain error in prosecution for corruption of a minor on the basis of sexual conduct with a person who was 13 years of age or older but less than 16 years of age and compelling prostitution on the basis that defendant induced, procured, solicited, or requested a minor to engage in sexual activity for hire, where victim testified that he was able to identify the date once he reviewed his old medical records and remembered the context within which the events occurred, and lack of specific dates did not serve as a material detriment to defendant, who appeared to maintain that no sexual activity ever occurred during the time frame when any victim was a minor. State v. Blankenburg (Ohio App. 12 Dist., 03-26-2012) 197 Ohio App.3d 201, 966 N.E.2d 958, 2012-Ohio-1289, appeal not allowed 132 Ohio St.3d 1514, 974 N.E.2d 112, 2012-Ohio-4021, denial of post-conviction relief reversed 2012-Ohio-6175, 2012 WL 6738255. Criminal Law ⇐ 1032(5)

2941.30 Amending an indictment

Notes of Decisions

3. Allowable amendments

Defendant was not prejudiced by the State's amendment to the indictment prior to trial to accurately reflect the proper county for each offense, in prosecution involving numerous alleged sexual offenses occurring in three counties; the amendment did not affect a material element of the offenses, and the State's bill of particulars had already identified the city in which each offense occurred. State v. Ahmed (Ohio App. 8 Dist., Cuyahoga, 06-16-2005) No. 84220, 2005-Ohio-2999, 2005 WL 1406282, Unreported, appeal not allowed 107 Ohio St.3d 1424, 837 N.E.2d 1208, 2005-Ohio-6124, appeal after new sentencing hearing 2007-Ohio-2639, 2007 WL 1559293, appeal not allowed 115 Ohio St.3d 1474, 875 N.E.2d 628, 2007-Ohio-5735, motion to reopen denied 2007-Ohio-6649, 2007 WL 4341217, appeal not allowed 117 Ohio St.3d 1427, 882 N.E.2d 446, 2008-Ohio-969, certiorari denied 129 S.Ct. 144, 555 U.S. 824, 172 L.Ed.2d 39, certiorari denied 128 S.Ct. 1716, 552 U.S. 1280, 170 L.Ed.2d 514, motion to reopen denied 2008-Ohio-217, 2008 WL 192151, appeal not allowed 118 Ohio St.3d 1462, 888 N.E.2d 1114, 2008-Ohio-2823, certiorari denied 129 S.Ct. 509, 555 U.S. 996, 172 L.Ed.2d 360. Indictment And Information ⇐ 159(3)

CONVICTS

2941.401 Request by a prisoner for trial on pending charges

Notes of Decisions

½. Scope of statute

Ohio speedy-trial statute governing requests by state prisoners for trial on pending charges did not apply to defendant who sought dismissal of a criminal case against him in Ohio on speedy-trial grounds, where defendant was in prison in Kentucky in the custody of the federal government. State v. Barrett (Ohio App. 8 Dist., 10-21-2010) 191 Ohio App.3d 245, 945 N.E.2d 1070, 2010-Ohio-5139. Criminal Law ⇐ 577.11(4)

1. Notice to prisoner of pending charge

An inmate's awareness of a pending indictment and of his right to request trial on the pending charges does not satisfy the notification requirements of statute requiring a warden or prison superintendent to notify a prisoner in writing of the source and contents of any untried indictment, and of his right to make a request for final disposition thereof. State v. Dillon (Ohio, 07-18-2007) 114 Ohio St.3d 154, 870 N.E.2d 1149, 2007-Ohio-3617. Criminal Law ⚷ 577.11(3)

Warden's failure to promptly inform inmate in writing of indictment and his right to request trial violated statute requiring warden or prison superintendent to notify prisoner in writing of source and contents of any untried indictment, and of his right to make a request for final disposition thereof. State v. Dillon (Ohio, 07-18-2007) 114 Ohio St.3d 154, 870 N.E.2d 1149, 2007-Ohio-3617. Criminal Law ⚷ 577.11(3)

Inmate's signing of detainer notifying him that he was wanted by county sheriff upon his release did not satisfy notification requirements of statute requiring warden or prison superintendent to notify prisoner in writing of source and contents of any untried indictment, and of his right to make a request for final disposition thereof, as the detainer did not provide notice of the contents of the indictment or of inmate's right to request speedy disposition of the pending charges. State v. Dillon (Ohio, 07-18-2007) 114 Ohio St.3d 154, 870 N.E.2d 1149, 2007-Ohio-3617. Criminal Law ⚷ 577.11(3)

Prosecutor's oral advisement to inmate that there was a pending indictment against him and that inmate had a duty to demand trial within 180 days did not satisfy statute requiring warden or prison superintendent to notify inmate in writing of source and contents of any untried indictment, and of his right to make a request for final disposition thereof. State v. Dillon (Ohio, 07-18-2007) 114 Ohio St.3d 154, 870 N.E.2d 1149, 2007-Ohio-3617. Criminal Law ⚷ 577.11(3)

2. Request for final disposition

Defendant who had been incarcerated on an unrelated charge substantially complied with statute governing the speedy trial rights of an imprisoned defendant such that he was entitled to dismissal on speedy trial grounds of charge of operating a vehicle under the influence, where defendant sent a letter to the appropriate prosecutor's office and court, notifying them of his location of imprisonment and demanding a final disposition, letter was stamped and signed by prison authorities, defendant attached to the letter the federal court judgment which contained the terms of his sentence, including the dates he was to be imprisoned, and certificate of service indicated that the letter was received. State v. Antos (Ohio App. 8 Dist., Cuyahoga, 02-01-2007) No. 88091, 2007-Ohio-415, 2007 WL 274304, Unreported, appeal not allowed 114 Ohio St.3d 1480, 870 N.E.2d 732, 2007-Ohio-3699. Criminal Law ⚷ 577.10(10)

Days that defendant was in prison for a previous conviction should not have been counted when computing speedy trial time, where defendant failed to request a final disposition of the pending case to trigger the one hundred and eighty day speedy trial requirement under controlling statute. State v. Stewart (Ohio App. 2 Dist., Montgomery, 08-11-2006) No. 21462, 2006-Ohio-4164, 2006 WL 2336629, Unreported. Criminal Law ⚷ 577.11(3)

State prisoner substantially complied with notification procedures set forth in statute governing speedy trial rights of an imprisoned defendant, thus triggering state's responsibility to bring him to trial within 180–day period; although prisoner's motion for speedy trial was not initially served upon proper prosecutor and appropriate court, and he failed to prove that warden received his notice and request for final disposition, State's response in opposition to prisoner's motion proved that notice and request were "cause[d] to be delivered" to it by response date, at latest, and because State was served with notice and request, and was aware of prisoner's status in facility, it was not prejudiced from his failure to prove that warden received notice. State v. Moore (Ohio App. 3 Dist., 11-03-2014) 23 N.E.3d 206, 2014-Ohio-4879. Criminal Law ⚷ 577.10(10); Criminal Law ⚷ 577.11(1)

3. Tolling speedy trial period

Defendant's speedy trial period was not tolled between date capias warrant was issued due to defendant's nonappearance at hearing and date defendant filed motion to dismiss on speedy trial grounds, even though defendant was incarcerated in another county, where both defendant and his attorney informed the court and the prosecutor of defendant's whereabouts, and State failed to exercise reasonable diligence in securing defendant's availability, such as by requesting a transport order. Cleveland Metroparks v. Signorelli (Ohio App. 8 Dist., Cuyahoga, 07-24-2008) No. 90157, 2008-Ohio-3675, 2008 WL 2837779, Unreported. Criminal Law ⚷ 577.11(4)

Delay caused by grant of defense counsel's motion for continuance was attributable to defendant for purposes of determining whether defendant was properly brought to trial within 180 days under statute governing prisoners' speedy trial rights. State v. Shepherd (Ohio App. 11 Dist., Ashtabula, 09-30-2004) No. 2003-A-0031, 2004-Ohio-5306, 2004 WL 2803407, Unreported, denial of post-conviction relief reversed 2011-Ohio-2451, 2011 WL 2112516. Criminal Law ⚷ 577.10(8)

Speedy trial statute governing requests for trial by a prisoner, and not general speedy trial statute, controlled speedy trial period for defendant who was already incarcerated for a separate offense. State v. Pesci (Ohio App. 11 Dist., Lake, 12-20-2002) No. 2001-L-026, 2002-Ohio-7131, 2002 WL 31866167, Unreported, appeal not allowed 98 Ohio St.3d 1566, 787 N.E.2d 1231, 2003-Ohio-2242, appeal from denial of post-conviction relief dismissed 2008-Ohio-1660, 2008 WL 919628, denial of post-conviction relief affirmed 2009-Ohio-6385, 2009 WL 4547766. Criminal Law ⚷ 577.5

In calculating speedy trial period for defendant who was already incarcerated for another offense, time was tolled for defendant's motions to dismiss and motion to suppress. State v. Pesci (Ohio App. 11 Dist., Lake, 12-20-2002) No. 2001-L-026, 2002-Ohio-7131, 2002 WL 31866167, Unreported, appeal not allowed 98 Ohio St.3d 1566, 787 N.E.2d 1231, 2003-Ohio-2242, appeal from denial of post-conviction relief dismissed 2008-Ohio-1660, 2008 WL 919628, denial of post-conviction relief affirmed 2009-Ohio-6385, 2009 WL 4547766. Criminal Law ⚬ 577.10(8)

State's duty to inform defendant who was already incarcerated for a separate offense of his right to make a demand for a speedy disposition was triggered on date of arraignment, and thus, 180-day statutory time limit for bringing defendant to trial commenced on date of arraignment, where warden did not notify defendant of his right to demand a speedy disposition. State v. Pesci (Ohio App. 11 Dist., Lake, 12-20-2002) No. 2001-L-026, 2002-Ohio-7131, 2002 WL 31866167, Unreported, appeal not allowed 98 Ohio St.3d 1566, 787 N.E.2d 1231, 2003-Ohio-2242, appeal from denial of post-conviction relief dismissed 2008-Ohio-1660, 2008 WL 919628, denial of post-conviction relief affirmed 2009-Ohio-6385, 2009 WL 4547766. Criminal Law ⚬ 577.8(2)

Speedy trial period began to run, for purposes of charges of burglary and other offenses against incarcerated defendant, when warden was requested to serve indictment on defendant. State v. Dillon (Ohio, 07-18-2007) 114 Ohio St.3d 154, 870 N.E.2d 1149, 2007-Ohio-3617. Criminal Law ⚬ 577.11(3)

MISCELLANEOUS PROVISIONS

2941.47 Summons on indictments against corporations

Notes of Decisions

Constitutional issues 2

1. Corporate officers' responsibilities

Statute that addresses prosecutions instituted by indictment or information against corporations in the court of common pleas, and directs the clerk of that court to enter a "not guilty" plea on behalf of a corporation that has failed to appear, does not authorize a trial of a corporation in absentia in a criminal proceeding that is initiated by affidavit or complaint in a municipal court.' Cleveland v. Washington Mut. Bank (Ohio, 05-26-2010) 125 Ohio St.3d 541, 929 N.E.2d 1039, 2010-Ohio-2219, on remand 2010-Ohio-2957, 2010 WL 2560074. Corporations And Business Organizations ⚬ 2623

Prosecution of corporate defendant on complaint charging misdemeanor building and housing code violations could not proceed in absentia, when defendant had never appeared in case. Cleveland v. Washington Mut. Bank (Ohio App. 8 Dist., 12-31-2008) 179 Ohio App.3d 692, 903 N.E.2d 384, 2008-Ohio-6956, appeal allowed 122 Ohio St.3d 1409, 907 N.E.2d 1193, 2009-Ohio-2751, affirmed and remanded 125 Ohio St.3d 541, 929 N.E.2d 1039, 2010-Ohio-2219, on remand 2010-Ohio-2957, 2010 WL 2560074. Criminal Law ⚬ 636(1)

2. Constitutional issues

Trial court's conducting of trial in absentia of corporate property owner for building and housing code violations did not violate owner's right to confrontation; owner was informed that trial would proceed if a corporate representative failed to appear, and owner never moved for a continuance or otherwise informed trial court that it was attempting to obtain counsel before the trial date. Cleveland v. Destiny Ventures, L.L.C. (Ohio App. 8 Dist., Cuyahoga, 09-11-2008) No. 91018, 2008-Ohio-4587, 2008 WL 4175026, Unreported, stay granted 120 Ohio St.3d 1439, 897 N.E.2d 670, 2008-Ohio-6376, appeal allowed 121 Ohio St.3d 1407, 902 N.E.2d 32, 2009-Ohio-805, reversed 125 Ohio St.3d 540, 929 N.E.2d 1038, 2010-Ohio-2320. Criminal Law ⚬ 662.70

2941.49 Indictment to be served on accused

Notes of Decisions

2. Service of indictment

Alleged failure to properly serve indictment did not rise to level of plain error, where defendant received copy of indictment, court read charges to defendant, defendant stated he understood charges, and defendant proceeded to plead guilty. State v. Turner (Ohio App. 8 Dist., Cuyahoga, 09-18-2003) No. 81449, 2003-Ohio-4933, 2003 WL 22145816, Unreported, appeal not allowed 101 Ohio St.3d 1422, 802 N.E.2d 154, 2004-Ohio-123. Criminal Law ⚬ 1035(2)

Defendant waived proper service of indictment, where defendant waived right to copy, notice, and reading of indictment at his arraignment and defendant pleaded guilty to charges. State v. Turner (Ohio App. 8 Dist., Cuyahoga, 09-18-2003) No. 81449, 2003-Ohio-4933, 2003 WL 22145816, Unreported, appeal not allowed 101 Ohio St.3d 1422, 802 N.E.2d 154, 2004-Ohio-123. Criminal Law ⚬ 627(7)

2941.51 Person represented shall pay for part of costs if able

(A) Counsel appointed to a case or selected by an indigent person under division (E) of section 120.16 or division (E) of section 120.26 of the Revised Code, or otherwise appointed by the court, except for counsel appointed by the court to provide legal representation for a person charged with a violation of an ordinance of a municipal corporation, shall be paid for their services by the county the compensation and expenses that the trial court approves. Each request for payment shall be accompanied by a financial disclosure form and an affidavit of indigency that are completed by the indigent person on forms prescribed by the state public defender. Compensation and expenses shall not exceed the amounts fixed by the board of county commissioners pursuant to division (B) of this section.

(B) The board of county commissioners shall establish a schedule of fees by case or on an hourly basis to be paid by the county for legal services provided by appointed counsel. Prior to establishing such schedule, the board shall request the bar association or associations of the county to submit a proposed schedule for cases other than capital cases. The schedule submitted shall be subject to the review, amendment, and approval of the board of county commissioners, except with respect to capital cases. With respect to capital cases, the schedule shall provide for fees by case or on an hourly basis to be paid to counsel in the amount or at the rate set by the supreme court pursuant to division (D) of section 120.33 of the Revised Code, and the board of county commissioners shall approve that amount or rate.

With respect to capital cases, counsel shall be paid compensation and expenses in accordance with the amount or at the rate set by the supreme court pursuant to division (D) of section 120.33 of the Revised Code.

(C) In a case where counsel have been appointed to conduct an appeal under Chapter 120. of the Revised Code, such compensation shall be fixed by the court of appeals or the supreme court, as provided in divisions (A) and (B) of this section.

(D) The fees and expenses approved by the court under this section shall not be taxed as part of the costs and shall be paid by the county. However, if the person represented has, or reasonably may be expected to have, the means to meet some part of the cost of the services rendered to the person, the person shall pay the county an amount that the person reasonably can be expected to pay. Pursuant to section 120.04 of the Revised Code, the county shall pay to the state public defender a percentage of the payment received from the person in an amount proportionate to the percentage of the costs of the person's case that were paid to the county by the state public defender pursuant to this section. The money paid to the state public defender shall be credited to the client payment fund created pursuant to division (B)(5) of section 120.04 of the Revised Code.

(E) The county auditor shall draw a warrant on the county treasurer for the payment of such counsel in the amount fixed by the court, plus the expenses that the court fixes and certifies to the auditor. The county auditor shall report periodically, but not less than annually, to the board of county commissioners and to the Ohio public defender commission the amounts paid out pursuant to the approval of the court under this section, separately stating costs and expenses that are reimbursable under section 120.35 of the Revised Code. The board, after review and approval of the auditor's report, may then certify it to the state public defender for reimbursement. The request for reimbursement shall be accompanied by a financial disclosure form completed by each indigent person for whom counsel was provided on a form prescribed by the state public defender. The state public defender shall review the report and, in accordance with the standards, guidelines, and maximums established pursuant to divisions (B)(7) and (8) of section 120.04 of the Revised Code, pay fifty per cent of the total cost, other than costs and expenses that are reimbursable under section 120.35 of the Revised Code, if any, of paying appointed counsel in each county and pay fifty per cent of costs and expenses that are reimbursable under section 120.35 of the Revised Code, if any, to the board.

(F) If any county system for paying appointed counsel fails to maintain the standards for the conduct of the system established by the rules of the Ohio public defender commission pursuant to divisions (B) and (C) of section 120.03 of the Revised Code or the standards established by the state public defender pursuant to division (B)(7) of section 120.04 of the Revised Code, the commission shall notify the board of county commissioners of the county that the county system for paying appointed counsel has failed to comply with its rules. Unless the board corrects the conduct of its appointed counsel system to comply with the rules within ninety days after the date of the notice, the state public defender may deny all or part of the county's reimbursement from the state provided for in this section.

(2014 H 663, eff. 3-23-15; 1999 H 283, eff. 9–29–99; 1997 H 215, eff. 9–29–97; 1995 H 117, eff. 6–30–95; 1985 H 201, eff. 7–1–85; 1984 S 271; 1983 H 291; 1975 H 164; 132 v H 1; 131 v H 362; 128 v 54; 1953 H 1; GC 13439–3)

Uncodified Law

2014 H 663, § 7, eff. 3–23–15, reads:

(A) As used in this section, "lethal injection" means the application of a lethal injection of a drug or a combination of drugs in carrying out a sentence of death.

(B) The intent of the General Assembly in enacting this act is to protect the identities of persons who assist the Department of Rehabilitation and Correction in carrying out a court-ordered sentence of death by lethal injection, in order to protect those persons from harassment and potential physical harm.

(C) It is the intent of the General Assembly in enacting this act to enable the Department of Rehabilitation and Correction to obtain the necessary assistance of persons in carrying out a court-ordered sentence of death by lethal injection or the drugs needed to administer such a sentence.

Historical and Statutory Notes

Amendment Note: 2014 H 663 rewrote division (B), which prior thereto read:

"(B) The board of county commissioners shall establish a schedule of fees by case or on an hourly basis to be paid by the county for legal services provided by appointed counsel. Prior to establishing such schedule, the board shall request the bar association or associations of the county to submit a proposed schedule. The schedule submitted shall be subject to the review, amendment, and approval of the board of county commissioners."

Ohio Administrative Code References

Reimbursement to the counties in capital cases, see OAC 120–1–13

Research References

Encyclopedias

OH Jur. 3d Civil Servants and Other Public Officers and Employees § 504, Duties Regarding Reimbursement of Costs.

OH Jur. 3d Criminal Law: Procedure § 108, Payment of Assigned Counsel.

OH Jur. 3d Criminal Law: Procedure § 109, Payment of Assigned Counsel--Reimbursement by Accused.

OH Jur. 3d Criminal Law: Procedure § 2692, State Payment of Criminal Costs.

Treatises and Practice Aids

Katz & Giannelli, Baldwin's Ohio Practice Criminal Law § 119:6, Financial Sanctions.

Katz & Giannelli, Baldwin's Ohio Practice Criminal Law § 151:1, Affidavit of Defendant's Indigency and Request for Appointment of Counsel.

Katz & Giannelli, Baldwin's Ohio Practice Criminal Law § 151:8, Entry Allowing Counsel Fee in Assigned Case.

Painter & Pollis, Ohio Appellate Practice App. M, Local Appellate Rules.

Notes of Decisions

1. Constitutional issues

Upon conviction for murder, trial court committed reversible error by imposing on defendant costs of confinement and attorney fees of court-appointed counsel without making an affirmative determination on the record that defendant had, or reasonably could be expected to have, the means to pay such fees. State v. Johnson (Ohio App. 6 Dist., Lucas, 03-24-2006) No. L-04-1221, 2006-Ohio-1406, 2006 WL 751348, Unreported, appeal not allowed 110 Ohio St.3d 1441, 852 N.E.2d 189, 2006-Ohio-3862, habeas corpus dismissed 597 F.Supp.2d 747. Costs ⚿ 314; Criminal Law ⚿ 1177.6; Prisons ⚿ 417

2. Reimbursement for cost of assigned counsel

Trial court's failure to make any finding on record that indigent defendant was able to pay costs of court-appointed counsel required reversal of portion of judgment of conviction that imposed costs of court-appointed counsel and remand for further proceedings. State v. Knight (Ohio App. 6 Dist., Sandusky, 09-15-2006) No. S-05-007, 2006-Ohio-4807, 2006 WL 2641738, Unreported. Criminal Law ⚿ 1181.5(6)

Record demonstrated that trial court properly considered whether defendant had or reasonably could be expected to have means to pay all or part of costs of legal services rendered to him before ordering him to pay costs; trial court asked defendant if defendant owned an interest in any real estate, defendant informed court that he owned a house which he intended to sell as soon as possible, and court noted that defendant had been gainfully employed his entire adult life. State v. Estes (Ohio App. 12 Dist., Preble, 10-06-2003) No. CA2002-05-008, 2003-Ohio-5283, 2003 WL 22283503, Unreported, denial of post-conviction relief affirmed 2005-Ohio-5478, 2005 WL 2626194, appeal not allowed 108 Ohio St.3d 1488, 843 N.E.2d 794, 2006-Ohio-962, habeas corpus denied 2009 WL 1362680. Costs ⚖ 314

Sentencing order requiring defendant to pay fees of appointed counsel was plain error in absence of affirmative determination on record that defendant had, or reasonably could be expected to have, means to pay all or some part of costs; after accepting defendant's plea, trial court immediately proceeded to impose sentence, and trial court had no presentence investigation report (PSI) from which to glean information necessary to order payment of counsel costs. State v. Isbell (Ohio App. 12 Dist., Butler, 09-08-2003) No. CA2002-07-160, 2003-Ohio-4751, 2003 WL 22073131, Unreported. Costs ⚖ 314; Criminal Law ⚖ 1042.6

3. Compensation of counsel

Sentencing court must enter a finding that the criminal defendant has the means to pay some part of the cost of attorney services rendered to him and that the determination of ability to pay must be supported by evidence in the record. State v. Williams (Ohio App. 6 Dist., 03-01-2013) 987 N.E.2d 322, 2013-Ohio-726, appeal not allowed 135 Ohio St.3d 1461, 988 N.E.2d 580, 2013-Ohio-2285. Costs ⚖ 314

5. Appeals

Arguable issue existed for appeal in trial court's imposition of costs of court-appointed counsel, and thus defendant's appeal was not wholly frivolous for purposes of defense counsel's request to withdraw pursuant to *Anders v. California,* where there was no indication in the record that defendant had the ability to pay the costs of court-appointed counsel. State v. Knight (Ohio App. 6 Dist., Sandusky, 08-19-2005) No. S-05-007, 2005-Ohio-4347, 2005 WL 2008144, Unreported, appeal decided 2006-Ohio-4807, 2006 WL 2641738. Criminal Law ⚖ 1833(3)

CHAPTER 2943

ARRAIGNMENT; PLEAS

PLEAS

Section

PLEAS

2943.03 Pleas to indictment

Notes of Decisions

1. Constitutional issues

Right to counsel, effective assistance, plea hearing, appearance via speaker phone, habeas corpus relief, see Wright v. Van Patten, 2008, 128 S.Ct. 743.

3. Guilty plea

The law of the case doctrine prevented the Court of Appeals from vacating its prior decision, which vacated defendant's plea to murder, and reinstating defendant's prior plea agreement; the decision of the appellate court in a prior appeal will be followed in a later appeal in the same case in the same court, and defendant failed to demonstrate an extraordinary circumstance that would allow the Court of Appeals to question the finality of its former decision. State v. Prom (Ohio App. 12 Dist., Butler, 05-09-2005) No. CA2004-07-174, 2005-Ohio-2272, 2005 WL 1077238, Unreported, appeal not allowed 106 Ohio St.3d 1536, 835 N.E.2d 384, 2005-Ohio-5146, reconsideration denied 107 Ohio St.3d 1686, 839 N.E.2d 405, 2005-Ohio-6480, habeas corpus denied 2009 WL 1270463. Criminal Law ⚖ 1180

Trial court was not required to enforce defendant's original plea agreement, which was vacated on appeal when her plea to the lesser charge of murder was set aside; the state was allowed to charge defendant with aggravated murder, which defendant was originally indicted for, after her plea was vacated on appeal, since the charge was within the limits of the original indictment. State v. Prom (Ohio App. 12 Dist., Butler, 05-09-2005) No. CA2004-07-174, 2005-Ohio-2272, 2005 WL 1077238, Unreported, appeal not allowed 106 Ohio

St.3d 1536, 835 N.E.2d 384, 2005-Ohio-5146, reconsideration denied 107 Ohio St.3d 1686, 839 N.E.2d 405, 2005-Ohio-6480, habeas corpus denied 2009 WL 1270463. Criminal Law ⚷ 273.1(2)

Defense counsel did not render ineffective assistance of counsel by allowing a heavily medicated defendant to enter guilty pleas to attempted rape and gross sexual imposition, as guilty pleas were entered knowing and voluntarily, as demonstrated by defendant's assurance to trial court that the drugs did not alter his understanding of what was happening. State v. Richter (Ohio App. 11 Dist., Lake, 12-15-2003) No. 2002-L-080, 2003-Ohio-6734, 2003 WL 22941222, Unreported, motion for delayed appeal granted 102 Ohio St.3d 1420, 807 N.E.2d 366, 2004-Ohio-2003, appeal not allowed 103 Ohio St.3d 1425, 814 N.E.2d 489, 2004-Ohio-4524, denial of post-conviction relief affirmed 2004-Ohio-6682, 2004 WL 2860401, appeal not allowed 105 Ohio St.3d 1518, 826 N.E.2d 315, 2005-Ohio-1880, appeal not allowed 106 Ohio St.3d 1509, 833 N.E.2d 1250, 2005-Ohio-4605, habeas corpus dismissed 2007 WL 2572250. Criminal Law ⚷ 1920

Defendant entered his guilty plea to one count of attempted rape and three counts of gross sexual imposition knowingly and voluntarily, even though he was medicated at time of plea hearing; trial court asked defendant if drugs caused him to be lethargic or unable to understand what was happening, to which defendant replied they did not, and provided trial court the correct date and time, before entering a verbal plea of guilty to each charge and signing the guilty plea form. State v. Richter (Ohio App. 11 Dist., Lake, 12-15-2003) No. 2002-L-080, 2003-Ohio-6734, 2003 WL 22941222, Unreported, motion for delayed appeal granted 102 Ohio St.3d 1420, 807 N.E.2d 366, 2004-Ohio-2003, appeal not allowed 103 Ohio St.3d 1425, 814 N.E.2d 489, 2004-Ohio-4524, denial of post-conviction relief affirmed 2004-Ohio-6682, 2004 WL 2860401, appeal not allowed 105 Ohio St.3d 1518, 826 N.E.2d 315, 2005-Ohio-1880, appeal not allowed 106 Ohio St.3d 1509, 833 N.E.2d 1250, 2005-Ohio-4605, habeas corpus dismissed 2007 WL 2572250. Criminal Law ⚷ 273(2)

Trial court could not allow defendant charged with subsequent-offense domestic violence to enter partial guilty plea to single element of having a prior conviction for domestic violence, and subsequently grant defendant's motion in limine to exclude evidence of the prior conviction; under statute and rules governing entry of guilty pleas, defendant could not plead guilty to fewer than all elements charged in indictment, and prior conviction was not merely a sentencing factor but instead was an element of the offense regarding which a bifurcated proceeding was prohibited. State v. Bibler (Ohio App. 3 Dist., 08-04-2014) 17 N.E.3d 1154, 2014-Ohio-3375. Criminal Law ⚷ 273(4.1); Criminal Law ⚷ 632(4)

Defendant's guilty plea to three counts of aggravated murder with death specifications was knowing and intelligent, despite claim that trial court did not ensure that defendant understood the nature of the charges against him, specifically that the trial court should have explained to him the legal definitions of "purposely" and "prior calculation and design"; record of plea hearing contained express representations by defendant and his counsel that the nature of the charges had been explained to him and that he understood them. State v. Fitzpatrick (Ohio, 07-07-2004) 102 Ohio St.3d 321, 810 N.E.2d 927, 2004-Ohio-3167, reconsideration denied 103 Ohio St.3d 1429, 814 N.E.2d 491, 2004-Ohio-4524, denial of post-conviction relief affirmed 2004-Ohio-5615, 2004 WL 2367987, appeal not allowed 105 Ohio St.3d 1499, 825 N.E.2d 623, 2005-Ohio-1666, motion to reopen denied 105 Ohio St.3d 1436, 822 N.E.2d 808, 2005-Ohio-531, certiorari denied 125 S.Ct. 2930, 545 U.S. 1130, 162 L.Ed.2d 869, habeas corpus denied 2009 WL 3734143, certificate of appealability granted in part, denied in part 2010 WL 2761578, affirmed 723 F.3d 624, certiorari denied 134 S.Ct. 1939, 188 L.Ed.2d 965. Criminal Law ⚷ 273.1(4)

Defendant's guilty plea to three counts of aggravated murder with death specifications was voluntary, knowing, and intelligent, despite claim that plea colloquy was inadequate; trial court informed defendant that by pleading guilty, he would waive his privilege against self-incrimination and his rights to confront the State's witnesses before a jury, to subpoena witnesses for the guilt phase, to a jury trial, and to require the State to prove to a jury that he was guilty beyond a reasonable doubt. State v. Fitzpatrick (Ohio, 07-07-2004) 102 Ohio St.3d 321, 810 N.E.2d 927, 2004-Ohio-3167, reconsideration denied 103 Ohio St.3d 1429, 814 N.E.2d 491, 2004-Ohio-4524, denial of post-conviction relief affirmed 2004-Ohio-5615, 2004 WL 2367987, appeal not allowed 105 Ohio St.3d 1499, 825 N.E.2d 623, 2005-Ohio-1666, motion to reopen denied 105 Ohio St.3d 1436, 822 N.E.2d 808, 2005-Ohio-531, certiorari denied 125 S.Ct. 2930, 545 U.S. 1130, 162 L.Ed.2d 869, habeas corpus denied 2009 WL 3734143, certificate of appealability granted in part, denied in part 2010 WL 2761578, affirmed 723 F.3d 624, certiorari denied 134 S.Ct. 1939, 188 L.Ed.2d 965. Criminal Law ⚷ 273.1(4)

2943.031 Court advising defendants on possibility of deportation, exclusion, or denial of naturalization prior to accepting pleas

United States Supreme Court

Counsel,

Padilla rule requiring counsel to advise noncitizen client of deportation consequences of guilty plea does not apply retroactively, see Chaidez v. U.S., 2013, 133 S.Ct. 1103, 185 L.Ed.2d 149. Courts ⚷100(1)

Notes of Decisions

1. Constitutional issues—In general

Defendant's plea of guilty to three counts of trafficking in drugs was not entered into knowingly, intelligently, and voluntarily, where defendant was noncitizen and plea court's advisement of immigration consequences did not satisfy statutory requirements. State v. Lucente (Ohio App. 7 Dist., Mahoning, 03-29-2005) No. 03 MA 216, 2005-Ohio-1657, 2005 WL 775886, Unreported, appeal not allowed 106 Ohio St.3d 1507, 833 N.E.2d 1249, 2005-Ohio-4605. Criminal Law ⚷ 273.1(4)

Even if defense counsel's incorrect advice to defendant prior to his guilty plea to offense of attempting to carry a concealed weapon that the plea would not result in defendant being deported might have fallen below acceptable standards, defendant did not show that he was prejudiced thereby, and, thus, counsel did not render ineffective assistance; trial court clearly explained to defendant that he could be deported after counsel gave his incorrect advice, and, had defendant gone to trial, there was nothing to suggest that he would not have been found guilty. State v. Sok (Ohio App. 1 Dist., 02-23-2007) 170 Ohio App.3d 777, 869 N.E.2d 60, 2007-Ohio-729, appeal not allowed 114 Ohio St.3d 1480, 870 N.E.2d 732, 2007-Ohio-3699. Criminal Law ⚷ 1920

4. Withdrawal of plea—In general

Trial court is required to set aside a conviction and withdraw a guilty plea if defendant establishes that the court failed to provide the warnings described in the statute requiring trial court to advise defendant of immigration consequences of his plea. State v. Sok (Ohio App. 1 Dist., 02-23-2007) 170 Ohio App.3d 777, 869 N.E.2d 60, 2007-Ohio-729, appeal not allowed 114 Ohio St.3d 1480, 870 N.E.2d 732, 2007-Ohio-3699. Criminal Law ⚷ 1482

A defendant who has not received the statutorily-required advisement that he may be deported if he is not a United States citizen and is convicted after pleading guilty may move to set aside the judgment and withdraw his guilty plea; the motion and an appeal from the denial of the motion provide the exclusive remedies for an alleged violation of the provision. State ex rel. McDonald v. Mitrovich (Ohio, 04-04-2007) 113 Ohio St.3d 167, 863 N.E.2d 172, 2007-Ohio-1258. Criminal Law ⚷ 274(3.1)

After inmate exhausted his exclusive remedies for trial court's failure to give him statutorily-required advisement that he could be deported if he was convicted after pleading guilty, by filing motion to withdraw plea and appealing denial of the motion, he could not obtain relief by petition for writ of mandamus. State ex rel. McDonald v. Mitrovich (Ohio, 04-04-2007) 113 Ohio St.3d 167, 863 N.E.2d 172, 2007-Ohio-1258. Mandamus ⚷ 4(4)

6. —— Res judicata, withdrawal of plea

Post-sentencing motion to withdraw guilty plea based upon sentencing court's failure to comply with statute governing advisements to noncitizens of immigration consequences of guilty pleas was not barred on grounds of res judicata by movant's failure directly to appeal such defect in plea process. State v. Lucente (Ohio App. 7 Dist., Mahoning, 03-29-2005) No. 03 MA 216, 2005-Ohio-1657, 2005 WL 775886, Unreported, appeal not allowed 106 Ohio St.3d 1507, 833 N.E.2d 1249, 2005-Ohio-4605. Criminal Law ⚷ 274(9)

7. —— Timeliness, withdrawal of plea

Defendant's motion to withdraw guilty plea, based upon plea court's failure to comply with statutory requirements in advising him of potential immigration consequences of his plea, filed five months after imposition of sentence and four months after initiation of deportation proceedings, was not so untimely as to warrant denial of motion. State v. Lucente (Ohio App. 7 Dist., Mahoning, 03-29-2005) No. 03 MA 216, 2005-Ohio-1657, 2005 WL 775886, Unreported, appeal not allowed 106 Ohio St.3d 1507, 833 N.E.2d 1249, 2005-Ohio-4605. Criminal Law ⚷ 274(9)

9. Court's duty to inform—In general

Fact that state's plea agreement with noncitizen defendant was based in part upon dismissal of charges against defendant's brother did not negate responsibility of plea court to comply with statute governing advisements to noncitizens of immigration consequences of guilty pleas. State v. Lucente (Ohio App. 7 Dist., Mahoning, 03-29-2005) No. 03 MA 216, 2005-Ohio-1657, 2005 WL 775886, Unreported, appeal not allowed 106 Ohio St.3d 1507, 833 N.E.2d 1249, 2005-Ohio-4605. Criminal Law ⚷ 273.1(4)

Plea court's statements to noncitizen defendant at sentencing, following defendant's plea of guilty to three counts of trafficking in drugs, were insufficient to constitute substantial compliance with statute governing advisements to noncitizens of immigration consequences of guilty pleas, where statute required that defendant be informed of immigration consequences prior to acceptance of his plea. State v. Lucente (Ohio App. 7 Dist., Mahoning, 03-29-2005) No. 03 MA 216, 2005-Ohio-1657, 2005 WL 775886, Unreported, appeal not allowed 106 Ohio St.3d 1507, 833 N.E.2d 1249, 2005-Ohio-4605. Criminal Law ⚷ 273.1(4); Sentencing And Punishment ⚷ 422

Plea court was required to advise noncitizen defendant of immigration consequences of his guilty plea, where prior to accepting plea, court asked defendant if he was United States citizen and defendant responded that he was not, signed plea agreement filed with court indicated that defendant was not United States citizen, and guilty plea to crime with which defendant was charged, namely, trafficking in drugs, could result in defendant's deportation. State v. Lucente (Ohio App. 7 Dist., Mahoning, 03-29-2005) No. 03 MA 216, 2005-Ohio-1657, 2005 WL 775886, Unreported, appeal not allowed 106 Ohio St.3d 1507, 833 N.E.2d 1249, 2005-Ohio-4605. Criminal Law ⚷ 273.1(4)

Appellate court would presume regularity in trial court's plea proceedings and find that it fully advised noncitizen defendant during his plea hearing of the potential for deportation on convictions for receiving stolen property, drug trafficking, and drug possession, as required by statute, where defendant failed to file a transcript of his plea hearing with his appeal. State v. Lababidi (Ohio App. 8 Dist., 01-26-2012) 969 N.E.2d 335, 2012-Ohio-267. Criminal Law ⚷ 1144.4

Court of Appeals could not presume regularity in trial court proceedings, but instead was required to presume that defendant had not been advised of the immigration consequences of pleading no-contest to domestic violence charges, and thus defendant's no-contest plea was required to be vacated; defendant stated in affidavit that he had pleaded no contest, that there was no record of proceedings, and that no one had given him statutorily-required immigration advisories, and existing record of proceedings was in conflict as to whether defendant had pleaded no contest or whether defendant had pleaded not guilty and been convicted after a bench trial. Cleveland Hts. v. Roland (Ohio App. 8 Dist., 01-19-2012) 197 Ohio App.3d 661, 968 N.E.2d 564, 2012-Ohio-170. Criminal Law ⚷ 1109(3); Criminal Law ⚷ 1144.4

Statutory provision requiring defendant to be advised of possible deportation consequences has no application when defendant pleads not guilty and is found guilty following jury trial. State v. Arnold (Ohio App. 2 Dist., Clark, 09-20-2002) No. 02CA0002, 2002-Ohio-4977, 2002 WL 31105404, Unreported, denial of post-conviction relief reversed 2008-Ohio-6720, 2008 WL 5273273. Criminal Law ⚷ 300

Under the doctrine of res judicata, the defendant's claim that his guilty plea was not knowing or voluntary, due to the trial court's alleged failure to inform the defendant that a plea would have deportation consequences, merged with the judgment of conviction, and the defendant's failure to directly appeal the judgment precluded his relitigation of the issue by way of a postconviction proceeding. State v. Idowu (Ohio App. 1 Dist., Hamilton, 06-28-2002) No. C-010646, 2002-Ohio-3302, 2002 WL 1393653, Unreported, appeal not allowed 97 Ohio St.3d 1424, 777 N.E.2d 277, 2002-Ohio-5820. Criminal Law ⚷ 1427; Judgment ⚷ 751

10. —— Deficient counsel, court's duty to inform

Trial court's delivery of warning as to immigration consequences of guilty plea did not necessarily cure trial counsel's alleged deficiency, as element of ineffective assistance, in purportedly giving defendant erroneous advice prior to her guilty plea that conviction would not adversely affect her immigration status. State v. Yahya (Ohio App. 10 Dist., Franklin, 11-22-2011) No. 10AP-1190, 2011-Ohio-6090, 2011 WL 5868794, Unreported. Criminal Law ⚷ 1920

11. —— Personally addressing defendant, court's duty to inform

Defendant's no contest plea to felonious assault was not knowing or voluntary, where the trial court failed to inform defendant as to the maximum penalties for felonious assault, and the court failed to advise defendant that the sentence would include a mandatory term of postrelease control. State v. Johnson (Ohio App. 5 Dist., Licking, 03-21-2008) No. 07 CA 35, 2008-Ohio-1348, 2008 WL 757918, Unreported. Criminal Law ⚷ 275.4(1)

Statutory duty to notify defendant of immigration consequences of his plea belongs to trial court, not counsel. State v. Sok (Ohio App. 1 Dist., 02-23-2007) 170 Ohio App.3d 777, 869 N.E.2d 60, 2007-Ohio-729, appeal not allowed 114 Ohio St.3d 1480, 870 N.E.2d 732, 2007-Ohio-3699. Criminal Law ⚷ 273.1(4)

12. —— Review, court's duty to inform

Defendant waived all appellate review other than for plain error of his contention that trial court failed to advise him of immigration consequences of his guilty plea, by failing to raise such issue before trial court. State v. Encarnacion (Ohio App. 12 Dist., Butler, 12-27-2004) No. CA2003-09-225, 2004-Ohio-7043, 2004 WL 2980594, Unreported, on remand 2005 WL 5939996. Criminal Law ⚷ 1031(4)

Following remand upon appellate reversal of trial court's order denying defendant's motion to withdraw his guilty plea, based on court of appeal's determination that trial court failed to properly advise defendant of immigration consequences of plea, trial court properly conducted proceedings on remand according to the law as set out in an intervening decision by the supreme court, rather than as set out by court of appeals, where intervening supreme court decision provided a roadmap for the proper application of the law with respect to advising defendant of immigration consequences of plea. State v. Encarnacion (Ohio App. 12 Dist., 08-28-2006) 168 Ohio App.3d 577, 861 N.E.2d 152, 2006-Ohio-4425. Criminal Law ⚷ 1192

13. —— Written advisement, court's duty to inform

Written advisement of potential immigration consequences of noncitizen defendant's guilty plea, without more, was insufficient to constitute substantial compliance with statute governing advisements to noncitizens of immigration consequences of guilty pleas, where statute required court to personally address defendant and inform him of such consequences. State v. Lucente (Ohio App. 7 Dist., Mahoning, 03-29-2005) No. 03 MA 216, 2005-Ohio-1657, 2005 WL 775886, Unreported, appeal not allowed 106 Ohio St.3d 1507, 833 N.E.2d 1249, 2005-Ohio-4605. Criminal Law ⚷ 273.1(4)

14. —— Use of statutory language, court's duty to inform

Plea court's advisement to noncitizen defendant of immigration consequences of his guilty plea to multiple counts of trafficking in drugs did not substantially comply with statutory requirements, where court stated only that prosecutor had advised that defendant's plea would not likely result in deportation, that court had allotted funds to defense counsel to obtain advice in that regard from attorney who was specialist in that field, and that if such attorney advised that deportation was possibility, court would permit defendant to withdraw plea and go to trial. State v. Lucente (Ohio App. 7 Dist., Mahoning, 03-29-2005) No. 03 MA 216, 2005-Ohio-1657, 2005 WL 775886, Unreported, appeal not allowed 106 Ohio St.3d 1507, 833 N.E.2d 1249, 2005-Ohio-4605. Criminal Law ⚷ 273.1(4)

Trial court's advisement to noncitizen drug defendant with respect to immigration consequences of his guilty plea amounted to plain error, where advisement did not substantially comply with requirements of applicable statute, trial court's failure adequately to inform defendant was obvious defect in proceedings, and such failure affected defendant's substantial rights. State v. Encarnacion (Ohio App. 12 Dist., Butler, 12-27-2004) No. CA2003-09-225, 2004-Ohio-7043, 2004 WL 2980594, Unreported, on remand 2005 WL 5939996. Criminal Law ⚷ 1031(4)

Defendant was not entitled to withdraw guilty plea based on trial court's failure to provide a verbatim recital of the statutorily-required language advising defendant of immigration consequences of plea, where defendant was informed of the possibility that his conviction could result in deportation, defendant told the trial court that he understood that he could be deported as a result of the conviction, there was no evidence to indicate defendant would have pleaded otherwise had he been notified of complete immigration consequences of guilty plea, there was no evidence that defendant had any desire or need to seek readmission should he be deported, and defendant did not provide any evidence that he was not a citizen of the United States. State v. Encarnacion (Ohio App. 12 Dist., 08-28-2006) 168 Ohio App.3d 577, 861 N.E.2d 152, 2006-Ohio-4425. Criminal Law ⚷ 274(3.1)

Upon motion to withdraw guilty plea based on trial court's failure to provide a verbatim recital of the statutorily-required language advising defendant of immigration consequences of plea, trial court must exercise its discretion to determine whether there was substantial compliance under the statute; this discretion refers to the trial court's decisions regarding whether the statutory elements have been established, the timeliness of defendant's motion, and whether the defendant was prejudiced by the court's alleged failure. State v. Encarnacion (Ohio App. 12 Dist., 08-28-2006) 168 Ohio App.3d 577, 861 N.E.2d 152, 2006-Ohio-4425. Criminal Law ⚷ 274(3.1)

15. Federal provisions

Sentence of 63 months' imprisonment, imposed upon defendant who pled guilty to illegal reentry after deportation, was reasonable, where sentence was within properly calculated advisory guidelines range and sentencing court considered statutory sentencing factors. U.S. v. Rodriquez-Gomez (C.A.6 (Ohio), 06-25-2007) No. 06-3540, 238 Fed. Appx. 86, 2007 WL 1837306, Unreported. Aliens, Immigration, And Citizenship ⚷ 799

2943.032 Court to inform defendant prison term may be administratively extended for offenses committed during term before accepting plea

Prior to accepting a guilty plea or a plea of no contest to an indictment, information, or complaint that charges a felony, the court shall inform the defendant personally that, if the defendant pleads guilty or no contest to the felony so charged or any other felony, if the court imposes a prison term upon the defendant for the felony, and if the offender violates the conditions of a post-release control sanction imposed by the parole board upon the completion of the stated prison term, the parole board may impose upon the offender a residential sanction that includes a new prison term of up to nine months.

(2008 H 130, eff. 4-7-09; 1995 S 2, eff. 7–1–96)

Uncodified Law

2008 H 130, § 5, eff. 4–7–09, reads:

The items of law contained in this act, and their applications, are severable. If any item of law contained in this act, or if any application of any item of law contained in this act, is held invalid, the invalidity does not affect other items of law contained in this act and their applications that can be given effect without the invalid item of law or application.

Historical and Statutory Notes

Amendment Note: 2008 H 130 rewrote this section, which prior thereto read:

"Prior to accepting a guilty plea or a plea of no contest to an indictment, information, or complaint that charges a felony, the court shall inform the defendant personally that, if the defendant pleads guilty or no contest to the felony so charged or any other felony and if the court imposes a prison term upon the defendant for the felony, all of the following apply:

"(A) The parole board may extend the stated prison term if the defendant commits any criminal offense under the law of this state or the United States while serving the prison term.

"(B) Any such extension will be done administratively as part of the defendant's sentence in accordance with section 2967.11 of the Revised Code and may be for thirty, sixty, or ninety days for each violation.

"(C) All such extensions of the stated prison term for all violations during the course of the term may not exceed one-half of the term's duration.

"(D) The sentence imposed for the felony automatically includes any such extension of the stated prison term by the parole board.

"(E) If the offender violates the conditions of a post-release control sanction imposed by the parole board upon the completion of the stated prison term, the parole board may impose upon the offender a residential sanction that includes a new prison term up to nine months."

Research References

Encyclopedias

OH Jur. 3d Criminal Law: Procedure § 1010, Felony Cases, Generally.

OH Jur. 3d Criminal Law: Procedure § 1050, Plea by Noncitizen.

Treatises and Practice Aids

Katz & Giannelli, Baldwin's Ohio Practice Criminal Law § 144:1, Plea of Guilty.

Katz & Giannelli, Baldwin's Ohio Practice Criminal Law § 144:2, No Contest Plea.

Katz & Giannelli, Baldwin's Ohio Practice Criminal Law § 43:11, Understanding the Penalty.

Notes of Decisions

Manifest injustice 4

3. Post release control

Trial court was not statutorily required to inform murder defendant at sentencing hearing of possible consequences of his violation of post-release control sanction, where defendant did not plead guilty or no contest, but rather was convicted by a jury. State v. Reid (Ohio App. 2 Dist., Montgomery, 06-15-2012) No. 24841, 2012-Ohio-2666, 2012 WL 2196350, Unreported, motion for delayed appeal granted 133 Ohio St.3d 1410, 975 N.E.2d 1028, 2012-Ohio-4650, cause dismissed 133 Ohio St.3d 1481, 978 N.E.2d 206, 2012-Ohio-5276. Sentencing and Punishment ⚷ 354

Res judicata did not bar defendant's argument on appeal from denial of her motion to withdraw her guilty plea after remand that she did not knowingly enter her guilty plea because trial court failed to advise her of postrelease control, where appellate court, in original appeal, found plain error in trial court's failure to advise defendant of postrelease control. State v. Smith (Ohio App. 8 Dist., Cuyahoga, 08-17-2006) No. 87253, 2006-Ohio-4271, 2006 WL 2374357, Unreported, appeal not allowed 112 Ohio St.3d 1443, 860 N.E.2d 767, 2007-Ohio-152. Judgment ⚷ 751

Defendant did not knowingly enter her plea of guilty to aggravated vehicular homicide, where trial court did not advise defendant of postrelease control before it accepted plea. State v. Smith (Ohio App. 8 Dist., Cuyahoga, 08-17-2006) No. 87253, 2006-Ohio-4271, 2006 WL 2374357, Unreported, appeal not allowed 112 Ohio St.3d 1443, 860 N.E.2d 767, 2007-Ohio-152. Criminal Law ⚷ 273.1(4)

Trial court's failure to address post-release control issue as it pertained to offenses to which defendant was pleading guilty, attempted theft of a motor vehicle and felonious assault, rendered guilty plea invalid; post-release control constituted portion of maximum penalty involved, without which explanation defendant could not fully understand the consequences of his plea. State v. Douglas (Ohio App. 8 Dist., Cuyahoga, 02-09-2006) No. 85525, No. 85526, 2006-Ohio-536, 2006 WL 302134, Unreported, appeal after new trial 2007-Ohio-2625, 2007 WL 1559545, motion to reopen granted 2007-Ohio-5941, 2007 WL 3286902, appeal after new sentencing hearing 2009-Ohio-1068, 2009 WL 626090, appeal not allowed 122 Ohio St.3d 1481, 910 N.E.2d 479, 2009-Ohio-3625, habeas corpus denied 2011 WL 666715, motion to reopen denied 2012-Ohio-3799, 2012 WL 3629603, motion to reopen denied 2008-Ohio-3133, 2008 WL 2536061. Criminal Law ⚷ 273.1(4)

4. Manifest injustice

A noncitizen criminal defendant is not required to show manifest injustice when seeking to withdraw a guilty plea. State v. Lababidi (Ohio App. 8

Dist., 01-26-2012) 969 N.E.2d 335, 2012-Ohio-267. Criminal Law ⚷ 274(3.1)

2943.033 Notice of firearm prohibitions

(A) As used in this section, "person living as a spouse" means a person who is living or has lived with the defendant in a common law marital relationship, who otherwise is cohabiting with the defendant, or who otherwise has cohabited with the defendant within five years prior to the date of the alleged commission of the act in question.

(B) The notice required under division (C) of this section shall be provided to a defendant when the alleged victim is any of the following:

(1) A spouse, person living as a spouse, or former spouse of the defendant;

(2) A parent or child of the defendant;

(3) A parent or child of a spouse, person living as a spouse, or former spouse of the defendant;

(4) The natural parent of any child of whom the defendant is the other natural or putative natural parent.

(C) Prior to accepting a guilty plea or plea of no contest to an indictment, information, or complaint that charges a person with a misdemeanor offense of violence, the court shall inform the defendant either personally or in writing that under 18 U.S.C. 922(g)(9) it may be unlawful for the person to ship, transport, purchase, or possess a firearm or ammunition as a result of any conviction for a misdemeanor offense of violence. The plea may not be vacated based on a failure to inform the person so charged regarding the restrictions under 18 U.S.C. 922(g)(9).

(2008 H 562, eff. 6–24–08)

Research References

Treatises and Practice Aids

Adrine & Ruden, Ohio Domestic Violence Law App. B, Rules of Superintendence for the Courts of Ohio.

Adrine & Ruden, Ohio Domestic Violence Law § 18:11, Firearm Offenses Under VAWA.

Adrine & Ruden, Ohio Domestic Violence Law § 18:13, Domestic Violence and Firearm Prohibition.

2943.04 Form of plea

Notes of Decisions

1. Guilty pleas

Defendant's guilty plea to kidnapping and rape was knowingly, voluntarily, and intelligently entered; although defendant argued that trial judge's discussion of evidence and penalties attached to counts coupled with his direct recommendation that defendant "should consider a plea" had a coercive effect that rendered his plea involuntary, trial judge's comments taken in their entirety did not reveal belief by judge that trial would be futile or that judge would be biased against defendant at trial. State v. Jabbaar (Ohio App. 8 Dist., 04-25-2013) 991 N.E.2d 290, 2013-Ohio-1655, motion to reopen denied 2013-Ohio-2897, 2013 WL 3421794, motion for delayed appeal denied 137 Ohio St.3d 1457, 1 N.E.3d 424, 2013-Ohio-4657. Criminal Law ⚷ 273.1(2)

5. Variance of plea from charge in indictment

Trial court's plain error in accepting defendant's guilty plea on charge of receiving stolen property, in violation of rule prohibiting amendment of indictment when the amendment changes the identity of the offense, was invited error, and thus did not warrant reversal of conviction, since defendant negotiated for the amended indictment and agreed to plead guilty to the amended charge. State v. Rohrbaugh (Ohio, 07-20-2010) 126 Ohio St.3d 421, 934 N.E.2d 920, 2010-Ohio-3286. Criminal Law ⚷ 1137(8)

Trial court's plain error, in accepting defendant's guilty plea on charge of receiving stolen property, in violation of rule prohibiting amendment of indictment when the amendment changes the identity of the offense, did not cause a miscarriage of justice and thus did not require reversal of conviction; defendant was not prejudiced by the amendment to the indictment, but gained a benefit when the prosecution dismissed six charges against him, amended charge of receiving stolen property and the original charge of breaking and entering were both felonies of the fifth degree, and defendant was represented by counsel and signed a statement that he had reviewed and understood the amended indictment. State v. Rohrbaugh (Ohio, 07-20-2010) 126 Ohio St.3d 421, 934 N.E.2d 920, 2010-Ohio-3286. Criminal Law ⇐ 1032(1)

Trial court's acceptance of defendant's plea of guilty to charge of receiving stolen property changed the name or identity of the crime charged in the indictment, breaking and entering, in violation of rule governing amendment of indictment, was plain error. State v. Rohrbaugh (Ohio, 07-20-2010) 126 Ohio St.3d 421, 934 N.E.2d 920, 2010-Ohio-3286. Criminal Law ⇐ 1032(1); Indictment and Information ⇐ 159(2)

CHAPTER 2945

TRIAL

PRELIMINARY PROVISIONS

Section

TRIAL BY COURT

TRIAL PROCEDURE

TRIAL BY JURY

INSANITY

WITNESSES

Cross References

Authority of department of mental health and addiction services, see 5119.141

Mental health and addiction services director, see 5119.10

PRELIMINARY PROVISIONS

2945.02 Setting and continuing cases

Notes of Decisions

5. —— Availability of witnesses, continuance denied

Trial court acted within its discretion in refusing to grant defendant's request for a further continuance, despite defendant's claim that such continuance was necessary to secure testimony of eyewitnesses; defendant's request for continuance occurred during trial, trial court provided a two-hour continuance, and defendant failed to indicate how eyewitnesses would have testified. State v. Rose (Ohio App. 8 Dist., Cuyahoga, 04-29-2004) No. 82635, 2004-Ohio-2151, 2004 WL 906022, Unreported, appeal not allowed 103 Ohio St.3d 1464, 815 N.E.2d 679, 2004-Ohio-5056, habeas corpus denied 2009 WL 1212478. Criminal Law ⚷ 649(2)

Trial court acted within its discretion in refusing to grant continuance when murder defendant's arson expert died two days before defense began presentation of its case; delay in middle of trial would have placed jurors out of court's control for great deal of time, and defense called another expert who had inspected home with expert who died. State v. Franklin (Ohio, 10-16-2002) 97 Ohio St.3d 1, 776 N.E.2d 26, 2002-Ohio-5304, denial of post-conviction relief affirmed 2002-Ohio-2370, 2002 WL 1000415, appeal not allowed 98 Ohio St.3d 1422, 782 N.E.2d 77, 2003-Ohio-259, reconsideration denied 101 Ohio St.3d 1462, 804 N.E.2d 37, 2004-Ohio-823, appeal not allowed 108 Ohio St.3d 1475, 842 N.E.2d 1054, 2006-Ohio-665, certiorari denied 127 S.Ct. 362, 549 U.S. 878, 166

L.Ed.2d 136, reconsideration denied 97 Ohio St.3d 1486, 780 N.E.2d 288, 2002-Ohio-6866, stay granted 97 Ohio St.3d 1491, 780 N.E.2d 597, 2002-Ohio-7045, certiorari denied 123 S.Ct. 2249, 539 U.S. 905, 156 L.Ed.2d 115, denial of post-conviction relief affirmed 2005-Ohio-1361, 2005 WL 678925, appeal not allowed 106 Ohio St.3d 1464, 830 N.E.2d 1170, 2005-Ohio-3490, certiorari denied 126 S.Ct. 1352, 546 U.S. 1179, 164 L.Ed.2d 64, habeas corpus denied 2009 WL 649581, subsequent determination 2009 WL 2243384, certificate of appealability granted in part, denied in part 2009 WL 5167764, affirmed 695 F.3d 439. Criminal Law ⚷ 594(1)

Trial court acted within its discretion in refusing to grant continuance when murder defendant's arson expert died two days before defense began presentation of its case; delay in middle of trial would have placed jurors out of court's control for great deal of time, and defense called another expert who had inspected home with expert who died. State v. Franklin (Ohio, 10-16-2002) 97 Ohio St.3d 1, 776 N.E.2d 26, 2002-Ohio-5304, denial of post-conviction relief affirmed 2002-Ohio-2370, 2002 WL 1000415, appeal not allowed 98 Ohio St.3d 1422, 782 N.E.2d 77, 2003-Ohio-259, reconsideration denied 101 Ohio St.3d 1462, 804 N.E.2d 37, 2004-Ohio-823, appeal not allowed 108 Ohio St.3d 1475, 842 N.E.2d 1054, 2006-Ohio-665, certiorari denied 127 S.Ct. 362, 549 U.S. 878, 166 L.Ed.2d 136, reconsideration denied 97 Ohio St.3d 1486, 780 N.E.2d 288, 2002-Ohio-6866, stay granted 97 Ohio St.3d 1491, 780 N.E.2d 597, 2002-Ohio-7045, certiorari denied 123 S.Ct. 2249, 539 U.S. 905, 156 L.Ed.2d 115, denial of post-conviction relief affirmed 2005-Ohio-1361, 2005 WL 678925, appeal not allowed 106 Ohio St.3d 1464, 830 N.E.2d 1170, 2005-Ohio-3490, certiorari denied 126 S.Ct. 1352, 546 U.S. 1179, 164 L.Ed.2d 64, habeas corpus denied 2009 WL 649581, subsequent determination 2009 WL 2243384, certificate of appealability granted in part, denied in part 2009 WL 5167764, affirmed 695 F.3d 439. Criminal Law ⚷ 594(1)

9. —— Timeliness of motion, continuance denied

Trial court denial of defendant's motion for a continuance of capital murder trial, which was made on the day before voir dire began, was not an abuse of discretion; defendant gave counsel a list of approximately 60 witnesses the day before voir dire began, the list did not contain addresses or telephone numbers for the witnesses, the witness list contained a number of people who lived in Pakistan, and defendant did not offer a summary of what the testimony of the witnesses would have been. State v. Ahmed (Ohio, 08-25-2004) 103 Ohio St.3d 27, 813 N.E.2d 637, 2004-Ohio-4190, reconsideration denied 103 Ohio St.3d 1496, 816 N.E.2d 1081, 2004-Ohio-5605, certiorari denied 125 S.Ct. 1703, 544 U.S. 952, 161 L.Ed.2d 531, rehearing denied, rehearing denied 125 S.Ct. 2901, 545 U.S. 1124, 162 L.Ed.2d 312, denial of post-conviction relief affirmed 2006-Ohio-7069, 2006 WL 3849862, appeal not allowed 113 Ohio St.3d 1513, 866 N.E.2d 512, 2007-Ohio-2208, motion to reopen denied 118 Ohio St.3d 1406, 886 N.E.2d 870, 2008-Ohio-2340. Criminal Law ⚷ 590(1)

11. Speedy trial

Continuance of 49 days for Government to procure witness served ends of justice and thus, was excludable from 70-day speedy trial period governing prosecution for conspiracy to distribute and possess with intent to distribute controlled substance and unlawful use of communications facility; Government learned of witness ten days before scheduled date of trial, witness was in state custody in Louisiana, and therefore continuance was necessary to procure witness, transport him to Ohio, appoint counsel for witness, and to interview him, and witness would have provided either important corroborating evidence for Government's case or exculpatory evidence for defendant. U.S. v. Nelson (C.A.6 (Ohio), 06-20-2007) No. 06-3027, 238 Fed. Appx. 65, 2007 WL 1805669, Unreported. Criminal Law ⚷ 577.10(6)

2945.03 Control of trial

Notes of Decisions

---

1. Relevant and material evidence

While statute grants prosecution and defense opportunity to conduct a reasonable examination of prospective jurors, trial court reserves right and responsibility to control proceedings, and must limit trial to relevant and material matters with a view toward expeditious and effective ascertainment of truth. State v. Getsy (Ohio, 12-23-1998) 84 Ohio St.3d 180, 702 N.E.2d 866, 1998-Ohio-533, reconsideration denied 84 Ohio St.3d 1488, 705 N.E.2d 368, certiorari denied 119 S.Ct. 2407, 527 U.S. 1042, 144 L.Ed.2d 805, dismissal of post-conviction relief affirmed 1999 WL 1073682, dismissed, appeal not allowed 88 Ohio St.3d 1425, 723 N.E.2d 1113, habeas corpus granted 456 F.3d 575, rehearing granted, opinion vacated, denial of habeas corpus affirmed 495 F.3d 295. Jury ⚷ 131(1)

Trial court did not improperly limit voir dire of prospective jurors during capital murder prosecution; while court attempted to keep voir dire moving, counsel were rarely limited in questioning jurors, and court did not unreasonably or arbitrarily restrict examination of individual jurors. State v. Getsy (Ohio, 12-23-1998) 84 Ohio St.3d 180, 702 N.E.2d 866, 1998-Ohio-533, reconsideration denied 84 Ohio St.3d 1488, 705 N.E.2d 368, certiorari denied 119 S.Ct. 2407, 527 U.S. 1042, 144 L.Ed.2d 805, dismissal of post-conviction relief affirmed

1999 WL 1073682, dismissed, appeal not allowed 88 Ohio St.3d 1425, 723 N.E.2d 1113, habeas corpus granted 456 F.3d 575, rehearing granted, opinion vacated, denial of habeas corpus affirmed 495 F.3d 295. Jury ⚿ 131(4)

2. Fair trial—In general

Time limit on voir dire imposed by trial judge, allotting each side one-half hour to question each prospective juror, did not deprive defendant of the requisite latitude in voir dire questioning so as to amount to an abuse of discretion; defense counsel did not object to the time allotment or request more time to question a juror during voir dire, and trial court's statement to defense counsel that he had fourteen minutes left in questioning that juror was in response to defense counsel's inquiry as to the time. State v. Cornwell (Ohio, 09-22-1999) 86 Ohio St.3d 560, 715 N.E.2d 1144, 1999-Ohio-125, stay granted 87 Ohio St.3d 1414, 717 N.E.2d 714, stay revoked 98 Ohio St.3d 1475, 784 N.E.2d 709, 2003-Ohio-980, certiorari denied 120 S.Ct. 1200, 528 U.S. 1172, 145 L.Ed.2d 1103, denial of post-conviction relief affirmed 2002-Ohio-5177, 2002 WL 31160861, appeal not allowed 98 Ohio St.3d 1413, 781 N.E.2d 1020, 2003-Ohio-60, denial of habeas corpus affirmed 2009 WL 605232. Jury ⚿ 131(4)

5. —— Judge's comments, fair trial

Trial court's allegedly berating comments to defense counsel, which were at times biting, did not violate defendant's constitutional right to fair trial; trial court admonished both the state and defense counsel equally, trial court gave cautionary instruction to jury regarding court's comments to counsel both after the comments were made and before jury deliberations began, and trial court's remarks in no way directly or even impliedly expressed an opinion as to merits of case, and instead, trial court was trying to limit defense counsel's cross-examination to relevant and material matters in order to keep the proceedings moving. State v. Jackson (Ohio App. 11 Dist., Ashtabula, 12-31-2008) No. 2007-A-0079, 2008-Ohio-6976, 2008 WL 5428259, Unreported, stay granted 120 Ohio St.3d 1523, 901 N.E.2d 244, 2009-Ohio-614, appeal allowed 121 Ohio St.3d 1449, 904 N.E.2d 900, 2009-Ohio-1820, remanded 122 Ohio St.3d 1235, 913 N.E.2d 453, 2009-Ohio-4087, reconsideration denied 123 Ohio St.3d 1426, 123 Ohio St.3d 1427, 914 N.E.2d 1066, 2009-Ohio-5340, on remand 2010-Ohio-820, 2010 WL 759193. Criminal Law ⚿ 655(5)

Trial court's restrictions on and interruptions of voir dire did not impair capital murder defendant's ability to use peremptory challenges effectively to remove prospective jurors or otherwise impair his defense, where trial court was not unduly restrictive, but rather balanced its obligation to control inquiry with according counsel latitude in questioning prospective jurors, and where court's only restrictions on particular areas of inquiry were well within its discretion. State v. Gross (Ohio, 10-30-2002) 97 Ohio St.3d 121, 776 N.E.2d 1061, 2002-Ohio-5524, reconsideration denied 97 Ohio St.3d 1486, 780 N.E.2d 288, 2002-Ohio-6866, certiorari denied 123 S.Ct. 2079, 538 U.S. 1037, 155 L.Ed.2d 1068, rehearing denied 124 S.Ct. 20, 539 U.S. 976, 156 L.Ed.2d 685, denial of post-conviction relief affirmed 2003-Ohio-6295, 2003 WL 22765845, appeal not allowed 102 Ohio St.3d 1410, 806 N.E.2d 562, 2004-Ohio-1763, certiorari denied 125 S.Ct. 165, 543 U.S. 888, 160 L.Ed.2d 149, dismissal of post-conviction relief affirmed 2006-Ohio-6941, 2006 WL 3804532, appeal not allowed 113 Ohio St.3d 1468, 864 N.E.2d 654, 2007-Ohio-1722, habeas corpus dismissed 2008 WL 4702181, motion to amend denied 2008 WL 4889626, certificate of appealability denied 2008 WL 5190017, affirmed 426 Fed.Appx. 349, 2011 WL 1597659. Jury ⚿ 131(4)

6. —— Media coverage, fair trial

While the presence of the media in the courtroom may address the societal need for public trials, it cannot act as an absolute substitute where it cannot be determined from the record that the media was present for the entire duration of the closure. Drummond v. Houk (N.D.Ohio, 12-31-2010) 761 F.Supp.2d 638, affirmed 728 F.3d 520, vacated 134 S.Ct. 1934, 188 L.Ed.2d 957. Criminal Law ⚿ 635.3

7. —— Closure of courtroom, fair trial

Ohio state trial court did not set forth reviewable findings justifying partial closure of courtroom during capital murder trial related to alleged gang–related activities, as required for closure to avoid violation of defendant's Sixth Amendment right to public trial; no witness testified as to any specific threat, only potential juror who felt threatened was dismissed for cause during jury selection, perpetrators of two prior courtroom incidents were known to court but were not specifically excluded from courtroom, and there were no incidents on morning that court ordered closure. Drummond v. Houk (N.D.Ohio, 12-31-2010) 761 F.Supp.2d 638, affirmed 728 F.3d 520, vacated 134 S.Ct. 1934, 188 L.Ed.2d 957. Criminal Law ⚿ 635.11(5)

Ohio state trial court did not adequately consider alternatives prior to ordering partial closure of courtroom during capital murder trial related to alleged gang–related activities, as required for closure to avoid violation of defendant's Sixth Amendment right to public trial; court provided only flat rejection, without explanation, of proposed alternative of allowing defendant's family to attend and, although perpetrators of two courtroom incidents were known to court, it did not consider simply excluding those two individuals. Drummond v. Houk (N.D.Ohio, 12-31-2010) 761 F.Supp.2d 638, affirmed 728 F.3d 520, vacated 134 S.Ct. 1934, 188 L.Ed.2d 957. Criminal Law ⚿ 635.9(3); Criminal Law ⚿ 635.9(5)

Partial closure of courtroom during Ohio capital murder trial related to alleged gang–related activities was more broad than necessary to ensure that jurors and witnesses were protected from violence and retaliation by courtroom spectators; court made no specific findings as to who felt threatened by whom, provided no reason to explain exclusion of defendant's family members, and, although duration of closure was limited to one cross–examination and two full examinations, court did not consider importance of that testimony in making its decision. Drummond v. Houk (N.D.Ohio, 12-31-2010) 761 F.Supp.2d 638, affirmed 728 F.3d 520, vacated 134 S.Ct. 1934, 188 L.Ed.2d 957. Criminal Law ⚷ 635.6(4); Criminal Law ⚷ 635.9(3)

Ohio state trial court made only blanket assertion of need to protect jurors and witnesses from potential violence and retaliation by courtroom spectators in capital murder trial related to alleged gang-related activities, and thus court did not have substantial interest required to warrant partial closure of courtroom; court made no specific inquiries on record about who was feeling threatened by whom, one juror who could be identified as having been threatened was dismissed for cause and did not participate at trial, and perpetrators of two incidents were known to court and could have been individually excluded from courtroom. Drummond v. Houk (N.D.Ohio, 12-31-2010) 761 F.Supp.2d 638, affirmed 728 F.3d 520, vacated 134 S.Ct. 1934, 188 L.Ed.2d 957. Criminal Law ⚷ 635.6(4); Criminal Law ⚷ 635.9(3)

TRIAL BY COURT

2945.05 Defendant may waive jury trial

Notes of Decisions

Waiver to be in open court 15

---

1. Constitutional issues—In general

Defendant's waiver of jury trial, made on the record during meeting in judge's chambers prior to beginning of assault trial, was not made in "open court" and thus not valid under statute governing waiver, since statutory open-court requirement was strict and prophylactic. State v. Burnside (Ohio App. 2 Dist., 03-26-2010) 2010 -Ohio- 1235, 2010 WL 1138963. Jury ⚷ 29(6)

While it may be better practice for the trial judge to enumerate all the possible implications of a waiver of a jury, there is no error in failing to do so. State v. Sanders (Ohio App. 10 Dist., 07-22-2010) 188 Ohio App.3d 452, 935 N.E.2d 905, 2010-Ohio-3433, appeal not allowed 127 Ohio St.3d 1462, 938 N.E.2d 364, 2010-Ohio-6008, reconsideration denied 127 Ohio St.3d 1551, 941 N.E.2d 806, 2011-Ohio-647. Jury ⚷ 29(6)

A defendant need not have a complete or technical understanding of the jury-trial right in order to knowingly and intelligently waive it. State v. Sanders (Ohio App. 10 Dist., 07-22-2010) 188 Ohio App.3d 452, 935 N.E.2d 905, 2010-Ohio-3433, appeal not allowed 127 Ohio St.3d 1462, 938 N.E.2d 364, 2010-Ohio-6008, reconsideration denied 127 Ohio St.3d 1551, 941 N.E.2d 806, 2011-Ohio-647. Jury ⚷ 29(6)

2. —— Effective assistance of counsel, constitutional issues

Habeas petitioner's appellate counsel was not constitutionally ineffective for failing to challenge petitioner's jury waiver on appeal, as required to establish cause for procedural default of petitioner's claim that his waiver was not voluntary, knowingly, and intelligently made; trial court did inquire as to whether petitioner voluntarily signed jury waiver, and petitioner's second trial attorney, who was in the jail cell with petitioner when he signed the jury waiver form, testified that he explained to petitioner that only three individuals were needed to convict him as opposed to a 12 member jury. Haliym v. Mitchell (C.A.6 (Ohio), 07-13-2007) 492 F.3d 680, rehearing and rehearing en banc denied. Habeas Corpus ⚷ 406

Ohio Supreme Court's decision denying habeas petitioner's untimely application to reopen appeal from judgment of conviction and sentence based on claim of ineffective assistance of appellate counsel, finding that there was "no genuine issue," was a decision on the merits, and therefore petitioner was not barred from demonstrating that his appellate counsel's failure to raise the issue constituted cause for the procedural default of his claim challenging the validity of petitioner's waiver of right to a jury trial. Haliym v. Mitchell (C.A.6 (Ohio), 07-13-2007) 492 F.3d 680, rehearing and rehearing en banc denied. Habeas Corpus ⚷ 423

Appellate counsel's failure to challenge trial court's jurisdiction based on the court's failure to file signed jury waiver form was not constitutionally ineffective, as would warrant habeas relief; although current Ohio law required strict compliance with rule requiring that waiver of trial by jury must be filed by the court in order for court to have jurisdiction, at the time of defendant's appeal, the necessity of strict compliance with the rule was uncertain. Haliym v. Mitchell (C.A.6 (Ohio), 07-13-2007) 492 F.3d 680, rehearing and rehearing en banc denied. Habeas Corpus ⚷ 486(5)

4. —— Duty of court, procedure for written waiver

Trial court fulfilled statutory requirements related to waiver of jury trial right; jury waiver was filed before state rested its case and well before jury verdict, trial court asked defendant whether he understood what he was doing and whether he wanted to waive jury trial, defendant responded affirmatively, and court informed defendant of potential punishment. State v. Lowe (Ohio App. 8 Dist., Cuyahoga, 09-02-2004) No. 82997, 2004-Ohio-4622, 2004 WL 1944785, Unreported, appeal not allowed 104 Ohio St.3d 1461, 821 N.E.2d 578, 2005-Ohio-204, motion to reopen denied 2005-Ohio-5986, 2005 WL 3007146, habeas corpus denied in part, dismissed in part 2008 WL 728365. Jury ⚷ 29(6)

Trial court's failure to strictly comply with mandates of code governing waiver of jury trials by failing to afford pro se defendant opportunity to consult with attorney prior to his waiver of jury trial amounted to prejudicial error. State v. Reese (Ohio App. 11 Dist., Trumbull, 12-31-2003) No. 2002-T-0068, 2004-Ohio-341, 2003 WL 23097097, Unreported, stay granted 101 Ohio St.3d 1457, 803 N.E.2d 830, 2004-Ohio-642, appeal allowed 102 Ohio St.3d 1457, 809 N.E.2d 32, 2004-Ohio-2569, reversed 106 Ohio St.3d 65, 831 N.E.2d 983, 2005-Ohio-3806, habeas corpus denied 2007 WL 2733842. Criminal Law ⚷ 1166(1)

Trial court's failure to strictly comply with mandates of code governing waiver of jury trials by failing to afford pro se defendant opportunity to consult with attorney prior to his waiver of jury trial resulted in an improper waiver. State v. Reese (Ohio App. 11 Dist., Trumbull, 12-31-2003) No. 2002-T-0068, 2004-Ohio-341, 2003 WL 23097097, Unreported, stay granted 101 Ohio St.3d 1457, 803 N.E.2d 830, 2004-Ohio-642, appeal allowed 102 Ohio St.3d 1457, 809 N.E.2d 32, 2004-Ohio-2569, reversed 106 Ohio St.3d 65, 831 N.E.2d 983, 2005-Ohio-3806, habeas corpus denied 2007 WL 2733842. Jury ⚷ 29(6)

Trial court failed to strictly comply with mandates of code governing waiver of jury trials by failing to afford pro se defendant opportunity to consult with attorney prior to his waiver of jury trial. State v. Reese (Ohio App. 11 Dist., Trumbull, 12-31-2003) No. 2002-T-0068, 2004-Ohio-341, 2003 WL 23097097, Unreported, stay granted 101 Ohio St.3d 1457, 803 N.E.2d 830, 2004-Ohio-642, appeal allowed 102 Ohio St.3d 1457, 809 N.E.2d 32, 2004-Ohio-2569, reversed 106 Ohio St.3d 65, 831 N.E.2d 983, 2005-Ohio-3806, habeas corpus denied 2007 WL 2733842. Jury ⚷ 29(6)

Trial court fulfilled all the statutory requirements for defendant's waiving trial by jury, and thus, court had jurisdiction to try the defendant without a jury; defendant signed his jury waiver before the beginning of his trial, defendant's counsel stated in open court that defendant was willing to waive trial by jury, defendant acknowledged the waiver and stated in open court that he was willing to waive trial by jury, and trial court filed the signed jury waiver eight days later and included it as part of the record. State v. Huber (Ohio App. 8 Dist., Cuyahoga, 10-24-2002) No. 80616, 2002-Ohio-5839, 2002 WL 31401616, Unreported, appeal not allowed 98 Ohio St.3d 1490, 785 N.E.2d 473, 2003-Ohio-1189, motion to reopen denied 2003-Ohio-3210, 2003 WL 21419177, on remand 2004 WL 5578185, motion to reopen denied 2004-Ohio-3951, 2004 WL 1681261, appeal after new sentencing hearing 2005-Ohio-2625, 2005 WL 1245629. Jury ⚷ 29(6)

Procedural requirements for waiving the right to a trial by jury are satisfied as long as the signed writing waiving the right has been made a part of the record and the waiver is reaffirmed in open court. State v. Strickland (Ohio App. 8 Dist., 08-06-2009) 183 Ohio App.3d 602, 918 N.E.2d 170, 2009-Ohio-3906, appeal not allowed 124 Ohio St.3d 1416, 919 N.E.2d 215, 2009-Ohio-6816, habeas corpus denied 2012 WL 2119304. Jury ⚷ 29(6)

Trial court complied at bench trial with requirements for waiver of right to trial by jury, where trial court read written jury waiver form to defendant and defendant confirmed that he wanted to waive trial by jury, written waiver was made part of the record, waiver bore defendant's signature attested to by defense counsel, and neither defendant nor defense counsel objected to commencement of trial or asserted at trial that defendant had not signed the form. State v. Strickland (Ohio App. 8 Dist., 08-06-2009) 183 Ohio App.3d 602, 918 N.E.2d 170, 2009-Ohio-3906, appeal not allowed 124 Ohio St.3d 1416, 919 N.E.2d 215, 2009-Ohio-6816, habeas corpus denied 2012 WL 2119304. Jury ⚷ 29(6)

To satisfy the statutory "in open court" requirement for waiver of a jury trial, there must be some evidence in the record that the defendant, while in the courtroom and in the presence of counsel, if any, acknowledged the jury waiver to the trial court. State v. Lomax (Ohio, 09-05-2007) 114 Ohio St.3d 350, 872 N.E.2d 279, 2007-Ohio-4277. Jury ⚷ 29(6)

A waiver of the right to a trial by jury must not only be made in writing, signed by the defendant, and filed as a part of the record, but must also be made in open court. State v. Lomax (Ohio, 09-05-2007) 114 Ohio St.3d 350, 872 N.E.2d 279, 2007-Ohio-4277. Jury ⚷ 29(6)

Trial court's passing reference to a jury waiver was insufficient to meet statutory requirement that a waiver of the right to a jury trial must be made in open court, where court's only reference to waiver was its statement "since there's going to be a jury waiver," when inquiring whether the State would make an opening statement. State v. Lomax (Ohio, 09-05-2007) 114 Ohio St.3d 350, 872 N.E.2d 279, 2007-Ohio-4277. Jury ⚷ 29(6)

A trial court does not need to engage in an extended colloquy with a defendant in order to comply with the statutory requirement that a jury waiver be made in open court; however, there must be some evidence in the record of the proceedings that the defendant acknowledged the waiver to the trial court while in the presence of counsel, if any. State v. Lomax (Ohio, 09-05-2007) 114 Ohio St.3d 350, 872 N.E.2d 279, 2007-Ohio-4277. Jury ⚷ 29(6)

A written waiver of the right to trial by jury is presumptively voluntary, knowing, and intelligent. State v. Lomax (Ohio, 09-05-2007) 114 Ohio St.3d 350, 872 N.E.2d 279, 2007-Ohio-4277. Jury ⚷ 29(6)

Requiring a colloquy between the trial court and a defendant who wishes to waive the right to a jury trial ensures voluntary, knowing, and intelligent waivers, promotes judicial economy by avoiding challenges to the validity of waivers on appeal, and emphasizes to the defendant the seriousness of the decision, and while the questioning of the defendant does not need to be extensive, it must at least be sufficient to show that the waiver is knowing, voluntary, and intelligent. State v. Lomax (Ohio App. 1 Dist., 03-24-2006) 166 Ohio App.3d 555, 852 N.E.2d 205, 2006-Ohio-1373, appeal allowed 110 Ohio St.3d 1438, 852 N.E.2d 187, 2006-Ohio-3862, affirmed 114 Ohio St.3d 350, 872 N.E.2d 279, 2007-Ohio-4277. Jury ⚷ 29(6)

5. —— Execution of waiver form, procedure for written waiver

Defendant failed to show that his waiver of his right to a jury trial with respect to the charge of having a weapon under disability was not voluntarily, knowingly, and intelligently made; record contained defendant's written waiver of a jury trial, and defendant did not dispute that this written waiver was properly executed. State v. Daniel (Ohio App. 10 Dist., Franklin, 08-31-2006) No. 05AP-564, No. 05AP-683, 2006-Ohio-4627, 2006 WL 2573500, Unreported, motion to certify allowed 112 Ohio St.3d 1417, 859 N.E.2d 557, 2006-Ohio-6712, appeal allowed 112 Ohio St.3d 1418, 859 N.E.2d 558, 2006-Ohio-6712, certified question answered, affirmed 116 Ohio St.3d 31, 876 N.E.2d 528, 2007-Ohio-5551, habeas corpus denied 2009 WL 1212262, appeal from denial of post-conviction relief dismissed 2009-Ohio-2082, 2009 WL 1175623, denial of post-conviction relief affirmed 2009-Ohio-2161, 2009 WL 1263653, appeal not allowed 122 Ohio St.3d 1505, 912 N.E.2d 109, 2009-Ohio-4233, habeas corpus dismissed 2009 WL 2058591, habeas corpus dismissed 2009 WL 2591676, certificate of appealability denied 2009 WL 4283207, habeas corpus dismissed 2010 WL 1416992, habeas corpus dismissed 2010 WL 3258395, habeas corpus dismissed 2012 WL 2562428, certificate of appealability denied 2012 WL 4442740. Jury ⚷ 29(6)

Defendant was not required to execute written waiver of right to jury trial in open court, and waiver executed in writing prior to entering courtroom and acknowledged by him in open court as knowing, intelligent and voluntary, was satisfactory. State v. Johnson (Ohio App. 8 Dist., Cuyahoga, 08-12-2004) No. 83117, 2004-Ohio-4229, 2004 WL 1795318, Unreported, appeal not allowed 104 Ohio St.3d 1461, 821 N.E.2d 577, 2005-Ohio-204, habeas corpus denied 2007 WL 2128344. Jury ⚷ 29(6)

Trial court's failure to execute defendant's waiver of trial by jury in open court, or to file a contemporaneous journal entry that noted defendant's waiver, did not render waiver of jury trial invalid; statute only required that a signed waiver form be filed. State v. Phillips (Ohio App. 8 Dist., Cuyahoga, 02-05-2004) No. 82886, 2004-Ohio-484, 2004 WL 226120, Unreported, appeal not allowed 103 Ohio St.3d 1404, 812 N.E.2d 1287, 2004-Ohio-3980, habeas corpus denied 2008 WL 141928. Jury ⚷ 29(6)

7. —— Jurisdiction, procedure for written waiver

Trial court lacked jurisdiction to conduct bench trial on charge for possession of methamphetamine, where defendant did not execute written waiver of right to jury trial. State v. Henson (Ohio App. 4 Dist., Highland, 05-31-2006) No. 05CA13, 2006-Ohio-2861, 2006 WL 1544728, Unreported. Jury ⚷ 29(6)

Three-judge panel lacked subject matter jurisdiction to accept defendant's guilty pleas to two counts of aggravated murder with mass murder and felony murder specifications, as both counts still contained death penalty specifications, and defendant had not signed waiver of his right to jury trial. State v. Carley (Ohio App. 8 Dist., 09-25-2000) 139 Ohio App.3d 841, 745 N.E.2d 1122, on remand 2002 WL 34271327. Criminal Law ⚷ 273(4.1); Jury ⚷ 29(4)

9. —— Time requirements, procedure for written waiver

Defendant validly waived his right to jury trial, even though waiver was not signed in open court and waiver may not have been filed until trial was over; trial court conducted lengthy colloquy with defendant regarding his waiver of jury trial at forefront of trial, and waiver was in writing, signed by defendant, filed and journalized in the case, and made a part of the record. State v. Kiriazis (Ohio App. 8 Dist., Cuyahoga, 02-05-2004) No. 82887, 2004-Ohio-502, 2004 WL 231478, Unreported, appeal not allowed 102 Ohio St.3d 1485, 810 N.E.2d 968, 2004-Ohio-3069, habeas corpus denied 2007 WL 4355355, affirmed 410 Fed.Appx. 958, 2011 WL 504191. Jury ⚷ 29(6)

Habeas petitioner's claim that trial court was without jurisdiction to try him because jury waiver form was not filed with the court was procedurally defaulted; petitioner did not raise his improperly filed jury waiver claim on direct appeal, as required by Ohio procedural law, and instead raised the claim for the first time in his post-conviction proceedings. Haliym v. Mitchell (C.A.6 (Ohio), 07-13-2007) 492 F.3d 680, rehearing and rehearing en banc denied. Habeas Corpus ⚷ 366

12. Capital cases

Record did not support capital murder defendant's claim that his jury waiver was not knowing, intelligent and voluntary due to fact that he was accidentally shocked with stun belt on morning of trial and was on medication as a result; record did not indicate voltage level of stun belt, court took recess after stun belt incident for remainder of morning, defendant's three attorneys, one of whom was a physician, never indicated that defendant would not be able to waive his right to jury, and defense counsel never asked court to revisit jury waiver issue. State v. Filiaggi (Ohio, 07-29-1999) 86 Ohio St.3d 230, 714 N.E.2d 867, 1999-Ohio-99, certiorari denied 120 S.Ct. 821, 528 U.S. 1090, 145

L.Ed.2d 691, denial of habeas corpus affirmed 445 F.3d 851. Jury ⚖ 29(6)

14. Bench trial

Trial court's mere reference that there was going to be jury waiver, without some colloquy with defendant to determine whether waiver was knowing, voluntary and intelligent, did not establish that waiver of right to jury trial was made in open court, as required to confer trial court with jurisdiction to conduct bench trial in prosecution for murder. State v. Lomax (Ohio App. 1 Dist., 03-24-2006) 166 Ohio App.3d 555, 852 N.E.2d 205, 2006-Ohio-1373, appeal allowed 110 Ohio St.3d 1438, 852 N.E.2d 187, 2006-Ohio-3862, affirmed 114 Ohio St.3d 350, 872 N.E.2d 279, 2007-Ohio-4277. Jury ⚖ 29(6)

Habeas petitioner's claim that his election to waive his right to a jury and instead be tried by a three-judge court was not knowing, voluntary, and intelligent was procedurally defaulted; petitioner failed to comply with Ohio's rule requiring that such a claim must be raised on direct appeal. Haliym v. Mitchell (C.A.6 (Ohio), 07-13-2007) 492 F.3d 680, rehearing and rehearing en banc denied. Habeas Corpus ⚖ 366

15. Waiver to be in open court

Trial court satisfied the "open court" requirement in statute governing jury-trial waivers by stating to defendant in open court that it was court's understanding that defendant had waived his right to a jury trial and would like to have the court decide the case, to which defendant responded "yes"; trial court was not required to engage in further questioning about defendant's understanding of his rights or to inform defendant of his jury-trial rights. State v. Sanders (Ohio App. 10 Dist., 07-22-2010) 188 Ohio App.3d 452, 935 N.E.2d 905, 2010-Ohio-3433, appeal not allowed 127 Ohio St.3d 1462, 938 N.E.2d 364, 2010-Ohio-6008, reconsideration denied 127 Ohio St.3d 1551, 941 N.E.2d 806, 2011-Ohio-647. Jury ⚖ 29(6)

2945.06 Jurisdiction of judge when jury trial is waived; three–judge court

Law Review and Journal Commentaries

"Oh, by the way . . . ": Why the Supreme court of Ohio lost its way in State of Ohio v. Fischer, 128 Ohio St. 3d 92 (2010). Ryan J. McGraw, 80 U. Cin. L. Rev. 567 (2011).

Notes of Decisions

2. —— Habeas corpus relief, constitutional issues

Any Fourteenth Amendment violation in state court's failure to make independent findings prior to entering sentence on defendant's state court guilty plea, in accordance with order of federal district court, did not render judgment invalid for purposes of running of filing period for federal habeas petition. Frazier v. Moore (C.A.6 (Ohio), 10-17-2007) No. 06-4532, 252 Fed.Appx. 1, 2007 WL 3037256, Unreported. Habeas Corpus ⚖ 603.5

Assuming that state trial court judgment entering sentence following defendant's plea of guilty to aggravated murder and in accordance with order of federal district court was defective under state law by reason of having been entered by one judge rather than panel of three judges, such acceptance was nevertheless sufficient to constitute "judgment" for purposes of statute of limitations for filing federal petition for writ of habeas corpus, where prior to entry of such judgment defendant reaffirmed his plea and again waived his right to jury trial, and state court expressly accepted that plea was knowing, voluntary, and intelligent. Frazier v. Moore (C.A.6 (Ohio), 10-17-2007) No. 06-4532, 252 Fed.Appx. 1, 2007 WL 3037256, Unreported. Habeas Corpus ⚖ 603.5

5. Waiver—In general

Defendant waived any challenge to judge presiding over case selecting three-judge panel, rather than presiding judge of the common pleas court selecting the panel, in capital murder prosecution, where defendant never objection to the selection process. State v. Osie (Ohio, 07-10-2014) 140 Ohio St.3d 131, 16 N.E.3d 588, 2014-Ohio-2966. Criminal Law ⚖ 1035(1)

State waived objection to petitioner's presentation of theory not raised in state postconviction proceedings to support claim that his waiver of jury, in favor of three-judge panel, for capital murder trial was ineffective, by telling district court that it did not object to new testimony of neuropsychologist supporting claim. Sowell v. Bradshaw (C.A.6 (Ohio), 06-23-2004) 372 F.3d 821, rehearing en banc denied, certiorari denied 125 S.Ct. 1645, 544 U.S. 925, 161 L.Ed.2d 485, on remand 557 F.Supp.2d 843. Habeas Corpus ⚖ 816

7. —— Jurisdiction, waiver

Three-judge panel lacked subject matter jurisdiction to accept defendant's guilty pleas to two counts of aggravated murder with mass murder and felony murder specifications, as both counts still contained death penalty specifications, and defendant had not signed waiver of his right to jury trial. State v. Carley (Ohio App. 8 Dist., 09-25-2000) 139 Ohio App.3d 841, 745 N.E.2d 1122, on remand 2002 WL 34271327. Criminal Law ⚖ 273(4.1); Jury ⚖ 29(4)

9. Three-judge panel—In general

Judge's unobjected-to appointment of other two judges of three-judge panel, rather than reserving appointment decision for Presiding Judge or Chief Justice of Common Pleas Court or Chief Justice of Supreme Court, was not plain error in capital murder prosecution in which defendant waived jury trial; defendant could not show that appointment of different members to three-judge panel would have changed outcome of proceeding, both of panelists served as members of County Court of Common Pleas, and nothing suggested that either was ineligible or unqualified to hear case. State v. Wesson (Ohio, 10-23-2013) 137 Ohio St.3d 309, 999 N.E.2d 557, 2013-Ohio-4575, motion to stay mandate denied, reconsideration denied 137 Ohio St.3d 1444, 999 N.E.2d 698, 2013-Ohio-5678, certiorari denied 134 S.Ct. 2311, 189 L.Ed.2d 191. Criminal Law ⚷ 260.4

Judge who was appointed to preside over defendant's trial and who was neither presiding judge nor chief justice of County Court of Common Pleas lacked authority to designate the other two members of the three-judge panel in capital murder prosecution in which defendant waived a jury; judge was required to reserve appointment decision for Presiding Judge or Chief Justice of Common Pleas Court or Chief Justice of the Supreme Court. State v. Wesson (Ohio, 10-23-2013) 137 Ohio St.3d 309, 999 N.E.2d 557, 2013-Ohio-4575, motion to stay mandate denied, reconsideration denied 137 Ohio St.3d 1444, 999 N.E.2d 698, 2013-Ohio-5678, certiorari denied 134 S.Ct. 2311, 189 L.Ed.2d 191. Courts ⚷ 70; Criminal Law ⚷ 247

When a defendant pleads guilty to aggravated murder in a capital case, a three-judge panel is required. State v. Parker (Ohio, 06-26-2002) 95 Ohio St.3d 524, 769 N.E.2d 846, 2002-Ohio-2833, reconsideration denied 96 Ohio St.3d 1489, 774 N.E.2d 764, 2002-Ohio-4478, habeas corpus dismissed 2009 WL 803597. Criminal Law ⚷ 273(4.1)

10. —— Culpability hearing, three-judge panel

Three-judge panel fully complied with statutory requirements when conducting hearing to determine guilt and to pronounce sentence following defendant's guilty plea to two counts of aggravated murder, where panel heard testimony and accepted exhibits regarding offenses to which defendant had pled. State v. Hughes (Ohio App. 8 Dist., Cuyahoga, 01-16-2003) No. 81019, 2003-Ohio-166, 2003 WL 125252, Unreported, appeal not allowed 99 Ohio St.3d 1436, 789 N.E.2d 1117, 2003-Ohio-2902, habeas corpus denied 2007 WL 2834636, motion to amend denied 2007 WL 3376653, denial of post-conviction relief affirmed 2013-Ohio-1566, 2013 WL 1697495. Criminal Law ⚷ 273(4.1)

11. —— Duty of court, three-judge panel

The failure of a court to convene a three-judge court in a capital murder case, as required by statute, does not constitute a lack of subject-matter jurisdiction that renders the trial court's judgment void ab initio and subject to collateral attack by extraordinary writ. State ex rel. Ketterer v. Oney (Ohio, 05-09-2007) 113 Ohio St.3d 306, 865 N.E.2d 44, 2007-Ohio-1954. Sentencing And Punishment ⚷ 1774

In capital murder case in which defendant waived jury, three-judge panel was to determine all charges against defendant, including those for non-capital offenses, and defendant could not waive three-judge panel as to non-capital charges; thus, where presiding judge alone had determined all non-capital charges against defendant, remand was necessary to permit three-judge panel to decide those charges. State v. Filiaggi (Ohio, 07-29-1999) 86 Ohio St.3d 230, 714 N.E.2d 867, 1999-Ohio-99, certiorari denied 120 S.Ct. 821, 528 U.S. 1090, 145 L.Ed.2d 691, denial of habeas corpus affirmed 445 F.3d 851. Criminal Law ⚷ 249; Criminal Law ⚷ 260.12

12. —— Jurisdiction, three-judge panel

Presiding judge of the common pleas court, rather than judge presiding over the trial, selected three-judge panel, as required by statute, in capital murder prosecution, where, although the judge presiding over the trial presided over the hearing at which the panel members were drawn, the presiding judge of the common pleas court signed the journal entry that actually appointed the panel members. State v. Osie (Ohio, 07-10-2014) 140 Ohio St.3d 131, 16 N.E.3d 588, 2014-Ohio-2966. Courts ⚷ 70

Statutory three-judge-panel requirement for capital cases in which defendant has waived his right to a jury is a jurisdictional matter that cannot be waived. State v. Parker (Ohio, 06-26-2002) 95 Ohio St.3d 524, 769 N.E.2d 846, 2002-Ohio-2833, reconsideration denied 96 Ohio St.3d 1489, 774 N.E.2d 764, 2002-Ohio-4478, habeas corpus dismissed 2009 WL 803597. Criminal Law ⚷ 254.1

13. —— Rights of defendant, three-judge panel

Capital defendant who opted to be tried before a three-judge panel rather than a jury waived for appellate review his challenge to judge's appointment of the other two judges of the panel, rather than reserving appointment decision for Presiding Judge or Chief Justice of Common Pleas Court or Chief Justice of Supreme Court; defendant executed an amended jury waiver in open court immediately after judge explained that he would designate members of panel, and journal entry confirmed that court had constituted panel as selected and approved by counsel for defendant, and defendant never objected to the procedure. State v. Wesson (Ohio, 10-23-2013) 137 Ohio St.3d 309, 999 N.E.2d 557, 2013-Ohio-4575, motion to stay mandate denied, reconsideration denied 137 Ohio St.3d 1444, 999 N.E.2d 698, 2013-Ohio-5678, certiorari denied 134 S.Ct. 2311, 189 L.Ed.2d 191. Criminal Law ⚷ 260.4

An alleged violation of the statute, providing for trial by three-judge court if jury trial is waived, is not cognizable in an extraordinary writ action, and may be remedied only in a direct appeal from a criminal conviction. State ex rel. Ketterer v. Oney (Ohio, 05-09-2007) 113 Ohio St.3d 306, 865 N.E.2d 44, 2007-Ohio-1954. Prohibition ⚷ 3(4)

Defendant charged with a crime punishable by death who had waived his right to trial by jury had to have his case heard and decided by a three-judge panel, even though the state agreed that it would not seek the death penalty, as the state did not delete the death penalty specification, such that defendant was still charged with offense punishable with death, and therefore, a single trial judge lacked authority to accept defendant's plea; abrogating *State v Griffin,* 73 Ohio App.3d 546, 597 N.E.2d 1178. State v. Parker (Ohio, 06-26-2002) 95 Ohio St.3d 524, 769 N.E.2d 846, 2002-Ohio-2833, reconsideration denied 96 Ohio St.3d 1489, 774 N.E.2d 764, 2002-Ohio-4478, habeas corpus dismissed 2009 WL 803597. Criminal Law ⚿ 273(4.1)

15. Guilty plea

Statutory requirements applicable to guilty pleas in death penalty cases were not applicable to defendant who, although initially on trial for aggravated murder in death penalty case, pled guilty to lesser offense of murder that did not contain a death penalty specification. State v. Moncrief (Ohio App. 10 Dist., Franklin, 09-11-2008) No. 08AP-153, 2008-Ohio-4594, 2008 WL 4174106, Unreported, appeal not allowed 120 Ohio St.3d 1508, 900 N.E.2d 624, 2009-Ohio-361, habeas corpus denied 2012 WL 3078682, affirmed, denial of post-conviction relief affirmed 2013-Ohio-4571, 2013 WL 5636129. Criminal Law ⚿ 273(4.1)

Trial court was not required to convene three-judge panel when it accepted defendant's guilty pleas to murder, kidnapping, aggravated burglary, and two counts of felonious assault; statute requiring convening of three-judge panel if defendant has been charged with crime punishable by death or has pleaded guilty to aggravated murder did not apply in defendant's case, as defendant was no longer charged with offense punishable by death at time he entered his guilty pleas. State v. West (Ohio App. 9 Dist., Lorain, 03-09-2005) No. 04CA008554, 2005-Ohio-990, 2005 WL 544820, Unreported, appeal not allowed 106 Ohio St.3d 1484, 832 N.E.2d 737, 2005-Ohio-3978, habeas corpus denied 2007 WL 2780506. Criminal Law ⚿ 273(4.1)

Although trial court received defendant's guilty plea to aggravated murder before dismissing death specifications, court considered the plea to be tendered only, and it was only subsequent to court's proper dismissal of death specifications, that court "accepted" defendant's plea and entered its finding of guilt as to the remaining counts and specifications, and consequently, when court entered its finding of guilt, defendant was no longer charged with an offense punishable by death, and therefore, statute providing that, if accused is charged with offense punishable with death, he shall be tried by a court to be composed of three judges was not applicable, and thus, single judge possessed jurisdiction to take the plea. State v. Jones (Ohio App. 6 Dist., Williams, 03-07-2003) No. WM-02-012, 2003-Ohio-1037, 2003 WL 859506, Unreported, appeal not allowed 116 Ohio St.3d 1414, 876 N.E.2d 970, 2007-Ohio-6140, habeas corpus dismissed 2008 WL 4849319. Criminal Law ⚿ 273(4.1)

The state is required to prove guilt of an aggravated-murder charge with death specifications even when an accused pleads guilty. State v. Ketterer (Ohio, 10-25-2006) 111 Ohio St.3d 70, 855 N.E.2d 48, 2006-Ohio-5283, reconsideration denied 112 Ohio St.3d 1409, 858 N.E.2d 819, 2006-Ohio-6447, appeal reopened 113 Ohio St.3d 1463, 864 N.E.2d 650, 2007-Ohio-1722, on remand 2007 WL 4286446, certiorari denied 127 S.Ct. 2266, 550 U.S. 942, 167 L.Ed.2d 1105. Criminal Law ⚿ 273.2(2); Sentencing And Punishment ⚿ 1754

16. Single-judge court

Petitioner for postconviction relief from capital murder conviction had adequate remedy, by way of appeal from single judge's ruling on the petition, as to denial, by single judge, of his motion to reconvene, for purposes of ruling on the petition, the three-judge trial court panel that had sentenced him to death, and thus, petitioner was not entitled to writ of prohibition. State ex rel. Ketterer v. Oney (Ohio, 05-09-2007) 113 Ohio St.3d 306, 865 N.E.2d 44, 2007-Ohio-1954. Prohibition ⚿ 3(4)

Alleged violation of statute governing waiver of jury trials, arising from acceptance of a guilty plea in a capital case by a single judge rather than a three-judge panel, was not a proper subject for habeas corpus relief and could be remedied only in a direct appeal from a criminal conviction. State ex rel. Frazier v. Brigano (Ohio, 05-12-2004) 102 Ohio St.3d 148, 807 N.E.2d 346, 2004-Ohio-2139, certiorari denied 125 S.Ct. 340, 543 U.S. 934, 160 L.Ed.2d 238. Habeas Corpus ⚿ 475.1

Although death penalty was never available as a sentencing option for 16-year-old defendant, due to his age, prosecution charging defendant with aggravated murder and aggravated robbery with specifications that would have made him eligible for the death penalty had he been an adult was required to be heard by a three-judge panel, as jurisdictional matter that could not be waived. State v. Koger (Ohio App. 6 Dist., 02-07-2003) 151 Ohio App.3d 534, 784 N.E.2d 780, 2003-Ohio-576, appeal allowed 99 Ohio St.3d 1451, 790 N.E.2d 1217, 2003-Ohio-3396, affirmed 102 Ohio St.3d 263, 809 N.E.2d 661, 2004-Ohio-2824, appeal after new trial 2007-Ohio-2398, 2007 WL 1452796. Criminal Law ⚿ 250; Sentencing And Punishment ⚿ 1643

TRIAL PROCEDURE

2945.10 Order of proceedings of trial

The trial of an issue upon an indictment or information shall proceed before the trial court or jury as follows:

(A) Counsel for the state must first state the case for the prosecution, and may briefly state the evidence by which the counsel for the state expects to sustain it.

(B) The defendant or the defendant's counsel must then state the defense, and may briefly state the evidence which the defendant or the defendant's counsel expects to offer in support of it.

(C) The state must first produce its evidence and the defendant shall then produce the defendant's evidence.

(D) The state will then be confined to rebutting evidence, but the court, for good reason, in furtherance of justice, may permit evidence to be offered by either side out of its order.

(E) When the evidence is concluded, one of the following applies regarding jury instructions:

(1) In a capital case that is being heard by a jury, the court shall prepare written instructions to the jury on the points of law, shall provide copies of the written instructions to the jury before orally instructing the jury, and shall permit the jury to retain and consult the instructions during the court's presentation of the oral instructions and during the jury's deliberations.

(2) In a case that is not a capital case, either party may request instructions to the jury on the points of law, which instructions shall be reduced to writing if either party requests it.

(F) When the evidence is concluded, unless the case is submitted without argument, the counsel for the state shall commence, the defendant or the defendant's counsel follow, and the counsel for the state conclude the argument to the jury.

(G) The court, after the argument is concluded and before proceeding with other business, shall forthwith charge the jury. Such charge shall be reduced to writing by the court if either party requests it before the argument to the jury is commenced. Such charge, or other charge or instruction provided for in this section, when so written and given, shall not be orally qualified, modified, or explained to the jury by the court. Written charges and instructions shall be taken by the jury in their retirement and returned with their verdict into court and remain on file with the papers of the case.

The court may deviate from the order of proceedings listed in this section.

(2014 H 663, eff. 3-23-15; 1953 H 1, eff. 10–1–53; GC 13442–8)

Uncodified Law

2014 H 663, § 7, eff. 3–23–15, reads:

(A) As used in this section, "lethal injection" means the application of a lethal injection of a drug or a combination of drugs in carrying out a sentence of death.

(B) The intent of the General Assembly in enacting this act is to protect the identities of persons who assist the Department of Rehabilitation and Correction in carrying out a court-ordered sentence of death by lethal injection, in order to protect those persons from harassment and potential physical harm.

(C) It is the intent of the General Assembly in enacting this act to enable the Department of Rehabilitation and Correction to obtain the necessary assistance of persons in carrying out a court-ordered sentence of death by lethal injection or the drugs needed to administer such a sentence.

Historical and Statutory Notes

Amendment Note: 2014 H 663 rewrote this section, which prior thereto read:

"The trial of an issue upon an indictment or information shall proceed before the trial court or jury as follows:

"(A) Counsel for the state must first state the case for the prosecution, and may briefly state the evidence by which he expects to sustain it.

"(B) The defendant or his counsel must then state his defense, and may briefly state the evidence which he expects to offer in support of it.

"(C) The state must first produce its evidence and the defendant shall then produce his evidence.

"(D) The state will then be confined to rebutting evidence, but the court, for good reason, in furtherance of justice, may permit evidence to be offered by either side out of its order.

"(E) When the evidence is concluded, either party may request instructions to the jury on the points of law, which instructions shall be reduced to writing if either party requests it.

"(F) When the evidence is concluded, unless the case is submitted without argument, the counsel for the state shall commence, the defendant or his counsel follow, and the counsel for the state conclude the argument to the jury.

"(G) The court, after the argument is concluded and before proceeding with other business, shall forthwith charge the jury. Such charge shall be reduced to writing by the court if either party requests it before the argument to the jury is commenced. Such charge, or other charge or instruction provided for in this section, when so written and given, shall not be orally qualified, modified, or explained to the jury by the court. Written charges and instructions shall be taken by the jury in their retirement and returned with their verdict into court and remain on file with the papers of the case.

"The court may deviate from the order of proceedings listed in this section."

Research References

ALR Library

169 ALR 315, Comment Note.--Duty in Instructing Jury in Criminal Prosecution to Explain and Define Offense Charged.

Encyclopedias

OH Jur. 3d Criminal Law: Procedure § 1249, Deviation from Order of Trial Proceedings.

OH Jur. 3d Criminal Law: Procedure § 1396, Generally; Transcripts; Written Charges and Instructions.

Treatises and Practice Aids

Katz & Giannelli, Baldwin's Ohio Practice Criminal Law § 68:2, Rules of Evidence.

Katz & Giannelli, Baldwin's Ohio Practice Criminal Law § 68:9, Closing Argument.

Giannelli, Baldwin's Ohio Practice Evidence R 611, Mode and Order of Interrogation and Presentation.

Hennenberg & Reinhart, Ohio Criminal Defense Motions F 8:4, Motion for Alternating Voir Dire--Jury-Related Motions.

Hennenberg & Reinhart, Ohio Criminal Defense Motions F 13:33, Motion to Allow the Defense to Argue Last and for Not Less Than Four (4) Hours--Death Penalty Motions.

Law Review and Journal Commentaries

Last attorney to the jury box is a rotten egg: Overcoming psychological hurdles in the order of presentation at trial. Hyatt Browning Shirkey, 8 Ohio St. J. Crim. L. 581 (2011).

The use of secret evidence by government lawyers: balancing defendants' rights with national security concerns. Comment, 52 Clev St L Rev 571 (2004–05).

Notes of Decisions

3. Statements of case

Trial court did not abuse its discretion by permitting state to supplement its opening statement after its initial opening statement failed to state charges against drug possession defendant and did not contain facts that would constitute prima facie evidence of guilt; state had relied on trial court's reading of indictment to prospective jurors at commencement of case, and at most, state's failure to state its case more completely was accidental or inadvertent. State v. Crane (Ohio App. 12 Dist., 08-25-2014) 17 N.E.3d 1252, 2014-Ohio-3657. Criminal Law ⚷ 2069

4. Introduction of evidence

Trial court acted within its discretion, at close of state's rebuttal case in capital murder prosecution, in refusing to admit reports of defense mental health experts; appropriate time for defense counsel to have requested admission of the reports was during defense's case. State v. Filiaggi (Ohio, 07-29-1999) 86 Ohio St.3d 230, 714 N.E.2d 867, 1999-Ohio-99, certiorari denied 120 S.Ct. 821, 528 U.S. 1090, 145 L.Ed.2d 691, denial of habeas corpus affirmed 445 F.3d 851. Criminal Law ⚷ 680(1)

5. Argument—In general

Assuming Fifth Amendment right not to put forth any evidence in corroboration of defendant's testimony exists, prosecutor's closing argument comment that defendant offered version of events that was completely unsupported by anything else did not violate such right, where prosecutor did not comment on defendant's failure to offer corroborating testimony, but simply indicated that defendant's testimony was not consistent with other testimony. State v. McSwain (Ohio App. 8 Dist., Cuyahoga, 06-24-2004) No. 83394, 2004-Ohio-3292, 2004 WL 1402700, Unreported, appeal not allowed 104 Ohio St.3d 1425, 819 N.E.2d 709, 2004-Ohio-6585, certiorari denied 125 S.Ct. 2269, 544 U.S. 1040, 161 L.Ed.2d 1072, on subsequent appeal 2008-Ohio-3661, 2008 WL 2833937, appeal not allowed 120 Ohio St.3d 1457, 898 N.E.2d 970, 2008-Ohio-6813, habeas corpus denied 2011 WL 3490152. Criminal Law ⚷ 2136

Once robbery defendant waived his right against self-incrimination by testifying, his credibility was at issue and could properly be challenged by charge of recent fabrication. State v. McSwain (Ohio App. 8 Dist., Cuyahoga, 06-24-2004) No. 83394, 2004-Ohio-3292, 2004 WL 1402700, Unreported, appeal not allowed 104 Ohio St.3d 1425, 819 N.E.2d 709, 2004-Ohio-6585, certiorari denied 125 S.Ct. 2269, 544 U.S. 1040, 161 L.Ed.2d 1072, on subsequent appeal 2008-Ohio-3661, 2008 WL 2833937, appeal not allowed 120 Ohio St.3d 1457, 898 N.E.2d 970, 2008-Ohio-6813, habeas corpus denied 2011 WL 3490152. Witnesses ⚷ 337(1)

Defendant failed to object to prosecutor's remarks during closing argument of murder trial and thus waived all but plain error. State v. Brandy (Ohio App. 10 Dist., Franklin, 04-10-2003) No. 02AP-832, 2003-Ohio-1836, 2003 WL 1848761, Unreported, appeal not allowed 99 Ohio St.3d 1515, 792 N.E.2d 201, 2003-Ohio-3957, denial of post-conviction relief affirmed 2007-Ohio-1505, 2007 WL 949439, appeal not allowed 114 Ohio St.3d 1511, 872 N.E.2d 952, 2007-Ohio-4285. Criminal Law ⚷ 1037.1(1)

Prosecutor's comment during closing argument of murder trial comparing defendant's actions in shooting victim to that of a dog hunting someone or something down, while it may have been a bit harsh, was merely an attempt by the prosecutor to explain to the jury defendant's actions and fell into the latitude afforded counsel during closing argument. State v. Brandy (Ohio App. 10 Dist., Franklin, 04-10-2003) No. 02AP-832, 2003-Ohio-1836, 2003 WL 1848761, Unreported, appeal not allowed 99 Ohio St.3d 1515, 792 N.E.2d 201, 2003-Ohio-3957, denial of post-conviction relief affirmed 2007-Ohio-1505, 2007 WL 949439, appeal not allowed 114 Ohio St.3d 1511, 872 N.E.2d 952, 2007-Ohio-4285. Criminal Law ⚷ 2149

Prosecutor's comments during closing argument of murder trial that defendant should not have escaped punishment for aggravated murder by alleging sudden passion or fit of rage and words alone were not enough to allow someone to escape their punishment for aggravated murder were not prejudicial, where defense counsel objected, trial court sustained objection, and trial court gave a curative instruction. State v. Brandy (Ohio App. 10 Dist., Franklin, 04-10-2003) No. 02AP-832, 2003-Ohio-1836, 2003 WL 1848761, Unreported, appeal not allowed 99 Ohio St.3d 1515, 792 N.E.2d 201, 2003-Ohio-3957, denial of post-conviction relief affirmed 2007-Ohio-1505, 2007 WL 949439, appeal not allowed 114 Ohio St.3d 1511, 872 N.E.2d 952, 2007-Ohio-4285. Criminal Law ⚷ 2209

Prosecutor can respond in argument to issues raised by an accused. State v. Cassano (Ohio, 08-07-2002) 96 Ohio St.3d 94, 772 N.E.2d 81, 2002-Ohio-3751, reconsideration denied 96 Ohio St.3d 1517, 775 N.E.2d 858, 2002-Ohio-4950, certiorari denied 123 S.Ct. 1359, 537 U.S. 1235, 155 L.Ed.2d 201, denial of post-conviction relief vacated 2008-Ohio-1045, 2008 WL 638190. Criminal Law ⚷ 2165

Prosecutor's statements during penalty phase closing argument in capital murder prosecution, to effect that future events might require abandoning single-cell policy of super-maximum security facility in which defendant was presently housed, or might require transfer of some of its inmates to other prisons, was proper rebuttal of defense argument that defendant would be restricted to single cell if given life sentence, defense assertions that defendant no longer represented danger since he would be under close scrutiny at his present facility, and defendant's optimistic speculation that his current conditions of confinement would continue indefinitely. State v. Cassano (Ohio, 08-07-2002) 96 Ohio St.3d 94, 772 N.E.2d 81, 2002-Ohio-3751, reconsideration denied 96 Ohio St.3d 1517, 775 N.E.2d 858, 2002-Ohio-4950, certiorari denied 123 S.Ct. 1359, 537 U.S. 1235, 155 L.Ed.2d 201, denial of post-conviction relief vacated 2008-Ohio-1045, 2008 WL 638190. Sentencing And Punishment ⚷ 1780(2)

6. —— Fair trial, argument

Prosecutor's comment during closing argument in a prosecution for possession with intent to distribute pseudoephedrine, asserting that defendant testified he was selling to "buying groups," and that there was no evidence other than from defendant's lips that there were buying groups, was supported by the evidence at trial, and thus, was not improper; defendant was the only person at trial who used the words "buying groups" when testifying, and the records showed no evidence of buying groups. U.S. v. Merkosky (C.A.6 (Ohio), 06-14-2005) No. 02-4332, 135 Fed.Appx. 828, 2005 WL 1400201, Unreported, appeal after new sentencing hearing 237 Fed.Appx. 66, 2007 WL 1880595, post-conviction relief denied 2008 WL 5169640. Criminal Law ⚷ 2111

Prosecutor's closing argument comment that only jury could correct injustices done to victims, when viewed in context of entire argument, was not prejudicial to defendant, who was convicted of kidnapping, aggravated robbery, aggravated burglary, and felonious assault, where such appeal to jury's sympathies was modest and prosecutor asked jury to use reason and common sense. State v. McSwain (Ohio App. 8 Dist., Cuyahoga, 06-24-2004) No. 83394, 2004-Ohio-3292, 2004 WL 1402700, Unreported, appeal not allowed 104 Ohio St.3d 1425, 819 N.E.2d 709, 2004-Ohio-6585, certiorari denied 125 S.Ct. 2269, 544 U.S. 1040, 161 L.Ed.2d 1072, on subsequent appeal 2008-Ohio-3661, 2008 WL 2833937, appeal not allowed 120 Ohio St.3d 1457, 898 N.E.2d 970, 2008-Ohio-6813, habeas corpus denied 2011 WL 3490152. Criminal Law ⚷ 2146

Claim that prosecutor's closing argument comment that only jury could correct injustices done to victims was improper could only be reviewed for plain error, where defendant failed at trial to object to such comment. State v. McSwain (Ohio App. 8 Dist., Cuyahoga, 06-24-2004) No. 83394, 2004-Ohio-3292, 2004 WL 1402700, Unreported, appeal not allowed 104 Ohio St.3d 1425, 819 N.E.2d 709, 2004-Ohio-6585, certiorari denied 125 S.Ct. 2269, 544 U.S. 1040, 161 L.Ed.2d 1072, on subsequent appeal 2008-Ohio-3661, 2008 WL 2833937, appeal not allowed 120 Ohio St.3d 1457, 898 N.E.2d 970, 2008-Ohio-6813, habeas corpus denied 2011 WL 3490152. Criminal Law ⚷ 1037.1(2)

Three comments made by prosecutor during closing arguments, when read in full context, were neither materially prejudicial nor did they deny defendant convicted of murder and possession of cocaine a fair trial, but were an attempt by prosecutor to convince jury that defendant's defense of voluntary manslaughter must be rejected; prosecutor asked jury what else could defendant have said but that his actions were merely voluntary manslaughter, and prosecutor stated that defendant's claim that victim and his wife who were attempting to buy drugs from defendant had time to hide drugs and money on their person or in body cavities was "ridiculous." State v. Brandy (Ohio App. 10 Dist., Franklin, 04-10-2003) No. 02AP-832, 2003-Ohio-1836, 2003 WL 1848761, Unreported, appeal not allowed 99 Ohio St.3d 1515, 792 N.E.2d 201, 2003-Ohio-3957, denial of post-conviction relief affirmed 2007-Ohio-1505, 2007 WL 949439, appeal not allowed 114 Ohio St.3d 1511, 872 N.E.2d 952, 2007-Ohio-4285. Criminal Law ⚿ 1171.1(3)

Prosecutor's characterization of murder defendant as a "drug dealer extraordinaire" was not plain error, where characterization was based on evidence presented at trial during which defendant admitted to a life of drug dealing. State v. Brandy (Ohio App. 10 Dist., Franklin, 04-10-2003) No. 02AP-832, 2003-Ohio-1836, 2003 WL 1848761, Unreported, appeal not allowed 99 Ohio St.3d 1515, 792 N.E.2d 201, 2003-Ohio-3957, denial of post-conviction relief affirmed 2007-Ohio-1505, 2007 WL 949439, appeal not allowed 114 Ohio St.3d 1511, 872 N.E.2d 952, 2007-Ohio-4285. Criminal Law ⚿ 1037.1(2)

7. —— Prosecutorial misconduct, argument

Prosecutor's comment during rebuttal closing argument that, under defense counsel's own argument to effect that inconsistencies between eyewitness' testimony indicated that they were liars, defense counsel's misspelling of word would make him a liar, did not constitute impermissible denigration of defense counsel, in trial for aggravated murder, murder, and aggravated robbery; rather, prosecutor's comment was in response to defense counsel's assertion that eyewitnesses were liars and to expose weakness in counsel's argument, and prosecutor quickly pointed out that defense counsel was not liar but had simply made mistake. State v. Huges (Ohio App. 1 Dist., Hamilton, 05-20-2005) No. C-030489, 2005-Ohio-2453, 2005 WL 1190715, Unreported, habeas corpus dismissed 2014 WL 4704585. Criminal Law ⚿ 2179

Prosecutor during closing argument of rape trial did not interject her personal beliefs about the veracity of victim's testimony, but rather merely argued that the evidence supported the theory that victim did not lie or concoct her story of abuse by her father, the defendant, and thus prosecutor did not commit misconduct. State v. Geboy (Ohio App. 3 Dist., 08-30-2001) 145 Ohio App.3d 706, 764 N.E.2d 451, 2001-Ohio-2214, appeal not allowed 94 Ohio St.3d 1410, 759 N.E.2d 787, appeal after new trial 2003-Ohio-343, 2003 WL 178616, appeal not allowed 99 Ohio St.3d 1412, 788 N.E.2d 648, 2003-Ohio-2454, grant of habeas corpus reversed in part 489 F.3d 752. Criminal Law ⚿ 2098(3)

8. Instructions—In general

Court's failure to include written jury instructions in record in drug offense prosecution was harmless error; defendant pointed to no prejudice from court's failure to include instructions in record, and neither party objected to court's instructions as read to jury. State v. Hudson (Ohio App. 8 Dist., Cuyahoga, 03-28-2002) No. 79010, 2002-Ohio-1408, 2002 WL 472304, Unreported, appeal after new sentencing hearing 2004-Ohio-1452, 2004 WL 583925. Criminal Law ⚿ 1109(3)

10. —— After argument, instructions

Defendant's substantial rights were not violated when the trial court provided the jury with written instructions on self defense and later provided additional oral instructions on self defense during jury deliberations, in prosecution for felonious assault; the trial court was not prohibited from answering the jury's question during deliberations. State v. Hibbard (Ohio App. 12 Dist., Butler, 09-29-2003) No. CA2002-05-129, 2003-Ohio-5104, 2003 WL 22227350, Unreported, on remand 2004 WL 5481578. Assault And Battery ⚿ 96(3); Criminal Law ⚿ 863(2)

11. —— Written or oral, instructions

Claim that trial court erred by failing to include written jury instructions in record, as required by rule, did not constitute plain error in felonious assault prosecution, where trial court fully and completely instructed jury prior to deliberations, parties had opportunity to review proposed written instructions, and neither party alleged variation between oral instructions and proposed written instructions. State v. Smith (Ohio App. 8 Dist., Cuyahoga, 07-01-2004) No. 82710, 2004-Ohio-3479, 2004 WL 1472081, Unreported, appeal not allowed 104 Ohio St.3d 1409, 818 N.E.2d 711, 2004-Ohio-6364, habeas corpus granted in part 562 F.Supp.2d 912. Criminal Law ⚿ 1038.1(6)

12. Questions from jurors to witnesses—In general

Court's response to jury request for read-back of testimony by asking jury to consider whether it still wanted read-back in light of court's answers to jury's other questions was not inappropriate. O'Hara v. Brigano (C.A.6 (Ohio), 08-21-2007) 499 F.3d 492. Criminal Law ⚿ 859

13. —— Discretion of court, questions from jurors to witnesses

The decision to allow jurors to question witnesses is a matter within the discretion of the trial court and should not be disturbed on appeal absent an abuse of that discretion. State v. Fisher (Ohio, 06-11-2003) 99 Ohio St.3d 127, 789 N.E.2d 222, 2003-Ohio-2761, denial of post-conviction relief affirmed 2005-Ohio-4065, 2005 WL 1869692, appeal not allowed 107 Ohio St.3d 1684, 839 N.E.2d 404, 2005-Ohio-6480, stay allowed 2006 WL 871194, habeas corpus dismissed 2007 WL 682392. Criminal Law ⚿ 1153.18(1); Witnesses ⚿ 246(1)

Practice of allowing jurors to question witnesses is matter committed to discretion of trial court; to minimize danger of prejudice, however, trial courts that permit juror questioning should: (1) require jurors to submit their questions to court in writing; (2) ensure that jurors do not display or discuss a question with other jurors until court reads question to witness; (3) provide counsel an opportunity to object to each question at sidebar or outside presence of jury; (4) instruct jurors that they should not draw adverse inferences from court's refusal to allow certain questions; and (5) allow counsel to ask follow-up questions of witnesses. State v. Fisher (Ohio, 06-11-2003) 99 Ohio St.3d 127, 789 N.E.2d 222, 2003-Ohio-2761, denial of post-conviction relief affirmed 2005-Ohio-4065, 2005 WL 1869692, appeal not allowed 107 Ohio St.3d 1684, 839 N.E.2d 404, 2005-Ohio-6480, stay allowed 2006 WL 871194, habeas corpus dismissed 2007 WL 682392. Witnesses ⚿ 246(1)

15. —— Objections, questions from jurors to witnesses

A trial judge should rule on any objections to juror questions when counsel objects at sidebar, including any objection that a question from a juror touches on a matter that counsel purposefully avoided as a matter of litigation strategy, and that, if asked, will cause particular prejudice to the party. State v. Fisher (Ohio, 06-11-2003) 99 Ohio St.3d 127, 789 N.E.2d 222, 2003-Ohio-2761, denial of post-conviction relief affirmed 2005-Ohio-4065, 2005 WL 1869692, appeal not allowed 107 Ohio St.3d 1684, 839 N.E.2d 404, 2005-Ohio-6480, stay allowed 2006 WL 871194, habeas corpus dismissed 2007 WL 682392. Witnesses ⚿ 246(1)

2945.11 Charge to the jury as to law and fact

Notes of Decisions

1. Constitutional issues

Failure of appellate counsel to assign as error trial court's failure to instruct jury concerning defendant's history of marijuana use, as mitigating factor in capital sentencing, was not ineffective assistance of counsel; reasonable appellate counsel could have decided that history of marijuana use was of such little mitigation value that any error in failing to so instruct jury was harmless. State v. McGuire (Ohio, 12-10-1997) 80 Ohio St.3d 390, 686 N.E.2d 1112, 1997-Ohio-335, reconsideration denied 81 Ohio St.3d 1433, 689 N.E.2d 52, dismissal of post-conviction relief affirmed 1998 WL 191415, dismissed, appeal not allowed 83 Ohio St.3d 1428, 699 N.E.2d 945, certiorari denied 119 S.Ct. 85, 525 U.S. 831, 142 L.Ed.2d 66, denial of post-conviction relief affirmed 2001 WL 409424, dismissed, appeal not allowed 93 Ohio St.3d 1411, 754 N.E.2d 259, habeas corpus denied 2007 WL 1893902. Criminal Law ⚿ 1969

2. Instructions—In general

Jury instruction in capital murder prosecution with respect to inference from manner in which defendant made use of deadly weapon did not create impermissible mandatory presumption, where court's use of "may" adequately communicated that jury was free to accept or reject permissive inference; language "purpose to cause the death may be inferred from the use of the weapon" did not communicate conclusive presumption relieving state of its burden of persuasion on criminal intent. State v. Gross (Ohio, 10-30-2002) 97 Ohio St.3d 121, 776 N.E.2d 1061, 2002-Ohio-5524, reconsideration denied 97 Ohio St.3d 1486, 780 N.E.2d 288, 2002-Ohio-6866, certiorari denied 123 S.Ct. 2079, 538 U.S. 1037, 155 L.Ed.2d 1068, rehearing denied 124 S.Ct. 20, 539 U.S. 976, 156 L.Ed.2d 685, denial of post-conviction relief affirmed 2003-Ohio-6295, 2003 WL 22765845, appeal not allowed 102 Ohio St.3d 1410, 806 N.E.2d 562, 2004-Ohio-1763, certiorari denied 125 S.Ct. 165, 543 U.S. 888, 160 L.Ed.2d 149, dismissal of post-conviction relief affirmed 2006-Ohio-6941, 2006 WL 3804532, appeal not allowed 113 Ohio St.3d 1468, 864 N.E.2d 654, 2007-Ohio-1722, habeas corpus dismissed 2008 WL 4702181, motion to amend denied 2008 WL 4889626, certificate of appealability denied 2008 WL 5190017, affirmed 426 Fed. Appx. 349, 2011 WL 1597659. Homicide ⚿ 1388

Trial court's action in informing jury of parties' stipulation of fact as to amount of crack cocaine involved in each transaction with which defendant was charged did not improperly remove matter of fact, credibility determination, or determination of weight of evidence from jury's consideration. State v. Sloan (Ohio App. 8 Dist., Cuyahoga, 05-30-2002) No. 79832, 2002-Ohio-2669, 2002 WL 1265578, Unreported, appeal not allowed 97 Ohio St.3d 1423, 777 N.E.2d 277, 2002-Ohio-5820. Criminal Law ⚿ 763(1)

3. —— When required, instructions

Trial court had statutory duty to charge jury on alibi and its failure to do so was reversible error, where defendant filed timely notice of alibi, presented evidence to support the claim, and relied on alibi as his sole defense. State v. Walton (Ohio App. 2 Dist., Montgomery, 04-21-2006) No. 20615, 2006-Ohio-1974, 2006 WL 1047467, Unreported. Criminal Law ⚿ 775(2); Criminal Law ⚿ 1173.2(3)

4. —— When not required, instructions

Defendant was not entitled to a jury instruction on criminal trespass, as a lesser-included offense of aggravated burglary; victim testified that defendant and co-defendants possessed guns, that they physically attacked second victim, and that defendant threatened to kill the victims. State v. Garrett (Ohio App. 12 Dist., Butler, 09-22-2003) No. CA2002-05-111, 2003-Ohio-5000, 2003 WL 22170186, Unreported, appeal not allowed 101 Ohio St.3d 1423, 802 N.E.2d 154, 2004-Ohio-123, habeas corpus denied 2007 WL 315093. Criminal Law ⚿ 795(2.35)

Erroneous giving of instruction on duty to retreat in connection with capital murder defendant's claim of self-defense did not prejudice defendant and was harmless, where no reasonable jury could have believed that defendant acted in self-defense; defendant's own testimony established that he had been the aggressor in fatal encounter, had no basis for bona fide belief that he was in imminent danger of death or great bodily harm, and repeatedly stabbed victim after victim had ceased to pose any conceivable threat. State v. Cassano (Ohio, 08-07-2002) 96 Ohio St.3d 94, 772 N.E.2d 81, 2002-Ohio-3751, reconsideration denied 96 Ohio St.3d 1517, 775 N.E.2d 858, 2002-Ohio-4950, certiorari denied 123 S.Ct. 1359, 537 U.S. 1235, 155 L.Ed.2d 201, denial of post-conviction relief vacated 2008-Ohio-1045, 2008 WL 638190. Criminal Law ⚿ 1172.1(4)

Instruction that would have relieved defendant in murder prosecution of criminal responsibility for death of cellmate after stabbing incident, if there was gross or willful maltreatment by medical personnel who attended to cellmate that was shown to be an independent intervening cause of death, was not warranted; pattern instructions adequately instructed on intervening cause and independent intervening cause of death, there was no evidence that cellmate was victim of gross or willful maltreatment, and defense expert agreed with coroner that attack by defendant was cause of death. State v. Hanna (Ohio, 05-22-2002) 95 Ohio St.3d 285, 767 N.E.2d 678, 2002-Ohio-2221, reconsideration denied 96 Ohio St.3d 1441, 770 N.E.2d 1050, 2002-Ohio-3344, certiorari denied 123 S.Ct. 554, 537 U.S. 1036, 154 L.Ed.2d 455, habeas corpus dismissed 2009 WL 485487, certificate of appealability granted in part, denied in part 2009 WL 2876260, affirmed 694 F.3d 596, rehearing and rehearing en banc denied. Criminal Law ⚿ 829(3)

Giving of jury instruction that defined causation in terms of foreseeability was not prejudicial error in aggravated murder prosecution arising from incident in which defendant thrust shank into sleeping cellmate's eye, where trial court provided jury with extensive instructions on the state's burden of proof and the requirement to prove purpose to kill both before and after giving foreseeability instruction. State v. Hanna (Ohio, 05-22-2002) 95 Ohio St.3d 285, 767 N.E.2d 678, 2002-Ohio-2221, reconsideration denied 96 Ohio St.3d 1441, 770 N.E.2d 1050, 2002-Ohio-3344, certiorari denied 123 S.Ct. 554, 537 U.S. 1036, 154 L.Ed.2d 455, habeas corpus dismissed 2009 WL 485487, certificate of appealability granted in part, denied in part 2009 WL 2876260, affirmed 694 F.3d 596, rehearing and rehearing en banc denied. Criminal Law ⚿ 1172.1(3)

6. —— Charge relating to punishment, instructions

Penalty phase instruction in capital murder prosecution, stating that "whenever all 12 of you agree upon your verdict, you will complete the verdict form, sign it in ink, and summons the bailiff," was not misleading, despite defendant's contention that it failed to convey that single juror could vote so as to require life sentence, where instruction was intended merely to inform jurors that all of them had to sign verdict form, and where court gave defendant's requested instruction explicitly recognizing that single juror could preclude imposition of death penalty. State v. Cassano (Ohio, 08-07-2002) 96 Ohio St.3d 94, 772 N.E.2d 81, 2002-Ohio-3751, reconsideration denied 96 Ohio St.3d 1517, 775 N.E.2d 858, 2002-Ohio-4950, certiorari denied 123 S.Ct. 1359, 537 U.S. 1235, 155 L.Ed.2d 201, denial of post-conviction relief vacated 2008-Ohio-1045, 2008 WL 638190. Sentencing And Punishment ⚿ 1780(3)

Penalty phase instruction in capital murder prosecution, stating that sentencing jury's weighing of evidence was "unlikely" to be disturbed and that it "should expect its sentence verdict to be carried out" was accurate reflection of state law and did not diminish jury's overall sense of responsibility for its verdict; in fact, court's strongly worded admonition as to importance of jury's verdict reinforced jury's sense of importance of its responsibility. State v. Cassano (Ohio, 08-07-2002) 96 Ohio St.3d 94, 772 N.E.2d 81, 2002-Ohio-3751, reconsideration denied 96 Ohio St.3d 1517, 775 N.E.2d 858, 2002-Ohio-4950, certiorari denied 123 S.Ct. 1359, 537 U.S. 1235, 155 L.Ed.2d 201, denial of post-conviction relief vacated 2008-Ohio-1045, 2008 WL 638190. Sentencing And Punishment ⚿ 1780(3)

2945.12 When accused may be tried in his absence

Notes of Decisions

2. Presence of defendant required

Prosecution of corporate defendant on complaint charging misdemeanor building and housing code violations could not proceed in absentia, when defendant had never appeared in case. Cleveland v. Washington Mut. Bank (Ohio App. 8 Dist., 12-31-2008) 179 Ohio App.3d 692, 903 N.E.2d 384, 2008-Ohio-6956, appeal allowed 122 Ohio St.3d 1409, 907 N.E.2d 1193, 2009-Ohio-2751, affirmed and remanded 125 Ohio St.3d 541, 929 N.E.2d 1039, 2010-Ohio-2219, on remand 2010-Ohio-2957, 2010 WL 2560074. Criminal Law ⚿ 636(1)

2945.13 Joint trials in felony cases

Notes of Decisions

4. —— Burden of showing cause, joinder

Two jointly indicted persons shall be tried together unless the prosecutor or one of the defendants applies for separate trials and shows good cause; the burden of establishing good cause is on the defendant requesting a separate trial and the granting or denial of such separate trial request rests within the sound discretion of the trial court. State v. Fannin (Ohio App. 8 Dist., Cuyahoga, 08-15-2002) No. 80014, 2002-Ohio-4180, 2002 WL 1878860, Unreported, appeal not allowed 98 Ohio St.3d 1412, 781 N.E.2d 1020, 2003-Ohio-60, motion to reopen denied 2008-Ohio-136, 2008 WL 152454. Criminal Law ⚷ 622.6(3)

2945.15 Discharge of defendant

Notes of Decisions

1. Motion for acquittal

A verdict that convicts a defendant of one crime and acquits him of another, when the first crime requires proof of the second, may not be disturbed merely because the two findings are irreconcilable. State v. Gardner (Ohio, 06-18-2008) 118 Ohio St.3d 420, 889 N.E.2d 995, 2008-Ohio-2787, on remand 2010-Ohio-6479, 2010 WL 5550244. Criminal Law ⚷ 878(4)

2945.16 View of the premises

Notes of Decisions

1. Discretion of court

Denial of capital murder defendant's motion for jury view of emergency berm area on highway where shooting occurred, which defendant sought in attempt to show that visual and auditory distractions of highway had prevented her from recognizing the man with whom she was involved in sexual relationship as shooter, and that she had not lied when she denied knowing who had shot her husband, was not abuse of discretion, given inherent dangers of conducting jury view next to heavily trafficked highway, and given that defendant was allowed to present testimony of reconstruction expert, who went to the emergency berm area under traffic conditions similar to those existing at time of shooting. U.S. v. Moonda (C.A.6 (Ohio), 09-29-2009) No. 07-4191, 347 Fed.Appx. 192, 2009 WL 3109834, Unreported. Criminal Law ⚷ 860

The trial judge's presence on the bus with the jury when they visited crime scene did not constitute plain error, in capital murder prosecution; there was no evidence that unauthorized communications occurred between the judge and jury on the bus ride to crime scene. State v. Were (Ohio, 06-17-2008) 118 Ohio St.3d 448, 890 N.E.2d 263, 2008-Ohio-2762, certiorari denied 129 S.Ct. 606, 555 U.S. 1036, 172 L.Ed.2d 464, denial of post-conviction relief affirmed 2009-Ohio-4494, 2009 WL 2768021, appeal not allowed 124 Ohio St.3d 1443, 920 N.E.2d 374, 2010-Ohio-188. Criminal Law ⚷ 1039

Trial court did not abuse its discretion in granting State's motion for a daytime jury view of the crime scene, during prosecution in which defendant was convicted of aggravated vehicular assault and vehicular assault, even though accident occurred at night; trial court stated safety concerns as a reason why the jury view should be conducted during the day, and the "other reasons" mentioned by the court could have included the additional expense and impracticality of gathering the jury, the court and its staff, counsel, and sheriff's deputies after dark. State v. Didion (Ohio App. 3 Dist., 09-04-2007) 173 Ohio App.3d 130, 877 N.E.2d 725, 2007-Ohio-4494. Criminal Law ⚷ 651(1)

Denial in capital murder prosecution of defense request for jury view of cell in correctional facility where charged killing occurred, to demonstrate how difficult it would have been for defendant to intentionally stab cellmate in the eye, was not abuse of discretion; trial court noted inherent problems of security and possible prejudice to case via other inmates and determined that dimensions and all aspects of cell could be fully presented to jury with aid of diagrams and photographs, and defendant failed to present any diagrams of cell during trial. State v. Hanna (Ohio, 05-22-2002) 95 Ohio St.3d 285, 767 N.E.2d 678, 2002-Ohio-2221, reconsideration denied 96 Ohio St.3d 1441, 770 N.E.2d 1050, 2002-Ohio-3344, certiorari denied 123 S.Ct. 554, 537 U.S. 1036, 154 L.Ed.2d 455, habeas corpus dismissed 2009 WL 485487, certificate of appealability granted in part, denied in part 2009 WL 2876260, affirmed 694 F.3d 596, rehearing and rehearing en banc denied. Criminal Law ⚷ 651(1)

2. Premises subject to view

Magistrate's decision to permit a view of property owner's premises by the court in connection with suit brought against owner by township zoning inspector seeking order permanently enjoining owner from using his property in violation of zoning resolution, pursuant to statute permitting court to order such a view, did not violate owner's Fourth Amendment rights; the view of owner's property was conducted under the auspices of the court, which concluded that such a view was reasonable, the magistrate, parties, and opposing counsel conducted a view of the outside of owner's property, and what a person chose voluntarily to expose to public view thereby lost its Fourth Amendment protection. Monus v. Day (Ohio App. 7 Dist., Mahoning, 06-13-2011) No. 10 MA 35, 2011-Ohio-3170, 2011 WL 2552728, Unreported, appeal not allowed 130 Ohio St.3d 1417, 956 N.E.2d 309, 2011-Ohio-5605, reconsideration denied 130 Ohio St.3d 1500, 958 N.E.2d 961, 2011-Ohio-6556. Searches and Seizures ⚿ 47.1; Zoning and Planning ⚿ 1796

3. Presence of accused

Denial of defendant's request to be present when the jury viewed the crime scene did not violate due process or constitute plain error; defendant waived the right to attend the jury view in open court, and defendant could not show that he was materially prejudiced by his absence from the jury view. State v. Were (Ohio, 06-17-2008) 118 Ohio St.3d 448, 890 N.E.2d 263, 2008-Ohio-2762, certiorari denied 129 S.Ct. 606, 555 U.S. 1036, 172 L.Ed.2d 464, denial of post-conviction relief affirmed 2009-Ohio-4494, 2009 WL 2768021, appeal not allowed 124 Ohio St.3d 1443, 920 N.E.2d 374, 2010-Ohio-188. Constitutional Law ⚿ 4614; Criminal Law ⚿ 1035(3)

Trial court's refusal to allow capital murder defendant to be present at jury view of crime scene, defendant's prison cell, did not deprive defendant of due process. State v. Cassano (Ohio, 08-07-2002) 96 Ohio St.3d 94, 772 N.E.2d 81, 2002-Ohio-3751, reconsideration denied 96 Ohio St.3d 1517, 775 N.E.2d 858, 2002-Ohio-4950, certiorari denied 123 S.Ct. 1359, 537 U.S. 1235, 155 L.Ed.2d 201, denial of post-conviction relief vacated 2008-Ohio-1045, 2008 WL 638190. Constitutional Law ⚿ 4614; Criminal Law ⚿ 636(5)

Capital murder defendant had statutory right to be present in person during jury view of crime scene, despite expressed concern of court and prison officials with respect to probable duration of the jury view, requirement that prison in which murder had occurred would have been required to be locked down during jury view, and fact that defendant would have been unshackled in his cell during jury view. State v. Cassano (Ohio, 08-07-2002) 96 Ohio St.3d 94, 772 N.E.2d 81, 2002-Ohio-3751, reconsideration denied 96 Ohio St.3d 1517, 775 N.E.2d 858, 2002-Ohio-4950, certiorari denied 123 S.Ct. 1359, 537 U.S. 1235, 155 L.Ed.2d 201, denial of post-conviction relief vacated 2008-Ohio-1045, 2008 WL 638190. Criminal Law ⚿ 636(5)

Trial court's refusal to allow capital murder defendant to be present at jury view of crime scene, defendant's prison cell, did not materially prejudice defendant, where jury view was neither evidence nor critical stage of proceedings, and court authorized defendant, his counsel, and any agent to view crime scene before trial. State v. Cassano (Ohio, 08-07-2002) 96 Ohio St.3d 94, 772 N.E.2d 81, 2002-Ohio-3751, reconsideration denied 96 Ohio St.3d 1517, 775 N.E.2d 858, 2002-Ohio-4950, certiorari denied 123 S.Ct. 1359, 537 U.S. 1235, 155 L.Ed.2d 201, denial of post-conviction relief vacated 2008-Ohio-1045, 2008 WL 638190. Criminal Law ⚿ 1166.14

TRIAL BY JURY

2945.17 Right of trial by jury

Law Review and Journal Commentaries

Ten ways to engage a jury. Alphonse A. Gerhardstein and George F. Moeller, 20 Ohio Law 30 (September/October 2006).

Notes of Decisions

1. Constitutional issues—In general

Defendant who was charged with one count of assault, a first degree misdemeanor, which included the possibility of imprisonment, was entitled to a trial by jury, and thus trial court's failure to inform defendant during the initial appearance of her right to a jury trial invalidated her conviction. State v. Bates (Ohio App. 11 Dist., Ashtabula, 07-21-2006) No. 2005-A-0078, 2006-Ohio-3777, 2006 WL 2042774, Unreported. Jury ⚿ 22(2); Jury ⚿ 29(3)

2945.21 Peremptory challenges in capital cases

Law Review and Journal Commentaries

The "Tainted decision-making approach": A solution for the mixed messages Batson gets from employment discrimination. Note, 56 Case W Res L Rev 769 (Spring 2006).

Notes of Decisions

1. Constitutional issues—In general

Failure to excuse, for cause, a prospective juror for capital murder trial who stated early in her voir dire that a defendant who took a life should get death and that she did not think she could consider a life sentence, but who later retreated from and ultimately abandoned that position, did not violate defendant's Sixth Amendment right to impartial jury, where the prospective juror ultimately did not sit on the jury because defendant used a peremptory challenge against her, and defendant did not exhaust his peremptory challenges. State v. Hale (Ohio, 07-15-2008) 119 Ohio St.3d 118, 892 N.E.2d 864, 2008-Ohio-3426, reconsideration denied 119 Ohio St.3d 1450, 893 N.E.2d 519, 2008-Ohio-4487, certiorari denied 129 S.Ct. 1906, 556 U.S. 1168, 173 L.Ed.2d 1061. Criminal Law ⚿ 1166.18

Trial judge's refusal to question prospective jurors about specific contents of news reports to which they had been exposed did not violate defendant's Sixth Amendment right to an impartial jury during aggravated murder prosecution, where all jurors had heard about case, but each stated they had not formed an opinion on the case, could disregard media accounts, and could decide case based solely on evidence presented at trial. Joseph v. Coyle (C.A.6 (Ohio), 11-09-2006) 469 F.3d 441, certiorari denied 127 S.Ct. 1827, 549 U.S. 1280, 167 L.Ed.2d 321, subsequent habeas corpus proceeding 2008-Ohio-1138, 2008 WL 697377, motion to certify allowed 118 Ohio St.3d 1504, 889 N.E.2d 1023, 2008-Ohio-3369, appeal allowed 118 Ohio St.3d 1505, 889 N.E.2d 1024, 2008-Ohio-3369, affirmed in part, reversed in part 125 Ohio St.3d 76, 926 N.E.2d 278, 2010-Ohio-954. Habeas Corpus ⚿ 496

Criminal defendant is not constitutionally entitled to a jury representative and proportionate of every age group, or ethnic group, or educated, or noneducated, group in the district in which the trial is held, and has no affirmative equal protection right to a jury of a particular racial, gender or age composition. U.S. v. Maxwell (C.A.6 (Ohio), 11-17-1998) 160 F.3d 1071, denial of post-conviction relief affirmed 193 Fed.Appx. 479, 2006 WL 2457072, certiorari denied 127 S.Ct. 2081, 167 L.Ed.2d 801, rehearing denied 127 S.Ct. 2454, 167 L.Ed.2d 1149. Constitutional Law ⚿ 3105; Constitutional Law ⚿ 3295; Constitutional Law ⚿ 3427; Constitutional Law ⚿ 3830; Jury ⚿ 33(1.10); Jury ⚿ 33(1.20)

2. —— Gender discrimination, constitutional issues

Prosecutors can exercise peremptory challenges for any reason, without inquiry, and without court's control, except that jurors cannot be excluded on basis of race or gender. State v. Reynolds (Ohio, 01-14-1998) 80 Ohio St.3d 670, 687 N.E.2d 1358, 1998-Ohio-171, certiorari denied 118 S.Ct. 2328, 524 U.S. 930, 141 L.Ed.2d 702, denial of post-conviction relief affirmed 1999 WL 980568, dismissed, appeal not allowed 88 Ohio St.3d 1425, 723 N.E.2d 1113, denial of habeas corpus affirmed 2007 WL 2323850. Jury ⚿ 33(5.15)

3. —— Ineffective assistance of counsel, constitutional issues

For purposes of ineffective assistance claim, trial counsel's decision in capital case to use peremptory challenge, rather than raise for-cause challenge, to remove prospective juror who said he was biased against defense to some degree but would decide case only on the evidence and would accord defendant the usual presumption of innocence was tactical decision that fell well within range of professionally reasonably judgments. State v. Jones (Ohio, 04-18-2001) 91 Ohio St.3d 335, 744 N.E.2d 1163, 2001-Ohio-57, reconsideration denied 92 Ohio St.3d 1418, 748 N.E.2d 550, stay granted 92 Ohio St.3d 1421, 748 N.E.2d 1142, certiorari denied 122 S.Ct. 483, 534 U.S. 1004, 151 L.Ed.2d 396, denial of post-conviction relief affirmed 2002-Ohio-2074, 2002 WL 737074, appeal not allowed 96 Ohio St.3d 1495, 774 N.E.2d 767, 2002-Ohio-4534, stay revoked 99 Ohio St.3d 1415, 788 N.E.2d 1098, 2003-Ohio-2526, motion to reopen denied 108 Ohio St.3d 1409, 841 N.E.2d 315, 2006-Ohio-179, habeas corpus denied 489 F.Supp.2d 786. Criminal Law ⚿ 1901

4. —— Racial discrimination, constitutional issues

Removal for cause of prospective juror who stated during voir dire that he was racist and that he felt he could not be fair to prosecution in view of negative experiences with law enforcement was not abuse of discretion, in trial for aiding and abetting bank robbery and other crimes, absent any showing that jury that was actually seated was biased. U.S. v. Parks (C.A.6 (Ohio), 05-16-2008) No. 06-4218, 278 Fed.Appx. 527, 2008 WL 2091427, Unreported, certiorari denied 129 S.Ct. 322, 555 U.S. 933, 172 L.Ed.2d 233, post-conviction relief denied 2010 WL 1741519. Jury ⚿ 97(1); Jury ⚿ 97(2)

Prosecutor's proffered race-neutral explanation for use of peremptory challenge to exclude only African-American member of jury pool in drug prosecution was valid and nonpretextual, where prospective juror was school teacher for same school district attended by defendant and defendant's roommate and had previously testified for a student in a robbery case, and prosecutor was member of school board in which prospective juror taught. State v. Barker (Ohio App. 7 Dist., Jefferson, 03-27-2006) No. 05-JE-21, 2006-Ohio-1472, 2006 WL 771724, Unreported, motion for delayed appeal denied 111 Ohio St.3d 1468, 855 N.E.2d 1257, 2006-Ohio-5625, appeal not allowed 114 Ohio St.3d 1483, 870 N.E.2d 734, 2007-Ohio-3699. Jury ⚿ 33(5.15)

Drug defendant established prima facie case of racial discrimination in state's exercise of peremptory challenges, where state challenged only African-American prospective juror in jury pool. State v. Barker (Ohio App. 7 Dist., Jefferson, 03-27-2006)

No. 05-JE-21, 2006-Ohio-1472, 2006 WL 771724, Unreported, motion for delayed appeal denied 111 Ohio St.3d 1468, 855 N.E.2d 1257, 2006-Ohio-5625, appeal not allowed 114 Ohio St.3d 1483, 870 N.E.2d 734, 2007-Ohio-3699. Jury ⚷ 33(5.15)

State's representation that African-American juror's body language suggested that he didn't want to be there constituted a race-neutral reason for striking him, rebutting a prima facie case of racial discrimination for purposes of *Batson* challenge. State v. Brown (Ohio App. 8 Dist., Cuyahoga, 12-16-2004) No. 84059, 2004-Ohio-6862, 2004 WL 2914987, Unreported, motion for delayed appeal denied 106 Ohio St.3d 1409, 830 N.E.2d 343, 2005-Ohio-3154, denial of post-conviction relief affirmed 2011-Ohio-345, 2011 WL 315754. Jury ⚷ 33(5.15)

Defendant established a prima facie case of racial discrimination, for purposes of *Batson* challenge, where 75% of available African-American jurors had been excluded by peremptory challenges. State v. Brown (Ohio App. 8 Dist., Cuyahoga, 12-16-2004) No. 84059, 2004-Ohio-6862, 2004 WL 2914987, Unreported, motion for delayed appeal denied 106 Ohio St.3d 1409, 830 N.E.2d 343, 2005-Ohio-3154, denial of post-conviction relief affirmed 2011-Ohio-345, 2011 WL 315754. Jury ⚷ 33(5.15)

State's representation that African-American juror acknowledged that he did not want to be a juror because of pressing business matters constituted a race-neutral reason for striking him, rebutting any prima facie case of racial discrimination for purposes of *Batson* challenge. State v. Brown (Ohio App. 8 Dist., Cuyahoga, 12-16-2004) No. 84059, 2004-Ohio-6862, 2004 WL 2914987, Unreported, motion for delayed appeal denied 106 Ohio St.3d 1409, 830 N.E.2d 343, 2005-Ohio-3154, denial of post-conviction relief affirmed 2011-Ohio-345, 2011 WL 315754. Jury ⚷ 33(5.15)

State's representation that African-American juror had a relative who had been prosecuted by the assistant prosecuting attorney constituted a race-neutral reason for striking him, rebutting any prima facie case of racial discrimination for purposes of *Batson* challenge. State v. Brown (Ohio App. 8 Dist., Cuyahoga, 12-16-2004) No. 84059, 2004-Ohio-6862, 2004 WL 2914987, Unreported, motion for delayed appeal denied 106 Ohio St.3d 1409, 830 N.E.2d 343, 2005-Ohio-3154, denial of post-conviction relief affirmed 2011-Ohio-345, 2011 WL 315754. Jury ⚷ 33(5.15)

Defense counsel's assertion that prosecutor had "kicked two blacks off the jury" was insufficient to establish a prima facie case of racial discrimination, for purposes of *Batson* challenge. State v. Brown (Ohio App. 8 Dist., Cuyahoga, 12-16-2004) No. 84059, 2004-Ohio-6862, 2004 WL 2914987, Unreported, motion for delayed appeal denied 106 Ohio St.3d 1409, 830 N.E.2d 343, 2005-Ohio-3154, denial of post-conviction relief affirmed 2011-Ohio-345, 2011 WL 315754. Jury ⚷ 33(5.15)

For purposes of *Batson*, record supported finding that State provided race-neutral explanation for using three of its peremptory challenges to exclude African-Americans from jury; State claimed that first juror was struck because he had a criminal conviction and was unemployed, that second juror was struck because he worked at the same company as defendant's mother, and that third juror was struck because she knew the alleged victims. State v. Taylor (Ohio App. 1 Dist., Hamilton, 03-26-2004) No. C-020475, 2004-Ohio-1494, 2004 WL 596128, Unreported, appeal not allowed 103 Ohio St.3d 1406, 812 N.E.2d 1289, 2004-Ohio-3980, habeas corpus denied 2007 WL 2477705. Jury ⚷ 33(5.15)

Defendant was not required to show a pattern of discriminatory peremptory challenges in order to raise *Batson* challenge to state's exercise of peremptory strike against African-American prospective juror. State v. Graves (Ohio App. 6 Dist., Lucas, 05-09-2003) No. L-02-1053, 2003-Ohio-2359, 2003 WL 21040652, Unreported, appeal not allowed 100 Ohio St.3d 1410, 796 N.E.2d 537, 2003-Ohio-4948, denial of post-conviction relief affirmed 2007-Ohio-4713, 2007 WL 2683569, appeal not allowed 116 Ohio St.3d 1479, 879 N.E.2d 786, 2008-Ohio-153. Jury ⚷ 33(5.15)

Attorney's allegedly ineffective failure to use peremptory strike to excuse juror who admitted during voir dire that she would give more weight to police officers' testimony since her son was police officer did not prejudice defendant in prosecution for committing felonious assault, carrying concealed weapon, having a weapon while under disability, and tampering with evidence; no police officer witnessed the shooting, and although the arresting officer testified that he saw defendant holding his hand to his side while running away and that a few minutes later his partner found a gun in the grass nearby, insufficient evidence supported the conviction for carrying a concealed weapon, no reasonable probability existed that the tampering verdict would have been different if attorney had excused the juror. State v. Harris (Ohio App. 6 Dist., Lucas, 08-02-2002) No. L-01-1419, 2002-Ohio-3968, 2002 WL 1781152, Unreported, appeal not allowed 97 Ohio St.3d 1470, 779 N.E.2d 236, 2002-Ohio-6347, denial of habeas corpus affirmed 198 Fed.Appx. 448, 2006 WL 2711942. Criminal Law ⚷ 1901

After the defendant establishes a prima facie case of race discrimination in prosecutor's use of peremptory challenge, for purposes of proving an equal protection violation, the issue is the facial validity of the prosecutor's explanation for the challenge; unless a discriminatory intent is inherent in the prosecutor's explanation, the reason offered will be deemed race neutral. State v. Manns (Ohio App. 2 Dist., 11-03-2006) 169 Ohio App.3d 687, 864 N.E.2d 657, 2006-Ohio-5802, appeal not allowed 113 Ohio St.3d 1466, 864 N.E.2d 653, 2007-Ohio-1722. Constitutional Law ⚷ 3309

To satisfy burden of articulating a race-neutral explanation for peremptory challenge, for purposes of determining whether prosecutor's use of the challenge violated defendant's equal protection rights, the prosecutor's explanation for striking the prospective juror is not required to be persuasive, or even plausible. State v. Manns (Ohio App. 2 Dist., 11-03-2006) 169 Ohio App.3d 687, 864 N.E.2d 657, 2006-Ohio-5802, appeal not allowed 113 Ohio St.3d 1466, 864 N.E.2d 653, 2007-Ohio-1722. Constitutional Law ⚿ 3309

A state denies a black defendant equal protection when it puts her on trial before a jury from which members of her race have been purposefully excluded; therefore, the Equal Protection Clause forbids the prosecutor to challenge potential jurors solely on account of their race or on the assumption that black jurors as a group will be unable impartially to consider the State's case against a black defendant. State v. Manns (Ohio App. 2 Dist., 11-03-2006) 169 Ohio App.3d 687, 864 N.E.2d 657, 2006-Ohio-5802, appeal not allowed 113 Ohio St.3d 1466, 864 N.E.2d 653, 2007-Ohio-1722. Constitutional Law ⚿ 3306; Constitutional Law ⚿ 3309

Capital murder defendant failed to establish that prosecutor had impermissible discriminatory motive, in violation of *Batson*, for exercise of peremptory strike against black prospective juror; prosecutor gave race-neutral explanation that juror was stricken because he was opposed to death penalty, prosecutor did not exercise peremptory strikes against any other black jurors, and prosecutor's challenges for cause to two black jurors were well-supported by record and upheld by trial court. State v. White (Ohio, 05-12-1999) 85 Ohio St.3d 433, 709 N.E.2d 140, 1999-Ohio-281, denial of post-conviction relief affirmed 1999 WL 394938, dismissed, appeal not allowed 87 Ohio St.3d 1418, 717 N.E.2d 1105, certiorari denied 120 S.Ct. 345, 528 U.S. 938, 145 L.Ed.2d 270, post-conviction relief denied 2005 WL 5775899, affirmed 2005-Ohio-6990, 2005 WL 3556634, appeal allowed 109 Ohio St.3d 1493, 848 N.E.2d 857, 2006-Ohio-2762, reversed 118 Ohio St.3d 12, 885 N.E.2d 905, 2008-Ohio-1623. Jury ⚿ 33(5.15)

While presence of one or more black persons on a jury certainly does not preclude a finding of discrimination by prosecution in exercise of peremptory strikes against other black prospective jurors, fact may be taken into account as one that suggests that prosecution did not seek to rid the jury of persons of a particular race. State v. White (Ohio, 05-12-1999) 85 Ohio St.3d 433, 709 N.E.2d 140, 1999-Ohio-281, denial of post-conviction relief affirmed 1999 WL 394938, dismissed, appeal not allowed 87 Ohio St.3d 1418, 717 N.E.2d 1105, certiorari denied 120 S.Ct. 345, 528 U.S. 938, 145 L.Ed.2d 270, post-conviction relief denied 2005 WL 5775899, affirmed 2005-Ohio-6990, 2005 WL 3556634, appeal allowed 109 Ohio St.3d 1493, 848 N.E.2d 857, 2006-Ohio-2762, reversed 118 Ohio St.3d 12, 885 N.E.2d 905, 2008-Ohio-1623. Jury ⚿ 33(5.15)

State trial and appellate courts' denial of defendant's *Batson* challenge was not an unreasonable application of clearly established federal law, and therefore, federal habeas relief was not warranted; the trial court, albeit in abbreviated fashion, adequately and reasonably conveyed its decision that the prosecution's race-neutral, demeanor-based justification for the peremptory strike of juror was credible and that defendant failed to carry his burden on the ultimate issue of purposeful discrimination, and, likewise, the appellate court acknowledged the prosecution's assertion that the juror's body language indicated disinterest, noted that the trial court, after appropriate inquiry, rejected the notion that the prosecutor's challenge was pretextual, and, concluded independently that nothing in the prosecutor's explanation showed that he chose to exclude jurors on the basis of race. Braxton v. Gansheimer (C.A.6 (Ohio), 04-02-2009) 561 F.3d 453. Habeas Corpus ⚿ 496

On *Batson* claim, fact that a prosecutor's reasons may be founded on nothing more than a trial lawyer's instincts about a prospective juror does not diminish the scope of acceptable invocation of peremptory challenges, so long as they are the actual reasons for the prosecutor's actions. Braxton v. Gansheimer (C.A.6 (Ohio), 04-02-2009) 561 F.3d 453. Jury ⚿ 33(5.15)

If the defendant successfully makes a prima facie showing of a *Batson* violation, the burden shifts to the government to come forward with a neutral explanation for its peremptory challenges, which requires a justification for its strikes that does not deny equal protection, but requirements for such a justification are not rigorous. U.S. v. Maxwell (C.A.6 (Ohio), 11-17-1998) 160 F.3d 1071, denial of post-conviction relief affirmed 193 Fed.Appx. 479, 2006 WL 2457072, certiorari denied 127 S.Ct. 2081, 167 L.Ed.2d 801, rehearing denied 127 S.Ct. 2454, 167 L.Ed.2d 1149. Jury ⚿ 33(5.15)

State court capital murder defendant was not required to establish pattern of discriminatory strikes of prospective jurors in order to sustain challenge to strike of particular prospective juror as unlawfully discriminatory on basis of race. Stallings v. Bagley (N.D.Ohio, 03-31-2008) 561 F.Supp.2d 821. Jury ⚿ 33(5.15)

State court capital murder defendant failed to make prima facie showing that prosecutor's exercise of peremptory challenge to remove one African-American veniremember was based on race, for purposes of federal habeas petition, where prosecutor did not waive defendant's initial burden, trial court found no pattern of discrimination, defense counsel suggested no other grounds from which inference of discrimination might arise, defendant did not explain how later strikes were exercised or whether he renewed his original challenge in face of later strikes, and defendant provided no detail beyond that provided by trial court regarding racial composition of original venire, or even of final panel. Stallings v. Bagley (N.D.Ohio, 03-31-2008) 561 F.Supp.2d 821. Jury ⚿ 33(5.15)

Jury selection, peremptory challenges, race discrimination, pretext, prospective juror's student teaching status, see Snyder v. Louisiana, 2008, 128 S.Ct. 1203.

Habeas corpus, peremptory challenge, demeanor based explanation for challenge. Thaler v. Haynes, (U.S., 02-22-2010) 130 S.Ct. 1171.

5. Procedure—In general

Apart from excluding jurors based on race or gender, prosecutors can exercise peremptory challenge for any reason, without inquiry, and without court's control. State v. Biros (Ohio, 05-14-1997) 78 Ohio St.3d 426, 678 N.E.2d 891, 1997-Ohio-204, reconsideration denied 79 Ohio St.3d 1451, 680 N.E.2d 1023, certiorari denied 118 S.Ct. 574, 522 U.S. 1002, 139 L.Ed.2d 413, denial of post-conviction relief affirmed 1999 WL 391090, dismissed, appeal not allowed 87 Ohio St.3d 1406, 716 N.E.2d 1168, denial of post-conviction relief affirmed 93 Ohio St.3d 250, 754 N.E.2d 805, 2001-Ohio-1339, grant of habeas corpus reversed 422 F.3d 379, rehearing and rehearing en banc denied, certiorari denied 127 S.Ct. 125, 166 L.Ed.2d 93, certiorari denied 127 S.Ct. 714, 166 L.Ed.2d 552, habeas corpus dismissed 2007 WL 852041. Jury ⚿ 33(5.15); Jury ⚿ 135

There was no equal protection violation in prosecutor's use of peremptory strikes against prospective jurors who were 18 and 21 years old respectively, though the government conceded that age was a primary reason for its peremptory challenges. U.S. v. Maxwell (C.A.6 (Ohio), 11-17-1998) 160 F.3d 1071, denial of post-conviction relief affirmed 193 Fed.Appx. 479, 2006 WL 2457072, certiorari denied 127 S.Ct. 2081, 167 L.Ed.2d 801, rehearing denied 127 S.Ct. 2454, 167 L.Ed.2d 1149. Constitutional Law ⚿ 3105; Jury ⚿ 33(5.15)

7. —— Juror's aversion to death penalty, procedure

Prosecution in capital murder case could properly exercise peremptorily challenges against two prospective jurors who expressed or indicated some aversion to death penalty. State v. Biros (Ohio, 05-14-1997) 78 Ohio St.3d 426, 678 N.E.2d 891, 1997-Ohio-204, reconsideration denied 79 Ohio St.3d 1451, 680 N.E.2d 1023, certiorari denied 118 S.Ct. 574, 522 U.S. 1002, 139 L.Ed.2d 413, denial of post-conviction relief affirmed 1999 WL 391090, dismissed, appeal not allowed 87 Ohio St.3d 1406, 716 N.E.2d 1168, denial of post-conviction relief affirmed 93 Ohio St.3d 250, 754 N.E.2d 805, 2001-Ohio-1339, grant of habeas corpus reversed 422 F.3d 379, rehearing and rehearing en banc denied, certiorari denied 127 S.Ct. 125, 166 L.Ed.2d 93, certiorari denied 127 S.Ct. 714, 166 L.Ed.2d 552, habeas corpus dismissed 2007 WL 852041. Jury ⚿ 33(5.15)

Striking of four prospective jurors for cause based on determination that they were substantially impaired in their ability to impose the death penalty was warranted, and did not result in biased jury, in capital murder case; one juror told the trial court that he definitely did not think he could sign a death penalty recommendation, even if aggravating factors outweighed mitigating factors, another juror stated that she would not recommend a death sentence under any circumstances, the two others stated that they could not sign a verdict recommending the death penalty, and although defense counsel was permitted to follow up with additional questions to try to rehabilitate the jurors, the jurors' responses to the additional questions confirmed each juror's unwillingness to sign a death verdict. Bedford v. Collins (C.A.6 (Ohio), 06-04-2009) 567 F.3d 225, rehearing and rehearing en banc denied, certiorari denied 130 S.Ct. 2344, 559 U.S. 1058, 176 L.Ed.2d 577. Jury ⚿ 108

8. —— Race or gender discrimination, procedure

State's reason for exercising peremptory challenge against African-American prospective juror was race-based, and thus, its use of the challenge was improper; State's assumption or belief was because this juror was African American, and her child was involved in an accident with a sport utility vehicle (SUV), she then must or may have been associated with a group of African Americans that had protested against prosecutor, and implicit in this explanation was the juror's race itself. State v. Manns (Ohio App. 2 Dist., 11-03-2006) 169 Ohio App.3d 687, 864 N.E.2d 657, 2006-Ohio-5802, appeal not allowed 113 Ohio St.3d 1466, 864 N.E.2d 653, 2007-Ohio-1722. Constitutional Law ⚿ 3309; Jury ⚿ 33(5.15)

State's facially race-neutral reason for peremptory strike of African-American juror, that juror's initial voir dire silence contradicted his subsequent voir dire testimony, relating to whether he had any relatives with convictions, thus calling into doubt juror's honesty or objectivity, was not pretext for racial discrimination under *Batson*. State v. Williams (Ohio App. 2 Dist., Montgomery, 06-24-2005) No. 19963, 2005-Ohio-3172, 2005 WL 1490140, Unreported, motion for delayed appeal denied 110 Ohio St.3d 1436, 852 N.E.2d 186, 2006-Ohio-3862, appeal not allowed 111 Ohio St.3d 1431, 855 N.E.2d 496, 2006-Ohio-5351, appeal not allowed 111 Ohio St.3d 1434, 855 N.E.2d 498, 2006-Ohio-5351, habeas corpus denied 2011 WL 1113242. Jury ⚿ 33(5.15)

Responses given by African–American juror to questions advanced by State provided adequate race-neutral grounds for State to exercise peremptory challenge, as required under *Batson*; juror indicated that he had unresolved issues with respect to police harassing him and his family and that he probably could not set aside his feelings when weighing the testimony of a police officer. State v. Parsons (Ohio App. 2 Dist., Montgomery, 04-29-2005) No. 20476, 2005-Ohio-2017, 2005 WL 994583, Unreported, motion for delayed appeal denied 110 Ohio St.3d 1437, 852 N.E.2d 186, 2006-Ohio-3862, habeas corpus denied 2007 WL 2874422. Jury ⚿ 33(5.15)

Prosecution's proffered race-neutral reasons for exercising peremptory challenge against sole African-American prospective juror in murder prosecution were viable and nonpretextual, and exercise of peremptory challenge did not amount to impermissible discrimination, where prospective juror's nephew had been victim of unsolved murder, and prospective juror was at time of trial commencing treatment for sleep apnea; prospective juror's medical condition could have caused him to be inattentive to proceedings, and crimes of which other prospective jurors or their family members had been victims did not include murder. State v. Herron (Ohio App. 2 Dist., Montgomery, 02-20-2004) No. 19894, 2004-Ohio-773, 2004 WL 315232, Unreported, motion for delayed appeal denied 107 Ohio St.3d 1404, 836 N.E.2d 1226, 2005-Ohio-5859, denial of post-conviction relief affirmed 2008-Ohio-5362, 2008 WL 4599609, appeal not allowed 121 Ohio St.3d 1426, 903 N.E.2d 325, 2009-Ohio-1296, habeas corpus dismissed 2010 WL 749651. Jury ⚿ 33(5.15)

Capital murder defendant failed to carry his burden of proving intentional discrimination in prosecutor's use of peremptory challenge to remove African–American juror; defendant offered no evidence of discriminatory intent to counter prosecutor's racially neutral reasons for peremptorily challenging juror, which included reference in her juror questionnaire to story involving a miscarriage of justice and the lynching of an innocent man, her nodding her head in response to question whether jurors felt pressure to return a certain verdict due to community views, and her mannerisms showing she was offended by prosecutor's asking whether she was inconvenienced by jury selection process. State v. Bryan (Ohio, 03-17-2004) 101 Ohio St.3d 272, 804 N.E.2d 433, 2004-Ohio-971, motion granted 102 Ohio St.3d 1437, 807 N.E.2d 937, 2004-Ohio-2226, reconsideration denied 102 Ohio St.3d 1449, 808 N.E.2d 399, 2004-Ohio-2263, motion to reopen denied 103 Ohio St.3d 1490, 816 N.E.2d 1078, 2004-Ohio-5605, reconsideration stricken 103 Ohio St.3d 1529, 817 N.E.2d 891, 2004-Ohio-6040, appeal from dismissal of post-conviction relief dismissed 2006-Ohio-5022, 2006 WL 2773646, dismissal of post-conviction relief affirmed 2010-Ohio-2088, 2010 WL 1918606, appeal not allowed 127 Ohio St.3d 1461, 938 N.E.2d 363, 2010-Ohio-6008. Jury ⚿ 33(5.15)

There was no *Batson* violation in the prosecution's peremptory strike of only remaining black member of jury venire; prosecutor provided race-neutral reasons for strike by noting that venire member was a guidance counselor, and that in his experience, guidance counselors were overly sympathetic with defendants, that venire member stated that she was particularly busy at the time, and the prosecutor noted her "misgivings" about serving, and that she knew one of the defendants' lawyers from his high school days and also knew that lawyer's parents well. U.S. v. Maxwell (C.A.6 (Ohio), 11-17-1998) 160 F.3d 1071, denial of post-conviction relief affirmed 193 Fed.Appx. 479, 2006 WL 2457072, certiorari denied 127 S.Ct. 2081, 167 L.Ed.2d 801, rehearing denied 127 S.Ct. 2454, 167 L.Ed.2d 1149. Jury ⚿ 33(5.15)

African American petitioner failed to raise prima facie case of discrimination based on prosecutor's use of a peremptory challenge to exclude a single African American (among four peremptory challenges exercised) where he failed to show that the relevant circumstances raised an inference of purposeful discrimination. Montgomery v. Bagley (N.D.Ohio, 03-31-2007) 482 F.Supp.2d 919, affirmed 581 F.3d 440, rehearing granted, opinion vacated, reversed 654 F.3d 668, certiorari denied 132 S.Ct. 2376, 182 L.Ed.2d 1026. Jury ⚿ 33(5.15)

2945.24 Selecting juries for criminal cases

In all criminal cases, a jury summoned and impaneled under Chapter 2313. of the Revised Code shall try the accused.

(2012 H 268, eff. 5-22-12; 1993 H 41, eff. 9–27–93; 1981 S 1; 1976 H 133; 1953 H 1; GC 13443–5)

Historical and Statutory Notes

Amendment Note: 2012 H 268 substituted "Chapter 2313." for "section 2313.01 to 2313.47".

Research References

Encyclopedias

OH Jur. 3d Criminal Law: Procedure § 1206, Selecting Jury.

OH Jur. 3d Jury § 170, Generally; Definitions.

Notes of Decisions

1. Cross–section of community

Mere fact that African–American defendant was convicted by all-white jury did not mean that requirement for venire containing fair cross-section of community had been violated; defendant made no showing as to composition of venire, lack of fair and reasonable representation by African–Americans in venire, or systematic exclusion of African–Americans from venire. U.S. v. Anthony (C.A.6 (Ohio), 04-15-2002) No. 00-4118, No. 00-4215, 39 Fed.Appx. 91, 2002 WL 562669, Unreported, habeas corpus denied 2009 WL 3270483. Jury ⚿ 33(1.15)

2945.25 Causes of challenging of jurors

Law Review and Journal Commentaries

Unfair and can't be fixed: The machinery of death in Ohio. Alice Lynd, 44 U. Tol. L. Rev. 1, 2012).

Notes of Decisions

1. Cross-section of community

Mere fact that African–American defendant was convicted by all-white jury did not mean that requirement for venire containing fair cross-section of community had been violated; defendant made no showing as to composition of venire, lack of fair and reasonable representation by African–Americans in venire, or systematic exclusion of African–Americans from venire. U.S. v. Anthony (C.A.6 (Ohio), 04-15-2002) No. 00-4118, No. 00-4215, 39 Fed.Appx. 91, 2002 WL 562669, Unreported, habeas corpus denied 2009 WL 3270483. Jury ⚬ 33(1.15)

2. Bias or enmity—In general

Removal for cause of prospective juror who stated during voir dire that he was racist and that he felt he could not be fair to prosecution in view of negative experiences with law enforcement was not abuse of discretion, in trial for aiding and abetting bank robbery and other crimes, absent any showing that jury that was actually seated was biased. U.S. v. Parks (C.A.6 (Ohio), 05-16-2008) No. 06-4218, 278 Fed.Appx. 527, 2008 WL 2091427, Unreported, certiorari denied 129 S.Ct. 322, 555 U.S. 933, 172 L.Ed.2d 233, post-conviction relief denied 2010 WL 1741519. Jury ⚬ 97(1); Jury ⚬ 97(2)

Fact that some or all jurors seated in capital murder prosecution had heard of defendant's case prior to trial, without more, did not obviate their stated willingness to function as impartial jurors. State v. Gross (Ohio, 10-30-2002) 97 Ohio St.3d 121, 776 N.E.2d 1061, 2002-Ohio-5524, reconsideration denied 97 Ohio St.3d 1486, 780 N.E.2d 288, 2002-Ohio-6866, certiorari denied 123 S.Ct. 2079, 538 U.S. 1037, 155 L.Ed.2d 1068, rehearing denied 124 S.Ct. 20, 539 U.S. 976, 156 L.Ed.2d 685, denial of post-conviction relief affirmed 2003-Ohio-6295, 2003 WL 22765845, appeal not allowed 102 Ohio St.3d 1410, 806 N.E.2d 562, 2004-Ohio-1763, certiorari denied 125 S.Ct. 165, 543 U.S. 888, 160 L.Ed.2d 149, dismissal of post-conviction relief affirmed 2006-Ohio-6941, 2006 WL 3804532, appeal not allowed 113 Ohio St.3d 1468, 864 N.E.2d 654, 2007-Ohio-1722, habeas corpus dismissed 2008 WL 4702181, motion to amend denied 2008 WL 4889626, certificate of appealability denied 2008 WL 5190017, affirmed 426 Fed.Appx. 349, 2011 WL 1597659. Jury ⚬ 100

Trial court's failure sua sponte to excuse for cause a prospective juror who testified during voir dire that he had discussed case with his ex-father-in-law, the former chief of police of city where murder occurred and that prospective juror was biased against the defense to some degree was not error in capital case, where juror also stated that he would try to disregard conversation in question, would decide the case only on the evidence, and would accord defendant the usual presumption of innocence. State v. Jones (Ohio, 04-18-2001) 91 Ohio St.3d 335, 744 N.E.2d 1163, 2001-Ohio-57, reconsideration denied 92 Ohio St.3d 1418, 748 N.E.2d 550, stay granted 92 Ohio St.3d 1421, 748 N.E.2d 1142, certiorari denied 122 S.Ct. 483, 534 U.S. 1004, 151 L.Ed.2d 396, denial of post-conviction relief affirmed 2002-Ohio-2074, 2002 WL 737074, appeal not allowed 96 Ohio St.3d 1495, 774 N.E.2d 767, 2002-Ohio-4534, stay revoked 99 Ohio St.3d 1415, 788 N.E.2d 1098, 2003-Ohio-2526, motion to reopen denied 108 Ohio St.3d 1409, 841 N.E.2d 315, 2006-Ohio-179, habeas corpus denied 489 F.Supp.2d 786. Jury ⚬ 103(6); Jury ⚬ 109

Petitioner was not prejudiced by his counsel's failure to object to the venire and the trial court's failure to conduct adequate inquiry of the prospective jurors that overheard another prospective juror's comment that she had read about the case and believed petitioner to be guilty; the person who made the remark may not have sat on petitioner's jury, and petitioner's counsel thoroughly voir dired all prospective jurors as to their bias, prejudice or preconceived opinions based on pretrial publicity or out-of-court discussions. Adams v. Bradshaw (N.D.Ohio, 04-24-2007) 484 F.Supp.2d 753, opinion after remand from court of appeals 2009 WL 2922042, stay granted, motion to certify appeal granted 2010 WL 816532, subsequent determination 2010 WL 1964904, affirmed 644 F.3d 481, on remand 2013 WL 3991867. Criminal Law ⚬ 1166.16; Criminal Law ⚬ 1901

Jury selection, peremptory challenges, race discrimination, pretext, prospective juror's student teaching status, see Snyder v. Louisiana, 2008, 128 S.Ct. 1203.

3. —— Ability to render impartial verdict, bias or enmity

Fact that prospective juror in murder trial heard gunshots on the night of the murders did not make her unsuitable as a juror, and thus trial court's denial of defendant's challenge for cause to the juror was not plain error; juror was not subpoenaed as a witness, fact that shots were fired outside the residence of one of the victims was never in dispute, and juror assured court that she would be fair and impartial and decide the case based on the evidence. State v. Trimble (Ohio, 06-30-2009) 122 Ohio St.3d 297, 911 N.E.2d 242, 2009-Ohio-2961, certiorari denied 130 S.Ct. 752, 558 U.S. 1055, 175 L.Ed.2d 526. Criminal Law ⚬ 1035(5)

In cases involving pretrial publicity, relevant question is not whether the community remembered the case, but whether the jurors had such fixed opinions that they could not judge impartially the guilt of the defendant.; it is sufficient if the juror can lay aside his impression or opinion and render a verdict based on the evidence presented in court. Adams v. Bradshaw (N.D.Ohio, 04-24-2007) 484 F.Supp.2d 753, opinion after remand from court of appeals 2009 WL 2922042, stay granted, motion to certify appeal granted 2010 WL 816532, subsequent determination 2010 WL 1964904, affirmed 644 F.3d 481, on remand 2013 WL 3991867. Criminal Law ⚷ 126(1)

4. Scruples as to death penalty—In general

Trial court properly excused for cause, in capital prosecution, juror who equivocated as to whether she would follow instructions on the death penalty; although juror told defense counsel that she "would consider" instructions on death penalty, juror was opposed to the death penalty and told prosecutor, "I honestly can't say" when asked whether she would follow trial court's instructions on the death penalty. State v. Neyland (Ohio, 05-08-2014) 139 Ohio St.3d 353, 12 N.E.3d 1112, 2014-Ohio-1914, reconsideration denied 140 Ohio St.3d 1418, 15 N.E.3d 886, 2014-Ohio-3785. Jury ⚷ 108

Trial court properly excluded for cause, in capital murder prosecution, prospective jurors expressing strong views against death penalty, while declining to excuse for cause prospective jurors expressing strong views in favor thereof; excluded jurors all indicated inability to impose the death penalty, retained jurors all indicated their ability to follow the law, instructions and evidence, and those retained jurors specifically challenged never sat on the jury. State v. Stallings (Ohio, 07-19-2000) 89 Ohio St.3d 280, 731 N.E.2d 159, 2000-Ohio-164, stay granted 89 Ohio St.3d 1483, 733 N.E.2d 1184, stay revoked 93 Ohio St.3d 1455, 756 N.E.2d 674, certiorari denied 122 S.Ct. 89, 534 U.S. 836, 151 L.Ed.2d 51, post-conviction relief denied 2004 WL 5388150, affirmed 2004-Ohio-4571, 2004 WL 1932869, appeal not allowed 104 Ohio St.3d 1460, 821 N.E.2d 577, 2005-Ohio-204, habeas corpus granted in part, denied in part 561 F.Supp.2d 821. Jury ⚷ 108

Prospective jurors were properly excluded in capital case because, although jurors equivocated in their answers, all they indicated that they could not follow the law and impose the death sentence, even if appropriate. Getsy v. Mitchell (C.A.6 (Ohio), 08-02-2006) 456 F.3d 575, rehearing granted, opinion vacated. Jury ⚷ 108

Allegation that state court misapplied statutory standard for excusal of jurors involved only issue of state law, which was not cognizable in federal habeas corpus proceeding. Frazier v. Mitchell (N.D.Ohio, 01-05-2001) 188 F.Supp.2d 798, reversed in part 343 F.3d 780, opinion supplemented on denial of rehearing 348 F.3d 174, rehearing and suggestion for rehearing en banc denied, certiorari denied 124 S.Ct. 2815, 541 U.S. 1095, 159 L.Ed.2d 261. Habeas Corpus ⚷ 496

5. —— Beliefs preventing impartiality, scruples as to death penalty

Trial court properly excused for cause, in capital prosecution, juror who provided equivocal responses on her ability to follow the trial court's instructions on the death penalty; although juror stated that she would follow the instructions on the death penalty, "[i]f legally I have to do it," juror opposed the death penalty and had responded "No" when asked whether she could "consider fairly" the court's instructions on the death penalty. State v. Neyland (Ohio, 05-08-2014) 139 Ohio St.3d 353, 12 N.E.3d 1112, 2014-Ohio-1914, reconsideration denied 140 Ohio St.3d 1418, 15 N.E.3d 886, 2014-Ohio-3785. Jury ⚷ 108

Trial court did not abuse its discretion in capital murder trial by excusing for cause prospective juror who stated she did not think that the death penalty was appropriate in any case but that she could consider imposing a death sentence, where juror stated she could not assure the court that her beliefs on death penalty would not have impaired her ability to serve as a juror. State v. Leonard (Ohio, 12-08-2004) 104 Ohio St.3d 54, 818 N.E.2d 229, 2004-Ohio-6235, denial of post-conviction relief affirmed 2007-Ohio-7095, 2007 WL 4562881, appeal not allowed 118 Ohio St.3d 1506, 889 N.E.2d 1025, 2008-Ohio-3369, certiorari denied 129 S.Ct. 734, 555 U.S. 1075, 172 L.Ed.2d 736. Jury ⚷ 108

Trial court did not abuse its discretion in capital murder trial by excusing for cause prospective juror who initially stated she could consider imposing death sentence, where juror later stated that she did not feel it was right to "deliberately take the life of another except in self-defense," and that her views against capital punishment were strongly held and that she was opposed to it in all cases, including defendant's case. State v. Leonard (Ohio, 12-08-2004) 104 Ohio St.3d 54, 818 N.E.2d 229, 2004-Ohio-6235, denial of post-conviction relief affirmed 2007-Ohio-7095, 2007 WL 4562881, appeal not allowed 118 Ohio St.3d 1506, 889 N.E.2d 1025, 2008-Ohio-3369, certiorari denied 129 S.Ct. 734, 555 U.S. 1075, 172 L.Ed.2d 736. Jury ⚷ 108

Trial court did not abuse its discretion in capital murder trial by failing to excuse for cause prospective juror who stated she strongly favored death penalty in most murder cases with very few exceptions, where upon further questioning, juror stated she could put aside her views and follow the judge's instructions, and stated she could fairly and impartially weigh the mitigation evidence before deciding on appropriate penalty. State v. Leonard (Ohio, 12-08-2004) 104 Ohio St.3d 54, 818 N.E.2d 229, 2004-Ohio-6235, denial of post-conviction relief affirmed 2007-Ohio-7095, 2007 WL 4562881, appeal not allowed 118 Ohio St.3d 1506, 889 N.E.2d 1025, 2008-Ohio-3369, certiorari denied 129 S.Ct. 734, 555 U.S. 1075, 172 L.Ed.2d 736. Jury ⚷ 108

Excusing two prospective jurors for cause was not an abuse of discretion in capital murder prosecution, even though defense counsel was able to elicit somewhat contradictory viewpoints from jurors during his examination, where first juror expressed her opposition to the death penalty because of Biblical teachings and indicated she did not want to sign the death-penalty verdict form, and second juror said she could not support the death penalty and doubted if she could sign the death-penalty verdict. State v. Bryan (Ohio, 03-17-2004) 101 Ohio St.3d 272, 804 N.E.2d 433, 2004-Ohio-971, motion granted 102 Ohio St.3d 1437, 807 N.E.2d 937, 2004-Ohio-2226, reconsideration denied 102 Ohio St.3d 1449, 808 N.E.2d 399, 2004-Ohio-2263, motion to reopen denied 103 Ohio St.3d 1490, 816 N.E.2d 1078, 2004-Ohio-5605, reconsideration stricken 103 Ohio St.3d 1529, 817 N.E.2d 891, 2004-Ohio-6040, appeal from dismissal of post-conviction relief dismissed 2006-Ohio-5022, 2006 WL 2773646, dismissal of post-conviction relief affirmed 2010-Ohio-2088, 2010 WL 1918606, appeal not allowed 127 Ohio St.3d 1461, 938 N.E.2d 363, 2010-Ohio-6008. Jury ⚷ 108

Finding that prospective juror's views regarding death penalty would prevent or substantial impair performance of his duties, thus warranting his removal for cause in capital murder prosecution, was supported by evidence that juror had stated that he opposed capital punishment, that it would be "difficult" for him to follow law as instructed if that would entail recommending death, and that his views would apparently substantially impair his ability to convict, even though juror later appeared to contradict those statements. State v. White (Ohio, 05-12-1999) 85 Ohio St.3d 433, 709 N.E.2d 140, 1999-Ohio-281, denial of post-conviction relief affirmed 1999 WL 394938, dismissed, appeal not allowed 87 Ohio St.3d 1418, 717 N.E.2d 1105, certiorari denied 120 S.Ct. 345, 528 U.S. 938, 145 L.Ed.2d 270, post-conviction relief denied 2005 WL 5775899, affirmed 2005-Ohio-6990, 2005 WL 3556634, appeal allowed 109 Ohio St.3d 1493, 848 N.E.2d 857, 2006-Ohio-2762, reversed 118 Ohio St.3d 12, 885 N.E.2d 905, 2008-Ohio-1623. Jury ⚷ 132

6. —— Mere opposition to death penalty, scruples as to death penalty

Capital defendant failed to establish that defense counsel rendered ineffective assistance of counsel during voir dire by declining to ask juror any questions on individual voir dire and by not challenging her for cause; defense counsel could have concluded that juror "would be favorable for the defense," as her voir dire suggested that she was less than a strong supporter of capital punishment, she stated repeatedly that she had no opinion about the death penalty, and when asked whether she could return a death sentence, juror initially answered that she did not know, although she ultimately decided that she could. State v. Mundt (Ohio, 10-03-2007) 115 Ohio St.3d 22, 873 N.E.2d 828, 2007-Ohio-4836. Criminal Law ⚷ 1901

Trial court did not abuse its discretion in capital murder trial by excusing for cause prospective juror who initially stated she could consider imposing death sentence, where while juror stated after further questioning, that she was not against the death penalty, she stated that she did not feel comfortable being the one to do it and ultimately stated she did not believe she could sign a death verdict. State v. Leonard (Ohio, 12-08-2004) 104 Ohio St.3d 54, 818 N.E.2d 229, 2004-Ohio-6235, denial of post-conviction relief affirmed 2007-Ohio-7095, 2007 WL 4562881, appeal not allowed 118 Ohio St.3d 1506, 889 N.E.2d 1025, 2008-Ohio-3369, certiorari denied 129 S.Ct. 734, 555 U.S. 1075, 172 L.Ed.2d 736. Jury ⚷ 108

Exclusion from capital jury of prospective jurors opposed to the death penalty was not unconstitutional. State v. Lynch (Ohio, 05-14-2003) 98 Ohio St.3d 514, 787 N.E.2d 1185, 2003-Ohio-2284, motion denied 99 Ohio St.3d 1402, 788 N.E.2d 641, 2003-Ohio-2382, certiorari denied 124 S.Ct. 405, 540 U.S. 955, 157 L.Ed.2d 291, denial of post-conviction relief affirmed 2006-Ohio-5076, 2006 WL 2788504, appeal not allowed 112 Ohio St.3d 1491, 862 N.E.2d 118, 2007-Ohio-724, habeas corpus denied 2011 WL 4537890, motion to amend denied 2012 WL 404871. Jury ⚷ 33(2.15)

7. —— Procedure on voir dire, scruples as to death penalty

Defense counsel's hypothetical voir dire question, asking jurors how they would proceed in the sentencing phase if they found capital defendant guilty, was not a concession of guilt, for purposes of claim of ineffective assistance of counsel; trial counsel's hypothetical question was designed to ascertain which jurors would automatically impose a death sentence upon conviction simply because the crime was heinous, without considering the mitigating factors. State v. Mundt (Ohio, 10-03-2007) 115 Ohio St.3d 22, 873 N.E.2d 828, 2007-Ohio-4836. Criminal Law ⚷ 1901; Jury ⚷ 131(13)

Capital defendant failed to prove that trial counsel rendered ineffective assistance during voir dire by failing to challenge juror for cause and in failing to remove juror with a peremptory challenge; taken as a whole, juror's voir dire responses made clear that she was not an automatic-death-penalty juror and would consider mitigating circumstances. State v. Mundt (Ohio, 10-03-2007) 115 Ohio St.3d 22, 873 N.E.2d 828, 2007-Ohio-4836. Criminal Law ⚷ 1901

Trial court did not abuse its discretion during voir dire of capital murder trial by denying trial counsel's request for sequestered voir dire; trial court did permit counsel to individually question prospective jurors, and although jurors were not sequestered, the trial court gave each juror the opportunity to be questioned in private if they were uncomfortable discussing their views in a group setting. State v. Leonard (Ohio, 12-08-2004) 104 Ohio St.3d 54, 818 N.E.2d 229, 2004-Ohio-6235, denial of post-conviction relief affirmed 2007-Ohio-7095, 2007 WL 4562881, appeal not allowed 118 Ohio St.3d 1506, 889 N.E.2d 1025, 2008-Ohio-3369, certiorari denied 129 S.Ct. 734, 555 U.S. 1075, 172 L.Ed.2d 736. Jury ⚷ 131(13)

Trial court did not abuse its discretion during voir dire of capital murder trial by precluding trial counsel from using hypothetical question, of whether juror "would impose the death sentence in a case like Timothy McVeigh's" to determine a juror's death-penalty position; trial counsel was permitted to thoroughly explore prospective jurors' views, and defendant failed to show that the trial court unreasonably or arbitrarily restricted counsel's examination. State v. Leonard (Ohio, 12-08-2004) 104 Ohio St.3d 54, 818 N.E.2d 229, 2004-Ohio-6235, denial of post-conviction relief affirmed 2007-Ohio-7095, 2007 WL 4562881, appeal not allowed 118 Ohio St.3d 1506, 889 N.E.2d 1025, 2008-Ohio-3369, certiorari denied 129 S.Ct. 734, 555 U.S. 1075, 172 L.Ed.2d 736. Jury ⚷ 131(13)

Rejecting capital murder defendant's challenge for cause against juror who initially said that she could not impose a penalty less severe than death was not an abuse of discretion; although juror was confused by initial questioning, her follow-up responses demonstrated her willingness to follow the law, evaluate mitigating factors, and consider a lesser sentence under appropriate circumstances. State v. Bryan (Ohio, 03-17-2004) 101 Ohio St.3d 272, 804 N.E.2d 433, 2004-Ohio-971, motion granted 102 Ohio St.3d 1437, 807 N.E.2d 937, 2004-Ohio-2226, reconsideration denied 102 Ohio St.3d 1449, 808 N.E.2d 399, 2004-Ohio-2263, motion to reopen denied 103 Ohio St.3d 1490, 816 N.E.2d 1078, 2004-Ohio-5605, reconsideration stricken 103 Ohio St.3d 1529, 817 N.E.2d 891, 2004-Ohio-6040, appeal from dismissal of post-conviction relief dismissed 2006-Ohio-5022, 2006 WL 2773646, dismissal of post-conviction relief affirmed 2010-Ohio-2088, 2010 WL 1918606, appeal not allowed 127 Ohio St.3d 1461, 938 N.E.2d 363, 2010-Ohio-6008. Jury ⚷ 108

In capital murder trial, court acted within its discretion in refusing to excuse for cause juror who indicated that she favored the death penalty but indicated that she would listen to all the evidence and would require state to prove that aggravating circumstances outweighed mitigating factors. State v. Smith (Ohio, 12-13-2002) 97 Ohio St.3d 367, 780 N.E.2d 221, 2002-Ohio-6659, reconsideration denied 97 Ohio St.3d 1500, 780 N.E.2d 1023, 2002-Ohio-7367, stay granted 98 Ohio St.3d 1417, 782 N.E.2d 73, 2003-Ohio-189, certiorari denied 123 S.Ct. 2255, 539 U.S. 907, 156 L.Ed.2d 118, habeas corpus denied 2007 WL 2840379, affirmed 591 F.3d 517, rehearing and rehearing en banc denied, certiorari denied 131 S.Ct. 185, 178 L.Ed.2d 111. Jury ⚷ 108

Denial in capital case of for-cause challenge to prospective juror who testified during voir dire that, according to his religious beliefs, one who takes the life of another should "automatically" lose his own life was not error, where prospective juror further testified that he would follow the law and that he was capable of considering a penalty less than death. State v. Jones (Ohio, 04-18-2001) 91 Ohio St.3d 335, 744 N.E.2d 1163, 2001-Ohio-57, reconsideration denied 92 Ohio St.3d 1418, 748 N.E.2d 550, stay granted 92 Ohio St.3d 1421, 748 N.E.2d 1142, certiorari denied 122 S.Ct. 483, 534 U.S. 1004, 151 L.Ed.2d 396, denial of post-conviction relief affirmed 2002-Ohio-2074, 2002 WL 737074, appeal not allowed 96 Ohio St.3d 1495, 774 N.E.2d 767, 2002-Ohio-4534, stay revoked 99 Ohio St.3d 1415, 788 N.E.2d 1098, 2003-Ohio-2526, motion to reopen denied 108 Ohio St.3d 1409, 841 N.E.2d 315, 2006-Ohio-179, habeas corpus denied 489 F.Supp.2d 786. Jury ⚷ 108

Inclusion in capital murder prosecution of juror who initially stated in voir dire that she "believed in" the death penalty because someone who took another person's life should give his life up, and that this principle should apply "in every case," did not violate defendant's right to fair and impartial jury, where juror later stated in voir dire that she had been confused by earlier questions, insisted she would follow the law and the court's directions, and specifically indicated she could consider mitigating circumstances that might warrant a lesser sentence. State v. Treesh (Ohio, 01-03-2001) 90 Ohio St.3d 460, 739 N.E.2d 749, 2001-Ohio-4, stay granted 91 Ohio St.3d 1435, 742 N.E.2d 135, certiorari denied 121 S.Ct. 2247, 533 U.S. 904, 150 L.Ed.2d 234, habeas corpus denied 2007 WL 1039081. Jury ⚷ 108

Defendant's counsel in capital murder case was not ineffective in failing to examine prospective jurors during voir dire to determine whether they were capable of considering all mitigating factors; counsel did ask veniremen whether they could consider mitigating circumstances, as opposed to automatically imposing death penalty, and counsel could reasonably decide that it was unnecessary to ask prospective jurors whether they would find specific factors to be mitigating. State v. McGuire (Ohio, 12-10-1997) 80 Ohio St.3d 390, 686 N.E.2d 1112, 1997-Ohio-335, reconsideration denied 81 Ohio St.3d 1433, 689 N.E.2d 52, dismissal of post-conviction relief affirmed 1998 WL 191415, dismissed, appeal not allowed 83 Ohio St.3d 1428, 699 N.E.2d 945, certiorari denied 119 S.Ct. 85, 525 U.S. 831, 142 L.Ed.2d 66, denial of post-conviction relief affirmed 2001 WL 409424, dismissed, appeal not allowed 93 Ohio St.3d 1411, 754 N.E.2d 259, habeas corpus denied 2007 WL 1893902. Criminal Law ⚷ 1901

Prosecution in capital murder case could properly exercise peremptorily challenges against two prospective jurors who expressed or indicated some aversion to death penalty. State v. Biros (Ohio, 05-14-1997) 78 Ohio St.3d 426, 678 N.E.2d 891, 1997-Ohio-204, reconsideration denied 79 Ohio St.3d 1451, 680 N.E.2d 1023, certiorari denied 118 S.Ct. 574, 522 U.S. 1002, 139 L.Ed.2d 413, denial of post-conviction relief affirmed 1999 WL 391090, dismissed, appeal not allowed 87 Ohio St.3d 1406, 716 N.E.2d 1168, denial of post-conviction relief affirmed 93 Ohio St.3d 250, 754 N.E.2d 805, 2001-Ohio-1339, grant of habeas corpus reversed

422 F.3d 379, rehearing and rehearing en banc denied, certiorari denied 127 S.Ct. 125, 166 L.Ed.2d 93, certiorari denied 127 S.Ct. 714, 166 L.Ed.2d 552, habeas corpus dismissed 2007 WL 852041. Jury ⚷ 33(5.15)

10. Other causes of unsuitability

Trial court reasonably exercised its discretion by excusing prospective juror, who had a scheduling conflict, from serving in capital murder trial. State v. Thompson (Ohio, 10-29-2014) 141 Ohio St.3d 254, 23 N.E.3d 1096, 2014-Ohio-4751. Jury ⚷ 75(2)

Trial court abused its discretion in failing to excuse a hearing-impaired juror for cause, in prosecution for aggravated vehicular homicide and involuntary manslaughter; juror candidly acknowledged that she could understand what someone was saying only if she could see them, and, consequently, it was unknown whether juror received all testimony, and juror could not adequately evaluate taped 911 call, which was offered to provide evidence of whether defendant's speech and conversation with dispatcher and Coast Guard indicated elements of crimes charged, namely, purposefulness and recklessness. State v. Speer (Ohio App. 6 Dist., 12-31-2008) 180 Ohio App.3d 230, 904 N.E.2d 956, 2008-Ohio-6947, affirmed 124 Ohio St.3d 564, 925 N.E.2d 584, 2010-Ohio-649. Jury ⚷ 40

11. Exercising challenges for cause

The constitutional standard for determining when a prospective juror may be excluded for cause based upon his or her views on capital punishment is whether the juror's views would prevent or substantially impair the performance of his duties as a juror in accordance with his instructions and oath. State v. Neyland (Ohio, 05-08-2014) 139 Ohio St.3d 353, 12 N.E.3d 1112, 2014-Ohio-1914, reconsideration denied 140 Ohio St.3d 1418, 15 N.E.3d 886, 2014-Ohio-3785. Jury ⚷ 108

Trial court properly excused for cause, in capital prosecution, prospective juror who refused to promise to follow the trial court's instructions and reserved the right to consider engaging in juror nullification in some circumstances. State v. Neyland (Ohio, 05-08-2014) 139 Ohio St.3d 353, 12 N.E.3d 1112, 2014-Ohio-1914, reconsideration denied 140 Ohio St.3d 1418, 15 N.E.3d 886, 2014-Ohio-3785. Jury ⚷ 105(4)

In deciding a challenge for cause to a prospective juror on the basis of a physical impairment, the court must determine, in light of the specific evidence to be presented, whether any reasonable and effective accommodation can be made to enable the juror to serve; in making that determination, the court must balance the public interest in equal access to jury service against the right of the accused to a fair trial, the latter being the predominant concern of the court. State v. Speer (Ohio, 03-03-2010) 124 Ohio St.3d 564, 925 N.E.2d 584, 2010-Ohio-649. Jury ⚷ 40

Trial court did not improperly deny challenges for cause, in capital murder prosecution, involving jurors who stated that they could not consider mitigating evidence and would automatically vote to recommend death penalty, and thus did not prejudicially affect defendant's use of peremptory challenges; many jurors challenged on such grounds in fact indicated willingness and ability to follow the law in sentencing phase, trial court excused for cause any prospective juror who did express inability to consider mitigation evidence, and defendant failed to identify any remaining prospective juror against whom he was required to exercise peremptory challenge to his prejudice. State v. Gross (Ohio, 10-30-2002) 97 Ohio St.3d 121, 776 N.E.2d 1061, 2002-Ohio-5524, reconsideration denied 97 Ohio St.3d 1486, 780 N.E.2d 288, 2002-Ohio-6866, certiorari denied 123 S.Ct. 2079, 538 U.S. 1037, 155 L.Ed.2d 1068, rehearing denied 124 S.Ct. 20, 539 U.S. 976, 156 L.Ed.2d 685, denial of post-conviction relief affirmed 2003-Ohio-6295, 2003 WL 22765845, appeal not allowed 102 Ohio St.3d 1410, 806 N.E.2d 562, 2004-Ohio-1763, certiorari denied 125 S.Ct. 165, 543 U.S. 888, 160 L.Ed.2d 149, dismissal of post-conviction relief affirmed 2006-Ohio-6941, 2006 WL 3804532, appeal not allowed 113 Ohio St.3d 1468, 864 N.E.2d 654, 2007-Ohio-1722, habeas corpus dismissed 2008 WL 4702181, motion to amend denied 2008 WL 4889626, certificate of appealability denied 2008 WL 5190017, affirmed 426 Fed.Appx. 349, 2011 WL 1597659. Jury ⚷ 108; Jury ⚷ 135

Capital murder defendant who waived his final peremptory challenge had no basis to complain of trial court's refusal to excuse for cause prospective jurors who expressed strong views in favor of imposition of death penalty. State v. Stallings (Ohio, 07-19-2000) 89 Ohio St.3d 280, 731 N.E.2d 159, 2000-Ohio-164, stay granted 89 Ohio St.3d 1483, 733 N.E.2d 1184, stay revoked 93 Ohio St.3d 1455, 756 N.E.2d 674, certiorari denied 122 S.Ct. 89, 534 U.S. 836, 151 L.Ed.2d 51, post-conviction relief denied 2004 WL 5388150, affirmed 2004-Ohio-4571, 2004 WL 1932869, appeal not allowed 104 Ohio St.3d 1460, 821 N.E.2d 577, 2005-Ohio-204, habeas corpus granted in part, denied in part 561 F.Supp.2d 821. Criminal Law ⚷ 1166.18

Time limit on voir dire imposed by trial judge, allotting each side one-half hour to question each prospective juror, did not deprive defendant of the requisite latitude in voir dire questioning so as to amount to an abuse of discretion; defense counsel did not object to the time allotment or request more time to question a juror during voir dire, and trial court's statement to defense counsel that he had fourteen minutes left in questioning that juror was in response to defense counsel's inquiry as to the time. State v. Cornwell (Ohio, 09-22-1999) 86 Ohio St.3d 560, 715 N.E.2d 1144, 1999-Ohio-125, stay granted 87 Ohio St.3d 1414, 717 N.E.2d 714, stay revoked 98 Ohio St.3d 1475, 784 N.E.2d 709, 2003-Ohio-980, certiorari denied 120 S.Ct. 1200, 528 U.S. 1172, 145 L.Ed.2d 1103, denial of post-conviction relief affirmed 2002-Ohio-5177, 2002 WL 31160861, appeal not allowed 98 Ohio St.3d

1413, 781 N.E.2d 1020, 2003-Ohio-60, denial of habeas corpus affirmed 2009 WL 605232. Jury ⚷ 131(4)

Habeas petitioner failed to fairly present his federal constitutional challenge to exclusion of prospective juror who expressed reservations about capital punishment to the state courts where his discussion of federal case law and citation to United States Supreme Court cases was only for the express purpose of distinguishing them in urging the state courts to ignore them in favor of state statutory law. Sheppard v. Bagley (S.D.Ohio, 03-04-2009) 604 F.Supp.2d 1003, affirmed 657 F.3d 338, rehearing and rehearing en banc denied, certiorari denied 132 S.Ct. 2751, 183 L.Ed.2d 623, motion for relief from judgment denied 2013 WL 146342, certificate of appealability 2013 WL 1346138. Habeas Corpus ⚷ 383

2945.26 Challenge for cause

Notes of Decisions

1. Constitutional issues

Failure of counsel to challenge, for cause, prospective juror who had known the murder victim did not constitute deficient performance and was not prejudicial, as elements of ineffective assistance of counsel; counsel had strong tactical reasons for wanting the prospective juror to sit on the jury, i.e., her religious beliefs emphasized "thou shall not judge" and she believed her religion would deem it a sin to vote for a death sentence, and for those very reasons, the prosecution repeatedly, but unsuccessfully, challenged her for cause. State v. Hale (Ohio, 07-15-2008) 119 Ohio St.3d 118, 892 N.E.2d 864, 2008-Ohio-3426, reconsideration denied 119 Ohio St.3d 1450, 893 N.E.2d 519, 2008-Ohio-4487, certiorari denied 129 S.Ct. 1906, 556 U.S. 1168, 173 L.Ed.2d 1061. Criminal Law ⚷ 1901

Defense counsel's failure to challenge for cause a juror who had taken paralegal classes taught by the prosecutor was not ineffective assistance in capital murder prosecution; such a challenge would not likely have succeeded in view of that juror's testimony that her past affiliation with prosecutor's paralegal course would not impair her ability to render a fair and impartial verdict. State v. Treesh (Ohio, 01-03-2001) 90 Ohio St.3d 460, 739 N.E.2d 749, 2001-Ohio-4, stay granted 91 Ohio St.3d 1435, 742 N.E.2d 135, certiorari denied 121 S.Ct. 2247, 533 U.S. 904, 150 L.Ed.2d 234, habeas corpus denied 2007 WL 1039081. Criminal Law ⚷ 1901

Defense counsel's failure in capital murder prosecution to challenge for cause a juror who admitted exposure to some newspaper articles about the case and admitted that she favored the death penalty " [w]hen it's warranted" was not ineffective assistance; such a challenge would not likely have been granted in view of juror's additional statements that she had not formed an opinion about the case and that she could fairly and impartially weigh the evidence presented. State v. Treesh (Ohio, 01-03-2001) 90 Ohio St.3d 460, 739 N.E.2d 749, 2001-Ohio-4, stay granted 91 Ohio St.3d 1435, 742 N.E.2d 135, certiorari denied 121 S.Ct. 2247, 533 U.S. 904, 150 L.Ed.2d 234, habeas corpus denied 2007 WL 1039081. Criminal Law ⚷ 1901

The seating of a biased juror who should have been dismissed for cause requires reversal of the conviction. Franklin v. Anderson (C.A.6 (Ohio), 01-09-2006) 434 F.3d 412, rehearing and rehearing en banc denied, certiorari denied 127 S.Ct. 941, 549 U.S. 1156, 166 L.Ed.2d 781. Criminal Law ⚷ 1166.16; Jury ⚷ 97(1)

Failure to remove biased jurors taints the entire trial, and therefore the resulting conviction must be overturned. Franklin v. Anderson (C.A.6 (Ohio), 01-09-2006) 434 F.3d 412, rehearing and rehearing en banc denied, certiorari denied 127 S.Ct. 941, 549 U.S. 1156, 166 L.Ed.2d 781. Criminal Law ⚷ 1166.16; Jury ⚷ 97(1)

Petitioner's right to impartial jury was not violated by trial court's failure to excuse for cause two jurors who were acquainted with police officers who testified at petitioner's murder where jurors indicated their ability to set aside their impressions or opinions and to fairly and impartially consider the case on the evidence presented and law as instructed by the trial court. Montgomery v. Bagley (N.D.Ohio, 03-31-2007) 482 F.Supp.2d 919, affirmed 581 F.3d 440, rehearing granted, opinion vacated, reversed 654 F.3d 668, certiorari denied 132 S.Ct. 2376, 182 L.Ed.2d 1026. Jury ⚷ 33(2.10); Jury ⚷ 90

Jury selection, peremptory challenges, race discrimination, pretext, prospective juror's student teaching status, see Snyder v. Louisiana, 2008, 128 S.Ct. 1203.

2. Record of ruling on challenge

Prospective juror, who had worked at same company as one victim approximately 10 years prior to trial, was not subject to discharge for cause in prosecution for theft from the elderly and robbery, where victim had worked for company part–time and had had very little interaction with juror, and juror stated that she could remain fair and impartial and that her association with victim would not affect her consideration of case. State v. Lester (Ohio App. 1 Dist., Hamilton, 07-18-2008) No. C-070383, 2008-Ohio-3570, 2008 WL 2781033, Unreported, appeal allowed 120 Ohio St.3d 1416, 897 N.E.2d 652, 2008-Ohio-6166, motion to dismiss appeal denied 121 Ohio St.3d 1209, 901 N.E.2d 1290, 2009-Ohio-478, reversed 123 Ohio St.3d 396, 916 N.E.2d 1038, 2009-Ohio-4225. Jury ⚷ 97(2)

Trial court did not abuse its discretion in capital murder case by overruling defendant's challenge for cause to prospective juror who gave contradictory statements in his questionnaire and on voir dire with respect to whether death penalty for robbery-murder should be automatic, where juror clearly stated that he could set his personal opinions aside, follow whatever instructions the trial court would give, and weigh the mitigating factors. State v. Perez (Ohio, 12-02-2009) 124 Ohio St.3d 122, 920 N.E.2d 104, 2009-Ohio-6179, reconsideration denied 124 Ohio St.3d 1446, 920 N.E.2d 375, 2010-Ohio-188, certiorari denied 130 S.Ct. 3516, 561 U.S. 1031, 177 L.Ed.2d 1101. Jury ⚖ 108

Trial court's failure to sustain defense challenge for cause against prospective juror whose husband had been correctional officer at prison where defendant was incarcerated at time of murder, and who favored death penalty, believed justice system was "too slow," and did not think it was "fair" for her to sit on jury, was not abuse of discretion, where juror's husband had been assigned to another facility, and juror stated that her husband's employment would not "taint" her view of evidence, and that she would be fair to both sides, keep open mind, consider all options, and follow the court's instructions, and that she would not automatically vote for death penalty. State v. Cassano (Ohio, 08-07-2002) 96 Ohio St.3d 94, 772 N.E.2d 81, 2002-Ohio-3751, reconsideration denied 96 Ohio St.3d 1517, 775 N.E.2d 858, 2002-Ohio-4950, certiorari denied 123 S.Ct. 1359, 537 U.S. 1235, 155 L.Ed.2d 201, denial of post-conviction relief vacated 2008-Ohio-1045, 2008 WL 638190. Jury ⚖ 97(2); Jury ⚖ 104.1; Jury ⚖ 108

3. Waiver of challenges

Capital murder defendant's failure to challenge for cause prospective juror who stated during voir dire that he believed that murder in cold blood and murders for hire merited "automatic death sentence" and that those who use gun to commit crime resulting in death should receive death penalty waived appellate review of any issue as to that juror's selection. State v. Stallings (Ohio, 07-19-2000) 89 Ohio St.3d 280, 731 N.E.2d 159, 2000-Ohio-164, stay granted 89 Ohio St.3d 1483, 733 N.E.2d 1184, stay revoked 93 Ohio St.3d 1455, 756 N.E.2d 674, certiorari denied 122 S.Ct. 89, 534 U.S. 836, 151 L.Ed.2d 51, post-conviction relief denied 2004 WL 5388150, affirmed 2004-Ohio-4571, 2004 WL 1932869, appeal not allowed 104 Ohio St.3d 1460, 821 N.E.2d 577, 2005-Ohio-204, habeas corpus granted in part, denied in part 561 F.Supp.2d 821. Criminal Law ⚖ 1166.16

2945.27 Examination of jurors by the court

Notes of Decisions

2. Examination by court

Trial court in a capital murder prosecution was not required to conduct sua sponte a further inquiry in response to casual comment by an unknown prospective juror suggesting a preconceived opinion of guilt in a jury-selection waiting room. State v. Adams (Ohio, 11-17-2004) 103 Ohio St.3d 508, 817 N.E.2d 29, 2004-Ohio-5845, reconsideration denied 104 Ohio St.3d 1442, 819 N.E.2d 1124, 2004-Ohio-7033, certiorari denied 125 S.Ct. 2271, 544 U.S. 1040, 161 L.Ed.2d 1072, habeas corpus denied 2007 WL 671296, habeas corpus denied 484 F.Supp.2d 753, opinion after remand from court of appeals 2009 WL 2922042, stay granted, motion to certify appeal granted 2010 WL 816532, subsequent determination 2010 WL 1964904, affirmed 644 F.3d 481, on remand 2013 WL 3991867. Jury ⚖ 133

Casual comment by an unknown prospective juror suggesting a preconceived opinion of guilt in a jury-selection waiting room did not prejudice defendant in capital murder prosecution; when this unknown person made the remark, no jury had been seated or sworn, the person and prospective jurors who heard it may not have sat on the jury, and the trial court and counsel conducted thorough and individual voir dire of all prospective jurors in order to uncover any bias, prejudice, or preconceived opinions based on pretrial publicity or out-of-court discussions. State v. Adams (Ohio, 11-17-2004) 103 Ohio St.3d 508, 817 N.E.2d 29, 2004-Ohio-5845, reconsideration denied 104 Ohio St.3d 1442, 819 N.E.2d 1124, 2004-Ohio-7033, certiorari denied 125 S.Ct. 2271, 544 U.S. 1040, 161 L.Ed.2d 1072, habeas corpus denied 2007 WL 671296, habeas corpus denied 484 F.Supp.2d 753, opinion after remand from court of appeals 2009 WL 2922042, stay granted, motion to certify appeal granted 2010 WL 816532, subsequent determination 2010 WL 1964904, affirmed 644 F.3d 481, on remand 2013 WL 3991867. Criminal Law ⚖ 1166.16

Trial court's restrictions on and interruptions of voir dire did not impair capital murder defendant's ability to use peremptory challenges effectively to remove prospective jurors or otherwise impair his defense, where trial court was not unduly restrictive, but rather balanced its obligation to control inquiry with according counsel latitude in questioning prospective jurors, and where court's only restrictions on particular areas of inquiry were well within its discretion. State v. Gross (Ohio, 10-30-2002) 97 Ohio St.3d 121, 776 N.E.2d 1061, 2002-Ohio-5524, reconsideration denied 97 Ohio St.3d 1486, 780 N.E.2d 288, 2002-Ohio-6866, certiorari denied 123 S.Ct. 2079, 538 U.S. 1037, 155 L.Ed.2d 1068, rehearing denied 124 S.Ct. 20, 539 U.S. 976, 156 L.Ed.2d 685, denial of post-conviction relief affirmed 2003-Ohio-6295, 2003 WL 22765845, appeal not allowed 102 Ohio St.3d 1410, 806 N.E.2d 562, 2004-Ohio-1763, certiorari denied 125 S.Ct. 165, 543 U.S. 888, 160 L.Ed.2d 149, dismissal of post-conviction relief affirmed 2006-Ohio-6941, 2006 WL 3804532, appeal not allowed 113 Ohio St.3d 1468, 864 N.E.2d 654, 2007-Ohio-1722, habeas corpus dismissed 2008 WL 4702181, motion to amend denied 2008 WL 4889626, certificate of appealability denied 2008 WL 5190017, affirmed

426 Fed.Appx. 349, 2011 WL 1597659. Jury ⚩ 131(4)

While statute grants prosecution and defense opportunity to conduct a reasonable examination of prospective jurors, trial court reserves right and responsibility to control proceedings, and must limit trial to relevant and material matters with a view toward expeditious and effective ascertainment of truth. State v. Getsy (Ohio, 12-23-1998) 84 Ohio St.3d 180, 702 N.E.2d 866, 1998-Ohio-533, reconsideration denied 84 Ohio St.3d 1488, 705 N.E.2d 368, certiorari denied 119 S.Ct. 2407, 527 U.S. 1042, 144 L.Ed.2d 805, dismissal of post-conviction relief affirmed 1999 WL 1073682, dismissed, appeal not allowed 88 Ohio St.3d 1425, 723 N.E.2d 1113, habeas corpus granted 456 F.3d 575, rehearing granted, opinion vacated, denial of habeas corpus affirmed 495 F.3d 295. Jury ⚩ 131(1)

Trial court did not improperly limit voir dire of prospective jurors during capital murder prosecution; while court attempted to keep voir dire moving, counsel were rarely limited in questioning jurors, and court did not unreasonably or arbitrarily restrict examination of individual jurors. State v. Getsy (Ohio, 12-23-1998) 84 Ohio St.3d 180, 702 N.E.2d 866, 1998-Ohio-533, reconsideration denied 84 Ohio St.3d 1488, 705 N.E.2d 368, certiorari denied 119 S.Ct. 2407, 527 U.S. 1042, 144 L.Ed.2d 805, dismissal of post-conviction relief affirmed 1999 WL 1073682, dismissed, appeal not allowed 88 Ohio St.3d 1425, 723 N.E.2d 1113, habeas corpus granted 456 F.3d 575, rehearing granted, opinion vacated, denial of habeas corpus affirmed 495 F.3d 295. Jury ⚩ 131(4)

Trial court's introduction of several visiting judges during voir dire in capital murder prosecution was not plain error. State v. Keenan (Ohio, 02-25-1998) 81 Ohio St.3d 133, 689 N.E.2d 929, 1998-Ohio-459, reconsideration denied 81 Ohio St.3d 1503, 691 N.E.2d 1062, certiorari denied 119 S.Ct. 146, 525 U.S. 860, 142 L.Ed.2d 119, rehearing denied 119 S.Ct. 581, 525 U.S. 1035, 142 L.Ed.2d 484, denial of post-conviction relief affirmed 2001 WL 91129, dismissed, appeal not allowed 92 Ohio St.3d 1429, 749 N.E.2d 756, habeas corpus dismissed 262 F.Supp.2d 818, motion to amend denied 262 F.Supp.2d 826, vacated and remanded 400 F.3d 417, on remand 2007 WL 838923, dismissal of post-conviction relief affirmed 2006-Ohio-6031, 2006 WL 3317922, appeal not allowed 114 Ohio St.3d 1508, 872 N.E.2d 950, 2007-Ohio-4285. Criminal Law ⚩ 1035(6)

Prospective juror's comments during general voir dire, based on his experience as police officer, that detective to be called as witness by state was truthful, and that prosecutor was efficient, did not taint jurors; remarks were tempered by prosecutor's response that the other jurors did not know detective and would have to evaluate his testimony based on what he said in court, and his statement that what happened in the past regarding prosecutor was in the past and this case would have to be decided based on evidence presented. State v. Reynolds (Ohio, 01-14-1998) 80 Ohio St.3d 670, 687 N.E.2d 1358, 1998-Ohio-171, certiorari denied 118 S.Ct. 2328, 524 U.S. 930, 141 L.Ed.2d 702, denial of post-conviction relief affirmed 1999 WL 980568, dismissed, appeal not allowed 88 Ohio St.3d 1425, 723 N.E.2d 1113, denial of habeas corpus affirmed 2007 WL 2323850. Jury ⚩ 133

Juror was partial or biased, and thus should not have served as juror in death penalty case, where juror's statements at voir dire indicated after she was corrected three times by judge that she so completely misunderstood presumption of innocence and burden of proof that she could not have made fair assessment of evidence of defendant's guilt; although juror assured counsel and judge that she would consider all of evidence before making decision, she also seemed to expect some of that evidence to come from defendant by way of proof of his innocence. Franklin v. Anderson (C.A.6 (Ohio), 01-09-2006) 434 F.3d 412, rehearing and rehearing en banc denied, certiorari denied 127 S.Ct. 941, 549 U.S. 1156, 166 L.Ed.2d 781. Jury ⚩ 107

Trial judge's decision, that juror's statement at jury viewing and her subsequent statements in conversation with judge did not indicate bias, was fairly supported by record, and presumed correct on federal habeas review, where juror's statements could have been understood in way that did not indicate bias, juror stated unequivocally that she had not made up her mind about guilt of death penalty defendant, and trial judge specifically stated that he believed that she could be impartial and fair after discussing matter with juror, observing her demeanor, and listening to her responses. Franklin v. Anderson (C.A.6 (Ohio), 01-09-2006) 434 F.3d 412, rehearing and rehearing en banc denied, certiorari denied 127 S.Ct. 941, 549 U.S. 1156, 166 L.Ed.2d 781. Habeas Corpus ⚩ 770

Trial court's decision to not dismiss juror constituted manifest error, and his factual finding that juror was not impartial did not merit presumption of correctness on federal habeas review that normally was due trial court factual findings, where record indicated that juror gave definite impression five times that she could not faithfully apply the law concerning burden of proof because she failed to understand it, and she still insisted with her last statement that death penalty defendant had to be proven innocent even after she was corrected by judge three times. Franklin v. Anderson (C.A.6 (Ohio), 01-09-2006) 434 F.3d 412, rehearing and rehearing en banc denied, certiorari denied 127 S.Ct. 941, 549 U.S. 1156, 166 L.Ed.2d 781. Habeas Corpus ⚩ 496; Habeas Corpus ⚩ 770

Trial counsel could reasonably withhold objection to trial court's repeated references during voir dire to murder victim's severed hands because such questioning would illuminate which jurors had been exposed to prejudicial pre-trial publicity. Hartman v. Bagley (N.D.Ohio, 08-31-2004) 333 F.Supp.2d 632, affirmed 492 F.3d 347, rehearing and rehearing en banc denied, certiorari denied 128 S.Ct. 2971, 554 U.S. 924, 171 L.Ed.2d 897, motion for relief from judgment denied 2012 WL 5290292. Criminal Law ⚖ 1901

Trial judge's statements during voir dire, admonishing defense counsel not to engage in trickery when questioning prospective jurors about presumption of innocence, were not prejudicial to defendant's right to fair trial; judge specifically stated during its colloquy that defendant should be presumed innocent and later charged jury to disregard anything he might have said that might have given jury a sense of how judge felt about facts of case. Henderson v. Collins (S.D.Ohio, 08-04-1999) 101 F.Supp.2d 866, affirmed in part, vacated in part 262 F.3d 615, rehearing en banc denied, certiorari denied 122 S.Ct. 1572, 535 U.S. 1002, 152 L.Ed.2d 492, on subsequent appeal 184 Fed.Appx. 518, 2006 WL 1675074, certiorari denied 127 S.Ct. 992, 549 U.S. 1138, 166 L.Ed.2d 749. Criminal Law ⚖ 655(5)

3. Examination by counsel

Voir dire on affirmative defense of duress was not warranted in criminal proceedings for armed bank robbery; all of the questions proposed by the defendant either asked the prospective jurors for irrelevant information, misstated or did not completely state the elements of the claimed defense, or covered areas otherwise adequately covered by the permitted voir dire. U.S. v. Hernandez (C.A.6 (Ohio), 08-21-2007) No. 06-3013, 232 Fed.Appx. 561, 2007 WL 2386563, Unreported. Jury ⚖ 131(8)

Defense counsel's failure to request voir dire on racial bias was not ineffective assistance, in capital murder prosecution, as it did not appear that racial bias permeated case, there were witnesses, including defendant and his brother, who did not mention race as motivating factor in parking-lot fight or in shooting, and, because defendant and person he killed were of same race, defense counsel might have reasonably concluded that race was not an important factor. State v. Conway (Ohio, 03-08-2006) 108 Ohio St.3d 214, 842 N.E.2d 996, 2006-Ohio-791, motion to reopen denied 110 Ohio St.3d 1461, 852 N.E.2d 1211, 2006-Ohio-4288, certiorari denied 127 S.Ct. 122, 549 U.S. 853, 166 L.Ed.2d 91. Criminal Law ⚖ 1901

Trial court did not unduly limit defense counsel's opportunity to question prospective jurors during voir dire regarding their views about capital punishment; although court precluded counsel from questioning prospective jurors about their views on specific mitigating factors, it allowed defense counsel to ask prospective jurors whether they would automatically vote for the death penalty, whether they were willing to fairly consider all mitigating factors raised by the defense, as well as all available sentencing options, and whether they would evaluate all evidence before making a sentencing determination. State v. Cunningham (Ohio, 12-29-2004) 105 Ohio St.3d 197, 824 N.E.2d 504, 2004-Ohio-7007, certiorari denied 126 S.Ct. 110, 546 U.S. 851, 163 L.Ed.2d 122, habeas corpus denied 2010 WL 5092705, vacated and remanded 756 F.3d 477, on remand 2014 WL 5341703. Jury ⚖ 131(8)

Defendant could not show prejudice in trial court's decision to limit counsel's opportunity to question prospective jurors during voir dire regarding their views about capital punishment, where he approved the jury selected before exhausting his peremptory challenges. State v. Cunningham (Ohio, 12-29-2004) 105 Ohio St.3d 197, 824 N.E.2d 504, 2004-Ohio-7007, certiorari denied 126 S.Ct. 110, 546 U.S. 851, 163 L.Ed.2d 122, habeas corpus denied 2010 WL 5092705, vacated and remanded 756 F.3d 477, on remand 2014 WL 5341703. Criminal Law ⚖ 1166.18

Defense counsel's failure, in capital murder prosecution, to object to references during voir dire by prosecutor and court to incorrect standard for weighing aggravating and mitigating factors, did not demonstrate performance below objective standard of reasonable representation, as misquoting of the weighing process was common mistake and did not create reasonable probability that result of trial would have been different were it not for counsel's errors; jury was correctly instructed as to governing legal standard, and its signed verdict form reflected correct legal standard. State v. Stallings (Ohio, 07-19-2000) 89 Ohio St.3d 280, 731 N.E.2d 159, 2000-Ohio-164, stay granted 89 Ohio St.3d 1483, 733 N.E.2d 1184, stay revoked 93 Ohio St.3d 1455, 756 N.E.2d 674, certiorari denied 122 S.Ct. 89, 534 U.S. 836, 151 L.Ed.2d 51, post-conviction relief denied 2004 WL 5388150, affirmed 2004-Ohio-4571, 2004 WL 1932869, appeal not allowed 104 Ohio St.3d 1460, 821 N.E.2d 577, 2005-Ohio-204, habeas corpus granted in part, denied in part 561 F.Supp.2d 821. Criminal Law ⚖ 1901

5. Pretrial publicity

Defendant charged with aggravated murder was not prejudiced by voir dire of prospective jurors regarding pretrial media publicity regarding his case; although most prospective jurors acknowledged some familiarity with the case, jurors were questioned as to whether they had formed any fixed opinions and whether they could deliberate in a fair and impartial manner based solely on the evidence presented at trial, trial court readily excused members of the venire who had formed fixed opinions due to pretrial publicity, and all jurors empanelled stated that they could set aside any pretrial opinions and render a fair and impartial verdict. State v. Jackson (Ohio, 11-23-2005) 107 Ohio St.3d 53, 836 N.E.2d 1173, 2005-Ohio-5981, reconsideration denied 108 Ohio St.3d 1418, 841 N.E.2d 321, 2006-Ohio-179, certiorari denied 126 S.Ct. 2940, 548 U.S. 912, 165 L.Ed.2d 964, motion to reopen denied 110 Ohio St.3d 1435, 852 N.E.2d 185, 2006-Ohio-3862, habeas corpus denied 2008 WL 1946790, affirmed 687 F.3d 723, certiorari denied 133 S.Ct. 1243, 185 L.Ed.2d 190. Jury ⚖ 103(14); Jury ⚖ 131(7)

Trial court's voir dire of prospective jurors in capital murder prosecution was adequate to permit court to rule on challenges for cause and to ascertain that all seated jurors would serve impartially, despite fact that some or all jurors seated had heard of case prior to trial; trial court conducted probing inquiry that addressed issues of prospective jurors' personal knowledge of individuals involved in case and influence of media reports, and permitted counsel for both sides to question the prospective jurors, and in course of such examination, all empanelled jurors indicated that they would be able to perform their duties as demanded by law. State v. Gross (Ohio, 10-30-2002) 97 Ohio St.3d 121, 776 N.E.2d 1061, 2002-Ohio-5524, reconsideration denied 97 Ohio St.3d 1486, 780 N.E.2d 288, 2002-Ohio-6866, certiorari denied 123 S.Ct. 2079, 538 U.S. 1037, 155 L.Ed.2d 1068, rehearing denied 124 S.Ct. 20, 539 U.S. 976, 156 L.Ed.2d 685, denial of post-conviction relief affirmed 2003-Ohio-6295, 2003 WL 22765845, appeal not allowed 102 Ohio St.3d 1410, 806 N.E.2d 562, 2004-Ohio-1763, certiorari denied 125 S.Ct. 165, 543 U.S. 888, 160 L.Ed.2d 149, dismissal of post-conviction relief affirmed 2006-Ohio-6941, 2006 WL 3804532, appeal not allowed 113 Ohio St.3d 1468, 864 N.E.2d 654, 2007-Ohio-1722, habeas corpus dismissed 2008 WL 4702181, motion to amend denied 2008 WL 4889626, certificate of appealability denied 2008 WL 5190017, affirmed 426 Fed.Appx. 349, 2011 WL 1597659. Jury ⚿ 131(7)

Voir dire adequately addressed issue of pretrial publicity in prosecution for aggravated murder of peace officer, and such publicity did not prejudice defendant or violate his right to fair trial, where voir dire covered three days and 450 pages of transcript, involved questioning by court and counsel of prospective jurors who were familiar with case, and resulted in several exclusions. State v. White (Ohio, 05-20-1998) 82 Ohio St.3d 16, 693 N.E.2d 772, 1998-Ohio-363, stay granted 82 Ohio St.3d 1445, 695 N.E.2d 267, stay revoked 85 Ohio St.3d 1453, 708 N.E.2d 1008, reconsideration denied 82 Ohio St.3d 1469, 696 N.E.2d 226, reconsideration denied 82 Ohio St.3d 1470, 696 N.E.2d 226, dismissal of post-conviction relief affirmed 1998 WL 515944, dismissed, appeal not allowed 84 Ohio St.3d 1445, 703 N.E.2d 326, reconsideration denied 84 Ohio St.3d 1489, 705 N.E.2d 368, certiorari denied 119 S.Ct. 623, 525 U.S. 1057, 142 L.Ed.2d 562, denial of habeas corpus affirmed in part, reversed in part 431 F.3d 517, rehearing denied, rehearing and rehearing en banc denied, certiorari denied 127 S.Ct. 578, 166 L.Ed.2d 457, certiorari denied 127 S.Ct. 581, 166 L.Ed.2d 434, dismissal of post-conviction relief affirmed 2007-Ohio-3424, 2007 WL 1934731. Criminal Law ⚿ 633.32

Pretrial publicity does not inevitably lead to unfair trial, even if it is pervasive and adverse. State v. White (Ohio, 05-20-1998) 82 Ohio St.3d 16, 693 N.E.2d 772, 1998-Ohio-363, stay granted 82 Ohio St.3d 1445, 695 N.E.2d 267, stay revoked 85 Ohio St.3d 1453, 708 N.E.2d 1008, reconsideration denied 82 Ohio St.3d 1469, 696 N.E.2d 226, reconsideration denied 82 Ohio St.3d 1470, 696 N.E.2d 226, dismissal of post-conviction relief affirmed 1998 WL 515944, dismissed, appeal not allowed 84 Ohio St.3d 1445, 703 N.E.2d 326, reconsideration denied 84 Ohio St.3d 1489, 705 N.E.2d 368, certiorari denied 119 S.Ct. 623, 525 U.S. 1057, 142 L.Ed.2d 562, denial of habeas corpus affirmed in part, reversed in part 431 F.3d 517, rehearing denied, rehearing and rehearing en banc denied, certiorari denied 127 S.Ct. 578, 166 L.Ed.2d 457, certiorari denied 127 S.Ct. 581, 166 L.Ed.2d 434, dismissal of post-conviction relief affirmed 2007-Ohio-3424, 2007 WL 1934731. Criminal Law ⚿ 633.32

Fact that prospective jurors have been exposed to pretrial publicity does not, in and of itself, demonstrate prejudice to defendant. State v. White (Ohio, 05-20-1998) 82 Ohio St.3d 16, 693 N.E.2d 772, 1998-Ohio-363, stay granted 82 Ohio St.3d 1445, 695 N.E.2d 267, stay revoked 85 Ohio St.3d 1453, 708 N.E.2d 1008, reconsideration denied 82 Ohio St.3d 1469, 696 N.E.2d 226, reconsideration denied 82 Ohio St.3d 1470, 696 N.E.2d 226, dismissal of post-conviction relief affirmed 1998 WL 515944, dismissed, appeal not allowed 84 Ohio St.3d 1445, 703 N.E.2d 326, reconsideration denied 84 Ohio St.3d 1489, 705 N.E.2d 368, certiorari denied 119 S.Ct. 623, 525 U.S. 1057, 142 L.Ed.2d 562, denial of habeas corpus affirmed in part, reversed in part 431 F.3d 517, rehearing denied, rehearing and rehearing en banc denied, certiorari denied 127 S.Ct. 578, 166 L.Ed.2d 457, certiorari denied 127 S.Ct. 581, 166 L.Ed.2d 434, dismissal of post-conviction relief affirmed 2007-Ohio-3424, 2007 WL 1934731. Criminal Law ⚿ 1163(2)

If record on voir dire establishes that prospective veniremen have been exposed to pretrial publicity but affirmed they would judge defendant solely on law and evidence presented at trial, it is not error to empanel such veniremen. State v. White (Ohio, 05-20-1998) 82 Ohio St.3d 16, 693 N.E.2d 772, 1998-Ohio-363, stay granted 82 Ohio St.3d 1445, 695 N.E.2d 267, stay revoked 85 Ohio St.3d 1453, 708 N.E.2d 1008, reconsideration denied 82 Ohio St.3d 1469, 696 N.E.2d 226, reconsideration denied 82 Ohio St.3d 1470, 696 N.E.2d 226, dismissal of post-conviction relief affirmed 1998 WL 515944, dismissed, appeal not allowed 84 Ohio St.3d 1445, 703 N.E.2d 326, reconsideration denied 84 Ohio St.3d 1489, 705 N.E.2d 368, certiorari denied 119 S.Ct. 623, 525 U.S. 1057, 142 L.Ed.2d 562, denial of habeas corpus affirmed in part, reversed in part 431 F.3d 517, rehearing denied, rehearing and rehearing en banc denied, certiorari denied 127 S.Ct. 578, 166 L.Ed.2d 457, certiorari denied 127 S.Ct. 581, 166 L.Ed.2d 434, dismissal of post-conviction relief affirmed 2007-Ohio-3424, 2007 WL 1934731. Jury ⚿ 103(14)

Public trial, exclusion of public from voir dire. Presley v. Georgia, (U.S., 01-19-2010) 130 S.Ct. 721.

6. Beliefs as to death penalty

Trial court did not improperly deny challenges for cause, in capital murder prosecution, involving jurors who stated that they could not consider mitigating evidence and would automatically vote to recommend death penalty, and thus did not prejudicially affect defendant's use of peremptory challenges; many jurors challenged on such grounds in fact indicated willingness and ability to follow the law in sentencing phase, trial court excused for cause any prospective juror who did express inability to consider mitigation evidence, and defendant failed to identify any remaining prospective juror against whom he was required to exercise peremptory challenge to his prejudice. State v. Gross (Ohio, 10-30-2002) 97 Ohio St.3d 121, 776 N.E.2d 1061, 2002-Ohio-5524, reconsideration denied 97 Ohio St.3d 1486, 780 N.E.2d 288, 2002-Ohio-6866, certiorari denied 123 S.Ct. 2079, 538 U.S. 1037, 155 L.Ed.2d 1068, rehearing denied 124 S.Ct. 20, 539 U.S. 976, 156 L.Ed.2d 685, denial of post-conviction relief affirmed 2003-Ohio-6295, 2003 WL 22765845, appeal not allowed 102 Ohio St.3d 1410, 806 N.E.2d 562, 2004-Ohio-1763, certiorari denied 125 S.Ct. 165, 543 U.S. 888, 160 L.Ed.2d 149, dismissal of post-conviction relief affirmed 2006-Ohio-6941, 2006 WL 3804532, appeal not allowed 113 Ohio St.3d 1468, 864 N.E.2d 654, 2007-Ohio-1722, habeas corpus dismissed 2008 WL 4702181, motion to amend denied 2008 WL 4889626, certificate of appealability denied 2008 WL 5190017, affirmed 426 Fed.Appx. 349, 2011 WL 1597659. Jury ⚷ 108; Jury ⚷ 135

Trial court did not abuse its discretion by excusing from capital murder trial prospective juror who opposed the death penalty even for Hitler and juror who was adamant in stating that the death penalty was against his religion and that it was up to God to take a life. State v. Fears (Ohio, 09-08-1999) 86 Ohio St.3d 329, 715 N.E.2d 136, 1999-Ohio-111, reconsideration denied 87 Ohio St.3d 1421, 717 N.E.2d 1107, stay granted 87 Ohio St.3d 1423, 718 N.E.2d 441, denial of post-conviction relief affirmed 1999 WL 1032592, dismissed, appeal not allowed 88 Ohio St.3d 1444, 725 N.E.2d 284, certiorari denied 120 S.Ct. 1535, 529 U.S. 1039, 146 L.Ed.2d 349, habeas corpus denied 2008 WL 2782888. Jury ⚷ 108

Trial court did not abuse its discretion in capital murder trial by excusing juror who unequivocally stated she could "never be involved in the decision whether or not someone lives or dies unless it's self-defense," though juror had earlier expressed reservations about serving due to child-care difficulties and had initially felt she could return a death recommendation. State v. Fears (Ohio, 09-08-1999) 86 Ohio St.3d 329, 715 N.E.2d 136, 1999-Ohio-111, reconsideration denied 87 Ohio St.3d 1421, 717 N.E.2d 1107, stay granted 87 Ohio St.3d 1423, 718 N.E.2d 441, denial of post-conviction relief affirmed 1999 WL 1032592, dismissed, appeal not allowed 88 Ohio St.3d 1444, 725 N.E.2d 284, certiorari denied 120 S.Ct. 1535, 529 U.S. 1039, 146 L.Ed.2d 349, habeas corpus denied 2008 WL 2782888. Jury ⚷ 108

Trial court did not commit plain error, during individual voir dire questioning of capital murder prosecution, by asking each juror if he or she could join in signing verdict form which recommended imposition of death penalty. State v. Goff (Ohio, 06-17-1998) 82 Ohio St.3d 123, 694 N.E.2d 916, 1998-Ohio-369, reconsideration denied 82 Ohio St.3d 1483, 696 N.E.2d 1089, certiorari denied 119 S.Ct. 2402, 527 U.S. 1039, 144 L.Ed.2d 800, dismissal of post-conviction relief affirmed 2001 WL 208845, dismissed, appeal not allowed 92 Ohio St.3d 1430, 749 N.E.2d 756, habeas corpus denied 2006 WL 3590369, certificate of appealability granted in part, denied in part 2007 WL 2601096. Criminal Law ⚷ 1035(5)

2945.28 Form of oath to jury; effect of form on validity of impanelment

Notes of Decisions

2. Administration of oath

Trial court's failure to strictly comply with statute requiring that trial court or clerk of court of common pleas administer oath to jurors did not require reversal of verdict, absent showing that capital murder defendant had been prejudiced due to fact that bailiff had administered oath to jurors. State v. Conway (Ohio, 03-08-2006) 108 Ohio St.3d 214, 842 N.E.2d 996, 2006-Ohio-791, motion to reopen denied 110 Ohio St.3d 1461, 852 N.E.2d 1211, 2006-Ohio-4288, certiorari denied 127 S.Ct. 122, 549 U.S. 853, 166 L.Ed.2d 91. Criminal Law ⚷ 1166.19

Fact that bailiff administered oath to jurors, instead of trial court or clerk of court of common pleas, as required by statute, was at most a statutory violation, not constitutional error, and, as such, no structural error occurred with respect to bailiff administering oath, in capital murder prosecution. State v. Conway (Ohio, 03-08-2006) 108 Ohio St.3d 214, 842 N.E.2d 996, 2006-Ohio-791, motion to reopen denied 110 Ohio St.3d 1461, 852 N.E.2d 1211, 2006-Ohio-4288, certiorari denied 127 S.Ct. 122, 549 U.S. 853, 166 L.Ed.2d 91. Jury ⚷ 148(1)

Capital murder defendant waived on appeal all but plain error with respect to whether trial court's having bailiff, rather than clerk of court of common pleas administer oath to jurors prejudiced him, as he did not object at time bailiff administered oath. State v. Conway (Ohio, 03-08-2006) 108 Ohio St.3d 214, 842 N.E.2d 996, 2006-Ohio-791, motion to reopen denied 110 Ohio St.3d 1461, 852 N.E.2d 1211, 2006-Ohio-4288, certiorari denied 127 S.Ct. 122, 549 U.S. 853, 166 L.Ed.2d 91. Criminal Law ⚷ 1035(6)

2945.29 Jurors becoming unable to perform duties

Notes of Decisions

2. Discharge of juror

Trial court acted within its discretion removing juror from jury on the ground that juror's objective participation in the trial had been compromised by her encounter with courtroom spectator; juror was crying as she discussed the encounter, juror became concerned with how parties would react to verdict, and juror was afraid for her safety. State v. Reid (Ohio App. 2 Dist., Montgomery, 08-01-2003) No. 19352, 2003-Ohio-4087, 2003 WL 21771782, Unreported, motion for delayed appeal denied 100 Ohio St.3d 1530, 800 N.E.2d 47, 2003-Ohio-6458, appeal not allowed 101 Ohio St.3d 1491, 805 N.E.2d 541, 2004-Ohio-1293, habeas corpus dismissed 2008 WL 355597. Criminal Law ⚷ 868

Trial court acted within its discretion in a prosecution for domestic assault in replacing a juror who complained to a bailiff that trial court was inconsiderate for making the jury wait for two hours, even though, after a dialogue with trial court, the juror settled down and indicated that he could continue; trial court, in dismissing the juror, explained that it did not want jury duty to upset the juror because the juror was almost 74 years old and he indicated that he had just had aortic aneurysm surgery two weeks earlier and had been "cut all the way up." State v. Clay (Ohio App. 8 Dist., 03-19-2009) 181 Ohio App.3d 563, 910 N.E.2d 14, 2009-Ohio-1235, appeal not allowed 122 Ohio St.3d 1482, 910 N.E.2d 480, 2009-Ohio-3625, reconsideration denied 122 Ohio St.3d 1525, 913 N.E.2d 459, 2009-Ohio-4776. Jury ⚷ 149

3. Excuse for cause after jury sworn

Statute and criminal rule governing replacement of seated juror unable to perform his or her duties with alternate juror after jury has been sworn and trial had commenced did not apply to trial court's replacement of seated juror with prospective juror from general venire pool, rather than alternate juror, prior to jury being sworn. State v. Mock (Ohio App. 7 Dist., 06-09-2010) 187 Ohio App.3d 599, 933 N.E.2d 270, 2010-Ohio-2747. Jury ⚷ 149

2945.31 Separation of jurors

Notes of Decisions

1. Pretrial publicity

Trial court's refusal to sequester jury throughout course of trial did not deprive capital murder defendant of fair trial, where court routinely admonished jury not to discuss case or to read any news accounts related thereto; trial court was in best position to gauge atmosphere of trial proceedings and to evaluate whether its instructions sufficed over sequestration, and pretrial publicity fell well short of justifying change of venue. State v. Gross (Ohio, 10-30-2002) 97 Ohio St.3d 121, 776 N.E.2d 1061, 2002-Ohio-5524, reconsideration denied 97 Ohio St.3d 1486, 780 N.E.2d 288, 2002-Ohio-6866, certiorari denied 123 S.Ct. 2079, 538 U.S. 1037, 155 L.Ed.2d 1068, rehearing denied 124 S.Ct. 20, 539 U.S. 976, 156 L.Ed.2d 685, denial of post-conviction relief affirmed 2003-Ohio-6295, 2003 WL 22765845, appeal not allowed 102 Ohio St.3d 1410, 806 N.E.2d 562, 2004-Ohio-1763, certiorari denied 125 S.Ct. 165, 543 U.S. 888, 160 L.Ed.2d 149, dismissal of post-conviction relief affirmed 2006-Ohio-6941, 2006 WL 3804532, appeal not allowed 113 Ohio St.3d 1468, 864 N.E.2d 654, 2007-Ohio-1722, habeas corpus dismissed 2008 WL 4702181, motion to amend denied 2008 WL 4889626, certificate of appealability denied 2008 WL 5190017, affirmed 426 Fed.Appx. 349, 2011 WL 1597659. Criminal Law ⚷ 665(1)

2945.33 Keeping and conduct of jury after case submitted

Notes of Decisions

2. Allowing jurors to separate

Trial court was not required to permit jurors to smoke during guilt or penalty phase deliberations in capital murder prosecution; there was only one smoker on jury, defendant's claim that this juror suffered from nicotine withdrawal such as might have affected length of deliberations was completely speculative, jury's simple request "can we smoke" did not indicate any type of emergency, and, in any event, jurors could not, pursuant to statute and rule, take smoking breaks outside jury room after submission of case. State v. Elmore (Ohio, 12-13-2006) 111 Ohio St.3d 515, 857 N.E.2d 547, 2006-Ohio-6207, certiorari denied 127 S.Ct. 2974, 551 U.S. 1133, 168 L.Ed.2d 707, appeal after new sentencing hearing 122 Ohio St.3d 472, 912 N.E.2d 582, 2009-Ohio-3478, certiorari denied 130 S.Ct. 1025, 558 U.S. 1096, 175 L.Ed.2d 627, motion to reopen denied 124 Ohio St.3d 1439, 920 N.E.2d 370, 2010-Ohio-188, denial of post-conviction relief affirmed 2014-Ohio-3674, 2014 WL 4180275. Criminal Law ⚷ 857(1); Sentencing And Punishment ⚷ 1779(3)

3. Improper communications

Trial court's error in answering a jury question during deliberations, through the bailiff, without the presence of defendant and her attorney was harmless; despite the obvious error in procedure, the bailiff's statement in chambers clearly reflected that she was asked by the court to refer the jury to the multiple counts instruction and that, at the court's instruction, she merely informed the jury that they should refer to that instruction. State v. Manns (Ohio App. 2 Dist., 11-03-2006) 169 Ohio App.3d 687, 864 N.E.2d 657, 2006-Ohio-5802, appeal not allowed 113 Ohio St.3d 1466, 864 N.E.2d 653, 2007-Ohio-1722. Criminal Law ⚯ 1174(1)

Trial court erred when it, through the bailiff, answered a jury question during deliberations without the presence of defendant and her attorney. State v. Manns (Ohio App. 2 Dist., 11-03-2006) 169 Ohio App.3d 687, 864 N.E.2d 657, 2006-Ohio-5802, appeal not allowed 113 Ohio St.3d 1466, 864 N.E.2d 653, 2007-Ohio-1722. Criminal Law ⚯ 863(1)

Fact that the trial court received information from the jury regarding its numerical division during deliberations did not warrant mistrial; while the trial judge asked the jury to clarify an earlier statement, he in no manner asked the jury for its numerical division, but rather, in earlier instructions he explicitly informed the jury not to provide the status of their deliberations to the court. State v. Villa (Ohio App. 9 Dist., Lorain, 09-05-2006) No. 05CA008773, 2006-Ohio-4529, 2006 WL 2527964, Unreported, appeal not allowed 112 Ohio St.3d 1445, 860 N.E.2d 768, 2007-Ohio-152, certiorari denied 127 S.Ct. 2885, 550 U.S. 973, 167 L.Ed.2d 1159, appeal not allowed 114 Ohio St.3d 1428, 868 N.E.2d 681, 2007-Ohio-2904, dismissal of post-conviction relief affirmed 2009-Ohio-5055, 2009 WL 3068397, habeas corpus denied 2012 WL 1435725. Criminal Law ⚯ 864

Supplementary charge urging the jurors to continue their deliberations after having reached an impasse, and attempt to reach a verdict on murder charge was not impermissibly coercive; charge was neutral in that it did not single out jurors in the minority, and fact that the jury continued deliberations through half of another day after the charge was given suggested that the jury felt uncoerced in continuing deliberations. Bonnell v. Mitchel (N.D.Ohio, 02-04-2004) 301 F.Supp.2d 698, affirmed 212 Fed.Appx. 517, 2007 WL 62628, certiorari denied 128 S.Ct. 710, 552 U.S. 1064, 169 L.Ed.2d 558. Criminal Law ⚯ 865(1.5)

4. Alternate juror

Jury's guilty verdict and imposition of death penalty in capital murder trial was not result of juror bias and/or misconduct; any speculative influence that alternate juror may have had on jury via communications prior to deliberation would have been entirely internal, alternate did not participate in actual jury deliberations, and court did not have opportunity to conclude whether alternate was biased. U.S. v. Lawrence (S.D.Ohio, 11-16-2006) 477 F.Supp.2d 864, vacated in part 555 F.3d 254, rehearing and rehearing en banc denied, certiorari denied 130 S.Ct. 1879, 559 U.S. 1009, 176 L.Ed.2d 368, affirmed in part 735 F.3d 385, petition for certiorari filed 135 S.Ct. 753. Criminal Law ⚯ 857(1)

2945.34 Admonition if jurors separate during trial

Notes of Decisions

1. Sufficiency of admonition

Trial court's failure to admonish the jury every time the court recessed the jury was not plain error at homicide trial; court adequately admonished the jury on many occasions throughout trial, and defendant did not argue how he was prejudiced by any omission. State v. Wilson (Ohio App. 8 Dist., 04-09-2009) 182 Ohio App.3d 171, 912 N.E.2d 133, 2009-Ohio-1681, motion for delayed appeal granted 123 Ohio St.3d 1505, 917 N.E.2d 809, 2009-Ohio-6210, cause dismissed 124 Ohio St.3d 1424, 919 N.E.2d 748, 2010-Ohio-20, motion to reopen denied 2010-Ohio-2080, 2010 WL 1910117, appeal after new sentencing hearing 2010-Ohio-2466, 2010 WL 2201735, appeal allowed, reversed 2010-Ohio-6285, 2010 WL 5392818. Criminal Law ⚯ 1039

2945.36 For what cause jury may be discharged

Notes of Decisions

6. Reconvened jury

Trial court's act of reconvening jury to return a second verdict on involuntary manslaughter charge, after jury returned a defective verdict on such charge and was discharged, constituted error. State v. Davis (Ohio App. 2 Dist., Clark, 09-12-2003) No. 2002-CA-43, 2003-Ohio-4839, 2003 WL 22110297, Unreported, cause dismissed 100 Ohio St.3d 1480, 798 N.E.2d 616, 2003-Ohio-5993. Criminal Law ⚯ 889

Defendant's claim, that original jury deliberations concerning involuntary manslaughter charge were improper due to presence of two different verdict forms, was rendered moot, where defendant's conviction and sentence for involuntary manslaughter charge were to be vacated. State v. Davis (Ohio App. 2 Dist., Clark, 09-12-2003) No. 2002-CA-43, 2003-Ohio-4839, 2003 WL 22110297, Unreported, cause dismissed 100 Ohio St.3d 1480, 798 N.E.2d 616, 2003-Ohio-5993. Criminal Law ⚯ 1134.26

Defendant did not waive claim that trial court erred in reconvening jury to return a second verdict on involuntary manslaughter charge after jury returned a defective verdict on such charge and was discharged, where defendant never consented to the jury's re-deliberating the case after the jury had been discharged, but rather asserted position that defective verdict should be set aside, and that the charge should be dismissed. State v. Davis (Ohio App. 2 Dist., Clark, 09-12-2003) No. 2002-CA-43, 2003-Ohio-4839, 2003 WL 22110297, Unreported, cause dismissed 100 Ohio St.3d 1480, 798 N.E.2d 616, 2003-Ohio-5993. Criminal Law ⚿ 1039

7. Retrial; speedy trial

Defendant waived claim that his retrial following hung jury in his first trial was "jurisdictionally unauthorized" because trial court discharged the jury in the first trial without stating the reasons for doing so in the journal, as required by statute, where defendant failed to raise that objection before his second trial. State ex rel. Bevins v. Cooper (Ohio, 02-20-2014) 138 Ohio St.3d 275, 6 N.E.3d 33, 2014-Ohio-544, reconsideration denied 138 Ohio St.3d 1471, 6 N.E.3d 1206, 2014-Ohio-1674. Criminal Law ⚿ 1039

INSANITY

2945.37 Competence to stand trial; raising of issue; procedures; municipal courts

(A) As used in sections 2945.37 to 2945.402 of the Revised Code:

(1) "Prosecutor" means a prosecuting attorney or a city director of law, village solicitor, or similar chief legal officer of a municipal corporation who has authority to prosecute a criminal case that is before the court or the criminal case in which a defendant in a criminal case has been found incompetent to stand trial or not guilty by reason of insanity.

(2) "Examiner" means either of the following:

(a) A psychiatrist or a licensed clinical psychologist who satisfies the criteria of division (I) of section 5122.01 of the Revised Code or is employed by a certified forensic center designated by the department of mental health and addiction services to conduct examinations or evaluations.

(b) For purposes of a separate mental retardation evaluation that is ordered by a court pursuant to division (H) of section 2945.371 of the Revised Code, a psychologist designated by the director of developmental disabilities pursuant to that section to conduct that separate mental retardation evaluation.

(3) "Nonsecured status" means any unsupervised, off-grounds movement or trial visit from a hospital or institution, or any conditional release, that is granted to a person who is found incompetent to stand trial and is committed pursuant to section 2945.39 of the Revised Code or to a person who is found not guilty by reason of insanity and is committed pursuant to section 2945.40 of the Revised Code.

(4) "Unsupervised, off-grounds movement" includes only off-grounds privileges that are unsupervised and that have an expectation of return to the hospital or institution on a daily basis.

(5) "Trial visit" means a patient privilege of a longer stated duration of unsupervised community contact with an expectation of return to the hospital or institution at designated times.

(6) "Conditional release" means a commitment status under which the trial court at any time may revoke a person's conditional release and order the rehospitalization or reinstitutionalization of the person as described in division (A) of section 2945.402 of the Revised Code and pursuant to which a person who is found incompetent to stand trial or a person who is found not guilty by reason of insanity lives and receives treatment in the community for a period of time that does not exceed the maximum prison term or term of imprisonment that the person could have received for the offense in question had the person been convicted of the offense instead of being found incompetent to stand trial on the charge of the offense or being found not guilty by reason of insanity relative to the offense.

(7) "Licensed clinical psychologist," "mentally ill person subject to court order," and "psychiatrist" have the same meanings as in section 5122.01 of the Revised Code.

(8) "Mentally retarded person subject to institutionalization by court order" has the same meaning as in section 5123.01 of the Revised Code.

(B) In a criminal action in a court of common pleas, a county court, or a municipal court, the court, prosecutor, or defense may raise the issue of the defendant's competence to stand trial. If the issue is raised before the trial has commenced, the court shall hold a hearing on the issue as provided in this section. If the issue is raised after the trial has commenced, the court shall hold a hearing on the issue only for good cause shown or on the court's own motion.

(C) The court shall conduct the hearing required or authorized under division (B) of this section within thirty days after the issue is raised, unless the defendant has been referred for evaluation in which case the court shall conduct the hearing within ten days after the filing of the report of the evaluation or, in the case of a defendant who is ordered by the court pursuant to division (H) of section 2945.371 of the Revised Code to undergo a separate mental retardation evaluation conducted by a psychologist designated by the director of developmental disabilities, within ten days after the filing of the report of the separate mental retardation evaluation under that division. A hearing may be continued for good cause.

(D) The defendant shall be represented by counsel at the hearing conducted under division (C) of this section. If the defendant is unable to obtain counsel, the court shall appoint counsel under Chapter 120. of the Revised Code or under the authority recognized in division (C) of section 120.06, division (E) of section 120.16, division (E) of section 120.26, or section 2941.51 of the Revised Code before proceeding with the hearing.

(E) The prosecutor and defense counsel may submit evidence on the issue of the defendant's competence to stand trial. A written report of the evaluation of the defendant may be admitted into evidence at the hearing by stipulation, but, if either the prosecution or defense objects to its admission, the report may be admitted under sections 2317.36 to 2317.38 of the Revised Code or any other applicable statute or rule.

(F) The court shall not find a defendant incompetent to stand trial solely because the defendant is receiving or has received treatment as a voluntary or involuntary mentally ill patient under Chapter 5122. or a voluntary or involuntary mentally retarded resident under Chapter 5123. of the Revised Code or because the defendant is receiving or has received psychotropic drugs or other medication, even if the defendant might become incompetent to stand trial without the drugs or medication.

(G) A defendant is presumed to be competent to stand trial. If, after a hearing, the court finds by a preponderance of the evidence that, because of the defendant's present mental condition, the defendant is incapable of understanding the nature and objective of the proceedings against the defendant or of assisting in the defendant's defense, the court shall find the defendant incompetent to stand trial and shall enter an order authorized by section 2945.38 of the Revised Code.

(H) Municipal courts shall follow the procedures set forth in sections 2945.37 to 2945.402 of the Revised Code. Except as provided in section 2945.371 of the Revised Code, a municipal court shall not order an evaluation of the defendant's competence to stand trial or the defendant's mental condition at the time of the commission of the offense to be conducted at any hospital operated by the department of mental health and addiction services. Those evaluations shall be performed through community resources including, but not limited to, certified forensic centers, court probation departments, and community mental health services providers. All expenses of the evaluations shall be borne by the legislative authority of the municipal court, as defined in section 1901.03 of the Revised Code, and shall be taxed as costs in the case. If a defendant is found incompetent to stand trial or not guilty by reason of insanity, a municipal court may commit the defendant as provided in sections 2945.38 to 2945.402 of the Revised Code.

(2014 S 43, eff. 9-17-14; 2013 H 83, eff. 3-20-14; 2013 H 59, eff. 9-29-13; 2009 S 79, eff. 10-6-09; 1996 S 285, eff. 7-1-97; 1988 S 156, eff. 7-1-89; 1981 H 694; 1980 S 297; 1978 H 565)

Historical and Statutory Notes

Amendment Note: 2014 S 43 substituted "mentally ill person subject to court order" for "mentally ill person subject to hospitalization by court order" in division (A)(7).

Amendment Note: 2013 H 83 substituted "division (I) of section 5122.01" for "division (I)(1) of section 5122.01" in division (A)(2)(a).

Amendment Note: 2013 H 59, in division (A)(2)(a), and (H), in the second sentence, inserted "and addiction services" following "mental health"; and in division (H); in the third sentence, substituted "services providers" for "agencies".

Amendment Note: 2009 S 79 deleted "mental retardation and" from "director of mental retardation and developmental disabilities" throughout.

Cross References

Fees and costs, municipal courts, see 2746.07

Ohio Administrative Code References

Community forensic psychiatric centers, see OAC 5122–32–01

Research References

ALR Library

70 ALR 5th 1, Adequacy of Defense Counsel's Representation of Criminal Client--Issues of Incompetency.

Encyclopedias

OH Jur. 3d Criminal Law: Procedure § 45, Competency Hearing; Psychiatric Examination.

OH Jur. 3d Criminal Law: Procedure § 415, Effect of Failure to Demand Speedy Trial.

OH Jur. 3d Criminal Law: Procedure § 1158, Presumption of Competence.

OH Jur. 3d Criminal Law: Procedure § 1160, Right to Hearing on Competency.

OH Jur. 3d Criminal Law: Procedure § 1161, Time for Hearing.

OH Jur. 3d Criminal Law: Procedure § 1162, Right to Counsel.

OH Jur. 3d Criminal Law: Procedure § 1163, Conduct of Hearing.

OH Jur. 3d Criminal Law: Procedure § 1168, Additional Evaluation Upon Indication of Mental Retardation.

OH Jur. 3d Criminal Law: Procedure § 1171, Finding of Incompetency.

OH Jur. 3d Criminal Law: Procedure § 1865, Rights of Person Found Not Guilty by Reason of Insanity.

OH Jur. 3d Family Law § 1643, Generally; Statutory Authorization.

OH Jur. 3d Family Law § 1680, Burden of Proof.

Treatises and Practice Aids

Klein, Darling, & Terez, Baldwin's Ohio Practice Civil Practice § 1:53, Civ. R. 1(C)(6): Commitment of the Mentally Ill--Proceedings Under RC 2945.38 and RC 2945.40.

Katz & Giannelli, Baldwin's Ohio Practice Criminal Law § 54:1, Introduction.

Katz & Giannelli, Baldwin's Ohio Practice Criminal Law § 54:2, Right to a Competency Hearing.

Katz & Giannelli, Baldwin's Ohio Practice Criminal Law § 54:3, Competency Standard.

Katz & Giannelli, Baldwin's Ohio Practice Criminal Law § 54:4, Mental Evaluation.

Katz & Giannelli, Baldwin's Ohio Practice Criminal Law § 54:5, Burden of Proof.

Katz & Giannelli, Baldwin's Ohio Practice Criminal Law § 54:6, Counsel, Waiver, and Guilty Pleas.

Katz & Giannelli, Baldwin's Ohio Practice Criminal Law § 54:7, Competency Hearing.

Katz & Giannelli, Baldwin's Ohio Practice Criminal Law § 106:8, Possession of Deadly Weapon While Under Detention.

Katz & Giannelli, Baldwin's Ohio Practice Criminal Law § 144:5, Plea of Not Guilty by Reason of Insanity at Arraignment.

Katz & Giannelli, Baldwin's Ohio Practice Criminal Law § 144:6, Entry on Plea of Not Guilty by Reason of Insanity.

Katz & Giannelli, Baldwin's Ohio Practice Criminal Law § 144:7, Plea of Not Guilty by Reason of Insanity After Arraignment.

Katz & Giannelli, Baldwin's Ohio Practice Criminal Law § 144:8, Acceptance of Plea of Not Guilty by Reason of Insanity After Arraignment.

Katz & Giannelli, Baldwin's Ohio Practice Criminal Law § 110:21, Escape.

Katz & Giannelli, Baldwin's Ohio Practice Criminal Law § 144:10, Entry Finding Defendant [Competent/Incompetent] to Stand Trial.

Carlin, Baldwin's Ohio Prac. Merrick-Rippner Probate Law § 3:6, Subject Matter--Specific Areas--Fiduciaries.

Carlin, Baldwin's Ohio Prac. Merrick-Rippner Probate Law § 3:14, Scope--Exclusive and Concurrent Jurisdiction.

Carlin, Baldwin's Ohio Prac. Merrick-Rippner Probate Law § 102:49, Hearings on Nonsecured Status and Termination of Commitment of Persons Found NGRI or Incompetent to Stand Trial.

Carlin, Baldwin's Ohio Prac. Merrick-Rippner Probate Law § 109:53, Adjudicatory Hearings--Mental Competency to Stand Trial.

Hennenberg & Reinhart, Ohio Criminal Defense Motions F 13:6, Motion for Order Granting Independent Psychiatric Evaluation at the State's Expense--Death Penalty Motions.

Hennenberg & Reinhart, Ohio Criminal Defense Motions F 5:25, Motion for Psychiatric Evaluation to Determine Defendant's Competency to Stand Trial--Pretrial Motions.

Hennenberg & Reinhart, Ohio Criminal Defense Motions F 5:26, Motion for Order Permitting

Psychiatric Evaluation at State's Expense--Pretrial Motions.
Adrine & Ruden, Ohio Domestic Violence Law App. A, Ohio Revised Code (Selected Provisions).
Giannelli & Yeomans Salvador, Ohio Juvenile Law § 19:3, Mental Competency.

Law Review and Journal Commentaries

The incompetency of courts and legislature: addressing linguistically deprived deaf defendants. Eric Eckes, 75 U. Cin. L. Rev. 1649 (Summer 2007).

Inconsistent methods for the adjudication of alleged mentally retarded individuals: a comparison of Ohio's and Georgia's post-Atkins frameworks for determining mental retardation. Scott R. Poe, 54 Clev. St. L. Rev. 405 (2006).

Notes of Decisions

1. Constitutional issues—In general

The right to a competency hearing rises to the level of a constitutional guarantee where the record contains sufficient indicia of incompetence such that an inquiry is necessary to ensure the defendant's right to a fair trial. State v. Skatzes (Ohio, 12-08-2004) 104 Ohio St.3d 195, 819 N.E.2d 215, 2004-Ohio-6391, denial of post-conviction relief affirmed 2008-Ohio-5387, 2008 WL 4603303, appeal not allowed 121 Ohio St.3d 1439, 903 N.E.2d 1222, 2009-Ohio-1638. Criminal Law ⚷ 625.10(2.1)

The right to a competency hearing rises to the level of a constitutional guarantee where the record contains sufficient indicia of incompetence, such that an inquiry into the defendant's competency is necessary to ensure the defendant's right to a fair trial. State v. Ahmed (Ohio, 08-25-2004) 103 Ohio St.3d 27, 813 N.E.2d 637, 2004-Ohio-4190, reconsideration denied 103 Ohio St.3d 1496, 816 N.E.2d 1081, 2004-Ohio-5605, certiorari denied 125 S.Ct. 1703, 544 U.S. 952, 161 L.Ed.2d 531, rehearing denied, rehearing denied 125 S.Ct. 2901, 545 U.S. 1124, 162 L.Ed.2d 312, denial of post-conviction relief affirmed 2006-Ohio-7069, 2006 WL 3849862, appeal not allowed 113 Ohio St.3d 1513, 866 N.E.2d 512, 2007-Ohio-2208, motion to reopen denied 118 Ohio St.3d 1406, 886 N.E.2d 870, 2008-Ohio-2340. Criminal Law ⚷ 625.10(2.1)

Failure to hold competency hearing in capital murder trial was constitutional error requiring reversal of conviction, where defendant asked for hearing on several occasions, defense counsel represented numerous times that they believed defendant was incompetent, counsel filed two separate motions to withdraw based on defendant's bizarre behavior, and defendant filed six pro se motions to dismiss counsel which alleged, among other things, that his attorneys had threatened his life and were conspiring with the prosecution. State v. Were (Ohio, 02-06-2002) 94 Ohio St.3d 173, 761 N.E.2d 591, 2002-Ohio-481, appeal after new trial 2005-Ohio-376, 2005 WL 267671, remanded 106 Ohio St.3d 1529, 835 N.E.2d 379, 2005-Ohio-5146, on remand 2006-Ohio-3511, 2006 WL 1867840. Criminal Law ⚷ 1166(12)

2. —— Due process, constitutional issues

At change-of-plea and sentencing hearing, at which defendant asked to change his plea from not guilty of misdemeanor first-degree domestic violence, which had been charged in original complaint, to no-contest to charge in amended complaint of misdemeanor first-degree assault, trial court was required to act sua sponte to order a competency evaluation; it had been disclosed at arraignment hearing that defendant was a full-time charge of a facility for persons with mental retardation and developmental disabilities and that an evaluation of defendant and medication monitoring had been scheduled at a hospital, and at plea colloquy, defendant stated "what's going on" and stated that he had not had adequate time to speak to his attorney and that he wanted additional time, which he did not receive. State v. Hartman (Ohio App. 3 Dist., 12-10-2007) 174 Ohio App.3d 244, 881 N.E.2d 891, 2007-Ohio-6555. Criminal Law ⚷ 625.10(3)

Trial court's failure to hold a hearing on the issue of defendant's competency to stand trial was harmless error and did not interfere with defendant's due process right to a fair trial; there was insufficient indicia that defendant was incompetent or unable to understand the nature of the proceedings against him and assist in his defense, given that defendant extensively and coherently discussed issues and options on the record and made choices on those options both before and after his violent outburst in the courtroom, and he presented closing arguments on his own behalf. State v. Murphy (Ohio App. 12 Dist., 09-04-2007) 173 Ohio App.3d 221, 877 N.E.2d 1034, 2007-Ohio-4535, appeal not allowed 116 Ohio St.3d 1507, 880 N.E.2d 483, 2008-Ohio-381. Constitutional Law ⚷ 4783(2); Criminal Law ⚷ 625.10(2.1); Criminal Law ⚷ 1035(2)

A person who lacks the capacity to understand the nature and object of the proceedings against him, to consult with counsel, and to assist in preparing his defense may not, under due process principles, be subjected to a trial. State v. Skatzes (Ohio, 12-08-2004) 104 Ohio St.3d 195, 819 N.E.2d 215, 2004-Ohio-6391, denial of post-conviction relief affirmed 2008-Ohio-5387, 2008 WL 4603303, appeal not allowed 121 Ohio St.3d 1439, 903

N.E.2d 1222, 2009-Ohio-1638. Constitutional Law ⚯ 4782

A person who lacks the capacity to understand the nature and object of the proceedings against him, to consult with counsel, and to assist in preparing his defense may not be subjected to a trial; fundamental principles of due process prohibit trial of a criminal defendant who is legally incompetent. State v. Adams (Ohio, 11-17-2004) 103 Ohio St.3d 508, 817 N.E.2d 29, 2004-Ohio-5845, reconsideration denied 104 Ohio St.3d 1442, 819 N.E.2d 1124, 2004-Ohio-7033, certiorari denied 125 S.Ct. 2271, 544 U.S. 1040, 161 L.Ed.2d 1072, habeas corpus denied 2007 WL 671296, habeas corpus denied 484 F.Supp.2d 753, opinion after remand from court of appeals 2009 WL 2922042, stay granted, motion to certify appeal granted 2010 WL 816532, subsequent determination 2010 WL 1964904, affirmed 644 F.3d 481, on remand 2013 WL 3991867. Constitutional Law ⚯ 4782; Criminal Law ⚯ 625(1)

Evincing a decision to waive the presentation of mitigating evidence, and thereby to invite a death sentence, does not by itself call the capital defendant's competency into question; rather, a trial court must conduct a hearing or determine a defendant's competency, even in the absence of a request by the defendant's counsel, if the defendant displays indicia of incompetence or has a history of mental instability sufficient to create a bona fide doubt as to the defendant's competency to stand trial, plead guilty, or waive other fundamental constitutional rights. Cowans v. Bagley (S.D.Ohio, 09-30-2008) 624 F.Supp.2d 709, affirmed 639 F.3d 241, rehearing and rehearing en banc denied. Sentencing and Punishment ⚯ 1782; Sentencing and Punishment ⚯ 1794

Trial court did not violate defendant's due process rights by failing to hold competency hearing prior to sentencing defendant who pleaded guilty to multiple counts of felony robbery, since record did not contain sufficient indicia of incompetence; even if defendant suffered from emotional problems and drug addiction, he exhibited an understanding of the nature and objective of the proceedings against him, exhibited ability to consult with his attorney and to assist with his defense, pre-sentencing investigation stated that defendant had not been diagnosed with any mental disability, and that he had reported no past or present suicidal or homicidal attempts or ideations, and defendant told court that he had no mental condition which would make it difficult for him to understand his legal rights. State v. Rodeffer (Ohio App. 2 Dist., 12-27-2013) 5 N.E.3d 1069, 2013-Ohio-5759. Constitutional Law ⚯ 4783(2); Sentencing and Punishment ⚯ 268

5. —— Ineffective assistance of counsel, constitutional issues

Defense counsel's failure to insist on second competency evaluation of murder defendant fell within realm of reasonable professional assistance and did not amount to ineffective assistance of counsel, where counsel requested that defendant be evaluated by Court Diagnostic and Treatment Center, and report prepared following such evaluation concluded that defendant was not suffering from emotional disturbance of psychotic proportions, was mildly mentally retarded, was able to understand nature and objectives of proceedings, and was capable of assisting attorney in his own defense. State v. Womack (Ohio App. 6 Dist., Lucas, 05-27-2005) No. L-04-1092, 2005-Ohio-2689, 2005 WL 1283687, Unreported, motion for delayed appeal denied 106 Ohio St.3d 1530, 835 N.E.2d 380, 2005-Ohio-5146, habeas corpus dismissed 2008 WL 123867. Criminal Law ⚯ 1900

Counsel's decision to stipulate to the content of three competency evaluations and not cross-examine these experts or otherwise challenge the competence of defendant was grounded on a reasoned tactical judgment and was not ineffective assistance in capital murder prosecution; the reports were comprehensive and satisfied the statutory requirements, no expert diagnosed any psychosis or mental limitations that would affect the competence to stand trial although all three experts reported that defendant had abused drugs and alcohol, personal requests by defendant demonstrated his understanding of the trial process and his ability to assist his defense, and his complaints about lawyers' tactical decisions established that he understood the trial process and was fully engaged in his defense. State v. Adams (Ohio, 11-17-2004) 103 Ohio St.3d 508, 817 N.E.2d 29, 2004-Ohio-5845, reconsideration denied 104 Ohio St.3d 1442, 819 N.E.2d 1124, 2004-Ohio-7033, certiorari denied 125 S.Ct. 2271, 544 U.S. 1040, 161 L.Ed.2d 1072, habeas corpus denied 2007 WL 671296, habeas corpus denied 484 F.Supp.2d 753, opinion after remand from court of appeals 2009 WL 2922042, stay granted, motion to certify appeal granted 2010 WL 816532, subsequent determination 2010 WL 1964904, affirmed 644 F.3d 481, on remand 2013 WL 3991867. Criminal Law ⚯ 1900

7. Raising issue of competence—In general

A defendant is presumed to be competent to stand trial, and the burden is on the defendant to prove by a preponderance of the evidence that he is not competent. State v. Neyland (Ohio, 05-08-2014) 139 Ohio St.3d 353, 12 N.E.3d 1112, 2014-Ohio-1914, reconsideration denied 140 Ohio St.3d 1418, 15 N.E.3d 886, 2014-Ohio-3785. Criminal Law ⚯ 625.15

Defendant was entitled to a hearing to determine his competency to stand trial on charges of harassment with a bodily substance, since defendant raised issue of competency before commencement of trial. State v. Hinkston (Ohio App. 4 Dist., 05-26-2009) 2009 -Ohio- 2631, 2009 WL 1581140. Criminal Law ⚯ 625.10(3)

For the purpose of a challenge of a defendant's competence to stand trial, a defendant may be emotionally disturbed or even psychotic and still be capable of understanding the charges against him and of assisting his counsel. State v. Ahmed (Ohio, 08-25-2004) 103 Ohio St.3d 27, 813 N.E.2d 637, 2004-Ohio-4190, reconsideration denied 103 Ohio

St.3d 1496, 816 N.E.2d 1081, 2004-Ohio-5605, certiorari denied 125 S.Ct. 1703, 544 U.S. 952, 161 L.Ed.2d 531, rehearing denied, rehearing denied 125 S.Ct. 2901, 545 U.S. 1124, 162 L.Ed.2d 312, denial of post-conviction relief affirmed 2006-Ohio-7069, 2006 WL 3849862, appeal not allowed 113 Ohio St.3d 1513, 866 N.E.2d 512, 2007-Ohio-2208, motion to reopen denied 118 Ohio St.3d 1406, 886 N.E.2d 870, 2008-Ohio-2340. Mental Health ⚷ 432

Capital murder defendant failed to establish that he was incompetent to stand trial; although clinical psychologist who evaluated defendant prior to trial wavered on issue of whether defendant was capable of going forward with trial due to his mental and emotional state following incident in which he was accidentally shocked by stun belt, he testified that defendant was able to understand the nature and object of the proceedings against him, to consult with his attorneys, and to assist in his defense, and several correctional guards indicated that defendant was acting normally. Filiaggi v. Bagley (C.A.6 (Ohio), 04-14-2006) 445 F.3d 851. Criminal Law ⚷ 625.15

8. —— Duty of court, raising issue of competence

Trial court's ruling in delinquency proceeding that 15-year-old juvenile was competent to stand trial, on complaint alleging rape, was supported by sufficient evidence; juvenile told court he understood he had been charged with "wrong doing" and charge was rape, and court appointed evaluator testified that juvenile possessed borderline IQ, a reasonable potential to understand, and, while he suffered from confused thinking, he could marginally assist in own defense. In re Childress (Ohio App. 5 Dist., Licking, 12-31-2008) No. 2008CA00057, 2008-Ohio-7001, 2008 WL 5427983, Unreported. Infants ⚷ 2539

The decision as to whether to hold a competency hearing once trial has commenced is in the trial court's discretion. State v. Skatzes (Ohio, 12-08-2004) 104 Ohio St.3d 195, 819 N.E.2d 215, 2004-Ohio-6391, denial of post-conviction relief affirmed 2008-Ohio-5387, 2008 WL 4603303, appeal not allowed 121 Ohio St.3d 1439, 903 N.E.2d 1222, 2009-Ohio-1638. Criminal Law ⚷ 625.10(1)

Capital murder defendant was not entitled to present rebuttal evidence on the issue of whether he established good cause to a hold a competency hearing; statute governing a request for a competency hearing did not require the court to hold a hearing to determine good cause or allow the presentation of rebuttal testimony, and defendant never made an offer of proof to demonstrate that he had reliable rebuttal evidence. State v. Ahmed (Ohio, 08-25-2004) 103 Ohio St.3d 27, 813 N.E.2d 637, 2004-Ohio-4190, reconsideration denied 103 Ohio St.3d 1496, 816 N.E.2d 1081, 2004-Ohio-5605, certiorari denied 125 S.Ct. 1703, 544 U.S. 952, 161 L.Ed.2d 531, rehearing denied, rehearing denied 125 S.Ct. 2901, 545 U.S. 1124, 162 L.Ed.2d 312, denial of post-conviction relief affirmed 2006-Ohio-7069, 2006 WL 3849862, appeal not allowed 113 Ohio St.3d 1513, 866 N.E.2d 512, 2007-Ohio-2208, motion to reopen denied 118 Ohio St.3d 1406, 886 N.E.2d 870, 2008-Ohio-2340. Criminal Law ⚷ 625.15

The trial court was not required to sua sponte order a competency evaluation for capital murder defendant; defendant made a pro se request for a competency evaluation during trial, jail personnel testified that defendant never complained of any medical, mental, or psychological condition prior to filing his motion, the court noted that defendant used correct legal terms in his pro se motion for a competency evaluation, and defendant assisted counsel subsequent to filing the motion. State v. Ahmed (Ohio, 08-25-2004) 103 Ohio St.3d 27, 813 N.E.2d 637, 2004-Ohio-4190, reconsideration denied 103 Ohio St.3d 1496, 816 N.E.2d 1081, 2004-Ohio-5605, certiorari denied 125 S.Ct. 1703, 544 U.S. 952, 161 L.Ed.2d 531, rehearing denied, rehearing denied 125 S.Ct. 2901, 545 U.S. 1124, 162 L.Ed.2d 312, denial of post-conviction relief affirmed 2006-Ohio-7069, 2006 WL 3849862, appeal not allowed 113 Ohio St.3d 1513, 866 N.E.2d 512, 2007-Ohio-2208, motion to reopen denied 118 Ohio St.3d 1406, 886 N.E.2d 870, 2008-Ohio-2340. Criminal Law ⚷ 625.10(4)

Capital murder defendant's decision to forego presentation of mitigation evidence, without more, did not require trial court to sua sponte inquire into his competence; trial court's assessment that defendant's disruptive conduct, which required his removal from courtroom on several occasions, evidenced pique rather than mental instability, was entitled to deference, defense counsel made no suggestion that defendant might lack competence to waive mitigation, and defendant's behavior did not inherently raise questions concerning his capacity to understand difference between life and death, to fully comprehend ramifications of his decision, or to reason logically. State v. Cowans (Ohio, 10-20-1999) 87 Ohio St.3d 68, 717 N.E.2d 298, 1999-Ohio-250, reconsideration denied 87 Ohio St.3d 1462, 720 N.E.2d 543, certiorari denied 120 S.Ct. 1839, 529 U.S. 1102, 146 L.Ed.2d 782, habeas corpus denied 2008 WL 4452578. Sentencing And Punishment ⚷ 1792

9. Psychiatric examination

Denial of defendant's motion for a psychiatric examination, which defendant alleged that he needed in order to investigate and prepare a motion to suppress evidence, was not error; during hearing on defendant's motion defendant informed the court that he understood the possible sentence he faced, he understood the crimes he was charged with, and he understood the burden of proof, police detective testified that he provided defendant with his *Miranda* rights, defendant seemed attentive during their interview, defendant reviewed and signed his statement, defendant did not exhibit any unusual behavior during the interview, and that he was not suspicious about defendant's mental health, and defendant's confession to police was voluntary. State v. Woodley (Ohio App. 8 Dist., Cuyahoga,

04-17-2003) No. 80732, 2003-Ohio-1950, 2003 WL 1900935, Unreported, appeal not allowed 100 Ohio St.3d 1425, 797 N.E.2d 92, 2003-Ohio-5232, habeas corpus denied 2008 WL 2048209, affirmed 451 Fed. Appx. 529, 2011 WL 6355204. Mental Health ⚿ 434

Capital murder defendant failed to establish that a preponderance of the evidence proved that she was not competent to stand trial during her resentencing; court-appointed psychologist who conducted competency evaluation on defendant testified that defendant had the ability to understand the sentencing process and to understand what the alternatives available were to her as well as to provide her counsel with any mitigating circumstances, should she desire to do so, and psychologist concluded that based on defendant's ability to interact with him and to provide information and a coherent account of her perceptions about the situation, she would be able to do so with her defense counsel as well. State v. Roberts (Ohio, 10-22-2013) 137 Ohio St.3d 230, 998 N.E.2d 1100, 2013-Ohio-4580. Sentencing and Punishment ⚿ 1793

Indicia of incompetence did not rise to a level that demanded a hearing or an evaluation, and thus, trial court did not abuse its discretion by denying counsel's motion for a competency evaluation in capital murder prosecution; defendant's refusal to heed his counsel's advice and his abandoned request to fire his counsel did not indicate that he was unable to understand nature of charges and proceedings or gravity of situation, or that he could not assist in his defense, and defendant, in his responses to court, expressed his understanding of nature of charges against him, possibility of death penalty, and ramifications of representing himself. State v. Johnson (Ohio, 12-13-2006) 112 Ohio St.3d 210, 858 N.E.2d 1144, 2006-Ohio-6404, reconsideration denied 112 Ohio St.3d 1472, 861 N.E.2d 145, 2007-Ohio-388, denial of post-conviction relief affirmed 2007-Ohio-1685, 2007 WL 1098106, appeal not allowed 115 Ohio St.3d 1439, 875 N.E.2d 101, 2007-Ohio-5567, certiorari denied 128 S.Ct. 74, 552 U.S. 836, 169 L.Ed.2d 55, habeas corpus dismissed in part 2009 WL 3124423, application for writ of habeas corpus held in abeyance 2012 WL 628507, denial of post-conviction relief affirmed 2013-Ohio-1398, 2013 WL 1400607. Criminal Law ⚿ 625.10(2.1); Mental Health ⚿ 434

10. Sufficiency of evidence—In general

A defendant is competent to stand trial if he has sufficient present ability to consult with his lawyer with a reasonable degree of rational understanding, and whether he has a rational as well as factual understanding of the proceedings against him. State v. Hess (Ohio App. 4 Dist., 07-14-2014) 17 N.E.3d 15, 2014-Ohio-3193. Mental Health ⚿ 432

Juvenile court could not rely on psychological report that was not a part of the record in finding that juvenile was competent to stand trial in delinquency proceeding for acts that would have constituted burglary, conveying a weapon in a school safety zone, and gross sexual imposition if committed by an adult; although court had carefully attempted to ensure that juvenile's right not to be tried while incompetent was respected, and although court commented on the report, the report was never introduced or formally admitted into evidence. In re Braden (Ohio App. 1 Dist., 06-20-2008) 176 Ohio App.3d 616, 893 N.E.2d 213, 2008-Ohio-2981. Infants ⚿ 2539

Defendant's decision to exercise his constitutional right to testify on his own behalf did not provide good cause for competency hearing during guilt phase of capital murder trial; defendant attempted to rebut the abundant testimony elicited against him. State v. Skatzes (Ohio, 12-08-2004) 104 Ohio St.3d 195, 819 N.E.2d 215, 2004-Ohio-6391, denial of post-conviction relief affirmed 2008-Ohio-5387, 2008 WL 4603303, appeal not allowed 121 Ohio St.3d 1439, 903 N.E.2d 1222, 2009-Ohio-1638. Criminal Law ⚿ 625.10(2.1)

Allegations that defendant did not understand consequences of answering questions with speculative responses during his trial testimony, that his use of colloquial phrases such as "I reckon" subjected him to ridicule by prosecutor, that he lost a significant amount of weight pending trial, and that he had been suffering from stress and confusion at time of prison takeover by inmates, did not provide good cause for competency hearing during guilt phase of capital murder trial, relating to prison riot and takeover. State v. Skatzes (Ohio, 12-08-2004) 104 Ohio St.3d 195, 819 N.E.2d 215, 2004-Ohio-6391, denial of post-conviction relief affirmed 2008-Ohio-5387, 2008 WL 4603303, appeal not allowed 121 Ohio St.3d 1439, 903 N.E.2d 1222, 2009-Ohio-1638. Criminal Law ⚿ 625.10(3)

Defendant's characterization of himself as "paranoid," fact he was known by the nickname "Crazy George," and his inability during his testimony to remember events from prison riot, did not provide good cause for competency evaluation, during guilt phase of capital murder trial relating to prison riot; such facts were not directly related to defendant's ability to understand nature of proceedings against him and to assist in his own defense. State v. Skatzes (Ohio, 12-08-2004) 104 Ohio St.3d 195, 819 N.E.2d 215, 2004-Ohio-6391, denial of post-conviction relief affirmed 2008-Ohio-5387, 2008 WL 4603303, appeal not allowed 121 Ohio St.3d 1439, 903 N.E.2d 1222, 2009-Ohio-1638. Mental Health ⚿ 434

Defendant was not entitled to competency hearing after commencement of trial; defendant's competency had been considered at pretrial competency hearing, and defendant's erratic behavior at trial, which included belching loudly and interrupting judge, illustrated pattern of rudeness rather than incompetency. State v. Franklin (Ohio, 10-16-2002) 97 Ohio St.3d 1, 776 N.E.2d 26, 2002-Ohio-5304, denial of post-conviction relief affirmed 2002-Ohio-2370, 2002 WL 1000415, appeal not allowed 98 Ohio St.3d 1422, 782 N.E.2d 77, 2003-Ohio-259, reconsideration denied 101 Ohio St.3d 1462, 804 N.E.2d 37, 2004-Ohio-823, appeal not allowed 108 Ohio St.3d 1475, 842 N.E.2d 1054, 2006-Ohio-665, certiorari denied 127 S.Ct. 362, 549 U.S. 878, 166 L.Ed.2d 136, reconsideration denied 97 Ohio St.3d 1486, 780 N.E.2d 288, 2002-Ohio-6866, stay granted 97 Ohio St.3d 1491, 780 N.E.2d 597, 2002-Ohio-7045, certiorari denied 123 S.Ct. 2249, 539 U.S. 905, 156 L.Ed.2d 115, denial of post-conviction relief affirmed 2005-Ohio-1361, 2005 WL 678925, appeal not allowed 106 Ohio St.3d 1464, 830 N.E.2d 1170, 2005-Ohio-3490, certiorari denied 126 S.Ct. 1352, 546 U.S. 1179, 164 L.Ed.2d 64, habeas corpus denied 2009 WL 649581, subsequent determination 2009 WL 2243384, certificate of appealability granted in part, denied in part 2009 WL 5167764, affirmed 695 F.3d 439. Criminal Law ⇨ 625(3); Criminal Law ⇨ 625.10(3)

Capital murder defendant who requested pretrial hearing on competency was entitled to hearing, and thus trial court could not determine competency without hearing, although defendant refused to speak with competency examiners; defendant was found competent, without the benefit of a psychiatric evaluation, based on examiners' opinion that his refusal of examination was part of a deliberate ploy to disrupt trial proceedings and that he was competent, and defendant did not stipulate to that report. State v. Were (Ohio, 02-06-2002) 94 Ohio St.3d 173, 761 N.E.2d 591, 2002-Ohio-481, appeal after new trial 2005-Ohio-376, 2005 WL 267671, remanded 106 Ohio St.3d 1529, 835 N.E.2d 379, 2005-Ohio-5146, on remand 2006-Ohio-3511, 2006 WL 1867840. Criminal Law ⇨ 625.10(1)

Capital murder defendant did not carry his burden of proving incompetence to stand trial, though doctor wavered on issue of whether defendant was capable of going forward with trial due to his mental/emotional state following incidents in which he was accidentally shocked by stun belt and correctional officers attempted to restrain him, where doctor testified that defendant was competent to stand trial, and defendant still came to trial after stun belt incident and waived his right to jury trial and sat through a half a day of testimony. State v. Filiaggi (Ohio, 07-29-1999) 86 Ohio St.3d 230, 714 N.E.2d 867, 1999-Ohio-99, certiorari denied 120 S.Ct. 821, 528 U.S. 1090, 145 L.Ed.2d 691, denial of habeas corpus affirmed 445 F.3d 851. Criminal Law ⇨ 625.15

11. —— Indicia of incompetence, sufficiency of evidence

Defendant's claim that earlier evaluation would have revealed his incompetency rested upon speculation and had no basis in record, in capital murder prosecution; court, between guilt and penalty phases of trial, granted counsel's renewed motion for mental evaluation and competency hearing, and although appointed defense psychologist opined that in stressful situations, anger and suspiciousness could contribute to extreme agitation and possible atypical perception, evidence failed to address defendant's competency, and failed to suggest what defendant's competency would have been four days earlier, when defendant believed he should have been evaluated. State v. Johnson (Ohio, 12-13-2006) 112 Ohio St.3d 210, 858 N.E.2d 1144, 2006-Ohio-6404, reconsideration denied 112 Ohio St.3d 1472, 861 N.E.2d 145, 2007-Ohio-388, denial of post-conviction relief affirmed 2007-Ohio-1685, 2007 WL 1098106, appeal not allowed 115 Ohio St.3d 1439, 875 N.E.2d 101, 2007-Ohio-5567, certiorari denied 128 S.Ct. 74, 552 U.S. 836, 169 L.Ed.2d 55, habeas corpus dismissed in part 2009 WL 3124423, application for writ of habeas corpus held in abeyance 2012 WL 628507, denial of post-conviction relief affirmed 2013-Ohio-1398, 2013 WL 1400607. Criminal Law ⇨ 625.15

Evidence of a criminal defendant's irrational behavior, his demeanor at trial, and any prior medical opinion on competence to stand trial all are relevant in determining whether further inquiry is required, but even one of these factors standing alone may, in some circumstances, be sufficient. Cowans v. Bagley (S.D.Ohio, 09-30-2008) 624 F.Supp.2d 709, affirmed 639 F.3d 241, rehearing and rehearing en banc denied. Criminal Law ⇨ 625.10(2.1)

Disruptive behavior alone, especially when prompted by anger at certain aspects of the proceedings against him as opposed to mental disease or defect, is insufficient to establish a criminal defendant's incompetency or even necessarily raise questions as to his competency. Cowans v. Bagley (S.D.Ohio, 09-30-2008) 624 F.Supp.2d 709, affirmed 639 F.3d 241, rehearing and rehearing en banc denied. Criminal Law ⇨ 625.10(2.1); Mental Health ⇨ 432

In capital murder proceedings, defendant's brief outburst during pre-trial hearing and distrust defendant harbored towards his lawyers were insufficient indicia of incompetency to warrant an evaluation; the outburst was limited to a single comment that did not pervade the entire hearing, and defendant's distrust of appointed counsel did not render him unable to consult with them or to understand the trial proceedings. Jones v. Bradshaw (N.D.Ohio, 05-21-2007) 489 F.Supp.2d 786. Criminal Law ⇨ 625.10(3)

12. —— Indicia of competence, sufficiency of evidence

Credible and reliable evidence supported conclusion that defendant was legally competent to stand trial for capital murder of corrections officer; prison employees who had numerous interactions with defendant testified that his behavior was always responsive and appropriate. State v. Were (Ohio App. 1 Dist., Hamilton, 02-04-2005) No. C-030485, 2005-Ohio-376, 2005 WL 267671, Unreported, remanded 106 Ohio St.3d 1529, 835 N.E.2d 379, 2005-Ohio-5146, on remand 2006-Ohio-3511, 2006 WL 1867840. Criminal Law ⇨ 625.15

Defendant was not rendered incompetent to enter guilty plea to aggravated murder due to fact that he was taking antidepressant medication, even though defendant stated during plea hearing that medication caused confusion, where defendant also stated that he took medication twice daily but did not take it on morning of hearing and that there was nothing affecting his ability to understand plea proceedings, defendant engaged in lengthy colloquy with trial court, and there was no evidence that medication was causing confusion when defendant pleaded guilty. State v. Doak (Ohio App. 7 Dist., Columbiana, 03-22-2004) No. 03 CO 15, No. 03 CO 31, 2004-Ohio-1548, 2004 WL 614851, Unreported, appeal not allowed 103 Ohio St.3d 1406, 812 N.E.2d 1288, 2004-Ohio-3980, habeas corpus dismissed 2006 WL 2869560, habeas corpus dismissed 2007 WL 1100436. Criminal Law ⚷ 273(2)

Trial court determination that defendant was competent to stand trial for capital murder was not an abuse of discretion; trial court determined that clinical psychologist's opinion that defendant was not competent to stand trial was not credible based on expert's education, experience, and how he arrived at his opinions, and expert's testimony that defendant was incompetent due to his inability to cooperate with counsel was undermined by several in-court statements made by defendant and the pro-se motions filed by defendant. State v. Were (Ohio, 06-17-2008) 118 Ohio St.3d 448, 890 N.E.2d 263, 2008-Ohio-2762, certiorari denied 129 S.Ct. 606, 555 U.S. 1036, 172 L.Ed.2d 464, denial of post-conviction relief affirmed 2009-Ohio-4494, 2009 WL 2768021, appeal not allowed 124 Ohio St.3d 1443, 920 N.E.2d 374, 2010-Ohio-188. Criminal Law ⚷ 625.15

Trial court acted within its discretion, in capital murder case, in denying defense counsel's motion for new trial which was based on claim that defendant was not competent to stand trial; presiding judge considered the additional medical evidence submitted by defendant, and judge's determination that defendant was competent to stand trial was properly based on court's own observations, as well as unrefuted representations of correctional officers who observed defendant showering, eating meals and conversing with other inmates, correctional officers and his attorneys. State v. Filiaggi (Ohio, 07-29-1999) 86 Ohio St.3d 230, 714 N.E.2d 867, 1999-Ohio-99, certiorari denied 120 S.Ct. 821, 528 U.S. 1090, 145 L.Ed.2d 691, denial of habeas corpus affirmed 445 F.3d 851. Criminal Law ⚷ 913(1)

13. Speedy trial

A defendant may be emotionally disturbed or even psychotic and still be capable of understanding the charges against him and of assisting his counsel. State v. Johnson (Ohio, 12-13-2006) 112 Ohio St.3d 210, 858 N.E.2d 1144, 2006-Ohio-6404, reconsideration denied 112 Ohio St.3d 1472, 861 N.E.2d 145, 2007-Ohio-388, denial of post-conviction relief affirmed 2007-Ohio-1685, 2007 WL 1098106, appeal not allowed 115 Ohio St.3d 1439, 875 N.E.2d 101, 2007-Ohio-5567, certiorari denied 128 S.Ct. 74, 552 U.S. 836, 169 L.Ed.2d 55, habeas corpus dismissed in part 2009 WL 3124423, application for writ of habeas corpus held in abeyance 2012 WL 628507, denial of post-conviction relief affirmed 2013-Ohio-1398, 2013 WL 1400607. Mental Health ⚷ 432

14. Insanity defense

The test to determine competency to stand trial differs from the test to determine whether a defendant is not guilty by reason of insanity. State v. Hess (Ohio App. 4 Dist., 07-14-2014) 17 N.E.3d 15, 2014-Ohio-3193. Criminal Law ⚷ 48; Mental Health ⚷ 432

18. Review

Trial court did not abuse its discretion by declining to order mid-trial competency hearing in prosecution for unlawful sexual conduct with a minor, as defendant's conduct and demeanor during trial did not provide the court with good cause to question defendant's competency; despite appellate counsel's contentions that defendant appeared to be asleep during trial, began laughing uncontrollably during trial, and did not appear to understand his rights at trial, defendant had been found competent in two pre-trial competency hearings, and defendant's behavior did not indicate that he was suffering from mental condition that would have caused him to be incapable of understanding the nature of the proceedings against him or assisting in his own defense. State v. Ellison (Ohio App. 8 Dist., 11-07-2013) 1 N.E.3d 824, 2013-Ohio-4909. Criminal Law ⚷ 625.10(3)

2945.371 Evaluations of mental condition

(A) If the issue of a defendant's competence to stand trial is raised or if a defendant enters a plea of not guilty by reason of insanity, the court may order one or more evaluations of the defendant's present mental condition or, in the case of a plea of not guilty by reason of insanity, of the defendant's mental condition at the time of the offense charged. An examiner shall conduct the evaluation.

(B) If the court orders more than one evaluation under division (A) of this section, the prosecutor and the defendant may recommend to the court an examiner whom each prefers to perform one of the evaluations. If a defendant enters a plea of not guilty by reason of insanity and if the court does not designate an examiner recommended by the defendant, the court shall inform the defendant that the defendant may have independent expert evaluation and that, if the defendant is unable to obtain independent expert evaluation, it will be obtained for the defendant at public expense if the defendant is indigent.

(C) If the court orders an evaluation under division (A) of this section, the defendant shall be available at the times and places established by the examiners who are to conduct the evaluation. The court may order a defendant who has been released on bail or recognizance to submit to an evaluation under this section. If a defendant who has been released on bail or recognizance refuses to submit to a complete evaluation, the court may amend the conditions of bail or recognizance and order the sheriff to take the defendant into custody and deliver the defendant to a center, program, or facility operated or certified by the department of mental health and addiction services or the department of developmental disabilities where the defendant may be held for evaluation for a reasonable period of time not to exceed twenty days.

(D) A defendant who has not been released on bail or recognizance may be evaluated at the defendant's place of detention. Upon the request of the examiner, the court may order the sheriff to transport the defendant to a program or facility operated or certified by the department of mental health and addiction services or the department of developmental disabilities, where the defendant may be held for evaluation for a reasonable period of time not to exceed twenty days, and to return the defendant to the place of detention after the evaluation. A municipal court may make an order under this division only upon the request of a certified forensic center examiner.

(E) If a court orders the evaluation to determine a defendant's mental condition at the time of the offense charged, the court shall inform the examiner of the offense with which the defendant is charged.

(F) In conducting an evaluation of a defendant's mental condition at the time of the offense charged, the examiner shall consider all relevant evidence. If the offense charged involves the use of force against another person, the relevant evidence to be considered includes, but is not limited to, any evidence that the defendant suffered, at the time of the commission of the offense, from the "battered woman syndrome."

(G) The examiner shall file a written report with the court within thirty days after entry of a court order for evaluation, and the court shall provide copies of the report to the prosecutor and defense counsel. The report shall include all of the following:

(1) The examiner's findings;

(2) The facts in reasonable detail on which the findings are based;

(3) If the evaluation was ordered to determine the defendant's competence to stand trial, all of the following findings or recommendations that are applicable:

(a) Whether the defendant is capable of understanding the nature and objective of the proceedings against the defendant or of assisting in the defendant's defense;

(b) If the examiner's opinion is that the defendant is incapable of understanding the nature and objective of the proceedings against the defendant or of assisting in the defendant's defense, whether the defendant presently is mentally ill or mentally retarded and, if the examiner's opinion is that the defendant presently is mentally retarded, whether the defendant appears to be a mentally retarded person subject to institutionalization by court order;

(c) If the examiner's opinion is that the defendant is incapable of understanding the nature and objective of the proceedings against the defendant or of assisting in the defendant's defense, the examiner's opinion as to the likelihood of the defendant becoming capable of understanding the nature and objective of the proceedings against the defendant and of assisting in the defendant's defense within one year if the defendant is provided with a course of treatment;

(d) If the examiner's opinion is that the defendant is incapable of understanding the nature and objective of the proceedings against the defendant or of assisting in the defendant's defense and that the defendant presently is mentally ill or mentally retarded, the examiner's recommendation as to the least restrictive placement or commitment alternative, consistent with the defendant's treatment needs for restoration to competency and with the safety of the community.

(4) If the evaluation was ordered to determine the defendant's mental condition at the time of the offense charged, the examiner's findings as to whether the defendant, at the time of the

offense charged, did not know, as a result of a severe mental disease or defect, the wrongfulness of the defendant's acts charged.

(H) If the examiner's report filed under division (G) of this section indicates that in the examiner's opinion the defendant is incapable of understanding the nature and objective of the proceedings against the defendant or of assisting in the defendant's defense and that in the examiner's opinion the defendant appears to be a mentally retarded person subject to institutionalization by court order, the court shall order the defendant to undergo a separate mental retardation evaluation conducted by a psychologist designated by the director of developmental disabilities. Divisions (C) to (F) of this section apply in relation to a separate mental retardation evaluation conducted under this division. The psychologist appointed under this division to conduct the separate mental retardation evaluation shall file a written report with the court within thirty days after the entry of the court order requiring the separate mental retardation evaluation, and the court shall provide copies of the report to the prosecutor and defense counsel. The report shall include all of the information described in divisions (G)(1) to (4) of this section. If the court orders a separate mental retardation evaluation of a defendant under this division, the court shall not conduct a hearing under divisions (B) to (H) of section 2945.37 of the Revised Code regarding that defendant until a report of the separate mental retardation evaluation conducted under this division has been filed. Upon the filing of that report, the court shall conduct the hearing within the period of time specified in division (C) of section 2945.37 of the Revised Code.

(I) An examiner appointed under divisions (A) and (B) of this section or under division (H) of this section to evaluate a defendant to determine the defendant's competence to stand trial also may be appointed to evaluate a defendant who has entered a plea of not guilty by reason of insanity, but an examiner of that nature shall prepare separate reports on the issue of competence to stand trial and the defense of not guilty by reason of insanity.

(J) No statement that a defendant makes in an evaluation or hearing under divisions (A) to (H) of this section relating to the defendant's competence to stand trial or to the defendant's mental condition at the time of the offense charged shall be used against the defendant on the issue of guilt in any criminal action or proceeding, but, in a criminal action or proceeding, the prosecutor or defense counsel may call as a witness any person who evaluated the defendant or prepared a report pursuant to a referral under this section. Neither the appointment nor the testimony of an examiner appointed under this section precludes the prosecutor or defense counsel from calling other witnesses or presenting other evidence on competency or insanity issues.

(K) Persons appointed as examiners under divisions (A) and (B) of this section or under division (H) of this section shall be paid a reasonable amount for their services and expenses, as certified by the court. The certified amount shall be paid by the county in the case of county courts and courts of common pleas and by the legislative authority, as defined in section 1901.03 of the Revised Code, in the case of municipal courts.

(2013 H 59, eff. 9-29-13; 2012 H 487, eff. 6-11-12; 2011 H 153, eff. 9-29-11; 2009 S 79, eff. 10-6-09; 2001 S 122, eff. 2-20-02; 1996 S 285, eff. 7-1-97; 1980 H 965, eff. 4-9-81; 1980 H 900, S 297; 1978 H 565)

Historical and Statutory Notes

Amendment Note: 2013 H 59, in divisions (C) and (D), inserted "and addiction services" following "mental health".

Amendment Note: 2012 H 487 deleted division (G)(3)(e); and made other nonsubstantive changes. Prior to deletion, division (G)(3)(e) read:

"(e) If the defendant is charged with a misdemeanor offense that is not an offense of violence and the examiner's opinion is that the defendant is incapable of understanding the nature and objective of the proceedings against the defendant or of assisting in the defendant's defense and that the defendant is presently mentally ill or mentally retarded, the examiner's recommendation as to whether the defendant is amenable to engagement in mental health treatment or developmental disability services."

Amendment Note: 2011 H 153, in division (D) inserted "or certified" before "by the department", in division (G)(3)(d) substituted "placement or commitment" for "treatment", and added division (G)(3)(e).

Amendment Note: 2009 S 79 deleted "mental retardation and" from "department of mental retardation and developmental disabilities" and from "director of mental retardation and developmental disabilities" throughout.

Ohio Administrative Code References

Community forensic psychiatric centers, see OAC 5122–32–01

Forensic evaluation service, see OAC 5122–29–07

Patient rights, participation and education, see OAC 5122–14–11

Procedure for reporting incompetency records, see OAC 109:5–3–01

Research References

Encyclopedias

OH Jur. 3d Criminal Law: Procedure § 1166, Time and Place of Evaluation.

OH Jur. 3d Criminal Law: Procedure § 1167, Evaluation Report.

OH Jur. 3d Criminal Law: Procedure § 1168, Additional Evaluation Upon Indication of Mental Retardation.

OH Jur. 3d Criminal Law: Procedure § 1169, Use of Statements Made by Defendant in Evaluation; Examiner as Witness.

OH Jur. 3d Criminal Law: Procedure § 1712, Number of Witnesses.

OH Jur. 3d Criminal Law: Substantive Principles and Offenses § 210, Examiner's Evaluation and Report.

OH Jur. 3d Criminal Law: Substantive Principles and Offenses § 211, Use of Statements Against Defendant.

OH Jur. 3d Evidence and Witnesses § 626, Expert Opinion.

Treatises and Practice Aids

Katz & Giannelli, Baldwin's Ohio Practice Criminal Law § 54:1, Introduction.

Katz & Giannelli, Baldwin's Ohio Practice Criminal Law § 54:4, Mental Evaluation.

Katz & Giannelli, Baldwin's Ohio Practice Criminal Law § 54:8, Findings.

Katz & Giannelli, Baldwin's Ohio Practice Criminal Law § 77:6, Experts--Insanity.

Katz & Giannelli, Baldwin's Ohio Practice Criminal Law § 77:8, Experts--Competency to Stand Trial.

Katz & Giannelli, Baldwin's Ohio Practice Criminal Law § 87:9, Examination of Accused.

Katz & Giannelli, Baldwin's Ohio Practice Criminal Law § 106:8, Possession of Deadly Weapon While Under Detention.

Katz & Giannelli, Baldwin's Ohio Practice Criminal Law § 144:5, Plea of Not Guilty by Reason of Insanity at Arraignment.

Katz & Giannelli, Baldwin's Ohio Practice Criminal Law § 144:6, Entry on Plea of Not Guilty by Reason of Insanity.

Katz & Giannelli, Baldwin's Ohio Practice Criminal Law § 144:7, Plea of Not Guilty by Reason of Insanity After Arraignment.

Katz & Giannelli, Baldwin's Ohio Practice Criminal Law § 144:8, Acceptance of Plea of Not Guilty by Reason of Insanity After Arraignment.

Katz & Giannelli, Baldwin's Ohio Practice Criminal Law § 144:9, Entry Ordering Inquiry Into Competence of Defendant.

Katz & Giannelli, Baldwin's Ohio Practice Criminal Law § 87:11, Evidence Issues.

Katz & Giannelli, Baldwin's Ohio Practice Criminal Law § 87:13, Defense Experts.

Katz & Giannelli, Baldwin's Ohio Practice Criminal Law § 110:21, Escape.

Carlin, Baldwin's Ohio Prac. Merrick-Rippner Probate Law § 102:47, Initial Treatment for Persons Found Incompetent to Stand Trial; Maximum Duration.

Hennenberg & Reinhart, Ohio Criminal Defense Motions F 13:6, Motion for Order Granting Independent Psychiatric Evaluation at the State's Expense--Death Penalty Motions.

Hennenberg & Reinhart, Ohio Criminal Defense Motions F 5:25, Motion for Psychiatric Evaluation to Determine Defendant's Competency to Stand Trial--Pretrial Motions.

Hennenberg & Reinhart, Ohio Criminal Defense Motions F 5:26, Motion for Order Permitting Psychiatric Evaluation at State's Expense--Pretrial Motions.

Adrine & Ruden, Ohio Domestic Violence Law § 4:6, Violation of a Protection Order.

Adrine & Ruden, Ohio Domestic Violence Law App. A, Ohio Revised Code (Selected Provisions).

Notes of Decisions

4. Psychiatric evaluations—In general

Denial of defendant's motion for a psychiatric examination, which defendant alleged that he needed in order to investigate and prepare a motion to suppress evidence, was not error; during hearing on defendant's motion defendant informed the court that he understood the possible sentence he faced, he understood the crimes he was charged with, and he understood the burden of proof, police detective testified that he provided defendant with his *Miranda* rights, defendant seemed attentive during their interview, defendant reviewed and signed his statement, defendant did not exhibit any unusual behavior during the interview, and that he was not suspicious about defendant's mental health, and defendant's confession to police was voluntary. State v. Woodley (Ohio App. 8 Dist., Cuyahoga, 04-17-2003) No. 80732, 2003-Ohio-1950, 2003 WL 1900935, Unreported, appeal not allowed 100 Ohio St.3d 1425, 797 N.E.2d 92, 2003-Ohio-5232, habeas corpus denied 2008 WL 2048209, affirmed 451 Fed. Appx. 529, 2011 WL 6355204. Mental Health ⚯ 434

Defendant who had raised level of his competency to stand trial through initial entry of plea of not guilty by reason of insanity could not avoid mental examinations ordered by court pursuant to statute. State v. White (Ohio, 05-12-1999) 85 Ohio St.3d 433, 709 N.E.2d 140, 1999-Ohio-281, denial of post-conviction relief affirmed 1999 WL 394938, dismissed, appeal not allowed 87 Ohio St.3d 1418, 717 N.E.2d 1105, certiorari denied 120 S.Ct. 345, 528 U.S. 938, 145 L.Ed.2d 270, post-conviction relief denied 2005 WL 5775899, affirmed 2005-Ohio-6990, 2005 WL 3556634, appeal allowed 109 Ohio St.3d 1493, 848 N.E.2d 857, 2006-Ohio-2762, reversed 118 Ohio St.3d 12, 885 N.E.2d 905, 2008-Ohio-1623. Mental Health ⚿ 434

7. Evidence, admissibility

Trial court properly ordered defendant's disclosure to the state of videotape of defendant's psychiatric examination; defense counsel filed a motion asking that psychiatrist have complete access to defendant for the purposes of a medical examination and evaluation, including having a videographer present at psychiatrist's discretion, and defendant had entered a plea of not guilty by reason of insanity on aggravated arson charge. State v. Henry (Ohio App. 11 Dist., Lake, 03-13-2009) No. 2007-L-142, 2009-Ohio-1138, 2009 WL 653051, Unreported, appeal not allowed 122 Ohio St.3d 1481, 910 N.E.2d 479, 2009-Ohio-3625, certiorari denied 130 S.Ct. 1519, 559 U.S. 946, 176 L.Ed.2d 125, denial of post-conviction relief affirmed 2010-Ohio-1446, 2010 WL 1254361, appeal not allowed 126 Ohio St.3d 1547, 932 N.E.2d 340, 2010-Ohio-3855, habeas corpus denied 2014 WL 763234. Criminal Law ⚿ 627.5(3)

In murder prosecution, any error was harmless in trial court's admission of statements allegedly made by defendant during competency evaluation, where the evidence of defendant's guilt was overwhelming. State v. Taylor (Ohio App. 1 Dist., Hamilton, 03-26-2004) No. C-020475, 2004-Ohio-1494, 2004 WL 596128, Unreported, appeal not allowed 103 Ohio St.3d 1406, 812 N.E.2d 1289, 2004-Ohio-3980, habeas corpus denied 2007 WL 2477705. Criminal Law ⚿ 1169.12

Defendant in aggravated murder prosecution waived his physician/patient privilege as to his psychiatric condition when he placed his mental health at issue by entering a plea of not guilty by reason of insanity. State v. Hancock (Ohio App. 12 Dist., Warren, 03-31-2003) No. CA2001-12-115, No. CA2001-12-116, No. CA2002-01-004, 2003-Ohio-1616, 2003 WL 1689612, Unreported, appeal not allowed 99 Ohio St.3d 1513, 792 N.E.2d 200, 2003-Ohio-3957, on remand 2003 WL 25672096. Privileged Communications And Confidentiality ⚿ 323

Clinical psychologist's testimony that defendant was feigning mental illness was inadmissible during state's case-in-chief under statute that prohibited admission of defendant's statement in an evaluation of his competence to stand trial or his mental condition at the time of offense, in prosecution for aggravated murder with a firearm specification, aggravated robbery, and having a weapon while under a disability, where defendant abandoned his assertion that he was incompetent to stand trial and his not guilty by reason of insanity defense. State v. Harris (Ohio, 01-22-2015) 2015-Ohio-166, 2015 WL 266924. Criminal Law ⚿ 411.71

Defendant's admission to court-appointed forensic psychiatrist that he "tied [victim] up and strangled him" was not offered as substantive evidence of guilt, but was relevant, in trial for capital murder, to determination of whether defendant had capacity to know wrongfulness of killing victim, for purposes of insanity defense. State v. Hancock (Ohio, 02-01-2006) 108 Ohio St.3d 57, 840 N.E.2d 1032, 2006-Ohio-160, reconsideration denied 108 Ohio St.3d 1513, 844 N.E.2d 857, 2006-Ohio-1329, on remand 2007 WL 4477699. Homicide ⚿ 1041

Court-appointed forensic psychiatrist's opinion that defendant was not insane but was malingering did not violate psychiatrist-patient privilege based on claim that psychiatrist had relied on information acquired from other mental health care professionals who had examined defendant, in trial for aggravated murder; psychiatrist did not testify as to communications made to him by defendant, and court-appointed psychiatrist was required to consider all relevant evidence in forming opinion. State v. Hancock (Ohio, 02-01-2006) 108 Ohio St.3d 57, 840 N.E.2d 1032, 2006-Ohio-160, reconsideration denied 108 Ohio St.3d 1513, 844 N.E.2d 857, 2006-Ohio-1329, on remand 2007 WL 4477699. Criminal Law ⚿ 486(6); Privileged Communications And Confidentiality ⚿ 308; Privileged Communications And Confidentiality ⚿ 310

Defendant's statements to doctor, who was not court-appointed, during defendant's mental evaluation were inadmissible hearsay with respect to issue of guilt. State v. Franklin (Ohio, 10-16-2002) 97 Ohio St.3d 1, 776 N.E.2d 26, 2002-Ohio-5304, denial of post-conviction relief affirmed 2002-Ohio-2370, 2002 WL 1000415, appeal not allowed 98 Ohio St.3d 1422, 782 N.E.2d 77, 2003-Ohio-259, reconsideration denied 101 Ohio St.3d 1462, 804 N.E.2d 37, 2004-Ohio-823, appeal not allowed 108 Ohio St.3d 1475, 842 N.E.2d 1054, 2006-Ohio-665, certiorari denied 127 S.Ct. 362, 549 U.S. 878, 166 L.Ed.2d 136, reconsideration denied 97 Ohio St.3d 1486, 780 N.E.2d 288, 2002-Ohio-6866, stay granted 97 Ohio St.3d 1491, 780 N.E.2d 597, 2002-Ohio-7045, certiorari denied 123 S.Ct. 2249, 539 U.S. 905, 156 L.Ed.2d 115, denial of post-conviction relief affirmed 2005-Ohio-1361, 2005 WL 678925, appeal not allowed 106 Ohio St.3d 1464, 830 N.E.2d 1170, 2005-Ohio-3490, certiorari denied 126 S.Ct. 1352, 546 U.S. 1179, 164 L.Ed.2d 64, habeas corpus denied 2009 WL 649581, subsequent determination 2009 WL 2243384, certificate of appealability granted in part, denied in part 2009 WL 5167764, affirmed 695 F.3d 439. Criminal Law ⚿ 411.71; Criminal Law ⚿ 419(1.5)

2945.38 Effect of findings; treatment or continuing evaluation and treatment of incompetent; medication; disposition of defendant; report; additional hearings; discharge

(A) If the issue of a defendant's competence to stand trial is raised and if the court, upon conducting the hearing provided for in section 2945.37 of the Revised Code, finds that the defendant is competent to stand trial, the defendant shall be proceeded against as provided by law. If the court finds the defendant competent to stand trial and the defendant is receiving psychotropic drugs or other medication, the court may authorize the continued administration of the drugs or medication or other appropriate treatment in order to maintain the defendant's competence to stand trial, unless the defendant's attending physician advises the court against continuation of the drugs, other medication, or treatment.

(B)(1)(a) If, after taking into consideration all relevant reports, information, and other evidence, the court finds that the defendant is incompetent to stand trial and that there is a substantial probability that the defendant will become competent to stand trial within one year if the defendant is provided with a course of treatment, the court shall order the defendant to undergo treatment. If the defendant has been charged with a felony offense and if, after taking into consideration all relevant reports, information, and other evidence, the court finds that the defendant is incompetent to stand trial, but the court is unable at that time to determine whether there is a substantial probability that the defendant will become competent to stand trial within one year if the defendant is provided with a course of treatment, the court shall order continuing evaluation and treatment of the defendant for a period not to exceed four months to determine whether there is a substantial probability that the defendant will become competent to stand trial within one year if the defendant is provided with a course of treatment.

(b) The court order for the defendant to undergo treatment or continuing evaluation and treatment under division (B)(1)(a) of this section shall specify that the defendant, if determined to require mental health treatment or continuing evaluation and treatment, either shall be committed to the department of mental health and addiction services for treatment or continuing evaluation and treatment at a hospital, facility, or agency, as determined to be clinically appropriate by the department of mental health and addiction services or shall be committed to a facility certified by the department of mental health and addiction services as being qualified to treat mental illness, to a public or community mental health facility, or to a psychiatrist or another mental health professional for treatment or continuing evaluation and treatment. Prior to placing the defendant, the department of mental health and addiction services shall obtain court approval for that placement following a hearing. The court order for the defendant to undergo treatment or continuing evaluation and treatment under division (B)(1)(a) of this section shall specify that the defendant, if determined to require treatment or continuing evaluation and treatment for mental retardation, shall receive treatment or continuing evaluation and treatment at an institution or facility operated by the department of developmental disabilities, at a facility certified by the department of developmental disabilities as being qualified to treat mental retardation, at a public or private mental retardation facility, or by a psychiatrist or another mental retardation professional. In any case, the order may restrict the defendant's freedom of movement as the court considers necessary. The prosecutor in the defendant's case shall send to the chief clinical officer of the hospital, facility, or agency where the defendant is placed by the department of mental health and addiction services, or to the managing officer of the institution, the director of the program or facility, or the person to which the defendant is committed, copies of relevant police reports and other background information that pertains to the defendant and is available to the prosecutor unless the prosecutor determines that the release of any of the information in the police reports or any of the other background information to unauthorized persons would interfere with the effective prosecution of any person or would create a substantial risk of harm to any person.

In determining the place of commitment, the court shall consider the extent to which the person is a danger to the person and to others, the need for security, and the type of crime involved and shall order the least restrictive alternative available that is consistent with public safety and treatment goals. In weighing these factors, the court shall give preference to protecting public safety.

(c) If the defendant is found incompetent to stand trial, if the chief clinical officer of the hospital, facility, or agency where the defendant is placed, or the managing officer of the institution, the director of the program or facility, or the person to which the defendant is committed for treatment or continuing evaluation and treatment under division (B)(1)(b) of this section determines that medication is necessary to restore the defendant's competency to stand trial, and if the defendant lacks the capacity to give informed consent or refuses medication, the chief clinical officer of the hospital, facility, or agency where the defendant is placed, or the managing officer of the institution, the director of the program or facility, or the person to which the defendant is committed for treatment or continuing evaluation and treatment may petition the court for authorization for the involuntary administration of medication. The court shall hold a hearing on the petition within five days of the filing of the petition if the petition was filed in a municipal court or a county court regarding an incompetent defendant charged with a misdemeanor or within ten days of the filing of the petition if the petition was filed in a court of common pleas regarding an incompetent defendant charged with a felony offense. Following the hearing, the court may authorize the involuntary administration of medication or may dismiss the petition.

(2) If the court finds that the defendant is incompetent to stand trial and that, even if the defendant is provided with a course of treatment, there is not a substantial probability that the defendant will become competent to stand trial within one year, the court shall order the discharge of the defendant, unless upon motion of the prosecutor or on its own motion, the court either seeks to retain jurisdiction over the defendant pursuant to section 2945.39 of the Revised Code or files an affidavit in the probate court for the civil commitment of the defendant pursuant to Chapter 5122. or 5123. of the Revised Code alleging that the defendant is a mentally ill person subject to court order or a mentally retarded person subject to institutionalization by court order. If an affidavit is filed in the probate court, the trial court shall send to the probate court copies of all written reports of the defendant's mental condition that were prepared pursuant to section 2945.371 of the Revised Code.

The trial court may issue the temporary order of detention that a probate court may issue under section 5122.11 or 5123.71 of the Revised Code, to remain in effect until the probable cause or initial hearing in the probate court. Further proceedings in the probate court are civil proceedings governed by Chapter 5122. or 5123. of the Revised Code.

(C) No defendant shall be required to undergo treatment, including any continuing evaluation and treatment, under division (B)(1) of this section for longer than whichever of the following periods is applicable:

(1) One year, if the most serious offense with which the defendant is charged is one of the following offenses:

(a) Aggravated murder, murder, or an offense of violence for which a sentence of death or life imprisonment may be imposed;

(b) An offense of violence that is a felony of the first or second degree;

(c) A conspiracy to commit, an attempt to commit, or complicity in the commission of an offense described in division (C)(1)(a) or (b) of this section if the conspiracy, attempt, or complicity is a felony of the first or second degree.

(2) Six months, if the most serious offense with which the defendant is charged is a felony other than a felony described in division (C)(1) of this section;

(3) Sixty days, if the most serious offense with which the defendant is charged is a misdemeanor of the first or second degree;

(4) Thirty days, if the most serious offense with which the defendant is charged is a misdemeanor of the third or fourth degree, a minor misdemeanor, or an unclassified misdemeanor.

(D) Any defendant who is committed pursuant to this section shall not voluntarily admit the defendant or be voluntarily admitted to a hospital or institution pursuant to section 5122.02, 5122.15, 5123.69, or 5123.76 of the Revised Code.

(E) Except as otherwise provided in this division, a defendant who is charged with an offense and is committed by the court under this section to the department of mental health and addiction services or is committed to an institution or facility for the treatment of mental retardation shall not be granted unsupervised on-grounds movement, supervised off-grounds movement, or nonsecured status except in accordance with the court order. The court may grant a defendant supervised off-grounds movement to obtain medical treatment or specialized habilitation treatment services if the person who supervises the treatment or the continuing evaluation and treatment of the defendant ordered under division (B)(1)(a) of this section informs the court that the treatment or continuing evaluation and treatment cannot be provided at the hospital or facility where the defendant is placed by the department of mental health and addiction services or the institution or facility to which the defendant is committed. The chief clinical officer of the hospital or facility where the defendant is placed by the department of mental health and addiction services or the managing officer of the institution or director of the facility to which the defendant is committed, or a designee of any of those persons, may grant a defendant movement to a medical facility for an emergency medical situation with appropriate supervision to ensure the safety of the defendant, staff, and community during that emergency medical situation. The chief clinical officer of the hospital or facility where the defendant is placed by the department of mental health and addiction services or the managing officer of the institution or director of the facility to which the defendant is committed shall notify the court within twenty-four hours of the defendant's movement to the medical facility for an emergency medical situation under this division.

(F) The person who supervises the treatment or continuing evaluation and treatment of a defendant ordered to undergo treatment or continuing evaluation and treatment under division (B)(1)(a) of this section shall file a written report with the court at the following times:

(1) Whenever the person believes the defendant is capable of understanding the nature and objective of the proceedings against the defendant and of assisting in the defendant's defense;

(2) For a felony offense, fourteen days before expiration of the maximum time for treatment as specified in division (C) of this section and fourteen days before the expiration of the maximum time for continuing evaluation and treatment as specified in division (B)(1)(a) of this section, and, for a misdemeanor offense, ten days before the expiration of the maximum time for treatment, as specified in division (C) of this section;

(3) At a minimum, after each six months of treatment;

(4) Whenever the person who supervises the treatment or continuing evaluation and treatment of a defendant ordered under division (B)(1)(a) of this section believes that there is not a substantial probability that the defendant will become capable of understanding the nature and objective of the proceedings against the defendant or of assisting in the defendant's defense even if the defendant is provided with a course of treatment.

(G) A report under division (F) of this section shall contain the examiner's findings, the facts in reasonable detail on which the findings are based, and the examiner's opinion as to the defendant's capability of understanding the nature and objective of the proceedings against the defendant and of assisting in the defendant's defense. If, in the examiner's opinion, the defendant remains incapable of understanding the nature and objective of the proceedings against the defendant and of assisting in the defendant's defense and there is a substantial probability that the defendant will become capable of understanding the nature and objective of the proceedings against the defendant and of assisting in the defendant's defense if the defendant is provided with a course of treatment, if in the examiner's opinion the defendant remains mentally ill or mentally retarded, and if the maximum time for treatment as specified in division (C) of this section has not expired, the report also shall contain the examiner's recommendation as to the least restrictive placement or commitment alternative that is consistent with the defendant's treatment needs for restoration to competency and with the safety of the community. The court shall provide copies of the report to the prosecutor and defense counsel.

(H) If a defendant is committed pursuant to division (B)(1) of this section, within ten days after the treating physician of the defendant or the examiner of the defendant who is employed or retained by the treating facility advises that there is not a substantial probability that the defendant will become capable of understanding the nature and objective of the proceedings against the defendant or of assisting in the defendant's defense even if the defendant is provided with a course of treatment, within ten days after the expiration of the maximum time for treatment as specified in division (C) of this section, within ten days after the expiration of the maximum time for continuing evaluation and treatment as specified in division (B)(1)(a) of this section, within thirty days after a defendant's request for a hearing that is made after six months of treatment, or within thirty days after being advised by the treating physician or examiner that the defendant is competent to stand trial, whichever is the earliest, the court shall conduct another hearing to determine if the defendant is competent to stand trial and shall do whichever of the following is applicable:

(1) If the court finds that the defendant is competent to stand trial, the defendant shall be proceeded against as provided by law.

(2) If the court finds that the defendant is incompetent to stand trial, but that there is a substantial probability that the defendant will become competent to stand trial if the defendant is provided with a course of treatment, and the maximum time for treatment as specified in division (C) of this section has not expired, the court, after consideration of the examiner's recommendation, shall order that treatment be continued, may change the facility or program at which the treatment is to be continued, and shall specify whether the treatment is to be continued at the same or a different facility or program.

(3) If the court finds that the defendant is incompetent to stand trial, if the defendant is charged with an offense listed in division (C)(1) of this section, and if the court finds that there is not a substantial probability that the defendant will become competent to stand trial even if the defendant is provided with a course of treatment, or if the maximum time for treatment relative to that offense as specified in division (C) of this section has expired, further proceedings shall be as provided in sections 2945.39, 2945.401, and 2945.402 of the Revised Code.

(4) If the court finds that the defendant is incompetent to stand trial, if the most serious offense with which the defendant is charged is a misdemeanor or a felony other than a felony listed in division (C)(1) of this section, and if the court finds that there is not a substantial probability that the defendant will become competent to stand trial even if the defendant is provided with a course of treatment, or if the maximum time for treatment relative to that offense as specified in division (C) of this section has expired, the court shall dismiss the indictment, information, or complaint against the defendant. A dismissal under this division is not a bar to further prosecution based on the same conduct. The court shall discharge the defendant unless the court or prosecutor files an affidavit in probate court for civil commitment pursuant to Chapter 5122. or 5123. of the Revised Code. If an affidavit for civil commitment is filed, the court may detain the defendant for ten days pending civil commitment. All of the following provisions apply to persons charged with a misdemeanor or a felony other than a felony listed in division (C)(1) of this section who are committed by the probate court subsequent to the court's or prosecutor's filing of an affidavit for civil commitment under authority of this division:

(a) The chief clinical officer of the entity, hospital, or facility, the managing officer of the institution, the director of the program, or the person to which the defendant is committed or admitted shall do all of the following:

(i) Notify the prosecutor, in writing, of the discharge of the defendant, send the notice at least ten days prior to the discharge unless the discharge is by the probate court, and state in the notice the date on which the defendant will be discharged;

(ii) Notify the prosecutor, in writing, when the defendant is absent without leave or is granted unsupervised, off-grounds movement, and send this notice promptly after the discovery of the absence without leave or prior to the granting of the unsupervised, off-grounds movement, whichever is applicable;

(iii) Notify the prosecutor, in writing, of the change of the defendant's commitment or admission to voluntary status, send the notice promptly upon learning of the change to voluntary status, and state in the notice the date on which the defendant was committed or admitted on a voluntary status.

(b) Upon receiving notice that the defendant will be granted unsupervised, off-grounds movement, the prosecutor either shall re-indict the defendant or promptly notify the court that the prosecutor does not intend to prosecute the charges against the defendant.

(I) If a defendant is convicted of a crime and sentenced to a jail or workhouse, the defendant's sentence shall be reduced by the total number of days the defendant is confined for evaluation to determine the defendant's competence to stand trial or treatment under this section and sections 2945.37 and 2945.371 of the Revised Code or by the total number of days the defendant is confined for evaluation to determine the defendant's mental condition at the time of the offense charged.

(2014 S 43, eff. 9-17-14; 2013 H 59, eff. 9-29-13; 2012 H 487, eff. 6-11-12; 2011 H 153, eff. 9-29-11; 2009 S 79, eff. 10-6-09; 2001 S 122, eff. 2-20-02; 1996 S 285, eff. 7-1-97; 1996 S 269, eff. 7-1-96; 1988 S 156, eff. 7-1-89; 1980 H 965, H 900, S 297; 1978 H 565; 1975 S 185; 1953 H 1; GC 13441-2)

Uncodified Law

2013 H 59, § 327.20.20, eff. 6-30-13, reads:

(A) Effective July 1, 2013, all records and reports, other than court journal entries or court docket entries, identifying a person and pertaining to the person's mental health condition, assessment, provision of care or treatment, or payment for assessment, care, or treatment that are maintained in connection with any services certified by the Department of Mental Health and Addiction Services, or any hospitals or facilities licensed or operated by the Department, shall be kept confidential and shall not be disclosed by any person, with the following exceptions:

(1) If the person identified, or the person's legal guardian, if any, or if the person is a minor, the person's parent or legal guardian, consents.

(2) When disclosure is provided for in Chapters 340., 5119., or 5122. of the Revised Code or in accordance with other provisions of state or federal law authorizing such disclosure.

(3) Hospitals, boards of alcohol, drug addiction, and mental health services, licensed facilities, and community mental health services providers may release necessary information to insurers and other third-party payers, including government entities responsible for processing and authorizing payment, to obtain payment for goods and services furnished to the person.

(4) Pursuant to a court order signed by a judge;

(5) A person shall be granted access to the person's own psychiatric and medical records unless access specifically is restricted in a person's treatment plan for clear treatment reasons.

(6) The Department of Mental Health and Addiction Services may exchange psychiatric records and other pertinent information with community mental health services providers and boards of alcohol, drug addiction, and mental health services relating to the person's care or services. Records and information that may be exchanged pursuant to this division shall be limited to medication history, physical health status and history, financial status, summary of course of treatment, summary of treatment needs, and a discharge summary, if any.

(7) The Department of Mental Health and Addiction Services, hospitals, and community providers operated by the Department, hospitals licensed by the Department under section 5119.20 (5119.33) of the Revised Code and community mental health services providers may exchange psychiatric records and other pertinent information with payers and other providers of treatment and health services if the purpose of the exchange is to facilitate continuity of care for the person or for the emergency treatment of the person.

(8) The Department of Mental Health and Addiction Services and community mental health services providers may exchange psychiatric records and other pertinent information with boards of alcohol, drug addiction, and mental health services for purposes of any board function set forth in Chapter 340. of the Revised Code. Boards of alcohol, drug addiction, and mental health services shall not access or use any personal information from the Department or providers except as required or permitted by this section, or Chapters 340. and 5122. of the Revised Code for purposes related to payment, care coordination, health care operations, program and service evaluation, reporting activities, research, system administration, oversight, or other authorized purposes.

(9) A person's family member who is involved in the provision, planning, and monitoring of services to the person may receive medication information, a summary of the person's diagnosis and prognosis, and a list of the services and personnel available to assist the person and the person's family, if the person's treatment provider determines that the disclosure would be in the best interests of the person. No such disclosure shall be made unless the person is notified first and receives the information and does not object to the disclosure.

(10) Community mental health services providers may exchange psychiatric records and certain other

information with the board of alcohol, drug addiction, and mental health services and other providers in order to provide services to a person involuntarily committed to a board. Release of records under this division shall be limited to medication history, physical health status and history, financial status, summary of course of treatment, summary of treatment needs, and discharge summary, if any.

(11) Information may be disclosed to the executor or the administrator of an estate of a deceased person when the information is necessary to administer the estate.

(12) Information may be disclosed to staff members of the appropriate board or to staff members designated by the Director of Mental Health and Addiction Services for the purpose of evaluating the quality, effectiveness, and efficiency of services and determining if the services meet minimum standards. Information obtained during such evaluations shall not be retained with the name of any person.

(13) Records pertaining to the person's diagnosis, course of treatment, treatment needs, and prognosis shall be disclosed and released to the appropriate prosecuting attorney if the person was committed pursuant to section 2945.38, 2945.39, 2945.40, 2945.401, or 2945.402 of the Revised Code, or to the attorney designated by the board for proceedings pursuant to involuntary commitment under Chapter 5122. of the Revised Code.

(14) The Department of Mental Health and Addiction Services may exchange psychiatric hospitalization records, other mental health treatment records, and other pertinent information with the Department of Rehabilitation and Correction and with the Department of Youth Services to ensure continuity of care for inmates and offenders who are receiving mental health services in an institution of the Department of Rehabilitation and Correction or the Department of Youth Services and may exchange psychiatric hospitalization records, other mental health treatment records, and other pertinent information with boards of alcohol, drug addiction, and mental health services and community mental health services providers to ensure continuity of care for inmates or offenders who are receiving mental health services in an institution and are scheduled for release within six months. The release of records under this division is limited to records regarding an inmate's or offender's medication history, physical health status and history, summary of course of treatment, summary of treatment needs, and a discharge summary, if any.

(15) A community mental health services provider that ceases to operate may transfer to either a community mental health services provider that assumes its caseload or to the board of alcohol, drug addiction, and mental health services of the service district in which the person resided at the time services were most recently provided any treatment records that have not been transferred elsewhere at the person's request.

(B) Before records are disclosed pursuant to divisions (A)(3), (6), or (10) of this section, the custodian of the records shall attempt to obtain the consent of the person in question for the disclosure.

(C) No person shall reveal the content of a medical record of a person except as authorized by the law.

(D) Portions of appropriation items 333321, Central Administration, 333416, Research Program Evaluation, 333605, Medicaid/Medicare—Refunds, 333606, Demonstration Grants—Administration, 333608, Federal Miscellaneous—Administration, 333609, Central Office Opening, 333611, Non-Federal Miscellaneous, 333612, Social Services Block Grant—Administration, 333613, Federal Grants—Administration, 333614, Mental Health Block Grant—Administration, 333618, Substance Abuse Block Grant—Administration, 333621, Family and Children First Administration, 333623, Statewide Treatment and Prevention—Administration, 333629, Problem Gambling and Casino Addictions—Administration, 333632, Mental Health Operating—Refunds, 333608, Federal Miscellaneous—Administration, 333640, Education and Conferences, 333641, Problem Gambling Services—Administration, 333639, Administrative Reimbursement, 334605, Medicaid/Medicare—Hospitals, 334608, Federal Miscellaneous—Hospitals, 334609, Hospital—Operating Expenses, 334613, Federal Letter of Credit, 334620, Special Education, 334632, Mental Health Operating—Hospitals, 335405, Family and Children First, 335406, Prevention and Wellness, 335421, Continuum of Care Services, 335422, Criminal Justice Services, 335604, Community Mental Health Projects, 335506, Residential State Supplement, 335608, Federal Miscellaneous, 335606, Demonstration Grants, 335612, Social Services Block Grant, 335613, Federal Grant—Community Mental Health Subsidy, 335614, Mental Health Block Grant, 335615, Behavioral Health Care, 335618, Substance Abuse Block Grant, 335623, Statewide Treatment and Prevention, 335629, Problem Gambling and Casino Addictions, 335638, Race to the Top—Early Learning Challenge Grant, 335900, Indigent Drivers Alcohol Treatment, 336601, Office of Support Services, 652609, Medicaid Legacy Costs Support, 652635, Community Medicaid Legacy Costs, and 652636, Community Medicaid Legacy Support, may be used to pay for the Department and community mental health system functions that operate under the confidentiality provisions enumerated above.

Historical and Statutory Notes

Amendment Note: 2014 S 43 substituted "mentally ill person subject to court order" for "mentally ill person subject to hospitalization by court order" in division (B)(2).

Amendment Note: 2013 H 59, in division (B)(1)(b), in five places, and in division (E), in four places, inserted "and addiction services" following "mental health".

Amendment Note: 2012 H 487, rewrote division (B)(1)(b); in division (B)(1)(c), inserted "program or" following both occurrences of "the director of the"; deleted division (B)(1)(d); in division (E), deleted "with restrictions on the defendant's freedom of movement" preceding, and substituted "mental retardation" for "developmental disabilities" following, "or is committed to an institution or facility for the treatment of "; rewrote division (H)(2); and in division (H)(4)(a), inserted "the director of the program," following "managing officer of the institution,". Prior to amendment, divisions (B)(1)(b), (B)(1)(d), and (H)(2) read:

"[(B)(1)](b) The court order for the defendant to undergo treatment or continuing evaluation and treatment under division (B)(1)(a) of this section shall specify that the defendant, if determined to require mental health treatment or continuing evaluation and treatment, shall be committed to the department of mental health for treatment or continuing evaluation and treatment at a hospital, facility, or agency, as determined to be clinically appropriate by the department of mental health and, if determined to require treatment or continuing evaluation and treatment for a developmental disability, shall receive treatment or continuing evaluation and treatment at an institution or facility operated by the department of developmental disabilities, at a facility certified by the department of developmental disabilities as being qualified to treat mental retardation, at a public or private community mental retardation facility, or by a mental retardation professional. The order may restrict the defendant's freedom of movement as the court considers necessary. The prosecutor in the defendant's case shall send to the chief clinical officer of the hospital, facility, or agency where the defendant is placed by the department of mental health, or to the managing officer of the institution, the director of the facility, or the person to which the defendant is committed, copies of relevant police reports and other background information that pertains to the defendant and is available to the prosecutor unless the prosecutor determines that the release of any of the information in the police reports or any of the other background information to unauthorized persons would interfere with the effective prosecution of any person or would create a substantial risk of harm to any person.

"In committing the defendant to the department of mental health, the court shall consider the extent to which the person is a danger to the person and to others, the need for security, and the type of crime involved and, if the court finds that restrictions on the defendant's freedom of movement are necessary, shall specify the least restrictive limitations on the person's freedom of movement determined to be necessary to protect public safety. In determining commitment alternatives for defendants determined to require treatment or continuing evaluation and treatment for developmental disabilities, the court shall consider the extent to which the person is a danger to the person and to others, the need for security, and the type of crime involved and shall order the least restrictive alternative available that is consistent with public safety and treatment goals. In weighing these factors, the court shall give preference to protecting public safety."

"[(B)(1)](d) If the defendant is charged with a misdemeanor offense that is not an offense of violence, the prosecutor may hold the charges in abeyance while the defendant engages in mental health treatment or developmental disability services."

"[(H)](2) If the court finds that the defendant is incompetent to stand trial, but that there is a substantial probability that the defendant will become competent to stand trial if the defendant is provided with a course of treatment, and the maximum time for treatment as specified in division (C) of this section has not expired, the court, after consideration of the examiner's recommendation, shall order that treatment be continued, may change the least restrictive limitations on the defendant's freedom of movement, and, if applicable, shall specify whether the treatment for developmental disabilities is to be continued at the same or a different facility or institution."

Amendment Note: 2011 H 153, added division (B)(1)(d); in division (G) substituted "placement or commitment" for "treatment" in the second sentence; in division (H)(2) substituted "least restrictive limitations on the defendant's freedom of movement, and, if applicable, shall specify whether the treatment for developmental disabilities" for "facility or program at which the treatment is to be continued and shall specify whether the treatment", and "institution" for "program"; in division (H)(4)(a), inserted "entity," before "hospital" and deleted ", the director of the program" after "institution"; and rewrote divisions (B)(1)(b), (B)(1)(c), and (E) which read:

"(b) The court order for the defendant to undergo treatment or continuing evaluation and treatment under division (B)(1)(a) of this section shall specify that the treatment or continuing evaluation and treatment shall occur at a facility operated by the department of mental health or the department of developmental disabilities, at a facility certified by either of those departments as being qualified to treat mental illness or mental retardation, at a public or private community mental health or mental retardation facility, or by a psychiatrist or another mental health or mental retardation professional. The order may restrict the defendant's freedom of movement as the court considers necessary. The prosecutor in the defendant's case shall send to the chief clinical officer of the hospital or facility, the managing officer of the institution, the director of the program, or the person to which the defendant is committed copies of relevant police reports and other background information that pertains to the defendant and is available to the prosecutor unless the prosecutor determines that the release of any of the information in the police reports or any of the other background information to unauthorized persons would interfere with the effective prosecution of any person or would create a substantial risk of harm to any person.

"In determining placement alternatives, the court shall consider the extent to which the person is a danger to the person and to others, the need for security, and the type of crime involved and shall order the least restrictive alternative available that is consistent with public safety and treatment goals. In weighing these factors, the court shall give preference to protecting public safety."

"(c) If the defendant is found incompetent to stand trial, if the chief clinical officer of the hospital or facility, the managing officer of the institution, the director of the program, or the person to which the defendant is committed for treatment or continuing evaluation and treatment under division (B)(1)(b) of this section determines that medication is necessary to restore the defendant's competency to stand trial, and if the defendant lacks the capacity to give informed consent or refuses medication, the chief clinical officer, managing officer, director, or person to which the defendant is committed for treatment or continuing evaluation and treatment may petition the court for authorization for the involuntary administration of medication. The court shall hold a hearing on the petition within five days of the filing of the petition if the petition was filed in a municipal court or a county court regarding an incompetent defendant charged with a misdemeanor or within ten days of the filing of the petition if the petition was filed in a court of common pleas regarding an incompetent defendant charged with a felony offense. Following the hearing, the court may authorize the involuntary administration of medication or may dismiss the petition."

"(E) Except as otherwise provided in this division, a defendant who is charged with an offense and is committed to a hospital or other institution by the court under this section shall not be granted unsupervised on-grounds movement, supervised off-grounds movement, or nonsecured status. The court may grant a defendant supervised off-grounds movement to obtain medical treatment or specialized habilitation treatment services if the person who supervises the treatment or the continuing evaluation and treatment of the defendant ordered under division (B)(1)(a) of this section informs the court that the treatment or continuing evaluation and treatment cannot be provided at the hospital or the institution to which the defendant is committed. The chief clinical officer of the hospital or the managing officer of the institution to which the defendant is committed or a designee of either of those persons may grant a defendant movement to a medical facility for an emergency medical situation with appropriate supervision to ensure the safety of the defendant, staff, and community during that emergency medical situation. The chief clinical officer of the hospital or the managing officer of the institution shall notify the court within twenty-four hours of the defendant's movement to the medical facility for an emergency medical situation under this division."

Amendment Note: 2009 S 79 deleted "mental retardation and" from "department of mental retardation and developmental disabilities" in division (B)(1)(b).

Cross References

Records pertaining to person's mental health condition confidential, exceptions, see 5119.28

Research References

Encyclopedias

OH Jur. 3d Criminal Law: Procedure § 1170, Finding of Competency.

OH Jur. 3d Criminal Law: Procedure § 1172, Order to Undergo Treatment.

OH Jur. 3d Criminal Law: Procedure § 1173, Place for Treatment.

OH Jur. 3d Criminal Law: Procedure § 1174, Authorization of Medication.

OH Jur. 3d Criminal Law: Procedure § 1176, Restrictions on Movement.

OH Jur. 3d Criminal Law: Procedure § 1177, Time Restrictions on Treatment.

OH Jur. 3d Criminal Law: Procedure § 1178, Reports Regarding Treatment.

OH Jur. 3d Criminal Law: Procedure § 1179, Hearing and Further Action.

OH Jur. 3d Criminal Law: Procedure § 2190, What Constitutes a Final Judgment or Order--"Substantial Right," "Provisional Remedy," and "Ancillary Proceeding" Defined.

OH Jur. 3d Incompetent Persons § 53, Admission of Involuntary Patients.

OH Jur. 3d Incompetent Persons § 192, Definitions.

Treatises and Practice Aids

Klein, Darling, & Terez, Baldwin's Ohio Practice Civil Practice § 1:53, Civ. R. 1(C)(6): Commitment of the Mentally Ill--Proceedings Under RC 2945.38 and RC 2945.40.

Katz & Giannelli, Baldwin's Ohio Practice Criminal Law § 54:1, Introduction.

Katz & Giannelli, Baldwin's Ohio Practice Criminal Law § 54:8, Findings.

Katz & Giannelli, Baldwin's Ohio Practice Criminal Law § 80:4, Final Judgment-Order Rule.

Katz & Giannelli, Baldwin's Ohio Practice Criminal Law § 106:8, Possession of Deadly Weapon While Under Detention.

Katz & Giannelli, Baldwin's Ohio Practice Criminal Law § 144:5, Plea of Not Guilty by Reason of Insanity at Arraignment.
Katz & Giannelli, Baldwin's Ohio Practice Criminal Law § 144:9, Entry Ordering Inquiry Into Competence of Defendant.
Katz & Giannelli, Baldwin's Ohio Practice Criminal Law § 80:23, Prosecution Appeals.
Katz & Giannelli, Baldwin's Ohio Practice Criminal Law § 110:21, Escape.
Katz & Giannelli, Baldwin's Ohio Practice Criminal Law § 144:10, Entry Finding Defendant [Competent/Incompetent] to Stand Trial.
Carlin, Baldwin's Ohio Prac. Merrick-Rippner Probate Law § 102:47, Initial Treatment for Persons Found Incompetent to Stand Trial; Maximum Duration.
Carlin, Baldwin's Ohio Prac. Merrick-Rippner Probate Law § 102:48, Further Commitment of Persons Found Incompetent to Stand Trial.
Carlin, Baldwin's Ohio Prac. Merrick-Rippner Probate Law § 102:59, Consent to Treatment (RC 5122.271)--Psychotropic Medication.
Carlin, Baldwin's Ohio Prac. Merrick-Rippner Probate Law § 102:60, Confidentiality of Records (RC 5122.31).
Adrine & Ruden, Ohio Domestic Violence Law § 4:6, Violation of a Protection Order.
Adrine & Ruden, Ohio Domestic Violence Law App. A, Ohio Revised Code (Selected Provisions).

Notes of Decisions

5. —— Administration of medication, competency to stand trial

Evidence did not support finding that defendant was competent to stand trial on charge of assaulting a police officer following an incident occurring while defendant was being held in jail on another charge; expert's evaluation report was based on a single interview and stated generalized conclusions, expert referenced previous irrelevant competency evaluations of defendant conducted in prior years, defendant's own mental health provider found defendant incompetent based on extensive evaluation and treatment, defendant's failure of focus and comprehension was apparent at plea hearing and sentencing, and defendant's inability to understand legal issues involved was related to her mental health and medication issues. State v. Nickell (Ohio App. 6 Dist., Wood, 03-31-2008) No. WD-07-015, 2008-Ohio-1571, 2008 WL 853539, Unreported. Criminal Law ⚷ 625.15

One year time period for a defendant to become competent to stand trial or else have the charges against him dismissed was tolled after the date the State petitioned for an order authorizing the involuntary administration of medication to defendant and during the time period that defendant appealed the order granting the involuntary administration of medication. State v. Barker (Ohio App. 2 Dist., Montgomery, 09-07-2007) No. 21438, 2007-Ohio-4612, 2007 WL 2568352, Unreported. Mental Health ⚷ 432

Trial court was required to specifically find, before it authorized the involuntary administration of medication to defendant to restore competency, that the medications were substantially unlikely to have side effects that would interfere significantly with defendant's ability to assist with his defense. State v. McClelland (Ohio App. 10 Dist., Franklin, 03-01-2007) No. 06AP-1236, 2007-Ohio-841, 2007 WL 611234, Unreported. Mental Health ⚷ 436.1

Trial court's failure to specifically find that the involuntary administration of medications to defendant were substantially unlikely to have side effects that would interfere significantly with defendant's ability to assist with his defense, prior to authorizing involuntary medication of defendant for the purpose of competency restoration, required reversal of order authorizing such medication. State v. McClelland (Ohio App. 10 Dist., Franklin, 03-01-2007) No. 06AP-1236, 2007-Ohio-841, 2007 WL 611234, Unreported. Mental Health ⚷ 436.1

Mental health facility's letter to trial court, requesting involuntary medication of defendant committed for purposes of competency restoration, was properly treated by court as petition for involuntary medication pursuant to applicable statute. State v. Upshaw (Ohio App. 2 Dist., 04-07-2006) 166 Ohio App.3d 95, 849 N.E.2d 91, 2006-Ohio-1819. Mental Health ⚷ 436.1

Finding that involuntary medication of defendant committed for purposes of competency restoration was necessary to further state's interest in defendant's prosecution, required to support issuance of order authorizing involuntary medication, required trial court to find that any alternative, less intrusive treatments were unlikely to achieve substantially same results, and to consider less intrusive means for administering drugs before considering more intrusive methods. State v. Upshaw (Ohio App. 2 Dist., 04-07-2006) 166 Ohio App.3d 95, 849 N.E.2d 91, 2006-Ohio-1819. Mental Health ⚷ 436.1

Finding that involuntary medication of defendant committed for purposes of competency restoration would significantly further state's interest in defendant's prosecution, required to support issuance of order authorizing involuntary medication, required trial court to find that administration of drugs was substantially likely to render defendant competent to stand trial, and was substantially unlikely to have side effects interfering significantly with defendant's ability to assist counsel in conducting a trial defense, thereby rendering trial unfair. State v. Upshaw (Ohio App. 2 Dist., 04-07-2006) 166 Ohio App.3d 95, 849 N.E.2d 91, 2006-Ohio-1819. Mental Health ⚷ 436.1

Trial court was required to find, prior to authorizing involuntary medication of defendant committed for purposes of competency restoration, that treatment proposed by mental health facility was medically appropriate, was substantially unlikely to have side effects undermining fairness of trial, and, taking account of less intrusive alternatives, was necessary significantly to further important governmental trial-related interests. State v. Upshaw (Ohio App. 2 Dist., 04-07-2006) 166 Ohio App.3d 95, 849 N.E.2d 91, 2006-Ohio-1819. Mental Health ⚷ 436.1

7. —— Duty of court, competency to stand trial

Trial court's ruling in delinquency proceeding that 15-year-old juvenile was competent to stand trial, on complaint alleging rape, was supported by sufficient evidence; juvenile told court he understood he had been charged with "wrong doing" and charge was rape, and court appointed evaluator testified that juvenile possessed borderline IQ, a reasonable potential to understand, and, while he suffered from confused thinking, he could marginally assist in own defense. In re Childress (Ohio App. 5 Dist., Licking, 12-31-2008) No. 2008CA00057, 2008-Ohio-7001, 2008 WL 5427983, Unreported. Infants ⚷ 2539

Trial court abused its discretion, in hearing on mental health facility's petition for involuntary medication of defendant committed for purposes of competency restoration, in denying defendant's request for brief continuance to present testimony of his treating psychiatrist. State v. Upshaw (Ohio App. 2 Dist., 04-07-2006) 166 Ohio App.3d 95, 849 N.E.2d 91, 2006-Ohio-1819. Mental Health ⚷ 436.1

8. —— Time requirements, competency to stand trial

Statute providing for dismissal of an indictment when an incompetent defendant's treatment exceeds 60 days did not require dismissal of an indictment for violation of a protective order even though 60 days had elapsed since defendant was ordered to undergo treatment after he was found incompetent to stand trial, where defendant had undergone less than 60 days of treatment. Cleveland v. Allen (Ohio App. 8 Dist., Cuyahoga, 02-26-2009) No. 91233, 2009-Ohio-860, 2009 WL 478285, Unreported, appeal not allowed 122 Ohio St.3d 1505, 912 N.E.2d 109, 2009-Ohio-4233. Criminal Law ⚷ 303.30(1)

Until an incompetent individual is found to be mentally competent, a criminal action must be halted, assuming that competency is restorable within the statutory period; if the possibility of restoration does not exist, the criminal matter may be dismissed in favor of probate civil commitment. State v. Upshaw (Ohio, 08-30-2006) 110 Ohio St.3d 189, 852 N.E.2d 711, 2006-Ohio-4253. Mental Health ⚷ 432; Mental Health ⚷ 436.1

2945.39 Civil commitment; expiration of time for treatment; jurisdiction; hearing; reports

(A) If a defendant who is charged with an offense described in division (C)(1) of section 2945.38 of the Revised Code is found incompetent to stand trial, after the expiration of the maximum time for treatment as specified in division (C) of that section or after the court finds that there is not a substantial probability that the defendant will become competent to stand trial even if the defendant is provided with a course of treatment, one of the following applies:

(1) The court or the prosecutor may file an affidavit in probate court for civil commitment of the defendant in the manner provided in Chapter 5122. or 5123. of the Revised Code. If the court or prosecutor files an affidavit for civil commitment, the court may detain the defendant for ten days pending civil commitment. If the probate court commits the defendant subsequent to the court's or prosecutor's filing of an affidavit for civil commitment, the chief clinical officer of the entity, hospital, or facility, the managing officer of the institution, the director of the program, or the person to which the defendant is committed or admitted shall send to the prosecutor the notices described in divisions (H)(4)(a)(i) to (iii) of section 2945.38 of the Revised Code within the periods of time and under the circumstances specified in those divisions.

(2) On the motion of the prosecutor or on its own motion, the court may retain jurisdiction over the defendant if, at a hearing, the court finds both of the following by clear and convincing evidence:

(a) The defendant committed the offense with which the defendant is charged.

(b) The defendant is a mentally ill person subject to court order or a mentally retarded person subject to institutionalization by court order.

(B) In making its determination under division (A)(2) of this section as to whether to retain jurisdiction over the defendant, the court may consider all relevant evidence, including, but not limited to, any relevant psychiatric, psychological, or medical testimony or reports, the acts constituting the offense charged, and any history of the defendant that is relevant to the defendant's ability to conform to the law.

(C) If the court conducts a hearing as described in division (A)(2) of this section and if the court does not make both findings described in divisions (A)(2)(a) and (b) of this section by clear and convincing evidence, the court shall dismiss the indictment, information, or complaint against the defendant. Upon the dismissal, the court shall discharge the defendant unless the court or prosecutor files an affidavit in probate court for civil commitment of the defendant pursuant to Chapter 5122. or 5123. of the Revised Code. If the court or prosecutor files an affidavit for civil commitment, the court may order that the defendant be detained for up to ten days pending the civil commitment. If the probate court commits the defendant subsequent to the court's or prosecutor's filing of an affidavit for civil commitment, the chief clinical officer of the entity, hospital, or facility, the managing officer of the institution, the director of the program, or the person to which the defendant is committed or admitted shall send to the prosecutor the notices described in divisions (H)(4)(a)(i) to (iii) of section 2945.38 of the Revised Code within the periods of time and under the circumstances specified in those divisions. A dismissal of charges under this division is not a bar to further criminal proceedings based on the same conduct.

(D)(1) If the court conducts a hearing as described in division (A)(2) of this section and if the court makes the findings described in divisions (A)(2)(a) and (b) of this section by clear and convincing evidence, the court shall commit the defendant, if determined to require mental health treatment, either to the department of mental health and addiction services for treatment at a hospital, facility, or agency as determined clinically appropriate by the department of mental health and addiction services or to another medical or psychiatric facility, as appropriate. Prior to placing the defendant, the department of mental health and addiction services shall obtain court approval for that placement. If the court conducts such a hearing and if it makes those findings by clear and convincing evidence, the court shall commit the defendant, if determined to require treatment for mental retardation, to a facility operated by the department of developmental disabilities, or another facility, as appropriate. In determining the place of commitment, the court shall consider the extent to which the person is a danger to the person and to others, the need for security, and the type of crime involved and shall order the least restrictive alternative available that is consistent with public safety and the welfare of the defendant. In weighing these factors, the court shall give preference to protecting public safety.

(2) If a court makes a commitment of a defendant under division (D)(1) of this section, the prosecutor shall send to the hospital, facility, or agency where the defendant is placed by the department of mental health and addiction services or to the defendant's place of commitment all reports of the defendant's current mental condition and, except as otherwise provided in this division, any other relevant information, including, but not limited to, a transcript of the hearing held pursuant to division (A)(2) of this section, copies of relevant police reports, and copies of any prior arrest and conviction records that pertain to the defendant and that the prosecutor possesses. The prosecutor shall send the reports of the defendant's current mental condition in every case of commitment, and, unless the prosecutor determines that the release of any of the other relevant information to unauthorized persons would interfere with the effective prosecution of any person or would create a substantial risk of harm to any person, the prosecutor also shall send the other relevant information. Upon admission of a defendant committed under division (D)(1) of this section, the place of commitment shall send to the board of alcohol, drug addiction, and mental health services or the community mental health board serving the county in which the charges against the defendant were filed a copy of all reports of the defendant's current mental condition and a copy of the other relevant information provided by the prosecutor under this division, including, if provided, a transcript of the hearing held pursuant to division (A)(2) of this section, the relevant police reports, and the prior arrest and conviction records that pertain to the defendant and that the prosecutor possesses.

(3) If a court makes a commitment under division (D)(1) of this section, all further proceedings shall be in accordance with sections 2945.401 and 2945.402 of the Revised Code.

(2014 S 43, eff. 9-17-14; 2013 H 59, eff. 9-29-13; 2012 H 487, eff. 6-11-12; 2011 H 153, eff. 9-29-11; 2009 S 79, eff. 10-6-09; 2001 S 122, eff. 2-20-02; 1996 S 285, eff. 7-1-97)

Uncodified Law

2013 H 59, § 327.20.20: See Uncodified Law under RC 2945.38.

Historical and Statutory Notes

Amendment Note: 2014 S 43 substituted "mentally ill person subject to court order" for "mentally ill person subject to hospitalization by court order" in division (A)(2)(b).

Amendment Note: 2013 H 59, in division (D)(1), in three places, and division (D)(2), in the first sentence, inserted "and addiction services" following "mental health".

Amendment Note: 2012 H 487, in division (A)(1) and division (C), inserted "the director of the program," following "the managing officer of the institution,"; rewrote division (D)(1); and added the third sentence to division (D)(2). Prior to amendment, division (D)(1) read:

"(D)(1) If the court conducts a hearing as described in division (A)(2) of this section and if the court makes the findings described in divisions (A)(2)(a) and (b) of this section by clear and convincing evidence, the court shall commit the defendant, if determined to require mental health treatment, to the department of mental health for treatment at a hospital, facility, or agency as determined clinically appropriate by the department of mental health or, if determined to require treatment for developmental disabilities, to a facility operated by the department of developmental disabilities, or another facility, as appropriate. In committing the defendant to the department of mental health, the court shall specify the least restrictive limitations on the defendant's freedom of movement determined to be necessary to protect public safety. In determining the place and nature of the commitment to a facility operated by the department of developmental disabilities or another facility for treatment of developmental disabilities, the court shall order the least restrictive commitment alternative available that is consistent with public safety and the welfare of the defendant. In weighing these factors, the court shall give preference to protecting public safety."

Amendment Note: 2011 H 153, in divisions (A)(1) and (C) substituted "entity hospital or facility" for "hospital, or facility" and deleted "the director of the program," before "managing officer of the institution,", and rewrote division (D) which read:

"(D)(1) If the court conducts a hearing as described in division (A)(2) of this section and if the court makes the findings described in divisions (A)(2)(a) and (b) of this section by clear and convincing evidence, the court shall commit the defendant to a hospital operated by the department of mental health, a facility operated by the department of developmental disabilities, or another medical or psychiatric facility, as appropriate. In determining the place and nature of the commitment, the court shall order the least restrictive commitment alternative available that is consistent with public safety and the welfare of the defendant. In weighing these factors, the court shall give preference to protecting public safety.

"(2) If a court makes a commitment of a defendant under division (D)(1) of this section, the prosecutor shall send to the place of commitment all reports of the defendant's current mental condition and, except as otherwise provided in this division, any other relevant information, including, but not limited to, a transcript of the hearing held pursuant to division (A)(2) of this section, copies of relevant police reports, and copies of any prior arrest and conviction records that pertain to the defendant and that the prosecutor possesses. The prosecutor shall send the reports of the defendant's current mental condition in every case of commitment, and, unless the prosecutor determines that the release of any of the other relevant information to unauthorized persons would interfere with the effective prosecution of any person or would create a substantial risk of harm to any person, the prosecutor also shall send the other relevant information. Upon admission of a defendant committed under division (D)(1) of this section, the place of commitment shall send to the board of alcohol, drug addiction, and mental health services or the community mental health board serving the county in which the charges against the defendant were filed a copy of all reports of the defendant's current mental condition and a copy of the other relevant information provided by the prosecutor under this division, including, if provided, a transcript of the hearing held pursuant to division (A)(2) of this section, the relevant police reports, and the prior arrest and conviction records that pertain to the defendant and that the prosecutor possesses."

Amendment Note: 2009 S 79 deleted "mental retardation and" from "department of mental retardation and developmental disabilities" in division (D)(1).

Cross References

Boards of alcohol, drug addiction, and mental health services, reports, statements, agreements, tracking and monitoring, see 340.08

Records pertaining to person's mental health condition confidential, exceptions, see 5119.28

Ohio Administrative Code References

Community forensic psychiatric centers, see OAC 5122–32–01

Research References

ALR Library

72 ALR 5th 109, Adequacy of Defense Counsel's Representation of Criminal Client--Pretrial Conduct or Conduct at Unspecified Time Regarding Issues of Insanity.

Encyclopedias

OH Jur. 3d Criminal Law: Procedure § 1179, Hearing and Further Action.

OH Jur. 3d Criminal Law: Procedure § 1183, Required Reports and Action.

OH Jur. 3d Incompetent Persons § 192, Definitions.

Treatises and Practice Aids

Katz & Giannelli, Baldwin's Ohio Practice Criminal Law § 54:1, Introduction.

Katz & Giannelli, Baldwin's Ohio Practice Criminal Law § 54:8, Findings.

Katz & Giannelli, Baldwin's Ohio Practice Criminal Law § 77:6, Experts--Insanity.

Katz & Giannelli, Baldwin's Ohio Practice Criminal Law § 106:8, Possession of Deadly Weapon While Under Detention.

Katz & Giannelli, Baldwin's Ohio Practice Criminal Law § 110:21, Escape.

Giannelli, Baldwin's Ohio Practice Evidence R 702, Testimony by Experts.

Carlin, Baldwin's Ohio Prac. Merrick-Rippner Probate Law § 102:18, Involuntary Admission--Notice and Assessment Requirements for All Involuntary Patients.

Carlin, Baldwin's Ohio Prac. Merrick-Rippner Probate Law § 102:42, Jurisdiction Over Commitments in Criminal Cases.

Carlin, Baldwin's Ohio Prac. Merrick-Rippner Probate Law § 102:43, Voluntary Status of Persons Committed by Criminal.

Carlin, Baldwin's Ohio Prac. Merrick-Rippner Probate Law § 102:44, Commencement of Commitment Proceedings in Criminal Cases.

Carlin, Baldwin's Ohio Prac. Merrick-Rippner Probate Law § 102:47, Initial Treatment for Persons Found Incompetent to Stand Trial; Maximum Duration.

Carlin, Baldwin's Ohio Prac. Merrick-Rippner Probate Law § 102:48, Further Commitment of Persons Found Incompetent to Stand Trial.

Carlin, Baldwin's Ohio Prac. Merrick-Rippner Probate Law § 102:49, Hearings on Nonsecured Status and Termination of Commitment of Persons Found NGRI or Incompetent to Stand Trial.

Hennenberg & Reinhart, Ohio Criminal Defense Motions F 13:6, Motion for Order Granting Independent Psychiatric Evaluation at the State's Expense--Death Penalty Motions.

Hennenberg & Reinhart, Ohio Criminal Defense Motions F 5:12, Defendant's Written Plea of Not Guilty by Reason of Insanity--Pretrial Motions.

Hennenberg & Reinhart, Ohio Criminal Defense Motions F 5:25, Motion for Psychiatric Evaluation to Determine Defendant's Competency to Stand Trial--Pretrial Motions.

Hennenberg & Reinhart, Ohio Criminal Defense Motions F 5:26, Motion for Order Permitting Psychiatric Evaluation at State's Expense--Pretrial Motions.

Adrine & Ruden, Ohio Domestic Violence Law § 4:6, Violation of a Protection Order.

Adrine & Ruden, Ohio Domestic Violence Law App. A, Ohio Revised Code (Selected Provisions).

Adrine & Ruden, Ohio Domestic Violence Law § 15:17, Presenting Evidence of Domestic Violence--Use of Domestic Violence Experts.

Notes of Decisions

1. Constitutional issues

Statute, allowing trial court to exercise continuing jurisdiction over a defendant charged with a violent felony after the defendant has been found to be incompetent to stand trial and who remains incompetent after expiration of one-year time frame for restoring competency, had a rational relation to the legitimate state goal of restraining mentally ill persons subject to hospitalization who have committed a serious crime, and thus did not violate equal protection rights of defendant in rape prosecution who was subject to trial court's continuing jurisdiction under statute. State v. Williams (Ohio, 06-08-2010) 126 Ohio St.3d 65, 930 N.E.2d 770, 2010-Ohio-2453. Constitutional Law ⚷ 3143; Mental Health ⚷ 433(1)

Statute governing civil commitment of defendant charged with violent felony and determined incompetent to stand trial that was substantially more restrictive than other civil commitments, that imposed more procedures for transferring defendant to less restrictive commitment, and which required court approval in addition to review by local forensic center prior to termination of commitment violated equal protection; although state had interest in confining individuals who were mentally ill and dangerous, statute did not apply to persons already convicted of violent offense or had history of committing same offense but were not under indictment, and there was no reasonable basis for providing more onerous procedures for terminating commitment, with attendant delay, since State had no interest in continuing commitment once it was determined that defendant was no longer mentally ill. State v. Williams (Ohio App. 2 Dist., 11-26-2008) 179 Ohio App.3d 584, 902 N.E.2d

1042, 2008-Ohio-6245, stay granted 120 Ohio St.3d 1485, 900 N.E.2d 197, 2009-Ohio-278, appeal allowed 121 Ohio St.3d 1438, 903 N.E.2d 1222, 2009-Ohio-1638, reversed 126 Ohio St.3d 65, 930 N.E.2d 770, 2010-Ohio-2453. Constitutional Law ⚷ 3143; Mental Health ⚷ 433(1)

Statute allowing for incompetent defendant's indefinite commitment until expiration of prison term applicable to charge for rape, and retention of indictment, after one-year period for restoration of competency had expired, without civil commitment proceedings, violated due process; maximum period of time of commitment, in this case ten years, bore no relationship to need to protect society from dangerous mentally ill persons, in that defendant could be released after ten years while still dangerous person, and it was fundamentally unfair for incompetent defendant have charges pending indefinitely when there was little hope he may be brought to trial and be exonerated. State v. Williams (Ohio App. 2 Dist., 11-26-2008) 179 Ohio App.3d 584, 902 N.E.2d 1042, 2008-Ohio-6245, stay granted 120 Ohio St.3d 1485, 900 N.E.2d 197, 2009-Ohio-278, appeal allowed 121 Ohio St.3d 1438, 903 N.E.2d 1222, 2009-Ohio-1638, reversed 126 Ohio St.3d 65, 930 N.E.2d 770, 2010-Ohio-2453. Constitutional Law ⚷ 4337; Mental Health ⚷ 433(1)

Statute that allowed trial court to retain jurisdiction over defendant charged with violent felony and found incompetent to stand trial if it found by clear and convincing evidence that defendant committed act for which he was charged violated due process right to have crime proven beyond reasonable doubt. State v. Williams (Ohio App. 2 Dist., 11-26-2008) 179 Ohio App.3d 584, 902 N.E.2d 1042, 2008-Ohio-6245, stay granted 120 Ohio St.3d 1485, 900 N.E.2d 197, 2009-Ohio-278, appeal allowed 121 Ohio St.3d 1438, 903 N.E.2d 1222, 2009-Ohio-1638, reversed 126 Ohio St.3d 65, 930 N.E.2d 770, 2010-Ohio-2453. Constitutional Law ⚷ 4335; Mental Health ⚷ 433(1)

Statute that allowed trial court to retain jurisdiction over defendant charged with violent felony and found incompetent to stand trial if it found by clear and convincing evidence that defendant committed act for which he was charged and that defendant was mentally ill was criminal in nature, for purposes of determining whether statute deprived defendant of due process and equal protection; statute was part of penal code, placement in mental health facility, changes to placement, and review hearings on defendant's mental status are all part of ongoing criminal case, defendant faced trial on charged offense if he was later found to be competent to stand trial, and period of commitment coincided with maximum sentence for offense. State v. Williams (Ohio App. 2 Dist., 11-26-2008) 179 Ohio App.3d 584, 902 N.E.2d 1042, 2008-Ohio-6245, stay granted 120 Ohio St.3d 1485, 900 N.E.2d 197, 2009-Ohio-278, appeal allowed 121 Ohio St.3d 1438, 903 N.E.2d 1222, 2009-Ohio-1638, reversed 126 Ohio St.3d 65, 930 N.E.2d 770, 2010-Ohio-2453. Constitutional Law ⚷ 3142; Constitutional Law ⚷ 4335; Mental Health ⚷ 433(1)

4. Psychiatric examination

Defendant who had raised level of his competency to stand trial through initial entry of plea of not guilty by reason of insanity could not avoid mental examinations ordered by court pursuant to statute. State v. White (Ohio, 05-12-1999) 85 Ohio St.3d 433, 709 N.E.2d 140, 1999-Ohio-281, denial of post-conviction relief affirmed 1999 WL 394938, dismissed, appeal not allowed 87 Ohio St.3d 1418, 717 N.E.2d 1105, certiorari denied 120 S.Ct. 345, 528 U.S. 938, 145 L.Ed.2d 270, post-conviction relief denied 2005 WL 5775899, affirmed 2005-Ohio-6990, 2005 WL 3556634, appeal allowed 109 Ohio St.3d 1493, 848 N.E.2d 857, 2006-Ohio-2762, reversed 118 Ohio St.3d 12, 885 N.E.2d 905, 2008-Ohio-1623. Mental Health ⚷ 434

2945.392 Battered woman syndrome

Notes of Decisions

Constitutional issues 1

---

1. Constitutional issues

State court's determination that female prisoner convicted of murdering husband with firearm was not deprived of effective assistance of counsel on "battered woman syndrome" defense was not contrary to or unreasonable application of United States Supreme Court precedent; expert witness's allegedly disappointing testimony on syndrome did not relate to counsel's decision to rely on that expert, and state court was not obligated to consider validity of expert's opinion. Manning v. Rogers (C.A.6 (Ohio), 05-24-2006) No. 04-4019, 183 Fed. Appx. 521, 2006 WL 1478518, Unreported. Habeas Corpus ⚷ 486(4)

2945.40 Verdict of not guilty by reason of insanity; effects; procedures; hearings; rights; commitment

(A) If a person is found not guilty by reason of insanity, the verdict shall state that finding, and the trial court shall conduct a full hearing to determine whether the person is a mentally ill person subject to court order or a mentally retarded person subject to institutionalization by court order. Prior to the hearing, if the trial judge believes that there is probable cause that the person found not guilty by reason of insanity is a mentally ill person subject to court order or mentally retarded person subject to institutionalization by court order, the trial judge may issue a temporary order of detention for that person to remain in effect for ten court days or until the hearing, whichever occurs first.

Any person detained pursuant to a temporary order of detention issued under this division shall be held in a suitable facility, taking into consideration the place and type of confinement prior to and during trial.

(B) The court shall hold the hearing under division (A) of this section to determine whether the person found not guilty by reason of insanity is a mentally ill person subject to court order or a mentally retarded person subject to institutionalization by court order within ten court days after the finding of not guilty by reason of insanity. Failure to conduct the hearing within the ten-day period shall cause the immediate discharge of the respondent, unless the judge grants a continuance for not longer than ten court days for good cause shown or for any period of time upon motion of the respondent.

(C) If a person is found not guilty by reason of insanity, the person has the right to attend all hearings conducted pursuant to sections 2945.37 to 2945.402 of the Revised Code. At any hearing conducted pursuant to one of those sections, the court shall inform the person that the person has all of the following rights:

(1) The right to be represented by counsel and to have that counsel provided at public expense if the person is indigent, with the counsel to be appointed by the court under Chapter 120. of the Revised Code or under the authority recognized in division (C) of section 120.06, division (E) of section 120.16, division (E) of section 120.26, or section 2941.51 of the Revised Code;

(2) The right to have independent expert evaluation and to have that independent expert evaluation provided at public expense if the person is indigent;

(3) The right to subpoena witnesses and documents, to present evidence on the person's behalf, and to cross-examine witnesses against the person;

(4) The right to testify in the person's own behalf and to not be compelled to testify;

(5) The right to have copies of any relevant medical or mental health document in the custody of the state or of any place of commitment other than a document for which the court finds that the release to the person of information contained in the document would create a substantial risk of harm to any person.

(D) The hearing under division (A) of this section shall be open to the public, and the court shall conduct the hearing in accordance with the Rules of Civil Procedure. The court shall make and maintain a full transcript and record of the hearing proceedings. The court may consider all relevant evidence, including, but not limited to, any relevant psychiatric, psychological, or medical testimony or reports, the acts constituting the offense in relation to which the person was found not guilty by reason of insanity, and any history of the person that is relevant to the person's ability to conform to the law.

(E) Upon completion of the hearing under division (A) of this section, if the court finds there is not clear and convincing evidence that the person is a mentally ill person subject to court order or a mentally retarded person subject to institutionalization by court order, the court shall discharge the person, unless a detainer has been placed upon the person by the department of rehabilitation and correction, in which case the person shall be returned to that department.

(F) If, at the hearing under division (A) of this section, the court finds by clear and convincing evidence that the person is a mentally ill person subject to court order, the court shall commit the person either to the department of mental health and addiction services for treatment in a hospital, facility, or agency as determined clinically appropriate by the department of mental health and addiction services or to another medical or psychiatric facility, as appropriate. Prior to placing the defendant, the department of mental health and addiction services shall obtain court approval for that placement. If, at the hearing under division (A) of this section, the court determines by clear and convincing evidence that the person requires treatment for mental retardation, it shall commit the person to a facility operated by the department of developmental disabilities or another facility, as appropriate. Further proceedings shall be in accordance with sections 2945.401 and 2945.402 of the Revised Code. In determining the place of commitment, the court shall consider the extent to which the person is a danger to the person and to others, the need for security, and the type of crime involved and shall order the least restrictive alternative available that is consistent with public safety and the welfare of the person. In weighing these factors, the court shall give preference to protecting public safety.

(G) If a court makes a commitment of a person under division (F) of this section, the prosecutor shall send to the hospital, facility, or agency where the person is placed by the department of mental health and addiction services or to the defendant's place of commitment all reports of the person's current mental condition, and, except as otherwise provided in this division, any other relevant information, including, but not limited to, a transcript of the hearing held pursuant to division (A) of this section, copies of relevant police reports, and copies of any prior arrest and conviction records that pertain to the person and that the prosecutor possesses. The prosecutor shall send the reports of the person's current mental condition in every case of commitment, and, unless the prosecutor determines that the release of any of the other relevant information to unauthorized persons would interfere with the effective prosecution of any person or would create a substantial risk of harm to any person, the prosecutor also shall send the other relevant information. Upon admission of a person committed under division (F) of this section, the place of commitment shall send to the board of alcohol, drug addiction, and mental health services or the community mental health board serving the county in which the charges against the person were filed a copy of all reports of the person's current mental condition and a copy of the other relevant information provided by the prosecutor under this division, including, if provided, a transcript of the hearing held pursuant to division (A) of this section, the relevant police reports, and the prior arrest and conviction records that pertain to the person and that the prosecutor possesses.

(H) A person who is committed pursuant to this section shall not voluntarily admit the person or be voluntarily admitted to a hospital or institution pursuant to section 5122.02, 5122.15, 5123.69, or 5123.76 of the Revised Code.

(2014 S 43, eff. 9-17-14; 2013 H 59, eff. 9-29-13; 2012 H 487, eff. 6-11-12; 2011 H 153, eff. 9-29-11; 2009 S 79, eff. 10-6-09; 1996 S 285, eff. 7–1–97; 1996 H 567, eff. 10–29–96; 1994 H 571, eff. 10–6–94; 1990 S 24, eff. 7–24–90; 1988 S 156; 1981 H 1; 1980 H 965, S 297; 1978 H 565)

Uncodified Law

2013 H 59, § 327.20.20: See Uncodified Law under RC 2945.38.

Historical and Statutory Notes

Amendment Note: 2014 S 43 substituted "mentally ill person subject to court order" for "mentally ill person subject to hospitalization by court order" throughout.

Amendment Note: 2013 H 59, in division (F), in three places, and in division (G), in one place, inserted "and addiction services" following "mental health".

Amendment Note: 2012 H 487, rewrote division (F); and added the third sentence to division (G). Prior to amendment, division (F) read:

"(F) If, at the hearing under division (A) of this section, the court finds by clear and convincing evidence that the person is a mentally ill person subject to hospitalization by court order, the court shall commit the person to the department of mental health for placement in a hospital, facility, or agency as determined clinically appropriate by the department of mental health. If, at the hearing under division (A) of this section, the court finds by clear and convincing evidence that the person is a mentally retarded person subject to institutionalization by court order, it shall commit the person to a facility operated by the department of developmental disabilities or another facility, as appropriate. Further proceedings shall be in accordance with sections 2945.401 and 2945.402 of the Revised Code. In committing the person to the department of mental health, the court shall specify the least restrictive limitations to the defendant's freedom of movement determined to be necessary to protect public safety. In determining the place and nature of the commitment of a mentally retarded person subject to institutionalization by court order, the court shall order the least restrictive commitment alternative available that is consistent with public safety and the welfare of the person. In weighing these factors, the court shall give preference to protecting public safety."

Amendment Note: 2011 H 153 rewrote divisions (F) and (G) which read:

"(F) If, at the hearing under division (A) of this section, the court finds by clear and convincing evidence that the person is a mentally ill person subject to hospitalization by court order or a mentally retarded person subject to institutionalization by court order, it shall commit the person to a hospital operated by the department of mental health, a facility operated by the department of developmental disabilities, or another medical or psychiatric facility, as appropriate, and further proceedings shall be in accordance with sections 2945.401 and 2945.402 of the Revised Code. In determining the place and nature of the commitment, the court shall order the least restrictive commitment alternative available that is consistent with public safety and the welfare of the person. In weighing these factors, the court shall give preference to protecting public safety."

"(G) If a court makes a commitment of a person under division (F) of this section, the prosecutor shall send to the place of commitment all reports of the person's current mental condition, and, except as otherwise provided in this division, any other relevant information, including, but not limited to, a transcript of the hearing held pursuant to division (A) of this section, copies of relevant police reports, and copies of any prior arrest and conviction records that pertain to the person and that the prosecutor possesses. The prosecutor shall send the reports of the person's current mental condition in every case of commitment, and, unless the prosecutor determines that the release of any of the other relevant information to unauthorized persons would interfere with the effective prosecution of any person or would create a substantial risk of harm to any person, the prosecutor also shall send the other relevant information. Upon admission of a person committed under division (F) of this section, the place of commitment shall send to the board of alcohol, drug addiction, and mental health services or the community mental health board serving the county in which the charges against the person were filed a copy of all reports of the person's current mental condition and a copy of the other relevant information provided by the prosecutor under this division, including, if provided, a transcript of the hearing held pursuant to division (A) of this section, the relevant police reports, and the prior arrest and conviction records that pertain to the person and that the prosecutor possesses."

Amendment Note: 2009 S 79 deleted "mental retardation and" from "department of mental retardation and developmental disabilities" in division (F); and substituted "section" for "sections" after "pursuant to" in division (H).

Cross References

Boards of alcohol, drug addiction, and mental health services, reports, statements, agreements, tracking and monitoring, see 340.08

Records pertaining to person's mental health condition confidential, exceptions, see 5119.28

Ohio Administrative Code References

Forensic evaluation service, see OAC 5122–29–07

Research References

ALR Library

43 ALR 5th 777, Propriety of Transferring Patient Found Not Guilty by Reason of Insanity to Less Restrictive Confinement.

Encyclopedias

OH Jur. 3d Criminal Law: Procedure § 1864, Timing of Hearing.

OH Jur. 3d Criminal Law: Procedure § 1865, Rights of Person Found Not Guilty by Reason of Insanity.

OH Jur. 3d Criminal Law: Procedure § 1866, Discharge of Person.

OH Jur. 3d Criminal Law: Procedure § 1868, Nature of Commitment.

OH Jur. 3d Criminal Law: Procedure § 1870, Conditional Release--Violation of Terms; Hearing.

OH Jur. 3d Criminal Law: Procedure § 1871, Continued Commitment; Termination.

OH Jur. 3d Incompetent Persons § 53, Admission of Involuntary Patients.

OH Jur. 3d Incompetent Persons § 104, Discharge by Chief Clinical Officer.

OH Jur. 3d Incompetent Persons § 183, Evidence.

OH Jur. 3d Incompetent Persons § 192, Definitions.

Treatises and Practice Aids

Klein, Darling, & Terez, Baldwin's Ohio Practice Civil Practice § 1:53, Civ. R. 1(C)(6): Commitment of the Mentally Ill--Proceedings Under RC 2945.38 and RC 2945.40.

Katz & Giannelli, Baldwin's Ohio Practice Criminal Law § 54:8, Findings.

Katz & Giannelli, Baldwin's Ohio Practice Criminal Law § 65:6, Return of Verdict.

Katz & Giannelli, Baldwin's Ohio Practice Criminal Law § 106:8, Possession of Deadly Weapon While Under Detention.

Katz & Giannelli, Baldwin's Ohio Practice Criminal Law § 87:15, Acquittal Consequences.

Katz & Giannelli, Baldwin's Ohio Practice Criminal Law § 110:21, Escape.

Katz & Giannelli, Baldwin's Ohio Practice Criminal Law § 144:11, Order for Detention and Hearing Following Verdict of Not Guilty by Reason of Insanity.

Katz & Giannelli, Baldwin's Ohio Practice Criminal Law § 148:36, Verdict of Not Guilty by Reason of Insanity..

Carlin, Baldwin's Ohio Prac. Merrick-Rippner Probate Law § 102:18, Involuntary Admission--Notice and Assessment Requirements for All Involuntary Patients.

Carlin, Baldwin's Ohio Prac. Merrick-Rippner Probate Law § 102:42, Jurisdiction Over Commitments in Criminal Cases.

Carlin, Baldwin's Ohio Prac. Merrick-Rippner Probate Law § 102:43, Voluntary Status of Persons Committed by Criminal.

Carlin, Baldwin's Ohio Prac. Merrick-Rippner Probate Law § 102:44, Commencement of Commitment Proceedings in Criminal Cases.

Carlin, Baldwin's Ohio Prac. Merrick-Rippner Probate Law § 102:45, Full Hearing for Persons Found NGRI.

Carlin, Baldwin's Ohio Prac. Merrick-Rippner Probate Law § 102;46, Disposition of Persons Committed by Court Order After Finding of NGRI.

Carlin, Baldwin's Ohio Prac. Merrick-Rippner Probate Law § 102:49, Hearings on Nonsecured Status and Termination of Commitment of Persons Found NGRI or Incompetent to Stand Trial.

Adrine & Ruden, Ohio Domestic Violence Law § 4:6, Violation of a Protection Order.

Adrine & Ruden, Ohio Domestic Violence Law App. A, Ohio Revised Code (Selected Provisions).

Notes of Decisions

5. Hearing on disposition

Patient who had been found not guilty of burglary by reason of insanity was entitled by statute to appointment of an independent expert at state's cost for hearing on his alleged violation of his conditional release. State v. Werner (Ohio App. 6 Dist., 07-28-2006) 168 Ohio App.3d 272, 859 N.E.2d 986, 2006-Ohio-3866. Mental Health ⚷ 440

7. Evidence

Competent, credible evidence supported conclusion that patient who had been found not guilty of burglary by reason of insanity was mentally ill and subject to hospitalization; there were expert testimony and multiple reports that patient had a mood disorder coupled with polysubstance dependence, whenever patient was exposed to the least permissive atmosphere, he returned to drugs, and he minimized the problem, suggesting little insight and a high risk of relapse. State v. Werner (Ohio App. 6 Dist., 07-28-2006) 168 Ohio App.3d 272, 859 N.E.2d 986, 2006-Ohio-3866. Mental Health ⚷ 439.1

8. Commitment, treatment and release

Trial court was required to make findings concerning whether the defendant had or did not have the capacity to give or withhold informed consent regarding his treatment, whether it was in defendant's best interest to take the medication, in other words, the benefits of the medication outweighed the side effects, and that no less intrusive treatment will be as effective in treating his mental illness, before the court could order forced administration of antipsychotic medications to defendant, who had been found not guilty by reason of mental illness. State v. Rowe (Ohio App. 3 Dist., Union, 04-17-2006) No. 14-05-31, No. 14-05-46, 2006-Ohio-1883, 2006 WL 988532, Unreported. Mental Health ⚷ 439.1

Defendant was entitled to appointment of an independent psychologist to conduct an examination before the trial court ordered the forced administration of medications; statute provided that defendants, who had been found not guilty by reason of insanity, were entitled "the right to have independent expert evaluation," and defendant had been found not guilty by reason of insanity. State v. Rowe (Ohio App. 3 Dist., Union, 04-17-2006) No. 14-05-31, No. 14-05-46, 2006-Ohio-1883, 2006 WL 988532, Unreported. Mental Health ⚷ 439.1

2945.401 Nonsecured status or termination of commitment; reports on competence; jurisdiction; hearing

(A) A defendant found incompetent to stand trial and committed pursuant to section 2945.39 of the Revised Code or a person found not guilty by reason of insanity and committed pursuant to section 2945.40 of the Revised Code shall remain subject to the jurisdiction of the trial court pursuant to that commitment, and to the provisions of this section, until the final termination of the commitment as described in division (J)(1) of this section. If the jurisdiction is terminated under this division because of the final termination of the commitment resulting from the expiration of the maximum prison term or term of imprisonment described in division (J)(1)(b) of this section, the court or prosecutor may file an affidavit for the civil commitment of the defendant or person pursuant to Chapter 5122. or 5123. of the Revised Code.

(B) A hearing conducted under any provision of sections 2945.37 to 2945.402 of the Revised Code shall not be conducted in accordance with Chapters 5122. and 5123. of the Revised Code. Any person who is committed pursuant to section 2945.39 or 2945.40 of the Revised Code shall not voluntarily admit the person or be voluntarily admitted to a hospital or institution pursuant to section 5122.02, 5122.15, 5123.69, or 5123.76 of the Revised Code. All other provisions of Chapters 5122. and 5123. of the Revised Code regarding hospitalization or institutionalization shall apply to the extent they are not in conflict with this chapter. A commitment under section 2945.39 or 2945.40 of the Revised Code shall not be terminated and the conditions of the commitment shall not be changed except as otherwise provided in division (D)(2) of this section with respect to a mentally retarded person subject to institutionalization by court order or except by order of the trial court.

(C) The department of mental health and addiction services or the institution, facility, or program to which a defendant or person has been committed under section 2945.39 or 2945.40 of the Revised Code shall report in writing to the trial court, at the times specified in this division, as to whether the defendant or person remains a mentally ill person subject to court order or a mentally retarded person subject to institutionalization by court order and, in the case of a defendant committed under section 2945.39 of the Revised Code, as to whether the defendant remains incompetent to stand trial. The department, institution, facility, or program shall make the reports after the initial six months of treatment and every two years after the initial report is made. The trial court shall provide copies of the reports to the prosecutor and to the counsel for the defendant or person. Within thirty days after its receipt pursuant to this division of a report from the department, institution, facility, or program, the trial court shall hold a hearing on the continued commitment of the defendant or person or on any changes in the conditions of the commitment of the defendant or person. The defendant or person may request a change in the conditions of confinement, and the trial court shall conduct a hearing on that request if six months or more have elapsed since the most recent hearing was conducted under this section.

(D)(1) Except as otherwise provided in division (D)(2) of this section, when a defendant or person has been committed under section 2945.39 or 2945.40 of the Revised Code, at any time after evaluating the risks to public safety and the welfare of the defendant or person, the designee of the department of mental health and addiction services or the managing officer of the institution or director of the facility or program to which the defendant or person is committed may recommend a termination of the defendant's or person's commitment or a change in the conditions of the defendant's or person's commitment.

Except as otherwise provided in division (D)(2) of this section, if the designee of the department of mental health and addiction services recommends on-grounds unsupervised movement, off-grounds supervised movement, or nonsecured status for the defendant or person or termination of the defendant's or person's commitment, the following provisions apply:

(a) If the department's designee recommends on-grounds unsupervised movement or off-grounds supervised movement, the department's designee shall file with the trial court an application for approval of the movement and shall send a copy of the application to the prosecutor. Within fifteen days after receiving the application, the prosecutor may request a hearing on the application and, if a hearing is requested, shall so inform the department's designee. If the prosecutor does not request a hearing within the fifteen-day period, the trial court shall approve the application by entering its order approving the requested movement or, within five days after the expiration of the fifteen-day period, shall set a date for a hearing on the application. If the prosecutor requests a hearing on the application within the fifteen-day period, the trial court shall hold a hearing on the application within thirty days after the hearing is requested. If the trial court, within five days after the expiration of the fifteen-day period, sets a date for a hearing on the application, the trial court shall hold the hearing within thirty days after setting the hearing date. At least fifteen days before any hearing is held under this division, the trial court shall give the prosecutor written notice of the date, time, and place of the hearing. At the conclusion of each hearing conducted under this division, the trial court either shall approve or disapprove the application and shall enter its order accordingly.

(b) If the department's designee recommends termination of the defendant's or person's commitment at any time or if the department's designee recommends the first of any nonsecured status for the defendant or person, the department's designee shall send written notice of this recommendation to the trial court and to the local forensic center. The local forensic center shall evaluate the committed defendant or person and, within thirty days after its receipt of the written notice, shall submit to the trial court and the department's designee a written report of the evaluation. The trial court shall provide a copy of the department's designee's written notice and of the local forensic center's written report to the prosecutor and to the counsel for the defendant or person. Upon the local forensic center's submission of the report to the trial court and the department's designee, all of the following apply:

(i) If the forensic center disagrees with the recommendation of the department's designee, it shall inform the department's designee and the trial court of its decision and the reasons for the decision. The department's designee, after consideration of the forensic center's decision, shall either withdraw, proceed with, or modify and proceed with the recommendation. If the department's designee proceeds with, or modifies and proceeds with, the recommendation, the department's designee shall proceed in accordance with division (D)(1)(b)(iii) of this section.

(ii) If the forensic center agrees with the recommendation of the department's designee, it shall inform the department's designee and the trial court of its decision and the reasons for the decision, and the department's designee shall proceed in accordance with division (D)(1)(b)(iii) of this section.

(iii) If the forensic center disagrees with the recommendation of the department's designee and the department's designee proceeds with, or modifies and proceeds with, the recommendation or if the forensic center agrees with the recommendation of the department's designee, the department's designee shall work with community mental health services providers, programs, facilities, or boards of alcohol, drug addiction, and mental health services or community mental health boards to develop a plan to implement the recommendation. If the defendant or person is on medication, the plan shall include, but shall not be limited to, a system to monitor the defendant's or person's compliance with the prescribed medication treatment plan. The system shall include a schedule that clearly states when the defendant or person shall report for a medication compliance check. The medication compliance checks shall be based upon the effective duration of the prescribed medication, taking into account the route by which it is taken, and shall be scheduled at intervals sufficiently close together to detect a potential increase in mental illness symptoms that the medication is intended to prevent.

The department's designee, after consultation with the board of alcohol, drug addiction, and mental health services or the community mental health board serving the area, shall send the recommendation and plan developed under division (D)(1)(b)(iii) of this section, in writing, to the trial court, the prosecutor, and the counsel for the committed defendant or person. The trial court shall conduct a hearing on the recommendation and plan developed under division (D)(1)(b)(iii) of this section. Divisions (D)(1)(c) and (d) and (E) to (J) of this section apply regarding the hearing.

(c) If the department's designee's recommendation is for nonsecured status or termination of commitment, the prosecutor may obtain an independent expert evaluation of the defendant's or person's mental condition, and the trial court may continue the hearing on the recommendation for a period of not more than thirty days to permit time for the evaluation.

The prosecutor may introduce the evaluation report or present other evidence at the hearing in accordance with the Rules of Evidence.

(d) The trial court shall schedule the hearing on a department's designee's recommendation for nonsecured status or termination of commitment and shall give reasonable notice to the prosecutor and the counsel for the defendant or person. Unless continued for independent evaluation at the prosecutor's request or for other good cause, the hearing shall be held within thirty days after the trial court's receipt of the recommendation and plan.

(2)(a) Division (D)(1) of this section does not apply to on-grounds unsupervised movement of a defendant or person who has been committed under section 2945.39 or 2945.40 of the Revised Code, who is a mentally retarded person subject to institutionalization by court order, and who is being provided residential habilitation, care, and treatment in a facility operated by the department of developmental disabilities.

(b) If, pursuant to section 2945.39 of the Revised Code, the trial court commits a defendant who is found incompetent to stand trial and who is a mentally retarded person subject to institutionalization by court order, if the defendant is being provided residential habilitation, care, and treatment in a facility operated by the department of developmental disabilities, if an individual who is conducting a survey for the department of health to determine the facility's compliance with the certification requirements of the medicaid program cites the defendant's receipt of the residential habilitation, care, and treatment in the facility as being inappropriate under the certification requirements, if the defendant's receipt of the residential habilitation, care, and treatment in the facility potentially jeopardizes the facility's continued receipt of federal medicaid moneys, and if as a result of the citation the chief clinical officer of the facility determines that the conditions of the defendant's commitment should be changed, the department of developmental disabilities may cause the defendant to be removed from the particular facility and, after evaluating the risks to public safety and the welfare of the defendant and after determining whether another type of placement is consistent with the certification requirements, may place the defendant in another facility that the department selects as an appropriate facility for the defendant's continued receipt of residential habilitation, care, and treatment and that is a no less secure setting than the facility in which the defendant had been placed at the time of the citation. Within three days after the defendant's removal and alternative placement under the circumstances described in division (D)(2)(b) of this section, the department of developmental disabilities shall notify the trial court and the prosecutor in writing of the removal and alternative placement.

The trial court shall set a date for a hearing on the removal and alternative placement, and the hearing shall be held within twenty-one days after the trial court's receipt of the notice from the department of developmental disabilities. At least ten days before the hearing is held, the trial court shall give the prosecutor, the department of developmental disabilities, and the counsel for the defendant written notice of the date, time, and place of the hearing. At the hearing, the trial court shall consider the citation issued by the individual who conducted the survey for the department of health to be prima-facie evidence of the fact that the defendant's commitment to the particular facility was inappropriate under the certification requirements of the medicaid program and potentially jeopardizes the particular facility's continued receipt of federal medicaid moneys. At the conclusion of the hearing, the trial court may approve or disapprove the defendant's removal and alternative placement. If the trial court approves the defendant's removal and alternative placement, the department of developmental disabilities may continue the defendant's alternative placement. If the trial court disapproves the defendant's removal and alternative placement, it shall enter an order modifying the defendant's removal and alternative placement, but that order shall not require the department of developmental disabilities to replace the defendant for purposes of continued residential habilitation, care, and treatment in the facility associated with the citation issued by the individual who conducted the survey for the department of health.

(E) In making a determination under this section regarding nonsecured status or termination of commitment, the trial court shall consider all relevant factors, including, but not limited to, all of the following:

(1) Whether, in the trial court's view, the defendant or person currently represents a substantial risk of physical harm to the defendant or person or others;

(2) Psychiatric and medical testimony as to the current mental and physical condition of the defendant or person;

(3) Whether the defendant or person has insight into the defendant's or person's condition so that the defendant or person will continue treatment as prescribed or seek professional assistance as needed;

(4) The grounds upon which the state relies for the proposed commitment;

(5) Any past history that is relevant to establish the defendant's or person's degree of conformity to the laws, rules, regulations, and values of society;

(6) If there is evidence that the defendant's or person's mental illness is in a state of remission, the medically suggested cause and degree of the remission and the probability that the defendant or person will continue treatment to maintain the remissive state of the defendant's or person's illness should the defendant's or person's commitment conditions be altered.

(F) At any hearing held pursuant to division (C) or (D)(1) or (2) of this section, the defendant or the person shall have all the rights of a defendant or person at a commitment hearing as described in section 2945.40 of the Revised Code.

(G) In a hearing held pursuant to division (C) or (D)(1) of this section, the prosecutor has the burden of proof as follows:

(1) For a recommendation of termination of commitment, to show by clear and convincing evidence that the defendant or person remains a mentally ill person subject to court order or a mentally retarded person subject to institutionalization by court order;

(2) For a recommendation for a change in the conditions of the commitment to a less restrictive status, to show by clear and convincing evidence that the proposed change represents a threat to public safety or a threat to the safety of any person.

(H) In a hearing held pursuant to division (C) or (D)(1) or (2) of this section, the prosecutor shall represent the state or the public interest.

(I) At the conclusion of a hearing conducted under division (D)(1) of this section regarding a recommendation from the designee of the department of mental health and addiction services, managing officer of the institution, or director of a facility or program, the trial court may approve, disapprove, or modify the recommendation and shall enter an order accordingly.

(J)(1) A defendant or person who has been committed pursuant to section 2945.39 or 2945.40 of the Revised Code continues to be under the jurisdiction of the trial court until the final termination of the commitment. For purposes of division (J) of this section, the final termination of a commitment occurs upon the earlier of one of the following:

(a) The defendant or person no longer is a mentally ill person subject to court order or a mentally retarded person subject to institutionalization by court order, as determined by the trial court;

(b) The expiration of the maximum prison term or term of imprisonment that the defendant or person could have received if the defendant or person had been convicted of the most serious offense with which the defendant or person is charged or in relation to which the defendant or person was found not guilty by reason of insanity;

(c) The trial court enters an order terminating the commitment under the circumstances described in division (J)(2)(a)(ii) of this section.

(2)(a) If a defendant is found incompetent to stand trial and committed pursuant to section 2945.39 of the Revised Code, if neither of the circumstances described in divisions (J)(1)(a) and (b) of this section applies to that defendant, and if a report filed with the trial court pursuant to division (C) of this section indicates that the defendant presently is competent to stand trial or if, at any other time during the period of the defendant's commitment, the prosecutor, the counsel for the defendant, or the designee of the department of mental health and addiction services or the managing officer of the institution or director of the facility or program to which the defendant is committed files an application with the trial court alleging that the defendant presently is competent to stand trial and requesting a hearing on the competency issue or the trial court otherwise has reasonable cause to believe that the defendant presently is competent to stand trial and determines on its own motion to hold a hearing on the competency issue, the trial court shall schedule a hearing on the competency of the defendant to stand trial, shall give the prosecutor, the counsel for the defendant, and the department's designee or the managing officer of the institution or the director of the facility to which the defendant is committed notice of the date, time, and place of the hearing at least fifteen days before the hearing, and shall conduct the hearing within thirty days of the filing of the application or of its own motion. If, at the conclusion of the hearing, the trial court determines that the defendant presently is capable of understanding the nature and objective of the proceedings against the defendant and of assisting in the defendant's defense, the trial court shall order that the defendant is competent to stand trial and shall be proceeded against as provided by law with respect to the applicable offenses described in division (C)(1) of section 2945.38 of the Revised Code and shall enter whichever of the following additional orders is appropriate:

(i) If the trial court determines that the defendant remains a mentally ill person subject to court order or a mentally retarded person subject to institutionalization by court order, the trial court shall order that the defendant's commitment to the department of mental health and addiction services or to an institution, facility, or program for the treatment of mental retardation be continued during the pendency of the trial on the applicable offenses described in division (C)(1) of section 2945.38 of the Revised Code.

(ii) If the trial court determines that the defendant no longer is a mentally ill person subject to court order or a mentally retarded person subject to institutionalization by court order, the trial court shall order that the defendant's commitment to the department of mental health and addiction services or to an institution, facility, or program for the treatment of mental retardation shall not be continued during the pendency of the trial on the applicable offenses described in division (C)(1) of section 2945.38 of the Revised Code. This order shall be a final termination of the commitment for purposes of division (J)(1)(c) of this section.

(b) If, at the conclusion of the hearing described in division (J)(2)(a) of this section, the trial court determines that the defendant remains incapable of understanding the nature and objective of the proceedings against the defendant or of assisting in the defendant's defense, the trial court shall order that the defendant continues to be incompetent to stand trial, that the defendant's commitment to the department of mental health and addiction services or to an institution, facility, or program for the treatment of mental retardation shall be continued, and that the defendant remains subject to the jurisdiction of the trial court pursuant to that commitment, and to the provisions of this section, until the final termination of the commitment as described in division (J)(1) of this section.

(2014 S 43, eff. 9-17-14; 2013 H 59, eff. 9-29-13; 2012 H 487, eff. 6-11-12; 2011 H 153, eff. 9-29-11; 2009 S 79, eff. 10-6-09; 1996 S 285, eff. 7-1-97)

Uncodified Law

2013 H 59, § 327.20.20: See Uncodified Law under RC 2945.38.

Historical and Statutory Notes

Amendment Note: 2014 S 43 substituted "mentally ill person subject to court order" for "mentally ill person subject to hospitalization by court order" throughout.

Amendment Note: 2013 H 59, in division (C), in one place, in division (D)(1), in two places, and in divisions (I), (J)(2)(a), (J)(2)(a)(i), (J)(2)(a)(ii), and (J)(2)(b), inserted "and addiction services" following "mental health"; in division (D)(1)(b)(iii), substituted "services providers" for "agencies"; and in division (D)(2)(b), deleted "under Chapter 5111. of the Revised Code and Title XIX of the 'Social Security Act,' 49 Stat. 620 (1935), 42 U.S.C.A. 301, as amended," following "requirements of the medicaid program" in two places.

Amendment Note: 2012 H 487, in division (C), the first paragraph of division (D)(1), and division (I) inserted "or program" following every occurrence of "facility"; in division (D)(1)(b)(iii), inserted "or community mental health boards" following "and mental health services"; in the undesignated paragraph following division (D)(1)(b)(iii), inserted ", after consultation with the board of alcohol, drug addiction, and mental health services or the community mental health board serving the area," following "The department's designee"; in division (E)(3), deleted "dependant's" following "insight into the"; in division (J)(2)(a), inserted "or program" following the first occurrence of "director of the facility"; and in divisions (J)(2)(a)(i), (J)(2)(a)(ii), and (J)(2)(b), substituted ", or program for the treatment of mental retardation" for "for the treatment of developmental disabilities"; and made other nonsubstantive changes.

Amendment Note: 2011 H 153 rewrote divisions (C), (D)(1), (I), and (J)(2), which read:

"(C) The hospital, facility, or program to which a defendant or person has been committed under section 2945.39 or 2945.40 of the Revised Code shall report in writing to the trial court, at the times specified in this division, as to whether the defendant or person remains a mentally ill person subject to hospitalization by court order or a mentally retarded person subject to institutionalization by court order and, in the case of a defendant committed under section 2945.39 of the Revised Code, as to whether the defendant remains incompetent to stand trial. The hospital, facility, or program shall make the reports after the initial six months of treatment and every two years after the initial report is made. The trial court shall provide copies of the reports to the prosecutor and to the counsel for the defendant or person. Within thirty days after its receipt pursuant to this division of a report from a hospital, facility, or program, the trial court shall hold a hearing on the continued commitment of the defendant or person or on any changes in the conditions of the commitment of the defendant or person. The defendant or person may request a change in the conditions of confinement, and the trial court shall conduct a hearing on that request if six months or more have elapsed since the most recent hearing was conducted under this section.

"(D)(1) Except as otherwise provided in division (D)(2) of this section, when a defendant or person has been committed under section 2945.39 or 2945.40 of the Revised Code, at any time after evaluating the risks to public safety and the welfare of the defendant or person, the chief clinical officer of the hospital, facility, or program to which the defendant or person is committed may recommend a termination of the defendant's or person's commitment or a change in the conditions of the defendant's or person's commitment.

"Except as otherwise provided in division (D)(2) of this section, if the chief clinical officer recommends on-grounds unsupervised movement, off-grounds supervised movement, or nonsecured status for the defendant or person or termination of the defendant's or person's commitment, the following provisions apply:

"(a) If the chief clinical officer recommends on-grounds unsupervised movement or off-grounds supervised movement, the chief clinical officer shall file with the trial court an application for approval of the movement and shall send a copy of the application to the prosecutor. Within fifteen days after receiving the application, the prosecutor may request a hearing on the application and, if a hearing is requested, shall so inform the chief clinical officer. If the prosecutor does not request a hearing within the fifteen-day period, the trial court shall approve the application by entering its order approving the requested movement or, within five days after the expiration of the fifteen-day period, shall set a date for a hearing on the application. If the prosecutor requests a hearing on the application within the fifteen-day period, the trial court shall hold a hearing on the application within thirty days after the hearing is requested. If the trial court, within five days after the expiration of the fifteen-day period, sets a date for a hearing on the application, the trial court shall hold the hearing within thirty days after setting the hearing date. At least fifteen days before any hearing is held under this division, the trial court shall give the prosecutor written notice of the date, time, and place of the hearing. At the conclusion of each hearing conducted under this division, the trial court either shall approve or disapprove the application and shall enter its order accordingly.

"(b) If the chief clinical officer recommends termination of the defendant's or person's commitment at any time or if the chief clinical officer recommends the first of any nonsecured status for the defendant or person, the chief clinical officer shall send written notice of this recommendation to the trial court and to the local forensic center. The local forensic center shall evaluate the committed defendant or person and, within thirty days after its receipt of the written notice, shall submit to the trial court and the chief clinical officer a written report of the evaluation. The trial court shall provide a copy of the chief clinical officer's written notice and of the local forensic center's written report to the prosecutor and to the counsel for the defendant or person. Upon the local forensic center's submission of the report to the trial court and the chief clinical officer, all of the following apply:

"(i) If the forensic center disagrees with the recommendation of the chief clinical officer, it shall inform the chief clinical officer and the trial court of its decision and the reasons for the decision. The chief clinical officer, after consideration of the forensic center's decision, shall either withdraw, proceed with, or modify and proceed with the recommendation. If the chief clinical officer proceeds with, or modifies and proceeds with, the recommendation, the chief clinical officer shall proceed in accordance with division (D)(1)(b)(iii) of this section.

"(ii) If the forensic center agrees with the recommendation of the chief clinical officer, it shall inform the chief clinical officer and the trial court of its decision and the reasons for the decision, and the chief clinical officer shall proceed in accordance with division (D)(1)(b)(iii) of this section.

"(iii) If the forensic center disagrees with the recommendation of the chief clinical officer and the chief clinical officer proceeds with, or modifies and proceeds with, the recommendation or if the forensic center agrees with the recommendation of the chief clinical officer, the chief clinical officer shall work with the board of alcohol, drug addiction, and mental health services or community mental health board serving the area, as appropriate, to develop a plan to implement the recommendation. If the defendant or person is on medication, the plan shall include, but shall not be limited to, a system to monitor the defendant's or person's compliance with the prescribed medication treatment plan. The system shall include a schedule that clearly states when the defendant or person shall report for a medication compliance check. The medication compliance checks shall be based upon the effective duration of the prescribed medication, taking into account the route by which it is taken, and shall be scheduled at intervals sufficiently close together to detect a potential increase in mental illness symptoms that the medication is intended to prevent.

"The chief clinical officer, after consultation with the board of alcohol, drug addiction, and mental health services or the community mental health board serving the area, shall send the recommendation and plan developed under division (D)(1)(b)(iii) of this section, in writing, to the trial court, the prosecutor and the counsel for the committed defendant or person. The trial court shall conduct a hearing on the recommendation and plan developed under division (D)(1)(b)(iii) of this section. Divisions (D)(1)(c) and (d) and (E) to (J) of this section apply regarding the hearing.

"(c) If the chief clinical officer's recommendation is for nonsecured status or termination of commitment, the prosecutor may obtain an independent expert evaluation of the defendant's or person's mental condition, and the trial court may continue the hearing on the recommendation for a period of not more than thirty days to permit time for the evaluation.

"The prosecutor may introduce the evaluation report or present other evidence at the hearing in accordance with the Rules of Evidence.

"(d) The trial court shall schedule the hearing on a chief clinical officer's recommendation for nonsecured status or termination of commitment and shall give reasonable notice to the prosecutor and the counsel for the defendant or person. Unless continued for independent evaluation at the prosecutor's request or for other good cause, the hearing shall be held within thirty days after the trial court's receipt of the recommendation and plan."

"(I) At the conclusion of a hearing conducted under division (D)(1) of this section regarding a recommendation from the chief clinical officer of a hospital, program, or facility, the trial court may approve, disapprove, or modify the recommendation and shall enter an order accordingly."

"[J](2)(a) If a defendant is found incompetent to stand trial and committed pursuant to section 2945.39 of the Revised Code, if neither of the circumstances described in divisions (J)(1)(a) and (b) of this section applies to that defendant, and if a report filed with the trial court pursuant to division (C) of this section indicates that the defendant presently is competent to stand trial or if, at any other time during the period of the defendant's commitment, the prosecutor, the counsel for the defendant, or the chief clinical officer of the hospital, facility, or program to which the defendant is committed files an application with the trial court alleging that the defendant presently is competent to stand trial and requesting a hearing on the competency issue or the trial court otherwise has reasonable cause to believe that the defendant presently is competent to stand trial and determines on its own motion to hold a hearing on the competency issue, the trial court shall schedule a hearing on the competency of the defendant to stand trial, shall give the prosecutor, the counsel for the defendant, and the chief clinical officer notice of the date, time, and place of the hearing at least fifteen days before the hearing, and shall conduct the hearing within thirty days of the filing of the application or of its own motion. If, at the conclusion of the hearing, the trial court determines that the defendant presently is capable of understanding the nature and objective of the proceedings against the defendant and of assisting in the defendant's defense, the trial court shall order that the defendant is competent to stand trial and shall be proceeded against as provided by law with respect to the applicable offenses described in division (C)(1) of section 2945.38 of the Revised Code and shall enter whichever of the following additional orders is appropriate:

"(i) If the trial court determines that the defendant remains a mentally ill person subject to hospitalization by court order or a mentally retarded person subject to institutionalization by court order, the trial court shall order that the defendant's commitment to the hospital, facility, or program be continued during the pendency of the trial on the applicable offenses described in division (C)(1) of section 2945.38 of the Revised Code.

"(ii) If the trial court determines that the defendant no longer is a mentally ill person subject to hospitalization by court order or a mentally retarded person subject to institutionalization by court order, the trial court shall order that the defendant's commitment to the hospital, facility, or program shall not be continued during the pendency of the trial on the applicable offenses described in division (C)(1) of section 2945.38 of the Revised Code. This order shall be a final termination of the commitment for purposes of division (J)(1)(c) of this section.

"(b) If, at the conclusion of the hearing described in division (J)(2)(a) of this section, the trial court determines that the defendant remains incapable of understanding the nature and objective of the proceedings against the defendant or of assisting in the defendant's defense, the trial court shall order that the defendant continues to be incompetent to stand trial, that the defendant's commitment to the hospital, facility, or program shall be continued, and that the defendant remains subject to the jurisdiction of the trial court pursuant to that commitment, and to the provisions of this section, until the final termination of the commitment as described in division (J)(1) of this section."

Amendment Note: 2009 S 79 deleted "mental retardation and" from "department of mental retardation and developmental disabilities" throughout; and made nonsubstantive changes.

Cross References

Records pertaining to person's mental health condition confidential, exceptions, see 5119.28

Ohio Administrative Code References

Forensic evaluation service, see OAC 5122–29–07

Research References

Encyclopedias

OH Jur. 3d Criminal Law: Procedure § 1179, Hearing and Further Action.
OH Jur. 3d Criminal Law: Procedure § 1183, Required Reports and Action.
OH Jur. 3d Criminal Law: Procedure § 1184, Termination of Commitment.
OH Jur. 3d Criminal Law: Procedure § 1869, Conditional Release.
OH Jur. 3d Criminal Law: Procedure § 1871, Continued Commitment; Termination.
OH Jur. 3d Incompetent Persons § 192, Definitions.

Treatises and Practice Aids

Katz & Giannelli, Baldwin's Ohio Practice Criminal Law § 54:8, Findings.
Katz & Giannelli, Baldwin's Ohio Practice Criminal Law § 106:8, Possession of Deadly Weapon While Under Detention.
Katz & Giannelli, Baldwin's Ohio Practice Criminal Law § 87:15, Acquittal Consequences.
Katz & Giannelli, Baldwin's Ohio Practice Criminal Law § 110:21, Escape.
Carlin, Baldwin's Ohio Prac. Merrick-Rippner Probate Law § 102:18, Involuntary Admission--Notice and Assessment Requirements for All Involuntary Patients.
Carlin, Baldwin's Ohio Prac. Merrick-Rippner Probate Law § 102:42, Jurisdiction Over Commitments in Criminal Cases.
Carlin, Baldwin's Ohio Prac. Merrick-Rippner Probate Law § 102:43, Voluntary Status of Persons Committed by Criminal.
Carlin, Baldwin's Ohio Prac. Merrick-Rippner Probate Law § 102:44, Commencement of Commitment Proceedings in Criminal Cases.
Carlin, Baldwin's Ohio Prac. Merrick-Rippner Probate Law § 102:49, Hearings on Nonsecured Status and Termination of Commitment of Persons Found NGRI or Incompetent to Stand Trial.
Carlin, Baldwin's Ohio Prac. Merrick-Rippner Probate Law § 102:50, Conditional Release.
Carlin, Baldwin's Ohio Prac. Merrick-Rippner Probate Law § 102:51, Review Hearings--Review Process for Persons Found Incompetent and NGRI.
Carlin, Baldwin's Ohio Prac. Merrick-Rippner Probate Law § 102:52, Discharge for Persons Found Incompetent or NGRI.
Adrine & Ruden, Ohio Domestic Violence Law App. A, Ohio Revised Code (Selected Provisions).

2945.402 Conditional release

(A) In approving a conditional release, the trial court may set any conditions on the release with respect to the treatment, evaluation, counseling, or control of the defendant or person that the court considers necessary to protect the public safety and the welfare of the defendant or person. The trial court may revoke a defendant's or person's conditional release and order reinstatement of the previous placement or reinstitutionalization at any time the conditions of the release have not been satisfied, provided that the revocation shall be in accordance with this section.

(B) A conditional release is a commitment. The hearings on continued commitment as described in section 2945.401 of the Revised Code apply to a defendant or person on conditional release.

(C) A person, agency, or facility that is assigned to monitor a defendant or person on conditional release immediately shall notify the trial court on learning that the defendant or person being monitored has violated the terms of the conditional release. Upon learning of any violation of the terms of the conditional release, the trial court may issue a temporary order of detention or, if necessary, an arrest warrant for the defendant or person. Within ten court days after the defendant's or person's detention or arrest, the trial court shall conduct a hearing to determine whether the conditional release should be modified or terminated. At the hearing, the defendant or person shall have the same rights as are described in division (C) of section 2945.40 of the Revised Code. The trial court may order a continuance of the ten-court-day period for no longer than ten days for good cause shown or for any period on motion of the defendant or person. If the trial court fails to conduct the hearing within the ten-court-day period and does not order a continuance in accordance with this division, the defendant or person shall be restored to the prior conditional release status.

(D) The trial court shall give all parties reasonable notice of a hearing conducted under this section. At the hearing, the prosecutor shall present the case demonstrating that the defendant or person violated the terms of the conditional release. If the court finds by a preponderance of the evidence that the defendant or person violated the terms of the conditional release, the court may continue, modify, or terminate the conditional release and shall enter its order accordingly.

(E)(1) If a court approves a conditional release, the court shall report the approval and information pertaining to the release to the local law enforcement agency. The local law enforcement agency shall enter the approval and information into the national crime information center supervised release file through the law enforcement automated data system. The information required by divisions (E)(1)(c) and (d) of this section shall be entered into the file's miscellaneous field. The information reported and entered shall include all of the following:

(a) The name of the court providing the information;

(b) The offense or offenses with which the defendant or person was charged;

(c) Whether the person was found not guilty by reason of insanity or incompetent to stand trial with no substantial probability of becoming competent even with a course of treatment;

(d) The reason for the conditional release;

(e) Any other information required for the entry of information into the national crime information center supervised release file.

(2) Information entered into the national crime information center supervised release file pursuant to this section shall remain in the file until the termination of the conditional release or commitment.

(3) If a defendant or person about whom information is entered into the national crime information center supervised release file pursuant to division (E)(1) of this section has contact with a law enforcement agency after the information is entered, the agency shall report the contact to the department of mental health and addiction services and, if the terms of the release require the defendant or person to receive mental health treatment, to the person, office, or agency providing the treatment.

(4) As used in division (E) of this section, "local law enforcement agency" means the police department of a municipal corporation in which the offense with which a releasee was charged allegedly occurred or, if the offense did not allegedly occur in a municipal corporation, the sheriff of the county in which the offense allegedly occurred.

(2014 H 483, eff. 9-15-14; 2013 S 7, eff. 9-4-13; 2011 H 153, eff. 9-29-11; 1996 S 285, eff. 7–1–97)

Uncodified Law

2013 H 59, § 327.20.20: See Uncodified Law under RC 2945.38.

2013 S 7, § 3, eff. 9–4–13, reads:

This act shall be known as the Deputy Suzanne Hopper Act.

Historical and Statutory Notes

Amendment Note: 2014 H 483 inserted "and addiction services" in division (E)(3).

Amendment Note: 2013 S 7 added division (E).

Amendment Note: 2011 H 129, in division (A) substituted "reinstatement of the previous placement" for "rehospitalization".

Cross References

Records pertaining to person's mental health condition confidential, exceptions, see 5119.28

Research References

Encyclopedias

OH Jur. 3d Criminal Law: Procedure § 1179, Hearing and Further Action.

OH Jur. 3d Criminal Law: Procedure § 1183, Required Reports and Action.

OH Jur. 3d Criminal Law: Procedure § 1865, Rights of Person Found Not Guilty by Reason of Insanity.

OH Jur. 3d Criminal Law: Procedure § 1869, Conditional Release.

OH Jur. 3d Criminal Law: Procedure § 1870, Conditional Release--Violation of Terms; Hearing.

OH Jur. 3d Incompetent Persons § 192, Definitions.

Treatises and Practice Aids

Katz & Giannelli, Baldwin's Ohio Practice Criminal Law § 106:8, Possession of Deadly Weapon While Under Detention.

Katz & Giannelli, Baldwin's Ohio Practice Criminal Law § 110:21, Escape.

Carlin, Baldwin's Ohio Prac. Merrick-Rippner Probate Law § 102:18, Involuntary Admission--Notice and Assessment Requirements for All Involuntary Patients.

Carlin, Baldwin's Ohio Prac. Merrick-Rippner Probate Law § 102:43, Voluntary Status of Persons Committed by Criminal.

Carlin, Baldwin's Ohio Prac. Merrick-Rippner Probate Law § 102:50, Conditional Release.

Adrine & Ruden, Ohio Domestic Violence Law App. A, Ohio Revised Code (Selected Provisions).

Notes of Decisions

Hearing 1

---

1. Hearing

The trial court's denial of defendant's motion for a continuance of hearing to determine whether to revoke defendant's conditional release was not an abuse of discretion; defendant requested a continuance to allow his new counsel more time to prepare and investigate the case three days before the hearing. State v. Rowe (Ohio App. 3 Dist., Union, 04-17-2006) No. 14-05-31, No. 14-05-46, 2006-Ohio-1883, 2006 WL 988532, Unreported. Sentencing And Punishment ⚷ 2025

The trial court substantially complied with statute that required a hearing to be conducted on a violation of conditional release within 10 days of the violation of conditional release, even though defendant's conditional release was not explicitly revoked until more than one month after defendant allegedly violated the terms of his conditional release; the trial court conducted a hearing on the alleged violation the day after the violation was reported, and at that hearing the court ordered defendant to be returned to healthcare facility until further order by the court. State v. Rowe (Ohio App. 3 Dist., Union, 04-17-2006) No. 14-05-31, No. 14-05-46, 2006-Ohio-1883, 2006 WL 988532, Unreported. Sentencing And Punishment ⚷ 2025

WITNESSES

2945.41 Rules applicable in criminal cases

Law Review and Journal Commentaries

Voluntary client testimony as a privilege waiver: Is Ohio's law caught in a time warp? David B. Alden and Matthew P. Silversten, 59 Clev. St. L. Rev. 1 (2011).

2945.42 Competency of witnesses

Notes of Decisions

3. —— Spouses testifying against one another, impeachment of witness

Defendant's wife was permitted to testify about spousal communications she had with defendant, during prosecution for rape and sexual battery, where the communications were specifically in regards to the acts of rape and sexual assault against the couples' daughter. State v. Wilson (Ohio App. 3 Dist., Putnam, 04-24-2006) No. 12-05-20, 2006-Ohio-2000, 2006 WL 1062103, Unreported, appeal not allowed 111 Ohio St.3d 1412, 854 N.E.2d 1092, 2006-Ohio-5083, appeal not allowed 115 Ohio St.3d 1476, 875 N.E.2d 629, 2007-Ohio-5735, habeas corpus denied 2008 WL 4534140, affirmed 382 Fed.Appx. 471, 2010 WL 2587942, certiorari denied 131 S.Ct. 576, 178 L.Ed.2d 421. Privileged Communications And Confidentiality ⚷ 65; Witnesses ⚷ 52(7)

Once it has been determined that a witness is married to the defendant, the trial court must instruct the witness on spousal competency and make a finding on the record that he or she voluntarily chose to testify; failure to do so constitutes reversible plain error. State v. Brown (Ohio, 10-03-2007) 115 Ohio St.3d 55, 873 N.E.2d 858, 2007-Ohio-4837, reconsideration denied 116 Ohio St.3d 1442, 877 N.E.2d 992, 2007-Ohio-6518, appeal after new trial 2010-Ohio-2460, 2010 WL 2202962, appeal not allowed 126 Ohio St.3d 1601, 935 N.E.2d 47, 2010-Ohio-4928. Criminal Law ⚷ 1170.5(1); Witnesses ⚷ 79(1)

Evidence was sufficient to support finding that defendant and witness were legally married, thus requiring affirmative determination on the record that the spouse elected to testify for state; although witness stated she and defendant were never married, defendant and witness had obtained marriage license, license included a certification that a minister solemnized the marriage on the same day it was issued, defendant's mother testified that she attended marriage ceremony, witness named defendant as her husband in life insurance policy, and defendant identified himself as witness's husband in letters from prison. State v. Brown (Ohio, 10-03-2007)

115 Ohio St.3d 55, 873 N.E.2d 858, 2007-Ohio-4837, reconsideration denied 116 Ohio St.3d 1442, 877 N.E.2d 992, 2007-Ohio-6518, appeal after new trial 2010-Ohio-2460, 2010 WL 2202962, appeal not allowed 126 Ohio St.3d 1601, 935 N.E.2d 47, 2010-Ohio-4928. Marriage ⚿ 50(1); Witnesses ⚿ 78

Accused may not assert a privilege to preclude a spouse from testifying with respect to a crime committed against a third person, where the crime is committed in the known presence of such third person, as well as in the presence of the testifying spouse. State v. Brown (Ohio, 10-03-2007) 115 Ohio St.3d 55, 873 N.E.2d 858, 2007-Ohio-4837, reconsideration denied 116 Ohio St.3d 1442, 877 N.E.2d 992, 2007-Ohio-6518, appeal after new trial 2010-Ohio-2460, 2010 WL 2202962, appeal not allowed 126 Ohio St.3d 1601, 935 N.E.2d 47, 2010-Ohio-4928. Witnesses ⚿ 52(7)

Spousal privilege cannot be waived unilaterally and allows a defendant to prevent his or her spouse from testifying unless one of the statute's exceptions applies. State v. Brown (Ohio, 10-03-2007) 115 Ohio St.3d 55, 873 N.E.2d 858, 2007-Ohio-4837, reconsideration denied 116 Ohio St.3d 1442, 877 N.E.2d 992, 2007-Ohio-6518, appeal after new trial 2010-Ohio-2460, 2010 WL 2202962, appeal not allowed 126 Ohio St.3d 1601, 935 N.E.2d 47, 2010-Ohio-4928. Witnesses ⚿ 52(1); Witnesses ⚿ 75; Witnesses ⚿ 76(3)

4. Privileged communications between spouses

Admission of testimony from murder defendant's wife, in violation of Ohio's marital privilege statute, did not rise to the level of a due process violation so as to warrant federal habeas relief; the privilege did not have a grounding in the concepts that underpinned the constitutional guarantee of due process, but was based on principles of marital peace and preservation. Sandoval v. Toledo Correctional Inst. (C.A.6 (Ohio), 11-30-2010) No. 07-4216, 409 Fed.Appx. 847, 2010 WL 4908260, Unreported, certiorari denied 131 S.Ct. 2887, 179 L.Ed.2d 1199. Constitutional Law ⚿ 4674; Habeas Corpus ⚿ 490(1)

Because threats did not constitute confidential marital communications and because defendant was charged with committing a crime against his spouse, the trial court did not abuse its discretion by compelling the testimony of defendant's wife; spousal privilege statute did not shield wife's testimony regarding defendant's threats toward her or the crimes he allegedly committed against her. Portsmouth v. Wrage (Ohio App. 4 Dist., Scioto, 07-02-2009) No. 08CA3237, 2009-Ohio-3390, 2009 WL 2003386, Unreported. Privileged Communications and Confidentiality ⚿ 74; Witnesses ⚿ 61(1)

Exception to spousal privilege set forth in spousal privilege statute in cases of personal injury by either the husband or wife to the other was not rendered inapplicable in prosecution of defendant for kidnapping his wife, in which defendant sought to assert privilege, on basis that actual personal injury was not an essential element of kidnapping, as statute in no way provided that injury to testifying spouse had to be an element of crime of which defendant spouse was charged, and, thus, it was irrelevant whether wife suffered her injuries while she was actually restrained by defendant or whether she sustained injuries as part of defendant's continuous course of conduct of which his restraint of wife was a part. State v. Purvis (Ohio App. 9 Dist., Medina, 03-31-2006) No. 05CA0053-M, 2006-Ohio-1555, 2006 WL 826349, Unreported. Privileged Communications And Confidentiality ⚿ 65

Defendant could not assert spousal privilege to preclude his wife's testimony in prosecution charging him with kidnapping her, even though kidnapping was not specifically listed as an exception under spousal privilege statute, as defendant's actions toward wife were not "confidential communications" within purpose of statute. State v. Purvis (Ohio App. 9 Dist., Medina, 03-31-2006) No. 05CA0053-M, 2006-Ohio-1555, 2006 WL 826349, Unreported. Privileged Communications And Confidentiality ⚿ 71

Defendant and his wife were not "in coverture" at the time he made self-implicating statements to wife, and thus the spousal privilege did not apply to preclude wife from testifying during prosecution of defendant for aggravated arson; at the time defendant made the statements defendant and wife were in the process of obtaining a divorce, they did not live together, and defendant lived with his girlfriend. State v. Reed (Ohio App. 11 Dist., 12-15-2014) 2014-Ohio-5463, 2014 WL 7014498. Privileged Communications and Confidentiality ⚿ 67

The traditional justification for the spousal privilege is the underlying principle that it is necessary to promote peace and marital harmony. State v. Reed (Ohio App. 11 Dist., 12-15-2014) 2014-Ohio-5463, 2014 WL 7014498. Privileged Communications and Confidentiality ⚿ 63

Spousal privilege did not apply to statements of defendant's wife that were made prior to their marriage. State v. Jones (Ohio, 12-06-2012) 135 Ohio St.3d 10, 984 N.E.2d 948, 2012-Ohio-5677. Privileged Communications and Confidentiality ⚿ 82

Detective's primary purpose in questioning of defendant's wife was to obtain information about victim's murder, and, thus, her statements were testimonial under the Confrontation Clause in capital murder trial, although some of the facts tended to demonstrate that defendant appeared to pose a threat to wife, who was hysterical when detective arrived at wife's home, kept running back and forth, looking out widows, pacing, and making sure no one was coming, where detective was not dispatched to an active crime scene, victim's body was found the previous day in a different location, no gun was involved in the murder, and detective's arrival at wife's home greatly reduced any immediate threat to her. State v. Jones (Ohio, 12-06-2012)

135 Ohio St.3d 10, 984 N.E.2d 948, 2012-Ohio-5677. Criminal Law ⚷ 662.8

Spousal privilege is wholly inapplicable to the testimony of a third party. State v. Jones (Ohio, 12-06-2012) 135 Ohio St.3d 10, 984 N.E.2d 948, 2012-Ohio-5677. Privileged Communications and Confidentiality ⚷ 81

Testimony of defendant's wife did not violate defendant's spousal privilege in capital murder trial, where wife was not asked, and did not testify as to, the communication between her and defendant. State v. Jones (Ohio, 12-06-2012) 135 Ohio St.3d 10, 984 N.E.2d 948, 2012-Ohio-5677. Privileged Communications and Confidentiality ⚷ 72

The spousal privilege cannot be waived unilaterally and allows a defendant to prevent his or her spouse from testifying as to privileged communications unless one of the statute's exceptions applies. State v. Jones (Ohio, 12-06-2012) 135 Ohio St.3d 10, 984 N.E.2d 948, 2012-Ohio-5677. Privileged Communications and Confidentiality ⚷ 85

Criminal acts against the other spouse are not within the reach of the spousal privilege. State v. Greaves (Ohio App. 6 Dist., 05-04-2012) 971 N.E.2d 987, 2012-Ohio-1989. Privileged Communications and Confidentiality ⚷ 71

A provably-made threat is not a "confidential communication" under spousal privilege statute, regardless of whether a third party was present to hear it. State v. Greaves (Ohio App. 6 Dist., 05-04-2012) 971 N.E.2d 987, 2012-Ohio-1989. Privileged Communications and Confidentiality ⚷ 74

The ostensible purpose of the spousal privilege, in protecting intimate exchanges, is to promote marital peace and harmony. State v. Greaves (Ohio App. 6 Dist., 05-04-2012) 971 N.E.2d 987, 2012-Ohio-1989. Privileged Communications and Confidentiality ⚷ 63

Verbal threats and violent acts between spouses are not marital "confidences" which the spousal privilege was intended to shield from courtroom disclosure. State v. Greaves (Ohio App. 6 Dist., 05-04-2012) 971 N.E.2d 987, 2012-Ohio-1989. Privileged Communications and Confidentiality ⚷ 71; Privileged Communications and Confidentiality ⚷ 74

In assessing whether a communication was confidential in order to qualify for spousal privilege, courts look to the language used, the nature of the message, the circumstances under which it was delivered, and other relevant facts. State v. Greaves (Ohio App. 6 Dist., 05-04-2012) 971 N.E.2d 987, 2012-Ohio-1989. Privileged Communications and Confidentiality ⚷ 80

For spousal communication to be privileged, the communication at issue must be confidential. State v. Greaves (Ohio App. 6 Dist., 05-04-2012) 971 N.E.2d 987, 2012-Ohio-1989. Privileged Communications and Confidentiality ⚷ 80

The right to invoke the spousal privilege, where it exists, belongs to the nontestifying spouse. State v. Greaves (Ohio App. 6 Dist., 05-04-2012) 971 N.E.2d 987, 2012-Ohio-1989. Privileged Communications and Confidentiality ⚷ 84

Defendant's alleged criminal acts of threatening his wife while brandishing a firearm, resulting in charges of using a weapon while intoxicated and domestic violence, did not involve confidential communication between defendant and his wife as contemplated by spousal privilege statute, and thus, State could compel wife's testimony at trial. State v. Greaves (Ohio App. 6 Dist., 05-04-2012) 971 N.E.2d 987, 2012-Ohio-1989. Privileged Communications and Confidentiality ⚷ 71; Privileged Communications and Confidentiality ⚷ 74

Marital-communications privilege applicable in criminal proceedings belongs to the nontestifying spouse. State v. Perez (Ohio, 12-02-2009) 124 Ohio St.3d 122, 920 N.E.2d 104, 2009-Ohio-6179, reconsideration denied 124 Ohio St.3d 1446, 920 N.E.2d 375, 2010-Ohio-188, certiorari denied 130 S.Ct. 3516, 561 U.S. 1031, 177 L.Ed.2d 1101. Privileged Communications and Confidentiality ⚷ 84

Admission in aggravated murder prosecution of taped jailhouse conversations between defendant and his wife, who was cooperating with police, did not violate marital-communications privilege, as those conversations were introduced only through the tape recordings and not through wife's testimony. State v. Perez (Ohio, 12-02-2009) 124 Ohio St.3d 122, 920 N.E.2d 104, 2009-Ohio-6179, reconsideration denied 124 Ohio St.3d 1446, 920 N.E.2d 375, 2010-Ohio-188, certiorari denied 130 S.Ct. 3516, 561 U.S. 1031, 177 L.Ed.2d 1101. Privileged Communications and Confidentiality ⚷ 70(3)

Cumulative effect of State's failure to disclose police reports indicating that someone other than defendant had claimed responsibility for the murders, and defense counsel's ineffective assistance in failing to obtain ruling on applicability of spousal privilege, warranted new trial in murder prosecution. State v. Brown (Ohio, 10-03-2007) 115 Ohio St.3d 55, 873 N.E.2d 858, 2007-Ohio-4837, reconsideration denied 116 Ohio St.3d 1442, 877 N.E.2d 992, 2007-Ohio-6518, appeal after new trial 2010-Ohio-2460, 2010 WL 2202962, appeal not allowed 126 Ohio St.3d 1601, 935 N.E.2d 47, 2010-Ohio-4928. Criminal Law ⚷ 1186.1; Criminal Law ⚷ 1905; Criminal Law ⚷ 1926; Criminal Law ⚷ 2001

Trial counsel's failure to request a formal decision on whether defendant and state's witness were actually married, such that spousal privilege would apply, was ineffective assistance of counsel in murder prosecution; although existence of marriage was disputed, evidence supported finding that defendant and witness were legally married, witness's testimony was central to issue of prior calculation and design necessary to support the death penalty, and prosecution's death penalty case would have been significantly weakened had witness been properly advised that it was her choice to testify, and had she chosen not to testify. State v. Brown (Ohio, 10-03-2007) 115 Ohio St.3d 55, 873 N.E.2d 858, 2007-Ohio-4837, reconsideration denied 116 Ohio

St.3d 1442, 877 N.E.2d 992, 2007-Ohio-6518, appeal after new trial 2010-Ohio-2460, 2010 WL 2202962, appeal not allowed 126 Ohio St.3d 1601, 935 N.E.2d 47, 2010-Ohio-4928. Criminal Law ⚿ 1926

2945.43 Defendant may testify

Notes of Decisions

2. Comment on defendant's silence

In prosecution for conspiracy to possess with intent to distribute cocaine and marijuana and using a communication facility to facilitate commission of a drug trafficking offense, trial court correctly presumed that defendant waived his right to testify on his own behalf, and court was therefore under no duty to inquire as to whether defendant's waiver was knowing and intelligent, since defendant did nothing to alert the trial court of his desire to testify. U.S. v. Stover (C.A.6 (Ohio), 01-30-2007) 474 F.3d 904, rehearing denied, post-conviction relief denied 2007 WL 928643, certiorari denied 128 S.Ct. 142, 552 U.S. 860, 169 L.Ed.2d 98, rehearing denied 128 S.Ct. 697, 552 U.S. 1057, 169 L.Ed.2d 544. Witnesses ⚿ 88

2945.44 Court of common pleas to grant transactional immunity; procedure; exceptions

(A) In any criminal proceeding in this state or in any criminal or civil proceeding brought pursuant to Chapter 2981. of the Revised Code, if a witness refuses to answer or produce information on the basis of the witness's privilege against self-incrimination, the court of common pleas of the county in which the proceeding is being held, unless it finds that to do so would not further the administration of justice, shall compel the witness to answer or produce the information, if both of the following apply:

(1) The prosecuting attorney of the county in which the proceedings are being held makes a written request to the court of common pleas to order the witness to answer or produce the information, notwithstanding the witness's claim of privilege;

(2) The court of common pleas informs the witness that by answering, or producing the information the witness will receive immunity under division (B) of this section.

(B) If, but for this section, the witness would have been privileged to withhold an answer or any information given in any criminal proceeding, and the witness complies with an order under division (A) of this section compelling the witness to give an answer or produce any information, the witness shall not be prosecuted or subjected to any criminal penalty in the courts of this state for or on account of any transaction or matter concerning which, in compliance with the order, the witness gave an answer or produced any information.

(C) A witness granted immunity under this section may be subjected to a criminal penalty for any violation of section 2921.11, 2921.12, or 2921.13 of the Revised Code, or for contempt committed in answering, failing to answer, or failing to produce information in compliance with the order.

(2006 H 241, eff. 7–1–07; 1985 H 5, eff. 1–1–86; 1978 H 491)

Research References

ALR Library

29 ALR 5th 1, Propriety, Under State Constitutional Provisions, of Granting Use or Transactional Immunity for Compelled Incriminating Testimony--Post-Kastigar Cases.

Encyclopedias

OH Jur. 3d Contempt § 34, Refusal to be Sworn or to Testify.

OH Jur. 3d Criminal Law: Procedure § 1718, Granting of Immunity.

OH Jur. 3d Criminal Law: Substantive Principles and Offenses § 154, Examination of Witnesses Concerning Felony Prior to Arrest.

OH Jur. 3d Criminal Law: Substantive Principles and Offenses § 219, Effect at Retrial.

OH Jur. 3d Criminal Law: Substantive Principles and Offenses § 992, Effect of Perjury While Testifying Under Grant of Immunity.

OH Jur. 3d Evidence and Witnesses § 677, Statutes Providing Transactional Immunity.

Treatises and Practice Aids

Katz & Giannelli, Baldwin's Ohio Practice Criminal Law § 41:6, Self-Incrimination--Immunity.

Katz & Giannelli, Baldwin's Ohio Practice Criminal Law § 69:6, Limits on Cross-Examination.

Katz & Giannelli, Baldwin's Ohio Practice Criminal Law § 70:5, Immunity.

Katz & Giannelli, Baldwin's Ohio Practice Criminal Law § 79:8, Newly Discovered Evidence.
Katz & Giannelli, Baldwin's Ohio Practice Criminal Law § 82:5, Rules of Construction.
Katz & Giannelli, Baldwin's Ohio Practice Criminal Law § 102:6, Coercion.
Katz & Giannelli, Baldwin's Ohio Practice Criminal Law § 110:6, Perjury.
Katz & Giannelli, Baldwin's Ohio Practice Criminal Law § 141:12, Motion for an Immunity Order.
Giannelli, Baldwin's Ohio Practice Evidence R 611, Mode and Order of Interrogation and Presentation.
Giannelli, Baldwin's Ohio Practice Evidence § 501.4, Ohio Statutory Privileges.
Carlin, Baldwin's Ohio Prac. Merrick-Rippner Probate Law § 109:124, Contempt of Court in Juvenile Proceedings.
Adrine & Ruden, Ohio Domestic Violence Law § 14:6, Law Enforcement Policies and Procedures.
Giannelli & Yeomans Salvador, Ohio Juvenile Law App. B, Rules of Juvenile Procedure.
Giannelli & Yeomans Salvador, Ohio Juvenile Law § 26:7, Contempt.
Giannelli & Yeomans Salvador, Ohio Juvenile Law § 48:4, Contempt.

Notes of Decisions

6. Transactional or use immunity

Trial court did not abuse its discretion at drug trial by refusing to grant defense witness, who testified that defendant was not involved in his sale of drugs to undercover police officer and then invoked his Fifth Amendment rights before he could be cross-examined, immunity from prosecution; trial court lacked authority to grant immunity at defendant's request, immunity for witnesses turning state's evidence typically required testimony implicating, rather than exculpating, defendant, prosecution had no advance knowledge of witness's identity or what his testimony would be, and prosecution did not coerce witness into invoking Fifth Amendment. State v. Perry (Ohio App. 8 Dist., Cuyahoga, 01-06-2005) No. 84397, 2005-Ohio-27, 2005 WL 23357, Unreported, appeal not allowed 105 Ohio St.3d 1564, 828 N.E.2d 118, 2005-Ohio-2447, habeas corpus conditionally granted 619 F.Supp.2d 390. Witnesses ⚷ 304(4)

2945.46 Attendance of witness enforced

Notes of Decisions

1. In general

Confrontation rights, admission of videotaped statement, new criminal rule prohibiting admission of out-of-court statements, retroactivity, postconviction relief, see Danforth v. Minnesota, 2008, 128 S.Ct. 1029.

2945.47 Testimony of prisoners in criminal proceedings

Cross References

Fees and costs, all courts, criminal cases, juvenile cases, and some civil actions related to criminal cases, see 2746.02

2945.481 Deposition of child sex offense victim; presence of defendant; additional depositions; videotaped deposition; admissibility of deposition; televised or recorded testimony

Notes of Decisions

Procedural issues 5
Victim, construed 4

---

2. Right to confront witnesses—In general

Statutory procedures by which defendant's minor daughter testified via closed-circuit camera in physical presence of judge, prosecutor, and defense counsel ensured reliability of adversarial system in prosecution for rape of daughter and did not violate Confrontation Clauses, where defendant and jurors could watch and listen to daughter's responses and observe her demeanor, defense counsel cross-examined daughter and remained in communication with defendant by way of a cell phone, and defense counsel went back into courtroom and conferred in person with defendant before concluding cross-examination and then stated on the record that defendant wished no further inquiry of daughter. State v. Knauff (Ohio App. 4 Dist., Adams, 05-24-2011) No. 10CA900, 2011-Ohio-2725, 2011 WL 2225022, Unreported, appeal not allowed 129 Ohio St.3d 1507, 955 N.E.2d 388, 2011-Ohio-5358, dismissal of post-conviction relief affirmed 2014-Ohio-308, 2014 WL 346691, appeal not allowed 139 Ohio St.3d 1406, 9 N.E.3d 1063, 2014-Ohio-2245. Criminal Law ⚷ 662.65

Allowing four-year-old victim's brother to testify by remote video from outside the courtroom did not violate defendant's right to confront witnesses against him in rape prosecution, where defendant had ample opportunity to cross-examine victim's brother and to see him over the video feed. State v. Lukacs (Ohio App. 1 Dist., 05-28-2010) 188 Ohio App.3d 597, 936 N.E.2d 506, 2010-Ohio-2364, appeal not allowed 126 Ohio St.3d 1599, 935 N.E.2d 45, 2010-Ohio-4928. Criminal Law ⚿ 662.65

Confrontation rights, admission of videotaped statement, new criminal rule prohibiting admission of out-of-court statements, retroactivity, postconviction relief, see Danforth v. Minnesota, 2008, 128 S.Ct. 1029.

3. —— Emotional harm to victim, right to confront witnesses

There is no significant legal distinction between "extreme fear" and "serious emotional trauma, as statutory bases for finding necessity of closed-circuit television testimony by an alleged child sex abuse victim. State v. Knauff (Ohio App. 4 Dist., Adams, 05-24-2011) No. 10CA900, 2011-Ohio-2725, 2011 WL 2225022, Unreported, appeal not allowed 129 Ohio St.3d 1507, 955 N.E.2d 388, 2011-Ohio-5358, dismissal of post-conviction relief affirmed 2014-Ohio-308, 2014 WL 346691, appeal not allowed 139 Ohio St.3d 1406, 9 N.E.3d 1063, 2014-Ohio-2245. Witnesses ⚿ 228

A finding of "extreme fear" meets the minimum showing of emotional trauma, as basis for testimony by alleged child sex abuse victim by way of closed-circuit television, and advances the important public policies of preventing further trauma to the child sex abuse witness and of ensuring reliability of testimonial evidence. State v. Knauff (Ohio App. 4 Dist., Adams, 05-24-2011) No. 10CA900, 2011-Ohio-2725, 2011 WL 2225022, Unreported, appeal not allowed 129 Ohio St.3d 1507, 955 N.E.2d 388, 2011-Ohio-5358, dismissal of post-conviction relief affirmed 2014-Ohio-308, 2014 WL 346691, appeal not allowed 139 Ohio St.3d 1406, 9 N.E.3d 1063, 2014-Ohio-2245. Witnesses ⚿ 228

Permitting child victim to testify outside physical presence of defendant without satisfying statutory requirements for such procedure did not constitute plain error in rape prosecution, where defendant failed to demonstrate that, but for such error, outcome of proceeding would have been different. State v. McConnell (Ohio App. 2 Dist., Montgomery, 08-13-2004) No. 19993, 2004-Ohio-4263, 2004 WL 1802142, Unreported, appeal not allowed 104 Ohio St.3d 1427, 819 N.E.2d 710, 2004-Ohio-6585, appeal not allowed 139 Ohio St.3d 1484, 12 N.E.3d 1230, 2014-Ohio-3195. Criminal Law ⚿ 1036.10

Claim that trial court improperly permitted child victim to testify outside physical presence of rape defendant without satisfying statutory requirements for such procedure could only be reviewed on appeal for plain error, where, at trial, defendant failed to object to victim testifying outside presence of defendant. State v. McConnell (Ohio App. 2 Dist., Montgomery, 08-13-2004) No. 19993, 2004-Ohio-4263, 2004 WL 1802142, Unreported, appeal not allowed 104 Ohio St.3d 1427, 819 N.E.2d 710, 2004-Ohio-6585, appeal not allowed 139 Ohio St.3d 1484, 12 N.E.3d 1230, 2014-Ohio-3195. Criminal Law ⚿ 1036.10

Statutory requirements for permitting child victim to testify outside room in which proceeding is being conducted, that child is unable to communicate about offense because of extreme fear and that there is substantial likelihood that child victim will suffer serious emotional trauma from testifying in physical presence of defendant, were not satisfied in rape prosecution, where child testified that she was scared to see defendant, which made her feel sad, and psychologist testified that if would be difficult for child to testify in front of defendant and that child would suffer emotional trauma if required to testify, but psychologist did not indicate that child would suffer serious emotional trauma. State v. McConnell (Ohio App. 2 Dist., Montgomery, 08-13-2004) No. 19993, 2004-Ohio-4263, 2004 WL 1802142, Unreported, appeal not allowed 104 Ohio St.3d 1427, 819 N.E.2d 710, 2004-Ohio-6585, appeal not allowed 139 Ohio St.3d 1484, 12 N.E.3d 1230, 2014-Ohio-3195. Witnesses ⚿ 228

4. Victim, construed

A child who witnesses the sexual abuse of another child can be a "victim" within the meaning of the statute that permits a court to allow a victim of certain offenses who is under the age of 13 to testify from a room outside the courtroom and to have the testimony televised for viewing by the jury in the courtroom. State v. Lukacs (Ohio App. 1 Dist., 05-28-2010) 188 Ohio App.3d 597, 936 N.E.2d 506, 2010-Ohio-2364, appeal not allowed 126 Ohio St.3d 1599, 935 N.E.2d 45, 2010-Ohio-4928. Witnesses ⚿ 228

5. Procedural issues

Trial court's failure to follow the procedures set forth in statute for determining the necessity of allowing four-year-old victim's brother to testify by remote video from outside the courtroom did not rise to level of plain error in rape prosecution; the findings necessary for allowing testimony by remote video would have been supported by the record. State v. Lukacs (Ohio App. 1 Dist., 05-28-2010) 188 Ohio App.3d 597, 936 N.E.2d 506, 2010-Ohio-2364, appeal not allowed 126 Ohio St.3d 1599, 935 N.E.2d 45, 2010-Ohio-4928. Criminal Law ⚿ 1036.10

2945.49 Testimony of deceased or absent witness; videotaped testimony of child victim

Law Review and Journal Commentaries

Suddenly, everything has changed: The testimonial approach to admission of hearsay statements under Michigan v. Bryant and beyond. Michael Richardson, 80 U. Cin. L. Rev. 945.

Notes of Decisions

2. Admissibility of prior recorded statement—In general

Confrontation rights, admission of videotaped statement, new criminal rule prohibiting admission of out-of-court statements, retroactivity, postconviction relief, see Danforth v. Minnesota, 2008, 128 S.Ct. 1029.

2945.50 Deposition in criminal cases

Law Review and Journal Commentaries

Two windows into innocence. George C. Thomas III, 7 Ohio St. J. Crim. L. 575 (2010).

Notes of Decisions

1. Constitutional issues

Confrontation rights, admission of videotaped statement, new criminal rule prohibiting admission of out-of-court statements, retroactivity, postconviction relief, see Danforth v. Minnesota, 2008, 128 S.Ct. 1029.

2945.53 Right of accused to examine witness

Law Review and Journal Commentaries

The use of secret evidence by government lawyers: balancing defendants' rights with national security concerns. Comment, 52 Clev St L Rev 571 (2004–05).

Notes of Decisions

In general 1

---

1. In general

Any error under confrontation clause in Ohio state court's limitation of defendant's cross–examination of state witness as to charges pending against witness was harmless in capital murder trial; witness was not clearly "key witness," and defendant was still allowed to develop theory that witness was viable suspect in murder. Drummond v. Houk (N.D.Ohio, 12-31-2010) 761 F.Supp.2d 638, affirmed 728 F.3d 520, vacated 134 S.Ct. 1934, 188 L.Ed.2d 957. Criminal Law ⚷ 1168(2)

Ohio state court acted reasonably under confrontation clause in limiting defendant's cross–examination of two state witnesses, with regard to pending charges against witnesses, in capital murder trial; charges against one witnesses had already been dropped at time of his testimony, and charges against other witness were 12 years old at time of his testimony and defendant was aware that prosecutor intended to dismiss those charges based on lack of evidence, so that neither witness had incentive to curry favor with state. Drummond v. Houk (N.D.Ohio, 12-31-2010) 761 F.Supp.2d 638, affirmed 728 F.3d 520, vacated 134 S.Ct. 1934, 188 L.Ed.2d 957. Criminal Law ⚷ 662.7

Confrontation rights, admission of videotaped statement, new criminal rule prohibiting admission of out-of-court statements, retroactivity, postconviction relief, see Danforth v. Minnesota, 2008, 128 S.Ct. 1029.

2945.54 Conduct of examination

Notes of Decisions

In general 1

1. In general

Confrontation rights, admission of videotaped statement, new criminal rule prohibiting admission of out-of-court statements, retroactivity, postconviction relief, see Danforth v. Minnesota, 2008, 128 S.Ct. 1029.

2945.55 Testimony of previous identification

Notes of Decisions

1. Constitutional issues—Due process

In prosecution for interference with commerce by robbery and carrying a firearm in relation to a crime of violence, out-of-court identification made from photo array by manager of store that was robbed was not impermissibly suggestive, as required to establish due process violation in admission of evidence of the identification; detective who conducted the pretrial identification provided a reasonable explanation why the background color of defendant's picture differed from the other pictures used in the array, and the store manager gave no indication that either the color of the background or the fact that defendant's picture was the only one showing both rows of teeth drew her attention to the picture. U.S. v. McComb (C.A.6 (Ohio), 10-03-2007) No. 06-3116, 249 Fed.Appx. 429, 2007 WL 2859743, Unreported, post-conviction relief dismissed 2009 WL 1542741, certificate of appealability denied 2009 WL 2132628. Constitutional Law ⚷ 4658(4); Criminal Law ⚷ 339.7(4)

In prosecution for interference with commerce by robbery and carrying firearm in relation to crime of violence, even if out-of-court identification made from photo array by manager of store that was robbed was impermissibly suggestive, totality of circumstances indicated that identification was sufficiently reliable that there was no due process violation in admission of evidence of identification; store manager testified that at time of robbery, defendant was standing three to four feet from her face, and that she remembered defendant because he exited and re-entered store several times throughout day and she had conversed with him multiple times before robbery began, and manager identified defendant in photo array nearly one month after robbery occurred. U.S. v. McComb (C.A.6 (Ohio), 10-03-2007) No. 06-3116, 249 Fed.Appx. 429, 2007 WL 2859743, Unreported, post-conviction relief dismissed 2009 WL 1542741, certificate of appealability denied 2009 WL 2132628. Constitutional Law ⚷ 4658(4); Criminal Law ⚷ 339.10(9)

Defendant's speedy trial rights were not violated, in prosecution for insurance fraud and falsification; defendant was not in jail pending trial, she waived her right to a speedy trial for five months, and she was granted ten continuances. State v. Hinson (Ohio App. 8 Dist., Cuyahoga, 07-27-2006) No. 87132, 2006-Ohio-3831, 2006 WL 2096589, Unreported, appeal not allowed 112 Ohio St.3d 1421, 859 N.E.2d 559, 2006-Ohio-6712. Criminal Law ⚷ 577.10(8); Criminal Law ⚷ 577.10(9)

Photo array used by police when victim identified defendant was not impermissibly suggestive and did not violate defendant's due process rights, even though defendant argued that he was the only light-skinned African-American in the photo array; victim testified that she concentrated on the eyes of the persons in the array, all of the individuals in the array had braids and facial hair, the victim was shown a array of photos that did not contain defendant's picture and she did not select any of the individuals from that array, victim testified that she clearly saw the intruder's face when his mask fell, and she was definite in her identification. State v. Johnson (Ohio App. 9 Dist., Summit, 03-22-2006) No. 22688, 2006-Ohio-1313, 2006 WL 709044, Unreported, appeal not allowed 110 Ohio St.3d 1442, 852 N.E.2d 190, 2006-Ohio-3862, habeas corpus denied 2008 WL 4452748. Constitutional Law ⚷ 4658(4); Criminal Law ⚷ 339.7(4)

Witness's pre-trial identification of defendant was unnecessarily suggestive, for purposes of determining whether witness's identification of defendant violated due process, where the defendant was the only one in the line-up who was bandaged and dressed in prison clothing. Haliym v. Mitchell (C.A.6 (Ohio), 07-13-2007) 492 F.3d 680, rehearing and rehearing en banc denied. Constitutional Law ⚷ 4658(2); Criminal Law ⚷ 339.8(4)

2. —— Effective assistance of counsel, constitutional issues

Defense counsel did not render ineffective assistance in robbery prosecution by failing to move to suppress victims' pretrial identifications of defendant, even though defendant argued that identifications were unreliable; defendant did not argue that photographic lineup was unduly suggestive, nothing suggested that photographic lineup was unduly suggestive, in that photographs were of young black males with roughly same build, clothing, and haircuts, and victims positively identified defendant at trial. State v. Harris (Ohio App. 2 Dist., Montgomery, 06-30-2004) No. CIV.A. 19796, 2004-Ohio-3570, 2004 WL 1506227, Unreported, appeal not allowed 110 Ohio St.3d 1443, 852

N.E.2d 190, 2006-Ohio-3862, habeas corpus denied 2008 WL 4951789. Criminal Law ⚷ 1930

3. Identification procedure generally

State appellate court's determination that show-up identifications of petitioner were not so suggestive as to create very substantial likelihood of irreparable misidentification was neither contrary to, nor unreasonable application of, clearly established federal law, and, thus, petitioner was not entitled to federal habeas relief on his due process claim; even assuming process by which witnesses observed petitioner while he was standing between two officers and with no other suspects was unduly suggestive, their identification testimony was reliable, in that it was based on clearly witnessing petitioner at crime scene. Gross v. Warden, Lebanon Correctional Inst. (C.A.6 (Ohio), 04-27-2011) No. 08-4727, 426 Fed.Appx. 349, 2011 WL 1597659, Unreported. Habeas Corpus ⚷ 490(2)

Victim's pretrial identifications of defendant and codefendants as perpetrators of aggravated burglary were reliable; although identifications were made several months after crime occurred, victim had good look at codefendant when he was standing inside victim's laundry room with gun, victim saw codefendant again when he was running down driveway, victim saw second codefendant open door of van so that codefendant could get in, victim had good look at defendant when he pointed gun at her, descriptions of defendant and codefendants given by victim were similar to appearances of defendant and codefendants, and victim was certain of her identifications. State v. West (Ohio App. 8 Dist., Cuyahoga, 09-30-2004) No. 83779, 2004-Ohio-5212, 2004 WL 2340180, Unreported, motion for delayed appeal denied 105 Ohio St.3d 1437, 822 N.E.2d 809, 2005-Ohio-531, motion for delayed appeal denied 106 Ohio St.3d 1480, 832 N.E.2d 734, 2005-Ohio-3978, habeas corpus denied 2007 WL 3024459. Criminal Law ⚷ 339.10(11)

Identification process was no more suggestive that typical photographic lineup, and thus, trial court properly declined to suppress first witness's identification testimony in murder prosecution, where police officer's testimony offered no evidence that she purposely left case folder on table when she left room to entice witnesses to view photographs and first witness testified that she joined second witness in squad room after being individually interviewed at police station, that she spotted "lineup pictures" on table nearby after police officer left room, that witnesses were "nosy" and looked through photographs, and that she identified defendant as person she observed on night of shooting. State v. Nix (Ohio App. 1 Dist., Hamilton, 10-15-2004) No. C-030696, 2004-Ohio-5502, 2004 WL 2315035, Unreported, motion for delayed appeal denied 105 Ohio St.3d 1496, 825 N.E.2d 621, 2005-Ohio-1666, habeas corpus denied 2007 WL 2326866. Criminal Law ⚷ 339.10(2)

Victim's out-of-court identification of defendant in "cold stand," or one-on-one show up, was reliable, and thus was admissible in prosecution for aggravated robbery, kidnapping, and having weapon while under disability; victim had sufficient opportunity to view attacker at time of crime, victim's attention was not diverted, his description of man who robbed him was consistent with appearance of defendant at cold stand, victim was certain defendant and his assailant were one and same person, and victim's identification arose from his unaided earlier identification that helped police find defendant. State v. Dowdell (Ohio App. 8 Dist., Cuyahoga, 10-14-2004) No. 83829, 2004-Ohio-5487, 2004 WL 2306678, Unreported, appeal not allowed 105 Ohio St.3d 1441, 822 N.E.2d 812, 2005-Ohio-531, habeas corpus denied 2007 WL 1299269. Criminal Law ⚷ 339.8(5)

Victim's "cold stand" identification of defendant as perpetrator, which was conducted approximately one hour after robbery, was reliable, where victim had sufficient opportunity to view perpetrator at time of robbery, victim's attention was not diverted, victim's description of perpetrator was consistent with defendant's appearance during such show-up identification procedure, and victim was certain that defendant was perpetrator. State v. Lowe (Ohio App. 8 Dist., Cuyahoga, 09-02-2004) No. 82997, 2004-Ohio-4622, 2004 WL 1944785, Unreported, appeal not allowed 104 Ohio St.3d 1461, 821 N.E.2d 578, 2005-Ohio-204, motion to reopen denied 2005-Ohio-5986, 2005 WL 3007146, habeas corpus denied in part, dismissed in part 2008 WL 728365. Criminal Law ⚷ 339.8(6)

Victim's identification of defendant as the burglar was sufficient to support defendant's conviction for burglary, where victim testified that he chased burglar from his home, threw his camera at burglar, who then turned around and met him face-to-face in fairly well lit area. State v. Pesci (Ohio App. 11 Dist., Lake, 12-20-2002) No. 2001-L-026, 2002-Ohio-7131, 2002 WL 31866167, Unreported, appeal not allowed 98 Ohio St.3d 1566, 787 N.E.2d 1231, 2003-Ohio-2242, appeal from denial of post-conviction relief dismissed 2008-Ohio-1660, 2008 WL 919628, denial of post-conviction relief affirmed 2009-Ohio-6385, 2009 WL 4547766. Burglary ⚷ 41(6)

First step of two-step process to determine the admissibility of identification testimony focuses only upon whether the identification procedure was impermissibly suggestive. State v. Williams (Ohio App. 8 Dist., 06-28-2007) 172 Ohio App.3d 646, 876 N.E.2d 991, 2007-Ohio-3266. Criminal Law ⚷ 339.6

Victim's identification of defendant as armed robber was unreliable; victim identified defendant, who was under light, through window of police car from a distance of 20 feet, identification took place approximately two and a half hours after incident, and although victim stated he was "100% certain" of identification, victim's opportunity to view robber was exceedingly short, late at night, and occurred under frightening circumstances since robber held gun to victim's head, victim saw side of robber's face out of corner of his eye and then he saw him from rear as robber was crossing street, and car in which defendant was arrested inconsistent with description given by victim. State v. Williams (Ohio App. 8 Dist., 06-28-2007) 172 Ohio App.3d 646, 876 N.E.2d 991, 2007-Ohio-3266. Criminal Law ⚷ 339.8(6)

Circumstances of show-up identifications of capital murder defendant by two witnesses, in which witnesses, sitting in separate police cars, identified defendant as he stood with his hands behind his back between two officers, although suggestive, were not so suggestive as to create very substantial likelihood of irreparable misidentification, where both witnesses had time to view defendant during commission of crimes, focused their attention on him, described him prior to show-up identification, were confident in their respective identifications, and identified defendant mere hours after witnessing crime. State v. Gross (Ohio, 10-30-2002) 97 Ohio St.3d 121, 776 N.E.2d 1061, 2002-Ohio-5524, reconsideration denied 97 Ohio St.3d 1486, 780 N.E.2d 288, 2002-Ohio-6866, certiorari denied 123 S.Ct. 2079, 538 U.S. 1037, 155 L.Ed.2d 1068, rehearing denied 124 S.Ct. 20, 539 U.S. 976, 156 L.Ed.2d 685, denial of post-conviction relief affirmed 2003-Ohio-6295, 2003 WL 22765845, appeal not allowed 102 Ohio St.3d 1410, 806 N.E.2d 562, 2004-Ohio-1763, certiorari denied 125 S.Ct. 165, 543 U.S. 888, 160 L.Ed.2d 149, dismissal of post-conviction relief affirmed 2006-Ohio-6941, 2006 WL 3804532, appeal not allowed 113 Ohio St.3d 1468, 864 N.E.2d 654, 2007-Ohio-1722, habeas corpus dismissed 2008 WL 4702181, motion to amend denied 2008 WL 4889626, certificate of appealability denied 2008 WL 5190017, affirmed 426 Fed. Appx. 349, 2011 WL 1597659. Criminal Law ⚷ 339.8(5)

Despite impermissibly suggestive pretrial identification procedure in which defendant was by far the youngest participant in five person line-up and dressed in ill-fitting jail jumpsuit, witness's identification of defendant as kidnapper was sufficiently reliable; at trial witness testified that he was working as security guard near intersection where defendant allegedly abducted victim, witness heard woman screaming and saw a man pick her up and throw her into back of van, witness identified defendant as that man, witness was 40 to 150 feet away and was focused on event as it occurred, and witness was able to describe defendant's clothing and appearance of his hair. Jells v. Mitchell (C.A.6 (Ohio), 08-18-2008) 538 F.3d 478, rehearing and rehearing en banc denied, writ denied 2011 WL 1257306. Criminal Law ⚷ 339.8(4); Criminal Law ⚷ 339.10(8)

4. "Impermissibly suggestive" test

Victim's pretrial identification of defendant during one-man show-up was sufficiently reliable to be admissible despite suggestiveness inherent in such identification procedure, even though police officer might have exacerbated inherent suggestiveness when he told victim that he had "a person of interest" at whom he wanted her to look, and victim had not mentioned several pronounced scars on defendant's face when she described robber to officer; officer's remark was no more than a reason for asking victim to look at man in custody, victim simply did not mention defendant's facial scars, and victim promptly and positively identified defendant two hours after incident. State v. Parrish (Ohio App. 2 Dist., Montgomery, 08-11-2006) No. 21206, 2006-Ohio-4161, 2006 WL 2336529, Unreported, motion for delayed appeal denied 112 Ohio St.3d 1417, 859 N.E.2d 557, 2006-Ohio-6712, habeas corpus denied 2008 WL 471543. Criminal Law ⚷ 339.8(6)

Single-photograph identification system used by arresting officer to identify defendant was so impermissibly suggestive as to give rise to substantial likelihood of irreparable misidentification, where officer had limited opportunity to view suspect and was unable to identify his clothing, facial features, or characteristics, and officer's identification of defendant was unreliable under totality of circumstances. State v. Bates (Ohio App. 8 Dist., Cuyahoga, 06-30-2005) No. 84654, 2005-Ohio-3411, 2005 WL 1541008, Unreported, stay granted 106 Ohio St.3d 1530, 835 N.E.2d 380, 2005-Ohio-5146, appeal allowed 107 Ohio St.3d 1422, 837 N.E.2d 1207, 2005-Ohio-6124, appeal dismissed as improvidently granted 110 Ohio St.3d 1230, 850 N.E.2d 1208, 2006-Ohio-3667. Criminal Law ⚷ 339.7(4)

Photographic array from which murder defendant was identified was not impermissibly suggestive or likely to cause irreparable misidentification, even though defendant was the only person in array who was present at scene of fatal shooting; each of four witnesses testified that they observed shooting and the shooter, witnesses described defendant's appearance, three of four witnesses identified defendant by name, and witness's identified defendant's photograph immediately and unequivocally. State v. Cheers (Ohio App. 9 Dist., Lorain, 12-08-2004) No. 04CA008465, 2004-Ohio-6533, 2004 WL 2806345, Unreported, appeal not allowed 105 Ohio St.3d 1501, 825 N.E.2d 624, 2005-Ohio-1666, habeas corpus dismissed 2007 WL 4190463. Criminal Law ⚷ 339.7(3)

Inclusion in photographic lineup from which witness identified burglary defendant of only one individual with reddish blond hair did not render lineup impermissibly suggestive, where two other individuals in lineup had blond hair, and witness further testified that hair color was not basis of his identification of defendant. State v. Elersic (Ohio App. 11 Dist., Lake, 09-30-2004) No. 2002-L-172, 2004-Ohio-5301, 2004 WL 2804809, Unreported, appeal not allowed 105 Ohio St.3d 1407, 821 N.E.2d 1027, 2005-Ohio-279, habeas corpus denied 2008 WL 618647, denial of post-conviction relief affirmed 2008-Ohio-2121, 2008 WL 1932109. Criminal Law ⚷ 339.7(4)

Assuming that photographic lineup from which witness identified burglary defendant was rendered unduly suggestive by inclusion therein of only one individual with reddish blond hair, such suggestiveness did not render identification inadmissible, where witness' identification of defendant was otherwise reliable; witness had opportunity to speak face to face with defendant when defendant attempted to purchase remote control for stolen stereo system from him, witness had been notified by police to be on lookout for individual inquiring about such a remote control, witness' description of defendant was accurate, and witness testified that he was 100 percent certain of his identification. State v. Elersic (Ohio App. 11 Dist., Lake, 09-30-2004) No. 2002-L-172, 2004-Ohio-5301, 2004 WL 2804809, Unreported, appeal not allowed 105 Ohio St.3d 1407, 821 N.E.2d 1027, 2005-Ohio-279, habeas corpus denied 2008 WL 618647, denial of post-conviction relief affirmed 2008-Ohio-2121, 2008 WL 1932109. Criminal Law ⚿ 339.7(4)

Photographic array containing six pictures of African-American men with similar facial features and similar skin tone was not unduly suggestive, even though defendant clearly had long hair; three other men clearly had hair long enough to be braided, the other two men had hair of an indeterminate length, and all men had facial hair. State v. Hayes (Ohio App. 6 Dist., Lucas, 12-03-2004) No. L-03-1221, No. L-03-1222, 2004-Ohio-6460, 2004 WL 2785290, Unreported, appeal not allowed 105 Ohio St.3d 1516, 826 N.E.2d 314, 2005-Ohio-1880, habeas corpus denied 2008 WL 596097. Criminal Law ⚿ 339.7(4)

Photographic array from which victim identified defendant was not impermissibly suggestive, even though defendant argued that other five black males depicted in array differed in complexion and hairstyle; defendant did not stand out as unique in array, and differences in complexion and hairstyle were not so drastic as to render array impermissibly suggestive. State v. Jennings (Ohio App. 9 Dist., Summit, 10-13-2004) No. 22016, 2004-Ohio-5447, 2004 WL 2292776, Unreported, appeal not allowed 105 Ohio St.3d 1441, 822 N.E.2d 812, 2005-Ohio-531, habeas corpus dismissed 2006 WL 2864367, objections overruled 2007 WL 315858. Criminal Law ⚿ 339.7(4)

Murder defendant, an African-American male who wore a mustache and goatee, failed to demonstrate that photographic array was impermissibly suggestive, where array contained photographs of African-American men of approximately the same age with varying styles of short to medium length hair, at least four of the individuals appeared to have some facial hair, and police did not indicate to any of the witnesses whether the suspected killer was included in the array. State v. Taylor (Ohio App. 1 Dist., Hamilton, 03-26-2004) No. C-020475, 2004-Ohio-1494, 2004 WL 596128, Unreported, appeal not allowed 103 Ohio St.3d 1406, 812 N.E.2d 1289, 2004-Ohio-3980, habeas corpus denied 2007 WL 2477705. Criminal Law ⚿ 339.7(4)

Eyewitness identifications of murder defendant were not result of impermissibly suggestive practices, despite investigating detectives' use of "loose" photo of defendant, where eyewitnesses to murder included victim's teen-aged sons, defense counsel had ample opportunity to cross-examine these witnesses, at least one witness stated he was familiar with defendant from the neighborhood and knew him by his "street name," witnesses were able to identify defendant when presented with his picture in addition to describing his general appearance on night in question, and two witnesses testified that they had seen defendant in neighborhood prior to the night of the murder. State v. Crosby (Ohio App. 8 Dist., Cuyahoga, 12-31-2003) No. 81779, 2003-Ohio-7236, 2003 WL 23095998, Unreported, appeal not allowed 103 Ohio St.3d 1404, 812 N.E.2d 1287, 2004-Ohio-3980, motion to reopen denied 2005-Ohio-5684, 2005 WL 2789454, habeas corpus dismissed 2007 WL 838062, subsequent determination 2007 WL 1299238, habeas corpus dismissed 2013 WL 1773820. Criminal Law ⚿ 339.7(3)

Victim's pretrial identification of defendant as burglar he chased from his home was not unnecessarily suggestive and prejudicial, even though confrontation was at night, victim could not identify object burglar carried, and his description to police did not mention facial stubble and indicated that burglar's age was 12 years younger than defendant's age, considering that victim had face-to-face encounter under streetlight, victim's description matched defendant's height, weight, clothing, and hair color, identification occurred without any encouragement from officers and within two hours of crime, and victim stated he was "100% sure" defendant was burglar. State v. Pesci (Ohio App. 11 Dist., Lake, 12-20-2002) No. 2001-L-026, 2002-Ohio-7131, 2002 WL 31866167, Unreported, appeal not allowed 98 Ohio St.3d 1566, 787 N.E.2d 1231, 2003-Ohio-2242, appeal from denial of post-conviction relief dismissed 2008-Ohio-1660, 2008 WL 919628, denial of post-conviction relief affirmed 2009-Ohio-6385, 2009 WL 4547766. Criminal Law ⚿ 339.8(6)

One-on-one showup employed by police to identify robbery defendant was not unduly suggestive and thus victim's identification of defendant as robber was admissible, where victim, who was a taxi cab driver, had clearly viewed his passengers at the time they requested the cab ride and during the ride, at which times they were in proximity to driver, driver identified defendant as one of the robbers shortly after driver was robbed, and driver testified that there was no hesitation in his mind that he had properly identified defendant. State v. Sargent (Ohio App. 1 Dist., 12-22-2006) 169 Ohio App.3d 679, 864 N.E.2d 155, 2006-Ohio-6823, appeal not allowed 113 Ohio St.3d 1491, 865 N.E.2d 915, 2007-Ohio-1986. Criminal Law ⚿ 339.8(6)

6. Photo array

Even assuming that pretrial identification process, in which witnesses identified murder defendant from a photo array, was unduly suggestive, the witnesses' identifications were reliable under the totality of the circumstances; the five witnesses testified that they each had a clear, unobstructed view of defendant when they saw his face, each witness was certain of his or her identification of defendant as the perpetrator, and each of the witnesses identified defendant within two weeks of the crime, several within 48 hours of the crime. State v. Villa (Ohio App. 9 Dist., Lorain, 09-05-2006) No. 05CA008773, 2006-Ohio-4529, 2006 WL 2527964, Unreported, appeal not allowed 112 Ohio St.3d 1445, 860 N.E.2d 768, 2007-Ohio-152, certiorari denied 127 S.Ct. 2885, 550 U.S. 973, 167 L.Ed.2d 1159, appeal not allowed 114 Ohio St.3d 1428, 868 N.E.2d 681, 2007-Ohio-2904, dismissal of post-conviction relief affirmed 2009-Ohio-5055, 2009 WL 3068397, habeas corpus denied 2012 WL 1435725. Criminal Law ⚷ 339.10(8)

Pretrial identification process, in which witnesses identified defendant from a photo array, was not unduly suggestive; photo array contained six photos, each individual in the array appeared to have been in the same age range as defendant and the same ethnicity, and while the lighting in defendant's photo was different, such was true of all of the photos. State v. Villa (Ohio App. 9 Dist., Lorain, 09-05-2006) No. 05CA008773, 2006-Ohio-4529, 2006 WL 2527964, Unreported, appeal not allowed 112 Ohio St.3d 1445, 860 N.E.2d 768, 2007-Ohio-152, certiorari denied 127 S.Ct. 2885, 550 U.S. 973, 167 L.Ed.2d 1159, appeal not allowed 114 Ohio St.3d 1428, 868 N.E.2d 681, 2007-Ohio-2904, dismissal of post-conviction relief affirmed 2009-Ohio-5055, 2009 WL 3068397, habeas corpus denied 2012 WL 1435725. Criminal Law ⚷ 339.7(4)

Pretrial identification procedure involving photographic lineup was not unduly suggestive, where police officer selected computer-produced photographs that most closely resembled defendant and arranged them in six-picture photospread, read to victim standard instructions on viewing photospread, which included admonition that picture of perpetrator might or might not be included in photospread, and did not tell victim who to select or even suggest that perpetrator was included in photospread, and victim immediately identified defendant as perpetrator. State v. Parrish (Ohio App. 2 Dist., Montgomery, 08-11-2006) No. 21206, 2006-Ohio-4161, 2006 WL 2336529, Unreported, motion for delayed appeal denied 112 Ohio St.3d 1417, 859 N.E.2d 557, 2006-Ohio-6712, habeas corpus denied 2008 WL 471543. Criminal Law ⚷ 339.7(3); Criminal Law ⚷ 339.7(4)

For purposes of determining admissibility of out-of-court identification of defendant by arresting officer, officer's identification of defendant through single-photograph identification system was unreliable, where officer failed to identify defendant in their first face-to-face encounter, prior to out-of-court identification at issue, and was in possession of additional information suggesting that defendant was perpetrator at time of out-of-court identification, defendant and his identical twin brother were depicted in photograph found in vehicle allegedly abandoned by defendant, officer did not testify that defendant resembled his twin, two black males were observed in vehicle, and less suggestive identification procedure was available. State v. Bates (Ohio App. 8 Dist., Cuyahoga, 06-30-2005) No. 84654, 2005-Ohio-3411, 2005 WL 1541008, Unreported, stay granted 106 Ohio St.3d 1530, 835 N.E.2d 380, 2005-Ohio-5146, appeal allowed 107 Ohio St.3d 1422, 837 N.E.2d 1207, 2005-Ohio-6124, appeal dismissed as improvidently granted 110 Ohio St.3d 1230, 850 N.E.2d 1208, 2006-Ohio-3667. Criminal Law ⚷ 339.7(4)

For purposes of determining admissibility of out-of-court identification of defendant by arresting officer, single-photograph identification system used by officer to identify defendant was unduly suggestive; officer testified that he had had limited opportunity to observe suspect, suspect escaped, and there were two black males in vehicle chased by him, and that at time suspect exited vehicle, officer was 25 to 35 feet away from him and could not identify his clothing, facial features, or characteristics. State v. Bates (Ohio App. 8 Dist., Cuyahoga, 06-30-2005) No. 84654, 2005-Ohio-3411, 2005 WL 1541008, Unreported, stay granted 106 Ohio St.3d 1530, 835 N.E.2d 380, 2005-Ohio-5146, appeal allowed 107 Ohio St.3d 1422, 837 N.E.2d 1207, 2005-Ohio-6124, appeal dismissed as improvidently granted 110 Ohio St.3d 1230, 850 N.E.2d 1208, 2006-Ohio-3667. Criminal Law ⚷ 339.7(4)

Evidence was sufficient to support defendant's conviction for aggravated robbery; eyewitness identified defendant before trial in photographic array, eyewitness testified at trial that she saw defendant walking on sidewalk outside store, that she then saw defendant enter store and walk to the end of the service counter, during which time eyewitness was able to see defendant's face for about 20 to 30 seconds without any obstructions, and eyewitness testified that defendant pulled gun and ordered eyewitness to get on the ground, at which point eyewitness heard defendant open two cash drawers and complain about how little money was there. State v. Tonn (Ohio App. 2 Dist., Greene, 04-29-2005) No. 2004-CA-36, No. 2004-CA-37, 2005-Ohio-2021, 2005 WL 994692, Unreported, denial of post-conviction relief affirmed 2010-Ohio-385, 2010 WL 415416. Robbery ⚷ 24.40

That eyewitness to robbery misidentified defendant's eye color and erroneously stated that defendant had freckles on her forehead did not render her pretrial identification of defendant from photographic array unreliable, where eyewitness testified at trial that she had an unobstructed view of defendant at the crime scene for 20 to 30 seconds and was "one hundred and twenty percent" sure defendant had robbed her. State v. Tonn (Ohio App. 2 Dist., Greene, 04-29-2005) No. 2004-CA-36, No. 2004-CA-37, 2005-Ohio-2021, 2005 WL 994692, Unreported, denial of post-conviction relief affirmed 2010-Ohio-385, 2010 WL 415416. Criminal Law ⚷ 339.7(1)

Victim's pretrial identification of defendant from an allegedly suggestive photographic array was reliable, even though victim was not able to see robber's entire face during robbery and four months had elapsed between time of robbery and the identification; victim looked at robber during entire holdup, which lasted 30 to 60 seconds, victim described robber as a large African-American man with long hair, which accurately described defendant, victim was very certain that defendant was robber, and victim identified defendant in under 30 seconds. State v. Hayes (Ohio App. 6 Dist., Lucas, 12-03-2004) No. L-03-1221, No. L-03-1222, 2004-Ohio-6460, 2004 WL 2785290, Unreported, appeal not allowed 105 Ohio St.3d 1516, 826 N.E.2d 314, 2005-Ohio-1880, habeas corpus denied 2008 WL 596097. Criminal Law ⚿ 339.7(3)

Evidence supported defendant's convictions for aggravated murder and complicity of murder; although witness failed to identify defendant in photographic array immediately following shooting, witness identified defendant from photographic array several months after shooting as person holding gun at time of murder, eyewitness made positive identification of defendant's codefendant shortly after shooting, and defendant testified he was with codefendant on night of shooting. State v. Sailor (Ohio App. 8 Dist., Cuyahoga, 09-30-2004) No. 83552, 2004-Ohio-5207, 2004 WL 2340113, Unreported, appeal not allowed 105 Ohio St.3d 1464, 824 N.E.2d 92, 2005-Ohio-1024, habeas corpus denied 2007 WL 4248182, motion to amend denied 2008 WL 1752147. Homicide ⚿ 1181

Witness's in-court identification of defendant as shooter was reliable and admissible in murder prosecution; although witness failed to identify defendant in photographic array immediately following shooting, witness had opportunity to view defendant at time of shooting, witness accurately described defendant to police, witness identified defendant from photographic array several months after shooting, and witness spoke to detective upon seeing defendant in courtroom to identify defendant as the shooter. State v. Sailor (Ohio App. 8 Dist., Cuyahoga, 09-30-2004) No. 83552, 2004-Ohio-5207, 2004 WL 2340113, Unreported, appeal not allowed 105 Ohio St.3d 1464, 824 N.E.2d 92, 2005-Ohio-1024, habeas corpus denied 2007 WL 4248182, motion to amend denied 2008 WL 1752147. Criminal Law ⚿ 339.9(3)

Identification of defendant by victim from photographic array was not so unreliable as to give rise to very substantial likelihood of irreparable misidentification, as required for reversal based on allegedly impermissibly suggestive identification procedure given that victim identified defendant at trial; victim had ample opportunity to view defendant both during and after attack, victim provided police with accurate description of defendant's race, height, weight, age, hair length, hair color, skin tone, and complexion, victim identified defendant from array within seconds, and only four days had passed between attack and presentation of array. State v. Jennings (Ohio App. 9 Dist., Summit, 10-13-2004) No. 22016, 2004-Ohio-5447, 2004 WL 2292776, Unreported, appeal not allowed 105 Ohio St.3d 1441, 822 N.E.2d 812, 2005-Ohio-531, habeas corpus dismissed 2006 WL 2864367, objections overruled 2007 WL 315858. Criminal Law ⚿ 339.10(8); Criminal Law ⚿ 339.10(10)

Circumstances of out-of-court identifications of capital murder defendant by juvenile eyewitnesses were not unduly suggestive, despite defendant's contention that state subjected juveniles to numerous viewings of defendant or defendant's photograph before photographic arrays and in-court identifications; investigators showed juveniles between 30 and 100 photographs, made no suggestions or comments to juveniles, did not rush them, and did not tell them whether they had chosen defendant's photograph, and any encounters juveniles might have had with media reports or with defendant in courtroom went to weight to be given identifications rather than their admissibility. State v. Gross (Ohio, 10-30-2002) 97 Ohio St.3d 121, 776 N.E.2d 1061, 2002-Ohio-5524, reconsideration denied 97 Ohio St.3d 1486, 780 N.E.2d 288, 2002-Ohio-6866, certiorari denied 123 S.Ct. 2079, 538 U.S. 1037, 155 L.Ed.2d 1068, rehearing denied 124 S.Ct. 20, 539 U.S. 976, 156 L.Ed.2d 685, denial of post-conviction relief affirmed 2003-Ohio-6295, 2003 WL 22765845, appeal not allowed 102 Ohio St.3d 1410, 806 N.E.2d 562, 2004-Ohio-1763, certiorari denied 125 S.Ct. 165, 543 U.S. 888, 160 L.Ed.2d 149, dismissal of post-conviction relief affirmed 2006-Ohio-6941, 2006 WL 3804532, appeal not allowed 113 Ohio St.3d 1468, 864 N.E.2d 654, 2007-Ohio-1722, habeas corpus dismissed 2008 WL 4702181, motion to amend denied 2008 WL 4889626, certificate of appealability denied 2008 WL 5190017, affirmed 426 Fed.Appx. 349, 2011 WL 1597659. Criminal Law ⚿ 339.7(4)

Pretrial procedure during which eyewitness identified defendant in a photographic array was not unduly suggestive, as could warrant exclusion of eyewitness's in-court identification of defendant as the shooter, in capital murder trial; even if the identification was unreliable, since eyewitness was in the hospital on morphine at the time of the initial pretrial identification, the police in no way suggested that any of the particular persons in the six-photo array were involved in the shooting, and eyewitness identified defendant's photo in three separate identifications. Cornwell v. Bradshaw (C.A.6 (Ohio), 03-11-2009) 559 F.3d 398, rehearing and rehearing en banc denied, certiorari denied 130 S.Ct. 1141, 558 U.S. 1151, 175 L.Ed.2d 978. Criminal Law ⚿ 339.7(3)

Photo arrays from which witness identified petitioner as person she had seen chasing intended third victim from scene of double murder were not impermissibly suggestive; mere fact that petitioner's photo contained writing in different colored ink than other photos was immaterial, depiction of petitioner in two different arrays was not impermissible, since different photos were used, and variations in age and facial hair were not so great that witness's attention necessarily and unavoidably would have been focused on petitioner's photo. Davie v. Mitchell (N.D.Ohio, 08-06-2003) 291 F.Supp.2d 573, motion to amend denied, certificate of appealability granted in part, denied in part 324 F.Supp.2d 862, affirmed 547 F.3d 297, rehearing and rehearing en banc denied, certiorari denied 130

S.Ct. 503, 558 U.S. 996, 175 L.Ed.2d 357. Criminal Law ⚷ 339.7(4)

PROOF

2945.59 Proof of defendant's motive

Notes of Decisions

Photographs 34.5

---

9. Admissibility of prior acts—In general

Probation officer's testimony during murder trial, in which he stated that defendant was subject to numerous conditions as part of his probation and that defendant's conduct prior to the murder was in violation of these conditions, violated the general rule against other bad acts evidence; assuming probation officer's testimony did show that defendant had a guilty conscience about going to a bar, about drinking alcoholic beverages, and about being in the presence of illegal drugs, these things had nothing to do with his criminal state of mind regarding the murder. State v. Anderson (Ohio App. 7 Dist., Mahoning, 09-01-2006) No. 03MA252, 2006-Ohio-4618, 2006 WL 2573785, Unreported, appeal not allowed 112 Ohio St.3d 1443, 860 N.E.2d 767, 2007-Ohio-152. Criminal Law ⚷ 368.28

For prior acts evidence to be admissible, there must be substantial evidence that the accused committed the act. State v. Moore (Ohio App. 8 Dist., 05-03-2012) 970 N.E.2d 1098, 2012-Ohio-1958, appeal not allowed 133 Ohio St.3d 1413, 975 N.E.2d 1030, 2012-Ohio-4650, appeal after new sentencing hearing 24 N.E.3d 1197, 2014-Ohio-5135, cause dismissed 141 Ohio St.3d 1433, 23 N.E.3d 1178, 2015-Ohio-168, stay denied 141 Ohio St.3d 1452, 23 N.E.3d 1195, 2015-Ohio-239. Criminal Law ⚷ 374.20(2)

For prior acts evidence to be admissible, the evidence must be relevant to proving the guilt of the offense in question. State v. Moore (Ohio App. 8 Dist., 05-03-2012) 970 N.E.2d 1098, 2012-Ohio-1958, appeal not allowed 133 Ohio St.3d 1413, 975 N.E.2d 1030, 2012-Ohio-4650, appeal after new sentencing hearing 24 N.E.3d 1197, 2014-Ohio-5135, cause dismissed 141 Ohio St.3d 1433, 23 N.E.3d 1178, 2015-Ohio-168, stay denied 141 Ohio St.3d 1452, 23 N.E.3d 1195, 2015-Ohio-239. Criminal Law ⚷ 368.9

To be admissible, the other acts evidence must tend to show by substantial proof one or more of motive, opportunity, intent, preparation, plan, knowledge, identity, or absence of mistake or accident. State v. Blankenburg (Ohio App. 12 Dist., 03-26-2012) 197 Ohio App.3d 201, 966 N.E.2d 958, 2012-Ohio-1289, appeal not allowed 132 Ohio St.3d 1514, 974 N.E.2d 112, 2012-Ohio-4021, denial of post-conviction relief reversed 2012-Ohio-6175, 2012 WL 6738255. Criminal Law ⚷ 368.4

Other-acts evidence that defendant swung a board at a third party after assaulting victim was admissible at a trial for felonious assault as inextricably related to or within the context and circumstances of the charged offense, where the third party intervened in the assault of victim by defendant, defendant responded by picking up a board and swinging it at the third party, and less than five minutes later, a law enforcement officer arrived at the scene and saw defendant with the board still in his hand. State v. Perkins (Ohio App. 2 Dist., 10-22-2010) 191 Ohio App.3d 263, 945 N.E.2d 1083, 2010-Ohio-5161. Criminal Law ⚷ 368.75

Statutory list of proper purposes for which evidence of other crimes, wrongs, or acts may be admissible is not exclusive; and, evidence of other crimes, wrongs or acts may be admissible for any purpose material to the issue of guilt or innocence, as long as it is not being introduced for the purpose of showing the accused's propensity to commit bad acts. State v. Boles (Ohio App. 2 Dist., 01-29-2010) 187 Ohio App.3d 345, 932 N.E.2d 345, 2010-Ohio-278, appeal not allowed 125 Ohio St.3d 1448, 927 N.E.2d 1128, 2010-Ohio-2510, appeal not allowed 126 Ohio St.3d 1619, 935 N.E.2d 856, 2010-Ohio-5101. Criminal Law ⚷ 368.4; Criminal Law ⚷ 368.5

Admissibility of other acts evidence is carefully limited because of the substantial danger that the jury will convict the defendant solely because it assumes that the defendant has a propensity to commit criminal acts, or deserves punishment regardless of whether he or she committed the crime charged in the indictment. State v. Kaufman (Ohio App. 7 Dist., 03-31-2010) 187 Ohio App.3d 50, 931 N.E.2d 143, 2010-Ohio-1536, appeal not allowed 126 Ohio St.3d 1546, 932 N.E.2d 340, 2010-Ohio-3855. Criminal Law ⚷ 368.1

10. —— Identity, admissibility of prior acts

Evidence that three digital scales were found in defendant's home when a search warrant was executed two weeks after his arrest for trafficking in crack cocaine was admissible as "other act" evidence to show identity, plan, or intent to engage in drug trafficking. State v. Lather (Ohio App. 6 Dist., 05-18-2007) 171 Ohio App.3d 708, 872 N.E.2d 991, 2007-Ohio-2399, stay denied 114 Ohio St.3d 1470, 870 N.E.2d 165, 2007-Ohio-3616, appeal not allowed 115 Ohio St.3d 1423, 874 N.E.2d 539, 2007-Ohio-5056. Criminal Law ⚷ 371.33; Criminal Law ⚷ 372.33; Criminal Law ⚷ 373.22

11. —— Propensity, admissibility of prior acts

Witness' testimony that he had seen defendant "in the past," with revolver was "other crimes" evidence that was not offered for any permissible purpose but merely showed defendant's propensity to commit charged aggravated murder and aggravated robbery; reference to revolver was due to speculation that, because no bullet casings were recovered from crime scene, gun used was revolver, no revolver was ever recovered, there was no connection between witness' revolver that was admitted into evidence and crime, and there was no evidence that defendant possessed revolver either on night of shooting or any time near shooting. State v. Williams (Ohio App. 8 Dist., Cuyahoga, 10-27-2011) No. 95796, 2011-Ohio-5483, 2011 WL 5116501, Unreported. Criminal Law ⚷ 368.28; Criminal Law ⚷ 368.36

Rule and statute prohibiting admission of other acts evidence to prove the character of a person to show that the person acted in conformity with his character on a particular occasion, but allowing admission of it to prove motive, opportunity, intent, preparation, plan, knowledge, identity, or absence of mistake or accident, do not require that the other acts be similar to the crime charged, as long as the prior act tends to show one of the enumerated factors. State v. Blankenburg (Ohio App. 12 Dist., 03-26-2012) 197 Ohio App.3d 201, 966 N.E.2d 958, 2012-Ohio-1289, appeal not allowed 132 Ohio St.3d 1514, 974 N.E.2d 112, 2012-Ohio-4021, denial of post-conviction relief reversed 2012-Ohio-6175, 2012 WL 6738255. Criminal Law ⚷ 368.4; Criminal Law ⚷ 373.8

The trial court has broad discretion with regard to admission of other acts evidence under rule and statute prohibiting admission of other acts evidence to prove the character of a person to show that the person acted in conformity with his character on a particular occasion, but allowing admission of it to prove motive, opportunity, intent, preparation, plan, knowledge, identity, or absence of mistake or accident, and under the rape shield law, where applicable; a reviewing court should not disturb evidentiary decisions in the absence of an abuse of discretion that has created material prejudice. State v. Blankenburg (Ohio App. 12 Dist., 03-26-2012) 197 Ohio App.3d 201, 966 N.E.2d 958, 2012-Ohio-1289, appeal not allowed 132 Ohio St.3d 1514, 974 N.E.2d 112, 2012-Ohio-4021, denial of post-conviction relief reversed 2012-Ohio-6175, 2012 WL 6738255. Criminal Law ⚷ 368.2; Criminal Law ⚷ 1153.5

In prosecution for ten counts of trafficking in drugs based on defendant physician's alleged conduct in illegally prescribing drugs to three patients, evidence that defendant engaged in the same wrongful conduct when he treated over 200 other patients was inadmissible other-acts evidence; evidence was not probative of whether defendant knowingly failed to act in accordance with law when treating the three patients, but merely portrayed conforming conduct to demonstrate a propensity to commit the crimes charged. State v. Nucklos (Ohio App. 2 Dist., 03-09-2007) 171 Ohio App.3d 38, 869 N.E.2d 674, 2007-Ohio-1025, appeal allowed 114 Ohio St.3d 1507, 872 N.E.2d 949, 2007-Ohio-4285, reconsideration denied 115 Ohio St.3d 1445, 875 N.E.2d 104, 2007-Ohio-5567, affirmed 121 Ohio St.3d 332, 904 N.E.2d 512, 2009-Ohio-792. Criminal Law ⚷ 368.21

Evidence that a loaded shotgun was found in defendant physician's office was not "extrinsic" to his alleged offense of trafficking in drugs, for purposes of requirement that extrinsic acts not be used to suggest that the accused has the propensity to act in a certain manner; although defendant did not use the loaded shotgun to write the prescriptions for patients, shotgun was in defendant's office while those patients were examined and treated, such that it was not separated by time and space from the criminal offenses. State v. Nucklos (Ohio App. 2 Dist., 03-09-2007) 171 Ohio App.3d 38, 869 N.E.2d 674, 2007-Ohio-1025, appeal allowed 114 Ohio St.3d 1507, 872 N.E.2d 949, 2007-Ohio-4285, reconsideration denied 115 Ohio St.3d 1445, 875 N.E.2d 104, 2007-Ohio-5567, affirmed 121 Ohio St.3d 332, 904 N.E.2d 512, 2009-Ohio-792. Criminal Law ⚷ 368.78

12. —— Remoteness, admissibility of prior acts

"Other acts" testimony concerning defendant's sexual abuse of two young boys was inadmissible during prosecution for, inter alia, unlawful sexual conduct with a minor and rape; the other acts admitted during defendant's case occurred over ten years before the acts alleged in the indictment, and thus, they were not inextricably related to the crimes charged, and were chronologically and factually separate occurrences. State v. Miley (Ohio App. 5 Dist., Richland, 09-08-2006) No. 2005-CA-67, No. 2006-CA-14, 2006-Ohio-4670, 2006 WL 2589816, Unreported, appeal not allowed 112 Ohio St.3d 1420, 859 N.E.2d 558, 2006-Ohio-6712, appeal after new trial 2009-Ohio-570, 2009 WL 321192. Criminal Law ⚷ 368.63; Criminal Law ⚷ 373.21

For prior acts evidence to be admissible, the prior act must not be too remote and must be closely related in time and nature to the offense charged; if the act is too distant in time or too removed in method or type, it has no permissible value. State v. Moore (Ohio App. 8 Dist., 05-03-2012) 970 N.E.2d 1098, 2012-Ohio-1958, appeal not allowed 133 Ohio St.3d 1413, 975 N.E.2d 1030, 2012-Ohio-4650, appeal after new sentencing hearing 24 N.E.3d 1197, 2014-Ohio-5135, cause dismissed 141 Ohio St.3d 1433, 23 N.E.3d 1178, 2015-Ohio-168, stay denied 141 Ohio St.3d 1452, 23 N.E.3d 1195, 2015-Ohio-239. Criminal Law ⚷ 373.8; Criminal Law ⚷ 373.15; Criminal Law ⚷ 373.20; Criminal Law ⚷ 373.21

To be admissible, prior acts must not be too remote and must be closely related in nature, time, and place to the offense charged. State v. Goodson (Ohio App. 8 Dist., 02-17-2011) 192 Ohio App.3d 246, 948 N.E.2d 988, 2011-Ohio-722, appeal not allowed 128 Ohio St.3d 1557, 949 N.E.2d 43,

2011-Ohio-2905, on reconsideration 130 Ohio St.3d 82, 955 N.E.2d 982, 2011-Ohio-4729, on remand 2011-Ohio-5820, 2011 WL 5506083. Criminal Law ⚷ 373.8; Criminal Law ⚷ 373.21

13. —— Absence of mistake or accident, admissibility of prior acts

Evidence of prior convictions for arson and domestic violence was relevant to show intent, absence of mistake or accident, or defendant's scheme, plan, or system in committing instant aggravated arson and domestic violence; in prior arson, defendant had set fire to clothing belonging to his wife and children, no accelerant was used in either fire, smoke detectors had been disabled in both fires, and alleged victim was same in both incidents of domestic assault. State v. Sines (Ohio App. 5 Dist., Stark, 04-17-2006) No. 2005CA00181, 2006-Ohio-1956, 2006 WL 1044445, Unreported. Criminal Law ⚷ 373.12; Criminal Law ⚷ 373.13; Criminal Law ⚷ 373.14; Criminal Law ⚷ 373.15

14. —— Scheme, plan or system, admissibility of prior acts

Evidence that defendant had previously engaged in oral sex with another 16-year-old boy was inadmissible to show intent, in prosecution for rape, unlawful sexual conduct with a minor, kidnapping, and gross sexual imposition; defendant's consensual sexual relationship with a boy 12 years prior to the alleged abuse in the case did not demonstrate defendant's purpose to achieve sexual gratification with victim. State v. Williams (Ohio App. 8 Dist., 11-03-2011) 195 Ohio App.3d 807, 961 N.E.2d 1200, 2011-Ohio-5650, appeal allowed 131 Ohio St.3d 1472, 962 N.E.2d 803, 2012-Ohio-896, reversed 134 Ohio St.3d 521, 983 N.E.2d 1278, 2012-Ohio-5695, reconsideration granted 133 Ohio St.3d 1512, 979 N.E.2d 1290, 2012-Ohio-6209, on remand 2013-Ohio-4471, 2013 WL 5603592. Criminal Law ⚷ 371.49

Evidence that defendant had previously engaged in oral sex with another 16-year-old boy was inadmissible to show defendant's "scheme, plan, or system," in prosecution for rape, unlawful sexual conduct with a minor, kidnapping, and gross sexual imposition; the State never claimed that the perpetrator's identity was at issue, and the sexual acts with the other boy were not a background act that formed the foundation of the crime charged, as they occurred more than a decade before the alleged abuse at issue, and, therefore, they were chronologically and factually separate occurrences. State v. Williams (Ohio App. 8 Dist., 11-03-2011) 195 Ohio App.3d 807, 961 N.E.2d 1200, 2011-Ohio-5650, appeal allowed 131 Ohio St.3d 1472, 962 N.E.2d 803, 2012-Ohio-896, reversed 134 Ohio St.3d 521, 983 N.E.2d 1278, 2012-Ohio-5695, reconsideration granted 133 Ohio St.3d 1512, 979 N.E.2d 1290, 2012-Ohio-6209, on remand 2013-Ohio-4471, 2013 WL 5603592. Criminal Law ⚷ 370.25

Witness's testimony, regarding alleged other acts of sexual imposition committed by defendant, was admissible to prove defendant's motive, plan, scheme or opportunity to commit gross sexual imposition and sexual imposition against victim; witness's testimony was reasonably offered to prove defendant's motive to inappropriately touch younger woman for purpose of sexual gratification, defendant's touchings of witness and victim were both accompanied by comments about women's breasts, and witness's testimony served to prove defendant's plan and opportunity. State v. Guenther (Ohio App. 9 Dist., Lorain, 02-22-2006) No. 05CA008663, 2006-Ohio-767, 2006 WL 401309, Unreported, appeal not allowed 110 Ohio St.3d 1412, 850 N.E.2d 73, 2006-Ohio-3306, denial of post-conviction relief affirmed in part, reversed in part 2007-Ohio-681, 2007 WL 507064. Criminal Law ⚷ 371.22; Criminal Law ⚷ 371.49

Probative value of evidence that defendant sexually abused his biological daughters, which was relevant to prove pattern of conduct, was not substantially outweighed by possibility of unfair prejudice in rape prosecution in which step-daughter was victim. State v. Russell (Ohio App. 8 Dist., Cuyahoga, 09-23-2004) No. 83699, 2004-Ohio-5031, 2004 WL 2340125, Unreported, appeal not allowed 105 Ohio St.3d 1452, 823 N.E.2d 457, 2005-Ohio-763, motion to reopen denied 2005-Ohio-2998, 2005 WL 1406347, appeal not allowed 106 Ohio St.3d 1537, 835 N.E.2d 384, 2005-Ohio-5146, habeas corpus dismissed 2008 WL 2600006. Criminal Law ⚷ 338(7)

Evidence that defendant sexually abused his biological daughters was admissible in rape prosecution in which step-daughter was victim to prove defendant's pattern of conduct, where state showed that defendant chose females of filial position to him who were under age of 12 and that defendant began touching them in progressively sexual manner. State v. Russell (Ohio App. 8 Dist., Cuyahoga, 09-23-2004) No. 83699, 2004-Ohio-5031, 2004 WL 2340125, Unreported, appeal not allowed 105 Ohio St.3d 1452, 823 N.E.2d 457, 2005-Ohio-763, motion to reopen denied 2005-Ohio-2998, 2005 WL 1406347, appeal not allowed 106 Ohio St.3d 1537, 835 N.E.2d 384, 2005-Ohio-5146, habeas corpus dismissed 2008 WL 2600006. Criminal Law ⚷ 370.25; Criminal Law ⚷ 373.10; Criminal Law ⚷ 373.13

Trial court did not abuse its discretion in drug prosecution by admitting evidence of defendant's prior involvement with drugs as evidence of a " common scheme or plan," where a defense strategy was to question whether detective focused a drug investigation on defendant only because detective previously had attempted unsuccessfully to have defendant prosecuted. State v. Washington (Ohio App. 8 Dist., Cuyahoga, 10-24-2002) No. 80418, 2002-Ohio-5834, 2002 WL 31401558, Unreported, appeal not allowed 98 Ohio St.3d 1491, 785 N.E.2d 473, 2003-Ohio-1189, dismissal of habeas corpus affirmed 101 Ohio St.3d 131, 802 N.E.2d 655, 2004-Ohio-298, appeal not allowed 102 Ohio St.3d 1413, 806 N.E.2d 564, 2004-Ohio-1763, habeas corpus denied 2007 WL 1592088. Criminal Law ⚷ 370.9

Other bad acts evidence, in form of testimony of defendant's daughter that defendant had locked up and restrained daughter during daughter's childhood, was admissible in unlawful restraint and kidnapping prosecution arising out of defendant's placement of chain and padlock around defendant's son's ankle; evidence was offered to rebut defendant's argument that her intent had not been to restrain son but to simply communicate with him and influence his behavior. State v. Hornschemeier (Ohio App. 1 Dist., 06-27-2012) 973 N.E.2d 779, 2012-Ohio-2860, appeal not allowed 133 Ohio St.3d 1426, 976 N.E.2d 915, 2012-Ohio-4902. Criminal Law ⚷ 371.42; Criminal Law ⚷ 372.56

Evidence of defendant's previous threat to his wife, that he would burn her house down if she ever left, and defendant's solicitation of third party to burn his wife's car and trailer were admissible to show defendant's motive, intent, plan, and identity in prosecution for aggravated arson. State v. Holdcroft (Ohio App. 3 Dist., 07-02-2012) 973 N.E.2d 334, 2012-Ohio-3066, appeal allowed 133 Ohio St.3d 1410, 975 N.E.2d 1029, 2012-Ohio-4650, reversed 137 Ohio St.3d 526, 1 N.E.3d 382, 2013-Ohio-5014. Criminal Law ⚷ 368.17

Statute under which State may introduce evidence of other acts to establish motive or intent, the absence of mistake or accident, or the defendant's scheme, plan, or system even if such evidence may show or tend to show the commission of another crime is to be strictly construed against the state, and to be conservatively applied by a trial court; thus, evidence of other acts may be admissible if the evidence is offered for a purpose other than to show the accused's propensity to act in conformity with the accused's character, such as to commit a certain type of crime. State v. Moore (Ohio App. 8 Dist., 05-03-2012) 970 N.E.2d 1098, 2012-Ohio-1958, appeal not allowed 133 Ohio St.3d 1413, 975 N.E.2d 1030, 2012-Ohio-4650, appeal after new sentencing hearing 24 N.E.3d 1197, 2014-Ohio-5135, cause dismissed 141 Ohio St.3d 1433, 23 N.E.3d 1178, 2015-Ohio-168, stay denied 141 Ohio St.3d 1452, 23 N.E.3d 1195, 2015-Ohio-239. Criminal Law ⚷ 368.1; Criminal Law ⚷ 368.5

Defendant's statement to police in which he made references to prior bad acts was admissible in its entirety in that the other acts were relevant for the purpose of demonstrating his identity and presence at the scene by highlighting his criminal relationship and history with an accomplice, in prosecution for robbery and kidnapping. State v. Moore (Ohio App. 8 Dist., 05-03-2012) 970 N.E.2d 1098, 2012-Ohio-1958, appeal not allowed 133 Ohio St.3d 1413, 975 N.E.2d 1030, 2012-Ohio-4650, appeal after new sentencing hearing 24 N.E.3d 1197, 2014-Ohio-5135, cause dismissed 141 Ohio St.3d 1433, 23 N.E.3d 1178, 2015-Ohio-168, stay denied 141 Ohio St.3d 1452, 23 N.E.3d 1195, 2015-Ohio-239. Criminal Law ⚷ 372.42; Criminal Law ⚷ 372.48; Criminal Law ⚷ 372.54; Criminal Law ⚷ 372.59

Evidence of defendant's scheme, plan, or system is relevant if the other acts form part of the immediate background of the alleged act which forms the foundation of the crime charged in the indictment; it would be virtually impossible to prove that the accused committed the crime charged without also introducing evidence of the other acts. State v. Kaufman (Ohio App. 7 Dist., 03-31-2010) 187 Ohio App.3d 50, 931 N.E.2d 143, 2010-Ohio-1536, appeal not allowed 126 Ohio St.3d 1546, 932 N.E.2d 340, 2010-Ohio-3855. Criminal Law ⚷ 370.1

16. —— Judicial admissions, admissibility of prior acts

Trial court abused its discretion during retrial in murder prosecution in allowing witness to testify that defendant had attacked her approximately four months before the murder; trial judge declared a mistrial during the first trial when this prior attack was merely mentioned by another witness, although the trial judge tried to distinguish the way the issue was presented in the two trials, the record did not reveal any fact or argument that had changed by the time he made his second ruling, the evidence establishing the prior attack was relatively weak, there were some significant dissimilarities between the two crimes, and the trial court did not provide any limiting instructions to the jury when the witness testified. State v. Anderson (Ohio App. 7 Dist., Mahoning, 09-01-2006) No. 03MA252, 2006-Ohio-4618, 2006 WL 2573785, Unreported, appeal not allowed 112 Ohio St.3d 1443, 860 N.E.2d 767, 2007-Ohio-152. Criminal Law ⚷ 368.54

18. Prior acts admissible—In general

There are two situations in which other-acts evidence is admissible to show a defendant's scheme, plan, or system, namely to show: (1) the background of the alleged crime, or (2) identity. State v. Blankenburg (Ohio App. 12 Dist., 03-26-2012) 197 Ohio App.3d 201, 966 N.E.2d 958, 2012-Ohio-1289, appeal not allowed 132 Ohio St.3d 1514, 974 N.E.2d 112, 2012-Ohio-4021, denial of post-conviction relief reversed 2012-Ohio-6175, 2012 WL 6738255. Criminal Law ⚷ 370.1; Criminal Law ⚷ 372.28; Criminal Law ⚷ 372.55

In order for other acts to be admissible to show motive, the other acts must be of a character so related to the offense for which the defendant is on trial that they have a logical connection therewith and may reasonably disclose a motive or purpose for the commission of such offense. State v. Blankenburg (Ohio App. 12 Dist., 03-26-2012) 197 Ohio App.3d 201, 966 N.E.2d 958, 2012-Ohio-1289, appeal not allowed 132 Ohio St.3d 1514, 974 N.E.2d 112, 2012-Ohio-4021, denial of post-conviction relief reversed 2012-Ohio-6175, 2012 WL 6738255. Criminal Law ⚷ 371.1

Evidence of other acts by a defendant is admissible only when it tends to show one of the matters enumerated in applicable statute and rule and only when the evidence is relevant to prove that the defendant is guilty of the offense in question. State v. Essa (Ohio App. 8 Dist., 05-26-2011) 194 Ohio App.3d 208, 955 N.E.2d 429, 2011-Ohio-2513, appeal not allowed 130 Ohio St.3d 1416, 956 N.E.2d 308, 2011-Ohio-5605. Criminal Law ⚷ 368.4; Criminal Law ⚷ 368.9

Proffered evidence of prior acts must be relevant and its probative value must outweigh its potential for unfair prejudice. State v. Goodson (Ohio App. 8 Dist., 02-17-2011) 192 Ohio App.3d 246, 948 N.E.2d 988, 2011-Ohio-722, appeal not allowed 128 Ohio St.3d 1557, 949 N.E.2d 43, 2011-Ohio-2905, on reconsideration 130 Ohio St.3d 82, 955 N.E.2d 982, 2011-Ohio-4729, on remand 2011-Ohio-5820, 2011 WL 5506083. Criminal Law ⚷ 368.9; Criminal Law ⚷ 368.13

Trial court did not abuse its discretion when it admitted evidence of the surveillance of the defendant and prior arrest as other acts of defendant; such evidence was admissible for the purpose of proof of motive, opportunity, intent, preparation, plan, knowledge, identity, or absence of mistake or accident, and court provided the jury with a corrective instruction to disregard the question as to whether a scale was found in the defendant's vehicle. State v. Fannin (Ohio App. 8 Dist., Cuyahoga, 08-15-2002) No. 80014, 2002-Ohio-4180, 2002 WL 1878860, Unreported, appeal not allowed 98 Ohio St.3d 1412, 781 N.E.2d 1020, 2003-Ohio-60, motion to reopen denied 2008-Ohio-136, 2008 WL 152454. Criminal Law ⚷ 368.21

22. —— Drug offenses, prior acts admissible

Testimony in prosecution for possession of controlled substances concerning defendants' practice of using old prescription bottles to make drugs they were selling appear to be legal, tending to show that defendants engaged in drug trafficking, was admissible as evidence of defendants' modus operandi in ongoing scheme, plan, or system, where drug trafficking was offense of same nature as charged offenses. State v. Dunham (Ohio App. 4 Dist., Scioto, 07-15-2005) No. 04CA2931, 2005-Ohio-3642, 2005 WL 1684674, Unreported, stay denied 106 Ohio St.3d 1517, 834 N.E.2d 821, 2005-Ohio-4807, motion for delayed appeal granted 106 Ohio St.3d 1542, 835 N.E.2d 725, 2005-Ohio-5343, appeal not allowed 108 Ohio St.3d 1437, 842 N.E.2d 63, 2006-Ohio-421. Criminal Law ⚷ 373.15

Other-acts evidence of defendant's prior arrests for possession of methamphetamine and lab equipment was admissible to show intent, in trial for illegal assembly or possession of chemicals for manufacture of drugs. State v. Kolvek (Ohio App. 9 Dist., Summit, 07-14-2004) No. 21752, 2004-Ohio-3706, 2004 WL 1562573, Unreported, appeal not allowed 103 Ohio St.3d 1528, 817 N.E.2d 410, 2004-Ohio-5852, appeal not allowed 104 Ohio St.3d 1441, 819 N.E.2d 1124, 2004-Ohio-7033, habeas corpus denied 2009 WL 891759. Criminal Law ⚷ 371.33

24. —— Murder, prior acts admissible

"Other acts" evidence was relevant and admissible in kidnapping and murder prosecution for the purpose of proving motive, where according to the state's theory, victim was killed because he witnessed a shooting that involved defendant and his companion, and victim's murder was part of an overall scheme that involved killing witnesses that could potentially implicate companion in criminal activities. State v. Horton (Ohio App. 10 Dist., Franklin, 02-08-2005) No. 03AP-665, 2005-Ohio-458, 2005 WL 289466, Unreported, appeal not allowed 106 Ohio St.3d 1415, 830 N.E.2d 347, 2005-Ohio-3154, appeal not allowed 108 Ohio St.3d 1490, 843 N.E.2d 795, 2006-Ohio-962, habeas corpus dismissed 2008 WL 687136, certificate of appealability 2008 WL 824300, motion for relief from judgment denied 2012 WL 3777431. Criminal Law ⚷ 371.13

Evidence of child victim's malnourished and underdeveloped condition, his suspected "behavior attachment" issues, and defendant mother's referring to victim as the "bad one," and "hard head," among other contemptuous epithets, was relevant to prove motive and intent in murder prosecution. State v. Terry (Ohio App. 8 Dist., 10-30-2014) 23 N.E.3d 188, 2014-Ohio-4804. Criminal Law ⚷ 371.13; Criminal Law ⚷ 371.40

25. —— Sexual offenses, prior acts admissible

Rule and statute prohibiting admission of other acts evidence to prove the character of a person to show that the person acted in conformity with his character on a particular occasion, but allowing admission of it to prove motive, opportunity, intent, preparation, plan, knowledge, identity, or absence of mistake or accident must be strictly construed against admissibility. State v. Blankenburg (Ohio App. 12 Dist., 03-26-2012) 197 Ohio App.3d 201, 966 N.E.2d 958, 2012-Ohio-1289, appeal not allowed 132 Ohio St.3d 1514, 974 N.E.2d 112, 2012-Ohio-4021, denial of post-conviction relief reversed 2012-Ohio-6175, 2012 WL 6738255. Criminal Law ⚷ 368.1

26. Prior acts inadmissible—In general

The admissibility of other-acts evidence is carefully limited because of the substantial danger that the jury will convict the defendant solely because it assumes that the defendant has a propensity to commit criminal acts or deserves punishment regardless of whether he or she committed the crime charged in the indictment. State v. Goodson (Ohio App. 8 Dist., 02-17-2011) 192 Ohio App.3d 246, 948 N.E.2d 988, 2011-Ohio-722, appeal not allowed 128 Ohio St.3d 1557, 949 N.E.2d 43, 2011-Ohio-2905, on reconsideration 130 Ohio St.3d 82, 955 N.E.2d 982, 2011-Ohio-4729, on remand 2011-Ohio-5820, 2011 WL 5506083. Criminal Law ⚷ 368.5

30. —— Drug offenses, prior acts inadmissible

Trial court error in prosecution of defendant for trafficking in ecstasy, in admitting prior bad acts evidence that defendant had previously been found at locations where police had found ecstasy, was not harmless, even though trial court gave jury a limiting instruction on proper use of evidence to show knowledge or lack of mistake; little evidence existed to convict defendant of possession of drugs, let alone drug trafficking, extensive testimony was offered on the prior bad acts, and defendant was convicted of charges involving ecstasy but acquitted of charges involving other drugs. State v. Ben (Ohio App. 8 Dist., 01-28-2010) 185 Ohio App.3d 832, 925 N.E.2d 1045, 2010-Ohio-238, appeal not allowed 125 Ohio St.3d 1450, 927 N.E.2d 1129, 2010-Ohio-2510. Criminal Law ⚿ 1169.11

34.5. Photographs

Prejudicial effect of the admission as other acts evidence of photographs of clothed buttocks or groin region of teenage boys and shirtless teenage boys, videotape of boys wrestling, and expert testimony regarding nature of child erotica did not outweigh their probative value in prosecution for aggravated trafficking in drugs, gross sexual imposition, and various other drug- and sex-related crimes, where the other acts evidence provided the motive or explained why the defendant, who was a respected local physician, acted in the manner in which he did with some of his minor patients and provided evidence of his preparation, scheme, plan, or system in committing the offenses. State v. Blankenburg (Ohio App. 12 Dist., 03-26-2012) 197 Ohio App.3d 201, 966 N.E.2d 958, 2012-Ohio-1289, appeal not allowed 132 Ohio St.3d 1514, 974 N.E.2d 112, 2012-Ohio-4021, denial of post-conviction relief reversed 2012-Ohio-6175, 2012 WL 6738255. Criminal Law ⚿ 370.25; Criminal Law ⚿ 371.22

There was substantial proof that defendant possessed photographic equipment and photographs of clothed buttocks or groin regions of teenage boys, or of shirtless teenage boys, most of whom were athletes, and, thus, pediatrician's expert testimony on nature of child erotica could rely on the photographs in prosecution for aggravated trafficking in drugs, gross sexual imposition, and various other drug- and sex-related crimes. State v. Blankenburg (Ohio App. 12 Dist., 03-26-2012) 197 Ohio App.3d 201, 966 N.E.2d 958, 2012-Ohio-1289, appeal not allowed 132 Ohio St.3d 1514, 974 N.E.2d 112, 2012-Ohio-4021, denial of post-conviction relief reversed 2012-Ohio-6175, 2012 WL 6738255. Criminal Law ⚿ 374.20(3); Criminal Law ⚿ 486(5)

38. —— Plain errors, review

Admission of "other acts" testimony concerning defendant's sexual abuse of two young boys during prosecution for, inter alia, unlawful sexual conduct with a minor and rape constituted prejudicial error, and, hence, defendant was entitled to a new trial. State v. Miley (Ohio App. 5 Dist., Richland, 09-08-2006) No. 2005-CA-67, No. 2006-CA-14, 2006-Ohio-4670, 2006 WL 2589816, Unreported, appeal not allowed 112 Ohio St.3d 1420, 859 N.E.2d 558, 2006-Ohio-6712, appeal after new trial 2009-Ohio-570, 2009 WL 321192. Criminal Law ⚿ 1169.11

39. —— Prejudice, review

Trial court erred in finding that the probative value of evidence that defendant had previously engaged in oral sex with another 16-year-old boy outweighed any prejudicial effect, in prosecution for rape, unlawful sexual conduct with a minor, kidnapping, and gross sexual imposition; there was testimony that the victim was a troubled teenager, no physical evidence of sexual abuse was found, and the case essentially hinged on the credibility of the witnesses. State v. Williams (Ohio App. 8 Dist., 11-03-2011) 195 Ohio App.3d 807, 961 N.E.2d 1200, 2011-Ohio-5650, appeal allowed 131 Ohio St.3d 1472, 962 N.E.2d 803, 2012-Ohio-896, reversed 134 Ohio St.3d 521, 983 N.E.2d 1278, 2012-Ohio-5695, reconsideration granted 133 Ohio St.3d 1512, 979 N.E.2d 1290, 2012-Ohio-6209, on remand 2013-Ohio-4471, 2013 WL 5603592. Criminal Law ⚿ 368.37

41. —— Harmless errors, review

Cumulative effect of errors arising out of prosecutor's misstatement about witness' testimony, admission of purely speculative witness testimony about what he "put together" about what happened when witness had no personal knowledge, admission of revolver that had no connection to crime, and admission of witness' testimony that he had seen defendant with revolver "in the past," which was not offered for any permissible purpose, was not harmless, in trial for aggravated murder and aggravated robbery, insofar as State's case was based entirely on circumstantial evidence and was heavily reliant on testimony of witness who had initially lied to police and only came forward after DNA evidence placed him at scene of crime. State v. Williams (Ohio App. 8 Dist., Cuyahoga, 10-27-2011) No. 95796, 2011-Ohio-5483, 2011 WL 5116501, Unreported. Criminal Law ⚿ 1186.1

Any error in trial court's admission of child victim's malnourished condition and defendant mother's contemptuous epithets for victim was harmless in murder prosecution, as the state presented substantial other evidence of defendant's guilt. State v. Terry (Ohio App. 8 Dist., 10-30-2014) 23 N.E.3d 188, 2014-Ohio-4804. Criminal Law ⚿ 1169.11

BILL OF EXCEPTIONS

2945.67 When prosecutor may appeal; when public defender to oppose

Law Review and Journal Commentaries

Government Appeals in Criminal Cases: The Myth of Asymmetry. Anne Bowen Poulin, 77 U. Cin. L. Rev. 1 (Fall 2008).

Notes of Decisions

1. Constitutional issues

Judge who presided over state's civil nuisance case brought against exotic dancing club lacked authority to order state to return computer seized pursuant to search warrant issued by grand jury judge in connection with criminal investigation of club, even though other seized evidence had been presented in nuisance suit; search warrant docket remained open and assigned to grand jury judge, computer was not used in nuisance trial, rule required property seized under warrant to be kept for use as evidence by court that issued warrant or by law enforcement agency that executed warrant, and, thus, it would be contradictory for judge who presided over nuisance trial to order release of criminal evidence seized pursuant to a criminal search. State ex rel. Gains v. Go Go Girls Cabaret, Inc. (Ohio App. 7 Dist., 03-02-2010) No. 09 MA 146, 2010 -Ohio- 870, 2010 WL 779997, Unreported. Searches and Seizures ⚷ 84

The double jeopardy clause precluded the State from appealing the trial court's post-verdict ruling on the sufficiency of the evidence or retrying defendant for theft; the trial court's post-verdict finding that the State failed to present sufficient evidence on an essential element of the charge was the equivalent of an acquittal, and thus jeopardy attached and barred retrial. State v. Snowden (Ohio App. 11 Dist., Ashtabula, 12-12-2008) No. 2008-A-0014, 2008-Ohio-6554, 2008 WL 5205102, Unreported, appeal not allowed 121 Ohio St.3d 1441, 903 N.E.2d 1224, 2009-Ohio-1638. Double Jeopardy ⚷ 103

The Court of Appeals lacked jurisdiction to hear state's appeal from trial court order granting criminal defendant's motion to suppress evidence, which was granted on the finding that defendant was not arrested with probable cause, where the trial court order did not specify which evidence was suppressed as a result of the determination. Tallmadge v. Barker (Ohio App. 9 Dist., Summit, 05-07-2008) No. 23961, 2008-Ohio-2154, 2008 WL 1961217, Unreported. Criminal Law ⚷ 1024(1)

Following determination that state had proved the complaint beyond a reasonable doubt and that child was delinquent by having committed rape, juvenile court's decision to dismiss complaint in the best interest of the child was a "final verdict" to which double jeopardy attached, and thus state was barred from appealing. In re N.I. (Ohio App. 8 Dist., 11-24-2010) 191 Ohio App.3d 97, 944 N.E.2d 1214, 2010-Ohio-5791. Double Jeopardy ⚷ 33

Issue of whether trial court erred in granting defendant's motion for judgment of acquittal as to charge of obstructing official business based on defendant not having previously been arraigned on charge was subject to appellate review, though issue was moot, given that double jeopardy barred retrial, as issue was substantive, in that trial court, by granting motion on basis that defendant was not arraigned, created material element to charge, imposing duty on state to prove issue, state was not appealing from final verdict itself, but was appealing from ruling that resulted in judgment of acquittal, and issue was capable of repetition yet evading review, in that without review, it was possible that district's trial courts would continue to grant a directed verdict on basis that there was some defect in the arraignment. State v. Bickel (Ohio App. 9 Dist., 06-02-2008) 178 Ohio App.3d 535, 899 N.E.2d 154, 2008-Ohio-5747. Criminal Law ⚷ 1134.26

2. In general

The state, in criminal and juvenile-delinquency proceedings, may appeal as of right an order that (1) grants a motion to dismiss all or any part of an indictment, complaint, or information, (2) grants a motion to suppress evidence, (3) grants a motion for the return of seized property, and (4) grants postconviction relief; further, with the exception of final verdicts, the state may appeal any other decision in a criminal or juvenile delinquency proceeding by leave of the appellate court. State v. Jackson (Ohio App. 9 Dist., 03-07-2011) 192 Ohio App.3d 617, 949 N.E.2d 1070, 2011-Ohio-986. Criminal Law ⚷ 1024(1); Criminal Law ⚷ 1024(2); Criminal Law ⚷ 1072; Infants ⚷ 2889

Among orders that the State may appeal by leave of court, under statute specifying orders in criminal cases that the State may appeal, are certain evidentiary rulings, orders granting a new trial on motion of a defendant, and substantive law rulings which result in a judgment of acquittal so long as the judgment itself is not appealed. State v. Ross (Ohio, 12-28-2010) 128 Ohio St.3d 283, 943 N.E.2d 992, 2010-Ohio-6282. Criminal Law ⚷ 1024(1); Criminal Law ⚷ 1024(5); Criminal Law ⚷ 1024(7)

State could not appeal as a matter of right the trial court's decision to issue a nunc pro tunc order in a criminal case. State v. Jama (Ohio App. 10 Dist., 09-30-2010) 189 Ohio App.3d 687, 939

N.E.2d 1309, 2010-Ohio-4739. Criminal Law ⚷ 1024(1)

State could appeal, as a matter of right, trial court's decision to strike one of three prior convictions for driving under the influence (DUI) in prosecution for DUI, as prior conviction enhanced current DUI violation from a first degree misdemeanor to a fourth degree felony, such that striking prior conviction affected an essential element of the current charge. State v. Skala (Ohio App. 8 Dist., Cuyahoga, 06-13-2002) No. 80331, 2002-Ohio-2962, 2002 WL 1308629, Unreported, appeal not allowed 97 Ohio St.3d 1422, 777 N.E.2d 276, 2002-Ohio-5820. Criminal Law ⚷ 1024(1)

5. Juvenile court

State was not authorized to pursue discretionary appeal of trial court's order granting juvenile's motion to suppress evidence, where state had failed to file interlocutory appeal pursuant to juvenile rule governing state's right to appeal motion to suppress; procedure for filing interlocutory appeal of suppression order was mandatory, since existence of an interlocutory appeal was necessary to ensure a fair trial for both juvenile and state, and also served judicial economy. In re M.M. (Ohio, 04-17-2013) 135 Ohio St.3d 375, 987 N.E.2d 652, 2013-Ohio-1495. Infants ⚷ 2887; Infants ⚷ 2889

In a case where double jeopardy barred review of juvenile court's dismissal of complaint following adjudication in the best interest of child, state's appeal did not raise a substantive legal issue capable of repetition that did not affect the verdict, and thus appellate court would not address state's arguments; state did not explicitly point to a legal question it wanted answered, but instead argued that the trial court abused its discretion in dismissing the complaint for myriad reasons, and addressing the alleged abuse of discretion reasons would require appellate court to engage in a factual analysis of the case. In re N.I. (Ohio App. 8 Dist., 11-24-2010) 191 Ohio App.3d 97, 944 N.E.2d 1214, 2010-Ohio-5791. Infants ⚷ 2907

6. Dismissal of charges or indictment

Dismissal was warranted of the State's appeal of order dismissing juvenile complaint due to lack of subject matter jurisdiction; State's complaint alleged unruliness, not delinquency, and thus the dismissal was not one of the circumstances from which the State had an absolute right of appeal under statute, and, since the dismissal was without prejudice, it was not a final, appealable order. In re A.E. (Ohio App. 10 Dist., Franklin, 09-09-2008) No. 08AP-59, 2008-Ohio-4552, 2008 WL 4151626, Unreported. Infants ⚷ 2878; Infants ⚷ 2903

Municipal court's journal entry granting drunk driving defendant's motion to suppress results of breath testing instrument was a final, appealable order; court's determination was not a tentative or precautionary ruling. State v. Canino (Ohio App. 11 Dist., 02-19-2013) 986 N.E.2d 1112, 2013-Ohio-551. Criminal Law ⚷ 1023(3)

A pretrial challenge to a breath test in a prosecution for operating a vehicle while under the influence (OVI), if granted, destroys the state's case and the state is permitted to appeal. State v. Canino (Ohio App. 11 Dist., 02-19-2013) 986 N.E.2d 1112, 2013-Ohio-551. Criminal Law ⚷ 1024(1)

Trial court's ruling on motorist's motion in limine to exclude any testimony regarding the result of his blood alcohol test, granting motion, ordering that breath test result not be admitted at trial, and dismissing charge for per se operating a vehicle while under the influence (OVI), was a final, appealable order; regardless of label of motion, it was motion to suppress since it resulted in exclusion of evidence that was essential to prove per se OVI charge. State v. Carter (Ohio App. 11 Dist., 12-03-2012) 983 N.E.2d 855, 2012-Ohio-5583. Criminal Law ⚷ 1023(3)

Trial court's modification of the jury verdict to reduce defendant's rape conviction to a conviction for attempted rape, following trial and after the introduction of newly discovered evidence, was not the functional equivalent of a dismissal of rape charge in the indictment, for purposes of determining whether state could appeal the order as of right. State ex rel. Steffen v. Court of Appeals, First Appellate Dist. (Ohio, 06-03-2010) 126 Ohio St.3d 405, 934 N.E.2d 906, 2010-Ohio-2430. Criminal Law ⚷ 1024(5)

Trial court's discharge of defendant who was acquitted of felonious assault but as to whom there was a hung jury on the offense of complicity to felonious assault, on the ground that there was no charging document charging defendant with complicity, constituted the dismissal of part of an indictment, and thus State could appeal as a matter of right, without seeking leave; complicity was inherent in the charged offense, and was activated by the giving of jury instruction on complicity. State v. Christian (Ohio App. 7 Dist., 09-10-2009) 184 Ohio App.3d 1, 919 N.E.2d 271, 2009-Ohio-4811, appeal not allowed 124 Ohio St.3d 1492, 922 N.E.2d 227, 2010-Ohio-670, habeas corpus denied 2012 WL 1658307, affirmed 739 F.3d 294. Criminal Law ⚷ 1024(2)

Pursuant to statute providing that prosecuting attorney may appeal as matter of right "any" decision of trial court which grants motion to dismiss all or any part of indictment, state may appeal dismissal of indictment, whether dismissal is with or without prejudice. State v. Craig (Ohio, 10-31-2007) 116 Ohio St.3d 135, 876 N.E.2d 957, 2007-Ohio-5752, on remand 2008-Ohio-3978, 2008 WL 3134809. Criminal Law ⚷ 1024(2)

9. —— Suppression, evidence

The ruling of the trial court at a hearing on a motion to suppress evidence prevails at trial and is, therefore, automatically appealable by the state. State v. Canino (Ohio App. 11 Dist., 02-19-2013) 986 N.E.2d 1112, 2013-Ohio-551. Criminal Law ⚷ 1024(1)

A ruling pursuant to a motion in limine is generally considered a tentative and interlocutory ruling to which finality does not attach, for purposes of State's statutory right to appeal; however, the determination of whether a motion is a motion to suppress or a motion in limine does not depend on what it is labeled, but instead depends on the type of relief it seeks to obtain. State v. Rouse (Ohio App. 11 Dist., 12-03-2012) 983 N.E.2d 845, 2012-Ohio-5584. Criminal Law ⚷ 1023(3)

Defendant's motion in limine which sought permanent exclusion of breath test results unless State presented predicate evidence establishing scientific reliability of breath test machine was equivalent of motion to suppress breath test machine results, and thus, State had statutory right to appeal from order excluding test results, in trial for operating motor vehicle while intoxicated; trial court expressly stated that matter was before it on defendant's motion to suppress, defendant did not object to court's ruling or dispute finality of order on appeal. State v. Rouse (Ohio App. 11 Dist., 12-03-2012) 983 N.E.2d 845, 2012-Ohio-5584. Criminal Law ⚷ 1023(3)

Municipal court's journal entry granting motorist's motion to suppress/motion in limine with respect to the results of breath testing instrument was a final, appealable order; court's ruling was not a tentative or precautionary ruling, but determined that motorist's breath test would not be admitted during trial, and any doubt as to finality of ruling was removed by court's dismissal of charge of operating a vehicle with a prohibited breath alcohol concentration. State v. Miller (Ohio App. 11 Dist., 12-03-2012) 983 N.E.2d 837, 2012-Ohio-5585. Criminal Law ⚷ 1023(2)

If trial court's order, on remand after affirmance of trial court's earlier order granting murder defendant's motion to suppress his confession, denying State's motion to vacate the suppression order was appealable at all, it was appealable as a discretionary appeal, as opposed to being appealable as of right. State v. Tate (Ohio App. 7 Dist., 11-06-2008) 179 Ohio App.3d 135, 900 N.E.2d 1067, 2008-Ohio-5820. Criminal Law ⚷ 1024(1)

10. Leave of court

State could not appeal as of right motion in limine prohibiting State from presenting evidence as to meaning of field sobriety tests absent expert testimony and limiting evidence related to tests as to arresting officers personal observations, in trial for driving under influence (DUI) and related offenses, but instead, was required to obtain leave to appeal, insofar as motion in limine was preliminary, temporary ruling on evidence which had to be proffered at trial in order to preserve issue for appellate review, and comment during opening statement was not evidence. State v. Phipps (Ohio App. 3 Dist., Auglaize, 02-13-2006) No. 2-05-19, 2006-Ohio-602, 2006 WL 319220, Unreported. Criminal Law ⚷ 1024(1)

Appellate court has discretion to determine which cases the state should be granted leave to appeal. State v. Jackson (Ohio App. 9 Dist., 03-07-2011) 192 Ohio App.3d 617, 949 N.E.2d 1070, 2011-Ohio-986. Criminal Law ⚷ 1072

Court of Appeals would grant State's motion for leave to appeal trial court's decision to issue nunc pro tunc order to amend verdict in criminal case, where State was not appealing the merits of the final verdict, order played a significant role in the case, and appeal provided an opportunity to resolve uncertainty about the proper use of nunc pro tunc orders. State v. Jama (Ohio App. 10 Dist., 09-30-2010) 189 Ohio App.3d 687, 939 N.E.2d 1309, 2010-Ohio-4739. Criminal Law ⚷ 1072

State was not required to seek leave of court before pursuing appeal from county court's grant of defendant's motion to dismiss criminal complaint. State v. Landers (Ohio App. 4 Dist., 08-05-2010) 188 Ohio App.3d 786, 936 N.E.2d 1026, 2010-Ohio-3709. Criminal Law ⚷ 1023(8)

13. Final verdict

State was statutorily precluded from appealing verdict acquitting defendant on seven-year firearm specification in prosecution for felonious assault, because state was challenging a final verdict of acquittal rather than a substantive legal issue. State v. Tinsley (Ohio App. 8 Dist., Cuyahoga, 05-13-2010) No. 92335, No. 92339, 2010-Ohio-2083, 2010 WL 1910297, Unreported, motion for delayed appeal granted 126 Ohio St.3d 1543, 932 N.E.2d 338, 2010-Ohio-3855, appeal not allowed 126 Ohio St.3d 1616, 935 N.E.2d 854, 2010-Ohio-5101. Criminal Law ⚷ 1024(5)

In virtually all circumstances, finality does not attach when a motion in limine is granted; however, any motion that seeks to obtain a judgment suppressing evidence, even if not labeled a motion to suppress, is a "motion to suppress" for purposes of the statute and the rule governing appeals by the state in a criminal case where the motion, if granted, effectively destroys the ability of the state to prosecute. State v. Schrock (Ohio App. 11 Dist., 02-08-2013) 986 N.E.2d 1068, 2013-Ohio-441. Criminal Law ⚷ 632(4); Criminal Law ⚷ 1024(1)

Order granting a motion in limine in which defendant sought a determination that the results from a breath-test machine were not admissible at a trial for operating a vehicle under the influence (OVI) of alcohol was a final, appealable order; trial court's ruling that the results were inadmissible effectively gutted the state's case and destroyed the state's ability to try the case, and the motion in limine was thus a motion to suppress for purposes of the statute and the rule governing appeals by the state in a criminal case. State v. Schrock (Ohio App. 11 Dist., 02-08-2013) 986 N.E.2d 1068, 2013-Ohio-441. Criminal Law ⚷ 1024(1)

The trial court's judgment of acquittal for lack of venue was not appealable as a matter of right or by leave to appeal; the judgment of acquittal was a final verdict that was not appealable. State v. Hampton (Ohio, 12-06-2012) 134 Ohio St.3d 447, 983 N.E.2d 324, 2012-Ohio-5688, reconsideration denied 133 Ohio St.3d 1512, 979 N.E.2d 1289, 2012-Ohio-6209. Criminal Law ⚷ 1024(5)

14. Correction of sentence

Statutory bar against appeal by state of sentence imposed for aggravated murder did not preclude appellate court from reviewing state's claims that trial court failed to follow proper procedure at penalty phase of capital case when it imposed sentence of life without parole and that trial court made incorrect evidentiary rulings at penalty phase. State v. Hancock (Ohio App. 12 Dist., Warren, 03-31-2003) No. CA2001-12-115, No. CA2001-12-116, No. CA2002-01-004, 2003-Ohio-1616, 2003 WL 1689612, Unreported, appeal not allowed 99 Ohio St.3d 1513, 792 N.E.2d 200, 2003-Ohio-3957, on remand 2003 WL 25672096. Criminal Law ⚷ 1023(11)

State could appeal as a matter of right the trial court's decision to sentence defendant to community control despite the statutory presumption of prison. State v. Jama (Ohio App. 10 Dist., 09-30-2010) 189 Ohio App.3d 687, 939 N.E.2d 1309, 2010 -Ohio- 4739. Criminal Law ⚷ 1024(9)

15. Extraordinary writs in lieu of appeal

Seeking leave of the court of appeals and filing a motion to stay discovery order in criminal case provided adequate remedy at law, and, thus, prosecutor was not entitled to writ of prohibition against enforcement of order to requiring prosecutor to provide all police reports and witness statements to defense counsel in a capital case. State ex rel. Mason v. Burnside (Ohio, 12-20-2007) 117 Ohio St.3d 1, 881 N.E.2d 224, 2007-Ohio-6754. Prohibition ⚷ 3(4)

16. Interlocutory appeals

State's notice of appeal of trial court's denial of its motion for reconsideration as to decision to hold defendant's sentence for felonious assault conviction in abeyance, which conviction arose from defendant's guilty plea, was filed pursuant to rule governing appeals for decisions other than final verdicts, and thus, the notice was timely, although it was filed more than 30 days after the court's sentencing order; the trial court's order was interlocutory and a proper subject to a motion for reconsideration. State v. Ford (Ohio App. 9 Dist., Summit, 12-29-2006) No. 23269, 2006-Ohio-6961, 2006 WL 3825194, Unreported. Criminal Law ⚷ 1081(4.1)

Trial court's order granting defendant's pretrial motion to suppress results of breath test destroyed State's case and thus could be appealed under statute allowing a prosecuting attorney to appeal a decision granting a motion to suppress evidence under certain circumstances, when there is no reasonable possibility of effective prosecution in the absence of the suppressed evidence, in prosecution for operating a vehicle while under the influence (OVI). State v. Mason (Ohio App. 11 Dist., 06-17-2013) 994 N.E.2d 36, 2013-Ohio-2612. Criminal Law ⚷ 1024(1)

17. Substantive review

State has no absolute right of appeal in a criminal matter unless specifically granted such right by statute. State v. Awkal (Ohio App. 8 Dist., 08-30-2012) 974 N.E.2d 200, 2012-Ohio-3970, appeal not allowed 141 Ohio St.3d 1421, 21 N.E.3d 1114, 2014-Ohio-5567. Criminal Law ⚷ 1024(1)

State did not have right to appeal from trial court's determination that death-sentence defendant was incompetent for purposes of execution; proceeding below was actually request for competency determination, even though proceeding was captioned as petition for postconviction relief, and court ruled on it as if it was petition, court's use of wrong terminology in ruling on motion did not constitute grounds for appeal, and did not change character of court's action or order, and legislature did not intend to provide state with ability to appeal. State v. Awkal (Ohio App. 8 Dist., 08-30-2012) 974 N.E.2d 200, 2012-Ohio-3970, appeal not allowed 141 Ohio St.3d 1421, 21 N.E.3d 1114, 2014-Ohio-5567. Sentencing and Punishment ⚷ 1788(2)

Sentencing guidelines, appellate review, nonguidelines sentence, abuse of discretion standard, see Gall v. U.S., 2007, 128 S.Ct. 586.

SCHEDULE OF TRIAL AND HEARINGS

2945.71 Time within which hearing or trial must be held

Notes of Decisions

1. Constitutional issues—In general

Defendant's statutory right to a speedy trial was not violated in child pornography prosecution, where trial was delayed due to defendant's motions for continuances, and it was not required that requests for continuances be reasonable in order to toll the statutory speedy trial time period. State of Ohio v. Timothy M. Glass (Ohio App. 10 Dist., Franklin, 12-08-2011) No. 10AP-558, 2011-Ohio-6287, 2011 WL 6147023, Unreported, motion for delayed appeal granted 131 Ohio St.3d 1497, 964 N.E.2d 438, 2012-Ohio-1501, appeal not allowed 132 Ohio St.3d 1481, 971 N.E.2d 960, 2012-Ohio-3334, habeas corpus denied 2014 WL 4829464. Criminal Law ⚷ 577.10(8)

Defendant established prima facie claim that right to speedy trial had been violated in prosecution for gross sexual imposition; state was statutorily required to bring defendant to trial within 270 days, state had used 268 days before scheduled trial date, and trial did not begin until two months after scheduled trial date. State v. Ange (Ohio App. 11 Dist., Portage, 05-09-2008) No. 2007-P-0108, 2008-Ohio-2314, 2008 WL 2042836, Unreported. Criminal Law ⚷ 577.16(8)

Defendant's speedy trial rights were not violated, in prosecution for insurance fraud and falsification; defendant was not in jail pending trial, she waived her right to a speedy trial for five months, and she was granted ten continuances. State v. Hinson (Ohio App. 8 Dist., Cuyahoga, 07-27-2006) No. 87132, 2006-Ohio-3831, 2006 WL 2096589, Unreported, appeal not allowed 112 Ohio St.3d 1421, 859 N.E.2d 559, 2006-Ohio-6712. Criminal Law ⚷ 577.10(8); Criminal Law ⚷ 577.10(9)

Incarcerated defendant's constitutional right to a speedy trial was adequately protected by speedy trial statute. State v. Pesci (Ohio App. 11 Dist., Lake, 12-20-2002) No. 2001-L-026, 2002-Ohio-7131, 2002 WL 31866167, Unreported, appeal not allowed 98 Ohio St.3d 1566, 787 N.E.2d 1231, 2003-Ohio-2242, appeal from denial of post-conviction relief dismissed 2008-Ohio-1660, 2008 WL 919628, denial of post-conviction relief affirmed 2009-Ohio-6385, 2009 WL 4547766. Criminal Law ⚷ 577.4

Ohio's speedy trial statutes constitute a rational effort to implement the constitutional right to a speedy trial and will be strictly enforced. State v. Ramey (Ohio App. 2 Dist., 12-28-2012) 986 N.E.2d 462, 2012-Ohio-6187. Criminal Law ⚷ 577.5

State failed to act with reasonable diligence to secure defendant's availability for trial on charges for kidnapping, felonious assault, and attempted murder, as required to toll statutory speedy trial period; defendant returned to Michigan home following release from incarceration where officials knew he was from and he lived there under his own name, State failed to secure Governor's Warrant in timely manner when defendant refused to waive extradition, and all pursuit of defendant ceased until he was pulled over for traffic violation ten years after his release. State v. Major (Ohio App. 6 Dist., 12-12-2008) 180 Ohio App.3d 29, 903 N.E.2d 1272, 2008-Ohio-6534, appeal not allowed 121 Ohio St.3d 1474, 905 N.E.2d 654, 2009-Ohio-2045. Criminal Law ⚷ 577.12(1)

Delay of 79 days following defendant's revocation of prior unlimited waiver of speedy-trial rights was not reasonable, and violated defendant's right to speedy trial in prosecution for criminal trespass, a fourth-degree misdemeanor. Toledo v. Sauger (Ohio App. 6 Dist., 11-07-2008) 179 Ohio App.3d 285, 901 N.E.2d 826, 2008-Ohio-5810. Criminal Law ⚷ 577.10(9); Criminal Law ⚷ 577.15(1)

The speedy trial statute is constitutional, mandatory, and must be strictly construed against the state. State v. Kist (Ohio App. 11 Dist., 09-14-2007) 173 Ohio App.3d 158, 877 N.E.2d 747, 2007-Ohio-4773. Criminal Law ⚷ 577.5

Trial court's notices and sua sponte orders for continuance in defendant's first-degree misdemeanor trial did not toll the statutory 90-day period in which defendant was to receive a trial, such that defendant's right to speedy trial was violated, where the notices and orders scheduled trial beyond the 90-day time limit and the reasons for the continuance were not stated by journal entry prior to the expiration of the 90-day period. State v. Kist (Ohio App. 11 Dist., 09-14-2007) 173 Ohio App.3d 158, 877 N.E.2d 747, 2007-Ohio-4773. Criminal Law ⚷ 577.13

A defendant's right to a speedy trial may be waived provided that such waiver is either expressed in writing or made in open court on the record. State v. Masters (Ohio App. 3 Dist., 08-20-2007) 172 Ohio App.3d 666, 876 N.E.2d 1007, 2007-Ohio-4229, appeal allowed 116 Ohio St.3d 1455, 878 N.E.2d 33, 2007-Ohio-6803, appeal dismissed as improvidently allowed 118 Ohio St.3d 1205, 886 N.E.2d 864, 2008-Ohio-1964. Criminal Law ⚷ 577.10(9)

State prisoner's allegations that his rights under Ohio's Speedy Trial Act were violated, and that state court's nunc pro tunc tolling entry in his case was improper under applicable Ohio precedents, raised issues of state law only, and therefore, claims were not cognizable on federal habeas petition; state court of appeals relied solely on state statutory requirements and case law in determining that nunc pro tunc entry was proper and that prisoner was tried within state statutory speedy trial limits. Bennett v. Warden, Lebanon Correctional Inst. (S.D.Ohio, 03-15-2011) 782 F.Supp.2d 466. Habeas Corpus ⚷ 479; Habeas Corpus ⚷ 503.1

2. —— Due process or equal protection, constitutional issues

Second prosecutions brought against defendants violated their constitutional right to a speedy trial, warranting dismissal of second indictment; first defendant did not even make her first appearance until almost a full year after the defendants' initial arrest, and State failed to show it exercised reasonable diligence during the time of the outstanding capiases so as to toll the speedy trial time. State v. Lloyd (Ohio App. 8 Dist., Cuyahoga, 03-23-2006) No. 86501, No. 86502, 2006-Ohio-1356, 2006 WL 728682, Unreported. Criminal Law ⚷ 577.13; Criminal Law ⚷ 577.15(3)

3. —— Effective assistance of counsel, constitutional issues

Defense counsel's failure to move for dismissal of case based upon violation of defendant's right to a speedy trial, prior to counsel's execution of time waiver, was ineffective assistance of counsel, in domestic violence prosecution; a motion to dismiss on speedy trial grounds would have resulted in dismissal of case, meaning defendant was prejudiced by counsel's ineffectiveness. State v. Gray (Ohio App. 2 Dist., Montgomery, 08-31-2007) No. 20980, 2007-Ohio-4549, 2007 WL 2502505, Unreported. Criminal Law ⚷ 1904

Defense counsel's failure to file motion to dismiss all charges against defendant based upon supposed violation of his speedy trial rights was not ineffective assistance of counsel, at trial in which defendant was convicted of complicity to commit aggravated murder and kidnapping; language contained in defendant's written waiver of his speedy trial rights did not contain limiting language as to period in which trial was to commence, and waiver was therefore unlimited in duration, and defendant never reinvoked his speedy trial rights, but rather filed three motions for continuances. State v. Green (Ohio App. 7 Dist., Mahoning, 06-13-2003) No. 01 CA 54, 2003-Ohio-3074, 2003 WL 21373172, Unreported, motion for delayed appeal granted 100 Ohio St.3d 1407, 796 N.E.2d 535, 2003-Ohio-4948, dismissal of post-conviction relief affirmed 2003-Ohio-5142, 2003 WL 22231592, motion to reopen denied 2003-Ohio-5442, 2003 WL 22332000, appeal not allowed 100 Ohio St.3d 1544, 800 N.E.2d 750, 2003-Ohio-6879, denial of post-conviction relief reversed 2006-Ohio-3097, 2006 WL 1680044, appeal not allowed 111 Ohio St.3d 1416, 854 N.E.2d 1094, 2006-Ohio-5083. Criminal Law ⚷ 1904

Defendant could not demonstrate that his counsel was ineffective for failing to move to dismiss charges against him for failure to provide him with a speedy trial because appellate court, on the record before it, could not determine when the speedy trial time began to run. State v. Thompson (Ohio App. 8 Dist., Cuyahoga, 10-31-2002) No. 79334, 2002-Ohio-5957, 2002 WL 31426356, Unreported, dismissal of post-conviction relief affirmed 2002-Ohio-6845, 2002 WL 31771437, appeal not allowed 100 Ohio St.3d 1506, 799 N.E.2d 186, 2003-Ohio-6161, appeal not allowed 98 Ohio St.3d 1512, 786 N.E.2d 62, 2003-Ohio-1572, reconsideration denied 99 Ohio St.3d 1414, 788 N.E.2d 649, 2003-Ohio-2454, motion to reopen denied 2003-Ohio-4336, 2003 WL 21954760, as amended nunc pro tunc, appeal not allowed 100 Ohio St.3d 1509, 799 N.E.2d 187, 2003-Ohio-6161, habeas corpus denied 2007 WL 2080454. Criminal Law ⚷ 1119(1)

4. Construction with other laws

For purposes of bringing an accused to trial, the speedy trial statute and the constitutional guarantees found in the United States and Ohio constitutions are coextensive. State v. Braden (Ohio App. 11 Dist., 12-27-2011) 197 Ohio App.3d 534, 968 N.E.2d 49, 2011-Ohio-6691. Criminal Law ⚷ 577.4; Criminal Law ⚷ 577.5

Speedy-trial claim involves a mixed question of law and fact. State v. Counts (Ohio App. 5 Dist., 01-07-2007) 170 Ohio App.3d 339, 867 N.E.2d 432, 2007-Ohio-117. Criminal Law ⚷ 735

5. Strict construction

State's speedy trial statute was implemented to incorporate the constitutional protection of the right to a speedy trial provided in the United States and Ohio Constitutions and, as such, that statute must be strictly construed against the State. State v. Large (Ohio App. 2 Dist., 01-09-2015) 2015-Ohio-33, 2015 WL 132453. Criminal Law ⚷ 577.2; Criminal Law ⚷ 577.5

The prosecution and the trial courts have a mandatory duty to try an accused within the time frame provided by statute that designates specific time requirements for the state to bring an accused to trial; strict compliance with the statute is required. State v. Ramey (Ohio, 06-28-2012) 132 Ohio St.3d 309, 971 N.E.2d 937, 2012-Ohio-2904, on remand 986 N.E.2d 462, 2012-Ohio-6187. Criminal Law ⚷ 577.5; Criminal Law ⚷ 577.7

Speedy trial statute is mandatory, constitutional, and must be construed strictly against the state. State v. Braden (Ohio App. 11 Dist., 12-27-2011) 197 Ohio App.3d 534, 968 N.E.2d 49, 2011-Ohio-6691. Criminal Law ⚷ 577.5

The Ohio speedy trial statute must be construed strictly against the state. State v. Masters (Ohio App. 3 Dist., 08-20-2007) 172 Ohio App.3d 666, 876 N.E.2d 1007, 2007-Ohio-4229, appeal allowed 116 Ohio St.3d 1455, 878 N.E.2d 33, 2007-Ohio-6803, appeal dismissed as improvidently allowed 118 Ohio St.3d 1205, 886 N.E.2d 864, 2008-Ohio-1964. Criminal Law ⚷ 577.5

6. Purpose

Speedy trial statute did not apply to criminal conviction that had been overturned on appeal on grounds that the trial court exceeded its jurisdiction in imposing sentence. State ex rel. Lisboa v. McCafferty (Ohio App. 8 Dist., Cuyahoga, 08-24-2009) No. 93051, 2009-Ohio-4377, 2009 WL 2625254, Unreported, cause dismissed 123 Ohio St.3d 1514, 917 N.E.2d 815, 2009-Ohio-6351, reconsideration denied 123 Ohio St.3d 1527, 918 N.E.2d 528, 2009-Ohio-6668. Criminal Law ⚷ 577.14

Prejudice to a defendant from the delay in bringing him to trial may fairly be presumed simply because everyone knows that memories fade, evidence is lost, and the burden of anxiety upon any criminal defendant increases with the passing months and years. State v. Major (Ohio App. 6 Dist., 12-12-2008) 180 Ohio App.3d 29, 903 N.E.2d 1272, 2008-Ohio-6534, appeal not allowed 121 Ohio St.3d 1474, 905 N.E.2d 654, 2009-Ohio-2045. Criminal Law ⚷ 577.16(4); Criminal Law ⚷ 577.16(8)

8. Mandatory nature of section

The Ohio speedy trial statute is mandatory. State v. Masters (Ohio App. 3 Dist., 08-20-2007) 172 Ohio App.3d 666, 876 N.E.2d 1007, 2007-Ohio-4229, appeal allowed 116 Ohio St.3d 1455, 878 N.E.2d 33, 2007-Ohio-6803, appeal dismissed as improvidently allowed 118 Ohio St.3d 1205, 886 N.E.2d 864, 2008-Ohio-1964. Criminal Law ⚷ 577.5

9. Held in jail

Statute, requiring that each day an accused is held in jail in lieu of bail pending trial be counted as three days for purposes of calculating when the accused should be brought to trial, did not apply to calculation of prisoner's jail time served for purposes of claim for additional jail-time credit against his prison sentence. Pruitt v. Cook (Ohio, 10-30-2013) 137 Ohio St.3d 296, 998 N.E.2d 1159, 2013-Ohio-4734, reconsideration denied 137 Ohio St.3d 1444, 999 N.E.2d 698, 2013-Ohio-5678. Sentencing and Punishment ⚷ 1158

11. Burden of proof

Once a criminal defendant shows that he was not brought to trial within the statutory speedy trial period, the accused presents a prima facie case for dismissal; at that point, the burden shifts to the state to demonstrate that sufficient time was tolled or extended under the statute. State v. Braden (Ohio App. 11 Dist., 12-27-2011) 197 Ohio App.3d 534, 968 N.E.2d 49, 2011-Ohio-6691. Criminal Law ⚷ 577.16(8)

The state had the burden of demonstrating the existence of a statutory ground for extending the 270-day statutory speedy-trial limit for bringing defendant to trial on felony charges of unauthorized use of a motor vehicle, where defendant and the state stipulated at a hearing on defendant's motion to dismiss that defendant had not been brought to trial within the time limit. State v. Stokes (Ohio App. 12 Dist., 05-02-2011) 193 Ohio App.3d 549, 952 N.E.2d 1192, 2011-Ohio-2104. Criminal Law ⚷ 577.16(8)

Once a criminal defendant shows that he was not brought to trial within the permissible period under the state speedy trial statute, the defendant presents a prima facie case for release, and the burden shifts to the state to demonstrate that sufficient time was tolled or extended under the statute. State v. Masters (Ohio App. 3 Dist., 08-20-2007) 172 Ohio App.3d 666, 876 N.E.2d 1007, 2007-Ohio-4229, appeal allowed 116 Ohio St.3d 1455, 878 N.E.2d 33, 2007-Ohio-6803, appeal dismissed as improvidently allowed 118 Ohio St.3d 1205, 886 N.E.2d 864, 2008-Ohio-1964. Criminal Law ⚷ 577.16(8)

12. Presumption of prejudice

Prejudice to a defendant from the delay in bringing him to trial may fairly be presumed simply because everyone knows that memories fade, evidence is lost, and the burden of anxiety upon any criminal defendant increases with the passing months and years. State v. Major (Ohio App. 6 Dist., 12-12-2008) 180 Ohio App.3d 29, 903 N.E.2d 1272, 2008-Ohio-6534, appeal not allowed 121 Ohio St.3d 1474, 905 N.E.2d 654, 2009-Ohio-2045. Criminal Law ⚷ 577.16(4); Criminal Law ⚷ 577.16(8)

14. Juvenile or delinquency proceedings

Juvenile defendant's statutory 90-day speedy trial period began to run on date that state filed its notice of intent to seek a serious youthful offender (SYO) dispositional sentence. In re D.S. (Ohio App. 8 Dist., Cuyahoga, 05-17-2012) No. 97757, 2012-Ohio-2213, 2012 WL 1806854, Unreported, appeal allowed 133 Ohio St.3d 1410, 975 N.E.2d 1029, 2012-Ohio-4650, appeal dismissed as improvidently allowed 136 Ohio St.3d 303, 995 N.E.2d 209, 2013-Ohio-3687. Infants ⚷ 2575

16. Extradition proceedings

Ohio court would not determine whether Missouri courts violated defendant's speedy trial rights regarding the prosecution of defendant in Missouri, where defendant was arrested and charged in Ohio for aiding or abetting aggravated robbery with a gun specification, but was extradited to Missouri to face outstanding charges there before his trial in Ohio. State v. Davis (Ohio App. 5 Dist., Richland, 05-15-2002) No. 01 CA 67, 2002-Ohio-2502, 2002 WL 999322, Unreported, appeal not allowed 99 Ohio St.3d 1438, 789 N.E.2d 1118, 2003-Ohio-2902, denial of post-conviction relief affirmed 2007-Ohio-923, 2007 WL 658565. Criminal Law ⚷ 577.11(4)

21. Retrials

Time between mistrial, which was necessitated because state sought to amend date in indictment, and new trial was to be counted against defendant's speedy trial time, as state waited to amend date in indictment until trial had already begun, which meant that defendant could no longer present his alibi as planned, and state had notice of alibi beforehand. State v. Brown (Ohio App. 7 Dist., Mahoning, 06-07-2005) No. 03-MA-32, 2005-Ohio-2939, 2005 WL 1385715, Unreported, appeal not allowed 106 Ohio St.3d 1558, 836 N.E.2d 582, 2005-Ohio-5531, habeas corpus denied 2007 WL 3342717, affirmed 656 F.3d 325, rehearing and rehearing en banc denied, certiorari denied 133 S.Ct. 1452, 185 L.Ed.2d 360. Criminal Law ⚷ 577.14

Defendant's speedy trial rights were not violated, even though it took the State 149 days to bring defendant to trial after defendant's no contest plea to driving under the influence (DUI) was vacated and the case was remanded for trial; defendant was required to be brought to trial on remand within a reasonable period of time, and less than one year was not presumptively prejudicial. State v. Hull (Ohio App. 7 Dist., Mahoning, 03-30-2005) No. 04 MA 2, 2005-Ohio-1659, 2005 WL 775885, Unreported, motion to certify allowed 106 Ohio St.3d 1479, 832 N.E.2d 733, 2005-Ohio-3978, appeal allowed 106 Ohio St.3d 1482, 832 N.E.2d 736, 2005-Ohio-3978, affirmed 110 Ohio St.3d 183, 852 N.E.2d 706, 2006-Ohio-4252. Criminal Law ⚷ 577.14; Criminal Law ⚷ 577.15(1)

23. When time begins to run

Thirty-day speedy trial time period for minor misdemeanor speed charge began to run on date on which case was transferred at defendant's request from mayor's court to county municipal court, as opposed to date of summons 13 days earlier. Dublin v. Streb (Ohio App. 10 Dist., Franklin, 07-29-2008) No. 07AP-995, 2008-Ohio-3766, 2008 WL 2896612, Unreported. Criminal Law ⚷ 577.8(2)

24. Computing time generally—In general

Misdemeanor charge of assault arose from same facts as original felony charge of aggravated burglary, and thus, speedy trial time began to run when defendant was arrested on the felony charge rather than the later date on which complaint was filed on assault charge and defendant was formally notified of the charge; the facts from which the misdemeanor charge arose were known to the State at the time defendant was charged with a felony. State v. Large (Ohio App. 2 Dist., 01-09-2015) 2015-Ohio-33, 2015 WL 132453. Criminal Law ⚷ 577.14

Defendant stipulated that only 62 speedy trial days had passed, and therefore his actual term of incarceration (433 days) was irrelevant to the legal analysis of his claim of a speedy trial violation in murder prosecution. State v. Lewis (Ohio App. 8 Dist., 08-16-2012) 976 N.E.2d 258, 2012-Ohio-3684, appeal not allowed 134 Ohio St.3d 1485, 984 N.E.2d 29, 2013-Ohio-902. Criminal Law ⚷ 577.15(1)

Statutory grounds for extensions of time of statutory speedy-trial limits are to be strictly construed against the state. State v. Stokes (Ohio App. 12 Dist., 05-02-2011) 193 Ohio App.3d 549, 952 N.E.2d 1192, 2011-Ohio-2104. Criminal Law ⚷ 577.13

26. —— Arrest, computing time generally

Date of defendant's first arrest was triggering event that started running of speedy trial time, for purposes of computing how much time has run under speedy trial statute, in prosecution for deception to obtain drugs. State v. Azbell (Ohio App. 5 Dist., Richland, 08-23-2005) No. 2005CA0004, 2005-Ohio-4405, 2005 WL 2045024, Unreported, appeal allowed 108 Ohio St.3d 1412, 841 N.E.2d 317, 2006-Ohio-179, reversed 112 Ohio St.3d 300, 859 N.E.2d 532, 2006-Ohio-6552, rehearing denied, reconsideration denied 112 Ohio St.3d 1495, 862 N.E.2d 120, 2007-Ohio-724. Criminal Law ⚷ 577.8(2)

State was required to bring defendant, charged with felonies and incarcerated from date of arrest to entry of pleas, to trial within 90 days of his arrest. State v. Smith (Ohio App. 2 Dist., Clark, 11-12-2004) No. 2003 CA 93, 2004-Ohio-6062, 2004 WL 2588269, Unreported, motion for delayed appeal denied 105 Ohio St.3d 1450, 823 N.E.2d 455, 2005-Ohio-763, motion for delayed appeal denied 105 Ohio St.3d 1496, 825 N.E.2d 621, 2005-Ohio-1666, appeal not allowed 110 Ohio St.3d 1468, 852 N.E.2d 1215, 2006-Ohio-4288, habeas corpus dismissed 2007 WL 2080463, subsequent determination 2007 WL 2120515. Criminal Law ⚷ 577.11(1); Criminal Law ⚷ 577.15(3)

Once a defendant against whom a felony charge is pending establishes that 270 days have elapsed since the defendant's arrest or service of summons, the defendant has established a prima facie case for discharge under a statutory speedy-trial provision. State v. Stokes (Ohio App. 12 Dist., 05-02-2011) 193 Ohio App.3d 549, 952 N.E.2d 1192, 2011-Ohio-2104. Criminal Law ⚷ 577.16(8)

Day of arrest is not included when computing the 270-day limit for bringing to trial a person against whom a felony charge is pending. State v. Stokes (Ohio App. 12 Dist., 05-02-2011) 193 Ohio App.3d 549, 952 N.E.2d 1192, 2011-Ohio-2104. Time ⚷ 9(11)

Under a statutory speedy-trial provision, a person against whom a felony charge is pending must be brought to trial within 270 days after the person's arrest or service of summons. State v. Stokes (Ohio App. 12 Dist., 05-02-2011) 193 Ohio App.3d 549, 952 N.E.2d 1192, 2011-Ohio-2104. Criminal Law ⚷ 577.5; Criminal Law ⚷ 577.15(3)

For purposes of computing time under speedy trial statute, each day an accused is held in jail in lieu of bond counts as three days, but the date of arrest is not included. State v. Pilgrim (Ohio App. 10 Dist., 10-08-2009) 184 Ohio App.3d 675, 922 N.E.2d 248, 2009-Ohio-5357, motion for delayed appeal granted 124 Ohio St.3d 1441, 920 N.E.2d 372, 2010-Ohio-188, appeal not allowed 125 Ohio St.3d 1437, 927 N.E.2d 10, 2010-Ohio-2212, reconsideration denied 126 Ohio St.3d 1517, 930 N.E.2d 334, 2010-Ohio-3331, habeas corpus dismissed 2012 WL 554477. Criminal Law ⚷ 577.8(1)

Day of arrest does not count for purposes of speedy trial claim. State v. Donkers (Ohio App. 11 Dist., 03-30-2007) 170 Ohio App.3d 509, 867 N.E.2d 903, 2007-Ohio-1557. Criminal Law ⚷ 577.8(1)

27. —— Service of summons, computing time generally

The date of service does not count against the state for purposes of determining whether a defendant's right to a speedy trial has been violated. State v. Kist (Ohio App. 11 Dist., 09-14-2007) 173 Ohio App.3d 158, 877 N.E.2d 747, 2007-Ohio-4773. Criminal Law ⚷ 577.12(1)

28. —— Arraignment or indictment, computing time generally

Defendant's guilty plea to original indictment for sexual battery terminated his statutory right to a speedy trial, and thus defendant's speedy trial rights were not violated by alleged delay of over 300 days between defendant's arrest and his no-contest plea to reinstated indictment; guilty plea acted as original trial proceeding satisfying statutory requirement that defendant be brought to trial within 270-day period. State v. Castro (Ohio App. 8 Dist., 06-05-2014) 13 N.E.3d 720, 2014-Ohio-2398, appeal not allowed 140 Ohio St.3d 1455, 17 N.E.3d 600, 2014-Ohio-4414. Criminal Law ⚷ 577.14

Charge was not pending against defendant, for the purpose of calculating speedy-trial time, until defendant was arrested on an indictment, even though defendant had been previously been arrested on the same charge; at defendant's initial arrest she was taken to the police station, questioned, and released, she was not charged with any offense, and she was not released on bail or recognizance. (Per Lundberg Stratton, J., with two judges concurring and one judge concurring separately.) State v. Azbell (Ohio, 12-20-2006) 112 Ohio St.3d 300, 859 N.E.2d 532, 2006-Ohio-6552, rehearing denied, reconsideration denied 112 Ohio St.3d 1495, 862 N.E.2d 120, 2007-Ohio-724. Criminal Law ⚷ 577.8(2)

30. —— Additional charges or refiling of indictment, computing time generally

When new and additional charges arise from the same facts as did the original charge and the state knew of such facts at the time of the initial indictment, the time within which trial is to begin on the additional charge is subject to the same statutory limitations period that is applied to the original charge. State v. Large (Ohio App. 2 Dist., 01-09-2015) 2015-Ohio-33, 2015 WL 132453. Criminal Law ⚿ 577.14

Defendant's speedy-trial time started over in prosecution for gross sexual imposition and rape when defendant was rearrested on bench warrant; defendant failed to appear at pretrial status conference, failed to appear for stipulated polygraph test, and failed to remain in contact with his attorney. State v. Counts (Ohio App. 5 Dist., 01-07-2007) 170 Ohio App.3d 339, 867 N.E.2d 432, 2007-Ohio-117. Criminal Law ⚿ 577.8(2)

Thirty-day clock under Speedy Trial Act, which requires that defendant be indicted within 30 days of his arrest, is reset by the dismissal of an outstanding indictment by the government where no further restraint on the defendant's freedom remains after that dismissal. U.S. v. DeJohn (C.A.6 (Ohio), 05-13-2004) 368 F.3d 533, rehearing en banc denied, certiorari denied 125 S.Ct. 510, 543 U.S. 988, 160 L.Ed.2d 373, post-conviction relief denied in part 2008 WL 5076827. Criminal Law ⚿ 577.14; Indictment And Information ⚿ 7

Thirty-day period under Speedy Trial Act in which to indict defendant after his arrest did not continue to run after dismissal of indictment against defendants, where no restraints were thereafter placed on their freedom, and thus reindictment 45 days after dismissal of initial indictment did not violate Speedy Trial Act. U.S. v. DeJohn (C.A.6 (Ohio), 05-13-2004) 368 F.3d 533, rehearing en banc denied, certiorari denied 125 S.Ct. 510, 543 U.S. 988, 160 L.Ed.2d 373, post-conviction relief denied in part 2008 WL 5076827. Indictment And Information ⚿ 7

33. Tolling—In general

Delay of 552 days between the date of defendant's arrest and the filing of defendant's motion for discovery constituted a violation of defendant's statutory right to speedy trial; tolling provision, which extended the period of time to bring an accused to trial by excluding any period of time that the accused was unavailable for trial, as long as the prosecution exercised reasonable diligence to secure the accused's availability, did not apply to toll the speedy trial time as there was no evidence that defendant attempted to avoid prosecution, and the prosecution merely entered the defendant's arrest warrant into the National Crime Information Center (NCIC) database and took no further action to locate defendant. State v. Baker (Ohio App. 12 Dist., Fayette, 02-17-2009) No. CA2008-03-008, 2009-Ohio-674, 2009 WL 372362, Unreported. Criminal Law ⚿ 577.11(2)

Trial court met 30-day statutory speedy trial deadline for misdemeanor speed charge, even assuming that no time was tolled as result of defendant's motions to dismiss, where 16 days passed prior to originally scheduled trial date, speedy trial time was tolled during a continuance requested by defendant, and eight days passed from defendant's motion to dismiss filed on rescheduled trial date and trial court's subsequent determination of guilt from no contest plea. Dublin v. Streb (Ohio App. 10 Dist., Franklin, 07-29-2008) No. 07AP-995, 2008-Ohio-3766, 2008 WL 2896612, Unreported. Criminal Law ⚿ 577.10(8); Criminal Law ⚿ 577.13

No tolling time would be attributed to discovery request that defendant made ten days prior to start of statutory 30–day speedy trial period for misdemeanor traffic charge. Dublin v. Streb (Ohio App. 10 Dist., Franklin, 07-29-2008) No. 07AP-995, 2008-Ohio-3766, 2008 WL 2896612, Unreported. Criminal Law ⚿ 577.10(8)

Asserted unavailability of citing officer on scheduled date of trial on misdemeanor traffic offense did not apply to toll statutory speedy-trial period during continuance granted at city's request, where there were no record documents, transcripts, or journal entries confirming why the trial court granted the continuance. Dublin v. Streb (Ohio App. 10 Dist., Franklin, 07-29-2008) No. 07AP-995, 2008-Ohio-3766, 2008 WL 2896612, Unreported. Criminal Law ⚿ 577.13

City's failure in prosecution for misdemeanor traffic charge to produce requested laser speed-reading device, operations manual, and calibration records for discovery did not preclude statutory speedy trial period from tolling during continuance requested by defendant, where defendant had opportunity to inspect the items at police department prior to scheduled date of trial but failed to do so. Dublin v. Streb (Ohio App. 10 Dist., Franklin, 07-29-2008) No. 07AP-995, 2008-Ohio-3766, 2008 WL 2896612, Unreported. Criminal Law ⚿ 577.10(8)

If the defendant can establish a prima facie case for a speedy trial violation by demonstrating that the trial was held past the time limit set by statute for the crime with which the defendant is charged, the burden shifts to the State to establish that some exceptions applied to toll the time and to make the trial timely; if the State does not meet its burden, the defendant must be discharged. State v. Large (Ohio App. 2 Dist., 01-09-2015) 2015-Ohio-33, 2015 WL 132453. Criminal Law ⚿ 577.16(2); Criminal Law ⚿ 577.16(8)

Speedy-trial time for trying defendant for drug offenses was tolled for at least 191 days, and thus bringing defendant to trial 161 days after expiration of the 90-day speedy-trial period did not violate defendant's right to a speedy trial. State v. Gartrell (Ohio App. 3 Dist., 11-24-2014) 24 N.E.3d 680, 2014-Ohio-5203. Criminal Law ⚿ 577.15(1)

41. —— Continuances, tolling

Assuming validity of murder defendant's pro se motion to revoke express written speedy trial waiver, 116-day delay between filing of such motion and defendant's being brought to trial was reasonable, where speedy trial time was tolled by trial court's sua sponte continuances for civil jury, defendant's motion for bill of particulars and request for discovery, and period between withdrawal of defendant's attorney and appointment of new counsel. State v. Love (Ohio App. 7 Dist., Mahoning, 03-27-2006) No. 02 CA 245, 2006-Ohio-1762, 2006 WL 890994, Unreported, appeal not allowed 110 Ohio St.3d 1465, 852 N.E.2d 1214, 2006-Ohio-4288. Criminal Law ⚿ 577.10(7); Criminal Law ⚿ 577.10(8)

Time period during which trial court granted continuance due to trial schedule conflict involving counsel for burglary defendant tolled constitutional and statutory speedy trial time periods. State v. Ossman (Ohio App. 5 Dist., Licking, 08-16-2004) No. 03 CA 92, 2004-Ohio-4302, 2004 WL 1827813, Unreported, appeal reopened 2006-Ohio-720, 2006 WL 367122, appeal not allowed 109 Ohio St.3d 1506, 849 N.E.2d 1028, 2006-Ohio-2998, habeas corpus dismissed 2007 WL 2110494. Criminal Law ⚿ 577.10(7)

Counsel's request for continuance because of schedule conflict tolled running of 270-day speedy trial period, even if defendant objected to continuance. State v. Wade (Ohio App. 10 Dist., Franklin, 07-29-2004) No. 03AP-774, 2004-Ohio-3974, 2004 WL 1688434, Unreported, stay granted 103 Ohio St.3d 1476, 816 N.E.2d 253, 2004-Ohio-5405, appeal not allowed 104 Ohio St.3d 1427, 819 N.E.2d 709, 2004-Ohio-6585, appeal not allowed 104 Ohio St.3d 1462, 821 N.E.2d 578, 2005-Ohio-204, appeal after new trial 2008-Ohio-543, 2008 WL 366143, on reconsideration 2008-Ohio-1797, 2008 WL 1723671, appeal not allowed 119 Ohio St.3d 1408, 891 N.E.2d 769, 2008-Ohio-3880, appeal not allowed 119 Ohio St.3d 1415, 891 N.E.2d 772, 2008-Ohio-3880, certiorari denied 129 S.Ct. 921, 555 U.S. 1126, 173 L.Ed.2d 158, appeal not allowed 120 Ohio St.3d 1491, 900 N.E.2d 200, 2009-Ohio-278. Criminal Law ⚿ 577.10(8)

Fifty-one-day period of a continuance after trial court granted a motion by defendant's initial counsel to withdraw and appointed new counsel in a prosecution for felony drug offenses was reasonable, and thus the speedy-trial clock was tolled during the period, where trial court granted the continuance to allow new counsel time to prepare for trial. State v. Gartrell (Ohio App. 3 Dist., 11-24-2014) 24 N.E.3d 680, 2014-Ohio-5203. Criminal Law ⚿ 577.10(8)

"Sua sponte continuances" are continuances granted other than on an accused's own motion and toll the speedy-trial time as long as the record reflects that the period of the continuance was reasonable. State v. Gartrell (Ohio App. 3 Dist., 11-24-2014) 24 N.E.3d 680, 2014-Ohio-5203. Criminal Law ⚿ 577.13

An accused's motion to continue a trial does not unconditionally extend the time limit in which the accused must be brought to trial; rather, the speedy-trial time limit is merely extended by the time necessary in light of the reason for delay. State v. Gartrell (Ohio App. 3 Dist., 11-24-2014) 24 N.E.3d 680, 2014-Ohio-5203. Criminal Law ⚿ 577.10(8)

Sixty-eight-day period of a continuance requested by defendant was not longer than necessary in a prosecution for felony drug offenses, such that the speedy-trial clock was tolled during the period, and because the period included the date of trial court's decision on defendant's motion to suppress, the decision did not restart the clock even if it normally would have. State v. Gartrell (Ohio App. 3 Dist., 11-24-2014) 24 N.E.3d 680, 2014-Ohio-5203. Criminal Law ⚿ 577.10(8)

42. —— Discovery, tolling

Time period during which burglary defendant's discovery request was pending tolled constitutional and statutory speedy trial time periods. State v. Ossman (Ohio App. 5 Dist., Licking, 08-16-2004) No. 03 CA 92, 2004-Ohio-4302, 2004 WL 1827813, Unreported, appeal reopened 2006-Ohio-720, 2006 WL 367122, appeal not allowed 109 Ohio St.3d 1506, 849 N.E.2d 1028, 2006-Ohio-2998, habeas corpus dismissed 2007 WL 2110494. Criminal Law ⚿ 577.10(8)

Speedy-trial period to bring defendant to trial on drug charges was tolled for 30 days following defendant's request for a bill of particulars and discovery, but not for the entire 67 days that state took to respond to request, absent a showing of special circumstances to justify the long delay; 30 days was reasonable amount of time for state to respond and thus toll speedy-trial period. State v. Ford (Ohio App. 1 Dist., 01-16-2009) 2009 -Ohio- 146, 2009 WL 104658. Criminal Law ⚿ 577.10(8); Criminal Law ⚿ 577.12(1)

Defendant's right to a speedy trial was not violated, even though roughly a year elapsed between the day defendant was served with the summons and complaint and defendant's trial; defendant filed four motions for continuances, which were granted, which tolled the speedy trial time, defendant's discovery demand tolled the speedy trial time, defendant filed a jury demand after much of the speedy trial had passed, the court explained that defendant's jury demand was filed two weeks prior to the scheduled bench trial and the expiration of his speedy-trial time and that it was unreasonable for defendant to expect a jury trial to be scheduled on such short notice, and the court listed the other cases it had scheduled for trial on the same day when it continued the case due to an overscheduled docket. State v. Marbury (Ohio App. 2 Dist., 02-25-2011) 192 Ohio App.3d 210, 948 N.E.2d 531, 2011 -Ohio- 879. Criminal Law ⚿ 577.10(7); Criminal Law ⚿ 577.10(8); Criminal Law ⚿ 577.10(10); Criminal Law ⚿ 577.15(4)

Defendant's second demand for discovery did not toll statutory speedy trial period, where state had already provided discovery and had no additional discovery to provide. State v. Dankworth (Ohio App. 2 Dist., 05-25-2007) 172 Ohio App.3d 159, 873 N.E.2d 902, 2007-Ohio-2588, appeal allowed 115 Ohio St.3d 1439, 875 N.E.2d 101, 2007-Ohio-5567, appeal dismissed as improvidently allowed 118 Ohio St.3d 1210, 887 N.E.2d 351, 2008-Ohio-2234. Criminal Law ⚿ 577.10(8)

43. —— Motions, tolling

Juvenile defendant's motion for transcripts of probable cause hearing did not toll statutory 90-day speedy trial period, in prosecution to impose on defendant a serious youthful offender (SYO) dispositional sentence, where motion was granted on the record the same day. In re D.S. (Ohio App. 8 Dist., Cuyahoga, 05-17-2012) No. 97757, 2012-Ohio-2213, 2012 WL 1806854, Unreported, appeal allowed 133 Ohio St.3d 1410, 975 N.E.2d 1029, 2012-Ohio-4650, appeal dismissed as improvidently allowed 136 Ohio St.3d 303, 995 N.E.2d 209, 2013-Ohio-3687. Infants ⚿ 2575

Trial court's continuance of proceedings, after granting juvenile defendant's motion for transcripts of the probable cause hearing, did not toll statutory 90-day speedy trial period in prosecution to impose on defendant a serious youthful offender (SYO) dispositional sentence, where trial court did not indicate the reason for the continuance. In re D.S. (Ohio App. 8 Dist., Cuyahoga, 05-17-2012) No. 97757, 2012-Ohio-2213, 2012 WL 1806854, Unreported, appeal allowed 133 Ohio St.3d 1410, 975 N.E.2d 1029, 2012-Ohio-4650, appeal dismissed as improvidently allowed 136 Ohio St.3d 303, 995 N.E.2d 209, 2013-Ohio-3687. Infants ⚿ 2575

Defendant's filing of motion to dismiss indictments based on speedy trial violation tolled speedy trial time until trial court ruled on motion. State v. Hawkins (Ohio App. 11 Dist., Portage, 12-31-2002) No. 2001-P-0060, 2002-Ohio-7347, 2002 WL 31895118, Unreported, appeal not allowed 98 Ohio St.3d 1567, 787 N.E.2d 1231, 2003-Ohio-2242, habeas corpus denied 2006 WL 2481987, certificate of appealability granted in part, denied in part 2006 WL 2990518, affirmed 286 Fed.Appx. 896, 2008 WL 2611339. Criminal Law ⚿ 577.13

Defendant's filing of motion to suppress evidence tolled speedy trial time until trial court ruled on motion. State v. Hawkins (Ohio App. 11 Dist., Portage, 12-31-2002) No. 2001-P-0060, 2002-Ohio-7347, 2002 WL 31895118, Unreported, appeal not allowed 98 Ohio St.3d 1567, 787 N.E.2d 1231, 2003-Ohio-2242, habeas corpus denied 2006 WL 2481987, certificate of appealability granted in part, denied in part 2006 WL 2990518, affirmed 286 Fed.Appx. 896, 2008 WL 2611339. Criminal Law ⚿ 577.13

Ninety-day speedy trial period for jailed defendant was not automatically tolled when co-defendant filed pretrial motion to suppress evidence; statute listing events and circumstances extending speedy trial period did not include filing of pretrial motions by a co-defendant. State v. Ramey (Ohio, 06-28-2012) 132 Ohio St.3d 309, 971 N.E.2d 937, 2012-Ohio-2904, on remand 986 N.E.2d 462, 2012-Ohio-6187. Criminal Law ⚿ 577.10(5)

Five months was an unreasonable amount of time for trial court to rule on defendant's motion to sever, and thus speedy-trial period to bring defendant to trial on charge of having a gun under a disability was not tolled for entire five months, even though defendant failed to petition court to rule on motion. State v. Ford (Ohio App. 1 Dist., 01-16-2009) 180 Ohio App.3d 636, 906 N.E.2d 1155, 2009-Ohio-146. Criminal Law ⚿ 577.10(7)

44. —— Refiling of charges, tolling

Failure of juvenile defendant to respond to prosecution's request for discovery before defendant's statutory 90-day speedy trial rights began to run, when state filed its notice of intent to seek a serious youthful offender (SYO) dispositional sentence, did not toll running of the speedy-trial time; state's discovery request was made well before defendant's right to speedy trial was effectuated, and state was not delayed in its preparation for trial by defendant's failure to respond to its request for discovery, but rather, any delay in case was attributed to state, which had held defendant in detention for 87 days before he was arraigned. In re D.S. (Ohio App. 8 Dist., Cuyahoga, 05-17-2012) No. 97757, 2012-Ohio-2213, 2012 WL 1806854, Unreported, appeal allowed 133 Ohio St.3d 1410, 975 N.E.2d 1029, 2012-Ohio-4650, appeal dismissed as improvidently allowed 136 Ohio St.3d 303, 995 N.E.2d 209, 2013-Ohio-3687. Infants ⚿ 2575

45. —— Appeals, tolling

Constitutional and statutory speedy trial time periods were tolled from time Court of Appeals issued decision in first appeal, which reversed trial court's decision, until time expired for parties to appeal to Supreme Court. State v. Ossman (Ohio App. 5 Dist., Licking, 08-16-2004) No. 03 CA 92, 2004-Ohio-4302, 2004 WL 1827813, Unreported, appeal reopened 2006-Ohio-720, 2006 WL 367122, appeal not allowed 109 Ohio St.3d 1506, 849 N.E.2d 1028, 2006-Ohio-2998, habeas corpus dismissed 2007 WL 2110494. Criminal Law ⚿ 577.14

47. —— Amendment or reduction of charges, revised or additional charges generally

When an original charge is reduced to a lesser charge that carries a shorter speedy trial time limit, the speedy trial deadline will be the earlier of: (1) the speedy trial deadline for the original charge, applied from the date of the original charge, or (2) the speedy trial deadline for the lesser charge applied from the date that the original charge was reduced to the lesser charge. State v. Kist (Ohio App. 11 Dist., 09-14-2007) 173 Ohio App.3d 158, 877 N.E.2d 747, 2007-Ohio-4773. Criminal Law ⚿ 577.14

49. —— Probation or parole violations, revised or additional charges generally

Statutory triple count provisions did not apply to require trial of defendant within 90 days after his arrest, where defendant was also being held prior to trial pursuant to valid parole holder. State v. Stadmire (Ohio App. 8 Dist., Cuyahoga, 02-27-2003) No. 81188, 2003-Ohio-873, 2003 WL 549912, Unreported, motion for delayed appeal denied 114 Ohio St.3d 1408, 867 N.E.2d 842, 2007-Ohio-2632. Criminal Law ⚷ 577.11(3)

50. Triple-count mechanism—In general

"Triple-count" provision of speedy trial statute did not apply to defendant held in jail in lieu of bail following arrest in connection with four unrelated acts of criminal conduct, involving at least three separate victims, on four separate dates. State v. Dankworth (Ohio App. 2 Dist., 05-25-2007) 172 Ohio App.3d 159, 873 N.E.2d 902, 2007-Ohio-2588, appeal allowed 115 Ohio St.3d 1439, 875 N.E.2d 101, 2007-Ohio-5567, appeal dismissed as improvidently allowed 118 Ohio St.3d 1210, 887 N.E.2d 351, 2008-Ohio-2234. Criminal Law ⚷ 577.11(3)

The date bond is posted and the defendant is released counts as a day in jail for triple-time purposes upon speedy trial claim. State v. Donkers (Ohio App. 11 Dist., 03-30-2007) 170 Ohio App.3d 509, 867 N.E.2d 903, 2007-Ohio-1557. Criminal Law ⚷ 577.11(1)

A detainer filed by the United States Bureau of Immigration and Customs Enforcement that does not purport to hold a defendant in custody does not nullify the triple-count provision of Ohio's speedy-trial statutes, which requires each day of custody to count as three days when a defendant is held in jail in lieu of bail. State v. Sanchez (Ohio, 09-13-2006) 110 Ohio St.3d 274, 853 N.E.2d 283, 2006-Ohio-4478. Criminal Law ⚷ 577.11(1)

Noncitizen defendant was not being held in custody by detainer filed by United States Bureau of Immigration and Customs Enforcement, and thus each day that defendant was held in jail on pending charges in lieu of bail counted as three days under triple-count provision of Ohio's speedy-trial statutes, which applied only if defendant was held in jail solely on pending charges; issuance of detainer did not result in defendant's present confinement by immigration authority but, instead, served to declare government's intention to seek future custody. State v. Sanchez (Ohio, 09-13-2006) 110 Ohio St.3d 274, 853 N.E.2d 283, 2006-Ohio-4478. Criminal Law ⚷ 577.11(1)

52. —— Pending charges, triple-count mechanism

Defendant who remained in jail pending trial on drug and other charges, and against whom probation officer placed a holder, was not held solely on the pending charges, and thus State's failure to bring defendant to trial within 90 days did not violate defendant's speedy trial rights pursuant to speedy trial provision triple counting days for which a defendant is held solely on the pending charges, even though the holder was also based on the pending charges; placement of holder meant that defendant would not have been released from jail if he posted bail, and probation violation was separate cause with different scope of inquiry. State v. McGhee (Ohio App. 4 Dist., Lawrence, 03-30-2005) No. 04CA15, 2005-Ohio-1585, 2005 WL 737581, Unreported, appeal after new sentencing hearing 2006-Ohio-6623, 2006 WL 3691664. Criminal Law ⚷ 577.11(1)

Speedy trial statute, providing that each day during which the accused is held in jail in lieu of bail on the pending charge shall be counted as three days for purposes of computing time within which accused must be afforded a preliminary hearing and brought to trial, applies only to those defendants who are held in jail solely on the pending charge; days will not be counted triply if a defendant is also being held for additional charges. State v. Dankworth (Ohio App. 2 Dist., 05-25-2007) 172 Ohio App.3d 159, 873 N.E.2d 902, 2007-Ohio-2588, appeal allowed 115 Ohio St.3d 1439, 875 N.E.2d 101, 2007-Ohio-5567, appeal dismissed as improvidently allowed 118 Ohio St.3d 1210, 887 N.E.2d 351, 2008-Ohio-2234. Criminal Law ⚷ 577.11(1); Criminal Law ⚷ 577.11(3)

Criminal charges arising out of the same criminal incident and brought simultaneously will always be deemed to have a "common litigation history" for the purposes of establishing incarceration solely on the "pending charge" within the meaning of the triple-count provision of the speedy trial statute, even if they are prosecuted in separate jurisdictions. State v. Parker (Ohio, 04-18-2007) 113 Ohio St.3d 207, 863 N.E.2d 1032, 2007-Ohio-1534. Criminal Law ⚷ 577.11(1)

Pretrial incarceration of defendant on three separate complaints constituted incarceration on the "pending charge," for purposes of the triple-count provision of the speedy trial statute, and thus defendant was entitled to credit for three days for each day in jail in lieu of bail on pending charge, although charges were pending in separate courts; the charges against defendant shared a common litigation history, given that all three complaints related to the same occurrence, resulting in defendant's arrest. State v. Parker (Ohio, 04-18-2007) 113 Ohio St.3d 207, 863 N.E.2d 1032, 2007-Ohio-1534. Criminal Law ⚷ 577.11(1)

53. —— Additional or unrelated charges, triple-count mechanism

Defendant charged with 42 fourth-degree misdemeanor violations of state tattooing statutes, arising out of multiple acts or transactions, was entitled to discharge on statutory grounds after he had been held in jail in lieu of bail for 30 days, where statute defining maximum periods of imprisonment on misdemeanor charges clearly and unambiguously applied to both single and multiple misdemeanor charges, series of related and unrelated offenses were brought in one charging instrument, and all charges were brought under same case number and combined before single judge for trial. State v. Skaggs (Ohio App. 10 Dist., Franklin, 03-28-2006) No. 05AP-554, 2006-Ohio-1476, 2006 WL 772027, Unreported. Criminal Law ⚷ 577.16(1)

Triple-count provision of speedy trial statute, pursuant to which each day that the accused is held in jail in lieu of bail counts as three days, did not apply to time defendant spent in jail, where record contained a holder from another state, and defendant was wanted on open warrants in other jurisdictions. State v. Brewster (Ohio App. 1 Dist., Hamilton, 06-11-2004) No. C-030024, No. C-030025, 2004-Ohio-2993, 2004 WL 1284008, Unreported, motion for delayed appeal denied 103 Ohio St.3d 1490, 816 N.E.2d 1078, 2004-Ohio-5605, habeas corpus denied 2007 WL 2688425. Criminal Law ⚿ 577.11(1); Criminal Law ⚿ 577.11(3)

Defendant's right to a speedy trial was not violated; statutory provision providing that each day during which defendant is held in jail in lieu of bail on pending charges is counted as three days for speedy trial purposes, was not applicable to defendant, as defendant was in jail on separate unrelated charges following arrest for current charges, and defendant's cases went to trial within 270 days from date of first indictment. State v. Johnson (Ohio App. 8 Dist., Cuyahoga, 06-19-2003) No. 81692, No. 81693, 2003-Ohio-3241, 2003 WL 21419631, Unreported, appeal not allowed 100 Ohio St.3d 1433, 797 N.E.2d 513, 2003-Ohio-5396, denial of habeas corpus affirmed 493 Fed.Appx. 666, 2012 WL 3241545. Criminal Law ⚿ 577.11(3)

Provision of speedy trial statute providing that, if a person is charged with multiple charges of different degrees, the speedy trial time is based on the highest degree of the offense charged, did not apply to extend speedy trial time for alleged misdemeanor assault offense from 90 days to the 270-day speedy trial deadline for the original felony charge of aggravated burglary, which was dismissed; felony case terminated when grand jury returned a no true bill, after which new misdemeanor charges arising from the same incident were filed. State v. Large (Ohio App. 2 Dist., 01-09-2015) 2015-Ohio-33, 2015 WL 132453. Criminal Law ⚿ 577.14

Where defendant held in jail in lieu of bond was charged with several unrelated offenses in a multiple-count indictment and all counts were to be tried in a single trial, the indictment would be treated as a single charge, and defendant was entitled to the triple-count provision of speedy trial statute. State v. Dankworth (Ohio App. 2 Dist., 05-25-2007) 172 Ohio App.3d 159, 873 N.E.2d 902, 2007-Ohio-2588, appeal allowed 115 Ohio St.3d 1439, 875 N.E.2d 101, 2007-Ohio-5567, appeal dismissed as improvidently allowed 118 Ohio St.3d 1210, 887 N.E.2d 351, 2008-Ohio-2234. Criminal Law ⚿ 577.11(1)

54. —— Probation or parole violations, triple-count mechanism

Defendant's entitlement to triple counting of days held in jail, for purposes of 270-day speedy trial period, ceased from date of probation holder. State v. Wade (Ohio App. 10 Dist., Franklin, 07-29-2004) No. 03AP-774, 2004-Ohio-3974, 2004 WL 1688434, Unreported, stay granted 103 Ohio St.3d 1476, 816 N.E.2d 253, 2004-Ohio-5405, appeal not allowed 104 Ohio St.3d 1427, 819 N.E.2d 709, 2004-Ohio-6585, appeal not allowed 104 Ohio St.3d 1462, 821 N.E.2d 578, 2005-Ohio-204, appeal after new trial 2008-Ohio-543, 2008 WL 366143, on reconsideration 2008-Ohio-1797, 2008 WL 1723671, appeal not allowed 119 Ohio St.3d 1408, 891 N.E.2d 769, 2008-Ohio-3880, appeal not allowed 119 Ohio St.3d 1415, 891 N.E.2d 772, 2008-Ohio-3880, certiorari denied 129 S.Ct. 921, 555 U.S. 1126, 173 L.Ed.2d 158, appeal not allowed 120 Ohio St.3d 1491, 900 N.E.2d 200, 2009-Ohio-278. Criminal Law ⚿ 577.8(1)

56. Delays generally—Trial date schedule

Neither defendant's statutory nor constitutional rights to a speedy trial were violated in prosecution for non-support of dependents; defendant's motion for recusal tolled the speedy trial time, and while his motion for recusal remained pending, defendant requested that the trial date be rescheduled and sought a stay of the proceedings pending the outcome of his federal litigation. State v. Galluzzo (Ohio App. 2 Dist., Champaign, 01-20-2006) No. 2004 CA 25, 2006-Ohio-309, 2006 WL 202599, Unreported, appeal not allowed 109 Ohio St.3d 1482, 847 N.E.2d 1227, 2006-Ohio-2466, certiorari denied 127 S.Ct. 950, 549 U.S. 1124, 166 L.Ed.2d 725. Criminal Law ⚿ 577.10(8)

57. —— Defendant's fault, delays generally

Period of delay between date on which plea hearing was held and date for which trial was rescheduled was chargeable to defendant for purposes of speedy trial statute, in drug prosecution, as, after hearing commenced, defendant changed his mind about entering a guilty plea to a lesser charge and offered instead to plead no contest to the reduced charge, which constituted a period of delay necessitated by reason of a plea in bar chargeable to defendant under statute. State v. Baker (Ohio App. 12 Dist., Fayette, 05-22-2006) No. CA2005-05-017, 2006-Ohio-2516, 2006 WL 1381698, Unreported. Criminal Law ⚿ 577.10(8)

Time spent determining motions filed by defendant would be counted against defendant for purposes of speedy trial statute. State v. Brewster (Ohio App. 1 Dist., Hamilton, 06-11-2004) No. C-030024, No. C-030025, 2004-Ohio-2993, 2004 WL 1284008, Unreported, motion for delayed appeal denied 103 Ohio St.3d 1490, 816 N.E.2d 1078, 2004-Ohio-5605, habeas corpus denied 2007 WL 2688425. Criminal Law ⚿ 577.10(8)

Delay of 391 days from date defendant was arrested until date of guilty plea did not violate his constitutional and statutory speedy trial rights; defendant filed multiple motions for continuance and numerous other motions, including two motions to suppress, a motion to withdraw counsel, several discovery motions, and a motion for a transcript at State's expense. State v. Crayton (Ohio App. 8 Dist., Cuyahoga, 05-08-2003) No. 81257, 2003-Ohio-2299, 2003 WL 21027500, Unreported, as amended nunc pro tunc, appeal not allowed 100 Ohio St.3d 1411, 796 N.E.2d 538, 2003-Ohio-4948, motion to reopen denied 2004-Ohio-6293, 2004 WL 2677641, habeas corpus denied in part, dismissed in part 2007 WL 4248129. Criminal Law ⚿ 577.15(3)

A court should not allow defendants to use their slipperiness to claim the protection of statutory speedy-trial time limitations; a contrary rule would permit an accused on bail to avoid prosecution permanently by providing an inaccurate address or by refusing mail notice for hearing, unless the state makes additional extraordinary efforts to locate him. State v. Stokes (Ohio App. 12 Dist., 05-02-2011) 193 Ohio App.3d 549, 952 N.E.2d 1192, 2011-Ohio-2104. Criminal Law ⚷ 577.10(8)

Delay of over two years from defendant's first appearance of record to his arrest in Florida was occasioned by defendant's neglect or improper act, as a statutory ground for extending the 270-day limit for bringing defendant to trial on felony charges of unauthorized use of a motor vehicle; defendant had sufficient notice of the pendency of charges to require that he continue to make himself readily available to the court and his attorney, which would include providing a reliable address, and defendant furnished an address that became unreliable for at least the time that he spent in Florida and, despite several appearances in court, failed to notify the court of any changes therein. State v. Stokes (Ohio App. 12 Dist., 05-02-2011) 193 Ohio App.3d 549, 952 N.E.2d 1192, 2011-Ohio-2104. Criminal Law ⚷ 577.10(8); Criminal Law ⚷ 577.15(1)

58. —— Competency examinations, delays generally

Statutory speedy-trial time applicable to defendant was tolled from the time that defendant was found incompetent to stand trial to the time that he was found competent. Cleveland v. Allen (Ohio App. 8 Dist., Cuyahoga, 02-26-2009) No. 91233, 2009-Ohio-860, 2009 WL 478285, Unreported, appeal not allowed 122 Ohio St.3d 1505, 912 N.E.2d 109, 2009-Ohio-4233. Criminal Law ⚷ 577.11(6)

59. —— Suppression of evidence, delays generally

Ninety-five day period between defendant's indictment and commencement of his trial did not violate defendant's Sixth Amendment right to speedy trial, even if period would have exceeded limit under state law had defendant's attorney not filed motion to suppress that he withdrew on day of hearing, absent showing of prejudice. Hilliard v. Hudson (N.D.Ohio, 03-02-2009) 599 F.Supp.2d 921. Criminal Law ⚷ 577.15(4); Criminal Law ⚷ 577.16(4)

61. —— Justified, delays generally

Delays of 16 and 14 days resulting from trial court's involvement in capital case was reasonable, for purposes of tolling statutory speedy trial time in defendant's theft prosecution. State v. Miller (Ohio App. 10 Dist., Franklin, 09-26-2006) No. 06AP-36, 2006-Ohio-4988, 2006 WL 2733241, Unreported. Criminal Law ⚷ 577.10(7)

Delay of 56 days between date on which defendant filed his motion to suppress evidence and date on which trial court ruled on motion was chargeable to defendant for purposes of speedy trial statute, as time trial court spent ruling on motion was not unreasonable or unjustified by record, and it fell within rule requiring court to rule on motion within 120 days from date motion was filed. State v. Baker (Ohio App. 12 Dist., Fayette, 05-22-2006) No. CA2005-05-017, 2006-Ohio-2516, 2006 WL 1381698, Unreported. Criminal Law ⚷ 577.10(8)

Delay of approximately one year from the time defendant was arrested for murder until the time he was brought to trial did not violate his statutory right to a speedy trial; time period during which defendant's mental competence to stand trial was being determined was tolled, and the trial began 136 days after defendant withdrew his waiver of speedy trial time. State v. Florence (Ohio App. 2 Dist., Montgomery, 08-19-2005) No. 20439, 2005-Ohio-4508, 2005 WL 2083079, Unreported, appeal not allowed 107 Ohio St.3d 1700, 840 N.E.2d 205, 2005-Ohio-6763, appeal not allowed 109 Ohio St.3d 1427, 846 N.E.2d 535, 2006-Ohio-1967, habeas corpus dismissed 2010 WL 1882132. Criminal Law ⚷ 577.11(6); Criminal Law ⚷ 577.15(3)

Delay of three years in issuing indictment charging defendant with burglary with firearm specification did not implicate defendant's constitutional right to speedy trial, despite fact that prior charge against defendant of receiving stolen property, which also carried firearm specification, involved same gun and some of the same witnesses, where charges stemmed from separate acts, defendant suffered no actual prejudice as result of delay, indictment issued within applicable statute of limitations, and defendant was tried within statutory speedy trial period. State v. Elersic (Ohio App. 11 Dist., Lake, 09-30-2004) No. 2002-L-172, 2004-Ohio-5301, 2004 WL 2804809, Unreported, appeal not allowed 105 Ohio St.3d 1407, 821 N.E.2d 1027, 2005-Ohio-279, habeas corpus denied 2008 WL 618647, denial of post-conviction relief affirmed 2008-Ohio-2121, 2008 WL 1932109. Indictment And Information ⚷ 7

Defendant's constitutional and statutory right to speedy trial was not violated; after time was excluded from speedy trial calculation due to defendant's waiver of his right to speedy trial, his filing of request for bill of particulars, his filing of various motions, and his request for a continuance, total time counted against State was 73 days, which was within the 90 days State was required to bring defendant to trial. State v. McKinney (Ohio App. 3 Dist., Defiance, 10-18-2004) No. 4-04-12, 2004-Ohio-5518, 2004 WL 2334318, Unreported, motion for delayed appeal granted 104 Ohio St.3d 1459, 821 N.E.2d 576, 2005-Ohio-204, appeal not allowed 105 Ohio St.3d 1561, 828 N.E.2d 116, 2005-Ohio-2447, reconsideration denied 106 Ohio St.3d 1488, 832 N.E.2d 740, 2005-Ohio-3978, denial of post-conviction relief affirmed 2011-Ohio-3521, 2011 WL 2750943, appeal not allowed 130 Ohio St.3d 1476, 957 N.E.2d 1168, 2011-Ohio-6124. Criminal Law ⚷ 577.15(1)

Defendant was brought to trial well within the 270-day speedy trial period for persons charged with felonies; defendant spent seven days in jail before trial, which constituted 21 days under the triple credit rule, and an additional 137 days expired before defendant was brought to trial, totaling 158 days. State v. Humphrey (Ohio App. 2 Dist., Clark, 05-30-2003) No. CIV.A. 02CA0025, 2003-Ohio-2825, 2003 WL 21267255, Unreported, motion for delayed appeal denied 101 Ohio St.3d 1485, 805 N.E.2d 537, 2004-Ohio-1293, appeal not allowed 102 Ohio St.3d 1533, 811 N.E.2d 1152, 2004-Ohio-3580, habeas corpus dismissed 2007 WL 2120510. Criminal Law ⚷ 577.8(1); Criminal Law ⚷ 577.15(1)

For purposes of speedy trial calculation for defendant who was unable to post bond and remained in jail pending trial, 89 days elapsed between the date of defendant's arrest and the date on which trial began, and thus defendant was brought to trial within the 90-day statutory period. State v. Brownlow (Ohio App. 3 Dist., Allen, 04-10-2003) No. 1-02-73, 2003-Ohio-1819, 2003 WL 1834504, Unreported, appeal not allowed 105 Ohio St.3d 1472, 824 N.E.2d 541, 2005-Ohio-1186, habeas corpus denied 2007 WL 3101715. Criminal Law ⚷ 577.15(3)

Defendant's right to a speedy trial was not violated, even though defendant claimed his new trial following remand was held beyond applicable time limit; although approximately two months passed after reversal of defendant's original convictions, defendant had not requested any action in the meantime, and defendant's newly-assigned counsel almost immediately took steps to familiarize himself with his client's cases. State v. Washington (Ohio App. 8 Dist., Cuyahoga, 10-24-2002) No. 80418, 2002-Ohio-5834, 2002 WL 31401558, Unreported, appeal not allowed 98 Ohio St.3d 1491, 785 N.E.2d 473, 2003-Ohio-1189, dismissal of habeas corpus affirmed 101 Ohio St.3d 131, 802 N.E.2d 655, 2004-Ohio-298, appeal not allowed 102 Ohio St.3d 1413, 806 N.E.2d 564, 2004-Ohio-1763, habeas corpus denied 2007 WL 1592088. Criminal Law ⚷ 577.14

62. —— Unjustified, delays generally

Delay of 252 days between date defendant filed his motion seeking reconsideration of trial court's denial of his motion to suppress evidence and date trial court issued its ruling was not justified, as record failed to demonstrate that trial court needed any more than the 120-day period set forth in rule to rule on motion, and, as such, only 120 days of delay was chargeable to defendant, for purposes of speedy trial statute. State v. Baker (Ohio App. 12 Dist., Fayette, 05-22-2006) No. CA2005-05-017, 2006-Ohio-2516, 2006 WL 1381698, Unreported. Criminal Law ⚷ 577.10(8); Criminal Law ⚷ 577.12(1)

Defendant's failure to respond to State's discovery request did not toll period between date State filed its motion for reciprocal discovery and date defendant filed his response, and thus, defendant's statutory right to speedy trial was violated; there was no evidence presented that State was prejudiced in any way, nor did they avail themselves of a motion to compel as facilitated by criminal rules. State v. Palmer (Ohio App. 11 Dist., Portage, 12-16-2005) No. 2004-P-0106, 2005-Ohio-6710, 2005 WL 3476650, Unreported, stay granted 108 Ohio St.3d 1435, 842 N.E.2d 61, 2006-Ohio-421, motion to certify allowed 109 Ohio St.3d 1403, 845 N.E.2d 521, 2006-Ohio-1703, appeal allowed 109 Ohio St.3d 1405, 845 N.E.2d 522, 2006-Ohio-1703, reversed 112 Ohio St.3d 457, 860 N.E.2d 1011, 2007-Ohio-374. Criminal Law ⚷ 577.10(8)

State's delay of 41 days in sending DNA samples to laboratory for testing was unreasonable, and, as such, 41 days were to be counted against defendant's speedy trial time; in its motion to continue, state represented to trial court that it had requested a "rush" on the DNA testing, and thus state should have sent DNA sample out within days of filing its motion. State v. Brown (Ohio App. 7 Dist., Mahoning, 06-07-2005) No. 03-MA-32, 2005-Ohio-2939, 2005 WL 1385715, Unreported, appeal not allowed 106 Ohio St.3d 1558, 836 N.E.2d 582, 2005-Ohio-5531, habeas corpus denied 2007 WL 3342717, affirmed 656 F.3d 325, rehearing and rehearing en banc denied, certiorari denied 133 S.Ct. 1452, 185 L.Ed.2d 360. Criminal Law ⚷ 577.12(1)

63. Continuances generally—In general

To obtain a reversal of a conviction on the basis of a violation of the Speedy Trial Act, when a district court exercises its discretion to grant a continuance for the ends of justice, a defendant must show actual prejudice. U.S. v. Stewart (C.A.6 (Ohio), 12-06-2010) 628 F.3d 246, post-conviction relief denied 2012 WL 1745076. Criminal Law ⚷ 1166(7)

Defendant's written consent to a continuance is not a statutory requirement under the Speedy Trial Act's ends-of-justice provision. U.S. v. Stewart (C.A.6 (Ohio), 12-06-2010) 628 F.3d 246, post-conviction relief denied 2012 WL 1745076. Criminal Law ⚷ 577.13

District Court was within its discretion in granting motion for continuance filed by defendant's attorney, even absent defendant's written consent, where the court properly considered the Speedy Trial Act's ends-of-justice factors, explained on the record why granting continuance outweighed best interests of public and of defendant in having a speedy trial, and recognized that defendant's counsel needed additional time to analyze complex issues involved in the case and to prepare a defense. U.S. v. Stewart (C.A.6 (Ohio), 12-06-2010) 628 F.3d 246, post-conviction relief denied 2012 WL 1745076. Criminal Law ⚷ 577.13

64. —— Journal entries, continuances generally

Unjournalized continuance granted at defendant's own request extended the time provided by state's speedy trial statute for bringing defendant to trial. State v. Richardson (Ohio App. 2 Dist., Clark, 10-22-2004) No. 03CA92, 2004-Ohio-5815, 2004 WL 2445347, Unreported, appeal not allowed

105 Ohio St.3d 1464, 824 N.E.2d 92, 2005-Ohio-1024, appeal not allowed 108 Ohio St.3d 1473, 842 N.E.2d 1053, 2006-Ohio-665, habeas corpus dismissed 2008 WL 755261. Criminal Law ⚷ 577.13

Trial court's grant of several continuances, mostly requested by and for the benefit of defendant, did not violate defendant's speedy trial right, even though trial court did not place in its journal entries the reasons for continuances; rationale of court was not required when continuance was requested by defendant, and statutory time limitation would not have been exceeded but for defendant's requested continuances. State v. Phillips (Ohio App. 8 Dist., Cuyahoga, 02-05-2004) No. 82886, 2004-Ohio-484, 2004 WL 226120, Unreported, appeal not allowed 103 Ohio St.3d 1404, 812 N.E.2d 1287, 2004-Ohio-3980, habeas corpus denied 2008 WL 141928. Criminal Law ⚷ 577.10(8)

65. —— Withdrawal of counsel, continuances generally

Trial court did not violate defendant's statutory right to a speedy trial when it allowed his trial counsel to withdraw just prior to trial and then continued the matter so that defendant could acquire new counsel; defendant agreed that he wanted to have counsel represent him at trial. State v. Mustard (Ohio App. 4 Dist., Pike, 09-14-2004) No. 04CA724, 2004-Ohio-4917, 2004 WL 2072454, Unreported, appeal not allowed 105 Ohio St.3d 1438, 822 N.E.2d 810, 2005-Ohio-531, habeas corpus dismissed 2006 WL 783452, dismissal of post-conviction relief affirmed 2007-Ohio-1183, 2007 WL 778952. Criminal Law ⚷ 577.10(8)

66. —— Reasonableness, continuances generally

Trial court's second continuance of trial date due to second straight absence of same witness was not reasonable for purposes of speedy trial statute, absent a hearing and a record to support reasonableness of request, and, thus, continuance was chargeable to state, in drug prosecution. State v. Baker (Ohio App. 12 Dist., Fayette, 05-22-2006) No. CA2005-05-017, 2006-Ohio-2516, 2006 WL 1381698, Unreported. Criminal Law ⚷ 577.12(1); Criminal Law ⚷ 577.13

Trial court's decision to continue trial beyond 270-day statutory speedy trial date was reasonable and necessary under the circumstances, in drug prosecution; state sought continuance on basis that one of its key witnesses was unavailable for trial on date scheduled, and although state did not offer reason for witness' unavailability, it was first continuance sought by state, and defendant had already requested and received a continuance of his own. State v. Baker (Ohio App. 12 Dist., Fayette, 05-22-2006) No. CA2005-05-017, 2006-Ohio-2516, 2006 WL 1381698, Unreported. Criminal Law ⚷ 577.13

Journal entry on trial court's sua sponte continuance of trial stating that "case to be set out of time on first available date due to ct schedule," without more, was not reasonable continuance, as required to toll 30-day period governing prosecution for misdemeanor speeding and towing violation. Toledo v. Murray (Ohio App. 6 Dist., 10-25-2013) 999 N.E.2d 1230, 2013-Ohio-4747. Criminal Law ⚷ 577.10(4)

After reversal of Court of Appeals' affirmance of denial of defendant's motion to dismiss robbery and assault charges on speedy trial grounds, remand was required for Court of Appeals to determine reasonableness of extension of trial date of jailed defendant beyond 90-day speedy trial period, pursuant to statutory speedy trial exception for period of a reasonable continuance granted other than upon defendant's own motion. State v. Ramey (Ohio, 06-28-2012) 132 Ohio St.3d 309, 971 N.E.2d 937, 2012-Ohio-2904, on remand 986 N.E.2d 462, 2012-Ohio-6187. Criminal Law ⚷ 1181.5(3.1)

Proper remedy for State's discovery violation in criminal prosecution in municipal court, in which prosecution, the day before trial was scheduled to begin, defense counsel did not have bank statements which had been requested pursuant to counsel's discovery demand for all matters discoverable under criminal procedure rules, was to grant a short continuance so that detective or prosecutor could transmit the bank statements to defense counsel, rather than to dismiss the case with prejudice, where discovery violation was apparently inadvertent, defendant had waived her statutory speedy trial rights, and continuance requested by prosecutor was first request by either party for continuance of either pretrial date or trial date. State v. Johnson (Ohio App. 2 Dist., 11-22-2006) 169 Ohio App.3d 552, 863 N.E.2d 1088, 2006-Ohio-6227, appeal not allowed 113 Ohio St.3d 1443, 863 N.E.2d 658, 2007-Ohio-1266. Criminal Law ⚷ 627.8(6)

Reversal of defendant's conviction on four counts arising out of an armed bank robbery, on basis of alleged violation of the Speedy Trial Act's ends-of-justice provision, was not warranted, absent showing of actual prejudice to defendant; three-month delay that allowed defense counsel adequate time to prepare for trial did not prejudice defendant, even if the delay afforded government more time to prepare its case against him. U.S. v. Stewart (C.A.6 (Ohio), 12-06-2010) 628 F.3d 246, post-conviction relief denied 2012 WL 1745076. Criminal Law ⚷ 1166(7)

Trial court's order rescheduling defendant's trial on minor misdemeanor charge eighteen days following the expiration of the speedy trial time limit due to a pending jury trial was not unreasonable, and thus speedy trial statute was tolled during period of continuance. State v. Berner (Ohio App. 9 Dist., Medina, 06-19-2002) No. 3275-M, 2002-Ohio-3024, 2002 WL 1363686, Unreported, appeal not allowed 97 Ohio St.3d 1422, 777 N.E.2d 276, 2002-Ohio-5820. Criminal Law ⚷ 577.10(7)

For purposes of tolling speedy trial statute, reasonableness of continuance requested by the state on basis that necessary witness was unavailable for trial was satisfactorily evidenced by defendant's failure to object when the continuance was granted.

State v. Berner (Ohio App. 9 Dist., Medina, 06-19-2002) No. 3275-M, 2002-Ohio-3024, 2002 WL 1363686, Unreported, appeal not allowed 97 Ohio St.3d 1422, 777 N.E.2d 276, 2002-Ohio-5820. Criminal Law ⚿ 577.10(6)

67. —— Calculation, continuances generally

Time period during which trial court granted continuance due to burglary defendant's failure to appear in court was included in calculating whether defendant's constitutional and statutory speedy trial rights were violated. State v. Ossman (Ohio App. 5 Dist., Licking, 08-16-2004) No. 03 CA 92, 2004-Ohio-4302, 2004 WL 1827813, Unreported, appeal reopened 2006-Ohio-720, 2006 WL 367122, appeal not allowed 109 Ohio St.3d 1506, 849 N.E.2d 1028, 2006-Ohio-2998, habeas corpus dismissed 2007 WL 2110494. Criminal Law ⚿ 577.11(2)

For purposes of statutory speedy trial calculation, period of time which elapsed between filing of defendant's notice for continuance and the new trial date set by trial court was excluded from speedy trial period. State v. Humphrey (Ohio App. 2 Dist., Clark, 06-27-2003) No. 2002 CA 30, 2003-Ohio-3401, 2003 WL 21487780, Unreported, motion for delayed appeal denied 103 Ohio St.3d 1490, 816 N.E.2d 1078, 2004-Ohio-5605, habeas corpus denied 2008 WL 5412444. Criminal Law ⚿ 577.10(8)

68. —— Allowed, continuances generally

Delay of approximately one year between arrest and trial did not violate right to speedy trial; continuances were warranted due to scheduling conflicts and delay was not unreasonable. State v. Wade (Ohio App. 10 Dist., Franklin, 07-29-2004) No. 03AP-774, 2004-Ohio-3974, 2004 WL 1688434, Unreported, stay granted 103 Ohio St.3d 1476, 816 N.E.2d 253, 2004-Ohio-5405, appeal not allowed 104 Ohio St.3d 1427, 819 N.E.2d 709, 2004-Ohio-6585, appeal not allowed 104 Ohio St.3d 1462, 821 N.E.2d 578, 2005-Ohio-204, appeal after new trial 2008-Ohio-543, 2008 WL 366143, on reconsideration 2008-Ohio-1797, 2008 WL 1723671, appeal not allowed 119 Ohio St.3d 1408, 891 N.E.2d 769, 2008-Ohio-3880, appeal not allowed 119 Ohio St.3d 1415, 891 N.E.2d 772, 2008-Ohio-3880, certiorari denied 129 S.Ct. 921, 555 U.S. 1126, 173 L.Ed.2d 158, appeal not allowed 120 Ohio St.3d 1491, 900 N.E.2d 200, 2009-Ohio-278. Criminal Law ⚿ 577.15(3)

70. —— Chargeable against defendant, continuances generally

Delay of nearly 11 months between defendant's arrest and his trial, during which time he was held without bond, did not violate his statutory right to a speedy trial; much of delay was the result of defendant's pretrial motions and requests for continuances. State v. Milam (Ohio App. 8 Dist., Cuyahoga, 09-14-2006) No. 86268, 2006-Ohio-4742, 2006 WL 2639448, Unreported, appeal not allowed 112 Ohio St.3d 1472, 861 N.E.2d 145, 2007-Ohio-388, motion to reopen denied 2007-Ohio-1590, 2007 WL 1018660, appeal after new sentencing hearing 2008-Ohio-3144, 2008 WL 2534925, appeal not allowed 120 Ohio St.3d 1487, 900 N.E.2d 198, 2009-Ohio-278, habeas corpus denied 2011 WL 6026707. Criminal Law ⚿ 577.10(8); Criminal Law ⚿ 577.15(3)

When calculating the time within which defendant must be brought to trial, trial delay resulting from defendant's motion for a continuance in a previous case applied to subsequent case in which different charges were filed based on the same underlying facts and circumstances of the previous case. State v. Blackburn (Ohio, 04-23-2008) 118 Ohio St.3d 163, 887 N.E.2d 319, 2008-Ohio-1823. Criminal Law ⚿ 577.14

Defendant's motion to continue trial tolled statutory speedy-trial time period in prosecution for gross sexual imposition and rape. State v. Counts (Ohio App. 5 Dist., 01-07-2007) 170 Ohio App.3d 339, 867 N.E.2d 432, 2007-Ohio-117. Criminal Law ⚿ 577.10(8)

71. —— Chargeable against state, continuances generally

Delay in bringing defendant to trial as result of trial court's sua sponte entry of continuance and reassignment of trial date, without issuance of reasons, was chargeable against State rather than defendant for speedy trial purposes, such that 552-day delay in bringing defendant to trial violated his statutory speedy trial rights, in prosecution for aggravated robbery; delay period included triple-count tally under provision of speedy trial statute whereby three days were counted for each day during which defendant was held in jail in lieu of bail on the pending charge. State v. Pollock (Ohio App. 4 Dist., Ross, 06-13-2012) No. 11CA3267, 2012-Ohio-2819, 2012 WL 2367371, Unreported. Criminal Law ⚿ 577.12(1); Criminal Law ⚿ 577.15(1)

Trial court's decision to continue trial beyond 270-day statutory speedy trial date per state's fourth request for continuance, on basis of unavailability of state's witness, was not reasonable, and, thus, continuance was chargeable to state, in drug prosecution; state failed to offer any reasonable explanation for not having witnesses it needed to prosecute case for the fourth time. State v. Baker (Ohio App. 12 Dist., Fayette, 05-22-2006) No. CA2005-05-017, 2006-Ohio-2516, 2006 WL 1381698, Unreported. Criminal Law ⚿ 577.12(1); Criminal Law ⚿ 577.13

Trial court's decision to continue trial beyond 270-day statutory speedy trial date at state's request, on basis of unavailability of two of state's witnesses, was not reasonable, and, thus, continuance was chargeable to state, in drug prosecution; state made no effort to explain why it was unable to procure witnesses' attendance at trial, or why it was unable to procure attendance of witnesses it needed to try its case on three straight occasions, which provided a strong indication that state did not use due diligence to secure attendance of witnesses at trial. State v. Baker (Ohio App. 12 Dist., Fayette,

05-22-2006) No. CA2005-05-017, 2006-Ohio-2516, 2006 WL 1381698, Unreported. Criminal Law ⚷ 577.12(1); Criminal Law ⚷ 577.13

Trial court's sua sponte continuance of trial was chargeable against state, for purposes of speedy trial statute, in drug prosecution, as trial court failed to explain its reasons for sua sponte continuing trial, and reasons were not apparent from the record. State v. Baker (Ohio App. 12 Dist., Fayette, 05-22-2006) No. CA2005-05-017, 2006-Ohio-2516, 2006 WL 1381698, Unreported. Criminal Law ⚷ 577.12(1)

Continuances at request of the parties, continuance for purposes of determining defendant's mental competency to stand trial, and continuances at request of court were not attributable to the State for purposes of determining speedy trial time period. State v. Tullis (Ohio App. 10 Dist., Franklin, 05-05-2005) No. 04AP-333, 2005-Ohio-2205, 2005 WL 1055977, Unreported, appeal not allowed 106 Ohio St.3d 1510, 833 N.E.2d 1250, 2005-Ohio-4605, habeas corpus dismissed 2007 WL 4171635. Criminal Law ⚷ 577.10(7); Criminal Law ⚷ 577.10(8)

When a continuance granted to the state or granted by the trial court sua sponte is not supported by an explanation, the time must be charged to the state for speedy trial purposes. State v. Hohenberger (Ohio App. 6 Dist., 08-27-2010) 189 Ohio App.3d 346, 938 N.E.2d 419, 2010-Ohio-4053, appeal not allowed 127 Ohio St.3d 1505, 939 N.E.2d 1267, 2011-Ohio-19. Criminal Law ⚷ 577.12(1)

The 34-day pretrial continuance granted to state was chargeable to state for statutory speedy trial purposes, where the trial court's order granting state's motion to continue provided no explanation for the continuance, though a journal entry issued after expiration of the speedy-trial period provided a reason for the continuance. State v. Hohenberger (Ohio App. 6 Dist., 08-27-2010) 189 Ohio App.3d 346, 938 N.E.2d 419, 2010-Ohio-4053, appeal not allowed 127 Ohio St.3d 1505, 939 N.E.2d 1267, 2011-Ohio-19. Criminal Law ⚷ 577.12(1)

74. Waiver by defendant—In general

Defendant was not entitled to a discharge for delay in bringing him to trial and the trial court properly denied his motion to dismiss for alleged speedy trial violations, where defense counsel had signed a waiver of time limits without limitation, and at no time did the defendant file a formal written objection to any further continuances or a demand for trial. State v. Clark (Ohio App. 3 Dist., 11-03-2014) 23 N.E.3d 218, 2014-Ohio-4873. Criminal Law ⚷ 577.10(9); Criminal Law ⚷ 577.10(10)

A criminal defendant may waive speedy trial rights. State v. Ramey (Ohio, 06-28-2012) 132 Ohio St.3d 309, 971 N.E.2d 937, 2012-Ohio-2904, on remand 986 N.E.2d 462, 2012-Ohio-6187. Criminal Law ⚷ 577.10(9)

75. —— Conditional or limited, waiver by defendant

Language of speedy trial time waiver, that defendant agreed to have trial postponed beyond the 90-day period "to allow his counsel opportunity to prepare for trial," was not qualifying language limiting the duration of the waiver to the time period of defendant's trial preparation. State v. Maisch (Ohio App. 3 Dist., 11-26-2007) 173 Ohio App.3d 724, 880 N.E.2d 153, 2007-Ohio-6230. Criminal Law ⚷ 577.10(9)

77. —— Knowingly, intelligently and voluntarily, waiver by defendant

Defendant validly waived his statutory and constitutional rights to speedy trial on attempted murder and other charges prior to being extradited to Pennsylvania and being incarcerated there, and thus state did not violate defendant's speedy trial rights by failing to prosecute defendant until six years later, after defendant's release from prison in Pennsylvania; waiver stated that defendant had been given sufficient opportunity to consult with an attorney or to question court about time limitations and effects of waiving them, stated that defendant understood his speedy trial rights and that he knowingly, intelligently and voluntarily waived any and all applicable restrictions and limitations, waiver was unlimited in duration, and defendant never filed a demand for trial. State v. Braden (Ohio App. 11 Dist., 12-27-2011) 197 Ohio App.3d 534, 968 N.E.2d 49, 2011-Ohio-6691. Criminal Law ⚷ 577.10(9)

An accused or his counsel may waive the constitutional and statutory right to a speedy trial if the waiver is made knowingly and voluntarily. State v. Birr (Ohio App. 6 Dist., 02-18-2011) 192 Ohio App.3d 514, 949 N.E.2d 589, 2011-Ohio-796. Criminal Law ⚷ 577.10(9)

78. —— Failure to raise claim, waiver by defendant

For purposes of appellate review, murder defendant waived claim that he was denied speedy trial, where defendant failed to raise claim in trial court. State v. Shakoor (Ohio App. 7 Dist., Mahoning, 09-23-2003) No. 01CA121, 2003-Ohio-5140, 2003 WL 22231582, Unreported, denial of post-conviction relief affirmed 2010-Ohio-6386, 2010 WL 5541697. Criminal Law ⚷ 1035(1)

Defendant was precluded from raising speedy trial issue on appeal, where he failed to move for dismissal or discharge for a violation of his speedy trial rights, either orally or in writing, during or prior to trial. State v. Humphrey (Ohio App. 2 Dist., Clark, 05-30-2003) No. CIV.A. 02CA0025, 2003-Ohio-2825, 2003 WL 21267255, Unreported, motion for delayed appeal denied 101 Ohio St.3d 1485, 805 N.E.2d 537, 2004-Ohio-1293, appeal not allowed 102 Ohio St.3d 1533, 811 N.E.2d 1152, 2004-Ohio-3580, habeas corpus dismissed 2007 WL 2120510. Criminal Law ⚷ 1044.1(1)

Defendant waived on appeal claim that the District Court violated his speedy-trial rights by not properly considering factors set out in the Speedy Trial Act when it granted motion for a continuance filed by his attorney prior to his first trial, where he did not raise the claim before his trial began. U.S. v. Stewart (C.A.6 (Ohio), 12-06-2010) 628 F.3d 246, post-conviction relief denied 2012 WL 1745076. Criminal Law ⚷ 1035(1)

81. —— Continuances, waiver by defendant

Defendant's motion to dismiss, based on state speedy-trial statute, revoked or withdrew his prior waiver of speedy trial rights in his motion for continuance, so that time for bringing defendant to trial could no longer be tolled. State v. Masters (Ohio App. 3 Dist., 08-20-2007) 172 Ohio App.3d 666, 876 N.E.2d 1007, 2007-Ohio-4229, appeal allowed 116 Ohio St.3d 1455, 878 N.E.2d 33, 2007-Ohio-6803, appeal dismissed as improvidently allowed 118 Ohio St.3d 1205, 886 N.E.2d 864, 2008-Ohio-1964. Criminal Law ⚷ 577.10(9)

82. —— Writing, waiver by defendant

Murder defendant failed to demonstrate that he was denied his right to speedy trial, even though time between arrest and trial was one and one-half years, where defendant signed unlimited waiver of speedy trial rights and did not later file written objection and demand for trial. State v. Shakoor (Ohio App. 7 Dist., Mahoning, 09-23-2003) No. 01CA121, 2003-Ohio-5140, 2003 WL 22231582, Unreported, denial of post-conviction relief affirmed 2010-Ohio-6386, 2010 WL 5541697. Criminal Law ⚷ 577.10(9); Criminal Law ⚷ 577.10(10); Criminal Law ⚷ 577.15(3)

Defendant waived his right to a speedy trial, where defendant signed a form which waived his right to a speedy trial, and the waiver was filed with the trial court. State v. Woodley (Ohio App. 8 Dist., Cuyahoga, 04-17-2003) No. 80732, 2003-Ohio-1950, 2003 WL 1900935, Unreported, appeal not allowed 100 Ohio St.3d 1425, 797 N.E.2d 92, 2003-Ohio-5232, habeas corpus denied 2008 WL 2048209, affirmed 451 Fed.Appx. 529, 2011 WL 6355204. Criminal Law ⚷ 577.10(9)

Defendant did not waive his right to speedy trial by indicating to trial court that he would file motions to suppress and to sever trial from co-defendant, and then failing to file such motions; defendant did not execute a written waiver of speedy-trial rights and his actions were not an express waiver in open court on the record. State v. Ramey (Ohio, 06-28-2012) 132 Ohio St.3d 309, 971 N.E.2d 937, 2012-Ohio-2904, on remand 986 N.E.2d 462, 2012-Ohio-6187. Criminal Law ⚷ 577.10(9)

To be effective, an accused's waiver of his or her constitutional and statutory rights to a speedy trial must be expressed in writing or made in open court on the record. State v. Ramey (Ohio, 06-28-2012) 132 Ohio St.3d 309, 971 N.E.2d 937, 2012-Ohio-2904, on remand 986 N.E.2d 462, 2012-Ohio-6187. Criminal Law ⚷ 577.10(9)

Journal entries recording defendant's written waivers, though counsel, of time requirements for trial were sufficient to show that defendant validly waived his speedy trial rights, in prosecution for domestic violence and aggravated menacing. State v. Birr (Ohio App. 6 Dist., 02-18-2011) 192 Ohio App.3d 514, 949 N.E.2d 589, 2011-Ohio-796. Criminal Law ⚷ 577.10(9)

Where a defendant files an express written waiver of unlimited duration, the defendant is not entitled to discharge for violation of his right to a speedy trial unless the defendant files a formal written objection to any further continuances and makes a demand for trial, following which the state must bring him to trial within a reasonable time. State v. Maisch (Ohio App. 3 Dist., 11-26-2007) 173 Ohio App.3d 724, 880 N.E.2d 153, 2007-Ohio-6230. Criminal Law ⚷ 577.10(9); Criminal Law ⚷ 577.10(10)

84. —— Additional charges or refiling of indictment, waiver by defendant

Defendant's waiver of the statutory speedy trial time on initial charge against him for disorderly conduct did not apply to the subsequent charge against him for menacing that was filed after the waiver, as both charges arose out of the same facts, the state knew of these facts at the time of the initial indictment, and, thus, speedy trial time within which trial was to begin on menacing charge was subject to same speedy trial period that applied to disorderly conduct charge. State v. Carthon (Ohio App. 2 Dist., 01-20-2012) 197 Ohio App.3d 677, 968 N.E.2d 576, 2012-Ohio-196. Criminal Law ⚷ 577.14

In situations where an accused waives his right to speedy trial as to an initial charge, the waiver does not apply to a subsequently filed charge which arises out of the same facts as the former charge, when the later charge is brought after a nolle prosequi is entered as to the first charge. State v. Hohenberger (Ohio App. 6 Dist., 08-27-2010) 189 Ohio App.3d 346, 938 N.E.2d 419, 2010-Ohio-4053, appeal not allowed 127 Ohio St.3d 1505, 939 N.E.2d 1267, 2011-Ohio-19. Criminal Law ⚷ 577.14

If an accused waives his right to speedy trial as to an initial charge, the waiver carries over to a subsequently filed charge if it is a lesser included offense of the initial charge or the initial indictment was defective in that it was missing an element, such as mens rea. State v. Hohenberger (Ohio App. 6 Dist., 08-27-2010) 189 Ohio App.3d 346, 938 N.E.2d 419, 2010-Ohio-4053, appeal not allowed 127 Ohio St.3d 1505, 939 N.E.2d 1267, 2011-Ohio-19. Criminal Law ⚷ 577.14

Reversal of defendant's conviction for vehicular assault, based on appellate court's determination that defendant's waiver of his statutory speedy trial rights for a charge of aggravated vehicular assault did not carry over to the later charge of vehicular assault, also required reversal of defendant's conviction for domestic violence, and remand for new trial on the domestic violence, due to the unfairly prejudicial effect, with respect to the domestic violence charge, of the extensive testimony at trial about the vehicular assault, i.e., that defendant allegedly struck the victim, who was his wife, with his vehicle, causing severe injuries to the victim, after he had committed the alleged acts underlying the domestic violence charge. State v. Hohenberger (Ohio App. 6 Dist., 08-27-2010) 189 Ohio App.3d 346, 938 N.E.2d 419, 2010-Ohio-4053, appeal not allowed 127 Ohio St.3d 1505, 939 N.E.2d 1267, 2011-Ohio-19. Criminal Law ⚿ 1186.1

Defendant's waiver of his statutory speedy trial rights, with respect to aggravated vehicular assault charge based on driving under the influence (DUI), did not carry over to later charge, by indictment, of vehicular assault based on recklessness, where vehicular assault was not a lesser included offense of aggravated vehicular assault; defendant would not have contemplated the element of recklessness at the time he signed the speedy-trial waiver in conjunction with the aggravated vehicular assault charge. State v. Hohenberger (Ohio App. 6 Dist., 08-27-2010) 189 Ohio App.3d 346, 938 N.E.2d 419, 2010-Ohio-4053, appeal not allowed 127 Ohio St.3d 1505, 939 N.E.2d 1267, 2011-Ohio-19. Criminal Law ⚿ 577.14

85. Dismissal of charges or discharge

Trial court was under no obligation to issue findings of fact in support of order denying defendant's motion to dismiss criminal charge on speedy trial grounds when a request for such findings had not been timely made by defendant. State ex rel. Mack v. Ambrose (Ohio App. 8 Dist., Cuyahoga, 07-27-2009) No. 93454, 2009-Ohio-3746, 2009 WL 2331847, Unreported. Criminal Law ⚿ 577.16(10)

Felony charge of trafficking in cocaine was pending against defendant from the date of his arrest, for the purpose of calculating speedy-trial time, where defendant was indicted for the offense before the complaint was dismissed in the municipal court. State v. Baker (Ohio App. 12 Dist., Fayette, 02-17-2009) No. CA2008-03-008, 2009-Ohio-674, 2009 WL 372362, Unreported. Criminal Law ⚿ 577.14

Defendant's statutory right to speedy trial was violated, and, thus, defendant was entitled to dismissal of drug charge against him; trial court continued trial four times at state's request, the last of which it failed to journalize before expiration of statutory speedy trial time limit, and, as a result of these continuances, it took 740 days, or more than two years, after date of defendant's arrest to bring him to trial, which was facially unreasonable. State v. Baker (Ohio App. 12 Dist., Fayette, 05-22-2006) No. CA2005-05-017, 2006-Ohio-2516, 2006 WL 1381698, Unreported. Criminal Law ⚿ 577.16(1)

When a misdemeanor charge is filed and then voluntarily dismissed, the speedy-trial time that elapsed with respect to the dismissed charge must be added to the speedy-trial time that elapsed with respect to a misdemeanor charge filed thereafter, if the subsequent charge arises from the same set of circumstances as the dismissed charge, unless the subsequent charge was based on new and additional facts of which the state had no knowledge when the dismissed charge was filed. State v. Dillon (Ohio App. 2 Dist., 02-06-2009) 2009 -Ohio- 530, 2009 WL 282072. Criminal Law ⚿ 577.14

Defense counsel's failure to move for dismissal of menacing charge against defendant on statutory speedy trial grounds prejudiced defendant, and, thus, was ineffective assistance, as such a motion would have resulted in dismissal of the charge, given that defendant's waiver of statutory speedy trial time on earlier charge filed against him for disorderly conduct did not apply to the later-filed menacing charge, and speedy trial time on the menacing charge had expired. State v. Carthon (Ohio App. 2 Dist., 01-20-2012) 197 Ohio App.3d 677, 968 N.E.2d 576, 2012-Ohio-196. Criminal Law ⚿ 1904

86. Appeals generally

Trial court's decision to dismiss supplemental indictment against defendant on statutory speedy trial grounds on basis that it was based on same facts as original indictment and was subject to same 270-day speedy trial time as original indictment, based on evidence that was not part of record, rather than holding evidentiary hearing on issue, precluded appellate review, as it was unclear how trial court determined that indictments were based on the same facts, and the only relevant "facts" in the record were the two indictments, which facially appeared to be based on different facts. State v. Martinez (Ohio App. 9 Dist., Lorain, 08-07-2006) No. 05CA008845, 2006-Ohio-4021, 2006 WL 2241513, Unreported. Criminal Law ⚿ 1118

Defendant waived appellate review of his claim that he was not brought to trial on felony charges within time provided by speedy trial statute and, therefore, should have been discharged, where record did not indicate that issue of speedy trial was raised to trial court. State v. Kolvek (Ohio App. 9 Dist., Summit, 07-14-2004) No. 21752, 2004-Ohio-3706, 2004 WL 1562573, Unreported, appeal not allowed 103 Ohio St.3d 1528, 817 N.E.2d 410, 2004-Ohio-5852, appeal not allowed 104 Ohio St.3d 1441, 819 N.E.2d 1124, 2004-Ohio-7033, habeas corpus denied 2009 WL 891759. Criminal Law ⚿ 1035(1)

Defendant waived for appellate review question as to whether his speedy trial rights were violated, where defendant failed to raise issue at trial, in which he was ultimately convicted of complicity to commit aggravated murder and kidnapping. State v. Green (Ohio App. 7 Dist., Mahoning, 06-13-2003) No. 01 CA 54, 2003-Ohio-3074, 2003 WL 21373172, Unreported, motion for delayed appeal granted 100 Ohio St.3d 1407, 796 N.E.2d 535, 2003-Ohio-4948, dismissal of post-conviction relief affirmed 2003-Ohio-5142, 2003 WL 22231592, motion to reopen denied 2003-Ohio-5442, 2003 WL 22332000, appeal not allowed 100 Ohio St.3d 1544, 800 N.E.2d 750, 2003-Ohio-6879, denial of post-conviction relief reversed 2006-Ohio-3097, 2006 WL 1680044, appeal not allowed 111 Ohio St.3d 1416, 854 N.E.2d 1094, 2006-Ohio-5083. Criminal Law ⚿ 1035(1)

Postconviction review, rather than direct appeal, was appropriate remedy for defendant's claim that trial counsel was ineffective for failing to assert speedy trial violation, in prosecution for felonious assault. State v. Mock (Ohio App. 7 Dist., 06-09-2010) 2010 -Ohio- 2747, 2010 WL 2392808. Criminal Law ⚷ 1134.47(3)

Court of Appeals would disregard defendant's claim that state's "machinations" in the indicting and charging process had to be taken into consideration when deciding whether the delay in bringing him to trial was unreasonable, even though defendant raised a speedy trial argument on appeal; defendant did not separately argue the claim or cite legal authority to support the proposition, and arguing irregularities or abuse of the grand jury process was markedly different from arguing alleged speedy trial violations. State v. Kelly (Ohio App. 8 Dist., 09-21-2006) 970 N.E.2d 986, 2006-Ohio-4879, superseded 2006-Ohio-5902, 2006 WL 3233895, appeal not allowed 113 Ohio St.3d 1416, 862 N.E.2d 844, 2007-Ohio-1036, appeal after new sentencing hearing 2007-Ohio-6838, 2007 WL 4445405, motion for delayed appeal denied 117 Ohio St.3d 1496, 885 N.E.2d 953, 2008-Ohio-2028. Criminal Law ⚷ 1043(3)

An appellate court's review of a speedy-trial issue involves a mixed question of law and fact; the appellate court defers to the trial court's findings of fact as long as the findings are supported by competent, credible evidence, but the appellate court independently reviews whether the trial court properly applied the law to those facts. State v. Stokes (Ohio App. 12 Dist., 05-02-2011) 193 Ohio App.3d 549, 952 N.E.2d 1192, 2011-Ohio-2104. Criminal Law ⚷ 1134.42; Criminal Law ⚷ 1158.18

The standard of review upon an appeal raising a statutory speedy trial issue is to count the expired days as directed by the speedy trial statutes. State v. Hohenberger (Ohio App. 6 Dist., 08-27-2010) 189 Ohio App.3d 346, 938 N.E.2d 419, 2010-Ohio-4053, appeal not allowed 127 Ohio St.3d 1505, 939 N.E.2d 1267, 2011-Ohio-19. Criminal Law ⚷ 1134.11

In an appeal raising a statutory speedy trial issue, if any ambiguity exists as to the counting of the expired days as directed by the speedy trial statutes, the appellate court will construe the record in the defendant's favor. State v. Hohenberger (Ohio App. 6 Dist., 08-27-2010) 189 Ohio App.3d 346, 938 N.E.2d 419, 2010-Ohio-4053, appeal not allowed 127 Ohio St.3d 1505, 939 N.E.2d 1267, 2011-Ohio-19. Criminal Law ⚷ 1144.7

Even if an appearance of a violation of the speedy trial statute appears on the face of the record, the failure to raise the question of such a violation denies the State the opportunity to establish that tolling of the statute occurred; consequently, the proper approach is the filing of a postconviction-relief petition alleging ineffective assistance of counsel. State v. Mock (Ohio App. 7 Dist., 06-09-2010) 187 Ohio App.3d 599, 933 N.E.2d 270, 2010-Ohio-2747. Criminal Law ⚷ 1118; Criminal Law ⚷ 1519(7)

Delay of 87 days between Supreme Court's denial of further review of decision of Court of Appeals, which reversed defendant's murder conviction on basis that trial court should have granted mistrial, and date on which defendant moved to dismiss indictment in connection with retrial, was not unreasonable, and thus did not violate defendant's speedy trial rights; delay stemmed in part from time needed to reassign matter to new judge, defendant filed several pretrial motions which caused delay, and defendant's ability to prepare his defense was not prejudiced by delay. State v. Girts (Ohio App. 8 Dist., 07-24-1997) 121 Ohio App.3d 539, 700 N.E.2d 395, dismissed, appeal not allowed 80 Ohio St.3d 1424, 685 N.E.2d 237, reconsideration denied 80 Ohio St.3d 1472, 687 N.E.2d 299, denial of postconviction relief affirmed 2000 WL 1739293, appeal not allowed 91 Ohio St.3d 1481, 744 N.E.2d 1194, habeas corpus denied 2005 WL 1637862, reversed and remanded 2007 WL 2481018. Criminal Law ⚷ 577.14

Time for computing reasonableness of delay in commencing retrial of defendant, whose murder conviction was reversed by Court of Appeals on ground that trial court should have granted mistrial, commenced from time Supreme Court refused further appeal, rather than time of reversal; while Court of Appeals had reversed unanimously, that fact did not prevent state from exercising its right to seek further review. State v. Girts (Ohio App. 8 Dist., 07-24-1997) 121 Ohio App.3d 539, 700 N.E.2d 395, dismissed, appeal not allowed 80 Ohio St.3d 1424, 685 N.E.2d 237, reconsideration denied 80 Ohio St.3d 1472, 687 N.E.2d 299, denial of postconviction relief affirmed 2000 WL 1739293, appeal not allowed 91 Ohio St.3d 1481, 744 N.E.2d 1194, habeas corpus denied 2005 WL 1637862, reversed and remanded 2007 WL 2481018. Criminal Law ⚷ 577.14

2945.72 Extension of time for hearing or trial

Notes of Decisions

1. Constitutional issues

Defendant's speedy trial rights were not violated, in prosecution for insurance fraud and falsification; defendant was not in jail pending trial, she waived her right to a speedy trial for five months, and she was granted ten continuances. State v. Hinson (Ohio App. 8 Dist., Cuyahoga, 07-27-2006) No. 87132, 2006-Ohio-3831, 2006 WL 2096589, Unreported, appeal not allowed 112 Ohio St.3d 1421, 859 N.E.2d 559, 2006-Ohio-6712. Criminal Law ⚷ 577.10(8); Criminal Law ⚷ 577.10(9)

Assuming validity of murder defendant's pro se motion to revoke express written speedy trial waiver, 116-day delay between filing of such motion and defendant's being brought to trial was reasonable, where speedy trial time was tolled by trial court's sua sponte continuances for civil jury, defendant's motion for bill of particulars and request for discovery, and period between withdrawal of defendant's attorney and appointment of new counsel. State v. Love (Ohio App. 7 Dist., Mahoning, 03-27-2006) No. 02 CA 245, 2006-Ohio-1762, 2006 WL 890994, Unreported, appeal not allowed 110 Ohio St.3d 1465, 852 N.E.2d 1214, 2006-Ohio-4288. Criminal Law ⚷ 577.10(7); Criminal Law ⚷ 577.10(8)

Trial court's grant of several continuances, mostly requested by and for the benefit of defendant, did not violate defendant's speedy trial right, even though trial court did not place in its journal entries the reasons for continuances; rationale of court was not required when continuance was requested by defendant, and statutory time limitation would not have been exceeded but for defendant's requested continuances. State v. Phillips (Ohio App. 8 Dist., Cuyahoga, 02-05-2004) No. 82886, 2004-Ohio-484, 2004 WL 226120, Unreported, appeal not allowed 103 Ohio St.3d 1404, 812 N.E.2d 1287, 2004-Ohio-3980, habeas corpus denied 2008 WL 141928. Criminal Law ⚷ 577.10(8)

Dismissal of indictment with prejudice, based on rationale that speedy trial period was purportedly about to end when state moved for continuance, was plain error compromising state's substantial right to have a criminal trial conducted according to proper procedure; defendant's motion to suppress extended speedy-trial time, prior unjournalized continuances did not affirmatively demonstrate a constitutional violation of speedy-trial rights in absence of pre-indictment incarceration, and trial court accordingly had obligation to hear and determine the cause submitted for adjudication. State v. Lindsey (Ohio App. 2 Dist., 08-14-2009) 2009 -Ohio- 4124, 2009 WL 2490019.

3. Strict construction

Statutory extensions of time to bring an accused to trial are to be strictly construed, and not liberalized in favor of the state. State v. Ramey (Ohio, 06-28-2012) 132 Ohio St.3d 309, 971 N.E.2d 937, 2012-Ohio-2904, on remand 986 N.E.2d 462, 2012-Ohio-6187. Criminal Law ⚷ 577.13

Statutory grounds for extensions of time of statutory speedy-trial limits are to be strictly construed against the state. State v. Stokes (Ohio App. 12 Dist., 05-02-2011) 193 Ohio App.3d 549, 952 N.E.2d 1192, 2011-Ohio-2104. Criminal Law ⚷ 577.13

5. Extradition proceedings

Time period between defendant's arrest in Missouri and arraignment on assault and attempted murder charges was not attributable to the State under speedy trial statute, absent evidence that prosecution failed to exercise diligence in seeking custody of defendant. State v. Tullis (Ohio App. 10 Dist., Franklin, 05-05-2005) No. 04AP-333, 2005-Ohio-2205, 2005 WL 1055977, Unreported, appeal not allowed 106 Ohio St.3d 1510, 833 N.E.2d 1250, 2005-Ohio-4605, habeas corpus dismissed 2007 WL 4171635. Criminal Law ⚷ 577.11(5)

6. Running of time period

Felony charge of trafficking in cocaine was pending against defendant from the date of his arrest, for the purpose of calculating speedy-trial time, where defendant was indicted for the offense before the complaint was dismissed in the municipal court. State v. Baker (Ohio App. 12 Dist., Fayette, 02-17-2009) No. CA2008-03-008, 2009-Ohio-674, 2009 WL 372362, Unreported. Criminal Law ⚷ 577.14

Delay of 552 days between the date of defendant's arrest and the filing of defendant's motion for discovery constituted a violation of defendant's statutory right to speedy trial; tolling provision, which extended the period of time to bring an accused to trial by excluding any period of time that the accused was unavailable for trial, as long as the prosecution exercised reasonable diligence to secure the accused's availability, did not apply to toll the speedy trial time as there was no evidence that defendant attempted to avoid prosecution, and the prosecution merely entered the defendant's arrest warrant into the National Crime Information Center (NCIC) database and took no further action to locate defendant. State v. Baker (Ohio App. 12 Dist., Fayette, 02-17-2009) No. CA2008-03-008, 2009-Ohio-674, 2009 WL 372362, Unreported. Criminal Law ⚷ 577.11(2)

Defendant's right to speedy trial was not implicated by delay of over one year between his arrest and entry of his no-contest plea to felony charges, where all but 68 days of such period was tolled for speedy trial purposes. State v. Smith (Ohio App. 2 Dist., Clark, 11-12-2004) No. 2003 CA 93, 2004-Ohio-6062, 2004 WL 2588269, Unreported, motion for delayed appeal denied 105 Ohio St.3d 1450, 823 N.E.2d 455, 2005-Ohio-763, motion for delayed appeal denied 105 Ohio St.3d 1496, 825 N.E.2d 621, 2005-Ohio-1666, appeal not allowed 110 Ohio St.3d 1468, 852 N.E.2d 1215, 2006-Ohio-4288, habeas corpus dismissed 2007 WL 2080463, subsequent determination 2007 WL 2120515. Criminal Law ⚷ 577.10(8)

Period of 19 days that the state used to respond to defendant's demand for discovery and request for a bill of particulars was reasonable and tolled the statutory speedy-trial time requirements for that length of time. State v. Pilgrim (Ohio App. 10 Dist., 10-08-2009) 184 Ohio App.3d 675, 922 N.E.2d 248, 2009-Ohio-5357, motion for delayed appeal granted 124 Ohio St.3d 1441, 920 N.E.2d 372, 2010-Ohio-188, appeal not allowed 125 Ohio St.3d 1437, 927 N.E.2d 10, 2010-Ohio-2212, reconsideration denied 126 Ohio St.3d 1517, 930 N.E.2d 334, 2010-Ohio-3331, habeas corpus dismissed 2012 WL 554477. Criminal Law ⚷ 577.10(8)

Speedy-trial time for fourth-degree misdemeanor prosecution was not tolled by trial court's sua sponte grant of continuance due to trial judge's medical leave, where journal entry of continuance was not made prior to expiration of speedy-trial time period. Toledo v. Sauger (Ohio App. 6 Dist., 11-07-2008) 179 Ohio App.3d 285, 901 N.E.2d 826, 2008-Ohio-5810. Criminal Law ⚷ 577.13

For purposes of tolling of statutory speedy-trial time, a trial court shall determine the date by which a defendant should reasonably have responded to a reciprocal discovery request based on the totality of facts and circumstances of the case, including the time established for response by local rule, if applicable. State v. Palmer (Ohio, 02-14-2007) 112 Ohio St.3d 457, 860 N.E.2d 1011, 2007-Ohio-374. Criminal Law ⚷ 577.10(8)

Defendant's response to State's reciprocal discovery request, which response was that defendant had nothing to disclose and that defendant acknowledged his duty to supplement his response should that circumstance change, could have been prepared much earlier than 60 days after State's request, and thus, trial court did not abuse its discretion in tolling the running of statutory speedy-trial time after 30 days had passed from service of State's request. State v. Palmer (Ohio, 02-14-2007) 112 Ohio St.3d 457, 860 N.E.2d 1011, 2007-Ohio-374. Criminal Law ⚷ 577.10(8)

7. Triple-count mechanism

Statements of defense counsel at hearing on defendant's motion to dismiss constituted acknowledgement that defendant was being held on both pending rape charges and a parole holder, and, as such, defendant was not entitled to invoke triple-count provision of speedy trial statute requiring each day to be counted as three days, if accused was being held in jail in lieu of bail on pending charge, even though trial court made no findings of fact supporting denial of speedy trial motion, as defendant never requested findings of fact. State v. Brown (Ohio App. 7 Dist., Mahoning, 06-07-2005) No. 03-MA-32, 2005-Ohio-2939, 2005 WL 1385715, Unreported, appeal not allowed 106 Ohio St.3d 1558, 836 N.E.2d 582, 2005-Ohio-5531, habeas corpus denied 2007 WL 3342717, affirmed 656 F.3d 325, rehearing and rehearing en banc denied, certiorari denied 133 S.Ct. 1452, 185 L.Ed.2d 360. Criminal Law ⚷ 577.11(1); Criminal Law ⚷ 577.16(10)

Defendant's right to a speedy trial was not violated; statutory provision providing that each day during which defendant is held in jail in lieu of bail on pending charges is counted as three days for speedy trial purposes, was not applicable to defendant, as defendant was in jail on separate unrelated charges following arrest for current charges, and defendant's cases went to trial within 270 days from date of first indictment. State v. Johnson (Ohio App. 8 Dist., Cuyahoga, 06-19-2003) No. 81692, No. 81693, 2003-Ohio-3241, 2003 WL 21419631, Unreported, appeal not allowed 100 Ohio St.3d 1433, 797 N.E.2d 513, 2003-Ohio-5396, denial of habeas corpus affirmed 493 Fed.Appx. 666, 2012 WL 3241545. Criminal Law ⚷ 577.11(3)

8. Unavailability of accused

Defendant's speedy trial period was not tolled between date capias warrant was issued due to defendant's nonappearance at hearing and date defendant filed motion to dismiss on speedy trial grounds, even though defendant was incarcerated in another county, where both defendant and his attorney informed the court and the prosecutor of defendant's whereabouts, and State failed to exercise reasonable diligence in securing defendant's availability, such as by requesting a transport order. Cleveland Metroparks v. Signorelli (Ohio App. 8 Dist., Cuyahoga, 07-24-2008) No. 90157, 2008-Ohio-3675, 2008 WL 2837779, Unreported. Criminal Law ⚷ 577.11(4)

Proceedings to extradite defendant to another state were "pending," though defendant signed a waiver of extradition, and thus, the time for bringing defendant to trial in Ohio on charge of aiding or abetting aggravated robbery with a gun specification, for speedy trial purposes, was extended while defendant was unavailable for trial. State v. Davis (Ohio App. 5 Dist., Richland, 05-15-2002) No. 01 CA 67, 2002-Ohio-2502, 2002 WL 999322, Unreported, appeal not allowed 99 Ohio St.3d 1438, 789 N.E.2d 1118, 2003-Ohio-2902, denial of post-conviction relief affirmed 2007-Ohio-923, 2007 WL 658565. Criminal Law ⚷ 577.11(4)

9. Mental or physical disabilities

Delay of approximately one year from the time defendant was arrested for murder until the time he was brought to trial did not violate his statutory right to a speedy trial; time period during which defendant's mental competence to stand trial was being determined was tolled, and the trial began 136 days after defendant withdrew his waiver of speedy trial time. State v. Florence (Ohio App. 2 Dist., Montgomery, 08-19-2005) No. 20439, 2005-Ohio-4508, 2005 WL 2083079, Unreported, appeal not allowed 107 Ohio St.3d 1700, 840 N.E.2d 205, 2005-Ohio-6763, appeal not allowed 109 Ohio St.3d 1427, 846 N.E.2d 535, 2006-Ohio-1967, habeas corpus dismissed 2010 WL 1882132. Criminal Law ⚷ 577.11(6); Criminal Law ⚷ 577.15(3)

11. Motions or requests of accused—In general

Period of delay between date on which plea hearing was held and date for which trial was rescheduled was chargeable to defendant for purposes of speedy trial statute, in drug prosecution, as, after hearing commenced, defendant changed his mind about entering a guilty plea to a lesser charge and offered instead to plead no contest to the reduced charge, which constituted a period of delay necessitated by reason of a plea in bar chargeable to defendant under statute. State v. Baker (Ohio App. 12 Dist., Fayette, 05-22-2006) No. CA2005-05-017, 2006-Ohio-2516, 2006 WL 1381698, Unreported. Criminal Law ⚷ 577.10(8)

Fifty-one-day period of a continuance after trial court granted a motion by defendant's initial counsel to withdraw and appointed new counsel in a prosecution for felony drug offenses was reasonable, and thus the speedy-trial clock was tolled during the period, where trial court granted the continuance to allow new counsel time to prepare for trial. State v. Gartrell (Ohio App. 3 Dist., 11-24-2014) 24 N.E.3d 680, 2014-Ohio-5203. Criminal Law ⚷ 577.10(8)

Assault defendant's request for a jury view tolled statutory speedy trial time period; the speedy trial time was tolled for any proceeding or action made or instituted by the accused, request for a jury view was a proceeding instituted by the accused, and request for a jury view was a substantive issue requiring the State to file a response and for the trial court to weigh the issues. State v. Sinkovitz (Ohio App. 4 Dist., 10-06-2014) 20 N.E.3d 1206, 2014-Ohio-4492. Criminal Law ⚷ 577.10(8)

Speedy-trial period to bring defendant to trial on drug charges was tolled for 30 days following defendant's request for a bill of particulars and discovery, but not for the entire 67 days that state took to respond to request, absent a showing of special circumstances to justify the long delay; 30 days was reasonable amount of time for state to respond and thus toll speedy-trial period. State v. Ford (Ohio App. 1 Dist., 01-16-2009) 2009 -Ohio- 146, 2009 WL 104658. Criminal Law ⚷ 577.10(8); Criminal Law ⚷ 577.12(1)

Defendant's right to a speedy trial was not violated, even though roughly a year elapsed between the day defendant was served with the summons and complaint and defendant's trial; defendant filed four motions for continuances, which were granted, which tolled the speedy trial time, defendant's discovery demand tolled the speedy trial time, defendant filed a jury demand after much of the speedy trial had passed, the court explained that defendant's jury demand was filed two weeks prior to the scheduled bench trial and the expiration of his speedy-trial time and that it was unreasonable for defendant to expect a jury trial to be scheduled on such short notice, and the court listed the other cases it had scheduled for trial on the same day when it continued the case due to an overscheduled docket. State v. Marbury (Ohio App. 2 Dist., 02-25-2011) 192 Ohio App.3d 210, 948 N.E.2d 531, 2011 -Ohio- 879. Criminal Law ⚷ 577.10(7); Criminal Law ⚷ 577.10(8); Criminal Law ⚷ 577.10(10); Criminal Law ⚷ 577.15(4)

Five months was an unreasonable amount of time for trial court to rule on defendant's motion to sever, and thus speedy-trial period to bring defendant to trial on charge of having a gun under a disability was not tolled for entire five months, even though defendant failed to petition court to rule on motion. State v. Ford (Ohio App. 1 Dist., 01-16-2009) 180 Ohio App.3d 636, 906 N.E.2d 1155, 2009-Ohio-146. Criminal Law ⚷ 577.10(7)

12. —— Competency evaluation, motions or requests of accused

Statutory speedy-trial time applicable to defendant was tolled from the time that defendant was found incompetent to stand trial to the time that he was found competent. Cleveland v. Allen (Ohio App. 8 Dist., Cuyahoga, 02-26-2009) No. 91233, 2009-Ohio-860, 2009 WL 478285, Unreported, appeal not allowed 122 Ohio St.3d 1505, 912 N.E.2d 109, 2009-Ohio-4233. Criminal Law ⚷ 577.11(6)

13. —— Discovery, motions or requests of accused

Delay of 11 days resulting from defendant's request for discovery and bill of particulars was reasonable, for purposes of tolling statutory speedy trial time. State v. Miller (Ohio App. 10 Dist., Franklin, 09-26-2006) No. 06AP-36, 2006-Ohio-4988, 2006 WL 2733241, Unreported. Criminal Law ⚷ 577.10(8)

Defendant's demand for discovery and request for a bill of particulars was a tolling event for purposes of speedy trial statute. State v. Pilgrim (Ohio App. 10 Dist., 10-08-2009) 184 Ohio App.3d 675, 922 N.E.2d 248, 2009-Ohio-5357, motion for delayed appeal granted 124 Ohio St.3d 1441, 920 N.E.2d 372, 2010-Ohio-188, appeal not allowed 125 Ohio St.3d 1437, 927 N.E.2d 10, 2010-Ohio-2212, reconsideration denied 126 Ohio St.3d 1517, 930 N.E.2d 334, 2010-Ohio-3331, habeas corpus dismissed 2012 WL 554477. Criminal Law ⚷ 577.10(8)

Defendant's request for discovery tolled statutory speedy-trial time period in prosecution for gross sexual imposition and rape. State v. Counts (Ohio App. 5 Dist., 01-07-2007) 170 Ohio App.3d 339, 867 N.E.2d 432, 2007-Ohio-117. Criminal Law ⚷ 577.10(8)

14. —— Continuance, motions or requests of accused

Delay of 20 days resulting from parties' request for continuance was reasonable, for purposes of tolling statutory speedy trial time. State v. Miller (Ohio App. 10 Dist., Franklin, 09-26-2006) No. 06AP-36, 2006-Ohio-4988, 2006 WL 2733241, Unreported. Criminal Law ⚷ 577.10(8)

Delay of nearly 11 months between defendant's arrest and his trial, during which time he was held without bond, did not violate his statutory right to a speedy trial; much of delay was the result of defendant's pretrial motions and requests for continuances. State v. Milam (Ohio App. 8 Dist., Cuyahoga, 09-14-2006) No. 86268, 2006-Ohio-4742, 2006 WL 2639448, Unreported, appeal not allowed 112 Ohio St.3d 1472, 861 N.E.2d 145, 2007-Ohio-388, motion to reopen denied 2007-Ohio-1590, 2007 WL 1018660, appeal after new sentencing hearing 2008-Ohio-3144, 2008 WL 2534925, appeal not allowed 120 Ohio St.3d 1487, 900 N.E.2d 198, 2009-Ohio-278, habeas corpus denied 2011 WL 6026707. Criminal Law ⚷ 577.10(8); Criminal Law ⚷ 577.15(3)

Period of continuances granted on defendant's own motion tolled speedy trial time, in rape prosecution. State v. Brown (Ohio App. 7 Dist., Mahoning, 06-07-2005) No. 03-MA-32, 2005-Ohio-2939, 2005 WL 1385715, Unreported, appeal not allowed 106 Ohio St.3d 1558, 836 N.E.2d 582, 2005-Ohio-5531, habeas corpus denied 2007 WL 3342717, affirmed 656 F.3d 325, rehearing and rehearing en banc denied, certiorari denied 133 S.Ct. 1452, 185 L.Ed.2d 360. Criminal Law ⚷ 577.10(8)

Statutory speedy trial period was tolled, in prosecution for grand theft of a motor vehicle, aggravated robbery, having weapon while under disability, carrying concealed weapon, and failure to comply with signal of police officer, during continuance of trial date on joint motion of defendant and co-defendant after co-defendant was involved in automobile accident. State v. Smith (Ohio App. 2 Dist., Clark, 11-12-2004) No. 2003 CA 93, 2004-Ohio-6062, 2004 WL 2588269, Unreported, motion for delayed appeal denied 105 Ohio St.3d 1450, 823 N.E.2d 455, 2005-Ohio-763, motion for delayed appeal denied 105 Ohio St.3d 1496, 825 N.E.2d 621, 2005-Ohio-1666, appeal not allowed 110 Ohio St.3d 1468, 852 N.E.2d 1215, 2006-Ohio-4288, habeas corpus dismissed 2007 WL 2080463, subsequent determination 2007 WL 2120515. Criminal Law ⚷ 577.10(5)

Statutory speedy trial period was tolled, in prosecution for grand theft of a motor vehicle, aggravated robbery, having weapon while under disability, carrying concealed weapon, and failure to comply with signal of police officer, during continuance of trial date on motion filed by counsel for defendant, despite defendant's claim that he did not concur in such motion and that speedy trial clock therefore should not have been tolled; defense counsel, appointed three weeks before first scheduled trial date, was entitled to request continuance in order to obtain more time to prepare for trial without defendant's agreement, and defendant was bound thereby. State v. Smith (Ohio App. 2 Dist., Clark, 11-12-2004) No. 2003 CA 93, 2004-Ohio-6062, 2004 WL 2588269, Unreported, motion for delayed appeal denied 105 Ohio St.3d 1450, 823 N.E.2d 455, 2005-Ohio-763, motion for delayed appeal denied 105 Ohio St.3d 1496, 825 N.E.2d 621, 2005-Ohio-1666, appeal not allowed 110 Ohio St.3d 1468, 852 N.E.2d 1215, 2006-Ohio-4288, habeas corpus dismissed 2007 WL 2080463, subsequent determination 2007 WL 2120515. Criminal Law ⚷ 577.10(8)

For purposes of statutory speedy trial calculation, period of time which elapsed between filing of defendant's notice for continuance and the new trial date set by trial court was excluded from speedy trial period. State v. Humphrey (Ohio App. 2 Dist., Clark, 06-27-2003) No. 2002 CA 30, 2003-Ohio-3401, 2003 WL 21487780, Unreported, motion for delayed appeal denied 103 Ohio St.3d 1490, 816 N.E.2d 1078, 2004-Ohio-5605, habeas corpus denied 2008 WL 5412444. Criminal Law ⚷ 577.10(8)

Sixty-eight-day period of a continuance requested by defendant was not longer than necessary in a prosecution for felony drug offenses, such that the speedy-trial clock was tolled during the period, and because the period included the date of trial court's decision on defendant's motion to suppress, the decision did not restart the clock even if it normally would have. State v. Gartrell (Ohio App. 3 Dist., 11-24-2014) 24 N.E.3d 680, 2014-Ohio-5203. Criminal Law ⚷ 577.10(8)

An accused's motion to continue a trial does not unconditionally extend the time limit in which the accused must be brought to trial; rather, the speedy-trial time limit is merely extended by the time necessary in light of the reason for delay. State v. Gartrell (Ohio App. 3 Dist., 11-24-2014) 24 N.E.3d 680, 2014-Ohio-5203. Criminal Law ⚷ 577.10(8)

The requirement that, in order to toll the statutory speedy trial period, a sua sponte continuance must be entered with the reasons therefor by journal entry prior to the expiration of the statutory time limits prevents attempts to revive the statutory speedy trial time after it has expired. State v. Ramey (Ohio App. 2 Dist., 12-28-2012) 986 N.E.2d 462, 2012-Ohio-6187. Criminal Law ⚷ 577.13

When a trial court exercises its discretion to continue a defendant's period for trial beyond the statutory speedy trial period, under statutory speedy trial exception for period of a continuance granted other than upon defendant's own motion, the continuance must be reasonable. State v. Ramey (Ohio, 06-28-2012) 132 Ohio St.3d 309, 971 N.E.2d 937, 2012-Ohio-2904, on remand 986 N.E.2d 462, 2012-Ohio-6187. Criminal Law ⚷ 577.13

After reversal of Court of Appeals' affirmance of denial of defendant's motion to dismiss robbery and assault charges on speedy trial grounds, remand was required for Court of Appeals to determine reasonableness of extension of trial date of jailed defendant beyond 90-day speedy trial period, pursuant to statutory speedy trial exception for period of a reasonable continuance granted other than upon defendant's own motion. State v. Ramey (Ohio, 06-28-2012) 132 Ohio St.3d 309, 971 N.E.2d 937, 2012-Ohio-2904, on remand 986 N.E.2d 462, 2012-Ohio-6187. Criminal Law ⚷ 1181.5(3.1)

Delay caused by defense counsel's agreement to continuance would be counted against defendant for purposes of speedy-trial statute, even though defendant did not personally agree to a continuance or waive his right to speedy trial for that period of time. State v. Pilgrim (Ohio App. 10 Dist., 10-08-2009) 184 Ohio App.3d 675, 922 N.E.2d 248, 2009-Ohio-5357, motion for delayed appeal granted 124 Ohio St.3d 1441, 920 N.E.2d 372, 2010-Ohio-188, appeal not allowed 125 Ohio St.3d 1437, 927 N.E.2d 10, 2010-Ohio-2212, reconsideration denied 126 Ohio St.3d 1517, 930 N.E.2d 334, 2010-Ohio-3331, habeas corpus dismissed 2012 WL 554477. Criminal Law ⚷ 577.13

When calculating the time within which defendant must be brought to trial, trial delay resulting from defendant's motion for a continuance in a previous case applied to subsequent case in which different charges were filed based on the same underlying facts and circumstances of the previous case. State v. Blackburn (Ohio, 04-23-2008) 118 Ohio St.3d 163, 887 N.E.2d 319, 2008-Ohio-1823. Criminal Law ⚿ 577.14

15. —— Suppression of evidence, motions or requests of accused

Delay of 252 days between date defendant filed his motion seeking reconsideration of trial court's denial of his motion to suppress evidence and date trial court issued its ruling was not justified, as record failed to demonstrate that trial court needed any more than the 120-day period set forth in rule to rule on motion, and, as such, only 120 days of delay was chargeable to defendant, for purposes of speedy trial statute. State v. Baker (Ohio App. 12 Dist., Fayette, 05-22-2006) No. CA2005-05-017, 2006-Ohio-2516, 2006 WL 1381698, Unreported. Criminal Law ⚿ 577.10(8); Criminal Law ⚿ 577.12(1)

Delay of 56 days between date on which defendant filed his motion to suppress evidence and date on which trial court ruled on motion was chargeable to defendant for purposes of speedy trial statute, as time trial court spent ruling on motion was not unreasonable or unjustified by record, and it fell within rule requiring court to rule on motion within 120 days from date motion was filed. State v. Baker (Ohio App. 12 Dist., Fayette, 05-22-2006) No. CA2005-05-017, 2006-Ohio-2516, 2006 WL 1381698, Unreported. Criminal Law ⚿ 577.10(8)

Ninety-day speedy trial period for jailed defendant was not automatically tolled when co-defendant filed pretrial motion to suppress evidence; statute listing events and circumstances extending speedy trial period did not include filing of pretrial motions by a co-defendant. State v. Ramey (Ohio, 06-28-2012) 132 Ohio St.3d 309, 971 N.E.2d 937, 2012-Ohio-2904, on remand 986 N.E.2d 462, 2012-Ohio-6187. Criminal Law ⚿ 577.10(5)

Speedy trial statute was tolled in aggravated robbery case for the 71 days that elapsed from when defendant filed his motion to suppress until date decision was rendered, where codefendant joined motion, state filed its opposition, a two day hearing was held, and court was also presiding over an aggravated murder trial that lasted in excess of a week. State v. Littlefield (Ohio App. 3 Dist., Marion, 06-28-2002) No. 9-02-03, 2002-Ohio-3399, 2002 WL 1433772, Unreported, appeal not allowed 97 Ohio St.3d 1424, 777 N.E.2d 277, 2002-Ohio-5820. Criminal Law ⚿ 577.10(7); Criminal Law ⚿ 577.10(8)

18. —— Procedural requirements, motions of court or prosecutor

Trial court's failure to journalize two orders setting new trial dates until after previous dates had passed did not result in statutory speedy trial clock continuing to run. State v. Smith (Ohio App. 2 Dist., Clark, 11-12-2004) No. 2003 CA 93, 2004-Ohio-6062, 2004 WL 2588269, Unreported, motion for delayed appeal denied 105 Ohio St.3d 1450, 823 N.E.2d 455, 2005-Ohio-763, motion for delayed appeal denied 105 Ohio St.3d 1496, 825 N.E.2d 621, 2005-Ohio-1666, appeal not allowed 110 Ohio St.3d 1468, 852 N.E.2d 1215, 2006-Ohio-4288, habeas corpus dismissed 2007 WL 2080463, subsequent determination 2007 WL 2120515. Criminal Law ⚿ 577.10(7)

19. —— Reasonable continuances, motions of court or prosecutor

Trial court did not violate defendant's statutory right to a speedy trial when it allowed his trial counsel to withdraw just prior to trial and then continued the matter so that defendant could acquire new counsel; defendant agreed that he wanted to have counsel represent him at trial. State v. Mustard (Ohio App. 4 Dist., Pike, 09-14-2004) No. 04CA724, 2004-Ohio-4917, 2004 WL 2072454, Unreported, appeal not allowed 105 Ohio St.3d 1438, 822 N.E.2d 810, 2005-Ohio-531, habeas corpus dismissed 2006 WL 783452, dismissal of post-conviction relief affirmed 2007-Ohio-1183, 2007 WL 778952. Criminal Law ⚿ 577.10(8)

"Sua sponte continuances" are continuances granted other than on an accused's own motion and toll the speedy-trial time as long as the record reflects that the period of the continuance was reasonable. State v. Gartrell (Ohio App. 3 Dist., 11-24-2014) 24 N.E.3d 680, 2014-Ohio-5203. Criminal Law ⚿ 577.13

For a sua sponte continuance to toll the statutory speedy trial time, the record must reflect that the period of the continuance was reasonable; to satisfy this standard, the trial court must enter the order of continuance and the reasons therefor by journal entry prior to the expiration of the statutory time limits for bringing the defendant to trial. State v. Ramey (Ohio App. 2 Dist., 12-28-2012) 986 N.E.2d 462, 2012-Ohio-6187. Criminal Law ⚿ 577.13

It is permissible for a trial court to grant the State a continuance of a trial date beyond the statutory speedy trial time limit if the continuance is reasonable and necessary under the circumstances, and in these circumstances, the concept of "reasonable" must be strictly construed against the State; if the continuance is not reasonable, it must be charged against the State for speedy trial purposes. State v. Ramey (Ohio App. 2 Dist., 12-28-2012) 986 N.E.2d 462, 2012-Ohio-6187. Criminal Law ⚿ 577.13

Trial court's setting of trial date beyond statutory speedy trial period for defendant, based on codefendant's filing of motion to suppress, was not reasonable, and thus did not toll statutory speedy trial period as to defendant, regardless of defense counsel's acquiescence to trial date; defendant did not file motion, codefendant's motion to suppress did not relate to or affect defendant in any way, and defendant's counsel did not affirmatively request that trial date be set outside statutory speedy trial period. State v. Ramey (Ohio App. 2 Dist.,

12-28-2012) 986 N.E.2d 462, 2012-Ohio-6187. Criminal Law ⚷ 577.13

When defense counsel merely acquiesces to a continuance of the trial date set by the court but does not affirmatively lodge a motion for a continuance, the continuance is entered "other than upon the accused's own motion," and thus must be reasonable in order to toll defendant's statutory right to speedy trial. State v. Ramey (Ohio App. 2 Dist., 12-28-2012) 986 N.E.2d 462, 2012-Ohio-6187. Criminal Law ⚷ 577.13

Trial court's order rescheduling defendant's trial on minor misdemeanor charge eighteen days following the expiration of the speedy trial time limit due to a pending jury trial was not unreasonable, and thus speedy trial statute was tolled during period of continuance. State v. Berner (Ohio App. 9 Dist., Medina, 06-19-2002) No. 3275-M, 2002-Ohio-3024, 2002 WL 1363686, Unreported, appeal not allowed 97 Ohio St.3d 1422, 777 N.E.2d 276, 2002-Ohio-5820. Criminal Law ⚷ 577.10(7)

For purposes of tolling speedy trial statute, reasonableness of continuance requested by the state on basis that necessary witness was unavailable for trial was satisfactorily evidenced by defendant's failure to object when the continuance was granted. State v. Berner (Ohio App. 9 Dist., Medina, 06-19-2002) No. 3275-M, 2002-Ohio-3024, 2002 WL 1363686, Unreported, appeal not allowed 97 Ohio St.3d 1422, 777 N.E.2d 276, 2002-Ohio-5820. Criminal Law ⚷ 577.10(6)

20. —— Unreasonable continuances, motions of court or prosecutor

Delay in bringing defendant to trial as result of trial court's sua sponte entry of continuance and reassignment of trial date, without issuance of reasons, was chargeable against State rather than defendant for speedy trial purposes, such that 552-day delay in bringing defendant to trial violated his statutory speedy trial rights, in prosecution for aggravated robbery; delay period included triple-count tally under provision of speedy trial statute whereby three days were counted for each day during which defendant was held in jail in lieu of bail on the pending charge. State v. Pollock (Ohio App. 4 Dist., Ross, 06-13-2012) No. 11CA3267, 2012-Ohio-2819, 2012 WL 2367371, Unreported. Criminal Law ⚷ 577.12(1); Criminal Law ⚷ 577.15(1)

Trial court's sua sponte continuance of trial was chargeable against state, for purposes of speedy trial statute, in drug prosecution, as trial court failed to explain its reasons for sua sponte continuing trial, and reasons were not apparent from the record. State v. Baker (Ohio App. 12 Dist., Fayette, 05-22-2006) No. CA2005-05-017, 2006-Ohio-2516, 2006 WL 1381698, Unreported. Criminal Law ⚷ 577.12(1)

Journal entry on trial court's sua sponte continuance of trial stating that "case to be set out of time on first available date due to ct schedule," without more, was not reasonable continuance, as required to toll 30-day period governing prosecution for misdemeanor speeding and towing violation. Toledo v. Murray (Ohio App. 6 Dist., 10-25-2013) 999 N.E.2d 1230, 2013-Ohio-4747. Criminal Law ⚷ 577.10(4)

21. Proceedings instituted by accused

Holding of *State v. Brown*, that requests for discovery toll running of speedy trial clock, applied to defendant's case, though *Brown* was decided after defendant's motion for discovery was filed, as appellate court had applied tolling rule of *Brown* to requests for discovery and bills of particulars that had been filed before *Brown* was decided. State v. Brown (Ohio App. 7 Dist., Mahoning, 06-07-2005) No. 03-MA-32, 2005-Ohio-2939, 2005 WL 1385715, Unreported, appeal not allowed 106 Ohio St.3d 1558, 836 N.E.2d 582, 2005-Ohio-5531, habeas corpus denied 2007 WL 3342717, affirmed 656 F.3d 325, rehearing and rehearing en banc denied, certiorari denied 133 S.Ct. 1452, 185 L.Ed.2d 360. Courts ⚷ 100(1)

Statutory speedy trial period was tolled, in prosecution for grand theft of a motor vehicle, aggravated robbery, having weapon while under disability, carrying concealed weapon, and failure to comply with signal of police officer, during pendency of defendant's numerous pre-trial motions. State v. Smith (Ohio App. 2 Dist., Clark, 11-12-2004) No. 2003 CA 93, 2004-Ohio-6062, 2004 WL 2588269, Unreported, motion for delayed appeal denied 105 Ohio St.3d 1450, 823 N.E.2d 455, 2005-Ohio-763, motion for delayed appeal denied 105 Ohio St.3d 1496, 825 N.E.2d 621, 2005-Ohio-1666, appeal not allowed 110 Ohio St.3d 1468, 852 N.E.2d 1215, 2006-Ohio-4288, habeas corpus dismissed 2007 WL 2080463, subsequent determination 2007 WL 2120515. Criminal Law ⚷ 577.10(8)

22. Neglect or improper acts of accused

Defendant's failure to respond to State's discovery request did not toll period between date State filed its motion for reciprocal discovery and date defendant filed his response, and thus, defendant's statutory right to speedy trial was violated; there was no evidence presented that State was prejudiced in any way, nor did they avail themselves of a motion to compel as facilitated by criminal rules. State v. Palmer (Ohio App. 11 Dist., Portage, 12-16-2005) No. 2004-P-0106, 2005-Ohio-6710, 2005 WL 3476650, Unreported, stay granted 108 Ohio St.3d 1435, 842 N.E.2d 61, 2006-Ohio-421, motion to certify allowed 109 Ohio St.3d 1403, 845 N.E.2d 521, 2006-Ohio-1703, appeal allowed 109 Ohio St.3d 1405, 845 N.E.2d 522, 2006-Ohio-1703, reversed 112 Ohio St.3d 457, 860 N.E.2d 1011, 2007-Ohio-374. Criminal Law ⚷ 577.10(8)

Defendant's unsuccessful attempts to contact his court-appointed counsel while he was in jail and awaiting trial on charges of felony forgery were not neglectful or improper, and thus statutory speedy trial period was not tolled between date on which counsel was appointed and date on which counsel first communicated with defendant; because counsel was not aware that defendant was in jail at time of appointment, and because county public defender's office did not accept collect phone calls from jail, defendant wrote letter to his court-appointed counsel informing her that he was in jail and would like to be released on bond, but counsel placed letter in another client's file, was not aware of its contents, and did not communicate with defendant until court date over one month later. State v. Chisolm (Ohio App. 9 Dist., 09-16-2013) 998 N.E.2d 816, 2013-Ohio-3965, appeal not allowed 138 Ohio St.3d 1415, 3 N.E.3d 1216, 2014-Ohio-566. Criminal Law ⚿ 577.10(8)

Delay of over two years from defendant's first appearance of record to his arrest in Florida was occasioned by defendant's neglect or improper act, as a statutory ground for extending the 270-day limit for bringing defendant to trial on felony charges of unauthorized use of a motor vehicle; defendant had sufficient notice of the pendency of charges to require that he continue to make himself readily available to the court and his attorney, which would include providing a reliable address, and defendant furnished an address that became unreliable for at least the time that he spent in Florida and, despite several appearances in court, failed to notify the court of any changes therein. State v. Stokes (Ohio App. 12 Dist., 05-02-2011) 193 Ohio App.3d 549, 952 N.E.2d 1192, 2011-Ohio-2104. Criminal Law ⚿ 577.10(8); Criminal Law ⚿ 577.15(1)

23. Burden of proof

An accused who claims that his speedy trial rights were violated bears the burden to rebut the presumption that the delay resulting from a sua sponte continuance was reasonable by demonstrating that the period of delay was not necessitated by his own motion or action, and it is not sufficient merely to point out that his statutory speedy trial time otherwise expired. State v. Ramey (Ohio App. 2 Dist., 12-28-2012) 986 N.E.2d 462, 2012-Ohio-6187. Criminal Law ⚿ 577.13; Criminal Law ⚿ 577.16(8)

The state had the burden of demonstrating the existence of a statutory ground for extending the 270-day statutory speedy-trial limit for bringing defendant to trial on felony charges of unauthorized use of a motor vehicle, where defendant and the state stipulated at a hearing on defendant's motion to dismiss that defendant had not been brought to trial within the time limit. State v. Stokes (Ohio App. 12 Dist., 05-02-2011) 193 Ohio App.3d 549, 952 N.E.2d 1192, 2011-Ohio-2104. Criminal Law ⚿ 577.16(8)

31. Appeal

An appellate court's review of a speedy-trial issue involves a mixed question of law and fact; the appellate court defers to the trial court's findings of fact as long as the findings are supported by competent, credible evidence, but the appellate court independently reviews whether the trial court properly applied the law to those facts. State v. Stokes (Ohio App. 12 Dist., 05-02-2011) 193 Ohio App.3d 549, 952 N.E.2d 1192, 2011-Ohio-2104. Criminal Law ⚿ 1134.42; Criminal Law ⚿ 1158.18

2945.73 Discharge for delay in trial

Notes of Decisions

1. Constitutional issues

Defendant was not entitled to appellate review of claim that his speedy trial rights were violated in prosecution for involuntary manslaughter and felonious assault, where he did not file motion to dismiss on speedy trial grounds or otherwise bring matter to trial court's attention. State v. Triplett (Ohio App. 8 Dist., 02-24-2011) 192 Ohio App.3d 600, 949 N.E.2d 1058, 2011-Ohio-816, appeal not allowed 128 Ohio St.3d 1558, 949 N.E.2d 44, 2011-Ohio-2905. Criminal Law ⚿ 1035(1); Criminal Law ⚿ 1044.1(1)

Defendant's speedy trial rights were not violated, in prosecution for insurance fraud and falsification; defendant was not in jail pending trial, she waived her right to a speedy trial for five months, and she was granted ten continuances. State v. Hinson (Ohio App. 8 Dist., Cuyahoga, 07-27-2006) No. 87132, 2006-Ohio-3831, 2006 WL 2096589, Unreported, appeal not allowed 112 Ohio St.3d 1421, 859 N.E.2d 559, 2006-Ohio-6712. Criminal Law ⚿ 577.10(8); Criminal Law ⚿ 577.10(9)

Assuming validity of murder defendant's pro se motion to revoke express written speedy trial waiver, 116-day delay between filing of such motion and defendant's being brought to trial was reasonable, where speedy trial time was tolled by trial court's sua sponte continuances for civil jury, defendant's motion for bill of particulars and request for discovery, and period between withdrawal of defendant's attorney and appointment of new counsel. State v. Love (Ohio App. 7 Dist., Mahoning, 03-27-2006) No. 02 CA 245, 2006-Ohio-1762, 2006 WL 890994, Unreported, appeal not allowed 110 Ohio St.3d 1465, 852 N.E.2d 1214, 2006-Ohio-4288. Criminal Law ⚿ 577.10(7); Criminal Law ⚿ 577.10(8)

The trial court's failure to provide defendant with a preliminary hearing did not entitle defendant to a dismissal of the murder charges against him; defendant failed to file a motion to dismiss before the grand jury returned an indictment against him, and defendant failed to assert that the denial of a preliminary hearing violated equal protection until four months after the indictment was issued. State v. Zaffino (Ohio App. 9 Dist., Summit, 12-31-2003) No. 21514, 2003-Ohio-7202, 2003 WL 23095392, Unreported, appeal not allowed 102 Ohio St.3d 1459, 809 N.E.2d 32, 2004-Ohio-2569, habeas corpus dismissed 2006 WL 2360902, denial of post-conviction relief affirmed 2012-Ohio-1176, 2012 WL 983143. Criminal Law ⚿ 223

Dismissal of inmate's habeas corpus petition asserting speedy trial and double jeopardy claims was warranted; speedy trial and double jeopardy claims were not cognizable in habeas corpus and were to be addressed on appeal. Boles v. Knab (Ohio, 10-04-2011) 130 Ohio St.3d 339, 958 N.E.2d 554, 2011-Ohio-5049. Habeas Corpus ⚷ 291

Delay of 79 days following defendant's revocation of prior unlimited waiver of speedy-trial rights was not reasonable, and violated defendant's right to speedy trial in prosecution for criminal trespass, a fourth-degree misdemeanor. Toledo v. Sauger (Ohio App. 6 Dist., 11-07-2008) 179 Ohio App.3d 285, 901 N.E.2d 826, 2008-Ohio-5810. Criminal Law ⚷ 577.10(9); Criminal Law ⚷ 577.15(1)

A defendant establishes a prima facie case for dismissal on speedy trial grounds once the statutory time limit has expired; at that point, the state has the burden to demonstrate any extension of the time limit. State v. Dubose (Ohio App. 7 Dist., 12-31-2007) 174 Ohio App.3d 637, 884 N.E.2d 75, 2007-Ohio-7217, appeal not allowed 118 Ohio St.3d 1433, 887 N.E.2d 1202, 2008-Ohio-2595. Criminal Law ⚷ 577.16(8)

2. In general

Continuances at request of the parties, continuance for purposes of determining defendant's mental competency to stand trial, and continuances at request of court were not attributable to the State for purposes of determining speedy trial time period. State v. Tullis (Ohio App. 10 Dist., Franklin, 05-05-2005) No. 04AP-333, 2005-Ohio-2205, 2005 WL 1055977, Unreported, appeal not allowed 106 Ohio St.3d 1510, 833 N.E.2d 1250, 2005-Ohio-4605, habeas corpus dismissed 2007 WL 4171635. Criminal Law ⚷ 577.10(7); Criminal Law ⚷ 577.10(8)

10. Running of time period

Defendant charged with 42 fourth-degree misdemeanor violations of state tattooing statutes, arising out of multiple acts or transactions, was entitled to discharge on statutory grounds after he had been held in jail in lieu of bail for 30 days, where statute defining maximum periods of imprisonment on misdemeanor charges clearly and unambiguously applied to both single and multiple misdemeanor charges, series of related and unrelated offenses were brought in one charging instrument, and all charges were brought under same case number and combined before single judge for trial. State v. Skaggs (Ohio App. 10 Dist., Franklin, 03-28-2006) No. 05AP-554, 2006-Ohio-1476, 2006 WL 772027, Unreported. Criminal Law ⚷ 577.16(1)

12. Burden of proof

In a speedy trial challenge, once a defendant demonstrates that he was not brought to trial within the applicable statutory limit, he has established a prima facie case for dismissal; the burden then shifts to the state to demonstrate that, as a result of tolling or extension of the statutory time limit, the right to a speedy trial has not been violated. State v. Kist (Ohio App. 11 Dist., 09-14-2007) 173 Ohio App.3d 158, 877 N.E.2d 747, 2007-Ohio-4773. Criminal Law ⚷ 577.16(8)

13. Right to speedy trial denied

Defendant's failure to respond to State's discovery request did not toll period between date State filed its motion for reciprocal discovery and date defendant filed his response, and thus, defendant's statutory right to speedy trial was violated; there was no evidence presented that State was prejudiced in any way, nor did they avail themselves of a motion to compel as facilitated by criminal rules. State v. Palmer (Ohio App. 11 Dist., Portage, 12-16-2005) No. 2004-P-0106, 2005-Ohio-6710, 2005 WL 3476650, Unreported, stay granted 108 Ohio St.3d 1435, 842 N.E.2d 61, 2006-Ohio-421, motion to certify allowed 109 Ohio St.3d 1403, 845 N.E.2d 521, 2006-Ohio-1703, appeal allowed 109 Ohio St.3d 1405, 845 N.E.2d 522, 2006-Ohio-1703, reversed 112 Ohio St.3d 457, 860 N.E.2d 1011, 2007-Ohio-374. Criminal Law ⚷ 577.10(8)

16. Appeal

Defendant waived appellate review of his claim that he was not brought to trial on felony charges within time provided by speedy trial statute and, therefore, should have been discharged, where record did not indicate that issue of speedy trial was raised to trial court. State v. Kolvek (Ohio App. 9 Dist., Summit, 07-14-2004) No. 21752, 2004-Ohio-3706, 2004 WL 1562573, Unreported, appeal not allowed 103 Ohio St.3d 1528, 817 N.E.2d 410, 2004-Ohio-5852, appeal not allowed 104 Ohio St.3d 1441, 819 N.E.2d 1124, 2004-Ohio-7033, habeas corpus denied 2009 WL 891759. Criminal Law ⚷ 1035(1)

An appellate court's review of a speedy-trial issue involves a mixed question of law and fact; the appellate court defers to the trial court's findings of fact as long as the findings are supported by competent, credible evidence, but the appellate court independently reviews whether the trial court properly applied the law to those facts. State v. Stokes (Ohio App. 12 Dist., 05-02-2011) 193 Ohio App.3d 549, 952 N.E.2d 1192, 2011-Ohio-2104. Criminal Law ⚷ 1134.42; Criminal Law ⚷ 1158.18

17. Waiver

Defendant was precluded from raising speedy trial issue on appeal, where he failed to move for dismissal or discharge for a violation of his speedy trial rights, either orally or in writing, during or prior to trial. State v. Humphrey (Ohio App. 2 Dist., Clark, 05-30-2003) No. CIV.A. 02CA0025, 2003-Ohio-2825, 2003 WL 21267255, Unreported, motion for delayed appeal denied 101 Ohio St.3d 1485, 805 N.E.2d 537, 2004-Ohio-1293, appeal not allowed 102 Ohio St.3d 1533, 811 N.E.2d 1152, 2004-Ohio-3580, habeas corpus dismissed 2007 WL 2120510. Criminal Law ⚷ 1044.1(1)

Defendant waived any violation of his speedy trial rights; trial counsel filed a limited waiver of speedy trial rights and thereafter specifically waived defendant's speedy trial rights without any limitation in connection with a motion for a continuance, counsel later filed a motion to dismiss based on a violation of speedy trial rights without attempting to withdraw the earlier unlimited waiver, and newly-appointed counsel sought dismissal during trial on speedy-trial grounds but never attempted to withdraw the waiver before the commencement of trial as required to bring any potential error to the court's attention. State v. Dubose (Ohio App. 7 Dist., 12-31-2007) 174 Ohio App.3d 637, 884 N.E.2d 75, 2007-Ohio-7217, appeal not allowed 118 Ohio St.3d 1433, 887 N.E.2d 1202, 2008-Ohio-2595. Criminal Law ⚷ 577.10(9)

DEGREE OF OFFENSE

2945.74 Defendant may be convicted of lesser offense

Notes of Decisions

---

1. Constitutional issues

A conviction for a lesser included offense does not deprive an offender of his constitutional right to presentment or indictment by the grand jury, because by indicting the offender for the greater offense, the jury has necessarily considered each of the essential elements of the lesser offense. State v. Evans (Ohio, 07-07-2009) 122 Ohio St.3d 381, 911 N.E.2d 889, 2009-Ohio-2974, reconsideration denied 122 Ohio St.3d 1507, 912 N.E.2d 110, 2009-Ohio-4233, habeas corpus denied 2012 WL 2599968. Indictment and Information ⚷ 191(.5)

Ohio trial court's refusal to give two additional lesser-included offense instructions, one for involuntary manslaughter by simple assault and one for reckless murder, did not violate defendant's due process rights; defendant was convicted of involuntary manslaughter, which was a lesser-included offense of felony murder charge for which jury was instructed. Talley v. Hageman (N.D.Ohio, 06-24-2008) 619 F.Supp.2d 407. Constitutional Law ⚷ 4637; Homicide ⚷ 1456; Homicide ⚷ 1457

4. Evidence of lesser offenses

Domestic violence, under state statute and under city ordinance using language identical to state statute, which statute required family member to be aware of offender's threat and of offender's intent to cause him or her imminent harm, could not, as statutorily defined, ever be committed without minor misdemeanor disorderly conduct, as defined by state statute, also being committed, as element for disorderly conduct to qualify as lesser included offense; offender could not cause family member to believe that offender would cause imminent physical harm to family member without also recklessly causing inconvenience, annoyance, or alarm, as element of minor misdemeanor disorderly conduct. Shaker Hts. v. Mosely (Ohio, 05-16-2007) 113 Ohio St.3d 329, 865 N.E.2d 859, 2007-Ohio-2072. Indictment And Information ⚷ 191(.5)

8. —— Instructions, jury

Defendant did not present evidence of serious provocation occasioned by victims and, thus, was not entitled in trial for felonious assault to jury instruction on lesser-included offense of aggravated assault, even though victim allegedly threw coins in defendant's face; defendant testified that he was not in fit of rage, was not angry, and was cool, calm, and collected. State v. Crim (Ohio App. 8 Dist., Cuyahoga, 05-20-2004) No. 82347, 2004-Ohio-2553, 2004 WL 1118719, Unreported, appeal after new sentencing hearing 2005-Ohio-4129, 2005 WL 1910669, appeal allowed 107 Ohio St.3d 1696, 840 N.E.2d 202, 2005-Ohio-6763, reversed 109 Ohio St.3d 450, 849 N.E.2d 1, 2006-Ohio-2626, appeal after new sentencing hearing 2007-Ohio-4486, 2007 WL 2472443, appeal not allowed 116 Ohio St.3d 1507, 880 N.E.2d 483, 2008-Ohio-381, reconsideration denied 117 Ohio St.3d 1462, 884 N.E.2d 69, 2008-Ohio-1635, appeal after new sentencing hearing 2007-Ohio-5859, 2007 WL 3208590, appeal after new sentencing hearing 2009-Ohio-1085, 2009 WL 626333, appeal after new sentencing hearing 2008-Ohio-3805, 2008 WL 2931534, appeal not allowed 120 Ohio St.3d 1454, 898 N.E.2d 968, 2008-Ohio-6813, motion to reopen denied 2009-Ohio-2701, 2009 WL 1618237, appeal not allowed 122 Ohio St.3d 1524, 913 N.E.2d 459, 2009-Ohio-4776, habeas corpus denied 2006 WL 2164673, motion for delayed appeal denied 125 Ohio St.3d 1436, 927 N.E.2d 9, 2010-Ohio-2212. Assault And Battery ⚷ 96(1)

Even though an offense may be statutorily defined as a lesser included offense of another, a jury instruction on such lesser included offense is required only where the evidence presented at trial would reasonably support both an acquittal on the crime charged and a conviction upon the lesser included offense. State v. Wine (Ohio, 09-25-2014) 140 Ohio St.3d 409, 18 N.E.3d 1207, 2014-Ohio-3948. Criminal Law ⚷ 795(2.20)

It is the quality of the evidence offered, not the strategy of the defendant, that determines whether a lesser-included-offense instruction should be given to a jury. State v. Wine (Ohio, 09-25-2014) 140 Ohio St.3d 409, 18 N.E.3d 1207, 2014-Ohio-3948. Criminal Law ⚷ 795(2.1)

The law, the evidence presented, and the discretion of the trial judge play a role in whether lesser-included-offense jury instructions are appropriate. State v. Wine (Ohio, 09-25-2014) 140 Ohio St.3d 409, 18 N.E.3d 1207, 2014-Ohio-3948. Criminal Law ⚷ 795(1); Criminal Law ⚷ 795(2.1)

Defendant who presents an "all or nothing" defense in a criminal trial does not have the right to control whether a jury receives instructions on lesser-included offenses. State v. Wine (Ohio, 09-25-2014) 140 Ohio St.3d 409, 18 N.E.3d 1207, 2014-Ohio-3948. Criminal Law ⚩ 795(1)

Evidence did not support jury instruction on lesser-included offenses of reckless homicide or involuntary manslaughter, in prosecution for aggravated murder arising out of death of defendant's infant from head injuries; no jury would reasonably have concluded that the two separate blunt force injuries suffered by infant were inflicted recklessly. State v. Grube (Ohio App. 4 Dist., 02-07-2013) 987 N.E.2d 287, 2013-Ohio-692, appeal not allowed 135 Ohio St.3d 1459, 988 N.E.2d 579, 2013-Ohio-2285. Homicide ⚩ 1456; Homicide ⚩ 1458

If the evidence is such that a jury could reasonably find the defendant not guilty of the charged offense, but could convict the defendant of the lesser included offense, then the judge should instruct the jury on the lesser offense. Shaker Hts. v. Mosely (Ohio, 05-16-2007) 113 Ohio St.3d 329, 865 N.E.2d 859, 2007-Ohio-2072. Criminal Law ⚩ 795(2.1)

10. Sentencing

Following trial court's grant of defendant's motion to vacate perjury conviction and find defendant guilty of lesser-included offense of falsification, trial court was authorized to impose sentence for falsification, where motion to vacate was filed before the sentence for perjury was journalized, and sentence for falsification was within misdemeanor sentencing scheme. State v. Knight (Ohio App. 6 Dist., Sandusky, 08-19-2005) No. S-05-007, 2005-Ohio-4347, 2005 WL 2008144, Unreported, appeal decided 2006-Ohio-4807, 2006 WL 2641738. Criminal Law ⚩ 1663

11. Specific offenses—In general

Minor misdemeanor disorderly conduct, which was an offense under state statute, was a lesser included offense of domestic violence under state statute and under city ordinance using language identical to state domestic violence statute. Shaker Hts. v. Mosely (Ohio, 05-16-2007) 113 Ohio St.3d 329, 865 N.E.2d 859, 2007-Ohio-2072. Indictment And Information ⚩ 191(.5)

Domestic violence, under state statute and under city ordinance using language identical to state domestic violence statute, contained an element not required to prove minor misdemeanor disorderly conduct under state statute, as element for disorderly conduct to qualify as lesser included offense; domestic violence, but not disorderly conduct, must be committed against a family member. Shaker Hts. v. Mosely (Ohio, 05-16-2007) 113 Ohio St.3d 329, 865 N.E.2d 859, 2007-Ohio-2072. Indictment And Information ⚩ 191(.5)

Minor misdemeanor disorderly conduct, which was an offense under state statute, carried lesser penalty than domestic violence under state statute and under city ordinance using language identical to state domestic violence statute, as element for being lesser included offense; domestic violence under state statute ranged from first-degree misdemeanor to fourth-degree misdemeanor depending on defendant's criminal history, domestic violence under city ordinance was first-degree misdemeanor, and minor misdemeanor carried lesser penalty than first-degree to fourth-degree misdemeanors. Shaker Hts. v. Mosely (Ohio, 05-16-2007) 113 Ohio St.3d 329, 865 N.E.2d 859, 2007-Ohio-2072. Indictment And Information ⚩ 191(.5)

14. —— Homicide and assault, specific offenses

Trial court was not required to convene three-judge panel when it accepted defendant's guilty pleas to murder, kidnapping, aggravated burglary, and two counts of felonious assault; statute requiring convening of three-judge panel if defendant has been charged with crime punishable by death or has pleaded guilty to aggravated murder did not apply in defendant's case, as defendant was no longer charged with offense punishable by death at time he entered his guilty pleas. State v. West (Ohio App. 9 Dist., Lorain, 03-09-2005) No. 04CA008554, 2005-Ohio-990, 2005 WL 544820, Unreported, appeal not allowed 106 Ohio St.3d 1484, 832 N.E.2d 737, 2005-Ohio-3978, habeas corpus denied 2007 WL 2780506. Criminal Law ⚩ 273(4.1)

Assault was not lesser-included offense of misdemeanor domestic violence, although all of the elements required to prove assault were required to prove domestic violence, domestic violence further required proof of defendant's status as a family or household member, and a domestic violence conviction carried additional consequences, including enhanced bail considerations and possibility of having a second offense become a felony; the additional consequences were not penalties, and misdemeanor domestic-violence and assault charges each carried an identical maximum penalty of six months in jail and a $1,000 fine. State v. Daugherty (Ohio App. 2 Dist., 03-10-2006) 166 Ohio App.3d 551, 852 N.E.2d 202, 2006-Ohio-1133. Indictment And Information ⚩ 191(.5)

18. —— Disorderly conduct, specific offenses

Disorderly conduct, persist after warning to desist, was not a lesser-included offense of domestic violence, and thus, juvenile could not be adjudicated delinquent based on disorderly conduct, which was not charged in delinquency petition; disorderly conduct contained an additional element, persisting in disorderly conduct after reasonable warning or request to desist, which was not required to prove domestic violence. In re S.W. (Ohio App. 2 Dist., Montgomery, 10-14-2011) No. 24525, 2011-Ohio-5291, 2011 WL 4863972, Unreported. Indictment And Information ⚩ 191(.5); Infants ⚩ 2560

2945.75 Degree of offense; charge and verdict; prior convictions

(A) When the presence of one or more additional elements makes an offense one of more serious degree:

(1) The affidavit, complaint, indictment, or information either shall state the degree of the offense which the accused is alleged to have committed, or shall allege such additional element or elements. Otherwise, such affidavit, complaint, indictment, or information is effective to charge only the least degree of the offense.

(2) A guilty verdict shall state either the degree of the offense of which the offender is found guilty, or that such additional element or elements are present. Otherwise, a guilty verdict constitutes a finding of guilty of the least degree of the offense charged.

(B)(1) Whenever in any case it is necessary to prove a prior conviction, a certified copy of the entry of judgment in such prior conviction together with evidence sufficient to identify the defendant named in the entry as the offender in the case at bar, is sufficient to prove such prior conviction.

(2) Whenever in any case it is necessary to prove a prior conviction of an offense for which the registrar of motor vehicles maintains a record, a certified copy of the record that shows the name, date of birth, and social security number of the accused is prima-facie evidence of the identity of the accused and prima-facie evidence of all prior convictions shown on the record. The accused may offer evidence to rebut the prima-facie evidence of the accused's identity and the evidence of prior convictions. Proof of a prior conviction of an offense for which the registrar maintains a record may also be proved as provided in division (B)(1) of this section.

(3) If the defendant claims a constitutional defect in any prior conviction, the defendant has the burden of proving the defect by a preponderance of the evidence.

(2008 S 17, eff. 9–30–08; 2006 H 461, eff. 4–4–07; 1972 H 511, eff. 1–1–74)

Historical and Statutory Notes

Amendment Note: 2008 S 17 added division (B)(3).

Amendment Note: 2006 H 461 redesignated division (B) as division (B)(1) and added division (B)(2).

Research References

Encyclopedias

OH Jur. 3d Criminal Law: Procedure § 897, Stating Degree of Offense.

OH Jur. 3d Criminal Law: Procedure § 1458, Elements of Offense--Prior Conviction.

OH Jur. 3d Criminal Law: Procedure § 1769, Other Crimes Committed by Accused.

OH Jur. 3d Criminal Law: Procedure § 1785, Errors and Irregularities in Verdict.

OH Jur. 3d Criminal Law: Procedure § 1873, Specification as Prerequisite to Enhanced Penalty; State's Burden of Proof; Proof of Prior Conviction.

OH Jur. 3d Criminal Law: Substantive Principles and Offenses § 786, Determining Amount of Damage.

OH Jur. 3d Family Law § 1694, Weight and Sufficiency; Circumstantial Evidence.

Treatises and Practice Aids

Klein, Darling, & Terez, Baldwin's Ohio Practice Civil Practice § 44:3, Authentication of Official Record or Entry Under Civ. R. 44(A)--Domestic Record or Entry.

Klein, Darling, & Terez, Baldwin's Ohio Practice Civil Practice § 44:8, Proof by Any Other Method Authorized by Law--Revised Code Provisions.

Katz & Giannelli, Baldwin's Ohio Practice Criminal Law § 40:5, Nature and Contents.

Katz & Giannelli, Baldwin's Ohio Practice Criminal Law § 65:6, Return of Verdict.

Katz & Giannelli, Baldwin's Ohio Practice Criminal Law § 65:7, Lesser Included Offenses.

Katz & Giannelli, Baldwin's Ohio Practice Criminal Law § 118:14, Repeat Violent Offenders.

Katz & Giannelli, Baldwin's Ohio Practice Criminal Law § 148:31, Jury Verdict.

Katz & Giannelli, Baldwin's Ohio Practice Criminal Law § 148:32, Verdict of Guilty and Finding of Value of Property.

Katz & Giannelli, Baldwin's Ohio Practice Criminal Law § 148:33, Verdict of Guilty on One Count.

Katz & Giannelli, Baldwin's Ohio Practice Criminal Law § 148:34, Verdict of Guilty of Inferior Degree or of Lesser Included Offense.

Giannelli, Baldwin's Ohio Practice Evidence R 609, Impeachment by Evidence of Conviction of Crime.

Giannelli, Baldwin's Ohio Practice Evidence R 802, Hearsay Rule.

Giannelli, Baldwin's Ohio Practice Evidence R 902, Self-Authentication.

Carlin, Baldwin's Ohio Prac. Merrick-Rippner Probate Law § 109:59, Adjudicatory Hearings--Proof Beyond a Reasonable Doubt.

Adrine & Ruden, Ohio Domestic Violence Law § 2:7, Felony Violations.

Adrine & Ruden, Ohio Domestic Violence Law § 5:21, Case Preparation--Hearsay Exceptions--Judgment of Previous Conviction.

Adrine & Ruden, Ohio Domestic Violence Law § 16:19, Hearsay Exceptions--Judgment of Previous Conviction.

Weiler & Weiler, Ohio Driving Under the Influence § 11:9, Proof of Prior Convictions--Acceptable Methods.

Weiler & Weiler, Ohio Driving Under the Influence § 2:12, Felony--Method of Charging--RC 2941.1413 Specification.

Weiler & Weiler, Ohio Driving Under the Influence § 10:15, Admissibility of Leads.

Weiler & Weiler, Ohio Driving Under the Influence § 11:10, Proof of Prior Convictions--Acceptable Methods--Foundation.

Weiler & Weiler, Ohio Driving Under the Influence § 11:11, Proof of Prior Convictions--Acceptable Methods--Weight of the Evidence.

Weiler & Weiler, Ohio Driving Under the Influence § 11:14, Proof of Prior Convictions--Misdemeanors--As Sentencing Factor.

Weiler & Weiler, Ohio Driving Under the Influence § 11:16, Proof of Prior Convictions--Felonies--Stipulation of Prior Convictions.

Weiler & Weiler, Ohio Driving Under the Influence § 11:23, Collateral Attack on Prior Convictions--Constitutional Grounds--Lack of Counsel and Effective Waiver of Counsel--Burden of Proof.

Weiler & Weiler, Ohio Driving Under the Influence § 13:29, Verdict Forms.

Giannelli & Yeomans Salvador, Ohio Juvenile Law § 11:8, Delinquency Complaints.

Notes of Decisions

1. Constitutional issues

Imposition of sentence for receiving stolen property as fourth-degree felony based on trial court's finding that property involved was a firearm or dangerous ordinance violated defendant's Sixth Amendment right to a jury trial; jury's verdict, which did not include a finding that property involved was a firearm or dangerous ordinance, allowed sentencing only as first-degree misdemeanor. State v. Lacey (Ohio App. 5 Dist., Richland, 08-16-2006) No. 2005-CA-119, 2006-Ohio-4290, 2006 WL 2382763, Unreported, appeal after new sentencing hearing 2007-Ohio-6110, 2007 WL 3408257, appeal not allowed 117 Ohio St.3d 1459, 884 N.E.2d 67, 2008-Ohio-1635. Jury ⚿ 34(7)

2. In general

Verdict form was sufficient to convict defendant of aggravated menacing, even though it failed to state either the degree of the offense or the aggravating element; city charged defendant with aggravated menacing, city did not charge any penalty enhancements, and city charged defendant with and the jury found him guilty of the least degree (first-degree misdemeanor) of the offense (aggravated menacing). Portsmouth v. Wrage (Ohio App. 4 Dist., Scioto, 07-02-2009) No. 08CA3237, 2009-Ohio-3390, 2009 WL 2003386, Unreported. Criminal Law ⚿ 798.5

Neither the complaint nor the verdict form stated the degree of defendant's disorderly conduct offense or included an additional element elevating the offense from a minor misdemeanor to a fourth-degree misdemeanor, as required by statute, and, thus, defendant could be convicted only of minor misdemeanor disorderly conduct. State v. Carthon (Ohio App. 2 Dist., 01-20-2012) 197 Ohio App.3d 677, 968 N.E.2d 576, 2012-Ohio-196. Criminal Law ⚿ 881(2); Criminal Law ⚿ 883

3. Indictment generally

Indictment charging defendant with robbery was not required to include the value of property alleged to be stolen in order for defendant's subsequent conviction, on the lesser-included offense of theft, to be valid; indictment was sufficient to put defendant on notice of all lesser included offenses, together with any of the special, statutory findings dictated by the evidence produced in the case. State v. Smith (Ohio, 03-04-2009) 121 Ohio St.3d 409, 905 N.E.2d 151, 2009-Ohio-787. Indictment and Information ⚿ 188

4. Jury verdict generally

Verdict form convicting defendant of failure to comply with the order of a police officer, and, in doing so, causing a substantial risk of harm to persons or property, was not deficient on the basis that it failed to state that the offense was a third degree felony, as the element that elevated the crime to a third degree felony was the fact that defendant caused a substantial risk of physical harm to person/property, and this language was included in the jury verdict. State v. McDonald (Ohio App. 4 Dist., Lawrence, 03-29-2012) No. 11CA1, 2012-Ohio-1528, 2012 WL 1142677, Unreported, motion to certify allowed 132 Ohio St.3d 1512, 974 N.E.2d 111, 2012-Ohio-4021, reversed 137 Ohio St.3d 517, 1 N.E.3d 374, 2013-Ohio-5042. Criminal Law ⚿ 798.5

Defendant could be convicted of the minimum degree or offense level for engaging in a pattern of corrupt activity and conspiracy given jury's failure to specify a degree on its verdict form. State v. Ross (Ohio App. 9 Dist., Lorain, 02-13-2012) No. 09CA009742, 2012-Ohio-536, 2012 WL 440821, Unreported, appeal not allowed 132 Ohio St.3d 1423, 969 N.E.2d 271, 2012-Ohio-2729, habeas corpus dismissed 2014 WL 3053304. Criminal Law ⚿ 883

Verdict form on which jury stated that it found defendant guilty of felonious assault under the statutory provision alleged in the indictment, which was a first-degree felony because victim was a peace officer, could only support a conviction for felonious assault as a second-degree felony, given that the verdict form failed to identify the degree of the offense or the aggravating element that victim was a peace officer, such that the verdict form, under the statute governing guilty verdicts in cases where the presence of one or more additional elements made an offense one of more serious degree, constituted a finding of the least degree of the offense charged, which was a second-degree felony. State v. Barnette (Ohio App. 7 Dist., 12-05-2014) 2014-Ohio-5405, 2014 WL 6901011. Criminal Law ⚷ 798.5

Verdict determining that defendant was guilty of failure to comply with the order or signal of a police officer, and finding that defendant had caused a substantial risk of serious physical harm to persons or property, could not support a third-degree felony conviction, but could only support a misdemeanor conviction, under statute requiring a verdict form to include either the degree of the offense of which the defendant is convicted or a statement that an aggravating element has been found to justify convicting a defendant of a greater degree of a criminal offense; verdict failed to set forth the degree of the offense and also failed to find that the risk occurred when defendant was in willful flight from a police officer. State v. McDonald (Ohio, 11-20-2013) 137 Ohio St.3d 517, 1 N.E.3d 374, 2013-Ohio-5042. Obstructing Justice ⚷ 159; Obstructing Justice ⚷ 175

A verdict form signed by a jury must include either the degree of the offense of which the defendant is convicted or a statement that an aggravating element has been found to justify convicting a defendant of a greater degree of a criminal offense. State v. Bondurant (Ohio App. 4 Dist., 10-17-2012) 982 N.E.2d 1261, 2012-Ohio-4912, appeal allowed 134 Ohio St.3d 1467, 983 N.E.2d 367, 2013-Ohio-553, appeal not allowed 136 Ohio St.3d 1451, 991 N.E.2d 257, 2013-Ohio-3210, reversed 139 Ohio St.3d 247, 11 N.E.3d 252, 2014-Ohio-1932. Criminal Law ⚷ 883

Jury's verdict form for conviction for engaging in a pattern of corrupt activity identified offense level, a first-degree felony, and thus, jury was not required to make a specific finding of an aggravating element, that one of the incidents of corrupt activity was a first, second or third-degree felony, to elevate defendant's conviction. State v. Bondurant (Ohio App. 4 Dist., 10-17-2012) 982 N.E.2d 1261, 2012-Ohio-4912, appeal allowed 134 Ohio St.3d 1467, 983 N.E.2d 367, 2013-Ohio-553, appeal not allowed 136 Ohio St.3d 1451, 991 N.E.2d 257, 2013-Ohio-3210, reversed 139 Ohio St.3d 247, 11 N.E.3d 252, 2014-Ohio-1932. Criminal Law ⚷ 883

Verdict forms for complicity to commit burglary were insufficient to convict defendant of second degree felonies; verdict form contained neither the degree of the offense nor the aggravating elements of burglary. State v. Haller (Ohio App. 3 Dist., 11-13-2012) 982 N.E.2d 111, 2012-Ohio-5233, appeal not allowed 134 Ohio St.3d 1508, 984 N.E.2d 1102, 2013-Ohio-1123. Criminal Law ⚷ 798.5

Verdict constituted a finding of guilty of the least degree of offense of which defendant was found guilty, which was third degree burglary; although statute governing offense contained separate subparts with distinct offense levels, and verdict did not include degree of offense of which defendant was found guilty or additional element that enhanced offense, verdict expressly stated that defendant was found guilty of "burglary," and least serious degree of burglary as set forth in statute was a felony of the third degree. State v. Wells (Ohio App. 11 Dist., 09-28-2012) 978 N.E.2d 609, 2012-Ohio-4459, motion for delayed appeal denied 134 Ohio St.3d 1447, 982 N.E.2d 727, 2013-Ohio-347. Criminal Law ⚷ 883

Defendant's failure to raise at trial the defect in jury's verdict form did not result in waiver of defendant's argument on appeal that defendant could only be convicted of drug possession as a third-degree misdemeanor, rather than a third-degree felony, when verdict form did not comply with statutory requirement of either including the degree of the offense or a statement that aggravating circumstances were found to justify a conviction of the greater offense. State v. Moore (Ohio App. 4 Dist., 04-22-2010) 188 Ohio App.3d 726, 936 N.E.2d 981, 2010-Ohio-1848. Criminal Law ⚷ 1038.1(3.1)

Jury verdict form that found defendant "guilty of trafficking in crack cocaine" as charged in indictment was guilty verdict on fourth-degree trafficking in crack cocaine, even though indictment charged offense as first-degree based on aggravating factor that crack exceeded ten grams but was less than 25 grams in weight and that offense was committed within vicinity of school; although jury noted it found that crime was committed in vicinity of school, jury verdict form did not contain applicable code section citation to first-degree offense, nor indicate that jury made any findings regarding weight. State v. Ligon (Ohio App. 3 Dist., 11-24-2008) 179 Ohio App.3d 544, 902 N.E.2d 1011, 2008-Ohio-6085. Criminal Law ⚷ 883

A verdict form signed by a jury must include either the degree of the offense of which the defendant is convicted or a statement that an aggravating element has been found to justify convicting a defendant of a greater degree of a criminal offense. State v. Pelfrey (Ohio, 02-07-2007) 112 Ohio St.3d 422, 860 N.E.2d 735, 2007-Ohio-256. Criminal Law ⚷ 883

5. Sentencing generally

Evidence was sufficient to support conviction for trafficking in marijuana as a misdemeanor, rather than as a fifth degree felony; statute required the jury verdict form to indicate the degree of the offense, and since the jury failed to indicate the degree of the offense, defendant could only be convicted of the least degree of the offense charged. State v. Taylor (Ohio App. 11 Dist.,

08-27-2012) 974 N.E.2d 175, 2012-Ohio-3890. Controlled Substances ⇨ 82

When an individual is convicted but the trier of fact fails to find sufficient evidence to support an enhancement provision, a guilty verdict constitutes a finding of guilty of the least degree of the offense charged. State v. Lee (Ohio App. 12 Dist., 12-20-2010) 191 Ohio App.3d 219, 945 N.E.2d 595, 2010-Ohio-6276. Criminal Law ⇨ 1159.5

In order for defendant's conviction, for interference with child custody, to be enhanced from first-degree misdemeanor to fifth-degree felony, jury verdict form either had to contain language setting forth the enhancing element of removal of child from state, or it had to set forth the degree of the offense as fifth-degree felony. State v. Vitteritto (Ohio App. 3 Dist., 10-15-2007) 173 Ohio App.3d 532, 879 N.E.2d 243, 2007-Ohio-5478. Criminal Law ⇨ 798.5

6. Prior convictions—In general

Defendant's stipulated prior convictions for misdemeanor marijuana possession were not constitutionally defective, and, thus, could serve to establish "disability" element of offense of having a weapon under a disability; while defendant was able to establish, by means of trial court's judicial notice, that the prior convictions were uncounseled, he made no showing that he had not validly waived his right to counsel in the prior proceedings, and neither of judge's sheets for prior convictions reflected the imposition of a sentence of incarceration. State v. Williams (Ohio App. 1 Dist., 12-09-2011) 197 Ohio App.3d 505, 968 N.E.2d 27, 2011-Ohio-6267. Weapons ⇨ 180(1)

9. —— Burden of proof, prior convictions

Statute governing proof of a prior conviction that is being used to make an offense one of more serious degree sets forth one way to provide sufficient proof of a prior conviction, but does not provide the only method to prove it. State v. Gwen (Ohio, 11-01-2012) 134 Ohio St.3d 284, 982 N.E.2d 626, 2012-Ohio-5046. Criminal Law ⇨ 374.26

When, pursuant to statute governing use of prior conviction to increase degree of offense, the state chooses to offer judgment entries to prove the element of prior domestic-violence convictions to increase the offense level of a later domestic-violence charge, the judgments must comply with rule setting forth required contents of judgment of conviction; abrogating *State v. McCumbers*, 2010 WL 5141281. R.C. State v. Gwen (Ohio, 11-01-2012) 134 Ohio St.3d 284, 982 N.E.2d 626, 2012-Ohio-5046. Assault and Battery ⇨ 83(1); Criminal Law ⇨ 374.26

When the state, in using a prior conviction to make an offense one of more serious degree, chooses to prove the prior offense not through a guilty plea, but via a conviction, and the defendant does not stipulate to the fact of the conviction, the judgment entry of conviction offered must contain the fact of the conviction, the sentence, the judge's signature, and the time stamp indicating the entry upon the journal by the clerk. State v. Gwen (Ohio, 11-01-2012) 134 Ohio St.3d 284, 982 N.E.2d 626, 2012-Ohio-5046. Criminal Law ⇨ 374.26

In order to prove a prior conviction as the basis for enhancing a charged offense, the State must present both a certified copy of the prior judgment and evidence that the defendant named in the prior judgment is the defendant in the case at bar. State v. Tate (Ohio App. 8 Dist., 09-20-2012) 982 N.E.2d 94, 2012-Ohio-4276, appeal allowed 134 Ohio St.3d 1466, 983 N.E.2d 367, 2013-Ohio-553, reversed 138 Ohio St.3d 139, 4 N.E.3d 1016, 2014-Ohio-44. Sentencing and Punishment ⇨ 1381(2); Sentencing and Punishment ⇨ 1381(6)

It is defendant's burden to prove a constitutional defect in a prior conviction, as an element of an offense, by a preponderance of the evidence; if defendant cannot discharge this burden, the court presumes the constitutional regularity of the prior proceeding. State v. Williams (Ohio App. 1 Dist., 12-09-2011) 197 Ohio App.3d 505, 968 N.E.2d 27, 2011-Ohio-6267. Criminal Law ⇨ 323; Criminal Law ⇨ 328

10. —— Instructions, prior convictions

Trial court's failure to instruct jury, concerning how to consider stipulation to certified copy of driving under influence (DUI) defendant's prior felony DUI in final instruction, did not constitute plain error, where court noted in preliminary instructions that if attorneys agreed to any facts such agreement would be brought to the jurors' attention, and they could then regard such fact as conclusively proved without necessity of further evidence of such fact, and defendant testified that he had previously been convicted of a felony DUI offense upon a plea of guilty. State v. McMannis (Ohio App. 5 Dist., Stark, 04-14-2003) No. 2002CA00258, 2003-Ohio-1901, 2003 WL 1874723, Unreported, motion for delayed appeal denied 107 Ohio St.3d 1405, 836 N.E.2d 1226, 2005-Ohio-5859, reconsideration denied 108 Ohio St.3d 1419, 841 N.E.2d 322, 2006-Ohio-179, habeas corpus dismissed 2008 WL 2323491. Criminal Law ⇨ 1042.5

Trial court's alleged failure to properly inform jury of the level of the offense, when defining driving under the influence (DUI) defendant's prior DUI conviction to the jury, did not constitute plain error, where court properly instructed jurors that they must make a finding that defendant had been previously convicted of a felony DUI offense. State v. McMannis (Ohio App. 5 Dist., Stark, 04-14-2003) No. 2002CA00258, 2003-Ohio-1901, 2003 WL 1874723, Unreported, motion for delayed appeal denied 107 Ohio St.3d 1405, 836 N.E.2d 1226, 2005-Ohio-5859, reconsideration denied 108 Ohio St.3d 1419, 841 N.E.2d 322, 2006-Ohio-179, habeas corpus dismissed 2008 WL 2323491. Criminal Law ⇨ 1042.5

11. —— Verdict form, prior convictions

For purposes of error preservation, defendant had no duty to inform trial court that verdict form, as drawn, charged him with receiving stolen property as first-degree misdemeanor rather than as fourth-degree felony; incorrect verdict form prejudiced the state, not defendant, and thus the state had responsibility of informing trial court of error. State v. Lacey (Ohio App. 5 Dist., Richland, 08-16-2006) No. 2005-CA-119, 2006-Ohio-4290, 2006 WL 2382763, Unreported, appeal after new sentencing hearing 2007-Ohio-6110, 2007 WL 3408257, appeal not allowed 117 Ohio St.3d 1459, 884 N.E.2d 67, 2008-Ohio-1635. Criminal Law ⚩ 1038.1(3.1)

Failure of verdict form, on which jury made additional finding of prior driving under the influence (DUI) conviction, to contain the word "felony" or phrase "as previously charged in the indictment," did not prevent DUI defendant from being convicted of greater third-degree felony offense, where verdict form stated defendant was found guilty of DUI offense as charged in indictment, evidence was undisputed that prior conviction was felony DUI, state introduced a certified copy of prior conviction, defendant testified that he pleaded guilty to prior felony DUI, and trial court instructed jurors that they must find beyond reasonable doubt that defendant had been convicted of felony DUI. State v. McMannis (Ohio App. 5 Dist., Stark, 04-14-2003) No. 2002CA00258, 2003-Ohio-1901, 2003 WL 1874723, Unreported, motion for delayed appeal denied 107 Ohio St.3d 1405, 836 N.E.2d 1226, 2005-Ohio-5859, reconsideration denied 108 Ohio St.3d 1419, 841 N.E.2d 322, 2006-Ohio-179, habeas corpus dismissed 2008 WL 2323491. Automobiles ⚩ 358

A failure to strictly comply with requirement that a verdict form signed by a jury include either the degree of the offense of which the defendant is convicted, or a statement that an aggravating element has been found to justify convicting defendant of a greater degree of a criminal offense, does not render a judgment void. State v. Hines (Ohio App. 3 Dist., 06-27-2011) 193 Ohio App.3d 660, 953 N.E.2d 387, 2011-Ohio-3125, appeal not allowed 130 Ohio St.3d 1437, 957 N.E.2d 299, 2011-Ohio-5883. Criminal Law ⚩ 883

12. —— Admissibility of evidence, prior convictions

Defendant's Bureau of Motor Vehicles (BMV) transcript was not properly authenticated and, thus, did not qualify as a certified record that could be used as evidence of a prior felony operating a vehicle under the influence (OVI) to support specification that elevated defendant's new OVI conviction to a third-degree felony, unless transcript was self-authenticating; no individual or employee of BMV was identified on document as certifying the record, there was no signature, notarization, or affidavit attesting to record's authenticity, and prosecution attempted to introduce defendant's BMV record through testimony of arresting officer, who was not an individual capable of authenticating the record because he had no personal knowledge of the contents of the exhibit. State v. Lee (Ohio App. 12 Dist., 12-20-2010) 191 Ohio App.3d 219, 945 N.E.2d 595, 2010-Ohio-6276. Criminal Law ⚩ 444.12

Defendant's Bureau of Motor Vehicles (BMV) transcript was not properly authenticated and, thus, did not qualify as a self-authenticating record that could be used as evidence of a prior felony operating a vehicle under the influence (OVI) to support specification that elevated defendant's new OVI conviction to a third-degree felony; record bore no official seal of the state motor vehicle registrar, record bore no signature, and there was no indication on the record that a custodian or authorized individual certified the record. State v. Lee (Ohio App. 12 Dist., 12-20-2010) 191 Ohio App.3d 219, 945 N.E.2d 595, 2010-Ohio-6276. Criminal Law ⚩ 444.12

13. —— Sufficiency of evidence, prior convictions

Jury's finding with respect to charge of possessing firearm while under a disability, that defendant had prior conviction involving illegal possession, use, sale, administration, distribution, or trafficking in any drug of abuse, was not against manifest weight of evidence; defendant stipulated to the identification of him as the person named in certified copy of judgment entry of conviction and sentence for trafficking in cocaine and possession of cocaine, and trial court instructed jury in accordance with that stipulation. State v. Smith (Ohio App. 9 Dist., Summit, 03-19-2003) No. 21069, 2003-Ohio-1306, 2003 WL 1240403, Unreported, appeal not allowed 99 Ohio St.3d 1455, 790 N.E.2d 1219, 2003-Ohio-3396, habeas corpus dismissed 2006 WL 2233211, denial of post-conviction relief affirmed 180 Ohio App.3d 684, 906 N.E.2d 1191, 2009-Ohio-335, habeas corpus dismissed 2009-Ohio-1857, 2009 WL 1041443, affirmed 123 Ohio St.3d 145, 914 N.E.2d 1036, 2009-Ohio-4691. Weapons ⚩ 293(4)

Defense counsel's stipulation to the authenticity of defendant's two prior domestic violence convictions established defendant's identity to sustain his conviction for felony domestic violence, an element of which was that defendant have two or more prior domestic violence convictions; wording of stipulation revealed that defendant stipulated that he was the individual referenced in certified copies of convictions that were entered into evidence, and defense counsel requested that jury be instructed that evidence was received that "defendant" had two prior convictions for domestic violence. State v. Tate (Ohio, 01-15-2014) 138 Ohio St.3d 139, 4 N.E.3d 1016, 2014-Ohio-44. Assault and Battery ⚩ 91.8

Defendant's stipulation to authenticity of prior conviction for domestic violence, without more, was insufficient to show that prior convictions for individual with same name as defendant were prior convictions for defendant, as required for prior convictions to serve as predicate offenses to enhance domestic violence charge to felony, where records of prior convictions did not have any unique identifier, such as social security number or birth date, to ensure that prior convictions were for defendant. State v. Tate (Ohio App. 8 Dist., 09-20-2012) 982 N.E.2d 94, 2012-Ohio-4276, appeal allowed 134 Ohio St.3d 1466, 983 N.E.2d 367, 2013-Ohio-553, reversed 138 Ohio St.3d 139, 4 N.E.3d 1016, 2014-Ohio-44. Sentencing and Punishment ⚿ 1381(6)

Evidence was sufficient to show that defendant had five prior convictions of operating a motor vehicle under the influence of alcohol (OVI), as required to support conviction for fourth degree felony OVI; supervisor of reinstatement and keeper of records at the Bureau of Motor Vehicles testified that defendant had five prior OVI convictions and testified as to the specific dates of the prior convictions, and certified copy of a defendant's driving record was introduced that listed defendant's prior convictions. State v. Simin (Ohio App. 9 Dist., 09-26-2012) 977 N.E.2d 714, 2012-Ohio-4389. Automobiles ⚿ 359.6

Stipulated exhibits containing complaint and journal entry of prior domestic-violence adjudication were sufficient evidence of prior adjudication to support charge of domestic violence as a fourth-degree felony as to subsequent incident; although the exhibit itself did not include the charge or case number upon which juvenile had been adjudicated, there was no dispute as to the correlation in the stipulated exhibits. In re D.N. (Ohio App. 8 Dist., 10-27-2011) 195 Ohio App.3d 552, 960 N.E.2d 1063, 2011-Ohio-5494. Infants ⚿ 2636

POST TRIAL PROCEDURE

2945.77 Polling jury

Notes of Decisions

2. Disagreements

Trial court acted within its discretion in denying defendant's motion for mistrial and, instead, ordering further deliberations upon discovering, when polling jury, that guilty verdict was not unanimous. State v. Williams (Ohio App. 8 Dist., Cuyahoga, 10-21-2004) No. 83423, 2004-Ohio-5592, 2004 WL 2361981, Unreported, appeal not allowed 105 Ohio St.3d 1470, 824 N.E.2d 540, 2005-Ohio-1186, habeas corpus denied 2007 WL 1160293. Criminal Law ⚿ 867.18

6. Review

In deciding whether there has been an abuse of discretion by a trial court in determining whether to grant a mistrial when a juror states that his or her verdict was compromised, Supreme Court will not second-guess that determination absent an abuse of discretion. State v. Brown (Ohio, 10-08-2003) 100 Ohio St.3d 51, 796 N.E.2d 506, 2003-Ohio-5059, stay granted 798 N.E.2d 615, 2003-Ohio-5993, certiorari denied 124 S.Ct. 1516, 540 U.S. 1224, 158 L.Ed.2d 162, habeas corpus denied 2006 WL 533405, affirmed 531 F.3d 433, rehearing and rehearing en banc denied, certiorari denied 129 S.Ct. 1617, 173 L.Ed.2d 1002, denial of post-conviction relief affirmed 186 Ohio App.3d 309, 927 N.E.2d 1133, 2010-Ohio-405, appeal not allowed 124 Ohio St.3d 1467, 920 N.E.2d 993, 2010-Ohio-355. Criminal Law ⚿ 1155

2945.79 Causes for new trial

Notes of Decisions

1. Constitutional issues

Trial court's decision to sua sponte declare mistrial, over defendant's objection, in prosecution for aggravated robbery and aggravated burglary was based on manifest necessity, so that retrial of defendant was not barred by double jeopardy clause; terrorist attacks of September 11, 2001, occurred on second day of trial, courthouse was evacuated and closed that day, judge was concerned about jurors' ability to concentrate on serious charges against defendant in light of breaking national news and, while judge considered instructing jurors to return next day, he did not do so because he did not know if courthouse would be open and he remained concerned about jurors' ability to concentrate. State v. Walls (Ohio App. 6 Dist., Lucas, 01-31-2003) No. L-01-1492, 2003-Ohio-493, 2003 WL 220460, Unreported, appeal not allowed 99 Ohio St.3d 1435, 789 N.E.2d 1117, 2003-Ohio-2902, habeas corpus granted 418 F.Supp.2d 962, reversed 490 F.3d 432, rehearing and rehearing en banc denied. Double Jeopardy ⚿ 99

Prosecutor's improper comments during closing arguments, in which prosecutor referred to defendant's post-arrest silence, constituted harmless error; improper comments were only a small portion of the closing argument, an inference of guilt was not stressed to jury when viewing the context of entire closing argument, and evidence of guilt was overwhelming. State v. Thomas (Ohio App. 1 Dist., Hamilton, 12-31-2002) No. C-010724, 2002-Ohio-7333, 2002 WL 31894850, Unreported, appeal not allowed 98 Ohio St.3d 1515, 786 N.E.2d 64, 2003-Ohio-1572, on reconsideration 2009-Ohio-971, 2009 WL 565511, stay granted 123 Ohio St.3d 1469, 915 N.E.2d 1252, 2009-Ohio-5704, vacated 124 Ohio St.3d 412, 922 N.E.2d 964, 2010-Ohio-577. Criminal Law ⚿ 1171.3

If one or more jurors are sleeping, the right to a jury trial has been impaired. State v. Majid (Ohio App. 8 Dist., 06-25-2009) 182 Ohio App.3d 730, 914

N.E.2d 1113, 2009-Ohio-3075, appeal not allowed 123 Ohio St.3d 1509, 917 N.E.2d 812, 2009-Ohio-6210, appeal after new trial 2012-Ohio-1192, 2012 WL 986127, appeal not allowed 132 Ohio St.3d 1464, 969 N.E.2d 1231, 2012-Ohio-3054. Criminal Law ⚿ 855(1)

Counsel did not perform deficiently, as element of ineffective assistance of counsel, in failing to request the dismissal and replacement of juror who was contacted at softball game, before guilt-phase opening statements in aggravated murder trial, by brother of murder victim's boyfriend, where nothing that was said during juror's brief conversation with brother would have supported a defense challenge to the juror. State v. Frazier (Ohio, 10-10-2007) 115 Ohio St.3d 139, 873 N.E.2d 1263, 2007-Ohio-5048, certiorari denied 128 S.Ct. 2077, 553 U.S. 1015, 170 L.Ed.2d 811, denial of post-conviction relief affirmed 2008-Ohio-5027, 2008 WL 4408645, appeal not allowed 121 Ohio St.3d 1425, 903 N.E.2d 325, 2009-Ohio-1296, motion to reopen denied 126 Ohio St.3d 1541, 932 N.E.2d 336, 2010-Ohio-3855, habeas corpus denied 2011 WL 5086443. Criminal Law ⚿ 1937

Prosecutor did not improperly vouch for state witness's testimony by telling her that she was doing a good job; prosecutor was simply reassuring witness in the midst of her difficult testimony. State v. Smith (Ohio, 12-13-2002) 97 Ohio St.3d 367, 780 N.E.2d 221, 2002-Ohio-6659, reconsideration denied 97 Ohio St.3d 1500, 780 N.E.2d 1023, 2002-Ohio-7367, stay granted 98 Ohio St.3d 1417, 782 N.E.2d 73, 2003-Ohio-189, certiorari denied 123 S.Ct. 2255, 539 U.S. 907, 156 L.Ed.2d 118, habeas corpus denied 2007 WL 2840379, affirmed 591 F.3d 517, rehearing and rehearing en banc denied, certiorari denied 131 S.Ct. 185, 178 L.Ed.2d 111. Criminal Law ⚿ 2098(5)

Prosecutor's question during closing argument, "Did he claim accident, that he didn't do this on purpose?", was not an improper comment on defendant's failure to testify; comment showed how evidence supported fact that defendant purposely committed crimes in question. State v. Smith (Ohio, 12-13-2002) 97 Ohio St.3d 367, 780 N.E.2d 221, 2002-Ohio-6659, reconsideration denied 97 Ohio St.3d 1500, 780 N.E.2d 1023, 2002-Ohio-7367, stay granted 98 Ohio St.3d 1417, 782 N.E.2d 73, 2003-Ohio-189, certiorari denied 123 S.Ct. 2255, 539 U.S. 907, 156 L.Ed.2d 118, habeas corpus denied 2007 WL 2840379, affirmed 591 F.3d 517, rehearing and rehearing en banc denied, certiorari denied 131 S.Ct. 185, 178 L.Ed.2d 111. Criminal Law ⚿ 2132(2)

Prosecutor's statement during closing argument that murder defendant was "seated right over there next to his counsel" was not an improper attempt to denigrate defendant and his trial counsel; prosecutor was merely pointing out defendant to jury as a means of emphasizing that it was he who committed the crimes. State v. Smith (Ohio, 12-13-2002) 97 Ohio St.3d 367, 780 N.E.2d 221, 2002-Ohio-6659, reconsideration denied 97 Ohio St.3d 1500, 780 N.E.2d 1023, 2002-Ohio-7367, stay granted 98 Ohio St.3d 1417, 782 N.E.2d 73, 2003-Ohio-189, certiorari denied 123 S.Ct. 2255, 539 U.S. 907, 156 L.Ed.2d 118, habeas corpus denied 2007 WL 2840379, affirmed 591 F.3d 517, rehearing and rehearing en banc denied, certiorari denied 131 S.Ct. 185, 178 L.Ed.2d 111. Criminal Law ⚿ 2143; Criminal Law ⚿ 2153

State trial court's refusal to grant mistrial after juror mentioned to bailiff some concern about precautions that were being taken as jurors entered and exited courtroom for aggravated murder trial did not deny petitioner a fair trial, in violation of due process; petitioner's counsel opposed any questioning of jurors as to whether any concerns prevented them from being fair and impartial, and court noted that juror in question had raised no specific incidents or circumstances, but was simply inquiring as to better way for jurors to enter and leave courtroom. Benge v. Johnson (S.D.Ohio, 03-31-2004) 312 F.Supp.2d 978, affirmed 474 F.3d 236, rehearing and rehearing en banc denied, certiorari denied 128 S.Ct. 626, 552 U.S. 1028, 169 L.Ed.2d 404. Constitutional Law ⚿ 4761; Criminal Law ⚿ 848; Criminal Law ⚿ 855(7)

State trial court's refusal to grant mistrial after victim's son attempted to assault petitioner in hallway outside courtroom during lunch recess at aggravated murder trial did not deny petitioner a fair trial, in violation of due process; no juror witnessed incident, and only juror who had any awareness of it expressly indicated that his ability to be fair and impartial had not been impaired. Benge v. Johnson (S.D.Ohio, 03-31-2004) 312 F.Supp.2d 978, affirmed 474 F.3d 236, rehearing and rehearing en banc denied, certiorari denied 128 S.Ct. 626, 552 U.S. 1028, 169 L.Ed.2d 404. Constitutional Law ⚿ 4601; Criminal Law ⚿ 659

State trial court's refusal to grant mistrial after member of victim's family left courtroom in tears during police officer's testimony did not deny petitioner a fair trial, in violation of due process; trial necessarily involved testimony describing victim's brutal death, a matter which was not in dispute, and fact that family member became upset during testimony describing circumstances of victim's death would not necessarily have prejudiced jury. Benge v. Johnson (S.D.Ohio, 03-31-2004) 312 F.Supp.2d 978, affirmed 474 F.3d 236, rehearing and rehearing en banc denied, certiorari denied 128 S.Ct. 626, 552 U.S. 1028, 169 L.Ed.2d 404. Constitutional Law ⚿ 4601; Criminal Law ⚿ 659

7. —— Testimony, mistrials

Witness's testimony that defendant was convicted felon did not warrant mistrial in assault prosecution, where curative instruction was given providing that testimony should not be considered and evidence of guilt was overwhelming. State v. Elko (Ohio App. 8 Dist., Cuyahoga, 09-30-2004) No. 83641, 2004-Ohio-5209, 2004 WL 2340258, Unreported, appeal not allowed 105 Ohio St.3d 1441, 822 N.E.2d 811, 2005-Ohio-540, denial of post-conviction relief affirmed 2007-Ohio-2638, 2007

WL 1559297, habeas corpus dismissed 2008 WL 728367. Criminal Law ⚷ 867.12(7)

Prosecutor's questioning of state witness, which elicited testimony that murder defendant said he "got that M.F.er," did not warrant mistrial, where witness's name was provided on original witness list, defendant received copy of tape recorded interview in which individual discussed defendant's alleged confession to witness, defendant interviewed witness prior to trial, and court instructed jury to disregard witness's testimony. State v. Woodward (Ohio App. 10 Dist., Franklin, 08-24-2004) No. 03AP-398, 2004-Ohio-4418, 2004 WL 1879037, Unreported, cause dismissed 103 Ohio St.3d 1489, 816 N.E.2d 1077, 2004-Ohio-5606, reconsideration denied 104 Ohio St.3d 1428, 819 N.E.2d 710, 2004-Ohio-6585, denial of post-conviction relief affirmed 2009-Ohio-4213, 2009 WL 2579503. Criminal Law ⚷ 867.12(4)

Witness's testimony in capital murder prosecution that, on night victim was murdered, she did not go inside victim's home after dropping victim off from work because defendant was home, did not violate court order that precluded witness from testifying about why she felt victim had fear of defendant, and thus defendant was not entitled to mistrial based on such testimony; witness's testimony did not reasonably relate to victim's fear, but rather, the most likely inference was simply that victim felt that inviting witness inside would be awkward because defendant was there, and at trial, prosecutor recognized that witness was somebody who was avoiding defendant. State v. Brinkley (Ohio, 04-13-2005) 105 Ohio St.3d 231, 824 N.E.2d 959, 2005-Ohio-1507, motion to reopen denied 106 Ohio St.3d 1529, 835 N.E.2d 379, 2005-Ohio-5146, habeas corpus denied 866 F.Supp.2d 747, amended in part 2012 WL 1537661. Criminal Law ⚷ 867.12(7)

Mistrial was not warranted in murder trial when head and leg of doll came off as coroner demonstrated way in which young victim was injured; incident was accidental, and prosecutor in no way tried to inflame passions of jury. State v. Smith (Ohio, 12-13-2002) 97 Ohio St.3d 367, 780 N.E.2d 221, 2002-Ohio-6659, reconsideration denied 97 Ohio St.3d 1500, 780 N.E.2d 1023, 2002-Ohio-7367, stay granted 98 Ohio St.3d 1417, 782 N.E.2d 73, 2003-Ohio-189, certiorari denied 123 S.Ct. 2255, 539 U.S. 907, 156 L.Ed.2d 118, habeas corpus denied 2007 WL 2840379, affirmed 591 F.3d 517, rehearing and rehearing en banc denied, certiorari denied 131 S.Ct. 185, 178 L.Ed.2d 111. Criminal Law ⚷ 867.14(2)

8. —— Outside evidence, mistrials

Juror's overhearing of question from nonparticipating attorney to bailiff on second day of deliberations as to how long it took jury to convict defendant did not warrant mistrial, in prosecution for complicity to commit aggravated robbery; bailiff immediately notified trial court, trial court questioned juror, bailiff and attorney involved, juror had not discussed comment with any other juror, and juror assured trial court that he could put matter out of his mind. State v. Gordon (Ohio App. 5 Dist., Stark, 07-18-2005) No. 2005CA00031, 2005-Ohio-3638, 2005 WL 1682658, Unreported, motion for delayed appeal granted 107 Ohio St.3d 1420, 837 N.E.2d 1206, 2005-Ohio-6124, appeal not allowed 108 Ohio St.3d 1509, 844 N.E.2d 855, 2006-Ohio-1329, appeal not allowed 109 Ohio St.3d 1408, 845 N.E.2d 524, 2006-Ohio-1703, habeas corpus denied 2007 WL 1231770. Criminal Law ⚷ 855(7)

9. —— Failure to produce evidence, mistrials

Prosecution's failure to disclose until trial existence of audiotaped discussion in which sergeant told detective that individual said specific person was in area when shots were fired did not warrant mistrial in murder prosecution, where disclosure was made toward beginning of trial, court ordered prosecution to immediately provide defendant with audiotape, court recessed so that defendant could locate and interview individual, and court granted defendant leave to place individual on witness list, but defendant failed to do so. State v. Woodward (Ohio App. 10 Dist., Franklin, 08-24-2004) No. 03AP-398, 2004-Ohio-4418, 2004 WL 1879037, Unreported, cause dismissed 103 Ohio St.3d 1489, 816 N.E.2d 1077, 2004-Ohio-5606, reconsideration denied 104 Ohio St.3d 1428, 819 N.E.2d 710, 2004-Ohio-6585, denial of post-conviction relief affirmed 2009-Ohio-4213, 2009 WL 2579503. Criminal Law ⚷ 627.8(6)

10. —— Prosecutorial comments, mistrials

Defendant was entitled to a mistrial after the prosecution mentioned defendant in connection with a polygraph test, in violation of an order in limine during prosecution for aggravated murder; after the court provided a curative instruction the jury submitted seven written questions asking the court if defendant had submitted to a polygraph test, and the evidence presented against defendant was full of inconsistencies and did not constitute overwhelming proof of guilt. State v. Doren (Ohio App. 6 Dist., Wood, 01-16-2009) No. WD-06-064, 2009-Ohio-1667, 2009 WL 105639, Unreported, appeal after new trial 2011-Ohio-5903, 2011 WL 5561817. Criminal Law ⚷ 2194

Prosecutor's comments during closing argument, that it was defendant, and not other witnesses, who mentioned lipstick being on his shirt, and suggesting that photocopy of receipt from automobile supply store was forgery, did not entitle defendant to mistrial in prosecution for rape, attempted rape, and gross sexual imposition; review of transcript indicated that it was defendant's attorney who claimed that defendant's shirt had lipstick on it, and defense made much of exculpatory nature of photocopied receipt prior to prosecutor's remarks. State v. Starcher (Ohio App. 9 Dist., Medina, 12-10-2003) No. 03CA0014-M, 2003-Ohio-6588, 2003 WL 22900642, Unreported, motion for delayed appeal denied 103 Ohio St.3d 1403, 812 N.E.2d 1287, 2004-Ohio-3980, habeas corpus dismissed 2006 WL 1515659, reconsideration denied 2007 WL 275971, denial of post-conviction relief affirmed 2006-Ohio-5955, 2006 WL 3257508, appeal not allowed 112 Ohio St.3d 1494, 862 N.E.2d 119, 2007-Ohio-724, habeas corpus denied 2008-Ohio-5042, 2008 WL 4416517. Criminal Law ⊂⊃ 2199

11. —— Jurors sleeping, mistrials

A juror who sleeps through much of the trial testimony cannot be expected to perform his duties and would warrant removal of juror. State v. Majid (Ohio App. 8 Dist., 06-25-2009) 182 Ohio App.3d 730, 914 N.E.2d 1113, 2009-Ohio-3075, appeal not allowed 123 Ohio St.3d 1509, 917 N.E.2d 812, 2009-Ohio-6210, appeal after new trial 2012-Ohio-1192, 2012 WL 986127, appeal not allowed 132 Ohio St.3d 1464, 969 N.E.2d 1231, 2012-Ohio-3054. Jury ⊂⊃ 149

Sleeping is a form of juror misconduct. State v. Majid (Ohio App. 8 Dist., 06-25-2009) 182 Ohio App.3d 730, 914 N.E.2d 1113, 2009-Ohio-3075, appeal not allowed 123 Ohio St.3d 1509, 917 N.E.2d 812, 2009-Ohio-6210, appeal after new trial 2012-Ohio-1192, 2012 WL 986127, appeal not allowed 132 Ohio St.3d 1464, 969 N.E.2d 1231, 2012-Ohio-3054. Criminal Law ⊂⊃ 855(1)

13. —— Discretion of court, mistrials

Trial court denial of defendant's motion for a mistrial, based on a previously undisclosed witness testifying at trial, was not an abuse of discretion; State learned of witness after trial had commenced, State subpoenaed the witness immediately, and defense counsel was provided several days to prepare and review the witnesses and testimony. State v. Wooden (Ohio App. 9 Dist., Summit, 04-16-2003) No. 21138, 2003-Ohio-1917, 2003 WL 1877631, Unreported, motion for delayed appeal denied 100 Ohio St.3d 1543, 800 N.E.2d 750, 2003-Ohio-6879, denial of post-conviction relief affirmed in part, vacated in part 2011-Ohio-4942, 2011 WL 4469523. Criminal Law ⊂⊃ 629.5(1)

Defendant who did not speak English was not entitled to mistrial based on alleged errors made by translator; although a second translator asserted that there were errors being made in translation, answers provided by defendant and codefendant were responsive, second translator stated that translation problems were not major, and second translator was unable to provide examples of material errors. State v. Negash (Ohio App. 10 Dist., 01-18-2007) 170 Ohio App.3d 86, 866 N.E.2d 39, 2007-Ohio-165. Criminal Law ⊂⊃ 867.10

18. Irregularities

Allowing juror to ask detective about the discrepancy between testimony of victim's friend that there were two robbers and detective's testimony mentioning three names, and allowing detective to answer that the third person acted as a lookout, was not plain error, in prosecution for aggravated robbery; the question and answer did not relate to defendant, and thus, the question and answer did not affect the outcome of the trial. State v. Davis (Ohio App. 8 Dist., Cuyahoga, 06-20-2002) No. 80364, 2002-Ohio-3104, 2002 WL 1348136, Unreported, appeal allowed 97 Ohio St.3d 1413, 777 N.E.2d 269, 2002-Ohio-5601, affirmed 99 Ohio St.3d 142, 789 N.E.2d 235, 2003-Ohio-2770, certiorari denied 124 S.Ct. 575, 540 U.S. 1021, 157 L.Ed.2d 438. Criminal Law ⊂⊃ 1036.10

20. —— False or misleading testimony, misconduct generally

Proper remedy for defendant who sustained material prejudice, in drug trial, from law-enforcement officer's false and misleading testimony at suppression hearing was remand for new trial, rather than dismissal of charges against defendant. State v. Williams (Ohio App. 12 Dist., Butler, 08-04-2003) No. CA2002-09-233, 2003-Ohio-4114, 2003 WL 21783683, Unreported, on remand 2004 WL 5481579. Criminal Law ⊂⊃ 1181.5(7)

Defendant was materially prejudiced and, thus, denied fair trial, in prosecution for trafficking in cocaine, by law-enforcement officer's false and misleading testimony at suppression hearing that confidential informant had not been searched prior to controlled drug buy; the testimony created impression that defense counsel could have shown reasonable doubt simply by establishing that the state lacked proof that informant did not already possess cocaine at time of the drug buy, another officer stated during trial that he carefully searched informant prior to the drug buy, and the false testimony might have caused defendant to reject favorable plea bargain. State v. Williams (Ohio App. 12 Dist., Butler, 08-04-2003) No. CA2002-09-233, 2003-Ohio-4114, 2003 WL 21783683, Unreported, on remand 2004 WL 5481579. Criminal Law ⊂⊃ 1168(2)

Defendant was materially prejudiced and, thus, denied fair trial, in prosecution for trafficking in cocaine, by law-enforcement officer's attempt at suppression hearing to mislead defense counsel by making it appear that two confidential informants had been used during controlled drug buy; counsel was left with impression that neither informant would testify at trial and, thus, might have believed that this gave him opportunity to argue reasonable doubt, opportunity disappeared when it became clear at trial that second informant to which officer had referred was another officer, who testified, and the misleading testimony might have caused defendant to reject favorable plea bargain. State v. Williams (Ohio App. 12 Dist., Butler, 08-04-2003) No. CA2002-09-233, 2003-Ohio-4114, 2003 WL 21783683, Unreported, on remand 2004 WL 5481579. Criminal Law ⊂⊃ 1168(2)

21. —— Jurors, misconduct generally

Trial court's failure to dismiss and replace a juror who was contacted at softball game, before guilt-phase opening statements in aggravated murder trial, by brother of murder victim's boyfriend, was not plain error; juror said she was not affected by the contact, and defendant's claim that juror might have had additional contact with brother was totally speculative. State v. Frazier (Ohio, 10-10-2007) 115 Ohio St.3d 139, 873 N.E.2d 1263,

2007-Ohio-5048, certiorari denied 128 S.Ct. 2077, 553 U.S. 1015, 170 L.Ed.2d 811, denial of post-conviction relief affirmed 2008-Ohio-5027, 2008 WL 4408645, appeal not allowed 121 Ohio St.3d 1425, 903 N.E.2d 325, 2009-Ohio-1296, motion to reopen denied 126 Ohio St.3d 1541, 932 N.E.2d 336, 2010-Ohio-3855, habeas corpus denied 2011 WL 5086443. Criminal Law ⚷ 1039

Capital murder defendant's allegation of guilt phase juror's out-of-court misconduct was insufficient to warrant or require replacement of allegedly offending juror with alternate; defendant's nephew testified that he overheard juror, from distance of 25 to 30 feet away at crowded public event, respond to question concerning trial by saying that "it shouldn't be much longer because I think he's guilty," juror at issue testified that he had done no more than confirm that he was a juror in defendant's trial and specifically denied that he had told anyone that he had made up his mind about the case, and ultimate issue for the court was one of credibility. State v. Gross (Ohio, 10-30-2002) 97 Ohio St.3d 121, 776 N.E.2d 1061, 2002-Ohio-5524, reconsideration denied 97 Ohio St.3d 1486, 780 N.E.2d 288, 2002-Ohio-6866, certiorari denied 123 S.Ct. 2079, 538 U.S. 1037, 155 L.Ed.2d 1068, rehearing denied 124 S.Ct. 20, 539 U.S. 976, 156 L.Ed.2d 685, denial of post-conviction relief affirmed 2003-Ohio-6295, 2003 WL 22765845, appeal not allowed 102 Ohio St.3d 1410, 806 N.E.2d 562, 2004-Ohio-1763, certiorari denied 125 S.Ct. 165, 543 U.S. 888, 160 L.Ed.2d 149, dismissal of post-conviction relief affirmed 2006-Ohio-6941, 2006 WL 3804532, appeal not allowed 113 Ohio St.3d 1468, 864 N.E.2d 654, 2007-Ohio-1722, habeas corpus dismissed 2008 WL 4702181, motion to amend denied 2008 WL 4889626, certificate of appealability denied 2008 WL 5190017, affirmed 426 Fed. Appx. 349, 2011 WL 1597659. Criminal Law ⚷ 855(8)

Trial court may not examine alternate jurors following receipt of a verdict in order to determine existence, extent, or effect of juror or alternate misconduct. State v. Gross (Ohio, 10-30-2002) 97 Ohio St.3d 121, 776 N.E.2d 1061, 2002-Ohio-5524, reconsideration denied 97 Ohio St.3d 1486, 780 N.E.2d 288, 2002-Ohio-6866, certiorari denied 123 S.Ct. 2079, 538 U.S. 1037, 155 L.Ed.2d 1068, rehearing denied 124 S.Ct. 20, 539 U.S. 976, 156 L.Ed.2d 685, denial of post-conviction relief affirmed 2003-Ohio-6295, 2003 WL 22765845, appeal not allowed 102 Ohio St.3d 1410, 806 N.E.2d 562, 2004-Ohio-1763, certiorari denied 125 S.Ct. 165, 543 U.S. 888, 160 L.Ed.2d 149, dismissal of post-conviction relief affirmed 2006-Ohio-6941, 2006 WL 3804532, appeal not allowed 113 Ohio St.3d 1468, 864 N.E.2d 654, 2007-Ohio-1722, habeas corpus dismissed 2008 WL 4702181, motion to amend denied 2008 WL 4889626, certificate of appealability denied 2008 WL 5190017, affirmed 426 Fed. Appx. 349, 2011 WL 1597659. Criminal Law ⚷ 874

Brief encounter between three jurors and material witness in capital murder prosecution outside courtroom did not require mistrial or replacement of jurors involved, absent any showing of prejudice to defendant resulting from encounter; incident was momentary, witness' comment to jurors was his personal opinion as to appropriateness of the death penalty, not fact, only two jurors heard the remark, and each of the three jurors declared unequivocally that they would not be affected by the event. State v. Stallings (Ohio, 07-19-2000) 89 Ohio St.3d 280, 731 N.E.2d 159, 2000-Ohio-164, stay granted 89 Ohio St.3d 1483, 733 N.E.2d 1184, stay revoked 93 Ohio St.3d 1455, 756 N.E.2d 674, certiorari denied 122 S.Ct. 89, 534 U.S. 836, 151 L.Ed.2d 51, post-conviction relief denied 2004 WL 5388150, affirmed 2004-Ohio-4571, 2004 WL 1932869, appeal not allowed 104 Ohio St.3d 1460, 821 N.E.2d 577, 2005-Ohio-204, habeas corpus granted in part, denied in part 561 F.Supp.2d 821. Criminal Law ⚷ 855(8); Jury ⚷ 149

24. —— Threats, coercion or intimidation, prosecutorial misconduct

Prosecutor's statement to capital murder defendant's accomplice, indicating that accomplice's plea bargain could be set aside if he failed to cooperate as provided for therein, did not amount to improper threats, coercion or intimidation causing accomplice to refuse to testify on defendant's behalf, where accomplice refused to talk to defendant's counsel and indicated that he would invoke the Fifth Amendment if called to testify, and prosecutor's statement merely reiterated terms of accomplice's plea agreement. State v. Jackson (Ohio, 08-15-2001) 92 Ohio St.3d 436, 751 N.E.2d 946, 2001-Ohio-1266, reconsideration denied 93 Ohio St.3d 1453, 756 N.E.2d 116, motion to reopen denied 94 Ohio St.3d 1426, 761 N.E.2d 44, denial of post-conviction relief affirmed 2002-Ohio-3330, 2002 WL 1379001, appeal not allowed 97 Ohio St.3d 1423, 777 N.E.2d 277, 2002-Ohio-5820, habeas corpus denied 2007 WL 2890388, certificate of appealability granted in part, denied in part 2008 WL 755097, entered nunc pro tunc 2008 WL 926572. Criminal Law ⚷ 2020

27. —— Testimony, prosecutorial misconduct

State did not commit prosecutorial misconduct, much less promote plain error, by asking police officers, as witnesses to shooting of fellow police officer, questions that led to their emotional display of crying on the witness stand, where State did nothing to prompt or elicit emotional displays, and reactions by witnesses was expected in light of their close professional relationship with permanently injured officer. State v. Twitty (Ohio App. 2 Dist., Montgomery, 10-18-2002) No. 18749, 2002-Ohio-5595, 2002 WL 31341561, Unreported, appeal not allowed 98 Ohio St.3d 1475, 784 N.E.2d 708, 2003-Ohio-904, appeal not allowed 98 Ohio St.3d 1478, 784 N.E.2d 711, 2003-Ohio-974, habeas corpus denied 2006 WL 2728694. Criminal Law ⚷ 1037.1(2)

Prosecutor's questions to state's firearms expert in capital murder prosecution, asking whether expert's ballistics work could be double-checked by other experts should the need arise, were permissible to show that expert's opinion was unchallenged, and did not amount to improper bolstering of expert's opinion. State v. Jackson (Ohio, 08-15-2001) 92 Ohio St.3d 436, 751 N.E.2d 946, 2001-Ohio-1266, reconsideration denied 93 Ohio St.3d 1453, 756 N.E.2d 116, motion to reopen denied 94 Ohio St.3d 1426, 761 N.E.2d 44, denial of post-conviction relief affirmed 2002-Ohio-3330, 2002 WL 1379001, appeal not allowed 97 Ohio St.3d 1423, 777 N.E.2d 277, 2002-Ohio-5820, habeas corpus denied 2007 WL 2890388, certificate of appealability granted in part, denied in part 2008 WL 755097, entered nunc pro tunc 2008 WL 926572. Criminal Law ⚖ 2098(4)

State's direct examination of capital murder defendant's accomplice, and of police detective, eliciting testimony that accomplice's plea agreement required him to provide truthful testimony, was not improper prosecutorial vouching for credibility of accomplice; rather, prosecutor was attempting to establish existence of plea agreement and fact that, as part of such agreement, accomplice had agreed to tell the truth. State v. Jackson (Ohio, 08-15-2001) 92 Ohio St.3d 436, 751 N.E.2d 946, 2001-Ohio-1266, reconsideration denied 93 Ohio St.3d 1453, 756 N.E.2d 116, motion to reopen denied 94 Ohio St.3d 1426, 761 N.E.2d 44, denial of post-conviction relief affirmed 2002-Ohio-3330, 2002 WL 1379001, appeal not allowed 97 Ohio St.3d 1423, 777 N.E.2d 277, 2002-Ohio-5820, habeas corpus denied 2007 WL 2890388, certificate of appealability granted in part, denied in part 2008 WL 755097, entered nunc pro tunc 2008 WL 926572. Criminal Law ⚖ 2098(5)

28. —— Opening or closing arguments, prosecutorial misconduct

Any error in prosecutor's crying during opening statement, in prosecution for kidnapping and rape, did not rise to level of prejudicial error necessary to require finding that defendant was deprived of fair trial, where jury clearly was not swayed or influenced by prosecutor's action. State v. Flannery (Ohio App. 5 Dist., Richland, 04-01-2005) No. 03-CA-24, 2005-Ohio-1614, 2005 WL 750077, Unreported, appeal not allowed 106 Ohio St.3d 1486, 832 N.E.2d 738, 2005-Ohio-3978, habeas corpus denied 2008 WL 1787155, affirmed 397 Fed.Appx. 189, 2010 WL 3927075. Criminal Law ⚖ 1171.2

Prosecutor's comments during closing arguments of aggravated murder prosecution, in which prosecutor told the jury that defendant had left the victim to die, was not improper; comment was fair statement of evidence presented. State v. Tenace (Ohio App. 6 Dist., Lucas, 06-30-2003) No. L-00-1002, 2003-Ohio-3458, 2003 WL 21500249, Unreported, dismissal of post-conviction relief affirmed 2006-Ohio-1226, 2006 WL 664327, appeal not allowed 110 Ohio St.3d 1464, 852 N.E.2d 1213, 2006-Ohio-4288, affirmed in part, reversed in part 109 Ohio St.3d 255, 847 N.E.2d 386, 2006-Ohio-2417, denial of post-conviction relief affirmed 109 Ohio St.3d 451, 849 N.E.2d 1, 2006-Ohio-2987. Criminal Law ⚖ 2095

Even if prosecutor's statements during opening and closing statements of aggravated murder prosecution, in which prosecutor stated that victim had massive damage, and that only reason massive damage was inflicted upon victim was to cause victim's death, constituted an exaggeration of evidence, such statements did not rise to level of plain error; evidence indicated that defendant intended to kill victim and amount of damage defendant inflicted upon victim would not have been the only evidence needed to prove defendant's intent to kill. State v. Tenace (Ohio App. 6 Dist., Lucas, 06-30-2003) No. L-00-1002, 2003-Ohio-3458, 2003 WL 21500249, Unreported, dismissal of post-conviction relief affirmed 2006-Ohio-1226, 2006 WL 664327, appeal not allowed 110 Ohio St.3d 1464, 852 N.E.2d 1213, 2006-Ohio-4288, affirmed in part, reversed in part 109 Ohio St.3d 255, 847 N.E.2d 386, 2006-Ohio-2417, denial of post-conviction relief affirmed 109 Ohio St.3d 451, 849 N.E.2d 1, 2006-Ohio-2987. Criminal Law ⚖ 1037.1(2)

Prosecutor's statements during opening and closing statements of aggravated murder prosecution, in which prosecutor stated that victim had massive damage, and that only reason massive damage was inflicted upon victim was to cause victim's death, was not improper, even though coroner never testified that amount of injury suffered by victim was inflicted for purpose of causing death; fact that it may not have taken much force to cause victim's death did not minimize consequence of victim's various injuries. State v. Tenace (Ohio App. 6 Dist., Lucas, 06-30-2003) No. L-00-1002, 2003-Ohio-3458, 2003 WL 21500249, Unreported, dismissal of post-conviction relief affirmed 2006-Ohio-1226, 2006 WL 664327, appeal not allowed 110 Ohio St.3d 1464, 852 N.E.2d 1213, 2006-Ohio-4288, affirmed in part, reversed in part 109 Ohio St.3d 255, 847 N.E.2d 386, 2006-Ohio-2417, denial of post-conviction relief affirmed 109 Ohio St.3d 451, 849 N.E.2d 1, 2006-Ohio-2987. Criminal Law ⚖ 2117

Prosecutor's statements that murder victim was "actually speaking to you through the evidence in this case" and that victim was "crying out to you" were within the wide latitude allowed by a prosecutor in closing argument. State v. Smith (Ohio, 12-13-2002) 97 Ohio St.3d 367, 780 N.E.2d 221, 2002-Ohio-6659, reconsideration denied 97 Ohio St.3d 1500, 780 N.E.2d 1023, 2002-Ohio-7367, stay granted 98 Ohio St.3d 1417, 782 N.E.2d 73, 2003-Ohio-189, certiorari denied 123 S.Ct. 2255, 539 U.S. 907, 156 L.Ed.2d 118, habeas corpus denied 2007 WL 2840379, affirmed 591 F.3d 517, rehearing and rehearing en banc denied, certiorari denied 131 S.Ct. 185, 178 L.Ed.2d 111. Criminal Law ⚖ 2146

Prosecutor's comment during closing argument that murder defendant "gets happiness out of molesting, raping a six-month old baby" was a permissible comment addressing sexual motivation specification. State v. Smith (Ohio, 12-13-2002) 97 Ohio

St.3d 367, 780 N.E.2d 221, 2002-Ohio-6659, reconsideration denied 97 Ohio St.3d 1500, 780 N.E.2d 1023, 2002-Ohio-7367, stay granted 98 Ohio St.3d 1417, 782 N.E.2d 73, 2003-Ohio-189, certiorari denied 123 S.Ct. 2255, 539 U.S. 907, 156 L.Ed.2d 118, habeas corpus denied 2007 WL 2840379, affirmed 591 F.3d 517, rehearing and rehearing en banc denied, certiorari denied 131 S.Ct. 185, 178 L.Ed.2d 111. Criminal Law ⚷ 2149

Prosecutor did not commit misconduct during closing argument by characterizing murder as a ten- to thirty-minute beating; expert testified that the attack lasted that long. State v. Smith (Ohio, 12-13-2002) 97 Ohio St.3d 367, 780 N.E.2d 221, 2002-Ohio-6659, reconsideration denied 97 Ohio St.3d 1500, 780 N.E.2d 1023, 2002-Ohio-7367, stay granted 98 Ohio St.3d 1417, 782 N.E.2d 73, 2003-Ohio-189, certiorari denied 123 S.Ct. 2255, 539 U.S. 907, 156 L.Ed.2d 118, habeas corpus denied 2007 WL 2840379, affirmed 591 F.3d 517, rehearing and rehearing en banc denied, certiorari denied 131 S.Ct. 185, 178 L.Ed.2d 111. Criminal Law ⚷ 2149

Prosecutor's references to murder defendant in opening statement as a "baby murderer" and a "baby molester" were not improper comments; evidence supported such characterization. State v. Smith (Ohio, 12-13-2002) 97 Ohio St.3d 367, 780 N.E.2d 221, 2002-Ohio-6659, reconsideration denied 97 Ohio St.3d 1500, 780 N.E.2d 1023, 2002-Ohio-7367, stay granted 98 Ohio St.3d 1417, 782 N.E.2d 73, 2003-Ohio-189, certiorari denied 123 S.Ct. 2255, 539 U.S. 907, 156 L.Ed.2d 118, habeas corpus denied 2007 WL 2840379, affirmed 591 F.3d 517, rehearing and rehearing en banc denied, certiorari denied 131 S.Ct. 185, 178 L.Ed.2d 111. Criminal Law ⚷ 2152

Test for prosecutorial misconduct in closing argument is whether remarks were improper and, if so, whether they prejudicially affected defendant's substantial rights. State v. White (Ohio, 05-20-1998) 82 Ohio St.3d 16, 693 N.E.2d 772, 1998-Ohio-363, stay granted 82 Ohio St.3d 1445, 695 N.E.2d 267, stay revoked 85 Ohio St.3d 1453, 708 N.E.2d 1008, reconsideration denied 82 Ohio St.3d 1469, 696 N.E.2d 226, reconsideration denied 82 Ohio St.3d 1470, 696 N.E.2d 226, dismissal of post-conviction relief affirmed 1998 WL 515944, dismissed, appeal not allowed 84 Ohio St.3d 1445, 703 N.E.2d 326, reconsideration denied 84 Ohio St.3d 1489, 705 N.E.2d 368, certiorari denied 119 S.Ct. 623, 525 U.S. 1057, 142 L.Ed.2d 562, denial of habeas corpus affirmed in part, reversed in part 431 F.3d 517, rehearing denied, rehearing and rehearing en banc denied, certiorari denied 127 S.Ct. 578, 166 L.Ed.2d 457, certiorari denied 127 S.Ct. 581, 166 L.Ed.2d 434, dismissal of post-conviction relief affirmed 2007-Ohio-3424, 2007 WL 1934731. Criminal Law ⚷ 2073

29. —— Plain errors, prosecutorial misconduct

State did not commit prosecutorial misconduct, much less promote plain error, by virtue of fact that the courtroom was packed with police officers at time defendant's shooting victim, a police officer, testified to events surrounding her shooting and resulting permanent paralysis; eyewitness testimony that defendant shot officer was such compelling direct evidence that such display of police solidarity added little to it, and record failed to demonstrate that State had anything to do with it. State v. Twitty (Ohio App. 2 Dist., Montgomery, 10-18-2002) No. 18749, 2002-Ohio-5595, 2002 WL 31341561, Unreported, appeal not allowed 98 Ohio St.3d 1475, 784 N.E.2d 708, 2003-Ohio-904, appeal not allowed 98 Ohio St.3d 1478, 784 N.E.2d 711, 2003-Ohio-974, habeas corpus denied 2006 WL 2728694. Criminal Law ⚷ 1037.1(1)

Trial judge's apparent act of wiping tear from her eye at conclusion of testimony of shooting victim, a police officer, wherein officer described shooting and her resulting permanent paralysis, did not constitute prosecutorial misconduct, much less plain error, where judge's conduct did not implicate any misconduct on part of State, and, even if judge did wipe tear from her eye, she instructed jury to disregard anything the court might have said or done that they believed reflected the court's opinion about the case. State v. Twitty (Ohio App. 2 Dist., Montgomery, 10-18-2002) No. 18749, 2002-Ohio-5595, 2002 WL 31341561, Unreported, appeal not allowed 98 Ohio St.3d 1475, 784 N.E.2d 708, 2003-Ohio-904, appeal not allowed 98 Ohio St.3d 1478, 784 N.E.2d 711, 2003-Ohio-974, habeas corpus denied 2006 WL 2728694. Criminal Law ⚷ 1037.1(1)

Prosecutor's so-called "theatrics" of displaying large photograph of slain police officer in uniform on easel in full view of jury, hanging officer's blood-soaked and tattered uniform on witness stand, and demonstrating disgust toward defendant by using latex gloves to handle defendant's clothing were not plain error in aggravated murder prosecution, particularly since these events were not reflected in transcript and defendant's motion to correct record was overruled. State v. White (Ohio, 05-20-1998) 82 Ohio St.3d 16, 693 N.E.2d 772, 1998-Ohio-363, stay granted 82 Ohio St.3d 1445, 695 N.E.2d 267, stay revoked 85 Ohio St.3d 1453, 708 N.E.2d 1008, reconsideration denied 82 Ohio St.3d 1469, 696 N.E.2d 226, reconsideration denied 82 Ohio St.3d 1470, 696 N.E.2d 226, dismissal of post-conviction relief affirmed 1998 WL 515944, dismissed, appeal not allowed 84 Ohio St.3d 1445, 703 N.E.2d 326, reconsideration denied 84 Ohio St.3d 1489, 705 N.E.2d 368, certiorari denied 119 S.Ct. 623, 525 U.S. 1057, 142 L.Ed.2d 562, denial of habeas corpus affirmed in part, reversed in part 431 F.3d 517, rehearing denied, rehearing and rehearing en banc denied, certiorari denied 127 S.Ct. 578, 166 L.Ed.2d 457, certiorari denied 127 S.Ct. 581, 166 L.Ed.2d 434, dismissal of post-conviction relief affirmed 2007-Ohio-3424, 2007 WL 1934731. Criminal Law ⚷ 1037.1(2); Criminal Law ⚷ 1037.1(3)

Alleged instances of prosecutorial misconduct could be reviewed only for plain error where defense counsel made no objections at trial. State v. White (Ohio, 05-20-1998) 82 Ohio St.3d 16, 693

N.E.2d 772, 1998-Ohio-363, stay granted 82 Ohio St.3d 1445, 695 N.E.2d 267, stay revoked 85 Ohio St.3d 1453, 708 N.E.2d 1008, reconsideration denied 82 Ohio St.3d 1469, 696 N.E.2d 226, reconsideration denied 82 Ohio St.3d 1470, 696 N.E.2d 226, dismissal of post-conviction relief affirmed 1998 WL 515944, dismissed, appeal not allowed 84 Ohio St.3d 1445, 703 N.E.2d 326, reconsideration denied 84 Ohio St.3d 1489, 705 N.E.2d 368, certiorari denied 119 S.Ct. 623, 525 U.S. 1057, 142 L.Ed.2d 562, denial of habeas corpus affirmed in part, reversed in part 431 F.3d 517, rehearing denied, rehearing and rehearing en banc denied, certiorari denied 127 S.Ct. 578, 166 L.Ed.2d 457, certiorari denied 127 S.Ct. 581, 166 L.Ed.2d 434, dismissal of post-conviction relief affirmed 2007-Ohio-3424, 2007 WL 1934731. Criminal Law ⚷ 1037.1(1)

30. Errors of law

Where a verdict is not sustained by sufficient evidence or is contrary to law, but there is evidence that defendant is guilty of a lesser degree or a lesser included offense, the court may modify the verdict or finding accordingly, without granting or ordering a new trial. State v. Johnson (Ohio App. 2 Dist., 07-16-2010) 188 Ohio App.3d 438, 935 N.E.2d 895, 2010-Ohio-3345, appeal not allowed 127 Ohio St.3d 1462, 938 N.E.2d 363, 2010-Ohio-6008. Criminal Law ⚷ 1184(3)

31. Newly discovered evidence

Juror statements and exposure to media reports are not evidence. State v. Gross (Ohio, 10-30-2002) 97 Ohio St.3d 121, 776 N.E.2d 1061, 2002-Ohio-5524, reconsideration denied 97 Ohio St.3d 1486, 780 N.E.2d 288, 2002-Ohio-6866, certiorari denied 123 S.Ct. 2079, 538 U.S. 1037, 155 L.Ed.2d 1068, rehearing denied 124 S.Ct. 20, 539 U.S. 976, 156 L.Ed.2d 685, denial of post-conviction relief affirmed 2003-Ohio-6295, 2003 WL 22765845, appeal not allowed 102 Ohio St.3d 1410, 806 N.E.2d 562, 2004-Ohio-1763, certiorari denied 125 S.Ct. 165, 543 U.S. 888, 160 L.Ed.2d 149, dismissal of post-conviction relief affirmed 2006-Ohio-6941, 2006 WL 3804532, appeal not allowed 113 Ohio St.3d 1468, 864 N.E.2d 654, 2007-Ohio-1722.

2945.80 Application for new trial

Validity

For validity of this section, see State v. Ray, 2006 WL 3055694, 2006-Ohio-5640, (Ohio App. 3 Dist.).

Notes of Decisions

1. In general

Criminal rule governing timing of motion for new trial controls over conflicting statute governing timing of motion for new trial. State v. Ray (Ohio App. 3 Dist., Union, 10-30-2006) No. 14-05-39, 2006-Ohio-5640, 2006 WL 3055694, Unreported, appeal not allowed 113 Ohio St.3d 1441, 863 N.E.2d 657, 2007-Ohio-1266. Criminal Law ⚷ 951(1)

2945.82 New trial

Notes of Decisions

2. Mention of previous trial at retrial

Statute providing that accused, upon being awarded new trial on appeal, shall stand for trial as though there had been no previous trial, does not preclude any mention of previous trial at new trial; rather, it means simply that there is no requirement for new indictment or information when case is remanded for retrial. State v. Keenan (Ohio, 02-25-1998) 81 Ohio St.3d 133, 689 N.E.2d 929, 1998-Ohio-459, reconsideration denied 81 Ohio St.3d 1503, 691 N.E.2d 1062, certiorari denied 119 S.Ct. 146, 525 U.S. 860, 142 L.Ed.2d 119, rehearing denied 119 S.Ct. 581, 525 U.S. 1035, 142 L.Ed.2d 484, denial of post-conviction relief affirmed 2001 WL 91129, dismissed, appeal not allowed 92 Ohio St.3d 1429, 749 N.E.2d 756, habeas corpus dismissed 262 F.Supp.2d 818, motion to amend denied 262 F.Supp.2d 826, vacated and remanded 400 F.3d 417, on remand 2007 WL 838923, dismissal of post-conviction relief affirmed 2006-Ohio-6031, 2006 WL 3317922, appeal not allowed 114 Ohio St.3d 1508, 872 N.E.2d 950, 2007-Ohio-4285. Criminal Law ⚷ 965; Criminal Law ⚷ 1192

2945.83 When new trial shall not be granted

Notes of Decisions

3. Evidence

Improper admission of prior bad acts evidence affects a defendant's substantial rights so that a new trial is required when: (1) there is prejudice to the defendant, (2) error was not harmless beyond a reasonable doubt, and (3) if the improper evidence is excised from the record, the remaining evidence is sufficient. State v. Morris (Ohio, 11-20-2014) 141 Ohio St.3d 399, 24 N.E.3d 1153, 2014-Ohio-5052. Criminal Law ⚷ 1169.11

Government's failure to disclose information about key government witness's continued drug trafficking after he cooperated with government by making controlled purchases of crack cocaine from defendant until after trial in which defendant was convicted of selling crack cocaine did not entitle defendant to new trial; trial record was replete with testimony undermining witness's credibility, defense counsel in closing argument described witness as admitted crack dealer, admitted drug defendant, admitted person who was there to gain something in return for his testimony, and recidivist who continued to sell drugs after receiving favorable dispositions on previous charges, and district court instructed jury to assess witness's testimony with more caution than that of other witnesses. U.S. v. Heriot (C.A.6 (Ohio), 07-26-2007) 496 F.3d 601, rehearing and rehearing en banc denied, certiorari denied 128 S.Ct. 1752, 552 U.S. 1302, 170 L.Ed.2d 550. Criminal Law ⚷ 919(1)

CHAPTER 2947

JUDGMENT; SENTENCE

SENTENCING

SENTENCING

2947.051 Victim impact statement for use in sentencing

Cross References

80% release procedure, see 2967.19

Notes of Decisions

1. Constitutional issues

State, rather than federal habeas petitioner, bore burden of producing victim impact statements and related documents for federal habeas review in connection with petitioner's claim that he was denied due process through sentencing determination which rested in part upon materially false information, and had to suffer consequences of any continued failure to do so. Stewart v. Erwin (C.A.6 (Ohio), 10-09-2007) 503 F.3d 488, on remand 544 F.Supp.2d 655. Habeas Corpus ⚷ 710

Remand was required, on appeal from denial of federal habeas relief, for determinations as to whether state appellate court unreasonably concluded that factual predicate was lacking for petitioner's claim that he was denied due process through sentencing determination which rested in part upon materially false information, and, if due process violation occurred, whether it was harmless error, given that the record contained some support for contention that sentencing decision was impermissibly influenced by materially false or misleading information in victim impact statements which were withheld from petitioner and his counsel, but did not contain victim impact statements and other documents essential to meaningful review. Stewart v. Erwin (C.A.6 (Ohio), 10-09-2007) 503 F.3d 488, on remand 544 F.Supp.2d 655. Habeas Corpus ⚷ 864(5)

There was no clearly established federal law entitling non-capital defendant to opportunity to review, rebut, and explain all of the information relied upon by state trial court in determining his sentence, and therefore state courts did not act contrary to clearly established federal law or unreasonably apply such law, as required for federal habeas relief, when they rejected defendant's claim of due process entitlement to disclosure of victim impact statements used in his sentencing. Stewart v. Erwin (C.A.6 (Ohio), 10-09-2007) 503 F.3d 488, on remand 544 F.Supp.2d 655. Habeas Corpus ⚷ 505

On federal habeas review of petitioner's due process challenge to trial court's withholding of victim impact statements considered at sentencing, deference was owed only to result reached by state appellate court, and not its reasoning, since that court rejected claim without articulating basis in federal law for doing so, and federal courts were thus required to conduct independent review of the record and law to determine whether state court's ruling comported with requirements of federal habeas statute. Stewart v. Erwin (C.A.6 (Ohio), 10-09-2007) 503 F.3d 488, on remand 544 F.Supp.2d 655. Habeas Corpus ⚖ 770

2. Victim impact evidence

In prosecution for multiple sex offenses involving young teenage victims, trial court's failure to permit defendant to view victim impact statements did not constitute plain error, where trial court placed on the record those aspects of the victim impact statements on which it relied to impose sentence, and thus court in effect advised defendant of the content of the statements and further gave defendant the opportunity to respond. State v. Randlett (Ohio App. 10 Dist., Franklin, 12-18-2003) No. 03AP-385, No. 03AP-388, No. 03AP-386, No. 03AP-387, 2003-Ohio-6934, 2003 WL 22976553, Unreported, appeal not allowed 102 Ohio St.3d 1447, 808 N.E.2d 398, 2004-Ohio-2263, habeas corpus dismissed 2006 WL 1805937, certificate of appealability denied 2006 WL 2519991, appeal not allowed 110 Ohio St.3d 1443, 852 N.E.2d 190, 2006-Ohio-3862. Criminal Law ⚖ 1042.3(2)

Record supported finding that trial court did not consider and weigh victim-impact statements in determining sentence in capital murder trial; record indicated that trial court had already accepted the jury's penalty verdict and had sentenced defendant to death before hearing any victim-impact statements. State v. Leonard (Ohio, 12-08-2004) 104 Ohio St.3d 54, 818 N.E.2d 229, 2004-Ohio-6235, denial of post-conviction relief affirmed 2007-Ohio-7095, 2007 WL 4562881, appeal not allowed 118 Ohio St.3d 1506, 889 N.E.2d 1025, 2008-Ohio-3369, certiorari denied 129 S.Ct. 734, 555 U.S. 1075, 172 L.Ed.2d 736. Sentencing And Punishment ⚖ 1763

To extent that incidental mention, in capital murder prosecution, of fact that victim's son, like victim a police officer, had arrived at murder scene shortly after shooting, could be said to constitute victim impact evidence, its admission did not prejudice defendant, where reference to victim's son was not detailed, not inflammatory, and not focus of witness' testimony. State v. Gross (Ohio, 10-30-2002) 97 Ohio St.3d 121, 776 N.E.2d 1061, 2002-Ohio-5524, reconsideration denied 97 Ohio St.3d 1486, 780 N.E.2d 288, 2002-Ohio-6866, certiorari denied 123 S.Ct. 2079, 538 U.S. 1037, 155 L.Ed.2d 1068, rehearing denied 124 S.Ct. 20, 539 U.S. 976, 156 L.Ed.2d 685, denial of post-conviction relief affirmed 2003-Ohio-6295, 2003 WL 22765845, appeal not allowed 102 Ohio St.3d 1410, 806 N.E.2d 562, 2004-Ohio-1763, certiorari denied 125 S.Ct. 165, 543 U.S. 888, 160 L.Ed.2d 149, dismissal of post-conviction relief affirmed 2006-Ohio-6941, 2006 WL 3804532, appeal not allowed 113 Ohio St.3d 1468, 864 N.E.2d 654, 2007-Ohio-1722, habeas corpus dismissed 2008 WL 4702181, motion to amend denied 2008 WL 4889626, certificate of appealability denied 2008 WL 5190017, affirmed 426 Fed.Appx. 349, 2011 WL 1597659. Criminal Law ⚖ 1169.1(3)

Emotional responses of witnesses in guilt phase of capital murder prosecution did not amount to improper victim impact evidence. State v. Gross (Ohio, 10-30-2002) 97 Ohio St.3d 121, 776 N.E.2d 1061, 2002-Ohio-5524, reconsideration denied 97 Ohio St.3d 1486, 780 N.E.2d 288, 2002-Ohio-6866, certiorari denied 123 S.Ct. 2079, 538 U.S. 1037, 155 L.Ed.2d 1068, rehearing denied 124 S.Ct. 20, 539 U.S. 976, 156 L.Ed.2d 685, denial of post-conviction relief affirmed 2003-Ohio-6295, 2003 WL 22765845, appeal not allowed 102 Ohio St.3d 1410, 806 N.E.2d 562, 2004-Ohio-1763, certiorari denied 125 S.Ct. 165, 543 U.S. 888, 160 L.Ed.2d 149, dismissal of post-conviction relief affirmed 2006-Ohio-6941, 2006 WL 3804532, appeal not allowed 113 Ohio St.3d 1468, 864 N.E.2d 654, 2007-Ohio-1722, habeas corpus dismissed 2008 WL 4702181, motion to amend denied 2008 WL 4889626, certificate of appealability denied 2008 WL 5190017, affirmed 426 Fed.Appx. 349, 2011 WL 1597659. Homicide ⚖ 984

Autopsy photographs, eyewitness' testimony to effect that upon her arrival at murder scene, victim had rolled over and looked at her before he died, and victim's clothes and personal belongings were all admissible in both guilt and penalty phases of capital murder prosecution, despite defendant's contention that they amounted to impermissible victim impact evidence, where all such evidence and testimony established circumstances of the crime. State v. Gross (Ohio, 10-30-2002) 97 Ohio St.3d 121, 776 N.E.2d 1061, 2002-Ohio-5524, reconsideration denied 97 Ohio St.3d 1486, 780 N.E.2d 288, 2002-Ohio-6866, certiorari denied 123 S.Ct. 2079, 538 U.S. 1037, 155 L.Ed.2d 1068, rehearing denied 124 S.Ct. 20, 539 U.S. 976, 156 L.Ed.2d 685, denial of post-conviction relief affirmed 2003-Ohio-6295, 2003 WL 22765845, appeal not allowed 102 Ohio St.3d 1410, 806 N.E.2d 562, 2004-Ohio-1763, certiorari denied 125 S.Ct. 165, 543 U.S. 888, 160 L.Ed.2d 149, dismissal of post-conviction relief affirmed 2006-Ohio-6941, 2006 WL 3804532, appeal not allowed 113 Ohio St.3d 1468, 864 N.E.2d 654, 2007-Ohio-1722, habeas corpus dismissed 2008 WL 4702181, motion to amend denied 2008 WL 4889626, certificate of appealability denied 2008 WL 5190017, affirmed 426 Fed.Appx. 349, 2011 WL 1597659. Homicide ⚖ 997; Homicide ⚖ 998; Sentencing And Punishment ⚖ 1759

Just because a victim impact statement is included in a presentence investigation report (PSI) does not mean that a defendant will have access to it, and thus statutes governing victim impact statements and PSIs do not violate a defendant's right to equal protection of the laws on the ground that statutes can produce a classification between defendants who receive sentencing information and those that do not because some victim impact statements are opted out of PSI. State v. Stewart (Ohio App. 12 Dist., 08-12-2002) 149 Ohio App.3d 1, 775 N.E.2d 563, 2002-Ohio-4124, appeal not allowed 98

Ohio St.3d 1409, 781 N.E.2d 1018, 2003-Ohio-60, habeas corpus dismissed 2005 WL 5835544, reversed 503 F.3d 488, on remand 544 F.Supp.2d 655, denial of post-conviction relief reversed 2011-Ohio-2211, 2011 WL 1837543. Constitutional Law ⚷ 3808; Sentencing And Punishment ⚷ 206

Trial court's refusal to allow defendant access to victim impact statements did not violate due process. State v. Stewart (Ohio App. 12 Dist., 08-12-2002) 149 Ohio App.3d 1, 775 N.E.2d 563, 2002-Ohio-4124, appeal not allowed 98 Ohio St.3d 1409, 781 N.E.2d 1018, 2003-Ohio-60, habeas corpus dismissed 2005 WL 5835544, reversed 503 F.3d 488, on remand 544 F.Supp.2d 655, denial of post-conviction relief reversed 2011-Ohio-2211, 2011 WL 1837543. Constitutional Law ⚷ 4716; Sentencing And Punishment ⚷ 244

Defendant was not entitled to access to victim impact statements, although trial court considered those statements, as the facts ultimately relied upon by the trial court in sentencing defendant were otherwise reflected in the psychological evaluations and the presentence investigation report (PSI). State v. Stewart (Ohio App. 12 Dist., 08-12-2002) 149 Ohio App.3d 1, 775 N.E.2d 563, 2002-Ohio-4124, appeal not allowed 98 Ohio St.3d 1409, 781 N.E.2d 1018, 2003-Ohio-60, habeas corpus dismissed 2005 WL 5835544, reversed 503 F.3d 488, on remand 544 F.Supp.2d 655, denial of post-conviction relief reversed 2011-Ohio-2211, 2011 WL 1837543. Sentencing And Punishment ⚷ 244

2947.06 Testimony after verdict to mitigate penalty; reports confidential

Cross References

Fees and costs, all courts, criminal cases, juvenile cases, and some civil actions related to criminal cases, see 2746.02

2947.09 Blocking of motor vehicle registration or transfer of registration for failure to pay fine or costs; forms

(A) If a person is charged with an offense in a court of common pleas, including a juvenile court, and either fails to appear in court at the required time and place to answer the charge or pleads guilty to or is found guilty of the offense or is adjudicated a delinquent child or juvenile traffic offender based on the offense and fails within the time allowed by the court to pay any fine or costs imposed by the court, the court may enter information relative to the person's failure to pay any outstanding amount of the fine or costs on a form prescribed or approved by the registrar of motor vehicles pursuant to division (B) of this section and send the form to the registrar. Upon receipt of the form, the registrar shall take any measures necessary to ensure that neither the registrar nor any deputy registrar accepts any application for the registration or transfer of registration of any motor vehicle owned or leased by the person. However, for a motor vehicle leased by the person, the registrar shall not implement this requirement until the registrar adopts procedures for that implementation under section 4503.39 of the Revised Code.

The period of denial relating to the issuance or transfer of a certificate of registration for a motor vehicle imposed under this section remains in effect until the person pays any fine or costs imposed by the court relative to the offense. When the fine or costs have been paid in full, the court shall inform the registrar of the payment by entering information relative to the payment on a notice of payment form prescribed or approved by the registrar pursuant to division (B) of this section and sending the form to the registrar.

(B) The registrar shall prescribe and make available to courts of common pleas forms to be used for a notice to the registrar of failure to pay fines or costs and a notice to the registrar of payment of fines or costs under division (A) of this section. The registrar may approve the use of other forms for these purposes.

The registrar may require that any of the forms prescribed or approved pursuant to this section be transmitted to the registrar electronically. If the registrar requires electronic transmission, the registrar shall not be required to give effect to any form that is not transmitted electronically.

(2014 S 143, eff. 9-19-14; 2012 H 197, eff. 3-22-13)

Historical and Statutory Notes

Ed. Note: Former RC 2947.09 repealed by 1972 H 511, eff. 1-1-74; 1970 S 460; 1953 H 1; GC 13451-6.

Amendment Note: 2014 S 143 rewrote division (A), which prior thereto read:

"(A) If a person is charged with an offense in a court of common pleas and either fails to appear in court at the required time and place to answer the charge or pleads guilty to or is found guilty of the offense and fails within the time allowed by the court to pay any fine or costs imposed by the court, unless the court previously has given written notice to the person, the court shall send the person a notice by ordinary mail at the person's last known address stating that there is a balance due, specifying the amount of the balance due, and directing the person to contact the court clerk's office within ten days of the date of the notice. The notice shall include the sentence: 'WARNING: Failure to timely respond to this notice may result in the blocking of your motor vehicle registration or transfer of registration!' To avoid a block on the person's motor vehicle registration or transfer of registration, the person may enter into a written agreement with the court to pay the balance due in installments or to perform community service in lieu of payment. The agreement shall include the sentence: 'WARNING: Failure to comply with the payment schedule or to complete your community service requirement may result in the blocking of your motor vehicle registration or transfer of registration!'

"If a person does not enter into an agreement under this division or if a person fails to comply with an agreement entered into under this division, the court may enter information relative to the person's failure to pay any outstanding amount of the fine or costs on a form prescribed or approved by the registrar pursuant to division (B) of this section and send the form to the registrar. Upon receipt of the form, the registrar shall take any measures necessary to ensure that neither the registrar nor any deputy registrar accepts any application for the registration or transfer of registration of any motor vehicle owned or leased by the person. However, for a motor vehicle leased by the person, the registrar shall not implement this requirement until the registrar adopts procedures for that implementation under section 4503.39 of the Revised Code.

"The period of denial relating to the issuance or transfer of a certificate of registration for a motor vehicle imposed under this section remains in effect until the person pays any fine or costs imposed by the court relative to the offense. When the fine or costs have been paid in full, the court shall inform the registrar of the payment by entering information relative to the payment on a notice of payment form prescribed or approved by the registrar pursuant to division (B) of this section and sending the form to the registrar."

Research References

Encyclopedias

OH Jur. 3d Criminal Law: Procedure § 1906, Range of Available Sentences that May be Imposed for Felonies, Generally.

2947.14 Satisfaction of fine and costs; determination of ability to pay must precede commitment; hearing on change of circumstances

Notes of Decisions

4. Hearing

Trial court was not required to hold a hearing on defendant's ability to pay $10,000 fine, before imposing fine for defendant's building and housing code violations. Cleveland v. Leneghan (Ohio App. 8 Dist., 03-12-2009) 181 Ohio App.3d 378, 909 N.E.2d 148, 2009-Ohio-1086. Fines ⚷ 1.5

Trial court was required to hold a hearing regarding defendant's ability to pay $10,000 fine for building and housing code violations, before incarcerating him for failure to pay. Cleveland v. Leneghan (Ohio App. 8 Dist., 03-12-2009) 181 Ohio App.3d 378, 909 N.E.2d 148, 2009-Ohio-1086. Fines ⚷ 11

5. Credit for pretrial detention

Trial court was required to determine on remand whether defendant was entitled to a credit for four days confinement at a rate of $50 per day against the $158 monetary sanction imposed by the court in his misdemeanor traffic violation case, or whether the jail time credit was applied against sentences that were imposed for other charges for which defendant was also confined for at the same time; the credit only applied to one sentence imposed. State v. Green (Ohio App. 2 Dist., Montgomery, 06-23-2006) No. 21082, 2006-Ohio-3196, 2006 WL 1719753, Unreported. Fines ⚷ 1.5; Sentencing And Punishment ⚷ 1157

6. Criminal sanction

A fine imposed as a sentence or a part of a sentence is not a civil sanction subject only to collection by the methods provided for the collection of civil judgment; instead, it is a criminal sanction. State v. Moore (Ohio, 11-29-2012) 135 Ohio St.3d 151, 985 N.E.2d 432, 2012-Ohio-5479, appeal after new sentencing hearing 2014-Ohio-5682, 2014 WL 7339138. Fines ⚩ 2

MISCELLANEOUS PROVISIONS

2947.23 Judgment for costs and jury fees; community service upon failure to pay

(A)(1)(a) In all criminal cases, including violations of ordinances, the judge or magistrate shall include in the sentence the costs of prosecution, including any costs under section 2947.231 of the Revised Code, and render a judgment against the defendant for such costs. If the judge or magistrate imposes a community control sanction or other nonresidential sanction, the judge or magistrate, when imposing the sanction, shall notify the defendant of both of the following:

(i) If the defendant fails to pay that judgment or fails to timely make payments towards that judgment under a payment schedule approved by the court, the court may order the defendant to perform community service until the judgment is paid or until the court is satisfied that the defendant is in compliance with the approved payment schedule.

(ii) If the court orders the defendant to perform the community service, the defendant will receive credit upon the judgment at the specified hourly credit rate per hour of community service performed, and each hour of community service performed will reduce the judgment by that amount.

(b) The failure of a judge or magistrate to notify the defendant pursuant to division (A)(1)(a) of this section does not negate or limit the authority of the court to order the defendant to perform community service if the defendant fails to pay the judgment described in that division or to timely make payments toward that judgment under an approved payment plan.

(2) The following shall apply in all criminal cases:

(a) If a jury has been sworn at the trial of a case, the fees of the jurors shall be included in the costs, which shall be paid to the public treasury from which the jurors were paid.

(b) If a jury has not been sworn at the trial of a case because of a defendant's failure to appear without good cause or because the defendant entered a plea of guilty or no contest less than twenty-four hours before the scheduled commencement of the trial, the costs incurred in summoning jurors for that particular trial may be included in the costs of prosecution. If the costs incurred in summoning jurors are assessed against the defendant, those costs shall be paid to the public treasury from which the jurors were paid.

(B) If a judge or magistrate has reason to believe that a defendant has failed to pay the judgment described in division (A) of this section or has failed to timely make payments towards that judgment under a payment schedule approved by the judge or magistrate, the judge or magistrate shall hold a hearing to determine whether to order the offender to perform community service for that failure. The judge or magistrate shall notify both the defendant and the prosecuting attorney of the place, time, and date of the hearing and shall give each an opportunity to present evidence. If, after the hearing, the judge or magistrate determines that the defendant has failed to pay the judgment or to timely make payments under the payment schedule and that imposition of community service for the failure is appropriate, the judge or magistrate may order the offender to perform community service until the judgment is paid or until the judge or magistrate is satisfied that the offender is in compliance with the approved payment schedule. If the judge or magistrate orders the defendant to perform community service under this division, the defendant shall receive credit upon the judgment at the specified hourly credit rate per hour of community service performed, and each hour of community service performed shall reduce the judgment by that amount. Except for the credit and reduction provided in this division, ordering an offender to perform community service under this division does not lessen the amount of the judgment and does not preclude the state from taking any other action to execute the judgment.

(C) The court retains jurisdiction to waive, suspend, or modify the payment of the costs of prosecution, including any costs under section 2947.231 of the Revised Code, at the time of sentencing or at any time thereafter.

(D) As used in this section:

(1) "Case" means a prosecution of all of the charges that result from the same act, transaction, or series of acts or transactions and that are given the same case type designator and case number under Rule 43 of the Rules of Superintendence for the Courts of Ohio or any successor to that rule.

(2) "Specified hourly credit rate" means an hourly credit rate set by the judge or magistrate, which shall not be less than the wage rate that is specified in 26 U.S.C.A. 206(a)(1) under the federal Fair Labor Standards Act of 1938, that then is in effect, and that an employer subject to that provision must pay per hour to each of the employer's employees who is subject to that provision.

(2014 S 143, eff. 9-19-14; 2012 H 247, eff. 3-22-13; 2012 S 337, eff. 9-28-12; 2012 H 268, eff. 5-22-12; 2008 H 283, eff. 9–12–08; 2004 S 71, eff. 5–18–05; 2002 H 271, eff. 3–24–03; 1953 H 1, eff. 10–1–53; GC 13451–18)

Historical and Statutory Notes

Amendment Note: 2014 S 143 deleted "in an amount of not more than forty hours per month" after "perform community service" in division (A)(1)(a)(i) and in the third sentence of division (B); and inserted "an hourly credit rate set by the judge or magistrate, which shall not be less than" in division (D)(2).

Amendment Note: 2012 H 247 rewrote this section. See *Baldwin's Ohio Legislative Service Annotated*, or the OH–LEGIS or OH–LEGIS–OLD database on Westlaw for prior version of this section.

Amendment Note: 2012 S 337, rewrote division (A)(1), which prior thereto read:

"(A)(1) In all criminal cases, including violations of ordinances, the judge or magistrate shall include in the sentence the costs of prosecution, including any costs under section 2947.231 of the Revised Code, and render a judgment against the defendant for such costs. At the time the judge or magistrate imposes sentence, the judge or magistrate shall notify the defendant of both of the following:

"(a) If the defendant fails to pay that judgment or fails to timely make payments towards that judgment under a payment schedule approved by the court, the court may order the defendant to perform community service in an amount of not more than forty hours per month until the judgment is paid or until the court is satisfied that the defendant is in compliance with the approved payment schedule.

"(b) If the court orders the defendant to perform the community service, the defendant will receive credit upon the judgment at the specified hourly credit rate per hour of community service performed, and each hour of community service performed will reduce the judgment by that amount."

Amendment Note: 2012 H 268 inserted "or because the defendant entered a plea of guilty or no contest less than twenty-four hours before the scheduled commencement of the trial" in division (A)(2)(b).

Amendment Note: 2008 H 283 added ", including any costs under section 2947.231 of the Revised Code," in division (A)(1).

Cross References

Fees and costs, all courts, criminal cases, juvenile cases, and some civil actions related to criminal cases, see 2746.02

Research References

Encyclopedias

OH Jur. 3d Criminal Law: Procedure § 1922, Financial Sanctions and Fines.

OH Jur. 3d Criminal Law: Procedure § 1942, Costs and Jury Fees, Generally.

OH Jur. 3d Criminal Law: Procedure § 1984, Suspension of Sentence on Defendant's Payment of Attorney's Fees or Court Costs.

OH Jur. 3d Criminal Law: Procedure § 2000, Financial Sanctions.

OH Jur. 3d Criminal Law: Procedure § 2016, Community Service.

OH Jur. 3d Criminal Law: Procedure § 2076, Imprisonment for Failure to Pay Fine--Community Service.

OH Jur. 3d Criminal Law: Procedure § 2680, Judgment for Costs and Jury Fees.

Treatises and Practice Aids

Katz & Giannelli, Baldwin's Ohio Practice Criminal Law § 61:5, Indigent Defendants.

Katz & Giannelli, Baldwin's Ohio Practice Criminal Law § 119:6, Financial Sanctions.
Katz & Giannelli, Baldwin's Ohio Practice Criminal Law § 123:10, Financial Sanctions.
Weiler & Weiler, Ohio Driving Under the Influence App. A, Ohio Revised Code--Selected Provisions.

Notes of Decisions

1. Jury costs

Appropriate remedy for trial court's failure at resentencing for felonious assault to inform defendant that court costs included jury fees and that he could be ordered to perform community service if he failed to pay court costs was reversal of imposition of court costs and remand for proper imposition of costs in accordance with statute governing same, and not modification of sentence to prohibit any future order of community service if defendant failed to pay costs. State v. Weathers (Ohio App. 12 Dist., 03-25-2013) 988 N.E.2d 16, 2013-Ohio-1104. Criminal Law ⚷ 1181.5(8)

At resentencing for felonious assault, trial court was required to inform defendant that court costs included jury fees, and that if he failed to pay court costs, he could be ordered to perform community service. State v. Weathers (Ohio App. 12 Dist., 03-25-2013) 988 N.E.2d 16, 2013-Ohio-1104. Costs ⚷ 314

3. Miscellaneous court costs

The court's imposition of court costs is not erroneous due to the court's failure to specify the amount of court costs at sentencing; the calculation of the amount of court costs is a ministerial act and the itemized bill may be calculated later. State v. Lux (Ohio App. 2 Dist., Miami, 01-13-2012) No. 2010 CA 30, 2012-Ohio-112, 2012 WL 114188, Unreported. Costs ⚷ 314

Trial court had the authority to order indigent defendant, convicted of sexual battery, to pay costs. State v. Cloud (Ohio App. 7 Dist., Columbiana, 03-18-2005) No. 01 CO 64, 2005-Ohio-1331, 2005 WL 678767, Unreported, appeal allowed 106 Ohio St.3d 1482, 832 N.E.2d 736, 2005-Ohio-3978, cause dismissed 112 Ohio St.3d 1483, 862 N.E.2d 111, 2007-Ohio-723. Costs ⚷ 302

Any error in trial court's failure to notify defendant, during sentencing for multiple counts of pandering sexually-oriented material involving a minor, that trial court could order defendant to perform community service to satisfy any outstanding court costs was harmless, where amendments to statute no longer required trial court to give the notification in cases where the defendant was sentenced to a term of incarceration, and amended statute would apply at resentencing. State v. Liuzzo (Ohio App. 8 Dist., 07-09-2014) 15 N.E.3d 424, 2014-Ohio-3030. Criminal Law ⚷ 1177.3(2)

Any error in trial court's imposition of costs in sentencing defendant, following guilty plea to sex offenses, was moot, where appellate court was remanding case for resentencing based on other argument, and statute providing for imposition of costs had been amended since original judgment. State v. Jirousek (Ohio App. 11 Dist., 12-02-2013) 2 N.E.3d 981, 2013-Ohio-5267, appeal not allowed 139 Ohio St.3d 1472, 11 N.E.3d 1194, 2014-Ohio-3012. Criminal Law ⚷ 1134.26

Appropriate remedy for trial court's error in failing to provide notice to defendant at his sentencing hearing on his convictions for rape and other offenses of the consequences of his failure to pay court costs was remand for resentencing so that proper notification could be provided, which did not include any elimination of requirement that he had to perform community service if he did not pay court costs. State v. Jeffery (Ohio App. 2 Dist., 02-15-2013) 986 N.E.2d 1093, 2013-Ohio-504. Criminal Law ⚷ 1181.5(8); Criminal Law ⚷ 1192

The expenses which may be taxed as costs in a criminal case are those directly related to the court proceedings and are identified by a specific statutory authorization. State v. Blankenburg (Ohio App. 12 Dist., 03-26-2012) 197 Ohio App.3d 201, 966 N.E.2d 958, 2012-Ohio-1289, appeal not allowed 132 Ohio St.3d 1514, 974 N.E.2d 112, 2012-Ohio-4021, denial of post-conviction relief reversed 2012-Ohio-6175, 2012 WL 6738255. Costs ⚷ 303

The clerk of courts is responsible for generating an itemized bill of the court costs that are included in sentencing entry. State v. Blankenburg (Ohio App. 12 Dist., 03-26-2012) 197 Ohio App.3d 201, 966 N.E.2d 958, 2012-Ohio-1289, appeal not allowed 132 Ohio St.3d 1514, 974 N.E.2d 112, 2012-Ohio-4021, denial of post-conviction relief reversed 2012-Ohio-6175, 2012 WL 6738255. Costs ⚷ 314

Issue of court costs imposed in sentencing entry was not ripe for review, where there was nothing in the record to indicate whether the proper procedure was being followed or whether the prosecution costs had been reduced to judgment. State v. Blankenburg (Ohio App. 12 Dist., 03-26-2012) 197 Ohio App.3d 201, 966 N.E.2d 958, 2012-Ohio-1289, appeal not allowed 132 Ohio St.3d 1514, 974 N.E.2d 112, 2012-Ohio-4021, denial of post-conviction relief reversed 2012-Ohio-6175, 2012 WL 6738255. Criminal Law ⚷ 1134.25

Remand to municipal court was warranted for purpose of clarifying its imposition of costs regarding convictions for speeding and operating a motor vehicle while intoxicated; from the record, Supreme Court was unable to segregate costs of prosecution assessed in case from special-projects fees imposed by municipal court rule. Middleburg Hts. v. Quinones (Ohio, 12-31-2008) 120 Ohio St.3d 534, 900

N.E.2d 1005, 2008-Ohio-6811. Criminal Law ⚷ 260.12

Court of Appeals would not consider, on defendant's appeal from felonious assault conviction, the issue of trial court's failure to inform defendant, at time sentence was imposed, that she could be ordered to perform community service if she failed to pay court costs, where defendant did not raise this issue in her assignment of error regarding court costs, and the issue was not ripe for adjudication, given that defendant had not suffered any prejudice. State v. Ward (Ohio App. 4 Dist., 09-13-2006) 168 Ohio App.3d 701, 861 N.E.2d 823, 2006-Ohio-4847. Criminal Law ⚷ 1129(1)

Trial court has authority to impose court costs upon indigent defendant; statute requires court to include costs as part of sentence and, while second statute provides collection mechanism only for non-indigent defendants, nothing in second statute prohibits court from collecting costs from indigent defendant. State v. Haynie (Ohio App. 3 Dist., 05-17-2004) 157 Ohio App.3d 708, 813 N.E.2d 686, 2004-Ohio-2452, appeal allowed 103 Ohio St.3d 1477, 816 N.E.2d 253, 2004-Ohio-5405, reconsideration denied 104 Ohio St.3d 1428, 819 N.E.2d 710, 2004-Ohio-6585, affirmed 105 Ohio St.3d 133, 823 N.E.2d 448, 2005-Ohio-785, denial of post-conviction relief affirmed 2013-Ohio-3777, 2013 WL 4737247, appeal not allowed 138 Ohio St.3d 1433, 4 N.E.3d 1051, 2014-Ohio-889. Costs ⚷ 302

5. Ability to pay

Trial court was not required to consider defendant's present and future ability to pay before imposing court costs upon defendant's conviction for gross sexual imposition; court costs were not financial sanctions of the sort requiring ability-to-pay analysis. State v. Lux (Ohio App. 2 Dist., Miami, 01-13-2012) No. 2010 CA 30, 2012-Ohio-112, 2012 WL 114188, Unreported. Costs ⚷ 292; Costs ⚷ 314

Trial court was required to impose costs of prosecution for sexual battery, regardless of defendant's indigency status. State v. Dickinson (Ohio App. 7 Dist., Columbiana, 11-26-2004) No. 03 CO 52, 2004-Ohio-6373, 2004 WL 2726057, Unreported, appeal not allowed 105 Ohio St.3d 1499, 825 N.E.2d 623, 2005-Ohio-1666, habeas corpus denied 2009 WL 396049. Costs ⚷ 292

Statute governing trial court's authority to impose costs on defendant convicted of felony did not prohibit court from assessing costs to indigent defendant as part of sentence. State v. Vasquez (Ohio App. 10 Dist., Franklin, 07-22-2004) No. 03AP-460, 2004-Ohio-3880, 2004 WL 1631610, Unreported, affirmed 104 Ohio St.3d 507, 820 N.E.2d 370, 2004-Ohio-7016, denial of post-conviction relief affirmed 2009-Ohio-1189, 2009 WL 690533, appeal not allowed 122 Ohio St.3d 1521, 913 N.E.2d 457, 2009-Ohio-4776, habeas corpus dismissed 2010 WL 597782. Costs ⚷ 302

Nothing prevented trial court from assessing defendant court costs by virtue of his indigent status, upon his conviction for multiple theft-related offenses and engaging in corrupt activity; imposition of court costs was not an infringement of defendant's rights nor did it violate any statute. State v. Glavic (Ohio App. 11 Dist., Lake, 12-22-2003) No. 2001-L-177, No. 2001-L-179, 2003-Ohio-6961, 2003 WL 22994557, Unreported, motion for delayed appeal granted 102 Ohio St.3d 1444, 808 N.E.2d 396, 2004-Ohio-2263, appeal allowed 103 Ohio St.3d 1442, 814 N.E.2d 869, 2004-Ohio-4626, appeal not allowed 104 Ohio St.3d 1411, 818 N.E.2d 711, 2004-Ohio-6364, affirmed 105 Ohio St.3d 131, 823 N.E.2d 447, 2005-Ohio-31, habeas corpus denied 2007 WL 1959213, appeal not allowed 107 Ohio St.3d 1411, 836 N.E.2d 1230, 2005-Ohio-5859. Costs ⚷ 302

Record demonstrated that trial court properly considered whether defendant had or reasonably could be expected to have means to pay all or part of costs of legal services rendered to him before ordering him to pay costs; trial court asked defendant if defendant owned an interest in any real estate, defendant informed court that he owned a house which he intended to sell as soon as possible, and court noted that defendant had been gainfully employed his entire adult life. State v. Estes (Ohio App. 12 Dist., Preble, 10-06-2003) No. CA2002-05-008, 2003-Ohio-5283, 2003 WL 22283503, Unreported, denial of post-conviction relief affirmed 2005-Ohio-5478, 2005 WL 2626194, appeal not allowed 108 Ohio St.3d 1488, 843 N.E.2d 794, 2006-Ohio-962, habeas corpus denied 2009 WL 1362680. Costs ⚷ 314

Trial court was not required to consider defendant's ability to pay costs of prosecution before ordering defendant to pay such costs. State v. Estes (Ohio App. 12 Dist., Preble, 10-06-2003) No. CA2002-05-008, 2003-Ohio-5283, 2003 WL 22283503, Unreported, denial of post-conviction relief affirmed 2005-Ohio-5478, 2005 WL 2626194, appeal not allowed 108 Ohio St.3d 1488, 843 N.E.2d 794, 2006-Ohio-962, habeas corpus denied 2009 WL 1362680. Costs ⚷ 292

The trial court adequately considered defendant's ability to pay fines and court costs, as required by statute, before imposing fines and court costs; the court stated it considered defendant's pre-sentence investigation report (PSI), and the PSI indicated that defendant was close to graduating from university with a degree in business administration. State v. Taylor (Ohio App. 11 Dist., 08-27-2012) 974 N.E.2d 175, 2012-Ohio-3890. Costs ⚷ 314; Fines ⚷ 1.5

A defendant's financial status is irrelevant to the imposition of court costs. State v. Clevenger (Ohio, 08-22-2007) 114 Ohio St.3d 258, 871 N.E.2d 589, 2007-Ohio-4006. Costs ⚷ 292

Trial court was not required to consider defendant's present or future ability to pay before assessing court costs. State v. Ward (Ohio App. 4 Dist., 09-13-2006) 168 Ohio App.3d 701, 861 N.E.2d 823, 2006-Ohio-4847. Costs ⚷ 314

6. Court's authority

Claim on appeal challenging trial court's imposition of court costs absent notification that any failure to pay could be addressed by an order to perform community service was ripe for review, in prosecution for gross sexual imposition. State v. Lux (Ohio App. 2 Dist., Miami, 01-13-2012) No. 2010 CA 30, 2012-Ohio-112, 2012 WL 114188, Unreported. Criminal Law ⚷ 1134.25

Claim challenging trial court's imposition of court costs absent notification that any failure to pay could be addressed by an order to perform community service was rendered moot upon defendant's completion of one-year prison sentence; Court of Appeals nevertheless recognized trial court's inability to order defendant to perform community service in the event he failed to pay costs. State v. Lux (Ohio App. 2 Dist., Miami, 01-13-2012) No. 2010 CA 30, 2012-Ohio-112, 2012 WL 114188, Unreported. Costs ⚷ 320; Criminal Law ⚷ 1134.26

Trial court's failure to inform defendant convicted of complicity to burglary that community service could be imposed if he failed to pay his court costs was clearly and convincingly contrary to law; court was required to inform defendant that community service could be imposed if he failed to pay court costs, and notification was mandatory. State v. Moss (Ohio App. 4 Dist., 03-19-2010) 186 Ohio App.3d 787, 930 N.E.2d 838, 2010-Ohio-1135. Costs ⚷ 314; Costs ⚷ 320

Trial court's error, in failing to inform defendant convicted of complicity to burglary that community service could be imposed if he failed to pay his court costs, was ripe for appellate review. State v. Moss (Ohio App. 4 Dist., 03-19-2010) 186 Ohio App.3d 787, 930 N.E.2d 838, 2010-Ohio-1135. Criminal Law ⚷ 1134.25

Trial court erred by imposing costs on defendant when it dismissed city's criminal complaint alleging that defendant failed to make municipal tax returns, notwithstanding city's assertion that purported settlement agreement required defendant to pay costs upon dismissal of complaint, absent evidence of settlement agreement in record or prerequisite conviction. Cleveland Hts. v. Machlup (Ohio App. 8 Dist., Cuyahoga, 12-10-2009) No. 93086, 2009-Ohio-6468, 2009 WL 4695440, Unreported. Costs ⚷ 292

Trial court's failure to inform defendant, after imposing court costs at defendant's sentencing hearing, that defendant's failure to pay such costs could result in imposition of community service or that he would receive credit toward the costs from any community service ordered and performed, was error requiring reversal of imposition of costs and remand for imposition in accordance with notification requirement. State v. Shover (Ohio App. 9 Dist., 02-05-2014) 8 N.E.3d 358, 2014-Ohio-373, appeal not allowed 139 Ohio St.3d 1406, 9 N.E.3d 1063, 2014-Ohio-2245. Costs ⚷ 314; Criminal Law ⚷ 1181.5(8)

Remand was required, on appeal from conviction of aggravated robbery and kidnapping, to permit sentencing court to inform defendant of possibility of court-ordered community service. State v. Foxx (Ohio App. 2 Dist., 01-24-2014) 7 N.E.3d 615, 2014-Ohio-235. Criminal Law ⚷ 1181.5(8)

Trial court was required to notify defendant that a failure to pay court costs could result in a court order to perform community service, in prosecution for felonious assault; State conceded issue on appeal. State v. Crews (Ohio App. 2 Dist., 10-19-2012) 980 N.E.2d 536, 2012-Ohio-4854, appeal not allowed 134 Ohio St.3d 1507, 984 N.E.2d 1101, 2013-Ohio-1123. Costs ⚷ 314; Costs ⚷ 320

Remand for resentencing was warranted, where the trial court imposed court costs against defendant but failed to comply with statute that required a judge to notify the defendant that if defendant failed to make payments towards the costs the court could order defendant to perform community service, and that of community services imposed the court would receive credit against the judgment at the specified hourly rate per hour of community service performed. State v. Taylor (Ohio App. 11 Dist., 08-27-2012) 974 N.E.2d 175, 2012-Ohio-3890. Costs ⚷ 314; Criminal Law ⚷ 1181.5(8)

A sentencing court's failure to inform a defendant that community service could be imposed if defendant fails to pay the costs of prosecution or court costs presents an issue ripe for review, even if the record does not show that the defendant has failed to pay such costs or that the trial court has ordered the defendant to perform community service as a result of failure to pay; statute states that court "shall notify" at the time judge imposes sentence, which clearly registers an intent that this notice is mandatory and that a court is to provide this notice at sentencing; abrogating *State v. Smith*, 2011 WL 882182. R.C. State v. Smith (Ohio, 03-01-2012) 131 Ohio St.3d 297, 964 N.E.2d 423, 2012-Ohio-781. Criminal Law ⚷ 1134.25

The trial court erred when it imposed court costs in the sentencing journal entry without first addressing court costs at defendant's sentencing hearing. State v. Butler (Ohio App. 8 Dist., 03-17-2011) 192 Ohio App.3d 623, 949 N.E.2d 1075, 2011-Ohio-1233, appeal not allowed 129 Ohio St.3d 1477, 953 N.E.2d 843, 2011-Ohio-4751. Sentencing and Punishment ⚷ 1139

Trial court's error in imposing court costs in its sentencing entry without orally notifying defendant that it was imposing court costs on him did not void the defendant's entire sentence, but mandated remand to trial court for the limited purpose of allowing defendant to move the court for a waiver of the payment of court costs. State v. Joseph (Ohio, 03-18-2010) 125 Ohio St.3d 76, 926 N.E.2d 278, 2010-Ohio-954. Criminal Law ⚷ 1181.5(8)

Trial court's failure to advise aggravated robbery defendant that he risked being required to perform community service if he failed to pay court costs did not constitute plain error; issue was not ripe for review as long as defendant remained incarcerated and court did not impose an order of community service, and state had over 15 years to garnish defendant's inmate account or defendant had over 15 years to pay his costs voluntarily. State v. Barkley (Ohio App. 10 Dist., 10-20-2009) 185 Ohio App.3d 686, 925 N.E.2d 626, 2009-Ohio-5549, appeal not allowed 124 Ohio St.3d 1477, 921 N.E.2d 248, 2010-Ohio-354, habeas corpus dismissed 2012 WL 2883717. Criminal Law ⚿ 1042.6

"Costs" may be defined as being the statutory fees to which officers, witnesses, jurors, and others are entitled for their services in an action or prosecution, and which the statutes authorize to be taxed and included in the judgment or sentence. Middleburg Hts. v. Quinones (Ohio, 12-31-2008) 120 Ohio St.3d 534, 900 N.E.2d 1005, 2008-Ohio-6811. Costs ⚿ 146; Costs ⚿ 303

Statute imposing mandatory obligation on trial judges in all criminal cases to include in the sentence the costs of prosecution and to render a judgment therefor does not authorize imposition of costs for each offense committed. Middleburg Hts. v. Quinones (Ohio, 12-31-2008) 120 Ohio St.3d 534, 900 N.E.2d 1005, 2008-Ohio-6811. Costs ⚿ 292

Trial court was required to order defendant convicted of first-degree misdemeanor of knowingly filing a false financial disclosure statement to pay the costs of prosecution. State v. Perz (Ohio App. 6 Dist., 08-03-2007) 173 Ohio App.3d 99, 877 N.E.2d 702, 2007-Ohio-3962. Costs ⚿ 304

Because the imposition of prosecutorial costs is mandatory, the trial court is not required to hold a hearing or otherwise determine an offender's ability to pay before ordering him to pay costs. State v. Perz (Ohio App. 6 Dist., 08-03-2007) 173 Ohio App.3d 99, 877 N.E.2d 702, 2007-Ohio-3962. Costs ⚿ 314

Costs of prosecution that trial court is required to order defendant to pay are limited to those expenses directly related to the court proceedings. State v. Perz (Ohio App. 6 Dist., 08-03-2007) 173 Ohio App.3d 99, 877 N.E.2d 702, 2007-Ohio-3962. Costs ⚿ 304

Costs of prosecution that trial court is required to order defendant to pay include fees of officers and court personnel, including clerks of court, jury fees, witness fees, interpreters fees, and fees of psychologists and psychiatrists. State v. Perz (Ohio App. 6 Dist., 08-03-2007) 173 Ohio App.3d 99, 877 N.E.2d 702, 2007-Ohio-3962. Costs ⚿ 304

A trial court may not suspend court costs previously imposed on a criminal defendant absent statutory authority. State v. Clevenger (Ohio, 08-22-2007) 114 Ohio St.3d 258, 871 N.E.2d 589, 2007-Ohio-4006. Costs ⚿ 319

A trial court may waive the payment of court costs previously imposed on a criminal defendant only upon statutory authority and only if the defendant moves for waiver of such costs at the time of sentencing. State v. Clevenger (Ohio, 08-22-2007) 114 Ohio St.3d 258, 871 N.E.2d 589, 2007-Ohio-4006. Costs ⚿ 319

Trial court's assessment of court costs against defendant, in prosecution on felony charge of breaking and entering, was res judicata, where defendant did not raise the issue of costs either at the initial sentencing hearing or at the subsequent hearing on the probation violation. State v. Clevenger (Ohio, 08-22-2007) 114 Ohio St.3d 258, 871 N.E.2d 589, 2007-Ohio-4006. Judgment ⚿ 751

Trial court lacked authority to suspend portion of defendant's sentence that imposed court costs in prosecution on felony charge of breaking and entering. State v. Clevenger (Ohio, 08-22-2007) 114 Ohio St.3d 258, 871 N.E.2d 589, 2007-Ohio-4006. Costs ⚿ 319

7. Assistance of counsel

Counsel's failure to seek to withdraw guilty plea did not prejudice defendant, and therefore did not constitute ineffective assistance of counsel in burglary prosecution in which defendant pleaded guilty, where there was nothing to suggest that trial court would have allowed defendant to withdraw his guilty plea. State v. Siler (Ohio App. 11 Dist., Ashtabula, 05-13-2011) No. 2010-A-0025, 2011-Ohio-2326, 2011 WL 1938500, Unreported. Criminal Law ⚿ 1920

Defense counsel's failure to move the sentencing court to waive the imposition of court costs on defendant at his sentencing on his conviction for aggravated vehicular homicide constituted deficient performance that prejudiced defendant, and thus was ineffective assistance; defendant was determined to be indigent and was appointed counsel for trial, there was nothing in the record to indicate that defendant's circumstances had changed at the time of sentencing, and the court did not impose a fine at sentencing, based upon its assessment of defendant's inability to pay a fine. State v. Rowe (Ohio App. 4 Dist., 11-29-2011) 197 Ohio App.3d 10, 965 N.E.2d 1047, 2011-Ohio-6614, motion for delayed appeal denied 131 Ohio St.3d 1497, 964 N.E.2d 438, 2012-Ohio-1501. Criminal Law ⚿ 1957

2947.231 Dangerous drug convictions; sentence to include costs

If a business entity described in division (B)(1)(j) or (k) of section 4729.51 of the Revised Code pleads guilty or no contest to or is found guilty of any criminal offense, the judge or magistrate shall include in the sentence any costs incurred by the state board of pharmacy in an investigation leading to the plea or conviction. Investigative costs include staff salaries, administrative costs, travel expenses, attorney's fees, and any other reasonable expense incurred by the board. The board shall set forth the costs the entity is required to pay in an itemized statement provided to the judge or magistrate.

(2008 H 283, eff. 9-12-08)

Research References

Encyclopedias

OH Jur. 3d Criminal Law: Procedure § 1942, Costs and Jury Fees, Generally.

OH Jur. 3d Criminal Law: Procedure § 2673, Items and Amounts Taxable, Generally.

OH Jur. 3d Criminal Law: Procedure § 2680, Judgment for Costs and Jury Fees.

CHAPTER 2949

EXECUTION OF SENTENCE

EXECUTION OF SENTENCE GENERALLY

EXECUTION OF SENTENCE GENERALLY

2949.05 Execution of sentence or judgment

Notes of Decisions

1. Execution of sentence

Trial court did not have authority or jurisdiction to resentence defendant after Court of Appeals rendered decision upholding validity of trial court's original sentencing decision and defendant was transferred to penal institution of executive branch. State v. Harrold (Ohio App. 9 Dist., Summit, 06-30-2004) No. 21797, 2004-Ohio-3423, 2004 WL 1462991, Unreported, on reconsideration 2004-Ohio-4450, 2004 WL 1882660. Sentencing And Punishment ⚩ 2282

2949.08 Confinement of convicts; reduction of sentence for confinement prior to conviction

(A) When a person who is convicted of or pleads guilty to a felony is sentenced to a community residential sanction in a community-based correctional facility pursuant to section 2929.16 of the Revised Code or when a person who is convicted of or pleads guilty to a felony or a misdemeanor is sentenced to a term of imprisonment in a jail, the judge or magistrate shall order the person into the custody of the sheriff or constable, and the sheriff or constable shall deliver the person with the record of the person's conviction to the jailer, administrator, or keeper, in whose custody the person shall remain until the term of imprisonment expires or the person is otherwise legally discharged.

(B) The record of the person's conviction shall specify the total number of days, if any, that the person was confined for any reason arising out of the offense for which the person was convicted and sentenced prior to delivery to the jailer, administrator, or keeper under this section. The record shall be used to determine any reduction of sentence under division (C) of this section.

(C)(1) If the person is sentenced to a jail for a felony or a misdemeanor, the jailer in charge of a jail shall reduce the sentence of a person delivered into the jailer's custody pursuant to division (A) of this section by the total number of days the person was confined for any reason arising out of the offense for which the person was convicted and sentenced, including confinement in lieu of bail while awaiting trial, confinement for examination to determine the person's competence to stand trial or to determine sanity, confinement while awaiting transportation to the place where the person is to serve the sentence, and confinement in a juvenile facility.

(2) If the person is sentenced to a community-based correctional facility for a felony, the total amount of time that a person shall be confined in a community-based correctional facility, in a jail, and for any reason arising out of the offense for which the person was convicted and sentenced prior to delivery to the jailer, administrator, or keeper shall not exceed the maximum prison term available for that offense. Any term in a jail shall be reduced first pursuant to division (C)(1) of this section by the total number of days the person was confined prior to delivery to the jailer, administrator, or keeper. Only after the term in a jail has been entirely reduced may the term in a community-based correctional facility be reduced pursuant to this division. This division does not affect the limitations placed on the duration of a term in a jail or a community-based correctional facility under divisions (A)(1), (2), and (3) of section 2929.16 of the Revised Code.

(D) For purposes of divisions (B) and (C) of this section, a person shall be considered to have been confined for a day if the person was confined for any period or periods of time totaling more than eight hours during that day.

(E) As used in this section, "community-based correctional facility" and "jail" have the same meanings as in section 2929.01 of the Revised Code.

(2012 S 337, eff. 9-28-12; 1999 S 107, eff. 3-23-00; 1979 S 23, eff. 3-27-80; 1953 H 1; GC 13454-1)

Historical and Statutory Notes

Amendment Note: 2012 S 337, in division (C)(1), deleted "and" preceding, and inserted ", and confinement in a juvenile facility" following, "confinement while awaiting transportation to the place where the person is to serve the sentence".

Research References

Encyclopedias

OH Jur. 3d Criminal Law: Procedure § 2079, Confinement Upon Conviction.

OH Jur. 3d Criminal Law: Procedure § 2080, Credit for Time Served.

OH Jur. 3d Criminal Law: Procedure § 2082, Delivery of Convict to Reception Facility.

OH Jur. 3d Criminal Law: Procedure § 2084, Credit for Time Served.

Treatises and Practice Aids

Katz & Giannelli, Baldwin's Ohio Practice Criminal Law § 115:5, Equal Protection in Sentencing.

Katz & Giannelli, Baldwin's Ohio Practice Criminal Law § 119:8, Violations of Community Control Sanctions.

Adrine & Ruden, Ohio Domestic Violence Law App. A, Ohio Revised Code (Selected Provisions).

Weiler & Weiler, Ohio Driving Under the Influence § 14:21, Credit for Time Served.

Notes of Decisions

1. Credit for jail time

Restriction on defendant's movements imposed by the electronic monitoring condition of community control, requiring defendant to abide by curfew as set by probation officer, did not so severely restrain defendant that he was subjected to "confinement" for purposes of calculating credit for time served, where, other than the curfew restriction, defendant had unfettered liberty to leave his house on his own volition. State v. Williams (Ohio App. 3 Dist., Hancock, 12-27-2011) No. 5-11-26, 2011-Ohio-6698, 2011 WL 6882915, Unreported. Sentencing and Punishment ⚷ 1170

Trial judge was required to state in journal entry the number of jail time credit days to which defendant was entitled for domestic violence conviction. State ex rel. Jones v. McMonagle (Ohio App. 8 Dist., Cuyahoga, 03-31-2009) No. 92401, 2009-Ohio-1601, 2009 WL 867624, Unreported. Sentencing and Punishment ⚷ 1157

County sheriff had no legal duty to calculate preconviction jail time credit or forward any calculation to the Ohio Department of Rehabilitation and Corrections as to prisoner, and therefore, prisoner was not entitled to a writ of mandamus compelling such action, even though he was entitled to preconviction jail time credit. State ex rel. Marich v. McFaul (Ohio App. 8 Dist., Cuyahoga, 03-04-2008) No. 90882, 2008-Ohio-2161, 2008 WL 1973472, Unreported. Mandamus ⚷ 73(1); Sentencing and Punishment ⚷ 1159

Trial court was required to determine on remand whether defendant was entitled to a credit for four days confinement at a rate of $50 per day against the $158 monetary sanction imposed by the court in his misdemeanor traffic violation case, or whether the jail time credit was applied against sentences that were imposed for other charges for which defendant was also confined for at the same time; the credit only applied to one sentence imposed. State v. Green (Ohio App. 2 Dist., Montgomery, 06-23-2006) No. 21082, 2006-Ohio-3196, 2006 WL 1719753, Unreported. Fines ⚷ 1.5; Sentencing And Punishment ⚷ 1157

Time-served credit is not limited to preconviction confinement. State v. Blankenship (Ohio App. 10 Dist., 03-31-2011) 192 Ohio App.3d 639, 949 N.E.2d 1087, 2011-Ohio-1601, appeal not allowed 129 Ohio St.3d 1453, 951 N.E.2d 1048, 2011-Ohio-4217. Sentencing And Punishment ⚷ 1157

A person convicted of a misdemeanor offense is not entitled to time-served credit for time spent under electronically monitored house arrest (EMHA) as a condition of postconviction probation. State v. Blankenship (Ohio App. 10 Dist., 03-31-2011) 192 Ohio App.3d 639, 949 N.E.2d 1087, 2011-Ohio-1601, appeal not allowed 129 Ohio St.3d 1453, 951 N.E.2d 1048, 2011-Ohio-4217. Sentencing And Punishment ⚷ 1170

3. Mandamus to compel sentence reduction

Mandamus petition seeking to compel trial court to grant inmate's motion for 378 days of jail time credit was defective, thus justifying denial of relief, as petition was not supported with an affidavit specifying details of claim, it was improperly captioned, and inmate failed to file certified statement from his prison cashier setting forth balance in his private account for each of the preceding six months. Leonard v. State (Ohio App. 8 Dist., Cuyahoga, 11-06-2009) No. 93872, 2009-Ohio-5971, 2009 WL 3772794, Unreported. Mandamus ⚷ 154(2); Mandamus ⚷ 155(1)

Inmate who sought mandamus relief to compel trial court to grant his motion for 378 days of jail time credit, as opposed to the 127 days of credit that court had granted, had adequate remedy at law through appeal, and, thus, was not entitled to mandamus relief, as court fulfilled its duty by specifying the number of days of jail-time credit in an entry, and its granting of credit was an exercise of discretion. Leonard v. State (Ohio App. 8 Dist., Cuyahoga, 11-06-2009) No. 93872, 2009-Ohio-5971, 2009 WL 3772794, Unreported. Mandamus ⚷ 4(4)

4. Work release

A trial court has discretion to impose a term of electronically monitored house arrest (EMHA) longer than the maximum jail term available for the offense, so long as the court heeds the cumulative five-year restriction for all community-control sanctions. State v. Blankenship (Ohio App. 10 Dist., 03-31-2011) 192 Ohio App.3d 639, 949 N.E.2d 1087, 2011-Ohio-1601, appeal not allowed 129 Ohio St.3d 1453, 951 N.E.2d 1048, 2011-Ohio-4217. Sentencing And Punishment ⚷ 1945

5. Transportation of prisoner

Except as provided in RC 2949.08(A), a county sheriff is not responsible for transporting between the county jail and a municipal court within the county a person arrested for a misdemeanor and confined in the county jail. Pursuant to RC 1901.32(A)(6), a person arrested for a misdemeanor and confined in the county jail is to be transported between the county jail and a municipal court within the county by a bailiff or deputy bailiff of the court unless RC 2949.08(A) applies. Pursuant to RC 1901.32(A)(5), when a municipal court requires it, a person arrested for a misdemeanor and confined in the county jail may be transported between the county jail and the court by a police officer of a municipal corporation or constable of a township located within the territory of the court, as an ex officio deputy bailiff of the court, unless RC 2949.08(A) applies. OAG 2010-018, 2010 WL 2757430.

2949.091 Fees and costs

(A)(1)(a) The court in which any person is convicted of or pleads guilty to any offense shall impose one of the following sums as costs in the case in addition to any other court costs that the court is required by law to impose upon the offender:

(i) Thirty dollars if the offense is a felony;

(ii) Twenty dollars if the offense is a misdemeanor other than a traffic offense that is not a moving violation;

(iii) Ten dollars if the offense is a traffic offense that is not a moving violation, excluding parking violations.

(b) All moneys collected pursuant to division (A)(1)(a) of this section during a month shall be transmitted on or before the twentieth day of the following month by the clerk of the court to the treasurer of state and deposited by the treasurer of state to the credit of the indigent defense support fund established under section 120.08 of the Revised Code. The court shall not waive the payment of the additional thirty-, twenty-, or ten-dollar court costs, unless the court determines that the offender is indigent and waives the payment of all court costs imposed upon the indigent offender.

(2)(a) The juvenile court in which a child is found to be a delinquent child or a juvenile traffic offender for an act that, if committed by an adult, would be an offense, shall impose one of the following sums as costs in the case in addition to any other court costs that the court is required or permitted by law to impose upon the delinquent child or juvenile traffic offender:

(i) Thirty dollars if the offense is a felony;

(ii) Twenty dollars if the offense is a misdemeanor other than a traffic offense that is not a moving violation;

(iii) Ten dollars if the offense is a traffic offense that is not a moving violation, excluding parking violations.

(b) All moneys collected pursuant to division (A)(2)(a) of this section during a month shall be transmitted on or before the twentieth day of the following month by the clerk of the court to the treasurer of state and deposited by the treasurer of state to the credit of the indigent defense support fund established under section 120.08 of the Revised Code. The thirty-, twenty-, or ten-dollar court costs shall be collected in all cases unless the court determines the juvenile is indigent and waives the payment of all court costs, or enters an order on its journal stating that it has determined that the juvenile is indigent, that no other court costs are to be taxed in the case, and that the payment of the thirty-, twenty-, or ten-dollar court costs is waived.

(B) Whenever a person is charged with any offense described in division (A)(1) of this section, the court shall add to the amount of the bail the thirty, twenty, or ten dollars required to be paid by division (A)(1) of this section. The thirty, twenty, or ten dollars shall be retained by the clerk of the court until the person is convicted, pleads guilty, forfeits bail, is found not guilty, or has the charges dismissed. If the person is convicted, pleads guilty, or forfeits bail, the clerk shall transmit the thirty, twenty, or ten dollars on or before the twentieth day of the month following the month in which the person was convicted, pleaded guilty, or forfeited bail to the treasurer of state, who shall deposit it to the credit of the indigent defense support fund established under section 120.08 of the Revised Code. If the person is found not guilty or the charges are dismissed, the clerk shall return the thirty, twenty, or ten dollars to the person.

(C) No person shall be placed or held in a detention facility for failing to pay the additional thirty-, twenty-, or ten-dollar court costs or bail that are required to be paid by this section.

(D) As used in this section:

(1) "Moving violation" and "bail" have the same meanings as in section 2743.70 of the Revised Code.

(2) "Detention facility" has the same meaning as in section 2921.01 of the Revised Code.

(3) "Case" has the same meaning as in section 2947.23 of the Revised Code.

(2012 H 247, eff. 3-22-13; 2009 H 1, eff. 10-16-09; 2003 H 95, eff. 9–26–03; 1998 H 426, eff. 7–22–98; 1991 H 298, eff. 7–26–91; 1990 S 131; 1989 H 111; 1987 H 171; 1983 H 291)

Historical and Statutory Notes

Amendment Note: 2012 H 247 added division (D)(3).

Amendment Note: 2009 H 1 rewrote the section, which prior to amendment read:

"(A)(1) The court in which any person is convicted of or pleads guilty to any offense other than a traffic offense that is not a moving violation, shall impose the sum of fifteen dollars as costs in the case in addition to any other court costs that the court is required by law to impose upon the offender. All such moneys collected during a month shall be transmitted on or before the twentieth day of the following month by the clerk of the court to the treasurer of state and deposited by the treasurer of state into the general revenue fund. The court shall not waive the payment of the additional fifteen dollars court costs, unless the court determines that the offender is indigent and waives the payment of all court costs imposed upon the indigent offender.

"(2) The juvenile court, in which a child is found to be a delinquent child or a juvenile traffic offender for an act which, if committed by an adult, would be an offense other than a traffic offense that is not a moving violation, shall impose the sum of fifteen dollars as costs in the case in addition to any other court costs that the court is required or permitted by law to impose upon the delinquent child or juvenile traffic offender. All such moneys collected during a month shall be transmitted on or before the twentieth day of the following month by the clerk of the court to the treasurer of state and deposited by the treasurer of state into the general revenue fund. The fifteen dollars court costs shall be collected in all cases unless the court determines the juvenile is indigent and waives the payment of all court costs, or enters an order on its journal stating that it has determined that the juvenile is indigent, that no other court costs are to be taxed in the case, and that the payment of the fifteen dollars court costs is waived.

"(B) Whenever a person is charged with any offense other than a traffic offense that is not a moving violation and posts bail, the court shall add to the amount of the bail the fifteen thirty, twenty, or ten dollars required to be paid by division (A)(1) of this section. The fifteen dollars shall be retained by the clerk of the court until the person is convicted, pleads guilty, forfeits bail, is found not guilty, or has the charges dismissed. If the person is convicted, pleads guilty, or forfeits bail, the clerk shall transmit the fifteen dollars on or before the twentieth day of the month following the month in which the person was convicted, pleaded guilty, or forfeited bail to the treasurer of state, who shall deposit it into of the general revenue fund. If the person is found not guilty or the charges are dismissed, the clerk shall return the fifteen dollars to the person.

"(C) No person shall be placed or held in a detention facility for failing to pay the additional fifteen dollars court costs or bail that are required to be paid by this section.

"(D) As used in this section:

"(1) 'Moving violation' and 'bail' have the same meanings as in section 2743.70 of the Revised Code.

"(2) 'Detention facility' has the same meaning as in section 2921.01 of the Revised Code."

Cross References

Fees and costs, all courts, criminal cases, juvenile cases, and some civil actions related to criminal cases, see 2746.02

Ohio Administrative Code References

Reparations rotary reporting for courts, see OAC 113–1–06

Research References

Encyclopedias

OH Jur. 3d Courts and Judges § 110, Generally; Acts Within Scope of Jurisdiction.

OH Jur. 3d Criminal Law: Procedure § 2677, Additional Court Costs.

OH Jur. 3d Criminal Law: Procedure § 2688, Waiver of Payment.

Treatises and Practice Aids

Giannelli & Yeomans Salvador, Ohio Juvenile Law App. A, Ohio Revised Code--Selected Provisions.

Notes of Decisions

Constitutional issues 6

1. Costs assessed per case

Trial court was required to impose certain fees on defendant who was convicted of domestic violence, and, thus, inclusion in written sentence entry of financial sanction of the cost of prosecution was not an unlawful additional sanction included in the sentencing entry, although trial court did not impose it at sentencing hearing. State v. Jackson (Ohio App. 3 Dist., 04-08-2013) 990 N.E.2d 184, 2013-Ohio-1390. Costs ⚷ 314; Sentencing and Punishment ⚷ 1139

6. Constitutional issues

Certification of class of persons, who served time in the county jail for failure to pay a fine, without being given an indigency hearing, and who were represented by a county public defender, was warranted, in §§ 1983 action asserting that the alleged policy or custom of the county public defender's office in failing to seek indigency hearings on behalf of criminal defendants facing jail time for unpaid fines violated due process; named plaintiff was typical of the class, in that he was jailed for failing to pay a court-ordered fine and his public defender did not seek indigency hearing prior to his incarceration, and action asserted a single factual theory of wrongdoing for the entire class, based on a single legal claim for all the class members, so that the commonality and predominance requirements for certification were satisfied. Powers v. Hamilton County Public Defender Com'n (C.A.6 (Ohio), 08-29-2007) 501 F.3d 592, rehearing and rehearing en banc denied, certiorari denied 129 S.Ct. 44, 555 U.S. 813, 172 L.Ed.2d 21. Federal Civil Procedure ⚿ 186.10

2949.092 Waiver of additional court costs

If a person is convicted of or pleads guilty to an offense and the court specifically is required, pursuant to section 2743.70, 2949.091, 2949.093, or 2949.094 of the Revised Code or pursuant to any other section of the Revised Code to impose a specified sum of money as costs in the case in addition to any other costs that the court is required or permitted by law to impose in the case, the court shall not waive the payment of the specified additional court costs that the section of the Revised Code specifically requires the court to impose unless the court determines that the offender is indigent and the court waives the payment of all court costs imposed upon the offender.

(2008 H 562, eff. 9–23–08; 2005 H 66, eff. 9–29–05; 1990 S 131, eff. 7–25–90)

Historical and Statutory Notes

Amendment Note: 2008 H 562 substituted "2949.093, or 2949.094" for "or 2949.093".

Cross References

Fees and costs, all courts, criminal cases, juvenile cases, and some civil actions related to criminal cases, see 2746.02

Research References

Encyclopedias

OH Jur. 3d Criminal Law: Procedure § 2688, Waiver of Payment.

Notes of Decisions

---

3. In general

If the defendant fails to make a motion to waive court costs at the time of sentencing, the issue is waived and the matter of costs are res judicata. State v. Rowe (Ohio App. 4 Dist., 11-29-2011) 197 Ohio App.3d 10, 965 N.E.2d 1047, 2011-Ohio-6614, motion for delayed appeal denied 131 Ohio St.3d 1497, 964 N.E.2d 438, 2012-Ohio-1501. Judgment ⚿ 751

The sentencing court may grant a waiver of court costs only if the defendant makes a motion at the time of sentencing. State v. Rowe (Ohio App. 4 Dist., 11-29-2011) 197 Ohio App.3d 10, 965 N.E.2d 1047, 2011-Ohio-6614, motion for delayed appeal denied 131 Ohio St.3d 1497, 964 N.E.2d 438, 2012-Ohio-1501. Costs ⚿ 314

4. Assistance of counsel

Defense counsel's failure to move the sentencing court to waive the imposition of court costs on defendant at his sentencing on his conviction for aggravated vehicular homicide constituted deficient performance that prejudiced defendant, and thus was ineffective assistance; defendant was determined to be indigent and was appointed counsel for trial, there was nothing in the record to indicate that defendant's circumstances had changed at the time of sentencing, and the court did not impose a fine at sentencing, based upon its assessment of defendant's inability to pay a fine. State v. Rowe (Ohio App. 4 Dist., 11-29-2011) 197 Ohio App.3d 10, 965 N.E.2d 1047, 2011-Ohio-6614, motion for delayed appeal denied 131 Ohio St.3d 1497, 964 N.E.2d 438, 2012-Ohio-1501. Criminal Law ⚿ 1957

2949.093 Participation in criminal justice regional information system; requirements; funding

Cross References

Fees and costs, all courts, criminal cases, juvenile cases, and some civil actions related to criminal cases, see 2746.02

Notes of Decisions

Funding 1
Liability 2

1. Funding

RC 2949.093 requires a municipal court to impose the additional court cost established by a board of county commissioners per moving violation adjudicated or otherwise processed by the court in a case when a person is convicted of, or pleads guilty to, more than one moving violation in a case. (2007 Op. Att'y Gen. No. 2007-030, 2007 WL 4923602, approved and followed). OAG 2013-025, 2013 WL 3971414.

The additional court cost established by a board of county commissioners pursuant to R.C. 2949.093 is to be charged per moving violation adjudicated or otherwise processed by a municipal court in a case when a person is convicted of or pleads guilty to more than one moving violation in a case. OAG 07–030.

2. Liability

Whether a municipal court or municipal court clerk is civilly liable for damages for failing to collect the additional court cost established by a board of county commissioners pursuant to RC 2949.093 is a question that cannot be answered by means of an Attorney General opinion. OAG 2013-025, 2013 WL 3971414.

2949.094 Additional court costs for moving violations

(A) The court in which any person is convicted of or pleads guilty to any moving violation shall impose an additional court cost of ten dollars upon the offender. The court shall not waive the payment of the ten dollars unless the court determines that the offender is indigent and waives the payment of all court costs imposed upon the indigent offender.

The clerk of the court shall transmit thirty-five per cent of all additional court costs collected pursuant to this division during a month on or before the twenty-third day of the following month to the state treasury of which ninety-seven per cent shall be credited to the drug law enforcement fund created under section 5502.68 of the Revised Code and the remaining three per cent shall be credited to the justice program services fund created under section 5502.67 of the Revised Code. The clerk shall transmit fifteen per cent of all additional court costs so collected during a month on or before the twenty-third day of the following month to the county or municipal indigent drivers alcohol treatment fund under the control of that court, as created by the county or municipal corporation under division (H) of section 4511.191 of the Revised Code. The clerk shall transmit fifty per cent of all additional court costs so collected during a month on or before the twenty-third day of the following month to the state treasury to be credited to the indigent defense support fund created pursuant to section 120.08 of the Revised Code.

(B) The juvenile court in which a child is found to be a juvenile traffic offender for an act that is a moving violation shall impose an additional court cost of ten dollars upon the juvenile traffic offender. The juvenile court shall not waive the payment of the ten dollars unless the court determines that the juvenile is indigent and waives the payment of all court costs imposed upon the indigent offender.

The clerk of the court shall transmit thirty-five per cent of all additional court costs collected pursuant to this division during a month on or before the twenty-third day of the following month to the state treasury of which ninety-seven per cent shall be credited to the drug law enforcement fund created under section 5502.68 of the Revised Code and the remaining three per cent shall be credited to the justice program services fund created under section 5502.67 of the Revised Code. The clerk shall transmit fifteen per cent of all additional court costs so collected during a month on or before the twenty-third day of the following month to the county juvenile indigent drivers alcohol treatment fund under the control of that court, as created by the county under division (H) of section 4511.191 of the Revised Code. The clerk shall transmit fifty per cent of all additional court costs so collected during a month on or before the twenty-third day of the following month to the state treasury to be credited to the indigent defense support fund created pursuant to section 120.08 of the Revised Code.

(C) Whenever a person is charged with any offense that is a moving violation and posts bail, the court shall add to the amount of the bail the ten dollars required to be paid by division (A) of this section. The clerk of the court shall retain the ten dollars until the person is convicted, pleads guilty, forfeits bail, is found not guilty, or has the charges dismissed. If the person is convicted, pleads guilty, or forfeits bail, the clerk shall transmit three dollars and fifty cents out of the ten dollars to the state treasury of which ninety-seven per cent shall be credited to the drug law enforcement fund created under section 5502.68 of the Revised Code and the remaining three per cent shall be credited to the justice program services fund created under section 5502.67 of the Revised Code, the clerk shall transmit one dollar and fifty cents out of the ten dollars to the county, municipal, or county juvenile indigent drivers alcohol treatment fund under the control of that court, as created by the county or municipal corporation under division (H) of section 4511.191 of the Revised Code, and the clerk shall transmit five dollars out of the ten dollars to the state treasury to be credited to the indigent defense support fund created under section 120.08 of the Revised Code. If the person is found not guilty or the charges are dismissed, the clerk shall return the ten dollars to the person.

(D) No person shall be placed or held in a detention facility for failing to pay the court cost or bail that is required to be paid by this section.

(E) As used in this section:

(1) "Bail" and "moving violation" have the same meanings as in section 2949.093 of the Revised Code.

(2) "Detention facility" has the same meaning as in section 2921.01 of the Revised Code.

(3) "Division of criminal justice services" means the division of criminal justice services of the department of public safety, created by section 5502.62 of the Revised Code.

(2009 H 2, eff. 7-1-09; 2008 H 215, eff. 4-7-09; 2008 H 562, eff. 9–23–08)

Historical and Statutory Notes

Amendment Note: 2009 H 2 substituted "state treasury of which ninety-seven per cent shall be credited to" for "division of criminal justice services, and the division of criminal justice services shall deposit the money so transmitted into" throughout; and inserted "and the remaining three percent shall be credited to the justice program services fund created under section 5502.67 of the Revised Code" at the end of the first sentences in the undesignated paragraphs of divisions (A) and (B) and after "Code" in the third sentence of division (C).

Cross References

Chemical tests for determining alcoholic content of blood, procedures, see 4511.191

Drug law enforcement fund, see 5501.68

Fees and costs, all courts, criminal cases, juvenile cases, and some civil actions related to criminal cases, see 2746.02

Indigent defense support fund, see 120.08

Justice program services fund, see 5502.67

Ohio Administrative Code References

Reparations rotary reporting for courts, see OAC 113–1–06

Research References

Encyclopedias

OH Jur. 3d Criminal Law: Procedure § 2677, Additional Court Costs.

OH Jur. 3d Criminal Law: Procedure § 2688, Waiver of Payment.

Treatises and Practice Aids

Weiler & Weiler, Ohio Driving Under the Influence App. A, Ohio Revised Code--Selected Provisions.

2949.111 Priority of assignment of payments to satisfaction of costs, restitution, fines, and probation fees

(A) As used in this section:

(1) "Court costs" means any assessment that the court requires an offender to pay to defray the costs of operating the court.

(2) "State fines or costs" means any costs imposed or forfeited bail collected by the court under section 2743.70 of the Revised Code for deposit into the reparations fund or under section 2949.091 of the Revised Code for deposit into the indigent defense support fund established under section 120.08 of the Revised Code and all fines, penalties, and forfeited bail collected by the court and paid to a law library association under section 307.515 of the Revised Code.

(3) "Reimbursement" means any reimbursement for the costs of confinement that the court orders an offender to pay pursuant to section 2929.28 of the Revised Code, any supervision fee, any fee for the costs of house arrest with electronic monitoring that an offender agrees to pay, any reimbursement for the costs of an investigation or prosecution that the court orders an offender to pay pursuant to section 2929.71 of the Revised Code, or any other costs that the court orders an offender to pay.

(4) "Supervision fees" means any fees that a court, pursuant to sections 2929.18, 2929.28, and 2951.021 of the Revised Code, requires an offender who is under a community control sanction to pay for supervision services.

(5) "Community control sanction" has the same meaning as in section 2929.01 of the Revised Code.

(B) Unless the court, in accordance with division (C) of this section, enters in the record of the case a different method of assigning payments, if a person who is charged with a misdemeanor is convicted of or pleads guilty to the offense, if the court orders the offender to pay any combination of court costs, state fines or costs, restitution, a conventional fine, or any reimbursement, and if the offender makes any payment of any of them to a clerk of court, the clerk shall assign the offender's payment in the following manner:

(1) If the court ordered the offender to pay any court costs, the offender's payment shall be assigned toward the satisfaction of those court costs until they have been entirely paid.

(2) If the court ordered the offender to pay any state fines or costs and if all of the court costs that the court ordered the offender to pay have been paid, the remainder of the offender's payment shall be assigned on a pro rata basis toward the satisfaction of the state fines or costs until they have been entirely paid.

(3) If the court ordered the offender to pay any restitution and if all of the court costs and state fines or costs that the court ordered the offender to pay have been paid, the remainder of the offender's payment shall be assigned toward the satisfaction of the restitution until it has been entirely paid.

(4) If the court ordered the offender to pay any fine and if all of the court costs, state fines or costs, and restitution that the court ordered the offender to pay have been paid, the remainder of the offender's payment shall be assigned toward the satisfaction of the fine until it has been entirely paid.

(5) If the court ordered the offender to pay any reimbursement and if all of the court costs, state fines or costs, restitution, and fines that the court ordered the offender to pay have been paid, the remainder of the offender's payment shall be assigned toward the satisfaction of the reimbursements until they have been entirely paid.

(C) If a person who is charged with a misdemeanor is convicted of or pleads guilty to the offense and if the court orders the offender to pay any combination of court costs, state fines or costs, restitution, fines, or reimbursements, the court, at the time it orders the offender to make those payments, may prescribe an order of payments that differs from the order set forth in division (B) of this section by entering in the record of the case the order so prescribed. If a different order is entered in the record, on receipt of any payment, the clerk of the court shall assign the payment in the manner prescribed by the court.

(2009 H 1, § 110.10, eff. 1–1–10; 2008 H 420, eff. 1-1-10; 2009 H 1, § 101.01, eff. 10–16–09; 2002 H 490, eff. 1–1–04; 2002 H 170, eff. 9–6–02; 1995 S 2, eff. 7–1–96; 1994 H 406, eff. 11–11–94)

Historical and Statutory Notes

Amendment Note: 2009 H 1 substituted "indigent defense support fund established under section 120.08 of the Revised Code" for "general revenue fund" in division (A)(2).

Amendment Note: 2008 H 420 substituted "section 307.515" for "sections 3375.50 to 3375.53" in division (A)(2).

Research References

Encyclopedias

OH Jur. 3d Criminal Law: Procedure § 1922, Financial Sanctions and Fines.

OH Jur. 3d Criminal Law: Procedure § 1936, Fines.

OH Jur. 3d Criminal Law: Procedure § 2007, Financial Sanctions.

OH Jur. 3d Criminal Law: Procedure § 2698, Collection of Costs in Misdemeanor Cases; Fines.

Treatises and Practice Aids

Weiler & Weiler, Ohio Driving Under the Influence App. A, Ohio Revised Code--Selected Provisions.

COSTS AND TRANSPORTATION OF CONVICTS

2949.12 Conveying convicted felon to reception facility

Unless the execution of sentence is suspended or the convicted felon has less than thirty days to serve in prison and the department of rehabilitation and correction, the county sheriff, and the court agree otherwise, a convicted felon who is sentenced to serve a term of imprisonment in a state correctional institution shall be conveyed, within five days after sentencing, excluding Saturdays, Sundays, and legal holidays, by the sheriff of the county in which the conviction was had to the facility that is designated by the department of rehabilitation and correction for the reception of convicted felons. The sheriff shall deliver the convicted felon into the custody of the managing officer of the reception facility and, at that time, unless the department and the sheriff have agreed to electronically processed prisoner commitment, shall present the managing officer with a copy of the convicted felon's sentence that clearly describes each offense for which the felon was sentenced to a correctional institution, designates each section of the Revised Code that the felon violated and that resulted in the felon's conviction and sentence to a correctional institution, designates the sentence imposed for each offense for which the felon was sentenced to a correctional institution, and, pursuant to section 2967.191 of the Revised Code, specifies the total number of days, if any, that the felon was confined for any reason prior to conviction and sentence. The sheriff, at that time, also shall present the managing officer with a copy of the indictment. The clerk of the court of common pleas shall furnish the copies of the sentence and indictment. In the case of a person under the age of eighteen years who is certified to the court of common pleas by the juvenile court, the clerk of the court of common pleas also shall attach a copy of the certification to the copy of the indictment.

The convicted felon shall be assigned to an institution or designated to be housed in a county, multicounty, municipal, municipal-county, or multicounty-municipal jail or workhouse, if authorized pursuant to section 5120.161 of the Revised Code, shall be conveyed to the institution, jail, or workhouse, and shall be kept within the institution, jail, or workhouse until the term of the felon's imprisonment expires, the felon is pardoned, paroled, or placed under a post-release control sanction, or the felon is transferred under laws permitting the transfer of prisoners. If the execution of the felon's sentence is suspended, and the judgment thereafter affirmed, the felon shall be conveyed, in the same manner as if the execution of the felon's sentence had not been suspended, to the reception facility as soon as practicable after the judge directs the execution of sentence. The trial judge or other judge of the court, in the judge's discretion and for good cause shown, may extend the time of the conveyance.

(2008 H 130, eff. 4-7-09; 1995 S 2, eff. 7–1–96; 1994 H 571, eff. 10–6–94; 1988 H 708, eff. 4–19–88; 1987 H 261, H 455, S 6, § 3; 1984 S 172, § 1, 3; 1983 S 210; 1982 H 269, § 4, S 199; 1976 H 685; 1973 S 254; 1953 H 1; GC 13455–1)

Uncodified Law

2008 H 130, § 5, eff. 4–7–09, reads:

The items of law contained in this act, and their applications, are severable. If any item of law contained in this act, or if any application of any item of law contained in this act, is held invalid, the invalidity does not affect other items of law contained in this act and their applications that can be given effect without the invalid item of law or application.

Historical and Statutory Notes

Amendment Note: 2008 H 130 inserted "or the convicted felon has less than thirty days to serve in prison and the department of rehabilitation and correction, the county sheriff, and the court agree otherwise" after "suspended" in the first sentence and inserted "unless the department and the sheriff have agreed to electronically processed prisoner commitment," after "at that time," in the second sentence of the first undesignated paragraph.

Research References

Encyclopedias

OH Jur. 3d Criminal Law: Procedure § 2082, Delivery of Convict to Reception Facility.

OH Jur. 3d Criminal Law: Procedure § 2083, Assignment to Local Jail or Workhouse.

OH Jur. 3d Penal and Correctional Institutions § 71, Managing Officer--Qualifications and Duties.

Treatises and Practice Aids

Hennenberg & Reinhart, Ohio Criminal Defense Motions F 10:32, Motion for Order Granting Defendant Credit for Time Served--Post-Trial Motions.

Notes of Decisions

3. Journal entry of sentence

Trial judge was required to state in journal entry the number of jail time credit days to which defendant was entitled for domestic violence conviction. State ex rel. Jones v. McMonagle (Ohio App. 8 Dist., Cuyahoga, 03-31-2009) No. 92401, 2009-Ohio-1601, 2009 WL 867624, Unreported. Sentencing and Punishment ⚷ 1157

4. Time for transporting prisoner

Statutory requirement that convicted felon must be conveyed to prison within five-day period following sentencing is merely directory in nature and may not be used to invalidate a defendant's sentence or prevent its enforcement. Thompson v. Gansheimer (Ohio, 12-19-2007) 116 Ohio St.3d 349, 879 N.E.2d 199, 2007-Ohio-6666. Sentencing And Punishment ⚷ 1155

5. Jail time credit

County sheriff had no legal duty to calculate preconviction jail time credit or forward any calculation to the Ohio Department of Rehabilitation and Corrections as to prisoner, and therefore, prisoner was not entitled to a writ of mandamus compelling such action, even though he was entitled to preconviction jail time credit. State ex rel. Marich v. McFaul (Ohio App. 8 Dist., Cuyahoga, 03-04-2008) No. 90882, 2008-Ohio-2161, 2008 WL 1973472, Unreported. Mandamus ⚷ 73(1); Sentencing and Punishment ⚷ 1159

2949.14 Cost bill in case of felony

Upon conviction of a nonindigent person for a felony, the clerk of the court of common pleas shall make and certify under the clerk's hand and seal of the court, a complete itemized bill of the costs made in such prosecution, including the sum paid by the board of county commissioners, certified by the county auditor, for the arrest and return of the person on the requisition of the governor, or on the request of the governor to the president of the United States, or on the return of the fugitive by a designated agent pursuant to a waiver of extradition except in cases of parole violation. The clerk shall attempt to collect the costs from the person convicted.

(2011 H 153, eff. 9-29-11; 1983 H 291, eff. 7–1–83; 132 v S 447; 1953 H 1; GC 13455–3)

Historical and Statutory Notes

Amendment Note: 2011 H 153 substituted "the clerk's" for "his" in the first sentence, and substituted "The" for "Such bill of costs shall be presented by such clerk to the prosecuting attorney, who shall examine each item therein charged and certify to it if correct and legal. Upon certification by the prosecuting attorney, the" before "clerk shall attempt" in the last sentence.

Research References

Encyclopedias

OH Jur. 3d Civil Servants and Other Public Officers and Employees § 491, Postconviction Responsibilities.
OH Jur. 3d Courts and Judges § 216, Seal.
OH Jur. 3d Criminal Law: Procedure § 2675, Extradition; Cost Bill in Case of Felony.
OH Jur. 3d Criminal Law: Procedure § 2697, Collection of Costs in Felony Cases; Payment by State.

Treatises and Practice Aids

Katz & Giannelli, Baldwin's Ohio Practice Criminal Law § 119:6, Financial Sanctions.

Notes of Decisions

1. Cost items

Nothing prevented trial court from assessing defendant court costs by virtue of his indigent status, upon his conviction for multiple theft-related offenses and engaging in corrupt activity; imposition of court costs was not an infringement of defendant's rights nor did it violate any statute. State v. Glavic (Ohio App. 11 Dist., Lake, 12-22-2003) No. 2001-L-177, No. 2001-L-179, 2003-Ohio-6961, 2003 WL 22994557, Unreported, motion for delayed appeal granted 102 Ohio St.3d 1444, 808 N.E.2d 396, 2004-Ohio-2263, appeal allowed 103 Ohio St.3d 1442, 814 N.E.2d 869, 2004-Ohio-4626, appeal not allowed 104 Ohio St.3d 1411, 818 N.E.2d 711, 2004-Ohio-6364, affirmed 105 Ohio St.3d 131, 823 N.E.2d 447, 2005-Ohio-31, habeas corpus denied 2007 WL 1959213, appeal not allowed 107 Ohio St.3d 1411, 836 N.E.2d 1230, 2005-Ohio-5859. Costs ⚿ 302

Error in trial court's order for defendant who was convicted of domestic battery to pay restitution to county sheriff's office for expenses associated with his extradition from a state to which defendant had fled before sentencing hearing, which trial court did not have statutory authority to do, was not harmless, even though the state argued that extradition expenses could be considered as part of trial court's order for costs of prosecution; nothing showed that procedures to collect extradition costs as part of costs of prosecution were followed, such costs were payable to clerk of court and not sheriff's office, and trial court clearly deemed extradition expenses as restitution. State v. Toler (Ohio App. 3 Dist., 12-26-2007) 174 Ohio App.3d 335, 882 N.E.2d 28, 2007-Ohio-6967. Criminal Law ⚿ 1177.3(5)

Trial court has authority to impose court costs upon indigent defendant; statute requires court to include costs as part of sentence and, while second statute provides collection mechanism only for non-indigent defendants, nothing in second statute prohibits court from collecting costs from indigent defendant. State v. Haynie (Ohio App. 3 Dist., 05-17-2004) 157 Ohio App.3d 708, 813 N.E.2d 686, 2004-Ohio-2452, appeal allowed 103 Ohio St.3d 1477, 816 N.E.2d 253, 2004-Ohio-5405, reconsideration denied 104 Ohio St.3d 1428, 819 N.E.2d 710, 2004-Ohio-6585, affirmed 105 Ohio St.3d 133, 823 N.E.2d 448, 2005-Ohio-785, denial of post-conviction relief affirmed 2013-Ohio-3777, 2013 WL 4737247, appeal not allowed 138 Ohio St.3d 1433, 4 N.E.3d 1051, 2014-Ohio-889. Costs ⚿ 302

3. Ability to pay

Trial court was required to impose costs of prosecution for sexual battery, regardless of defendant's indigency status. State v. Dickinson (Ohio App. 7 Dist., Columbiana, 11-26-2004) No. 03 CO 52, 2004-Ohio-6373, 2004 WL 2726057, Unreported, appeal not allowed 105 Ohio St.3d 1499, 825 N.E.2d 623, 2005-Ohio-1666, habeas corpus denied 2009 WL 396049. Costs ⚿ 292

2949.17 Transportation of prisoners; expenses

(A) The sheriff may take one guard for every two convicted felons to be transported to a correctional institution. The trial judge may authorize a larger number of guards upon written application of the sheriff, in which case a transcript of the order of the judge shall be certified by the clerk of the court of common pleas under the seal of the court, and the sheriff shall deliver the order with the convict to the person in charge of the correctional institution.

(B) In order to obtain reimbursement for the county for the expenses of transportation for indigent convicted felons, the clerk of the court of common pleas shall prepare a transportation cost bill for each indigent convicted felon transported pursuant to this section for an amount equal to not less than one dollar a mile from the county seat to the state correctional institution and return for each prisoner. The number of miles shall be computed by the usual route of travel. The clerk's duties under this division are subject to division (B) of section 2949.19 of the Revised Code.

(2009 H 1, eff. 10-16-09; 1999 H 283, eff. 9–29–99; 1994 H 571, eff. 10–6–94; 1983 H 291, eff. 7–1–83; 1981 H 694; 1979 H 204; 128 v 542; 1953 H 1; GC 13455–6)

Historical and Statutory Notes

Amendment Note: 2009 H 1 substituted "not less than one dollar" for "ten cents" and deleted "the sheriff and each of the guards and five cents a mile from the county seat to the state correctional institution for" prior to "each prisoner" in division (B).

Research References

Encyclopedias

OH Jur. 3d Civil Servants and Other Public Officers and Employees § 504, Duties Regarding Reimbursement of Costs.

OH Jur. 3d Criminal Law: Procedure § 2676, Transportation of Prisoners.

OH Jur. 3d Criminal Law: Procedure § 2692, State Payment of Criminal Costs.

OH Jur. 3d Police, Sheriffs, and Related Officers § 51, Other Sheriff's Fees.

DEATH SENTENCE

2949.22 Execution of death sentence

Validity

For stay of implementation of order of execution, see In re Ohio Execution Protocol Litigation, 840 F.Supp.2d 1044, 2012 WL 84548 (S.D. Ohio 2012).

Notes of Decisions

1. Constitutional issues

Challenge to electrocution was moot because electrocution was no longer authorized to carry out the death penalty. State v. Adams (Ohio, 11-17-2004) 103 Ohio St.3d 508, 817 N.E.2d 29, 2004-Ohio-5845, reconsideration denied 104 Ohio St.3d 1442, 819 N.E.2d 1124, 2004-Ohio-7033, certiorari denied 125 S.Ct. 2271, 544 U.S. 1040, 161 L.Ed.2d 1072, habeas corpus denied 2007 WL 671296, habeas corpus denied 484 F.Supp.2d 753, opinion after remand from court of appeals 2009 WL 2922042, stay granted, motion to certify appeal granted 2010 WL 816532, subsequent determination 2010 WL 1964904, affirmed 644 F.3d 481, on remand 2013 WL 3991867. Sentencing And Punishment ⚷ 1788(5)

Ohio statute requiring that "death sentence shall be executed by causing the application to the person, upon whom the sentence was imposed, of a lethal injection of a drug or combination of drugs of sufficient dosage to quickly and painlessly cause death" creates no cause of action to enforce any right to quick and painless death, enforceable under due process clause. Cooey v. Strickland (C.A.6 (Ohio), 05-12-2010) 604 F.3d 939, certiorari denied 130 S.Ct. 3272, 559 U.S. 1118, 176 L.Ed.2d 945. Civil Rights ⚷ 1721; Constitutional Law ⚷ 4746; Sentencing and Punishment ⚷ 1796

Risk of improper implementation of state's one-drug lethal injection protocol, which called for intravenous (IV) injection of thiopental sodium, did not render protocol cruel and unusual in violation of the Eighth Amendment. Cooey v. Strickland (C.A.6 (Ohio), 12-07-2009) 589 F.3d 210, rehearing en banc denied 588 F.3d 1124, for denial of stay of execution, see 130 S.Ct. 826, 558 U.S. 1087, 175 L.Ed.2d 580. Sentencing and Punishment ⚷ 1796

Lack of an explicit ban on the use of cut-down procedures, which entailed making an incision into an arm or leg to gain intravenous (IV) access, did not render state's one-drug lethal injection protocol cruel and unusual in violation of the Eighth Amendment; director of state department of rehabilitation and correction stated that procedure would not be used, and protocol indicated that intramuscular injection was to be utilized if the execution team found prisoner's veins difficult to access, which implied that this intramuscular procedure, and not cut-down, would be employed should execution team find peripheral IV injection impossible. Cooey v. Strickland (C.A.6 (Ohio), 12-07-2009) 589 F.3d 210, rehearing en banc denied 588 F.3d 1124, for denial of stay of execution, see 130 S.Ct. 826, 558 U.S. 1087, 175 L.Ed.2d 580. Sentencing and Punishment ⚷ 1796

State's back-up lethal injection procedure, which called for intramuscular injection of hydromorphone and midazolam should execution team fail to find veins suitable for intravenous (IV) injection of thiopental sodium, did not pose substantial risk of severe pain, as would violate Eighth Amendment, despite risk of side effects such as nausea and vomiting; midazolam was anti-emetic medication that would counteract many side effects of hydromorphone, and expert testified that prisoner would lose consciousness within two to four minutes of first administration of midazolam, would therefore be unlikely to aspirate, and would not suffer pain even if he did vomit because he would be unconscious. Cooey v. Strickland (C.A.6 (Ohio), 12-07-2009) 589 F.3d 210, rehearing en banc denied

588 F.3d 1124, for denial of stay of execution, see 130 S.Ct. 826, 558 U.S. 1087, 175 L.Ed.2d 580. Sentencing and Punishment ⚖ 1796

State's failure to adopt proposed, allegedly more humane alternative of using a central line in back-up lethal injection procedure should execution team fail to find veins suitable for intravenous (IV) injection did not render state's chosen intramuscular injection backup procedure cruel and unusual in violation of the Eighth Amendment; mere existence of an alternative was insufficient to render chosen protocol cruel and unusual, and expert testified that central line had a far greater capability of causing severe injury and pain. Cooey v. Strickland (C.A.6 (Ohio), 12-07-2009) 589 F.3d 210, rehearing en banc denied 588 F.3d 1124, for denial of stay of execution, see 130 S.Ct. 826, 558 U.S. 1087, 175 L.Ed.2d 580. Sentencing and Punishment ⚖ 1796

Ohio statute providing that a death sentence was to be executed by causing the application of a drug of sufficient dosage to quickly and painlessly cause death did not create a liberty and property interest in a quick and painless execution protected by the substantive component of the Due Process Clause of the Fourteenth Amendment. Cooey v. Strickland (C.A.6 (Ohio), 12-07-2009) 589 F.3d 210, rehearing en banc denied 588 F.3d 1124, for denial of stay of execution, see 130 S.Ct. 826, 558 U.S. 1087, 175 L.Ed.2d 580. Constitutional Law ⚖ 4746; Sentencing and Punishment ⚖ 1796

Even assuming that Antiterrorism and Effective Death Penalty Act's (AEDPA) limitations provisions applied to inmate's § 1983 challenge to Ohio's lethal injection method of execution, decision of an Ohio court of common pleas that potentially painful three-drug lethal-injection protocol violated the Fifth and Fourteenth Amendments was not a newly-recognized right by the Supreme Court, for purposes of AEDPA provision permitting a habeas petitioner to file one year from when the Supreme Court recognizes a new, retroactive constitutional right. Broom v. Strickland (C.A.6 (Ohio), 09-01-2009) 579 F.3d 553, certiorari denied 130 S.Ct. 636, 558 U.S. 1030, 175 L.Ed.2d 489. Habeas Corpus ⚖ 603.11

Supreme Court's decision in *Baze v. Rees* did not create a new Eighth Amendment right to challenge lethal injection as a means of execution, and thus did not trigger a new accrual date for death row inmate's § 1983 claim challenging Ohio's lethal-injection protocol; *Baze* clarified the standards that should apply to the merits of Eighth Amendment protocol challenges. Getsy v. Strickland (C.A.6 (Ohio), 08-13-2009) 577 F.3d 309, certiorari denied 130 S.Ct. 40, 557 U.S. 958, 174 L.Ed.2d 618, rehearing en banc denied 577 F.3d 320. Limitation of Actions ⚖ 58(1)

Prisoner's cause of action that state's lethal injection protocol would violate his Fourteenth Amendment due process right by depriving him of a property interest in a quick and painless death accrued, and statute of limitations began to run, on date of enactment of state statute providing for such quick and painless death. Cooey v. Strickland (C.A.6 (Ohio), 10-09-2008) 544 F.3d 588, certiorari denied 129 S.Ct. 394, 555 U.S. 940, 172 L.Ed.2d 282. Limitation of Actions ⚖ 58(1)

State death row inmate's Eighth Amendment claim, alleging that proposed lethal injection protocol would constitute cruel and unusual punishment, was cognizable under §§ 1983 and did not have to be presented in petition for writ of habeas corpus, since challenge was to specific protocol rather than a general challenge to execution. Cooey v. Strickland (C.A.6 (Ohio), 03-02-2007) 479 F.3d 412, rehearing denied 489 F.3d 775, certiorari denied 128 S.Ct. 2047, 553 U.S. 1006, 170 L.Ed.2d 796, certiorari denied 128 S.Ct. 2047, 553 U.S. 1014, 170 L.Ed.2d 811, rehearing denied 128 S.Ct. 2927, 553 U.S. 1103, 171 L.Ed.2d 859. Civil Rights ⚖ 1088(5); Civil Rights ⚖ 1311

Limitations period for state death row inmate's §§ 1983 claim, alleging that proposed lethal injection protocol would constitute cruel and unusual punishment, began to run no later than date when challenged protocol became state's exclusive execution method, which was well after triggering event of affirmance of death penalty on direct review; limitations period did not commence later, when inmate's execution became imminent and all state and federal postconviction remedies had been exhausted, or when inmate obtained actual knowledge of publicly available information concerning protocol's exclusivity. Cooey v. Strickland (C.A.6 (Ohio), 03-02-2007) 479 F.3d 412, rehearing denied 489 F.3d 775, certiorari denied 128 S.Ct. 2047, 553 U.S. 1006, 170 L.Ed.2d 796, certiorari denied 128 S.Ct. 2047, 553 U.S. 1014, 170 L.Ed.2d 811, rehearing denied 128 S.Ct. 2927, 553 U.S. 1103, 171 L.Ed.2d 859. Limitation Of Actions ⚖ 58(1); Limitation Of Actions ⚖ 95(15)

Motion to vacate stay of scheduled execution granted by district court pending determination of constitutionality of Ohio's protocol for lethal injection would be transferred to another panel in deference to that panel's knowledge of underlying merits of stay motion and its prior resolution of a stay motion to ensure uniform application of federal law and promote judicial economy. Cooey v. Strickland (C.A.6 (Ohio), 01-16-2007) 474 F.3d 268. Courts ⚖ 50

Lethal injection was a constitutional method of execution. Adams v. Bradshaw (N.D.Ohio, 04-24-2007) 484 F.Supp.2d 753, opinion after remand from court of appeals 2009 WL 2922042, stay granted, motion to certify appeal granted 2010 WL 816532, subsequent determination 2010 WL 1964904, affirmed 644 F.3d 481, on remand 2013 WL 3991867. Sentencing And Punishment ⚖ 1796

Preliminary injunction staying state inmate's execution was warranted in §§ 1983 action challenging Ohio's lethal injection protocol on Eighth Amendment grounds, inasmuch as inmate intervened in action immediately after his cause of action accrued and thus did not delay in seeking relief, mounting evidence called into question Ohio's lethal injection protocol and same or similar protocols of other states and inmate, at the least, demonstrated stronger likelihood of success on the merits than plaintiffs who preceded him, there was unacceptable risk that inmate could suffer unnecessary and excruciating pain while being executed, harm from injunction to state's interests would be minimal in light of both state's ability to correct protocol's flaws and delay in case due to state's interlocutory appeal, and injunctive relief served public interests. Cooey v. Taft (S.D.Ohio, 04-28-2006) 430 F.Supp.2d 702. Civil Rights ⚷ 1457(5)

Cruel and unusual punishment, death penalty, three drug lethal injection, risk of improper administration, resulting pain. Baze v. Rees, 2008, 128 S.Ct. 1520, 170 L.Ed.2d 420.

Civil rights action cognizable, death row inmates, lethal injection, cruel and unusual punishment, Hill v. McDonough, 2006, 126 S.Ct. 2096.

2. Lethal injection option

Trial judge's order of "death by electrocution" did not preclude capital murder defendant's statutory right to elect lethal injection, especially considering the trial judge's express statement that defendant's execution comply with statute affording defendant the lethal injection option. State v. Bey (Ohio, 05-19-1999) 85 Ohio St.3d 487, 709 N.E.2d 484, 1999-Ohio-283, reconsideration denied 86 Ohio St.3d 1421, 711 N.E.2d 1014, certiorari denied 120 S.Ct. 587, 528 U.S. 1049, 145 L.Ed.2d 488, dismissal of habeas corpus affirmed 2007 WL 2768300. Sentencing And Punishment ⚷ 1796

The Ohio statute providing that a death sentence shall be executed by causing the application of a drug of sufficient dosage to quickly and painlessly cause death creates no cause of action to enforce any right to a quick and painless death. Cooey v. Strickland (C.A.6 (Ohio), 12-07-2009) 589 F.3d 210, rehearing en banc denied 588 F.3d 1124, for denial of stay of execution, see 130 S.Ct. 826, 558 U.S. 1087, 175 L.Ed.2d 580. Action ⚷ 5

Continuing-violations doctrine did not toll the statute of limitations applicable to inmate's § 1983 challenge to Ohio's lethal-injection method of execution; Ohio's adoption of its lethal-injection protocol was not continued wrongful conduct, only the continued risk of future harm. Broom v. Strickland (C.A.6 (Ohio), 09-01-2009) 579 F.3d 553, certiorari denied 130 S.Ct. 636, 558 U.S. 1030, 175 L.Ed.2d 489. Limitation of Actions ⚷ 58(1)

State death row inmate failed to demonstrate any basis upon which Court of Appeals should exercise its equitable power to stay his execution to permit him to pursue appeal from order denying his motion to intervene in §§ 1983 Eighth Amendment action brought by another inmate against state officials, challenging state's three-drug lethal injection protocol; inmate, who did not exhaust his administrative remedies as was required under the Prison Litigation Reform Act (PLRA), failed to demonstrate any likelihood that he could succeed on merits of his motion to intervene, and state had strong interest in proceeding with its judgment. Cooey v. Strickland (C.A.6 (Ohio), 04-23-2007) 484 F.3d 424. Sentencing And Punishment ⚷ 1798

3. Accrual of limitations period

Even if Court of Appeals' decision in *Cooey II*, holding that suits challenging Ohio's lethal injection protocol accrue for limitations purposes when Ohio adopted lethal injection as the sole method of execution, announced a new rule of law, decision applied retroactively to inmate's intervenor complaint in that action. Broom v. Strickland (C.A.6 (Ohio), 09-01-2009) 579 F.3d 553, certiorari denied 130 S.Ct. 636, 558 U.S. 1030, 175 L.Ed.2d 489. Courts ⚷ 100(1)

What happened to death row inmate's criminal case while on collateral review was irrelevant to accrual of his § 1983 claim challenging Ohio's lethal-injection protocol. Getsy v. Strickland (C.A.6 (Ohio), 08-13-2009) 577 F.3d 309, certiorari denied 130 S.Ct. 40, 557 U.S. 958, 174 L.Ed.2d 618, rehearing en banc denied 577 F.3d 320. Limitation of Actions ⚷ 105(2)

Modifications to Ohio's lethal-injection protocol did not create a new date of accrual for death row inmate's § 1983 claim challenging Ohio's lethal-injection protocol, where inmate failed to make a prima facie showing that the modifications would likely subject him to extreme pain based on either new evidence or on existing evidence that had already been proffered in support of his core complaints. Getsy v. Strickland (C.A.6 (Ohio), 08-13-2009) 577 F.3d 309, certiorari denied 130 S.Ct. 40, 557 U.S. 958, 174 L.Ed.2d 618, rehearing en banc denied 577 F.3d 320. Limitation of Actions ⚷ 58(1)

The two-year limitations period applicable to death row inmate's § 1983 claim challenging Ohio's lethal-injection protocol began to accrue when Ohio adopted lethal injection as the sole method of execution, where direct review in state court had ended earlier, when Supreme Court denied petition for writ of certiorari from state court decision affirming his conviction. Getsy v. Strickland (C.A.6 (Ohio), 08-13-2009) 577 F.3d 309, certiorari denied 130 S.Ct. 40, 557 U.S. 958, 174 L.Ed.2d 618, rehearing en banc denied 577 F.3d 320. Limitation of Actions ⚷ 58(1)

2949.221 Confidentiality of information concerning lethal injections

(A) As used in this section:

(1) "Person" has the same meaning as in section 1.59 of the Revised Code.

(2) "Licensing authority" means an entity, board, department, commission, association, or agency that issues a license to a person or entity.

(3) "Public office" has the same meaning as in section 117.01 of the Revised Code.

(B) If, at any time prior to the day that is twenty-four months after the effective date of this section, a person manufactures, compounds, imports, transports, distributes, supplies, prescribes, prepares, administers, uses, or tests any of the compounding equipment or components, the active pharmaceutical ingredients, the drugs or combination of drugs, the medical supplies, or the medical equipment used in the application of a lethal injection of a drug or combination of drugs in the administration of a death sentence by lethal injection as provided for in division (A) of section 2949.22 of the Revised Code, notwithstanding any provision of law to the contrary, all of the following apply regarding any information or record in the possession of any public office that identifies or reasonably leads to the identification of the person and the person's participation in any activity described in this division:

(1) The information or record shall be classified as confidential, is privileged under law, and is not subject to disclosure by any person, state agency, governmental entity, board, or commission or any political subdivision as a public record under section 149.43 of the Revised Code or otherwise.

(2) The information or record shall not be subject to disclosure by or during any judicial proceeding, inquiry, or process, except as described in division (B)(4) of this section or in section 2949.222 of the Revised Code.

(3) The information or record shall not be subject to discovery, subpoena, or any other means of legal compulsion for disclosure to any person or entity, except as described in division (B)(4) of this section or in section 2949.222 of the Revised Code.

(4)(a) If the information or record pertains to the manufacture, compounding, importing, transportation, distribution, or supplying of any of the items or materials described in division (B) of this section, the person or entity that maintains the information or record shall disclose the information or record to the Ohio ethics commission and the commission may use the information or record, subject to division (B)(1) of this section, only to confirm the following:

(i) That the relationship between the person and the department of rehabilitation and correction is consistent with and complies with the ethics laws of this state;

(ii) That at the time of the specified conduct, the person has all licenses required under the laws of this state to engage in that conduct and the licenses are valid.

(b) If the Ohio ethics commission receives any information or record pursuant to division (B)(4)(a) of this section, the commission shall complete its use of the information or record for the purposes described in that division within fourteen days of its receipt and shall promptly report its findings to the director of rehabilitation and correction.

(C)(1) If, at any time prior to the day that is twenty-four months after the effective date of this section, an employee or former employee of the department of rehabilitation and correction or any other individual selected or designated by the director of the department participates or participated in the administration of a sentence of death by lethal injection, as provided for in division (A) of section 2949.22 of the Revised Code, subject to division (C)(2) of this section and notwithstanding any other provision of law to the contrary, the protections and limitations specified in divisions (B)(1), (2), and (3) of this section shall apply regarding any information or record in the possession of any public office that identifies or reasonably leads to the identification of the employee, former employee, or other individual and the employee's, former employee's, or individual's participation in the administration of the sentence of death by lethal injection described in this division.

(2) Division (C)(1) of this section does not apply with respect to information or a record that identifies or reasonably leads to the identification of the director of rehabilitation and correction or the warden of the state correctional institution in which the administration of the sentence of death takes place.

(D) The protections and limitations specified in divisions (B)(1), (2), and (3) of this section regarding information and records that identify or may reasonably lead to the identification of a person described in divisions (B) or (C) of this section and the person's participation in any activity described in the particular division are rights that shall be recognized as follows:

(1) With respect to a person that is an individual, without any requirement for the person to take any action or specifically apply for recognition of such rights.

(2) With respect to a person that is not an individual, the rights do not exist unless the person requests to have the rights recognized by applying in writing to the director of rehabilitation and correction.

The director of rehabilitation and correction by rule shall establish the procedure according to which a person who is not an individual may apply in writing for the rights described in divisions (B)(1), (2), and (3) of this section. The director shall approve an application that is submitted in compliance with the rules. A person whose application is approved is entitled to the rights for twenty years after the person ceases the qualifying activity as contemplated by the first paragraph of division (B) of this section. The director shall notify any person, who is not an individual and who is entitled to the rights, of the application procedures.

(E) If a person or entity that, at any time prior to the day that is twenty-four months after the effective date of this section, participates in, consults regarding, performs any function with respect to, including any activity described in division (B) of this section, or provides any expert opinion testimony regarding an execution by lethal injection conducted in accordance with division (A) of section 2949.22 of the Revised Code is licensed by a licensing authority, notwithstanding any provision of law to the contrary, the licensing authority shall not do any of the following as a result of that participation, consultation, performance, activity, or testimony by the person or entity:

(1) Challenge, reprimand, suspend, or revoke the person's or entity's license;

(2) Take any disciplinary action against the person or entity or the person's or entity's licensure.

(F) A person may not, without the approval of the director of rehabilitation and correction, knowingly disclose the identity and participation in an activity described in the particular division of any person to whom division (B) of this section applies and that is made confidential, privileged, and not subject to disclosure under that division or of an employee, former employee, or other individual to whom division (C)(1) of this section applies and that is made confidential, privileged, and not subject to disclosure under that division. Any person, employee, former employee, or individual whose identity and participation in a specified activity is disclosed in violation of this division has a civil cause of action against any person who discloses the identity and participation in the activity in violation of this division. In a civil action brought under this division, the plaintiff is entitled to recover from the defendant actual damages, punitive or exemplary damages upon a showing of a willful violation of this division, and reasonable attorney's fees and court costs.

(G) If division (B), (C), or (D) of this section applies to a person with respect to any conduct or activity of the person occurring at a time prior to the day that is twenty-four months after the effective date of this section, the expiration of that twenty-four month period does not affect, add to, or diminish the protections and limitations specified in division (B) or (C), division (D), and division (E) of this section with respect to their application to that person.

(2014 H 663, eff. 3-23-15)

Uncodified Law

2014 H 663, § 7, eff. 3–23–15, reads:

(A) As used in this section, "lethal injection" means the application of a lethal injection of a drug or a combination of drugs in carrying out a sentence of death.

(B) The intent of the General Assembly in enacting this act is to protect the identities of persons who assist the Department of Rehabilitation and Correction in carrying out a court-ordered sentence of death by lethal injection, in order to protect those persons from harassment and potential physical harm.

(C) It is the intent of the General Assembly in enacting this act to enable the Department of Rehabilitation and Correction to obtain the necessary assistance of persons in carrying out a court-ordered sentence of death by lethal injection or the drugs needed to administer such a sentence.

2949.222 Sealing of records containing information concerning lethal injections

(A) As used in this section, "seal a record" means to remove a record from the main file of similar records and to secure it in a separate file that contains only sealed records accessible only to the court.

(B) The court promptly shall order the immediate sealing of records containing information described in division (B) or (C) of section 2949.221 of the Revised Code and the person's participation in any activity described in the particular division, whenever the records come into the court's possession.

(C) If a record containing information described in division (B) or (C) of section 2949.221 of the Revised Code and the person's participation in any activity described in the particular division, is subpoenaed or requested by a court order, the director of rehabilitation and correction shall provide the record. If the court determines that the record is necessary for just adjudication, the court shall order the director to appear at a private hearing with a copy of the record and any other relevant evidence. The information is not otherwise subject to disclosure unless the court, through clear and convincing evidence presented in the private hearing, finds that the person whose identity is protected appears to have acted unlawfully with respect to the person's involvement in the administration of a lethal injection as contemplated by the first paragraph of division (B) and by division (C)(1) of section 2949.221 of the Revised Code.

(2014 H 663, eff. 3-23-15)

Uncodified Law

2014 H 663, § 7, eff. 3–23–15, reads:

(A) As used in this section, "lethal injection" means the application of a lethal injection of a drug or a combination of drugs in carrying out a sentence of death.

(B) The intent of the General Assembly in enacting this act is to protect the identities of persons who assist the Department of Rehabilitation and Correction in carrying out a court-ordered sentence of death by lethal injection, in order to protect those persons from harassment and potential physical harm.

(C) It is the intent of the General Assembly in enacting this act to enable the Department of Rehabilitation and Correction to obtain the necessary assistance of persons in carrying out a court-ordered sentence of death by lethal injection or the drugs needed to administer such a sentence.

2949.25 Attendance at execution

Notes of Decisions

1. Broadcasting of event

Allegedly improper statement of trial court judge, authorizing authorities in charge of executing death sentence to permit media representatives to broadcast execution, was of no force, where it was not incorporated into trial court's journal entries. State v. Keenan (Ohio, 02-25-1998) 81 Ohio St.3d 133, 689 N.E.2d 929, 1998-Ohio-459, reconsideration denied 81 Ohio St.3d 1503, 691 N.E.2d 1062, certiorari denied 119 S.Ct. 146, 525 U.S. 860, 142 L.Ed.2d 119, rehearing denied 119 S.Ct. 581, 525 U.S. 1035, 142 L.Ed.2d 484, denial of post-conviction relief affirmed 2001 WL 91129, dismissed, appeal not allowed 92 Ohio St.3d 1429, 749 N.E.2d 756, habeas corpus dismissed 262 F.Supp.2d 818, motion to amend denied 262 F.Supp.2d 826, vacated and remanded 400 F.3d 417, on remand 2007 WL 838923, dismissal of post-conviction relief affirmed 2006-Ohio-6031, 2006 WL 3317922, appeal not allowed 114 Ohio St.3d 1508, 872 N.E.2d 950, 2007-Ohio-4285. Criminal Law ⚿ 655(1)

2949.28 Inquiry on sanity of convict

Notes of Decisions

1. Constitutional issues

State did not have right to appeal from trial court's determination that death-sentence defendant was incompetent for purposes of execution; proceeding below was actually request for competency determination, even though proceeding was captioned as petition for postconviction relief, and court ruled on it as if it was petition, court's use of wrong terminology in ruling on motion did not constitute grounds for appeal, and did not change character of court's action or order, and legislature did not intend to provide state with ability to appeal. State v. Awkal (Ohio App. 8 Dist., 08-30-2012) 974 N.E.2d 200, 2012-Ohio-3970, appeal not allowed 141 Ohio St.3d 1421, 21 N.E.3d 1114, 2014-Ohio-5567. Sentencing and Punishment ⚿ 1788(2)

Because inmate did not demonstrate probable cause to believe that he was insane under statute allowing for suspension of death sentence for insane inmates, he had necessarily not made a substantial threshold showing of insanity that entitled him to a hearing under the due process clause to the federal constitution. Bedford v. State (Ohio App. 1 Dist., 05-16-2011) 194 Ohio App.3d 570, 957 N.E.2d 336, 2011-Ohio-2352, appeal denied 128 Ohio St.3d 1494, 947 N.E.2d 177, 2011-Ohio-2355. Constitutional Law ⚿ 4786; Sentencing and Punishment ⚿ 1794

There was no probable cause to believe that inmate could not understand the nature of the death penalty and why it was imposed upon him so as to warrant suspension of death sentence pursuant to inmate's notice of insanity. Bedford v. State (Ohio App. 1 Dist., 05-16-2011) 194 Ohio App.3d 570, 957 N.E.2d 336, 2011-Ohio-2352, appeal denied 128 Ohio St.3d 1494, 947 N.E.2d 177, 2011-Ohio-2355. Sentencing and Punishment ⚿ 1794

Court of appeals would grant state's motion to expand record to include an affidavit from a neuroradiologist who reviewed petitioner's MRI results, for purposes of petitioner's motion for relief from judgment of denial of habeas petition alleging that counsel's failure to present evidence of organic brain impairment in death penalty prosecution was ineffective assistance of counsel; the state acted diligently in informing the district court of the MRI and in attempting to present the relevant materials to the district court, and, the MRI results were plainly relevant to the court's determination of whether a stay of execution was warranted. Smith v. Anderson (C.A.6 (Ohio), 03-06-2005) 402 F.3d 718, rehearing en banc denied, certiorari denied 125 S.Ct. 1609, 544 U.S. 913, 161 L.Ed.2d 293. Habeas Corpus ⚿ 823

2. Test of insanity

In the context of statutes allowing for suspension of death sentence if inmate is insane, a showing of probable cause requires the production of sufficient evidence to establish that there is reason to believe that the convict is insane. Bedford v. State (Ohio App. 1 Dist., 05-16-2011) 194 Ohio App.3d 570, 957 N.E.2d 336, 2011-Ohio-2352, appeal denied 128 Ohio St.3d 1494, 947 N.E.2d 177, 2011-Ohio-2355. Sentencing and Punishment ⚿ 1794

3. Final appealable order

Trial court's determination that death-sentence defendant was incompetent for purposes of execution did not constitute a final, appealable order, and thus, appellate court was without jurisdiction to hear state's appeal; state did not have substantial right that was affected by court's order, court's decision did not affect defendant's underlying conviction of guilt or sentence of death, and finding of incompetency did not prevent court from finding in future that defendant was competent after he received ordered medical treatment. State v. Awkal (Ohio App. 8 Dist., 08-30-2012) 974 N.E.2d 200, 2012-Ohio-3970, appeal not allowed 141 Ohio St.3d 1421, 21 N.E.3d 1114, 2014-Ohio-5567. Sentencing and Punishment ⚿ 1788(2)

2949.29 Proceedings on the insanity inquiry

Notes of Decisions

1. Constitutional issues

Because inmate did not demonstrate probable cause to believe that he was insane under statute allowing for suspension of death sentence for insane inmates, he had necessarily not made a substantial threshold showing of insanity that entitled him to a hearing under the due process clause to the federal constitution. Bedford v. State (Ohio App. 1 Dist., 05-16-2011) 194 Ohio App.3d 570, 957 N.E.2d 336, 2011-Ohio-2352, appeal denied 128 Ohio St.3d 1494, 947 N.E.2d 177, 2011-Ohio-2355. Constitutional Law ⚿ 4786; Sentencing and Punishment ⚿ 1794

2. Nature of proceeding

There was no probable cause to believe that inmate could not understand the nature of the death penalty and why it was imposed upon him so as to warrant suspension of death sentence pursuant to inmate's notice of insanity. Bedford v. State (Ohio App. 1 Dist., 05-16-2011) 194 Ohio App.3d 570, 957 N.E.2d 336, 2011-Ohio-2352, appeal denied 128 Ohio St.3d 1494, 947 N.E.2d 177, 2011-Ohio-2355. Sentencing and Punishment ⚿ 1794

In the context of statutes allowing for suspension of death sentence if inmate is insane, a showing of probable cause requires the production of sufficient evidence to establish that there is reason to believe that the convict is insane. Bedford v. State (Ohio App. 1 Dist., 05-16-2011) 194 Ohio App.3d 570, 957 N.E.2d 336, 2011-Ohio-2352, appeal denied 128 Ohio St.3d 1494, 947 N.E.2d 177, 2011-Ohio-2355. Sentencing and Punishment ⚿ 1794